THE
ROYAL
ANCESTRY
BIBLE

a 3,400 pedigree chart compilation
(plus index and appendix)

containing

Royal Ancestors
of
300 Colonial American Families

who are themselves ancestors of 70 million Americans

Vol. 2

Michel L. Call

Michel L. Call
P. O. Box 11488
Salt Lake City, Utah 84147
E-mail – royalancestors@hotmail.com

Heritage Creations

Library of Congress Control Number 2005931452

International Standard Book Number 1-933194-22-7 (3 Volumes)

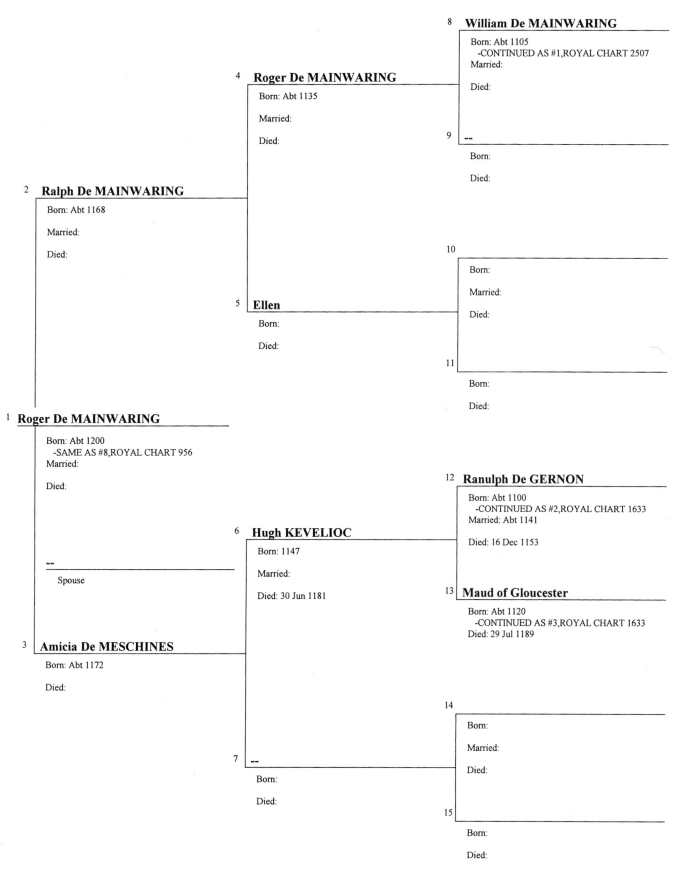

8 William De MAINWARING
Born: Abt 1105
-CONTINUED AS #1,ROYAL CHART 2507
Married:

Died:

4 Roger De MAINWARING
Born: Abt 1135

Married:

Died:

9 --
Born:

Died:

2 Ralph De MAINWARING
Born: Abt 1168

Married:

Died:

10
Born:

Married:

Died:

5 Ellen
Born:

Died:

11
Born:

Died:

1 Roger De MAINWARING
Born: Abt 1200
-SAME AS #8,ROYAL CHART 956
Married:

Died:

12 Ranulph De GERNON
Born: Abt 1100
-CONTINUED AS #2,ROYAL CHART 1633
Married: Abt 1141

Died: 16 Dec 1153

6 Hugh KEVELIOC
Born: 1147

Married:

Died: 30 Jun 1181

13 Maud of Gloucester
Born: Abt 1120
-CONTINUED AS #3,ROYAL CHART 1633
Died: 29 Jul 1189

--
Spouse

3 Amicia De MESCHINES
Born: Abt 1172

Died:

14
Born:

Married:

Died:

7 --
Born:

Died:

15
Born:

Died:

Sources include: *The Genealogist* 7-8, pp. 34-73.

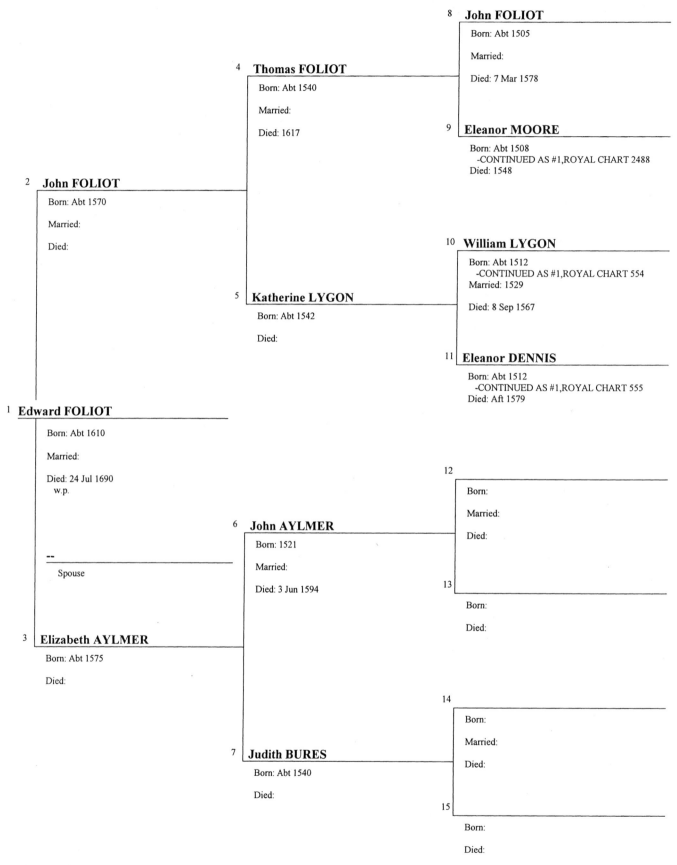

8 **John FOLIOT**

Born: Abt 1505

Married:

Died: 7 Mar 1578

4 **Thomas FOLIOT**

Born: Abt 1540

Married:

Died: 1617

9 **Eleanor MOORE**

Born: Abt 1508
  -CONTINUED AS #1,ROYAL CHART 2488
Died: 1548

2 **John FOLIOT**

Born: Abt 1570

Married:

Died:

10 **William LYGON**

Born: Abt 1512
  -CONTINUED AS #1,ROYAL CHART 554
Married: 1529

Died: 8 Sep 1567

5 **Katherine LYGON**

Born: Abt 1542

Died:

11 **Eleanor DENNIS**

Born: Abt 1512
  -CONTINUED AS #1,ROYAL CHART 555
Died: Aft 1579

1 **Edward FOLIOT**

Born: Abt 1610

Married:

Died: 24 Jul 1690
  w.p.

--
  Spouse

12

Born:

Married:

Died:

6 **John AYLMER**

Born: 1521

Married:

Died: 3 Jun 1594

13

Born:

Died:

3 **Elizabeth AYLMER**

Born: Abt 1575

Died:

14

Born:

Married:

Died:

7 **Judith BURES**

Born: Abt 1540

Died:

15

Born:

Died:

Sources include: Richardson *Plantagenet* (2004), pp. 337 (Foliot), 448-449 (Ligon); Faris--Ligon; Faris 2--Ligon 3; *Magna Charta* 70.

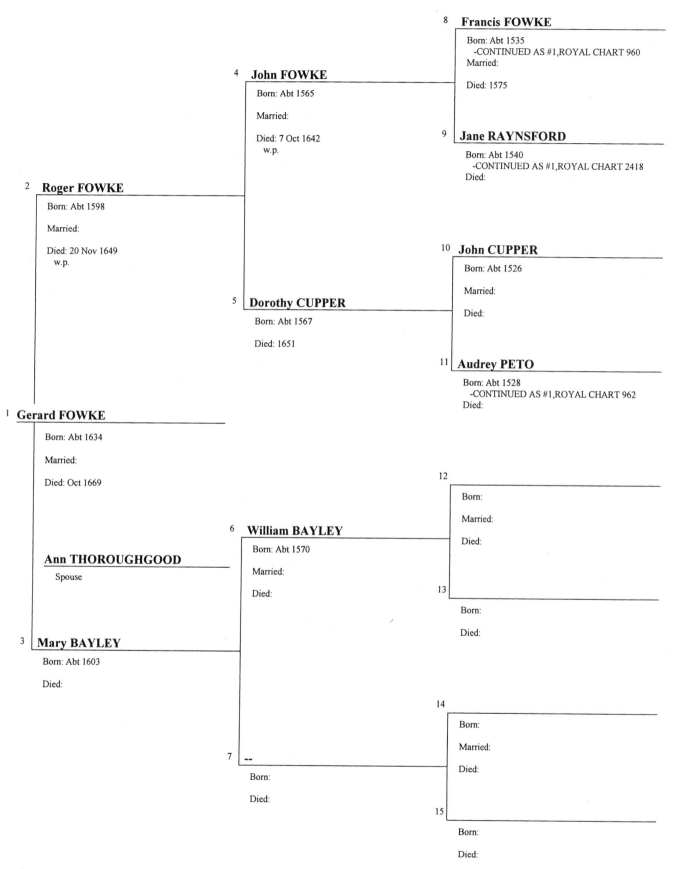

8 **Francis FOWKE**

Born: Abt 1535
   -CONTINUED AS #1,ROYAL CHART 960
Married:

Died: 1575

4 **John FOWKE**

Born: Abt 1565

Married:

Died: 7 Oct 1642
   w.p.

9 **Jane RAYNSFORD**

Born: Abt 1540
   -CONTINUED AS #1,ROYAL CHART 2418
Died:

2 **Roger FOWKE**

Born: Abt 1598

Married:

Died: 20 Nov 1649
   w.p.

10 **John CUPPER**

Born: Abt 1526

Married:

Died:

5 **Dorothy CUPPER**

Born: Abt 1567

Died: 1651

11 **Audrey PETO**

Born: Abt 1528
   -CONTINUED AS #1,ROYAL CHART 962
Died:

1 **Gerard FOWKE**

Born: Abt 1634

Married:

Died: Oct 1669

12

Born:

Married:

Died:

6 **William BAYLEY**

Born: Abt 1570
Married:

Died:

13

Born:

Died:

Ann THOROUGHGOOD

   Spouse

3 **Mary BAYLEY**

Born: Abt 1603

Died:

14

Born:

Married:

Died:

7 --

Born:

Died:

15

Born:

Died:

Sources include: Roberts *500*, pp. 363-364; Consultation with Douglas Richardson; LDS records.

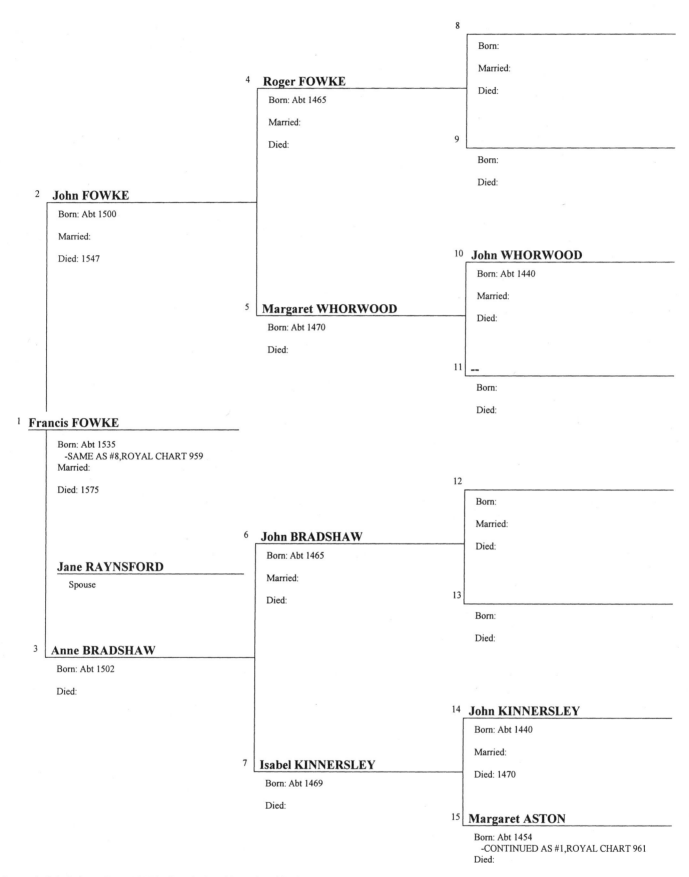

8

Born:

Married:

Died:

4 **Roger FOWKE**

Born: Abt 1465

Married:

Died:

9

Born:

Died:

2 **John FOWKE**

Born: Abt 1500

Married:

Died: 1547

10 **John WHORWOOD**

Born: Abt 1440

Married:

Died:

5 **Margaret WHORWOOD**

Born: Abt 1470

Died:

11 **--**

Born:

Died:

1 **Francis FOWKE**

Born: Abt 1535
-SAME AS #8,ROYAL CHART 959
Married:

Died: 1575

Jane RAYNSFORD

Spouse

12

Born:

Married:

Died:

6 **John BRADSHAW**

Born: Abt 1465

Married:

Died:

13

Born:

Died:

3 **Anne BRADSHAW**

Born: Abt 1502

Died:

14 **John KINNERSLEY**

Born: Abt 1440

Married:

Died: 1470

7 **Isabel KINNERSLEY**

Born: Abt 1469

Died:

15 **Margaret ASTON**

Born: Abt 1454
-CONTINUED AS #1,ROYAL CHART 961
Died:

Sources include: Roberts *500*, pp. 363-364; Consultation with Douglas Richardson.

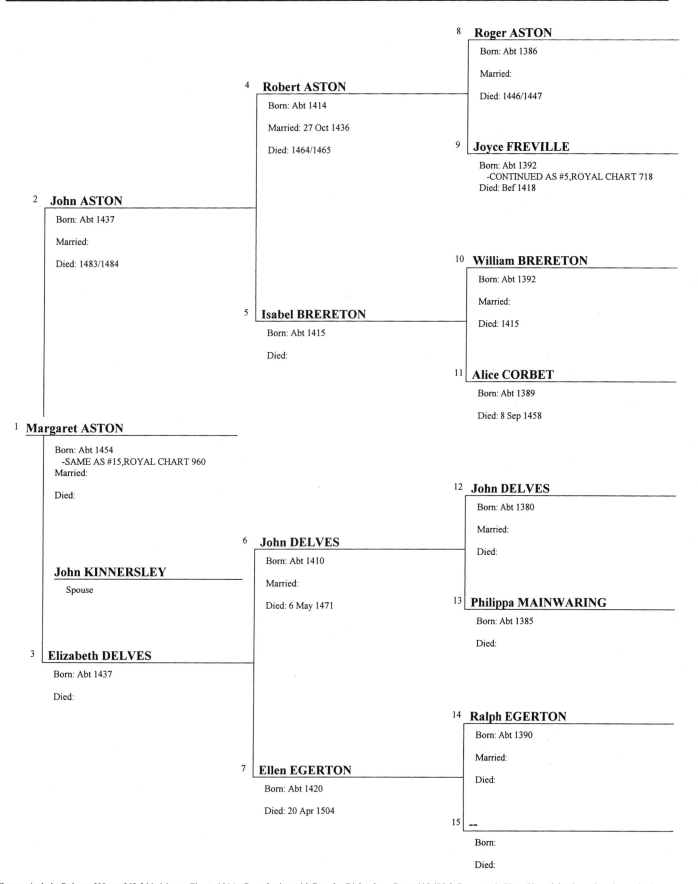

8 Roger ASTON

Born: Abt 1386

Married:

Died: 1446/1447

4 Robert ASTON

Born: Abt 1414

Married: 27 Oct 1436

Died: 1464/1465

9 Joyce FREVILLE

Born: Abt 1392
   -CONTINUED AS #5, ROYAL CHART 718
Died: Bef 1418

2 John ASTON

Born: Abt 1437

Married:

Died: 1483/1484

10 William BRERETON

Born: Abt 1392

Married:

Died: 1415

5 Isabel BRERETON

Born: Abt 1415

Died:

11 Alice CORBET

Born: Abt 1389

Died: 8 Sep 1458

1 Margaret ASTON

Born: Abt 1454
   -SAME AS #15, ROYAL CHART 960
Married:

Died:

12 John DELVES

Born: Abt 1380

Married:

Died:

6 John DELVES

Born: Abt 1410

Married:

Died: 6 May 1471

13 Philippa MAINWARING

Born: Abt 1385

Died:

John KINNERSLEY

Spouse

3 Elizabeth DELVES

Born: Abt 1437

Died:

14 Ralph EGERTON

Born: Abt 1390

Married:

Died:

7 Ellen EGERTON

Born: Abt 1420

Died: 20 Apr 1504

15 --

Born:

Died:

Sources include: Roberts *500*, pp. 363-364; *Magna Charta* 101A; Consultation with Douglas Richardson; Paget 418 (#6 & 7 ancestry). Note: Very tight chronology is required to get the Kinnersley descent that is claimed from the above Aston and Delves lines. More work appears to be needed. The connection may be questionable.

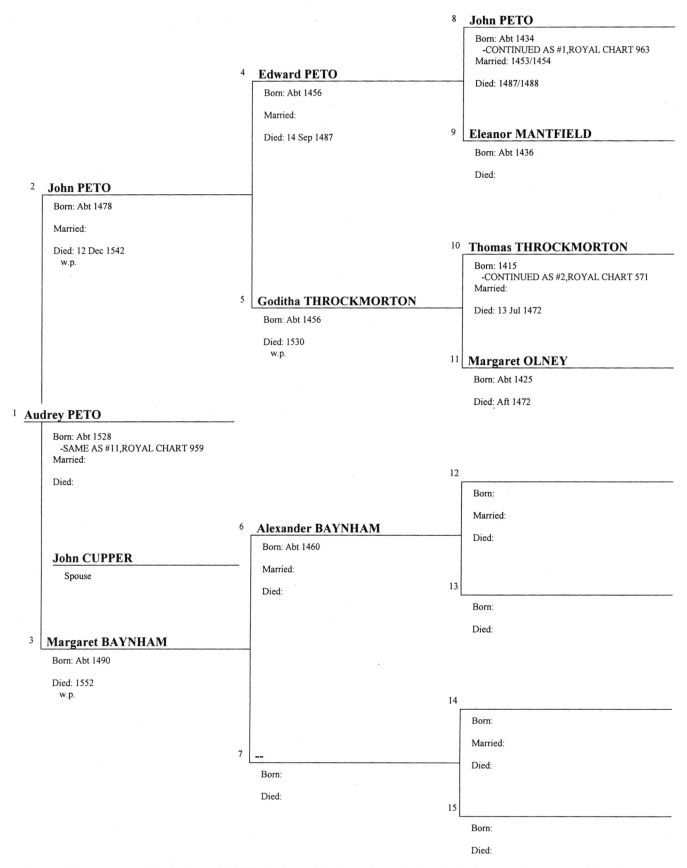

8 John PETO

Born: Abt 1434
-CONTINUED AS #1,ROYAL CHART 963
Married: 1453/1454

Died: 1487/1488

4 Edward PETO

Born: Abt 1456

Married:

Died: 14 Sep 1487

9 Eleanor MANTFIELD

Born: Abt 1436

Died:

2 John PETO

Born: Abt 1478

Married:

Died: 12 Dec 1542
w.p.

10 Thomas THROCKMORTON

Born: 1415
-CONTINUED AS #2,ROYAL CHART 571
Married:

Died: 13 Jul 1472

5 Goditha THROCKMORTON

Born: Abt 1456

Died: 1530
w.p.

11 Margaret OLNEY

Born: Abt 1425

Died: Aft 1472

1 Audrey PETO

Born: Abt 1528
-SAME AS #11,ROYAL CHART 959
Married:

Died:

John CUPPER

Spouse

12

Born:

Married:

Died:

6 Alexander BAYNHAM

Born: Abt 1460

Married:

Died:

13

Born:

Died:

3 Margaret BAYNHAM

Born: Abt 1490

Died: 1552
w.p.

14

Born:

Married:

Died:

7 --

Born:

Died:

15

Born:

Died:

Sources include: Richardson *Magna Carta* (April 2005), pp. 661-662 (Peyto); Faris preliminary baronial manuscript (1998), p. 1244 (Peyto); Roberts *500*, pp. 363-364; *AAP*, p. 218.
Note: Peto is also given as Peyto.

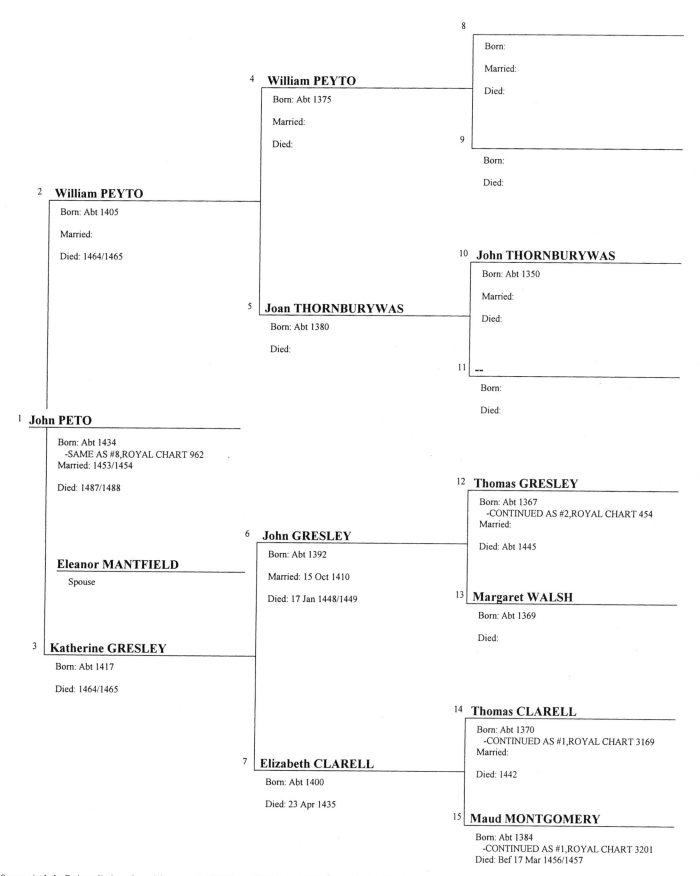

8

Born:

Married:

Died:

4 William PEYTO

Born: Abt 1375

Married:

Died:

9

Born:

Died:

2 William PEYTO

Born: Abt 1405

Married:

Died: 1464/1465

10 John THORNBURYWAS

Born: Abt 1350

Married:

Died:

5 Joan THORNBURYWAS

Born: Abt 1380

Died:

11 --

Born:

Died:

1 John PETO

Born: Abt 1434
  -SAME AS #8,ROYAL CHART 962
Married: 1453/1454

Died: 1487/1488

12 Thomas GRESLEY

Born: Abt 1367
  -CONTINUED AS #2,ROYAL CHART 454
Married:

Died: Abt 1445

6 John GRESLEY

Born: Abt 1392

Married: 15 Oct 1410

Died: 17 Jan 1448/1449

13 Margaret WALSH

Born: Abt 1369

Died:

Eleanor MANTFIELD

Spouse

3 Katherine GRESLEY

Born: Abt 1417

Died: 1464/1465

14 Thomas CLARELL

Born: Abt 1370
  -CONTINUED AS #1,ROYAL CHART 3169
Married:

Died: 1442

7 Elizabeth CLARELL

Born: Abt 1400

Died: 23 Apr 1435

15 Maud MONTGOMERY

Born: Abt 1384
  -CONTINUED AS #1,ROYAL CHART 3201
Died: Bef 17 Mar 1456/1457

Sources include: Faris preliminary baronial manuscript (1998), pp. 1244 (Peyto), 739 (Gresley), 356 (Clarell); Roberts *500*, pp. 363-364; LDS records.

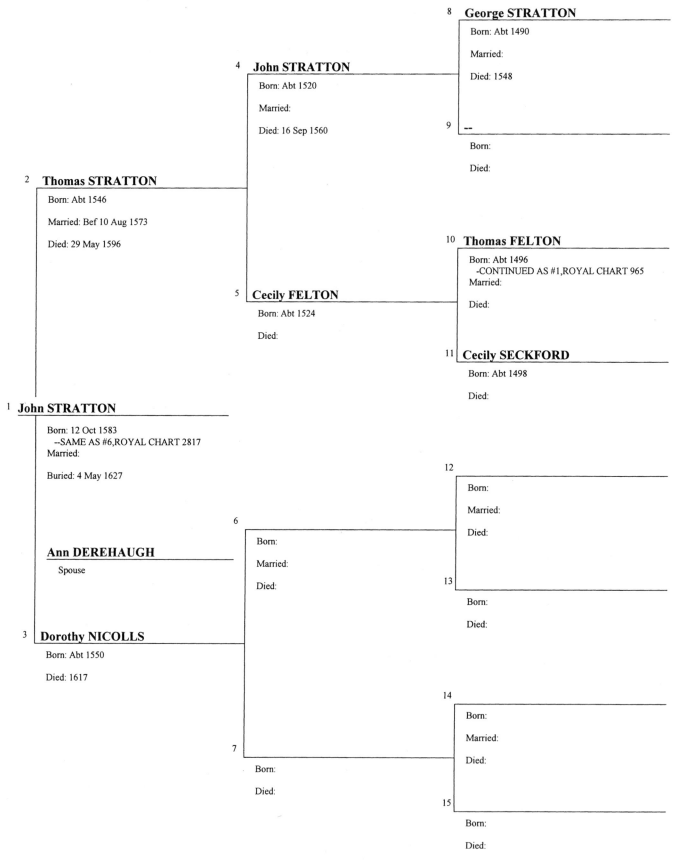

8 **George STRATTON**

Born: Abt 1490

Married:

Died: 1548

4 **John STRATTON**

Born: Abt 1520

Married:

Died: 16 Sep 1560

9 **--**

Born:

Died:

2 **Thomas STRATTON**

Born: Abt 1546

Married: Bef 10 Aug 1573

Died: 29 May 1596

10 **Thomas FELTON**

Born: Abt 1496
  -CONTINUED AS #1,ROYAL CHART 965
Married:

Died:

5 **Cecily FELTON**

Born: Abt 1524

Died:

11 **Cecily SECKFORD**

Born: Abt 1498

Died:

1 **John STRATTON**

Born: 12 Oct 1583
  --SAME AS #6,ROYAL CHART 2817
Married:

Buried: 4 May 1627

12

Born:

Married:

Died:

6

Born:

Married:

Died:

13

Born:

Died:

Ann DEREHAUGH
  Spouse

3 **Dorothy NICOLLS**

Born: Abt 1550

Died: 1617

14

Born:

Married:

Died:

7

Born:

Died:

15

Born:

Died:

Sources include: Roberts *500*, pp. 425-426; LDS records.

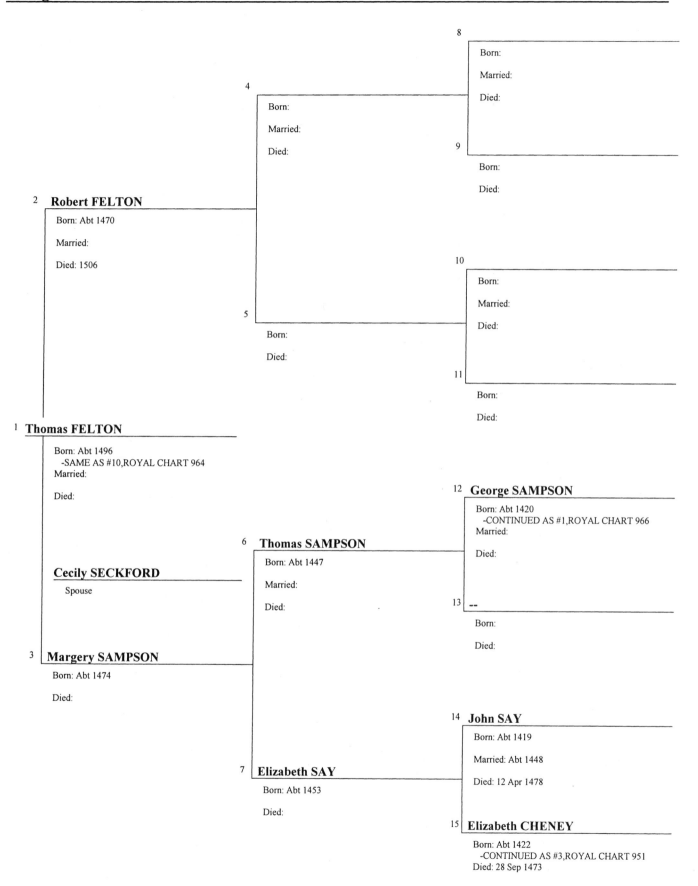

8

Born:

Married:

Died:

4

Born:

Married:

Died:

9

Born:

Died:

2 **Robert FELTON**

Born: Abt 1470

Married:

Died: 1506

10

Born:

Married:

Died:

5

Born:

Died:

11

Born:

Died:

1 **Thomas FELTON**

Born: Abt 1496
-SAME AS #10,ROYAL CHART 964
Married:

Died:

12 **George SAMPSON**

Born: Abt 1420
-CONTINUED AS #1,ROYAL CHART 966
Married:

Died:

6 **Thomas SAMPSON**

Born: Abt 1447

Married:

Died:

13 **--**

Born:

Died:

Cecily SECKFORD

Spouse

3 **Margery SAMPSON**

Born: Abt 1474

Died:

14 **John SAY**

Born: Abt 1419

Married: Abt 1448

Died: 12 Apr 1478

7 **Elizabeth SAY**

Born: Abt 1453

Died:

15 **Elizabeth CHENEY**

Born: Abt 1422
-CONTINUED AS #3,ROYAL CHART 951
Died: 28 Sep 1473

Sources include: Roberts *500*, pp. 425-426; Roberts *600* (2004), pp. 528-529; Consultation with Douglas Richardson (August 2004); Richardson *Plantagenet* (2004), pp. 206-207
Cheyne (#7 identification & ancestry).

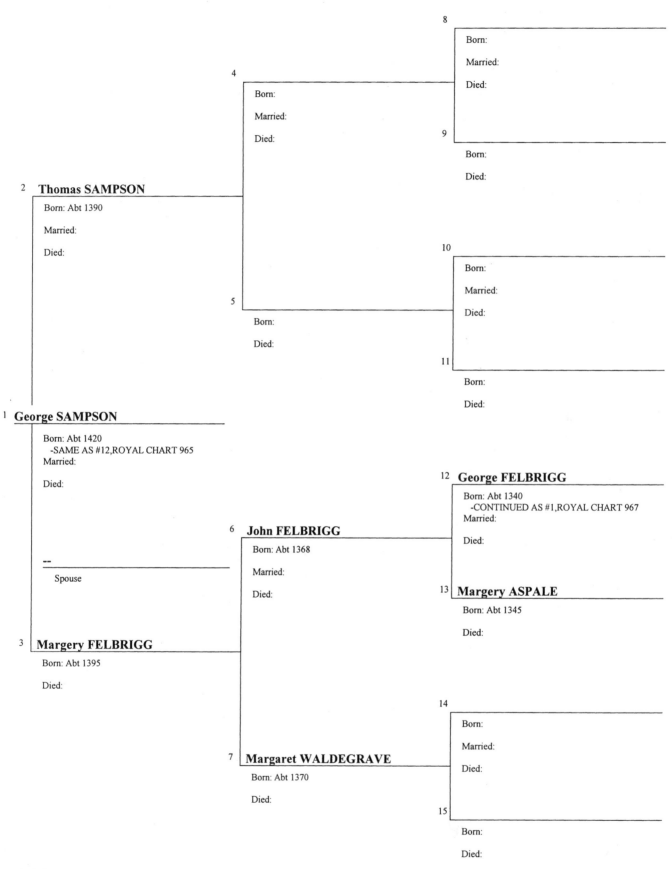

8
Born:
Married:
Died:

4
Born:
Married:
Died:

9
Born:
Died:

2 Thomas SAMPSON
Born: Abt 1390
Married:
Died:

10
Born:
Married:
Died:

5
Born:
Died:

11
Born:
Died:

1 George SAMPSON
Born: Abt 1420
 -SAME AS #12,ROYAL CHART 965
Married:
Died:

12 George FELBRIGG
Born: Abt 1340
 -CONTINUED AS #1,ROYAL CHART 967
Married:
Died:

6 John FELBRIGG
Born: Abt 1368
Married:
Died:

13 Margery ASPALE
Born: Abt 1345
Died:

--
Spouse

3 Margery FELBRIGG
Born: Abt 1395
Died:

14
Born:
Married:
Died:

7 Margaret WALDEGRAVE
Born: Abt 1370
Died:

15
Born:
Died:

Sources include: Roberts *500*, pp. 425-426.

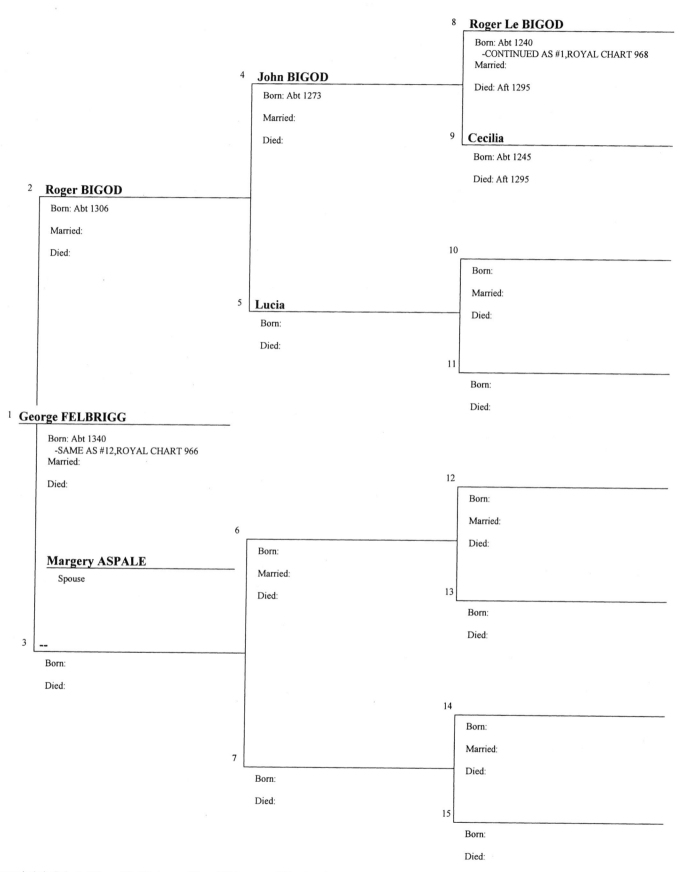

8 Roger Le BIGOD

Born: Abt 1240
-CONTINUED AS #1,ROYAL CHART 968
Married:

Died: Aft 1295

4 John BIGOD

Born: Abt 1273

Married:

Died:

9 Cecilia

Born: Abt 1245

Died: Aft 1295

2 Roger BIGOD

Born: Abt 1306

Married:

Died:

10

Born:

Married:

Died:

5 Lucia

Born:

Died:

11

Born:

Died:

1 George FELBRIGG

Born: Abt 1340
-SAME AS #12,ROYAL CHART 966
Married:

Died:

12

Born:

Married:

Died:

6

Born:

Married:

Died:

13

Born:

Died:

Margery ASPALE

Spouse

3 --

Born:

Died:

14

Born:

Married:

Died:

7

Born:

Died:

15

Born:

Died:

Sources include: Roberts *500*, pp. 425-426; *Ancestral Roots* 232 (ancestry of #8). Note: #2 & 4 -- Bigod alias Felbrigg.

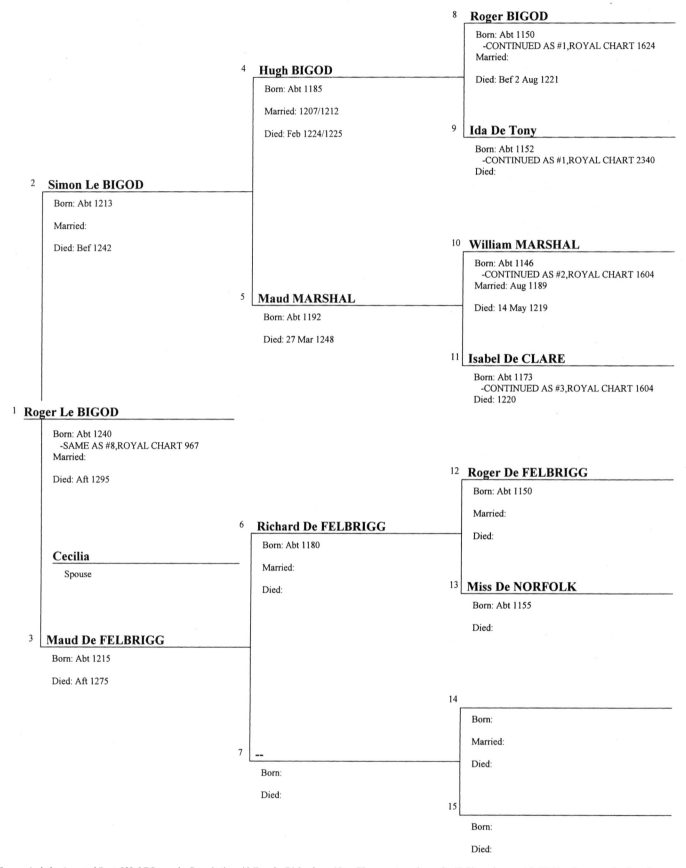

8 **Roger BIGOD**

Born: Abt 1150
-CONTINUED AS #1,ROYAL CHART 1624
Married:

Died: Bef 2 Aug 1221

4 **Hugh BIGOD**

Born: Abt 1185

Married: 1207/1212

Died: Feb 1224/1225

9 **Ida De Tony**

Born: Abt 1152
-CONTINUED AS #1,ROYAL CHART 2340
Died:

2 **Simon Le BIGOD**

Born: Abt 1213

Married:

Died: Bef 1242

10 **William MARSHAL**

Born: Abt 1146
-CONTINUED AS #2,ROYAL CHART 1604
Married: Aug 1189

Died: 14 May 1219

5 **Maud MARSHAL**

Born: Abt 1192

Died: 27 Mar 1248

11 **Isabel De CLARE**

Born: Abt 1173
-CONTINUED AS #3,ROYAL CHART 1604
Died: 1220

1 **Roger Le BIGOD**

Born: Abt 1240
-SAME AS #8,ROYAL CHART 967
Married:

Died: Aft 1295

12 **Roger De FELBRIGG**

Born: Abt 1150

Married:

Died:

6 **Richard De FELBRIGG**

Born: Abt 1180

Married:

Died:

13 **Miss De NORFOLK**

Born: Abt 1155

Died:

Cecilia

Spouse

3 **Maud De FELBRIGG**

Born: Abt 1215

Died: Aft 1275

14

Born:

Married:

Died:

7 **--**

Born:

Died:

15

Born:

Died:

Sources include: *Ancestral Roots* 232; LDS records; Consultation with Douglas Richardson. Note: The parentage shown for #2 Simon is uncertain. Neither Paget nor the *Complete Peerage* claims a son Simon for #4 & 5 Hugh & Maud.

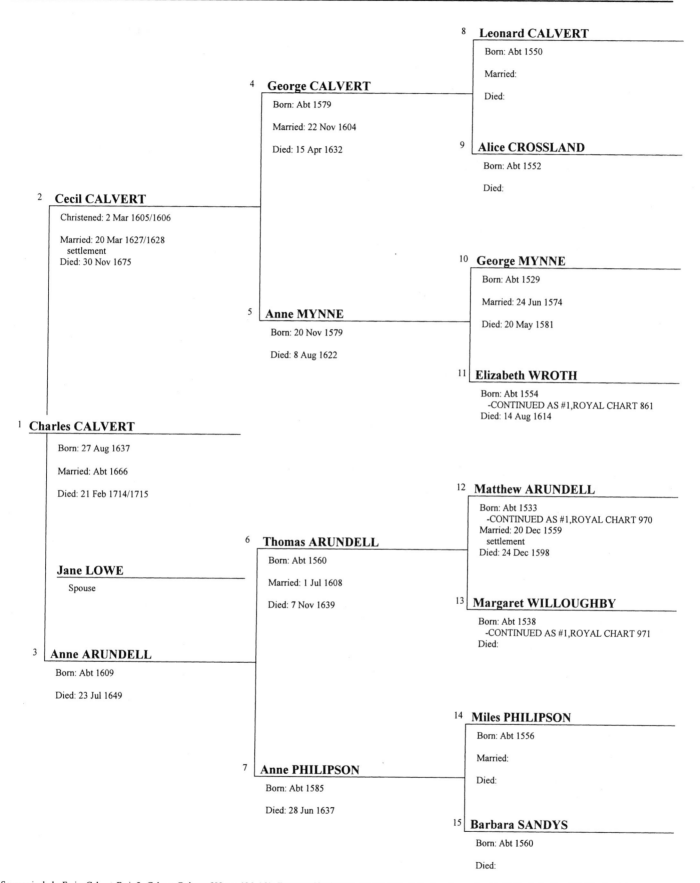

8 Leonard CALVERT
Born: Abt 1550
Married:
Died:

9 Alice CROSSLAND
Born: Abt 1552
Died:

4 George CALVERT
Born: Abt 1579
Married: 22 Nov 1604
Died: 15 Apr 1632

2 Cecil CALVERT
Christened: 2 Mar 1605/1606
Married: 20 Mar 1627/1628
  settlement
Died: 30 Nov 1675

10 George MYNNE
Born: Abt 1529
Married: 24 Jun 1574
Died: 20 May 1581

11 Elizabeth WROTH
Born: Abt 1554
  -CONTINUED AS #1,ROYAL CHART 861
Died: 14 Aug 1614

5 Anne MYNNE
Born: 20 Nov 1579
Died: 8 Aug 1622

1 Charles CALVERT
Born: 27 Aug 1637
Married: Abt 1666
Died: 21 Feb 1714/1715

Jane LOWE
  Spouse

12 Matthew ARUNDELL
Born: Abt 1533
  -CONTINUED AS #1,ROYAL CHART 970
Married: 20 Dec 1559
  settlement
Died: 24 Dec 1598

13 Margaret WILLOUGHBY
Born: Abt 1538
  -CONTINUED AS #1,ROYAL CHART 971
Died:

6 Thomas ARUNDELL
Born: Abt 1560
Married: 1 Jul 1608
Died: 7 Nov 1639

3 Anne ARUNDELL
Born: Abt 1609
Died: 23 Jul 1649

14 Miles PHILIPSON
Born: Abt 1556
Married:
Died:

15 Barbara SANDYS
Born: Abt 1560
Died:

7 Anne PHILIPSON
Born: Abt 1585
Died: 28 Jun 1637

Sources include: Faris--Calvert, Faris 2--Calvert; Roberts *500*, pp. 136, 161; *Emperor Charlemagne* 1:146-147. Note: Jane Lowe (b. abt. 1637), 2nd wife of #1 Charles Calvert, was daughter of Vincent Lowe (b. 1594) & Anne Cavendish (b. abt. 1596), continued chart 1336, #4 & 5. Charles and Jane above had a son Benedict Leonard Calvert (b. 21 Mar 1678/1679) who married Charlotte Lee (b. 13 Mar 1678), daughter of Charlotte Fitzroy (b. 5 Sep 1664; md. Edward Henry Lee), continued under E. Lee in Appendix.

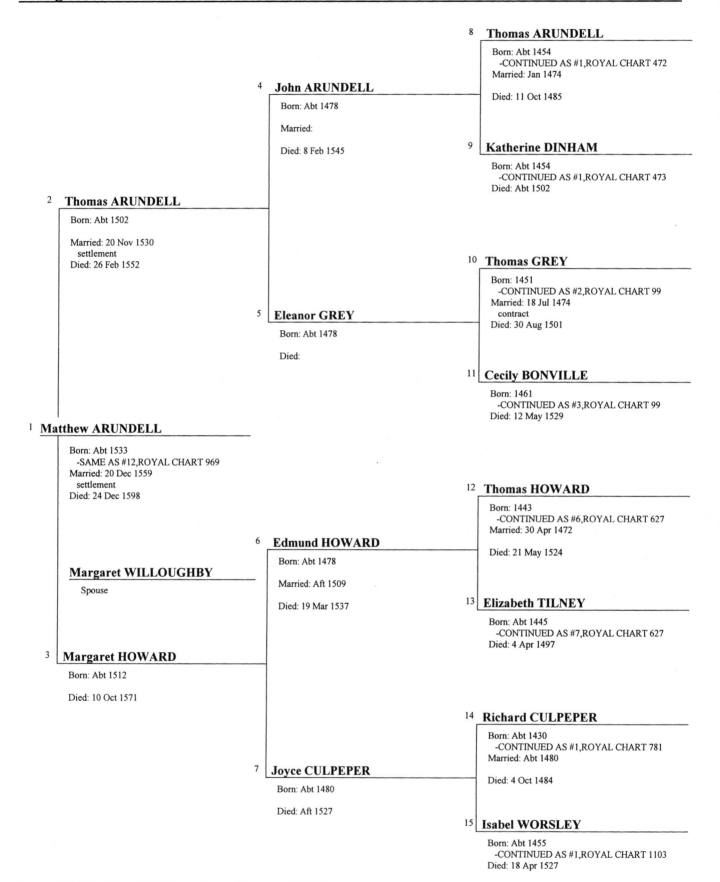

Pedigree Chart

8 **Thomas ARUNDELL**
Born: Abt 1454
-CONTINUED AS #1,ROYAL CHART 472
Married: Jan 1474

Died: 11 Oct 1485

4 **John ARUNDELL**
Born: Abt 1478

Married:

Died: 8 Feb 1545

9 **Katherine DINHAM**
Born: Abt 1454
-CONTINUED AS #1,ROYAL CHART 473
Died: Abt 1502

2 **Thomas ARUNDELL**
Born: Abt 1502

Married: 20 Nov 1530
settlement
Died: 26 Feb 1552

10 **Thomas GREY**
Born: 1451
-CONTINUED AS #2,ROYAL CHART 99
Married: 18 Jul 1474
contract
Died: 30 Aug 1501

5 **Eleanor GREY**
Born: Abt 1478

Died:

11 **Cecily BONVILLE**
Born: 1461
-CONTINUED AS #3,ROYAL CHART 99
Died: 12 May 1529

1 **Matthew ARUNDELL**
Born: Abt 1533
-SAME AS #12,ROYAL CHART 969
Married: 20 Dec 1559
settlement
Died: 24 Dec 1598

12 **Thomas HOWARD**
Born: 1443
-CONTINUED AS #6,ROYAL CHART 627
Married: 30 Apr 1472

Died: 21 May 1524

6 **Edmund HOWARD**
Born: Abt 1478

Married: Aft 1509

Died: 19 Mar 1537

13 **Elizabeth TILNEY**
Born: Abt 1445
-CONTINUED AS #7,ROYAL CHART 627
Died: 4 Apr 1497

Margaret WILLOUGHBY
Spouse

3 **Margaret HOWARD**
Born: Abt 1512

Died: 10 Oct 1571

14 **Richard CULPEPER**
Born: Abt 1430
-CONTINUED AS #1,ROYAL CHART 781
Married: Abt 1480

Died: 4 Oct 1484

7 **Joyce CULPEPER**
Born: Abt 1480

Died: Aft 1527

15 **Isabel WORSLEY**
Born: Abt 1455
-CONTINUED AS #1,ROYAL CHART 1103
Died: 18 Apr 1527

Sources include: Faris--Calvert; Faris 2--Calvert; *Emperor Charlemagne* 1:146-147.

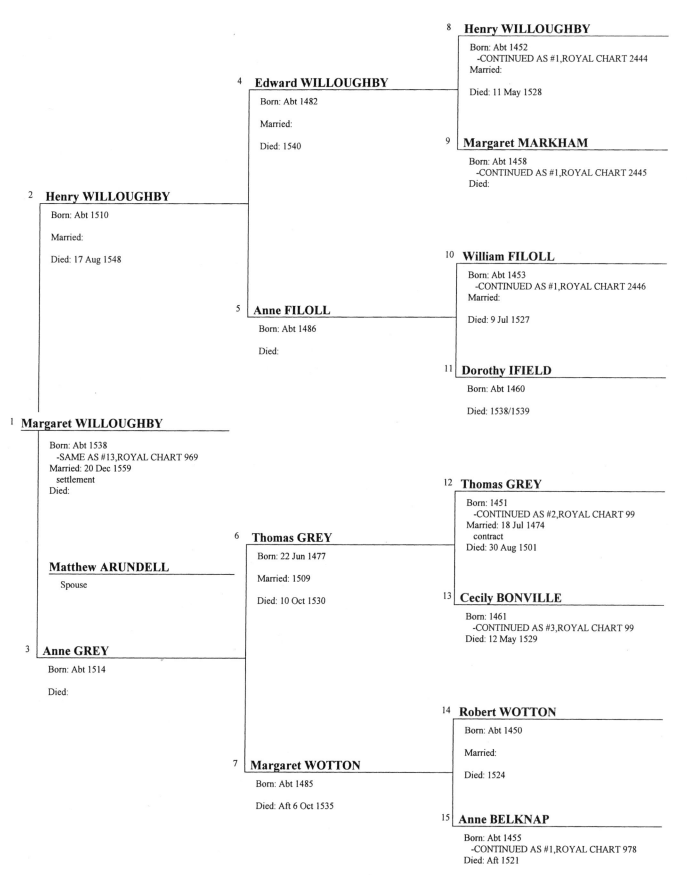

8 Henry WILLOUGHBY

Born: Abt 1452
  -CONTINUED AS #1,ROYAL CHART 2444
Married:

Died: 11 May 1528

4 Edward WILLOUGHBY

Born: Abt 1482

Married:

Died: 1540

9 Margaret MARKHAM

Born: Abt 1458
  -CONTINUED AS #1,ROYAL CHART 2445
Died:

2 Henry WILLOUGHBY

Born: Abt 1510

Married:

Died: 17 Aug 1548

10 William FILOLL

Born: Abt 1453
  -CONTINUED AS #1,ROYAL CHART 2446
Married:

Died: 9 Jul 1527

5 Anne FILOLL

Born: Abt 1486

Died:

11 Dorothy IFIELD

Born: Abt 1460

Died: 1538/1539

1 Margaret WILLOUGHBY

Born: Abt 1538
  -SAME AS #13,ROYAL CHART 969
Married: 20 Dec 1559
  settlement
Died:

Matthew ARUNDELL

Spouse

12 Thomas GREY

Born: 1451
  -CONTINUED AS #2,ROYAL CHART 99
Married: 18 Jul 1474
  contract
Died: 30 Aug 1501

6 Thomas GREY

Born: 22 Jun 1477

Married: 1509

Died: 10 Oct 1530

13 Cecily BONVILLE

Born: 1461
  -CONTINUED AS #3,ROYAL CHART 99
Died: 12 May 1529

3 Anne GREY

Born: Abt 1514

Died:

14 Robert WOTTON

Born: Abt 1450

Married:

Died: 1524

7 Margaret WOTTON

Born: Abt 1485

Died: Aft 6 Oct 1535

15 Anne BELKNAP

Born: Abt 1455
  -CONTINUED AS #1,ROYAL CHART 978
Died: Aft 1521

Sources include: Faris--Grey; Paget 188, 460; Consultation with Douglas Richardson.

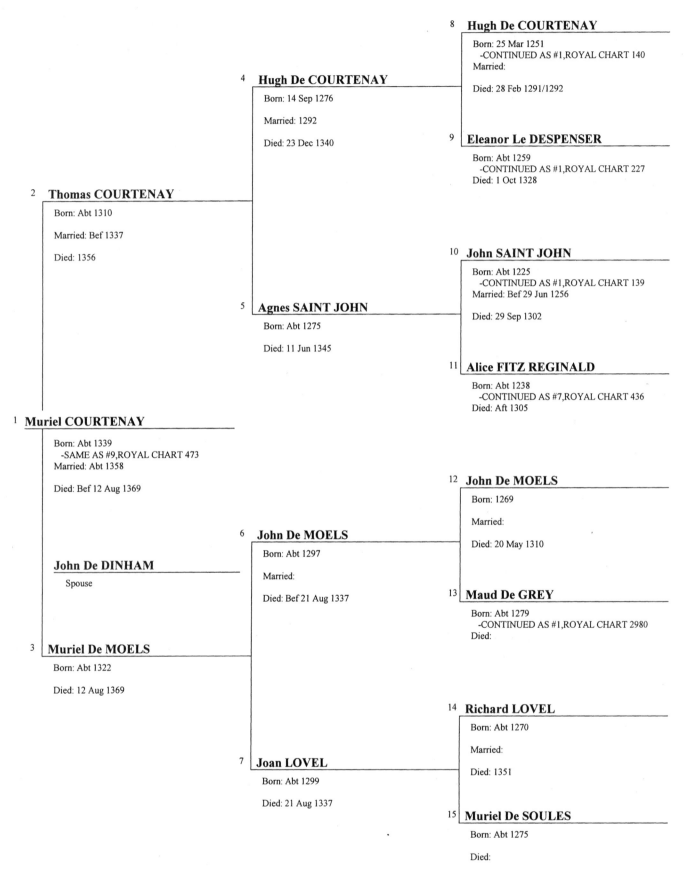

8 Hugh De COURTENAY

Born: 25 Mar 1251
-CONTINUED AS #1,ROYAL CHART 140
Married:

Died: 28 Feb 1291/1292

4 Hugh De COURTENAY

Born: 14 Sep 1276

Married: 1292

Died: 23 Dec 1340

9 Eleanor Le DESPENSER

Born: Abt 1259
-CONTINUED AS #1,ROYAL CHART 227
Died: 1 Oct 1328

2 Thomas COURTENAY

Born: Abt 1310

Married: Bef 1337

Died: 1356

10 John SAINT JOHN

Born: Abt 1225
-CONTINUED AS #1,ROYAL CHART 139
Married: Bef 29 Jun 1256

Died: 29 Sep 1302

5 Agnes SAINT JOHN

Born: Abt 1275

Died: 11 Jun 1345

11 Alice FITZ REGINALD

Born: Abt 1238
-CONTINUED AS #7,ROYAL CHART 436
Died: Aft 1305

1 Muriel COURTENAY

Born: Abt 1339
-SAME AS #9,ROYAL CHART 473
Married: Abt 1358

Died: Bef 12 Aug 1369

12 John De MOELS

Born: 1269

Married:

Died: 20 May 1310

6 John De MOELS

Born: Abt 1297

Married:

Died: Bef 21 Aug 1337

13 Maud De GREY

Born: Abt 1279
-CONTINUED AS #1,ROYAL CHART 2980
Died:

John De DINHAM

Spouse

3 Muriel De MOELS

Born: Abt 1322

Died: 12 Aug 1369

14 Richard LOVEL

Born: Abt 1270

Married:

Died: 1351

7 Joan LOVEL

Born: Abt 1299

Died: 21 Aug 1337

15 Muriel De SOULES

Born: Abt 1275

Died:

Sources include: Richardson *Plantagenet* (2004), pp. 274 (Dinham), 501-502 (Moels); *Ancestral Roots* 214-33; LDS records.

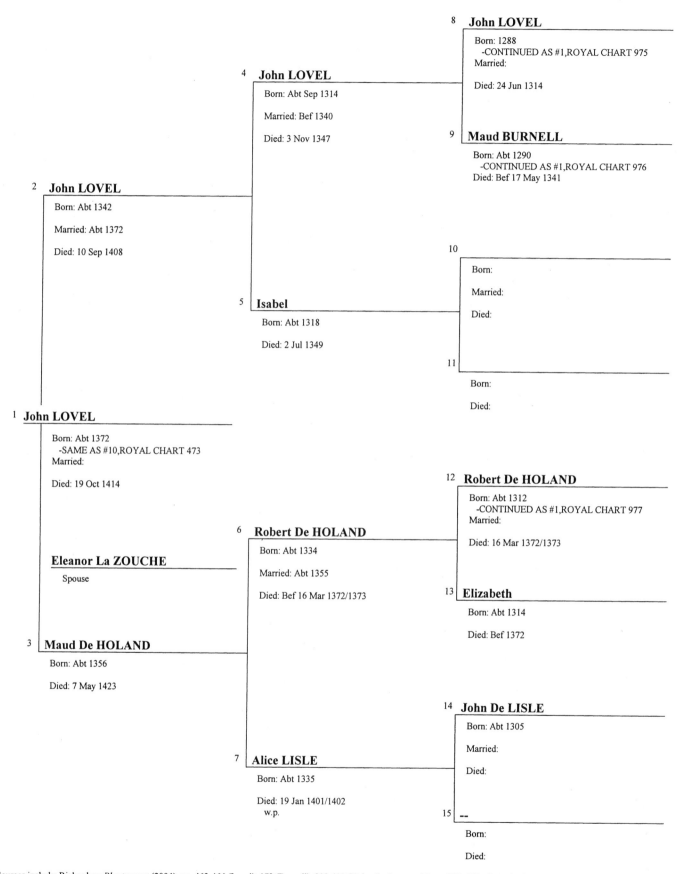

8 John LOVEL

Born: 1288
    -CONTINUED AS #1,ROYAL CHART 975
Married:

Died: 24 Jun 1314

4 John LOVEL

Born: Abt Sep 1314

Married: Bef 1340

Died: 3 Nov 1347

9 Maud BURNELL

Born: Abt 1290
    -CONTINUED AS #1,ROYAL CHART 976
Died: Bef 17 May 1341

2 John LOVEL

Born: Abt 1342

Married: Abt 1372

Died: 10 Sep 1408

10

Born:

Married:

Died:

5 Isabel

Born: Abt 1318

Died: 2 Jul 1349

11

Born:

Died:

1 John LOVEL

Born: Abt 1372
    -SAME AS #10,ROYAL CHART 473
Married:

Died: 19 Oct 1414

12 Robert De HOLAND

Born: Abt 1312
    -CONTINUED AS #1,ROYAL CHART 977
Married:

Died: 16 Mar 1372/1373

6 Robert De HOLAND

Born: Abt 1334

Married: Abt 1355

Died: Bef 16 Mar 1372/1373

13 Elizabeth

Born: Abt 1314

Died: Bef 1372

Eleanor La ZOUCHE

Spouse

3 Maud De HOLAND

Born: Abt 1356

Died: 7 May 1423

14 John De LISLE

Born: Abt 1305

Married:

Died:

7 Alice LISLE

Born: Abt 1335

Died: 19 Jan 1401/1402
w.p.

15 --

Born:

Died:

Sources include: Richardson *Plantagenet* (2004), pp. 463-464 (Lovel), 172 (Burnell), 399-400 (Holand); *Ancestral Roots* 215, 47A; Consultation with Douglas Richardson.

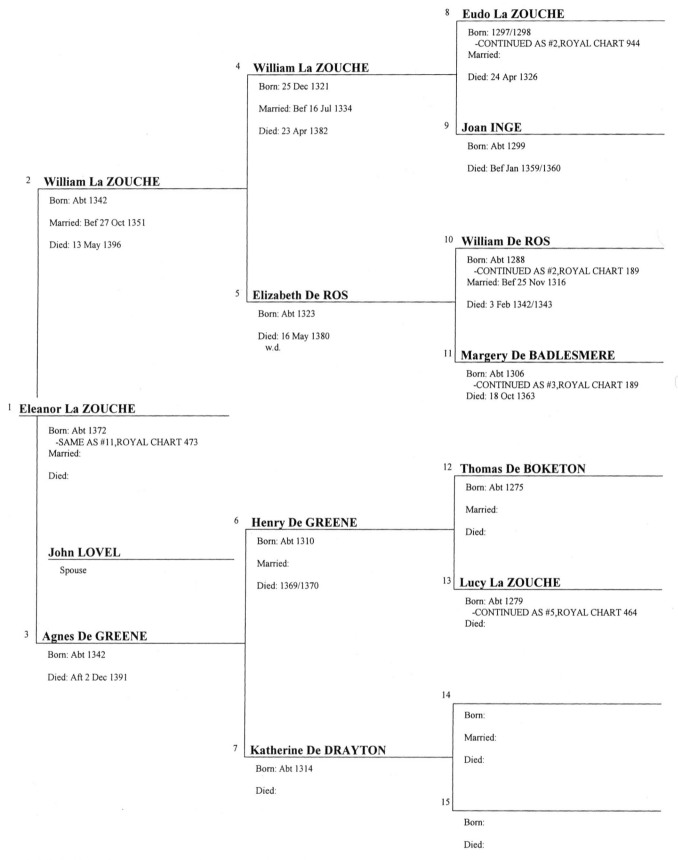

8   **Eudo La ZOUCHE**

Born: 1297/1298
   -CONTINUED AS #2,ROYAL CHART 944
Married:

Died: 24 Apr 1326

4   **William La ZOUCHE**

Born: 25 Dec 1321

Married: Bef 16 Jul 1334

Died: 23 Apr 1382

9   **Joan INGE**

Born: Abt 1299

Died: Bef Jan 1359/1360

2   **William La ZOUCHE**

Born: Abt 1342

Married: Bef 27 Oct 1351

Died: 13 May 1396

10   **William De ROS**

Born: Abt 1288
   -CONTINUED AS #2,ROYAL CHART 189
Married: Bef 25 Nov 1316

Died: 3 Feb 1342/1343

5   **Elizabeth De ROS**

Born: Abt 1323

Died: 16 May 1380
w.d.

11   **Margery De BADLESMERE**

Born: Abt 1306
   -CONTINUED AS #3,ROYAL CHART 189
Died: 18 Oct 1363

1   **Eleanor La ZOUCHE**

Born: Abt 1372
   -SAME AS #11,ROYAL CHART 473
Married:

Died:

12   **Thomas De BOKETON**

Born: Abt 1275

Married:

Died:

6   **Henry De GREENE**

Born: Abt 1310

Married:

Died: 1369/1370

John LOVEL

Spouse

13   **Lucy La ZOUCHE**

Born: Abt 1279
   -CONTINUED AS #5,ROYAL CHART 464
Died:

3   **Agnes De GREENE**

Born: Abt 1342

Died: Aft 2 Dec 1391

14

Born:

Married:

Died:

7   **Katherine De DRAYTON**

Born: Abt 1314

Died:

15

Born:

Died:

Sources include: Faris-Richardson preliminary Magna Carta manuscript (June 2000), pp. 551-552 (Zouche); Faris preliminary baronial manuscript (1998), pp. 731 (Green), 515 (Drayton); *Ancestral Roots* 212; LDS records. Note: The parentage of #7 Katherine is disputed. The cited Magna Carta manuscript gives her as daughter of Simon De Drayton. The baronial manuscript gives her as daughter of John Drayton & Phillipa De Arderne and shows descent from Aubrey II De Vere & Adeliza De Clare (chart 1665, #2 & 3).

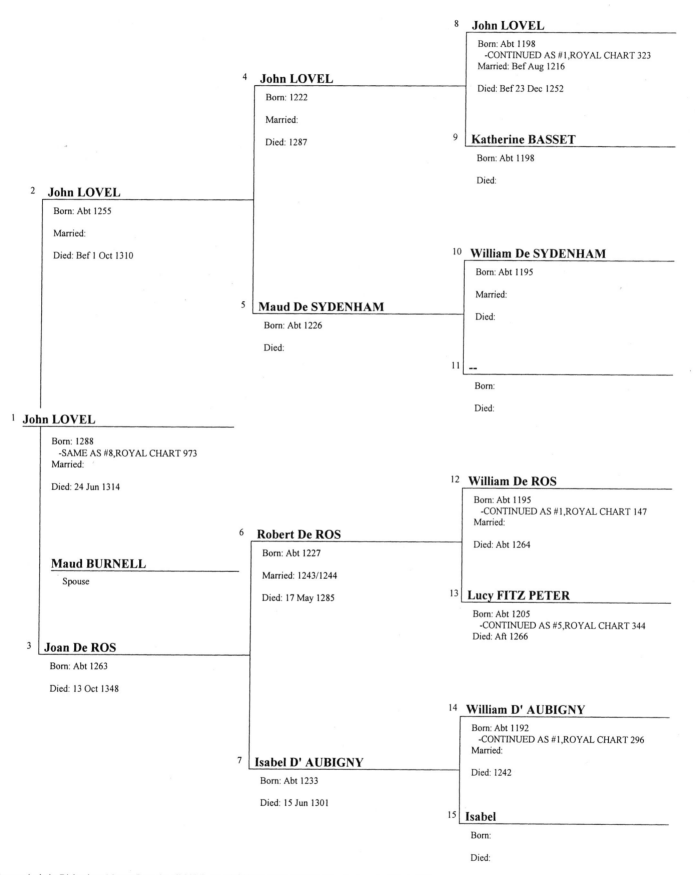

8 John LOVEL

Born: Abt 1198
 -CONTINUED AS #1,ROYAL CHART 323
Married: Bef Aug 1216

Died: Bef 23 Dec 1252

4 John LOVEL

Born: 1222

Married:

Died: 1287

9 Katherine BASSET

Born: Abt 1198

Died:

2 John LOVEL

Born: Abt 1255

Married:

Died: Bef 1 Oct 1310

10 William De SYDENHAM

Born: Abt 1195

Married:

Died:

5 Maud De SYDENHAM

Born: Abt 1226

Died:

11 --

Born:

Died:

1 John LOVEL

Born: 1288
 -SAME AS #8,ROYAL CHART 973
Married:

Died: 24 Jun 1314

12 William De ROS

Born: Abt 1195
 -CONTINUED AS #1,ROYAL CHART 147
Married:

Died: Abt 1264

6 Robert De ROS

Born: Abt 1227

Married: 1243/1244

Died: 17 May 1285

13 Lucy FITZ PETER

Born: Abt 1205
 -CONTINUED AS #5,ROYAL CHART 344
Died: Aft 1266

Maud BURNELL

Spouse

3 Joan De ROS

Born: Abt 1263

Died: 13 Oct 1348

14 William D' AUBIGNY

Born: Abt 1192
 -CONTINUED AS #1,ROYAL CHART 296
Married:

Died: 1242

7 Isabel D' AUBIGNY

Born: Abt 1233

Died: 15 Jun 1301

15 Isabel

Born:

Died:

Sources include: Richardson *Magna Carta* (April 2005), pp. 525-526 (Lovel), 705-706 (Roos); *Ancestral Roots* 215.

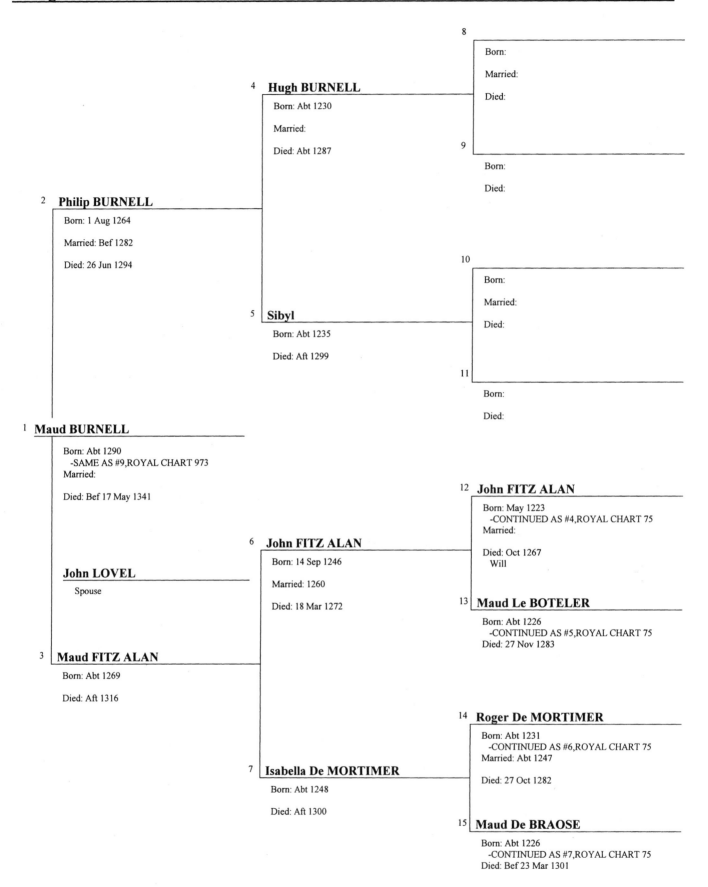

8

Born:

Married:

Died:

4 Hugh BURNELL

Born: Abt 1230

Married:

Died: Abt 1287

9

Born:

Died:

2 Philip BURNELL

Born: 1 Aug 1264

Married: Bef 1282

Died: 26 Jun 1294

10

Born:

Married:

Died:

5 Sibyl

Born: Abt 1235

Died: Aft 1299

11

Born:

Died:

1 Maud BURNELL

Born: Abt 1290
-SAME AS #9,ROYAL CHART 973
Married:

Died: Bef 17 May 1341

12 John FITZ ALAN

Born: May 1223
-CONTINUED AS #4,ROYAL CHART 75
Married:

Died: Oct 1267
Will

6 John FITZ ALAN

Born: 14 Sep 1246

Married: 1260

Died: 18 Mar 1272

13 Maud Le BOTELER

Born: Abt 1226
-CONTINUED AS #5,ROYAL CHART 75
Died: 27 Nov 1283

John LOVEL

Spouse

3 Maud FITZ ALAN

Born: Abt 1269

Died: Aft 1316

14 Roger De MORTIMER

Born: Abt 1231
-CONTINUED AS #6,ROYAL CHART 75
Married: Abt 1247

Died: 27 Oct 1282

7 Isabella De MORTIMER

Born: Abt 1248

Died: Aft 1300

15 Maud De BRAOSE

Born: Abt 1226
-CONTINUED AS #7,ROYAL CHART 75
Died: Bef 23 Mar 1301

Sources include: Richardson *Plantagenet* (2004), pp. 171-172 (Burnell), 314-315 (Fitz Alan), 521 (Mortimer); Faris-Richardson 3 (July 2002 preliminary)--Burnell, Fitz Alan; Faris preliminary baronial manuscript (1998), p. 269 (Burnell); *Ancestral Roots* 215-30, 149.

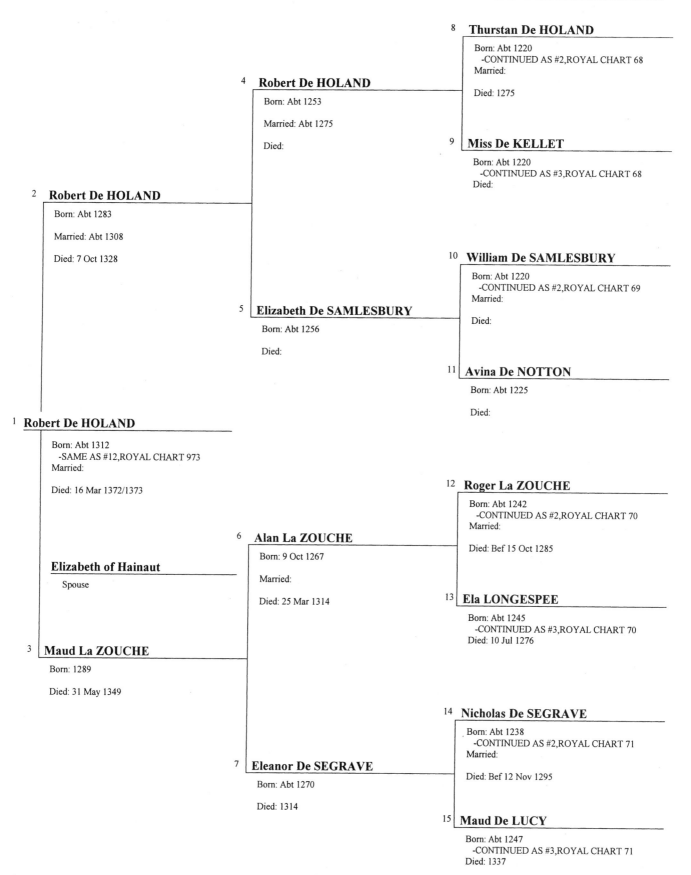

8 Thurstan De HOLAND

Born: Abt 1220
 -CONTINUED AS #2,ROYAL CHART 68
Married:

Died: 1275

4 Robert De HOLAND

Born: Abt 1253

Married: Abt 1275

Died:

9 Miss De KELLET

Born: Abt 1220
 -CONTINUED AS #3,ROYAL CHART 68
Died:

2 Robert De HOLAND

Born: Abt 1283

Married: Abt 1308

Died: 7 Oct 1328

10 William De SAMLESBURY

Born: Abt 1220
 -CONTINUED AS #2,ROYAL CHART 69
Married:

Died:

5 Elizabeth De SAMLESBURY

Born: Abt 1256

Died:

11 Avina De NOTTON

Born: Abt 1225

Died:

1 Robert De HOLAND

Born: Abt 1312
 -SAME AS #12,ROYAL CHART 973
Married:

Died: 16 Mar 1372/1373

12 Roger La ZOUCHE

Born: Abt 1242
 -CONTINUED AS #2,ROYAL CHART 70
Married:

Died: Bef 15 Oct 1285

6 Alan La ZOUCHE

Born: 9 Oct 1267

Married:

Died: 25 Mar 1314

13 Ela LONGESPEE

Born: Abt 1245
 -CONTINUED AS #3,ROYAL CHART 70
Died: 10 Jul 1276

Elizabeth of Hainaut

Spouse

3 Maud La ZOUCHE

Born: 1289

Died: 31 May 1349

14 Nicholas De SEGRAVE

Born: Abt 1238
 -CONTINUED AS #2,ROYAL CHART 71
Married:

Died: Bef 12 Nov 1295

7 Eleanor De SEGRAVE

Born: Abt 1270

Died: 1314

15 Maud De LUCY

Born: Abt 1247
 -CONTINUED AS #3,ROYAL CHART 71
Died: 1337

Sources include: *Ancestral Roots* 47A, 32-30.

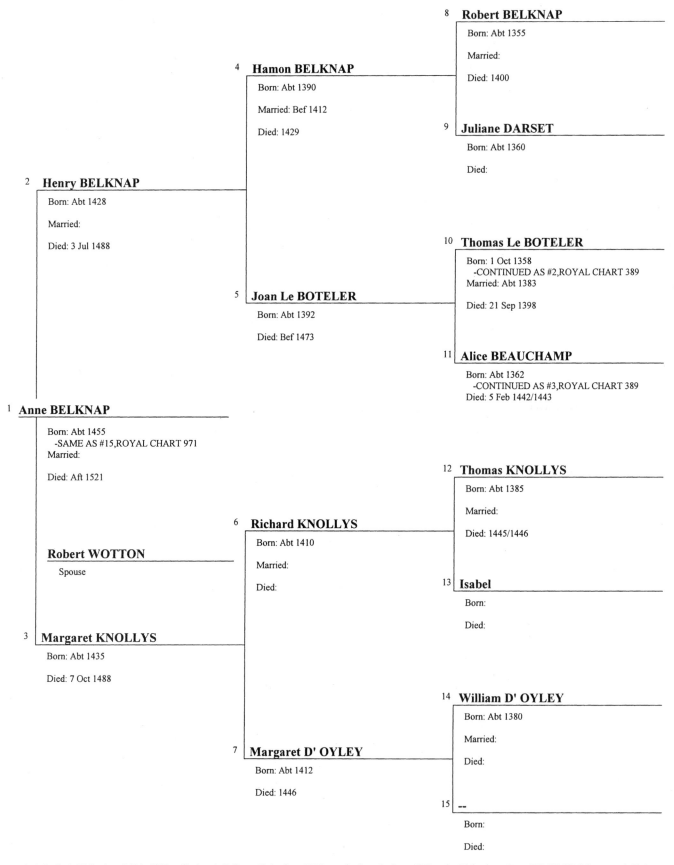

8 **Robert BELKNAP**

Born: Abt 1355

Married:

Died: 1400

4 **Hamon BELKNAP**

Born: Abt 1390

Married: Bef 1412

Died: 1429

9 **Juliane DARSET**

Born: Abt 1360

Died:

2 **Henry BELKNAP**

Born: Abt 1428

Married:

Died: 3 Jul 1488

10 **Thomas Le BOTELER**

Born: 1 Oct 1358
  -CONTINUED AS #2,ROYAL CHART 389
Married: Abt 1383

Died: 21 Sep 1398

5 **Joan Le BOTELER**

Born: Abt 1392

Died: Bef 1473

11 **Alice BEAUCHAMP**

Born: Abt 1362
  -CONTINUED AS #3,ROYAL CHART 389
Died: 5 Feb 1442/1443

1 **Anne BELKNAP**

Born: Abt 1455
  -SAME AS #15,ROYAL CHART 971
Married:

Died: Aft 1521

12 **Thomas KNOLLYS**

Born: Abt 1385

Married:

Died: 1445/1446

6 **Richard KNOLLYS**

Born: Abt 1410

Married:

Died:

13 **Isabel**

Born:

Died:

Robert WOTTON

Spouse

3 **Margaret KNOLLYS**

Born: Abt 1435

Died: 7 Oct 1488

14 **William D' OYLEY**

Born: Abt 1380

Married:

Died:

7 **Margaret D' OYLEY**

Born: Abt 1412

Died: 1446

15 **--**

Born:

Died:

Sources include: Faris-Richardson 3 (July 2002 preliminary)--Belknap; Faris--Grey; LDS records; Consultation with Douglas Richardson; Paget 398-399 (#2 & 3 ancestry); Faris preliminary baronial manuscript (1998), pp. 911-912 Knollys (#3 ancestry).

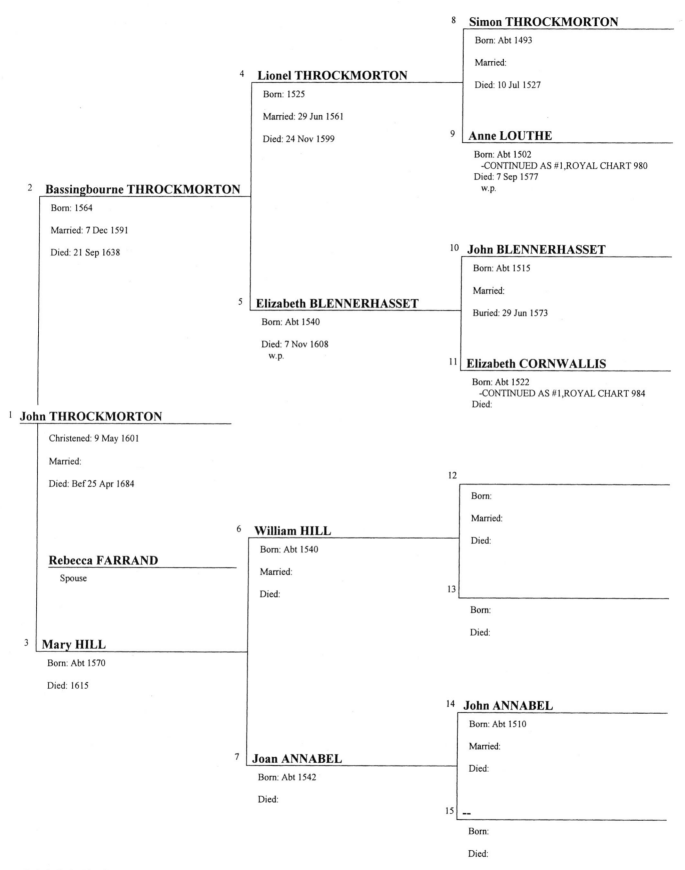

8 Simon THROCKMORTON

Born: Abt 1493

Married:

Died: 10 Jul 1527

4 Lionel THROCKMORTON

Born: 1525

Married: 29 Jun 1561

Died: 24 Nov 1599

9 Anne LOUTHE

Born: Abt 1502
  -CONTINUED AS #1, ROYAL CHART 980
Died: 7 Sep 1577
w.p.

2 Bassingbourne THROCKMORTON

Born: 1564

Married: 7 Dec 1591

Died: 21 Sep 1638

10 John BLENNERHASSET

Born: Abt 1515

Married:

Buried: 29 Jun 1573

5 Elizabeth BLENNERHASSET

Born: Abt 1540

Died: 7 Nov 1608
w.p.

11 Elizabeth CORNWALLIS

Born: Abt 1522
  -CONTINUED AS #1, ROYAL CHART 984
Died:

1 John THROCKMORTON

Christened: 9 May 1601

Married:

Died: Bef 25 Apr 1684

12

Born:

Married:

Died:

6 William HILL

Born: Abt 1540

Married:

Died:

13

Born:

Died:

Rebecca FARRAND

Spouse

3 Mary HILL

Born: Abt 1570

Died: 1615

14 John ANNABEL

Born: Abt 1510

Married:

Died:

7 Joan ANNABEL

Born: Abt 1542

Died:

15 --

Born:

Died:

Sources include: Faris--Throckmorton; *Ancestral Roots* 208; Roberts *AAP*, p. 225; *Blood Royal* 5:1008-12; *TAG* 77:229-234 (wife of #1 John).

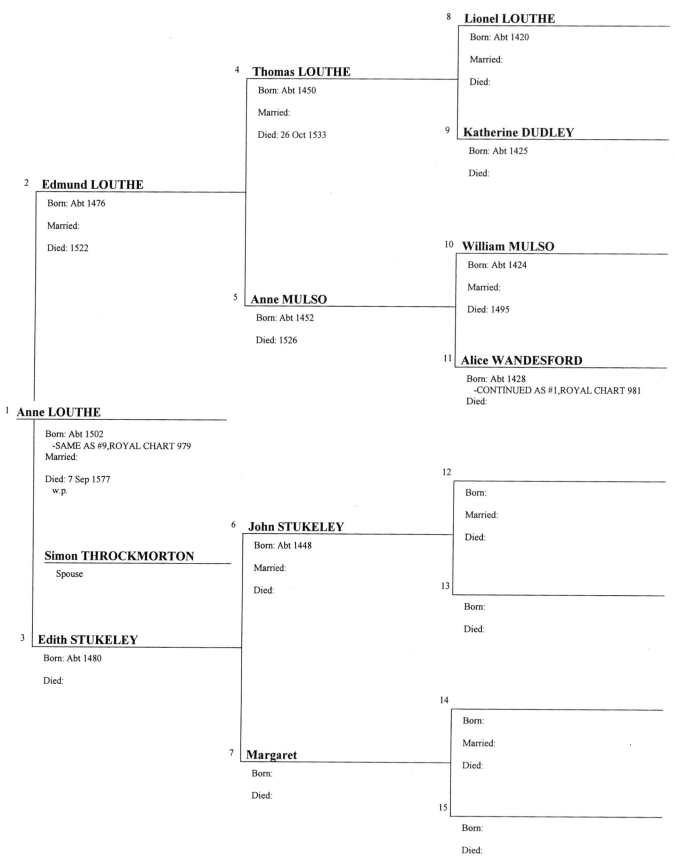

8 **Lionel LOUTHE**
Born: Abt 1420
Married:
Died:

4 **Thomas LOUTHE**
Born: Abt 1450
Married:
Died: 26 Oct 1533

9 **Katherine DUDLEY**
Born: Abt 1425
Died:

2 **Edmund LOUTHE**
Born: Abt 1476
Married:
Died: 1522

10 **William MULSO**
Born: Abt 1424
Married:
Died: 1495

5 **Anne MULSO**
Born: Abt 1452
Died: 1526

11 **Alice WANDESFORD**
Born: Abt 1428
-CONTINUED AS #1,ROYAL CHART 981
Died:

1 **Anne LOUTHE**
Born: Abt 1502
-SAME AS #9,ROYAL CHART 979
Married:
Died: 7 Sep 1577
w.p.

Simon THROCKMORTON
Spouse

12
Born:
Married:
Died:

6 **John STUKELEY**
Born: Abt 1448
Married:
Died:

13
Born:
Died:

3 **Edith STUKELEY**
Born: Abt 1480
Died:

14
Born:
Married:
Died:

7 **Margaret**
Born:
Died:

15
Born:
Died:

Sources include: *Ancestral Roots* 208; *Blood Royal* 5:1011; Consultation with Douglas Richardson.

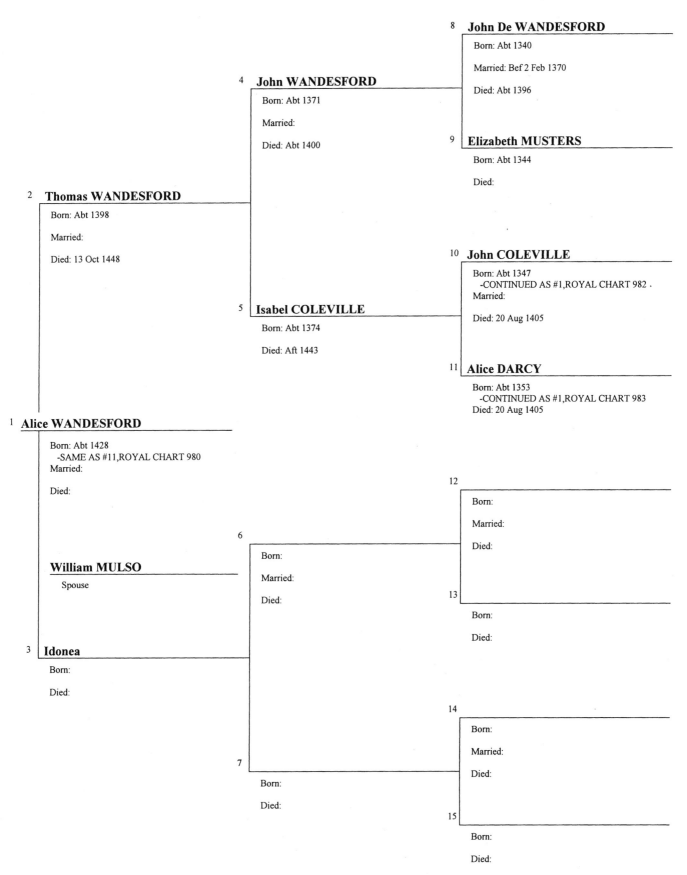

8 **John De WANDESFORD**

Born: Abt 1340

Married: Bef 2 Feb 1370

Died: Abt 1396

4 **John WANDESFORD**

Born: Abt 1371

Married:

Died: Abt 1400

9 **Elizabeth MUSTERS**

Born: Abt 1344

Died:

2 **Thomas WANDESFORD**

Born: Abt 1398

Married:

Died: 13 Oct 1448

10 **John COLEVILLE**

Born: Abt 1347
   -CONTINUED AS #1,ROYAL CHART 982 .
Married:

Died: 20 Aug 1405

5 **Isabel COLEVILLE**

Born: Abt 1374

Died: Aft 1443

11 **Alice DARCY**

Born: Abt 1353
   -CONTINUED AS #1,ROYAL CHART 983
Died: 20 Aug 1405

1 **Alice WANDESFORD**

Born: Abt 1428
   -SAME AS #11,ROYAL CHART 980
Married:

Died:

William MULSO

   Spouse

12

Born:

Married:

Died:

6

Born:

Married:

Died:

13

Born:

Died:

3 **Idonea**

Born:

Died:

14

Born:

Married:

Died:

7

Born:

Died:

15

Born:

Died:

Sources include: *Ancestral Roots* 208; *Magna Charta* 117; LDS records; *Blood Royal* 5:1011.

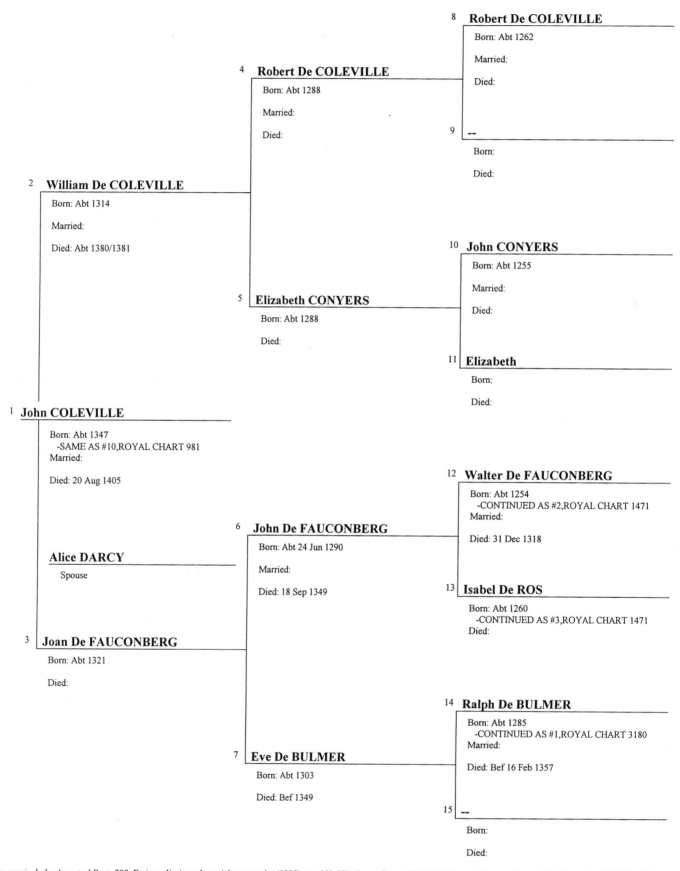

8 **Robert De COLEVILLE**
Born: Abt 1262
Married:
Died:

4 **Robert De COLEVILLE**
Born: Abt 1288
Married:
Died:

9 --
Born:
Died:

2 **William De COLEVILLE**
Born: Abt 1314
Married:
Died: Abt 1380/1381

10 **John CONYERS**
Born: Abt 1255
Married:
Died:

5 **Elizabeth CONYERS**
Born: Abt 1288
Died:

11 **Elizabeth**
Born:
Died:

1 **John COLEVILLE**
Born: Abt 1347
-SAME AS #10,ROYAL CHART 981
Married:
Died: 20 Aug 1405

12 **Walter De FAUCONBERG**
Born: Abt 1254
-CONTINUED AS #2,ROYAL CHART 1471
Married:
Died: 31 Dec 1318

6 **John De FAUCONBERG**
Born: Abt 24 Jun 1290
Married:
Died: 18 Sep 1349

13 **Isabel De ROS**
Born: Abt 1260
-CONTINUED AS #3,ROYAL CHART 1471
Died:

Alice DARCY
Spouse

3 **Joan De FAUCONBERG**
Born: Abt 1321
Died:

14 **Ralph De BULMER**
Born: Abt 1285
-CONTINUED AS #1,ROYAL CHART 3180
Married:
Died: Bef 16 Feb 1357

7 **Eve De BULMER**
Born: Abt 1303
Died: Bef 1349

15 --
Born:
Died:

Sources include: *Ancestral Roots* 208; Faris preliminary baronial manuscript (1998), pp. 569-570 (Fauconberg), 257-258 (Bulmer); *Magna Charta* 117; *Blood Royal* 5:1011; LDS records. Note: #7 Eve is also claimed as daughter of William Bulmer.

2 John DARCY

Born: 1317

Married: Abt 7 Jan 1344/1345

Died: 5 Mar 1355/1356

4 John DARCY

Born: Abt 1275

Married:

Died: 30 May 1347

8 Roger DARCY

Born: Abt 1240
-CONTINUED AS #1,ROYAL CHART 3182
Married:

Died: Bef 12 May 1284

9 Isabel D' ATON

Born: Abt 1250

Died:

5 Emmeline HERON

Born: Abt 1289

Died: Abt 1328

10 Walter HERON

Born: Abt 1260

Married: 27 Oct 1284

Died: Bef 1296

11 Alice De HASTINGS

Born: Abt 1265
-CONTINUED AS #1,ROYAL CHART 3204
Died:

1 Alice DARCY

Born: Abt 1353
-SAME AS #11,ROYAL CHART 981
Married:

Died: 20 Aug 1405

John COLEVILLE

Spouse

3 Elizabeth De MEINILL

Born: 15 Oct 1331

Died: 9 Jul 1368

6 Nicholas De MEINILL

Born: Abt 1303

Married:

Died: Bef 20 Nov 1341

12 Nicholas De MEYNELL

Born: 6 Dec 1274

Married:

Died: 26 Apr 1322

13 Lucy De THWENGE

Born: 24 Mar 1278/1279
-CONTINUED AS #3,ROYAL CHART 3325
Died: 8 Jan 1346/1347

7 Alice De ROS

Born: Abt 1310

Died: Bef 4 Jul 1344

14 William De ROS

Born: Abt 1288
-CONTINUED AS #2,ROYAL CHART 337
Married:

Died: 3 Feb 1342/1343

15 --

Born:

Died:

Sources include: Faris preliminary baronial manuscript (1998), pp. 462-463, 467 (Darcy), 846-847 (Heron); Faris-Richardson preliminary Magna Carta manuscript (June 2000), pp. 162-163 (Darcy); *Ancestral Roots* 208; LDS records.

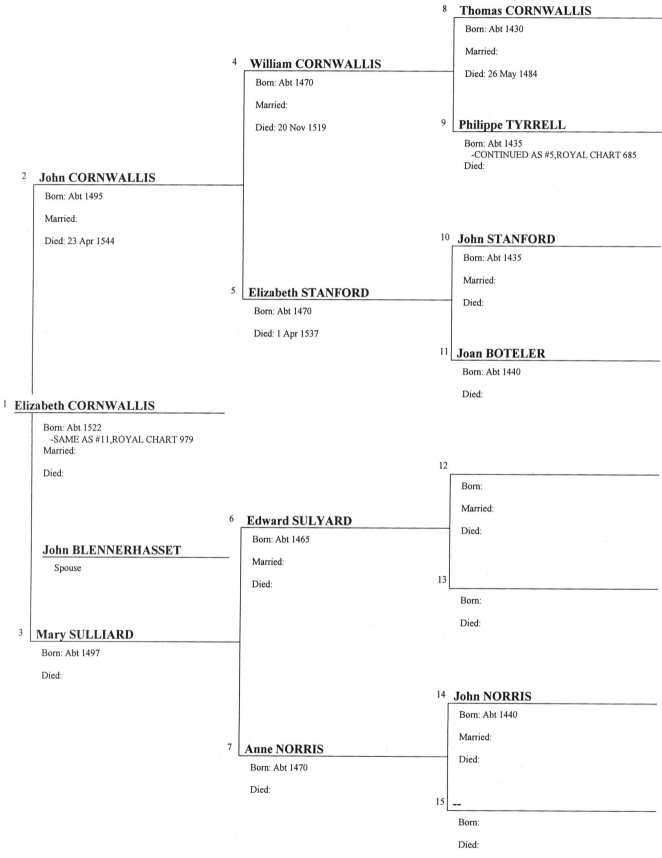

8 **Thomas CORNWALLIS**

Born: Abt 1430

Married:

Died: 26 May 1484

4 **William CORNWALLIS**

Born: Abt 1470

Married:

Died: 20 Nov 1519

9 **Philippe TYRRELL**

Born: Abt 1435
   -CONTINUED AS #5,ROYAL CHART 685
Died:

2 **John CORNWALLIS**

Born: Abt 1495

Married:

Died: 23 Apr 1544

10 **John STANFORD**

Born: Abt 1435

Married:

Died:

5 **Elizabeth STANFORD**

Born: Abt 1470

Died: 1 Apr 1537

11 **Joan BOTELER**

Born: Abt 1440

Died:

1 **Elizabeth CORNWALLIS**

Born: Abt 1522
   -SAME AS #11,ROYAL CHART 979
Married:

Died:

12

Born:

Married:

Died:

6 **Edward SULYARD**

Born: Abt 1465

Married:

Died:

13

Born:

Died:

John BLENNERHASSET

Spouse

3 **Mary SULLIARD**

Born: Abt 1497

Died:

14 **John NORRIS**

Born: Abt 1440

Married:

Died:

7 **Anne NORRIS**

Born: Abt 1470

Died:

15 **--**

Born:

Died:

Sources include: Richardson *Plantagenet* (2004), pp. 711 (Throckmorton), 252-253 (Dade); Faris--Throckmorton, Dade; Faris 2--Dade.

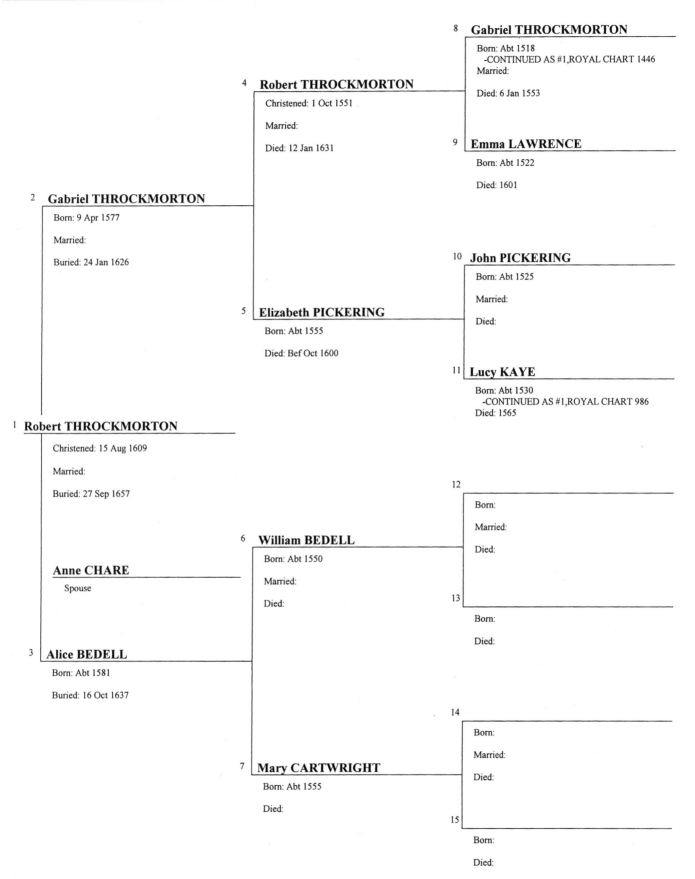

8 Gabriel THROCKMORTON

Born: Abt 1518
  -CONTINUED AS #1,ROYAL CHART 1446
Married:

Died: 6 Jan 1553

4 Robert THROCKMORTON

Christened: 1 Oct 1551

Married:

Died: 12 Jan 1631

9 Emma LAWRENCE

Born: Abt 1522

Died: 1601

2 Gabriel THROCKMORTON

Born: 9 Apr 1577

Married:

Buried: 24 Jan 1626

10 John PICKERING

Born: Abt 1525

Married:

Died:

5 Elizabeth PICKERING

Born: Abt 1555

Died: Bef Oct 1600

11 Lucy KAYE

Born: Abt 1530
  -CONTINUED AS #1,ROYAL CHART 986
Died: 1565

1 Robert THROCKMORTON

Christened: 15 Aug 1609

Married:

Buried: 27 Sep 1657

12

Born:

Married:

Died:

Anne CHARE

Spouse

6 William BEDELL

Born: Abt 1550

Married:

Died:

13

Born:

Died:

3 Alice BEDELL

Born: Abt 1581

Buried: 16 Oct 1637

14

Born:

Married:

Died:

7 Mary CARTWRIGHT

Born: Abt 1555

Died:

15

Born:

Died:

Sources include: *Magna Charta* 8B; Roberts *500*, pp. 340-341; *Blood Royal* 5:124-125; LDS records.

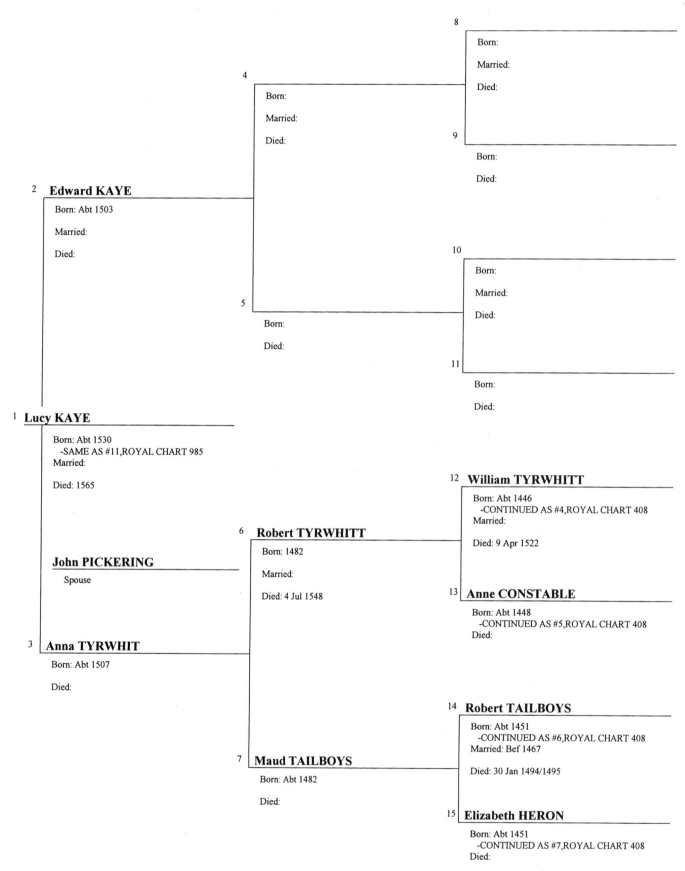

8

Born:

Married:

Died:

4

Born:

Married:

Died:

9

Born:

Died:

2 Edward KAYE

Born: Abt 1503

Married:

Died:

10

Born:

Married:

Died:

5

Born:

Died:

11

Born:

Died:

1 Lucy KAYE

Born: Abt 1530
  -SAME AS #11,ROYAL CHART 985
Married:

Died: 1565

12 William TYRWHITT

Born: Abt 1446
  -CONTINUED AS #4,ROYAL CHART 408
Married:

Died: 9 Apr 1522

6 Robert TYRWHITT

Born: 1482

Married:

Died: 4 Jul 1548

13 Anne CONSTABLE

Born: Abt 1448
  -CONTINUED AS #5,ROYAL CHART 408
Died:

John PICKERING

Spouse

3 Anna TYRWHIT

Born: Abt 1507

Died:

14 Robert TAILBOYS

Born: Abt 1451
  -CONTINUED AS #6,ROYAL CHART 408
Married: Bef 1467

Died: 30 Jan 1494/1495

7 Maud TAILBOYS

Born: Abt 1482

Died:

15 Elizabeth HERON

Born: Abt 1451
  -CONTINUED AS #7,ROYAL CHART 408
Died:

Sources include: Roberts *500*, pp. 340-341; *Blood Royal* 5:124-125. Note: #2 Edward is not the Edward born 11 May 1558, son of John Kaye and Dorothy Mauleverer, as claimed in *Blood Royal* 5:125. John and Dorothy appear on chart 854.

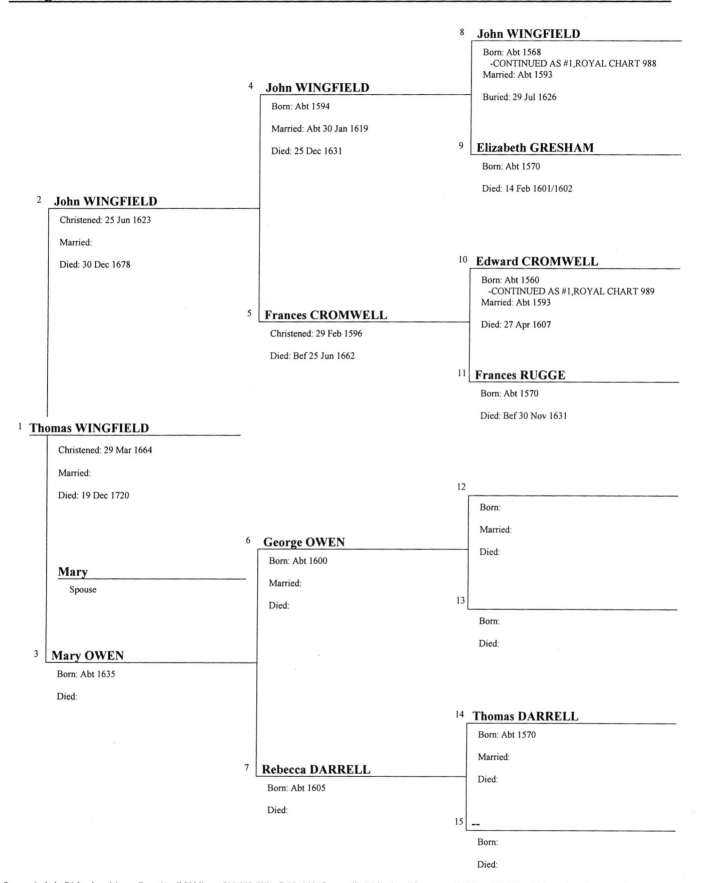

8 John WINGFIELD

Born: Abt 1568
-CONTINUED AS #1,ROYAL CHART 988
Married: Abt 1593

Buried: 29 Jul 1626

4 John WINGFIELD

Born: Abt 1594

Married: Abt 30 Jan 1619

Died: 25 Dec 1631

9 Elizabeth GRESHAM

Born: Abt 1570

Died: 14 Feb 1601/1602

2 John WINGFIELD

Christened: 25 Jun 1623

Married:

Died: 30 Dec 1678

10 Edward CROMWELL

Born: Abt 1560
-CONTINUED AS #1,ROYAL CHART 989
Married: Abt 1593

Died: 27 Apr 1607

5 Frances CROMWELL

Christened: 29 Feb 1596

Died: Bef 25 Jun 1662

11 Frances RUGGE

Born: Abt 1570

Died: Bef 30 Nov 1631

1 Thomas WINGFIELD

Christened: 29 Mar 1664

Married:

Died: 19 Dec 1720

Mary

Spouse

12

Born:

Married:

Died:

6 George OWEN

Born: Abt 1600

Married:

Died:

13

Born:

Died:

3 Mary OWEN

Born: Abt 1635

Died:

14 Thomas DARRELL

Born: Abt 1570

Married:

Died:

7 Rebecca DARRELL

Born: Abt 1605

Died:

15 --

Born:

Died:

Sources include: Richardson *Magna Carta* (April 2005), pp. 901-902 (Wingfield), 248 (Cromwell); Richardson *Plantagenet* (2004), p. 770 (Wingfield); Faris--Wingfield; *Blood Royal* 5:33-40. Note: #1 Thomas had 2 wives, both named Mary --.

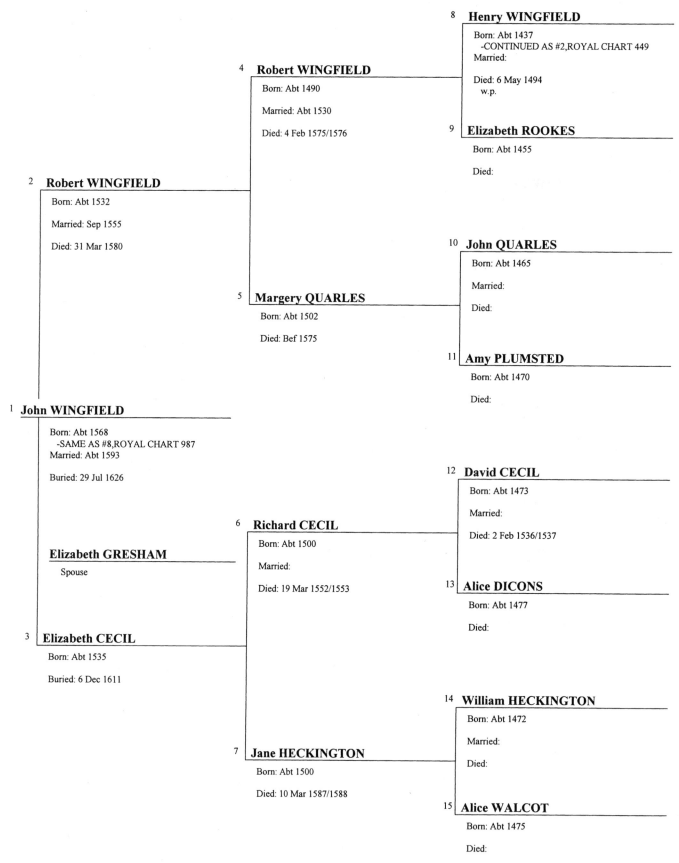

8 **Henry WINGFIELD**

Born: Abt 1437
-CONTINUED AS #2,ROYAL CHART 449
Married:

Died: 6 May 1494
w.p.

4 **Robert WINGFIELD**

Born: Abt 1490

Married: Abt 1530

Died: 4 Feb 1575/1576

9 **Elizabeth ROOKES**

Born: Abt 1455

Died:

2 **Robert WINGFIELD**

Born: Abt 1532

Married: Sep 1555

Died: 31 Mar 1580

10 **John QUARLES**

Born: Abt 1465

Married:

Died:

5 **Margery QUARLES**

Born: Abt 1502

Died: Bef 1575

11 **Amy PLUMSTED**

Born: Abt 1470

Died:

1 **John WINGFIELD**

Born: Abt 1568
-SAME AS #8,ROYAL CHART 987
Married: Abt 1593

Buried: 29 Jul 1626

12 **David CECIL**

Born: Abt 1473

Married:

Died: 2 Feb 1536/1537

6 **Richard CECIL**

Born: Abt 1500

Married:

Died: 19 Mar 1552/1553

Elizabeth GRESHAM

Spouse

13 **Alice DICONS**

Born: Abt 1477

Died:

3 **Elizabeth CECIL**

Born: Abt 1535

Buried: 6 Dec 1611

14 **William HECKINGTON**

Born: Abt 1472

Married:

Died:

7 **Jane HECKINGTON**

Born: Abt 1500

Died: 10 Mar 1587/1588

15 **Alice WALCOT**

Born: Abt 1475

Died:

Sources include: Faris--Letheringham; Faris 2--Wingfield; Faris preliminary baronial manuscript (1998), pp. 305-306 (Cecil).

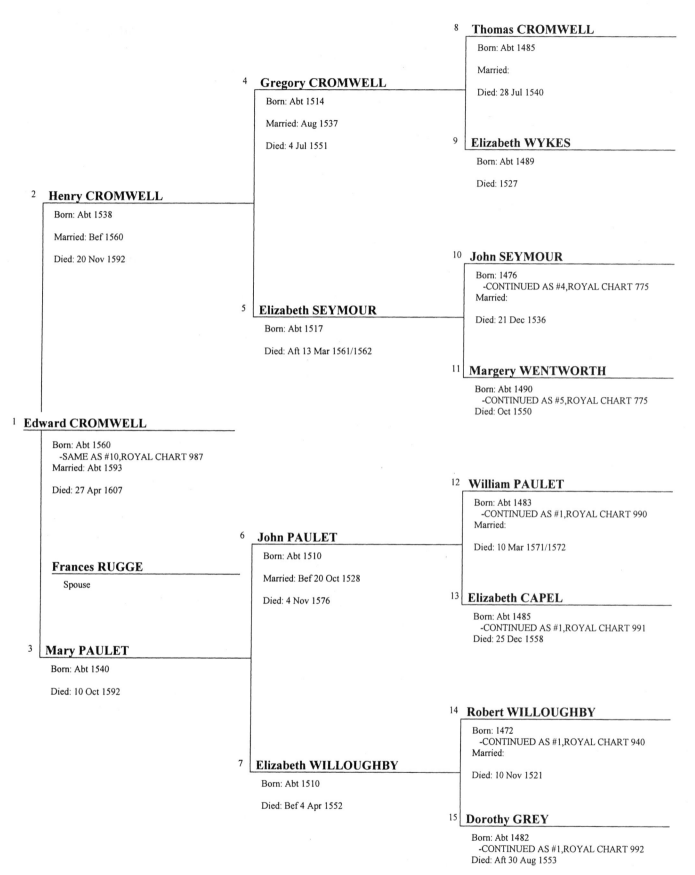

8 Thomas CROMWELL
Born: Abt 1485
Married:
Died: 28 Jul 1540

4 Gregory CROMWELL
Born: Abt 1514
Married: Aug 1537
Died: 4 Jul 1551

9 Elizabeth WYKES
Born: Abt 1489
Died: 1527

2 Henry CROMWELL
Born: Abt 1538
Married: Bef 1560
Died: 20 Nov 1592

10 John SEYMOUR
Born: 1476
 -CONTINUED AS #4,ROYAL CHART 775
Married:
Died: 21 Dec 1536

5 Elizabeth SEYMOUR
Born: Abt 1517
Died: Aft 13 Mar 1561/1562

11 Margery WENTWORTH
Born: Abt 1490
 -CONTINUED AS #5,ROYAL CHART 775
Died: Oct 1550

1 Edward CROMWELL
Born: Abt 1560
 -SAME AS #10,ROYAL CHART 987
Married: Abt 1593
Died: 27 Apr 1607

12 William PAULET
Born: Abt 1483
 -CONTINUED AS #1,ROYAL CHART 990
Married:
Died: 10 Mar 1571/1572

6 John PAULET
Born: Abt 1510
Married: Bef 20 Oct 1528
Died: 4 Nov 1576

13 Elizabeth CAPEL
Born: Abt 1485
 -CONTINUED AS #1,ROYAL CHART 991
Died: 25 Dec 1558

Frances RUGGE
Spouse

3 Mary PAULET
Born: Abt 1540
Died: 10 Oct 1592

14 Robert WILLOUGHBY
Born: 1472
 -CONTINUED AS #1,ROYAL CHART 940
Married:
Died: 10 Nov 1521

7 Elizabeth WILLOUGHBY
Born: Abt 1510
Died: Bef 4 Apr 1552

15 Dorothy GREY
Born: Abt 1482
 -CONTINUED AS #1,ROYAL CHART 992
Died: Aft 30 Aug 1553

Sources include: Richardson *Magna Carta* (April 2005), pp. 247-248 (Cromwell), 653-654 (Paulet); Faris 2--Cromwell, Paulet; Faris--Wingfield, Paulet; Roberts *500*, pp. 219-221.

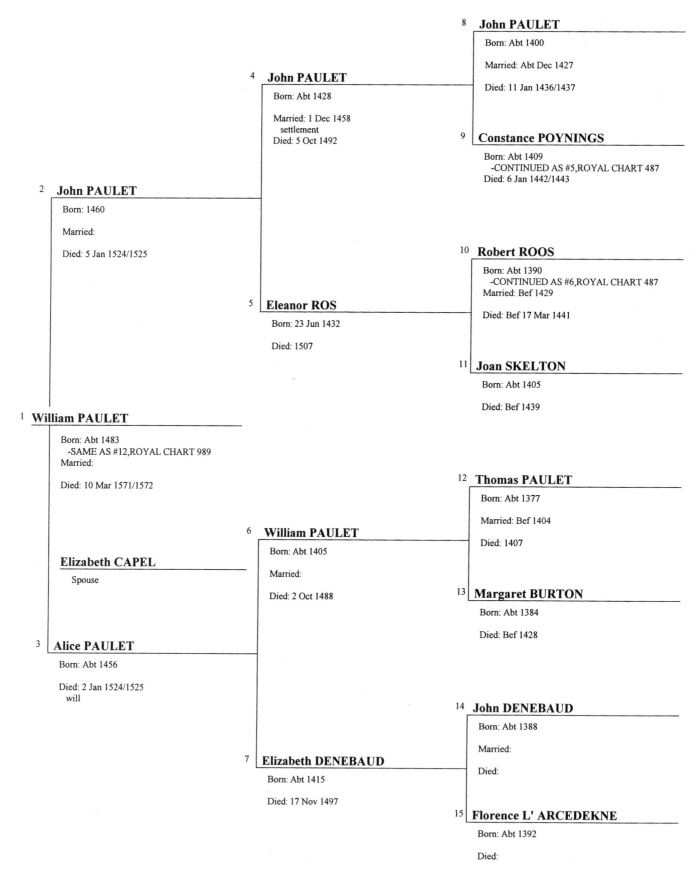

8 John PAULET

Born: Abt 1400

Married: Abt Dec 1427

Died: 11 Jan 1436/1437

4 John PAULET

Born: Abt 1428

Married: 1 Dec 1458
settlement
Died: 5 Oct 1492

9 Constance POYNINGS

Born: Abt 1409
-CONTINUED AS #5,ROYAL CHART 487
Died: 6 Jan 1442/1443

2 John PAULET

Born: 1460

Married:

Died: 5 Jan 1524/1525

10 Robert ROOS

Born: Abt 1390
-CONTINUED AS #6,ROYAL CHART 487
Married: Bef 1429

Died: Bef 17 Mar 1441

5 Eleanor ROS

Born: 23 Jun 1432

Died: 1507

11 Joan SKELTON

Born: Abt 1405

Died: Bef 1439

1 William PAULET

Born: Abt 1483
-SAME AS #12,ROYAL CHART 989
Married:

Died: 10 Mar 1571/1572

Elizabeth CAPEL

Spouse

12 Thomas PAULET

Born: Abt 1377

Married: Bef 1404

Died: 1407

6 William PAULET

Born: Abt 1405

Married:

Died: 2 Oct 1488

13 Margaret BURTON

Born: Abt 1384

Died: Bef 1428

3 Alice PAULET

Born: Abt 1456

Died: 2 Jan 1524/1525
will

14 John DENEBAUD

Born: Abt 1388

Married:

Died:

7 Elizabeth DENEBAUD

Born: Abt 1415

Died: 17 Nov 1497

15 Florence L' ARCEDEKNE

Born: Abt 1392

Died:

Sources include: Faris 2--Paulet; Roberts *500*, pp. 219-221; LDS records.

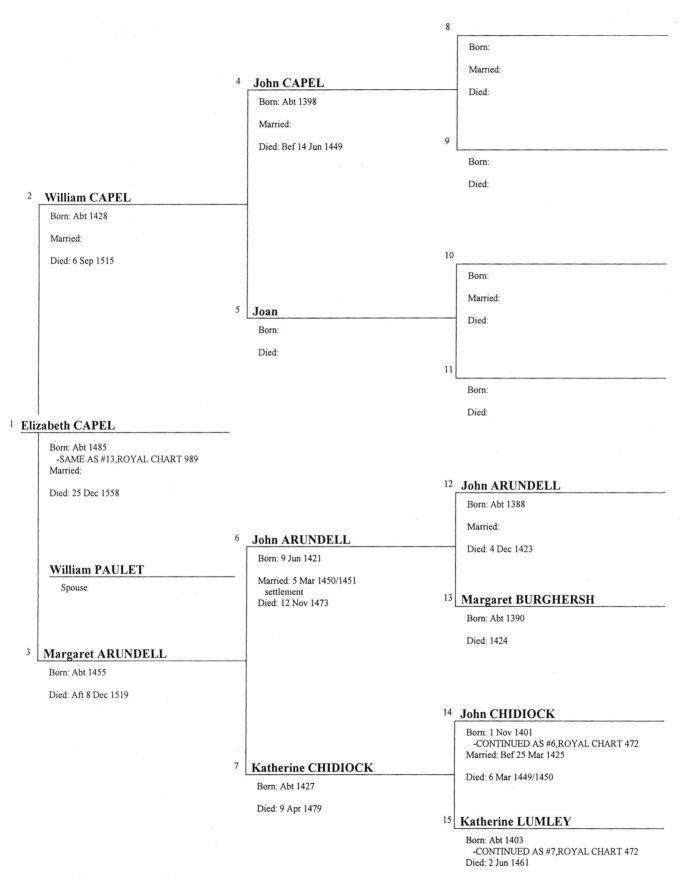

8

Born:

Married:

Died:

4 **John CAPEL**

Born: Abt 1398

Married:

Died: Bef 14 Jun 1449

9

Born:

Died:

2 **William CAPEL**

Born: Abt 1428

Married:

Died: 6 Sep 1515

10

Born:

Married:

Died:

5 **Joan**

Born:

Died:

11

Born:

Died:

1 **Elizabeth CAPEL**

Born: Abt 1485
  -SAME AS #13,ROYAL CHART 989
Married:

Died: 25 Dec 1558

12 **John ARUNDELL**

Born: Abt 1388

Married:

Died: 4 Dec 1423

6 **John ARUNDELL**

Born: 9 Jun 1421

Married: 5 Mar 1450/1451
  settlement
Died: 12 Nov 1473

13 **Margaret BURGHERSH**

Born: Abt 1390

Died: 1424

William PAULET

Spouse

3 **Margaret ARUNDELL**

Born: Abt 1455

Died: Aft 8 Dec 1519

14 **John CHIDIOCK**

Born: 1 Nov 1401
  -CONTINUED AS #6,ROYAL CHART 472
Married: Bef 25 Mar 1425

Died: 6 Mar 1449/1450

7 **Katherine CHIDIOCK**

Born: Abt 1427

Died: 9 Apr 1479

15 **Katherine LUMLEY**

Born: Abt 1403
  -CONTINUED AS #7,ROYAL CHART 472
Died: 2 Jun 1461

Sources include: Faris 2--Paulet 6; Faris--Paulet 5; LDS records; Roberts *500*, pp. 354-355 (ancestry of #3).

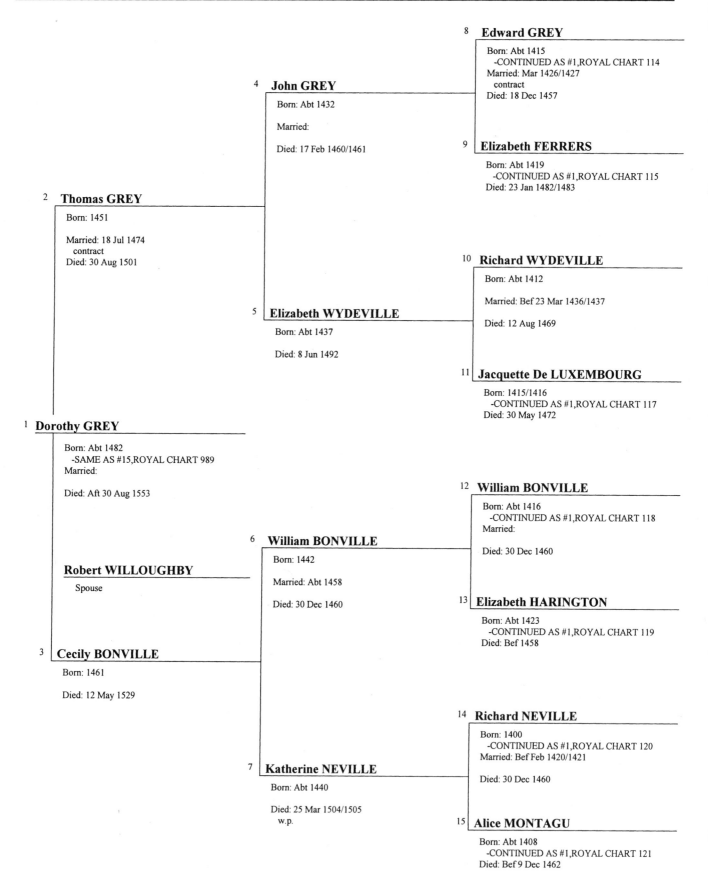

8 Edward GREY
Born: Abt 1415
-CONTINUED AS #1,ROYAL CHART 114
Married: Mar 1426/1427
contract
Died: 18 Dec 1457

4 John GREY
Born: Abt 1432
Married:
Died: 17 Feb 1460/1461

9 Elizabeth FERRERS
Born: Abt 1419
-CONTINUED AS #1,ROYAL CHART 115
Died: 23 Jan 1482/1483

2 Thomas GREY
Born: 1451
Married: 18 Jul 1474
contract
Died: 30 Aug 1501

10 Richard WYDEVILLE
Born: Abt 1412
Married: Bef 23 Mar 1436/1437
Died: 12 Aug 1469

5 Elizabeth WYDEVILLE
Born: Abt 1437
Died: 8 Jun 1492

11 Jacquette De LUXEMBOURG
Born: 1415/1416
-CONTINUED AS #1,ROYAL CHART 117
Died: 30 May 1472

1 Dorothy GREY
Born: Abt 1482
-SAME AS #15,ROYAL CHART 989
Married:
Died: Aft 30 Aug 1553

Robert WILLOUGHBY
Spouse

12 William BONVILLE
Born: Abt 1416
-CONTINUED AS #1,ROYAL CHART 118
Married:
Died: 30 Dec 1460

6 William BONVILLE
Born: 1442
Married: Abt 1458
Died: 30 Dec 1460

13 Elizabeth HARINGTON
Born: Abt 1423
-CONTINUED AS #1,ROYAL CHART 119
Died: Bef 1458

3 Cecily BONVILLE
Born: 1461
Died: 12 May 1529

14 Richard NEVILLE
Born: 1400
-CONTINUED AS #1,ROYAL CHART 120
Married: Bef Feb 1420/1421
Died: 30 Dec 1460

7 Katherine NEVILLE
Born: Abt 1440
Died: 25 Mar 1504/1505
w.p.

15 Alice MONTAGU
Born: Abt 1408
-CONTINUED AS #1,ROYAL CHART 121
Died: Bef 9 Dec 1462

Sources include: Faris--Paulet, Grey.

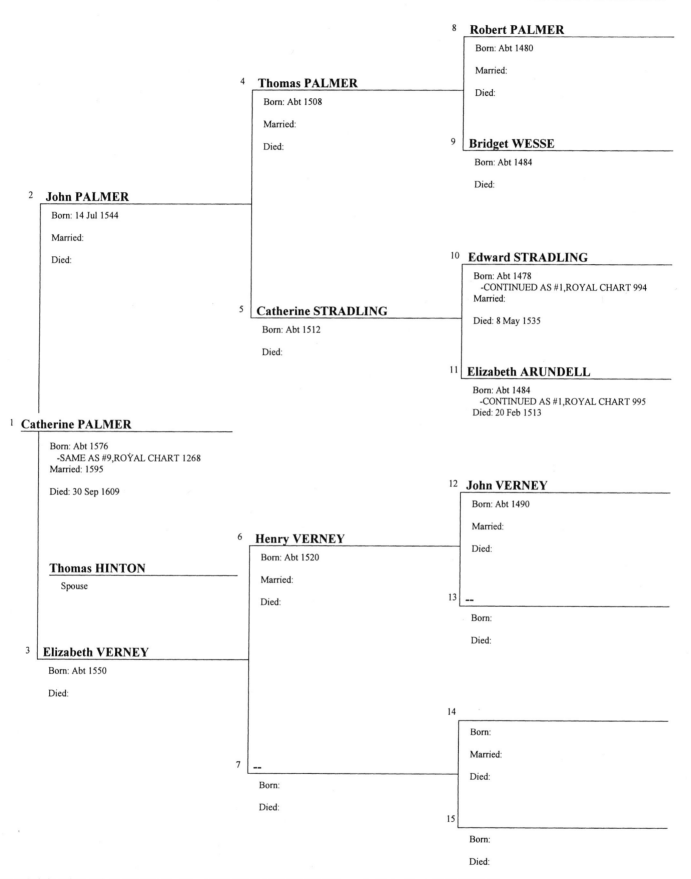

8 **Robert PALMER**

Born: Abt 1480

Married:

Died:

4 **Thomas PALMER**

Born: Abt 1508

Married:

Died:

9 **Bridget WESSE**

Born: Abt 1484

Died:

2 **John PALMER**

Born: 14 Jul 1544

Married:

Died:

10 **Edward STRADLING**

Born: Abt 1478
  -CONTINUED AS #1,ROYAL CHART 994
Married:

Died: 8 May 1535

5 **Catherine STRADLING**

Born: Abt 1512

Died:

11 **Elizabeth ARUNDELL**

Born: Abt 1484
  -CONTINUED AS #1,ROYAL CHART 995
Died: 20 Feb 1513

1 **Catherine PALMER**

Born: Abt 1576
  -SAME AS #9,ROYAL CHART 1268
Married: 1595

Died: 30 Sep 1609

Thomas HINTON

Spouse

12 **John VERNEY**

Born: Abt 1490

Married:

Died:

6 **Henry VERNEY**

Born: Abt 1520

Married:

Died:

13 **--**

Born:

Died:

3 **Elizabeth VERNEY**

Born: Abt 1550

Died:

14

Born:

Married:

Died:

7 **--**

Born:

Died:

15

Born:

Died:

Sources include: Roberts *500*, pp. 134-135; *Blood Royal* 5:237-238, 368-369, 177-178; LDS records; *Magna Charta* 27-12 (#10 & 11).

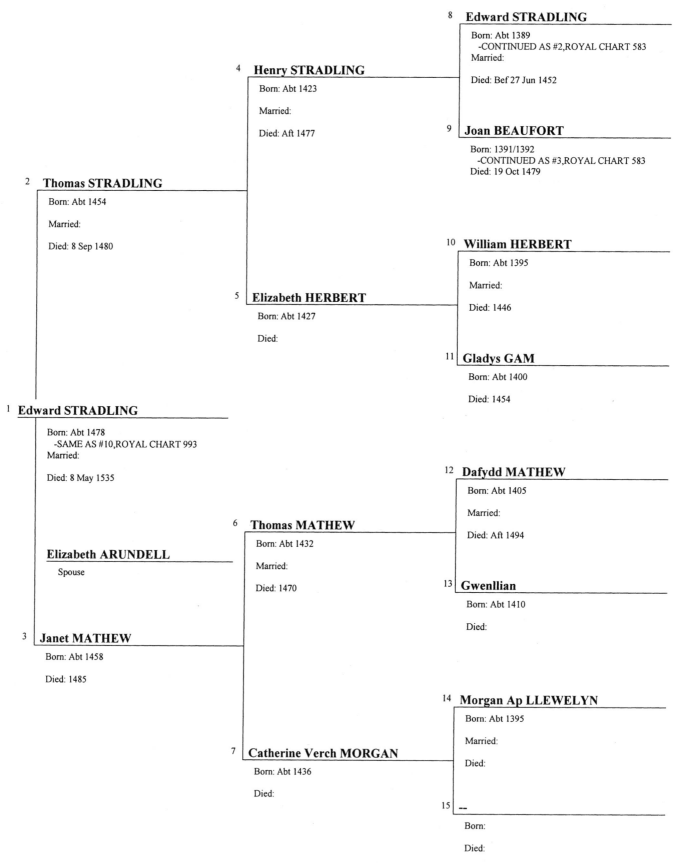

8 Edward STRADLING
Born: Abt 1389
  -CONTINUED AS #2,ROYAL CHART 583
Married:

Died: Bef 27 Jun 1452

4 Henry STRADLING
Born: Abt 1423

Married:

Died: Aft 1477

9 Joan BEAUFORT
Born: 1391/1392
  -CONTINUED AS #3,ROYAL CHART 583
Died: 19 Oct 1479

2 Thomas STRADLING
Born: Abt 1454

Married:

Died: 8 Sep 1480

10 William HERBERT
Born: Abt 1395

Married:

Died: 1446

5 Elizabeth HERBERT
Born: Abt 1427

Died:

11 Gladys GAM
Born: Abt 1400

Died: 1454

1 Edward STRADLING
Born: Abt 1478
  -SAME AS #10,ROYAL CHART 993
Married:

Died: 8 May 1535

12 Dafydd MATHEW
Born: Abt 1405

Married:

Died: Aft 1494

6 Thomas MATHEW
Born: Abt 1432

Married:

Died: 1470

13 Gwenllian
Born: Abt 1410

Died:

Elizabeth ARUNDELL
Spouse

3 Janet MATHEW
Born: Abt 1458

Died: 1485

14 Morgan Ap LLEWELYN
Born: Abt 1395

Married:

Died:

7 Catherine Verch MORGAN
Born: Abt 1436

Died:

15 --
Born:

Died:

Sources include: Roberts *500*, pp. 134-135; LDS records.

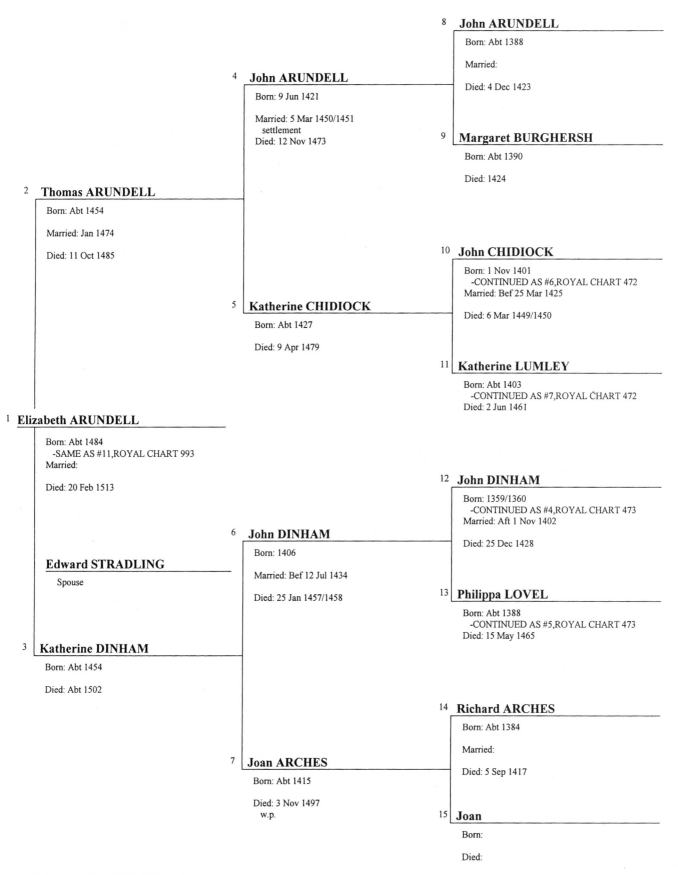

8 John ARUNDELL
Born: Abt 1388
Married:
Died: 4 Dec 1423

4 John ARUNDELL
Born: 9 Jun 1421
Married: 5 Mar 1450/1451
    settlement
Died: 12 Nov 1473

9 Margaret BURGHERSH
Born: Abt 1390
Died: 1424

2 Thomas ARUNDELL
Born: Abt 1454
Married: Jan 1474
Died: 11 Oct 1485

10 John CHIDIOCK
Born: 1 Nov 1401
    -CONTINUED AS #6,ROYAL CHART 472
Married: Bef 25 Mar 1425
Died: 6 Mar 1449/1450

5 Katherine CHIDIOCK
Born: Abt 1427
Died: 9 Apr 1479

11 Katherine LUMLEY
Born: Abt 1403
    -CONTINUED AS #7,ROYAL CHART 472
Died: 2 Jun 1461

1 Elizabeth ARUNDELL
Born: Abt 1484
    -SAME AS #11,ROYAL CHART 993
Married:
Died: 20 Feb 1513

12 John DINHAM
Born: 1359/1360
    -CONTINUED AS #4,ROYAL CHART 473
Married: Aft 1 Nov 1402
Died: 25 Dec 1428

6 John DINHAM
Born: 1406
Married: Bef 12 Jul 1434
Died: 25 Jan 1457/1458

13 Philippa LOVEL
Born: Abt 1388
    -CONTINUED AS #5,ROYAL CHART 473
Died: 15 May 1465

Edward STRADLING
Spouse

3 Katherine DINHAM
Born: Abt 1454
Died: Abt 1502

14 Richard ARCHES
Born: Abt 1384
Married:
Died: 5 Sep 1417

7 Joan ARCHES
Born: Abt 1415
Died: 3 Nov 1497
    w.p.

15 Joan
Born:
Died:

Sources include: *Magna Charta* 27-12; LDS records.

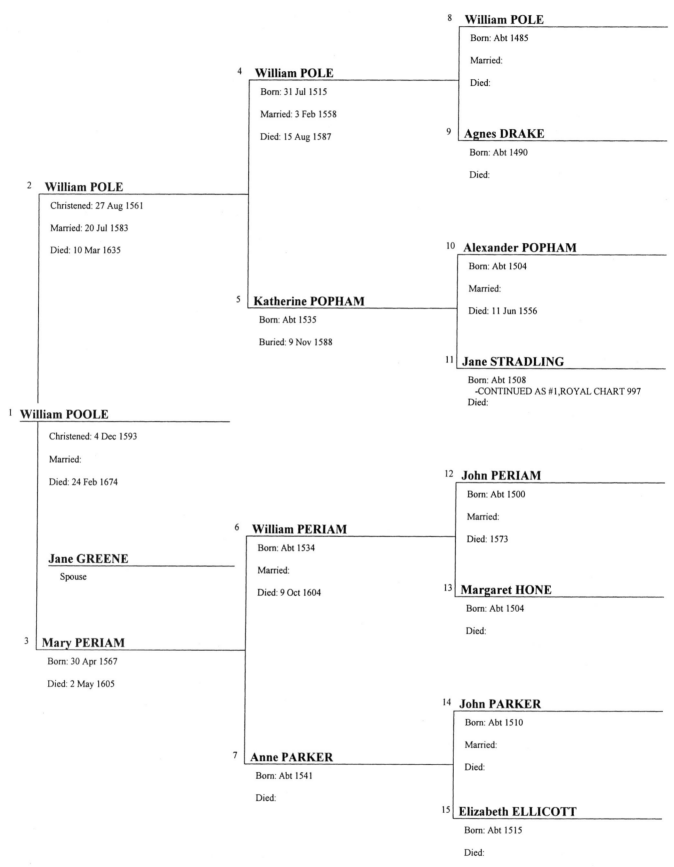

8 William POLE
Born: Abt 1485
Married:
Died:

9 Agnes DRAKE
Born: Abt 1490
Died:

4 William POLE
Born: 31 Jul 1515
Married: 3 Feb 1558
Died: 15 Aug 1587

2 William POLE
Christened: 27 Aug 1561
Married: 20 Jul 1583
Died: 10 Mar 1635

10 Alexander POPHAM
Born: Abt 1504
Married:
Died: 11 Jun 1556

11 Jane STRADLING
Born: Abt 1508
-CONTINUED AS #1, ROYAL CHART 997
Died:

5 Katherine POPHAM
Born: Abt 1535
Buried: 9 Nov 1588

1 William POOLE
Christened: 4 Dec 1593
Married:
Died: 24 Feb 1674

Jane GREENE
Spouse

12 John PERIAM
Born: Abt 1500
Married:
Died: 1573

13 Margaret HONE
Born: Abt 1504
Died:

6 William PERIAM
Born: Abt 1534
Married:
Died: 9 Oct 1604

3 Mary PERIAM
Born: 30 Apr 1567
Died: 2 May 1605

14 John PARKER
Born: Abt 1510
Married:
Died:

15 Elizabeth ELLICOTT
Born: Abt 1515
Died:

7 Anne PARKER
Born: Abt 1541
Died:

Sources include: Richardson *Plantagenet* (2004), pp. 80-82 (Beaufort); Faris 2--Poole; *Magna Charta* 27; Roberts *500*, pp. 134-135; LDS records.

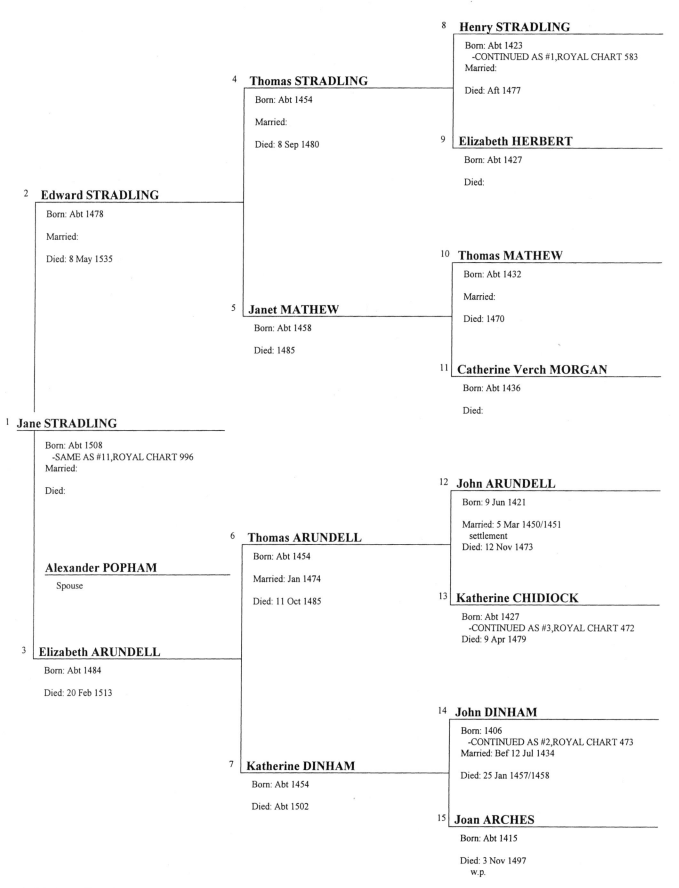

8 Henry STRADLING
Born: Abt 1423
-CONTINUED AS #1,ROYAL CHART 583
Married:

Died: Aft 1477

4 Thomas STRADLING
Born: Abt 1454

Married:

Died: 8 Sep 1480

9 Elizabeth HERBERT
Born: Abt 1427

Died:

2 Edward STRADLING
Born: Abt 1478

Married:

Died: 8 May 1535

10 Thomas MATHEW
Born: Abt 1432

Married:

Died: 1470

5 Janet MATHEW
Born: Abt 1458

Died: 1485

11 Catherine Verch MORGAN
Born: Abt 1436

Died:

1 Jane STRADLING
Born: Abt 1508
-SAME AS #11,ROYAL CHART 996
Married:

Died:

Alexander POPHAM
Spouse

12 John ARUNDELL
Born: 9 Jun 1421

Married: 5 Mar 1450/1451
settlement
Died: 12 Nov 1473

6 Thomas ARUNDELL
Born: Abt 1454

Married: Jan 1474

Died: 11 Oct 1485

13 Katherine CHIDIOCK
Born: Abt 1427
-CONTINUED AS #3,ROYAL CHART 472
Died: 9 Apr 1479

3 Elizabeth ARUNDELL
Born: Abt 1484

Died: 20 Feb 1513

14 John DINHAM
Born: 1406
-CONTINUED AS #2,ROYAL CHART 473
Married: Bef 12 Jul 1434

Died: 25 Jan 1457/1458

7 Katherine DINHAM
Born: Abt 1454

Died: Abt 1502

15 Joan ARCHES
Born: Abt 1415

Died: 3 Nov 1497
w.p.

Sources include: *Magna Charta* 27; Roberts *500*, pp. 134-135; LDS records.

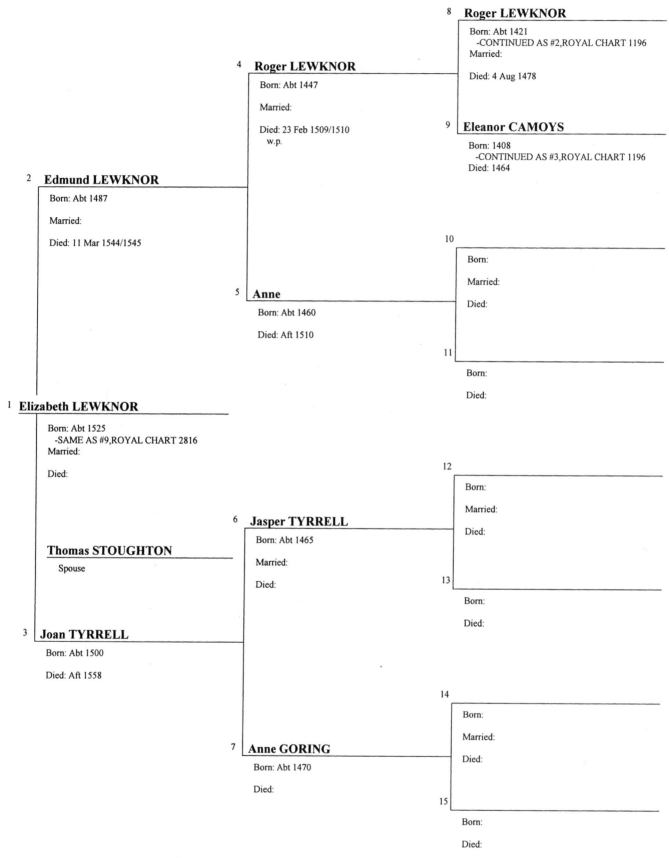

8 **Roger LEWKNOR**

Born: Abt 1421
　-CONTINUED AS #2,ROYAL CHART 1196
Married:

Died: 4 Aug 1478

4 **Roger LEWKNOR**

Born: Abt 1447

Married:

Died: 23 Feb 1509/1510
　w.p.

9 **Eleanor CAMOYS**

Born: 1408
　-CONTINUED AS #3,ROYAL CHART 1196
Died: 1464

2 **Edmund LEWKNOR**

Born: Abt 1487

Married:

Died: 11 Mar 1544/1545

10

Born:

Married:

Died:

5 **Anne**

Born: Abt 1460

Died: Aft 1510

11

Born:

Died:

1 **Elizabeth LEWKNOR**

Born: Abt 1525
　-SAME AS #9,ROYAL CHART 2816
Married:

Died:

12

Born:

Married:

Died:

6 **Jasper TYRRELL**

Born: Abt 1465

Married:

Died:

13

Born:

Died:

Thomas STOUGHTON

Spouse

3 **Joan TYRRELL**

Born: Abt 1500

Died: Aft 1558

14

Born:

Married:

Died:

7 **Anne GORING**

Born: Abt 1470

Died:

15

Born:

Died:

Sources include: Richardson *Magna Carta* (April 2005), pp. 787-788 (Stoughton), 511-512 (Lewknor); MPGL 1304, 10076; *Royal Ancestors* (1989), Section I, p. 119 Otis; Roberts *600* (2004), p. 376; *NEHGR* 5:350; *TAG* 29:200; Edith B. Sumner, *Descendants of Thomas Farr* (1959), pp. 268- 269; Correspondence from J.C.S. Durand of Salt Lake City; Consultation with Douglas Richardson. Note: #5 is claimed to be Mary West (1st wife of #4 Roger), daughter of Reynold West & Margaret Thorley (see chart 593, #6 & 7; see also Richardson *Plantagenet* (2004), p. 402). This is unacceptable chronologically. Richardson believes that #5 was a later wife (probably Anne), whose parentage is unknown.

Pedigree Chart

Chart 999

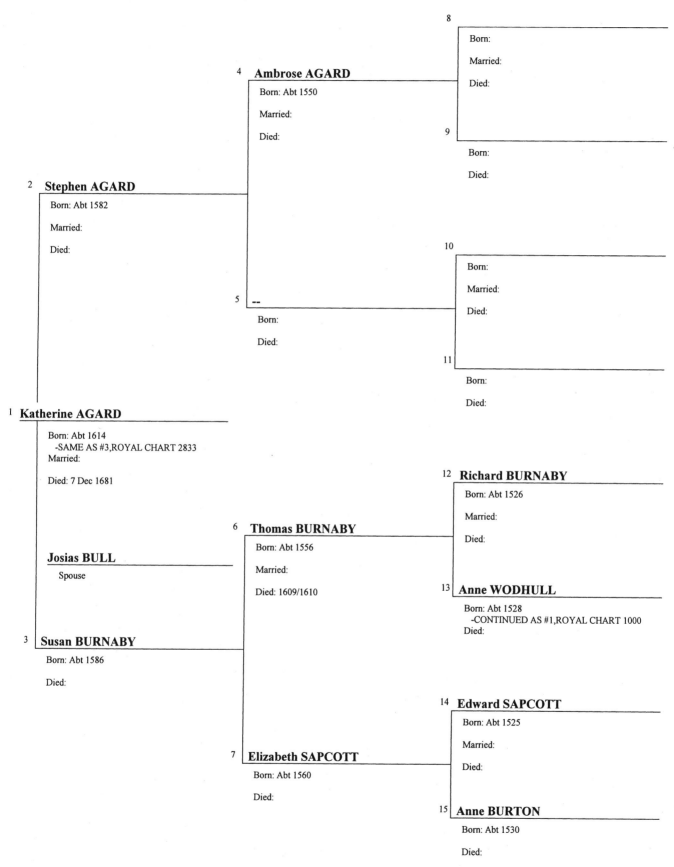

8
Born:
Married:
Died:

4 Ambrose AGARD
Born: Abt 1550
Married:
Died:

9
Born:
Died:

2 Stephen AGARD
Born: Abt 1582
Married:
Died:

10
Born:
Married:
Died:

5 --
Born:
Died:

11
Born:
Died:

1 Katherine AGARD
Born: Abt 1614
-SAME AS #3,ROYAL CHART 2833
Married:
Died: 7 Dec 1681

12 Richard BURNABY
Born: Abt 1526
Married:
Died:

6 Thomas BURNABY
Born: Abt 1556
Married:
Died: 1609/1610

Josias BULL
Spouse

13 Anne WODHULL
Born: Abt 1528
-CONTINUED AS #1,ROYAL CHART 1000
Died:

3 Susan BURNABY
Born: Abt 1586
Died:

14 Edward SAPCOTT
Born: Abt 1525
Married:
Died:

7 Elizabeth SAPCOTT
Born: Abt 1560
Died:

15 Anne BURTON
Born: Abt 1530
Died:

Sources include: Faris--Bull.

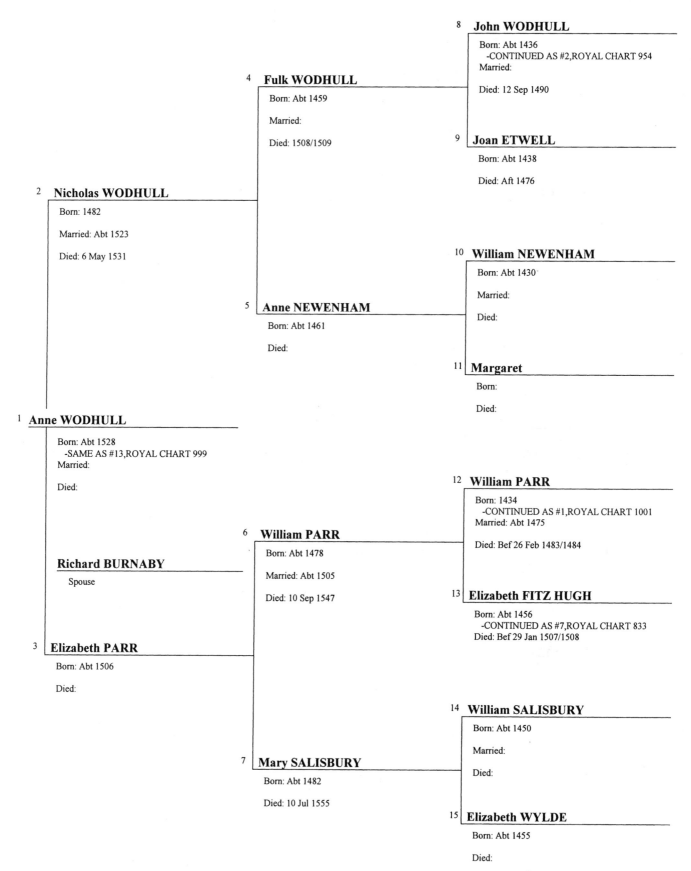

8 John WODHULL

Born: Abt 1436
-CONTINUED AS #2,ROYAL CHART 954
Married:

Died: 12 Sep 1490

4 Fulk WODHULL

Born: Abt 1459

Married:

Died: 1508/1509

9 Joan ETWELL

Born: Abt 1438

Died: Aft 1476

2 Nicholas WODHULL

Born: 1482

Married: Abt 1523

Died: 6 May 1531

10 William NEWENHAM

Born: Abt 1430

Married:

Died:

5 Anne NEWENHAM

Born: Abt 1461

Died:

11 Margaret

Born:

Died:

1 Anne WODHULL

Born: Abt 1528
-SAME AS #13,ROYAL CHART 999
Married:

Died:

12 William PARR

Born: 1434
-CONTINUED AS #1,ROYAL CHART 1001
Married: Abt 1475

Died: Bef 26 Feb 1483/1484

6 William PARR

Born: Abt 1478

Married: Abt 1505

Died: 10 Sep 1547

Richard BURNABY

Spouse

13 Elizabeth FITZ HUGH

Born: Abt 1456
-CONTINUED AS #7,ROYAL CHART 833
Died: Bef 29 Jan 1507/1508

3 Elizabeth PARR

Born: Abt 1506

Died:

14 William SALISBURY

Born: Abt 1450

Married:

Died:

7 Mary SALISBURY

Born: Abt 1482

Died: 10 Jul 1555

15 Elizabeth WYLDE

Born: Abt 1455

Died:

Sources include: Faris--Bull; *Emperor Charlemagne* 1:235-237.

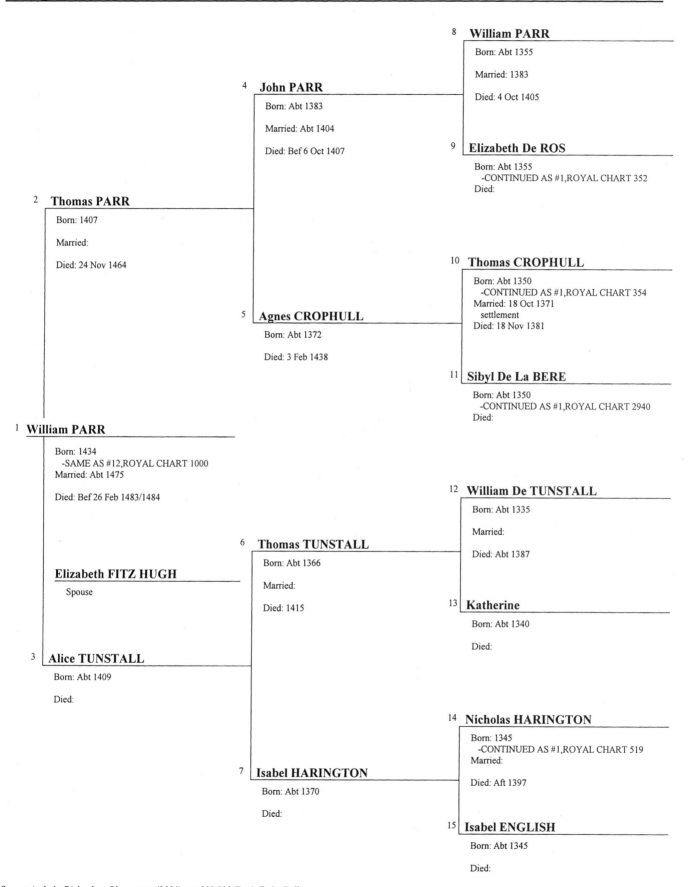

8 William PARR

Born: Abt 1355

Married: 1383

Died: 4 Oct 1405

4 John PARR

Born: Abt 1383

Married: Abt 1404

Died: Bef 6 Oct 1407

9 Elizabeth De ROS

Born: Abt 1355
-CONTINUED AS #1,ROYAL CHART 352
Died:

2 Thomas PARR

Born: 1407

Married:

Died: 24 Nov 1464

10 Thomas CROPHULL

Born: Abt 1350
-CONTINUED AS #1,ROYAL CHART 354
Married: 18 Oct 1371
settlement
Died: 18 Nov 1381

5 Agnes CROPHULL

Born: Abt 1372

Died: 3 Feb 1438

11 Sibyl De La BERE

Born: Abt 1350
-CONTINUED AS #1,ROYAL CHART 2940
Died:

1 William PARR

Born: 1434
-SAME AS #12,ROYAL CHART 1000
Married: Abt 1475

Died: Bef 26 Feb 1483/1484

12 William De TUNSTALL

Born: Abt 1335

Married:

Died: Abt 1387

6 Thomas TUNSTALL

Born: Abt 1366

Married:

Died: 1415

13 Katherine

Born: Abt 1340

Died:

Elizabeth FITZ HUGH

Spouse

3 Alice TUNSTALL

Born: Abt 1409

Died:

14 Nicholas HARINGTON

Born: 1345
-CONTINUED AS #1,ROYAL CHART 519
Married:

Died: Aft 1397

7 Isabel HARINGTON

Born: Abt 1370

Died:

15 Isabel ENGLISH

Born: Abt 1345

Died:

Sources include: Richardson *Plantagenet* (2004), pp. 565-566 (Parr); Faris--Bull.

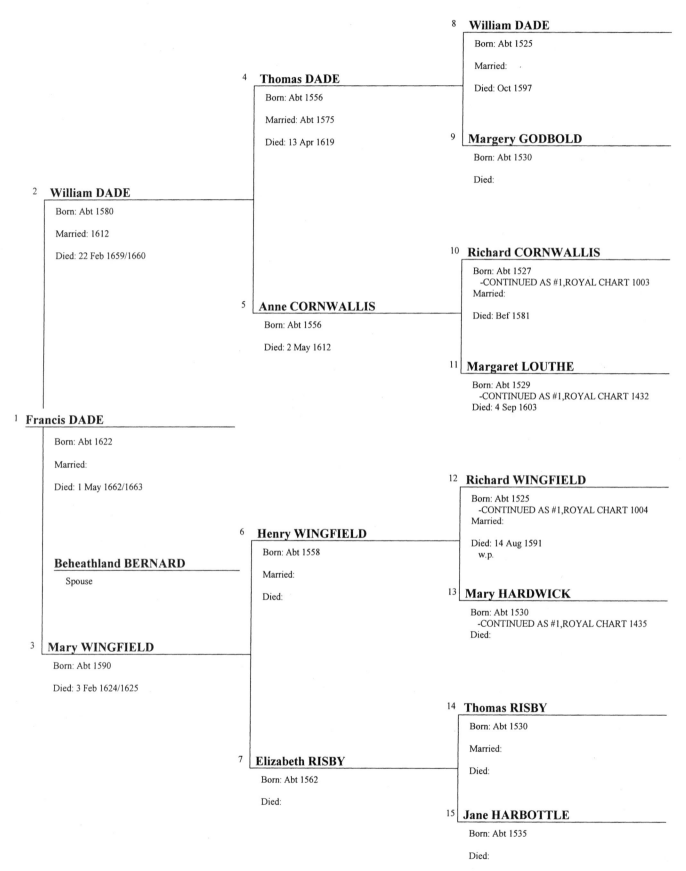

8 **William DADE**

Born: Abt 1525

Married:

Died: Oct 1597

4 **Thomas DADE**

Born: Abt 1556

Married: Abt 1575

Died: 13 Apr 1619

9 **Margery GODBOLD**

Born: Abt 1530

Died:

2 **William DADE**

Born: Abt 1580

Married: 1612

Died: 22 Feb 1659/1660

10 **Richard CORNWALLIS**

Born: Abt 1527
-CONTINUED AS #1,ROYAL CHART 1003
Married:

Died: Bef 1581

5 **Anne CORNWALLIS**

Born: Abt 1556

Died: 2 May 1612

11 **Margaret LOUTHE**

Born: Abt 1529
-CONTINUED AS #1,ROYAL CHART 1432
Died: 4 Sep 1603

1 **Francis DADE**

Born: Abt 1622

Married:

Died: 1 May 1662/1663

12 **Richard WINGFIELD**

Born: Abt 1525
-CONTINUED AS #1,ROYAL CHART 1004
Married:

Died: 14 Aug 1591
w.p.

6 **Henry WINGFIELD**

Born: Abt 1558

Married:

Died:

13 **Mary HARDWICK**

Born: Abt 1530
-CONTINUED AS #1,ROYAL CHART 1435
Died:

Beheathland BERNARD

Spouse

3 **Mary WINGFIELD**

Born: Abt 1590

Died: 3 Feb 1624/1625

14 **Thomas RISBY**

Born: Abt 1530

Married:

Died:

7 **Elizabeth RISBY**

Born: Abt 1562

Died:

15 **Jane HARBOTTLE**

Born: Abt 1535

Died:

Sources include: Faris--Dade.

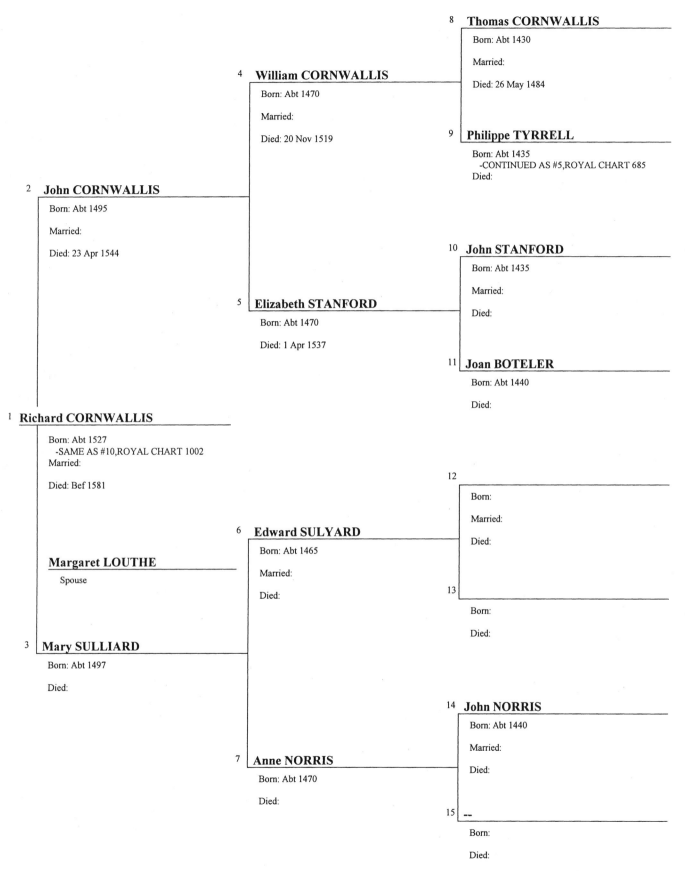

8 **Thomas CORNWALLIS**

Born: Abt 1430

Married:

Died: 26 May 1484

4 **William CORNWALLIS**

Born: Abt 1470

Married:

Died: 20 Nov 1519

9 **Philippe TYRRELL**

Born: Abt 1435
    -CONTINUED AS #5,ROYAL CHART 685
Died:

2 **John CORNWALLIS**

Born: Abt 1495

Married:

Died: 23 Apr 1544

10 **John STANFORD**

Born: Abt 1435

Married:

Died:

5 **Elizabeth STANFORD**

Born: Abt 1470

Died: 1 Apr 1537

11 **Joan BOTELER**

Born: Abt 1440

Died:

1 **Richard CORNWALLIS**

Born: Abt 1527
    -SAME AS #10,ROYAL CHART 1002
Married:

Died: Bef 1581

12

Born:

Married:

Died:

Margaret LOUTHE

Spouse

6 **Edward SULYARD**

Born: Abt 1465

Married:

Died:

13

Born:

Died:

3 **Mary SULLIARD**

Born: Abt 1497

Died:

14 **John NORRIS**

Born: Abt 1440

Married:

Died:

7 **Anne NORRIS**

Born: Abt 1470

Died:

15 **--**

Born:

Died:

Sources include: Richardson *Plantagenet* (2004), pp. 252-253 (Dade); Faris 2--Dade; Faris--Dade.

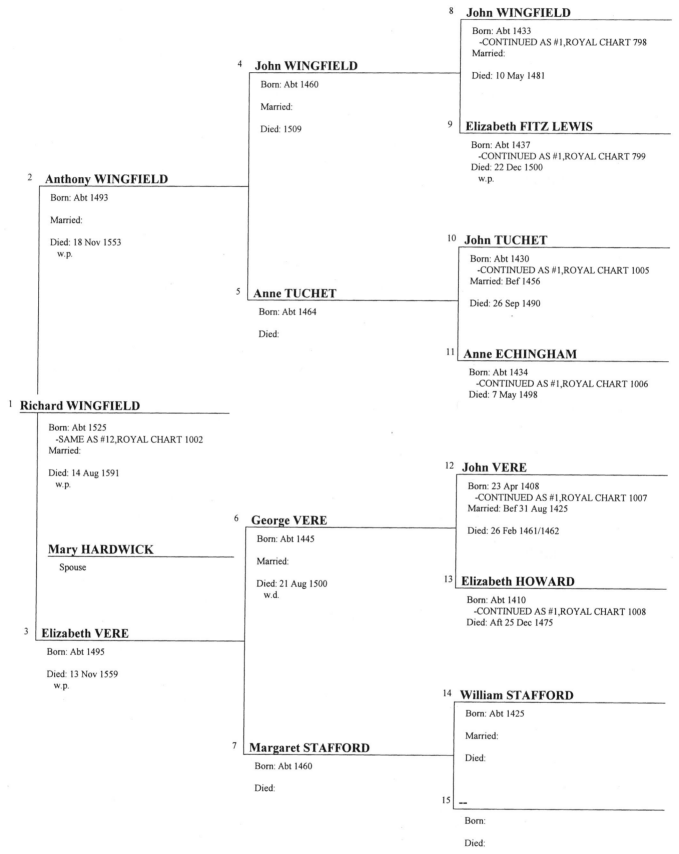

8 **John WINGFIELD**
Born: Abt 1433
  -CONTINUED AS #1,ROYAL CHART 798
Married:

Died: 10 May 1481

4 **John WINGFIELD**
Born: Abt 1460

Married:

Died: 1509

9 **Elizabeth FITZ LEWIS**
Born: Abt 1437
  -CONTINUED AS #1,ROYAL CHART 799
Died: 22 Dec 1500
w.p.

2 **Anthony WINGFIELD**
Born: Abt 1493

Married:

Died: 18 Nov 1553
w.p.

10 **John TUCHET**
Born: Abt 1430
  -CONTINUED AS #1,ROYAL CHART 1005
Married: Bef 1456

Died: 26 Sep 1490

5 **Anne TUCHET**
Born: Abt 1464

Died:

11 **Anne ECHINGHAM**
Born: Abt 1434
  -CONTINUED AS #1,ROYAL CHART 1006
Died: 7 May 1498

1 **Richard WINGFIELD**
Born: Abt 1525
  -SAME AS #12,ROYAL CHART 1002
Married:

Died: 14 Aug 1591
w.p.

12 **John VERE**
Born: 23 Apr 1408
  -CONTINUED AS #1,ROYAL CHART 1007
Married: Bef 31 Aug 1425

Died: 26 Feb 1461/1462

6 **George VERE**
Born: Abt 1445

Married:

Died: 21 Aug 1500
w.d.

13 **Elizabeth HOWARD**
Born: Abt 1410
  -CONTINUED AS #1,ROYAL CHART 1008
Died: Aft 25 Dec 1475

Mary HARDWICK
Spouse

3 **Elizabeth VERE**
Born: Abt 1495

Died: 13 Nov 1559
w.p.

14 **William STAFFORD**
Born: Abt 1425

Married:

Died:

7 **Margaret STAFFORD**
Born: Abt 1460

Died:

15 **--**
Born:

Died:

Sources include: Faris--Hankford, Tuchet.

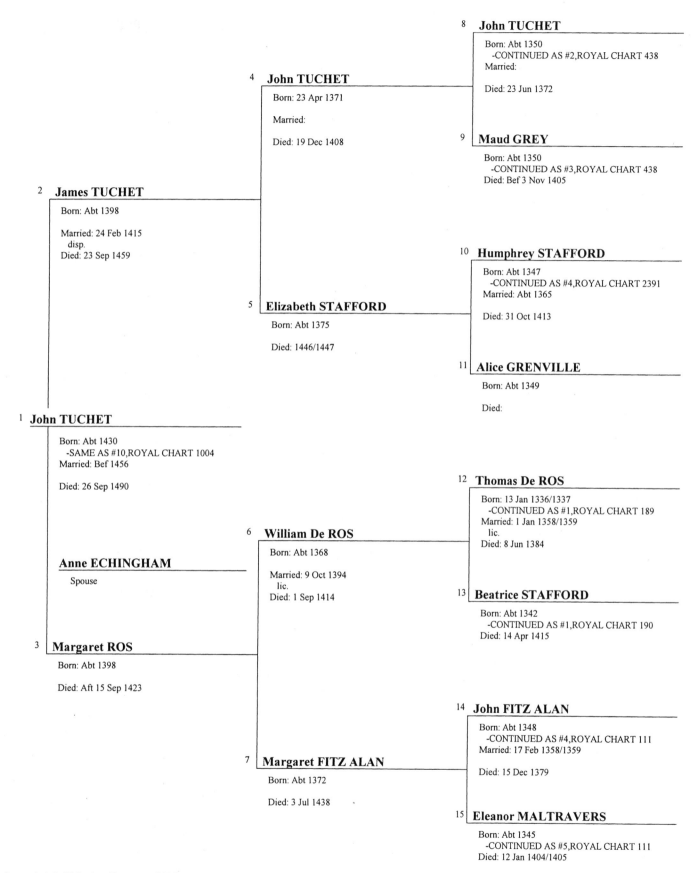

8 | John TUCHET
Born: Abt 1350
-CONTINUED AS #2,ROYAL CHART 438
Married:

Died: 23 Jun 1372

4 | John TUCHET
Born: 23 Apr 1371

Married:

Died: 19 Dec 1408

9 | Maud GREY
Born: Abt 1350
-CONTINUED AS #3,ROYAL CHART 438
Died: Bef 3 Nov 1405

2 | James TUCHET
Born: Abt 1398

Married: 24 Feb 1415
disp.
Died: 23 Sep 1459

10 | Humphrey STAFFORD
Born: Abt 1347
-CONTINUED AS #4,ROYAL CHART 2391
Married: Abt 1365

Died: 31 Oct 1413

5 | Elizabeth STAFFORD
Born: Abt 1375

Died: 1446/1447

11 | Alice GRENVILLE
Born: Abt 1349

Died:

1 | John TUCHET
Born: Abt 1430
-SAME AS #10,ROYAL CHART 1004
Married: Bef 1456

Died: 26 Sep 1490

12 | Thomas De ROS
Born: 13 Jan 1336/1337
-CONTINUED AS #1,ROYAL CHART 189
Married: 1 Jan 1358/1359
lic.
Died: 8 Jun 1384

6 | William De ROS
Born: Abt 1368

Married: 9 Oct 1394
lic.
Died: 1 Sep 1414

13 | Beatrice STAFFORD
Born: Abt 1342
-CONTINUED AS #1,ROYAL CHART 190
Died: 14 Apr 1415

Anne ECHINGHAM
Spouse

3 | Margaret ROS
Born: Abt 1398

Died: Aft 15 Sep 1423

14 | John FITZ ALAN
Born: Abt 1348
-CONTINUED AS #4,ROYAL CHART 111
Married: 17 Feb 1358/1359

Died: 15 Dec 1379

7 | Margaret FITZ ALAN
Born: Abt 1372

Died: 3 Jul 1438

15 | Eleanor MALTRAVERS
Born: Abt 1345
-CONTINUED AS #5,ROYAL CHART 111
Died: 12 Jan 1404/1405

Sources include: Richardson *Plantagenet* (2004), pp. 721-724 (Tuchet), 612-614 (Roos); Faris--Tuchet; Faris 2--Roos (#3 ancestry), Tuchet 9 (#5 Elizabeth); Consultation with Douglas Richardson (#5 ancestry). Note: #1 is also called John Audley.

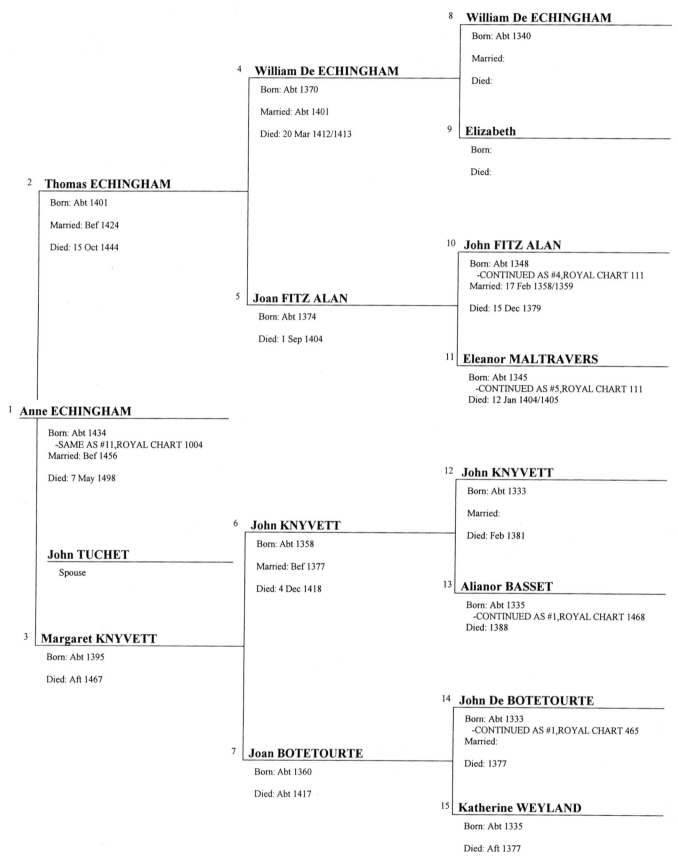

8 **William De ECHINGHAM**

Born: Abt 1340

Married:

Died:

4 **William De ECHINGHAM**

Born: Abt 1370

Married: Abt 1401

Died: 20 Mar 1412/1413

9 **Elizabeth**

Born:

Died:

2 **Thomas ECHINGHAM**

Born: Abt 1401

Married: Bef 1424

Died: 15 Oct 1444

10 **John FITZ ALAN**

Born: Abt 1348
  -CONTINUED AS #4,ROYAL CHART 111
Married: 17 Feb 1358/1359

Died: 15 Dec 1379

5 **Joan FITZ ALAN**

Born: Abt 1374

Died: 1 Sep 1404

11 **Eleanor MALTRAVERS**

Born: Abt 1345
  -CONTINUED AS #5,ROYAL CHART 111
Died: 12 Jan 1404/1405

1 **Anne ECHINGHAM**

Born: Abt 1434
  -SAME AS #11,ROYAL CHART 1004
Married: Bef 1456

Died: 7 May 1498

12 **John KNYVETT**

Born: Abt 1333

Married:

Died: Feb 1381

6 **John KNYVETT**

Born: Abt 1358

Married: Bef 1377

Died: 4 Dec 1418

John TUCHET

Spouse

13 **Alianor BASSET**

Born: Abt 1335
  -CONTINUED AS #1,ROYAL CHART 1468
Died: 1388

3 **Margaret KNYVETT**

Born: Abt 1395

Died: Aft 1467

14 **John De BOTETOURTE**

Born: Abt 1333
  -CONTINUED AS #1,ROYAL CHART 465
Married:

Died: 1377

7 **Joan BOTETOURTE**

Born: Abt 1360

Died: Abt 1417

15 **Katherine WEYLAND**

Born: Abt 1335

Died: Aft 1377

Sources include: Faris--Tuchet, Echingham; Faris 2--Echingham; *Ancestral Roots* 188, 216A (#6 & 7 ancestry).

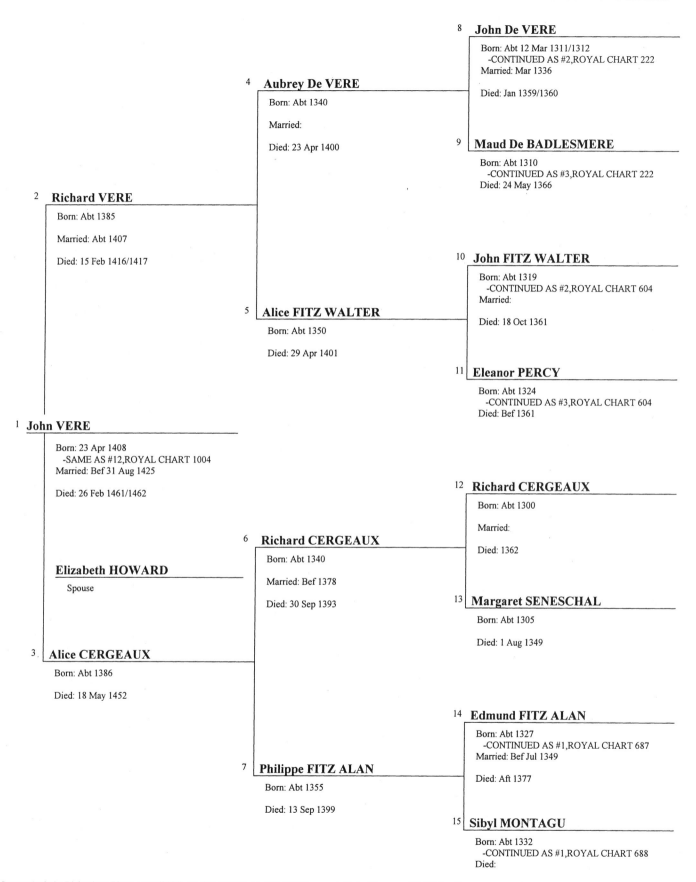

8 **John De VERE**

Born: Abt 12 Mar 1311/1312
    -CONTINUED AS #2,ROYAL CHART 222
Married: Mar 1336

Died: Jan 1359/1360

4 **Aubrey De VERE**

Born: Abt 1340

Married:

Died: 23 Apr 1400

9 **Maud De BADLESMERE**

Born: Abt 1310
    -CONTINUED AS #3,ROYAL CHART 222
Died: 24 May 1366

2 **Richard VERE**

Born: Abt 1385

Married: Abt 1407

Died: 15 Feb 1416/1417

10 **John FITZ WALTER**

Born: Abt 1319
    -CONTINUED AS #2,ROYAL CHART 604
Married:

Died: 18 Oct 1361

5 **Alice FITZ WALTER**

Born: Abt 1350

Died: 29 Apr 1401

11 **Eleanor PERCY**

Born: Abt 1324
    -CONTINUED AS #3,ROYAL CHART 604
Died: Bef 1361

1 **John VERE**

Born: 23 Apr 1408
    -SAME AS #12,ROYAL CHART 1004
Married: Bef 31 Aug 1425

Died: 26 Feb 1461/1462

12 **Richard CERGEAUX**

Born: Abt 1300

Married:

Died: 1362

6 **Richard CERGEAUX**

Born: Abt 1340

Married: Bef 1378

Died: 30 Sep 1393

13 **Margaret SENESCHAL**

Born: Abt 1305

Died: 1 Aug 1349

Elizabeth HOWARD

Spouse

3 **Alice CERGEAUX**

Born: Abt 1386

Died: 18 May 1452

14 **Edmund FITZ ALAN**

Born: Abt 1327
    -CONTINUED AS #1,ROYAL CHART 687
Married: Bef Jul 1349

Died: Aft 1377

7 **Philippe FITZ ALAN**

Born: Abt 1355

Died: 13 Sep 1399

15 **Sibyl MONTAGU**

Born: Abt 1332
    -CONTINUED AS #1,ROYAL CHART 688
Died:

Sources include: Richardson *Plantagenet* (2004), pp. 737-738 (Vere), 646-647 (Sergeaux); Faris--Cergeaux, Fitz Walter 11.

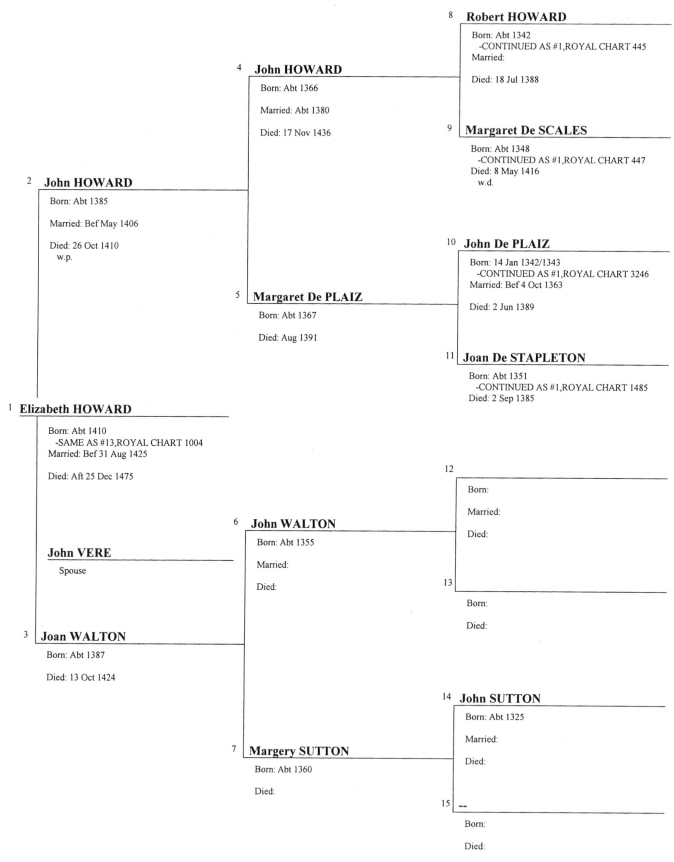

8 Robert HOWARD

Born: Abt 1342
-CONTINUED AS #1,ROYAL CHART 445
Married:

Died: 18 Jul 1388

4 John HOWARD

Born: Abt 1366

Married: Abt 1380

Died: 17 Nov 1436

9 Margaret De SCALES

Born: Abt 1348
-CONTINUED AS #1,ROYAL CHART 447
Died: 8 May 1416
w.d.

2 John HOWARD

Born: Abt 1385

Married: Bef May 1406

Died: 26 Oct 1410
w.p.

10 John De PLAIZ

Born: 14 Jan 1342/1343
-CONTINUED AS #1,ROYAL CHART 3246
Married: Bef 4 Oct 1363

Died: 2 Jun 1389

5 Margaret De PLAIZ

Born: Abt 1367

Died: Aug 1391

11 Joan De STAPLETON

Born: Abt 1351
-CONTINUED AS #1,ROYAL CHART 1485
Died: 2 Sep 1385

1 Elizabeth HOWARD

Born: Abt 1410
-SAME AS #13,ROYAL CHART 1004
Married: Bef 31 Aug 1425

Died: Aft 25 Dec 1475

John VERE

Spouse

12

Born:

Married:

Died:

6 John WALTON

Born: Abt 1355

Married:

Died:

13

Born:

Died:

3 Joan WALTON

Born: Abt 1387

Died: 13 Oct 1424

14 John SUTTON

Born: Abt 1325

Married:

Died:

7 Margery SUTTON

Born: Abt 1360

Died:

15 --

Born:

Died:

Sources include: Consultation with Douglas Richardson; Faris--Cergeaux 6; LDS records.

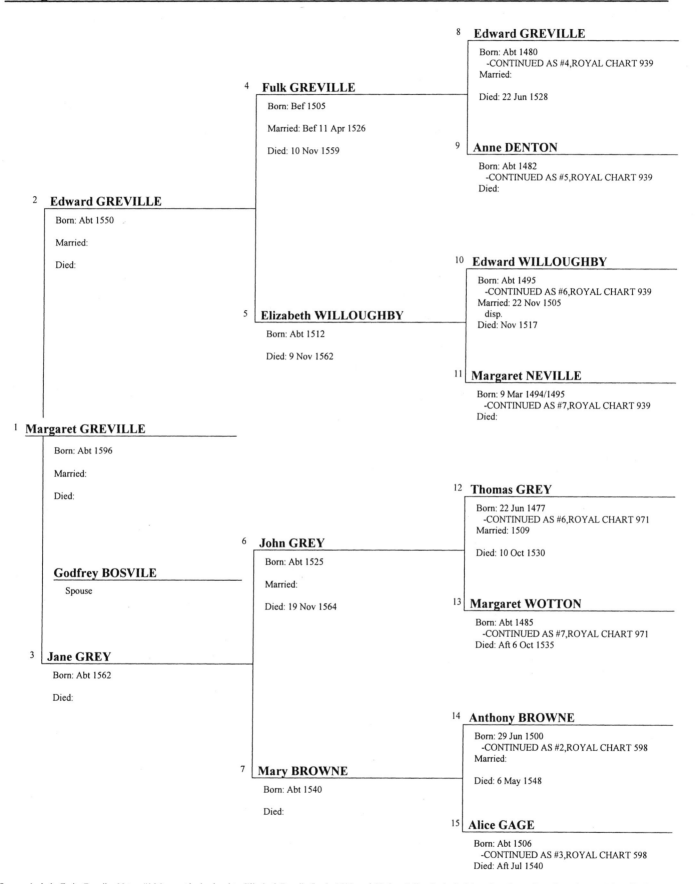

2 Edward GREVILLE
Born: Abt 1550
Married:
Died:

4 Fulk GREVILLE
Born: Bef 1505
Married: Bef 11 Apr 1526
Died: 10 Nov 1559

8 Edward GREVILLE
Born: Abt 1480
 -CONTINUED AS #4,ROYAL CHART 939
Married:
Died: 22 Jun 1528

9 Anne DENTON
Born: Abt 1482
 -CONTINUED AS #5,ROYAL CHART 939
Died:

5 Elizabeth WILLOUGHBY
Born: Abt 1512
Died: 9 Nov 1562

10 Edward WILLOUGHBY
Born: Abt 1495
 -CONTINUED AS #6,ROYAL CHART 939
Married: 22 Nov 1505
 disp.
Died: Nov 1517

11 Margaret NEVILLE
Born: 9 Mar 1494/1495
 -CONTINUED AS #7,ROYAL CHART 939
Died:

1 Margaret GREVILLE
Born: Abt 1596
Married:
Died:

Godfrey BOSVILE
Spouse

3 Jane GREY
Born: Abt 1562
Died:

6 John GREY
Born: Abt 1525
Married:
Died: 19 Nov 1564

12 Thomas GREY
Born: 22 Jun 1477
 -CONTINUED AS #6,ROYAL CHART 971
Married: 1509
Died: 10 Oct 1530

13 Margaret WOTTON
Born: Abt 1485
 -CONTINUED AS #7,ROYAL CHART 971
Died: Aft 6 Oct 1535

7 Mary BROWNE
Born: Abt 1540
Died:

14 Anthony BROWNE
Born: 29 Jun 1500
 -CONTINUED AS #2,ROYAL CHART 598
Married:
Died: 6 May 1548

15 Alice GAGE
Born: Abt 1506
 -CONTINUED AS #3,ROYAL CHART 598
Died: Aft Jul 1540

Sources include: Faris--Bosvile. Notes: #1 Margaret had a daughter Elizabeth Bosvile (b. abt 1617; md. Herbert Pelham) who had American descendants through a son Edward Pelham (b. abt 1652; md. Freelove Arnold). See chart 3301 for the ancestry of Godfrey Bosvile, husband of #1 Margaret.

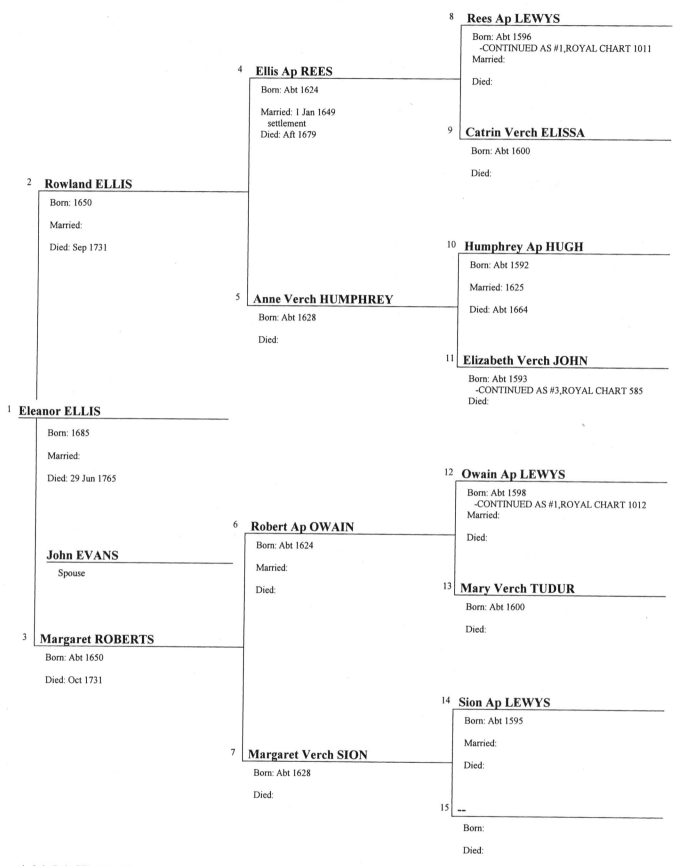

8 **Rees Ap LEWYS**

Born: Abt 1596
-CONTINUED AS #1,ROYAL CHART 1011
Married:

Died:

4 **Ellis Ap REES**

Born: Abt 1624

Married: 1 Jan 1649
settlement
Died: Aft 1679

9 **Catrin Verch ELISSA**

Born: Abt 1600

Died:

2 **Rowland ELLIS**

Born: 1650

Married:

Died: Sep 1731

10 **Humphrey Ap HUGH**

Born: Abt 1592

Married: 1625

Died: Abt 1664

5 **Anne Verch HUMPHREY**

Born: Abt 1628

Died:

11 **Elizabeth Verch JOHN**

Born: Abt 1593
-CONTINUED AS #3,ROYAL CHART 585
Died:

1 **Eleanor ELLIS**

Born: 1685

Married:

Died: 29 Jun 1765

12 **Owain Ap LEWYS**

Born: Abt 1598
-CONTINUED AS #1,ROYAL CHART 1012
Married:

Died:

6 **Robert Ap OWAIN**

Born: Abt 1624

Married:

Died:

John EVANS

Spouse

13 **Mary Verch TUDUR**

Born: Abt 1600

Died:

3 **Margaret ROBERTS**

Born: Abt 1650

Died: Oct 1731

14 **Sion Ap LEWYS**

Born: Abt 1595

Married:

Died:

7 **Margaret Verch SION**

Born: Abt 1628

Died:

15 **--**

Born:

Died:

Sources include: Faris--Ellis. Note: John Evans (b. abt 1685; husband of #1) was son of Cadwalader Evans (b. abt 1655; md. Ellen Morris), son of John Ap Evan (b. abt 1630), son of Evan Robert Lewis (b. abt 1600) & Jane Verch Cadwaladr (b. abt 1605), cont. in Appendix under Lewis. Ellen Morris (b. abt 1660) was daughter of Eleanor Williams (b. abt 1628; md. John Morris), daughter of Ellis Williams (b. abt 1600) & Margaret John, cont. in Appendix under Williams.

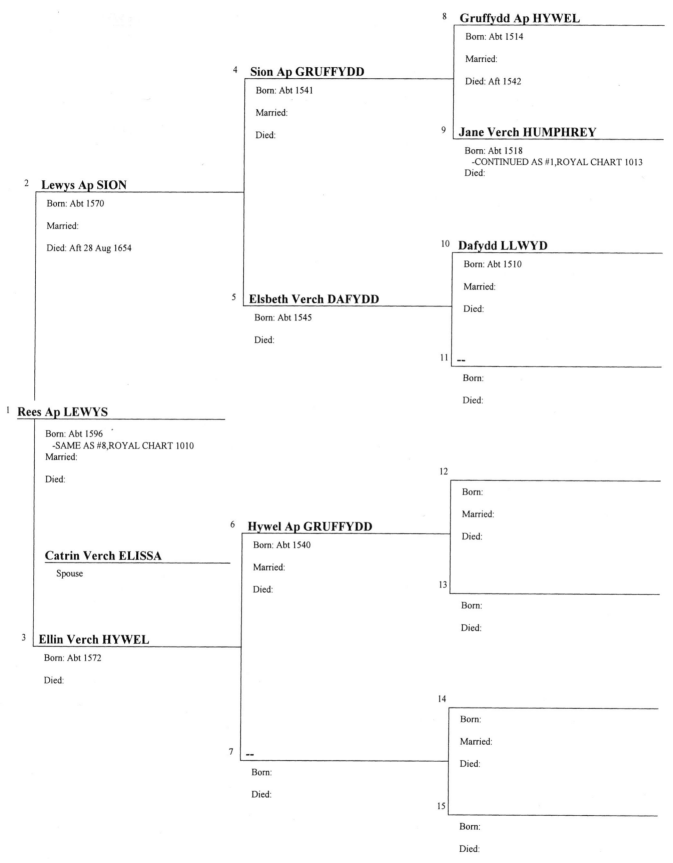

8 **Gruffydd Ap HYWEL**
Born: Abt 1514
Married:
Died: Aft 1542

4 **Sion Ap GRUFFYDD**
Born: Abt 1541
Married:
Died:

9 **Jane Verch HUMPHREY**
Born: Abt 1518
-CONTINUED AS #1,ROYAL CHART 1013
Died:

2 **Lewys Ap SION**
Born: Abt 1570
Married:
Died: Aft 28 Aug 1654

10 **Dafydd LLWYD**
Born: Abt 1510
Married:
Died:

5 **Elsbeth Verch DAFYDD**
Born: Abt 1545
Died:

11 **--**
Born:
Died:

1 **Rees Ap LEWYS**
Born: Abt 1596
-SAME AS #8,ROYAL CHART 1010
Married:
Died:

12
Born:
Married:
Died:

6 **Hywel Ap GRUFFYDD**
Born: Abt 1540
Married:
Died:

13
Born:
Died:

Catrin Verch ELISSA
Spouse

3 **Ellin Verch HYWEL**
Born: Abt 1572
Died:

14
Born:
Married:
Died:

7 **--**
Born:
Died:

15
Born:
Died:

Sources include: Faris--Ellis.

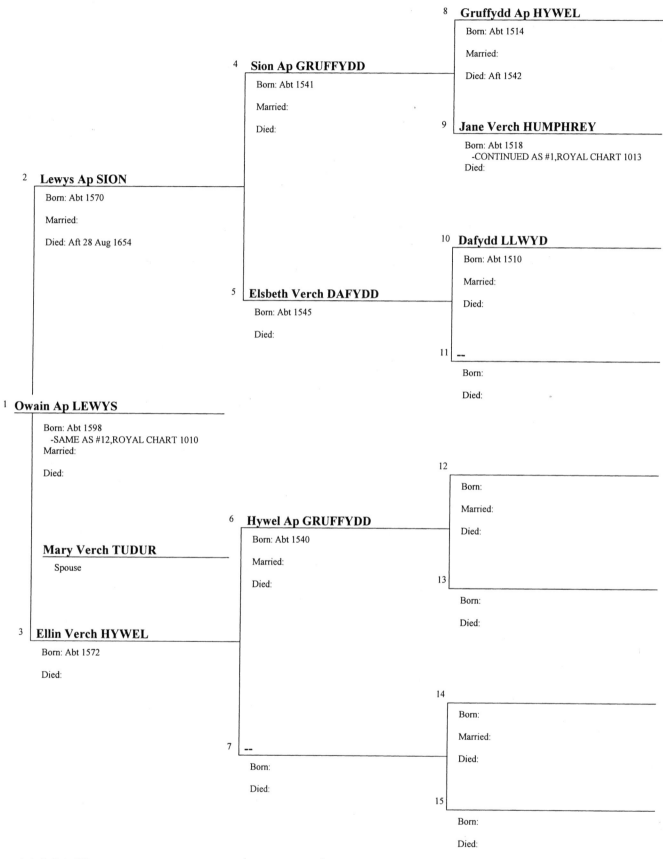

8 **Gruffydd Ap HYWEL**

Born: Abt 1514

Married:

Died: Aft 1542

4 **Sion Ap GRUFFYDD**

Born: Abt 1541

Married:

Died:

9 **Jane Verch HUMPHREY**

Born: Abt 1518
  -CONTINUED AS #1,ROYAL CHART 1013
Died:

2 **Lewys Ap SION**

Born: Abt 1570

Married:

Died: Aft 28 Aug 1654

10 **Dafydd LLWYD**

Born: Abt 1510

Married:

Died:

5 **Elsbeth Verch DAFYDD**

Born: Abt 1545

Died:

11 **--**

Born:

Died:

1 **Owain Ap LEWYS**

Born: Abt 1598
  -SAME AS #12,ROYAL CHART 1010
Married:

Died:

12

Born:

Married:

Died:

6 **Hywel Ap GRUFFYDD**

Born: Abt 1540

Married:

Died:

13

Born:

Died:

Mary Verch TUDUR

Spouse

3 **Ellin Verch HYWEL**

Born: Abt 1572

Died:

14

Born:

Married:

Died:

7 **--**

Born:

Died:

15

Born:

Died:

Sources include: Faris--Ellis.

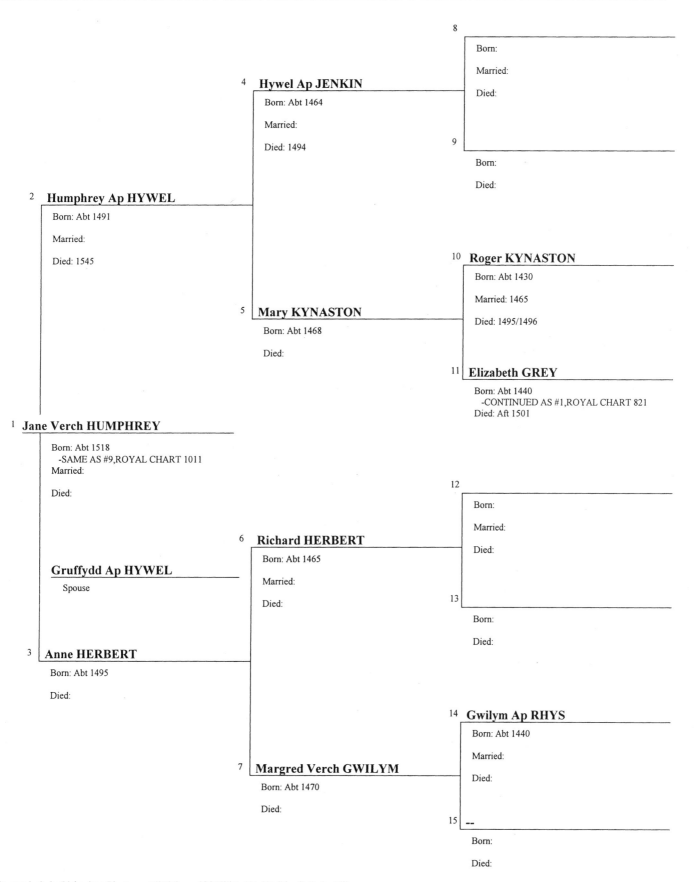

2 Humphrey Ap HYWEL

Born: Abt 1491

Married:

Died: 1545

4 Hywel Ap JENKIN

Born: Abt 1464

Married:

Died: 1494

8

Born:

Married:

Died:

9

Born:

Died:

5 Mary KYNASTON

Born: Abt 1468

Died:

10 Roger KYNASTON

Born: Abt 1430

Married: 1465

Died: 1495/1496

11 Elizabeth GREY

Born: Abt 1440
  -CONTINUED AS #1,ROYAL CHART 821
Died: Aft 1501

1 Jane Verch HUMPHREY

Born: Abt 1518
  -SAME AS #9,ROYAL CHART 1011
Married:

Died:

Gruffydd Ap HYWEL

Spouse

3 Anne HERBERT

Born: Abt 1495

Died:

6 Richard HERBERT

Born: Abt 1465

Married:

Died:

12

Born:

Married:

Died:

13

Born:

Died:

7 Margred Verch GWILYM

Born: Abt 1470

Died:

14 Gwilym Ap RHYS

Born: Abt 1440

Married:

Died:

15 --

Born:

Died:

Sources include: Richardson *Plantagenet* (2004), pp. 286 (Ellis), 454-455 (Lloyd); Faris--Ellis.

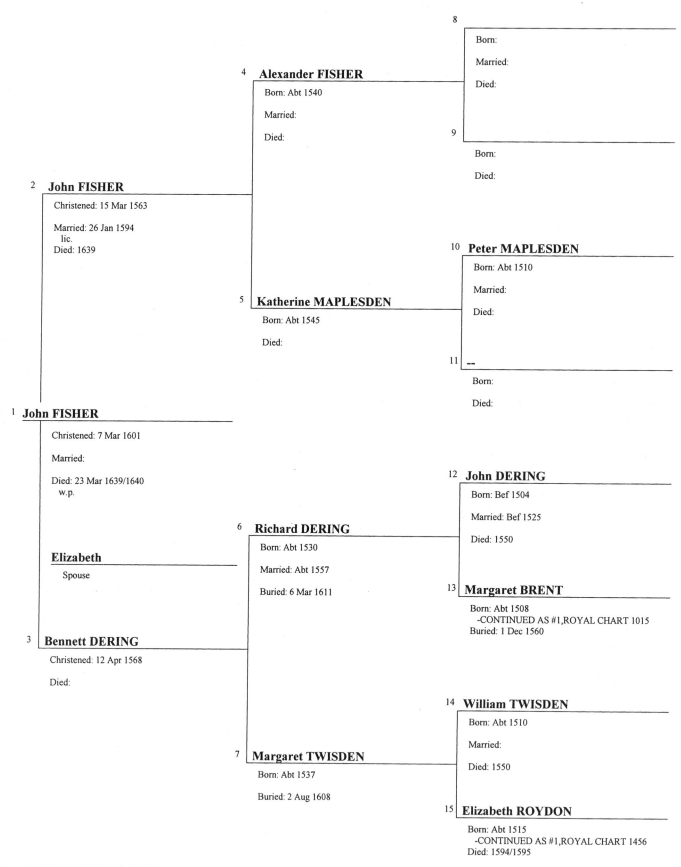

8

Born:

Married:

Died:

4 Alexander FISHER

Born: Abt 1540

Married:

Died:

9

Born:

Died:

2 John FISHER

Christened: 15 Mar 1563

Married: 26 Jan 1594
lic.
Died: 1639

10 Peter MAPLESDEN

Born: Abt 1510

Married:

Died:

5 Katherine MAPLESDEN

Born: Abt 1545

Died:

11 --

Born:

Died:

1 John FISHER

Christened: 7 Mar 1601

Married:

Died: 23 Mar 1639/1640
w.p.

Elizabeth

Spouse

12 John DERING

Born: Bef 1504

Married: Bef 1525

Died: 1550

6 Richard DERING

Born: Abt 1530

Married: Abt 1557

Buried: 6 Mar 1611

13 Margaret BRENT

Born: Abt 1508
-CONTINUED AS #1,ROYAL CHART 1015
Buried: 1 Dec 1560

3 Bennett DERING

Christened: 12 Apr 1568

Died:

14 William TWISDEN

Born: Abt 1510

Married:

Died: 1550

7 Margaret TWISDEN

Born: Abt 1537

Buried: 2 Aug 1608

15 Elizabeth ROYDON

Born: Abt 1515
-CONTINUED AS #1,ROYAL CHART 1456
Died: 1594/1595

Sources include: Faris 2--Fisher; Faris--Fisher. Note: #1 John had American descendants through a son Philip Fisher (b. abt 1637; md. Elizabeth Maddox).

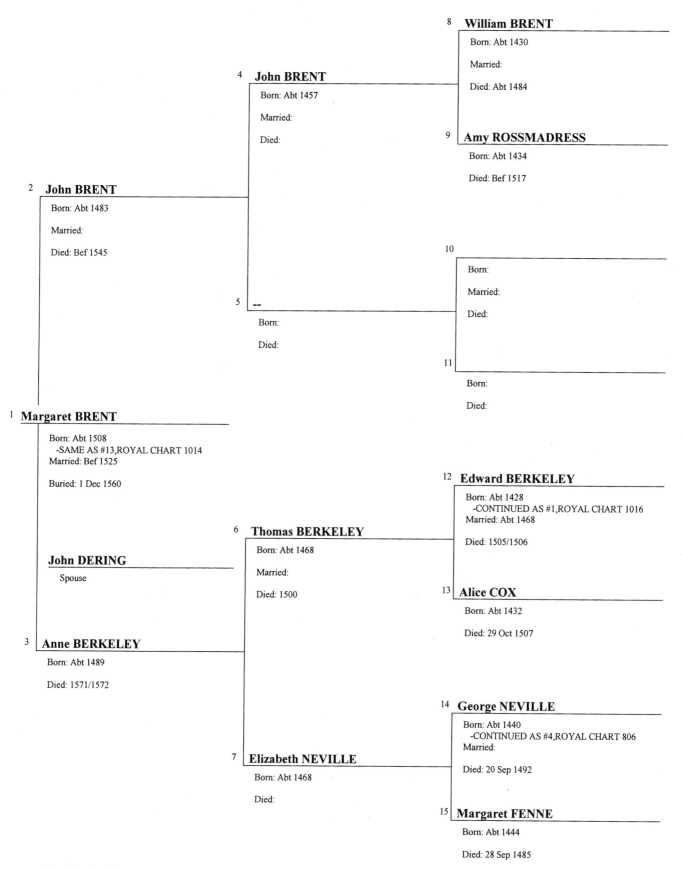

8 William BRENT
Born: Abt 1430
Married:
Died: Abt 1484

4 John BRENT
Born: Abt 1457
Married:
Died:

9 Amy ROSSMADRESS
Born: Abt 1434
Died: Bef 1517

2 John BRENT
Born: Abt 1483
Married:
Died: Bef 1545

10
Born:
Married:
Died:

5 --
Born:
Died:

11
Born:
Died:

1 Margaret BRENT
Born: Abt 1508
-SAME AS #13,ROYAL CHART 1014
Married: Bef 1525
Buried: 1 Dec 1560

12 Edward BERKELEY
Born: Abt 1428
-CONTINUED AS #1,ROYAL CHART 1016
Married: Abt 1468
Died: 1505/1506

6 Thomas BERKELEY
Born: Abt 1468
Married:
Died: 1500

13 Alice COX
Born: Abt 1432
Died: 29 Oct 1507

John DERING
Spouse

3 Anne BERKELEY
Born: Abt 1489
Died: 1571/1572

14 George NEVILLE
Born: Abt 1440
-CONTINUED AS #4,ROYAL CHART 806
Married:
Died: 20 Sep 1492

7 Elizabeth NEVILLE
Born: Abt 1468
Died:

15 Margaret FENNE
Born: Abt 1444
Died: 28 Sep 1485

Sources include: Faris--Fisher; LDS records.

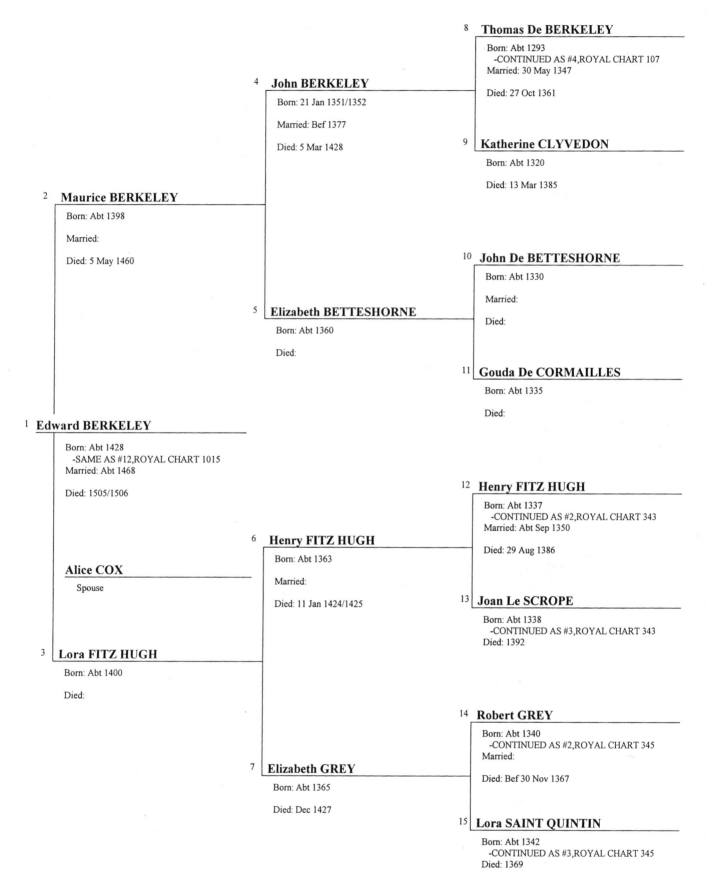

8 Thomas De BERKELEY

Born: Abt 1293
 -CONTINUED AS #4,ROYAL CHART 107
Married: 30 May 1347

Died: 27 Oct 1361

4 John BERKELEY

Born: 21 Jan 1351/1352

Married: Bef 1377

Died: 5 Mar 1428

9 Katherine CLYVEDON

Born: Abt 1320

Died: 13 Mar 1385

2 Maurice BERKELEY

Born: Abt 1398

Married:

Died: 5 May 1460

10 John De BETTESHORNE

Born: Abt 1330

Married:

Died:

5 Elizabeth BETTESHORNE

Born: Abt 1360

Died:

11 Gouda De CORMAILLES

Born: Abt 1335

Died:

1 Edward BERKELEY

Born: Abt 1428
 -SAME AS #12,ROYAL CHART 1015
Married: Abt 1468

Died: 1505/1506

12 Henry FITZ HUGH

Born: Abt 1337
 -CONTINUED AS #2,ROYAL CHART 343
Married: Abt Sep 1350

Died: 29 Aug 1386

6 Henry FITZ HUGH

Born: Abt 1363

Married:

Died: 11 Jan 1424/1425

13 Joan Le SCROPE

Born: Abt 1338
 -CONTINUED AS #3,ROYAL CHART 343
Died: 1392

Alice COX

Spouse

3 Lora FITZ HUGH

Born: Abt 1400

Died:

14 Robert GREY

Born: Abt 1340
 -CONTINUED AS #2,ROYAL CHART 345
Married:

Died: Bef 30 Nov 1367

7 Elizabeth GREY

Born: Abt 1365

Died: Dec 1427

15 Lora SAINT QUINTIN

Born: Abt 1342
 -CONTINUED AS #3,ROYAL CHART 345
Died: 1369

Sources include: Consultation with Douglas Richardson; LDS records.

Pedigree Chart

Chart 1017

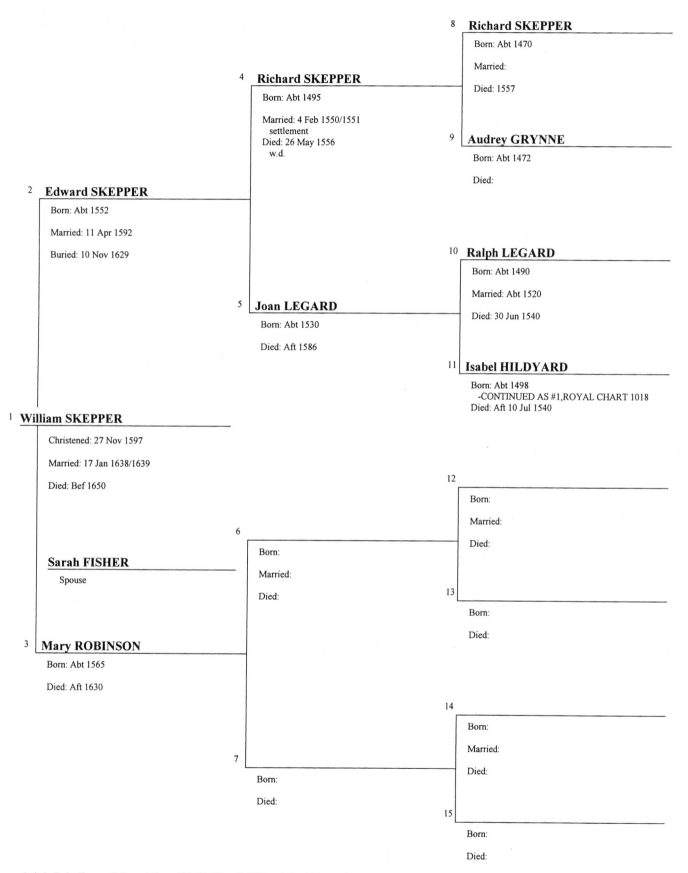

8   **Richard SKEPPER**

Born: Abt 1470

Married:

Died: 1557

4   **Richard SKEPPER**

Born: Abt 1495

Married: 4 Feb 1550/1551
settlement
Died: 26 May 1556
w.d.

9   **Audrey GRYNNE**

Born: Abt 1472

Died:

2   **Edward SKEPPER**

Born: Abt 1552

Married: 11 Apr 1592

Buried: 10 Nov 1629

10   **Ralph LEGARD**

Born: Abt 1490

Married: Abt 1520

Died: 30 Jun 1540

5   **Joan LEGARD**

Born: Abt 1530

Died: Aft 1586

11   **Isabel HILDYARD**

Born: Abt 1498
-CONTINUED AS #1, ROYAL CHART 1018
Died: Aft 10 Jul 1540

1   **William SKEPPER**

Christened: 27 Nov 1597

Married: 17 Jan 1638/1639

Died: Bef 1650

12

Born:

Married:

Died:

6

Born:

Married:

Died:

13

Born:

Died:

Sarah FISHER

Spouse

3   **Mary ROBINSON**

Born: Abt 1565

Died: Aft 1630

14

Born:

Married:

Died:

7

Born:

Died:

15

Born:

Died:

Sources include: Faris--Skepper; Roberts *AAP*, pp. 196-197. Note: #1 William & Sarah have MPGL descendants through a daughter Sarah Skipper (b. abt 1640; md. Walter Fairfield).

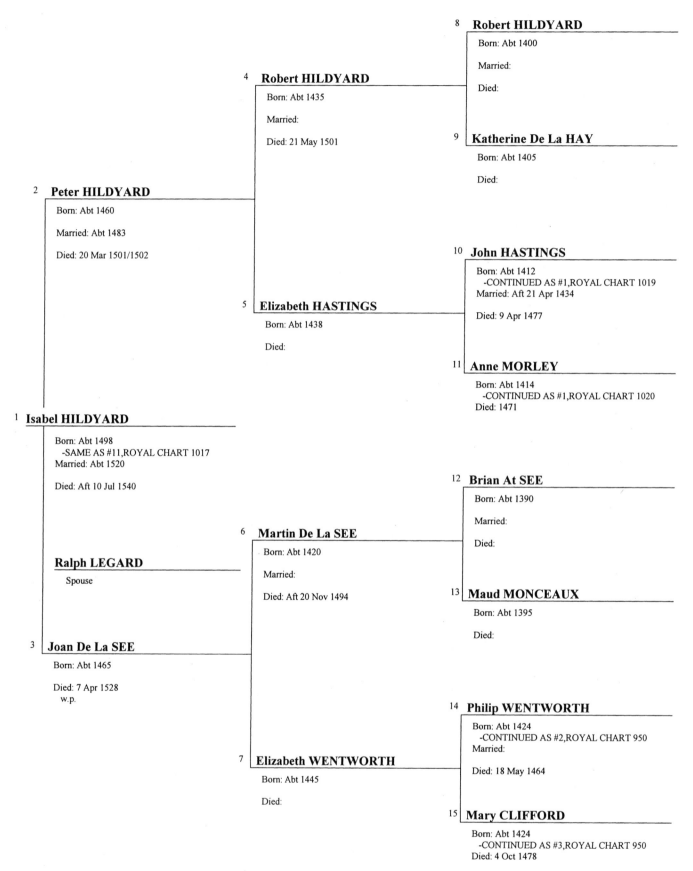

8　**Robert HILDYARD**

Born: Abt 1400

Married:

Died:

4　**Robert HILDYARD**

Born: Abt 1435

Married:

Died: 21 May 1501

9　**Katherine De La HAY**

Born: Abt 1405

Died:

2　**Peter HILDYARD**

Born: Abt 1460

Married: Abt 1483

Died: 20 Mar 1501/1502

10　**John HASTINGS**

Born: Abt 1412
　-CONTINUED AS #1,ROYAL CHART 1019
Married: Aft 21 Apr 1434

Died: 9 Apr 1477

5　**Elizabeth HASTINGS**

Born: Abt 1438

Died:

11　**Anne MORLEY**

Born: Abt 1414
　-CONTINUED AS #1,ROYAL CHART 1020
Died: 1471

1　**Isabel HILDYARD**

Born: Abt 1498
　-SAME AS #11,ROYAL CHART 1017
Married: Abt 1520

Died: Aft 10 Jul 1540

12　**Brian At SEE**

Born: Abt 1390

Married:

Died:

6　**Martin De La SEE**

Born: Abt 1420

Married:

Died: Aft 20 Nov 1494

13　**Maud MONCEAUX**

Born: Abt 1395

Died:

Ralph LEGARD

Spouse

3　**Joan De La SEE**

Born: Abt 1465

Died: 7 Apr 1528
w.p.

14　**Philip WENTWORTH**

Born: Abt 1424
　-CONTINUED AS #2,ROYAL CHART 950
Married:

Died: 18 May 1464

7　**Elizabeth WENTWORTH**

Born: Abt 1445

Died:

15　**Mary CLIFFORD**

Born: Abt 1424
　-CONTINUED AS #3,ROYAL CHART 950
Died: 4 Oct 1478

Sources include: Faris--Skepper; Roberts *AAP*, pp. 196-197.

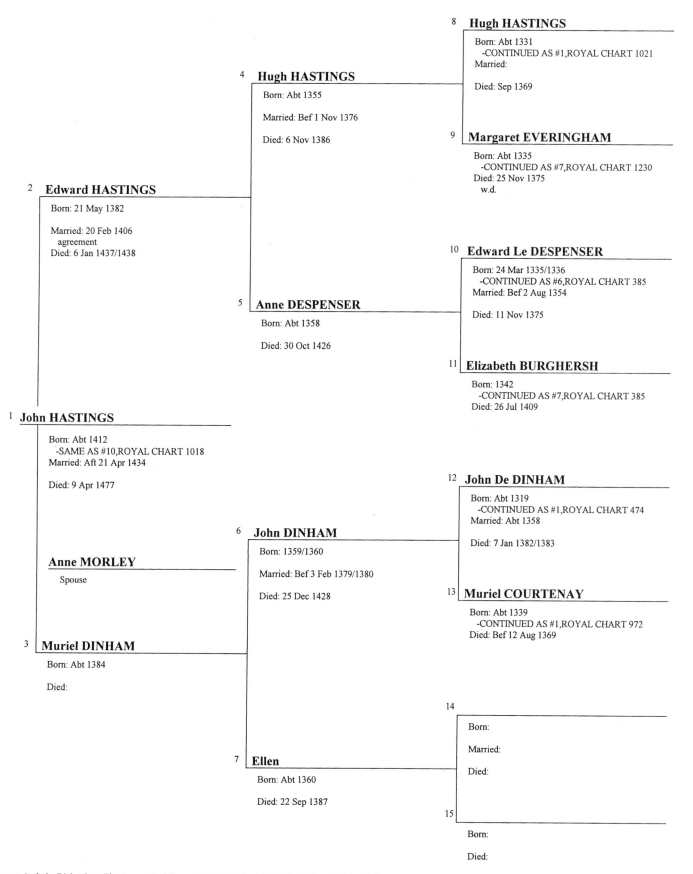

8 Hugh HASTINGS

Born: Abt 1331
-CONTINUED AS #1,ROYAL CHART 1021
Married:

Died: Sep 1369

4 Hugh HASTINGS

Born: Abt 1355

Married: Bef 1 Nov 1376

Died: 6 Nov 1386

9 Margaret EVERINGHAM

Born: Abt 1335
-CONTINUED AS #7,ROYAL CHART 1230
Died: 25 Nov 1375
w.d.

2 Edward HASTINGS

Born: 21 May 1382

Married: 20 Feb 1406
agreement
Died: 6 Jan 1437/1438

10 Edward Le DESPENSER

Born: 24 Mar 1335/1336
-CONTINUED AS #6,ROYAL CHART 385
Married: Bef 2 Aug 1354

Died: 11 Nov 1375

5 Anne DESPENSER

Born: Abt 1358

Died: 30 Oct 1426

11 Elizabeth BURGHERSH

Born: 1342
-CONTINUED AS #7,ROYAL CHART 385
Died: 26 Jul 1409

1 John HASTINGS

Born: Abt 1412
-SAME AS #10,ROYAL CHART 1018
Married: Aft 21 Apr 1434

Died: 9 Apr 1477

12 John De DINHAM

Born: Abt 1319
-CONTINUED AS #1,ROYAL CHART 474
Married: Abt 1358

Died: 7 Jan 1382/1383

6 John DINHAM

Born: 1359/1360

Married: Bef 3 Feb 1379/1380

Died: 25 Dec 1428

13 Muriel COURTENAY

Born: Abt 1339
-CONTINUED AS #1,ROYAL CHART 972
Died: Bef 12 Aug 1369

Anne MORLEY

Spouse

3 Muriel DINHAM

Born: Abt 1384

Died:

14

Born:

Married:

Died:

7 Ellen

Born: Abt 1360

Died: 22 Sep 1387

15

Born:

Died:

Sources include: Richardson *Plantagenet* (2004), pp. 288-290 (Elsing), 274-275 (Dinham); Faris--Elsing.

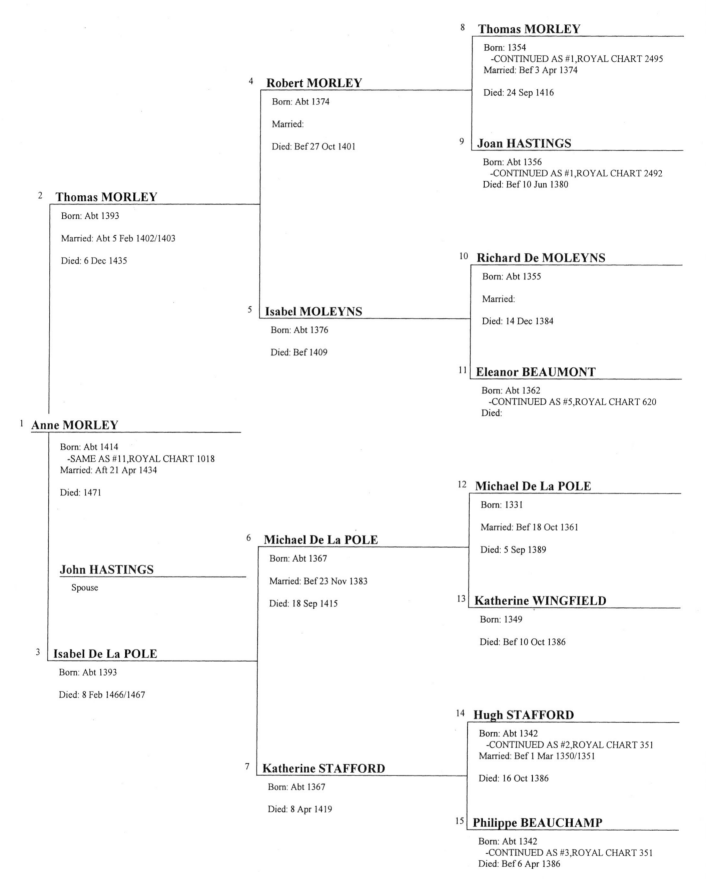

8 Thomas MORLEY

Born: 1354
-CONTINUED AS #1,ROYAL CHART 2495
Married: Bef 3 Apr 1374

Died: 24 Sep 1416

4 Robert MORLEY

Born: Abt 1374

Married:

Died: Bef 27 Oct 1401

9 Joan HASTINGS

Born: Abt 1356
-CONTINUED AS #1,ROYAL CHART 2492
Died: Bef 10 Jun 1380

2 Thomas MORLEY

Born: Abt 1393

Married: Abt 5 Feb 1402/1403

Died: 6 Dec 1435

10 Richard De MOLEYNS

Born: Abt 1355

Married:

Died: 14 Dec 1384

5 Isabel MOLEYNS

Born: Abt 1376

Died: Bef 1409

11 Eleanor BEAUMONT

Born: Abt 1362
-CONTINUED AS #5,ROYAL CHART 620
Died:

1 Anne MORLEY

Born: Abt 1414
-SAME AS #11,ROYAL CHART 1018
Married: Aft 21 Apr 1434

Died: 1471

12 Michael De La POLE

Born: 1331

Married: Bef 18 Oct 1361

Died: 5 Sep 1389

6 Michael De La POLE

Born: Abt 1367

Married: Bef 23 Nov 1383

Died: 18 Sep 1415

13 Katherine WINGFIELD

Born: 1349

Died: Bef 10 Oct 1386

John HASTINGS

Spouse

3 Isabel De La POLE

Born: Abt 1393

Died: 8 Feb 1466/1467

14 Hugh STAFFORD

Born: Abt 1342
-CONTINUED AS #2,ROYAL CHART 351
Married: Bef 1 Mar 1350/1351

Died: 16 Oct 1386

7 Katherine STAFFORD

Born: Abt 1367

Died: 8 Apr 1419

15 Philippe BEAUCHAMP

Born: Abt 1342
-CONTINUED AS #3,ROYAL CHART 351
Died: Bef 6 Apr 1386

Sources include: Richardson *Plantagenet* (2004), pp. 517-518 (Morley), 687-688 (Stonor); Faris--Elsing, Pole; Faris 2--Morley.

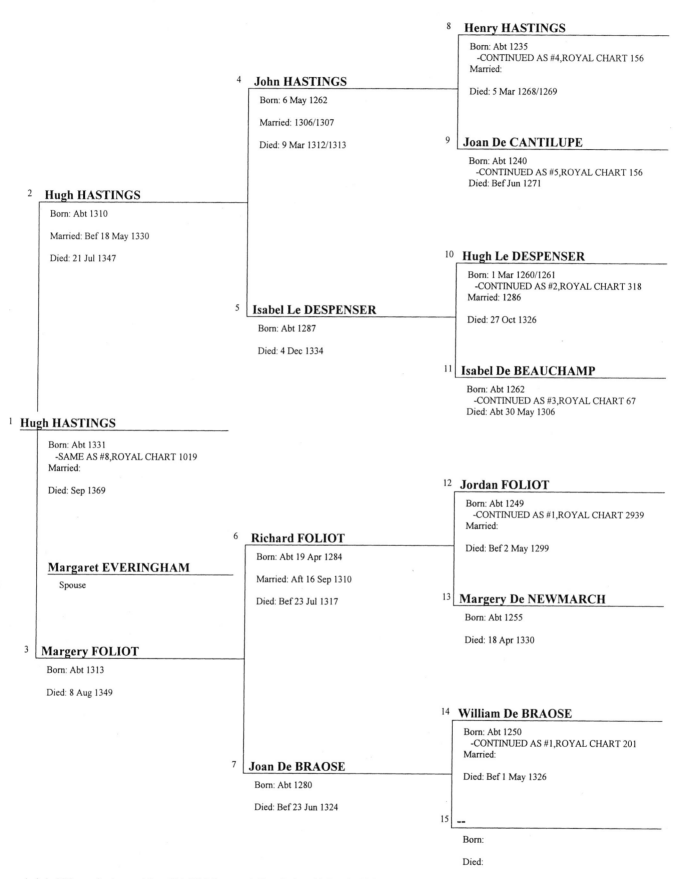

8 Henry HASTINGS
Born: Abt 1235
-CONTINUED AS #4,ROYAL CHART 156
Married:

Died: 5 Mar 1268/1269

4 John HASTINGS
Born: 6 May 1262

Married: 1306/1307

Died: 9 Mar 1312/1313

9 Joan De CANTILUPE
Born: Abt 1240
-CONTINUED AS #5,ROYAL CHART 156
Died: Bef Jun 1271

2 Hugh HASTINGS
Born: Abt 1310

Married: Bef 18 May 1330

Died: 21 Jul 1347

10 Hugh Le DESPENSER
Born: 1 Mar 1260/1261
-CONTINUED AS #2,ROYAL CHART 318
Married: 1286

Died: 27 Oct 1326

5 Isabel Le DESPENSER
Born: Abt 1287

Died: 4 Dec 1334

11 Isabel De BEAUCHAMP
Born: Abt 1262
-CONTINUED AS #3,ROYAL CHART 67
Died: Abt 30 May 1306

1 Hugh HASTINGS
Born: Abt 1331
-SAME AS #8,ROYAL CHART 1019
Married:

Died: Sep 1369

12 Jordan FOLIOT
Born: Abt 1249
-CONTINUED AS #1,ROYAL CHART 2939
Married:

Died: Bef 2 May 1299

6 Richard FOLIOT
Born: Abt 19 Apr 1284

Married: Aft 16 Sep 1310

Died: Bef 23 Jul 1317

13 Margery De NEWMARCH
Born: Abt 1255

Died: 18 Apr 1330

Margaret EVERINGHAM
Spouse

3 Margery FOLIOT
Born: Abt 1313

Died: 8 Aug 1349

14 William De BRAOSE
Born: Abt 1250
-CONTINUED AS #1,ROYAL CHART 201
Married:

Died: Bef 1 May 1326

7 Joan De BRAOSE
Born: Abt 1280

Died: Bef 23 Jun 1324

15 --
Born:

Died:

Sources include: LDS records; *Ancestral Roots* 93A (#4 & 5 ancestry); Consultation with Douglas Richardson.

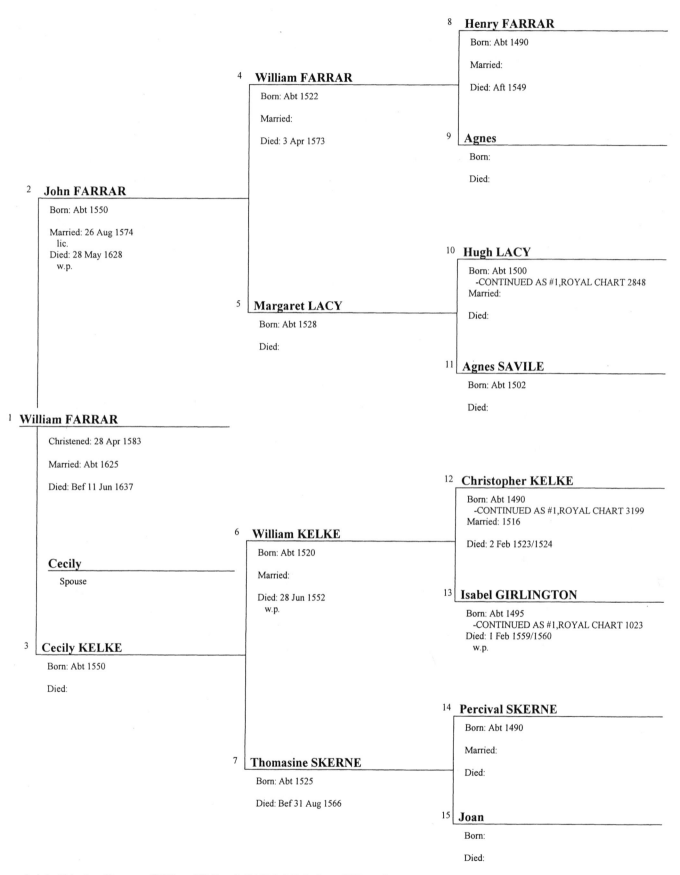

8 **Henry FARRAR**
Born: Abt 1490
Married:
Died: Aft 1549

4 **William FARRAR**
Born: Abt 1522
Married:
Died: 3 Apr 1573

9 **Agnes**
Born:
Died:

2 **John FARRAR**
Born: Abt 1550
Married: 26 Aug 1574
lic.
Died: 28 May 1628
w.p.

10 **Hugh LACY**
Born: Abt 1500
-CONTINUED AS #1,ROYAL CHART 2848
Married:
Died:

5 **Margaret LACY**
Born: Abt 1528
Died:

11 **Agnes SAVILE**
Born: Abt 1502
Died:

1 **William FARRAR**
Christened: 28 Apr 1583
Married: Abt 1625
Died: Bef 11 Jun 1637

12 **Christopher KELKE**
Born: Abt 1490
-CONTINUED AS #1,ROYAL CHART 3199
Married: 1516
Died: 2 Feb 1523/1524

6 **William KELKE**
Born: Abt 1520
Married:
Died: 28 Jun 1552
w.p.

13 **Isabel GIRLINGTON**
Born: Abt 1495
-CONTINUED AS #1,ROYAL CHART 1023
Died: 1 Feb 1559/1560
w.p.

Cecily
Spouse

3 **Cecily KELKE**
Born: Abt 1550
Died:

14 **Percival SKERNE**
Born: Abt 1490
Married:
Died:

7 **Thomasine SKERNE**
Born: Abt 1525
Died: Bef 31 Aug 1566

15 **Joan**
Born:
Died:

Sources include: Richardson *Plantagenet* (2004), pp. 303 (Farrar), 414 (Kelke); Faris--Farrar; LDS records.

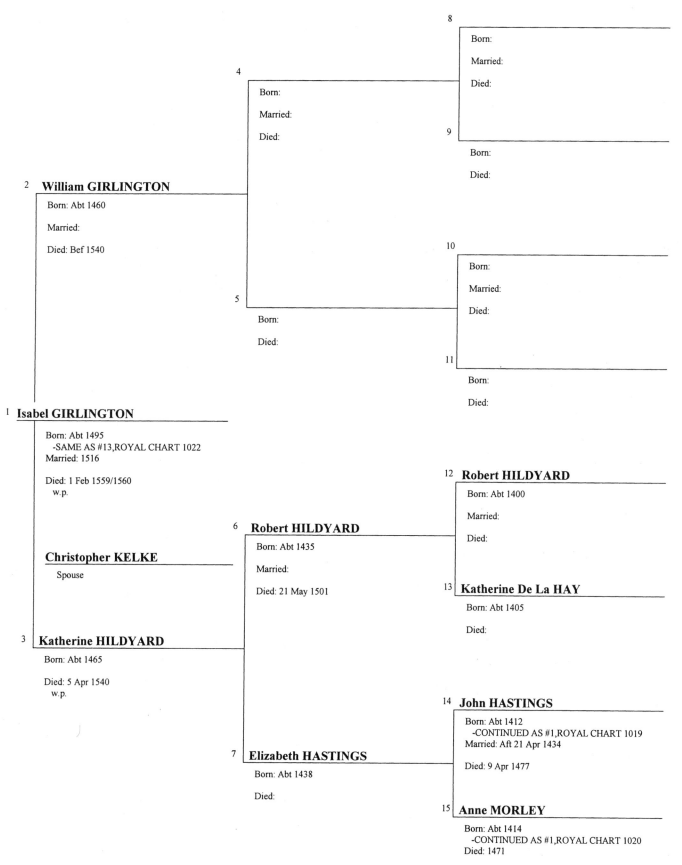

8

Born:

Married:

Died:

4

Born:

Married:

Died:

9

Born:

Died:

2   William GIRLINGTON

Born: Abt 1460

Married:

Died: Bef 1540

10

Born:

Married:

Died:

5

Born:

Died:

11

Born:

Died:

1   Isabel GIRLINGTON

Born: Abt 1495
  -SAME AS #13,ROYAL CHART 1022
Married: 1516

Died: 1 Feb 1559/1560
  w.p.

12   Robert HILDYARD

Born: Abt 1400

Married:

Died:

6   Robert HILDYARD

Born: Abt 1435

Married:

Died: 21 May 1501

Christopher KELKE

Spouse

13   Katherine De La HAY

Born: Abt 1405

Died:

3   Katherine HILDYARD

Born: Abt 1465

Died: 5 Apr 1540
  w.p.

14   John HASTINGS

Born: Abt 1412
  -CONTINUED AS #1,ROYAL CHART 1019
Married: Aft 21 Apr 1434

Died: 9 Apr 1477

7   Elizabeth HASTINGS

Born: Abt 1438

Died:

15   Anne MORLEY

Born: Abt 1414
  -CONTINUED AS #1,ROYAL CHART 1020
Died: 1471

Sources include: Faris--Girlington.

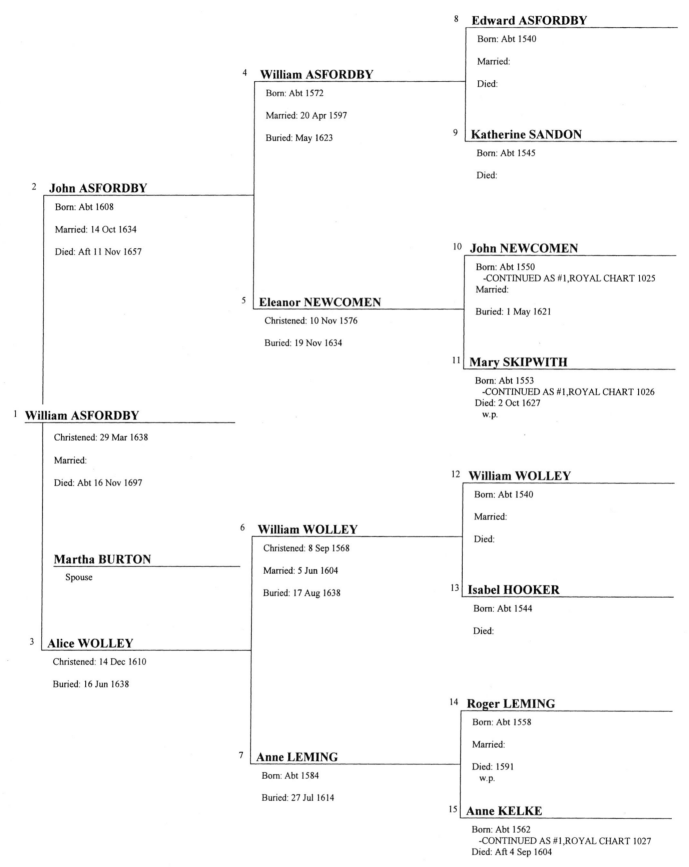

8 Edward ASFORDBY
Born: Abt 1540
Married:
Died:

4 William ASFORDBY
Born: Abt 1572
Married: 20 Apr 1597
Buried: May 1623

9 Katherine SANDON
Born: Abt 1545
Died:

2 John ASFORDBY
Born: Abt 1608
Married: 14 Oct 1634
Died: Aft 11 Nov 1657

10 John NEWCOMEN
Born: Abt 1550
-CONTINUED AS #1,ROYAL CHART 1025
Married:
Buried: 1 May 1621

5 Eleanor NEWCOMEN
Christened: 10 Nov 1576
Buried: 19 Nov 1634

11 Mary SKIPWITH
Born: Abt 1553
-CONTINUED AS #1,ROYAL CHART 1026
Died: 2 Oct 1627
w.p.

1 William ASFORDBY
Christened: 29 Mar 1638
Married:
Died: Abt 16 Nov 1697

12 William WOLLEY
Born: Abt 1540
Married:
Died:

6 William WOLLEY
Christened: 8 Sep 1568
Married: 5 Jun 1604
Buried: 17 Aug 1638

13 Isabel HOOKER
Born: Abt 1544
Died:

Martha BURTON
Spouse

3 Alice WOLLEY
Christened: 14 Dec 1610
Buried: 16 Jun 1638

14 Roger LEMING
Born: Abt 1558
Married:
Died: 1591
w.p.

7 Anne LEMING
Born: Abt 1584
Buried: 27 Jul 1614

15 Anne KELKE
Born: Abt 1562
-CONTINUED AS #1,ROYAL CHART 1027
Died: Aft 4 Sep 1604

Sources include: Faris--Asfordby, Girlington.

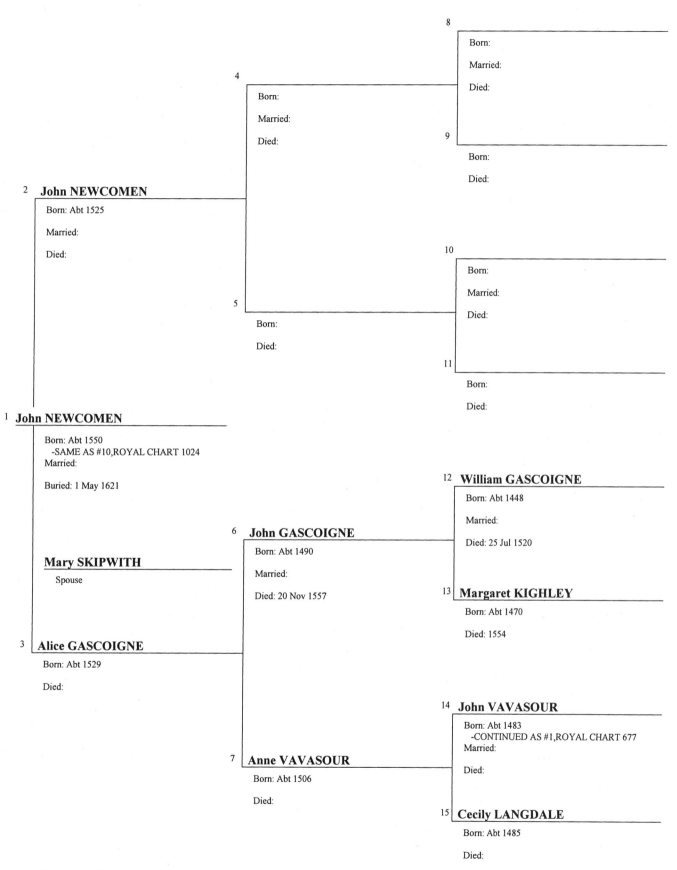

8

Born:

Married:

Died:

4

Born:

Married:

Died:

9

Born:

Died:

2   **John NEWCOMEN**

Born: Abt 1525

Married:

Died:

10

Born:

Married:

Died:

5

Born:

Died:

11

Born:

Died:

1   **John NEWCOMEN**

Born: Abt 1550
   -SAME AS #10,ROYAL CHART 1024
Married:

Buried: 1 May 1621

12   **William GASCOIGNE**

Born: Abt 1448

Married:

Died: 25 Jul 1520

6   **John GASCOIGNE**

Born: Abt 1490

Married:

Died: 20 Nov 1557

13   **Margaret KIGHLEY**

Born: Abt 1470

Died: 1554

Mary SKIPWITH

Spouse

3   **Alice GASCOIGNE**

Born: Abt 1529

Died:

14   **John VAVASOUR**

Born: Abt 1483
   -CONTINUED AS #1,ROYAL CHART 677
Married:

Died:

7   **Anne VAVASOUR**

Born: Abt 1506

Died:

15   **Cecily LANGDALE**

Born: Abt 1485

Died:

Sources include: Faris--Asfordby; LDS records.

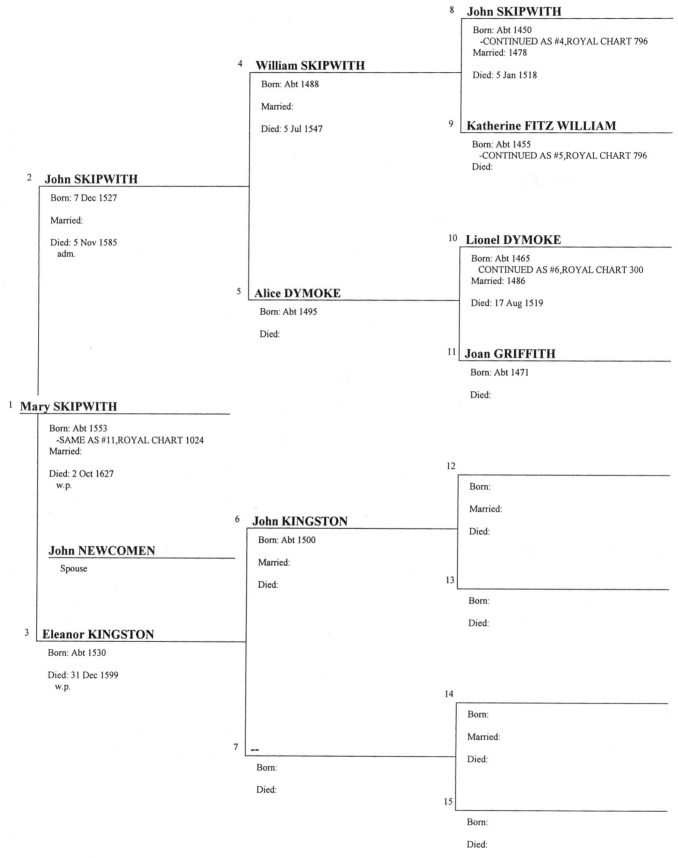

8 John SKIPWITH

Born: Abt 1450
-CONTINUED AS #4,ROYAL CHART 796
Married: 1478

Died: 5 Jan 1518

4 William SKIPWITH

Born: Abt 1488

Married:

Died: 5 Jul 1547

9 Katherine FITZ WILLIAM

Born: Abt 1455
-CONTINUED AS #5,ROYAL CHART 796
Died:

2 John SKIPWITH

Born: 7 Dec 1527

Married:

Died: 5 Nov 1585
adm.

10 Lionel DYMOKE

Born: Abt 1465
CONTINUED AS #6,ROYAL CHART 300
Married: 1486

Died: 17 Aug 1519

5 Alice DYMOKE

Born: Abt 1495

Died:

11 Joan GRIFFITH

Born: Abt 1471

Died:

1 Mary SKIPWITH

Born: Abt 1553
-SAME AS #11,ROYAL CHART 1024
Married:

Died: 2 Oct 1627
w.p.

John NEWCOMEN

Spouse

12

Born:

Married:

Died:

6 John KINGSTON

Born: Abt 1500

Married:

Died:

13

Born:

Died:

3 Eleanor KINGSTON

Born: Abt 1530

Died: 31 Dec 1599
w.p.

14

Born:

Married:

Died:

7 --

Born:

Died:

15

Born:

Died:

Sources include: Faris 2--Skipwith; Faris--Asfordby.

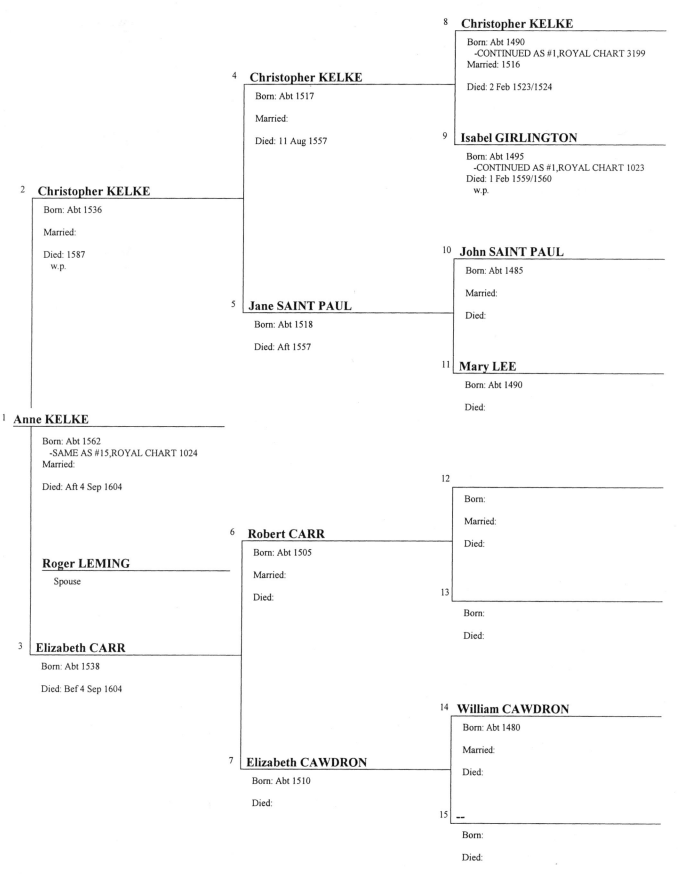

8 **Christopher KELKE**

Born: Abt 1490
   -CONTINUED AS #1,ROYAL CHART 3199
Married: 1516

Died: 2 Feb 1523/1524

4 **Christopher KELKE**

Born: Abt 1517

Married:

Died: 11 Aug 1557

9 **Isabel GIRLINGTON**

Born: Abt 1495
   -CONTINUED AS #1,ROYAL CHART 1023
Died: 1 Feb 1559/1560
w.p.

2 **Christopher KELKE**

Born: Abt 1536

Married:

Died: 1587
w.p.

10 **John SAINT PAUL**

Born: Abt 1485

Married:

Died:

5 **Jane SAINT PAUL**

Born: Abt 1518

Died: Aft 1557

11 **Mary LEE**

Born: Abt 1490

Died:

1 **Anne KELKE**

Born: Abt 1562
   -SAME AS #15,ROYAL CHART 1024
Married:

Died: Aft 4 Sep 1604

12

Born:

Married:

Died:

Roger LEMING

Spouse

6 **Robert CARR**

Born: Abt 1505

Married:

Died:

13

Born:

Died:

3 **Elizabeth CARR**

Born: Abt 1538

Died: Bef 4 Sep 1604

14 **William CAWDRON**

Born: Abt 1480

Married:

Died:

7 **Elizabeth CAWDRON**

Born: Abt 1510

Died:

15 **--**

Born:

Died:

Sources include: Richardson *Plantagenet* (2004), pp. 414-415 (Kelke); Faris 2--Kelke; Faris--Girlington.

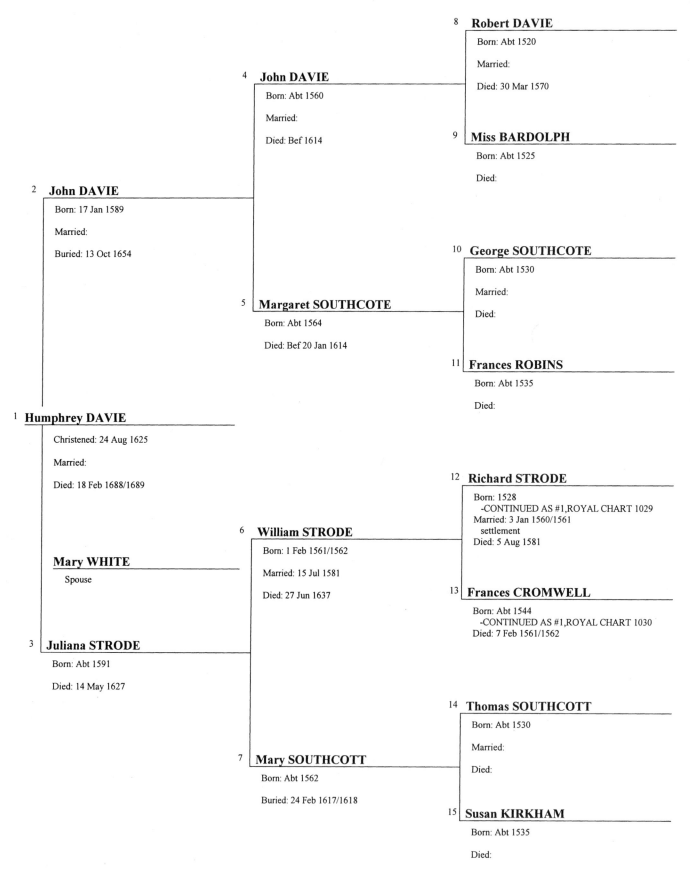

8 | Robert DAVIE
Born: Abt 1520
Married:
Died: 30 Mar 1570

4 | John DAVIE
Born: Abt 1560
Married:
Died: Bef 1614

9 | Miss BARDOLPH
Born: Abt 1525
Died:

2 | John DAVIE
Born: 17 Jan 1589
Married:
Buried: 13 Oct 1654

10 | George SOUTHCOTE
Born: Abt 1530
Married:
Died:

5 | Margaret SOUTHCOTE
Born: Abt 1564
Died: Bef 20 Jan 1614

11 | Frances ROBINS
Born: Abt 1535
Died:

1 | Humphrey DAVIE
Christened: 24 Aug 1625
Married:
Died: 18 Feb 1688/1689

Mary WHITE
Spouse

12 | Richard STRODE
Born: 1528
  -CONTINUED AS #1,ROYAL CHART 1029
Married: 3 Jan 1560/1561
  settlement
Died: 5 Aug 1581

6 | William STRODE
Born: 1 Feb 1561/1562
Married: 15 Jul 1581
Died: 27 Jun 1637

13 | Frances CROMWELL
Born: Abt 1544
  -CONTINUED AS #1,ROYAL CHART 1030
Died: 7 Feb 1561/1562

3 | Juliana STRODE
Born: Abt 1591
Died: 14 May 1627

14 | Thomas SOUTHCOTT
Born: Abt 1530
Married:
Died:

7 | Mary SOUTHCOTT
Born: Abt 1562
Buried: 24 Feb 1617/1618

15 | Susan KIRKHAM
Born: Abt 1535
Died:

Sources include: Faris 2--Davie; Faris--Davie; LDS records.

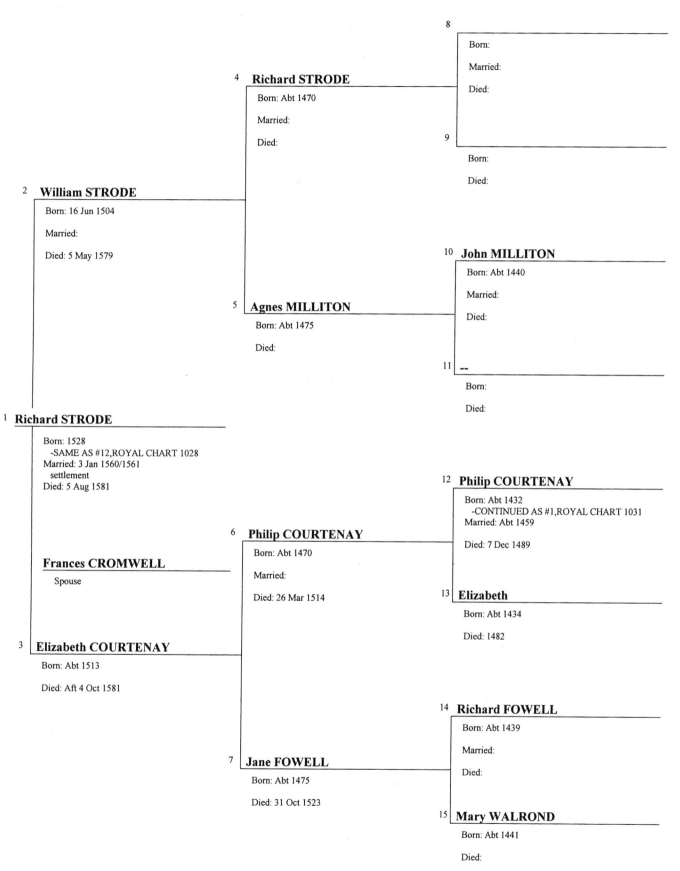

8

Born:

Married:

Died:

4 **Richard STRODE**

Born: Abt 1470

Married:

Died:

9

Born:

Died:

2 **William STRODE**

Born: 16 Jun 1504

Married:

Died: 5 May 1579

10 **John MILLITON**

Born: Abt 1440

Married:

Died:

5 **Agnes MILLITON**

Born: Abt 1475

Died:

11 **--**

Born:

Died:

1 **Richard STRODE**

Born: 1528
    -SAME AS #12,ROYAL CHART 1028
Married: 3 Jan 1560/1561
    settlement
Died: 5 Aug 1581

12 **Philip COURTENAY**

Born: Abt 1432
    -CONTINUED AS #1,ROYAL CHART 1031
Married: Abt 1459

Died: 7 Dec 1489

6 **Philip COURTENAY**

Born: Abt 1470

Married:

Died: 26 Mar 1514

13 **Elizabeth**

Born: Abt 1434

Died: 1482

Frances CROMWELL

Spouse

3 **Elizabeth COURTENAY**

Born: Abt 1513

Died: Aft 4 Oct 1581

14 **Richard FOWELL**

Born: Abt 1439

Married:

Died:

7 **Jane FOWELL**

Born: Abt 1475

Died: 31 Oct 1523

15 **Mary WALROND**

Born: Abt 1441

Died:

Sources include: Faris 2--Davie; Faris--Davie, Courtenay; LDS records.

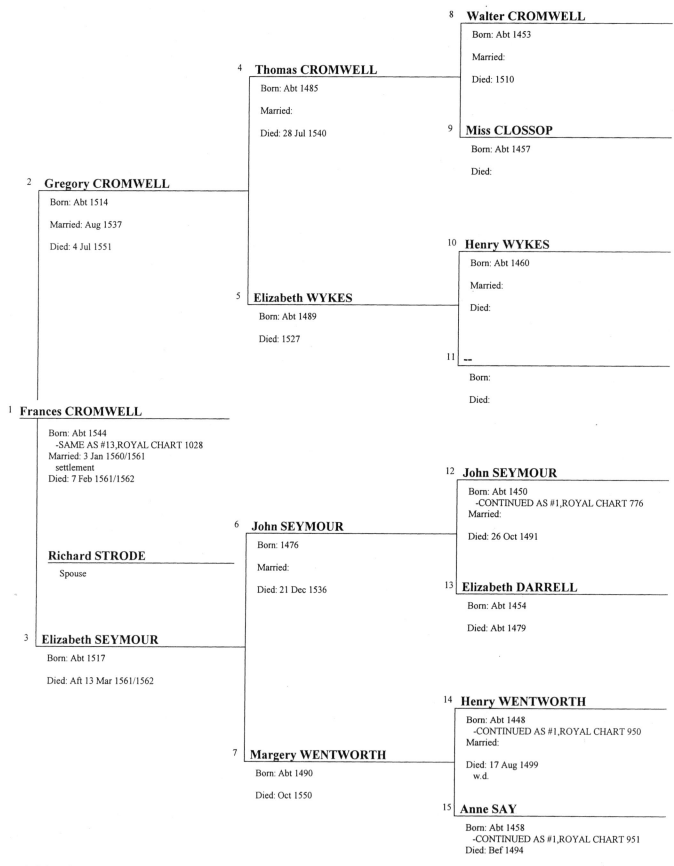

2 Gregory CROMWELL

Born: Abt 1514

Married: Aug 1537

Died: 4 Jul 1551

4 Thomas CROMWELL

Born: Abt 1485

Married:

Died: 28 Jul 1540

8 Walter CROMWELL

Born: Abt 1453

Married:

Died: 1510

9 Miss CLOSSOP

Born: Abt 1457

Died:

5 Elizabeth WYKES

Born: Abt 1489

Died: 1527

10 Henry WYKES

Born: Abt 1460

Married:

Died:

11 --

Born:

Died:

1 Frances CROMWELL

Born: Abt 1544
   -SAME AS #13,ROYAL CHART 1028
Married: 3 Jan 1560/1561
   settlement
Died: 7 Feb 1561/1562

Richard STRODE

Spouse

3 Elizabeth SEYMOUR

Born: Abt 1517

Died: Aft 13 Mar 1561/1562

6 John SEYMOUR

Born: 1476

Married:

Died: 21 Dec 1536

12 John SEYMOUR

Born: Abt 1450
   -CONTINUED AS #1,ROYAL CHART 776
Married:

Died: 26 Oct 1491

13 Elizabeth DARRELL

Born: Abt 1454

Died: Abt 1479

7 Margery WENTWORTH

Born: Abt 1490

Died: Oct 1550

14 Henry WENTWORTH

Born: Abt 1448
   -CONTINUED AS #1,ROYAL CHART 950
Married:

Died: 17 Aug 1499
   w.d.

15 Anne SAY

Born: Abt 1458
   -CONTINUED AS #1,ROYAL CHART 951
Died: Bef 1494

Sources include: Faris--Davie; Faris 2--Rodney.

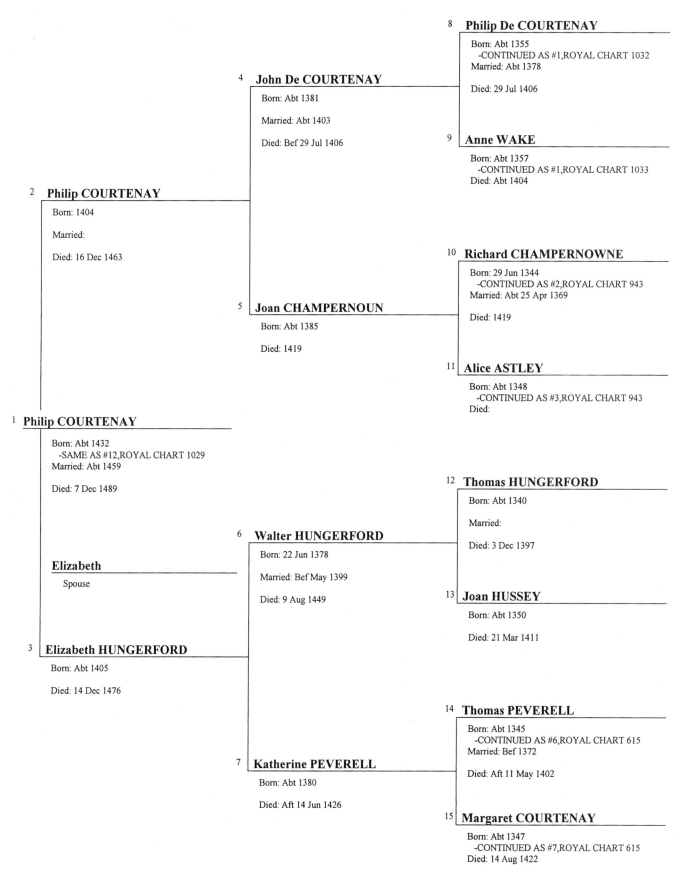

2 Philip COURTENAY

Born: 1404

Married:

Died: 16 Dec 1463

4 John De COURTENAY

Born: Abt 1381

Married: Abt 1403

Died: Bef 29 Jul 1406

5 Joan CHAMPERNOUN

Born: Abt 1385

Died: 1419

8 Philip De COURTENAY

Born: Abt 1355
  -CONTINUED AS #1,ROYAL CHART 1032
Married: Abt 1378

Died: 29 Jul 1406

9 Anne WAKE

Born: Abt 1357
  -CONTINUED AS #1,ROYAL CHART 1033
Died: Abt 1404

10 Richard CHAMPERNOWNE

Born: 29 Jun 1344
  -CONTINUED AS #2,ROYAL CHART 943
Married: Abt 25 Apr 1369

Died: 1419

11 Alice ASTLEY

Born: Abt 1348
  -CONTINUED AS #3,ROYAL CHART 943
Died:

1 Philip COURTENAY

Born: Abt 1432
  -SAME AS #12,ROYAL CHART 1029
Married: Abt 1459

Died: 7 Dec 1489

Elizabeth

Spouse

3 Elizabeth HUNGERFORD

Born: Abt 1405

Died: 14 Dec 1476

6 Walter HUNGERFORD

Born: 22 Jun 1378

Married: Bef May 1399

Died: 9 Aug 1449

7 Katherine PEVERELL

Born: Abt 1380

Died: Aft 14 Jun 1426

12 Thomas HUNGERFORD

Born: Abt 1340

Married:

Died: 3 Dec 1397

13 Joan HUSSEY

Born: Abt 1350

Died: 21 Mar 1411

14 Thomas PEVERELL

Born: Abt 1345
  -CONTINUED AS #6,ROYAL CHART 615
Married: Bef 1372

Died: Aft 11 May 1402

15 Margaret COURTENAY

Born: Abt 1347
  -CONTINUED AS #7,ROYAL CHART 615
Died: 14 Aug 1422

Sources include: Richardson *Plantagenet* (2004), pp. 257-258 (Davie), 406-407 (Hungerford); Faris 2--Davie; Faris--Courtenay; *Ancestral Roots* 51.

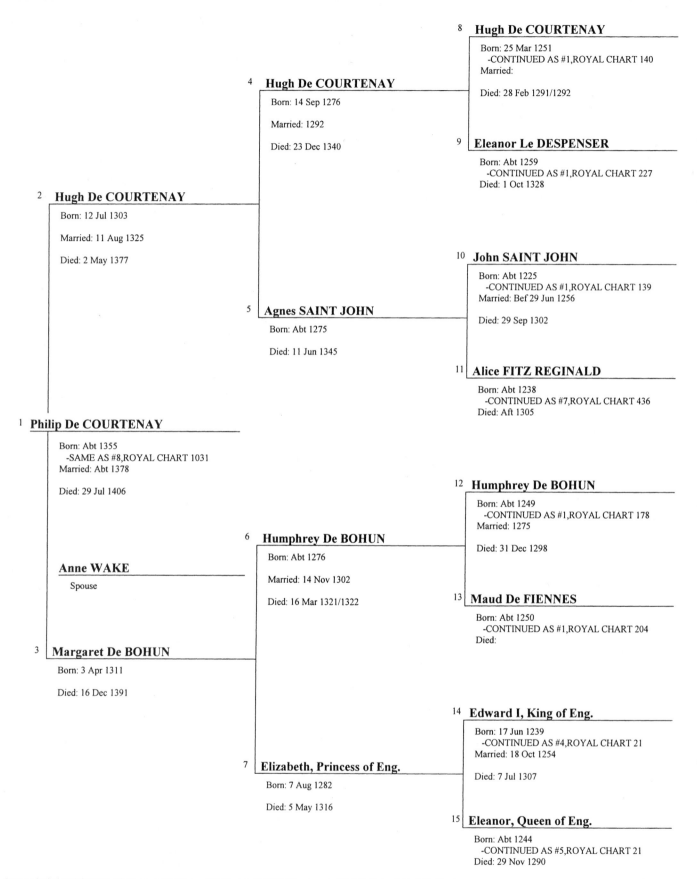

Pedigree Chart

8 **Hugh De COURTENAY**

Born: 25 Mar 1251
-CONTINUED AS #1,ROYAL CHART 140
Married:

Died: 28 Feb 1291/1292

4 **Hugh De COURTENAY**

Born: 14 Sep 1276

Married: 1292

Died: 23 Dec 1340

9 **Eleanor Le DESPENSER**

Born: Abt 1259
-CONTINUED AS #1,ROYAL CHART 227
Died: 1 Oct 1328

2 **Hugh De COURTENAY**

Born: 12 Jul 1303

Married: 11 Aug 1325

Died: 2 May 1377

10 **John SAINT JOHN**

Born: Abt 1225
-CONTINUED AS #1,ROYAL CHART 139
Married: Bef 29 Jun 1256

Died: 29 Sep 1302

5 **Agnes SAINT JOHN**

Born: Abt 1275

Died: 11 Jun 1345

11 **Alice FITZ REGINALD**

Born: Abt 1238
-CONTINUED AS #7,ROYAL CHART 436
Died: Aft 1305

1 **Philip De COURTENAY**

Born: Abt 1355
-SAME AS #8,ROYAL CHART 1031
Married: Abt 1378

Died: 29 Jul 1406

12 **Humphrey De BOHUN**

Born: Abt 1249
-CONTINUED AS #1,ROYAL CHART 178
Married: 1275

Died: 31 Dec 1298

6 **Humphrey De BOHUN**

Born: Abt 1276

Married: 14 Nov 1302

Died: 16 Mar 1321/1322

Anne WAKE

Spouse

13 **Maud De FIENNES**

Born: Abt 1250
-CONTINUED AS #1,ROYAL CHART 204
Died:

3 **Margaret De BOHUN**

Born: 3 Apr 1311

Died: 16 Dec 1391

14 **Edward I, King of Eng.**

Born: 17 Jun 1239
-CONTINUED AS #4,ROYAL CHART 21
Married: 18 Oct 1254

Died: 7 Jul 1307

7 **Elizabeth, Princess of Eng.**

Born: 7 Aug 1282

Died: 5 May 1316

15 **Eleanor, Queen of Eng.**

Born: Abt 1244
-CONTINUED AS #5,ROYAL CHART 21
Died: 29 Nov 1290

Sources include: Richardson *Plantagenet* (2004), pp. 257 (Davie), 238-239 (Courtenay), 120-122 (Bohun); Faris 2--Courtenay.

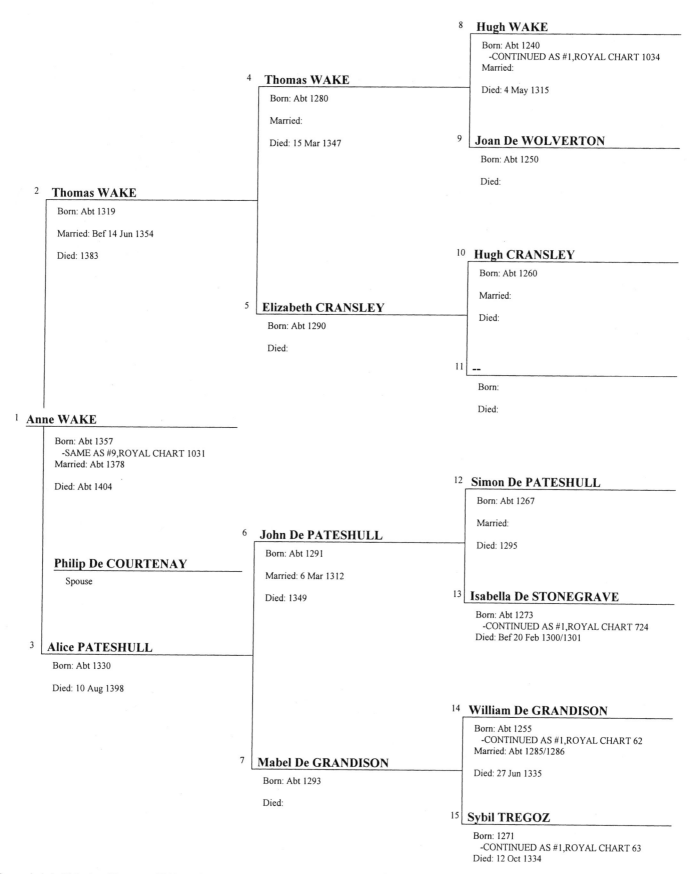

Hugh WAKE

Born: Abt 1240
-CONTINUED AS #1,ROYAL CHART 1034
Married:

Died: 4 May 1315

4 **Thomas WAKE**

Born: Abt 1280

Married:

Died: 15 Mar 1347

9 **Joan De WOLVERTON**

Born: Abt 1250

Died:

2 **Thomas WAKE**

Born: Abt 1319

Married: Bef 14 Jun 1354

Died: 1383

10 **Hugh CRANSLEY**

Born: Abt 1260

Married:

Died:

5 **Elizabeth CRANSLEY**

Born: Abt 1290

Died:

11 **--**

Born:

Died:

1 **Anne WAKE**

Born: Abt 1357
-SAME AS #9,ROYAL CHART 1031
Married: Abt 1378

Died: Abt 1404

12 **Simon De PATESHULL**

Born: Abt 1267

Married:

Died: 1295

6 **John De PATESHULL**

Born: Abt 1291

Married: 6 Mar 1312

Died: 1349

13 **Isabella De STONEGRAVE**

Born: Abt 1273
-CONTINUED AS #1,ROYAL CHART 724
Died: Bef 20 Feb 1300/1301

Philip De COURTENAY

Spouse

3 **Alice PATESHULL**

Born: Abt 1330

Died: 10 Aug 1398

14 **William De GRANDISON**

Born: Abt 1255
-CONTINUED AS #1,ROYAL CHART 62
Married: Abt 1285/1286

Died: 27 Jun 1335

7 **Mabel De GRANDISON**

Born: Abt 1293

Died:

15 **Sybil TREGOZ**

Born: 1271
-CONTINUED AS #1,ROYAL CHART 63
Died: 12 Oct 1334

Sources include: Richardson *Plantagenet* (2004), pp. 257 (Davie), 568-569 (Pateshulle); Faris--Courtenay 9; LDS records.

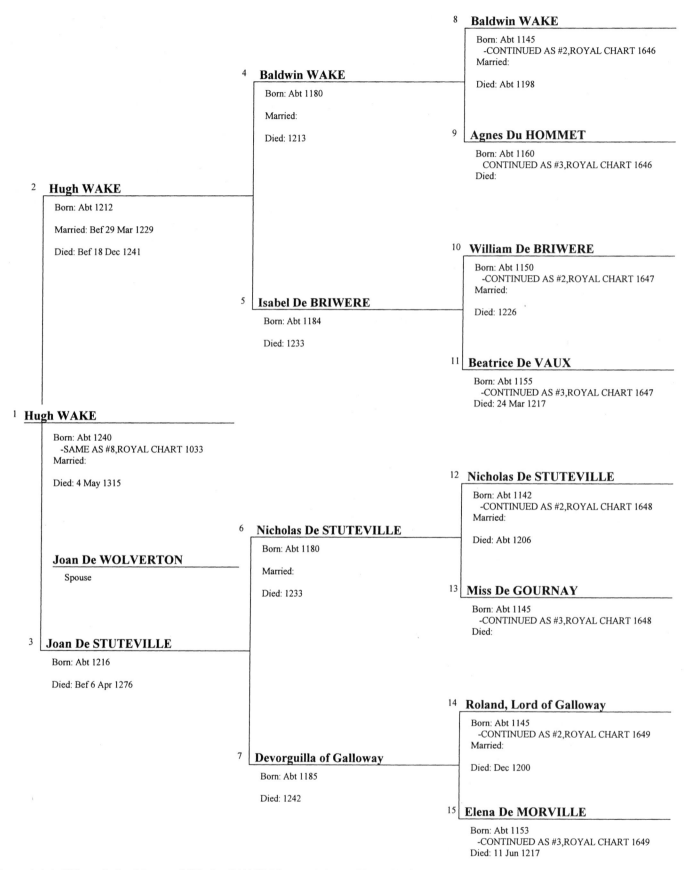

8 Baldwin WAKE

Born: Abt 1145
 -CONTINUED AS #2,ROYAL CHART 1646
Married:

Died: Abt 1198

4 Baldwin WAKE

Born: Abt 1180

Married:

Died: 1213

9 Agnes Du HOMMET

Born: Abt 1160
 CONTINUED AS #3,ROYAL CHART 1646
Died:

2 Hugh WAKE

Born: Abt 1212

Married: Bef 29 Mar 1229

Died: Bef 18 Dec 1241

10 William De BRIWERE

Born: Abt 1150
 -CONTINUED AS #2,ROYAL CHART 1647
Married:

Died: 1226

5 Isabel De BRIWERE

Born: Abt 1184

Died: 1233

11 Beatrice De VAUX

Born: Abt 1155
 -CONTINUED AS #3,ROYAL CHART 1647
Died: 24 Mar 1217

1 Hugh WAKE

Born: Abt 1240
 -SAME AS #8,ROYAL CHART 1033
Married:

Died: 4 May 1315

12 Nicholas De STUTEVILLE

Born: Abt 1142
 -CONTINUED AS #2,ROYAL CHART 1648
Married:

Died: Abt 1206

6 Nicholas De STUTEVILLE

Born: Abt 1180

Married:

Died: 1233

13 Miss De GOURNAY

Born: Abt 1145
 -CONTINUED AS #3,ROYAL CHART 1648
Died:

Joan De WOLVERTON

Spouse

3 Joan De STUTEVILLE

Born: Abt 1216

Died: Bef 6 Apr 1276

14 Roland, Lord of Galloway

Born: Abt 1145
 -CONTINUED AS #2,ROYAL CHART 1649
Married:

Died: Dec 1200

7 Devorguilla of Galloway

Born: Abt 1185

Died: 1242

15 Elena De MORVILLE

Born: Abt 1153
 -CONTINUED AS #3,ROYAL CHART 1649
Died: 11 Jun 1217

Sources include: LDS records; *Royal Ancestors* (1989), chart 11346 (#2 & 3 ancestry); *Ancestral Roots* 184A (#2 & 3 ancestry).

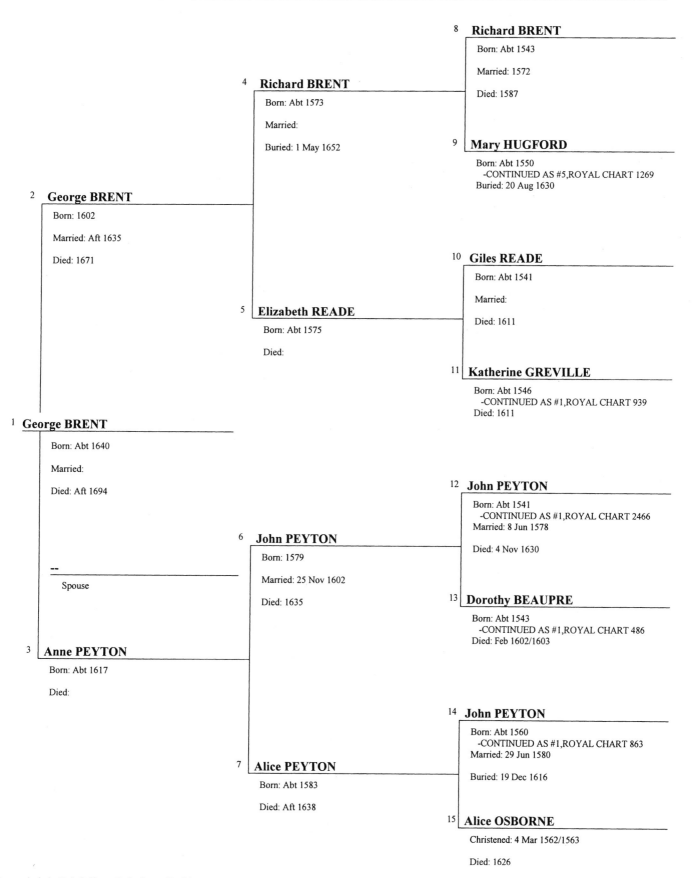

8 Richard BRENT

Born: Abt 1543

Married: 1572

Died: 1587

4 Richard BRENT

Born: Abt 1573

Married:

Buried: 1 May 1652

9 Mary HUGFORD

Born: Abt 1550
-CONTINUED AS #5,ROYAL CHART 1269
Buried: 20 Aug 1630

2 George BRENT

Born: 1602

Married: Aft 1635

Died: 1671

10 Giles READE

Born: Abt 1541

Married:

Died: 1611

5 Elizabeth READE

Born: Abt 1575

Died:

11 Katherine GREVILLE

Born: Abt 1546
-CONTINUED AS #1,ROYAL CHART 939
Died: 1611

1 George BRENT

Born: Abt 1640

Married:

Died: Aft 1694

--

Spouse

12 John PEYTON

Born: Abt 1541
-CONTINUED AS #1,ROYAL CHART 2466
Married: 8 Jun 1578

Died: 4 Nov 1630

6 John PEYTON

Born: 1579

Married: 25 Nov 1602

Died: 1635

13 Dorothy BEAUPRE

Born: Abt 1543
-CONTINUED AS #1,ROYAL CHART 486
Died: Feb 1602/1603

3 Anne PEYTON

Born: Abt 1617

Died:

14 John PEYTON

Born: Abt 1560
-CONTINUED AS #1,ROYAL CHART 863
Married: 29 Jun 1580

Buried: 19 Dec 1616

7 Alice PEYTON

Born: Abt 1583

Died: Aft 1638

15 Alice OSBORNE

Christened: 4 Mar 1562/1563

Died: 1626

Sources include: Faris 2--Brent; Faris--Brent, Hasilden.

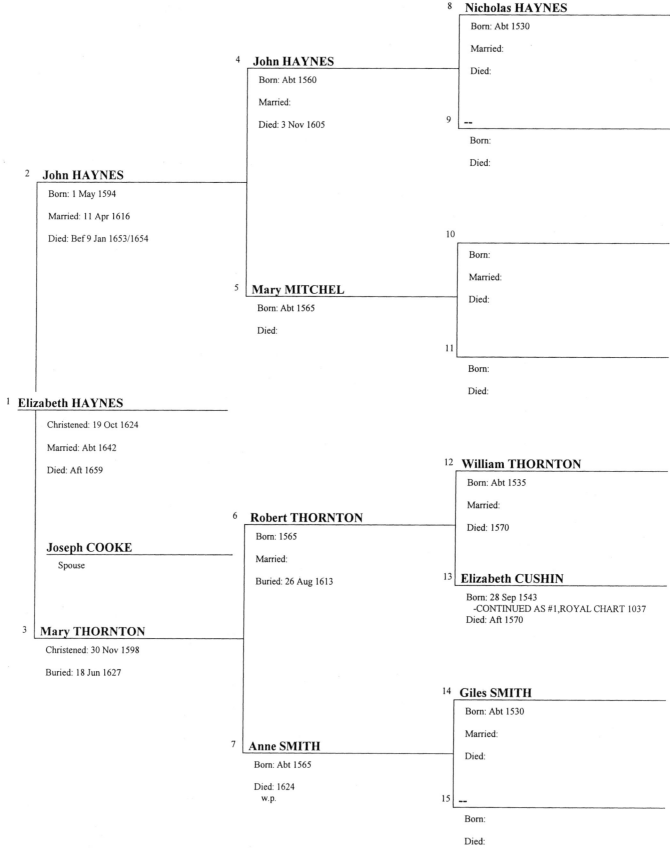

8 Nicholas HAYNES
Born: Abt 1530
Married:
Died:

4 John HAYNES
Born: Abt 1560
Married:
Died: 3 Nov 1605

9 --
Born:
Died:

2 John HAYNES
Born: 1 May 1594
Married: 11 Apr 1616
Died: Bef 9 Jan 1653/1654

10
Born:
Married:
Died:

5 Mary MITCHEL
Born: Abt 1565
Died:

11
Born:
Died:

1 Elizabeth HAYNES
Christened: 19 Oct 1624
Married: Abt 1642
Died: Aft 1659

12 William THORNTON
Born: Abt 1535
Married:
Died: 1570

6 Robert THORNTON
Born: 1565
Married:
Buried: 26 Aug 1613

13 Elizabeth CUSHIN
Born: 28 Sep 1543
-CONTINUED AS #1,ROYAL CHART 1037
Died: Aft 1570

Joseph COOKE
Spouse

3 Mary THORNTON
Christened: 30 Nov 1598
Buried: 18 Jun 1627

14 Giles SMITH
Born: Abt 1530
Married:
Died:

7 Anne SMITH
Born: Abt 1565
Died: 1624
w.p.

15 --
Born:
Died:

Sources include: Richardson *Plantagenet* (2004), pp. 392-393 (Haynes); Faris--Haynes; LDS records. Note: #1 Elizabeth had American descendants through a son Joseph Cooke (b. 27 Dec. 1643; md. Martha Stedman).

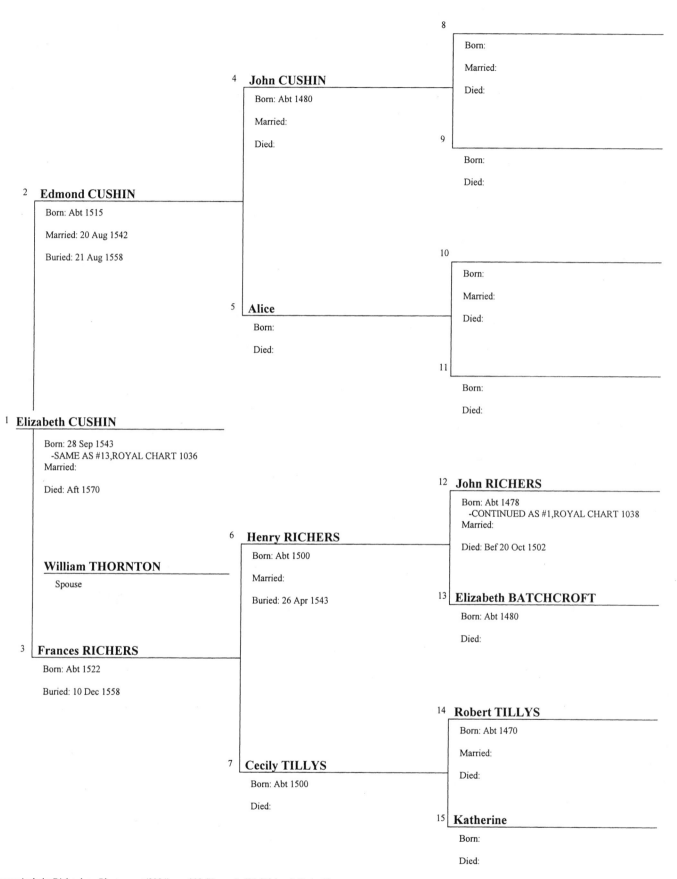

8

John CUSHIN
Born: Abt 1480
Married:
Died:

Born:
Married:
Died:

9
Born:
Died:

2   **Edmond CUSHIN**
Born: Abt 1515
Married: 20 Aug 1542
Buried: 21 Aug 1558

10
Born:
Married:
Died:

5   **Alice**
Born:
Died:

11
Born:
Died:

1   **Elizabeth CUSHIN**
Born: 28 Sep 1543
  -SAME AS #13,ROYAL CHART 1036
Married:

Died: Aft 1570

12   **John RICHERS**
Born: Abt 1478
  -CONTINUED AS #1,ROYAL CHART 1038
Married:

Died: Bef 20 Oct 1502

6   **Henry RICHERS**
Born: Abt 1500
Married:
Buried: 26 Apr 1543

13   **Elizabeth BATCHCROFT**
Born: Abt 1480
Died:

William THORNTON
Spouse

3   **Frances RICHERS**
Born: Abt 1522
Buried: 10 Dec 1558

14   **Robert TILLYS**
Born: Abt 1470
Married:
Died:

7   **Cecily TILLYS**
Born: Abt 1500
Died:

15   **Katherine**
Born:
Died:

Sources include: Richardson *Plantagenet* (2004), pp. 392 (Haynes), 608 (Richers); Faris--Haynes.

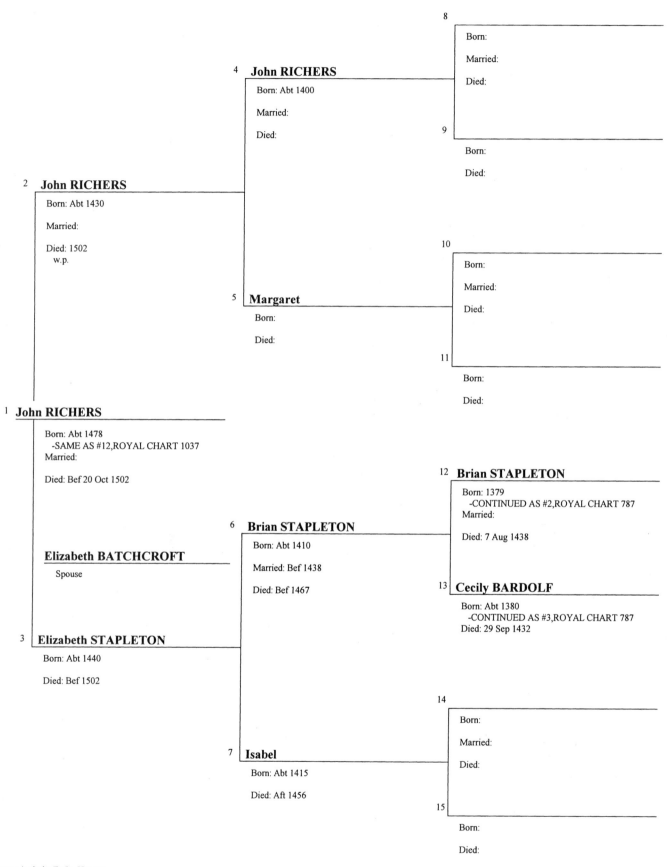

8

Born:

Married:

Died:

4 **John RICHERS**

Born: Abt 1400

Married:

Died:

9

Born:

Died:

2 **John RICHERS**

Born: Abt 1430

Married:

Died: 1502
w.p.

10

Born:

Married:

Died:

5 **Margaret**

Born:

Died:

11

Born:

Died:

1 **John RICHERS**

Born: Abt 1478
-SAME AS #12,ROYAL CHART 1037
Married:

Died: Bef 20 Oct 1502

12 **Brian STAPLETON**

Born: 1379
-CONTINUED AS #2,ROYAL CHART 787
Married:

Died: 7 Aug 1438

6 **Brian STAPLETON**

Born: Abt 1410

Married: Bef 1438

Died: Bef 1467

13 **Cecily BARDOLF**

Born: Abt 1380
-CONTINUED AS #3,ROYAL CHART 787
Died: 29 Sep 1432

Elizabeth BATCHCROFT

Spouse

3 **Elizabeth STAPLETON**

Born: Abt 1440

Died: Bef 1502

14

Born:

Married:

Died:

7 **Isabel**

Born: Abt 1415

Died: Aft 1456

15

Born:

Died:

Sources include: Faris--Haynes.

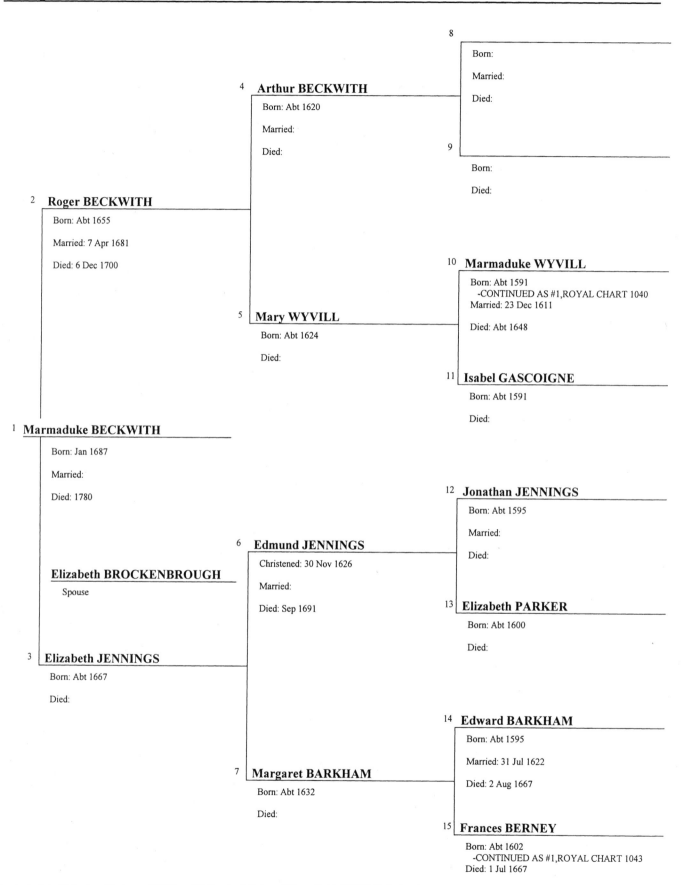

4 Arthur BECKWITH

Born: Abt 1620

Married:

Died:

8

Born:

Married:

Died:

9

Born:

Died:

2 Roger BECKWITH

Born: Abt 1655

Married: 7 Apr 1681

Died: 6 Dec 1700

10 Marmaduke WYVILL

Born: Abt 1591
 -CONTINUED AS #1,ROYAL CHART 1040
Married: 23 Dec 1611

Died: Abt 1648

5 Mary WYVILL

Born: Abt 1624

Died:

11 Isabel GASCOIGNE

Born: Abt 1591

Died:

1 Marmaduke BECKWITH

Born: Jan 1687

Married:

Died: 1780

12 Jonathan JENNINGS

Born: Abt 1595

Married:

Died:

6 Edmund JENNINGS

Christened: 30 Nov 1626

Married:

Died: Sep 1691

13 Elizabeth PARKER

Born: Abt 1600

Died:

Elizabeth BROCKENBROUGH

Spouse

3 Elizabeth JENNINGS

Born: Abt 1667

Died:

14 Edward BARKHAM

Born: Abt 1595

Married: 31 Jul 1622

Died: 2 Aug 1667

7 Margaret BARKHAM

Born: Abt 1632

Died:

15 Frances BERNEY

Born: Abt 1602
 -CONTINUED AS #1,ROYAL CHART 1043
Died: 1 Jul 1667

Sources include: Richardson *Plantagenet* (2004), p. 413 (Jennings); Roberts *500*, pp. 40-44, 287-288; Faris--Jennings; Faris 2--Jennings.

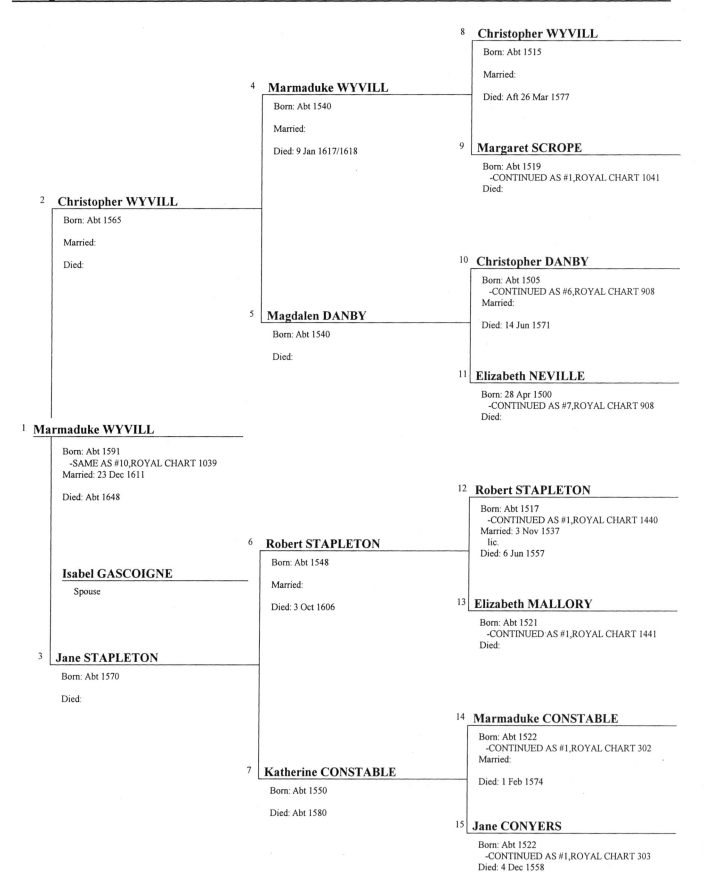

8 Christopher WYVILL
Born: Abt 1515
Married:
Died: Aft 26 Mar 1577

4 Marmaduke WYVILL
Born: Abt 1540
Married:
Died: 9 Jan 1617/1618

9 Margaret SCROPE
Born: Abt 1519
-CONTINUED AS #1,ROYAL CHART 1041
Died:

2 Christopher WYVILL
Born: Abt 1565
Married:
Died:

10 Christopher DANBY
Born: Abt 1505
-CONTINUED AS #6,ROYAL CHART 908
Married:
Died: 14 Jun 1571

5 Magdalen DANBY
Born: Abt 1540
Died:

11 Elizabeth NEVILLE
Born: 28 Apr 1500
-CONTINUED AS #7,ROYAL CHART 908
Died:

1 Marmaduke WYVILL
Born: Abt 1591
-SAME AS #10,ROYAL CHART 1039
Married: 23 Dec 1611
Died: Abt 1648

12 Robert STAPLETON
Born: Abt 1517
-CONTINUED AS #1,ROYAL CHART 1440
Married: 3 Nov 1537
lic.
Died: 6 Jun 1557

6 Robert STAPLETON
Born: Abt 1548
Married:
Died: 3 Oct 1606

13 Elizabeth MALLORY
Born: Abt 1521
-CONTINUED AS #1,ROYAL CHART 1441
Died:

Isabel GASCOIGNE
Spouse

3 Jane STAPLETON
Born: Abt 1570
Died:

14 Marmaduke CONSTABLE
Born: Abt 1522
-CONTINUED AS #1,ROYAL CHART 302
Married:
Died: 1 Feb 1574

7 Katherine CONSTABLE
Born: Abt 1550
Died: Abt 1580

15 Jane CONYERS
Born: Abt 1522
-CONTINUED AS #1,ROYAL CHART 303
Died: 4 Dec 1558

Sources include: Roberts *500*, pp. 40-44; *Blood Royal* 2, pp. 532-533; LDS records; Faris 2--Stapleton (#6 & 7 ancestry).

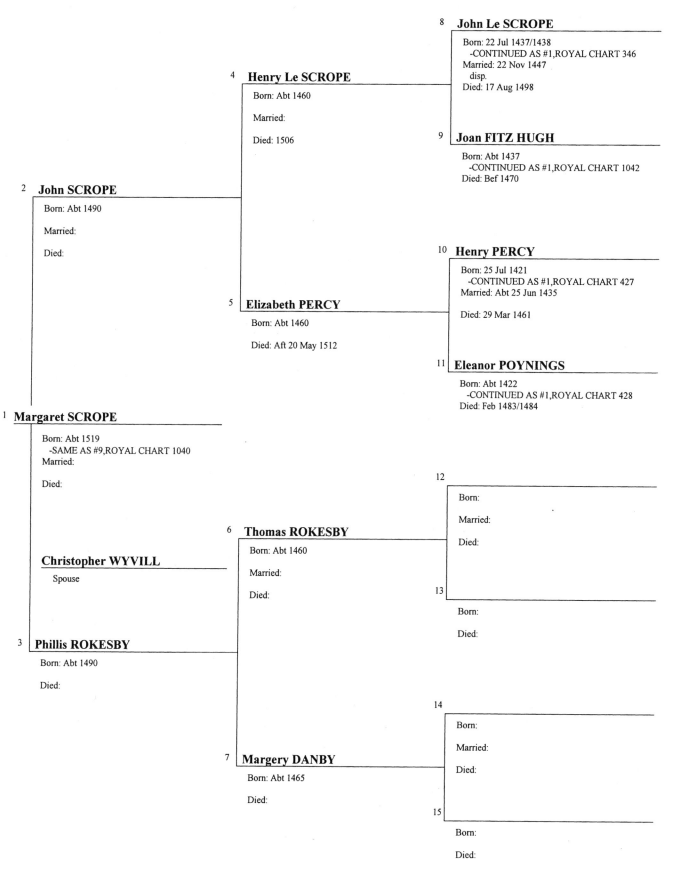

8 John Le SCROPE

Born: 22 Jul 1437/1438
  -CONTINUED AS #1,ROYAL CHART 346
Married: 22 Nov 1447
  disp.
Died: 17 Aug 1498

4 Henry Le SCROPE

Born: Abt 1460

Married:

Died: 1506

9 Joan FITZ HUGH

Born: Abt 1437
  -CONTINUED AS #1,ROYAL CHART 1042
Died: Bef 1470

2 John SCROPE

Born: Abt 1490

Married:

Died:

10 Henry PERCY

Born: 25 Jul 1421
  -CONTINUED AS #1,ROYAL CHART 427
Married: Abt 25 Jun 1435

Died: 29 Mar 1461

5 Elizabeth PERCY

Born: Abt 1460

Died: Aft 20 May 1512

11 Eleanor POYNINGS

Born: Abt 1422
  -CONTINUED AS #1,ROYAL CHART 428
Died: Feb 1483/1484

1 Margaret SCROPE

Born: Abt 1519
  -SAME AS #9,ROYAL CHART 1040
Married:

Died:

12

Born:

Married:

Died:

6 Thomas ROKESBY

Born: Abt 1460

Married:

Died:

Christopher WYVILL

Spouse

13

Born:

Died:

3 Phillis ROKESBY

Born: Abt 1490

Died:

14

Born:

Married:

Died:

7 Margery DANBY

Born: Abt 1465

Died:

15

Born:

Died:

Sources include: *Blood Royal* 2, pp. 532-533; LDS records.

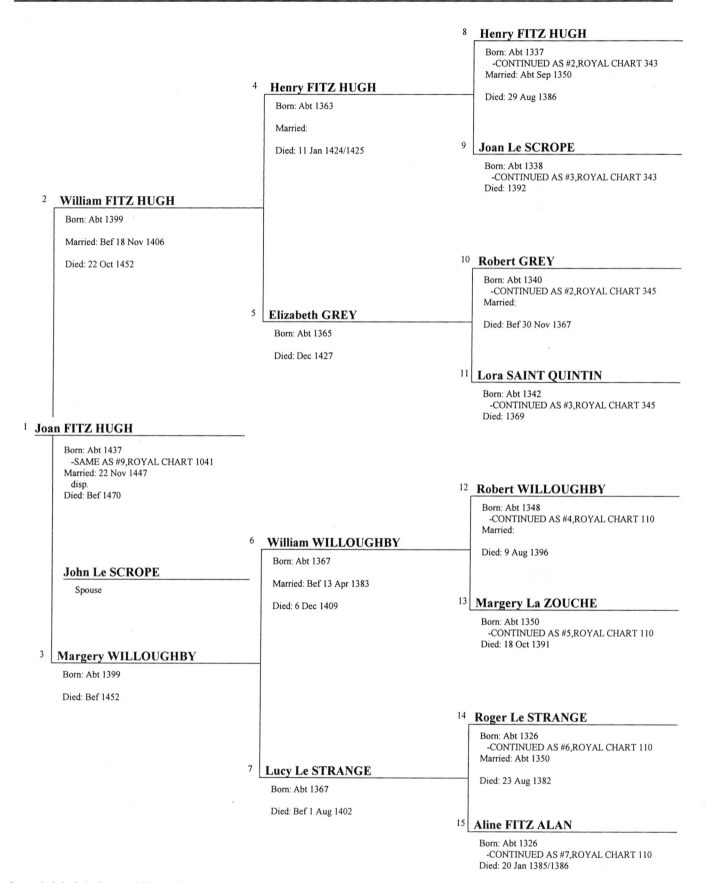

8 Henry FITZ HUGH

Born: Abt 1337
-CONTINUED AS #2,ROYAL CHART 343
Married: Abt Sep 1350

Died: 29 Aug 1386

4 Henry FITZ HUGH

Born: Abt 1363

Married:

Died: 11 Jan 1424/1425

9 Joan Le SCROPE

Born: Abt 1338
-CONTINUED AS #3,ROYAL CHART 343
Died: 1392

2 William FITZ HUGH

Born: Abt 1399

Married: Bef 18 Nov 1406

Died: 22 Oct 1452

10 Robert GREY

Born: Abt 1340
-CONTINUED AS #2,ROYAL CHART 345
Married:

Died: Bef 30 Nov 1367

5 Elizabeth GREY

Born: Abt 1365

Died: Dec 1427

11 Lora SAINT QUINTIN

Born: Abt 1342
-CONTINUED AS #3,ROYAL CHART 345
Died: 1369

1 Joan FITZ HUGH

Born: Abt 1437
-SAME AS #9,ROYAL CHART 1041
Married: 22 Nov 1447
disp.
Died: Bef 1470

12 Robert WILLOUGHBY

Born: Abt 1348
-CONTINUED AS #4,ROYAL CHART 110
Married:

Died: 9 Aug 1396

6 William WILLOUGHBY

Born: Abt 1367

Married: Bef 13 Apr 1383

Died: 6 Dec 1409

13 Margery La ZOUCHE

Born: Abt 1350
-CONTINUED AS #5,ROYAL CHART 110
Died: 18 Oct 1391

John Le SCROPE

Spouse

3 Margery WILLOUGHBY

Born: Abt 1399

Died: Bef 1452

14 Roger Le STRANGE

Born: Abt 1326
-CONTINUED AS #6,ROYAL CHART 110
Married: Abt 1350

Died: 23 Aug 1382

7 Lucy Le STRANGE

Born: Abt 1367

Died: Bef 1 Aug 1402

15 Aline FITZ ALAN

Born: Abt 1326
-CONTINUED AS #7,ROYAL CHART 110
Died: 20 Jan 1385/1386

Sources include: Faris--Scrope 5; LDS records.

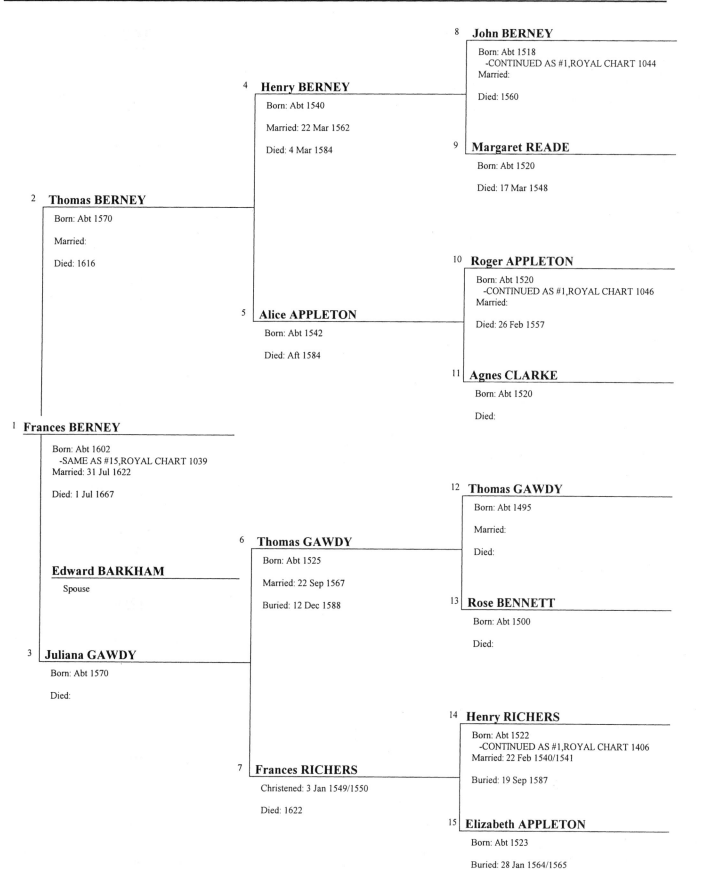

8 **John BERNEY**

Born: Abt 1518
  -CONTINUED AS #1, ROYAL CHART 1044
Married:

Died: 1560

4 **Henry BERNEY**

Born: Abt 1540

Married: 22 Mar 1562

Died: 4 Mar 1584

9 **Margaret READE**

Born: Abt 1520

Died: 17 Mar 1548

2 **Thomas BERNEY**

Born: Abt 1570

Married:

Died: 1616

10 **Roger APPLETON**

Born: Abt 1520
  -CONTINUED AS #1, ROYAL CHART 1046
Married:

Died: 26 Feb 1557

5 **Alice APPLETON**

Born: Abt 1542

Died: Aft 1584

11 **Agnes CLARKE**

Born: Abt 1520

Died:

1 **Frances BERNEY**

Born: Abt 1602
  -SAME AS #15, ROYAL CHART 1039
Married: 31 Jul 1622

Died: 1 Jul 1667

12 **Thomas GAWDY**

Born: Abt 1495

Married:

Died:

6 **Thomas GAWDY**

Born: Abt 1525

Married: 22 Sep 1567

Buried: 12 Dec 1588

Edward BARKHAM

Spouse

13 **Rose BENNETT**

Born: Abt 1500

Died:

3 **Juliana GAWDY**

Born: Abt 1570

Died:

14 **Henry RICHERS**

Born: Abt 1522
  -CONTINUED AS #1, ROYAL CHART 1406
Married: 22 Feb 1540/1541

Buried: 19 Sep 1587

7 **Frances RICHERS**

Christened: 3 Jan 1549/1550

Died: 1622

15 **Elizabeth APPLETON**

Born: Abt 1523

Buried: 28 Jan 1564/1565

Sources include: Richardson *Plantagenet* (2004), pp. 412-413 (Jennings), 609 (Richers); Faris 2--Jennings, Richers; Faris--Jennings; Roberts *500*, pp. 287-288; LDS records.

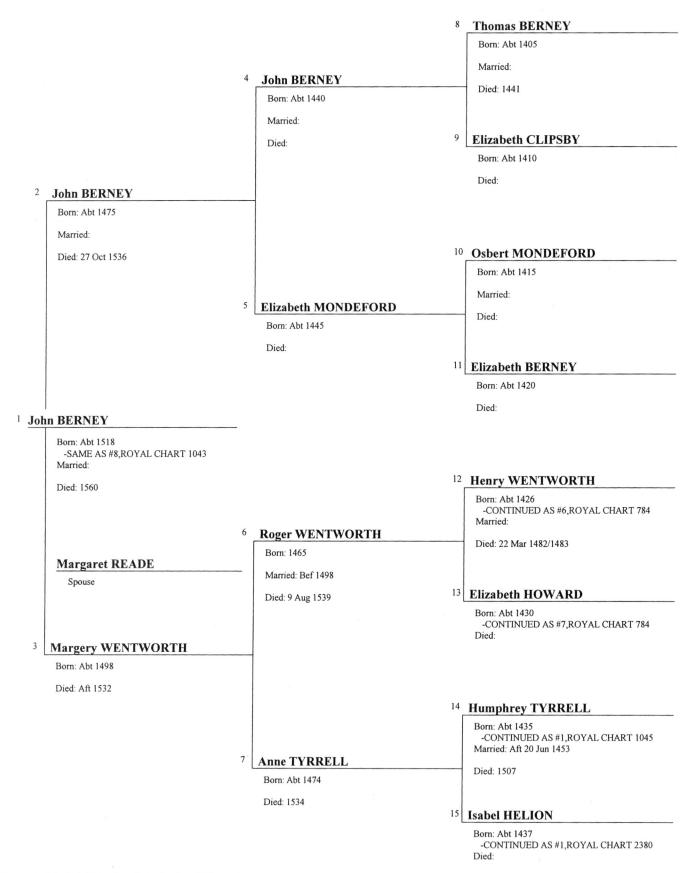

8 **Thomas BERNEY**

Born: Abt 1405

Married:

Died: 1441

4 **John BERNEY**

Born: Abt 1440

Married:

Died:

9 **Elizabeth CLIPSBY**

Born: Abt 1410

Died:

2 **John BERNEY**

Born: Abt 1475

Married:

Died: 27 Oct 1536

10 **Osbert MONDEFORD**

Born: Abt 1415

Married:

Died:

5 **Elizabeth MONDEFORD**

Born: Abt 1445

Died:

11 **Elizabeth BERNEY**

Born: Abt 1420

Died:

1 **John BERNEY**

Born: Abt 1518
-SAME AS #8,ROYAL CHART 1043
Married:

Died: 1560

12 **Henry WENTWORTH**

Born: Abt 1426
-CONTINUED AS #6,ROYAL CHART 784
Married:

Died: 22 Mar 1482/1483

6 **Roger WENTWORTH**

Born: 1465

Married: Bef 1498

Died: 9 Aug 1539

13 **Elizabeth HOWARD**

Born: Abt 1430
-CONTINUED AS #7,ROYAL CHART 784
Died:

Margaret READE

Spouse

3 **Margery WENTWORTH**

Born: Abt 1498

Died: Aft 1532

14 **Humphrey TYRRELL**

Born: Abt 1435
-CONTINUED AS #1,ROYAL CHART 1045
Married: Aft 20 Jun 1453

Died: 1507

7 **Anne TYRRELL**

Born: Abt 1474

Died: 1534

15 **Isabel HELION**

Born: Abt 1437
-CONTINUED AS #1,ROYAL CHART 2380
Died:

Sources include: Faris 2--Jennings; Faris--Jennings; LDS records.

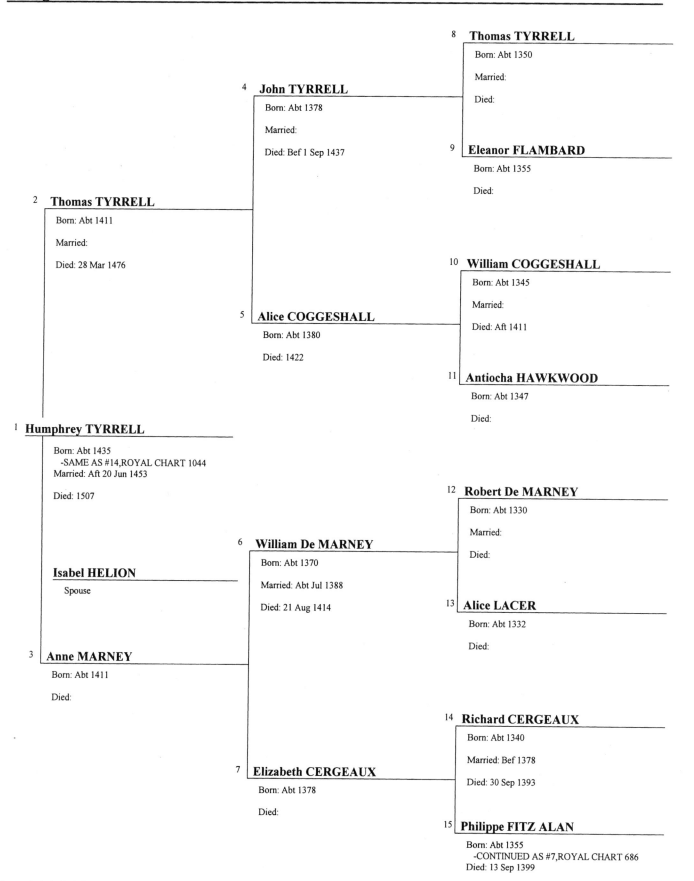

8 **Thomas TYRRELL**
Born: Abt 1350
Married:
Died:

4 **John TYRRELL**
Born: Abt 1378
Married:
Died: Bef 1 Sep 1437

9 **Eleanor FLAMBARD**
Born: Abt 1355
Died:

2 **Thomas TYRRELL**
Born: Abt 1411
Married:
Died: 28 Mar 1476

10 **William COGGESHALL**
Born: Abt 1345
Married:
Died: Aft 1411

5 **Alice COGGESHALL**
Born: Abt 1380
Died: 1422

11 **Antiocha HAWKWOOD**
Born: Abt 1347
Died:

1 **Humphrey TYRRELL**
Born: Abt 1435
  -SAME AS #14,ROYAL CHART 1044
Married: Aft 20 Jun 1453
Died: 1507

12 **Robert De MARNEY**
Born: Abt 1330
Married:
Died:

6 **William De MARNEY**
Born: Abt 1370
Married: Abt Jul 1388
Died: 21 Aug 1414

13 **Alice LACER**
Born: Abt 1332
Died:

Isabel HELION
Spouse

3 **Anne MARNEY**
Born: Abt 1411
Died:

14 **Richard CERGEAUX**
Born: Abt 1340
Married: Bef 1378
Died: 30 Sep 1393

7 **Elizabeth CERGEAUX**
Born: Abt 1378
Died:

15 **Philippe FITZ ALAN**
Born: Abt 1355
  -CONTINUED AS #7,ROYAL CHART 686
Died: 13 Sep 1399

Sources include: Faris 2--Jennings; Faris--Jennings; Faris preliminary baronial manuscript (1998), pp. 1559-61 (Tyrrell), 385 (Coggeshall).

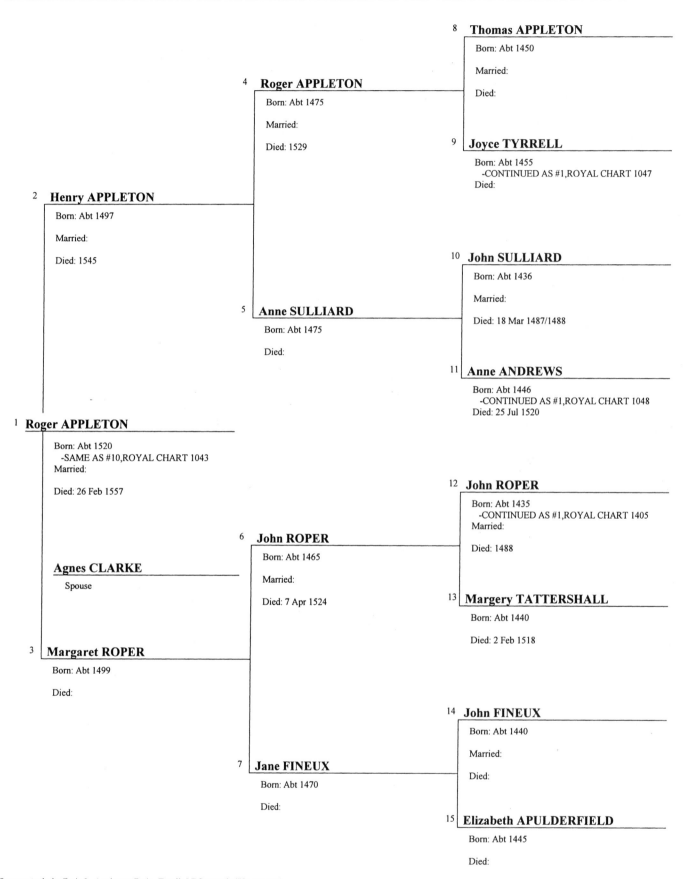

8 **Thomas APPLETON**

Born: Abt 1450

Married:

Died:

4 **Roger APPLETON**

Born: Abt 1475

Married:

Died: 1529

9 **Joyce TYRRELL**

Born: Abt 1455
-CONTINUED AS #1,ROYAL CHART 1047
Died:

2 **Henry APPLETON**

Born: Abt 1497

Married:

Died: 1545

10 **John SULLIARD**

Born: Abt 1436

Married:

Died: 18 Mar 1487/1488

5 **Anne SULLIARD**

Born: Abt 1475

Died:

11 **Anne ANDREWS**

Born: Abt 1446
-CONTINUED AS #1,ROYAL CHART 1048
Died: 25 Jul 1520

1 **Roger APPLETON**

Born: Abt 1520
-SAME AS #10,ROYAL CHART 1043
Married:

Died: 26 Feb 1557

12 **John ROPER**

Born: Abt 1435
-CONTINUED AS #1,ROYAL CHART 1405
Married:

Died: 1488

6 **John ROPER**

Born: Abt 1465

Married:

Died: 7 Apr 1524

13 **Margery TATTERSHALL**

Born: Abt 1440

Died: 2 Feb 1518

Agnes CLARKE

Spouse

3 **Margaret ROPER**

Born: Abt 1499

Died:

14 **John FINEUX**

Born: Abt 1440

Married:

Died:

7 **Jane FINEUX**

Born: Abt 1470

Died:

15 **Elizabeth APULDERFIELD**

Born: Abt 1445

Died:

Sources include: Faris 2--Appleton; Faris--Tyrell; LDS records (#3 ancestry).

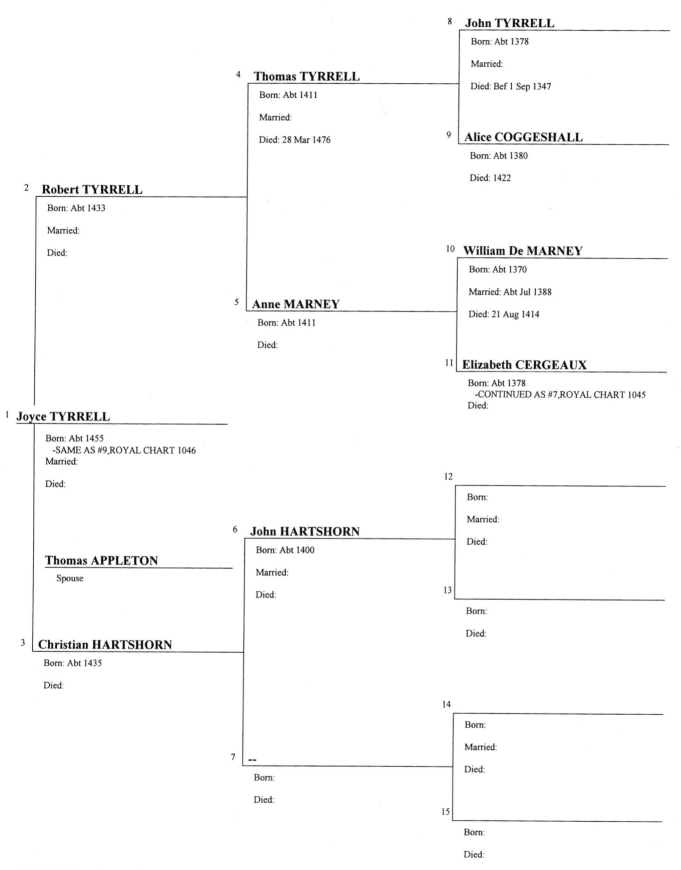

8 John TYRRELL

Born: Abt 1378

Married:

Died: Bef 1 Sep 1347

4 Thomas TYRRELL

Born: Abt 1411

Married:

Died: 28 Mar 1476

9 Alice COGGESHALL

Born: Abt 1380

Died: 1422

2 Robert TYRRELL

Born: Abt 1433

Married:

Died:

10 William De MARNEY

Born: Abt 1370

Married: Abt Jul 1388

Died: 21 Aug 1414

5 Anne MARNEY

Born: Abt 1411

Died:

11 Elizabeth CERGEAUX

Born: Abt 1378
 -CONTINUED AS #7,ROYAL CHART 1045
Died:

1 Joyce TYRRELL

Born: Abt 1455
 -SAME AS #9,ROYAL CHART 1046
Married:

Died:

Thomas APPLETON

Spouse

12

Born:

Married:

Died:

6 John HARTSHORN

Born: Abt 1400

Married:

Died:

13

Born:

Died:

3 Christian HARTSHORN

Born: Abt 1435

Died:

14

Born:

Married:

Died:

7 --

Born:

Died:

15

Born:

Died:

Sources include: Faris 2--Appleton, Jennings; Faris--Tyrrell.

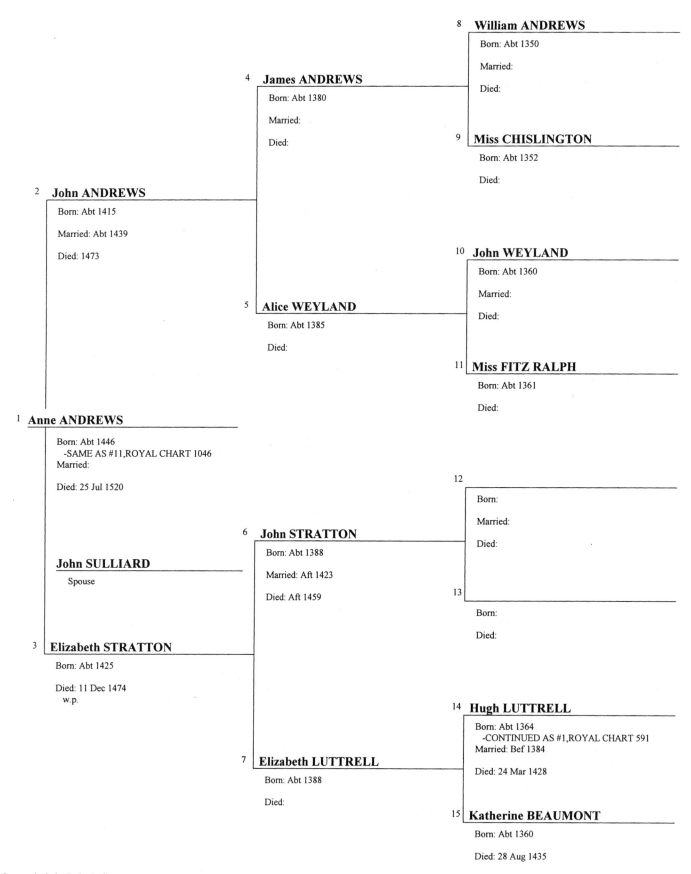

8 **William ANDREWS**
Born: Abt 1350
Married:
Died:

4 **James ANDREWS**
Born: Abt 1380
Married:
Died:

9 **Miss CHISLINGTON**
Born: Abt 1352
Died:

2 **John ANDREWS**
Born: Abt 1415
Married: Abt 1439
Died: 1473

10 **John WEYLAND**
Born: Abt 1360
Married:
Died:

5 **Alice WEYLAND**
Born: Abt 1385
Died:

11 **Miss FITZ RALPH**
Born: Abt 1361
Died:

1 **Anne ANDREWS**
Born: Abt 1446
-SAME AS #11,ROYAL CHART 1046
Married:
Died: 25 Jul 1520

12
Born:
Married:
Died:

6 **John STRATTON**
Born: Abt 1388
Married: Aft 1423
Died: Aft 1459

13
Born:
Died:

John SULLIARD
Spouse

3 **Elizabeth STRATTON**
Born: Abt 1425
Died: 11 Dec 1474
w.p.

14 **Hugh LUTTRELL**
Born: Abt 1364
-CONTINUED AS #1,ROYAL CHART 591
Married: Bef 1384
Died: 24 Mar 1428

7 **Elizabeth LUTTRELL**
Born: Abt 1388
Died:

15 **Katherine BEAUMONT**
Born: Abt 1360
Died: 28 Aug 1435

Sources include: Faris--Ludlow.

Pedigree Chart

Chart 1049

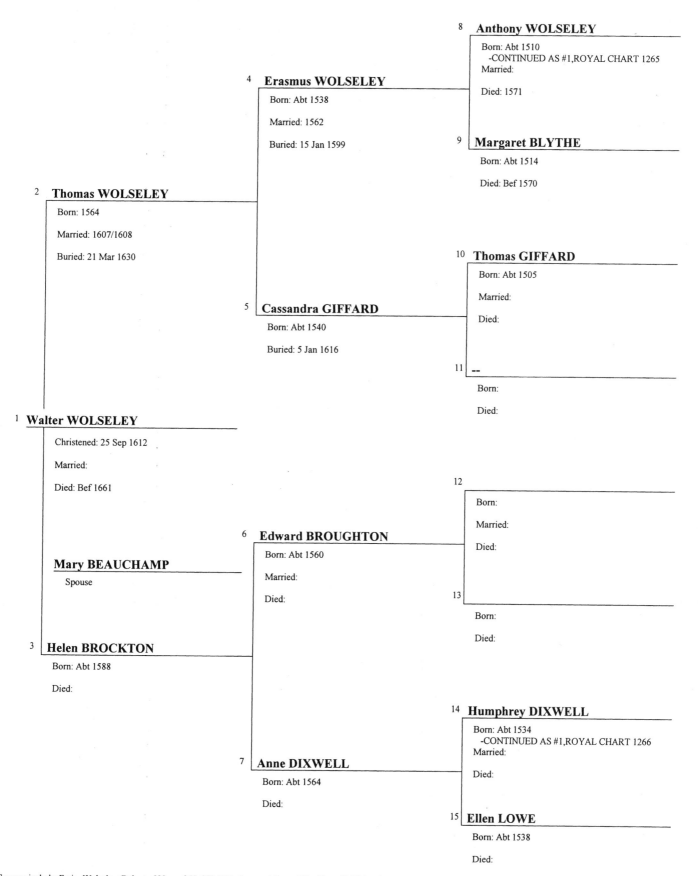

8 **Anthony WOLSELEY**
Born: Abt 1510
  -CONTINUED AS #1,ROYAL CHART 1265
Married:

Died: 1571

4 **Erasmus WOLSELEY**
Born: Abt 1538
Married: 1562
Buried: 15 Jan 1599

9 **Margaret BLYTHE**
Born: Abt 1514

Died: Bef 1570

2 **Thomas WOLSELEY**
Born: 1564
Married: 1607/1608
Buried: 21 Mar 1630

10 **Thomas GIFFARD**
Born: Abt 1505
Married:

Died:

5 **Cassandra GIFFARD**
Born: Abt 1540
Buried: 5 Jan 1616

11 **--**
Born:

Died:

1 **Walter WOLSELEY**
Christened: 25 Sep 1612
Married:
Died: Bef 1661

12
Born:
Married:
Died:

6 **Edward BROUGHTON**
Born: Abt 1560
Married:
Died:

13
Born:
Died:

Mary BEAUCHAMP
Spouse

3 **Helen BROCKTON**
Born: Abt 1588
Died:

14 **Humphrey DIXWELL**
Born: Abt 1534
  -CONTINUED AS #1,ROYAL CHART 1266
Married:

Died:

7 **Anne DIXWELL**
Born: Abt 1564
Died:

15 **Ellen LOWE**
Born: Abt 1538

Died:

Sources include: Faris--Wolseley; Roberts *500*, pp. 258, 373-375; *Ancestral Roots* 81B. Note: #1 Walter has American descendants through a daughter Mary Wolseley (b. abt 1645; md. Roger Brooke).

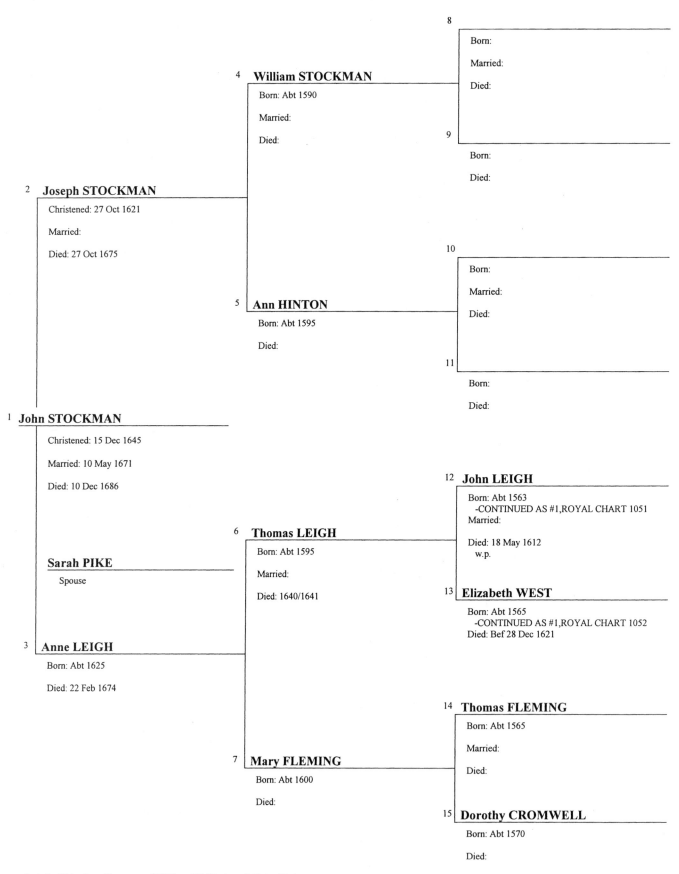

8

Born:

Married:

Died:

4 William STOCKMAN

Born: Abt 1590

Married:

Died:

9

Born:

Died:

2 Joseph STOCKMAN

Christened: 27 Oct 1621

Married:

Died: 27 Oct 1675

10

Born:

Married:

Died:

5 Ann HINTON

Born: Abt 1595

Died:

11

Born:

Died:

1 John STOCKMAN

Christened: 15 Dec 1645

Married: 10 May 1671

Died: 10 Dec 1686

12 John LEIGH

Born: Abt 1563
-CONTINUED AS #1,ROYAL CHART 1051
Married:

Died: 18 May 1612
w.p.

6 Thomas LEIGH

Born: Abt 1595

Married:

Died: 1640/1641

13 Elizabeth WEST

Born: Abt 1565
-CONTINUED AS #1,ROYAL CHART 1052
Died: Bef 28 Dec 1621

Sarah PIKE

Spouse

3 Anne LEIGH

Born: Abt 1625

Died: 22 Feb 1674

14 Thomas FLEMING

Born: Abt 1565

Married:

Died:

7 Mary FLEMING

Born: Abt 1600

Died:

15 Dorothy CROMWELL

Born: Abt 1570

Died:

Sources include: Richardson *Plantagenet* (2004), p. 687 (Stockman); Faris--Stockman.

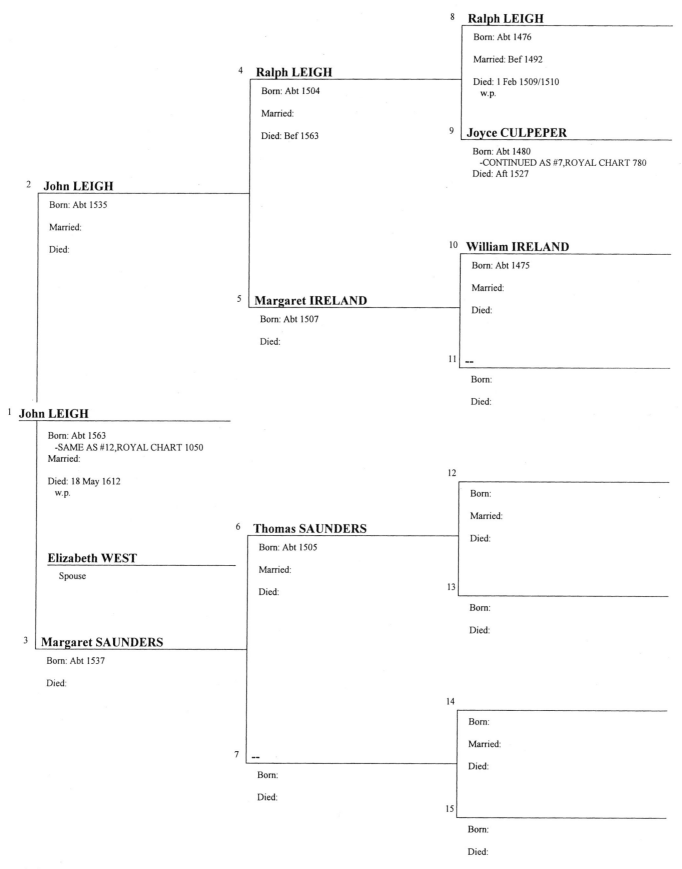

8 Ralph LEIGH
Born: Abt 1476
Married: Bef 1492
Died: 1 Feb 1509/1510
w.p.

4 Ralph LEIGH
Born: Abt 1504
Married:
Died: Bef 1563

9 Joyce CULPEPER
Born: Abt 1480
-CONTINUED AS #7,ROYAL CHART 780
Died: Aft 1527

2 John LEIGH
Born: Abt 1535
Married:
Died:

10 William IRELAND
Born: Abt 1475
Married:
Died:

5 Margaret IRELAND
Born: Abt 1507
Died:

11 --
Born:
Died:

1 John LEIGH
Born: Abt 1563
-SAME AS #12,ROYAL CHART 1050
Married:
Died: 18 May 1612
w.p.

Elizabeth WEST
Spouse

12
Born:
Married:
Died:

6 Thomas SAUNDERS
Born: Abt 1505
Married:
Died:

13
Born:
Died:

3 Margaret SAUNDERS
Born: Abt 1537
Died:

14
Born:
Married:
Died:

7 --
Born:
Died:

15
Born:
Died:

Sources include: Richardson *Plantagenet* (2004), pp. 686-687 (Stockman); Faris--Stockman.

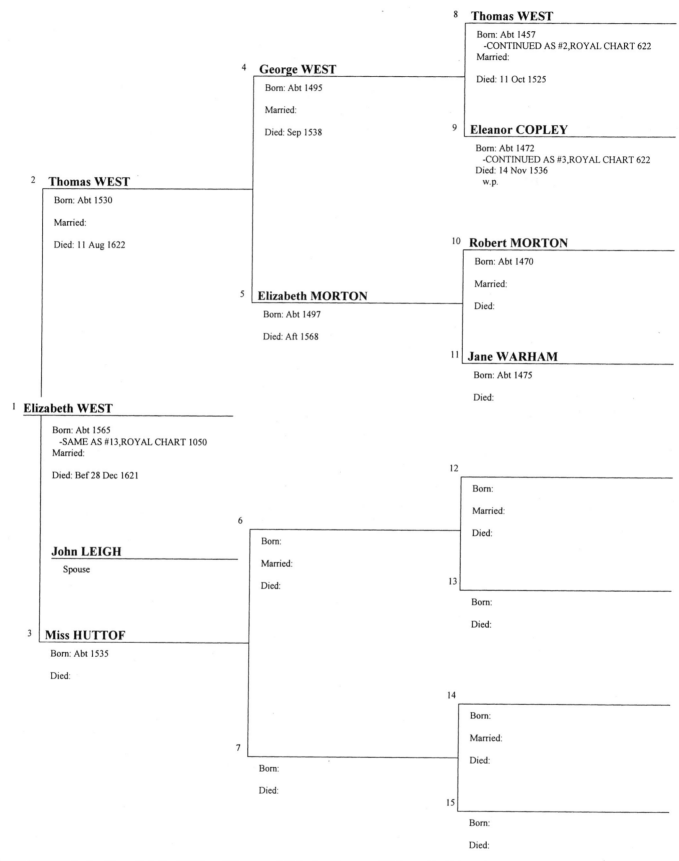

8 **Thomas WEST**

Born: Abt 1457
 -CONTINUED AS #2,ROYAL CHART 622
Married:

Died: 11 Oct 1525

4 **George WEST**

Born: Abt 1495

Married:

Died: Sep 1538

9 **Eleanor COPLEY**

Born: Abt 1472
 -CONTINUED AS #3,ROYAL CHART 622
Died: 14 Nov 1536
w.p.

2 **Thomas WEST**

Born: Abt 1530

Married:

Died: 11 Aug 1622

10 **Robert MORTON**

Born: Abt 1470

Married:

Died:

5 **Elizabeth MORTON**

Born: Abt 1497

Died: Aft 1568

11 **Jane WARHAM**

Born: Abt 1475

Died:

1 **Elizabeth WEST**

Born: Abt 1565
 -SAME AS #13,ROYAL CHART 1050
Married:

Died: Bef 28 Dec 1621

12

Born:

Married:

Died:

6

Born:

Married:

Died:

13

Born:

Died:

John LEIGH

Spouse

3 **Miss HUTTOF**

Born: Abt 1535

Died:

14

Born:

Married:

Died:

7

Born:

Died:

15

Born:

Died:

Sources include: Richardson *Magna Carta* (April 2005), pp. 887-888 (West); Richardson *Plantagenet* (2004), pp. 403-404 (Humphrey); Faris--Humphrey; Faris 2--Humphrey.

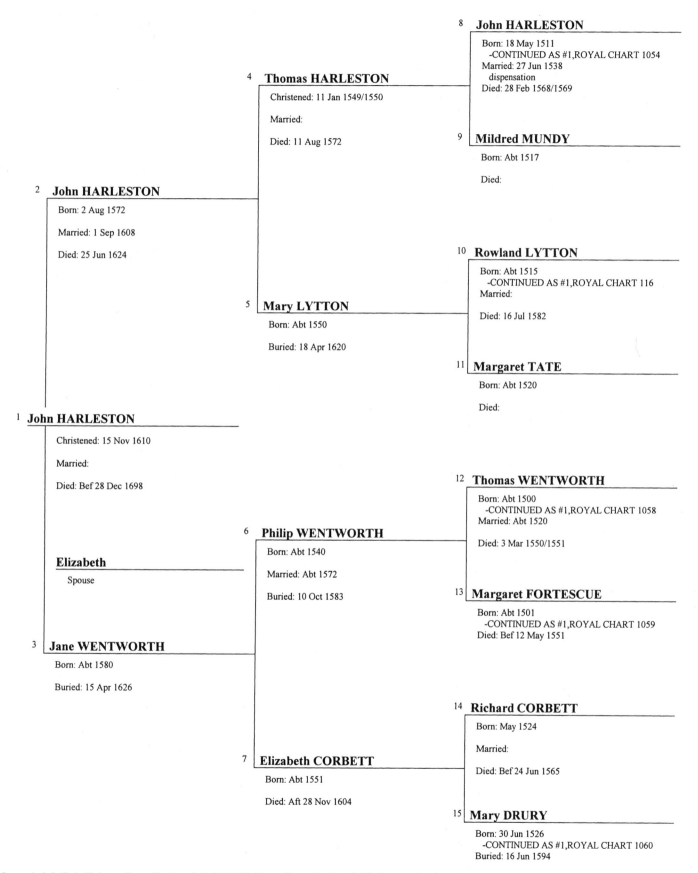

8 John HARLESTON

Born: 18 May 1511
-CONTINUED AS #1,ROYAL CHART 1054
Married: 27 Jun 1538
dispensation
Died: 28 Feb 1568/1569

4 Thomas HARLESTON

Christened: 11 Jan 1549/1550

Married:

Died: 11 Aug 1572

9 Mildred MUNDY

Born: Abt 1517

Died:

2 John HARLESTON

Born: 2 Aug 1572

Married: 1 Sep 1608

Died: 25 Jun 1624

10 Rowland LYTTON

Born: Abt 1515
-CONTINUED AS #1,ROYAL CHART 116
Married:

Died: 16 Jul 1582

5 Mary LYTTON

Born: Abt 1550

Buried: 18 Apr 1620

11 Margaret TATE

Born: Abt 1520

Died:

1 John HARLESTON

Christened: 15 Nov 1610

Married:

Died: Bef 28 Dec 1698

Elizabeth

Spouse

12 Thomas WENTWORTH

Born: Abt 1500
-CONTINUED AS #1,ROYAL CHART 1058
Married: Abt 1520

Died: 3 Mar 1550/1551

6 Philip WENTWORTH

Born: Abt 1540

Married: Abt 1572

Buried: 10 Oct 1583

13 Margaret FORTESCUE

Born: Abt 1501
-CONTINUED AS #1,ROYAL CHART 1059
Died: Bef 12 May 1551

3 Jane WENTWORTH

Born: Abt 1580

Buried: 15 Apr 1626

14 Richard CORBETT

Born: May 1524

Married:

Died: Bef 24 Jun 1565

7 Elizabeth CORBETT

Born: Abt 1551

Died: Aft 28 Nov 1604

15 Mary DRURY

Born: 30 Jun 1526
-CONTINUED AS #1,ROYAL CHART 1060
Buried: 16 Jun 1594

Sources include: Faris–Harleston, Drury; *The Genealogist* 9:163-185; *Magna Charta* 4A. Note: #1 John has American descendants through two children: John Harleston (b. abt 1665; md. Elizabeth Willis) of SC, parents of John Harleston (b. 19 Jan 1708/1709; md. Hannah Child); Elizabeth Harleston (b. abt 1672; md. Elias Ball) of SC.

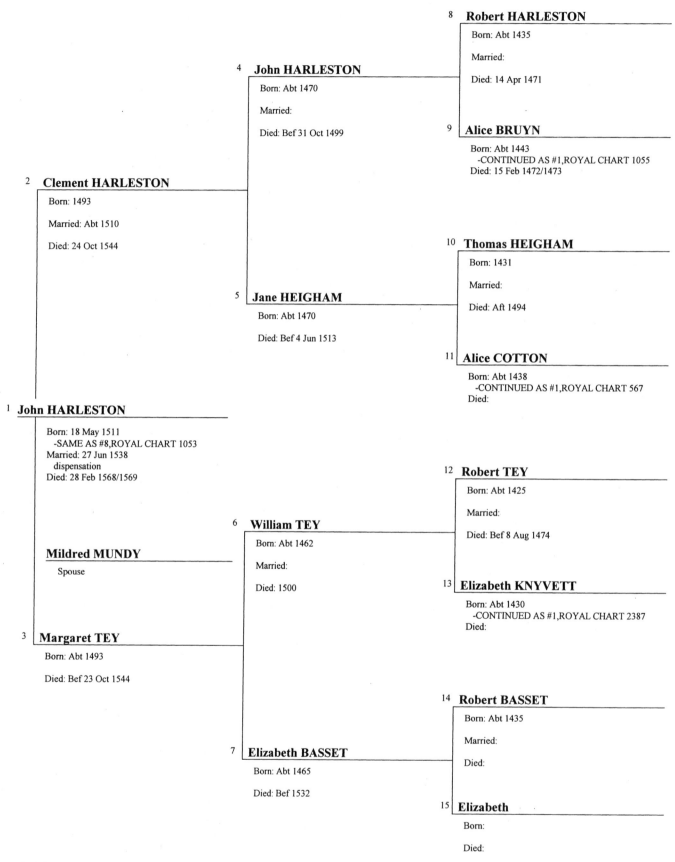

8 **Robert HARLESTON**

Born: Abt 1435

Married:

Died: 14 Apr 1471

4 **John HARLESTON**

Born: Abt 1470

Married:

Died: Bef 31 Oct 1499

9 **Alice BRUYN**

Born: Abt 1443
  -CONTINUED AS #1,ROYAL CHART 1055
Died: 15 Feb 1472/1473

2 **Clement HARLESTON**

Born: 1493

Married: Abt 1510

Died: 24 Oct 1544

10 **Thomas HEIGHAM**

Born: 1431

Married:

Died: Aft 1494

5 **Jane HEIGHAM**

Born: Abt 1470

Died: Bef 4 Jun 1513

11 **Alice COTTON**

Born: Abt 1438
  -CONTINUED AS #1,ROYAL CHART 567
Died:

1 **John HARLESTON**

Born: 18 May 1511
  -SAME AS #8,ROYAL CHART 1053
Married: 27 Jun 1538
  dispensation
Died: 28 Feb 1568/1569

12 **Robert TEY**

Born: Abt 1425

Married:

Died: Bef 8 Aug 1474

6 **William TEY**

Born: Abt 1462

Married:

Died: 1500

Mildred MUNDY

Spouse

13 **Elizabeth KNYVETT**

Born: Abt 1430
  -CONTINUED AS #1,ROYAL CHART 2387
Died:

3 **Margaret TEY**

Born: Abt 1493

Died: Bef 23 Oct 1544

14 **Robert BASSET**

Born: Abt 1435

Married:

Died:

7 **Elizabeth BASSET**

Born: Abt 1465

Died: Bef 1532

15 **Elizabeth**

Born:

Died:

Sources include: Consultation with Douglas Richardson; *The Genealogist* 9:163-177; *Magna Charta* 4A; LDS records.

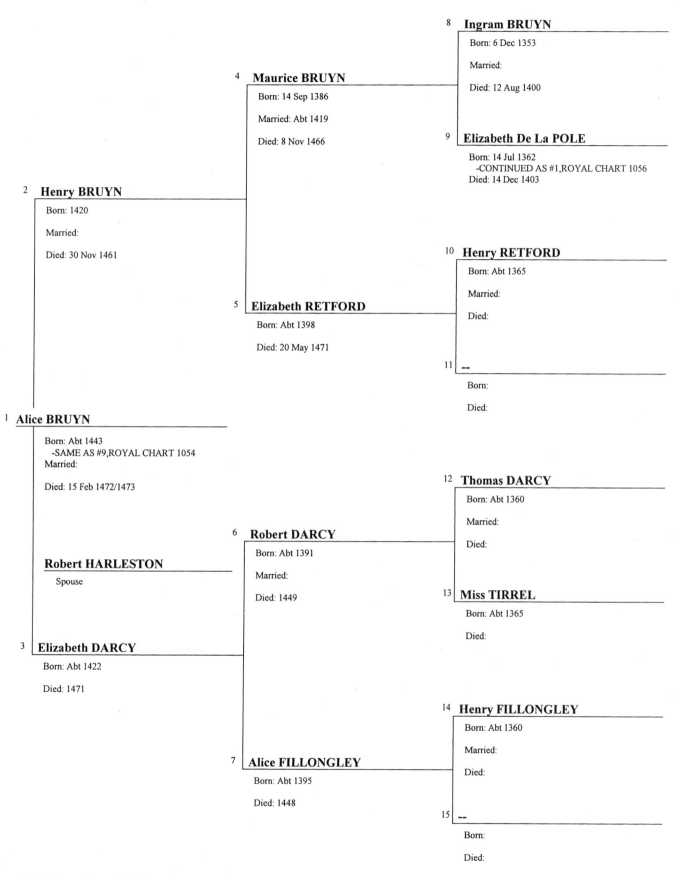

8   Ingram BRUYN

Born: 6 Dec 1353

Married:

Died: 12 Aug 1400

4   Maurice BRUYN

Born: 14 Sep 1386

Married: Abt 1419

Died: 8 Nov 1466

9   Elizabeth De La POLE

Born: 14 Jul 1362
    -CONTINUED AS #1,ROYAL CHART 1056
Died: 14 Dec 1403

2   Henry BRUYN

Born: 1420

Married:

Died: 30 Nov 1461

10   Henry RETFORD

Born: Abt 1365

Married:

Died:

5   Elizabeth RETFORD

Born: Abt 1398

Died: 20 May 1471

11   --

Born:

Died:

1   Alice BRUYN

Born: Abt 1443
    -SAME AS #9,ROYAL CHART 1054
Married:

Died: 15 Feb 1472/1473

12   Thomas DARCY

Born: Abt 1360

Married:

Died:

6   Robert DARCY

Born: Abt 1391

Married:

Died: 1449

13   Miss TIRREL

Born: Abt 1365

Died:

Robert HARLESTON

Spouse

3   Elizabeth DARCY

Born: Abt 1422

Died: 1471

14   Henry FILLONGLEY

Born: Abt 1360

Married:

Died:

7   Alice FILLONGLEY

Born: Abt 1395

Died: 1448

15   --

Born:

Died:

Sources include: *Magna Charta* 4A; LDS records.

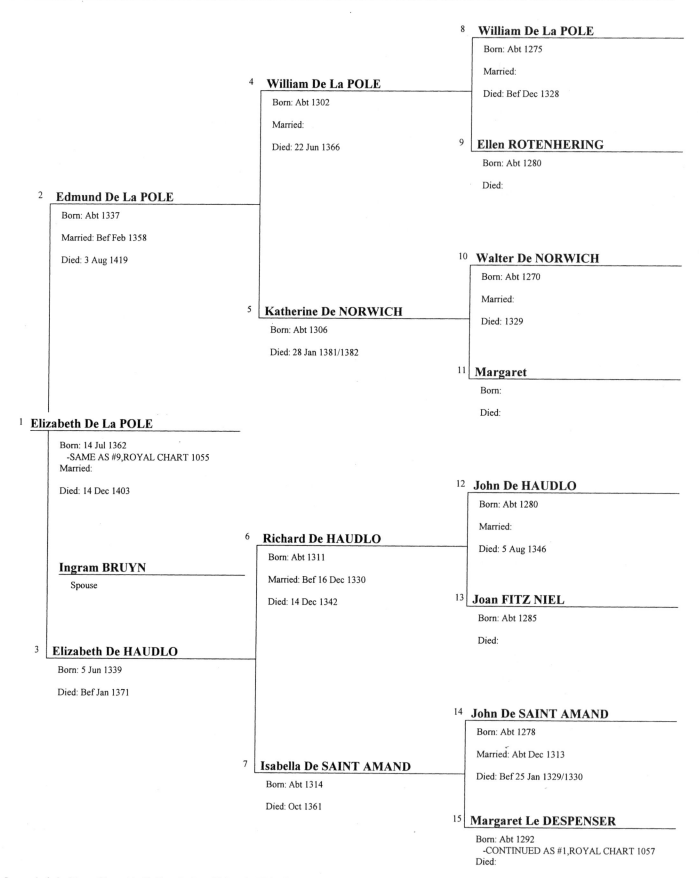

8 William De La POLE
Born: Abt 1275
Married:
Died: Bef Dec 1328

4 William De La POLE
Born: Abt 1302
Married:
Died: 22 Jun 1366

9 Ellen ROTENHERING
Born: Abt 1280
Died:

2 Edmund De La POLE
Born: Abt 1337
Married: Bef Feb 1358
Died: 3 Aug 1419

10 Walter De NORWICH
Born: Abt 1270
Married:
Died: 1329

5 Katherine De NORWICH
Born: Abt 1306
Died: 28 Jan 1381/1382

11 Margaret
Born:
Died:

1 Elizabeth De La POLE
Born: 14 Jul 1362
-SAME AS #9,ROYAL CHART 1055
Married:
Died: 14 Dec 1403

12 John De HAUDLO
Born: Abt 1280
Married:
Died: 5 Aug 1346

6 Richard De HAUDLO
Born: Abt 1311
Married: Bef 16 Dec 1330
Died: 14 Dec 1342

Ingram BRUYN
Spouse

13 Joan FITZ NIEL
Born: Abt 1285
Died:

3 Elizabeth De HAUDLO
Born: 5 Jun 1339
Died: Bef Jan 1371

14 John De SAINT AMAND
Born: Abt 1278
Married: Abt Dec 1313
Died: Bef 25 Jan 1329/1330

7 Isabella De SAINT AMAND
Born: Abt 1314
Died: Oct 1361

15 Margaret Le DESPENSER
Born: Abt 1292
-CONTINUED AS #1,ROYAL CHART 1057
Died:

Sources include: *Magna Charta* 4A, 10; Consultation with Douglas Richardson; LDS records.

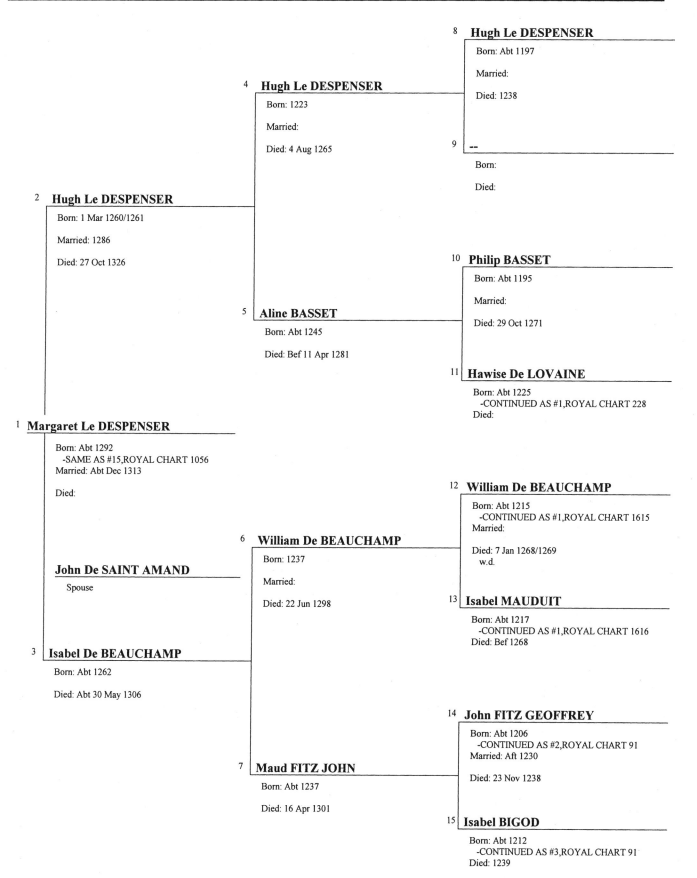

8 **Hugh Le DESPENSER**

Born: Abt 1197

Married:

Died: 1238

4 **Hugh Le DESPENSER**

Born: 1223

Married:

Died: 4 Aug 1265

9 **--**

Born:

Died:

2 **Hugh Le DESPENSER**

Born: 1 Mar 1260/1261

Married: 1286

Died: 27 Oct 1326

10 **Philip BASSET**

Born: Abt 1195

Married:

Died: 29 Oct 1271

5 **Aline BASSET**

Born: Abt 1245

Died: Bef 11 Apr 1281

11 **Hawise De LOVAINE**

Born: Abt 1225
-CONTINUED AS #1,ROYAL CHART 228
Died:

1 **Margaret Le DESPENSER**

Born: Abt 1292
-SAME AS #15,ROYAL CHART 1056
Married: Abt Dec 1313

Died:

12 **William De BEAUCHAMP**

Born: Abt 1215
-CONTINUED AS #1,ROYAL CHART 1615
Married:

Died: 7 Jan 1268/1269
w.d.

6 **William De BEAUCHAMP**

Born: 1237

Married:

Died: 22 Jun 1298

John De SAINT AMAND

Spouse

13 **Isabel MAUDUIT**

Born: Abt 1217
-CONTINUED AS #1,ROYAL CHART 1616
Died: Bef 1268

3 **Isabel De BEAUCHAMP**

Born: Abt 1262

Died: Abt 30 May 1306

14 **John FITZ GEOFFREY**

Born: Abt 1206
-CONTINUED AS #2,ROYAL CHART 91
Married: Aft 1230

Died: 23 Nov 1238

7 **Maud FITZ JOHN**

Born: Abt 1237

Died: 16 Apr 1301

15 **Isabel BIGOD**

Born: Abt 1212
-CONTINUED AS #3,ROYAL CHART 91
Died: 1239

Sources include: Faris-Richardson preliminary Magna Carta manuscript (June 2000), pp. 171-172 (Despenser), 32-33 (Beauchamp); Faris preliminary baronial manuscript (1998), pp. 495-497 (Despenser); *Magna Charta* 4A; *Ancestral Roots* 74 (#3 ancestry).

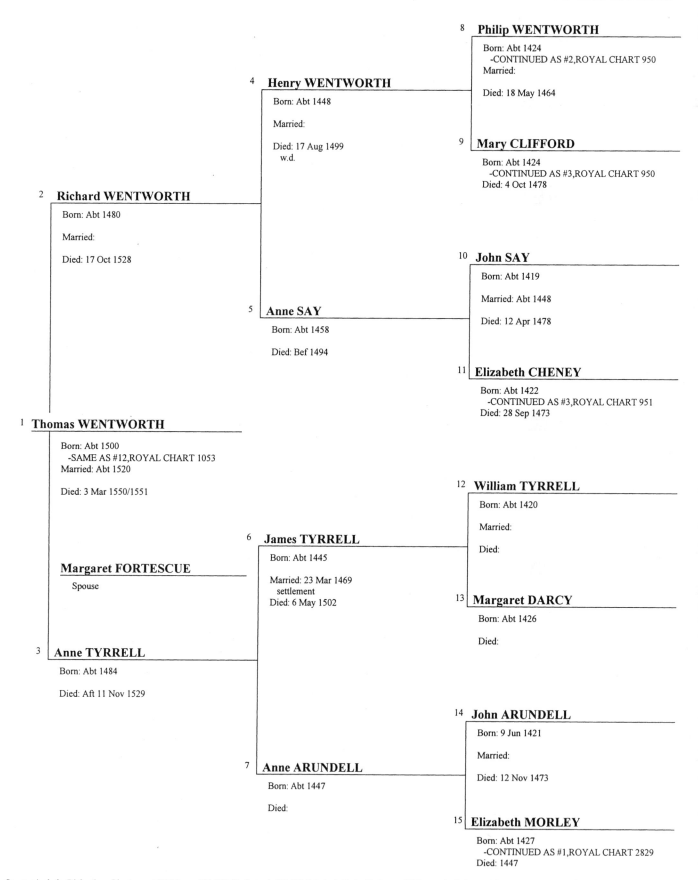

8 Philip WENTWORTH

Born: Abt 1424
  -CONTINUED AS #2,ROYAL CHART 950
Married:

Died: 18 May 1464

4 Henry WENTWORTH

Born: Abt 1448

Married:

Died: 17 Aug 1499
  w.d.

9 Mary CLIFFORD

Born: Abt 1424
  -CONTINUED AS #3,ROYAL CHART 950
Died: 4 Oct 1478

2 Richard WENTWORTH

Born: Abt 1480

Married:

Died: 17 Oct 1528

10 John SAY

Born: Abt 1419

Married: Abt 1448

Died: 12 Apr 1478

5 Anne SAY

Born: Abt 1458

Died: Bef 1494

11 Elizabeth CHENEY

Born: Abt 1422
  -CONTINUED AS #3,ROYAL CHART 951
Died: 28 Sep 1473

1 Thomas WENTWORTH

Born: Abt 1500
  -SAME AS #12,ROYAL CHART 1053
Married: Abt 1520

Died: 3 Mar 1550/1551

12 William TYRRELL

Born: Abt 1420

Married:

Died:

6 James TYRRELL

Born: Abt 1445

Married: 23 Mar 1469
  settlement
Died: 6 May 1502

13 Margaret DARCY

Born: Abt 1426

Died:

Margaret FORTESCUE

Spouse

3 Anne TYRRELL

Born: Abt 1484

Died: Aft 11 Nov 1529

14 John ARUNDELL

Born: 9 Jun 1421

Married:

Died: 12 Nov 1473

7 Anne ARUNDELL

Born: Abt 1447

Died:

15 Elizabeth MORLEY

Born: Abt 1427
  -CONTINUED AS #1,ROYAL CHART 2829
Died: 1447

Sources include: Richardson *Plantagenet* (2004), pp. 380-382 (Harleston), 518-519 (Morley); Faris--Harleston; LDS records; Roberts *500* (600) updated manuscript (November 2000), pp. 324-325 (#7 ancestry).

Pedigree Chart

Chart 1059

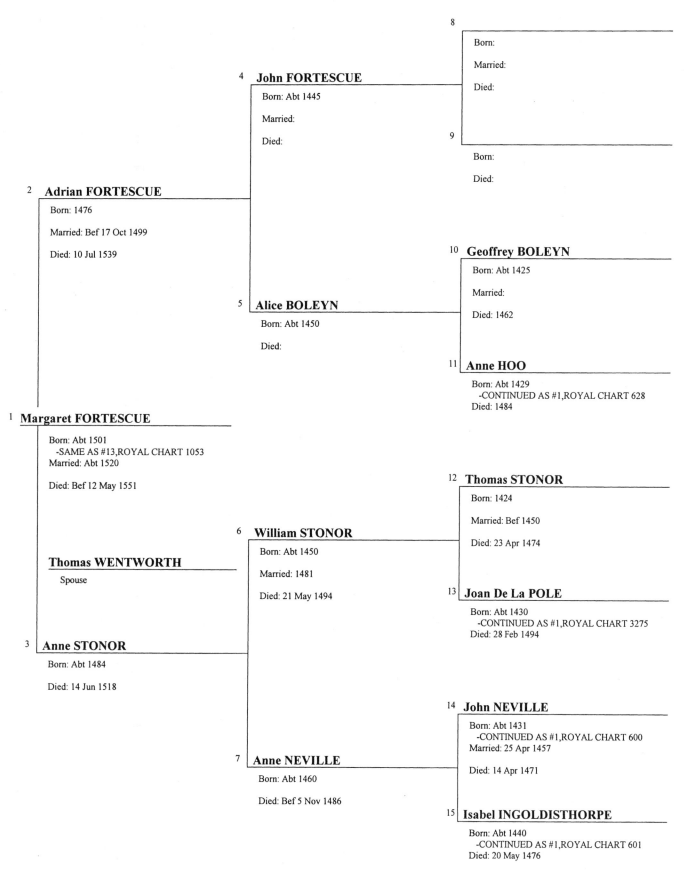

8

4 John FORTESCUE

Born: Abt 1445

Married:

Died:

Born:

Married:

Died:

9

Born:

Died:

2 Adrian FORTESCUE

Born: 1476

Married: Bef 17 Oct 1499

Died: 10 Jul 1539

10 Geoffrey BOLEYN

Born: Abt 1425

Married:

Died: 1462

5 Alice BOLEYN

Born: Abt 1450

Died:

11 Anne HOO

Born: Abt 1429
-CONTINUED AS #1,ROYAL CHART 628
Died: 1484

1 Margaret FORTESCUE

Born: Abt 1501
-SAME AS #13,ROYAL CHART 1053
Married: Abt 1520

Died: Bef 12 May 1551

12 Thomas STONOR

Born: 1424

Married: Bef 1450

Died: 23 Apr 1474

6 William STONOR

Born: Abt 1450

Married: 1481

Died: 21 May 1494

Thomas WENTWORTH

Spouse

13 Joan De La POLE

Born: Abt 1430
-CONTINUED AS #1,ROYAL CHART 3275
Died: 28 Feb 1494

3 Anne STONOR

Born: Abt 1484

Died: 14 Jun 1518

14 John NEVILLE

Born: Abt 1431
-CONTINUED AS #1,ROYAL CHART 600
Married: 25 Apr 1457

Died: 14 Apr 1471

7 Anne NEVILLE

Born: Abt 1460

Died: Bef 5 Nov 1486

15 Isabel INGOLDISTHORPE

Born: Abt 1440
-CONTINUED AS #1,ROYAL CHART 601
Died: 20 May 1476

Sources include: Faris 2--Cherleton; Faris--Harleston, Monthermer; LDS records (#11).

8 **Roger DRURY**
Born: Abt 1425
Married:
Died: 31 Jan 1497/1498

4 **Robert DRURY**
Born: Abt 1455
Married:
Died: 2 Mar 1535/1536

9 **Felice DENSTON**
Born: Abt 1430
Died:

2 **William DRURY**
Born: Abt 1500
Married:
Died: 11 Jan 1557/1558

10 **William CALTHORPE**
Born: 30 Jan 1409/1410
Married: Bef 7 Mar 1463/1464
Died: 15 Nov 1494

5 **Anne CALTHORPE**
Born: Abt 1465
Died:

11 **Elizabeth STAPLETON**
Born: Abt 1441
-CONTINUED AS #7,ROYAL CHART 786
Died: 18 Feb 1504/1505

1 **Mary DRURY**
Born: 30 Jun 1526
-SAME AS #15,ROYAL CHART 1053
Married:
Buried: 16 Jun 1594

12 **John SOTHILL**
Born: Abt 1450
Married: Abt 1475
Died: 7 Oct 1494
w.p.

6 **Henry SOTHILL**
Born: Abt 1478
Married:
Died: 16 May 1506
w.p.

13 **Elizabeth PLUMPTON**
Born: Abt 1461
-CONTINUED AS #3,ROYAL CHART 873
Died: 21 Sep 1506

Richard CORBETT
Spouse

3 **Elizabeth SOTHILL**
Born: Abt 1505
Died: 19 May 1575

14 **Richard EMPSON**
Born: Abt 1450
Married:
Died: 1510

7 **Joan EMPSON**
Born: Abt 1480
Died:

15 **Jane**
Born:
Died:

Sources include: Faris 2--Drury, Sothill; Faris--Drury.

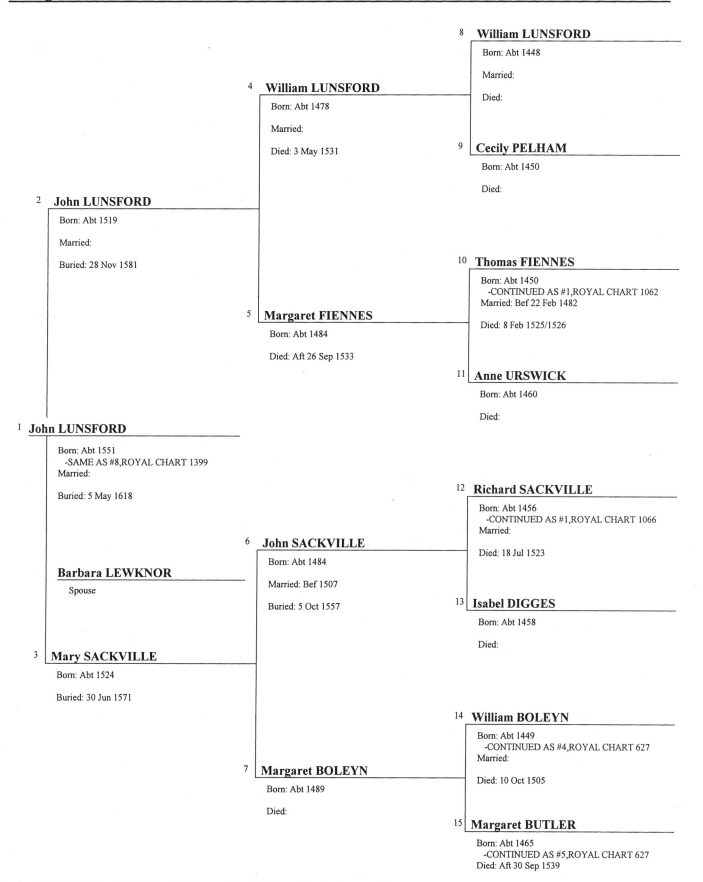

8 William LUNSFORD

Born: Abt 1448

Married:

Died:

4 William LUNSFORD

Born: Abt 1478

Married:

Died: 3 May 1531

9 Cecily PELHAM

Born: Abt 1450

Died:

2 John LUNSFORD

Born: Abt 1519

Married:

Buried: 28 Nov 1581

10 Thomas FIENNES

Born: Abt 1450
  -CONTINUED AS #1,ROYAL CHART 1062
Married: Bef 22 Feb 1482

Died: 8 Feb 1525/1526

5 Margaret FIENNES

Born: Abt 1484

Died: Aft 26 Sep 1533

11 Anne URSWICK

Born: Abt 1460

Died:

1 John LUNSFORD

Born: Abt 1551
  -SAME AS #8,ROYAL CHART 1399
Married:

Buried: 5 May 1618

12 Richard SACKVILLE

Born: Abt 1456
  -CONTINUED AS #1,ROYAL CHART 1066
Married:

Died: 18 Jul 1523

6 John SACKVILLE

Born: Abt 1484

Married: Bef 1507

Buried: 5 Oct 1557

13 Isabel DIGGES

Born: Abt 1458

Died:

Barbara LEWKNOR

Spouse

3 Mary SACKVILLE

Born: Abt 1524

Buried: 30 Jun 1571

14 William BOLEYN

Born: Abt 1449
  -CONTINUED AS #4,ROYAL CHART 627
Married:

Died: 10 Oct 1505

7 Margaret BOLEYN

Born: Abt 1489

Died:

15 Margaret BUTLER

Born: Abt 1465
  -CONTINUED AS #5,ROYAL CHART 627
Died: Aft 30 Sep 1539

Sources include: Faris 2--Lunsford; Faris--Lunsford; *Magna Charta* 88A. Note: The claim in *Magna Charta* and in LDS records that #8 William was a great-grandson of Thomas De Echingham (b. abt 1401) & Margaret Knyvett (cont. chart 593, #4 & 5) is too tight chronologically and appears to be incorrect.

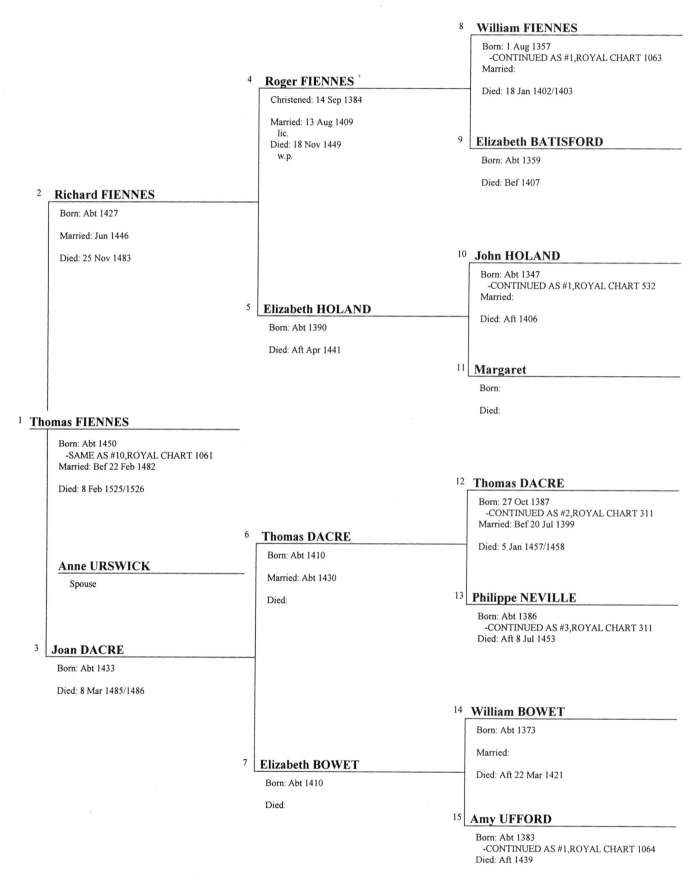

8 William FIENNES

Born: 1 Aug 1357
 -CONTINUED AS #1,ROYAL CHART 1063
Married:

Died: 18 Jan 1402/1403

4 Roger FIENNES

Christened: 14 Sep 1384

Married: 13 Aug 1409
lic.
Died: 18 Nov 1449
w.p.

9 Elizabeth BATISFORD

Born: Abt 1359

Died: Bef 1407

2 Richard FIENNES

Born: Abt 1427

Married: Jun 1446

Died: 25 Nov 1483

10 John HOLAND

Born: Abt 1347
 -CONTINUED AS #1,ROYAL CHART 532
Married:

Died: Aft 1406

5 Elizabeth HOLAND

Born: Abt 1390

Died: Aft Apr 1441

11 Margaret

Born:

Died:

1 Thomas FIENNES

Born: Abt 1450
 -SAME AS #10,ROYAL CHART 1061
Married: Bef 22 Feb 1482

Died: 8 Feb 1525/1526

12 Thomas DACRE

Born: 27 Oct 1387
 -CONTINUED AS #2,ROYAL CHART 311
Married: Bef 20 Jul 1399

Died: 5 Jan 1457/1458

6 Thomas DACRE

Born: Abt 1410

Married: Abt 1430

Died:

13 Philippe NEVILLE

Born: Abt 1386
 -CONTINUED AS #3,ROYAL CHART 311
Died: Aft 8 Jul 1453

Anne URSWICK

Spouse

3 Joan DACRE

Born: Abt 1433

Died: 8 Mar 1485/1486

14 William BOWET

Born: Abt 1373

Married:

Died: Aft 22 Mar 1421

7 Elizabeth BOWET

Born: Abt 1410

Died:

15 Amy UFFORD

Born: Abt 1383
 -CONTINUED AS #1,ROYAL CHART 1064
Died: Aft 1439

Sources include: Richardson *Plantagenet* (2004), pp. 642-643 (Say), 399-400 (Holand), 250-251 (Dacre); Faris 2--Fiennes; Faris--Lunsford; *Magna Charta* 8A; Consultation with Douglas Richardson.

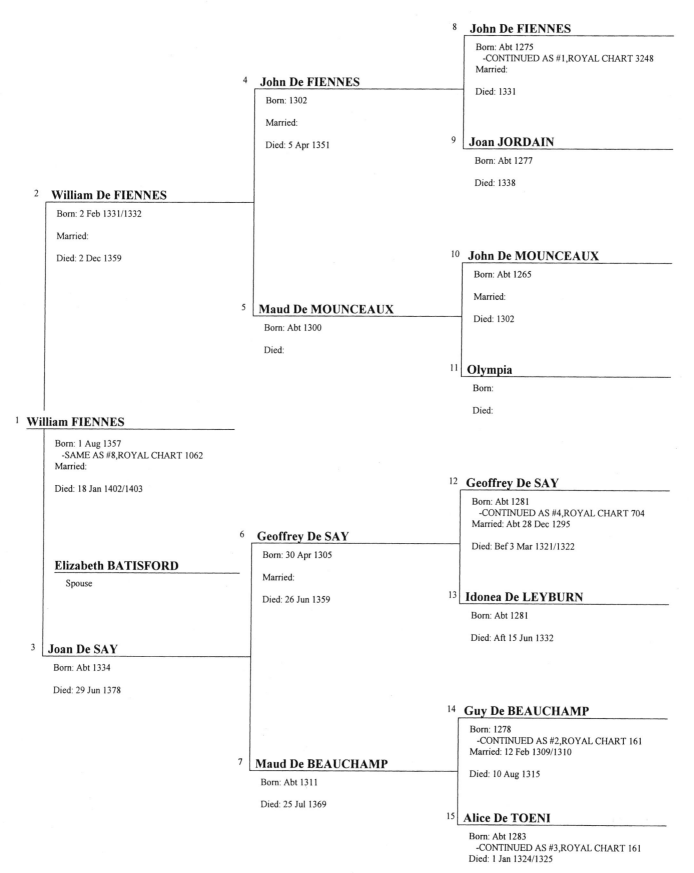

8 **John De FIENNES**

Born: Abt 1275
 -CONTINUED AS #1,ROYAL CHART 3248
Married:

Died: 1331

4 **John De FIENNES**

Born: 1302

Married:

Died: 5 Apr 1351

9 **Joan JORDAIN**

Born: Abt 1277

Died: 1338

2 **William De FIENNES**

Born: 2 Feb 1331/1332

Married:

Died: 2 Dec 1359

10 **John De MOUNCEAUX**

Born: Abt 1265

Married:

Died: 1302

5 **Maud De MOUNCEAUX**

Born: Abt 1300

Died:

11 **Olympia**

Born:

Died:

1 **William FIENNES**

Born: 1 Aug 1357
 -SAME AS #8,ROYAL CHART 1062
Married:

Died: 18 Jan 1402/1403

12 **Geoffrey De SAY**

Born: Abt 1281
 -CONTINUED AS #4,ROYAL CHART 704
Married: Abt 28 Dec 1295

Died: Bef 3 Mar 1321/1322

6 **Geoffrey De SAY**

Born: 30 Apr 1305

Married:

Died: 26 Jun 1359

Elizabeth BATISFORD

Spouse

13 **Idonea De LEYBURN**

Born: Abt 1281

Died: Aft 15 Jun 1332

3 **Joan De SAY**

Born: Abt 1334

Died: 29 Jun 1378

14 **Guy De BEAUCHAMP**

Born: 1278
 -CONTINUED AS #2,ROYAL CHART 161
Married: 12 Feb 1309/1310

Died: 10 Aug 1315

7 **Maud De BEAUCHAMP**

Born: Abt 1311

Died: 25 Jul 1369

15 **Alice De TOENI**

Born: Abt 1283
 -CONTINUED AS #3,ROYAL CHART 161
Died: 1 Jan 1324/1325

Sources include: Faris-Richardson preliminary Magna Carta manuscript (June 2000), pp. 339 (Lunsford), 465 (Say), 33-35 (Beauchamp); Paget (1957) 210:2; *Magna Charta* 16C.

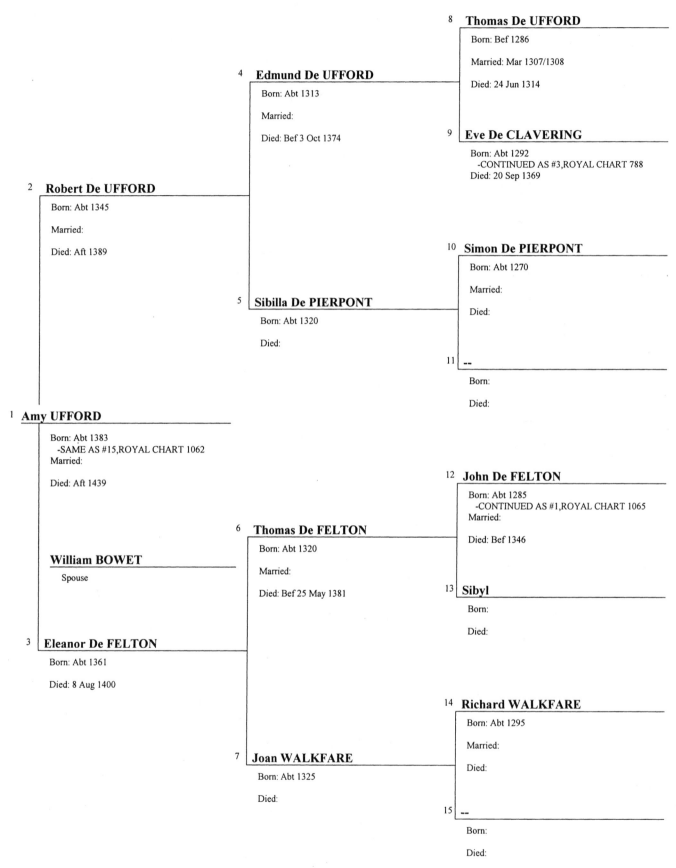

8 Thomas De UFFORD
Born: Bef 1286
Married: Mar 1307/1308
Died: 24 Jun 1314

4 Edmund De UFFORD
Born: Abt 1313
Married:
Died: Bef 3 Oct 1374

9 Eve De CLAVERING
Born: Abt 1292
-CONTINUED AS #3,ROYAL CHART 788
Died: 20 Sep 1369

2 Robert De UFFORD
Born: Abt 1345
Married:
Died: Aft 1389

10 Simon De PIERPONT
Born: Abt 1270
Married:
Died:

5 Sibilla De PIERPONT
Born: Abt 1320
Died:

11 --
Born:
Died:

1 Amy UFFORD
Born: Abt 1383
-SAME AS #15,ROYAL CHART 1062
Married:
Died: Aft 1439

12 John De FELTON
Born: Abt 1285
-CONTINUED AS #1,ROYAL CHART 1065
Married:
Died: Bef 1346

6 Thomas De FELTON
Born: Abt 1320
Married:
Died: Bef 25 May 1381

13 Sibyl
Born:
Died:

William BOWET
Spouse

3 Eleanor De FELTON
Born: Abt 1361
Died: 8 Aug 1400

14 Richard WALKFARE
Born: Abt 1295
Married:
Died:

7 Joan WALKFARE
Born: Abt 1325
Died:

15 --
Born:
Died:

Sources include: Richardson *Magna Carta* (April 2005), pp. 213-215 (Clavering); Faris preliminary baronial manuscript (1998), pp. 1564-65 (Ufford), 1252-53 (Pierpont); *Magna Charta* 49A, 137A.

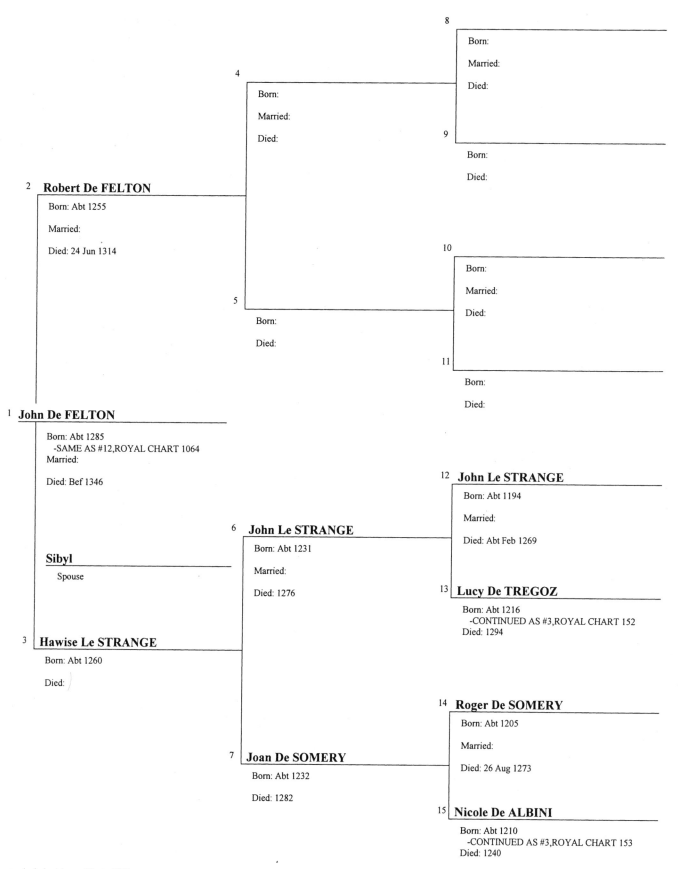

8
Born:
Married:
Died:

4
Born:
Married:
Died:

9
Born:
Died:

2 **Robert De FELTON**
Born: Abt 1255
Married:
Died: 24 Jun 1314

10
Born:
Married:
Died:

5
Born:
Died:

11
Born:
Died:

1 **John De FELTON**
Born: Abt 1285
  -SAME AS #12,ROYAL CHART 1064
Married:
Died: Bef 1346

12 **John Le STRANGE**
Born: Abt 1194
Married:
Died: Abt Feb 1269

6 **John Le STRANGE**
Born: Abt 1231
Married:
Died: 1276

13 **Lucy De TREGOZ**
Born: Abt 1216
  -CONTINUED AS #3,ROYAL CHART 152
Died: 1294

Sibyl
Spouse

3 **Hawise Le STRANGE**
Born: Abt 1260
Died:

14 **Roger De SOMERY**
Born: Abt 1205
Married:
Died: 26 Aug 1273

7 **Joan De SOMERY**
Born: Abt 1232
Died: 1282

15 **Nicole De ALBINI**
Born: Abt 1210
  -CONTINUED AS #3,ROYAL CHART 153
Died: 1240

Sources include: *Magna Charta* 137A.

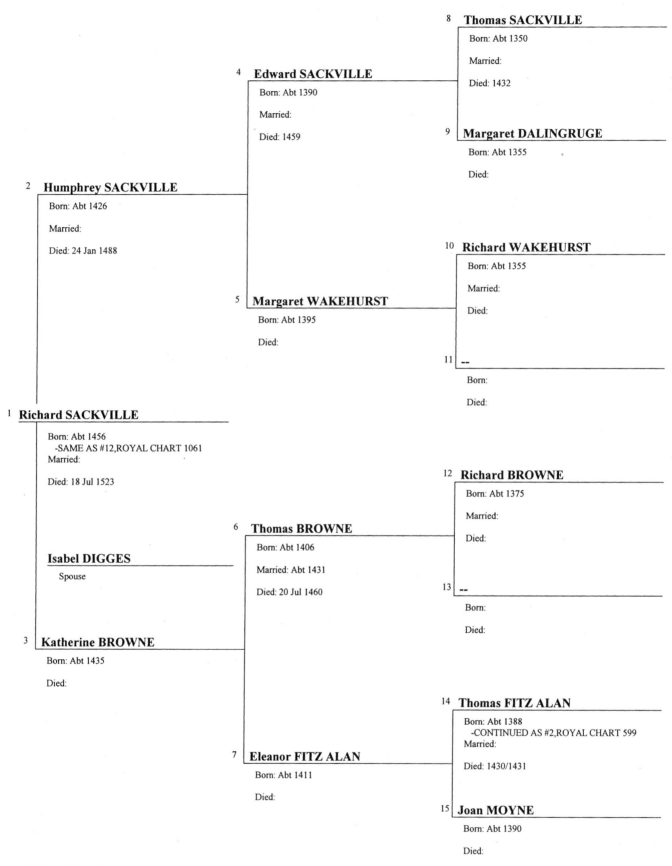

8 | **Thomas SACKVILLE**
Born: Abt 1350
Married:
Died: 1432

4 | **Edward SACKVILLE**
Born: Abt 1390
Married:
Died: 1459

9 | **Margaret DALINGRUGE**
Born: Abt 1355
Died:

2 | **Humphrey SACKVILLE**
Born: Abt 1426
Married:
Died: 24 Jan 1488

10 | **Richard WAKEHURST**
Born: Abt 1355
Married:
Died:

5 | **Margaret WAKEHURST**
Born: Abt 1395
Died:

11 | **--**
Born:
Died:

1 | **Richard SACKVILLE**
Born: Abt 1456
-SAME AS #12,ROYAL CHART 1061
Married:
Died: 18 Jul 1523

12 | **Richard BROWNE**
Born: Abt 1375
Married:
Died:

6 | **Thomas BROWNE**
Born: Abt 1406
Married: Abt 1431
Died: 20 Jul 1460

Isabel DIGGES
Spouse

13 | **--**
Born:
Died:

3 | **Katherine BROWNE**
Born: Abt 1435
Died:

14 | **Thomas FITZ ALAN**
Born: Abt 1388
-CONTINUED AS #2,ROYAL CHART 599
Married:
Died: 1430/1431

7 | **Eleanor FITZ ALAN**
Born: Abt 1411
Died:

15 | **Joan MOYNE**
Born: Abt 1390
Died:

Sources include: LDS records.

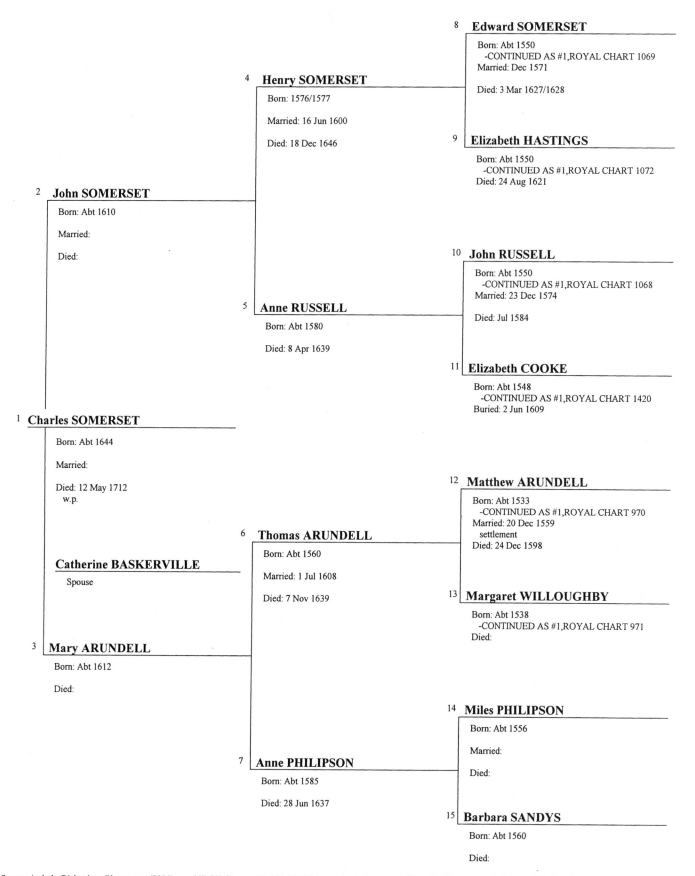

8 Edward SOMERSET

Born: Abt 1550
-CONTINUED AS #1,ROYAL CHART 1069
Married: Dec 1571

Died: 3 Mar 1627/1628

4 Henry SOMERSET

Born: 1576/1577

Married: 16 Jun 1600

Died: 18 Dec 1646

9 Elizabeth HASTINGS

Born: Abt 1550
-CONTINUED AS #1,ROYAL CHART 1072
Died: 24 Aug 1621

2 John SOMERSET

Born: Abt 1610

Married:

Died:

10 John RUSSELL

Born: Abt 1550
-CONTINUED AS #1,ROYAL CHART 1068
Married: 23 Dec 1574

Died: Jul 1584

5 Anne RUSSELL

Born: Abt 1580

Died: 8 Apr 1639

11 Elizabeth COOKE

Born: Abt 1548
-CONTINUED AS #1,ROYAL CHART 1420
Buried: 2 Jun 1609

1 Charles SOMERSET

Born: Abt 1644

Married:

Died: 12 May 1712
w.p.

12 Matthew ARUNDELL

Born: Abt 1533
-CONTINUED AS #1,ROYAL CHART 970
Married: 20 Dec 1559
settlement
Died: 24 Dec 1598

6 Thomas ARUNDELL

Born: Abt 1560

Married: 1 Jul 1608

Died: 7 Nov 1639

13 Margaret WILLOUGHBY

Born: Abt 1538
-CONTINUED AS #1,ROYAL CHART 971
Died:

Catherine BASKERVILLE

Spouse

3 Mary ARUNDELL

Born: Abt 1612

Died:

14 Miles PHILIPSON

Born: Abt 1556

Married:

Died:

7 Anne PHILIPSON

Born: Abt 1585

Died: 28 Jun 1637

15 Barbara SANDYS

Born: Abt 1560

Died:

Sources include: Richardson *Plantagenet* (2004), pp. 667-669 (Somerset), 182-183 (Calvert); Faris--Somerset. Note: #1 Charles was the father of Maria Johanna Somerset (b. abt 1670; md. Richard Smith), who was mother of Charles Somerset Smith (b. Feb 1698), both of MD.

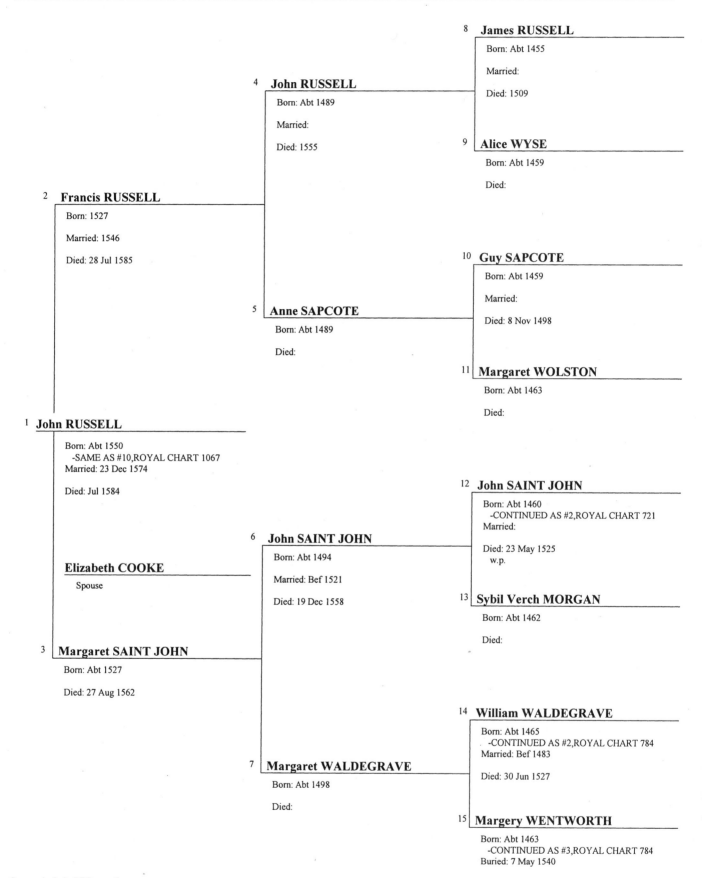

8 **James RUSSELL**

Born: Abt 1455

Married:

Died: 1509

4 **John RUSSELL**

Born: Abt 1489

Married:

Died: 1555

9 **Alice WYSE**

Born: Abt 1459

Died:

2 **Francis RUSSELL**

Born: 1527

Married: 1546

Died: 28 Jul 1585

10 **Guy SAPCOTE**

Born: Abt 1459

Married:

Died: 8 Nov 1498

5 **Anne SAPCOTE**

Born: Abt 1489

Died:

11 **Margaret WOLSTON**

Born: Abt 1463

Died:

1 **John RUSSELL**

Born: Abt 1550
 -SAME AS #10,ROYAL CHART 1067
Married: 23 Dec 1574

Died: Jul 1584

12 **John SAINT JOHN**

Born: Abt 1460
 -CONTINUED AS #2,ROYAL CHART 721
Married:

Died: 23 May 1525
 w.p.

6 **John SAINT JOHN**

Born: Abt 1494

Married: Bef 1521

Died: 19 Dec 1558

13 **Sybil Verch MORGAN**

Born: Abt 1462

Died:

Elizabeth COOKE

Spouse

3 **Margaret SAINT JOHN**

Born: Abt 1527

Died: 27 Aug 1562

14 **William WALDEGRAVE**

Born: Abt 1465
 -CONTINUED AS #2,ROYAL CHART 784
Married: Bef 1483

Died: 30 Jun 1527

7 **Margaret WALDEGRAVE**

Born: Abt 1498

Died:

15 **Margery WENTWORTH**

Born: Abt 1463
 -CONTINUED AS #3,ROYAL CHART 784
Buried: 7 May 1540

Sources include: LDS records.

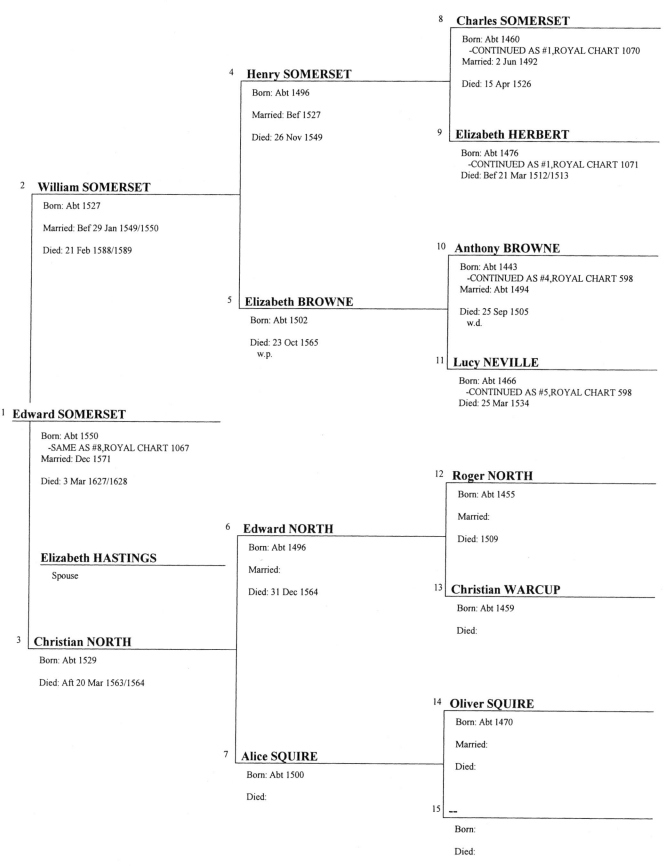

2 William SOMERSET

Born: Abt 1527

Married: Bef 29 Jan 1549/1550

Died: 21 Feb 1588/1589

4 Henry SOMERSET

Born: Abt 1496

Married: Bef 1527

Died: 26 Nov 1549

8 Charles SOMERSET

Born: Abt 1460
-CONTINUED AS #1,ROYAL CHART 1070
Married: 2 Jun 1492

Died: 15 Apr 1526

9 Elizabeth HERBERT

Born: Abt 1476
-CONTINUED AS #1,ROYAL CHART 1071
Died: Bef 21 Mar 1512/1513

5 Elizabeth BROWNE

Born: Abt 1502

Died: 23 Oct 1565
w.p.

10 Anthony BROWNE

Born: Abt 1443
-CONTINUED AS #4,ROYAL CHART 598
Married: Abt 1494

Died: 25 Sep 1505
w.d.

11 Lucy NEVILLE

Born: Abt 1466
-CONTINUED AS #5,ROYAL CHART 598
Died: 25 Mar 1534

1 Edward SOMERSET

Born: Abt 1550
-SAME AS #8,ROYAL CHART 1067
Married: Dec 1571

Died: 3 Mar 1627/1628

Elizabeth HASTINGS

Spouse

3 Christian NORTH

Born: Abt 1529

Died: Aft 20 Mar 1563/1564

6 Edward NORTH

Born: Abt 1496

Married:

Died: 31 Dec 1564

12 Roger NORTH

Born: Abt 1455

Married:

Died: 1509

13 Christian WARCUP

Born: Abt 1459

Died:

7 Alice SQUIRE

Born: Abt 1500

Died:

14 Oliver SQUIRE

Born: Abt 1470

Married:

Died:

15 --

Born:

Died:

Sources include: Faris--Beaufort; LDS records.

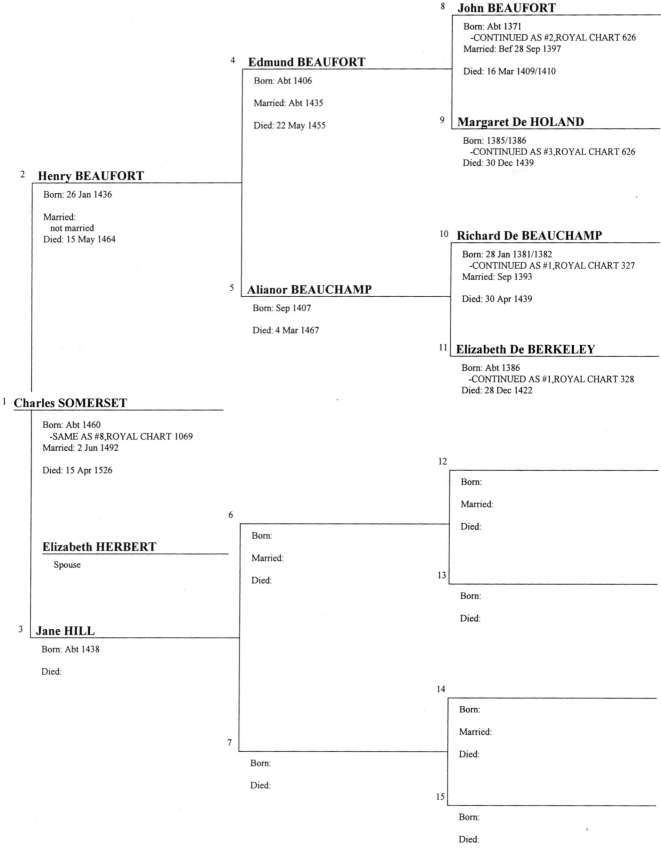

8 John BEAUFORT

Born: Abt 1371
  -CONTINUED AS #2,ROYAL CHART 626
Married: Bef 28 Sep 1397

Died: 16 Mar 1409/1410

4 Edmund BEAUFORT

Born: Abt 1406

Married: Abt 1435

Died: 22 May 1455

9 Margaret De HOLAND

Born: 1385/1386
  -CONTINUED AS #3,ROYAL CHART 626
Died: 30 Dec 1439

2 Henry BEAUFORT

Born: 26 Jan 1436

Married:
  not married
Died: 15 May 1464

10 Richard De BEAUCHAMP

Born: 28 Jan 1381/1382
  -CONTINUED AS #1,ROYAL CHART 327
Married: Sep 1393

Died: 30 Apr 1439

5 Alianor BEAUCHAMP

Born: Sep 1407

Died: 4 Mar 1467

11 Elizabeth De BERKELEY

Born: Abt 1386
  -CONTINUED AS #1,ROYAL CHART 328
Died: 28 Dec 1422

1 Charles SOMERSET

Born: Abt 1460
  -SAME AS #8,ROYAL CHART 1069
Married: 2 Jun 1492

Died: 15 Apr 1526

12

Born:

Married:

Died:

6

Born:

Married:

Died:

13

Born:

Died:

Elizabeth HERBERT

Spouse

3 Jane HILL

Born: Abt 1438

Died:

14

Born:

Married:

Died:

7

Born:

Died:

15

Born:

Died:

Sources include: Faris--Beaufort.

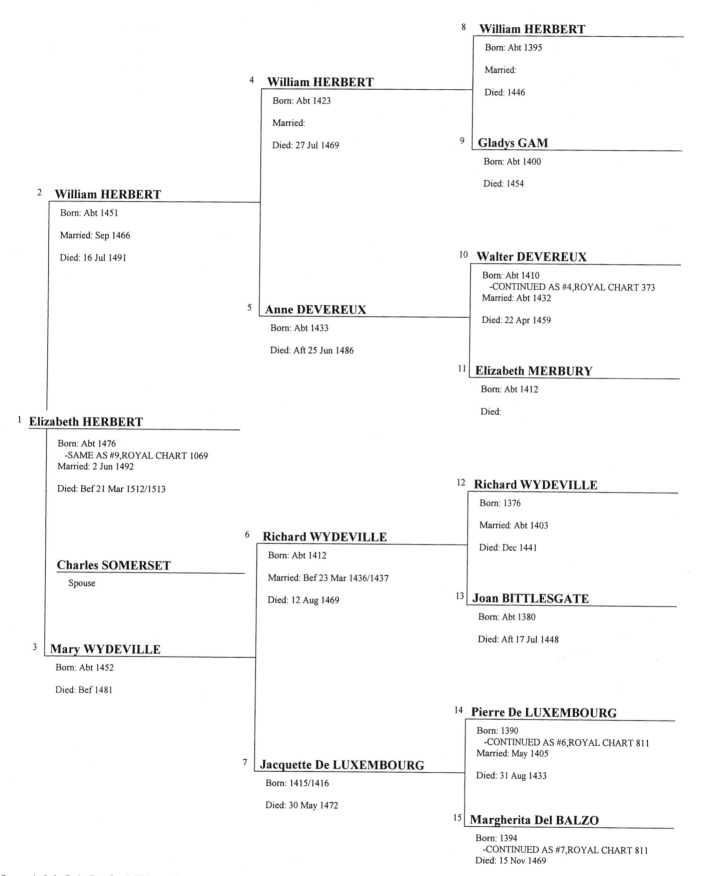

8 William HERBERT
Born: Abt 1395
Married:
Died: 1446

4 William HERBERT
Born: Abt 1423
Married:
Died: 27 Jul 1469

9 Gladys GAM
Born: Abt 1400
Died: 1454

2 William HERBERT
Born: Abt 1451
Married: Sep 1466
Died: 16 Jul 1491

10 Walter DEVEREUX
Born: Abt 1410
-CONTINUED AS #4,ROYAL CHART 373
Married: Abt 1432
Died: 22 Apr 1459

5 Anne DEVEREUX
Born: Abt 1433
Died: Aft 25 Jun 1486

11 Elizabeth MERBURY
Born: Abt 1412
Died:

1 Elizabeth HERBERT
Born: Abt 1476
-SAME AS #9,ROYAL CHART 1069
Married: 2 Jun 1492
Died: Bef 21 Mar 1512/1513

12 Richard WYDEVILLE
Born: 1376
Married: Abt 1403
Died: Dec 1441

6 Richard WYDEVILLE
Born: Abt 1412
Married: Bef 23 Mar 1436/1437
Died: 12 Aug 1469

13 Joan BITTLESGATE
Born: Abt 1380
Died: Aft 17 Jul 1448

Charles SOMERSET
Spouse

3 Mary WYDEVILLE
Born: Abt 1452
Died: Bef 1481

14 Pierre De LUXEMBOURG
Born: 1390
-CONTINUED AS #6,ROYAL CHART 811
Married: May 1405
Died: 31 Aug 1433

7 Jacquette De LUXEMBOURG
Born: 1415/1416
Died: 30 May 1472

15 Margherita Del BALZO
Born: 1394
-CONTINUED AS #7,ROYAL CHART 811
Died: 15 Nov 1469

Sources include: Faris--Beaufort 7; LDS records.

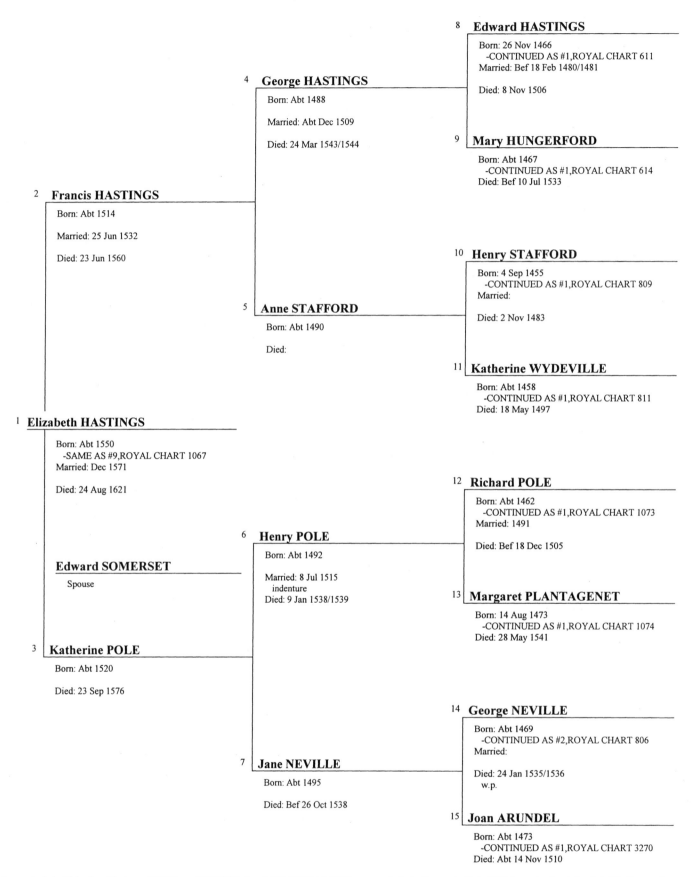

8 Edward HASTINGS
Born: 26 Nov 1466
-CONTINUED AS #1,ROYAL CHART 611
Married: Bef 18 Feb 1480/1481

Died: 8 Nov 1506

4 George HASTINGS
Born: Abt 1488

Married: Abt Dec 1509

Died: 24 Mar 1543/1544

9 Mary HUNGERFORD
Born: Abt 1467
-CONTINUED AS #1,ROYAL CHART 614
Died: Bef 10 Jul 1533

2 Francis HASTINGS
Born: Abt 1514

Married: 25 Jun 1532

Died: 23 Jun 1560

10 Henry STAFFORD
Born: 4 Sep 1455
-CONTINUED AS #1,ROYAL CHART 809
Married:

Died: 2 Nov 1483

5 Anne STAFFORD
Born: Abt 1490

Died:

11 Katherine WYDEVILLE
Born: Abt 1458
-CONTINUED AS #1,ROYAL CHART 811
Died: 18 May 1497

1 Elizabeth HASTINGS
Born: Abt 1550
-SAME AS #9,ROYAL CHART 1067
Married: Dec 1571

Died: 24 Aug 1621

12 Richard POLE
Born: Abt 1462
-CONTINUED AS #1,ROYAL CHART 1073
Married: 1491

Died: Bef 18 Dec 1505

6 Henry POLE
Born: Abt 1492

Married: 8 Jul 1515
  indenture
Died: 9 Jan 1538/1539

Edward SOMERSET
  Spouse

13 Margaret PLANTAGENET
Born: 14 Aug 1473
-CONTINUED AS #1,ROYAL CHART 1074
Died: 28 May 1541

3 Katherine POLE
Born: Abt 1520

Died: 23 Sep 1576

14 George NEVILLE
Born: Abt 1469
-CONTINUED AS #2,ROYAL CHART 806
Married:

Died: 24 Jan 1535/1536
w.p.

7 Jane NEVILLE
Born: Abt 1495

Died: Bef 26 Oct 1538

15 Joan ARUNDEL
Born: Abt 1473
-CONTINUED AS #1,ROYAL CHART 3270
Died: Abt 14 Nov 1510

Sources include: Richardson *Plantagenet* (2004), pp. 386-388 (Hastings), 585-587 (Pole), 95 (Bergavenny); Faris--Somerset. Note: #13 Margaret, when beheaded at the Tower of London 28 May 1541, was the last of the Plantagenets.

Pedigree Chart

Chart 1073

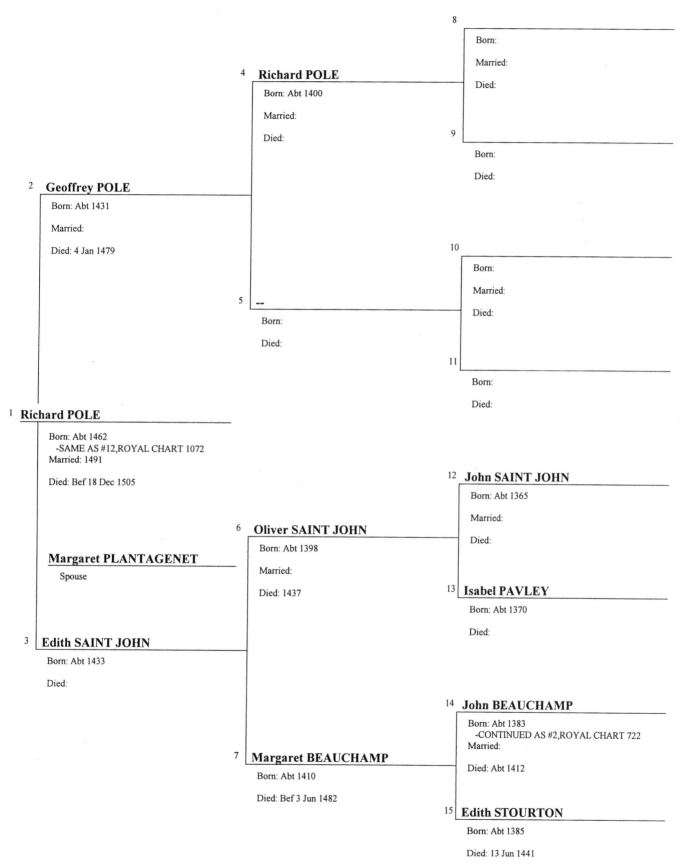

8

Born:

Married:

Died:

4   **Richard POLE**

Born: Abt 1400

Married:

Died:

9

Born:

Died:

2   **Geoffrey POLE**

Born: Abt 1431

Married:

Died: 4 Jan 1479

10

Born:

Married:

Died:

5   **--**

Born:

Died:

11

Born:

Died:

1   **Richard POLE**

Born: Abt 1462
   -SAME AS #12,ROYAL CHART 1072
Married: 1491

Died: Bef 18 Dec 1505

12   **John SAINT JOHN**

Born: Abt 1365

Married:

Died:

6   **Oliver SAINT JOHN**

Born: Abt 1398

Married:

Died: 1437

13   **Isabel PAVLEY**

Born: Abt 1370

Died:

Margaret PLANTAGENET

Spouse

3   **Edith SAINT JOHN**

Born: Abt 1433

Died:

14   **John BEAUCHAMP**

Born: Abt 1383
   -CONTINUED AS #2,ROYAL CHART 722
Married:

Died: Abt 1412

7   **Margaret BEAUCHAMP**

Born: Abt 1410

Died: Bef 3 Jun 1482

15   **Edith STOURTON**

Born: Abt 1385

Died: 13 Jun 1441

Sources include: Richardson *Plantagenet* (2004), pp. 626-628 (St. John); *Ancestral Roots* 225-37, 85; Faris--Somerset 7; Faris 2--Pole 5, Tudor 6 (#7 ancestry); LDS records.

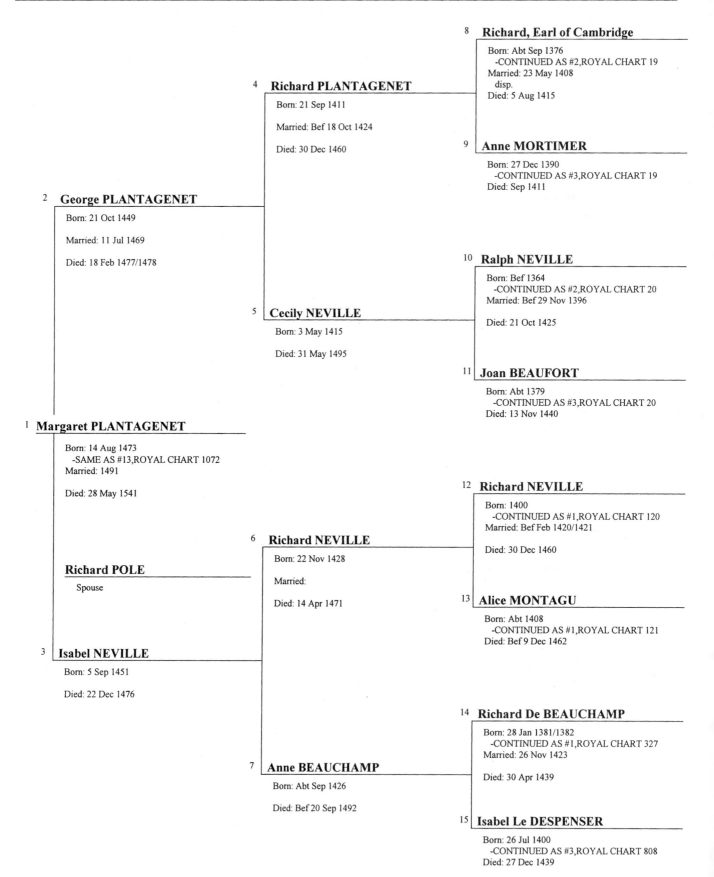

8 | **Richard, Earl of Cambridge**
Born: Abt Sep 1376
-CONTINUED AS #2,ROYAL CHART 19
Married: 23 May 1408
disp.
Died: 5 Aug 1415

4 | **Richard PLANTAGENET**
Born: 21 Sep 1411
Married: Bef 18 Oct 1424
Died: 30 Dec 1460

9 | **Anne MORTIMER**
Born: 27 Dec 1390
-CONTINUED AS #3,ROYAL CHART 19
Died: Sep 1411

2 | **George PLANTAGENET**
Born: 21 Oct 1449
Married: 11 Jul 1469
Died: 18 Feb 1477/1478

10 | **Ralph NEVILLE**
Born: Bef 1364
-CONTINUED AS #2,ROYAL CHART 20
Married: Bef 29 Nov 1396
Died: 21 Oct 1425

5 | **Cecily NEVILLE**
Born: 3 May 1415
Died: 31 May 1495

11 | **Joan BEAUFORT**
Born: Abt 1379
-CONTINUED AS #3,ROYAL CHART 20
Died: 13 Nov 1440

1 | **Margaret PLANTAGENET**
Born: 14 Aug 1473
-SAME AS #13,ROYAL CHART 1072
Married: 1491
Died: 28 May 1541

12 | **Richard NEVILLE**
Born: 1400
-CONTINUED AS #1,ROYAL CHART 120
Married: Bef Feb 1420/1421
Died: 30 Dec 1460

6 | **Richard NEVILLE**
Born: 22 Nov 1428
Married:
Died: 14 Apr 1471

Richard POLE
Spouse

13 | **Alice MONTAGU**
Born: Abt 1408
-CONTINUED AS #1,ROYAL CHART 121
Died: Bef 9 Dec 1462

3 | **Isabel NEVILLE**
Born: 5 Sep 1451
Died: 22 Dec 1476

14 | **Richard De BEAUCHAMP**
Born: 28 Jan 1381/1382
-CONTINUED AS #1,ROYAL CHART 327
Married: 26 Nov 1423
Died: 30 Apr 1439

7 | **Anne BEAUCHAMP**
Born: Abt Sep 1426
Died: Bef 20 Sep 1492

15 | **Isabel Le DESPENSER**
Born: 26 Jul 1400
-CONTINUED AS #3,ROYAL CHART 808
Died: 27 Dec 1439

Sources include: Faris--Somerset, York, Monthermer.

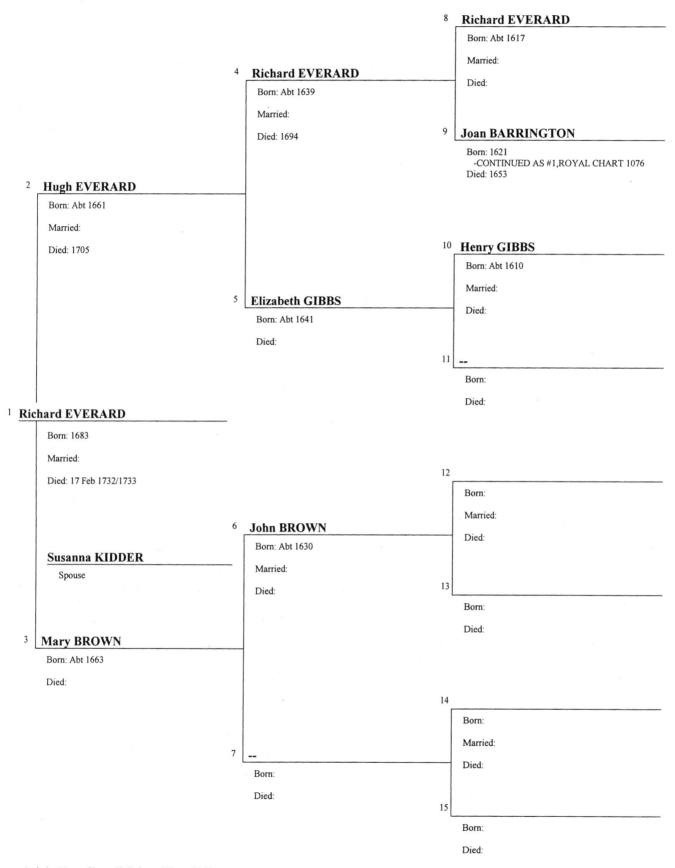

8 **Richard EVERARD**

Born: Abt 1617

Married:

Died:

4 **Richard EVERARD**

Born: Abt 1639

Married:

Died: 1694

9 **Joan BARRINGTON**

Born: 1621
  -CONTINUED AS #1,ROYAL CHART 1076
Died: 1653

2 **Hugh EVERARD**

Born: Abt 1661

Married:

Died: 1705

10 **Henry GIBBS**

Born: Abt 1610

Married:

Died:

5 **Elizabeth GIBBS**

Born: Abt 1641

Died:

11 **--**

Born:

Died:

1 **Richard EVERARD**

Born: 1683

Married:

Died: 17 Feb 1732/1733

12

Born:

Married:

Died:

6 **John BROWN**

Born: Abt 1630

Married:

Died:

13

Born:

Died:

Susanna KIDDER

Spouse

3 **Mary BROWN**

Born: Abt 1663

Died:

14

Born:

Married:

Died:

7 **--**

Born:

Died:

15

Born:

Died:

Sources include: *Magna Charta* 62; Roberts *500*, pp. 35-39.

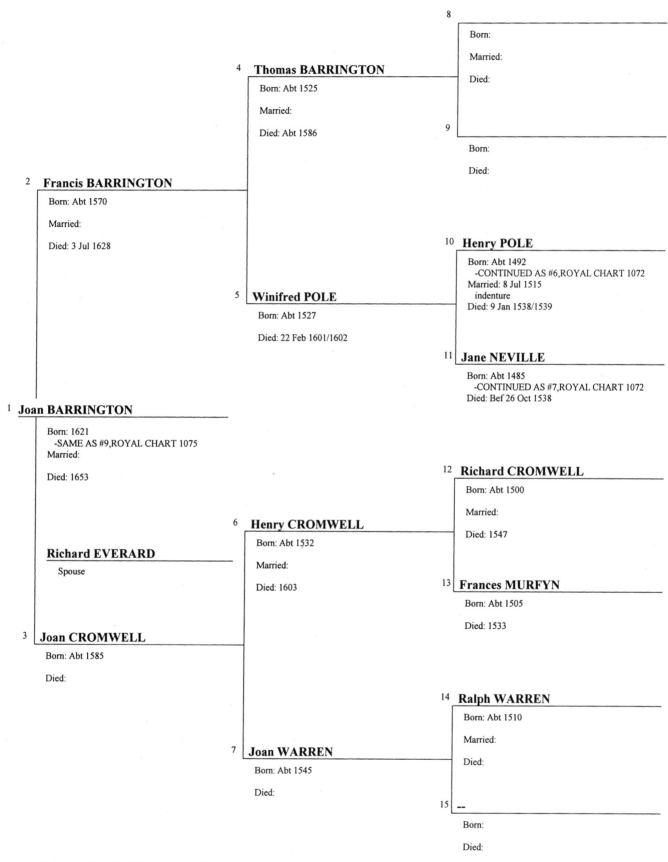

8

Born:

Married:

Died:

4 Thomas BARRINGTON

Born: Abt 1525

Married:

Died: Abt 1586

9

Born:

Died:

2 Francis BARRINGTON

Born: Abt 1570

Married:

Died: 3 Jul 1628

10 Henry POLE

Born: Abt 1492
   -CONTINUED AS #6,ROYAL CHART 1072
Married: 8 Jul 1515
   indenture
Died: 9 Jan 1538/1539

5 Winifred POLE

Born: Abt 1527

Died: 22 Feb 1601/1602

11 Jane NEVILLE

Born: Abt 1485
   -CONTINUED AS #7,ROYAL CHART 1072
Died: Bef 26 Oct 1538

1 Joan BARRINGTON

Born: 1621
   -SAME AS #9,ROYAL CHART 1075
Married:

Died: 1653

12 Richard CROMWELL

Born: Abt 1500

Married:

Died: 1547

6 Henry CROMWELL

Born: Abt 1532

Married:

Died: 1603

Richard EVERARD

Spouse

13 Frances MURFYN

Born: Abt 1505

Died: 1533

3 Joan CROMWELL

Born: Abt 1585

Died:

14 Ralph WARREN

Born: Abt 1510

Married:

Died:

7 Joan WARREN

Born: Abt 1545

Died:

15 --

Born:

Died:

Sources include: *Magna Charta* 62; Roberts *500*, pp. 35-39; LDS records. Note: #12 Richard Cromwell or Williams.

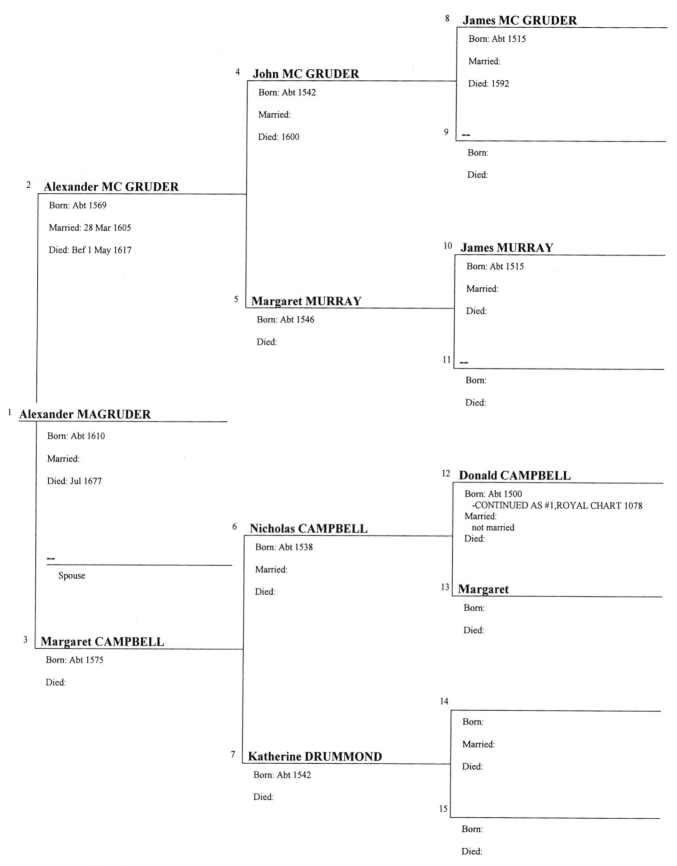

8 **James MC GRUDER**
Born: Abt 1515
Married:
Died: 1592

4 **John MC GRUDER**
Born: Abt 1542
Married:
Died: 1600

9 **--**
Born:
Died:

2 **Alexander MC GRUDER**
Born: Abt 1569
Married: 28 Mar 1605
Died: Bef 1 May 1617

10 **James MURRAY**
Born: Abt 1515
Married:
Died:

5 **Margaret MURRAY**
Born: Abt 1546
Died:

11 **--**
Born:
Died:

1 **Alexander MAGRUDER**
Born: Abt 1610
Married:
Died: Jul 1677

12 **Donald CAMPBELL**
Born: Abt 1500
    -CONTINUED AS #1, ROYAL CHART 1078
Married:
    not married
Died:

6 **Nicholas CAMPBELL**
Born: Abt 1538
Married:
Died:

13 **Margaret**
Born:
Died:

--
Spouse

3 **Margaret CAMPBELL**
Born: Abt 1575
Died:

14
Born:
Married:
Died:

7 **Katherine DRUMMOND**
Born: Abt 1542
Died:

15
Born:
Died:

Sources include: Roberts *500*, p. 99; LDS records.

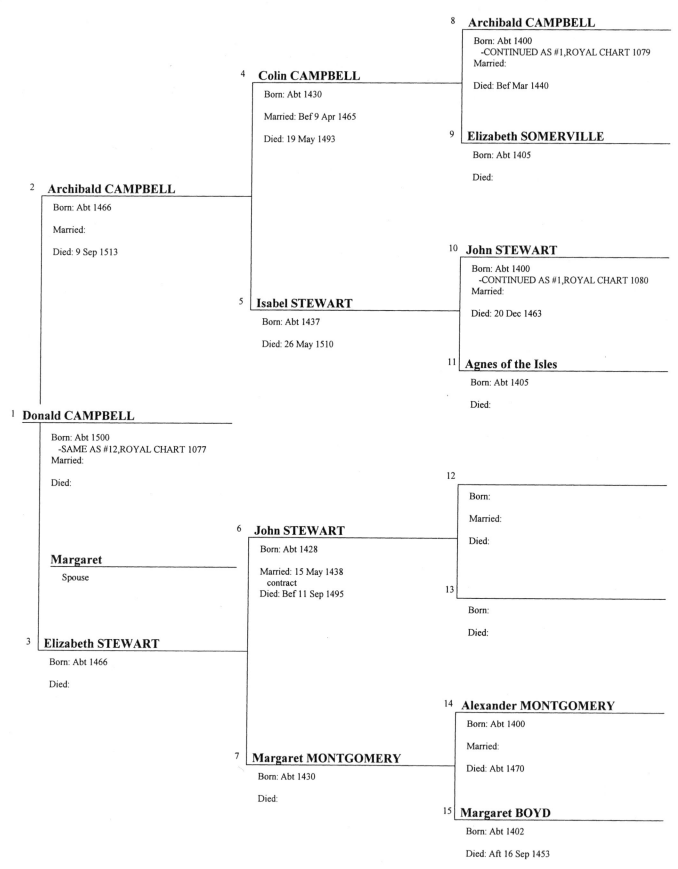

8 **Archibald CAMPBELL**

Born: Abt 1400
  -CONTINUED AS #1,ROYAL CHART 1079
Married:

Died: Bef Mar 1440

4 **Colin CAMPBELL**

Born: Abt 1430

Married: Bef 9 Apr 1465

Died: 19 May 1493

9 **Elizabeth SOMERVILLE**

Born: Abt 1405

Died:

2 **Archibald CAMPBELL**

Born: Abt 1466

Married:

Died: 9 Sep 1513

10 **John STEWART**

Born: Abt 1400
  -CONTINUED AS #1,ROYAL CHART 1080
Married:

Died: 20 Dec 1463

5 **Isabel STEWART**

Born: Abt 1437

Died: 26 May 1510

11 **Agnes of the Isles**

Born: Abt 1405

Died:

1 **Donald CAMPBELL**

Born: Abt 1500
  -SAME AS #12,ROYAL CHART 1077
Married:

Died:

12

Born:

Married:

Died:

6 **John STEWART**

Born: Abt 1428

Married: 15 May 1438
  contract
Died: Bef 11 Sep 1495

13

Born:

Died:

Margaret

Spouse

3 **Elizabeth STEWART**

Born: Abt 1466

Died:

14 **Alexander MONTGOMERY**

Born: Abt 1400

Married:

Died: Abt 1470

7 **Margaret MONTGOMERY**

Born: Abt 1430

Died:

15 **Margaret BOYD**

Born: Abt 1402

Died: Aft 16 Sep 1453

Sources include: Roberts *500*, p. 99; *Magna Charta* 41D, 15A.

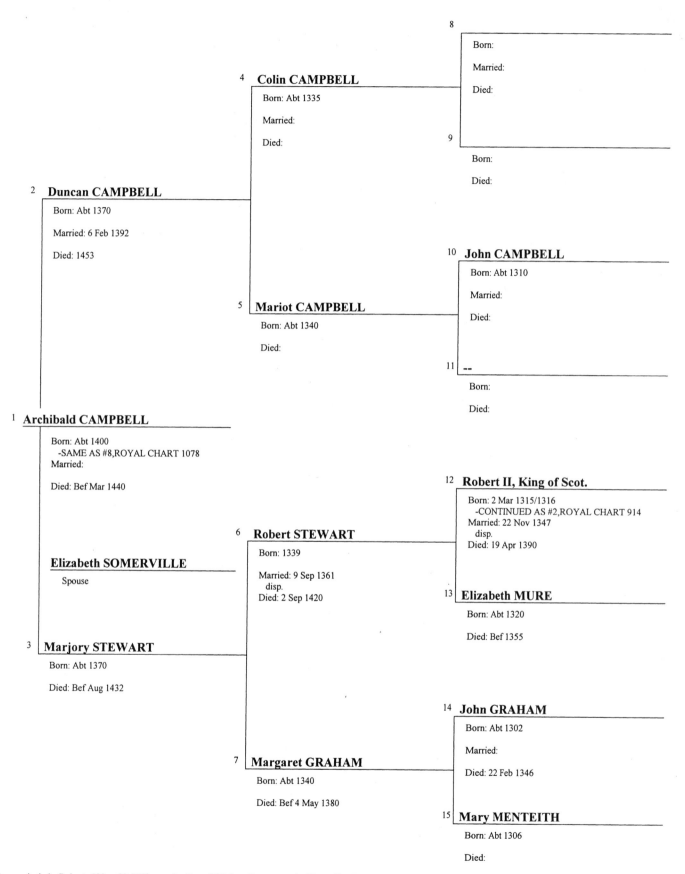

8

Colin CAMPBELL 4

Born: Abt 1335

Married:

Died:

Born:

Married:

Died:

9

Born:

Died:

Duncan CAMPBELL 2

Born: Abt 1370

Married: 6 Feb 1392

Died: 1453

10 **John CAMPBELL**

Born: Abt 1310

Married:

Died:

Mariot CAMPBELL 5

Born: Abt 1340

Died:

11 **--**

Born:

Died:

Archibald CAMPBELL 1

Born: Abt 1400
  -SAME AS #8,ROYAL CHART 1078
Married:

Died: Bef Mar 1440

12 **Robert II, King of Scot.**

Born: 2 Mar 1315/1316
  -CONTINUED AS #2,ROYAL CHART 914
Married: 22 Nov 1347
disp.
Died: 19 Apr 1390

Robert STEWART 6

Born: 1339

Married: 9 Sep 1361
disp.
Died: 2 Sep 1420

13 **Elizabeth MURE**

Born: Abt 1320

Died: Bef 1355

Elizabeth SOMERVILLE

Spouse

Marjory STEWART 3

Born: Abt 1370

Died: Bef Aug 1432

14 **John GRAHAM**

Born: Abt 1302

Married:

Died: 22 Feb 1346

Margaret GRAHAM 7

Born: Abt 1340

Died: Bef 4 May 1380

15 **Mary MENTEITH**

Born: Abt 1306

Died:

Sources include: Roberts *500*, p. 99; LDS records. Note: #6 Robert Stewart was legitimated by his parents marriage about eight years after his birth.

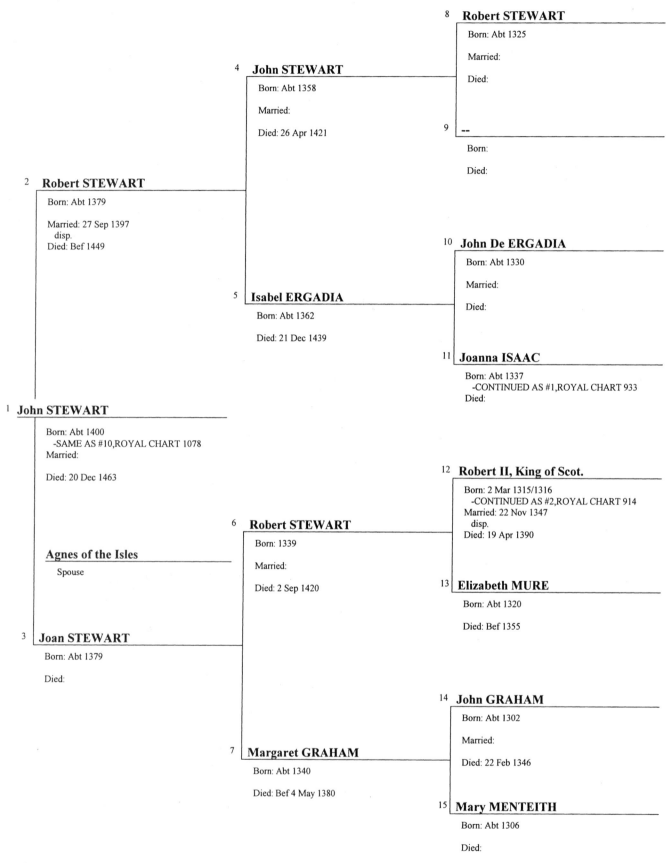

8 Robert STEWART

Born: Abt 1325

Married:

Died:

4 John STEWART

Born: Abt 1358

Married:

Died: 26 Apr 1421

9 --

Born:

Died:

2 Robert STEWART

Born: Abt 1379

Married: 27 Sep 1397
disp.
Died: Bef 1449

10 John De ERGADIA

Born: Abt 1330

Married:

Died:

5 Isabel ERGADIA

Born: Abt 1362

Died: 21 Dec 1439

11 Joanna ISAAC

Born: Abt 1337
  -CONTINUED AS #1,ROYAL CHART 933
Died:

1 John STEWART

Born: Abt 1400
  -SAME AS #10,ROYAL CHART 1078
Married:

Died: 20 Dec 1463

12 Robert II, King of Scot.

Born: 2 Mar 1315/1316
  -CONTINUED AS #2,ROYAL CHART 914
Married: 22 Nov 1347
  disp.
Died: 19 Apr 1390

6 Robert STEWART

Born: 1339

Married:

Died: 2 Sep 1420

13 Elizabeth MURE

Born: Abt 1320

Died: Bef 1355

Agnes of the Isles

Spouse

3 Joan STEWART

Born: Abt 1379

Died:

14 John GRAHAM

Born: Abt 1302

Married:

Died: 22 Feb 1346

7 Margaret GRAHAM

Born: Abt 1340

Died: Bef 4 May 1380

15 Mary MENTEITH

Born: Abt 1306

Died:

Sources include: Roberts *500*, p. 99; *Magna Charta* 41D, 42A.

Pedigree Chart

Chart 1081

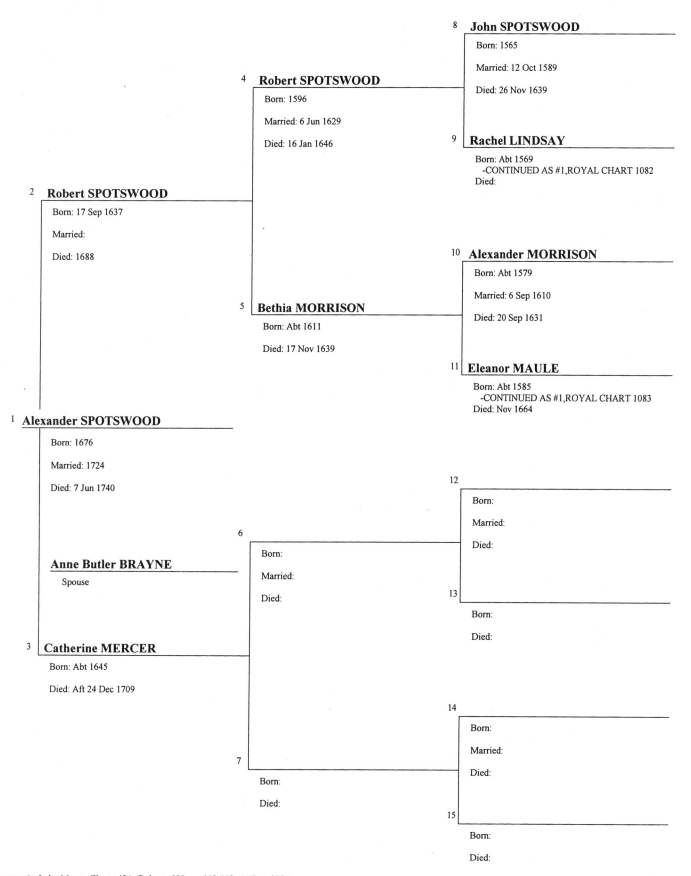

8 John SPOTSWOOD

Born: 1565

Married: 12 Oct 1589

Died: 26 Nov 1639

4 Robert SPOTSWOOD

Born: 1596

Married: 6 Jun 1629

Died: 16 Jan 1646

9 Rachel LINDSAY

Born: Abt 1569
  -CONTINUED AS #1,ROYAL CHART 1082
Died:

2 Robert SPOTSWOOD

Born: 17 Sep 1637

Married:

Died: 1688

10 Alexander MORRISON

Born: Abt 1579

Married: 6 Sep 1610

Died: 20 Sep 1631

5 Bethia MORRISON

Born: Abt 1611

Died: 17 Nov 1639

11 Eleanor MAULE

Born: Abt 1585
  -CONTINUED AS #1,ROYAL CHART 1083
Died: Nov 1664

1 Alexander SPOTSWOOD

Born: 1676

Married: 1724

Died: 7 Jun 1740

12

Born:

Married:

Died:

6

Born:

Married:

Died:

13

Born:

Died:

Anne Butler BRAYNE

Spouse

3 Catherine MERCER

Born: Abt 1645

Died: Aft 24 Dec 1709

14

Born:

Married:

Died:

7

Born:

Died:

15

Born:

Died:

Sources include: *Magna Charta* 43A; Roberts *500*, pp. 112-113; *AAP*, p. 229.

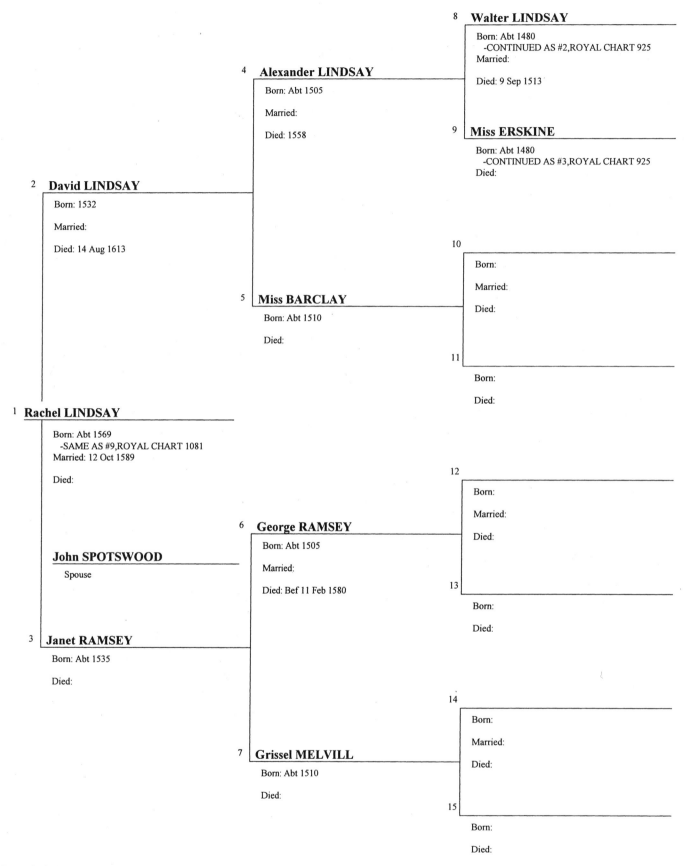

Chart details

2 David LINDSAY
Born: 1532
Married:
Died: 14 Aug 1613

4 Alexander LINDSAY
Born: Abt 1505
Married:
Died: 1558

8 Walter LINDSAY
Born: Abt 1480
  -CONTINUED AS #2,ROYAL CHART 925
Married:
Died: 9 Sep 1513

9 Miss ERSKINE
Born: Abt 1480
  -CONTINUED AS #3,ROYAL CHART 925
Died:

5 Miss BARCLAY
Born: Abt 1510
Died:

10
Born:
Married:
Died:

11
Born:
Died:

1 Rachel LINDSAY
Born: Abt 1569
  -SAME AS #9,ROYAL CHART 1081
Married: 12 Oct 1589
Died:

John SPOTSWOOD
Spouse

3 Janet RAMSEY
Born: Abt 1535
Died:

6 George RAMSEY
Born: Abt 1505
Married:
Died: Bef 11 Feb 1580

12
Born:
Married:
Died:

13
Born:
Died:

7 Grissel MELVILL
Born: Abt 1510
Died:

14
Born:
Married:
Died:

15
Born:
Died:

Sources include: *Magna Charta* 43A.

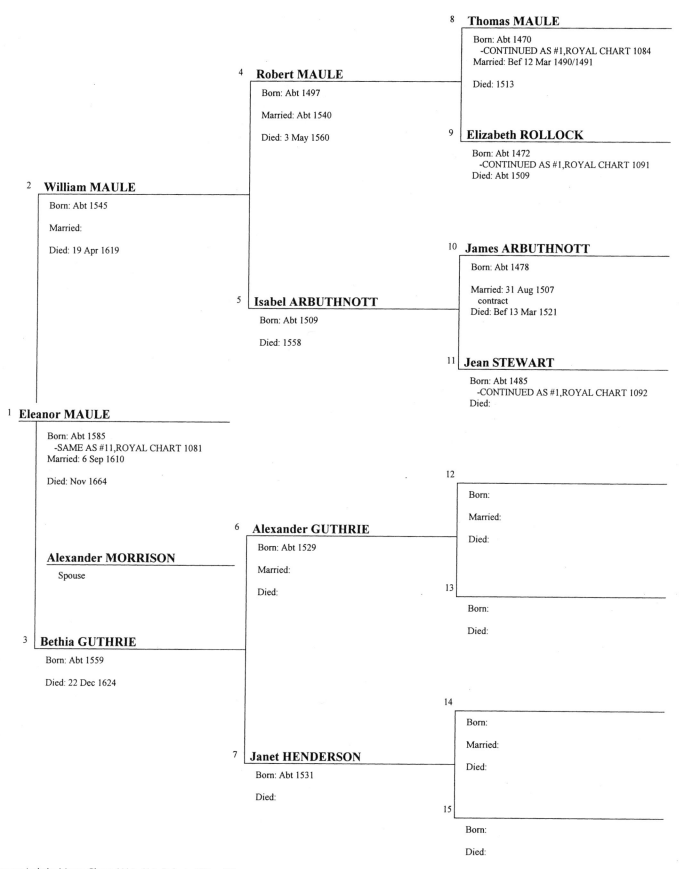

8 Thomas MAULE
Born: Abt 1470
-CONTINUED AS #1,ROYAL CHART 1084
Married: Bef 12 Mar 1490/1491

Died: 1513

4 Robert MAULE
Born: Abt 1497

Married: Abt 1540

Died: 3 May 1560

9 Elizabeth ROLLOCK
Born: Abt 1472
-CONTINUED AS #1,ROYAL CHART 1091
Died: Abt 1509

2 William MAULE
Born: Abt 1545

Married:

Died: 19 Apr 1619

10 James ARBUTHNOTT
Born: Abt 1478

Married: 31 Aug 1507
contract
Died: Bef 13 Mar 1521

5 Isabel ARBUTHNOTT
Born: Abt 1509

Died: 1558

11 Jean STEWART
Born: Abt 1485
-CONTINUED AS #1,ROYAL CHART 1092
Died:

1 Eleanor MAULE
Born: Abt 1585
-SAME AS #11,ROYAL CHART 1081
Married: 6 Sep 1610

Died: Nov 1664

Alexander MORRISON
Spouse

12
Born:

Married:

Died:

6 Alexander GUTHRIE
Born: Abt 1529

Married:

Died:

13
Born:

Died:

3 Bethia GUTHRIE
Born: Abt 1559

Died: 22 Dec 1624

14
Born:

Married:

Died:

7 Janet HENDERSON
Born: Abt 1531

Died:

15
Born:

Died:

Sources include: *Magna Charta* 111A, 41A; Roberts *500*, p. 112.

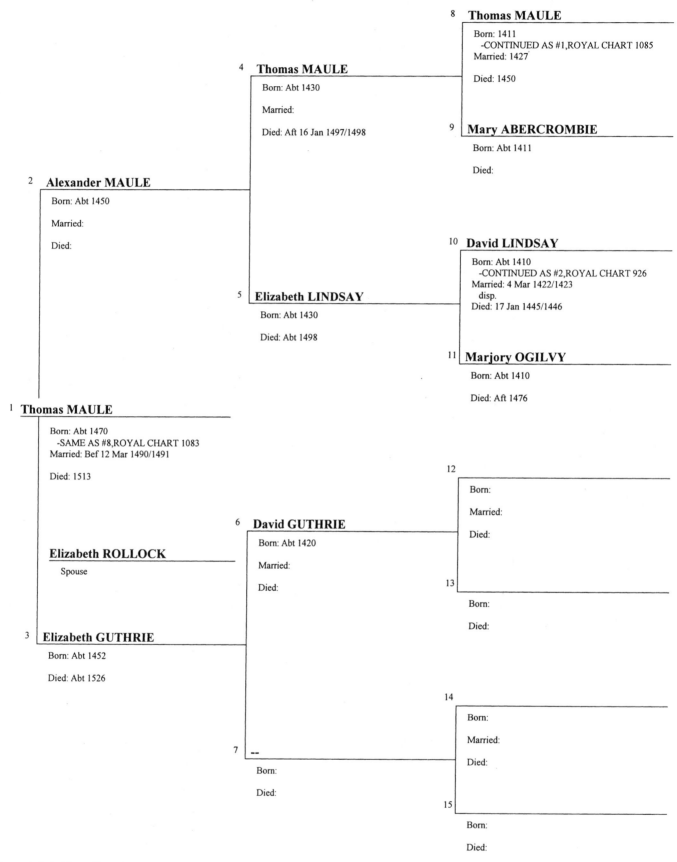

8 Thomas MAULE

Born: 1411
 -CONTINUED AS #1,ROYAL CHART 1085
Married: 1427

Died: 1450

4 Thomas MAULE

Born: Abt 1430

Married:

Died: Aft 16 Jan 1497/1498

9 Mary ABERCROMBIE

Born: Abt 1411

Died:

2 Alexander MAULE

Born: Abt 1450

Married:

Died:

10 David LINDSAY

Born: Abt 1410
 -CONTINUED AS #2,ROYAL CHART 926
Married: 4 Mar 1422/1423
 disp.
Died: 17 Jan 1445/1446

5 Elizabeth LINDSAY

Born: Abt 1430

Died: Abt 1498

11 Marjory OGILVY

Born: Abt 1410

Died: Aft 1476

1 Thomas MAULE

Born: Abt 1470
 -SAME AS #8,ROYAL CHART 1083
Married: Bef 12 Mar 1490/1491

Died: 1513

12

Born:

Married:

Died:

6 David GUTHRIE

Born: Abt 1420

Married:

Died:

13

Born:

Died:

Elizabeth ROLLOCK

Spouse

3 Elizabeth GUTHRIE

Born: Abt 1452

Died: Abt 1526

14

Born:

Married:

Died:

7 --

Born:

Died:

15

Born:

Died:

Sources include: *Magna Charta* 111A.

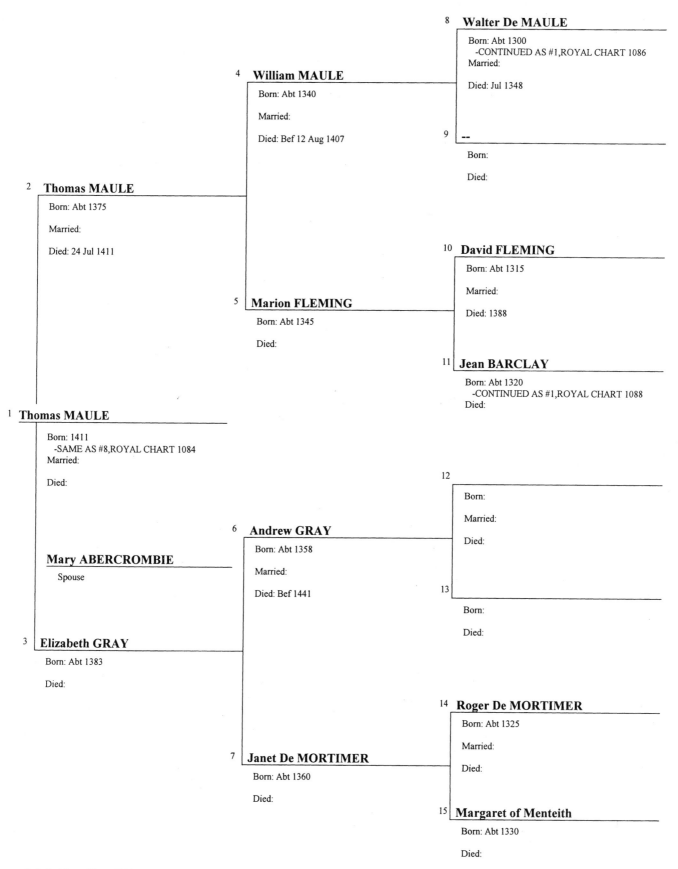

8 Walter De MAULE

Born: Abt 1300
-CONTINUED AS #1,ROYAL CHART 1086
Married:

Died: Jul 1348

4 William MAULE

Born: Abt 1340

Married:

Died: Bef 12 Aug 1407

9 --

Born:

Died:

2 Thomas MAULE

Born: Abt 1375

Married:

Died: 24 Jul 1411

10 David FLEMING

Born: Abt 1315

Married:

Died: 1388

5 Marion FLEMING

Born: Abt 1345

Died:

11 Jean BARCLAY

Born: Abt 1320
-CONTINUED AS #1,ROYAL CHART 1088
Died:

1 Thomas MAULE

Born: 1411
-SAME AS #8,ROYAL CHART 1084
Married:

Died:

12

Born:

Married:

Died:

6 Andrew GRAY

Born: Abt 1358

Married:

Died: Bef 1441

13

Born:

Died:

Mary ABERCROMBIE

Spouse

3 Elizabeth GRAY

Born: Abt 1383

Died:

14 Roger De MORTIMER

Born: Abt 1325

Married:

Died:

7 Janet De MORTIMER

Born: Abt 1360

Died:

15 Margaret of Menteith

Born: Abt 1330

Died:

Sources include: *Magna Charta* 111A.

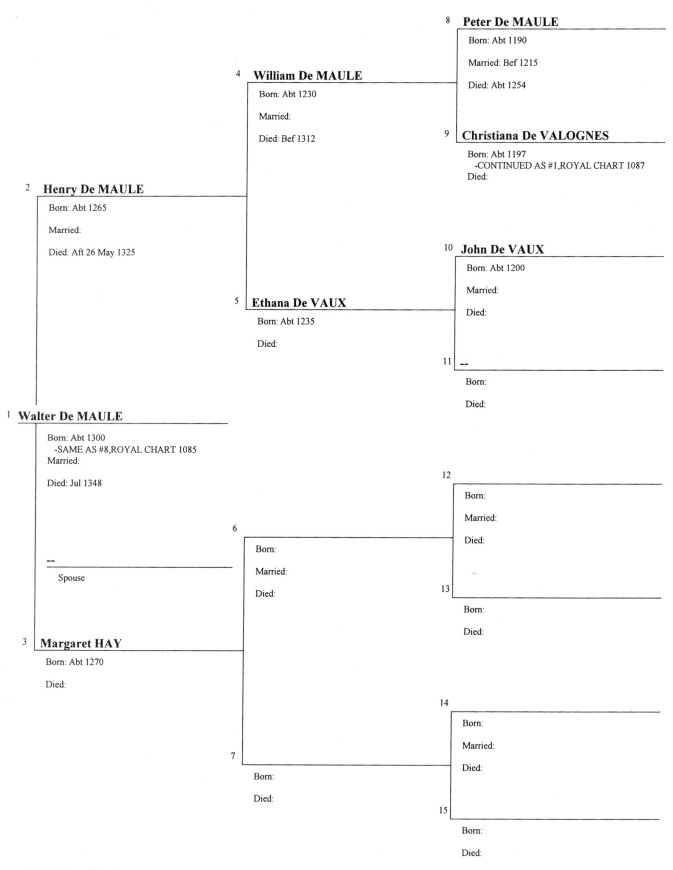

8 **Peter De MAULE**

Born: Abt 1190

Married: Bef 1215

Died: Abt 1254

4 **William De MAULE**

Born: Abt 1230

Married:

Died: Bef 1312

9 **Christiana De VALOGNES**

Born: Abt 1197
-CONTINUED AS #1, ROYAL CHART 1087
Died:

2 **Henry De MAULE**

Born: Abt 1265

Married:

Died: Aft 26 May 1325

10 **John De VAUX**

Born: Abt 1200

Married:

Died:

5 **Ethana De VAUX**

Born: Abt 1235

Died:

11 **--**

Born:

Died:

1 **Walter De MAULE**

Born: Abt 1300
-SAME AS #8, ROYAL CHART 1085
Married:

Died: Jul 1348

12

Born:

Married:

Died:

6

Born:

Married:

Died:

13

Born:

Died:

--

Spouse

3 **Margaret HAY**

Born: Abt 1270

Died:

14

Born:

Married:

Died:

7

Born:

Died:

15

Born:

Died:

Sources include: *Magna Charta* 111A.

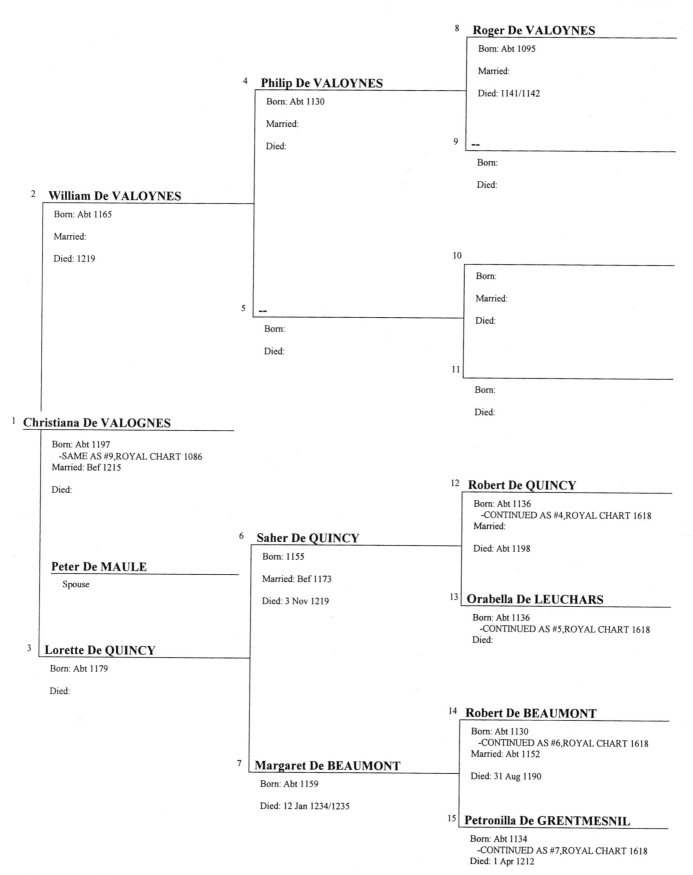

2 William De VALOYNES
Born: Abt 1165
Married:
Died: 1219

1 Christiana De VALOGNES
Born: Abt 1197
 -SAME AS #9,ROYAL CHART 1086
Married: Bef 1215

Died:

Peter De MAULE
Spouse

3 Lorette De QUINCY
Born: Abt 1179

Died:

4 Philip De VALOYNES
Born: Abt 1130
Married:
Died:

5 --
Born:
Died:

6 Saher De QUINCY
Born: 1155
Married: Bef 1173
Died: 3 Nov 1219

7 Margaret De BEAUMONT
Born: Abt 1159
Died: 12 Jan 1234/1235

8 Roger De VALOYNES
Born: Abt 1095
Married:
Died: 1141/1142

9 --
Born:
Died:

10
Born:
Married:
Died:

11
Born:
Died:

12 Robert De QUINCY
Born: Abt 1136
 -CONTINUED AS #4,ROYAL CHART 1618
Married:
Died: Abt 1198

13 Orabella De LEUCHARS
Born: Abt 1136
 -CONTINUED AS #5,ROYAL CHART 1618
Died:

14 Robert De BEAUMONT
Born: Abt 1130
 -CONTINUED AS #6,ROYAL CHART 1618
Married: Abt 1152
Died: 31 Aug 1190

15 Petronilla De GRENTMESNIL
Born: Abt 1134
 -CONTINUED AS #7,ROYAL CHART 1618
Died: 1 Apr 1212

Sources include: Faris preliminary baronial manuscript (1998), pp. 1074 (Maule), 1574-75 (Valoynes); *Magna Charta* 111A; *Royal Ancestors* (1989), charts 11442-43 (#6 & 7 ancestry).

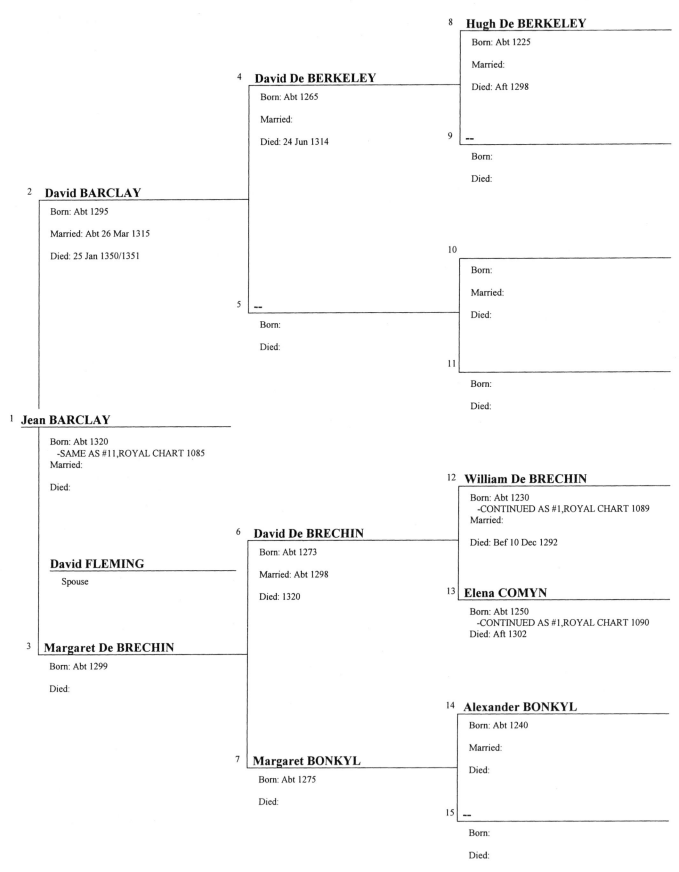

8 Hugh De BERKELEY

Born: Abt 1225

Married:

Died: Aft 1298

4 David De BERKELEY

Born: Abt 1265

Married:

Died: 24 Jun 1314

9 --

Born:

Died:

2 David BARCLAY

Born: Abt 1295

Married: Abt 26 Mar 1315

Died: 25 Jan 1350/1351

10

Born:

Married:

Died:

5 --

Born:

Died:

11

Born:

Died:

1 Jean BARCLAY

Born: Abt 1320
-SAME AS #11,ROYAL CHART 1085
Married:

Died:

12 William De BRECHIN

Born: Abt 1230
-CONTINUED AS #1,ROYAL CHART 1089
Married:

Died: Bef 10 Dec 1292

6 David De BRECHIN

Born: Abt 1273

Married: Abt 1298

Died: 1320

13 Elena COMYN

Born: Abt 1250
-CONTINUED AS #1,ROYAL CHART 1090
Died: Aft 1302

David FLEMING

Spouse

3 Margaret De BRECHIN

Born: Abt 1299

Died:

14 Alexander BONKYL

Born: Abt 1240

Married:

Died:

7 Margaret BONKYL

Born: Abt 1275

Died:

15 --

Born:

Died:

Sources include: *Magna Charta* 108A; LDS records (#4 & 8).

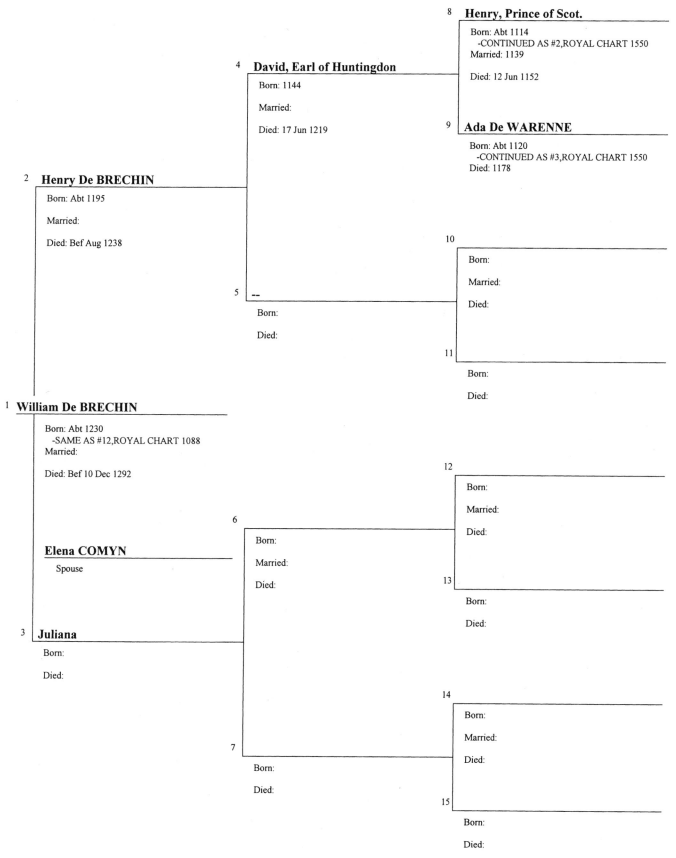

8 Henry, Prince of Scot.

Born: Abt 1114
-CONTINUED AS #2,ROYAL CHART 1550
Married: 1139

Died: 12 Jun 1152

4 David, Earl of Huntingdon

Born: 1144

Married:

Died: 17 Jun 1219

9 Ada De WARENNE

Born: Abt 1120
-CONTINUED AS #3,ROYAL CHART 1550
Died: 1178

2 Henry De BRECHIN

Born: Abt 1195

Married:

Died: Bef Aug 1238

10

Born:

Married:

Died:

5 --

Born:

Died:

11

Born:

Died:

1 William De BRECHIN

Born: Abt 1230
-SAME AS #12,ROYAL CHART 1088
Married:

Died: Bef 10 Dec 1292

12

Born:

Married:

Died:

6

Born:

Married:

Died:

13

Born:

Died:

Elena COMYN

Spouse

3 Juliana

Born:

Died:

14

Born:

Married:

Died:

7

Born:

Died:

15

Born:

Died:

Sources include: *Magna Charta* 108A.

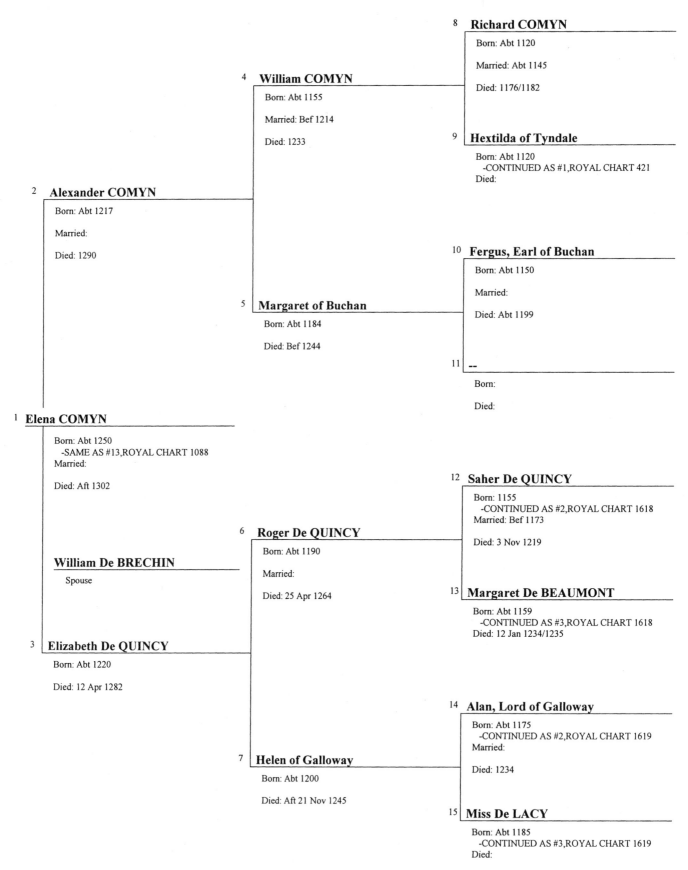

8 Richard COMYN

Born: Abt 1120

Married: Abt 1145

Died: 1176/1182

4 William COMYN

Born: Abt 1155

Married: Bef 1214

Died: 1233

9 Hextilda of Tyndale

Born: Abt 1120
  -CONTINUED AS #1,ROYAL CHART 421
Died:

2 Alexander COMYN

Born: Abt 1217

Married:

Died: 1290

10 Fergus, Earl of Buchan

Born: Abt 1150

Married:

Died: Abt 1199

5 Margaret of Buchan

Born: Abt 1184

Died: Bef 1244

11 --

Born:

Died:

1 Elena COMYN

Born: Abt 1250
  -SAME AS #13,ROYAL CHART 1088
Married:

Died: Aft 1302

12 Saher De QUINCY

Born: 1155
  -CONTINUED AS #2,ROYAL CHART 1618
Married: Bef 1173

Died: 3 Nov 1219

6 Roger De QUINCY

Born: Abt 1190

Married:

Died: 25 Apr 1264

13 Margaret De BEAUMONT

Born: Abt 1159
  -CONTINUED AS #3,ROYAL CHART 1618
Died: 12 Jan 1234/1235

William De BRECHIN

Spouse

3 Elizabeth De QUINCY

Born: Abt 1220

Died: 12 Apr 1282

14 Alan, Lord of Galloway

Born: Abt 1175
  -CONTINUED AS #2,ROYAL CHART 1619
Married:

Died: 1234

7 Helen of Galloway

Born: Abt 1200

Died: Aft 21 Nov 1245

15 Miss De LACY

Born: Abt 1185
  -CONTINUED AS #3,ROYAL CHART 1619
Died:

Sources include: *Magna Charta* 108A.

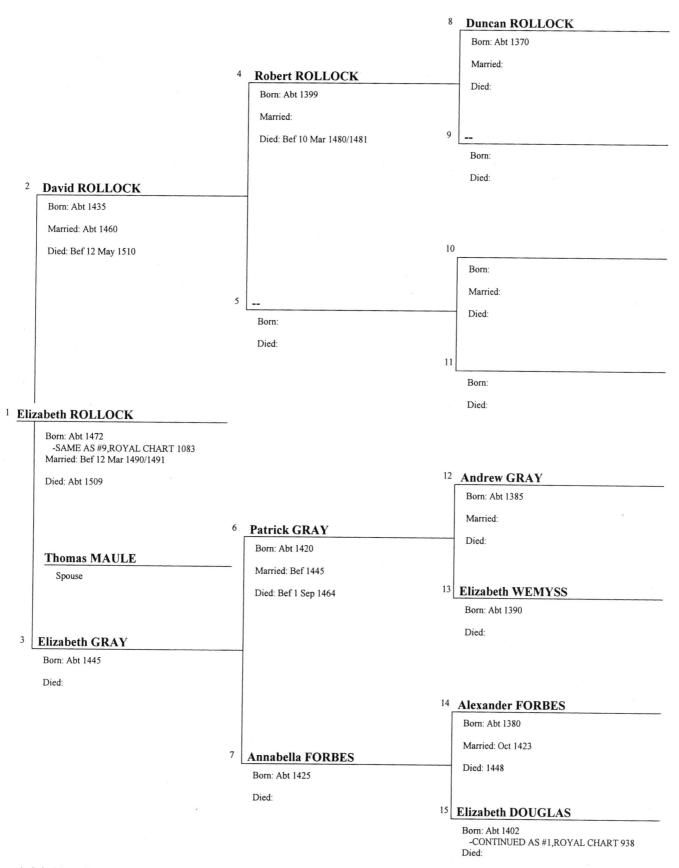

8 Duncan ROLLOCK
Born: Abt 1370
Married:
Died:

4 Robert ROLLOCK
Born: Abt 1399
Married:
Died: Bef 10 Mar 1480/1481

9 --
Born:
Died:

2 David ROLLOCK
Born: Abt 1435
Married: Abt 1460
Died: Bef 12 May 1510

10
Born:
Married:
Died:

5 --
Born:
Died:

11
Born:
Died:

1 Elizabeth ROLLOCK
Born: Abt 1472
 -SAME AS #9,ROYAL CHART 1083
Married: Bef 12 Mar 1490/1491
Died: Abt 1509

12 Andrew GRAY
Born: Abt 1385
Married:
Died:

6 Patrick GRAY
Born: Abt 1420
Married: Bef 1445
Died: Bef 1 Sep 1464

13 Elizabeth WEMYSS
Born: Abt 1390
Died:

Thomas MAULE
Spouse

3 Elizabeth GRAY
Born: Abt 1445
Died:

14 Alexander FORBES
Born: Abt 1380
Married: Oct 1423
Died: 1448

7 Annabella FORBES
Born: Abt 1425
Died:

15 Elizabeth DOUGLAS
Born: Abt 1402
 -CONTINUED AS #1,ROYAL CHART 938
Died:

Sources include: *Magna Charta* 41A; LDS records (#4 & 8).

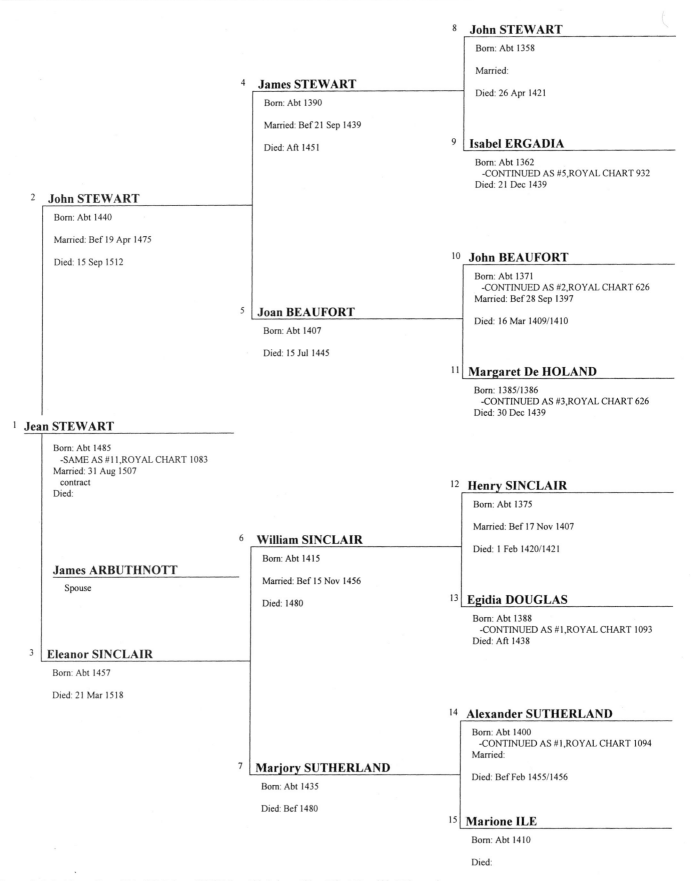

8 **John STEWART**

Born: Abt 1358

Married:

Died: 26 Apr 1421

4 **James STEWART**

Born: Abt 1390

Married: Bef 21 Sep 1439

Died: Aft 1451

9 **Isabel ERGADIA**

Born: Abt 1362
   -CONTINUED AS #5,ROYAL CHART 932
Died: 21 Dec 1439

2 **John STEWART**

Born: Abt 1440

Married: Bef 19 Apr 1475

Died: 15 Sep 1512

10 **John BEAUFORT**

Born: Abt 1371
   -CONTINUED AS #2,ROYAL CHART 626
Married: Bef 28 Sep 1397

Died: 16 Mar 1409/1410

5 **Joan BEAUFORT**

Born: Abt 1407

Died: 15 Jul 1445

11 **Margaret De HOLAND**

Born: 1385/1386
   -CONTINUED AS #3,ROYAL CHART 626
Died: 30 Dec 1439

1 **Jean STEWART**

Born: Abt 1485
   -SAME AS #11,ROYAL CHART 1083
Married: 31 Aug 1507
   contract
Died:

12 **Henry SINCLAIR**

Born: Abt 1375

Married: Bef 17 Nov 1407

Died: 1 Feb 1420/1421

6 **William SINCLAIR**

Born: Abt 1415

Married: Bef 15 Nov 1456

Died: 1480

James ARBUTHNOTT

Spouse

13 **Egidia DOUGLAS**

Born: Abt 1388
   -CONTINUED AS #1,ROYAL CHART 1093
Died: Aft 1438

3 **Eleanor SINCLAIR**

Born: Abt 1457

Died: 21 Mar 1518

14 **Alexander SUTHERLAND**

Born: Abt 1400
   -CONTINUED AS #1,ROYAL CHART 1094
Married:

Died: Bef Feb 1455/1456

7 **Marjory SUTHERLAND**

Born: Abt 1435

Died: Bef 1480

15 **Marione ILE**

Born: Abt 1410

Died:

Sources include: *Magna Charta* 91A, 41C; Roberts *600* (2004), p. 138; Roberts *500*, p. 112; *AAP*, p. 229; LDS records.

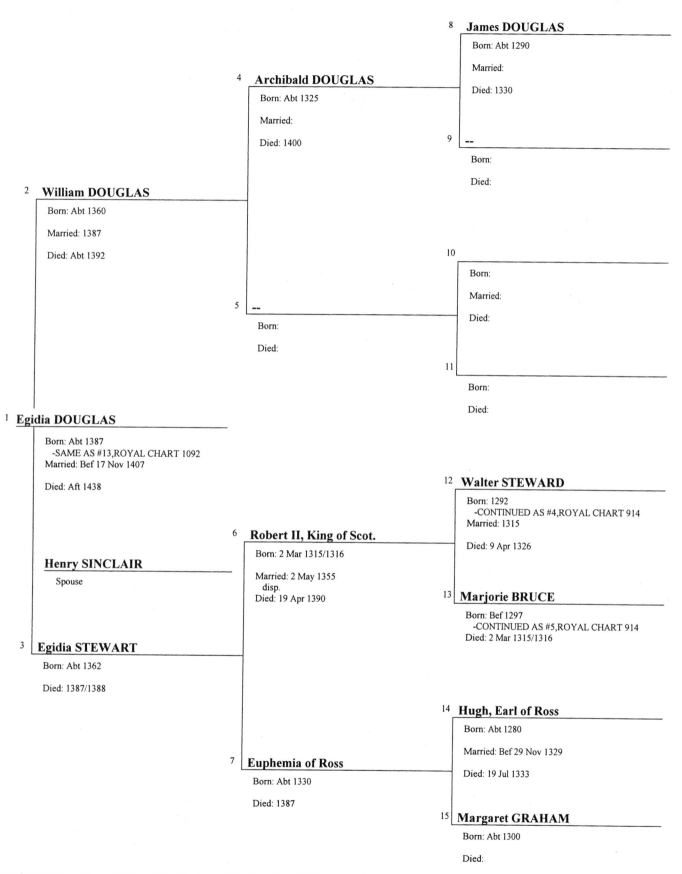

8 James DOUGLAS

Born: Abt 1290

Married:

Died: 1330

4 Archibald DOUGLAS

Born: Abt 1325

Married:

Died: 1400

9 --

Born:

Died:

2 William DOUGLAS

Born: Abt 1360

Married: 1387

Died: Abt 1392

10

Born:

Married:

Died:

5 --

Born:

Died:

11

Born:

Died:

1 Egidia DOUGLAS

Born: Abt 1387
  -SAME AS #13,ROYAL CHART 1092
Married: Bef 17 Nov 1407

Died: Aft 1438

Henry SINCLAIR

Spouse

12 Walter STEWARD

Born: 1292
  -CONTINUED AS #4,ROYAL CHART 914
Married: 1315

Died: 9 Apr 1326

6 Robert II, King of Scot.

Born: 2 Mar 1315/1316

Married: 2 May 1355
  disp.
Died: 19 Apr 1390

13 Marjorie BRUCE

Born: Bef 1297
  -CONTINUED AS #5,ROYAL CHART 914
Died: 2 Mar 1315/1316

3 Egidia STEWART

Born: Abt 1362

Died: 1387/1388

14 Hugh, Earl of Ross

Born: Abt 1280

Married: Bef 29 Nov 1329

Died: 19 Jul 1333

7 Euphemia of Ross

Born: Abt 1330

Died: 1387

15 Margaret GRAHAM

Born: Abt 1300

Died:

Sources include: *Magna Charta* 41C; Ernest Flagg Henderson III, Pedigree Chart BTJK (ancestry of #4 Archibald).

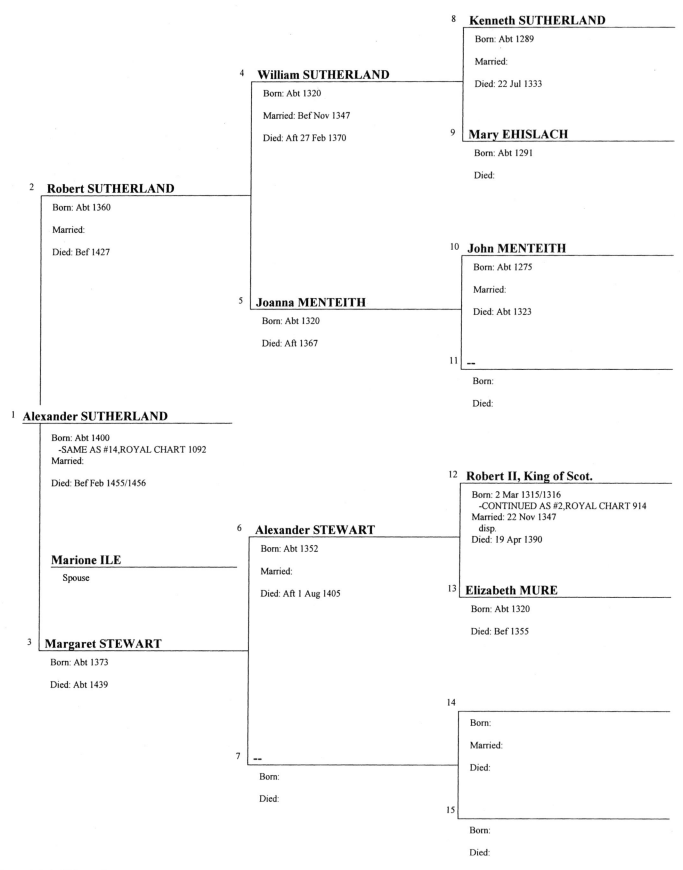

8 **Kenneth SUTHERLAND**

Born: Abt 1289

Married:

Died: 22 Jul 1333

4 **William SUTHERLAND**

Born: Abt 1320

Married: Bef Nov 1347

Died: Aft 27 Feb 1370

9 **Mary EHISLACH**

Born: Abt 1291

Died:

2 **Robert SUTHERLAND**

Born: Abt 1360

Married:

Died: Bef 1427

10 **John MENTEITH**

Born: Abt 1275

Married:

Died: Abt 1323

5 **Joanna MENTEITH**

Born: Abt 1320

Died: Aft 1367

11 **--**

Born:

Died:

1 **Alexander SUTHERLAND**

Born: Abt 1400
 -SAME AS #14,ROYAL CHART 1092
Married:

Died: Bef Feb 1455/1456

12 **Robert II, King of Scot.**

Born: 2 Mar 1315/1316
 -CONTINUED AS #2,ROYAL CHART 914
Married: 22 Nov 1347
 disp.
Died: 19 Apr 1390

6 **Alexander STEWART**

Born: Abt 1352

Married:

Died: Aft 1 Aug 1405

Marione ILE

Spouse

13 **Elizabeth MURE**

Born: Abt 1320

Died: Bef 1355

3 **Margaret STEWART**

Born: Abt 1373

Died: Abt 1439

14

Born:

Married:

Died:

7 **--**

Born:

Died:

15

Born:

Died:

Sources include: LDS records.

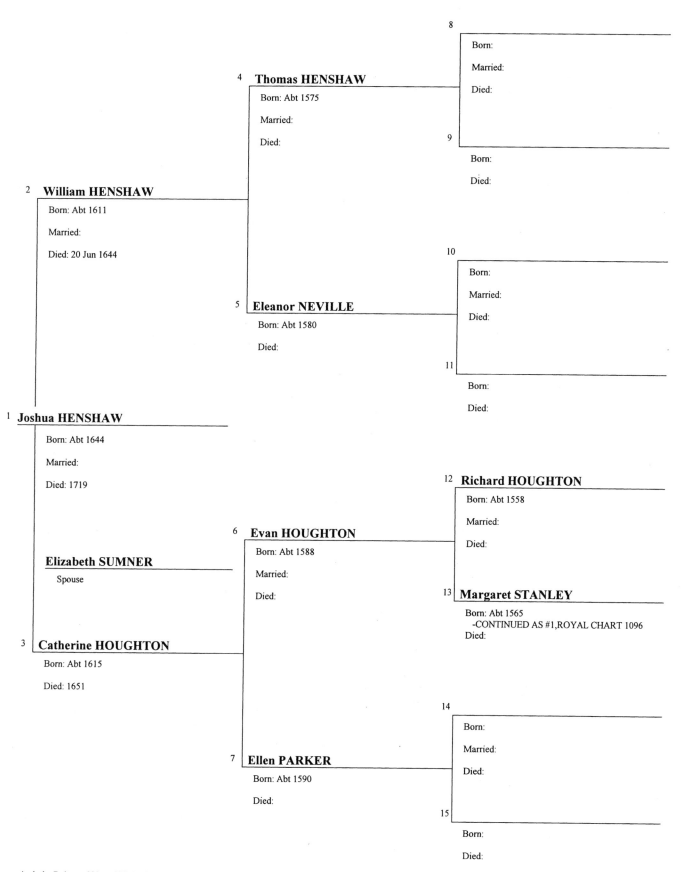

8

Thomas HENSHAW
Born: Abt 1575
Married:
Died:

Born:
Married:
Died:

9

Born:
Died:

2 **William HENSHAW**
Born: Abt 1611
Married:
Died: 20 Jun 1644

10

Born:
Married:
Died:

5 **Eleanor NEVILLE**
Born: Abt 1580
Died:

11

Born:
Died:

1 **Joshua HENSHAW**
Born: Abt 1644
Married:
Died: 1719

12 **Richard HOUGHTON**
Born: Abt 1558
Married:
Died:

6 **Evan HOUGHTON**
Born: Abt 1588
Married:
Died:

Elizabeth SUMNER
Spouse

13 **Margaret STANLEY**
Born: Abt 1565
-CONTINUED AS #1,ROYAL CHART 1096
Died:

3 **Catherine HOUGHTON**
Born: Abt 1615
Died: 1651

14

Born:
Married:
Died:

7 **Ellen PARKER**
Born: Abt 1590
Died:

15

Born:
Died:

Sources include: Roberts *500*, p. 177; LDS records.

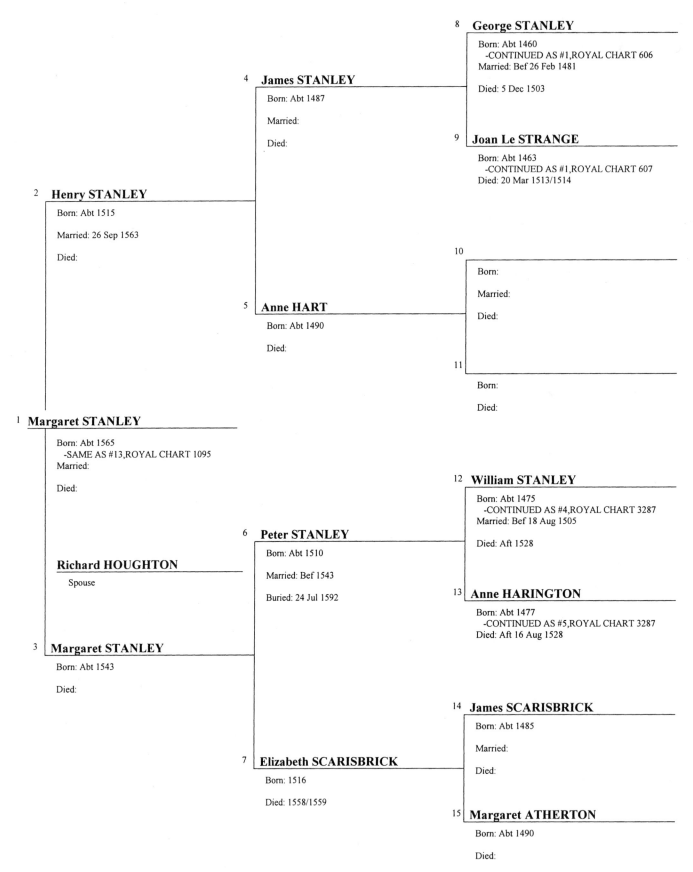

8 George STANLEY

Born: Abt 1460
  -CONTINUED AS #1,ROYAL CHART 606
Married: Bef 26 Feb 1481

Died: 5 Dec 1503

4 James STANLEY

Born: Abt 1487

Married:

Died:

9 Joan Le STRANGE

Born: Abt 1463
  -CONTINUED AS #1,ROYAL CHART 607
Died: 20 Mar 1513/1514

2 Henry STANLEY

Born: Abt 1515

Married: 26 Sep 1563

Died:

10

Born:

Married:

Died:

5 Anne HART

Born: Abt 1490

Died:

11

Born:

Died:

1 Margaret STANLEY

Born: Abt 1565
  -SAME AS #13,ROYAL CHART 1095
Married:

Died:

12 William STANLEY

Born: Abt 1475
  -CONTINUED AS #4,ROYAL CHART 3287
Married: Bef 18 Aug 1505

Died: Aft 1528

6 Peter STANLEY

Born: Abt 1510

Married: Bef 1543

Buried: 24 Jul 1592

13 Anne HARINGTON

Born: Abt 1477
  -CONTINUED AS #5,ROYAL CHART 3287
Died: Aft 16 Aug 1528

Richard HOUGHTON

Spouse

3 Margaret STANLEY

Born: Abt 1543

Died:

14 James SCARISBRICK

Born: Abt 1485

Married:

Died:

7 Elizabeth SCARISBRICK

Born: 1516

Died: 1558/1559

15 Margaret ATHERTON

Born: Abt 1490

Died:

Sources include: Roberts *500*, p. 177; Richardson *Plantagenet* (2004), pp. 291-292 Eltonhead (#3 ancestry); LDS records. Note: #1 Margaret may have been an illegitimate daughter of #2 Henry.

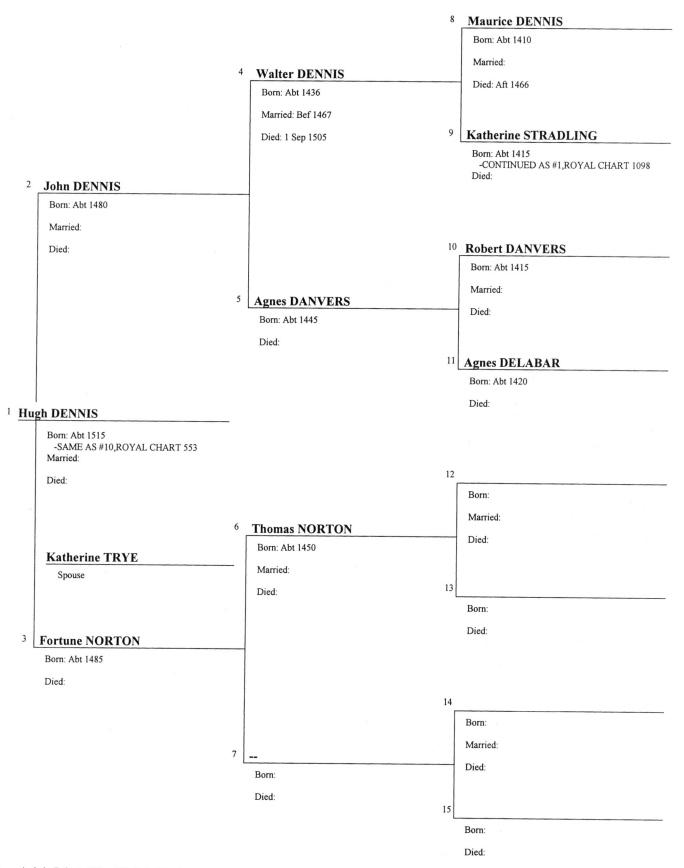

8 **Maurice DENNIS**

Born: Abt 1410

Married:

Died: Aft 1466

4 **Walter DENNIS**

Born: Abt 1436

Married: Bef 1467

Died: 1 Sep 1505

9 **Katherine STRADLING**

Born: Abt 1415
-CONTINUED AS #1, ROYAL CHART 1098
Died:

2 **John DENNIS**

Born: Abt 1480

Married:

Died:

10 **Robert DANVERS**

Born: Abt 1415

Married:

Died:

5 **Agnes DANVERS**

Born: Abt 1445

Died:

11 **Agnes DELABAR**

Born: Abt 1420

Died:

1 **Hugh DENNIS**

Born: Abt 1515
-SAME AS #10, ROYAL CHART 553
Married:

Died:

12

Born:

Married:

Died:

6 **Thomas NORTON**

Born: Abt 1450

Married:

Died:

13

Born:

Died:

Katherine TRYE

Spouse

3 **Fortune NORTON**

Born: Abt 1485

Died:

14

Born:

Married:

Died:

7 **--**

Born:

Died:

15

Born:

Died:

Sources include: Roberts *500*, p. 204; Faris--Trye 3.

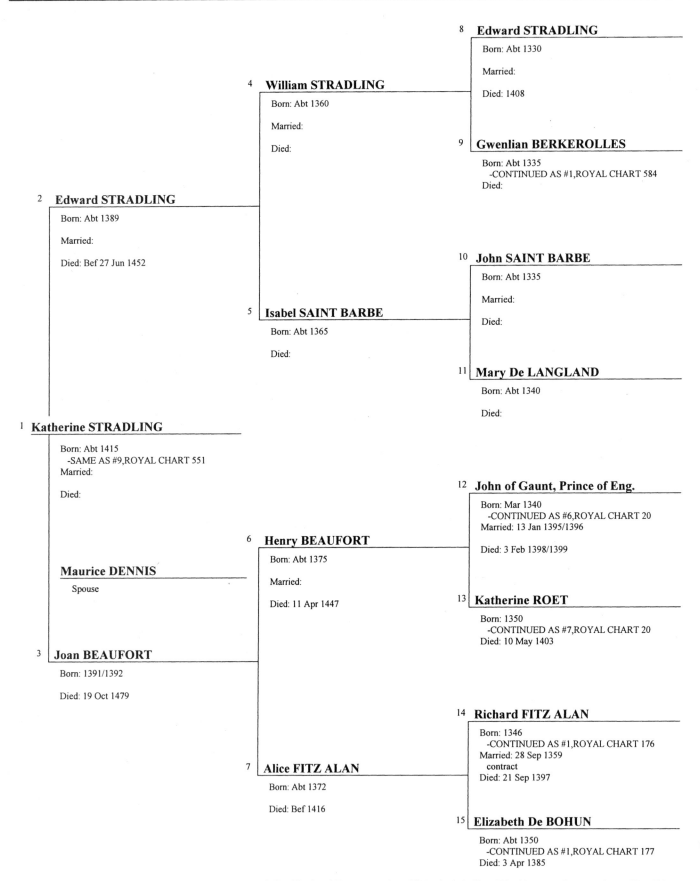

8 **Edward STRADLING**
Born: Abt 1330
Married:
Died: 1408

4 **William STRADLING**
Born: Abt 1360
Married:
Died:

9 **Gwenlian BERKEROLLES**
Born: Abt 1335
-CONTINUED AS #1,ROYAL CHART 584
Died:

2 **Edward STRADLING**
Born: Abt 1389
Married:
Died: Bef 27 Jun 1452

10 **John SAINT BARBE**
Born: Abt 1335
Married:
Died:

5 **Isabel SAINT BARBE**
Born: Abt 1365
Died:

11 **Mary De LANGLAND**
Born: Abt 1340
Died:

1 **Katherine STRADLING**
Born: Abt 1415
-SAME AS #9,ROYAL CHART 551
Married:
Died:

12 **John of Gaunt, Prince of Eng.**
Born: Mar 1340
-CONTINUED AS #6,ROYAL CHART 20
Married: 13 Jan 1395/1396
Died: 3 Feb 1398/1399

6 **Henry BEAUFORT**
Born: Abt 1375
Married:
Died: 11 Apr 1447

13 **Katherine ROET**
Born: 1350
-CONTINUED AS #7,ROYAL CHART 20
Died: 10 May 1403

Maurice DENNIS
Spouse

3 **Joan BEAUFORT**
Born: 1391/1392
Died: 19 Oct 1479

14 **Richard FITZ ALAN**
Born: 1346
-CONTINUED AS #1,ROYAL CHART 176
Married: 28 Sep 1359
  contract
Died: 21 Sep 1397

7 **Alice FITZ ALAN**
Born: Abt 1372
Died: Bef 1416

15 **Elizabeth De BOHUN**
Born: Abt 1350
-CONTINUED AS #1,ROYAL CHART 177
Died: 3 Apr 1385

Sources include: Consultation with Douglas Richardson, December 2003 (identification of #3 Joan as mother of #1 Katherine); Chart 583 with sources & note; Roberts *500*, p. 204.

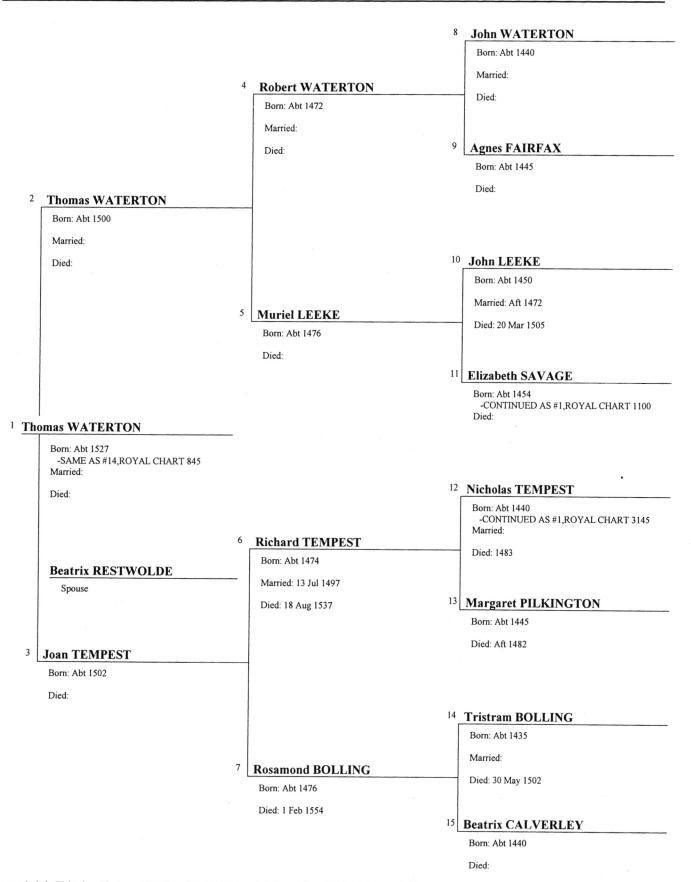

8 John WATERTON
Born: Abt 1440
Married:
Died:

4 Robert WATERTON
Born: Abt 1472
Married:
Died:

9 Agnes FAIRFAX
Born: Abt 1445
Died:

2 Thomas WATERTON
Born: Abt 1500
Married:
Died:

10 John LEEKE
Born: Abt 1450
Married: Aft 1472
Died: 20 Mar 1505

5 Muriel LEEKE
Born: Abt 1476
Died:

11 Elizabeth SAVAGE
Born: Abt 1454
-CONTINUED AS #1,ROYAL CHART 1100
Died:

1 Thomas WATERTON
Born: Abt 1527
-SAME AS #14,ROYAL CHART 845
Married:
Died:

12 Nicholas TEMPEST
Born: Abt 1440
-CONTINUED AS #1,ROYAL CHART 3145
Married:
Died: 1483

6 Richard TEMPEST
Born: Abt 1474
Married: 13 Jul 1497
Died: 18 Aug 1537

13 Margaret PILKINGTON
Born: Abt 1445
Died: Aft 1482

Beatrix RESTWOLDE
Spouse

3 Joan TEMPEST
Born: Abt 1502
Died:

14 Tristram BOLLING
Born: Abt 1435
Married:
Died: 30 May 1502

7 Rosamond BOLLING
Born: Abt 1476
Died: 1 Feb 1554

15 Beatrix CALVERLEY
Born: Abt 1440
Died:

Sources include: Richardson *Plantagenet* (2004), pp. 755-756 (Waterton); Roberts *500*, pp. 238-239; LDS records (#3 ancestry). Note: #15 Beatrix was daughter of Walter Calverley & Elizabeth Markenfield, whose ancestry is incorrectly given by Roberts *600* (2004), pp. 399-400. The marriage covenant for Walter & Elizabeth was dated 1 Mar 1415. See Faris preliminary baronial manuscript (1998), pp. 285 (Calverley), 1054 (Markenfield). See also note chart 475.

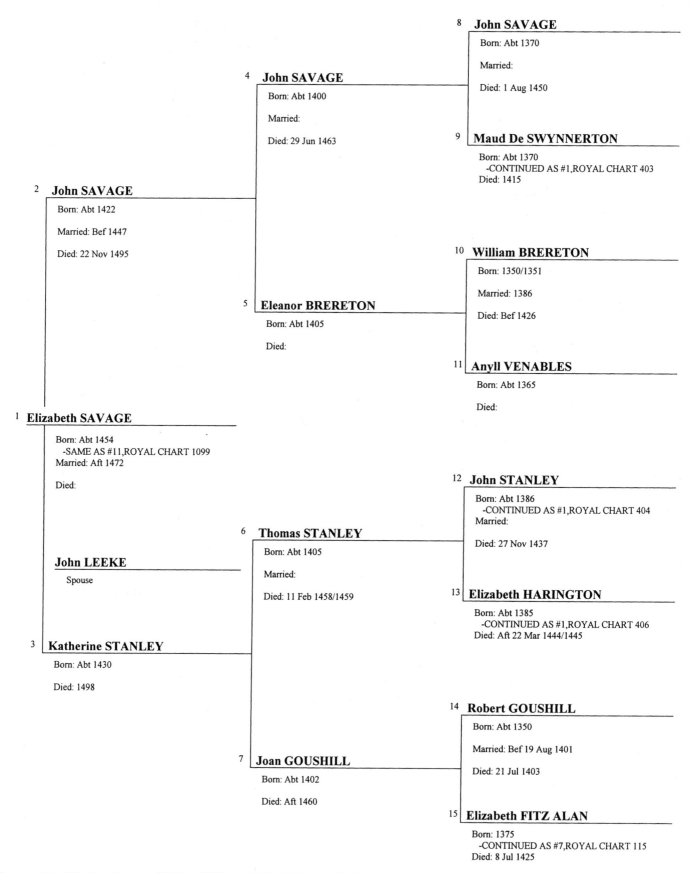

8 John SAVAGE
Born: Abt 1370
Married:
Died: 1 Aug 1450

4 John SAVAGE
Born: Abt 1400
Married:
Died: 29 Jun 1463

9 Maud De SWYNNERTON
Born: Abt 1370
-CONTINUED AS #1,ROYAL CHART 403
Died: 1415

2 John SAVAGE
Born: Abt 1422
Married: Bef 1447
Died: 22 Nov 1495

10 William BRERETON
Born: 1350/1351
Married: 1386
Died: Bef 1426

5 Eleanor BRERETON
Born: Abt 1405
Died:

11 Anyll VENABLES
Born: Abt 1365
Died:

1 Elizabeth SAVAGE
Born: Abt 1454
-SAME AS #11,ROYAL CHART 1099
Married: Aft 1472
Died:

12 John STANLEY
Born: Abt 1386
-CONTINUED AS #1,ROYAL CHART 404
Married:
Died: 27 Nov 1437

6 Thomas STANLEY
Born: Abt 1405
Married:
Died: 11 Feb 1458/1459

13 Elizabeth HARINGTON
Born: Abt 1385
-CONTINUED AS #1,ROYAL CHART 406
Died: Aft 22 Mar 1444/1445

John LEEKE
Spouse

3 Katherine STANLEY
Born: Abt 1430
Died: 1498

14 Robert GOUSHILL
Born: Abt 1350
Married: Bef 19 Aug 1401
Died: 21 Jul 1403

7 Joan GOUSHILL
Born: Abt 1402
Died: Aft 1460

15 Elizabeth FITZ ALAN
Born: 1375
-CONTINUED AS #7,ROYAL CHART 115
Died: 8 Jul 1425

Sources include: Richardson *Plantagenet* (2004), pp. 755 (Waterton), 637-639 (Savage), 678-680 (Stanley); Roberts *500*, pp. 238-239; Chart 371 & sources.

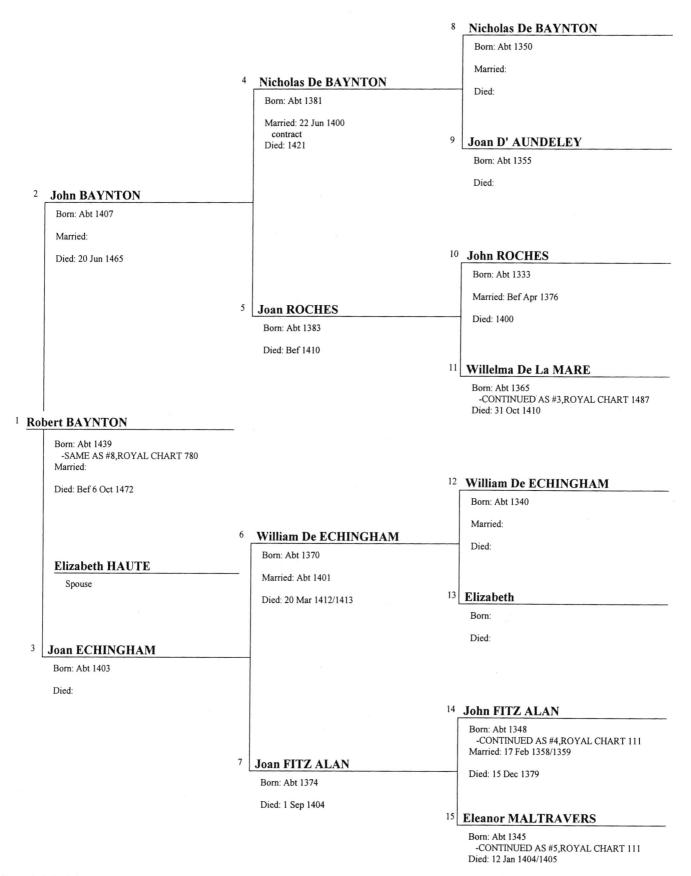

8 **Nicholas De BAYNTON**

Born: Abt 1350

Married:

Died:

4 **Nicholas De BAYNTON**

Born: Abt 1381

Married: 22 Jun 1400
  contract
Died: 1421

9 **Joan D' AUNDELEY**

Born: Abt 1355

Died:

2 **John BAYNTON**

Born: Abt 1407

Married:

Died: 20 Jun 1465

10 **John ROCHES**

Born: Abt 1333

Married: Bef Apr 1376

Died: 1400

5 **Joan ROCHES**

Born: Abt 1383

Died: Bef 1410

11 **Willelma De La MARE**

Born: Abt 1365
  -CONTINUED AS #3,ROYAL CHART 1487
Died: 31 Oct 1410

1 **Robert BAYNTON**

Born: Abt 1439
  -SAME AS #8,ROYAL CHART 780
Married:

Died: Bef 6 Oct 1472

12 **William De ECHINGHAM**

Born: Abt 1340

Married:

Died:

6 **William De ECHINGHAM**

Born: Abt 1370

Married: Abt 1401

Died: 20 Mar 1412/1413

13 **Elizabeth**

Born:

Died:

Elizabeth HAUTE

Spouse

3 **Joan ECHINGHAM**

Born: Abt 1403

Died:

14 **John FITZ ALAN**

Born: Abt 1348
  -CONTINUED AS #4,ROYAL CHART 111
Married: 17 Feb 1358/1359

Died: 15 Dec 1379

7 **Joan FITZ ALAN**

Born: Abt 1374

Died: 1 Sep 1404

15 **Eleanor MALTRAVERS**

Born: Abt 1345
  -CONTINUED AS #5,ROYAL CHART 111
Died: 12 Jan 1404/1405

Sources include: Faris--Baynton; Consultation with Douglas Richardson.

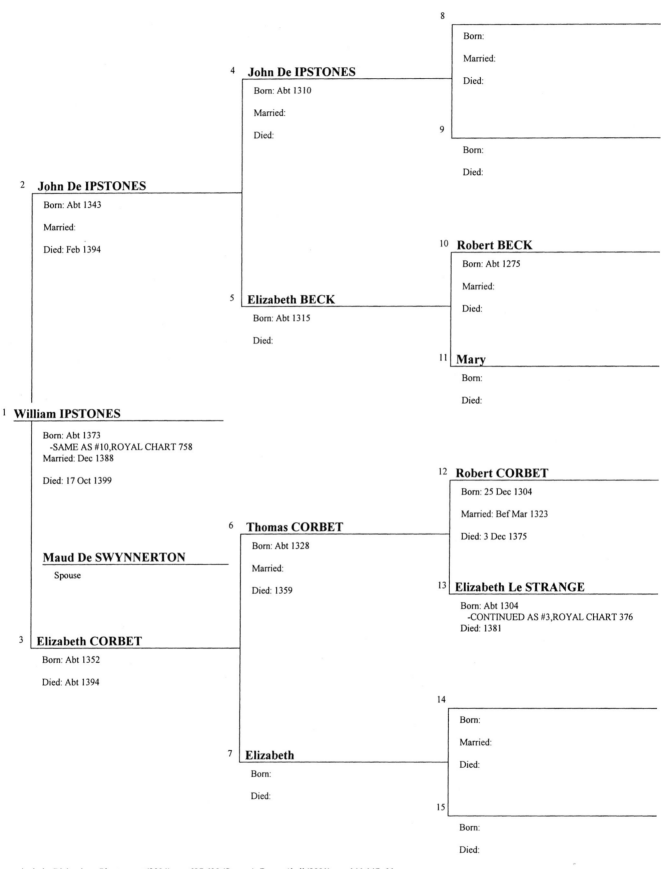

8

Born:

Married:

Died:

4 **John De IPSTONES**

Born: Abt 1310

Married:

Died:

9

Born:

Died:

2 **John De IPSTONES**

Born: Abt 1343

Married:

Died: Feb 1394

10 **Robert BECK**

Born: Abt 1275

Married:

Died:

5 **Elizabeth BECK**

Born: Abt 1315

Died:

11 **Mary**

Born:

Died:

1 **William IPSTONES**

Born: Abt 1373
  -SAME AS #10,ROYAL CHART 758
Married: Dec 1388

Died: 17 Oct 1399

12 **Robert CORBET**

Born: 25 Dec 1304

Married: Bef Mar 1323

Died: 3 Dec 1375

6 **Thomas CORBET**

Born: Abt 1328

Married:

Died: 1359

13 **Elizabeth Le STRANGE**

Born: Abt 1304
  -CONTINUED AS #3,ROYAL CHART 376
Died: 1381

Maud De SWYNNERTON

Spouse

3 **Elizabeth CORBET**

Born: Abt 1352

Died: Abt 1394

14

Born:

Married:

Died:

7 **Elizabeth**

Born:

Died:

15

Born:

Died:

Sources include: Richardson *Plantagenet* (2004), pp. 637-638 (Savage); Boyer *Abell* (2001), pp. 146-147, 66.

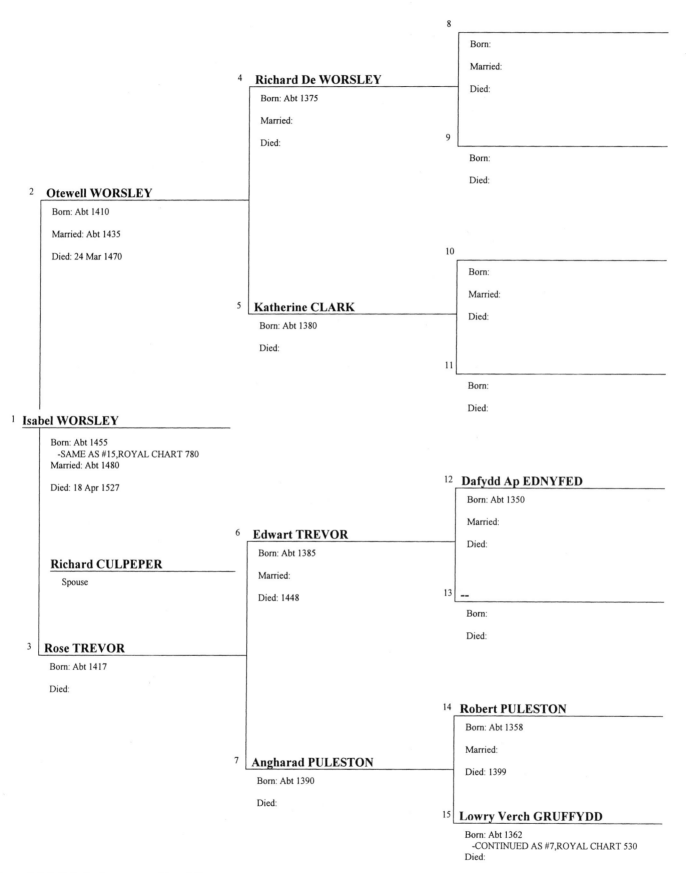

8

Born:

Married:

Died:

4 **Richard De WORSLEY**

Born: Abt 1375

Married:

Died:

9

Born:

Died:

2 **Otewell WORSLEY**

Born: Abt 1410

Married: Abt 1435

Died: 24 Mar 1470

10

Born:

Married:

Died:

5 **Katherine CLARK**

Born: Abt 1380

Died:

11

Born:

Died:

1 **Isabel WORSLEY**

Born: Abt 1455
-SAME AS #15,ROYAL CHART 780
Married: Abt 1480

Died: 18 Apr 1527

12 **Dafydd Ap EDNYFED**

Born: Abt 1350

Married:

Died:

6 **Edwart TREVOR**

Born: Abt 1385

Married:

Died: 1448

13 **--**

Born:

Died:

Richard CULPEPER

Spouse

3 **Rose TREVOR**

Born: Abt 1417

Died:

14 **Robert PULESTON**

Born: Abt 1358

Married:

Died: 1399

7 **Angharad PULESTON**

Born: Abt 1390

Died:

15 **Lowry Verch GRUFFYDD**

Born: Abt 1362
-CONTINUED AS #7,ROYAL CHART 530
Died:

Sources include: Faris--Stockman; *Ancestral Roots* 249.

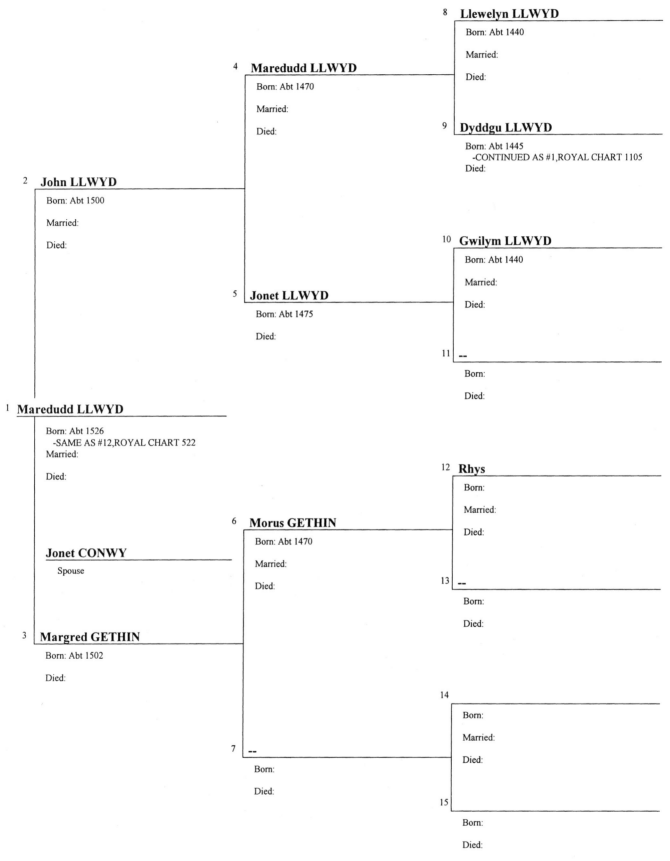

8 **Llewelyn LLWYD**
Born: Abt 1440
Married:
Died:

4 **Maredudd LLWYD**
Born: Abt 1470
Married:
Died:

9 **Dyddgu LLWYD**
Born: Abt 1445
-CONTINUED AS #1,ROYAL CHART 1105
Died:

2 **John LLWYD**
Born: Abt 1500
Married:
Died:

10 **Gwilym LLWYD**
Born: Abt 1440
Married:
Died:

5 **Jonet LLWYD**
Born: Abt 1475
Died:

11 **--**
Born:
Died:

1 **Maredudd LLWYD**
Born: Abt 1526
-SAME AS #12,ROYAL CHART 522
Married:
Died:

12 **Rhys**
Born:
Married:
Died:

6 **Morus GETHIN**
Born: Abt 1470
Married:
Died:

Jonet CONWY
Spouse

13 **--**
Born:
Died:

3 **Margred GETHIN**
Born: Abt 1502
Died:

14
Born:
Married:
Died:

7 **--**
Born:
Died:

15
Born:
Died:

Sources include: Roberts *500*, pp. 321-322.

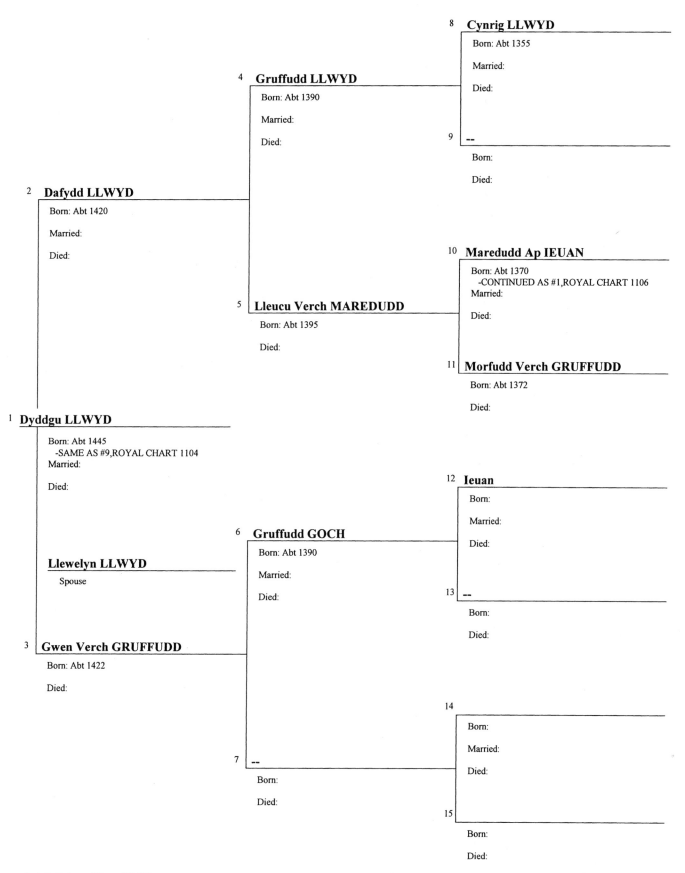

8 Cynrig LLWYD

Born: Abt 1355

Married:

Died:

4 Gruffudd LLWYD

Born: Abt 1390

Married:

Died:

9 --

Born:

Died:

2 Dafydd LLWYD

Born: Abt 1420

Married:

Died:

10 Maredudd Ap IEUAN

Born: Abt 1370
    -CONTINUED AS #1,ROYAL CHART 1106
Married:

Died:

5 Lleucu Verch MAREDUDD

Born: Abt 1395

Died:

11 Morfudd Verch GRUFFUDD

Born: Abt 1372

Died:

1 Dyddgu LLWYD

Born: Abt 1445
    -SAME AS #9,ROYAL CHART 1104
Married:

Died:

12 Ieuan

Born:

Married:

Died:

Llewelyn LLWYD

Spouse

6 Gruffudd GOCH

Born: Abt 1390

Married:

Died:

13 --

Born:

Died:

3 Gwen Verch GRUFFUDD

Born: Abt 1422

Died:

14

Born:

Married:

Died:

7 --

Born:

Died:

15

Born:

Died:

Sources include: Roberts *500*, pp. 321-322.

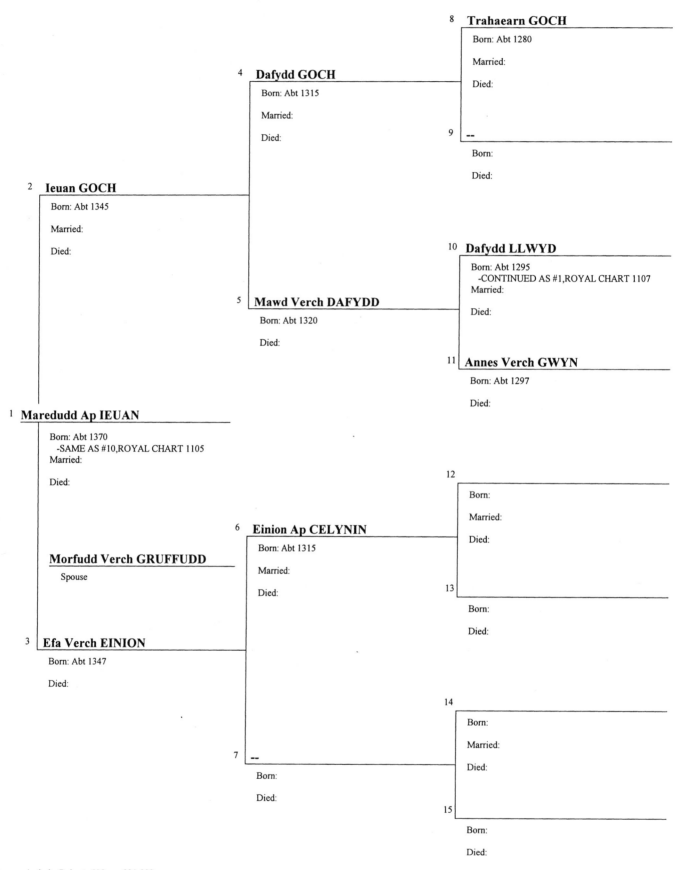

8 **Trahaearn GOCH**

Born: Abt 1280

Married:

Died:

4 **Dafydd GOCH**

Born: Abt 1315

Married:

Died:

9 --

Born:

Died:

2 **Ieuan GOCH**

Born: Abt 1345

Married:

Died:

10 **Dafydd LLWYD**

Born: Abt 1295
    -CONTINUED AS #1,ROYAL CHART 1107
Married:

Died:

5 **Mawd Verch DAFYDD**

Born: Abt 1320

Died:

11 **Annes Verch GWYN**

Born: Abt 1297

Died:

1 **Maredudd Ap IEUAN**

Born: Abt 1370
    -SAME AS #10,ROYAL CHART 1105
Married:

Died:

12

Born:

Married:

Died:

6 **Einion Ap CELYNIN**

Born: Abt 1315

Married:

Died:

13

Born:

Died:

Morfudd Verch GRUFFUDD

Spouse

3 **Efa Verch EINION**

Born: Abt 1347

Died:

14

Born:

Married:

Died:

7 --

Born:

Died:

15

Born:

Died:

Sources include: Roberts *500*, pp. 321-322.

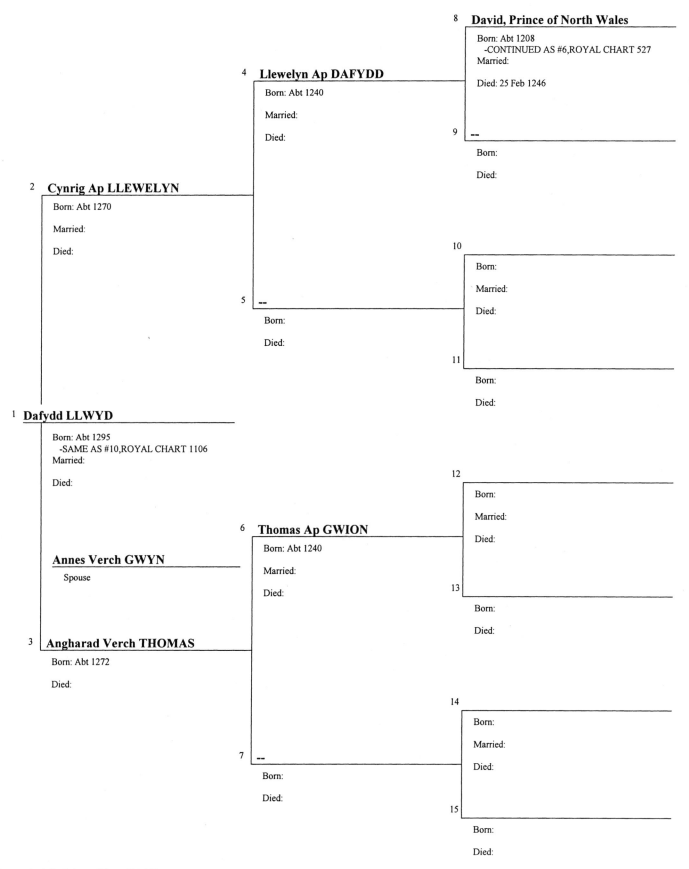

8 **David, Prince of North Wales**

Born: Abt 1208
  -CONTINUED AS #6,ROYAL CHART 527
Married:

Died: 25 Feb 1246

4 **Llewelyn Ap DAFYDD**

Born: Abt 1240

Married:

Died:

9 --

Born:

Died:

2 **Cynrig Ap LLEWELYN**

Born: Abt 1270

Married:

Died:

10

Born:

Married:

Died:

5 --

Born:

Died:

11

Born:

Died:

1 **Dafydd LLWYD**

Born: Abt 1295
  -SAME AS #10,ROYAL CHART 1106
Married:

Died:

12

Born:

Married:

Died:

6 **Thomas Ap GWION**

Born: Abt 1240

Married:

Died:

13

Born:

Died:

Annes Verch GWYN

Spouse

3 **Angharad Verch THOMAS**

Born: Abt 1272

Died:

14

Born:

Married:

Died:

7 --

Born:

Died:

15

Born:

Died:

Sources include: Roberts *500*, pp. 321-322.

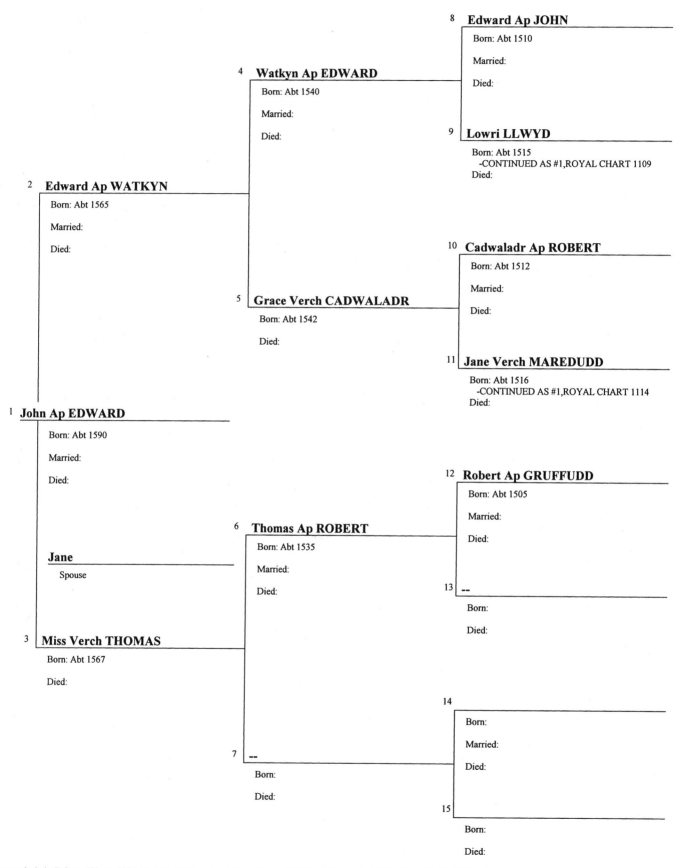

8 **Edward Ap JOHN**

Born: Abt 1510

Married:

Died:

4 **Watkyn Ap EDWARD**

Born: Abt 1540

Married:

Died:

9 **Lowri LLWYD**

Born: Abt 1515
  -CONTINUED AS #1,ROYAL CHART 1109
Died:

2 **Edward Ap WATKYN**

Born: Abt 1565

Married:

Died:

10 **Cadwaladr Ap ROBERT**

Born: Abt 1512

Married:

Died:

5 **Grace Verch CADWALADR**

Born: Abt 1542

Died:

11 **Jane Verch MAREDUDD**

Born: Abt 1516
  -CONTINUED AS #1,ROYAL CHART 1114
Died:

1 **John Ap EDWARD**

Born: Abt 1590

Married:

Died:

12 **Robert Ap GRUFFUDD**

Born: Abt 1505

Married:

Died:

6 **Thomas Ap ROBERT**

Born: Abt 1535

Married:

Died:

13 **--**

Born:

Died:

Jane

Spouse

3 **Miss Verch THOMAS**

Born: Abt 1567

Died:

14

Born:

Married:

Died:

7 **--**

Born:

Died:

15

Born:

Died:

Sources include: Roberts *500*, pp. 308-310. Note: PA immigrant descendants of #1 John & Jane include John Evans (b. abt 1666; md. Mary Hughes), son of Evan Ap Edward (b. abt 1646), son of Edward Ap John (b. abt 1618), son of #1 John & Jane above.

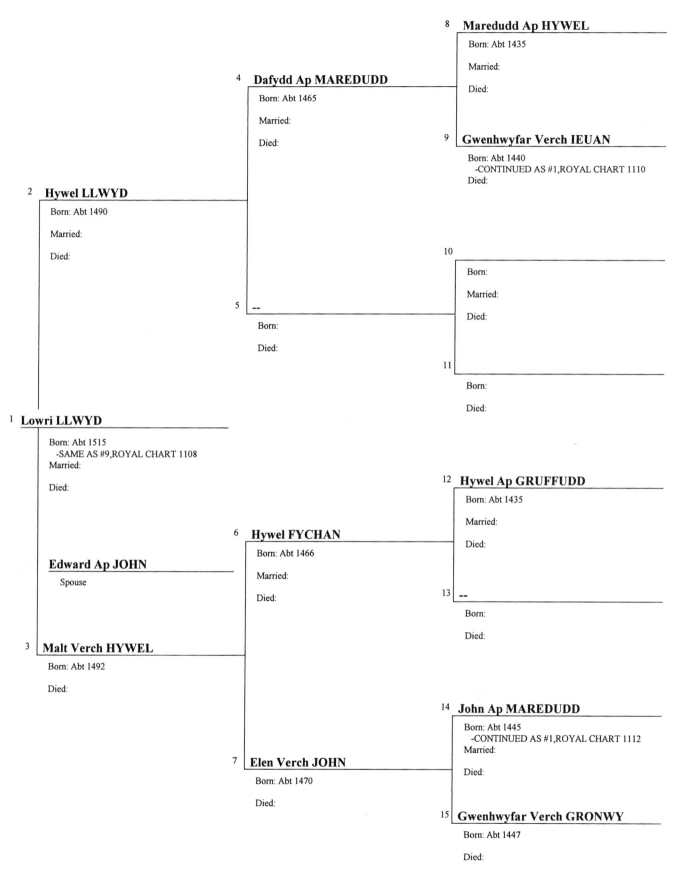

8 **Maredudd Ap HYWEL**

Born: Abt 1435

Married:

Died:

4 **Dafydd Ap MAREDUDD**

Born: Abt 1465

Married:

Died:

9 **Gwenhwyfar Verch IEUAN**

Born: Abt 1440
  -CONTINUED AS #1,ROYAL CHART 1110
Died:

2 **Hywel LLWYD**

Born: Abt 1490

Married:

Died:

10

Born:

Married:

Died:

5 --

Born:

Died:

11

Born:

Died:

1 **Lowri LLWYD**

Born: Abt 1515
  -SAME AS #9,ROYAL CHART 1108
Married:

Died:

12 **Hywel Ap GRUFFUDD**

Born: Abt 1435

Married:

Died:

6 **Hywel FYCHAN**

Born: Abt 1466

Married:

Died:

Edward Ap JOHN

Spouse

13 --

Born:

Died:

3 **Malt Verch HYWEL**

Born: Abt 1492

Died:

14 **John Ap MAREDUDD**

Born: Abt 1445
  -CONTINUED AS #1,ROYAL CHART 1112
Married:

Died:

7 **Elen Verch JOHN**

Born: Abt 1470

Died:

15 **Gwenhwyfar Verch GRONWY**

Born: Abt 1447

Died:

Sources include: Roberts *500*, pp. 308-310, 326-327.

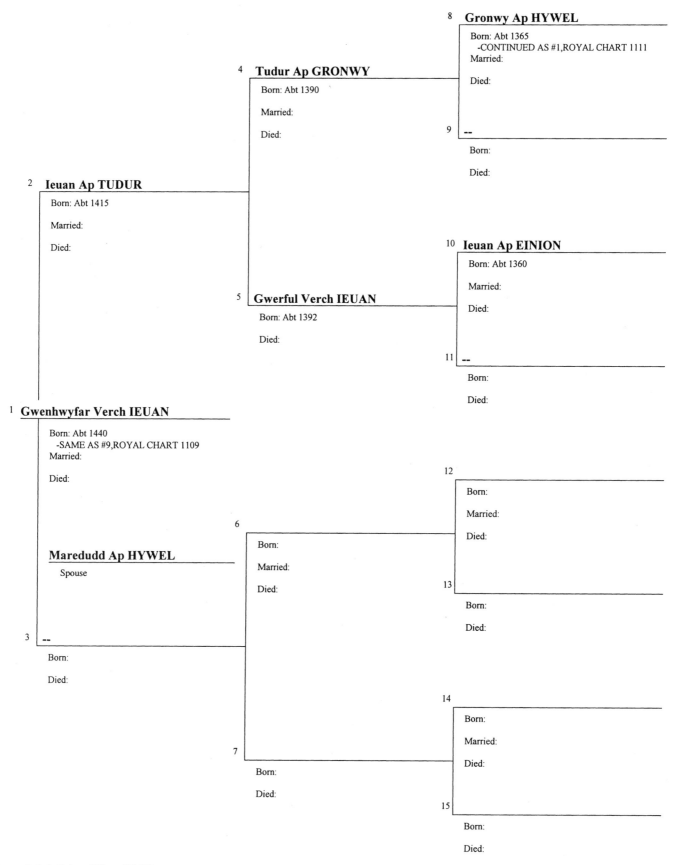

8 **Gronwy Ap HYWEL**

Born: Abt 1365
-CONTINUED AS #1,ROYAL CHART 1111
Married:

Died:

4 **Tudur Ap GRONWY**

Born: Abt 1390

Married:

Died:

9 --

Born:

Died:

2 **Ieuan Ap TUDUR**

Born: Abt 1415

Married:

Died:

10 **Ieuan Ap EINION**

Born: Abt 1360

Married:

Died:

5 **Gwerful Verch IEUAN**

Born: Abt 1392

Died:

11 --

Born:

Died:

1 **Gwenhwyfar Verch IEUAN**

Born: Abt 1440
-SAME AS #9,ROYAL CHART 1109
Married:

Died:

12

Born:

Married:

Died:

6

Born:

Married:

Died:

13

Born:

Died:

Maredudd Ap HYWEL

Spouse

14

Born:

Married:

Died:

3 --

Born:

Died:

7

Born:

Died:

15

Born:

Died:

Sources include: Roberts *500*, pp. 326-327.

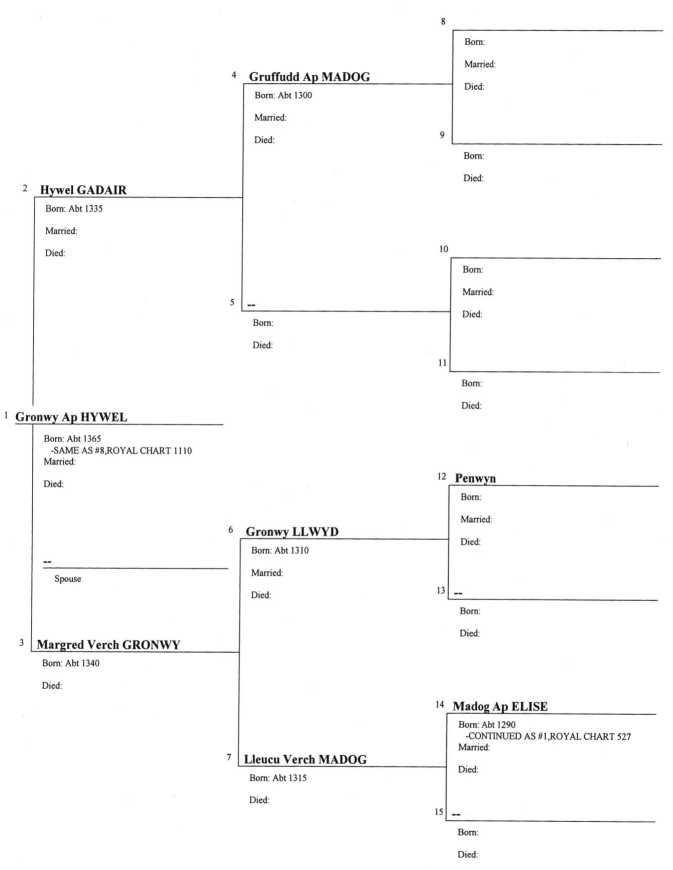

8

Born:

Married:

Died:

4 Gruffudd Ap MADOG

Born: Abt 1300

Married:

Died:

9

Born:

Died:

2 Hywel GADAIR

Born: Abt 1335

Married:

Died:

10

Born:

Married:

Died:

5 --

Born:

Died:

11

Born:

Died:

1 Gronwy Ap HYWEL

Born: Abt 1365
   -SAME AS #8,ROYAL CHART 1110
Married:

Died:

12 Penwyn

Born:

Married:

Died:

6 Gronwy LLWYD

Born: Abt 1310

Married:

Died:

13 --

Born:

Died:

--

Spouse

3 Margred Verch GRONWY

Born: Abt 1340

Died:

14 Madog Ap ELISE

Born: Abt 1290
   -CONTINUED AS #1,ROYAL CHART 527
Married:

Died:

7 Lleucu Verch MADOG

Born: Abt 1315

Died:

15 --

Born:

Died:

Sources include: Roberts *500*, pp. 326-327.

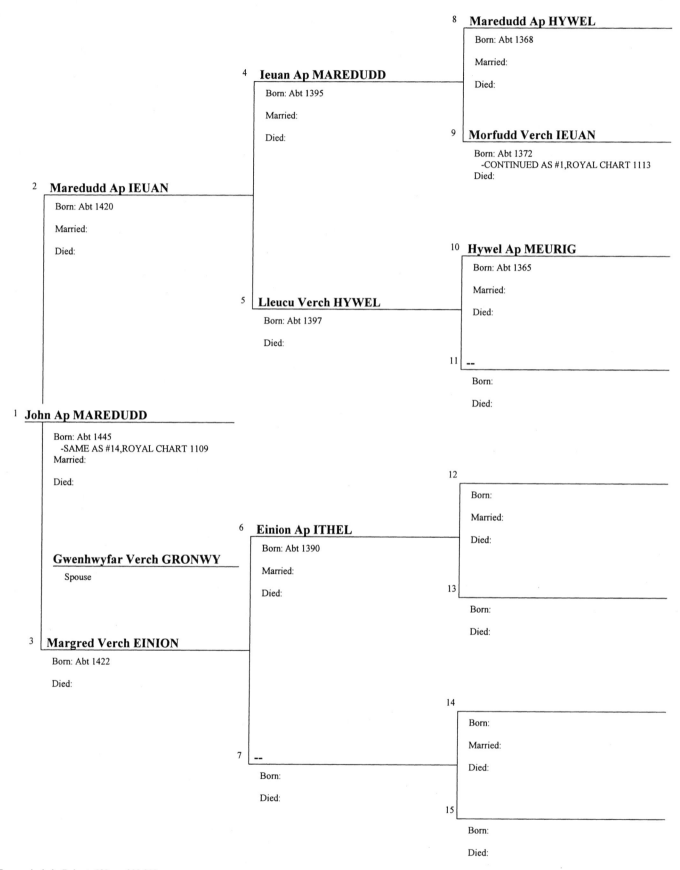

8 **Maredudd Ap HYWEL**

Born: Abt 1368

Married:

Died:

4 **Ieuan Ap MAREDUDD**

Born: Abt 1395

Married:

Died:

9 **Morfudd Verch IEUAN**

Born: Abt 1372
  -CONTINUED AS #1,ROYAL CHART 1113
Died:

2 **Maredudd Ap IEUAN**

Born: Abt 1420

Married:

Died:

10 **Hywel Ap MEURIG**

Born: Abt 1365

Married:

Died:

5 **Lleucu Verch HYWEL**

Born: Abt 1397

Died:

11 **--**

Born:

Died:

1 **John Ap MAREDUDD**

Born: Abt 1445
  -SAME AS #14,ROYAL CHART 1109
Married:

Died:

12

Born:

Married:

Died:

6 **Einion Ap ITHEL**

Born: Abt 1390

Married:

Died:

13

Born:

Died:

Gwenhwyfar Verch GRONWY

Spouse

3 **Margred Verch EINION**

Born: Abt 1422

Died:

14

Born:

Married:

Died:

7 **--**

Born:

Died:

15

Born:

Died:

Sources include: Roberts *500*, pp. 308-310.

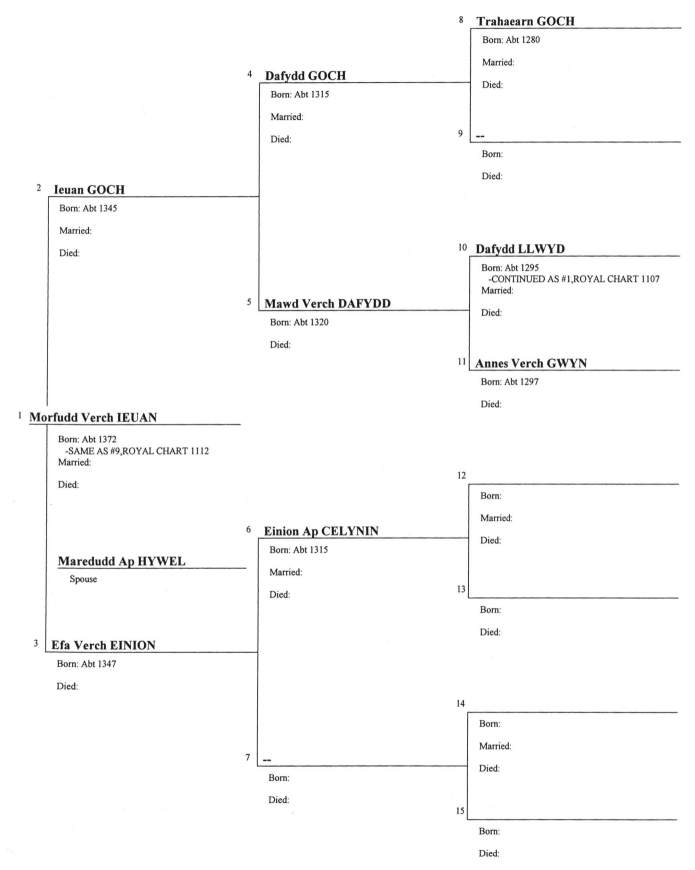

8 Trahaearn GOCH
Born: Abt 1280
Married:
Died:

4 Dafydd GOCH
Born: Abt 1315
Married:
Died:

9 --
Born:
Died:

2 Ieuan GOCH
Born: Abt 1345
Married:
Died:

10 Dafydd LLWYD
Born: Abt 1295
   -CONTINUED AS #1,ROYAL CHART 1107
Married:
Died:

5 Mawd Verch DAFYDD
Born: Abt 1320
Died:

11 Annes Verch GWYN
Born: Abt 1297
Died:

1 Morfudd Verch IEUAN
Born: Abt 1372
   -SAME AS #9,ROYAL CHART 1112
Married:
Died:

12
Born:
Married:
Died:

6 Einion Ap CELYNIN
Born: Abt 1315
Married:
Died:

Maredudd Ap HYWEL
Spouse

13
Born:
Died:

3 Efa Verch EINION
Born: Abt 1347
Died:

14
Born:
Married:
Died:

7 --
Born:
Died:

15
Born:
Died:

Sources include: Roberts *500*, pp. 308-310.

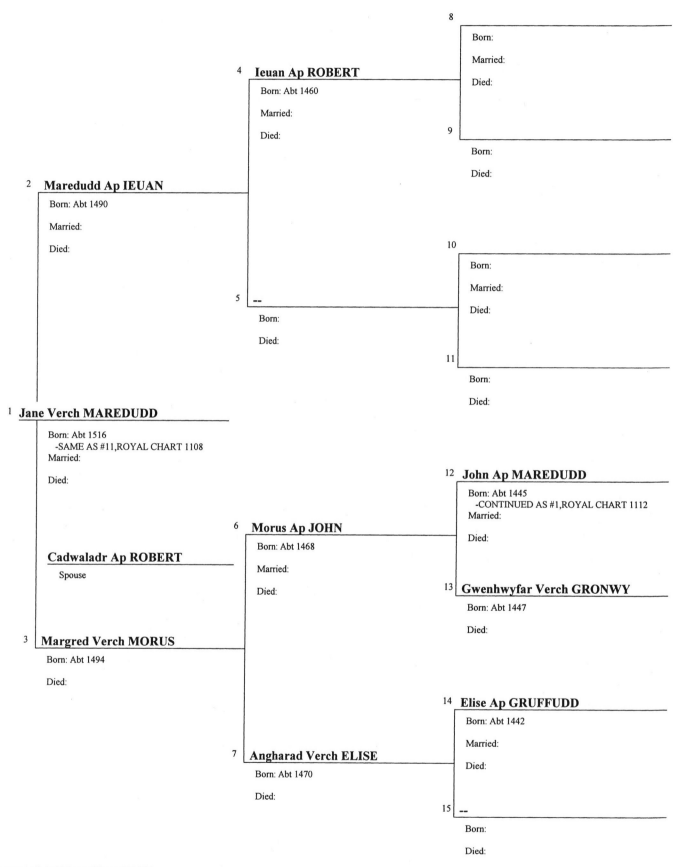

8

Born:

Married:

Died:

4 **Ieuan Ap ROBERT**

Born: Abt 1460

Married:

Died:

9

Born:

Died:

2 **Maredudd Ap IEUAN**

Born: Abt 1490

Married:

Died:

10

Born:

Married:

Died:

5 --

Born:

Died:

11

Born:

Died:

1 **Jane Verch MAREDUDD**

Born: Abt 1516
-SAME AS #11,ROYAL CHART 1108
Married:

Died:

12 **John Ap MAREDUDD**

Born: Abt 1445
-CONTINUED AS #1,ROYAL CHART 1112
Married:

Died:

6 **Morus Ap JOHN**

Born: Abt 1468

Married:

Died:

13 **Gwenhwyfar Verch GRONWY**

Born: Abt 1447

Died:

Cadwaladr Ap ROBERT

Spouse

3 **Margred Verch MORUS**

Born: Abt 1494

Died:

14 **Elise Ap GRUFFUDD**

Born: Abt 1442

Married:

Died:

7 **Angharad Verch ELISE**

Born: Abt 1470

Died:

15 --

Born:

Died:

Sources include: Roberts *500*, pp. 328-329.

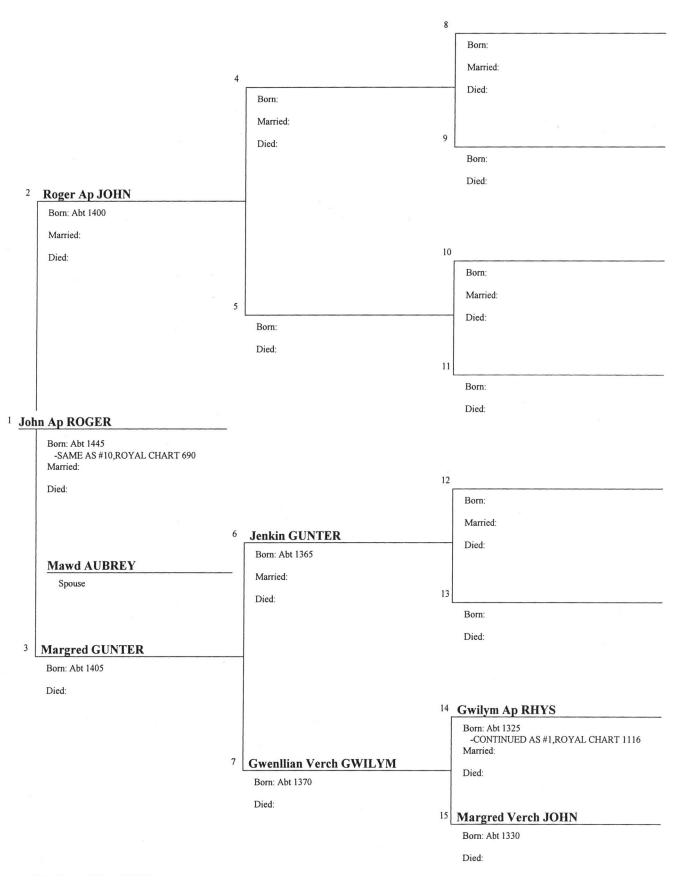

8

Born:

Married:

Died:

4

Born:

Married:

Died:

9

Born:

Died:

2 **Roger Ap JOHN**

Born: Abt 1400

Married:

Died:

5

Born:

Died:

10

Born:

Married:

Died:

11

Born:

Died:

1 **John Ap ROGER**

Born: Abt 1445
-SAME AS #10,ROYAL CHART 690
Married:

Died:

12

Born:

Married:

Died:

6 **Jenkin GUNTER**

Born: Abt 1365

Married:

Died:

13

Born:

Died:

Mawd AUBREY

Spouse

3 **Margred GUNTER**

Born: Abt 1405

Died:

14 **Gwilym Ap RHYS**

Born: Abt 1325
-CONTINUED AS #1,ROYAL CHART 1116
Married:

Died:

7 **Gwenllian Verch GWILYM**

Born: Abt 1370

Died:

15 **Margred Verch JOHN**

Born: Abt 1330

Died:

Sources include: Roberts *500*, pp. 387-388.

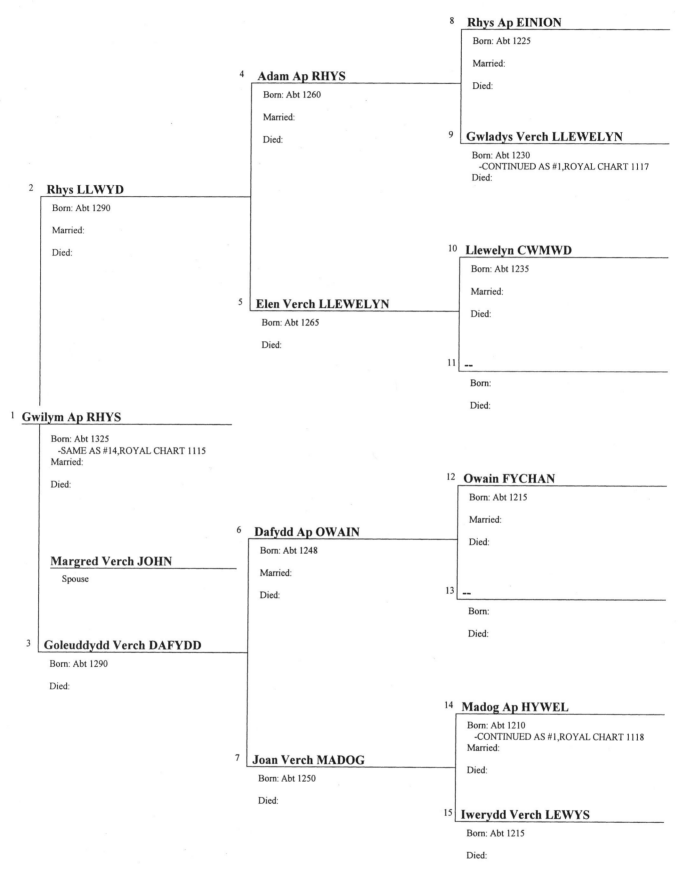

8 **Rhys Ap EINION**

Born: Abt 1225

Married:

Died:

4 **Adam Ap RHYS**

Born: Abt 1260

Married:

Died:

9 **Gwladys Verch LLEWELYN**

Born: Abt 1230
　　-CONTINUED AS #1,ROYAL CHART 1117
Died:

2 **Rhys LLWYD**

Born: Abt 1290

Married:

Died:

10 **Llewelyn CWMWD**

Born: Abt 1235

Married:

Died:

5 **Elen Verch LLEWELYN**

Born: Abt 1265

Died:

11 **--**

Born:

Died:

1 **Gwilym Ap RHYS**

Born: Abt 1325
　　-SAME AS #14,ROYAL CHART 1115
Married:

Died:

12 **Owain FYCHAN**

Born: Abt 1215

Married:

Died:

6 **Dafydd Ap OWAIN**

Born: Abt 1248

Married:

Died:

Margred Verch JOHN

Spouse

13 **--**

Born:

Died:

3 **Goleuddydd Verch DAFYDD**

Born: Abt 1290

Died:

14 **Madog Ap HYWEL**

Born: Abt 1210
　　-CONTINUED AS #1,ROYAL CHART 1118
Married:

Died:

7 **Joan Verch MADOG**

Born: Abt 1250

Died:

15 **Iwerydd Verch LEWYS**

Born: Abt 1215

Died:

Sources include: Roberts *500*, pp. 387-388.

Pedigree Chart

Chart 1117

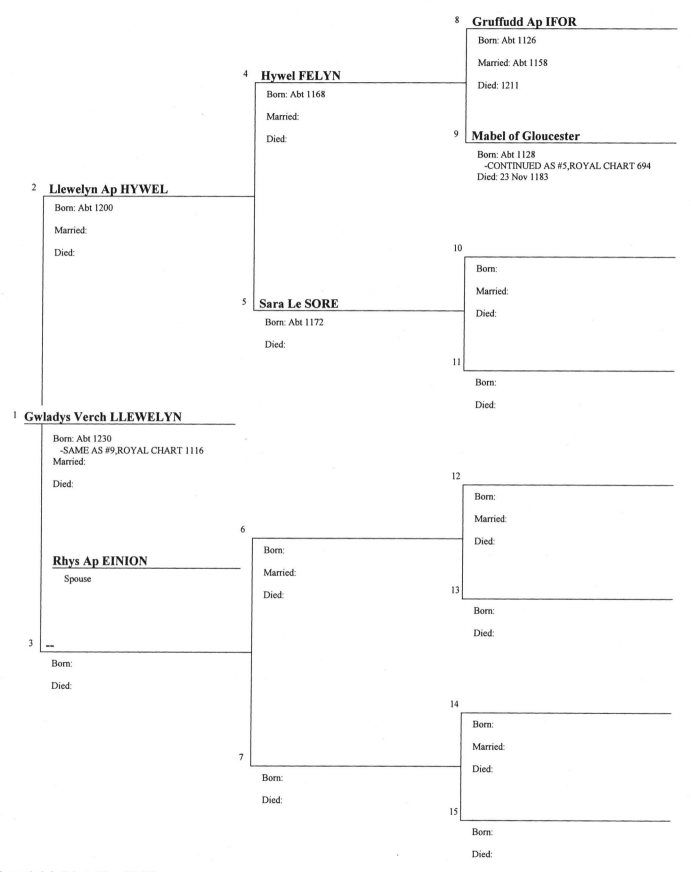

8 **Gruffudd Ap IFOR**

Born: Abt 1126

Married: Abt 1158

Died: 1211

4 **Hywel FELYN**

Born: Abt 1168

Married:

Died:

9 **Mabel of Gloucester**

Born: Abt 1128
  -CONTINUED AS #5,ROYAL CHART 694
Died: 23 Nov 1183

2 **Llewelyn Ap HYWEL**

Born: Abt 1200

Married:

Died:

10

Born:

Married:

Died:

5 **Sara Le SORE**

Born: Abt 1172

Died:

11

Born:

Died:

1 **Gwladys Verch LLEWELYN**

Born: Abt 1230
  -SAME AS #9,ROYAL CHART 1116
Married:

Died:

12

Born:

Married:

Died:

6

Born:

Married:

Died:

13

Born:

Died:

Rhys Ap EINION

Spouse

3 **--**

Born:

Died:

14

Born:

Married:

Died:

7

Born:

Died:

15

Born:

Died:

Sources include: Roberts *500*, pp 387-388.

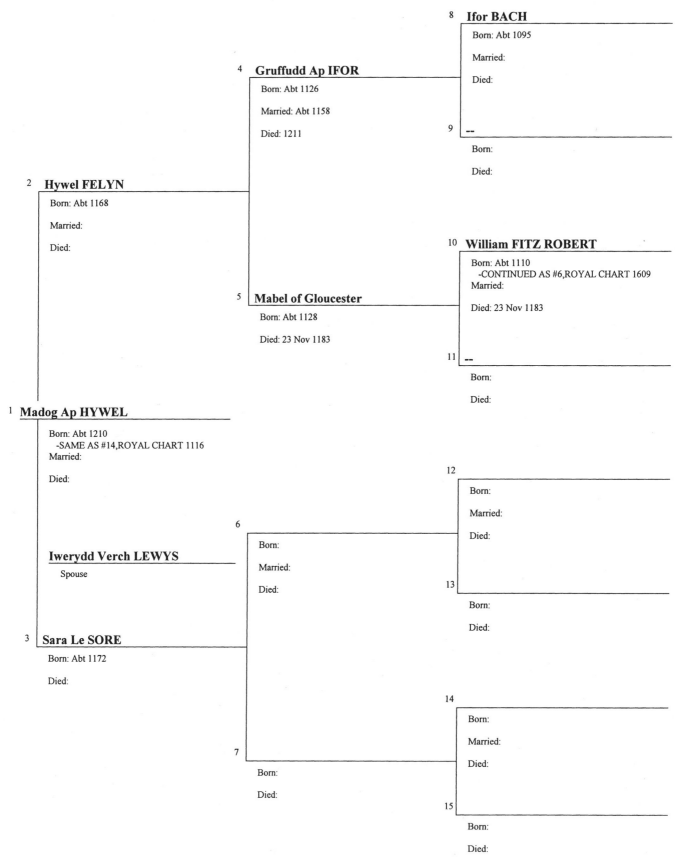

8 **Ifor BACH**

Born: Abt 1095

Married:

Died:

4 **Gruffudd Ap IFOR**

Born: Abt 1126

Married: Abt 1158

Died: 1211

9 --

Born:

Died:

2 **Hywel FELYN**

Born: Abt 1168

Married:

Died:

10 **William FITZ ROBERT**

Born: Abt 1110
  -CONTINUED AS #6,ROYAL CHART 1609
Married:

Died: 23 Nov 1183

5 **Mabel of Gloucester**

Born: Abt 1128

Died: 23 Nov 1183

11 --

Born:

Died:

1 **Madog Ap HYWEL**

Born: Abt 1210
  -SAME AS #14,ROYAL CHART 1116
Married:

Died:

12

Born:

Married:

Died:

6

Born:

Married:

Died:

13

Born:

Died:

Iwerydd Verch LEWYS

Spouse

3 **Sara Le SORE**

Born: Abt 1172

Died:

14

Born:

Married:

Died:

7

Born:

Died:

15

Born:

Died:

Sources include: Roberts *500*, pp. 387-388.

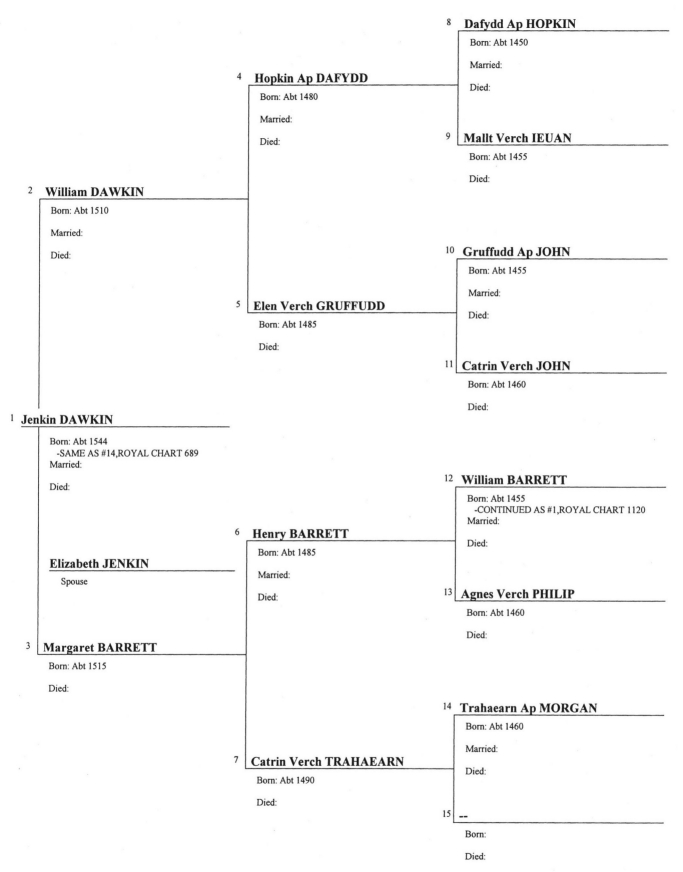

8 Dafydd Ap HOPKIN

Born: Abt 1450

Married:

Died:

4 Hopkin Ap DAFYDD

Born: Abt 1480

Married:

Died:

9 Mallt Verch IEUAN

Born: Abt 1455

Died:

2 William DAWKIN

Born: Abt 1510

Married:

Died:

10 Gruffudd Ap JOHN

Born: Abt 1455

Married:

Died:

5 Elen Verch GRUFFUDD

Born: Abt 1485

Died:

11 Catrin Verch JOHN

Born: Abt 1460

Died:

1 Jenkin DAWKIN

Born: Abt 1544
-SAME AS #14,ROYAL CHART 689
Married:

Died:

12 William BARRETT

Born: Abt 1455
-CONTINUED AS #1,ROYAL CHART 1120
Married:

Died:

6 Henry BARRETT

Born: Abt 1485

Married:

Died:

13 Agnes Verch PHILIP

Born: Abt 1460

Died:

Elizabeth JENKIN

Spouse

3 Margaret BARRETT

Born: Abt 1515

Died:

14 Trahaearn Ap MORGAN

Born: Abt 1460

Married:

Died:

7 Catrin Verch TRAHAEARN

Born: Abt 1490

Died:

15 --

Born:

Died:

Sources include: Roberts *500*, pp. 387-388; Faris preliminary baronial manuscript (1998), pp. 479 (Dawkin), 129 (Bleddyn).

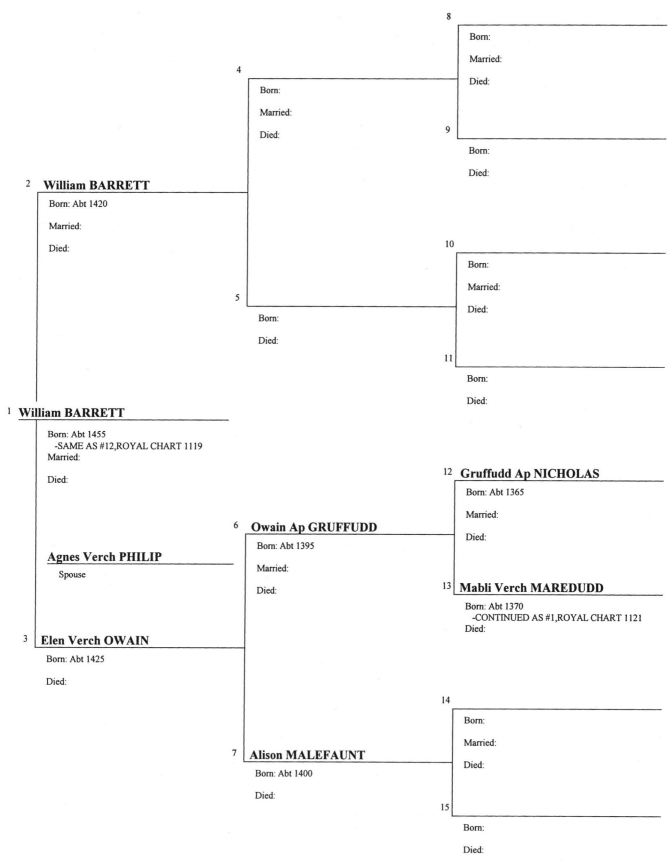

8

4

Born:

Married:

Died:

Born:

Married:

Died:

9

Born:

Died:

2 William BARRETT

Born: Abt 1420

Married:

Died:

10

Born:

Married:

Died:

5

Born:

Died:

11

Born:

Died:

1 William BARRETT

Born: Abt 1455
  -SAME AS #12,ROYAL CHART 1119
Married:

Died:

12 Gruffudd Ap NICHOLAS

Born: Abt 1365

Married:

Died:

6 Owain Ap GRUFFUDD

Born: Abt 1395

Married:

Died:

13 Mabli Verch MAREDUDD

Born: Abt 1370
  -CONTINUED AS #1,ROYAL CHART 1121
Died:

Agnes Verch PHILIP

Spouse

3 Elen Verch OWAIN

Born: Abt 1425

Died:

14

Born:

Married:

Died:

7 Alison MALEFAUNT

Born: Abt 1400

Died:

15

Born:

Died:

Sources include: Roberts 500 pp 387-388

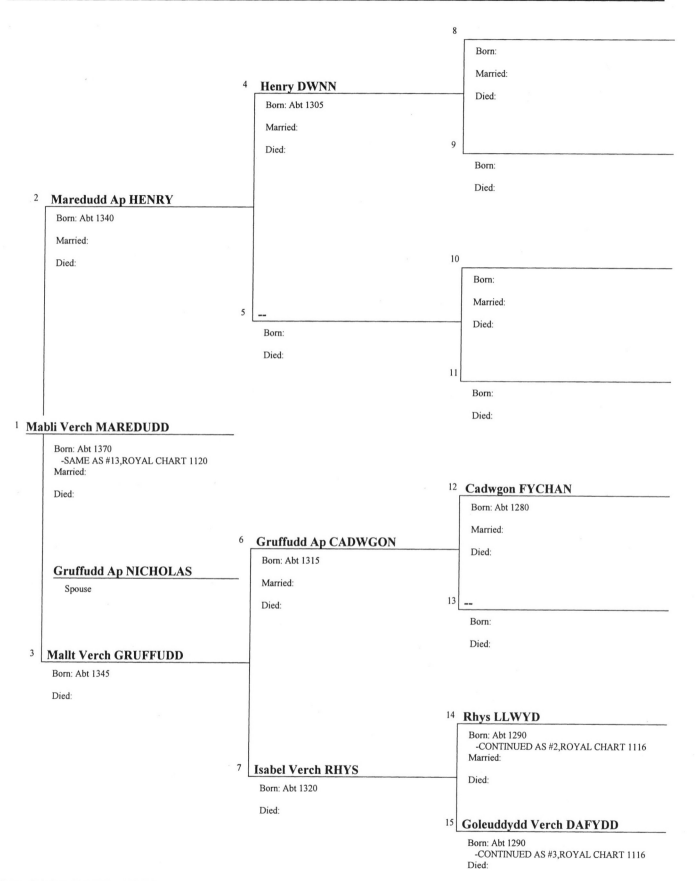

8

Born:

Married:

Died:

4   **Henry DWNN**

Born: Abt 1305

Married:

Died:

9

Born:

Died:

2   **Maredudd Ap HENRY**

Born: Abt 1340

Married:

Died:

10

Born:

Married:

Died:

5   --

Born:

Died:

11

Born:

Died:

1   **Mabli Verch MAREDUDD**

Born: Abt 1370
   -SAME AS #13, ROYAL CHART 1120
Married:

Died:

12   **Cadwgon FYCHAN**

Born: Abt 1280

Married:

Died:

6   **Gruffudd Ap CADWGON**

Born: Abt 1315

Married:

Died:

Gruffudd Ap NICHOLAS

Spouse

13   --

Born:

Died:

3   **Mallt Verch GRUFFUDD**

Born: Abt 1345

Died:

14   **Rhys LLWYD**

Born: Abt 1290
   -CONTINUED AS #2, ROYAL CHART 1116
Married:

Died:

7   **Isabel Verch RHYS**

Born: Abt 1320

Died:

15   **Goleuddydd Verch DAFYDD**

Born: Abt 1290
   -CONTINUED AS #3, ROYAL CHART 1116
Died:

Sources include: Roberts *500*, pp. 387-388.

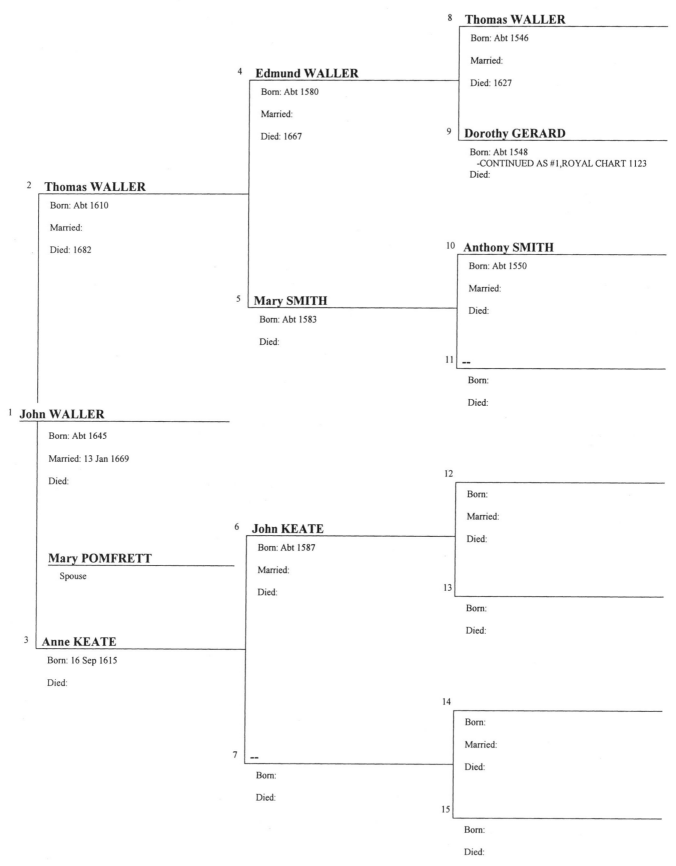

8 **Thomas WALLER**

Born: Abt 1546

Married:

Died: 1627

4 **Edmund WALLER**

Born: Abt 1580

Married:

Died: 1667

9 **Dorothy GERARD**

Born: Abt 1548

-CONTINUED AS #1,ROYAL CHART 1123
Died:

2 **Thomas WALLER**

Born: Abt 1610

Married:

Died: 1682

10 **Anthony SMITH**

Born: Abt 1550

Married:

Died:

5 **Mary SMITH**

Born: Abt 1583

Died:

11 **--**

Born:

Died:

1 **John WALLER**

Born: Abt 1645

Married: 13 Jan 1669

Died:

12

Born:

Married:

Died:

6 **John KEATE**

Born: Abt 1587

Married:

Died:

13

Born:

Died:

Mary POMFRETT

Spouse

3 **Anne KEATE**

Born: 16 Sep 1615

Died:

14

Born:

Married:

Died:

7 **--**

Born:

Died:

15

Born:

Died:

Sources include: Roberts *500*, pp. 330-333; *AAP*, p. 221; LDS records.

Pedigree Chart

Chart 1123

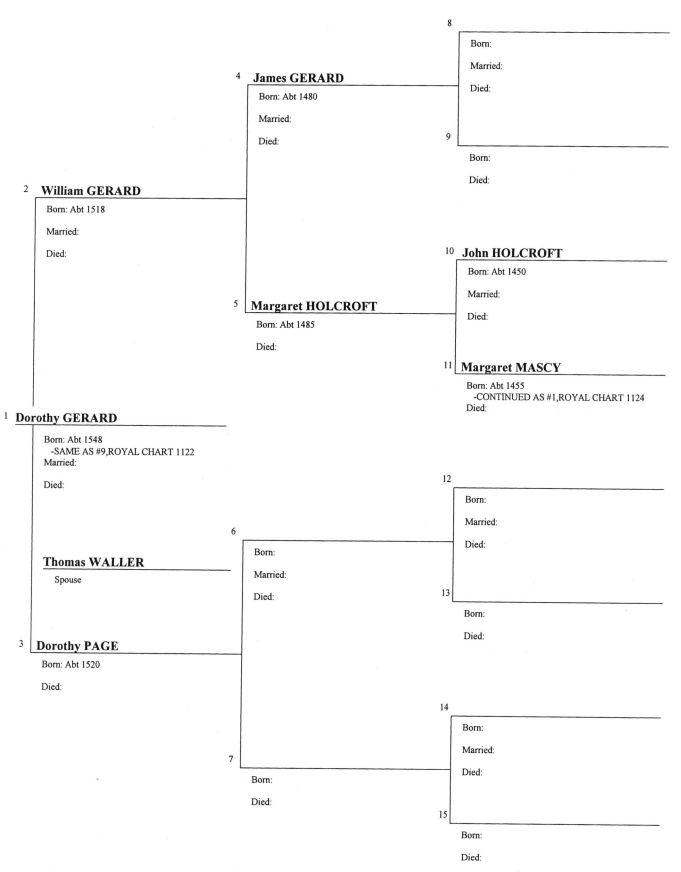

8

Born:

Married:

Died:

4 **James GERARD**

Born: Abt 1480

Married:

Died:

9

Born:

Died:

2 **William GERARD**

Born: Abt 1518

Married:

Died:

10 **John HOLCROFT**

Born: Abt 1450

Married:

Died:

5 **Margaret HOLCROFT**

Born: Abt 1485

Died:

11 **Margaret MASCY**

Born: Abt 1455
  -CONTINUED AS #1,ROYAL CHART 1124
Died:

1 **Dorothy GERARD**

Born: Abt 1548
  -SAME AS #9,ROYAL CHART 1122
Married:

Died:

12

Born:

Married:

Died:

6

Born:

Married:

Died:

Thomas WALLER

Spouse

13

Born:

Died:

3 **Dorothy PAGE**

Born: Abt 1520

Died:

14

Born:

Married:

Died:

7

Born:

Died:

15

Born:

Died:

Sources include: Roberts *500*, pp. 330-333.

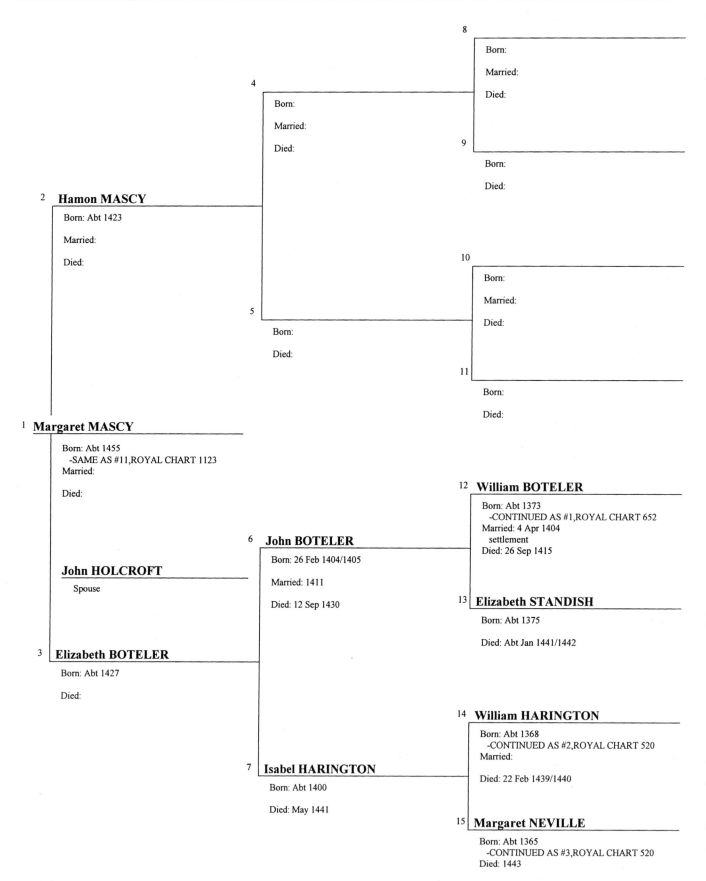

8

Born:

Married:

Died:

4

Born:

Married:

Died:

9

Born:

Died:

2 **Hamon MASCY**

Born: Abt 1423

Married:

Died:

10

Born:

Married:

Died:

5

Born:

Died:

11

Born:

Died:

1 **Margaret MASCY**

Born: Abt 1455
-SAME AS #11,ROYAL CHART 1123
Married:

Died:

12 **William BOTELER**

Born: Abt 1373
-CONTINUED AS #1,ROYAL CHART 652
Married: 4 Apr 1404
settlement
Died: 26 Sep 1415

6 **John BOTELER**

Born: 26 Feb 1404/1405

Married: 1411

Died: 12 Sep 1430

13 **Elizabeth STANDISH**

Born: Abt 1375

Died: Abt Jan 1441/1442

John HOLCROFT

Spouse

3 **Elizabeth BOTELER**

Born: Abt 1427

Died:

14 **William HARINGTON**

Born: Abt 1368
-CONTINUED AS #2,ROYAL CHART 520
Married:

Died: 22 Feb 1439/1440

7 **Isabel HARINGTON**

Born: Abt 1400

Died: May 1441

15 **Margaret NEVILLE**

Born: Abt 1365
-CONTINUED AS #3,ROYAL CHART 520
Died: 1443

Sources include: Roberts *500*, pp. 330-333; *Ancestral Roots* 46.

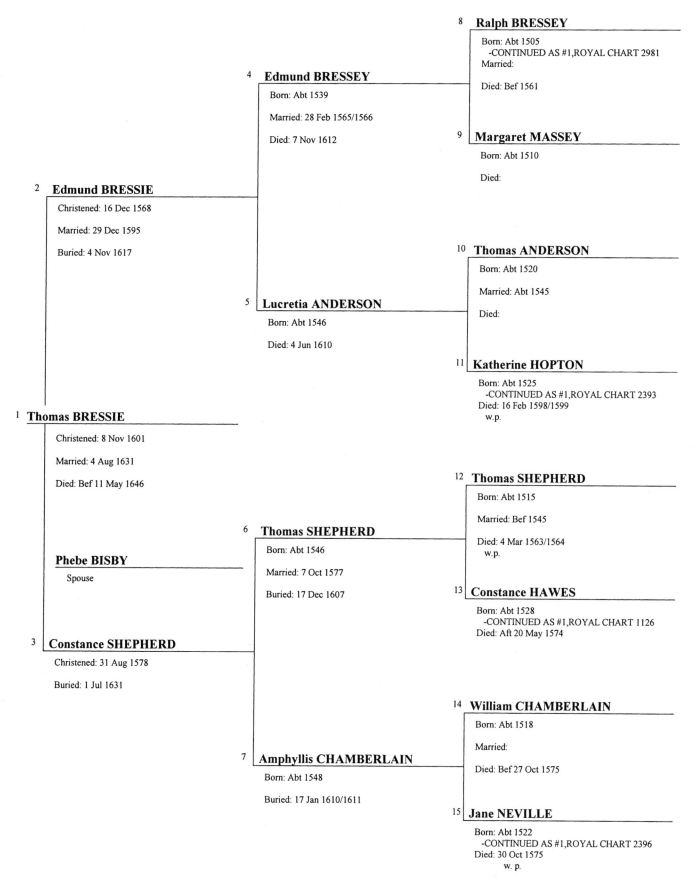

8 Ralph BRESSEY
Born: Abt 1505
-CONTINUED AS #1,ROYAL CHART 2981
Married:

Died: Bef 1561

4 Edmund BRESSEY
Born: Abt 1539

Married: 28 Feb 1565/1566

Died: 7 Nov 1612

9 Margaret MASSEY
Born: Abt 1510

Died:

2 Edmund BRESSIE
Christened: 16 Dec 1568

Married: 29 Dec 1595

Buried: 4 Nov 1617

10 Thomas ANDERSON
Born: Abt 1520

Married: Abt 1545

Died:

5 Lucretia ANDERSON
Born: Abt 1546

Died: 4 Jun 1610

11 Katherine HOPTON
Born: Abt 1525
-CONTINUED AS #1,ROYAL CHART 2393
Died: 16 Feb 1598/1599
w.p.

1 Thomas BRESSIE
Christened: 8 Nov 1601

Married: 4 Aug 1631

Died: Bef 11 May 1646

12 Thomas SHEPHERD
Born: Abt 1515

Married: Bef 1545

Died: 4 Mar 1563/1564
w.p.

6 Thomas SHEPHERD
Born: Abt 1546

Married: 7 Oct 1577

Buried: 17 Dec 1607

13 Constance HAWES
Born: Abt 1528
-CONTINUED AS #1,ROYAL CHART 1126
Died: Aft 20 May 1574

Phebe BISBY
Spouse

3 Constance SHEPHERD
Christened: 31 Aug 1578

Buried: 1 Jul 1631

14 William CHAMBERLAIN
Born: Abt 1518

Married:

Died: Bef 27 Oct 1575

7 Amphyllis CHAMBERLAIN
Born: Abt 1548

Buried: 17 Jan 1610/1611

15 Jane NEVILLE
Born: Abt 1522
-CONTINUED AS #1,ROYAL CHART 2396
Died: 30 Oct 1575
w. p.

Sources include: Richardson *Plantagenet* (2004), pp. 153-154 (Bressey), 649 (Sheppard); Roberts *600* (2004), pp. 403-404; Roberts *500*, pp. 334-335; *AAP*, p. 224; *Magna Charta* 122D. Note: #1--Bressie, Bressey, Bracy, Bracie; #7 & 14--Chamberlayne alias Spicer.

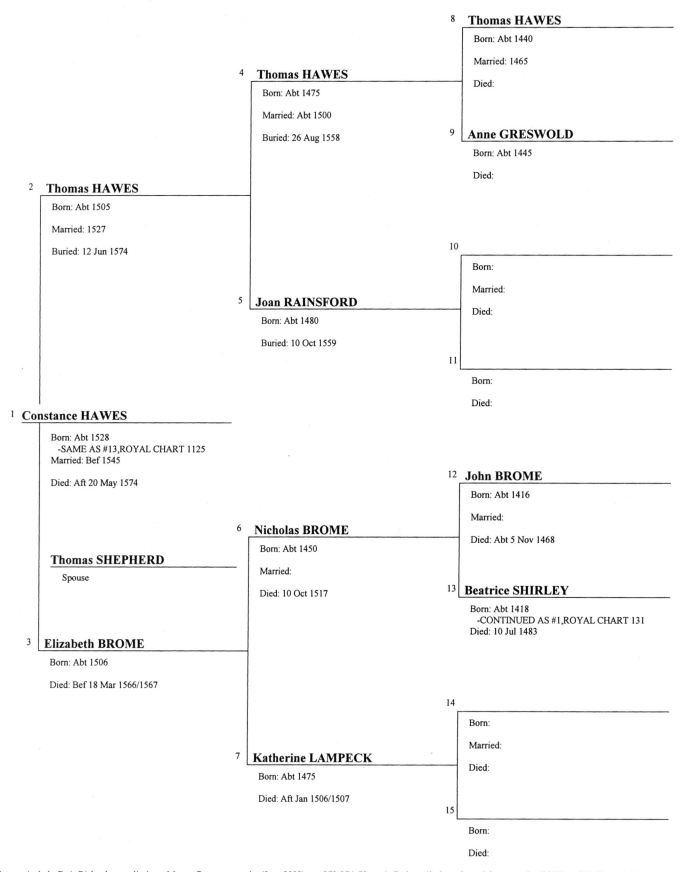

8 Thomas HAWES

Born: Abt 1440

Married: 1465

Died:

4 Thomas HAWES

Born: Abt 1475

Married: Abt 1500

Buried: 26 Aug 1558

9 Anne GRESWOLD

Born: Abt 1445

Died:

2 Thomas HAWES

Born: Abt 1505

Married: 1527

Buried: 12 Jun 1574

10

Born:

Married:

Died:

5 Joan RAINSFORD

Born: Abt 1480

Buried: 10 Oct 1559

11

Born:

Died:

1 Constance HAWES

Born: Abt 1528
-SAME AS #13,ROYAL CHART 1125
Married: Bef 1545

Died: Aft 20 May 1574

12 John BROME

Born: Abt 1416

Married:

Died: Abt 5 Nov 1468

6 Nicholas BROME

Born: Abt 1450

Married:

Died: 10 Oct 1517

Thomas SHEPHERD

Spouse

13 Beatrice SHIRLEY

Born: Abt 1418
-CONTINUED AS #1,ROYAL CHART 131
Died: 10 Jul 1483

3 Elizabeth BROME

Born: Abt 1506

Died: Bef 18 Mar 1566/1567

14

Born:

Married:

Died:

7 Katherine LAMPECK

Born: Abt 1475

Died: Aft Jan 1506/1507

15

Born:

Died:

Sources include: Faris-Richardson preliminary Magna Carta manuscript (June 2000), pp. 273-274 (Hawes); Faris preliminary baronial manuscript (1998), p. 840 (Hawes); *Magna Charta* 122D; Roberts *500*, pp. 334-335.

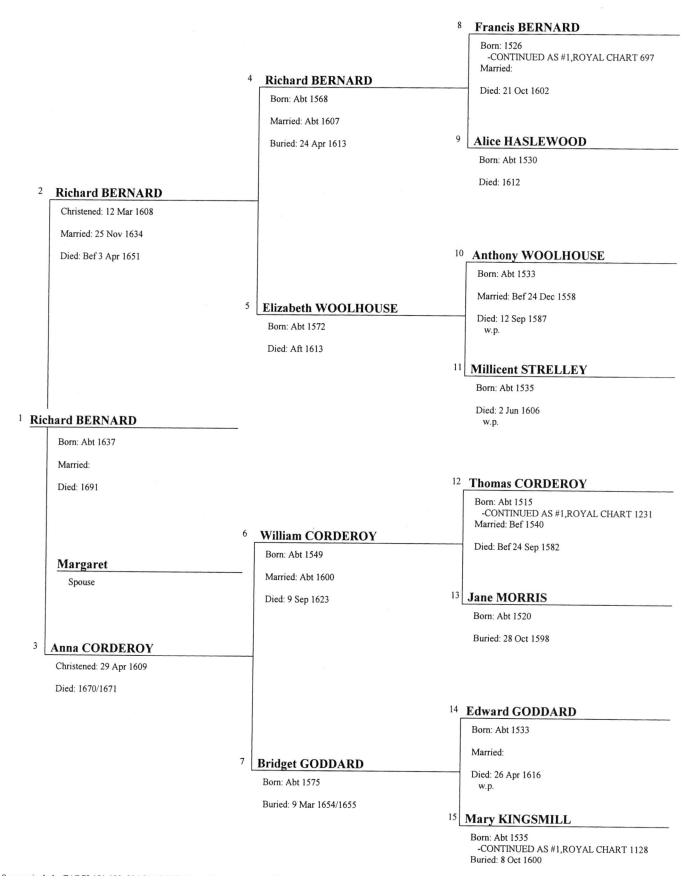

8 **Francis BERNARD**

Born: 1526
-CONTINUED AS #1, ROYAL CHART 697
Married:

Died: 21 Oct 1602

4 **Richard BERNARD**

Born: Abt 1568

Married: Abt 1607

Buried: 24 Apr 1613

9 **Alice HASLEWOOD**

Born: Abt 1530

Died: 1612

2 **Richard BERNARD**

Christened: 12 Mar 1608

Married: 25 Nov 1634

Died: Bef 3 Apr 1651

10 **Anthony WOOLHOUSE**

Born: Abt 1533

Married: Bef 24 Dec 1558

Died: 12 Sep 1587
w.p.

5 **Elizabeth WOOLHOUSE**

Born: Abt 1572

Died: Aft 1613

11 **Millicent STRELLEY**

Born: Abt 1535

Died: 2 Jun 1606
w.p.

1 **Richard BERNARD**

Born: Abt 1637

Married:

Died: 1691

12 **Thomas CORDEROY**

Born: Abt 1515
-CONTINUED AS #1, ROYAL CHART 1231
Married: Bef 1540

Died: Bef 24 Sep 1582

6 **William CORDEROY**

Born: Abt 1549

Married: Abt 1600

Died: 9 Sep 1623

13 **Jane MORRIS**

Born: Abt 1520

Buried: 28 Oct 1598

Margaret

Spouse

3 **Anna CORDEROY**

Christened: 29 Apr 1609

Died: 1670/1671

14 **Edward GODDARD**

Born: Abt 1533

Married:

Died: 26 Apr 1616
w.p.

7 **Bridget GODDARD**

Born: Abt 1575

Buried: 9 Mar 1654/1655

15 **Mary KINGSMILL**

Born: Abt 1535
-CONTINUED AS #1, ROYAL CHART 1128
Buried: 8 Oct 1600

Sources include: *TAG* 73:181-193, 294-311 (1998); Faris--Bernard; *Magna Charta* 46; Roberts *500*, pp. 382-384; MPGL 6606, 10132-34; LDS records; *Blood Royal* 5:285, 742-744.

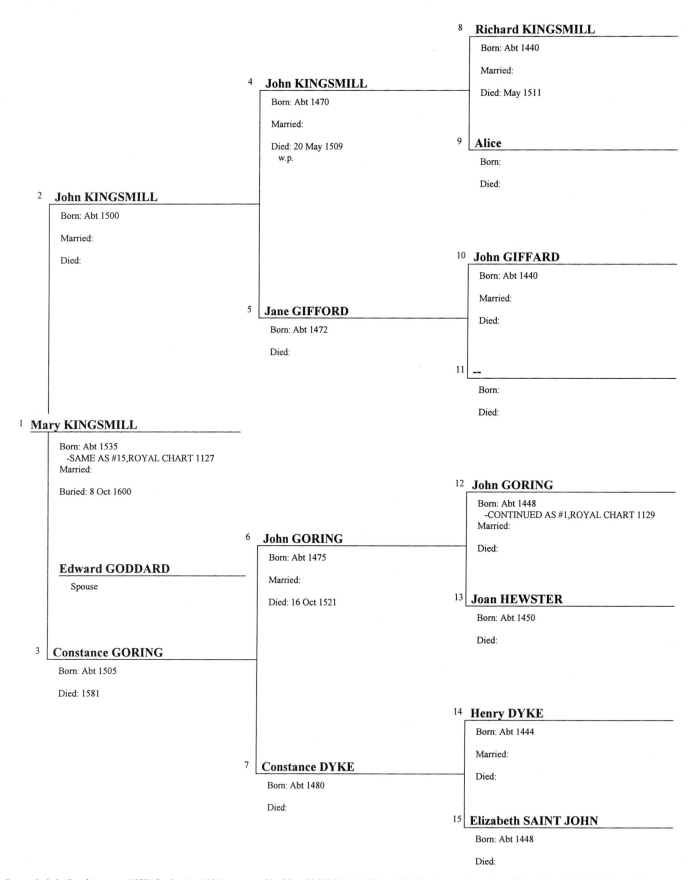

8 Richard KINGSMILL
Born: Abt 1440
Married:
Died: May 1511

4 John KINGSMILL
Born: Abt 1470
Married:
Died: 20 May 1509
w.p.

9 Alice
Born:
Died:

2 John KINGSMILL
Born: Abt 1500
Married:
Died:

10 John GIFFARD
Born: Abt 1440
Married:
Died:

5 Jane GIFFORD
Born: Abt 1472
Died:

11 --
Born:
Died:

1 Mary KINGSMILL
Born: Abt 1535
    -SAME AS #15,ROYAL CHART 1127
Married:
Buried: 8 Oct 1600

12 John GORING
Born: Abt 1448
    -CONTINUED AS #1,ROYAL CHART 1129
Married:
Died:

6 John GORING
Born: Abt 1475
Married:
Died: 16 Oct 1521

13 Joan HEWSTER
Born: Abt 1450
Died:

Edward GODDARD
Spouse

3 Constance GORING
Born: Abt 1505
Died: 1581

14 Henry DYKE
Born: Abt 1444
Married:
Died:

7 Constance DYKE
Born: Abt 1480
Died:

15 Elizabeth SAINT JOHN
Born: Abt 1448
Died:

Sources include: *Royal Ancestors* (1989), Section 1, p. 103 Ironmonger; *Blood Royal* 5:585; Roberts *500*, pp. 382-384; chart on descendants of John Giffard of Itchell; Faris preliminary baronial manuscript (1998), pp. 908 (Kingsmill), 722-723 (Goring).

Pedigree Chart

Chart 1129

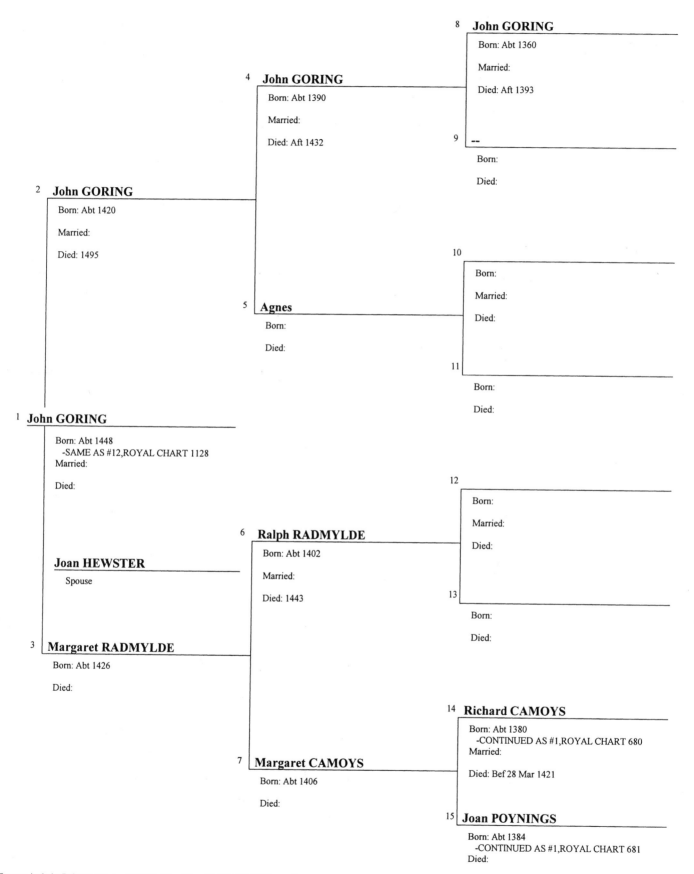

8   **John GORING**

Born: Abt 1360

Married:

Died: Aft 1393

4   **John GORING**

Born: Abt 1390

Married:

Died: Aft 1432

9   **--**

Born:

Died:

2   **John GORING**

Born: Abt 1420

Married:

Died: 1495

10

Born:

Married:

Died:

5   **Agnes**

Born:

Died:

11

Born:

Died:

1   **John GORING**

Born: Abt 1448
   -SAME AS #12,ROYAL CHART 1128
Married:

Died:

12

Born:

Married:

Died:

6   **Ralph RADMYLDE**

Born: Abt 1402

Married:

Died: 1443

13

Born:

Died:

Joan HEWSTER

Spouse

3   **Margaret RADMYLDE**

Born: Abt 1426

Died:

14   **Richard CAMOYS**

Born: Abt 1380
   -CONTINUED AS #1,ROYAL CHART 680
Married:

Died: Bef 28 Mar 1421

7   **Margaret CAMOYS**

Born: Abt 1406

Died:

15   **Joan POYNINGS**

Born: Abt 1384
   -CONTINUED AS #1,ROYAL CHART 681
Died:

Sources include: Roberts *500*, pp. 382-384; *Blood Royal* 5:582-585; LDS records.

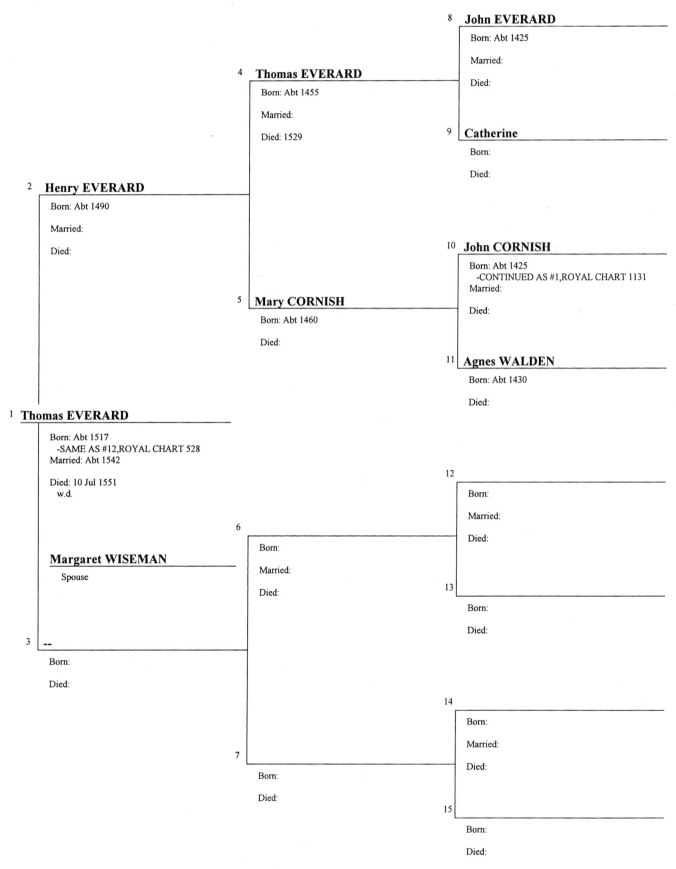

8 **John EVERARD**
Born: Abt 1425
Married:
Died:

4 **Thomas EVERARD**
Born: Abt 1455
Married:
Died: 1529

9 **Catherine**
Born:
Died:

2 **Henry EVERARD**
Born: Abt 1490
Married:
Died:

10 **John CORNISH**
Born: Abt 1425
　-CONTINUED AS #1,ROYAL CHART 1131
Married:
Died:

5 **Mary CORNISH**
Born: Abt 1460
Died:

11 **Agnes WALDEN**
Born: Abt 1430
Died:

1 **Thomas EVERARD**
Born: Abt 1517
　-SAME AS #12,ROYAL CHART 528
Married: Abt 1542
Died: 10 Jul 1551
　w.d.

Margaret WISEMAN
Spouse

12
Born:
Married:
Died:

6
Born:
Married:
Died:

13
Born:
Died:

3 **--**
Born:
Died:

14
Born:
Married:
Died:

7
Born:
Died:

15
Born:
Died:

Sources include: Roberts *500*, pp. 458-460; *AAP*, pp. 199-200; LDS records; Jacobus, *Granberry*, pp. 351-352.

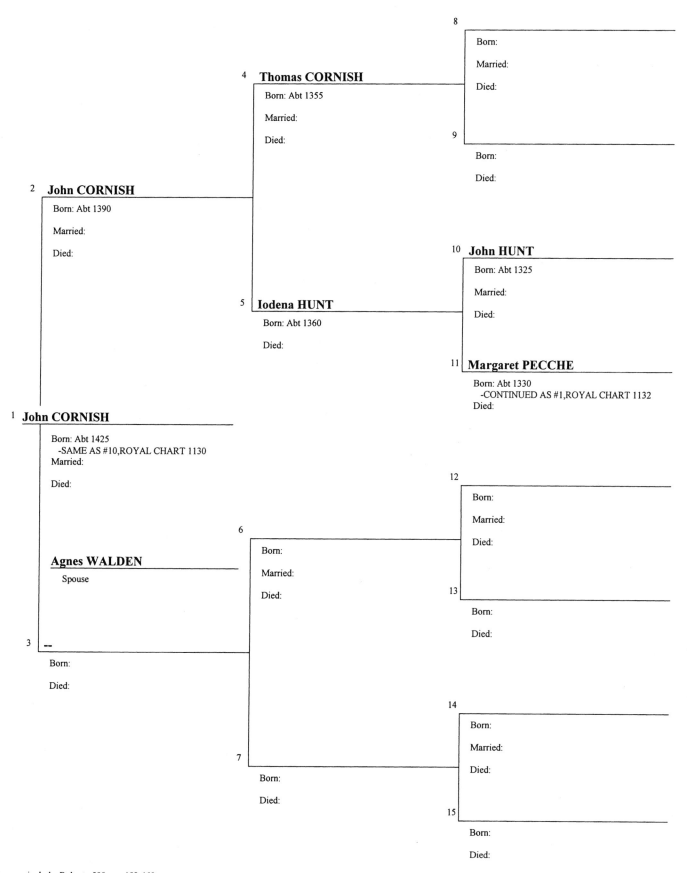

8

Born:

Married:

Died:

4   **Thomas CORNISH**

Born: Abt 1355

Married:

Died:

9

Born:

Died:

2   **John CORNISH**

Born: Abt 1390

Married:

Died:

10   **John HUNT**

Born: Abt 1325

Married:

Died:

5   **Iodena HUNT**

Born: Abt 1360

Died:

11   **Margaret PECCHE**

Born: Abt 1330
   -CONTINUED AS #1,ROYAL CHART 1132
Died:

1   **John CORNISH**

Born: Abt 1425
   -SAME AS #10,ROYAL CHART 1130
Married:

Died:

Agnes WALDEN

Spouse

12

Born:

Married:

Died:

6

Born:

Married:

Died:

13

Born:

Died:

3   **--**

Born:

Died:

14

Born:

Married:

Died:

7

Born:

Died:

15

Born:

Died:

Sources include: Roberts *500*, pp. 458-460.

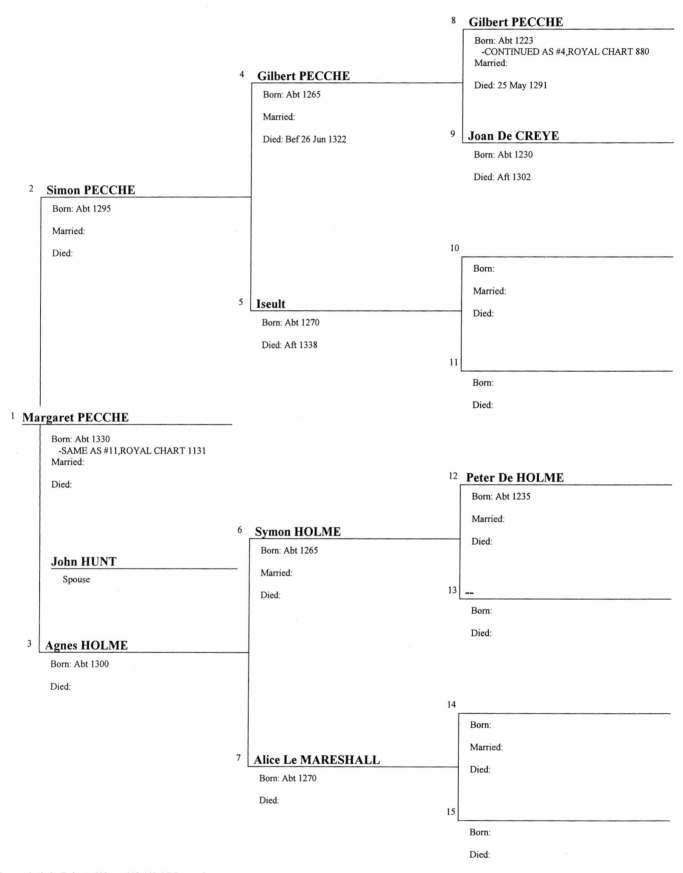

8 **Gilbert PECCHE**

Born: Abt 1223
 -CONTINUED AS #4,ROYAL CHART 880
Married:

Died: 25 May 1291

4 **Gilbert PECCHE**

Born: Abt 1265

Married:

Died: Bef 26 Jun 1322

9 **Joan De CREYE**

Born: Abt 1230

Died: Aft 1302

2 **Simon PECCHE**

Born: Abt 1295

Married:

Died:

10

Born:

Married:

Died:

5 **Iseult**

Born: Abt 1270

Died: Aft 1338

11

Born:

Died:

1 **Margaret PECCHE**

Born: Abt 1330
 -SAME AS #11,ROYAL CHART 1131
Married:

Died:

12 **Peter De HOLME**

Born: Abt 1235

Married:

Died:

John HUNT

Spouse

6 **Symon HOLME**

Born: Abt 1265

Married:

Died:

13 **--**

Born:

Died:

3 **Agnes HOLME**

Born: Abt 1300

Died:

14

Born:

Married:

Died:

7 **Alice Le MARESHALL**

Born: Abt 1270

Died:

15

Born:

Died:

Sources include: Roberts *500*, pp. 458-460; LDS records.

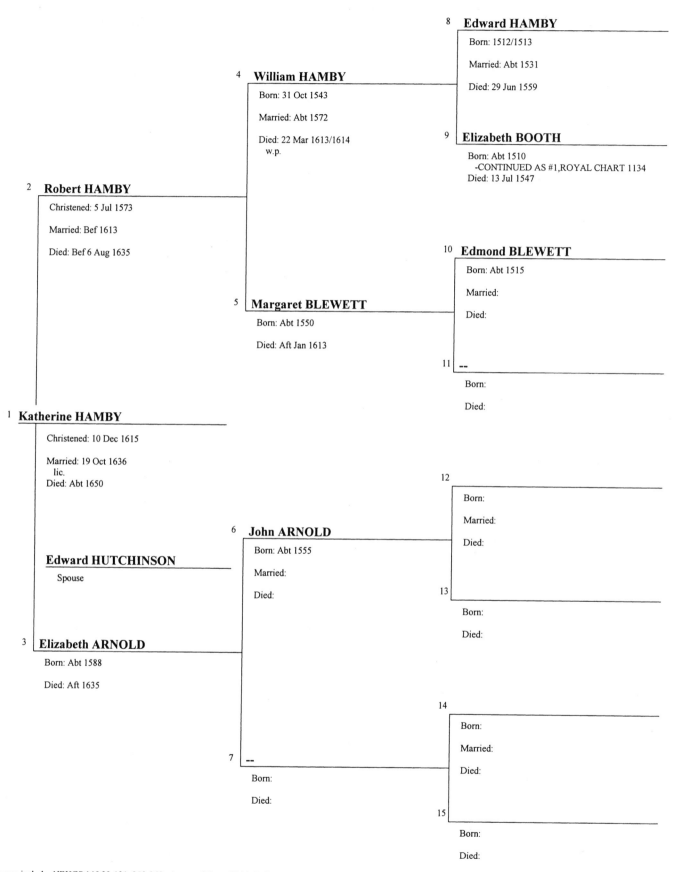

8 **Edward HAMBY**

Born: 1512/1513

Married: Abt 1531

Died: 29 Jun 1559

4 **William HAMBY**

Born: 31 Oct 1543

Married: Abt 1572

Died: 22 Mar 1613/1614
w.p.

9 **Elizabeth BOOTH**

Born: Abt 1510
-CONTINUED AS #1,ROYAL CHART 1134
Died: 13 Jul 1547

2 **Robert HAMBY**

Christened: 5 Jul 1573

Married: Bef 1613

Died: Bef 6 Aug 1635

10 **Edmond BLEWETT**

Born: Abt 1515

Married:

Died:

5 **Margaret BLEWETT**

Born: Abt 1550

Died: Aft Jan 1613

11 **--**

Born:

Died:

1 **Katherine HAMBY**

Christened: 10 Dec 1615

Married: 19 Oct 1636
lic.
Died: Abt 1650

12

Born:

Married:

Died:

6 **John ARNOLD**

Born: Abt 1555

Married:

Died:

13

Born:

Died:

Edward HUTCHINSON

Spouse

3 **Elizabeth ARNOLD**

Born: Abt 1588

Died: Aft 1635

14

Born:

Married:

Died:

7 **--**

Born:

Died:

15

Born:

Died:

Sources include: *NEHGR* 145:99-121, 258-268; *Ancestral Roots* 224A; Roberts *AAP*, p. 206. Note: Edward Hutchinson, husband of #1, was son of Anne Marbury, whose line is continued on chart 452.

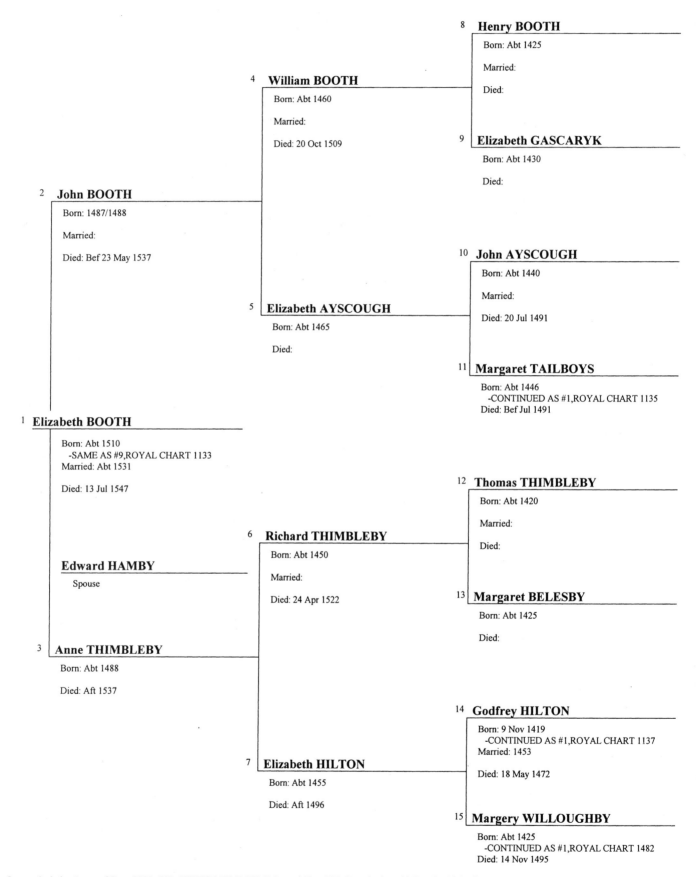

8 Henry BOOTH

Born: Abt 1425

Married:

Died:

4 William BOOTH

Born: Abt 1460

Married:

Died: 20 Oct 1509

9 Elizabeth GASCARYK

Born: Abt 1430

Died:

2 John BOOTH

Born: 1487/1488

Married:

Died: Bef 23 May 1537

10 John AYSCOUGH

Born: Abt 1440

Married:

Died: 20 Jul 1491

5 Elizabeth AYSCOUGH

Born: Abt 1465

Died:

11 Margaret TAILBOYS

Born: Abt 1446
  -CONTINUED AS #1,ROYAL CHART 1135
Died: Bef Jul 1491

1 Elizabeth BOOTH

Born: Abt 1510
  -SAME AS #9,ROYAL CHART 1133
Married: Abt 1531

Died: 13 Jul 1547

12 Thomas THIMBLEBY

Born: Abt 1420

Married:

Died:

6 Richard THIMBLEBY

Born: Abt 1450

Married:

Died: 24 Apr 1522

Edward HAMBY

Spouse

13 Margaret BELESBY

Born: Abt 1425

Died:

3 Anne THIMBLEBY

Born: Abt 1488

Died: Aft 1537

14 Godfrey HILTON

Born: 9 Nov 1419
  -CONTINUED AS #1,ROYAL CHART 1137
Married: 1453

Died: 18 May 1472

7 Elizabeth HILTON

Born: Abt 1455

Died: Aft 1496

15 Margery WILLOUGHBY

Born: Abt 1425
  -CONTINUED AS #1,ROYAL CHART 1482
Died: 14 Nov 1495

Sources include: *Ancestral Roots* 224A, 74A; *NEHGR* 145:265-268; Roberts *AAP*, p. 206; Consultation with Douglas Richardson.

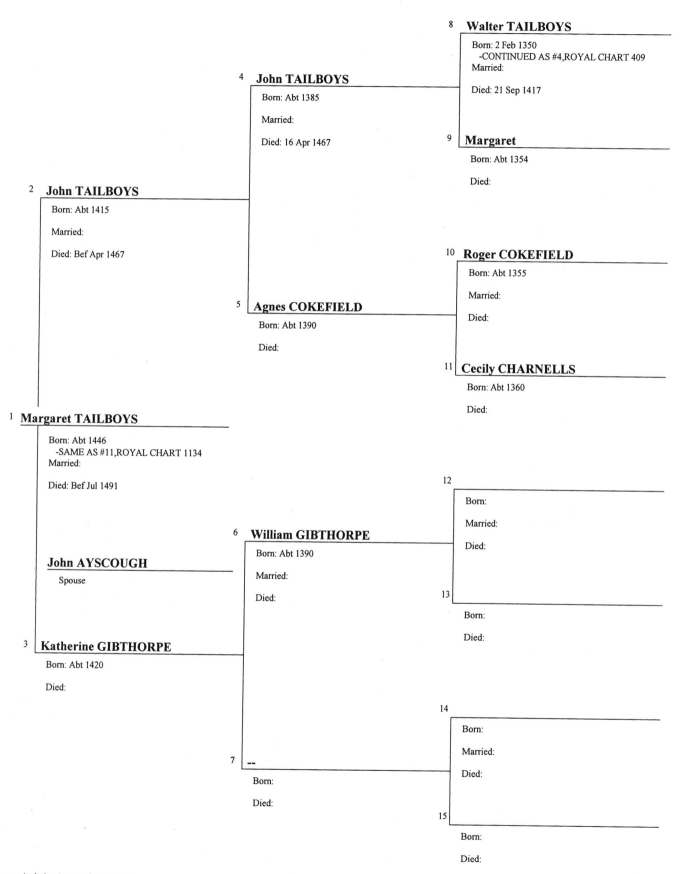

8 Walter TAILBOYS

Born: 2 Feb 1350
-CONTINUED AS #4, ROYAL CHART 409
Married:

Died: 21 Sep 1417

4 John TAILBOYS

Born: Abt 1385

Married:

Died: 16 Apr 1467

9 Margaret

Born: Abt 1354

Died:

2 John TAILBOYS

Born: Abt 1415

Married:

Died: Bef Apr 1467

10 Roger COKEFIELD

Born: Abt 1355

Married:

Died:

5 Agnes COKEFIELD

Born: Abt 1390

Died:

11 Cecily CHARNELLS

Born: Abt 1360

Died:

1 Margaret TAILBOYS

Born: Abt 1446
-SAME AS #11, ROYAL CHART 1134
Married:

Died: Bef Jul 1491

John AYSCOUGH

Spouse

12

Born:

Married:

Died:

6 William GIBTHORPE

Born: Abt 1390

Married:

Died:

13

Born:

Died:

3 Katherine GIBTHORPE

Born: Abt 1420

Died:

14

Born:

Married:

Died:

7 ---

Born:

Died:

15

Born:

Died:

Sources include: *Ancestral Roots* 224A.

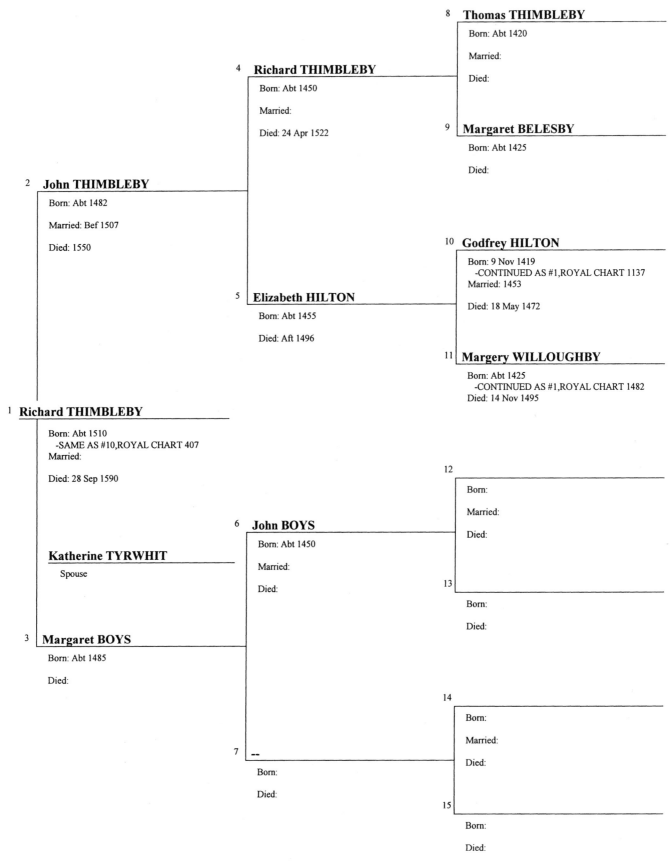

8 Thomas THIMBLEBY

Born: Abt 1420

Married:

Died:

4 Richard THIMBLEBY

Born: Abt 1450

Married:

Died: 24 Apr 1522

9 Margaret BELESBY

Born: Abt 1425

Died:

2 John THIMBLEBY

Born: Abt 1482

Married: Bef 1507

Died: 1550

10 Godfrey HILTON

Born: 9 Nov 1419
 -CONTINUED AS #1,ROYAL CHART 1137
Married: 1453

Died: 18 May 1472

5 Elizabeth HILTON

Born: Abt 1455

Died: Aft 1496

11 Margery WILLOUGHBY

Born: Abt 1425
 -CONTINUED AS #1,ROYAL CHART 1482
Died: 14 Nov 1495

1 Richard THIMBLEBY

Born: Abt 1510
 -SAME AS #10,ROYAL CHART 407
Married:

Died: 28 Sep 1590

12

Born:

Married:

Died:

6 John BOYS

Born: Abt 1450

Married:

Died:

13

Born:

Died:

Katherine TYRWHIT

Spouse

3 Margaret BOYS

Born: Abt 1485

Died:

14

Born:

Married:

Died:

7 --

Born:

Died:

15

Born:

Died:

Sources include: Consultation with Douglas Richardson; LDS records; *Ancestral Roots* 74A (#5 ancestry).

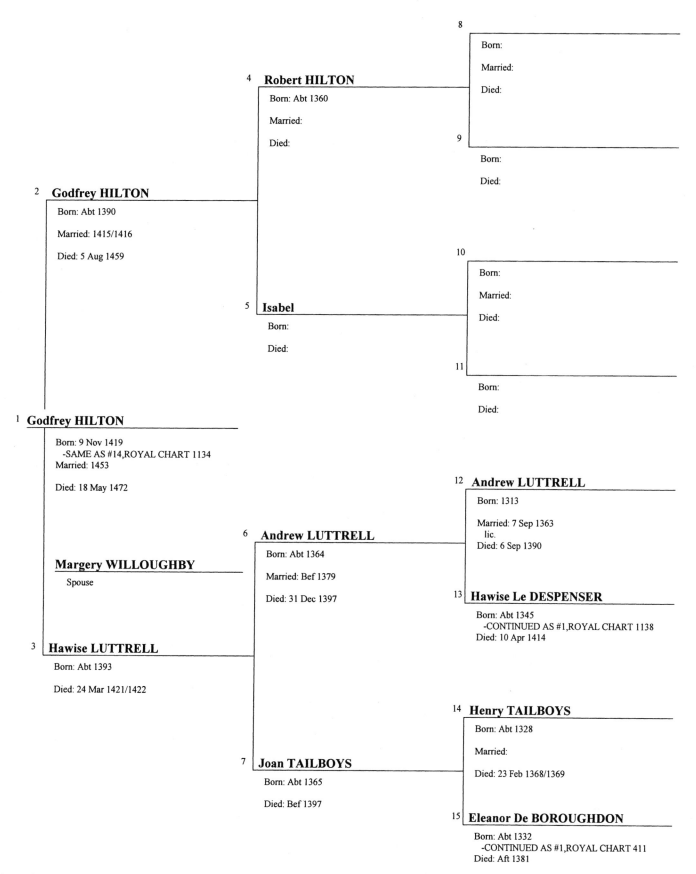

8

Born:

Married:

Died:

4 | **Robert HILTON**

Born: Abt 1360

Married:

Died:

9

Born:

Died:

2 | **Godfrey HILTON**

Born: Abt 1390

Married: 1415/1416

Died: 5 Aug 1459

10

Born:

Married:

Died:

5 | **Isabel**

Born:

Died:

11

Born:

Died:

1 | **Godfrey HILTON**

Born: 9 Nov 1419
  -SAME AS #14,ROYAL CHART 1134
Married: 1453

Died: 18 May 1472

12 | **Andrew LUTTRELL**

Born: 1313

Married: 7 Sep 1363
lic.
Died: 6 Sep 1390

6 | **Andrew LUTTRELL**

Born: Abt 1364

Married: Bef 1379

Died: 31 Dec 1397

13 | **Hawise Le DESPENSER**

Born: Abt 1345
  -CONTINUED AS #1,ROYAL CHART 1138
Died: 10 Apr 1414

Margery WILLOUGHBY

Spouse

3 | **Hawise LUTTRELL**

Born: Abt 1393

Died: 24 Mar 1421/1422

14 | **Henry TAILBOYS**

Born: Abt 1328

Married:

Died: 23 Feb 1368/1369

7 | **Joan TAILBOYS**

Born: Abt 1365

Died: Bef 1397

15 | **Eleanor De BOROUGHDON**

Born: Abt 1332
  -CONTINUED AS #1,ROYAL CHART 411
Died: Aft 1381

Sources include: *Ancestral Roots* 74A; Roberts *AAP*, p. 206; Consultation with Douglas Richardson.

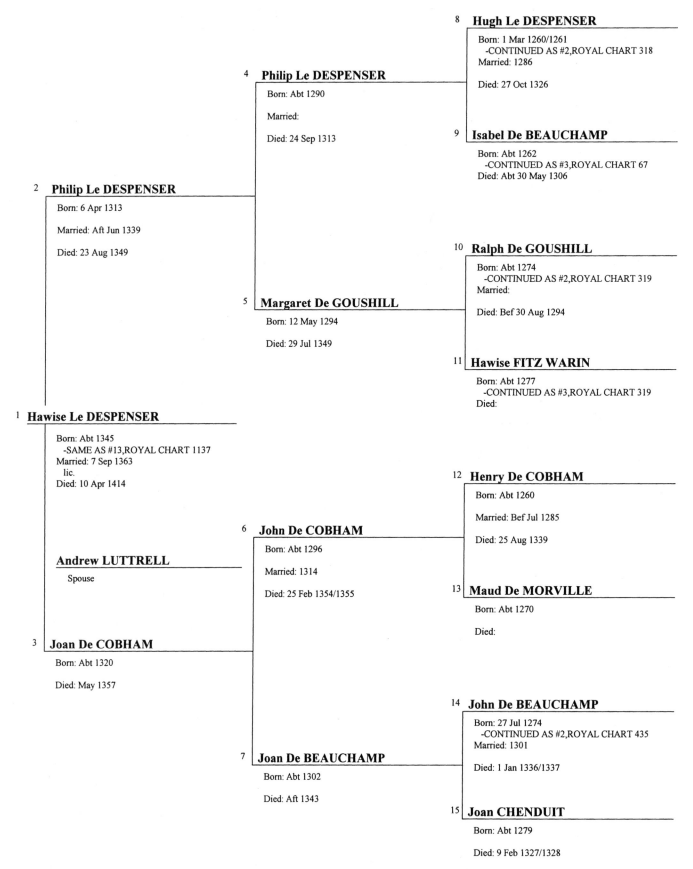

Pedigree Chart Chart 1138

8 **Hugh Le DESPENSER**
Born: 1 Mar 1260/1261
-CONTINUED AS #2,ROYAL CHART 318
Married: 1286
Died: 27 Oct 1326

4 **Philip Le DESPENSER**
Born: Abt 1290
Married:
Died: 24 Sep 1313

9 **Isabel De BEAUCHAMP**
Born: Abt 1262
-CONTINUED AS #3,ROYAL CHART 67
Died: Abt 30 May 1306

2 **Philip Le DESPENSER**
Born: 6 Apr 1313
Married: Aft Jun 1339
Died: 23 Aug 1349

10 **Ralph De GOUSHILL**
Born: Abt 1274
-CONTINUED AS #2,ROYAL CHART 319
Married:
Died: Bef 30 Aug 1294

5 **Margaret De GOUSHILL**
Born: 12 May 1294
Died: 29 Jul 1349

11 **Hawise FITZ WARIN**
Born: Abt 1277
-CONTINUED AS #3,ROYAL CHART 319
Died:

1 **Hawise Le DESPENSER**
Born: Abt 1345
-SAME AS #13,ROYAL CHART 1137
Married: 7 Sep 1363
lic.
Died: 10 Apr 1414

12 **Henry De COBHAM**
Born: Abt 1260
Married: Bef Jul 1285
Died: 25 Aug 1339

6 **John De COBHAM**
Born: Abt 1296
Married: 1314
Died: 25 Feb 1354/1355

Andrew LUTTRELL
Spouse

13 **Maud De MORVILLE**
Born: Abt 1270
Died:

3 **Joan De COBHAM**
Born: Abt 1320
Died: May 1357

14 **John De BEAUCHAMP**
Born: 27 Jul 1274
-CONTINUED AS #2,ROYAL CHART 435
Married: 1301
Died: 1 Jan 1336/1337

7 **Joan De BEAUCHAMP**
Born: Abt 1302
Died: Aft 1343

15 **Joan CHENDUIT**
Born: Abt 1279
Died: 9 Feb 1327/1328

Sources include: *Ancestral Roots* 74A; *NEHGR* 145:268; Faris preliminary baronial manuscript (1998), pp. 381-382 (Cobham); Consultation with Douglas Richardson.

Pedigree Chart

Chart 1139

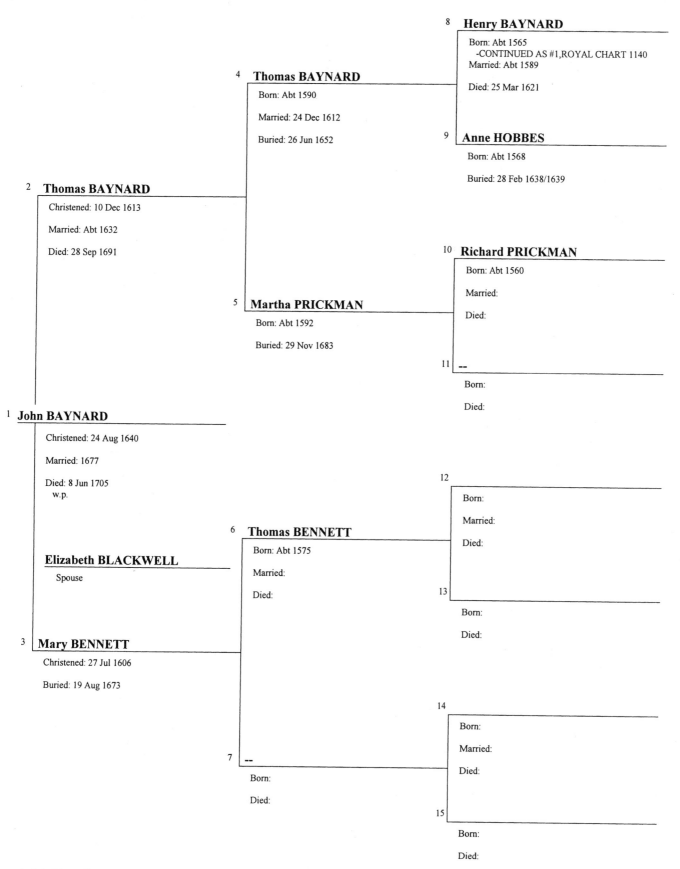

8   **Henry BAYNARD**

Born: Abt 1565
  -CONTINUED AS #1,ROYAL CHART 1140
Married: Abt 1589

Died: 25 Mar 1621

4   **Thomas BAYNARD**

Born: Abt 1590

Married: 24 Dec 1612

Buried: 26 Jun 1652

9   **Anne HOBBES**

Born: Abt 1568

Buried: 28 Feb 1638/1639

2   **Thomas BAYNARD**

Christened: 10 Dec 1613

Married: Abt 1632

Died: 28 Sep 1691

10   **Richard PRICKMAN**

Born: Abt 1560

Married:

Died:

5   **Martha PRICKMAN**

Born: Abt 1592

Buried: 29 Nov 1683

11   **--**

Born:

Died:

1   **John BAYNARD**

Christened: 24 Aug 1640

Married: 1677

Died: 8 Jun 1705
  w.p.

Elizabeth BLACKWELL
   Spouse

12

Born:

Married:

Died:

6   **Thomas BENNETT**

Born: Abt 1575

Married:

Died:

13

Born:

Died:

3   **Mary BENNETT**

Christened: 27 Jul 1606

Buried: 19 Aug 1673

14

Born:

Married:

Died:

7   **--**

Born:

Died:

15

Born:

Died:

Sources include: *Magna Charta* 90A; Roberts *500*, pp. 345-347.

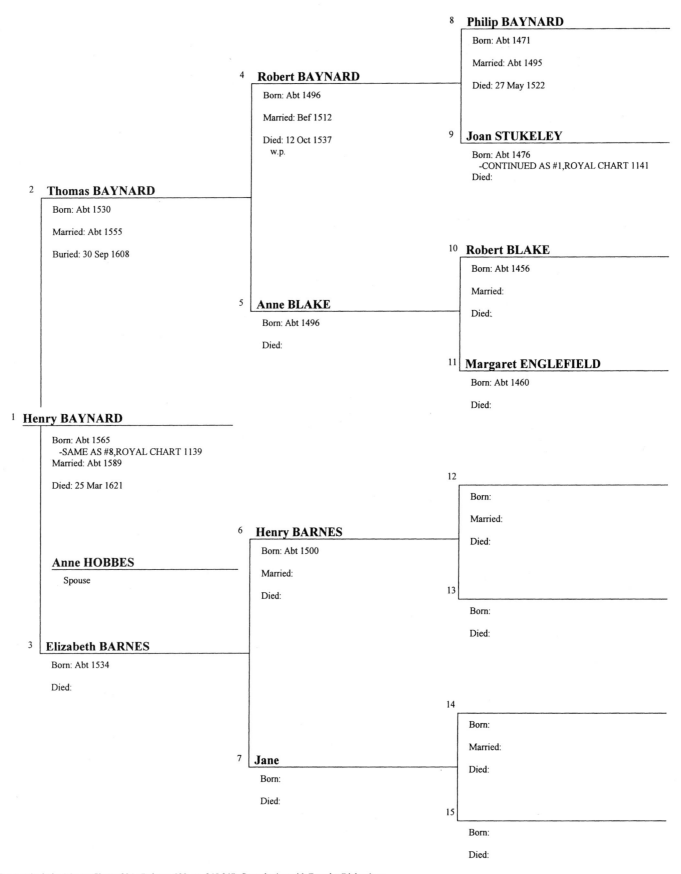

8 Philip BAYNARD

Born: Abt 1471

Married: Abt 1495

Died: 27 May 1522

4 Robert BAYNARD

Born: Abt 1496

Married: Bef 1512

Died: 12 Oct 1537
w.p.

9 Joan STUKELEY

Born: Abt 1476
 -CONTINUED AS #1, ROYAL CHART 1141
Died:

2 Thomas BAYNARD

Born: Abt 1530

Married: Abt 1555

Buried: 30 Sep 1608

10 Robert BLAKE

Born: Abt 1456

Married:

Died:

5 Anne BLAKE

Born: Abt 1496

Died:

11 Margaret ENGLEFIELD

Born: Abt 1460

Died:

1 Henry BAYNARD

Born: Abt 1565
 -SAME AS #8, ROYAL CHART 1139
Married: Abt 1589

Died: 25 Mar 1621

12

Born:

Married:

Died:

6 Henry BARNES

Born: Abt 1500

Married:

Died:

Anne HOBBES

Spouse

13

Born:

Died:

3 Elizabeth BARNES

Born: Abt 1534

Died:

14

Born:

Married:

Died:

7 Jane

Born:

Died:

15

Born:

Died:

Sources include: *Magna Charta* 90A; Roberts *500*, pp. 345-347; Consultation with Douglas Richardson.

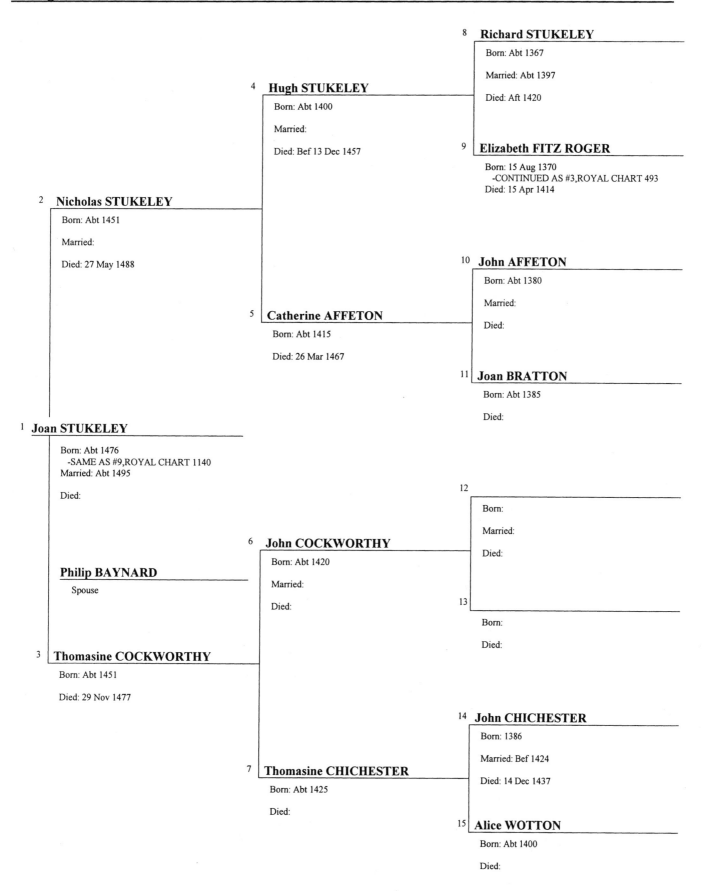

8 Richard STUKELEY

Born: Abt 1367

Married: Abt 1397

Died: Aft 1420

4 Hugh STUKELEY

Born: Abt 1400

Married:

Died: Bef 13 Dec 1457

9 Elizabeth FITZ ROGER

Born: 15 Aug 1370
  -CONTINUED AS #3,ROYAL CHART 493
Died: 15 Apr 1414

2 Nicholas STUKELEY

Born: Abt 1451

Married:

Died: 27 May 1488

10 John AFFETON

Born: Abt 1380

Married:

Died:

5 Catherine AFFETON

Born: Abt 1415

Died: 26 Mar 1467

11 Joan BRATTON

Born: Abt 1385

Died:

1 Joan STUKELEY

Born: Abt 1476
  -SAME AS #9,ROYAL CHART 1140
Married: Abt 1495

Died:

12

Born:

Married:

Died:

6 John COCKWORTHY

Born: Abt 1420

Married:

Died:

13

Born:

Died:

Philip BAYNARD

Spouse

3 Thomasine COCKWORTHY

Born: Abt 1451

Died: 29 Nov 1477

14 John CHICHESTER

Born: 1386

Married: Bef 1424

Died: 14 Dec 1437

7 Thomasine CHICHESTER

Born: Abt 1425

Died:

15 Alice WOTTON

Born: Abt 1400

Died:

Sources include: Faris preliminary baronial manuscript (1998), pp. 1471-72 (Stukeley), 340 (Chichester); *Magna Charta* 90A; *Ancestral Roots* 261; Roberts *500*, pp. 345-347.

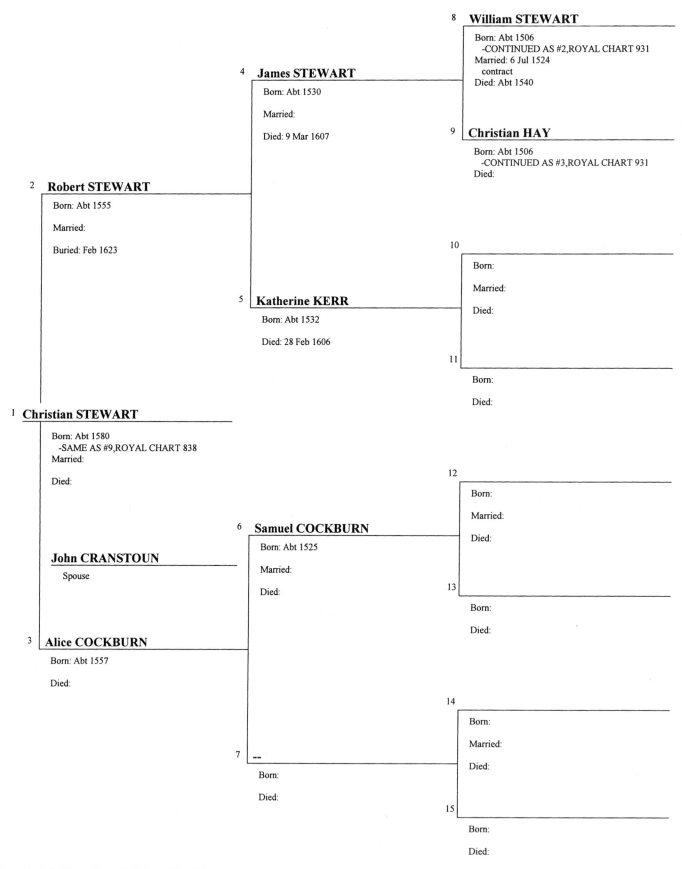

8 **William STEWART**

Born: Abt 1506
-CONTINUED AS #2,ROYAL CHART 931
Married: 6 Jul 1524
contract
Died: Abt 1540

4 **James STEWART**

Born: Abt 1530

Married:

Died: 9 Mar 1607

9 **Christian HAY**

Born: Abt 1506
-CONTINUED AS #3,ROYAL CHART 931
Died:

2 **Robert STEWART**

Born: Abt 1555

Married:

Buried: Feb 1623

10

Born:

Married:

Died:

5 **Katherine KERR**

Born: Abt 1532

Died: 28 Feb 1606

11

Born:

Died:

1 **Christian STEWART**

Born: Abt 1580
-SAME AS #9,ROYAL CHART 838
Married:

Died:

12

Born:

Married:

Died:

6 **Samuel COCKBURN**

Born: Abt 1525

Married:

Died:

John CRANSTOUN

Spouse

13

Born:

Died:

3 **Alice COCKBURN**

Born: Abt 1557

Died:

14

Born:

Married:

Died:

7 **--**

Born:

Died:

15

Born:

Died:

Sources include: *Magna Charta* 41; Roberts *500*, p. 111.

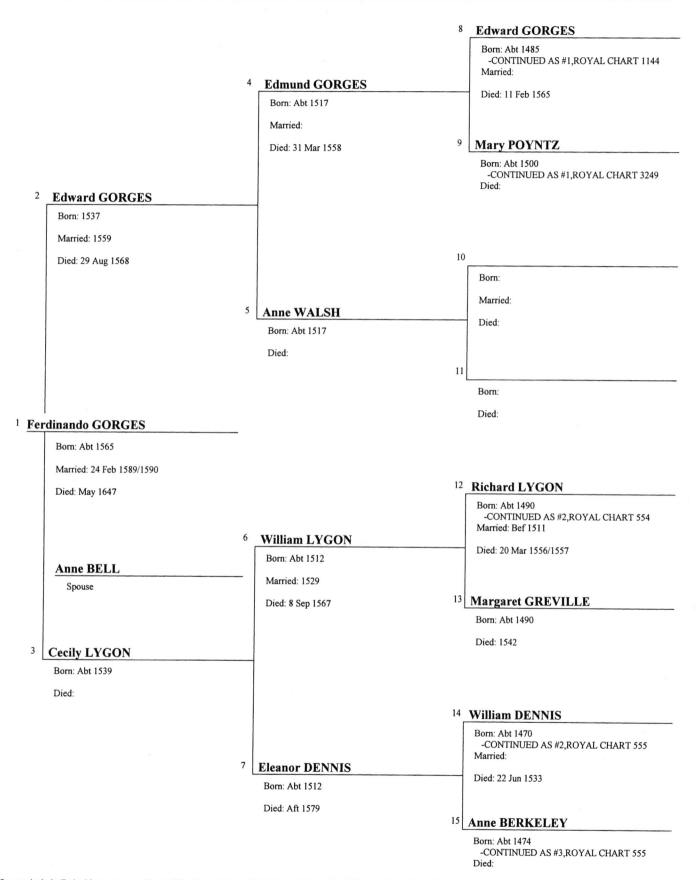

8 **Edward GORGES**
Born: Abt 1485
 -CONTINUED AS #1,ROYAL CHART 1144
Married:

Died: 11 Feb 1565

4 **Edmund GORGES**
Born: Abt 1517

Married:

Died: 31 Mar 1558

9 **Mary POYNTZ**
Born: Abt 1500
 -CONTINUED AS #1,ROYAL CHART 3249
Died:

2 **Edward GORGES**
Born: 1537

Married: 1559

Died: 29 Aug 1568

10
Born:

Married:

Died:

5 **Anne WALSH**
Born: Abt 1517

Died:

11
Born:

Died:

1 **Ferdinando GORGES**
Born: Abt 1565

Married: 24 Feb 1589/1590

Died: May 1647

12 **Richard LYGON**
Born: Abt 1490
 -CONTINUED AS #2,ROYAL CHART 554
Married: Bef 1511

Died: 20 Mar 1556/1557

6 **William LYGON**
Born: Abt 1512

Married: 1529

Died: 8 Sep 1567

13 **Margaret GREVILLE**
Born: Abt 1490

Died: 1542

Anne BELL
Spouse

3 **Cecily LYGON**
Born: Abt 1539

Died:

14 **William DENNIS**
Born: Abt 1470
 -CONTINUED AS #2,ROYAL CHART 555
Married:

Died: 22 Jun 1533

7 **Eleanor DENNIS**
Born: Abt 1512

Died: Aft 1579

15 **Anne BERKELEY**
Born: Abt 1474
 -CONTINUED AS #3,ROYAL CHART 555
Died:

Sources include: Faris--Ligon; *Ancestral Roots* 209; *Magna Charta* 29; Roberts *500*, pp. 204-206, 244. Note: See Bell in Appendix for a royal line for Anne Bell, first wife of #1. Roberts *500*, pp. 163, 244 gives royal descents for the other three wives of #1.

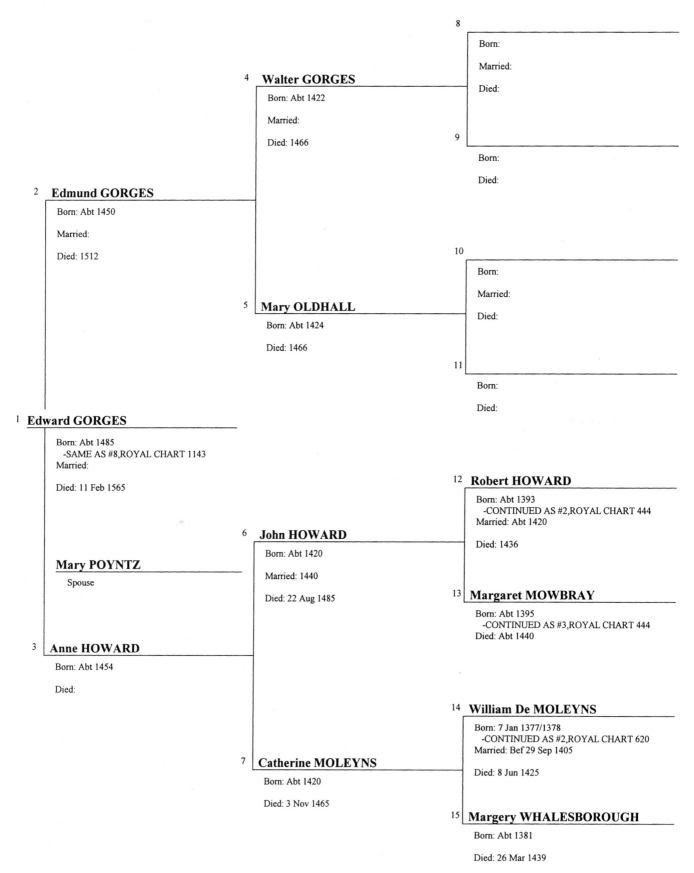

8

Born:

Married:

Died:

4 Walter GORGES

Born: Abt 1422

Married:

Died: 1466

9

Born:

Died:

2 Edmund GORGES

Born: Abt 1450

Married:

Died: 1512

10

Born:

Married:

Died:

5 Mary OLDHALL

Born: Abt 1424

Died: 1466

11

Born:

Died:

1 Edward GORGES

Born: Abt 1485
  -SAME AS #8,ROYAL CHART 1143
Married:

Died: 11 Feb 1565

12 Robert HOWARD

Born: Abt 1393
  -CONTINUED AS #2,ROYAL CHART 444
Married: Abt 1420

Died: 1436

6 John HOWARD

Born: Abt 1420

Married: 1440

Died: 22 Aug 1485

13 Margaret MOWBRAY

Born: Abt 1395
  -CONTINUED AS #3,ROYAL CHART 444
Died: Abt 1440

Mary POYNTZ

Spouse

3 Anne HOWARD

Born: Abt 1454

Died:

14 William De MOLEYNS

Born: 7 Jan 1377/1378
  -CONTINUED AS #2,ROYAL CHART 620
Married: Bef 29 Sep 1405

Died: 8 Jun 1425

7 Catherine MOLEYNS

Born: Abt 1420

Died: 3 Nov 1465

15 Margery WHALESBOROUGH

Born: Abt 1381

Died: 26 Mar 1439

Sources include: Roberts *500*, p. 244; LDS records.

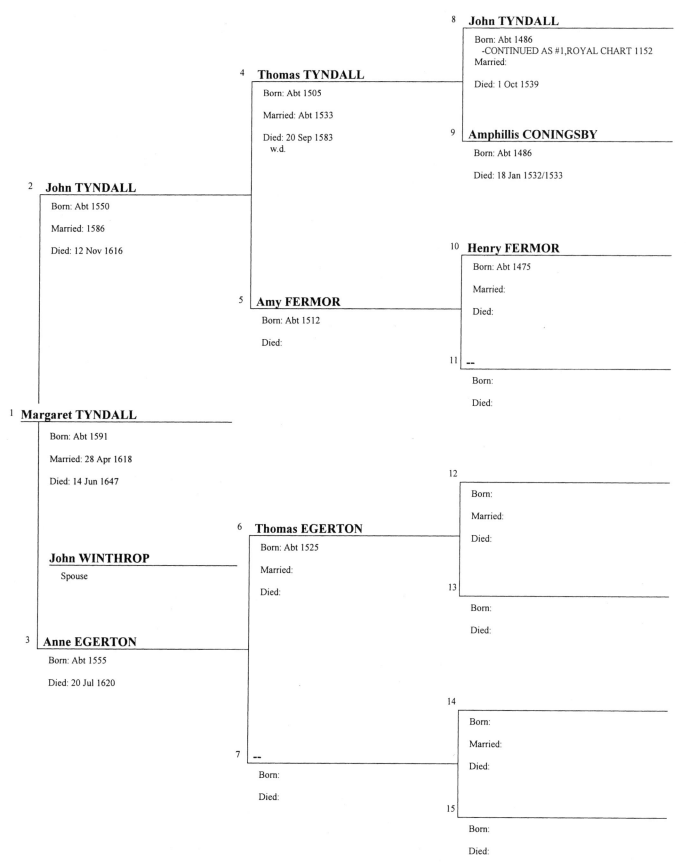

8 **John TYNDALL**

Born: Abt 1486
-CONTINUED AS #1, ROYAL CHART 1152
Married:

Died: 1 Oct 1539

4 **Thomas TYNDALL**

Born: Abt 1505

Married: Abt 1533

Died: 20 Sep 1583
w.d.

9 **Amphillis CONINGSBY**

Born: Abt 1486

Died: 18 Jan 1532/1533

2 **John TYNDALL**

Born: Abt 1550

Married: 1586

Died: 12 Nov 1616

10 **Henry FERMOR**

Born: Abt 1475

Married:

Died:

5 **Amy FERMOR**

Born: Abt 1512

Died:

11 **--**

Born:

Died:

1 **Margaret TYNDALL**

Born: Abt 1591

Married: 28 Apr 1618

Died: 14 Jun 1647

12

Born:

Married:

Died:

6 **Thomas EGERTON**

Born: Abt 1525

Married:

Died:

13

Born:

Died:

John WINTHROP

Spouse

3 **Anne EGERTON**

Born: Abt 1555

Died: 20 Jul 1620

14

Born:

Married:

Died:

7 **--**

Born:

Died:

15

Born:

Died:

Sources include: Richardson *Magna Carta* (April 2005), pp. 848-849 (Tyndall); Faris preliminary baronial manuscript (1998), pp. 1557-58 (Tyndal); *Ancestral Roots* 232; Roberts *500*, pp. 427-428. Note: The children of #1 Margaret include Deane Winthrop (chr. 23 Mar 1622-23; md. Sarah Glover).

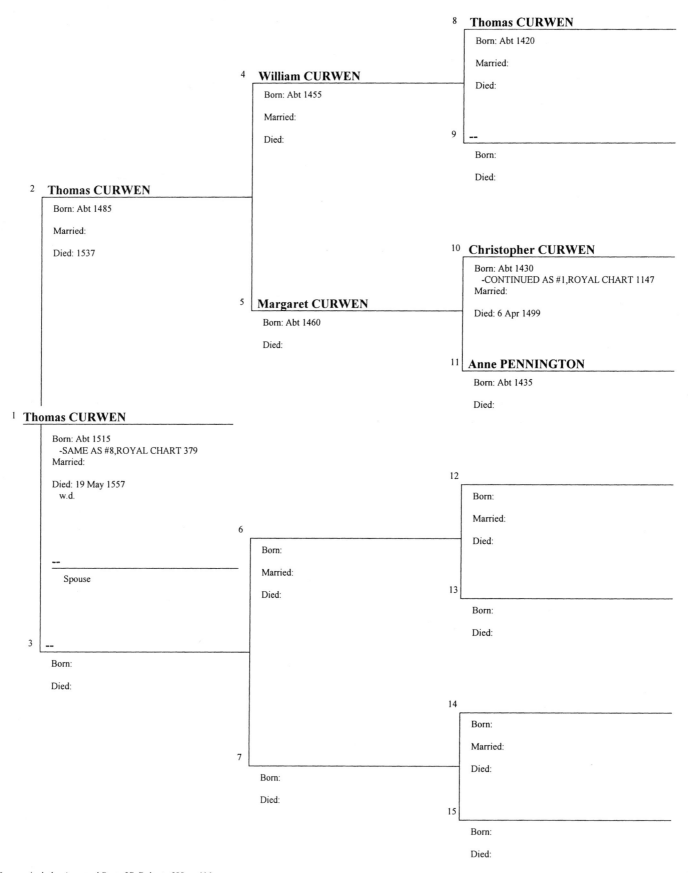

8 **Thomas CURWEN**
Born: Abt 1420
Married:
Died:

4 **William CURWEN**
Born: Abt 1455
Married:
Died:

9 --
Born:
Died:

2 **Thomas CURWEN**
Born: Abt 1485
Married:
Died: 1537

10 **Christopher CURWEN**
Born: Abt 1430
-CONTINUED AS #1,ROYAL CHART 1147
Married:
Died: 6 Apr 1499

5 **Margaret CURWEN**
Born: Abt 1460
Died:

11 **Anne PENNINGTON**
Born: Abt 1435
Died:

1 **Thomas CURWEN**
Born: Abt 1515
-SAME AS #8,ROYAL CHART 379
Married:
Died: 19 May 1557
w.d.

-- Spouse

12
Born:
Married:
Died:

6
Born:
Married:
Died:

13
Born:
Died:

3 --
Born:
Died:

14
Born:
Married:
Died:

7
Born:
Died:

15
Born:
Died:

Sources include: *Ancestral Roots* 37; Roberts *500*, p. 416.

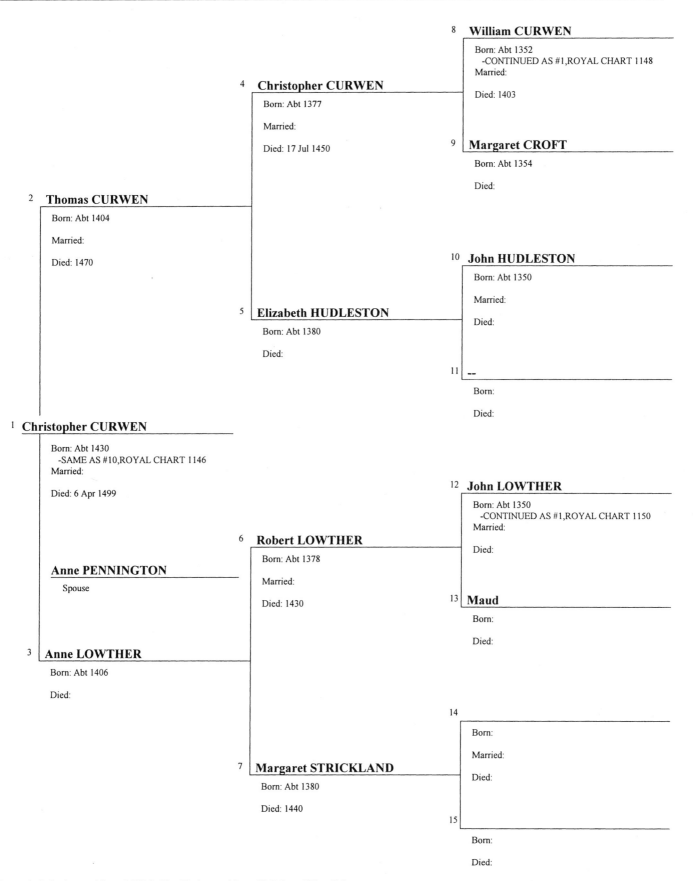

8 **William CURWEN**

Born: Abt 1352
-CONTINUED AS #1,ROYAL CHART 1148
Married:

Died: 1403

4 **Christopher CURWEN**

Born: Abt 1377

Married:

Died: 17 Jul 1450

9 **Margaret CROFT**

Born: Abt 1354

Died:

2 **Thomas CURWEN**

Born: Abt 1404

Married:

Died: 1470

10 **John HUDLESTON**

Born: Abt 1350

Married:

Died:

5 **Elizabeth HUDLESTON**

Born: Abt 1380

Died:

11 **--**

Born:

Died:

1 **Christopher CURWEN**

Born: Abt 1430
-SAME AS #10,ROYAL CHART 1146
Married:

Died: 6 Apr 1499

12 **John LOWTHER**

Born: Abt 1350
-CONTINUED AS #1,ROYAL CHART 1150
Married:

Died:

6 **Robert LOWTHER**

Born: Abt 1378

Married:

Died: 1430

13 **Maud**

Born:

Died:

Anne PENNINGTON

Spouse

3 **Anne LOWTHER**

Born: Abt 1406

Died:

14

Born:

Married:

Died:

7 **Margaret STRICKLAND**

Born: Abt 1380

Died: 1440

15

Born:

Died:

Sources include: *Ancestral Roots* 8 (2004), Line 37; *Ancestral Roots* 37; Roberts *500*, p. 416.

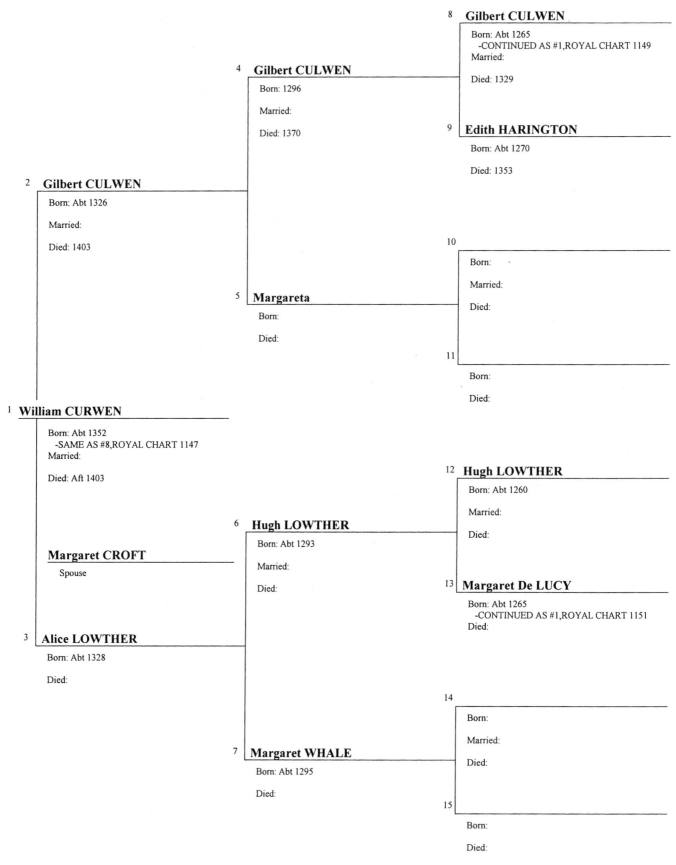

8 Gilbert CULWEN

Born: Abt 1265
-CONTINUED AS #1,ROYAL CHART 1149
Married:

Died: 1329

4 Gilbert CULWEN

Born: 1296

Married:

Died: 1370

9 Edith HARINGTON

Born: Abt 1270

Died: 1353

2 Gilbert CULWEN

Born: Abt 1326

Married:

Died: 1403

10

Born:

Married:

Died:

5 Margareta

Born:

Died:

11

Born:

Died:

1 William CURWEN

Born: Abt 1352
-SAME AS #8,ROYAL CHART 1147
Married:

Died: Aft 1403

Margaret CROFT

Spouse

12 Hugh LOWTHER

Born: Abt 1260

Married:

Died:

6 Hugh LOWTHER

Born: Abt 1293

Married:

Died:

13 Margaret De LUCY

Born: Abt 1265
-CONTINUED AS #1,ROYAL CHART 1151
Died:

3 Alice LOWTHER

Born: Abt 1328

Died:

14

Born:

Married:

Died:

7 Margaret WHALE

Born: Abt 1295

Died:

15

Born:

Died:

Sources include: *Ancestral Roots* 8 (2004), Line 37; *Ancestral Roots* 37; Roberts *500*, p. 416.

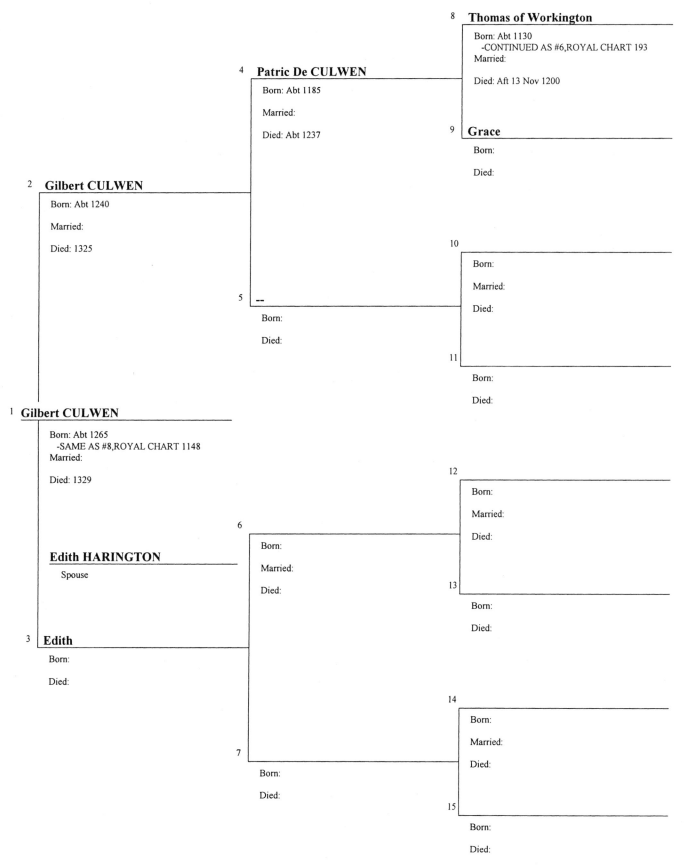

8 Thomas of Workington

Born: Abt 1130
   -CONTINUED AS #6,ROYAL CHART 193
Married:

Died: Aft 13 Nov 1200

4 Patric De CULWEN

Born: Abt 1185

Married:

Died: Abt 1237

9 Grace

Born:

Died:

2 Gilbert CULWEN

Born: Abt 1240

Married:

Died: 1325

10

Born:

Married:

Died:

5 --

Born:

Died:

11

Born:

Died:

1 Gilbert CULWEN

Born: Abt 1265
   -SAME AS #8,ROYAL CHART 1148
Married:

Died: 1329

12

Born:

Married:

Died:

6

Born:

Married:

Died:

13

Born:

Died:

Edith HARINGTON

Spouse

3 Edith

Born:

Died:

14

Born:

Married:

Died:

7

Born:

Died:

15

Born:

Died:

Sources include: *Ancestral Roots* 8 (2004), Line 37; *Ancestral Roots* 37.

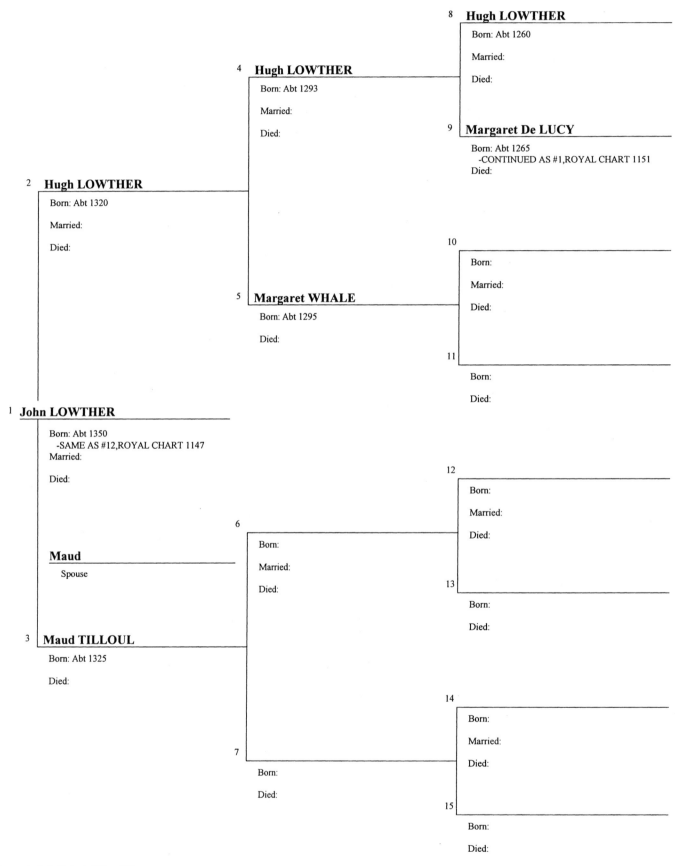

8 Hugh LOWTHER
Born: Abt 1260
Married:
Died:

4 Hugh LOWTHER
Born: Abt 1293
Married:
Died:

9 Margaret De LUCY
Born: Abt 1265
-CONTINUED AS #1,ROYAL CHART 1151
Died:

2 Hugh LOWTHER
Born: Abt 1320
Married:
Died:

10
Born:
Married:
Died:

5 Margaret WHALE
Born: Abt 1295
Died:

11
Born:
Died:

1 John LOWTHER
Born: Abt 1350
-SAME AS #12,ROYAL CHART 1147
Married:
Died:

12
Born:
Married:
Died:

6
Born:
Married:
Died:

13
Born:
Died:

Maud
Spouse

3 Maud TILLOUL
Born: Abt 1325
Died:

14
Born:
Married:
Died:

7
Born:
Died:

15
Born:
Died:

Sources include: Roberts *500*, p. 416.

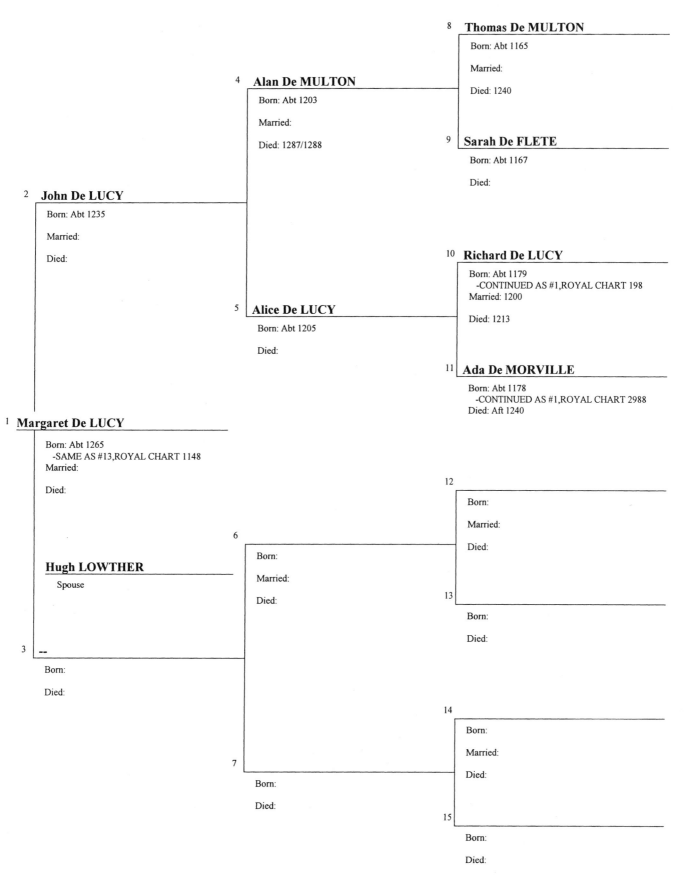

8 **Thomas De MULTON**

Born: Abt 1165

Married:

Died: 1240

4 **Alan De MULTON**

Born: Abt 1203

Married:

Died: 1287/1288

9 **Sarah De FLETE**

Born: Abt 1167

Died:

2 **John De LUCY**

Born: Abt 1235

Married:

Died:

10 **Richard De LUCY**

Born: Abt 1179
    -CONTINUED AS #1,ROYAL CHART 198
Married: 1200

Died: 1213

5 **Alice De LUCY**

Born: Abt 1205

Died:

11 **Ada De MORVILLE**

Born: Abt 1178
    -CONTINUED AS #1,ROYAL CHART 2988
Died: Aft 1240

1 **Margaret De LUCY**

Born: Abt 1265
    -SAME AS #13,ROYAL CHART 1148
Married:

Died:

12

Born:

Married:

Died:

6

Born:

Married:

Died:

Hugh LOWTHER

Spouse

13

Born:

Died:

3 --

Born:

Died:

14

Born:

Married:

Died:

7

Born:

Died:

15

Born:

Died:

Sources include: Roberts *500*, p. 416; Faris preliminary baronial manuscript (1998), p. 1149 (Multon).

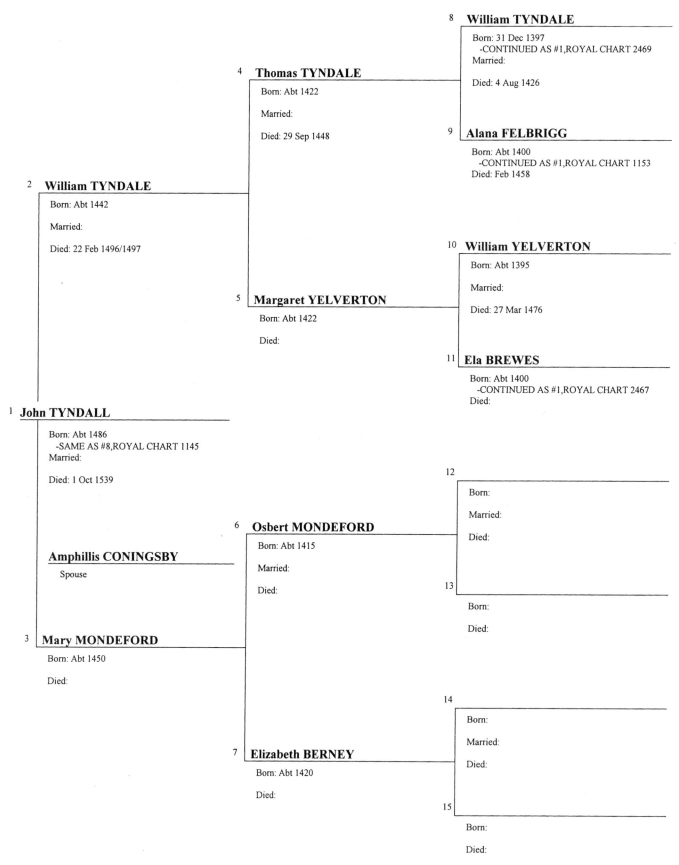

8 **William TYNDALE**

Born: 31 Dec 1397
-CONTINUED AS #1,ROYAL CHART 2469
Married:

Died: 4 Aug 1426

4 **Thomas TYNDALE**

Born: Abt 1422

Married:

Died: 29 Sep 1448

9 **Alana FELBRIGG**

Born: Abt 1400
-CONTINUED AS #1,ROYAL CHART 1153
Died: Feb 1458

2 **William TYNDALE**

Born: Abt 1442

Married:

Died: 22 Feb 1496/1497

10 **William YELVERTON**

Born: Abt 1395

Married:

Died: 27 Mar 1476

5 **Margaret YELVERTON**

Born: Abt 1422

Died:

11 **Ela BREWES**

Born: Abt 1400
-CONTINUED AS #1,ROYAL CHART 2467
Died:

1 **John TYNDALL**

Born: Abt 1486
-SAME AS #8,ROYAL CHART 1145
Married:

Died: 1 Oct 1539

12

Born:

Married:

Died:

6 **Osbert MONDEFORD**

Born: Abt 1415

Married:

Died:

13

Born:

Died:

Amphillis CONINGSBY

Spouse

3 **Mary MONDEFORD**

Born: Abt 1450

Died:

14

Born:

Married:

Died:

7 **Elizabeth BERNEY**

Born: Abt 1420

Died:

15

Born:

Died:

Sources include: Richardson *Magna Carta* (April 2005), pp. 848-849 (Tyndall), 918-919 (Yelverton); *Ancestral Roots* 232; Roberts *500*, pp. 427-428.

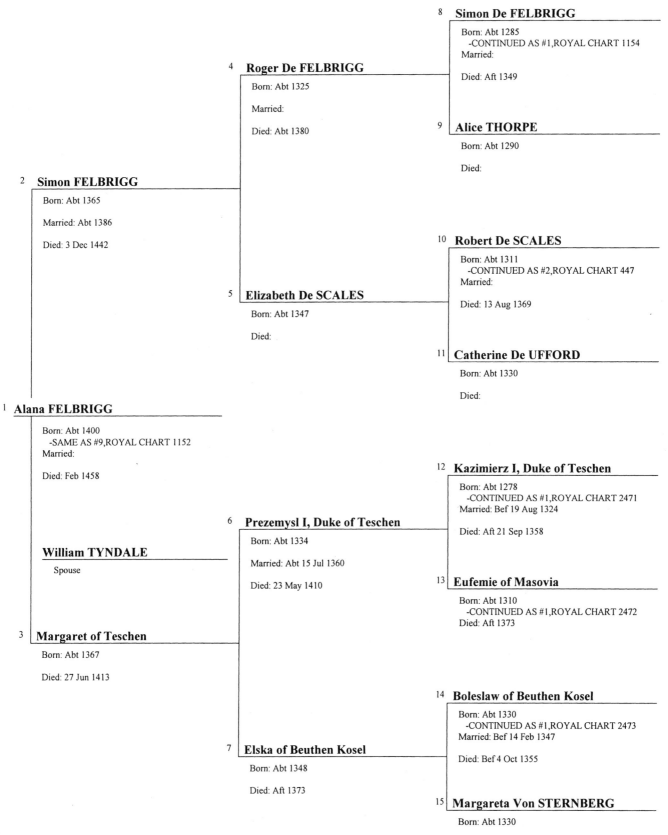

8 Simon De FELBRIGG

Born: Abt 1285
-CONTINUED AS #1,ROYAL CHART 1154
Married:

Died: Aft 1349

4 Roger De FELBRIGG

Born: Abt 1325

Married:

Died: Abt 1380

9 Alice THORPE

Born: Abt 1290

Died:

2 Simon FELBRIGG

Born: Abt 1365

Married: Abt 1386

Died: 3 Dec 1442

10 Robert De SCALES

Born: Abt 1311
-CONTINUED AS #2,ROYAL CHART 447
Married:

Died: 13 Aug 1369

5 Elizabeth De SCALES

Born: Abt 1347

Died:

11 Catherine De UFFORD

Born: Abt 1330

Died:

1 Alana FELBRIGG

Born: Abt 1400
-SAME AS #9,ROYAL CHART 1152
Married:

Died: Feb 1458

12 Kazimierz I, Duke of Teschen

Born: Abt 1278
-CONTINUED AS #1,ROYAL CHART 2471
Married: Bef 19 Aug 1324

Died: Aft 21 Sep 1358

6 Prezemysl I, Duke of Teschen

Born: Abt 1334

Married: Abt 15 Jul 1360

Died: 23 May 1410

13 Eufemie of Masovia

Born: Abt 1310
-CONTINUED AS #1,ROYAL CHART 2472
Died: Aft 1373

William TYNDALE

Spouse

3 Margaret of Teschen

Born: Abt 1367

Died: 27 Jun 1413

14 Boleslaw of Beuthen Kosel

Born: Abt 1330
-CONTINUED AS #1,ROYAL CHART 2473
Married: Bef 14 Feb 1347

Died: Bef 4 Oct 1355

7 Elska of Beuthen Kosel

Born: Abt 1348

Died: Aft 1373

15 Margareta Von STERNBERG

Born: Abt 1330

Died: Aft 5 Jun 1365

Sources include: Faris-Richardson preliminary Magna Carta manuscript (June 2000), pp. 197-198 (Felbrigg); Faris preliminary baronial manuscript (1998), pp. 571-572 (Felbrigg); LDS records; *Ancestral Roots* 232; Roberts *500*, pp. 427-428; Schwennicke 3:15-16 (#6 & 7 ancestry); *TAG* 79:283-291 (October 2004); Consultation with Douglas Richardson, March 2005. Note: The parentage shown above for #3 Margaret is uncertain and is challenged by Charles M. Hansen (*TAG* 79). Richardson still believes it may be correct, citing additional sources and the fact that #6 Prezemysl came to England.

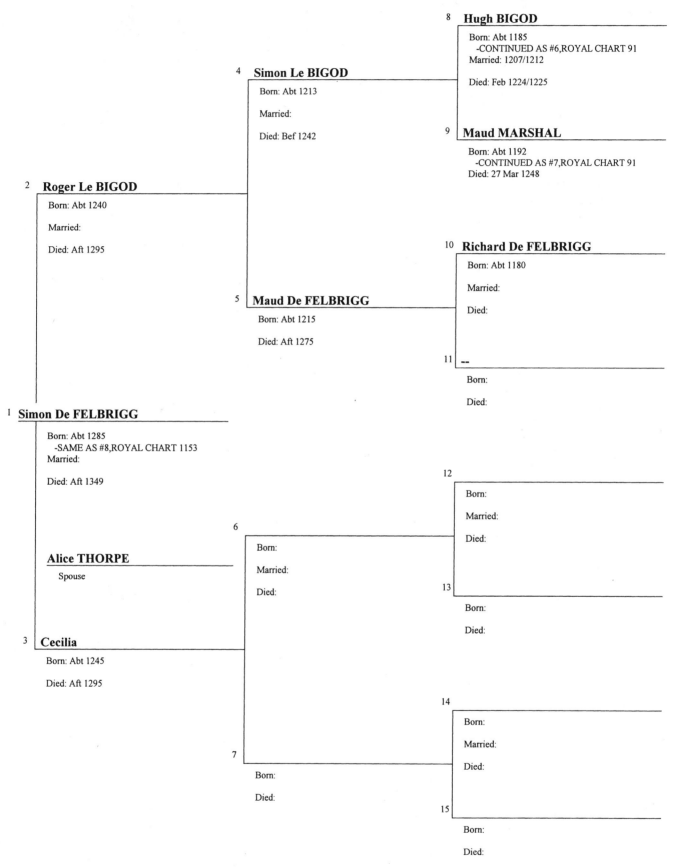

8   **Hugh BIGOD**

Born: Abt 1185
  -CONTINUED AS #6,ROYAL CHART 91
Married: 1207/1212

Died: Feb 1224/1225

4   **Simon Le BIGOD**

Born: Abt 1213

Married:

Died: Bef 1242

9   **Maud MARSHAL**

Born: Abt 1192
  -CONTINUED AS #7,ROYAL CHART 91
Died: 27 Mar 1248

2   **Roger Le BIGOD**

Born: Abt 1240

Married:

Died: Aft 1295

10   **Richard De FELBRIGG**

Born: Abt 1180

Married:

Died:

5   **Maud De FELBRIGG**

Born: Abt 1215

Died: Aft 1275

11   **--**

Born:

Died:

1   **Simon De FELBRIGG**

Born: Abt 1285
  -SAME AS #8,ROYAL CHART 1153
Married:

Died: Aft 1349

12

Born:

Married:

Died:

6

Born:

Married:

Died:

13

Born:

Died:

Alice THORPE

Spouse

14

Born:

Married:

Died:

3   **Cecilia**

Born: Abt 1245

Died: Aft 1295

7

Born:

Died:

15

Born:

Died:

Sources include: *Ancestral Roots* 232; Roberts *500*, pp. 427-428; LDS records; Consultation with Douglas Richardson. Note: The above ancestry shown for #1 Simon has been challenged and is uncertain. Neither Paget nor the *Complete Peerage* claims a son Simon for #8 & 9 Hugh & Maud.

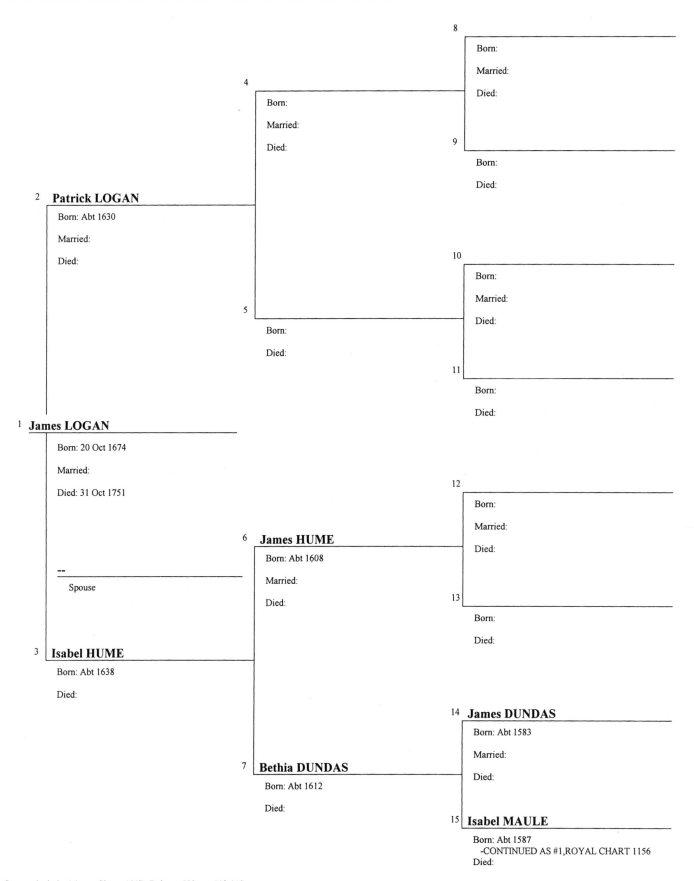

8

Born:

Married:

Died:

4

Born:

Married:

Died:

9

Born:

Died:

2 Patrick LOGAN

Born: Abt 1630

Married:

Died:

10

Born:

Married:

Died:

5

Born:

Died:

11

Born:

Died:

1 James LOGAN

Born: 20 Oct 1674

Married:

Died: 31 Oct 1751

12

Born:

Married:

Died:

6 James HUME

Born: Abt 1608

Married:

Died:

13

Born:

Died:

--

Spouse

3 Isabel HUME

Born: Abt 1638

Died:

14 James DUNDAS

Born: Abt 1583

Married:

Died:

7 Bethia DUNDAS

Born: Abt 1612

Died:

15 Isabel MAULE

Born: Abt 1587
    -CONTINUED AS #1, ROYAL CHART 1156
Died:

Sources include: *Magna Charta* 111B; Roberts *500*, pp. 112-113.

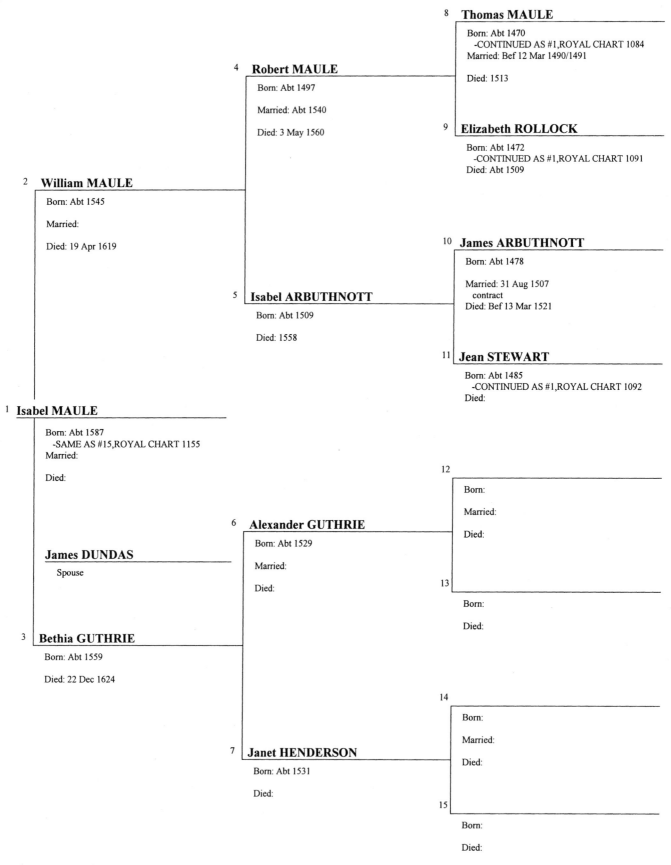

8 **Thomas MAULE**

Born: Abt 1470
-CONTINUED AS #1,ROYAL CHART 1084
Married: Bef 12 Mar 1490/1491

Died: 1513

4 **Robert MAULE**

Born: Abt 1497

Married: Abt 1540

Died: 3 May 1560

9 **Elizabeth ROLLOCK**

Born: Abt 1472
-CONTINUED AS #1,ROYAL CHART 1091
Died: Abt 1509

2 **William MAULE**

Born: Abt 1545

Married:

Died: 19 Apr 1619

10 **James ARBUTHNOTT**

Born: Abt 1478

Married: 31 Aug 1507
contract
Died: Bef 13 Mar 1521

5 **Isabel ARBUTHNOTT**

Born: Abt 1509

Died: 1558

11 **Jean STEWART**

Born: Abt 1485
-CONTINUED AS #1,ROYAL CHART 1092
Died:

1 **Isabel MAULE**

Born: Abt 1587
-SAME AS #15,ROYAL CHART 1155
Married:

Died:

12

Born:

Married:

Died:

6 **Alexander GUTHRIE**

Born: Abt 1529

Married:

Died:

13

Born:

Died:

James DUNDAS

Spouse

3 **Bethia GUTHRIE**

Born: Abt 1559

Died: 22 Dec 1624

14

Born:

Married:

Died:

7 **Janet HENDERSON**

Born: Abt 1531

Died:

15

Born:

Died:

Sources include: *Magna Charta* 111B; Roberts *500*, pp. 112-113.

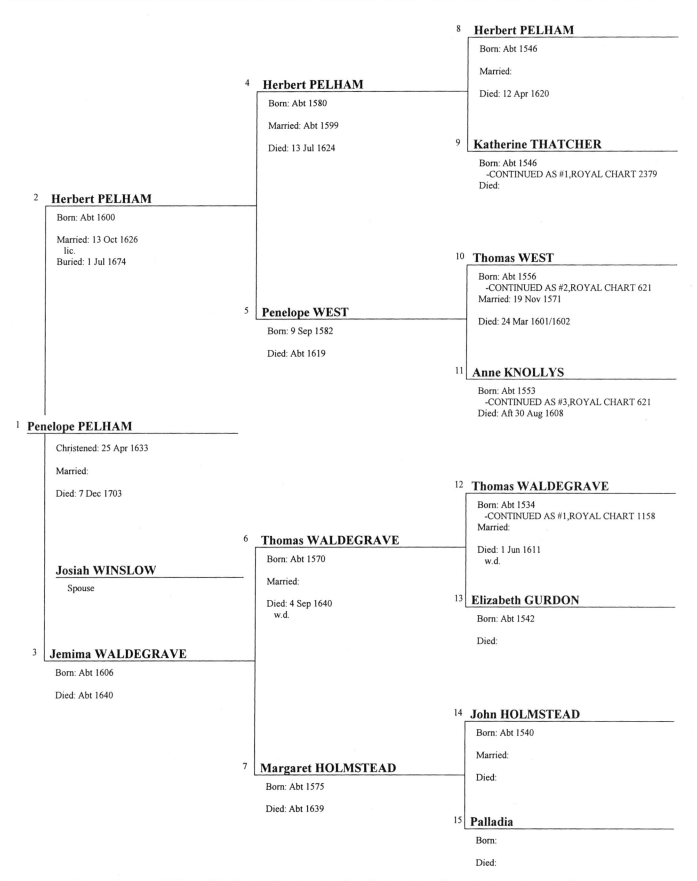

8 **Herbert PELHAM**

Born: Abt 1546

Married:

Died: 12 Apr 1620

4 **Herbert PELHAM**

Born: Abt 1580

Married: Abt 1599

Died: 13 Jul 1624

9 **Katherine THATCHER**

Born: Abt 1546
 -CONTINUED AS #1,ROYAL CHART 2379
Died:

2 **Herbert PELHAM**

Born: Abt 1600

Married: 13 Oct 1626
 lic.
Buried: 1 Jul 1674

10 **Thomas WEST**

Born: Abt 1556
 -CONTINUED AS #2,ROYAL CHART 621
Married: 19 Nov 1571

Died: 24 Mar 1601/1602

5 **Penelope WEST**

Born: 9 Sep 1582

Died: Abt 1619

11 **Anne KNOLLYS**

Born: Abt 1553
 -CONTINUED AS #3,ROYAL CHART 621
Died: Aft 30 Aug 1608

1 **Penelope PELHAM**

Christened: 25 Apr 1633

Married:

Died: 7 Dec 1703

12 **Thomas WALDEGRAVE**

Born: Abt 1534
 -CONTINUED AS #1,ROYAL CHART 1158
Married:

Died: 1 Jun 1611
 w.d.

6 **Thomas WALDEGRAVE**

Born: Abt 1570

Married:

Died: 4 Sep 1640
 w.d.

13 **Elizabeth GURDON**

Born: Abt 1542

Died:

Josiah WINSLOW

Spouse

3 **Jemima WALDEGRAVE**

Born: Abt 1606

Died: Abt 1640

14 **John HOLMSTEAD**

Born: Abt 1540

Married:

Died:

7 **Margaret HOLMSTEAD**

Born: Abt 1575

Died: Abt 1639

15 **Palladia**

Born:

Died:

Sources include: Richardson *Plantagenet* (2004), pp. 573 (Pelham), 166 (Bures); Faris--Pelham, Humphrey; *Magna Charta* 75A; *Ancestral Roots* 1; Roberts *500*, pp. 317-318.

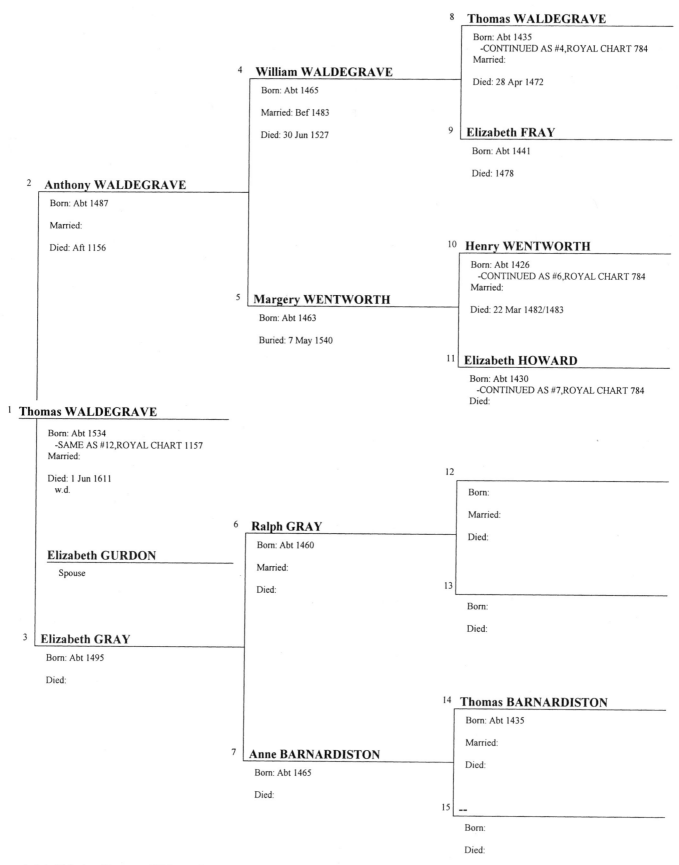

8 **Thomas WALDEGRAVE**

Born: Abt 1435
-CONTINUED AS #4,ROYAL CHART 784
Married:

Died: 28 Apr 1472

4 **William WALDEGRAVE**

Born: Abt 1465

Married: Bef 1483

Died: 30 Jun 1527

9 **Elizabeth FRAY**

Born: Abt 1441

Died: 1478

2 **Anthony WALDEGRAVE**

Born: Abt 1487

Married:

Died: Aft 1156

10 **Henry WENTWORTH**

Born: Abt 1426
-CONTINUED AS #6,ROYAL CHART 784
Married:

Died: 22 Mar 1482/1483

5 **Margery WENTWORTH**

Born: Abt 1463

Buried: 7 May 1540

11 **Elizabeth HOWARD**

Born: Abt 1430
-CONTINUED AS #7,ROYAL CHART 784
Died:

1 **Thomas WALDEGRAVE**

Born: Abt 1534
-SAME AS #12,ROYAL CHART 1157
Married:

Died: 1 Jun 1611
w.d.

12

Born:

Married:

Died:

6 **Ralph GRAY**

Born: Abt 1460

Married:

Died:

13

Born:

Died:

Elizabeth GURDON

Spouse

3 **Elizabeth GRAY**

Born: Abt 1495

Died:

14 **Thomas BARNARDISTON**

Born: Abt 1435

Married:

Died:

7 **Anne BARNARDISTON**

Born: Abt 1465

Died:

15 **--**

Born:

Died:

Sources include: Richardson *Plantagenet* (2004), pp. 165-166 (Bures), 740-741 (Waldegrave); *Magna Charta* 75A; Roberts *500*, pp. 317-318.

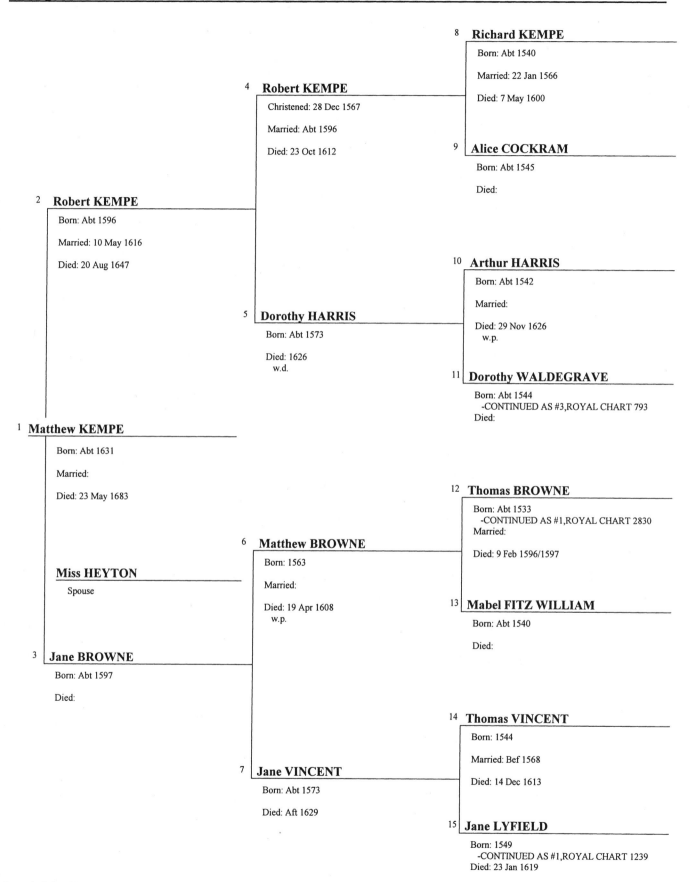

2 **Robert KEMPE**

Born: Abt 1596

Married: 10 May 1616

Died: 20 Aug 1647

4 **Robert KEMPE**

Christened: 28 Dec 1567

Married: Abt 1596

Died: 23 Oct 1612

8 **Richard KEMPE**

Born: Abt 1540

Married: 22 Jan 1566

Died: 7 May 1600

9 **Alice COCKRAM**

Born: Abt 1545

Died:

5 **Dorothy HARRIS**

Born: Abt 1573

Died: 1626
w.d.

10 **Arthur HARRIS**

Born: Abt 1542

Married:

Died: 29 Nov 1626
w.p.

11 **Dorothy WALDEGRAVE**

Born: Abt 1544
-CONTINUED AS #3,ROYAL CHART 793
Died:

1 **Matthew KEMPE**

Born: Abt 1631

Married:

Died: 23 May 1683

Miss HEYTON

Spouse

3 **Jane BROWNE**

Born: Abt 1597

Died:

6 **Matthew BROWNE**

Born: 1563

Married:

Died: 19 Apr 1608
w.p.

12 **Thomas BROWNE**

Born: Abt 1533
-CONTINUED AS #1,ROYAL CHART 2830
Married:

Died: 9 Feb 1596/1597

13 **Mabel FITZ WILLIAM**

Born: Abt 1540

Died:

7 **Jane VINCENT**

Born: Abt 1573

Died: Aft 1629

14 **Thomas VINCENT**

Born: 1544

Married: Bef 1568

Died: 14 Dec 1613

15 **Jane LYFIELD**

Born: 1549
-CONTINUED AS #1,ROYAL CHART 1239
Died: 23 Jan 1619

Sources include: Richardson *Plantagenet* (2004), pp. 415-416 (Kempe), 161-162 (Browne); Faris 2--Kempe; *Magna Charta* 75 (#4 & 5 ancestry); November 2000 research by Douglas Richardson (#3 ancestry); LDS records; *Visitations of Surrey* 43:9-10 (#3 ancestry); P.W. Hasler, *The House of Commons* (1558-1603) 1:501, 505 (Browne); 3:558-559 (Vincent).

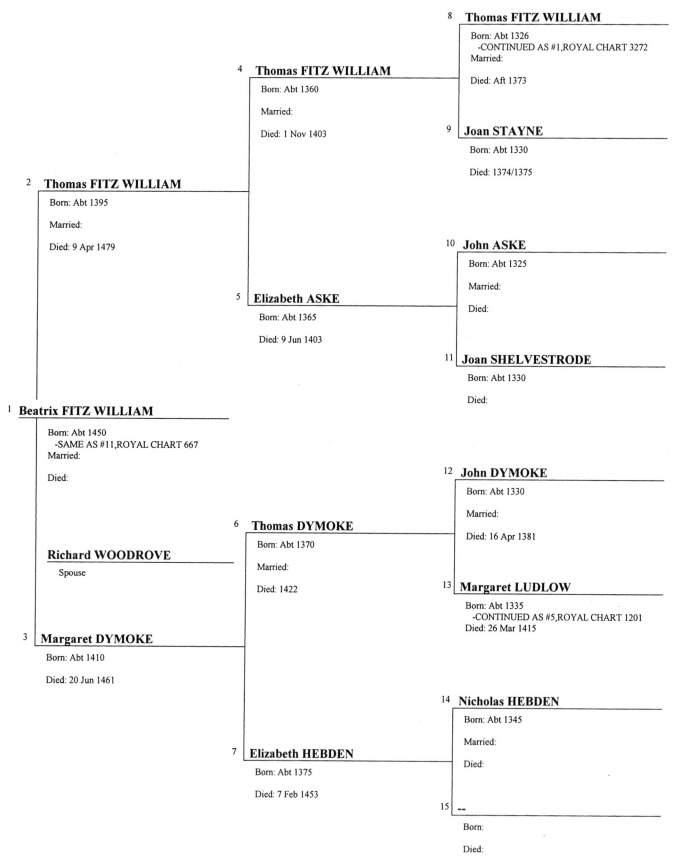

8 Thomas FITZ WILLIAM

Born: Abt 1326
-CONTINUED AS #1,ROYAL CHART 3272
Married:

Died: Aft 1373

4 Thomas FITZ WILLIAM

Born: Abt 1360

Married:

Died: 1 Nov 1403

9 Joan STAYNE

Born: Abt 1330

Died: 1374/1375

2 Thomas FITZ WILLIAM

Born: Abt 1395

Married:

Died: 9 Apr 1479

10 John ASKE

Born: Abt 1325

Married:

Died:

5 Elizabeth ASKE

Born: Abt 1365

Died: 9 Jun 1403

11 Joan SHELVESTRODE

Born: Abt 1330

Died:

1 Beatrix FITZ WILLIAM

Born: Abt 1450
-SAME AS #11,ROYAL CHART 667
Married:

Died:

12 John DYMOKE

Born: Abt 1330

Married:

Died: 16 Apr 1381

6 Thomas DYMOKE

Born: Abt 1370

Married:

Died: 1422

13 Margaret LUDLOW

Born: Abt 1335
-CONTINUED AS #5,ROYAL CHART 1201
Died: 26 Mar 1415

Richard WOODROVE

Spouse

3 Margaret DYMOKE

Born: Abt 1410

Died: 20 Jun 1461

14 Nicholas HEBDEN

Born: Abt 1345

Married:

Died:

7 Elizabeth HEBDEN

Born: Abt 1375

Died: 7 Feb 1453

15 --

Born:

Died:

Sources include: LDS records; *Emperor Charlemagne* 2:286; Roberts *500*, pp. 272-273; *AAP*, pp. 233-234; NEHGS *Nexus* 13:124. Note: #3 Margaret was <u>not</u> the daughter of Thomas Dymoke (b. abt 1428) & Margaret Welles, as claimed earlier. They were not married until 13 June 1457.

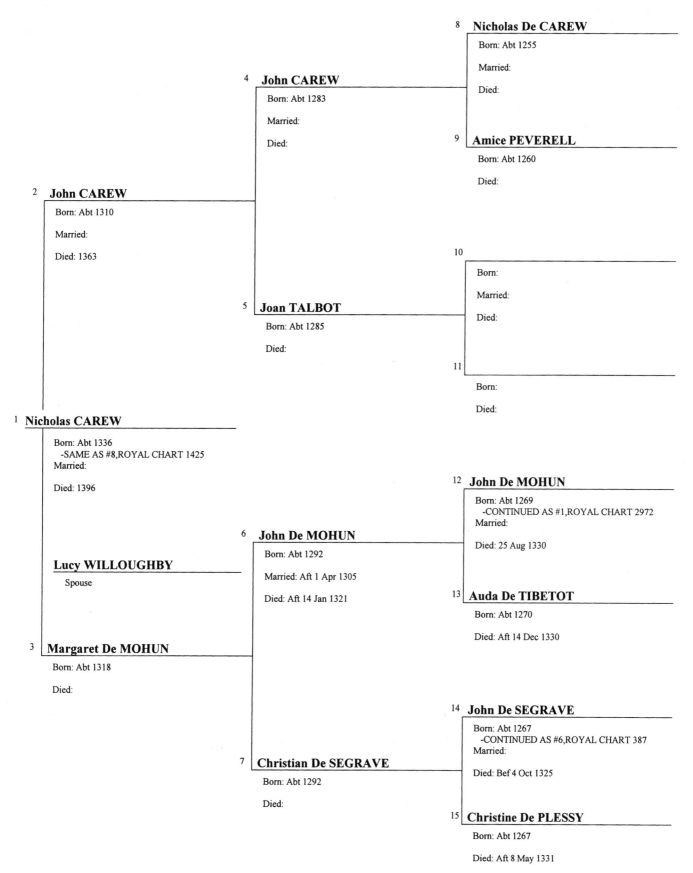

8 **Nicholas De CAREW**
Born: Abt 1255
Married:
Died:

4 **John CAREW**
Born: Abt 1283
Married:
Died:

9 **Amice PEVERELL**
Born: Abt 1260
Died:

2 **John CAREW**
Born: Abt 1310
Married:
Died: 1363

10
Born:
Married:
Died:

5 **Joan TALBOT**
Born: Abt 1285
Died:

11
Born:
Died:

1 **Nicholas CAREW**
Born: Abt 1336
  -SAME AS #8,ROYAL CHART 1425
Married:
Died: 1396

Lucy WILLOUGHBY
Spouse

12 **John De MOHUN**
Born: Abt 1269
  -CONTINUED AS #1,ROYAL CHART 2972
Married:
Died: 25 Aug 1330

6 **John De MOHUN**
Born: Abt 1292
Married: Aft 1 Apr 1305
Died: Aft 14 Jan 1321

13 **Auda De TIBETOT**
Born: Abt 1270
Died: Aft 14 Dec 1330

3 **Margaret De MOHUN**
Born: Abt 1318
Died:

14 **John De SEGRAVE**
Born: Abt 1267
  -CONTINUED AS #6,ROYAL CHART 387
Married:
Died: Bef 4 Oct 1325

7 **Christian De SEGRAVE**
Born: Abt 1292
Died:

15 **Christine De PLESSY**
Born: Abt 1267
Died: Aft 8 May 1331

Sources include: Faris preliminary baronial manuscript (1998), pp. 296 (Carew), 1096-97 (Mohun).

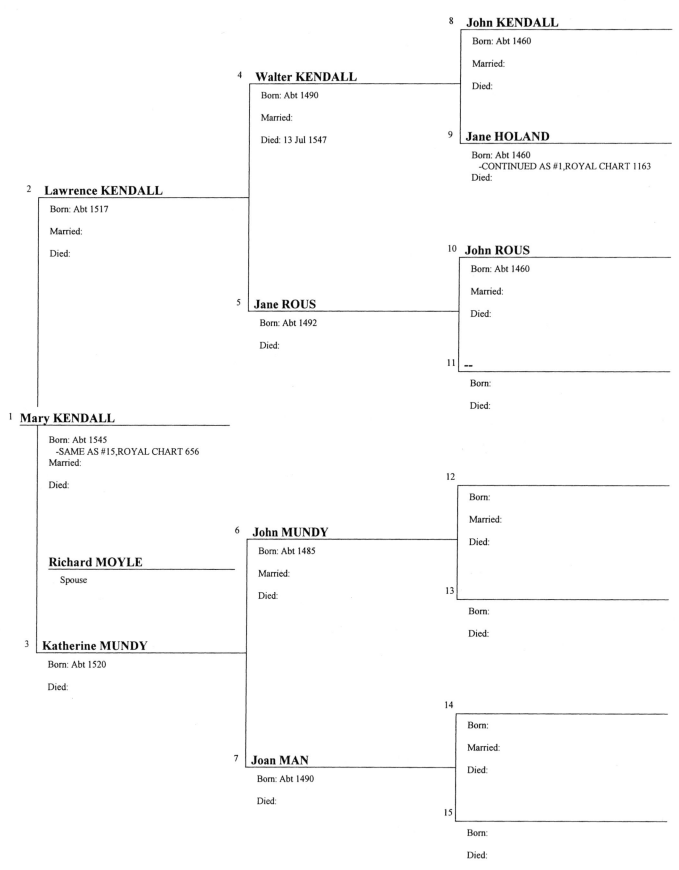

8 **John KENDALL**
Born: Abt 1460
Married:
Died:

4 **Walter KENDALL**
Born: Abt 1490
Married:
Died: 13 Jul 1547

9 **Jane HOLAND**
Born: Abt 1460
  -CONTINUED AS #1,ROYAL CHART 1163
Died:

2 **Lawrence KENDALL**
Born: Abt 1517
Married:
Died:

10 **John ROUS**
Born: Abt 1460
Married:
Died:

5 **Jane ROUS**
Born: Abt 1492
Died:

11 **--**
Born:
Died:

1 **Mary KENDALL**
Born: Abt 1545
  -SAME AS #15,ROYAL CHART 656
Married:
Died:

12
Born:
Married:
Died:

6 **John MUNDY**
Born: Abt 1485
Married:
Died:

Richard MOYLE
  Spouse

13
Born:
Died:

3 **Katherine MUNDY**
Born: Abt 1520
Died:

14
Born:
Married:
Died:

7 **Joan MAN**
Born: Abt 1490
Died:

15
Born:
Died:

Sources include: *TAG* 76:46-49 (Jan 2001); LDS records.

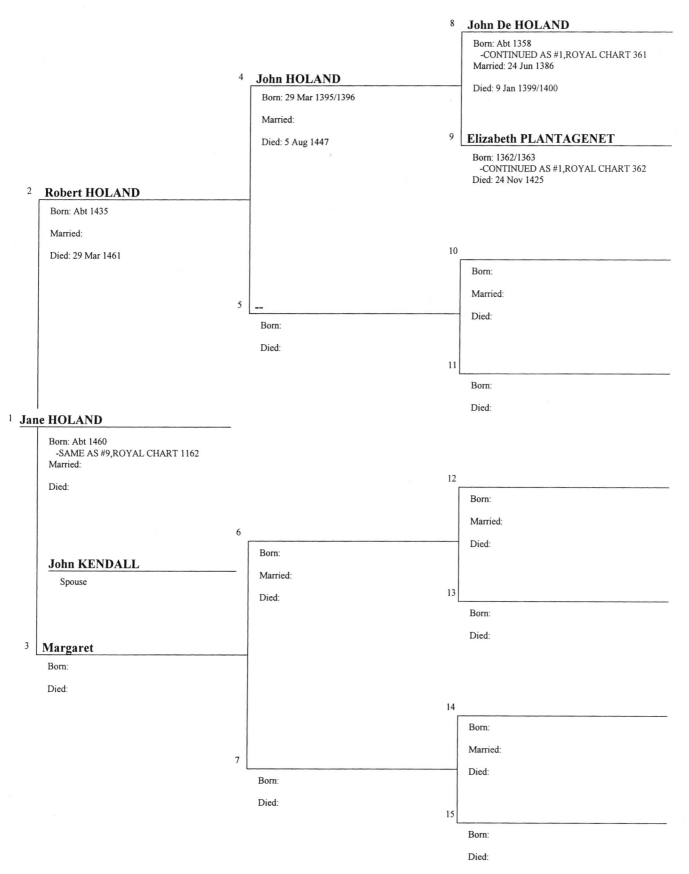

8 John De HOLAND

Born: Abt 1358
-CONTINUED AS #1,ROYAL CHART 361
Married: 24 Jun 1386

Died: 9 Jan 1399/1400

4 John HOLAND

Born: 29 Mar 1395/1396

Married:

Died: 5 Aug 1447

9 Elizabeth PLANTAGENET

Born: 1362/1363
-CONTINUED AS #1,ROYAL CHART 362
Died: 24 Nov 1425

2 Robert HOLAND

Born: Abt 1435

Married:

Died: 29 Mar 1461

10

Born:

Married:

Died:

5 --

Born:

Died:

11

Born:

Died:

1 Jane HOLAND

Born: Abt 1460
-SAME AS #9,ROYAL CHART 1162
Married:

Died:

12

Born:

Married:

Died:

6

Born:

Married:

Died:

John KENDALL

Spouse

13

Born:

Died:

3 Margaret

Born:

Died:

14

Born:

Married:

Died:

7

Born:

Died:

15

Born:

Died:

Sources include: Richardson *Plantagenet* (2004), pp. 299-301 (Exeter); *TAG* 76:46-49 (Jan 2001); Consultation with Douglas Richardson (May 2003); *Complete Peerage* 5:205-215.
Note: #2 Robert was called "bastard of Exeter". According to Douglas Richardson, this means he was the son of a duke. Chronology dictates that he was almost certainly the son of #4 John (died 1447), as shown. Robert was of age in 1458.

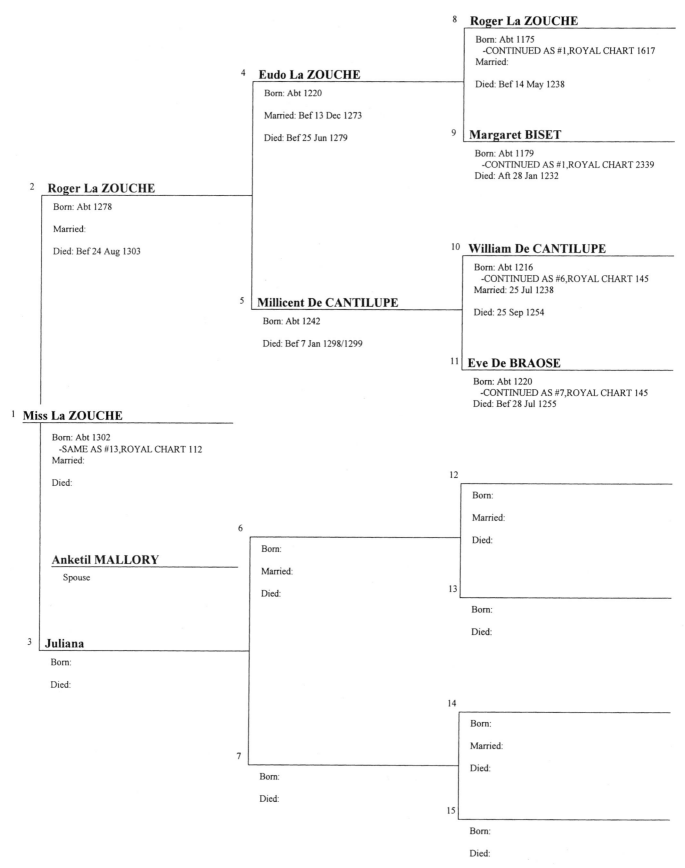

8 **Roger La ZOUCHE**

Born: Abt 1175
-CONTINUED AS #1,ROYAL CHART 1617
Married:

Died: Bef 14 May 1238

4 **Eudo La ZOUCHE**

Born: Abt 1220

Married: Bef 13 Dec 1273

Died: Bef 25 Jun 1279

9 **Margaret BISET**

Born: Abt 1179
-CONTINUED AS #1,ROYAL CHART 2339
Died: Aft 28 Jan 1232

2 **Roger La ZOUCHE**

Born: Abt 1278

Married:

Died: Bef 24 Aug 1303

10 **William De CANTILUPE**

Born: Abt 1216
-CONTINUED AS #6,ROYAL CHART 145
Married: 25 Jul 1238

Died: 25 Sep 1254

5 **Millicent De CANTILUPE**

Born: Abt 1242

Died: Bef 7 Jan 1298/1299

11 **Eve De BRAOSE**

Born: Abt 1220
-CONTINUED AS #7,ROYAL CHART 145
Died: Bef 28 Jul 1255

1 **Miss La ZOUCHE**

Born: Abt 1302
-SAME AS #13,ROYAL CHART 112
Married:

Died:

12

Born:

Married:

Died:

6

Born:

Married:

Died:

13

Born:

Died:

Anketil MALLORY

Spouse

3 **Juliana**

Born:

Died:

14

Born:

Married:

Died:

7

Born:

Died:

15

Born:

Died:

Sources include: *Genealogist's Magazine* 13:172; Paget (1957) 581:1-3; Faris preliminary baronial manuscript (1998), p. 1709-10 (Zouche); *TAG* 77:62-65 (January 2002); LDS records.

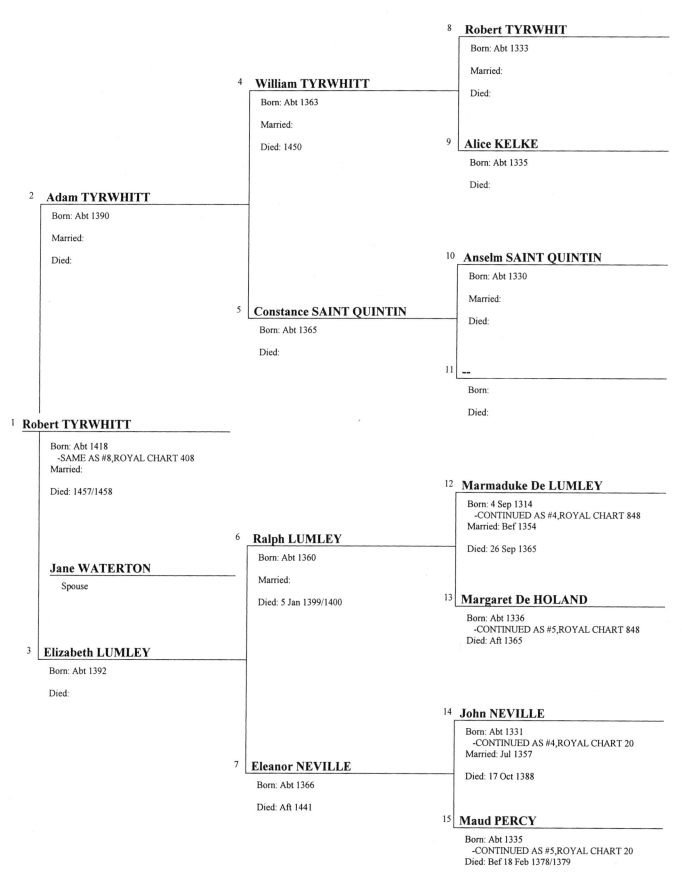

8 **Robert TYRWHIT**

Born: Abt 1333

Married:

Died:

4 **William TYRWHITT**

Born: Abt 1363

Married:

Died: 1450

9 **Alice KELKE**

Born: Abt 1335

Died:

2 **Adam TYRWHITT**

Born: Abt 1390

Married:

Died:

10 **Anselm SAINT QUINTIN**

Born: Abt 1330

Married:

Died:

5 **Constance SAINT QUINTIN**

Born: Abt 1365

Died:

11 **--**

Born:

Died:

1 **Robert TYRWHITT**

Born: Abt 1418
 -SAME AS #8,ROYAL CHART 408
Married:

Died: 1457/1458

12 **Marmaduke De LUMLEY**

Born: 4 Sep 1314
 -CONTINUED AS #4,ROYAL CHART 848
Married: Bef 1354

Died: 26 Sep 1365

6 **Ralph LUMLEY**

Born: Abt 1360

Married:

Died: 5 Jan 1399/1400

13 **Margaret De HOLAND**

Born: Abt 1336
 -CONTINUED AS #5,ROYAL CHART 848
Died: Aft 1365

Jane WATERTON

Spouse

3 **Elizabeth LUMLEY**

Born: Abt 1392

Died:

14 **John NEVILLE**

Born: Abt 1331
 -CONTINUED AS #4,ROYAL CHART 20
Married: Jul 1357

Died: 17 Oct 1388

7 **Eleanor NEVILLE**

Born: Abt 1366

Died: Aft 1441

15 **Maud PERCY**

Born: Abt 1335
 -CONTINUED AS #5,ROYAL CHART 20
Died: Bef 18 Feb 1378/1379

Sources include: Faris-Richardson preliminary Magna Carta manuscript (June 2000), pp. 459 (Saltonstall), 337-338 (Lumley); Faris preliminary baronial manuscript (1998), pp. 1562-63 (Tyrwhit).

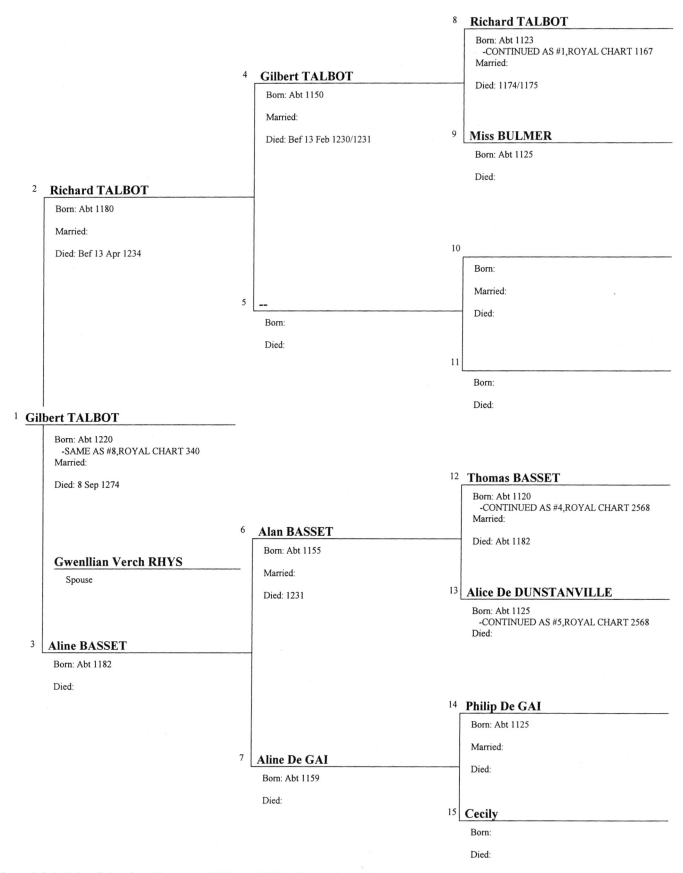

8 **Richard TALBOT**

Born: Abt 1123
-CONTINUED AS #1,ROYAL CHART 1167
Married:

Died: 1174/1175

4 **Gilbert TALBOT**

Born: Abt 1150

Married:

Died: Bef 13 Feb 1230/1231

9 **Miss BULMER**

Born: Abt 1125

Died:

2 **Richard TALBOT**

Born: Abt 1180

Married:

Died: Bef 13 Apr 1234

10

Born:

Married:

Died:

5 **--**

Born:

Died:

11

Born:

Died:

1 **Gilbert TALBOT**

Born: Abt 1220
-SAME AS #8,ROYAL CHART 340
Married:

Died: 8 Sep 1274

12 **Thomas BASSET**

Born: Abt 1120
-CONTINUED AS #4,ROYAL CHART 2568
Married:

Died: Abt 1182

6 **Alan BASSET**

Born: Abt 1155

Married:

Died: 1231

13 **Alice De DUNSTANVILLE**

Born: Abt 1125
-CONTINUED AS #5,ROYAL CHART 2568
Died:

Gwenllian Verch RHYS

Spouse

3 **Aline BASSET**

Born: Abt 1182

Died:

14 **Philip De GAI**

Born: Abt 1125

Married:

Died:

7 **Aline De GAI**

Born: Abt 1159

Died:

15 **Cecily**

Born:

Died:

Sources include: Faris preliminary baronial manuscript (1998), pp. 1492-93 (Talbot); Jacobus, *Bulkeley Genealogy*, p. 71.

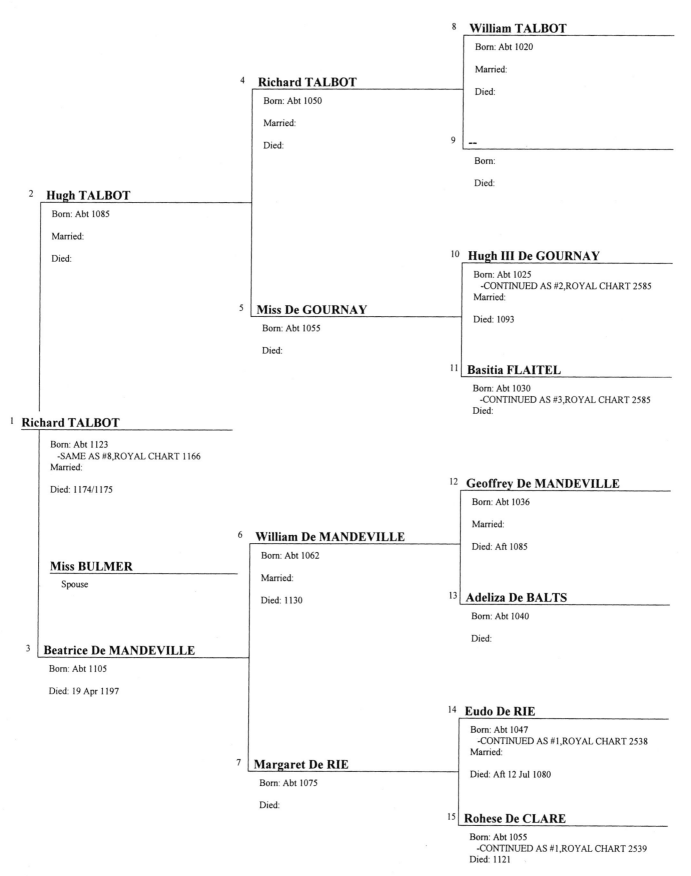

8 **William TALBOT**

Born: Abt 1020

Married:

Died:

4 **Richard TALBOT**

Born: Abt 1050

Married:

Died:

9 **--**

Born:

Died:

2 **Hugh TALBOT**

Born: Abt 1085

Married:

Died:

10 **Hugh III De GOURNAY**

Born: Abt 1025
-CONTINUED AS #2,ROYAL CHART 2585
Married:

Died: 1093

5 **Miss De GOURNAY**

Born: Abt 1055

Died:

11 **Basitia FLAITEL**

Born: Abt 1030
-CONTINUED AS #3,ROYAL CHART 2585
Died:

1 **Richard TALBOT**

Born: Abt 1123
-SAME AS #8,ROYAL CHART 1166
Married:

Died: 1174/1175

12 **Geoffrey De MANDEVILLE**

Born: Abt 1036

Married:

Died: Aft 1085

6 **William De MANDEVILLE**

Born: Abt 1062

Married:

Died: 1130

Miss BULMER

Spouse

13 **Adeliza De BALTS**

Born: Abt 1040

Died:

3 **Beatrice De MANDEVILLE**

Born: Abt 1105

Died: 19 Apr 1197

14 **Eudo De RIE**

Born: Abt 1047
-CONTINUED AS #1,ROYAL CHART 2538
Married:

Died: Aft 12 Jul 1080

7 **Margaret De RIE**

Born: Abt 1075

Died:

15 **Rohese De CLARE**

Born: Abt 1055
-CONTINUED AS #1,ROYAL CHART 2539
Died: 1121

Sources include: Faris preliminary baronial manuscript (1998), p. 1492 (Talbot); Jacobus, *Bulkeley Genealogy*, p. 71; LDS records (#3 ancestry). Note: #7 is not certain. See chart 1623 & notes.

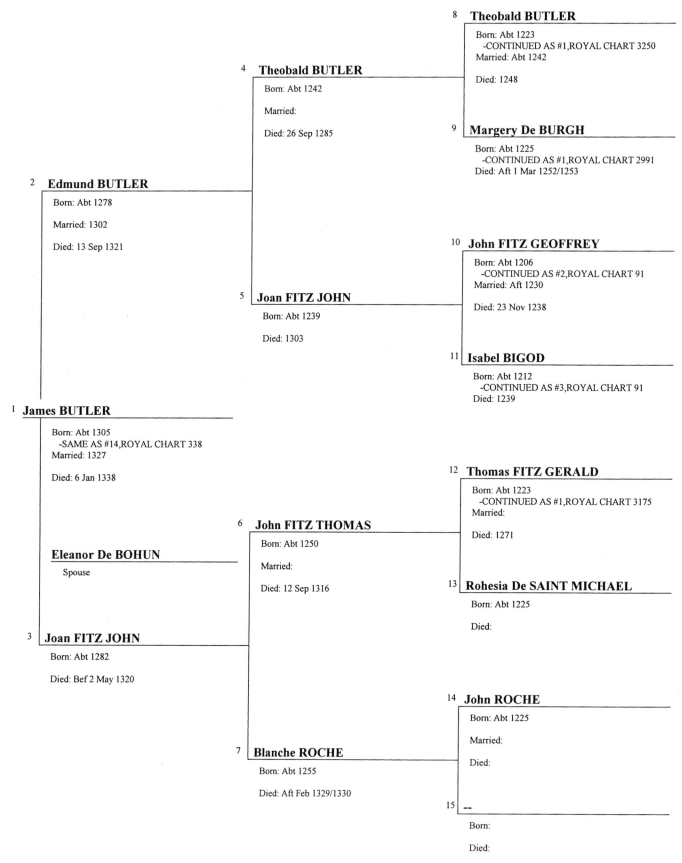

8 **Theobald BUTLER**

Born: Abt 1223
-CONTINUED AS #1,ROYAL CHART 3250
Married: Abt 1242

Died: 1248

4 **Theobald BUTLER**

Born: Abt 1242

Married:

Died: 26 Sep 1285

9 **Margery De BURGH**

Born: Abt 1225
-CONTINUED AS #1,ROYAL CHART 2991
Died: Aft 1 Mar 1252/1253

2 **Edmund BUTLER**

Born: Abt 1278

Married: 1302

Died: 13 Sep 1321

10 **John FITZ GEOFFREY**

Born: Abt 1206
-CONTINUED AS #2,ROYAL CHART 91
Married: Aft 1230

Died: 23 Nov 1238

5 **Joan FITZ JOHN**

Born: Abt 1239

Died: 1303

11 **Isabel BIGOD**

Born: Abt 1212
-CONTINUED AS #3,ROYAL CHART 91
Died: 1239

1 **James BUTLER**

Born: Abt 1305
-SAME AS #14,ROYAL CHART 338
Married: 1327

Died: 6 Jan 1338

12 **Thomas FITZ GERALD**

Born: Abt 1223
-CONTINUED AS #1,ROYAL CHART 3175
Married:

Died: 1271

6 **John FITZ THOMAS**

Born: Abt 1250

Married:

Died: 12 Sep 1316

13 **Rohesia De SAINT MICHAEL**

Born: Abt 1225

Died:

Eleanor De BOHUN

Spouse

3 **Joan FITZ JOHN**

Born: Abt 1282

Died: Bef 2 May 1320

14 **John ROCHE**

Born: Abt 1225

Married:

Died:

7 **Blanche ROCHE**

Born: Abt 1255

Died: Aft Feb 1329/1330

15 **--**

Born:

Died:

Sources include: Richardson *Plantagenet* (2004), pp. 176-177 (Butler); Faris-Richardson preliminary Magna Carta manuscript (June 2000), pp. 99 (Butler), 93-95 (Burgh); Boyer *Abell* (2001), pp. 48-49, 113-114; Faris--Butler; Faris preliminary baronial manuscript (1998), pp. 274-276 (Butler); Jacobus, *Bulkeley Genealogy*, p. 77.

8 **Hervey BAGOT**

Born: Abt 1145

Married:

Died: Bef 25 Aug 1214

4 **Hervey De STAFFORD**

Born: Abt 1183

Married:

Died: 12 May 1257

9 **Millicent De STAFFORD**

Born: Abt 1155

Died: Bef Jan 1224/1225

2 **Robert De STAFFORD**

Born: Abt 1215

Married:

Died: 4 Jun 1261

10 **William De FERRERS**

Born: Abt 1140
-CONTINUED AS #1,ROYAL CHART 2516
Married:

Died: Bef 21 Oct 1190

5 **Pernel De FERRERS**

Born: Abt 1185

Died:

11 **Sybil De BRAOSE**

Born: Abt 1152
-CONTINUED AS #1,ROYAL CHART 2517
Died: Aft 5 Feb 1227/1228

1 **Nicholas De STAFFORD**

Born: Abt 1255
-SAME AS #8,ROYAL CHART 134
Married:

Died: 1 Aug 1287

12 **Robert CORBET**

Born: Abt 1150

Married:

Died: Abt 1222

6 **Thomas CORBET**

Born: Abt 1190

Married:

Died: 1274

13 **Emma PANTOLPH**

Born: Abt 1162

Died:

Miss De LANGLEY

Spouse

3 **Alice CORBET**

Born: Abt 1225

Died:

14 **Roger De VAUTORT**

Born: Abt 1170

Married:

Died:

7 **Isabel De VAUTORT**

Born: Abt 1200

Died:

15 **--**

Born:

Died:

Sources include: Faris preliminary baronial manuscript (1998), pp. 1421-22 (Stafford), 410-411 (Corbet), 574 (Ferrers); LDS records.

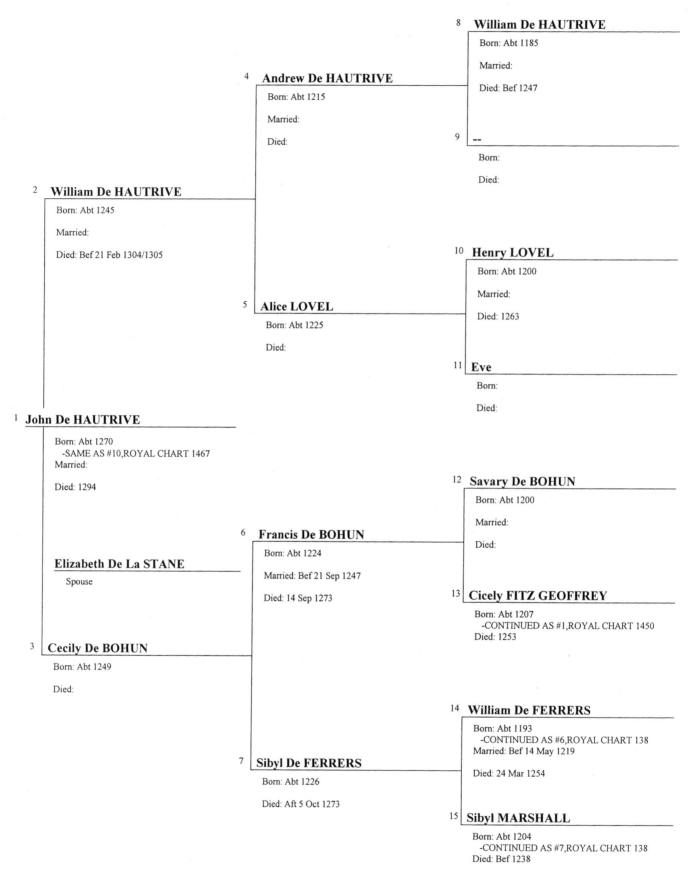

8 **William De HAUTRIVE**

Born: Abt 1185

Married:

Died: Bef 1247

4 **Andrew De HAUTRIVE**

Born: Abt 1215

Married:

Died:

9 **--**

Born:

Died:

2 **William De HAUTRIVE**

Born: Abt 1245

Married:

Died: Bef 21 Feb 1304/1305

10 **Henry LOVEL**

Born: Abt 1200

Married:

Died: 1263

5 **Alice LOVEL**

Born: Abt 1225

Died:

11 **Eve**

Born:

Died:

1 **John De HAUTRIVE**

Born: Abt 1270
-SAME AS #10,ROYAL CHART 1467
Married:

Died: 1294

12 **Savary De BOHUN**

Born: Abt 1200

Married:

Died:

6 **Francis De BOHUN**

Born: Abt 1224

Married: Bef 21 Sep 1247

Died: 14 Sep 1273

13 **Cicely FITZ GEOFFREY**

Born: Abt 1207
-CONTINUED AS #1,ROYAL CHART 1450
Died: 1253

Elizabeth De La STANE

Spouse

3 **Cecily De BOHUN**

Born: Abt 1249

Died:

14 **William De FERRERS**

Born: Abt 1193
-CONTINUED AS #6,ROYAL CHART 138
Married: Bef 14 May 1219

Died: 24 Mar 1254

7 **Sibyl De FERRERS**

Born: Abt 1226

Died: Aft 5 Oct 1273

15 **Sibyl MARSHALL**

Born: Abt 1204
-CONTINUED AS #7,ROYAL CHART 138
Died: Bef 1238

Sources include: Faris preliminary baronial manuscript (1998), pp. 838-839 (Hautrive), 136-137 (Bohun), 992-993 (Lovel); Chart 1449 & sources (#6 & 7 ancestry).

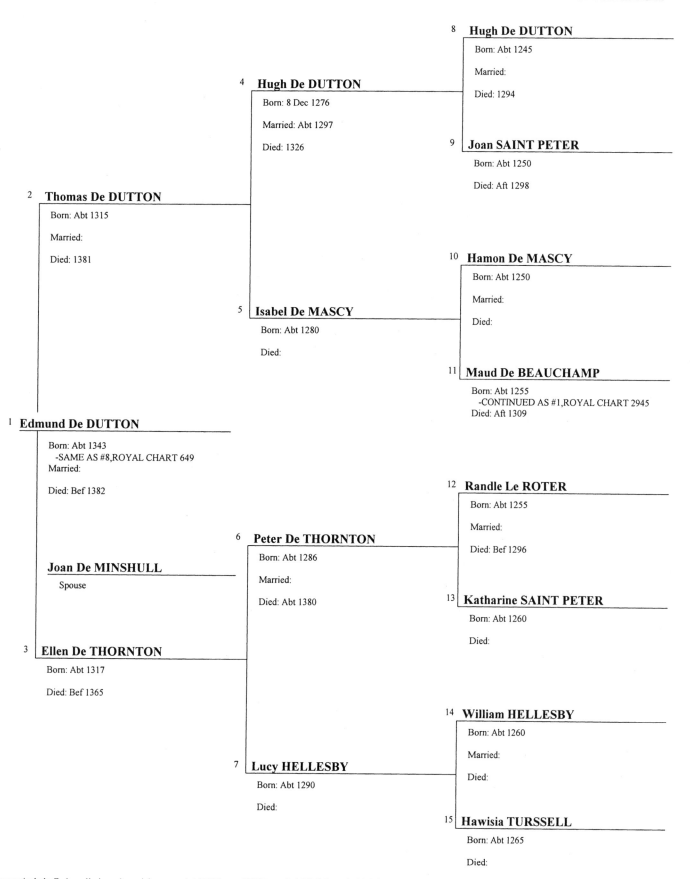

8   **Hugh De DUTTON**

Born: Abt 1245

Married:

Died: 1294

4   **Hugh De DUTTON**

Born: 8 Dec 1276

Married: Abt 1297

Died: 1326

9   **Joan SAINT PETER**

Born: Abt 1250

Died: Aft 1298

2   **Thomas De DUTTON**

Born: Abt 1315

Married:

Died: 1381

10   **Hamon De MASCY**

Born: Abt 1250

Married:

Died:

5   **Isabel De MASCY**

Born: Abt 1280

Died:

11   **Maud De BEAUCHAMP**

Born: Abt 1255
   -CONTINUED AS #1,ROYAL CHART 2945
Died: Aft 1309

1   **Edmund De DUTTON**

Born: Abt 1343
   -SAME AS #8,ROYAL CHART 649
Married:

Died: Bef 1382

12   **Randle Le ROTER**

Born: Abt 1255

Married:

Died: Bef 1296

6   **Peter De THORNTON**

Born: Abt 1286

Married:

Died: Abt 1380

13   **Katharine SAINT PETER**

Born: Abt 1260

Died:

Joan De MINSHULL

Spouse

3   **Ellen De THORNTON**

Born: Abt 1317

Died: Bef 1365

14   **William HELLESBY**

Born: Abt 1260

Married:

Died:

7   **Lucy HELLESBY**

Born: Abt 1290

Died:

15   **Hawisia TURSSELL**

Born: Abt 1265

Died:

Sources include: Faris preliminary baronial manuscript (1998), pp. 532 (Dutton), 1070 (Massey), 1512 (Thornton); Boyer *Abell* (2001), pp. 92-93, 249, 138. Notes: Boyer (citing Ormerod 2:791-796) gives #2 Thomas as the son of Ralph De Vernon & Matilda De Hatton. The Faris version is followed above. #5 is not certain and could be a 2nd wife Joan Holand. Isabel was a 1st wife.

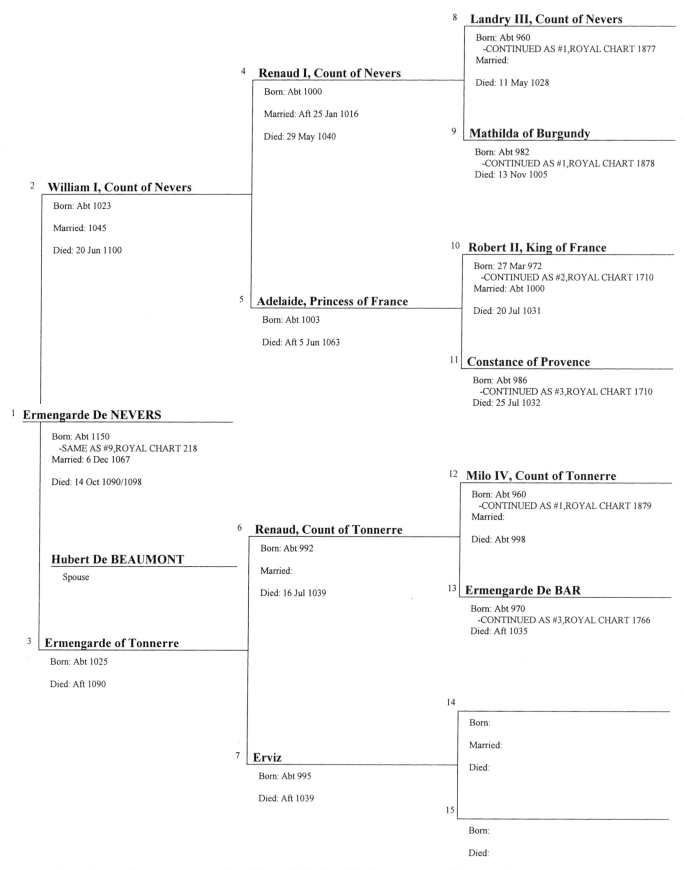

8 **Landry III, Count of Nevers**

Born: Abt 960
-CONTINUED AS #1,ROYAL CHART 1877
Married:

Died: 11 May 1028

4 **Renaud I, Count of Nevers**

Born: Abt 1000

Married: Aft 25 Jan 1016

Died: 29 May 1040

9 **Mathilda of Burgundy**

Born: Abt 982
-CONTINUED AS #1,ROYAL CHART 1878
Died: 13 Nov 1005

2 **William I, Count of Nevers**

Born: Abt 1023

Married: 1045

Died: 20 Jun 1100

10 **Robert II, King of France**

Born: 27 Mar 972
-CONTINUED AS #2,ROYAL CHART 1710
Married: Abt 1000

Died: 20 Jul 1031

5 **Adelaide, Princess of France**

Born: Abt 1003

Died: Aft 5 Jun 1063

11 **Constance of Provence**

Born: Abt 986
-CONTINUED AS #3,ROYAL CHART 1710
Died: 25 Jul 1032

1 **Ermengarde De NEVERS**

Born: Abt 1150
-SAME AS #9,ROYAL CHART 218
Married: 6 Dec 1067

Died: 14 Oct 1090/1098

12 **Milo IV, Count of Tonnerre**

Born: Abt 960
-CONTINUED AS #1,ROYAL CHART 1879
Married:

Died: Abt 998

6 **Renaud, Count of Tonnerre**

Born: Abt 992

Married:

Died: 16 Jul 1039

13 **Ermengarde De BAR**

Born: Abt 970
-CONTINUED AS #3,ROYAL CHART 1766
Died: Aft 1035

Hubert De BEAUMONT

Spouse

3 **Ermengarde of Tonnerre**

Born: Abt 1025

Died: Aft 1090

14

Born:

Married:

Died:

7 **Erviz**

Born: Abt 995

Died: Aft 1039

15

Born:

Died:

Sources include: Faris preliminary Charlemagne manuscript (June 1995), pp. 44, 204; Chart 1738 with sources & notes (#2 & 3 ancestry).

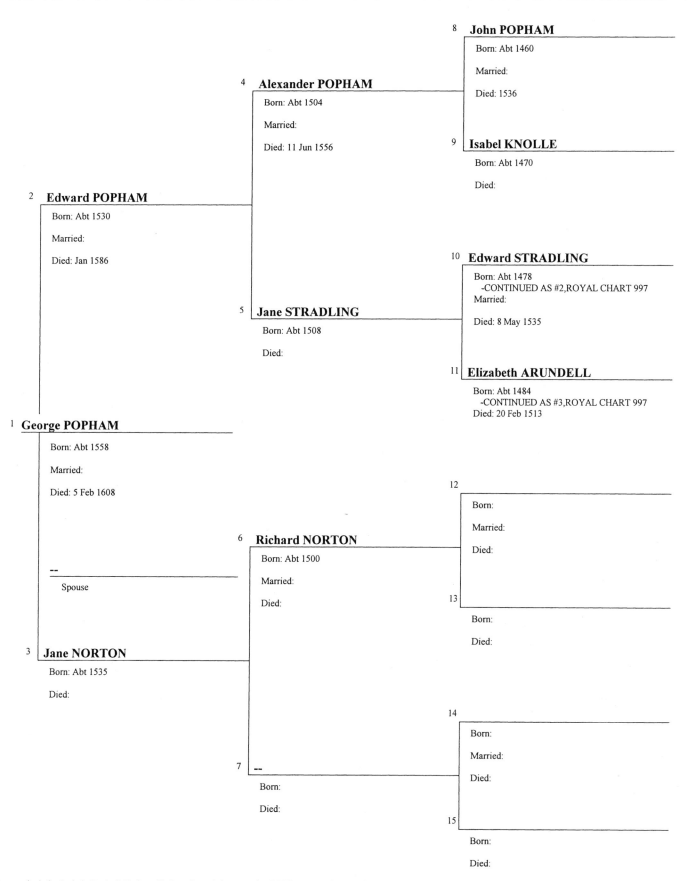

8 John POPHAM

Born: Abt 1460

Married:

Died: 1536

4 Alexander POPHAM

Born: Abt 1504

Married:

Died: 11 Jun 1556

9 Isabel KNOLLE

Born: Abt 1470

Died:

2 Edward POPHAM

Born: Abt 1530

Married:

Died: Jan 1586

10 Edward STRADLING

Born: Abt 1478
-CONTINUED AS #2,ROYAL CHART 997
Married:

Died: 8 May 1535

5 Jane STRADLING

Born: Abt 1508

Died:

11 Elizabeth ARUNDELL

Born: Abt 1484
-CONTINUED AS #3,ROYAL CHART 997
Died: 20 Feb 1513

1 George POPHAM

Born: Abt 1558

Married:

Died: 5 Feb 1608

12

Born:

Married:

Died:

--

Spouse

6 Richard NORTON

Born: Abt 1500

Married:

Died:

13

Born:

Died:

3 Jane NORTON

Born: Abt 1535

Died:

14

Born:

Married:

Died:

7 --

Born:

Died:

15

Born:

Died:

Sources include: Faris 2--Poole 3; Faris preliminary baronial manuscript (1998), p. 1270 (Popham); *Magna Charta* 27A; Roberts *500*, pp. 134-135.

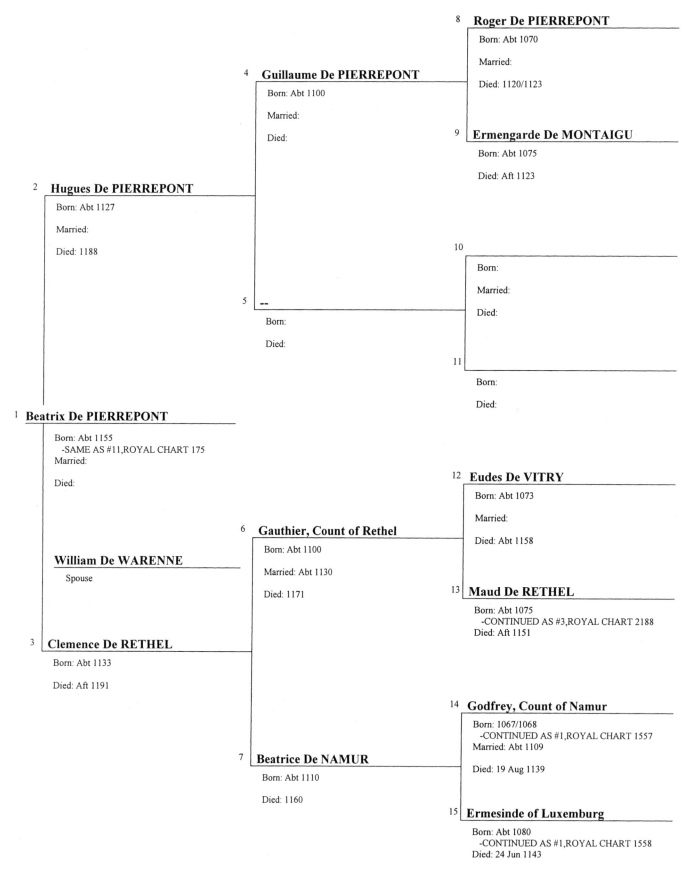

8 Roger De PIERREPONT

Born: Abt 1070

Married:

Died: 1120/1123

4 Guillaume De PIERREPONT

Born: Abt 1100

Married:

Died:

9 Ermengarde De MONTAIGU

Born: Abt 1075

Died: Aft 1123

2 Hugues De PIERREPONT

Born: Abt 1127

Married:

Died: 1188

10

Born:

Married:

Died:

5 --

Born:

Died:

11

Born:

Died:

1 Beatrix De PIERREPONT

Born: Abt 1155
-SAME AS #11,ROYAL CHART 175
Married:

Died:

12 Eudes De VITRY

Born: Abt 1073

Married:

Died: Abt 1158

6 Gauthier, Count of Rethel

Born: Abt 1100

Married: Abt 1130

Died: 1171

13 Maud De RETHEL

Born: Abt 1075
-CONTINUED AS #3,ROYAL CHART 2188
Died: Aft 1151

William De WARENNE

Spouse

3 Clemence De RETHEL

Born: Abt 1133

Died: Aft 1191

14 Godfrey, Count of Namur

Born: 1067/1068
-CONTINUED AS #1,ROYAL CHART 1557
Married: Abt 1109

Died: 19 Aug 1139

7 Beatrice De NAMUR

Born: Abt 1110

Died: 1160

15 Ermesinde of Luxemburg

Born: Abt 1080
-CONTINUED AS #1,ROYAL CHART 1558
Died: 24 Jun 1143

Sources include: Faris preliminary Charlemagne manuscript (June 1995), pp. 280-281; Schwennicke 3:678, 626.

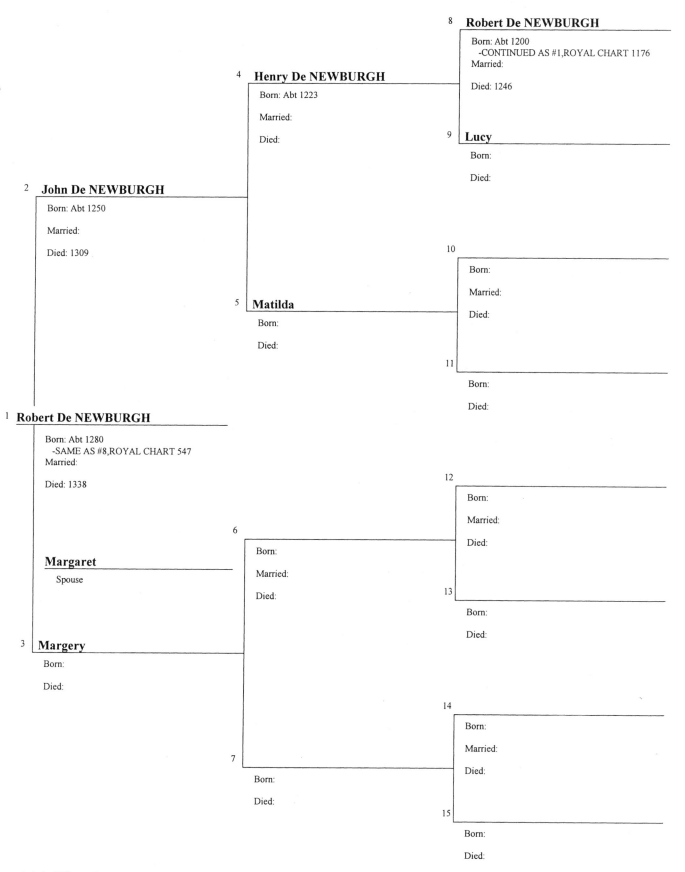

8 **Robert De NEWBURGH**

Born: Abt 1200
-CONTINUED AS #1,ROYAL CHART 1176
Married:

Died: 1246

4 **Henry De NEWBURGH**

Born: Abt 1223

Married:

Died:

9 **Lucy**

Born:

Died:

2 **John De NEWBURGH**

Born: Abt 1250

Married:

Died: 1309

10

Born:

Married:

Died:

5 **Matilda**

Born:

Died:

11

Born:

Died:

1 **Robert De NEWBURGH**

Born: Abt 1280
-SAME AS #8,ROYAL CHART 547
Married:

Died: 1338

12

Born:

Married:

Died:

6

Born:

Married:

Died:

13

Born:

Died:

Margaret

Spouse

3 **Margery**

Born:

Died:

14

Born:

Married:

Died:

7

Born:

Died:

15

Born:

Died:

Sources include: LDS records.

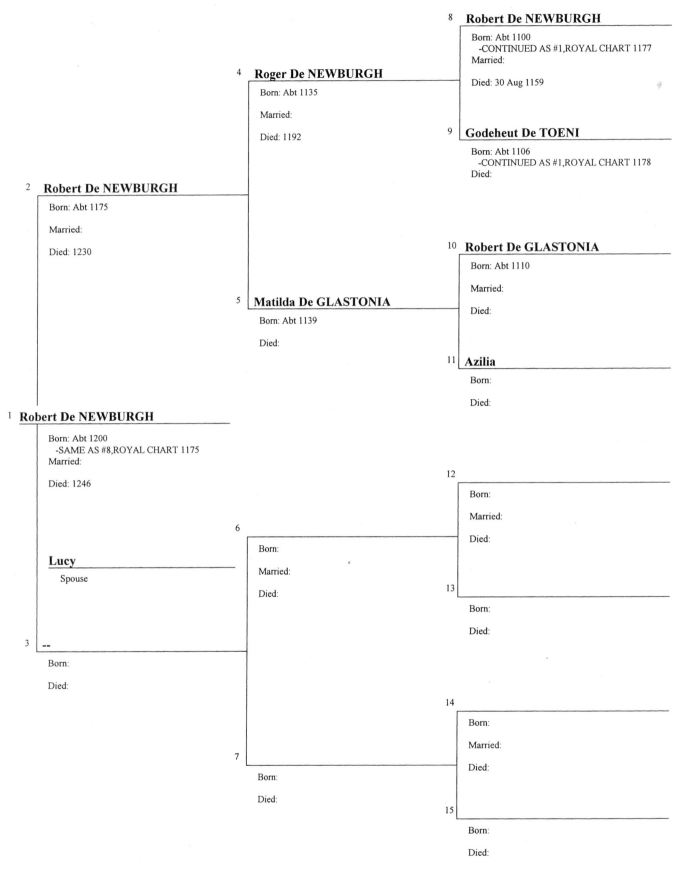

8 **Robert De NEWBURGH**

Born: Abt 1100
-CONTINUED AS #1,ROYAL CHART 1177
Married:

Died: 30 Aug 1159

4 **Roger De NEWBURGH**

Born: Abt 1135

Married:

Died: 1192

9 **Godeheut De TOENI**

Born: Abt 1106
-CONTINUED AS #1,ROYAL CHART 1178
Died:

2 **Robert De NEWBURGH**

Born: Abt 1175

Married:

Died: 1230

10 **Robert De GLASTONIA**

Born: Abt 1110

Married:

Died:

5 **Matilda De GLASTONIA**

Born: Abt 1139

Died:

11 **Azilia**

Born:

Died:

1 **Robert De NEWBURGH**

Born: Abt 1200
-SAME AS #8,ROYAL CHART 1175
Married:

Died: 1246

12

Born:

Married:

Died:

6

Born:

Married:

Died:

13

Born:

Died:

Lucy

Spouse

3 **--**

Born:

Died:

14

Born:

Married:

Died:

7

Born:

Died:

15

Born:

Died:

Sources include: LDS records.

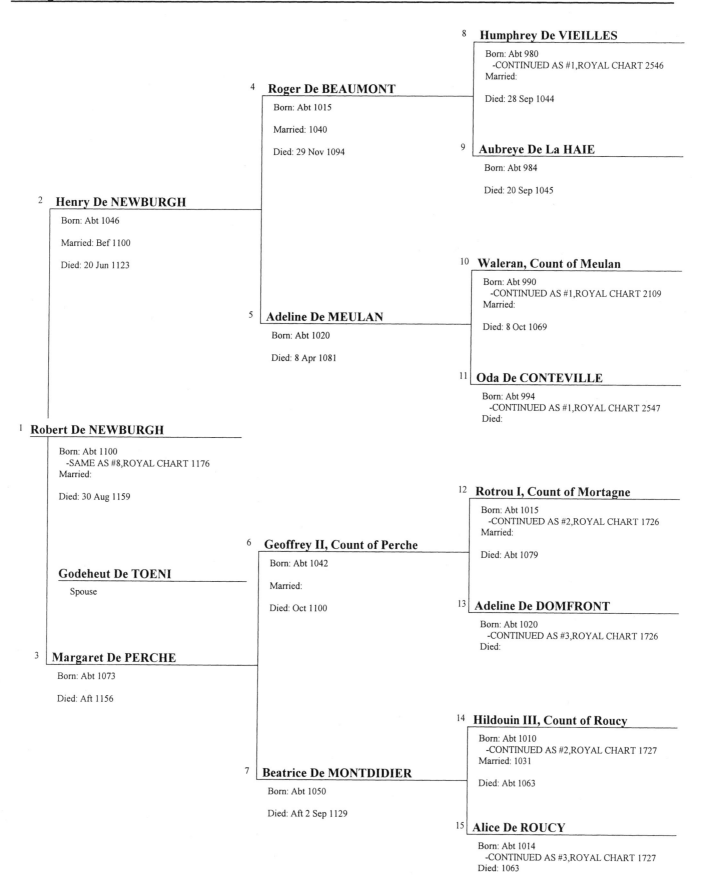

8 **Humphrey De VIEILLES**

Born: Abt 980
 -CONTINUED AS #1,ROYAL CHART 2546
Married:

Died: 28 Sep 1044

4 **Roger De BEAUMONT**

Born: Abt 1015

Married: 1040

Died: 29 Nov 1094

9 **Aubreye De La HAIE**

Born: Abt 984

Died: 20 Sep 1045

2 **Henry De NEWBURGH**

Born: Abt 1046

Married: Bef 1100

Died: 20 Jun 1123

10 **Waleran, Count of Meulan**

Born: Abt 990
 -CONTINUED AS #1,ROYAL CHART 2109
Married:

Died: 8 Oct 1069

5 **Adeline De MEULAN**

Born: Abt 1020

Died: 8 Apr 1081

11 **Oda De CONTEVILLE**

Born: Abt 994
 -CONTINUED AS #1,ROYAL CHART 2547
Died:

1 **Robert De NEWBURGH**

Born: Abt 1100
 -SAME AS #8,ROYAL CHART 1176
Married:

Died: 30 Aug 1159

12 **Rotrou I, Count of Mortagne**

Born: Abt 1015
 -CONTINUED AS #2,ROYAL CHART 1726
Married:

Died: Abt 1079

6 **Geoffrey II, Count of Perche**

Born: Abt 1042

Married:

Died: Oct 1100

Godeheut De TOENI

Spouse

13 **Adeline De DOMFRONT**

Born: Abt 1020
 -CONTINUED AS #3,ROYAL CHART 1726
Died:

3 **Margaret De PERCHE**

Born: Abt 1073

Died: Aft 1156

14 **Hildouin III, Count of Roucy**

Born: Abt 1010
 -CONTINUED AS #2,ROYAL CHART 1727
Married: 1031

Died: Abt 1063

7 **Beatrice De MONTDIDIER**

Born: Abt 1050

Died: Aft 2 Sep 1129

15 **Alice De ROUCY**

Born: Abt 1014
 -CONTINUED AS #3,ROYAL CHART 1727
Died: 1063

Sources include: LDS records; *Royal Ancestors* (1989), chart 11455 (#2 & 3 ancestry).

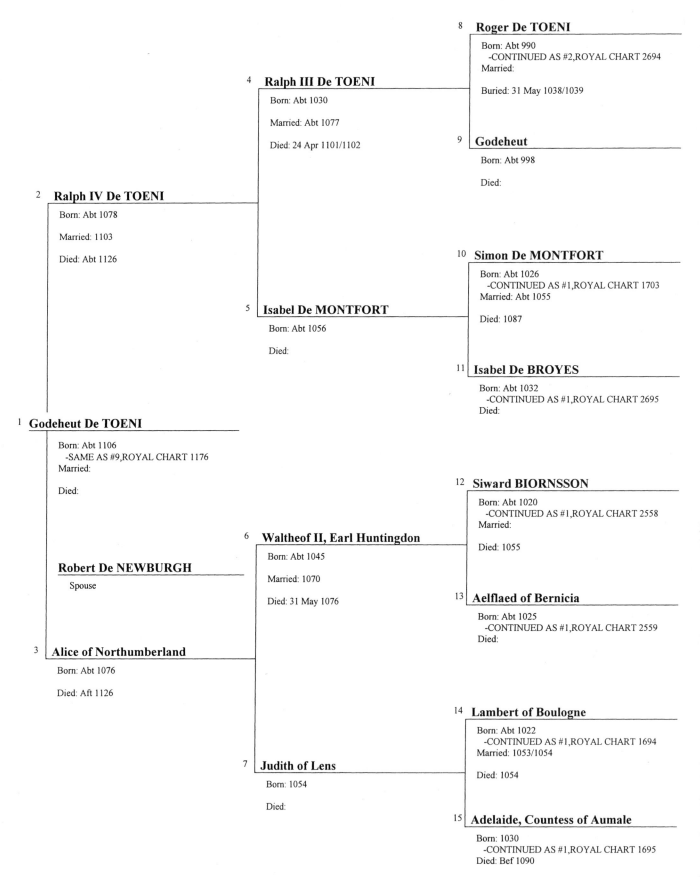

8 Roger De TOENI

Born: Abt 990
-CONTINUED AS #2,ROYAL CHART 2694
Married:

Buried: 31 May 1038/1039

4 Ralph III De TOENI

Born: Abt 1030

Married: Abt 1077

Died: 24 Apr 1101/1102

9 Godeheut

Born: Abt 998

Died:

2 Ralph IV De TOENI

Born: Abt 1078

Married: 1103

Died: Abt 1126

10 Simon De MONTFORT

Born: Abt 1026
-CONTINUED AS #1,ROYAL CHART 1703
Married: Abt 1055

Died: 1087

5 Isabel De MONTFORT

Born: Abt 1056

Died:

11 Isabel De BROYES

Born: Abt 1032
-CONTINUED AS #1,ROYAL CHART 2695
Died:

1 Godeheut De TOENI

Born: Abt 1106
-SAME AS #9,ROYAL CHART 1176
Married:

Died:

12 Siward BIORNSSON

Born: Abt 1020
-CONTINUED AS #1,ROYAL CHART 2558
Married:

Died: 1055

6 Waltheof II, Earl Huntingdon

Born: Abt 1045

Married: 1070

Died: 31 May 1076

13 Aelflaed of Bernicia

Born: Abt 1025
-CONTINUED AS #1,ROYAL CHART 2559
Died:

Robert De NEWBURGH

Spouse

3 Alice of Northumberland

Born: Abt 1076

Died: Aft 1126

14 Lambert of Boulogne

Born: Abt 1022
-CONTINUED AS #1,ROYAL CHART 1694
Married: 1053/1054

Died: 1054

7 Judith of Lens

Born: 1054

Died:

15 Adelaide, Countess of Aumale

Born: 1030
-CONTINUED AS #1,ROYAL CHART 1695
Died: Bef 1090

Sources include: LDS records; *Royal Ancestors* (1989), chart 11357 (#2 & 3 ancestry).

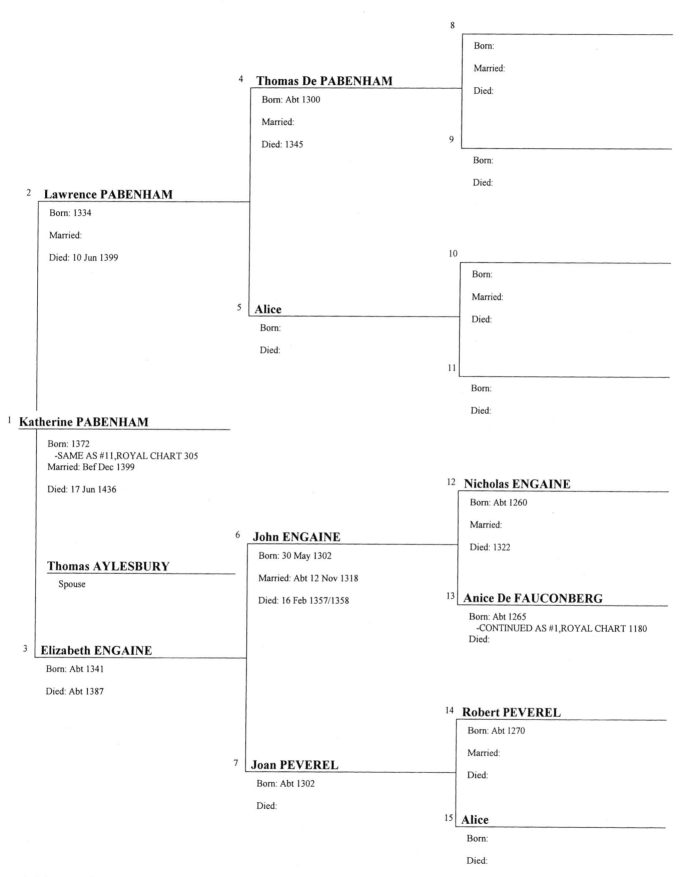

8

4 **Thomas De PABENHAM**
Born: Abt 1300
Married:
Died: 1345

Born:
Married:
Died:

9

Born:
Died:

2 **Lawrence PABENHAM**
Born: 1334
Married:
Died: 10 Jun 1399

10

Born:
Married:
Died:

5 **Alice**
Born:
Died:

11

Born:
Died:

1 **Katherine PABENHAM**
Born: 1372
   -SAME AS #11,ROYAL CHART 305
Married: Bef Dec 1399
Died: 17 Jun 1436

12 **Nicholas ENGAINE**
Born: Abt 1260
Married:
Died: 1322

6 **John ENGAINE**
Born: 30 May 1302
Married: Abt 12 Nov 1318
Died: 16 Feb 1357/1358

13 **Anice De FAUCONBERG**
Born: Abt 1265
   -CONTINUED AS #1,ROYAL CHART 1180
Died:

Thomas AYLESBURY
Spouse

3 **Elizabeth ENGAINE**
Born: Abt 1341
Died: Abt 1387

14 **Robert PEVEREL**
Born: Abt 1270
Married:
Died:

7 **Joan PEVEREL**
Born: Abt 1302
Died:

15 **Alice**
Born:
Died:

Sources include: *Ancestral Roots* 136.

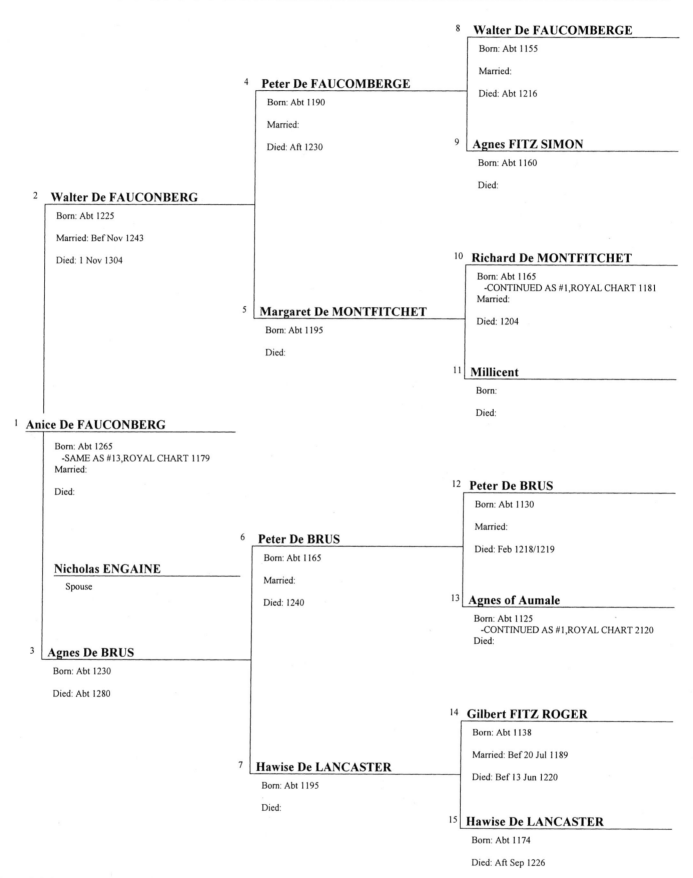

8 **Walter De FAUCOMBERGE**

Born: Abt 1155

Married:

Died: Abt 1216

4 **Peter De FAUCOMBERGE**

Born: Abt 1190

Married:

Died: Aft 1230

9 **Agnes FITZ SIMON**

Born: Abt 1160

Died:

2 **Walter De FAUCONBERG**

Born: Abt 1225

Married: Bef Nov 1243

Died: 1 Nov 1304

10 **Richard De MONTFITCHET**

Born: Abt 1165
  -CONTINUED AS #1,ROYAL CHART 1181
Married:

Died: 1204

5 **Margaret De MONTFITCHET**

Born: Abt 1195

Died:

11 **Millicent**

Born:

Died:

1 **Anice De FAUCONBERG**

Born: Abt 1265
  -SAME AS #13,ROYAL CHART 1179
Married:

Died:

12 **Peter De BRUS**

Born: Abt 1130

Married:

Died: Feb 1218/1219

6 **Peter De BRUS**

Born: Abt 1165

Married:

Died: 1240

13 **Agnes of Aumale**

Born: Abt 1125
  -CONTINUED AS #1,ROYAL CHART 2120
Died:

Nicholas ENGAINE

Spouse

3 **Agnes De BRUS**

Born: Abt 1230

Died: Abt 1280

14 **Gilbert FITZ ROGER**

Born: Abt 1138

Married: Bef 20 Jul 1189

Died: Bef 13 Jun 1220

7 **Hawise De LANCASTER**

Born: Abt 1195

Died:

15 **Hawise De LANCASTER**

Born: Abt 1174

Died: Aft Sep 1226

Sources include: *Ancestral Roots* 8 (2004), Line 136; *Ancestral Roots* 136, 184B; Faris preliminary baronial manuscript (1998), pp. 567-569 (Fauconberg), 246 (Brus). See note chart 353 regarding the death date of #6 Peter.

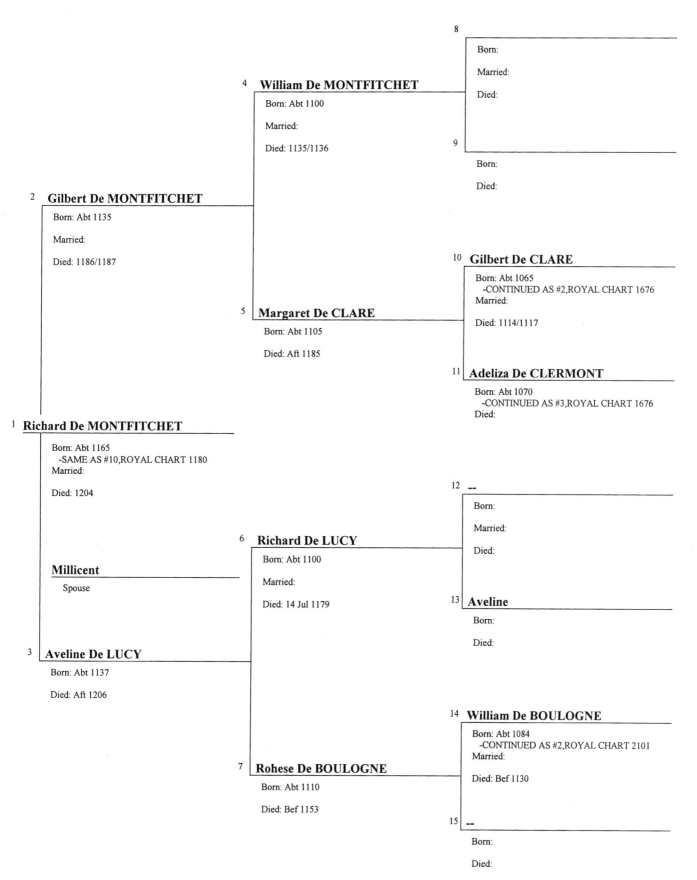

8

Born:

Married:

Died:

---

4 **William De MONTFITCHET**

Born: Abt 1100

Married:

Died: 1135/1136

9

Born:

Died:

---

2 **Gilbert De MONTFITCHET**

Born: Abt 1135

Married:

Died: 1186/1187

10 **Gilbert De CLARE**

Born: Abt 1065
  -CONTINUED AS #2,ROYAL CHART 1676
Married:

Died: 1114/1117

---

5 **Margaret De CLARE**

Born: Abt 1105

Died: Aft 1185

11 **Adeliza De CLERMONT**

Born: Abt 1070
  -CONTINUED AS #3,ROYAL CHART 1676
Died:

---

1 **Richard De MONTFITCHET**

Born: Abt 1165
  -SAME AS #10,ROYAL CHART 1180
Married:

Died: 1204

12 **--**

Born:

Married:

Died:

---

6 **Richard De LUCY**

Born: Abt 1100

Married:

Died: 14 Jul 1179

13 **Aveline**

Born:

Died:

Millicent

Spouse

---

3 **Aveline De LUCY**

Born: Abt 1137

Died: Aft 1206

14 **William De BOULOGNE**

Born: Abt 1084
  -CONTINUED AS #2,ROYAL CHART 2101
Married:

Died: Bef 1130

---

7 **Rohese De BOULOGNE**

Born: Abt 1110

Died: Bef 1153

15 **--**

Born:

Died:

Sources include: *Ancestral Roots* 184B; Research report by Douglas Richardson on the Lucy & Boulogne families (July 2004); LDS records. Note: #12 is claimed as Adrian De Lucy in LDS records. No evidence for the claim has been seen.

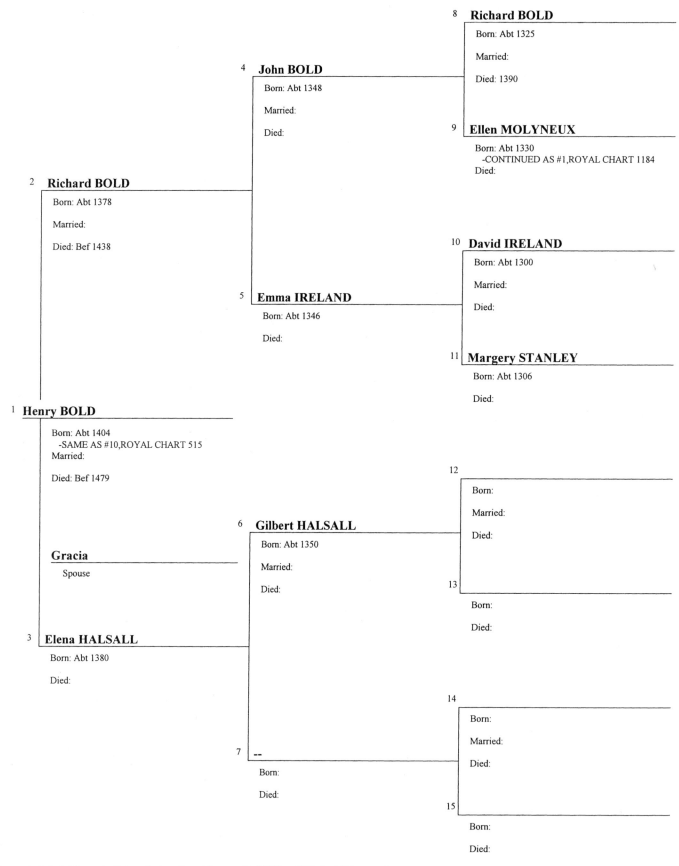

8 **Richard BOLD**

Born: Abt 1325

Married:

Died: 1390

4 **John BOLD**

Born: Abt 1348

Married:

Died:

9 **Ellen MOLYNEUX**

Born: Abt 1330
  -CONTINUED AS #1,ROYAL CHART 1184
Died:

2 **Richard BOLD**

Born: Abt 1378

Married:

Died: Bef 1438

10 **David IRELAND**

Born: Abt 1300

Married:

Died:

5 **Emma IRELAND**

Born: Abt 1346

Died:

11 **Margery STANLEY**

Born: Abt 1306

Died:

1 **Henry BOLD**

Born: Abt 1404
  -SAME AS #10,ROYAL CHART 515
Married:

Died: Bef 1479

12

Born:

Married:

Died:

6 **Gilbert HALSALL**

Born: Abt 1350

Married:

Died:

13

Born:

Died:

Gracia

Spouse

3 **Elena HALSALL**

Born: Abt 1380

Died:

14

Born:

Married:

Died:

7 **--**

Born:

Died:

15

Born:

Died:

Sources include: LDS records; Faris preliminary baronial manuscript (1998), p. 895 Ireland (#5 ancestry).

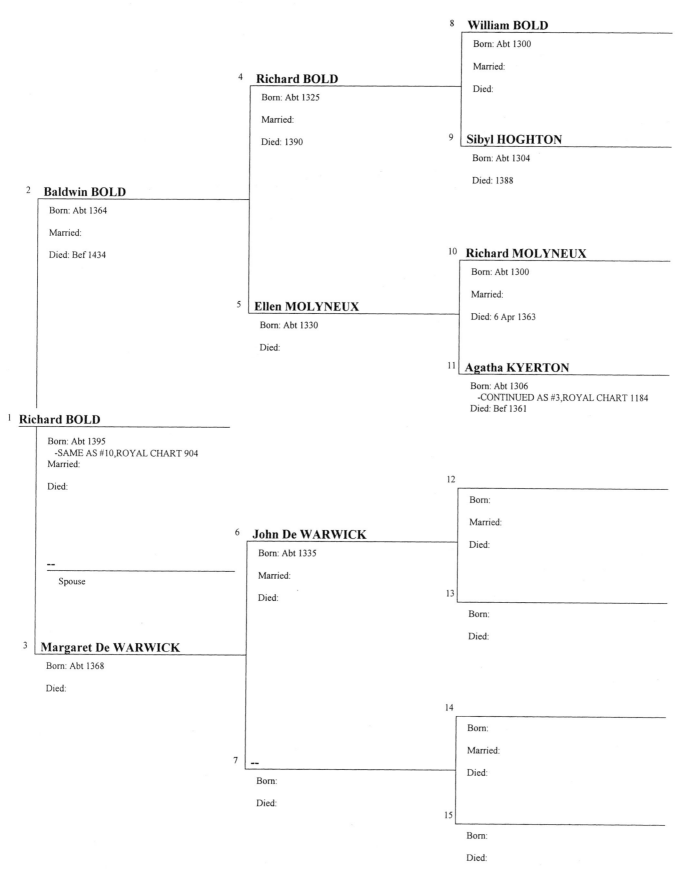

8 **William BOLD**

Born: Abt 1300

Married:

Died:

4 **Richard BOLD**

Born: Abt 1325

Married:

Died: 1390

9 **Sibyl HOGHTON**

Born: Abt 1304

Died: 1388

2 **Baldwin BOLD**

Born: Abt 1364

Married:

Died: Bef 1434

10 **Richard MOLYNEUX**

Born: Abt 1300

Married:

Died: 6 Apr 1363

5 **Ellen MOLYNEUX**

Born: Abt 1330

Died:

11 **Agatha KYERTON**

Born: Abt 1306
-CONTINUED AS #3,ROYAL CHART 1184
Died: Bef 1361

1 **Richard BOLD**

Born: Abt 1395
-SAME AS #10,ROYAL CHART 904
Married:

Died:

12

Born:

Married:

Died:

6 **John De WARWICK**

Born: Abt 1335

Married:

Died:

13

Born:

Died:

--
Spouse

3 **Margaret De WARWICK**

Born: Abt 1368

Died:

14

Born:

Married:

Died:

7 **--**

Born:

Died:

15

Born:

Died:

Sources include: LDS records.

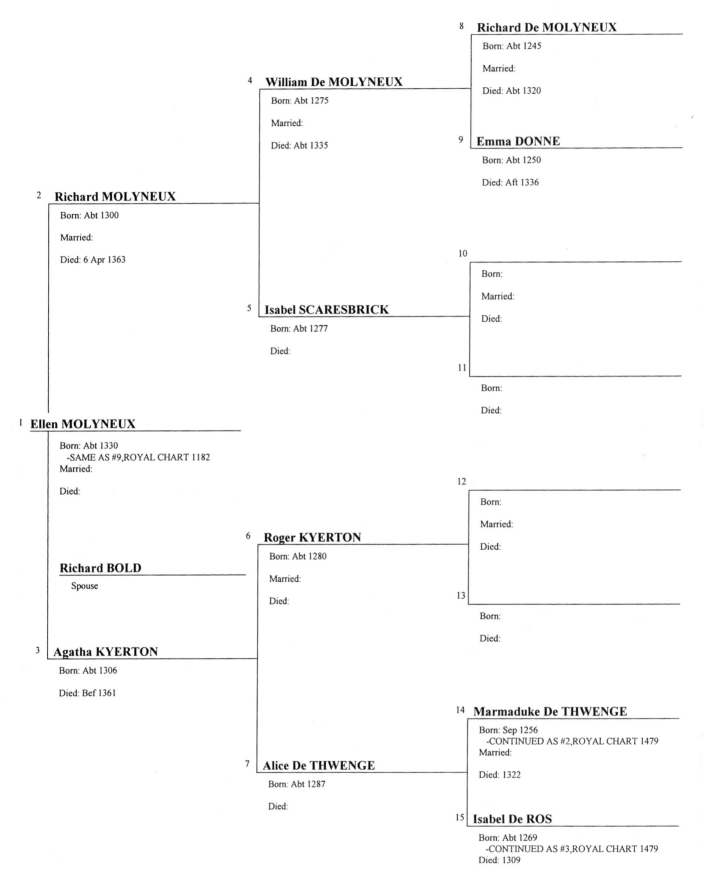

8 **Richard De MOLYNEUX**

Born: Abt 1245

Married:

Died: Abt 1320

4 **William De MOLYNEUX**

Born: Abt 1275

Married:

Died: Abt 1335

9 **Emma DONNE**

Born: Abt 1250

Died: Aft 1336

2 **Richard MOLYNEUX**

Born: Abt 1300

Married:

Died: 6 Apr 1363

10

Born:

Married:

Died:

5 **Isabel SCARESBRICK**

Born: Abt 1277

Died:

11

Born:

Died:

1 **Ellen MOLYNEUX**

Born: Abt 1330
  -SAME AS #9,ROYAL CHART 1182
Married:

Died:

12

Born:

Married:

Died:

6 **Roger KYERTON**

Born: Abt 1280

Married:

Died:

13

Born:

Died:

Richard BOLD

Spouse

3 **Agatha KYERTON**

Born: Abt 1306

Died: Bef 1361

14 **Marmaduke De THWENGE**

Born: Sep 1256
  -CONTINUED AS #2,ROYAL CHART 1479
Married:

Died: 1322

7 **Alice De THWENGE**

Born: Abt 1287

Died:

15 **Isabel De ROS**

Born: Abt 1269
  -CONTINUED AS #3,ROYAL CHART 1479
Died: 1309

Sources include: LDS records.

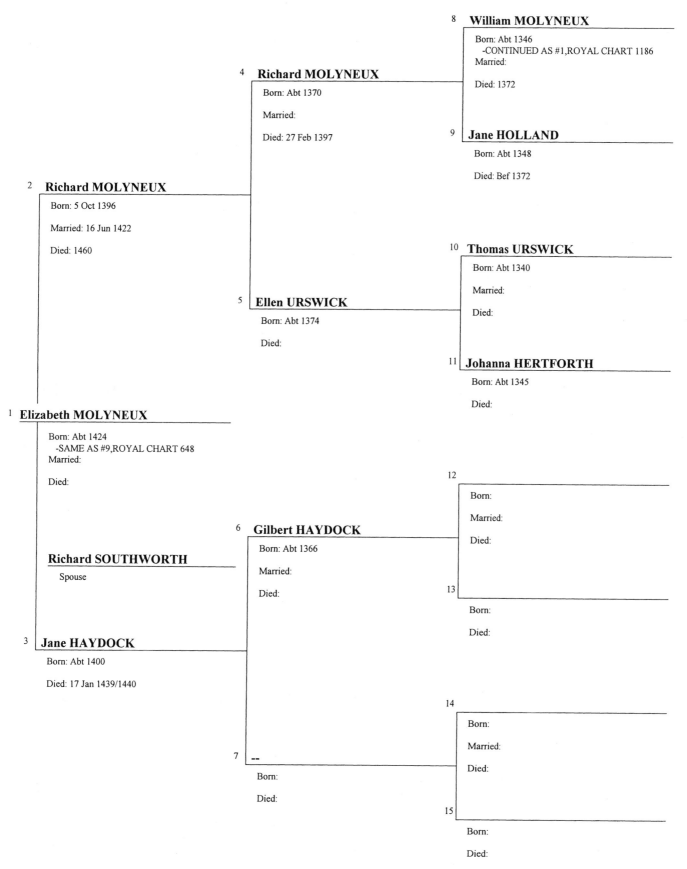

Pedigree Chart

8 **William MOLYNEUX**
Born: Abt 1346
-CONTINUED AS #1,ROYAL CHART 1186
Married:

Died: 1372

4 **Richard MOLYNEUX**
Born: Abt 1370

Married:

Died: 27 Feb 1397

9 **Jane HOLLAND**
Born: Abt 1348

Died: Bef 1372

2 **Richard MOLYNEUX**
Born: 5 Oct 1396

Married: 16 Jun 1422

Died: 1460

10 **Thomas URSWICK**
Born: Abt 1340

Married:

Died:

5 **Ellen URSWICK**
Born: Abt 1374

Died:

11 **Johanna HERTFORTH**
Born: Abt 1345

Died:

1 **Elizabeth MOLYNEUX**
Born: Abt 1424
-SAME AS #9,ROYAL CHART 648
Married:

Died:

12
Born:

Married:

Died:

6 **Gilbert HAYDOCK**
Born: Abt 1366

Married:

Died:

13
Born:

Died:

Richard SOUTHWORTH
Spouse

3 **Jane HAYDOCK**
Born: Abt 1400

Died: 17 Jan 1439/1440

14
Born:

Married:

Died:

7 **--**
Born:

Died:

15
Born:

Died:

Sources include: Weis, *Ancestry of Ensign Constant & Captain Thomas Southworth*, p. 31; LDS records.

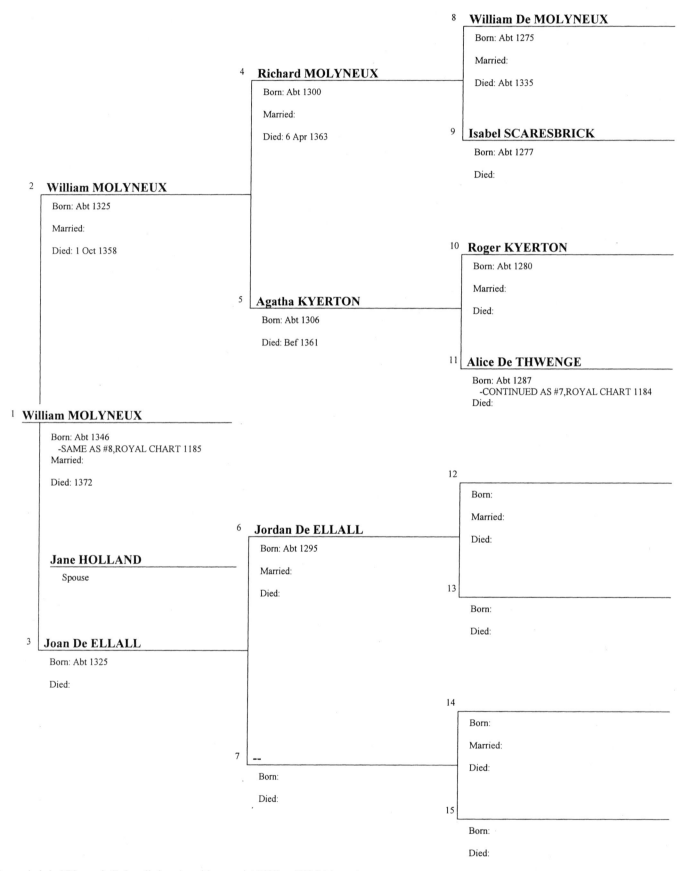

8 **William De MOLYNEUX**

Born: Abt 1275

Married:

Died: Abt 1335

4 **Richard MOLYNEUX**

Born: Abt 1300

Married:

Died: 6 Apr 1363

9 **Isabel SCARESBRICK**

Born: Abt 1277

Died:

2 **William MOLYNEUX**

Born: Abt 1325

Married:

Died: 1 Oct 1358

10 **Roger KYERTON**

Born: Abt 1280

Married:

Died:

5 **Agatha KYERTON**

Born: Abt 1306

Died: Bef 1361

11 **Alice De THWENGE**

Born: Abt 1287
-CONTINUED AS #7,ROYAL CHART 1184
Died:

1 **William MOLYNEUX**

Born: Abt 1346
-SAME AS #8,ROYAL CHART 1185
Married:

Died: 1372

12

Born:

Married:

Died:

6 **Jordan De ELLALL**

Born: Abt 1295

Married:

Died:

13

Born:

Died:

Jane HOLLAND

Spouse

3 **Joan De ELLALL**

Born: Abt 1325

Died:

14

Born:

Married:

Died:

7 **--**

Born:

Died:

15

Born:

Died:

Sources include: LDS records; Faris preliminary baronial manuscript (1998), p. 1098 (Molyneux).

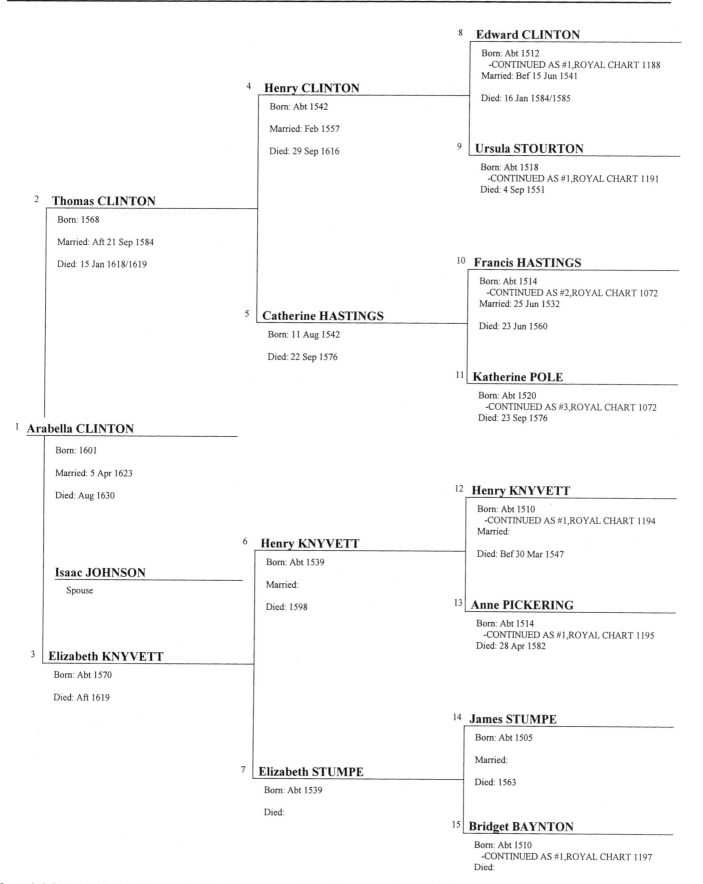

8 **Edward CLINTON**

Born: Abt 1512
-CONTINUED AS #1,ROYAL CHART 1188
Married: Bef 15 Jun 1541

Died: 16 Jan 1584/1585

4 **Henry CLINTON**

Born: Abt 1542

Married: Feb 1557

Died: 29 Sep 1616

9 **Ursula STOURTON**

Born: Abt 1518
-CONTINUED AS #1,ROYAL CHART 1191
Died: 4 Sep 1551

2 **Thomas CLINTON**

Born: 1568

Married: Aft 21 Sep 1584

Died: 15 Jan 1618/1619

10 **Francis HASTINGS**

Born: Abt 1514
-CONTINUED AS #2,ROYAL CHART 1072
Married: 25 Jun 1532

Died: 23 Jun 1560

5 **Catherine HASTINGS**

Born: 11 Aug 1542

Died: 22 Sep 1576

11 **Katherine POLE**

Born: Abt 1520
-CONTINUED AS #3,ROYAL CHART 1072
Died: 23 Sep 1576

1 **Arabella CLINTON**

Born: 1601

Married: 5 Apr 1623

Died: Aug 1630

12 **Henry KNYVETT**

Born: Abt 1510
-CONTINUED AS #1,ROYAL CHART 1194
Married:

Died: Bef 30 Mar 1547

6 **Henry KNYVETT**

Born: Abt 1539

Married:

Died: 1598

Isaac JOHNSON

Spouse

13 **Anne PICKERING**

Born: Abt 1514
-CONTINUED AS #1,ROYAL CHART 1195
Died: 28 Apr 1582

3 **Elizabeth KNYVETT**

Born: Abt 1570

Died: Aft 1619

14 **James STUMPE**

Born: Abt 1505

Married:

Died: 1563

7 **Elizabeth STUMPE**

Born: Abt 1539

Died:

15 **Bridget BAYNTON**

Born: Abt 1510
-CONTINUED AS #1,ROYAL CHART 1197
Died:

Sources include: *Ancestral Roots* 225; *Magna Charta* 57; LDS records. Notes: #1, 2, 4 & 8--Clinton or Fiennes. #2 & 3 have no proven American descendants, although claims have been made. At least five of their children took an active part in the settlement of New England. No other noble house in England "had more intimate connections with New England settlements and...a deeper interest in their success" (see *TAG* 15:122-125; 20:46-48).

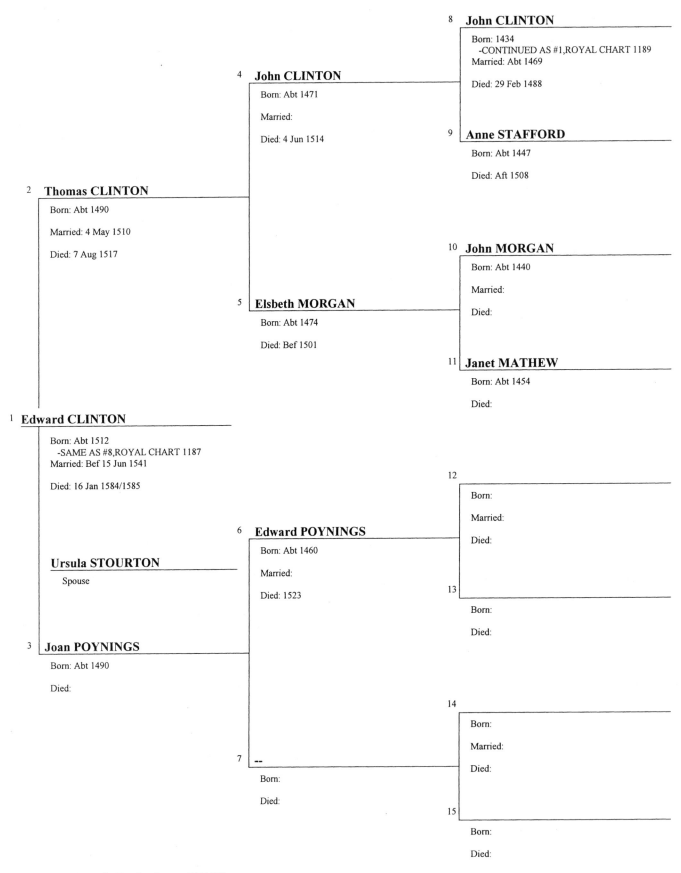

8 **John CLINTON**

Born: 1434
-CONTINUED AS #1,ROYAL CHART 1189
Married: Abt 1469

Died: 29 Feb 1488

4 **John CLINTON**

Born: Abt 1471

Married:

Died: 4 Jun 1514

9 **Anne STAFFORD**

Born: Abt 1447

Died: Aft 1508

2 **Thomas CLINTON**

Born: Abt 1490

Married: 4 May 1510

Died: 7 Aug 1517

10 **John MORGAN**

Born: Abt 1440

Married:

Died:

5 **Elsbeth MORGAN**

Born: Abt 1474

Died: Bef 1501

11 **Janet MATHEW**

Born: Abt 1454

Died:

1 **Edward CLINTON**

Born: Abt 1512
-SAME AS #8,ROYAL CHART 1187
Married: Bef 15 Jun 1541

Died: 16 Jan 1584/1585

12

Born:

Married:

Died:

6 **Edward POYNINGS**

Born: Abt 1460

Married:

Died: 1523

13

Born:

Died:

Ursula STOURTON

Spouse

3 **Joan POYNINGS**

Born: Abt 1490

Died:

14

Born:

Married:

Died:

7 **--**

Born:

Died:

15

Born:

Died:

Sources include: LDS records; *Complete Peerage* 3:316 (#9).

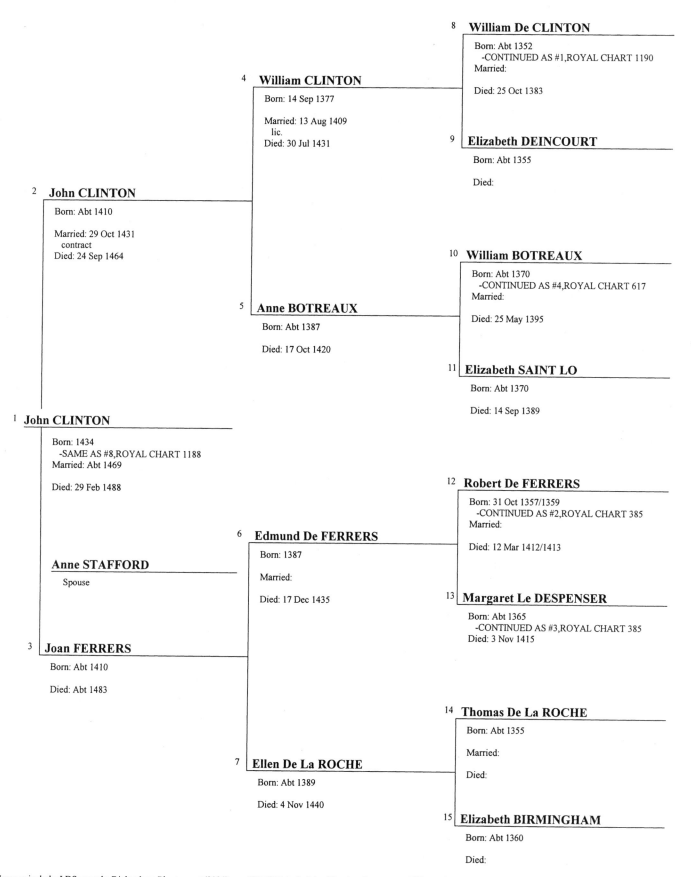

8 William De CLINTON

Born: Abt 1352
-CONTINUED AS #1,ROYAL CHART 1190
Married:

Died: 25 Oct 1383

4 William CLINTON

Born: 14 Sep 1377

Married: 13 Aug 1409
lic.
Died: 30 Jul 1431

9 Elizabeth DEINCOURT

Born: Abt 1355

Died:

2 John CLINTON

Born: Abt 1410

Married: 29 Oct 1431
contract
Died: 24 Sep 1464

10 William BOTREAUX

Born: Abt 1370
-CONTINUED AS #4,ROYAL CHART 617
Married:

Died: 25 May 1395

5 Anne BOTREAUX

Born: Abt 1387

Died: 17 Oct 1420

11 Elizabeth SAINT LO

Born: Abt 1370

Died: 14 Sep 1389

1 John CLINTON

Born: 1434
-SAME AS #8,ROYAL CHART 1188
Married: Abt 1469

Died: 29 Feb 1488

12 Robert De FERRERS

Born: 31 Oct 1357/1359
-CONTINUED AS #2,ROYAL CHART 385
Married:

Died: 12 Mar 1412/1413

6 Edmund De FERRERS

Born: 1387

Married:

Died: 17 Dec 1435

13 Margaret Le DESPENSER

Born: Abt 1365
-CONTINUED AS #3,ROYAL CHART 385
Died: 3 Nov 1415

Anne STAFFORD

Spouse

3 Joan FERRERS

Born: Abt 1410

Died: Abt 1483

14 Thomas De La ROCHE

Born: Abt 1355

Married:

Died:

7 Ellen De La ROCHE

Born: Abt 1389

Died: 4 Nov 1440

15 Elizabeth BIRMINGHAM

Born: Abt 1360

Died:

Sources include: LDS records; Richardson *Plantagenet* (2004), pp. 502-503 Moels (identification & ancestry of #5 Anne); Faris 2--Ferrers (#6 & 7 ancestry).

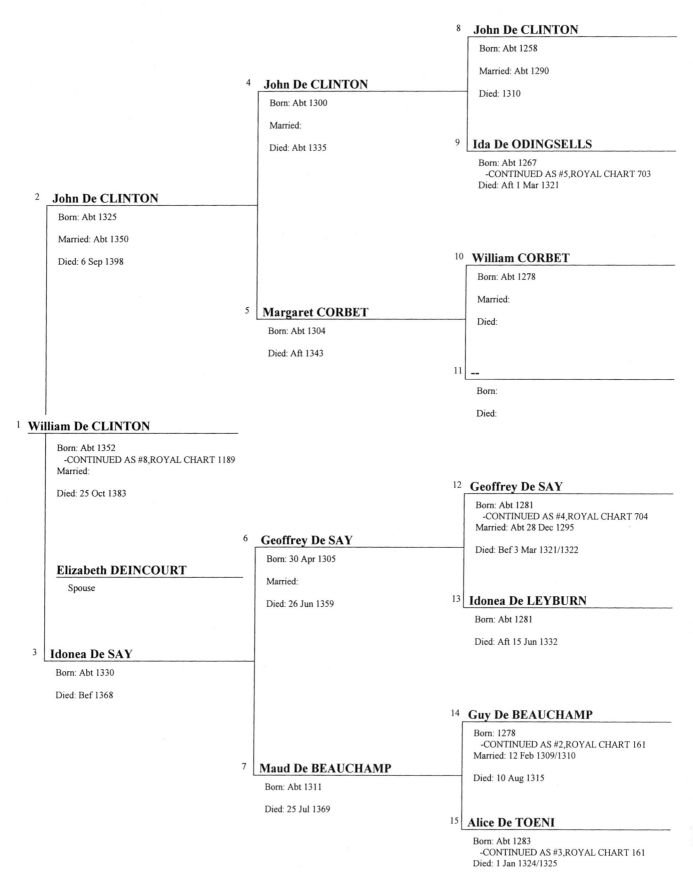

8 John De CLINTON

Born: Abt 1258

Married: Abt 1290

Died: 1310

4 John De CLINTON

Born: Abt 1300

Married:

Died: Abt 1335

9 Ida De ODINGSELLS

Born: Abt 1267
    -CONTINUED AS #5,ROYAL CHART 703
Died: Aft 1 Mar 1321

2 John De CLINTON

Born: Abt 1325

Married: Abt 1350

Died: 6 Sep 1398

10 William CORBET

Born: Abt 1278

Married:

Died:

5 Margaret CORBET

Born: Abt 1304

Died: Aft 1343

11 --

Born:

Died:

1 William De CLINTON

Born: Abt 1352
    -CONTINUED AS #8,ROYAL CHART 1189
Married:

Died: 25 Oct 1383

Elizabeth DEINCOURT

Spouse

12 Geoffrey De SAY

Born: Abt 1281
    -CONTINUED AS #4,ROYAL CHART 704
Married: Abt 28 Dec 1295

Died: Bef 3 Mar 1321/1322

6 Geoffrey De SAY

Born: 30 Apr 1305

Married:

Died: 26 Jun 1359

13 Idonea De LEYBURN

Born: Abt 1281

Died: Aft 15 Jun 1332

3 Idonea De SAY

Born: Abt 1330

Died: Bef 1368

14 Guy De BEAUCHAMP

Born: 1278
    -CONTINUED AS #2,ROYAL CHART 161
Married: 12 Feb 1309/1310

Died: 10 Aug 1315

7 Maud De BEAUCHAMP

Born: Abt 1311

Died: 25 Jul 1369

15 Alice De TOENI

Born: Abt 1283
    -CONTINUED AS #3,ROYAL CHART 161
Died: 1 Jan 1324/1325

Sources include: LDS records.

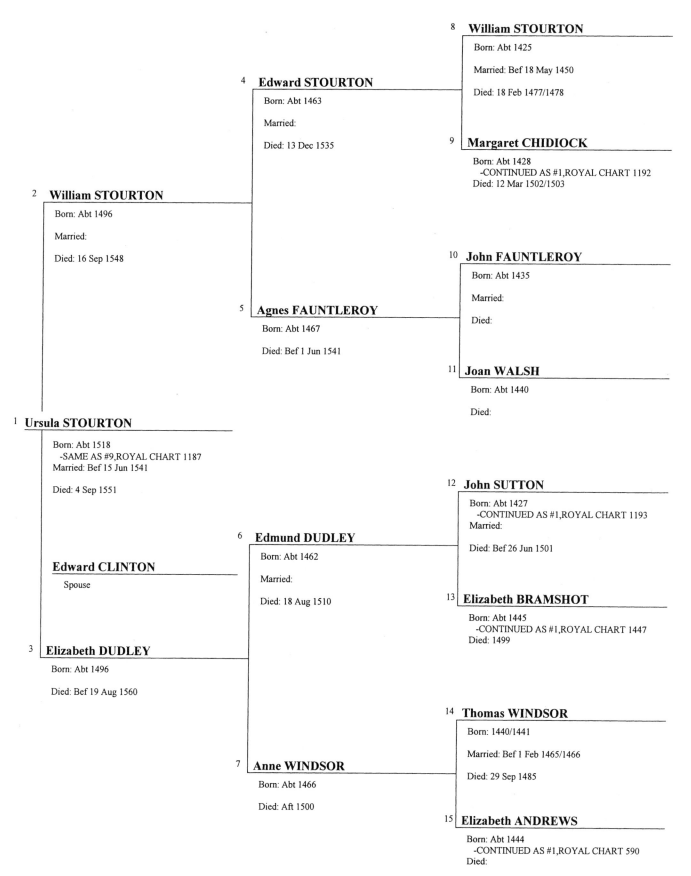

8 **William STOURTON**
Born: Abt 1425
Married: Bef 18 May 1450
Died: 18 Feb 1477/1478

4 **Edward STOURTON**
Born: Abt 1463
Married:
Died: 13 Dec 1535

9 **Margaret CHIDIOCK**
Born: Abt 1428
-CONTINUED AS #1,ROYAL CHART 1192
Died: 12 Mar 1502/1503

2 **William STOURTON**
Born: Abt 1496
Married:
Died: 16 Sep 1548

10 **John FAUNTLEROY**
Born: Abt 1435
Married:
Died:

5 **Agnes FAUNTLEROY**
Born: Abt 1467
Died: Bef 1 Jun 1541

11 **Joan WALSH**
Born: Abt 1440
Died:

1 **Ursula STOURTON**
Born: Abt 1518
-SAME AS #9,ROYAL CHART 1187
Married: Bef 15 Jun 1541
Died: 4 Sep 1551

12 **John SUTTON**
Born: Abt 1427
-CONTINUED AS #1,ROYAL CHART 1193
Married:
Died: Bef 26 Jun 1501

6 **Edmund DUDLEY**
Born: Abt 1462
Married:
Died: 18 Aug 1510

13 **Elizabeth BRAMSHOT**
Born: Abt 1445
-CONTINUED AS #1,ROYAL CHART 1447
Died: 1499

Edward CLINTON
Spouse

3 **Elizabeth DUDLEY**
Born: Abt 1496
Died: Bef 19 Aug 1560

14 **Thomas WINDSOR**
Born: 1440/1441
Married: Bef 1 Feb 1465/1466
Died: 29 Sep 1485

7 **Anne WINDSOR**
Born: Abt 1466
Died: Aft 1500

15 **Elizabeth ANDREWS**
Born: Abt 1444
-CONTINUED AS #1,ROYAL CHART 590
Died:

Sources include: Faris preliminary baronial manuscript (1998), pp. 1451-52 (Stourton), 520-521 (Dudley); *Ancestral Roots* 225-40; *Magna Charta* 149B (#6 ancestry); LDS records.

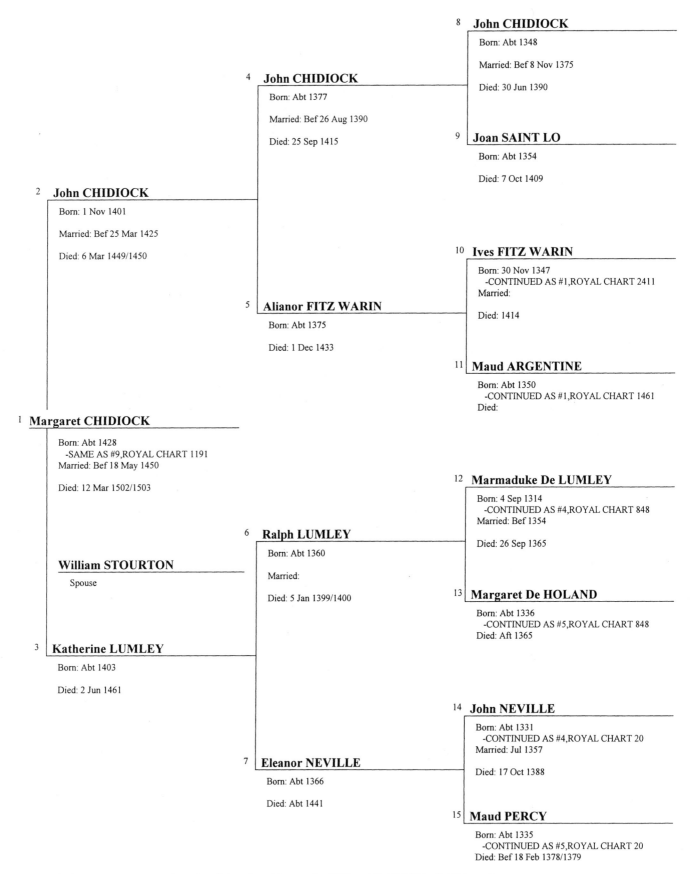

8 **John CHIDIOCK**
Born: Abt 1348
Married: Bef 8 Nov 1375
Died: 30 Jun 1390

4 **John CHIDIOCK**
Born: Abt 1377
Married: Bef 26 Aug 1390
Died: 25 Sep 1415

9 **Joan SAINT LO**
Born: Abt 1354
Died: 7 Oct 1409

2 **John CHIDIOCK**
Born: 1 Nov 1401
Married: Bef 25 Mar 1425
Died: 6 Mar 1449/1450

10 **Ives FITZ WARIN**
Born: 30 Nov 1347
-CONTINUED AS #1,ROYAL CHART 2411
Married:
Died: 1414

5 **Alianor FITZ WARIN**
Born: Abt 1375
Died: 1 Dec 1433

11 **Maud ARGENTINE**
Born: Abt 1350
-CONTINUED AS #1,ROYAL CHART 1461
Died:

1 **Margaret CHIDIOCK**
Born: Abt 1428
-SAME AS #9,ROYAL CHART 1191
Married: Bef 18 May 1450
Died: 12 Mar 1502/1503

12 **Marmaduke De LUMLEY**
Born: 4 Sep 1314
-CONTINUED AS #4,ROYAL CHART 848
Married: Bef 1354
Died: 26 Sep 1365

6 **Ralph LUMLEY**
Born: Abt 1360
Married:
Died: 5 Jan 1399/1400

William STOURTON
Spouse

13 **Margaret De HOLAND**
Born: Abt 1336
-CONTINUED AS #5,ROYAL CHART 848
Died: Aft 1365

3 **Katherine LUMLEY**
Born: Abt 1403
Died: 2 Jun 1461

14 **John NEVILLE**
Born: Abt 1331
-CONTINUED AS #4,ROYAL CHART 20
Married: Jul 1357
Died: 17 Oct 1388

7 **Eleanor NEVILLE**
Born: Abt 1366
Died: Abt 1441

15 **Maud PERCY**
Born: Abt 1335
-CONTINUED AS #5,ROYAL CHART 20
Died: Bef 18 Feb 1378/1379

Sources include: *Complete Peerage* 5:455-462; Faris preliminary baronial manuscript (1998), pp. 342-343 (Chideock); LDS records.

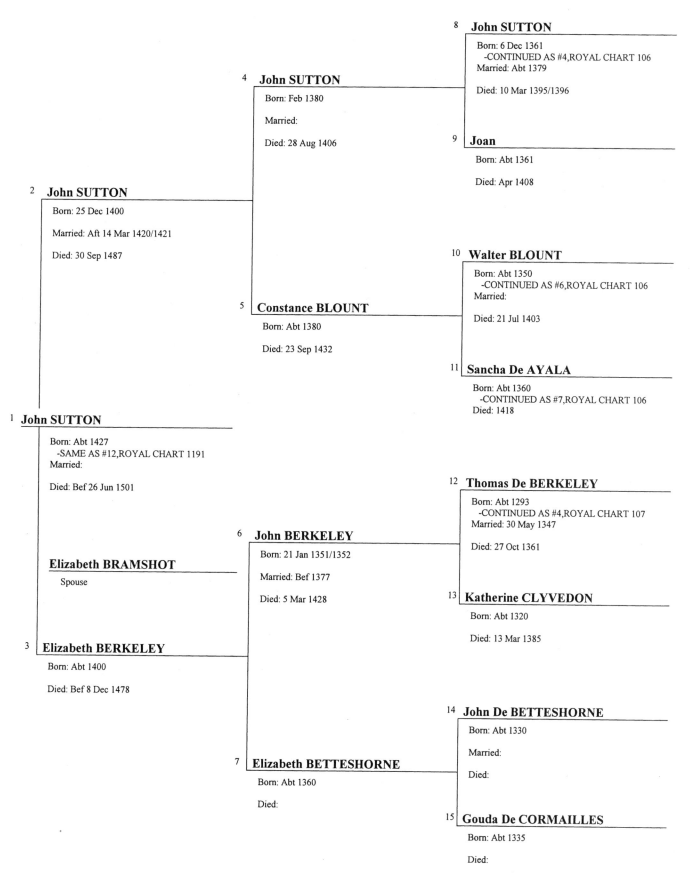

8 John SUTTON

Born: 6 Dec 1361
 -CONTINUED AS #4,ROYAL CHART 106
Married: Abt 1379

Died: 10 Mar 1395/1396

4 John SUTTON

Born: Feb 1380

Married:

Died: 28 Aug 1406

9 Joan

Born: Abt 1361

Died: Apr 1408

2 John SUTTON

Born: 25 Dec 1400

Married: Aft 14 Mar 1420/1421

Died: 30 Sep 1487

10 Walter BLOUNT

Born: Abt 1350
 -CONTINUED AS #6,ROYAL CHART 106
Married:

Died: 21 Jul 1403

5 Constance BLOUNT

Born: Abt 1380

Died: 23 Sep 1432

11 Sancha De AYALA

Born: Abt 1360
 -CONTINUED AS #7,ROYAL CHART 106
Died: 1418

1 John SUTTON

Born: Abt 1427
 -SAME AS #12,ROYAL CHART 1191
Married:

Died: Bef 26 Jun 1501

12 Thomas De BERKELEY

Born: Abt 1293
 -CONTINUED AS #4,ROYAL CHART 107
Married: 30 May 1347

Died: 27 Oct 1361

6 John BERKELEY

Born: 21 Jan 1351/1352

Married: Bef 1377

Died: 5 Mar 1428

13 Katherine CLYVEDON

Born: Abt 1320

Died: 13 Mar 1385

Elizabeth BRAMSHOT

Spouse

3 Elizabeth BERKELEY

Born: Abt 1400

Died: Bef 8 Dec 1478

14 John De BETTESHORNE

Born: Abt 1330

Married:

Died:

7 Elizabeth BETTESHORNE

Born: Abt 1360

Died:

15 Gouda De CORMAILLES

Born: Abt 1335

Died:

Sources include: *Magna Charta* 149B-11; LDS records.

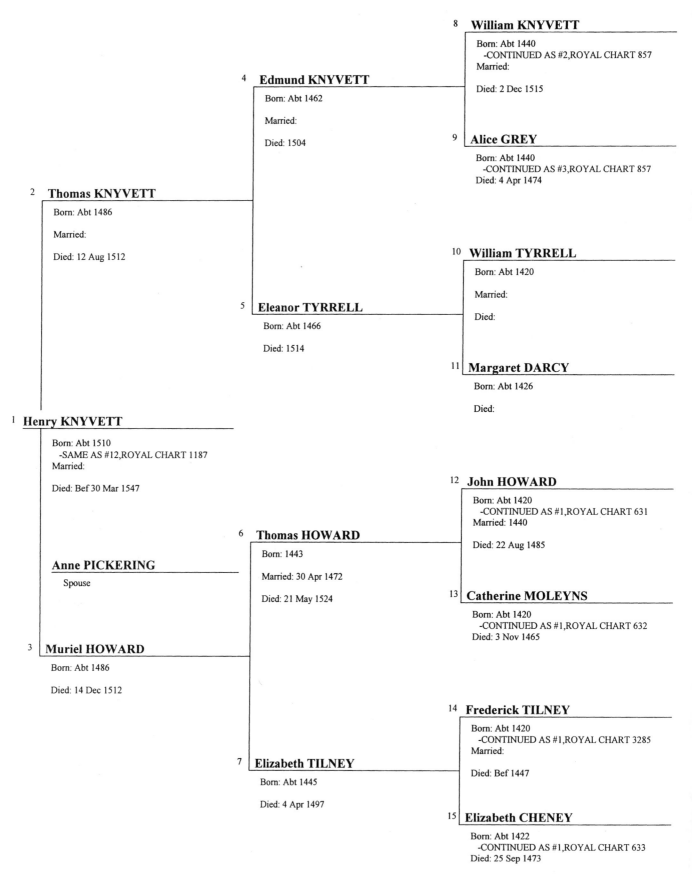

8 William KNYVETT

Born: Abt 1440
-CONTINUED AS #2,ROYAL CHART 857
Married:

Died: 2 Dec 1515

4 Edmund KNYVETT

Born: Abt 1462

Married:

Died: 1504

9 Alice GREY

Born: Abt 1440
-CONTINUED AS #3,ROYAL CHART 857
Died: 4 Apr 1474

2 Thomas KNYVETT

Born: Abt 1486

Married:

Died: 12 Aug 1512

10 William TYRRELL

Born: Abt 1420

Married:

Died:

5 Eleanor TYRRELL

Born: Abt 1466

Died: 1514

11 Margaret DARCY

Born: Abt 1426

Died:

1 Henry KNYVETT

Born: Abt 1510
-SAME AS #12,ROYAL CHART 1187
Married:

Died: Bef 30 Mar 1547

12 John HOWARD

Born: Abt 1420
-CONTINUED AS #1,ROYAL CHART 631
Married: 1440

Died: 22 Aug 1485

6 Thomas HOWARD

Born: 1443

Married: 30 Apr 1472

Died: 21 May 1524

Anne PICKERING

Spouse

13 Catherine MOLEYNS

Born: Abt 1420
-CONTINUED AS #1,ROYAL CHART 632
Died: 3 Nov 1465

3 Muriel HOWARD

Born: Abt 1486

Died: 14 Dec 1512

14 Frederick TILNEY

Born: Abt 1420
-CONTINUED AS #1,ROYAL CHART 3285
Married:

Died: Bef 1447

7 Elizabeth TILNEY

Born: Abt 1445

Died: 4 Apr 1497

15 Elizabeth CHENEY

Born: Abt 1422
-CONTINUED AS #1,ROYAL CHART 633
Died: 25 Sep 1473

Sources include: Faris preliminary baronial manuscript (1998), p. 918 (Knyvet); LDS records.

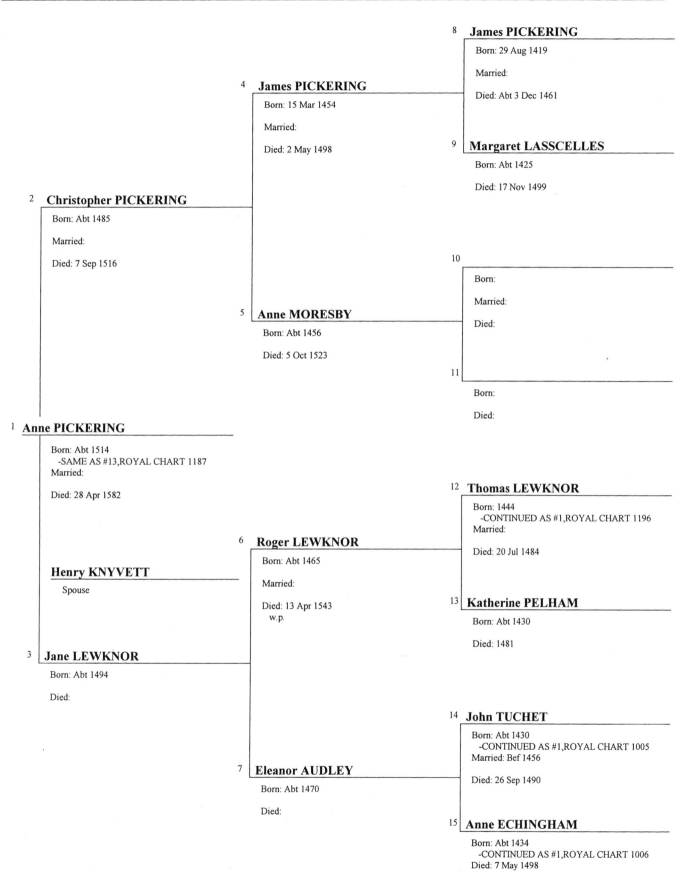

8 **James PICKERING**

Born: 29 Aug 1419

Married:

Died: Abt 3 Dec 1461

4 **James PICKERING**

Born: 15 Mar 1454

Married:

Died: 2 May 1498

9 **Margaret LASSCELLES**

Born: Abt 1425

Died: 17 Nov 1499

2 **Christopher PICKERING**

Born: Abt 1485

Married:

Died: 7 Sep 1516

10

Born:

Married:

Died:

5 **Anne MORESBY**

Born: Abt 1456

Died: 5 Oct 1523

11

Born:

Died:

1 **Anne PICKERING**

Born: Abt 1514
-SAME AS #13,ROYAL CHART 1187
Married:

Died: 28 Apr 1582

12 **Thomas LEWKNOR**

Born: 1444
-CONTINUED AS #1,ROYAL CHART 1196
Married:

Died: 20 Jul 1484

6 **Roger LEWKNOR**

Born: Abt 1465

Married:

Died: 13 Apr 1543
w.p.

13 **Katherine PELHAM**

Born: Abt 1430

Died: 1481

Henry KNYVETT

Spouse

3 **Jane LEWKNOR**

Born: Abt 1494

Died:

14 **John TUCHET**

Born: Abt 1430
-CONTINUED AS #1,ROYAL CHART 1005
Married: Bef 1456

Died: 26 Sep 1490

7 **Eleanor AUDLEY**

Born: Abt 1470

Died:

15 **Anne ECHINGHAM**

Born: Abt 1434
-CONTINUED AS #1,ROYAL CHART 1006
Died: 7 May 1498

Sources include: Faris preliminary baronial manuscript (1998), pp. 918 (Knyvet), 1251-52 (Pickering); Faris 2--Tuchet (#3 ancestry); LDS records. Note: The claim by Faris that #5 Anne was daughter of Christopher Moresby & Margaret Threlkeld, daughter of Lancelot Threlkeld & Margaret Bromflete (see chart 1440, #10 & 11) is unacceptable chronologically.

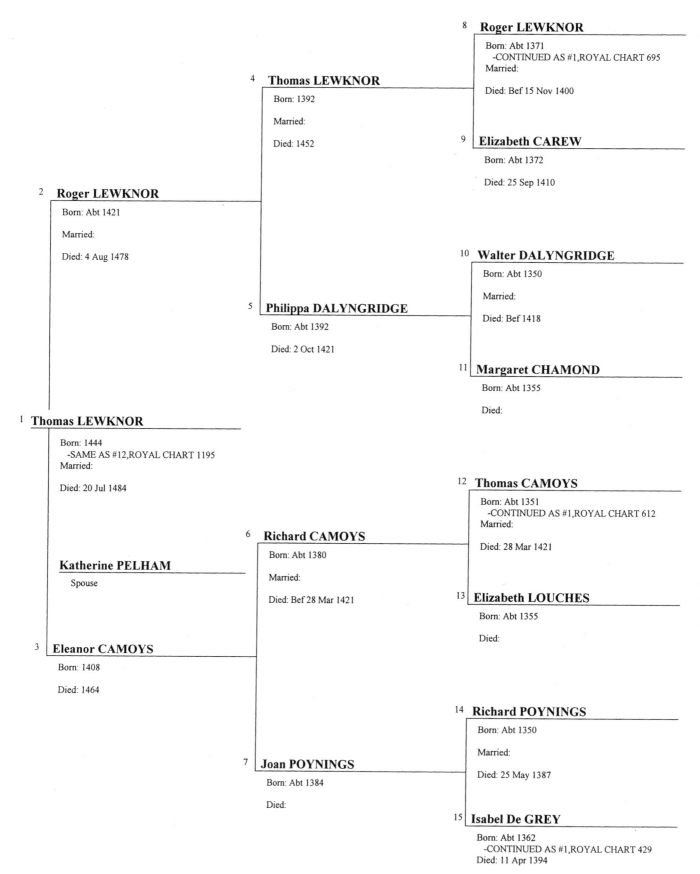

8 Roger LEWKNOR

Born: Abt 1371
-CONTINUED AS #1,ROYAL CHART 695
Married:

Died: Bef 15 Nov 1400

4 Thomas LEWKNOR

Born: 1392

Married:

Died: 1452

9 Elizabeth CAREW

Born: Abt 1372

Died: 25 Sep 1410

2 Roger LEWKNOR

Born: Abt 1421

Married:

Died: 4 Aug 1478

10 Walter DALYNGRIDGE

Born: Abt 1350

Married:

Died: Bef 1418

5 Philippa DALYNGRIDGE

Born: Abt 1392

Died: 2 Oct 1421

11 Margaret CHAMOND

Born: Abt 1355

Died:

1 Thomas LEWKNOR

Born: 1444
-SAME AS #12,ROYAL CHART 1195
Married:

Died: 20 Jul 1484

12 Thomas CAMOYS

Born: Abt 1351
-CONTINUED AS #1,ROYAL CHART 612
Married:

Died: 28 Mar 1421

6 Richard CAMOYS

Born: Abt 1380

Married:

Died: Bef 28 Mar 1421

13 Elizabeth LOUCHES

Born: Abt 1355

Died:

Katherine PELHAM

Spouse

3 Eleanor CAMOYS

Born: 1408

Died: 1464

14 Richard POYNINGS

Born: Abt 1350

Married:

Died: 25 May 1387

7 Joan POYNINGS

Born: Abt 1384

Died:

15 Isabel De GREY

Born: Abt 1362
-CONTINUED AS #1,ROYAL CHART 429
Died: 11 Apr 1394

Sources include: Consultation with Douglas Richardson; LDS records. Note: The parentage of #9 Elizabeth is disputed and uncertain.

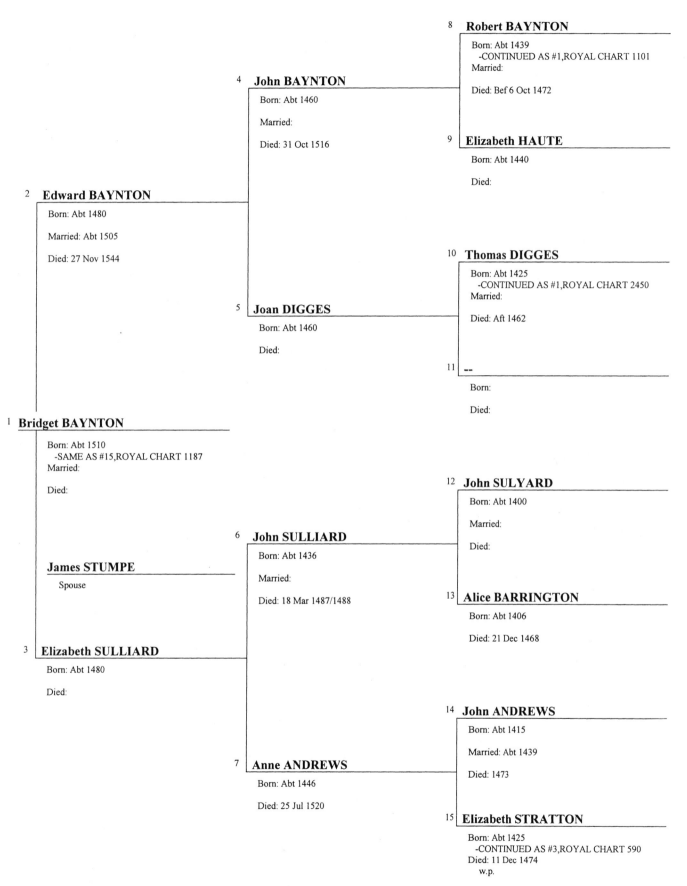

8 Robert BAYNTON

Born: Abt 1439
 -CONTINUED AS #1,ROYAL CHART 1101
Married:

Died: Bef 6 Oct 1472

4 John BAYNTON

Born: Abt 1460

Married:

Died: 31 Oct 1516

9 Elizabeth HAUTE

Born: Abt 1440

Died:

2 Edward BAYNTON

Born: Abt 1480

Married: Abt 1505

Died: 27 Nov 1544

10 Thomas DIGGES

Born: Abt 1425
 -CONTINUED AS #1,ROYAL CHART 2450
Married:

Died: Aft 1462

5 Joan DIGGES

Born: Abt 1460

Died:

11 --

Born:

Died:

1 Bridget BAYNTON

Born: Abt 1510
 -SAME AS #15,ROYAL CHART 1187
Married:

Died:

12 John SULYARD

Born: Abt 1400

Married:

Died:

6 John SULLIARD

Born: Abt 1436

Married:

Died: 18 Mar 1487/1488

13 Alice BARRINGTON

Born: Abt 1406

Died: 21 Dec 1468

James STUMPE

Spouse

3 Elizabeth SULLIARD

Born: Abt 1480

Died:

14 John ANDREWS

Born: Abt 1415

Married: Abt 1439

Died: 1473

7 Anne ANDREWS

Born: Abt 1446

Died: 25 Jul 1520

15 Elizabeth STRATTON

Born: Abt 1425
 -CONTINUED AS #3,ROYAL CHART 590
Died: 11 Dec 1474
 w.p.

Sources include: LDS records; Faris--Baynton, Ludlow; Faris preliminary baronial manuscript (1998), pp. 1479-80 (Sulyard).

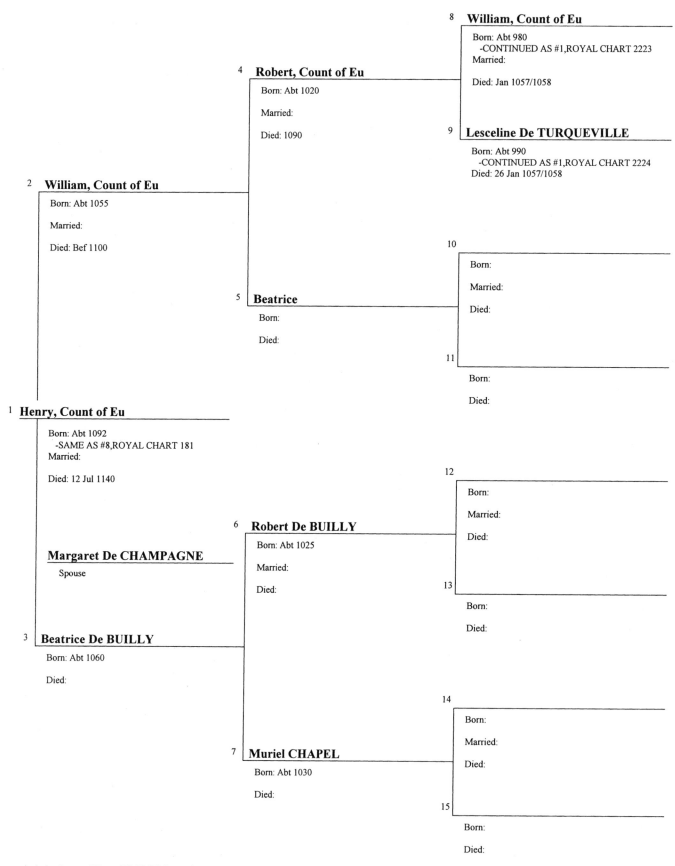

8 William, Count of Eu

Born: Abt 980
  -CONTINUED AS #1,ROYAL CHART 2223
Married:

Died: Jan 1057/1058

4 Robert, Count of Eu

Born: Abt 1020

Married:

Died: 1090

9 Lesceline De TURQUEVILLE

Born: Abt 990
  -CONTINUED AS #1,ROYAL CHART 2224
Died: 26 Jan 1057/1058

2 William, Count of Eu

Born: Abt 1055

Married:

Died: Bef 1100

10

Born:

Married:

Died:

5 Beatrice

Born:

Died:

11

Born:

Died:

1 Henry, Count of Eu

Born: Abt 1092
  -SAME AS #8,ROYAL CHART 181
Married:

Died: 12 Jul 1140

12

Born:

Married:

Died:

6 Robert De BUILLY

Born: Abt 1025

Married:

Died:

13

Born:

Died:

Margaret De CHAMPAGNE

Spouse

3 Beatrice De BUILLY

Born: Abt 1060

Died:

14

Born:

Married:

Died:

7 Muriel CHAPEL

Born: Abt 1030

Died:

15

Born:

Died:

Sources include: *Ancestral Roots* 139-25; LDS records.

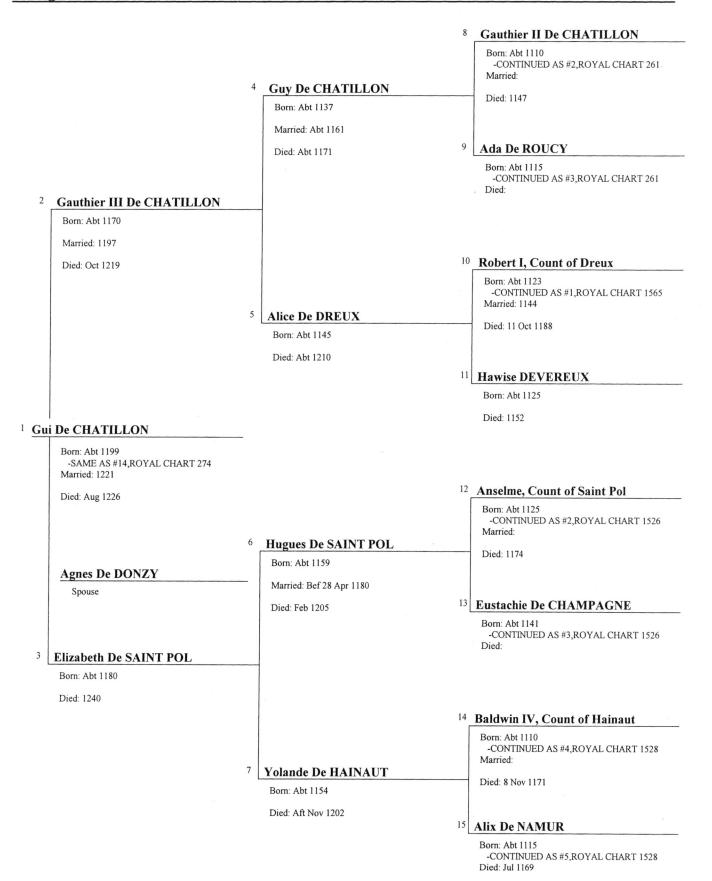

8 Gauthier II De CHATILLON
Born: Abt 1110
  -CONTINUED AS #2,ROYAL CHART 261
Married:

Died: 1147

4 Guy De CHATILLON
Born: Abt 1137

Married: Abt 1161

Died: Abt 1171

9 Ada De ROUCY
Born: Abt 1115
  -CONTINUED AS #3,ROYAL CHART 261
Died:

2 Gauthier III De CHATILLON
Born: Abt 1170

Married: 1197

Died: Oct 1219

10 Robert I, Count of Dreux
Born: Abt 1123
  -CONTINUED AS #1,ROYAL CHART 1565
Married: 1144

Died: 11 Oct 1188

5 Alice De DREUX
Born: Abt 1145

Died: Abt 1210

11 Hawise DEVEREUX
Born: Abt 1125

Died: 1152

1 Gui De CHATILLON
Born: Abt 1199
  -SAME AS #14,ROYAL CHART 274
Married: 1221

Died: Aug 1226

12 Anselme, Count of Saint Pol
Born: Abt 1125
  -CONTINUED AS #2,ROYAL CHART 1526
Married:

Died: 1174

6 Hugues De SAINT POL
Born: Abt 1159

Married: Bef 28 Apr 1180

Died: Feb 1205

Agnes De DONZY
Spouse

13 Eustachie De CHAMPAGNE
Born: Abt 1141
  -CONTINUED AS #3,ROYAL CHART 1526
Died:

3 Elizabeth De SAINT POL
Born: Abt 1180

Died: 1240

14 Baldwin IV, Count of Hainaut
Born: Abt 1110
  -CONTINUED AS #4,ROYAL CHART 1528
Married:

Died: 8 Nov 1171

7 Yolande De HAINAUT
Born: Abt 1154

Died: Aft Nov 1202

15 Alix De NAMUR
Born: Abt 1115
  -CONTINUED AS #5,ROYAL CHART 1528
Died: Jul 1169

Sources include: Faris preliminary Charlemagne manuscript (June 1995), pp. 148, 105, 243; Turton 184-185.

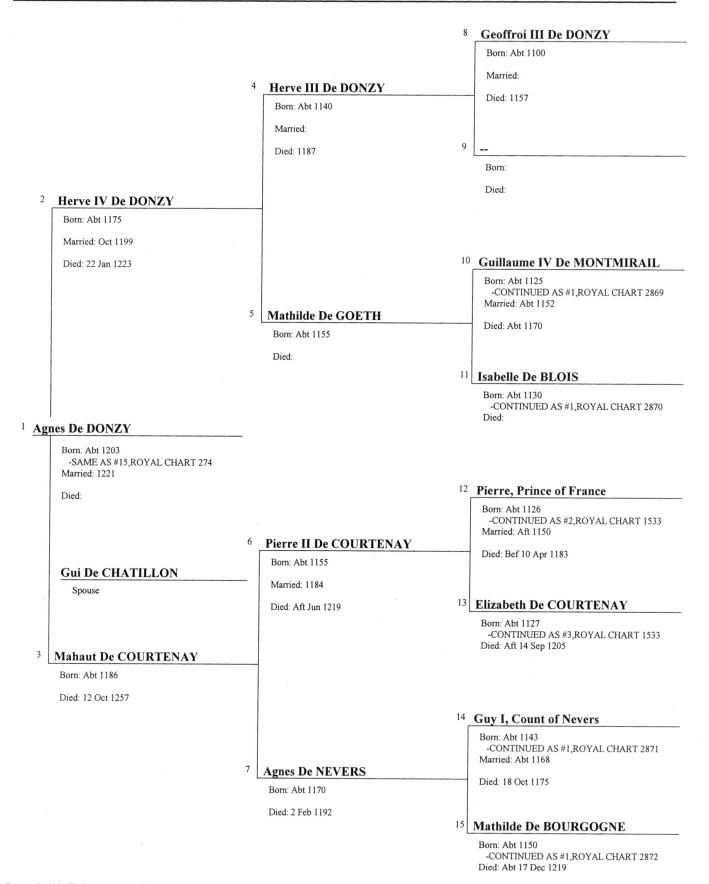

8 **Geoffroi III De DONZY**

Born: Abt 1100

Married:

Died: 1157

4 **Herve III De DONZY**

Born: Abt 1140

Married:

Died: 1187

9 **--**

Born:

Died:

2 **Herve IV De DONZY**

Born: Abt 1175

Married: Oct 1199

Died: 22 Jan 1223

10 **Guillaume IV De MONTMIRAIL**

Born: Abt 1125
  -CONTINUED AS #1,ROYAL CHART 2869
Married: Abt 1152

Died: Abt 1170

5 **Mathilde De GOETH**

Born: Abt 1155

Died:

11 **Isabelle De BLOIS**

Born: Abt 1130
  -CONTINUED AS #1,ROYAL CHART 2870
Died:

1 **Agnes De DONZY**

Born: Abt 1203
  -SAME AS #15,ROYAL CHART 274
Married: 1221

Died:

12 **Pierre, Prince of France**

Born: Abt 1126
  -CONTINUED AS #2,ROYAL CHART 1533
Married: Aft 1150

Died: Bef 10 Apr 1183

6 **Pierre II De COURTENAY**

Born: Abt 1155

Married: 1184

Died: Aft Jun 1219

13 **Elizabeth De COURTENAY**

Born: Abt 1127
  -CONTINUED AS #3,ROYAL CHART 1533
Died: Aft 14 Sep 1205

Gui De CHATILLON

Spouse

3 **Mahaut De COURTENAY**

Born: Abt 1186

Died: 12 Oct 1257

14 **Guy I, Count of Nevers**

Born: Abt 1143
  -CONTINUED AS #1,ROYAL CHART 2871
Married: Abt 1168

Died: 18 Oct 1175

7 **Agnes De NEVERS**

Born: Abt 1170

Died: 2 Feb 1192

15 **Mathilde De BOURGOGNE**

Born: Abt 1150
  -CONTINUED AS #1,ROYAL CHART 2872
Died: Abt 17 Dec 1219

Sources include: Faris preliminary Charlemagne manuscript (June 1995), pp. 148, 113; Schwennicke 3:435; Turton 203-204.

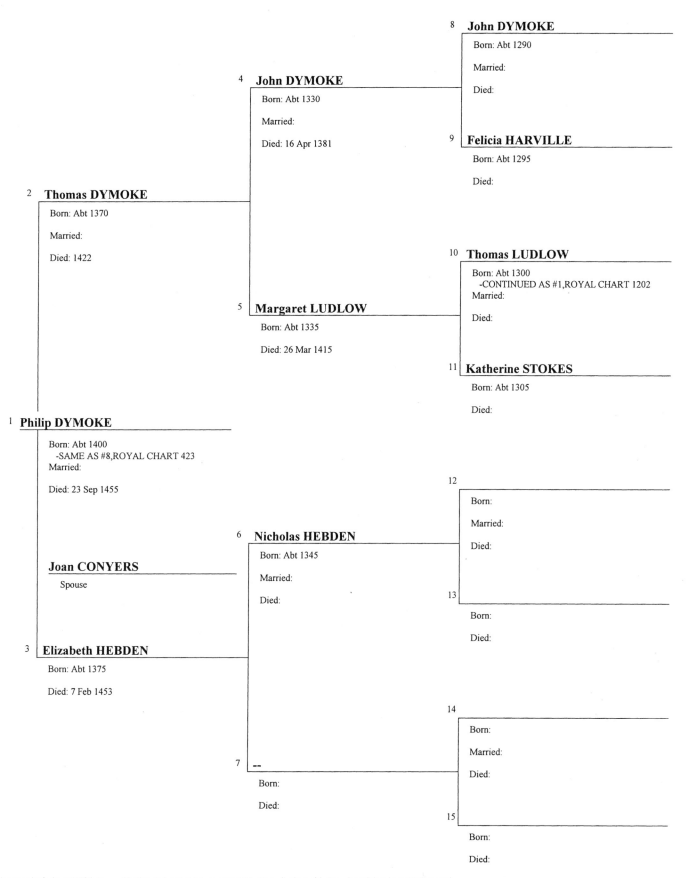

8 **John DYMOKE**
Born: Abt 1290
Married:
Died:

4 **John DYMOKE**
Born: Abt 1330
Married:
Died: 16 Apr 1381

9 **Felicia HARVILLE**
Born: Abt 1295
Died:

2 **Thomas DYMOKE**
Born: Abt 1370
Married:
Died: 1422

10 **Thomas LUDLOW**
Born: Abt 1300
  -CONTINUED AS #1,ROYAL CHART 1202
Married:
Died:

5 **Margaret LUDLOW**
Born: Abt 1335
Died: 26 Mar 1415

11 **Katherine STOKES**
Born: Abt 1305
Died:

1 **Philip DYMOKE**
Born: Abt 1400
  -SAME AS #8,ROYAL CHART 423
Married:
Died: 23 Sep 1455

12
Born:
Married:
Died:

6 **Nicholas HEBDEN**
Born: Abt 1345
Married:
Died:

13
Born:
Died:

Joan CONYERS
Spouse

3 **Elizabeth HEBDEN**
Born: Abt 1375
Died: 7 Feb 1453

14
Born:
Married:
Died:

7 **--**
Born:
Died:

15
Born:
Died:

Sources include: NEHGS *Nexus* 13:124; Roberts *AAP*, pp. 233-234; Consultation with Douglas Richardson; LDS records.

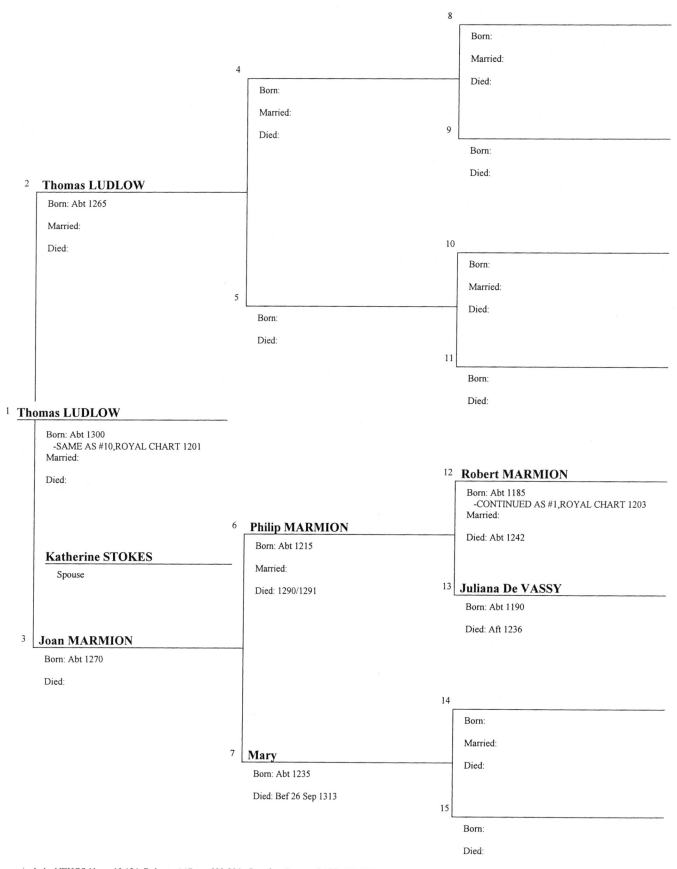

8

Born:

Married:

Died:

4

Born:

Married:

Died:

9

Born:

Died:

2 Thomas LUDLOW

Born: Abt 1265

Married:

Died:

10

Born:

Married:

Died:

5

Born:

Died:

11

Born:

Died:

1 Thomas LUDLOW

Born: Abt 1300
    -SAME AS #10,ROYAL CHART 1201
Married:

Died:

12 Robert MARMION

Born: Abt 1185
    -CONTINUED AS #1,ROYAL CHART 1203
Married:

Died: Abt 1242

6 Philip MARMION

Born: Abt 1215

Married:

Died: 1290/1291

13 Juliana De VASSY

Born: Abt 1190

Died: Aft 1236

Katherine STOKES

Spouse

3 Joan MARMION

Born: Abt 1270

Died:

14

Born:

Married:

Died:

7 Mary

Born: Abt 1235

Died: Bef 26 Sep 1313

15

Born:

Died:

Sources include: NEHGS *Nexus* 13:124; Roberts *AAP*, pp. 233-234; *Complete Peerage* 8:507, 510-514.

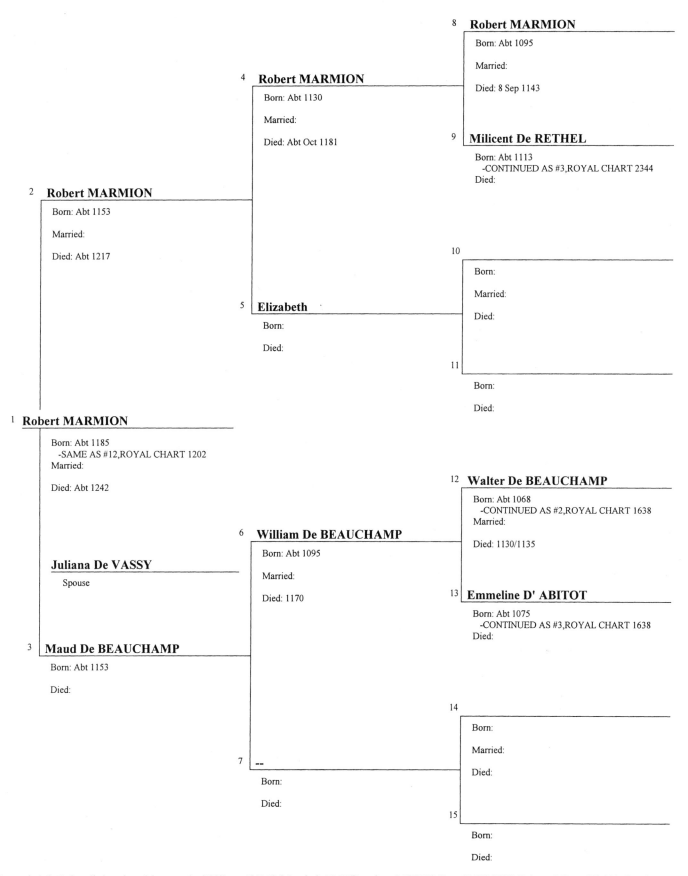

8 **Robert MARMION**

Born: Abt 1095

Married:

Died: 8 Sep 1143

4 **Robert MARMION**

Born: Abt 1130

Married:

Died: Abt Oct 1181

9 **Milicent De RETHEL**

Born: Abt 1113
  -CONTINUED AS #3,ROYAL CHART 2344
Died:

2 **Robert MARMION**

Born: Abt 1153

Married:

Died: Abt 1217

10

Born:

Married:

Died:

5 **Elizabeth**

Born:

Died:

11

Born:

Died:

1 **Robert MARMION**

Born: Abt 1185
  -SAME AS #12,ROYAL CHART 1202
Married:

Died: Abt 1242

12 **Walter De BEAUCHAMP**

Born: Abt 1068
  -CONTINUED AS #2,ROYAL CHART 1638
Married:

Died: 1130/1135

6 **William De BEAUCHAMP**

Born: Abt 1095

Married:

Died: 1170

13 **Emmeline D' ABITOT**

Born: Abt 1075
  -CONTINUED AS #3,ROYAL CHART 1638
Died:

Juliana De VASSY

Spouse

3 **Maud De BEAUCHAMP**

Born: Abt 1153

Died:

14

Born:

Married:

Died:

7 **--**

Born:

Died:

15

Born:

Died:

Sources include: Faris preliminary baronial manuscript (1998), pp. 1058-59 (Marmion), 56-57 (Beauchamp); NEHGS *Nexus* 13:124 (1996); Roberts *AAP*, pp. 233-234; *Complete Peerage* 8:505-510. Note: The ancestry suggested by Faris for #3 Maud, shown above, is not certain.

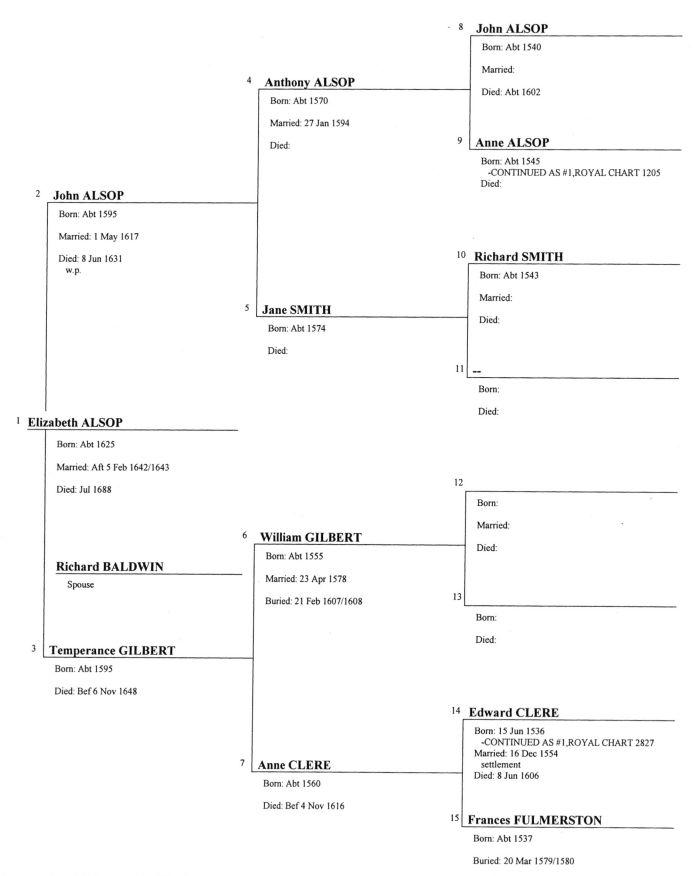

8 John ALSOP
Born: Abt 1540
Married:
Died: Abt 1602

4 Anthony ALSOP
Born: Abt 1570
Married: 27 Jan 1594
Died:

9 Anne ALSOP
Born: Abt 1545
-CONTINUED AS #1, ROYAL CHART 1205
Died:

2 John ALSOP
Born: Abt 1595
Married: 1 May 1617
Died: 8 Jun 1631
w.p.

10 Richard SMITH
Born: Abt 1543
Married:
Died:

5 Jane SMITH
Born: Abt 1574
Died:

11 --
Born:
Died:

1 Elizabeth ALSOP
Born: Abt 1625
Married: Aft 5 Feb 1642/1643
Died: Jul 1688

12
Born:
Married:
Died:

6 William GILBERT
Born: Abt 1555
Married: 23 Apr 1578
Buried: 21 Feb 1607/1608

13
Born:
Died:

Richard BALDWIN
Spouse

3 Temperance GILBERT
Born: Abt 1595
Died: Bef 6 Nov 1648

14 Edward CLERE
Born: 15 Jun 1536
-CONTINUED AS #1, ROYAL CHART 2827
Married: 16 Dec 1554
settlement
Died: 8 Jun 1606

7 Anne CLERE
Born: Abt 1560
Died: Bef 4 Nov 1616

15 Frances FULMERSTON
Born: Abt 1537
Buried: 20 Mar 1579/1580

Sources include: Faris-Richardson 3 (July 2002 preliminary)–Alsop; Roberts *AAP*, pp. 233-234; *500* (600) updated manuscript (November 2000), pp. 324-325; NEHGS *Nexus* 13:124; *Emperor Charlemagne* 2:18-21, 24-25; LDS records. Note: #1 Elizabeth has MPGL descendants through a son Theophilus Baldwin (b. 26 Apr 1659; md. Elizabeth Canfield).

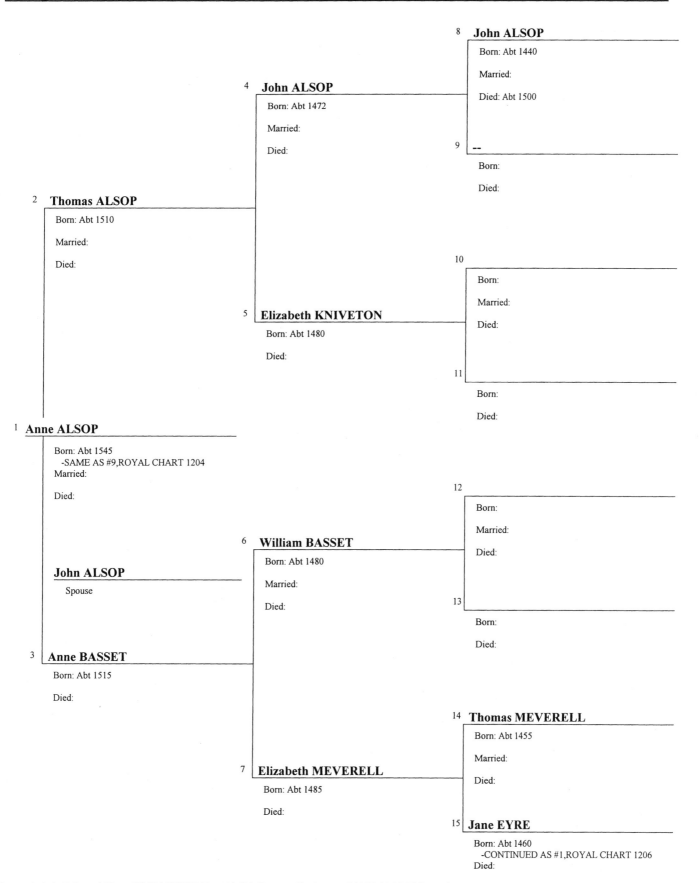

8 John ALSOP
Born: Abt 1440
Married:
Died: Abt 1500

4 John ALSOP
Born: Abt 1472
Married:
Died:

9 --
Born:
Died:

2 Thomas ALSOP
Born: Abt 1510
Married:
Died:

10
Born:
Married:
Died:

5 Elizabeth KNIVETON
Born: Abt 1480
Died:

11
Born:
Died:

1 Anne ALSOP
Born: Abt 1545
  -SAME AS #9,ROYAL CHART 1204
Married:
Died:

John ALSOP
Spouse

12
Born:
Married:
Died:

6 William BASSET
Born: Abt 1480
Married:
Died:

13
Born:
Died:

3 Anne BASSET
Born: Abt 1515
Died:

14 Thomas MEVERELL
Born: Abt 1455
Married:
Died:

7 Elizabeth MEVERELL
Born: Abt 1485
Died:

15 Jane EYRE
Born: Abt 1460
  -CONTINUED AS #1,ROYAL CHART 1206
Died:

Sources include: Roberts *AAP*, pp. 233-234; NEHGS *Nexus* 13:124; *Emperor Charlemagne* 2:18-21, 24-25; LDS records.

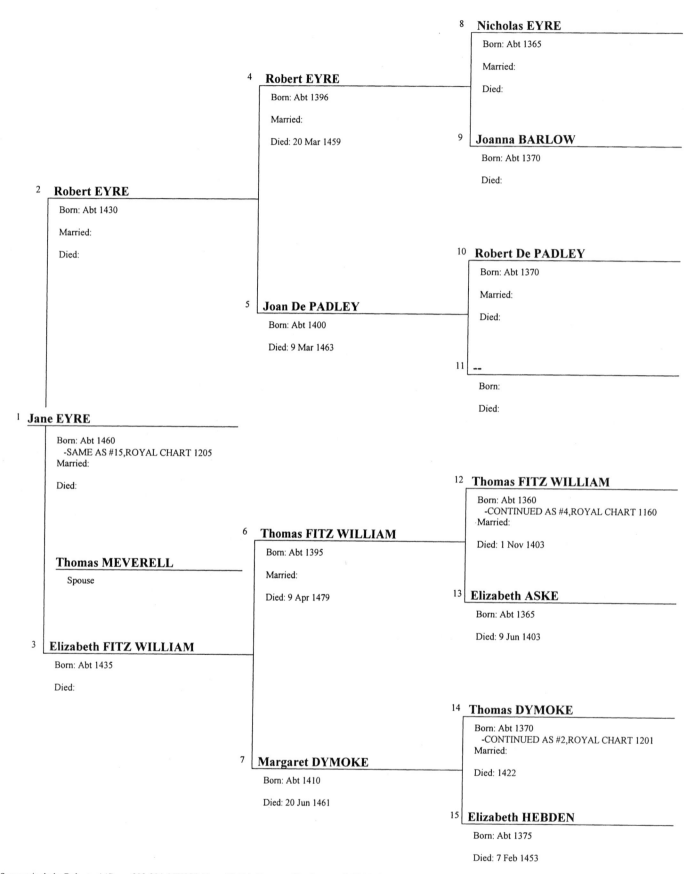

8 **Nicholas EYRE**

Born: Abt 1365

Married:

Died:

4 **Robert EYRE**

Born: Abt 1396

Married:

Died: 20 Mar 1459

9 **Joanna BARLOW**

Born: Abt 1370

Died:

2 **Robert EYRE**

Born: Abt 1430

Married:

Died:

10 **Robert De PADLEY**

Born: Abt 1370

Married:

Died:

5 **Joan De PADLEY**

Born: Abt 1400

Died: 9 Mar 1463

11 **--**

Born:

Died:

1 **Jane EYRE**

Born: Abt 1460
-SAME AS #15,ROYAL CHART 1205
Married:

Died:

12 **Thomas FITZ WILLIAM**

Born: Abt 1360
-CONTINUED AS #4,ROYAL CHART 1160
Married:

Died: 1 Nov 1403

6 **Thomas FITZ WILLIAM**

Born: Abt 1395

Married:

Died: 9 Apr 1479

13 **Elizabeth ASKE**

Born: Abt 1365

Died: 9 Jun 1403

Thomas MEVERELL

Spouse

3 **Elizabeth FITZ WILLIAM**

Born: Abt 1435

Died:

14 **Thomas DYMOKE**

Born: Abt 1370
-CONTINUED AS #2,ROYAL CHART 1201
Married:

Died: 1422

7 **Margaret DYMOKE**

Born: Abt 1410

Died: 20 Jun 1461

15 **Elizabeth HEBDEN**

Born: Abt 1375

Died: 7 Feb 1453

Sources include: Roberts *AAP*, pp. 233-234; NEHGS *Nexus* 13:124; *Emperor Charlemagne* 2:18-21, 24-25; LDS records.

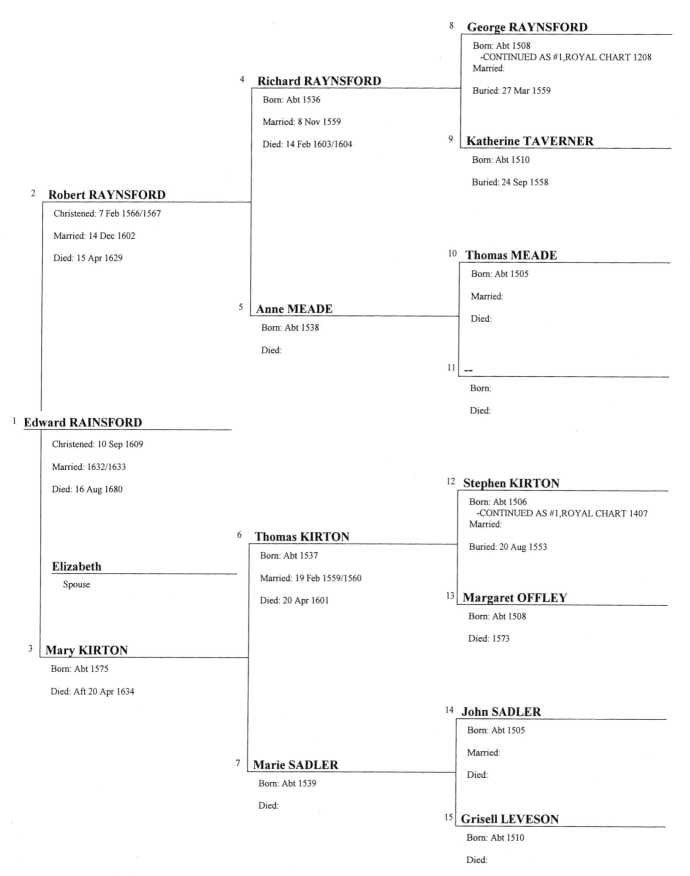

8 George **RAYNSFORD**

Born: Abt 1508
  -CONTINUED AS #1,ROYAL CHART 1208
Married:

Buried: 27 Mar 1559

4 Richard **RAYNSFORD**

Born: Abt 1536

Married: 8 Nov 1559

Died: 14 Feb 1603/1604

9 Katherine **TAVERNER**

Born: Abt 1510

Buried: 24 Sep 1558

2 Robert **RAYNSFORD**

Christened: 7 Feb 1566/1567

Married: 14 Dec 1602

Died: 15 Apr 1629

10 Thomas **MEADE**

Born: Abt 1505

Married:

Died:

5 Anne **MEADE**

Born: Abt 1538

Died:

11 --

Born:

Died:

1 Edward **RAINSFORD**

Christened: 10 Sep 1609

Married: 1632/1633

Died: 16 Aug 1680

12 Stephen **KIRTON**

Born: Abt 1506
  -CONTINUED AS #1,ROYAL CHART 1407
Married:

Buried: 20 Aug 1553

6 Thomas **KIRTON**

Born: Abt 1537

Married: 19 Feb 1559/1560

Died: 20 Apr 1601

13 Margaret **OFFLEY**

Born: Abt 1508

Died: 1573

Elizabeth

Spouse

3 Mary **KIRTON**

Born: Abt 1575

Died: Aft 20 Apr 1634

14 John **SADLER**

Born: Abt 1505

Married:

Died:

7 Marie **SADLER**

Born: Abt 1539

Died:

15 Grisell **LEVESON**

Born: Abt 1510

Died:

Sources include: *NEHGR* 154:219-226 (April 2000); 150:463; 139:225-238, 296-315; Faris 2--Raynsford; Roberts *AAP*, pp. 222-223; *500*, pp. 438-439; LDS records. Note: #1 Edward has MPGL descendants through a daughter Urania (Ranis) Raynsford (b. 4 Jun 1638; md. Josiah Belcher).

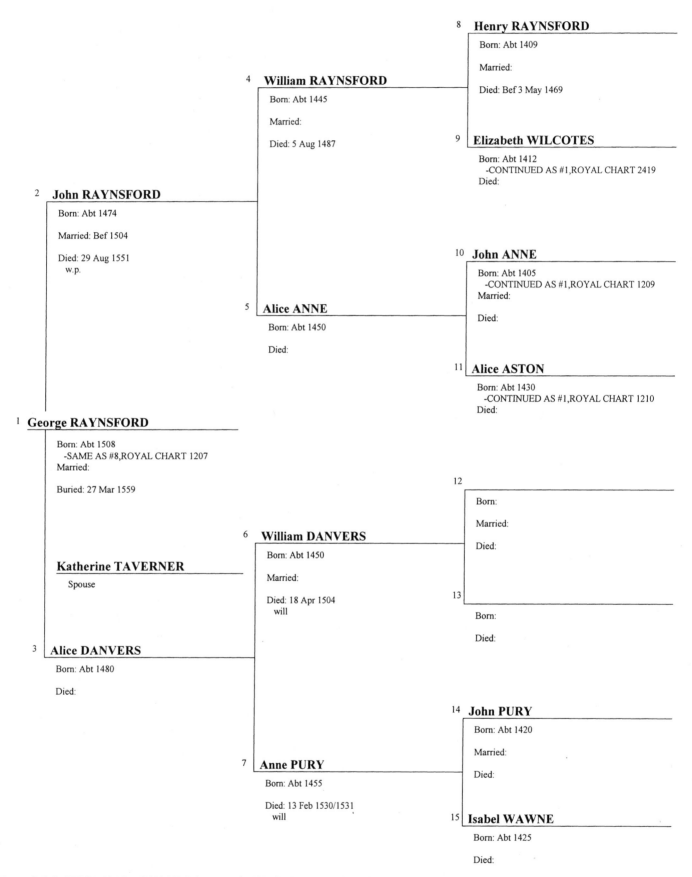

8 Henry RAYNSFORD

Born: Abt 1409

Married:

Died: Bef 3 May 1469

4 William RAYNSFORD

Born: Abt 1445

Married:

Died: 5 Aug 1487

9 Elizabeth WILCOTES

Born: Abt 1412
   -CONTINUED AS #1,ROYAL CHART 2419
Died:

2 John RAYNSFORD

Born: Abt 1474

Married: Bef 1504

Died: 29 Aug 1551
   w.p.

10 John ANNE

Born: Abt 1405
   -CONTINUED AS #1,ROYAL CHART 1209
Married:

Died:

5 Alice ANNE

Born: Abt 1450

Died:

11 Alice ASTON

Born: Abt 1430
   -CONTINUED AS #1,ROYAL CHART 1210
Died:

1 George RAYNSFORD

Born: Abt 1508
   -SAME AS #8,ROYAL CHART 1207
Married:

Buried: 27 Mar 1559

12

Born:

Married:

Died:

6 William DANVERS

Born: Abt 1450

Married:

Died: 18 Apr 1504
   will

13

Born:

Died:

Katherine TAVERNER

Spouse

3 Alice DANVERS

Born: Abt 1480

Died:

14 John PURY

Born: Abt 1420

Married:

Died:

7 Anne PURY

Born: Abt 1455

Died: 13 Feb 1530/1531
   will

15 Isabel WAWNE

Born: Abt 1425

Died:

Sources include: *NEHGR* 150:463; 139:225-238; Roberts *AAP*, pp. 222-223; *500*, pp. 438-439; LDS records. Note: The claim in *NEHGR* 139:230 that #6 William is son of John Danvers & Joan Bruley (of royal descent through her maternal Quatremain line) is no longer accepted.

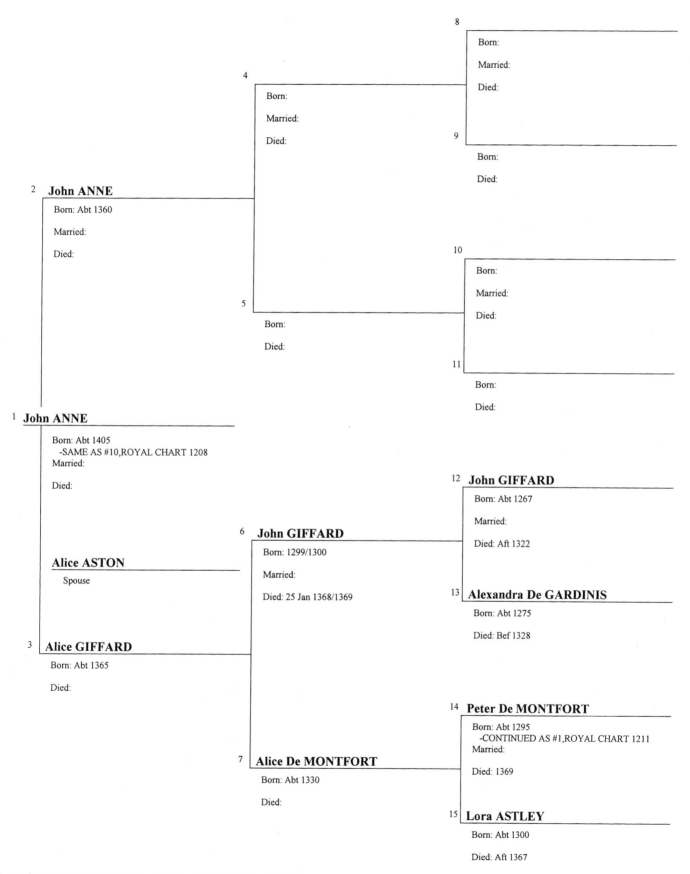

8
Born:
Married:
Died:

4
Born:
Married:
Died:

9
Born:
Died:

2 **John ANNE**
Born: Abt 1360
Married:
Died:

10
Born:
Married:
Died:

5
Born:
Died:

11
Born:
Died:

1 **John ANNE**
Born: Abt 1405
  -SAME AS #10,ROYAL CHART 1208
Married:
Died:

12 **John GIFFARD**
Born: Abt 1267
Married:
Died: Aft 1322

6 **John GIFFARD**
Born: 1299/1300
Married:
Died: 25 Jan 1368/1369

13 **Alexandra De GARDINIS**
Born: Abt 1275
Died: Bef 1328

Alice ASTON
Spouse

3 **Alice GIFFARD**
Born: Abt 1365
Died:

14 **Peter De MONTFORT**
Born: Abt 1295
  -CONTINUED AS #1,ROYAL CHART 1211
Married:
Died: 1369

7 **Alice De MONTFORT**
Born: Abt 1330
Died:

15 **Lora ASTLEY**
Born: Abt 1300
Died: Aft 1367

Sources include: *NEHGR* 150:463; Roberts *AAP*, pp. 222-223; *500*, pp. 438-439.

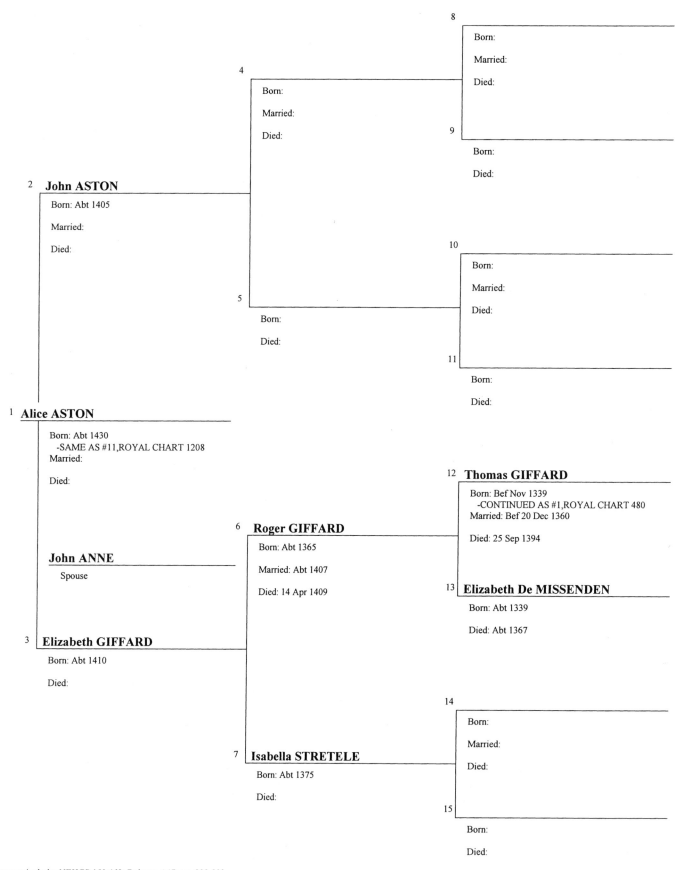

8

Born:

Married:

Died:

4

Born:

Married:

Died:

9

Born:

Died:

2 **John ASTON**

Born: Abt 1405

Married:

Died:

10

Born:

Married:

Died:

5

Born:

Died:

11

Born:

Died:

1 **Alice ASTON**

Born: Abt 1430
  -SAME AS #11,ROYAL CHART 1208
Married:

Died:

12 **Thomas GIFFARD**

Born: Bef Nov 1339
  -CONTINUED AS #1,ROYAL CHART 480
Married: Bef 20 Dec 1360

Died: 25 Sep 1394

6 **Roger GIFFARD**

Born: Abt 1365

Married: Abt 1407

Died: 14 Apr 1409

13 **Elizabeth De MISSENDEN**

Born: Abt 1339

Died: Abt 1367

John ANNE

Spouse

3 **Elizabeth GIFFARD**

Born: Abt 1410

Died:

14

Born:

Married:

Died:

7 **Isabella STRETELE**

Born: Abt 1375

Died:

15

Born:

Died:

Sources include: *NEHGR* 150:463; Roberts *AAP*, pp. 222-223.

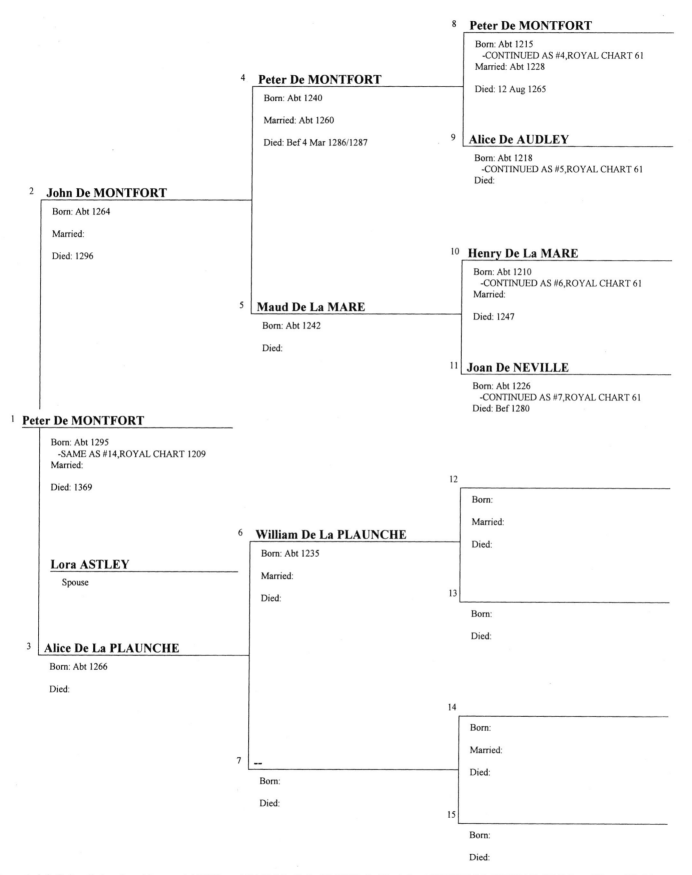

8 Peter De MONTFORT

Born: Abt 1215
  -CONTINUED AS #4,ROYAL CHART 61
Married: Abt 1228

Died: 12 Aug 1265

4 Peter De MONTFORT

Born: Abt 1240

Married: Abt 1260

Died: Bef 4 Mar 1286/1287

9 Alice De AUDLEY

Born: Abt 1218
  -CONTINUED AS #5,ROYAL CHART 61
Died:

2 John De MONTFORT

Born: Abt 1264

Married:

Died: 1296

10 Henry De La MARE

Born: Abt 1210
  -CONTINUED AS #6,ROYAL CHART 61
Married:

Died: 1247

5 Maud De La MARE

Born: Abt 1242

Died:

11 Joan De NEVILLE

Born: Abt 1226
  -CONTINUED AS #7,ROYAL CHART 61
Died: Bef 1280

1 Peter De MONTFORT

Born: Abt 1295
  -SAME AS #14,ROYAL CHART 1209
Married:

Died: 1369

Lora ASTLEY

Spouse

12

Born:

Married:

Died:

6 William De La PLAUNCHE

Born: Abt 1235

Married:

Died:

13

Born:

Died:

3 Alice De La PLAUNCHE

Born: Abt 1266

Died:

14

Born:

Married:

Died:

7 --

Born:

Died:

15

Born:

Died:

Sources include: Faris preliminary baronial manuscript (1998), pp. 1114-15 (Montfort), 485-486 (De La Mare); Paget (1957) 378:2-4; *NEHGR* 150:463; Roberts *500*, pp. 438-439; *AAP*, pp. 222-223; Consultation with Douglas Richardson (#2 & 3 ancestry).

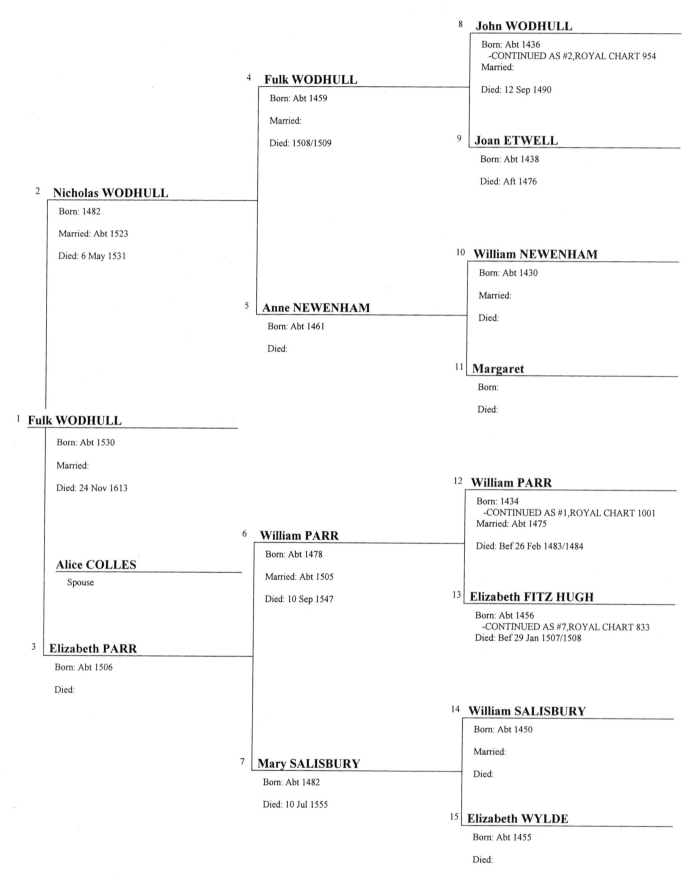

8 John WODHULL

Born: Abt 1436
-CONTINUED AS #2,ROYAL CHART 954
Married:

Died: 12 Sep 1490

4 Fulk WODHULL

Born: Abt 1459

Married:

Died: 1508/1509

9 Joan ETWELL

Born: Abt 1438

Died: Aft 1476

2 Nicholas WODHULL

Born: 1482

Married: Abt 1523

Died: 6 May 1531

10 William NEWENHAM

Born: Abt 1430

Married:

Died:

5 Anne NEWENHAM

Born: Abt 1461

Died:

11 Margaret

Born:

Died:

1 Fulk WODHULL

Born: Abt 1530

Married:

Died: 24 Nov 1613

12 William PARR

Born: 1434
-CONTINUED AS #1,ROYAL CHART 1001
Married: Abt 1475

Died: Bef 26 Feb 1483/1484

6 William PARR

Born: Abt 1478

Married: Abt 1505

Died: 10 Sep 1547

13 Elizabeth FITZ HUGH

Born: Abt 1456
-CONTINUED AS #7,ROYAL CHART 833
Died: Bef 29 Jan 1507/1508

Alice COLLES

Spouse

3 Elizabeth PARR

Born: Abt 1506

Died:

14 William SALISBURY

Born: Abt 1450

Married:

Died:

7 Mary SALISBURY

Born: Abt 1482

Died: 10 Jul 1555

15 Elizabeth WYLDE

Born: Abt 1455

Died:

Sources include: *TAG* 52:14-17; Faris--Bull. Note: #1 Fulk has long been claimed as the grandfather or great-grandfather of the colonist Richard Woodhull (md. Dorothy) of New York. The claim may be correct. However, an alternative identification for this Richard (Richard Odell or Wodell, chr. 17 Dec 1609, son of Thomas) has also been proposed. See *Ancestral Roots* 150; *Magna Charta* 118 (both older and recent editions); *Emperor Charlemagne* 1:235-240; Selleck, *One Branch of the Miner Family*, pp. 204-212; *TAG* 52:14-17; 59:90-92; *The Genealogist* 2:197-201; 7-8:102-104; MPGL chart 2898.

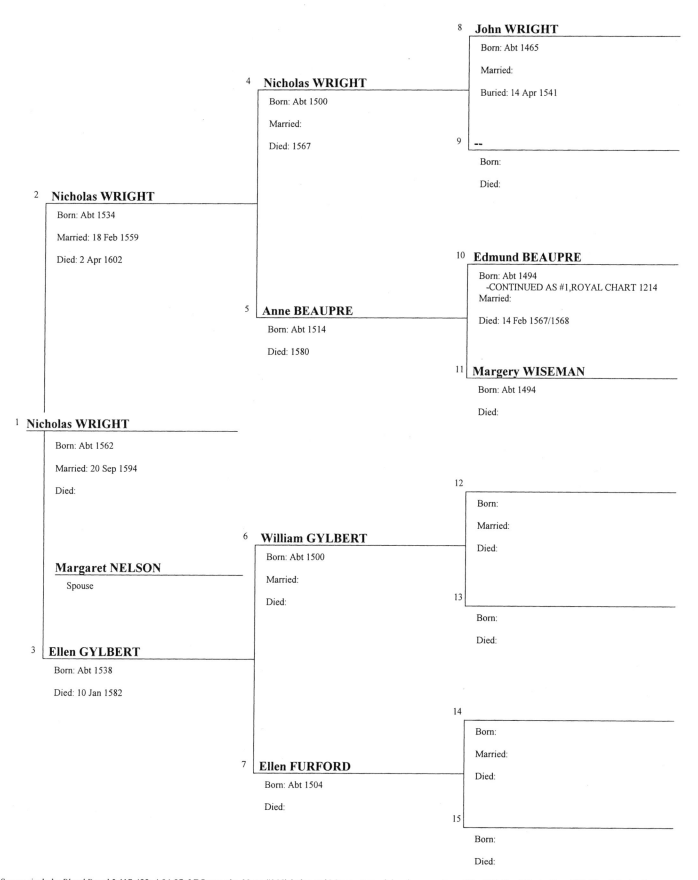

8 John WRIGHT
Born: Abt 1465
Married:
Buried: 14 Apr 1541

4 Nicholas WRIGHT
Born: Abt 1500
Married:
Died: 1567

9 --
Born:
Died:

2 Nicholas WRIGHT
Born: Abt 1534
Married: 18 Feb 1559
Died: 2 Apr 1602

10 Edmund BEAUPRE
Born: Abt 1494
    -CONTINUED AS #1,ROYAL CHART 1214
Married:
Died: 14 Feb 1567/1568

5 Anne BEAUPRE
Born: Abt 1514
Died: 1580

11 Margery WISEMAN
Born: Abt 1494
Died:

1 Nicholas WRIGHT
Born: Abt 1562
Married: 20 Sep 1594
Died:

12
Born:
Married:
Died:

6 William GYLBERT
Born: Abt 1500
Married:
Died:

13
Born:
Died:

Margaret NELSON
Spouse

3 Ellen GYLBERT
Born: Abt 1538
Died: 10 Jan 1582

14
Born:
Married:
Died:

7 Ellen FURFORD
Born: Abt 1504
Died:

15
Born:
Died:

Sources include: *Blood Royal* 5:417-422; 4:94-97; LDS records. Note: #1 Nicholas and Margaret are claimed as ancestors of the Wrights of Oyster Bay, NY. The claim has been classified by Walter Lee Sheppard as "unproven though possible" (*NGSQ* 67:187). *Blood Royal* 3:301-303 gives #6 William as the son of Catherine Tanfield (md. John Gylbert) and grandson of William Tanfield (born 1488/1489) & Isabell Staveley (cont. chart 432, #2 & 3). This is unlikely chronologically and is being rejected here.

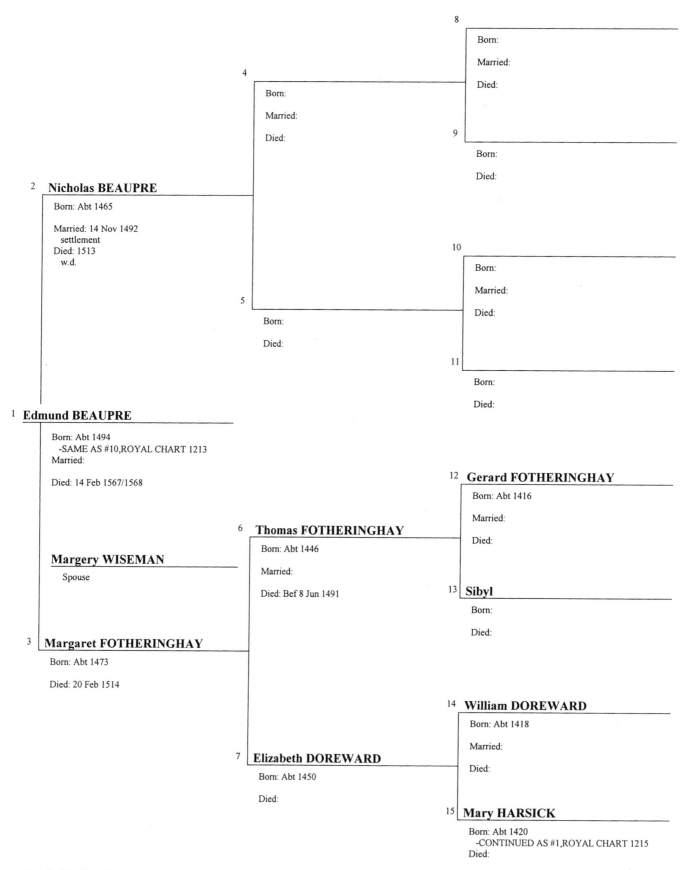

8

Born:

Married:

Died:

4

Born:

Married:

Died:

9

Born:

Died:

2 **Nicholas BEAUPRE**

Born: Abt 1465

Married: 14 Nov 1492
   settlement
Died: 1513
   w.d.

10

Born:

Married:

Died:

5

Born:

Died:

11

Born:

Died:

1 **Edmund BEAUPRE**

Born: Abt 1494
   -SAME AS #10,ROYAL CHART 1213
Married:

Died: 14 Feb 1567/1568

12 **Gerard FOTHERINGHAY**

Born: Abt 1416

Married:

Died:

6 **Thomas FOTHERINGHAY**

Born: Abt 1446

Married:

Died: Bef 8 Jun 1491

13 **Sibyl**

Born:

Died:

Margery WISEMAN

   Spouse

3 **Margaret FOTHERINGHAY**

Born: Abt 1473

Died: 20 Feb 1514

14 **William DOREWARD**

Born: Abt 1418

Married:

Died:

7 **Elizabeth DOREWARD**

Born: Abt 1450

Died:

15 **Mary HARSICK**

Born: Abt 1420
   -CONTINUED AS #1,ROYAL CHART 1215
Died:

Sources include: *Blood Royal* 5:417-422; 4:94-97; LDS records. Note: There are conflicting claims for the ancestry of #2 Nicholas.

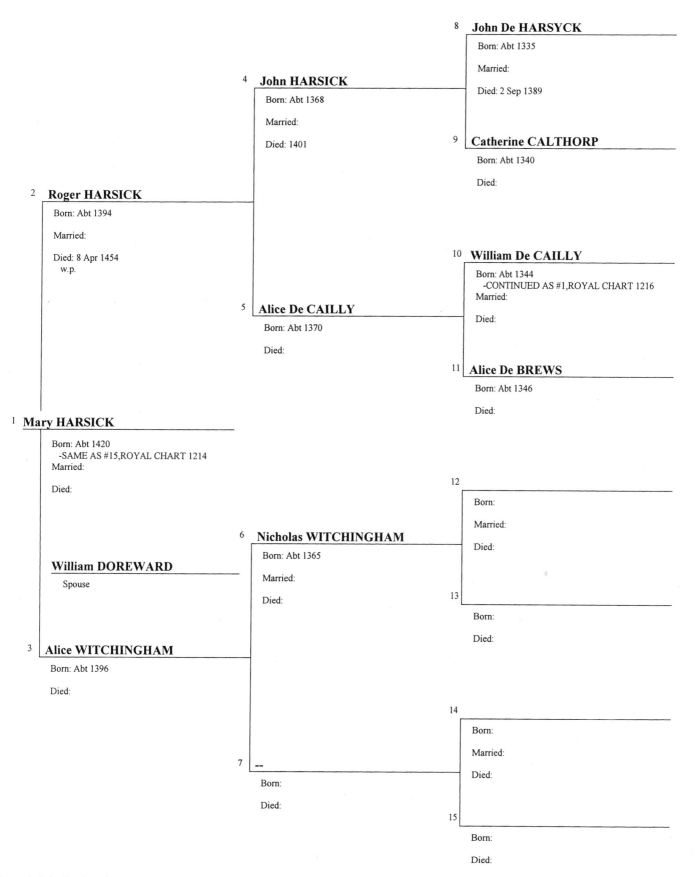

Pedigree Chart

Chart 1215

8 **John De HARSYCK**
Born: Abt 1335
Married:
Died: 2 Sep 1389

4 **John HARSICK**
Born: Abt 1368
Married:
Died: 1401

9 **Catherine CALTHORP**
Born: Abt 1340
Died:

2 **Roger HARSICK**
Born: Abt 1394
Married:
Died: 8 Apr 1454
w.p.

10 **William De CAILLY**
Born: Abt 1344
-CONTINUED AS #1,ROYAL CHART 1216
Married:
Died:

5 **Alice De CAILLY**
Born: Abt 1370
Died:

11 **Alice De BREWS**
Born: Abt 1346
Died:

1 **Mary HARSICK**
Born: Abt 1420
-SAME AS #15,ROYAL CHART 1214
Married:
Died:

12
Born:
Married:
Died:

6 **Nicholas WITCHINGHAM**
Born: Abt 1365
Married:
Died:

13
Born:
Died:

William DOREWARD
Spouse

3 **Alice WITCHINGHAM**
Born: Abt 1396
Died:

14
Born:
Married:
Died:

7 **--**
Born:
Died:

15
Born:
Died:

Sources include: *Blood Royal* 5:417-422; LDS records.

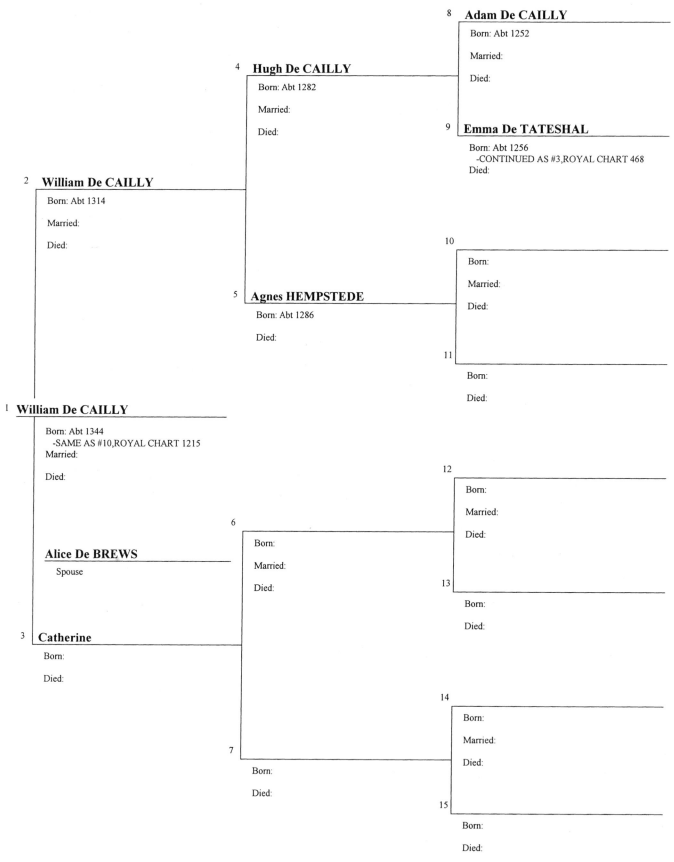

8 **Adam De CAILLY**

Born: Abt 1252

Married:

Died:

4 **Hugh De CAILLY**

Born: Abt 1282

Married:

Died:

9 **Emma De TATESHAL**

Born: Abt 1256
-CONTINUED AS #3,ROYAL CHART 468
Died:

2 **William De CAILLY**

Born: Abt 1314

Married:

Died:

10

Born:

Married:

Died:

5 **Agnes HEMPSTEDE**

Born: Abt 1286

Died:

11

Born:

Died:

1 **William De CAILLY**

Born: Abt 1344
-SAME AS #10,ROYAL CHART 1215
Married:

Died:

12

Born:

Married:

Died:

6

Born:

Married:

Died:

13

Born:

Died:

Alice De BREWS

Spouse

3 **Catherine**

Born:

Died:

14

Born:

Married:

Died:

7

Born:

Died:

15

Born:

Died:

Sources include: *Blood Royal* 5:417-422.

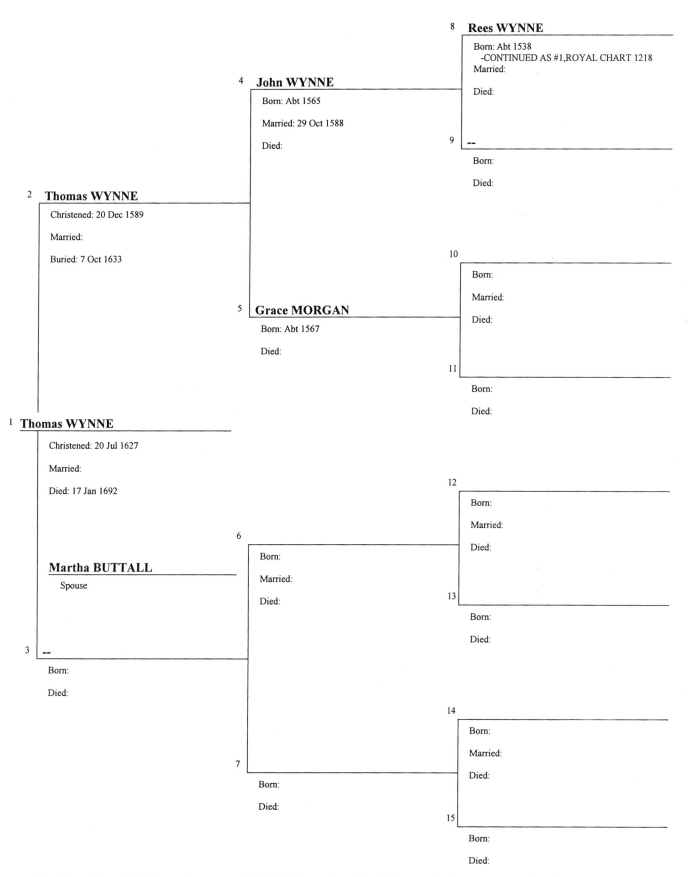

8 Rees WYNNE

Born: Abt 1538
   -CONTINUED AS #1,ROYAL CHART 1218
Married:

Died:

4 | John WYNNE

Born: Abt 1565

Married: 29 Oct 1588

Died:

9 | --

Born:

Died:

2 Thomas WYNNE

Christened: 20 Dec 1589

Married:

Buried: 7 Oct 1633

10

Born:

Married:

Died:

5 | Grace MORGAN

Born: Abt 1567

Died:

11

Born:

Died:

1 Thomas WYNNE

Christened: 20 Jul 1627

Married:

Died: 17 Jan 1692

12

Born:

Married:

Died:

6

Born:

Married:

Died:

13

Born:

Died:

Martha BUTTALL

Spouse

14

Born:

Married:

Died:

3 | --

Born:

Died:

7

Born:

Died:

15

Born:

Died:

Sources include: Roberts *500*, pp. 356-357; *Emperor Charlemagne* 2:329-330; *Welsh Founders of PA* 1:95-98. Notes: This line is not proven and is doubted by some (see NEHGS *Nexus* 13:130). Roberts *600* (2004) discusses these doubts (see p. lxxii) and drops the line. #1 Thomas has MPGL descendants through a daughter Mary Wynne (b. abt 1659; md. Edward Jones).

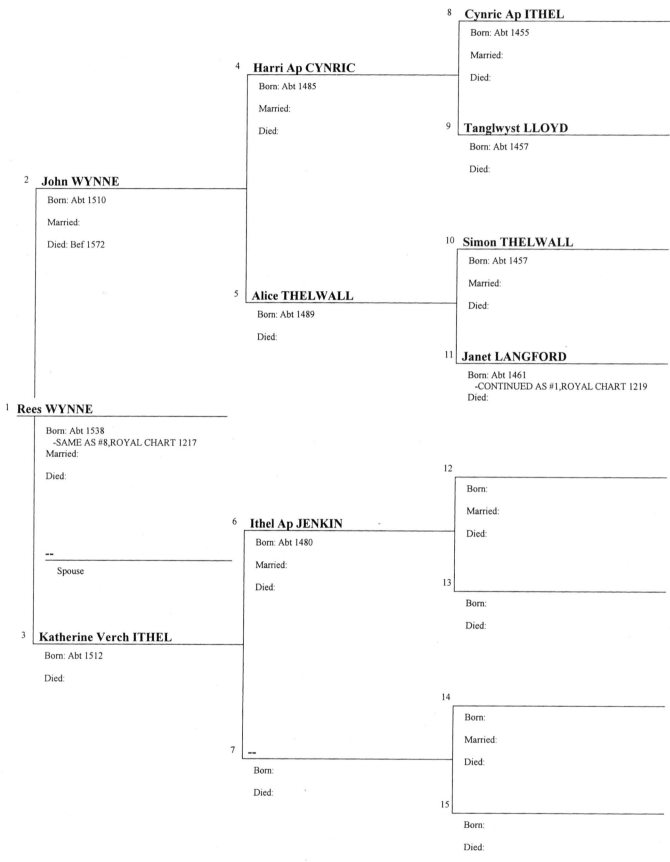

8 **Cynric Ap ITHEL**

Born: Abt 1455

Married:

Died:

4 **Harri Ap CYNRIC**

Born: Abt 1485

Married:

Died:

9 **Tanglwyst LLOYD**

Born: Abt 1457

Died:

2 **John WYNNE**

Born: Abt 1510

Married:

Died: Bef 1572

10 **Simon THELWALL**

Born: Abt 1457

Married:

Died:

5 **Alice THELWALL**

Born: Abt 1489

Died:

11 **Janet LANGFORD**

Born: Abt 1461
    -CONTINUED AS #1,ROYAL CHART 1219
Died:

1 **Rees WYNNE**

Born: Abt 1538
    -SAME AS #8,ROYAL CHART 1217
Married:

Died:

12

Born:

Married:

Died:

6 **Ithel Ap JENKIN**

Born: Abt 1480

Married:

Died:

13

Born:

Died:

--

Spouse

3 **Katherine Verch ITHEL**

Born: Abt 1512

Died:

14

Born:

Married:

Died:

7 **--**

Born:

Died:

15

Born:

Died:

Sources include: Roberts *500*, pp. 356-357; LDS records; *Emperor Charlemagne* 2:329-330; *Welsh Founders of PA* 1:95-98.

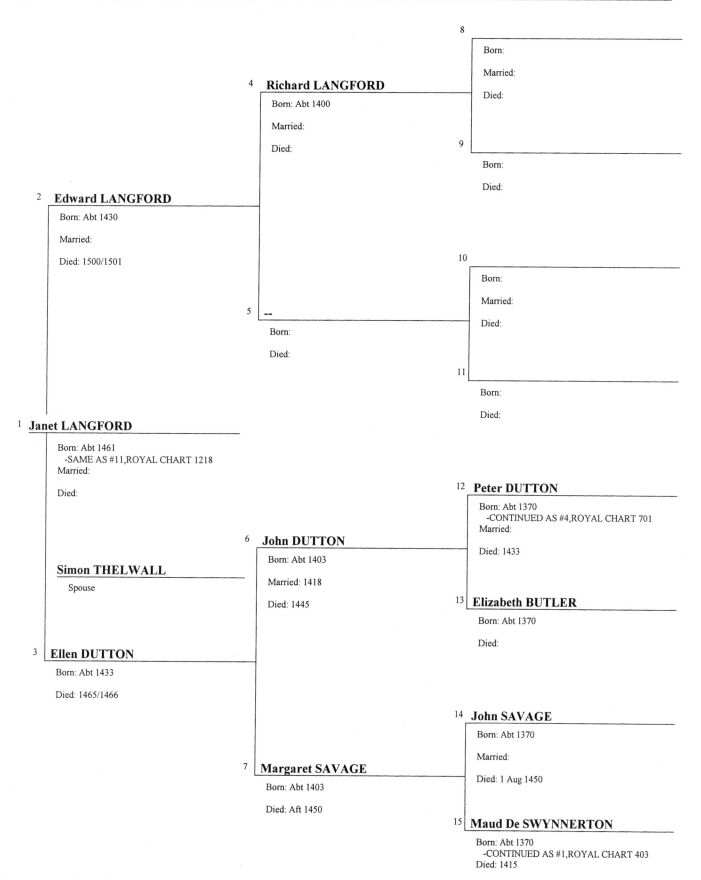

8

Born:

Married:

Died:

4 **Richard LANGFORD**

Born: Abt 1400

Married:

Died:

9

Born:

Died:

2 **Edward LANGFORD**

Born: Abt 1430

Married:

Died: 1500/1501

10

Born:

Married:

Died:

5 --

Born:

Died:

11

Born:

Died:

1 **Janet LANGFORD**

Born: Abt 1461
-SAME AS #11,ROYAL CHART 1218
Married:

Died:

12 **Peter DUTTON**

Born: Abt 1370
-CONTINUED AS #4,ROYAL CHART 701
Married:

Died: 1433

6 **John DUTTON**

Born: Abt 1403

Married: 1418

Died: 1445

13 **Elizabeth BUTLER**

Born: Abt 1370

Died:

Simon THELWALL

Spouse

3 **Ellen DUTTON**

Born: Abt 1433

Died: 1465/1466

14 **John SAVAGE**

Born: Abt 1370

Married:

Died: 1 Aug 1450

7 **Margaret SAVAGE**

Born: Abt 1403

Died: Aft 1450

15 **Maud De SWYNNERTON**

Born: Abt 1370
-CONTINUED AS #1,ROYAL CHART 403
Died: 1415

Sources include: Roberts *500*, pp. 356-357; *Emperor Charlemagne* 2:329-330; *Welsh Founders of PA* 1:95-98; LDS records.

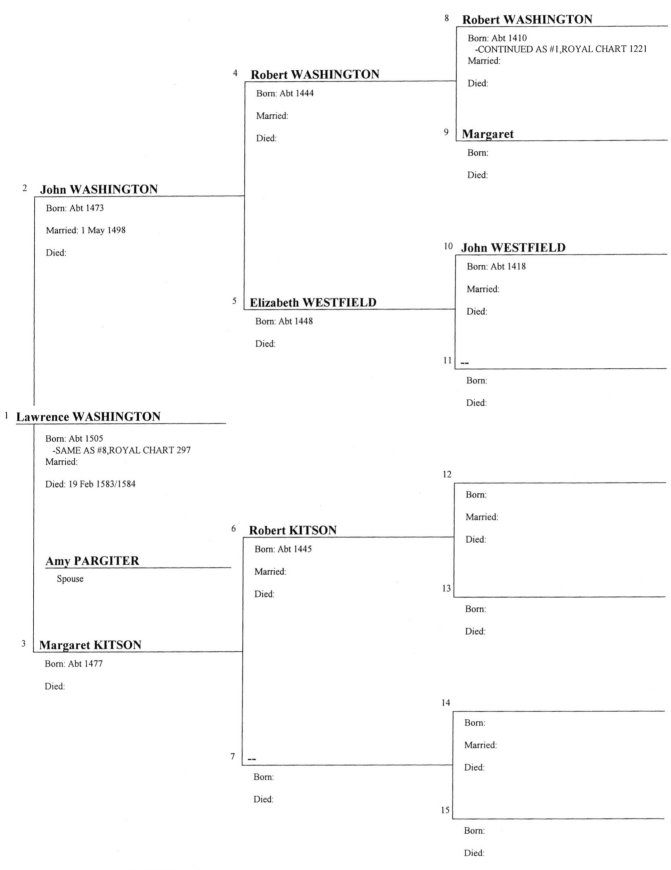

8 Robert WASHINGTON

Born: Abt 1410
-CONTINUED AS #1,ROYAL CHART 1221
Married:

Died:

4 Robert WASHINGTON

Born: Abt 1444

Married:

Died:

9 Margaret

Born:

Died:

2 John WASHINGTON

Born: Abt 1473

Married: 1 May 1498

Died:

10 John WESTFIELD

Born: Abt 1418

Married:

Died:

5 Elizabeth WESTFIELD

Born: Abt 1448

Died:

11 --

Born:

Died:

1 Lawrence WASHINGTON

Born: Abt 1505
-SAME AS #8,ROYAL CHART 297
Married:

Died: 19 Feb 1583/1584

12

Born:

Married:

Died:

6 Robert KITSON

Born: Abt 1445

Married:

Died:

13

Born:

Died:

Amy PARGITER

Spouse

3 Margaret KITSON

Born: Abt 1477

Died:

14

Born:

Married:

Died:

7 --

Born:

Died:

15

Born:

Died:

Sources include: Roberts *500*, pp. 442-443; LDS records.

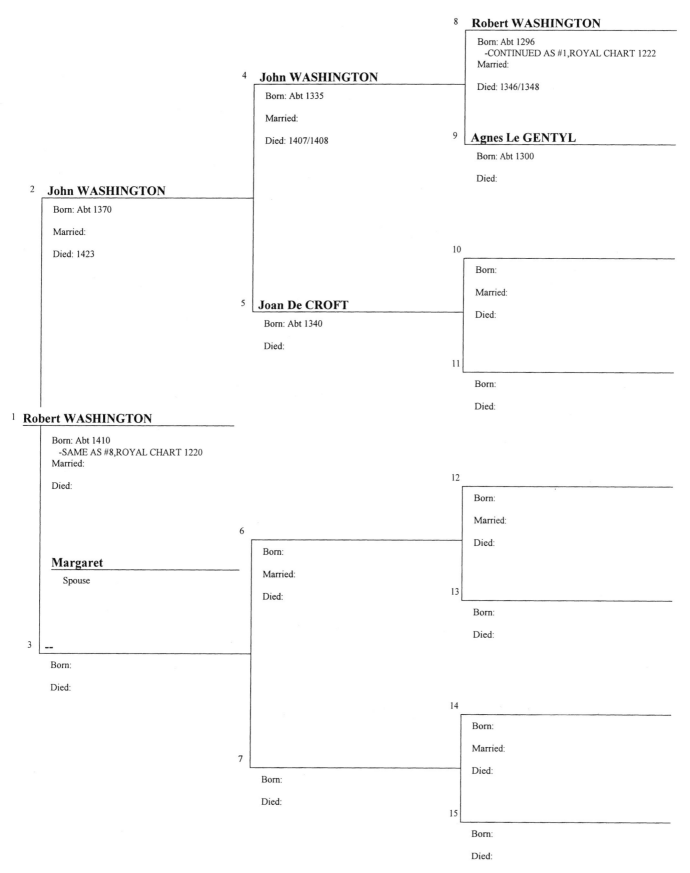

8 **Robert WASHINGTON**

Born: Abt 1296
-CONTINUED AS #1, ROYAL CHART 1222
Married:

Died: 1346/1348

4 **John WASHINGTON**

Born: Abt 1335

Married:

Died: 1407/1408

9 **Agnes Le GENTYL**

Born: Abt 1300

Died:

2 **John WASHINGTON**

Born: Abt 1370

Married:

Died: 1423

10

Born:

Married:

Died:

5 **Joan De CROFT**

Born: Abt 1340

Died:

11

Born:

Died:

1 **Robert WASHINGTON**

Born: Abt 1410
-SAME AS #8, ROYAL CHART 1220
Married:

Died:

12

Born:

Married:

Died:

6

Born:

Married:

Died:

13

Born:

Died:

Margaret

Spouse

3 **--**

Born:

Died:

14

Born:

Married:

Died:

7

Born:

Died:

15

Born:

Died:

Sources include: Roberts *500*, pp. 442-443; *Ancestral Roots* 41-28.

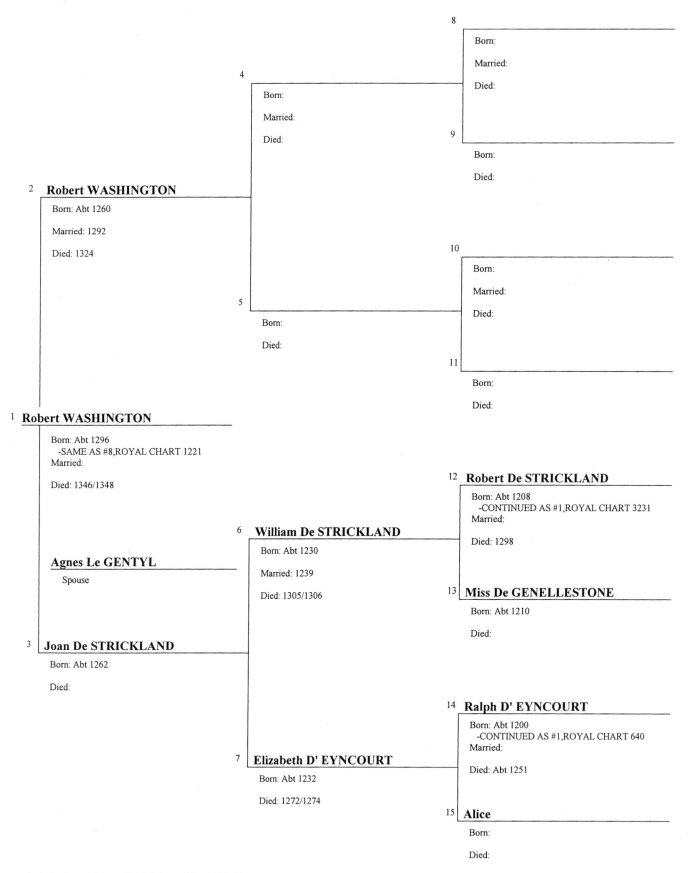

8

Born:

Married:

Died:

4

Born:

Married:

Died:

9

Born:

Died:

2 **Robert WASHINGTON**

Born: Abt 1260

Married: 1292

Died: 1324

10

Born:

Married:

Died:

5

Born:

Died:

11

Born:

Died:

1 **Robert WASHINGTON**

Born: Abt 1296
-SAME AS #8,ROYAL CHART 1221
Married:

Died: 1346/1348

12 **Robert De STRICKLAND**

Born: Abt 1208
-CONTINUED AS #1,ROYAL CHART 3231
Married:

Died: 1298

6 **William De STRICKLAND**

Born: Abt 1230

Married: 1239

Died: 1305/1306

13 **Miss De GENELLESTONE**

Born: Abt 1210

Died:

Agnes Le GENTYL

Spouse

3 **Joan De STRICKLAND**

Born: Abt 1262

Died:

14 **Ralph D' EYNCOURT**

Born: Abt 1200
-CONTINUED AS #1,ROYAL CHART 640
Married:

Died: Abt 1251

7 **Elizabeth D' EYNCOURT**

Born: Abt 1232

Died: 1272/1274

15 **Alice**

Born:

Died:

Sources include: *Ancestral Roots* 41-28; Roberts *500*, pp. 442-443.

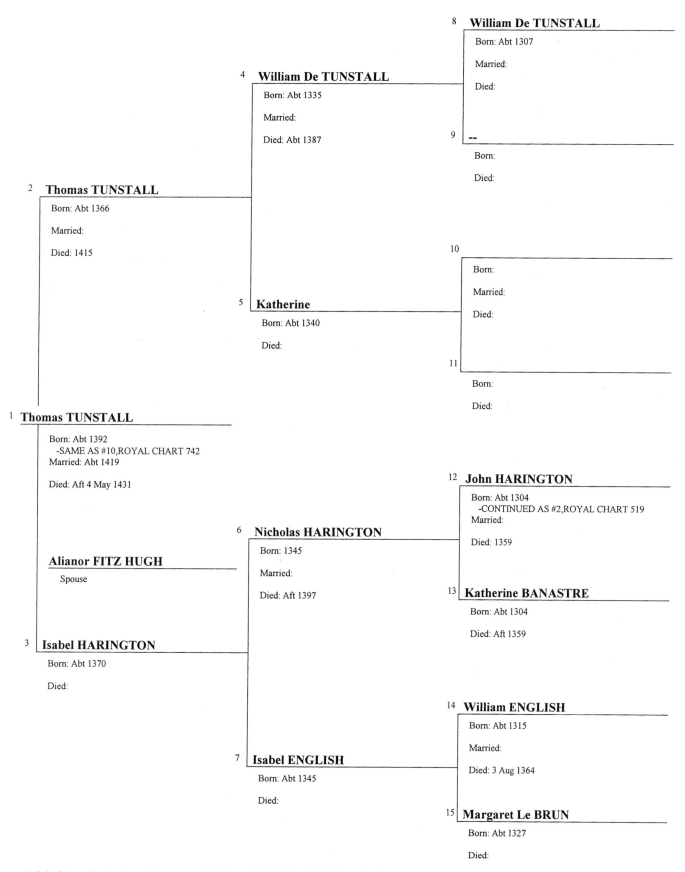

8 **William De TUNSTALL**

Born: Abt 1307

Married:

Died:

4 **William De TUNSTALL**

Born: Abt 1335

Married:

Died: Abt 1387

9 **--**

Born:

Died:

2 **Thomas TUNSTALL**

Born: Abt 1366

Married:

Died: 1415

10

Born:

Married:

Died:

5 **Katherine**

Born: Abt 1340

Died:

11

Born:

Died:

1 **Thomas TUNSTALL**

Born: Abt 1392
-SAME AS #10,ROYAL CHART 742
Married: Abt 1419

Died: Aft 4 May 1431

12 **John HARINGTON**

Born: Abt 1304
-CONTINUED AS #2,ROYAL CHART 519
Married:

Died: 1359

6 **Nicholas HARINGTON**

Born: 1345

Married:

Died: Aft 1397

13 **Katherine BANASTRE**

Born: Abt 1304

Died: Aft 1359

Alianor FITZ HUGH

Spouse

3 **Isabel HARINGTON**

Born: Abt 1370

Died:

14 **William ENGLISH**

Born: Abt 1315

Married:

Died: 3 Aug 1364

7 **Isabel ENGLISH**

Born: Abt 1345

Died:

15 **Margaret Le BRUN**

Born: Abt 1327

Died:

Sources include: Faris preliminary baronial manuscript (1998), pp. 1551-53 (Tunstall); LDS records; Faris--Darcy 10i; chart 903 & sources (#6 & 7 ancestry).

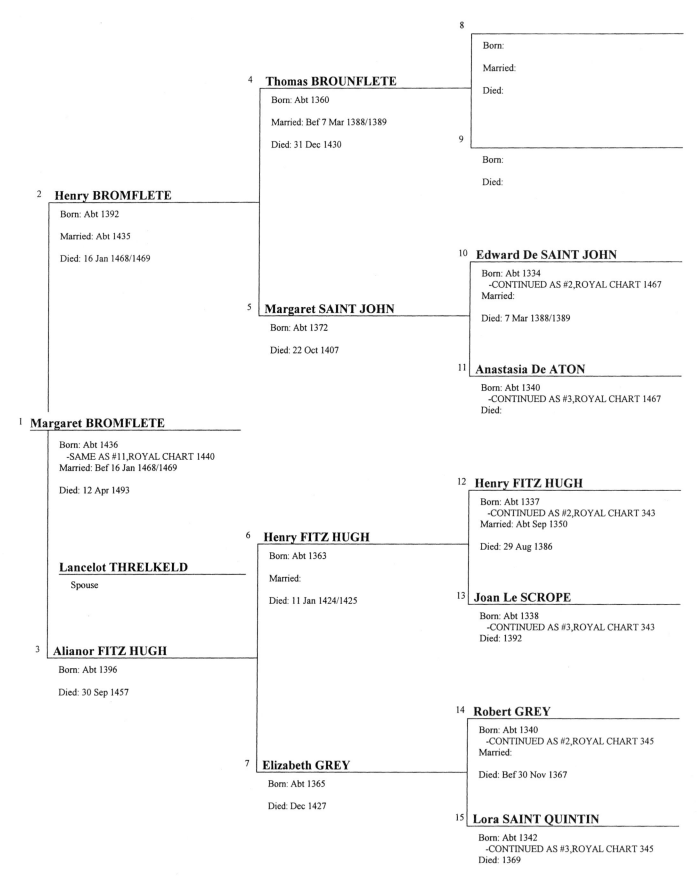

8

Born:

Married:

Died:

4 **Thomas BROUNFLETE**

Born: Abt 1360

Married: Bef 7 Mar 1388/1389

Died: 31 Dec 1430

9

Born:

Died:

2 **Henry BROMFLETE**

Born: Abt 1392

Married: Abt 1435

Died: 16 Jan 1468/1469

10 **Edward De SAINT JOHN**

Born: Abt 1334
    -CONTINUED AS #2,ROYAL CHART 1467
Married:

Died: 7 Mar 1388/1389

5 **Margaret SAINT JOHN**

Born: Abt 1372

Died: 22 Oct 1407

11 **Anastasia De ATON**

Born: Abt 1340
    -CONTINUED AS #3,ROYAL CHART 1467
Died:

1 **Margaret BROMFLETE**

Born: Abt 1436
    -SAME AS #11,ROYAL CHART 1440
Married: Bef 16 Jan 1468/1469

Died: 12 Apr 1493

12 **Henry FITZ HUGH**

Born: Abt 1337
    -CONTINUED AS #2,ROYAL CHART 343
Married: Abt Sep 1350

Died: 29 Aug 1386

6 **Henry FITZ HUGH**

Born: Abt 1363

Married:

Died: 11 Jan 1424/1425

13 **Joan Le SCROPE**

Born: Abt 1338
    -CONTINUED AS #3,ROYAL CHART 343
Died: 1392

Lancelot THRELKELD

Spouse

3 **Alianor FITZ HUGH**

Born: Abt 1396

Died: 30 Sep 1457

14 **Robert GREY**

Born: Abt 1340
    -CONTINUED AS #2,ROYAL CHART 345
Married:

Died: Bef 30 Nov 1367

7 **Elizabeth GREY**

Born: Abt 1365

Died: Dec 1427

15 **Lora SAINT QUINTIN**

Born: Abt 1342
    -CONTINUED AS #3,ROYAL CHART 345
Died: 1369

Sources include: *Complete Peerage* 12 (part 2):285-288; Consultation with Douglas Richardson; Faris 2--Darcy 9 (#3 marriages and ancestry).

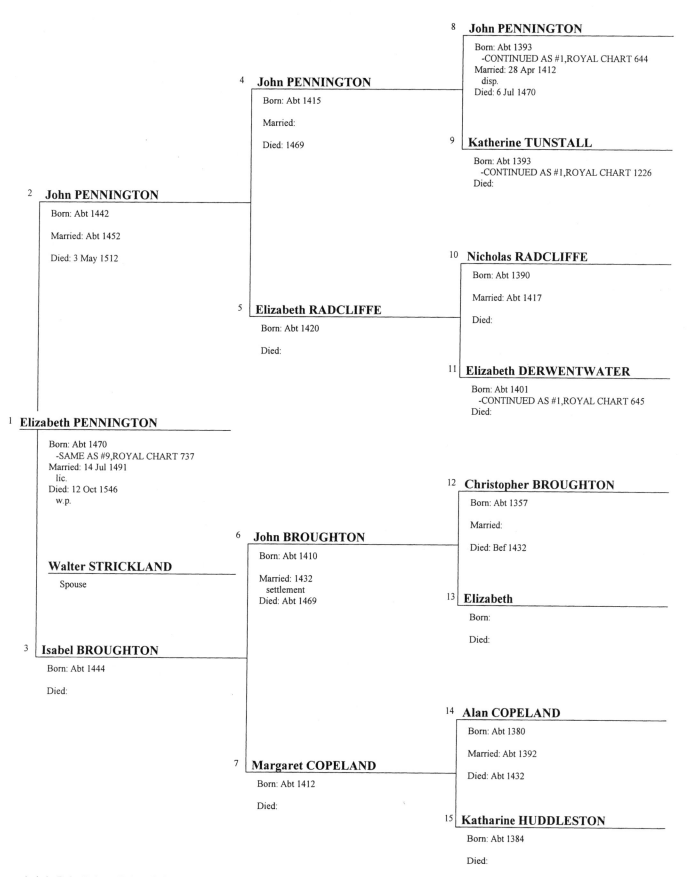

2 John PENNINGTON

Born: Abt 1442

Married: Abt 1452

Died: 3 May 1512

4 John PENNINGTON

Born: Abt 1415

Married:

Died: 1469

8 John PENNINGTON

Born: Abt 1393
 -CONTINUED AS #1,ROYAL CHART 644
Married: 28 Apr 1412
 disp.
Died: 6 Jul 1470

9 Katherine TUNSTALL

Born: Abt 1393
 -CONTINUED AS #1,ROYAL CHART 1226
Died:

5 Elizabeth RADCLIFFE

Born: Abt 1420

Died:

10 Nicholas RADCLIFFE

Born: Abt 1390

Married: Abt 1417

Died:

11 Elizabeth DERWENTWATER

Born: Abt 1401
 -CONTINUED AS #1,ROYAL CHART 645
Died:

1 Elizabeth PENNINGTON

Born: Abt 1470
 -SAME AS #9,ROYAL CHART 737
Married: 14 Jul 1491
 lic.
Died: 12 Oct 1546
 w.p.

Walter STRICKLAND

Spouse

3 Isabel BROUGHTON

Born: Abt 1444

Died:

6 John BROUGHTON

Born: Abt 1410

Married: 1432
 settlement
Died: Abt 1469

12 Christopher BROUGHTON

Born: Abt 1357

Married:

Died: Bef 1432

13 Elizabeth

Born:

Died:

7 Margaret COPELAND

Born: Abt 1412

Died:

14 Alan COPELAND

Born: Abt 1380

Married: Abt 1392

Died: Abt 1432

15 Katharine HUDDLESTON

Born: Abt 1384

Died:

Sources include: Faris--Carleton; Faris preliminary baronial manuscript (1998), pp. 1228 (Pennington), 235 (Broughton); LDS records.

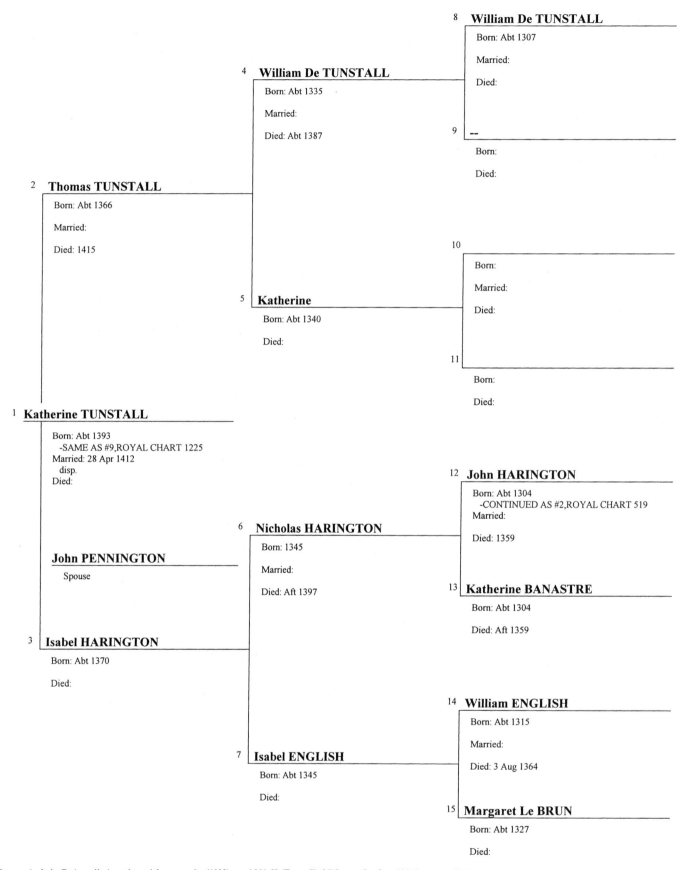

8 **William De TUNSTALL**

Born: Abt 1307

Married:

Died:

4 **William De TUNSTALL**

Born: Abt 1335

Married:

Died: Abt 1387

9 **--**

Born:

Died:

2 **Thomas TUNSTALL**

Born: Abt 1366

Married:

Died: 1415

10

Born:

Married:

Died:

5 **Katherine**

Born: Abt 1340

Died:

11

Born:

Died:

1 **Katherine TUNSTALL**

Born: Abt 1393
-SAME AS #9,ROYAL CHART 1225
Married: 28 Apr 1412
disp.
Died:

12 **John HARINGTON**

Born: Abt 1304
-CONTINUED AS #2,ROYAL CHART 519
Married:

Died: 1359

6 **Nicholas HARINGTON**

Born: 1345

Married:

Died: Aft 1397

13 **Katherine BANASTRE**

Born: Abt 1304

Died: Aft 1359

John PENNINGTON

Spouse

3 **Isabel HARINGTON**

Born: Abt 1370

Died:

14 **William ENGLISH**

Born: Abt 1315

Married:

Died: 3 Aug 1364

7 **Isabel ENGLISH**

Born: Abt 1345

Died:

15 **Margaret Le BRUN**

Born: Abt 1327

Died:

Sources include: Faris preliminary baronial manuscript (1998), pp. 1551-52 (Tunstall); LDS records; chart 903 & sources (#6 & 7 ancestry).

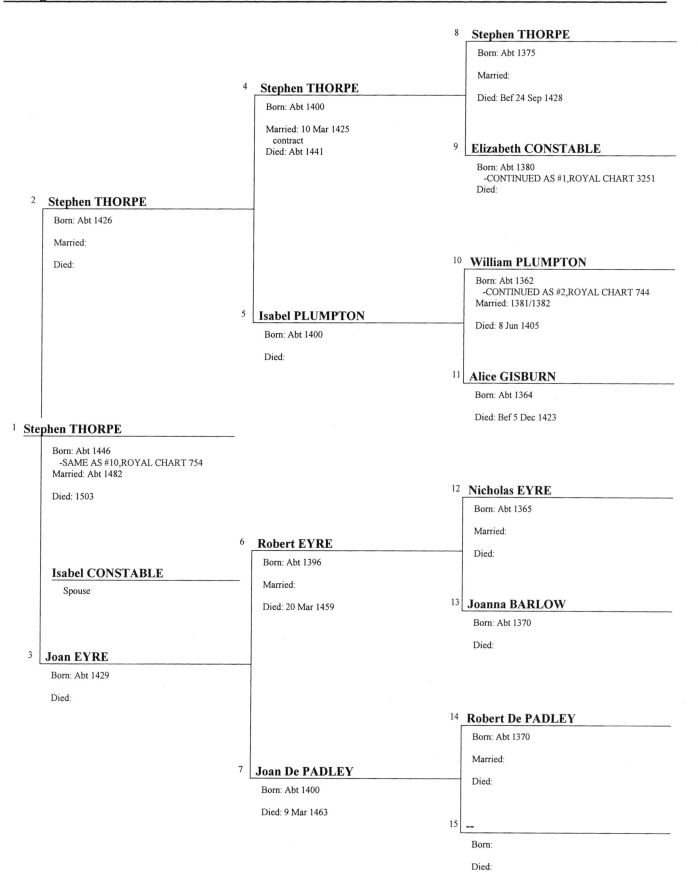

8 Stephen THORPE

Born: Abt 1375

Married:

Died: Bef 24 Sep 1428

4 Stephen THORPE

Born: Abt 1400

Married: 10 Mar 1425
  contract
Died: Abt 1441

9 Elizabeth CONSTABLE

Born: Abt 1380
  -CONTINUED AS #1,ROYAL CHART 3251
Died:

2 Stephen THORPE

Born: Abt 1426

Married:

Died:

10 William PLUMPTON

Born: Abt 1362
  -CONTINUED AS #2,ROYAL CHART 744
Married: 1381/1382

Died: 8 Jun 1405

5 Isabel PLUMPTON

Born: Abt 1400

Died:

11 Alice GISBURN

Born: Abt 1364

Died: Bef 5 Dec 1423

1 Stephen THORPE

Born: Abt 1446
  -SAME AS #10,ROYAL CHART 754
Married: Abt 1482

Died: 1503

12 Nicholas EYRE

Born: Abt 1365

Married:

Died:

6 Robert EYRE

Born: Abt 1396

Married:

Died: 20 Mar 1459

13 Joanna BARLOW

Born: Abt 1370

Died:

Isabel CONSTABLE

Spouse

3 Joan EYRE

Born: Abt 1429

Died:

14 Robert De PADLEY

Born: Abt 1370

Married:

Died:

7 Joan De PADLEY

Born: Abt 1400

Died: 9 Mar 1463

15 --

Born:

Died:

Sources include: Faris-Richardson preliminary Magna Carta manuscript (June 2000), pp. 399-400 (Newton), 426 (Plumpton); Faris preliminary baronial manuscript (1998), pp. 1515 (Thorpe), 564 (Eyre).

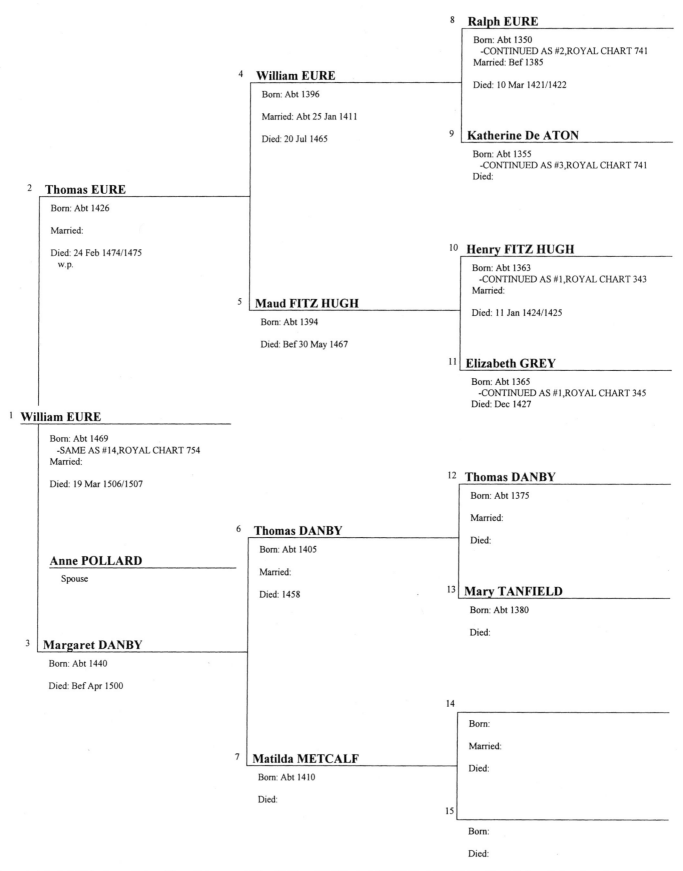

8 Ralph EURE

Born: Abt 1350
-CONTINUED AS #2,ROYAL CHART 741
Married: Bef 1385

Died: 10 Mar 1421/1422

4 William EURE

Born: Abt 1396

Married: Abt 25 Jan 1411

Died: 20 Jul 1465

9 Katherine De ATON

Born: Abt 1355
-CONTINUED AS #3,ROYAL CHART 741
Died:

2 Thomas EURE

Born: Abt 1426

Married:

Died: 24 Feb 1474/1475
w.p.

10 Henry FITZ HUGH

Born: Abt 1363
-CONTINUED AS #1,ROYAL CHART 343
Married:

Died: 11 Jan 1424/1425

5 Maud FITZ HUGH

Born: Abt 1394

Died: Bef 30 May 1467

11 Elizabeth GREY

Born: Abt 1365
-CONTINUED AS #1,ROYAL CHART 345
Died: Dec 1427

1 William EURE

Born: Abt 1469
-SAME AS #14,ROYAL CHART 754
Married:

Died: 19 Mar 1506/1507

12 Thomas DANBY

Born: Abt 1375

Married:

Died:

6 Thomas DANBY

Born: Abt 1405

Married:

Died: 1458

Anne POLLARD

Spouse

13 Mary TANFIELD

Born: Abt 1380

Died:

3 Margaret DANBY

Born: Abt 1440

Died: Bef Apr 1500

14

Born:

Married:

Died:

7 Matilda METCALF

Born: Abt 1410

Died:

15

Born:

Died:

Sources include: Faris-Richardson preliminary Magna Carta manuscript (June 2000), pp. 247 (Grimston), 192-193 (Eure), 210-211 (Fitz Hugh); Faris preliminary baronial manuscript (1998), pp. 557-559 (Eure), 457 (Danby); *NEHGR* 111:260-265.

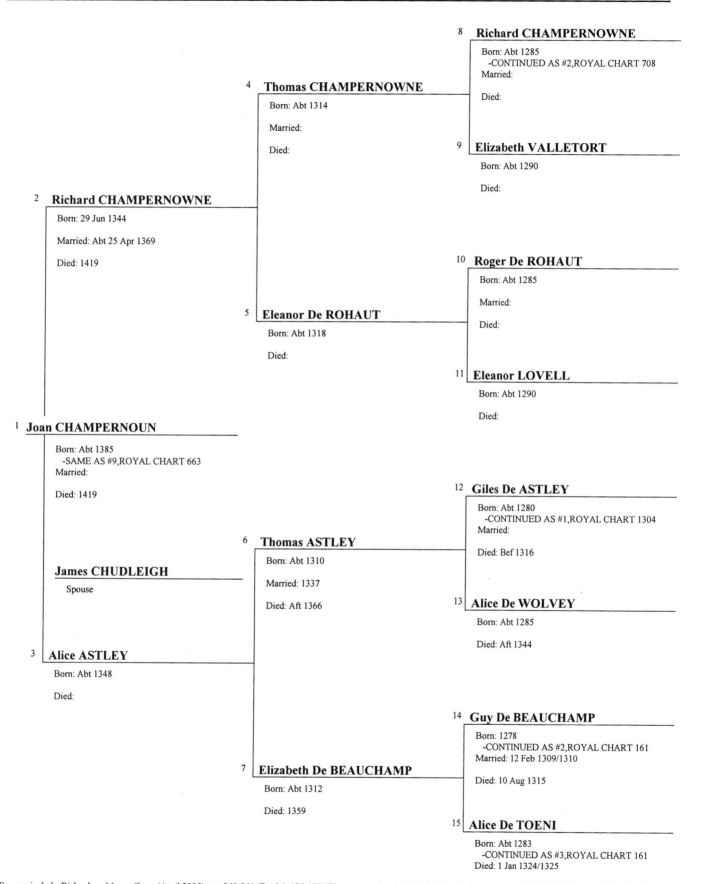

8 Richard CHAMPERNOWNE
Born: Abt 1285
-CONTINUED AS #2,ROYAL CHART 708
Married:

Died:

4 Thomas CHAMPERNOWNE
Born: Abt 1314

Married:

Died:

9 Elizabeth VALLETORT
Born: Abt 1290

Died:

2 Richard CHAMPERNOWNE
Born: 29 Jun 1344

Married: Abt 25 Apr 1369

Died: 1419

10 Roger De ROHAUT
Born: Abt 1285

Married:

Died:

5 Eleanor De ROHAUT
Born: Abt 1318

Died:

11 Eleanor LOVELL
Born: Abt 1290

Died:

1 Joan CHAMPERNOUN
Born: Abt 1385
-SAME AS #9,ROYAL CHART 663
Married:

Died: 1419

12 Giles De ASTLEY
Born: Abt 1280
-CONTINUED AS #1,ROYAL CHART 1304
Married:

Died: Bef 1316

6 Thomas ASTLEY
Born: Abt 1310

Married: 1337

Died: Aft 1366

13 Alice De WOLVEY
Born: Abt 1285

Died: Aft 1344

James CHUDLEIGH
Spouse

3 Alice ASTLEY
Born: Abt 1348

Died:

14 Guy De BEAUCHAMP
Born: 1278
-CONTINUED AS #2,ROYAL CHART 161
Married: 12 Feb 1309/1310

Died: 10 Aug 1315

7 Elizabeth De BEAUCHAMP
Born: Abt 1312

Died: 1359

15 Alice De TOENI
Born: Abt 1283
-CONTINUED AS #3,ROYAL CHART 161
Died: 1 Jan 1324/1325

Sources include: Richardson *Magna Carta* (April 2005), pp. 260-261 (Davie), 175-176 (Champernoun), 22 (Astley); Roberts *600* (2004), pp. 489-492; Roberts *500* (600) updated manuscript (November 2000), pp. 470, 468a; LDS records; *Ancestral Roots* 217-36; *Ancestral Roots* 8 (2004), Line 217. Note: *Ancestral Roots* 8 inserts an additional generation (Alexander Champernoun md. Joan Ferrers) between #1 & 2 above. This claim is chronologically difficult and appears to be incorrect. Richardson and Roberts both accept the version charted above. For Alexander & Joan, see chart 940, #12 & 13.

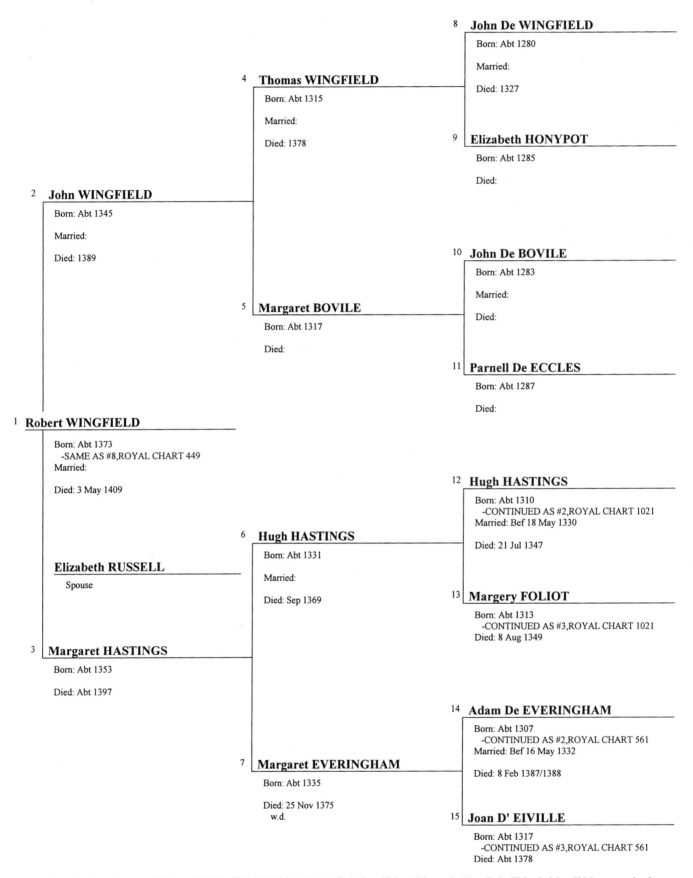

8   **John De WINGFIELD**

Born: Abt 1280

Married:

Died: 1327

4   **Thomas WINGFIELD**

Born: Abt 1315

Married:

Died: 1378

9   **Elizabeth HONYPOT**

Born: Abt 1285

Died:

2   **John WINGFIELD**

Born: Abt 1345

Married:

Died: 1389

10   **John De BOVILE**

Born: Abt 1283

Married:

Died:

5   **Margaret BOVILE**

Born: Abt 1317

Died:

11   **Parnell De ECCLES**

Born: Abt 1287

Died:

1   **Robert WINGFIELD**

Born: Abt 1373
  -SAME AS #8,ROYAL CHART 449
Married:

Died: 3 May 1409

12   **Hugh HASTINGS**

Born: Abt 1310
  -CONTINUED AS #2,ROYAL CHART 1021
Married: Bef 18 May 1330

Died: 21 Jul 1347

6   **Hugh HASTINGS**

Born: Abt 1331

Married:

Died: Sep 1369

Elizabeth RUSSELL

Spouse

13   **Margery FOLIOT**

Born: Abt 1313
  -CONTINUED AS #3,ROYAL CHART 1021
Died: 8 Aug 1349

3   **Margaret HASTINGS**

Born: Abt 1353

Died: Abt 1397

14   **Adam De EVERINGHAM**

Born: Abt 1307
  -CONTINUED AS #2,ROYAL CHART 561
Married: Bef 16 May 1332

Died: 8 Feb 1387/1388

7   **Margaret EVERINGHAM**

Born: Abt 1335

Died: 25 Nov 1375
w.d.

15   **Joan D' EIVILLE**

Born: Abt 1317
  -CONTINUED AS #3,ROYAL CHART 561
Died: Abt 1378

Sources include: Richardson *Plantagenet* (2004), pp. 768 (Wingfield), 288 (Elsing); Faris--Letheringham, Elsing; LDS records. Note: Faris--Elsing 8 claims #3 Margaret as daughter of Hugh Hastings & Anne Despencer (cont. chart 1019, #4 & 5). This does not work chronologically. It appears that #3 Margaret was the <u>daughter</u> (<u>not</u> granddaughter) of Hugh Hastings & Margaret Everingham, the version given in LDS records and in a Faris--Letheringham 9 note.

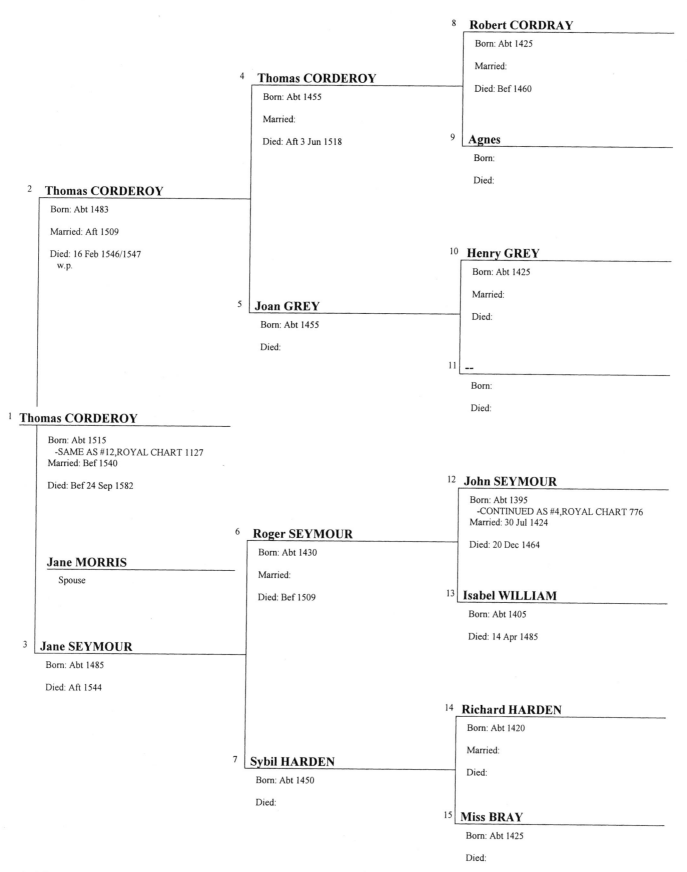

8 **Robert CORDRAY**

Born: Abt 1425

Married:

Died: Bef 1460

4 **Thomas CORDEROY**

Born: Abt 1455

Married:

Died: Aft 3 Jun 1518

9 **Agnes**

Born:

Died:

2 **Thomas CORDEROY**

Born: Abt 1483

Married: Aft 1509

Died: 16 Feb 1546/1547
  w.p.

10 **Henry GREY**

Born: Abt 1425

Married:

Died:

5 **Joan GREY**

Born: Abt 1455

Died:

11 **--**

Born:

Died:

1 **Thomas CORDEROY**

Born: Abt 1515
  -SAME AS #12,ROYAL CHART 1127
Married: Bef 1540

Died: Bef 24 Sep 1582

12 **John SEYMOUR**

Born: Abt 1395
  -CONTINUED AS #4,ROYAL CHART 776
Married: 30 Jul 1424

Died: 20 Dec 1464

6 **Roger SEYMOUR**

Born: Abt 1430

Married:

Died: Bef 1509

Jane MORRIS

Spouse

13 **Isabel WILLIAM**

Born: Abt 1405

Died: 14 Apr 1485

3 **Jane SEYMOUR**

Born: Abt 1485

Died: Aft 1544

14 **Richard HARDEN**

Born: Abt 1420

Married:

Died:

7 **Sybil HARDEN**

Born: Abt 1450

Died:

15 **Miss BRAY**

Born: Abt 1425

Died:

Sources include: *TAG* 73:181-193, 294-311 (1998); MPGL 6606, 10133; Consultation with Douglas Richardson. Note: #1, 2, & 4 are also given as Cordray.

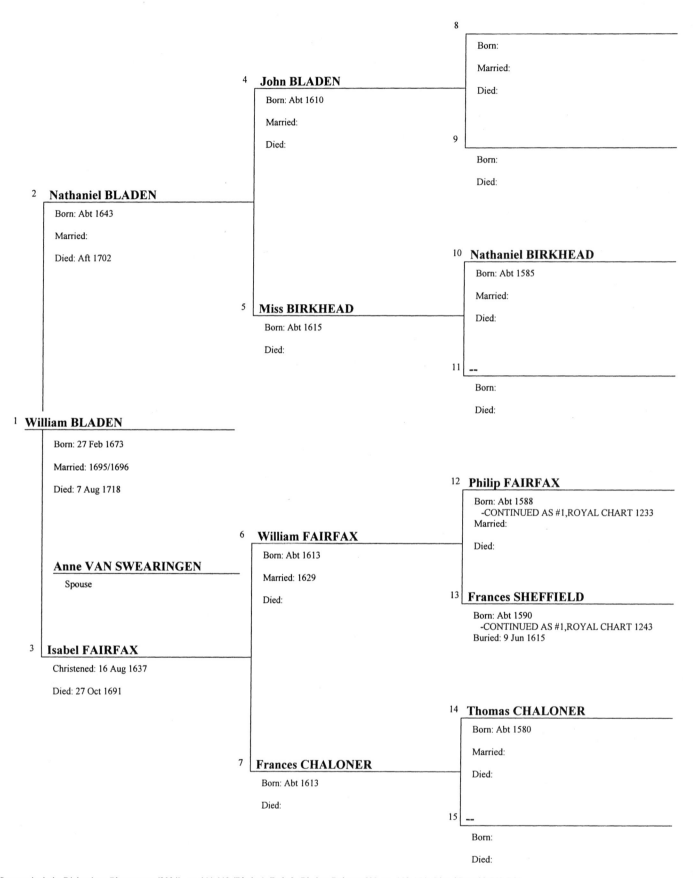

8

Born:

Married:

Died:

4   **John BLADEN**

Born: Abt 1610

Married:

Died:

9

Born:

Died:

2   **Nathaniel BLADEN**

Born: Abt 1643

Married:

Died: Aft 1702

10   **Nathaniel BIRKHEAD**

Born: Abt 1585

Married:

Died:

5   **Miss BIRKHEAD**

Born: Abt 1615

Died:

11   --

Born:

Died:

1   **William BLADEN**

Born: 27 Feb 1673

Married: 1695/1696

Died: 7 Aug 1718

12   **Philip FAIRFAX**

Born: Abt 1588
   -CONTINUED AS #1,ROYAL CHART 1233
Married:

Died:

6   **William FAIRFAX**

Born: Abt 1613

Married: 1629

Died:

13   **Frances SHEFFIELD**

Born: Abt 1590
   -CONTINUED AS #1,ROYAL CHART 1243
Buried: 9 Jun 1615

Anne VAN SWEARINGEN

Spouse

3   **Isabel FAIRFAX**

Christened: 16 Aug 1637

Died: 27 Oct 1691

14   **Thomas CHALONER**

Born: Abt 1580

Married:

Died:

7   **Frances CHALONER**

Born: Abt 1613

Died:

15   --

Born:

Died:

Sources include: Richardson *Plantagenet* (2004), pp. 111-112 (Bladen); Faris 2--Bladen; Roberts *500*, pp. 152-154; *Blood Royal* 2:763-764.

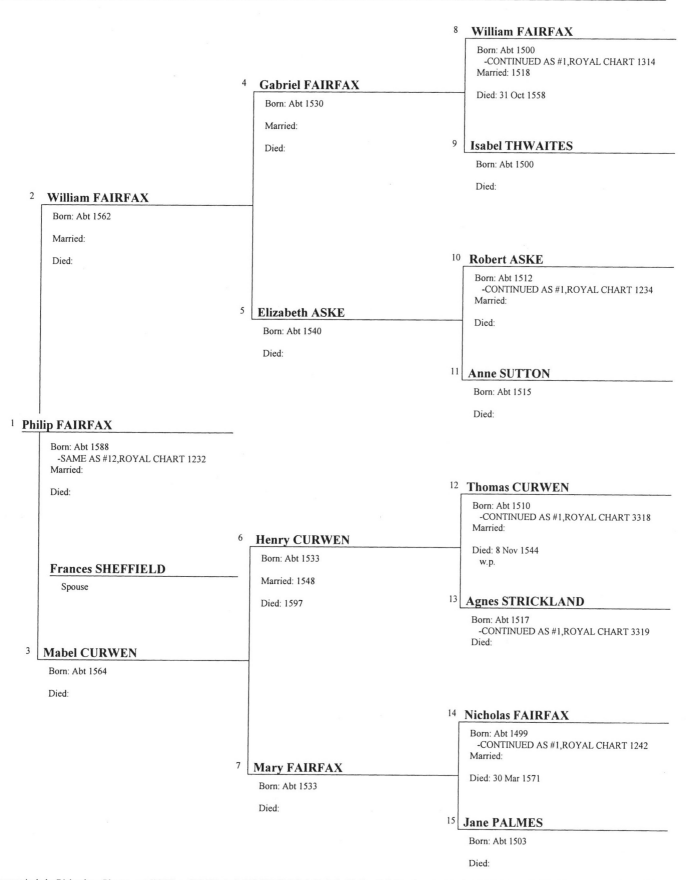

8 **William FAIRFAX**

Born: Abt 1500
-CONTINUED AS #1,ROYAL CHART 1314
Married: 1518

Died: 31 Oct 1558

4 **Gabriel FAIRFAX**

Born: Abt 1530

Married:

Died:

9 **Isabel THWAITES**

Born: Abt 1500

Died:

2 **William FAIRFAX**

Born: Abt 1562

Married:

Died:

10 **Robert ASKE**

Born: Abt 1512
-CONTINUED AS #1,ROYAL CHART 1234
Married:

Died:

5 **Elizabeth ASKE**

Born: Abt 1540

Died:

11 **Anne SUTTON**

Born: Abt 1515

Died:

1 **Philip FAIRFAX**

Born: Abt 1588
-SAME AS #12,ROYAL CHART 1232
Married:

Died:

12 **Thomas CURWEN**

Born: Abt 1510
-CONTINUED AS #1,ROYAL CHART 3318
Married:

Died: 8 Nov 1544
w.p.

6 **Henry CURWEN**

Born: Abt 1533

Married: 1548

Died: 1597

13 **Agnes STRICKLAND**

Born: Abt 1517
-CONTINUED AS #1,ROYAL CHART 3319
Died:

Frances SHEFFIELD

Spouse

3 **Mabel CURWEN**

Born: Abt 1564

Died:

14 **Nicholas FAIRFAX**

Born: Abt 1499
-CONTINUED AS #1,ROYAL CHART 1242
Married:

Died: 30 Mar 1571

7 **Mary FAIRFAX**

Born: Abt 1533

Died:

15 **Jane PALMES**

Born: Abt 1503

Died:

Sources include: Richardson *Plantagenet* (2004), p. 111 (Bladen), 302-303 (Fairfax); Faris 2--Bladen, Fairfax; *Ancestral Roots* 8 (2004), Line 37 (#6 & 7 ancestry); Roberts *500*, pp. 152-154. Note: Richardson gives #6 Henry as born in May 1528. This is very difficult chronologically.

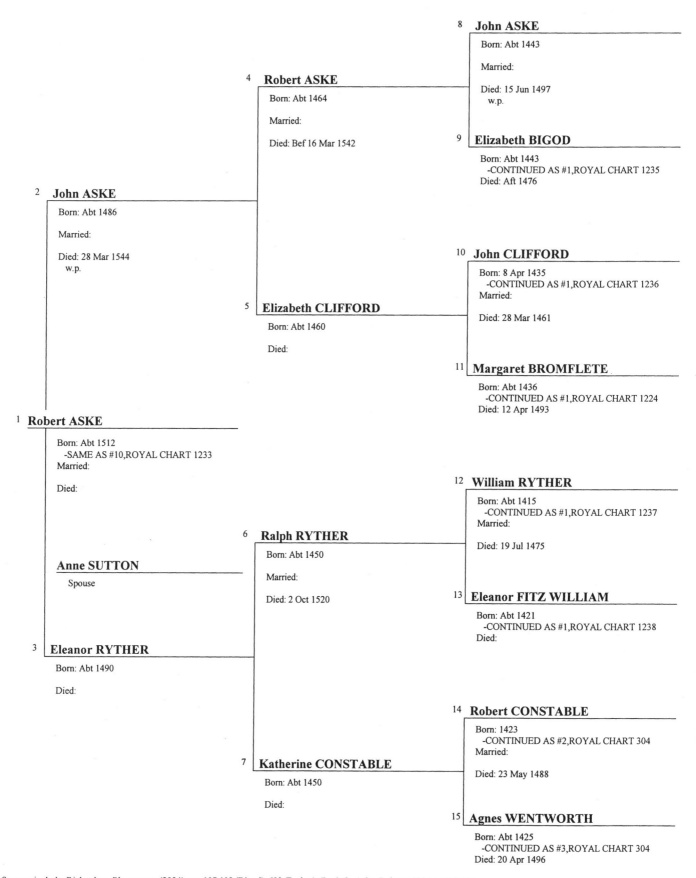

8 **John ASKE**
Born: Abt 1443
Married:
Died: 15 Jun 1497
w.p.

4 **Robert ASKE**
Born: Abt 1464
Married:
Died: Bef 16 Mar 1542

9 **Elizabeth BIGOD**
Born: Abt 1443
  -CONTINUED AS #1,ROYAL CHART 1235
Died: Aft 1476

2 **John ASKE**
Born: Abt 1486
Married:
Died: 28 Mar 1544
w.p.

10 **John CLIFFORD**
Born: 8 Apr 1435
  -CONTINUED AS #1,ROYAL CHART 1236
Married:
Died: 28 Mar 1461

5 **Elizabeth CLIFFORD**
Born: Abt 1460
Died:

11 **Margaret BROMFLETE**
Born: Abt 1436
  -CONTINUED AS #1,ROYAL CHART 1224
Died: 12 Apr 1493

1 **Robert ASKE**
Born: Abt 1512
  -SAME AS #10,ROYAL CHART 1233
Married:
Died:

12 **William RYTHER**
Born: Abt 1415
  -CONTINUED AS #1,ROYAL CHART 1237
Married:
Died: 19 Jul 1475

6 **Ralph RYTHER**
Born: Abt 1450
Married:
Died: 2 Oct 1520

13 **Eleanor FITZ WILLIAM**
Born: Abt 1421
  -CONTINUED AS #1,ROYAL CHART 1238
Died:

Anne SUTTON
Spouse

3 **Eleanor RYTHER**
Born: Abt 1490
Died:

14 **Robert CONSTABLE**
Born: 1423
  -CONTINUED AS #2,ROYAL CHART 304
Married:
Died: 23 May 1488

7 **Katherine CONSTABLE**
Born: Abt 1450
Died:

15 **Agnes WENTWORTH**
Born: Abt 1425
  -CONTINUED AS #3,ROYAL CHART 304
Died: 20 Apr 1496

Sources include: Richardson *Plantagenet* (2004), pp. 107-108 (Bigod), 623 (Ryther); Farris 2--Aske; Roberts *500*, pp. 152-154.

Pedigree Chart

Chart 1235

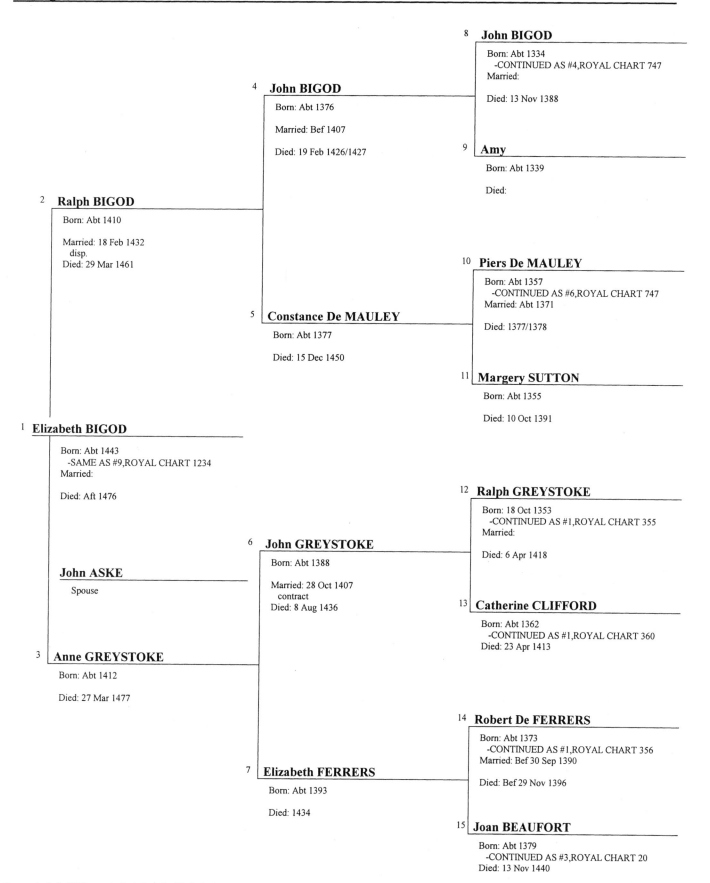

8 John BIGOD

Born: Abt 1334
-CONTINUED AS #4,ROYAL CHART 747
Married:

Died: 13 Nov 1388

4 John BIGOD

Born: Abt 1376

Married: Bef 1407

Died: 19 Feb 1426/1427

9 Amy

Born: Abt 1339

Died:

2 Ralph BIGOD

Born: Abt 1410

Married: 18 Feb 1432
disp.
Died: 29 Mar 1461

10 Piers De MAULEY

Born: Abt 1357
-CONTINUED AS #6,ROYAL CHART 747
Married: Abt 1371

Died: 1377/1378

5 Constance De MAULEY

Born: Abt 1377

Died: 15 Dec 1450

11 Margery SUTTON

Born: Abt 1355

Died: 10 Oct 1391

1 Elizabeth BIGOD

Born: Abt 1443
-SAME AS #9,ROYAL CHART 1234
Married:

Died: Aft 1476

12 Ralph GREYSTOKE

Born: 18 Oct 1353
-CONTINUED AS #1,ROYAL CHART 355
Married:

Died: 6 Apr 1418

6 John GREYSTOKE

Born: Abt 1388

Married: 28 Oct 1407
contract
Died: 8 Aug 1436

13 Catherine CLIFFORD

Born: Abt 1362
-CONTINUED AS #1,ROYAL CHART 360
Died: 23 Apr 1413

John ASKE

Spouse

3 Anne GREYSTOKE

Born: Abt 1412

Died: 27 Mar 1477

14 Robert De FERRERS

Born: Abt 1373
-CONTINUED AS #1,ROYAL CHART 356
Married: Bef 30 Sep 1390

Died: Bef 29 Nov 1396

7 Elizabeth FERRERS

Born: Abt 1393

Died: 1434

15 Joan BEAUFORT

Born: Abt 1379
-CONTINUED AS #3,ROYAL CHART 20
Died: 13 Nov 1440

Sources include: LDS records; Faris 2--Aske (#1 & 2), Greystoke (#6 & 7).

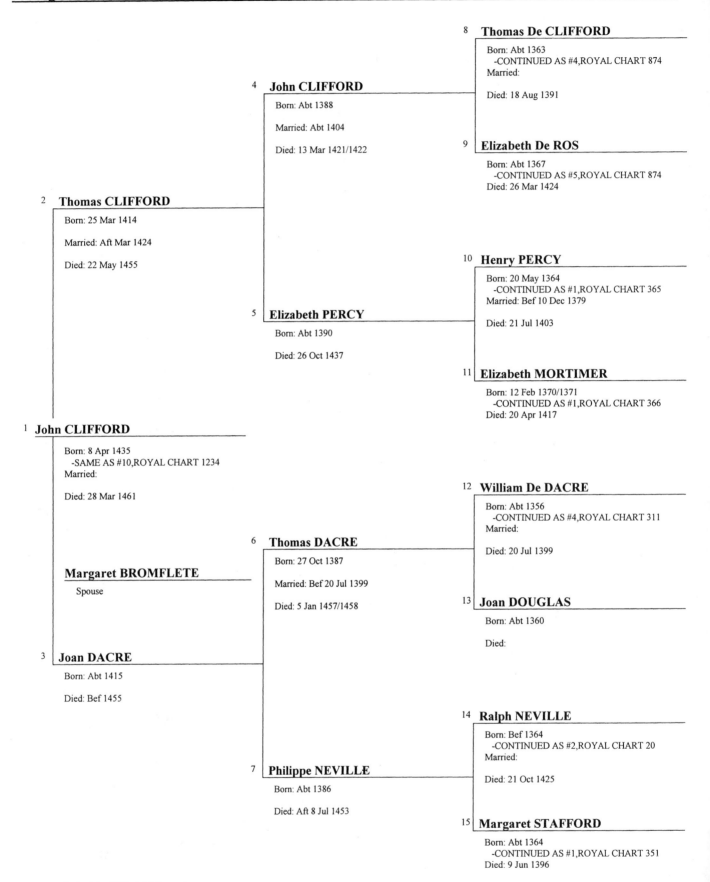

Pedigree Chart

8 **Thomas De CLIFFORD**
Born: Abt 1363
-CONTINUED AS #4,ROYAL CHART 874
Married:

Died: 18 Aug 1391

4 **John CLIFFORD**
Born: Abt 1388

Married: Abt 1404

Died: 13 Mar 1421/1422

9 **Elizabeth De ROS**
Born: Abt 1367
-CONTINUED AS #5,ROYAL CHART 874
Died: 26 Mar 1424

2 **Thomas CLIFFORD**
Born: 25 Mar 1414

Married: Aft Mar 1424

Died: 22 May 1455

10 **Henry PERCY**
Born: 20 May 1364
-CONTINUED AS #1,ROYAL CHART 365
Married: Bef 10 Dec 1379

Died: 21 Jul 1403

5 **Elizabeth PERCY**
Born: Abt 1390

Died: 26 Oct 1437

11 **Elizabeth MORTIMER**
Born: 12 Feb 1370/1371
-CONTINUED AS #1,ROYAL CHART 366
Died: 20 Apr 1417

1 **John CLIFFORD**
Born: 8 Apr 1435
-SAME AS #10,ROYAL CHART 1234
Married:

Died: 28 Mar 1461

12 **William De DACRE**
Born: Abt 1356
-CONTINUED AS #4,ROYAL CHART 311
Married:

Died: 20 Jul 1399

6 **Thomas DACRE**
Born: 27 Oct 1387

Married: Bef 20 Jul 1399

Died: 5 Jan 1457/1458

Margaret BROMFLETE
Spouse

13 **Joan DOUGLAS**
Born: Abt 1360

Died:

3 **Joan DACRE**
Born: Abt 1415

Died: Bef 1455

14 **Ralph NEVILLE**
Born: Bef 1364
-CONTINUED AS #2,ROYAL CHART 20
Married:

Died: 21 Oct 1425

7 **Philippe NEVILLE**
Born: Abt 1386

Died: Aft 8 Jul 1453

15 **Margaret STAFFORD**
Born: Abt 1364
-CONTINUED AS #1,ROYAL CHART 351
Died: 9 Jun 1396

Sources include: Faris 2--Clifford; LDS records.

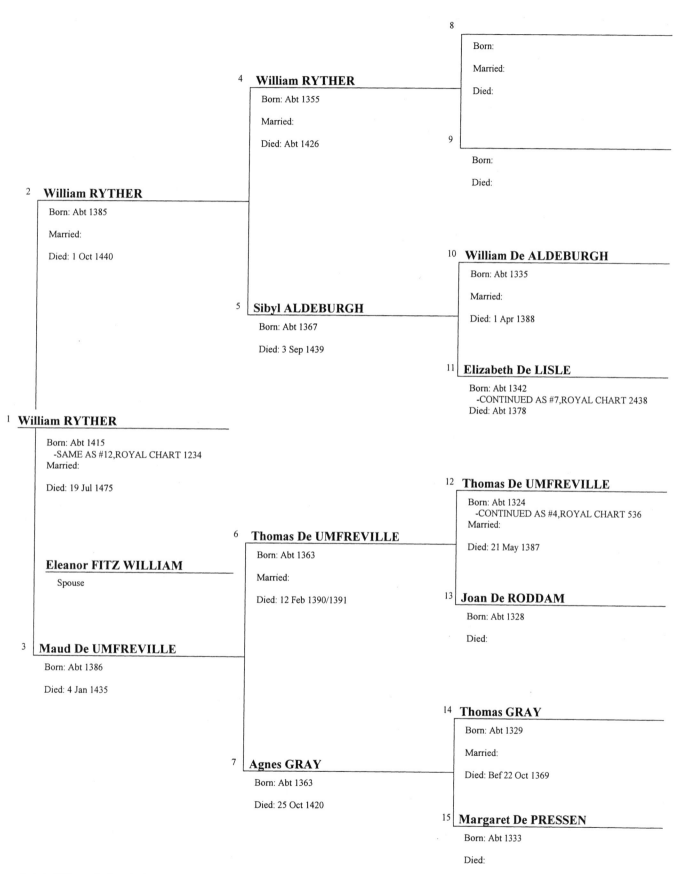

8

4 **William RYTHER**
Born: Abt 1355
Married:
Died: Abt 1426

Born:
Married:
Died:

9

Born:
Died:

2 **William RYTHER**
Born: Abt 1385
Married:
Died: 1 Oct 1440

10 **William De ALDEBURGH**
Born: Abt 1335
Married:
Died: 1 Apr 1388

5 **Sibyl ALDEBURGH**
Born: Abt 1367
Died: 3 Sep 1439

11 **Elizabeth De LISLE**
Born: Abt 1342
  -CONTINUED AS #7,ROYAL CHART 2438
Died: Abt 1378

1 **William RYTHER**
Born: Abt 1415
  -SAME AS #12,ROYAL CHART 1234
Married:
Died: 19 Jul 1475

12 **Thomas De UMFREVILLE**
Born: Abt 1324
  -CONTINUED AS #4,ROYAL CHART 536
Married:
Died: 21 May 1387

6 **Thomas De UMFREVILLE**
Born: Abt 1363
Married:
Died: 12 Feb 1390/1391

Eleanor FITZ WILLIAM
Spouse

13 **Joan De RODDAM**
Born: Abt 1328
Died:

3 **Maud De UMFREVILLE**
Born: Abt 1386
Died: 4 Jan 1435

14 **Thomas GRAY**
Born: Abt 1329
Married:
Died: Bef 22 Oct 1369

7 **Agnes GRAY**
Born: Abt 1363
Died: 25 Oct 1420

15 **Margaret De PRESSEN**
Born: Abt 1333
Died:

Sources include: LDS records; Consultation with Douglas Richardson; *Complete Peerage* 1:100-101 (#5 ancestry).

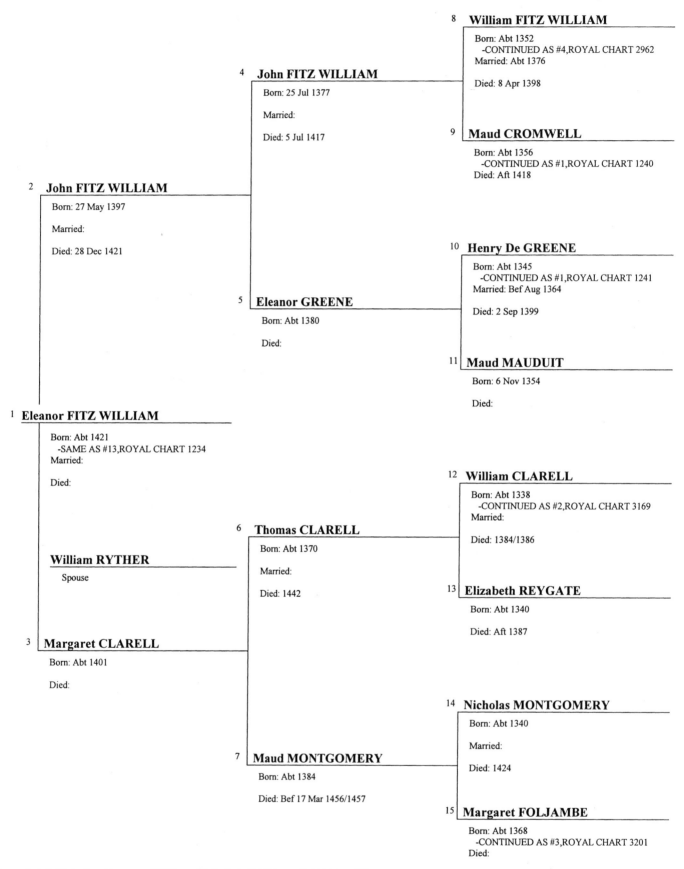

8 **William FITZ WILLIAM**

Born: Abt 1352
  -CONTINUED AS #4, ROYAL CHART 2962
Married: Abt 1376

Died: 8 Apr 1398

4 **John FITZ WILLIAM**

Born: 25 Jul 1377

Married:

Died: 5 Jul 1417

9 **Maud CROMWELL**

Born: Abt 1356
  -CONTINUED AS #1, ROYAL CHART 1240
Died: Aft 1418

2 **John FITZ WILLIAM**

Born: 27 May 1397

Married:

Died: 28 Dec 1421

10 **Henry De GREENE**

Born: Abt 1345
  -CONTINUED AS #1, ROYAL CHART 1241
Married: Bef Aug 1364

Died: 2 Sep 1399

5 **Eleanor GREENE**

Born: Abt 1380

Died:

11 **Maud MAUDUIT**

Born: 6 Nov 1354

Died:

1 **Eleanor FITZ WILLIAM**

Born: Abt 1421
  -SAME AS #13, ROYAL CHART 1234
Married:

Died:

12 **William CLARELL**

Born: Abt 1338
  -CONTINUED AS #2, ROYAL CHART 3169
Married:

Died: 1384/1386

6 **Thomas CLARELL**

Born: Abt 1370

Married:

Died: 1442

13 **Elizabeth REYGATE**

Born: Abt 1340

Died: Aft 1387

William RYTHER

Spouse

3 **Margaret CLARELL**

Born: Abt 1401

Died:

14 **Nicholas MONTGOMERY**

Born: Abt 1340

Married:

Died: 1424

7 **Maud MONTGOMERY**

Born: Abt 1384

Died: Bef 17 Mar 1456/1457

15 **Margaret FOLJAMBE**

Born: Abt 1368
  -CONTINUED AS #3, ROYAL CHART 3201
Died:

Sources include: Richardson *Plantagenet* (2004), pp. 623 (Ryther), 634 (Saltonstall), 332 (Fitz William); Paget (1957) 233:1-2; *Complete Peerage* 5:518-520 (#2 ancestry); Faris preliminary baronial manuscript (1998), p. 356 Clarell (#3 ancestry).

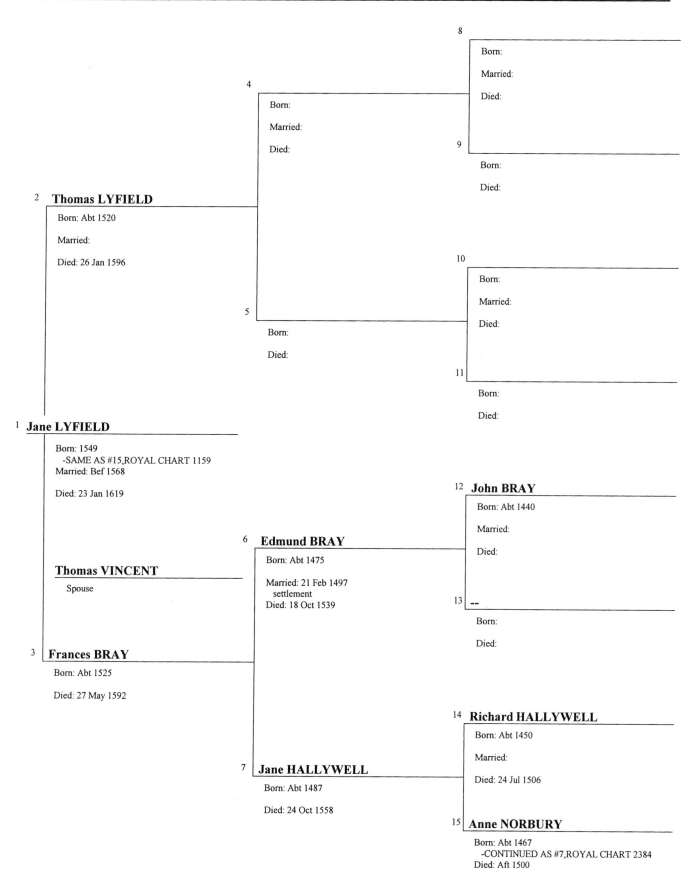

Thomas LYFIELD — 2
Born: Abt 1520
Married:
Died: 26 Jan 1596

4
Born:
Married:
Died:

8
Born:
Married:
Died:

9
Born:
Died:

5
Born:
Died:

10
Born:
Married:
Died:

11
Born:
Died:

Jane LYFIELD — 1
Born: 1549
    -SAME AS #15,ROYAL CHART 1159
Married: Bef 1568
Died: 23 Jan 1619

Thomas VINCENT
Spouse

Frances BRAY — 3
Born: Abt 1525
Died: 27 May 1592

6 — **Edmund BRAY**
Born: Abt 1475
Married: 21 Feb 1497
    settlement
Died: 18 Oct 1539

12 — **John BRAY**
Born: Abt 1440
Married:
Died:

13 — **--**
Born:
Died:

7 — **Jane HALLYWELL**
Born: Abt 1487
Died: 24 Oct 1558

14 — **Richard HALLYWELL**
Born: Abt 1450
Married:
Died: 24 Jul 1506

15 — **Anne NORBURY**
Born: Abt 1467
    -CONTINUED AS #7,ROYAL CHART 2384
Died: Aft 1500

Sources include: Research by Douglas Richardson (November 2000); P.W. Hasler, *The House of Commons* (1558-1603) 3:558-559 (Vincent), 2:503-504 (Lyfield); *Complete Peerage* 2:287-288.

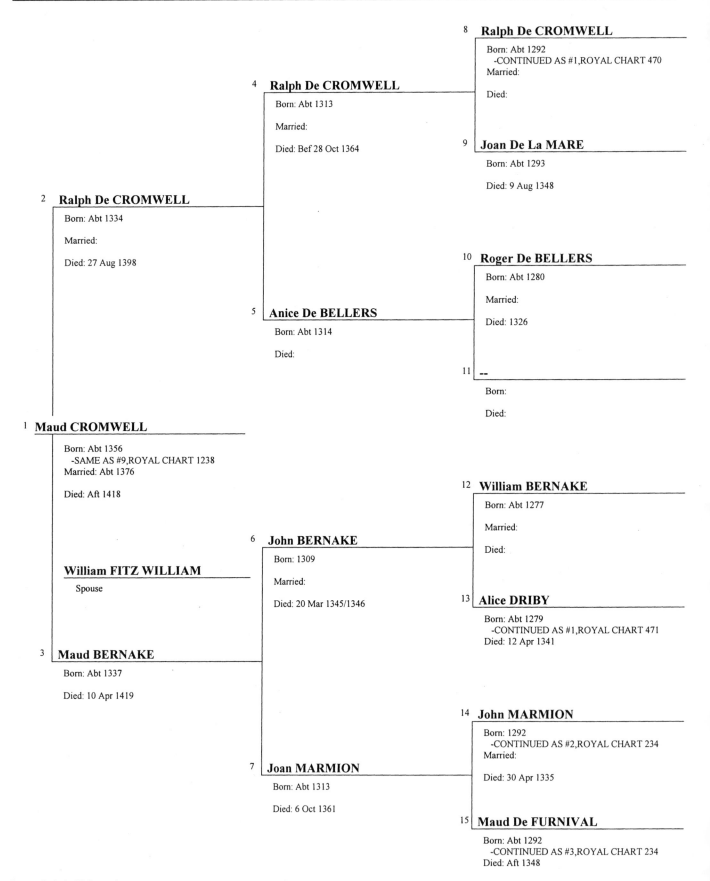

8 **Ralph De CROMWELL**

Born: Abt 1292
-CONTINUED AS #1,ROYAL CHART 470
Married:

Died:

4 **Ralph De CROMWELL**

Born: Abt 1313

Married:

Died: Bef 28 Oct 1364

9 **Joan De La MARE**

Born: Abt 1293

Died: 9 Aug 1348

2 **Ralph De CROMWELL**

Born: Abt 1334

Married:

Died: 27 Aug 1398

10 **Roger De BELLERS**

Born: Abt 1280

Married:

Died: 1326

5 **Anice De BELLERS**

Born: Abt 1314

Died:

11 **--**

Born:

Died:

1 **Maud CROMWELL**

Born: Abt 1356
-SAME AS #9,ROYAL CHART 1238
Married: Abt 1376

Died: Aft 1418

12 **William BERNAKE**

Born: Abt 1277

Married:

Died:

6 **John BERNAKE**

Born: 1309

Married:

Died: 20 Mar 1345/1346

13 **Alice DRIBY**

Born: Abt 1279
-CONTINUED AS #1,ROYAL CHART 471
Died: 12 Apr 1341

William FITZ WILLIAM

Spouse

3 **Maud BERNAKE**

Born: Abt 1337

Died: 10 Apr 1419

14 **John MARMION**

Born: 1292
-CONTINUED AS #2,ROYAL CHART 234
Married:

Died: 30 Apr 1335

7 **Joan MARMION**

Born: Abt 1313

Died: 6 Oct 1361

15 **Maud De FURNIVAL**

Born: Abt 1292
-CONTINUED AS #3,ROYAL CHART 234
Died: Aft 1348

Sources include: LDS records.

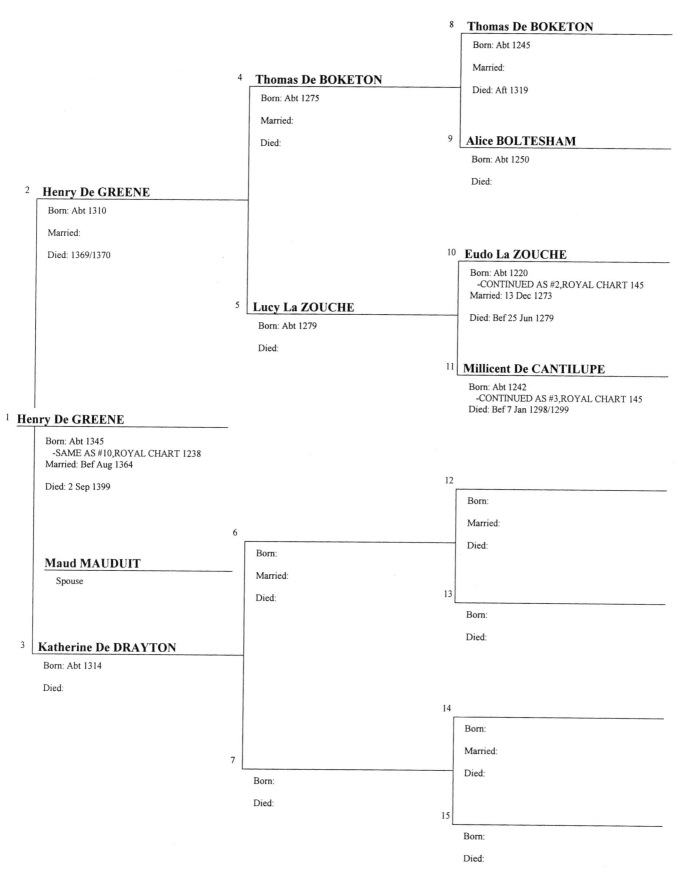

8 **Thomas De BOKETON**

Born: Abt 1245

Married:

Died: Aft 1319

4 **Thomas De BOKETON**

Born: Abt 1275

Married:

Died:

9 **Alice BOLTESHAM**

Born: Abt 1250

Died:

2 **Henry De GREENE**

Born: Abt 1310

Married:

Died: 1369/1370

10 **Eudo La ZOUCHE**

Born: Abt 1220
   -CONTINUED AS #2,ROYAL CHART 145
Married: 13 Dec 1273

Died: Bef 25 Jun 1279

5 **Lucy La ZOUCHE**

Born: Abt 1279

Died:

11 **Millicent De CANTILUPE**

Born: Abt 1242
   -CONTINUED AS #3,ROYAL CHART 145
Died: Bef 7 Jan 1298/1299

1 **Henry De GREENE**

Born: Abt 1345
   -SAME AS #10,ROYAL CHART 1238
Married: Bef Aug 1364

Died: 2 Sep 1399

12

Born:

Married:

Died:

6

Born:

Married:

Died:

13

Born:

Died:

Maud MAUDUIT

Spouse

3 **Katherine De DRAYTON**

Born: Abt 1314

Died:

14

Born:

Married:

Died:

7

Born:

Died:

15

Born:

Died:

Sources include: LDS records; Faris preliminary baronial manuscript (1998), pp. 731 Green, 515 Drayton (#2 & 3 ancestry). Note: The parentage of #3 Katherine is disputed. See chart 974 note.

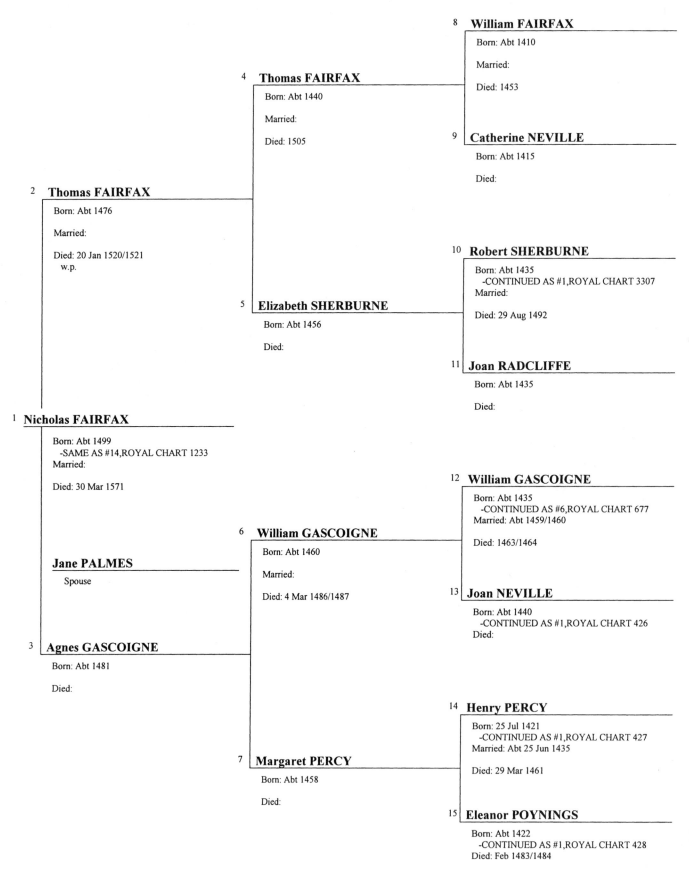

8 William FAIRFAX

Born: Abt 1410

Married:

Died: 1453

4 Thomas FAIRFAX

Born: Abt 1440

Married:

Died: 1505

9 Catherine NEVILLE

Born: Abt 1415

Died:

2 Thomas FAIRFAX

Born: Abt 1476

Married:

Died: 20 Jan 1520/1521
w.p.

10 Robert SHERBURNE

Born: Abt 1435
-CONTINUED AS #1,ROYAL CHART 3307
Married:

Died: 29 Aug 1492

5 Elizabeth SHERBURNE

Born: Abt 1456

Died:

11 Joan RADCLIFFE

Born: Abt 1435

Died:

1 Nicholas FAIRFAX

Born: Abt 1499
-SAME AS #14,ROYAL CHART 1233
Married:

Died: 30 Mar 1571

12 William GASCOIGNE

Born: Abt 1435
-CONTINUED AS #6,ROYAL CHART 677
Married: Abt 1459/1460

Died: 1463/1464

6 William GASCOIGNE

Born: Abt 1460

Married:

Died: 4 Mar 1486/1487

13 Joan NEVILLE

Born: Abt 1440
-CONTINUED AS #1,ROYAL CHART 426
Died:

Jane PALMES

Spouse

3 Agnes GASCOIGNE

Born: Abt 1481

Died:

14 Henry PERCY

Born: 25 Jul 1421
-CONTINUED AS #1,ROYAL CHART 427
Married: Abt 25 Jun 1435

Died: 29 Mar 1461

7 Margaret PERCY

Born: Abt 1458

Died:

15 Eleanor POYNINGS

Born: Abt 1422
-CONTINUED AS #1,ROYAL CHART 428
Died: Feb 1483/1484

Sources include: Faris 2--Fairfax; Richardson *Magna Carta* (April 2005), pp. 316-317 (Fairfax), 831-832 (Towneley); Roberts *500*, pp. 152-154; LDS records.

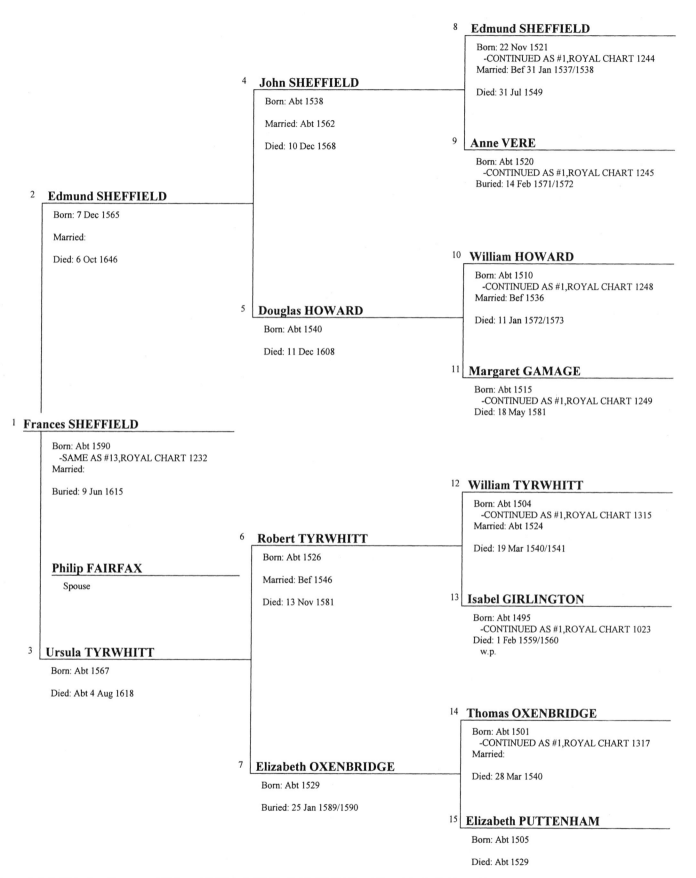

8 **Edmund SHEFFIELD**
Born: 22 Nov 1521
 -CONTINUED AS #1,ROYAL CHART 1244
Married: Bef 31 Jan 1537/1538

Died: 31 Jul 1549

4 **John SHEFFIELD**
Born: Abt 1538

Married: Abt 1562

Died: 10 Dec 1568

9 **Anne VERE**
Born: Abt 1520
 -CONTINUED AS #1,ROYAL CHART 1245
Buried: 14 Feb 1571/1572

2 **Edmund SHEFFIELD**
Born: 7 Dec 1565

Married:

Died: 6 Oct 1646

10 **William HOWARD**
Born: Abt 1510
 -CONTINUED AS #1,ROYAL CHART 1248
Married: Bef 1536

Died: 11 Jan 1572/1573

5 **Douglas HOWARD**
Born: Abt 1540

Died: 11 Dec 1608

11 **Margaret GAMAGE**
Born: Abt 1515
 -CONTINUED AS #1,ROYAL CHART 1249
Died: 18 May 1581

1 **Frances SHEFFIELD**
Born: Abt 1590
 -SAME AS #13,ROYAL CHART 1232
Married:

Buried: 9 Jun 1615

12 **William TYRWHITT**
Born: Abt 1504
 -CONTINUED AS #1,ROYAL CHART 1315
Married: Abt 1524

Died: 19 Mar 1540/1541

6 **Robert TYRWHITT**
Born: Abt 1526

Married: Bef 1546

Died: 13 Nov 1581

13 **Isabel GIRLINGTON**
Born: Abt 1495
 -CONTINUED AS #1,ROYAL CHART 1023
Died: 1 Feb 1559/1560
w.p.

Philip FAIRFAX
Spouse

3 **Ursula TYRWHITT**
Born: Abt 1567

Died: Abt 4 Aug 1618

14 **Thomas OXENBRIDGE**
Born: Abt 1501
 -CONTINUED AS #1,ROYAL CHART 1317
Married:

Died: 28 Mar 1540

7 **Elizabeth OXENBRIDGE**
Born: Abt 1529

Buried: 25 Jan 1589/1590

15 **Elizabeth PUTTENHAM**
Born: Abt 1505

Died: Abt 1529

Sources include: Richardson *Plantagenet* (2004), pp. 111 (Bladen), 648 (Sheffield), 733-734 (Tyrwhit); Faris 2--Sheffield, Tyrwhitt, *Blood Royal* 2:763-764.

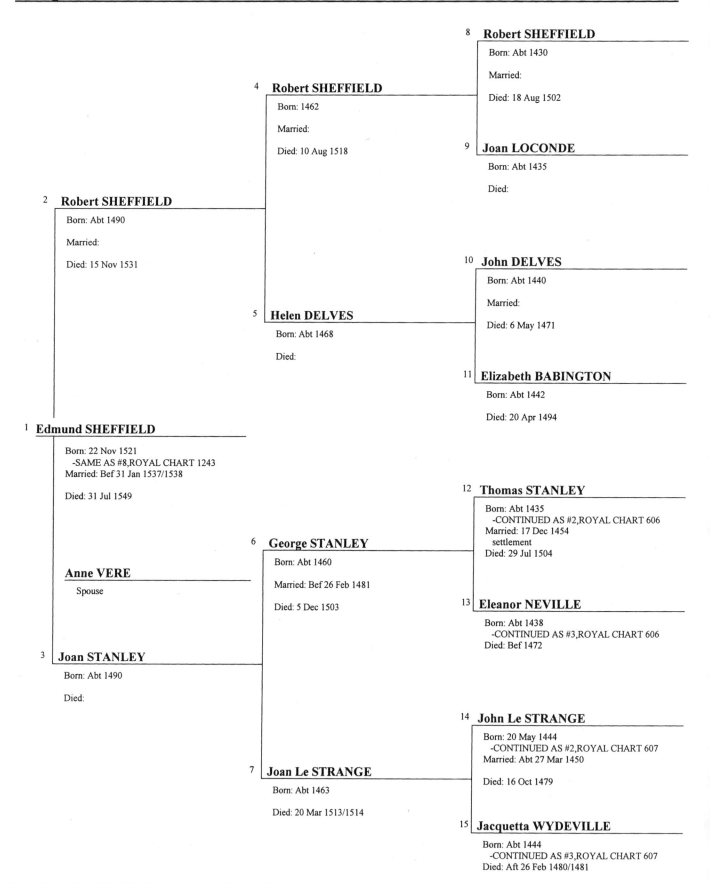

2 **Robert SHEFFIELD**

Born: Abt 1490

Married:

Died: 15 Nov 1531

4 **Robert SHEFFIELD**

Born: 1462

Married:

Died: 10 Aug 1518

8 **Robert SHEFFIELD**

Born: Abt 1430

Married:

Died: 18 Aug 1502

9 **Joan LOCONDE**

Born: Abt 1435

Died:

5 **Helen DELVES**

Born: Abt 1468

Died:

10 **John DELVES**

Born: Abt 1440

Married:

Died: 6 May 1471

11 **Elizabeth BABINGTON**

Born: Abt 1442

Died: 20 Apr 1494

1 **Edmund SHEFFIELD**

Born: 22 Nov 1521
    -SAME AS #8,ROYAL CHART 1243
Married: Bef 31 Jan 1537/1538

Died: 31 Jul 1549

Anne VERE

Spouse

3 **Joan STANLEY**

Born: Abt 1490

Died:

6 **George STANLEY**

Born: Abt 1460

Married: Bef 26 Feb 1481

Died: 5 Dec 1503

12 **Thomas STANLEY**

Born: Abt 1435
    -CONTINUED AS #2,ROYAL CHART 606
Married: 17 Dec 1454
    settlement
Died: 29 Jul 1504

13 **Eleanor NEVILLE**

Born: Abt 1438
    -CONTINUED AS #3,ROYAL CHART 606
Died: Bef 1472

7 **Joan Le STRANGE**

Born: Abt 1463

Died: 20 Mar 1513/1514

14 **John Le STRANGE**

Born: 20 May 1444
    -CONTINUED AS #2,ROYAL CHART 607
Married: Abt 27 Mar 1450

Died: 16 Oct 1479

15 **Jacquetta WYDEVILLE**

Born: Abt 1444
    -CONTINUED AS #3,ROYAL CHART 607
Died: Aft 26 Feb 1480/1481

Sources include: Faris 2--Sheffield; LDS records; Paget 182, 268, 447.

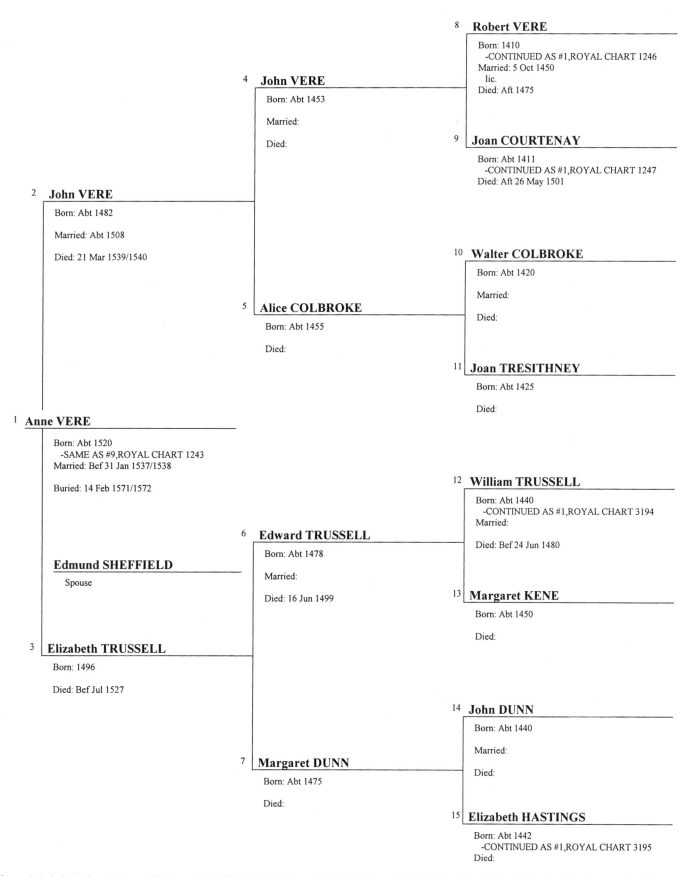

8 **Robert VERE**

Born: 1410
  -CONTINUED AS #1,ROYAL CHART 1246
Married: 5 Oct 1450
  lic.
Died: Aft 1475

4 **John VERE**

Born: Abt 1453

Married:

Died:

9 **Joan COURTENAY**

Born: Abt 1411
  -CONTINUED AS #1,ROYAL CHART 1247
Died: Aft 26 May 1501

2 **John VERE**

Born: Abt 1482

Married: Abt 1508

Died: 21 Mar 1539/1540

10 **Walter COLBROKE**

Born: Abt 1420

Married:

Died:

5 **Alice COLBROKE**

Born: Abt 1455

Died:

11 **Joan TRESITHNEY**

Born: Abt 1425

Died:

1 **Anne VERE**

Born: Abt 1520
  -SAME AS #9,ROYAL CHART 1243
Married: Bef 31 Jan 1537/1538

Buried: 14 Feb 1571/1572

12 **William TRUSSELL**

Born: Abt 1440
  -CONTINUED AS #1,ROYAL CHART 3194
Married:

Died: Bef 24 Jun 1480

6 **Edward TRUSSELL**

Born: Abt 1478

Married:

Died: 16 Jun 1499

13 **Margaret KENE**

Born: Abt 1450

Died:

Edmund SHEFFIELD

Spouse

3 **Elizabeth TRUSSELL**

Born: 1496

Died: Bef Jul 1527

14 **John DUNN**

Born: Abt 1440

Married:

Died:

7 **Margaret DUNN**

Born: Abt 1475

Died:

15 **Elizabeth HASTINGS**

Born: Abt 1442
  -CONTINUED AS #1,ROYAL CHART 3195
Died:

Sources include: Richardson *Plantagenet* (2004), pp. 648 (Sheffield), 370-371 (Haccombe), 719-720 (Trussell); Faris 2--Vere; Consultation with Douglas Richardson, June 2004 (#5 ancestry); LDS records (#7 ancestry).

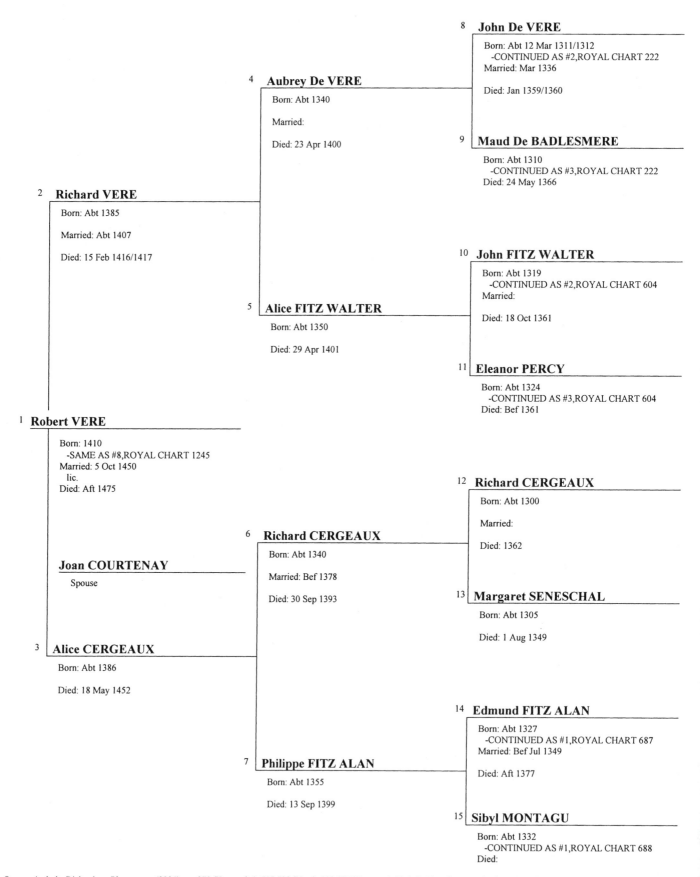

8   **John De VERE**

Born: Abt 12 Mar 1311/1312
  -CONTINUED AS #2,ROYAL CHART 222
Married: Mar 1336

Died: Jan 1359/1360

4   **Aubrey De VERE**

Born: Abt 1340

Married:

Died: 23 Apr 1400

9   **Maud De BADLESMERE**

Born: Abt 1310
  -CONTINUED AS #3,ROYAL CHART 222
Died: 24 May 1366

2   **Richard VERE**

Born: Abt 1385

Married: Abt 1407

Died: 15 Feb 1416/1417

10   **John FITZ WALTER**

Born: Abt 1319
  -CONTINUED AS #2,ROYAL CHART 604
Married:

Died: 18 Oct 1361

5   **Alice FITZ WALTER**

Born: Abt 1350

Died: 29 Apr 1401

11   **Eleanor PERCY**

Born: Abt 1324
  -CONTINUED AS #3,ROYAL CHART 604
Died: Bef 1361

1   **Robert VERE**

Born: 1410
  -SAME AS #8,ROYAL CHART 1245
Married: 5 Oct 1450
  lic.
Died: Aft 1475

12   **Richard CERGEAUX**

Born: Abt 1300

Married:

Died: 1362

6   **Richard CERGEAUX**

Born: Abt 1340

Married: Bef 1378

Died: 30 Sep 1393

13   **Margaret SENESCHAL**

Born: Abt 1305

Died: 1 Aug 1349

Joan COURTENAY

Spouse

3   **Alice CERGEAUX**

Born: Abt 1386

Died: 18 May 1452

14   **Edmund FITZ ALAN**

Born: Abt 1327
  -CONTINUED AS #1,ROYAL CHART 687
Married: Bef Jul 1349

Died: Aft 1377

7   **Philippe FITZ ALAN**

Born: Abt 1355

Died: 13 Sep 1399

15   **Sibyl MONTAGU**

Born: Abt 1332
  -CONTINUED AS #1,ROYAL CHART 688
Died:

Sources include: Richardson *Plantagenet* (2004), pp. 370 (Haccombe), 737-738 (Vere), 646-647 (Sergeaux); Faris 2--Vere (incorrectly gives #1 Robert as <u>grandson</u> of #2 & 3 above), Cergeaux.

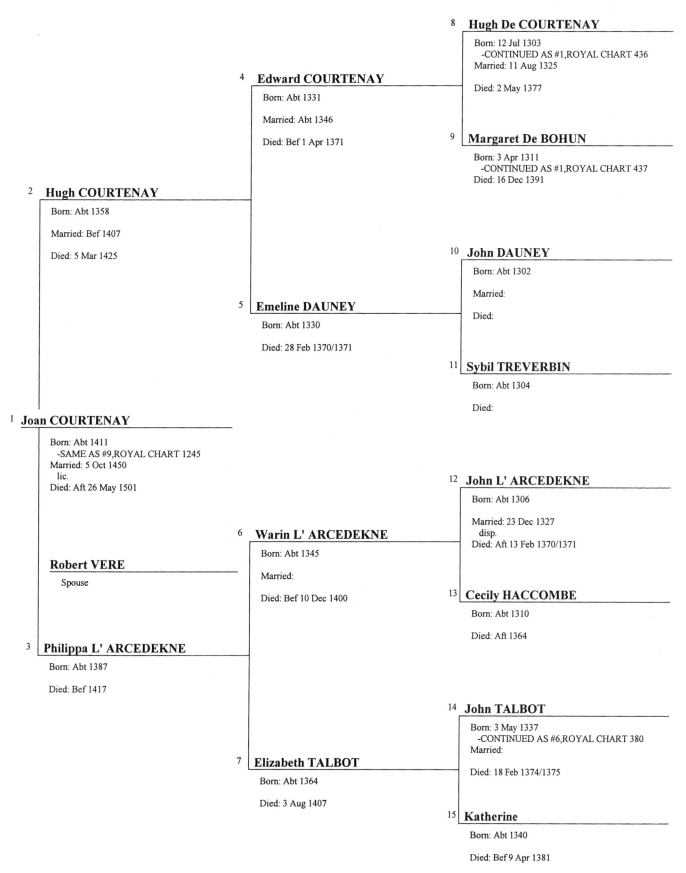

8 **Hugh De COURTENAY**

Born: 12 Jul 1303
-CONTINUED AS #1,ROYAL CHART 436
Married: 11 Aug 1325

Died: 2 May 1377

4 **Edward COURTENAY**

Born: Abt 1331

Married: Abt 1346

Died: Bef 1 Apr 1371

9 **Margaret De BOHUN**

Born: 3 Apr 1311
-CONTINUED AS #1,ROYAL CHART 437
Died: 16 Dec 1391

2 **Hugh COURTENAY**

Born: Abt 1358

Married: Bef 1407

Died: 5 Mar 1425

10 **John DAUNEY**

Born: Abt 1302

Married:

Died:

5 **Emeline DAUNEY**

Born: Abt 1330

Died: 28 Feb 1370/1371

11 **Sybil TREVERBIN**

Born: Abt 1304

Died:

1 **Joan COURTENAY**

Born: Abt 1411
-SAME AS #9,ROYAL CHART 1245
Married: 5 Oct 1450
lic.
Died: Aft 26 May 1501

12 **John L' ARCEDEKNE**

Born: Abt 1306

Married: 23 Dec 1327
disp.
Died: Aft 13 Feb 1370/1371

6 **Warin L' ARCEDEKNE**

Born: Abt 1345

Married:

Died: Bef 10 Dec 1400

Robert VERE

Spouse

13 **Cecily HACCOMBE**

Born: Abt 1310

Died: Aft 1364

3 **Philippa L' ARCEDEKNE**

Born: Abt 1387

Died: Bef 1417

14 **John TALBOT**

Born: 3 May 1337
-CONTINUED AS #6,ROYAL CHART 380
Married:

Died: 18 Feb 1374/1375

7 **Elizabeth TALBOT**

Born: Abt 1364

Died: 3 Aug 1407

15 **Katherine**

Born: Abt 1340

Died: Bef 9 Apr 1381

Sources include: Richardson *Plantagenet* (2004), pp. 370 (Haccombe), 238-241 (Courtenay), 607-608 (Richard's Castle); Faris 2--Courtenay; LDS records; *Ancestral Roots* 6-33.

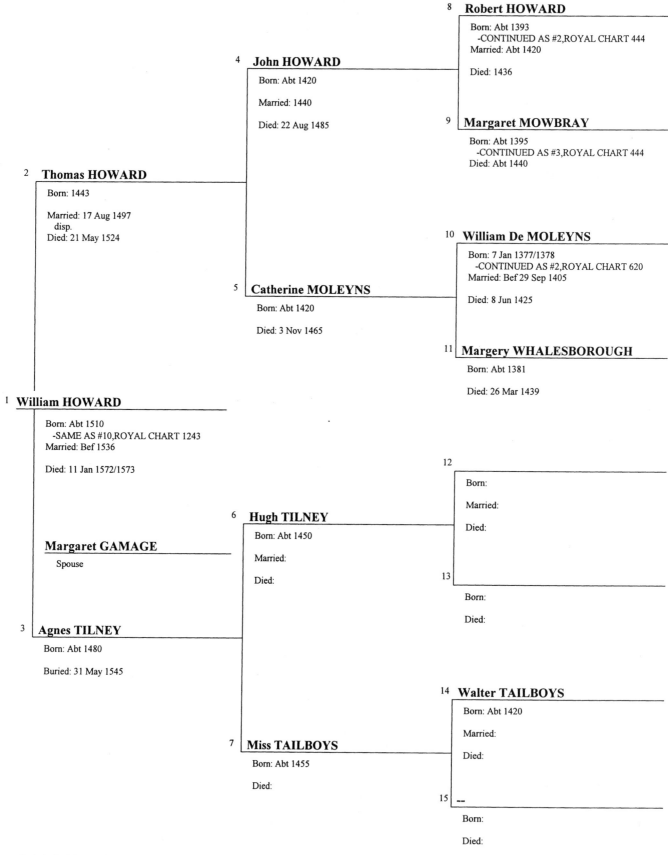

8 Robert HOWARD
Born: Abt 1393
-CONTINUED AS #2,ROYAL CHART 444
Married: Abt 1420

Died: 1436

4 John HOWARD
Born: Abt 1420

Married: 1440

Died: 22 Aug 1485

9 Margaret MOWBRAY
Born: Abt 1395
-CONTINUED AS #3,ROYAL CHART 444
Died: Abt 1440

2 Thomas HOWARD
Born: 1443

Married: 17 Aug 1497
disp.
Died: 21 May 1524

10 William De MOLEYNS
Born: 7 Jan 1377/1378
-CONTINUED AS #2,ROYAL CHART 620
Married: Bef 29 Sep 1405

Died: 8 Jun 1425

5 Catherine MOLEYNS
Born: Abt 1420

Died: 3 Nov 1465

11 Margery WHALESBOROUGH
Born: Abt 1381

Died: 26 Mar 1439

1 William HOWARD
Born: Abt 1510
-SAME AS #10,ROYAL CHART 1243
Married: Bef 1536

Died: 11 Jan 1572/1573

Margaret GAMAGE
Spouse

12
Born:

Married:

Died:

6 Hugh TILNEY
Born: Abt 1450

Married:

Died:

13
Born:

Died:

3 Agnes TILNEY
Born: Abt 1480

Buried: 31 May 1545

14 Walter TAILBOYS
Born: Abt 1420

Married:

Died:

7 Miss TAILBOYS
Born: Abt 1455

Died:

15 --
Born:

Died:

Sources include: Faris 2--Mowbray; LDS records.

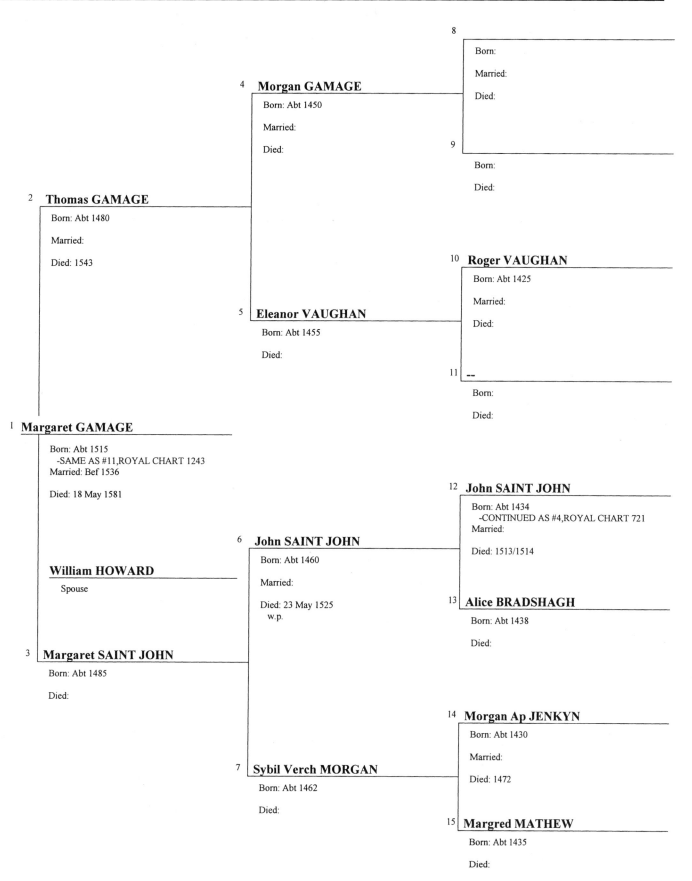

8
Born:
Married:
Died:

4 Morgan GAMAGE
Born: Abt 1450
Married:
Died:

9
Born:
Died:

2 Thomas GAMAGE
Born: Abt 1480
Married:
Died: 1543

10 Roger VAUGHAN
Born: Abt 1425
Married:
Died:

5 Eleanor VAUGHAN
Born: Abt 1455
Died:

11 --
Born:
Died:

1 Margaret GAMAGE
Born: Abt 1515
-SAME AS #11, ROYAL CHART 1243
Married: Bef 1536
Died: 18 May 1581

12 John SAINT JOHN
Born: Abt 1434
-CONTINUED AS #4, ROYAL CHART 721
Married:
Died: 1513/1514

6 John SAINT JOHN
Born: Abt 1460
Married:
Died: 23 May 1525
w.p.

13 Alice BRADSHAGH
Born: Abt 1438
Died:

William HOWARD
Spouse

3 Margaret SAINT JOHN
Born: Abt 1485
Died:

14 Morgan Ap JENKYN
Born: Abt 1430
Married:
Died: 1472

7 Sybil Verch MORGAN
Born: Abt 1462
Died:

15 Margred MATHEW
Born: Abt 1435
Died:

Sources include: Faris 2--Mowbray; Consultation with Douglas Richardson; *Ancestral Roots* 85 (#6 & 7 ancestry); *Magna Charta* 61 (#6 & 7 ancestry); LDS records.

8 John BERNARD
Born: Abt 1490
  -CONTINUED AS #2,ROYAL CHART 697
Married:
Died: 1549

4 Francis BERNARD
Born: 1526
Married:
Died: 21 Oct 1602

9 Cecily MUSCOTE
Born: Abt 1495
Died: 21 Sep 1557

2 Francis BERNARD
Born: 1558
Married:
Died: 1630

10 John HASLEWOOD
Born: Abt 1500
Married:
Died: 1550

5 Alice HASLEWOOD
Born: Abt 1530
Died: 1612

11 Katherine MARMION
Born: Abt 1503
Died: 15 May 1573

1 William BERNARD
Born: 1603
Married: Bef 1655
Died: 31 Mar 1665

12 John WOOLHOUSE
Born: Abt 1500
Married:
Died:

6 Anthony WOOLHOUSE
Born: Abt 1533
Married: Bef 24 Dec 1558
Died: 12 Sep 1587
  w.p.

13 Margaret BAKER
Born: Abt 1505
Died:

Lucy HIGGINSON
Spouse

3 Mary WOOLHOUSE
Born: Abt 1564
Died:

14 John STRELLEY
Born: Abt 1500
Married:
Died: 27 Nov 1559
  w.p.

7 Millicent STRELLEY
Born: Abt 1535
Died: 2 Jun 1606
  w.p.

15 Alice
Born:
Died:

Sources include: Faris--Bernard; *Blood Royal* 5:424-425; *Magna Charta* 46; Roberts *500*, pp. 144-145; LDS records.

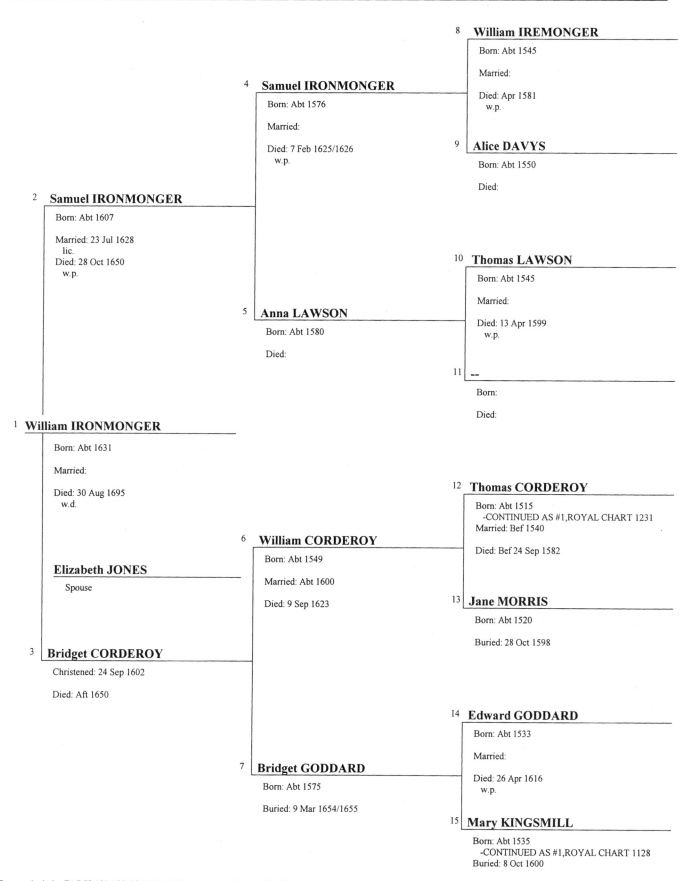

8 William IREMONGER
Born: Abt 1545
Married:
Died: Apr 1581
w.p.

4 Samuel IRONMONGER
Born: Abt 1576
Married:
Died: 7 Feb 1625/1626
w.p.

9 Alice DAVYS
Born: Abt 1550
Died:

2 Samuel IRONMONGER
Born: Abt 1607
Married: 23 Jul 1628
lic.
Died: 28 Oct 1650
w.p.

10 Thomas LAWSON
Born: Abt 1545
Married:
Died: 13 Apr 1599
w.p.

5 Anna LAWSON
Born: Abt 1580
Died:

11 --
Born:
Died:

1 William IRONMONGER
Born: Abt 1631
Married:
Died: 30 Aug 1695
w.d.

12 Thomas CORDEROY
Born: Abt 1515
-CONTINUED AS #1,ROYAL CHART 1231
Married: Bef 1540
Died: Bef 24 Sep 1582

6 William CORDEROY
Born: Abt 1549
Married: Abt 1600
Died: 9 Sep 1623

Elizabeth JONES
Spouse

13 Jane MORRIS
Born: Abt 1520
Buried: 28 Oct 1598

3 Bridget CORDEROY
Christened: 24 Sep 1602
Died: Aft 1650

14 Edward GODDARD
Born: Abt 1533
Married:
Died: 26 Apr 1616
w.p.

7 Bridget GODDARD
Born: Abt 1575
Buried: 9 Mar 1654/1655

15 Mary KINGSMILL
Born: Abt 1535
-CONTINUED AS #1,ROYAL CHART 1128
Buried: 8 Oct 1600

Sources include: *TAG* 73:181-193, 294-311 (1998); Roberts *500*, pp. 382-384; *Magna Charta* 46; *Blood Royal* 5:585, 742-744.

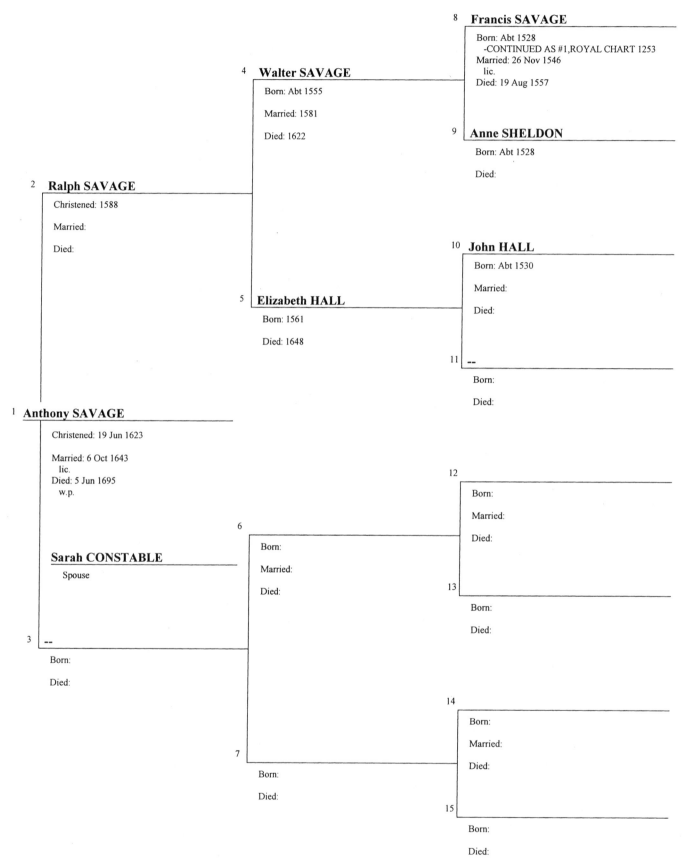

8 Francis SAVAGE

Born: Abt 1528
  -CONTINUED AS #1,ROYAL CHART 1253
Married: 26 Nov 1546
  lic.
Died: 19 Aug 1557

4 Walter SAVAGE

Born: Abt 1555

Married: 1581

Died: 1622

9 Anne SHELDON

Born: Abt 1528

Died:

2 Ralph SAVAGE

Christened: 1588

Married:

Died:

10 John HALL

Born: Abt 1530

Married:

Died:

5 Elizabeth HALL

Born: 1561

Died: 1648

11 --

Born:

Died:

1 Anthony SAVAGE

Christened: 19 Jun 1623

Married: 6 Oct 1643
  lic.
Died: 5 Jun 1695
  w.p.

Sarah CONSTABLE

Spouse

12

Born:

Married:

Died:

6

Born:

Married:

Died:

13

Born:

Died:

3 --

Born:

Died:

14

Born:

Married:

Died:

7

Born:

Died:

15

Born:

Died:

Sources include: Faris 2--Savage; Roberts *AAP*, pp. 11, 184; *500*, pp. 253-254.

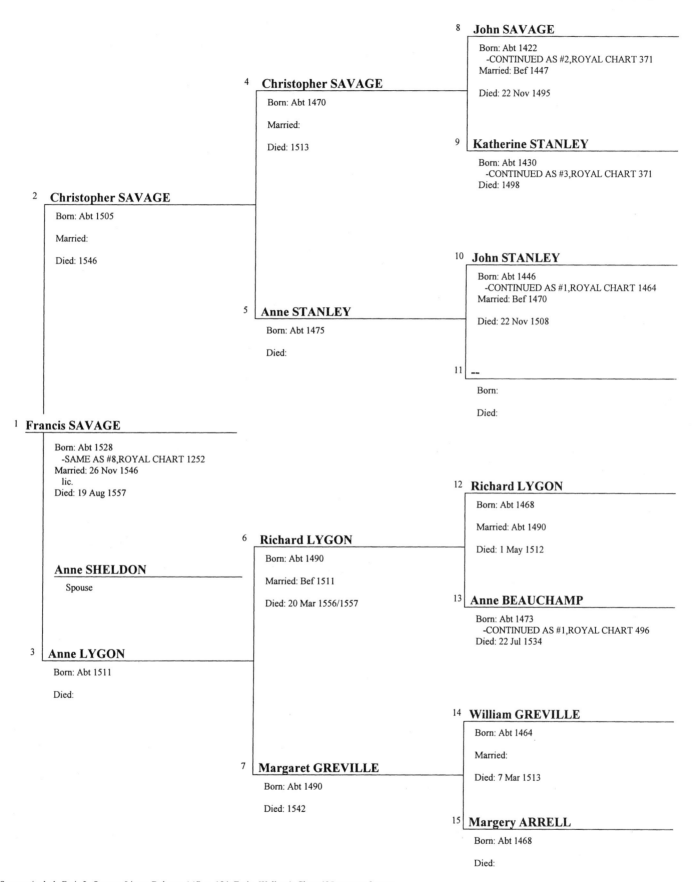

8 **John SAVAGE**

Born: Abt 1422
-CONTINUED AS #2,ROYAL CHART 371
Married: Bef 1447

Died: 22 Nov 1495

4 **Christopher SAVAGE**

Born: Abt 1470

Married:

Died: 1513

9 **Katherine STANLEY**

Born: Abt 1430
-CONTINUED AS #3,ROYAL CHART 371
Died: 1498

2 **Christopher SAVAGE**

Born: Abt 1505

Married:

Died: 1546

10 **John STANLEY**

Born: Abt 1446
-CONTINUED AS #1,ROYAL CHART 1464
Married: Bef 1470

Died: 22 Nov 1508

5 **Anne STANLEY**

Born: Abt 1475

Died:

11 **--**

Born:

Died:

1 **Francis SAVAGE**

Born: Abt 1528
-SAME AS #8,ROYAL CHART 1252
Married: 26 Nov 1546
lic.
Died: 19 Aug 1557

12 **Richard LYGON**

Born: Abt 1468

Married: Abt 1490

Died: 1 May 1512

6 **Richard LYGON**

Born: Abt 1490

Married: Bef 1511

Died: 20 Mar 1556/1557

13 **Anne BEAUCHAMP**

Born: Abt 1473
-CONTINUED AS #1,ROYAL CHART 496
Died: 22 Jul 1534

Anne SHELDON

Spouse

3 **Anne LYGON**

Born: Abt 1511

Died:

14 **William GREVILLE**

Born: Abt 1464

Married:

Died: 7 Mar 1513

7 **Margaret GREVILLE**

Born: Abt 1490

Died: 1542

15 **Margery ARRELL**

Born: Abt 1468

Died:

Sources include:Faris 2--Savage, Ligon; Roberts *AAP*, p. 184; Faris--Wyllys 4; Chart 495 sources & note.

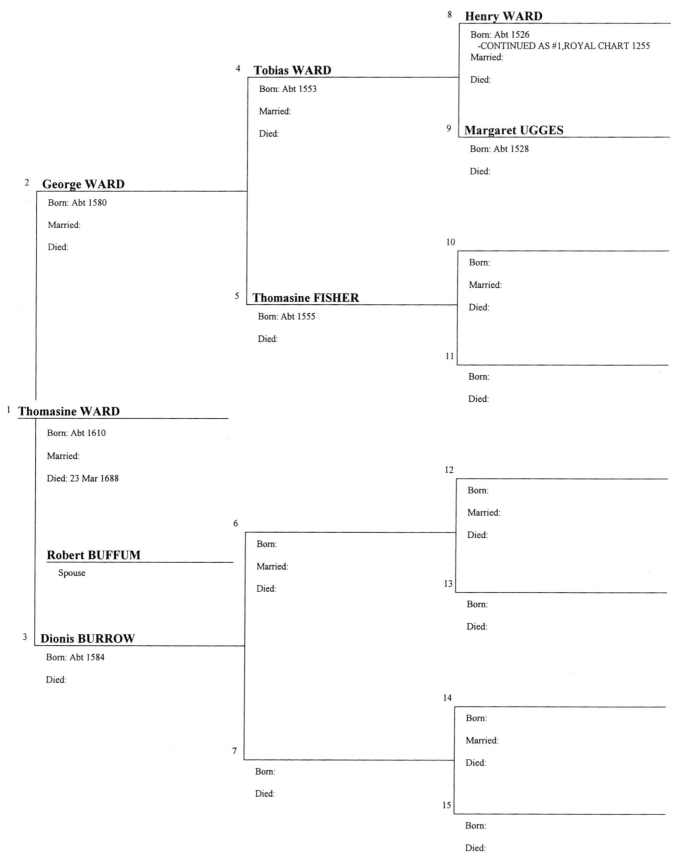

8 **Henry WARD**
Born: Abt 1526
-CONTINUED AS #1,ROYAL CHART 1255
Married:

Died:

9 **Margaret UGGES**
Born: Abt 1528

Died:

4 **Tobias WARD**
Born: Abt 1553

Married:

Died:

10
Born:

Married:

Died:

2 **George WARD**
Born: Abt 1580

Married:

Died:

5 **Thomasine FISHER**
Born: Abt 1555

Died:

11
Born:

Died:

1 **Thomasine WARD**
Born: Abt 1610

Married:

Died: 23 Mar 1688

12
Born:

Married:

Died:

6
Born:

Married:

Died:

13
Born:

Died:

Robert BUFFUM
Spouse

3 **Dionis BURROW**
Born: Abt 1584

Died:

7
Born:

Died:

14
Born:

Married:

Died:

15
Born:

Died:

Sources include: Roberts *500*, pp. 354-355. Notes: The parentage shown for #2 George is not proven but is highly probable. #1 Thomasine has MPGL descendants through a son Joshua Buffum (b. 22 Apr 1635; md. Damaris Pope).

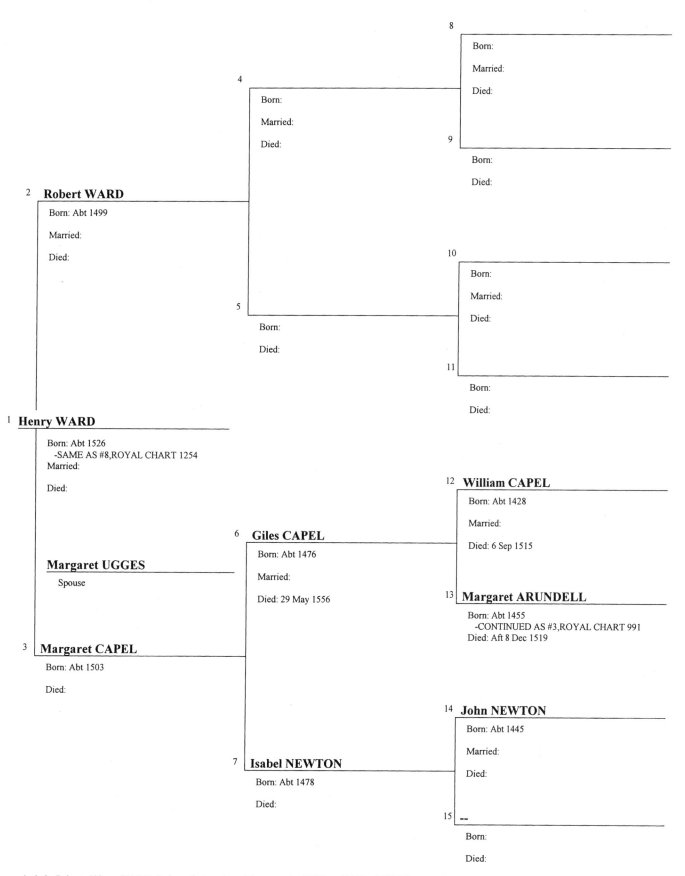

8

Born:

Married:

Died:

4

Born:

Married:

Died:

9

Born:

Died:

2　**Robert WARD**

Born: Abt 1499

Married:

Died:

10

Born:

Married:

Died:

5

Born:

Died:

11

Born:

Died:

1　**Henry WARD**

Born: Abt 1526
　-SAME AS #8,ROYAL CHART 1254
Married:

Died:

12　**William CAPEL**

Born: Abt 1428

Married:

Died: 6 Sep 1515

6　**Giles CAPEL**

Born: Abt 1476

Married:

Died: 29 May 1556

13　**Margaret ARUNDELL**

Born: Abt 1455
　-CONTINUED AS #3,ROYAL CHART 991
Died: Aft 8 Dec 1519

Margaret UGGES

Spouse

3　**Margaret CAPEL**

Born: Abt 1503

Died:

14　**John NEWTON**

Born: Abt 1445

Married:

Died:

7　**Isabel NEWTON**

Born: Abt 1478

Died:

15　**--**

Born:

Died:

Sources include: Roberts *500*, pp. 354-355; Faris preliminary baronial manuscript (1998), p. 295 Capel (#6 & 7 ancestry).

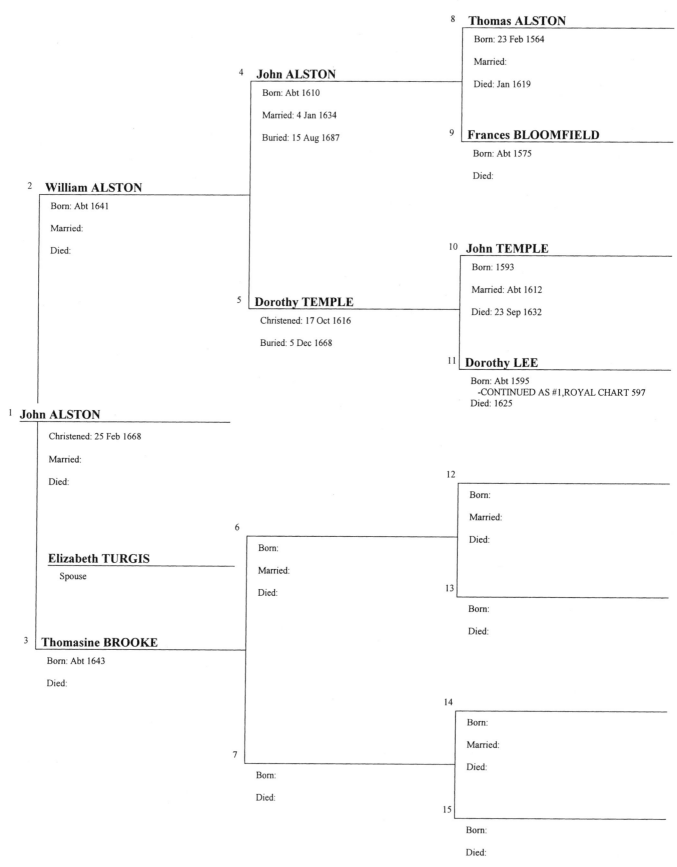

8 **Thomas ALSTON**
Born: 23 Feb 1564
Married:
Died: Jan 1619

4 **John ALSTON**
Born: Abt 1610
Married: 4 Jan 1634
Buried: 15 Aug 1687

9 **Frances BLOOMFIELD**
Born: Abt 1575
Died:

2 **William ALSTON**
Born: Abt 1641
Married:
Died:

10 **John TEMPLE**
Born: 1593
Married: Abt 1612
Died: 23 Sep 1632

5 **Dorothy TEMPLE**
Christened: 17 Oct 1616
Buried: 5 Dec 1668

11 **Dorothy LEE**
Born: Abt 1595
  -CONTINUED AS #1,ROYAL CHART 597
Died: 1625

1 **John ALSTON**
Christened: 25 Feb 1668
Married:
Died:

12
Born:
Married:
Died:

Elizabeth TURGIS
Spouse

6
Born:
Married:
Died:

13
Born:
Died:

3 **Thomasine BROOKE**
Born: Abt 1643
Died:

14
Born:
Married:
Died:

7
Born:
Died:

15
Born:
Died:

Sources include: Faris--Nelson; Roberts *500*, pp. 148-149; *Blood Royal* 2:19; 5:383-384; LDS records. Note: The above identification and ancestry of #1 John Alston of SC is probable but not proven.

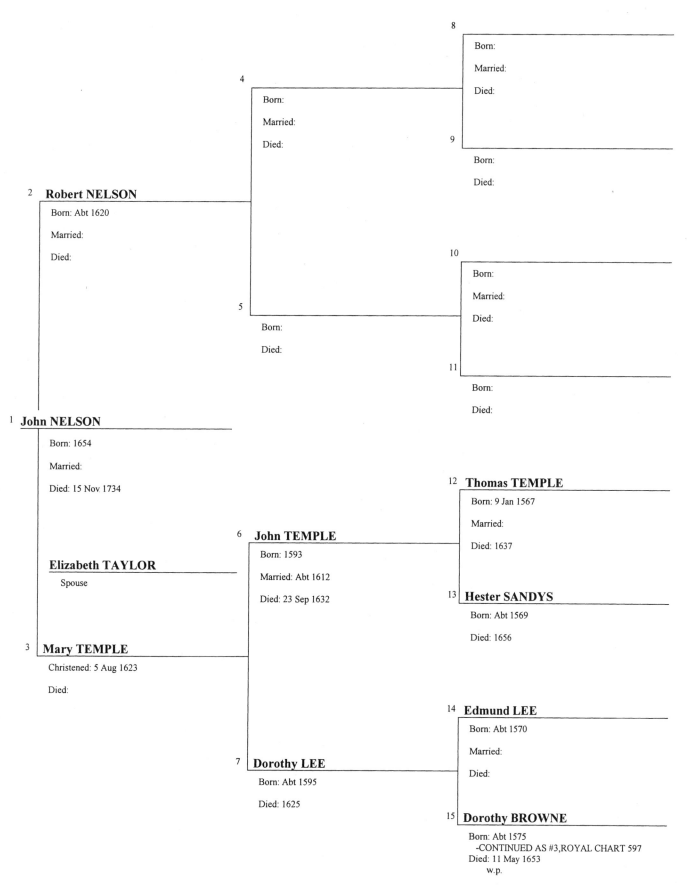

8
Born:
Married:
Died:

4
Born:
Married:
Died:

9
Born:
Died:

2 **Robert NELSON**
Born: Abt 1620
Married:
Died:

10
Born:
Married:
Died:

5
Born:
Died:

11
Born:
Died:

1 **John NELSON**
Born: 1654
Married:
Died: 15 Nov 1734

12 **Thomas TEMPLE**
Born: 9 Jan 1567
Married:
Died: 1637

6 **John TEMPLE**
Born: 1593
Married: Abt 1612
Died: 23 Sep 1632

13 **Hester SANDYS**
Born: Abt 1569
Died: 1656

Elizabeth TAYLOR
Spouse

3 **Mary TEMPLE**
Christened: 5 Aug 1623
Died:

14 **Edmund LEE**
Born: Abt 1570
Married:
Died:

7 **Dorothy LEE**
Born: Abt 1595
Died: 1625

15 **Dorothy BROWNE**
Born: Abt 1575
-CONTINUED AS #3,ROYAL CHART 597
Died: 11 May 1653
w.p.

Sources include: Faris--Nelson; Roberts *AAP*, pp. 202-203.

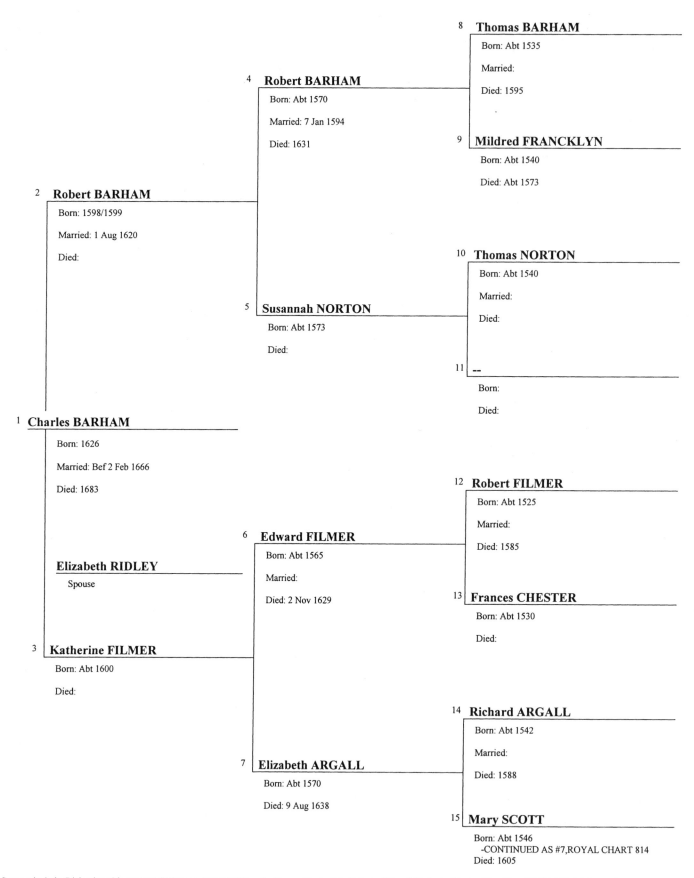

8 Thomas BARHAM

Born: Abt 1535

Married:

Died: 1595

4 Robert BARHAM

Born: Abt 1570

Married: 7 Jan 1594

Died: 1631

9 Mildred FRANCKLYN

Born: Abt 1540

Died: Abt 1573

2 Robert BARHAM

Born: 1598/1599

Married: 1 Aug 1620

Died:

10 Thomas NORTON

Born: Abt 1540

Married:

Died:

5 Susannah NORTON

Born: Abt 1573

Died:

11 --

Born:

Died:

1 Charles BARHAM

Born: 1626

Married: Bef 2 Feb 1666

Died: 1683

12 Robert FILMER

Born: Abt 1525

Married:

Died: 1585

6 Edward FILMER

Born: Abt 1565

Married:

Died: 2 Nov 1629

13 Frances CHESTER

Born: Abt 1530

Died:

Elizabeth RIDLEY

Spouse

3 Katherine FILMER

Born: Abt 1600

Died:

14 Richard ARGALL

Born: Abt 1542

Married:

Died: 1588

7 Elizabeth ARGALL

Born: Abt 1570

Died: 9 Aug 1638

15 Mary SCOTT

Born: Abt 1546
-CONTINUED AS #7,ROYAL CHART 814
Died: 1605

Sources include: Richardson *Plantagenet* (2004), pp. 310-311 (Filmer); *Magna Charta* 134; Roberts *500*, p. 242; Faris--Fleete; *Blood Royal* 5:792-793; LDS records.

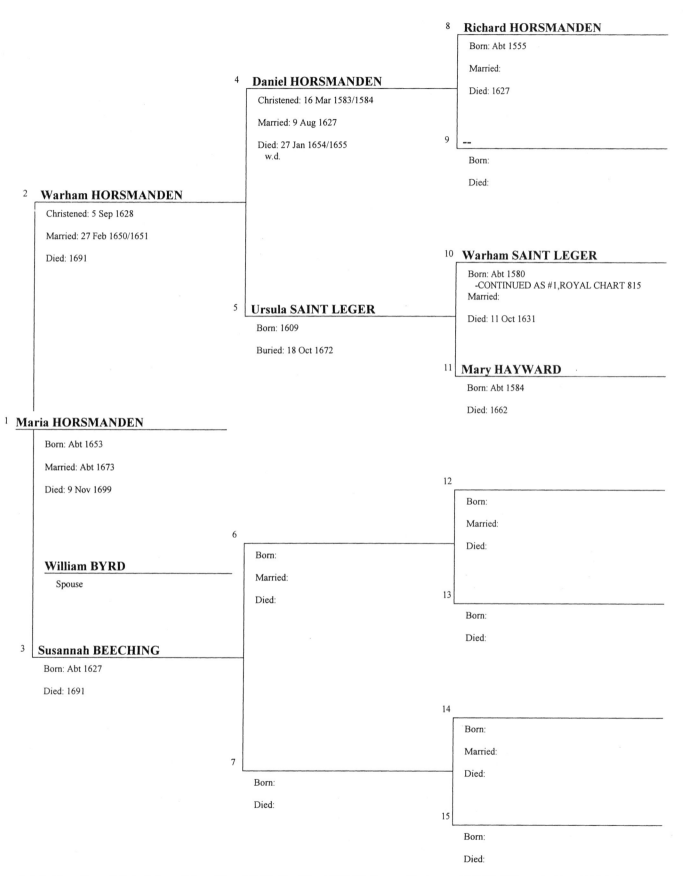

8 Richard HORSMANDEN

Born: Abt 1555

Married:

Died: 1627

4 Daniel HORSMANDEN

Christened: 16 Mar 1583/1584

Married: 9 Aug 1627

Died: 27 Jan 1654/1655
w.d.

9 --

Born:

Died:

2 Warham HORSMANDEN

Christened: 5 Sep 1628

Married: 27 Feb 1650/1651

Died: 1691

10 Warham SAINT LEGER

Born: Abt 1580
-CONTINUED AS #1,ROYAL CHART 815
Married:

Died: 11 Oct 1631

5 Ursula SAINT LEGER

Born: 1609

Buried: 18 Oct 1672

11 Mary HAYWARD

Born: Abt 1584

Died: 1662

1 Maria HORSMANDEN

Born: Abt 1653

Married: Abt 1673

Died: 9 Nov 1699

12

Born:

Married:

Died:

6

Born:

Married:

Died:

William BYRD

Spouse

13

Born:

Died:

3 Susannah BEECHING

Born: Abt 1627

Died: 1691

14

Born:

Married:

Died:

7

Born:

Died:

15

Born:

Died:

Sources include: *Magna Charta* 47; Faris--St. Leger; Roberts *500*, pp. 140-141; *Blood Royal* 5:880-881; *Emperor Charlemagne* 1:219-221; LDS records. Note: #1 Maria (or Mary)
had American descendants through a son William Byrd (b. 10 Mar 1674; d. 26 Aug 1744) of VA.

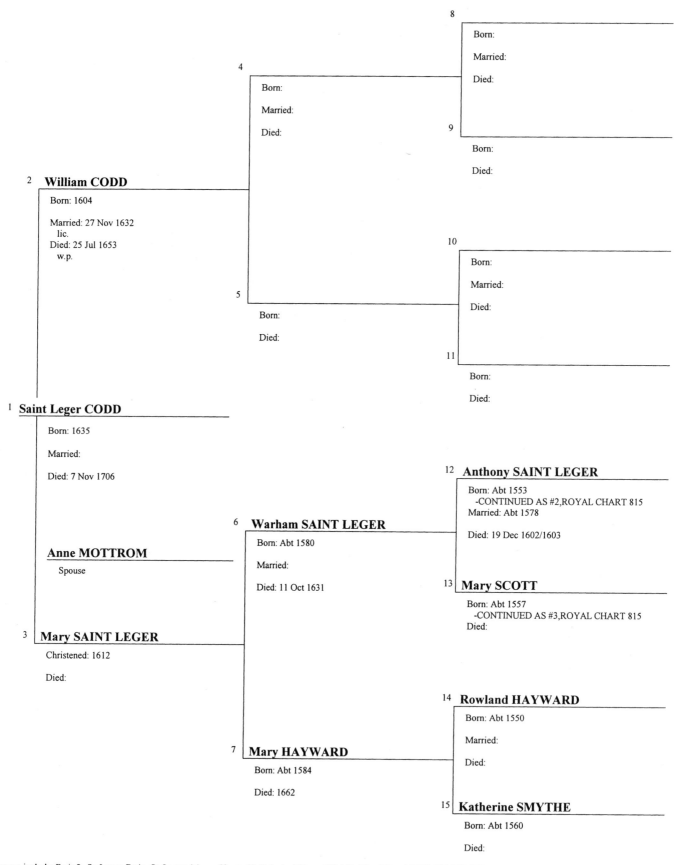

8

Born:

Married:

Died:

4

Born:

Married:

Died:

9

Born:

Died:

2 William CODD

Born: 1604

Married: 27 Nov 1632
lic.
Died: 25 Jul 1653
w.p.

10

Born:

Married:

Died:

5

Born:

Died:

11

Born:

Died:

1 Saint Leger CODD

Born: 1635

Married:

Died: 7 Nov 1706

12 Anthony SAINT LEGER

Born: Abt 1553
   -CONTINUED AS #2,ROYAL CHART 815
Married: Abt 1578

Died: 19 Dec 1602/1603

6 Warham SAINT LEGER

Born: Abt 1580

Married:

Died: 11 Oct 1631

13 Mary SCOTT

Born: Abt 1557
   -CONTINUED AS #3,ROYAL CHART 815
Died:

Anne MOTTROM

Spouse

3 Mary SAINT LEGER

Christened: 1612

Died:

14 Rowland HAYWARD

Born: Abt 1550

Married:

Died:

7 Mary HAYWARD

Born: Abt 1584

Died: 1662

15 Katherine SMYTHE

Born: Abt 1560

Died:

Sources include: Faris 2--St. Leger; Faris--St. Leger; *Magna Charta* 47; Roberts *500*, pp. 140-141; *Blood Royal* 5:304-306, 309-310.

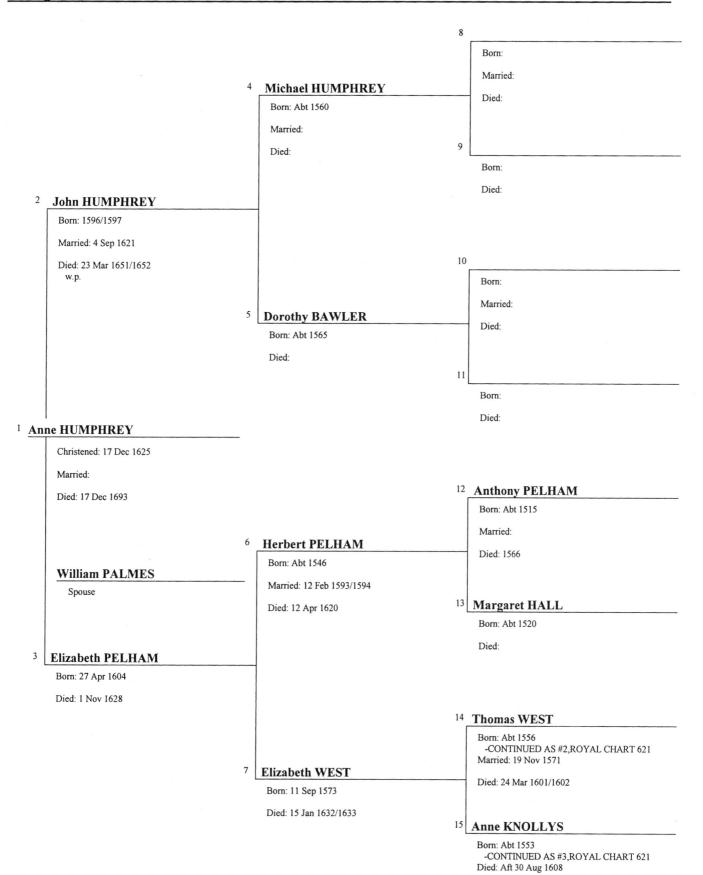

8

Born:

Married:

Died:

4 Michael HUMPHREY

Born: Abt 1560

Married:

Died:

9

Born:

Died:

2 John HUMPHREY

Born: 1596/1597

Married: 4 Sep 1621

Died: 23 Mar 1651/1652
w.p.

10

Born:

Married:

Died:

5 Dorothy BAWLER

Born: Abt 1565

Died:

11

Born:

Died:

1 Anne HUMPHREY

Christened: 17 Dec 1625

Married:

Died: 17 Dec 1693

12 Anthony PELHAM

Born: Abt 1515

Married:

Died: 1566

6 Herbert PELHAM

Born: Abt 1546

Married: 12 Feb 1593/1594

Died: 12 Apr 1620

13 Margaret HALL

Born: Abt 1520

Died:

William PALMES

Spouse

3 Elizabeth PELHAM

Born: 27 Apr 1604

Died: 1 Nov 1628

14 Thomas WEST

Born: Abt 1556
   -CONTINUED AS #2,ROYAL CHART 621
Married: 19 Nov 1571

Died: 24 Mar 1601/1602

7 Elizabeth WEST

Born: 11 Sep 1573

Died: 15 Jan 1632/1633

15 Anne KNOLLYS

Born: Abt 1553
   -CONTINUED AS #3,ROYAL CHART 621
Died: Aft 30 Aug 1608

Sources include: Richardson *Plantagenet* (2004), pp. 404-406 (Humphrey); Faris--Humphrey. Note: #1 Anne has MPGL descendants through a daughter Susanna Palmes (b. abt 1665; md. Samuel Avery).

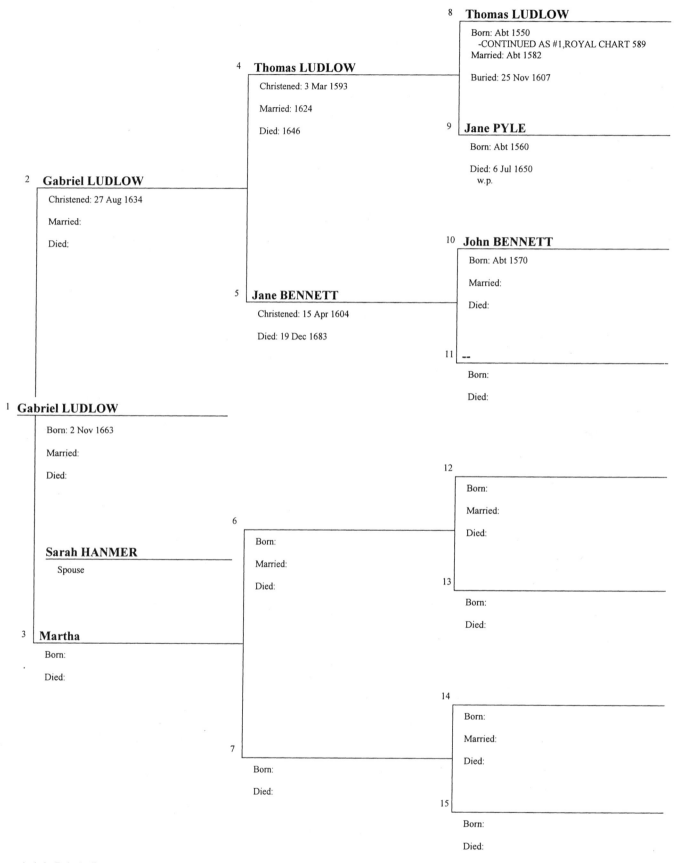

8 **Thomas LUDLOW**

Born: Abt 1550
-CONTINUED AS #1,ROYAL CHART 589
Married: Abt 1582

Buried: 25 Nov 1607

4 **Thomas LUDLOW**

Christened: 3 Mar 1593

Married: 1624

Died: 1646

9 **Jane PYLE**

Born: Abt 1560

Died: 6 Jul 1650
w.p.

2 **Gabriel LUDLOW**

Christened: 27 Aug 1634

Married:

Died:

10 **John BENNETT**

Born: Abt 1570

Married:

Died:

5 **Jane BENNETT**

Christened: 15 Apr 1604

Died: 19 Dec 1683

11 **--**

Born:

Died:

1 **Gabriel LUDLOW**

Born: 2 Nov 1663

Married:

Died:

12

Born:

Married:

Died:

6

Born:

Married:

Died:

13

Born:

Died:

Sarah HANMER
Spouse

3 **Martha**

Born:

Died:

14

Born:

Married:

Died:

7

Born:

Died:

15

Born:

Died:

Sources include: Faris--Ludlow.

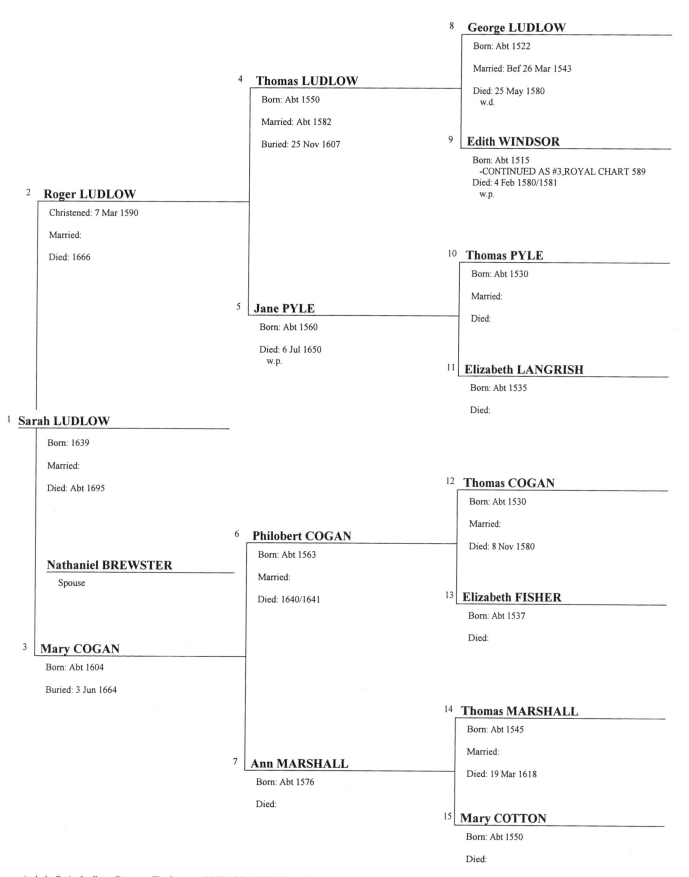

8 **George LUDLOW**
Born: Abt 1522
Married: Bef 26 Mar 1543
Died: 25 May 1580
w.d.

4 **Thomas LUDLOW**
Born: Abt 1550
Married: Abt 1582
Buried: 25 Nov 1607

9 **Edith WINDSOR**
Born: Abt 1515
-CONTINUED AS #3,ROYAL CHART 589
Died: 4 Feb 1580/1581
w.p.

2 **Roger LUDLOW**
Christened: 7 Mar 1590
Married:
Died: 1666

10 **Thomas PYLE**
Born: Abt 1530
Married:
Died:

5 **Jane PYLE**
Born: Abt 1560
Died: 6 Jul 1650
w.p.

11 **Elizabeth LANGRISH**
Born: Abt 1535
Died:

1 **Sarah LUDLOW**
Born: 1639
Married:
Died: Abt 1695

12 **Thomas COGAN**
Born: Abt 1530
Married:
Died: 8 Nov 1580

6 **Philobert COGAN**
Born: Abt 1563
Married:
Died: 1640/1641

13 **Elizabeth FISHER**
Born: Abt 1537
Died:

Nathaniel BREWSTER
Spouse

3 **Mary COGAN**
Born: Abt 1604
Buried: 3 Jun 1664

14 **Thomas MARSHALL**
Born: Abt 1545
Married:
Died: 19 Mar 1618

7 **Ann MARSHALL**
Born: Abt 1576
Died:

15 **Mary COTTON**
Born: Abt 1550
Died:

Sources include: Faris--Ludlow; *Emperor Charlemagne* 1:192, 196-197; LDS records.

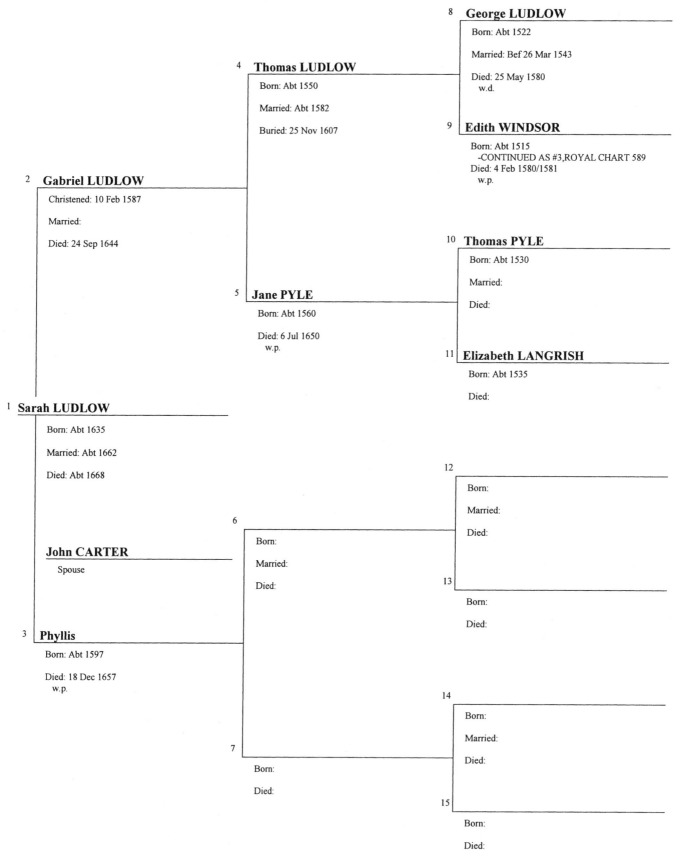

8 George LUDLOW
Born: Abt 1522
Married: Bef 26 Mar 1543
Died: 25 May 1580
w.d.

4 Thomas LUDLOW
Born: Abt 1550
Married: Abt 1582
Buried: 25 Nov 1607

9 Edith WINDSOR
Born: Abt 1515
-CONTINUED AS #3,ROYAL CHART 589
Died: 4 Feb 1580/1581
w.p.

2 Gabriel LUDLOW
Christened: 10 Feb 1587
Married:
Died: 24 Sep 1644

10 Thomas PYLE
Born: Abt 1530
Married:
Died:

5 Jane PYLE
Born: Abt 1560
Died: 6 Jul 1650
w.p.

11 Elizabeth LANGRISH
Born: Abt 1535
Died:

1 Sarah LUDLOW
Born: Abt 1635
Married: Abt 1662
Died: Abt 1668

12
Born:
Married:
Died:

6
Born:
Married:
Died:

13
Born:
Died:

John CARTER
Spouse

3 Phyllis
Born: Abt 1597
Died: 18 Dec 1657
w.p.

14
Born:
Married:
Died:

7
Born:
Died:

15
Born:
Died:

Sources include: Faris--Ludlow; Roberts *AAP*, pp. 16-19, 186-187; *Blood Royal* 5:165-167, 345-346. Note: #1 Sarah had a son Robert Carter (b. abt 1663; md. Elizabeth Landon), through whom both U.S. President Harrisons descend.

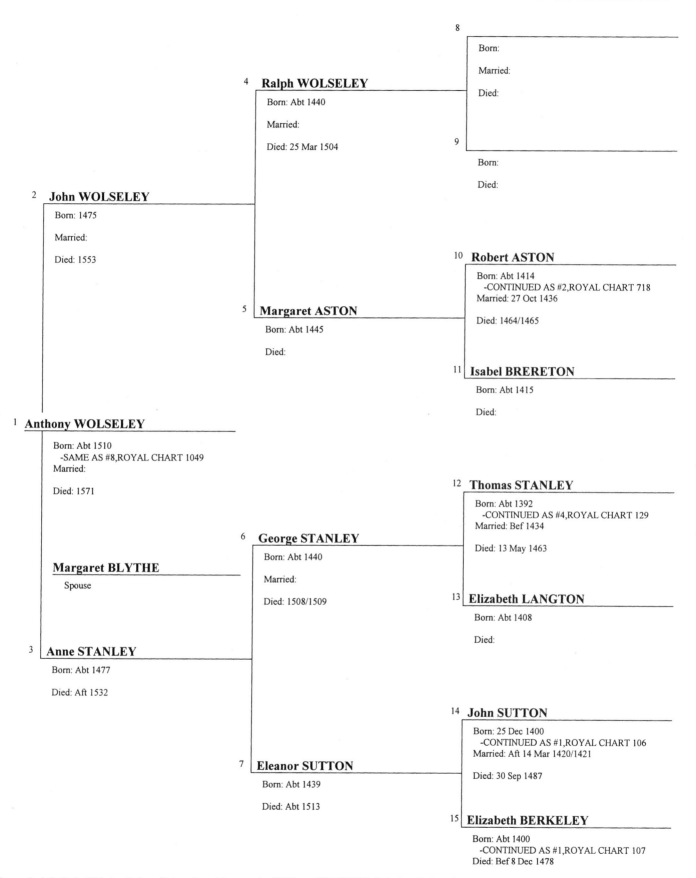

8

Born:

Married:

Died:

4 **Ralph WOLSELEY**

Born: Abt 1440

Married:

Died: 25 Mar 1504

9

Born:

Died:

2 **John WOLSELEY**

Born: 1475

Married:

Died: 1553

10 **Robert ASTON**

Born: Abt 1414
  -CONTINUED AS #2,ROYAL CHART 718
Married: 27 Oct 1436

Died: 1464/1465

5 **Margaret ASTON**

Born: Abt 1445

Died:

11 **Isabel BRERETON**

Born: Abt 1415

Died:

1 **Anthony WOLSELEY**

Born: Abt 1510
  -SAME AS #8,ROYAL CHART 1049
Married:

Died: 1571

12 **Thomas STANLEY**

Born: Abt 1392
  -CONTINUED AS #4,ROYAL CHART 129
Married: Bef 1434

Died: 13 May 1463

6 **George STANLEY**

Born: Abt 1440

Married:

Died: 1508/1509

Margaret BLYTHE

Spouse

13 **Elizabeth LANGTON**

Born: Abt 1408

Died:

3 **Anne STANLEY**

Born: Abt 1477

Died: Aft 1532

14 **John SUTTON**

Born: 25 Dec 1400
  -CONTINUED AS #1,ROYAL CHART 106
Married: Aft 14 Mar 1420/1421

Died: 30 Sep 1487

7 **Eleanor SUTTON**

Born: Abt 1439

Died: Abt 1513

15 **Elizabeth BERKELEY**

Born: Abt 1400
  -CONTINUED AS #1,ROYAL CHART 107
Died: Bef 8 Dec 1478

Sources include: Faris--Wolseley; Faris preliminary baronial manuscript (1998), pp. 1686-87 (Wolseley); Consultation with Douglas Richardson (#5 ancestry).

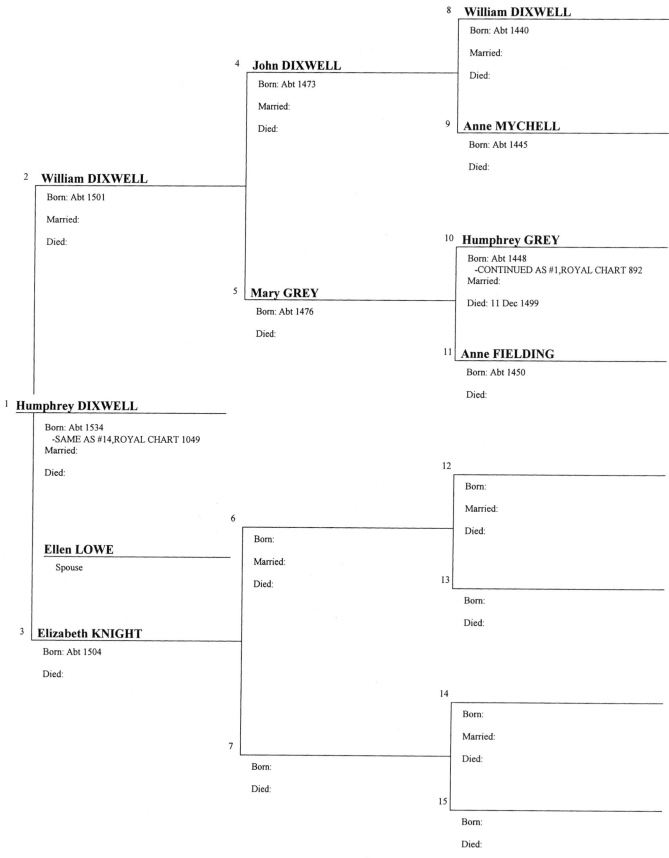

8 **William DIXWELL**

Born: Abt 1440

Married:

Died:

4 **John DIXWELL**

Born: Abt 1473

Married:

Died:

9 **Anne MYCHELL**

Born: Abt 1445

Died:

2 **William DIXWELL**

Born: Abt 1501

Married:

Died:

10 **Humphrey GREY**

Born: Abt 1448
-CONTINUED AS #1,ROYAL CHART 892
Married:

Died: 11 Dec 1499

5 **Mary GREY**

Born: Abt 1476

Died:

11 **Anne FIELDING**

Born: Abt 1450

Died:

1 **Humphrey DIXWELL**

Born: Abt 1534
-SAME AS #14,ROYAL CHART 1049
Married:

Died:

12

Born:

Married:

Died:

6

Born:

Married:

Died:

13

Born:

Died:

Ellen LOWE

Spouse

3 **Elizabeth KNIGHT**

Born: Abt 1504

Died:

14

Born:

Married:

Died:

7

Born:

Died:

15

Born:

Died:

Sources include: Roberts *500*, pp. 373-375; LDS records.

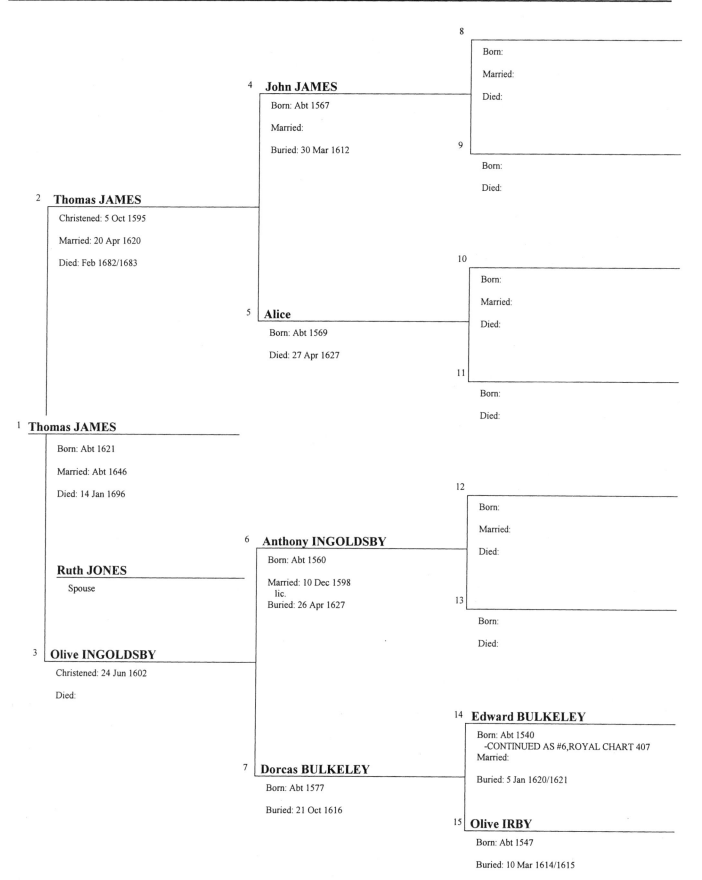

8

Born:

Married:

Died:

4 John JAMES

Born: Abt 1567

Married:

Buried: 30 Mar 1612

9

Born:

Died:

2 Thomas JAMES

Christened: 5 Oct 1595

Married: 20 Apr 1620

Died: Feb 1682/1683

10

Born:

Married:

Died:

5 Alice

Born: Abt 1569

Died: 27 Apr 1627

11

Born:

Died:

1 Thomas JAMES

Born: Abt 1621

Married: Abt 1646

Died: 14 Jan 1696

12

Born:

Married:

Died:

6 Anthony INGOLDSBY

Born: Abt 1560

Married: 10 Dec 1598 lic.
Buried: 26 Apr 1627

13

Born:

Died:

Ruth JONES

Spouse

3 Olive INGOLDSBY

Christened: 24 Jun 1602

Died:

14 Edward BULKELEY

Born: Abt 1540
-CONTINUED AS #6,ROYAL CHART 407
Married:

Buried: 5 Jan 1620/1621

7 Dorcas BULKELEY

Born: Abt 1577

Buried: 21 Oct 1616

15 Olive IRBY

Born: Abt 1547

Buried: 10 Mar 1614/1615

Sources include: *Ancestral Roots* 203, 31; *Blood Royal* 5:450-451; Jacobus, *Bulkeley Genealogy*; LDS records. Note: #1 Thomas has MPGL descendants through a daughter Ruth James (b. abt 1664; md. Thomas Harris).

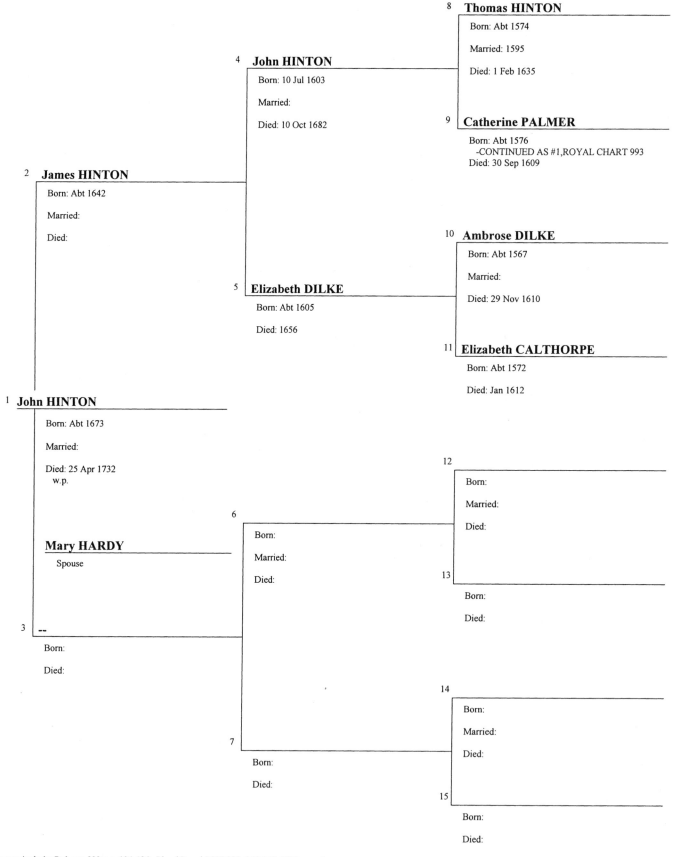

8 Thomas HINTON

Born: Abt 1574

Married: 1595

Died: 1 Feb 1635

4 John HINTON

Born: 10 Jul 1603

Married:

Died: 10 Oct 1682

9 Catherine PALMER

Born: Abt 1576
   -CONTINUED AS #1,ROYAL CHART 993
Died: 30 Sep 1609

2 James HINTON

Born: Abt 1642

Married:

Died:

10 Ambrose DILKE

Born: Abt 1567

Married:

Died: 29 Nov 1610

5 Elizabeth DILKE

Born: Abt 1605

Died: 1656

11 Elizabeth CALTHORPE

Born: Abt 1572

Died: Jan 1612

1 John HINTON

Born: Abt 1673

Married:

Died: 25 Apr 1732
   w.p.

Mary HARDY

Spouse

12

Born:

Married:

Died:

6

Born:

Married:

Died:

13

Born:

Died:

3 --

Born:

Died:

14

Born:

Married:

Died:

7

Born:

Died:

15

Born:

Died:

Sources include: Roberts *500*, pp. 134-135; *Blood Royal* 5:237-238, 368-369; LDS records.

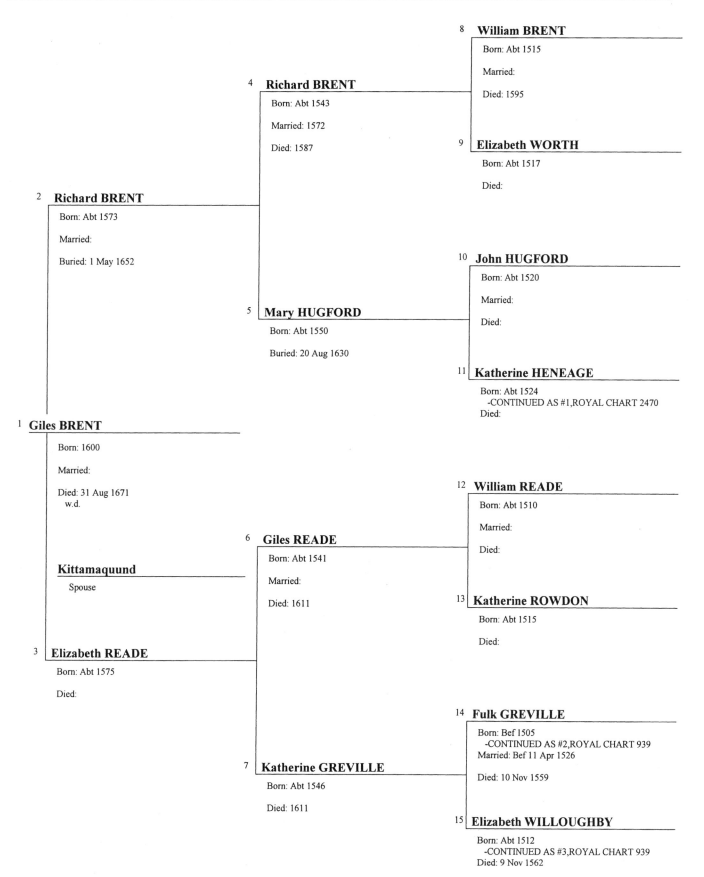

8 **William BRENT**
Born: Abt 1515
Married:
Died: 1595

4 **Richard BRENT**
Born: Abt 1543
Married: 1572
Died: 1587

9 **Elizabeth WORTH**
Born: Abt 1517
Died:

2 **Richard BRENT**
Born: Abt 1573
Married:
Buried: 1 May 1652

10 **John HUGFORD**
Born: Abt 1520
Married:
Died:

5 **Mary HUGFORD**
Born: Abt 1550
Buried: 20 Aug 1630

11 **Katherine HENEAGE**
Born: Abt 1524
-CONTINUED AS #1,ROYAL CHART 2470
Died:

1 **Giles BRENT**
Born: 1600
Married:
Died: 31 Aug 1671
w.d.

Kittamaquund
Spouse

12 **William READE**
Born: Abt 1510
Married:
Died:

6 **Giles READE**
Born: Abt 1541
Married:
Died: 1611

13 **Katherine ROWDON**
Born: Abt 1515
Died:

3 **Elizabeth READE**
Born: Abt 1575
Died:

14 **Fulk GREVILLE**
Born: Bef 1505
-CONTINUED AS #2,ROYAL CHART 939
Married: Bef 11 Apr 1526
Died: 10 Nov 1559

7 **Katherine GREVILLE**
Born: Abt 1546
Died: 1611

15 **Elizabeth WILLOUGHBY**
Born: Abt 1512
-CONTINUED AS #3,ROYAL CHART 939
Died: 9 Nov 1562

Sources include: Faris 2--Brent; Faris--Brent; Roberts *500*, pp. 132-133; *Blood Royal* 5:492-495; LDS records.

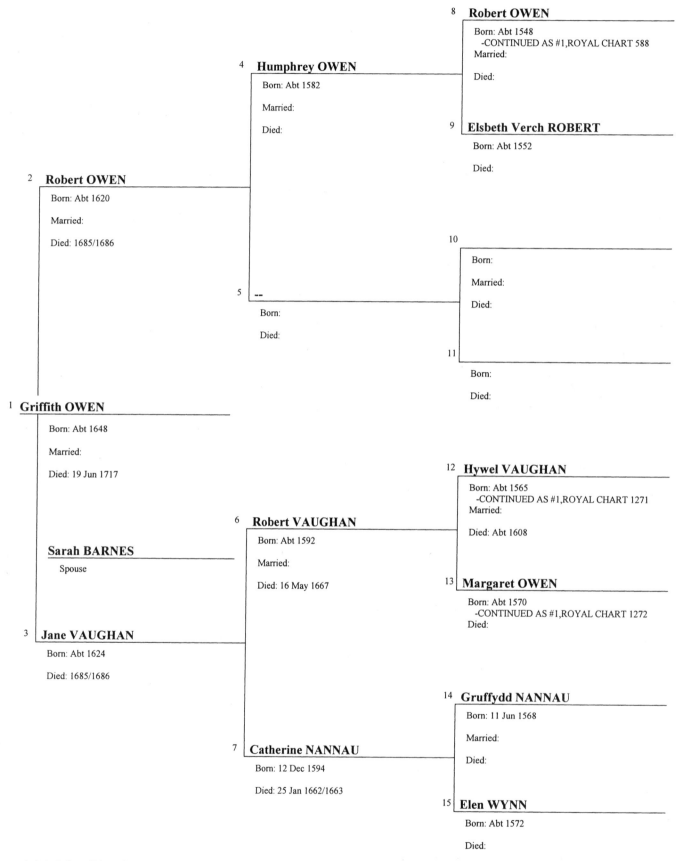

8 Robert OWEN

Born: Abt 1548
-CONTINUED AS #1,ROYAL CHART 588
Married:

Died:

4 Humphrey OWEN

Born: Abt 1582

Married:

Died:

9 Elsbeth Verch ROBERT

Born: Abt 1552

Died:

2 Robert OWEN

Born: Abt 1620

Married:

Died: 1685/1686

10

Born:

Married:

Died:

5 --

Born:

Died:

11

Born:

Died:

1 Griffith OWEN

Born: Abt 1648

Married:

Died: 19 Jun 1717

12 Hywel VAUGHAN

Born: Abt 1565
-CONTINUED AS #1,ROYAL CHART 1271
Married:

Died: Abt 1608

6 Robert VAUGHAN

Born: Abt 1592

Married:

Died: 16 May 1667

13 Margaret OWEN

Born: Abt 1570
-CONTINUED AS #1,ROYAL CHART 1272
Died:

Sarah BARNES

Spouse

3 Jane VAUGHAN

Born: Abt 1624

Died: 1685/1686

14 Gruffydd NANNAU

Born: 11 Jun 1568

Married:

Died:

7 Catherine NANNAU

Born: 12 Dec 1594

Died: 25 Jan 1662/1663

15 Elen WYNN

Born: Abt 1572

Died:

Sources include: Roberts *500*, p. 167; *Welsh Founders of PA*, pp. 50-53, including charts facing p. 52; *Utah Woolley Family*, p. 8; LDS records; MPGL 4305.

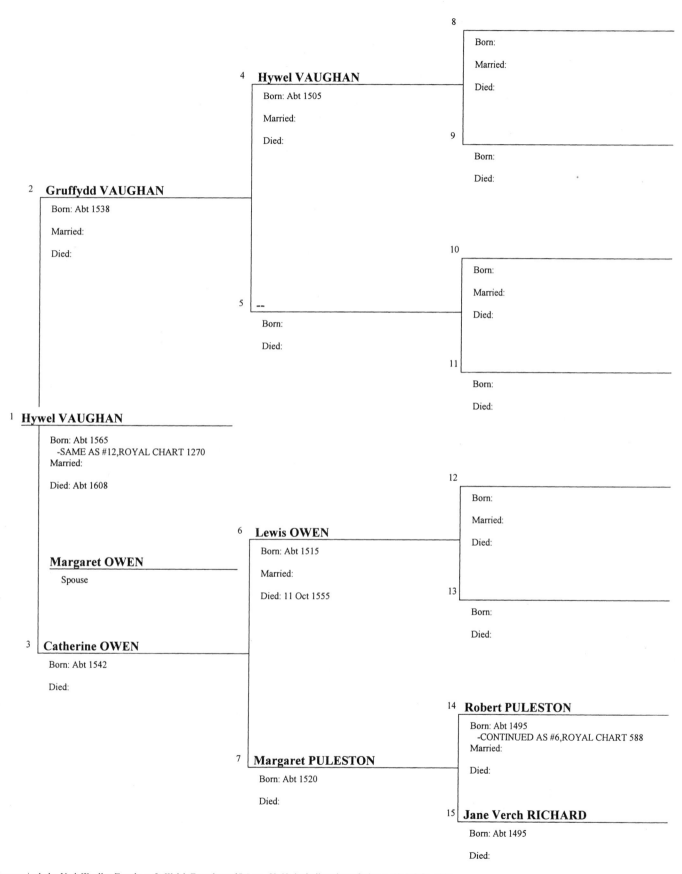

8

Born:

Married:

Died:

4 Hywel VAUGHAN

Born: Abt 1505

Married:

Died:

9

Born:

Died:

2 Gruffydd VAUGHAN

Born: Abt 1538

Married:

Died:

10

Born:

Married:

Died:

5 --

Born:

Died:

11

Born:

Died:

1 Hywel VAUGHAN

Born: Abt 1565
-SAME AS #12, ROYAL CHART 1270
Married:

Died: Abt 1608

12

Born:

Married:

Died:

6 Lewis OWEN

Born: Abt 1515

Married:

Died: 11 Oct 1555

13

Born:

Died:

Margaret OWEN

Spouse

3 Catherine OWEN

Born: Abt 1542

Died:

14 Robert PULESTON

Born: Abt 1495
-CONTINUED AS #6, ROYAL CHART 588
Married:

Died:

7 Margaret PULESTON

Born: Abt 1520

Died:

15 Jane Verch RICHARD

Born: Abt 1495

Died:

Sources include: *Utah Woolley Family*, p. 8; *Welsh Founders of PA*, pp. 50-53, including charts facing p. 52; MPGL 4305.

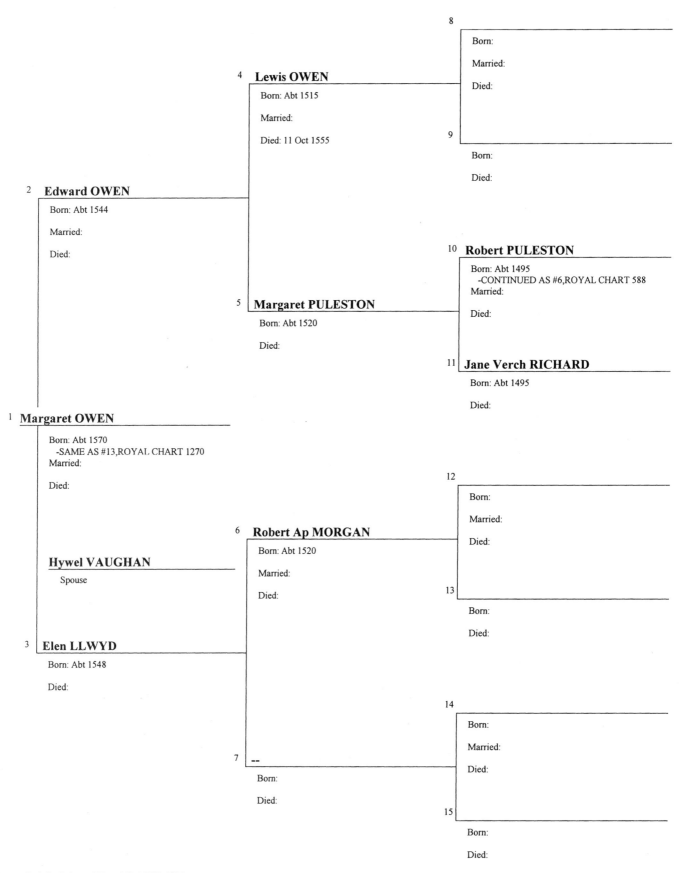

8

Born:

Married:

Died:

4 **Lewis OWEN**

Born: Abt 1515

Married:

Died: 11 Oct 1555

9

Born:

Died:

2 **Edward OWEN**

Born: Abt 1544

Married:

Died:

10 **Robert PULESTON**

Born: Abt 1495
  -CONTINUED AS #6,ROYAL CHART 588
Married:

Died:

5 **Margaret PULESTON**

Born: Abt 1520

Died:

11 **Jane Verch RICHARD**

Born: Abt 1495

Died:

1 **Margaret OWEN**

Born: Abt 1570
  -SAME AS #13,ROYAL CHART 1270
Married:

Died:

12

Born:

Married:

Died:

6 **Robert Ap MORGAN**

Born: Abt 1520

Married:

Died:

13

Born:

Died:

Hywel VAUGHAN

Spouse

3 **Elen LLWYD**

Born: Abt 1548

Died:

14

Born:

Married:

Died:

7 **--**

Born:

Died:

15

Born:

Died:

Sources include: Roberts *500*, p. 167; MPGL 4305.

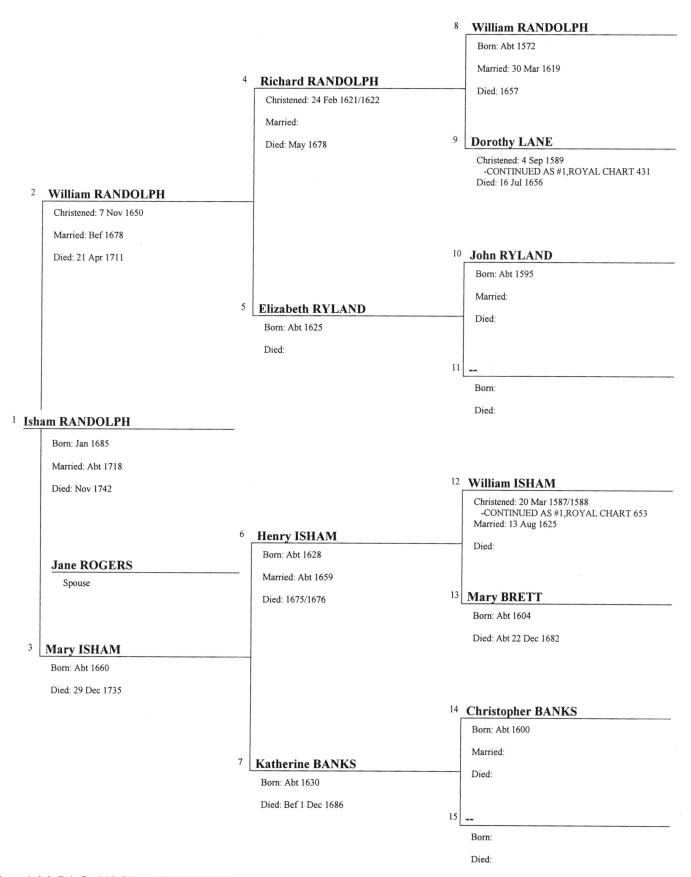

8 William RANDOLPH

Born: Abt 1572

Married: 30 Mar 1619

Died: 1657

4 Richard RANDOLPH

Christened: 24 Feb 1621/1622

Married:

Died: May 1678

9 Dorothy LANE

Christened: 4 Sep 1589
-CONTINUED AS #1,ROYAL CHART 431
Died: 16 Jul 1656

2 William RANDOLPH

Christened: 7 Nov 1650

Married: Bef 1678

Died: 21 Apr 1711

10 John RYLAND

Born: Abt 1595

Married:

Died:

5 Elizabeth RYLAND

Born: Abt 1625

Died:

11 --

Born:

Died:

1 Isham RANDOLPH

Born: Jan 1685

Married: Abt 1718

Died: Nov 1742

Jane ROGERS

Spouse

12 William ISHAM

Christened: 20 Mar 1587/1588
-CONTINUED AS #1,ROYAL CHART 653
Married: 13 Aug 1625

Died:

6 Henry ISHAM

Born: Abt 1628

Married: Abt 1659

Died: 1675/1676

13 Mary BRETT

Born: Abt 1604

Died: Abt 22 Dec 1682

3 Mary ISHAM

Born: Abt 1660

Died: 29 Dec 1735

14 Christopher BANKS

Born: Abt 1600

Married:

Died:

7 Katherine BANKS

Born: Abt 1630

Died: Bef 1 Dec 1686

15 --

Born:

Died:

Sources include: Faris--Randolph; Roberts *AAP*, pp. 7-9, 181-182, 217; *500*, p. 169; *Blood Royal* 5:106-110; LDS records. Note: #2 & 3 William & Mary have MPGL descendants through a daughter Elizabeth Randolph (b. abt 1680; md. Richard Bland). #6 & 7 Henry & Katherine have MPGL descendants through a daughter Anne Isham (b. abt 1665; md. Francis Epes).

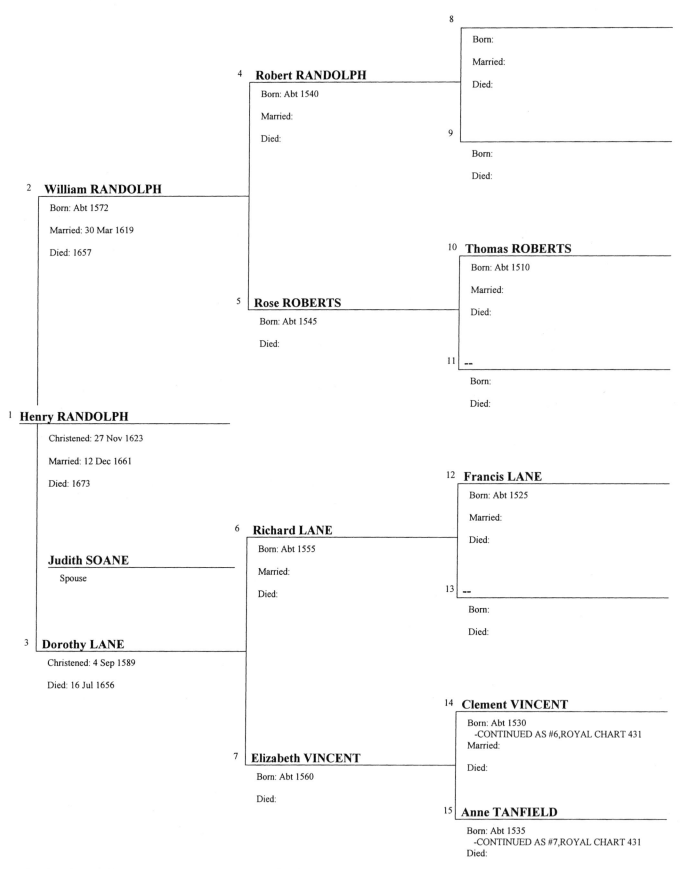

8

Robert RANDOLPH
Born: Abt 1540
Married:
Died:

Born:
Married:
Died:

9

Born:
Died:

2 **William RANDOLPH**
Born: Abt 1572
Married: 30 Mar 1619
Died: 1657

10 **Thomas ROBERTS**
Born: Abt 1510
Married:
Died:

5 **Rose ROBERTS**
Born: Abt 1545
Died:

11 --
Born:
Died:

1 **Henry RANDOLPH**
Christened: 27 Nov 1623
Married: 12 Dec 1661
Died: 1673

12 **Francis LANE**
Born: Abt 1525
Married:
Died:

6 **Richard LANE**
Born: Abt 1555
Married:
Died:

13 --
Born:
Died:

Judith SOANE
Spouse

3 **Dorothy LANE**
Christened: 4 Sep 1589
Died: 16 Jul 1656

14 **Clement VINCENT**
Born: Abt 1530
-CONTINUED AS #6,ROYAL CHART 431
Married:
Died:

7 **Elizabeth VINCENT**
Born: Abt 1560
Died:

15 **Anne TANFIELD**
Born: Abt 1535
-CONTINUED AS #7,ROYAL CHART 431
Died:

Sources include: Faris--Randolph. Note: #1 Henry has MPGL descendants through a son Henry Randolph (b. 16 Jan 1665-66; md. Sarah Swan).

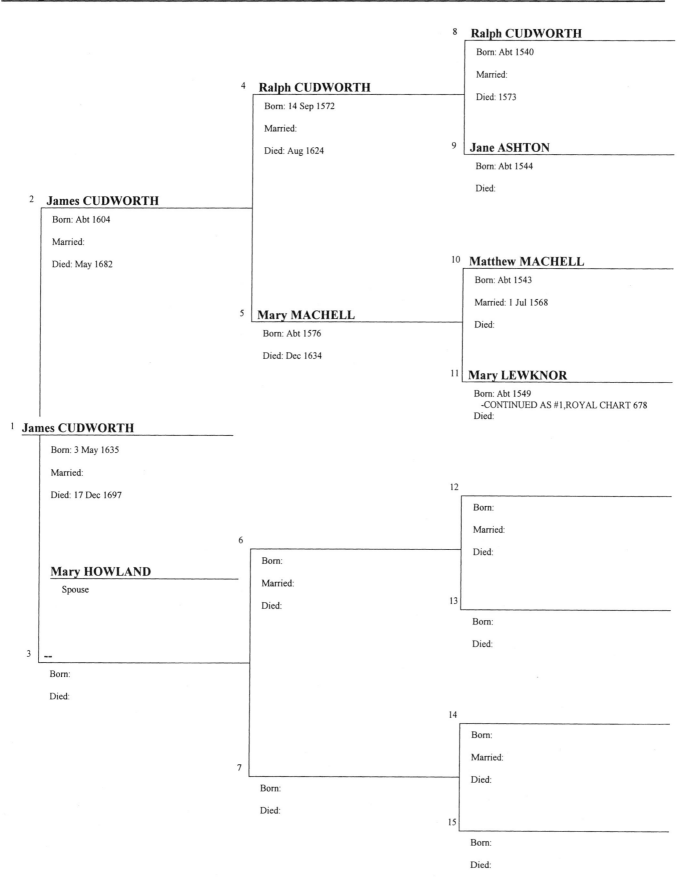

8 **Ralph CUDWORTH**

Born: Abt 1540

Married:

Died: 1573

4 **Ralph CUDWORTH**

Born: 14 Sep 1572

Married:

Died: Aug 1624

9 **Jane ASHTON**

Born: Abt 1544

Died:

2 **James CUDWORTH**

Born: Abt 1604

Married:

Died: May 1682

10 **Matthew MACHELL**

Born: Abt 1543

Married: 1 Jul 1568

Died:

5 **Mary MACHELL**

Born: Abt 1576

Died: Dec 1634

11 **Mary LEWKNOR**

Born: Abt 1549
    -CONTINUED AS #1,ROYAL CHART 678
Died:

1 **James CUDWORTH**

Born: 3 May 1635

Married:

Died: 17 Dec 1697

12

Born:

Married:

Died:

6

Born:

Married:

Died:

13

Born:

Died:

Mary HOWLAND

Spouse

3 --

Born:

Died:

14

Born:

Married:

Died:

7

Born:

Died:

15

Born:

Died:

Sources include: Roberts *500*, p. 270; NEHGS *Nexus* 13:130; Boyer, *How to Publish your Family History*, p. 59 (#1 & wife); MPGL 7776; LDS records. Notes: #5 Mary was probably the daughter of Matthew Machell & Mary Lewknor above, but this is not certain. Both #1 James and a sister Mary Cudworth (b. 23 Jul 1637; md. Robert Whitcomb) have MPGL descendants.

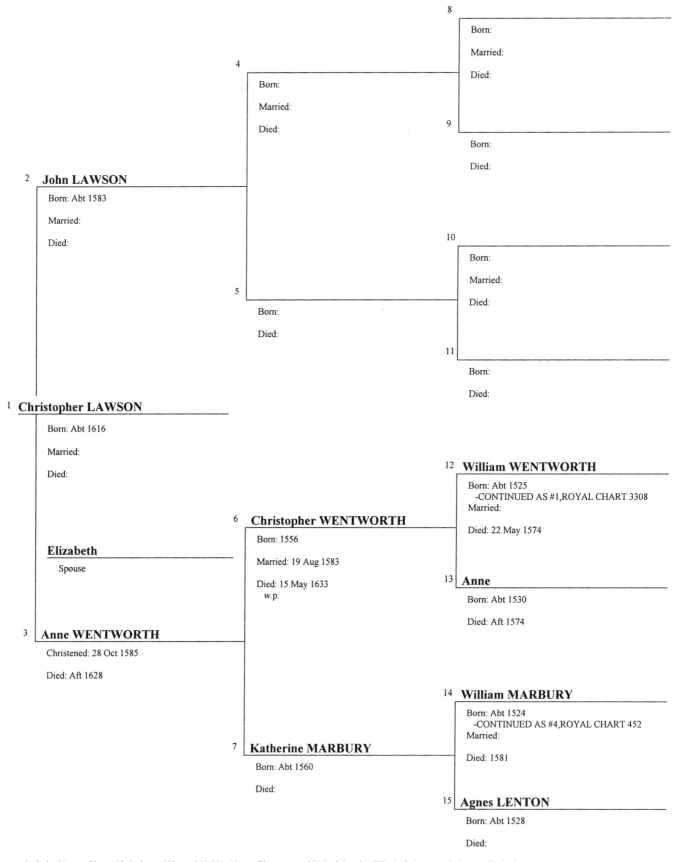

8

Born:

Married:

Died:

4

Born:

Married:

Died:

9

Born:

Died:

2 John LAWSON

Born: Abt 1583

Married:

Died:

10

Born:

Married:

Died:

5

Born:

Died:

11

Born:

Died:

¹ Christopher LAWSON

Born: Abt 1616

Married:

Died:

12 William WENTWORTH

Born: Abt 1525
  -CONTINUED AS #1,ROYAL CHART 3308
Married:

Died: 22 May 1574

6 Christopher WENTWORTH

Born: 1556

Married: 19 Aug 1583

Died: 15 May 1633
  w.p.

13 Anne

Born: Abt 1530

Died: Aft 1574

Elizabeth

Spouse

3 Anne WENTWORTH

Christened: 28 Oct 1585

Died: Aft 1628

14 William MARBURY

Born: Abt 1524
  -CONTINUED AS #4,ROYAL CHART 452
Married:

Died: 1581

7 Katherine MARBURY

Born: Abt 1560

Died:

15 Agnes LENTON

Born: Abt 1528

Died:

Sources include: *Magna Charta* 78; Roberts *500*. pp. 350-351. Notes: The spouse of #1 is claimed as Elizabeth James and also as Elizabeth Fitton.

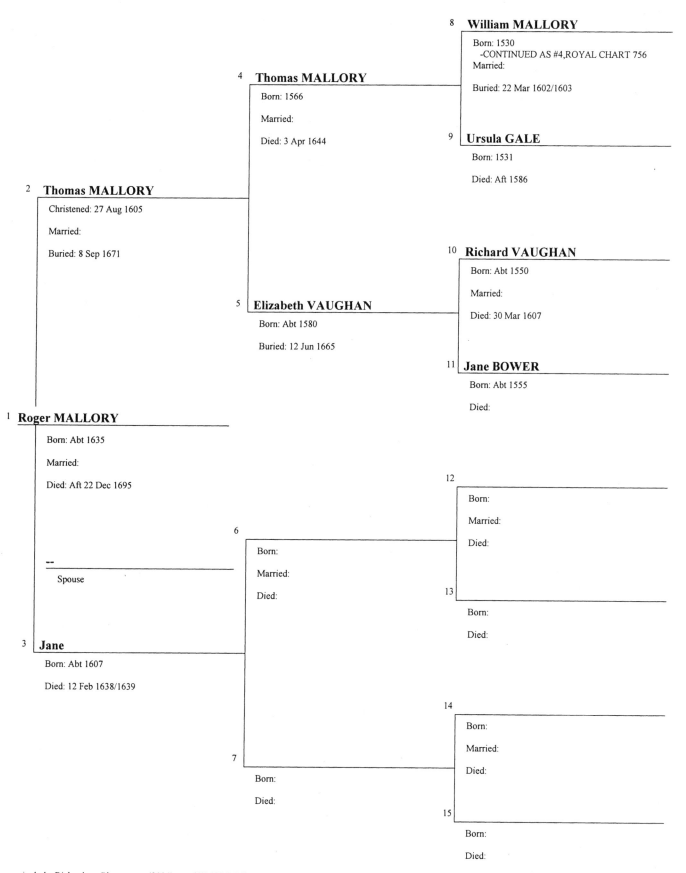

8 **William MALLORY**

Born: 1530
   -CONTINUED AS #4, ROYAL CHART 756
Married:

Buried: 22 Mar 1602/1603

4 **Thomas MALLORY**

Born: 1566

Married:

Died: 3 Apr 1644

9 **Ursula GALE**

Born: 1531

Died: Aft 1586

2 **Thomas MALLORY**

Christened: 27 Aug 1605

Married:

Buried: 8 Sep 1671

10 **Richard VAUGHAN**

Born: Abt 1550

Married:

Died: 30 Mar 1607

5 **Elizabeth VAUGHAN**

Born: Abt 1580

Buried: 12 Jun 1665

11 **Jane BOWER**

Born: Abt 1555

Died:

1 **Roger MALLORY**

Born: Abt 1635

Married:

Died: Aft 22 Dec 1695

--
   Spouse

12

Born:

Married:

Died:

6

Born:

Married:

Died:

13

Born:

Died:

3 **Jane**

Born: Abt 1607

Died: 12 Feb 1638/1639

14

Born:

Married:

Died:

7

Born:

Died:

15

Born:

Died:

Sources include: Richardson *Plantagenet* (2004), pp. 487-488 (Mallory); *Magna Charta* 109; Roberts *500*, pp. 313-314.

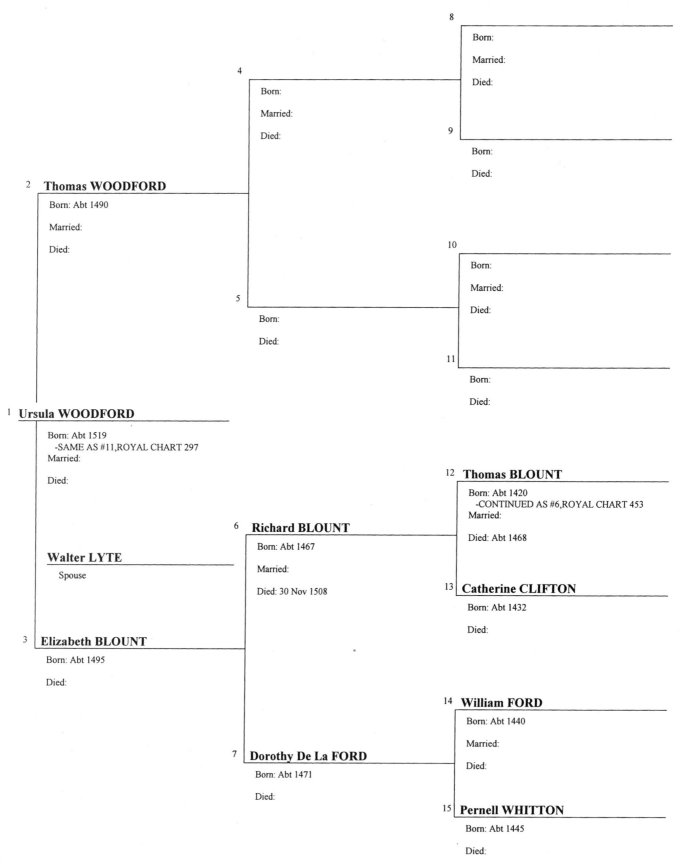

8

Born:

Married:

Died:

4

Born:

Married:

Died:

9

Born:

Died:

2   **Thomas WOODFORD**

Born: Abt 1490

Married:

Died:

10

Born:

Married:

Died:

5

Born:

Died:

11

Born:

Died:

1   **Ursula WOODFORD**

Born: Abt 1519
   -SAME AS #11,ROYAL CHART 297
Married:

Died:

12   **Thomas BLOUNT**

Born: Abt 1420
   -CONTINUED AS #6,ROYAL CHART 453
Married:

Died: Abt 1468

6   **Richard BLOUNT**

Born: Abt 1467

Married:

Died: 30 Nov 1508

13   **Catherine CLIFTON**

Born: Abt 1432

Died:

Walter LYTE

Spouse

3   **Elizabeth BLOUNT**

Born: Abt 1495

Died:

14   **William FORD**

Born: Abt 1440

Married:

Died:

7   **Dorothy De La FORD**

Born: Abt 1471

Died:

15   **Pernell WHITTON**

Born: Abt 1445

Died:

Sources include: Roberts *AAP*, pp. 365, 367; LDS records.

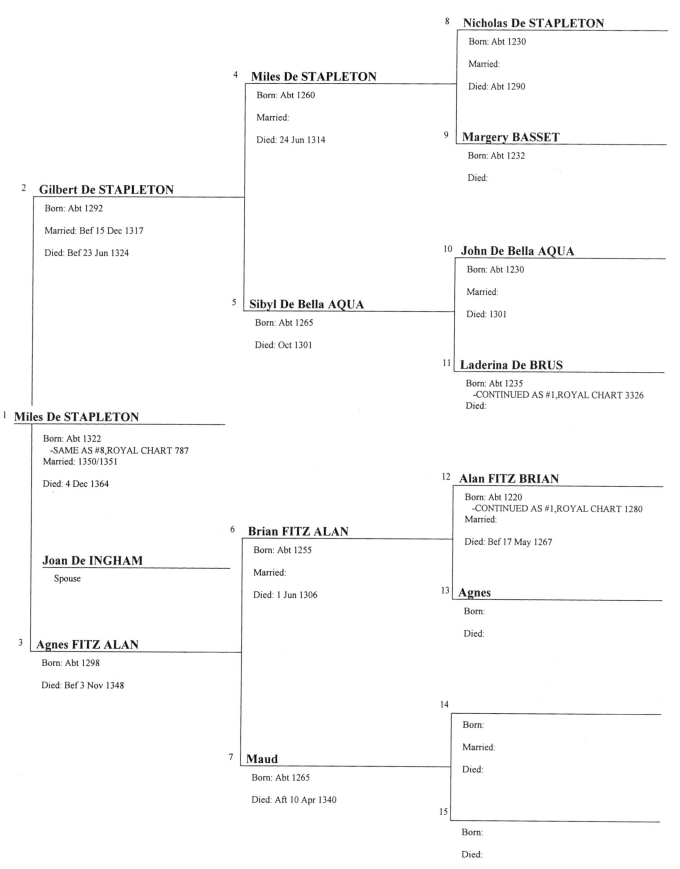

8 Nicholas De STAPLETON

Born: Abt 1230

Married:

Died: Abt 1290

4 Miles De STAPLETON

Born: Abt 1260

Married:

Died: 24 Jun 1314

9 Margery BASSET

Born: Abt 1232

Died:

2 Gilbert De STAPLETON

Born: Abt 1292

Married: Bef 15 Dec 1317

Died: Bef 23 Jun 1324

10 John De Bella AQUA

Born: Abt 1230

Married:

Died: 1301

5 Sibyl De Bella AQUA

Born: Abt 1265

Died: Oct 1301

11 Laderina De BRUS

Born: Abt 1235
  -CONTINUED AS #1,ROYAL CHART 3326
Died:

1 Miles De STAPLETON

Born: Abt 1322
  -SAME AS #8,ROYAL CHART 787
Married: 1350/1351

Died: 4 Dec 1364

12 Alan FITZ BRIAN

Born: Abt 1220
  -CONTINUED AS #1,ROYAL CHART 1280
Married:

Died: Bef 17 May 1267

6 Brian FITZ ALAN

Born: Abt 1255

Married:

Died: 1 Jun 1306

13 Agnes

Born:

Died:

Joan De INGHAM

Spouse

3 Agnes FITZ ALAN

Born: Abt 1298

Died: Bef 3 Nov 1348

14

Born:

Married:

Died:

7 Maud

Born: Abt 1265

Died: Aft 10 Apr 1340

15

Born:

Died:

Sources include: *Blood Royal* 5:70-73; LDS records.

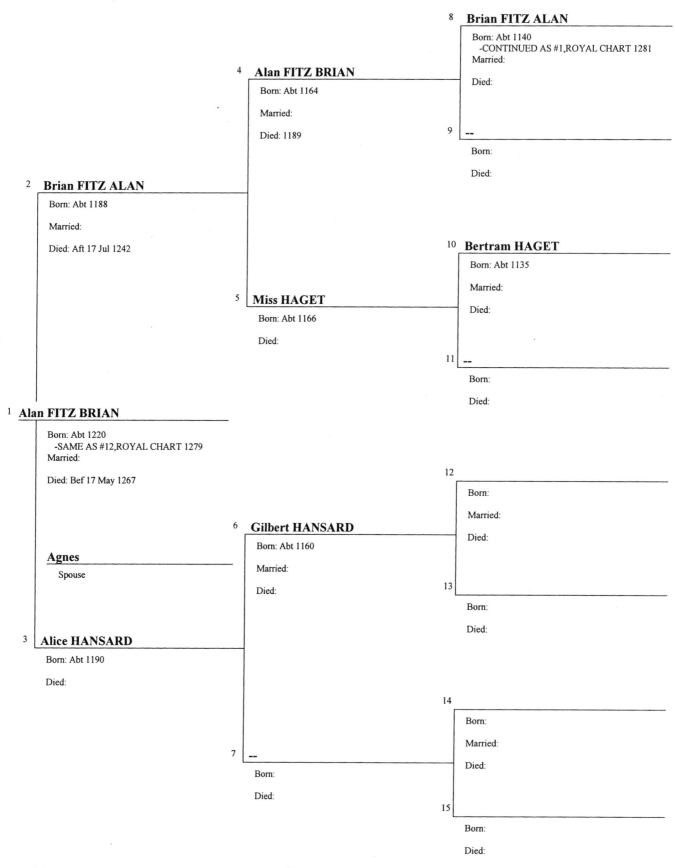

8 Brian FITZ ALAN

Born: Abt 1140
-CONTINUED AS #1,ROYAL CHART 1281
Married:

Died:

4 Alan FITZ BRIAN

Born: Abt 1164

Married:

Died: 1189

9 --

Born:

Died:

2 Brian FITZ ALAN

Born: Abt 1188

Married:

Died: Aft 17 Jul 1242

10 Bertram HAGET

Born: Abt 1135

Married:

Died:

5 Miss HAGET

Born: Abt 1166

Died:

11 --

Born:

Died:

1 Alan FITZ BRIAN

Born: Abt 1220
-SAME AS #12,ROYAL CHART 1279
Married:

Died: Bef 17 May 1267

12

Born:

Married:

Died:

6 Gilbert HANSARD

Born: Abt 1160

Married:

Died:

13

Born:

Died:

Agnes

Spouse

3 Alice HANSARD

Born: Abt 1190

Died:

14

Born:

Married:

Died:

7 --

Born:

Died:

15

Born:

Died:

Sources include: *Complete Peerage* 5:397; *Blood Royal* 5:70-73; Faris preliminary baronial manuscript (1998), p. 607 (Fitz Alan). Note: The identification of #8 Brian is disputed. *Complete Peerage* gives the line as shown above and on chart 1281. The Faris manuscript, citing *Carleton* (7-7-8, 7-7-3), gives #8 as Brian Fitz <u>Scolland</u>, claimed as steward instead of son of Earl Alan (see chart 1281, #2).

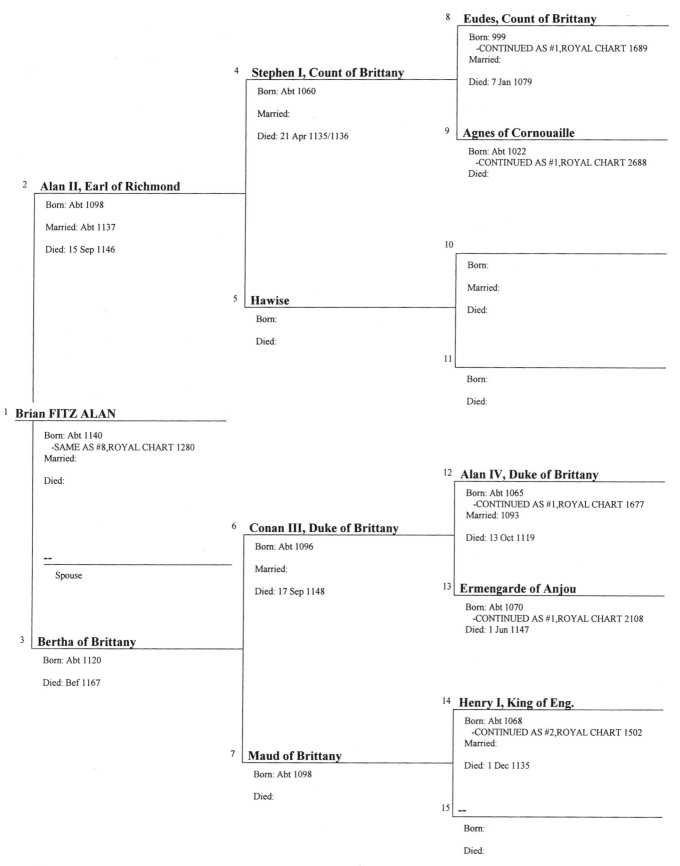

8 Eudes, Count of Brittany

Born: 999
  -CONTINUED AS #1,ROYAL CHART 1689
Married:

Died: 7 Jan 1079

4 Stephen I, Count of Brittany

Born: Abt 1060

Married:

Died: 21 Apr 1135/1136

9 Agnes of Cornouaille

Born: Abt 1022
  -CONTINUED AS #1,ROYAL CHART 2688
Died:

2 Alan II, Earl of Richmond

Born: Abt 1098

Married: Abt 1137

Died: 15 Sep 1146

10

Born:

Married:

Died:

5 Hawise

Born:

Died:

11

Born:

Died:

1 Brian FITZ ALAN

Born: Abt 1140
  -SAME AS #8,ROYAL CHART 1280
Married:

Died:

12 Alan IV, Duke of Brittany

Born: Abt 1065
  -CONTINUED AS #1,ROYAL CHART 1677
Married: 1093

Died: 13 Oct 1119

6 Conan III, Duke of Brittany

Born: Abt 1096

Married:

Died: 17 Sep 1148

13 Ermengarde of Anjou

Born: Abt 1070
  -CONTINUED AS #1,ROYAL CHART 2108
Died: 1 Jun 1147

--

Spouse

3 Bertha of Brittany

Born: Abt 1120

Died: Bef 1167

14 Henry I, King of Eng.

Born: Abt 1068
  -CONTINUED AS #2,ROYAL CHART 1502
Married:

Died: 1 Dec 1135

7 Maud of Brittany

Born: Abt 1098

Died:

15 --

Born:

Died:

Sources include: *Blood Royal* 5:70-73; *Royal Ancestors* (1989), chart 11490 (#2 & 3 ancestry).

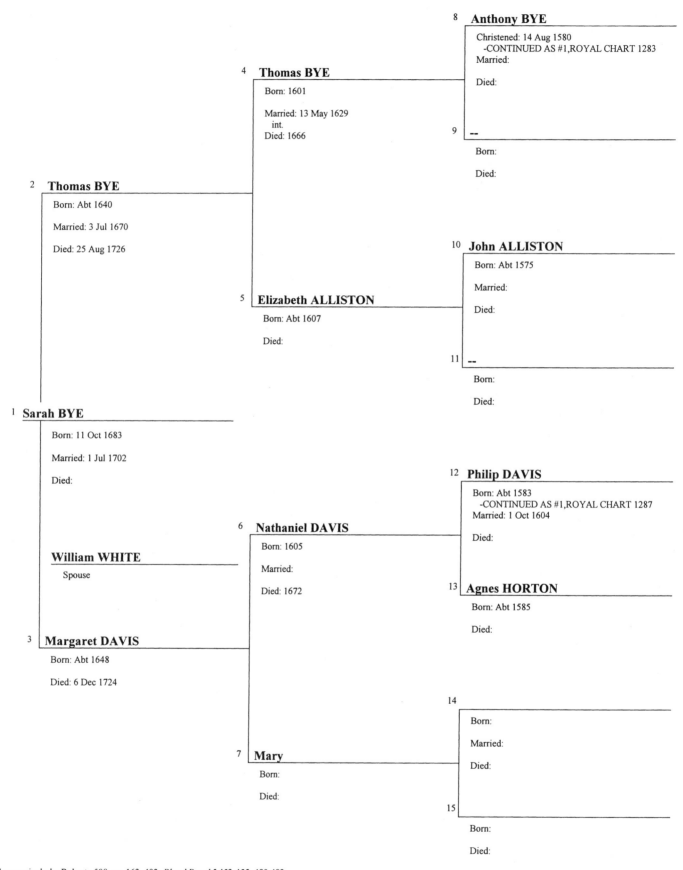

8 **Anthony BYE**

Christened: 14 Aug 1580
  -CONTINUED AS #1,ROYAL CHART 1283
Married:

Died:

4 **Thomas BYE**

Born: 1601

Married: 13 May 1629
  int.
Died: 1666

9 **--**

Born:

Died:

2 **Thomas BYE**

Born: Abt 1640

Married: 3 Jul 1670

Died: 25 Aug 1726

10 **John ALLISTON**

Born: Abt 1575

Married:

Died:

5 **Elizabeth ALLISTON**

Born: Abt 1607

Died:

11 **--**

Born:

Died:

1 **Sarah BYE**

Born: 11 Oct 1683

Married: 1 Jul 1702

Died:

12 **Philip DAVIS**

Born: Abt 1583
  -CONTINUED AS #1,ROYAL CHART 1287
Married: 1 Oct 1604

Died:

6 **Nathaniel DAVIS**

Born: 1605

Married:

Died: 1672

13 **Agnes HORTON**

Born: Abt 1585

Died:

William WHITE

Spouse

3 **Margaret DAVIS**

Born: Abt 1648

Died: 6 Dec 1724

14

Born:

Married:

Died:

7 **Mary**

Born:

Died:

15

Born:

Died:

Sources include: Roberts *500*, pp. 163, 403; *Blood Royal* 5:453-455, 480-482.

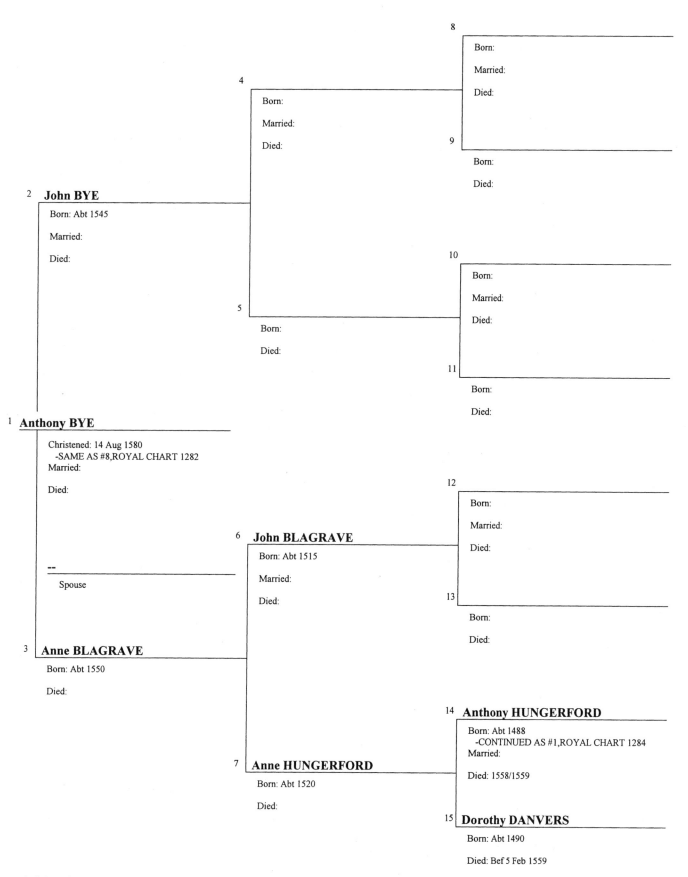

8

Born:

Married:

Died:

4

Born:

Married:

Died:

9

Born:

Died:

2 **John BYE**

Born: Abt 1545

Married:

Died:

10

Born:

Married:

Died:

5

Born:

Died:

11

Born:

Died:

1 **Anthony BYE**

Christened: 14 Aug 1580
-SAME AS #8,ROYAL CHART 1282
Married:

Died:

12

Born:

Married:

Died:

6 **John BLAGRAVE**

Born: Abt 1515

Married:

Died:

13

Born:

Died:

--

Spouse

3 **Anne BLAGRAVE**

Born: Abt 1550

Died:

14 **Anthony HUNGERFORD**

Born: Abt 1488
-CONTINUED AS #1,ROYAL CHART 1284
Married:

Died: 1558/1559

7 **Anne HUNGERFORD**

Born: Abt 1520

Died:

15 **Dorothy DANVERS**

Born: Abt 1490

Died: Bef 5 Feb 1559

Sources include: Roberts *500*, p. 403; *Blood Royal* 5:480-481.

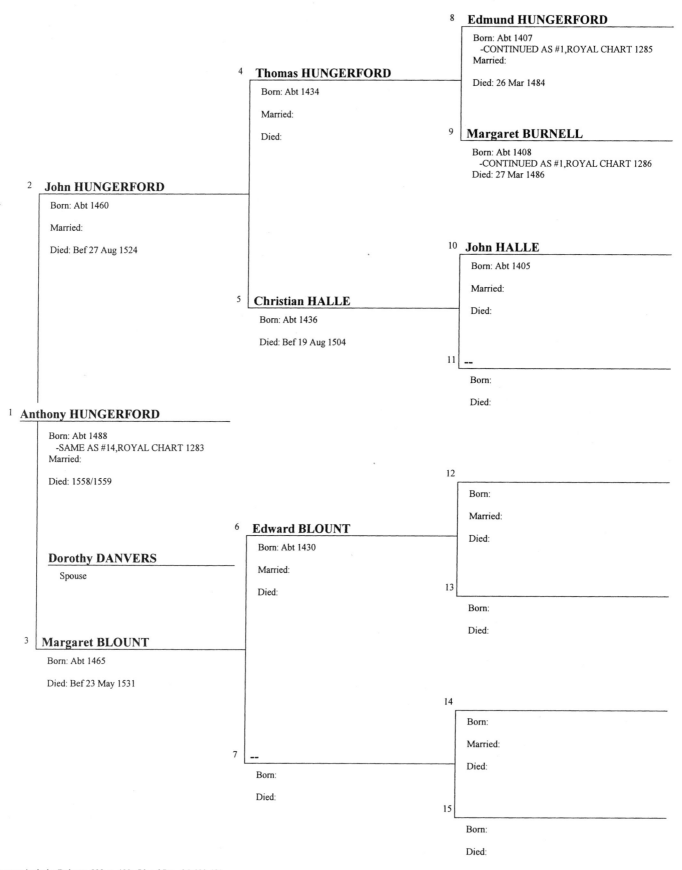

8 **Edmund HUNGERFORD**

Born: Abt 1407
-CONTINUED AS #1, ROYAL CHART 1285
Married:

Died: 26 Mar 1484

4 **Thomas HUNGERFORD**

Born: Abt 1434

Married:

Died:

9 **Margaret BURNELL**

Born: Abt 1408
-CONTINUED AS #1, ROYAL CHART 1286
Died: 27 Mar 1486

2 **John HUNGERFORD**

Born: Abt 1460

Married:

Died: Bef 27 Aug 1524

10 **John HALLE**

Born: Abt 1405

Married:

Died:

5 **Christian HALLE**

Born: Abt 1436

Died: Bef 19 Aug 1504

11 **--**

Born:

Died:

1 **Anthony HUNGERFORD**

Born: Abt 1488
-SAME AS #14, ROYAL CHART 1283
Married:

Died: 1558/1559

12

Born:

Married:

Died:

6 **Edward BLOUNT**

Born: Abt 1430

Married:

Died:

13

Born:

Died:

Dorothy DANVERS

Spouse

3 **Margaret BLOUNT**

Born: Abt 1465

Died: Bef 23 May 1531

14

Born:

Married:

Died:

7 **--**

Born:

Died:

15

Born:

Died:

Sources include: Roberts *500*, p. 403; *Blood Royal* 5:480-481.

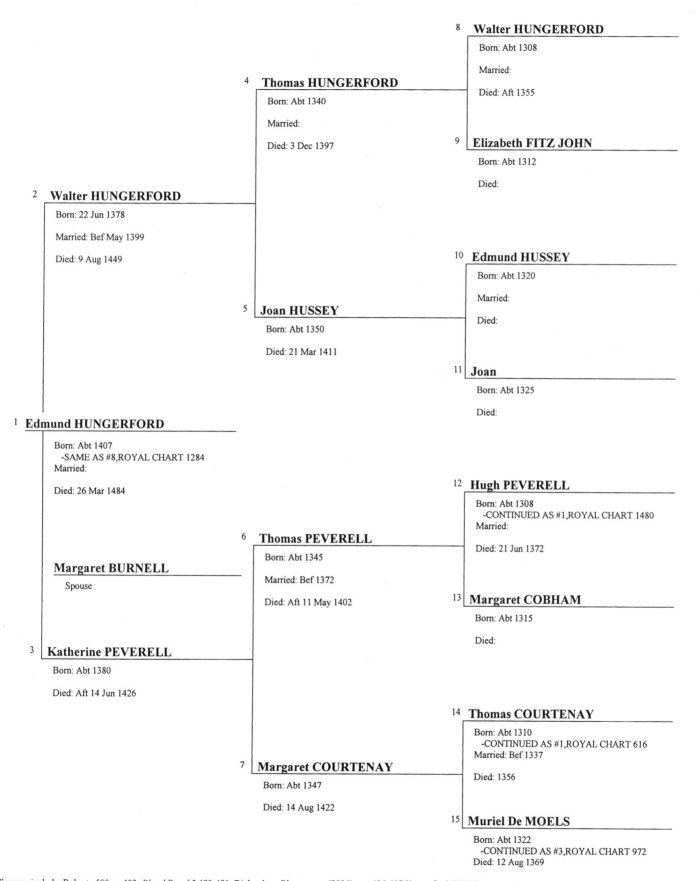

8 | **Walter HUNGERFORD**
Born: Abt 1308
Married:
Died: Aft 1355

4 | **Thomas HUNGERFORD**
Born: Abt 1340
Married:
Died: 3 Dec 1397

9 | **Elizabeth FITZ JOHN**
Born: Abt 1312
Died:

2 | **Walter HUNGERFORD**
Born: 22 Jun 1378
Married: Bef May 1399
Died: 9 Aug 1449

10 | **Edmund HUSSEY**
Born: Abt 1320
Married:
Died:

5 | **Joan HUSSEY**
Born: Abt 1350
Died: 21 Mar 1411

11 | **Joan**
Born: Abt 1325
Died:

1 | **Edmund HUNGERFORD**
Born: Abt 1407
-SAME AS #8, ROYAL CHART 1284
Married:
Died: 26 Mar 1484

12 | **Hugh PEVERELL**
Born: Abt 1308
-CONTINUED AS #1, ROYAL CHART 1480
Married:
Died: 21 Jun 1372

6 | **Thomas PEVERELL**
Born: Abt 1345
Married: Bef 1372
Died: Aft 11 May 1402

13 | **Margaret COBHAM**
Born: Abt 1315
Died:

Margaret BURNELL
Spouse

3 | **Katherine PEVERELL**
Born: Abt 1380
Died: Aft 14 Jun 1426

14 | **Thomas COURTENAY**
Born: Abt 1310
-CONTINUED AS #1, ROYAL CHART 616
Married: Bef 1337
Died: 1356

7 | **Margaret COURTENAY**
Born: Abt 1347
Died: 14 Aug 1422

15 | **Muriel De MOELS**
Born: Abt 1322
-CONTINUED AS #3, ROYAL CHART 972
Died: 12 Aug 1369

Sources include: Roberts *500*, p. 403; *Blood Royal* 5:480-481; Richardson *Plantagenet* (2004), pp. 406-407 Hungerford (#2 & 3 ancestry).

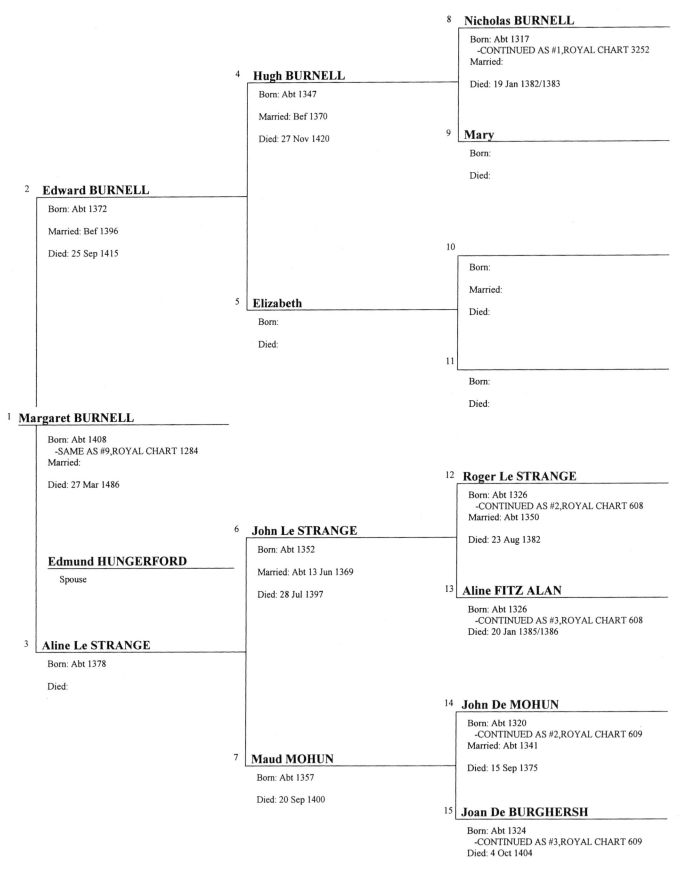

8 Nicholas BURNELL

Born: Abt 1317
  -CONTINUED AS #1,ROYAL CHART 3252
Married:

Died: 19 Jan 1382/1383

4 Hugh BURNELL

Born: Abt 1347

Married: Bef 1370

Died: 27 Nov 1420

9 Mary

Born:

Died:

2 Edward BURNELL

Born: Abt 1372

Married: Bef 1396

Died: 25 Sep 1415

10

Born:

Married:

Died:

5 Elizabeth

Born:

Died:

11

Born:

Died:

1 Margaret BURNELL

Born: Abt 1408
  -SAME AS #9,ROYAL CHART 1284
Married:

Died: 27 Mar 1486

12 Roger Le STRANGE

Born: Abt 1326
  -CONTINUED AS #2,ROYAL CHART 608
Married: Abt 1350

Died: 23 Aug 1382

6 John Le STRANGE

Born: Abt 1352

Married: Abt 13 Jun 1369

Died: 28 Jul 1397

13 Aline FITZ ALAN

Born: Abt 1326
  -CONTINUED AS #3,ROYAL CHART 608
Died: 20 Jan 1385/1386

Edmund HUNGERFORD

Spouse

3 Aline Le STRANGE

Born: Abt 1378

Died:

14 John De MOHUN

Born: Abt 1320
  -CONTINUED AS #2,ROYAL CHART 609
Married: Abt 1341

Died: 15 Sep 1375

7 Maud MOHUN

Born: Abt 1357

Died: 20 Sep 1400

15 Joan De BURGHERSH

Born: Abt 1324
  -CONTINUED AS #3,ROYAL CHART 609
Died: 4 Oct 1404

Sources include: Faris preliminary baronial manuscript (1998), pp. 882 (Hungerford), 269-270 (Burnell); Faris-Richardson 3 (July 2002 preliminary)--Burnell.

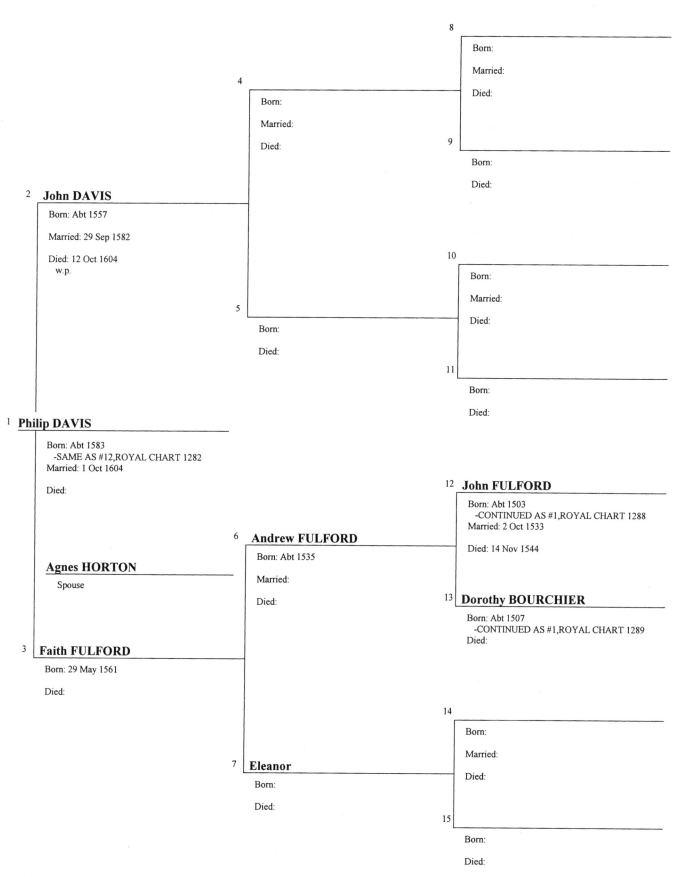

8

Born:

Married:

Died:

4

Born:

Married:

Died:

9

Born:

Died:

2 **John DAVIS**

Born: Abt 1557

Married: 29 Sep 1582

Died: 12 Oct 1604
w.p.

10

Born:

Married:

Died:

5

Born:

Died:

11

Born:

Died:

1 **Philip DAVIS**

Born: Abt 1583
-SAME AS #12,ROYAL CHART 1282
Married: 1 Oct 1604

Died:

12 **John FULFORD**

Born: Abt 1503
-CONTINUED AS #1,ROYAL CHART 1288
Married: 2 Oct 1533

Died: 14 Nov 1544

6 **Andrew FULFORD**

Born: Abt 1535

Married:

Died:

13 **Dorothy BOURCHIER**

Born: Abt 1507
-CONTINUED AS #1,ROYAL CHART 1289
Died:

Agnes HORTON

Spouse

3 **Faith FULFORD**

Born: 29 May 1561

Died:

14

Born:

Married:

Died:

7 **Eleanor**

Born:

Died:

15

Born:

Died:

Sources include: Faris preliminary baronial manuscript (1998), pp. 477-478 (Davis), 678-679 (Fulford); Roberts *500*, p. 163; *Blood Royal* 5:453-454; 4:230.

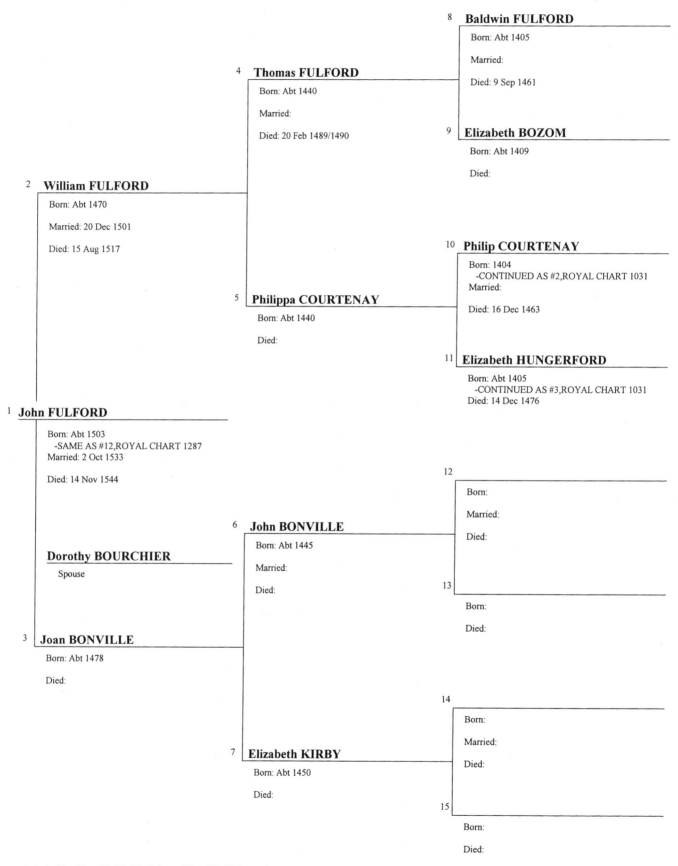

8   **Baldwin FULFORD**

Born: Abt 1405

Married:

Died: 9 Sep 1461

4   **Thomas FULFORD**

Born: Abt 1440

Married:

Died: 20 Feb 1489/1490

9 | **Elizabeth BOZOM**

Born: Abt 1409

Died:

2   **William FULFORD**

Born: Abt 1470

Married: 20 Dec 1501

Died: 15 Aug 1517

10   **Philip COURTENAY**

Born: 1404
  -CONTINUED AS #2,ROYAL CHART 1031
Married:

Died: 16 Dec 1463

5   **Philippa COURTENAY**

Born: Abt 1440

Died:

11 | **Elizabeth HUNGERFORD**

Born: Abt 1405
  -CONTINUED AS #3,ROYAL CHART 1031
Died: 14 Dec 1476

1   **John FULFORD**

Born: Abt 1503
  -SAME AS #12,ROYAL CHART 1287
Married: 2 Oct 1533

Died: 14 Nov 1544

12

Born:

Married:

Died:

6   **John BONVILLE**

Born: Abt 1445

Married:

Died:

13

Born:

Died:

Dorothy BOURCHIER

Spouse

3   **Joan BONVILLE**

Born: Abt 1478

Died:

14

Born:

Married:

Died:

7   **Elizabeth KIRBY**

Born: Abt 1450

Died:

15

Born:

Died:

Sources include: *Blood Royal* 5:453-454; Roberts *500*, p. 163; LDS records.

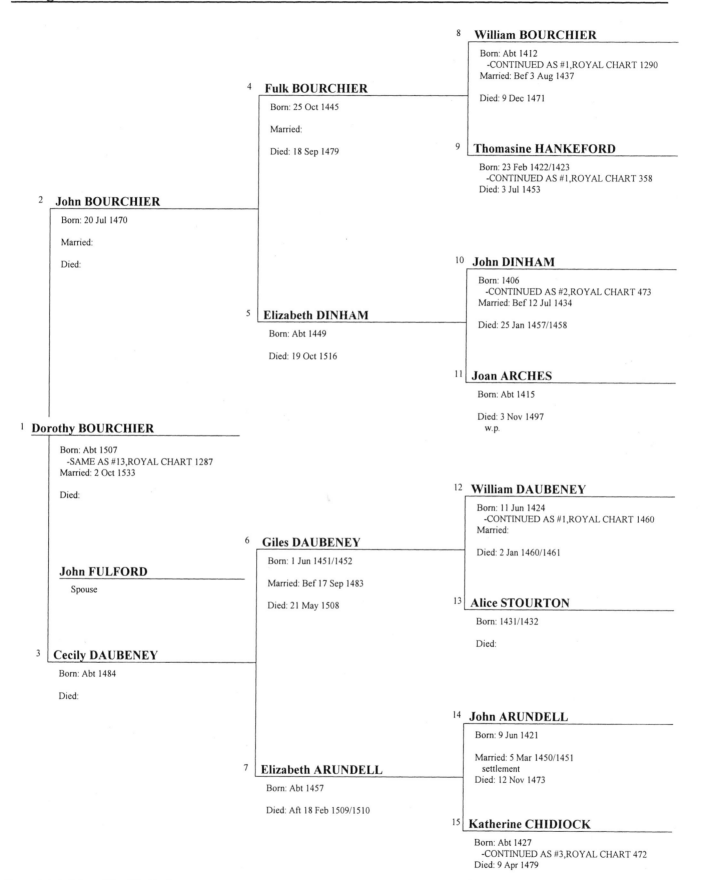

8 **William BOURCHIER**

Born: Abt 1412
-CONTINUED AS #1,ROYAL CHART 1290
Married: Bef 3 Aug 1437

Died: 9 Dec 1471

4 **Fulk BOURCHIER**

Born: 25 Oct 1445

Married:

Died: 18 Sep 1479

9 **Thomasine HANKEFORD**

Born: 23 Feb 1422/1423
-CONTINUED AS #1,ROYAL CHART 358
Died: 3 Jul 1453

2 **John BOURCHIER**

Born: 20 Jul 1470

Married:

Died:

10 **John DINHAM**

Born: 1406
-CONTINUED AS #2,ROYAL CHART 473
Married: Bef 12 Jul 1434

Died: 25 Jan 1457/1458

5 **Elizabeth DINHAM**

Born: Abt 1449

Died: 19 Oct 1516

11 **Joan ARCHES**

Born: Abt 1415

Died: 3 Nov 1497
w.p.

1 **Dorothy BOURCHIER**

Born: Abt 1507
-SAME AS #13,ROYAL CHART 1287
Married: 2 Oct 1533

Died:

12 **William DAUBENEY**

Born: 11 Jun 1424
-CONTINUED AS #1,ROYAL CHART 1460
Married:

Died: 2 Jan 1460/1461

6 **Giles DAUBENEY**

Born: 1 Jun 1451/1452

Married: Bef 17 Sep 1483

Died: 21 May 1508

13 **Alice STOURTON**

Born: 1431/1432

Died:

John FULFORD

Spouse

3 **Cecily DAUBENEY**

Born: Abt 1484

Died:

14 **John ARUNDELL**

Born: 9 Jun 1421

Married: 5 Mar 1450/1451
settlement
Died: 12 Nov 1473

7 **Elizabeth ARUNDELL**

Born: Abt 1457

Died: Aft 18 Feb 1509/1510

15 **Katherine CHIDIOCK**

Born: Abt 1427
-CONTINUED AS #3,ROYAL CHART 472
Died: 9 Apr 1479

Sources include: Roberts *500*, p. 163; *Blood Royal* 4:230; LDS records; *Complete Peerage* 4:92-105 (#6 ancestry).

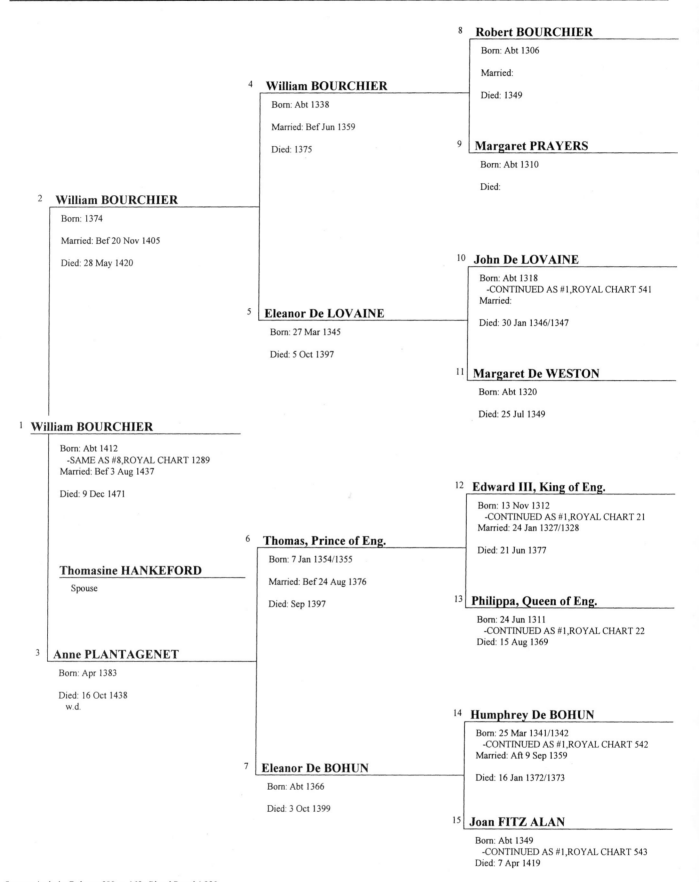

8 **Robert BOURCHIER**

Born: Abt 1306

Married:

Died: 1349

4 **William BOURCHIER**

Born: Abt 1338

Married: Bef Jun 1359

Died: 1375

9 **Margaret PRAYERS**

Born: Abt 1310

Died:

2 **William BOURCHIER**

Born: 1374

Married: Bef 20 Nov 1405

Died: 28 May 1420

10 **John De LOVAINE**

Born: Abt 1318
  -CONTINUED AS #1,ROYAL CHART 541
Married:

Died: 30 Jan 1346/1347

5 **Eleanor De LOVAINE**

Born: 27 Mar 1345

Died: 5 Oct 1397

11 **Margaret De WESTON**

Born: Abt 1320

Died: 25 Jul 1349

1 **William BOURCHIER**

Born: Abt 1412
  -SAME AS #8,ROYAL CHART 1289
Married: Bef 3 Aug 1437

Died: 9 Dec 1471

12 **Edward III, King of Eng.**

Born: 13 Nov 1312
  -CONTINUED AS #1,ROYAL CHART 21
Married: 24 Jan 1327/1328

Died: 21 Jun 1377

6 **Thomas, Prince of Eng.**

Born: 7 Jan 1354/1355

Married: Bef 24 Aug 1376

Died: Sep 1397

13 **Philippa, Queen of Eng.**

Born: 24 Jun 1311
  -CONTINUED AS #1,ROYAL CHART 22
Died: 15 Aug 1369

Thomasine HANKEFORD

Spouse

3 **Anne PLANTAGENET**

Born: Apr 1383

Died: 16 Oct 1438
w.d.

14 **Humphrey De BOHUN**

Born: 25 Mar 1341/1342
  -CONTINUED AS #1,ROYAL CHART 542
Married: Aft 9 Sep 1359

Died: 16 Jan 1372/1373

7 **Eleanor De BOHUN**

Born: Abt 1366

Died: 3 Oct 1399

15 **Joan FITZ ALAN**

Born: Abt 1349
  -CONTINUED AS #1,ROYAL CHART 543
Died: 7 Apr 1419

Sources include: Roberts *500*, p. 163; *Blood Royal* 4:230.

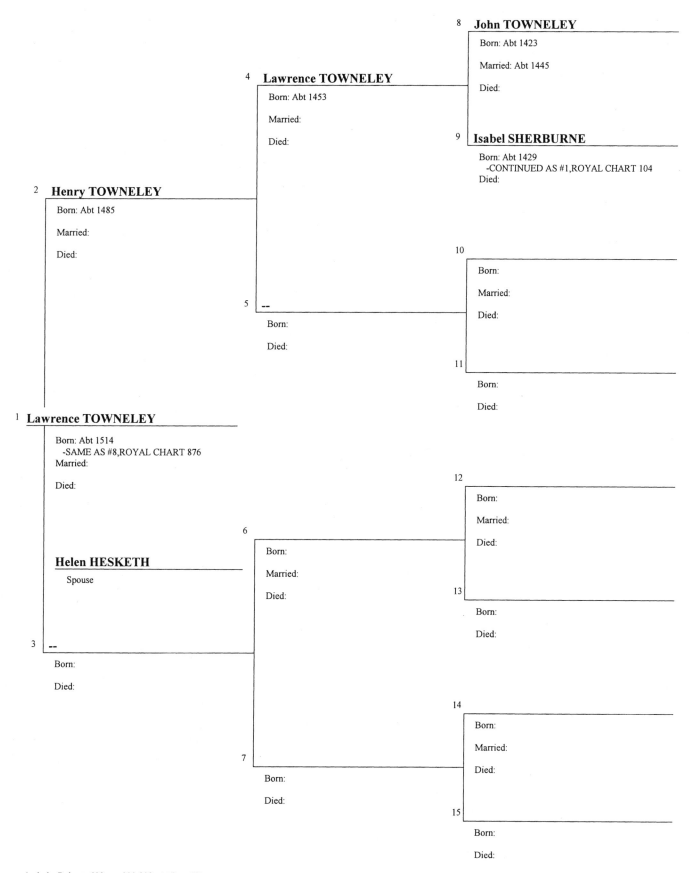

8 **John TOWNELEY**

Born: Abt 1423

Married: Abt 1445

Died:

4 **Lawrence TOWNELEY**

Born: Abt 1453

Married:

Died:

9 **Isabel SHERBURNE**

Born: Abt 1429
-CONTINUED AS #1,ROYAL CHART 104
Died:

2 **Henry TOWNELEY**

Born: Abt 1485

Married:

Died:

10

Born:

Married:

Died:

5 **--**

Born:

Died:

11

Born:

Died:

1 **Lawrence TOWNELEY**

Born: Abt 1514
-SAME AS #8,ROYAL CHART 876
Married:

Died:

12

Born:

Married:

Died:

6

Born:

Married:

Died:

13

Born:

Died:

Helen HESKETH

Spouse

3 **--**

Born:

Died:

14

Born:

Married:

Died:

7

Born:

Died:

15

Born:

Died:

Sources include: Roberts *500*, pp. 330-333; *AAP*, p. 181.

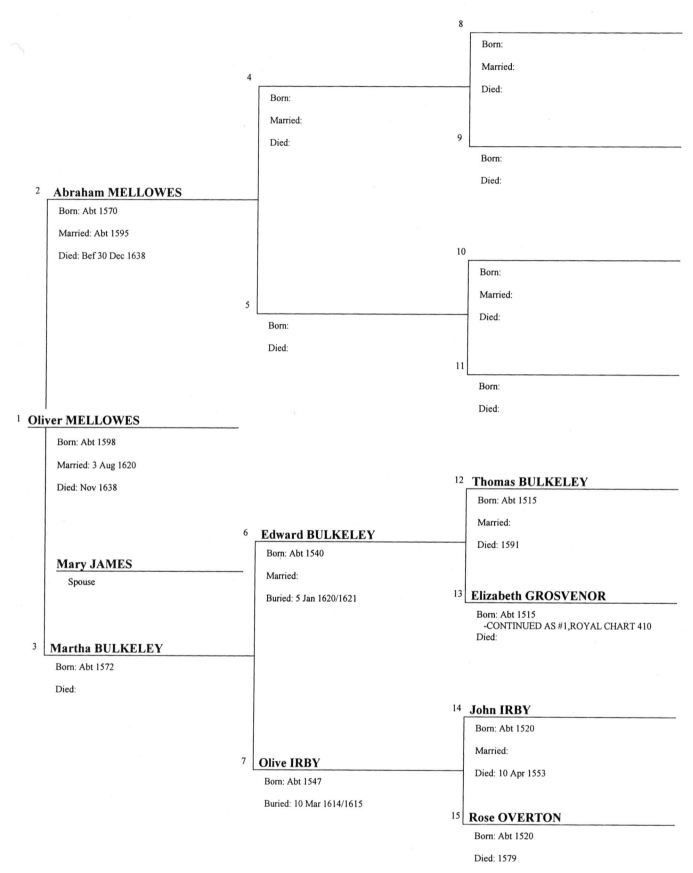

8

Born:

Married:

Died:

4

Born:

Married:

Died:

9

Born:

Died:

2 Abraham MELLOWES

Born: Abt 1570

Married: Abt 1595

Died: Bef 30 Dec 1638

10

Born:

Married:

Died:

5

Born:

Died:

11

Born:

Died:

1 Oliver MELLOWES

Born: Abt 1598

Married: 3 Aug 1620

Died: Nov 1638

12 Thomas BULKELEY

Born: Abt 1515

Married:

Died: 1591

6 Edward BULKELEY

Born: Abt 1540

Married:

Buried: 5 Jan 1620/1621

13 Elizabeth GROSVENOR

Born: Abt 1515
  -CONTINUED AS #1,ROYAL CHART 410
Died:

Mary JAMES

Spouse

3 Martha BULKELEY

Born: Abt 1572

Died:

14 John IRBY

Born: Abt 1520

Married:

Died: 10 Apr 1553

7 Olive IRBY

Born: Abt 1547

Buried: 10 Mar 1614/1615

15 Rose OVERTON

Born: Abt 1520

Died: 1579

Sources include: *Ancestral Roots* 31; Jacobus, *Bulkeley Genealogy.* Note: #1 Oliver has MPGL descendants through children John Mellowes (chr. 6 June 1622; md. Martha) and Elizabeth Mellowes (chr. 10 Dec 1625; md. Edward Wright). In addition to other descendants charted elsewhere in this volume, #6 & 7 Edward & Olive also had American descendants through a daughter Elizabeth Bulkeley (b. abt 1579; md. Richard Whittingham), parents of John Whittingham (chr. 29 Sep 1616; md. Martha Hubbard).

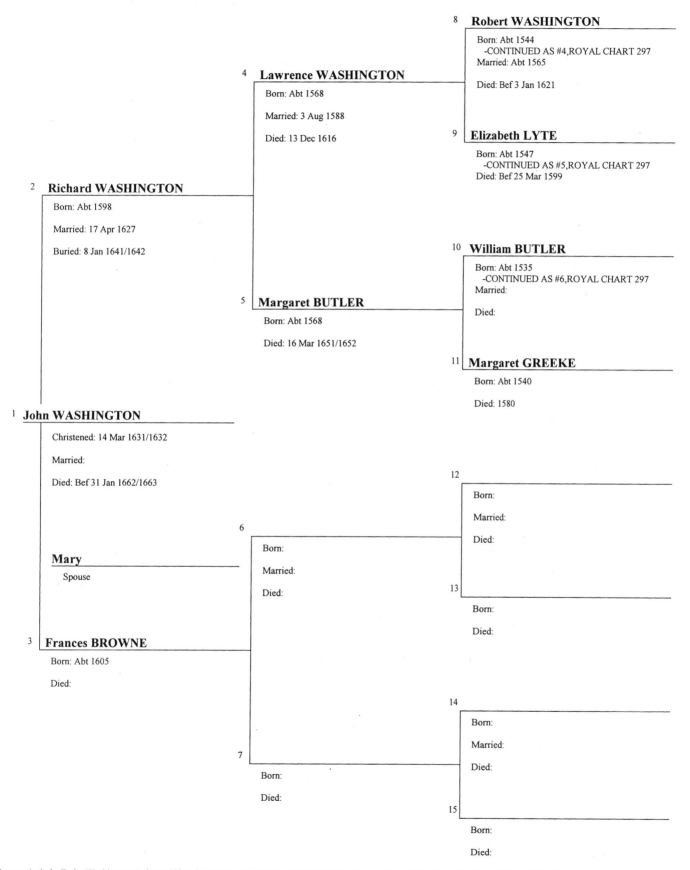

8 Robert WASHINGTON
Born: Abt 1544
 -CONTINUED AS #4, ROYAL CHART 297
Married: Abt 1565

Died: Bef 3 Jan 1621

4 Lawrence WASHINGTON
Born: Abt 1568

Married: 3 Aug 1588

Died: 13 Dec 1616

9 Elizabeth LYTE
Born: Abt 1547
 -CONTINUED AS #5, ROYAL CHART 297
Died: Bef 25 Mar 1599

2 Richard WASHINGTON
Born: Abt 1598

Married: 17 Apr 1627

Buried: 8 Jan 1641/1642

10 William BUTLER
Born: Abt 1535
 -CONTINUED AS #6, ROYAL CHART 297
Married:

Died:

5 Margaret BUTLER
Born: Abt 1568

Died: 16 Mar 1651/1652

11 Margaret GREEKE
Born: Abt 1540

Died: 1580

1 John WASHINGTON
Christened: 14 Mar 1631/1632

Married:

Died: Bef 31 Jan 1662/1663

12
Born:

Married:

Died:

6
Born:

Married:

Died:

13
Born:

Died:

Mary
Spouse

3 Frances BROWNE
Born: Abt 1605

Died:

14
Born:

Married:

Died:

7
Born:

Died:

15
Born:

Died:

Sources include: Faris--Washington; Roberts *500*, p. 243; *Magna Charta* 30. Note: #1 John had a son Richard Washington (b. 5 Sep 1660; md. Elizabeth Jordan).

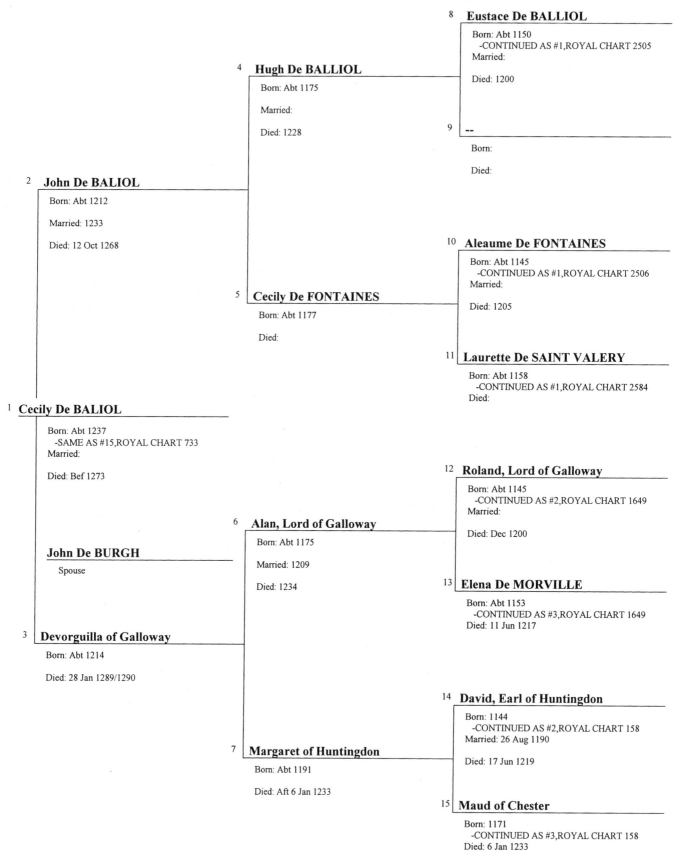

8 Eustace De BALLIOL

Born: Abt 1150
 -CONTINUED AS #1,ROYAL CHART 2505
Married:

Died: 1200

4 Hugh De BALLIOL

Born: Abt 1175

Married:

Died: 1228

9 --

Born:

Died:

2 John De BALIOL

Born: Abt 1212

Married: 1233

Died: 12 Oct 1268

10 Aleaume De FONTAINES

Born: Abt 1145
 -CONTINUED AS #1,ROYAL CHART 2506
Married:

Died: 1205

5 Cecily De FONTAINES

Born: Abt 1177

Died:

11 Laurette De SAINT VALERY

Born: Abt 1158
 -CONTINUED AS #1,ROYAL CHART 2584
Died:

1 Cecily De BALIOL

Born: Abt 1237
 -SAME AS #15,ROYAL CHART 733
Married:

Died: Bef 1273

12 Roland, Lord of Galloway

Born: Abt 1145
 -CONTINUED AS #2,ROYAL CHART 1649
Married:

Died: Dec 1200

6 Alan, Lord of Galloway

Born: Abt 1175

Married: 1209

Died: 1234

13 Elena De MORVILLE

Born: Abt 1153
 -CONTINUED AS #3,ROYAL CHART 1649
Died: 11 Jun 1217

John De BURGH

Spouse

3 Devorguilla of Galloway

Born: Abt 1214

Died: 28 Jan 1289/1290

14 David, Earl of Huntingdon

Born: 1144
 -CONTINUED AS #2,ROYAL CHART 158
Married: 26 Aug 1190

Died: 17 Jun 1219

7 Margaret of Huntingdon

Born: Abt 1191

Died: Aft 6 Jan 1233

15 Maud of Chester

Born: 1171
 -CONTINUED AS #3,ROYAL CHART 158
Died: 6 Jan 1233

Sources include: *Ancestral Roots* 94; Faris preliminary baronial manuscript (1998), pp. 21-22 (Balliol); *Magna Charta* 44-1; Turton 124; *Royal Ancestors* (1989), charts 11361, 11371 & notes; LDS records.

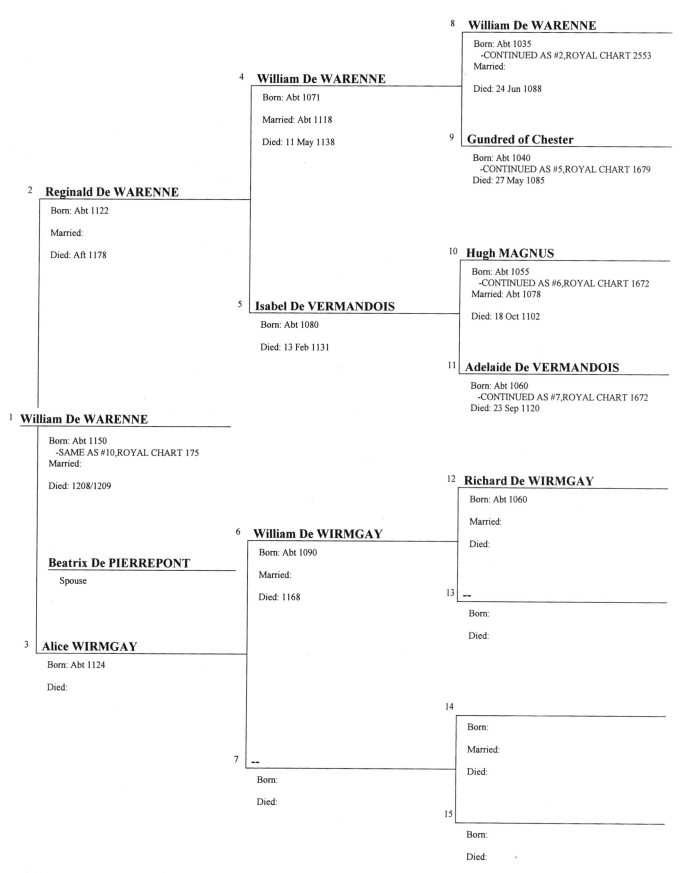

8 **William De WARENNE**

Born: Abt 1035
-CONTINUED AS #2,ROYAL CHART 2553
Married:

Died: 24 Jun 1088

4 **William De WARENNE**

Born: Abt 1071

Married: Abt 1118

Died: 11 May 1138

9 **Gundred of Chester**

Born: Abt 1040
-CONTINUED AS #5,ROYAL CHART 1679
Died: 27 May 1085

2 **Reginald De WARENNE**

Born: Abt 1122

Married:

Died: Aft 1178

10 **Hugh MAGNUS**

Born: Abt 1055
-CONTINUED AS #6,ROYAL CHART 1672
Married: Abt 1078

Died: 18 Oct 1102

5 **Isabel De VERMANDOIS**

Born: Abt 1080

Died: 13 Feb 1131

11 **Adelaide De VERMANDOIS**

Born: Abt 1060
-CONTINUED AS #7,ROYAL CHART 1672
Died: 23 Sep 1120

1 **William De WARENNE**

Born: Abt 1150
-SAME AS #10,ROYAL CHART 175
Married:

Died: 1208/1209

12 **Richard De WIRMGAY**

Born: Abt 1060

Married:

Died:

6 **William De WIRMGAY**

Born: Abt 1090

Married:

Died: 1168

13 **--**

Born:

Died:

Beatrix De PIERREPONT

Spouse

3 **Alice WIRMGAY**

Born: Abt 1124

Died:

14

Born:

Married:

Died:

7 **--**

Born:

Died:

15

Born:

Died:

Sources include: *Royal Ancestors* (1989), chart 11926; Turton 93.

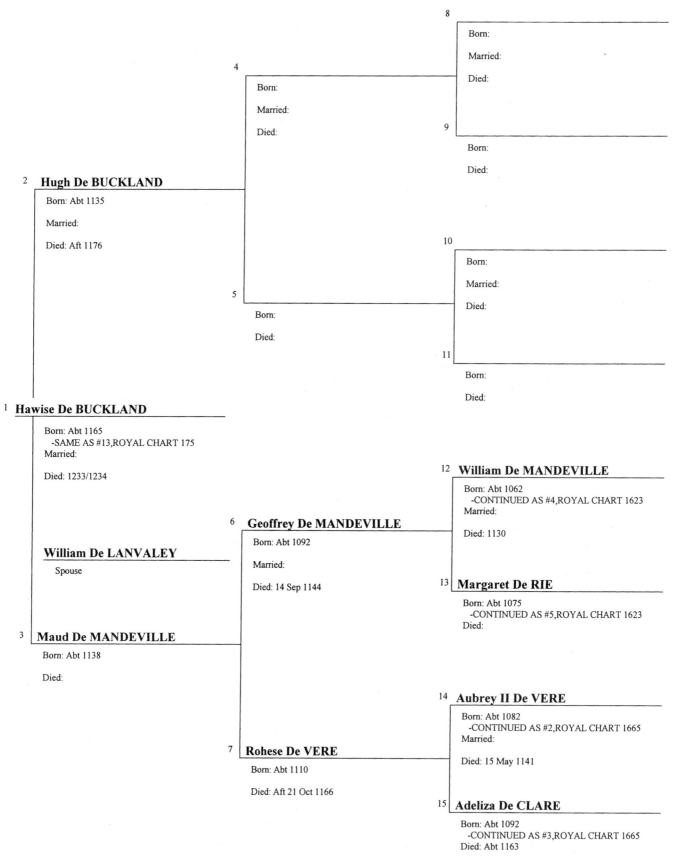

8

Born:

Married:

Died:

4

Born:

Married:

Died:

9

Born:

Died:

2 **Hugh De BUCKLAND**

Born: Abt 1135

Married:

Died: Aft 1176

10

Born:

Married:

Died:

5

Born:

Died:

11

Born:

Died:

1 **Hawise De BUCKLAND**

Born: Abt 1165
  -SAME AS #13,ROYAL CHART 175
Married:

Died: 1233/1234

12 **William De MANDEVILLE**

Born: Abt 1062
  -CONTINUED AS #4,ROYAL CHART 1623
Married:

Died: 1130

6 **Geoffrey De MANDEVILLE**

Born: Abt 1092

Married:

Died: 14 Sep 1144

13 **Margaret De RIE**

Born: Abt 1075
  -CONTINUED AS #5,ROYAL CHART 1623
Died:

William De LANVALEY

Spouse

3 **Maud De MANDEVILLE**

Born: Abt 1138

Died:

14 **Aubrey II De VERE**

Born: Abt 1082
  -CONTINUED AS #2,ROYAL CHART 1665
Married:

Died: 15 May 1141

7 **Rohese De VERE**

Born: Abt 1110

Died: Aft 21 Oct 1166

15 **Adeliza De CLARE**

Born: Abt 1092
  -CONTINUED AS #3,ROYAL CHART 1665
Died: Abt 1163

Sources include: *Magna Charta* 159; Faris preliminary baronial manuscript (1998), pp. 943-944 (Lanvaley). Note: The identification and parentage of #3 Maud is not certain.

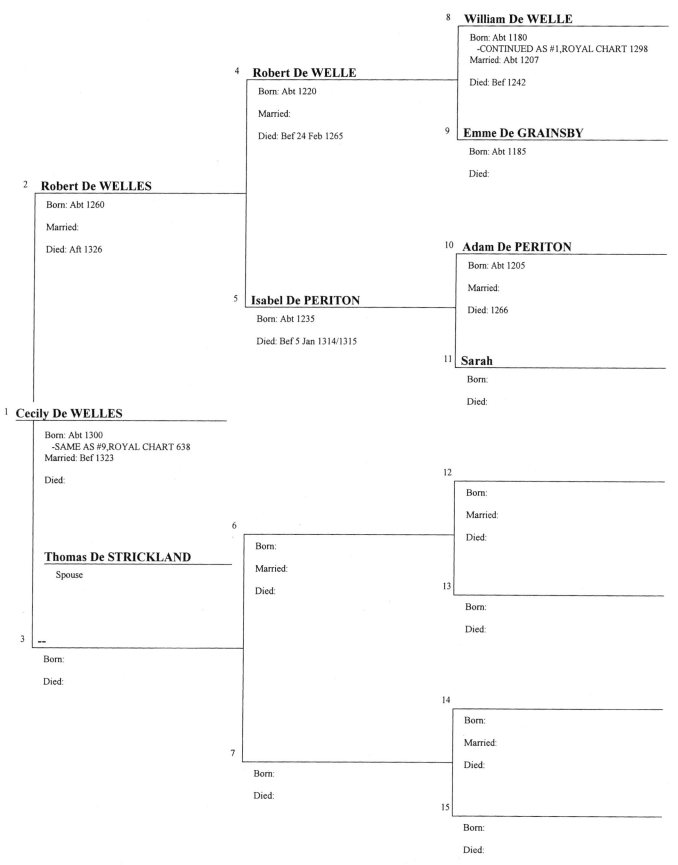

8 William De WELLE

Born: Abt 1180
    -CONTINUED AS #1,ROYAL CHART 1298
Married: Abt 1207

Died: Bef 1242

4 Robert De WELLE

Born: Abt 1220

Married:

Died: Bef 24 Feb 1265

9 Emme De GRAINSBY

Born: Abt 1185

Died:

2 Robert De WELLES

Born: Abt 1260

Married:

Died: Aft 1326

10 Adam De PERITON

Born: Abt 1205

Married:

Died: 1266

5 Isabel De PERITON

Born: Abt 1235

Died: Bef 5 Jan 1314/1315

11 Sarah

Born:

Died:

1 Cecily De WELLES

Born: Abt 1300
    -SAME AS #9,ROYAL CHART 638
Married: Bef 1323

Died:

12

Born:

Married:

Died:

6

Born:

Married:

Died:

Thomas De STRICKLAND

Spouse

13

Born:

Died:

3 --

Born:

Died:

14

Born:

Married:

Died:

7

Born:

Died:

15

Born:

Died:

Sources include: Faris preliminary baronial manuscript (1998), p. 1633 (Welles).

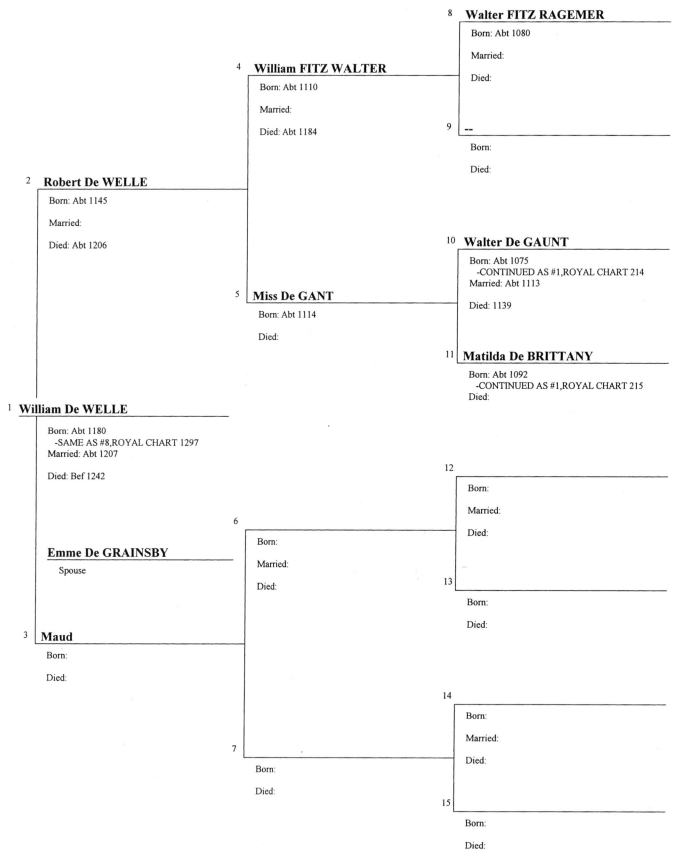

8 **Walter FITZ RAGEMER**

Born: Abt 1080

Married:

Died:

4 **William FITZ WALTER**

Born: Abt 1110

Married:

Died: Abt 1184

9 **--**

Born:

Died:

2 **Robert De WELLE**

Born: Abt 1145

Married:

Died: Abt 1206

10 **Walter De GAUNT**

Born: Abt 1075
    -CONTINUED AS #1,ROYAL CHART 214
Married: Abt 1113

Died: 1139

5 **Miss De GANT**

Born: Abt 1114

Died:

11 **Matilda De BRITTANY**

Born: Abt 1092
    -CONTINUED AS #1,ROYAL CHART 215
Died:

1 **William De WELLE**

Born: Abt 1180
    -SAME AS #8,ROYAL CHART 1297
Married: Abt 1207

Died: Bef 1242

12

Born:

Married:

Died:

Emme De GRAINSBY

Spouse

6

Born:

Married:

Died:

13

Born:

Died:

3 **Maud**

Born:

Died:

14

Born:

Married:

Died:

7

Born:

Died:

15

Born:

Died:

Sources include: Faris preliminary baronial manuscript (1998), pp. 1632-33 (Welles).

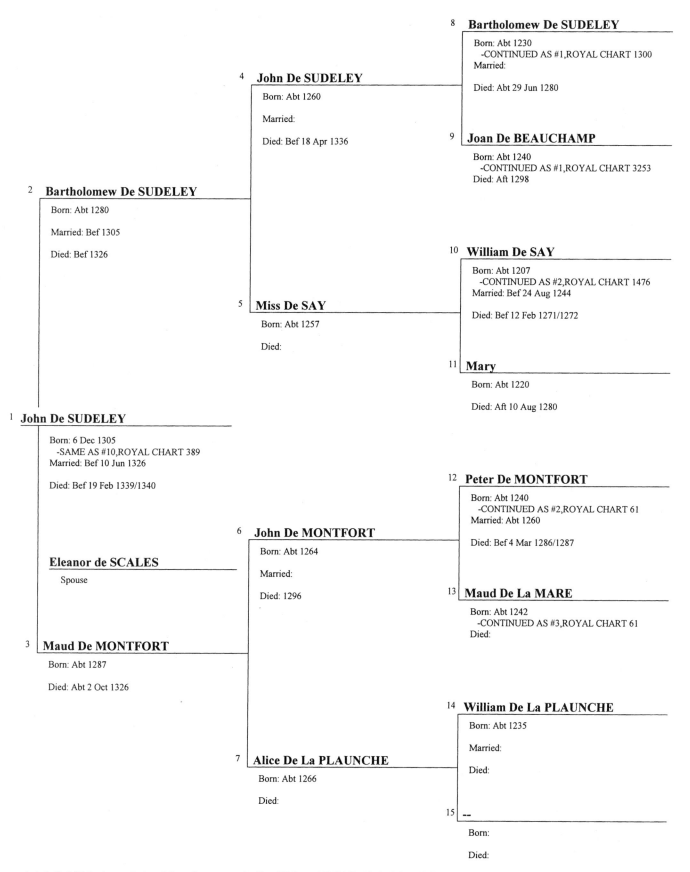

8 Bartholomew De SUDELEY

Born: Abt 1230
  -CONTINUED AS #1,ROYAL CHART 1300
Married:

Died: Abt 29 Jun 1280

4 John De SUDELEY

Born: Abt 1260

Married:

Died: Bef 18 Apr 1336

9 Joan De BEAUCHAMP

Born: Abt 1240
  -CONTINUED AS #1,ROYAL CHART 3253
Died: Aft 1298

2 Bartholomew De SUDELEY

Born: Abt 1280

Married: Bef 1305

Died: Bef 1326

10 William De SAY

Born: Abt 1207
  -CONTINUED AS #2,ROYAL CHART 1476
Married: Bef 24 Aug 1244

Died: Bef 12 Feb 1271/1272

5 Miss De SAY

Born: Abt 1257

Died:

11 Mary

Born: Abt 1220

Died: Aft 10 Aug 1280

1 John De SUDELEY

Born: 6 Dec 1305
  -SAME AS #10,ROYAL CHART 389
Married: Bef 10 Jun 1326

Died: Bef 19 Feb 1339/1340

12 Peter De MONTFORT

Born: Abt 1240
  -CONTINUED AS #2,ROYAL CHART 61
Married: Abt 1260

Died: Bef 4 Mar 1286/1287

6 John De MONTFORT

Born: Abt 1264

Married:

Died: 1296

Eleanor de SCALES

Spouse

13 Maud De La MARE

Born: Abt 1242
  -CONTINUED AS #3,ROYAL CHART 61
Died:

3 Maud De MONTFORT

Born: Abt 1287

Died: Abt 2 Oct 1326

14 William De La PLAUNCHE

Born: Abt 1235

Married:

Died:

7 Alice De La PLAUNCHE

Born: Abt 1266

Died:

15 --

Born:

Died:

Sources include: Faris-Richardson preliminary Magna Carta manuscript (June 2000), pp. 483-484 (Sudeley); Faris preliminary baronial manuscript (1998), pp. 1477 (Sudeley), 1114-15 (Montfort); *Ancestral Roots* 222; Roberts *500*, pp. 438-439 (#6 ancestry).

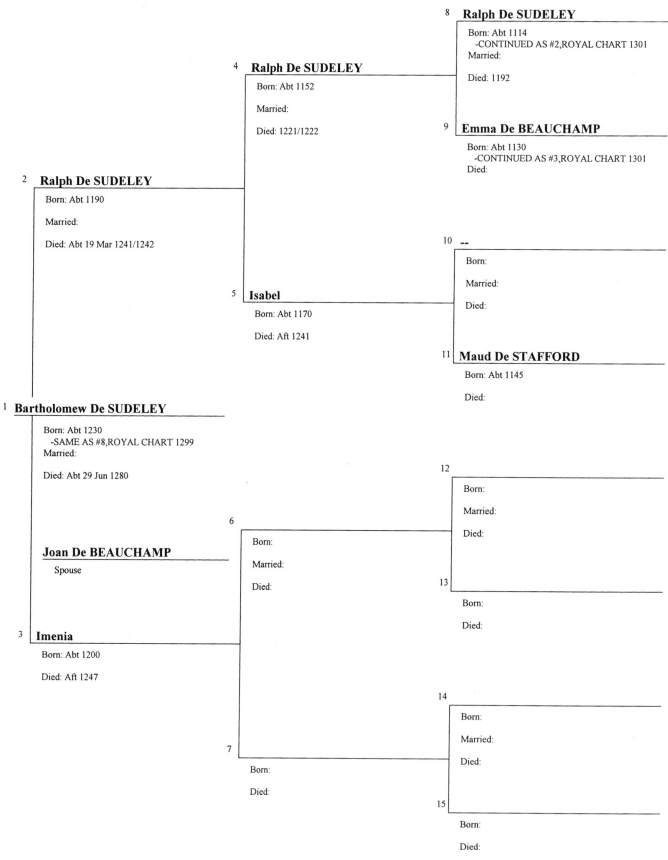

8 Ralph De SUDELEY

Born: Abt 1114
  -CONTINUED AS #2,ROYAL CHART 1301
Married:

Died: 1192

4 Ralph De SUDELEY

Born: Abt 1152

Married:

Died: 1221/1222

9 Emma De BEAUCHAMP

Born: Abt 1130
  -CONTINUED AS #3,ROYAL CHART 1301
Died:

2 Ralph De SUDELEY

Born: Abt 1190

Married:

Died: Abt 19 Mar 1241/1242

10 --

Born:

Married:

Died:

5 Isabel

Born: Abt 1170

Died: Aft 1241

11 Maud De STAFFORD

Born: Abt 1145

Died:

1 Bartholomew De SUDELEY

Born: Abt 1230
  -SAME AS #8,ROYAL CHART 1299
Married:

Died: Abt 29 Jun 1280

12

Born:

Married:

Died:

6

Born:

Married:

Died:

13

Born:

Died:

Joan De BEAUCHAMP

Spouse

3 Imenia

Born: Abt 1200

Died: Aft 1247

14

Born:

Married:

Died:

7

Born:

Died:

15

Born:

Died:

Sources include: *Ancestral Roots* 8 (2004), Line 222; *Ancestral Roots* 222; *Complete Peerage* 12 (part 1): 413-415; Faris preliminary baronial manuscript (1998), pp. 1476-77 (Sudeley).

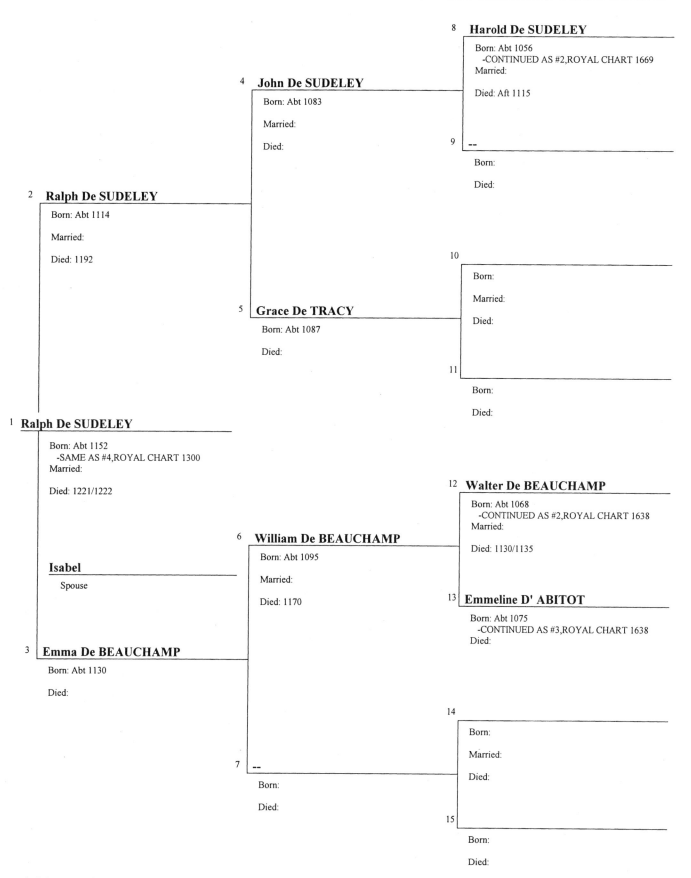

8 | **Harold De SUDELEY**
Born: Abt 1056
 -CONTINUED AS #2,ROYAL CHART 1669
Married:

Died: Aft 1115

4 | **John De SUDELEY**
Born: Abt 1083

Married:

Died:

9 | **--**
Born:

Died:

2 | **Ralph De SUDELEY**
Born: Abt 1114

Married:

Died: 1192

10 |
Born:

Married:

Died:

5 | **Grace De TRACY**
Born: Abt 1087

Died:

11 |
Born:

Died:

1 | **Ralph De SUDELEY**
Born: Abt 1152
 -SAME AS #4,ROYAL CHART 1300
Married:

Died: 1221/1222

Isabel
Spouse

12 | **Walter De BEAUCHAMP**
Born: Abt 1068
 -CONTINUED AS #2,ROYAL CHART 1638
Married:

Died: 1130/1135

6 | **William De BEAUCHAMP**
Born: Abt 1095

Married:

Died: 1170

13 | **Emmeline D' ABITOT**
Born: Abt 1075
 -CONTINUED AS #3,ROYAL CHART 1638
Died:

3 | **Emma De BEAUCHAMP**
Born: Abt 1130

Died:

14 |
Born:

Married:

Died:

7 | **--**
Born:

Died:

15 |
Born:

Died:

Sources include: *Ancestral Roots* 8 (2004), Lines 222, 235; *Ancestral Roots* 222, 235; Faris preliminary baronial manuscript (1998), pp. 1476-77 (Sudeley), 56-57 (Beauchamp).
Note: *Ancestral Roots* gives #7 as Bertha De Braose, daughter of William De Braose & Bertha De Gloucester (compare charts 1603, 1615). The claim is chronologically difficult. The Faris version is accepted here. *Ancestral Roots* 8 reinstates a previous claim that #5 Grace was daughter of William De Tracy and granddaughter of King Henry I (see chart 186). That claim is also chronologically difficult and is being rejected here.

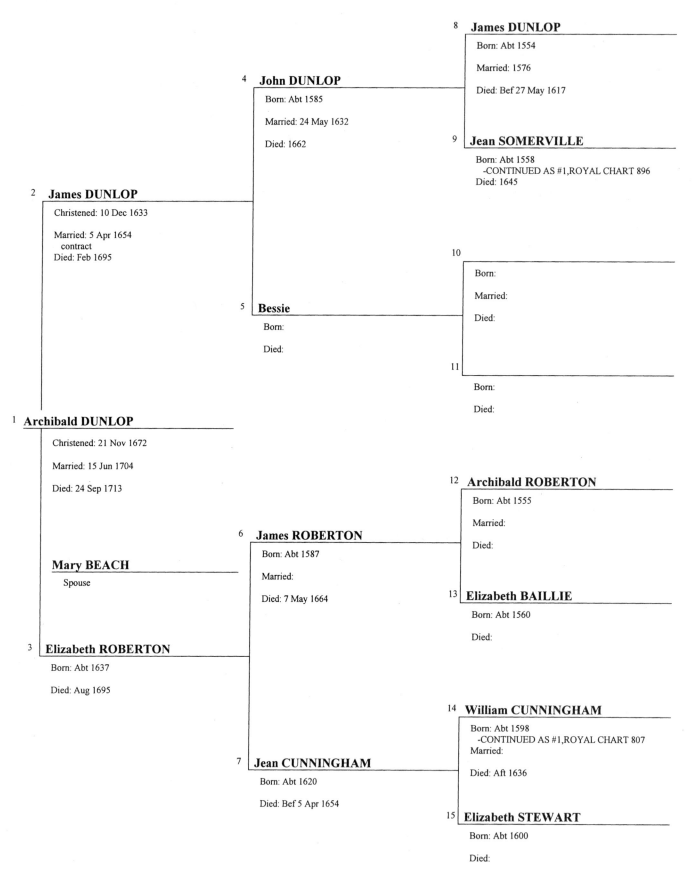

8 James DUNLOP

Born: Abt 1554

Married: 1576

Died: Bef 27 May 1617

4 John DUNLOP

Born: Abt 1585

Married: 24 May 1632

Died: 1662

9 Jean SOMERVILLE

Born: Abt 1558
 -CONTINUED AS #1,ROYAL CHART 896
Died: 1645

2 James DUNLOP

Christened: 10 Dec 1633

Married: 5 Apr 1654
 contract
Died: Feb 1695

10

Born:

Married:

Died:

5 Bessie

Born:

Died:

11

Born:

Died:

1 Archibald DUNLOP

Christened: 21 Nov 1672

Married: 15 Jun 1704

Died: 24 Sep 1713

12 Archibald ROBERTON

Born: Abt 1555

Married:

Died:

6 James ROBERTON

Born: Abt 1587

Married:

Died: 7 May 1664

13 Elizabeth BAILLIE

Born: Abt 1560

Died:

Mary BEACH

Spouse

3 Elizabeth ROBERTON

Born: Abt 1637

Died: Aug 1695

14 William CUNNINGHAM

Born: Abt 1598
 -CONTINUED AS #1,ROYAL CHART 807
Married:

Died: Aft 1636

7 Jean CUNNINGHAM

Born: Abt 1620

Died: Bef 5 Apr 1654

15 Elizabeth STEWART

Born: Abt 1600

Died:

Sources include: *NEHGR* 152:186-196 (1998); 154:321-324 (July 2000).

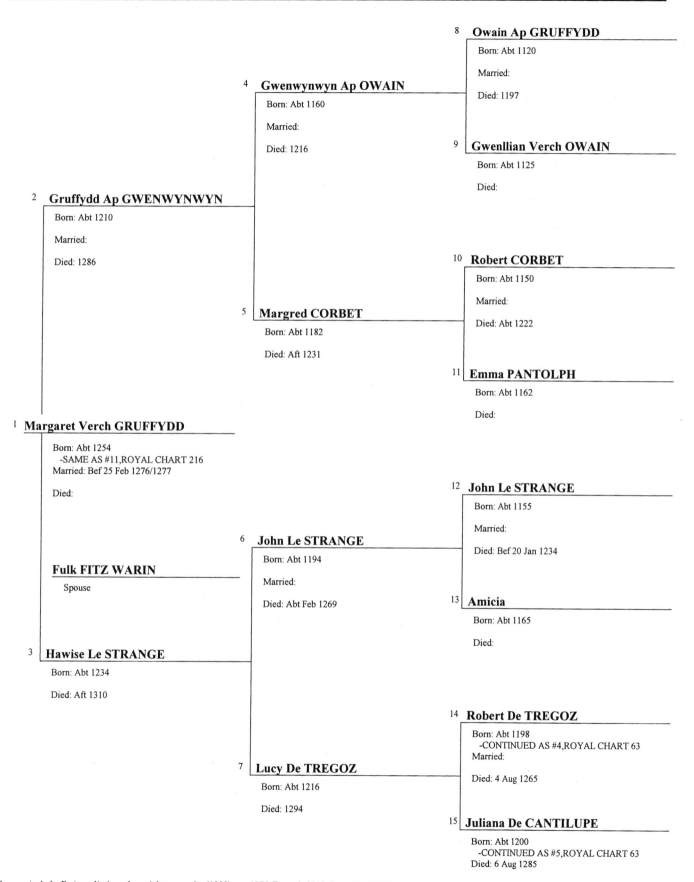

8 Owain Ap GRUFFYDD
Born: Abt 1120
Married:
Died: 1197

4 Gwenwynwyn Ap OWAIN
Born: Abt 1160
Married:
Died: 1216

9 Gwenllian Verch OWAIN
Born: Abt 1125
Died:

2 Gruffydd Ap GWENWYNWYN
Born: Abt 1210
Married:
Died: 1286

10 Robert CORBET
Born: Abt 1150
Married:
Died: Abt 1222

5 Margred CORBET
Born: Abt 1182
Died: Aft 1231

11 Emma PANTOLPH
Born: Abt 1162
Died:

1 Margaret Verch GRUFFYDD
Born: Abt 1254
-SAME AS #11,ROYAL CHART 216
Married: Bef 25 Feb 1276/1277
Died:

12 John Le STRANGE
Born: Abt 1155
Married:
Died: Bef 20 Jan 1234

6 John Le STRANGE
Born: Abt 1194
Married:
Died: Abt Feb 1269

13 Amicia
Born: Abt 1165
Died:

Fulk FITZ WARIN
Spouse

3 Hawise Le STRANGE
Born: Abt 1234
Died: Aft 1310

14 Robert De TREGOZ
Born: Abt 1198
-CONTINUED AS #4,ROYAL CHART 63
Married:
Died: 4 Aug 1265

7 Lucy De TREGOZ
Born: Abt 1216
Died: 1294

15 Juliana De CANTILUPE
Born: Abt 1200
-CONTINUED AS #5,ROYAL CHART 63
Died: 6 Aug 1285

Sources include: Faris preliminary baronial manuscript (1998), pp. 1276 (Powys), 1459 (Strange); *NEHGR* 140:227-228; LDS records (#2 & 3 ancestry).

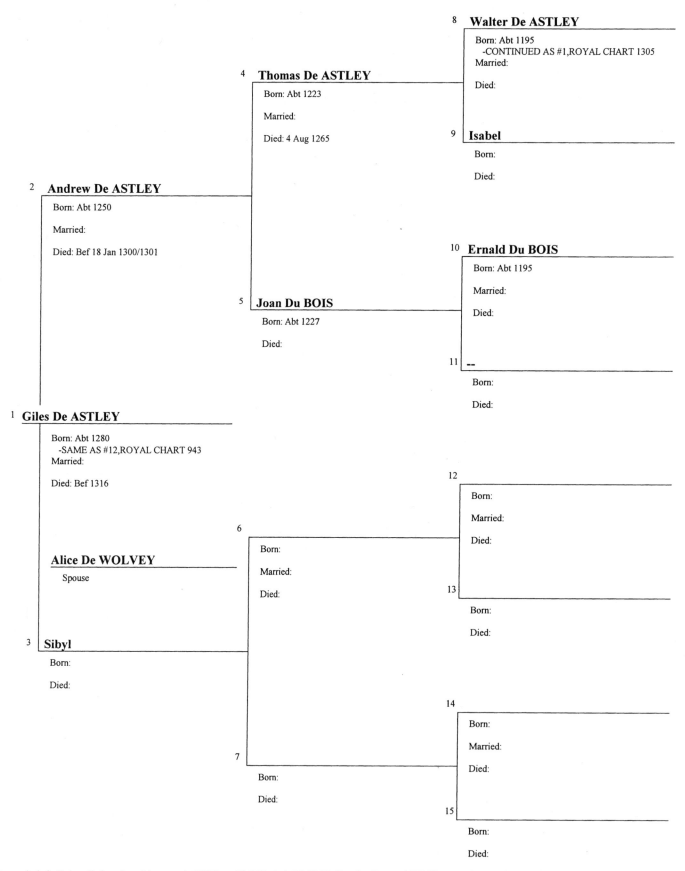

8 Walter De ASTLEY

Born: Abt 1195
-CONTINUED AS #1,ROYAL CHART 1305
Married:

Died:

4 Thomas De ASTLEY

Born: Abt 1223

Married:

Died: 4 Aug 1265

9 Isabel

Born:

Died:

2 Andrew De ASTLEY

Born: Abt 1250

Married:

Died: Bef 18 Jan 1300/1301

10 Ernald Du BOIS

Born: Abt 1195

Married:

Died:

5 Joan Du BOIS

Born: Abt 1227

Died:

11 --

Born:

Died:

1 Giles De ASTLEY

Born: Abt 1280
-SAME AS #12,ROYAL CHART 943
Married:

Died: Bef 1316

12

Born:

Married:

Died:

6

Born:

Married:

Died:

13

Born:

Died:

Alice De WOLVEY

Spouse

3 Sibyl

Born:

Died:

14

Born:

Married:

Died:

7

Born:

Died:

15

Born:

Died:

Sources include: Faris preliminary baronial manuscript (1998), pp. 13-14 (Astley), 144 (Bois); *Complete Peerage* 1:283 (#2 ancestry). Note: #10 Ernald appears to be the same person as Arnold De Bois (chart 322, #12).

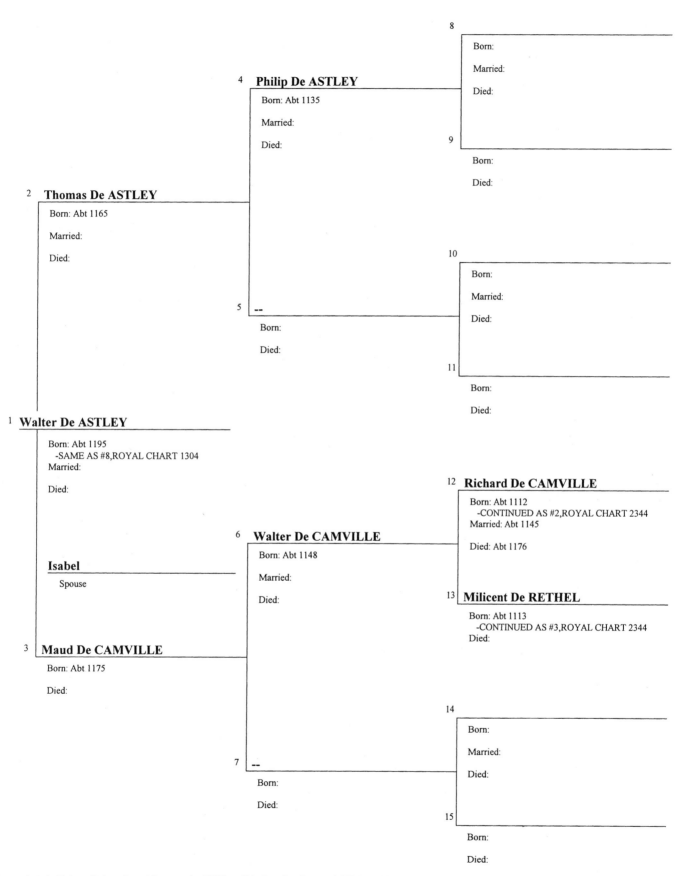

8

Born:

Married:

Died:

4 Philip De ASTLEY

Born: Abt 1135

Married:

Died:

9

Born:

Died:

2 Thomas De ASTLEY

Born: Abt 1165

Married:

Died:

10

Born:

Married:

Died:

5 --

Born:

Died:

11

Born:

Died:

1 Walter De ASTLEY

Born: Abt 1195
   -SAME AS #8,ROYAL CHART 1304
Married:

Died:

12 Richard De CAMVILLE

Born: Abt 1112
   -CONTINUED AS #2,ROYAL CHART 2344
Married: Abt 1145

Died: Abt 1176

6 Walter De CAMVILLE

Born: Abt 1148

Married:

Died:

13 Milicent De RETHEL

Born: Abt 1113
   -CONTINUED AS #3,ROYAL CHART 2344
Died:

Isabel

Spouse

3 Maud De CAMVILLE

Born: Abt 1175

Died:

14

Born:

Married:

Died:

7 --

Born:

Died:

15

Born:

Died:

Sources include: Faris preliminary baronial manuscript (1998), p. 113; *Complete Peerage* 1:283; Paget (1957) 115:2-3 (#3 ancestry).

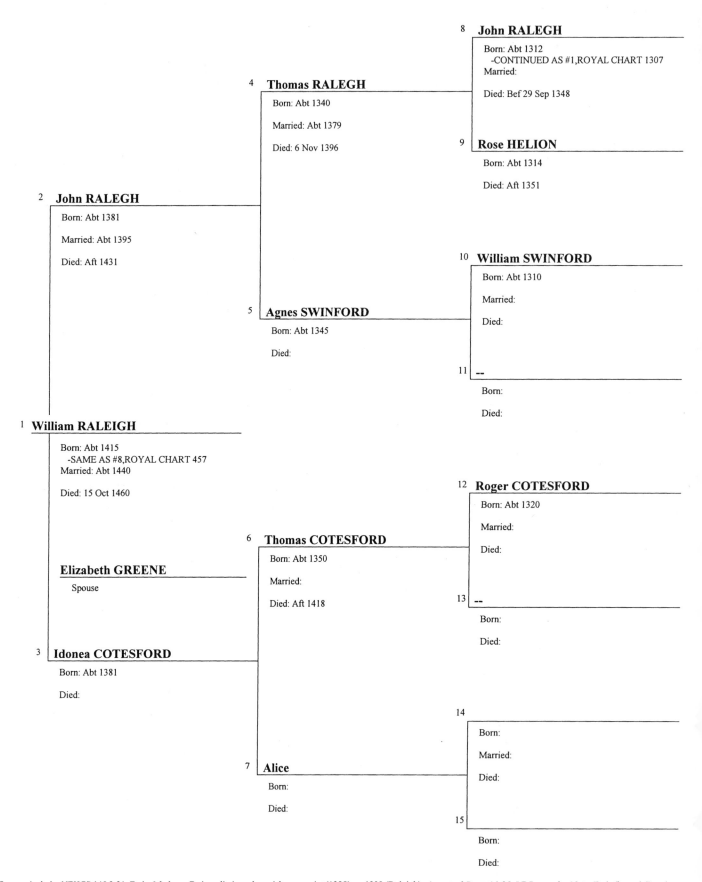

8 **John RALEGH**

Born: Abt 1312
    -CONTINUED AS #1,ROYAL CHART 1307
Married:

Died: Bef 29 Sep 1348

4 **Thomas RALEGH**

Born: Abt 1340

Married: Abt 1379

Died: 6 Nov 1396

9 **Rose HELION**

Born: Abt 1314

Died: Aft 1351

2 **John RALEGH**

Born: Abt 1381

Married: Abt 1395

Died: Aft 1431

10 **William SWINFORD**

Born: Abt 1310

Married:

Died:

5 **Agnes SWINFORD**

Born: Abt 1345

Died:

11 **--**

Born:

Died:

1 **William RALEIGH**

Born: Abt 1415
    -SAME AS #8,ROYAL CHART 457
Married: Abt 1440

Died: 15 Oct 1460

Elizabeth GREENE

Spouse

12 **Roger COTESFORD**

Born: Abt 1320

Married:

Died:

6 **Thomas COTESFORD**

Born: Abt 1350

Married:

Died: Aft 1418

13 **--**

Born:

Died:

3 **Idonea COTESFORD**

Born: Abt 1381

Died:

14

Born:

Married:

Died:

7 **Alice**

Born:

Died:

15

Born:

Died:

Sources include: *NEHGR* 145:3-21; Faris--Marbury; Faris preliminary baronial manuscript (1998), p. 1309 (Raleigh); *Ancestral Roots* 14-35; LDS records. Note: Faris (baronial) and LDS records insert an additional generation (Henry Raleigh md. Miss Bennet) between #2 John and #4 Thomas above. The *NEHGR* version is shown above.

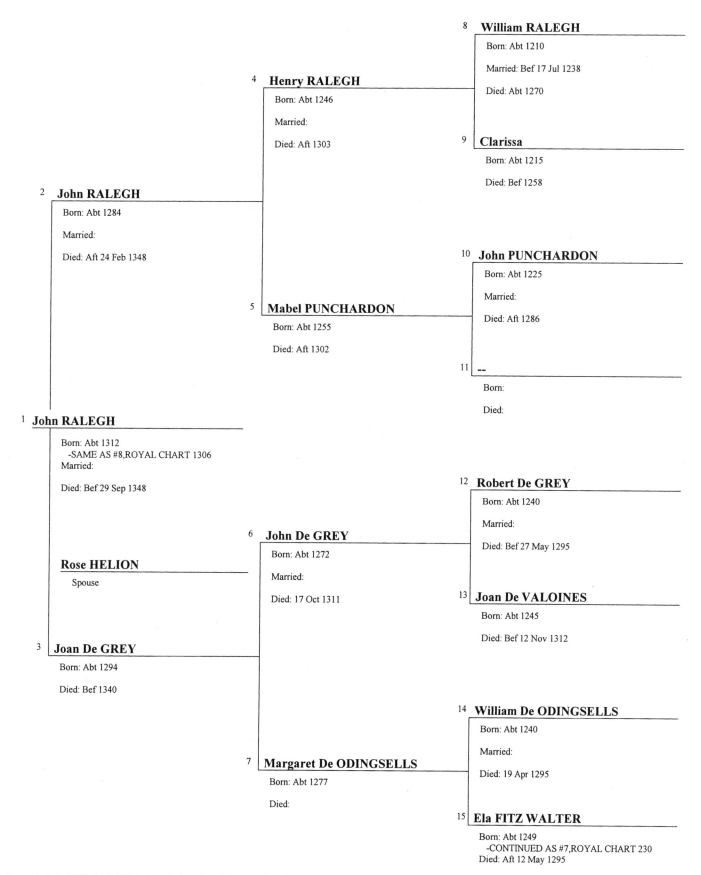

2 John RALEGH
Born: Abt 1284
Married:
Died: Aft 24 Feb 1348

4 Henry RALEGH
Born: Abt 1246
Married:
Died: Aft 1303

8 William RALEGH
Born: Abt 1210
Married: Bef 17 Jul 1238
Died: Abt 1270

9 Clarissa
Born: Abt 1215
Died: Bef 1258

5 Mabel PUNCHARDON
Born: Abt 1255
Died: Aft 1302

10 John PUNCHARDON
Born: Abt 1225
Married:
Died: Aft 1286

11 --
Born:
Died:

1 John RALEGH
Born: Abt 1312
-SAME AS #8,ROYAL CHART 1306
Married:
Died: Bef 29 Sep 1348

Rose HELION
Spouse

3 Joan De GREY
Born: Abt 1294
Died: Bef 1340

6 John De GREY
Born: Abt 1272
Married:
Died: 17 Oct 1311

12 Robert De GREY
Born: Abt 1240
Married:
Died: Bef 27 May 1295

13 Joan De VALOINES
Born: Abt 1245
Died: Bef 12 Nov 1312

7 Margaret De ODINGSELLS
Born: Abt 1277
Died:

14 William De ODINGSELLS
Born: Abt 1240
Married:
Died: 19 Apr 1295

15 Ela FITZ WALTER
Born: Abt 1249
-CONTINUED AS #7,ROYAL CHART 230
Died: Aft 12 May 1295

Sources include: *NEHGR* 145:3-21; Faris preliminary baronial manuscript (1998), p. 1309 (Raleigh); *Ancestral Roots* 30 (#6 & 7 ancestry). Note: Faris shows #4 as Walter, son of Henry, son of Peter De Raleigh (md. Margaret, daughter of Philip Daubeny). The *NEHGR* version is shown above.

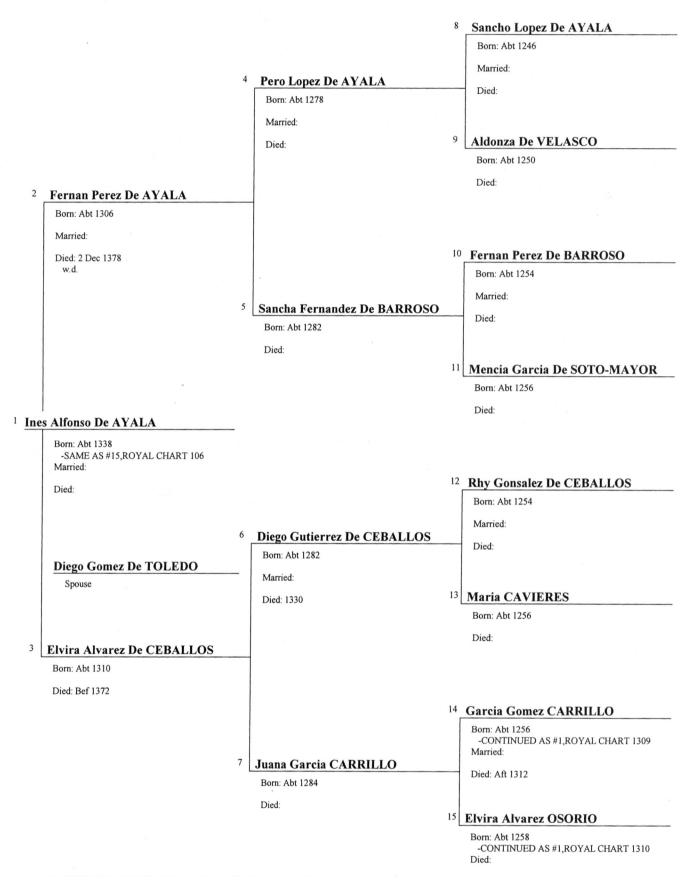

8 **Sancho Lopez De AYALA**

Born: Abt 1246

Married:

Died:

4 **Pero Lopez De AYALA**

Born: Abt 1278

Married:

Died:

9 **Aldonza De VELASCO**

Born: Abt 1250

Died:

2 **Fernan Perez De AYALA**

Born: Abt 1306

Married:

Died: 2 Dec 1378
w.d.

10 **Fernan Perez De BARROSO**

Born: Abt 1254

Married:

Died:

5 **Sancha Fernandez De BARROSO**

Born: Abt 1282

Died:

11 **Mencia Garcia De SOTO-MAYOR**

Born: Abt 1256

Died:

1 **Ines Alfonso De AYALA**

Born: Abt 1338
-SAME AS #15,ROYAL CHART 106
Married:

Died:

12 **Rhy Gonsalez De CEBALLOS**

Born: Abt 1254

Married:

Died:

6 **Diego Gutierrez De CEBALLOS**

Born: Abt 1282

Married:

Died: 1330

13 **Maria CAVIERES**

Born: Abt 1256

Died:

Diego Gomez De TOLEDO

Spouse

3 **Elvira Alvarez De CEBALLOS**

Born: Abt 1310

Died: Bef 1372

14 **Garcia Gomez CARRILLO**

Born: Abt 1256
-CONTINUED AS #1,ROYAL CHART 1309
Married:

Died: Aft 1312

7 **Juana Garcia CARRILLO**

Born: Abt 1284

Died:

15 **Elvira Alvarez OSORIO**

Born: Abt 1258
-CONTINUED AS #1,ROYAL CHART 1310
Died:

Sources include: *NEHGR* 152:36-48 (1998); LDS records. Note: #12 Rhy was son of Gonsalo Diaz De Ceballos & Antolina De Hoces (continued chart 53, #2 & 3), but no descent from English or French kings is apparent.

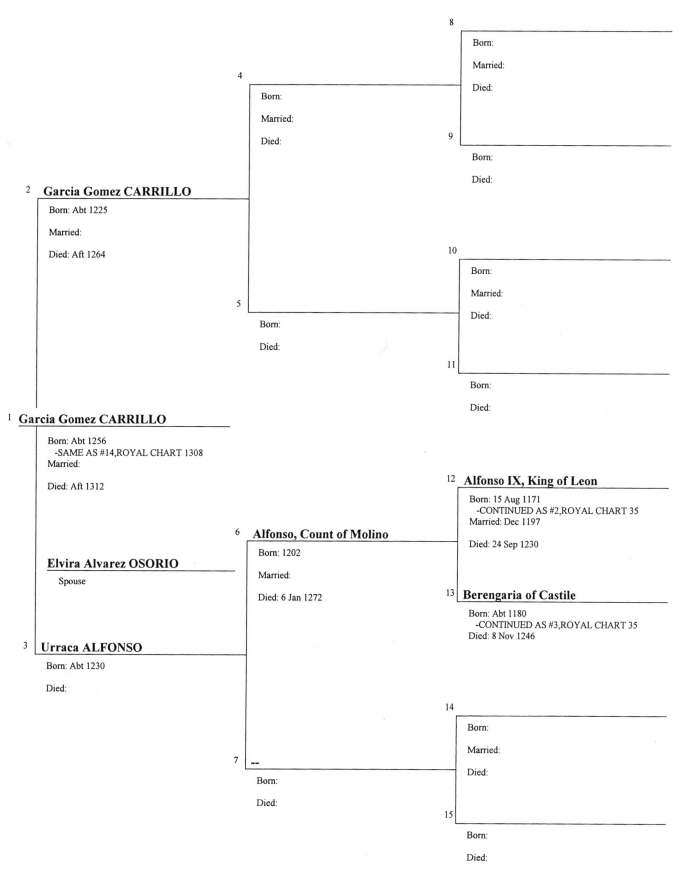

8

Born:

Married:

Died:

4

Born:

Married:

Died:

9

Born:

Died:

2 Garcia Gomez CARRILLO

Born: Abt 1225

Married:

Died: Aft 1264

10

Born:

Married:

Died:

5

Born:

Died:

11

Born:

Died:

1 Garcia Gomez CARRILLO

Born: Abt 1256
-SAME AS #14,ROYAL CHART 1308
Married:

Died: Aft 1312

12 Alfonso IX, King of Leon

Born: 15 Aug 1171
-CONTINUED AS #2,ROYAL CHART 35
Married: Dec 1197

Died: 24 Sep 1230

6 Alfonso, Count of Molino

Born: 1202

Married:

Died: 6 Jan 1272

13 Berengaria of Castile

Born: Abt 1180
-CONTINUED AS #3,ROYAL CHART 35
Died: 8 Nov 1246

Elvira Alvarez OSORIO

Spouse

3 Urraca ALFONSO

Born: Abt 1230

Died:

14

Born:

Married:

Died:

7 --

Born:

Died:

15

Born:

Died:

Sources include: *NEHGR* 152:36-48 (1998); Richardson *Plantagenet* (2004), pp. 190-191 Castile (#3 ancestry).

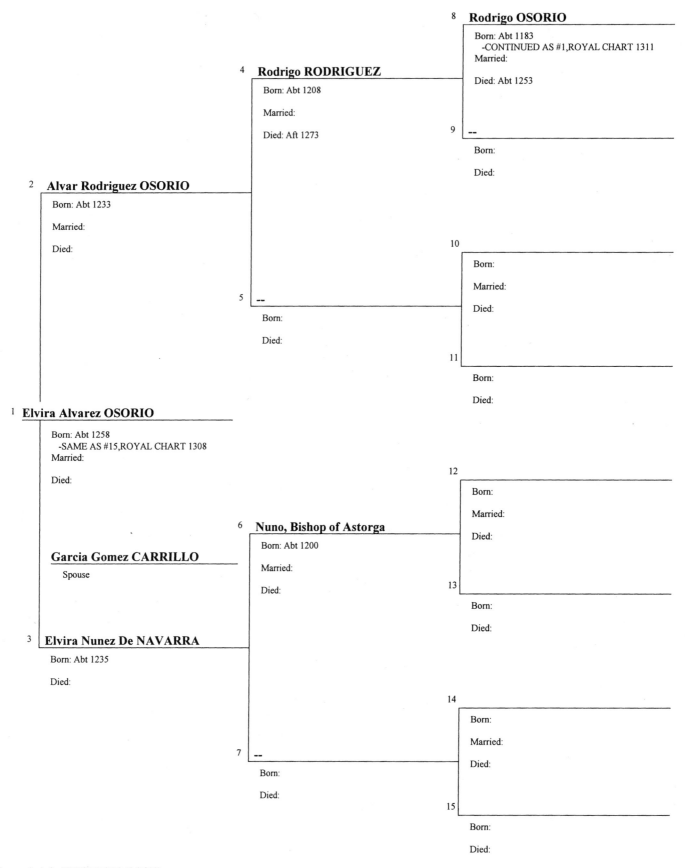

8 **Rodrigo OSORIO**

Born: Abt 1183
  -CONTINUED AS #1,ROYAL CHART 1311
Married:

Died: Abt 1253

4 **Rodrigo RODRIGUEZ**

Born: Abt 1208

Married:

Died: Aft 1273

9 --

Born:

Died:

2 **Alvar Rodriguez OSORIO**

Born: Abt 1233

Married:

Died:

10

Born:

Married:

Died:

5 --

Born:

Died:

11

Born:

Died:

1 **Elvira Alvarez OSORIO**

Born: Abt 1258
  -SAME AS #15,ROYAL CHART 1308
Married:

Died:

12

Born:

Married:

Died:

6 **Nuno, Bishop of Astorga**

Born: Abt 1200

Married:

Died:

13

Born:

Died:

Garcia Gomez CARRILLO

Spouse

3 **Elvira Nunez De NAVARRA**

Born: Abt 1235

Died:

14

Born:

Married:

Died:

7 --

Born:

Died:

15

Born:

Died:

Sources include: *NEHGR* 152:36-48 (1998).

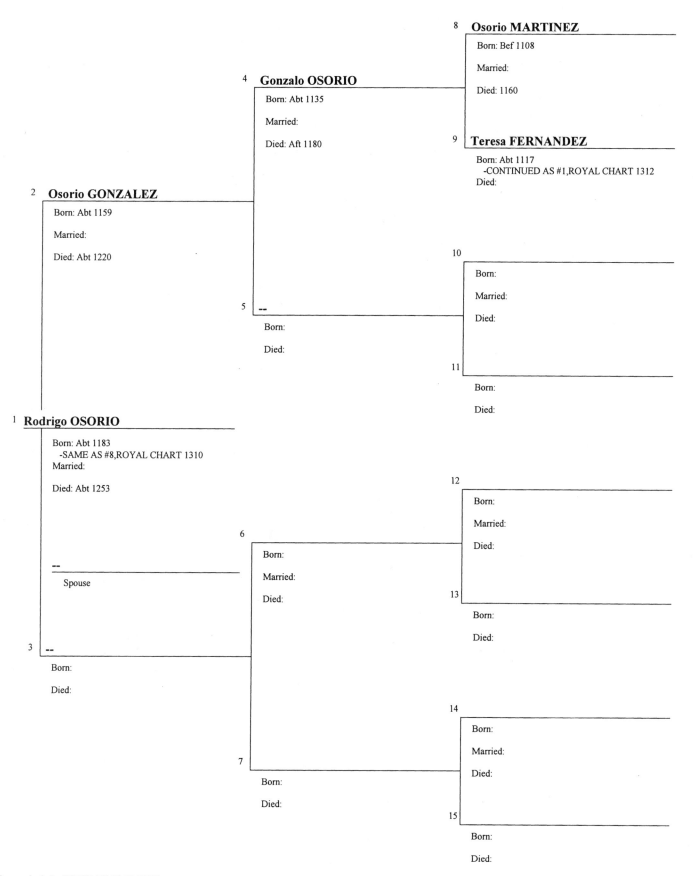

8 Osorio MARTINEZ
Born: Bef 1108
Married:
Died: 1160

4 Gonzalo OSORIO
Born: Abt 1135
Married:
Died: Aft 1180

9 Teresa FERNANDEZ
Born: Abt 1117
  -CONTINUED AS #1,ROYAL CHART 1312
Died:

2 Osorio GONZALEZ
Born: Abt 1159
Married:
Died: Abt 1220

10
Born:
Married:
Died:

5 --
Born:
Died:

11
Born:
Died:

1 Rodrigo OSORIO
Born: Abt 1183
  -SAME AS #8,ROYAL CHART 1310
Married:
Died: Abt 1253

12
Born:
Married:
Died:

6 --
Born:
Married:
Died:

13
Born:
Died:

--
  Spouse

3 --
Born:
Died:

14
Born:
Married:
Died:

7 --
Born:
Died:

15
Born:
Died:

Sources include: *NEHGR* 152:36-48 (1998).

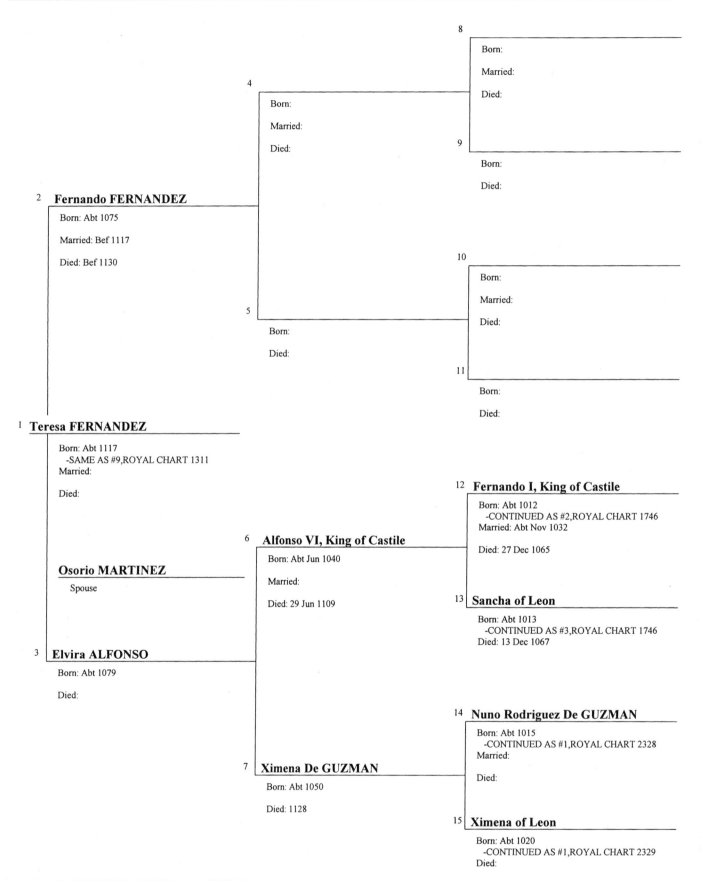

8
Born:
Married:
Died:

4
Born:
Married:
Died:

9
Born:
Died:

2 **Fernando FERNANDEZ**
Born: Abt 1075
Married: Bef 1117
Died: Bef 1130

10
Born:
Married:
Died:

5
Born:
Died:

11
Born:
Died:

1 **Teresa FERNANDEZ**
Born: Abt 1117
-SAME AS #9,ROYAL CHART 1311
Married:

Died:

12 **Fernando I, King of Castile**
Born: Abt 1012
-CONTINUED AS #2,ROYAL CHART 1746
Married: Abt Nov 1032

Died: 27 Dec 1065

6 **Alfonso VI, King of Castile**
Born: Abt Jun 1040
Married:
Died: 29 Jun 1109

13 **Sancha of Leon**
Born: Abt 1013
-CONTINUED AS #3,ROYAL CHART 1746
Died: 13 Dec 1067

Osorio MARTINEZ
Spouse

3 **Elvira ALFONSO**
Born: Abt 1079

Died:

14 **Nuno Rodriguez De GUZMAN**
Born: Abt 1015
-CONTINUED AS #1,ROYAL CHART 2328
Married:

Died:

7 **Ximena De GUZMAN**
Born: Abt 1050
Died: 1128

15 **Ximena of Leon**
Born: Abt 1020
-CONTINUED AS #1,ROYAL CHART 2329
Died:

Sources include: *NEHGR* 152:36-48 (1998); Moriarty 82 (#6 & 7 ancestry).

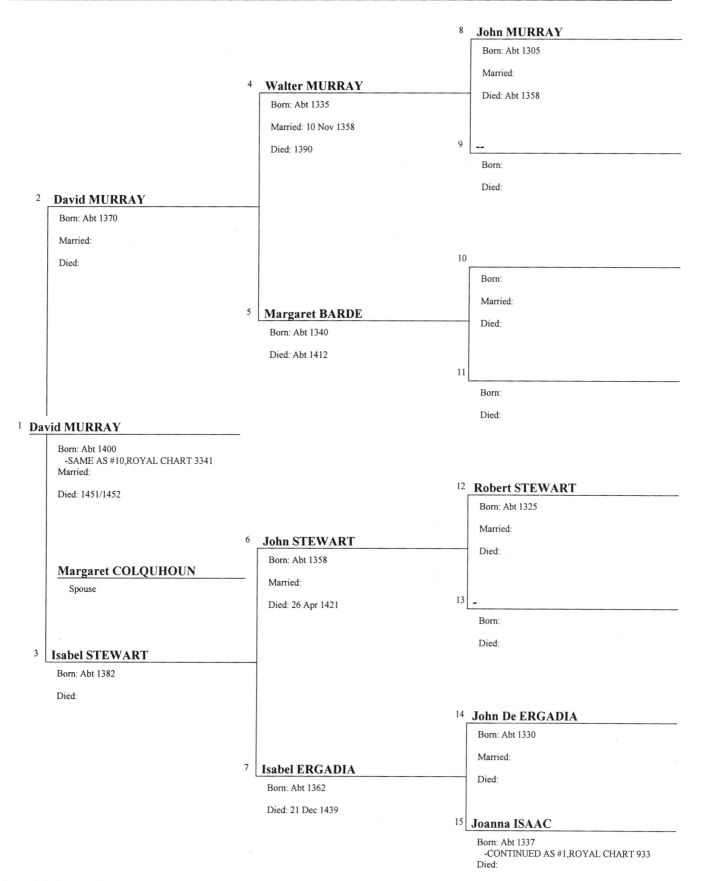

8 **John MURRAY**

Born: Abt 1305

Married:

Died: Abt 1358

4 **Walter MURRAY**

Born: Abt 1335

Married: 10 Nov 1358

Died: 1390

9 **--**

Born:

Died:

2 **David MURRAY**

Born: Abt 1370

Married:

Died:

10

Born:

Married:

Died:

5 **Margaret BARDE**

Born: Abt 1340

Died: Abt 1412

11

Born:

Died:

1 **David MURRAY**

Born: Abt 1400
-SAME AS #10,ROYAL CHART 3341
Married:

Died: 1451/1452

12 **Robert STEWART**

Born: Abt 1325

Married:

Died:

6 **John STEWART**

Born: Abt 1358

Married:

Died: 26 Apr 1421

Margaret COLQUHOUN

Spouse

13 **-**

Born:

Died:

3 **Isabel STEWART**

Born: Abt 1382

Died:

14 **John De ERGADIA**

Born: Abt 1330

Married:

Died:

7 **Isabel ERGADIA**

Born: Abt 1362

Died: 21 Dec 1439

15 **Joanna ISAAC**

Born: Abt 1337
-CONTINUED AS #1,ROYAL CHART 933
Died:

Sources include: Ernest Flagg Henderson III, Pedigree Chart BTJW; LDS records.

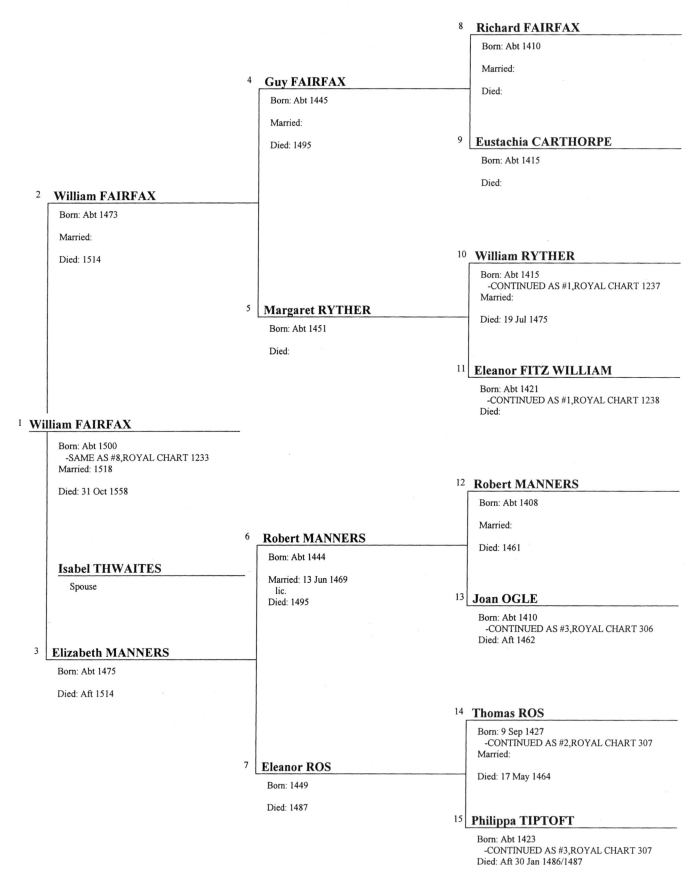

8 **Richard FAIRFAX**
Born: Abt 1410
Married:
Died:

4 **Guy FAIRFAX**
Born: Abt 1445
Married:
Died: 1495

9 **Eustachia CARTHORPE**
Born: Abt 1415
Died:

2 **William FAIRFAX**
Born: Abt 1473
Married:
Died: 1514

10 **William RYTHER**
Born: Abt 1415
-CONTINUED AS #1,ROYAL CHART 1237
Married:
Died: 19 Jul 1475

5 **Margaret RYTHER**
Born: Abt 1451
Died:

11 **Eleanor FITZ WILLIAM**
Born: Abt 1421
-CONTINUED AS #1,ROYAL CHART 1238
Died:

1 **William FAIRFAX**
Born: Abt 1500
-SAME AS #8,ROYAL CHART 1233
Married: 1518
Died: 31 Oct 1558

Isabel THWAITES
Spouse

12 **Robert MANNERS**
Born: Abt 1408
Married:
Died: 1461

6 **Robert MANNERS**
Born: Abt 1444
Married: 13 Jun 1469
lic.
Died: 1495

13 **Joan OGLE**
Born: Abt 1410
-CONTINUED AS #3,ROYAL CHART 306
Died: Aft 1462

3 **Elizabeth MANNERS**
Born: Abt 1475
Died: Aft 1514

14 **Thomas ROS**
Born: 9 Sep 1427
-CONTINUED AS #2,ROYAL CHART 307
Married:
Died: 17 May 1464

7 **Eleanor ROS**
Born: 1449
Died: 1487

15 **Philippa TIPTOFT**
Born: Abt 1423
-CONTINUED AS #3,ROYAL CHART 307
Died: Aft 30 Jan 1486/1487

Sources include: Richardson *Plantagenet* (2004), pp. 110-111 (Bladen), 489 (Manners); Faris 2--Bladen, Stapleton; LDS records.

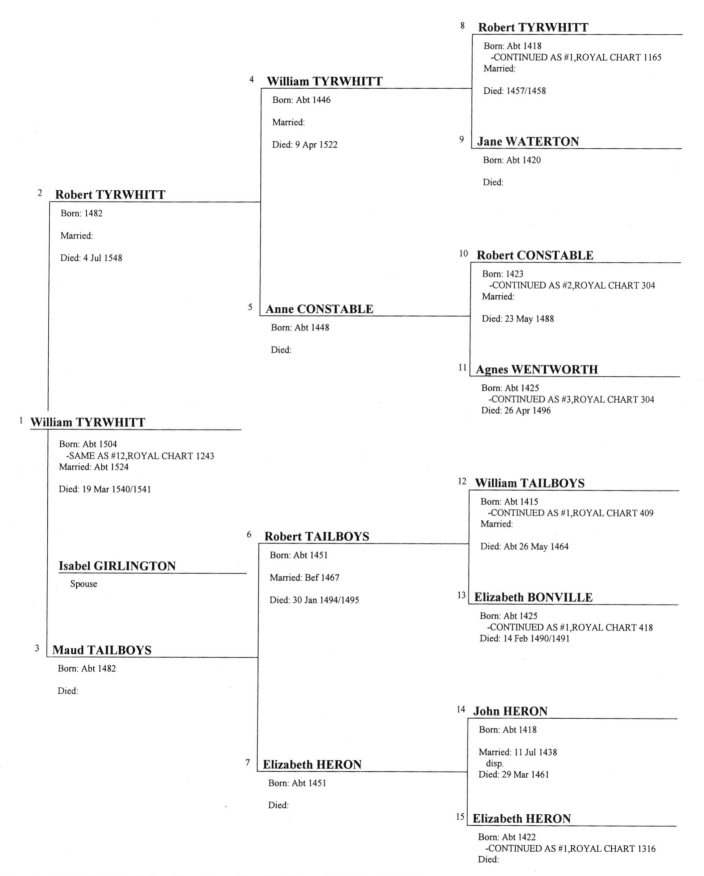

8 Robert TYRWHITT
Born: Abt 1418
 -CONTINUED AS #1,ROYAL CHART 1165
Married:

Died: 1457/1458

4 William TYRWHITT
Born: Abt 1446

Married:

Died: 9 Apr 1522

9 Jane WATERTON
Born: Abt 1420

Died:

2 Robert TYRWHITT
Born: 1482

Married:

Died: 4 Jul 1548

10 Robert CONSTABLE
Born: 1423
 -CONTINUED AS #2,ROYAL CHART 304
Married:

Died: 23 May 1488

5 Anne CONSTABLE
Born: Abt 1448

Died:

11 Agnes WENTWORTH
Born: Abt 1425
 -CONTINUED AS #3,ROYAL CHART 304
Died: 26 Apr 1496

1 William TYRWHITT
Born: Abt 1504
 -SAME AS #12,ROYAL CHART 1243
Married: Abt 1524

Died: 19 Mar 1540/1541

12 William TAILBOYS
Born: Abt 1415
 -CONTINUED AS #1,ROYAL CHART 409
Married:

Died: Abt 26 May 1464

6 Robert TAILBOYS
Born: Abt 1451

Married: Bef 1467

Died: 30 Jan 1494/1495

13 Elizabeth BONVILLE
Born: Abt 1425
 -CONTINUED AS #1,ROYAL CHART 418
Died: 14 Feb 1490/1491

Isabel GIRLINGTON
Spouse

3 Maud TAILBOYS
Born: Abt 1482

Died:

14 John HERON
Born: Abt 1418

Married: 11 Jul 1438
 disp.
Died: 29 Mar 1461

7 Elizabeth HERON
Born: Abt 1451

Died:

15 Elizabeth HERON
Born: Abt 1422
 -CONTINUED AS #1,ROYAL CHART 1316
Died:

Sources include: Faris 2--Tyrwhitt, Tailboys, Heron; *Ancestral Roots* 224; LDS records; *Blood Royal* 5:189-190, 522.

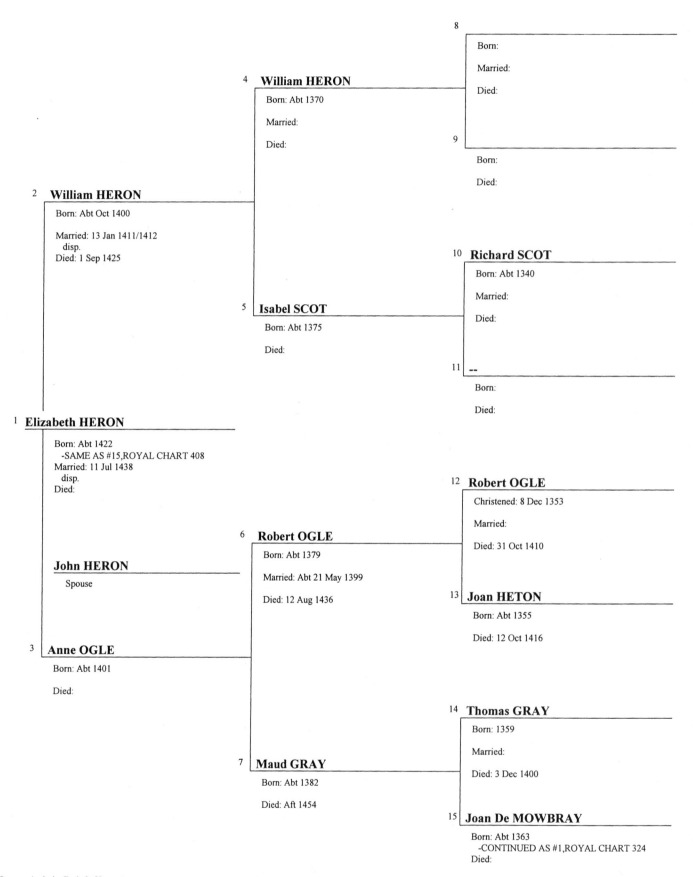

8

William HERON

Born: Abt 1370

Married:

Died:

Born:

Married:

Died:

9

Born:

Died:

2 **William HERON**

Born: Abt Oct 1400

Married: 13 Jan 1411/1412
  disp.
Died: 1 Sep 1425

10 **Richard SCOT**

Born: Abt 1340

Married:

Died:

5 **Isabel SCOT**

Born: Abt 1375

Died:

11 **--**

Born:

Died:

1 **Elizabeth HERON**

Born: Abt 1422
  -SAME AS #15,ROYAL CHART 408
Married: 11 Jul 1438
  disp.
Died:

12 **Robert OGLE**

Christened: 8 Dec 1353

Married:

Died: 31 Oct 1410

6 **Robert OGLE**

Born: Abt 1379

Married: Abt 21 May 1399

Died: 12 Aug 1436

13 **Joan HETON**

Born: Abt 1355

Died: 12 Oct 1416

John HERON

Spouse

3 **Anne OGLE**

Born: Abt 1401

Died:

14 **Thomas GRAY**

Born: 1359

Married:

Died: 3 Dec 1400

7 **Maud GRAY**

Born: Abt 1382

Died: Aft 1454

15 **Joan De MOWBRAY**

Born: Abt 1363
  -CONTINUED AS #1,ROYAL CHART 324
Died:

Sources include: Faris 2--Heron.

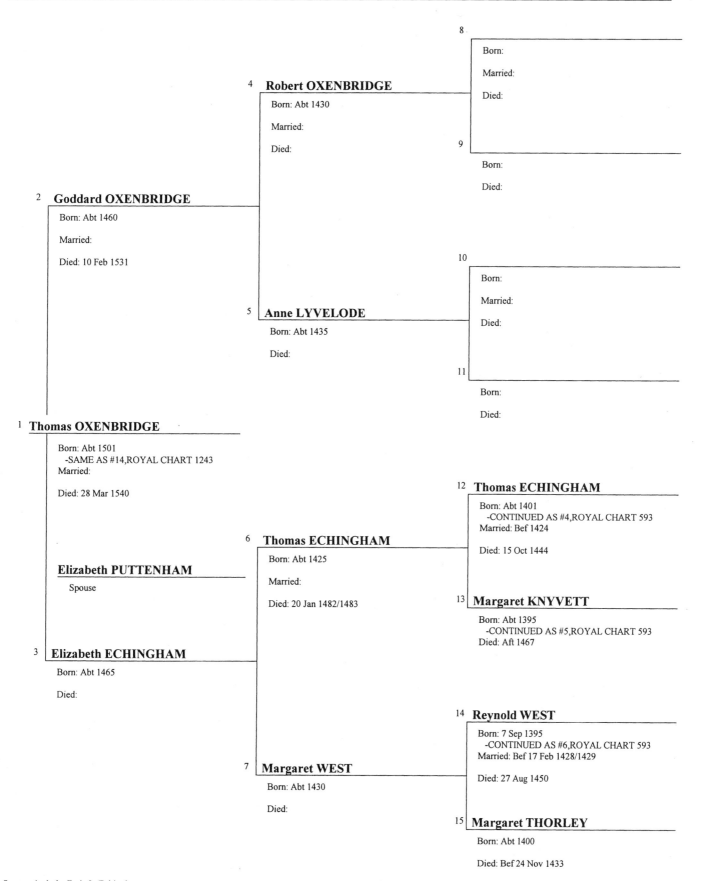

8

Born:

Married:

Died:

4 **Robert OXENBRIDGE**

Born: Abt 1430

Married:

Died:

9

Born:

Died:

2 **Goddard OXENBRIDGE**

Born: Abt 1460

Married:

Died: 10 Feb 1531

10

Born:

Married:

Died:

5 **Anne LYVELODE**

Born: Abt 1435

Died:

11

Born:

Died:

1 **Thomas OXENBRIDGE**

Born: Abt 1501
    -SAME AS #14,ROYAL CHART 1243
Married:

Died: 28 Mar 1540

12 **Thomas ECHINGHAM**

Born: Abt 1401
    -CONTINUED AS #4,ROYAL CHART 593
Married: Bef 1424

Died: 15 Oct 1444

6 **Thomas ECHINGHAM**

Born: Abt 1425

Married:

Died: 20 Jan 1482/1483

13 **Margaret KNYVETT**

Born: Abt 1395
    -CONTINUED AS #5,ROYAL CHART 593
Died: Aft 1467

Elizabeth PUTTENHAM

Spouse

3 **Elizabeth ECHINGHAM**

Born: Abt 1465

Died:

14 **Reynold WEST**

Born: 7 Sep 1395
    -CONTINUED AS #6,ROYAL CHART 593
Married: Bef 17 Feb 1428/1429

Died: 27 Aug 1450

7 **Margaret WEST**

Born: Abt 1430

Died:

15 **Margaret THORLEY**

Born: Abt 1400

Died: Bef 24 Nov 1433

Sources include: Faris 2--Echingham.

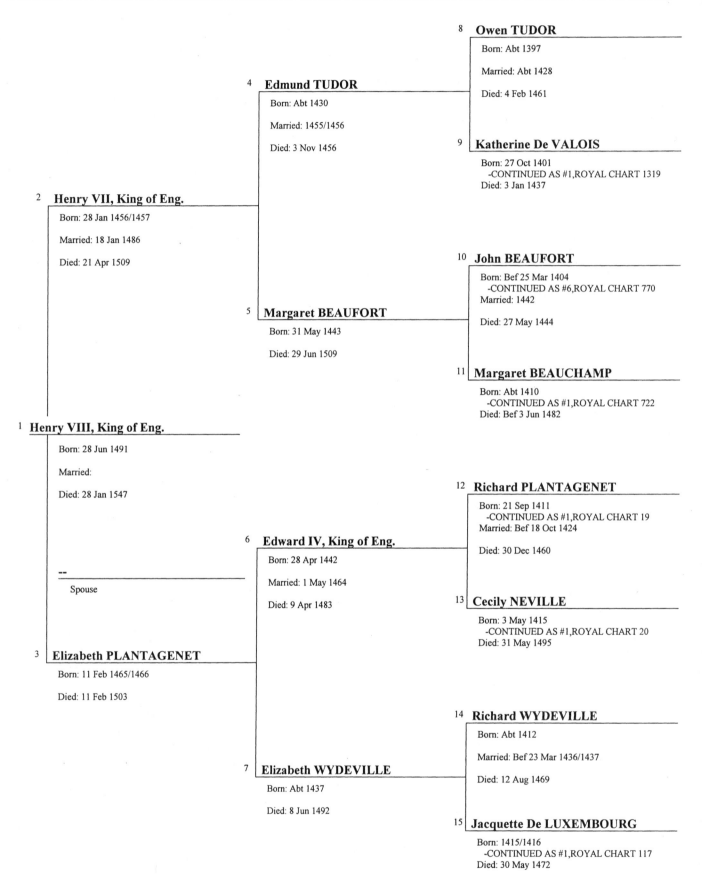

8 Owen TUDOR
Born: Abt 1397
Married: Abt 1428
Died: 4 Feb 1461

4 Edmund TUDOR
Born: Abt 1430
Married: 1455/1456
Died: 3 Nov 1456

9 Katherine De VALOIS
Born: 27 Oct 1401
-CONTINUED AS #1,ROYAL CHART 1319
Died: 3 Jan 1437

2 Henry VII, King of Eng.
Born: 28 Jan 1456/1457
Married: 18 Jan 1486
Died: 21 Apr 1509

10 John BEAUFORT
Born: Bef 25 Mar 1404
-CONTINUED AS #6,ROYAL CHART 770
Married: 1442
Died: 27 May 1444

5 Margaret BEAUFORT
Born: 31 May 1443
Died: 29 Jun 1509

11 Margaret BEAUCHAMP
Born: Abt 1410
-CONTINUED AS #1,ROYAL CHART 722
Died: Bef 3 Jun 1482

1 Henry VIII, King of Eng.
Born: 28 Jun 1491
Married:
Died: 28 Jan 1547

--
Spouse

12 Richard PLANTAGENET
Born: 21 Sep 1411
-CONTINUED AS #1,ROYAL CHART 19
Married: Bef 18 Oct 1424
Died: 30 Dec 1460

6 Edward IV, King of Eng.
Born: 28 Apr 1442
Married: 1 May 1464
Died: 9 Apr 1483

13 Cecily NEVILLE
Born: 3 May 1415
-CONTINUED AS #1,ROYAL CHART 20
Died: 31 May 1495

3 Elizabeth PLANTAGENET
Born: 11 Feb 1465/1466
Died: 11 Feb 1503

14 Richard WYDEVILLE
Born: Abt 1412
Married: Bef 23 Mar 1436/1437
Died: 12 Aug 1469

7 Elizabeth WYDEVILLE
Born: Abt 1437
Died: 8 Jun 1492

15 Jacquette De LUXEMBOURG
Born: 1415/1416
-CONTINUED AS #1,ROYAL CHART 117
Died: 30 May 1472

Sources include: Richardson *Plantagenet* (2004), pp. 724-731 (Tudor), 794-799 (York); Faris 2--Tudor, York, Lancaster 9; *Magna Charta* 161. Note: #1 Henry VIII had six wives and at least one mistress. He had a claimed mistress Mary Boleyn, wife of William Cary. Henry VIII might be the father of Mary's daughter Katherine Cary, who married Francis Knollys (see chart 621, #7).

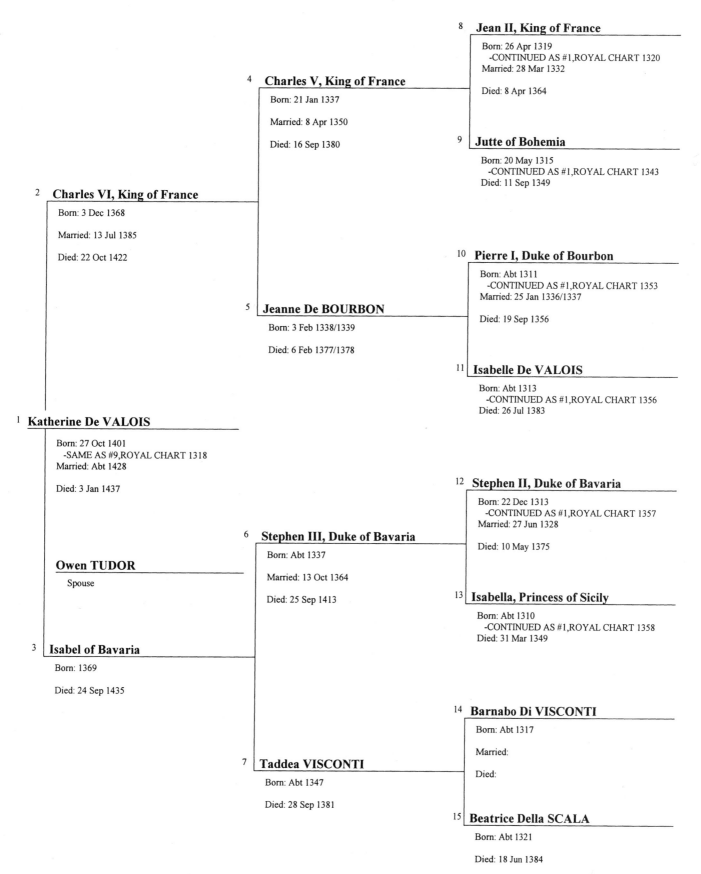

8 **Jean II, King of France**

Born: 26 Apr 1319
-CONTINUED AS #1,ROYAL CHART 1320
Married: 28 Mar 1332

Died: 8 Apr 1364

4 **Charles V, King of France**

Born: 21 Jan 1337

Married: 8 Apr 1350

Died: 16 Sep 1380

9 **Jutte of Bohemia**

Born: 20 May 1315
-CONTINUED AS #1,ROYAL CHART 1343
Died: 11 Sep 1349

2 **Charles VI, King of France**

Born: 3 Dec 1368

Married: 13 Jul 1385

Died: 22 Oct 1422

10 **Pierre I, Duke of Bourbon**

Born: Abt 1311
-CONTINUED AS #1,ROYAL CHART 1353
Married: 25 Jan 1336/1337

Died: 19 Sep 1356

5 **Jeanne De BOURBON**

Born: 3 Feb 1338/1339

Died: 6 Feb 1377/1378

11 **Isabelle De VALOIS**

Born: Abt 1313
-CONTINUED AS #1,ROYAL CHART 1356
Died: 26 Jul 1383

1 **Katherine De VALOIS**

Born: 27 Oct 1401
-SAME AS #9,ROYAL CHART 1318
Married: Abt 1428

Died: 3 Jan 1437

12 **Stephen II, Duke of Bavaria**

Born: 22 Dec 1313
-CONTINUED AS #1,ROYAL CHART 1357
Married: 27 Jun 1328

Died: 10 May 1375

6 **Stephen III, Duke of Bavaria**

Born: Abt 1337

Married: 13 Oct 1364

Died: 25 Sep 1413

Owen TUDOR

Spouse

13 **Isabella, Princess of Sicily**

Born: Abt 1310
-CONTINUED AS #1,ROYAL CHART 1358
Died: 31 Mar 1349

3 **Isabel of Bavaria**

Born: 1369

Died: 24 Sep 1435

14 **Barnabo Di VISCONTI**

Born: Abt 1317

Married:

Died:

7 **Taddea VISCONTI**

Born: Abt 1347

Died: 28 Sep 1381

15 **Beatrice Della SCALA**

Born: Abt 1321

Died: 18 Jun 1384

Sources include: Faris 2--Lancaster 9, Tudor 5; Schwennicke 2:22-23, 3:72, 1:24; LDS records.

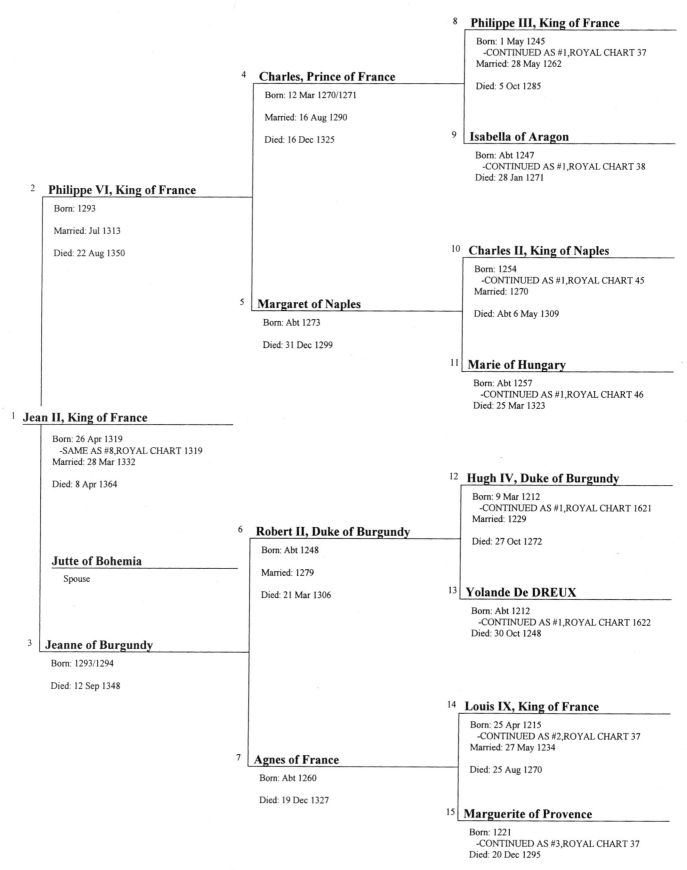

8 **Philippe III, King of France**

Born: 1 May 1245
 -CONTINUED AS #1,ROYAL CHART 37
Married: 28 May 1262

Died: 5 Oct 1285

4 **Charles, Prince of France**

Born: 12 Mar 1270/1271

Married: 16 Aug 1290

Died: 16 Dec 1325

9 **Isabella of Aragon**

Born: Abt 1247
 -CONTINUED AS #1,ROYAL CHART 38
Died: 28 Jan 1271

2 **Philippe VI, King of France**

Born: 1293

Married: Jul 1313

Died: 22 Aug 1350

10 **Charles II, King of Naples**

Born: 1254
 -CONTINUED AS #1,ROYAL CHART 45
Married: 1270

Died: Abt 6 May 1309

5 **Margaret of Naples**

Born: Abt 1273

Died: 31 Dec 1299

11 **Marie of Hungary**

Born: Abt 1257
 -CONTINUED AS #1,ROYAL CHART 46
Died: 25 Mar 1323

1 **Jean II, King of France**

Born: 26 Apr 1319
 -SAME AS #8,ROYAL CHART 1319
Married: 28 Mar 1332

Died: 8 Apr 1364

12 **Hugh IV, Duke of Burgundy**

Born: 9 Mar 1212
 -CONTINUED AS #1,ROYAL CHART 1621
Married: 1229

Died: 27 Oct 1272

6 **Robert II, Duke of Burgundy**

Born: Abt 1248

Married: 1279

Died: 21 Mar 1306

13 **Yolande De DREUX**

Born: Abt 1212
 -CONTINUED AS #1,ROYAL CHART 1622
Died: 30 Oct 1248

Jutte of Bohemia

Spouse

3 **Jeanne of Burgundy**

Born: 1293/1294

Died: 12 Sep 1348

14 **Louis IX, King of France**

Born: 25 Apr 1215
 -CONTINUED AS #2,ROYAL CHART 37
Married: 27 May 1234

Died: 25 Aug 1270

7 **Agnes of France**

Born: Abt 1260

Died: 19 Dec 1327

15 **Marguerite of Provence**

Born: 1221
 -CONTINUED AS #3,ROYAL CHART 37
Died: 20 Dec 1295

Sources include: Schwennicke 2:21-22, 12; *Royal Ancestors* (1989), chart 11202 (#4 & 5 ancestry).

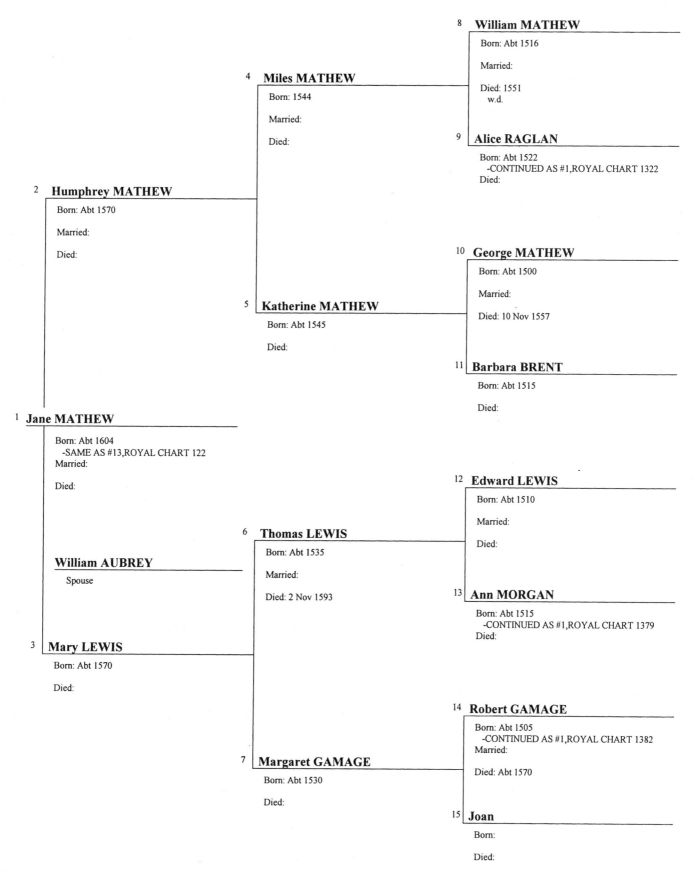

8 William MATHEW

Born: Abt 1516

Married:

Died: 1551
w.d.

4 Miles MATHEW

Born: 1544

Married:

Died:

9 Alice RAGLAN

Born: Abt 1522
  -CONTINUED AS #1,ROYAL CHART 1322
Died:

2 Humphrey MATHEW

Born: Abt 1570

Married:

Died:

10 George MATHEW

Born: Abt 1500

Married:

Died: 10 Nov 1557

5 Katherine MATHEW

Born: Abt 1545

Died:

11 Barbara BRENT

Born: Abt 1515

Died:

1 Jane MATHEW

Born: Abt 1604
  -SAME AS #13,ROYAL CHART 122
Married:

Died:

12 Edward LEWIS

Born: Abt 1510

Married:

Died:

6 Thomas LEWIS

Born: Abt 1535

Married:

Died: 2 Nov 1593

William AUBREY

Spouse

13 Ann MORGAN

Born: Abt 1515
  -CONTINUED AS #1,ROYAL CHART 1379
Died:

3 Mary LEWIS

Born: Abt 1570

Died:

14 Robert GAMAGE

Born: Abt 1505
  -CONTINUED AS #1,ROYAL CHART 1382
Married:

Died: Abt 1570

7 Margaret GAMAGE

Born: Abt 1530

Died:

15 Joan

Born:

Died:

Sources include: Faris 2--Aubrey; LDS records. Note: LDS records erroneously identify #15 as Joan, daughter of Philip Champernoun & Katherine Carew. That Joan married Anthony Denny (see chart 1383).

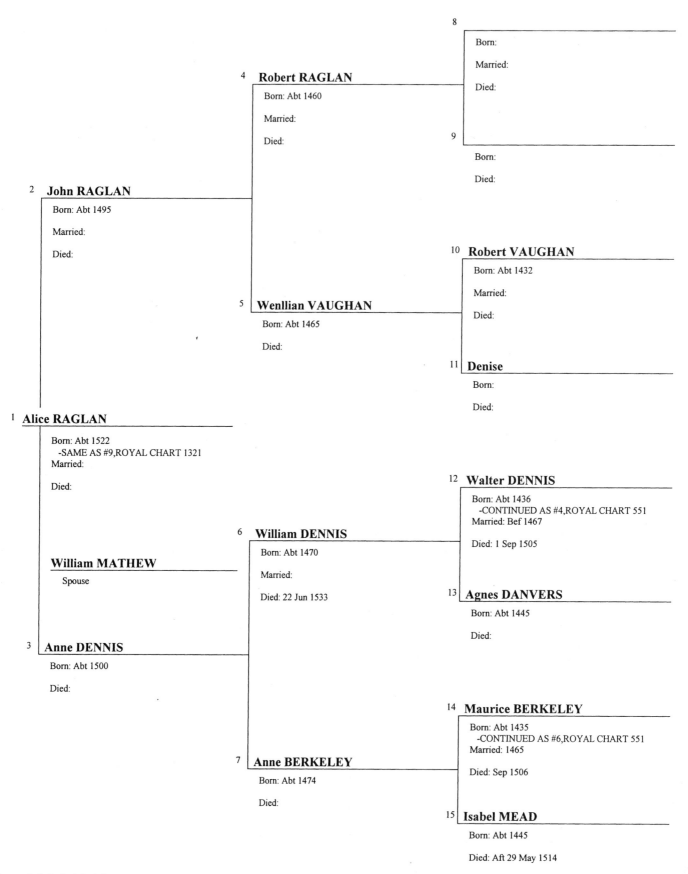

8

Born:

Married:

Died:

4 **Robert RAGLAN**

Born: Abt 1460

Married:

Died:

9

Born:

Died:

2 **John RAGLAN**

Born: Abt 1495

Married:

Died:

10 **Robert VAUGHAN**

Born: Abt 1432

Married:

Died:

5 **Wenllian VAUGHAN**

Born: Abt 1465

Died:

11 **Denise**

Born:

Died:

1 **Alice RAGLAN**

Born: Abt 1522
   -SAME AS #9,ROYAL CHART 1321
Married:

Died:

12 **Walter DENNIS**

Born: Abt 1436
   -CONTINUED AS #4,ROYAL CHART 551
Married: Bef 1467

Died: 1 Sep 1505

6 **William DENNIS**

Born: Abt 1470

Married:

Died: 22 Jun 1533

13 **Agnes DANVERS**

Born: Abt 1445

Died:

William MATHEW

Spouse

3 **Anne DENNIS**

Born: Abt 1500

Died:

14 **Maurice BERKELEY**

Born: Abt 1435
   -CONTINUED AS #6,ROYAL CHART 551
Married: 1465

Died: Sep 1506

7 **Anne BERKELEY**

Born: Abt 1474

Died:

15 **Isabel MEAD**

Born: Abt 1445

Died: Aft 29 May 1514

Sources include: Faris 2--Aubrey.

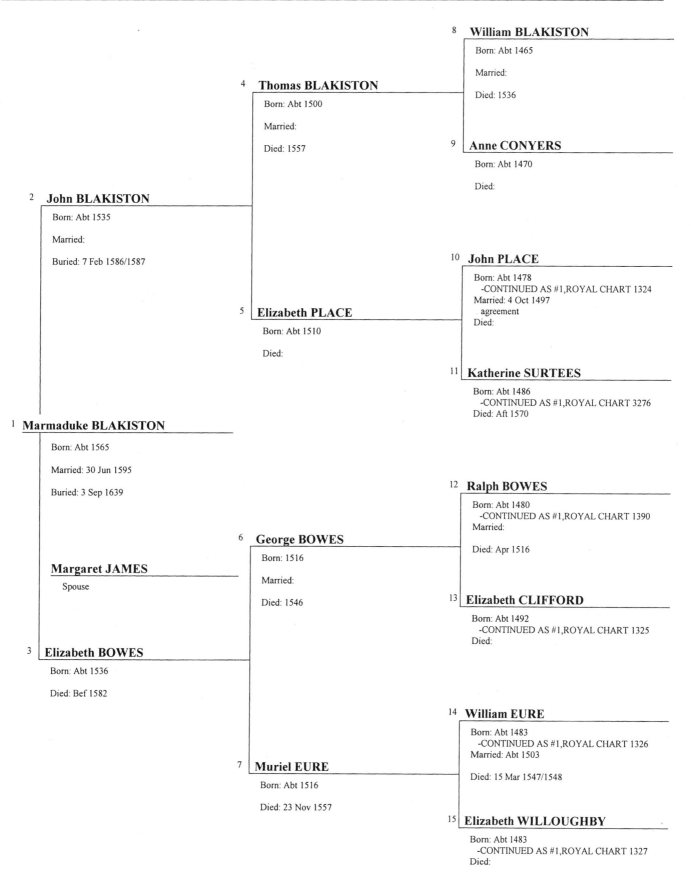

8 William BLAKISTON

Born: Abt 1465

Married:

Died: 1536

4 Thomas BLAKISTON

Born: Abt 1500

Married:

Died: 1557

9 Anne CONYERS

Born: Abt 1470

Died:

2 John BLAKISTON

Born: Abt 1535

Married:

Buried: 7 Feb 1586/1587

10 John PLACE

Born: Abt 1478
    -CONTINUED AS #1,ROYAL CHART 1324
Married: 4 Oct 1497
    agreement
Died:

5 Elizabeth PLACE

Born: Abt 1510

Died:

11 Katherine SURTEES

Born: Abt 1486
    -CONTINUED AS #1,ROYAL CHART 3276
Died: Aft 1570

1 Marmaduke BLAKISTON

Born: Abt 1565

Married: 30 Jun 1595

Buried: 3 Sep 1639

12 Ralph BOWES

Born: Abt 1480
    -CONTINUED AS #1,ROYAL CHART 1390
Married:

Died: Apr 1516

6 George BOWES

Born: 1516

Married:

Died: 1546

13 Elizabeth CLIFFORD

Born: Abt 1492
    -CONTINUED AS #1,ROYAL CHART 1325
Died:

Margaret JAMES

Spouse

3 Elizabeth BOWES

Born: Abt 1536

Died: Bef 1582

14 William EURE

Born: Abt 1483
    -CONTINUED AS #1,ROYAL CHART 1326
Married: Abt 1503

Died: 15 Mar 1547/1548

7 Muriel EURE

Born: Abt 1516

Died: 23 Nov 1557

15 Elizabeth WILLOUGHBY

Born: Abt 1483
    -CONTINUED AS #1,ROYAL CHART 1327
Died:

Sources include: Faris 2--Blakiston, Bowes. Note: #1 Marmaduke had a son George Blakiston (b. 1 Mar 1611; md. Barbara Lawson) who had American descendants in Maryland. #1 also had a son John Blakiston (chr. 21 Aug 1603; md. Susannah Charles), whose son Nehemiah Blakiston (b. abt. 1637; md. Elizabeth Gerard) left descendants in Maryland.

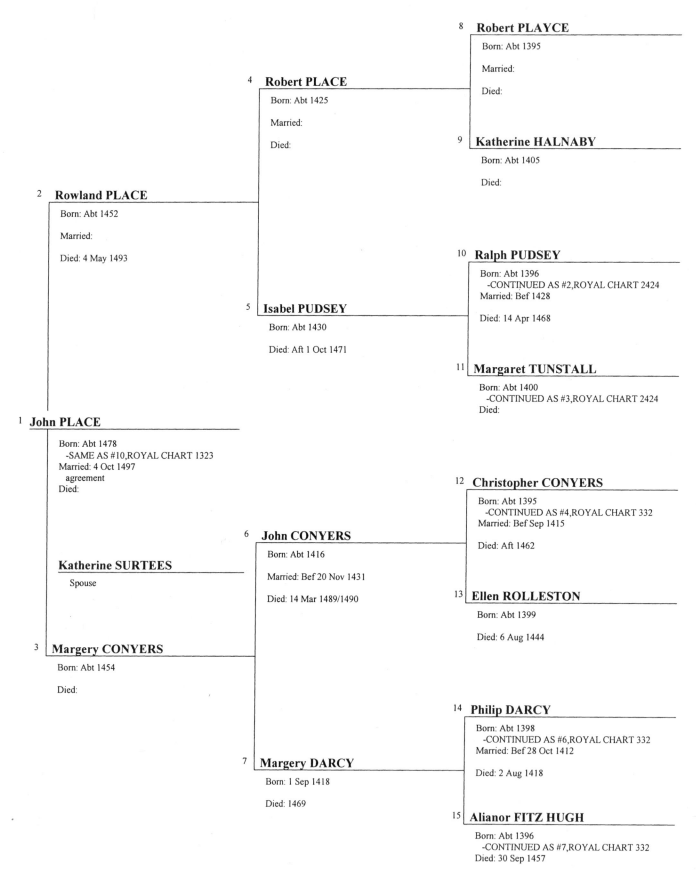

8 **Robert PLAYCE**
Born: Abt 1395
Married:
Died:

4 **Robert PLACE**
Born: Abt 1425
Married:
Died:

9 **Katherine HALNABY**
Born: Abt 1405
Died:

2 **Rowland PLACE**
Born: Abt 1452
Married:
Died: 4 May 1493

10 **Ralph PUDSEY**
Born: Abt 1396
   -CONTINUED AS #2,ROYAL CHART 2424
Married: Bef 1428
Died: 14 Apr 1468

5 **Isabel PUDSEY**
Born: Abt 1430
Died: Aft 1 Oct 1471

11 **Margaret TUNSTALL**
Born: Abt 1400
   -CONTINUED AS #3,ROYAL CHART 2424
Died:

1 **John PLACE**
Born: Abt 1478
   -SAME AS #10,ROYAL CHART 1323
Married: 4 Oct 1497
   agreement
Died:

12 **Christopher CONYERS**
Born: Abt 1395
   -CONTINUED AS #4,ROYAL CHART 332
Married: Bef Sep 1415
Died: Aft 1462

6 **John CONYERS**
Born: Abt 1416
Married: Bef 20 Nov 1431
Died: 14 Mar 1489/1490

Katherine SURTEES
Spouse

13 **Ellen ROLLESTON**
Born: Abt 1399
Died: 6 Aug 1444

3 **Margery CONYERS**
Born: Abt 1454
Died:

14 **Philip DARCY**
Born: Abt 1398
   -CONTINUED AS #6,ROYAL CHART 332
Married: Bef 28 Oct 1412
Died: 2 Aug 1418

7 **Margery DARCY**
Born: 1 Sep 1418
Died: 1469

15 **Alianor FITZ HUGH**
Born: Abt 1396
   -CONTINUED AS #7,ROYAL CHART 332
Died: 30 Sep 1457

Sources include: Richardson *Plantagenet* (2004), pp. 112-113 (Blakiston), 227 (Conyers), 597 (Pudsey); Faris 2--Blakiston.

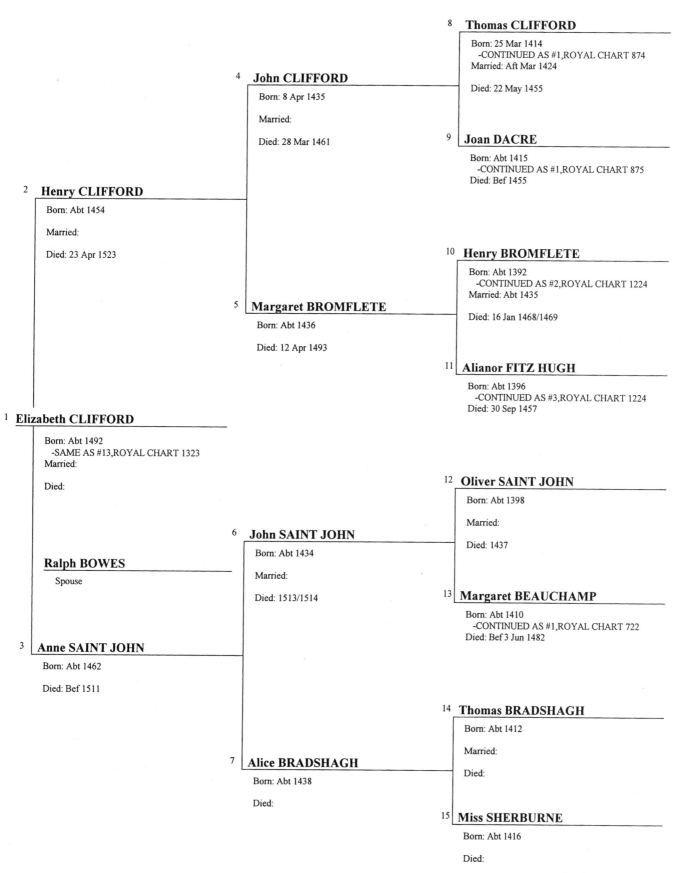

8 Thomas CLIFFORD

Born: 25 Mar 1414
-CONTINUED AS #1,ROYAL CHART 874
Married: Aft Mar 1424

Died: 22 May 1455

4 John CLIFFORD

Born: 8 Apr 1435

Married:

Died: 28 Mar 1461

9 Joan DACRE

Born: Abt 1415
-CONTINUED AS #1,ROYAL CHART 875
Died: Bef 1455

2 Henry CLIFFORD

Born: Abt 1454

Married:

Died: 23 Apr 1523

10 Henry BROMFLETE

Born: Abt 1392
-CONTINUED AS #2,ROYAL CHART 1224
Married: Abt 1435

Died: 16 Jan 1468/1469

5 Margaret BROMFLETE

Born: Abt 1436

Died: 12 Apr 1493

11 Alianor FITZ HUGH

Born: Abt 1396
-CONTINUED AS #3,ROYAL CHART 1224
Died: 30 Sep 1457

1 Elizabeth CLIFFORD

Born: Abt 1492
-SAME AS #13,ROYAL CHART 1323
Married:

Died:

12 Oliver SAINT JOHN

Born: Abt 1398

Married:

Died: 1437

6 John SAINT JOHN

Born: Abt 1434

Married:

Died: 1513/1514

Ralph BOWES

Spouse

13 Margaret BEAUCHAMP

Born: Abt 1410
-CONTINUED AS #1,ROYAL CHART 722
Died: Bef 3 Jun 1482

3 Anne SAINT JOHN

Born: Abt 1462

Died: Bef 1511

14 Thomas BRADSHAGH

Born: Abt 1412

Married:

Died:

7 Alice BRADSHAGH

Born: Abt 1438

Died:

15 Miss SHERBURNE

Born: Abt 1416

Died:

Sources include: Faris 2--Bowes, Clifford.

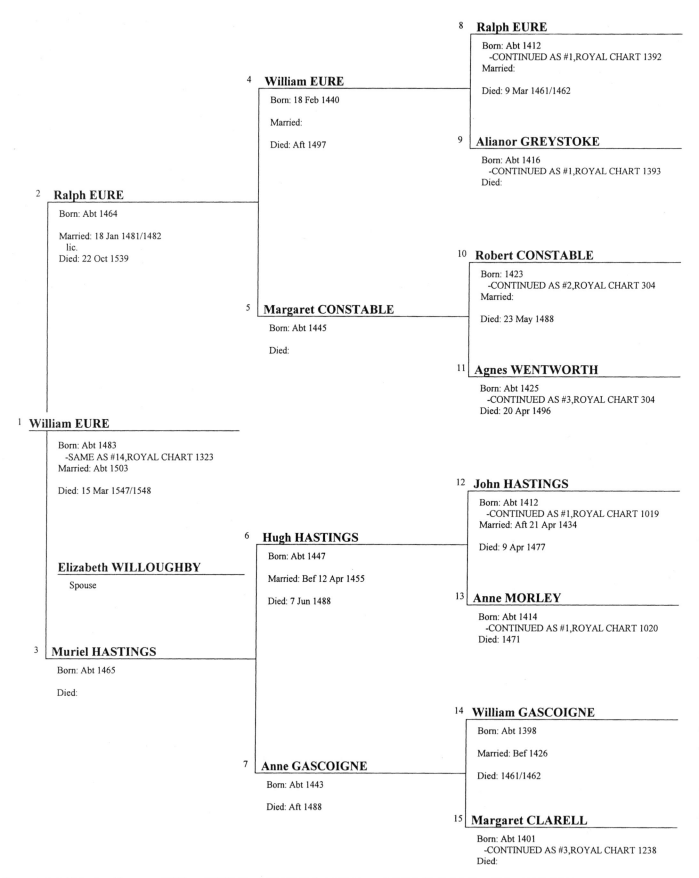

8 **Ralph EURE**

Born: Abt 1412
-CONTINUED AS #1,ROYAL CHART 1392
Married:

Died: 9 Mar 1461/1462

4 **William EURE**

Born: 18 Feb 1440

Married:

Died: Aft 1497

9 **Alianor GREYSTOKE**

Born: Abt 1416
-CONTINUED AS #1,ROYAL CHART 1393
Died:

2 **Ralph EURE**

Born: Abt 1464

Married: 18 Jan 1481/1482
lic.
Died: 22 Oct 1539

10 **Robert CONSTABLE**

Born: 1423
-CONTINUED AS #2,ROYAL CHART 304
Married:

Died: 23 May 1488

5 **Margaret CONSTABLE**

Born: Abt 1445

Died:

11 **Agnes WENTWORTH**

Born: Abt 1425
-CONTINUED AS #3,ROYAL CHART 304
Died: 20 Apr 1496

1 **William EURE**

Born: Abt 1483
-SAME AS #14,ROYAL CHART 1323
Married: Abt 1503

Died: 15 Mar 1547/1548

12 **John HASTINGS**

Born: Abt 1412
-CONTINUED AS #1,ROYAL CHART 1019
Married: Aft 21 Apr 1434

Died: 9 Apr 1477

6 **Hugh HASTINGS**

Born: Abt 1447

Married: Bef 12 Apr 1455

Died: 7 Jun 1488

Elizabeth WILLOUGHBY

Spouse

13 **Anne MORLEY**

Born: Abt 1414
-CONTINUED AS #1,ROYAL CHART 1020
Died: 1471

3 **Muriel HASTINGS**

Born: Abt 1465

Died:

14 **William GASCOIGNE**

Born: Abt 1398

Married: Bef 1426

Died: 1461/1462

7 **Anne GASCOIGNE**

Born: Abt 1443

Died: Aft 1488

15 **Margaret CLARELL**

Born: Abt 1401
-CONTINUED AS #3,ROYAL CHART 1238
Died:

Sources include: Richardson *Plantagenet* (2004), pp. 296-297 (Eure), 289-290 (Elsing), 634 Saltonstall (#14 & 15); Faris 2--Eure, Elsing; MPGL 10043.

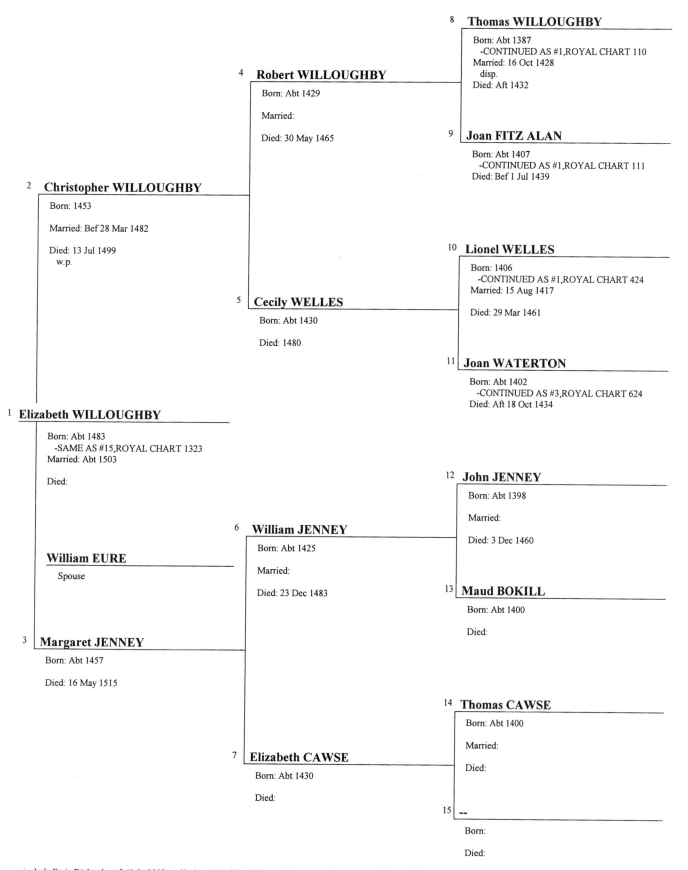

8 Thomas WILLOUGHBY
Born: Abt 1387
-CONTINUED AS #1,ROYAL CHART 110
Married: 16 Oct 1428
disp.
Died: Aft 1432

4 Robert WILLOUGHBY
Born: Abt 1429
Married:
Died: 30 May 1465

9 Joan FITZ ALAN
Born: Abt 1407
-CONTINUED AS #1,ROYAL CHART 111
Died: Bef 1 Jul 1439

2 Christopher WILLOUGHBY
Born: 1453
Married: Bef 28 Mar 1482
Died: 13 Jul 1499
w.p.

10 Lionel WELLES
Born: 1406
-CONTINUED AS #1,ROYAL CHART 424
Married: 15 Aug 1417
Died: 29 Mar 1461

5 Cecily WELLES
Born: Abt 1430
Died: 1480

11 Joan WATERTON
Born: Abt 1402
-CONTINUED AS #3,ROYAL CHART 624
Died: Aft 18 Oct 1434

1 Elizabeth WILLOUGHBY
Born: Abt 1483
-SAME AS #15,ROYAL CHART 1323
Married: Abt 1503
Died:

12 John JENNEY
Born: Abt 1398
Married:
Died: 3 Dec 1460

6 William JENNEY
Born: Abt 1425
Married:
Died: 23 Dec 1483

William EURE
Spouse

13 Maud BOKILL
Born: Abt 1400
Died:

3 Margaret JENNEY
Born: Abt 1457
Died: 16 May 1515

14 Thomas CAWSE
Born: Abt 1400
Married:
Died:

7 Elizabeth CAWSE
Born: Abt 1430
Died:

15 --
Born:
Died:

Sources include:Faris-Richardson 3 (July 2002 preliminary)--Willoughby; Faris 2--Eure, Willoughby; MPGL 10043.

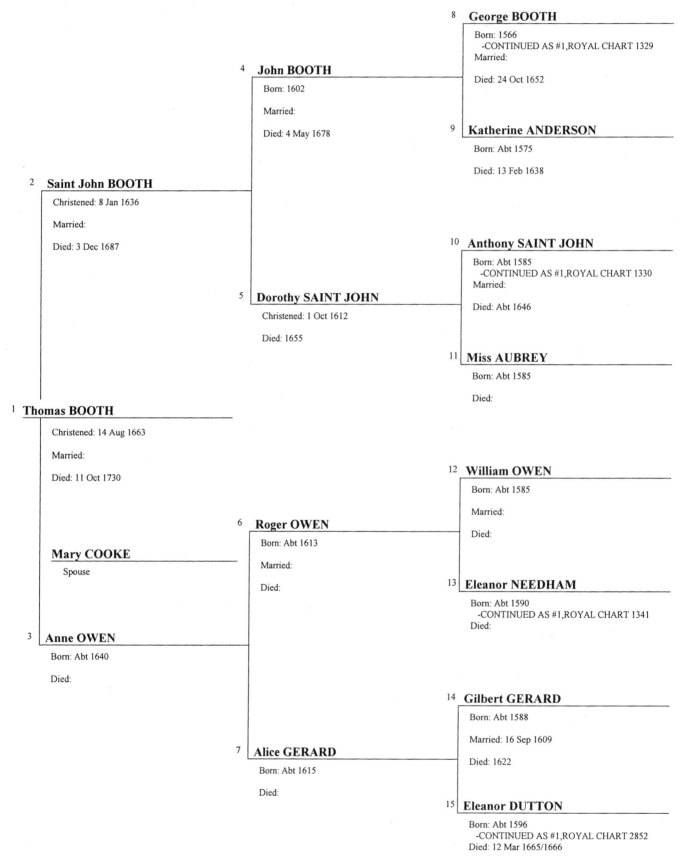

8 **George BOOTH**

Born: 1566
-CONTINUED AS #1,ROYAL CHART 1329
Married:

Died: 24 Oct 1652

4 **John BOOTH**

Born: 1602

Married:

Died: 4 May 1678

9 **Katherine ANDERSON**

Born: Abt 1575

Died: 13 Feb 1638

2 **Saint John BOOTH**

Christened: 8 Jan 1636

Married:

Died: 3 Dec 1687

10 **Anthony SAINT JOHN**

Born: Abt 1585
-CONTINUED AS #1,ROYAL CHART 1330
Married:

Died: Abt 1646

5 **Dorothy SAINT JOHN**

Christened: 1 Oct 1612

Died: 1655

11 **Miss AUBREY**

Born: Abt 1585

Died:

1 **Thomas BOOTH**

Christened: 14 Aug 1663

Married:

Died: 11 Oct 1730

12 **William OWEN**

Born: Abt 1585

Married:

Died:

6 **Roger OWEN**

Born: Abt 1613

Married:

Died:

13 **Eleanor NEEDHAM**

Born: Abt 1590
-CONTINUED AS #1,ROYAL CHART 1341
Died:

Mary COOKE

Spouse

3 **Anne OWEN**

Born: Abt 1640

Died:

14 **Gilbert GERARD**

Born: Abt 1588

Married: 16 Sep 1609

Died: 1622

7 **Alice GERARD**

Born: Abt 1615

Died:

15 **Eleanor DUTTON**

Born: Abt 1596
-CONTINUED AS #1,ROYAL CHART 2852
Died: 12 Mar 1665/1666

Sources include: Richardson *Plantagenet* (2004), pp. 129-130 (Booth), 116 (Bletsoe); *Blood Royal* 5:585, 744 (Cooke, Ironmonger); Faris 2--Booth; Roberts *500* (600) updated manuscript (November 2000), pp. 344-345. Note: Mary Cooke (b. abt. 1680), wife of #1 Thomas Booth, was dau. of Frances Ironmonger (b. abt. 1654; md. Mordecai Cooke), dau. of William Ironmonger (b. abt. 1631; md. Elizabeth Jones), cont. cht. 1251, #1.

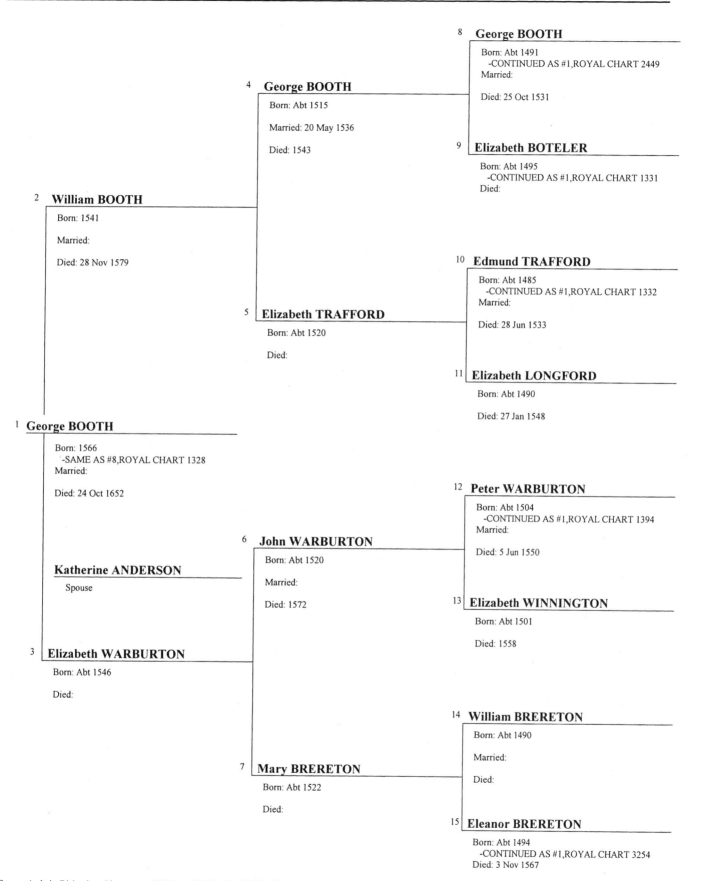

8 George BOOTH
Born: Abt 1491
-CONTINUED AS #1,ROYAL CHART 2449
Married:

Died: 25 Oct 1531

4 George BOOTH
Born: Abt 1515

Married: 20 May 1536

Died: 1543

9 Elizabeth BOTELER
Born: Abt 1495
-CONTINUED AS #1,ROYAL CHART 1331
Died:

2 William BOOTH
Born: 1541

Married:

Died: 28 Nov 1579

10 Edmund TRAFFORD
Born: Abt 1485
-CONTINUED AS #1,ROYAL CHART 1332
Married:

Died: 28 Jun 1533

5 Elizabeth TRAFFORD
Born: Abt 1520

Died:

11 Elizabeth LONGFORD
Born: Abt 1490

Died: 27 Jan 1548

1 George BOOTH
Born: 1566
-SAME AS #8,ROYAL CHART 1328
Married:

Died: 24 Oct 1652

Katherine ANDERSON
Spouse

12 Peter WARBURTON
Born: Abt 1504
-CONTINUED AS #1,ROYAL CHART 1394
Married:

Died: 5 Jun 1550

6 John WARBURTON
Born: Abt 1520

Married:

Died: 1572

13 Elizabeth WINNINGTON
Born: Abt 1501

Died: 1558

3 Elizabeth WARBURTON
Born: Abt 1546

Died:

14 William BRERETON
Born: Abt 1490

Married:

Died:

7 Mary BRERETON
Born: Abt 1522

Died:

15 Eleanor BRERETON
Born: Abt 1494
-CONTINUED AS #1,ROYAL CHART 3254
Died: 3 Nov 1567

Sources include: Richardson *Plantagenet* (2004), pp. 129 (Booth), 716 (Trafford), 460 (Longford); Faris 2--Booth; LDS records. Note: #11 Elizabeth was daughter of Ralph Longford (md. Mabel Ferrers) and a descendant of Nicholas De Longford & Alice Le Boteler (see chart 2994, #2 & 3).

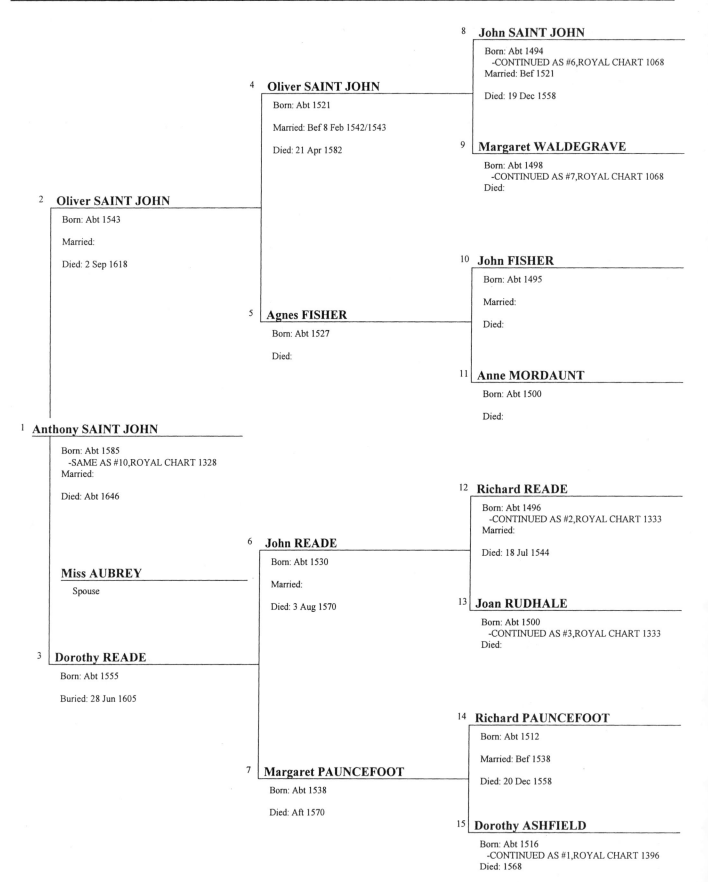

8 **John SAINT JOHN**

Born: Abt 1494
  -CONTINUED AS #6,ROYAL CHART 1068
Married: Bef 1521

Died: 19 Dec 1558

4 **Oliver SAINT JOHN**

Born: Abt 1521

Married: Bef 8 Feb 1542/1543

Died: 21 Apr 1582

9 **Margaret WALDEGRAVE**

Born: Abt 1498
  -CONTINUED AS #7,ROYAL CHART 1068
Died:

2 **Oliver SAINT JOHN**

Born: Abt 1543

Married:

Died: 2 Sep 1618

10 **John FISHER**

Born: Abt 1495

Married:

Died:

5 **Agnes FISHER**

Born: Abt 1527

Died:

11 **Anne MORDAUNT**

Born: Abt 1500

Died:

1 **Anthony SAINT JOHN**

Born: Abt 1585
  -SAME AS #10,ROYAL CHART 1328
Married:

Died: Abt 1646

12 **Richard READE**

Born: Abt 1496
  -CONTINUED AS #2,ROYAL CHART 1333
Married:

Died: 18 Jul 1544

6 **John READE**

Born: Abt 1530

Married:

Died: 3 Aug 1570

13 **Joan RUDHALE**

Born: Abt 1500
  -CONTINUED AS #3,ROYAL CHART 1333
Died:

Miss AUBREY

Spouse

3 **Dorothy READE**

Born: Abt 1555

Buried: 28 Jun 1605

14 **Richard PAUNCEFOOT**

Born: Abt 1512

Married: Bef 1538

Died: 20 Dec 1558

7 **Margaret PAUNCEFOOT**

Born: Abt 1538

Died: Aft 1570

15 **Dorothy ASHFIELD**

Born: Abt 1516
  -CONTINUED AS #1,ROYAL CHART 1396
Died: 1568

Sources include: Richardson *Plantagenet* (2004), pp. 114-116 (Bletsoe), 117 (Boddington); Faris 2--Booth, Saint John.

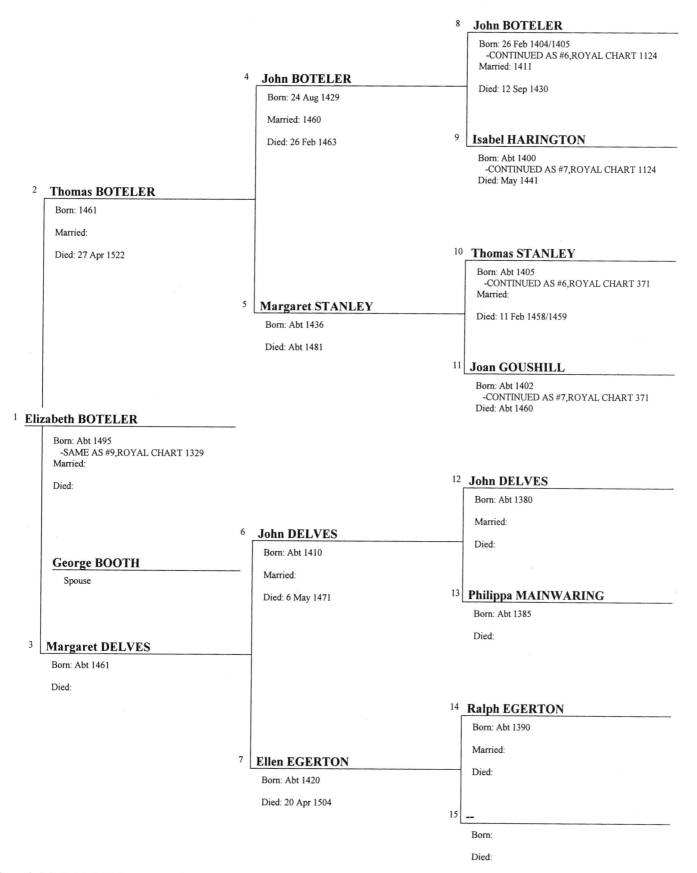

8 **John BOTELER**

Born: 26 Feb 1404/1405
-CONTINUED AS #6,ROYAL CHART 1124
Married: 1411

Died: 12 Sep 1430

4 **John BOTELER**

Born: 24 Aug 1429

Married: 1460

Died: 26 Feb 1463

9 **Isabel HARINGTON**

Born: Abt 1400
-CONTINUED AS #7,ROYAL CHART 1124
Died: May 1441

2 **Thomas BOTELER**

Born: 1461

Married:

Died: 27 Apr 1522

10 **Thomas STANLEY**

Born: Abt 1405
-CONTINUED AS #6,ROYAL CHART 371
Married:

Died: 11 Feb 1458/1459

5 **Margaret STANLEY**

Born: Abt 1436

Died: Abt 1481

11 **Joan GOUSHILL**

Born: Abt 1402
-CONTINUED AS #7,ROYAL CHART 371
Died: Abt 1460

1 **Elizabeth BOTELER**

Born: Abt 1495
-SAME AS #9,ROYAL CHART 1329
Married:

Died:

12 **John DELVES**

Born: Abt 1380

Married:

Died:

6 **John DELVES**

Born: Abt 1410

Married:

Died: 6 May 1471

13 **Philippa MAINWARING**

Born: Abt 1385

Died:

George BOOTH

Spouse

3 **Margaret DELVES**

Born: Abt 1461

Died:

14 **Ralph EGERTON**

Born: Abt 1390

Married:

Died:

7 **Ellen EGERTON**

Born: Abt 1420

Died: 20 Apr 1504

15 **--**

Born:

Died:

Sources include: Faris 2--Booth; Paget 418 (#6 & 7 ancestry).

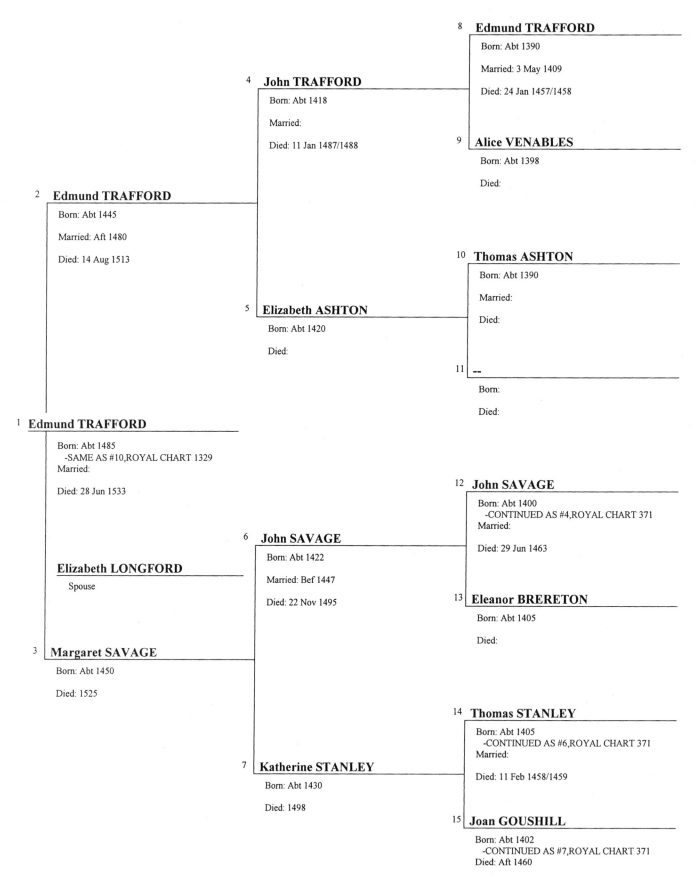

8 Edmund TRAFFORD
Born: Abt 1390
Married: 3 May 1409
Died: 24 Jan 1457/1458

4 John TRAFFORD
Born: Abt 1418
Married:
Died: 11 Jan 1487/1488

9 Alice VENABLES
Born: Abt 1398
Died:

2 Edmund TRAFFORD
Born: Abt 1445
Married: Aft 1480
Died: 14 Aug 1513

10 Thomas ASHTON
Born: Abt 1390
Married:
Died:

5 Elizabeth ASHTON
Born: Abt 1420
Died:

11 --
Born:
Died:

1 Edmund TRAFFORD
Born: Abt 1485
 -SAME AS #10,ROYAL CHART 1329
Married:
Died: 28 Jun 1533

12 John SAVAGE
Born: Abt 1400
 -CONTINUED AS #4,ROYAL CHART 371
Married:
Died: 29 Jun 1463

6 John SAVAGE
Born: Abt 1422
Married: Bef 1447
Died: 22 Nov 1495

13 Eleanor BRERETON
Born: Abt 1405
Died:

Elizabeth LONGFORD
Spouse

3 Margaret SAVAGE
Born: Abt 1450
Died: 1525

14 Thomas STANLEY
Born: Abt 1405
 -CONTINUED AS #6,ROYAL CHART 371
Married:
Died: 11 Feb 1458/1459

7 Katherine STANLEY
Born: Abt 1430
Died: 1498

15 Joan GOUSHILL
Born: Abt 1402
 -CONTINUED AS #7,ROYAL CHART 371
Died: Aft 1460

Sources include: Richardson *Plantagenet* (2004), pp. 715-716 (Trafford), 638-639 (Savage); Faris 2--Booth, Trafford; Faris preliminary baronial manuscript (1998), pp. 1538-41 (Trafford).

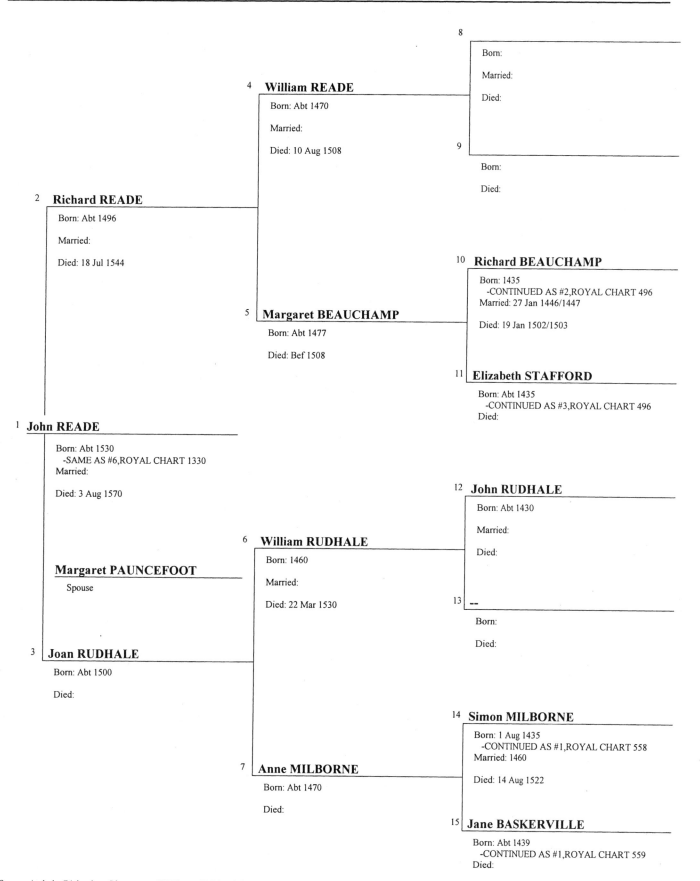

8

William READE
4
Born: Abt 1470

Married:

Died: 10 Aug 1508

Born:

Married:

Died:

9

Born:

Died:

2 **Richard READE**

Born: Abt 1496

Married:

Died: 18 Jul 1544

10 **Richard BEAUCHAMP**

Born: 1435
  -CONTINUED AS #2,ROYAL CHART 496
Married: 27 Jan 1446/1447

Died: 19 Jan 1502/1503

5 **Margaret BEAUCHAMP**

Born: Abt 1477

Died: Bef 1508

11 **Elizabeth STAFFORD**

Born: Abt 1435
  -CONTINUED AS #3,ROYAL CHART 496
Died:

1 **John READE**

Born: Abt 1530
  -SAME AS #6,ROYAL CHART 1330
Married:

Died: 3 Aug 1570

12 **John RUDHALE**

Born: Abt 1430

Married:

Died:

6 **William RUDHALE**

Born: 1460

Married:

Died: 22 Mar 1530

Margaret PAUNCEFOOT

Spouse

13 **--**

Born:

Died:

3 **Joan RUDHALE**

Born: Abt 1500

Died:

14 **Simon MILBORNE**

Born: 1 Aug 1435
  -CONTINUED AS #1,ROYAL CHART 558
Married: 1460

Died: 14 Aug 1522

7 **Anne MILBORNE**

Born: Abt 1470

Died:

15 **Jane BASKERVILLE**

Born: Abt 1439
  -CONTINUED AS #1,ROYAL CHART 559
Died:

Sources include: Richardson *Plantagenet* (2004), pp. 117 (Boddington), 500-501 (Milborne); Faris 2--St. John, Ligon.

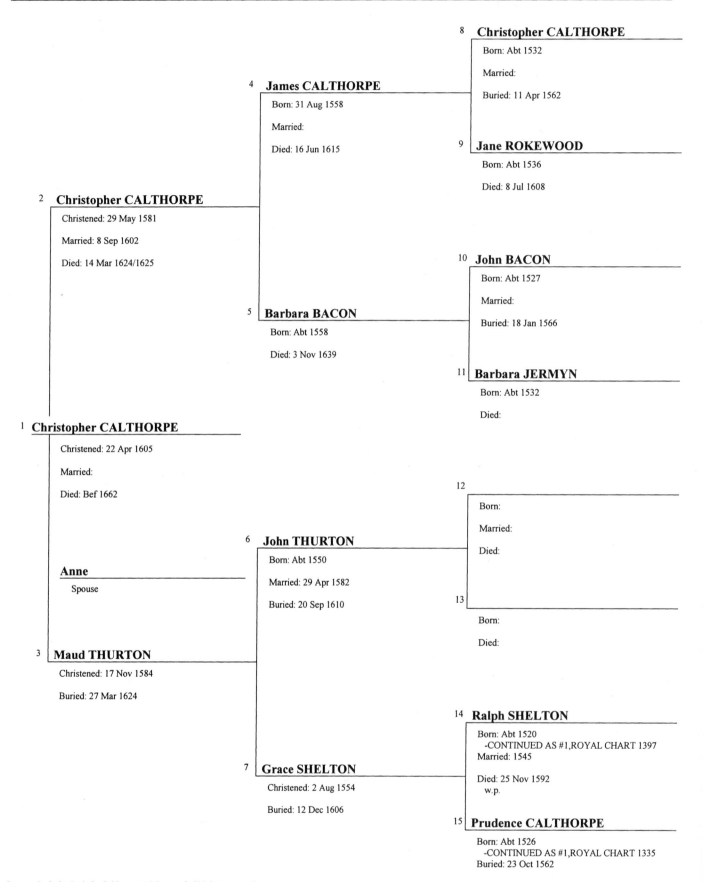

8 **Christopher CALTHORPE**
Born: Abt 1532
Married:
Buried: 11 Apr 1562

4 **James CALTHORPE**
Born: 31 Aug 1558
Married:
Died: 16 Jun 1615

9 **Jane ROKEWOOD**
Born: Abt 1536
Died: 8 Jul 1608

2 **Christopher CALTHORPE**
Christened: 29 May 1581
Married: 8 Sep 1602
Died: 14 Mar 1624/1625

10 **John BACON**
Born: Abt 1527
Married:
Buried: 18 Jan 1566

5 **Barbara BACON**
Born: Abt 1558
Died: 3 Nov 1639

11 **Barbara JERMYN**
Born: Abt 1532
Died:

1 **Christopher CALTHORPE**
Christened: 22 Apr 1605
Married:
Died: Bef 1662

12
Born:
Married:
Died:

6 **John THURTON**
Born: Abt 1550
Married: 29 Apr 1582
Buried: 20 Sep 1610

13
Born:
Died:

Anne
Spouse

3 **Maud THURTON**
Christened: 17 Nov 1584
Buried: 27 Mar 1624

14 **Ralph SHELTON**
Born: Abt 1520
    -CONTINUED AS #1,ROYAL CHART 1397
Married: 1545
Died: 25 Nov 1592
w.p.

7 **Grace SHELTON**
Christened: 2 Aug 1554
Buried: 12 Dec 1606

15 **Prudence CALTHORPE**
Born: Abt 1526
    -CONTINUED AS #1,ROYAL CHART 1335
Buried: 23 Oct 1562

Sources include: Faris 2--Calthorpe; LDS records (#4 & 5 ancestry).

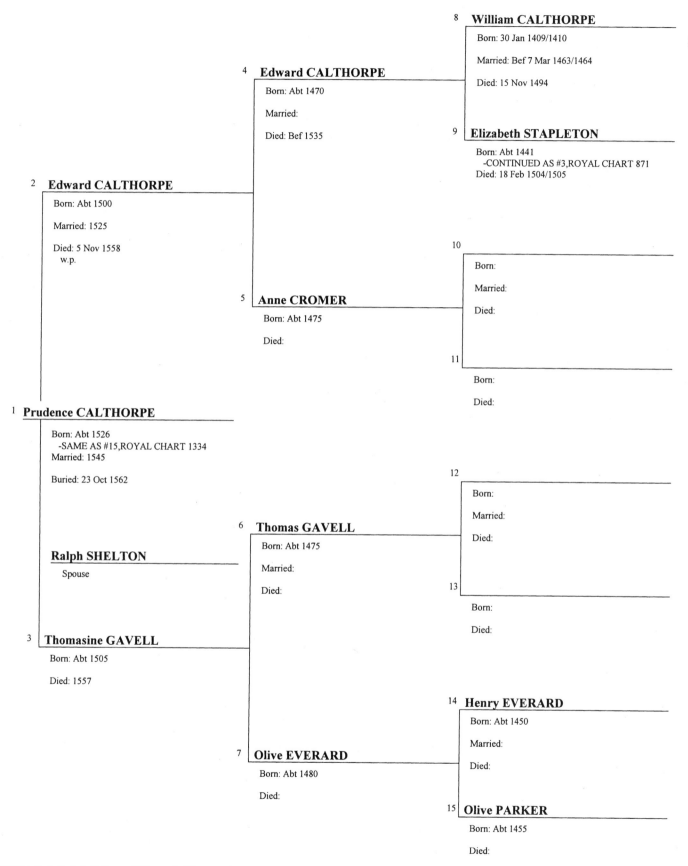

2 Edward CALTHORPE
Born: Abt 1500
Married: 1525
Died: 5 Nov 1558
w.p.

4 Edward CALTHORPE
Born: Abt 1470
Married:
Died: Bef 1535

8 William CALTHORPE
Born: 30 Jan 1409/1410
Married: Bef 7 Mar 1463/1464
Died: 15 Nov 1494

9 Elizabeth STAPLETON
Born: Abt 1441
-CONTINUED AS #3,ROYAL CHART 871
Died: 18 Feb 1504/1505

5 Anne CROMER
Born: Abt 1475
Died:

10
Born:
Married:
Died:

11
Born:
Died:

1 Prudence CALTHORPE
Born: Abt 1526
-SAME AS #15,ROYAL CHART 1334
Married: 1545
Buried: 23 Oct 1562

Ralph SHELTON
Spouse

3 Thomasine GAVELL
Born: Abt 1505
Died: 1557

6 Thomas GAVELL
Born: Abt 1475
Married:
Died:

12
Born:
Married:
Died:

13
Born:
Died:

7 Olive EVERARD
Born: Abt 1480
Died:

14 Henry EVERARD
Born: Abt 1450
Married:
Died:

15 Olive PARKER
Born: Abt 1455
Died:

Sources include: Faris 2--Calthorpe; LDS records (#7 ancestry).

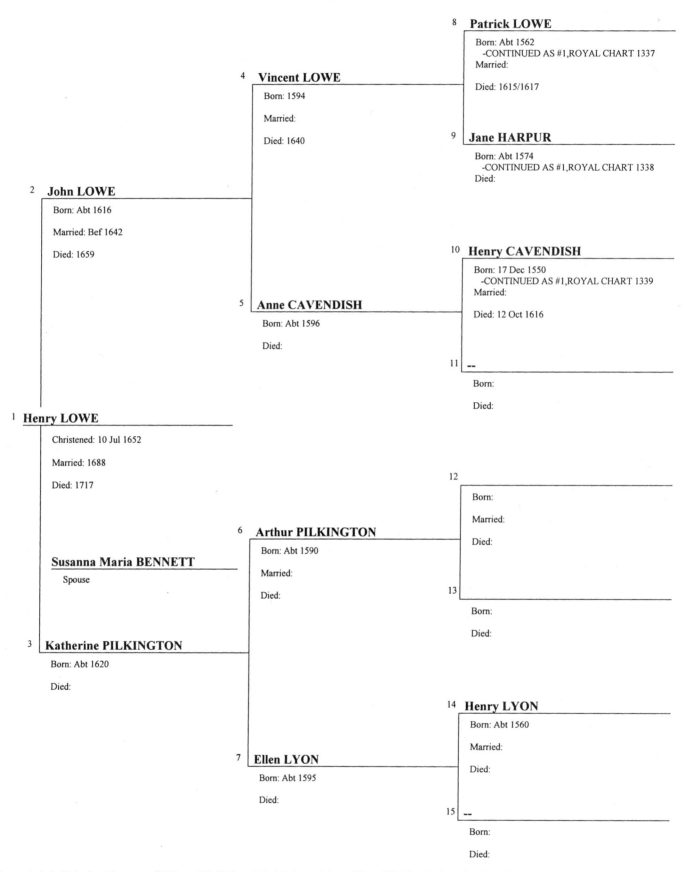

8 Patrick LOWE

Born: Abt 1562
-CONTINUED AS #1,ROYAL CHART 1337
Married:

Died: 1615/1617

4 Vincent LOWE

Born: 1594

Married:

Died: 1640

9 Jane HARPUR

Born: Abt 1574
-CONTINUED AS #1,ROYAL CHART 1338
Died:

2 John LOWE

Born: Abt 1616

Married: Bef 1642

Died: 1659

10 Henry CAVENDISH

Born: 17 Dec 1550
-CONTINUED AS #1,ROYAL CHART 1339
Married:

Died: 12 Oct 1616

5 Anne CAVENDISH

Born: Abt 1596

Died:

11 --

Born:

Died:

1 Henry LOWE

Christened: 10 Jul 1652

Married: 1688

Died: 1717

12

Born:

Married:

Died:

6 Arthur PILKINGTON

Born: Abt 1590

Married:

Died:

13

Born:

Died:

Susanna Maria BENNETT

Spouse

3 Katherine PILKINGTON

Born: Abt 1620

Died:

14 Henry LYON

Born: Abt 1560

Married:

Died:

7 Ellen LYON

Born: Abt 1595

Died:

15 --

Born:

Died:

Sources include: Richardson *Plantagenet* (2004), pp. 468-470 (Lowe); Faris 2--Lowe; Roberts *500*, pp. 161-162; *Blood Royal* 5:910-913. Note: Susanna Maria Bennett (spouse of #1) was dau. of Henrietta Maria Neale (b. 29 Apr 1647; md. Richard Bennett), dau. of James Neale & Anna Maria Gill, cont. cht. 893, #2 & 3).

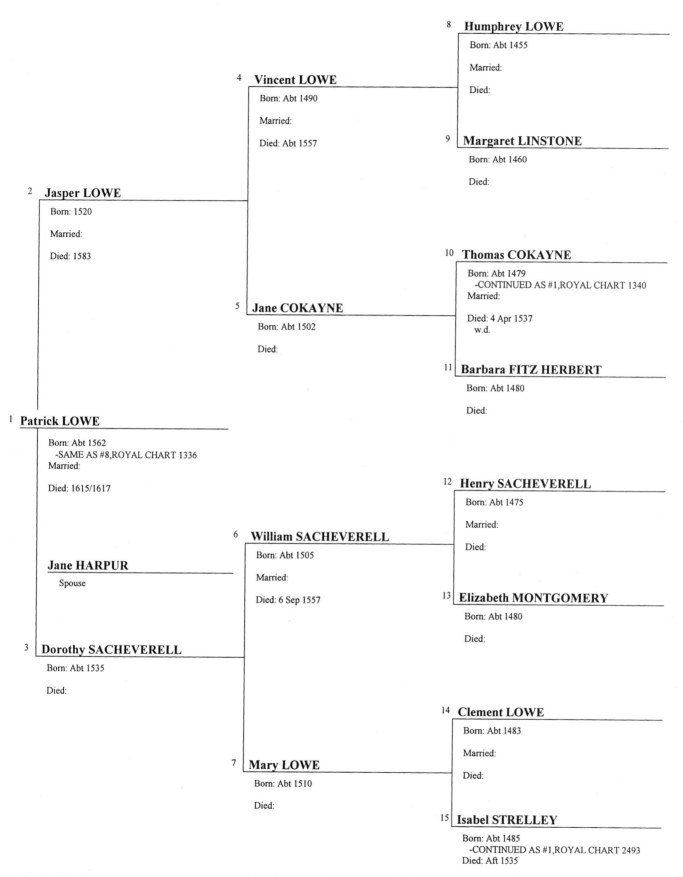

8 Humphrey LOWE

Born: Abt 1455

Married:

Died:

4 Vincent LOWE

Born: Abt 1490

Married:

Died: Abt 1557

9 Margaret LINSTONE

Born: Abt 1460

Died:

2 Jasper LOWE

Born: 1520

Married:

Died: 1583

10 Thomas COKAYNE

Born: Abt 1479
  -CONTINUED AS #1,ROYAL CHART 1340
Married:

Died: 4 Apr 1537
w.d.

5 Jane COKAYNE

Born: Abt 1502

Died:

11 Barbara FITZ HERBERT

Born: Abt 1480

Died:

1 Patrick LOWE

Born: Abt 1562
  -SAME AS #8,ROYAL CHART 1336
Married:

Died: 1615/1617

12 Henry SACHEVERELL

Born: Abt 1475

Married:

Died:

6 William SACHEVERELL

Born: Abt 1505

Married:

Died: 6 Sep 1557

13 Elizabeth MONTGOMERY

Born: Abt 1480

Died:

Jane HARPUR

Spouse

3 Dorothy SACHEVERELL

Born: Abt 1535

Died:

14 Clement LOWE

Born: Abt 1483

Married:

Died:

7 Mary LOWE

Born: Abt 1510

Died:

15 Isabel STRELLEY

Born: Abt 1485
  -CONTINUED AS #1,ROYAL CHART 2493
Died: Aft 1535

Sources include: Richardson *Plantagenet* (2004), pp. 468-469 (Lowe), 224-225 (Cokayne), 624 (Sacheverell); *Blood Royal* 5:912; Faris 2--Lowe (#1 of Magna Charta descent).

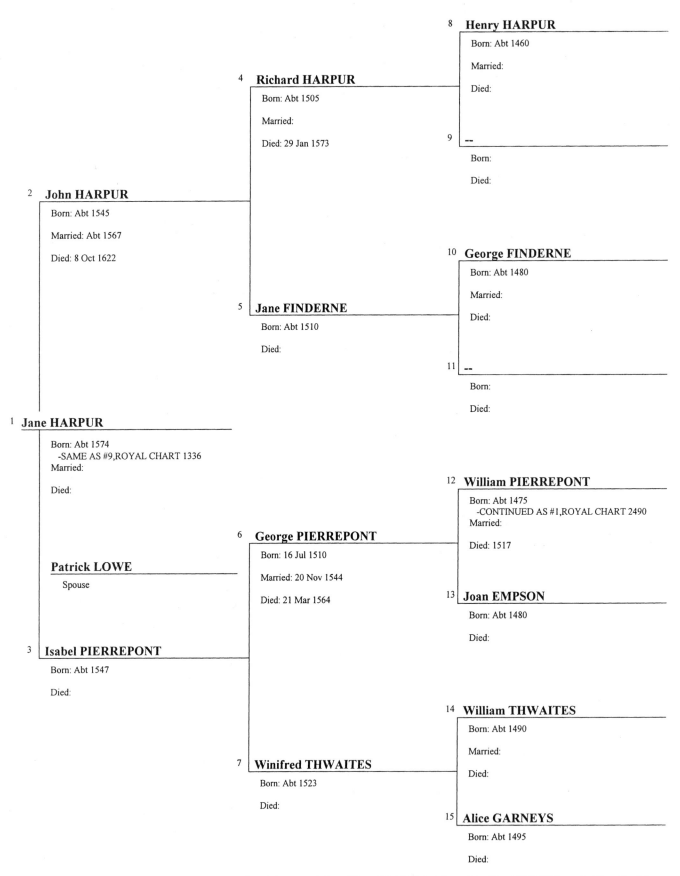

8 **Henry HARPUR**

Born: Abt 1460

Married:

Died:

4 **Richard HARPUR**

Born: Abt 1505

Married:

Died: 29 Jan 1573

9 **--**

Born:

Died:

2 **John HARPUR**

Born: Abt 1545

Married: Abt 1567

Died: 8 Oct 1622

10 **George FINDERNE**

Born: Abt 1480

Married:

Died:

5 **Jane FINDERNE**

Born: Abt 1510

Died:

11 **--**

Born:

Died:

1 **Jane HARPUR**

Born: Abt 1574
 -SAME AS #9,ROYAL CHART 1336
Married:

Died:

12 **William PIERREPONT**

Born: Abt 1475
 -CONTINUED AS #1,ROYAL CHART 2490
Married:

Died: 1517

Patrick LOWE

Spouse

6 **George PIERREPONT**

Born: 16 Jul 1510

Married: 20 Nov 1544

Died: 21 Mar 1564

13 **Joan EMPSON**

Born: Abt 1480

Died:

3 **Isabel PIERREPONT**

Born: Abt 1547

Died:

14 **William THWAITES**

Born: Abt 1490

Married:

Died:

7 **Winifred THWAITES**

Born: Abt 1523

Died:

15 **Alice GARNEYS**

Born: Abt 1495

Died:

Sources include: Richardson *Plantagenet* (2004), pp. 468 (Lowe), 583-584 (Pierrepont); Roberts *500*, pp. 161-162; Faris 2--Lowe; *Blood Royal* 5:912; LDS records. Note: The claim that #14 William descends from William Knyvett & Alice Grey (see chart 857) is corrected in Roberts *500* (600) updated manuscript (November 2000), pp. 186-187.

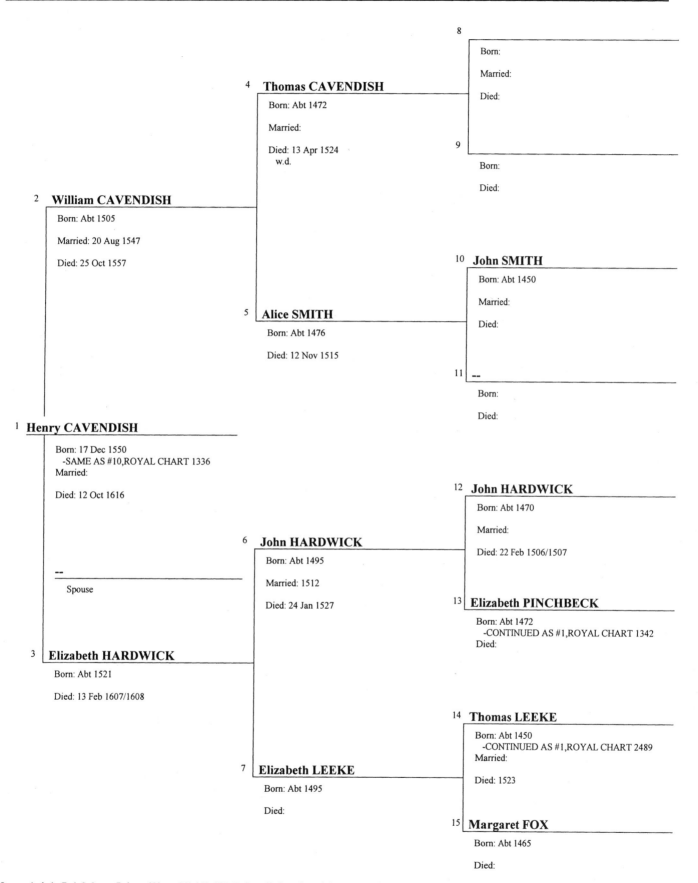

8

Born:

Married:

Died:

---

4   Thomas CAVENDISH

Born: Abt 1472

Married:

Died: 13 Apr 1524
w.d.

9

Born:

Died:

---

2   William CAVENDISH

Born: Abt 1505

Married: 20 Aug 1547

Died: 25 Oct 1557

10   John SMITH

Born: Abt 1450

Married:

Died:

---

5   Alice SMITH

Born: Abt 1476

Died: 12 Nov 1515

11   --

Born:

Died:

---

1   Henry CAVENDISH

Born: 17 Dec 1550
-SAME AS #10,ROYAL CHART 1336
Married:

Died: 12 Oct 1616

12   John HARDWICK

Born: Abt 1470

Married:

Died: 22 Feb 1506/1507

---

6   John HARDWICK

Born: Abt 1495

Married: 1512

Died: 24 Jan 1527

13   Elizabeth PINCHBECK

Born: Abt 1472
-CONTINUED AS #1,ROYAL CHART 1342
Died:

--

Spouse

---

3   Elizabeth HARDWICK

Born: Abt 1521

Died: 13 Feb 1607/1608

14   Thomas LEEKE

Born: Abt 1450
-CONTINUED AS #1,ROYAL CHART 2489
Married:

Died: 1523

---

7   Elizabeth LEEKE

Born: Abt 1495

Died:

15   Margaret FOX

Born: Abt 1465

Died:

Sources include: Faris 2–Lowe; Roberts *500*, pp. 161-162, 285; Faris preliminary baronial manuscript (1998), pp. 799-800 Hardwick (#3 ancestry); *Blood Royal* 5:912. Note: The claim by Roberts and by Faris (baronial) that #12 John descends from Elizabeth Goushill (chart 449, #5) through a 2nd husband William Hardwick is unacceptable chronologically. See also chart 1435 and note.

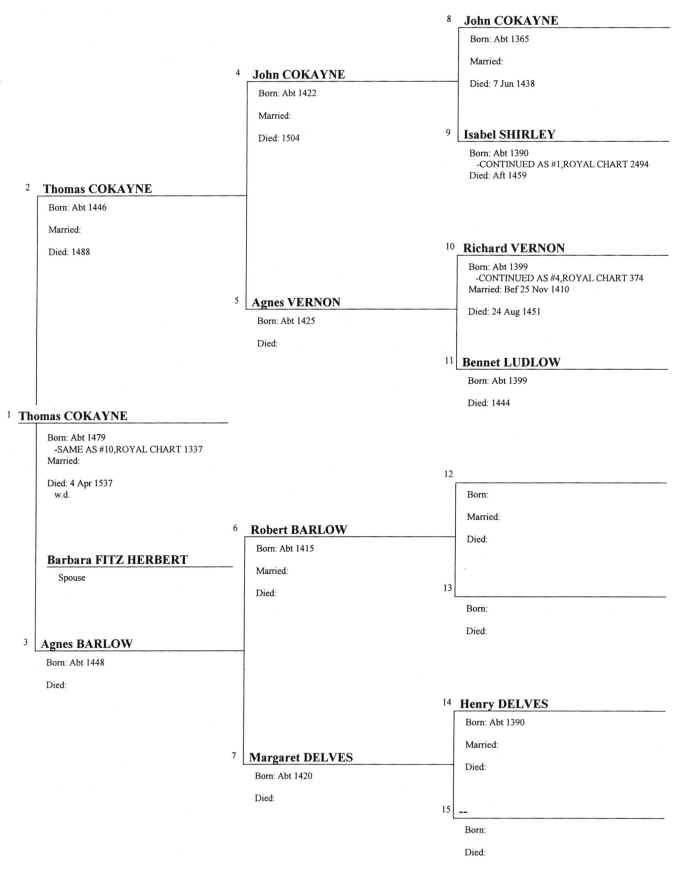

8 **John COKAYNE**

Born: Abt 1365

Married:

Died: 7 Jun 1438

4 **John COKAYNE**

Born: Abt 1422

Married:

Died: 1504

9 **Isabel SHIRLEY**

Born: Abt 1390
   -CONTINUED AS #1,ROYAL CHART 2494
Died: Aft 1459

2 **Thomas COKAYNE**

Born: Abt 1446

Married:

Died: 1488

10 **Richard VERNON**

Born: Abt 1399
   -CONTINUED AS #4,ROYAL CHART 374
Married: Bef 25 Nov 1410

Died: 24 Aug 1451

5 **Agnes VERNON**

Born: Abt 1425

Died:

11 **Bennet LUDLOW**

Born: Abt 1399

Died: 1444

1 **Thomas COKAYNE**

Born: Abt 1479
   -SAME AS #10,ROYAL CHART 1337
Married:

Died: 4 Apr 1537
  w.d.

12

Born:

Married:

Died:

6 **Robert BARLOW**

Born: Abt 1415

Married:

Died:

13

Born:

Died:

Barbara FITZ HERBERT

Spouse

3 **Agnes BARLOW**

Born: Abt 1448

Died:

14 **Henry DELVES**

Born: Abt 1390

Married:

Died:

7 **Margaret DELVES**

Born: Abt 1420

Died:

15 **--**

Born:

Died:

Sources include: Consultation with Douglas Richardson; *Blood Royal* 5:912; LDS records (#4 ancestry).

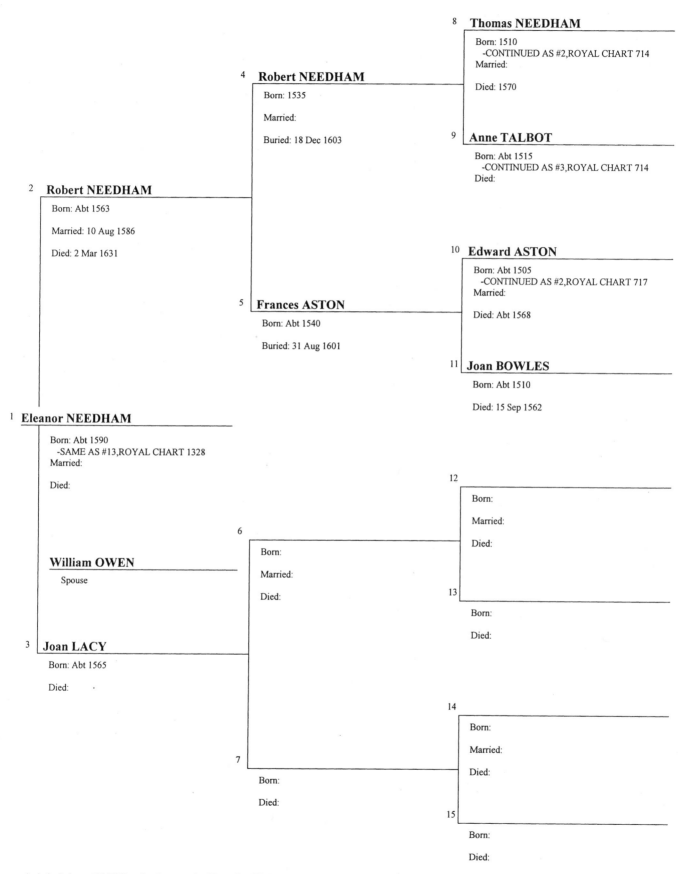

8 **Thomas NEEDHAM**

Born: 1510
-CONTINUED AS #2,ROYAL CHART 714
Married:

Died: 1570

4 **Robert NEEDHAM**

Born: 1535

Married:

Buried: 18 Dec 1603

9 **Anne TALBOT**

Born: Abt 1515
-CONTINUED AS #3,ROYAL CHART 714
Died:

2 **Robert NEEDHAM**

Born: Abt 1563

Married: 10 Aug 1586

Died: 2 Mar 1631

10 **Edward ASTON**

Born: Abt 1505
-CONTINUED AS #2,ROYAL CHART 717
Married:

Died: Abt 1568

5 **Frances ASTON**

Born: Abt 1540

Buried: 31 Aug 1601

11 **Joan BOWLES**

Born: Abt 1510

Died: 15 Sep 1562

1 **Eleanor NEEDHAM**

Born: Abt 1590
-SAME AS #13,ROYAL CHART 1328
Married:

Died:

12

Born:

Married:

Died:

6

Born:

Married:

Died:

13

Born:

Died:

William OWEN

Spouse

3 **Joan LACY**

Born: Abt 1565

Died:

14

Born:

Married:

Died:

7

Born:

Died:

15

Born:

Died:

Sources include: Roberts *500* (600) updated manuscript (November 2000), pp. 344-345.

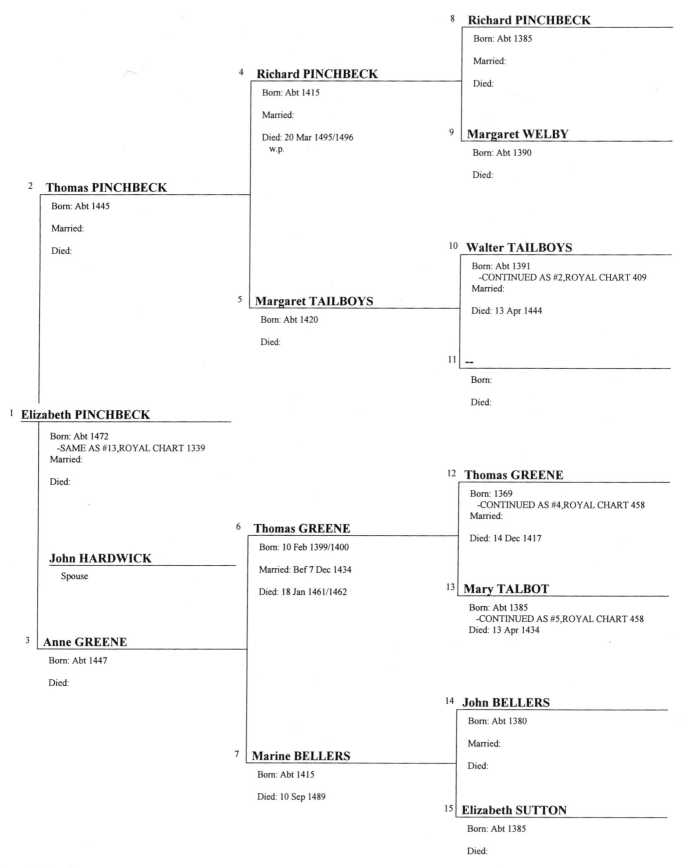

8 Richard PINCHBECK
Born: Abt 1385
Married:
Died:

4 Richard PINCHBECK
Born: Abt 1415
Married:
Died: 20 Mar 1495/1496
w.p.

9 Margaret WELBY
Born: Abt 1390
Died:

2 Thomas PINCHBECK
Born: Abt 1445
Married:
Died:

10 Walter TAILBOYS
Born: Abt 1391
-CONTINUED AS #2,ROYAL CHART 409
Married:
Died: 13 Apr 1444

5 Margaret TAILBOYS
Born: Abt 1420
Died:

11 --
Born:
Died:

1 Elizabeth PINCHBECK
Born: Abt 1472
-SAME AS #13,ROYAL CHART 1339
Married:
Died:

12 Thomas GREENE
Born: 1369
-CONTINUED AS #4,ROYAL CHART 458
Married:
Died: 14 Dec 1417

6 Thomas GREENE
Born: 10 Feb 1399/1400
Married: Bef 7 Dec 1434
Died: 18 Jan 1461/1462

John HARDWICK
Spouse

13 Mary TALBOT
Born: Abt 1385
-CONTINUED AS #5,ROYAL CHART 458
Died: 13 Apr 1434

3 Anne GREENE
Born: Abt 1447
Died:

14 John BELLERS
Born: Abt 1380
Married:
Died:

7 Marine BELLERS
Born: Abt 1415
Died: 10 Sep 1489

15 Elizabeth SUTTON
Born: Abt 1385
Died:

Sources include: Faris 2--Lowe, Greene; Faris-Richardson preliminary Magna Carta manuscript (June 2000), pp. 423 (Pinchbeck), 489-490 (Tailboys); Faris preliminary baronial manuscript (1998), p. 1254 (Pinchbeck).

Pedigree Chart

Chart 1343

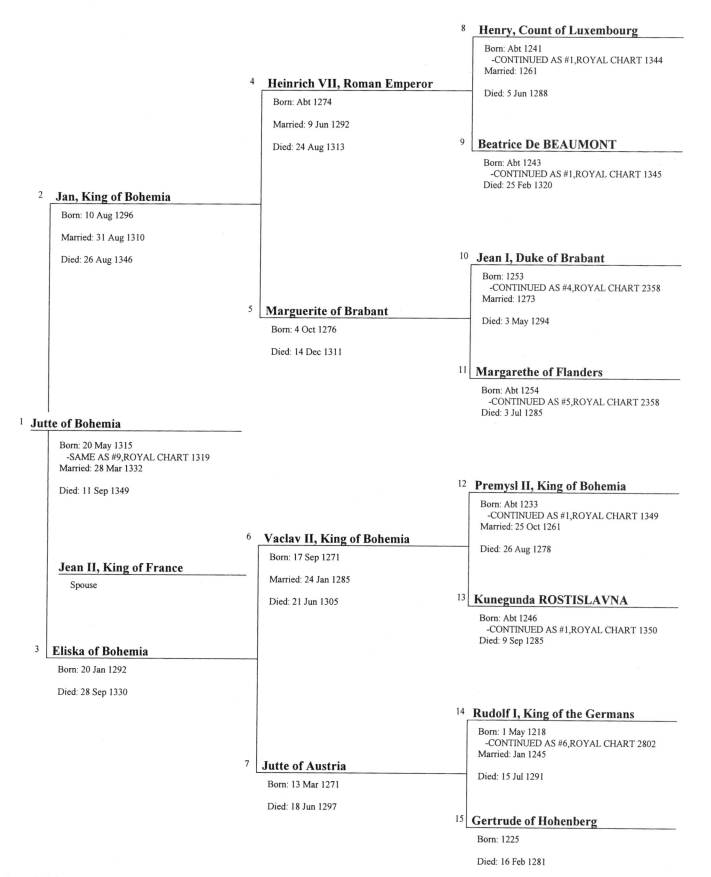

2 Jan, King of Bohemia

Born: 10 Aug 1296

Married: 31 Aug 1310

Died: 26 Aug 1346

4 Heinrich VII, Roman Emperor

Born: Abt 1274

Married: 9 Jun 1292

Died: 24 Aug 1313

8 Henry, Count of Luxembourg

Born: Abt 1241
-CONTINUED AS #1,ROYAL CHART 1344
Married: 1261

Died: 5 Jun 1288

9 Beatrice De BEAUMONT

Born: Abt 1243
-CONTINUED AS #1,ROYAL CHART 1345
Died: 25 Feb 1320

5 Marguerite of Brabant

Born: 4 Oct 1276

Died: 14 Dec 1311

10 Jean I, Duke of Brabant

Born: 1253
-CONTINUED AS #4,ROYAL CHART 2358
Married: 1273

Died: 3 May 1294

11 Margarethe of Flanders

Born: Abt 1254
-CONTINUED AS #5,ROYAL CHART 2358
Died: 3 Jul 1285

1 Jutte of Bohemia

Born: 20 May 1315
-SAME AS #9,ROYAL CHART 1319
Married: 28 Mar 1332

Died: 11 Sep 1349

Jean II, King of France

Spouse

3 Eliska of Bohemia

Born: 20 Jan 1292

Died: 28 Sep 1330

6 Vaclav II, King of Bohemia

Born: 17 Sep 1271

Married: 24 Jan 1285

Died: 21 Jun 1305

12 Premysl II, King of Bohemia

Born: Abt 1233
-CONTINUED AS #1,ROYAL CHART 1349
Married: 25 Oct 1261

Died: 26 Aug 1278

13 Kunegunda ROSTISLAVNA

Born: Abt 1246
-CONTINUED AS #1,ROYAL CHART 1350
Died: 9 Sep 1285

7 Jutte of Austria

Born: 13 Mar 1271

Died: 18 Jun 1297

14 Rudolf I, King of the Germans

Born: 1 May 1218
-CONTINUED AS #6,ROYAL CHART 2802
Married: Jan 1245

Died: 15 Jul 1291

15 Gertrude of Hohenberg

Born: 1225

Died: 16 Feb 1281

Sources include: LDS records; Schwennicke 1:96 (#5 ancestry), 1:56 (#3 ancestry).

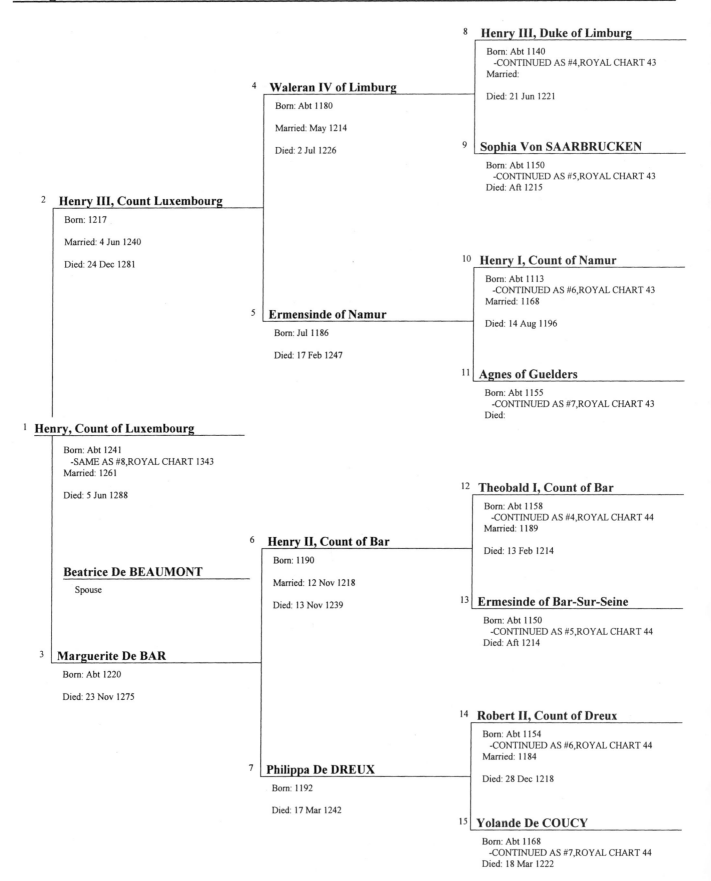

8 Henry III, Duke of Limburg

Born: Abt 1140
  -CONTINUED AS #4,ROYAL CHART 43
Married:

Died: 21 Jun 1221

4 Waleran IV of Limburg

Born: Abt 1180

Married: May 1214

Died: 2 Jul 1226

9 Sophia Von SAARBRUCKEN

Born: Abt 1150
  -CONTINUED AS #5,ROYAL CHART 43
Died: Aft 1215

2 Henry III, Count Luxembourg

Born: 1217

Married: 4 Jun 1240

Died: 24 Dec 1281

10 Henry I, Count of Namur

Born: Abt 1113
  -CONTINUED AS #6,ROYAL CHART 43
Married: 1168

Died: 14 Aug 1196

5 Ermensinde of Namur

Born: Jul 1186

Died: 17 Feb 1247

11 Agnes of Guelders

Born: Abt 1155
  -CONTINUED AS #7,ROYAL CHART 43
Died:

1 Henry, Count of Luxembourg

Born: Abt 1241
  -SAME AS #8,ROYAL CHART 1343
Married: 1261

Died: 5 Jun 1288

12 Theobald I, Count of Bar

Born: Abt 1158
  -CONTINUED AS #4,ROYAL CHART 44
Married: 1189

Died: 13 Feb 1214

6 Henry II, Count of Bar

Born: 1190

Married: 12 Nov 1218

Died: 13 Nov 1239

13 Ermesinde of Bar-Sur-Seine

Born: Abt 1150
  -CONTINUED AS #5,ROYAL CHART 44
Died: Aft 1214

Beatrice De BEAUMONT

Spouse

3 Marguerite De BAR

Born: Abt 1220

Died: 23 Nov 1275

14 Robert II, Count of Dreux

Born: Abt 1154
  -CONTINUED AS #6,ROYAL CHART 44
Married: 1184

Died: 28 Dec 1218

7 Philippa De DREUX

Born: 1192

Died: 17 Mar 1242

15 Yolande De COUCY

Born: Abt 1168
  -CONTINUED AS #7,ROYAL CHART 44
Died: 18 Mar 1222

Sources include: LDS records; *Royal Ancestors* (1989), chart 11202 (#2 & 3 ancestry).

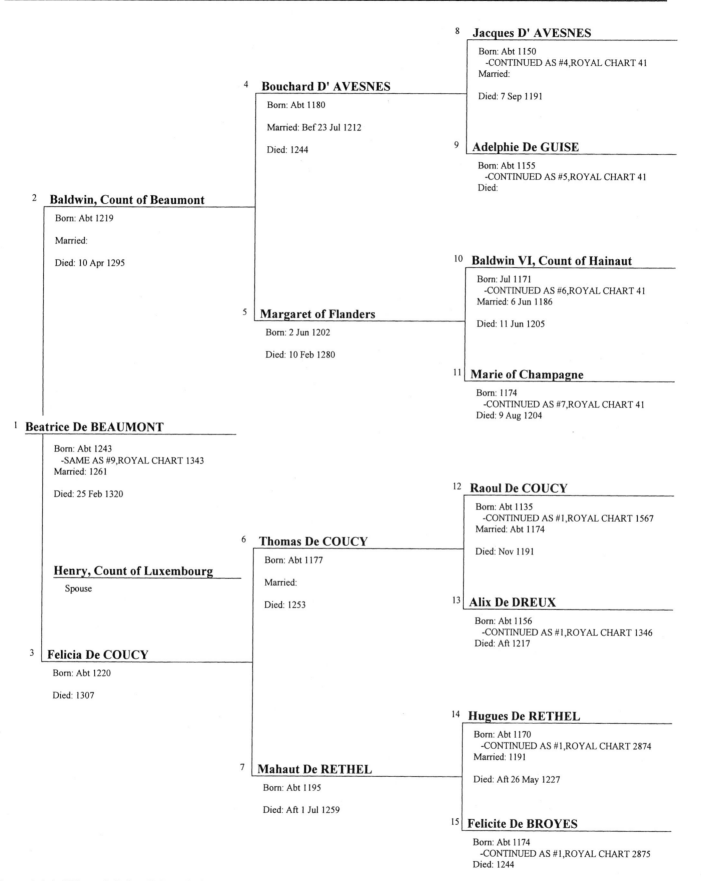

8 **Jacques D' AVESNES**

Born: Abt 1150
-CONTINUED AS #4,ROYAL CHART 41
Married:

Died: 7 Sep 1191

4 **Bouchard D' AVESNES**

Born: Abt 1180

Married: Bef 23 Jul 1212

Died: 1244

9 **Adelphie De GUISE**

Born: Abt 1155
-CONTINUED AS #5,ROYAL CHART 41
Died:

2 **Baldwin, Count of Beaumont**

Born: Abt 1219

Married:

Died: 10 Apr 1295

10 **Baldwin VI, Count of Hainaut**

Born: Jul 1171
-CONTINUED AS #6,ROYAL CHART 41
Married: 6 Jun 1186

Died: 11 Jun 1205

5 **Margaret of Flanders**

Born: 2 Jun 1202

Died: 10 Feb 1280

11 **Marie of Champagne**

Born: 1174
-CONTINUED AS #7,ROYAL CHART 41
Died: 9 Aug 1204

1 **Beatrice De BEAUMONT**

Born: Abt 1243
-SAME AS #9,ROYAL CHART 1343
Married: 1261

Died: 25 Feb 1320

12 **Raoul De COUCY**

Born: Abt 1135
-CONTINUED AS #1,ROYAL CHART 1567
Married: Abt 1174

Died: Nov 1191

6 **Thomas De COUCY**

Born: Abt 1177

Married:

Died: 1253

13 **Alix De DREUX**

Born: Abt 1156
-CONTINUED AS #1,ROYAL CHART 1346
Died: Aft 1217

Henry, Count of Luxembourg

Spouse

3 **Felicia De COUCY**

Born: Abt 1220

Died: 1307

14 **Hugues De RETHEL**

Born: Abt 1170
-CONTINUED AS #1,ROYAL CHART 2874
Married: 1191

Died: Aft 26 May 1227

7 **Mahaut De RETHEL**

Born: Abt 1195

Died: Aft 1 Jul 1259

15 **Felicite De BROYES**

Born: Abt 1174
-CONTINUED AS #1,ROYAL CHART 2875
Died: 1244

Sources include: LDS records; Faris preliminary Charlemagne manuscript (June 1995), p. 112 (#6 & 7 ancestry); *Royal Ancestors* (1989), charts 11315-16 (#4 & 5 ancestry).

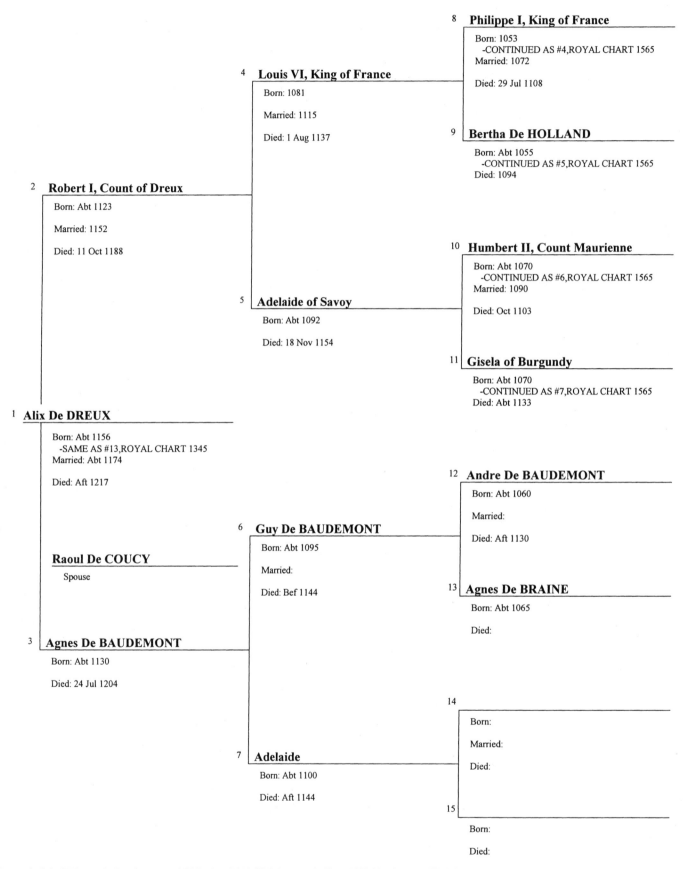

8 Philippe I, King of France
Born: 1053
  -CONTINUED AS #4,ROYAL CHART 1565
Married: 1072

Died: 29 Jul 1108

4 Louis VI, King of France
Born: 1081

Married: 1115

Died: 1 Aug 1137

9 Bertha De HOLLAND
Born: Abt 1055
  -CONTINUED AS #5,ROYAL CHART 1565
Died: 1094

2 Robert I, Count of Dreux
Born: Abt 1123

Married: 1152

Died: 11 Oct 1188

10 Humbert II, Count Maurienne
Born: Abt 1070
  -CONTINUED AS #6,ROYAL CHART 1565
Married: 1090

Died: Oct 1103

5 Adelaide of Savoy
Born: Abt 1092

Died: 18 Nov 1154

11 Gisela of Burgundy
Born: Abt 1070
  -CONTINUED AS #7,ROYAL CHART 1565
Died: Abt 1133

1 Alix De DREUX
Born: Abt 1156
  -SAME AS #13,ROYAL CHART 1345
Married: Abt 1174

Died: Aft 1217

12 Andre De BAUDEMONT
Born: Abt 1060

Married:

Died: Aft 1130

6 Guy De BAUDEMONT
Born: Abt 1095

Married:

Died: Bef 1144

Raoul De COUCY
Spouse

13 Agnes De BRAINE
Born: Abt 1065

Died:

3 Agnes De BAUDEMONT
Born: Abt 1130

Died: 24 Jul 1204

14
Born:

Married:

Died:

7 Adelaide
Born: Abt 1100

Died: Aft 1144

15
Born:

Died:

Sources include: LDS records; *Royal Ancestors* (1989), chart 11376 (#2 & 3 ancestry); Charts 1565-66 and sources (#2 & 3 ancestry).

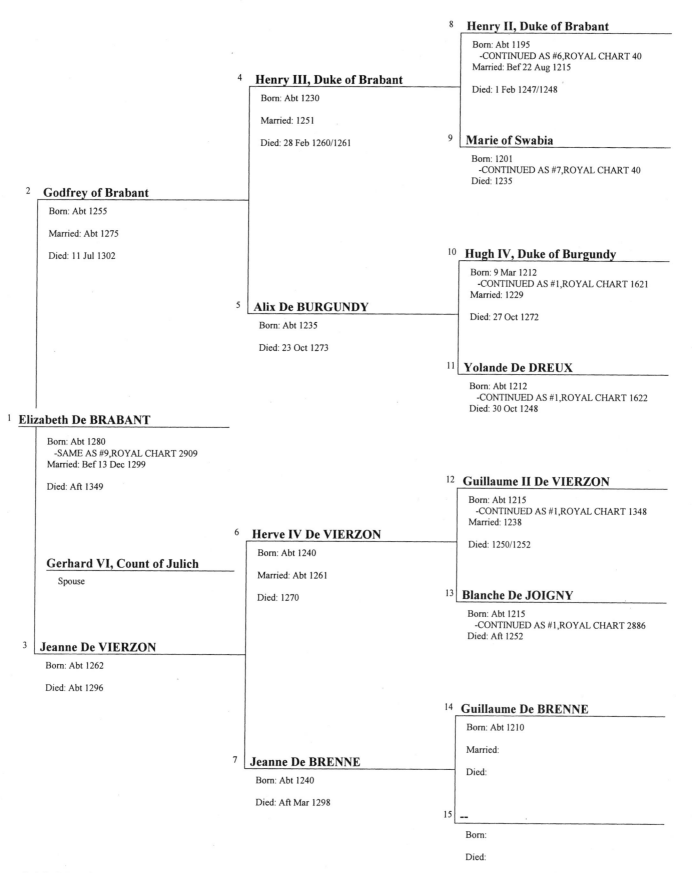

8 Henry II, Duke of Brabant

Born: Abt 1195
-CONTINUED AS #6,ROYAL CHART 40
Married: Bef 22 Aug 1215

Died: 1 Feb 1247/1248

4 Henry III, Duke of Brabant

Born: Abt 1230

Married: 1251

Died: 28 Feb 1260/1261

9 Marie of Swabia

Born: 1201
-CONTINUED AS #7,ROYAL CHART 40
Died: 1235

2 Godfrey of Brabant

Born: Abt 1255

Married: Abt 1275

Died: 11 Jul 1302

10 Hugh IV, Duke of Burgundy

Born: 9 Mar 1212
-CONTINUED AS #1,ROYAL CHART 1621
Married: 1229

Died: 27 Oct 1272

5 Alix De BURGUNDY

Born: Abt 1235

Died: 23 Oct 1273

11 Yolande De DREUX

Born: Abt 1212
-CONTINUED AS #1,ROYAL CHART 1622
Died: 30 Oct 1248

1 Elizabeth De BRABANT

Born: Abt 1280
-SAME AS #9,ROYAL CHART 2909
Married: Bef 13 Dec 1299

Died: Aft 1349

12 Guillaume II De VIERZON

Born: Abt 1215
-CONTINUED AS #1,ROYAL CHART 1348
Married: 1238

Died: 1250/1252

6 Herve IV De VIERZON

Born: Abt 1240

Married: Abt 1261

Died: 1270

13 Blanche De JOIGNY

Born: Abt 1215
-CONTINUED AS #1,ROYAL CHART 2886
Died: Aft 1252

Gerhard VI, Count of Julich

Spouse

3 Jeanne De VIERZON

Born: Abt 1262

Died: Abt 1296

14 Guillaume De BRENNE

Born: Abt 1210

Married:

Died:

7 Jeanne De BRENNE

Born: Abt 1240

Died: Aft Mar 1298

15 --

Born:

Died:

Sources include: Schwennicke 1:96, 13:158.

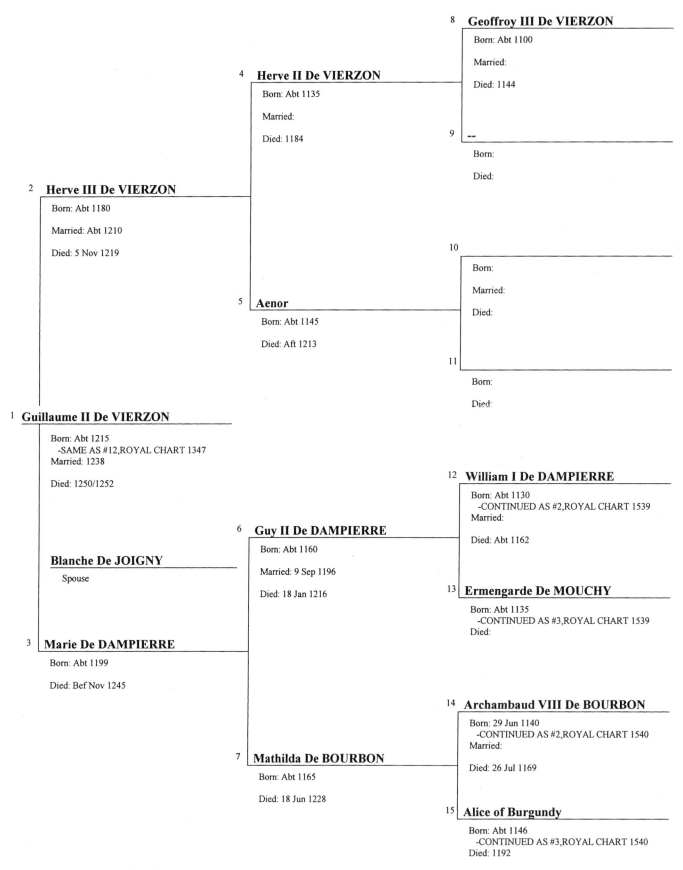

8　**Geoffroy III De VIERZON**
Born: Abt 1100
Married:
Died: 1144

4　**Herve II De VIERZON**
Born: Abt 1135
Married:
Died: 1184

9　**--**
Born:
Died:

2　**Herve III De VIERZON**
Born: Abt 1180
Married: Abt 1210
Died: 5 Nov 1219

10
Born:
Married:
Died:

5　**Aenor**
Born: Abt 1145
Died: Aft 1213

11
Born:
Died:

1　**Guillaume II De VIERZON**
Born: Abt 1215
　-SAME AS #12,ROYAL CHART 1347
Married: 1238
Died: 1250/1252

12　**William I De DAMPIERRE**
Born: Abt 1130
　-CONTINUED AS #2,ROYAL CHART 1539
Married:
Died: Abt 1162

6　**Guy II De DAMPIERRE**
Born: Abt 1160
Married: 9 Sep 1196
Died: 18 Jan 1216

13　**Ermengarde De MOUCHY**
Born: Abt 1135
　-CONTINUED AS #3,ROYAL CHART 1539
Died:

Blanche De JOIGNY
Spouse

3　**Marie De DAMPIERRE**
Born: Abt 1199
Died: Bef Nov 1245

14　**Archambaud VIII De BOURBON**
Born: 29 Jun 1140
　-CONTINUED AS #2,ROYAL CHART 1540
Married:
Died: 26 Jul 1169

7　**Mathilda De BOURBON**
Born: Abt 1165
Died: 18 Jun 1228

15　**Alice of Burgundy**
Born: Abt 1146
　-CONTINUED AS #3,ROYAL CHART 1540
Died: 1192

Sources include: Schwennicke 13:158, 3:51.

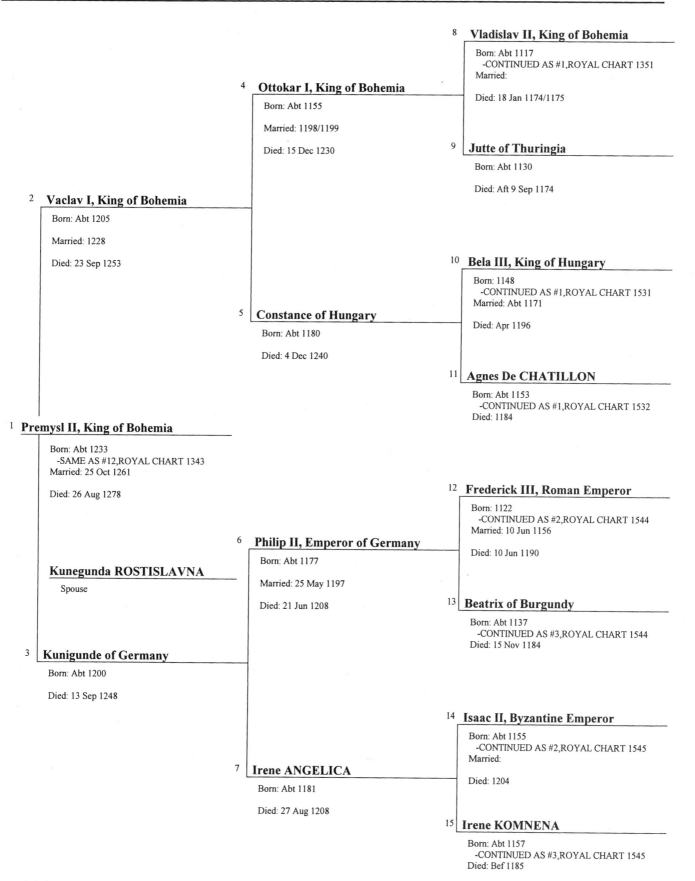

8 Vladislav II, King of Bohemia
Born: Abt 1117
 -CONTINUED AS #1,ROYAL CHART 1351
Married:

Died: 18 Jan 1174/1175

4 Ottokar I, King of Bohemia
Born: Abt 1155

Married: 1198/1199

Died: 15 Dec 1230

9 Jutte of Thuringia
Born: Abt 1130

Died: Aft 9 Sep 1174

2 Vaclav I, King of Bohemia
Born: Abt 1205

Married: 1228

Died: 23 Sep 1253

10 Bela III, King of Hungary
Born: 1148
 -CONTINUED AS #1,ROYAL CHART 1531
Married: Abt 1171

Died: Apr 1196

5 Constance of Hungary
Born: Abt 1180

Died: 4 Dec 1240

11 Agnes De CHATILLON
Born: Abt 1153
 -CONTINUED AS #1,ROYAL CHART 1532
Died: 1184

1 Premysl II, King of Bohemia
Born: Abt 1233
 -SAME AS #12,ROYAL CHART 1343
Married: 25 Oct 1261

Died: 26 Aug 1278

12 Frederick III, Roman Emperor
Born: 1122
 -CONTINUED AS #2,ROYAL CHART 1544
Married: 10 Jun 1156

Died: 10 Jun 1190

6 Philip II, Emperor of Germany
Born: Abt 1177

Married: 25 May 1197

Died: 21 Jun 1208

13 Beatrix of Burgundy
Born: Abt 1137
 -CONTINUED AS #3,ROYAL CHART 1544
Died: 15 Nov 1184

Kunegunda ROSTISLAVNA
Spouse

3 Kunigunde of Germany
Born: Abt 1200

Died: 13 Sep 1248

14 Isaac II, Byzantine Emperor
Born: Abt 1155
 -CONTINUED AS #2,ROYAL CHART 1545
Married:

Died: 1204

7 Irene ANGELICA
Born: Abt 1181

Died: 27 Aug 1208

15 Irene KOMNENA
Born: Abt 1157
 -CONTINUED AS #3,ROYAL CHART 1545
Died: Bef 1185

Sources include: Schwennicke 1:55-56; LDS records; *Royal Ancestors* (1989), chart 11314 (#6 & 7 ancestry); Von Isenburg 1:5 (#3 ancestry); 2:104 (#5 ancestry). Note: Schwennicke calls #2 Wenzel I.

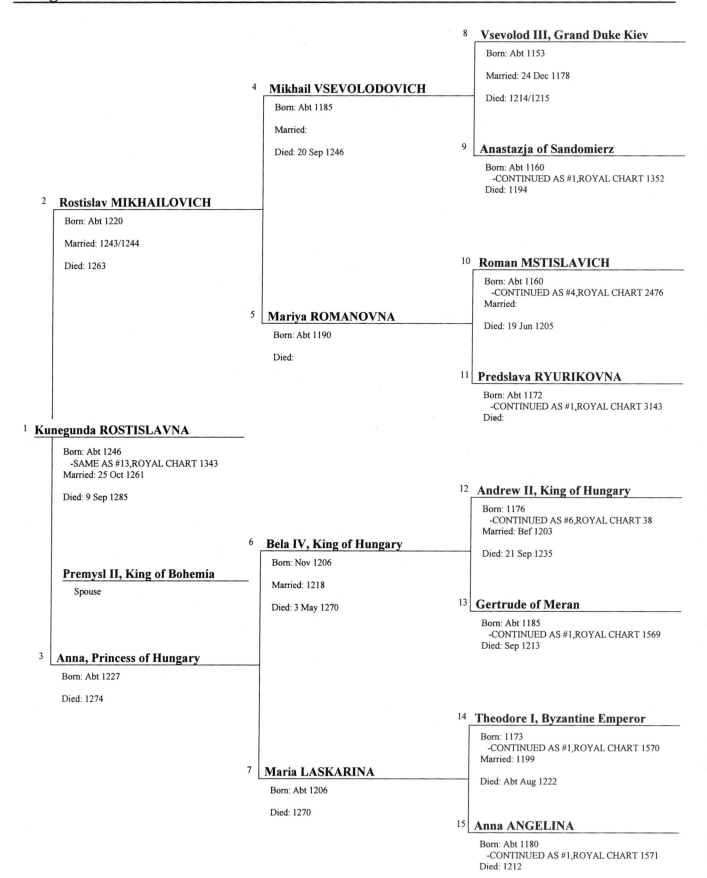

2 Rostislav MIKHAILOVICH

Born: Abt 1220

Married: 1243/1244

Died: 1263

4 Mikhail VSEVOLODOVICH

Born: Abt 1185

Married:

Died: 20 Sep 1246

8 Vsevolod III, Grand Duke Kiev

Born: Abt 1153

Married: 24 Dec 1178

Died: 1214/1215

9 Anastazja of Sandomierz

Born: Abt 1160
  -CONTINUED AS #1,ROYAL CHART 1352
Died: 1194

5 Mariya ROMANOVNA

Born: Abt 1190

Died:

10 Roman MSTISLAVICH

Born: Abt 1160
  -CONTINUED AS #4,ROYAL CHART 2476
Married:

Died: 19 Jun 1205

11 Predslava RYURIKOVNA

Born: Abt 1172
  -CONTINUED AS #1,ROYAL CHART 3143
Died:

1 Kunegunda ROSTISLAVNA

Born: Abt 1246
  -SAME AS #13,ROYAL CHART 1343
Married: 25 Oct 1261

Died: 9 Sep 1285

Premysl II, King of Bohemia

Spouse

3 Anna, Princess of Hungary

Born: Abt 1227

Died: 1274

6 Bela IV, King of Hungary

Born: Nov 1206

Married: 1218

Died: 3 May 1270

12 Andrew II, King of Hungary

Born: 1176
  -CONTINUED AS #6,ROYAL CHART 38
Married: Bef 1203

Died: 21 Sep 1235

13 Gertrude of Meran

Born: Abt 1185
  -CONTINUED AS #1,ROYAL CHART 1569
Died: Sep 1213

7 Maria LASKARINA

Born: Abt 1206

Died: 1270

14 Theodore I, Byzantine Emperor

Born: 1173
  -CONTINUED AS #1,ROYAL CHART 1570
Married: 1199

Died: Abt Aug 1222

15 Anna ANGELINA

Born: Abt 1180
  -CONTINUED AS #1,ROYAL CHART 1571
Died: 1212

Sources include: LDS records; Schwennicke 2:136 (#5 ancestry); *Royal Ancestors* (1989), chart 11319 (#6 & 7 ancestry).

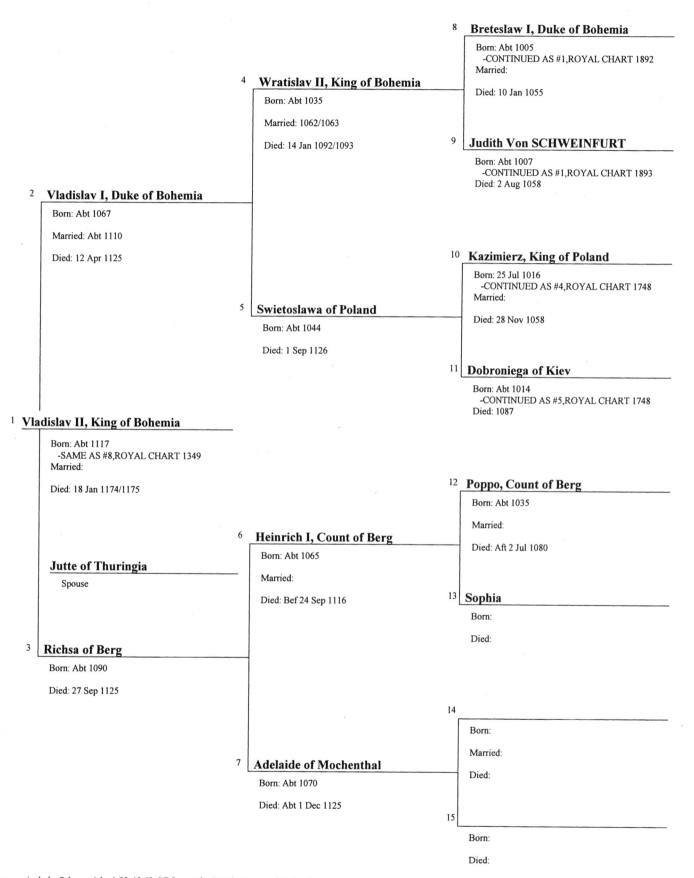

2 Vladislav I, Duke of Bohemia

Born: Abt 1067

Married: Abt 1110

Died: 12 Apr 1125

4 Wratislav II, King of Bohemia

Born: Abt 1035

Married: 1062/1063

Died: 14 Jan 1092/1093

8 Breteslaw I, Duke of Bohemia

Born: Abt 1005
     -CONTINUED AS #1,ROYAL CHART 1892
Married:

Died: 10 Jan 1055

9 Judith Von SCHWEINFURT

Born: Abt 1007
     -CONTINUED AS #1,ROYAL CHART 1893
Died: 2 Aug 1058

5 Swietoslawa of Poland

Born: Abt 1044

Died: 1 Sep 1126

10 Kazimierz, King of Poland

Born: 25 Jul 1016
     -CONTINUED AS #4,ROYAL CHART 1748
Married:

Died: 28 Nov 1058

11 Dobroniega of Kiev

Born: Abt 1014
     -CONTINUED AS #5,ROYAL CHART 1748
Died: 1087

1 Vladislav II, King of Bohemia

Born: Abt 1117
     -SAME AS #8,ROYAL CHART 1349
Married:

Died: 18 Jan 1174/1175

Jutte of Thuringia

Spouse

3 Richsa of Berg

Born: Abt 1090

Died: 27 Sep 1125

6 Heinrich I, Count of Berg

Born: Abt 1065

Married:

Died: Bef 24 Sep 1116

12 Poppo, Count of Berg

Born: Abt 1035

Married:

Died: Aft 2 Jul 1080

13 Sophia

Born:

Died:

7 Adelaide of Mochenthal

Born: Abt 1070

Died: Abt 1 Dec 1125

14

Born:

Married:

Died:

15

Born:

Died:

Sources include: Schwennicke 1:55, 12:62; LDS records; *Royal Ancestors* (1989), charts 11575-76 (#10 & 11), 11915 (#4 ancestry).

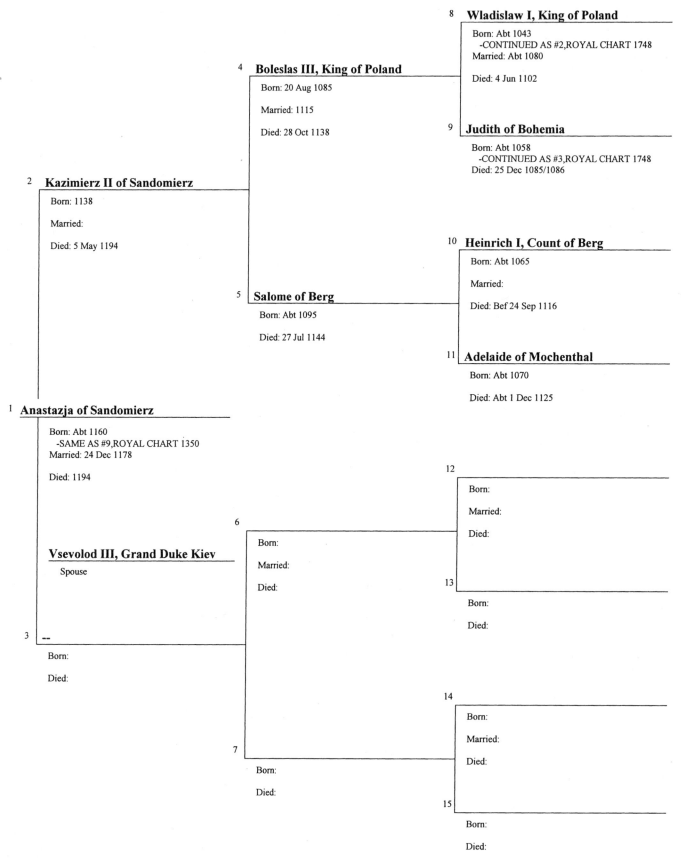

8 Wladislaw I, King of Poland
Born: Abt 1043
-CONTINUED AS #2,ROYAL CHART 1748
Married: Abt 1080

Died: 4 Jun 1102

4 Boleslas III, King of Poland
Born: 20 Aug 1085

Married: 1115

Died: 28 Oct 1138

9 Judith of Bohemia
Born: Abt 1058
-CONTINUED AS #3,ROYAL CHART 1748
Died: 25 Dec 1085/1086

2 Kazimierz II of Sandomierz
Born: 1138

Married:

Died: 5 May 1194

10 Heinrich I, Count of Berg
Born: Abt 1065

Married:

Died: Bef 24 Sep 1116

5 Salome of Berg
Born: Abt 1095

Died: 27 Jul 1144

11 Adelaide of Mochenthal
Born: Abt 1070

Died: Abt 1 Dec 1125

1 Anastazja of Sandomierz
Born: Abt 1160
-SAME AS #9,ROYAL CHART 1350
Married: 24 Dec 1178

Died: 1194

12
Born:

Married:

Died:

6
Born:

Married:

Died:

13
Born:

Died:

Vsevolod III, Grand Duke Kiev
Spouse

3 --
Born:

Died:

14
Born:

Married:

Died:

7
Born:

Died:

15
Born:

Died:

Sources include: LDS records; *Royal Ancestors* (1989), chart 11499 (#4 ancestry); Chart 1372 & sources (#4 & 5 ancestry).

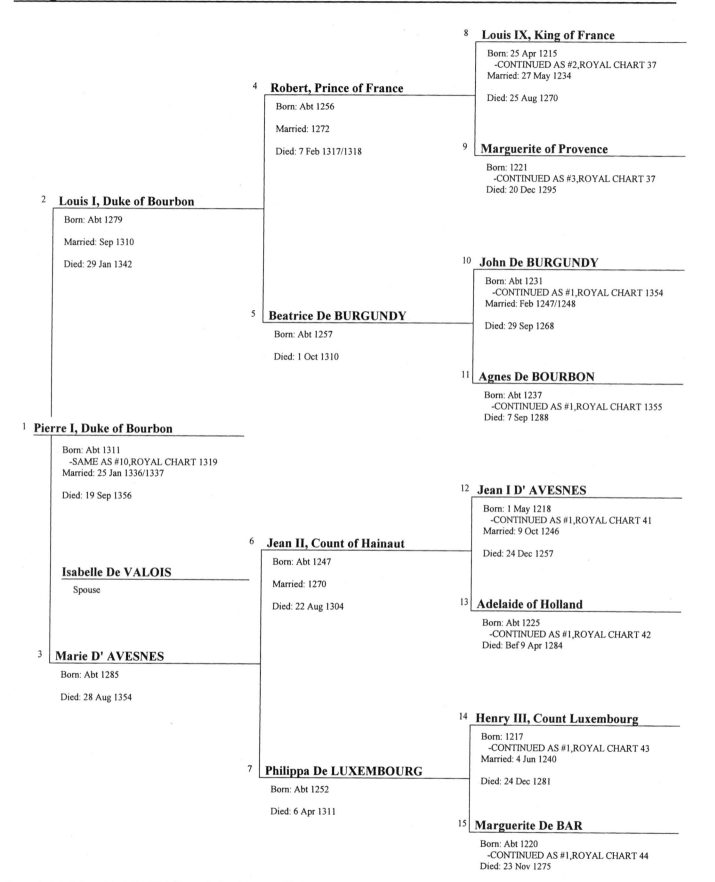

8 Louis IX, King of France
Born: 25 Apr 1215
    -CONTINUED AS #2,ROYAL CHART 37
Married: 27 May 1234

Died: 25 Aug 1270

4 Robert, Prince of France
Born: Abt 1256

Married: 1272

Died: 7 Feb 1317/1318

9 Marguerite of Provence
Born: 1221
    -CONTINUED AS #3,ROYAL CHART 37
Died: 20 Dec 1295

2 Louis I, Duke of Bourbon
Born: Abt 1279

Married: Sep 1310

Died: 29 Jan 1342

10 John De BURGUNDY
Born: Abt 1231
    -CONTINUED AS #1,ROYAL CHART 1354
Married: Feb 1247/1248

Died: 29 Sep 1268

5 Beatrice De BURGUNDY
Born: Abt 1257

Died: 1 Oct 1310

11 Agnes De BOURBON
Born: Abt 1237
    -CONTINUED AS #1,ROYAL CHART 1355
Died: 7 Sep 1288

1 Pierre I, Duke of Bourbon
Born: Abt 1311
    -SAME AS #10,ROYAL CHART 1319
Married: 25 Jan 1336/1337

Died: 19 Sep 1356

12 Jean I D' AVESNES
Born: 1 May 1218
    -CONTINUED AS #1,ROYAL CHART 41
Married: 9 Oct 1246

Died: 24 Dec 1257

6 Jean II, Count of Hainaut
Born: Abt 1247

Married: 1270

Died: 22 Aug 1304

13 Adelaide of Holland
Born: Abt 1225
    -CONTINUED AS #1,ROYAL CHART 42
Died: Bef 9 Apr 1284

Isabelle De VALOIS
Spouse

3 Marie D' AVESNES
Born: Abt 1285

Died: 28 Aug 1354

14 Henry III, Count Luxembourg
Born: 1217
    -CONTINUED AS #1,ROYAL CHART 43
Married: 4 Jun 1240

Died: 24 Dec 1281

7 Philippa De LUXEMBOURG
Born: Abt 1252

Died: 6 Apr 1311

15 Marguerite De BAR
Born: Abt 1220
    -CONTINUED AS #1,ROYAL CHART 44
Died: 23 Nov 1275

Sources include: Schwennicke 3:72, 2:21; LDS records; *Royal Ancestors* (1989), charts 11202 (#6 & 7 ancestry), 11309-10 (#8 & 9 ancestry).

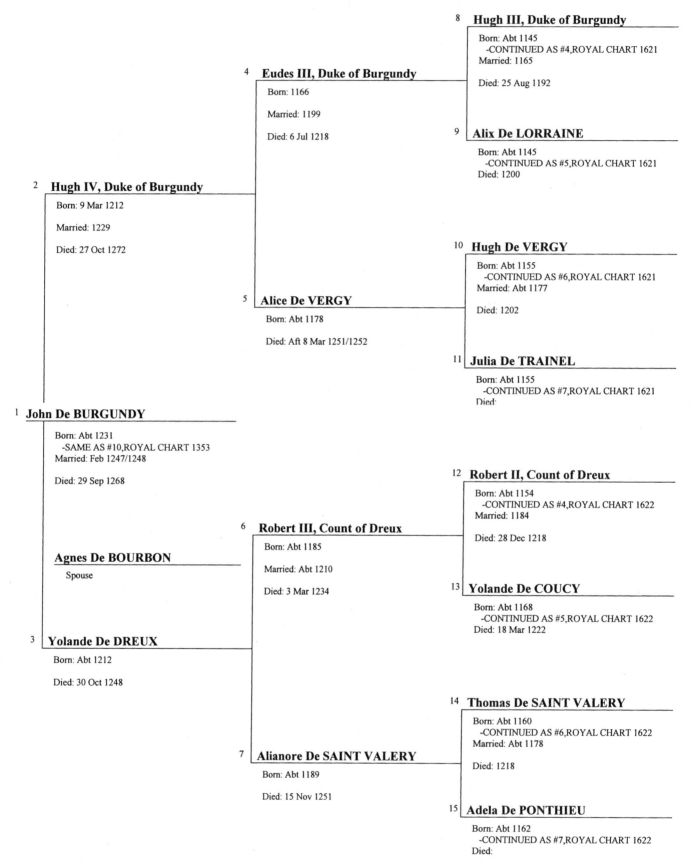

8 **Hugh III, Duke of Burgundy**

Born: Abt 1145
-CONTINUED AS #4,ROYAL CHART 1621
Married: 1165

Died: 25 Aug 1192

4 **Eudes III, Duke of Burgundy**

Born: 1166

Married: 1199

Died: 6 Jul 1218

9 **Alix De LORRAINE**

Born: Abt 1145
-CONTINUED AS #5,ROYAL CHART 1621
Died: 1200

2 **Hugh IV, Duke of Burgundy**

Born: 9 Mar 1212

Married: 1229

Died: 27 Oct 1272

10 **Hugh De VERGY**

Born: Abt 1155
-CONTINUED AS #6,ROYAL CHART 1621
Married: Abt 1177

Died: 1202

5 **Alice De VERGY**

Born: Abt 1178

Died: Aft 8 Mar 1251/1252

11 **Julia De TRAINEL**

Born: Abt 1155
-CONTINUED AS #7,ROYAL CHART 1621
Died:

1 **John De BURGUNDY**

Born: Abt 1231
-SAME AS #10,ROYAL CHART 1353
Married: Feb 1247/1248

Died: 29 Sep 1268

12 **Robert II, Count of Dreux**

Born: Abt 1154
-CONTINUED AS #4,ROYAL CHART 1622
Married: 1184

Died: 28 Dec 1218

6 **Robert III, Count of Dreux**

Born: Abt 1185

Married: Abt 1210

Died: 3 Mar 1234

13 **Yolande De COUCY**

Born: Abt 1168
-CONTINUED AS #5,ROYAL CHART 1622
Died: 18 Mar 1222

Agnes De BOURBON

Spouse

3 **Yolande De DREUX**

Born: Abt 1212

Died: 30 Oct 1248

14 **Thomas De SAINT VALERY**

Born: Abt 1160
-CONTINUED AS #6,ROYAL CHART 1622
Married: Abt 1178

Died: 1218

7 **Alianore De SAINT VALERY**

Born: Abt 1189

Died: 15 Nov 1251

15 **Adela De PONTHIEU**

Born: Abt 1162
-CONTINUED AS #7,ROYAL CHART 1622
Died:

Sources include: LDS records; *Royal Ancestors* (1989), chart 11345 and family group sheets; Charts 1621-22 and sources (#2 & 3 ancestry).

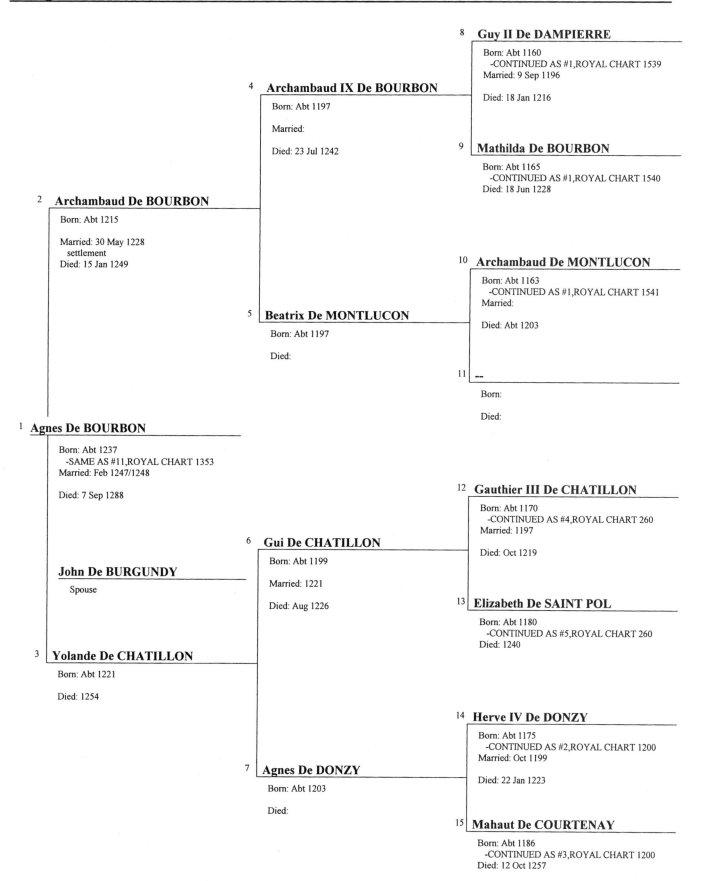

8 **Guy II De DAMPIERRE**

Born: Abt 1160
-CONTINUED AS #1,ROYAL CHART 1539
Married: 9 Sep 1196

Died: 18 Jan 1216

4 **Archambaud IX De BOURBON**

Born: Abt 1197

Married:

Died: 23 Jul 1242

9 **Mathilda De BOURBON**

Born: Abt 1165
-CONTINUED AS #1,ROYAL CHART 1540
Died: 18 Jun 1228

2 **Archambaud De BOURBON**

Born: Abt 1215

Married: 30 May 1228
settlement
Died: 15 Jan 1249

10 **Archambaud De MONTLUCON**

Born: Abt 1163
-CONTINUED AS #1,ROYAL CHART 1541
Married:

Died: Abt 1203

5 **Beatrix De MONTLUCON**

Born: Abt 1197

Died:

11 **--**

Born:

Died:

1 **Agnes De BOURBON**

Born: Abt 1237
-SAME AS #11,ROYAL CHART 1353
Married: Feb 1247/1248

Died: 7 Sep 1288

12 **Gauthier III De CHATILLON**

Born: Abt 1170
-CONTINUED AS #4,ROYAL CHART 260
Married: 1197

Died: Oct 1219

6 **Gui De CHATILLON**

Born: Abt 1199

Married: 1221

Died: Aug 1226

13 **Elizabeth De SAINT POL**

Born: Abt 1180
-CONTINUED AS #5,ROYAL CHART 260
Died: 1240

John De BURGUNDY

Spouse

3 **Yolande De CHATILLON**

Born: Abt 1221

Died: 1254

14 **Herve IV De DONZY**

Born: Abt 1175
-CONTINUED AS #2,ROYAL CHART 1200
Married: Oct 1199

Died: 22 Jan 1223

7 **Agnes De DONZY**

Born: Abt 1203

Died:

15 **Mahaut De COURTENAY**

Born: Abt 1186
-CONTINUED AS #3,ROYAL CHART 1200
Died: 12 Oct 1257

Sources include: Schwennicke 3:51; Faris preliminary Charlemagne manuscript (June 1995), pp. 60-61, 148-149 (#2 & 3 ancestry); Chart 274 with notes & sources (#2 & 3 ancestry).

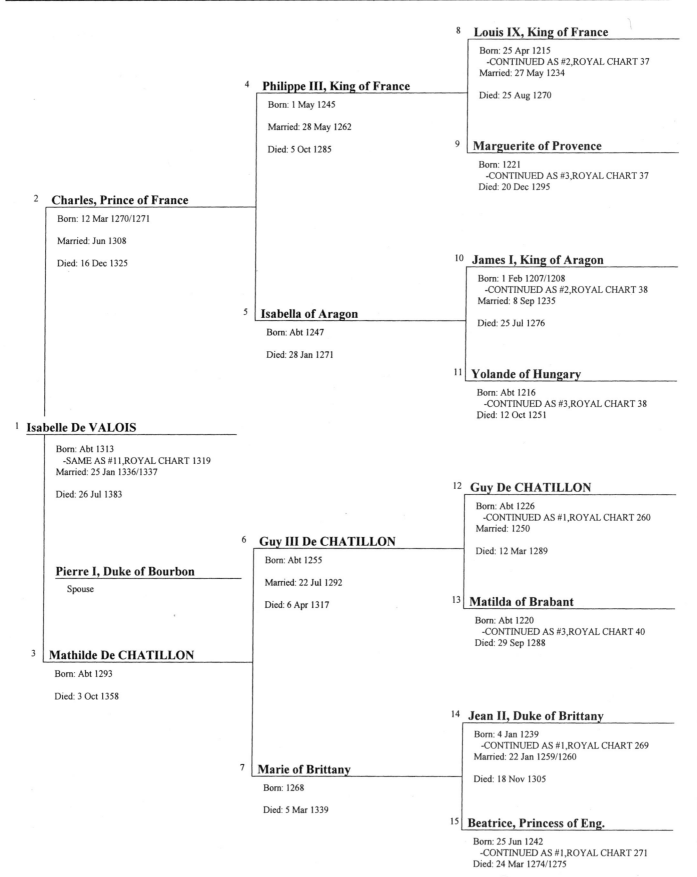

8 **Louis IX, King of France**
Born: 25 Apr 1215
-CONTINUED AS #2, ROYAL CHART 37
Married: 27 May 1234

Died: 25 Aug 1270

4 **Philippe III, King of France**
Born: 1 May 1245

Married: 28 May 1262

Died: 5 Oct 1285

9 **Marguerite of Provence**
Born: 1221
-CONTINUED AS #3, ROYAL CHART 37
Died: 20 Dec 1295

2 **Charles, Prince of France**
Born: 12 Mar 1270/1271

Married: Jun 1308

Died: 16 Dec 1325

10 **James I, King of Aragon**
Born: 1 Feb 1207/1208
-CONTINUED AS #2, ROYAL CHART 38
Married: 8 Sep 1235

Died: 25 Jul 1276

5 **Isabella of Aragon**
Born: Abt 1247

Died: 28 Jan 1271

11 **Yolande of Hungary**
Born: Abt 1216
-CONTINUED AS #3, ROYAL CHART 38
Died: 12 Oct 1251

1 **Isabelle De VALOIS**
Born: Abt 1313
-SAME AS #11, ROYAL CHART 1319
Married: 25 Jan 1336/1337

Died: 26 Jul 1383

12 **Guy De CHATILLON**
Born: Abt 1226
-CONTINUED AS #1, ROYAL CHART 260
Married: 1250

Died: 12 Mar 1289

6 **Guy III De CHATILLON**
Born: Abt 1255

Married: 22 Jul 1292

Died: 6 Apr 1317

Pierre I, Duke of Bourbon
Spouse

13 **Matilda of Brabant**
Born: Abt 1220
-CONTINUED AS #3, ROYAL CHART 40
Died: 29 Sep 1288

3 **Mathilde De CHATILLON**
Born: Abt 1293

Died: 3 Oct 1358

14 **Jean II, Duke of Brittany**
Born: 4 Jan 1239
-CONTINUED AS #1, ROYAL CHART 269
Married: 22 Jan 1259/1260

Died: 18 Nov 1305

7 **Marie of Brittany**
Born: 1268

Died: 5 Mar 1339

15 **Beatrice, Princess of Eng.**
Born: 25 Jun 1242
-CONTINUED AS #1, ROYAL CHART 271
Died: 24 Mar 1274/1275

Sources include: Schwennicke 2:22, 7:18; LDS records; Von Isenburg 2:16; Faris preliminary Charlemagne manuscript (June 1995), pp. 269, 93 (#2 & 3 ancestry); *Royal Ancestors* (1989), chart 11202 (#2 ancestry).

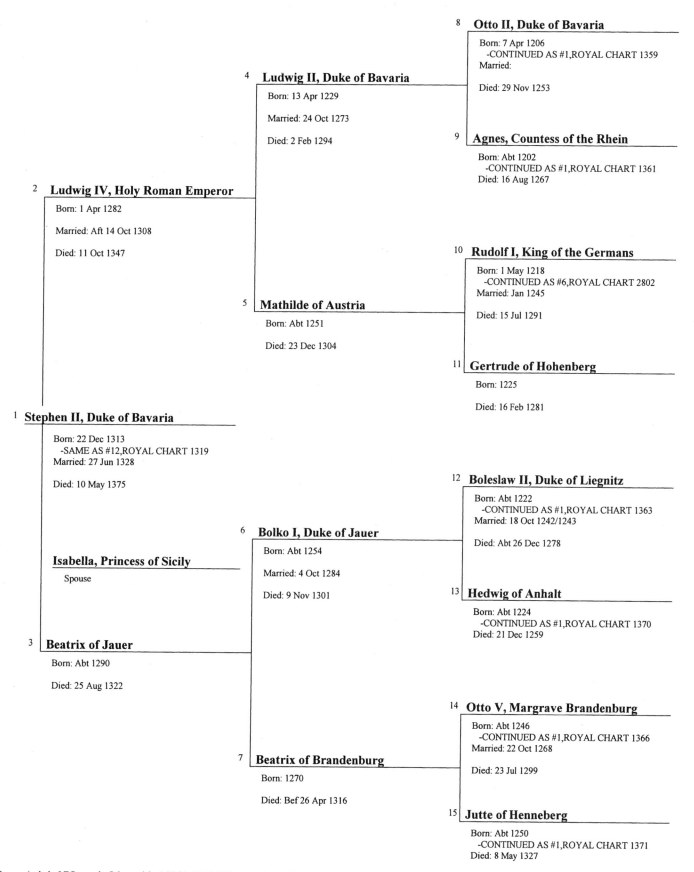

8 **Otto II, Duke of Bavaria**

Born: 7 Apr 1206
-CONTINUED AS #1,ROYAL CHART 1359
Married:

Died: 29 Nov 1253

4 **Ludwig II, Duke of Bavaria**

Born: 13 Apr 1229

Married: 24 Oct 1273

Died: 2 Feb 1294

9 **Agnes, Countess of the Rhein**

Born: Abt 1202
-CONTINUED AS #1,ROYAL CHART 1361
Died: 16 Aug 1267

2 **Ludwig IV, Holy Roman Emperor**

Born: 1 Apr 1282

Married: Aft 14 Oct 1308

Died: 11 Oct 1347

10 **Rudolf I, King of the Germans**

Born: 1 May 1218
-CONTINUED AS #6,ROYAL CHART 2802
Married: Jan 1245

Died: 15 Jul 1291

5 **Mathilde of Austria**

Born: Abt 1251

Died: 23 Dec 1304

11 **Gertrude of Hohenberg**

Born: 1225

Died: 16 Feb 1281

1 **Stephen II, Duke of Bavaria**

Born: 22 Dec 1313
-SAME AS #12,ROYAL CHART 1319
Married: 27 Jun 1328

Died: 10 May 1375

12 **Boleslaw II, Duke of Liegnitz**

Born: Abt 1222
-CONTINUED AS #1,ROYAL CHART 1363
Married: 18 Oct 1242/1243

Died: Abt 26 Dec 1278

6 **Bolko I, Duke of Jauer**

Born: Abt 1254

Married: 4 Oct 1284

Died: 9 Nov 1301

Isabella, Princess of Sicily

Spouse

13 **Hedwig of Anhalt**

Born: Abt 1224
-CONTINUED AS #1,ROYAL CHART 1370
Died: 21 Dec 1259

3 **Beatrix of Jauer**

Born: Abt 1290

Died: 25 Aug 1322

14 **Otto V, Margrave Brandenburg**

Born: Abt 1246
-CONTINUED AS #1,ROYAL CHART 1366
Married: 22 Oct 1268

Died: 23 Jul 1299

7 **Beatrix of Brandenburg**

Born: 1270

Died: Bef 26 Apr 1316

15 **Jutte of Henneberg**

Born: Abt 1250
-CONTINUED AS #1,ROYAL CHART 1371
Died: 8 May 1327

Sources include: LDS records; Schwennicke 1:23-24, 14, 12 (#10 ancestry), 144 (#11 ancestry); 3:12, 9 (corrected #3 ancestry); 1:69. Note: The parentage and ancestry of #3 Beatrix is disputed. LDS records and Schwennicke 1:24 give #3 as daughter of Henry (Henryk, Heinrich) of Glogau. Schwennicke 3:12 corrects this to Bolko I & Beatrix, as shown above.

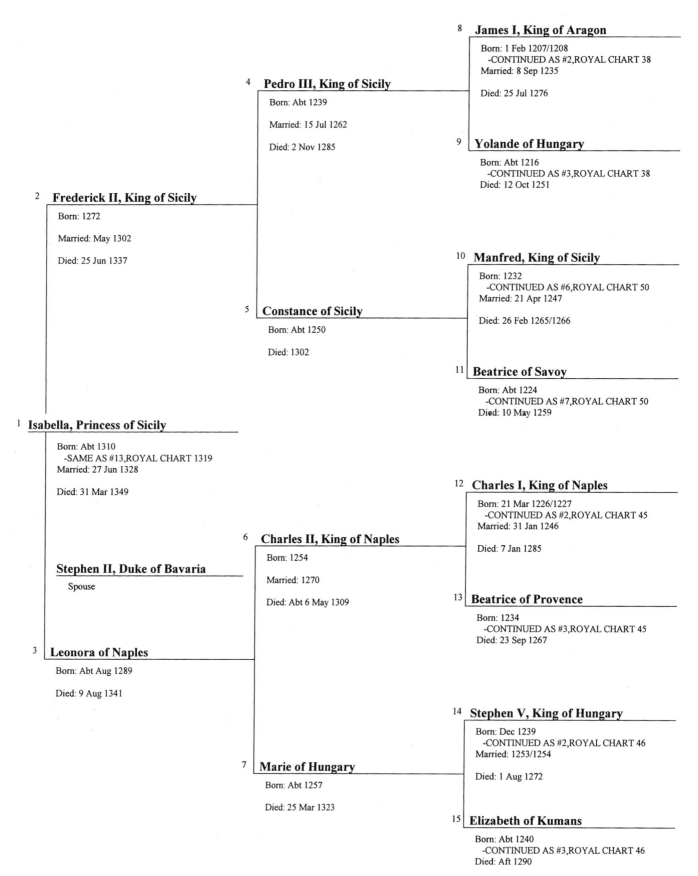

8 **James I, King of Aragon**

Born: 1 Feb 1207/1208
-CONTINUED AS #2,ROYAL CHART 38
Married: 8 Sep 1235

Died: 25 Jul 1276

4 **Pedro III, King of Sicily**

Born: Abt 1239

Married: 15 Jul 1262

Died: 2 Nov 1285

9 **Yolande of Hungary**

Born: Abt 1216
-CONTINUED AS #3,ROYAL CHART 38
Died: 12 Oct 1251

2 **Frederick II, King of Sicily**

Born: 1272

Married: May 1302

Died: 25 Jun 1337

10 **Manfred, King of Sicily**

Born: 1232
-CONTINUED AS #6,ROYAL CHART 50
Married: 21 Apr 1247

Died: 26 Feb 1265/1266

5 **Constance of Sicily**

Born: Abt 1250

Died: 1302

11 **Beatrice of Savoy**

Born: Abt 1224
-CONTINUED AS #7,ROYAL CHART 50
Died: 10 May 1259

1 **Isabella, Princess of Sicily**

Born: Abt 1310
-SAME AS #13,ROYAL CHART 1319
Married: 27 Jun 1328

Died: 31 Mar 1349

12 **Charles I, King of Naples**

Born: 21 Mar 1226/1227
-CONTINUED AS #2,ROYAL CHART 45
Married: 31 Jan 1246

Died: 7 Jan 1285

6 **Charles II, King of Naples**

Born: 1254

Married: 1270

Died: Abt 6 May 1309

13 **Beatrice of Provence**

Born: 1234
-CONTINUED AS #3,ROYAL CHART 45
Died: 23 Sep 1267

Stephen II, Duke of Bavaria

Spouse

3 **Leonora of Naples**

Born: Abt Aug 1289

Died: 9 Aug 1341

14 **Stephen V, King of Hungary**

Born: Dec 1239
-CONTINUED AS #2,ROYAL CHART 46
Married: 1253/1254

Died: 1 Aug 1272

7 **Marie of Hungary**

Born: Abt 1257

Died: 25 Mar 1323

15 **Elizabeth of Kumans**

Born: Abt 1240
-CONTINUED AS #3,ROYAL CHART 46
Died: Aft 1290

Sources include: Schwennicke 2:73, 70-71, 15; LDS records; Von Isenburg 2:45 (#2 ancestry); *Royal Ancestors* (1989), charts 11202 -03, 11324-25, family group sheets (#2 & 3 ancestry).

Pedigree Chart

Chart 1359

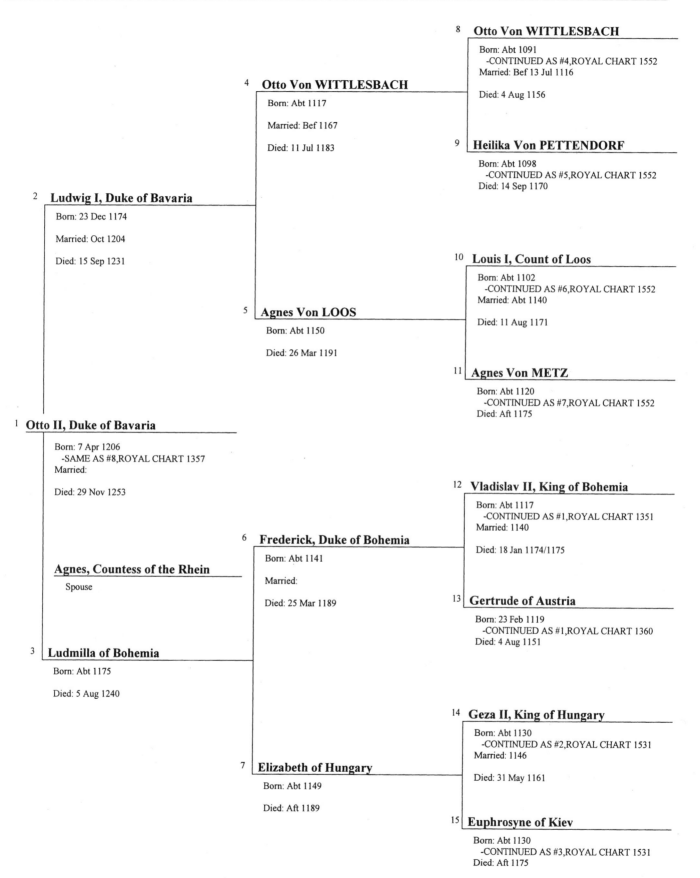

8 Otto Von **WITTLESBACH**

Born: Abt 1091
-CONTINUED AS #4,ROYAL CHART 1552
Married: Bef 13 Jul 1116

Died: 4 Aug 1156

4 Otto Von **WITTLESBACH**

Born: Abt 1117

Married: Bef 1167

Died: 11 Jul 1183

9 Heilika Von **PETTENDORF**

Born: Abt 1098
-CONTINUED AS #5,ROYAL CHART 1552
Died: 14 Sep 1170

2 Ludwig I, Duke of Bavaria

Born: 23 Dec 1174

Married: Oct 1204

Died: 15 Sep 1231

10 Louis I, Count of Loos

Born: Abt 1102
-CONTINUED AS #6,ROYAL CHART 1552
Married: Abt 1140

Died: 11 Aug 1171

5 Agnes Von **LOOS**

Born: Abt 1150

Died: 26 Mar 1191

11 Agnes Von **METZ**

Born: Abt 1120
-CONTINUED AS #7,ROYAL CHART 1552
Died: Aft 1175

1 Otto II, Duke of Bavaria

Born: 7 Apr 1206
-SAME AS #8,ROYAL CHART 1357
Married:

Died: 29 Nov 1253

12 Vladislav II, King of Bohemia

Born: Abt 1117
-CONTINUED AS #1,ROYAL CHART 1351
Married: 1140

Died: 18 Jan 1174/1175

6 Frederick, Duke of Bohemia

Born: Abt 1141

Married:

Died: 25 Mar 1189

13 Gertrude of Austria

Born: 23 Feb 1119
-CONTINUED AS #1,ROYAL CHART 1360
Died: 4 Aug 1151

Agnes, Countess of the Rhein

Spouse

3 Ludmilla of Bohemia

Born: Abt 1175

Died: 5 Aug 1240

14 Geza II, King of Hungary

Born: Abt 1130
-CONTINUED AS #2,ROYAL CHART 1531
Married: 1146

Died: 31 May 1161

7 Elizabeth of Hungary

Born: Abt 1149

Died: Aft 1189

15 Euphrosyne of Kiev

Born: Abt 1130
-CONTINUED AS #3,ROYAL CHART 1531
Died: Aft 1175

Sources include: Schwennicke 1:23, 55; LDS records; *Royal Ancestors* (1989), charts 11317 (#4 & 5 ancestry), 11492-93 (#14 & 15 ancestry).

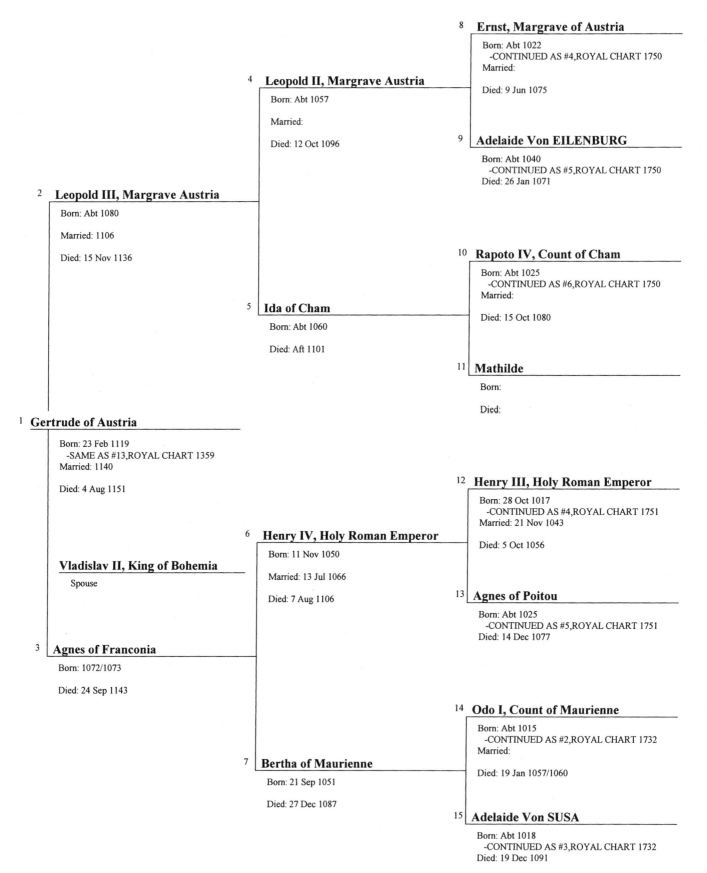

8 **Ernst, Margrave of Austria**

Born: Abt 1022
 -CONTINUED AS #4,ROYAL CHART 1750
Married:

Died: 9 Jun 1075

4 **Leopold II, Margrave Austria**

Born: Abt 1057

Married:

Died: 12 Oct 1096

9 **Adelaide Von EILENBURG**

Born: Abt 1040
 -CONTINUED AS #5,ROYAL CHART 1750
Died: 26 Jan 1071

2 **Leopold III, Margrave Austria**

Born: Abt 1080

Married: 1106

Died: 15 Nov 1136

10 **Rapoto IV, Count of Cham**

Born: Abt 1025
 -CONTINUED AS #6,ROYAL CHART 1750
Married:

Died: 15 Oct 1080

5 **Ida of Cham**

Born: Abt 1060

Died: Aft 1101

11 **Mathilde**

Born:

Died:

1 **Gertrude of Austria**

Born: 23 Feb 1119
 -SAME AS #13,ROYAL CHART 1359
Married: 1140

Died: 4 Aug 1151

12 **Henry III, Holy Roman Emperor**

Born: 28 Oct 1017
 -CONTINUED AS #4,ROYAL CHART 1751
Married: 21 Nov 1043

Died: 5 Oct 1056

6 **Henry IV, Holy Roman Emperor**

Born: 11 Nov 1050

Married: 13 Jul 1066

Died: 7 Aug 1106

Vladislav II, King of Bohemia

Spouse

13 **Agnes of Poitou**

Born: Abt 1025
 -CONTINUED AS #5,ROYAL CHART 1751
Died: 14 Dec 1077

3 **Agnes of Franconia**

Born: 1072/1073

Died: 24 Sep 1143

14 **Odo I, Count of Maurienne**

Born: Abt 1015
 -CONTINUED AS #2,ROYAL CHART 1732
Married:

Died: 19 Jan 1057/1060

7 **Bertha of Maurienne**

Born: 21 Sep 1051

Died: 27 Dec 1087

15 **Adelaide Von SUSA**

Born: Abt 1018
 -CONTINUED AS #3,ROYAL CHART 1732
Died: 19 Dec 1091

Sources include: LDS records; Von Isenburg 1:15; *Royal Ancestors* (1989), chart 11499.

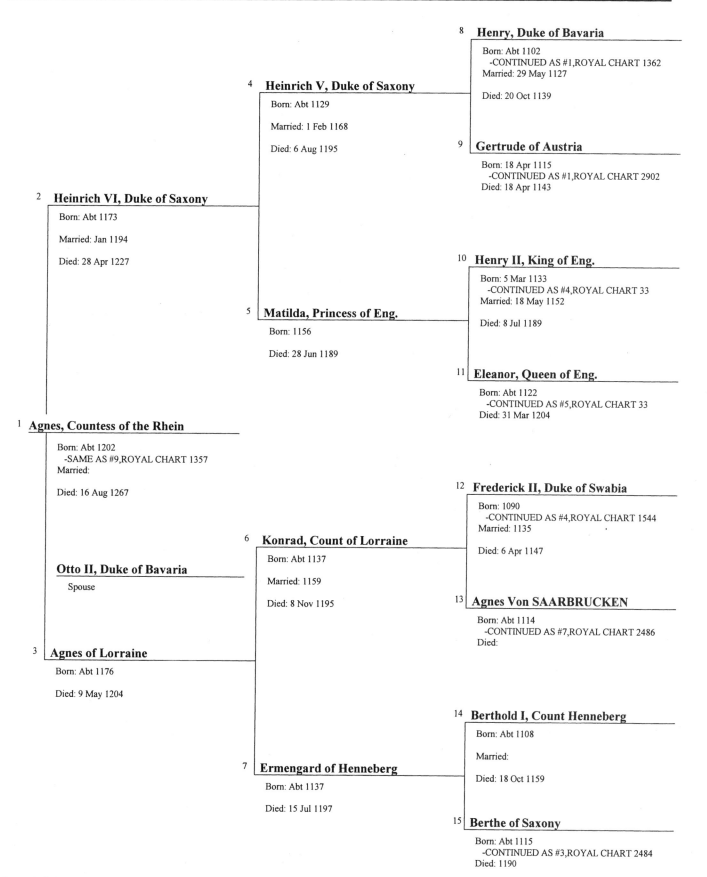

8 Henry, Duke of Bavaria

Born: Abt 1102
-CONTINUED AS #1,ROYAL CHART 1362
Married: 29 May 1127

Died: 20 Oct 1139

4 Heinrich V, Duke of Saxony

Born: Abt 1129

Married: 1 Feb 1168

Died: 6 Aug 1195

9 Gertrude of Austria

Born: 18 Apr 1115
-CONTINUED AS #1,ROYAL CHART 2902
Died: 18 Apr 1143

2 Heinrich VI, Duke of Saxony

Born: Abt 1173

Married: Jan 1194

Died: 28 Apr 1227

10 Henry II, King of Eng.

Born: 5 Mar 1133
-CONTINUED AS #4,ROYAL CHART 33
Married: 18 May 1152

Died: 8 Jul 1189

5 Matilda, Princess of Eng.

Born: 1156

Died: 28 Jun 1189

11 Eleanor, Queen of Eng.

Born: Abt 1122
-CONTINUED AS #5,ROYAL CHART 33
Died: 31 Mar 1204

1 Agnes, Countess of the Rhein

Born: Abt 1202
-SAME AS #9,ROYAL CHART 1357
Married:

Died: 16 Aug 1267

12 Frederick II, Duke of Swabia

Born: 1090
-CONTINUED AS #4,ROYAL CHART 1544
Married: 1135

Died: 6 Apr 1147

6 Konrad, Count of Lorraine

Born: Abt 1137

Married: 1159

Died: 8 Nov 1195

Otto II, Duke of Bavaria

Spouse

13 Agnes Von SAARBRUCKEN

Born: Abt 1114
-CONTINUED AS #7,ROYAL CHART 2486
Died:

3 Agnes of Lorraine

Born: Abt 1176

Died: 9 May 1204

14 Berthold I, Count Henneberg

Born: Abt 1108

Married:

Died: 18 Oct 1159

7 Ermengard of Henneberg

Born: Abt 1137

Died: 15 Jul 1197

15 Berthe of Saxony

Born: Abt 1115
-CONTINUED AS #3,ROYAL CHART 2484
Died: 1190

Sources include: Schwennicke 1:58, 5; 16:144; 6:152; 8:1316; LDS records.

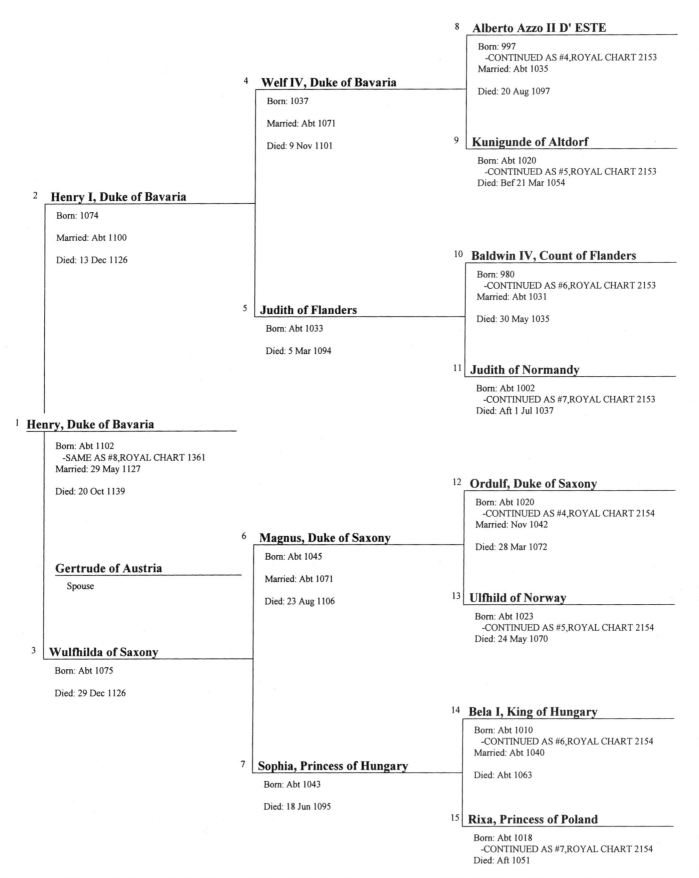

8 Alberto Azzo II D' ESTE

Born: 997
-CONTINUED AS #4,ROYAL CHART 2153
Married: Abt 1035

Died: 20 Aug 1097

4 Welf IV, Duke of Bavaria

Born: 1037

Married: Abt 1071

Died: 9 Nov 1101

9 Kunigunde of Altdorf

Born: Abt 1020
-CONTINUED AS #5,ROYAL CHART 2153
Died: Bef 21 Mar 1054

2 Henry I, Duke of Bavaria

Born: 1074

Married: Abt 1100

Died: 13 Dec 1126

10 Baldwin IV, Count of Flanders

Born: 980
-CONTINUED AS #6,ROYAL CHART 2153
Married: Abt 1031

Died: 30 May 1035

5 Judith of Flanders

Born: Abt 1033

Died: 5 Mar 1094

11 Judith of Normandy

Born: Abt 1002
-CONTINUED AS #7,ROYAL CHART 2153
Died: Aft 1 Jul 1037

1 Henry, Duke of Bavaria

Born: Abt 1102
-SAME AS #8,ROYAL CHART 1361
Married: 29 May 1127

Died: 20 Oct 1139

12 Ordulf, Duke of Saxony

Born: Abt 1020
-CONTINUED AS #4,ROYAL CHART 2154
Married: Nov 1042

Died: 28 Mar 1072

6 Magnus, Duke of Saxony

Born: Abt 1045

Married: Abt 1071

Died: 23 Aug 1106

Gertrude of Austria

Spouse

13 Ulfhild of Norway

Born: Abt 1023
-CONTINUED AS #5,ROYAL CHART 2154
Died: 24 May 1070

3 Wulfhilda of Saxony

Born: Abt 1075

Died: 29 Dec 1126

14 Bela I, King of Hungary

Born: Abt 1010
-CONTINUED AS #6,ROYAL CHART 2154
Married: Abt 1040

Died: Abt 1063

7 Sophia, Princess of Hungary

Born: Abt 1043

Died: 18 Jun 1095

15 Rixa, Princess of Poland

Born: Abt 1018
-CONTINUED AS #7,ROYAL CHART 2154
Died: Aft 1051

Sources include: LDS records; Von Isenburg 1:11; *Royal Ancestors* (1989), chart 11485. Note: The origin and parentage of #5 Judith (of Flanders?) is disputed. See note chart 2153.

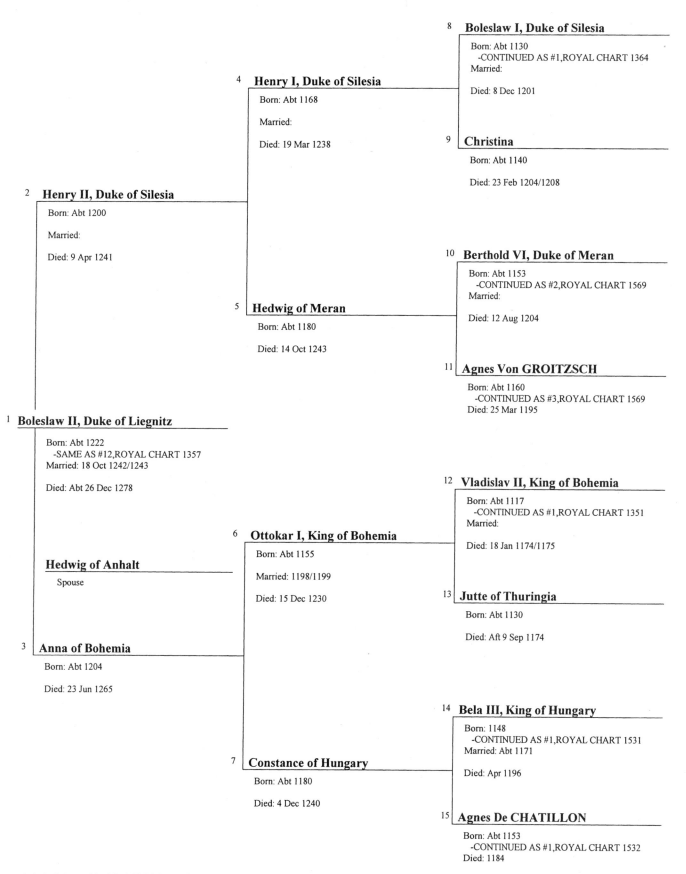

8 Boleslaw I, Duke of Silesia

Born: Abt 1130
-CONTINUED AS #1,ROYAL CHART 1364
Married:

Died: 8 Dec 1201

4 Henry I, Duke of Silesia

Born: Abt 1168

Married:

Died: 19 Mar 1238

9 Christina

Born: Abt 1140

Died: 23 Feb 1204/1208

2 Henry II, Duke of Silesia

Born: Abt 1200

Married:

Died: 9 Apr 1241

10 Berthold VI, Duke of Meran

Born: Abt 1153
-CONTINUED AS #2,ROYAL CHART 1569
Married:

Died: 12 Aug 1204

5 Hedwig of Meran

Born: Abt 1180

Died: 14 Oct 1243

11 Agnes Von GROITZSCH

Born: Abt 1160
-CONTINUED AS #3,ROYAL CHART 1569
Died: 25 Mar 1195

1 Boleslaw II, Duke of Liegnitz

Born: Abt 1222
-SAME AS #12,ROYAL CHART 1357
Married: 18 Oct 1242/1243

Died: Abt 26 Dec 1278

12 Vladislav II, King of Bohemia

Born: Abt 1117
-CONTINUED AS #1,ROYAL CHART 1351
Married:

Died: 18 Jan 1174/1175

6 Ottokar I, King of Bohemia

Born: Abt 1155

Married: 1198/1199

Died: 15 Dec 1230

13 Jutte of Thuringia

Born: Abt 1130

Died: Aft 9 Sep 1174

Hedwig of Anhalt

Spouse

3 Anna of Bohemia

Born: Abt 1204

Died: 23 Jun 1265

14 Bela III, King of Hungary

Born: 1148
-CONTINUED AS #1,ROYAL CHART 1531
Married: Abt 1171

Died: Apr 1196

7 Constance of Hungary

Born: Abt 1180

Died: 4 Dec 1240

15 Agnes De CHATILLON

Born: Abt 1153
-CONTINUED AS #1,ROYAL CHART 1532
Died: 1184

Sources include: Schwennicke 3:9, 1:56; LDS records; Von Isenburg 1:26a (#5 ancestry).

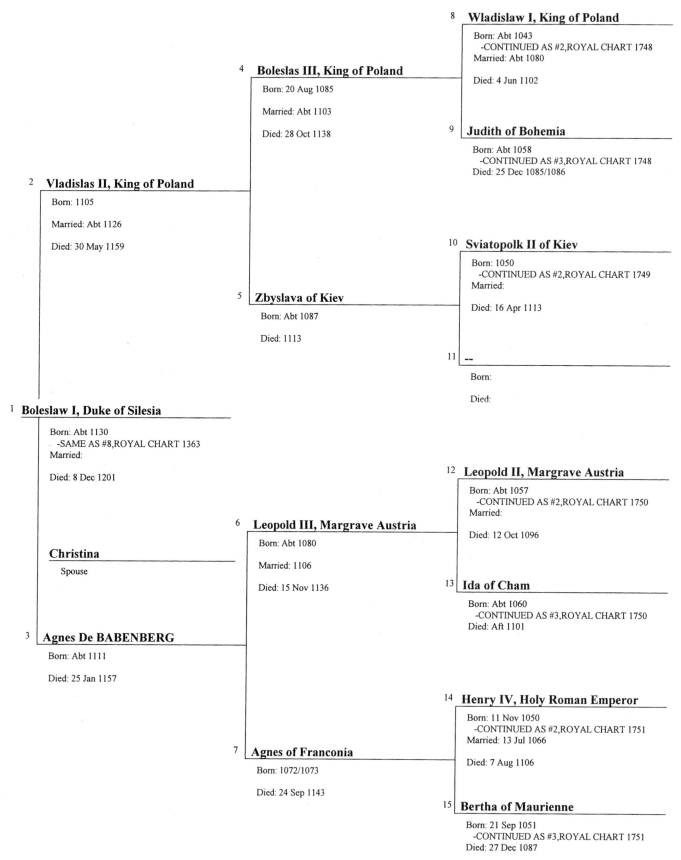

1 Boleslaw I, Duke of Silesia

Born: Abt 1130
-SAME AS #8,ROYAL CHART 1363
Married:

Died: 8 Dec 1201

Christina
Spouse

2 Vladislas II, King of Poland

Born: 1105

Married: Abt 1126

Died: 30 May 1159

3 Agnes De BABENBERG

Born: Abt 1111

Died: 25 Jan 1157

4 Boleslas III, King of Poland

Born: 20 Aug 1085

Married: Abt 1103

Died: 28 Oct 1138

5 Zbyslava of Kiev

Born: Abt 1087

Died: 1113

6 Leopold III, Margrave Austria

Born: Abt 1080

Married: 1106

Died: 15 Nov 1136

7 Agnes of Franconia

Born: 1072/1073

Died: 24 Sep 1143

8 Wladislaw I, King of Poland

Born: Abt 1043
-CONTINUED AS #2,ROYAL CHART 1748
Married: Abt 1080

Died: 4 Jun 1102

9 Judith of Bohemia

Born: Abt 1058
-CONTINUED AS #3,ROYAL CHART 1748
Died: 25 Dec 1085/1086

10 Sviatopolk II of Kiev

Born: 1050
-CONTINUED AS #2,ROYAL CHART 1749
Married:

Died: 16 Apr 1113

11 --

Born:

Died:

12 Leopold II, Margrave Austria

Born: Abt 1057
-CONTINUED AS #2,ROYAL CHART 1750
Married:

Died: 12 Oct 1096

13 Ida of Cham

Born: Abt 1060
-CONTINUED AS #3,ROYAL CHART 1750
Died: Aft 1101

14 Henry IV, Holy Roman Emperor

Born: 11 Nov 1050
-CONTINUED AS #2,ROYAL CHART 1751
Married: 13 Jul 1066

Died: 7 Aug 1106

15 Bertha of Maurienne

Born: 21 Sep 1051
-CONTINUED AS #3,ROYAL CHART 1751
Died: 27 Dec 1087

Sources include: Schwennicke 3:9; LDS records; Von Isenburg 1:191; *Royal Ancestors* (1989), chart 11499 (#2 & 3 ancestry); Faris preliminary Charlemagne manuscript (June 1995), pp. 58, 54, 27-28 (#2 & 3 ancestry).

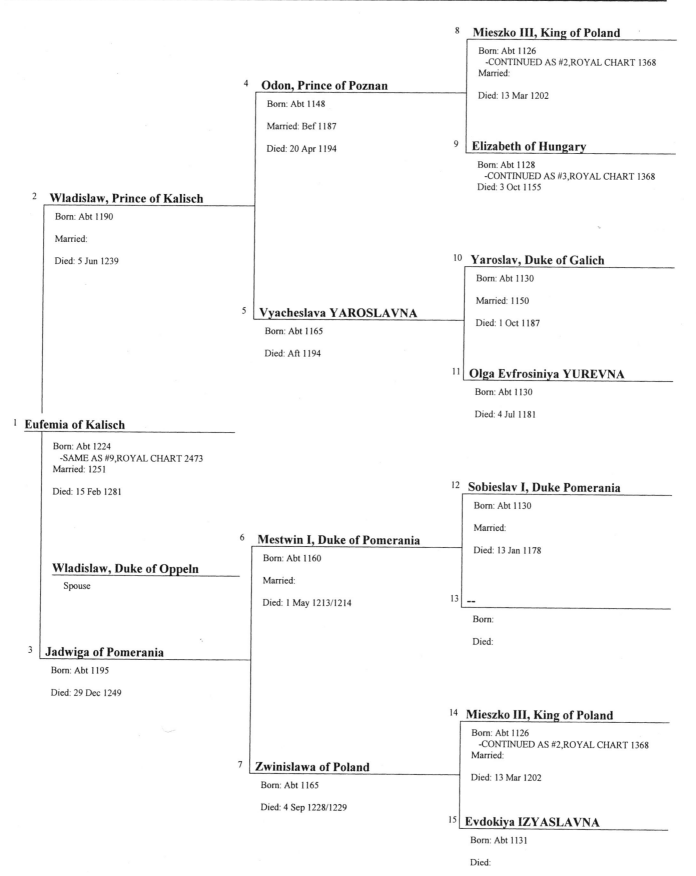

8 Mieszko III, King of Poland
Born: Abt 1126
-CONTINUED AS #2,ROYAL CHART 1368
Married:
Died: 13 Mar 1202

4 Odon, Prince of Poznan
Born: Abt 1148
Married: Bef 1187
Died: 20 Apr 1194

9 Elizabeth of Hungary
Born: Abt 1128
-CONTINUED AS #3,ROYAL CHART 1368
Died: 3 Oct 1155

2 Wladislaw, Prince of Kalisch
Born: Abt 1190
Married:
Died: 5 Jun 1239

10 Yaroslav, Duke of Galich
Born: Abt 1130
Married: 1150
Died: 1 Oct 1187

5 Vyacheslava YAROSLAVNA
Born: Abt 1165
Died: Aft 1194

11 Olga Evfrosiniya YUREVNA
Born: Abt 1130
Died: 4 Jul 1181

1 Eufemia of Kalisch
Born: Abt 1224
-SAME AS #9,ROYAL CHART 2473
Married: 1251
Died: 15 Feb 1281

12 Sobieslav I, Duke Pomerania
Born: Abt 1130
Married:
Died: 13 Jan 1178

6 Mestwin I, Duke of Pomerania
Born: Abt 1160
Married:
Died: 1 May 1213/1214

Wladislaw, Duke of Oppeln
Spouse

13 --
Born:
Died:

3 Jadwiga of Pomerania
Born: Abt 1195
Died: 29 Dec 1249

14 Mieszko III, King of Poland
Born: Abt 1126
-CONTINUED AS #2,ROYAL CHART 1368
Married:
Died: 13 Mar 1202

7 Zwinislawa of Poland
Born: Abt 1165
Died: 4 Sep 1228/1229

15 Evdokiya IZYASLAVNA
Born: Abt 1131
Died:

Sources include: LDS records; Schwennicke 2:120-121. Note: Schwennicke does not give parentage for #3 Jadwiga (Hedwig) and does not identify #7 Zwinislawa as a daughter of Mieszko III.

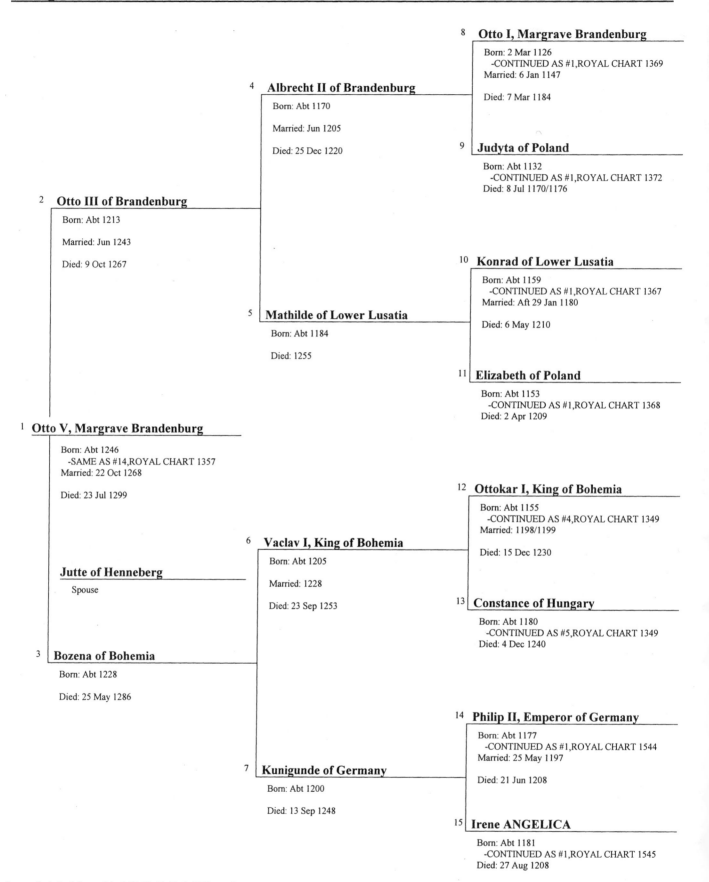

8 Otto I, Margrave Brandenburg

Born: 2 Mar 1126
  -CONTINUED AS #1,ROYAL CHART 1369
Married: 6 Jan 1147

Died: 7 Mar 1184

4 Albrecht II of Brandenburg

Born: Abt 1170

Married: Jun 1205

Died: 25 Dec 1220

9 Judyta of Poland

Born: Abt 1132
  -CONTINUED AS #1,ROYAL CHART 1372
Died: 8 Jul 1170/1176

2 Otto III of Brandenburg

Born: Abt 1213

Married: Jun 1243

Died: 9 Oct 1267

10 Konrad of Lower Lusatia

Born: Abt 1159
  -CONTINUED AS #1,ROYAL CHART 1367
Married: Aft 29 Jan 1180

Died: 6 May 1210

5 Mathilde of Lower Lusatia

Born: Abt 1184

Died: 1255

11 Elizabeth of Poland

Born: Abt 1153
  -CONTINUED AS #1,ROYAL CHART 1368
Died: 2 Apr 1209

1 Otto V, Margrave Brandenburg

Born: Abt 1246
  -SAME AS #14,ROYAL CHART 1357
Married: 22 Oct 1268

Died: 23 Jul 1299

12 Ottokar I, King of Bohemia

Born: Abt 1155
  -CONTINUED AS #4,ROYAL CHART 1349
Married: 1198/1199

Died: 15 Dec 1230

6 Vaclav I, King of Bohemia

Born: Abt 1205

Married: 1228

Died: 23 Sep 1253

13 Constance of Hungary

Born: Abt 1180
  -CONTINUED AS #5,ROYAL CHART 1349
Died: 4 Dec 1240

Jutte of Henneberg

Spouse

3 Bozena of Bohemia

Born: Abt 1228

Died: 25 May 1286

14 Philip II, Emperor of Germany

Born: Abt 1177
  -CONTINUED AS #1,ROYAL CHART 1544
Married: 25 May 1197

Died: 21 Jun 1208

7 Kunigunde of Germany

Born: Abt 1200

Died: 13 Sep 1248

15 Irene ANGELICA

Born: Abt 1181
  -CONTINUED AS #1,ROYAL CHART 1545
Died: 27 Aug 1208

Sources include: Schwennicke 1:68-69, 56, 41, 5; LDS records.

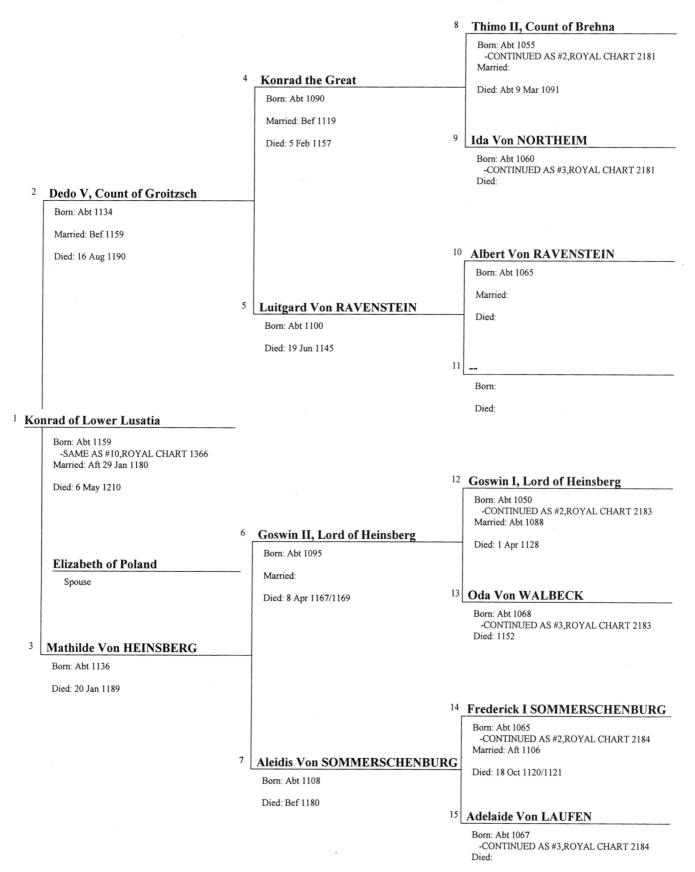

8 Thimo II, Count of Brehna
Born: Abt 1055
-CONTINUED AS #2,ROYAL CHART 2181
Married:

Died: Abt 9 Mar 1091

4 Konrad the Great
Born: Abt 1090

Married: Bef 1119

Died: 5 Feb 1157

9 Ida Von NORTHEIM
Born: Abt 1060
-CONTINUED AS #3,ROYAL CHART 2181
Died:

2 Dedo V, Count of Groitzsch
Born: Abt 1134

Married: Bef 1159

Died: 16 Aug 1190

10 Albert Von RAVENSTEIN
Born: Abt 1065

Married:

Died:

5 Luitgard Von RAVENSTEIN
Born: Abt 1100

Died: 19 Jun 1145

11 --
Born:

Died:

1 Konrad of Lower Lusatia
Born: Abt 1159
-SAME AS #10,ROYAL CHART 1366
Married: Aft 29 Jan 1180

Died: 6 May 1210

12 Goswin I, Lord of Heinsberg
Born: Abt 1050
-CONTINUED AS #2,ROYAL CHART 2183
Married: Abt 1088

Died: 1 Apr 1128

6 Goswin II, Lord of Heinsberg
Born: Abt 1095

Married:

Died: 8 Apr 1167/1169

Elizabeth of Poland
Spouse

13 Oda Von WALBECK
Born: Abt 1068
-CONTINUED AS #3,ROYAL CHART 2183
Died: 1152

3 Mathilde Von HEINSBERG
Born: Abt 1136

Died: 20 Jan 1189

14 Frederick I SOMMERSCHENBURG
Born: Abt 1065
-CONTINUED AS #2,ROYAL CHART 2184
Married: Aft 1106

Died: 18 Oct 1120/1121

7 Aleidis Von SOMMERSCHENBURG
Born: Abt 1108

Died: Bef 1180

15 Adelaide Von LAUFEN
Born: Abt 1067
-CONTINUED AS #3,ROYAL CHART 2184
Died:

Sources include: Schwennicke 1:41; 18:2 (#14 & 15); LDS records; Von Isenburg 1:43; *Royal Ancestors* (1989), charts 11899-900 (#2 & 3 ancestry); Stuart 8, 11 (#2 & 3 ancestry); Faris preliminary Charlemagne manuscript (June 1995), p. 282 (#2 & 3 ancestry).

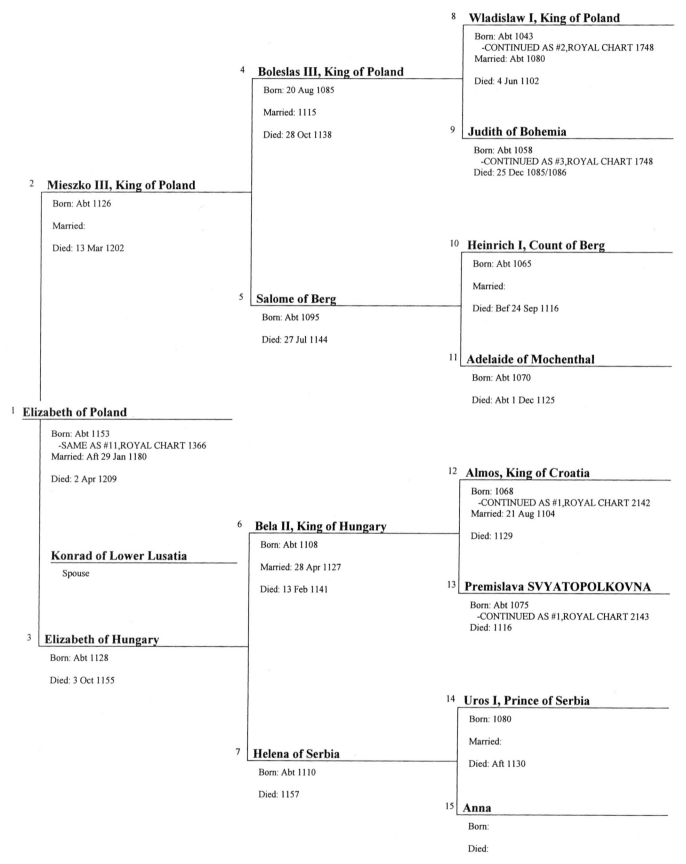

2 Mieszko III, King of Poland
Born: Abt 1126
Married:
Died: 13 Mar 1202

4 Boleslas III, King of Poland
Born: 20 Aug 1085
Married: 1115
Died: 28 Oct 1138

8 Wladislaw I, King of Poland
Born: Abt 1043
-CONTINUED AS #2,ROYAL CHART 1748
Married: Abt 1080
Died: 4 Jun 1102

9 Judith of Bohemia
Born: Abt 1058
-CONTINUED AS #3,ROYAL CHART 1748
Died: 25 Dec 1085/1086

5 Salome of Berg
Born: Abt 1095
Died: 27 Jul 1144

10 Heinrich I, Count of Berg
Born: Abt 1065
Married:
Died: Bef 24 Sep 1116

11 Adelaide of Mochenthal
Born: Abt 1070
Died: Abt 1 Dec 1125

1 Elizabeth of Poland
Born: Abt 1153
-SAME AS #11,ROYAL CHART 1366
Married: Aft 29 Jan 1180
Died: 2 Apr 1209

Konrad of Lower Lusatia
Spouse

3 Elizabeth of Hungary
Born: Abt 1128
Died: 3 Oct 1155

6 Bela II, King of Hungary
Born: Abt 1108
Married: 28 Apr 1127
Died: 13 Feb 1141

12 Almos, King of Croatia
Born: 1068
-CONTINUED AS #1,ROYAL CHART 2142
Married: 21 Aug 1104
Died: 1129

13 Premislava SVYATOPOLKOVNA
Born: Abt 1075
-CONTINUED AS #1,ROYAL CHART 2143
Died: 1116

7 Helena of Serbia
Born: Abt 1110
Died: 1157

14 Uros I, Prince of Serbia
Born: 1080
Married:
Died: Aft 1130

15 Anna
Born:
Died:

Sources include: Schwennicke 2:120-121, 154; 12:62; LDS records; Von Isenburg 2:104 (#3 ancestry); *Royal Ancestors* (1989), charts 11499 (#4 ancestry), 11492 (# 6 & 7 ancestry).
Note: LDS records and Von Isenburg give #3 Elizabeth as the daughter of #12 Almos. Schwennicke corrects this by adding an extra generation (Bela II) as accepted above.

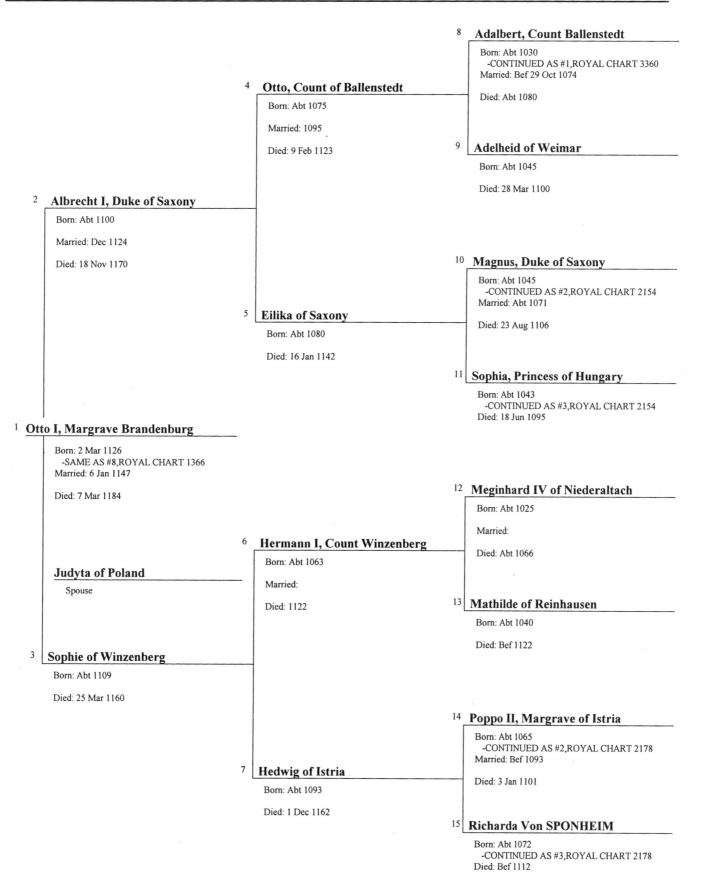

8 Adalbert, Count Ballenstedt
Born: Abt 1030
-CONTINUED AS #1,ROYAL CHART 3360
Married: Bef 29 Oct 1074

Died: Abt 1080

4 Otto, Count of Ballenstedt
Born: Abt 1075

Married: 1095

Died: 9 Feb 1123

9 Adelheid of Weimar
Born: Abt 1045

Died: 28 Mar 1100

2 Albrecht I, Duke of Saxony
Born: Abt 1100

Married: Dec 1124

Died: 18 Nov 1170

10 Magnus, Duke of Saxony
Born: Abt 1045
-CONTINUED AS #2,ROYAL CHART 2154
Married: Abt 1071

Died: 23 Aug 1106

5 Eilika of Saxony
Born: Abt 1080

Died: 16 Jan 1142

11 Sophia, Princess of Hungary
Born: Abt 1043
-CONTINUED AS #3,ROYAL CHART 2154
Died: 18 Jun 1095

1 Otto I, Margrave Brandenburg
Born: 2 Mar 1126
-SAME AS #8,ROYAL CHART 1366
Married: 6 Jan 1147

Died: 7 Mar 1184

12 Meginhard IV of Niederaltach
Born: Abt 1025

Married:

Died: Abt 1066

6 Hermann I, Count Winzenberg
Born: Abt 1063

Married:

Died: 1122

Judyta of Poland
Spouse

13 Mathilde of Reinhausen
Born: Abt 1040

Died: Bef 1122

3 Sophie of Winzenberg
Born: Abt 1109

Died: 25 Mar 1160

14 Poppo II, Margrave of Istria
Born: Abt 1065
-CONTINUED AS #2,ROYAL CHART 2178
Married: Bef 1093

Died: 3 Jan 1101

7 Hedwig of Istria
Born: Abt 1093

Died: 1 Dec 1162

15 Richarda Von SPONHEIM
Born: Abt 1072
-CONTINUED AS #3,ROYAL CHART 2178
Died: Bef 1112

Sources include: Schwennicke 1:68, 16:37; LDS records; Von Isenburg 1:10 (#5 ancestry); *Royal Ancestors* (1989), chart 11485 (#10 & 11 ancestry).

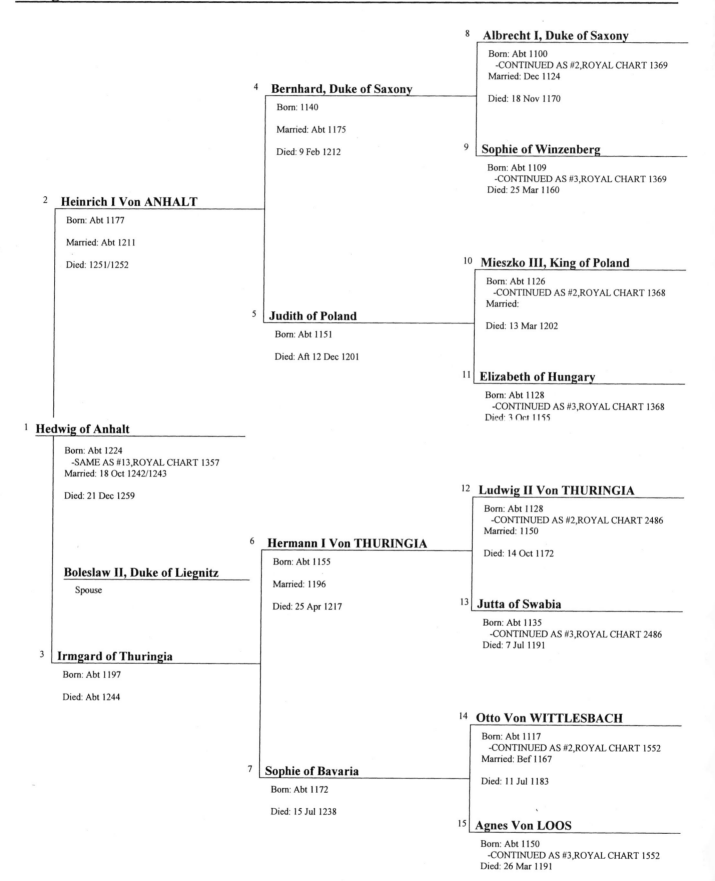

2 Heinrich I Von ANHALT

Born: Abt 1177

Married: Abt 1211

Died: 1251/1252

4 Bernhard, Duke of Saxony

Born: 1140

Married: Abt 1175

Died: 9 Feb 1212

8 **Albrecht I, Duke of Saxony**

Born: Abt 1100
    -CONTINUED AS #2,ROYAL CHART 1369
Married: Dec 1124

Died: 18 Nov 1170

9 **Sophie of Winzenberg**

Born: Abt 1109
    -CONTINUED AS #3,ROYAL CHART 1369
Died: 25 Mar 1160

5 Judith of Poland

Born: Abt 1151

Died: Aft 12 Dec 1201

10 **Mieszko III, King of Poland**

Born: Abt 1126
    -CONTINUED AS #2,ROYAL CHART 1368
Married:

Died: 13 Mar 1202

11 **Elizabeth of Hungary**

Born: Abt 1128
    -CONTINUED AS #3,ROYAL CHART 1368
Died: 3 Oct 1155

1 Hedwig of Anhalt

Born: Abt 1224
    -SAME AS #13,ROYAL CHART 1357
Married: 18 Oct 1242/1243

Died: 21 Dec 1259

Boleslaw II, Duke of Liegnitz

Spouse

3 Irmgard of Thuringia

Born: Abt 1197

Died: Abt 1244

6 Hermann I Von THURINGIA

Born: Abt 1155

Married: 1196

Died: 25 Apr 1217

12 **Ludwig II Von THURINGIA**

Born: Abt 1128
    -CONTINUED AS #2,ROYAL CHART 2486
Married: 1150

Died: 14 Oct 1172

13 **Jutta of Swabia**

Born: Abt 1135
    -CONTINUED AS #3,ROYAL CHART 2486
Died: 7 Jul 1191

7 Sophie of Bavaria

Born: Abt 1172

Died: 15 Jul 1238

14 **Otto Von WITTLESBACH**

Born: Abt 1117
    -CONTINUED AS #2,ROYAL CHART 1552
Married: Bef 1167

Died: 11 Jul 1183

15 **Agnes Von LOOS**

Born: Abt 1150
    -CONTINUED AS #3,ROYAL CHART 1552
Died: 26 Mar 1191

Sources include: Schwennicke 1:68, 40, 23; 2:120-121.

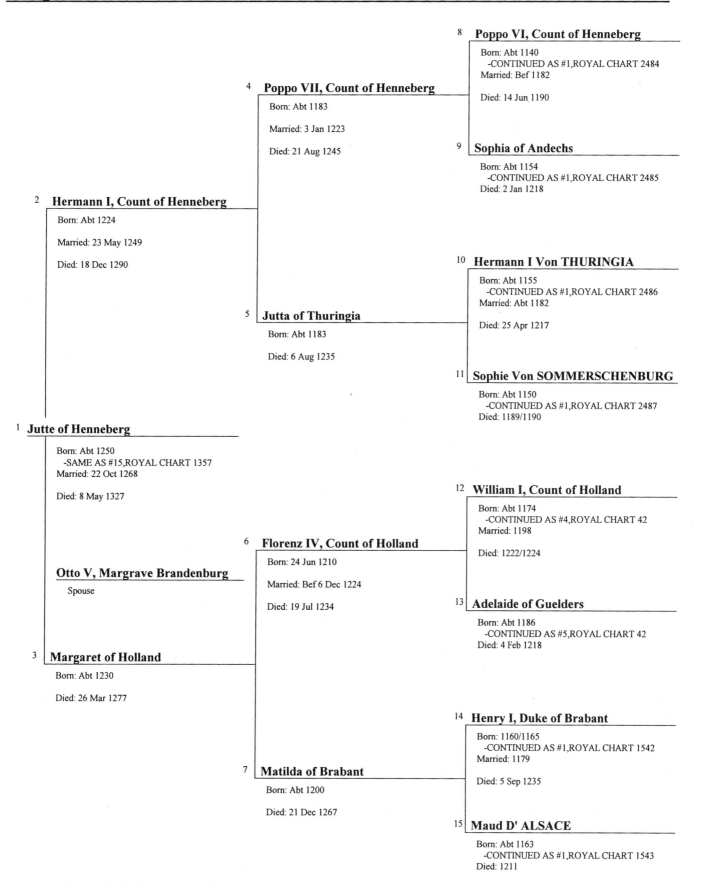

2 Hermann I, Count of Henneberg

Born: Abt 1224

Married: 23 May 1249

Died: 18 Dec 1290

1 Jutte of Henneberg

Born: Abt 1250
-SAME AS #15,ROYAL CHART 1357
Married: 22 Oct 1268

Died: 8 May 1327

Otto V, Margrave Brandenburg

Spouse

3 Margaret of Holland

Born: Abt 1230

Died: 26 Mar 1277

4 Poppo VII, Count of Henneberg

Born: Abt 1183

Married: 3 Jan 1223

Died: 21 Aug 1245

5 Jutta of Thuringia

Born: Abt 1183

Died: 6 Aug 1235

6 Florenz IV, Count of Holland

Born: 24 Jun 1210

Married: Bef 6 Dec 1224

Died: 19 Jul 1234

7 Matilda of Brabant

Born: Abt 1200

Died: 21 Dec 1267

8 Poppo VI, Count of Henneberg

Born: Abt 1140
-CONTINUED AS #1,ROYAL CHART 2484
Married: Bef 1182

Died: 14 Jun 1190

9 Sophia of Andechs

Born: Abt 1154
-CONTINUED AS #1,ROYAL CHART 2485
Died: 2 Jan 1218

10 Hermann I Von THURINGIA

Born: Abt 1155
-CONTINUED AS #1,ROYAL CHART 2486
Married: Abt 1182

Died: 25 Apr 1217

11 Sophie Von SOMMERSCHENBURG

Born: Abt 1150
-CONTINUED AS #1,ROYAL CHART 2487
Died: 1189/1190

12 William I, Count of Holland

Born: Abt 1174
-CONTINUED AS #4,ROYAL CHART 42
Married: 1198

Died: 1222/1224

13 Adelaide of Guelders

Born: Abt 1186
-CONTINUED AS #5,ROYAL CHART 42
Died: 4 Feb 1218

14 Henry I, Duke of Brabant

Born: 1160/1165
-CONTINUED AS #1,ROYAL CHART 1542
Married: 1179

Died: 5 Sep 1235

15 Maud D' ALSACE

Born: Abt 1163
-CONTINUED AS #1,ROYAL CHART 1543
Died: 1211

Sources include: Schwennicke 16:146, 144; 2:2; 1:96, 40; Faris preliminary Charlemagne manuscript (June 1995), pp. 159, 69 (#6 & 7 ancestry).

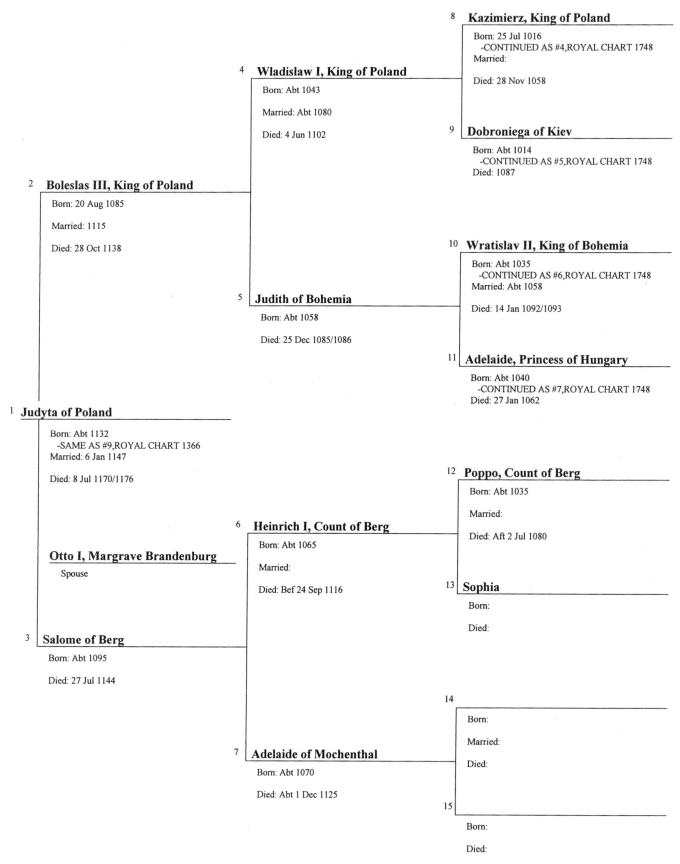

8   **Kazimierz, King of Poland**

Born: 25 Jul 1016
   -CONTINUED AS #4,ROYAL CHART 1748
Married:

Died: 28 Nov 1058

4   **Wladislaw I, King of Poland**

Born: Abt 1043

Married: Abt 1080

Died: 4 Jun 1102

9   **Dobroniega of Kiev**

Born: Abt 1014
   -CONTINUED AS #5,ROYAL CHART 1748
Died: 1087

2   **Boleslas III, King of Poland**

Born: 20 Aug 1085

Married: 1115

Died: 28 Oct 1138

10   **Wratislav II, King of Bohemia**

Born: Abt 1035
   -CONTINUED AS #6,ROYAL CHART 1748
Married: Abt 1058

Died: 14 Jan 1092/1093

5   **Judith of Bohemia**

Born: Abt 1058

Died: 25 Dec 1085/1086

11   **Adelaide, Princess of Hungary**

Born: Abt 1040
   -CONTINUED AS #7,ROYAL CHART 1748
Died: 27 Jan 1062

1   **Judyta of Poland**

Born: Abt 1132
   -SAME AS #9,ROYAL CHART 1366
Married: 6 Jan 1147

Died: 8 Jul 1170/1176

12   **Poppo, Count of Berg**

Born: Abt 1035

Married:

Died: Aft 2 Jul 1080

6   **Heinrich I, Count of Berg**

Born: Abt 1065

Married:

Died: Bef 24 Sep 1116

Otto I, Margrave Brandenburg

Spouse

13   **Sophia**

Born:

Died:

3   **Salome of Berg**

Born: Abt 1095

Died: 27 Jul 1144

14

Born:

Married:

Died:

7   **Adelaide of Mochenthal**

Born: Abt 1070

Died: Abt 1 Dec 1125

15

Born:

Died:

Sources include: Schwennicke 2:120, 12:62; LDS records; *Royal Ancestors* (1989), chart 11499 (#2 ancestry); Faris preliminary Charlemagne manuscript (June 1995), p. 54 (#2 & 3 ancestry).

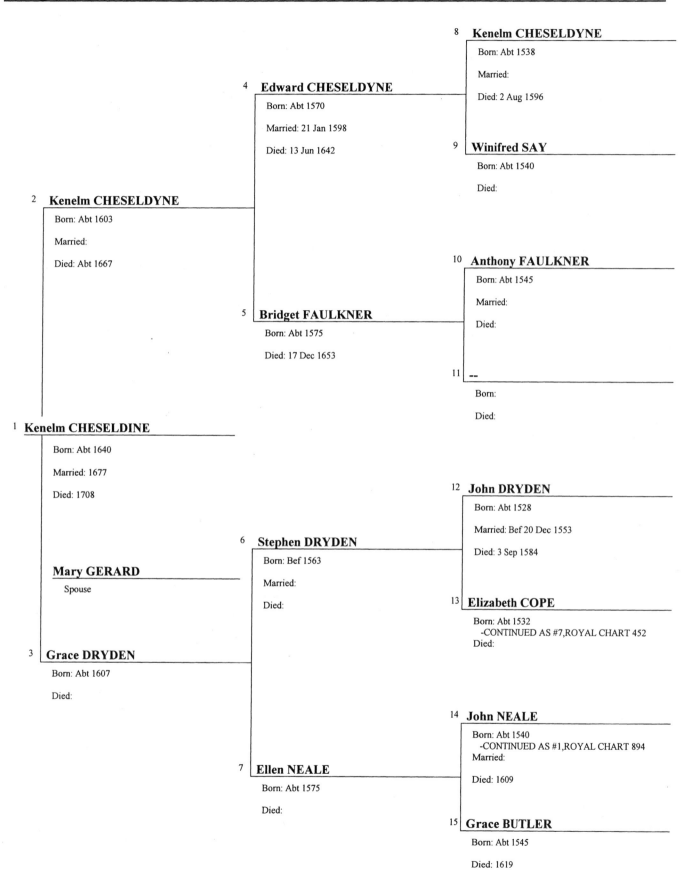

8 Kenelm CHESELDYNE
Born: Abt 1538
Married:
Died: 2 Aug 1596

4 Edward CHESELDYNE
Born: Abt 1570
Married: 21 Jan 1598
Died: 13 Jun 1642

9 Winifred SAY
Born: Abt 1540
Died:

2 Kenelm CHESELDYNE
Born: Abt 1603
Married:
Died: Abt 1667

10 Anthony FAULKNER
Born: Abt 1545
Married:
Died:

5 Bridget FAULKNER
Born: Abt 1575
Died: 17 Dec 1653

11 --
Born:
Died:

1 Kenelm CHESELDINE
Born: Abt 1640
Married: 1677
Died: 1708

Mary GERARD
Spouse

12 John DRYDEN
Born: Abt 1528
Married: Bef 20 Dec 1553
Died: 3 Sep 1584

6 Stephen DRYDEN
Born: Bef 1563
Married:
Died:

13 Elizabeth COPE
Born: Abt 1532
 -CONTINUED AS #7,ROYAL CHART 452
Died:

3 Grace DRYDEN
Born: Abt 1607
Died:

14 John NEALE
Born: Abt 1540
 -CONTINUED AS #1,ROYAL CHART 894
Married:
Died: 1609

7 Ellen NEALE
Born: Abt 1575
Died:

15 Grace BUTLER
Born: Abt 1545
Died: 1619

Sources include: Faris 2--Cheseldine; LDS records; Roberts *500* (600) updated manuscript (November 2000), p. 257 (#7 identification and parentage). Note: Mary Gerard (spouse of #1) was daughter of Thomas Gerard (chr. 10 Dec 1608; md. Susanna Snow). See chart 665 for his ancestry.

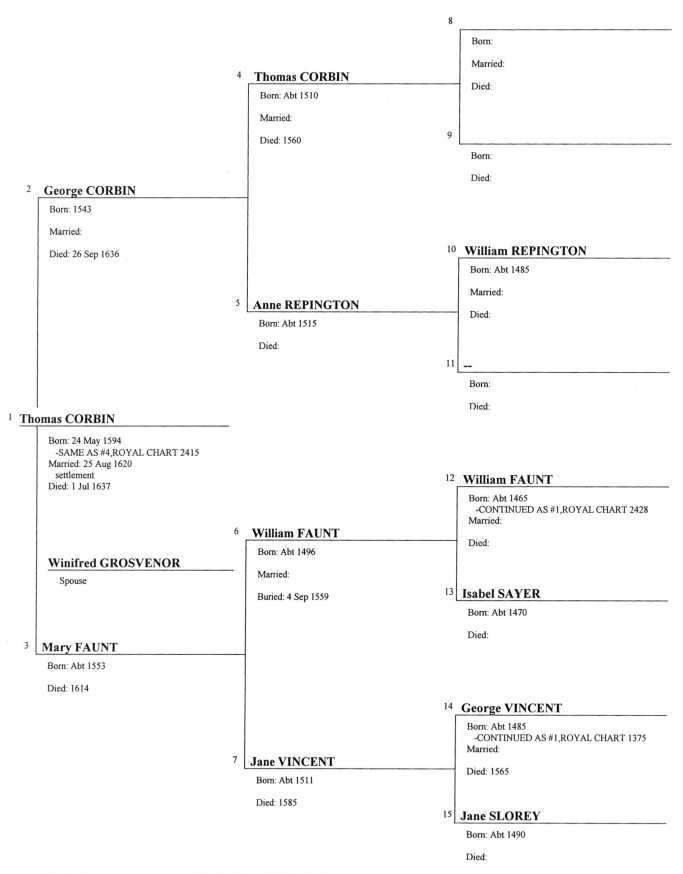

8

Born:

Married:

Died:

4 Thomas CORBIN

Born: Abt 1510

Married:

Died: 1560

9

Born:

Died:

2 George CORBIN

Born: 1543

Married:

Died: 26 Sep 1636

10 William REPINGTON

Born: Abt 1485

Married:

Died:

5 Anne REPINGTON

Born: Abt 1515

Died:

11 --

Born:

Died:

1 Thomas CORBIN

Born: 24 May 1594
  -SAME AS #4,ROYAL CHART 2415
Married: 25 Aug 1620
  settlement
Died: 1 Jul 1637

Winifred GROSVENOR

Spouse

12 William FAUNT

Born: Abt 1465
  -CONTINUED AS #1,ROYAL CHART 2428
Married:

Died:

6 William FAUNT

Born: Abt 1496

Married:

Buried: 4 Sep 1559

13 Isabel SAYER

Born: Abt 1470

Died:

3 Mary FAUNT

Born: Abt 1553

Died: 1614

14 George VINCENT

Born: Abt 1485
  -CONTINUED AS #1,ROYAL CHART 1375
Married:

Died: 1565

7 Jane VINCENT

Born: Abt 1511

Died: 1585

15 Jane SLOREY

Born: Abt 1490

Died:

Sources include: Richardson *Plantagenet* (2004), pp. 229-230 (Corbin); Faris 2--Corbin. Note: #15 is also given as Anne Slorey.

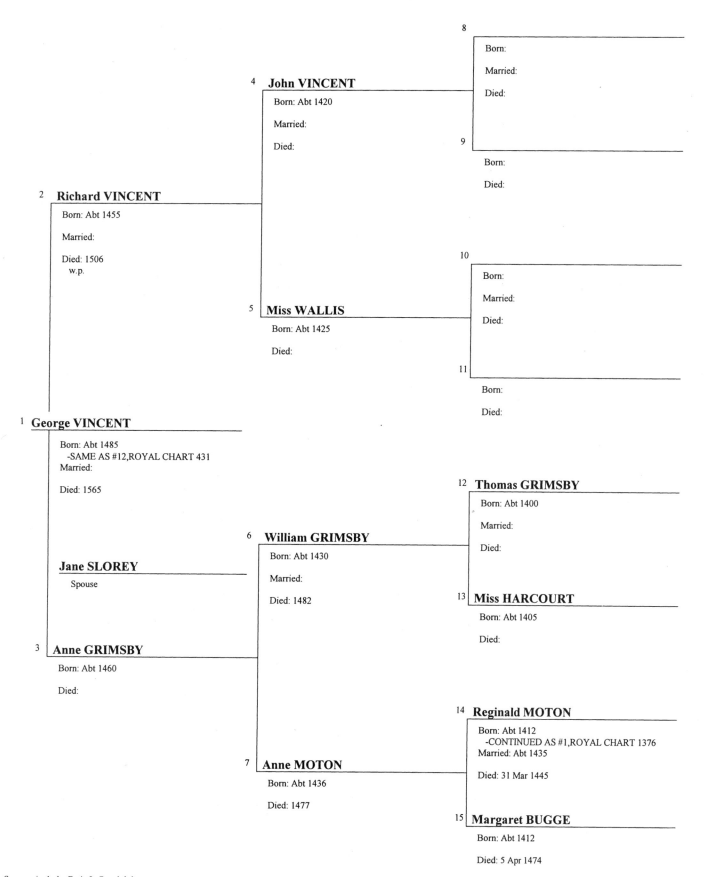

8

Born:

Married:

Died:

4   **John VINCENT**

Born: Abt 1420

Married:

Died: 9

Born:

Died:

2   **Richard VINCENT**

Born: Abt 1455

Married:

Died: 1506
        w.p.
                                                        10

Born:

Married:

Died:

5   **Miss WALLIS**

Born: Abt 1425

Died: 11

Born:

Died:

1   **George VINCENT**

Born: Abt 1485
     -SAME AS #12,ROYAL CHART 431
Married:

Died: 1565   12   **Thomas GRIMSBY**

Born: Abt 1400

Married:

Died:

6   **William GRIMSBY**

Born: Abt 1430

Married:

Died: 1482   13   **Miss HARCOURT**

Born: Abt 1405

Died:

Jane SLOREY

Spouse

3   **Anne GRIMSBY**

Born: Abt 1460

Died:
                                                        14   **Reginald MOTON**

Born: Abt 1412
     -CONTINUED AS #1,ROYAL CHART 1376
Married: Abt 1435

Died: 31 Mar 1445

7   **Anne MOTON**

Born: Abt 1436

Died: 1477   15   **Margaret BUGGE**

Born: Abt 1412

Died: 5 Apr 1474

Sources include: Faris 2--Randolph.

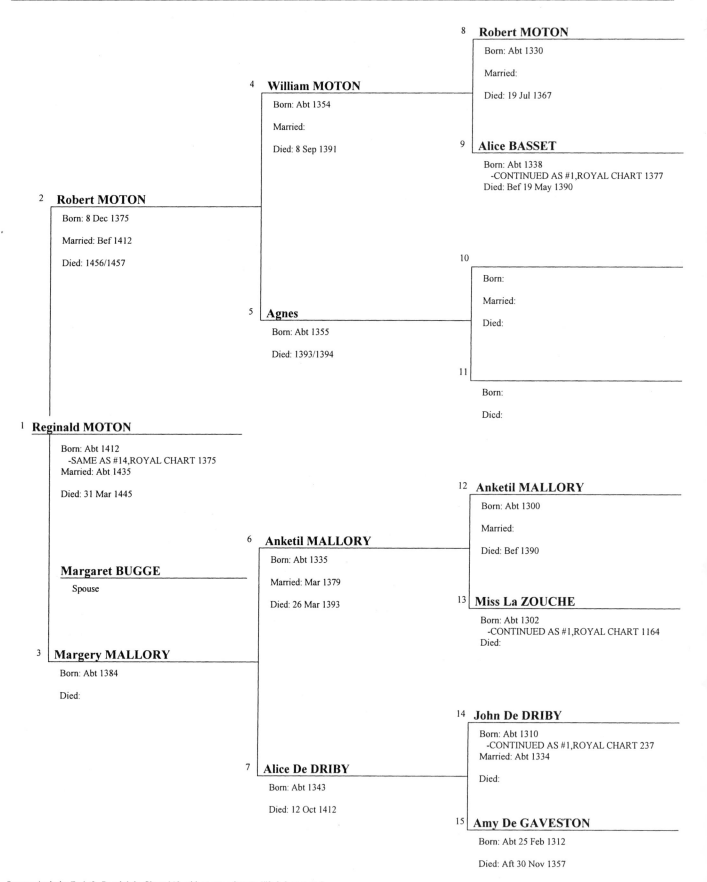

8 **Robert MOTON**
Born: Abt 1330
Married:
Died: 19 Jul 1367

4 **William MOTON**
Born: Abt 1354
Married:
Died: 8 Sep 1391

9 **Alice BASSET**
Born: Abt 1338
   -CONTINUED AS #1,ROYAL CHART 1377
Died: Bef 19 May 1390

2 **Robert MOTON**
Born: 8 Dec 1375
Married: Bef 1412
Died: 1456/1457

10
Born:
Married:
Died:

5 **Agnes**
Born: Abt 1355
Died: 1393/1394

11
Born:
Died:

1 **Reginald MOTON**
Born: Abt 1412
   -SAME AS #14,ROYAL CHART 1375
Married: Abt 1435
Died: 31 Mar 1445

12 **Anketil MALLORY**
Born: Abt 1300
Married:
Died: Bef 1390

6 **Anketil MALLORY**
Born: Abt 1335
Married: Mar 1379
Died: 26 Mar 1393

13 **Miss La ZOUCHE**
Born: Abt 1302
   -CONTINUED AS #1,ROYAL CHART 1164
Died:

Margaret BUGGE
Spouse

3 **Margery MALLORY**
Born: Abt 1384
Died:

14 **John De DRIBY**
Born: Abt 1310
   -CONTINUED AS #1,ROYAL CHART 237
Married: Abt 1334
Died:

7 **Alice De DRIBY**
Born: Abt 1343
Died: 12 Oct 1412

15 **Amy De GAVESTON**
Born: Abt 25 Feb 1312
Died: Aft 30 Nov 1357

Sources include: Faris 2--Randolph; Chart 112 with sources & note (#2 & 3 ancestry).

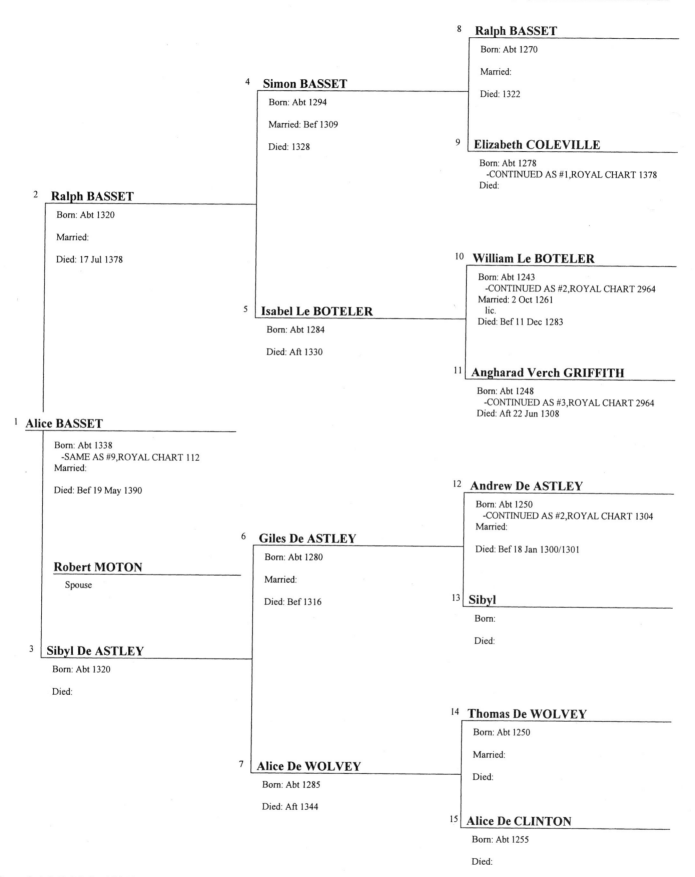

8 **Ralph BASSET**
Born: Abt 1270
Married:
Died: 1322

4 **Simon BASSET**
Born: Abt 1294
Married: Bef 1309
Died: 1328

9 **Elizabeth COLEVILLE**
Born: Abt 1278
-CONTINUED AS #1,ROYAL CHART 1378
Died:

2 **Ralph BASSET**
Born: Abt 1320
Married:
Died: 17 Jul 1378

10 **William Le BOTELER**
Born: Abt 1243
-CONTINUED AS #2,ROYAL CHART 2964
Married: 2 Oct 1261
lic.
Died: Bef 11 Dec 1283

5 **Isabel Le BOTELER**
Born: Abt 1284
Died: Aft 1330

11 **Angharad Verch GRIFFITH**
Born: Abt 1248
-CONTINUED AS #3,ROYAL CHART 2964
Died: Aft 22 Jun 1308

1 **Alice BASSET**
Born: Abt 1338
-SAME AS #9,ROYAL CHART 112
Married:
Died: Bef 19 May 1390

12 **Andrew De ASTLEY**
Born: Abt 1250
-CONTINUED AS #2,ROYAL CHART 1304
Married:
Died: Bef 18 Jan 1300/1301

6 **Giles De ASTLEY**
Born: Abt 1280
Married:
Died: Bef 1316

13 **Sibyl**
Born:
Died:

Robert MOTON
Spouse

3 **Sibyl De ASTLEY**
Born: Abt 1320
Died:

14 **Thomas De WOLVEY**
Born: Abt 1250
Married:
Died:

7 **Alice De WOLVEY**
Born: Abt 1285
Died: Aft 1344

15 **Alice De CLINTON**
Born: Abt 1255
Died:

Sources include: Faris 2--Randolph 10; Faris preliminary *Magna Carta* manuscript (June 2000), p. 441 (Randolph); Faris preliminary baronial manuscript (1998), pp. 178 (Boteler), 13-14 (Astley), 1689 (Wolvey); LDS records.

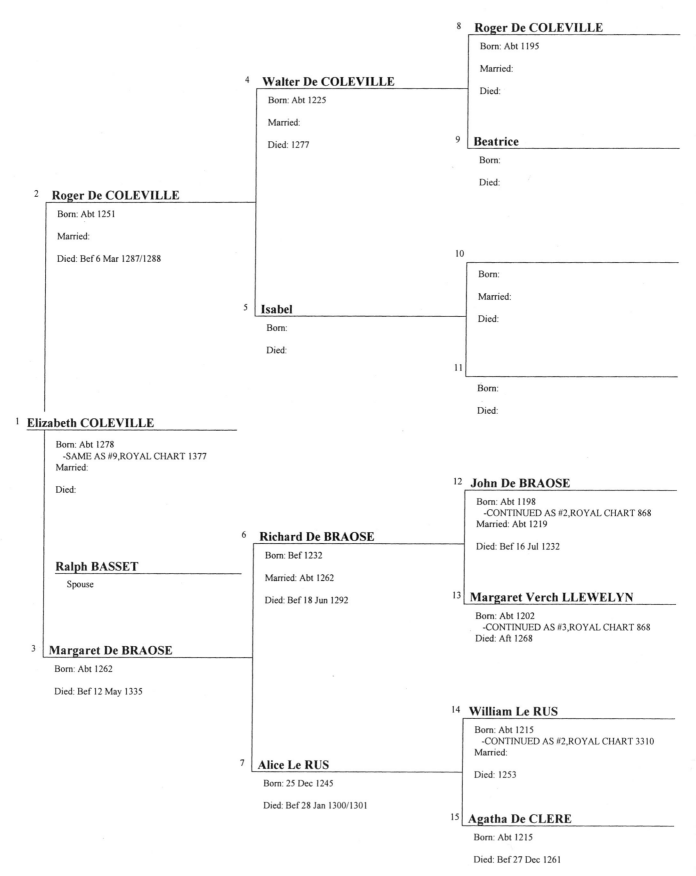

8 | **Roger De COLEVILLE**
Born: Abt 1195
Married:
Died:

4 | **Walter De COLEVILLE**
Born: Abt 1225
Married:
Died: 1277

9 | **Beatrice**
Born:
Died:

2 | **Roger De COLEVILLE**
Born: Abt 1251
Married:
Died: Bef 6 Mar 1287/1288

10
Born:
Married:
Died:

5 | **Isabel**
Born:
Died:

11
Born:
Died:

1 | **Elizabeth COLEVILLE**
Born: Abt 1278
  -SAME AS #9,ROYAL CHART 1377
Married:
Died:

Ralph BASSET
Spouse

12 | **John De BRAOSE**
Born: Abt 1198
  -CONTINUED AS #2,ROYAL CHART 868
Married: Abt 1219
Died: Bef 16 Jul 1232

6 | **Richard De BRAOSE**
Born: Bef 1232
Married: Abt 1262
Died: Bef 18 Jun 1292

13 | **Margaret Verch LLEWELYN**
Born: Abt 1202
  -CONTINUED AS #3,ROYAL CHART 868
Died: Aft 1268

3 | **Margaret De BRAOSE**
Born: Abt 1262
Died: Bef 12 May 1335

14 | **William Le RUS**
Born: Abt 1215
  -CONTINUED AS #2,ROYAL CHART 3310
Married:
Died: 1253

7 | **Alice Le RUS**
Born: 25 Dec 1245
Died: Bef 28 Jan 1300/1301

15 | **Agatha De CLERE**
Born: Abt 1215
Died: Bef 27 Dec 1261

Sources include: Faris-Richardson preliminary Magna Carta manuscript (June 2000), pp. 440-441 (Randolph), 101 (Calthorpe), 77 (Brewes); Faris preliminary baronial manuscript (1998), p. 386 (Coleville); *Magna Charta* 28A (#2 & 3 ancestry); *Ancestral Roots* 246-30 (#2 & 3 ancestry).

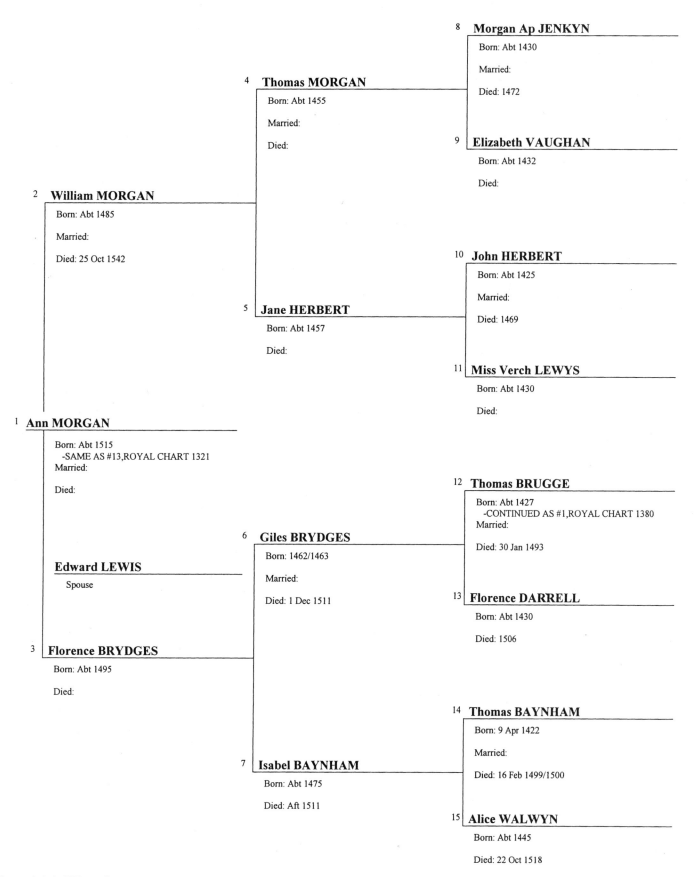

8 **Morgan Ap JENKYN**
Born: Abt 1430
Married:
Died: 1472

4 **Thomas MORGAN**
Born: Abt 1455
Married:
Died:

9 **Elizabeth VAUGHAN**
Born: Abt 1432
Died:

2 **William MORGAN**
Born: Abt 1485
Married:
Died: 25 Oct 1542

10 **John HERBERT**
Born: Abt 1425
Married:
Died: 1469

5 **Jane HERBERT**
Born: Abt 1457
Died:

11 **Miss Verch LEWYS**
Born: Abt 1430
Died:

1 **Ann MORGAN**
Born: Abt 1515
-SAME AS #13, ROYAL CHART 1321
Married:
Died:

Edward LEWIS
Spouse

12 **Thomas BRUGGE**
Born: Abt 1427
-CONTINUED AS #1, ROYAL CHART 1380
Married:
Died: 30 Jan 1493

6 **Giles BRYDGES**
Born: 1462/1463
Married:
Died: 1 Dec 1511

13 **Florence DARRELL**
Born: Abt 1430
Died: 1506

3 **Florence BRYDGES**
Born: Abt 1495
Died:

14 **Thomas BAYNHAM**
Born: 9 Apr 1422
Married:
Died: 16 Feb 1499/1500

7 **Isabel BAYNHAM**
Born: Abt 1475
Died: Aft 1511

15 **Alice WALWYN**
Born: Abt 1445
Died: 22 Oct 1518

Sources include: LDS records.

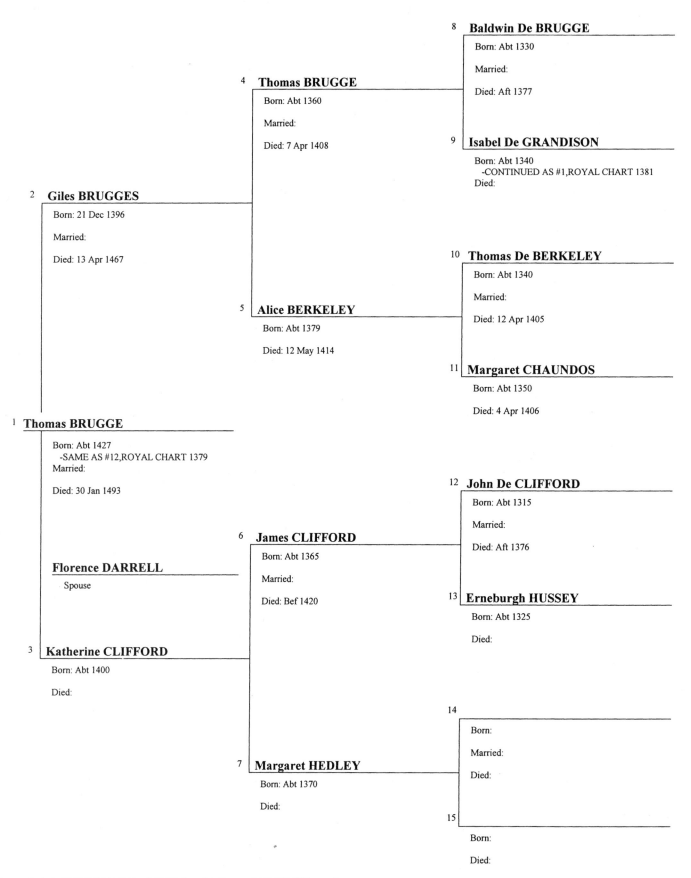

8 Baldwin De BRUGGE

Born: Abt 1330

Married:

Died: Aft 1377

4 Thomas BRUGGE

Born: Abt 1360

Married:

Died: 7 Apr 1408

9 Isabel De GRANDISON

Born: Abt 1340
   -CONTINUED AS #1,ROYAL CHART 1381
Died:

2 Giles BRUGGES

Born: 21 Dec 1396

Married:

Died: 13 Apr 1467

10 Thomas De BERKELEY

Born: Abt 1340

Married:

Died: 12 Apr 1405

5 Alice BERKELEY

Born: Abt 1379

Died: 12 May 1414

11 Margaret CHAUNDOS

Born: Abt 1350

Died: 4 Apr 1406

1 Thomas BRUGGE

Born: Abt 1427
   -SAME AS #12,ROYAL CHART 1379
Married:

Died: 30 Jan 1493

12 John De CLIFFORD

Born: Abt 1315

Married:

Died: Aft 1376

6 James CLIFFORD

Born: Abt 1365

Married:

Died: Bef 1420

13 Erneburgh HUSSEY

Born: Abt 1325

Died:

Florence DARRELL

   Spouse

3 Katherine CLIFFORD

Born: Abt 1400

Died:

14

Born:

Married:

Died:

7 Margaret HEDLEY

Born: Abt 1370

Died:

15

Born:

Died:

Sources include: *NEHGR* 156:140 (April 2002); *Complete Peerage* 3:150-152; LDS records.

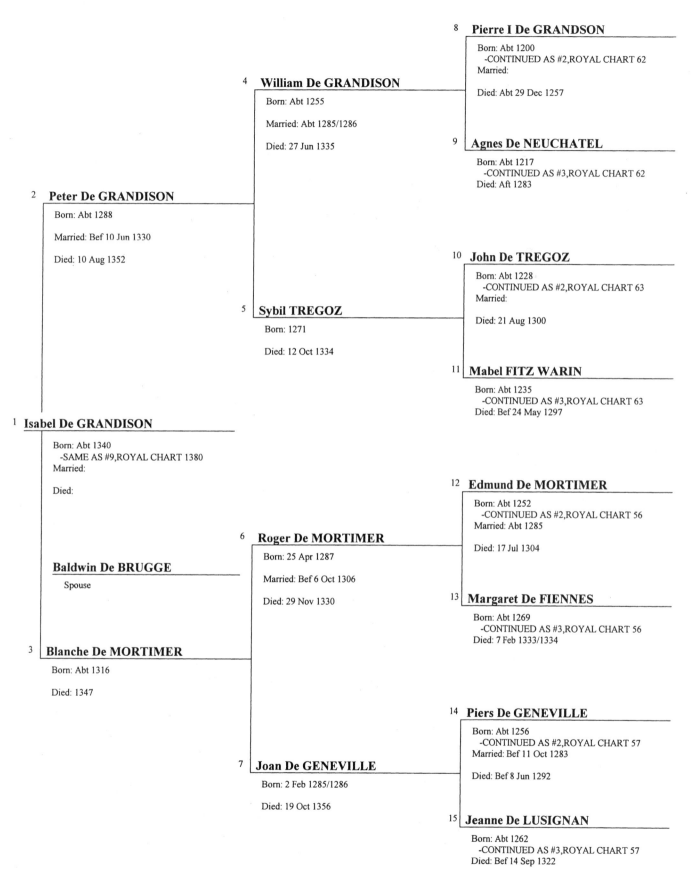

8 Pierre I De GRANDSON
Born: Abt 1200
  -CONTINUED AS #2,ROYAL CHART 62
Married:

Died: Abt 29 Dec 1257

4 **William De GRANDISON**
Born: Abt 1255

Married: Abt 1285/1286

Died: 27 Jun 1335

9 Agnes De NEUCHATEL
Born: Abt 1217
  -CONTINUED AS #3,ROYAL CHART 62
Died: Aft 1283

2 **Peter De GRANDISON**
Born: Abt 1288

Married: Bef 10 Jun 1330

Died: 10 Aug 1352

10 John De TREGOZ
Born: Abt 1228
  -CONTINUED AS #2,ROYAL CHART 63
Married:

Died: 21 Aug 1300

5 **Sybil TREGOZ**
Born: 1271

Died: 12 Oct 1334

11 Mabel FITZ WARIN
Born: Abt 1235
  -CONTINUED AS #3,ROYAL CHART 63
Died: Bef 24 May 1297

1 **Isabel De GRANDISON**
Born: Abt 1340
  -SAME AS #9,ROYAL CHART 1380
Married:

Died:

12 Edmund De MORTIMER
Born: Abt 1252
  -CONTINUED AS #2,ROYAL CHART 56
Married: Abt 1285

Died: 17 Jul 1304

6 **Roger De MORTIMER**
Born: 25 Apr 1287

Married: Bef 6 Oct 1306

Died: 29 Nov 1330

13 Margaret De FIENNES
Born: Abt 1269
  -CONTINUED AS #3,ROYAL CHART 56
Died: 7 Feb 1333/1334

Baldwin De BRUGGE
    Spouse

3 **Blanche De MORTIMER**
Born: Abt 1316

Died: 1347

14 Piers De GENEVILLE
Born: Abt 1256
  -CONTINUED AS #2,ROYAL CHART 57
Married: Bef 11 Oct 1283

Died: Bef 8 Jun 1292

7 **Joan De GENEVILLE**
Born: 2 Feb 1285/1286

Died: 19 Oct 1356

15 Jeanne De LUSIGNAN
Born: Abt 1262
  -CONTINUED AS #3,ROYAL CHART 57
Died: Bef 14 Sep 1322

Sources include: LDS records; Schwennicke 11:153-154 (#2 & 3 ancestry); *Royal Ancestors* (1989), chart 11205 & family group sheets (#2 & 3 ancestry).

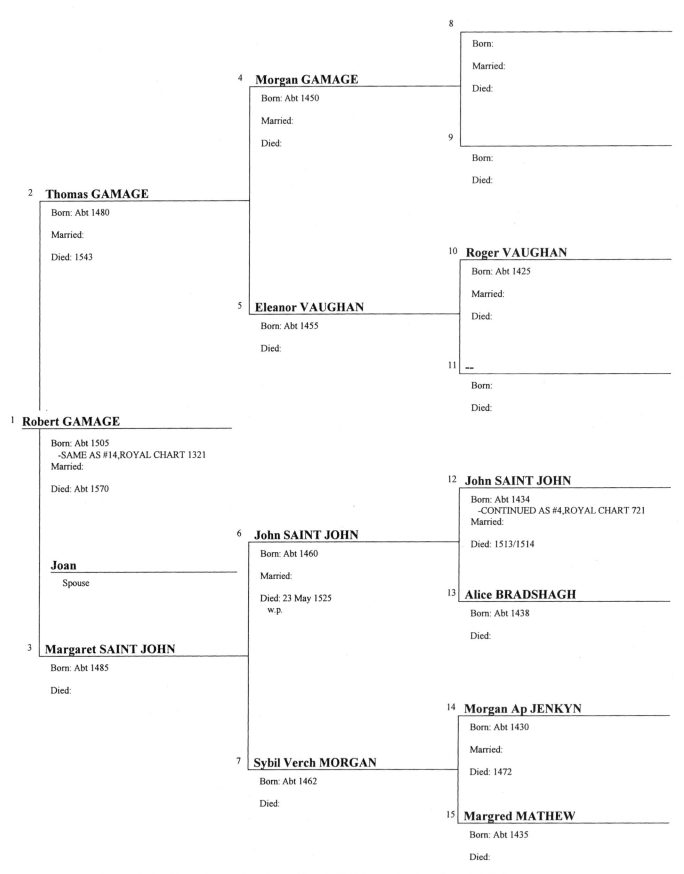

8
Born:
Married:
Died:

4 **Morgan GAMAGE**
Born: Abt 1450
Married:
Died:

9
Born:
Died:

2 **Thomas GAMAGE**
Born: Abt 1480
Married:
Died: 1543

10 **Roger VAUGHAN**
Born: Abt 1425
Married:
Died:

5 **Eleanor VAUGHAN**
Born: Abt 1455
Died:

11 **--**
Born:
Died:

1 **Robert GAMAGE**
Born: Abt 1505
  -SAME AS #14,ROYAL CHART 1321
Married:
Died: Abt 1570

12 **John SAINT JOHN**
Born: Abt 1434
  -CONTINUED AS #4,ROYAL CHART 721
Married:
Died: 1513/1514

6 **John SAINT JOHN**
Born: Abt 1460
Married:
Died: 23 May 1525
  w.p.

Joan
Spouse

13 **Alice BRADSHAGH**
Born: Abt 1438
Died:

3 **Margaret SAINT JOHN**
Born: Abt 1485
Died:

14 **Morgan Ap JENKYN**
Born: Abt 1430
Married:
Died: 1472

7 **Sybil Verch MORGAN**
Born: Abt 1462
Died:

15 **Margred MATHEW**
Born: Abt 1435
Died:

Sources include: LDS records; Consultation with Douglas Richardson; *Ancestral Roots* 85 (#6 & 7 ancestry); *Magna Charta* 61 (#6 & 7 ancestry).

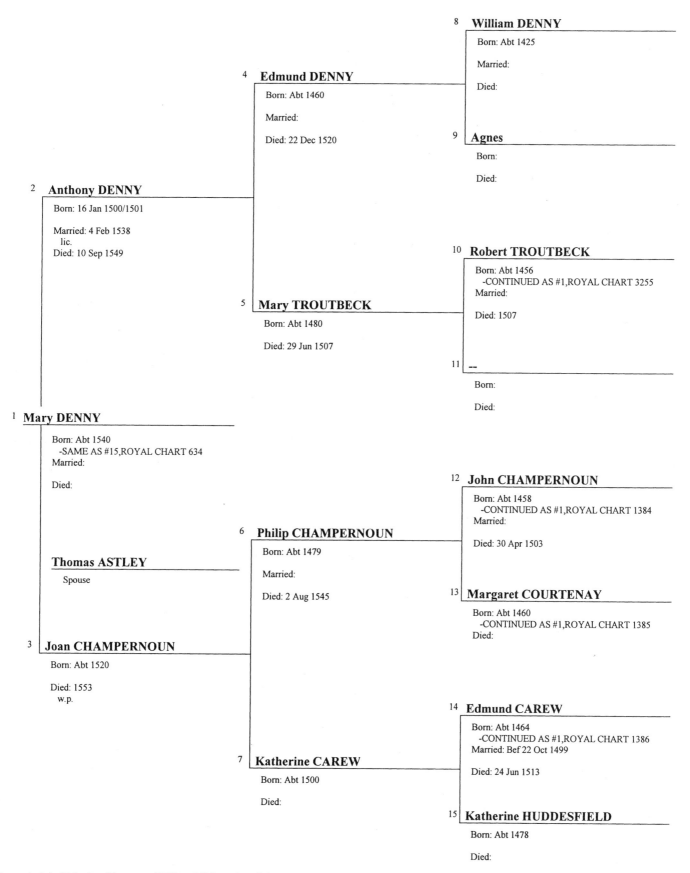

8 William **DENNY**

Born: Abt 1425

Married:

Died:

4 Edmund **DENNY**

Born: Abt 1460

Married:

Died: 22 Dec 1520

9 **Agnes**

Born:

Died:

2 Anthony **DENNY**

Born: 16 Jan 1500/1501

Married: 4 Feb 1538
lic.
Died: 10 Sep 1549

10 Robert **TROUTBECK**

Born: Abt 1456
    -CONTINUED AS #1,ROYAL CHART 3255
Married:

Died: 1507

5 Mary **TROUTBECK**

Born: Abt 1480

Died: 29 Jun 1507

11 **__**

Born:

Died:

1 Mary **DENNY**

Born: Abt 1540
    -SAME AS #15,ROYAL CHART 634
Married:

Died:

Thomas **ASTLEY**

Spouse

12 John **CHAMPERNOUN**

Born: Abt 1458
    -CONTINUED AS #1,ROYAL CHART 1384
Married:

Died: 30 Apr 1503

6 Philip **CHAMPERNOUN**

Born: Abt 1479

Married:

Died: 2 Aug 1545

13 Margaret **COURTENAY**

Born: Abt 1460
    -CONTINUED AS #1,ROYAL CHART 1385
Died:

3 Joan **CHAMPERNOUN**

Born: Abt 1520

Died: 1553
w.p.

14 Edmund **CAREW**

Born: Abt 1464
    -CONTINUED AS #1,ROYAL CHART 1386
Married: Bef 22 Oct 1499

Died: 24 Jun 1513

7 Katherine **CAREW**

Born: Abt 1500

Died:

15 Katherine **HUDDESFIELD**

Born: Abt 1478

Died:

Sources include: Richardson *Plantagenet* (2004), p. 265 (Denny); Faris 2--Denny; LDS records.

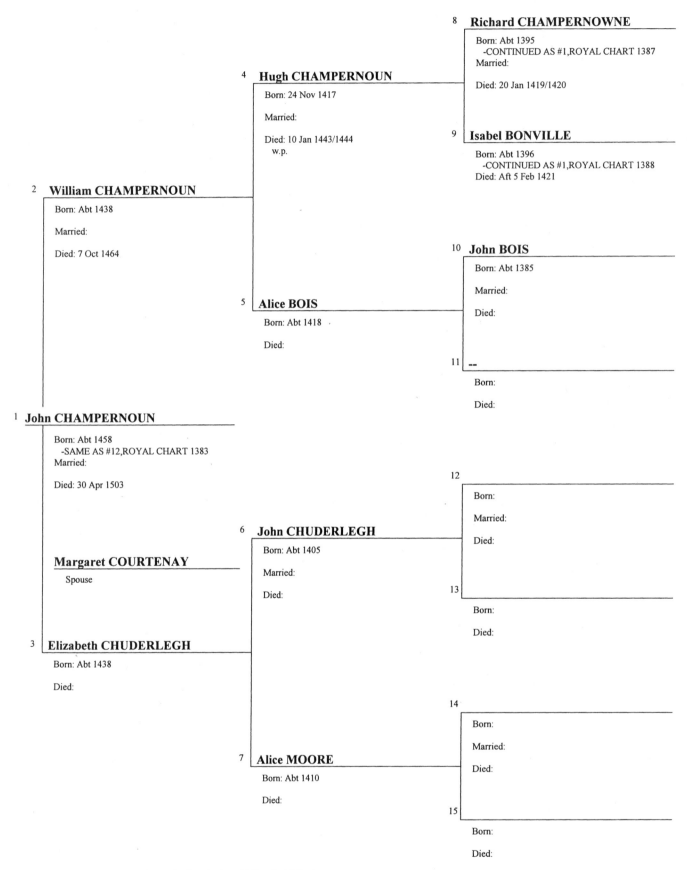

2 William CHAMPERNOUN

Born: Abt 1438

Married:

Died: 7 Oct 1464

4 Hugh CHAMPERNOUN

Born: 24 Nov 1417

Married:

Died: 10 Jan 1443/1444
w.p.

8 Richard CHAMPERNOWNE

Born: Abt 1395
-CONTINUED AS #1,ROYAL CHART 1387
Married:

Died: 20 Jan 1419/1420

9 Isabel BONVILLE

Born: Abt 1396
-CONTINUED AS #1,ROYAL CHART 1388
Died: Aft 5 Feb 1421

5 Alice BOIS

Born: Abt 1418

Died:

10 John BOIS

Born: Abt 1385

Married:

Died:

11 --

Born:

Died:

1 John CHAMPERNOUN

Born: Abt 1458
-SAME AS #12,ROYAL CHART 1383
Married:

Died: 30 Apr 1503

Margaret COURTENAY

Spouse

3 Elizabeth CHUDERLEGH

Born: Abt 1438

Died:

6 John CHUDERLEGH

Born: Abt 1405

Married:

Died:

12

Born:

Married:

Died:

13

Born:

Died:

7 Alice MOORE

Born: Abt 1410

Died:

14

Born:

Married:

Died:

15

Born:

Died:

Sources include: Faris 2--Denny 6; LDS records; Consultation with Douglas Richardson.

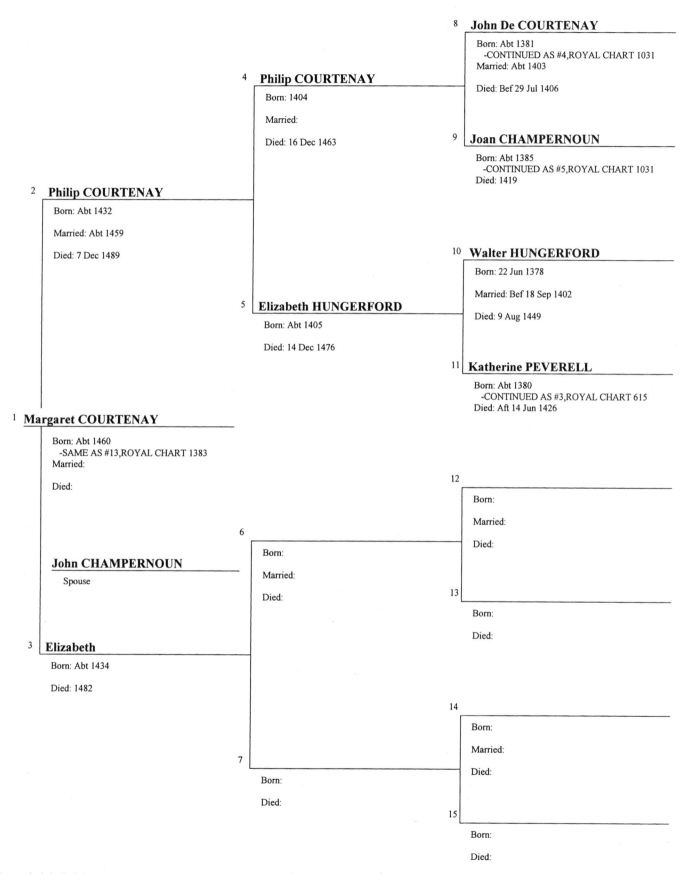

8 John De COURTENAY

Born: Abt 1381
    -CONTINUED AS #4,ROYAL CHART 1031
Married: Abt 1403

Died: Bef 29 Jul 1406

4 Philip COURTENAY

Born: 1404

Married:

Died: 16 Dec 1463

9 Joan CHAMPERNOUN

Born: Abt 1385
    -CONTINUED AS #5,ROYAL CHART 1031
Died: 1419

2 Philip COURTENAY

Born: Abt 1432

Married: Abt 1459

Died: 7 Dec 1489

10 Walter HUNGERFORD

Born: 22 Jun 1378

Married: Bef 18 Sep 1402

Died: 9 Aug 1449

5 Elizabeth HUNGERFORD

Born: Abt 1405

Died: 14 Dec 1476

11 Katherine PEVERELL

Born: Abt 1380
    -CONTINUED AS #3,ROYAL CHART 615
Died: Aft 14 Jun 1426

1 Margaret COURTENAY

Born: Abt 1460
    -SAME AS #13,ROYAL CHART 1383
Married:

Died:

12

Born:

Married:

Died:

6

Born:

Married:

Died:

John CHAMPERNOUN

Spouse

13

Born:

Died:

3 Elizabeth

Born: Abt 1434

Died: 1482

14

Born:

Married:

Died:

7

Born:

Died:

15

Born:

Died:

Sources include: Faris 2--Denny, Davie.

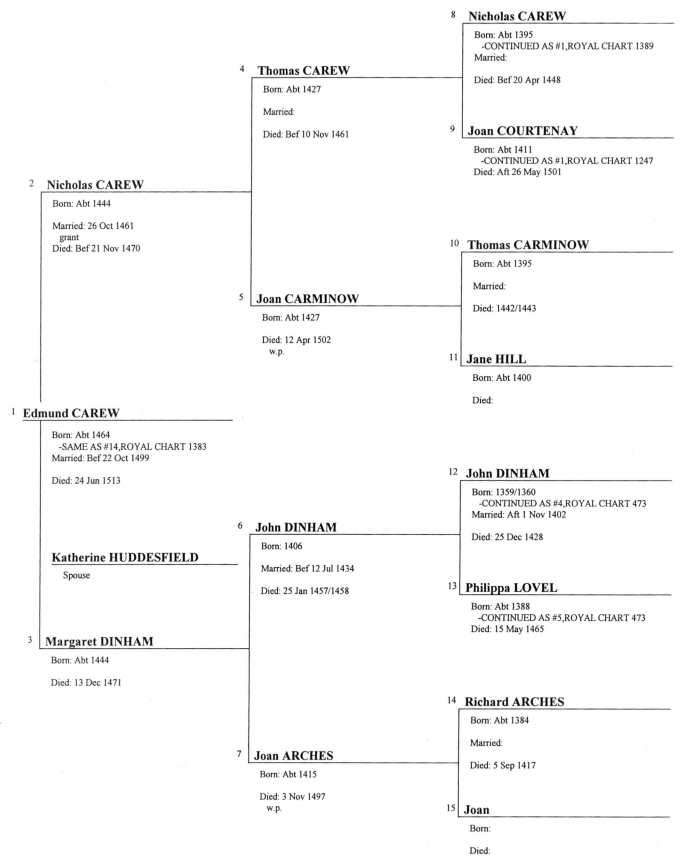

8 Nicholas CAREW
Born: Abt 1395
-CONTINUED AS #1,ROYAL CHART 1389
Married:

Died: Bef 20 Apr 1448

4 Thomas CAREW
Born: Abt 1427

Married:

Died: Bef 10 Nov 1461

9 Joan COURTENAY
Born: Abt 1411
-CONTINUED AS #1,ROYAL CHART 1247
Died: Aft 26 May 1501

2 Nicholas CAREW
Born: Abt 1444

Married: 26 Oct 1461
grant
Died: Bef 21 Nov 1470

10 Thomas CARMINOW
Born: Abt 1395

Married:

Died: 1442/1443

5 Joan CARMINOW
Born: Abt 1427

Died: 12 Apr 1502
w.p.

11 Jane HILL
Born: Abt 1400

Died:

1 Edmund CAREW
Born: Abt 1464
-SAME AS #14,ROYAL CHART 1383
Married: Bef 22 Oct 1499

Died: 24 Jun 1513

12 John DINHAM
Born: 1359/1360
-CONTINUED AS #4,ROYAL CHART 473
Married: Aft 1 Nov 1402

Died: 25 Dec 1428

6 John DINHAM
Born: 1406

Married: Bef 12 Jul 1434

Died: 25 Jan 1457/1458

13 Philippa LOVEL
Born: Abt 1388
-CONTINUED AS #5,ROYAL CHART 473
Died: 15 May 1465

Katherine HUDDESFIELD
Spouse

3 Margaret DINHAM
Born: Abt 1444

Died: 13 Dec 1471

14 Richard ARCHES
Born: Abt 1384

Married:

Died: 5 Sep 1417

7 Joan ARCHES
Born: Abt 1415

Died: 3 Nov 1497
w.p.

15 Joan
Born:

Died:

Sources include: Richardson *Plantagenet* (2004), pp. 184-186 (Carew), 274-275 (Dinham); Faris 2--Carew; *Ancestral Roots* 6, 214; *Magna Charta* 35; LDS records.

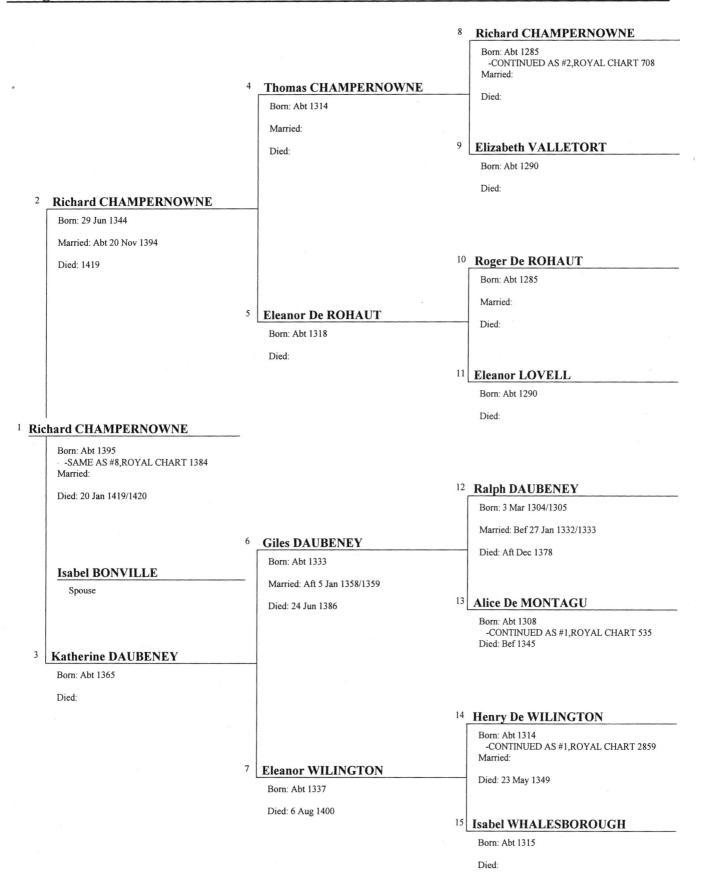

8 **Richard CHAMPERNOWNE**

Born: Abt 1285
-CONTINUED AS #2,ROYAL CHART 708
Married:

Died:

4 **Thomas CHAMPERNOWNE**

Born: Abt 1314

Married:

Died:

9 **Elizabeth VALLETORT**

Born: Abt 1290

Died:

2 **Richard CHAMPERNOWNE**

Born: 29 Jun 1344

Married: Abt 20 Nov 1394

Died: 1419

10 **Roger De ROHAUT**

Born: Abt 1285

Married:

Died:

5 **Eleanor De ROHAUT**

Born: Abt 1318

Died:

11 **Eleanor LOVELL**

Born: Abt 1290

Died:

1 **Richard CHAMPERNOWNE**

Born: Abt 1395
-SAME AS #8,ROYAL CHART 1384
Married:

Died: 20 Jan 1419/1420

12 **Ralph DAUBENEY**

Born: 3 Mar 1304/1305

Married: Bef 27 Jan 1332/1333

Died: Aft Dec 1378

6 **Giles DAUBENEY**

Born: Abt 1333

Married: Aft 5 Jan 1358/1359

Died: 24 Jun 1386

13 **Alice De MONTAGU**

Born: Abt 1308
-CONTINUED AS #1,ROYAL CHART 535
Died: Bef 1345

Isabel BONVILLE

Spouse

3 **Katherine DAUBENEY**

Born: Abt 1365

Died:

14 **Henry De WILINGTON**

Born: Abt 1314
-CONTINUED AS #1,ROYAL CHART 2859
Married:

Died: 23 May 1349

7 **Eleanor WILINGTON**

Born: Abt 1337

Died: 6 Aug 1400

15 **Isabel WHALESBOROUGH**

Born: Abt 1315

Died:

Sources include: Consultation with Douglas Richardson; LDS records; Roberts *500*, p. 396 (#2 ancestry); *Complete Peerage* 4:93-101 (#3 ancestry).

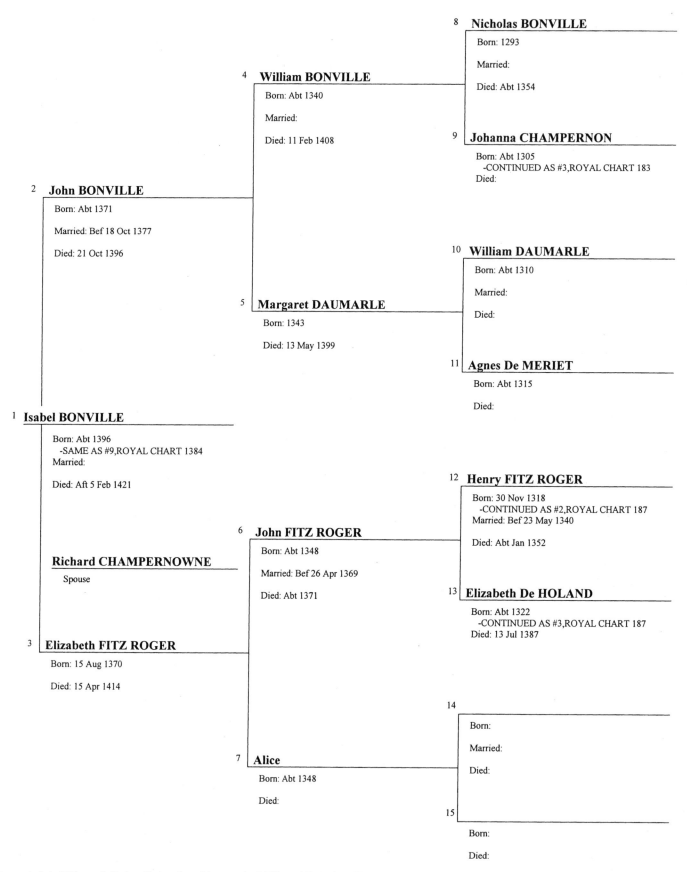

8 **Nicholas BONVILLE**

Born: 1293

Married:

Died: Abt 1354

4 **William BONVILLE**

Born: Abt 1340

Married:

Died: 11 Feb 1408

9 **Johanna CHAMPERNON**

Born: Abt 1305
-CONTINUED AS #3, ROYAL CHART 183
Died:

2 **John BONVILLE**

Born: Abt 1371

Married: Bef 18 Oct 1377

Died: 21 Oct 1396

10 **William DAUMARLE**

Born: Abt 1310

Married:

Died:

5 **Margaret DAUMARLE**

Born: 1343

Died: 13 May 1399

11 **Agnes De MERIET**

Born: Abt 1315

Died:

1 **Isabel BONVILLE**

Born: Abt 1396
-SAME AS #9, ROYAL CHART 1384
Married:

Died: Aft 5 Feb 1421

12 **Henry FITZ ROGER**

Born: 30 Nov 1318
-CONTINUED AS #2, ROYAL CHART 187
Married: Bef 23 May 1340

Died: Abt Jan 1352

6 **John FITZ ROGER**

Born: Abt 1348

Married: Bef 26 Apr 1369

Died: Abt 1371

13 **Elizabeth De HOLAND**

Born: Abt 1322
-CONTINUED AS #3, ROYAL CHART 187
Died: 13 Jul 1387

Richard CHAMPERNOWNE

Spouse

3 **Elizabeth FITZ ROGER**

Born: 15 Aug 1370

Died: 15 Apr 1414

14

Born:

Married:

Died:

7 **Alice**

Born: Abt 1348

Died:

15

Born:

Died:

Sources include: LDS records; Faris preliminary baronial manuscript (1998), pp. 150-151 (Bonville), 475 (Daumarle); *Ancestral Roots* 124A, 261 (#2 & 3 ancestry).

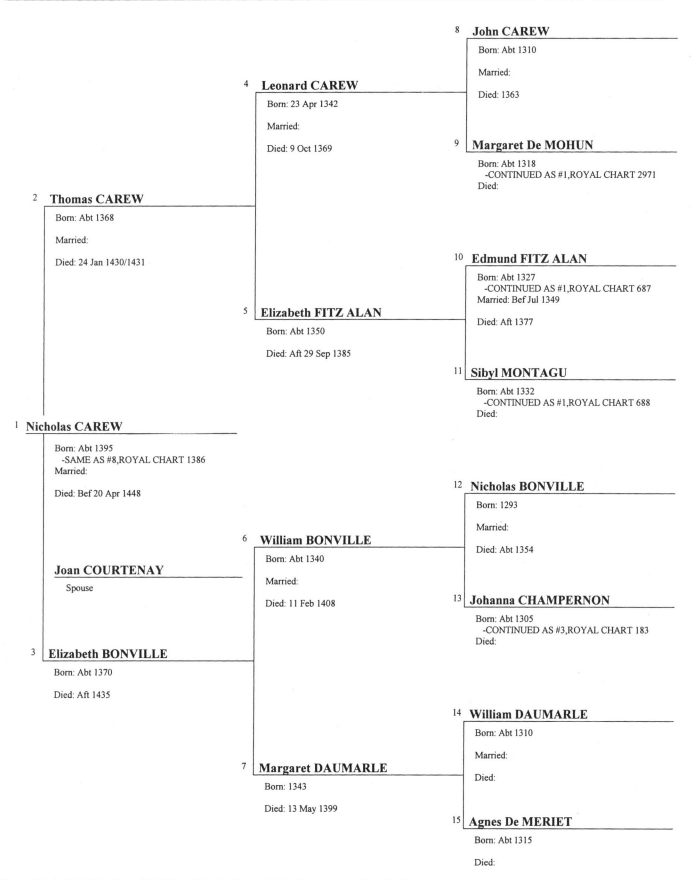

8 **John CAREW**
Born: Abt 1310
Married:
Died: 1363

4 **Leonard CAREW**
Born: 23 Apr 1342
Married:
Died: 9 Oct 1369

9 **Margaret De MOHUN**
Born: Abt 1318
-CONTINUED AS #1,ROYAL CHART 2971
Died:

2 **Thomas CAREW**
Born: Abt 1368
Married:
Died: 24 Jan 1430/1431

10 **Edmund FITZ ALAN**
Born: Abt 1327
-CONTINUED AS #1,ROYAL CHART 687
Married: Bef Jul 1349
Died: Aft 1377

5 **Elizabeth FITZ ALAN**
Born: Abt 1350
Died: Aft 29 Sep 1385

11 **Sibyl MONTAGU**
Born: Abt 1332
-CONTINUED AS #1,ROYAL CHART 688
Died:

1 **Nicholas CAREW**
Born: Abt 1395
-SAME AS #8,ROYAL CHART 1386
Married:
Died: Bef 20 Apr 1448

12 **Nicholas BONVILLE**
Born: 1293
Married:
Died: Abt 1354

6 **William BONVILLE**
Born: Abt 1340
Married:
Died: 11 Feb 1408

13 **Johanna CHAMPERNON**
Born: Abt 1305
-CONTINUED AS #3,ROYAL CHART 183
Died:

Joan COURTENAY
Spouse

3 **Elizabeth BONVILLE**
Born: Abt 1370
Died: Aft 1435

14 **William DAUMARLE**
Born: Abt 1310
Married:
Died:

7 **Margaret DAUMARLE**
Born: 1343
Died: 13 May 1399

15 **Agnes De MERIET**
Born: Abt 1315
Died:

Sources include: Faris-Richardson 3 (July 2002 preliminary)--Carew; Faris 2--Carew; *Ancestral Roots* 28, 124A.

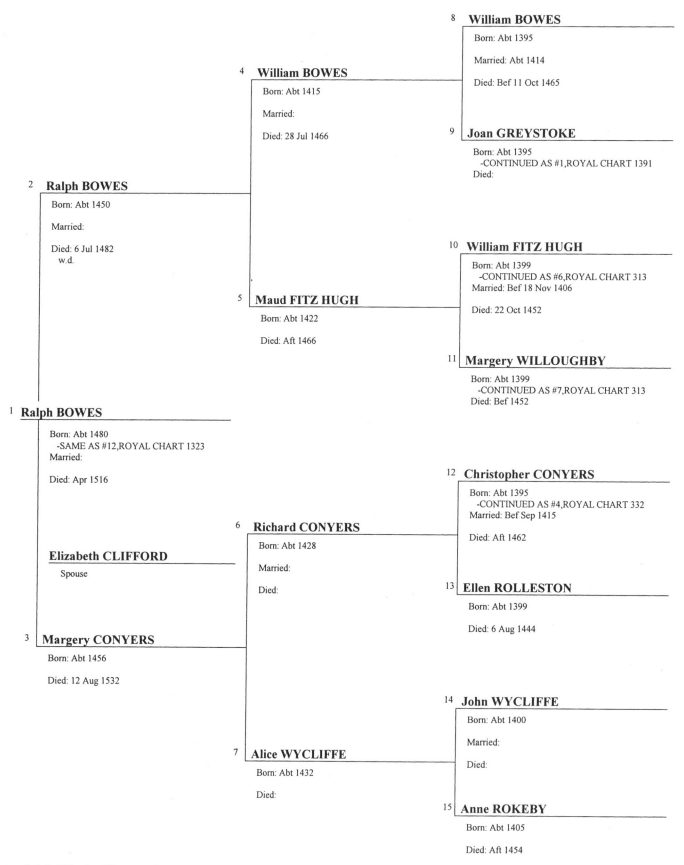

8 William BOWES

Born: Abt 1395

Married: Abt 1414

Died: Bef 11 Oct 1465

4 William BOWES

Born: Abt 1415

Married:

Died: 28 Jul 1466

9 Joan GREYSTOKE

Born: Abt 1395
    -CONTINUED AS #1,ROYAL CHART 1391
Died:

2 Ralph BOWES

Born: Abt 1450

Married:

Died: 6 Jul 1482
    w.d.

10 William FITZ HUGH

Born: Abt 1399
    -CONTINUED AS #6,ROYAL CHART 313
Married: Bef 18 Nov 1406

Died: 22 Oct 1452

5 Maud FITZ HUGH

Born: Abt 1422

Died: Aft 1466

11 Margery WILLOUGHBY

Born: Abt 1399
    -CONTINUED AS #7,ROYAL CHART 313
Died: Bef 1452

1 Ralph BOWES

Born: Abt 1480
    -SAME AS #12,ROYAL CHART 1323
Married:

Died: Apr 1516

12 Christopher CONYERS

Born: Abt 1395
    -CONTINUED AS #4,ROYAL CHART 332
Married: Bef Sep 1415

Died: Aft 1462

6 Richard CONYERS

Born: Abt 1428

Married:

Died:

13 Ellen ROLLESTON

Born: Abt 1399

Died: 6 Aug 1444

Elizabeth CLIFFORD

Spouse

3 Margery CONYERS

Born: Abt 1456

Died: 12 Aug 1532

14 John WYCLIFFE

Born: Abt 1400

Married:

Died:

7 Alice WYCLIFFE

Born: Abt 1432

Died:

15 Anne ROKEBY

Born: Abt 1405

Died: Aft 1454

Sources include: Richardson *Plantagenet* (2004), pp. 144-145 (Bowes), 325 (Fitz Hugh); MPGL 10044; LDS records.

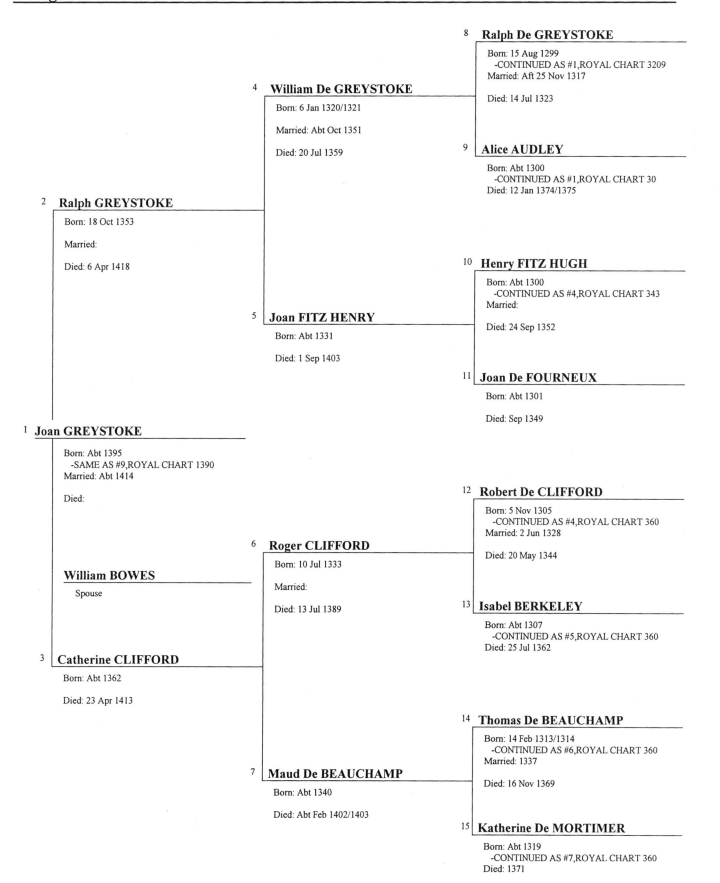

8   Ralph De GREYSTOKE

Born: 15 Aug 1299
   -CONTINUED AS #1,ROYAL CHART 3209
Married: Aft 25 Nov 1317

Died: 14 Jul 1323

4   William De GREYSTOKE

Born: 6 Jan 1320/1321

Married: Abt Oct 1351

Died: 20 Jul 1359

9   Alice AUDLEY

Born: Abt 1300
   -CONTINUED AS #1,ROYAL CHART 30
Died: 12 Jan 1374/1375

2   Ralph GREYSTOKE

Born: 18 Oct 1353

Married:

Died: 6 Apr 1418

10   Henry FITZ HUGH

Born: Abt 1300
   -CONTINUED AS #4,ROYAL CHART 343
Married:

Died: 24 Sep 1352

5   Joan FITZ HENRY

Born: Abt 1331

Died: 1 Sep 1403

11   Joan De FOURNEUX

Born: Abt 1301

Died: Sep 1349

1   Joan GREYSTOKE

Born: Abt 1395
   -SAME AS #9,ROYAL CHART 1390
Married: Abt 1414

Died:

12   Robert De CLIFFORD

Born: 5 Nov 1305
   -CONTINUED AS #4,ROYAL CHART 360
Married: 2 Jun 1328

Died: 20 May 1344

6   Roger CLIFFORD

Born: 10 Jul 1333

Married:

Died: 13 Jul 1389

William BOWES

Spouse

13   Isabel BERKELEY

Born: Abt 1307
   -CONTINUED AS #5,ROYAL CHART 360
Died: 25 Jul 1362

3   Catherine CLIFFORD

Born: Abt 1362

Died: 23 Apr 1413

14   Thomas De BEAUCHAMP

Born: 14 Feb 1313/1314
   -CONTINUED AS #6,ROYAL CHART 360
Married: 1337

Died: 16 Nov 1369

7   Maud De BEAUCHAMP

Born: Abt 1340

Died: Abt Feb 1402/1403

15   Katherine De MORTIMER

Born: Abt 1319
   -CONTINUED AS #7,ROYAL CHART 360
Died: 1371

Sources include: LDS records; *Emperor Charlemagne* 1:215-216; *Ancestral Roots* 202 (#3 ancestry).

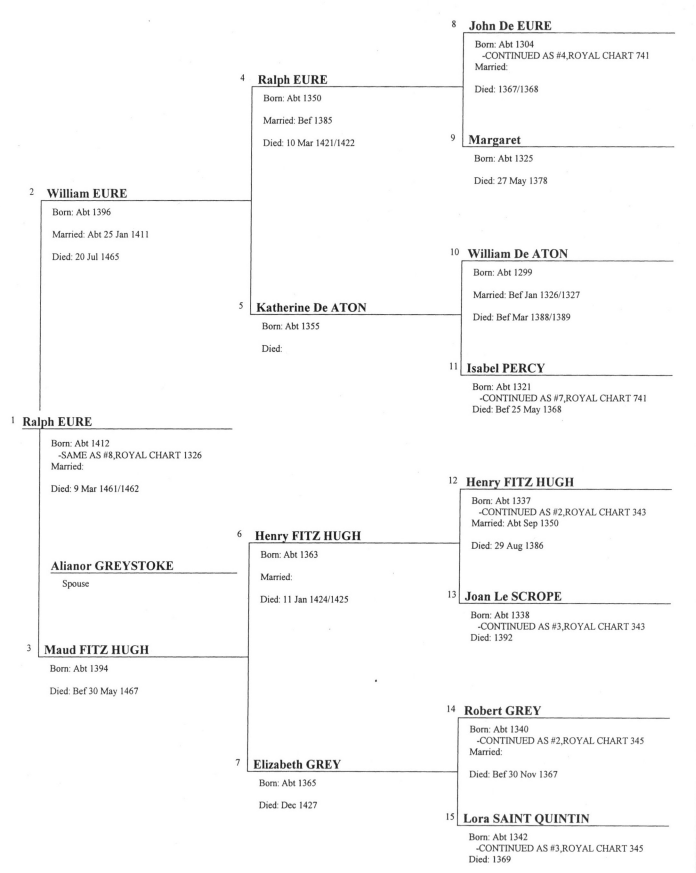

2 William EURE

Born: Abt 1396

Married: Abt 25 Jan 1411

Died: 20 Jul 1465

4 Ralph EURE

Born: Abt 1350

Married: Bef 1385

Died: 10 Mar 1421/1422

8 John De EURE

Born: Abt 1304
   -CONTINUED AS #4,ROYAL CHART 741
Married:

Died: 1367/1368

9 Margaret

Born: Abt 1325

Died: 27 May 1378

5 Katherine De ATON

Born: Abt 1355

Died:

10 William De ATON

Born: Abt 1299

Married: Bef Jan 1326/1327

Died: Bef Mar 1388/1389

11 Isabel PERCY

Born: Abt 1321
   -CONTINUED AS #7,ROYAL CHART 741
Died: Bef 25 May 1368

1 Ralph EURE

Born: Abt 1412
   -SAME AS #8,ROYAL CHART 1326
Married:

Died: 9 Mar 1461/1462

Alianor GREYSTOKE

Spouse

3 Maud FITZ HUGH

Born: Abt 1394

Died: Bef 30 May 1467

6 Henry FITZ HUGH

Born: Abt 1363

Married:

Died: 11 Jan 1424/1425

12 Henry FITZ HUGH

Born: Abt 1337
   -CONTINUED AS #2,ROYAL CHART 343
Married: Abt Sep 1350

Died: 29 Aug 1386

13 Joan Le SCROPE

Born: Abt 1338
   -CONTINUED AS #3,ROYAL CHART 343
Died: 1392

7 Elizabeth GREY

Born: Abt 1365

Died: Dec 1427

14 Robert GREY

Born: Abt 1340
   -CONTINUED AS #2,ROYAL CHART 345
Married:

Died: Bef 30 Nov 1367

15 Lora SAINT QUINTIN

Born: Abt 1342
   -CONTINUED AS #3,ROYAL CHART 345
Died: 1369

Sources include: Faris 2--Eure 6.

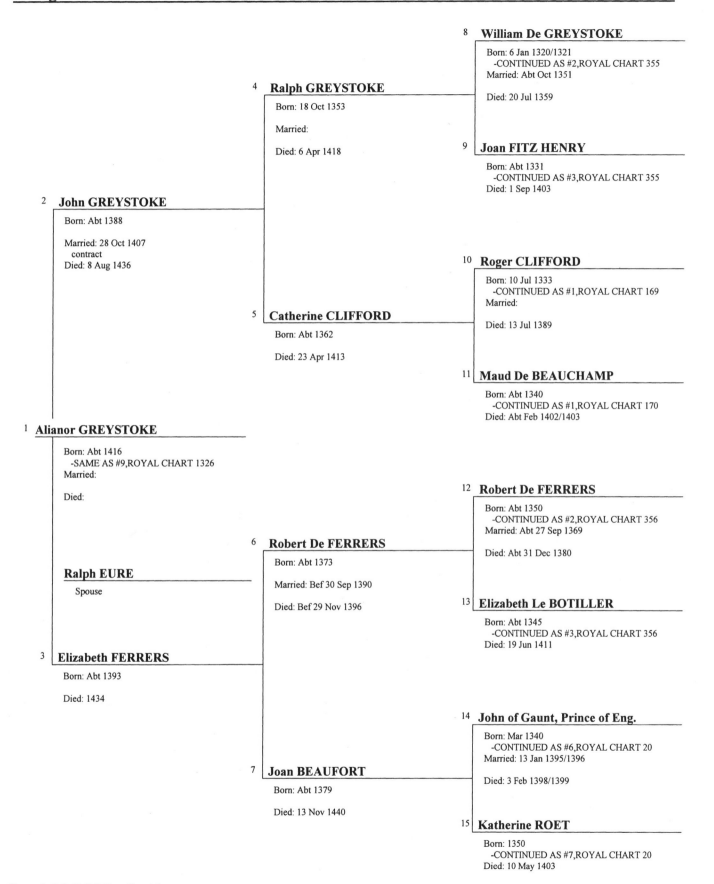

8 **William De GREYSTOKE**

Born: 6 Jan 1320/1321
  -CONTINUED AS #2,ROYAL CHART 355
Married: Abt Oct 1351

Died: 20 Jul 1359

4 **Ralph GREYSTOKE**

Born: 18 Oct 1353

Married:

Died: 6 Apr 1418

9 **Joan FITZ HENRY**

Born: Abt 1331
  -CONTINUED AS #3,ROYAL CHART 355
Died: 1 Sep 1403

2 **John GREYSTOKE**

Born: Abt 1388

Married: 28 Oct 1407
  contract
Died: 8 Aug 1436

10 **Roger CLIFFORD**

Born: 10 Jul 1333
  -CONTINUED AS #1,ROYAL CHART 169
Married:

Died: 13 Jul 1389

5 **Catherine CLIFFORD**

Born: Abt 1362

Died: 23 Apr 1413

11 **Maud De BEAUCHAMP**

Born: Abt 1340
  -CONTINUED AS #1,ROYAL CHART 170
Died: Abt Feb 1402/1403

1 **Alianor GREYSTOKE**

Born: Abt 1416
  -SAME AS #9,ROYAL CHART 1326
Married:

Died:

12 **Robert De FERRERS**

Born: Abt 1350
  -CONTINUED AS #2,ROYAL CHART 356
Married: Abt 27 Sep 1369

Died: Abt 31 Dec 1380

6 **Robert De FERRERS**

Born: Abt 1373

Married: Bef 30 Sep 1390

Died: Bef 29 Nov 1396

Ralph EURE

Spouse

13 **Elizabeth Le BOTILLER**

Born: Abt 1345
  -CONTINUED AS #3,ROYAL CHART 356
Died: 19 Jun 1411

3 **Elizabeth FERRERS**

Born: Abt 1393

Died: 1434

14 **John of Gaunt, Prince of Eng.**

Born: Mar 1340
  -CONTINUED AS #6,ROYAL CHART 20
Married: 13 Jan 1395/1396

Died: 3 Feb 1398/1399

7 **Joan BEAUFORT**

Born: Abt 1379

Died: 13 Nov 1440

15 **Katherine ROET**

Born: 1350
  -CONTINUED AS #7,ROYAL CHART 20
Died: 10 May 1403

Sources include: Faris 2--Eure, Greystoke.

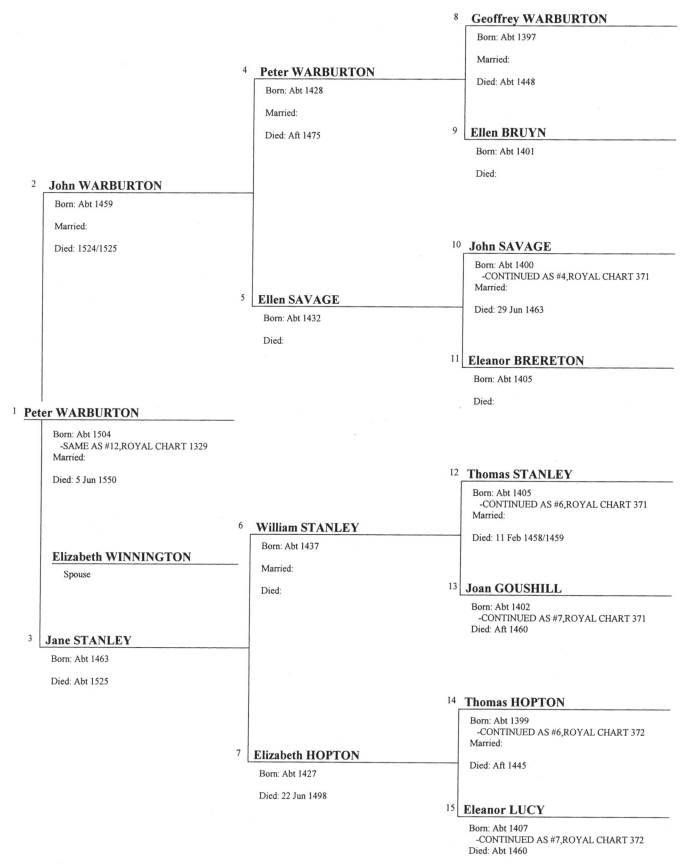

8 **Geoffrey WARBURTON**
Born: Abt 1397
Married:
Died: Abt 1448

4 **Peter WARBURTON**
Born: Abt 1428
Married:
Died: Aft 1475

9 **Ellen BRUYN**
Born: Abt 1401
Died:

2 **John WARBURTON**
Born: Abt 1459
Married:
Died: 1524/1525

10 **John SAVAGE**
Born: Abt 1400
  -CONTINUED AS #4,ROYAL CHART 371
Married:
Died: 29 Jun 1463

5 **Ellen SAVAGE**
Born: Abt 1432
Died:

11 **Eleanor BRERETON**
Born: Abt 1405
Died:

1 **Peter WARBURTON**
Born: Abt 1504
  -SAME AS #12,ROYAL CHART 1329
Married:
Died: 5 Jun 1550

12 **Thomas STANLEY**
Born: Abt 1405
  -CONTINUED AS #6,ROYAL CHART 371
Married:
Died: 11 Feb 1458/1459

6 **William STANLEY**
Born: Abt 1437
Married:
Died:

13 **Joan GOUSHILL**
Born: Abt 1402
  -CONTINUED AS #7,ROYAL CHART 371
Died: Aft 1460

Elizabeth WINNINGTON
Spouse

3 **Jane STANLEY**
Born: Abt 1463
Died: Abt 1525

14 **Thomas HOPTON**
Born: Abt 1399
  -CONTINUED AS #6,ROYAL CHART 372
Married:
Died: Aft 1445

7 **Elizabeth HOPTON**
Born: Abt 1427
Died: 22 Jun 1498

15 **Eleanor LUCY**
Born: Abt 1407
  -CONTINUED AS #7,ROYAL CHART 372
Died: Abt 1460

Sources include: LDS records; *Ancestral Roots* 56B-38 (#6 & 7).

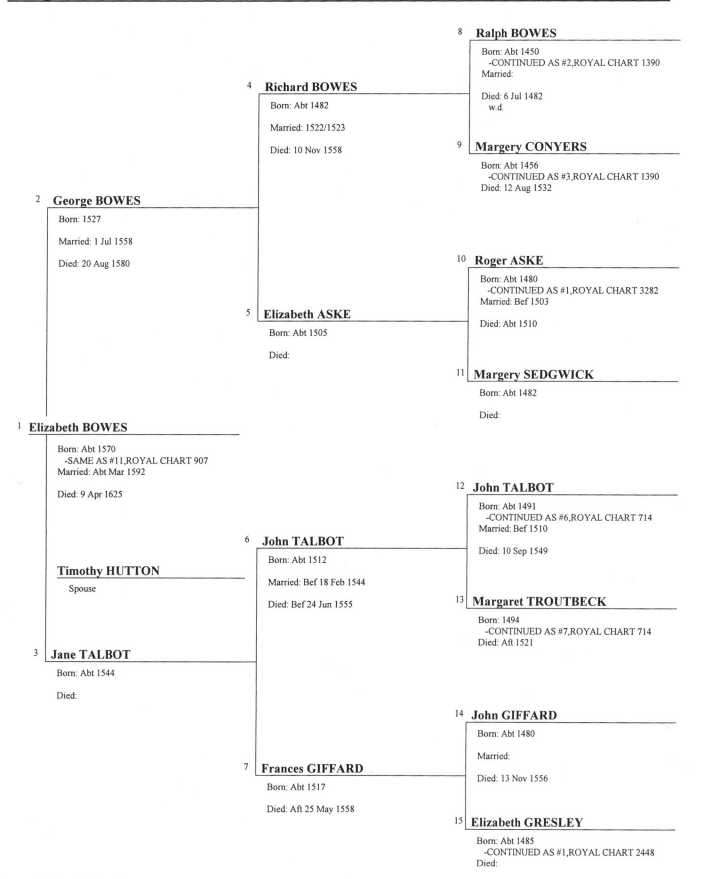

8 Ralph BOWES

Born: Abt 1450
  -CONTINUED AS #2,ROYAL CHART 1390
Married:

Died: 6 Jul 1482
w.d.

4 Richard BOWES

Born: Abt 1482

Married: 1522/1523

Died: 10 Nov 1558

9 Margery CONYERS

Born: Abt 1456
  -CONTINUED AS #3,ROYAL CHART 1390
Died: 12 Aug 1532

2 George BOWES

Born: 1527

Married: 1 Jul 1558

Died: 20 Aug 1580

10 Roger ASKE

Born: Abt 1480
  -CONTINUED AS #1,ROYAL CHART 3282
Married: Bef 1503

Died: Abt 1510

5 Elizabeth ASKE

Born: Abt 1505

Died:

11 Margery SEDGWICK

Born: Abt 1482

Died:

1 Elizabeth BOWES

Born: Abt 1570
  -SAME AS #11,ROYAL CHART 907
Married: Abt Mar 1592

Died: 9 Apr 1625

Timothy HUTTON

Spouse

12 John TALBOT

Born: Abt 1491
  -CONTINUED AS #6,ROYAL CHART 714
Married: Bef 1510

Died: 10 Sep 1549

6 John TALBOT

Born: Abt 1512

Married: Bef 18 Feb 1544

Died: Bef 24 Jun 1555

13 Margaret TROUTBECK

Born: 1494
  -CONTINUED AS #7,ROYAL CHART 714
Died: Aft 1521

3 Jane TALBOT

Born: Abt 1544

Died:

14 John GIFFARD

Born: Abt 1480

Married:

Died: 13 Nov 1556

7 Frances GIFFARD

Born: Abt 1517

Died: Aft 25 May 1558

15 Elizabeth GRESLEY

Born: Abt 1485
  -CONTINUED AS #1,ROYAL CHART 2448
Died:

Sources include: Richardson *Plantagenet* (2004), pp. 410-411 (Hutton), 706-707 (Talbot), 144-145 (Bowes), 695 (Strangeways).

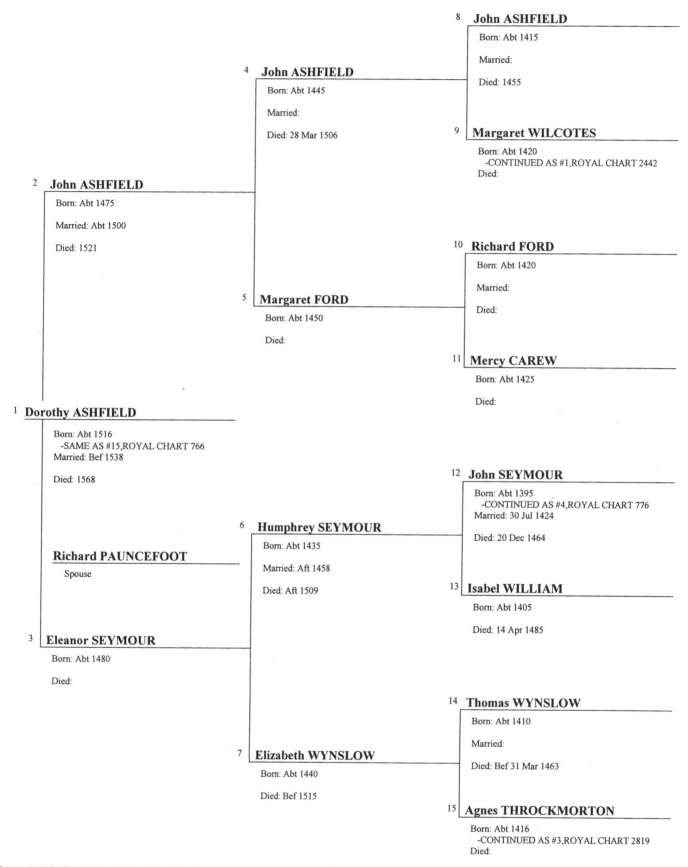

8 **John ASHFIELD**

Born: Abt 1415

Married:

Died: 1455

4 **John ASHFIELD**

Born: Abt 1445

Married:

Died: 28 Mar 1506

9 **Margaret WILCOTES**

Born: Abt 1420
-CONTINUED AS #1,ROYAL CHART 2442
Died:

2 **John ASHFIELD**

Born: Abt 1475

Married: Abt 1500

Died: 1521

10 **Richard FORD**

Born: Abt 1420

Married:

Died:

5 **Margaret FORD**

Born: Abt 1450

Died:

11 **Mercy CAREW**

Born: Abt 1425

Died:

1 **Dorothy ASHFIELD**

Born: Abt 1516
-SAME AS #15,ROYAL CHART 766
Married: Bef 1538

Died: 1568

12 **John SEYMOUR**

Born: Abt 1395
-CONTINUED AS #4,ROYAL CHART 776
Married: 30 Jul 1424

Died: 20 Dec 1464

6 **Humphrey SEYMOUR**

Born: Abt 1435

Married: Aft 1458

Died: Aft 1509

13 **Isabel WILLIAM**

Born: Abt 1405

Died: 14 Apr 1485

Richard PAUNCEFOOT

Spouse

3 **Eleanor SEYMOUR**

Born: Abt 1480

Died:

14 **Thomas WYNSLOW**

Born: Abt 1410

Married:

Died: Bef 31 Mar 1463

7 **Elizabeth WYNSLOW**

Born: Abt 1440

Died: Bef 1515

15 **Agnes THROCKMORTON**

Born: Abt 1416
-CONTINUED AS #3,ROYAL CHART 2819
Died:

Sources include: Consultation with Douglas Richardson; Faris 2--St. John 4; LDS records.

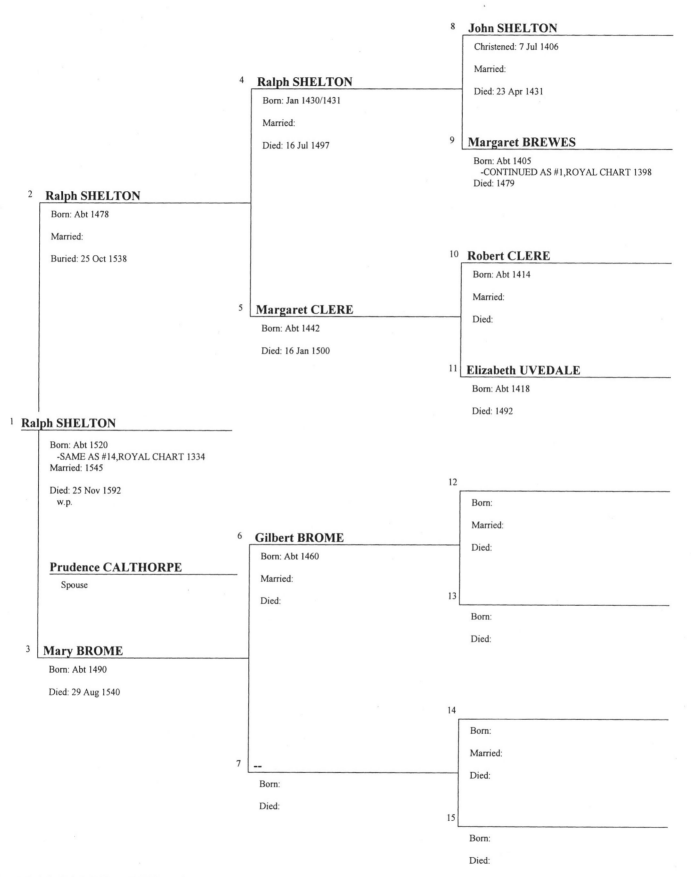

8 **John SHELTON**

Christened: 7 Jul 1406

Married:

Died: 23 Apr 1431

4 **Ralph SHELTON**

Born: Jan 1430/1431

Married:

Died: 16 Jul 1497

9 **Margaret BREWES**

Born: Abt 1405
  -CONTINUED AS #1,ROYAL CHART 1398
Died: 1479

2 **Ralph SHELTON**

Born: Abt 1478

Married:

Buried: 25 Oct 1538

10 **Robert CLERE**

Born: Abt 1414

Married:

Died:

5 **Margaret CLERE**

Born: Abt 1442

Died: 16 Jan 1500

11 **Elizabeth UVEDALE**

Born: Abt 1418

Died: 1492

1 **Ralph SHELTON**

Born: Abt 1520
  -SAME AS #14,ROYAL CHART 1334
Married: 1545

Died: 25 Nov 1592
  w.p.

12

Born:

Married:

Died:

6 **Gilbert BROME**

Born: Abt 1460

Married:

Died:

13

Born:

Died:

Prudence CALTHORPE

Spouse

3 **Mary BROME**

Born: Abt 1490

Died: 29 Aug 1540

14

Born:

Married:

Died:

7 **--**

Born:

Died:

15

Born:

Died:

Sources include: Faris 2--Calthorpe 3; LDS records.

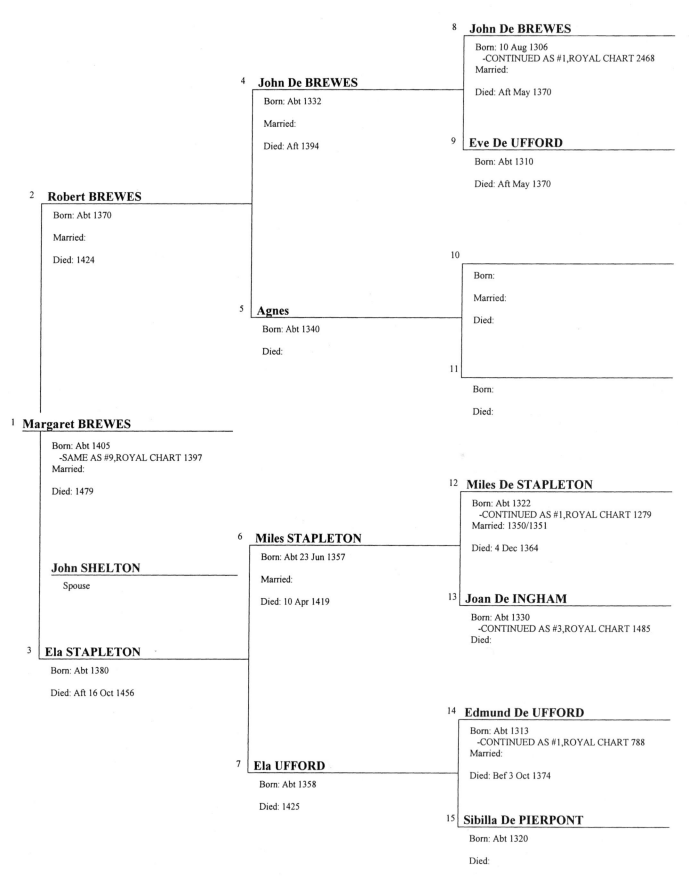

8 **John De BREWES**

Born: 10 Aug 1306
-CONTINUED AS #1,ROYAL CHART 2468
Married:

Died: Aft May 1370

4 **John De BREWES**

Born: Abt 1332

Married:

Died: Aft 1394

9 **Eve De UFFORD**

Born: Abt 1310

Died: Aft May 1370

2 **Robert BREWES**

Born: Abt 1370

Married:

Died: 1424

10

Born:

Married:

Died:

5 **Agnes**

Born: Abt 1340

Died:

11

Born:

Died:

1 **Margaret BREWES**

Born: Abt 1405
-SAME AS #9,ROYAL CHART 1397
Married:

Died: 1479

12 **Miles De STAPLETON**

Born: Abt 1322
-CONTINUED AS #1,ROYAL CHART 1279
Married: 1350/1351

Died: 4 Dec 1364

6 **Miles STAPLETON**

Born: Abt 23 Jun 1357

Married:

Died: 10 Apr 1419

13 **Joan De INGHAM**

Born: Abt 1330
-CONTINUED AS #3,ROYAL CHART 1485
Died:

John SHELTON

Spouse

3 **Ela STAPLETON**

Born: Abt 1380

Died: Aft 16 Oct 1456

14 **Edmund De UFFORD**

Born: Abt 1313
-CONTINUED AS #1,ROYAL CHART 788
Married:

Died: Bef 3 Oct 1374

7 **Ela UFFORD**

Born: Abt 1358

Died: 1425

15 **Sibilla De PIERPONT**

Born: Abt 1320

Died:

Sources include: Richardson *Magna Carta* (April 2005), pp. 166-167 (Calthorpe), 213-214 (Clavering); *Complete Peerage* 2:304-306 (#2 & 3 ancestry); Faris 2--Calthorpe 8 (#6 & 7 ancestry).

Pedigree Chart

Chart 1399

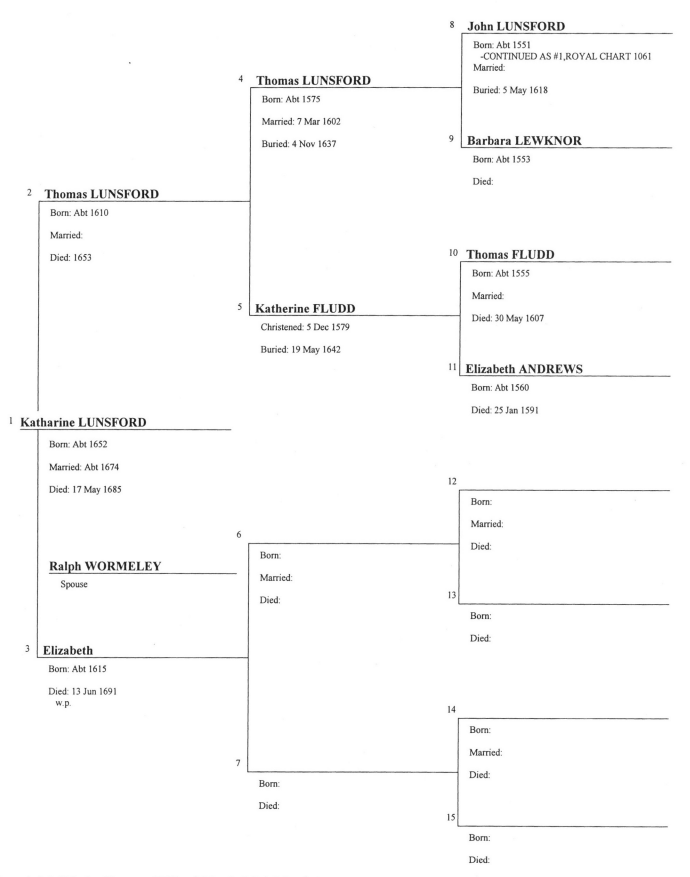

8 **John LUNSFORD**

Born: Abt 1551
   -CONTINUED AS #1,ROYAL CHART 1061
Married:

Buried: 5 May 1618

4 **Thomas LUNSFORD**

Born: Abt 1575

Married: 7 Mar 1602

Buried: 4 Nov 1637

9 **Barbara LEWKNOR**

Born: Abt 1553

Died:

2 **Thomas LUNSFORD**

Born: Abt 1610

Married:

Died: 1653

10 **Thomas FLUDD**

Born: Abt 1555

Married:

Died: 30 May 1607

5 **Katherine FLUDD**

Christened: 5 Dec 1579

Buried: 19 May 1642

11 **Elizabeth ANDREWS**

Born: Abt 1560

Died: 25 Jan 1591

1 **Katharine LUNSFORD**

Born: Abt 1652

Married: Abt 1674

Died: 17 May 1685

12

Born:

Married:

Died:

6

Born:

Married:

Died:

13

Born:

Died:

Ralph WORMELEY

Spouse

3 **Elizabeth**

Born: Abt 1615

Died: 13 Jun 1691
   w.p.

14

Born:

Married:

Died:

7

Born:

Died:

15

Born:

Died:

Sources include: Richardson *Plantagenet* (2004), p. 481 (Lunsford); Faris 2--Lunsford.

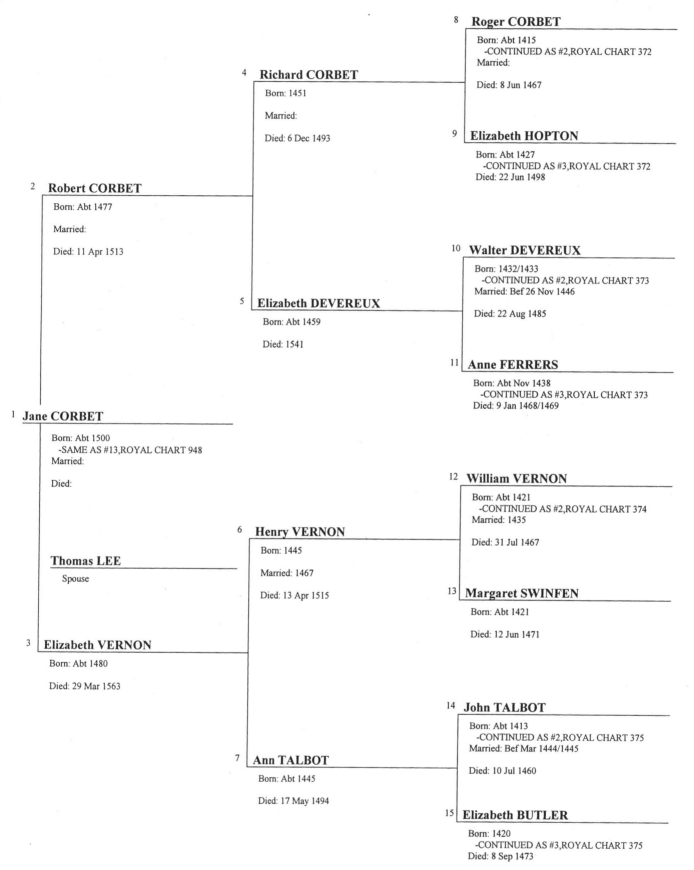

8 Roger CORBET

Born: Abt 1415
  -CONTINUED AS #2,ROYAL CHART 372
Married:

Died: 8 Jun 1467

4 Richard CORBET

Born: 1451

Married:

Died: 6 Dec 1493

9 Elizabeth HOPTON

Born: Abt 1427
  -CONTINUED AS #3,ROYAL CHART 372
Died: 22 Jun 1498

2 Robert CORBET

Born: Abt 1477

Married:

Died: 11 Apr 1513

10 Walter DEVEREUX

Born: 1432/1433
  -CONTINUED AS #2,ROYAL CHART 373
Married: Bef 26 Nov 1446

Died: 22 Aug 1485

5 Elizabeth DEVEREUX

Born: Abt 1459

Died: 1541

11 Anne FERRERS

Born: Abt Nov 1438
  -CONTINUED AS #3,ROYAL CHART 373
Died: 9 Jan 1468/1469

1 Jane CORBET

Born: Abt 1500
  -SAME AS #13,ROYAL CHART 948
Married:

Died:

12 William VERNON

Born: Abt 1421
  -CONTINUED AS #2,ROYAL CHART 374
Married: 1435

Died: 31 Jul 1467

6 Henry VERNON

Born: 1445

Married: 1467

Died: 13 Apr 1515

13 Margaret SWINFEN

Born: Abt 1421

Died: 12 Jun 1471

Thomas LEE

Spouse

3 Elizabeth VERNON

Born: Abt 1480

Died: 29 Mar 1563

14 John TALBOT

Born: Abt 1413
  -CONTINUED AS #2,ROYAL CHART 375
Married: Bef Mar 1444/1445

Died: 10 Jul 1460

7 Ann TALBOT

Born: Abt 1445

Died: 17 May 1494

15 Elizabeth BUTLER

Born: 1420
  -CONTINUED AS #3,ROYAL CHART 375
Died: 8 Sep 1473

Sources include: Richardson *Plantagenet* (2004), pp. 484 (Mackworth), 472-474 (Lucy), 705 (Talbot); Boyer *Abell* (2001), pp. 67-68, 260.

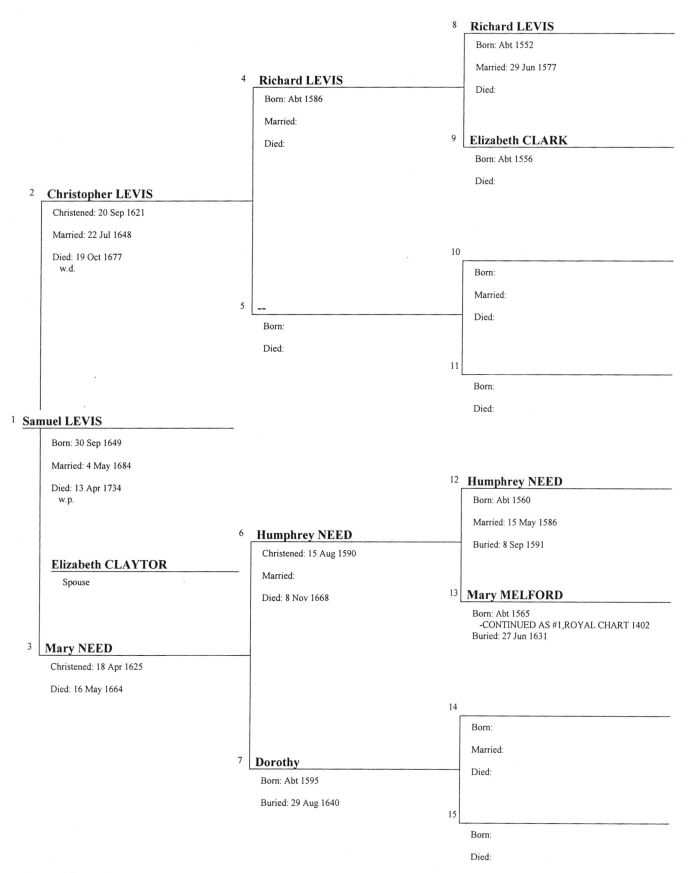

8 **Richard LEVIS**
Born: Abt 1552
Married: 29 Jun 1577
Died:

4 **Richard LEVIS**
Born: Abt 1586
Married:
Died:

9 **Elizabeth CLARK**
Born: Abt 1556
Died:

2 **Christopher LEVIS**
Christened: 20 Sep 1621
Married: 22 Jul 1648
Died: 19 Oct 1677
w.d.

10
Born:
Married:
Died:

5 **--**
Born:
Died:

11
Born:
Died:

1 **Samuel LEVIS**
Born: 30 Sep 1649
Married: 4 May 1684
Died: 13 Apr 1734
w.p.

Elizabeth CLAYTOR
Spouse

12 **Humphrey NEED**
Born: Abt 1560
Married: 15 May 1586
Buried: 8 Sep 1591

6 **Humphrey NEED**
Christened: 15 Aug 1590
Married:
Died: 8 Nov 1668

13 **Mary MELFORD**
Born: Abt 1565
-CONTINUED AS #1,ROYAL CHART 1402
Buried: 27 Jun 1631

3 **Mary NEED**
Christened: 18 Apr 1625
Died: 16 May 1664

14
Born:
Married:
Died:

7 **Dorothy**
Born: Abt 1595
Buried: 29 Aug 1640

15
Born:
Died:

Sources include: Richardson *Plantagenet* (2004), pp. 537-538 (Need); Faris 2--Levis; LDS records. Note: #6 Humphrey had a son Nathaniel Need (chr. 8 Jul 1622; md. Anne), who had a son Joseph Need (chr. 14 Feb 1648-49; md. Rebecca) of PA.

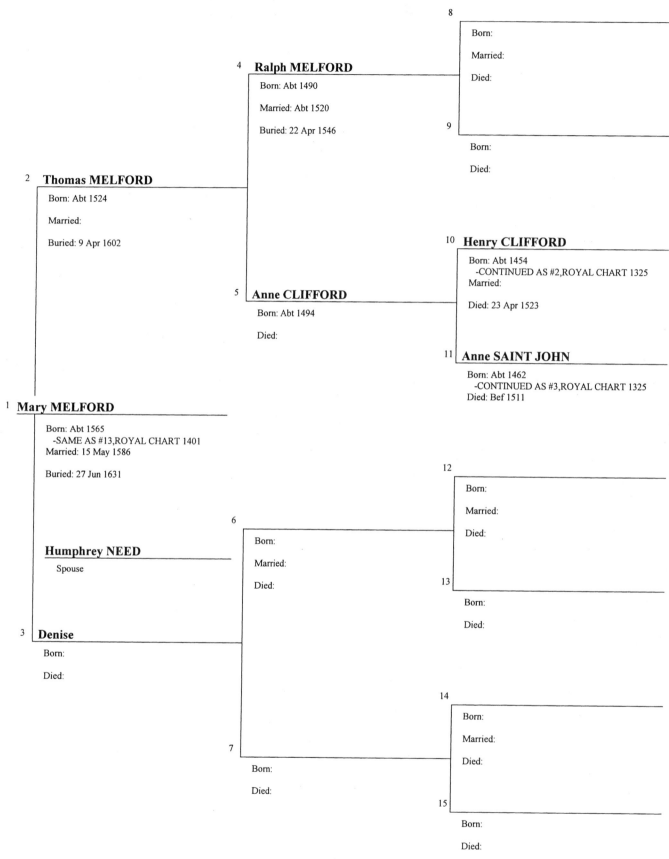

8

Born:

Married:

Died:

4 **Ralph MELFORD**

Born: Abt 1490

Married: Abt 1520

Buried: 22 Apr 1546

9

Born:

Died:

2 **Thomas MELFORD**

Born: Abt 1524

Married:

Buried: 9 Apr 1602

10 **Henry CLIFFORD**

Born: Abt 1454
    -CONTINUED AS #2,ROYAL CHART 1325
Married:

Died: 23 Apr 1523

5 **Anne CLIFFORD**

Born: Abt 1494

Died:

11 **Anne SAINT JOHN**

Born: Abt 1462
    -CONTINUED AS #3,ROYAL CHART 1325
Died: Bef 1511

1 **Mary MELFORD**

Born: Abt 1565
    -SAME AS #13,ROYAL CHART 1401
Married: 15 May 1586

Buried: 27 Jun 1631

12

Born:

Married:

Died:

6

Born:

Married:

Died:

13

Born:

Died:

Humphrey NEED

Spouse

3 **Denise**

Born:

Died:

14

Born:

Married:

Died:

7

Born:

Died:

15

Born:

Died:

Sources include: Faris 2--Levis.

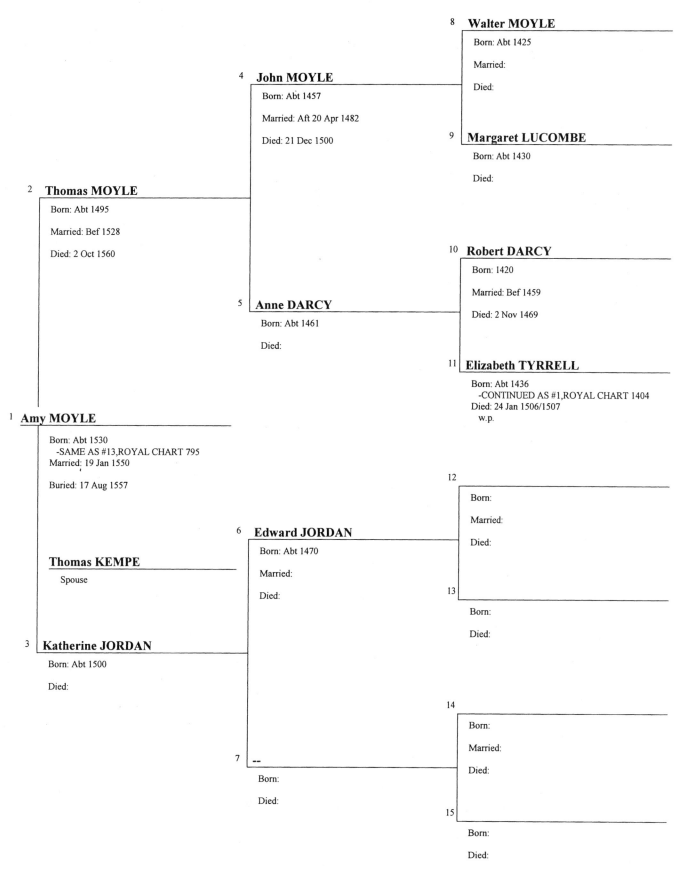

8   **Walter MOYLE**

Born: Abt 1425

Married:

Died:

4   **John MOYLE**

Born: Abt 1457

Married: Aft 20 Apr 1482

Died: 21 Dec 1500

9   **Margaret LUCOMBE**

Born: Abt 1430

Died:

2   **Thomas MOYLE**

Born: Abt 1495

Married: Bef 1528

Died: 2 Oct 1560

10   **Robert DARCY**

Born: 1420

Married: Bef 1459

Died: 2 Nov 1469

5   **Anne DARCY**

Born: Abt 1461

Died:

11   **Elizabeth TYRRELL**

Born: Abt 1436
    -CONTINUED AS #1,ROYAL CHART 1404
Died: 24 Jan 1506/1507
w.p.

1   **Amy MOYLE**

Born: Abt 1530
    -SAME AS #13,ROYAL CHART 795
Married: 19 Jan 1550

Buried: 17 Aug 1557

12

Born:

Married:

Died:

6   **Edward JORDAN**

Born: Abt 1470

Married:

Died:

13

Born:

Died:

Thomas KEMPE

Spouse

3   **Katherine JORDAN**

Born: Abt 1500

Died:

14

Born:

Married:

Died:

7   **--**

Born:

Died:

15

Born:

Died:

Sources include: Faris 2--Ollantigh 3, Moyle.

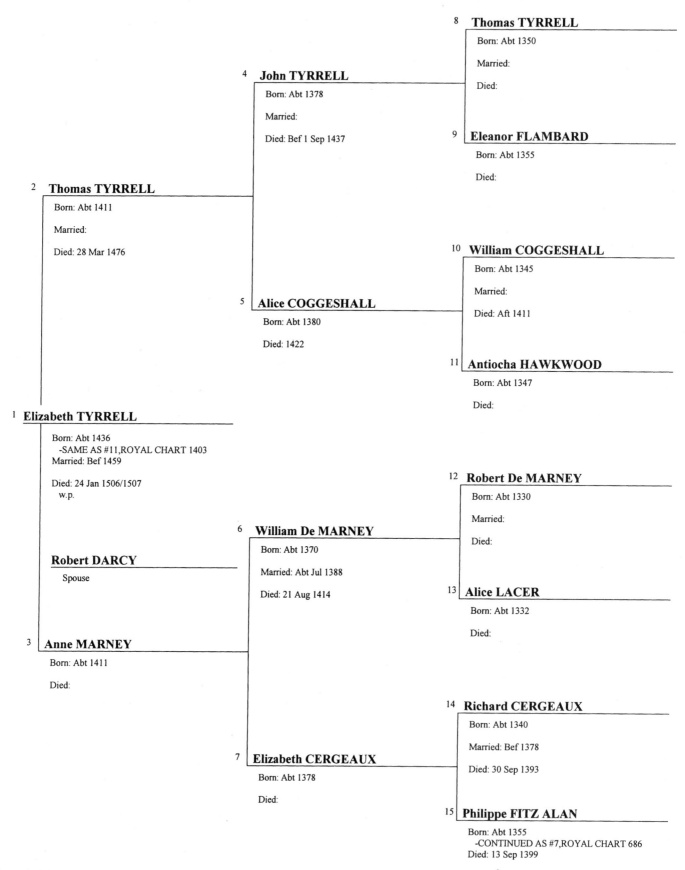

8   Thomas TYRRELL
Born: Abt 1350
Married:
Died:

4   John TYRRELL
Born: Abt 1378
Married:
Died: Bef 1 Sep 1437

9   Eleanor FLAMBARD
Born: Abt 1355
Died:

2   Thomas TYRRELL
Born: Abt 1411
Married:
Died: 28 Mar 1476

10   William COGGESHALL
Born: Abt 1345
Married:
Died: Aft 1411

5   Alice COGGESHALL
Born: Abt 1380
Died: 1422

11   Antiocha HAWKWOOD
Born: Abt 1347
Died:

1   Elizabeth TYRRELL
Born: Abt 1436
  -SAME AS #11,ROYAL CHART 1403
Married: Bef 1459

Died: 24 Jan 1506/1507
  w.p.

12   Robert De MARNEY
Born: Abt 1330
Married:
Died:

Robert DARCY
  Spouse

6   William De MARNEY
Born: Abt 1370
Married: Abt Jul 1388
Died: 21 Aug 1414

13   Alice LACER
Born: Abt 1332
Died:

3   Anne MARNEY
Born: Abt 1411
Died:

14   Richard CERGEAUX
Born: Abt 1340
Married: Bef 1378
Died: 30 Sep 1393

7   Elizabeth CERGEAUX
Born: Abt 1378
Died:

15   Philippe FITZ ALAN
Born: Abt 1355
  -CONTINUED AS #7,ROYAL CHART 686
Died: 13 Sep 1399

Sources include: Faris 2--St. Leger 6, Jennings; Faris preliminary baronial manuscript (1998), pp. 1559-61 (Tyrrell), 385 (Coggeshall).

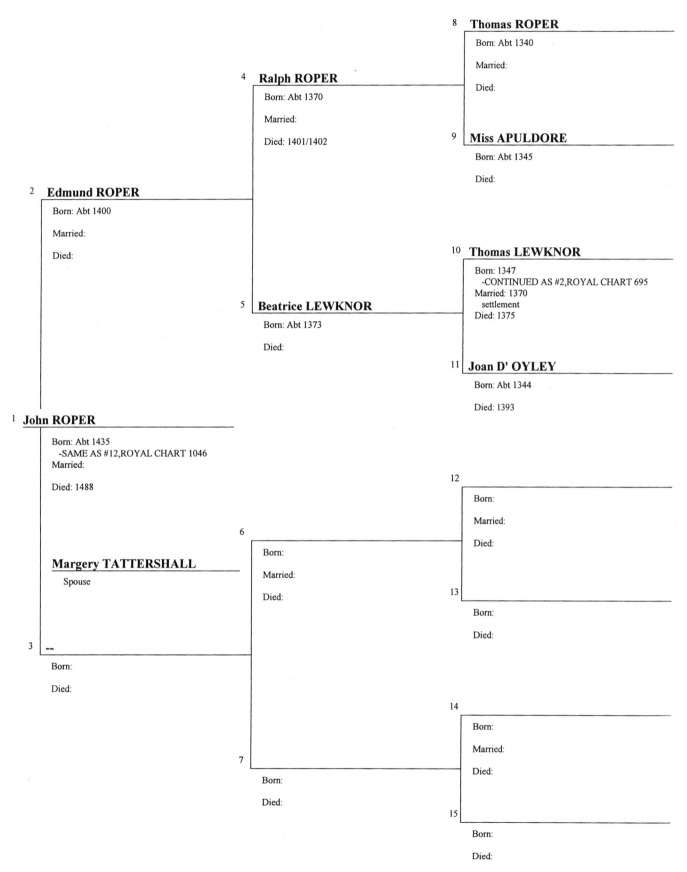

8 Thomas ROPER
Born: Abt 1340
Married:
Died:

4 Ralph ROPER
Born: Abt 1370
Married:
Died: 1401/1402

9 Miss APULDORE
Born: Abt 1345
Died:

2 Edmund ROPER
Born: Abt 1400
Married:
Died:

10 Thomas LEWKNOR
Born: 1347
    -CONTINUED AS #2,ROYAL CHART 695
Married: 1370
    settlement
Died: 1375

5 Beatrice LEWKNOR
Born: Abt 1373
Died:

11 Joan D' OYLEY
Born: Abt 1344
Died: 1393

1 John ROPER
Born: Abt 1435
    -SAME AS #12,ROYAL CHART 1046
Married:
Died: 1488

Margery TATTERSHALL
Spouse

3 --
Born:
Died:

6
Born:
Married:
Died:

12
Born:
Married:
Died:

13
Born:
Died:

7
Born:
Died:

14
Born:
Married:
Died:

15
Born:
Died:

Sources include: LDS records; Roberts *500*, pp. 431-434. Note: The parentage of #5 Beatrice is uncertain. Roberts erroneously calls her daughter of the Thomas Lewknor (grandson of #10 & 11 Thomas & Joan above) who married Philippa Dalyngridge (see them chart 1196). The version claimed in LDS records is tentatively accepted above.

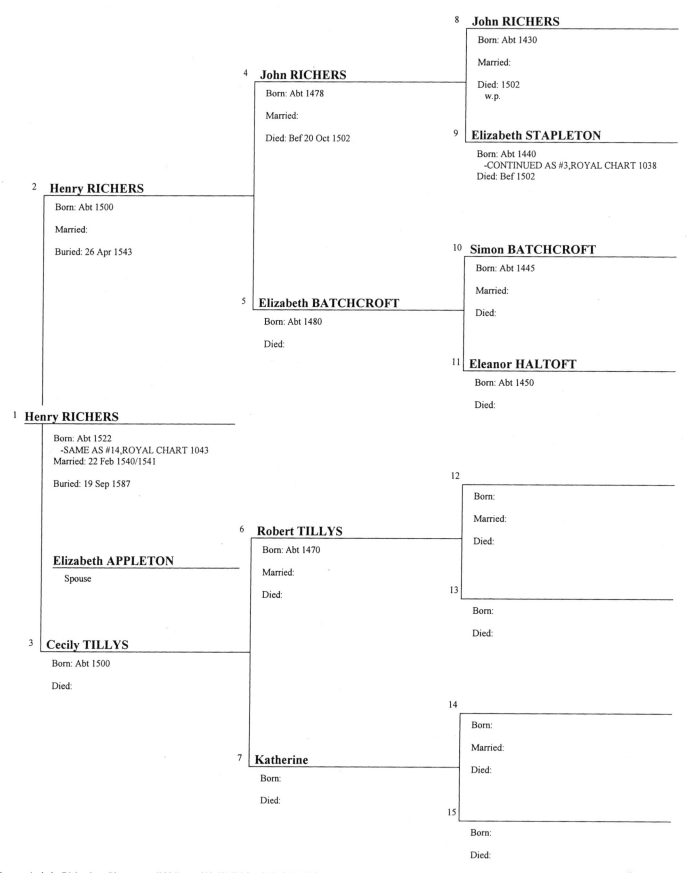

8 **John RICHERS**

Born: Abt 1430

Married:

Died: 1502
w.p.

4 **John RICHERS**

Born: Abt 1478

Married:

Died: Bef 20 Oct 1502

9 **Elizabeth STAPLETON**

Born: Abt 1440
    -CONTINUED AS #3,ROYAL CHART 1038
Died: Bef 1502

2 **Henry RICHERS**

Born: Abt 1500

Married:

Buried: 26 Apr 1543

10 **Simon BATCHCROFT**

Born: Abt 1445

Married:

Died:

5 **Elizabeth BATCHCROFT**

Born: Abt 1480

Died:

11 **Eleanor HALTOFT**

Born: Abt 1450

Died:

1 **Henry RICHERS**

Born: Abt 1522
    -SAME AS #14,ROYAL CHART 1043
Married: 22 Feb 1540/1541

Buried: 19 Sep 1587

12

Born:

Married:

Died:

6 **Robert TILLYS**

Born: Abt 1470

Married:

Died:

13

Born:

Died:

Elizabeth APPLETON

    Spouse

3 **Cecily TILLYS**

Born: Abt 1500

Died:

14

Born:

Married:

Died:

7 **Katherine**

Born:

Died:

15

Born:

Died:

Sources include: Richardson *Plantagenet* (2004), pp. 608-609 (Richers); Faris 2--Richers.

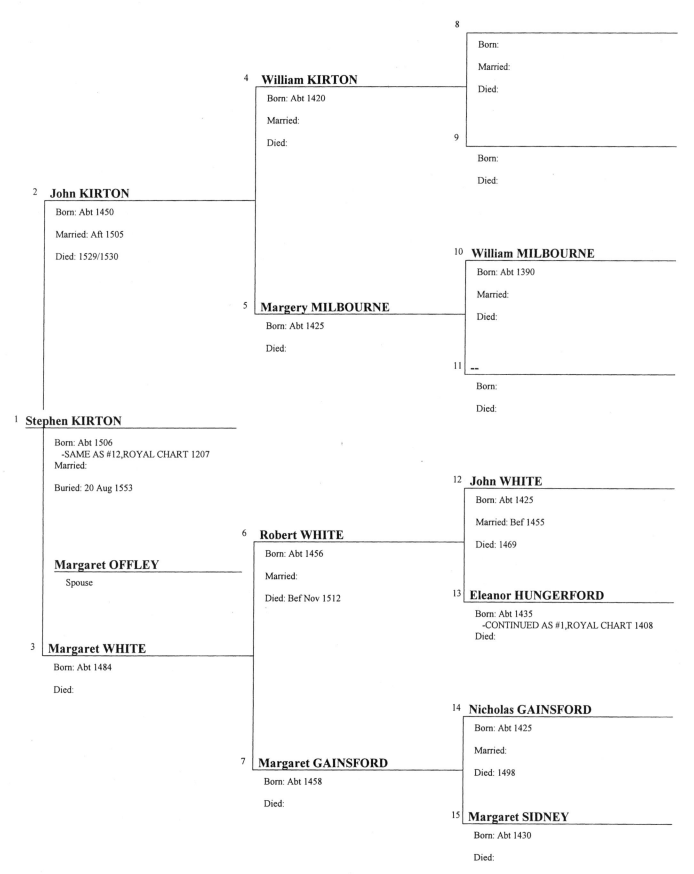

8

William KIRTON 4

Born: Abt 1420

Married:

Died:

Born:

Married:

Died:

9

Born:

Died:

John KIRTON 2

Born: Abt 1450

Married: Aft 1505

Died: 1529/1530

10 **William MILBOURNE**

Born: Abt 1390

Married:

Died:

Margery MILBOURNE 5

Born: Abt 1425

Died:

11 **--**

Born:

Died:

Stephen KIRTON 1

Born: Abt 1506
-SAME AS #12,ROYAL CHART 1207
Married:

Buried: 20 Aug 1553

12 **John WHITE**

Born: Abt 1425

Married: Bef 1455

Died: 1469

Robert WHITE 6

Born: Abt 1456

Married:

Died: Bef Nov 1512

13 **Eleanor HUNGERFORD**

Born: Abt 1435
-CONTINUED AS #1,ROYAL CHART 1408
Died:

Margaret OFFLEY

Spouse

Margaret WHITE 3

Born: Abt 1484

Died:

14 **Nicholas GAINSFORD**

Born: Abt 1425

Married:

Died: 1498

Margaret GAINSFORD 7

Born: Abt 1458

Died:

15 **Margaret SIDNEY**

Born: Abt 1430

Died:

Sources include: *NEHGR* 154:219-226 (April 2000); Faris 2--Raynsford.

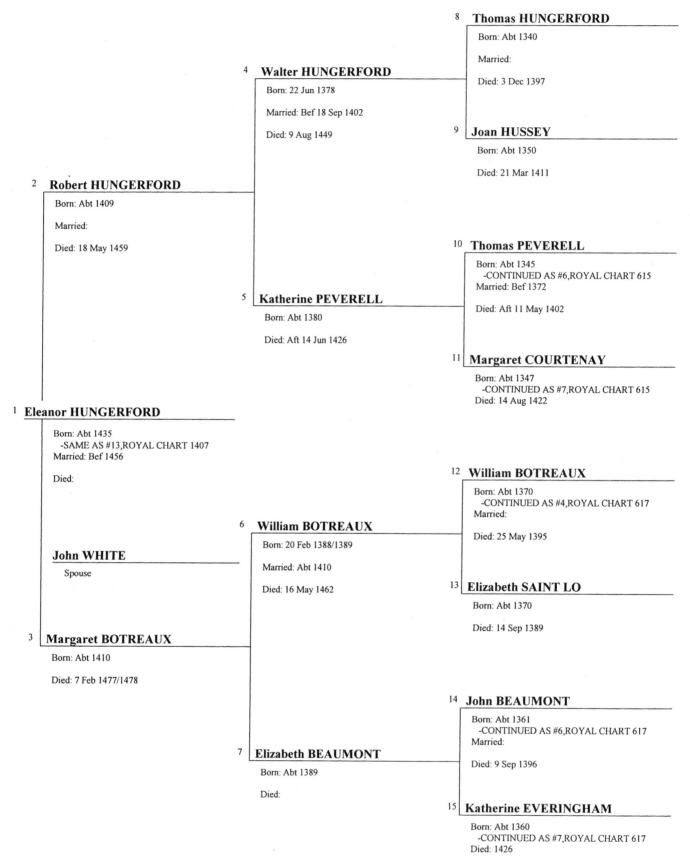

8 Thomas HUNGERFORD
Born: Abt 1340
Married:
Died: 3 Dec 1397

4 Walter HUNGERFORD
Born: 22 Jun 1378
Married: Bef 18 Sep 1402
Died: 9 Aug 1449

9 Joan HUSSEY
Born: Abt 1350
Died: 21 Mar 1411

2 Robert HUNGERFORD
Born: Abt 1409
Married:
Died: 18 May 1459

10 Thomas PEVERELL
Born: Abt 1345
 -CONTINUED AS #6,ROYAL CHART 615
Married: Bef 1372
Died: Aft 11 May 1402

5 Katherine PEVERELL
Born: Abt 1380
Died: Aft 14 Jun 1426

11 Margaret COURTENAY
Born: Abt 1347
 -CONTINUED AS #7,ROYAL CHART 615
Died: 14 Aug 1422

1 Eleanor HUNGERFORD
Born: Abt 1435
 -SAME AS #13,ROYAL CHART 1407
Married: Bef 1456
Died:

12 William BOTREAUX
Born: Abt 1370
 -CONTINUED AS #4,ROYAL CHART 617
Married:
Died: 25 May 1395

6 William BOTREAUX
Born: 20 Feb 1388/1389
Married: Abt 1410
Died: 16 May 1462

John WHITE
Spouse

13 Elizabeth SAINT LO
Born: Abt 1370
Died: 14 Sep 1389

3 Margaret BOTREAUX
Born: Abt 1410
Died: 7 Feb 1477/1478

14 John BEAUMONT
Born: Abt 1361
 -CONTINUED AS #6,ROYAL CHART 617
Married:
Died: 9 Sep 1396

7 Elizabeth BEAUMONT
Born: Abt 1389
Died:

15 Katherine EVERINGHAM
Born: Abt 1360
 -CONTINUED AS #7,ROYAL CHART 617
Died: 1426

Sources include: *NEHGR* 154:219-226 (April 2000); Faris 2--Raynsford.

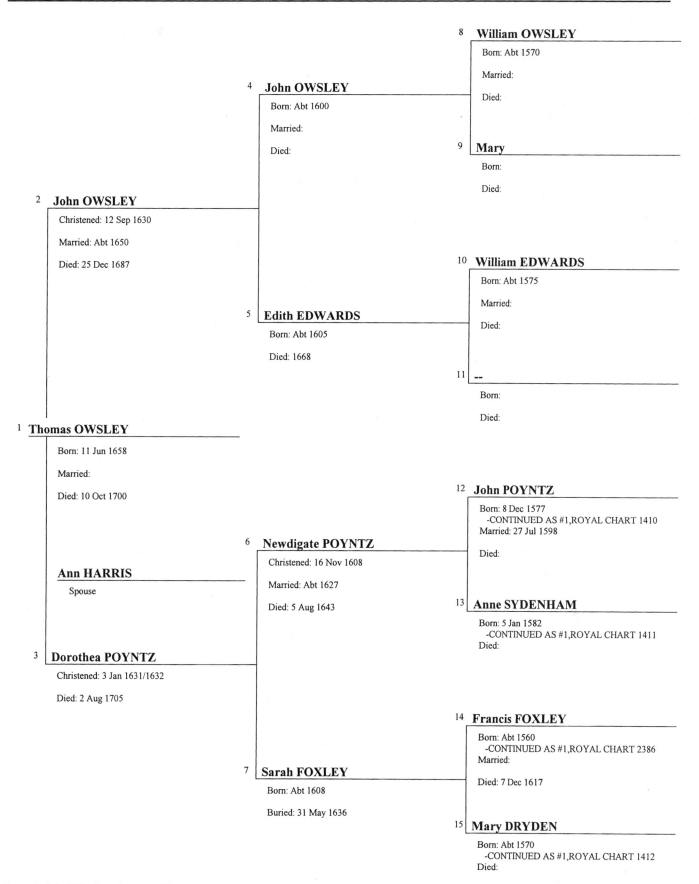

8   William OWSLEY

Born: Abt 1570

Married:

Died:

4   John OWSLEY

Born: Abt 1600

Married:

Died:

9   Mary

Born:

Died:

2   John OWSLEY

Christened: 12 Sep 1630

Married: Abt 1650

Died: 25 Dec 1687

10   William EDWARDS

Born: Abt 1575

Married:

Died:

5   Edith EDWARDS

Born: Abt 1605

Died: 1668

11   --

Born:

Died:

1   Thomas OWSLEY

Born: 11 Jun 1658

Married:

Died: 10 Oct 1700

Ann HARRIS

Spouse

12   John POYNTZ

Born: 8 Dec 1577
  -CONTINUED AS #1,ROYAL CHART 1410
Married: 27 Jul 1598

Died:

6   Newdigate POYNTZ

Christened: 16 Nov 1608

Married: Abt 1627

Died: 5 Aug 1643

13   Anne SYDENHAM

Born: 5 Jan 1582
  -CONTINUED AS #1,ROYAL CHART 1411
Died:

3   Dorothea POYNTZ

Christened: 3 Jan 1631/1632

Died: 2 Aug 1705

14   Francis FOXLEY

Born: Abt 1560
  -CONTINUED AS #1,ROYAL CHART 2386
Married:

Died: 7 Dec 1617

7   Sarah FOXLEY

Born: Abt 1608

Buried: 31 May 1636

15   Mary DRYDEN

Born: Abt 1570
  -CONTINUED AS #1,ROYAL CHART 1412
Died:

Sources include: Richardson *Plantagenet* (2004), pp. 560-561 (Owsley), 338 (Foxley); Faris 2--Owsley; Roberts *500*, p. 286; LDS records (#8 & 9).

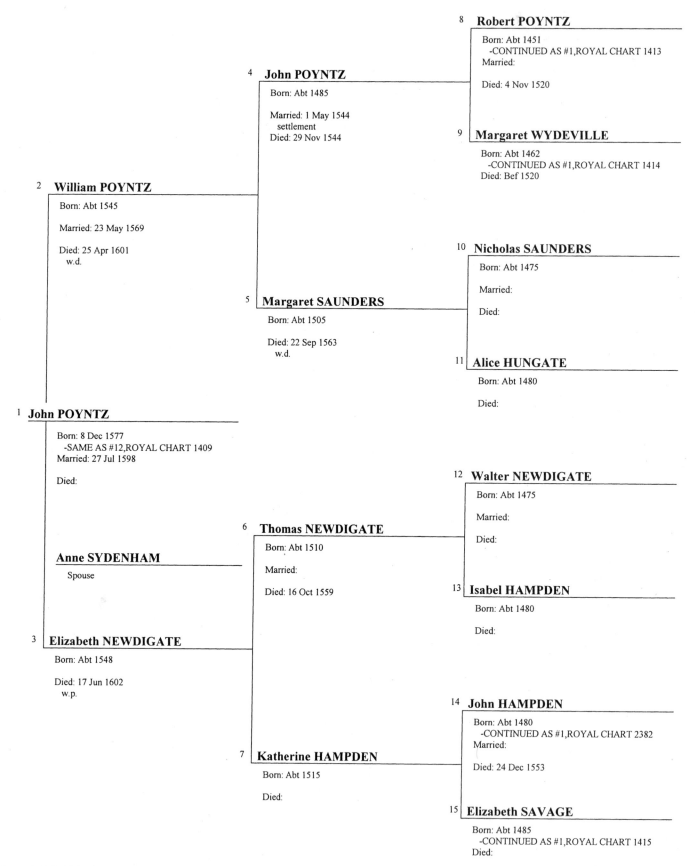

8 Robert POYNTZ

Born: Abt 1451
-CONTINUED AS #1,ROYAL CHART 1413
Married:

Died: 4 Nov 1520

4 John POYNTZ

Born: Abt 1485

Married: 1 May 1544
settlement
Died: 29 Nov 1544

9 Margaret WYDEVILLE

Born: Abt 1462
-CONTINUED AS #1,ROYAL CHART 1414
Died: Bef 1520

2 William POYNTZ

Born: Abt 1545

Married: 23 May 1569

Died: 25 Apr 1601
w.d.

10 Nicholas SAUNDERS

Born: Abt 1475

Married:

Died:

5 Margaret SAUNDERS

Born: Abt 1505

Died: 22 Sep 1563
w.d.

11 Alice HUNGATE

Born: Abt 1480

Died:

1 John POYNTZ

Born: 8 Dec 1577
-SAME AS #12,ROYAL CHART 1409
Married: 27 Jul 1598

Died:

12 Walter NEWDIGATE

Born: Abt 1475

Married:

Died:

6 Thomas NEWDIGATE

Born: Abt 1510

Married:

Died: 16 Oct 1559

13 Isabel HAMPDEN

Born: Abt 1480

Died:

Anne SYDENHAM

Spouse

3 Elizabeth NEWDIGATE

Born: Abt 1548

Died: 17 Jun 1602
w.p.

14 John HAMPDEN

Born: Abt 1480
-CONTINUED AS #1,ROYAL CHART 2382
Married:

Died: 24 Dec 1553

7 Katherine HAMPDEN

Born: Abt 1515

Died:

15 Elizabeth SAVAGE

Born: Abt 1485
-CONTINUED AS #1,ROYAL CHART 1415
Died:

Sources include: Richardson *Plantagenet* (2004), pp. 559-560 (Owsley), 784-785 (Wydeville); Faris 2--Owsley.

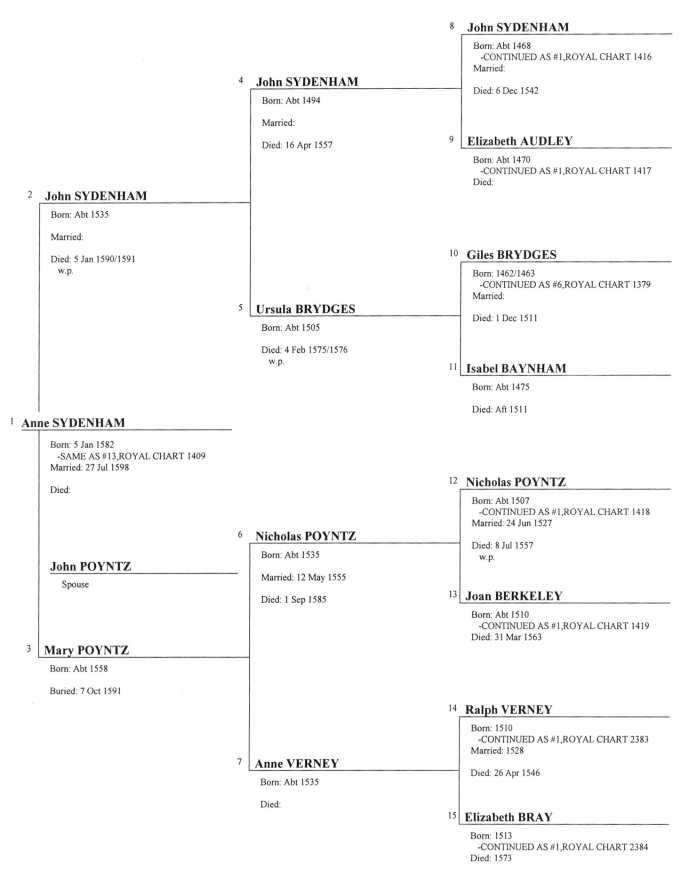

8 **John SYDENHAM**

Born: Abt 1468
-CONTINUED AS #1,ROYAL CHART 1416
Married:

Died: 6 Dec 1542

4 **John SYDENHAM**

Born: Abt 1494

Married:

Died: 16 Apr 1557

9 **Elizabeth AUDLEY**

Born: Abt 1470
-CONTINUED AS #1,ROYAL CHART 1417
Died:

2 **John SYDENHAM**

Born: Abt 1535

Married:

Died: 5 Jan 1590/1591
w.p.

10 **Giles BRYDGES**

Born: 1462/1463
-CONTINUED AS #6,ROYAL CHART 1379
Married:

Died: 1 Dec 1511

5 **Ursula BRYDGES**

Born: Abt 1505

Died: 4 Feb 1575/1576
w.p.

11 **Isabel BAYNHAM**

Born: Abt 1475

Died: Aft 1511

1 **Anne SYDENHAM**

Born: 5 Jan 1582
-SAME AS #13,ROYAL CHART 1409
Married: 27 Jul 1598

Died:

12 **Nicholas POYNTZ**

Born: Abt 1507
-CONTINUED AS #1,ROYAL CHART 1418
Married: 24 Jun 1527

Died: 8 Jul 1557
w.p.

6 **Nicholas POYNTZ**

Born: Abt 1535

Married: 12 May 1555

Died: 1 Sep 1585

13 **Joan BERKELEY**

Born: Abt 1510
-CONTINUED AS #1,ROYAL CHART 1419
Died: 31 Mar 1563

John POYNTZ

Spouse

3 **Mary POYNTZ**

Born: Abt 1558

Buried: 7 Oct 1591

14 **Ralph VERNEY**

Born: 1510
-CONTINUED AS #1,ROYAL CHART 2383
Married: 1528

Died: 26 Apr 1546

7 **Anne VERNEY**

Born: Abt 1535

Died:

15 **Elizabeth BRAY**

Born: 1513
-CONTINUED AS #1,ROYAL CHART 2384
Died: 1573

Sources include: Richardson *Plantagenet* (2004), pp. 560 (Owsley), 699-700 (Sydenham), 595-596 (Poyntz); Faris 2--Owsley, Poyntz; NEHGS *Nexus* 13:128 (#2 ancestry).

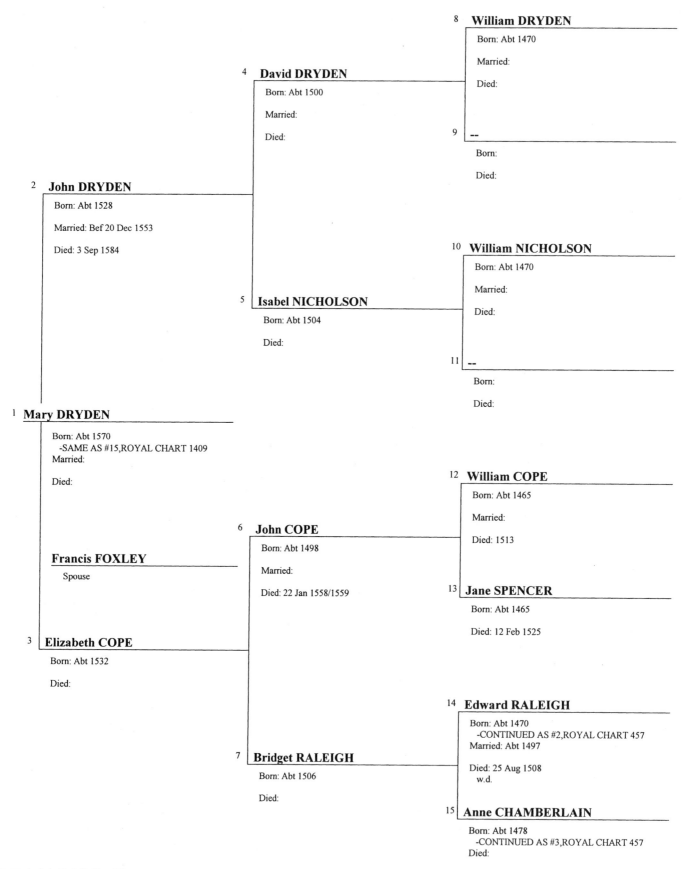

8 **William DRYDEN**

Born: Abt 1470

Married:

Died:

4 **David DRYDEN**

Born: Abt 1500

Married:

Died:

9 **--**

Born:

Died:

2 **John DRYDEN**

Born: Abt 1528

Married: Bef 20 Dec 1553

Died: 3 Sep 1584

10 **William NICHOLSON**

Born: Abt 1470

Married:

Died:

5 **Isabel NICHOLSON**

Born: Abt 1504

Died:

11 **--**

Born:

Died:

1 **Mary DRYDEN**

Born: Abt 1570
-SAME AS #15,ROYAL CHART 1409
Married:

Died:

12 **William COPE**

Born: Abt 1465

Married:

Died: 1513

6 **John COPE**

Born: Abt 1498

Married:

Died: 22 Jan 1558/1559

13 **Jane SPENCER**

Born: Abt 1465

Died: 12 Feb 1525

Francis FOXLEY

Spouse

3 **Elizabeth COPE**

Born: Abt 1532

Died:

14 **Edward RALEIGH**

Born: Abt 1470
-CONTINUED AS #2,ROYAL CHART 457
Married: Abt 1497

Died: 25 Aug 1508
w.d.

7 **Bridget RALEIGH**

Born: Abt 1506

Died:

15 **Anne CHAMBERLAIN**

Born: Abt 1478
-CONTINUED AS #3,ROYAL CHART 457
Died:

Sources include: Faris 2--Cheseldine.

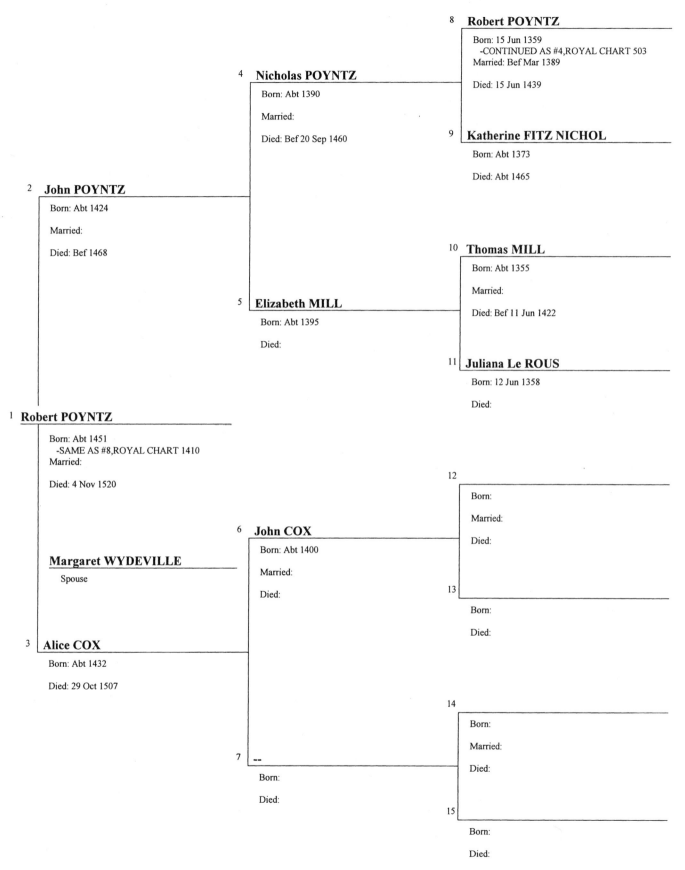

8 Robert POYNTZ

Born: 15 Jun 1359
-CONTINUED AS #4,ROYAL CHART 503
Married: Bef Mar 1389

Died: 15 Jun 1439

4 Nicholas POYNTZ

Born: Abt 1390

Married:

Died: Bef 20 Sep 1460

9 Katherine FITZ NICHOL

Born: Abt 1373

Died: Abt 1465

2 John POYNTZ

Born: Abt 1424

Married:

Died: Bef 1468

10 Thomas MILL

Born: Abt 1355

Married:

Died: Bef 11 Jun 1422

5 Elizabeth MILL

Born: Abt 1395

Died:

11 Juliana Le ROUS

Born: 12 Jun 1358

Died:

1 Robert POYNTZ

Born: Abt 1451
-SAME AS #8,ROYAL CHART 1410
Married:

Died: 4 Nov 1520

Margaret WYDEVILLE

Spouse

12

Born:

Married:

Died:

6 John COX

Born: Abt 1400

Married:

Died:

13

Born:

Died:

3 Alice COX

Born: Abt 1432

Died: 29 Oct 1507

14

Born:

Married:

Died:

7 --

Born:

Died:

15

Born:

Died:

Sources include: LDS records; *Ancestral Roots* 234A (#4 & 5 ancestry).

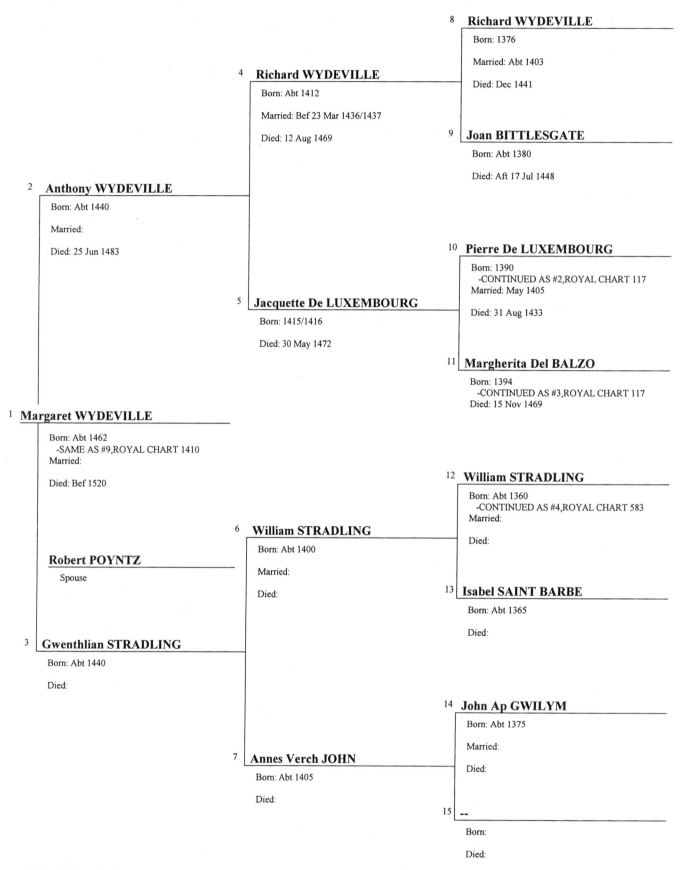

8 Richard WYDEVILLE
Born: 1376
Married: Abt 1403
Died: Dec 1441

4 Richard WYDEVILLE
Born: Abt 1412
Married: Bef 23 Mar 1436/1437
Died: 12 Aug 1469

9 Joan BITTLESGATE
Born: Abt 1380
Died: Aft 17 Jul 1448

2 Anthony WYDEVILLE
Born: Abt 1440
Married:
Died: 25 Jun 1483

10 Pierre De LUXEMBOURG
Born: 1390
  -CONTINUED AS #2,ROYAL CHART 117
Married: May 1405
Died: 31 Aug 1433

5 Jacquette De LUXEMBOURG
Born: 1415/1416
Died: 30 May 1472

11 Margherita Del BALZO
Born: 1394
  -CONTINUED AS #3,ROYAL CHART 117
Died: 15 Nov 1469

1 Margaret WYDEVILLE
Born: Abt 1462
  -SAME AS #9,ROYAL CHART 1410
Married:
Died: Bef 1520

12 William STRADLING
Born: Abt 1360
  -CONTINUED AS #4,ROYAL CHART 583
Married:
Died:

6 William STRADLING
Born: Abt 1400
Married:
Died:

13 Isabel SAINT BARBE
Born: Abt 1365
Died:

Robert POYNTZ
Spouse

3 Gwenthlian STRADLING
Born: Abt 1440
Died:

14 John Ap GWILYM
Born: Abt 1375
Married:
Died:

7 Annes Verch JOHN
Born: Abt 1405
Died:

15 --
Born:
Died:

Sources include: LDS records.

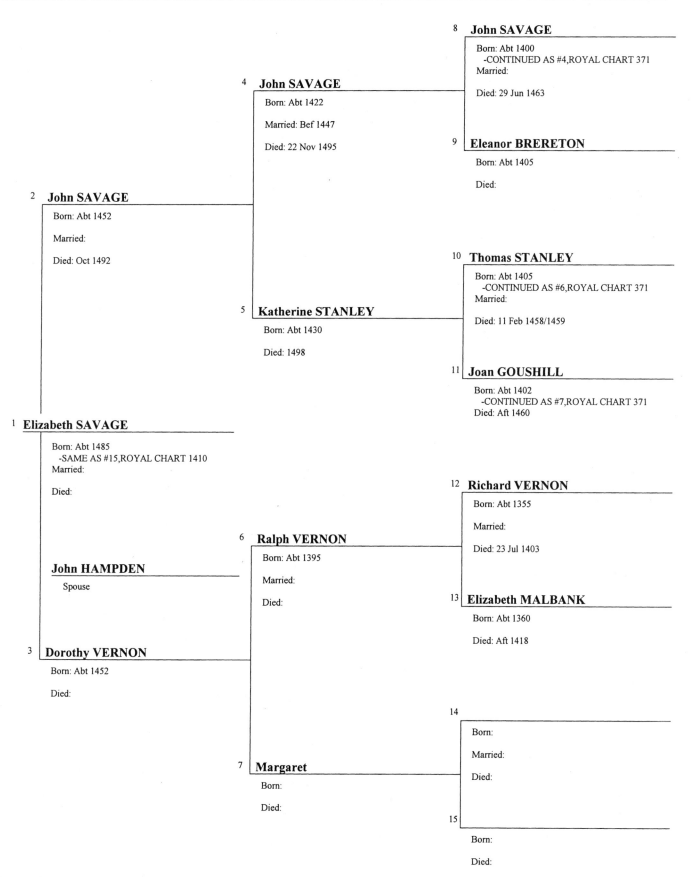

8 **John SAVAGE**

Born: Abt 1400
-CONTINUED AS #4,ROYAL CHART 371
Married:

Died: 29 Jun 1463

4 **John SAVAGE**

Born: Abt 1422

Married: Bef 1447

Died: 22 Nov 1495

9 **Eleanor BRERETON**

Born: Abt 1405

Died:

2 **John SAVAGE**

Born: Abt 1452

Married:

Died: Oct 1492

10 **Thomas STANLEY**

Born: Abt 1405
-CONTINUED AS #6,ROYAL CHART 371
Married:

Died: 11 Feb 1458/1459

5 **Katherine STANLEY**

Born: Abt 1430

Died: 1498

11 **Joan GOUSHILL**

Born: Abt 1402
-CONTINUED AS #7,ROYAL CHART 371
Died: Aft 1460

1 **Elizabeth SAVAGE**

Born: Abt 1485
-SAME AS #15,ROYAL CHART 1410
Married:

Died:

12 **Richard VERNON**

Born: Abt 1355

Married:

Died: 23 Jul 1403

6 **Ralph VERNON**

Born: Abt 1395

Married:

Died:

John HAMPDEN

Spouse

13 **Elizabeth MALBANK**

Born: Abt 1360

Died: Aft 1418

3 **Dorothy VERNON**

Born: Abt 1452

Died:

14

Born:

Married:

Died:

7 **Margaret**

Born:

Died:

15

Born:

Died:

Sources include: Faris 2--Owsley, Savage; Faris preliminary baronial manuscript (1998), pp. 1600-01 (Vernon). Note: The ancestry shown for #3 Dorothy appears to be uncertain because of chronological problems.

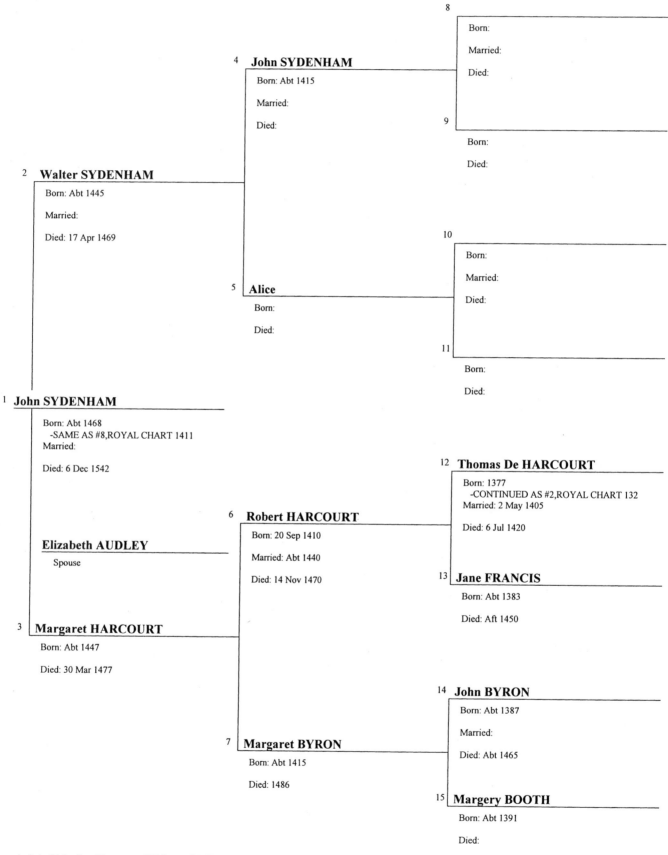

8

Born:

Married:

Died:

4 John SYDENHAM

Born: Abt 1415

Married:

Died:

9

Born:

Died:

2 Walter SYDENHAM

Born: Abt 1445

Married:

Died: 17 Apr 1469

10

Born:

Married:

Died:

5 Alice

Born:

Died:

11

Born:

Died:

1 John SYDENHAM

Born: Abt 1468
    -SAME AS #8,ROYAL CHART 1411
Married:

Died: 6 Dec 1542

Elizabeth AUDLEY

Spouse

12 Thomas De HARCOURT

Born: 1377
    -CONTINUED AS #2,ROYAL CHART 132
Married: 2 May 1405

Died: 6 Jul 1420

6 Robert HARCOURT

Born: 20 Sep 1410

Married: Abt 1440

Died: 14 Nov 1470

13 Jane FRANCIS

Born: Abt 1383

Died: Aft 1450

3 Margaret HARCOURT

Born: Abt 1447

Died: 30 Mar 1477

14 John BYRON

Born: Abt 1387

Married:

Died: Abt 1465

7 Margaret BYRON

Born: Abt 1415

Died: 1486

15 Margery BOOTH

Born: Abt 1391

Died:

Sources include: Richardson *Plantagenet* (2004), pp. 698-699 (Sydenham), 376-377 (Harcourt).

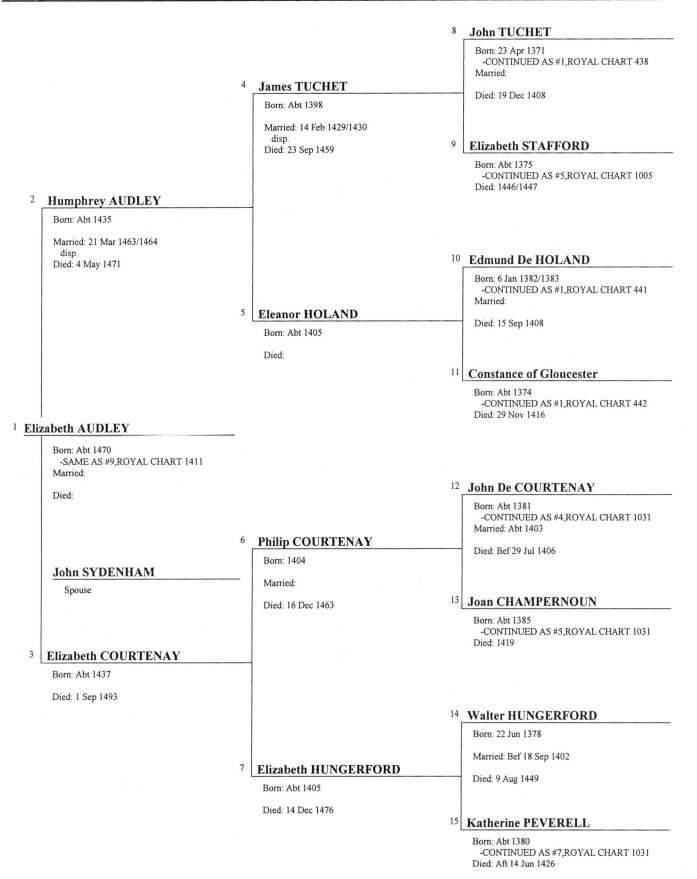

8 John TUCHET

Born: 23 Apr 1371
-CONTINUED AS #1,ROYAL CHART 438
Married:

Died: 19 Dec 1408

4 James TUCHET

Born: Abt 1398

Married: 14 Feb 1429/1430
disp.
Died: 23 Sep 1459

9 Elizabeth STAFFORD

Born: Abt 1375
-CONTINUED AS #5,ROYAL CHART 1005
Died: 1446/1447

2 Humphrey AUDLEY

Born: Abt 1435

Married: 21 Mar 1463/1464
disp.
Died: 4 May 1471

10 Edmund De HOLAND

Born: 6 Jan 1382/1383
-CONTINUED AS #1,ROYAL CHART 441
Married:

Died: 15 Sep 1408

5 Eleanor HOLAND

Born: Abt 1405

Died:

11 Constance of Gloucester

Born: Abt 1374
-CONTINUED AS #1,ROYAL CHART 442
Died: 29 Nov 1416

1 Elizabeth AUDLEY

Born: Abt 1470
-SAME AS #9,ROYAL CHART 1411
Married:

Died:

12 John De COURTENAY

Born: Abt 1381
-CONTINUED AS #4,ROYAL CHART 1031
Married: Abt 1403

Died: Bef 29 Jul 1406

6 Philip COURTENAY

Born: 1404

Married:

Died: 16 Dec 1463

13 Joan CHAMPERNOUN

Born: Abt 1385
-CONTINUED AS #5,ROYAL CHART 1031
Died: 1419

John SYDENHAM

Spouse

3 Elizabeth COURTENAY

Born: Abt 1437

Died: 1 Sep 1493

14 Walter HUNGERFORD

Born: 22 Jun 1378

Married: Bef 18 Sep 1402

Died: 9 Aug 1449

7 Elizabeth HUNGERFORD

Born: Abt 1405

Died: 14 Dec 1476

15 Katherine PEVERELL

Born: Abt 1380
-CONTINUED AS #7,ROYAL CHART 1031
Died: Aft 14 Jun 1426

Sources include: Richardson *Plantagenet* (2004), pp. 699 (Sydenham), 722-723 (Tuchet), 257-258 (Davie); NEHGS *Nexus* 13:128; Faris 2--Holand 6, Tuchet 9 (#4 & 5 ancestry).

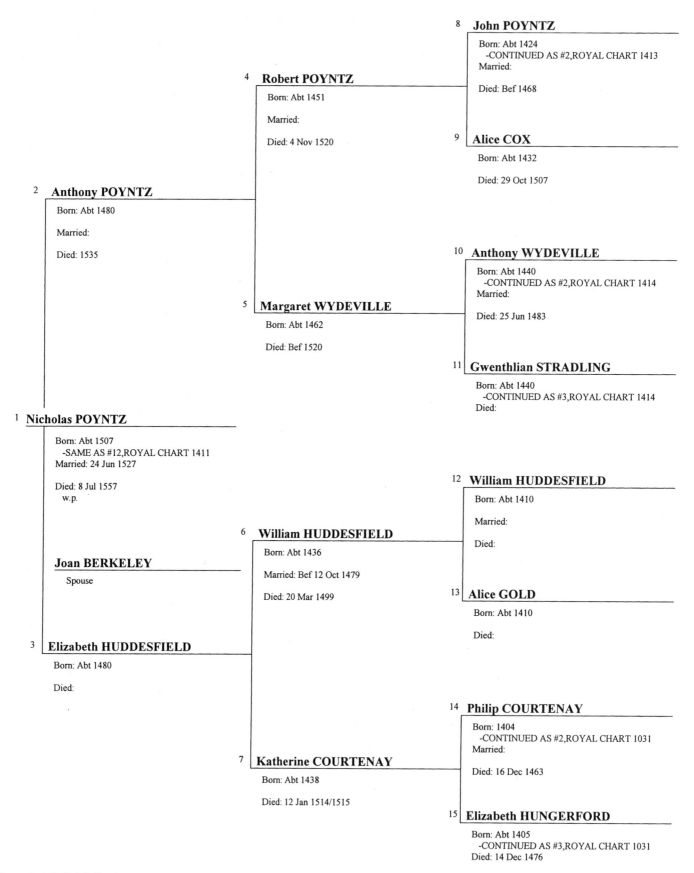

8 | **John POYNTZ**
Born: Abt 1424
 -CONTINUED AS #2,ROYAL CHART 1413
Married:

Died: Bef 1468

4 | **Robert POYNTZ**
Born: Abt 1451

Married:

Died: 4 Nov 1520

9 | **Alice COX**
Born: Abt 1432

Died: 29 Oct 1507

2 | **Anthony POYNTZ**
Born: Abt 1480

Married:

Died: 1535

10 | **Anthony WYDEVILLE**
Born: Abt 1440
 -CONTINUED AS #2,ROYAL CHART 1414
Married:

Died: 25 Jun 1483

5 | **Margaret WYDEVILLE**
Born: Abt 1462

Died: Bef 1520

11 | **Gwenthlian STRADLING**
Born: Abt 1440
 -CONTINUED AS #3,ROYAL CHART 1414
Died:

1 | **Nicholas POYNTZ**
Born: Abt 1507
 -SAME AS #12,ROYAL CHART 1411
Married: 24 Jun 1527

Died: 8 Jul 1557
 w.p.

12 | **William HUDDESFIELD**
Born: Abt 1410

Married:

Died:

6 | **William HUDDESFIELD**
Born: Abt 1436

Married: Bef 12 Oct 1479

Died: 20 Mar 1499

13 | **Alice GOLD**
Born: Abt 1410

Died:

Joan BERKELEY
Spouse

3 | **Elizabeth HUDDESFIELD**
Born: Abt 1480

Died:

14 | **Philip COURTENAY**
Born: 1404
 -CONTINUED AS #2,ROYAL CHART 1031
Married:

Died: 16 Dec 1463

7 | **Katherine COURTENAY**
Born: Abt 1438

Died: 12 Jan 1514/1515

15 | **Elizabeth HUNGERFORD**
Born: Abt 1405
 -CONTINUED AS #3,ROYAL CHART 1031
Died: 14 Dec 1476

Sources include: Faris 2--Poyntz.

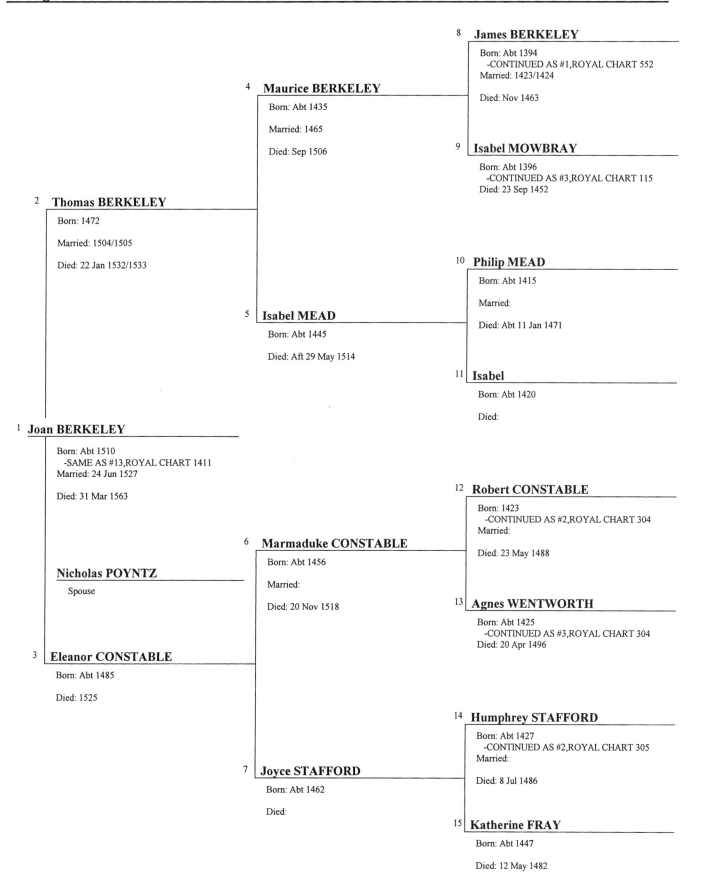

8 James BERKELEY

Born: Abt 1394
-CONTINUED AS #1,ROYAL CHART 552
Married: 1423/1424

Died: Nov 1463

4 Maurice BERKELEY

Born: Abt 1435

Married: 1465

Died: Sep 1506

9 Isabel MOWBRAY

Born: Abt 1396
-CONTINUED AS #3,ROYAL CHART 115
Died: 23 Sep 1452

2 Thomas BERKELEY

Born: 1472

Married: 1504/1505

Died: 22 Jan 1532/1533

10 Philip MEAD

Born: Abt 1415

Married:

Died: Abt 11 Jan 1471

5 Isabel MEAD

Born: Abt 1445

Died: Aft 29 May 1514

11 Isabel

Born: Abt 1420

Died:

1 Joan BERKELEY

Born: Abt 1510
-SAME AS #13,ROYAL CHART 1411
Married: 24 Jun 1527

Died: 31 Mar 1563

12 Robert CONSTABLE

Born: 1423
-CONTINUED AS #2,ROYAL CHART 304
Married:

Died: 23 May 1488

6 Marmaduke CONSTABLE

Born: Abt 1456

Married:

Died: 20 Nov 1518

13 Agnes WENTWORTH

Born: Abt 1425
-CONTINUED AS #3,ROYAL CHART 304
Died: 20 Apr 1496

Nicholas POYNTZ

Spouse

3 Eleanor CONSTABLE

Born: Abt 1485

Died: 1525

14 Humphrey STAFFORD

Born: Abt 1427
-CONTINUED AS #2,ROYAL CHART 305
Married:

Died: 8 Jul 1486

7 Joyce STAFFORD

Born: Abt 1462

Died:

15 Katherine FRAY

Born: Abt 1447

Died: 12 May 1482

Sources include: Faris 2--Berkeley.

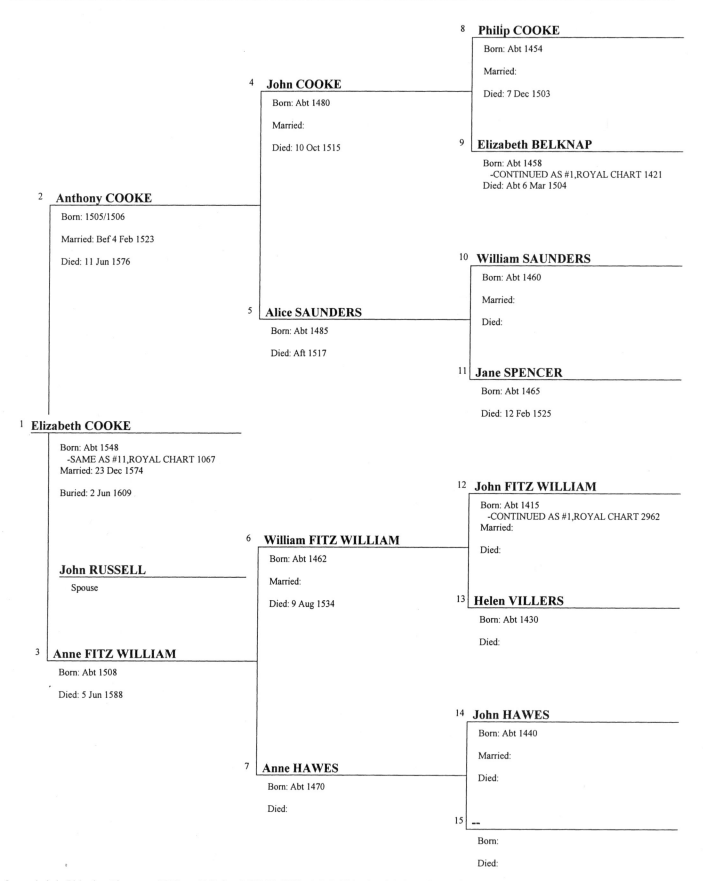

8 Philip COOKE

Born: Abt 1454

Married:

Died: 7 Dec 1503

4 John COOKE

Born: Abt 1480

Married:

Died: 10 Oct 1515

9 Elizabeth BELKNAP

Born: Abt 1458
-CONTINUED AS #1,ROYAL CHART 1421
Died: Abt 6 Mar 1504

2 Anthony COOKE

Born: 1505/1506

Married: Bef 4 Feb 1523

Died: 11 Jun 1576

10 William SAUNDERS

Born: Abt 1460

Married:

Died:

5 Alice SAUNDERS

Born: Abt 1485

Died: Aft 1517

11 Jane SPENCER

Born: Abt 1465

Died: 12 Feb 1525

1 Elizabeth COOKE

Born: Abt 1548
-SAME AS #11,ROYAL CHART 1067
Married: 23 Dec 1574

Buried: 2 Jun 1609

12 John FITZ WILLIAM

Born: Abt 1415
-CONTINUED AS #1,ROYAL CHART 2962
Married:

Died:

6 William FITZ WILLIAM

Born: Abt 1462

Married:

Died: 9 Aug 1534

13 Helen VILLERS

Born: Abt 1430

Died:

John RUSSELL

Spouse

3 Anne FITZ WILLIAM

Born: Abt 1508

Died: 5 Jun 1588

14 John HAWES

Born: Abt 1440

Married:

Died:

7 Anne HAWES

Born: Abt 1470

Died:

15 --

Born:

Died:

Sources include: Richardson *Plantagenet* (2004), pp. 91 (Belknap), 333 (Fitz William); Faris-Richardson 3 (July 2002 preliminary)--Belknap; Faris preliminary baronial manuscript (1998), p. 654 (Fitz William); Faris 2--Somerset 3 (#1 & 2); LDS records.

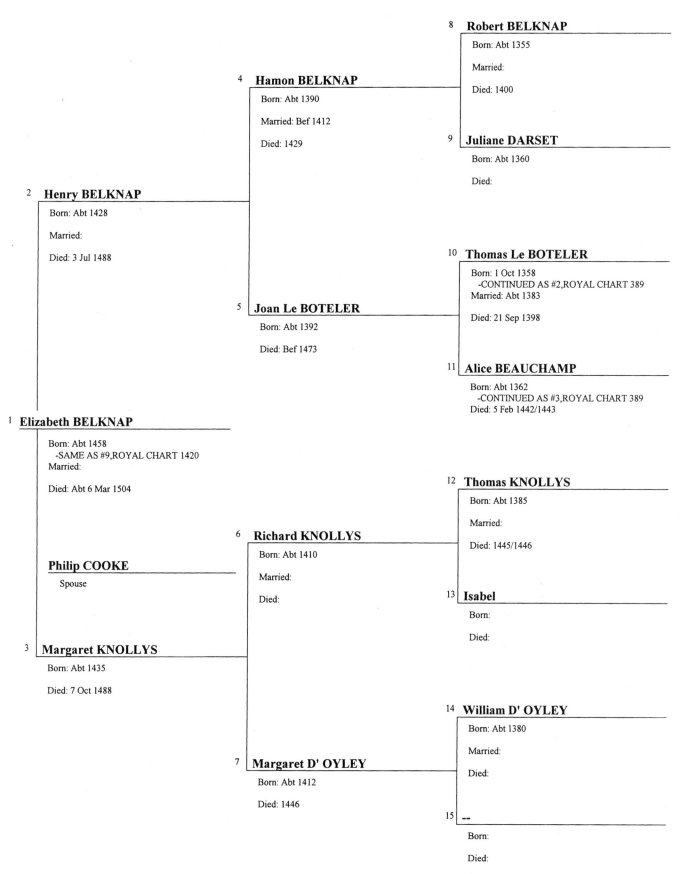

8 Robert BELKNAP

Born: Abt 1355

Married:

Died: 1400

4 Hamon BELKNAP

Born: Abt 1390

Married: Bef 1412

Died: 1429

9 Juliane DARSET

Born: Abt 1360

Died:

2 Henry BELKNAP

Born: Abt 1428

Married:

Died: 3 Jul 1488

10 Thomas Le BOTELER

Born: 1 Oct 1358
    -CONTINUED AS #2,ROYAL CHART 389
Married: Abt 1383

Died: 21 Sep 1398

5 Joan Le BOTELER

Born: Abt 1392

Died: Bef 1473

11 Alice BEAUCHAMP

Born: Abt 1362
    -CONTINUED AS #3,ROYAL CHART 389
Died: 5 Feb 1442/1443

1 Elizabeth BELKNAP

Born: Abt 1458
    -SAME AS #9,ROYAL CHART 1420
Married:

Died: Abt 6 Mar 1504

12 Thomas KNOLLYS

Born: Abt 1385

Married:

Died: 1445/1446

6 Richard KNOLLYS

Born: Abt 1410

Married:

Died:

13 Isabel

Born:

Died:

Philip COOKE

Spouse

3 Margaret KNOLLYS

Born: Abt 1435

Died: 7 Oct 1488

14 William D' OYLEY

Born: Abt 1380

Married:

Died:

7 Margaret D' OYLEY

Born: Abt 1412

Died: 1446

15 --

Born:

Died:

Sources include: Faris-Richardson 3 (July 2002 preliminary)--Belknap; LDS records; Consultation with Douglas Richardson; Paget 398-399 (#2 & 3 ancestry).

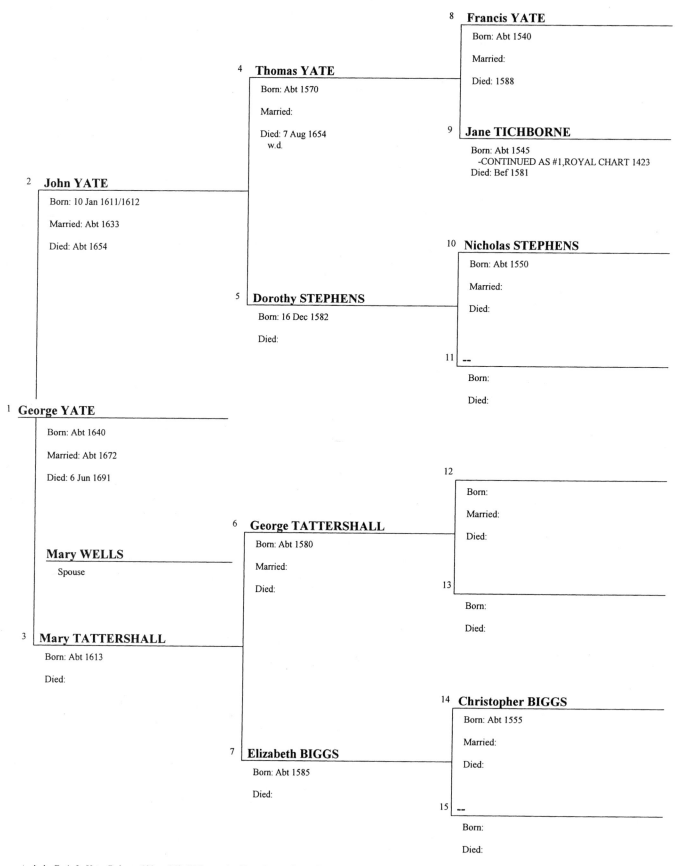

8   **Francis YATE**

Born: Abt 1540

Married:

Died: 1588

4   **Thomas YATE**

Born: Abt 1570

Married:

Died: 7 Aug 1654
     w.d.

9   **Jane TICHBORNE**

Born: Abt 1545
     -CONTINUED AS #1,ROYAL CHART 1423
Died: Bef 1581

2   **John YATE**

Born: 10 Jan 1611/1612

Married: Abt 1633

Died: Abt 1654

10   **Nicholas STEPHENS**

Born: Abt 1550

Married:

Died:

5   **Dorothy STEPHENS**

Born: 16 Dec 1582

Died:

11   **--**

Born:

Died:

1   **George YATE**

Born: Abt 1640

Married: Abt 1672

Died: 6 Jun 1691

Mary WELLS

Spouse

12

Born:

Married:

Died:

6   **George TATTERSHALL**

Born: Abt 1580

Married:

Died:

13

Born:

Died:

3   **Mary TATTERSHALL**

Born: Abt 1613

Died:

14   **Christopher BIGGS**

Born: Abt 1555

Married:

Died:

7   **Elizabeth BIGGS**

Born: Abt 1585

Died:

15   **--**

Born:

Died:

Sources include: Faris 2--Yate; Roberts *500*, p. 342; LDS records. Note: Descendants of #1 George used the name Yates.

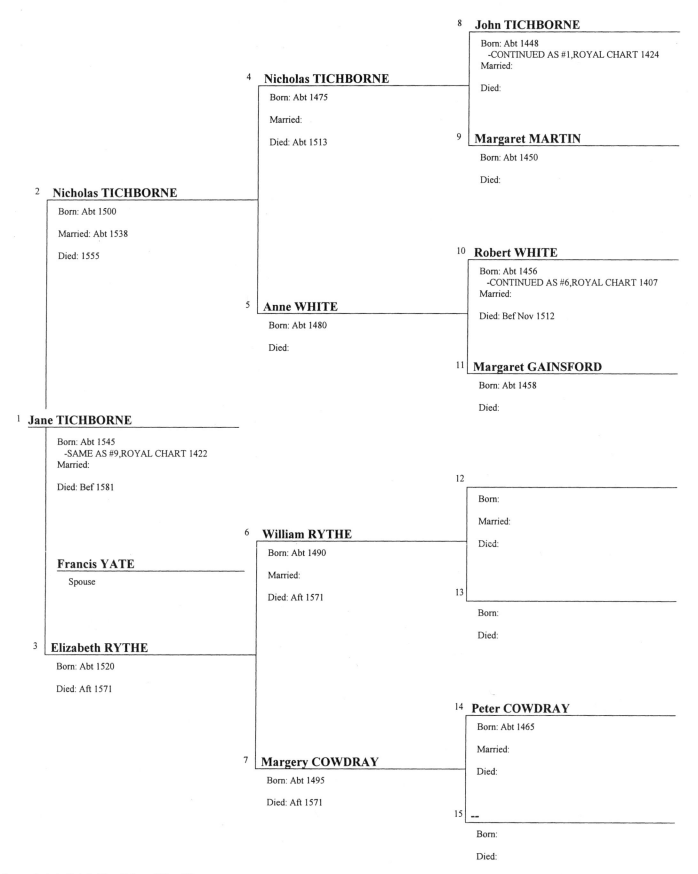

8 John TICHBORNE
Born: Abt 1448
-CONTINUED AS #1,ROYAL CHART 1424
Married:

Died:

4 Nicholas TICHBORNE
Born: Abt 1475

Married:

Died: Abt 1513

9 Margaret MARTIN
Born: Abt 1450

Died:

2 Nicholas TICHBORNE
Born: Abt 1500

Married: Abt 1538

Died: 1555

10 Robert WHITE
Born: Abt 1456
-CONTINUED AS #6,ROYAL CHART 1407
Married:

Died: Bef Nov 1512

5 Anne WHITE
Born: Abt 1480

Died:

11 Margaret GAINSFORD
Born: Abt 1458

Died:

1 Jane TICHBORNE
Born: Abt 1545
-SAME AS #9,ROYAL CHART 1422
Married:

Died: Bef 1581

Francis YATE
Spouse

12
Born:

Married:

Died:

6 William RYTHE
Born: Abt 1490

Married:

Died: Aft 1571

13
Born:

Died:

3 Elizabeth RYTHE
Born: Abt 1520

Died: Aft 1571

14 Peter COWDRAY
Born: Abt 1465

Married:

Died:

7 Margery COWDRAY
Born: Abt 1495

Died: Aft 1571

15 --
Born:

Died:

Sources include: Faris 2--Yate; Roberts *500*, p. 342.

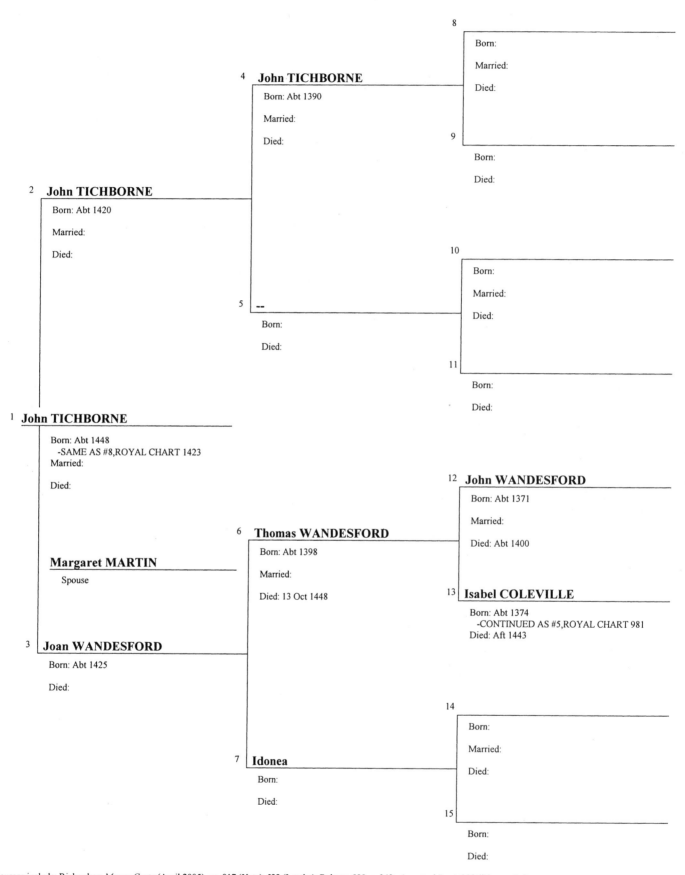

8

John TICHBORNE
Born: Abt 1390
Married:
Died:

Born:
Married:
Died:

9

Born:
Died:

2 **John TICHBORNE**
Born: Abt 1420
Married:
Died:

10

Born:
Married:
Died:

5 --
Born:
Died:

11

Born:
Died:

1 **John TICHBORNE**
Born: Abt 1448
-SAME AS #8,ROYAL CHART 1423
Married:
Died:

12 **John WANDESFORD**
Born: Abt 1371
Married:
Died: Abt 1400

6 **Thomas WANDESFORD**
Born: Abt 1398
Married:
Died: 13 Oct 1448

13 **Isabel COLEVILLE**
Born: Abt 1374
-CONTINUED AS #5,ROYAL CHART 981
Died: Aft 1443

Margaret MARTIN
Spouse

3 **Joan WANDESFORD**
Born: Abt 1425
Died:

14

Born:
Married:
Died:

7 **Idonea**
Born:
Died:

15

Born:
Died:

Sources include: Richardson *Magna Carta* (April 2005), pp. 917 (Yate), 522 (Louthe); Roberts *500*, p. 342; *Ancestral Roots* 208 (#6 ancestry).

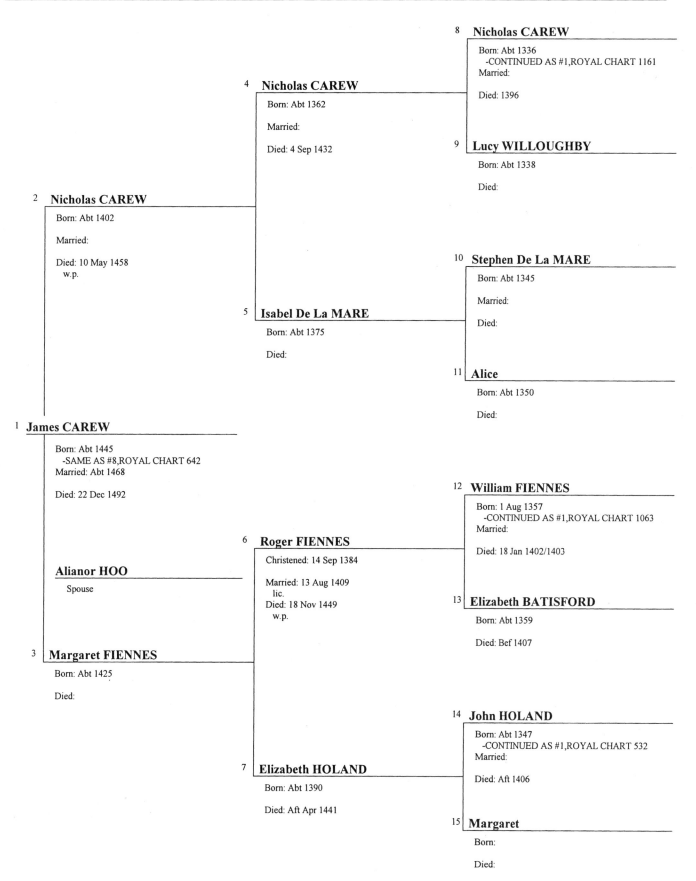

8 Nicholas CAREW

Born: Abt 1336
-CONTINUED AS #1,ROYAL CHART 1161
Married:

Died: 1396

4 Nicholas CAREW

Born: Abt 1362

Married:

Died: 4 Sep 1432

9 Lucy WILLOUGHBY

Born: Abt 1338

Died:

2 Nicholas CAREW

Born: Abt 1402

Married:

Died: 10 May 1458
w.p.

10 Stephen De La MARE

Born: Abt 1345

Married:

Died:

5 Isabel De La MARE

Born: Abt 1375

Died:

11 Alice

Born: Abt 1350

Died:

1 James CAREW

Born: Abt 1445
-SAME AS #8,ROYAL CHART 642
Married: Abt 1468

Died: 22 Dec 1492

12 William FIENNES

Born: 1 Aug 1357
-CONTINUED AS #1,ROYAL CHART 1063
Married:

Died: 18 Jan 1402/1403

6 Roger FIENNES

Christened: 14 Sep 1384

Married: 13 Aug 1409
lic.
Died: 18 Nov 1449
w.p.

13 Elizabeth BATISFORD

Born: Abt 1359

Died: Bef 1407

Alianor HOO

Spouse

3 Margaret FIENNES

Born: Abt 1425

Died:

14 John HOLAND

Born: Abt 1347
-CONTINUED AS #1,ROYAL CHART 532
Married:

Died: Aft 1406

7 Elizabeth HOLAND

Born: Abt 1390

Died: Aft Apr 1441

15 Margaret

Born:

Died:

Sources include: Richardson *Plantagenet* (2004), pp. 87-88 (Beddington), 642 (Say), 399-400 (Holand); Faris 2--Beddington; Faris preliminary baronial manuscript (1998), pp. 296-297 (Carew); Consultation with Douglas Richardson.

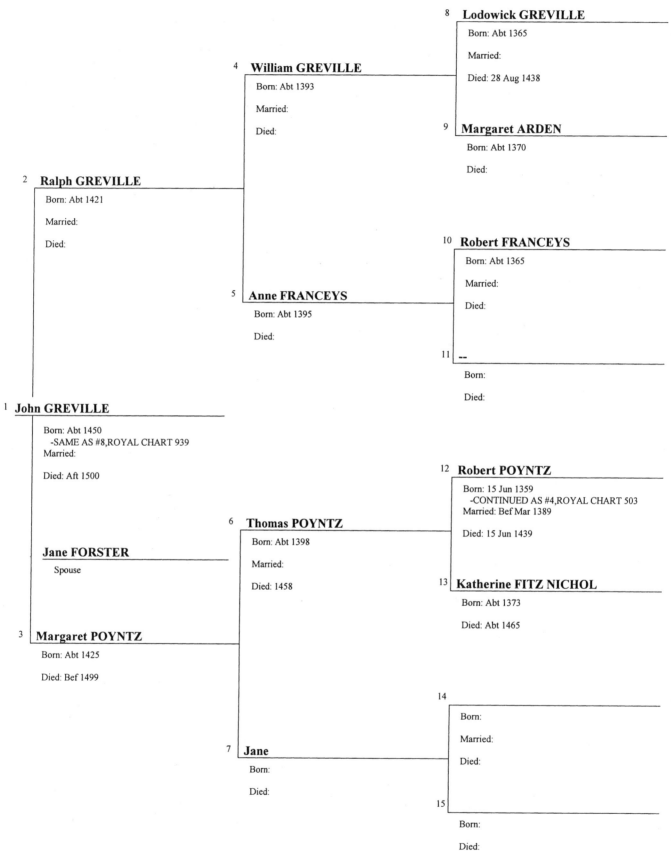

8 **Lodowick GREVILLE**
Born: Abt 1365
Married:
Died: 28 Aug 1438

4 **William GREVILLE**
Born: Abt 1393
Married:
Died:

9 **Margaret ARDEN**
Born: Abt 1370
Died:

2 **Ralph GREVILLE**
Born: Abt 1421
Married:
Died:

10 **Robert FRANCEYS**
Born: Abt 1365
Married:
Died:

5 **Anne FRANCEYS**
Born: Abt 1395
Died:

11 **--**
Born:
Died:

1 **John GREVILLE**
Born: Abt 1450
  -SAME AS #8,ROYAL CHART 939
Married:
Died: Aft 1500

12 **Robert POYNTZ**
Born: 15 Jun 1359
  -CONTINUED AS #4,ROYAL CHART 503
Married: Bef Mar 1389
Died: 15 Jun 1439

6 **Thomas POYNTZ**
Born: Abt 1398
Married:
Died: 1458

13 **Katherine FITZ NICHOL**
Born: Abt 1373
Died: Abt 1465

Jane FORSTER
Spouse

3 **Margaret POYNTZ**
Born: Abt 1425
Died: Bef 1499

14
Born:
Married:
Died:

7 **Jane**
Born:
Died:

15
Born:
Died:

Sources include: LDS records.

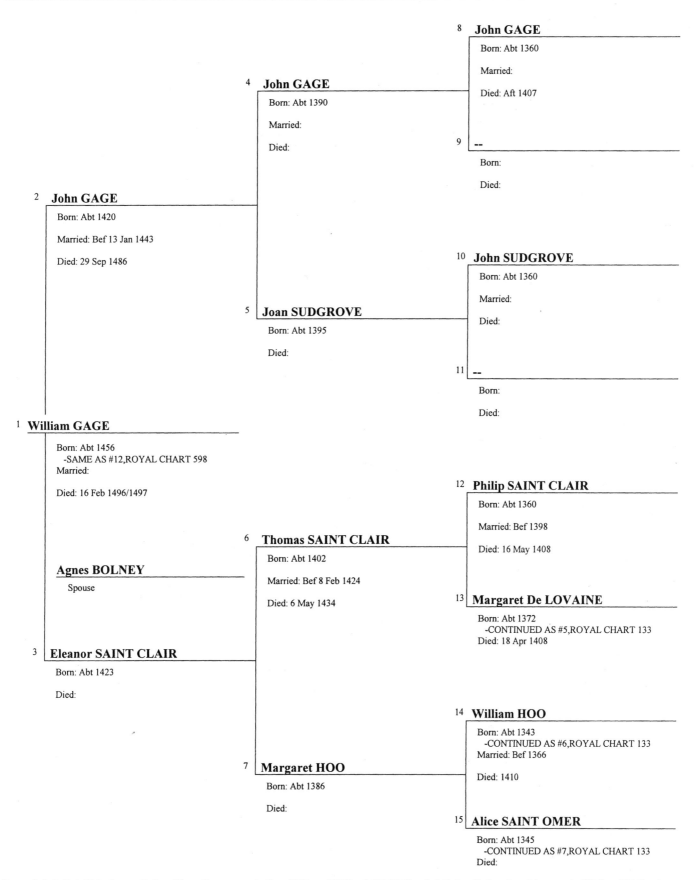

8 **John GAGE**
Born: Abt 1360
Married:
Died: Aft 1407

4 **John GAGE**
Born: Abt 1390
Married:
Died:

9 **--**
Born:
Died:

2 **John GAGE**
Born: Abt 1420
Married: Bef 13 Jan 1443
Died: 29 Sep 1486

10 **John SUDGROVE**
Born: Abt 1360
Married:
Died:

5 **Joan SUDGROVE**
Born: Abt 1395
Died:

11 **--**
Born:
Died:

1 **William GAGE**
Born: Abt 1456
-SAME AS #12,ROYAL CHART 598
Married:
Died: 16 Feb 1496/1497

Agnes BOLNEY
Spouse

12 **Philip SAINT CLAIR**
Born: Abt 1360
Married: Bef 1398
Died: 16 May 1408

6 **Thomas SAINT CLAIR**
Born: Abt 1402
Married: Bef 8 Feb 1424
Died: 6 May 1434

13 **Margaret De LOVAINE**
Born: Abt 1372
-CONTINUED AS #5,ROYAL CHART 133
Died: 18 Apr 1408

3 **Eleanor SAINT CLAIR**
Born: Abt 1423
Died:

14 **William HOO**
Born: Abt 1343
-CONTINUED AS #6,ROYAL CHART 133
Married: Bef 1366
Died: 1410

7 **Margaret HOO**
Born: Abt 1386
Died:

15 **Alice SAINT OMER**
Born: Abt 1345
-CONTINUED AS #7,ROYAL CHART 133
Died:

Sources include: Faris-Richardson preliminary Magna Carta manuscript (June 2000), pp. 232 (Gage), 327-328 (Lovaine); Faris preliminary baronial manuscript (1998), p. 685 (Gage); *NEHGR* 139:283-287 (#3 ancestry); *Ancestral Roots* 79 (#6 & 7 ancestry).

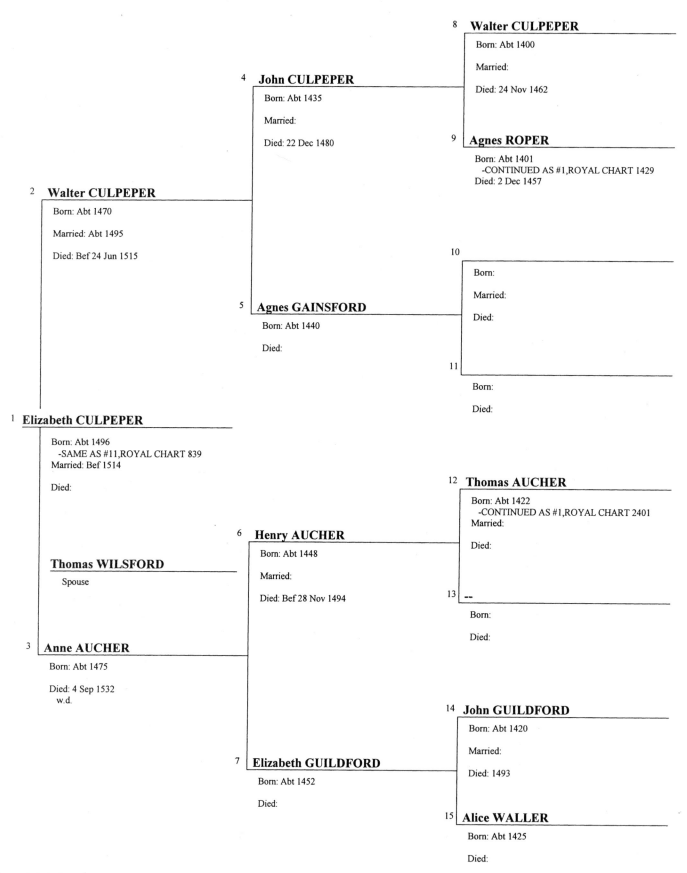

8 Walter CULPEPER

Born: Abt 1400

Married:

Died: 24 Nov 1462

4 John CULPEPER

Born: Abt 1435

Married:

Died: 22 Dec 1480

9 Agnes ROPER

Born: Abt 1401
   -CONTINUED AS #1,ROYAL CHART 1429
Died: 2 Dec 1457

2 Walter CULPEPER

Born: Abt 1470

Married: Abt 1495

Died: Bef 24 Jun 1515

10

Born:

Married:

Died:

5 Agnes GAINSFORD

Born: Abt 1440

Died:

11

Born:

Died:

1 Elizabeth CULPEPER

Born: Abt 1496
   -SAME AS #11,ROYAL CHART 839
Married: Bef 1514

Died:

12 Thomas AUCHER

Born: Abt 1422
   -CONTINUED AS #1,ROYAL CHART 2401
Married:

Died:

6 Henry AUCHER

Born: Abt 1448

Married:

Died: Bef 28 Nov 1494

13 --

Born:

Died:

Thomas WILSFORD

Spouse

3 Anne AUCHER

Born: Abt 1475

Died: 4 Sep 1532
w.d.

14 John GUILDFORD

Born: Abt 1420

Married:

Died: 1493

7 Elizabeth GUILDFORD

Born: Abt 1452

Died:

15 Alice WALLER

Born: Abt 1425

Died:

Sources include: Consultation with Douglas Richardson; Faris 2--Clarke 3 (#1 & 2; #1 of Magna Charta descent); Roberts *500*, pp. 431-434 (#2 ancestry); *Magna Charta* 16D (#3 ancestry); LDS records.

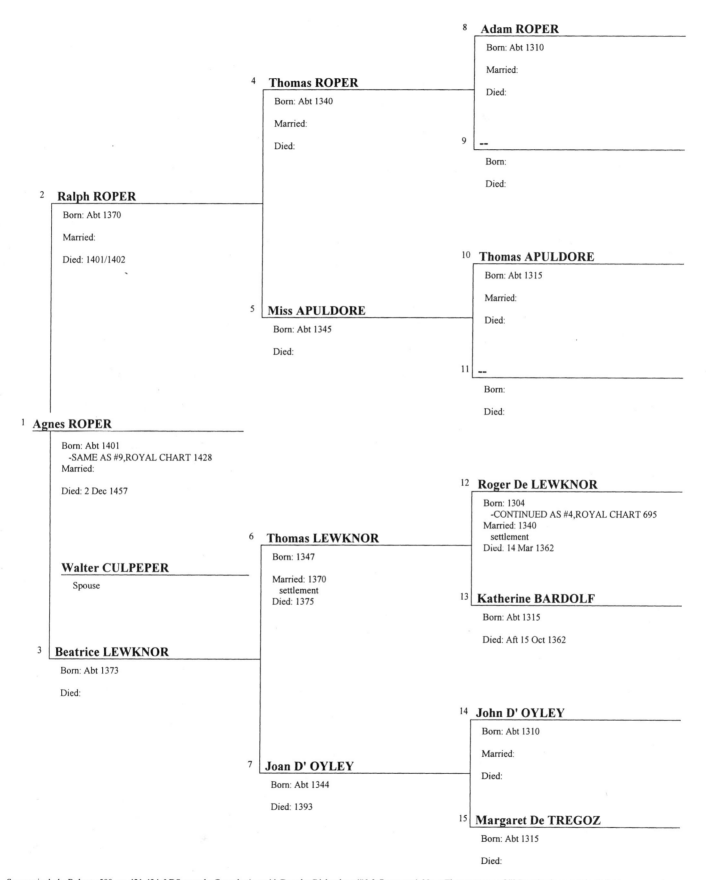

8 Adam ROPER
Born: Abt 1310
Married:
Died:

4 Thomas ROPER
Born: Abt 1340
Married:
Died:

9 --
Born:
Died:

2 Ralph ROPER
Born: Abt 1370
Married:
Died: 1401/1402

10 Thomas APULDORE
Born: Abt 1315
Married:
Died:

5 Miss APULDORE
Born: Abt 1345
Died:

11 --
Born:
Died:

1 Agnes ROPER
Born: Abt 1401
-SAME AS #9,ROYAL CHART 1428
Married:
Died: 2 Dec 1457

12 Roger De LEWKNOR
Born: 1304
-CONTINUED AS #4,ROYAL CHART 695
Married: 1340
    settlement
Died: 14 Mar 1362

6 Thomas LEWKNOR
Born: 1347
Married: 1370
    settlement
Died: 1375

13 Katherine BARDOLF
Born: Abt 1315
Died: Aft 15 Oct 1362

Walter CULPEPER
Spouse

3 Beatrice LEWKNOR
Born: Abt 1373
Died:

14 John D' OYLEY
Born: Abt 1310
Married:
Died:

7 Joan D' OYLEY
Born: Abt 1344
Died: 1393

15 Margaret De TREGOZ
Born: Abt 1315
Died:

Sources include: Roberts *500*, pp. 431-434; LDS records; Consultation with Douglas Richardson (#6 & 7 ancestry). Note: The parentage of #3 Beatrice is uncertain. Roberts erroneously calls her daughter of the Thomas Lewknor (grandson of #6 & 7 Thomas & Joan above) who married Philippa Dalyngridge (see them chart 1196). The version claimed in LDS records is tentatively accepted above.

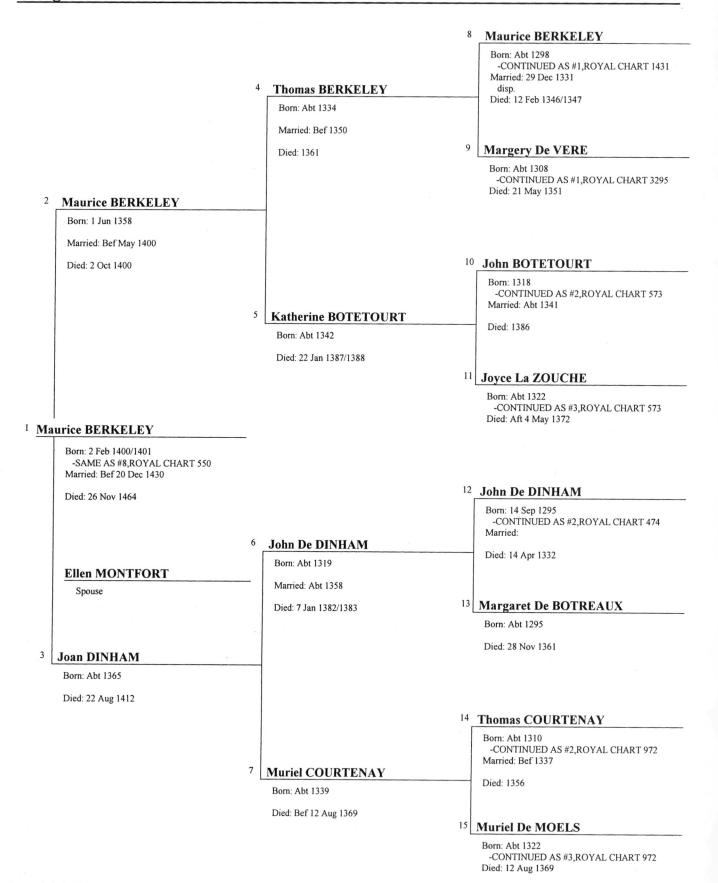

8 Maurice BERKELEY
Born: Abt 1298
 -CONTINUED AS #1,ROYAL CHART 1431
Married: 29 Dec 1331
 disp.
Died: 12 Feb 1346/1347

4 Thomas BERKELEY
Born: Abt 1334
Married: Bef 1350
Died: 1361

9 Margery De VERE
Born: Abt 1308
 -CONTINUED AS #1,ROYAL CHART 3295
Died: 21 May 1351

2 Maurice BERKELEY
Born: 1 Jun 1358
Married: Bef May 1400
Died: 2 Oct 1400

10 John BOTETOURT
Born: 1318
 -CONTINUED AS #2,ROYAL CHART 573
Married: Abt 1341
Died: 1386

5 Katherine BOTETOURT
Born: Abt 1342
Died: 22 Jan 1387/1388

11 Joyce La ZOUCHE
Born: Abt 1322
 -CONTINUED AS #3,ROYAL CHART 573
Died: Aft 4 May 1372

1 Maurice BERKELEY
Born: 2 Feb 1400/1401
 -SAME AS #8,ROYAL CHART 550
Married: Bef 20 Dec 1430
Died: 26 Nov 1464

12 John De DINHAM
Born: 14 Sep 1295
 -CONTINUED AS #2,ROYAL CHART 474
Married:
Died: 14 Apr 1332

6 John De DINHAM
Born: Abt 1319
Married: Abt 1358
Died: 7 Jan 1382/1383

13 Margaret De BOTREAUX
Born: Abt 1295
Died: 28 Nov 1361

Ellen MONTFORT
Spouse

3 Joan DINHAM
Born: Abt 1365
Died: 22 Aug 1412

14 Thomas COURTENAY
Born: Abt 1310
 -CONTINUED AS #2,ROYAL CHART 972
Married: Bef 1337
Died: 1356

7 Muriel COURTENAY
Born: Abt 1339
Died: Bef 12 Aug 1369

15 Muriel De MOELS
Born: Abt 1322
 -CONTINUED AS #3,ROYAL CHART 972
Died: 12 Aug 1369

Sources include: Richardson *Plantagenet* (2004), pp. 260-261 (Berkeley), 274 (Dinham).

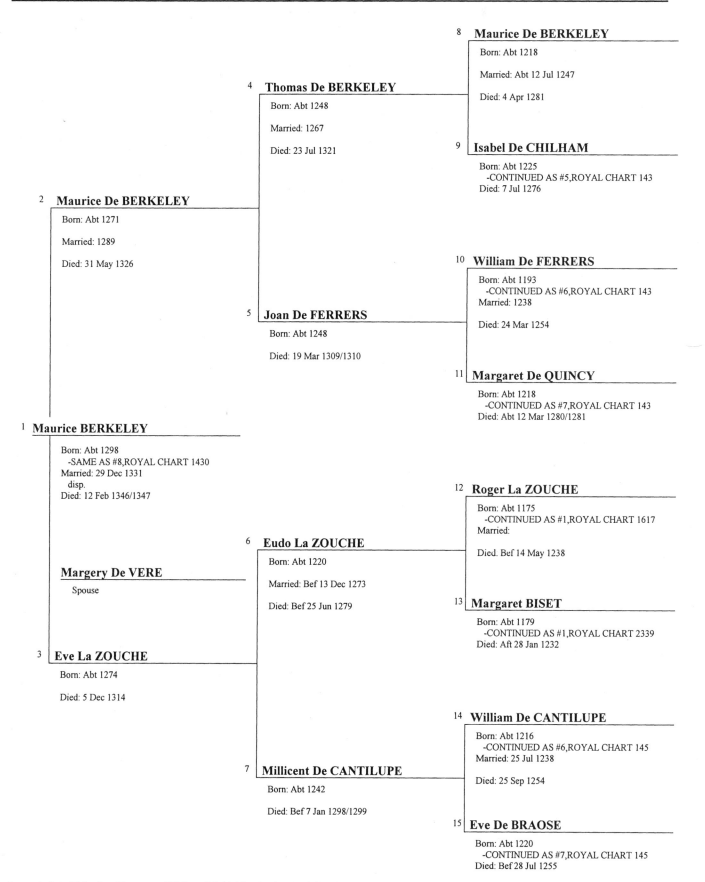

8 **Maurice De BERKELEY**

Born: Abt 1218

Married: Abt 12 Jul 1247

Died: 4 Apr 1281

4 **Thomas De BERKELEY**

Born: Abt 1248

Married: 1267

Died: 23 Jul 1321

9 **Isabel De CHILHAM**

Born: Abt 1225
  -CONTINUED AS #5,ROYAL CHART 143
Died: 7 Jul 1276

2 **Maurice De BERKELEY**

Born: Abt 1271

Married: 1289

Died: 31 May 1326

10 **William De FERRERS**

Born: Abt 1193
  -CONTINUED AS #6,ROYAL CHART 143
Married: 1238

Died: 24 Mar 1254

5 **Joan De FERRERS**

Born: Abt 1248

Died: 19 Mar 1309/1310

11 **Margaret De QUINCY**

Born: Abt 1218
  -CONTINUED AS #7,ROYAL CHART 143
Died: Abt 12 Mar 1280/1281

1 **Maurice BERKELEY**

Born: Abt 1298
  -SAME AS #8,ROYAL CHART 1430
Married: 29 Dec 1331
  disp.
Died: 12 Feb 1346/1347

12 **Roger La ZOUCHE**

Born: Abt 1175
  -CONTINUED AS #1,ROYAL CHART 1617
Married:

Died. Bef 14 May 1238

6 **Eudo La ZOUCHE**

Born: Abt 1220

Married: Bef 13 Dec 1273

Died: Bef 25 Jun 1279

13 **Margaret BISET**

Born: Abt 1179
  -CONTINUED AS #1,ROYAL CHART 2339
Died: Aft 28 Jan 1232

Margery De VERE

Spouse

3 **Eve La ZOUCHE**

Born: Abt 1274

Died: 5 Dec 1314

14 **William De CANTILUPE**

Born: Abt 1216
  -CONTINUED AS #6,ROYAL CHART 145
Married: 25 Jul 1238

Died: 25 Sep 1254

7 **Millicent De CANTILUPE**

Born: Abt 1242

Died: Bef 7 Jan 1298/1299

15 **Eve De BRAOSE**

Born: Abt 1220
  -CONTINUED AS #7,ROYAL CHART 145
Died: Bef 28 Jul 1255

Sources include: Richardson *Plantagenet* (2004), pp. 260 (Deighton), 96-97 (Berkeley); *Ancestral Roots* 26, 39 (#2 & 3 ancestry).

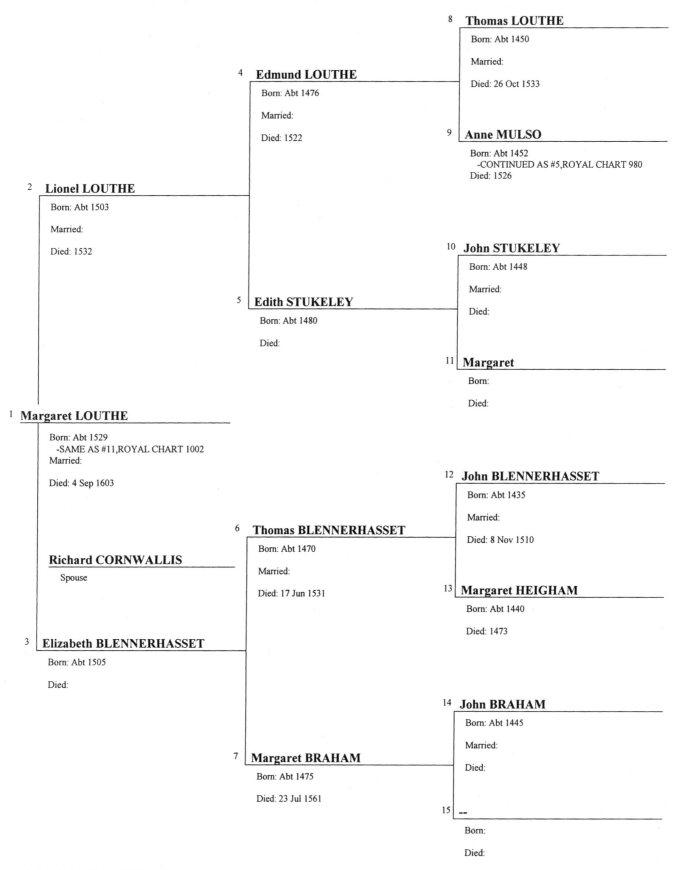

8 **Thomas LOUTHE**

Born: Abt 1450

Married:

Died: 26 Oct 1533

4 **Edmund LOUTHE**

Born: Abt 1476

Married:

Died: 1522

9 **Anne MULSO**

Born: Abt 1452
-CONTINUED AS #5,ROYAL CHART 980
Died: 1526

2 **Lionel LOUTHE**

Born: Abt 1503

Married:

Died: 1532

10 **John STUKELEY**

Born: Abt 1448

Married:

Died:

5 **Edith STUKELEY**

Born: Abt 1480

Died:

11 **Margaret**

Born:

Died:

1 **Margaret LOUTHE**

Born: Abt 1529
-SAME AS #11,ROYAL CHART 1002
Married:

Died: 4 Sep 1603

12 **John BLENNERHASSET**

Born: Abt 1435

Married:

Died: 8 Nov 1510

6 **Thomas BLENNERHASSET**

Born: Abt 1470

Married:

Died: 17 Jun 1531

Richard CORNWALLIS

Spouse

13 **Margaret HEIGHAM**

Born: Abt 1440

Died: 1473

3 **Elizabeth BLENNERHASSET**

Born: Abt 1505

Died:

14 **John BRAHAM**

Born: Abt 1445

Married:

Died:

7 **Margaret BRAHAM**

Born: Abt 1475

Died: 23 Jul 1561

15 **--**

Born:

Died:

Sources include: Faris 2--Dade 3; LDS records.

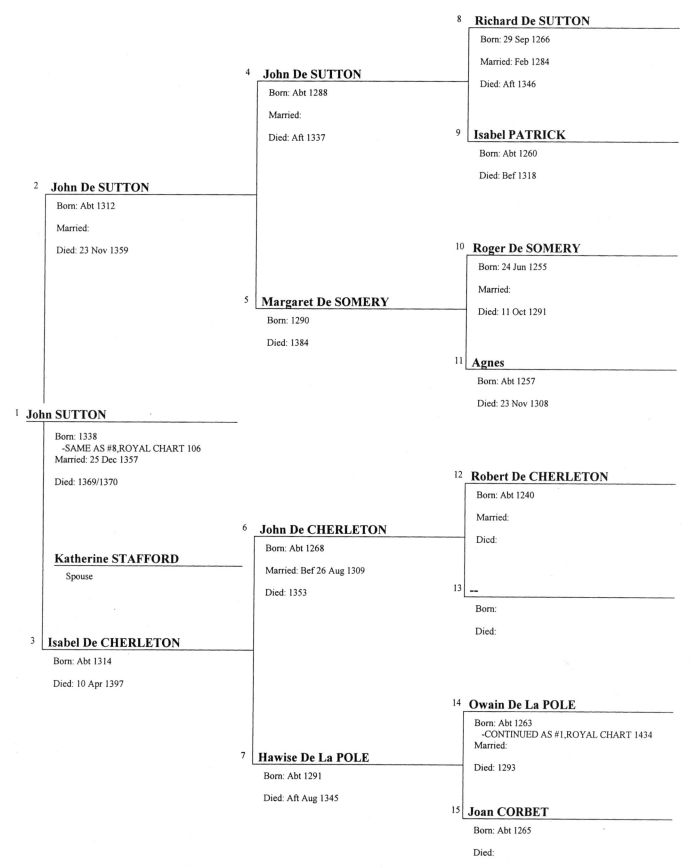

8 Richard De SUTTON
Born: 29 Sep 1266
Married: Feb 1284
Died: Aft 1346

4 John De SUTTON
Born: Abt 1288
Married:
Died: Aft 1337

9 Isabel PATRICK
Born: Abt 1260
Died: Bef 1318

2 John De SUTTON
Born: Abt 1312
Married:
Died: 23 Nov 1359

10 Roger De SOMERY
Born: 24 Jun 1255
Married:
Died: 11 Oct 1291

5 Margaret De SOMERY
Born: 1290
Died: 1384

11 Agnes
Born: Abt 1257
Died: 23 Nov 1308

1 John SUTTON
Born: 1338
-SAME AS #8,ROYAL CHART 106
Married: 25 Dec 1357
Died: 1369/1370

12 Robert De CHERLETON
Born: Abt 1240
Married:
Died:

6 John De CHERLETON
Born: Abt 1268
Married: Bef 26 Aug 1309
Died: 1353

Katherine STAFFORD
Spouse

13 --
Born:
Died:

3 Isabel De CHERLETON
Born: Abt 1314
Died: 10 Apr 1397

14 Owain De La POLE
Born: Abt 1263
-CONTINUED AS #1,ROYAL CHART 1434
Married:
Died: 1293

7 Hawise De La POLE
Born: Abt 1291
Died: Aft Aug 1345

15 Joan CORBET
Born: Abt 1265
Died:

Sources include: Faris preliminary baronial manuscript (1998), pp. 1481-82 (Sutton), 1413-14 (Somery), 333 (Cherleton), 412 (Corbet); Faris 2--Dudley 9; *Ancestral Roots* 81.

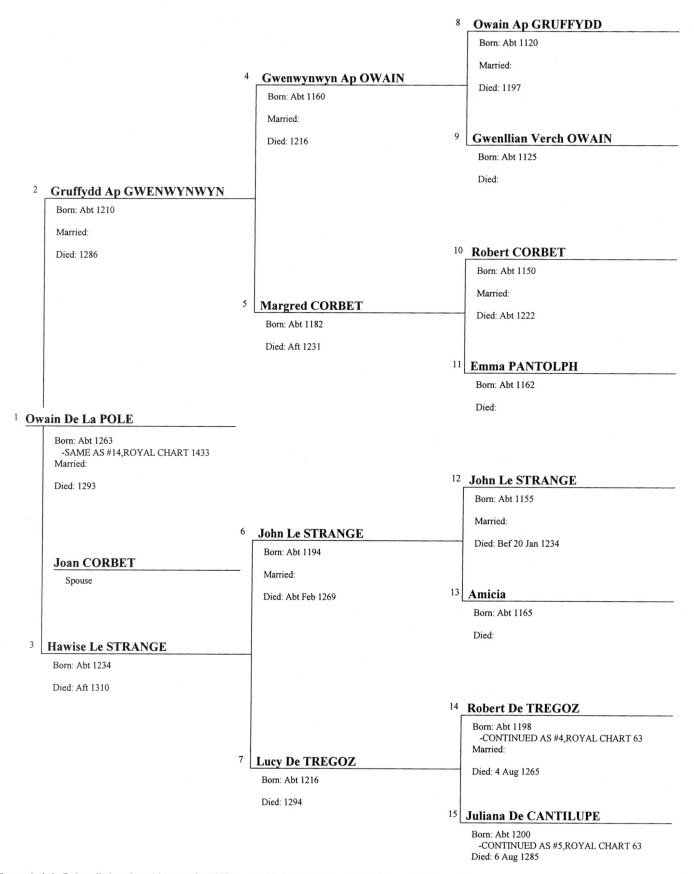

8 **Owain Ap GRUFFYDD**
Born: Abt 1120
Married:
Died: 1197

4 **Gwenwynwyn Ap OWAIN**
Born: Abt 1160
Married:
Died: 1216

9 **Gwenllian Verch OWAIN**
Born: Abt 1125
Died:

2 **Gruffydd Ap GWENWYNWYN**
Born: Abt 1210
Married:
Died: 1286

10 **Robert CORBET**
Born: Abt 1150
Married:
Died: Abt 1222

5 **Margred CORBET**
Born: Abt 1182
Died: Aft 1231

11 **Emma PANTOLPH**
Born: Abt 1162
Died:

1 **Owain De La POLE**
Born: Abt 1263
  -SAME AS #14,ROYAL CHART 1433
Married:
Died: 1293

Joan CORBET
Spouse

12 **John Le STRANGE**
Born: Abt 1155
Married:
Died: Bef 20 Jan 1234

6 **John Le STRANGE**
Born: Abt 1194
Married:
Died: Abt Feb 1269

13 **Amicia**
Born: Abt 1165
Died:

3 **Hawise Le STRANGE**
Born: Abt 1234
Died: Aft 1310

14 **Robert De TREGOZ**
Born: Abt 1198
  -CONTINUED AS #4,ROYAL CHART 63
Married:
Died: 4 Aug 1265

7 **Lucy De TREGOZ**
Born: Abt 1216
Died: 1294

15 **Juliana De CANTILUPE**
Born: Abt 1200
  -CONTINUED AS #5,ROYAL CHART 63
Died: 6 Aug 1285

Sources include: Faris preliminary baronial manuscript (1998), pp. 412 (Corbet), 1276 (Powys), 1459 (Strange); LDS records.

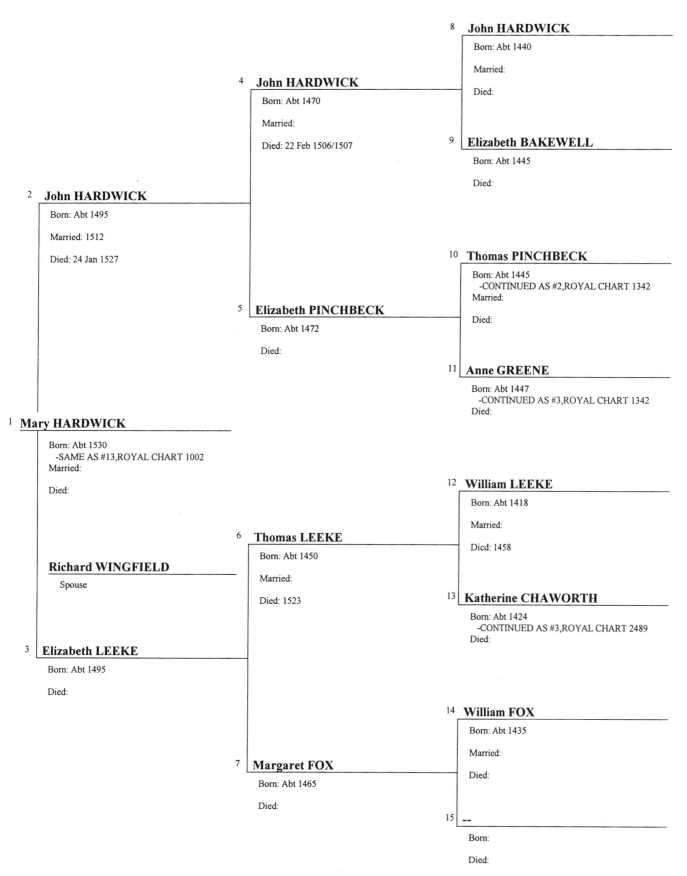

8 **John HARDWICK**

Born: Abt 1440

Married:

Died:

4 **John HARDWICK**

Born: Abt 1470

Married:

Died: 22 Feb 1506/1507

9 **Elizabeth BAKEWELL**

Born: Abt 1445

Died:

2 **John HARDWICK**

Born: Abt 1495

Married: 1512

Died: 24 Jan 1527

10 **Thomas PINCHBECK**

Born: Abt 1445
-CONTINUED AS #2,ROYAL CHART 1342
Married:

Died:

5 **Elizabeth PINCHBECK**

Born: Abt 1472

Died:

11 **Anne GREENE**

Born: Abt 1447
-CONTINUED AS #3,ROYAL CHART 1342
Died:

1 **Mary HARDWICK**

Born: Abt 1530
-SAME AS #13,ROYAL CHART 1002
Married:

Died:

Richard WINGFIELD

Spouse

12 **William LEEKE**

Born: Abt 1418

Married:

Died: 1458

6 **Thomas LEEKE**

Born: Abt 1450

Married:

Died: 1523

13 **Katherine CHAWORTH**

Born: Abt 1424
-CONTINUED AS #3,ROYAL CHART 2489
Died:

3 **Elizabeth LEEKE**

Born: Abt 1495

Died:

14 **William FOX**

Born: Abt 1435

Married:

Died:

7 **Margaret FOX**

Born: Abt 1465

Died:

15 **--**

Born:

Died:

Sources include: Faris 2--Hankford 3, Lowe; Faris preliminary baronial manuscript (1998), pp. 799-800 (Hardwick). Note: Roberts (*500*, p. 285) and Faris (baronial) give #8 John as son of Roger Hardwick (md. Nicola Barlow) and grandson of Elizabeth Goushill (see chart 449, #5) by a claimed 2nd husband William Hardwick. The claim is unacceptable chronologically.

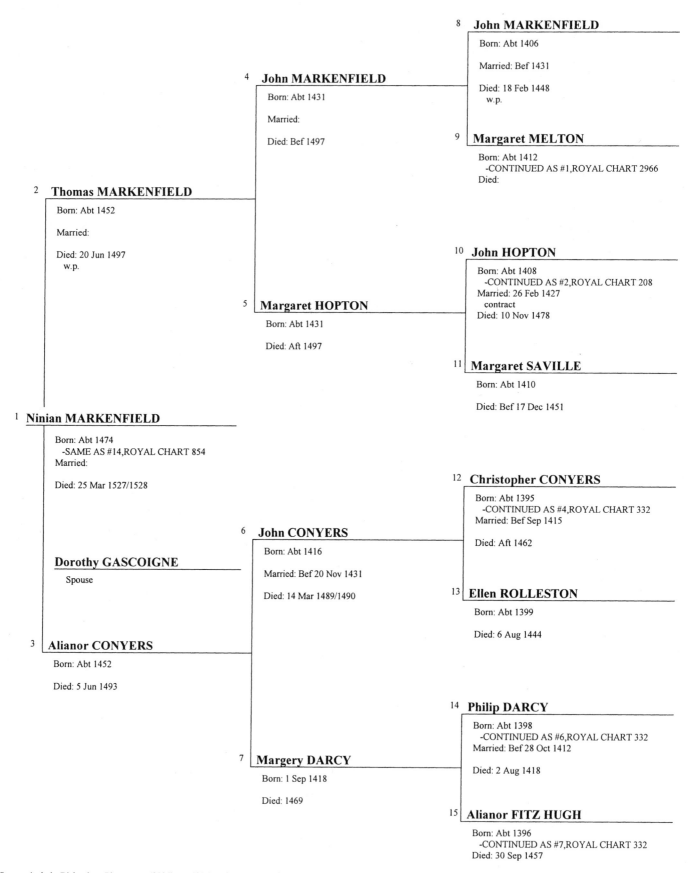

8 John MARKENFIELD
Born: Abt 1406
Married: Bef 1431
Died: 18 Feb 1448
w.p.

4 John MARKENFIELD
Born: Abt 1431
Married:
Died: Bef 1497

9 Margaret MELTON
Born: Abt 1412
-CONTINUED AS #1,ROYAL CHART 2966
Died:

2 Thomas MARKENFIELD
Born: Abt 1452
Married:
Died: 20 Jun 1497
w.p.

10 John HOPTON
Born: Abt 1408
-CONTINUED AS #2,ROYAL CHART 208
Married: 26 Feb 1427
contract
Died: 10 Nov 1478

5 Margaret HOPTON
Born: Abt 1431
Died: Aft 1497

11 Margaret SAVILLE
Born: Abt 1410
Died: Bef 17 Dec 1451

1 Ninian MARKENFIELD
Born: Abt 1474
-SAME AS #14,ROYAL CHART 854
Married:
Died: 25 Mar 1527/1528

12 Christopher CONYERS
Born: Abt 1395
-CONTINUED AS #4,ROYAL CHART 332
Married: Bef Sep 1415
Died: Aft 1462

6 John CONYERS
Born: Abt 1416
Married: Bef 20 Nov 1431
Died: 14 Mar 1489/1490

13 Ellen ROLLESTON
Born: Abt 1399
Died: 6 Aug 1444

Dorothy GASCOIGNE
Spouse

3 Alianor CONYERS
Born: Abt 1452
Died: 5 Jun 1493

14 Philip DARCY
Born: Abt 1398
-CONTINUED AS #6,ROYAL CHART 332
Married: Bef 28 Oct 1412
Died: 2 Aug 1418

7 Margery DARCY
Born: 1 Sep 1418
Died: 1469

15 Alianor FITZ HUGH
Born: Abt 1396
-CONTINUED AS #7,ROYAL CHART 332
Died: 30 Sep 1457

Sources include: Richardson *Plantagenet* (2004), pp. 498 (Mauleverer), 227 (Conyers); Faris 2--Mauleverer. Note: #8 John was son of Thomas Markenfield & Beatrice Sothill. Beatrice was daughter of either Henry or his brother John. Roberts *600* (p. 399) gives Beatrice as a great-granddaughter of William Fitz William & Maud Cromwell (cont. cht. 2962, #4 & 5), but this claim is unacceptable chronologically. See also note chart 475.

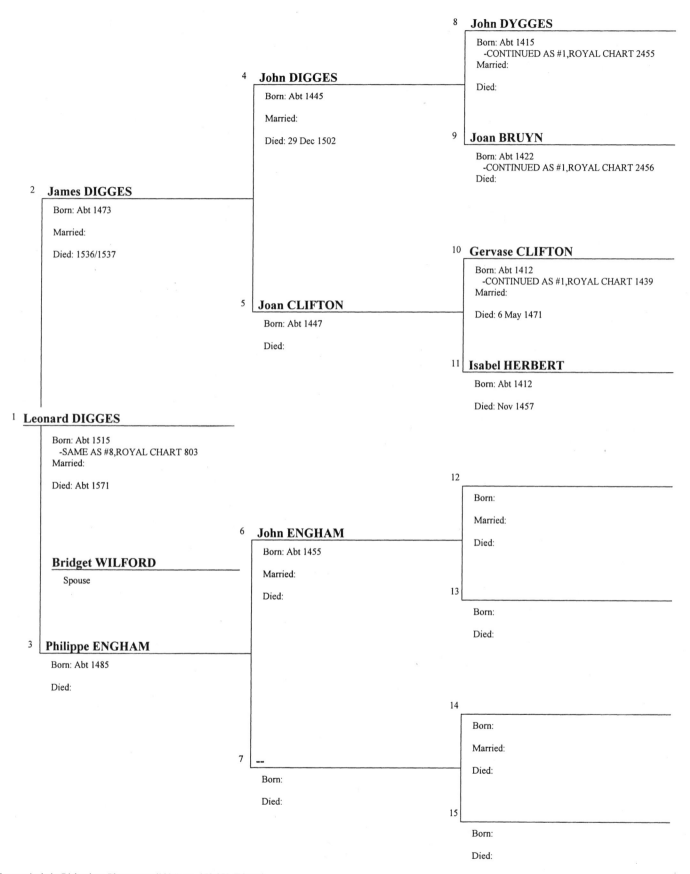

8 John DYGGES

Born: Abt 1415
-CONTINUED AS #1,ROYAL CHART 2455
Married:

Died:

4 John DIGGES

Born: Abt 1445

Married:

Died: 29 Dec 1502

9 Joan BRUYN

Born: Abt 1422
-CONTINUED AS #1,ROYAL CHART 2456
Died:

2 James DIGGES

Born: Abt 1473

Married:

Died: 1536/1537

10 Gervase CLIFTON

Born: Abt 1412
-CONTINUED AS #1,ROYAL CHART 1439
Married:

Died: 6 May 1471

5 Joan CLIFTON

Born: Abt 1447

Died:

11 Isabel HERBERT

Born: Abt 1412

Died: Nov 1457

1 Leonard DIGGES

Born: Abt 1515
-SAME AS #8,ROYAL CHART 803
Married:

Died: Abt 1571

12

Born:

Married:

Died:

6 John ENGHAM

Born: Abt 1455

Married:

Died:

13

Born:

Died:

Bridget WILFORD

Spouse

3 Philippe ENGHAM

Born: Abt 1485

Died:

14

Born:

Married:

Died:

7 --

Born:

Died:

15

Born:

Died:

Sources include: Richardson *Plantagenet* (2004), pp. 272-273 (Digges).

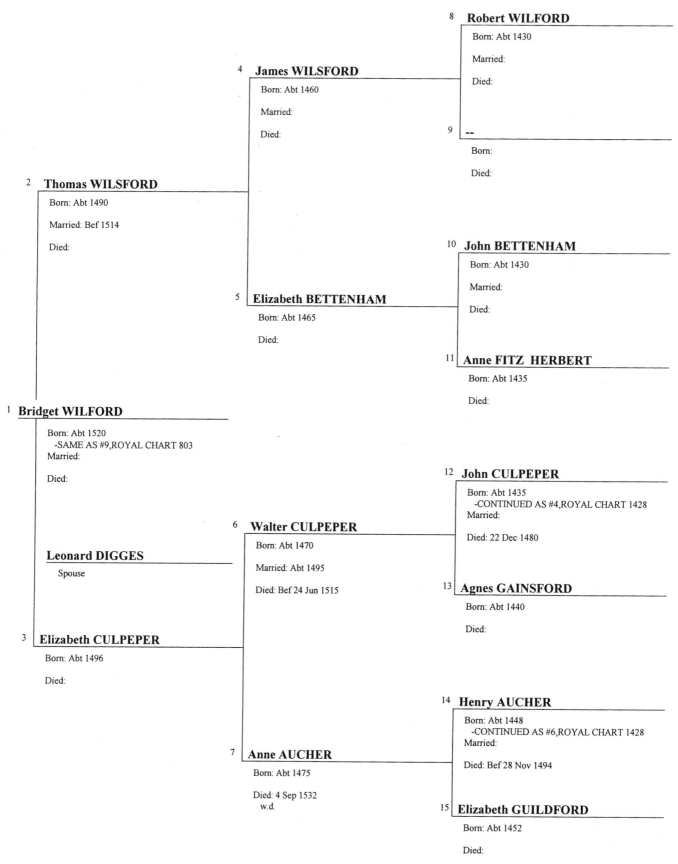

8 Robert WILFORD
Born: Abt 1430
Married:
Died:

9 --
Born:
Died:

4 James WILSFORD
Born: Abt 1460
Married:
Died:

10 John BETTENHAM
Born: Abt 1430
Married:
Died:

5 Elizabeth BETTENHAM
Born: Abt 1465
Died:

11 Anne FITZ HERBERT
Born: Abt 1435
Died:

2 Thomas WILSFORD
Born: Abt 1490
Married: Bef 1514
Died:

1 Bridget WILFORD
Born: Abt 1520
  -SAME AS #9,ROYAL CHART 803
Married:
Died:

Leonard DIGGES
Spouse

12 John CULPEPER
Born: Abt 1435
  -CONTINUED AS #4,ROYAL CHART 1428
Married:
Died: 22 Dec 1480

6 Walter CULPEPER
Born: Abt 1470
Married: Abt 1495
Died: Bef 24 Jun 1515

13 Agnes GAINSFORD
Born: Abt 1440
Died:

3 Elizabeth CULPEPER
Born: Abt 1496
Died:

14 Henry AUCHER
Born: Abt 1448
  -CONTINUED AS #6,ROYAL CHART 1428
Married:
Died: Bef 28 Nov 1494

7 Anne AUCHER
Born: Abt 1475
Died: 4 Sep 1532
w.d.

15 Elizabeth GUILDFORD
Born: Abt 1452
Died:

Sources include: Consultation with Douglas Richardson; Faris preliminary baronial manuscript (1998), pp. 1674-75 (Wilsford). Note: #8 was either Robert or Thomas, son of William Wilford & Margaret Cornu.

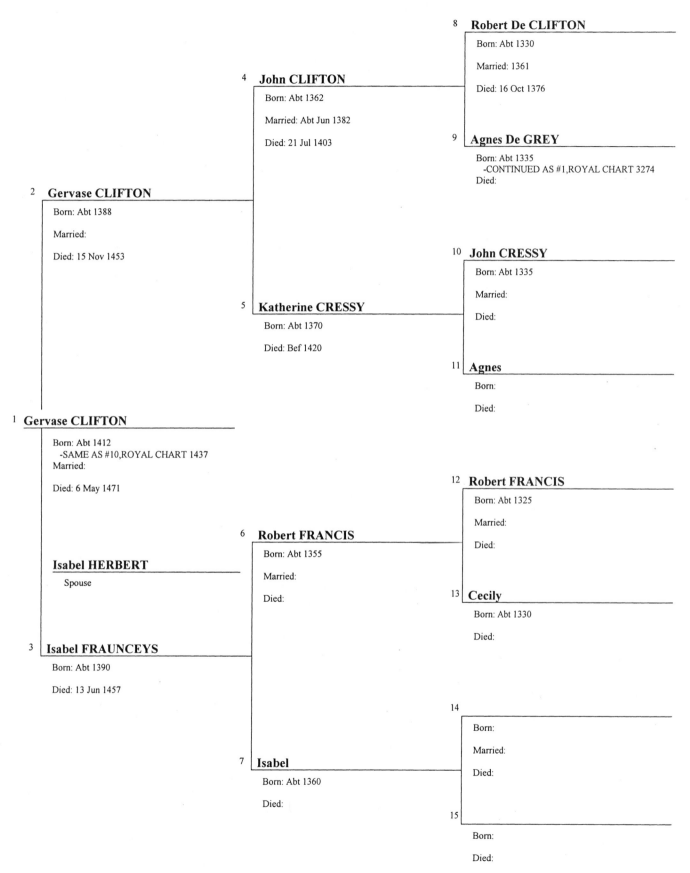

8 Robert De CLIFTON
Born: Abt 1330
Married: 1361
Died: 16 Oct 1376

4 John CLIFTON
Born: Abt 1362
Married: Abt Jun 1382
Died: 21 Jul 1403

9 Agnes De GREY
Born: Abt 1335
-CONTINUED AS #1,ROYAL CHART 3274
Died:

2 Gervase CLIFTON
Born: Abt 1388
Married:
Died: 15 Nov 1453

10 John CRESSY
Born: Abt 1335
Married:
Died:

5 Katherine CRESSY
Born: Abt 1370
Died: Bef 1420

11 Agnes
Born:
Died:

1 Gervase CLIFTON
Born: Abt 1412
-SAME AS #10,ROYAL CHART 1437
Married:
Died: 6 May 1471

12 Robert FRANCIS
Born: Abt 1325
Married:
Died:

6 Robert FRANCIS
Born: Abt 1355
Married:
Died:

13 Cecily
Born: Abt 1330
Died:

Isabel HERBERT
Spouse

3 Isabel FRAUNCEYS
Born: Abt 1390
Died: 13 Jun 1457

14
Born:
Married:
Died:

7 Isabel
Born: Abt 1360
Died:

15
Born:
Died:

Sources include: Richardson *Plantagenet* (2004), pp. 271-272 (Digges); Faris preliminary baronial manuscript (1998), pp. 668-669 (Francis).

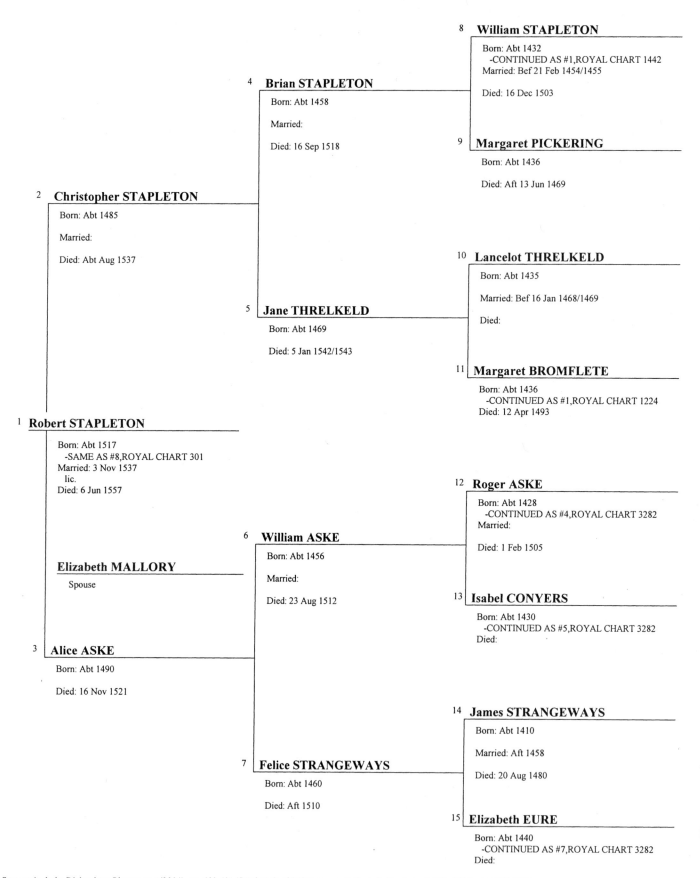

8 **William STAPLETON**

Born: Abt 1432
  -CONTINUED AS #1,ROYAL CHART 1442
Married: Bef 21 Feb 1454/1455

Died: 16 Dec 1503

4 **Brian STAPLETON**

Born: Abt 1458

Married:

Died: 16 Sep 1518

9 **Margaret PICKERING**

Born: Abt 1436

Died: Aft 13 Jun 1469

2 **Christopher STAPLETON**

Born: Abt 1485

Married:

Died: Abt Aug 1537

10 **Lancelot THRELKELD**

Born: Abt 1435

Married: Bef 16 Jan 1468/1469

Died:

5 **Jane THRELKELD**

Born: Abt 1469

Died: 5 Jan 1542/1543

11 **Margaret BROMFLETE**

Born: Abt 1436
  -CONTINUED AS #1,ROYAL CHART 1224
Died: 12 Apr 1493

1 **Robert STAPLETON**

Born: Abt 1517
  -SAME AS #8,ROYAL CHART 301
Married: 3 Nov 1537
  lic.
Died: 6 Jun 1557

12 **Roger ASKE**

Born: Abt 1428
  -CONTINUED AS #4,ROYAL CHART 3282
Married:

Died: 1 Feb 1505

6 **William ASKE**

Born: Abt 1456

Married:

Died: 23 Aug 1512

13 **Isabel CONYERS**

Born: Abt 1430
  -CONTINUED AS #5,ROYAL CHART 3282
Died:

Elizabeth MALLORY

Spouse

3 **Alice ASKE**

Born: Abt 1490

Died: 16 Nov 1521

14 **James STRANGEWAYS**

Born: Abt 1410

Married: Aft 1458

Died: 20 Aug 1480

7 **Felice STRANGEWAYS**

Born: Abt 1460

Died: Aft 1510

15 **Elizabeth EURE**

Born: Abt 1440
  -CONTINUED AS #7,ROYAL CHART 3282
Died:

Sources include: Richardson *Plantagenet* (2004), pp. 683-684 (Stapleton), 695 (Strangeways); Faris 2--Stapleton 3 (#1), Clifford 6 (#10 &11).

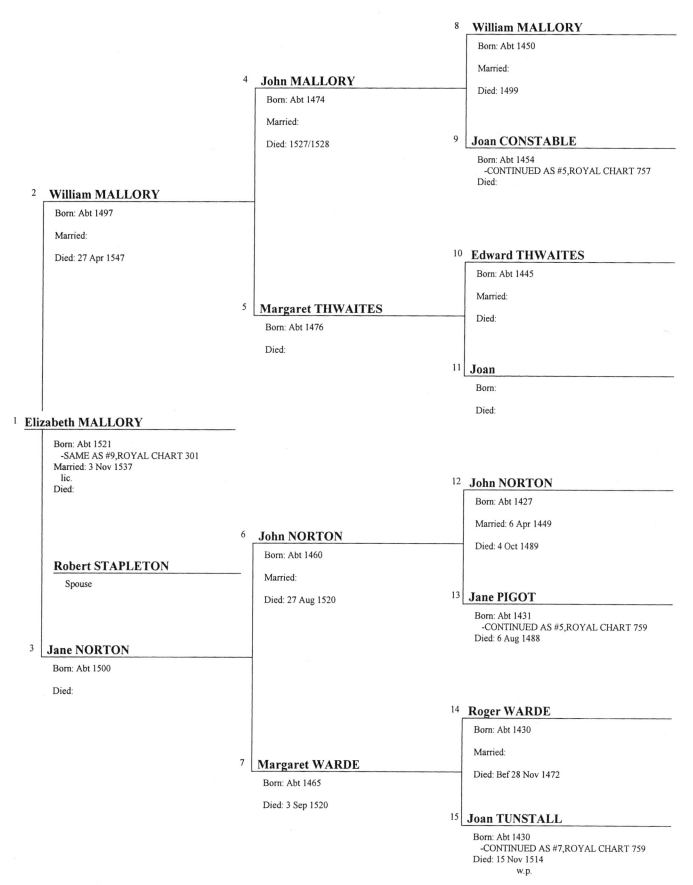

8 William MALLORY

Born: Abt 1450

Married:

Died: 1499

4 John MALLORY

Born: Abt 1474

Married:

Died: 1527/1528

9 Joan CONSTABLE

Born: Abt 1454
  -CONTINUED AS #5,ROYAL CHART 757
Died:

2 William MALLORY

Born: Abt 1497

Married:

Died: 27 Apr 1547

10 Edward THWAITES

Born: Abt 1445

Married:

Died:

5 Margaret THWAITES

Born: Abt 1476

Died:

11 Joan

Born:

Died:

1 Elizabeth MALLORY

Born: Abt 1521
  -SAME AS #9,ROYAL CHART 301
Married: 3 Nov 1537
  lic.
Died:

12 John NORTON

Born: Abt 1427

Married: 6 Apr 1449

Died: 4 Oct 1489

6 John NORTON

Born: Abt 1460

Married:

Died: 27 Aug 1520

13 Jane PIGOT

Born: Abt 1431
  -CONTINUED AS #5,ROYAL CHART 759
Died: 6 Aug 1488

Robert STAPLETON

Spouse

3 Jane NORTON

Born: Abt 1500

Died:

14 Roger WARDE

Born: Abt 1430

Married:

Died: Bef 28 Nov 1472

7 Margaret WARDE

Born: Abt 1465

Died: 3 Sep 1520

15 Joan TUNSTALL

Born: Abt 1430
  -CONTINUED AS #7,ROYAL CHART 759
Died: 15 Nov 1514
  w.p.

Sources include: Richardson *Plantagenet* (2004), pp. 684 (Stapleton), 487 (Mallory), 731-732 (Tunstall); Faris 2--Stapleton 3 (#1 & 2); *Magna Charta* 109 (#2 & 3 ancestry); Roberts *500*, pp. 313-314 (#2 ancestry).

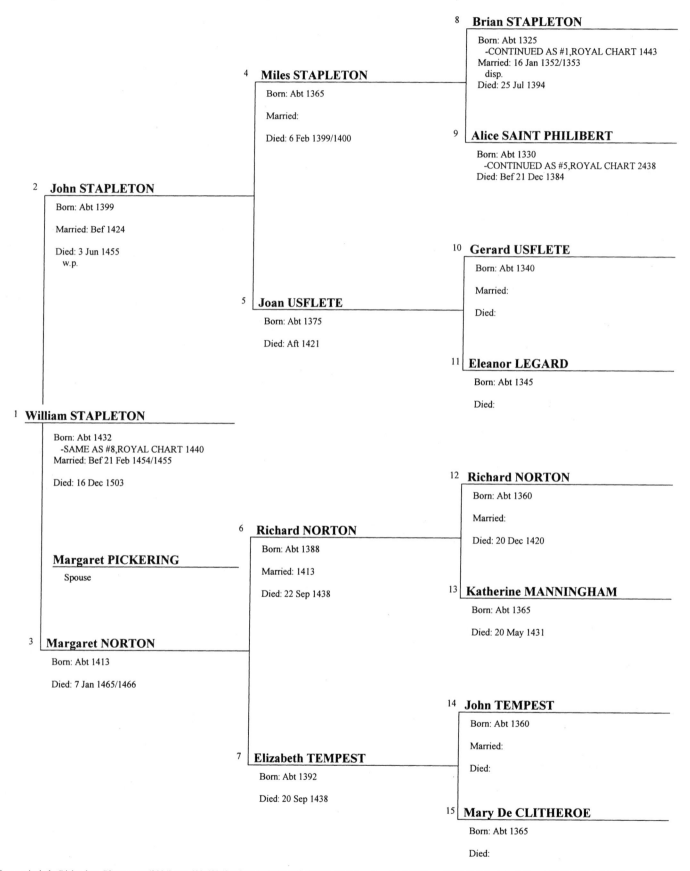

8 Brian STAPLETON

Born: Abt 1325
  -CONTINUED AS #1,ROYAL CHART 1443
Married: 16 Jan 1352/1353
  disp.
Died: 25 Jul 1394

4 Miles STAPLETON

Born: Abt 1365

Married:

Died: 6 Feb 1399/1400

9 Alice SAINT PHILIBERT

Born: Abt 1330
  -CONTINUED AS #5,ROYAL CHART 2438
Died: Bef 21 Dec 1384

2 John STAPLETON

Born: Abt 1399

Married: Bef 1424

Died: 3 Jun 1455
  w.p.

10 Gerard USFLETE

Born: Abt 1340

Married:

Died:

5 Joan USFLETE

Born: Abt 1375

Died: Aft 1421

11 Eleanor LEGARD

Born: Abt 1345

Died:

1 William STAPLETON

Born: Abt 1432
  -SAME AS #8,ROYAL CHART 1440
Married: Bef 21 Feb 1454/1455

Died: 16 Dec 1503

12 Richard NORTON

Born: Abt 1360

Married:

Died: 20 Dec 1420

6 Richard NORTON

Born: Abt 1388

Married: 1413

Died: 22 Sep 1438

13 Katherine MANNINGHAM

Born: Abt 1365

Died: 20 May 1431

Margaret PICKERING

Spouse

3 Margaret NORTON

Born: Abt 1413

Died: 7 Jan 1465/1466

14 John TEMPEST

Born: Abt 1360

Married:

Died:

7 Elizabeth TEMPEST

Born: Abt 1392

Died: 20 Sep 1438

15 Mary De CLITHEROE

Born: Abt 1365

Died:

Sources include: Richardson *Plantagenet* (2004), pp. 682-683 (Stapleton); Faris preliminary baronial manuscript (1998), pp. 1443-44 (Stapleton); Paget (1957) 505:1-2; LDS records.

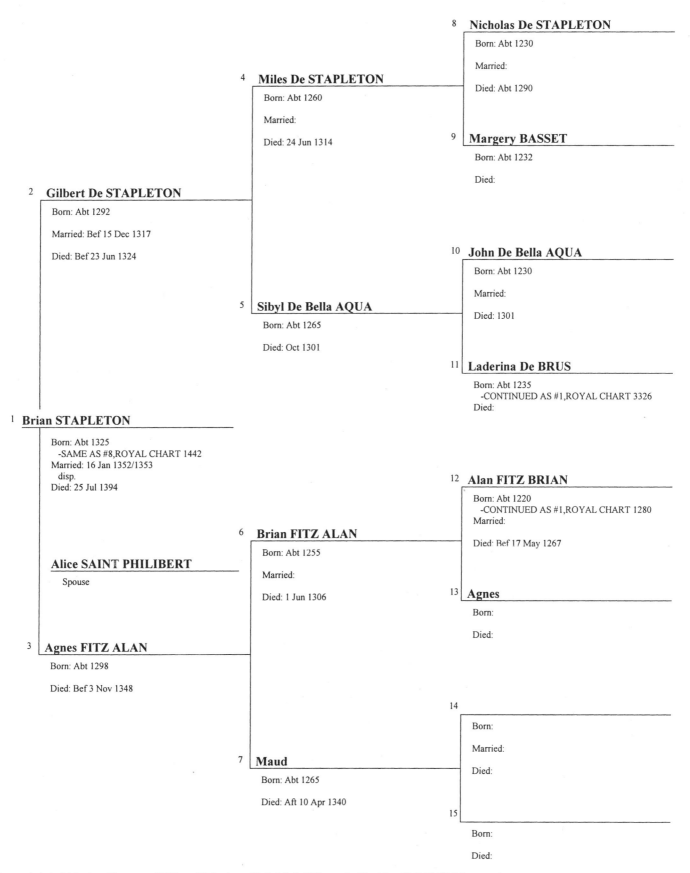

2 Gilbert De STAPLETON
Born: Abt 1292
Married: Bef 15 Dec 1317
Died: Bef 23 Jun 1324

4 Miles De STAPLETON
Born: Abt 1260
Married:
Died: 24 Jun 1314

8 Nicholas De STAPLETON
Born: Abt 1230
Married:
Died: Abt 1290

9 Margery BASSET
Born: Abt 1232
Died:

5 Sibyl De Bella AQUA
Born: Abt 1265
Died: Oct 1301

10 John De Bella AQUA
Born: Abt 1230
Married:
Died: 1301

11 Laderina De BRUS
Born: Abt 1235
-CONTINUED AS #1,ROYAL CHART 3326
Died:

1 Brian STAPLETON
Born: Abt 1325
-SAME AS #8,ROYAL CHART 1442
Married: 16 Jan 1352/1353
disp.
Died: 25 Jul 1394

Alice SAINT PHILIBERT
Spouse

3 Agnes FITZ ALAN
Born: Abt 1298
Died: Bef 3 Nov 1348

6 Brian FITZ ALAN
Born: Abt 1255
Married:
Died: 1 Jun 1306

12 Alan FITZ BRIAN
Born: Abt 1220
-CONTINUED AS #1,ROYAL CHART 1280
Married:
Died: Bef 17 May 1267

13 Agnes
Born:
Died:

7 Maud
Born: Abt 1265
Died: Aft 10 Apr 1340

14
Born:
Married:
Died:

15
Born:
Died:

Sources include: Richardson *Plantagenet* (2004), p. 682 Stapleton (#1, 2, 3 & 6); LDS records; *Blood Royal* 5:70-73 (#2 & 3 ancestry).

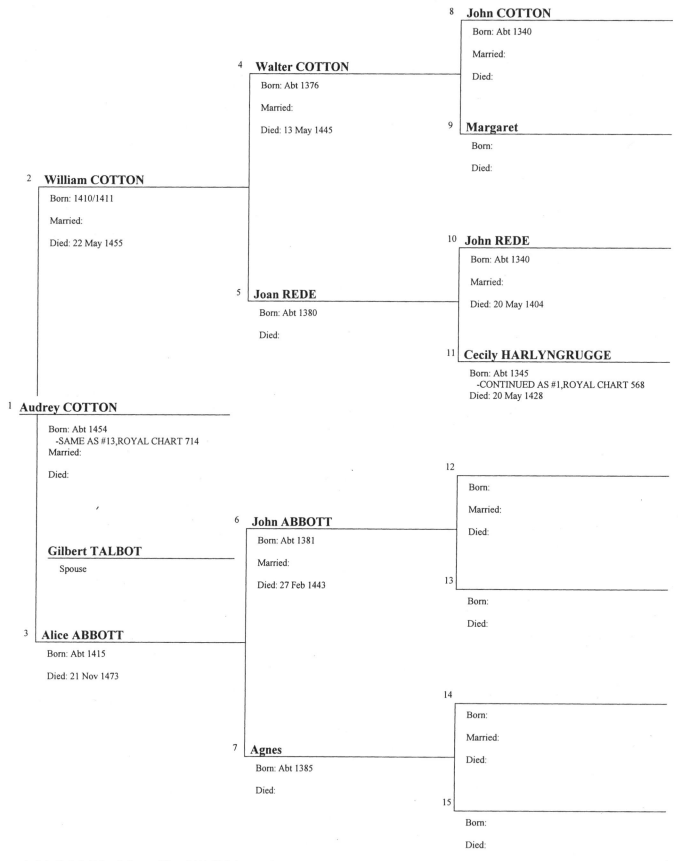

8 **John COTTON**

Born: Abt 1340

Married:

Died:

4 **Walter COTTON**

Born: Abt 1376

Married:

Died: 13 May 1445

9 **Margaret**

Born:

Died:

2 **William COTTON**

Born: 1410/1411

Married:

Died: 22 May 1455

10 **John REDE**

Born: Abt 1340

Married:

Died: 20 May 1404

5 **Joan REDE**

Born: Abt 1380

Died:

11 **Cecily HARLYNGRUGGE**

Born: Abt 1345
-CONTINUED AS #1,ROYAL CHART 568
Died: 20 May 1428

1 **Audrey COTTON**

Born: Abt 1454
-SAME AS #13,ROYAL CHART 714
Married:

Died:

12

Born:

Married:

Died:

6 **John ABBOTT**

Born: Abt 1381

Married:

Died: 27 Feb 1443

13

Born:

Died:

Gilbert TALBOT

Spouse

3 **Alice ABBOTT**

Born: Abt 1415

Died: 21 Nov 1473

14

Born:

Married:

Died:

7 **Agnes**

Born: Abt 1385

Died:

15

Born:

Died:

Sources include: Faris 2--Talbot 5; *Ancestral Roots* 246A (#2 & 3 ancestry).

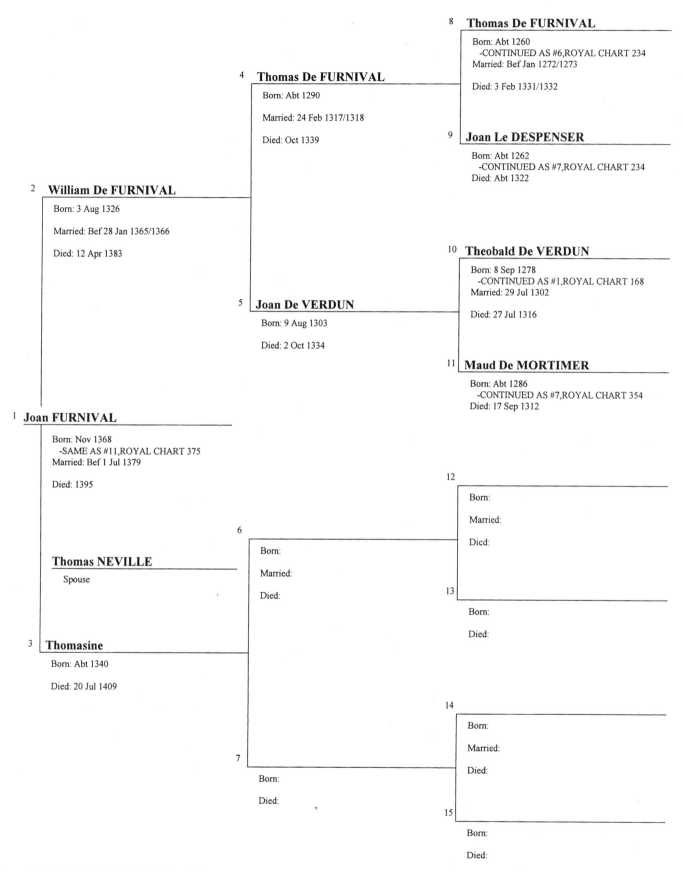

8 **Thomas De FURNIVAL**

Born: Abt 1260
-CONTINUED AS #6,ROYAL CHART 234
Married: Bef Jan 1272/1273

Died: 3 Feb 1331/1332

4 **Thomas De FURNIVAL**

Born: Abt 1290

Married: 24 Feb 1317/1318

Died: Oct 1339

9 **Joan Le DESPENSER**

Born: Abt 1262
-CONTINUED AS #7,ROYAL CHART 234
Died: Abt 1322

2 **William De FURNIVAL**

Born: 3 Aug 1326

Married: Bef 28 Jan 1365/1366

Died: 12 Apr 1383

10 **Theobald De VERDUN**

Born: 8 Sep 1278
-CONTINUED AS #1,ROYAL CHART 168
Married: 29 Jul 1302

Died: 27 Jul 1316

5 **Joan De VERDUN**

Born: 9 Aug 1303

Died: 2 Oct 1334

11 **Maud De MORTIMER**

Born: Abt 1286
-CONTINUED AS #7,ROYAL CHART 354
Died: 17 Sep 1312

1 **Joan FURNIVAL**

Born: Nov 1368
-SAME AS #11,ROYAL CHART 375
Married: Bef 1 Jul 1379

Died: 1395

12

Born:

Married:

Died:

6

Born:

Married:

Died:

13

Born:

Died:

Thomas NEVILLE

Spouse

3 **Thomasine**

Born: Abt 1340

Died: 20 Jul 1409

14

Born:

Married:

Died:

7

Born:

Died:

15

Born:

Died:

Sources include: Faris 2--Talbot 7 (#1 & 2); Vernon M. Norr, *Some Early English Pedigrees*, pp. 71-72; LDS records; *Ancestral Roots* 148A (#8 & 9 ancestry).

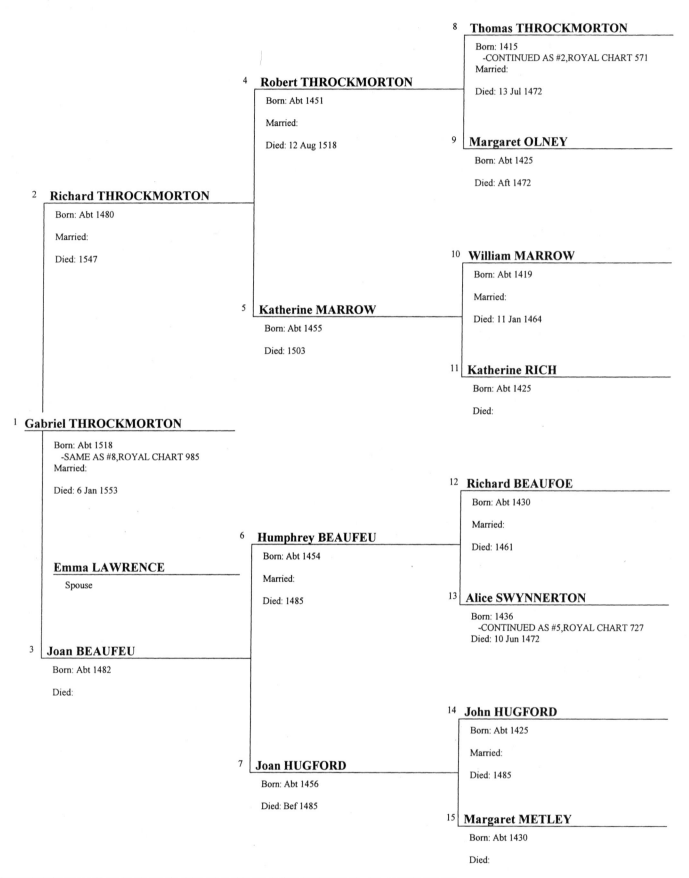

8 Thomas THROCKMORTON

Born: 1415
-CONTINUED AS #2,ROYAL CHART 571
Married:

Died: 13 Jul 1472

4 Robert THROCKMORTON

Born: Abt 1451

Married:

Died: 12 Aug 1518

9 Margaret OLNEY

Born: Abt 1425

Died: Aft 1472

2 Richard THROCKMORTON

Born: Abt 1480

Married:

Died: 1547

10 William MARROW

Born: Abt 1419

Married:

Died: 11 Jan 1464

5 Katherine MARROW

Born: Abt 1455

Died: 1503

11 Katherine RICH

Born: Abt 1425

Died:

1 Gabriel THROCKMORTON

Born: Abt 1518
-SAME AS #8,ROYAL CHART 985
Married:

Died: 6 Jan 1553

12 Richard BEAUFOE

Born: Abt 1430

Married:

Died: 1461

6 Humphrey BEAUFEU

Born: Abt 1454

Married:

Died: 1485

13 Alice SWYNNERTON

Born: 1436
-CONTINUED AS #5,ROYAL CHART 727
Died: 10 Jun 1472

Emma LAWRENCE

Spouse

3 Joan BEAUFEU

Born: Abt 1482

Died:

14 John HUGFORD

Born: Abt 1425

Married:

Died: 1485

7 Joan HUGFORD

Born: Abt 1456

Died: Bef 1485

15 Margaret METLEY

Born: Abt 1430

Died:

Sources include: *Magna Charta* 8B-18; *Maryland Genealogical Society Bulletin* 31:137-153; *Blood Royal* 5:883, 975-976.

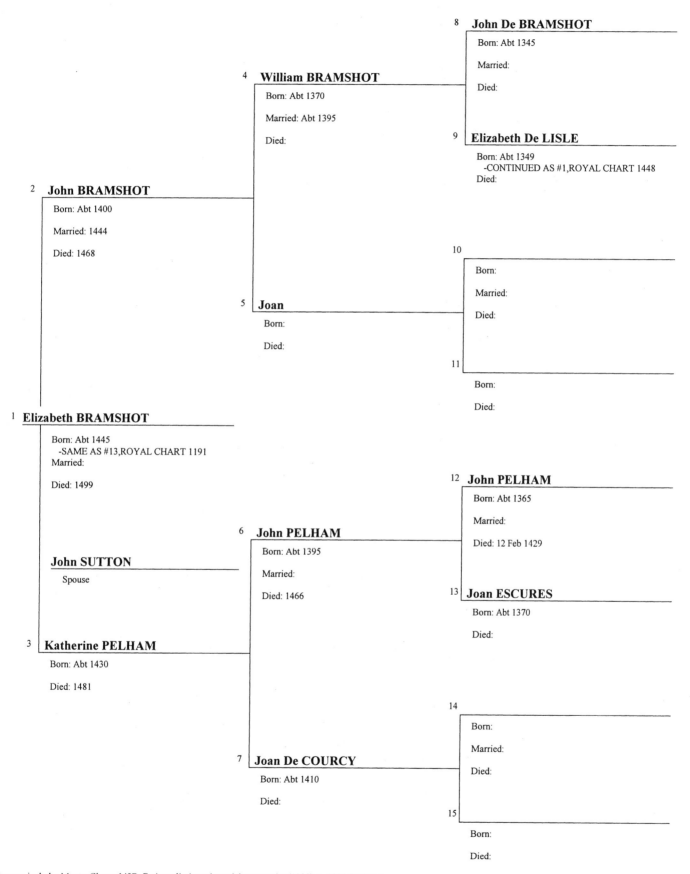

8 John De BRAMSHOT
Born: Abt 1345
Married:
Died:

4 William BRAMSHOT
Born: Abt 1370
Married: Abt 1395
Died:

9 Elizabeth De LISLE
Born: Abt 1349
-CONTINUED AS #1,ROYAL CHART 1448
Died:

2 John BRAMSHOT
Born: Abt 1400
Married: 1444
Died: 1468

10
Born:
Married:
Died:

5 Joan
Born:
Died:

11
Born:
Died:

1 Elizabeth BRAMSHOT
Born: Abt 1445
-SAME AS #13,ROYAL CHART 1191
Married:
Died: 1499

12 John PELHAM
Born: Abt 1365
Married:
Died: 12 Feb 1429

6 John PELHAM
Born: Abt 1395
Married:
Died: 1466

13 Joan ESCURES
Born: Abt 1370
Died:

John SUTTON
Spouse

3 Katherine PELHAM
Born: Abt 1430
Died: 1481

14
Born:
Married:
Died:

7 Joan De COURCY
Born: Abt 1410
Died:

15
Born:
Died:

Sources include: *Magna Charta* 149B; Faris preliminary baronial manuscript (1998), p. 1224 (Pelham).

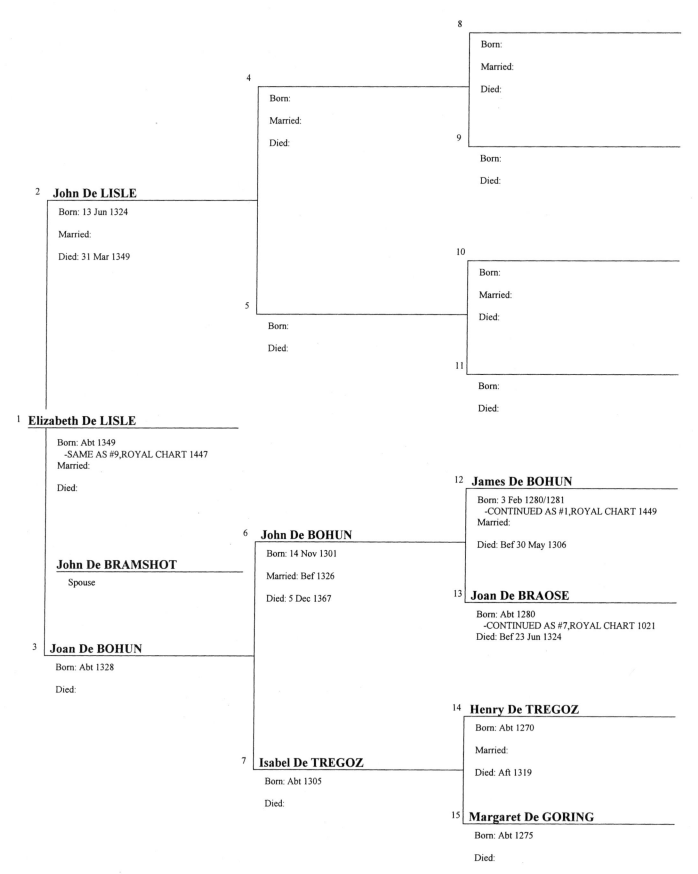

8

Born:

Married:

Died:

4

Born:

Married:

Died:

9

Born:

Died:

2 **John De LISLE**

Born: 13 Jun 1324

Married:

Died: 31 Mar 1349

10

Born:

Married:

Died:

5

Born:

Died:

11

Born:

Died:

1 **Elizabeth De LISLE**

Born: Abt 1349
-SAME AS #9,ROYAL CHART 1447
Married:

Died:

12 **James De BOHUN**

Born: 3 Feb 1280/1281
-CONTINUED AS #1,ROYAL CHART 1449
Married:

Died: Bef 30 May 1306

6 **John De BOHUN**

Born: 14 Nov 1301

Married: Bef 1326

Died: 5 Dec 1367

13 **Joan De BRAOSE**

Born: Abt 1280
-CONTINUED AS #7,ROYAL CHART 1021
Died: Bef 23 Jun 1324

John De BRAMSHOT

Spouse

3 **Joan De BOHUN**

Born: Abt 1328

Died:

14 **Henry De TREGOZ**

Born: Abt 1270

Married:

Died: Aft 1319

7 **Isabel De TREGOZ**

Born: Abt 1305

Died:

15 **Margaret De GORING**

Born: Abt 1275

Died:

Sources include: *Magna Charta* 149B; LDS records (#7 ancestry).

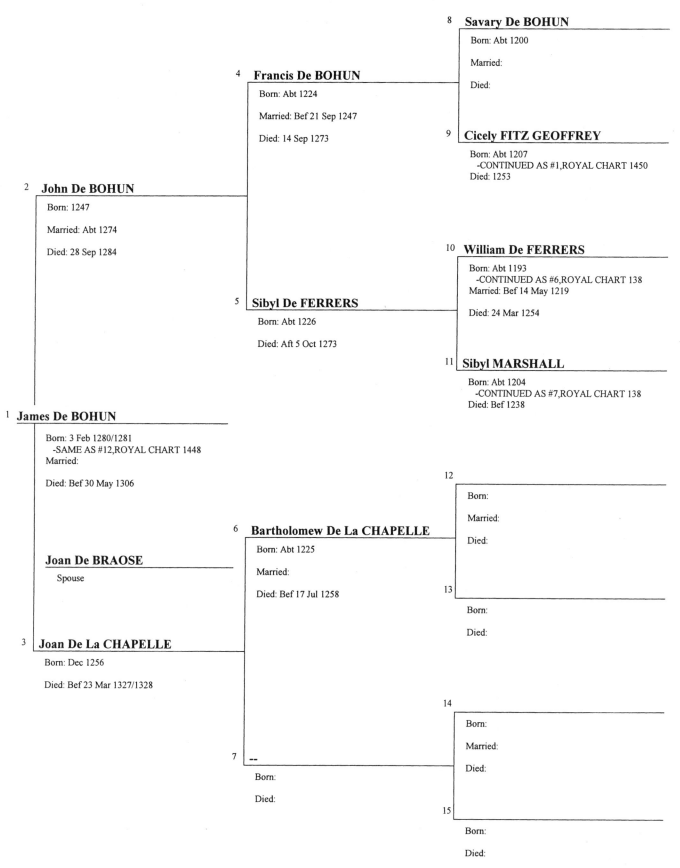

8 **Savary De BOHUN**
- Born: Abt 1200
- Married:
- Died:

4 **Francis De BOHUN**
- Born: Abt 1224
- Married: Bef 21 Sep 1247
- Died: 14 Sep 1273

9 **Cicely FITZ GEOFFREY**
- Born: Abt 1207
  -CONTINUED AS #1,ROYAL CHART 1450
- Died: 1253

2 **John De BOHUN**
- Born: 1247
- Married: Abt 1274
- Died: 28 Sep 1284

10 **William De FERRERS**
- Born: Abt 1193
  -CONTINUED AS #6,ROYAL CHART 138
- Married: Bef 14 May 1219
- Died: 24 Mar 1254

5 **Sibyl De FERRERS**
- Born: Abt 1226
- Died: Aft 5 Oct 1273

11 **Sibyl MARSHALL**
- Born: Abt 1204
  -CONTINUED AS #7,ROYAL CHART 138
- Died: Bef 1238

1 **James De BOHUN**
- Born: 3 Feb 1280/1281
  -SAME AS #12,ROYAL CHART 1448
- Married:
- Died: Bef 30 May 1306

12
- Born:
- Married:
- Died:

6 **Bartholomew De La CHAPELLE**
- Born: Abt 1225
- Married:
- Died: Bef 17 Jul 1258

13
- Born:
- Died:

Joan De BRAOSE
- Spouse

3 **Joan De La CHAPELLE**
- Born: Dec 1256
- Died: Bef 23 Mar 1327/1328

14
- Born:
- Married:
- Died:

7 **--**
- Born:
- Died:

15
- Born:
- Died:

Sources include: *Magna Charta* 149B; *Ancestral Roots* 127 (#10 & 11).

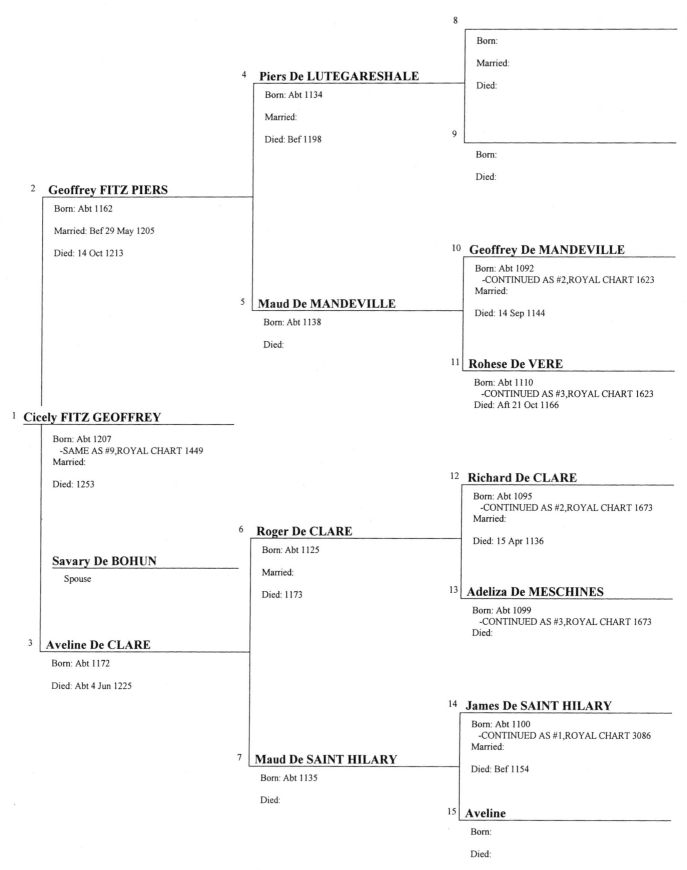

8

Piers De LUTEGARESHALE
4

Born:
Married:
Died:

Born: Abt 1134

Married:

Died: Bef 1198

9

Born:

Died:

2 **Geoffrey FITZ PIERS**

Born: Abt 1162

Married: Bef 29 May 1205

Died: 14 Oct 1213

10 **Geoffrey De MANDEVILLE**

Born: Abt 1092
  -CONTINUED AS #2,ROYAL CHART 1623
Married:

Died: 14 Sep 1144

5 **Maud De MANDEVILLE**

Born: Abt 1138

Died:

11 **Rohese De VERE**

Born: Abt 1110
  -CONTINUED AS #3,ROYAL CHART 1623
Died: Aft 21 Oct 1166

1 **Cicely FITZ GEOFFREY**

Born: Abt 1207
  -SAME AS #9,ROYAL CHART 1449
Married:

Died: 1253

12 **Richard De CLARE**

Born: Abt 1095
  -CONTINUED AS #2,ROYAL CHART 1673
Married:

Died: 15 Apr 1136

6 **Roger De CLARE**

Born: Abt 1125

Married:

Died: 1173

Savary De BOHUN

Spouse

13 **Adeliza De MESCHINES**

Born: Abt 1099
  -CONTINUED AS #3,ROYAL CHART 1673
Died:

3 **Aveline De CLARE**

Born: Abt 1172

Died: Abt 4 Jun 1225

14 **James De SAINT HILARY**

Born: Abt 1100
  -CONTINUED AS #1,ROYAL CHART 3086
Married:

Died: Bef 1154

7 **Maud De SAINT HILARY**

Born: Abt 1135

Died:

15 **Aveline**

Born:

Died:

Sources include: *Magna Charta* 149B-12; *Royal Ancestors* (1989), chart 11358 (#2 & 3 ancestry).

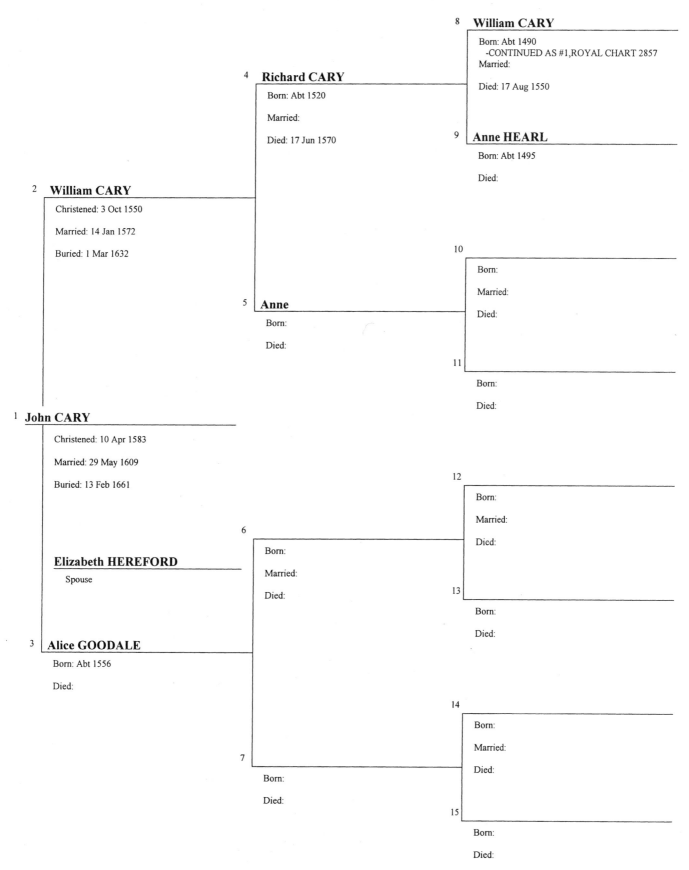

8 William CARY

Born: Abt 1490
   -CONTINUED AS #1,ROYAL CHART 2857
Married:

Died: 17 Aug 1550

4 Richard CARY

Born: Abt 1520

Married:

Died: 17 Jun 1570

9 Anne HEARL

Born: Abt 1495

Died:

2 William CARY

Christened: 3 Oct 1550

Married: 14 Jan 1572

Buried: 1 Mar 1632

10

Born:

Married:

Died:

5 Anne

Born:

Died:

11

Born:

Died:

1 John CARY

Christened: 10 Apr 1583

Married: 29 May 1609

Buried: 13 Feb 1661

12

Born:

Married:

Died:

6

Born:

Married:

Died:

Elizabeth HEREFORD

Spouse

13

Born:

Died:

3 Alice GOODALE

Born: Abt 1556

Died:

14

Born:

Married:

Died:

7

Born:

Died:

15

Born:

Died:

Sources include: Roberts *500* (600) updated manuscript (Novermber 2000), tentative section pp. 1-2. Notes: #1 John & Elizabeth may have been parents of John Cary (b. abt 1610; md. Elizabeth Godfrey) of MA, who left American and MPGL descendants. #1 John & Elizabeth had a son Thomas Cary (b. abt 1613; md. Susanna Limberey), father of John Cary (b. abt 1642, md. Jane Flood), father of Mary Cary (b. abt 1684; md. Nathaniel Harrison) of VA. #1 John also had a 2nd wife Alice Hobson by whom he had a son Miles Cary (chr. 30 Jan 1622; md. Anne Taylor) of VA. #2 & 3 William & Alice had another son James Cary (chr. 14 Apr 1600; md. Eleanor) of MA, who left American and MPGL descendants.

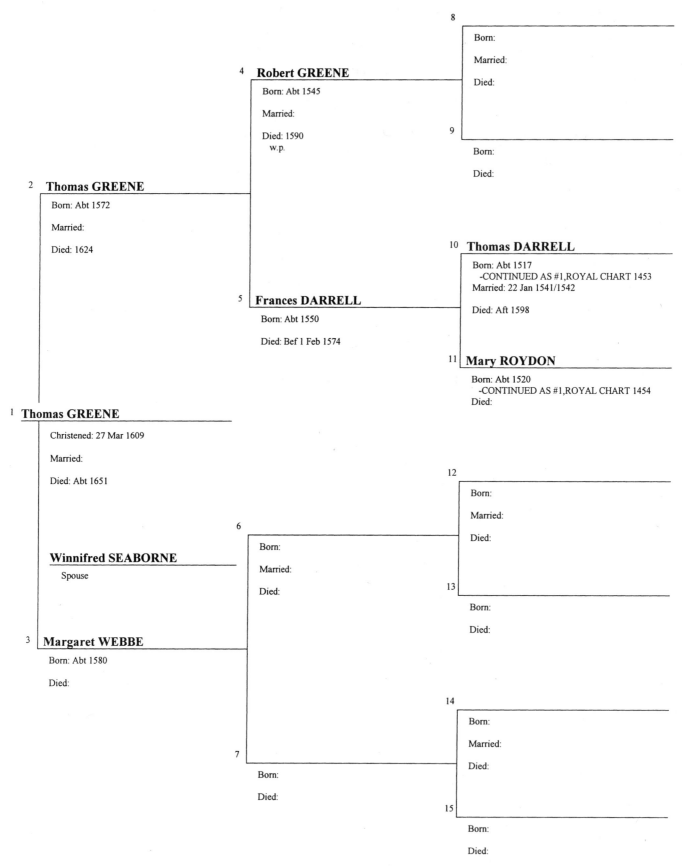

8

Born:

Married:

Died:

4   **Robert GREENE**

Born: Abt 1545

Married:

Died: 1590
w.p.

9

Born:

Died:

2   **Thomas GREENE**

Born: Abt 1572

Married:

Died: 1624

10   **Thomas DARRELL**

Born: Abt 1517
-CONTINUED AS #1,ROYAL CHART 1453
Married: 22 Jan 1541/1542

Died: Aft 1598

5   **Frances DARRELL**

Born: Abt 1550

Died: Bef 1 Feb 1574

11   **Mary ROYDON**

Born: Abt 1520
-CONTINUED AS #1,ROYAL CHART 1454
Died:

1   **Thomas GREENE**

Christened: 27 Mar 1609

Married:

Died: Abt 1651

12

Born:

Married:

Died:

6

Born:

Married:

Died:

Winnifred SEABORNE
Spouse

13

Born:

Died:

3   **Margaret WEBBE**

Born: Abt 1580

Died:

14

Born:

Married:

Died:

7

Born:

Died:

15

Born:

Died:

Sources include: *Magna Charta* 16 E.

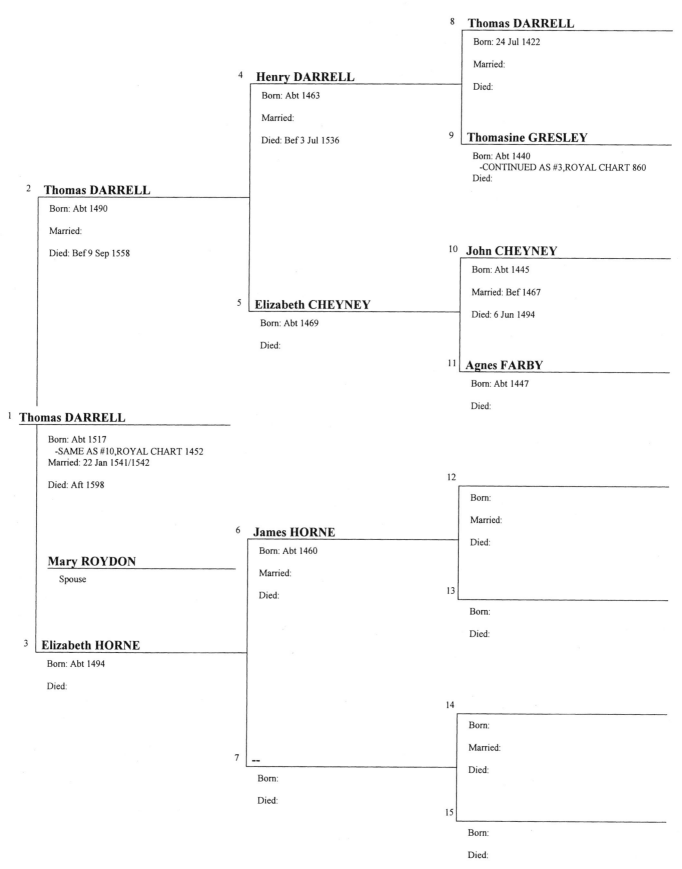

8   **Thomas DARRELL**

Born: 24 Jul 1422

Married:

Died:

4   **Henry DARRELL**

Born: Abt 1463

Married:

Died: Bef 3 Jul 1536

9   **Thomasine GRESLEY**

Born: Abt 1440
    -CONTINUED AS #3, ROYAL CHART 860
Died:

2   **Thomas DARRELL**

Born: Abt 1490

Married:

Died: Bef 9 Sep 1558

10   **John CHEYNEY**

Born: Abt 1445

Married: Bef 1467

Died: 6 Jun 1494

5   **Elizabeth CHEYNEY**

Born: Abt 1469

Died:

11   **Agnes FARBY**

Born: Abt 1447

Died:

1   **Thomas DARRELL**

Born: Abt 1517
    -SAME AS #10, ROYAL CHART 1452
Married: 22 Jan 1541/1542

Died: Aft 1598

Mary ROYDON

Spouse

12

Born:

Married:

Died:

6   **James HORNE**

Born: Abt 1460

Married:

Died:

13

Born:

Died:

3   **Elizabeth HORNE**

Born: Abt 1494

Died:

14

Born:

Married:

Died:

7   **--**

Born:

Died:

15

Born:

Died:

Sources include: LDS records.

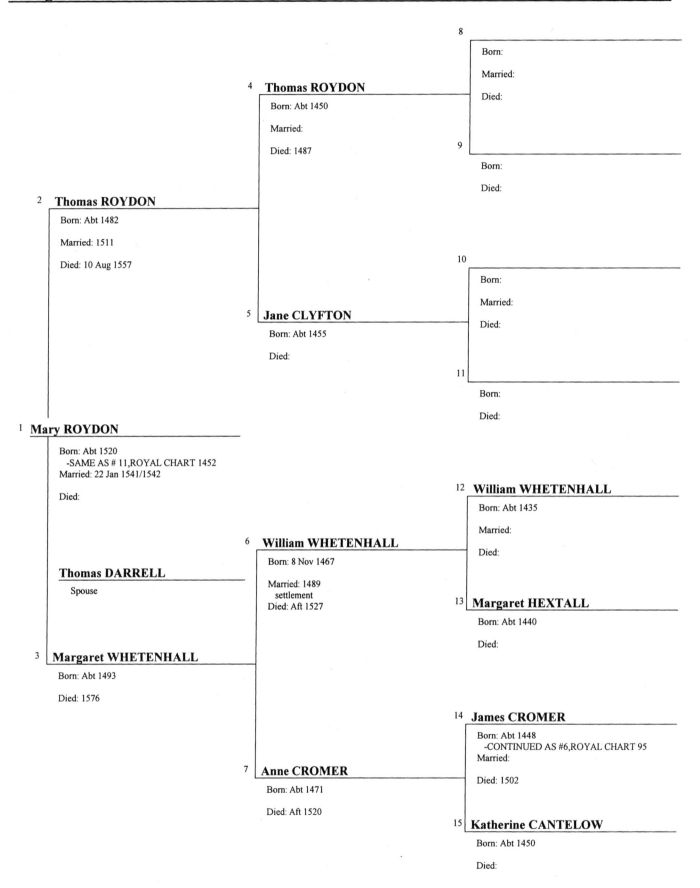

8

Born:

Married:

Died:

4 Thomas ROYDON

Born: Abt 1450

Married:

Died: 1487

9

Born:

Died:

2 Thomas ROYDON

Born: Abt 1482

Married: 1511

Died: 10 Aug 1557

10

Born:

Married:

Died:

5 Jane CLYFTON

Born: Abt 1455

Died:

11

Born:

Died:

1 Mary ROYDON

Born: Abt 1520
   -SAME AS # 11,ROYAL CHART 1452
Married: 22 Jan 1541/1542

Died:

12 William WHETENHALL

Born: Abt 1435

Married:

Died:

6 William WHETENHALL

Born: 8 Nov 1467

Married: 1489
   settlement
Died: Aft 1527

13 Margaret HEXTALL

Born: Abt 1440

Died:

Thomas DARRELL

Spouse

3 Margaret WHETENHALL

Born: Abt 1493

Died: 1576

14 James CROMER

Born: Abt 1448
   -CONTINUED AS #6,ROYAL CHART 95
Married:

Died: 1502

7 Anne CROMER

Born: Abt 1471

Died: Aft 1520

15 Katherine CANTELOW

Born: Abt 1450

Died:

Sources include: Consultation with Douglas Richardson; *Magna Charta* 16 E; LDS records; Roberts *500*, p. 430 (#7 ancestry).

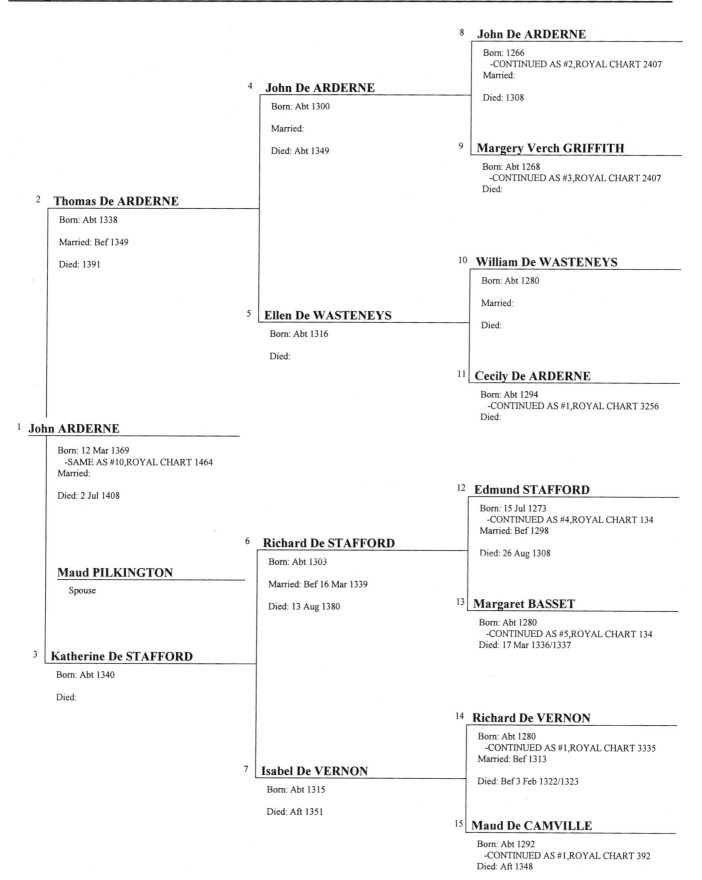

8 **John De ARDERNE**

Born: 1266
  -CONTINUED AS #2,ROYAL CHART 2407
Married:

Died: 1308

4 **John De ARDERNE**

Born: Abt 1300

Married:

Died: Abt 1349

9 **Margery Verch GRIFFITH**

Born: Abt 1268
  -CONTINUED AS #3,ROYAL CHART 2407
Died:

2 **Thomas De ARDERNE**

Born: Abt 1338

Married: Bef 1349

Died: 1391

10 **William De WASTENEYS**

Born: Abt 1280

Married:

Died:

5 **Ellen De WASTENEYS**

Born: Abt 1316

Died:

11 **Cecily De ARDERNE**

Born: Abt 1294
  -CONTINUED AS #1,ROYAL CHART 3256
Died:

1 **John ARDERNE**

Born: 12 Mar 1369
  -SAME AS #10,ROYAL CHART 1464
Married:

Died: 2 Jul 1408

12 **Edmund STAFFORD**

Born: 15 Jul 1273
  -CONTINUED AS #4,ROYAL CHART 134
Married: Bef 1298

Died: 26 Aug 1308

6 **Richard De STAFFORD**

Born: Abt 1303

Married: Bef 16 Mar 1339

Died: 13 Aug 1380

Maud PILKINGTON

Spouse

13 **Margaret BASSET**

Born: Abt 1280
  -CONTINUED AS #5,ROYAL CHART 134
Died: 17 Mar 1336/1337

3 **Katherine De STAFFORD**

Born: Abt 1340

Died:

14 **Richard De VERNON**

Born: Abt 1280
  -CONTINUED AS #1,ROYAL CHART 3335
Married: Bef 1313

Died: Bef 3 Feb 1322/1323

7 **Isabel De VERNON**

Born: Abt 1315

Died: Aft 1351

15 **Maud De CAMVILLE**

Born: Abt 1292
  -CONTINUED AS #1,ROYAL CHART 392
Died: Aft 1348

Sources include: Faris-Richardson preliminary Magna Carta manuscript (June 2000), pp. 4-6 (Arderne); Faris preliminary baronial manuscript (1998), p. 1628 (Wasteneys); LDS records.

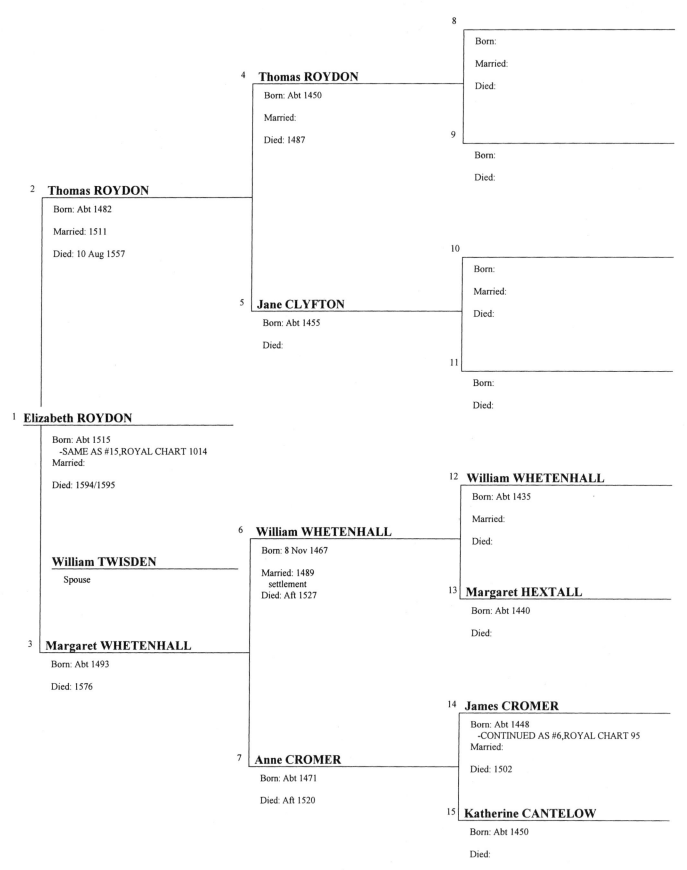

8

Born:

Married:

Died:

4 Thomas ROYDON

Born: Abt 1450

Married:

Died: 1487

9

Born:

Died:

2 Thomas ROYDON

Born: Abt 1482

Married: 1511

Died: 10 Aug 1557

10

Born:

Married:

Died:

5 Jane CLYFTON

Born: Abt 1455

Died:

11

Born:

Died:

1 Elizabeth ROYDON

Born: Abt 1515
-SAME AS #15,ROYAL CHART 1014
Married:

Died: 1594/1595

12 William WHETENHALL

Born: Abt 1435

Married:

Died:

6 William WHETENHALL

Born: 8 Nov 1467

Married: 1489
settlement
Died: Aft 1527

13 Margaret HEXTALL

Born: Abt 1440

Died:

William TWISDEN

Spouse

3 Margaret WHETENHALL

Born: Abt 1493

Died: 1576

14 James CROMER

Born: Abt 1448
-CONTINUED AS #6,ROYAL CHART 95
Married:

Died: 1502

7 Anne CROMER

Born: Abt 1471

Died: Aft 1520

15 Katherine CANTELOW

Born: Abt 1450

Died:

Sources include: Consultation with Douglas Richardson; *Magna Charta* 16E (#2 & 3 ancestry); LDS records.

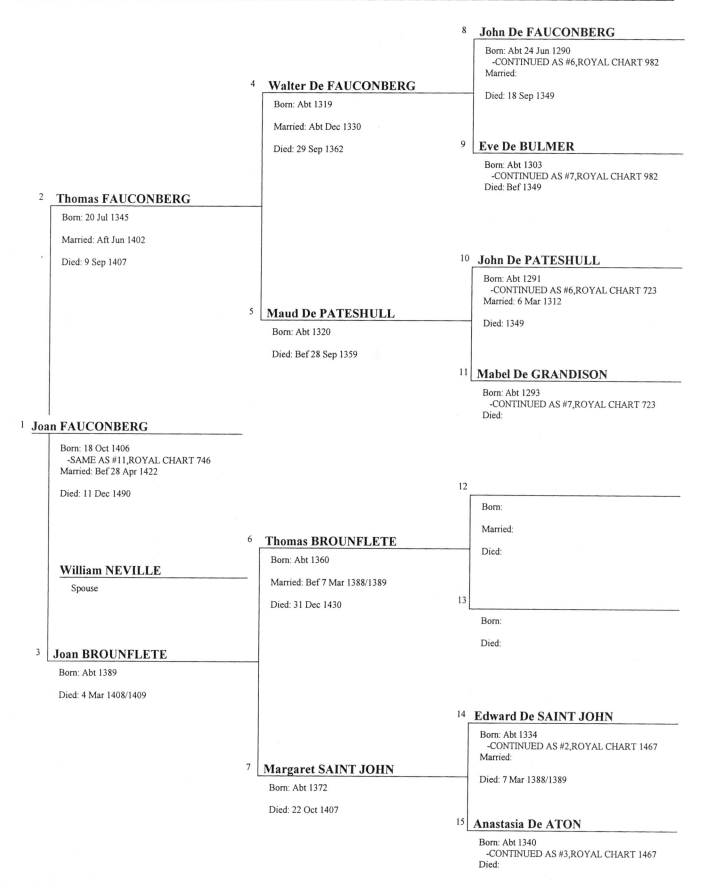

8 John De FAUCONBERG
Born: Abt 24 Jun 1290
-CONTINUED AS #6,ROYAL CHART 982
Married:

Died: 18 Sep 1349

4 Walter De FAUCONBERG
Born: Abt 1319

Married: Abt Dec 1330

Died: 29 Sep 1362

9 Eve De BULMER
Born: Abt 1303
-CONTINUED AS #7,ROYAL CHART 982
Died: Bef 1349

2 Thomas FAUCONBERG
Born: 20 Jul 1345

Married: Aft Jun 1402

Died: 9 Sep 1407

10 John De PATESHULL
Born: Abt 1291
-CONTINUED AS #6,ROYAL CHART 723
Married: 6 Mar 1312

Died: 1349

5 Maud De PATESHULL
Born: Abt 1320

Died: Bef 28 Sep 1359

11 Mabel De GRANDISON
Born: Abt 1293
-CONTINUED AS #7,ROYAL CHART 723
Died:

1 Joan FAUCONBERG
Born: 18 Oct 1406
-SAME AS #11,ROYAL CHART 746
Married: Bef 28 Apr 1422

Died: 11 Dec 1490

12
Born:

Married:

Died:

6 Thomas BROUNFLETE
Born: Abt 1360

Married: Bef 7 Mar 1388/1389

Died: 31 Dec 1430

13
Born:

Died:

William NEVILLE
Spouse

3 Joan BROUNFLETE
Born: Abt 1389

Died: 4 Mar 1408/1409

14 Edward De SAINT JOHN
Born: Abt 1334
-CONTINUED AS #2,ROYAL CHART 1467
Married:

Died: 7 Mar 1388/1389

7 Margaret SAINT JOHN
Born: Abt 1372

Died: 22 Oct 1407

15 Anastasia De ATON
Born: Abt 1340
-CONTINUED AS #3,ROYAL CHART 1467
Died:

Sources include: *Complete Peerage* 5:271-287; 12 (part 2):285 (#14 & 15); Consultation with Douglas Richardson.

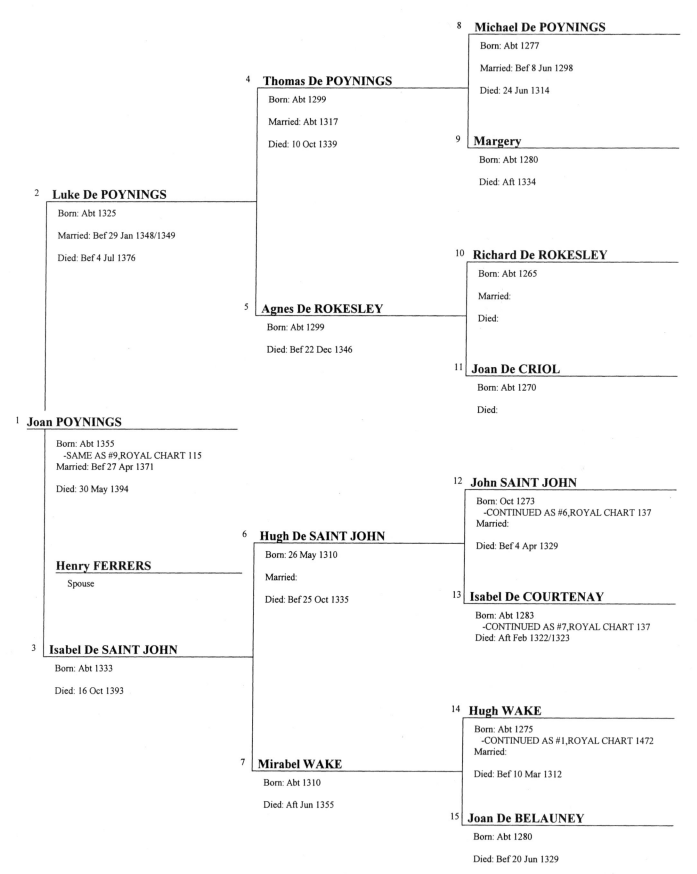

8 Michael De POYNINGS

Born: Abt 1277

Married: Bef 8 Jun 1298

Died: 24 Jun 1314

4 Thomas De POYNINGS

Born: Abt 1299

Married: Abt 1317

Died: 10 Oct 1339

9 Margery

Born: Abt 1280

Died: Aft 1334

2 Luke De POYNINGS

Born: Abt 1325

Married: Bef 29 Jan 1348/1349

Died: Bef 4 Jul 1376

10 Richard De ROKESLEY

Born: Abt 1265

Married:

Died:

5 Agnes De ROKESLEY

Born: Abt 1299

Died: Bef 22 Dec 1346

11 Joan De CRIOL

Born: Abt 1270

Died:

1 Joan POYNINGS

Born: Abt 1355
  -SAME AS #9,ROYAL CHART 115
Married: Bef 27 Apr 1371

Died: 30 May 1394

12 John SAINT JOHN

Born: Oct 1273
  -CONTINUED AS #6,ROYAL CHART 137
Married:

Died: Bef 4 Apr 1329

6 Hugh De SAINT JOHN

Born: 26 May 1310

Married:

Died: Bef 25 Oct 1335

13 Isabel De COURTENAY

Born: Abt 1283
  -CONTINUED AS #7,ROYAL CHART 137
Died: Aft Feb 1322/1323

Henry FERRERS

Spouse

3 Isabel De SAINT JOHN

Born: Abt 1333

Died: 16 Oct 1393

14 Hugh WAKE

Born: Abt 1275
  -CONTINUED AS #1,ROYAL CHART 1472
Married:

Died: Bef 10 Mar 1312

7 Mirabel WAKE

Born: Abt 1310

Died: Aft Jun 1355

15 Joan De BELAUNEY

Born: Abt 1280

Died: Bef 20 Jun 1329

Sources include: Faris 2--Clarke 8; Consultation with Douglas Richardson; *Complete Peerage* 10:665-668, 656-660; 11:325-330 (#2 & 3 ancestry).

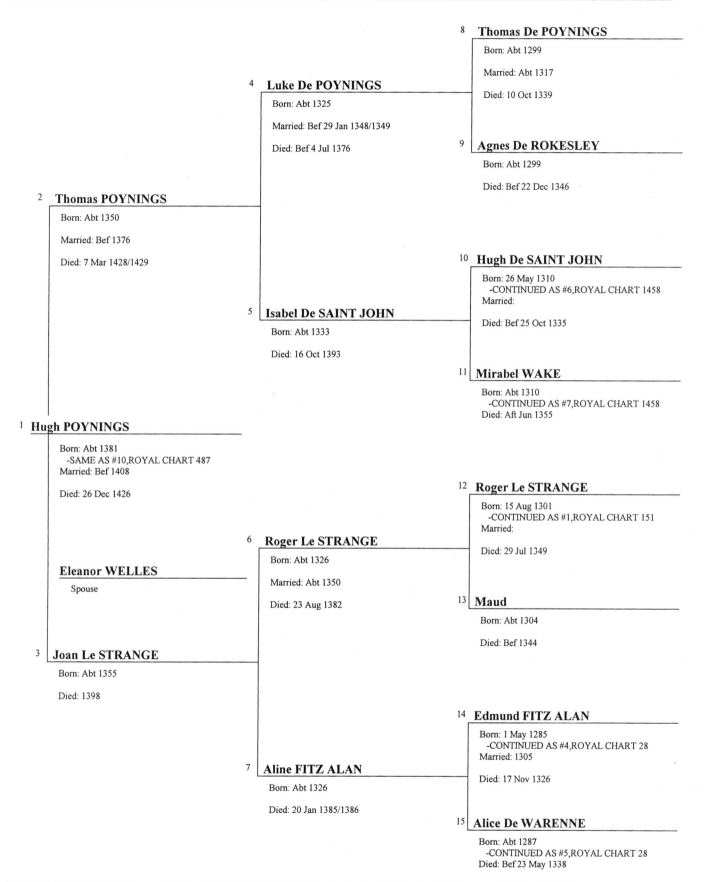

8 Thomas De POYNINGS

Born: Abt 1299

Married: Abt 1317

Died: 10 Oct 1339

4 Luke De POYNINGS

Born: Abt 1325

Married: Bef 29 Jan 1348/1349

Died: Bef 4 Jul 1376

9 Agnes De ROKESLEY

Born: Abt 1299

Died: Bef 22 Dec 1346

2 Thomas POYNINGS

Born: Abt 1350

Married: Bef 1376

Died: 7 Mar 1428/1429

10 Hugh De SAINT JOHN

Born: 26 May 1310
    -CONTINUED AS #6,ROYAL CHART 1458
Married:

Died: Bef 25 Oct 1335

5 Isabel De SAINT JOHN

Born: Abt 1333

Died: 16 Oct 1393

11 Mirabel WAKE

Born: Abt 1310
    -CONTINUED AS #7,ROYAL CHART 1458
Died: Aft Jun 1355

1 Hugh POYNINGS

Born: Abt 1381
    -SAME AS #10,ROYAL CHART 487
Married: Bef 1408

Died: 26 Dec 1426

12 Roger Le STRANGE

Born: 15 Aug 1301
    -CONTINUED AS #1,ROYAL CHART 151
Married:

Died: 29 Jul 1349

6 Roger Le STRANGE

Born: Abt 1326

Married: Abt 1350

Died: 23 Aug 1382

13 Maud

Born: Abt 1304

Died: Bef 1344

Eleanor WELLES

Spouse

3 Joan Le STRANGE

Born: Abt 1355

Died: 1398

14 Edmund FITZ ALAN

Born: 1 May 1285
    -CONTINUED AS #4,ROYAL CHART 28
Married: 1305

Died: 17 Nov 1326

7 Aline FITZ ALAN

Born: Abt 1326

Died: 20 Jan 1385/1386

15 Alice De WARENNE

Born: Abt 1287
    -CONTINUED AS #5,ROYAL CHART 28
Died: Bef 23 May 1338

Sources include: Richardson *Plantagenet* (2004), p. 569-571 (Paulet), 692-693 (Strange); Faris 2--Paulet 10; *Complete Peerage* 11:325-330, 10:665-668.

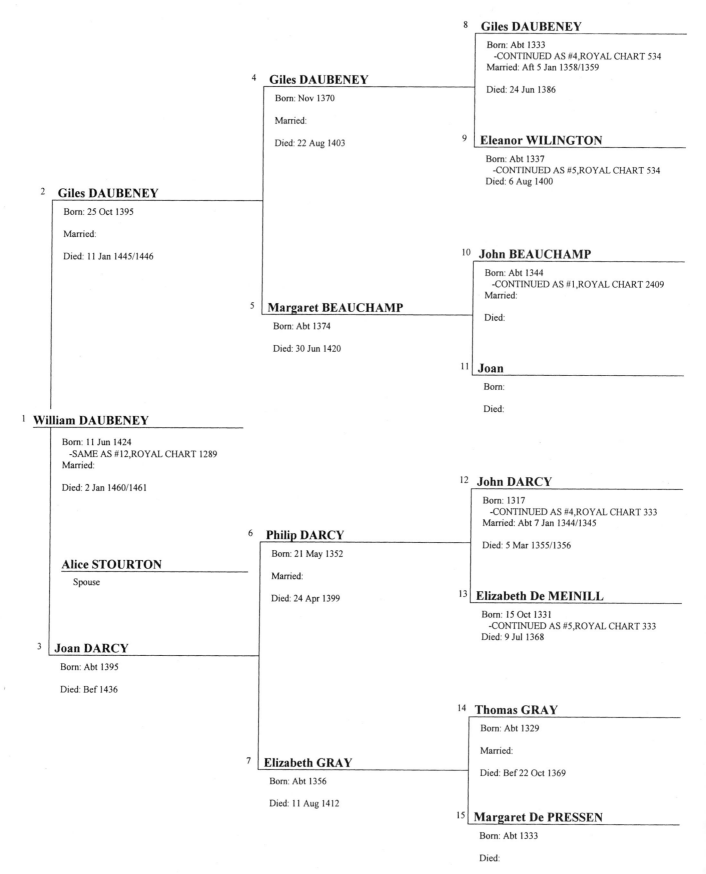

8 Giles DAUBENEY
Born: Abt 1333
 -CONTINUED AS #4,ROYAL CHART 534
Married: Aft 5 Jan 1358/1359

Died: 24 Jun 1386

4 Giles DAUBENEY
Born: Nov 1370

Married:

Died: 22 Aug 1403

9 Eleanor WILINGTON
Born: Abt 1337
 -CONTINUED AS #5,ROYAL CHART 534
Died: 6 Aug 1400

2 Giles DAUBENEY
Born: 25 Oct 1395

Married:

Died: 11 Jan 1445/1446

10 John BEAUCHAMP
Born: Abt 1344
 -CONTINUED AS #1,ROYAL CHART 2409
Married:

Died:

5 Margaret BEAUCHAMP
Born: Abt 1374

Died: 30 Jun 1420

11 Joan
Born:

Died:

1 William DAUBENEY
Born: 11 Jun 1424
 -SAME AS #12,ROYAL CHART 1289
Married:

Died: 2 Jan 1460/1461

12 John DARCY
Born: 1317
 -CONTINUED AS #4,ROYAL CHART 333
Married: Abt 7 Jan 1344/1345

Died: 5 Mar 1355/1356

6 Philip DARCY
Born: 21 May 1352

Married:

Died: 24 Apr 1399

13 Elizabeth De MEINILL
Born: 15 Oct 1331
 -CONTINUED AS #5,ROYAL CHART 333
Died: 9 Jul 1368

Alice STOURTON
Spouse

3 Joan DARCY
Born: Abt 1395

Died: Bef 1436

14 Thomas GRAY
Born: Abt 1329

Married:

Died: Bef 22 Oct 1369

7 Elizabeth GRAY
Born: Abt 1356

Died: 11 Aug 1412

15 Margaret De PRESSEN
Born: Abt 1333

Died:

Sources include: *Complete Peerage* 4:92-102.

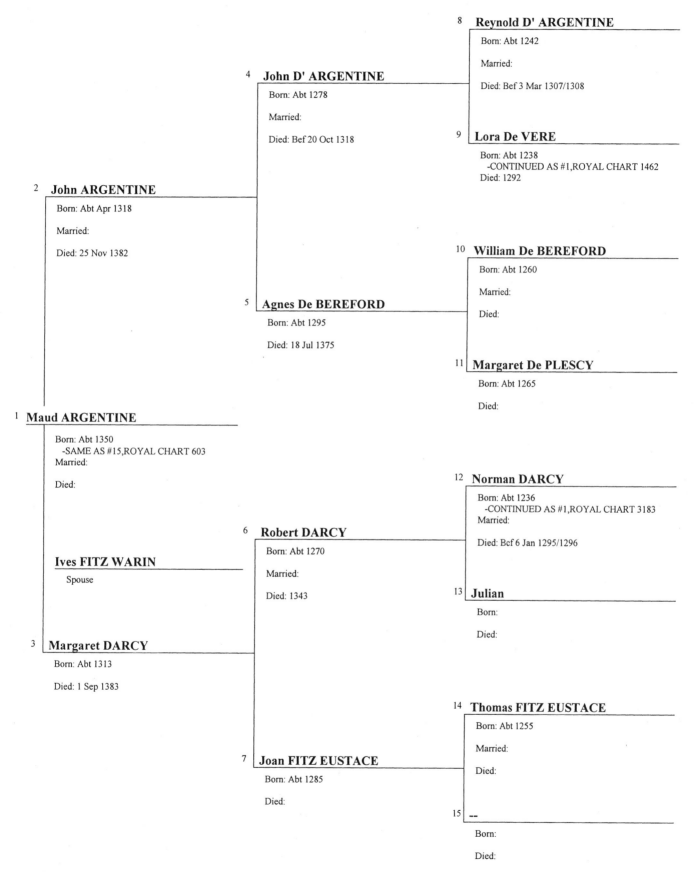

8 Reynold D' ARGENTINE

Born: Abt 1242

Married:

Died: Bef 3 Mar 1307/1308

4 John D' ARGENTINE

Born: Abt 1278

Married:

Died: Bef 20 Oct 1318

9 Lora De VERE

Born: Abt 1238
    -CONTINUED AS #1,ROYAL CHART 1462
Died: 1292

2 John ARGENTINE

Born: Abt Apr 1318

Married:

Died: 25 Nov 1382

10 William De BEREFORD

Born: Abt 1260

Married:

Died:

5 Agnes De BEREFORD

Born: Abt 1295

Died: 18 Jul 1375

11 Margaret De PLESCY

Born: Abt 1265

Died:

1 Maud ARGENTINE

Born: Abt 1350
    -SAME AS #15,ROYAL CHART 603
Married:

Died:

12 Norman DARCY

Born: Abt 1236
    -CONTINUED AS #1,ROYAL CHART 3183
Married:

Died: Bef 6 Jan 1295/1296

6 Robert DARCY

Born: Abt 1270

Married:

Died: 1343

13 Julian

Born:

Died:

Ives FITZ WARIN

Spouse

3 Margaret DARCY

Born: Abt 1313

Died: 1 Sep 1383

14 Thomas FITZ EUSTACE

Born: Abt 1255

Married:

Died:

7 Joan FITZ EUSTACE

Born: Abt 1285

Died:

15 --

Born:

Died:

Sources include: Faris-Richardson preliminary Magna Carta manuscript (June 2000), pp. 6-7 (Argentine); Faris preliminary baronial manuscript (1998), p. 467 (Darcy); *Complete Peerage* 1:196-197. Note: Ives (spouse of #1) is also called Ivo, Ioun or Eudes.

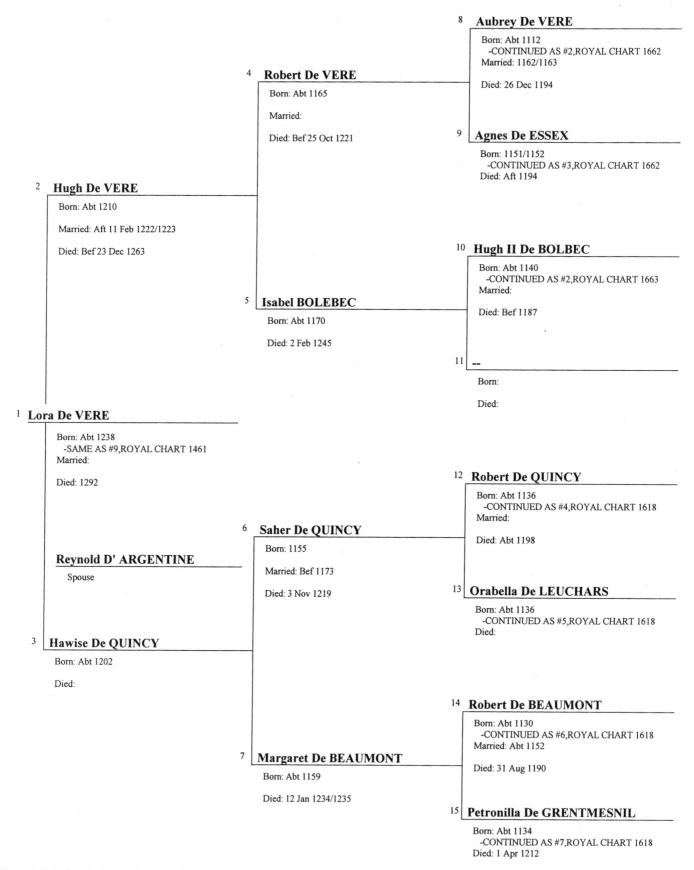

2 Hugh De VERE

Born: Abt 1210

Married: Aft 11 Feb 1222/1223

Died: Bef 23 Dec 1263

4 Robert De VERE

Born: Abt 1165

Married:

Died: Bef 25 Oct 1221

8 Aubrey De VERE

Born: Abt 1112
-CONTINUED AS #2,ROYAL CHART 1662
Married: 1162/1163

Died: 26 Dec 1194

9 Agnes De ESSEX

Born: 1151/1152
-CONTINUED AS #3,ROYAL CHART 1662
Died: Aft 1194

5 Isabel BOLEBEC

Born: Abt 1170

Died: 2 Feb 1245

10 Hugh II De BOLBEC

Born: Abt 1140
-CONTINUED AS #2,ROYAL CHART 1663
Married:

Died: Bef 1187

11 --

Born:

Died:

1 Lora De VERE

Born: Abt 1238
-SAME AS #9,ROYAL CHART 1461
Married:

Died: 1292

Reynold D' ARGENTINE

Spouse

3 Hawise De QUINCY

Born: Abt 1202

Died:

6 Saher De QUINCY

Born: 1155

Married: Bef 1173

Died: 3 Nov 1219

12 Robert De QUINCY

Born: Abt 1136
-CONTINUED AS #4,ROYAL CHART 1618
Married:

Died: Abt 1198

13 Orabella De LEUCHARS

Born: Abt 1136
-CONTINUED AS #5,ROYAL CHART 1618
Died:

7 Margaret De BEAUMONT

Born: Abt 1159

Died: 12 Jan 1234/1235

14 Robert De BEAUMONT

Born: Abt 1130
-CONTINUED AS #6,ROYAL CHART 1618
Married: Abt 1152

Died: 31 Aug 1190

15 Petronilla De GRENTMESNIL

Born: Abt 1134
-CONTINUED AS #7,ROYAL CHART 1618
Died: 1 Apr 1212

Sources include: Consultation with Douglas Richardson; *Complete Peerage* 1:196-197; Chart 78 & sources (#2 & 3 ancestry).

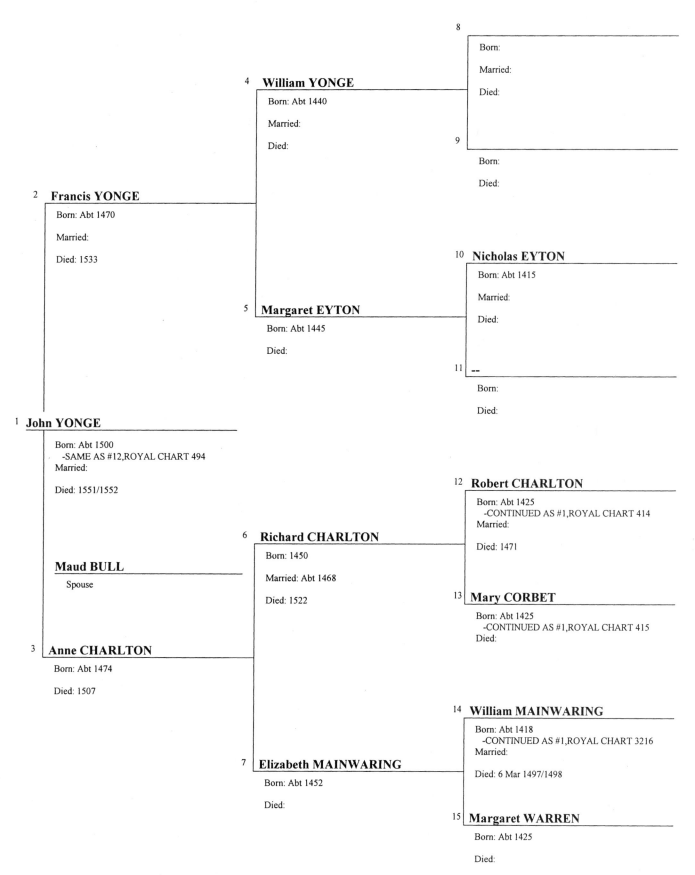

8

Born:

Married:

Died:

4 William YONGE

Born: Abt 1440

Married:

Died:

9

Born:

Died:

2 Francis YONGE

Born: Abt 1470

Married:

Died: 1533

10 Nicholas EYTON

Born: Abt 1415

Married:

Died:

5 Margaret EYTON

Born: Abt 1445

Died:

11 --

Born:

Died:

1 John YONGE

Born: Abt 1500
  -SAME AS #12,ROYAL CHART 494
Married:

Died: 1551/1552

12 Robert CHARLTON

Born: Abt 1425
  -CONTINUED AS #1,ROYAL CHART 414
Married:

Died: 1471

6 Richard CHARLTON

Born: 1450

Married: Abt 1468

Died: 1522

13 Mary CORBET

Born: Abt 1425
  -CONTINUED AS #1,ROYAL CHART 415
Died:

Maud BULL

Spouse

3 Anne CHARLTON

Born: Abt 1474

Died: 1507

14 William MAINWARING

Born: Abt 1418
  -CONTINUED AS #1,ROYAL CHART 3216
Married:

Died: 6 Mar 1497/1498

7 Elizabeth MAINWARING

Born: Abt 1452

Died:

15 Margaret WARREN

Born: Abt 1425

Died:

Sources include: Faris 2--Wyllys 2; Richardson *Plantagenet* (2004), pp. 760-761 (Willis), 805-806 (Zouche). Note: #6 & 7 are believed to have two daughters named Anne. See chart 410.

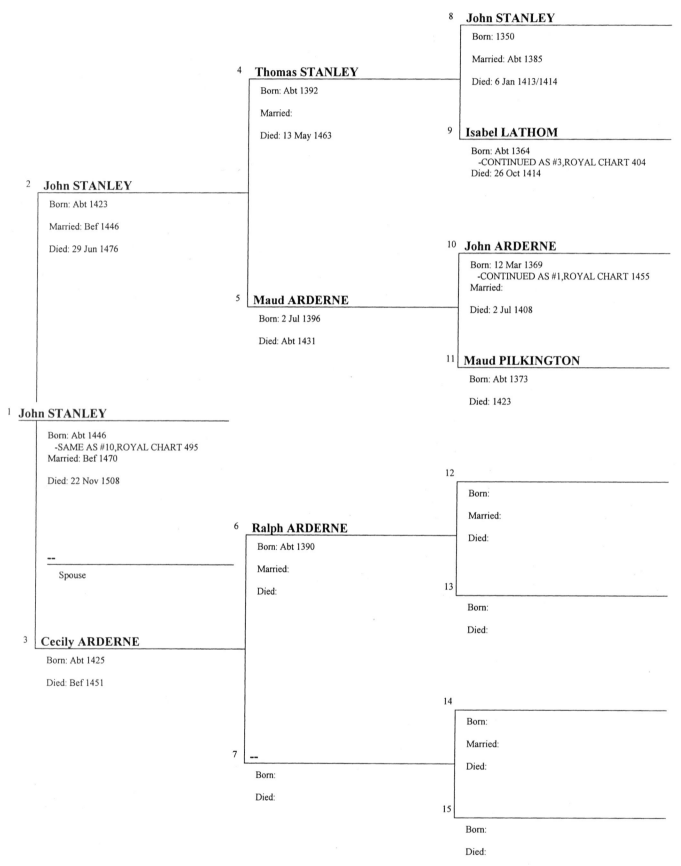

8 **John STANLEY**

Born: 1350

Married: Abt 1385

Died: 6 Jan 1413/1414

4 **Thomas STANLEY**

Born: Abt 1392

Married:

Died: 13 May 1463

9 **Isabel LATHOM**

Born: Abt 1364
  -CONTINUED AS #3,ROYAL CHART 404
Died: 26 Oct 1414

2 **John STANLEY**

Born: Abt 1423

Married: Bef 1446

Died: 29 Jun 1476

10 **John ARDERNE**

Born: 12 Mar 1369
  -CONTINUED AS #1,ROYAL CHART 1455
Married:

Died: 2 Jul 1408

5 **Maud ARDERNE**

Born: 2 Jul 1396

Died: Abt 1431

11 **Maud PILKINGTON**

Born: Abt 1373

Died: 1423

1 **John STANLEY**

Born: Abt 1446
  -SAME AS #10,ROYAL CHART 495
Married: Bef 1470

Died: 22 Nov 1508

12

Born:

Married:

Died:

6 **Ralph ARDERNE**

Born: Abt 1390

Married:

Died:

13

Born:

Died:

--

Spouse

3 **Cecily ARDERNE**

Born: Abt 1425

Died: Bef 1451

14

Born:

Married:

Died:

7 **--**

Born:

Died:

15

Born:

Died:

Sources include: Faris 2--Savage 5; Consultation with Douglas Richardson.

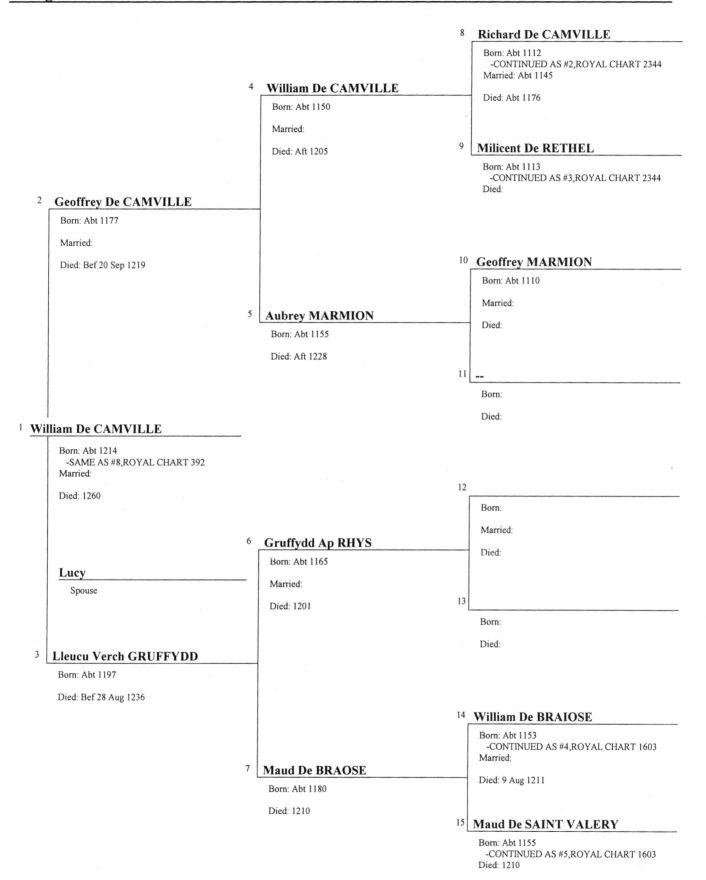

8 Richard De CAMVILLE

Born: Abt 1112
  -CONTINUED AS #2,ROYAL CHART 2344
Married: Abt 1145

Died: Abt 1176

4 William De CAMVILLE

Born: Abt 1150

Married:

Died: Aft 1205

9 Milicent De RETHEL

Born: Abt 1113
  -CONTINUED AS #3,ROYAL CHART 2344
Died:

2 Geoffrey De CAMVILLE

Born: Abt 1177

Married:

Died: Bef 20 Sep 1219

10 Geoffrey MARMION

Born: Abt 1110

Married:

Died:

5 Aubrey MARMION

Born: Abt 1155

Died: Aft 1228

11 --

Born:

Died:

1 William De CAMVILLE

Born: Abt 1214
  -SAME AS #8,ROYAL CHART 392
Married:

Died: 1260

12

Born:

Married:

Died:

6 Gruffydd Ap RHYS

Born: Abt 1165

Married:

Died: 1201

13

Born:

Died:

Lucy

Spouse

3 Lleucu Verch GRUFFYDD

Born: Abt 1197

Died: Bef 28 Aug 1236

14 William De BRAIOSE

Born: Abt 1153
  -CONTINUED AS #4,ROYAL CHART 1603
Married:

Died: 9 Aug 1211

7 Maud De BRAOSE

Born: Abt 1180

Died: 1210

15 Maud De SAINT VALERY

Born: Abt 1155
  -CONTINUED AS #5,ROYAL CHART 1603
Died: 1210

Sources include: Faris-Richardson preliminary Magna Carta manuscript (June 2000), pp. 103-104 (Camville); Consultation with Douglas Richardson, December 2004 (corrected ancestry of #3 Lleucu); Paget (1957) 115:2, 5; 116:1; *Complete Peerage* 3:3-5; Roberts *500* (600) updated manuscript (November 2000), p. 533 (#4 & 5 ancestry). Note: #8 Richard had a son Richard who is claimed by Paget to be the husband of #9 Milicent. The version shown above is accepted by Roberts and seems more likely correct.

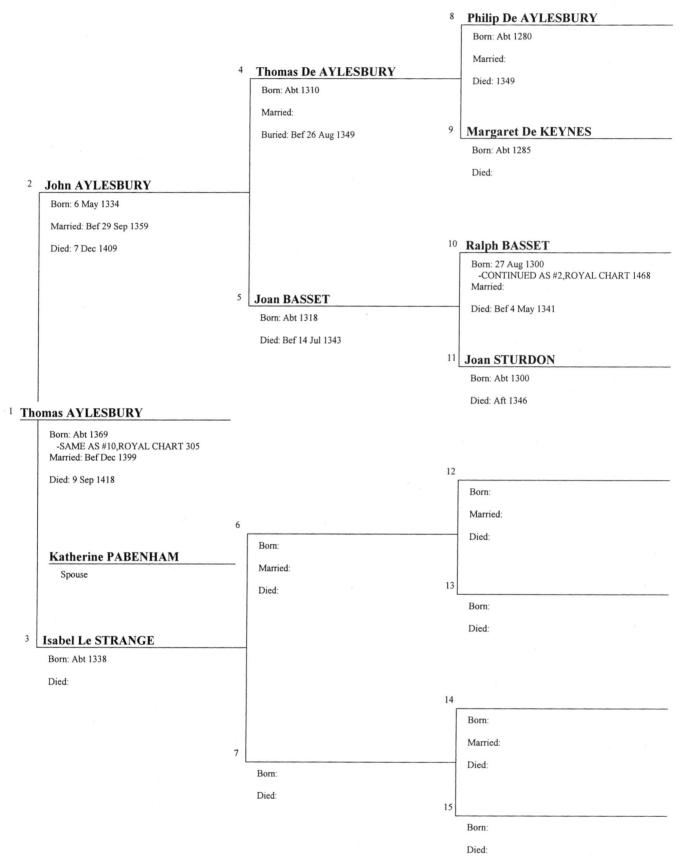

8 **Philip De AYLESBURY**

Born: Abt 1280

Married:

Died: 1349

4 **Thomas De AYLESBURY**

Born: Abt 1310

Married:

Buried: Bef 26 Aug 1349

9 **Margaret De KEYNES**

Born: Abt 1285

Died:

2 **John AYLESBURY**

Born: 6 May 1334

Married: Bef 29 Sep 1359

Died: 7 Dec 1409

10 **Ralph BASSET**

Born: 27 Aug 1300
   -CONTINUED AS #2,ROYAL CHART 1468
Married:

Died: Bef 4 May 1341

5 **Joan BASSET**

Born: Abt 1318

Died: Bef 14 Jul 1343

11 **Joan STURDON**

Born: Abt 1300

Died: Aft 1346

1 **Thomas AYLESBURY**

Born: Abt 1369
   -SAME AS #10,ROYAL CHART 305
Married: Bef Dec 1399

Died: 9 Sep 1418

12

Born:

Married:

Died:

6

Born:

Married:

Died:

13

Born:

Died:

Katherine PABENHAM

Spouse

3 **Isabel Le STRANGE**

Born: Abt 1338

Died:

14

Born:

Married:

Died:

7

Born:

Died:

15

Born:

Died:

Sources include: *Ancestral Roots* 187; *Magna Charta* 51; Consultation with Douglas Richardson. Note: #3 Isabel was <u>not</u> the daughter of Eble Le Strange, as claimed elsewhere.

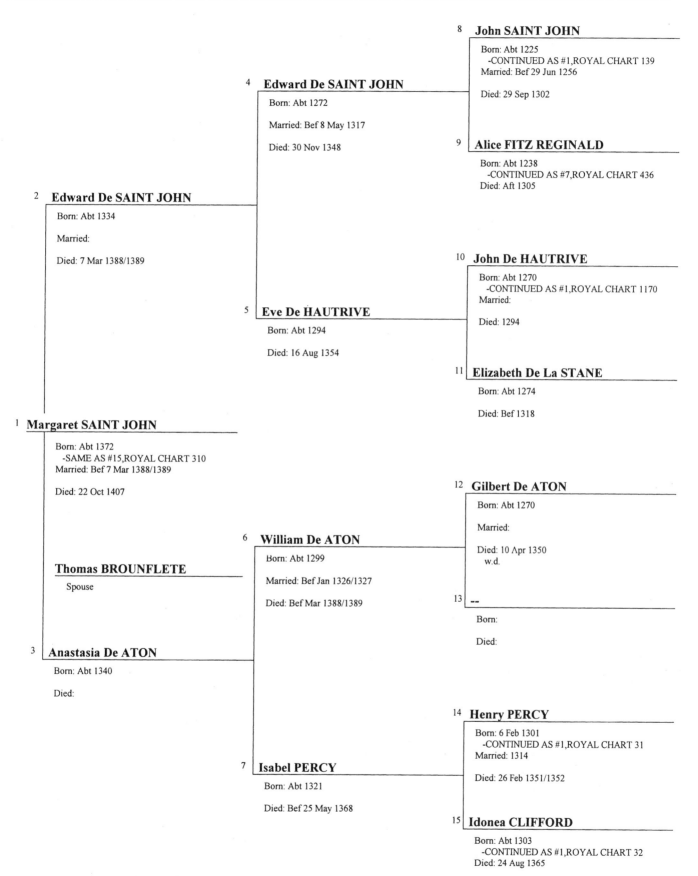

8 John SAINT JOHN
Born: Abt 1225
-CONTINUED AS #1,ROYAL CHART 139
Married: Bef 29 Jun 1256
Died: 29 Sep 1302

4 Edward De SAINT JOHN
Born: Abt 1272
Married: Bef 8 May 1317
Died: 30 Nov 1348

9 Alice FITZ REGINALD
Born: Abt 1238
-CONTINUED AS #7,ROYAL CHART 436
Died: Aft 1305

2 Edward De SAINT JOHN
Born: Abt 1334
Married:
Died: 7 Mar 1388/1389

10 John De HAUTRIVE
Born: Abt 1270
-CONTINUED AS #1,ROYAL CHART 1170
Married:
Died: 1294

5 Eve De HAUTRIVE
Born: Abt 1294
Died: 16 Aug 1354

11 Elizabeth De La STANE
Born: Abt 1274
Died: Bef 1318

1 Margaret SAINT JOHN
Born: Abt 1372
-SAME AS #15,ROYAL CHART 310
Married: Bef 7 Mar 1388/1389
Died: 22 Oct 1407

12 Gilbert De ATON
Born: Abt 1270
Married:
Died: 10 Apr 1350
w.d.

6 William De ATON
Born: Abt 1299
Married: Bef Jan 1326/1327
Died: Bef Mar 1388/1389

13 --
Born:
Died:

Thomas BROUNFLETE
Spouse

3 Anastasia De ATON
Born: Abt 1340
Died:

14 Henry PERCY
Born: 6 Feb 1301
-CONTINUED AS #1,ROYAL CHART 31
Married: 1314
Died: 26 Feb 1351/1352

7 Isabel PERCY
Born: Abt 1321
Died: Bef 25 May 1368

15 Idonea CLIFFORD
Born: Abt 1303
-CONTINUED AS #1,ROYAL CHART 32
Died: 24 Aug 1365

Sources include: Faris preliminary baronial manuscript (1998), pp. 1354-56 (St. John), 838-839 (Hautrive); Paget (1957) 480:2-4 (St. John), 13:1-8 (#11 Aubigny ancestry);
Consultation with Douglas Richardson; *Complete Peerage* 1:324-326 (#3 ancestry).

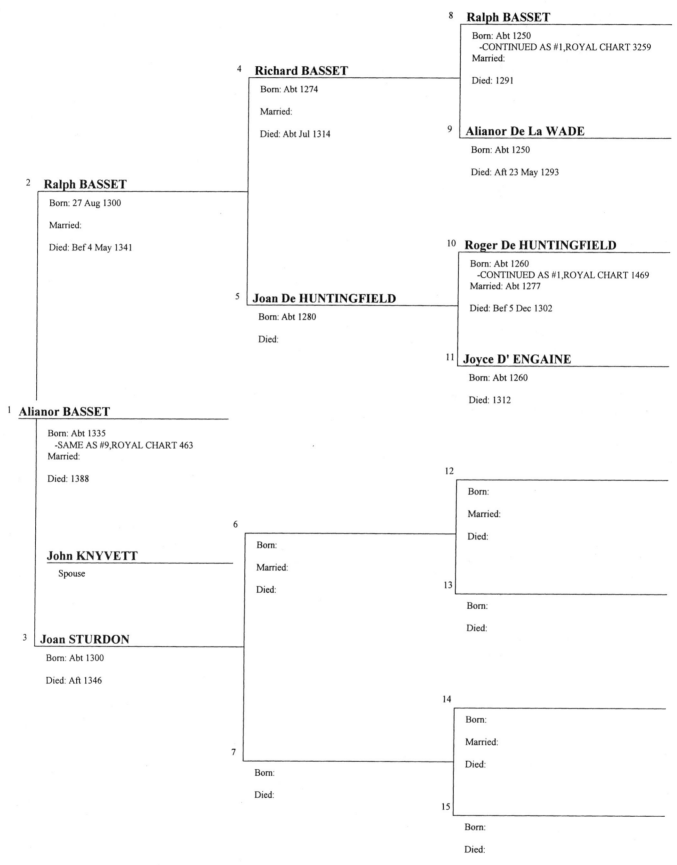

8 **Ralph BASSET**

Born: Abt 1250
  -CONTINUED AS #1,ROYAL CHART 3259
Married:

Died: 1291

4 **Richard BASSET**

Born: Abt 1274

Married:

Died: Abt Jul 1314

9 **Alianor De La WADE**

Born: Abt 1250

Died: Aft 23 May 1293

2 **Ralph BASSET**

Born: 27 Aug 1300

Married:

Died: Bef 4 May 1341

10 **Roger De HUNTINGFIELD**

Born: Abt 1260
  -CONTINUED AS #1,ROYAL CHART 1469
Married: Abt 1277

Died: Bef 5 Dec 1302

5 **Joan De HUNTINGFIELD**

Born: Abt 1280

Died:

11 **Joyce D' ENGAINE**

Born: Abt 1260

Died: 1312

1 **Alianor BASSET**

Born: Abt 1335
  -SAME AS #9,ROYAL CHART 463
Married:

Died: 1388

12

Born:

Married:

Died:

6

Born:

Married:

Died:

13

Born:

Died:

John KNYVETT

Spouse

3 **Joan STURDON**

Born: Abt 1300

Died: Aft 1346

14

Born:

Married:

Died:

7

Born:

Died:

15

Born:

Died:

Sources include: Faris preliminary baronial manuscript (1998), pp. 41-42 (Basset); Consultation with Douglas Richardson; *Ancestral Roots* 187; *Magna Charta* 51.

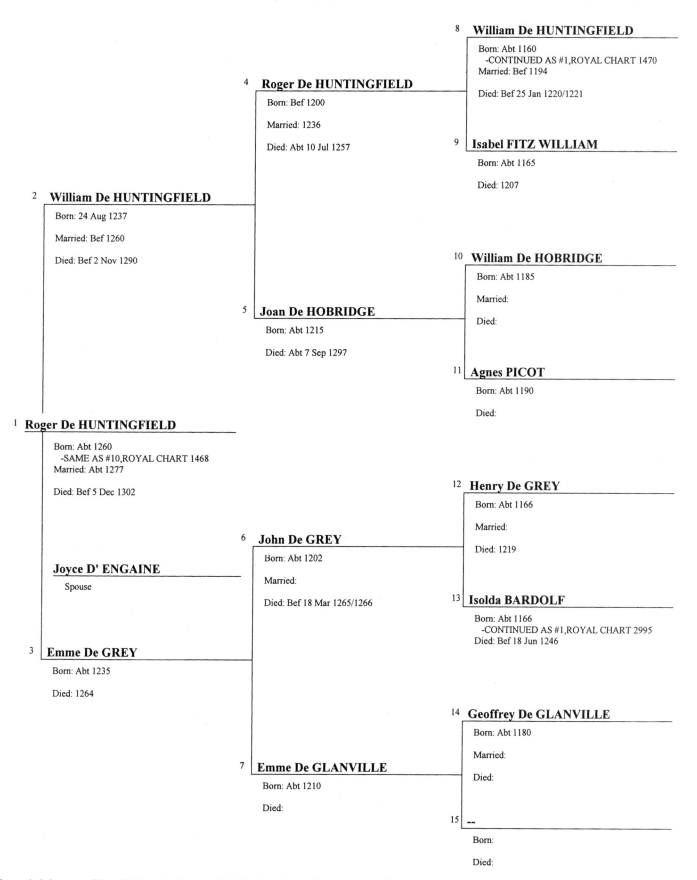

8 William De HUNTINGFIELD

Born: Abt 1160
  -CONTINUED AS #1,ROYAL CHART 1470
Married: Bef 1194

Died: Bef 25 Jan 1220/1221

4 Roger De HUNTINGFIELD

Born: Bef 1200

Married: 1236

Died: Abt 10 Jul 1257

9 Isabel FITZ WILLIAM

Born: Abt 1165

Died: 1207

2 William De HUNTINGFIELD

Born: 24 Aug 1237

Married: Bef 1260

Died: Bef 2 Nov 1290

10 William De HOBRIDGE

Born: Abt 1185

Married:

Died:

5 Joan De HOBRIDGE

Born: Abt 1215

Died: Abt 7 Sep 1297

11 Agnes PICOT

Born: Abt 1190

Died:

1 Roger De HUNTINGFIELD

Born: Abt 1260
  -SAME AS #10,ROYAL CHART 1468
Married: Abt 1277

Died: Bef 5 Dec 1302

12 Henry De GREY

Born: Abt 1166

Married:

Died: 1219

6 John De GREY

Born: Abt 1202

Married:

Died: Bef 18 Mar 1265/1266

13 Isolda BARDOLF

Born: Abt 1166
  -CONTINUED AS #1,ROYAL CHART 2995
Died: Bef 18 Jun 1246

Joyce D' ENGAINE

Spouse

3 Emme De GREY

Born: Abt 1235

Died: 1264

14 Geoffrey De GLANVILLE

Born: Abt 1180

Married:

Died:

7 Emme De GLANVILLE

Born: Abt 1210

Died:

15 --

Born:

Died:

Sources include: *Ancestral Roots* 187; *Complete Peerage* 6:664-671; *Magna Charta* 51; Consultation with Douglas Richardson; Faris preliminary baronial manuscript (1998), pp. 754, 742 (Grey); LDS records. Note: #6 John md. (1) Emme De Glanville & (2) Emma (Emme) De Cauz.

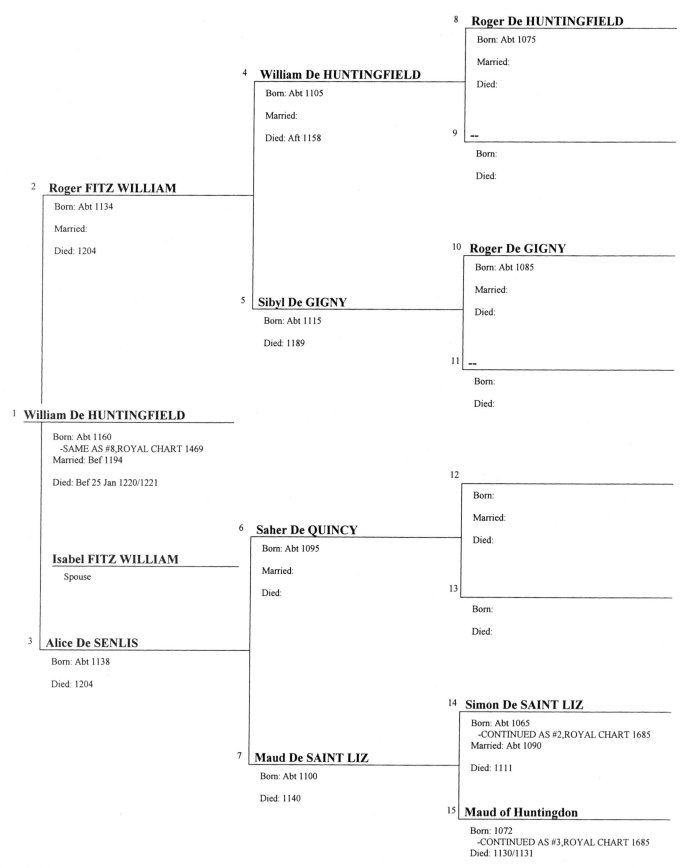

8 **Roger De HUNTINGFIELD**
Born: Abt 1075
Married:
Died:

4 **William De HUNTINGFIELD**
Born: Abt 1105
Married:
Died: Aft 1158

9 **--**
Born:
Died:

2 **Roger FITZ WILLIAM**
Born: Abt 1134
Married:
Died: 1204

10 **Roger De GIGNY**
Born: Abt 1085
Married:
Died:

5 **Sibyl De GIGNY**
Born: Abt 1115
Died: 1189

11 **--**
Born:
Died:

1 **William De HUNTINGFIELD**
Born: Abt 1160
  -SAME AS #8,ROYAL CHART 1469
Married: Bef 1194
Died: Bef 25 Jan 1220/1221

12
Born:
Married:
Died:

6 **Saher De QUINCY**
Born: Abt 1095
Married:
Died:

Isabel FITZ WILLIAM
Spouse

13
Born:
Died:

3 **Alice De SENLIS**
Born: Abt 1138
Died: 1204

14 **Simon De SAINT LIZ**
Born: Abt 1065
  -CONTINUED AS #2,ROYAL CHART 1685
Married: Abt 1090
Died: 1111

7 **Maud De SAINT LIZ**
Born: Abt 1100
Died: 1140

15 **Maud of Huntingdon**
Born: 1072
  -CONTINUED AS #3,ROYAL CHART 1685
Died: 1130/1131

Sources include: Faris-Richardson preliminary Magna Carta manuscript (June 2000), pp. 288-289 (Huntingfield); Faris preliminary baronial manuscript (1998), pp. 888 (Huntingfield), 1301 (Quincy); *Complete Peerage* 6:664-671; *Ancestral Roots* 187, 53-27, 148 (#7 ancestry).

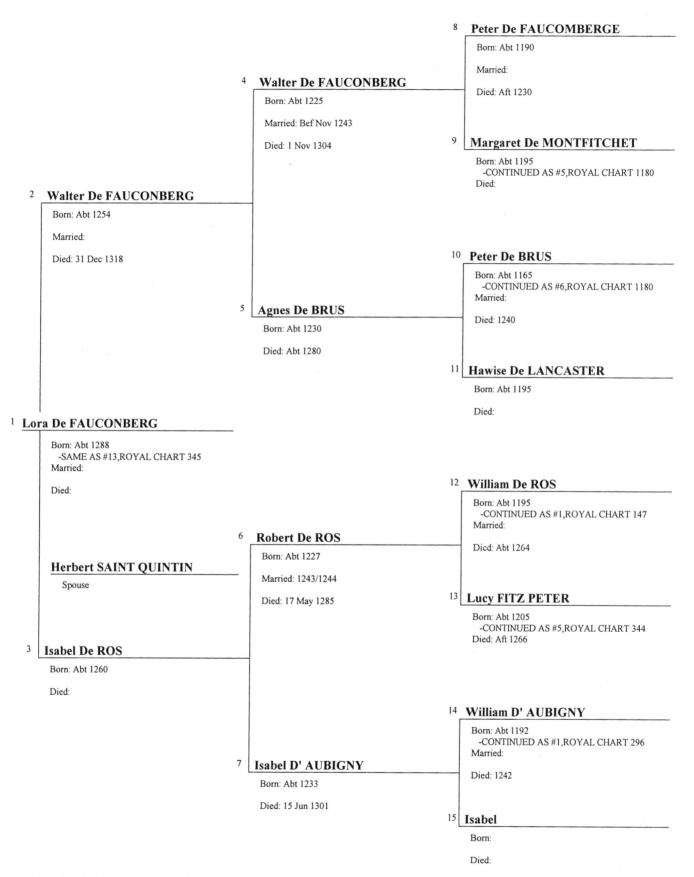

8 Peter De FAUCOMBERGE

Born: Abt 1190

Married:

Died: Aft 1230

4 Walter De FAUCONBERG

Born: Abt 1225

Married: Bef Nov 1243

Died: 1 Nov 1304

9 Margaret De MONTFITCHET

Born: Abt 1195
    -CONTINUED AS #5,ROYAL CHART 1180
Died:

2 Walter De FAUCONBERG

Born: Abt 1254

Married:

Died: 31 Dec 1318

10 Peter De BRUS

Born: Abt 1165
    -CONTINUED AS #6,ROYAL CHART 1180
Married:

Died: 1240

5 Agnes De BRUS

Born: Abt 1230

Died: Abt 1280

11 Hawise De LANCASTER

Born: Abt 1195

Died:

1 Lora De FAUCONBERG

Born: Abt 1288
    -SAME AS #13,ROYAL CHART 345
Married:

Died:

12 William De ROS

Born: Abt 1195
    -CONTINUED AS #1,ROYAL CHART 147
Married:

Died: Abt 1264

6 Robert De ROS

Born: Abt 1227

Married: 1243/1244

Died: 17 May 1285

13 Lucy FITZ PETER

Born: Abt 1205
    -CONTINUED AS #5,ROYAL CHART 344
Died: Aft 1266

Herbert SAINT QUINTIN

Spouse

3 Isabel De ROS

Born: Abt 1260

Died:

14 William D' AUBIGNY

Born: Abt 1192
    -CONTINUED AS #1,ROYAL CHART 296
Married:

Died: 1242

7 Isabel D' AUBIGNY

Born: Abt 1233

Died: 15 Jun 1301

15 Isabel

Born:

Died:

Sources include: Richardson *Magna Carta* (April 2005), pp. 318-319 Fauconberge, 705-706 Roos (#2 & 3 ancestry); *Ancestral Roots* 89 (#6 & 7 ancestry), 136 (#5 ancestry), 184B (#4 ancestry).

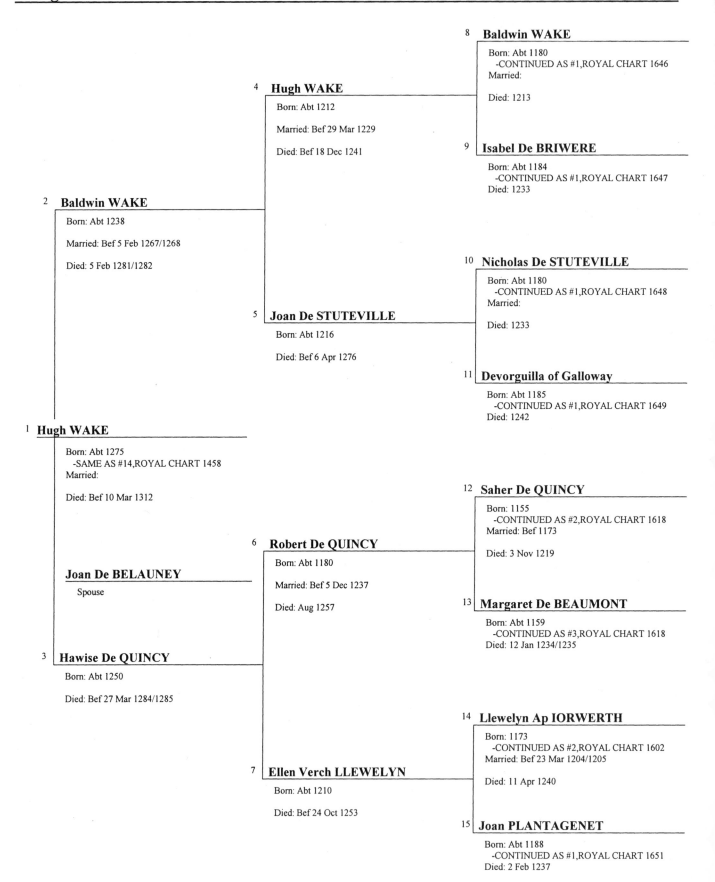

8 Baldwin WAKE

Born: Abt 1180
    -CONTINUED AS #1,ROYAL CHART 1646
Married:

Died: 1213

4 Hugh WAKE

Born: Abt 1212

Married: Bef 29 Mar 1229

Died: Bef 18 Dec 1241

9 Isabel De BRIWERE

Born: Abt 1184
    -CONTINUED AS #1,ROYAL CHART 1647
Died: 1233

2 Baldwin WAKE

Born: Abt 1238

Married: Bef 5 Feb 1267/1268

Died: 5 Feb 1281/1282

10 Nicholas De STUTEVILLE

Born: Abt 1180
    -CONTINUED AS #1,ROYAL CHART 1648
Married:

Died: 1233

5 Joan De STUTEVILLE

Born: Abt 1216

Died: Bef 6 Apr 1276

11 Devorguilla of Galloway

Born: Abt 1185
    -CONTINUED AS #1,ROYAL CHART 1649
Died: 1242

1 Hugh WAKE

Born: Abt 1275
    -SAME AS #14,ROYAL CHART 1458
Married:

Died: Bef 10 Mar 1312

12 Saher De QUINCY

Born: 1155
    -CONTINUED AS #2,ROYAL CHART 1618
Married: Bef 1173

Died: 3 Nov 1219

6 Robert De QUINCY

Born: Abt 1180

Married: Bef 5 Dec 1237

Died: Aug 1257

13 Margaret De BEAUMONT

Born: Abt 1159
    -CONTINUED AS #3,ROYAL CHART 1618
Died: 12 Jan 1234/1235

Joan De BELAUNEY

Spouse

3 Hawise De QUINCY

Born: Abt 1250

Died: Bef 27 Mar 1284/1285

14 Llewelyn Ap IORWERTH

Born: 1173
    -CONTINUED AS #2,ROYAL CHART 1602
Married: Bef 23 Mar 1204/1205

Died: 11 Apr 1240

7 Ellen Verch LLEWELYN

Born: Abt 1210

Died: Bef 24 Oct 1253

15 Joan PLANTAGENET

Born: Abt 1188
    -CONTINUED AS #1,ROYAL CHART 1651
Died: 2 Feb 1237

Sources include: Consultation with Douglas Richardson; Chart 73 & sources (#2 & 3 ancestry).

Pedigree Chart

Chart 1473

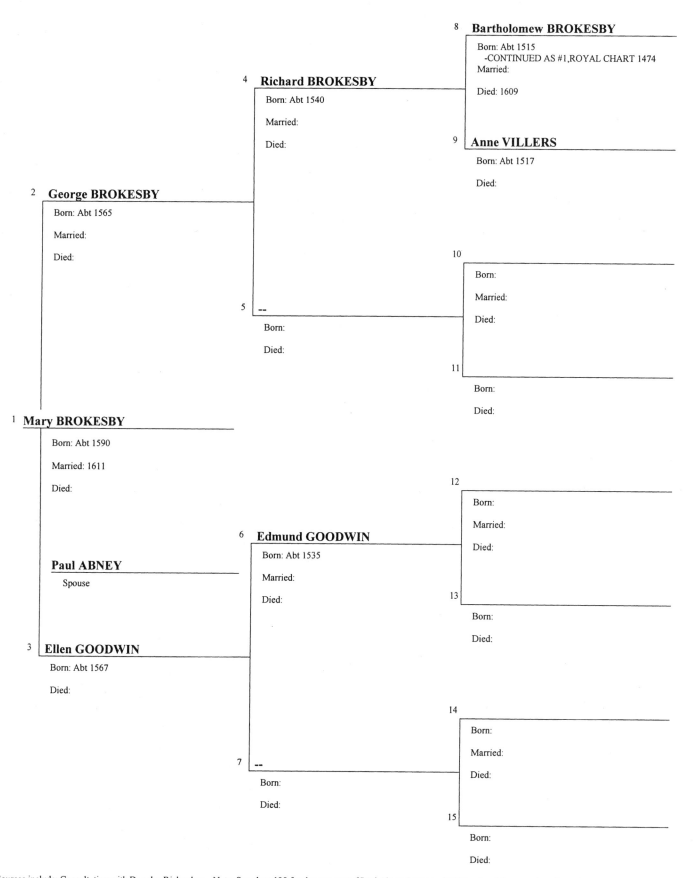

8 Bartholomew BROKESBY

Born: Abt 1515
-CONTINUED AS #1,ROYAL CHART 1474
Married:

Died: 1609

4 Richard BROKESBY

Born: Abt 1540

Married:

Died:

9 Anne VILLERS

Born: Abt 1517

Died:

2 George BROKESBY

Born: Abt 1565

Married:

Died:

10

Born:

Married:

Died:

5 --

Born:

Died:

11

Born:

Died:

1 Mary BROKESBY

Born: Abt 1590

Married: 1611

Died:

12

Born:

Married:

Died:

6 Edmund GOODWIN

Born: Abt 1535

Married:

Died:

13

Born:

Died:

Paul ABNEY

Spouse

3 Ellen GOODWIN

Born: Abt 1567

Died:

14

Born:

Married:

Died:

7 --

Born:

Died:

15

Born:

Died:

Sources include: Consultation with Douglas Richardson. Note: See chart 128 for the ancestry of Paul Abney (spouse of #1 Mary) and for some American descents.

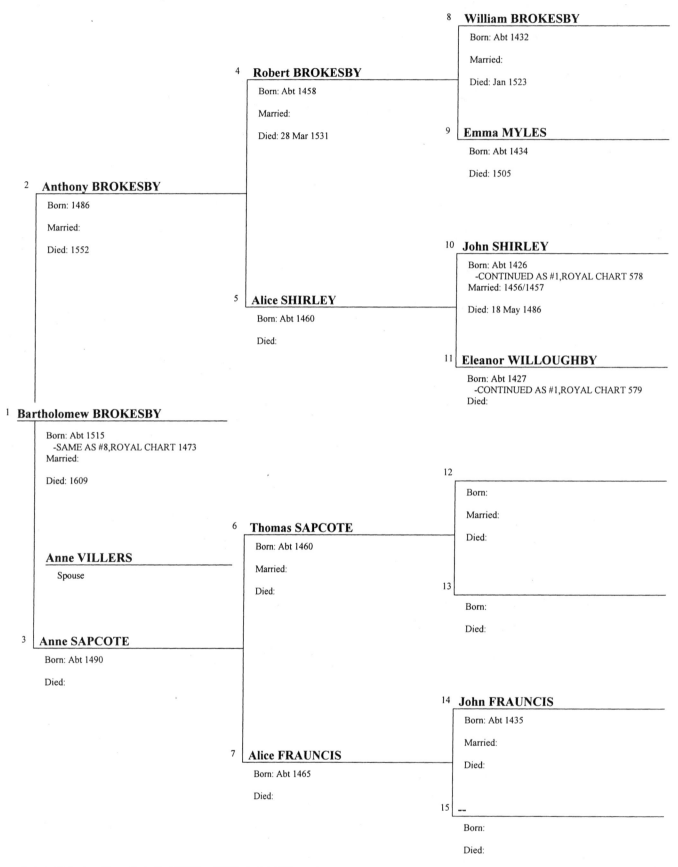

8 William BROKESBY
Born: Abt 1432
Married:
Died: Jan 1523

4 Robert BROKESBY
Born: Abt 1458
Married:
Died: 28 Mar 1531

9 Emma MYLES
Born: Abt 1434
Died: 1505

2 Anthony BROKESBY
Born: 1486
Married:
Died: 1552

10 John SHIRLEY
Born: Abt 1426
 -CONTINUED AS #1,ROYAL CHART 578
Married: 1456/1457
Died: 18 May 1486

5 Alice SHIRLEY
Born: Abt 1460
Died:

11 Eleanor WILLOUGHBY
Born: Abt 1427
 -CONTINUED AS #1,ROYAL CHART 579
Died:

1 Bartholomew BROKESBY
Born: Abt 1515
 -SAME AS #8,ROYAL CHART 1473
Married:
Died: 1609

12
Born:
Married:
Died:

6 Thomas SAPCOTE
Born: Abt 1460
Married:
Died:

13
Born:
Died:

Anne VILLERS
Spouse

3 Anne SAPCOTE
Born: Abt 1490
Died:

14 John FRAUNCIS
Born: Abt 1435
Married:
Died:

7 Alice FRAUNCIS
Born: Abt 1465
Died:

15 --
Born:
Died:

Sources include: Richardson *Magna Carta* (April 2005), p. 139 (Brokesby); LDS records.

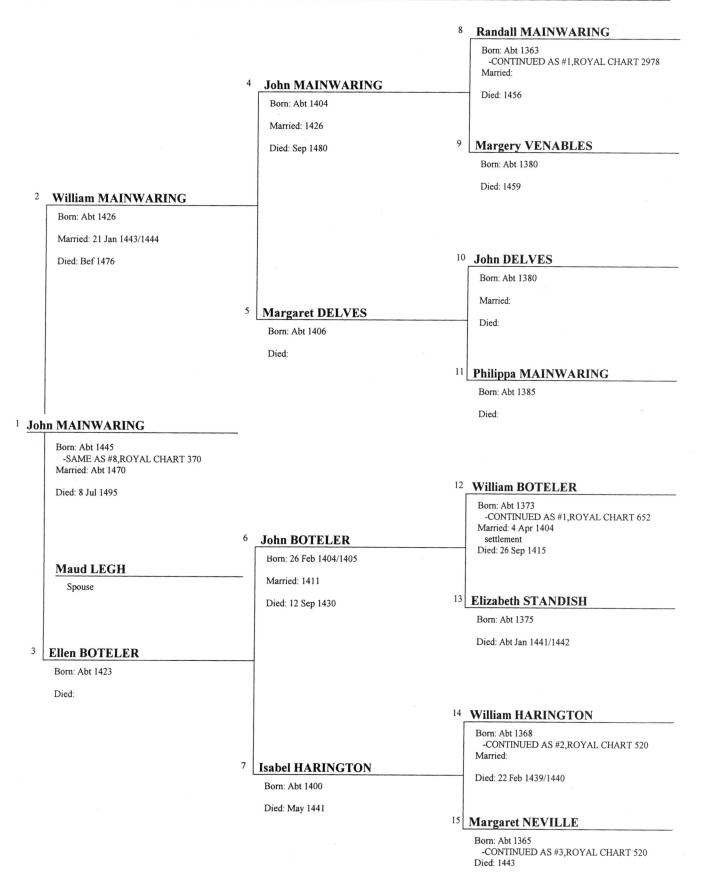

8 Randall MAINWARING

Born: Abt 1363
 -CONTINUED AS #1,ROYAL CHART 2978
Married:

Died: 1456

4 John MAINWARING

Born: Abt 1404

Married: 1426

Died: Sep 1480

9 Margery VENABLES

Born: Abt 1380

Died: 1459

2 William MAINWARING

Born: Abt 1426

Married: 21 Jan 1443/1444

Died: Bef 1476

10 John DELVES

Born: Abt 1380

Married:

Died:

5 Margaret DELVES

Born: Abt 1406

Died:

11 Philippa MAINWARING

Born: Abt 1385

Died:

1 John MAINWARING

Born: Abt 1445
 -SAME AS #8,ROYAL CHART 370
Married: Abt 1470

Died: 8 Jul 1495

Maud LEGH

Spouse

12 William BOTELER

Born: Abt 1373
 -CONTINUED AS #1,ROYAL CHART 652
Married: 4 Apr 1404
 settlement
Died: 26 Sep 1415

6 John BOTELER

Born: 26 Feb 1404/1405

Married: 1411

Died: 12 Sep 1430

13 Elizabeth STANDISH

Born: Abt 1375

Died: Abt Jan 1441/1442

3 Ellen BOTELER

Born: Abt 1423

Died:

14 William HARINGTON

Born: Abt 1368
 -CONTINUED AS #2,ROYAL CHART 520
Married:

Died: 22 Feb 1439/1440

7 Isabel HARINGTON

Born: Abt 1400

Died: May 1441

15 Margaret NEVILLE

Born: Abt 1365
 -CONTINUED AS #3,ROYAL CHART 520
Died: 1443

Sources include: Faris preliminary baronial manuscript (1998), pp. 1036-38 (Mainwaring); Consultation with Douglas Richardson; LDS records.

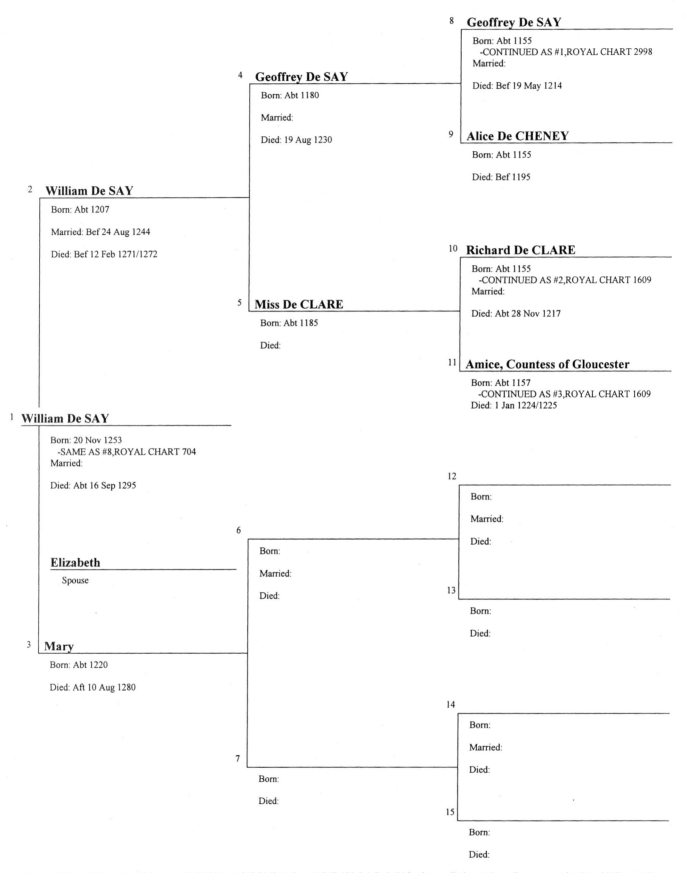

8 Geoffrey De SAY

Born: Abt 1155
 -CONTINUED AS #1,ROYAL CHART 2998
Married:

Died: Bef 19 May 1214

4 Geoffrey De SAY

Born: Abt 1180

Married:

Died: 19 Aug 1230

9 Alice De CHENEY

Born: Abt 1155

Died: Bef 1195

2 William De SAY

Born: Abt 1207

Married: Bef 24 Aug 1244

Died: Bef 12 Feb 1271/1272

10 Richard De CLARE

Born: Abt 1155
 -CONTINUED AS #2,ROYAL CHART 1609
Married:

Died: Abt 28 Nov 1217

5 Miss De CLARE

Born: Abt 1185

Died:

11 Amice, Countess of Gloucester

Born: Abt 1157
 -CONTINUED AS #3,ROYAL CHART 1609
Died: 1 Jan 1224/1225

1 William De SAY

Born: 20 Nov 1253
 -SAME AS #8,ROYAL CHART 704
Married:

Died: Abt 16 Sep 1295

Elizabeth
  Spouse

3 Mary

Born: Abt 1220

Died: Aft 10 Aug 1280

12

Born:

Married:

Died:

6

Born:

Married:

Died:

13

Born:

Died:

14

Born:

Married:

Died:

7

Born:

Died:

15

Born:

Died:

Sources include: Faris preliminary baronial manuscript (1998), pp. 1379-82 (Say); Paget (1957) 485: 2-4; Faris-Richardson preliminary Magna Carta manuscript (June 2000), pp. 463-465 (Say); *Magna Charta* 16A.

Pedigree Chart

Chart 1477

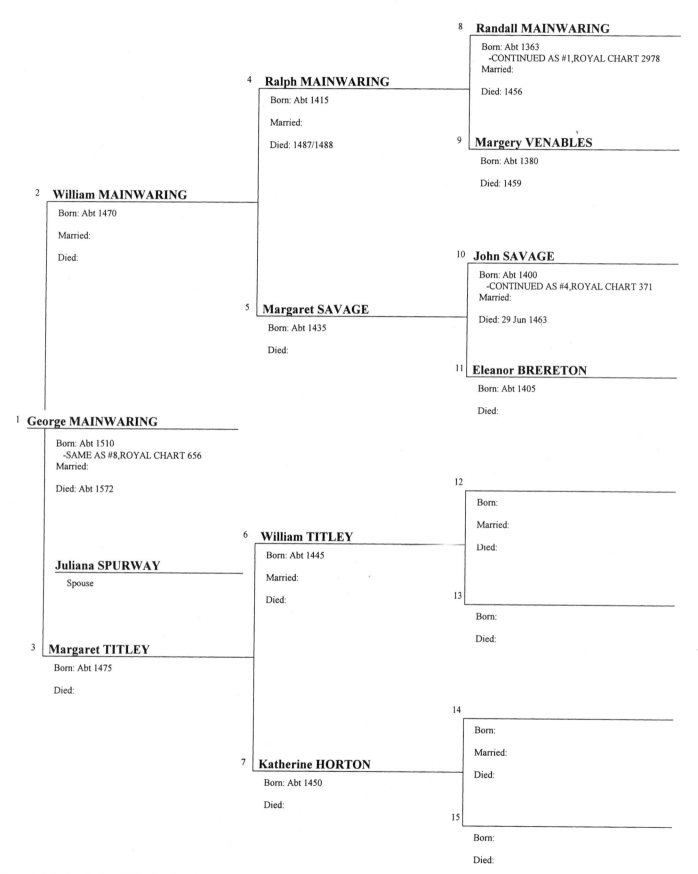

8   **Randall MAINWARING**

Born: Abt 1363
  -CONTINUED AS #1,ROYAL CHART 2978
Married:

Died: 1456

4   **Ralph MAINWARING**

Born: Abt 1415

Married:

Died: 1487/1488

9   **Margery VENABLES**

Born: Abt 1380

Died: 1459

2   **William MAINWARING**

Born: Abt 1470

Married:

Died:

10   **John SAVAGE**

Born: Abt 1400
  -CONTINUED AS #4,ROYAL CHART 371
Married:

Died: 29 Jun 1463

5   **Margaret SAVAGE**

Born: Abt 1435

Died:

11   **Eleanor BRERETON**

Born: Abt 1405

Died:

1   **George MAINWARING**

Born: Abt 1510
  -SAME AS #8,ROYAL CHART 656
Married:

Died: Abt 1572

12

Born:

Married:

Died:

6   **William TITLEY**

Born: Abt 1445

Married:

Died:

13

Born:

Died:

Juliana SPURWAY

Spouse

3   **Margaret TITLEY**

Born: Abt 1475

Died:

14

Born:

Married:

Died:

7   **Katherine HORTON**

Born: Abt 1450

Died:

15

Born:

Died:

Sources include: Consultation with Douglas Richardson. Note: #5 Margaret was likely the daughter of John & Eleanor above, but this is not certain.

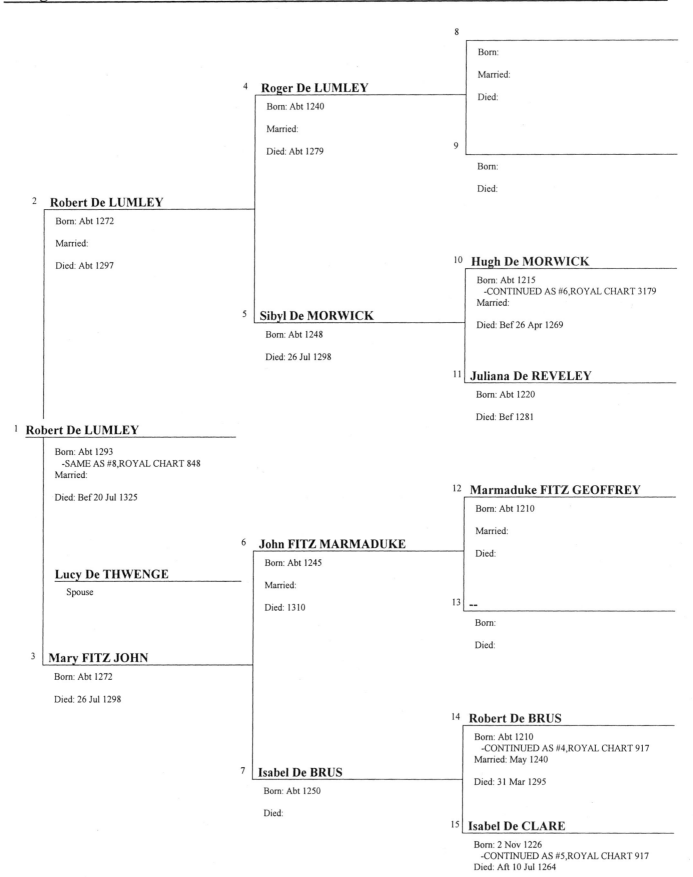

8

Born:

Married:

Died:

4 **Roger De LUMLEY**

Born: Abt 1240

Married:

Died: Abt 1279

9

Born:

Died:

2 **Robert De LUMLEY**

Born: Abt 1272

Married:

Died: Abt 1297

10 **Hugh De MORWICK**

Born: Abt 1215
-CONTINUED AS #6,ROYAL CHART 3179
Married:

Died: Bef 26 Apr 1269

5 **Sibyl De MORWICK**

Born: Abt 1248

Died: 26 Jul 1298

11 **Juliana De REVELEY**

Born: Abt 1220

Died: Bef 1281

1 **Robert De LUMLEY**

Born: Abt 1293
-SAME AS #8,ROYAL CHART 848
Married:

Died: Bef 20 Jul 1325

12 **Marmaduke FITZ GEOFFREY**

Born: Abt 1210

Married:

Died:

6 **John FITZ MARMADUKE**

Born: Abt 1245

Married:

Died: 1310

Lucy De THWENGE

Spouse

13 **--**

Born:

Died:

3 **Mary FITZ JOHN**

Born: Abt 1272

Died: 26 Jul 1298

14 **Robert De BRUS**

Born: Abt 1210
-CONTINUED AS #4,ROYAL CHART 917
Married: May 1240

Died: 31 Mar 1295

7 **Isabel De BRUS**

Born: Abt 1250

Died:

15 **Isabel De CLARE**

Born: 2 Nov 1226
-CONTINUED AS #5,ROYAL CHART 917
Died: Aft 10 Jul 1264

Sources include: Faris-Richardson preliminary Magna Carta manuscript (June 2000), pp. 336-337 (Lumley); Faris preliminary baronial manuscript (1998), pp. 1007-08 (Lumley); *Complete Peerage* 8:266-268.

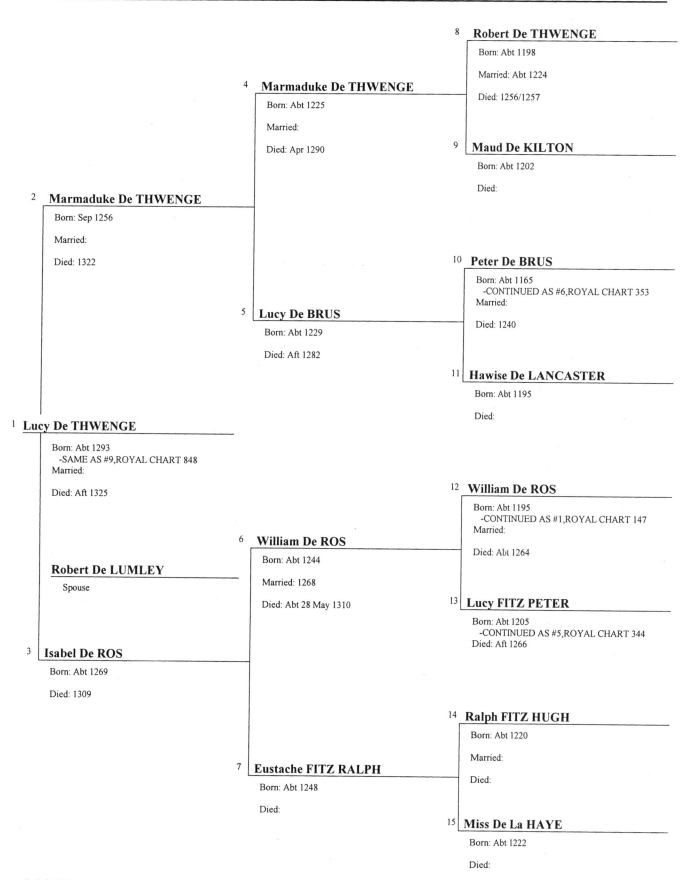

8 Robert De THWENGE
Born: Abt 1198
Married: Abt 1224
Died: 1256/1257

4 Marmaduke De THWENGE
Born: Abt 1225
Married:
Died: Apr 1290

9 Maud De KILTON
Born: Abt 1202
Died:

2 Marmaduke De THWENGE
Born: Sep 1256
Married:
Died: 1322

10 Peter De BRUS
Born: Abt 1165
-CONTINUED AS #6,ROYAL CHART 353
Married:
Died: 1240

5 Lucy De BRUS
Born: Abt 1229
Died: Aft 1282

11 Hawise De LANCASTER
Born: Abt 1195
Died:

1 Lucy De THWENGE
Born: Abt 1293
-SAME AS #9,ROYAL CHART 848
Married:
Died: Aft 1325

Robert De LUMLEY
Spouse

12 William De ROS
Born: Abt 1195
-CONTINUED AS #1,ROYAL CHART 147
Married:
Died: Abt 1264

6 William De ROS
Born: Abt 1244
Married: 1268
Died: Abt 28 May 1310

13 Lucy FITZ PETER
Born: Abt 1205
-CONTINUED AS #5,ROYAL CHART 344
Died: Aft 1266

3 Isabel De ROS
Born: Abt 1269
Died: 1309

14 Ralph FITZ HUGH
Born: Abt 1220
Married:
Died:

7 Eustache FITZ RALPH
Born: Abt 1248
Died:

15 Miss De La HAYE
Born: Abt 1222
Died:

Sources include: Richardson *Magna Carta* (April 2005), pp. 119-120 (Botreaux), 705 (Roos); Faris-Richardson preliminary Magna Carta manuscript (June 2000), pp. 67 (Botreaux), 447-448 (Roos); Faris preliminary baronial manuscript (1998), p. 1523 (Thwenge).

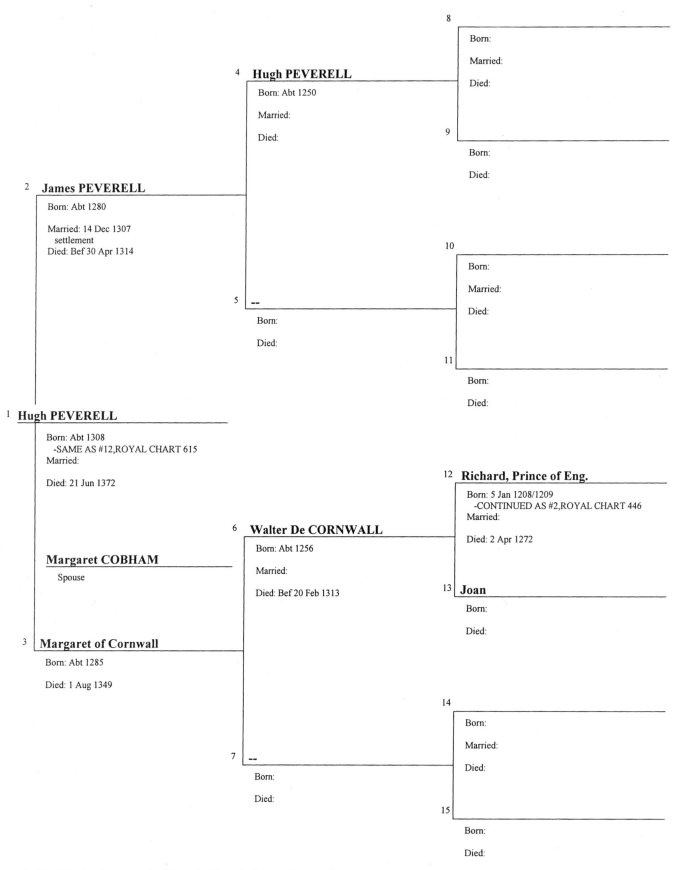

8

Born:

Married:

Died:

4   **Hugh PEVERELL**

Born: Abt 1250

Married:

Died:

9

Born:

Died:

2   **James PEVERELL**

Born: Abt 1280

Married: 14 Dec 1307
  settlement
Died: Bef 30 Apr 1314

10

Born:

Married:

Died:

5   --

Born:

Died:

11

Born:

Died:

1   **Hugh PEVERELL**

Born: Abt 1308
  -SAME AS #12,ROYAL CHART 615
Married:

Died: 21 Jun 1372

12   **Richard, Prince of Eng.**

Born: 5 Jan 1208/1209
  -CONTINUED AS #2,ROYAL CHART 446
Married:

Died: 2 Apr 1272

6   **Walter De CORNWALL**

Born: Abt 1256

Married:

Died: Bef 20 Feb 1313

13   **Joan**

Born:

Died:

Margaret COBHAM

Spouse

3   **Margaret of Cornwall**

Born: Abt 1285

Died: 1 Aug 1349

14

Born:

Married:

Died:

7   --

Born:

Died:

15

Born:

Died:

Sources include: Richardson *Plantagenet* (2004), pp. 406 (Hungerford), 230-232 (Cornwall).

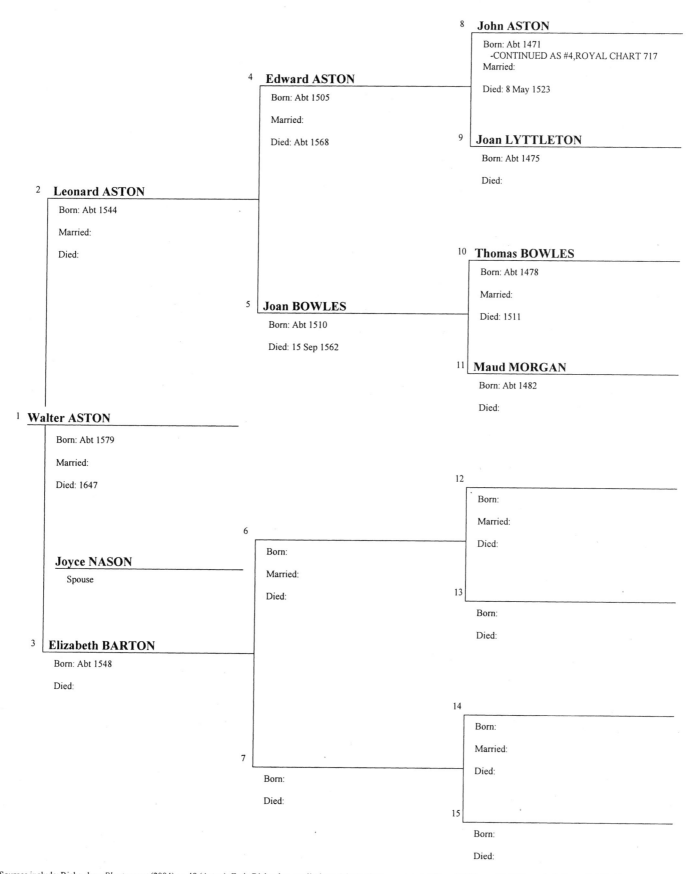

8 John ASTON
Born: Abt 1471
  -CONTINUED AS #4,ROYAL CHART 717
Married:

Died: 8 May 1523

4 Edward ASTON
Born: Abt 1505

Married:

Died: Abt 1568

9 Joan LYTTLETON
Born: Abt 1475

Died:

2 Leonard ASTON
Born: Abt 1544

Married:

Died:

10 Thomas BOWLES
Born: Abt 1478

Married:

Died: 1511

5 Joan BOWLES
Born: Abt 1510

Died: 15 Sep 1562

11 Maud MORGAN
Born: Abt 1482

Died:

1 Walter ASTON
Born: Abt 1579

Married:

Died: 1647

12
Born:

Married:

Died:

6
Born:

Married:

Died:

13
Born:

Died:

Joyce NASON
Spouse

3 Elizabeth BARTON
Born: Abt 1548

Died:

14
Born:

Married:

Died:

7
Born:

Died:

15
Born:

Died:

Sources include: Richardson *Plantagenet* (2004), p. 48 (Aston); Faris-Richardson preliminary Magna Carta manuscript (June 2000), pp. 15-16 (Aston); Roberts *600* (2004), pp. 435-436; *500*, pp. 361-362; *Magna Charta* 101; *Blood Royal* 5:253-257. Note: #1 Walter <u>might be</u> the father of the VA immigrant Walter Aston (b. 1606-07; md. Hannah Jordan). The claim is rejected by Paul C. Reed (*TAG* 76:234-236) but retained as a possibility by Roberts (2004). The issue is whether Walter (son of #1 Walter), who was in the West Indies in 1634 but returned to England, actually died in England or returned to VA in 1647 or later and died there, as claimed.

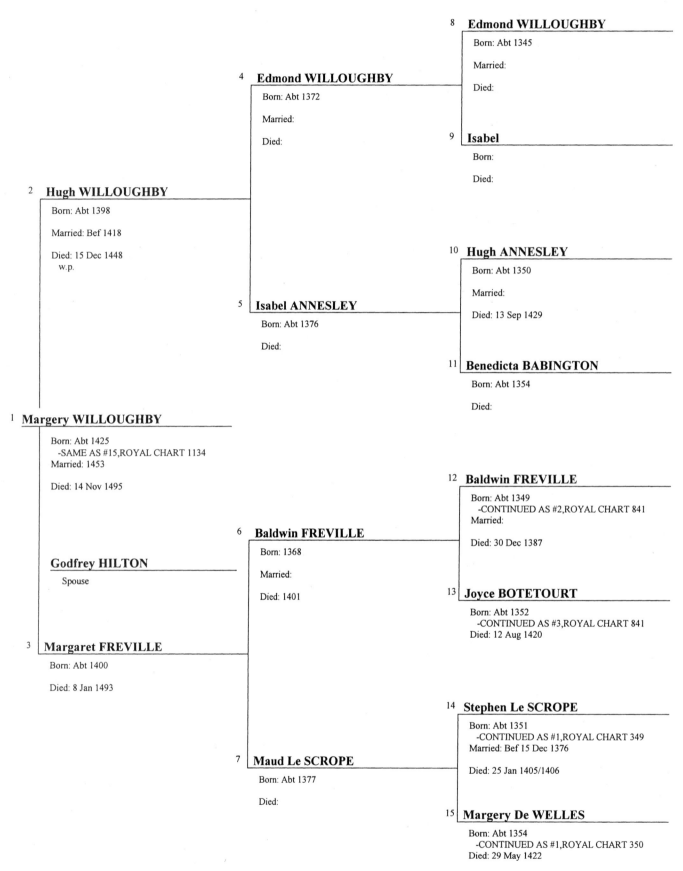

8 Edmond WILLOUGHBY
Born: Abt 1345
Married:
Died:

4 Edmond WILLOUGHBY
Born: Abt 1372
Married:
Died:

9 Isabel
Born:
Died:

2 Hugh WILLOUGHBY
Born: Abt 1398
Married: Bef 1418
Died: 15 Dec 1448
w.p.

10 Hugh ANNESLEY
Born: Abt 1350
Married:
Died: 13 Sep 1429

5 Isabel ANNESLEY
Born: Abt 1376
Died:

11 Benedicta BABINGTON
Born: Abt 1354
Died:

1 Margery WILLOUGHBY
Born: Abt 1425
-SAME AS #15,ROYAL CHART 1134
Married: 1453
Died: 14 Nov 1495

12 Baldwin FREVILLE
Born: Abt 1349
-CONTINUED AS #2,ROYAL CHART 841
Married:
Died: 30 Dec 1387

6 Baldwin FREVILLE
Born: 1368
Married:
Died: 1401

13 Joyce BOTETOURT
Born: Abt 1352
-CONTINUED AS #3,ROYAL CHART 841
Died: 12 Aug 1420

Godfrey HILTON
Spouse

3 Margaret FREVILLE
Born: Abt 1400
Died: 8 Jan 1493

14 Stephen Le SCROPE
Born: Abt 1351
-CONTINUED AS #1,ROYAL CHART 349
Married: Bef 15 Dec 1376
Died: 25 Jan 1405/1406

7 Maud Le SCROPE
Born: Abt 1377
Died:

15 Margery De WELLES
Born: Abt 1354
-CONTINUED AS #1,ROYAL CHART 350
Died: 29 May 1422

Sources include: Consultation with Douglas Richardson; Chart 579 & sources (#2 & 3 ancestry); LDS records; *Ancestral Roots* 230A, 216 (#3 ancestry).

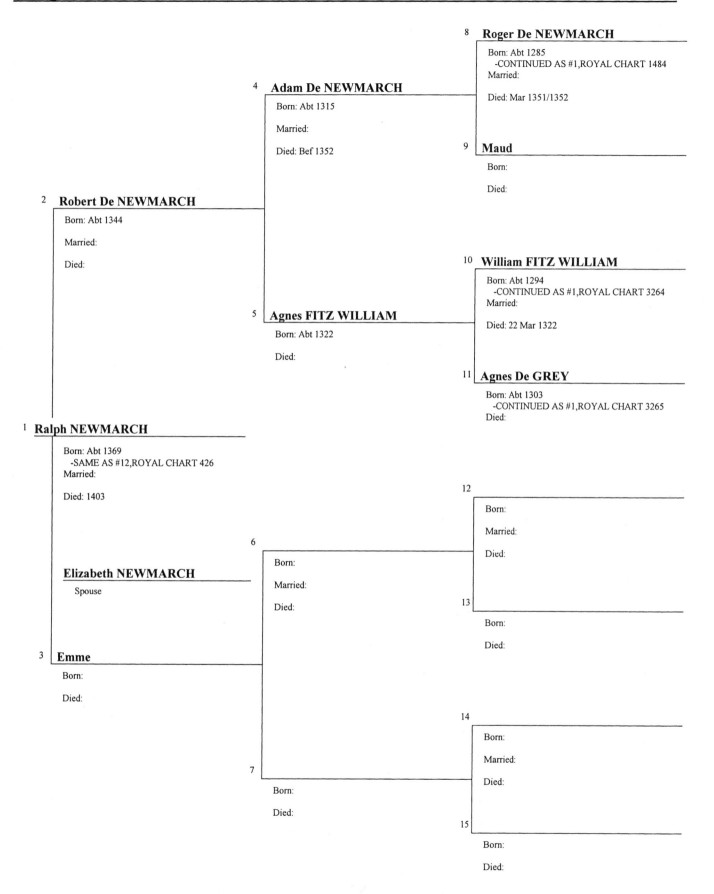

8 Roger De NEWMARCH
Born: Abt 1285
-CONTINUED AS #1,ROYAL CHART 1484
Married:

Died: Mar 1351/1352

4 Adam De NEWMARCH
Born: Abt 1315

Married:

Died: Bef 1352

9 Maud
Born:

Died:

2 Robert De NEWMARCH
Born: Abt 1344

Married:

Died:

10 William FITZ WILLIAM
Born: Abt 1294
-CONTINUED AS #1,ROYAL CHART 3264
Married:

Died: 22 Mar 1322

5 Agnes FITZ WILLIAM
Born: Abt 1322

Died:

11 Agnes De GREY
Born: Abt 1303
-CONTINUED AS #1,ROYAL CHART 3265
Died:

1 Ralph NEWMARCH
Born: Abt 1369
-SAME AS #12,ROYAL CHART 426
Married:

Died: 1403

12
Born:

Married:

Died:

6
Born:

Married:

Died:

13
Born:

Died:

Elizabeth NEWMARCH
Spouse

3 Emme
Born:

Died:

14
Born:

Married:

Died:

7
Born:

Died:

15
Born:

Died:

Sources include: Richardson *Plantagenet* (2004), p. 545 (Newmarch); Faris-Richardson preliminary Magna Carta manuscript (June 2000), p. 399 (Newmarch); Faris preliminary baronial manuscript (1998), pp. 1189 (Newmarch), 652 (Fitz William). Note: The parentage shown for #5 Agnes is not certain. She is also claimed as the <u>daughter</u> (instead of the granddaughter) of William Fitz William & Isabel Deincourt (see chart 3264, #2 & 3).

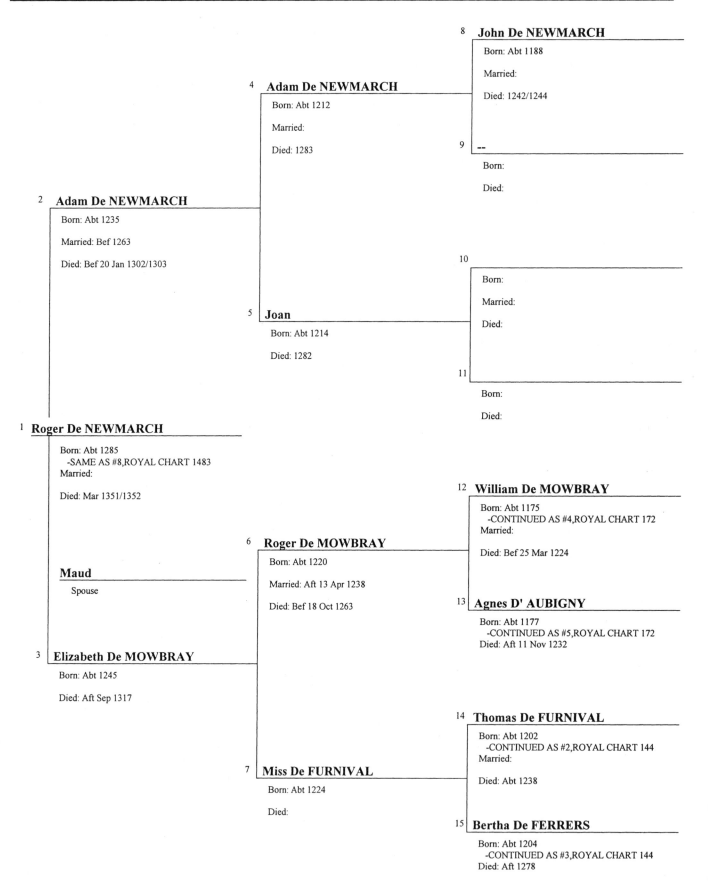

8 **John De NEWMARCH**

Born: Abt 1188

Married:

Died: 1242/1244

4 **Adam De NEWMARCH**

Born: Abt 1212

Married:

Died: 1283

9 **--**

Born:

Died:

2 **Adam De NEWMARCH**

Born: Abt 1235

Married: Bef 1263

Died: Bef 20 Jan 1302/1303

10

Born:

Married:

Died:

5 **Joan**

Born: Abt 1214

Died: 1282

11

Born:

Died:

1 **Roger De NEWMARCH**

Born: Abt 1285
-SAME AS #8,ROYAL CHART 1483
Married:

Died: Mar 1351/1352

12 **William De MOWBRAY**

Born: Abt 1175
-CONTINUED AS #4,ROYAL CHART 172
Married:

Died: Bef 25 Mar 1224

6 **Roger De MOWBRAY**

Born: Abt 1220

Married: Aft 13 Apr 1238

Died: Bef 18 Oct 1263

Maud

Spouse

13 **Agnes D' AUBIGNY**

Born: Abt 1177
-CONTINUED AS #5,ROYAL CHART 172
Died: Aft 11 Nov 1232

3 **Elizabeth De MOWBRAY**

Born: Abt 1245

Died: Aft Sep 1317

14 **Thomas De FURNIVAL**

Born: Abt 1202
-CONTINUED AS #2,ROYAL CHART 144
Married:

Died: Abt 1238

7 **Miss De FURNIVAL**

Born: Abt 1224

Died:

15 **Bertha De FERRERS**

Born: Abt 1204
-CONTINUED AS #3,ROYAL CHART 144
Died: Aft 1278

Sources include: Faris-Richardson preliminary Magna Carta manuscript (June 2000), pp. 398-399 (Newmarch), 383-384 (Mowbray); Faris preliminary baronial manuscript (1998), p. 1189 (Newmarch); Research report by Douglas Richardson on the Lucy & Boulogne families, August 2004 (#3 ancestry).

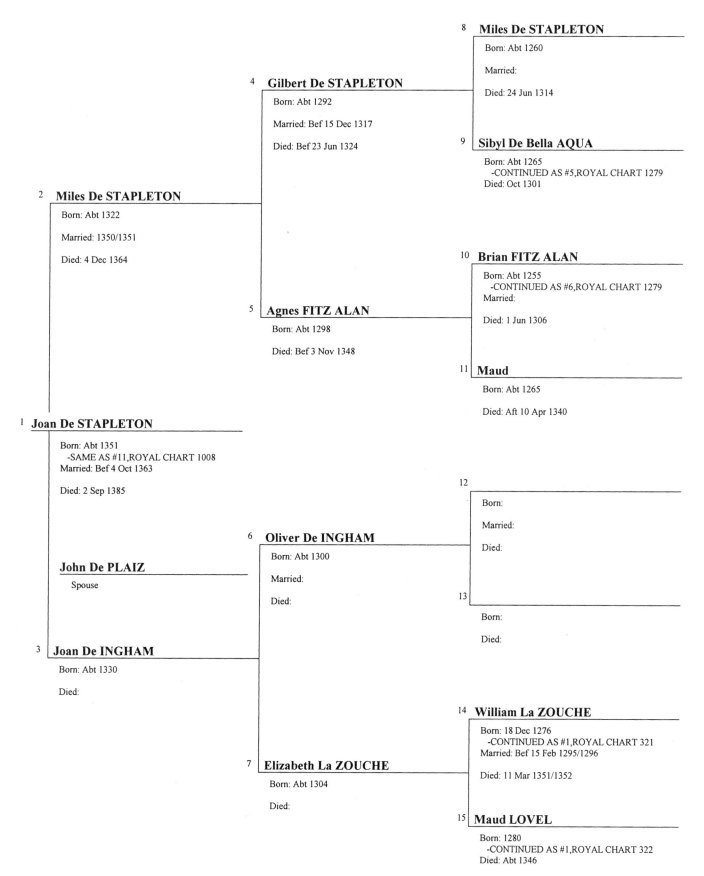

8 Miles De STAPLETON

Born: Abt 1260

Married:

Died: 24 Jun 1314

4 Gilbert De STAPLETON

Born: Abt 1292

Married: Bef 15 Dec 1317

Died: Bef 23 Jun 1324

9 Sibyl De Bella AQUA

Born: Abt 1265
  -CONTINUED AS #5,ROYAL CHART 1279
Died: Oct 1301

2 Miles De STAPLETON

Born: Abt 1322

Married: 1350/1351

Died: 4 Dec 1364

10 Brian FITZ ALAN

Born: Abt 1255
  -CONTINUED AS #6,ROYAL CHART 1279
Married:

Died: 1 Jun 1306

5 Agnes FITZ ALAN

Born: Abt 1298

Died: Bef 3 Nov 1348

11 Maud

Born: Abt 1265

Died: Aft 10 Apr 1340

1 Joan De STAPLETON

Born: Abt 1351
  -SAME AS #11,ROYAL CHART 1008
Married: Bef 4 Oct 1363

Died: 2 Sep 1385

12

Born:

Married:

Died:

6 Oliver De INGHAM

Born: Abt 1300

Married:

Died:

John De PLAIZ

Spouse

13

Born:

Died:

3 Joan De INGHAM

Born: Abt 1330

Died:

14 William La ZOUCHE

Born: 18 Dec 1276
  -CONTINUED AS #1,ROYAL CHART 321
Married: Bef 15 Feb 1295/1296

Died: 11 Mar 1351/1352

7 Elizabeth La ZOUCHE

Born: Abt 1304

Died:

15 Maud LOVEL

Born: 1280
  -CONTINUED AS #1,ROYAL CHART 322
Died: Abt 1346

Sources include: Faris preliminary baronial manuscript (1998), pp. 1438-39 (Stapleton), 1710-11 (Zouche); LDS records; *Blood Royal* 5:70-73 (#2 ancestry). Note: The parentage shown for #7 Elizabeth (or Isabel) is not certain.

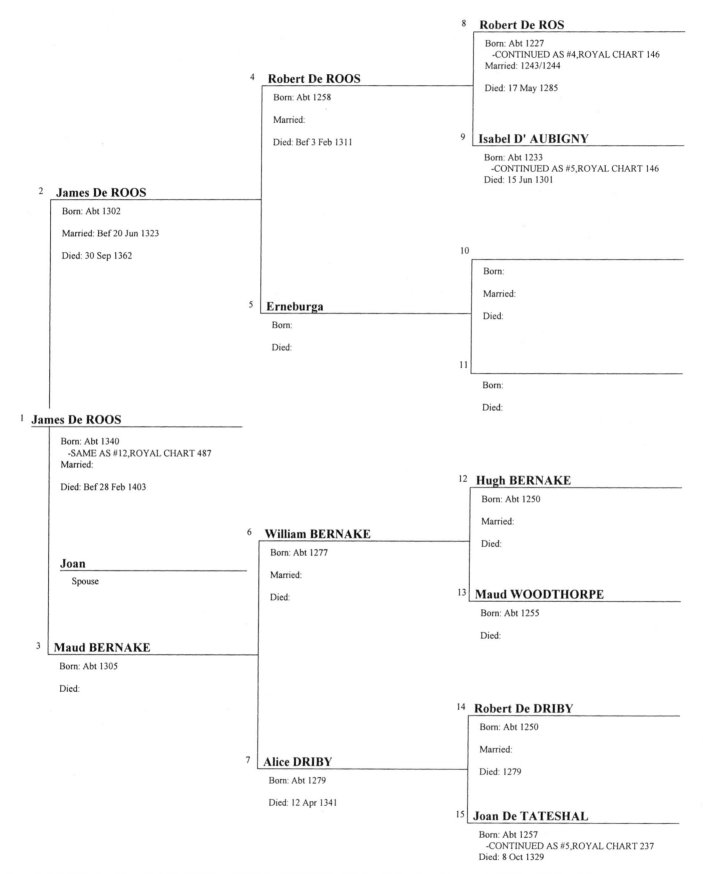

8 **Robert De ROS**

Born: Abt 1227
  -CONTINUED AS #4,ROYAL CHART 146
Married: 1243/1244

Died: 17 May 1285

4 **Robert De ROOS**

Born: Abt 1258

Married:

Died: Bef 3 Feb 1311

9 **Isabel D' AUBIGNY**

Born: Abt 1233
  -CONTINUED AS #5,ROYAL CHART 146
Died: 15 Jun 1301

2 **James De ROOS**

Born: Abt 1302

Married: Bef 20 Jun 1323

Died: 30 Sep 1362

10

Born:

Married:

Died:

5 **Erneburga**

Born:

Died:

11

Born:

Died:

1 **James De ROOS**

Born: Abt 1340
  -SAME AS #12,ROYAL CHART 487
Married:

Died: Bef 28 Feb 1403

12 **Hugh BERNAKE**

Born: Abt 1250

Married:

Died:

6 **William BERNAKE**

Born: Abt 1277

Married:

Died:

13 **Maud WOODTHORPE**

Born: Abt 1255

Died:

Joan

Spouse

3 **Maud BERNAKE**

Born: Abt 1305

Died:

14 **Robert De DRIBY**

Born: Abt 1250

Married:

Died: 1279

7 **Alice DRIBY**

Born: Abt 1279

Died: 12 Apr 1341

15 **Joan De TATESHAL**

Born: Abt 1257
  -CONTINUED AS #5,ROYAL CHART 237
Died: 8 Oct 1329

Sources include: Richardson *Magna Carta* (April 2005), pp. 369 (Gedney), 705-706 (Roos); Faris preliminary baronial manuscript (1998), p. 113 (Bernake).

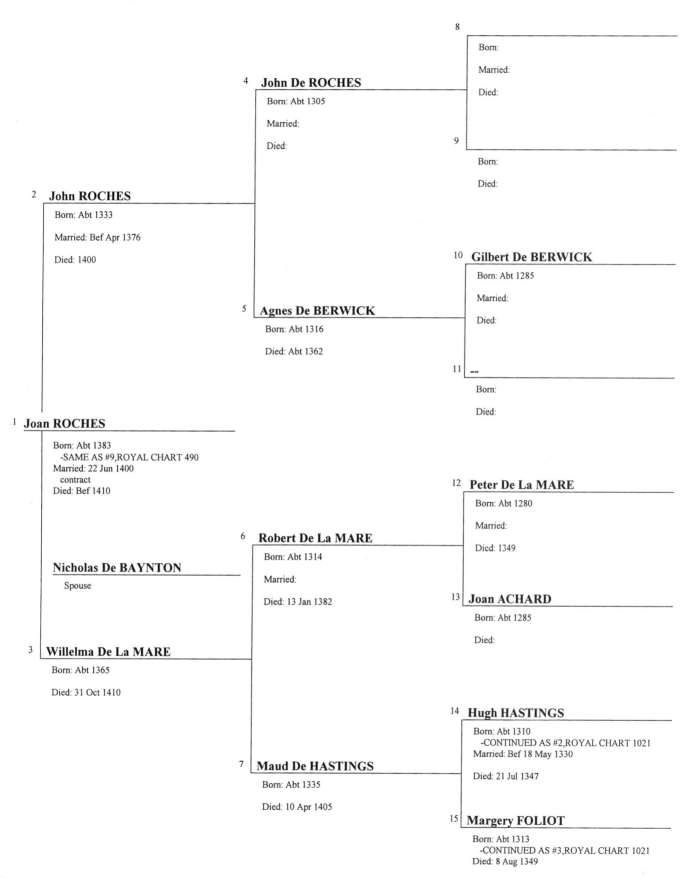

8

Born:

Married:

Died:

4 John De ROCHES

Born: Abt 1305

Married:

Died:

9

Born:

Died:

2 John ROCHES

Born: Abt 1333

Married: Bef Apr 1376

Died: 1400

10 Gilbert De BERWICK

Born: Abt 1285

Married:

Died:

5 Agnes De BERWICK

Born: Abt 1316

Died: Abt 1362

11 --

Born:

Died:

1 Joan ROCHES

Born: Abt 1383
-SAME AS #9,ROYAL CHART 490
Married: 22 Jun 1400
contract
Died: Bef 1410

Nicholas De BAYNTON

Spouse

12 Peter De La MARE

Born: Abt 1280

Married:

Died: 1349

6 Robert De La MARE

Born: Abt 1314

Married:

Died: 13 Jan 1382

13 Joan ACHARD

Born: Abt 1285

Died:

3 Willelma De La MARE

Born: Abt 1365

Died: 31 Oct 1410

14 Hugh HASTINGS

Born: Abt 1310
-CONTINUED AS #2,ROYAL CHART 1021
Married: Bef 18 May 1330

Died: 21 Jul 1347

7 Maud De HASTINGS

Born: Abt 1335

Died: 10 Apr 1405

15 Margery FOLIOT

Born: Abt 1313
-CONTINUED AS #3,ROYAL CHART 1021
Died: 8 Aug 1349

Sources include: Faris-Richardson preliminary Magna Carta manuscript (June 2000), pp. 31-32 (Baynton); Faris preliminary baronial manuscript (1998), pp. 1326-27 (Roche).

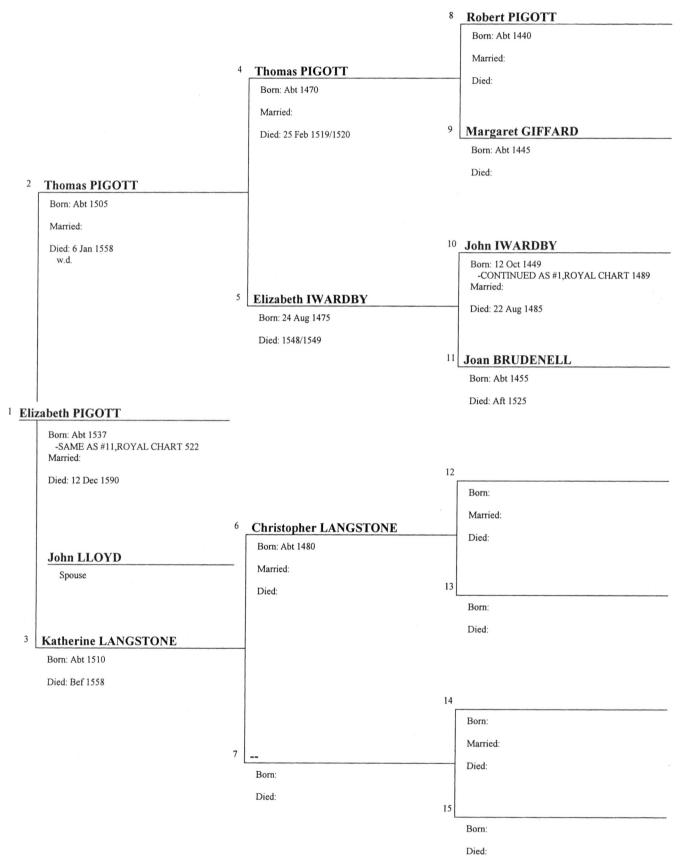

8 **Robert PIGOTT**

Born: Abt 1440

Married:

Died:

4 **Thomas PIGOTT**

Born: Abt 1470

Married:

Died: 25 Feb 1519/1520

9 **Margaret GIFFARD**

Born: Abt 1445

Died:

2 **Thomas PIGOTT**

Born: Abt 1505

Married:

Died: 6 Jan 1558
w.d.

10 **John IWARDBY**

Born: 12 Oct 1449
-CONTINUED AS #1,ROYAL CHART 1489
Married:

Died: 22 Aug 1485

5 **Elizabeth IWARDBY**

Born: 24 Aug 1475

Died: 1548/1549

11 **Joan BRUDENELL**

Born: Abt 1455

Died: Aft 1525

1 **Elizabeth PIGOTT**

Born: Abt 1537
-SAME AS #11,ROYAL CHART 522
Married:

Died: 12 Dec 1590

12

Born:

Married:

Died:

6 **Christopher LANGSTONE**

Born: Abt 1480

Married:

Died:

John LLOYD

Spouse

13

Born:

Died:

3 **Katherine LANGSTONE**

Born: Abt 1510

Died: Bef 1558

14

Born:

Married:

Died:

7 **--**

Born:

Died:

15

Born:

Died:

Sources include: Richardson *Plantagenet* (2004), pp. 787-788 (Yale).

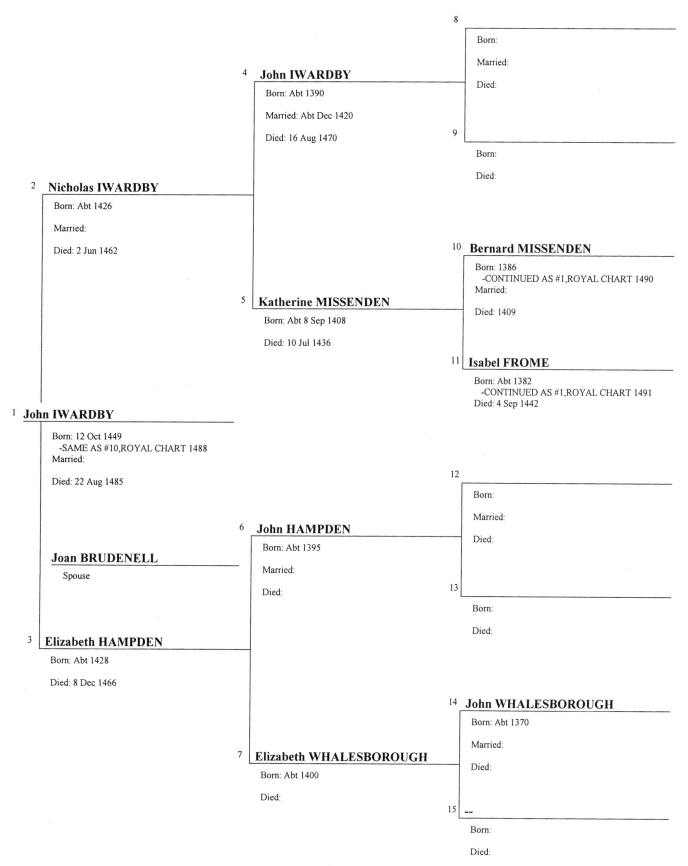

8

Born:

Married:

Died:

4 **John IWARDBY**

Born: Abt 1390

Married: Abt Dec 1420

Died: 16 Aug 1470

9

Born:

Died:

2 **Nicholas IWARDBY**

Born: Abt 1426

Married:

Died: 2 Jun 1462

10 **Bernard MISSENDEN**

Born: 1386
-CONTINUED AS #1,ROYAL CHART 1490
Married:

Died: 1409

5 **Katherine MISSENDEN**

Born: Abt 8 Sep 1408

Died: 10 Jul 1436

11 **Isabel FROME**

Born: Abt 1382
-CONTINUED AS #1,ROYAL CHART 1491
Died: 4 Sep 1442

1 **John IWARDBY**

Born: 12 Oct 1449
-SAME AS #10,ROYAL CHART 1488
Married:

Died: 22 Aug 1485

12

Born:

Married:

Died:

6 **John HAMPDEN**

Born: Abt 1395

Married:

Died:

13

Born:

Died:

Joan BRUDENELL

Spouse

3 **Elizabeth HAMPDEN**

Born: Abt 1428

Died: 8 Dec 1466

14 **John WHALESBOROUGH**

Born: Abt 1370

Married:

Died:

7 **Elizabeth WHALESBOROUGH**

Born: Abt 1400

Died:

15 **--**

Born:

Died:

Sources include: Richardson *Plantagenet* (2004), pp. 786-787 (Yale).

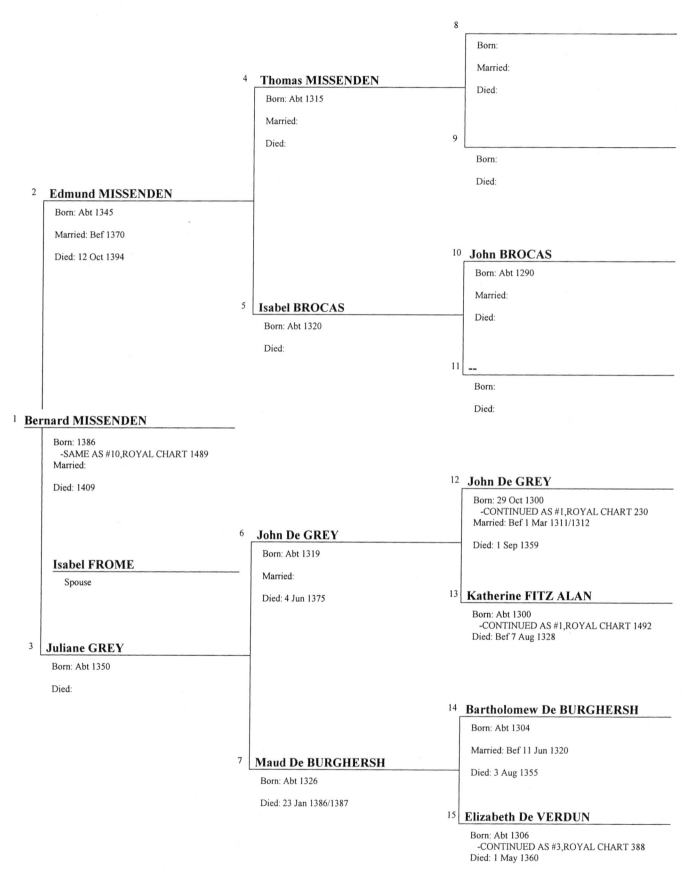

4 Thomas MISSENDEN
Born: Abt 1315
Married:
Died:

8
Born:
Married:
Died:

9
Born:
Died:

2 Edmund MISSENDEN
Born: Abt 1345
Married: Bef 1370
Died: 12 Oct 1394

5 Isabel BROCAS
Born: Abt 1320
Died:

10 John BROCAS
Born: Abt 1290
Married:
Died:

11 --
Born:
Died:

1 Bernard MISSENDEN
Born: 1386
    -SAME AS #10,ROYAL CHART 1489
Married:
Died: 1409

Isabel FROME
    Spouse

6 John De GREY
Born: Abt 1319
Married:
Died: 4 Jun 1375

12 John De GREY
Born: 29 Oct 1300
    -CONTINUED AS #1,ROYAL CHART 230
Married: Bef 1 Mar 1311/1312
Died: 1 Sep 1359

13 Katherine FITZ ALAN
Born: Abt 1300
    -CONTINUED AS #1,ROYAL CHART 1492
Died: Bef 7 Aug 1328

3 Juliane GREY
Born: Abt 1350
Died:

7 Maud De BURGHERSH
Born: Abt 1326
Died: 23 Jan 1386/1387

14 Bartholomew De BURGHERSH
Born: Abt 1304
Married: Bef 11 Jun 1320
Died: 3 Aug 1355

15 Elizabeth De VERDUN
Born: Abt 1306
    -CONTINUED AS #3,ROYAL CHART 388
Died: 1 May 1360

Sources include: Richardson *Plantagenet* (2004), pp. 786-787 (Yale), 554-555 (Oddingseles); Faris-Richardson preliminary Magna Carta manuscript (June 2000), pp. 546-547 (Yale), 97 (Burghersh). Note: The parentage shown for #7 Maud, given as probable in *Complete Peerage* 6:147-149, is based on weak evidence according to Richardson.

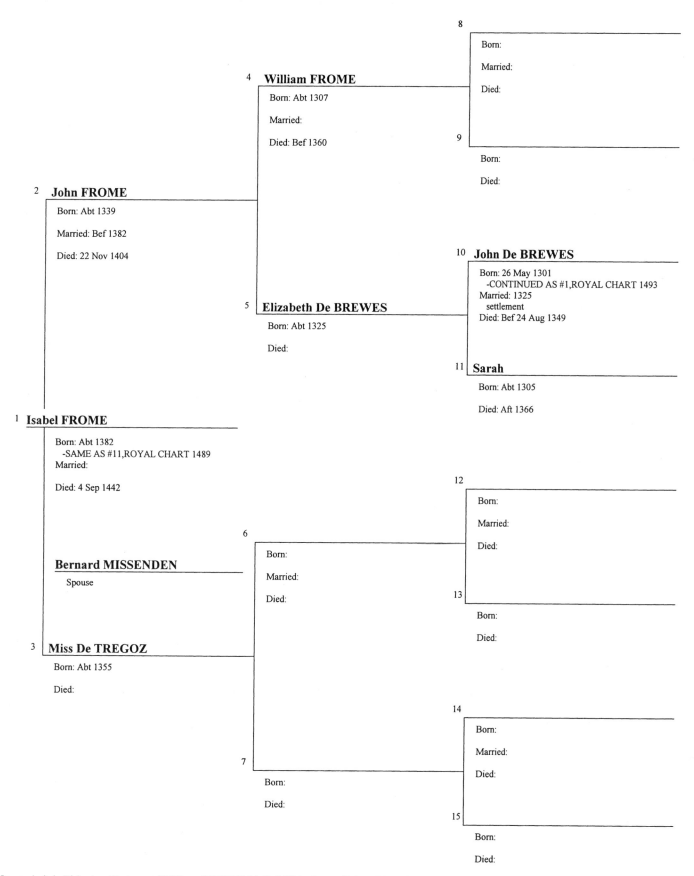

8

4 **William FROME**
Born: Abt 1307
Married:
Died: Bef 1360

Born:
Married:
Died:

9

Born:
Died:

2 **John FROME**
Born: Abt 1339
Married: Bef 1382
Died: 22 Nov 1404

10 **John De BREWES**
Born: 26 May 1301
  -CONTINUED AS #1, ROYAL CHART 1493
Married: 1325
  settlement
Died: Bef 24 Aug 1349

5 **Elizabeth De BREWES**
Born: Abt 1325
Died:

11 **Sarah**
Born: Abt 1305
Died: Aft 1366

1 **Isabel FROME**
Born: Abt 1382
  -SAME AS #11, ROYAL CHART 1489
Married:
Died: 4 Sep 1442

12

Born:
Married:
Died:

6
Born:
Married:
Died:

13

Born:
Died:

Bernard MISSENDEN
Spouse

3 **Miss De TREGOZ**
Born: Abt 1355
Died:

14

Born:
Married:
Died:

7
Born:
Died:

15

Born:
Died:

Sources include: Richardson *Plantagenet* (2004), pp. 786-787 (Yale); Faris-Richardson preliminary Magna Carta manuscript (June 2000), pp. 230-231 (Frome).

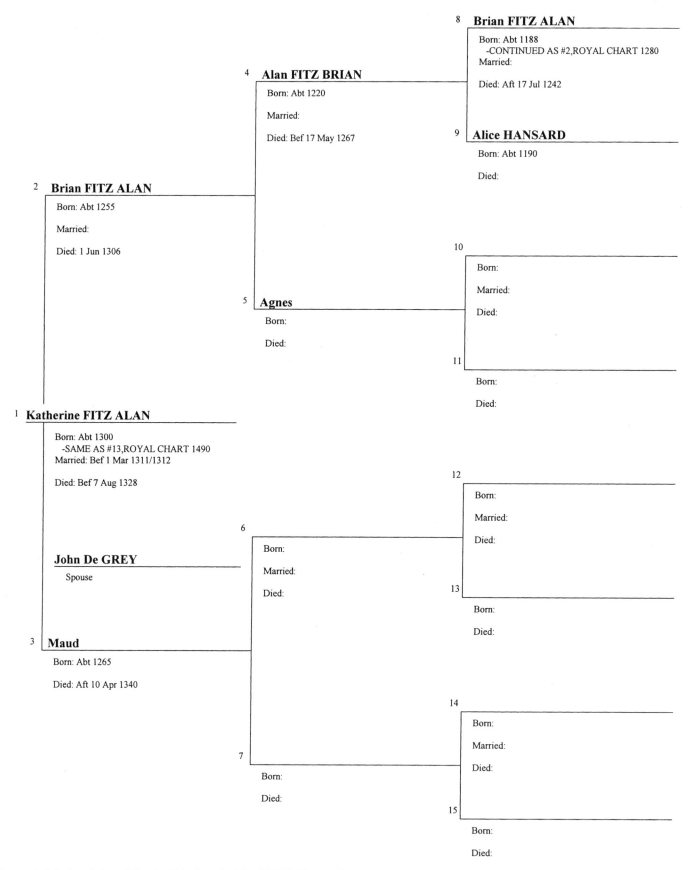

8 Brian FITZ ALAN

Born: Abt 1188
  -CONTINUED AS #2,ROYAL CHART 1280
Married:

Died: Aft 17 Jul 1242

4 Alan FITZ BRIAN

Born: Abt 1220

Married:

Died: Bef 17 May 1267

9 Alice HANSARD

Born: Abt 1190

Died:

2 Brian FITZ ALAN

Born: Abt 1255

Married:

Died: 1 Jun 1306

10

Born:

Married:

Died:

5 Agnes

Born:

Died:

11

Born:

Died:

1 Katherine FITZ ALAN

Born: Abt 1300
  -SAME AS #13,ROYAL CHART 1490
Married: Bef 1 Mar 1311/1312

Died: Bef 7 Aug 1328

12

Born:

Married:

Died:

6

Born:

Married:

Died:

13

Born:

Died:

John De GREY

Spouse

3 Maud

Born: Abt 1265

Died: Aft 10 Apr 1340

14

Born:

Married:

Died:

7

Born:

Died:

15

Born:

Died:

Sources include: Consultation with Douglas Richardson; *Blood Royal* 5:70-73 (#2 ancestry).

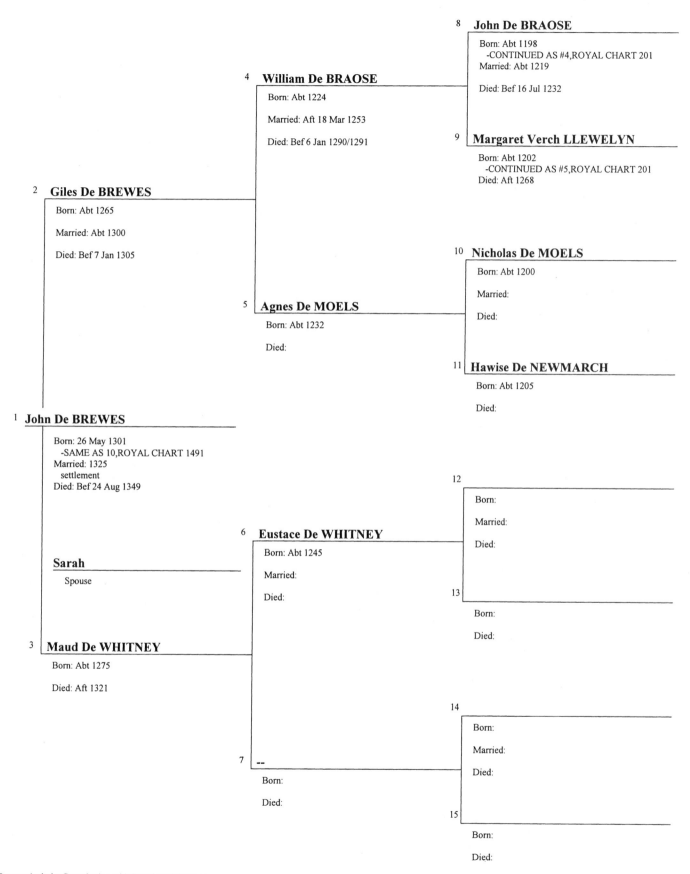

8 John De BRAOSE

Born: Abt 1198
  -CONTINUED AS #4,ROYAL CHART 201
Married: Abt 1219

Died: Bef 16 Jul 1232

4 William De BRAOSE

Born: Abt 1224

Married: Aft 18 Mar 1253

Died: Bef 6 Jan 1290/1291

9 Margaret Verch LLEWELYN

Born: Abt 1202
  -CONTINUED AS #5,ROYAL CHART 201
Died: Aft 1268

2 Giles De BREWES

Born: Abt 1265

Married: Abt 1300

Died: Bef 7 Jan 1305

10 Nicholas De MOELS

Born: Abt 1200

Married:

Died:

5 Agnes De MOELS

Born: Abt 1232

Died:

11 Hawise De NEWMARCH

Born: Abt 1205

Died:

1 John De BREWES

Born: 26 May 1301
  -SAME AS 10,ROYAL CHART 1491
Married: 1325
  settlement
Died: Bef 24 Aug 1349

12

Born:

Married:

Died:

6 Eustace De WHITNEY

Born: Abt 1245

Married:

Died:

13

Born:

Died:

Sarah

Spouse

3 Maud De WHITNEY

Born: Abt 1275

Died: Aft 1321

14

Born:

Married:

Died:

7 --

Born:

Died:

15

Born:

Died:

Sources include: Consultation with Douglas Richardson.

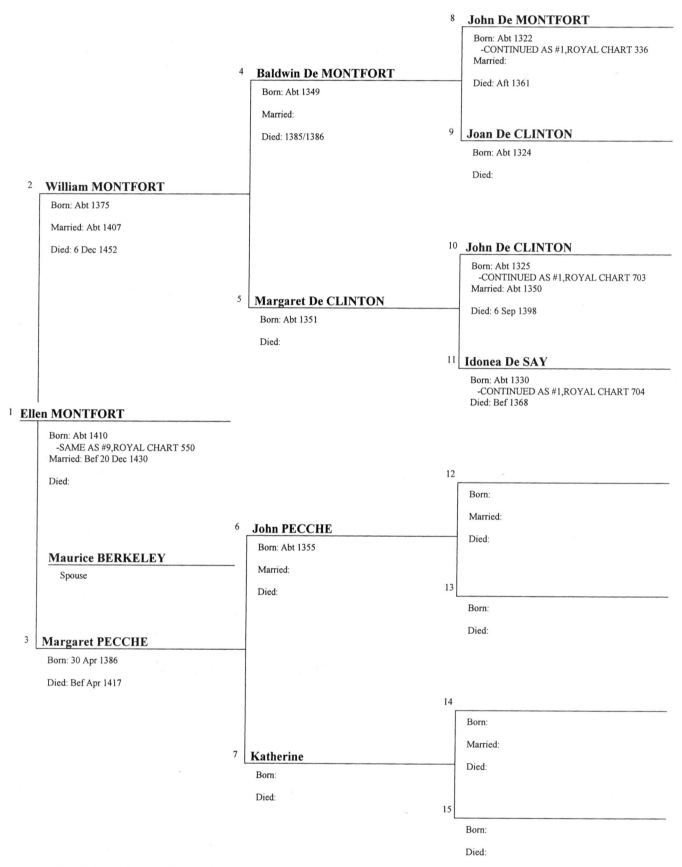

8 John De MONTFORT

Born: Abt 1322
-CONTINUED AS #1,ROYAL CHART 336
Married:

Died: Aft 1361

4 Baldwin De MONTFORT

Born: Abt 1349

Married:

Died: 1385/1386

9 Joan De CLINTON

Born: Abt 1324

Died:

2 William MONTFORT

Born: Abt 1375

Married: Abt 1407

Died: 6 Dec 1452

10 John De CLINTON

Born: Abt 1325
-CONTINUED AS #1,ROYAL CHART 703
Married: Abt 1350

Died: 6 Sep 1398

5 Margaret De CLINTON

Born: Abt 1351

Died:

11 Idonea De SAY

Born: Abt 1330
-CONTINUED AS #1,ROYAL CHART 704
Died: Bef 1368

1 Ellen MONTFORT

Born: Abt 1410
-SAME AS #9,ROYAL CHART 550
Married: Bef 20 Dec 1430

Died:

12

Born:

Married:

Died:

6 John PECCHE

Born: Abt 1355

Married:

Died:

13

Born:

Died:

Maurice BERKELEY

Spouse

3 Margaret PECCHE

Born: 30 Apr 1386

Died: Bef Apr 1417

14

Born:

Married:

Died:

7 Katherine

Born:

Died:

15

Born:

Died:

Sources include: Consultation with Douglas Richardson; *Ancestral Roots* 86.

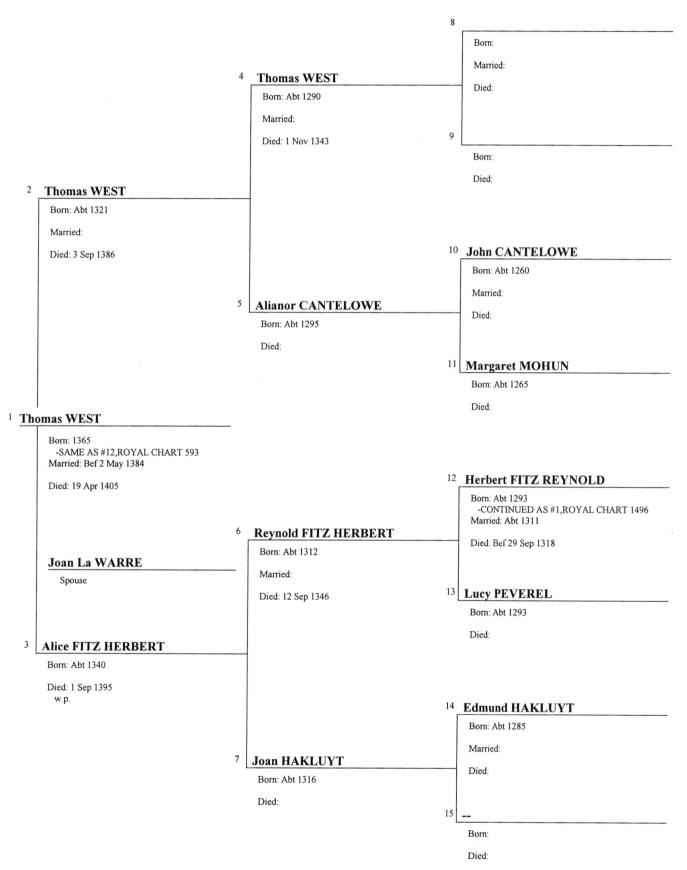

8
Born:
Married:
Died:

4 Thomas WEST
Born: Abt 1290
Married:
Died: 1 Nov 1343

9
Born:
Died:

2 Thomas WEST
Born: Abt 1321
Married:
Died: 3 Sep 1386

10 John CANTELOWE
Born: Abt 1260
Married:
Died:

5 Alianor CANTELOWE
Born: Abt 1295
Died:

11 Margaret MOHUN
Born: Abt 1265
Died:

1 Thomas WEST
Born: 1365
  -SAME AS #12,ROYAL CHART 593
Married: Bef 2 May 1384
Died: 19 Apr 1405

12 Herbert FITZ REYNOLD
Born: Abt 1293
  -CONTINUED AS #1,ROYAL CHART 1496
Married: Abt 1311
Died: Bef 29 Sep 1318

6 Reynold FITZ HERBERT
Born: Abt 1312
Married:
Died: 12 Sep 1346

Joan La WARRE
Spouse

13 Lucy PEVEREL
Born: Abt 1293
Died:

3 Alice FITZ HERBERT
Born: Abt 1340
Died: 1 Sep 1395
w.p.

14 Edmund HAKLUYT
Born: Abt 1285
Married:
Died:

7 Joan HAKLUYT
Born: Abt 1316
Died:

15 --
Born:
Died:

Sources include: Consultation with Douglas Richardson; LDS records.

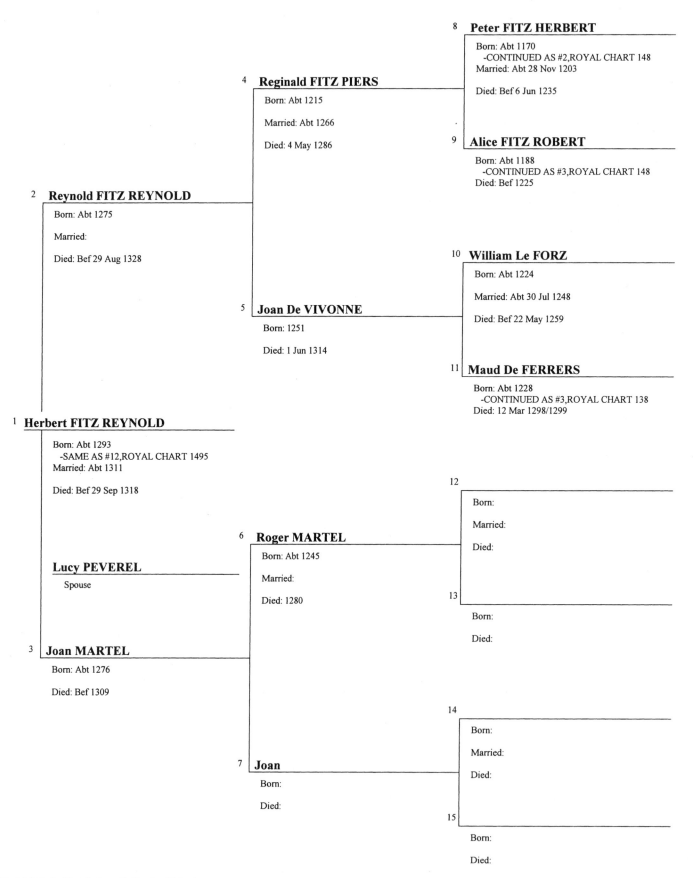

8   Peter FITZ HERBERT

Born: Abt 1170
 -CONTINUED AS #2,ROYAL CHART 148
Married: Abt 28 Nov 1203

Died: Bef 6 Jun 1235

4   Reginald FITZ PIERS

Born: Abt 1215

Married: Abt 1266

Died: 4 May 1286

9   Alice FITZ ROBERT

Born: Abt 1188
 -CONTINUED AS #3,ROYAL CHART 148
Died: Bef 1225

2   Reynold FITZ REYNOLD

Born: Abt 1275

Married:

Died: Bef 29 Aug 1328

10   William Le FORZ

Born: Abt 1224

Married: Abt 30 Jul 1248

Died: Bef 22 May 1259

5   Joan De VIVONNE

Born: 1251

Died: 1 Jun 1314

11   Maud De FERRERS

Born: Abt 1228
 -CONTINUED AS #3,ROYAL CHART 138
Died: 12 Mar 1298/1299

1   Herbert FITZ REYNOLD

Born: Abt 1293
 -SAME AS #12,ROYAL CHART 1495
Married: Abt 1311

Died: Bef 29 Sep 1318

12

Born:

Married:

Died:

6   Roger MARTEL

Born: Abt 1245

Married:

Died: 1280

13

Born:

Died:

Lucy PEVEREL

Spouse

3   Joan MARTEL

Born: Abt 1276

Died: Bef 1309

14

Born:

Married:

Died:

7   Joan

Born:

Died:

15

Born:

Died:

Sources include: Consultation with Douglas Richardson.

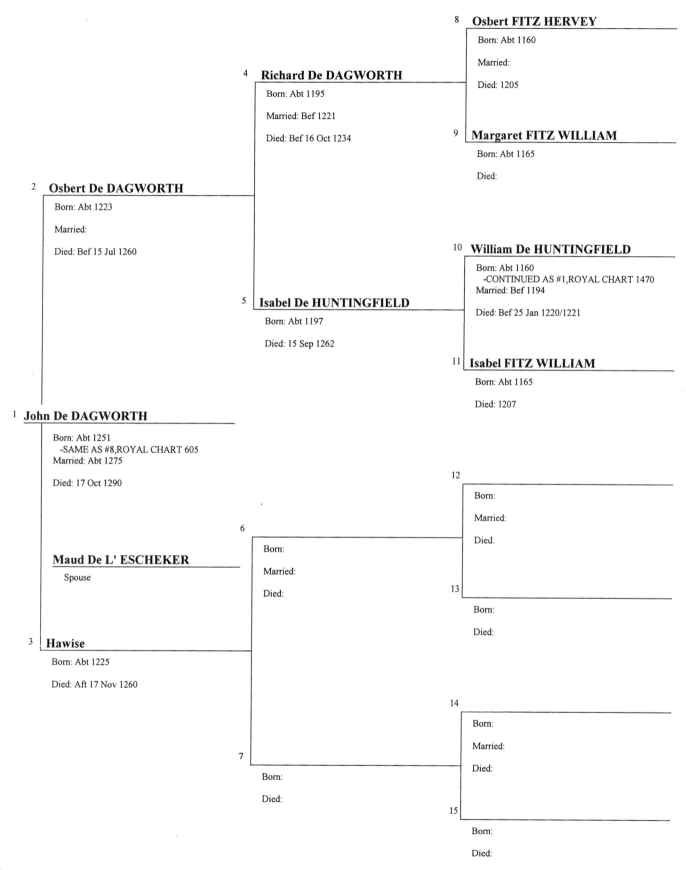

8 **Osbert FITZ HERVEY**
Born: Abt 1160
Married:
Died: 1205

4 **Richard De DAGWORTH**
Born: Abt 1195
Married: Bef 1221
Died: Bef 16 Oct 1234

9 **Margaret FITZ WILLIAM**
Born: Abt 1165
Died:

2 **Osbert De DAGWORTH**
Born: Abt 1223
Married:
Died: Bef 15 Jul 1260

10 **William De HUNTINGFIELD**
Born: Abt 1160
  -CONTINUED AS #1,ROYAL CHART 1470
Married: Bef 1194
Died: Bef 25 Jan 1220/1221

5 **Isabel De HUNTINGFIELD**
Born: Abt 1197
Died: 15 Sep 1262

11 **Isabel FITZ WILLIAM**
Born: Abt 1165
Died: 1207

1 **John De DAGWORTH**
Born: Abt 1251
  -SAME AS #8,ROYAL CHART 605
Married: Abt 1275
Died: 17 Oct 1290

12
Born:
Married:
Died.

6
Born:
Married:
Died:

13
Born:
Died:

Maud De L' ESCHEKER
Spouse

3 **Hawise**
Born: Abt 1225
Died: Aft 17 Nov 1260

14
Born:
Married:
Died:

7
Born:
Died:

15
Born:
Died:

Sources include: Consultation with Douglas Richardson.

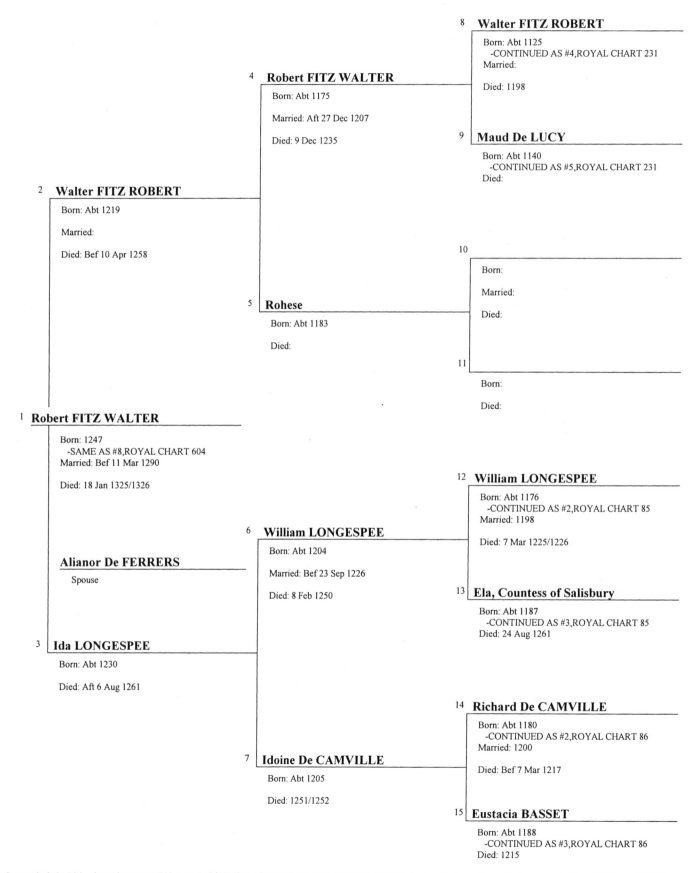

8 **Walter FITZ ROBERT**

Born: Abt 1125
-CONTINUED AS #4,ROYAL CHART 231
Married:

Died: 1198

4 **Robert FITZ WALTER**

Born: Abt 1175

Married: Aft 27 Dec 1207

Died: 9 Dec 1235

9 **Maud De LUCY**

Born: Abt 1140
-CONTINUED AS #5,ROYAL CHART 231
Died:

2 **Walter FITZ ROBERT**

Born: Abt 1219

Married:

Died: Bef 10 Apr 1258

10

Born:

Married:

Died:

5 **Rohese**

Born: Abt 1183

Died:

11

Born:

Died:

1 **Robert FITZ WALTER**

Born: 1247
-SAME AS #8,ROYAL CHART 604
Married: Bef 11 Mar 1290

Died: 18 Jan 1325/1326

12 **William LONGESPEE**

Born: Abt 1176
-CONTINUED AS #2,ROYAL CHART 85
Married: 1198

Died: 7 Mar 1225/1226

6 **William LONGESPEE**

Born: Abt 1204

Married: Bef 23 Sep 1226

Died: 8 Feb 1250

Alianor De FERRERS

Spouse

13 **Ela, Countess of Salisbury**

Born: Abt 1187
-CONTINUED AS #3,ROYAL CHART 85
Died: 24 Aug 1261

3 **Ida LONGESPEE**

Born: Abt 1230

Died: Aft 6 Aug 1261

14 **Richard De CAMVILLE**

Born: Abt 1180
-CONTINUED AS #2,ROYAL CHART 86
Married: 1200

Died: Bef 7 Mar 1217

7 **Idoine De CAMVILLE**

Born: Abt 1205

Died: 1251/1252

15 **Eustacia BASSET**

Born: Abt 1188
-CONTINUED AS #3,ROYAL CHART 86
Died: 1215

Sources include: Richardson *Plantagenet* (2004), pp. 326-327 (Fitz Walter), 456-460 (Longespee); Faris-Richardson preliminary Magna Carta manuscript (June 2000), pp. 218-220 (Fitz Walter); *Ancestral Roots* 30 (#3 ancestry). Note: #3 Ida is also claimed as daughter of #12 & 13 William & Ela.

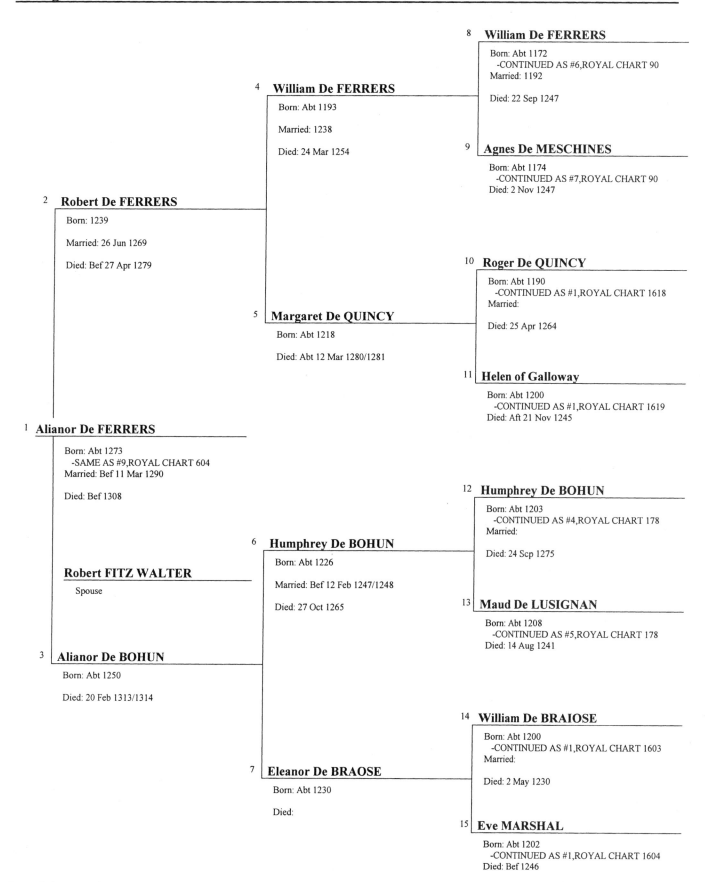

8 William De FERRERS

Born: Abt 1172
-CONTINUED AS #6,ROYAL CHART 90
Married: 1192

Died: 22 Sep 1247

4 William De FERRERS

Born: Abt 1193

Married: 1238

Died: 24 Mar 1254

9 Agnes De MESCHINES

Born: Abt 1174
-CONTINUED AS #7,ROYAL CHART 90
Died: 2 Nov 1247

2 Robert De FERRERS

Born: 1239

Married: 26 Jun 1269

Died: Bef 27 Apr 1279

10 Roger De QUINCY

Born: Abt 1190
-CONTINUED AS #1,ROYAL CHART 1618
Married:

Died: 25 Apr 1264

5 Margaret De QUINCY

Born: Abt 1218

Died: Abt 12 Mar 1280/1281

11 Helen of Galloway

Born: Abt 1200
-CONTINUED AS #1,ROYAL CHART 1619
Died: Aft 21 Nov 1245

1 Alianor De FERRERS

Born: Abt 1273
-SAME AS #9,ROYAL CHART 604
Married: Bef 11 Mar 1290

Died: Bef 1308

12 Humphrey De BOHUN

Born: Abt 1203
-CONTINUED AS #4,ROYAL CHART 178
Married:

Died: 24 Scp 1275

6 Humphrey De BOHUN

Born: Abt 1226

Married: Bef 12 Feb 1247/1248

Died: 27 Oct 1265

13 Maud De LUSIGNAN

Born: Abt 1208
-CONTINUED AS #5,ROYAL CHART 178
Died: 14 Aug 1241

Robert FITZ WALTER

Spouse

3 Alianor De BOHUN

Born: Abt 1250

Died: 20 Feb 1313/1314

14 William De BRAIOSE

Born: Abt 1200
-CONTINUED AS #1,ROYAL CHART 1603
Married:

Died: 2 May 1230

7 Eleanor De BRAOSE

Born: Abt 1230

Died:

15 Eve MARSHAL

Born: Abt 1202
-CONTINUED AS #1,ROYAL CHART 1604
Died: Bef 1246

Sources include: Consultation with Douglas Richardson; *Ancestral Roots* 57, 68 (#2 & 3 ancestry).

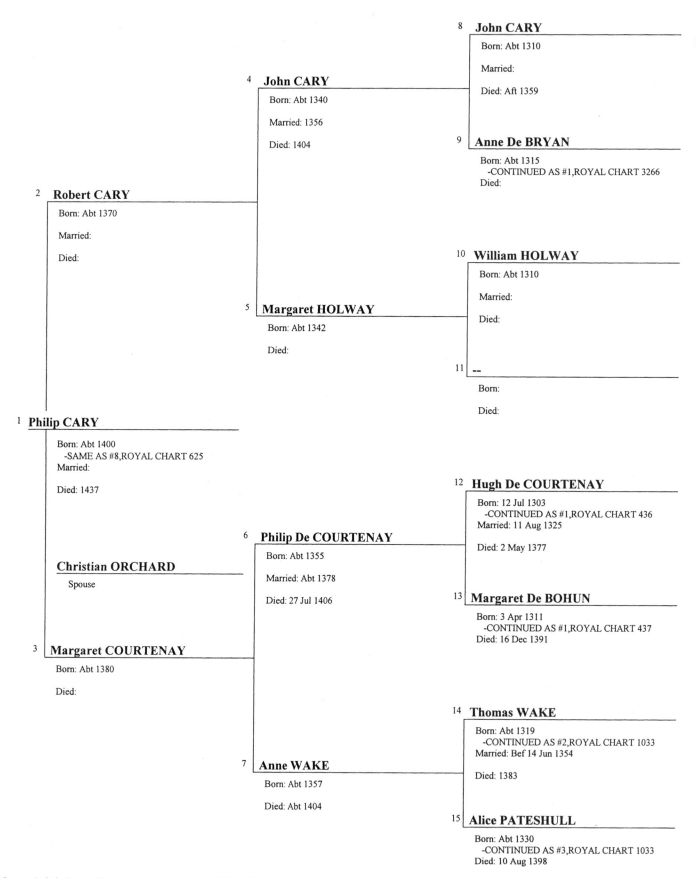

Chart 1500

8 **John CARY**

Born: Abt 1310

Married:

Died: Aft 1359

4 **John CARY**

Born: Abt 1340

Married: 1356

Died: 1404

9 **Anne De BRYAN**

Born: Abt 1315
  -CONTINUED AS #1,ROYAL CHART 3266
Died:

2 **Robert CARY**

Born: Abt 1370

Married:

Died:

10 **William HOLWAY**

Born: Abt 1310

Married:

Died:

5 **Margaret HOLWAY**

Born: Abt 1342

Died:

11 **--**

Born:

Died:

1 **Philip CARY**

Born: Abt 1400
  -SAME AS #8,ROYAL CHART 625
Married:

Died: 1437

12 **Hugh De COURTENAY**

Born: 12 Jul 1303
  -CONTINUED AS #1,ROYAL CHART 436
Married: 11 Aug 1325

Died: 2 May 1377

6 **Philip De COURTENAY**

Born: Abt 1355

Married: Abt 1378

Died: 27 Jul 1406

13 **Margaret De BOHUN**

Born: 3 Apr 1311
  -CONTINUED AS #1,ROYAL CHART 437
Died: 16 Dec 1391

Christian ORCHARD

Spouse

3 **Margaret COURTENAY**

Born: Abt 1380

Died:

14 **Thomas WAKE**

Born: Abt 1319
  -CONTINUED AS #2,ROYAL CHART 1033
Married: Bef 14 Jun 1354

Died: 1383

7 **Anne WAKE**

Born: Abt 1357

Died: Abt 1404

15 **Alice PATESHULL**

Born: Abt 1330
  -CONTINUED AS #3,ROYAL CHART 1033
Died: 10 Aug 1398

Sources include: Faris preliminary baronial manuscript (1998), p. 302 (Cary); Consultation with Douglas Richardson; Faris 2--Davie (#6 & 7 ancestry).

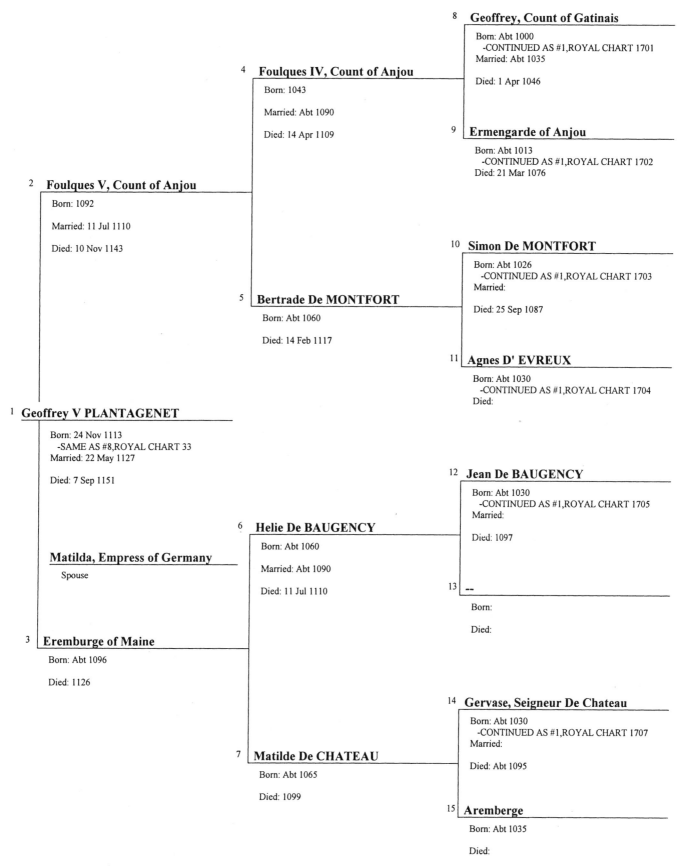

2 Foulques V, Count of Anjou

Born: 1092

Married: 11 Jul 1110

Died: 10 Nov 1143

4 Foulques IV, Count of Anjou

Born: 1043

Married: Abt 1090

Died: 14 Apr 1109

8 Geoffrey, Count of Gatinais

Born: Abt 1000
   -CONTINUED AS #1,ROYAL CHART 1701
Married: Abt 1035

Died: 1 Apr 1046

9 Ermengarde of Anjou

Born: Abt 1013
   -CONTINUED AS #1,ROYAL CHART 1702
Died: 21 Mar 1076

5 Bertrade De MONTFORT

Born: Abt 1060

Died: 14 Feb 1117

10 Simon De MONTFORT

Born: Abt 1026
   -CONTINUED AS #1,ROYAL CHART 1703
Married:

Died: 25 Sep 1087

11 Agnes D' EVREUX

Born: Abt 1030
   -CONTINUED AS #1,ROYAL CHART 1704
Died:

1 Geoffrey V PLANTAGENET

Born: 24 Nov 1113
   -SAME AS #8,ROYAL CHART 33
Married: 22 May 1127

Died: 7 Sep 1151

Matilda, Empress of Germany

Spouse

3 Eremburge of Maine

Born: Abt 1096

Died: 1126

6 Helie De BAUGENCY

Born: Abt 1060

Married: Abt 1090

Died: 11 Jul 1110

12 Jean De BAUGENCY

Born: Abt 1030
   -CONTINUED AS #1,ROYAL CHART 1705
Married:

Died: 1097

13 --

Born:

Died:

7 Matilde De CHATEAU

Born: Abt 1065

Died: 1099

14 Gervase, Seigneur De Chateau

Born: Abt 1030
   -CONTINUED AS #1,ROYAL CHART 1707
Married:

Died: Abt 1095

15 Aremberge

Born: Abt 1035

Died:

Sources include: *Royal Ancestors* 11301; Faris--Plantagenet 18; *Ancestral Roots* 118; Stuart 53, 313; Moriarty 1-4, 10-12.

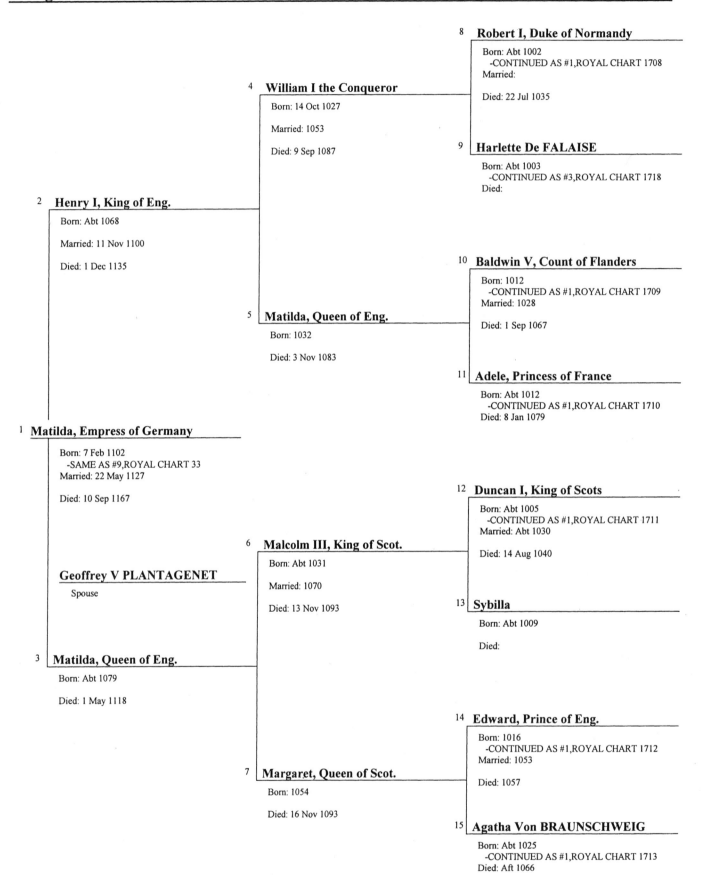

8 Robert I, Duke of Normandy

Born: Abt 1002
-CONTINUED AS #1,ROYAL CHART 1708
Married:

Died: 22 Jul 1035

4 William I the Conqueror

Born: 14 Oct 1027

Married: 1053

Died: 9 Sep 1087

9 Harlette De FALAISE

Born: Abt 1003
-CONTINUED AS #3,ROYAL CHART 1718
Died:

2 Henry I, King of Eng.

Born: Abt 1068

Married: 11 Nov 1100

Died: 1 Dec 1135

10 Baldwin V, Count of Flanders

Born: 1012
-CONTINUED AS #1,ROYAL CHART 1709
Married: 1028

Died: 1 Sep 1067

5 Matilda, Queen of Eng.

Born: 1032

Died: 3 Nov 1083

11 Adele, Princess of France

Born: Abt 1012
-CONTINUED AS #1,ROYAL CHART 1710
Died: 8 Jan 1079

1 Matilda, Empress of Germany

Born: 7 Feb 1102
-SAME AS #9,ROYAL CHART 33
Married: 22 May 1127

Died: 10 Sep 1167

12 Duncan I, King of Scots

Born: Abt 1005
-CONTINUED AS #1,ROYAL CHART 1711
Married: Abt 1030

Died: 14 Aug 1040

6 Malcolm III, King of Scot.

Born: Abt 1031

Married: 1070

Died: 13 Nov 1093

Geoffrey V PLANTAGENET

Spouse

13 Sybilla

Born: Abt 1009

Died:

3 Matilda, Queen of Eng.

Born: Abt 1079

Died: 1 May 1118

14 Edward, Prince of Eng.

Born: 1016
-CONTINUED AS #1,ROYAL CHART 1712
Married: 1053

Died: 1057

7 Margaret, Queen of Scot.

Born: 1054

Died: 16 Nov 1093

15 Agatha Von BRAUNSCHWEIG

Born: Abt 1025
-CONTINUED AS #1,ROYAL CHART 1713
Died: Aft 1066

Sources include: *Royal Ancestors* (1989), charts 11301, 11406; Faris--Plantagenet 18; *Ancestral Roots* 1, 121; Stuart 89, 165; Moriarty 13-15, 28-31; Faris preliminary Charlemagne manuscript (June 1995), p. 16 (#3 ancestry); *NEHGR* 150: 417-432, 152:215-235 (debate on #15 ancestry). Notes: The parentage of #13 Sybilla is disputed and uncertain. See Moriarty 30; *Ancestral Roots* 170-20; Stuart 165-32. The parentage of #15 Agatha is heavily disputed. The version argued in *NEHGR* 152 and accepted by Faris and Richardson is accepted here.

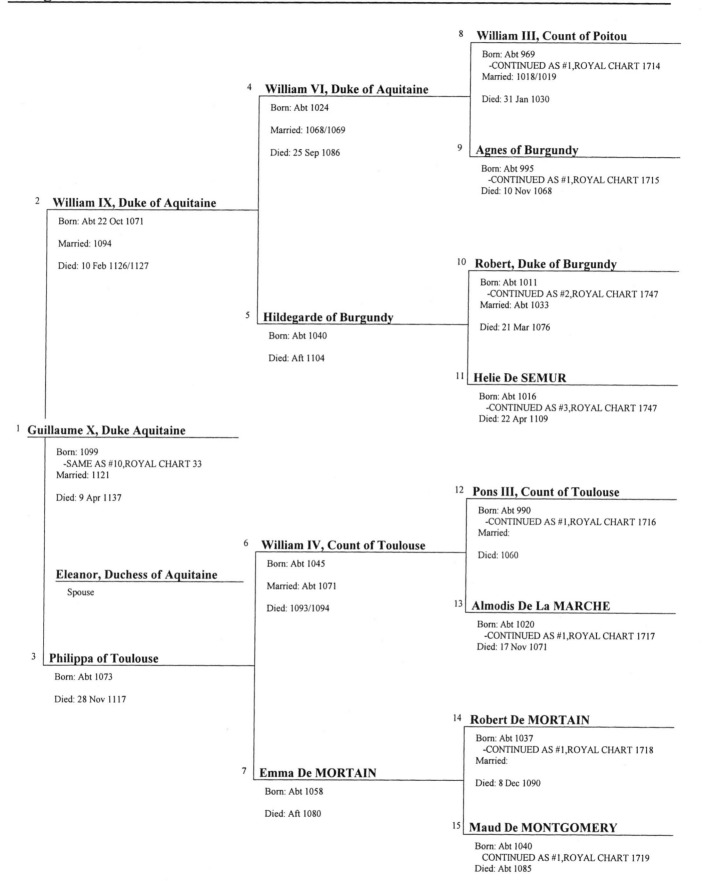

8 **William III, Count of Poitou**
Born: Abt 969
-CONTINUED AS #1,ROYAL CHART 1714
Married: 1018/1019

Died: 31 Jan 1030

4 **William VI, Duke of Aquitaine**
Born: Abt 1024

Married: 1068/1069

Died: 25 Sep 1086

9 **Agnes of Burgundy**
Born: Abt 995
-CONTINUED AS #1,ROYAL CHART 1715
Died: 10 Nov 1068

2 **William IX, Duke of Aquitaine**
Born: Abt 22 Oct 1071

Married: 1094

Died: 10 Feb 1126/1127

10 **Robert, Duke of Burgundy**
Born: Abt 1011
-CONTINUED AS #2,ROYAL CHART 1747
Married: Abt 1033

Died: 21 Mar 1076

5 **Hildegarde of Burgundy**
Born: Abt 1040

Died: Aft 1104

11 **Helie De SEMUR**
Born: Abt 1016
-CONTINUED AS #3,ROYAL CHART 1747
Died: 22 Apr 1109

1 **Guillaume X, Duke Aquitaine**
Born: 1099
-SAME AS #10,ROYAL CHART 33
Married: 1121

Died: 9 Apr 1137

12 **Pons III, Count of Toulouse**
Born: Abt 990
-CONTINUED AS #1,ROYAL CHART 1716
Married:

Died: 1060

6 **William IV, Count of Toulouse**
Born: Abt 1045

Married: Abt 1071

Died: 1093/1094

13 **Almodis De La MARCHE**
Born: Abt 1020
-CONTINUED AS #1,ROYAL CHART 1717
Died: 17 Nov 1071

Eleanor, Duchess of Aquitaine
Spouse

3 **Philippa of Toulouse**
Born: Abt 1073

Died: 28 Nov 1117

14 **Robert De MORTAIN**
Born: Abt 1037
-CONTINUED AS #1,ROYAL CHART 1718
Married:

Died: 8 Dec 1090

7 **Emma De MORTAIN**
Born: Abt 1058

Died: Aft 1080

15 **Maud De MONTGOMERY**
Born: Abt 1040
CONTINUED AS #1,ROYAL CHART 1719
Died: Abt 1085

Sources: *Royal Ancestors* 11301; Stuart 88; *Ancestral Roots* 110, 185; Moriarty 35-37, 40, 42, 44; Faris preliminary Charlemagne manuscript (June 1995), pp. 217-219. Notes: #1, 2, 4 & 8--William or Guillaume. #11 is disputed. Moriarty and others accept Helie De Semur (a 1st wife), as shown. Faris gives Ermengarde of Anjou (a 2nd wife), same person as #1, chart 1702.

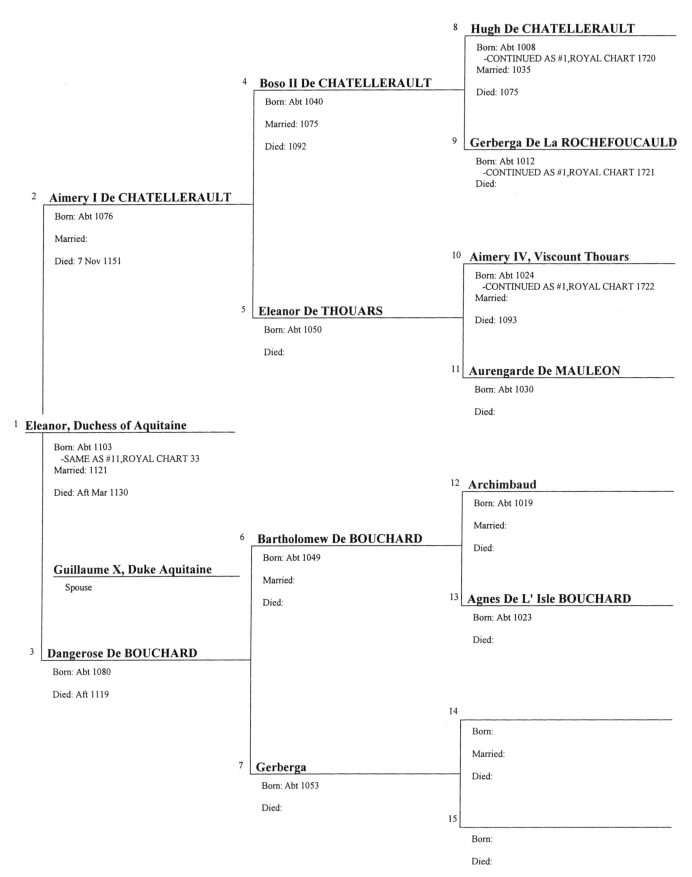

8 **Hugh De CHATELLERAULT**

Born: Abt 1008
 -CONTINUED AS #1,ROYAL CHART 1720
Married: 1035

Died: 1075

4 **Boso II De CHATELLERAULT**

Born: Abt 1040

Married: 1075

Died: 1092

9 **Gerberga De La ROCHEFOUCAULD**

Born: Abt 1012
 -CONTINUED AS #1,ROYAL CHART 1721
Died:

2 **Aimery I De CHATELLERAULT**

Born: Abt 1076

Married:

Died: 7 Nov 1151

10 **Aimery IV, Viscount Thouars**

Born: Abt 1024
 -CONTINUED AS #1,ROYAL CHART 1722
Married:

Died: 1093

5 **Eleanor De THOUARS**

Born: Abt 1050

Died:

11 **Aurengarde De MAULEON**

Born: Abt 1030

Died:

1 **Eleanor, Duchess of Aquitaine**

Born: Abt 1103
 -SAME AS #11,ROYAL CHART 33
Married: 1121

Died: Aft Mar 1130

12 **Archimbaud**

Born: Abt 1019

Married:

Died:

6 **Bartholomew De BOUCHARD**

Born: Abt 1049

Married:

Died:

13 **Agnes De L' Isle BOUCHARD**

Born: Abt 1023

Died:

Guillaume X, Duke Aquitaine

Spouse

3 **Dangerose De BOUCHARD**

Born: Abt 1080

Died: Aft 1119

14

Born:

Married:

Died:

7 **Gerberga**

Born: Abt 1053

Died:

15

Born:

Died:

Sources: *Royal Ancestors* (1989), chart 11301; Faris--Plantagenet 17; Stuart 159; *Ancestral Roots* 183; Moriarty 45-46; Paget 9; Kraentzler 1166; LDS records. Note: #3 & 6 -- De L' Isle Bouchard.

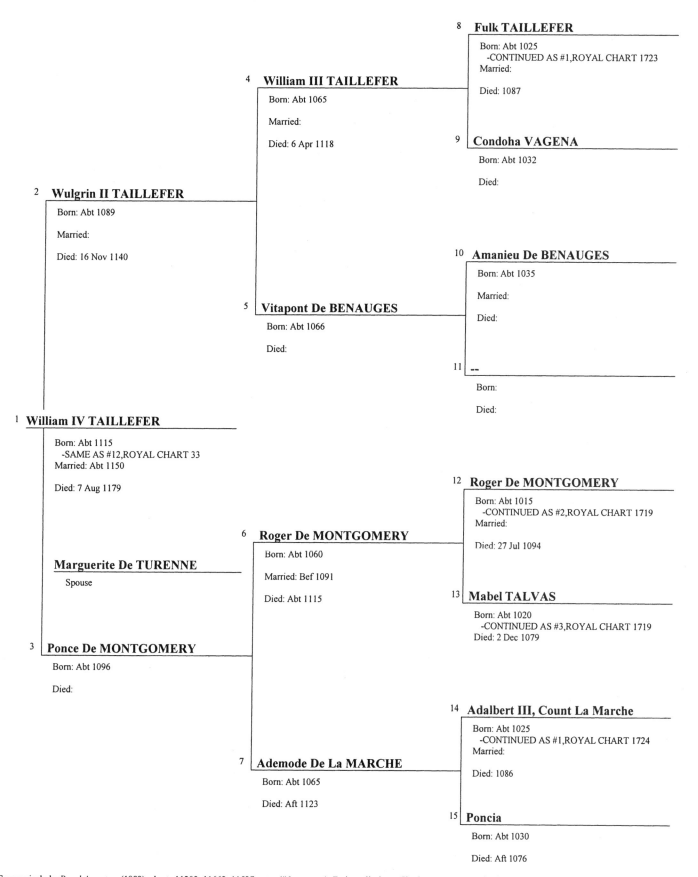

8 Fulk TAILLEFER

Born: Abt 1025
   -CONTINUED AS #1,ROYAL CHART 1723
Married:

Died: 1087

4 William III TAILLEFER

Born: Abt 1065

Married:

Died: 6 Apr 1118

9 Condoha VAGENA

Born: Abt 1032

Died:

2 Wulgrin II TAILLEFER

Born: Abt 1089

Married:

Died: 16 Nov 1140

10 Amanieu De BENAUGES

Born: Abt 1035

Married:

Died:

5 Vitapont De BENAUGES

Born: Abt 1066

Died:

11 --

Born:

Died:

1 William IV TAILLEFER

Born: Abt 1115
   -SAME AS #12,ROYAL CHART 33
Married: Abt 1150

Died: 7 Aug 1179

12 Roger De MONTGOMERY

Born: Abt 1015
   -CONTINUED AS #2,ROYAL CHART 1719
Married:

Died: 27 Jul 1094

6 Roger De MONTGOMERY

Born: Abt 1060

Married: Bef 1091

Died: Abt 1115

13 Mabel TALVAS

Born: Abt 1020
   -CONTINUED AS #3,ROYAL CHART 1719
Died: 2 Dec 1079

Marguerite De TURENNE

Spouse

3 Ponce De MONTGOMERY

Born: Abt 1096

Died:

14 Adalbert III, Count La Marche

Born: Abt 1025
   -CONTINUED AS #1,ROYAL CHART 1724
Married:

Died: 1086

7 Ademode De La MARCHE

Born: Abt 1065

Died: Aft 1123

15 Poncia

Born: Abt 1030

Died: Aft 1076

Sources include: *Royal Ancestors* (1989), charts 11302, 11662, 11527 notes (#6 ancestry); Faris preliminary Charlemagne manuscript (June 1995), pp. 18-19, 166; Stuart 87, 335; Moriarty 42, 45, 47; *Ancestral Roots* 153-26. Note: The parentage of #9 Condoha is disputed.

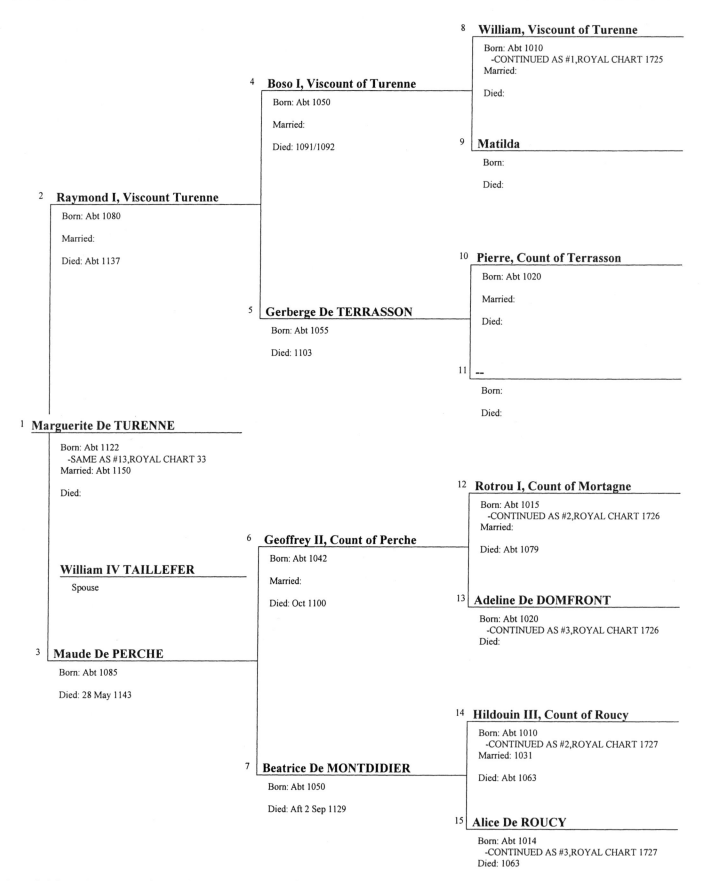

8 William, Viscount of Turenne

Born: Abt 1010
-CONTINUED AS #1,ROYAL CHART 1725
Married:

Died:

4 Boso I, Viscount of Turenne

Born: Abt 1050

Married:

Died: 1091/1092

9 Matilda

Born:

Died:

2 Raymond I, Viscount Turenne

Born: Abt 1080

Married:

Died: Abt 1137

10 Pierre, Count of Terrasson

Born: Abt 1020

Married:

Died:

5 Gerberge De TERRASSON

Born: Abt 1055

Died: 1103

11 --

Born:

Died:

1 Marguerite De TURENNE

Born: Abt 1122
-SAME AS #13,ROYAL CHART 33
Married: Abt 1150

Died:

William IV TAILLEFER

Spouse

12 Rotrou I, Count of Mortagne

Born: Abt 1015
-CONTINUED AS #2,ROYAL CHART 1726
Married:

Died: Abt 1079

6 Geoffrey II, Count of Perche

Born: Abt 1042

Married:

Died: Oct 1100

13 Adeline De DOMFRONT

Born: Abt 1020
-CONTINUED AS #3,ROYAL CHART 1726
Died:

3 Maude De PERCHE

Born: Abt 1085

Died: 28 May 1143

14 Hildouin III, Count of Roucy

Born: Abt 1010
-CONTINUED AS #2,ROYAL CHART 1727
Married: 1031

Died: Abt 1063

7 Beatrice De MONTDIDIER

Born: Abt 1050

Died: Aft 2 Sep 1129

15 Alice De ROUCY

Born: Abt 1014
-CONTINUED AS #3,ROYAL CHART 1727
Died: 1063

Sources include: *Royal Ancestors* 11302; *Ancestral Roots* 153; Moriarty 48; Faris preliminary Charlemagne manuscript (June 1995), pp. 19, 213; Paget 13; Stuart 156, 249. Note: #3 is also claimed as the daughter of Rotrou II (md. Maud, daughter of King Henry I of England by a concubine Edith) and the <u>granddaughter</u> of #6 & 7 Geoffrey and Beatrice.

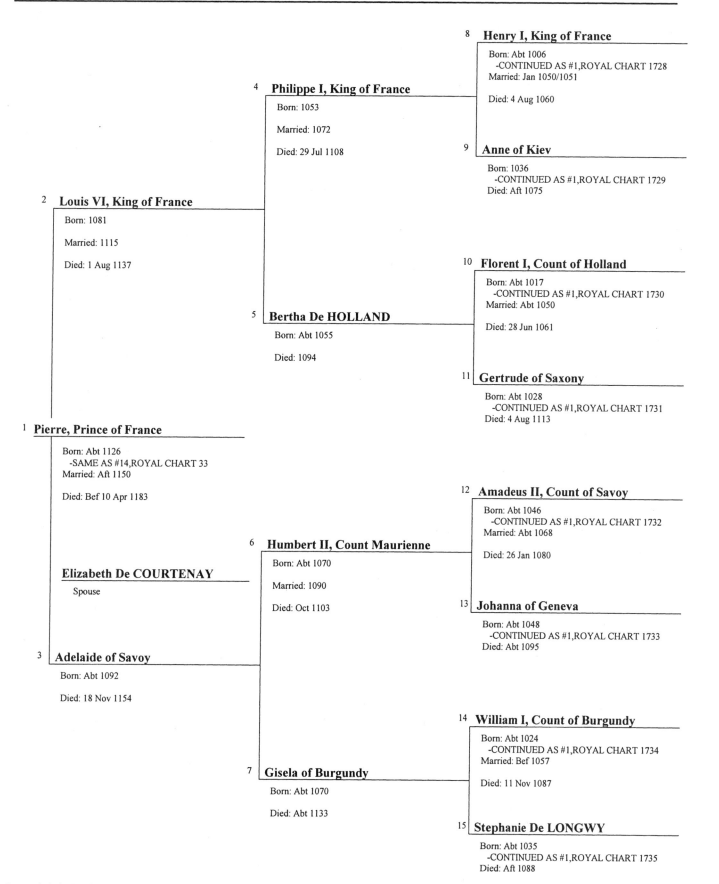

2 Louis VI, King of France

Born: 1081

Married: 1115

Died: 1 Aug 1137

4 Philippe I, King of France

Born: 1053

Married: 1072

Died: 29 Jul 1108

8 Henry I, King of France

Born: Abt 1006
-CONTINUED AS #1,ROYAL CHART 1728
Married: Jan 1050/1051

Died: 4 Aug 1060

9 Anne of Kiev

Born: 1036
-CONTINUED AS #1,ROYAL CHART 1729
Died: Aft 1075

5 Bertha De HOLLAND

Born: Abt 1055

Died: 1094

10 Florent I, Count of Holland

Born: Abt 1017
-CONTINUED AS #1,ROYAL CHART 1730
Married: Abt 1050

Died: 28 Jun 1061

11 Gertrude of Saxony

Born: Abt 1028
-CONTINUED AS #1,ROYAL CHART 1731
Died: 4 Aug 1113

1 Pierre, Prince of France

Born: Abt 1126
-SAME AS #14,ROYAL CHART 33
Married: Aft 1150

Died: Bef 10 Apr 1183

Elizabeth De COURTENAY

Spouse

3 Adelaide of Savoy

Born: Abt 1092

Died: 18 Nov 1154

6 Humbert II, Count Maurienne

Born: Abt 1070

Married: 1090

Died: Oct 1103

12 Amadeus II, Count of Savoy

Born: Abt 1046
-CONTINUED AS #1,ROYAL CHART 1732
Married: Abt 1068

Died: 26 Jan 1080

13 Johanna of Geneva

Born: Abt 1048
-CONTINUED AS #1,ROYAL CHART 1733
Died: Abt 1095

7 Gisela of Burgundy

Born: Abt 1070

Died: Abt 1133

14 William I, Count of Burgundy

Born: Abt 1024
-CONTINUED AS #1,ROYAL CHART 1734
Married: Bef 1057

Died: 11 Nov 1087

15 Stephanie De LONGWY

Born: Abt 1035
-CONTINUED AS #1,ROYAL CHART 1735
Died: Aft 1088

Sources include: *Royal Ancestors* 11302; *Ancestral Roots* 117, 101; Stuart 79, 134; Moriarty 62.

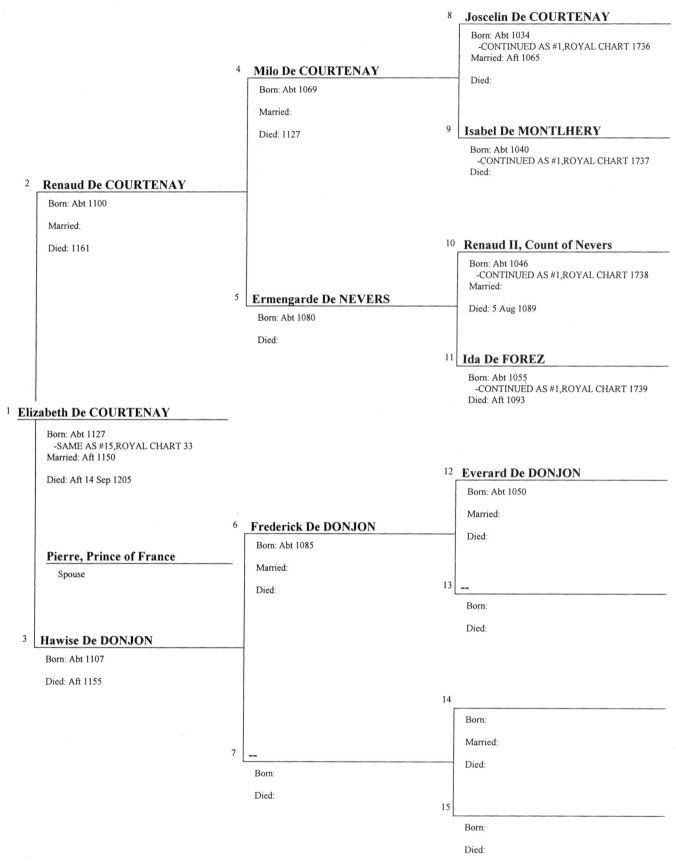

8 **Joscelin De COURTENAY**

Born: Abt 1034
-CONTINUED AS #1,ROYAL CHART 1736
Married: Aft 1065

Died:

4 **Milo De COURTENAY**

Born: Abt 1069

Married:

Died: 1127

9 **Isabel De MONTLHERY**

Born: Abt 1040
-CONTINUED AS #1,ROYAL CHART 1737
Died:

2 **Renaud De COURTENAY**

Born: Abt 1100

Married:

Died: 1161

10 **Renaud II, Count of Nevers**

Born: Abt 1046
-CONTINUED AS #1,ROYAL CHART 1738
Married:

Died: 5 Aug 1089

5 **Ermengarde De NEVERS**

Born: Abt 1080

Died:

11 **Ida De FOREZ**

Born: Abt 1055
-CONTINUED AS #1,ROYAL CHART 1739
Died: Aft 1093

1 **Elizabeth De COURTENAY**

Born: Abt 1127
-SAME AS #15,ROYAL CHART 33
Married: Aft 1150

Died: Aft 14 Sep 1205

12 **Everard De DONJON**

Born: Abt 1050

Married:

Died:

6 **Frederick De DONJON**

Born: Abt 1085

Married:

Died:

13 **--**

Born:

Died:

Pierre, Prince of France

Spouse

3 **Hawise De DONJON**

Born: Abt 1107

Died: Aft 1155

14

Born:

Married:

Died:

7 **--**

Born:

Died:

15

Born:

Died:

Sources include: *Royal Ancestors* 11302; Schwennicke 3:629; *Ancestral Roots* 8 (2004), Line 107; *Ancestral Roots* 107; Stuart 144; Moriarty 63; Faris preliminary Charlemagne manuscript (June 1995), pp. 113, 204-205. Note: #3 Hawise (Helvis, Havise, Hedwig) is also claimed to be a <u>sister</u> of Frederick or Guy De Donjon.

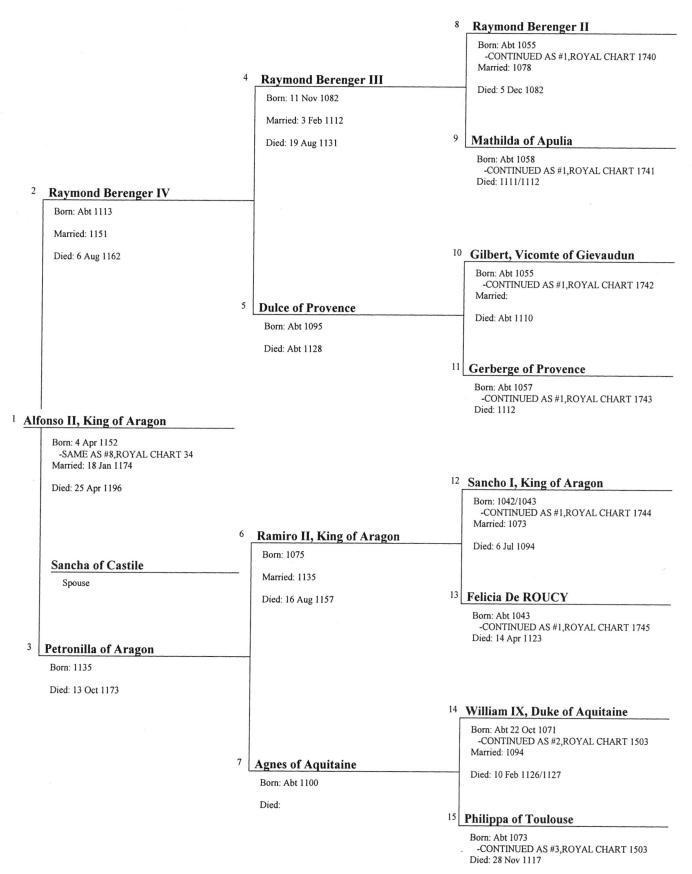

8 Raymond Berenger II

Born: Abt 1055
  -CONTINUED AS #1,ROYAL CHART 1740
Married: 1078

Died: 5 Dec 1082

4 Raymond Berenger III

Born: 11 Nov 1082

Married: 3 Feb 1112

Died: 19 Aug 1131

9 Mathilda of Apulia

Born: Abt 1058
  -CONTINUED AS #1,ROYAL CHART 1741
Died: 1111/1112

2 Raymond Berenger IV

Born: Abt 1113

Married: 1151

Died: 6 Aug 1162

10 Gilbert, Vicomte of Gievaudun

Born: Abt 1055
  -CONTINUED AS #1,ROYAL CHART 1742
Married:

Died: Abt 1110

5 Dulce of Provence

Born: Abt 1095

Died: Abt 1128

11 Gerberge of Provence

Born: Abt 1057
  -CONTINUED AS #1,ROYAL CHART 1743
Died: 1112

1 Alfonso II, King of Aragon

Born: 4 Apr 1152
  -SAME AS #8,ROYAL CHART 34
Married: 18 Jan 1174

Died: 25 Apr 1196

12 Sancho I, King of Aragon

Born: 1042/1043
  -CONTINUED AS #1,ROYAL CHART 1744
Married: 1073

Died: 6 Jul 1094

6 Ramiro II, King of Aragon

Born: 1075

Married: 1135

Died: 16 Aug 1157

Sancha of Castile

Spouse

13 Felicia De ROUCY

Born: Abt 1043
  -CONTINUED AS #1,ROYAL CHART 1745
Died: 14 Apr 1123

3 Petronilla of Aragon

Born: 1135

Died: 13 Oct 1173

14 William IX, Duke of Aquitaine

Born: Abt 22 Oct 1071
  -CONTINUED AS #2,ROYAL CHART 1503
Married: 1094

Died: 10 Feb 1126/1127

7 Agnes of Aquitaine

Born: Abt 1100

Died:

15 Philippa of Toulouse

Born: Abt 1073
  -CONTINUED AS #3,ROYAL CHART 1503
Died: 28 Nov 1117

Sources include: *Royal Ancestors* 11303; *Ancestral Roots* 111; Stuart 54, 95; Moriarty 68, 78; Faris preliminary Charlemagne manuscript (June 1995), pp. 36-37, 24.

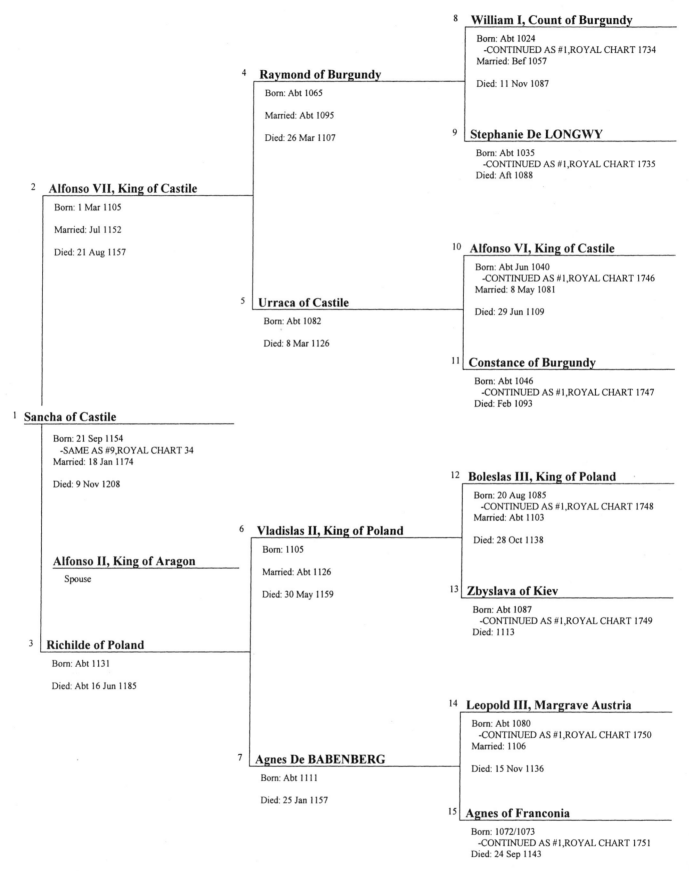

8 William I, Count of Burgundy

Born: Abt 1024
-CONTINUED AS #1,ROYAL CHART 1734
Married: Bef 1057

Died: 11 Nov 1087

4 Raymond of Burgundy

Born: Abt 1065

Married: Abt 1095

Died: 26 Mar 1107

9 Stephanie De LONGWY

Born: Abt 1035
-CONTINUED AS #1,ROYAL CHART 1735
Died: Aft 1088

2 Alfonso VII, King of Castile

Born: 1 Mar 1105

Married: Jul 1152

Died: 21 Aug 1157

10 Alfonso VI, King of Castile

Born: Abt Jun 1040
-CONTINUED AS #1,ROYAL CHART 1746
Married: 8 May 1081

Died: 29 Jun 1109

5 Urraca of Castile

Born: Abt 1082

Died: 8 Mar 1126

11 Constance of Burgundy

Born: Abt 1046
-CONTINUED AS #1,ROYAL CHART 1747
Died: Feb 1093

1 Sancha of Castile

Born: 21 Sep 1154
-SAME AS #9,ROYAL CHART 34
Married: 18 Jan 1174

Died: 9 Nov 1208

12 Boleslas III, King of Poland

Born: 20 Aug 1085
-CONTINUED AS #1,ROYAL CHART 1748
Married: Abt 1103

Died: 28 Oct 1138

6 Vladislas II, King of Poland

Born: 1105

Married: Abt 1126

Died: 30 May 1159

13 Zbyslava of Kiev

Born: Abt 1087
-CONTINUED AS #1,ROYAL CHART 1749
Died: 1113

Alfonso II, King of Aragon

Spouse

3 Richilde of Poland

Born: Abt 1131

Died: Abt 16 Jun 1185

14 Leopold III, Margrave Austria

Born: Abt 1080
-CONTINUED AS #1,ROYAL CHART 1750
Married: 1106

Died: 15 Nov 1136

7 Agnes De BABENBERG

Born: Abt 1111

Died: 25 Jan 1157

15 Agnes of Franconia

Born: 1072/1073
-CONTINUED AS #1,ROYAL CHART 1751
Died: 24 Sep 1143

Sources include: *Royal Ancestors* 11303; *Ancestral Roots* 116, 113, 147; Stuart 94, 378; Moriarty 81, 84; Faris preliminary Charlemagne manuscript (June 1995), pp. 99-100, 58, 54.

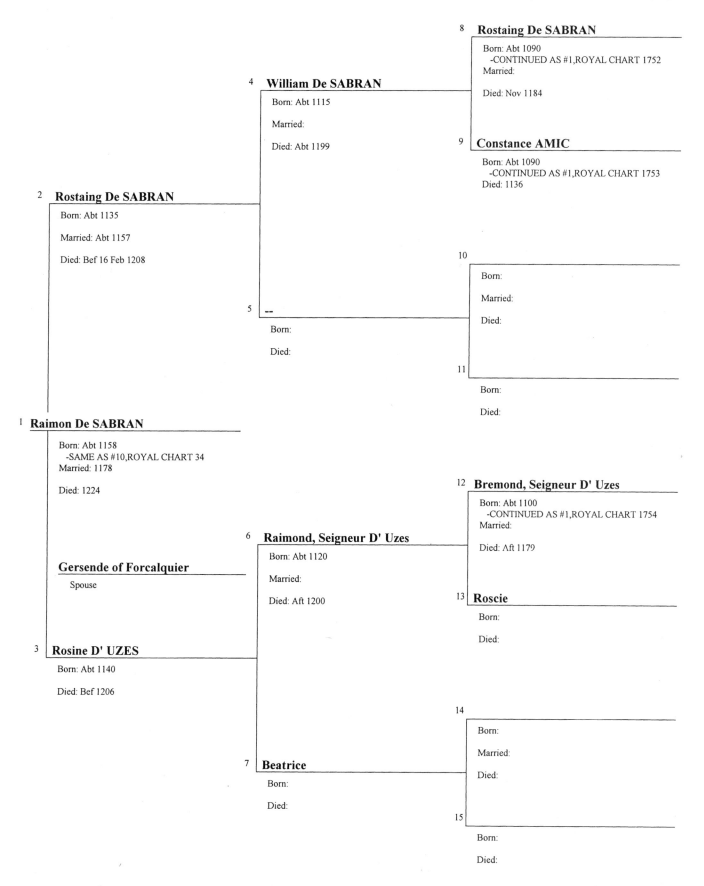

8 Rostaing De SABRAN

Born: Abt 1090
-CONTINUED AS #1,ROYAL CHART 1752
Married:

Died: Nov 1184

4 William De SABRAN

Born: Abt 1115

Married:

Died: Abt 1199

9 Constance AMIC

Born: Abt 1090
-CONTINUED AS #1,ROYAL CHART 1753
Died: 1136

2 Rostaing De SABRAN

Born: Abt 1135

Married: Abt 1157

Died: Bef 16 Feb 1208

10

Born:

Married:

Died:

5 --

Born:

Died:

11

Born:

Died:

1 Raimon De SABRAN

Born: Abt 1158
-SAME AS #10,ROYAL CHART 34
Married: 1178

Died: 1224

12 Bremond, Seigneur D' Uzes

Born: Abt 1100
-CONTINUED AS #1,ROYAL CHART 1754
Married:

Died: Aft 1179

6 Raimond, Seigneur D' Uzes

Born: Abt 1120

Married:

Died: Aft 1200

13 Roscie

Born:

Died:

Gersende of Forcalquier

Spouse

3 Rosine D' UZES

Born: Abt 1140

Died: Bef 1206

14

Born:

Married:

Died:

7 Beatrice

Born:

Died:

15

Born:

Died:

Sources include: *Royal Ancestors* 11303; Moriarty 98-100; Faris preliminary Charlemagne manuscript (June 1995), p. 31; Stuart 116, 193. Note: Stuart 116 gives #3 as Almode De Mevouillon and claims Rosine (#3 above) as a 2nd wife of #8 Rostaing. However, Stuart 116-28, 116-29, and 193-29 has serious conflicts. The version retained above agrees with Faris and Moriarty.

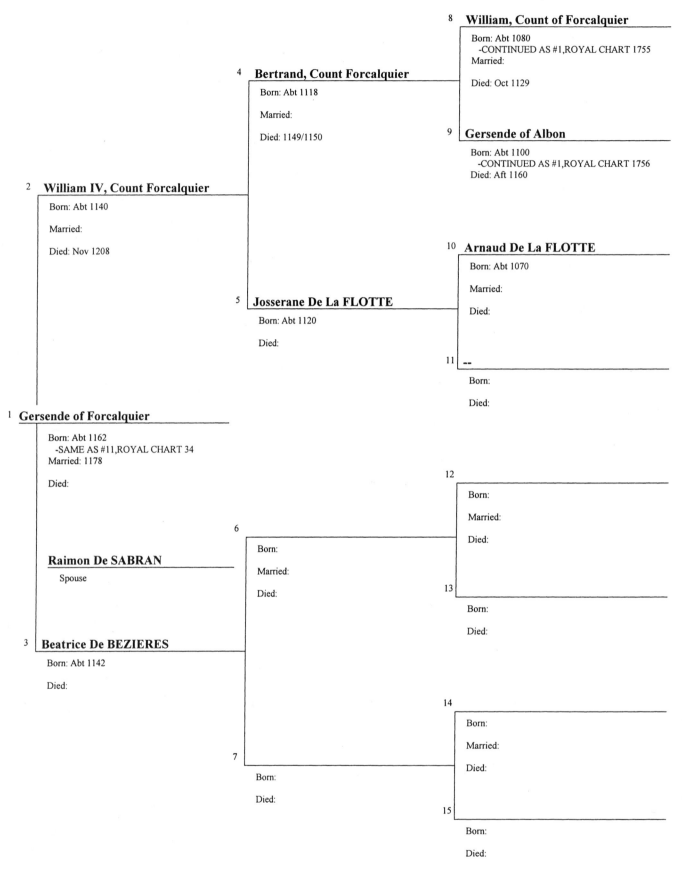

8 William, Count of Forcalquier

Born: Abt 1080
 -CONTINUED AS #1,ROYAL CHART 1755
Married:

Died: Oct 1129

4 Bertrand, Count Forcalquier

Born: Abt 1118

Married:

Died: 1149/1150

9 Gersende of Albon

Born: Abt 1100
 -CONTINUED AS #1,ROYAL CHART 1756
Died: Aft 1160

2 William IV, Count Forcalquier

Born: Abt 1140

Married:

Died: Nov 1208

10 Arnaud De La FLOTTE

Born: Abt 1070

Married:

Died:

5 Josserane De La FLOTTE

Born: Abt 1120

Died:

11 --

Born:

Died:

1 Gersende of Forcalquier

Born: Abt 1162
 -SAME AS #11,ROYAL CHART 34
Married: 1178

Died:

12

Born:

Married:

Died:

6

Born:

Married:

Died:

13

Born:

Died:

Raimon De SABRAN

Spouse

3 Beatrice De BEZIERES

Born: Abt 1142

Died:

14

Born:

Married:

Died:

7

Born:

Died:

15

Born:

Died:

Sources include: *Royal Ancestors* 11303; Stuart 195; Moriarty 100-101; Faris preliminary Charlemagne manuscript (June 1995), pp. 267-268. Note: #3 is also given as <u>Adelaide</u> De Bezieres.

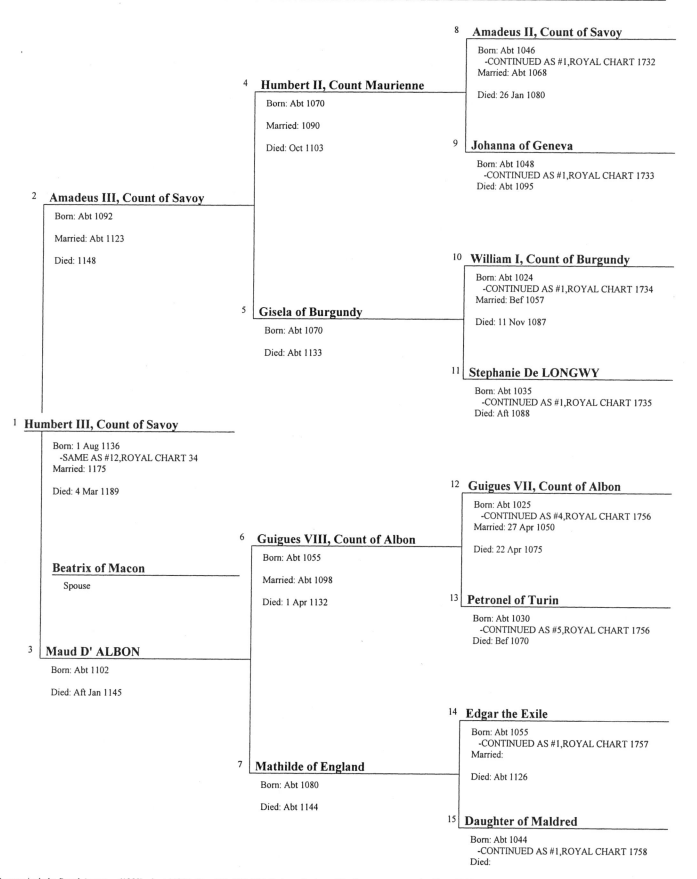

2 Amadeus III, Count of Savoy

Born: Abt 1092

Married: Abt 1123

Died: 1148

4 Humbert II, Count Maurienne

Born: Abt 1070

Married: 1090

Died: Oct 1103

8 Amadeus II, Count of Savoy

Born: Abt 1046
-CONTINUED AS #1,ROYAL CHART 1732
Married: Abt 1068

Died: 26 Jan 1080

9 Johanna of Geneva

Born: Abt 1048
-CONTINUED AS #1,ROYAL CHART 1733
Died: Abt 1095

5 Gisela of Burgundy

Born: Abt 1070

Died: Abt 1133

10 William I, Count of Burgundy

Born: Abt 1024
-CONTINUED AS #1,ROYAL CHART 1734
Married: Bef 1057

Died: 11 Nov 1087

11 Stephanie De LONGWY

Born: Abt 1035
-CONTINUED AS #1,ROYAL CHART 1735
Died: Aft 1088

1 Humbert III, Count of Savoy

Born: 1 Aug 1136
-SAME AS #12,ROYAL CHART 34
Married: 1175

Died: 4 Mar 1189

Beatrix of Macon

Spouse

3 Maud D' ALBON

Born: Abt 1102

Died: Aft Jan 1145

6 Guigues VIII, Count of Albon

Born: Abt 1055

Married: Abt 1098

Died: 1 Apr 1132

12 Guigues VII, Count of Albon

Born: Abt 1025
-CONTINUED AS #4,ROYAL CHART 1756
Married: 27 Apr 1050

Died: 22 Apr 1075

13 Petronel of Turin

Born: Abt 1030
-CONTINUED AS #5,ROYAL CHART 1756
Died: Bef 1070

7 Mathilde of England

Born: Abt 1080

Died: Abt 1144

14 Edgar the Exile

Born: Abt 1055
-CONTINUED AS #1,ROYAL CHART 1757
Married:

Died: Abt 1126

15 Daughter of Maldred

Born: Abt 1044
-CONTINUED AS #1,ROYAL CHART 1758
Died:

Sources include: *Royal Ancestors* (1989), chart 11304; Stuart 93, 192, 196; Faris preliminary Charlemagne manuscript (June 1995), pp. 246-247, 279; Moriarty 104, 102, 259-260. Note: #7 and ancestry is disputed. See Stuart 196, Faris 279 & 16, and Moriarty 102 & 259 notes. Moriarty concluded that #7 was probably the daughter of Edgar the Exile.

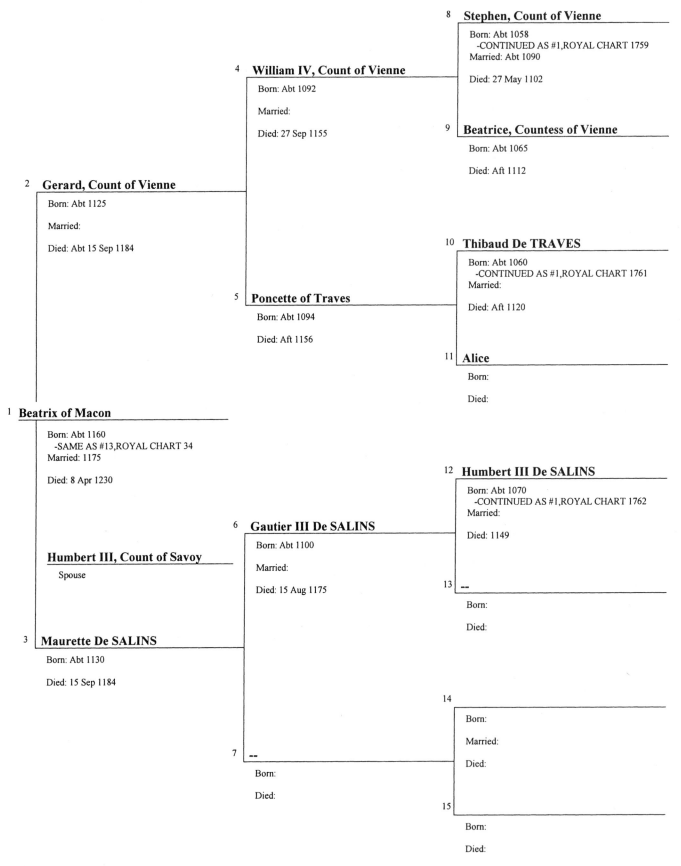

8 **Stephen, Count of Vienne**

Born: Abt 1058
-CONTINUED AS #1,ROYAL CHART 1759
Married: Abt 1090

Died: 27 May 1102

4 **William IV, Count of Vienne**

Born: Abt 1092

Married:

Died: 27 Sep 1155

9 **Beatrice, Countess of Vienne**

Born: Abt 1065

Died: Aft 1112

2 **Gerard, Count of Vienne**

Born: Abt 1125

Married:

Died: Abt 15 Sep 1184

10 **Thibaud De TRAVES**

Born: Abt 1060
-CONTINUED AS #1,ROYAL CHART 1761
Married:

Died: Aft 1120

5 **Poncette of Traves**

Born: Abt 1094

Died: Aft 1156

11 **Alice**

Born:

Died:

1 **Beatrix of Macon**

Born: Abt 1160
-SAME AS #13,ROYAL CHART 34
Married: 1175

Died: 8 Apr 1230

Humbert III, Count of Savoy

Spouse

12 **Humbert III De SALINS**

Born: Abt 1070
-CONTINUED AS #1,ROYAL CHART 1762
Married:

Died: 1149

6 **Gautier III De SALINS**

Born: Abt 1100

Married:

Died: 15 Aug 1175

13 **--**

Born:

Died:

3 **Maurette De SALINS**

Born: Abt 1130

Died: 15 Sep 1184

14

Born:

Married:

Died:

7 **--**

Born:

Died:

15

Born:

Died:

Sources include: *Royal Ancestors* 11304; Stuart 187, 189; Moriarty 105-106.

Pedigree Chart

Chart 1515

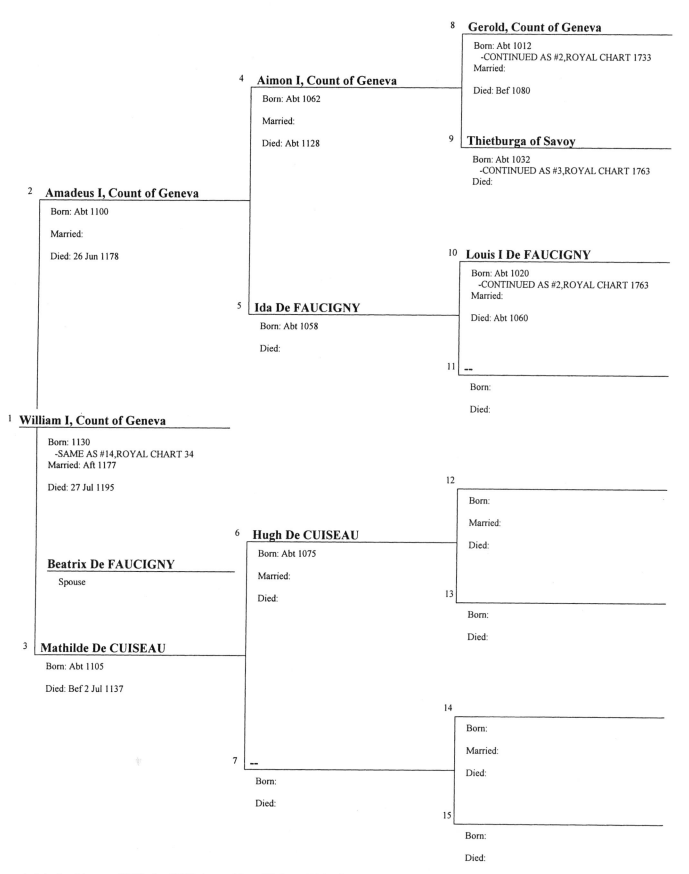

8 Gerold, Count of Geneva

Born: Abt 1012
  -CONTINUED AS #2,ROYAL CHART 1733
Married:

Died: Bef 1080

4 Aimon I, Count of Geneva

Born: Abt 1062

Married:

Died: Abt 1128

9 Thietburga of Savoy

Born: Abt 1032
  -CONTINUED AS #3,ROYAL CHART 1763
Died:

2 Amadeus I, Count of Geneva

Born: Abt 1100

Married:

Died: 26 Jun 1178

10 Louis I De FAUCIGNY

Born: Abt 1020
  -CONTINUED AS #2,ROYAL CHART 1763
Married:

Died: Abt 1060

5 Ida De FAUCIGNY

Born: Abt 1058

Died:

11 --

Born:

Died:

1 William I, Count of Geneva

Born: 1130
  -SAME AS #14,ROYAL CHART 34
Married: Aft 1177

Died: 27 Jul 1195

Beatrix De FAUCIGNY

Spouse

12

Born:

Married:

Died:

6 Hugh De CUISEAU

Born: Abt 1075

Married:

Died:

13

Born:

Died:

3 Mathilde De CUISEAU

Born: Abt 1105

Died: Bef 2 Jul 1137

14

Born:

Married:

Died:

7 --

Born:

Died:

15

Born:

Died:

Sources include: *Royal Ancestors* (1989), chart 11304; *Ancestral Roots* 133; Stuart 175; Moriarty 107; LDS records.

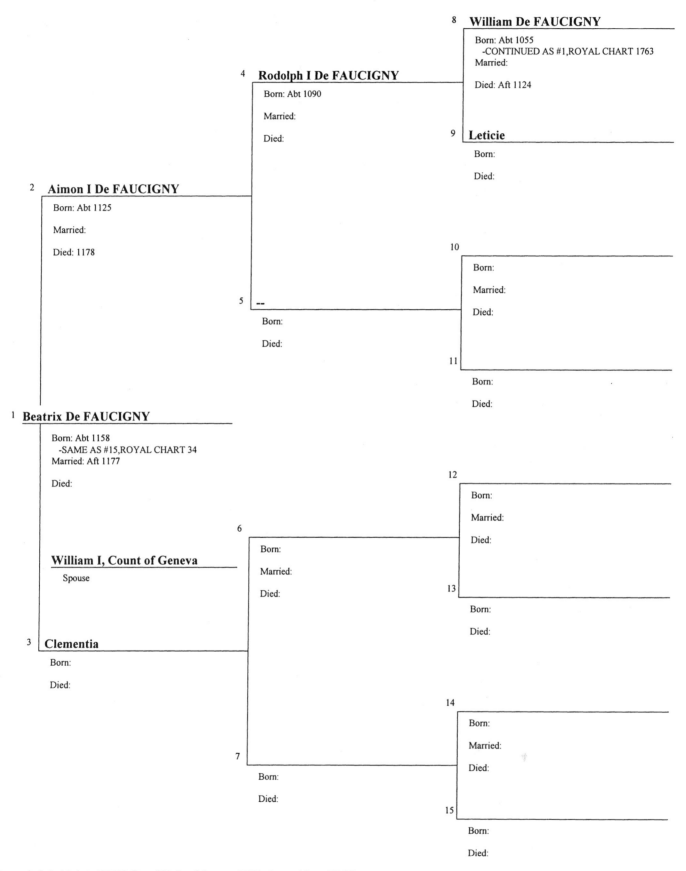

8 William De FAUCIGNY

Born: Abt 1055
  -CONTINUED AS #1,ROYAL CHART 1763
Married:

Died: Aft 1124

4 Rodolph I De FAUCIGNY

Born: Abt 1090

Married:

Died:

9 Leticie

Born:

Died:

2 Aimon I De FAUCIGNY

Born: Abt 1125

Married:

Died: 1178

10

Born:

Married:

Died:

5 --

Born:

Died:

11

Born:

Died:

1 Beatrix De FAUCIGNY

Born: Abt 1158
  -SAME AS #15,ROYAL CHART 34
Married: Aft 1177

Died:

12

Born:

Married:

Died:

6

Born:

Married:

Died:

13

Born:

Died:

William I, Count of Geneva

Spouse

3 Clementia

Born:

Died:

14

Born:

Married:

Died:

7

Born:

Died:

15

Born:

Died:

Sources include: Moriarty 107-108; Stuart 288; *Royal Ancestors* 11304; *Ancestral Roots* 133-25.

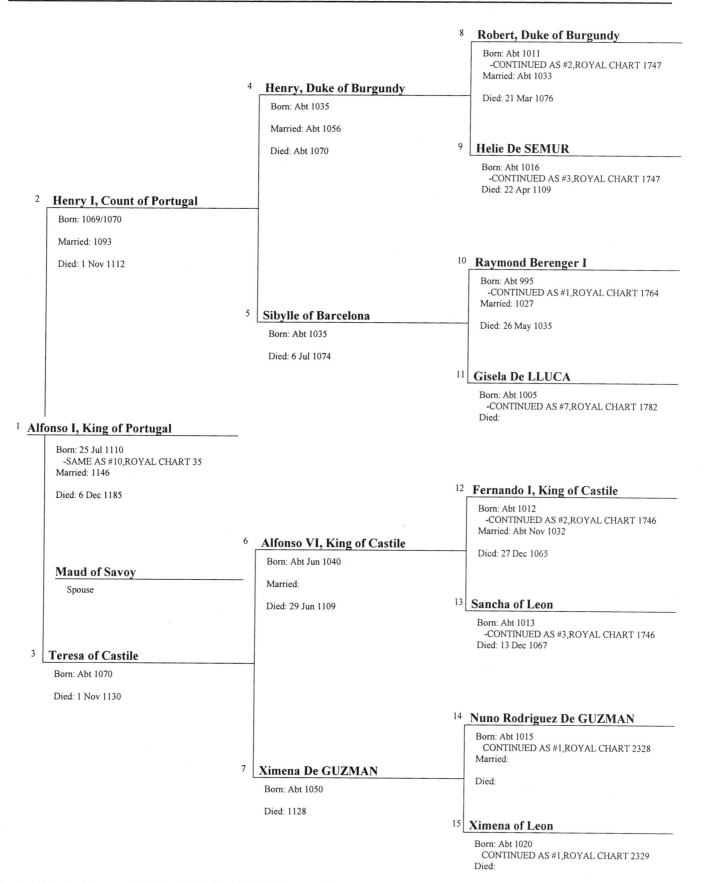

8 **Robert, Duke of Burgundy**

Born: Abt 1011
  -CONTINUED AS #2,ROYAL CHART 1747
Married: Abt 1033

Died: 21 Mar 1076

4 **Henry, Duke of Burgundy**

Born: Abt 1035

Married: Abt 1056

Died: Abt 1070

9 **Helie De SEMUR**

Born: Abt 1016
  -CONTINUED AS #3,ROYAL CHART 1747
Died: 22 Apr 1109

2 **Henry I, Count of Portugal**

Born: 1069/1070

Married: 1093

Died: 1 Nov 1112

10 **Raymond Berenger I**

Born: Abt 995
  -CONTINUED AS #1,ROYAL CHART 1764
Married: 1027

Died: 26 May 1035

5 **Sibylle of Barcelona**

Born: Abt 1035

Died: 6 Jul 1074

11 **Gisela De LLUCA**

Born: Abt 1005
  -CONTINUED AS #7,ROYAL CHART 1782
Died:

1 **Alfonso I, King of Portugal**

Born: 25 Jul 1110
  -SAME AS #10,ROYAL CHART 35
Married: 1146

Died: 6 Dec 1185

12 **Fernando I, King of Castile**

Born: Abt 1012
  -CONTINUED AS #2,ROYAL CHART 1746
Married: Abt Nov 1032

Died: 27 Dec 1065

6 **Alfonso VI, King of Castile**

Born: Abt Jun 1040

Married:

Died: 29 Jun 1109

13 **Sancha of Leon**

Born: Abt 1013
  -CONTINUED AS #3,ROYAL CHART 1746
Died: 13 Dec 1067

Maud of Savoy

Spouse

3 **Teresa of Castile**

Born: Abt 1070

Died: 1 Nov 1130

14 **Nuno Rodriguez De GUZMAN**

Born: Abt 1015
  CONTINUED AS #1,ROYAL CHART 2328
Married:

Died:

7 **Ximena De GUZMAN**

Born: Abt 1050

Died: 1128

15 **Ximena of Leon**

Born: Abt 1020
  CONTINUED AS #1,ROYAL CHART 2329
Died:

Sources include: *Royal Ancestors* 11305; *Stuart* 85, 430 (false); *TAG* 74:150; *Ancestral Roots* 112, 108; Moriarty 109, 83.

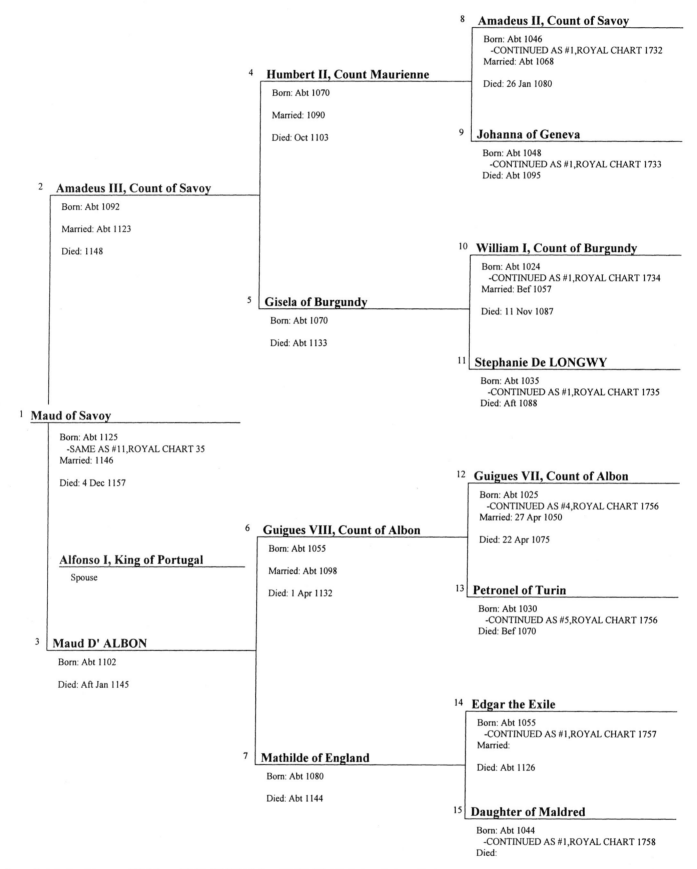

8 Amadeus II, Count of Savoy

Born: Abt 1046
-CONTINUED AS #1,ROYAL CHART 1732
Married: Abt 1068

Died: 26 Jan 1080

4 Humbert II, Count Maurienne

Born: Abt 1070

Married: 1090

Died: Oct 1103

9 Johanna of Geneva

Born: Abt 1048
-CONTINUED AS #1,ROYAL CHART 1733
Died: Abt 1095

2 Amadeus III, Count of Savoy

Born: Abt 1092

Married: Abt 1123

Died: 1148

10 William I, Count of Burgundy

Born: Abt 1024
-CONTINUED AS #1,ROYAL CHART 1734
Married: Bef 1057

Died: 11 Nov 1087

5 Gisela of Burgundy

Born: Abt 1070

Died: Abt 1133

11 Stephanie De LONGWY

Born: Abt 1035
-CONTINUED AS #1,ROYAL CHART 1735
Died: Aft 1088

1 Maud of Savoy

Born: Abt 1125
-SAME AS #11,ROYAL CHART 35
Married: 1146

Died: 4 Dec 1157

12 Guigues VII, Count of Albon

Born: Abt 1025
-CONTINUED AS #4,ROYAL CHART 1756
Married: 27 Apr 1050

Died: 22 Apr 1075

6 Guigues VIII, Count of Albon

Born: Abt 1055

Married: Abt 1098

Died: 1 Apr 1132

13 Petronel of Turin

Born: Abt 1030
-CONTINUED AS #5,ROYAL CHART 1756
Died: Bef 1070

Alfonso I, King of Portugal

Spouse

3 Maud D' ALBON

Born: Abt 1102

Died: Aft Jan 1145

14 Edgar the Exile

Born: Abt 1055
-CONTINUED AS #1,ROYAL CHART 1757
Married:

Died: Abt 1126

7 Mathilde of England

Born: Abt 1080

Died: Abt 1144

15 Daughter of Maldred

Born: Abt 1044
-CONTINUED AS #1,ROYAL CHART 1758
Died:

Sources include: *Royal Ancestors* 11305; Stuart 182, 93, 192, 196; Moriarty 104, 102, 259-260; Faris preliminary Charlemagne manuscript (June 1995), pp. 246-247, 279; Moriarty 104, 102, 259-260. Note: #7 and ancestry is disputed. See Stuart 196, Faris 279 & 16, and Moriarty 102 & 259 notes. Moriarty concluded that #7 was probably the daughter of Edgar the Exile.

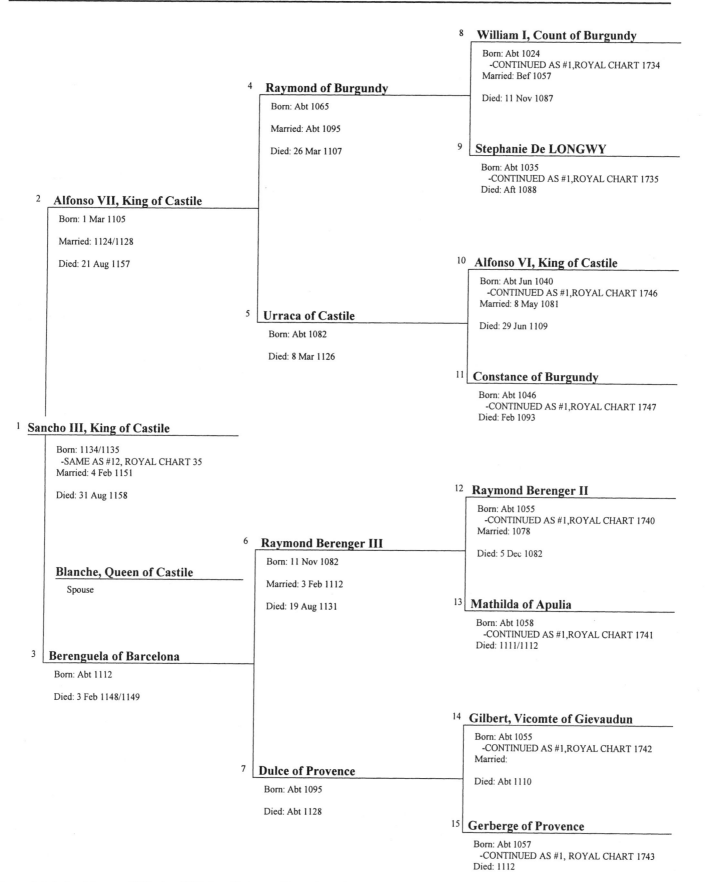

Pedigree Chart

8 **William I, Count of Burgundy**
Born: Abt 1024
  -CONTINUED AS #1,ROYAL CHART 1734
Married: Bef 1057

Died: 11 Nov 1087

4 **Raymond of Burgundy**
Born: Abt 1065

Married: Abt 1095

Died: 26 Mar 1107

9 **Stephanie De LONGWY**
Born: Abt 1035
  -CONTINUED AS #1,ROYAL CHART 1735
Died: Aft 1088

2 **Alfonso VII, King of Castile**
Born: 1 Mar 1105

Married: 1124/1128

Died: 21 Aug 1157

10 **Alfonso VI, King of Castile**
Born: Abt Jun 1040
  -CONTINUED AS #1,ROYAL CHART 1746
Married: 8 May 1081

Died: 29 Jun 1109

5 **Urraca of Castile**
Born: Abt 1082

Died: 8 Mar 1126

11 **Constance of Burgundy**
Born: Abt 1046
  -CONTINUED AS #1,ROYAL CHART 1747
Died: Feb 1093

1 **Sancho III, King of Castile**
Born: 1134/1135
  -SAME AS #12, ROYAL CHART 35
Married: 4 Feb 1151

Died: 31 Aug 1158

12 **Raymond Berenger II**
Born: Abt 1055
  -CONTINUED AS #1,ROYAL CHART 1740
Married: 1078

Died: 5 Dec 1082

6 **Raymond Berenger III**
Born: 11 Nov 1082

Married: 3 Feb 1112

Died: 19 Aug 1131

13 **Mathilda of Apulia**
Born: Abt 1058
  -CONTINUED AS #1,ROYAL CHART 1741
Died: 1111/1112

Blanche, Queen of Castile
Spouse

3 **Berenguela of Barcelona**
Born: Abt 1112

Died: 3 Feb 1148/1149

14 **Gilbert, Vicomte of Gievaudun**
Born: Abt 1055
  -CONTINUED AS #1,ROYAL CHART 1742
Married:

Died: Abt 1110

7 **Dulce of Provence**
Born: Abt 1095

Died: Abt 1128

15 **Gerberge of Provence**
Born: Abt 1057
  -CONTINUED AS #1, ROYAL CHART 1743
Died: 1112

Sources include: *Royal Ancestors* (1989), chart 11306; Stuart 83; *Ancestral Roots* 113; Moriarty 108, 81, 67-68.

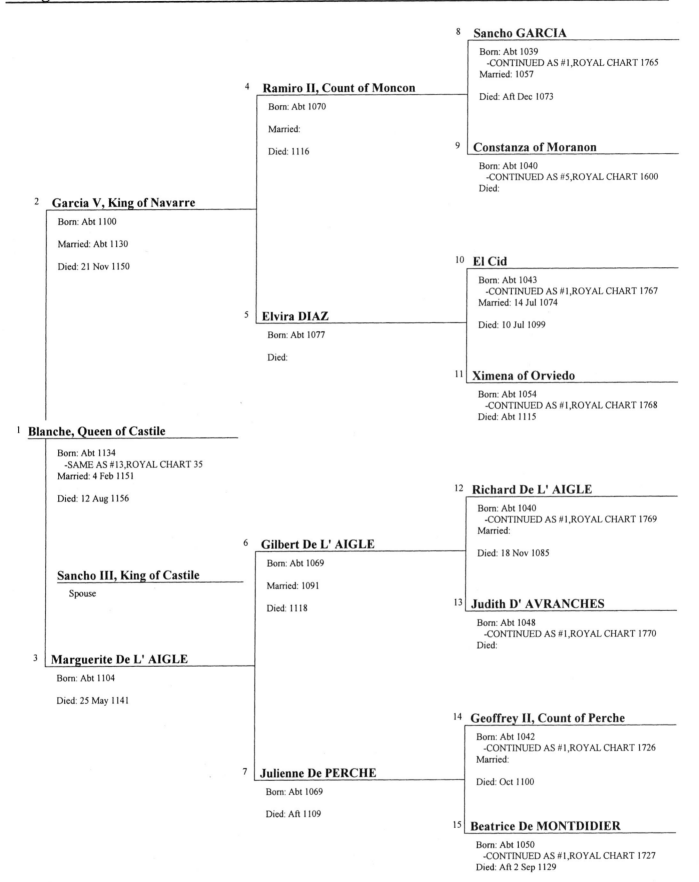

8 Sancho GARCIA

Born: Abt 1039
 -CONTINUED AS #1,ROYAL CHART 1765
Married: 1057

Died: Aft Dec 1073

4 Ramiro II, Count of Moncon

Born: Abt 1070

Married:

Died: 1116

9 Constanza of Moranon

Born: Abt 1040
 -CONTINUED AS #5,ROYAL CHART 1600
Died:

2 Garcia V, King of Navarre

Born: Abt 1100

Married: Abt 1130

Died: 21 Nov 1150

10 El Cid

Born: Abt 1043
 -CONTINUED AS #1,ROYAL CHART 1767
Married: 14 Jul 1074

Died: 10 Jul 1099

5 Elvira DIAZ

Born: Abt 1077

Died:

11 Ximena of Orviedo

Born: Abt 1054
 -CONTINUED AS #1,ROYAL CHART 1768
Died: Abt 1115

1 Blanche, Queen of Castile

Born: Abt 1134
 -SAME AS #13,ROYAL CHART 35
Married: 4 Feb 1151

Died: 12 Aug 1156

12 Richard De L' AIGLE

Born: Abt 1040
 -CONTINUED AS #1,ROYAL CHART 1769
Married:

Died: 18 Nov 1085

6 Gilbert De L' AIGLE

Born: Abt 1069

Married: 1091

Died: 1118

13 Judith D' AVRANCHES

Born: Abt 1048
 -CONTINUED AS #1,ROYAL CHART 1770
Died:

Sancho III, King of Castile

Spouse

3 Marguerite De L' AIGLE

Born: Abt 1104

Died: 25 May 1141

14 Geoffrey II, Count of Perche

Born: Abt 1042
 -CONTINUED AS #1,ROYAL CHART 1726
Married:

Died: Oct 1100

7 Julienne De PERCHE

Born: Abt 1069

Died: Aft 1109

15 Beatrice De MONTDIDIER

Born: Abt 1050
 -CONTINUED AS #1,ROYAL CHART 1727
Died: Aft 2 Sep 1129

Sources include: *Royal Ancestors* (1989), chart 11306; Stuart 151; *Ancestral Roots* 113A; Moriarty 109-110; *NEHGR* 117:94-96 (#5 ancestry); *TAG* 74:152 (#6 & 12). Notes: #10 "El Cid" is Rodrigo Diaz De Vivar (Bivar) or De Castro. There is disagreement on #8 & 9. The Stuart version is followed above.

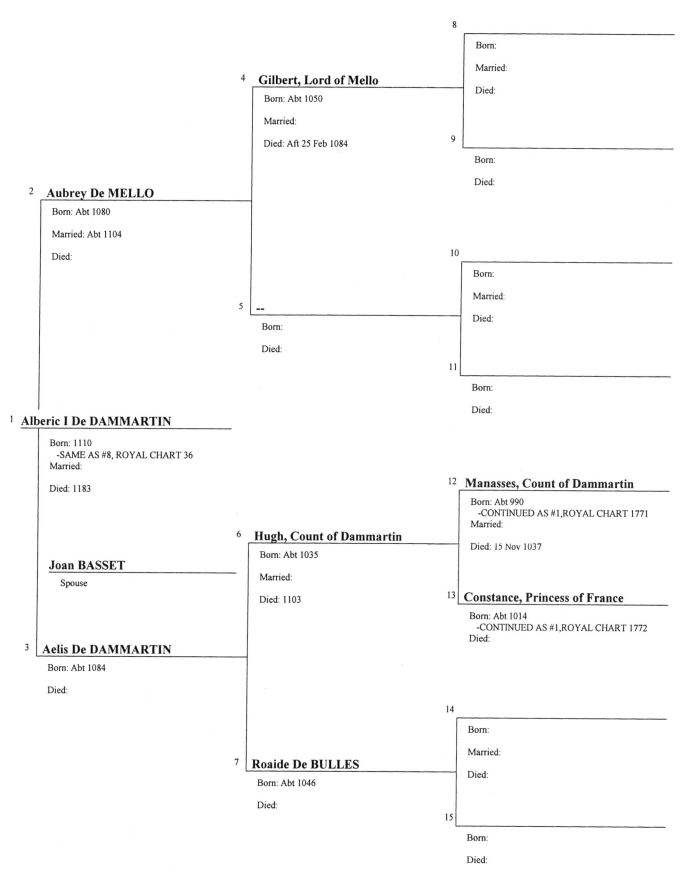

8
Born:
Married:
Died:

4 Gilbert, Lord of Mello
Born: Abt 1050
Married:
Died: Aft 25 Feb 1084

9
Born:
Died:

2 Aubrey De MELLO
Born: Abt 1080
Married: Abt 1104
Died:

10
Born:
Married:
Died:

5 --
Born:
Died:

11
Born:
Died:

1 Alberic I De DAMMARTIN
Born: 1110
-SAME AS #8, ROYAL CHART 36
Married:
Died: 1183

12 Manasses, Count of Dammartin
Born: Abt 990
-CONTINUED AS #1,ROYAL CHART 1771
Married:
Died: 15 Nov 1037

6 Hugh, Count of Dammartin
Born: Abt 1035
Married:
Died: 1103

13 Constance, Princess of France
Born: Abt 1014
-CONTINUED AS #1,ROYAL CHART 1772
Died:

Joan BASSET
Spouse

3 Aelis De DAMMARTIN
Born: Abt 1084
Died:

14
Born:
Married:
Died:

7 Roaide De BULLES
Born: Abt 1046
Died:

15
Born:
Died:

Sources include: Stuart 82, 397; LDS records; *Royal Ancestors* (1989), chart 11307; *The Genealogists' Magazine* 21:94 (#6 ancestry).

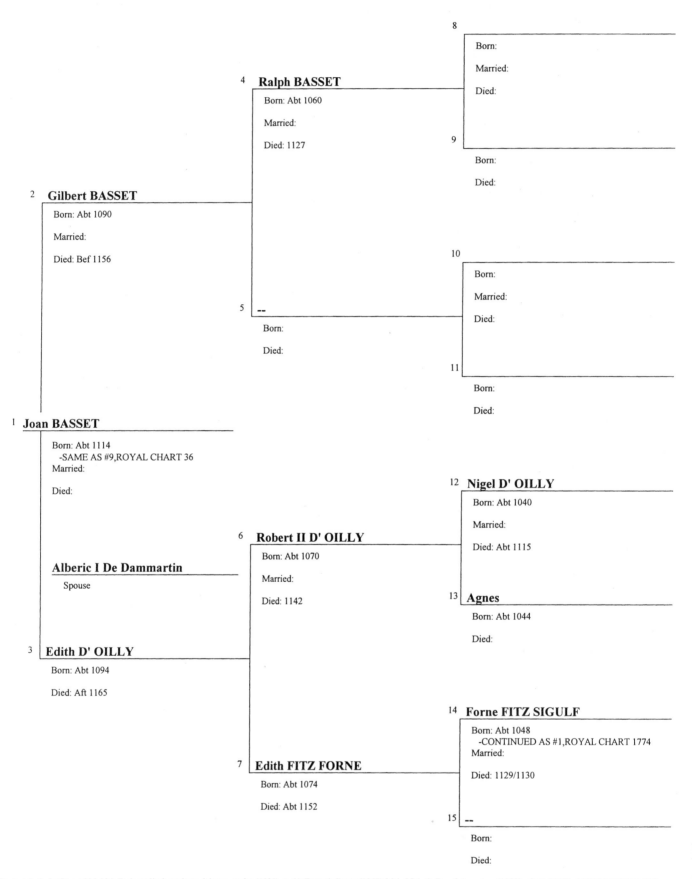

8

Born:

Married:

Died:

4 **Ralph BASSET**

Born: Abt 1060

Married:

Died: 1127

9

Born:

Died:

2 **Gilbert BASSET**

Born: Abt 1090

Married:

Died: Bef 1156

10

Born:

Married:

Died:

5 **--**

Born:

Died:

11

Born:

Died:

1 **Joan BASSET**

Born: Abt 1114
-SAME AS #9,ROYAL CHART 36
Married:

Died:

12 **Nigel D' OILLY**

Born: Abt 1040

Married:

Died: Abt 1115

6 **Robert II D' OILLY**

Born: Abt 1070

Married:

Died: 1142

13 **Agnes**

Born: Abt 1044

Died:

Alberic I De Dammartin

Spouse

3 **Edith D' OILLY**

Born: Abt 1094

Died: Aft 1165

14 **Forne FITZ SIGULF**

Born: Abt 1048
-CONTINUED AS #1,ROYAL CHART 1774
Married:

Died: 1129/1130

7 **Edith FITZ FORNE**

Born: Abt 1074

Died: Abt 1152

15 **--**

Born:

Died:

Sources include: Stuart 395-396; Faris preliminary baronial manuscript (1998), p. 41 (Basset); Paget (1957) 26:1, 27:1, 4; *Royal Ancestors* (1989), chart 11670; *NEHGR* 142:238-239; LDS records. Notes: The parentage of #2 Gilbert is not certain. He may have been brother instead of son of Ralph. #4 Ralph is claimed as son of Thurstan (living 1080) and might be grandson of Osmund Basset (living 1050).

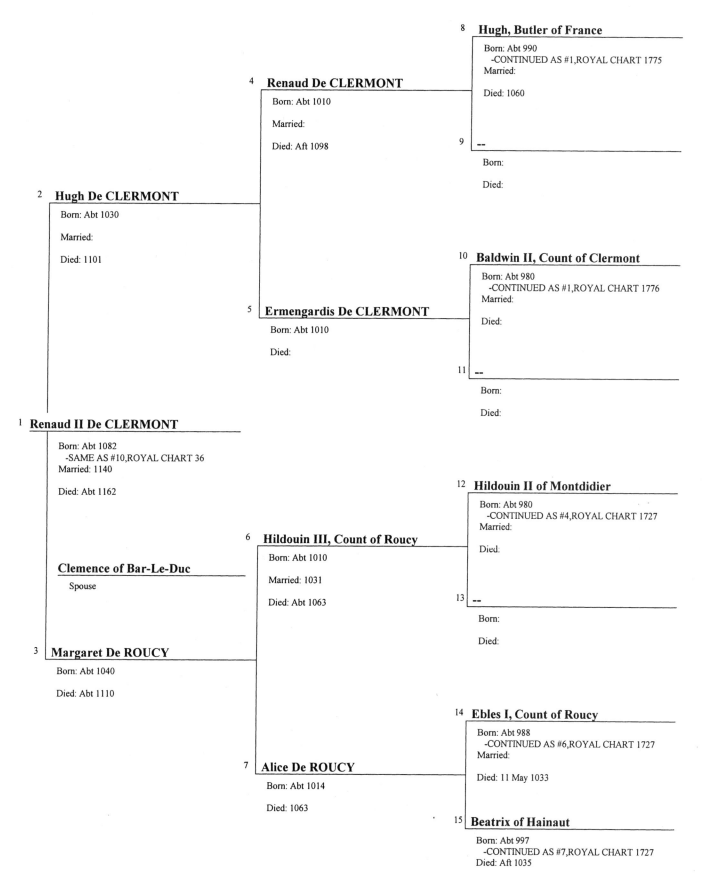

2 Hugh De CLERMONT

Born: Abt 1030

Married:

Died: 1101

4 Renaud De CLERMONT

Born: Abt 1010

Married:

Died: Aft 1098

8 Hugh, Butler of France

Born: Abt 990
  -CONTINUED AS #1,ROYAL CHART 1775
Married:

Died: 1060

9 --

Born:

Died:

5 Ermengardis De CLERMONT

Born: Abt 1010

Died:

10 Baldwin II, Count of Clermont

Born: Abt 980
  -CONTINUED AS #1,ROYAL CHART 1776
Married:

Died:

11 --

Born:

Died:

1 Renaud II De CLERMONT

Born: Abt 1082
  -SAME AS #10,ROYAL CHART 36
Married: 1140

Died: Abt 1162

Clemence of Bar-Le-Duc

Spouse

3 Margaret De ROUCY

Born: Abt 1040

Died: Abt 1110

6 Hildouin III, Count of Roucy

Born: Abt 1010

Married: 1031

Died: Abt 1063

12 Hildouin II of Montdidier

Born: Abt 980
  -CONTINUED AS #4,ROYAL CHART 1727
Married:

Died:

13 --

Born:

Died:

7 Alice De ROUCY

Born: Abt 1014

Died: 1063

14 Ebles I, Count of Roucy

Born: Abt 988
  -CONTINUED AS #6,ROYAL CHART 1727
Married:

Died: 11 May 1033

15 Beatrix of Hainaut

Born: Abt 997
  -CONTINUED AS #7,ROYAL CHART 1727
Died: Aft 1035

Sources include: Stuart 344; *Ancestral Roots* 144-25, 246; *Royal Ancestors* 11436; Turton 184.

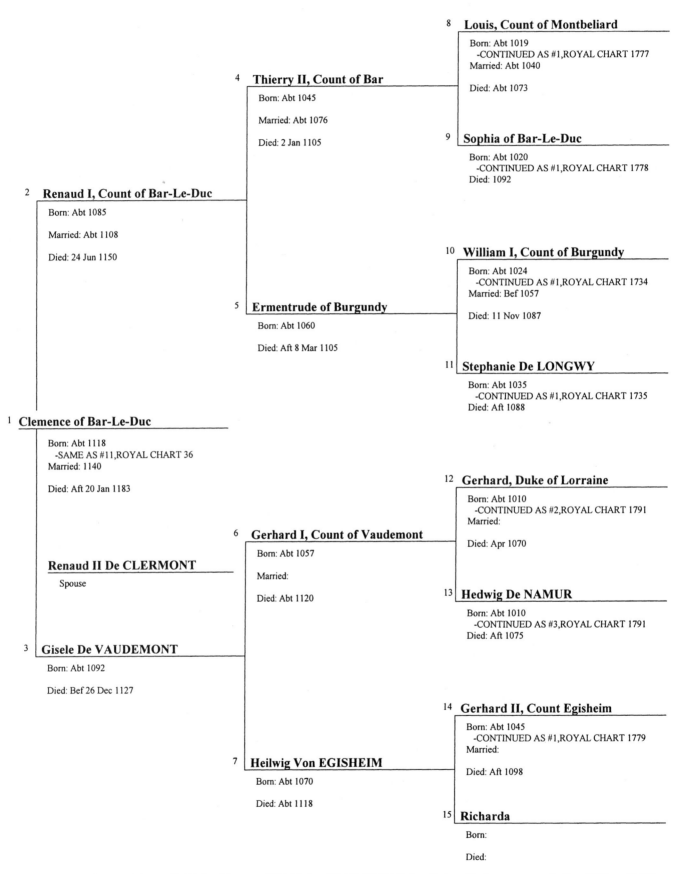

8 **Louis, Count of Montbeliard**

Born: Abt 1019
-CONTINUED AS #1,ROYAL CHART 1777
Married: Abt 1040

Died: Abt 1073

4 **Thierry II, Count of Bar**

Born: Abt 1045

Married: Abt 1076

Died: 2 Jan 1105

9 **Sophia of Bar-Le-Duc**

Born: Abt 1020
-CONTINUED AS #1,ROYAL CHART 1778
Died: 1092

2 **Renaud I, Count of Bar-Le-Duc**

Born: Abt 1085

Married: Abt 1108

Died: 24 Jun 1150

10 **William I, Count of Burgundy**

Born: Abt 1024
-CONTINUED AS #1,ROYAL CHART 1734
Married: Bef 1057

Died: 11 Nov 1087

5 **Ermentrude of Burgundy**

Born: Abt 1060

Died: Aft 8 Mar 1105

11 **Stephanie De LONGWY**

Born: Abt 1035
-CONTINUED AS #1,ROYAL CHART 1735
Died: Aft 1088

1 **Clemence of Bar-Le-Duc**

Born: Abt 1118
-SAME AS #11,ROYAL CHART 36
Married: 1140

Died: Aft 20 Jan 1183

12 **Gerhard, Duke of Lorraine**

Born: Abt 1010
-CONTINUED AS #2,ROYAL CHART 1791
Married:

Died: Apr 1070

6 **Gerhard I, Count of Vaudemont**

Born: Abt 1057

Married:

Died: Abt 1120

13 **Hedwig De NAMUR**

Born: Abt 1010
-CONTINUED AS #3,ROYAL CHART 1791
Died: Aft 1075

Renaud II De CLERMONT

Spouse

3 **Gisele De VAUDEMONT**

Born: Abt 1092

Died: Bef 26 Dec 1127

14 **Gerhard II, Count Egisheim**

Born: Abt 1045
-CONTINUED AS #1,ROYAL CHART 1779
Married:

Died: Aft 1098

7 **Heilwig Von EGISHEIM**

Born: Abt 1070

Died: Abt 1118

15 **Richarda**

Born:

Died:

Sources include: *Ancestral Roots* 144; Stuart 149, 246; *Royal Ancestors* 11434; Moriarty 112-113, 193-194; Faris preliminary Charlemagne manuscript (June 1995), pp. 34, 126.

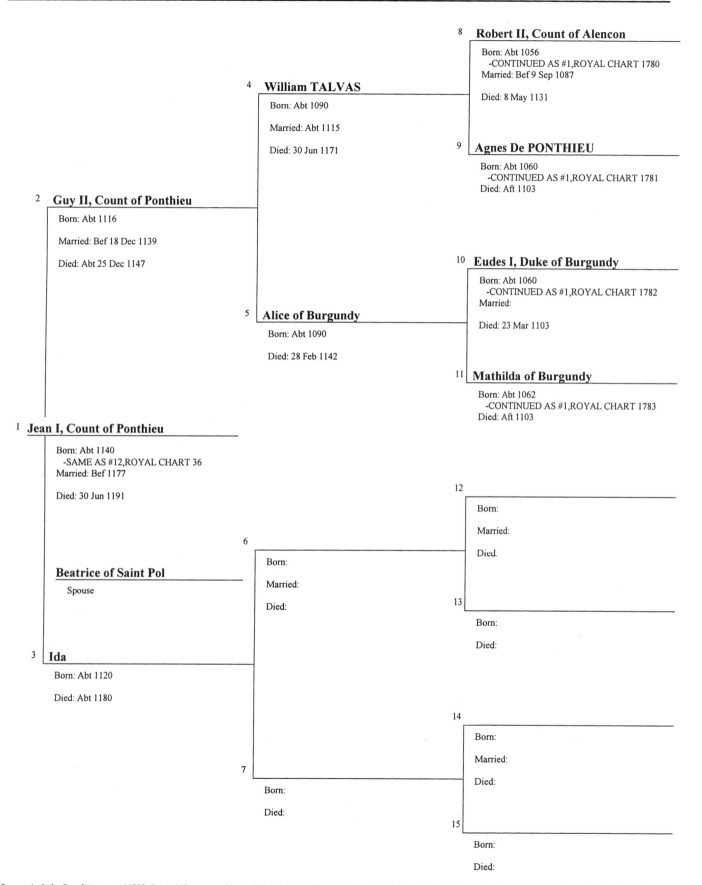

8 **Robert II, Count of Alencon**

Born: Abt 1056
  -CONTINUED AS #1,ROYAL CHART 1780
Married: Bef 9 Sep 1087

Died: 8 May 1131

4 **William TALVAS**

Born: Abt 1090

Married: Abt 1115

Died: 30 Jun 1171

9 **Agnes De PONTHIEU**

Born: Abt 1060
  -CONTINUED AS #1,ROYAL CHART 1781
Died: Aft 1103

2 **Guy II, Count of Ponthieu**

Born: Abt 1116

Married: Bef 18 Dec 1139

Died: Abt 25 Dec 1147

10 **Eudes I, Duke of Burgundy**

Born: Abt 1060
  -CONTINUED AS #1,ROYAL CHART 1782
Married:

Died: 23 Mar 1103

5 **Alice of Burgundy**

Born: Abt 1090

Died: 28 Feb 1142

11 **Mathilda of Burgundy**

Born: Abt 1062
  -CONTINUED AS #1,ROYAL CHART 1783
Died: Aft 1103

1 **Jean I, Count of Ponthieu**

Born: Abt 1140
  -SAME AS #12,ROYAL CHART 36
Married: Bef 1177

Died: 30 Jun 1191

12

Born:

Married:

Died:

6

Born:

Married:

Died:

13

Born:

Died:

Beatrice of Saint Pol

Spouse

3 **Ida**

Born: Abt 1120

Died: Abt 1180

14

Born:

Married:

Died:

7

Born:

Died:

15

Born:

Died:

Sources include: *Royal Ancestors* 11308; Stuart 148; *Ancestral Roots* 109; Moriarty 112-114; Schwennicke 3:638; Faris preliminary Charlemagne manuscript, pp. 220-221, 81. Note: #5 Alice is also called Helie, and #11 Mathilda is also called Sibylle.

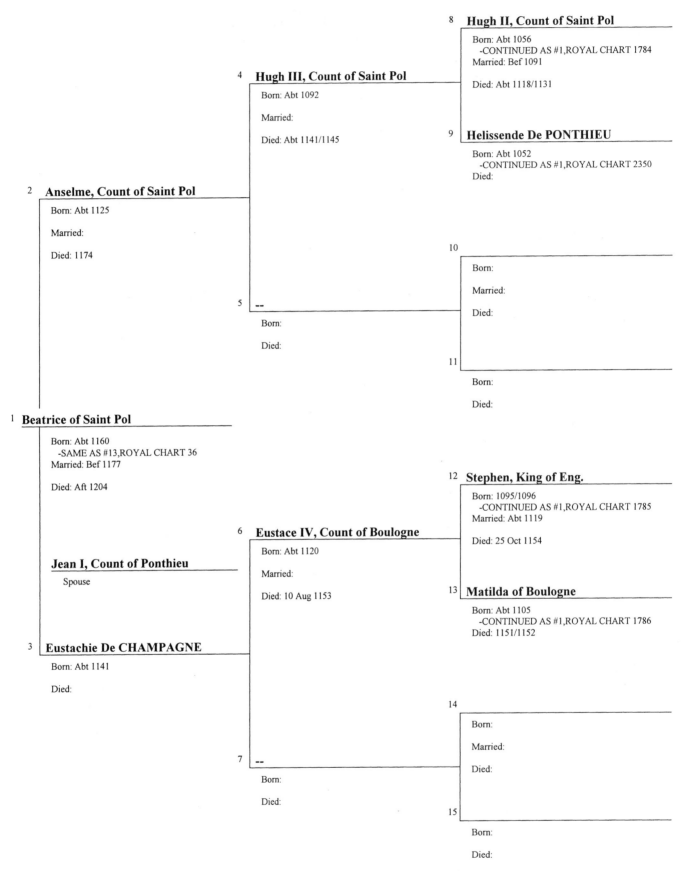

8 **Hugh II, Count of Saint Pol**

Born: Abt 1056
-CONTINUED AS #1,ROYAL CHART 1784
Married: Bef 1091

Died: Abt 1118/1131

4 **Hugh III, Count of Saint Pol**

Born: Abt 1092

Married:

Died: Abt 1141/1145

9 **Helissende De PONTHIEU**

Born: Abt 1052
-CONTINUED AS #1,ROYAL CHART 2350
Died:

2 **Anselme, Count of Saint Pol**

Born: Abt 1125

Married:

Died: 1174

10

Born:

Married:

Died:

5 --

Born:

Died:

11

Born:

Died:

1 **Beatrice of Saint Pol**

Born: Abt 1160
-SAME AS #13,ROYAL CHART 36
Married: Bef 1177

Died: Aft 1204

12 **Stephen, King of Eng.**

Born: 1095/1096
-CONTINUED AS #1,ROYAL CHART 1785
Married: Abt 1119

Died: 25 Oct 1154

6 **Eustace IV, Count of Boulogne**

Born: Abt 1120

Married:

Died: 10 Aug 1153

Jean I, Count of Ponthieu

Spouse

13 **Matilda of Boulogne**

Born: Abt 1105
-CONTINUED AS #1,ROYAL CHART 1786
Died: 1151/1152

3 **Eustachie De CHAMPAGNE**

Born: Abt 1141

Died:

14

Born:

Married:

Died:

7 --

Born:

Died:

15

Born:

Died:

Sources include: *Royal Ancestors* (1989), chart 11308; Stuart 242, 184; Schwennicke 3:622; *Ancestral Roots* 8 (2004), Lines 109, 169A; *Ancestral Roots* 109, 169A; Faris preliminary Charlemagne manuscript (June 1995), pp. 242-243; Moriarty 115; Richardson *Plantagenet* (2004), p. 8 (Plantagenet); Consultation with Douglas Richardson (March 2003, June 2005).
Notes: The maternal ancestry of #1 Beatrice is disputed. Richardson states that #3 was an unknown 1st wife, with Eustachie being a later 2nd wife. #7 was an unknown mistress of Eustace IV.

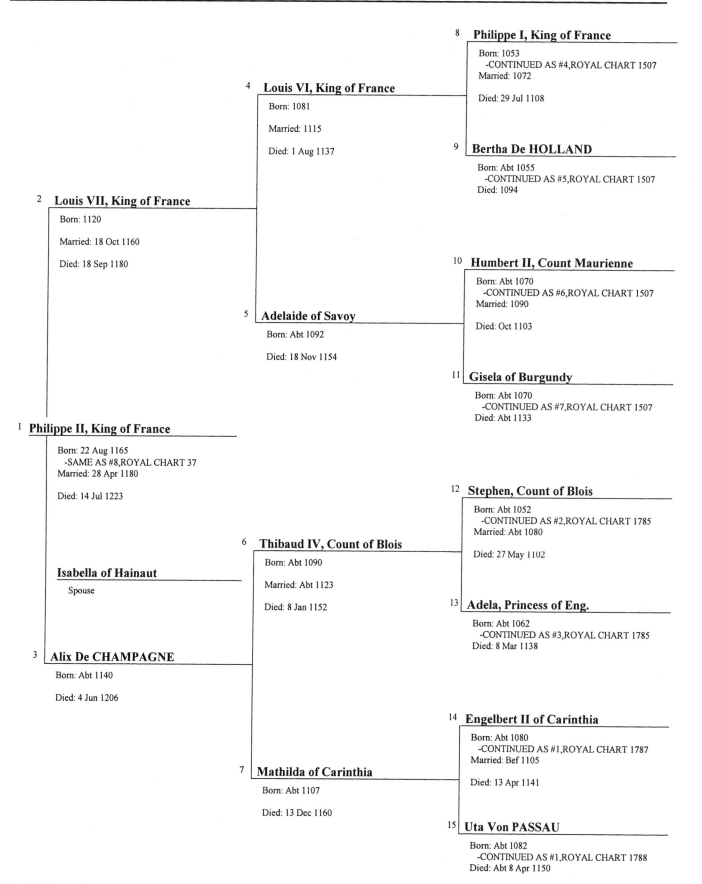

8 **Philippe I, King of France**

Born: 1053
-CONTINUED AS #4,ROYAL CHART 1507
Married: 1072

Died: 29 Jul 1108

4 **Louis VI, King of France**

Born: 1081

Married: 1115

Died: 1 Aug 1137

9 **Bertha De HOLLAND**

Born: Abt 1055
-CONTINUED AS #5,ROYAL CHART 1507
Died: 1094

2 **Louis VII, King of France**

Born: 1120

Married: 18 Oct 1160

Died: 18 Sep 1180

10 **Humbert II, Count Maurienne**

Born: Abt 1070
-CONTINUED AS #6,ROYAL CHART 1507
Married: 1090

Died: Oct 1103

5 **Adelaide of Savoy**

Born: Abt 1092

Died: 18 Nov 1154

11 **Gisela of Burgundy**

Born: Abt 1070
-CONTINUED AS #7,ROYAL CHART 1507
Died: Abt 1133

1 **Philippe II, King of France**

Born: 22 Aug 1165
-SAME AS #8,ROYAL CHART 37
Married: 28 Apr 1180

Died: 14 Jul 1223

12 **Stephen, Count of Blois**

Born: Abt 1052
-CONTINUED AS #2,ROYAL CHART 1785
Married: Abt 1080

Died: 27 May 1102

6 **Thibaud IV, Count of Blois**

Born: Abt 1090

Married: Abt 1123

Died: 8 Jan 1152

Isabella of Hainaut

Spouse

13 **Adela, Princess of Eng.**

Born: Abt 1062
-CONTINUED AS #3,ROYAL CHART 1785
Died: 8 Mar 1138

3 **Alix De CHAMPAGNE**

Born: Abt 1140

Died: 4 Jun 1206

14 **Engelbert II of Carinthia**

Born: Abt 1080
-CONTINUED AS #1,ROYAL CHART 1787
Married: Bef 1105

Died: 13 Apr 1141

7 **Mathilda of Carinthia**

Born: Abt 1107

Died: 13 Dec 1160

15 **Uta Von PASSAU**

Born: Abt 1082
-CONTINUED AS #1,ROYAL CHART 1788
Died: Abt 8 Apr 1150

Sources include: *Royal Ancestors* 11308-09; Stuart 70, 133; *Ancestral Roots* 101, 137; Moriarty 116-117, 120; Faris preliminary Charlemagne manuscript (June 1995), pp. 90-92, 50-52, 42.

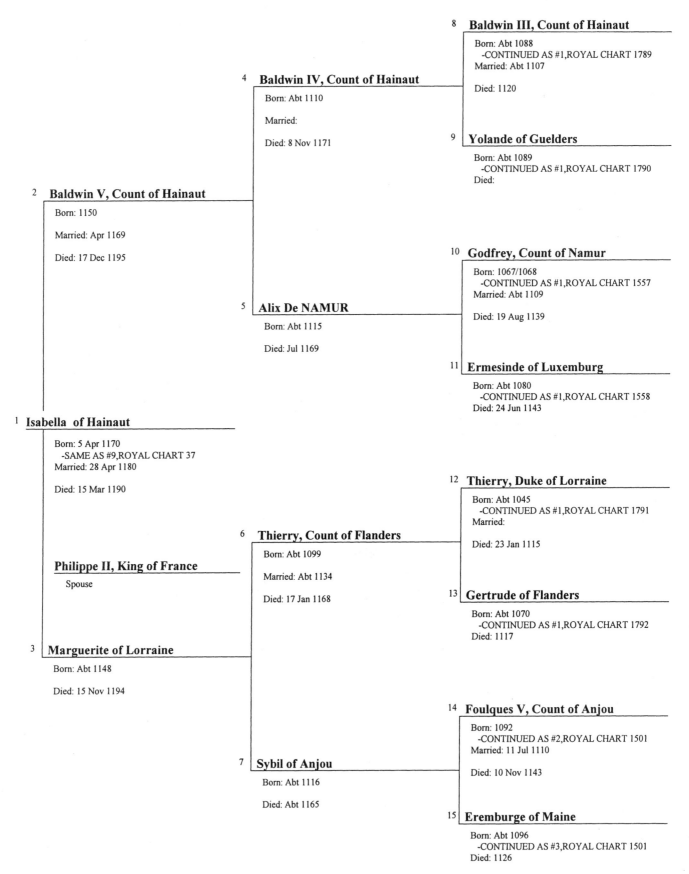

8 **Baldwin III, Count of Hainaut**

Born: Abt 1088
-CONTINUED AS #1,ROYAL CHART 1789
Married: Abt 1107

Died: 1120

4 **Baldwin IV, Count of Hainaut**

Born: Abt 1110

Married:

Died: 8 Nov 1171

9 **Yolande of Guelders**

Born: Abt 1089
-CONTINUED AS #1,ROYAL CHART 1790
Died:

2 **Baldwin V, Count of Hainaut**

Born: 1150

Married: Apr 1169

Died: 17 Dec 1195

10 **Godfrey, Count of Namur**

Born: 1067/1068
-CONTINUED AS #1,ROYAL CHART 1557
Married: Abt 1109

Died: 19 Aug 1139

5 **Alix De NAMUR**

Born: Abt 1115

Died: Jul 1169

11 **Ermesinde of Luxemburg**

Born: Abt 1080
-CONTINUED AS #1,ROYAL CHART 1558
Died: 24 Jun 1143

1 **Isabella of Hainaut**

Born: 5 Apr 1170
-SAME AS #9,ROYAL CHART 37
Married: 28 Apr 1180

Died: 15 Mar 1190

12 **Thierry, Duke of Lorraine**

Born: Abt 1045
-CONTINUED AS #1,ROYAL CHART 1791
Married:

Died: 23 Jan 1115

6 **Thierry, Count of Flanders**

Born: Abt 1099

Married: Abt 1134

Died: 17 Jan 1168

13 **Gertrude of Flanders**

Born: Abt 1070
-CONTINUED AS #1,ROYAL CHART 1792
Died: 1117

Philippe II, King of France

Spouse

3 **Marguerite of Lorraine**

Born: Abt 1148

Died: 15 Nov 1194

14 **Foulques V, Count of Anjou**

Born: 1092
-CONTINUED AS #2,ROYAL CHART 1501
Married: 11 Jul 1110

Died: 10 Nov 1143

7 **Sybil of Anjou**

Born: Abt 1116

Died: Abt 1165

15 **Eremburge of Maine**

Born: Abt 1096
-CONTINUED AS #3,ROYAL CHART 1501
Died: 1126

Sources include: *Royal Ancestors* 11309; Stuart 73, 132; *Ancestral Roots* 163-164; Moriarty 124.

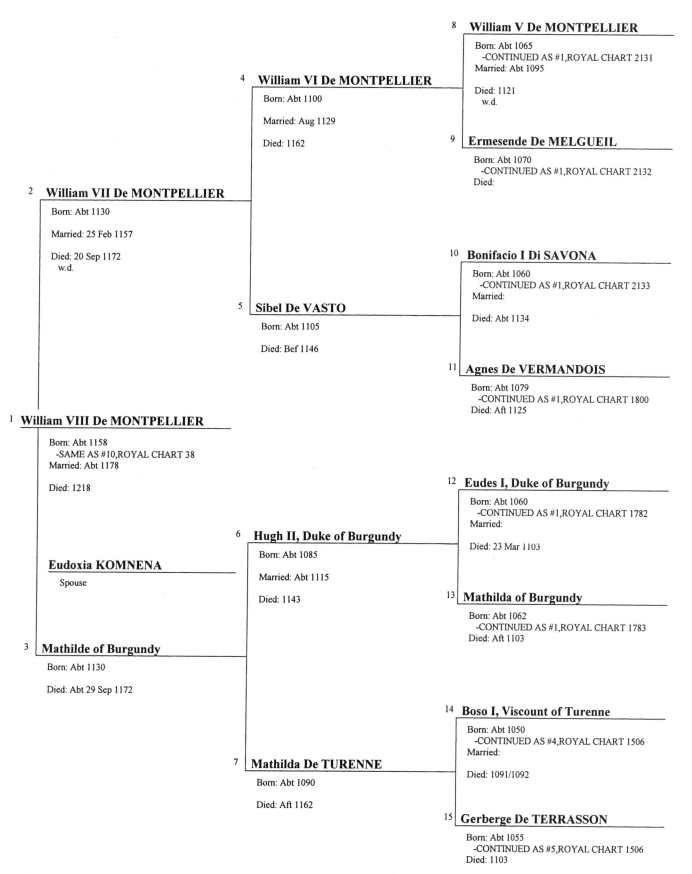

8 William V De MONTPELLIER
Born: Abt 1065
-CONTINUED AS #1,ROYAL CHART 2131
Married: Abt 1095

Died: 1121
w.d.

4 William VI De MONTPELLIER
Born: Abt 1100

Married: Aug 1129

Died: 1162

9 Ermesende De MELGUEIL
Born: Abt 1070
-CONTINUED AS #1,ROYAL CHART 2132
Died:

2 William VII De MONTPELLIER
Born: Abt 1130

Married: 25 Feb 1157

Died: 20 Sep 1172
w.d.

10 Bonifacio I Di SAVONA
Born: Abt 1060
-CONTINUED AS #1,ROYAL CHART 2133
Married:

Died: Abt 1134

5 Sibel De VASTO
Born: Abt 1105

Died: Bef 1146

11 Agnes De VERMANDOIS
Born: Abt 1079
-CONTINUED AS #1,ROYAL CHART 1800
Died: Aft 1125

1 William VIII De MONTPELLIER
Born: Abt 1158
-SAME AS #10,ROYAL CHART 38
Married: Abt 1178

Died: 1218

12 Eudes I, Duke of Burgundy
Born: Abt 1060
-CONTINUED AS #1,ROYAL CHART 1782
Married:

Died: 23 Mar 1103

6 Hugh II, Duke of Burgundy
Born: Abt 1085

Married: Abt 1115

Died: 1143

Eudoxia KOMNENA
Spouse

13 Mathilda of Burgundy
Born: Abt 1062
-CONTINUED AS #1,ROYAL CHART 1783
Died: Aft 1103

3 Mathilde of Burgundy
Born: Abt 1130

Died: Abt 29 Sep 1172

14 Boso I, Viscount of Turenne
Born: Abt 1050
-CONTINUED AS #4,ROYAL CHART 1506
Married:

Died: 1091/1092

7 Mathilda De TURENNE
Born: Abt 1090

Died: Aft 1162

15 Gerberge De TERRASSON
Born: Abt 1055
-CONTINUED AS #5,ROYAL CHART 1506
Died: 1103

Sources include: *Royal Ancestors* (1989), charts 11311, 11846-47; Stuart 150, 377; *Ancestral Roots* 105A-27; Moriarty 131-132; Turton 58.

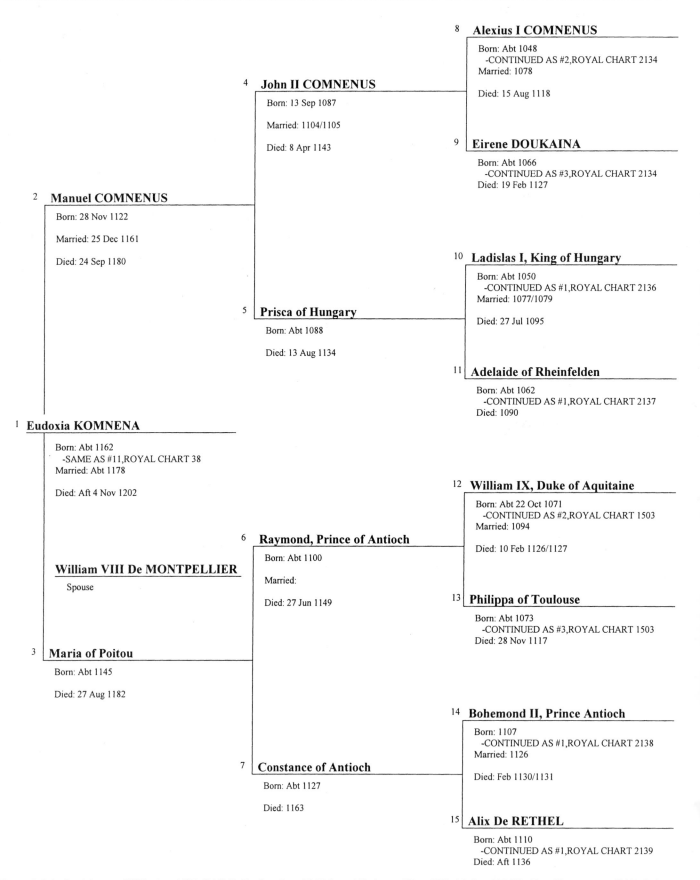

8 Alexius I COMNENUS
Born: Abt 1048
-CONTINUED AS #2,ROYAL CHART 2134
Married: 1078

Died: 15 Aug 1118

4 John II COMNENUS
Born: 13 Sep 1087
Married: 1104/1105
Died: 8 Apr 1143

9 Eirene DOUKAINA
Born: Abt 1066
-CONTINUED AS #3,ROYAL CHART 2134
Died: 19 Feb 1127

2 Manuel COMNENUS
Born: 28 Nov 1122
Married: 25 Dec 1161
Died: 24 Sep 1180

10 Ladislas I, King of Hungary
Born: Abt 1050
-CONTINUED AS #1,ROYAL CHART 2136
Married: 1077/1079
Died: 27 Jul 1095

5 Prisca of Hungary
Born: Abt 1088
Died: 13 Aug 1134

11 Adelaide of Rheinfelden
Born: Abt 1062
-CONTINUED AS #1,ROYAL CHART 2137
Died: 1090

1 Eudoxia KOMNENA
Born: Abt 1162
-SAME AS #11,ROYAL CHART 38
Married: Abt 1178

Died: Aft 4 Nov 1202

12 William IX, Duke of Aquitaine
Born: Abt 22 Oct 1071
-CONTINUED AS #2,ROYAL CHART 1503
Married: 1094
Died: 10 Feb 1126/1127

6 Raymond, Prince of Antioch
Born: Abt 1100
Married:
Died: 27 Jun 1149

13 Philippa of Toulouse
Born: Abt 1073
-CONTINUED AS #3,ROYAL CHART 1503
Died: 28 Nov 1117

William VIII De MONTPELLIER
Spouse

3 Maria of Poitou
Born: Abt 1145
Died: 27 Aug 1182

14 Bohemond II, Prince Antioch
Born: 1107
-CONTINUED AS #1,ROYAL CHART 2138
Married: 1126
Died: Feb 1130/1131

7 Constance of Antioch
Born: Abt 1127
Died: 1163

15 Alix De RETHEL
Born: Abt 1110
-CONTINUED AS #1,ROYAL CHART 2139
Died: Aft 1136

Sources include: *Royal Ancestors* (1989), charts 11311, 11848-49; *The Genealogist* 2:3-33; Stuart 111; *Ancestral Roots* 105A; Moriarty 137-138; Note: The parentage of #1 Eudoxia is uncertain and has been heavily debated. The version shown above is accepted by Moriarty and *Ancestral Roots*. Other versions agree on descent from #4 & 5 John & Prisca (Pyriska, Irene). *Ancestral Roots* 8 (2004), Line 105A switches from the Moriarty version shown above to the Schwennicke 2:177 version, which gives #1 Eudoxia as dau. of Alexius Comnenus (b. abt. 1136; d. 1183; md. Maria Dukas or Dukaina), son of Andronicus Comnenus (b. abt. 1108; md. Irene), cont. cht. 279, #1, son of #4 & 5 John II & Prisca above.

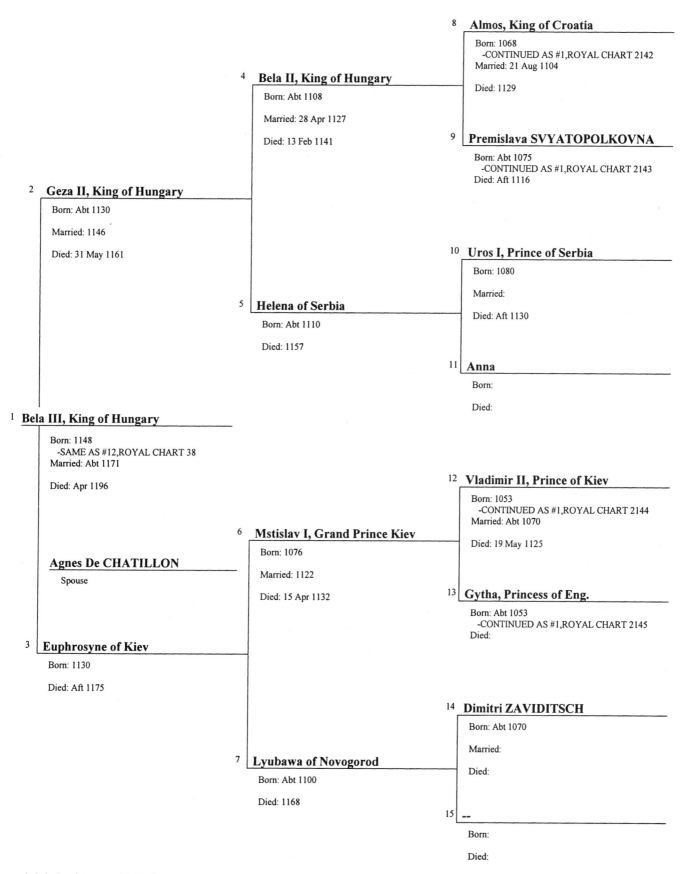

Pedigree Chart

8 **Almos, King of Croatia**
Born: 1068
-CONTINUED AS #1,ROYAL CHART 2142
Married: 21 Aug 1104

Died: 1129

4 **Bela II, King of Hungary**
Born: Abt 1108

Married: 28 Apr 1127

Died: 13 Feb 1141

9 **Premislava SVYATOPOLKOVNA**
Born: Abt 1075
-CONTINUED AS #1,ROYAL CHART 2143
Died: Aft 1116

2 **Geza II, King of Hungary**
Born: Abt 1130

Married: 1146

Died: 31 May 1161

10 **Uros I, Prince of Serbia**
Born: 1080

Married:

Died: Aft 1130

5 **Helena of Serbia**
Born: Abt 1110

Died: 1157

11 **Anna**
Born:

Died:

1 **Bela III, King of Hungary**
Born: 1148
-SAME AS #12,ROYAL CHART 38
Married: Abt 1171

Died: Apr 1196

12 **Vladimir II, Prince of Kiev**
Born: 1053
-CONTINUED AS #1,ROYAL CHART 2144
Married: Abt 1070

Died: 19 May 1125

6 **Mstislav I, Grand Prince Kiev**
Born: 1076

Married: 1122

Died: 15 Apr 1132

13 **Gytha, Princess of Eng.**
Born: Abt 1053
-CONTINUED AS #1,ROYAL CHART 2145
Died:

Agnes De CHATILLON
Spouse

3 **Euphrosyne of Kiev**
Born: 1130

Died: Aft 1175

14 **Dimitri ZAVIDITSCH**
Born: Abt 1070

Married:

Died:

7 **Lyubawa of Novogorod**
Born: Abt 1100

Died: 1168

15 **--**
Born:

Died:

Sources include: *Royal Ancestors* (1989), charts 11311, 11492-93; Schwennicke 2:154; *Ancestral Roots* 242; Stuart 51; Moriarty 143-145; *The Genealogist* 2:21-22, 26, 32; Von Isenburg 2:104; LDS records. Notes: #9 is disputed. Moriarty gives the mother of Bela II as Sophia Von Loos. The parentage and ancestry of both #10 & 11 Uros and Anna is also disputed and unclear.

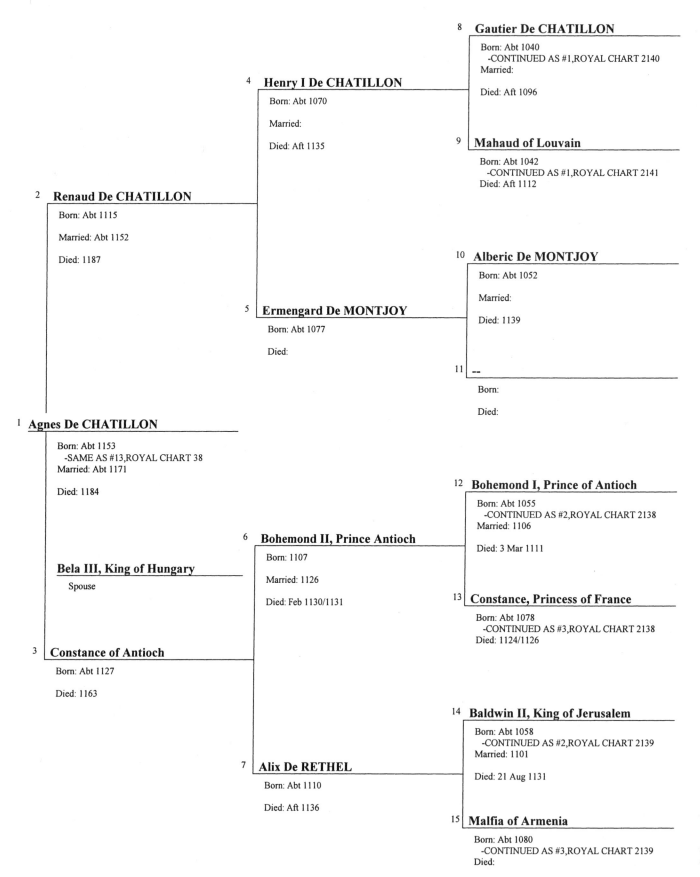

8 **Gautier De CHATILLON**

Born: Abt 1040
-CONTINUED AS #1,ROYAL CHART 2140
Married:

Died: Aft 1096

4 **Henry I De CHATILLON**

Born: Abt 1070

Married:

Died: Aft 1135

9 **Mahaud of Louvain**

Born: Abt 1042
-CONTINUED AS #1,ROYAL CHART 2141
Died: Aft 1112

2 **Renaud De CHATILLON**

Born: Abt 1115

Married: Abt 1152

Died: 1187

10 **Alberic De MONTJOY**

Born: Abt 1052

Married:

Died: 1139

5 **Ermengard De MONTJOY**

Born: Abt 1077

Died:

11 **--**

Born:

Died:

1 **Agnes De CHATILLON**

Born: Abt 1153
-SAME AS #13,ROYAL CHART 38
Married: Abt 1171

Died: 1184

12 **Bohemond I, Prince of Antioch**

Born: Abt 1055
-CONTINUED AS #2,ROYAL CHART 2138
Married: 1106

Died: 3 Mar 1111

6 **Bohemond II, Prince Antioch**

Born: 1107

Married: 1126

Died: Feb 1130/1131

13 **Constance, Princess of France**

Born: Abt 1078
-CONTINUED AS #3,ROYAL CHART 2138
Died: 1124/1126

Bela III, King of Hungary

Spouse

3 **Constance of Antioch**

Born: Abt 1127

Died: 1163

14 **Baldwin II, King of Jerusalem**

Born: Abt 1058
-CONTINUED AS #2,ROYAL CHART 2139
Married: 1101

Died: 21 Aug 1131

7 **Alix De RETHEL**

Born: Abt 1110

Died: Aft 1136

15 **Malfia of Armenia**

Born: Abt 1080
-CONTINUED AS #3,ROYAL CHART 2139
Died:

Sources include: *Royal Ancestors* (1989), charts 11311, 11494-95; Stuart 80, 99; Faris preliminary Charlemagne manuscript (June 1995), pp. 155-156; *Ancestral Roots* 103; Moriarty 142, 147, 262, 272-273. Note: The parentage of #2 Renaud is uncertain and disputed. Faris gives him as son of Geoffroi De Chatillon.

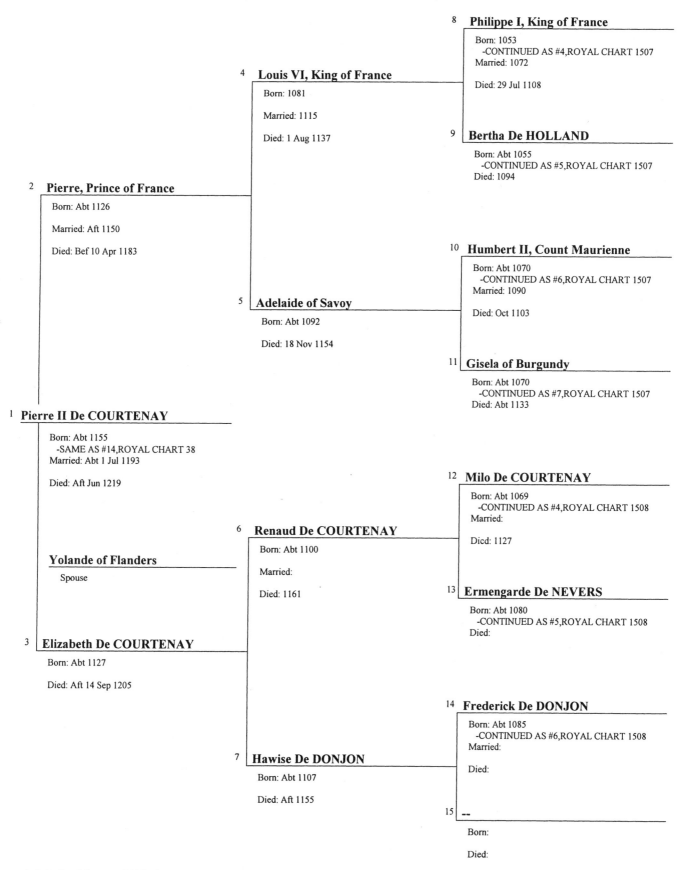

8 Philippe I, King of France
Born: 1053
 -CONTINUED AS #4,ROYAL CHART 1507
Married: 1072

Died: 29 Jul 1108

4 Louis VI, King of France
Born: 1081

Married: 1115

Died: 1 Aug 1137

9 Bertha De HOLLAND
Born: Abt 1055
 -CONTINUED AS #5,ROYAL CHART 1507
Died: 1094

2 Pierre, Prince of France
Born: Abt 1126

Married: Aft 1150

Died: Bef 10 Apr 1183

10 Humbert II, Count Maurienne
Born: Abt 1070
 -CONTINUED AS #6,ROYAL CHART 1507
Married: 1090

Died: Oct 1103

5 Adelaide of Savoy
Born: Abt 1092

Died: 18 Nov 1154

11 Gisela of Burgundy
Born: Abt 1070
 -CONTINUED AS #7,ROYAL CHART 1507
Died: Abt 1133

1 Pierre II De COURTENAY
Born: Abt 1155
 -SAME AS #14,ROYAL CHART 38
Married: Abt 1 Jul 1193

Died: Aft Jun 1219

12 Milo De COURTENAY
Born: Abt 1069
 -CONTINUED AS #4,ROYAL CHART 1508
Married:

Died: 1127

6 Renaud De COURTENAY
Born: Abt 1100

Married:

Died: 1161

13 Ermengarde De NEVERS
Born: Abt 1080
 -CONTINUED AS #5,ROYAL CHART 1508
Died:

Yolande of Flanders
Spouse

3 Elizabeth De COURTENAY
Born: Abt 1127

Died: Aft 14 Sep 1205

14 Frederick De DONJON
Born: Abt 1085
 -CONTINUED AS #6,ROYAL CHART 1508
Married:

Died:

7 Hawise De DONJON
Born: Abt 1107

Died: Aft 1155

15 --
Born:

Died:

Sources include: *Royal Ancestors* (1989), charts 11311, 11302; Stuart 79, 144; *Ancestral Roots* 107.

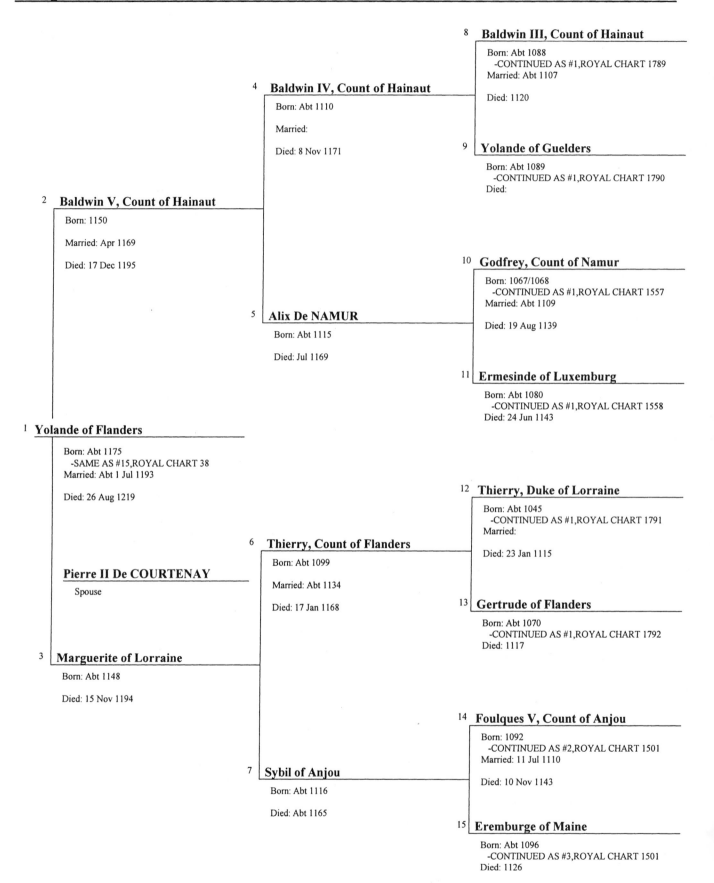

8 Baldwin III, Count of Hainaut

Born: Abt 1088
  -CONTINUED AS #1,ROYAL CHART 1789
Married: Abt 1107

Died: 1120

4 Baldwin IV, Count of Hainaut

Born: Abt 1110

Married:

Died: 8 Nov 1171

9 Yolande of Guelders

Born: Abt 1089
  -CONTINUED AS #1,ROYAL CHART 1790
Died:

2 Baldwin V, Count of Hainaut

Born: 1150

Married: Apr 1169

Died: 17 Dec 1195

10 Godfrey, Count of Namur

Born: 1067/1068
  -CONTINUED AS #1,ROYAL CHART 1557
Married: Abt 1109

Died: 19 Aug 1139

5 Alix De NAMUR

Born: Abt 1115

Died: Jul 1169

11 Ermesinde of Luxemburg

Born: Abt 1080
  -CONTINUED AS #1,ROYAL CHART 1558
Died: 24 Jun 1143

1 Yolande of Flanders

Born: Abt 1175
  -SAME AS #15,ROYAL CHART 38
Married: Abt 1 Jul 1193

Died: 26 Aug 1219

12 Thierry, Duke of Lorraine

Born: Abt 1045
  -CONTINUED AS #1,ROYAL CHART 1791
Married:

Died: 23 Jan 1115

6 Thierry, Count of Flanders

Born: Abt 1099

Married: Abt 1134

Died: 17 Jan 1168

13 Gertrude of Flanders

Born: Abt 1070
  -CONTINUED AS #1,ROYAL CHART 1792
Died: 1117

Pierre II De COURTENAY

Spouse

3 Marguerite of Lorraine

Born: Abt 1148

Died: 15 Nov 1194

14 Foulques V, Count of Anjou

Born: 1092
  -CONTINUED AS #2,ROYAL CHART 1501
Married: 11 Jul 1110

Died: 10 Nov 1143

7 Sybil of Anjou

Born: Abt 1116

Died: Abt 1165

15 Eremburge of Maine

Born: Abt 1096
  -CONTINUED AS #3,ROYAL CHART 1501
Died: 1126

Sources include: *Royal Ancestors* (1989), charts 11311, 11316; Stuart 79-27, 73, 132; *Ancestral Roots* 163A, 163, 164.

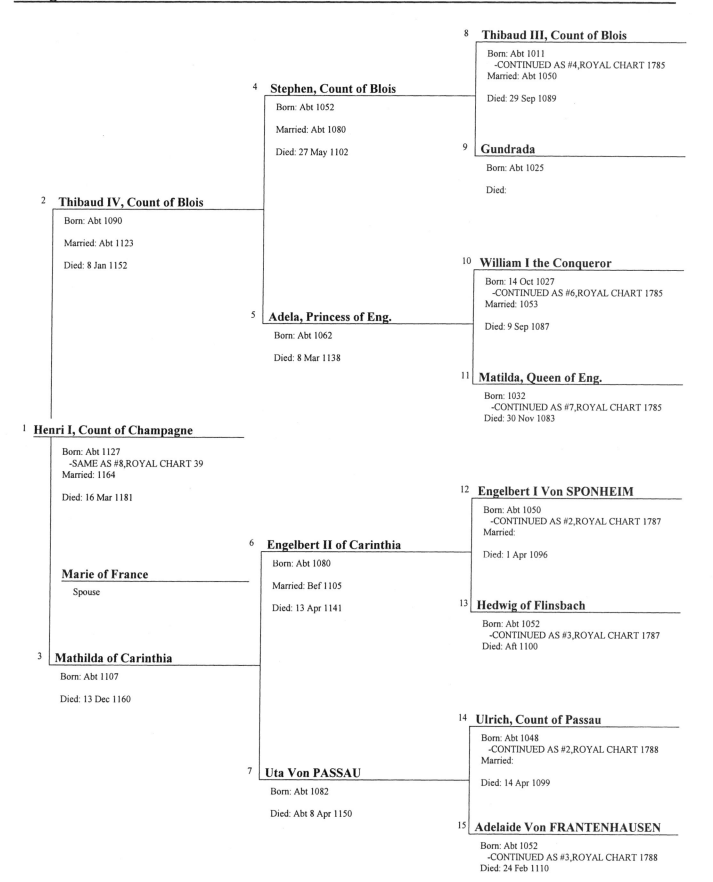

8 **Thibaud III, Count of Blois**

Born: Abt 1011
-CONTINUED AS #4,ROYAL CHART 1785
Married: Abt 1050

Died: 29 Sep 1089

4 **Stephen, Count of Blois**

Born: Abt 1052

Married: Abt 1080

Died: 27 May 1102

9 **Gundrada**

Born: Abt 1025

Died:

2 **Thibaud IV, Count of Blois**

Born: Abt 1090

Married: Abt 1123

Died: 8 Jan 1152

10 **William I the Conqueror**

Born: 14 Oct 1027
-CONTINUED AS #6,ROYAL CHART 1785
Married: 1053

Died: 9 Sep 1087

5 **Adela, Princess of Eng.**

Born: Abt 1062

Died: 8 Mar 1138

11 **Matilda, Queen of Eng.**

Born: 1032
-CONTINUED AS #7,ROYAL CHART 1785
Died: 30 Nov 1083

1 **Henri I, Count of Champagne**

Born: Abt 1127
-SAME AS #8,ROYAL CHART 39
Married: 1164

Died: 16 Mar 1181

12 **Engelbert I Von SPONHEIM**

Born: Abt 1050
-CONTINUED AS #2,ROYAL CHART 1787
Married:

Died: 1 Apr 1096

6 **Engelbert II of Carinthia**

Born: Abt 1080

Married: Bef 1105

Died: 13 Apr 1141

13 **Hedwig of Flinsbach**

Born: Abt 1052
-CONTINUED AS #3,ROYAL CHART 1787
Died: Aft 1100

Marie of France

Spouse

3 **Mathilda of Carinthia**

Born: Abt 1107

Died: 13 Dec 1160

14 **Ulrich, Count of Passau**

Born: Abt 1048
-CONTINUED AS #2,ROYAL CHART 1788
Married:

Died: 14 Apr 1099

7 **Uta Von PASSAU**

Born: Abt 1082

Died: Abt 8 Apr 1150

15 **Adelaide Von FRANTENHAUSEN**

Born: Abt 1052
-CONTINUED AS #3,ROYAL CHART 1788
Died: 24 Feb 1110

Sources include: *Royal Ancestors* (1989), chart 11312; Stuart 81, 228; Moriarty 117.

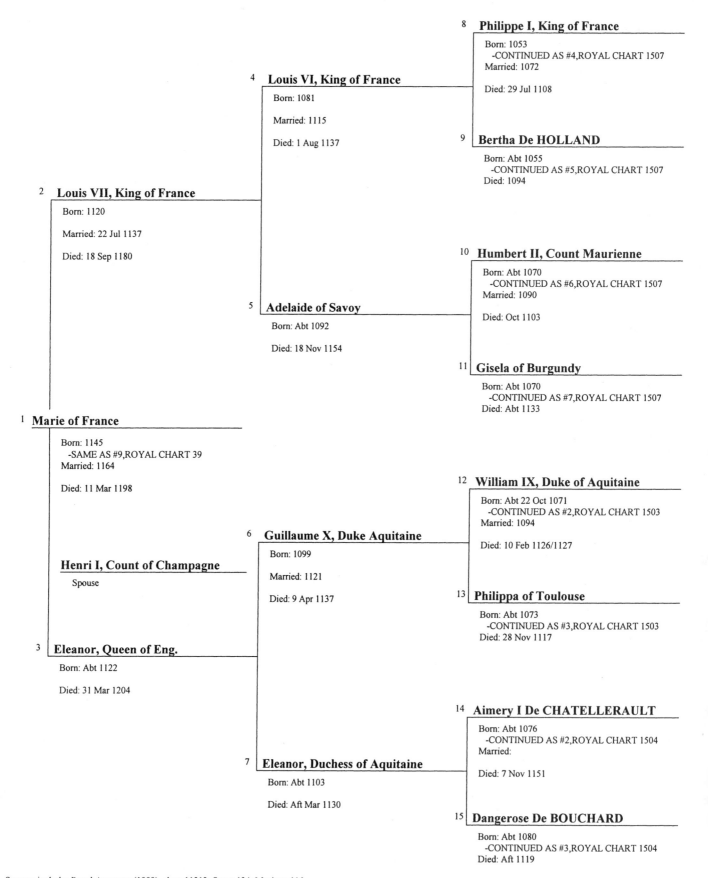

8   **Philippe I, King of France**

Born: 1053
    -CONTINUED AS #4,ROYAL CHART 1507
Married: 1072

Died: 29 Jul 1108

4   **Louis VI, King of France**

Born: 1081

Married: 1115

Died: 1 Aug 1137

9   **Bertha De HOLLAND**

Born: Abt 1055
    -CONTINUED AS #5,ROYAL CHART 1507
Died: 1094

2   **Louis VII, King of France**

Born: 1120

Married: 22 Jul 1137

Died: 18 Sep 1180

10   **Humbert II, Count Maurienne**

Born: Abt 1070
    -CONTINUED AS #6,ROYAL CHART 1507
Married: 1090

Died: Oct 1103

5   **Adelaide of Savoy**

Born: Abt 1092

Died: 18 Nov 1154

11   **Gisela of Burgundy**

Born: Abt 1070
    -CONTINUED AS #7,ROYAL CHART 1507
Died: Abt 1133

1   **Marie of France**

Born: 1145
    -SAME AS #9,ROYAL CHART 39
Married: 1164

Died: 11 Mar 1198

12   **William IX, Duke of Aquitaine**

Born: Abt 22 Oct 1071
    -CONTINUED AS #2,ROYAL CHART 1503
Married: 1094

Died: 10 Feb 1126/1127

6   **Guillaume X, Duke Aquitaine**

Born: 1099

Married: 1121

Died: 9 Apr 1137

Henri I, Count of Champagne

Spouse

13   **Philippa of Toulouse**

Born: Abt 1073
    -CONTINUED AS #3,ROYAL CHART 1503
Died: 28 Nov 1117

3   **Eleanor, Queen of Eng.**

Born: Abt 1122

Died: 31 Mar 1204

14   **Aimery I De CHATELLERAULT**

Born: Abt 1076
    -CONTINUED AS #2,ROYAL CHART 1504
Married:

Died: 7 Nov 1151

7   **Eleanor, Duchess of Aquitaine**

Born: Abt 1103

Died: Aft Mar 1130

15   **Dangerose De BOUCHARD**

Born: Abt 1080
    -CONTINUED AS #3,ROYAL CHART 1504
Died: Aft 1119

Sources include: *Royal Ancestors* (1989), chart 11312; Stuart 134; Moriarty 116.

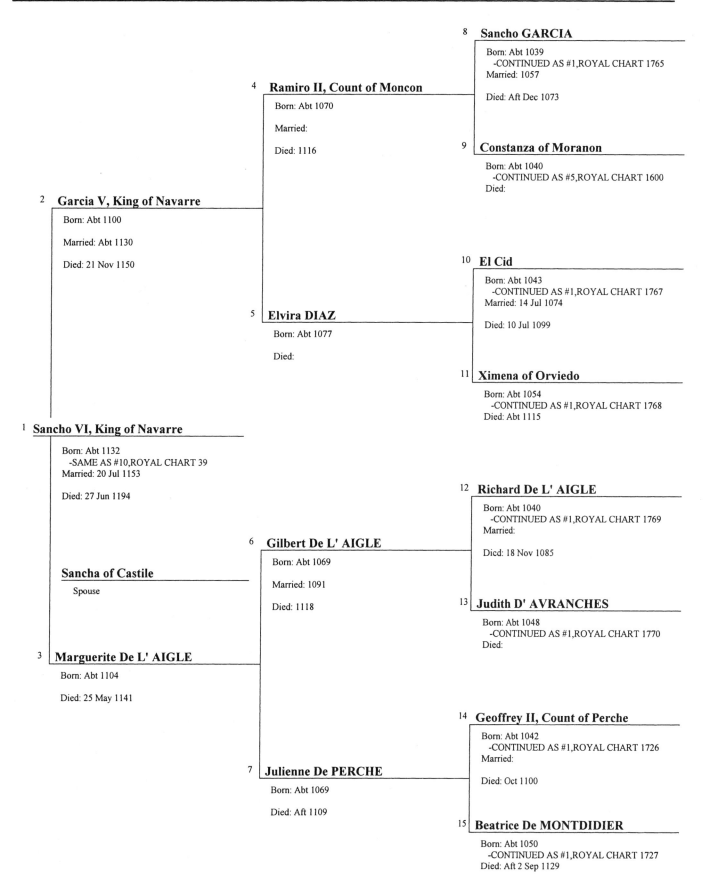

2 Garcia V, King of Navarre

Born: Abt 1100

Married: Abt 1130

Died: 21 Nov 1150

4 Ramiro II, Count of Moncon

Born: Abt 1070

Married:

Died: 1116

8 Sancho GARCIA

Born: Abt 1039
   -CONTINUED AS #1,ROYAL CHART 1765
Married: 1057

Died: Aft Dec 1073

9 Constanza of Moranon

Born: Abt 1040
   -CONTINUED AS #5,ROYAL CHART 1600
Died:

5 Elvira DIAZ

Born: Abt 1077

Died:

10 El Cid

Born: Abt 1043
   -CONTINUED AS #1,ROYAL CHART 1767
Married: 14 Jul 1074

Died: 10 Jul 1099

11 Ximena of Orviedo

Born: Abt 1054
   -CONTINUED AS #1,ROYAL CHART 1768
Died: Abt 1115

1 Sancho VI, King of Navarre

Born: Abt 1132
   -SAME AS #10,ROYAL CHART 39
Married: 20 Jul 1153

Died: 27 Jun 1194

Sancha of Castile

Spouse

3 Marguerite De L' AIGLE

Born: Abt 1104

Died: 25 May 1141

6 Gilbert De L' AIGLE

Born: Abt 1069

Married: 1091

Died: 1118

12 Richard De L' AIGLE

Born: Abt 1040
   -CONTINUED AS #1,ROYAL CHART 1769
Married:

Died: 18 Nov 1085

13 Judith D' AVRANCHES

Born: Abt 1048
   -CONTINUED AS #1,ROYAL CHART 1770
Died:

7 Julienne De PERCHE

Born: Abt 1069

Died: Aft 1109

14 Geoffrey II, Count of Perche

Born: Abt 1042
   -CONTINUED AS #1,ROYAL CHART 1726
Married:

Died: Oct 1100

15 Beatrice De MONTDIDIER

Born: Abt 1050
   -CONTINUED AS #1,ROYAL CHART 1727
Died: Aft 2 Sep 1129

Sources include: *Royal Ancestors* (1989), chart 11312; Stuart 86-28, 151, 178; Chart 1520 with sources and notes.

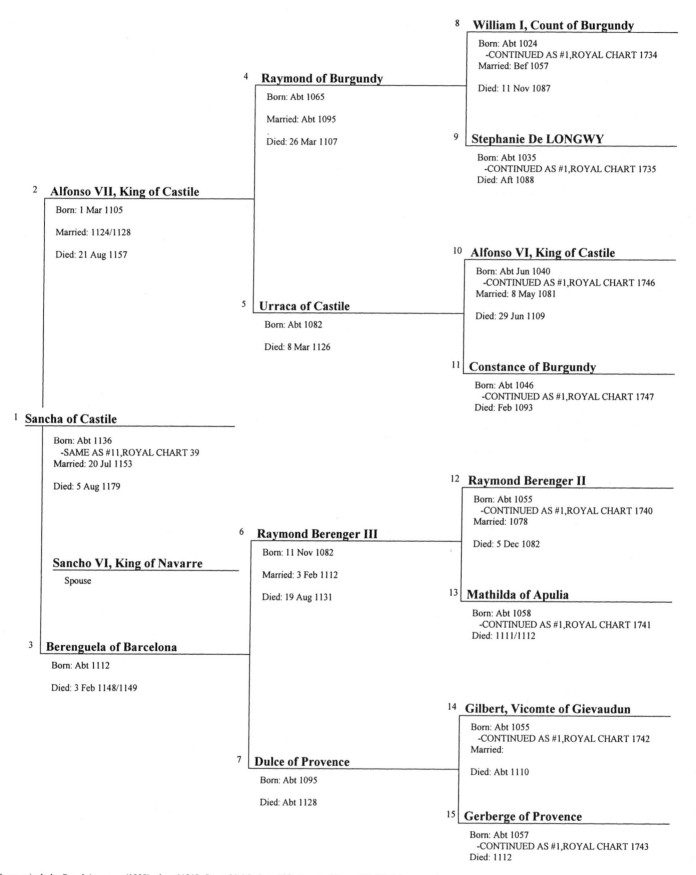

8 William I, Count of Burgundy

Born: Abt 1024
-CONTINUED AS #1,ROYAL CHART 1734
Married: Bef 1057

Died: 11 Nov 1087

4 Raymond of Burgundy

Born: Abt 1065

Married: Abt 1095

Died: 26 Mar 1107

9 Stephanie De LONGWY

Born: Abt 1035
-CONTINUED AS #1,ROYAL CHART 1735
Died: Aft 1088

2 Alfonso VII, King of Castile

Born: 1 Mar 1105

Married: 1124/1128

Died: 21 Aug 1157

10 Alfonso VI, King of Castile

Born: Abt Jun 1040
-CONTINUED AS #1,ROYAL CHART 1746
Married: 8 May 1081

Died: 29 Jun 1109

5 Urraca of Castile

Born: Abt 1082

Died: 8 Mar 1126

11 Constance of Burgundy

Born: Abt 1046
-CONTINUED AS #1,ROYAL CHART 1747
Died: Feb 1093

1 Sancha of Castile

Born: Abt 1136
-SAME AS #11,ROYAL CHART 39
Married: 20 Jul 1153

Died: 5 Aug 1179

12 Raymond Berenger II

Born: Abt 1055
-CONTINUED AS #1,ROYAL CHART 1740
Married: 1078

Died: 5 Dec 1082

6 Raymond Berenger III

Born: 11 Nov 1082

Married: 3 Feb 1112

Died: 19 Aug 1131

13 Mathilda of Apulia

Born: Abt 1058
-CONTINUED AS #1,ROYAL CHART 1741
Died: 1111/1112

Sancho VI, King of Navarre

Spouse

3 Berenguela of Barcelona

Born: Abt 1112

Died: 3 Feb 1148/1149

14 Gilbert, Vicomte of Gievaudun

Born: Abt 1055
-CONTINUED AS #1,ROYAL CHART 1742
Married:

Died: Abt 1110

7 Dulce of Provence

Born: Abt 1095

Died: Abt 1128

15 Gerberge of Provence

Born: Abt 1057
-CONTINUED AS #1,ROYAL CHART 1743
Died: 1112

Sources include: *Royal Ancestors* (1989), chart 11312; Stuart 86; Moriarty 108; *Ancestral Roots* 113 (#2 & 3 ancestry).

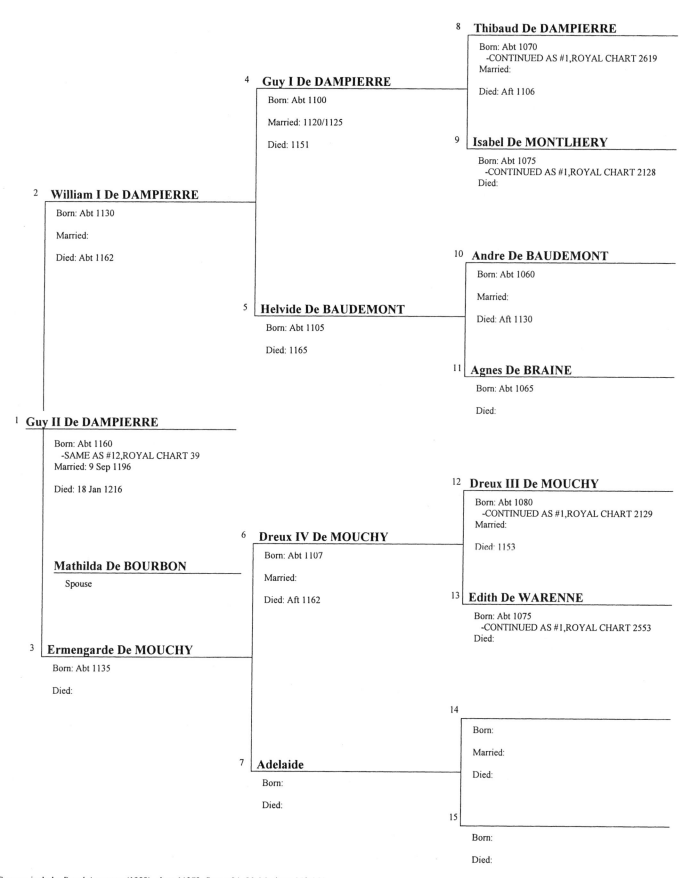

2 William I De DAMPIERRE

Born: Abt 1130

Married:

Died: Abt 1162

4 Guy I De DAMPIERRE

Born: Abt 1100

Married: 1120/1125

Died: 1151

8 Thibaud De DAMPIERRE

Born: Abt 1070
 -CONTINUED AS #1,ROYAL CHART 2619
Married:

Died: Aft 1106

9 Isabel De MONTLHERY

Born: Abt 1075
 -CONTINUED AS #1,ROYAL CHART 2128
Died:

5 Helvide De BAUDEMONT

Born: Abt 1105

Died: 1165

10 Andre De BAUDEMONT

Born: Abt 1060

Married:

Died: Aft 1130

11 Agnes De BRAINE

Born: Abt 1065

Died:

1 Guy II De DAMPIERRE

Born: Abt 1160
 -SAME AS #12,ROYAL CHART 39
Married: 9 Sep 1196

Died: 18 Jan 1216

Mathilda De BOURBON

Spouse

3 Ermengarde De MOUCHY

Born: Abt 1135

Died:

6 Dreux IV De MOUCHY

Born: Abt 1107

Married:

Died: Aft 1162

12 Dreux III De MOUCHY

Born: Abt 1080
 -CONTINUED AS #1,ROYAL CHART 2129
Married:

Died: 1153

13 Edith De WARENNE

Born: Abt 1075
 -CONTINUED AS #1,ROYAL CHART 2553
Died:

7 Adelaide

Born:

Died:

14

Born:

Married:

Died:

15

Born:

Died:

Sources include: *Royal Ancestors* (1989), chart 11372; Stuart 84, 56; Moriarty 149-151.

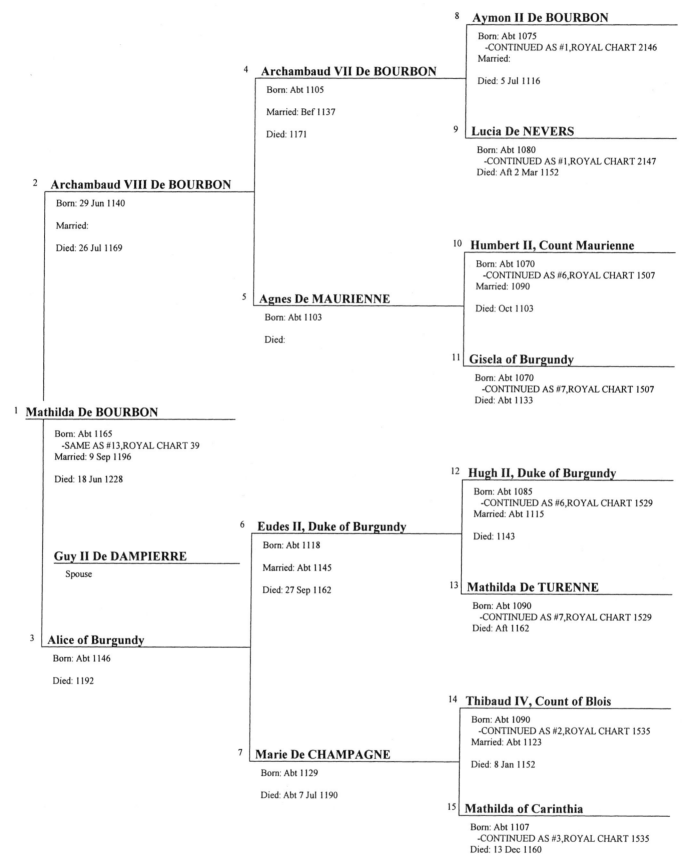

8 **Aymon II De BOURBON**

Born: Abt 1075
  -CONTINUED AS #1,ROYAL CHART 2146
Married:

Died: 5 Jul 1116

4 **Archambaud VII De BOURBON**

Born: Abt 1105

Married: Bef 1137

Died: 1171

9 **Lucia De NEVERS**

Born: Abt 1080
  -CONTINUED AS #1,ROYAL CHART 2147
Died: Aft 2 Mar 1152

2 **Archambaud VIII De BOURBON**

Born: 29 Jun 1140

Married:

Died: 26 Jul 1169

10 **Humbert II, Count Maurienne**

Born: Abt 1070
  -CONTINUED AS #6,ROYAL CHART 1507
Married: 1090

Died: Oct 1103

5 **Agnes De MAURIENNE**

Born: Abt 1103

Died:

11 **Gisela of Burgundy**

Born: Abt 1070
  -CONTINUED AS #7,ROYAL CHART 1507
Died: Abt 1133

1 **Mathilda De BOURBON**

Born: Abt 1165
  -SAME AS #13,ROYAL CHART 39
Married: 9 Sep 1196

Died: 18 Jun 1228

12 **Hugh II, Duke of Burgundy**

Born: Abt 1085
  -CONTINUED AS #6,ROYAL CHART 1529
Married: Abt 1115

Died: 1143

6 **Eudes II, Duke of Burgundy**

Born: Abt 1118

Married: Abt 1145

Died: 27 Sep 1162

13 **Mathilda De TURENNE**

Born: Abt 1090
  -CONTINUED AS #7,ROYAL CHART 1529
Died: Aft 1162

Guy II De DAMPIERRE

Spouse

3 **Alice of Burgundy**

Born: Abt 1146

Died: 1192

14 **Thibaud IV, Count of Blois**

Born: Abt 1090
  -CONTINUED AS #2,ROYAL CHART 1535
Married: Abt 1123

Died: 8 Jan 1152

7 **Marie De CHAMPAGNE**

Born: Abt 1129

Died: Abt 7 Jul 1190

15 **Mathilda of Carinthia**

Born: Abt 1107
  -CONTINUED AS #3,ROYAL CHART 1535
Died: 13 Dec 1160

Sources include: *Royal Ancestors* (1989), chart 11372; Stuart 84-28, 59-60; Moriarty 153; Faris preliminary Charlemagne manuscript (June 1995), pp. 60, 81-82.

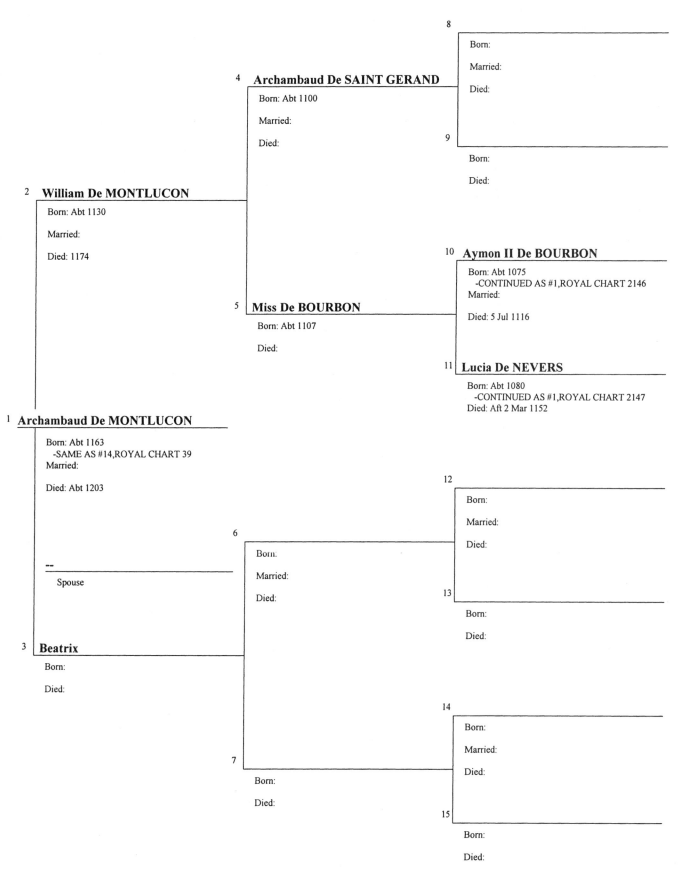

8

Born:

Married:

Died:

4 Archambaud De SAINT GERAND

Born: Abt 1100

Married:

Died:

9

Born:

Died:

2 William De MONTLUCON

Born: Abt 1130

Married:

Died: 1174

10 **Aymon II De BOURBON**

Born: Abt 1075
    -CONTINUED AS #1,ROYAL CHART 2146
Married:

Died: 5 Jul 1116

5 Miss De BOURBON

Born: Abt 1107

Died:

11 **Lucia De NEVERS**

Born: Abt 1080
    -CONTINUED AS #1,ROYAL CHART 2147
Died: Aft 2 Mar 1152

1 Archambaud De MONTLUCON

Born: Abt 1163
    -SAME AS #14,ROYAL CHART 39
Married:

Died: Abt 1203

12

Born:

Married:

Died:

6

Born:

Married:

Died:

13

Born:

Died:

--

Spouse

3 Beatrix

Born:

Died:

14

Born:

Married:

Died:

7

Born:

Died:

15

Born:

Died:

Sources include: *Royal Ancestors* (1989), charts 11372, 11929; Faris preliminary Charlemagne manuscript (June 1995), p. 191; Moriarty 151; Kraentzler 1242; Stuart 84-27 (#1 Archambaud). Note: The parentage of #2 William is disputed. The Faris version (following West Winter) is given above. Moriarty gives #2 as William II, son of William I, son of #4 Archambaud, where he ends the line without identifying a wife. Kraentzler claims #4 Archambaud as the grandson of Archambaud IV De Bourbon (see chart 2146).

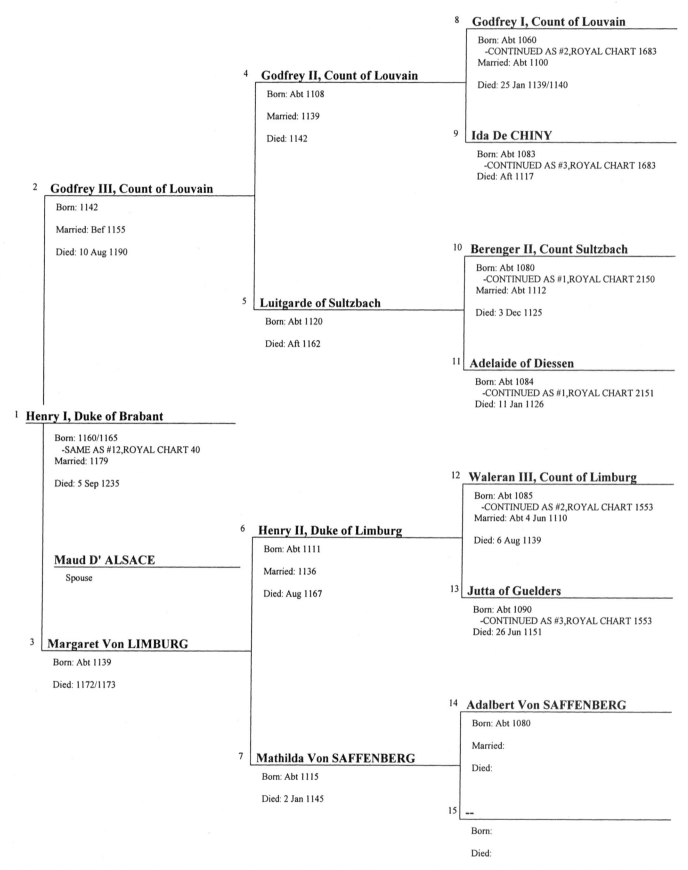

2 Godfrey III, Count of Louvain

Born: 1142

Married: Bef 1155

Died: 10 Aug 1190

4 Godfrey II, Count of Louvain

Born: Abt 1108

Married: 1139

Died: 1142

8 Godfrey I, Count of Louvain

Born: Abt 1060
  -CONTINUED AS #2,ROYAL CHART 1683
Married: Abt 1100

Died: 25 Jan 1139/1140

9 Ida De CHINY

Born: Abt 1083
  -CONTINUED AS #3,ROYAL CHART 1683
Died: Aft 1117

5 Luitgarde of Sultzbach

Born: Abt 1120

Died: Aft 1162

10 Berenger II, Count Sultzbach

Born: Abt 1080
  -CONTINUED AS #1,ROYAL CHART 2150
Married: Abt 1112

Died: 3 Dec 1125

11 Adelaide of Diessen

Born: Abt 1084
  -CONTINUED AS #1,ROYAL CHART 2151
Died: 11 Jan 1126

1 Henry I, Duke of Brabant

Born: 1160/1165
  -SAME AS #12,ROYAL CHART 40
Married: 1179

Died: 5 Sep 1235

Maud D' ALSACE

Spouse

3 Margaret Von LIMBURG

Born: Abt 1139

Died: 1172/1173

6 Henry II, Duke of Limburg

Born: Abt 1111

Married: 1136

Died: Aug 1167

12 Waleran III, Count of Limburg

Born: Abt 1085
  -CONTINUED AS #2,ROYAL CHART 1553
Married: Abt 4 Jun 1110

Died: 6 Aug 1139

13 Jutta of Guelders

Born: Abt 1090
  -CONTINUED AS #3,ROYAL CHART 1553
Died: 26 Jun 1151

7 Mathilda Von SAFFENBERG

Born: Abt 1115

Died: 2 Jan 1145

14 Adalbert Von SAFFENBERG

Born: Abt 1080

Married:

Died:

15 --

Born:

Died:

Sources include: *Royal Ancestors* (1989), charts 11367, 11373; Stuart 68, 62; Faris preliminary Charlemagne manuscript (June 1995), pp. 68-69, 174-175; *Ancestral Roots* 155; Moriarty 154, 160; Turton 170. Note: Moriarty extends #14 (Adalbert or Adolf) & #15 (given as Margaret Von Schwarzenburg), but Stuart deletes the claimed lines. Faris gives #15 as a 2nd wife Mechtild. Schwennicke 18:1 gives #7 Mathilda as dau. of Adolf (md. 1122 Margareta Von Schwarzenburg), son of Adalbert (d. 16 Dec 1109; md. Mathilde, d. 4 Dec 1110), son of Hermann Von Saffenberg (md. Gepa).

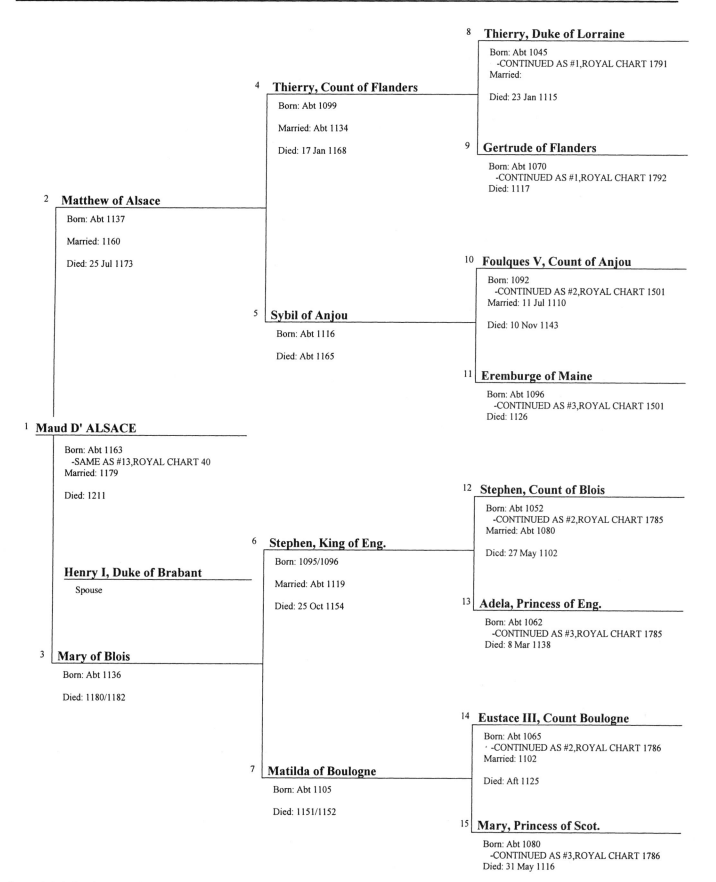

8 Thierry, Duke of Lorraine

Born: Abt 1045
  -CONTINUED AS #1,ROYAL CHART 1791
Married:

Died: 23 Jan 1115

4 Thierry, Count of Flanders

Born: Abt 1099

Married: Abt 1134

Died: 17 Jan 1168

9 Gertrude of Flanders

Born: Abt 1070
  -CONTINUED AS #1,ROYAL CHART 1792
Died: 1117

2 Matthew of Alsace

Born: Abt 1137

Married: 1160

Died: 25 Jul 1173

10 Foulques V, Count of Anjou

Born: 1092
  -CONTINUED AS #2,ROYAL CHART 1501
Married: 11 Jul 1110

Died: 10 Nov 1143

5 Sybil of Anjou

Born: Abt 1116

Died: Abt 1165

11 Eremburge of Maine

Born: Abt 1096
  -CONTINUED AS #3,ROYAL CHART 1501
Died: 1126

1 Maud D' ALSACE

Born: Abt 1163
  -SAME AS #13,ROYAL CHART 40
Married: 1179

Died: 1211

Henry I, Duke of Brabant

Spouse

12 Stephen, Count of Blois

Born: Abt 1052
  -CONTINUED AS #2,ROYAL CHART 1785
Married: Abt 1080

Dicd: 27 May 1102

6 Stephen, King of Eng.

Born: 1095/1096

Married: Abt 1119

Died: 25 Oct 1154

13 Adela, Princess of Eng.

Born: Abt 1062
  -CONTINUED AS #3,ROYAL CHART 1785
Died: 8 Mar 1138

3 Mary of Blois

Born: Abt 1136

Died: 1180/1182

14 Eustace III, Count Boulogne

Born: Abt 1065
  -CONTINUED AS #2,ROYAL CHART 1786
Married: 1102

Died: Aft 1125

7 Matilda of Boulogne

Born: Abt 1105

Died: 1151/1152

15 Mary, Princess of Scot.

Born: Abt 1080
  -CONTINUED AS #3,ROYAL CHART 1786
Died: 31 May 1116

Sources include: *Royal Ancestors* (1989), chart 11314; *Ancestral Roots* 165; Stuart 205.

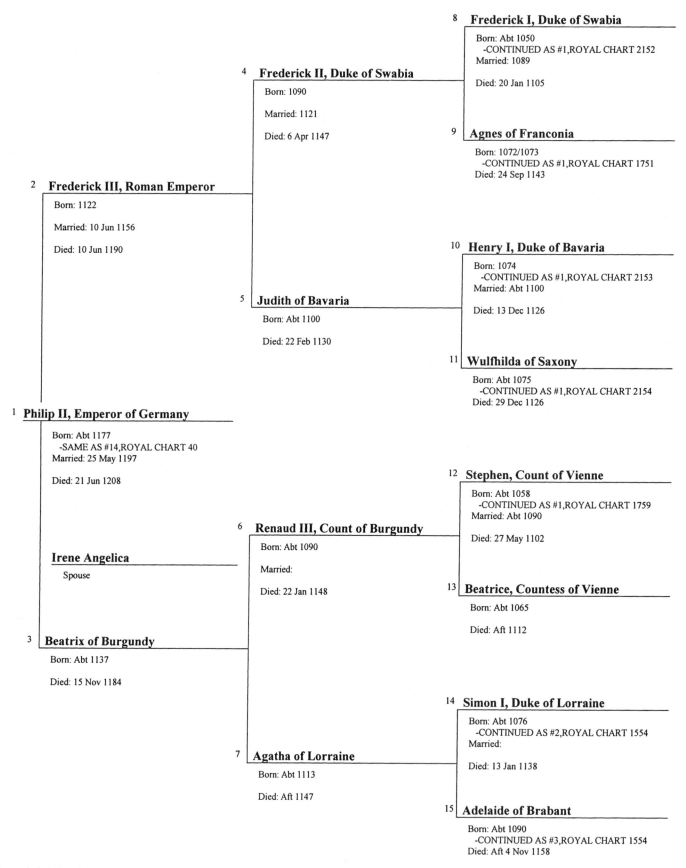

8 Frederick I, Duke of Swabia

Born: Abt 1050
 -CONTINUED AS #1,ROYAL CHART 2152
Married: 1089

Died: 20 Jan 1105

4 Frederick II, Duke of Swabia

Born: 1090

Married: 1121

Died: 6 Apr 1147

9 Agnes of Franconia

Born: 1072/1073
 -CONTINUED AS #1,ROYAL CHART 1751
Died: 24 Sep 1143

2 Frederick III, Roman Emperor

Born: 1122

Married: 10 Jun 1156

Died: 10 Jun 1190

10 Henry I, Duke of Bavaria

Born: 1074
 -CONTINUED AS #1,ROYAL CHART 2153
Married: Abt 1100

Died: 13 Dec 1126

5 Judith of Bavaria

Born: Abt 1100

Died: 22 Feb 1130

11 Wulfhilda of Saxony

Born: Abt 1075
 -CONTINUED AS #1,ROYAL CHART 2154
Died: 29 Dec 1126

1 Philip II, Emperor of Germany

Born: Abt 1177
 -SAME AS #14,ROYAL CHART 40
Married: 25 May 1197

Died: 21 Jun 1208

12 Stephen, Count of Vienne

Born: Abt 1058
 -CONTINUED AS #1,ROYAL CHART 1759
Married: Abt 1090

Died: 27 May 1102

6 Renaud III, Count of Burgundy

Born: Abt 1090

Married:

Died: 22 Jan 1148

13 Beatrice, Countess of Vienne

Born: Abt 1065

Died: Aft 1112

Irene Angelica

Spouse

3 Beatrix of Burgundy

Born: Abt 1137

Died: 15 Nov 1184

14 Simon I, Duke of Lorraine

Born: Abt 1076
 -CONTINUED AS #2,ROYAL CHART 1554
Married:

Died: 13 Jan 1138

7 Agatha of Lorraine

Born: Abt 1113

Died: Aft 1147

15 Adelaide of Brabant

Born: Abt 1090
 -CONTINUED AS #3,ROYAL CHART 1554
Died: Aft 4 Nov 1158

Sources include: *Royal Ancestors* (1989), chart 11314; *Ancestral Roots* 45; Faris preliminary Charlemagne manuscript (June 1995), pp. 141-142, 65; Stuart 125, 40-41; Moriarty 166, 171.

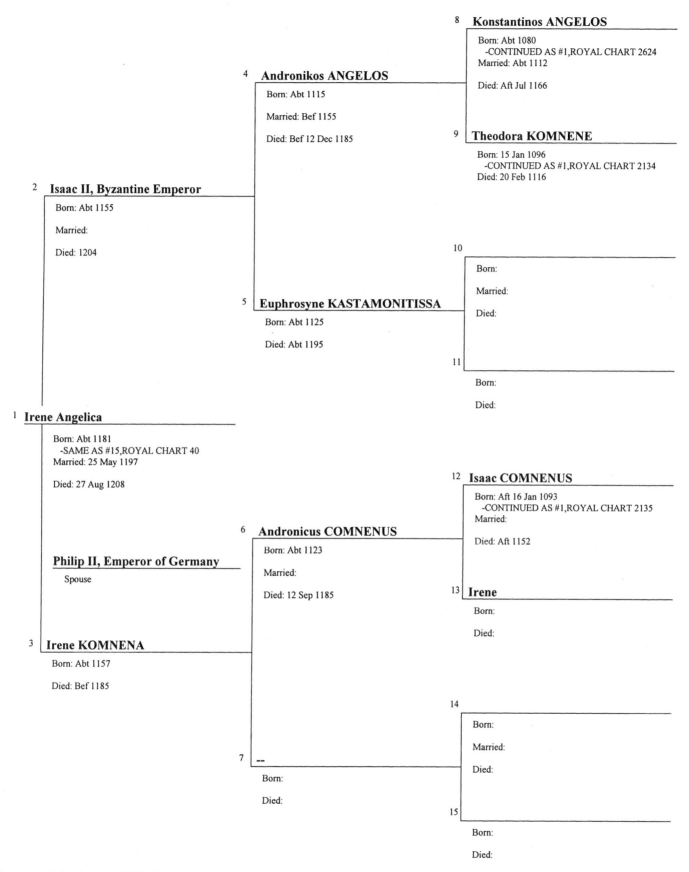

8 Konstantinos ANGELOS

Born: Abt 1080
-CONTINUED AS #1,ROYAL CHART 2624
Married: Abt 1112

Died: Aft Jul 1166

4 Andronikos ANGELOS

Born: Abt 1115

Married: Bef 1155

Died: Bef 12 Dec 1185

9 Theodora KOMNENE

Born: 15 Jan 1096
-CONTINUED AS #1,ROYAL CHART 2134
Died: 20 Feb 1116

2 Isaac II, Byzantine Emperor

Born: Abt 1155

Married:

Died: 1204

10

Born:

Married:

Died:

5 Euphrosyne KASTAMONITISSA

Born: Abt 1125

Died: Abt 1195

11

Born:

Died:

1 Irene Angelica

Born: Abt 1181
-SAME AS #15,ROYAL CHART 40
Married: 25 May 1197

Died: 27 Aug 1208

12 Isaac COMNENUS

Born: Aft 16 Jan 1093
-CONTINUED AS #1,ROYAL CHART 2135
Married:

Died: Aft 1152

6 Andronicus COMNENUS

Born: Abt 1123

Married:

Died: 12 Sep 1185

Philip II, Emperor of Germany

Spouse

13 Irene

Born:

Died:

3 Irene KOMNENA

Born: Abt 1157

Died: Bef 1185

14

Born:

Married:

Died:

7 --

Born:

Died:

15

Born:

Died:

Sources include: *Royal Ancestors* (1989), charts 11314, 11486, 11861; Stuart 215, 42; *The Genealogist* 2:3-33, 91 (parentage of #5 unknown); *Ancestral Roots* 45-27; Moriarty 174; Von Isenburg 2:142. Note: #6 Andronicus had 2 wives and 3 concubines. Which one of these was the mother of #3 Irene is disputed and uncertain.

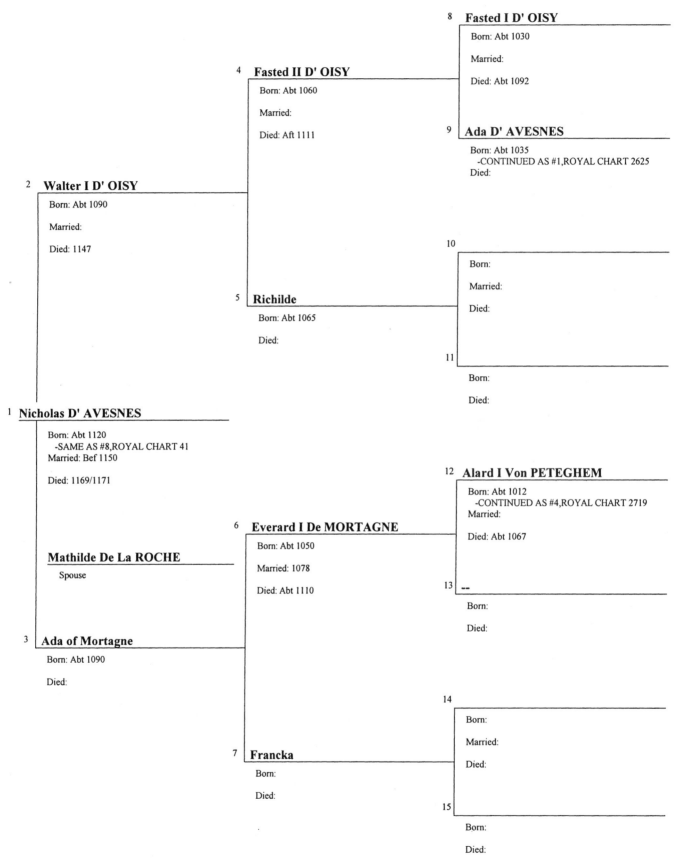

8 Fasted I D' OISY

Born: Abt 1030

Married:

Died: Abt 1092

---

4 Fasted II D' OISY

Born: Abt 1060

Married:

Died: Aft 1111

---

9 Ada D' AVESNES

Born: Abt 1035
  -CONTINUED AS #1,ROYAL CHART 2625
Died:

---

2 Walter I D' OISY

Born: Abt 1090

Married:

Died: 1147

10

Born:

Married:

Died:

---

5 Richilde

Born: Abt 1065

Died:

11

Born:

Died:

---

1 Nicholas D' AVESNES

Born: Abt 1120
  -SAME AS #8,ROYAL CHART 41
Married: Bef 1150

Died: 1169/1171

Mathilde De La ROCHE

Spouse

---

12 Alard I Von PETEGHEM

Born: Abt 1012
  -CONTINUED AS #4,ROYAL CHART 2719
Married:

Died: Abt 1067

---

6 Everard I De MORTAGNE

Born: Abt 1050

Married: 1078

Died: Abt 1110

---

13 --

Born:

Died:

---

3 Ada of Mortagne

Born: Abt 1090

Died:

14

Born:

Married:

Died:

---

7 Francka

Born:

Died:

15

Born:

Died:

Sources include: *Royal Ancestors* (1989), charts 11315, 11862-63; Stuart 50; Schwennicke 3:50, 7:88; Moriarty 175; Kraentzler 1078.

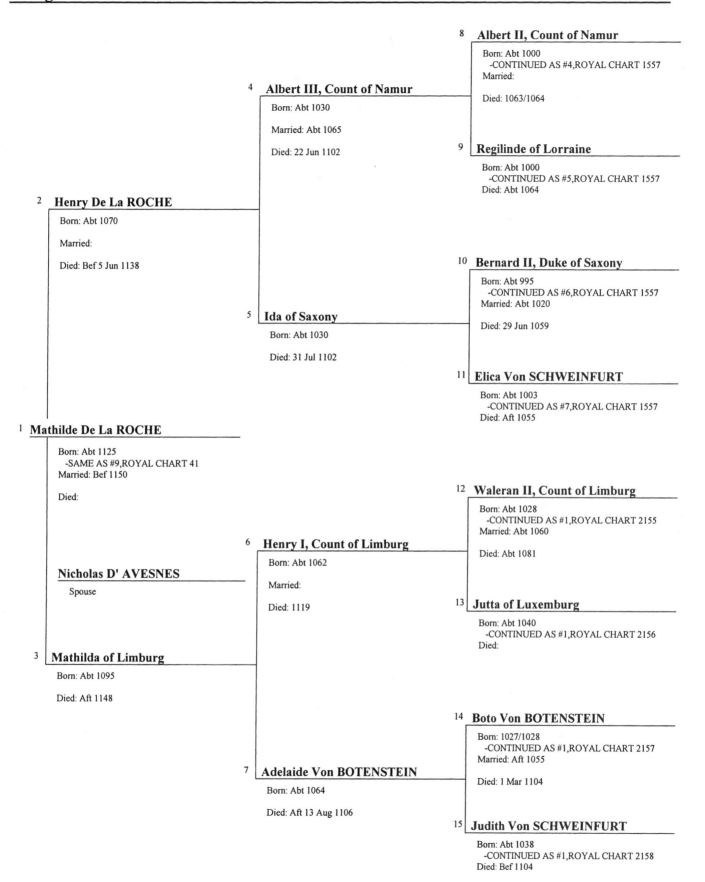

2 Henry De La ROCHE

Born: Abt 1070

Married:

Died: Bef 5 Jun 1138

4 Albert III, Count of Namur

Born: Abt 1030

Married: Abt 1065

Died: 22 Jun 1102

8 Albert II, Count of Namur

Born: Abt 1000
  -CONTINUED AS #4,ROYAL CHART 1557
Married:

Died: 1063/1064

9 Regilinde of Lorraine

Born: Abt 1000
  -CONTINUED AS #5,ROYAL CHART 1557
Died: Abt 1064

5 Ida of Saxony

Born: Abt 1030

Died: 31 Jul 1102

10 Bernard II, Duke of Saxony

Born: Abt 995
  -CONTINUED AS #6,ROYAL CHART 1557
Married: Abt 1020

Died: 29 Jun 1059

11 Elica Von SCHWEINFURT

Born: Abt 1003
  -CONTINUED AS #7,ROYAL CHART 1557
Died: Aft 1055

1 Mathilde De La ROCHE

Born: Abt 1125
  -SAME AS #9,ROYAL CHART 41
Married: Bef 1150

Died:

Nicholas D' AVESNES

Spouse

3 Mathilda of Limburg

Born: Abt 1095

Died: Aft 1148

6 Henry I, Count of Limburg

Born: Abt 1062

Married:

Died: 1119

12 Waleran II, Count of Limburg

Born: Abt 1028
  -CONTINUED AS #1,ROYAL CHART 2155
Married: Abt 1060

Died: Abt 1081

13 Jutta of Luxemburg

Born: Abt 1040
  -CONTINUED AS #1,ROYAL CHART 2156
Died:

7 Adelaide Von BOTENSTEIN

Born: Abt 1064

Died: Aft 13 Aug 1106

14 Boto Von BOTENSTEIN

Born: 1027/1028
  -CONTINUED AS #1,ROYAL CHART 2157
Married: Aft 1055

Died: 1 Mar 1104

15 Judith Von SCHWEINFURT

Born: Abt 1038
  -CONTINUED AS #1,ROYAL CHART 2158
Died: Bef 1104

Sources include: *Royal Ancestors* (1989), chart 11315; Moriarty 175-176, 128, 159-160; Stuart 50-28 (partially in error), 387; Turton 186; Collett family group sheets (Namur).
Note: There is disagreement on the ancestry shown for #6 & 7. It is agreed that #13 was Jutta of Luxemburg, but West Winter and others give #12 as an unknown count of Limburg, with #7 claimed as an unknown daughter of Waleran II by an unknown wife. Adelaide Von Botenstein is given as a 2nd childless wife of #6 Henry I. This scenario makes #3 Mathilda the maternal instead of the paternal granddaughter of Waleran II. This claim is presented and discussed by Faris in a preliminary Charlemagne manuscript (June 1995), pp. 29, 174, 26.

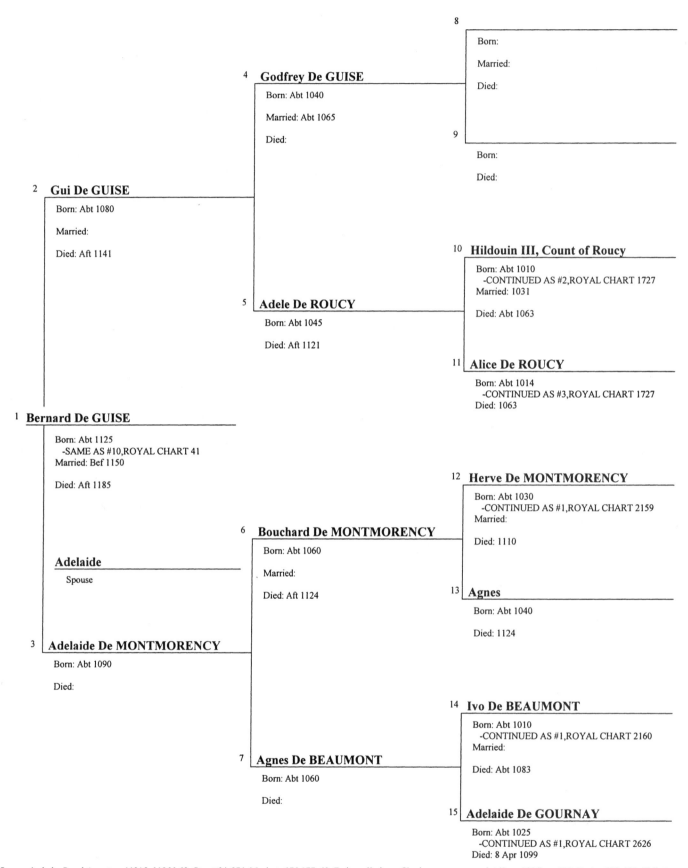

8

Born:

Married:

Died:

---

4 **Godfrey De GUISE**

Born: Abt 1040

Married: Abt 1065

Died:

9

Born:

Died:

---

2 **Gui De GUISE**

Born: Abt 1080

Married:

Died: Aft 1141

---

10 **Hildouin III, Count of Roucy**

Born: Abt 1010
-CONTINUED AS #2,ROYAL CHART 1727
Married: 1031

Died: Abt 1063

---

5 **Adele De ROUCY**

Born: Abt 1045

Died: Aft 1121

---

11 **Alice De ROUCY**

Born: Abt 1014
-CONTINUED AS #3,ROYAL CHART 1727
Died: 1063

---

1 **Bernard De GUISE**

Born: Abt 1125
-SAME AS #10,ROYAL CHART 41
Married: Bef 1150

Died: Aft 1185

---

12 **Herve De MONTMORENCY**

Born: Abt 1030
-CONTINUED AS #1,ROYAL CHART 2159
Married:

Died: 1110

---

6 **Bouchard De MONTMORENCY**

Born: Abt 1060

Married:

Died: Aft 1124

Adelaide

Spouse

---

13 **Agnes**

Born: Abt 1040

Died: 1124

---

3 **Adelaide De MONTMORENCY**

Born: Abt 1090

Died:

---

14 **Ivo De BEAUMONT**

Born: Abt 1010
-CONTINUED AS #1,ROYAL CHART 2160
Married:

Died: Abt 1083

---

7 **Agnes De BEAUMONT**

Born: Abt 1060

Died:

---

15 **Adelaide De GOURNAY**

Born: Abt 1025
-CONTINUED AS #1,ROYAL CHART 2626
Died: 8 Apr 1099

Sources include: *Royal Ancestors* 11315, 11866-68; Stuart 34, 274; Moriarty 176-177, 49; Faris preliminary Charlemagne manuscript (June 1995), p. 154; Turton 186, 191; Collett (family group sheet for #10 Hildouin). Notes: The parentage shown for #5 Adele (Ada) is disputed and uncertain. Stuart discontinues the line. Moriarty and Collett give the parentage as shown. Faris cites West Winter's claimed correction of Brandenburg and Winkhaus, claiming #5 as daughter of Wouter IV De Lens & Adele (Ada) De Roucy, but this Adele (Ada) appears to be the same person as #5 and to have married 2nd Walter De Ath (see chart 2115). Stuart and Moriarty also disagree on the parentage of #6 Bouchard. The Stuart version (which agrees with Winkhaus, as noted by Moriarty) is tentatively accepted here.

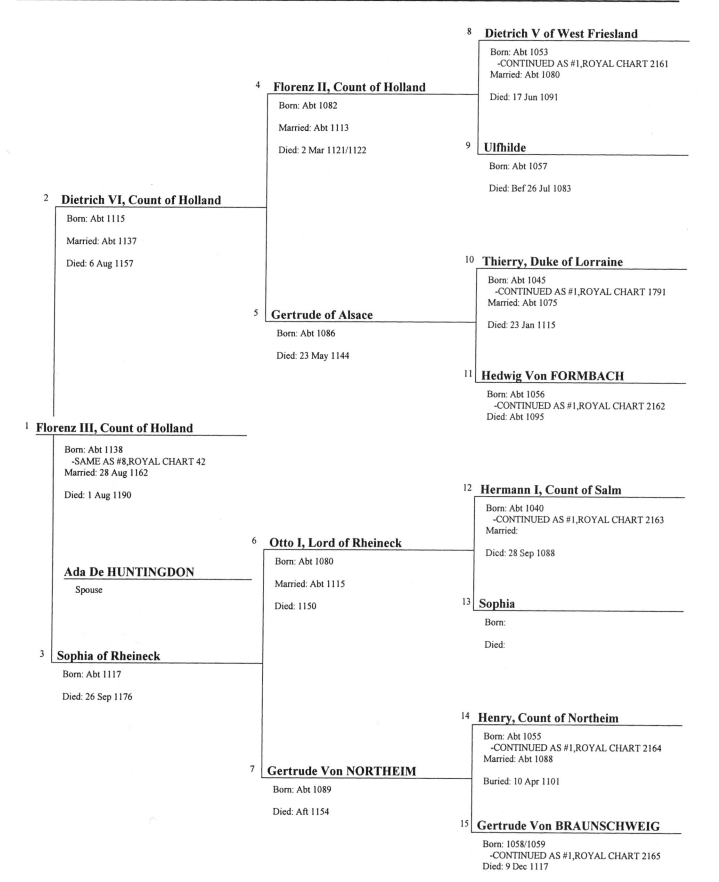

8 Dietrich V of West Friesland

Born: Abt 1053
  -CONTINUED AS #1,ROYAL CHART 2161
Married: Abt 1080

Died: 17 Jun 1091

4 Florenz II, Count of Holland

Born: Abt 1082

Married: Abt 1113

Died: 2 Mar 1121/1122

9 Ulfhilde

Born: Abt 1057

Died: Bef 26 Jul 1083

2 Dietrich VI, Count of Holland

Born: Abt 1115

Married: Abt 1137

Died: 6 Aug 1157

10 Thierry, Duke of Lorraine

Born: Abt 1045
  -CONTINUED AS #1,ROYAL CHART 1791
Married: Abt 1075

Died: 23 Jan 1115

5 Gertrude of Alsace

Born: Abt 1086

Died: 23 May 1144

11 Hedwig Von FORMBACH

Born: Abt 1056
  -CONTINUED AS #1,ROYAL CHART 2162
Died: Abt 1095

1 Florenz III, Count of Holland

Born: Abt 1138
  -SAME AS #8,ROYAL CHART 42
Married: 28 Aug 1162

Died: 1 Aug 1190

12 Hermann I, Count of Salm

Born: Abt 1040
  -CONTINUED AS #1,ROYAL CHART 2163
Married:

Died: 28 Sep 1088

6 Otto I, Lord of Rheineck

Born: Abt 1080

Married: Abt 1115

Died: 1150

13 Sophia

Born:

Died:

Ada De HUNTINGDON

Spouse

3 Sophia of Rheineck

Born: Abt 1117

Died: 26 Sep 1176

14 Henry, Count of Northeim

Born: Abt 1055
  -CONTINUED AS #1,ROYAL CHART 2164
Married: Abt 1088

Buried: 10 Apr 1101

7 Gertrude Von NORTHEIM

Born: Abt 1089

Died: Aft 1154

15 Gertrude Von BRAUNSCHWEIG

Born: 1058/1059
  -CONTINUED AS #1,ROYAL CHART 2165
Died: 9 Dec 1117

Sources include: *Royal Ancestors* (1989), chart 11317; Stuart 390-391; Moriarty 178.

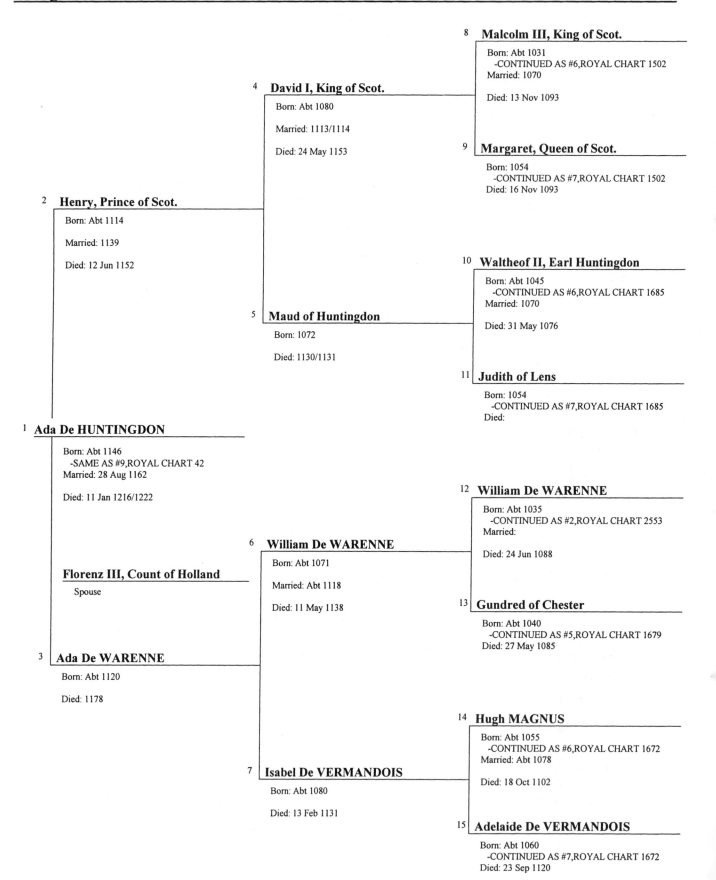

8 Malcolm III, King of Scot.

Born: Abt 1031
    -CONTINUED AS #6,ROYAL CHART 1502
Married: 1070

Died: 13 Nov 1093

4 David I, King of Scot.

Born: Abt 1080

Married: 1113/1114

Died: 24 May 1153

9 Margaret, Queen of Scot.

Born: 1054
    -CONTINUED AS #7,ROYAL CHART 1502
Died: 16 Nov 1093

2 Henry, Prince of Scot.

Born: Abt 1114

Married: 1139

Died: 12 Jun 1152

10 Waltheof II, Earl Huntingdon

Born: Abt 1045
    -CONTINUED AS #6,ROYAL CHART 1685
Married: 1070

Died: 31 May 1076

5 Maud of Huntingdon

Born: 1072

Died: 1130/1131

11 Judith of Lens

Born: 1054
    -CONTINUED AS #7,ROYAL CHART 1685
Died:

1 Ada De HUNTINGDON

Born: Abt 1146
    -SAME AS #9,ROYAL CHART 42
Married: 28 Aug 1162

Died: 11 Jan 1216/1222

12 William De WARENNE

Born: Abt 1035
    -CONTINUED AS #2,ROYAL CHART 2553
Married:

Died: 24 Jun 1088

6 William De WARENNE

Born: Abt 1071

Married: Abt 1118

Died: 11 May 1138

Florenz III, Count of Holland

Spouse

13 Gundred of Chester

Born: Abt 1040
    -CONTINUED AS #5,ROYAL CHART 1679
Died: 27 May 1085

3 Ada De WARENNE

Born: Abt 1120

Died: 1178

14 Hugh MAGNUS

Born: Abt 1055
    -CONTINUED AS #6,ROYAL CHART 1672
Married: Abt 1078

Died: 18 Oct 1102

7 Isabel De VERMANDOIS

Born: Abt 1080

Died: 13 Feb 1131

15 Adelaide De VERMANDOIS

Born: Abt 1060
    -CONTINUED AS #7,ROYAL CHART 1672
Died: 23 Sep 1120

Sources include: *Royal Ancestors* 11317, 11422-25; *Stuart* 72, 135; *Ancestral Roots* 100, 93, 170, 50.

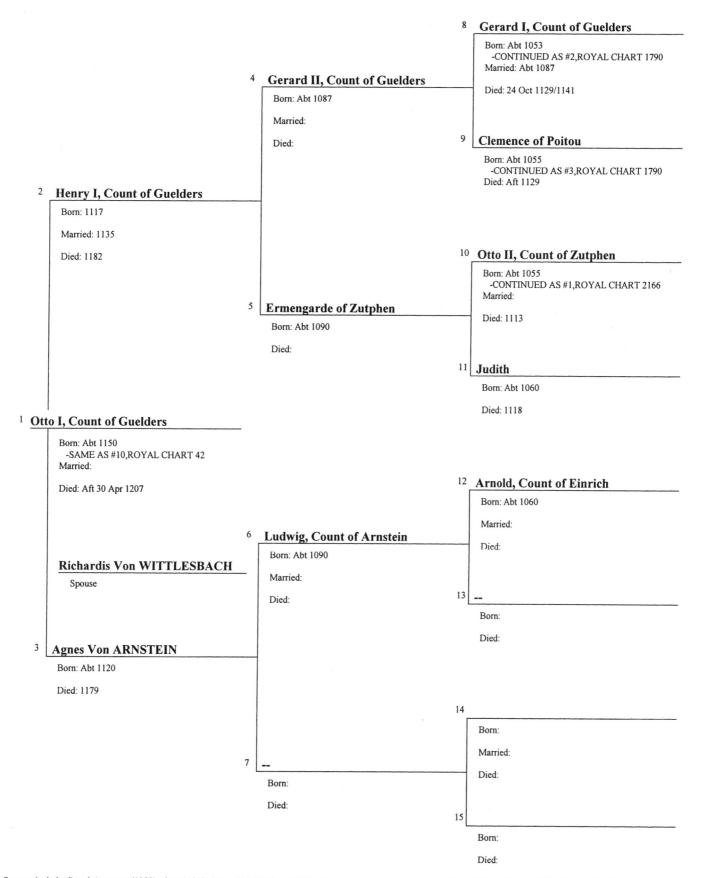

8 **Gerard I, Count of Guelders**

Born: Abt 1053
-CONTINUED AS #2,ROYAL CHART 1790
Married: Abt 1087

Died: 24 Oct 1129/1141

4 **Gerard II, Count of Guelders**

Born: Abt 1087

Married:

Died:

9 **Clemence of Poitou**

Born: Abt 1055
-CONTINUED AS #3,ROYAL CHART 1790
Died: Aft 1129

2 **Henry I, Count of Guelders**

Born: 1117

Married: 1135

Died: 1182

10 **Otto II, Count of Zutphen**

Born: Abt 1055
-CONTINUED AS #1,ROYAL CHART 2166
Married:

Died: 1113

5 **Ermengarde of Zutphen**

Born: Abt 1090

Died:

11 **Judith**

Born: Abt 1060

Died: 1118

1 **Otto I, Count of Guelders**

Born: Abt 1150
-SAME AS #10,ROYAL CHART 42
Married:

Died: Aft 30 Apr 1207

12 **Arnold, Count of Einrich**

Born: Abt 1060

Married:

Died:

6 **Ludwig, Count of Arnstein**

Born: Abt 1090

Married:

Died:

Richardis Von WITTLESBACH

Spouse

13 **--**

Born:

Died:

3 **Agnes Von ARNSTEIN**

Born: Abt 1120

Died: 1179

14

Born:

Married:

Died:

7 **--**

Born:

Died:

15

Born:

Died:

Sources include: *Royal Ancestors* (1989), chart 11317; Stuart 304; Moriarty 185 (omits one generation, erroneously making #2 Henry the son of #8 & 9 Gerard & Clemence).

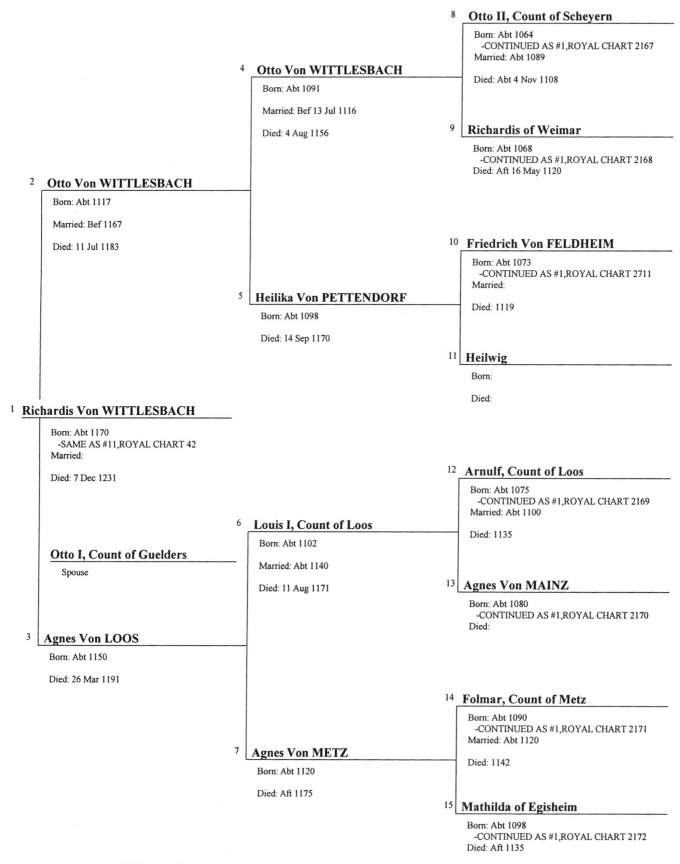

8 **Otto II, Count of Scheyern**

Born: Abt 1064
    -CONTINUED AS #1,ROYAL CHART 2167
Married: Abt 1089

Died: Abt 4 Nov 1108

4 **Otto Von WITTLESBACH**

Born: Abt 1091

Married: Bef 13 Jul 1116

Died: 4 Aug 1156

9 **Richardis of Weimar**

Born: Abt 1068
    -CONTINUED AS #1,ROYAL CHART 2168
Died: Aft 16 May 1120

2 **Otto Von WITTLESBACH**

Born: Abt 1117

Married: Bef 1167

Died: 11 Jul 1183

10 **Friedrich Von FELDHEIM**

Born: Abt 1073
    -CONTINUED AS #1,ROYAL CHART 2711
Married:

Died: 1119

5 **Heilika Von PETTENDORF**

Born: Abt 1098

Died: 14 Sep 1170

11 **Heilwig**

Born:

Died:

1 **Richardis Von WITTLESBACH**

Born: Abt 1170
    -SAME AS #11,ROYAL CHART 42
Married:

Died: 7 Dec 1231

Otto I, Count of Guelders

Spouse

12 **Arnulf, Count of Loos**

Born: Abt 1075
    -CONTINUED AS #1,ROYAL CHART 2169
Married: Abt 1100

Died: 1135

6 **Louis I, Count of Loos**

Born: Abt 1102

Married: Abt 1140

Died: 11 Aug 1171

13 **Agnes Von MAINZ**

Born: Abt 1080
    -CONTINUED AS #1,ROYAL CHART 2170
Died:

3 **Agnes Von LOOS**

Born: Abt 1150

Died: 26 Mar 1191

14 **Folmar, Count of Metz**

Born: Abt 1090
    -CONTINUED AS #1,ROYAL CHART 2171
Married: Abt 1120

Died: 1142

7 **Agnes Von METZ**

Born: Abt 1120

Died: Aft 1175

15 **Mathilda of Egisheim**

Born: Abt 1098
    -CONTINUED AS #1,ROYAL CHART 2172
Died: Aft 1135

Sources include: *Royal Ancestors* (1989), charts 11317, 11880-83; Stuart 307, 320; Moriarty 186-191; Faris preliminary Charlemagne manuscript (June 1995), pp. 286-287, 48-49, 215. Note: #5 Heilika is also claimed as the daughter of Frederick (Lord of Legenfeld) & Signa of Leige. The Faris version is accepted and shown above.

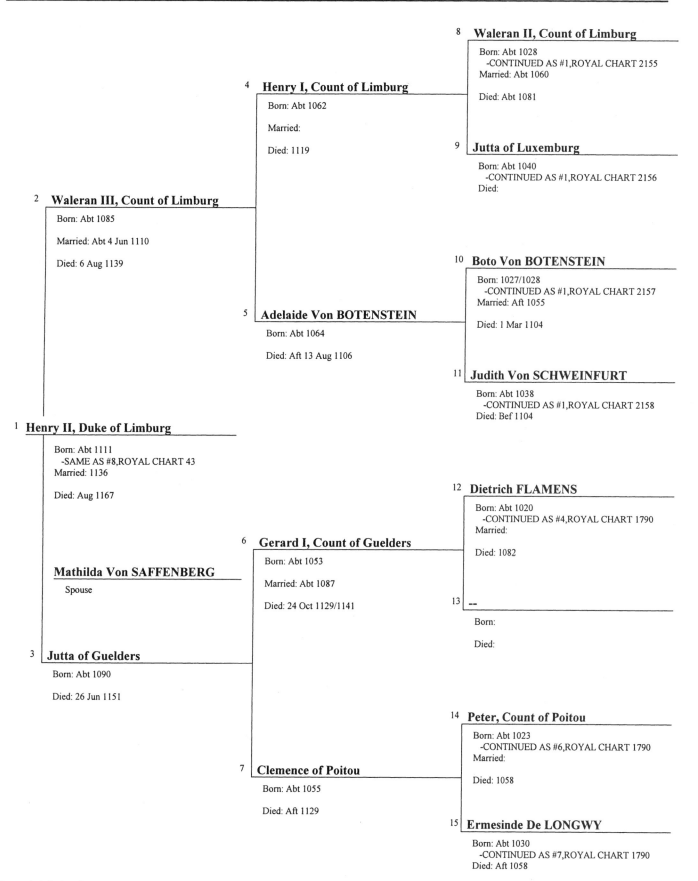

8 Waleran II, Count of Limburg

Born: Abt 1028
-CONTINUED AS #1,ROYAL CHART 2155
Married: Abt 1060

Died: Abt 1081

4 Henry I, Count of Limburg

Born: Abt 1062

Married:

Died: 1119

9 Jutta of Luxemburg

Born: Abt 1040
-CONTINUED AS #1,ROYAL CHART 2156
Died:

2 Waleran III, Count of Limburg

Born: Abt 1085

Married: Abt 4 Jun 1110

Died: 6 Aug 1139

10 Boto Von BOTENSTEIN

Born: 1027/1028
-CONTINUED AS #1,ROYAL CHART 2157
Married: Aft 1055

Died: 1 Mar 1104

5 Adelaide Von BOTENSTEIN

Born: Abt 1064

Died: Aft 13 Aug 1106

11 Judith Von SCHWEINFURT

Born: Abt 1038
-CONTINUED AS #1,ROYAL CHART 2158
Died: Bef 1104

1 Henry II, Duke of Limburg

Born: Abt 1111
-SAME AS #8,ROYAL CHART 43
Married: 1136

Died: Aug 1167

12 Dietrich FLAMENS

Born: Abt 1020
-CONTINUED AS #4,ROYAL CHART 1790
Married:

Died: 1082

6 Gerard I, Count of Guelders

Born: Abt 1053

Married: Abt 1087

Died: 24 Oct 1129/1141

13 --

Born:

Died:

Mathilda Von SAFFENBERG

Spouse

3 Jutta of Guelders

Born: Abt 1090

Died: 26 Jun 1151

14 Peter, Count of Poitou

Born: Abt 1023
-CONTINUED AS #6,ROYAL CHART 1790
Married:

Died: 1058

7 Clemence of Poitou

Born: Abt 1055

Died: Aft 1129

15 Ermesinde De LONGWY

Born: Abt 1030
-CONTINUED AS #7,ROYAL CHART 1790
Died: Aft 1058

Sources include: *Royal Ancestors* (1989), charts 11373, 11658, 11698, 11814; Stuart 62, 119; Faris preliminary Charlemagne manuscript (June 1995), pp. 173-174; Moriarty 159-160, 162, 127, 246, 36. Notes: The ancestry of #4 & 5 is disputed. See note chart 1547. The identification of #7 Clemence is not certain. #14 Peter is also called William.

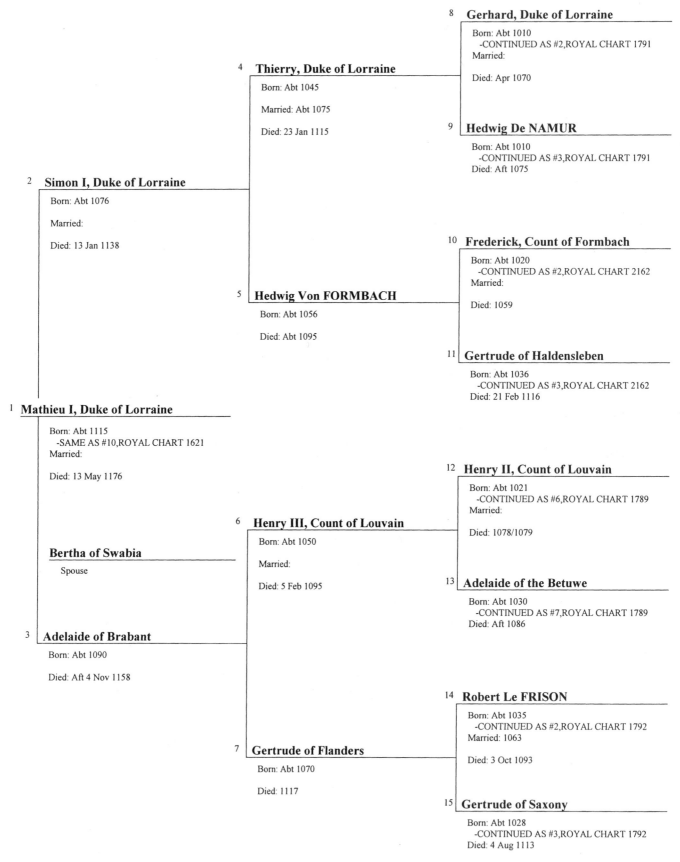

8 Gerhard, Duke of Lorraine
Born: Abt 1010
-CONTINUED AS #2,ROYAL CHART 1791
Married:

Died: Apr 1070

4 Thierry, Duke of Lorraine
Born: Abt 1045

Married: Abt 1075

Died: 23 Jan 1115

9 Hedwig De NAMUR
Born: Abt 1010
-CONTINUED AS #3,ROYAL CHART 1791
Died: Aft 1075

2 Simon I, Duke of Lorraine
Born: Abt 1076

Married:

Died: 13 Jan 1138

10 Frederick, Count of Formbach
Born: Abt 1020
-CONTINUED AS #2,ROYAL CHART 2162
Married:

Died: 1059

5 Hedwig Von FORMBACH
Born: Abt 1056

Died: Abt 1095

11 Gertrude of Haldensleben
Born: Abt 1036
-CONTINUED AS #3,ROYAL CHART 2162
Died: 21 Feb 1116

1 Mathieu I, Duke of Lorraine
Born: Abt 1115
-SAME AS #10,ROYAL CHART 1621
Married:

Died: 13 May 1176

12 Henry II, Count of Louvain
Born: Abt 1021
-CONTINUED AS #6,ROYAL CHART 1789
Married:

Died: 1078/1079

6 Henry III, Count of Louvain
Born: Abt 1050

Married:

Died: 5 Feb 1095

13 Adelaide of the Betuwe
Born: Abt 1030
-CONTINUED AS #7,ROYAL CHART 1789
Died: Aft 1086

Bertha of Swabia
Spouse

3 Adelaide of Brabant
Born: Abt 1090

Died: Aft 4 Nov 1158

14 Robert Le FRISON
Born: Abt 1035
-CONTINUED AS #2,ROYAL CHART 1792
Married: 1063

Died: 3 Oct 1093

7 Gertrude of Flanders
Born: Abt 1070

Died: 1117

15 Gertrude of Saxony
Born: Abt 1028
-CONTINUED AS #3,ROYAL CHART 1792
Died: 4 Aug 1113

Sources include: *Royal Ancestors* (1989), charts 11697, 11669; Faris preliminary Charlemagne manuscript (June 1995), pp. 2-3, 68; Turton 200; Moriarty 130 (#2 & 3 ancestry); Stuart 41 (#2 & 3 ancestry). Note: The statement by Moriarty, repeated by Stuart, that #3 Adelaide was perhaps the daughter of Baldwin II, Count of Hainaut (see chart 1789), is disputed by Faris, who states that #3 Adelaide was evidently the daughter of Henry (Heinrich) III & Gertrude, as tentatively accepted above.

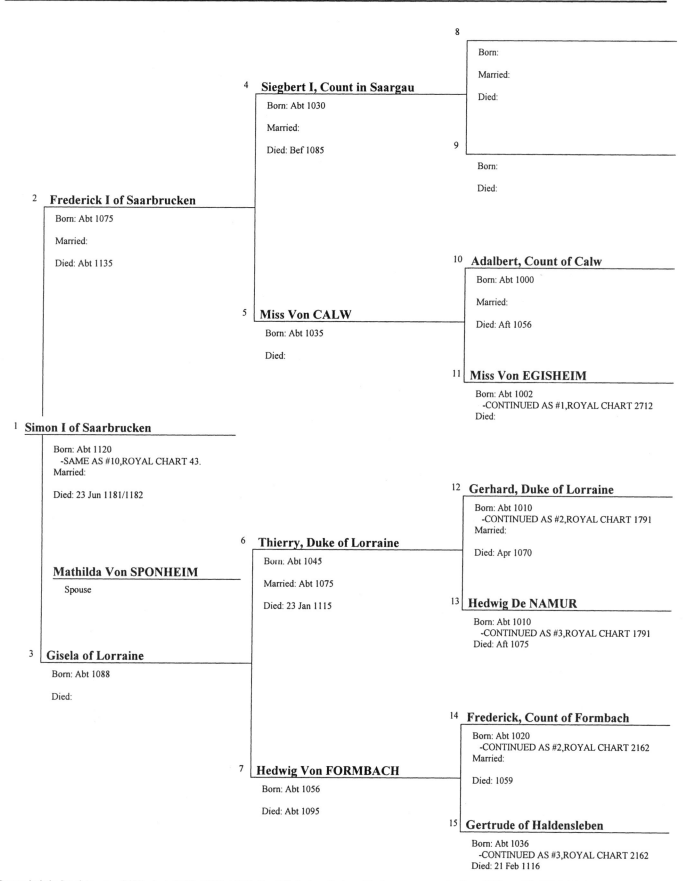

8

Born:

Married:

Died:

4 Siegbert I, Count in Saargau

Born: Abt 1030

Married:

Died: Bef 1085

9

Born:

Died:

2 Frederick I of Saarbrucken

Born: Abt 1075

Married:

Died: Abt 1135

10 Adalbert, Count of Calw

Born: Abt 1000

Married:

Died: Aft 1056

5 Miss Von CALW

Born: Abt 1035

Died:

11 Miss Von EGISHEIM

Born: Abt 1002
-CONTINUED AS #1,ROYAL CHART 2712
Died:

1 Simon I of Saarbrucken

Born: Abt 1120
-SAME AS #10,ROYAL CHART 43.
Married:

Died: 23 Jun 1181/1182

12 Gerhard, Duke of Lorraine

Born: Abt 1010
-CONTINUED AS #2,ROYAL CHART 1791
Married:

Died: Apr 1070

6 Thierry, Duke of Lorraine

Born: Abt 1045

Married: Abt 1075

Died: 23 Jan 1115

13 Hedwig De NAMUR

Born: Abt 1010
-CONTINUED AS #3,ROYAL CHART 1791
Died: Aft 1075

Mathilda Von SPONHEIM

Spouse

3 Gisela of Lorraine

Born: Abt 1088

Died:

14 Frederick, Count of Formbach

Born: Abt 1020
-CONTINUED AS #2,ROYAL CHART 2162
Married:

Died: 1059

7 Hedwig Von FORMBACH

Born: Abt 1056

Died: Abt 1095

15 Gertrude of Haldensleben

Born: Abt 1036
-CONTINUED AS #3,ROYAL CHART 2162
Died: 21 Feb 1116

Sources include: *Royal Ancestors* (1989), charts 11373, 11940, 11669; Stuart 23; Faris preliminary Charlemagne manuscript (June 1995), pp. 240, 136, 2; Moriarty 192. Notes: The ancestry shown for #2 Frederick & #3 Gisela is not certain. Faris is followed on the ancestry of #2. Moriarty gives #2 Frederick as son of Siegbert II and grandson of Siegbert I. Faris states that Siegbert I died before 1118, the date Moriarty gives for Siegbert II. Stuart states that Siegbert I is now known to be the father of Frederick. Stuart has been followed on the parentage of #3 Gisela. Moriarty gives an additional generation (Simon I -- see chart 1554) between #3 Gisela and #6 & 7 Thierry (Dietrich) & Hedwig (a 1st wife). Faris states that #3 Gisela was evidently the daughter of Thierry and his 2nd wife Gertrude of Flanders (see chart 1792 for her ancestry).

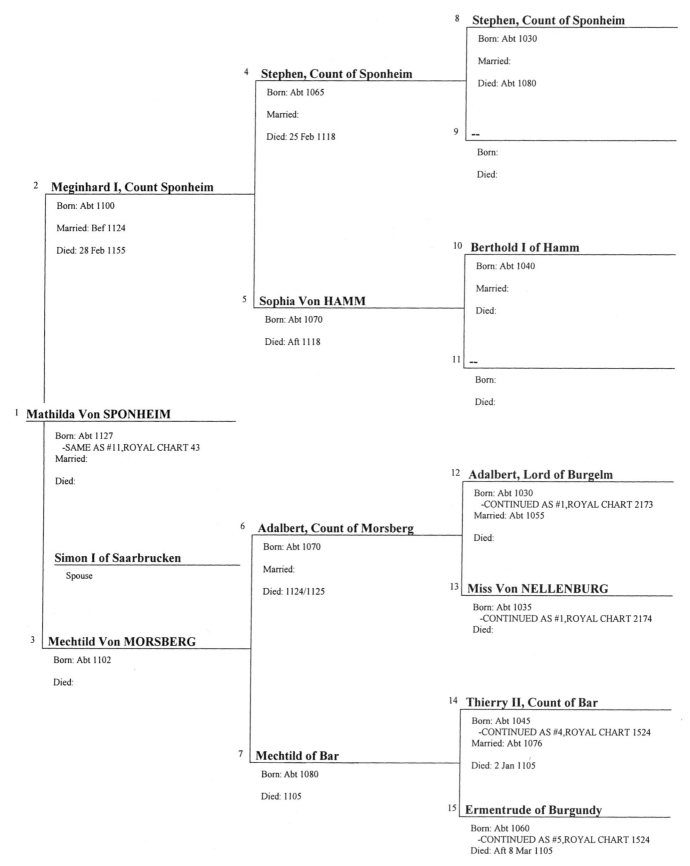

8 Stephen, Count of Sponheim

Born: Abt 1030

Married:

Died: Abt 1080

4 Stephen, Count of Sponheim

Born: Abt 1065

Married:

Died: 25 Feb 1118

9 --

Born:

Died:

2 Meginhard I, Count Sponheim

Born: Abt 1100

Married: Bef 1124

Died: 28 Feb 1155

10 Berthold I of Hamm

Born: Abt 1040

Married:

Died:

5 Sophia Von HAMM

Born: Abt 1070

Died: Aft 1118

11 --

Born:

Died:

1 Mathilda Von SPONHEIM

Born: Abt 1127
    -SAME AS #11,ROYAL CHART 43
Married:

Died:

Simon I of Saarbrucken

Spouse

12 Adalbert, Lord of Burgelm

Born: Abt 1030
    -CONTINUED AS #1,ROYAL CHART 2173
Married: Abt 1055

Died:

6 Adalbert, Count of Morsberg

Born: Abt 1070

Married:

Died: 1124/1125

13 Miss Von NELLENBURG

Born: Abt 1035
    -CONTINUED AS #1,ROYAL CHART 2174
Died:

3 Mechtild Von MORSBERG

Born: Abt 1102

Died:

14 Thierry II, Count of Bar

Born: Abt 1045
    -CONTINUED AS #4,ROYAL CHART 1524
Married: Abt 1076

Died: 2 Jan 1105

7 Mechtild of Bar

Born: Abt 1080

Died: 1105

15 Ermentrude of Burgundy

Born: Abt 1060
    -CONTINUED AS #5,ROYAL CHART 1524
Died: Aft 8 Mar 1105

Sources include: *Royal Ancestors* (1989), charts 11373, 11941-42; Stuart 365, 364; Moriarty 212-213. Note: The parentage shown for #1 Mathilda is not certain.

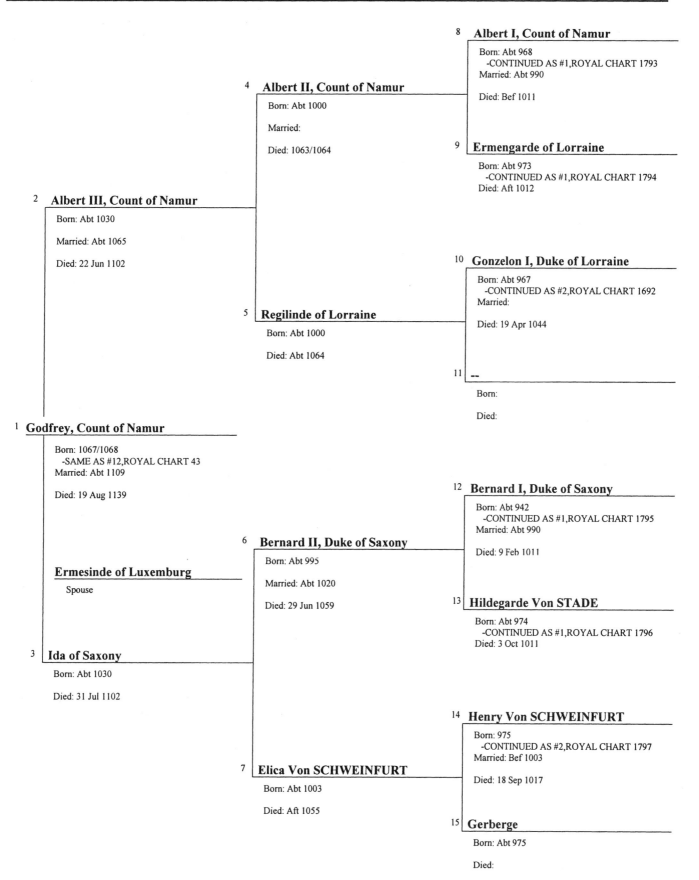

8 Albert I, Count of Namur

Born: Abt 968
-CONTINUED AS #1,ROYAL CHART 1793
Married: Abt 990

Died: Bef 1011

4 Albert II, Count of Namur

Born: Abt 1000

Married:

Died: 1063/1064

9 Ermengarde of Lorraine

Born: Abt 973
-CONTINUED AS #1,ROYAL CHART 1794
Died: Aft 1012

2 Albert III, Count of Namur

Born: Abt 1030

Married: Abt 1065

Died: 22 Jun 1102

10 Gonzelon I, Duke of Lorraine

Born: Abt 967
-CONTINUED AS #2,ROYAL CHART 1692
Married:

Died: 19 Apr 1044

5 Regilinde of Lorraine

Born: Abt 1000

Died: Abt 1064

11 --

Born:

Died:

1 Godfrey, Count of Namur

Born: 1067/1068
-SAME AS #12,ROYAL CHART 43
Married: Abt 1109

Died: 19 Aug 1139

12 Bernard I, Duke of Saxony

Born: Abt 942
-CONTINUED AS #1,ROYAL CHART 1795
Married: Abt 990

Died: 9 Feb 1011

6 Bernard II, Duke of Saxony

Born: Abt 995

Married: Abt 1020

Died: 29 Jun 1059

13 Hildegarde Von STADE

Born: Abt 974
-CONTINUED AS #1,ROYAL CHART 1796
Died: 3 Oct 1011

Ermesinde of Luxemburg

Spouse

3 Ida of Saxony

Born: Abt 1030

Died: 31 Jul 1102

14 Henry Von SCHWEINFURT

Born: 975
-CONTINUED AS #2,ROYAL CHART 1797
Married: Bef 1003

Died: 18 Sep 1017

7 Elica Von SCHWEINFURT

Born: Abt 1003

Died: Aft 1055

15 Gerberge

Born: Abt 975

Died:

Sources include: *Royal Ancestors* 11374, 11572-73; *Ancestral Roots* 246A, 149; Stuart 126, 120, 204, 312, 270, 102; Paget 5; Moriarty 56-57. Note: Stuart 270-34 & 204-34 conflicts on #7. All other sources agree on Elica (Elicia, Elicke). Stuart and Moriarty also disagree on the ancestry of #15 Gerberge.

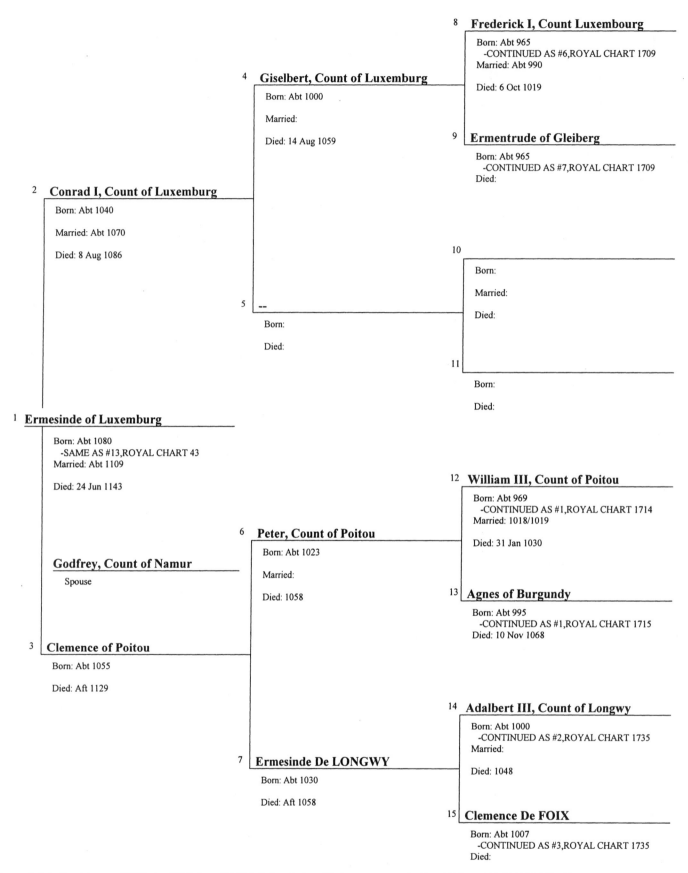

8 Frederick I, Count Luxembourg
Born: Abt 965
  -CONTINUED AS #6,ROYAL CHART 1709
Married: Abt 990

Died: 6 Oct 1019

4 Giselbert, Count of Luxemburg
Born: Abt 1000

Married:

Died: 14 Aug 1059

9 Ermentrude of Gleiberg
Born: Abt 965
  -CONTINUED AS #7,ROYAL CHART 1709
Died:

2 Conrad I, Count of Luxemburg
Born: Abt 1040

Married: Abt 1070

Died: 8 Aug 1086

10
Born:

Married:

Died:

5 --
Born:

Died:

11
Born:

Died:

1 Ermesinde of Luxemburg
Born: Abt 1080
  -SAME AS #13,ROYAL CHART 43
Married: Abt 1109

Died: 24 Jun 1143

12 William III, Count of Poitou
Born: Abt 969
  -CONTINUED AS #1,ROYAL CHART 1714
Married: 1018/1019

Died: 31 Jan 1030

6 Peter, Count of Poitou
Born: Abt 1023

Married:

Died: 1058

13 Agnes of Burgundy
Born: Abt 995
  -CONTINUED AS #1,ROYAL CHART 1715
Died: 10 Nov 1068

Godfrey, Count of Namur
Spouse

3 Clemence of Poitou
Born: Abt 1055

Died: Aft 1129

14 Adalbert III, Count of Longwy
Born: Abt 1000
  -CONTINUED AS #2,ROYAL CHART 1735
Married:

Died: 1048

7 Ermesinde De LONGWY
Born: Abt 1030

Died: Aft 1058

15 Clemence De FOIX
Born: Abt 1007
  -CONTINUED AS #3,ROYAL CHART 1735
Died:

Sources include: *Royal Ancestors* (1989), chart 11659; Stuart 126-30, 3; Faris preliminary Charlemagne manuscript (June 1995), pp. 201, 244-245, 217, 168-169; Moriarty 129, 36.
Notes: #6 Peter is also called William. Stuart and Faris agree with the parentage shown for #7 Ermesinde. Moriarty (36, 246) states her parentage is unknown.

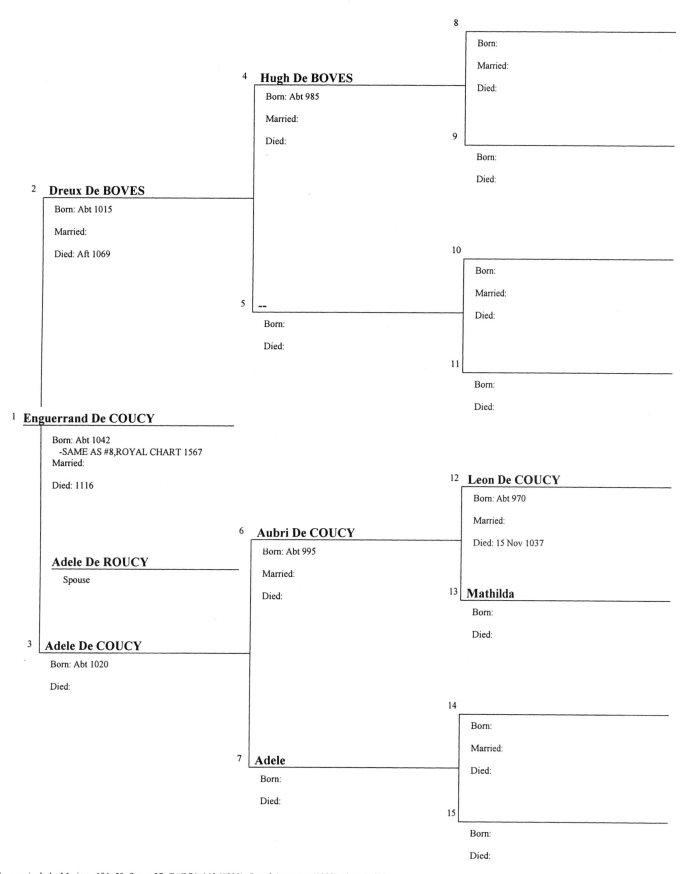

4 Hugh De BOVES
Born: Abt 985
Married:
Died:

8
Born:
Married:
Died:

9
Born:
Died:

2 Dreux De BOVES
Born: Abt 1015
Married:
Died: Aft 1069

5 --
Born:
Died:

10
Born:
Married:
Died:

11
Born:
Died:

1 Enguerrand De COUCY
Born: Abt 1042
 -SAME AS #8,ROYAL CHART 1567
Married:
Died: 1116

Adele De ROUCY
Spouse

3 Adele De COUCY
Born: Abt 1020
Died:

6 Aubri De COUCY
Born: Abt 995
Married:
Died:

12 Leon De COUCY
Born: Abt 970
Married:
Died: 15 Nov 1037

13 Mathilda
Born:
Died:

7 Adele
Born:
Died:

14
Born:
Married:
Died:

15
Born:
Died:

Sources include: Moriarty 196, 50; Stuart 37; *TAG* 74: 148 (1999); *Royal Ancestors* (1989), chart 11673.

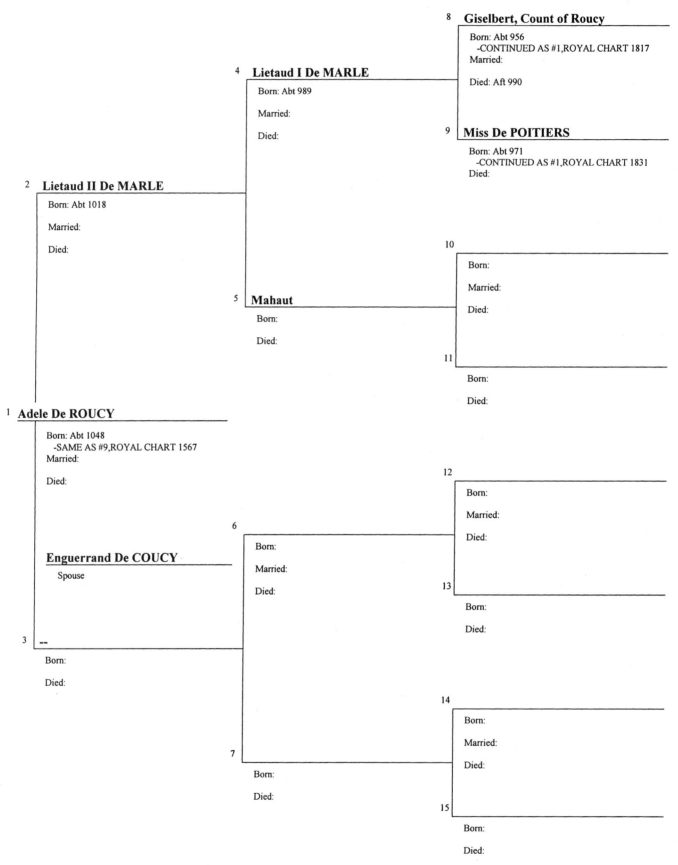

8 Giselbert, Count of Roucy

Born: Abt 956
  -CONTINUED AS #1,ROYAL CHART 1817
Married:

Died: Aft 990

4 Lietaud I De MARLE

Born: Abt 989

Married:

Died:

9 Miss De POITIERS

Born: Abt 971
  -CONTINUED AS #1,ROYAL CHART 1831
Died:

2 Lietaud II De MARLE

Born: Abt 1018

Married:

Died:

10

Born:

Married:

Died:

5 Mahaut

Born:

Died:

11

Born:

Died:

1 Adele De ROUCY

Born: Abt 1048
  -SAME AS #9,ROYAL CHART 1567
Married:

Died:

12

Born:

Married:

Died:

6

Born:

Married:

Died:

13

Born:

Died:

Enguerrand De COUCY

Spouse

3 --

Born:

Died:

14

Born:

Married:

Died:

7

Born:

Died:

15

Born:

Died:

Sources include: Stuart 6; Moriarty 50; Faris preliminary Charlemagne manuscript (June 1995), pp. 111, 235; *Royal Ancestors* (1989), chart 11673.

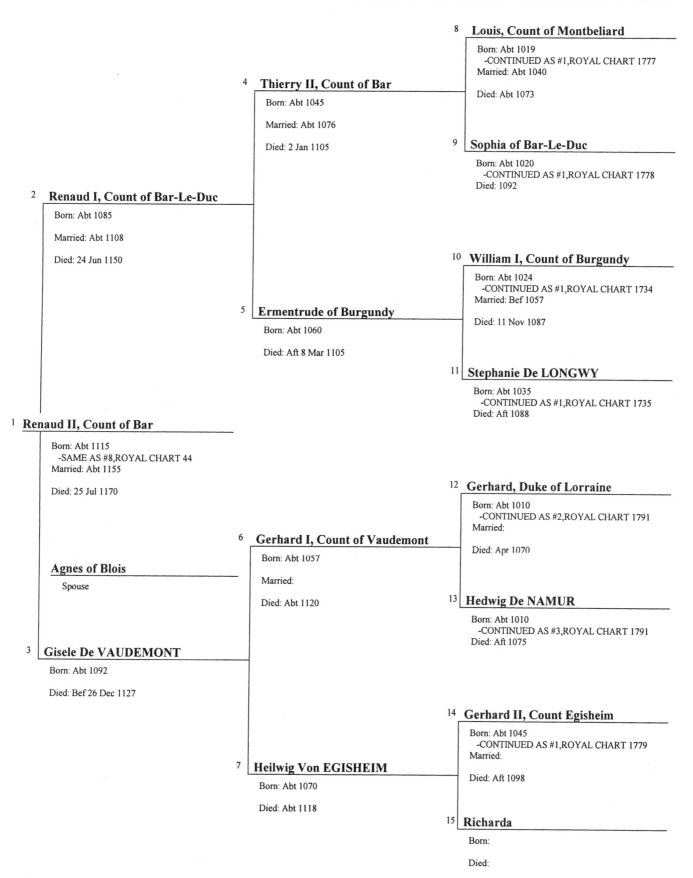

8 Louis, Count of Montbeliard
Born: Abt 1019
-CONTINUED AS #1,ROYAL CHART 1777
Married: Abt 1040

Died: Abt 1073

4 Thierry II, Count of Bar
Born: Abt 1045

Married: Abt 1076

Died: 2 Jan 1105

9 Sophia of Bar-Le-Duc
Born: Abt 1020
-CONTINUED AS #1,ROYAL CHART 1778
Died: 1092

2 Renaud I, Count of Bar-Le-Duc
Born: Abt 1085

Married: Abt 1108

Died: 24 Jun 1150

10 William I, Count of Burgundy
Born: Abt 1024
-CONTINUED AS #1,ROYAL CHART 1734
Married: Bef 1057

Died: 11 Nov 1087

5 Ermentrude of Burgundy
Born: Abt 1060

Died: Aft 8 Mar 1105

11 Stephanie De LONGWY
Born: Abt 1035
-CONTINUED AS #1,ROYAL CHART 1735
Died: Aft 1088

1 Renaud II, Count of Bar
Born: Abt 1115
-SAME AS #8,ROYAL CHART 44
Married: Abt 1155

Died: 25 Jul 1170

12 Gerhard, Duke of Lorraine
Born: Abt 1010
-CONTINUED AS #2,ROYAL CHART 1791
Married:

Died: Apr 1070

6 Gerhard I, Count of Vaudemont
Born: Abt 1057

Married:

Died: Abt 1120

13 Hedwig De NAMUR
Born: Abt 1010
-CONTINUED AS #3,ROYAL CHART 1791
Died: Aft 1075

Agnes of Blois
Spouse

3 Gisele De VAUDEMONT
Born: Abt 1092

Died: Bef 26 Dec 1127

14 Gerhard II, Count Egisheim
Born: Abt 1045
-CONTINUED AS #1,ROYAL CHART 1779
Married:

Died: Aft 1098

7 Heilwig Von EGISHEIM
Born: Abt 1070

Died: Abt 1118

15 Richarda
Born:

Died:

Sources include: *Royal Ancestors* (1989), chart 11375; Stuart 36, 149, 246; Moriarty 193-194; Faris preliminary Charlemagne manuscript (June 1995), pp. 34, 126.

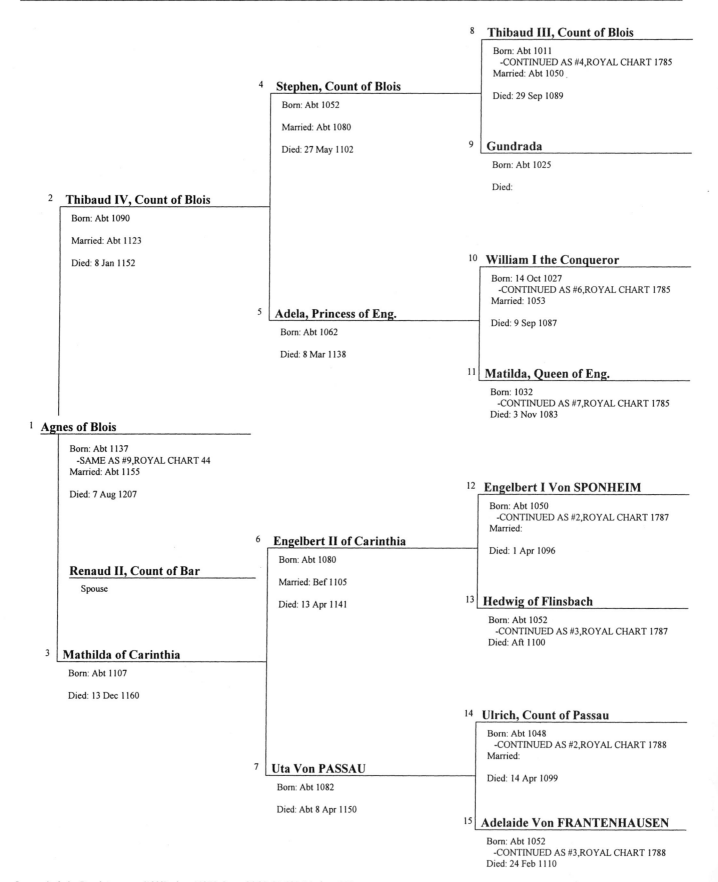

8 Thibaud III, Count of Blois

Born: Abt 1011
-CONTINUED AS #4,ROYAL CHART 1785
Married: Abt 1050

Died: 29 Sep 1089

4 Stephen, Count of Blois

Born: Abt 1052

Married: Abt 1080

Died: 27 May 1102

9 Gundrada

Born: Abt 1025

Died:

2 Thibaud IV, Count of Blois

Born: Abt 1090

Married: Abt 1123

Died: 8 Jan 1152

10 William I the Conqueror

Born: 14 Oct 1027
-CONTINUED AS #6,ROYAL CHART 1785
Married: 1053

Died: 9 Sep 1087

5 Adela, Princess of Eng.

Born: Abt 1062

Died: 8 Mar 1138

11 Matilda, Queen of Eng.

Born: 1032
-CONTINUED AS #7,ROYAL CHART 1785
Died: 3 Nov 1083

1 Agnes of Blois

Born: Abt 1137
-SAME AS #9,ROYAL CHART 44
Married: Abt 1155

Died: 7 Aug 1207

12 Engelbert I Von SPONHEIM

Born: Abt 1050
-CONTINUED AS #2,ROYAL CHART 1787
Married:

Died: 1 Apr 1096

6 Engelbert II of Carinthia

Born: Abt 1080

Married: Bef 1105

Died: 13 Apr 1141

Renaud II, Count of Bar

Spouse

13 Hedwig of Flinsbach

Born: Abt 1052
-CONTINUED AS #3,ROYAL CHART 1787
Died: Aft 1100

3 Mathilda of Carinthia

Born: Abt 1107

Died: 13 Dec 1160

14 Ulrich, Count of Passau

Born: Abt 1048
-CONTINUED AS #2,ROYAL CHART 1788
Married:

Died: 14 Apr 1099

7 Uta Von PASSAU

Born: Abt 1082

Died: Abt 8 Apr 1150

15 Adelaide Von FRANTENHAUSEN

Born: Abt 1052
-CONTINUED AS #3,ROYAL CHART 1788
Died: 24 Feb 1110

Sources include: *Royal Ancestors* (1989), chart 11375; Stuart 36-28, 81, 228; Moriarty 117.

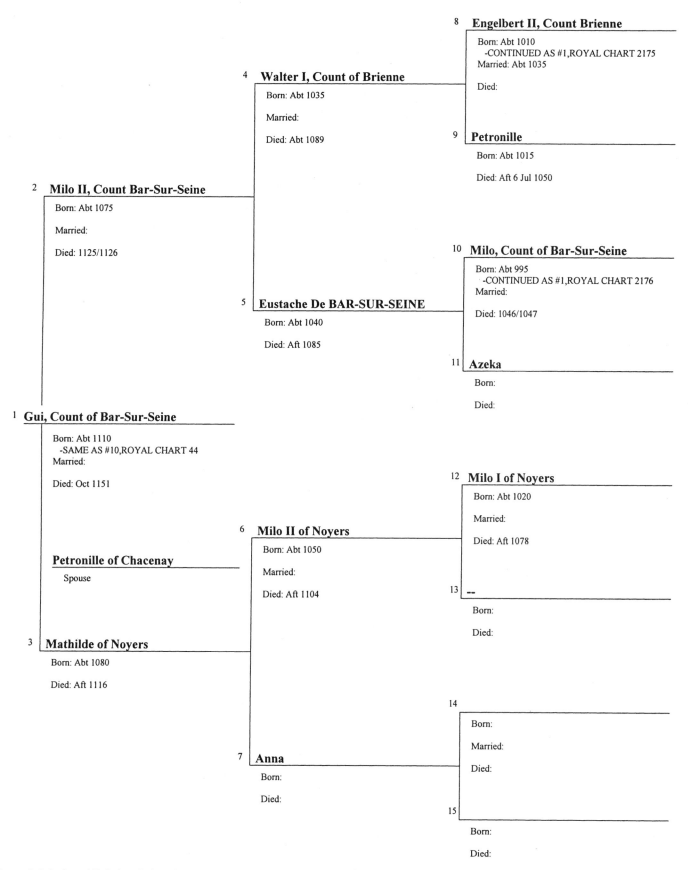

8   **Engelbert II, Count Brienne**

Born: Abt 1010
  -CONTINUED AS #1,ROYAL CHART 2175
Married: Abt 1035

Died:

4   **Walter I, Count of Brienne**

Born: Abt 1035

Married:

Died: Abt 1089

9   **Petronille**

Born: Abt 1015

Died: Aft 6 Jul 1050

2   **Milo II, Count Bar-Sur-Seine**

Born: Abt 1075

Married:

Died: 1125/1126

10   **Milo, Count of Bar-Sur-Seine**

Born: Abt 995
  -CONTINUED AS #1,ROYAL CHART 2176
Married:

Died: 1046/1047

5   **Eustache De BAR-SUR-SEINE**

Born: Abt 1040

Died: Aft 1085

11   **Azeka**

Born:

Died:

1   **Gui, Count of Bar-Sur-Seine**

Born: Abt 1110
  -SAME AS #10,ROYAL CHART 44
Married:

Died: Oct 1151

Petronille of Chacenay

Spouse

12   **Milo I of Noyers**

Born: Abt 1020

Married:

Died: Aft 1078

6   **Milo II of Noyers**

Born: Abt 1050

Married:

Died: Aft 1104

13   **--**

Born:

Died:

3   **Mathilde of Noyers**

Born: Abt 1080

Died: Aft 1116

14

Born:

Married:

Died:

7   **Anna**

Born:

Died:

15

Born:

Died:

Sources include: Stuart 383; Faris preliminary Charlemagne manuscript (June 1995), p. 72; Turton 168; *Royal Ancestors* (1989), charts 11375, 11901 (#4 & 5 ancestry).

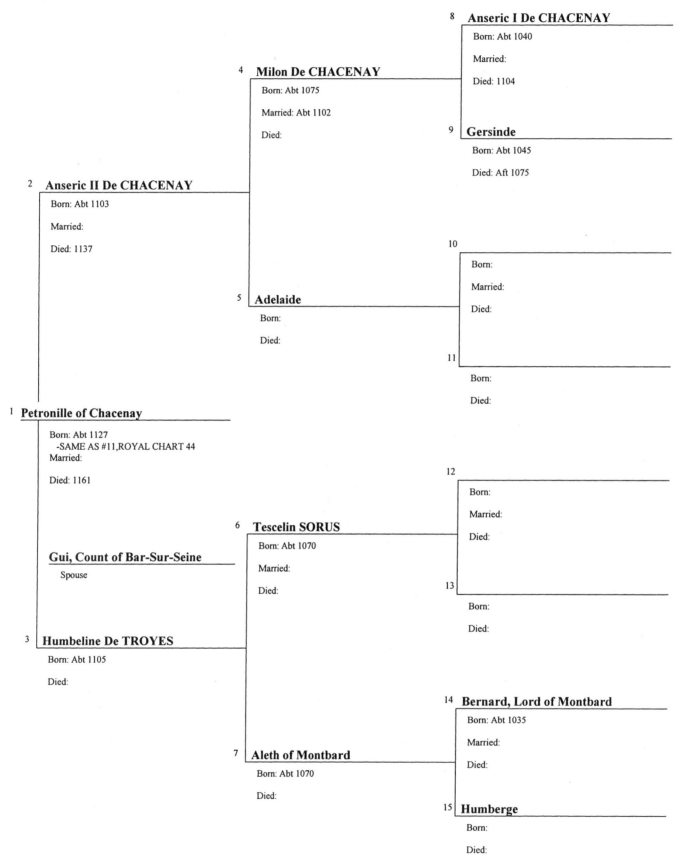

8 Anseric I De CHACENAY

Born: Abt 1040

Married:

Died: 1104

4 Milon De CHACENAY

Born: Abt 1075

Married: Abt 1102

Died:

9 Gersinde

Born: Abt 1045

Died: Aft 1075

2 Anseric II De CHACENAY

Born: Abt 1103

Married:

Died: 1137

10

Born:

Married:

Died:

5 Adelaide

Born:

Died:

11

Born:

Died:

1 Petronille of Chacenay

Born: Abt 1127
    -SAME AS #11,ROYAL CHART 44
Married:

Died: 1161

12

Born:

Married:

Died:

6 Tescelin SORUS

Born: Abt 1070

Married:

Died:

13

Born:

Died:

Gui, Count of Bar-Sur-Seine

Spouse

3 Humbeline De TROYES

Born: Abt 1105

Died:

14 Bernard, Lord of Montbard

Born: Abt 1035

Married:

Died:

7 Aleth of Montbard

Born: Abt 1070

Died:

15 Humberge

Born:

Died:

Sources include: Stuart 384-385; Turton 166; *Royal Ancestors* (1989), chart 11375.

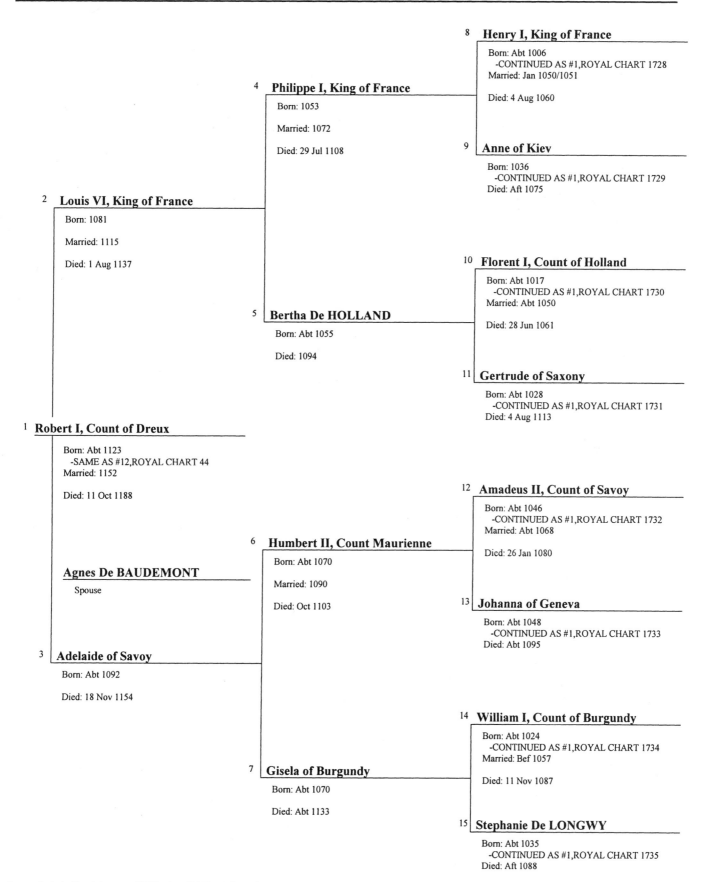

2 Louis VI, King of France
Born: 1081
Married: 1115
Died: 1 Aug 1137

4 Philippe I, King of France
Born: 1053
Married: 1072
Died: 29 Jul 1108

8 Henry I, King of France
Born: Abt 1006
-CONTINUED AS #1,ROYAL CHART 1728
Married: Jan 1050/1051
Died: 4 Aug 1060

9 Anne of Kiev
Born: 1036
-CONTINUED AS #1,ROYAL CHART 1729
Died: Aft 1075

5 Bertha De HOLLAND
Born: Abt 1055
Died: 1094

10 Florent I, Count of Holland
Born: Abt 1017
-CONTINUED AS #1,ROYAL CHART 1730
Married: Abt 1050
Died: 28 Jun 1061

11 Gertrude of Saxony
Born: Abt 1028
-CONTINUED AS #1,ROYAL CHART 1731
Died: 4 Aug 1113

1 Robert I, Count of Dreux
Born: Abt 1123
-SAME AS #12,ROYAL CHART 44
Married: 1152
Died: 11 Oct 1188

Agnes De BAUDEMONT
Spouse

3 Adelaide of Savoy
Born: Abt 1092
Died: 18 Nov 1154

6 Humbert II, Count Maurienne
Born: Abt 1070
Married: 1090
Died: Oct 1103

12 Amadeus II, Count of Savoy
Born: Abt 1046
-CONTINUED AS #1,ROYAL CHART 1732
Married: Abt 1068
Died: 26 Jan 1080

13 Johanna of Geneva
Born: Abt 1048
-CONTINUED AS #1,ROYAL CHART 1733
Died: Abt 1095

7 Gisela of Burgundy
Born: Abt 1070
Died: Abt 1133

14 William I, Count of Burgundy
Born: Abt 1024
-CONTINUED AS #1,ROYAL CHART 1734
Married: Bef 1057
Died: 11 Nov 1087

15 Stephanie De LONGWY
Born: Abt 1035
-CONTINUED AS #1,ROYAL CHART 1735
Died: Aft 1088

Sources include: *Royal Ancestors* (1989), chart 11376; Moriarty 195, 51; Stuart 124; *Ancestral Roots* 135.

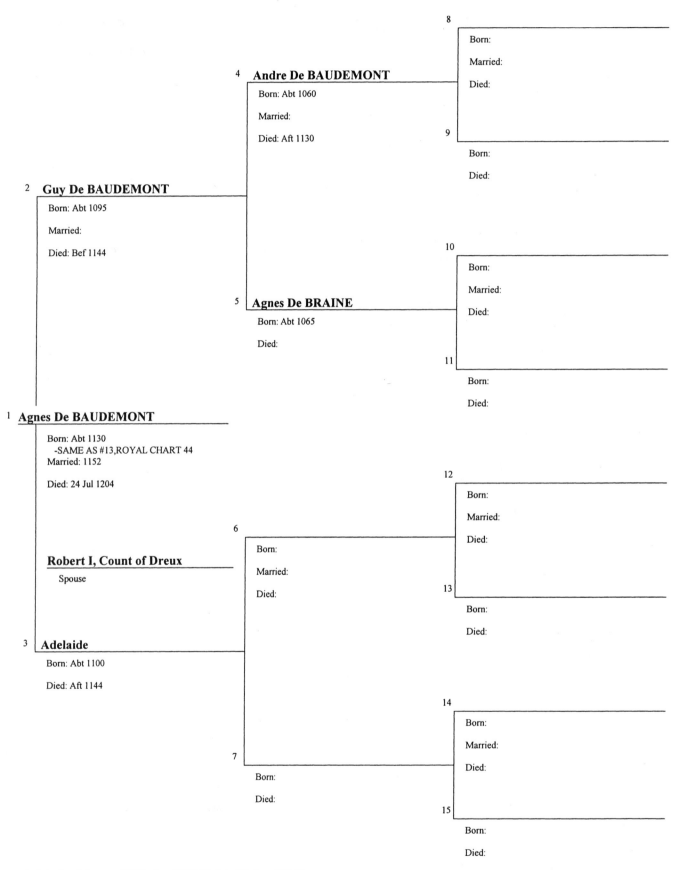

8

Born:

Married:

Died:

4 **Andre De BAUDEMONT**

Born: Abt 1060

Married:

Died: Aft 1130

9

Born:

Died:

2 **Guy De BAUDEMONT**

Born: Abt 1095

Married:

Died: Bef 1144

10

Born:

Married:

Died:

5 **Agnes De BRAINE**

Born: Abt 1065

Died:

11

Born:

Died:

1 **Agnes De BAUDEMONT**

Born: Abt 1130
-SAME AS #13,ROYAL CHART 44
Married: 1152

Died: 24 Jul 1204

12

Born:

Married:

Died:

6

Born:

Married:

Died:

13

Born:

Died:

Robert I, Count of Dreux

Spouse

3 **Adelaide**

Born: Abt 1100

Died: Aft 1144

14

Born:

Married:

Died:

7

Born:

Died:

15

Born:

Died:

Sources include: *Royal Ancestors* (1989), chart 11376; Moriarty 150; Stuart 124-30.

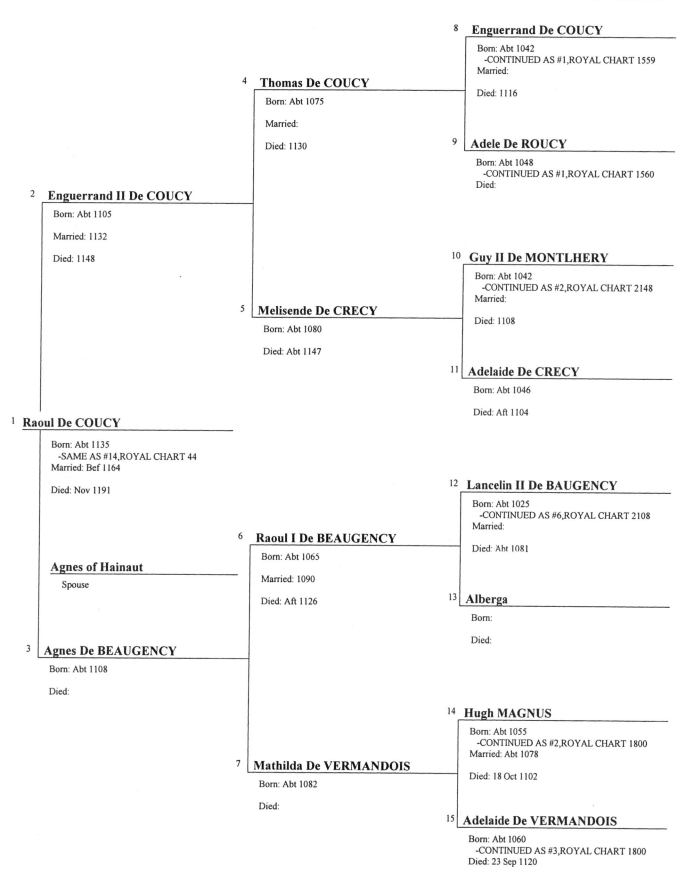

8 Enguerrand De COUCY
Born: Abt 1042
  -CONTINUED AS #1,ROYAL CHART 1559
Married:

Died: 1116

4 Thomas De COUCY
Born: Abt 1075

Married:

Died: 1130

9 Adele De ROUCY
Born: Abt 1048
  -CONTINUED AS #1,ROYAL CHART 1560
Died:

2 Enguerrand II De COUCY
Born: Abt 1105

Married: 1132

Died: 1148

10 Guy II De MONTLHERY
Born: Abt 1042
  -CONTINUED AS #2,ROYAL CHART 2148
Married:

Died: 1108

5 Melisende De CRECY
Born: Abt 1080

Died: Abt 1147

11 Adelaide De CRECY
Born: Abt 1046

Died: Aft 1104

1 Raoul De COUCY
Born: Abt 1135
  -SAME AS #14,ROYAL CHART 44
Married: Bef 1164

Died: Nov 1191

12 Lancelin II De BAUGENCY
Born: Abt 1025
  -CONTINUED AS #6,ROYAL CHART 2108
Married:

Died: Abt 1081

6 Raoul I De BEAUGENCY
Born: Abt 1065

Married: 1090

Died: Aft 1126

13 Alberga
Born:

Died:

Agnes of Hainaut
Spouse

3 Agnes De BEAUGENCY
Born: Abt 1108

Died:

14 Hugh MAGNUS
Born: Abt 1055
  -CONTINUED AS #2,ROYAL CHART 1800
Married: Abt 1078

Died: 18 Oct 1102

7 Mathilda De VERMANDOIS
Born: Abt 1082

Died:

15 Adelaide De VERMANDOIS
Born: Abt 1060
  -CONTINUED AS #3,ROYAL CHART 1800
Died: 23 Sep 1120

Sources include: *Royal Ancestors* (1989), chart 11376; Stuart 37, 4-5; Moriarty 196-197, 63; Faris preliminary Charlemagne manuscript (June 1995), pp. 111-112, 38-39; Turton 175; *Ancestral Roots* 135-28 (#1 Raoul). Note: The parentage shown for #5 Melisende is not certain. Faris gives #11 as Elisabeth De Montdidier.

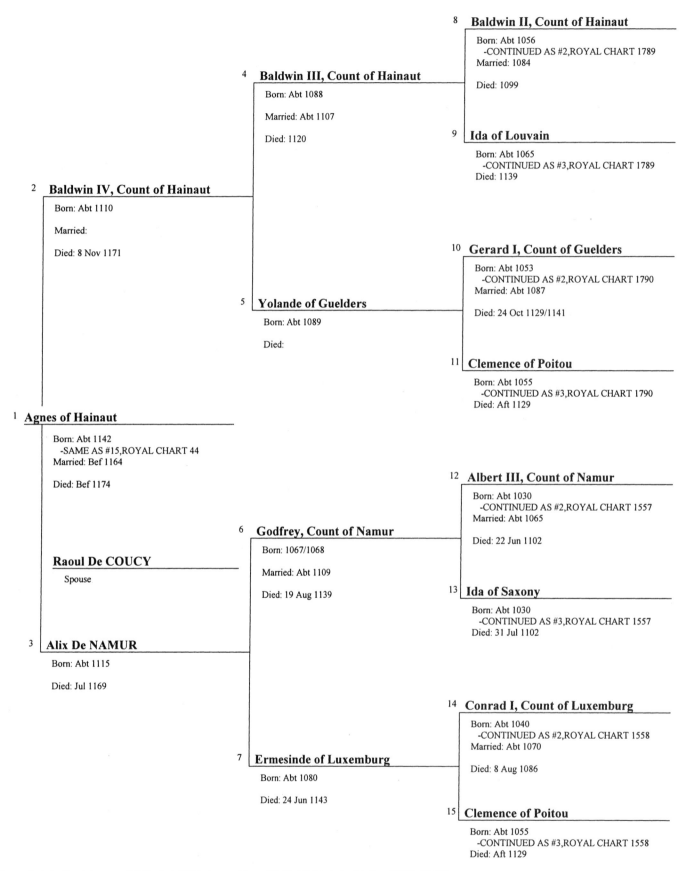

8 Baldwin II, Count of Hainaut
Born: Abt 1056
-CONTINUED AS #2,ROYAL CHART 1789
Married: 1084

Died: 1099

4 Baldwin III, Count of Hainaut
Born: Abt 1088

Married: Abt 1107

Died: 1120

9 Ida of Louvain
Born: Abt 1065
-CONTINUED AS #3,ROYAL CHART 1789
Died: 1139

2 Baldwin IV, Count of Hainaut
Born: Abt 1110

Married:

Died: 8 Nov 1171

10 Gerard I, Count of Guelders
Born: Abt 1053
-CONTINUED AS #2,ROYAL CHART 1790
Married: Abt 1087

Died: 24 Oct 1129/1141

5 Yolande of Guelders
Born: Abt 1089

Died:

11 Clemence of Poitou
Born: Abt 1055
-CONTINUED AS #3,ROYAL CHART 1790
Died: Aft 1129

1 Agnes of Hainaut
Born: Abt 1142
-SAME AS #15,ROYAL CHART 44
Married: Bef 1164

Died: Bef 1174

Raoul De COUCY
Spouse

12 Albert III, Count of Namur
Born: Abt 1030
-CONTINUED AS #2,ROYAL CHART 1557
Married: Abt 1065

Died: 22 Jun 1102

6 Godfrey, Count of Namur
Born: 1067/1068

Married: Abt 1109

Died: 19 Aug 1139

13 Ida of Saxony
Born: Abt 1030
-CONTINUED AS #3,ROYAL CHART 1557
Died: 31 Jul 1102

3 Alix De NAMUR
Born: Abt 1115

Died: Jul 1169

14 Conrad I, Count of Luxemburg
Born: Abt 1040
-CONTINUED AS #2,ROYAL CHART 1558
Married: Abt 1070

Died: 8 Aug 1086

7 Ermesinde of Luxemburg
Born: Abt 1080

Died: 24 Jun 1143

15 Clemence of Poitou
Born: Abt 1055
-CONTINUED AS #3,ROYAL CHART 1558
Died: Aft 1129

Sources include: *Royal Ancestors* (1989), chart 11376; *Ancestral Roots* 135-28, 163; Moriarty 124; Stuart 37-28, 73, 126.

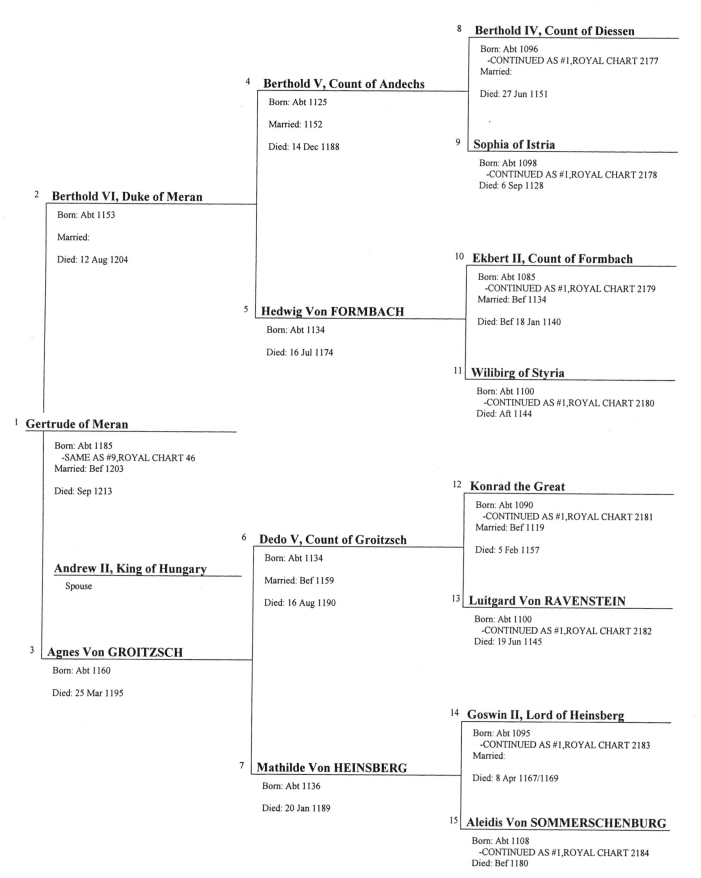

8 Berthold IV, Count of Diessen

Born: Abt 1096
-CONTINUED AS #1,ROYAL CHART 2177
Married:

Died: 27 Jun 1151

4 Berthold V, Count of Andechs

Born: Abt 1125

Married: 1152

Died: 14 Dec 1188

9 Sophia of Istria

Born: Abt 1098
-CONTINUED AS #1,ROYAL CHART 2178
Died: 6 Sep 1128

2 Berthold VI, Duke of Meran

Born: Abt 1153

Married:

Died: 12 Aug 1204

10 Ekbert II, Count of Formbach

Born: Abt 1085
-CONTINUED AS #1,ROYAL CHART 2179
Married: Bef 1134

Died: Bef 18 Jan 1140

5 Hedwig Von FORMBACH

Born: Abt 1134

Died: 16 Jul 1174

11 Wilibirg of Styria

Born: Abt 1100
-CONTINUED AS #1,ROYAL CHART 2180
Died: Aft 1144

1 Gertrude of Meran

Born: Abt 1185
-SAME AS #9,ROYAL CHART 46
Married: Bef 1203

Died: Sep 1213

12 Konrad the Great

Born: Abt 1090
-CONTINUED AS #1,ROYAL CHART 2181
Married: Bef 1119

Died: 5 Feb 1157

6 Dedo V, Count of Groitzsch

Born: Abt 1134

Married: Bef 1159

Died: 16 Aug 1190

Andrew II, King of Hungary

Spouse

13 Luitgard Von RAVENSTEIN

Born: Abt 1100
-CONTINUED AS #1,ROYAL CHART 2182
Died: 19 Jun 1145

3 Agnes Von GROITZSCH

Born: Abt 1160

Died: 25 Mar 1195

14 Goswin II, Lord of Heinsberg

Born: Abt 1095
-CONTINUED AS #1,ROYAL CHART 2183
Married:

Died: 8 Apr 1167/1169

7 Mathilde Von HEINSBERG

Born: Abt 1136

Died: 20 Jan 1189

15 Aleidis Von SOMMERSCHENBURG

Born: Abt 1108
-CONTINUED AS #1,ROYAL CHART 2184
Died: Bef 1180

Sources include: *Royal Ancestors* (1989), chart 11319; Stuart 7-8; Moriarty 198; *Ancestral Roots* 103-28; Schwennicke 1:36; Faris preliminary Charlemagne manuscript (June 1995), pp. 156, 288, 282. Note: #5 is also claimed as Hedwig Von Wittlesbach, daughter of Otto Von Wittlesbach & Heilika Von Pettendorf (see chart 1552, #4 & 5). Moriarty acknowledged that claim by Von Isenburg but retained the Formbach version as shown above.

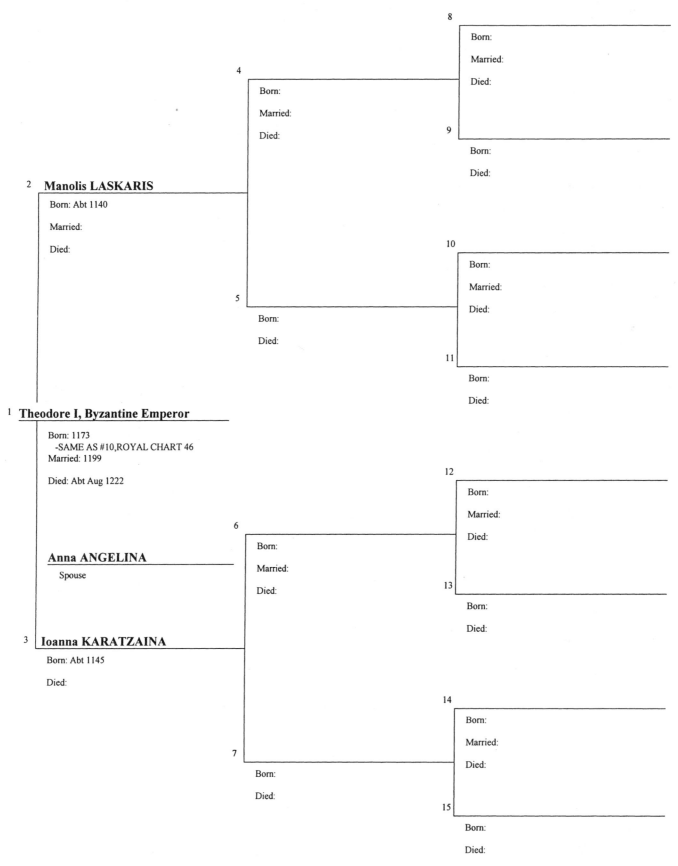

8

Born:

Married:

Died:

4

Born:

Married:

Died:

9

Born:

Died:

2 Manolis LASKARIS

Born: Abt 1140

Married:

Died:

10

Born:

Married:

Died:

5

Born:

Died:

11

Born:

Died:

1 Theodore I, Byzantine Emperor

Born: 1173
  -SAME AS #10,ROYAL CHART 46
Married: 1199

Died: Abt Aug 1222

12

Born:

Married:

Died:

6

Born:

Married:

Died:

13

Born:

Died:

Anna ANGELINA

Spouse

3 Ioanna KARATZAINA

Born: Abt 1145

Died:

14

Born:

Married:

Died:

7

Born:

Died:

15

Born:

Died:

Sources include: LDS records; Stuart 74-28; Moriarty 174 (#1 Theodore); *Royal Ancestors* (1989), chart 11319.

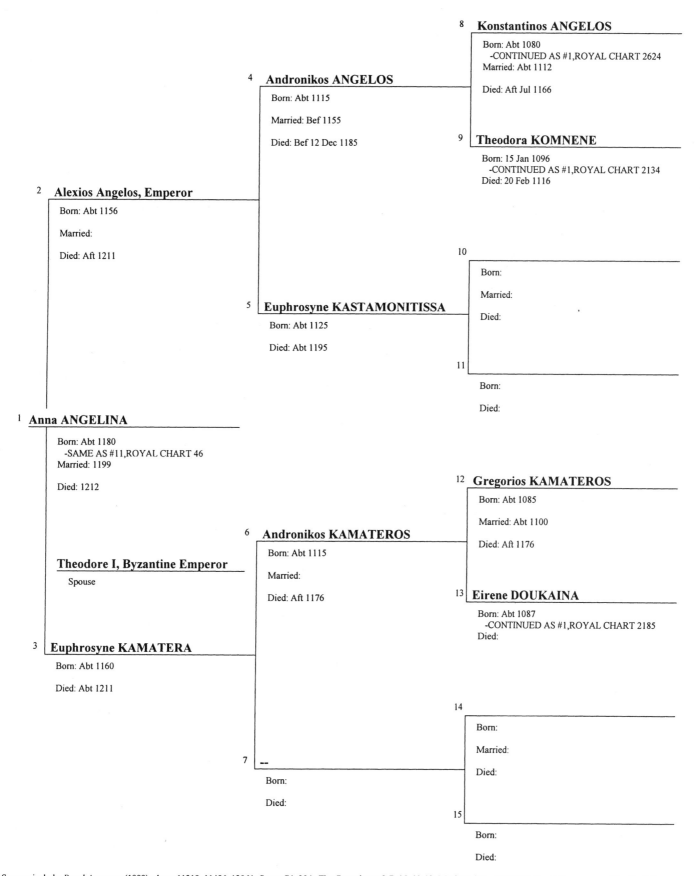

8 Konstantinos ANGELOS

Born: Abt 1080
 -CONTINUED AS #1,ROYAL CHART 2624
Married: Abt 1112

Died: Aft Jul 1166

4 Andronikos ANGELOS

Born: Abt 1115

Married: Bef 1155

Died: Bef 12 Dec 1185

9 Theodora KOMNENE

Born: 15 Jan 1096
 -CONTINUED AS #1,ROYAL CHART 2134
Died: 20 Feb 1116

2 Alexios Angelos, Emperor

Born: Abt 1156

Married:

Died: Aft 1211

10

Born:

Married:

Died:

5 Euphrosyne KASTAMONITISSA

Born: Abt 1125

Died: Abt 1195

11

Born:

Died:

1 Anna ANGELINA

Born: Abt 1180
 -SAME AS #11,ROYAL CHART 46
Married: 1199

Died: 1212

12 Gregorios KAMATEROS

Born: Abt 1085

Married: Abt 1100

Died: Aft 1176

6 Andronikos KAMATEROS

Born: Abt 1115

Married:

Died: Aft 1176

13 Eirene DOUKAINA

Born: Abt 1087
 -CONTINUED AS #1,ROYAL CHART 2185
Died:

Theodore I, Byzantine Emperor

Spouse

3 Euphrosyne KAMATERA

Born: Abt 1160

Died: Abt 1211

14

Born:

Married:

Died:

7 --

Born:

Died:

15

Born:

Died:

Sources include: *Royal Ancestors* (1989), charts 11319, 11486, 12061; Stuart 74, 394; *The Genealogist* 2:7, 15, 12-13; Moriarty 174. Note: #12 Gregorios was son of the Basileios (Emperor) Kamateros.

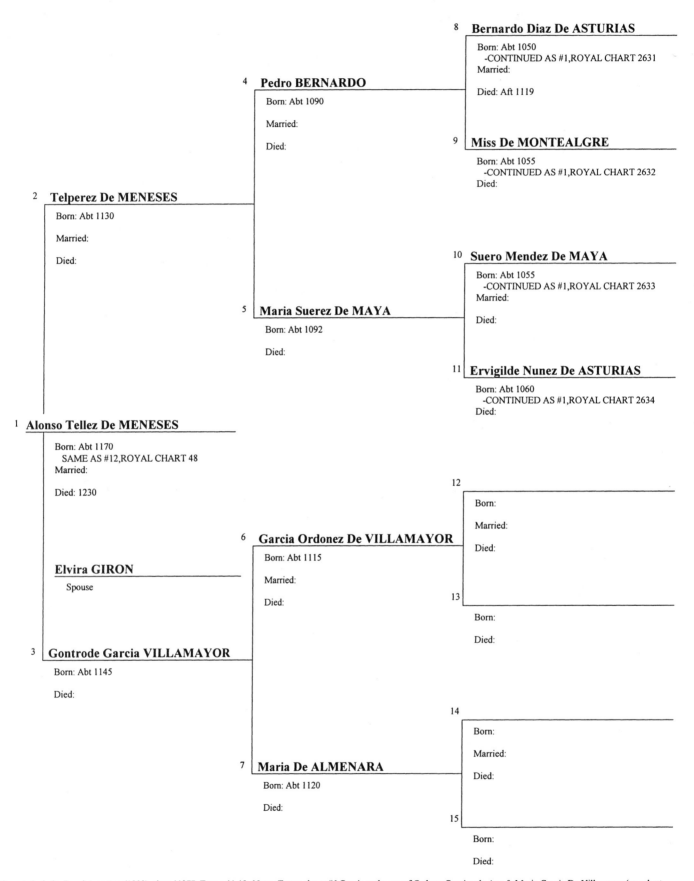

8 Bernardo Diaz De ASTURIAS
Born: Abt 1050
-CONTINUED AS #1, ROYAL CHART 2631
Married:

Died: Aft 1119

4 Pedro BERNARDO
Born: Abt 1090

Married:

Died:

9 Miss De MONTEALGRE
Born: Abt 1055
-CONTINUED AS #1, ROYAL CHART 2632
Died:

2 Telperez De MENESES
Born: Abt 1130

Married:

Died:

10 Suero Mendez De MAYA
Born: Abt 1055
-CONTINUED AS #1, ROYAL CHART 2633
Married:

Died:

5 Maria Suerez De MAYA
Born: Abt 1092

Died:

11 Ervigilde Nunez De ASTURIAS
Born: Abt 1060
-CONTINUED AS #1, ROYAL CHART 2634
Died:

1 Alonso Tellez De MENESES
Born: Abt 1170
SAME AS #12, ROYAL CHART 48
Married:

Died: 1230

12
Born:

Married:

Died:

6 Garcia Ordonez De VILLAMAYOR
Born: Abt 1115

Married:

Died:

13
Born:

Died:

Elvira GIRON
Spouse

3 Gontrode Garcia VILLAMAYOR
Born: Abt 1145

Died:

14
Born:

Married:

Died:

7 Maria De ALMENARA
Born: Abt 1120

Died:

15
Born:

Died:

Sources include: *Royal Ancestors* (1989), chart 11377; Turton 44-45. Notes: Turton shows #6 Garcia as the son of Ordono Garciez de Aza & Maria Garcia De Villamayor (see chart 1589, #2 & 3). The connection is unacceptable chronologically on the Villamayor side. The ancestry claimed by Turton for #7 Maria is not possible chronologically.

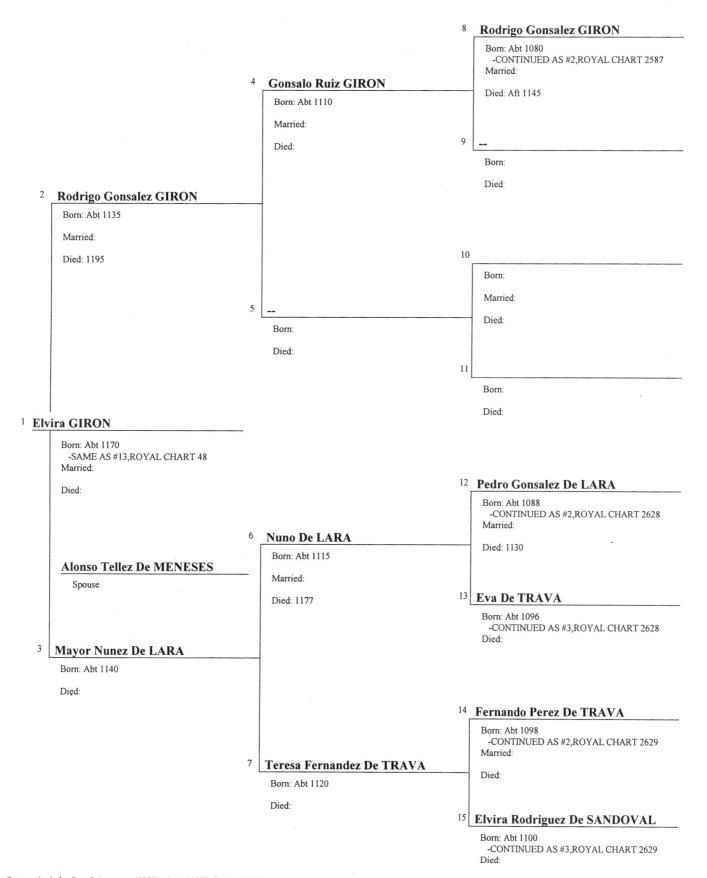

2 Rodrigo Gonsalez GIRON
Born: Abt 1135
Married:
Died: 1195

4 Gonsalo Ruiz GIRON
Born: Abt 1110
Married:
Died:

8 Rodrigo Gonsalez GIRON
Born: Abt 1080
 -CONTINUED AS #2,ROYAL CHART 2587
Married:

Died: Aft 1145

9 --
Born:

Died:

5 --
Born:
Died:

10
Born:
Married:
Died:

11
Born:
Died:

1 Elvira GIRON
Born: Abt 1170
 -SAME AS #13,ROYAL CHART 48
Married:

Died:

Alonso Tellez De MENESES
Spouse

3 Mayor Nunez De LARA
Born: Abt 1140

Died:

6 Nuno De LARA
Born: Abt 1115
Married:
Died: 1177

12 Pedro Gonsalez De LARA
Born: Abt 1088
 -CONTINUED AS #2,ROYAL CHART 2628
Married:

Died: 1130

13 Eva De TRAVA
Born: Abt 1096
 -CONTINUED AS #3,ROYAL CHART 2628
Died:

7 Teresa Fernandez De TRAVA
Born: Abt 1120
Died:

14 Fernando Perez De TRAVA
Born: Abt 1098
 -CONTINUED AS #2,ROYAL CHART 2629
Married:

Died:

15 Elvira Rodriguez De SANDOVAL
Born: Abt 1100
 -CONTINUED AS #3,ROYAL CHART 2629
Died:

Sources include: *Royal Ancestors* (1989), chart 11377; Turton 44, 54.

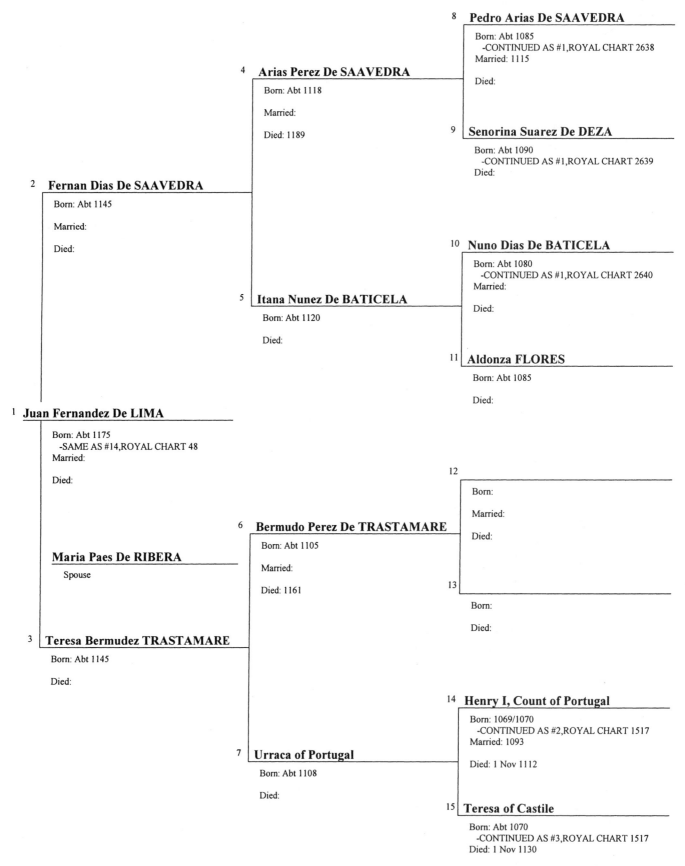

8 Pedro Arias De SAAVEDRA

Born: Abt 1085
-CONTINUED AS #1,ROYAL CHART 2638
Married: 1115

Died:

4 Arias Perez De SAAVEDRA

Born: Abt 1118

Married:

Died: 1189

9 Senorina Suarez De DEZA

Born: Abt 1090
-CONTINUED AS #1,ROYAL CHART 2639
Died:

2 Fernan Dias De SAAVEDRA

Born: Abt 1145

Married:

Died:

10 Nuno Dias De BATICELA

Born: Abt 1080
-CONTINUED AS #1,ROYAL CHART 2640
Married:

Died:

5 Itana Nunez De BATICELA

Born: Abt 1120

Died:

11 Aldonza FLORES

Born: Abt 1085

Died:

1 Juan Fernandez De LIMA

Born: Abt 1175
-SAME AS #14,ROYAL CHART 48
Married:

Died:

12

Born:

Married:

Died:

6 Bermudo Perez De TRASTAMARE

Born: Abt 1105

Married:

Died: 1161

Maria Paes De RIBERA

Spouse

13

Born:

Died:

3 Teresa Bermudez TRASTAMARE

Born: Abt 1145

Died:

14 Henry I, Count of Portugal

Born: 1069/1070
-CONTINUED AS #2,ROYAL CHART 1517
Married: 1093

Died: 1 Nov 1112

7 Urraca of Portugal

Born: Abt 1108

Died:

15 Teresa of Castile

Born: Abt 1070
-CONTINUED AS #3,ROYAL CHART 1517
Died: 1 Nov 1130

Sources include: *Royal Ancestors* (1989), chart 11377; Turton 47, 50; Kraentzler 1092. Note: There is disagreement on the parentage and ancestry of #6 Bermudo.

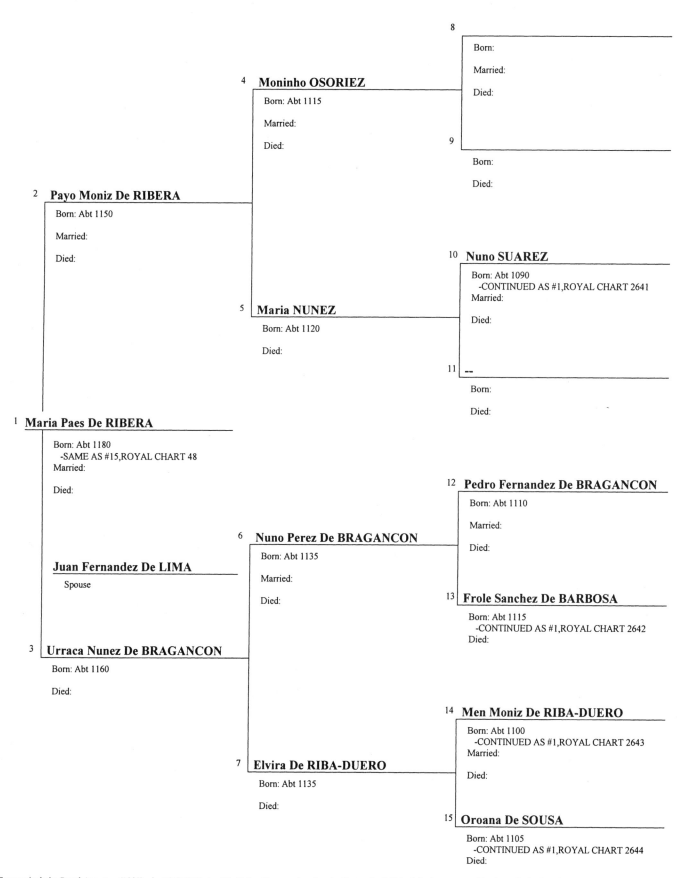

8

Born:

Married:

Died:

4 Moninho OSORIEZ

Born: Abt 1115

Married:

Died:

9

Born:

Died:

2 Payo Moniz De RIBERA

Born: Abt 1150

Married:

Died:

10 Nuno SUAREZ

Born: Abt 1090
  -CONTINUED AS #1,ROYAL CHART 2641
Married:

Died:

5 Maria NUNEZ

Born: Abt 1120

Died:

11 --

Born:

Died:

1 Maria Paes De RIBERA

Born: Abt 1180
  -SAME AS #15,ROYAL CHART 48
Married:

Died:

12 Pedro Fernandez De BRAGANCON

Born: Abt 1110

Married:

Died:

6 Nuno Perez De BRAGANCON

Born: Abt 1135

Married:

Died:

13 Frole Sanchez De BARBOSA

Born: Abt 1115
  -CONTINUED AS #1,ROYAL CHART 2642
Died:

Juan Fernandez De LIMA

Spouse

3 Urraca Nunez De BRAGANCON

Born: Abt 1160

Died:

14 Men Moniz De RIBA-DUERO

Born: Abt 1100
  -CONTINUED AS #1,ROYAL CHART 2643
Married:

Died:

7 Elvira De RIBA-DUERO

Born: Abt 1135

Died:

15 Oroana De SOUSA

Born: Abt 1105
  -CONTINUED AS #1,ROYAL CHART 2644
Died:

Sources include: *Royal Ancestors* (1989), chart 11377; Turton 48. Notes: The ancestry given by Turton for #4 Moninho is unacceptable chronologically. The ancestry given for #12 Pedro is not possible chronologically.

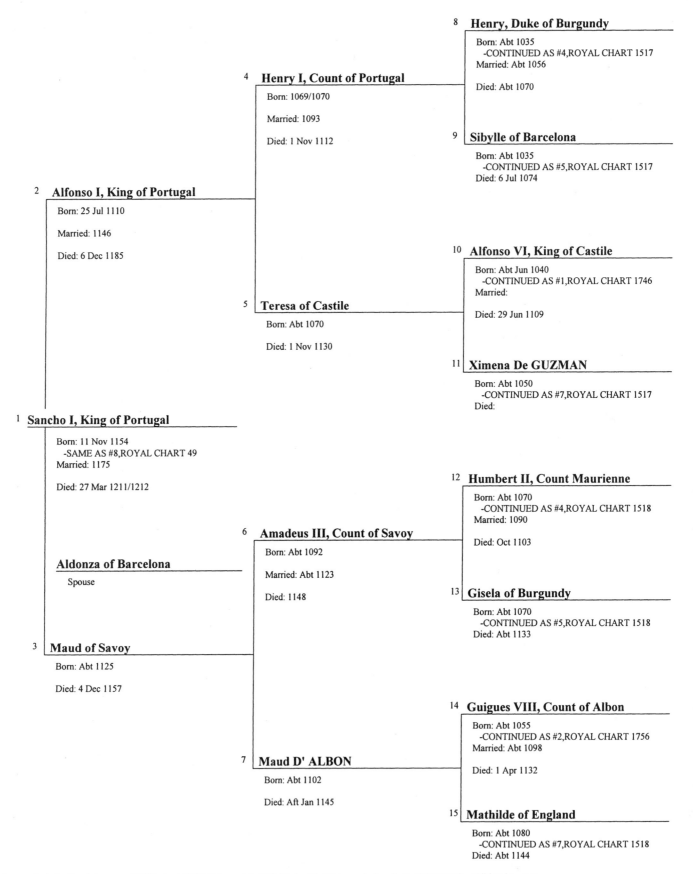

8 Henry, Duke of Burgundy

Born: Abt 1035
-CONTINUED AS #4,ROYAL CHART 1517
Married: Abt 1056

Died: Abt 1070

4 Henry I, Count of Portugal

Born: 1069/1070

Married: 1093

Died: 1 Nov 1112

9 Sibylle of Barcelona

Born: Abt 1035
-CONTINUED AS #5,ROYAL CHART 1517
Died: 6 Jul 1074

2 Alfonso I, King of Portugal

Born: 25 Jul 1110

Married: 1146

Died: 6 Dec 1185

10 Alfonso VI, King of Castile

Born: Abt Jun 1040
-CONTINUED AS #1,ROYAL CHART 1746
Married:

Died: 29 Jun 1109

5 Teresa of Castile

Born: Abt 1070

Died: 1 Nov 1130

11 Ximena De GUZMAN

Born: Abt 1050
-CONTINUED AS #7,ROYAL CHART 1517
Died:

1 Sancho I, King of Portugal

Born: 11 Nov 1154
-SAME AS #8,ROYAL CHART 49
Married: 1175

Died: 27 Mar 1211/1212

12 Humbert II, Count Maurienne

Born: Abt 1070
-CONTINUED AS #4,ROYAL CHART 1518
Married: 1090

Died: Oct 1103

6 Amadeus III, Count of Savoy

Born: Abt 1092

Married: Abt 1123

Died: 1148

13 Gisela of Burgundy

Born: Abt 1070
-CONTINUED AS #5,ROYAL CHART 1518
Died: Abt 1133

Aldonza of Barcelona

Spouse

3 Maud of Savoy

Born: Abt 1125

Died: 4 Dec 1157

14 Guigues VIII, Count of Albon

Born: Abt 1055
-CONTINUED AS #2,ROYAL CHART 1756
Married: Abt 1098

Died: 1 Apr 1132

7 Maud D' ALBON

Born: Abt 1102

Died: Aft Jan 1145

15 Mathilde of England

Born: Abt 1080
-CONTINUED AS #7,ROYAL CHART 1518
Died: Abt 1144

Sources include: *Royal Ancestors* (1989), chart 11322; Schwennicke 2:38; Turton 36; LDS records. See charts 1517-1518 for additional sources.

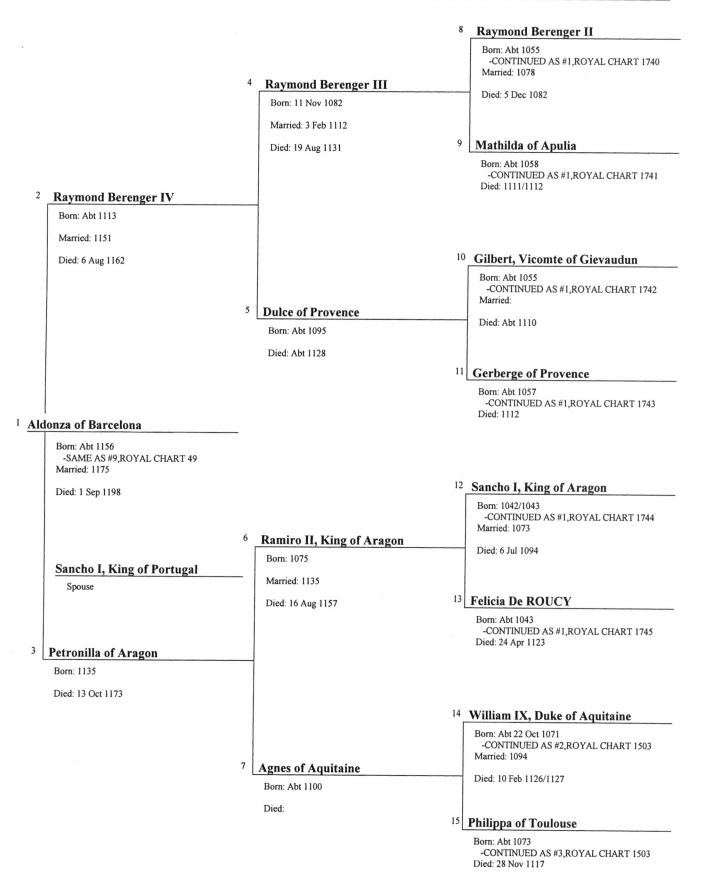

8 **Raymond Berenger II**

Born: Abt 1055
-CONTINUED AS #1,ROYAL CHART 1740
Married: 1078

Died: 5 Dec 1082

4 **Raymond Berenger III**

Born: 11 Nov 1082

Married: 3 Feb 1112

Died: 19 Aug 1131

9 **Mathilda of Apulia**

Born: Abt 1058
-CONTINUED AS #1,ROYAL CHART 1741
Died: 1111/1112

2 **Raymond Berenger IV**

Born: Abt 1113

Married: 1151

Died: 6 Aug 1162

10 **Gilbert, Vicomte of Gievaudun**

Born: Abt 1055
-CONTINUED AS #1,ROYAL CHART 1742
Married:

Died: Abt 1110

5 **Dulce of Provence**

Born: Abt 1095

Died: Abt 1128

11 **Gerberge of Provence**

Born: Abt 1057
-CONTINUED AS #1,ROYAL CHART 1743
Died: 1112

1 **Aldonza of Barcelona**

Born: Abt 1156
-SAME AS #9,ROYAL CHART 49
Married: 1175

Died: 1 Sep 1198

12 **Sancho I, King of Aragon**

Born: 1042/1043
-CONTINUED AS #1,ROYAL CHART 1744
Married: 1073

Died: 6 Jul 1094

6 **Ramiro II, King of Aragon**

Born: 1075

Married: 1135

Died: 16 Aug 1157

Sancho I, King of Portugal

Spouse

13 **Felicia De ROUCY**

Born: Abt 1043
-CONTINUED AS #1,ROYAL CHART 1745
Died: 24 Apr 1123

3 **Petronilla of Aragon**

Born: 1135

Died: 13 Oct 1173

14 **William IX, Duke of Aquitaine**

Born: Abt 22 Oct 1071
-CONTINUED AS #2,ROYAL CHART 1503
Married: 1094

Died: 10 Feb 1126/1127

7 **Agnes of Aquitaine**

Born: Abt 1100

Died:

15 **Philippa of Toulouse**

Born: Abt 1073
-CONTINUED AS #3,ROYAL CHART 1503
Died: 28 Nov 1117

Sources include: *Royal Ancestors* (1989), chart 11322; Turton 36; LDS records. See chart 1509 for additional sources.

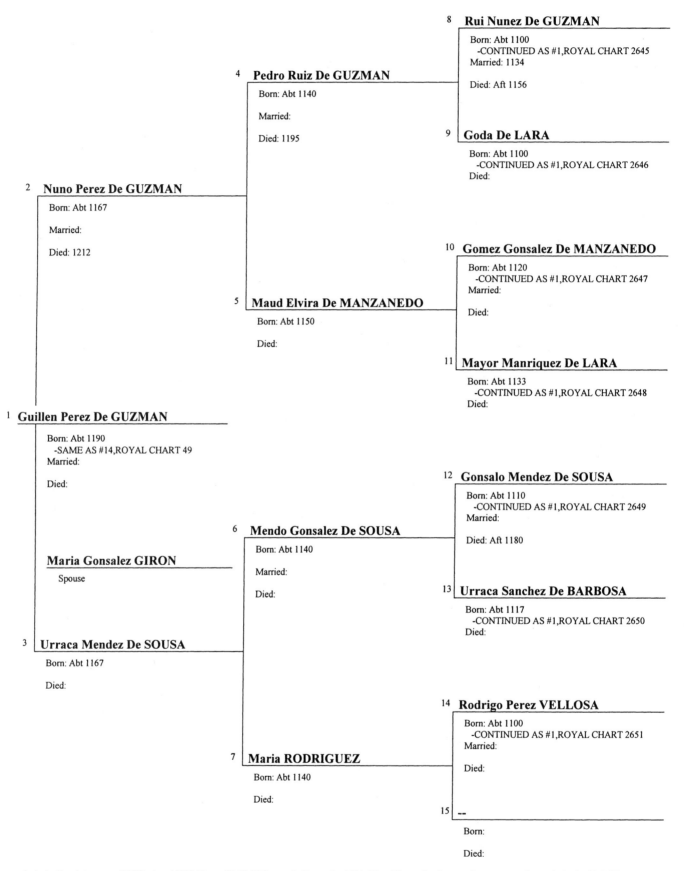

8 Rui Nunez De GUZMAN

Born: Abt 1100
-CONTINUED AS #1,ROYAL CHART 2645
Married: 1134

Died: Aft 1156

4 Pedro Ruiz De GUZMAN

Born: Abt 1140

Married:

Died: 1195

9 Goda De LARA

Born: Abt 1100
-CONTINUED AS #1,ROYAL CHART 2646
Died:

2 Nuno Perez De GUZMAN

Born: Abt 1167

Married:

Died: 1212

10 Gomez Gonsalez De MANZANEDO

Born: Abt 1120
-CONTINUED AS #1,ROYAL CHART 2647
Married:

Died:

5 Maud Elvira De MANZANEDO

Born: Abt 1150

Died:

11 Mayor Manriquez De LARA

Born: Abt 1133
-CONTINUED AS #1,ROYAL CHART 2648
Died:

1 Guillen Perez De GUZMAN

Born: Abt 1190
-SAME AS #14,ROYAL CHART 49
Married:

Died:

12 Gonsalo Mendez De SOUSA

Born: Abt 1110
-CONTINUED AS #1,ROYAL CHART 2649
Married:

Died: Aft 1180

6 Mendo Gonsalez De SOUSA

Born: Abt 1140

Married:

Died:

Maria Gonsalez GIRON

Spouse

13 Urraca Sanchez De BARBOSA

Born: Abt 1117
-CONTINUED AS #1,ROYAL CHART 2650
Died:

3 Urraca Mendez De SOUSA

Born: Abt 1167

Died:

14 Rodrigo Perez VELLOSA

Born: Abt 1100
-CONTINUED AS #1,ROYAL CHART 2651
Married:

Died:

7 Maria RODRIGUEZ

Born: Abt 1140

Died:

15 --

Born:

Died:

Sources include: *Royal Ancestors* (1989), chart 11323; Turton 51-53; LDS records; Kraentzler 1094. Note: Kraentzler disputes the parentage shown above for #1 Guillen.

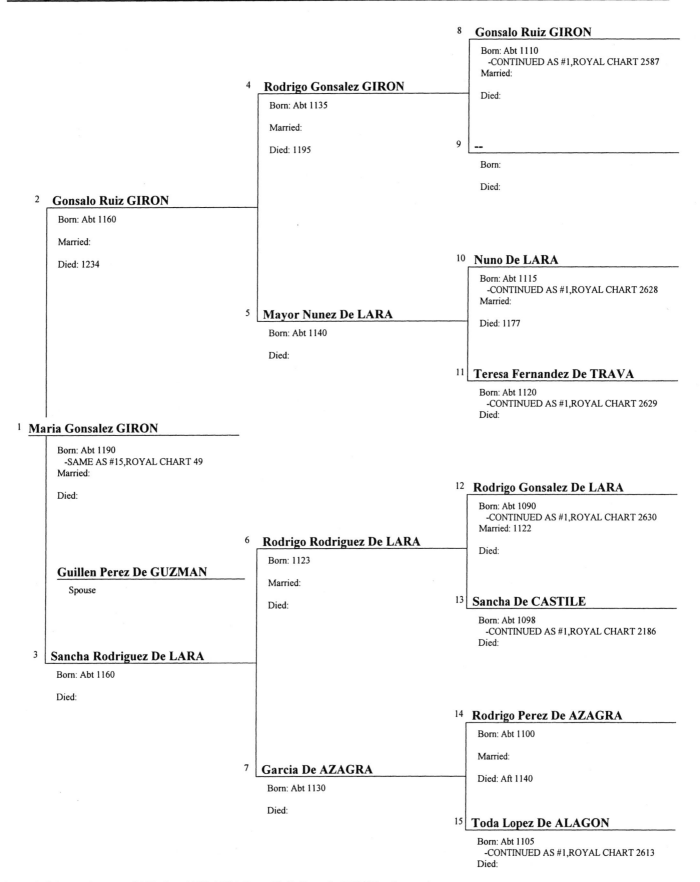

2 Gonsalo Ruiz GIRON

Born: Abt 1160

Married:

Died: 1234

4 Rodrigo Gonsalez GIRON

Born: Abt 1135

Married:

Died: 1195

8 Gonsalo Ruiz GIRON

Born: Abt 1110
 -CONTINUED AS #1,ROYAL CHART 2587
Married:

Died:

9 --

Born:

Died:

5 Mayor Nunez De LARA

Born: Abt 1140

Died:

10 Nuno De LARA

Born: Abt 1115
 -CONTINUED AS #1,ROYAL CHART 2628
Married:

Died: 1177

11 Teresa Fernandez De TRAVA

Born: Abt 1120
 -CONTINUED AS #1,ROYAL CHART 2629
Died:

1 Maria Gonsalez GIRON

Born: Abt 1190
 -SAME AS #15,ROYAL CHART 49
Married:

Died:

Guillen Perez De GUZMAN

Spouse

3 Sancha Rodriguez De LARA

Born: Abt 1160

Died:

6 Rodrigo Rodriguez De LARA

Born: 1123

Married:

Died:

12 Rodrigo Gonsalez De LARA

Born: Abt 1090
 -CONTINUED AS #1,ROYAL CHART 2630
Married: 1122

Died:

13 Sancha De CASTILE

Born: Abt 1098
 -CONTINUED AS #1,ROYAL CHART 2186
Died:

7 Garcia De AZAGRA

Born: Abt 1130

Died:

14 Rodrigo Perez De AZAGRA

Born: Abt 1100

Married:

Died: Aft 1140

15 Toda Lopez De ALAGON

Born: Abt 1105
 -CONTINUED AS #1,ROYAL CHART 2613
Died:

Sources include: *Royal Ancestors* (1989), charts 11323, 11386; Turton 54, 67; Kraentzler 1296 (#11 and ancestry).

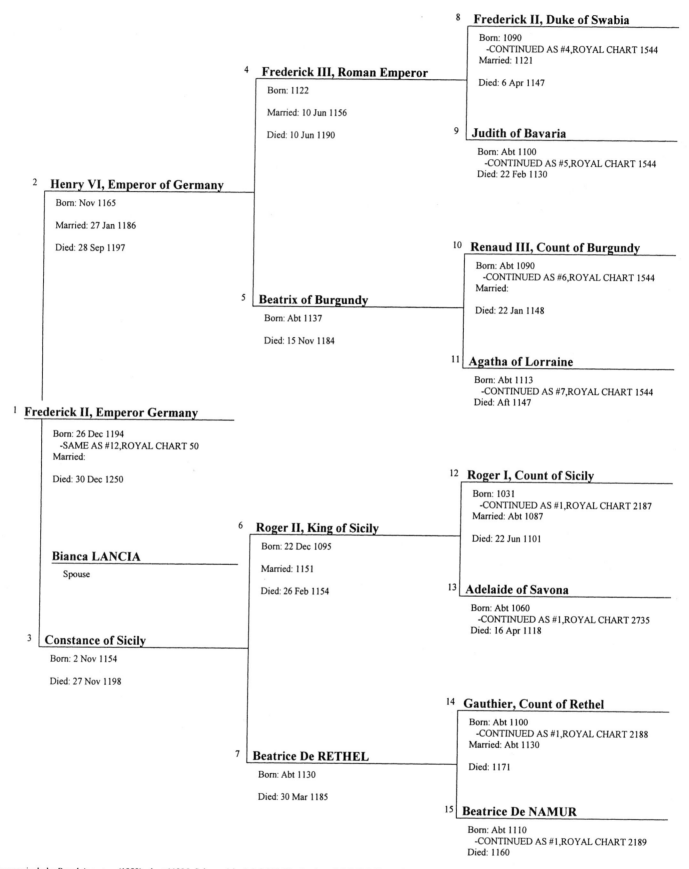

8 Frederick II, Duke of Swabia

Born: 1090
-CONTINUED AS #4,ROYAL CHART 1544
Married: 1121

Died: 6 Apr 1147

4 Frederick III, Roman Emperor

Born: 1122

Married: 10 Jun 1156

Died: 10 Jun 1190

9 Judith of Bavaria

Born: Abt 1100
-CONTINUED AS #5,ROYAL CHART 1544
Died: 22 Feb 1130

2 Henry VI, Emperor of Germany

Born: Nov 1165

Married: 27 Jan 1186

Died: 28 Sep 1197

10 Renaud III, Count of Burgundy

Born: Abt 1090
-CONTINUED AS #6,ROYAL CHART 1544
Married:

Died: 22 Jan 1148

5 Beatrix of Burgundy

Born: Abt 1137

Died: 15 Nov 1184

11 Agatha of Lorraine

Born: Abt 1113
-CONTINUED AS #7,ROYAL CHART 1544
Died: Aft 1147

1 Frederick II, Emperor Germany

Born: 26 Dec 1194
-SAME AS #12,ROYAL CHART 50
Married:

Died: 30 Dec 1250

12 Roger I, Count of Sicily

Born: 1031
-CONTINUED AS #1,ROYAL CHART 2187
Married: Abt 1087

Died: 22 Jun 1101

6 Roger II, King of Sicily

Born: 22 Dec 1095

Married: 1151

Died: 26 Feb 1154

13 Adelaide of Savona

Born: Abt 1060
-CONTINUED AS #1,ROYAL CHART 2735
Died: 16 Apr 1118

Bianca LANCIA

Spouse

3 Constance of Sicily

Born: 2 Nov 1154

Died: 27 Nov 1198

14 Gauthier, Count of Rethel

Born: Abt 1100
-CONTINUED AS #1,ROYAL CHART 2188
Married: Abt 1130

Died: 1171

7 Beatrice De RETHEL

Born: Abt 1130

Died: 30 Mar 1185

15 Beatrice De NAMUR

Born: Abt 1110
-CONTINUED AS #1,ROYAL CHART 2189
Died: 1160

Sources include: *Royal Ancestors* (1989), chart 11325; Schwennicke 1:5, 2:206; Von Isenburg 1:5, 2:117; Turton 36; LDS records (wrong on #7). Note: The parentage of #13 Adelaide (Adelheid) is disputed.

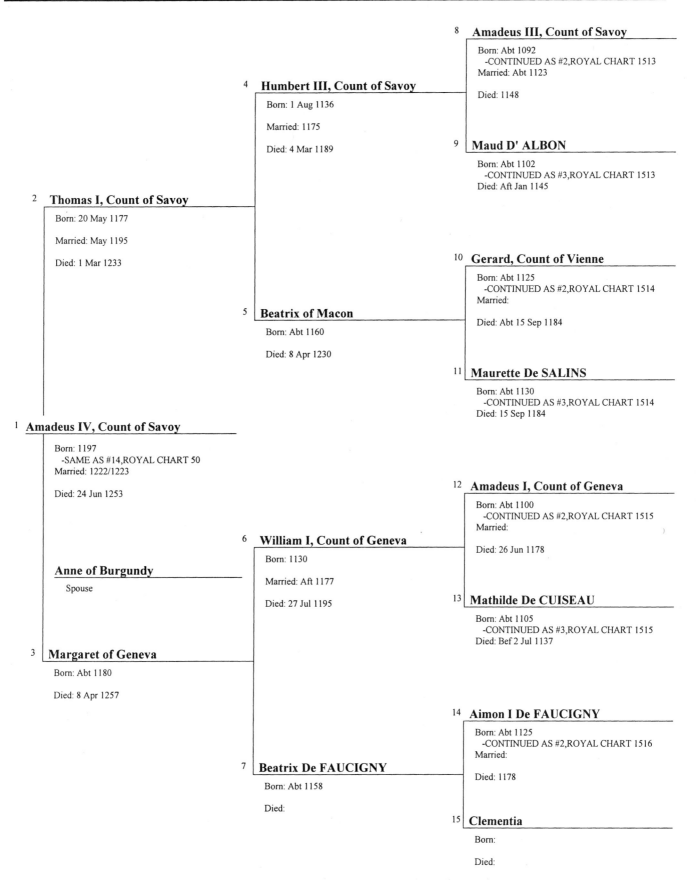

8 Amadeus III, Count of Savoy

Born: Abt 1092
  -CONTINUED AS #2,ROYAL CHART 1513
Married: Abt 1123

Died: 1148

4 Humbert III, Count of Savoy

Born: 1 Aug 1136

Married: 1175

Died: 4 Mar 1189

9 Maud D' ALBON

Born: Abt 1102
  -CONTINUED AS #3,ROYAL CHART 1513
Died: Aft Jan 1145

2 Thomas I, Count of Savoy

Born: 20 May 1177

Married: May 1195

Died: 1 Mar 1233

10 Gerard, Count of Vienne

Born: Abt 1125
  -CONTINUED AS #2,ROYAL CHART 1514
Married:

Died: Abt 15 Sep 1184

5 Beatrix of Macon

Born: Abt 1160

Died: 8 Apr 1230

11 Maurette De SALINS

Born: Abt 1130
  -CONTINUED AS #3,ROYAL CHART 1514
Died: 15 Sep 1184

1 Amadeus IV, Count of Savoy

Born: 1197
  -SAME AS #14,ROYAL CHART 50
Married: 1222/1223

Died: 24 Jun 1253

12 Amadeus I, Count of Geneva

Born: Abt 1100
  -CONTINUED AS #2,ROYAL CHART 1515
Married:

Died: 26 Jun 1178

6 William I, Count of Geneva

Born: 1130

Married: Aft 1177

Died: 27 Jul 1195

13 Mathilde De CUISEAU

Born: Abt 1105
  -CONTINUED AS #3,ROYAL CHART 1515
Died: Bef 2 Jul 1137

Anne of Burgundy

Spouse

3 Margaret of Geneva

Born: Abt 1180

Died: 8 Apr 1257

14 Aimon I De FAUCIGNY

Born: Abt 1125
  -CONTINUED AS #2,ROYAL CHART 1516
Married:

Died: 1178

7 Beatrix De FAUCIGNY

Born: Abt 1158

Died:

15 Clementia

Born:

Died:

Sources include: *Royal Ancestors* (1989), chart 11325; Faris preliminary Charlemagne manuscript (June 1995), pp. 247-248, 85-86; Turton 60; Stuart 93, 175 (#2 & 3 ancestry); Moriarty 104, 261 (#2 & 3 ancestry). Note: The spouse of #1 Amadeus IV is disputed. See note chart 1582.

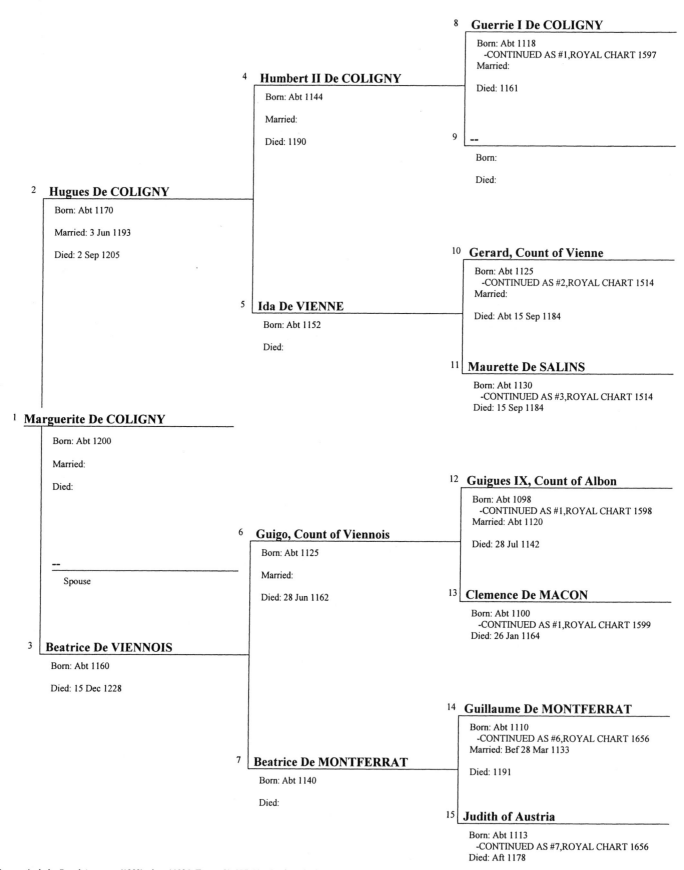

8 Guerrie I De COLIGNY

Born: Abt 1118
-CONTINUED AS #1,ROYAL CHART 1597
Married:

Died: 1161

4 Humbert II De COLIGNY

Born: Abt 1144

Married:

Died: 1190

9 --

Born:

Died:

2 Hugues De COLIGNY

Born: Abt 1170

Married: 3 Jun 1193

Died: 2 Sep 1205

10 Gerard, Count of Vienne

Born: Abt 1125
-CONTINUED AS #2,ROYAL CHART 1514
Married:

Died: Abt 15 Sep 1184

5 Ida De VIENNE

Born: Abt 1152

Died:

11 Maurette De SALINS

Born: Abt 1130
-CONTINUED AS #3,ROYAL CHART 1514
Died: 15 Sep 1184

1 Marguerite De COLIGNY

Born: Abt 1200

Married:

Died:

12 Guigues IX, Count of Albon

Born: Abt 1098
-CONTINUED AS #1,ROYAL CHART 1598
Married: Abt 1120

Died: 28 Jul 1142

6 Guigo, Count of Viennois

Born: Abt 1125

Married:

Died: 28 Jun 1162

13 Clemence De MACON

Born: Abt 1100
-CONTINUED AS #1,ROYAL CHART 1599
Died: 26 Jan 1164

--

Spouse

3 Beatrice De VIENNOIS

Born: Abt 1160

Died: 15 Dec 1228

14 Guillaume De MONTFERRAT

Born: Abt 1110
-CONTINUED AS #6,ROYAL CHART 1656
Married: Bef 28 Mar 1133

Died: 1191

7 Beatrice De MONTFERRAT

Born: Abt 1140

Died:

15 Judith of Austria

Born: Abt 1113
-CONTINUED AS #7,ROYAL CHART 1656
Died: Aft 1178

Sources include: *Royal Ancestors* (1989), chart 11325; Turton 61, 177; Von Isenburg 2:110, 24; Kraentzler 1096; Faris preliminary Charlemagne manuscript (June 1995), pp. 82-83, 279-280 (#2 & 3 ancestry); LDS records. Notes: #2 Hugues De Coligny was the 3rd husband of #3 Beatrice. Turton and Kraentzler claim #1 Marguerite as the daughter who married 1222-23 Amadeus IV (Count of Savoy) and died 1242-43. Chronologically, this is the more plausible version. Von Isenburg and Faris give the wife of Amadeus IV as Anne of Burgundy (daughter of #3 Beatrice by her 2nd husband Hugh III, Duke of Burgundy, who died 25 Aug 1192), the version tentatively accepted in this compilation (see charts 50, 76). The identification of #7 Beatrice (Beatrix) as a Montferrat is not certain.

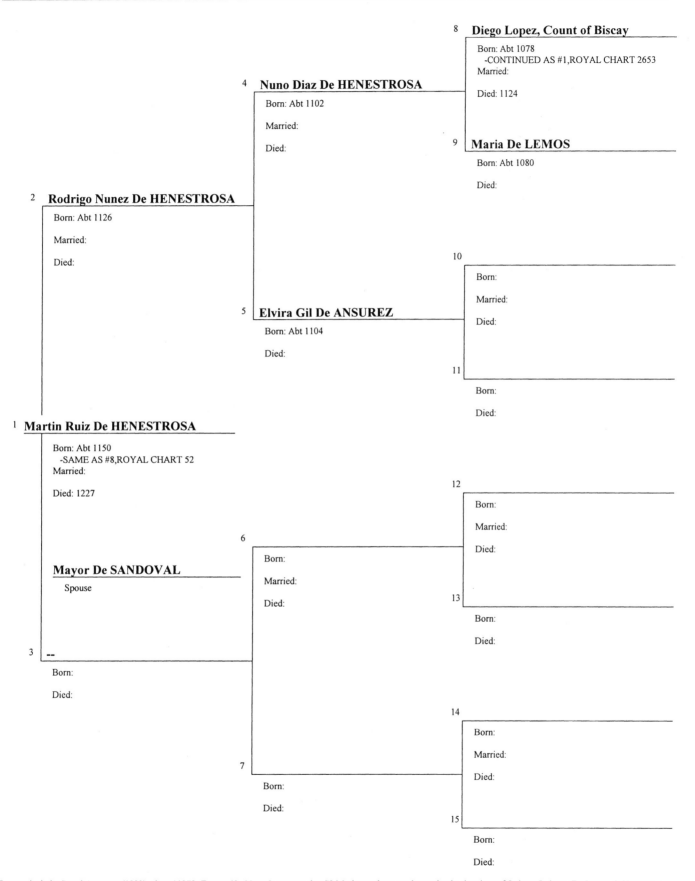

8 Diego Lopez, Count of Biscay
Born: Abt 1078
   -CONTINUED AS #1,ROYAL CHART 2653
Married:

Died: 1124

4 Nuno Diaz De HENESTROSA
Born: Abt 1102

Married:

Died:

9 Maria De LEMOS
Born: Abt 1080

Died:

2 Rodrigo Nunez De HENESTROSA
Born: Abt 1126

Married:

Died:

10
Born:

Married:

Died:

5 Elvira Gil De ANSUREZ
Born: Abt 1104

Died:

11
Born:

Died:

1 Martin Ruiz De HENESTROSA
Born: Abt 1150
   -SAME AS #8,ROYAL CHART 52
Married:

Died: 1227

12
Born:

Married:

Died:

6
Born:

Married:

Died:

Mayor De SANDOVAL
   Spouse

13
Born:

Died:

3 --
Born:

Died:

14
Born:

Married:

Died:

7
Born:

Died:

15
Born:

Died:

Sources include: *Royal Ancestors* (1989), chart 11379; Turton 62. Note: It appears that #9 Maria was born too late to be the daughter of Ordono Ordonez De Lemos & Urraca De Aza (see chart 1589, #8 & 9), as claimed by Turton, although this is possible.

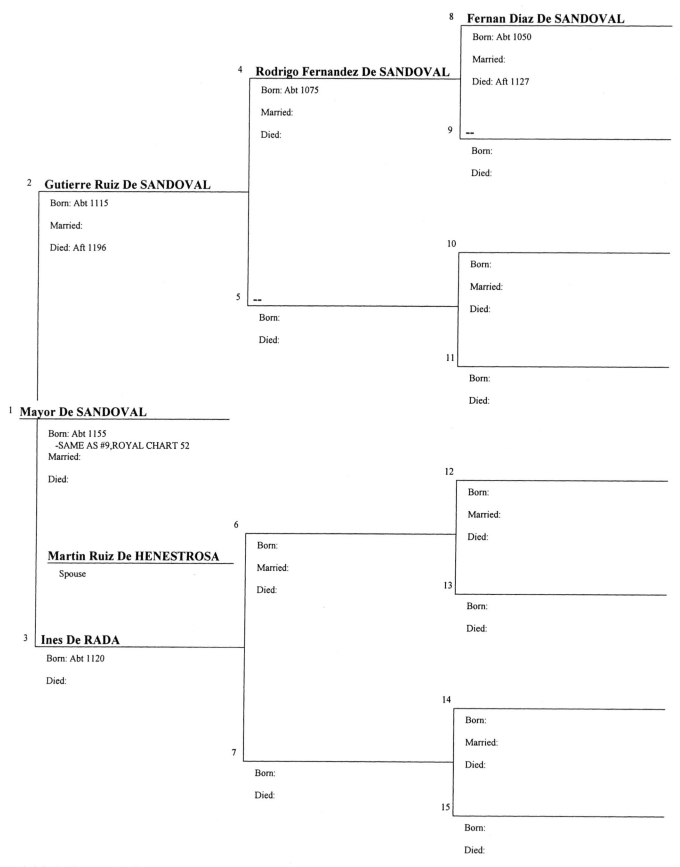

8 Fernan Diaz De SANDOVAL

Born: Abt 1050

Married:

Died: Aft 1127

4 Rodrigo Fernandez De SANDOVAL

Born: Abt 1075

Married:

Died:

9 --

Born:

Died:

2 Gutierre Ruiz De SANDOVAL

Born: Abt 1115

Married:

Died: Aft 1196

10

Born:

Married:

Died:

5 --

Born:

Died:

11

Born:

Died:

1 Mayor De SANDOVAL

Born: Abt 1155
-SAME AS #9,ROYAL CHART 52
Married:

Died:

12

Born:

Married:

Died:

6

Born:

Married:

Died:

13

Born:

Died:

Martin Ruiz De HENESTROSA

Spouse

3 Ines De RADA

Born: Abt 1120

Died:

14

Born:

Married:

Died:

7

Born:

Died:

15

Born:

Died:

Sources include: *Royal Ancestors* (1989), chart 11379; Turton 62. Note: #8 Fernan is claimed by Turton to be the son of Diego Gomez de Sandoval & Maria Rodriguez De Asturias (see chart 2636, #2 & 3). The claim is chronologically untenable.

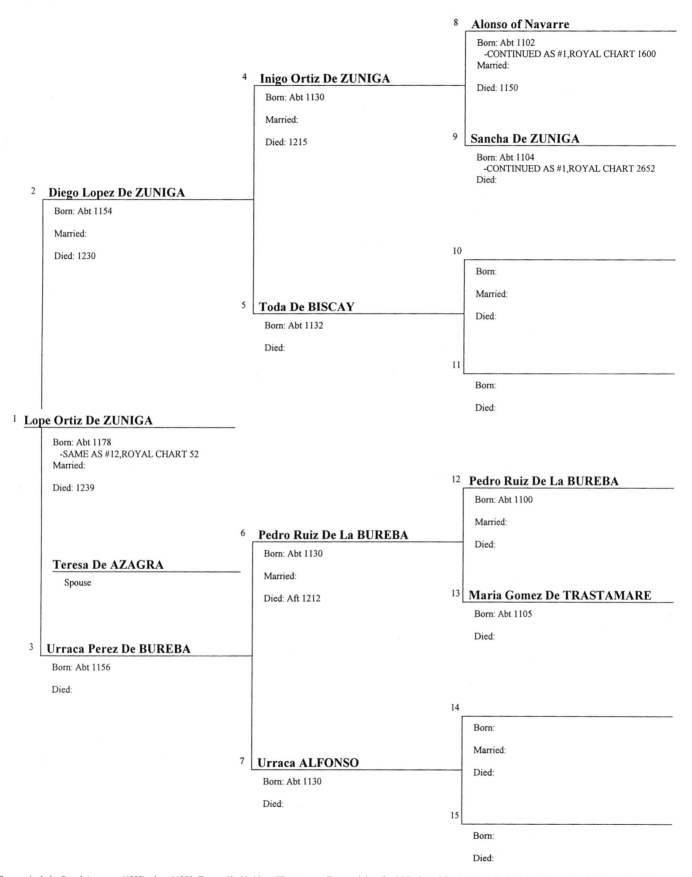

8 Alonso of Navarre

Born: Abt 1102
-CONTINUED AS #1,ROYAL CHART 1600
Married:

Died: 1150

4 Inigo Ortiz De ZUNIGA

Born: Abt 1130

Married:

Died: 1215

9 Sancha De ZUNIGA

Born: Abt 1104
-CONTINUED AS #1,ROYAL CHART 2652
Died:

2 Diego Lopez De ZUNIGA

Born: Abt 1154

Married:

Died: 1230

10

Born:

Married:

Died:

5 Toda De BISCAY

Born: Abt 1132

Died:

11

Born:

Died:

1 Lope Ortiz De ZUNIGA

Born: Abt 1178
-SAME AS #12,ROYAL CHART 52
Married:

Died: 1239

Teresa De AZAGRA

Spouse

12 Pedro Ruiz De La BUREBA

Born: Abt 1100

Married:

Died:

6 Pedro Ruiz De La BUREBA

Born: Abt 1130

Married:

Died: Aft 1212

13 Maria Gomez De TRASTAMARE

Born: Abt 1105

Died:

3 Urraca Perez De BUREBA

Born: Abt 1156

Died:

14

Born:

Married:

Died:

7 Urraca ALFONSO

Born: Abt 1130

Died:

15

Born:

Died:

Sources include: *Royal Ancestors* (1989), chart 11380; Turton 63, 66. Note: The ancestry Turton claims for #5 Toda and for #12 & 13 Pedro & Maria is chronologically untenable. He claims #5 Toda as daughter of Diego Lopez (Count of Biscay) & Toda Perez De Azagra, but it appears they were born too late (perhaps about 1150) to be parents of #5.

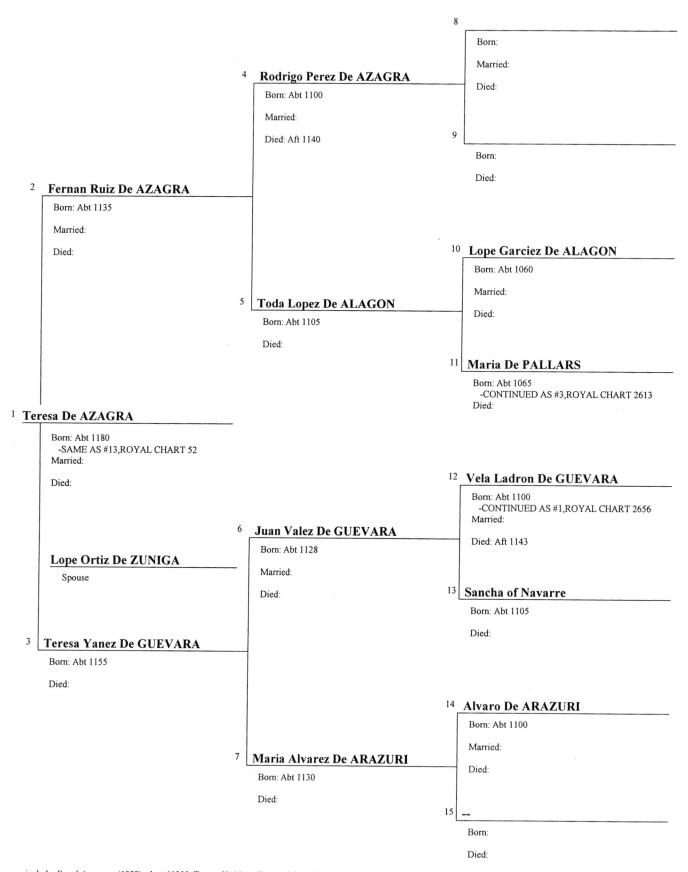

8

Born:

Married:

Died:

4   **Rodrigo Perez De AZAGRA**

Born: Abt 1100

Married:

Died: Aft 1140

9

Born:

Died:

2   **Fernan Ruiz De AZAGRA**

Born: Abt 1135

Married:

Died:

10   **Lope Garciez De ALAGON**

Born: Abt 1060

Married:

Died:

5   **Toda Lopez De ALAGON**

Born: Abt 1105

Died:

11   **Maria De PALLARS**

Born: Abt 1065
     -CONTINUED AS #3,ROYAL CHART 2613

Died:

1   **Teresa De AZAGRA**

Born: Abt 1180
     -SAME AS #13,ROYAL CHART 52

Married:

Died:

12   **Vela Ladron De GUEVARA**

Born: Abt 1100
     -CONTINUED AS #1,ROYAL CHART 2656

Married:

Died: Aft 1143

6   **Juan Valez De GUEVARA**

Born: Abt 1128

Married:

Died:

13   **Sancha of Navarre**

Born: Abt 1105

Died:

Lope Ortiz De ZUNIGA

Spouse

3   **Teresa Yanez De GUEVARA**

Born: Abt 1155

Died:

14   **Alvaro De ARAZURI**

Born: Abt 1100

Married:

Died:

7   **Maria Alvarez De ARAZURI**

Born: Abt 1130

Died:

15   --

Born:

Died:

Sources include: *Royal Ancestors* (1989), chart 11380; Turton 67. Note: Turton claims #13 Sancha as daughter of Garcia V, King of Navarre (see cht. 1520, #2) by his 2nd wife Urraca of Castile (md. 24 Jun 1144). This is incorrect and not chronologically possible. Schwennicke 2:56 shows they had a daughter Sancha who married twice but did <u>not</u> marry #12 Vela.

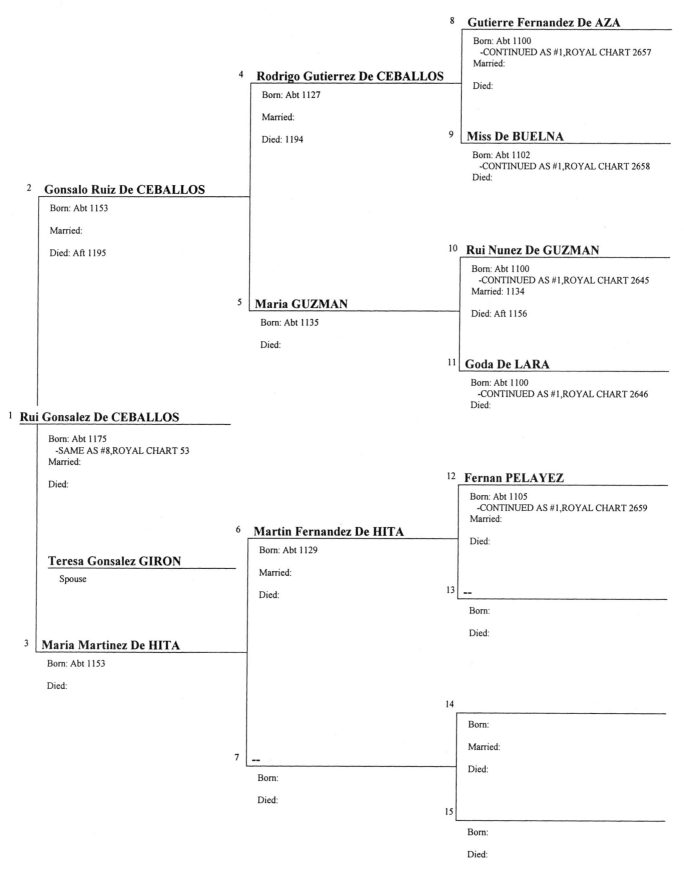

8 Gutierre Fernandez De AZA

Born: Abt 1100
-CONTINUED AS #1,ROYAL CHART 2657
Married:

Died:

4 Rodrigo Gutierrez De CEBALLOS

Born: Abt 1127

Married:

Died: 1194

9 Miss De BUELNA

Born: Abt 1102
-CONTINUED AS #1,ROYAL CHART 2658
Died:

2 Gonsalo Ruiz De CEBALLOS

Born: Abt 1153

Married:

Died: Aft 1195

10 Rui Nunez De GUZMAN

Born: Abt 1100
-CONTINUED AS #1,ROYAL CHART 2645
Married: 1134

Died: Aft 1156

5 Maria GUZMAN

Born: Abt 1135

Died:

11 Goda De LARA

Born: Abt 1100
-CONTINUED AS #1,ROYAL CHART 2646
Died:

1 Rui Gonsalez De CEBALLOS

Born: Abt 1175
-SAME AS #8,ROYAL CHART 53
Married:

Died:

Teresa Gonsalez GIRON

Spouse

12 Fernan PELAYEZ

Born: Abt 1105
-CONTINUED AS #1,ROYAL CHART 2659
Married:

Died:

6 Martin Fernandez De HITA

Born: Abt 1129

Married:

Died:

13 --

Born:

Died:

3 Maria Martinez De HITA

Born: Abt 1153

Died:

14

Born:

Married:

Died:

7 --

Born:

Died:

15

Born:

Died:

Sources include: *Royal Ancestors* (1989), chart 11381; Turton 68-69.

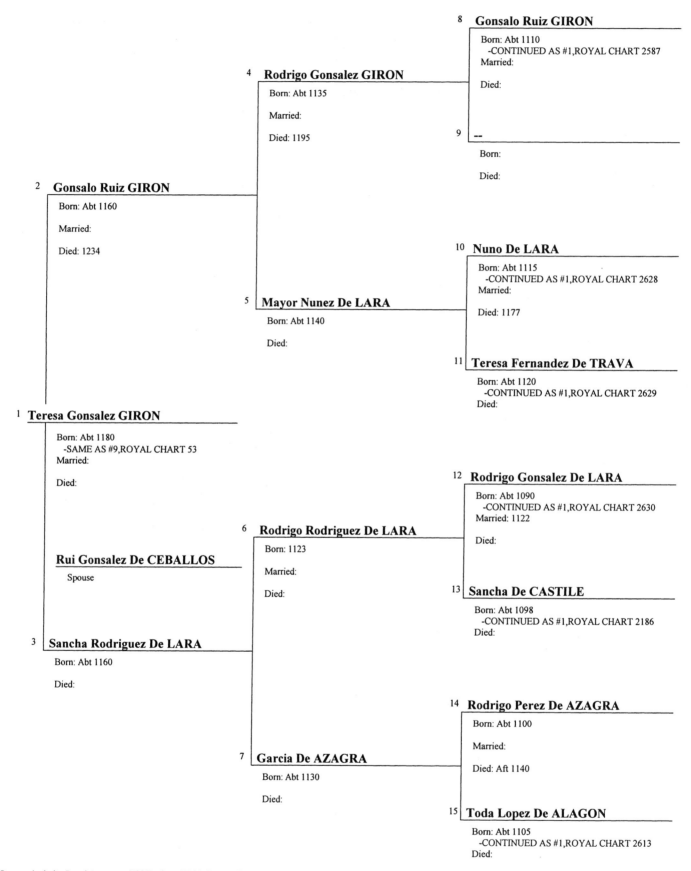

8 **Gonsalo Ruiz GIRON**

Born: Abt 1110
-CONTINUED AS #1,ROYAL CHART 2587
Married:

Died:

4 **Rodrigo Gonsalez GIRON**

Born: Abt 1135

Married:

Died: 1195

9 **--**

Born:

Died:

2 **Gonsalo Ruiz GIRON**

Born: Abt 1160

Married:

Died: 1234

10 **Nuno De LARA**

Born: Abt 1115
-CONTINUED AS #1,ROYAL CHART 2628
Married:

Died: 1177

5 **Mayor Nunez De LARA**

Born: Abt 1140

Died:

11 **Teresa Fernandez De TRAVA**

Born: Abt 1120
-CONTINUED AS #1,ROYAL CHART 2629
Died:

1 **Teresa Gonsalez GIRON**

Born: Abt 1180
-SAME AS #9,ROYAL CHART 53
Married:

Died:

12 **Rodrigo Gonsalez De LARA**

Born: Abt 1090
-CONTINUED AS #1,ROYAL CHART 2630
Married: 1122

Died:

6 **Rodrigo Rodriguez De LARA**

Born: 1123

Married:

Died:

Rui Gonsalez De CEBALLOS

Spouse

13 **Sancha De CASTILE**

Born: Abt 1098
-CONTINUED AS #1,ROYAL CHART 2186
Died:

3 **Sancha Rodriguez De LARA**

Born: Abt 1160

Died:

14 **Rodrigo Perez De AZAGRA**

Born: Abt 1100

Married:

Died: Aft 1140

7 **Garcia De AZAGRA**

Born: Abt 1130

Died:

15 **Toda Lopez De ALAGON**

Born: Abt 1105
-CONTINUED AS #1,ROYAL CHART 2613
Died:

Sources include: *Royal Ancestors* (1989), chart 11381; Turton 68, 54.

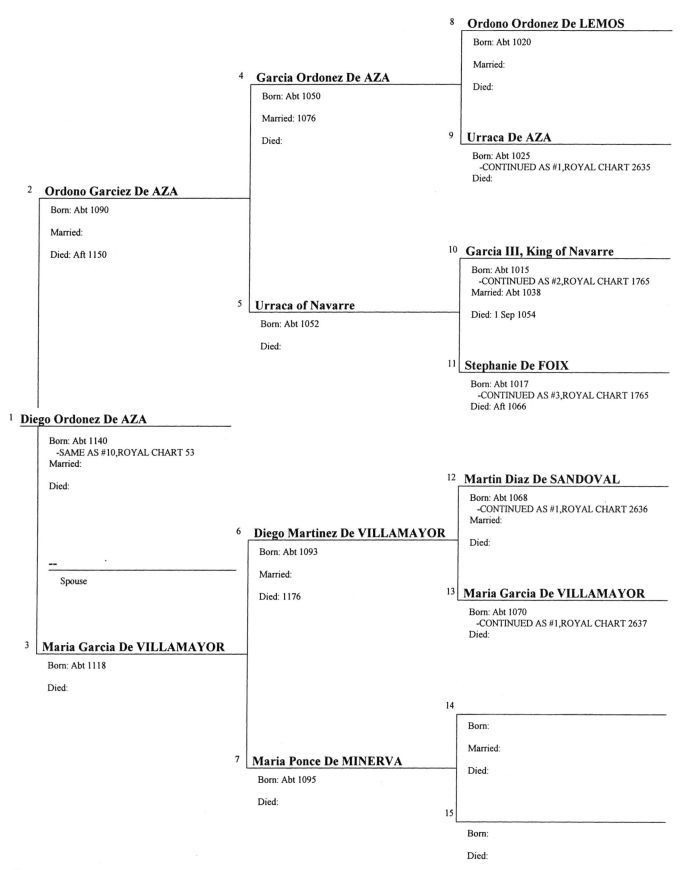

8 Ordono Ordonez De LEMOS

Born: Abt 1020

Married:

Died:

4 Garcia Ordonez De AZA

Born: Abt 1050

Married: 1076

Died:

9 Urraca De AZA

Born: Abt 1025
  -CONTINUED AS #1,ROYAL CHART 2635
Died:

2 Ordono Garciez De AZA

Born: Abt 1090

Married:

Died: Aft 1150

10 Garcia III, King of Navarre

Born: Abt 1015
  -CONTINUED AS #2,ROYAL CHART 1765
Married: Abt 1038

Died: 1 Sep 1054

5 Urraca of Navarre

Born: Abt 1052

Died:

11 Stephanie De FOIX

Born: Abt 1017
  -CONTINUED AS #3,ROYAL CHART 1765
Died: Aft 1066

1 Diego Ordonez De AZA

Born: Abt 1140
  -SAME AS #10,ROYAL CHART 53
Married:

Died:

--
Spouse

12 Martin Diaz De SANDOVAL

Born: Abt 1068
  -CONTINUED AS #1,ROYAL CHART 2636
Married:

Died:

6 Diego Martinez De VILLAMAYOR

Born: Abt 1093

Married:

Died: 1176

13 Maria Garcia De VILLAMAYOR

Born: Abt 1070
  -CONTINUED AS #1,ROYAL CHART 2637
Died:

3 Maria Garcia De VILLAMAYOR

Born: Abt 1118

Died:

14

Born:

Married:

Died:

7 Maria Ponce De MINERVA

Born: Abt 1095

Died:

15

Born:

Died:

Sources include: Turton 37, 45. Note: The parentage and ancestry claimed by Turton for #7 Maria is unacceptable chronologically.

8 Ansur Perez De VALLADOLID
Born: Abt 996
 -CONTINUED AS #1,ROYAL CHART 2660
Married:

Died:

4 Diego Ansurez De CIFONTES
Born: Abt 1035

Married:

Died:

9 Juliana De MONCON
Born: Abt 996
 -CONTINUED AS #1,ROYAL CHART 2661
Died:

2 Fruela Diaz De CIFONTES
Born: Abt 1065

Married: 1087

Died: Bef 1121

10 Pelayo Pelayez De CISNEROS
Born: Abt 990
 -CONTINUED AS #1,ROYAL CHART 2662
Married:

Died:

5 Maria Pelayez De CISNEROS
Born: Abt 1043

Died:

11 Mayor GONSALEZ
Born: Abt 1010

Died:

1 Ramiro Fruelaz De CIFONTES
Born: Abt 1110
 -SAME AS #8,ROYAL CHART 54
Married:

Died:

Elvira OSORIEZ
Spouse

12 Garcia III, King of Navarre
Born: Abt 1015
 -CONTINUED AS #2,ROYAL CHART 1765
Married: Abt 1038

Died: 1 Sep 1054

6 Ramiro, Prince of Navarre
Born: Abt 1043

Married:

Died: 6 Jan 1083

13 Stephanie De FOIX
Born: Abt 1017
 -CONTINUED AS #3,ROYAL CHART 1765
Died: Aft 1066

3 Estephania RAMIREZ
Born: Abt 1070

Died:

14 Gonzalo SALVADORES
Born: Abt 1015

Married:

Died:

7 Teresa GONZALEZ
Born: Abt 1045

Died:

15 Elvira
Born:

Died:

Sources include: *Royal Ancestors* (1989), chart 11383; Turton 71; Schwennicke 2:56 (corrected #3 ancestry). Notes: See note chart 1596 regarding #1 Ramiro and another claim that conflicts chronologically. The ancestry shown for #5 Maria seems uncertain. It requires a big stretch chronologically and dismissal of Turton's claim that #10 Pelayo was living as late as about 1111.

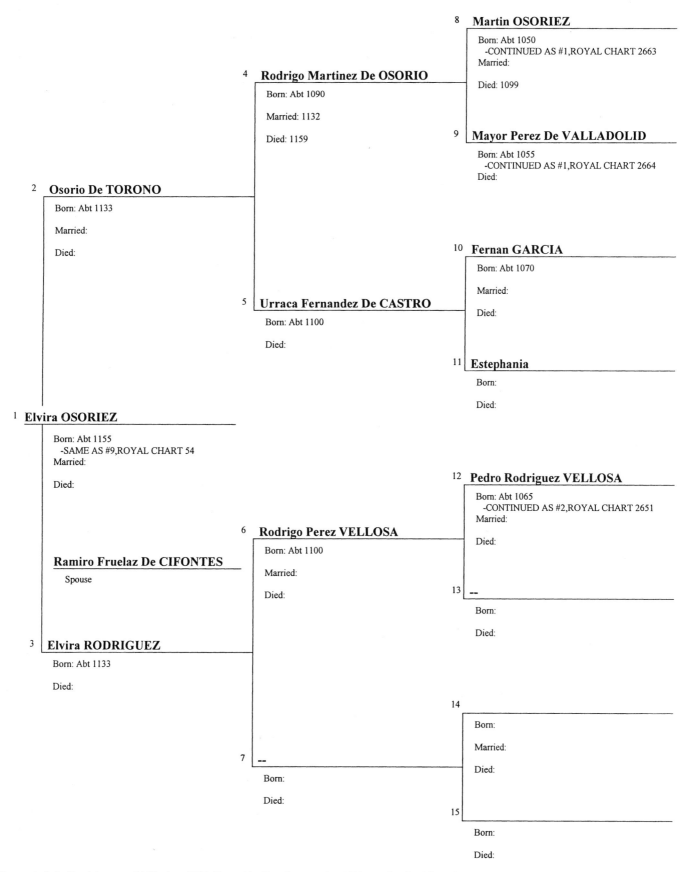

8 Martin OSORIEZ

Born: Abt 1050
 -CONTINUED AS #1,ROYAL CHART 2663
Married:

Died: 1099

4 Rodrigo Martinez De OSORIO

Born: Abt 1090

Married: 1132

Died: 1159

9 Mayor Perez De VALLADOLID

Born: Abt 1055
 -CONTINUED AS #1,ROYAL CHART 2664
Died:

2 Osorio De TORONO

Born: Abt 1133

Married:

Died:

10 Fernan GARCIA

Born: Abt 1070

Married:

Died:

5 Urraca Fernandez De CASTRO

Born: Abt 1100

Died:

11 Estephania

Born:

Died:

1 Elvira OSORIEZ

Born: Abt 1155
 -SAME AS #9,ROYAL CHART 54
Married:

Died:

12 Pedro Rodriguez VELLOSA

Born: Abt 1065
 -CONTINUED AS #2,ROYAL CHART 2651
Married:

Died:

6 Rodrigo Perez VELLOSA

Born: Abt 1100

Married:

Died:

13 --

Born:

Died:

Ramiro Fruelaz De CIFONTES

Spouse

3 Elvira RODRIGUEZ

Born: Abt 1133

Died:

14

Born:

Married:

Died:

7 --

Born:

Died:

15

Born:

Died:

Sources include: *Royal Ancestors* (1989), chart 11383; Turton 71. Note: See note chart 1596 regarding #1 Elvira and her husband Ramiro and another claim that conflicts chronologically.

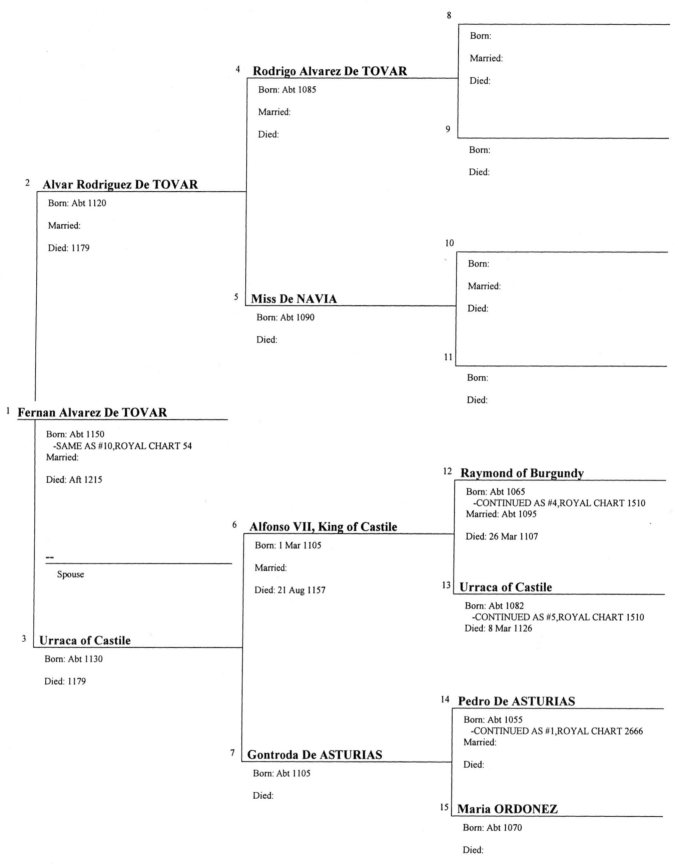

8

Born:

Married:

Died:

4 Rodrigo Alvarez De TOVAR

Born: Abt 1085

Married:

Died:

9

Born:

Died:

2 Alvar Rodriguez De TOVAR

Born: Abt 1120

Married:

Died: 1179

10

Born:

Married:

Died:

5 Miss De NAVIA

Born: Abt 1090

Died:

11

Born:

Died:

1 Fernan Alvarez De TOVAR

Born: Abt 1150
 -SAME AS #10,ROYAL CHART 54
Married:

Died: Aft 1215

12 Raymond of Burgundy

Born: Abt 1065
 -CONTINUED AS #4,ROYAL CHART 1510
Married: Abt 1095

Died: 26 Mar 1107

6 Alfonso VII, King of Castile

Born: 1 Mar 1105

Married:

Died: 21 Aug 1157

13 Urraca of Castile

Born: Abt 1082
 -CONTINUED AS #5,ROYAL CHART 1510
Died: 8 Mar 1126

--

Spouse

3 Urraca of Castile

Born: Abt 1130

Died: 1179

14 Pedro De ASTURIAS

Born: Abt 1055
 -CONTINUED AS #1,ROYAL CHART 2666
Married:

Died:

7 Gontroda De ASTURIAS

Born: Abt 1105

Died:

15 Maria ORDONEZ

Born: Abt 1070

Died:

Sources include: *Royal Ancestors* (1989), chart 11383; Turton 71, 38; Von Isenburg 2:47 (#3 ancestry).

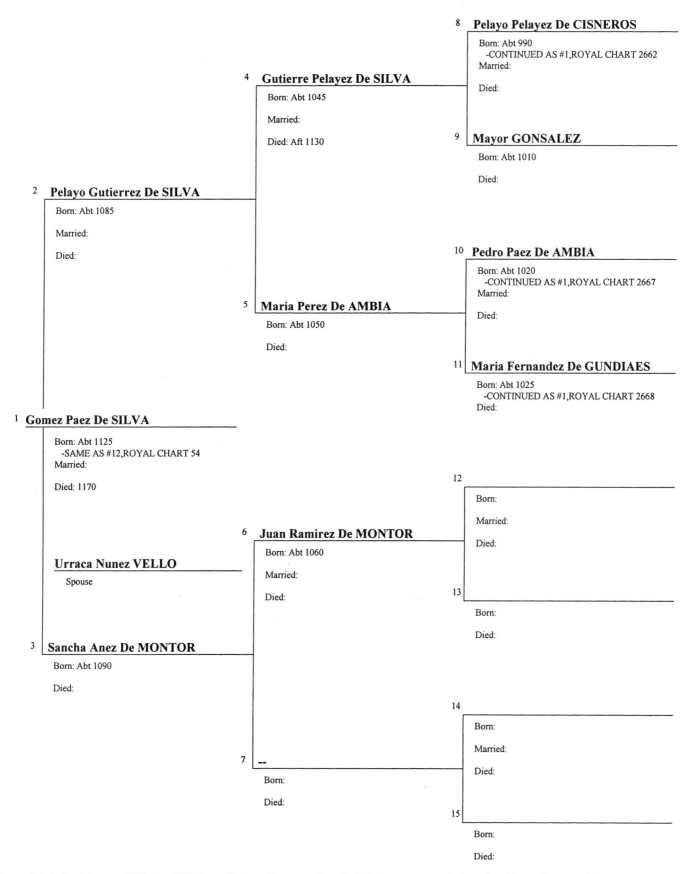

8 Pelayo Pelayez De CISNEROS

Born: Abt 990
-CONTINUED AS #1,ROYAL CHART 2662
Married:

Died:

4 Gutierre Pelayez De SILVA

Born: Abt 1045

Married:

Died: Aft 1130

9 Mayor GONSALEZ

Born: Abt 1010

Died:

2 Pelayo Gutierrez De SILVA

Born: Abt 1085

Married:

Died:

10 Pedro Paez De AMBIA

Born: Abt 1020
-CONTINUED AS #1,ROYAL CHART 2667
Married:

Died:

5 Maria Perez De AMBIA

Born: Abt 1050

Died:

11 Maria Fernandez De GUNDIAES

Born: Abt 1025
-CONTINUED AS #1,ROYAL CHART 2668
Died:

1 Gomez Paez De SILVA

Born: Abt 1125
-SAME AS #12,ROYAL CHART 54
Married:

Died: 1170

12

Born:

Married:

Died:

6 Juan Ramirez De MONTOR

Born: Abt 1060

Married:

Died:

13

Born:

Died:

Urraca Nunez VELLO

Spouse

3 Sancha Anez De MONTOR

Born: Abt 1090

Died:

14

Born:

Married:

Died:

7 --

Born:

Died:

15

Born:

Died:

Sources include: *Royal Ancestors* (1989), chart 11384; Turton 70. Notes: The ancestry shown for #4 Gutierre seems uncertain. It requires a big stretch chronologically and dismissal of Turton's claim that #8 Pelayo was living as late as about 1111. The claim by Turton that #6 Juan was son of Ramiro Frade and grandson of Frade Valdrique (living about 950) is chronologically untenable.

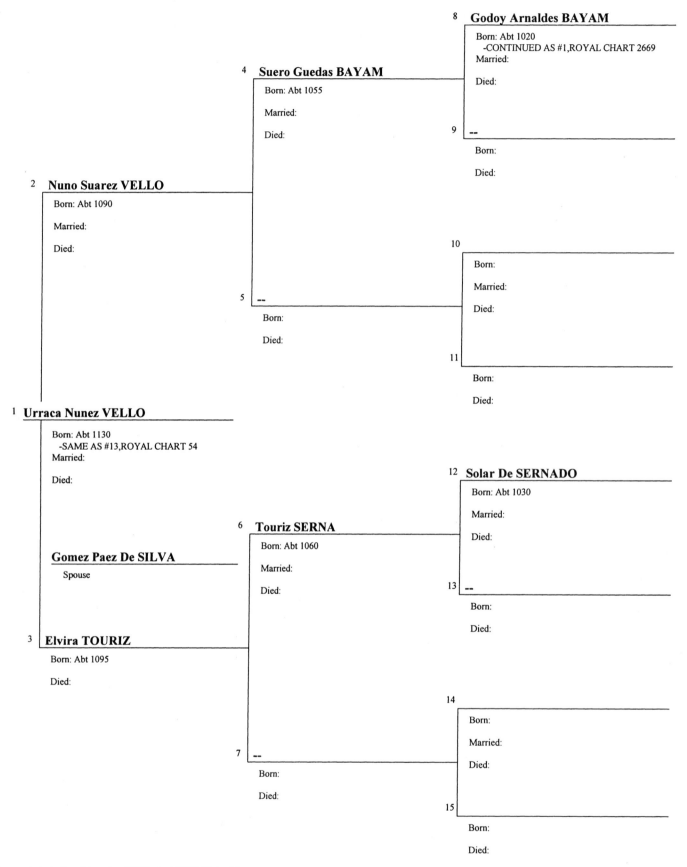

8 Godoy Arnaldes BAYAM

Born: Abt 1020
  -CONTINUED AS #1,ROYAL CHART 2669
Married:

Died:

4 Suero Guedas BAYAM

Born: Abt 1055

Married:

Died:

9 --

Born:

Died:

2 Nuno Suarez VELLO

Born: Abt 1090

Married:

Died:

10

Born:

Married:

Died:

5 --

Born:

Died:

11

Born:

Died:

1 Urraca Nunez VELLO

Born: Abt 1130
  -SAME AS #13,ROYAL CHART 54
Married:

Died:

12 Solar De SERNADO

Born: Abt 1030

Married:

Died:

6 Touriz SERNA

Born: Abt 1060

Married:

Died:

13 --

Born:

Died:

Gomez Paez De SILVA

Spouse

3 Elvira TOURIZ

Born: Abt 1095

Died:

14

Born:

Married:

Died:

7 --

Born:

Died:

15

Born:

Died:

Sources include: *Royal Ancestors* (1989), chart 11384; Turton 70.

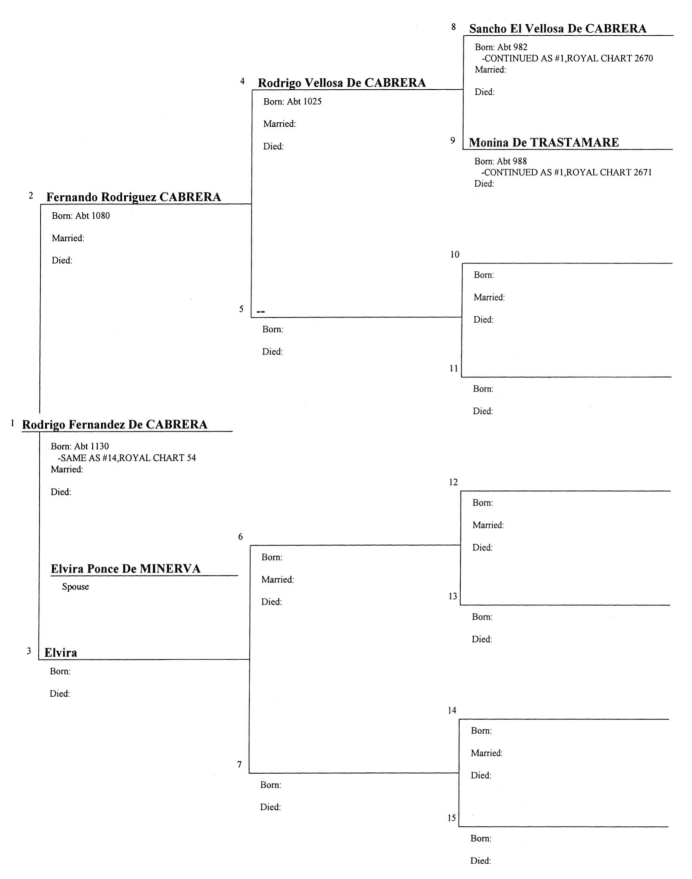

8 | **Sancho El Vellosa De CABRERA**

Born: Abt 982
-CONTINUED AS #1,ROYAL CHART 2670
Married:

Died:

4 | **Rodrigo Vellosa De CABRERA**

Born: Abt 1025

Married:

Died:

9 | **Monina De TRASTAMARE**

Born: Abt 988
-CONTINUED AS #1,ROYAL CHART 2671
Died:

2 | **Fernando Rodriguez CABRERA**

Born: Abt 1080

Married:

Died:

10

Born:

Married:

Died:

5 | **--**

Born:

Died:

11

Born:

Died:

1 | **Rodrigo Fernandez De CABRERA**

Born: Abt 1130
-SAME AS #14,ROYAL CHART 54
Married:

Died:

12

Born:

Married:

Died:

6

Born:

Married:

Died:

13

Born:

Died:

Elvira Ponce De MINERVA

Spouse

3 | **Elvira**

Born:

Died:

14

Born:

Married:

Died:

7

Born:

Died:

15

Born:

Died:

Sources include: *Royal Ancestors* (1989), chart 11384; Turton 70, 53.

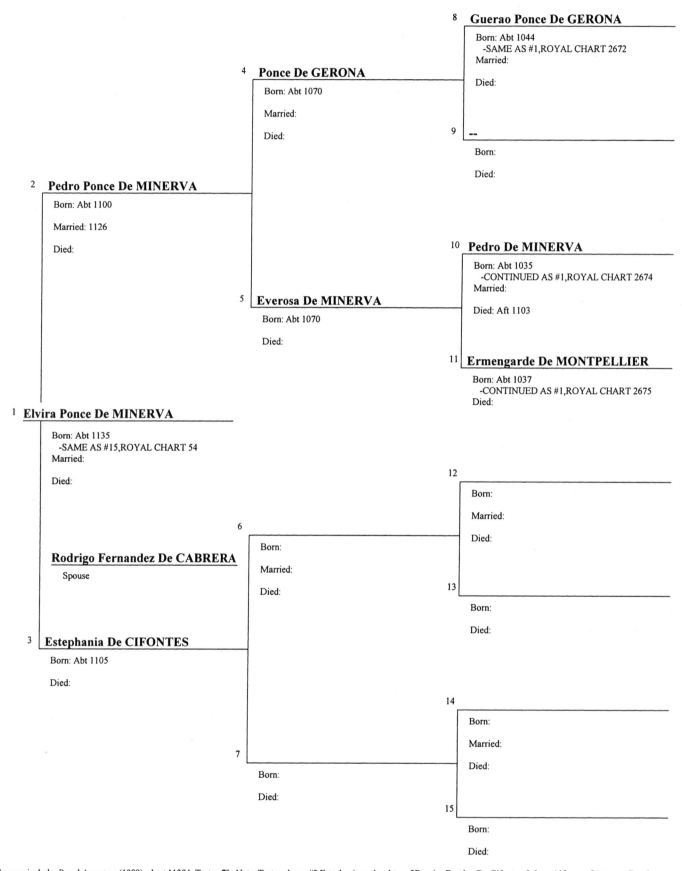

8 Guerao Ponce De GERONA

Born: Abt 1044
-SAME AS #1,ROYAL CHART 2672
Married:

Died:

4 Ponce De GERONA

Born: Abt 1070

Married:

Died:

9 --

Born:

Died:

2 Pedro Ponce De MINERVA

Born: Abt 1100

Married: 1126

Died:

10 Pedro De MINERVA

Born: Abt 1035
-CONTINUED AS #1,ROYAL CHART 2674
Married:

Died: Aft 1103

5 Everosa De MINERVA

Born: Abt 1070

Died:

11 Ermengarde De MONTPELLIER

Born: Abt 1037
-CONTINUED AS #1,ROYAL CHART 2675
Died:

1 Elvira Ponce De MINERVA

Born: Abt 1135
-SAME AS #15,ROYAL CHART 54
Married:

Died:

12

Born:

Married:

Died:

6

Born:

Married:

Died:

Rodrigo Fernandez De CABRERA

Spouse

13

Born:

Died:

3 Estephania De CIFONTES

Born: Abt 1105

Died:

14

Born:

Married:

Died:

7

Born:

Died:

15

Born:

Died:

Sources include: *Royal Ancestors* (1989), chart 11384; Turton 70. Note: Turton shows #3 Estephania as daughter of Ramiro Fruelaz De Cifontes & Inez Alfonso of Astorga. Ramiro is claimed to be the same person as #1, chart 1590 who married Elvira Osoriez as a 2nd wife (see also chart 1591). Chronologically, the claim shown on charts 1590-1591 and the claim for the parentage of #3 above cannot both be true. The 1590-1591 version is being tentatively retained.

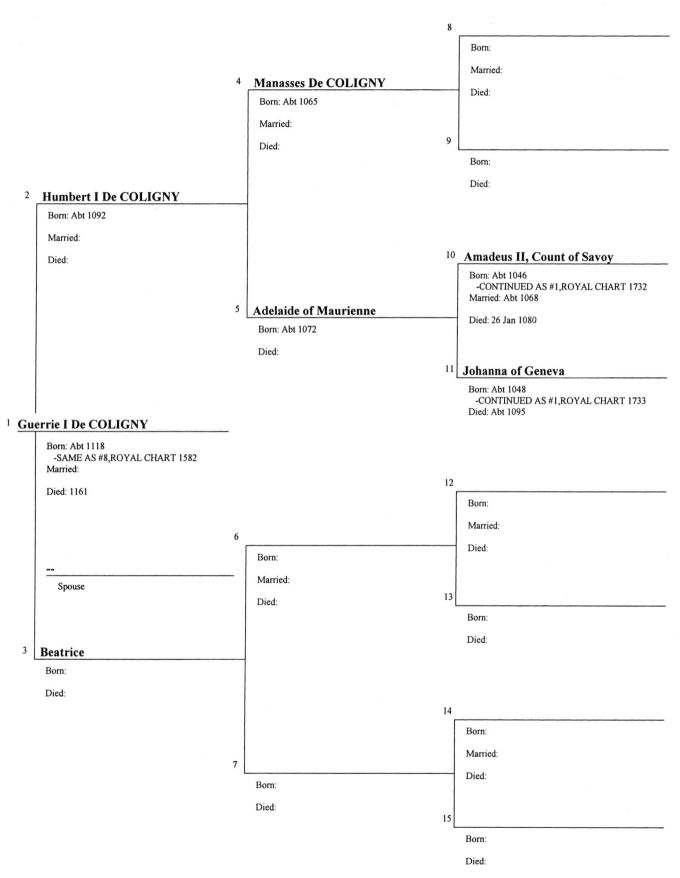

8

Born:

Married:

Died:

4 Manasses De COLIGNY

Born: Abt 1065

Married:

Died:

9

Born:

Died:

2 Humbert I De COLIGNY

Born: Abt 1092

Married:

Died:

10 Amadeus II, Count of Savoy

Born: Abt 1046
  -CONTINUED AS #1,ROYAL CHART 1732
Married: Abt 1068

Died: 26 Jan 1080

5 Adelaide of Maurienne

Born: Abt 1072

Died:

11 Johanna of Geneva

Born: Abt 1048
  -CONTINUED AS #1,ROYAL CHART 1733
Died: Abt 1095

1 Guerrie I De COLIGNY

Born: Abt 1118
  -SAME AS #8,ROYAL CHART 1582
Married:

Died: 1161

12

Born:

Married:

Died:

6

Born:

Married:

Died:

13

Born:

Died:

--

Spouse

3 Beatrice

Born:

Died:

14

Born:

Married:

Died:

7

Born:

Died:

15

Born:

Died:

Sources include: *Royal Ancestors* (1989), chart 11827; Turton 61.

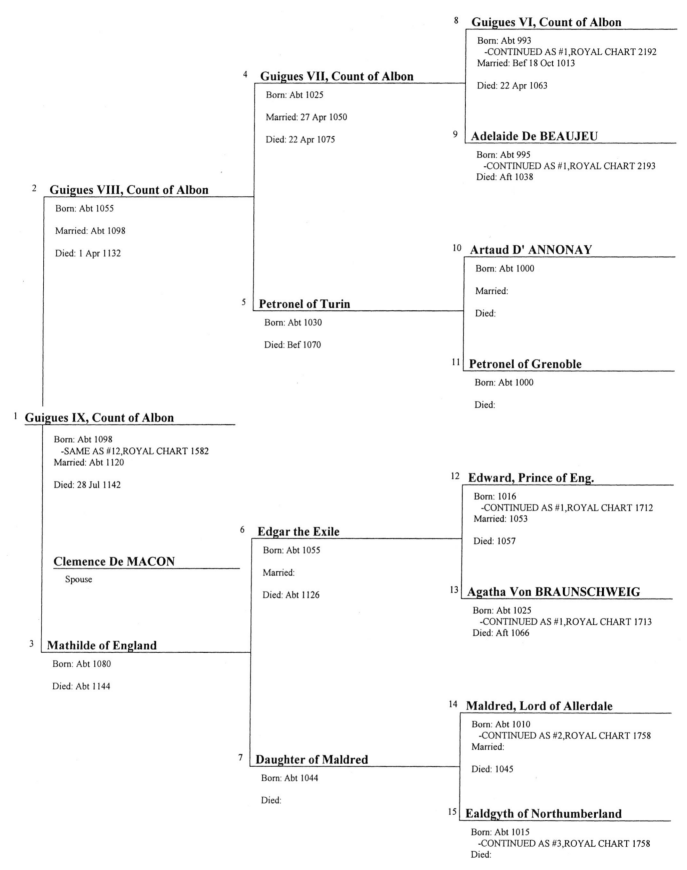

2 Guigues VIII, Count of Albon

Born: Abt 1055

Married: Abt 1098

Died: 1 Apr 1132

4 Guigues VII, Count of Albon

Born: Abt 1025

Married: 27 Apr 1050

Died: 22 Apr 1075

8 Guigues VI, Count of Albon

Born: Abt 993
 -CONTINUED AS #1,ROYAL CHART 2192
Married: Bef 18 Oct 1013

Died: 22 Apr 1063

9 Adelaide De BEAUJEU

Born: Abt 995
 -CONTINUED AS #1,ROYAL CHART 2193
Died: Aft 1038

5 Petronel of Turin

Born: Abt 1030

Died: Bef 1070

10 Artaud D' ANNONAY

Born: Abt 1000

Married:

Died:

11 Petronel of Grenoble

Born: Abt 1000

Died:

1 Guigues IX, Count of Albon

Born: Abt 1098
 -SAME AS #12,ROYAL CHART 1582
Married: Abt 1120

Died: 28 Jul 1142

Clemence De MACON

Spouse

3 Mathilde of England

Born: Abt 1080

Died: Abt 1144

6 Edgar the Exile

Born: Abt 1055

Married:

Died: Abt 1126

12 Edward, Prince of Eng.

Born: 1016
 -CONTINUED AS #1,ROYAL CHART 1712
Married: 1053

Died: 1057

13 Agatha Von BRAUNSCHWEIG

Born: Abt 1025
 -CONTINUED AS #1,ROYAL CHART 1713
Died: Aft 1066

7 Daughter of Maldred

Born: Abt 1044

Died:

14 Maldred, Lord of Allerdale

Born: Abt 1010
 -CONTINUED AS #2,ROYAL CHART 1758
Married:

Died: 1045

15 Ealdgyth of Northumberland

Born: Abt 1015
 -CONTINUED AS #3,ROYAL CHART 1758
Died:

Sources include: *Royal Ancestors* (1989), chart 11826; Faris preliminary Charlemagne manuscript (June 1995), pp. 278-279; Turton 177; Stuart 196; Moriarty 102. Note: The identification and ancestry of #3 Mathilde is disputed. See notes by Stuart 196, Faris 279 & 16, and Moriarty 102 & 259. Moriarty concluded that Mathilde was probably the daughter of Edgar the Exile.

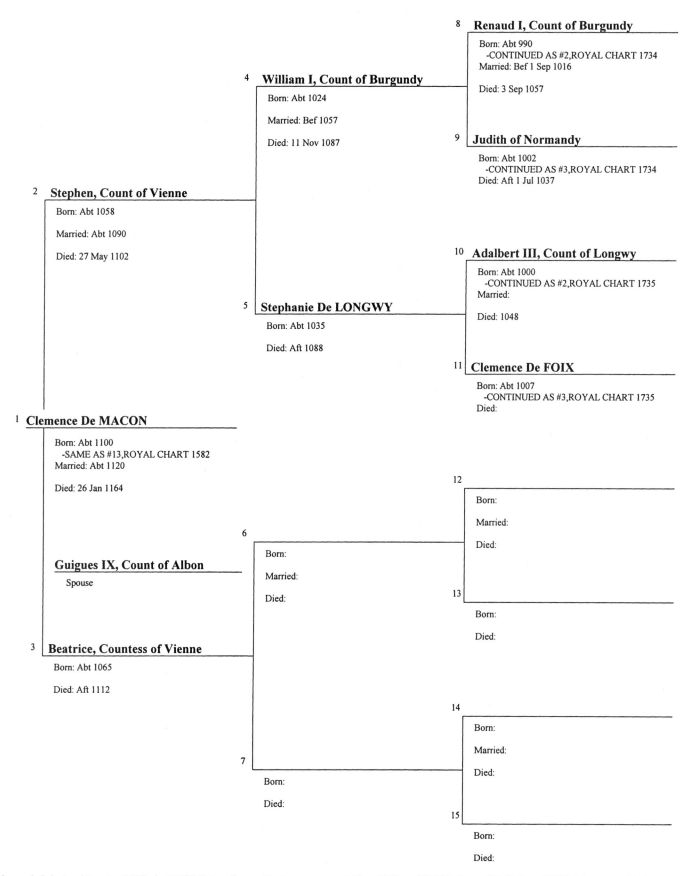

8 Renaud I, Count of Burgundy

Born: Abt 990
  -CONTINUED AS #2,ROYAL CHART 1734
Married: Bef 1 Sep 1016

Died: 3 Sep 1057

4 William I, Count of Burgundy

Born: Abt 1024

Married: Bef 1057

Died: 11 Nov 1087

9 Judith of Normandy

Born: Abt 1002
  -CONTINUED AS #3,ROYAL CHART 1734
Died: Aft 1 Jul 1037

2 Stephen, Count of Vienne

Born: Abt 1058

Married: Abt 1090

Died: 27 May 1102

10 Adalbert III, Count of Longwy

Born: Abt 1000
  -CONTINUED AS #2,ROYAL CHART 1735
Married:

Died: 1048

5 Stephanie De LONGWY

Born: Abt 1035

Died: Aft 1088

11 Clemence De FOIX

Born: Abt 1007
  -CONTINUED AS #3,ROYAL CHART 1735
Died:

1 Clemence De MACON

Born: Abt 1100
  -SAME AS #13,ROYAL CHART 1582
Married: Abt 1120

Died: 26 Jan 1164

12

Born:

Married:

Died:

6

Born:

Married:

Died:

Guigues IX, Count of Albon

Spouse

13

Born:

Died:

3 Beatrice, Countess of Vienne

Born: Abt 1065

Died: Aft 1112

14

Born:

Married:

Died:

7

Born:

Died:

15

Born:

Died:

Sources include: *Royal Ancestors* (1989), chart 11826; Faris preliminary Charlemagne manuscript (June 1995), pp. 279, 64-65; Turton 177, 42; Stuart 187 (#2 & 3 ancestry); Moriarty 105, 62 (#2 &3 ancestry). Note: The ancestry of #3 Beatrice (Beatrix) is disputed and uncertain.

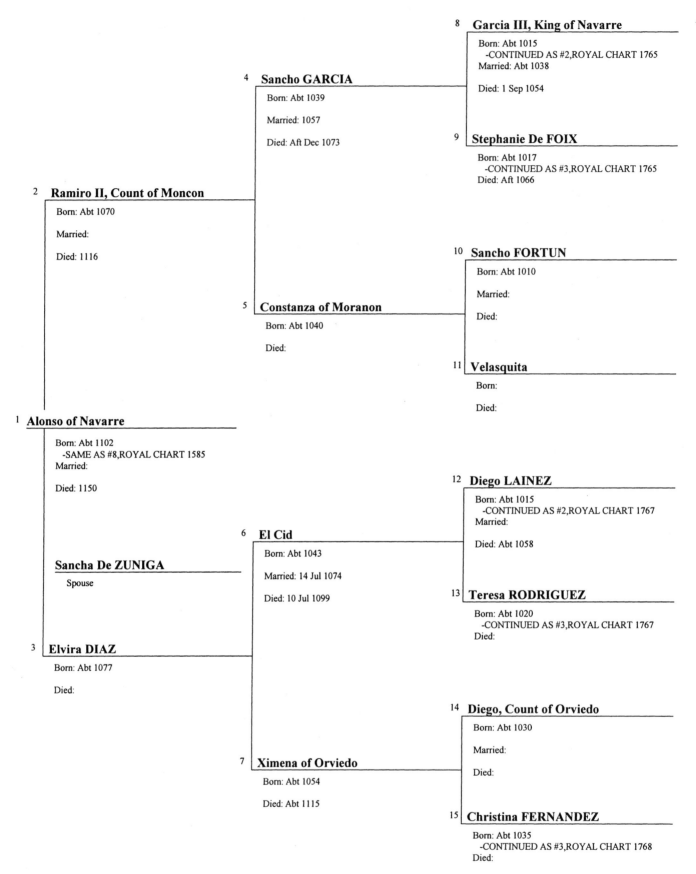

8 Garcia III, King of Navarre

Born: Abt 1015
-CONTINUED AS #2,ROYAL CHART 1765
Married: Abt 1038

Died: 1 Sep 1054

4 Sancho GARCIA

Born: Abt 1039

Married: 1057

Died: Aft Dec 1073

9 Stephanie De FOIX

Born: Abt 1017
-CONTINUED AS #3,ROYAL CHART 1765
Died: Aft 1066

2 Ramiro II, Count of Moncon

Born: Abt 1070

Married:

Died: 1116

10 Sancho FORTUN

Born: Abt 1010

Married:

Died:

5 Constanza of Moranon

Born: Abt 1040

Died:

11 Velasquita

Born:

Died:

1 Alonso of Navarre

Born: Abt 1102
-SAME AS #8,ROYAL CHART 1585
Married:

Died: 1150

12 Diego LAINEZ

Born: Abt 1015
-CONTINUED AS #2,ROYAL CHART 1767
Married:

Died: Abt 1058

6 El Cid

Born: Abt 1043

Married: 14 Jul 1074

Died: 10 Jul 1099

13 Teresa RODRIGUEZ

Born: Abt 1020
-CONTINUED AS #3,ROYAL CHART 1767
Died:

Sancha De ZUNIGA

Spouse

3 Elvira DIAZ

Born: Abt 1077

Died:

14 Diego, Count of Orviedo

Born: Abt 1030

Married:

Died:

7 Ximena of Orviedo

Born: Abt 1054

Died: Abt 1115

15 Christina FERNANDEZ

Born: Abt 1035
-CONTINUED AS #3,ROYAL CHART 1768
Died:

Sources include: Turton 63, 16; Stuart 151 (#2 & 3 ancestry); *NEHGR* 117:94-96 (#3 ancestry); Chart 1520 notes and sources.

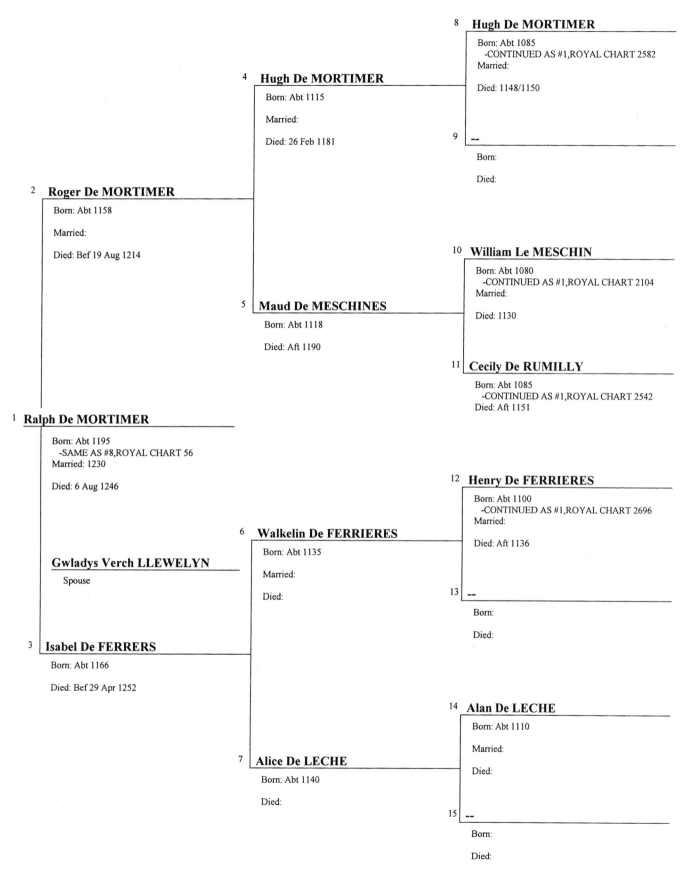

8 Hugh De MORTIMER

Born: Abt 1085
  -CONTINUED AS #1,ROYAL CHART 2582
Married:

Died: 1148/1150

4 Hugh De MORTIMER

Born: Abt 1115

Married:

Died: 26 Feb 1181

9 --

Born:

Died:

2 Roger De MORTIMER

Born: Abt 1158

Married:

Died: Bef 19 Aug 1214

10 William Le MESCHIN

Born: Abt 1080
  -CONTINUED AS #1,ROYAL CHART 2104
Married:

Died: 1130

5 Maud De MESCHINES

Born: Abt 1118

Died: Aft 1190

11 Cecily De RUMILLY

Born: Abt 1085
  -CONTINUED AS #1,ROYAL CHART 2542
Died: Aft 1151

1 Ralph De MORTIMER

Born: Abt 1195
  -SAME AS #8,ROYAL CHART 56
Married: 1230

Died: 6 Aug 1246

12 Henry De FERRIERES

Born: Abt 1100
  -CONTINUED AS #1,ROYAL CHART 2696
Married:

Died: Aft 1136

6 Walkelin De FERRIERES

Born: Abt 1135

Married:

Died:

13 --

Born:

Died:

Gwladys Verch LLEWELYN

Spouse

3 Isabel De FERRERS

Born: Abt 1166

Died: Bef 29 Apr 1252

14 Alan De LECHE

Born: Abt 1110

Married:

Died:

7 Alice De LECHE

Born: Abt 1140

Died:

15 --

Born:

Died:

Sources include: *Royal Ancestors* (1989), chart 11326 and notes; *Ancestral Roots* 132C; Faris preliminary baronial manuscript (1998), pp. 1126-28 (Mortimer), 586-587 (Ferrers or Ferrieres); Turton 76 (#7 & 14).

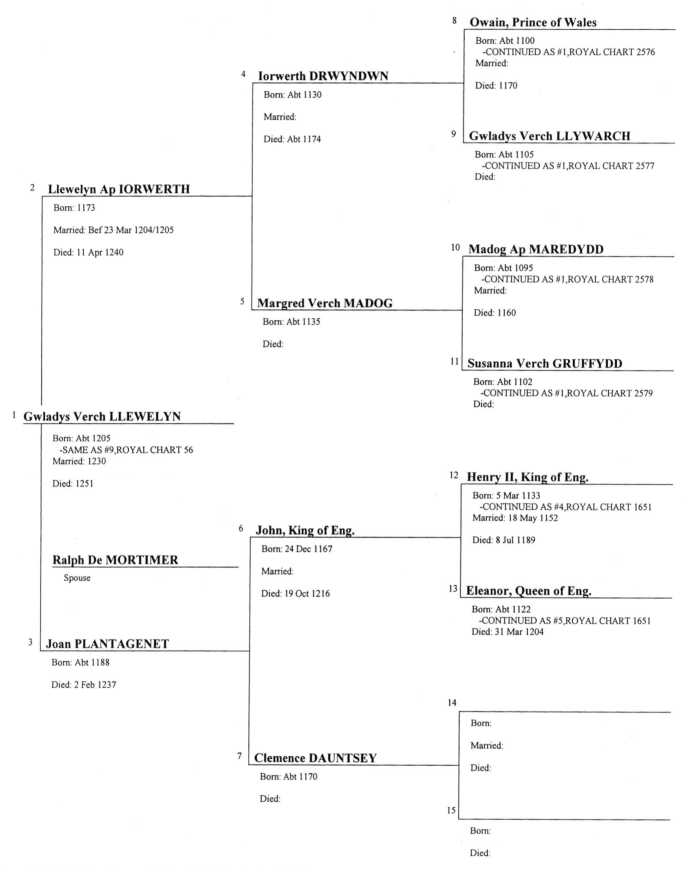

8 Owain, Prince of Wales

Born: Abt 1100
-CONTINUED AS #1,ROYAL CHART 2576
Married:

Died: 1170

4 Iorwerth DRWYNDWN

Born: Abt 1130

Married:

Died: Abt 1174

9 Gwladys Verch LLYWARCH

Born: Abt 1105
-CONTINUED AS #1,ROYAL CHART 2577
Died:

2 Llewelyn Ap IORWERTH

Born: 1173

Married: Bef 23 Mar 1204/1205

Died: 11 Apr 1240

10 Madog Ap MAREDYDD

Born: Abt 1095
-CONTINUED AS #1,ROYAL CHART 2578
Married:

Died: 1160

5 Margred Verch MADOG

Born: Abt 1135

Died:

11 Susanna Verch GRUFFYDD

Born: Abt 1102
-CONTINUED AS #1,ROYAL CHART 2579
Died:

1 Gwladys Verch LLEWELYN

Born: Abt 1205
-SAME AS #9,ROYAL CHART 56
Married: 1230

Died: 1251

12 Henry II, King of Eng.

Born: 5 Mar 1133
-CONTINUED AS #4,ROYAL CHART 1651
Married: 18 May 1152

Died: 8 Jul 1189

6 John, King of Eng.

Born: 24 Dec 1167

Married:

Died: 19 Oct 1216

13 Eleanor, Queen of Eng.

Born: Abt 1122
-CONTINUED AS #5,ROYAL CHART 1651
Died: 31 Mar 1204

Ralph De MORTIMER

Spouse

3 Joan PLANTAGENET

Born: Abt 1188

Died: 2 Feb 1237

14

Born:

Married:

Died:

7 Clemence DAUNTSEY

Born: Abt 1170

Died:

15

Born:

Died:

Sources include: Richardson *Plantagenet* (2004), pp. 520-521 (Mortimer), 742-744 (Wales), 3-11 (Plantagenet); *Royal Ancestors* (1989), charts 11326, 11347; *Ancestral Roots* 27, 176, 239; Turton 77, 128; Chart 1651 sources & note. Note: #3 (mother of Gwladys) is also claimed as a mistress Tangwystl Verch Llywarch. Richardson argues persuasively that Joan is the correct mother, as shown above.

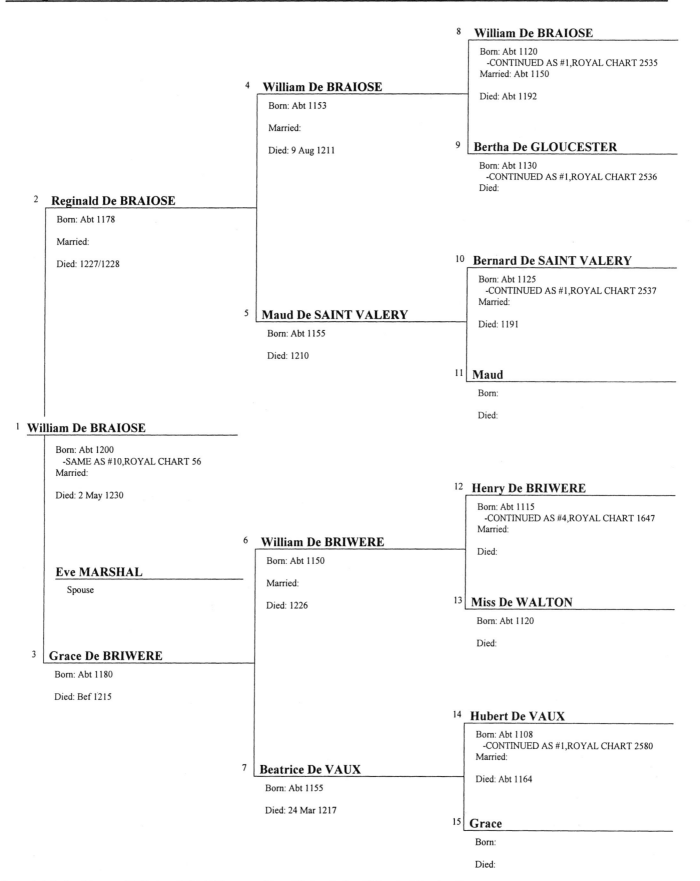

8 William De BRAIOSE

Born: Abt 1120
-CONTINUED AS #1,ROYAL CHART 2535
Married: Abt 1150

Died: Abt 1192

4 William De BRAIOSE

Born: Abt 1153

Married:

Died: 9 Aug 1211

9 Bertha De GLOUCESTER

Born: Abt 1130
-CONTINUED AS #1,ROYAL CHART 2536
Died:

2 Reginald De BRAIOSE

Born: Abt 1178

Married:

Died: 1227/1228

10 Bernard De SAINT VALERY

Born: Abt 1125
-CONTINUED AS #1,ROYAL CHART 2537
Married:

Died: 1191

5 Maud De SAINT VALERY

Born: Abt 1155

Died: 1210

11 Maud

Born:

Died:

1 William De BRAIOSE

Born: Abt 1200
-SAME AS #10,ROYAL CHART 56
Married:

Died: 2 May 1230

12 Henry De BRIWERE

Born: Abt 1115
-CONTINUED AS #4,ROYAL CHART 1647
Married:

Died:

6 William De BRIWERE

Born: Abt 1150

Married:

Died: 1226

13 Miss De WALTON

Born: Abt 1120

Died:

Eve MARSHAL

Spouse

3 Grace De BRIWERE

Born: Abt 1180

Died: Bef 1215

14 Hubert De VAUX

Born: Abt 1108
-CONTINUED AS #1,ROYAL CHART 2580
Married:

Died: Abt 1164

7 Beatrice De VAUX

Born: Abt 1155

Died: 24 Mar 1217

15 Grace

Born:

Died:

Sources include: *Royal Ancestors* (1989), charts 11326, 11430; *Ancestral Roots* 177; Consultation with Douglas Richardson (#7 parentage); Turton 133, 178 (ancestry of #5 Maud);
LDS records.

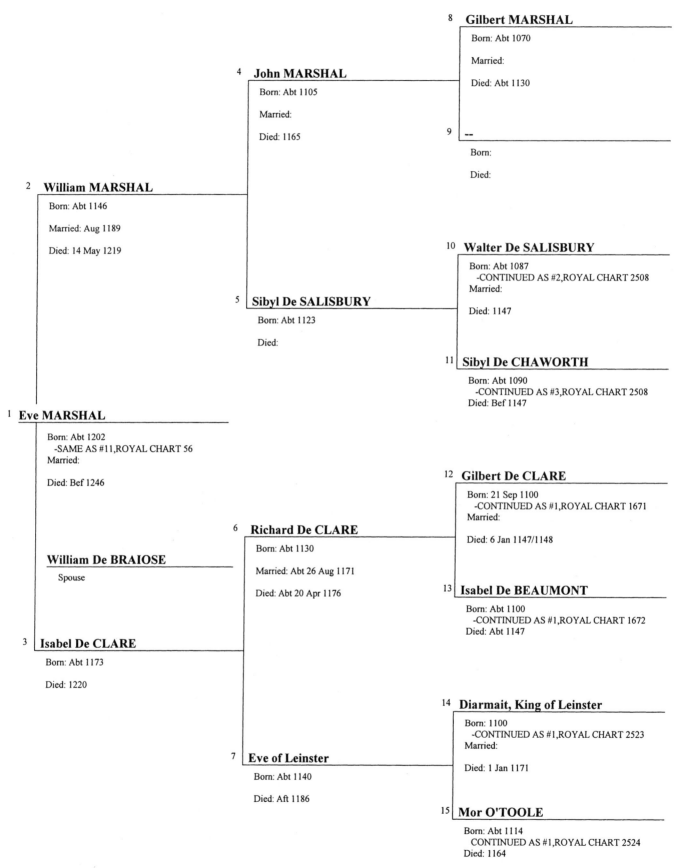

8 Gilbert MARSHAL
Born: Abt 1070
Married:
Died: Abt 1130

4 John MARSHAL
Born: Abt 1105
Married:
Died: 1165

9 --
Born:
Died:

2 William MARSHAL
Born: Abt 1146
Married: Aug 1189
Died: 14 May 1219

10 Walter De SALISBURY
Born: Abt 1087
  -CONTINUED AS #2,ROYAL CHART 2508
Married:
Died: 1147

5 Sibyl De SALISBURY
Born: Abt 1123
Died:

11 Sibyl De CHAWORTH
Born: Abt 1090
  -CONTINUED AS #3,ROYAL CHART 2508
Died: Bef 1147

1 Eve MARSHAL
Born: Abt 1202
  -SAME AS #11,ROYAL CHART 56
Married:
Died: Bef 1246

William De BRAIOSE
Spouse

12 Gilbert De CLARE
Born: 21 Sep 1100
  -CONTINUED AS #1,ROYAL CHART 1671
Married:
Died: 6 Jan 1147/1148

6 Richard De CLARE
Born: Abt 1130
Married: Abt 26 Aug 1171
Died: Abt 20 Apr 1176

13 Isabel De BEAUMONT
Born: Abt 1100
  -CONTINUED AS #1,ROYAL CHART 1672
Died: Abt 1147

3 Isabel De CLARE
Born: Abt 1173
Died: 1220

14 Diarmait, King of Leinster
Born: 1100
  -CONTINUED AS #1,ROYAL CHART 2523
Married:
Died: 1 Jan 1171

7 Eve of Leinster
Born: Abt 1140
Died: Aft 1186

15 Mor O'TOOLE
Born: Abt 1114
  CONTINUED AS #1,ROYAL CHART 2524
Died: 1164

Sources include: *Royal Ancestors* 11326, 11356; Faris preliminary baronial manuscript (1998), pp. 1064-65 (Marshal), 354-355 (Clare); *Ancestral Roots* 66, 175; *Magna Charta* 145-146; *The Genealogist* 1:4-27 (#7 ancestry). Note: The parentage and ancestry of #8 is disputed.

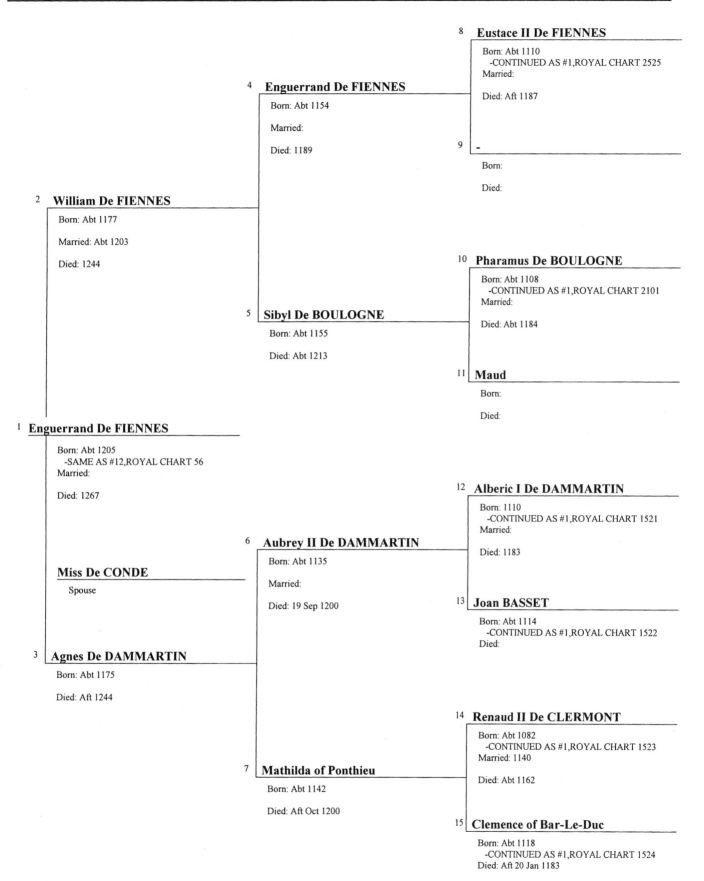

2 William De FIENNES

Born: Abt 1177

Married: Abt 1203

Died: 1244

4 Enguerrand De FIENNES

Born: Abt 1154

Married:

Died: 1189

8 Eustace II De FIENNES

Born: Abt 1110
 -CONTINUED AS #1,ROYAL CHART 2525
Married:

Died: Aft 1187

9 -

Born:

Died:

5 Sibyl De BOULOGNE

Born: Abt 1155

Died: Abt 1213

10 Pharamus De BOULOGNE

Born: Abt 1108
 -CONTINUED AS #1,ROYAL CHART 2101
Married:

Died: Abt 1184

11 Maud

Born:

Died:

1 Enguerrand De FIENNES

Born: Abt 1205
 -SAME AS #12,ROYAL CHART 56
Married:

Died: 1267

Miss De CONDE

Spouse

3 Agnes De DAMMARTIN

Born: Abt 1175

Died: Aft 1244

6 Aubrey II De DAMMARTIN

Born: Abt 1135

Married:

Died: 19 Sep 1200

12 Alberic I De DAMMARTIN

Born: 1110
 -CONTINUED AS #1,ROYAL CHART 1521
Married:

Died: 1183

13 Joan BASSET

Born: Abt 1114
 -CONTINUED AS #1,ROYAL CHART 1522
Died:

7 Mathilda of Ponthieu

Born: Abt 1142

Died: Aft Oct 1200

14 Renaud II De CLERMONT

Born: Abt 1082
 -CONTINUED AS #1,ROYAL CHART 1523
Married: 1140

Died: Abt 1162

15 Clemence of Bar-Le-Duc

Born: Abt 1118
 -CONTINUED AS #1,ROYAL CHART 1524
Died: Aft 20 Jan 1183

Sources include: *Royal Ancestors* (1989), chart 11327; *Ancestral Roots* 152, 158A, 144; Research report by Douglas Richardson on the Lucy & Boulogne families (July 2004); Faris preliminary Charlemagne manuscript (June 1995), pp. 152-153, 118; Turton 190.

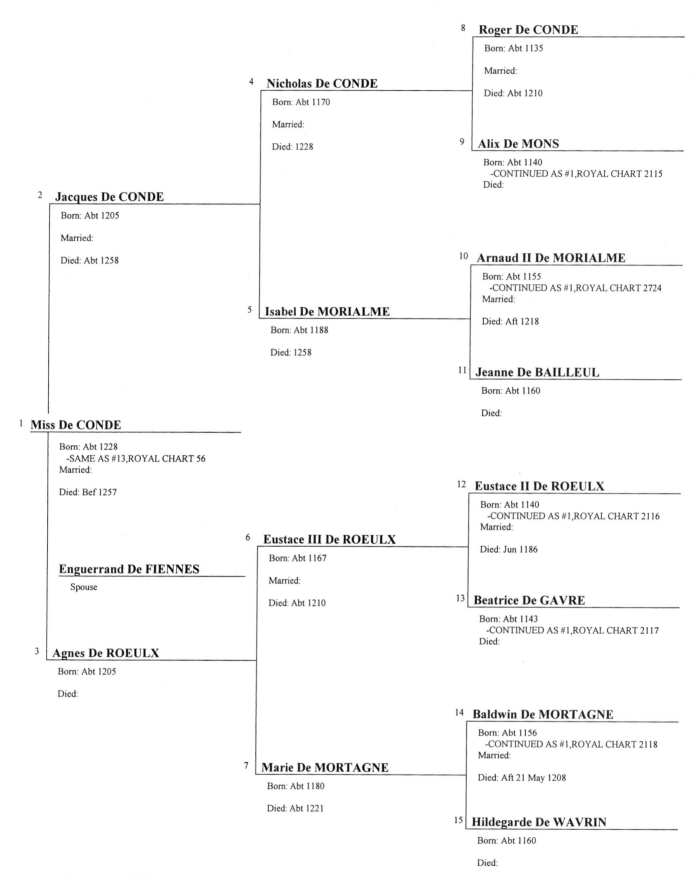

8 Roger De CONDE
Born: Abt 1135
Married:
Died: Abt 1210

4 Nicholas De CONDE
Born: Abt 1170
Married:
Died: 1228

9 Alix De MONS
Born: Abt 1140
  -CONTINUED AS #1,ROYAL CHART 2115
Died:

2 Jacques De CONDE
Born: Abt 1205
Married:
Died: Abt 1258

10 Arnaud II De MORIALME
Born: Abt 1155
  -CONTINUED AS #1,ROYAL CHART 2724
Married:
Died: Aft 1218

5 Isabel De MORIALME
Born: Abt 1188
Died: 1258

11 Jeanne De BAILLEUL
Born: Abt 1160
Died:

1 Miss De CONDE
Born: Abt 1228
  -SAME AS #13,ROYAL CHART 56
Married:
Died: Bef 1257

12 Eustace II De ROEULX
Born: Abt 1140
  -CONTINUED AS #1,ROYAL CHART 2116
Married:
Died: Jun 1186

6 Eustace III De ROEULX
Born: Abt 1167
Married:
Died: Abt 1210

13 Beatrice De GAVRE
Born: Abt 1143
  -CONTINUED AS #1,ROYAL CHART 2117
Died:

Enguerrand De FIENNES
Spouse

3 Agnes De ROEULX
Born: Abt 1205
Died:

14 Baldwin De MORTAGNE
Born: Abt 1156
  -CONTINUED AS #1,ROYAL CHART 2118
Married:
Died: Aft 21 May 1208

7 Marie De MORTAGNE
Born: Abt 1180
Died: Abt 1221

15 Hildegarde De WAVRIN
Born: Abt 1160
Died:

Sources include: *Royal Ancestors* (1989), charts 11327, 11957-60; Faris preliminary Charlemagne manuscript (June 1995), pp. 184-185, 232, 264-265; *Ancestral Roots* 152-28; Turton 167, 191; Kraentzler 1316-1319. Notes: The parentage of #1 Miss (or Isabel) De Conde is disputed. The Faris version is shown above. Richardson *Plantagenet* (2004), p. 155 (Brienne) also gives #1 as an unknown daughter of #2 Jacques. *Ancestral Roots* 8 (2004, Lines 152 & 158C, corrects itself and now gives #1 as Isabel, daughter of Nicholas De Conde & Isabel (Elizabeth) De Morialme (see #4 & 5 above). The parentage of #15 Hildegarde (Heldiardis) is disputed. See note chart 254 regarding #5 Isabel.

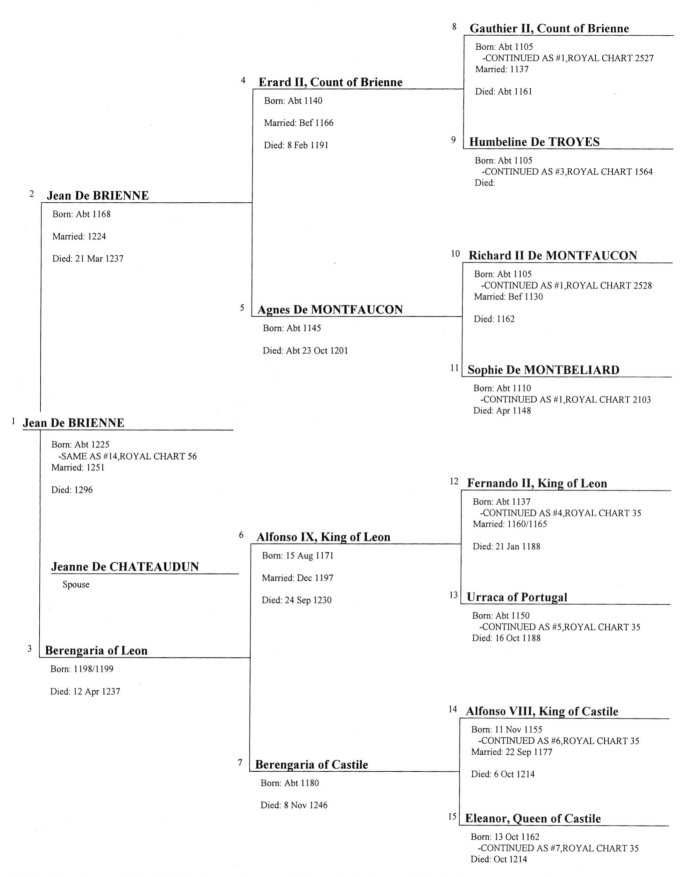

8 Gauthier II, Count of Brienne

Born: Abt 1105
-CONTINUED AS #1,ROYAL CHART 2527
Married: 1137

Died: Abt 1161

4 Erard II, Count of Brienne

Born: Abt 1140

Married: Bef 1166

Died: 8 Feb 1191

9 Humbeline De TROYES

Born: Abt 1105
-CONTINUED AS #3,ROYAL CHART 1564
Died:

2 Jean De BRIENNE

Born: Abt 1168

Married: 1224

Died: 21 Mar 1237

10 Richard II De MONTFAUCON

Born: Abt 1105
-CONTINUED AS #1,ROYAL CHART 2528
Married: Bef 1130

Died: 1162

5 Agnes De MONTFAUCON

Born: Abt 1145

Died: Abt 23 Oct 1201

11 Sophie De MONTBELIARD

Born: Abt 1110
-CONTINUED AS #1,ROYAL CHART 2103
Died: Apr 1148

1 Jean De BRIENNE

Born: Abt 1225
-SAME AS #14,ROYAL CHART 56
Married: 1251

Died: 1296

12 Fernando II, King of Leon

Born: Abt 1137
-CONTINUED AS #4,ROYAL CHART 35
Married: 1160/1165

Died: 21 Jan 1188

6 Alfonso IX, King of Leon

Born: 15 Aug 1171

Married: Dec 1197

Died: 24 Sep 1230

13 Urraca of Portugal

Born: Abt 1150
-CONTINUED AS #5,ROYAL CHART 35
Died: 16 Oct 1188

Jeanne De CHATEAUDUN

Spouse

3 Berengaria of Leon

Born: 1198/1199

Died: 12 Apr 1237

14 Alfonso VIII, King of Castile

Born: 11 Nov 1155
-CONTINUED AS #6,ROYAL CHART 35
Married: 22 Sep 1177

Died: 6 Oct 1214

7 Berengaria of Castile

Born: Abt 1180

Died: 8 Nov 1246

15 Eleanor, Queen of Castile

Born: 13 Oct 1162
-CONTINUED AS #7,ROYAL CHART 35
Died: Oct 1214

Sources include: *Royal Ancestors* (1989), chart 11327; Richardson *Plantagenet* (2004), pp. 154-155 (Brienne), 190-191 (Castile); Faris preliminary Charlemagne manuscript (June 1995), pp. 74-75, 236-237, 223; *Ancestral Roots* 120, 114; Turton 206.

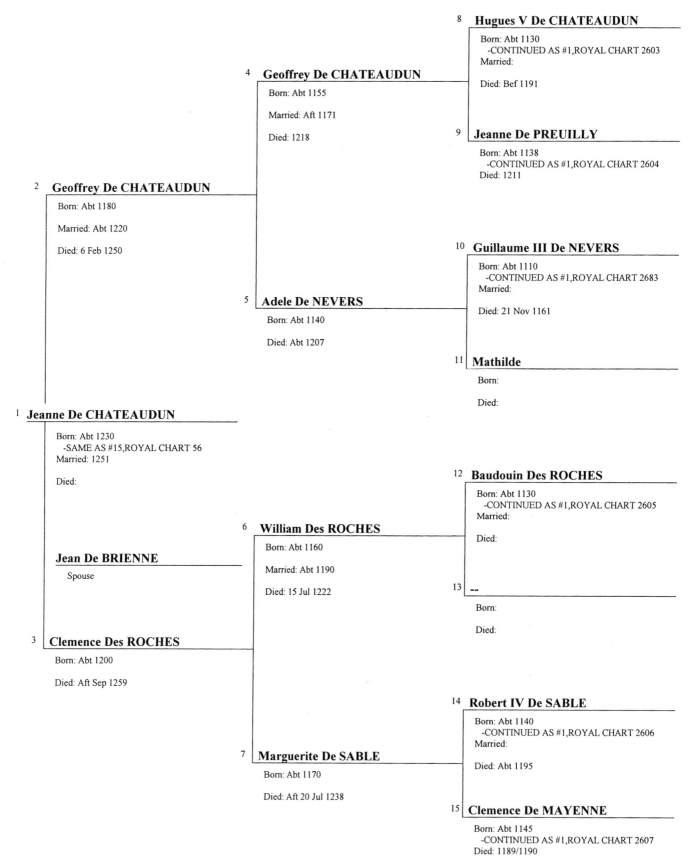

8 Hugues V De CHATEAUDUN
Born: Abt 1130
-CONTINUED AS #1,ROYAL CHART 2603
Married:

Died: Bef 1191

4 Geoffrey De CHATEAUDUN
Born: Abt 1155

Married: Aft 1171

Died: 1218

9 Jeanne De PREUILLY
Born: Abt 1138
-CONTINUED AS #1,ROYAL CHART 2604
Died: 1211

2 Geoffrey De CHATEAUDUN
Born: Abt 1180

Married: Abt 1220

Died: 6 Feb 1250

10 Guillaume III De NEVERS
Born: Abt 1110
-CONTINUED AS #1,ROYAL CHART 2683
Married:

Died: 21 Nov 1161

5 Adele De NEVERS
Born: Abt 1140

Died: Abt 1207

11 Mathilde
Born:

Died:

1 Jeanne De CHATEAUDUN
Born: Abt 1230
-SAME AS #15,ROYAL CHART 56
Married: 1251

Died:

Jean De BRIENNE
Spouse

12 Baudouin Des ROCHES
Born: Abt 1130
-CONTINUED AS #1,ROYAL CHART 2605
Married:

Died:

6 William Des ROCHES
Born: Abt 1160

Married: Abt 1190

Died: 15 Jul 1222

13 --
Born:

Died:

3 Clemence Des ROCHES
Born: Abt 1200

Died: Aft Sep 1259

14 Robert IV De SABLE
Born: Abt 1140
-CONTINUED AS #1,ROYAL CHART 2606
Married:

Died: Abt 1195

7 Marguerite De SABLE
Born: Abt 1170

Died: Aft 20 Jul 1238

15 Clemence De MAYENNE
Born: Abt 1145
-CONTINUED AS #1,ROYAL CHART 2607
Died: 1189/1190

Sources include: *Royal Ancestors* (1989), charts 11327, 11813-15; Faris preliminary Charlemagne manuscript (June 1995), pp. 75, 102-103, 205; Schwennicke 3:690, 718A-B; *Ancestral Roots* 120-30; Turton 167, 179-180. Note: Faris identifies #5 Adele as the same person who married 1st Renaud IV, Count of Joigny, who died in or after 1171 (see chart 2875). While tentatively accepted above, this claim is chronologically difficult and may be incorrect. Adele must have been born by about 1140 to make the Joigny descents work, but this appears to require her to be much older than her claimed 2nd husband Geoffrey (#4 above), by whom she had nine children.

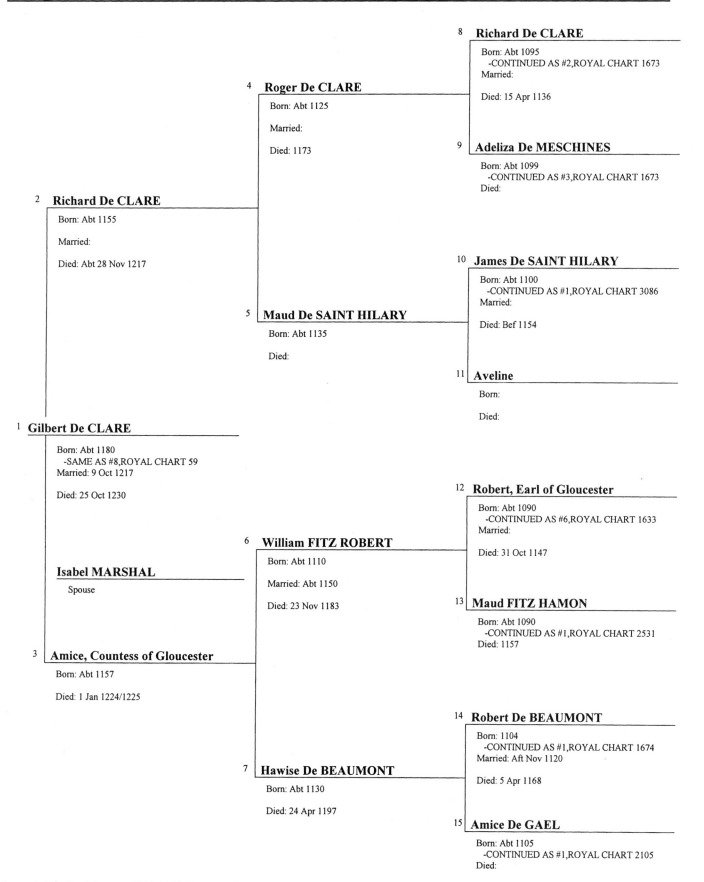

8 | **Richard De CLARE**

Born: Abt 1095
  -CONTINUED AS #2,ROYAL CHART 1673
Married:

Died: 15 Apr 1136

4 | **Roger De CLARE**

Born: Abt 1125

Married:

Died: 1173

9 | **Adeliza De MESCHINES**

Born: Abt 1099
  -CONTINUED AS #3,ROYAL CHART 1673
Died:

2 | **Richard De CLARE**

Born: Abt 1155

Married:

Died: Abt 28 Nov 1217

10 | **James De SAINT HILARY**

Born: Abt 1100
  -CONTINUED AS #1,ROYAL CHART 3086
Married:

Died: Bef 1154

5 | **Maud De SAINT HILARY**

Born: Abt 1135

Died:

11 | **Aveline**

Born:

Died:

1 | **Gilbert De CLARE**

Born: Abt 1180
  -SAME AS #8,ROYAL CHART 59
Married: 9 Oct 1217

Died: 25 Oct 1230

12 | **Robert, Earl of Gloucester**

Born: Abt 1090
  -CONTINUED AS #6,ROYAL CHART 1633
Married:

Died: 31 Oct 1147

6 | **William FITZ ROBERT**

Born: Abt 1110

Married: Abt 1150

Died: 23 Nov 1183

13 | **Maud FITZ HAMON**

Born: Abt 1090
  -CONTINUED AS #1,ROYAL CHART 2531
Died: 1157

Isabel MARSHAL

Spouse

3 | **Amice, Countess of Gloucester**

Born: Abt 1157

Died: 1 Jan 1224/1225

14 | **Robert De BEAUMONT**

Born: 1104
  -CONTINUED AS #1,ROYAL CHART 1674
Married: Aft Nov 1120

Died: 5 Apr 1168

7 | **Hawise De BEAUMONT**

Born: Abt 1130

Died: 24 Apr 1197

15 | **Amice De GAEL**

Born: Abt 1105
  -CONTINUED AS #1,ROYAL CHART 2105
Died:

Sources include: *Royal Ancestors* 11332, 11438-39; *Ancestral Roots* 63, 53.

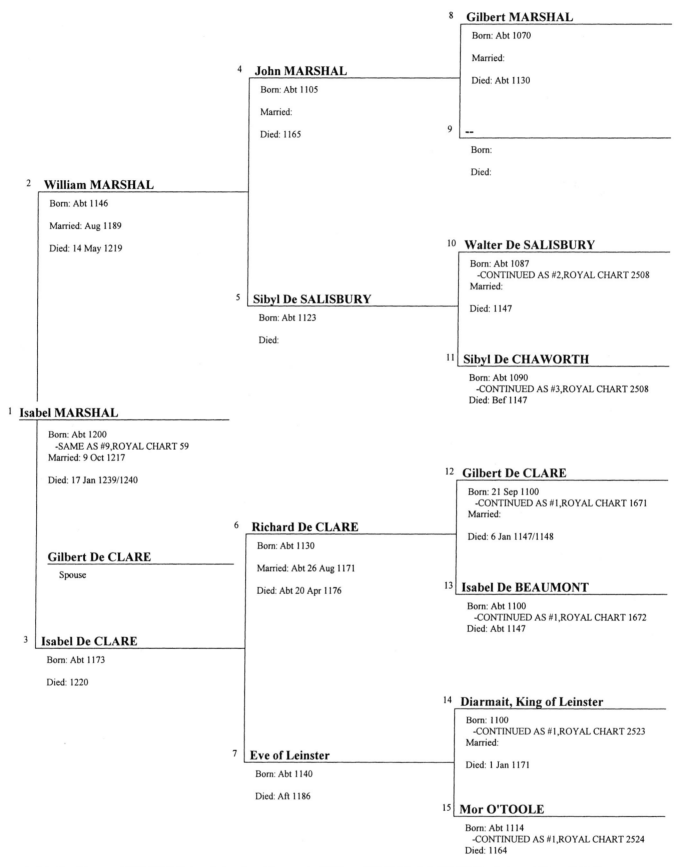

8 Gilbert MARSHAL

Born: Abt 1070

Married:

Died: Abt 1130

4 John MARSHAL

Born: Abt 1105

Married:

Died: 1165

9 --

Born:

Died:

2 William MARSHAL

Born: Abt 1146

Married: Aug 1189

Died: 14 May 1219

10 Walter De SALISBURY

Born: Abt 1087
-CONTINUED AS #2,ROYAL CHART 2508
Married:

Died: 1147

5 Sibyl De SALISBURY

Born: Abt 1123

Died:

11 Sibyl De CHAWORTH

Born: Abt 1090
-CONTINUED AS #3,ROYAL CHART 2508
Died: Bef 1147

1 Isabel MARSHAL

Born: Abt 1200
-SAME AS #9,ROYAL CHART 59
Married: 9 Oct 1217

Died: 17 Jan 1239/1240

12 Gilbert De CLARE

Born: 21 Sep 1100
-CONTINUED AS #1,ROYAL CHART 1671
Married:

Died: 6 Jan 1147/1148

6 Richard De CLARE

Born: Abt 1130

Married: Abt 26 Aug 1171

Died: Abt 20 Apr 1176

13 Isabel De BEAUMONT

Born: Abt 1100
-CONTINUED AS #1,ROYAL CHART 1672
Died: Abt 1147

Gilbert De CLARE

Spouse

3 Isabel De CLARE

Born: Abt 1173

Died: 1220

14 Diarmait, King of Leinster

Born: 1100
-CONTINUED AS #1,ROYAL CHART 2523
Married:

Died: 1 Jan 1171

7 Eve of Leinster

Born: Abt 1140

Died: Aft 1186

15 Mor O'TOOLE

Born: Abt 1114
-CONTINUED AS #1,ROYAL CHART 2524
Died: 1164

Sources include: *Royal Ancestors* 11332, 11356; Faris preliminary baronial manuscript (1998), pp. 1064-65 (Marshal), 354-355 (Clare); *Ancestral Roots* 63-28, 66.

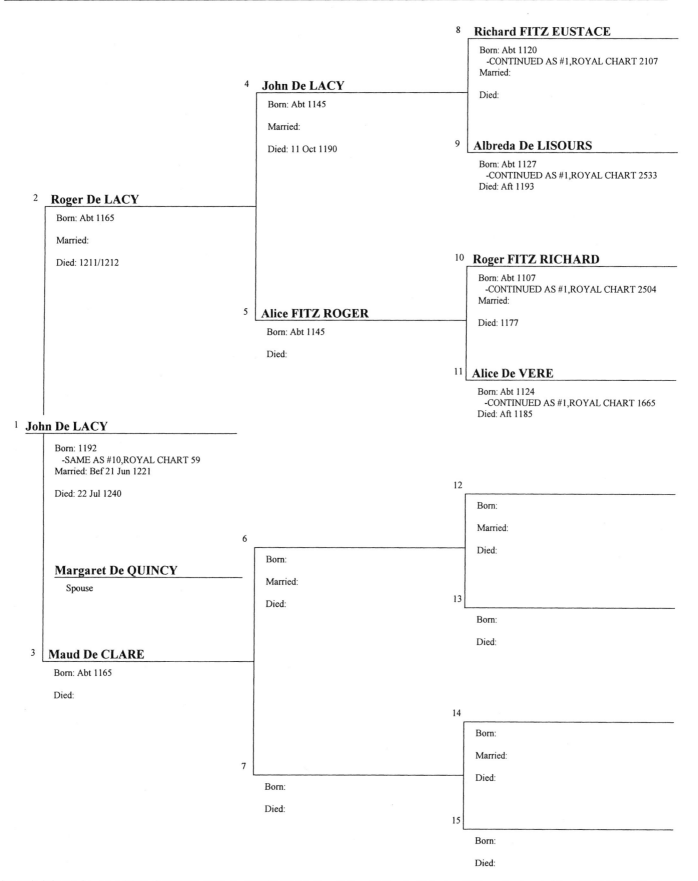

8   **Richard FITZ EUSTACE**

Born: Abt 1120
  -CONTINUED AS #1,ROYAL CHART 2107
Married:

Died:

9   **Albreda De LISOURS**

Born: Abt 1127
  -CONTINUED AS #1,ROYAL CHART 2533
Died: Aft 1193

4   **John De LACY**

Born: Abt 1145

Married:

Died: 11 Oct 1190

10   **Roger FITZ RICHARD**

Born: Abt 1107
  -CONTINUED AS #1,ROYAL CHART 2504
Married:

Died: 1177

11   **Alice De VERE**

Born: Abt 1124
  -CONTINUED AS #1,ROYAL CHART 1665
Died: Aft 1185

2   **Roger De LACY**

Born: Abt 1165

Married:

Died: 1211/1212

5   **Alice FITZ ROGER**

Born: Abt 1145

Died:

1   **John De LACY**

Born: 1192
  -SAME AS #10,ROYAL CHART 59
Married: Bef 21 Jun 1221

Died: 22 Jul 1240

Margaret De QUINCY

Spouse

12

Born:

Married:

Died:

13

Born:

Died:

6

Born:

Married:

Died:

3   **Maud De CLARE**

Born: Abt 1165

Died:

14

Born:

Married:

Died:

15

Born:

Died:

7

Born:

Died:

Sources include: *Royal Ancestors* (1989), charts 11332, 11391; Paget (1957) 311:1-2; Consultation with Douglas Richardson; LDS records; *Ancestral Roots* 54-29; *Magna Charta* 54; Turton 95; *Complete Peerage* 5:115 (footnote f); 10:117-118 (appendix J) -- identification and ancestry of #5 Alice. Note: The parentage of #3 is unknown. She was not the daughter of Richard & Amice, as erroneously claimed in LDS records. That Maud married only William De Braose. Compare chart 203.

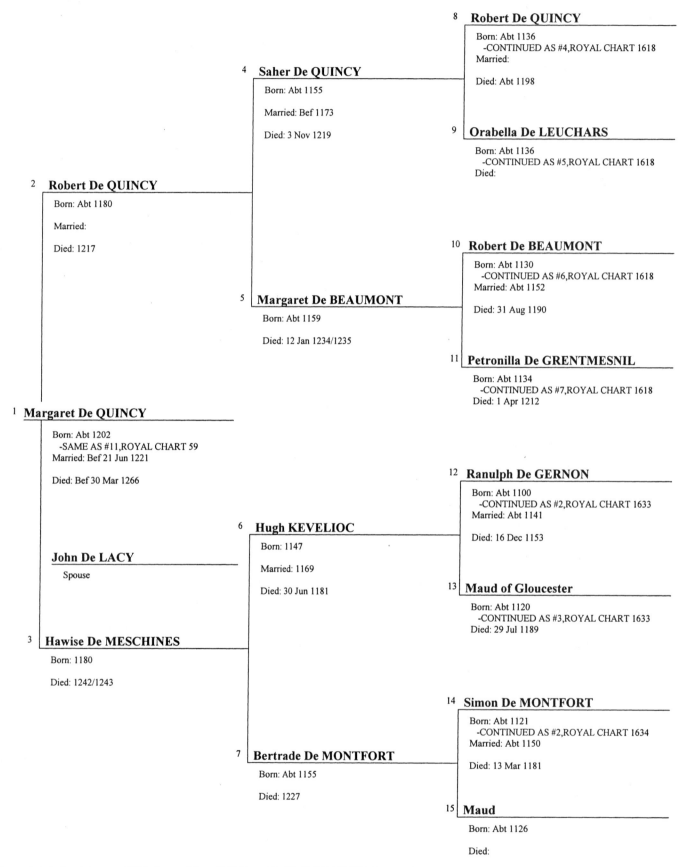

8 | **Robert De QUINCY**
Born: Abt 1136
  -CONTINUED AS #4,ROYAL CHART 1618
Married:

Died: Abt 1198

4 | **Saher De QUINCY**
Born: Abt 1155

Married: Bef 1173

Died: 3 Nov 1219

9 | **Orabella De LEUCHARS**
Born: Abt 1136
  -CONTINUED AS #5,ROYAL CHART 1618
Died:

2 | **Robert De QUINCY**
Born: Abt 1180

Married:

Died: 1217

10 | **Robert De BEAUMONT**
Born: Abt 1130
  -CONTINUED AS #6,ROYAL CHART 1618
Married: Abt 1152

Died: 31 Aug 1190

5 | **Margaret De BEAUMONT**
Born: Abt 1159

Died: 12 Jan 1234/1235

11 | **Petronilla De GRENTMESNIL**
Born: Abt 1134
  -CONTINUED AS #7,ROYAL CHART 1618
Died: 1 Apr 1212

1 | **Margaret De QUINCY**
Born: Abt 1202
  -SAME AS #11,ROYAL CHART 59
Married: Bef 21 Jun 1221

Died: Bef 30 Mar 1266

12 | **Ranulph De GERNON**
Born: Abt 1100
  -CONTINUED AS #2,ROYAL CHART 1633
Married: Abt 1141

Died: 16 Dec 1153

6 | **Hugh KEVELIOC**
Born: 1147

Married: 1169

Died: 30 Jun 1181

13 | **Maud of Gloucester**
Born: Abt 1120
  -CONTINUED AS #3,ROYAL CHART 1633
Died: 29 Jul 1189

John De LACY
Spouse

3 | **Hawise De MESCHINES**
Born: 1180

Died: 1242/1243

14 | **Simon De MONTFORT**
Born: Abt 1121
  -CONTINUED AS #2,ROYAL CHART 1634
Married: Abt 1150

Died: 13 Mar 1181

7 | **Bertrade De MONTFORT**
Born: Abt 1155

Died: 1227

15 | **Maud**
Born: Abt 1126

Died:

Sources include: *Royal Ancestors* 11332; *Ancestral Roots* 53-54; Turton 95, 100; *TAG* 73:308 (#6 & 7 ancestry).

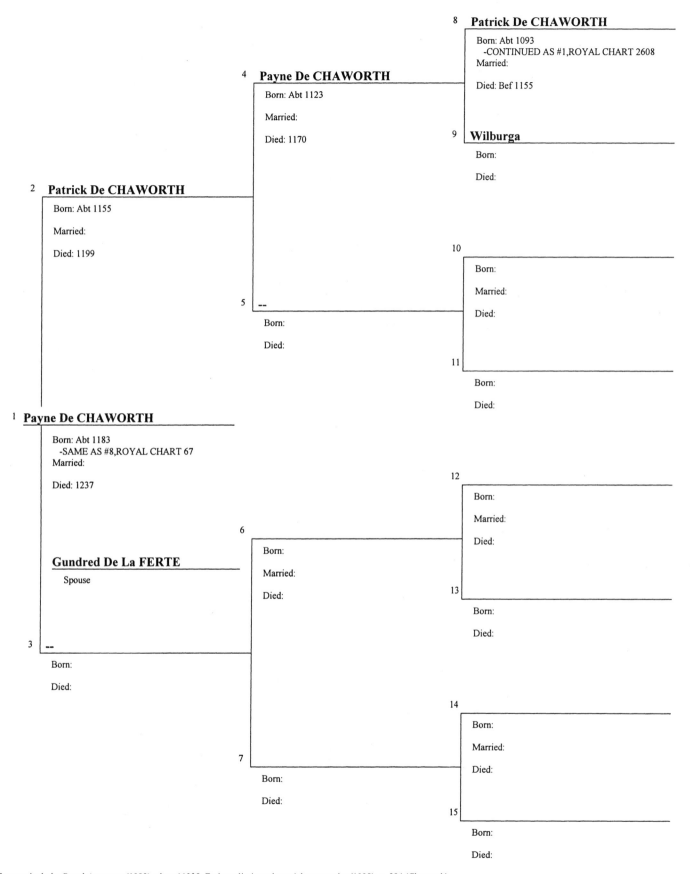

8 Patrick De CHAWORTH

Born: Abt 1093
  -CONTINUED AS #1,ROYAL CHART 2608
Married:

Died: Bef 1155

---

4 Payne De CHAWORTH

Born: Abt 1123

Married:

Died: 1170

---

9 Wilburga

Born:

Died:

---

2 Patrick De CHAWORTH

Born: Abt 1155

Married:

Died: 1199

10

Born:

Married:

Died:

---

5 --

Born:

Died:

11

Born:

Died:

---

1 Payne De CHAWORTH

Born: Abt 1183
  -SAME AS #8,ROYAL CHART 67
Married:

Died: 1237

12

Born:

Married:

Died:

6

Born:

Married:

Died:

13

Born:

Died:

Gundred De La FERTE

Spouse

---

3 --

Born:

Died:

14

Born:

Married:

Died:

7

Born:

Died:

15

Born:

Died:

Sources include: *Royal Ancestors* (1989), chart 11338; Faris preliminary baronial manuscript (1998), p. 324 (Chaworth).

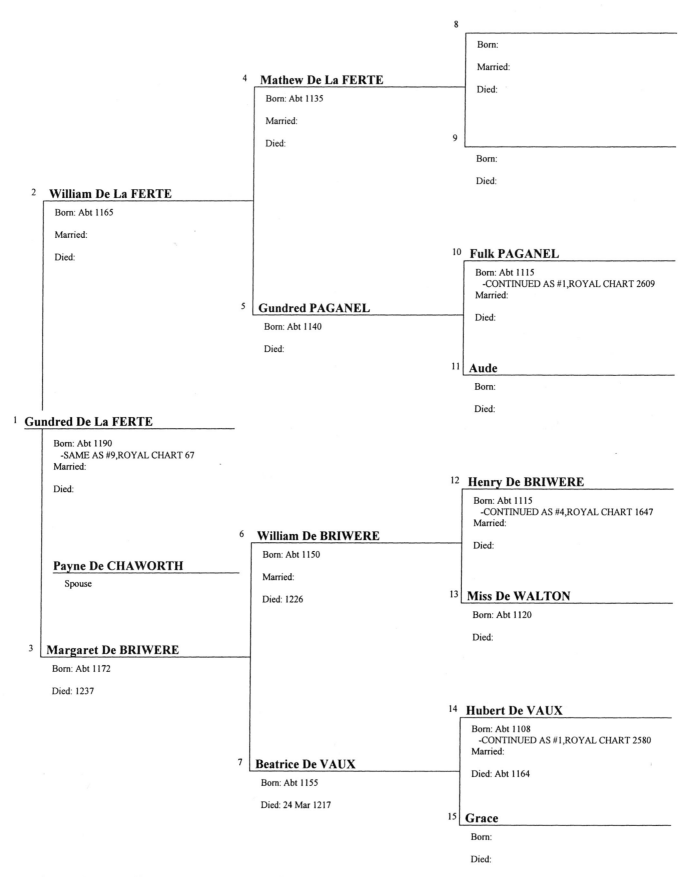

8

Born:

Married:

Died:

4 Mathew De La FERTE

Born: Abt 1135

Married:

Died:

9

Born:

Died:

2 William De La FERTE

Born: Abt 1165

Married:

Died:

10 Fulk PAGANEL

Born: Abt 1115
  -CONTINUED AS #1,ROYAL CHART 2609

Married:

Died:

5 Gundred PAGANEL

Born: Abt 1140

Died:

11 Aude

Born:

Died:

1 Gundred De La FERTE

Born: Abt 1190
  -SAME AS #9,ROYAL CHART 67

Married:

Died:

12 Henry De BRIWERE

Born: Abt 1115
  -CONTINUED AS #4,ROYAL CHART 1647

Married:

Died:

6 William De BRIWERE

Born: Abt 1150

Married:

Died: 1226

13 Miss De WALTON

Born: Abt 1120

Died:

Payne De CHAWORTH

Spouse

3 Margaret De BRIWERE

Born: Abt 1172

Died: 1237

14 Hubert De VAUX

Born: Abt 1108
  -CONTINUED AS #1,ROYAL CHART 2580

Married:

Died: Abt 1164

7 Beatrice De VAUX

Born: Abt 1155

Died: 24 Mar 1217

15 Grace

Born:

Died:

Sources include: *Royal Ancestors* (1989), chart 11338; Turton 116; Kraentzler 1131-32, 1149; Collett 21-7C; Consultation with Douglas Richardson (#7 parentage).

8 William De BEAUCHAMP

Born: Abt 1095
-CONTINUED AS #1,ROYAL CHART 1638
Married:

Died: 1170

4 William De BEAUCHAMP

Born: Abt 1143

Married:

Died: 1197

9 --

Born:

Died:

2 Walter De BEAUCHAMP

Born: Abt 1191

Married: Abt 10 Jul 1214

Died: 14 Apr 1236

10 William De BRAIOSE

Born: Abt 1153
-CONTINUED AS #4,ROYAL CHART 1603
Married:

Died: 9 Aug 1211

5 Bertha De BRAOSE

Born: Abt 1174

Died: .

11 Maud De SAINT VALERY

Born: Abt 1155
-CONTINUED AS #5,ROYAL CHART 1603
Died: 1210

1 William De BEAUCHAMP

Born: Abt 1215
-SAME AS #12,ROYAL CHART 67
Married:

Died: 7 Jan 1268/1269
w.d.

Isabel MAUDUIT

Spouse

12 Hugh De MORTIMER

Born: Abt 1115
-CONTINUED AS #4,ROYAL CHART 1601
Married:

Died: 26 Feb 1181

6 Roger De MORTIMER

Born: Abt 1158

Married:

Died: Bef 19 Aug 1214

13 Maud De MESCHINES

Born: Abt 1118
-CONTINUED AS #5,ROYAL CHART 1601
Died: Aft 1190

3 Joan De MORTIMER

Born: Abt 1196

Died: 1225

14 Walkelin De FERRIERES

Born: Abt 1135
-CONTINUED AS #6,ROYAL CHART 1601
Married:

Died:

7 Isabel De FERRERS

Born: Abt 1166

Died: Bef 29 Apr 1252

15 Alice De LECHE

Born: Abt 1140
-CONTINUED AS #7,ROYAL CHART 1601
Died:

Sources include: *Royal Ancestors* (1989), chart 11339; Paget (1957) 39:1-3; Faris preliminary baronial manuscript (1998), pp. 57-58 (Beauchamp), 217 (Breuse), 1127-28 (Mortimer), 586-587 (Ferrers or Ferrieres).

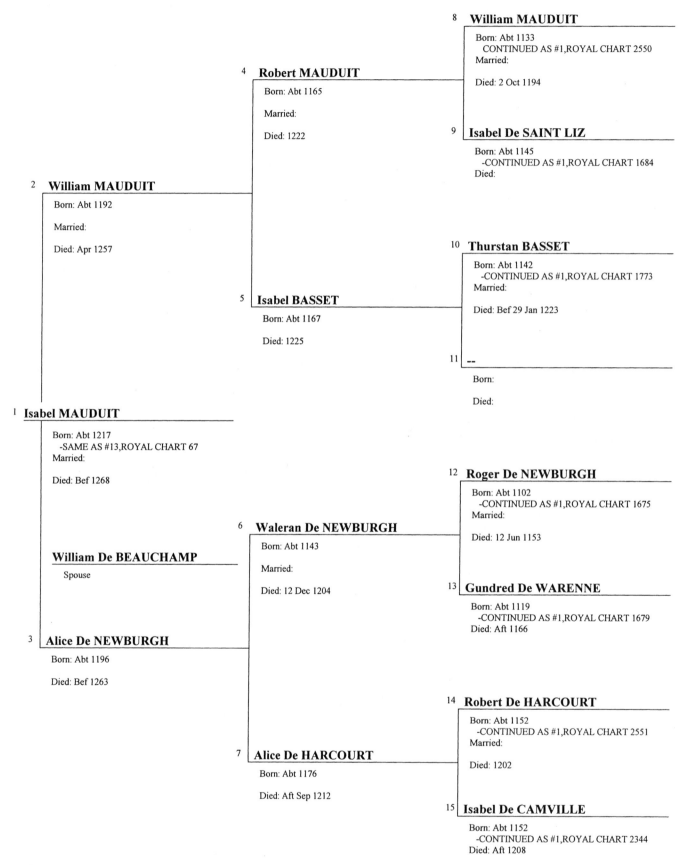

8 **William MAUDUIT**

Born: Abt 1133
   CONTINUED AS #1,ROYAL CHART 2550
Married:

Died: 2 Oct 1194

4 **Robert MAUDUIT**

Born: Abt 1165

Married:

Died: 1222

9 **Isabel De SAINT LIZ**

Born: Abt 1145
   -CONTINUED AS #1,ROYAL CHART 1684
Died:

2 **William MAUDUIT**

Born: Abt 1192

Married:

Died: Apr 1257

10 **Thurstan BASSET**

Born: Abt 1142
   -CONTINUED AS #1,ROYAL CHART 1773
Married:

Died: Bef 29 Jan 1223

5 **Isabel BASSET**

Born: Abt 1167

Died: 1225

11 **--**

Born:

Died:

1 **Isabel MAUDUIT**

Born: Abt 1217
   -SAME AS #13,ROYAL CHART 67
Married:

Died: Bef 1268

12 **Roger De NEWBURGH**

Born: Abt 1102
   -CONTINUED AS #1,ROYAL CHART 1675
Married:

Died: 12 Jun 1153

6 **Waleran De NEWBURGH**

Born: Abt 1143

Married:

Died: 12 Dec 1204

13 **Gundred De WARENNE**

Born: Abt 1119
   -CONTINUED AS #1,ROYAL CHART 1679
Died: Aft 1166

William De BEAUCHAMP

Spouse

3 **Alice De NEWBURGH**

Born: Abt 1196

Died: Bef 1263

14 **Robert De HARCOURT**

Born: Abt 1152
   -CONTINUED AS #1,ROYAL CHART 2551
Married:

Died: 1202

7 **Alice De HARCOURT**

Born: Abt 1176

Died: Aft Sep 1212

15 **Isabel De CAMVILLE**

Born: Abt 1152
   -CONTINUED AS #1,ROYAL CHART 2344
Died: Aft 1208

Sources include: *Royal Ancestors* (1989), chart 11339; *Ancestral Roots* 84; Paget (1957) 360:2-3, 26:1-2; Turton 117. Notes: *Ancestral Roots* 84-27 states that the maternal grandfather of #4 Robert was Simon De Saint Liz, died 1153.

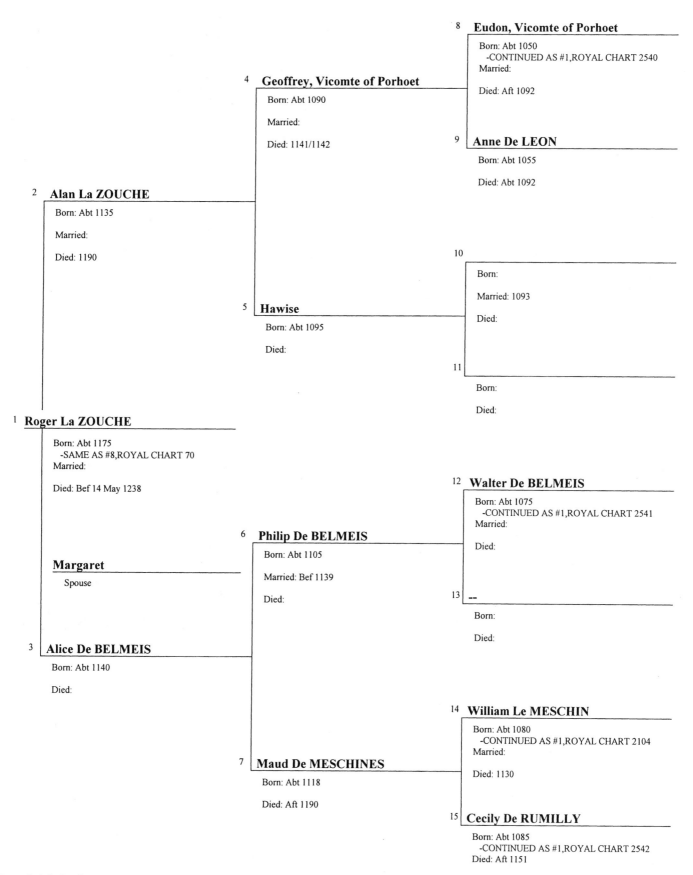

8 Eudon, Vicomte of Porhoet
Born: Abt 1050
-CONTINUED AS #1,ROYAL CHART 2540
Married:

Died: Aft 1092

4 Geoffrey, Vicomte of Porhoet
Born: Abt 1090

Married:

Died: 1141/1142

9 Anne De LEON
Born: Abt 1055

Died: Abt 1092

2 Alan La ZOUCHE
Born: Abt 1135

Married:

Died: 1190

10
Born:

Married: 1093

Died:

5 Hawise
Born: Abt 1095

Died:

11
Born:

Died:

1 Roger La ZOUCHE
Born: Abt 1175
-SAME AS #8,ROYAL CHART 70
Married:

Died: Bef 14 May 1238

12 Walter De BELMEIS
Born: Abt 1075
-CONTINUED AS #1,ROYAL CHART 2541
Married:

Died:

6 Philip De BELMEIS
Born: Abt 1105

Married: Bef 1139

Died:

13 --
Born:

Died:

Margaret
Spouse

3 Alice De BELMEIS
Born: Abt 1140

Died:

14 William Le MESCHIN
Born: Abt 1080
-CONTINUED AS #1,ROYAL CHART 2104
Married:

Died: 1130

7 Maud De MESCHINES
Born: Abt 1118

Died: Aft 1190

15 Cecily De RUMILLY
Born: Abt 1085
-CONTINUED AS #1,ROYAL CHART 2542
Died: Aft 1151

Sources include: *Royal Ancestors* 11342, 11458-61; *Ancestral Roots* 8 (2004), Line 39; *Ancestral Roots* 39, 132B; Schwennicke 10:13; Faris preliminary Charlemagne manuscript (June 1995), pp. 78-79 (#2 ancestry); Turton 98; Kraentzler 1339, 1309. Note: #5 Hawise has been claimed to be the daughter of Alan IV, Duke of Brittany & Ermengarde of Anjou (see chart 2124, #12 & 13). *Ancestral Roots* 8 drops the claim, and the claim is not recognized by Schwennicke (2:75 or 10:13) or by Mas Latrie (col. 1572), as noted by Faris in tentatively accepting the line.

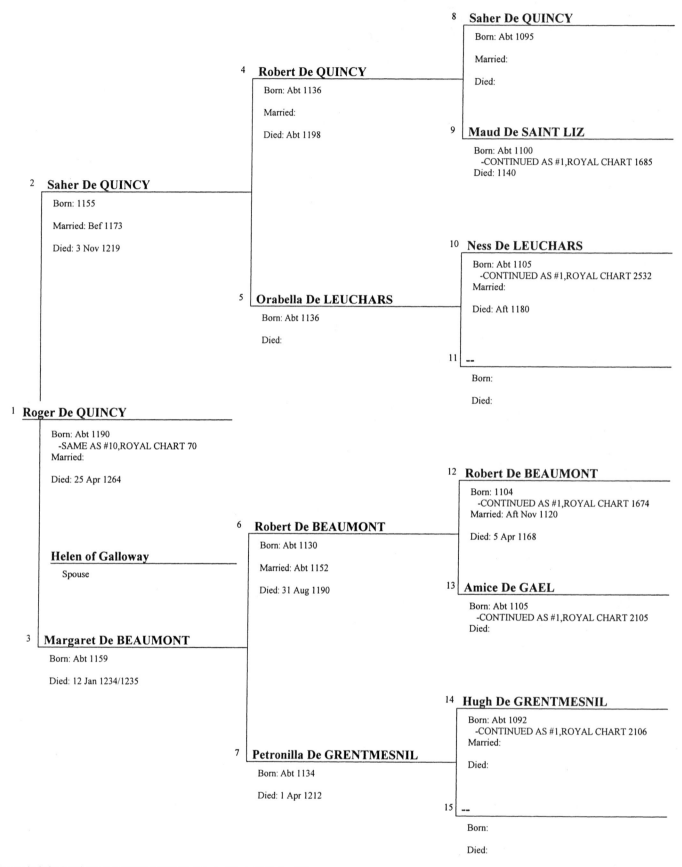

2 Saher De QUINCY
Born: 1155
Married: Bef 1173
Died: 3 Nov 1219

4 Robert De QUINCY
Born: Abt 1136
Married:
Died: Abt 1198

8 Saher De QUINCY
Born: Abt 1095
Married:
Died:

9 Maud De SAINT LIZ
Born: Abt 1100
  -CONTINUED AS #1,ROYAL CHART 1685
Died: 1140

5 Orabella De LEUCHARS
Born: Abt 1136
Died:

10 Ness De LEUCHARS
Born: Abt 1105
  -CONTINUED AS #1,ROYAL CHART 2532
Married:
Died: Aft 1180

11 --
Born:
Died:

1 Roger De QUINCY
Born: Abt 1190
  -SAME AS #10,ROYAL CHART 70
Married:
Died: 25 Apr 1264

Helen of Galloway
Spouse

3 Margaret De BEAUMONT
Born: Abt 1159
Died: 12 Jan 1234/1235

6 Robert De BEAUMONT
Born: Abt 1130
Married: Abt 1152
Died: 31 Aug 1190

12 Robert De BEAUMONT
Born: 1104
  -CONTINUED AS #1,ROYAL CHART 1674
Married: Aft Nov 1120
Died: 5 Apr 1168

13 Amice De GAEL
Born: Abt 1105
  -CONTINUED AS #1,ROYAL CHART 2105
Died:

7 Petronilla De GRENTMESNIL
Born: Abt 1134
Died: 1 Apr 1212

14 Hugh De GRENTMESNIL
Born: Abt 1092
  -CONTINUED AS #1,ROYAL CHART 2106
Married:
Died:

15 --
Born:
Died:

Sources include: *Royal Ancestors* 11342, 11442-43; *Ancestral Roots* 53; Turton 100.

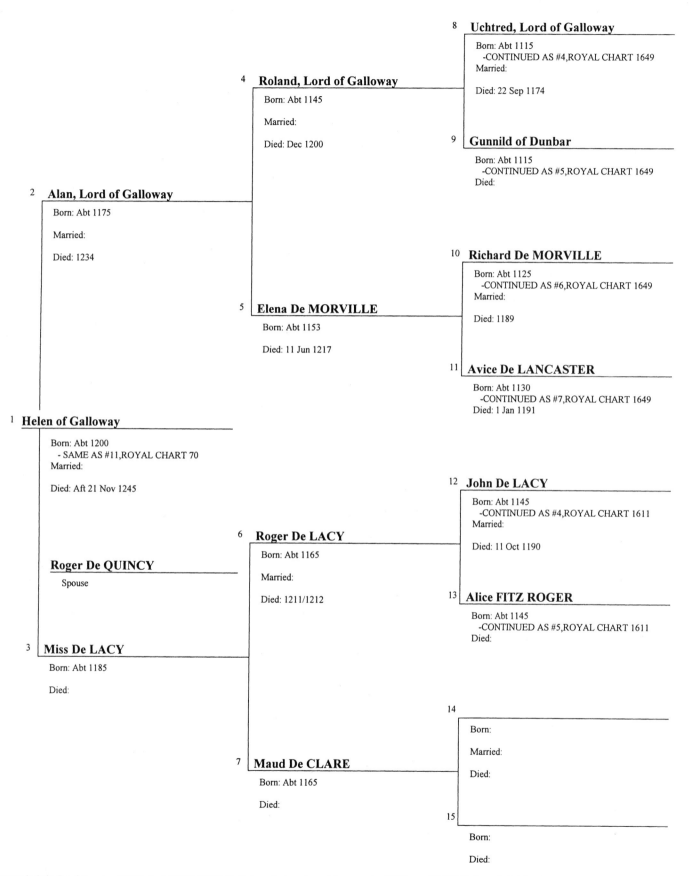

8 **Uchtred, Lord of Galloway**
Born: Abt 1115
   -CONTINUED AS #4,ROYAL CHART 1649
Married:

Died: 22 Sep 1174

4 **Roland, Lord of Galloway**
Born: Abt 1145

Married:

Died: Dec 1200

9 **Gunnild of Dunbar**
Born: Abt 1115
   -CONTINUED AS #5,ROYAL CHART 1649
Died:

2 **Alan, Lord of Galloway**
Born: Abt 1175

Married:

Died: 1234

10 **Richard De MORVILLE**
Born: Abt 1125
   -CONTINUED AS #6,ROYAL CHART 1649
Married:

Died: 1189

5 **Elena De MORVILLE**
Born: Abt 1153

Died: 11 Jun 1217

11 **Avice De LANCASTER**
Born: Abt 1130
   -CONTINUED AS #7,ROYAL CHART 1649
Died: 1 Jan 1191

1 **Helen of Galloway**
Born: Abt 1200
 - SAME AS #11,ROYAL CHART 70
Married:

Died: Aft 21 Nov 1245

12 **John De LACY**
Born: Abt 1145
   -CONTINUED AS #4,ROYAL CHART 1611
Married:

Died: 11 Oct 1190

6 **Roger De LACY**
Born: Abt 1165

Married:

Died: 1211/1212

Roger De QUINCY
Spouse

13 **Alice FITZ ROGER**
Born: Abt 1145
   -CONTINUED AS #5,ROYAL CHART 1611
Died:

3 **Miss De LACY**
Born: Abt 1185

Died:

14
Born:

Married:

Died:

7 **Maud De CLARE**
Born: Abt 1165

Died:

15
Born:

Died:

Sources include: *Royal Ancestors* (1989), charts 11342, 11462-63; Faris preliminary baronial manuscript (1998), pp. 686-687 (Galloway), 926-927 (Lacy); *Ancestral Roots* 38, 88; Turton 101. Notes: The parentage of #3 is disputed. The Faris (Richardson) version is accepted above. #1 is also called Ellen Fitz Alan and #2 Alan Fitz Roland.

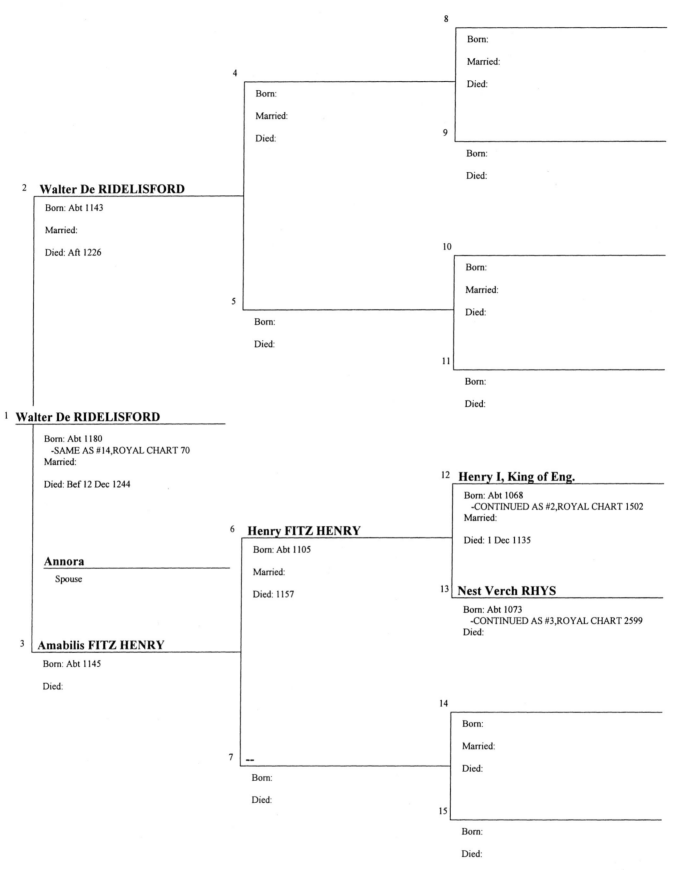

8

Born:

Married:

Died:

4

Born:

Married:

Died:

9

Born:

Died:

2 Walter De RIDELISFORD

Born: Abt 1143

Married:

Died: Aft 1226

10

Born:

Married:

Died:

5

Born:

Died:

11

Born:

Died:

1 Walter De RIDELISFORD

Born: Abt 1180
  -SAME AS #14,ROYAL CHART 70
Married:

Died: Bef 12 Dec 1244

12 Henry I, King of Eng.

Born: Abt 1068
  -CONTINUED AS #2,ROYAL CHART 1502
Married:

Died: 1 Dec 1135

6 Henry FITZ HENRY

Born: Abt 1105

Married:

Died: 1157

13 Nest Verch RHYS

Born: Abt 1073
  -CONTINUED AS #3,ROYAL CHART 2599
Died:

Annora

Spouse

3 Amabilis FITZ HENRY

Born: Abt 1145

Died:

14

Born:

Married:

Died:

7 --

Born:

Died:

15

Born:

Died:

Sources include: *Royal Ancestors* (1989), chart 11343; *Ancestral Roots* 33A.

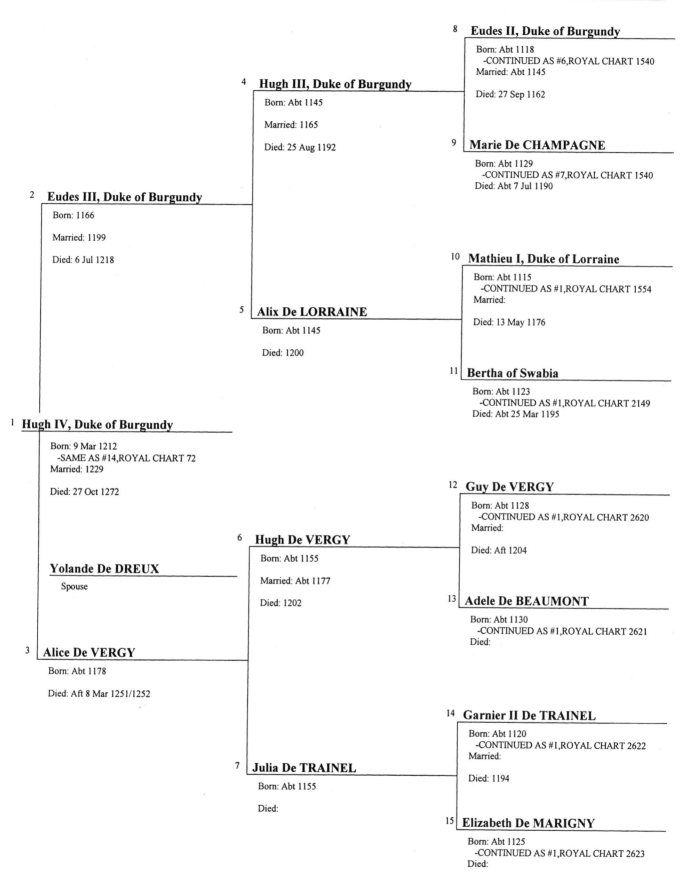

8 Eudes II, Duke of Burgundy

Born: Abt 1118
 -CONTINUED AS #6,ROYAL CHART 1540
Married: Abt 1145

Died: 27 Sep 1162

4 Hugh III, Duke of Burgundy

Born: Abt 1145

Married: 1165

Died: 25 Aug 1192

9 Marie De CHAMPAGNE

Born: Abt 1129
 -CONTINUED AS #7,ROYAL CHART 1540
Died: Abt 7 Jul 1190

2 Eudes III, Duke of Burgundy

Born: 1166

Married: 1199

Died: 6 Jul 1218

10 Mathieu I, Duke of Lorraine

Born: Abt 1115
 -CONTINUED AS #1,ROYAL CHART 1554
Married:

Died: 13 May 1176

5 Alix De LORRAINE

Born: Abt 1145

Died: 1200

11 Bertha of Swabia

Born: Abt 1123
 -CONTINUED AS #1,ROYAL CHART 2149
Died: Abt 25 Mar 1195

1 Hugh IV, Duke of Burgundy

Born: 9 Mar 1212
 -SAME AS #14,ROYAL CHART 72
Married: 1229

Died: 27 Oct 1272

12 Guy De VERGY

Born: Abt 1128
 -CONTINUED AS #1,ROYAL CHART 2620
Married:

Died: Aft 1204

6 Hugh De VERGY

Born: Abt 1155

Married: Abt 1177

Died: 1202

13 Adele De BEAUMONT

Born: Abt 1130
 -CONTINUED AS #1,ROYAL CHART 2621
Died:

Yolande De DREUX

Spouse

3 Alice De VERGY

Born: Abt 1178

Died: Aft 8 Mar 1251/1252

14 Garnier II De TRAINEL

Born: Abt 1120
 -CONTINUED AS #1,ROYAL CHART 2622
Married:

Died: 1194

7 Julia De TRAINEL

Born: Abt 1155

Died:

15 Elizabeth De MARIGNY

Born: Abt 1125
 -CONTINUED AS #1,ROYAL CHART 2623
Died:

Sources include: *Royal Ancestors* (1989), chart 11345; Faris preliminary Charlemagne manuscript (June 1995), pp. 82-83; Paget 18; *Tableaux Genealogiques des Souverans de la France* 26, 41; *Ancestral Roots* 155-28; Turton 200-201; LDS records; Kraentzler 1392-93 (#3 ancestry).

8 Robert I, Count of Dreux

Born: Abt 1123
-CONTINUED AS #1,ROYAL CHART 1565
Married: 1152

Died: 11 Oct 1188

4 Robert II, Count of Dreux

Born: Abt 1154

Married: 1184

Died: 28 Dec 1218

9 Agnes De BAUDEMONT

Born: Abt 1130
-CONTINUED AS #1,ROYAL CHART 1566
Died: 24 Jul 1204

2 Robert III, Count of Dreux

Born: Abt 1185

Married: Abt 1210

Died: 3 Mar 1234

10 Raoul De COUCY

Born: Abt 1135
-CONTINUED AS #1,ROYAL CHART 1567
Married: Bef 1164

Died: Nov 1191

5 Yolande De COUCY

Born: Abt 1168

Died: 18 Mar 1222

11 Agnes of Hainaut

Born: Abt 1142
-CONTINUED AS #1,ROYAL CHART 1568
Died: Bef 1174

1 Yolande De DREUX

Born: Abt 1212
-SAME AS #15,ROYAL CHART 72
Married: 1229

Died: 30 Oct 1248

12 Bernard De SAINT VALERY

Born: Abt 1125
-CONTINUED AS #2,ROYAL CHART 2584
Married:

Died: 1191

6 Thomas De SAINT VALERY

Born: Abt 1160

Married: Abt 1178

Died: 1218

13 Annora De SAINT JOHN

Born: Abt 1130
-CONTINUED AS #3,ROYAL CHART 2584
Died:

Hugh IV, Duke of Burgundy

Spouse

3 Alianore De SAINT VALERY

Born: Abt 1189

Died: 15 Nov 1251

14 Jean I, Count of Ponthieu

Born: Abt 1140
-CONTINUED AS #1,ROYAL CHART 1525
Married:

Died: 30 Jun 1191

7 Adela De PONTHIEU

Born: Abt 1162

Died:

15 Mathilda

Born:

Died:

Sources include: *Royal Ancestors* (1989), chart 11345; Paget 18, 177; Faris preliminary Charlemagne manuscript (June 1995), pp. 123-124, 221; *Ancestral Roots* 155-28; Turton 200, 178; Kraentzler 1394-95; Schwennicke 3:638 (#7 ancestry); Moriarty 113 (#7 ancestry). Note: #15 is disputed and uncertain. Moriarty gives Mathilda (1st wife) as the mother of Adela, as shown above. Adela is also claimed as the daughter of Beatrice of Saint Pol (3rd wife), whose ancestry is given on chart 1526, and of Laura (Laure) De St. Valery (2nd wife). Mathilda is more acceptable chronologically.

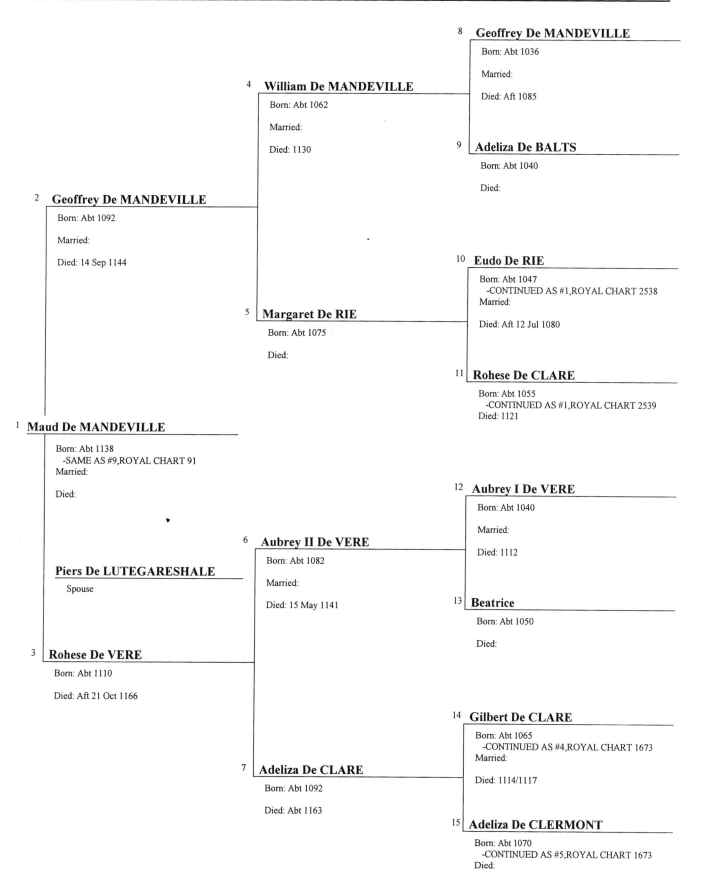

2 Geoffrey De MANDEVILLE
Born: Abt 1092
Married:
Died: 14 Sep 1144

4 William De MANDEVILLE
Born: Abt 1062
Married:
Died: 1130

8 Geoffrey De MANDEVILLE
Born: Abt 1036
Married:
Died: Aft 1085

9 Adeliza De BALTS
Born: Abt 1040
Died:

5 Margaret De RIE
Born: Abt 1075
Died:

10 Eudo De RIE
Born: Abt 1047
-CONTINUED AS #1,ROYAL CHART 2538
Married:
Died: Aft 12 Jul 1080

11 Rohese De CLARE
Born: Abt 1055
-CONTINUED AS #1,ROYAL CHART 2539
Died: 1121

1 Maud De MANDEVILLE
Born: Abt 1138
-SAME AS #9,ROYAL CHART 91
Married:
Died:

Piers De LUTEGARESHALE
Spouse

3 Rohese De VERE
Born: Abt 1110
Died: Aft 21 Oct 1166

6 Aubrey II De VERE
Born: Abt 1082
Married:
Died: 15 May 1141

12 Aubrey I De VERE
Born: Abt 1040
Married:
Died: 1112

13 Beatrice
Born: Abt 1050
Died:

7 Adeliza De CLARE
Born: Abt 1092
Died: Abt 1163

14 Gilbert De CLARE
Born: Abt 1065
-CONTINUED AS #4,ROYAL CHART 1673
Married:
Died: 1114/1117

15 Adeliza De CLERMONT
Born: Abt 1070
-CONTINUED AS #5,ROYAL CHART 1673
Died:

Sources include: *Royal Ancestors* (1989), chart 11457; *Magna Charta* 159; *Complete Peerage* 5:113-116 (#2 & 3 ancestry); Faris preliminary baronial manuscript (1998), p. 1047 Mandeville (#2 & 3 ancestry); *Ancestral Roots* 246D-25 (#6 & 7 ancestry); Turton 95; LDS records. Notes: Douglas Richardson questions that Maud, the wife of Piers De Lutegareshale (more properly called Peter the Forester, alias De Lutegareshale) was a Mandeville. The identity and ancestry shown for #5 is questionable. *Complete Peerage* 5:113-114 discusses the claim at length.'

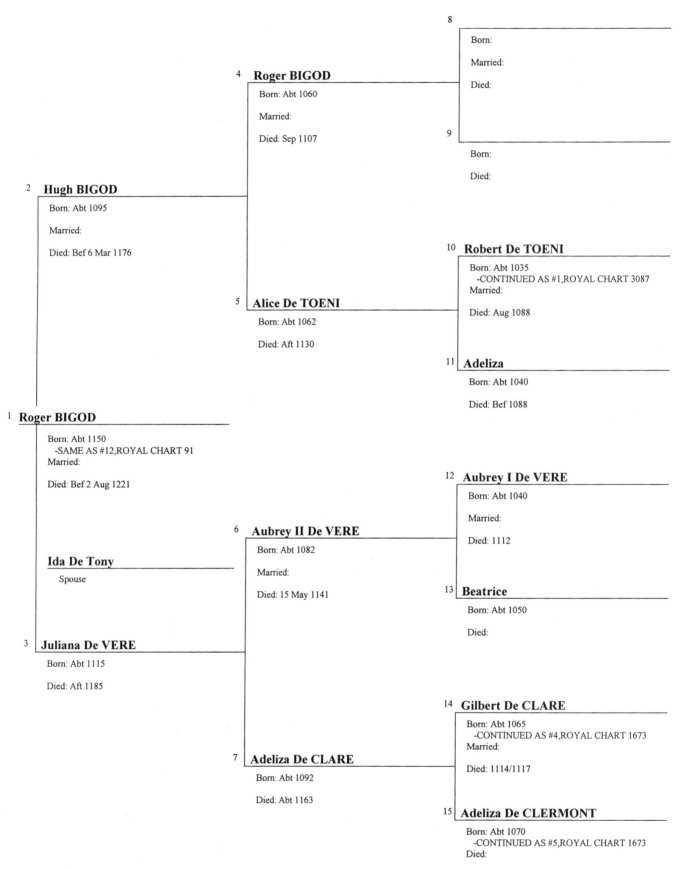

8

Born:

Married:

Died:

9

Born:

Died:

4 Roger BIGOD

Born: Abt 1060

Married:

Died: Sep 1107

10 Robert De TOENI

Born: Abt 1035
     -CONTINUED AS #1,ROYAL CHART 3087
Married:

Died: Aug 1088

11 Adeliza

Born: Abt 1040

Died: Bef 1088

2 Hugh BIGOD

Born: Abt 1095

Married:

Died: Bef 6 Mar 1176

5 Alice De TOENI

Born: Abt 1062

Died: Aft 1130

1 Roger BIGOD

Born: Abt 1150
     -SAME AS #12,ROYAL CHART 91
Married:

Died: Bef 2 Aug 1221

Ida De Tony

Spouse

12 Aubrey I De VERE

Born: Abt 1040

Married:

Died: 1112

13 Beatrice

Born: Abt 1050

Died:

6 Aubrey II De VERE

Born: Abt 1082

Married:

Died: 15 May 1141

3 Juliana De VERE

Born: Abt 1115

Died: Aft 1185

14 Gilbert De CLARE

Born: Abt 1065
     -CONTINUED AS #4,ROYAL CHART 1673
Married:

Died: 1114/1117

15 Adeliza De CLERMONT

Born: Abt 1070
     -CONTINUED AS #5,ROYAL CHART 1673
Died:

7 Adeliza De CLARE

Born: Abt 1092

Died: Abt 1163

Sources include: *Royal Ancestors* (1989), charts 11390, 11660 notes; Faris preliminary baronial manuscript (1998), pp. 122-123 (Bigod); Faris-Richardson preliminary Magna Carta manuscript (June 2000), p. 47 (Bigod); *Magna Charta* 155; *Complete Peerage* 9:575-578 (#2 ancestry); LDS records; *Ancestral Roots* 246D-25 (#6 &7 ancestry). Note: The parentage of #4 Roger is uncertain. Turton 138 may be incorrect on the claimed ancestry of #4 and is probably wrong in claiming a Grentmesnil line for #5. #5 Alice De Toeni (Tosny, Todeni) was a 2nd wife. #2 Hugh might be the son of a 1st wife Alice or Adelaide, whose parentage is unknown.

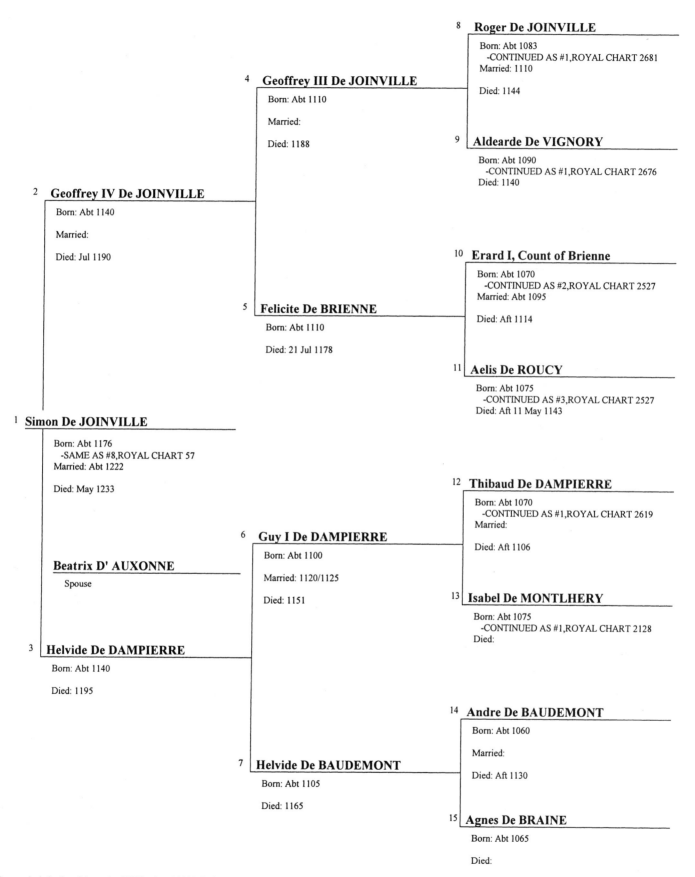

8 **Roger De JOINVILLE**
Born: Abt 1083
-CONTINUED AS #1,ROYAL CHART 2681
Married: 1110

Died: 1144

4 **Geoffrey III De JOINVILLE**
Born: Abt 1110

Married:

Died: 1188

9 **Aldearde De VIGNORY**
Born: Abt 1090
-CONTINUED AS #1,ROYAL CHART 2676
Died: 1140

2 **Geoffrey IV De JOINVILLE**
Born: Abt 1140

Married:

Died: Jul 1190

10 **Erard I, Count of Brienne**
Born: Abt 1070
-CONTINUED AS #2,ROYAL CHART 2527
Married: Abt 1095

Died: Aft 1114

5 **Felicite De BRIENNE**
Born: Abt 1110

Died: 21 Jul 1178

11 **Aelis De ROUCY**
Born: Abt 1075
-CONTINUED AS #3,ROYAL CHART 2527
Died: Aft 11 May 1143

1 **Simon De JOINVILLE**
Born: Abt 1176
-SAME AS #8,ROYAL CHART 57
Married: Abt 1222

Died: May 1233

12 **Thibaud De DAMPIERRE**
Born: Abt 1070
-CONTINUED AS #1,ROYAL CHART 2619
Married:

Died: Aft 1106

6 **Guy I De DAMPIERRE**
Born: Abt 1100

Married: 1120/1125

Died: 1151

13 **Isabel De MONTLHERY**
Born: Abt 1075
-CONTINUED AS #1,ROYAL CHART 2128
Died:

Beatrix D' AUXONNE
Spouse

3 **Helvide De DAMPIERRE**
Born: Abt 1140

Died: 1195

14 **Andre De BAUDEMONT**
Born: Abt 1060

Married:

Died: Aft 1130

7 **Helvide De BAUDEMONT**
Born: Abt 1105

Died: 1165

15 **Agnes De BRAINE**
Born: Abt 1065

Died:

Sources include: *Royal Ancestors* (1989), chart 11328; Faris preliminary Charlemagne manuscript (June 1995), pp. 162-163; Schwennicke 7:6; Turton 79; LDS records; Moriarty 149 (#3 ancestry); Stuart 84 (#6 & 7 ancestry).

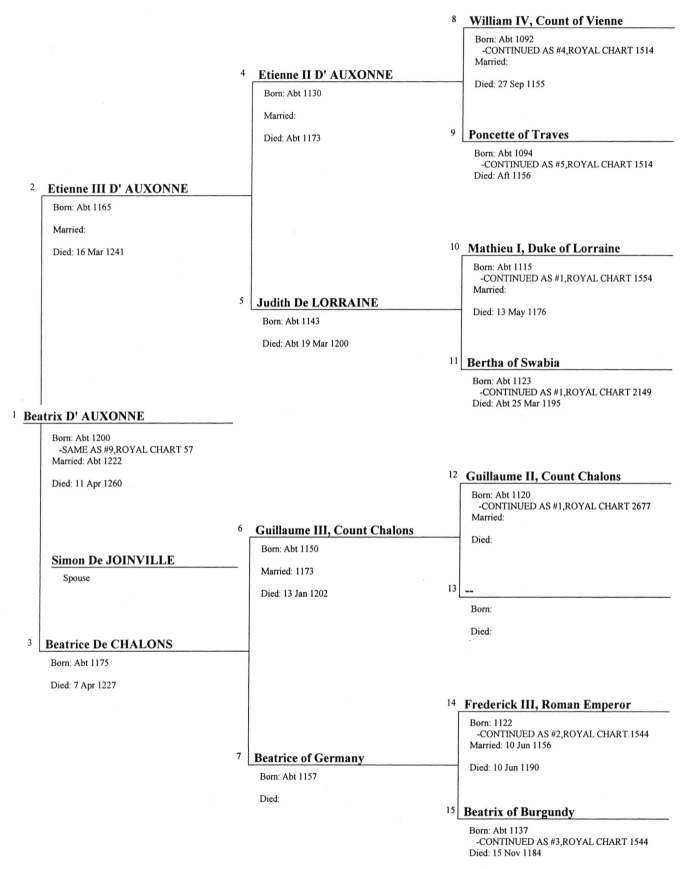

8 William IV, Count of Vienne

Born: Abt 1092
    -CONTINUED AS #4,ROYAL CHART 1514
Married:

Died: 27 Sep 1155

4 Etienne II D' AUXONNE

Born: Abt 1130

Married:

Died: Abt 1173

9 Poncette of Traves

Born: Abt 1094
    -CONTINUED AS #5,ROYAL CHART 1514
Died: Aft 1156

2 Etienne III D' AUXONNE

Born: Abt 1165

Married:

Died: 16 Mar 1241

10 Mathieu I, Duke of Lorraine

Born: Abt 1115
    -CONTINUED AS #1,ROYAL CHART 1554
Married:

Died: 13 May 1176

5 Judith De LORRAINE

Born: Abt 1143

Died: Abt 19 Mar 1200

11 Bertha of Swabia

Born: Abt 1123
    -CONTINUED AS #1,ROYAL CHART 2149
Died: Abt 25 Mar 1195

1 Beatrix D' AUXONNE

Born: Abt 1200
    -SAME AS #9,ROYAL CHART 57
Married: Abt 1222

Died: 11 Apr 1260

12 Guillaume II, Count Chalons

Born: Abt 1120
    -CONTINUED AS #1,ROYAL CHART 2677
Married:

Died:

6 Guillaume III, Count Chalons

Born: Abt 1150

Married: 1173

Died: 13 Jan 1202

13 --

Born:

Died:

Simon De JOINVILLE

Spouse

3 Beatrice De CHALONS

Born: Abt 1175

Died: 7 Apr 1227

14 Frederick III, Roman Emperor

Born: 1122
    -CONTINUED AS #2,ROYAL CHART 1544
Married: 10 Jun 1156

Died: 10 Jun 1190

7 Beatrice of Germany

Born: Abt 1157

Died:

15 Beatrix of Burgundy

Born: Abt 1137
    -CONTINUED AS #3,ROYAL CHART 1544
Died: 15 Nov 1184

Sources include: *Royal Ancestors* (1989), chart 11328; Faris preliminary Charlemagne manuscript (June 1995), pp. 65-66; Turton 80; Kraentzler 1329. Note: Turton claims Guillaume II (#12 above) as the father of #3 Beatrice and the husband of #7 Beatrice of Germany.

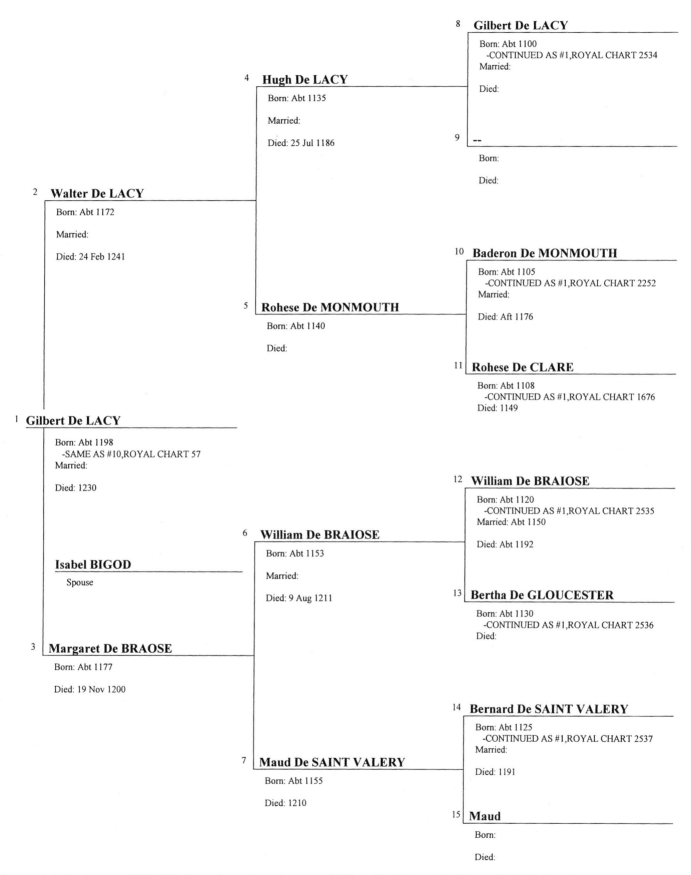

8 Gilbert De LACY
Born: Abt 1100
-CONTINUED AS #1,ROYAL CHART 2534
Married:

Died:

4 Hugh De LACY
Born: Abt 1135

Married:

Died: 25 Jul 1186

9 --
Born:

Died:

2 Walter De LACY
Born: Abt 1172

Married:

Died: 24 Feb 1241

10 Baderon De MONMOUTH
Born: Abt 1105
-CONTINUED AS #1,ROYAL CHART 2252
Married:

Died: Aft 1176

5 Rohese De MONMOUTH
Born: Abt 1140

Died:

11 Rohese De CLARE
Born: Abt 1108
-CONTINUED AS #1,ROYAL CHART 1676
Died: 1149

1 Gilbert De LACY
Born: Abt 1198
-SAME AS #10,ROYAL CHART 57
Married:

Died: 1230

12 William De BRAIOSE
Born: Abt 1120
-CONTINUED AS #1,ROYAL CHART 2535
Married: Abt 1150

Died: Abt 1192

6 William De BRAIOSE
Born: Abt 1153

Married:

Died: 9 Aug 1211

13 Bertha De GLOUCESTER
Born: Abt 1130
-CONTINUED AS #1,ROYAL CHART 2536
Died:

Isabel BIGOD
Spouse

3 Margaret De BRAOSE
Born: Abt 1177

Died: 19 Nov 1200

14 Bernard De SAINT VALERY
Born: Abt 1125
-CONTINUED AS #1,ROYAL CHART 2537
Married:

Died: 1191

7 Maud De SAINT VALERY
Born: Abt 1155

Died: 1210

15 Maud
Born:

Died:

Sources include: *Royal Ancestors* 11328, 11430; Faris preliminary baronial manuscript (1998), pp. 929-931 (Lacy), 1101 (Monmouth), 217-218 (Breuse).

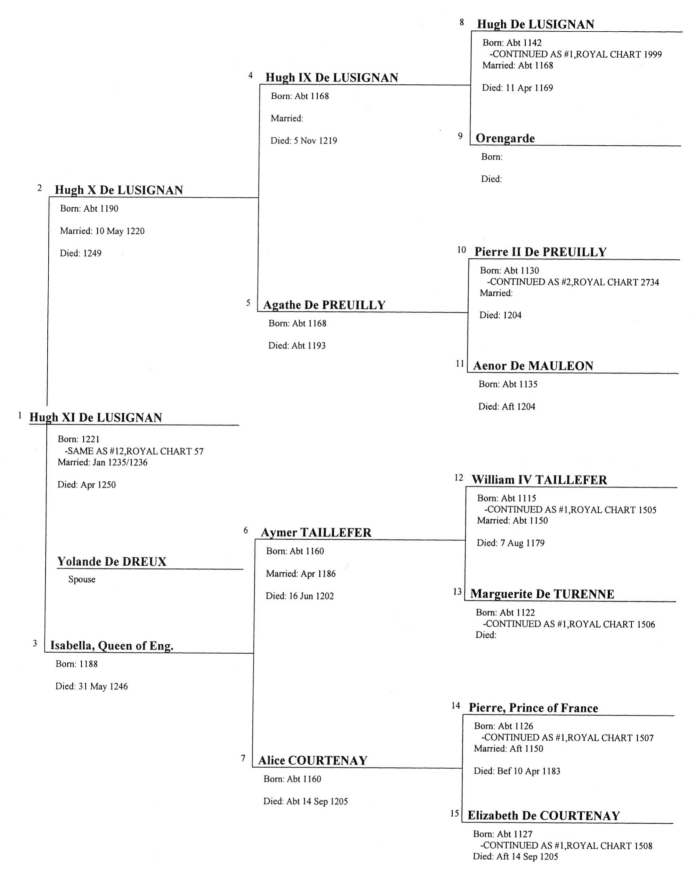

8 **Hugh De LUSIGNAN**

Born: Abt 1142
-CONTINUED AS #1,ROYAL CHART 1999
Married: Abt 1168

Died: 11 Apr 1169

4 **Hugh IX De LUSIGNAN**

Born: Abt 1168

Married:

Died: 5 Nov 1219

9 **Orengarde**

Born:

Died:

2 **Hugh X De LUSIGNAN**

Born: Abt 1190

Married: 10 May 1220

Died: 1249

10 **Pierre II De PREUILLY**

Born: Abt 1130
-CONTINUED AS #2,ROYAL CHART 2734
Married:

Died: 1204

5 **Agathe De PREUILLY**

Born: Abt 1168

Died: Abt 1193

11 **Aenor De MAULEON**

Born: Abt 1135

Died: Aft 1204

1 **Hugh XI De LUSIGNAN**

Born: 1221
-SAME AS #12,ROYAL CHART 57
Married: Jan 1235/1236

Died: Apr 1250

12 **William IV TAILLEFER**

Born: Abt 1115
-CONTINUED AS #1,ROYAL CHART 1505
Married: Abt 1150

Died: 7 Aug 1179

6 **Aymer TAILLEFER**

Born: Abt 1160

Married: Apr 1186

Died: 16 Jun 1202

13 **Marguerite De TURENNE**

Born: Abt 1122
-CONTINUED AS #1,ROYAL CHART 1506
Died:

Yolande De DREUX

Spouse

3 **Isabella, Queen of Eng.**

Born: 1188

Died: 31 May 1246

14 **Pierre, Prince of France**

Born: Abt 1126
-CONTINUED AS #1,ROYAL CHART 1507
Married: Aft 1150

Died: Bef 10 Apr 1183

7 **Alice COURTENAY**

Born: Abt 1160

Died: Abt 14 Sep 1205

15 **Elizabeth De COURTENAY**

Born: Abt 1127
-CONTINUED AS #1,ROYAL CHART 1508
Died: Aft 14 Sep 1205

Sources include: *Royal Ancestors* (1989), chart 11329; Faris preliminary Charlemagne manuscript (June 1995), pp. 171, 19; Schwennicke 3:816, 725; Faris preliminary baronial manuscript (1998), pp. 1016-17 (Lusignan); *Ancestral Roots* 117, 123-28.

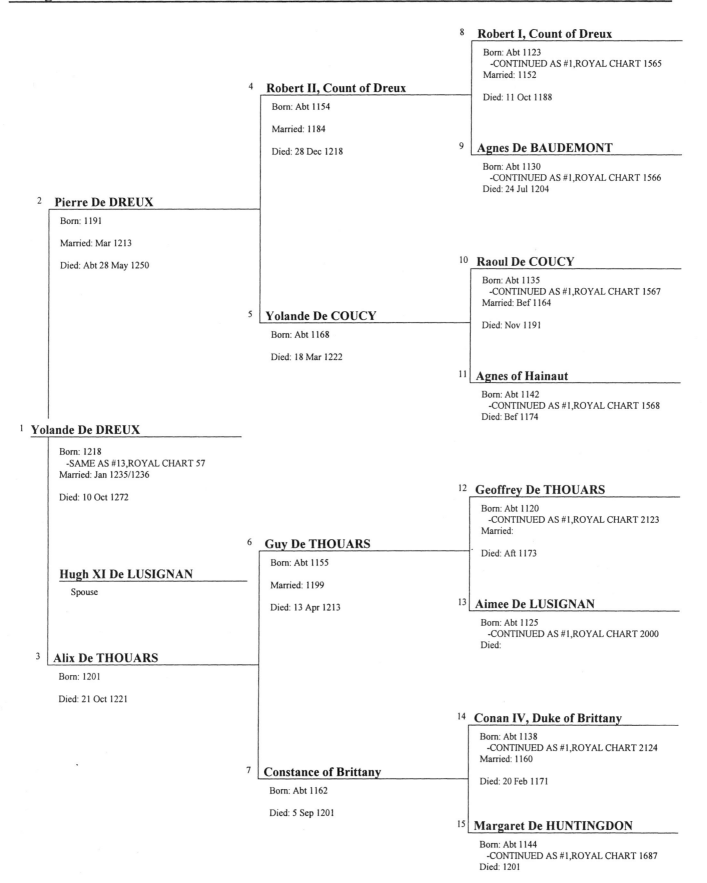

4 Robert II, Count of Dreux

Born: Abt 1154

Married: 1184

Died: 28 Dec 1218

8 Robert I, Count of Dreux

Born: Abt 1123
-CONTINUED AS #1,ROYAL CHART 1565
Married: 1152

Died: 11 Oct 1188

9 Agnes De BAUDEMONT

Born: Abt 1130
-CONTINUED AS #1,ROYAL CHART 1566
Died: 24 Jul 1204

2 Pierre De DREUX

Born: 1191

Married: Mar 1213

Died: Abt 28 May 1250

5 Yolande De COUCY

Born: Abt 1168

Died: 18 Mar 1222

10 Raoul De COUCY

Born: Abt 1135
-CONTINUED AS #1,ROYAL CHART 1567
Married: Bef 1164

Died: Nov 1191

11 Agnes of Hainaut

Born: Abt 1142
-CONTINUED AS #1,ROYAL CHART 1568
Died: Bef 1174

1 Yolande De DREUX

Born: 1218
-SAME AS #13,ROYAL CHART 57
Married: Jan 1235/1236

Died: 10 Oct 1272

Hugh XI De LUSIGNAN

Spouse

3 Alix De THOUARS

Born: 1201

Died: 21 Oct 1221

6 Guy De THOUARS

Born: Abt 1155

Married: 1199

Died: 13 Apr 1213

12 Geoffrey De THOUARS

Born: Abt 1120
-CONTINUED AS #1,ROYAL CHART 2123
Married:

Died: Aft 1173

13 Aimee De LUSIGNAN

Born: Abt 1125
-CONTINUED AS #1,ROYAL CHART 2000
Died:

7 Constance of Brittany

Born: Abt 1162

Died: 5 Sep 1201

14 Conan IV, Duke of Brittany

Born: Abt 1138
-CONTINUED AS #1,ROYAL CHART 2124
Married: 1160

Died: 20 Feb 1171

15 Margaret De HUNTINGDON

Born: Abt 1144
-CONTINUED AS #1,ROYAL CHART 1687
Died: 1201

Sources include: *Royal Ancestors* (1989), chart 11329; Faris preliminary Charlemagne manuscript (June 1995), pp. 171-172, 260-261, 123; *Ancestral Roots* 135, 96; *Complete Peerage* 10:794-797 (#3 ancestry); Schwennicke 3:810 (#3 ancestry).

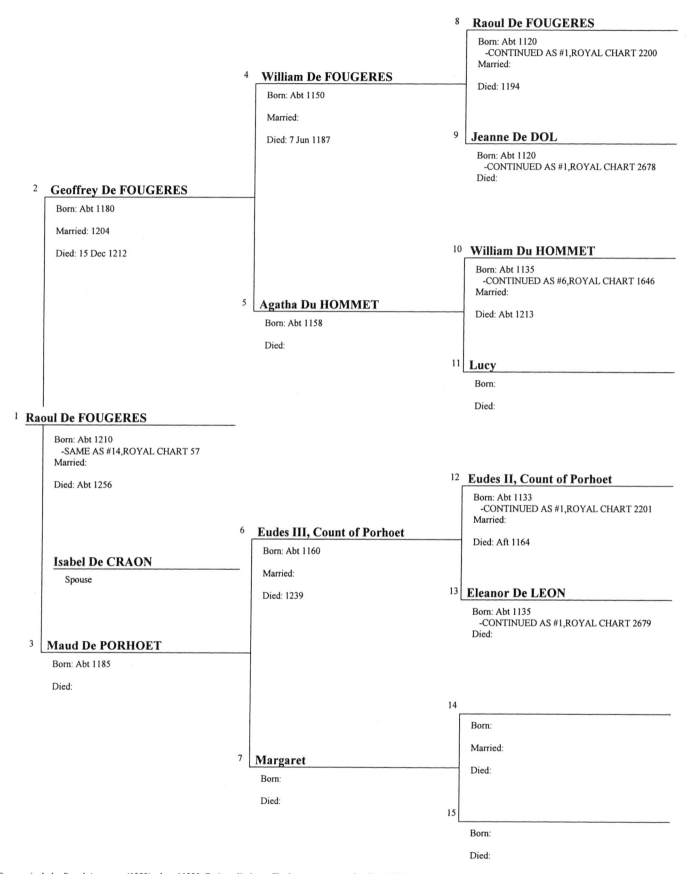

8 **Raoul De FOUGERES**

Born: Abt 1120
  -CONTINUED AS #1,ROYAL CHART 2200
Married:

Died: 1194

4 **William De FOUGERES**

Born: Abt 1150

Married:

Died: 7 Jun 1187

9 **Jeanne De DOL**

Born: Abt 1120
  -CONTINUED AS #1,ROYAL CHART 2678
Died:

2 **Geoffrey De FOUGERES**

Born: Abt 1180

Married: 1204

Died: 15 Dec 1212

10 **William Du HOMMET**

Born: Abt 1135
  -CONTINUED AS #6,ROYAL CHART 1646
Married:

Died: Abt 1213

5 **Agatha Du HOMMET**

Born: Abt 1158

Died:

11 **Lucy**

Born:

Died:

1 **Raoul De FOUGERES**

Born: Abt 1210
  -SAME AS #14,ROYAL CHART 57
Married:

Died: Abt 1256

12 **Eudes II, Count of Porhoet**

Born: Abt 1133
  -CONTINUED AS #1,ROYAL CHART 2201
Married:

Died: Aft 1164

6 **Eudes III, Count of Porhoet**

Born: Abt 1160

Married:

Died: 1239

13 **Eleanor De LEON**

Born: Abt 1135
  -CONTINUED AS #1,ROYAL CHART 2679
Died:

Isabel De CRAON

Spouse

3 **Maud De PORHOET**

Born: Abt 1185

Died:

14

Born:

Married:

Died:

7 **Margaret**

Born:

Died:

15

Born:

Died:

Sources include: *Royal Ancestors* (1989), chart 11329; Faris preliminary Charlemagne manuscript (June 1995), p. 139; *Ancestral Roots* 214A, 184A-6; Turton 82.

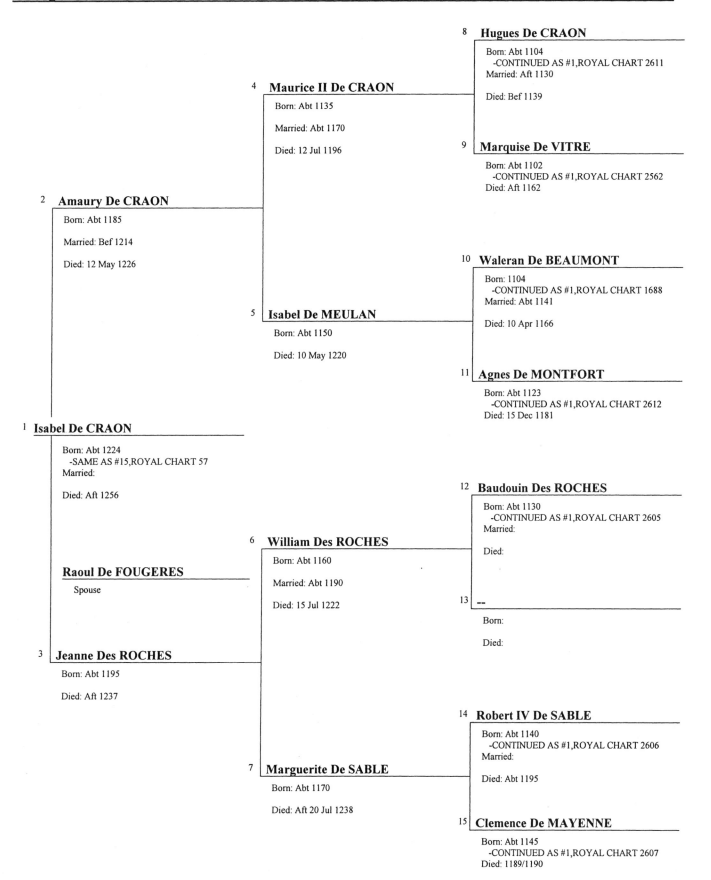

8 Hugues De CRAON

Born: Abt 1104
 -CONTINUED AS #1,ROYAL CHART 2611
Married: Aft 1130

Died: Bef 1139

4 Maurice II De CRAON

Born: Abt 1135

Married: Abt 1170

Died: 12 Jul 1196

9 Marquise De VITRE

Born: Abt 1102
 -CONTINUED AS #1,ROYAL CHART 2562
Died: Aft 1162

2 Amaury De CRAON

Born: Abt 1185

Married: Bef 1214

Died: 12 May 1226

10 Waleran De BEAUMONT

Born: 1104
 -CONTINUED AS #1,ROYAL CHART 1688
Married: Abt 1141

Died: 10 Apr 1166

5 Isabel De MEULAN

Born: Abt 1150

Died: 10 May 1220

11 Agnes De MONTFORT

Born: Abt 1123
 -CONTINUED AS #1,ROYAL CHART 2612
Died: 15 Dec 1181

1 Isabel De CRAON

Born: Abt 1224
 -SAME AS #15,ROYAL CHART 57
Married:

Died: Aft 1256

12 Baudouin Des ROCHES

Born: Abt 1130
 -CONTINUED AS #1,ROYAL CHART 2605
Married:

Died:

6 William Des ROCHES

Born: Abt 1160

Married: Abt 1190

Died: 15 Jul 1222

13 --

Born:

Died:

Raoul De FOUGERES

Spouse

3 Jeanne Des ROCHES

Born: Abt 1195

Died: Aft 1237

14 Robert IV De SABLE

Born: Abt 1140
 -CONTINUED AS #1,ROYAL CHART 2606
Married:

Died: Abt 1195

7 Marguerite De SABLE

Born: Abt 1170

Died: Aft 20 Jul 1238

15 Clemence De MAYENNE

Born: Abt 1145
 -CONTINUED AS #1,ROYAL CHART 2607
Died: 1189/1190

Sources include: *Royal Ancestors* (1989), chart 11329; Faris preliminary Charlemagne manuscript (June 1995), pp. 139, 115, 241; Schwennicke 3:719, 700; *Ancestral Roots* 214A-29; Turton 83; Kraentzler 1340-41.

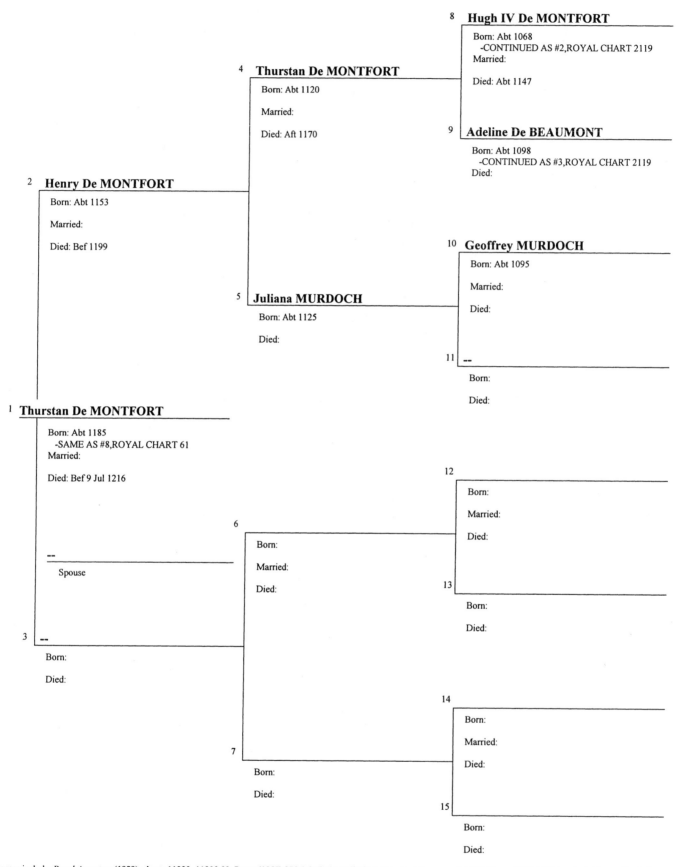

8 Hugh IV De MONTFORT

Born: Abt 1068
  -CONTINUED AS #2,ROYAL CHART 2119
Married:

Died: Abt 1147

4 Thurstan De MONTFORT

Born: Abt 1120

Married:

Died: Aft 1170

9 Adeline De BEAUMONT

Born: Abt 1098
  -CONTINUED AS #3,ROYAL CHART 2119
Died:

2 Henry De MONTFORT

Born: Abt 1153

Married:

Died: Bef 1199

10 Geoffrey MURDOCH

Born: Abt 1095

Married:

Died:

5 Juliana MURDOCH

Born: Abt 1125

Died:

11 --

Born:

Died:

1 Thurstan De MONTFORT

Born: Abt 1185
  -SAME AS #8,ROYAL CHART 61
Married:

Died: Bef 9 Jul 1216

12

Born:

Married:

Died:

6

Born:

Married:

Died:

13

Born:

Died:

**-- **

Spouse

3 --

Born:

Died:

14

Born:

Married:

Died:

7

Born:

Died:

15

Born:

Died:

Sources include: *Royal Ancestors* (1989), charts 11333, 11908-09; Paget (1957) 378:1-2; Faris preliminary baroronial manuscript (1998), pp. 1113-14 (Montfort); Turton 88; LDS records.

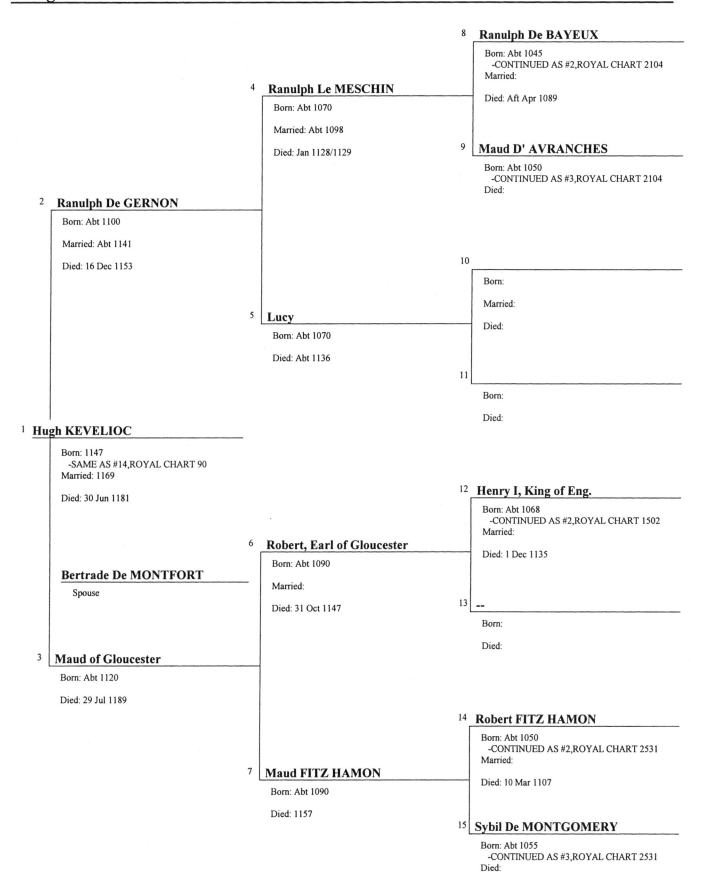

8 Ranulph De BAYEUX

Born: Abt 1045
-CONTINUED AS #2,ROYAL CHART 2104
Married:

Died: Aft Apr 1089

4 Ranulph Le MESCHIN

Born: Abt 1070

Married: Abt 1098

Died: Jan 1128/1129

9 Maud D' AVRANCHES

Born: Abt 1050
-CONTINUED AS #3,ROYAL CHART 2104
Died:

2 Ranulph De GERNON

Born: Abt 1100

Married: Abt 1141

Died: 16 Dec 1153

10

Born:

Married:

Died:

5 Lucy

Born: Abt 1070

Died: Abt 1136

11

Born:

Died:

1 Hugh KEVELIOC

Born: 1147
-SAME AS #14,ROYAL CHART 90
Married: 1169

Died: 30 Jun 1181

12 Henry I, King of Eng.

Born: Abt 1068
-CONTINUED AS #2,ROYAL CHART 1502
Married:

Died: 1 Dec 1135

6 Robert, Earl of Gloucester

Born: Abt 1090

Married:

Died: 31 Oct 1147

13 --

Born:

Died:

Bertrade De MONTFORT

Spouse

3 Maud of Gloucester

Born: Abt 1120

Died: 29 Jul 1189

14 Robert FITZ HAMON

Born: Abt 1050
-CONTINUED AS #2,ROYAL CHART 2531
Married:

Died: 10 Mar 1107

7 Maud FITZ HAMON

Born: Abt 1090

Died: 1157

15 Sybil De MONTGOMERY

Born: Abt 1055
-CONTINUED AS #3,ROYAL CHART 2531
Died:

Sources include: *Royal Ancestors* (1989), chart 11444; *Ancestral Roots* 125, 124; *TAG* 73:308; Roberts *500*, pp. 400-401; Turton 95, 94. Note: #6 Robert was illegitimate by an unknown mistress of Henry I.

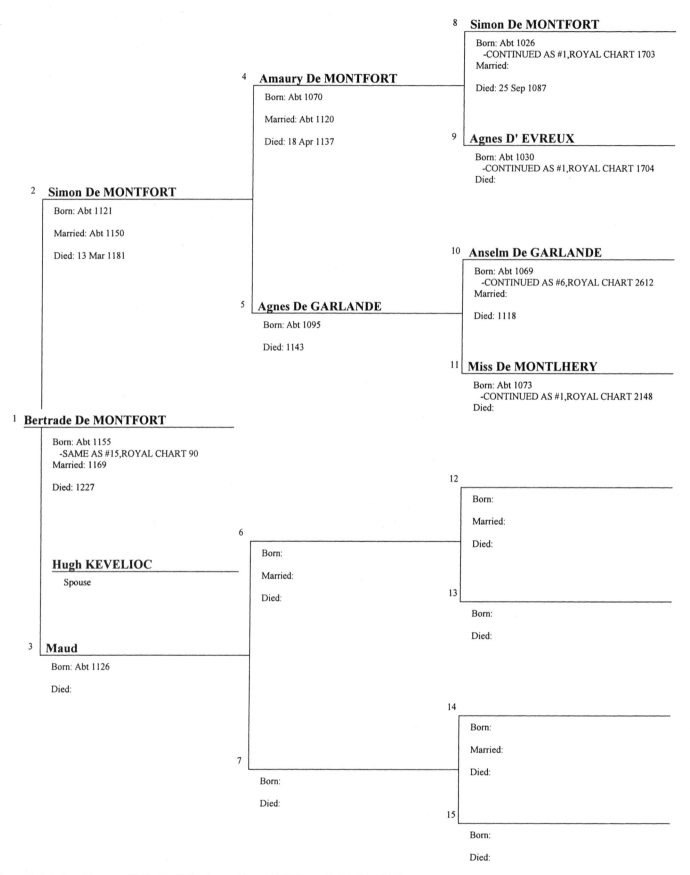

8 **Simon De MONTFORT**

Born: Abt 1026
  -CONTINUED AS #1,ROYAL CHART 1703
Married:

Died: 25 Sep 1087

4 **Amaury De MONTFORT**

Born: Abt 1070

Married: Abt 1120

Died: 18 Apr 1137

9 **Agnes D' EVREUX**

Born: Abt 1030
  -CONTINUED AS #1,ROYAL CHART 1704
Died:

2 **Simon De MONTFORT**

Born: Abt 1121

Married: Abt 1150

Died: 13 Mar 1181

10 **Anselm De GARLANDE**

Born: Abt 1069
  -CONTINUED AS #6,ROYAL CHART 2612
Married:

Died: 1118

5 **Agnes De GARLANDE**

Born: Abt 1095

Died: 1143

11 **Miss De MONTLHERY**

Born: Abt 1073
  -CONTINUED AS #1,ROYAL CHART 2148
Died:

1 **Bertrade De MONTFORT**

Born: Abt 1155
  -SAME AS #15,ROYAL CHART 90
Married: 1169

Died: 1227

12

Born:

Married:

Died:

6

Born:

Married:

Died:

13

Born:

Died:

Hugh KEVELIOC

Spouse

3 **Maud**

Born: Abt 1126

Died:

14

Born:

Married:

Died:

7

Born:

Died:

15

Born:

Died:

Sources include: *Royal Ancestors* (1989), chart 11445; *Ancestral Roots* 125-28; Turton 95, 230; *TAG* 73:308.

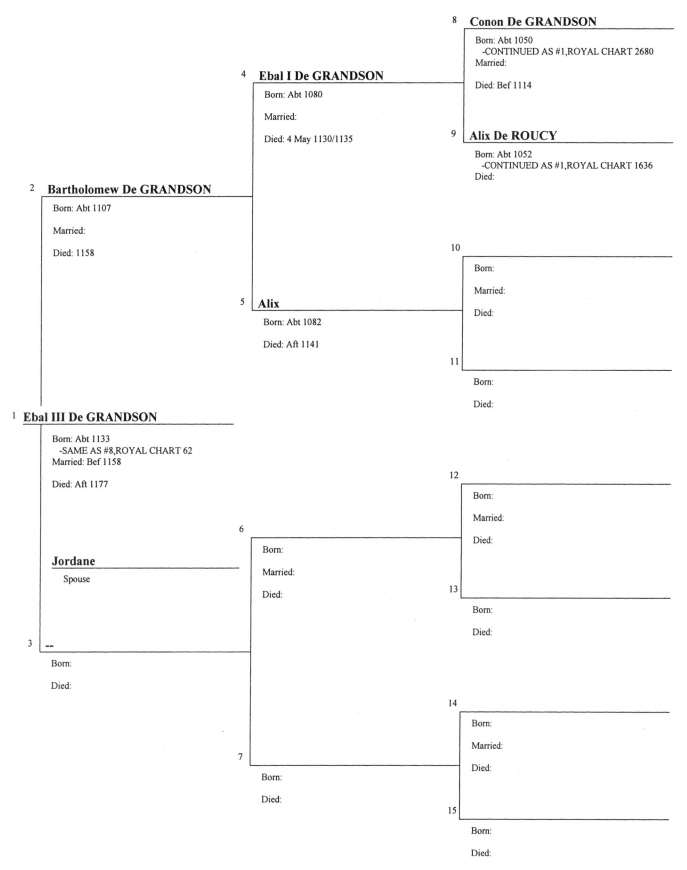

8 Conon De GRANDSON

Born: Abt 1050
   -CONTINUED AS #1,ROYAL CHART 2680
Married:

Died: Bef 1114

4 Ebal I De GRANDSON

Born: Abt 1080

Married:

Died: 4 May 1130/1135

9 Alix De ROUCY

Born: Abt 1052
   -CONTINUED AS #1,ROYAL CHART 1636
Died:

2 Bartholomew De GRANDSON

Born: Abt 1107

Married:

Died: 1158

10

Born:

Married:

Died:

5 Alix

Born: Abt 1082

Died: Aft 1141

11

Born:

Died:

1 Ebal III De GRANDSON

Born: Abt 1133
   -SAME AS #8,ROYAL CHART 62
Married: Bef 1158

Died: Aft 1177

12

Born:

Married:

Died:

6

Born:

Married:

Died:

13

Born:

Died:

Jordane

Spouse

3 --

Born:

Died:

14

Born:

Married:

Died:

7

Born:

Died:

15

Born:

Died:

Sources include: *Royal Ancestors* (1989), chart 11335; Faris preliminary Charlemagne manuscript (June 1995), pp. 150-151; Schwennicke 11:153.

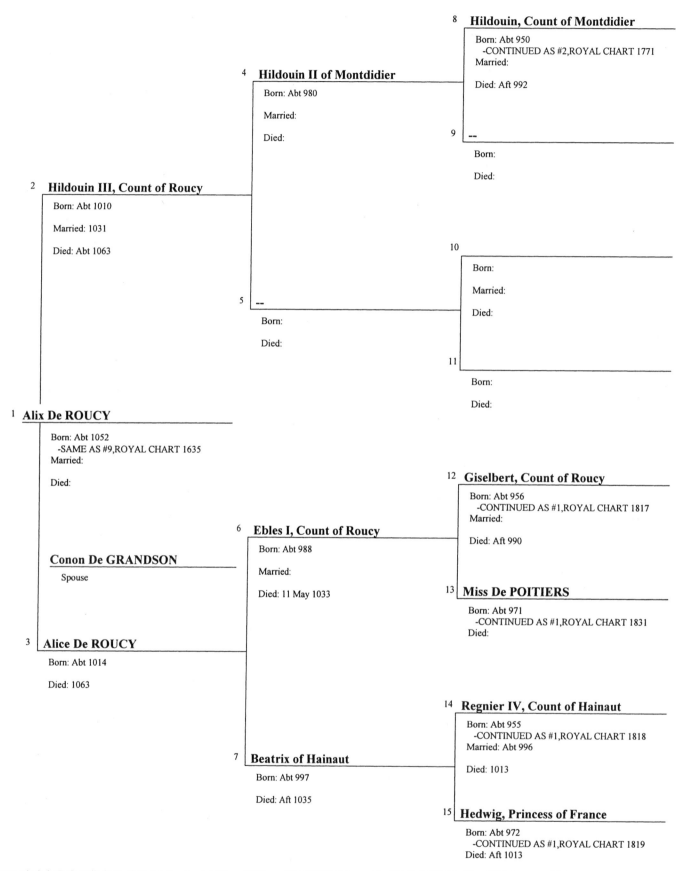

8 **Hildouin, Count of Montdidier**

Born: Abt 950
 -CONTINUED AS #2,ROYAL CHART 1771
Married:

Died: Aft 992

4 **Hildouin II of Montdidier**

Born: Abt 980

Married:

Died:

9 --

Born:

Died:

2 **Hildouin III, Count of Roucy**

Born: Abt 1010

Married: 1031

Died: Abt 1063

10

Born:

Married:

Died:

5 --

Born:

Died:

11

Born:

Died:

1 **Alix De ROUCY**

Born: Abt 1052
 -SAME AS #9,ROYAL CHART 1635
Married:

Died:

12 **Giselbert, Count of Roucy**

Born: Abt 956
 -CONTINUED AS #1,ROYAL CHART 1817
Married:

Died: Aft 990

6 **Ebles I, Count of Roucy**

Born: Abt 988

Married:

Died: 11 May 1033

13 **Miss De POITIERS**

Born: Abt 971
 -CONTINUED AS #1,ROYAL CHART 1831
Died:

Conon De GRANDSON

Spouse

3 **Alice De ROUCY**

Born: Abt 1014

Died: 1063

14 **Regnier IV, Count of Hainaut**

Born: Abt 955
 -CONTINUED AS #1,ROYAL CHART 1818
Married: Abt 996

Died: 1013

7 **Beatrix of Hainaut**

Born: Abt 997

Died: Aft 1035

15 **Hedwig, Princess of France**

Born: Abt 972
 -CONTINUED AS #1,ROYAL CHART 1819
Died: Aft 1013

Sources include: Faris preliminary Charlemagne manuscript (June 1995), pp. 150, 235-236; Schwennicke 11:153, 3:676-677; Chart 1727 & sources (#2 & 3 ancestry).

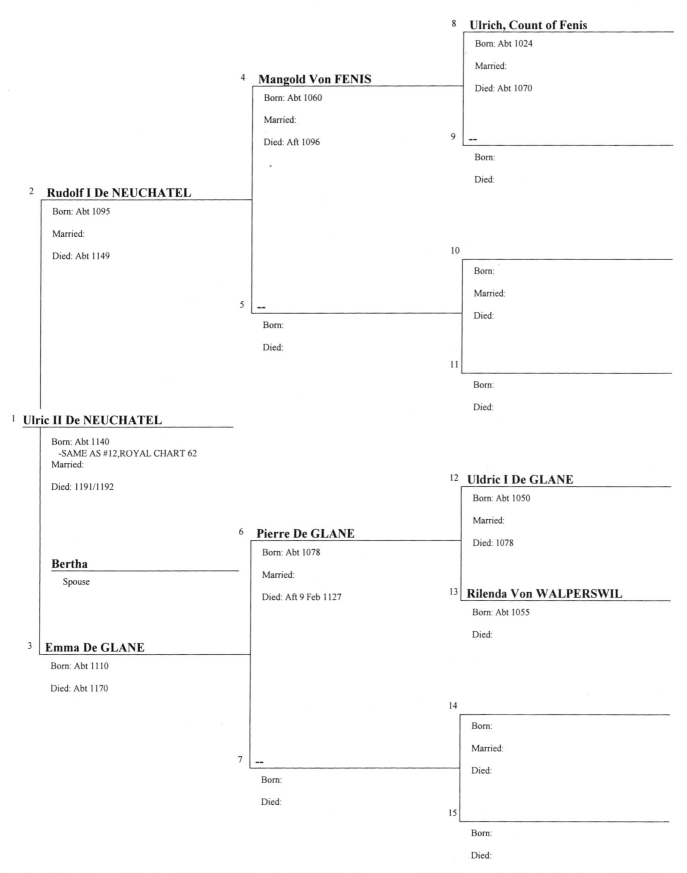

8   **Ulrich, Count of Fenis**

Born: Abt 1024

Married:

Died: Abt 1070

4   **Mangold Von FENIS**

Born: Abt 1060

Married:

Died: Aft 1096

9   --

Born:

Died:

2   **Rudolf I De NEUCHATEL**

Born: Abt 1095

Married:

Died: Abt 1149

10

Born:

Married:

Died:

5   --

Born:

Died:

11

Born:

Died:

1   **Ulric II De NEUCHATEL**

Born: Abt 1140
   -SAME AS #12,ROYAL CHART 62
Married:

Died: 1191/1192

Bertha

Spouse

12   **Uldric I De GLANE**

Born: Abt 1050

Married:

Died: 1078

6   **Pierre De GLANE**

Born: Abt 1078

Married:

Died: Aft 9 Feb 1127

13   **Rilenda Von WALPERSWIL**

Born: Abt 1055

Died:

3   **Emma De GLANE**

Born: Abt 1110

Died: Abt 1170

14

Born:

Married:

Died:

7   --

Born:

Died:

15

Born:

Died:

Sources include: *Royal Ancestors* (1989), charts 11335, 11977-78; Schwennicke 15:6, 19A. Note: The parentage of #2 Rudolf is not certain. #2 is also claimed as son of Ulric (died 1130), son of Rudolph (died abt. 1099), son of #8 Ulrich (Ulric) above. See Turton 89.

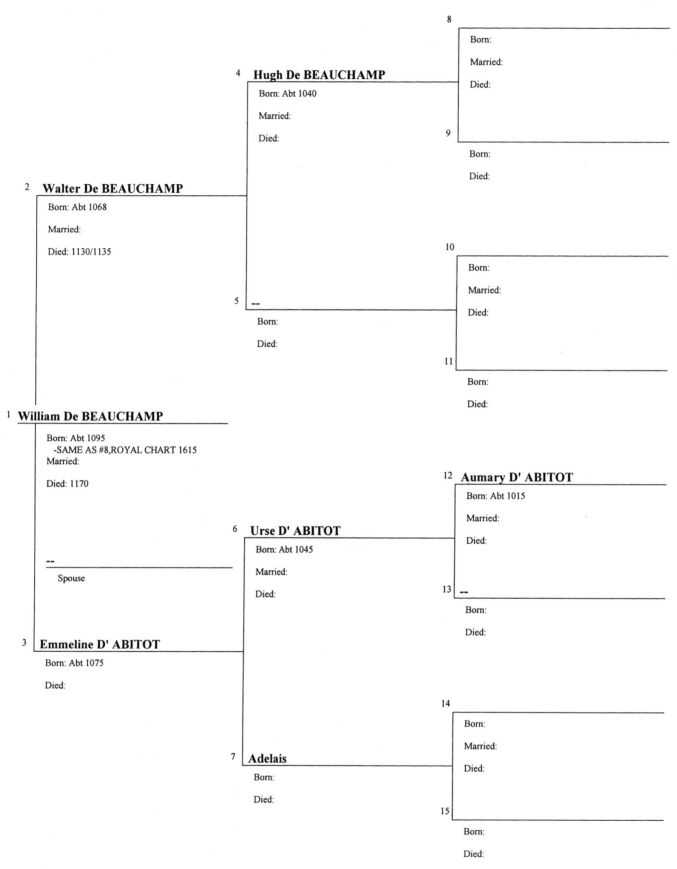

8

Born:

Married:

Died:

4 Hugh De BEAUCHAMP

Born: Abt 1040

Married:

Died:

9

Born:

Died:

2 Walter De BEAUCHAMP

Born: Abt 1068

Married:

Died: 1130/1135

10

Born:

Married:

Died:

5 --

Born:

Died:

11

Born:

Died:

1 William De BEAUCHAMP

Born: Abt 1095
 -SAME AS #8,ROYAL CHART 1615
Married:

Died: 1170

12 Aumary D' ABITOT

Born: Abt 1015

Married:

Died:

6 Urse D' ABITOT

Born: Abt 1045

Married:

Died:

13 --

Born:

Died:

--

Spouse

3 Emmeline D' ABITOT

Born: Abt 1075

Died:

14

Born:

Married:

Died:

7 Adelais

Born:

Died:

15

Born:

Died:

Sources include: *Royal Ancestors* (1989), chart 11450; Faris preliminary baronial manuscript (1998), pp. 56-57; Paget (1957) 39:1-2; Turton 117 (#12 Aumary, whom he gives as son of Gerard De Tankerville & Helesinde).

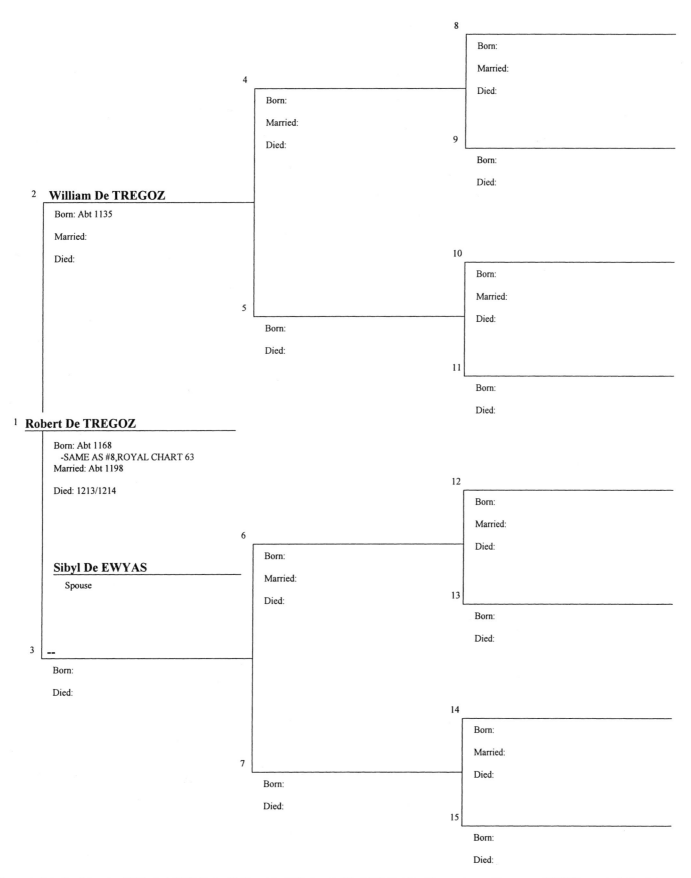

8

Born:

Married:

Died:

4

Born:

Married:

Died:

9

Born:

Died:

2 **William De TREGOZ**

Born: Abt 1135

Married:

Died:

10

Born:

Married:

Died:

5

Born:

Died:

11

Born:

Died:

1 **Robert De TREGOZ**

Born: Abt 1168
  -SAME AS #8,ROYAL CHART 63
Married: Abt 1198

Died: 1213/1214

12

Born:

Married:

Died:

6

Born:

Married:

Died:

13

Born:

Died:

Sibyl De EWYAS

Spouse

3 **--**

Born:

Died:

14

Born:

Married:

Died:

7

Born:

Died:

15

Born:

Died:

Sources include: *Royal Ancestors* (1989), chart 11336; Turton 90; Kraentzler 1109; *Ancestral Roots* 255-28. Note: The parentage and the spouse of #2 William are both disputed.

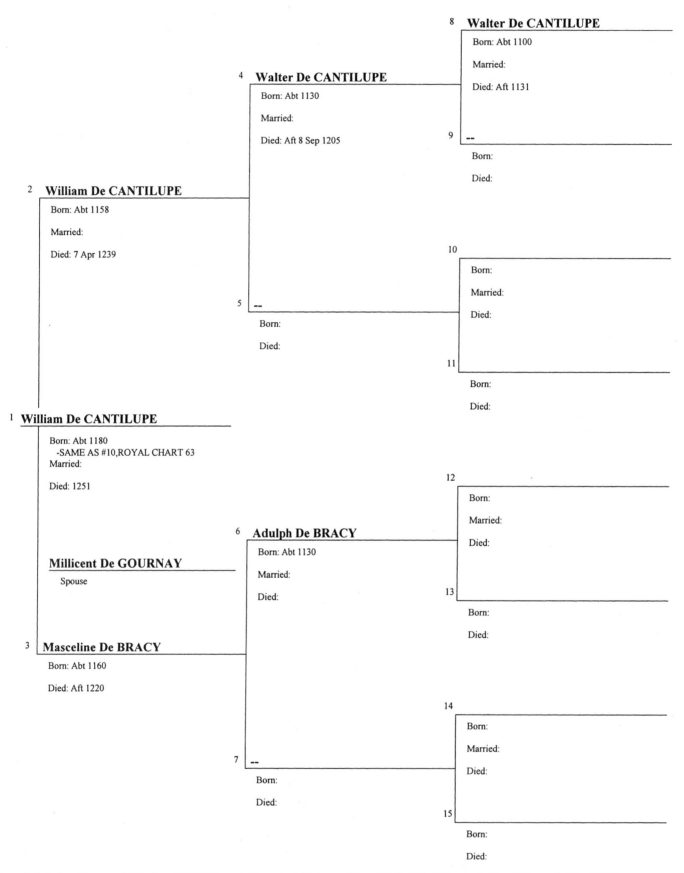

8 Walter De CANTILUPE

Born: Abt 1100

Married:

Died: Aft 1131

4 Walter De CANTILUPE

Born: Abt 1130

Married:

Died: Aft 8 Sep 1205

9 --

Born:

Died:

2 William De CANTILUPE

Born: Abt 1158

Married:

Died: 7 Apr 1239

10

Born:

Married:

Died:

5 --

Born:

Died:

11

Born:

Died:

1 William De CANTILUPE

Born: Abt 1180
  -SAME AS #10,ROYAL CHART 63
Married:

Died: 1251

12

Born:

Married:

Died:

6 Adulph De BRACY

Born: Abt 1130

Married:

Died:

13

Born:

Died:

Millicent De GOURNAY

Spouse

3 Masceline De BRACY

Born: Abt 1160

Died: Aft 1220

14

Born:

Married:

Died:

7 --

Born:

Died:

15

Born:

Died:

Sources include: *Royal Ancestors* (1989), chart 11336; LDS records; Kraentzler 1109; *Ancestral Roots* 255-29, 255A-29; Turton 90. Note: LDS records claim #2 William as son of Walter and grandson of Walter.

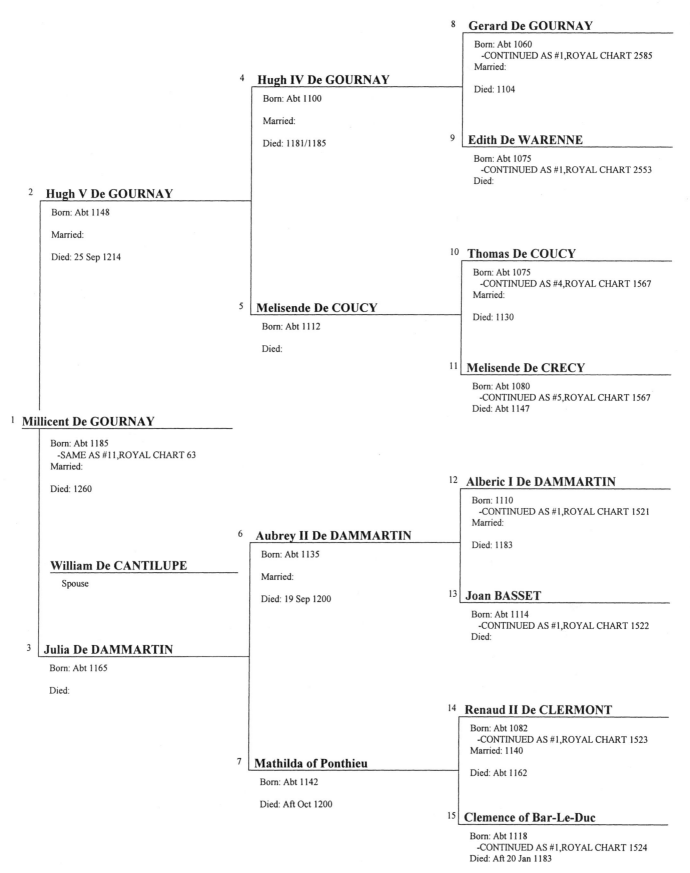

8 Gerard De GOURNAY
Born: Abt 1060
-CONTINUED AS #1,ROYAL CHART 2585
Married:
Died: 1104

4 Hugh IV De GOURNAY
Born: Abt 1100
Married:
Died: 1181/1185

9 Edith De WARENNE
Born: Abt 1075
-CONTINUED AS #1,ROYAL CHART 2553
Died:

2 Hugh V De GOURNAY
Born: Abt 1148
Married:
Died: 25 Sep 1214

10 Thomas De COUCY
Born: Abt 1075
-CONTINUED AS #4,ROYAL CHART 1567
Married:
Died: 1130

5 Melisende De COUCY
Born: Abt 1112
Died:

11 Melisende De CRECY
Born: Abt 1080
-CONTINUED AS #5,ROYAL CHART 1567
Died: Abt 1147

1 Millicent De GOURNAY
Born: Abt 1185
-SAME AS #11,ROYAL CHART 63
Married:
Died: 1260

William De CANTILUPE
Spouse

12 Alberic I De DAMMARTIN
Born: 1110
-CONTINUED AS #1,ROYAL CHART 1521
Married:
Died: 1183

6 Aubrey II De DAMMARTIN
Born: Abt 1135
Married:
Died: 19 Sep 1200

13 Joan BASSET
Born: Abt 1114
-CONTINUED AS #1,ROYAL CHART 1522
Died:

3 Julia De DAMMARTIN
Born: Abt 1165
Died:

14 Renaud II De CLERMONT
Born: Abt 1082
-CONTINUED AS #1,ROYAL CHART 1523
Married: 1140
Died: Abt 1162

7 Mathilda of Ponthieu
Born: Abt 1142
Died: Aft Oct 1200

15 Clemence of Bar-Le-Duc
Born: Abt 1118
-CONTINUED AS #1,ROYAL CHART 1524
Died: Aft 20 Jan 1183

Sources include: *Royal Ancestors* (1989), chart 11336; Faris preliminary Charlemagne manuscript (June 1995), pp. 149-150; Turton 90; Collett family group sheets; *Ancestral Roots* 255-29, 225A-29 (#1 & 2).

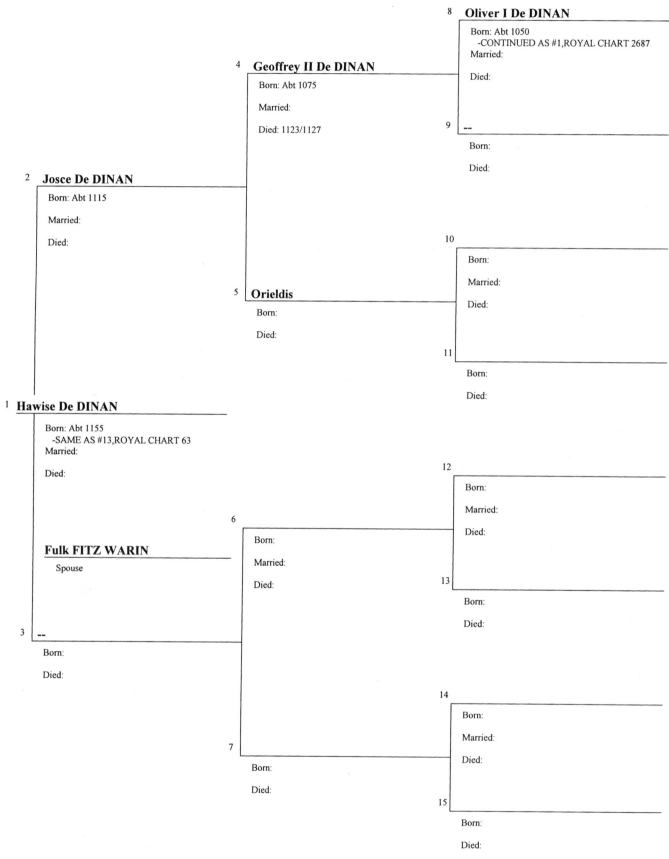

8 Oliver I De DINAN

Born: Abt 1050
-CONTINUED AS #1,ROYAL CHART 2687
Married:

Died:

4 Geoffrey II De DINAN

Born: Abt 1075

Married:

Died: 1123/1127

9 --

Born:

Died:

2 Josce De DINAN

Born: Abt 1115

Married:

Died:

10

Born:

Married:

Died:

5 Orieldis

Born:

Died:

11

Born:

Died:

1 Hawise De DINAN

Born: Abt 1155
-SAME AS #13,ROYAL CHART 63
Married:

Died:

12

Born:

Married:

Died:

6

Born:

Married:

Died:

13

Born:

Died:

Fulk FITZ WARIN

Spouse

3 --

Born:

Died:

14

Born:

Married:

Died:

7

Born:

Died:

15

Born:

Died:

Sources include: *Royal Ancestors* (1989), chart 11337; Turton 91, 126; Kraentzler 1110; *Ancestral Roots* 8 (2004), Line 214-25 (#4 & 5).

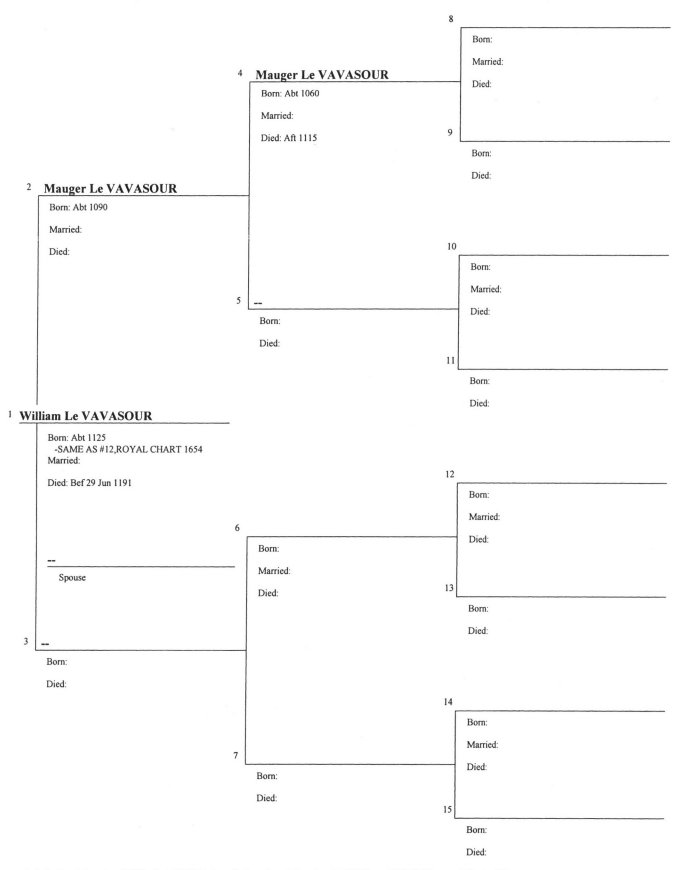

8

4 Mauger Le VAVASOUR

Born: Abt 1060

Married:

Died: Aft 1115

Born:

Married:

Died:

9

Born:

Died:

2 Mauger Le VAVASOUR

Born: Abt 1090

Married:

Died:

10

Born:

Married:

Died:

5 --

Born:

Died:

11

Born:

Died:

1 William Le VAVASOUR

Born: Abt 1125
   -SAME AS #12,ROYAL CHART 1654
Married:

Died: Bef 29 Jun 1191

12

Born:

Married:

Died:

6

Born:

Married:

Died:

13

Born:

Died:

--

Spouse

3 --

Born:

Died:

14

Born:

Married:

Died:

7

Born:

Died:

15

Born:

Died:

Sources include: *Royal Ancestors* (1989), chart 11337; Faris preliminary baronial manuscript (1998), pp. 1578-79 (Vavasour); Turton 108.

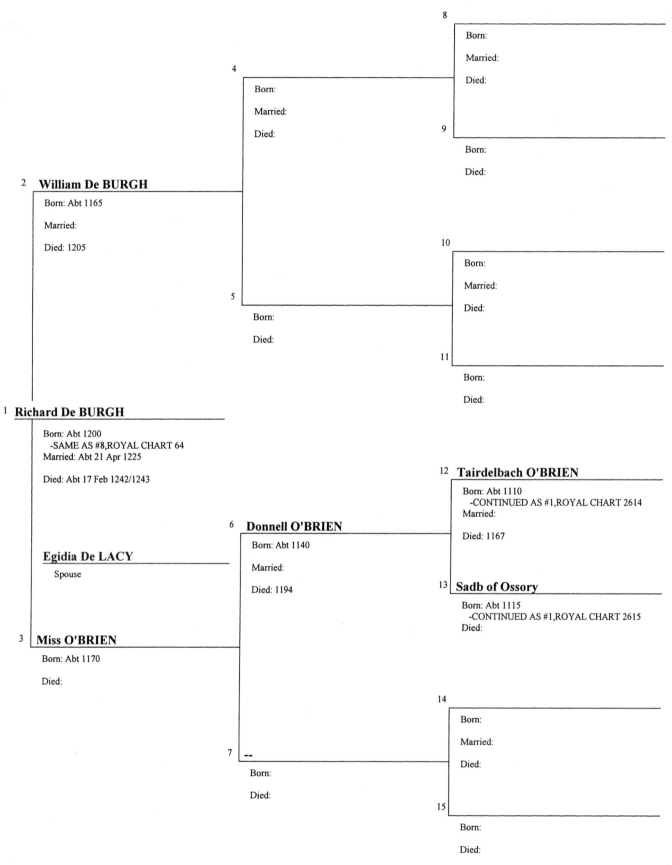

8

Born:

Married:

Died:

4

Born:

Married:

Died:

9

Born:

Died:

2 **William De BURGH**

Born: Abt 1165

Married:

Died: 1205

10

Born:

Married:

Died:

5

Born:

Died:

11

Born:

Died:

1 **Richard De BURGH**

Born: Abt 1200
  -SAME AS #8,ROYAL CHART 64
Married: Abt 21 Apr 1225

Died: Abt 17 Feb 1242/1243

12 **Tairdelbach O'BRIEN**

Born: Abt 1110
  -CONTINUED AS #1,ROYAL CHART 2614
Married:

Died: 1167

6 **Donnell O'BRIEN**

Born: Abt 1140

Married:

Died: 1194

Egidia De LACY

Spouse

13 **Sadb of Ossory**

Born: Abt 1115
  -CONTINUED AS #1,ROYAL CHART 2615
Died:

3 **Miss O'BRIEN**

Born: Abt 1170

Died:

14

Born:

Married:

Died:

7 **--**

Born:

Died:

15

Born:

Died:

Sources include: *Royal Ancestors* (1989), chart 11360; *Ancestral Roots* 177B-8; *TAG* 54:1-5 (#6 ancestry); Turton 92; Kraentzler 1111a; LDS records. Note: The parentage of #2 William is disputed.

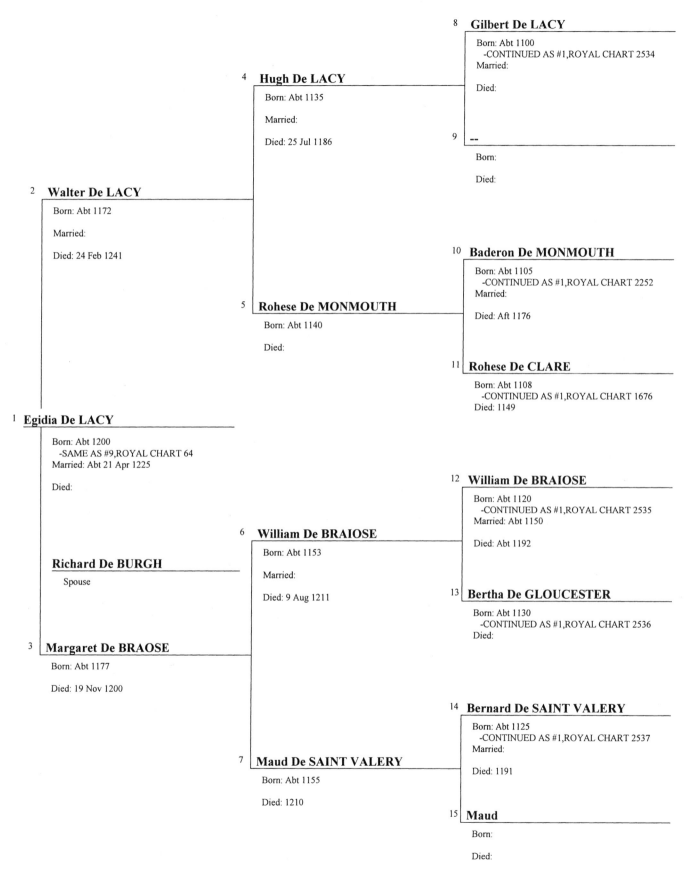

8 Gilbert De LACY
Born: Abt 1100
 -CONTINUED AS #1,ROYAL CHART 2534
Married:

Died:

4 Hugh De LACY
Born: Abt 1135

Married:

Died: 25 Jul 1186

9 --
Born:

Died:

2 Walter De LACY
Born: Abt 1172

Married:

Died: 24 Feb 1241

10 Baderon De MONMOUTH
Born: Abt 1105
 -CONTINUED AS #1,ROYAL CHART 2252
Married:

Died: Aft 1176

5 Rohese De MONMOUTH
Born: Abt 1140

Died:

11 Rohese De CLARE
Born: Abt 1108
 -CONTINUED AS #1,ROYAL CHART 1676
Died: 1149

1 Egidia De LACY
Born: Abt 1200
 -SAME AS #9,ROYAL CHART 64
Married: Abt 21 Apr 1225

Died:

12 William De BRAIOSE
Born: Abt 1120
 -CONTINUED AS #1,ROYAL CHART 2535
Married: Abt 1150

Died: Abt 1192

6 William De BRAIOSE
Born: Abt 1153

Married:

Died: 9 Aug 1211

13 Bertha De GLOUCESTER
Born: Abt 1130
 -CONTINUED AS #1,ROYAL CHART 2536
Died:

Richard De BURGH
Spouse

3 Margaret De BRAOSE
Born: Abt 1177

Died: 19 Nov 1200

14 Bernard De SAINT VALERY
Born: Abt 1125
 -CONTINUED AS #1,ROYAL CHART 2537
Married:

Died: 1191

7 Maud De SAINT VALERY
Born: Abt 1155

Died: 1210

15 Maud
Born:

Died:

Sources include: *Royal Ancestors* 11360; Faris preliminary baronial manuscript (1998), p. 929-930 (Lacy), 1101 (Monmouth), 217-218 (Breuse); *Ancestral Roots* 177B, 177A; *Complete Peerage* 12:171-172; Turton 92, 74; Kraentzler 1111a.

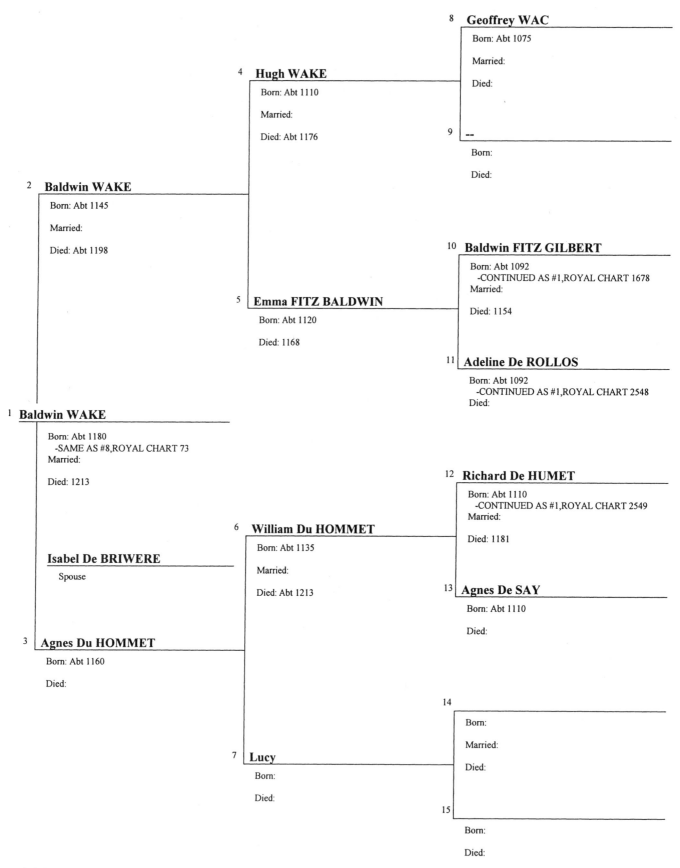

8 **Geoffrey WAC**
Born: Abt 1075
Married:
Died:

4 **Hugh WAKE**
Born: Abt 1110
Married:
Died: Abt 1176

9 **--**
Born:
Died:

2 **Baldwin WAKE**
Born: Abt 1145
Married:
Died: Abt 1198

10 **Baldwin FITZ GILBERT**
Born: Abt 1092
    -CONTINUED AS #1,ROYAL CHART 1678
Married:
Died: 1154

5 **Emma FITZ BALDWIN**
Born: Abt 1120
Died: 1168

11 **Adeline De ROLLOS**
Born: Abt 1092
    -CONTINUED AS #1,ROYAL CHART 2548
Died:

1 **Baldwin WAKE**
Born: Abt 1180
    -SAME AS #8,ROYAL CHART 73
Married:
Died: 1213

12 **Richard De HUMET**
Born: Abt 1110
    -CONTINUED AS #1,ROYAL CHART 2549
Married:
Died: 1181

6 **William Du HOMMET**
Born: Abt 1135
Married:
Died: Abt 1213

Isabel De BRIWERE
Spouse

13 **Agnes De SAY**
Born: Abt 1110
Died:

3 **Agnes Du HOMMET**
Born: Abt 1160
Died:

14
Born:
Married:
Died:

7 **Lucy**
Born:
Died:

15
Born:
Died:

Sources include: *Royal Ancestors* 11346; *Ancestral Roots* 184A; Turton 106 & Kraentzler 1338 (ancestry of #6 William; #13 Agnes claimed as either daughter or granddaughter of Jordan De Say & Lucy).

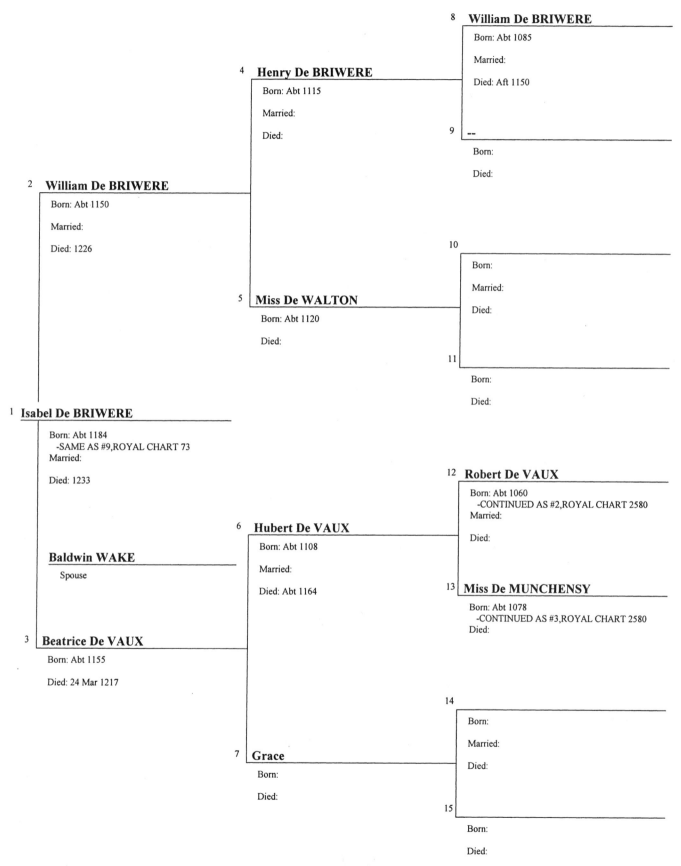

8 **William De BRIWERE**

Born: Abt 1085

Married:

Died: Aft 1150

4 **Henry De BRIWERE**

Born: Abt 1115

Married:

Died:

9 **--**

Born:

Died:

2 **William De BRIWERE**

Born: Abt 1150

Married:

Died: 1226

10

Born:

Married:

Died:

5 **Miss De WALTON**

Born: Abt 1120

Died:

11

Born:

Died:

1 **Isabel De BRIWERE**

Born: Abt 1184
    -SAME AS #9,ROYAL CHART 73
Married:

Died: 1233

Baldwin WAKE

Spouse

12 **Robert De VAUX**

Born: Abt 1060
    -CONTINUED AS #2,ROYAL CHART 2580
Married:

Died:

6 **Hubert De VAUX**

Born: Abt 1108

Married:

Died: Abt 1164

13 **Miss De MUNCHENSY**

Born: Abt 1078
    -CONTINUED AS #3,ROYAL CHART 2580
Died:

3 **Beatrice De VAUX**

Born: Abt 1155

Died: 24 Mar 1217

14

Born:

Married:

Died:

7 **Grace**

Born:

Died:

15

Born:

Died:

Sources include: *Royal Ancestors* (1989), charts 11346, 11354; Faris preliminary baronial manuscript (1998), pp. 226-227 (Briwerre), 1577-78 (Vaux); Consultation with Douglas Richardson (#3 parentage); *Ancestral Roots* 184A-7; Turton 106; LDS records. Note: There is disagreement on the parentage of #2 William and #8 William. #4 is also claimed as Richard, son of #8 William.

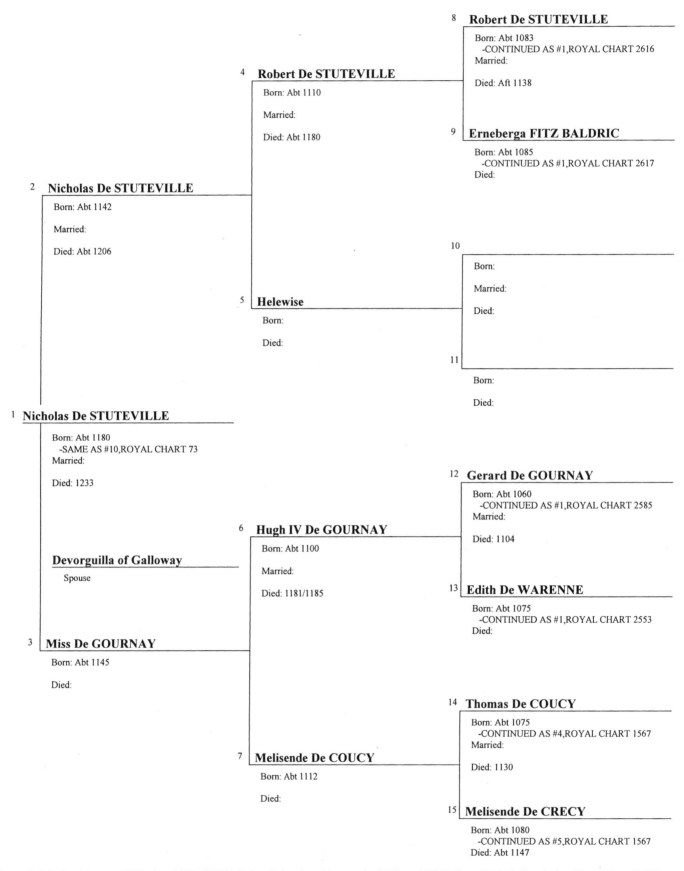

2 **Nicholas De STUTEVILLE**
Born: Abt 1142
Married:
Died: Abt 1206

4 **Robert De STUTEVILLE**
Born: Abt 1110
Married:
Died: Abt 1180

8 **Robert De STUTEVILLE**
Born: Abt 1083
-CONTINUED AS #1,ROYAL CHART 2616
Married:
Died: Aft 1138

9 **Erneberga FITZ BALDRIC**
Born: Abt 1085
-CONTINUED AS #1,ROYAL CHART 2617
Died:

5 **Helewise**
Born:
Died:

10
Born:
Married:
Died:

11
Born:
Died:

1 **Nicholas De STUTEVILLE**
Born: Abt 1180
-SAME AS #10,ROYAL CHART 73
Married:
Died: 1233

Devorguilla of Galloway
Spouse

3 **Miss De GOURNAY**
Born: Abt 1145
Died:

6 **Hugh IV De GOURNAY**
Born: Abt 1100
Married:
Died: 1181/1185

12 **Gerard De GOURNAY**
Born: Abt 1060
-CONTINUED AS #1,ROYAL CHART 2585
Married:
Died: 1104

13 **Edith De WARENNE**
Born: Abt 1075
-CONTINUED AS #1,ROYAL CHART 2553
Died:

7 **Melisende De COUCY**
Born: Abt 1112
Died:

14 **Thomas De COUCY**
Born: Abt 1075
-CONTINUED AS #4,ROYAL CHART 1567
Married:
Died: 1130

15 **Melisende De CRECY**
Born: Abt 1080
-CONTINUED AS #5,ROYAL CHART 1567
Died: Abt 1147

Sources include: *Royal Ancestors* (1989), charts 11346, 11672-73; Faris preliminary baronial manuscript (1998), pp. 1473-75 (Stuteville), including citation of Brandenburg (Teil III 653, p. 83) on Gournay line; *Ancestral Roots* 8 (2004), Line 270; *Ancestral Roots* 184A-8. Note: The claim in *Ancestral Roots* 8 that #3 was Gunnor D' Aubigny (2nd wife) appears to be in error. Paget (1957) 14:1 (Aubigny) & 511:7-8 (Stuteville) clearly shows that #1 Nicholas was son of the 1st wife (Gournay). Faris accepts the Gournay line, as shown.

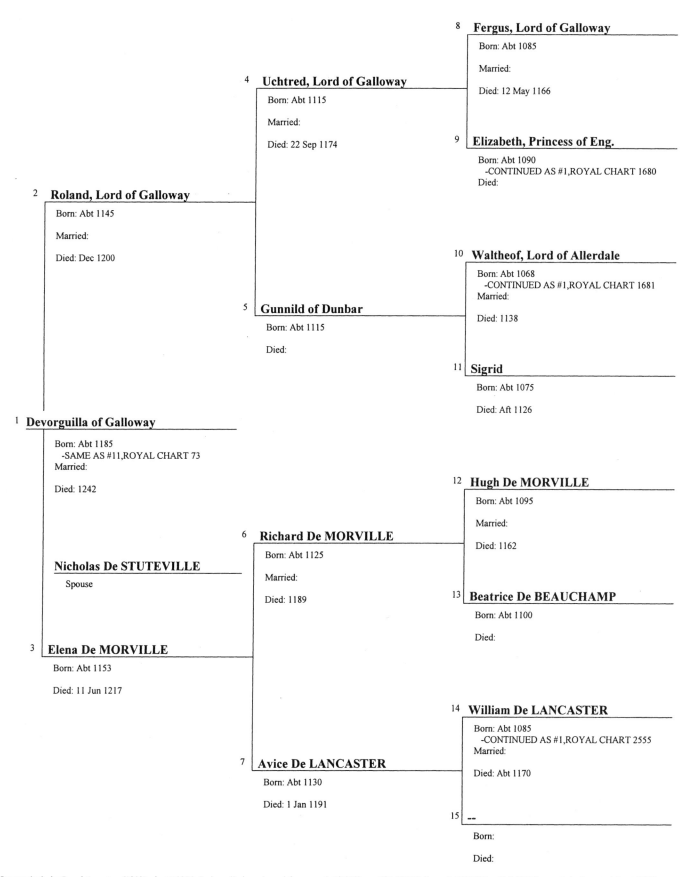

8 Fergus, Lord of Galloway

Born: Abt 1085

Married:

Died: 12 May 1166

4 Uchtred, Lord of Galloway

Born: Abt 1115

Married:

Died: 22 Sep 1174

9 Elizabeth, Princess of Eng.

Born: Abt 1090
-CONTINUED AS #1,ROYAL CHART 1680
Died:

2 Roland, Lord of Galloway

Born: Abt 1145

Married:

Died: Dec 1200

10 Waltheof, Lord of Allerdale

Born: Abt 1068
-CONTINUED AS #1,ROYAL CHART 1681
Married:

Died: 1138

5 Gunnild of Dunbar

Born: Abt 1115

Died:

11 Sigrid

Born: Abt 1075

Died: Aft 1126

1 Devorguilla of Galloway

Born: Abt 1185
-SAME AS #11,ROYAL CHART 73
Married:

Died: 1242

12 Hugh De MORVILLE

Born: Abt 1095

Married:

Died: 1162

6 Richard De MORVILLE

Born: Abt 1125

Married:

Died: 1189

13 Beatrice De BEAUCHAMP

Born: Abt 1100

Died:

Nicholas De STUTEVILLE

Spouse

3 Elena De MORVILLE

Born: Abt 1153

Died: 11 Jun 1217

14 William De LANCASTER

Born: Abt 1085
-CONTINUED AS #1,ROYAL CHART 2555
Married:

Died: Abt 1170

7 Avice De LANCASTER

Born: Abt 1130

Died: 1 Jan 1191

15 --

Born:

Died:

Sources include: *Royal Ancestors* (1989), chart 11346; Faris preliminary baronial manuscript (1998), pp. 686-687 (Galloway), 1136 (Morville), 932 (Lancaster); *Ancestral Roots* 184A-8, 38, 88-25, 121B.

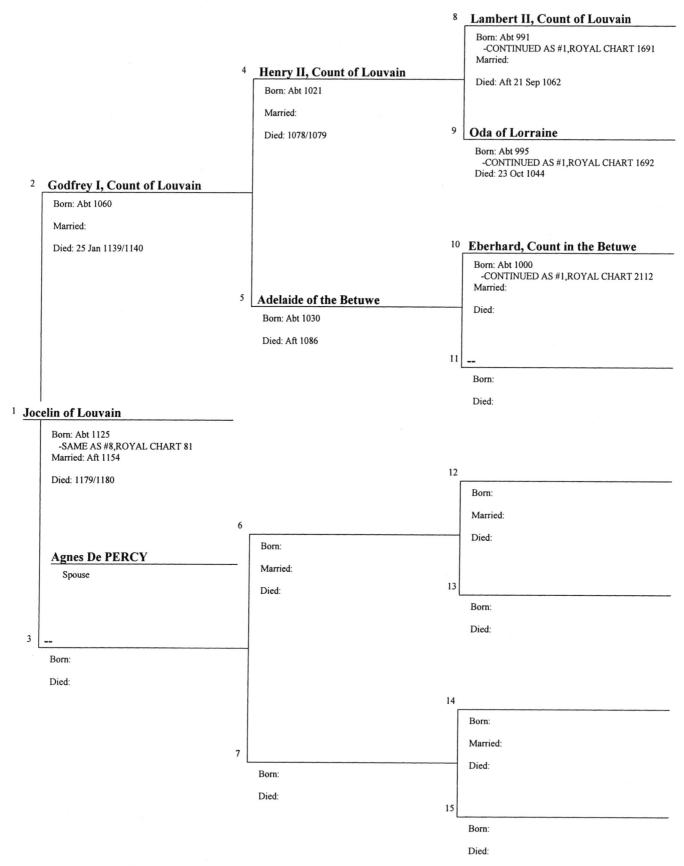

8 **Lambert II, Count of Louvain**

Born: Abt 991
-CONTINUED AS #1,ROYAL CHART 1691
Married:

Died: Aft 21 Sep 1062

4 **Henry II, Count of Louvain**

Born: Abt 1021

Married:

Died: 1078/1079

9 **Oda of Lorraine**

Born: Abt 995
-CONTINUED AS #1,ROYAL CHART 1692
Died: 23 Oct 1044

2 **Godfrey I, Count of Louvain**

Born: Abt 1060

Married:

Died: 25 Jan 1139/1140

10 **Eberhard, Count in the Betuwe**

Born: Abt 1000
-CONTINUED AS #1,ROYAL CHART 2112
Married:

Died:

5 **Adelaide of the Betuwe**

Born: Abt 1030

Died: Aft 1086

11 **--**

Born:

Died:

1 **Jocelin of Louvain**

Born: Abt 1125
-SAME AS #8,ROYAL CHART 81
Married: Aft 1154

Died: 1179/1180

12

Born:

Married:

Died:

6

Born:

Married:

Died:

13

Born:

Died:

Agnes De PERCY

Spouse

3 **--**

Born:

Died:

14

Born:

Married:

Died:

7

Born:

Died:

15

Born:

Died:

Sources include: *Royal Ancestors* (1989), chart 11353; *Ancestral Roots* 161. Note: #1 Jocelin was a natural son of Godfrey I by an unknown mistress.

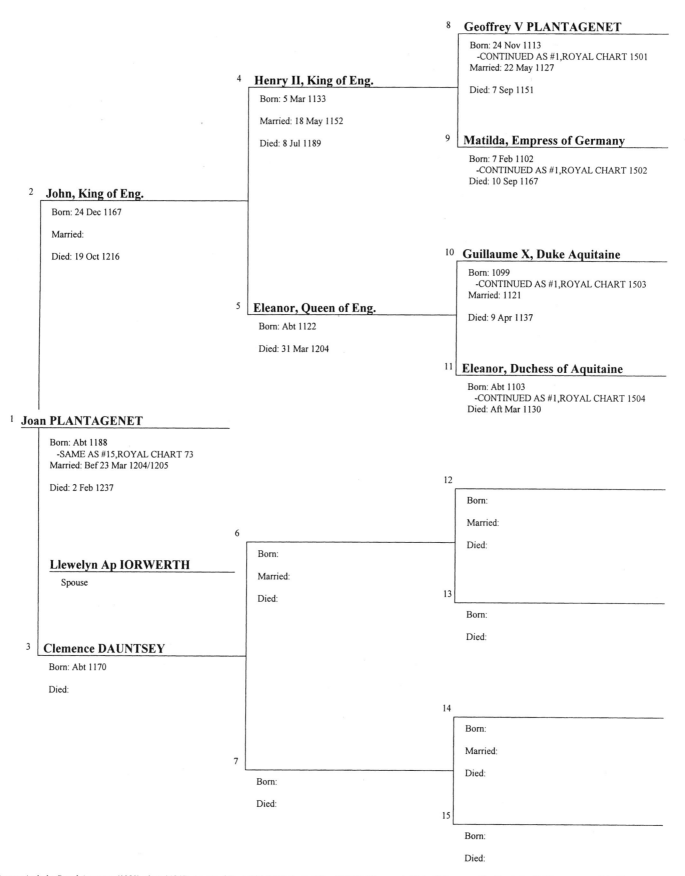

8 **Geoffrey V PLANTAGENET**

Born: 24 Nov 1113
-CONTINUED AS #1,ROYAL CHART 1501
Married: 22 May 1127

Died: 7 Sep 1151

4 **Henry II, King of Eng.**

Born: 5 Mar 1133

Married: 18 May 1152

Died: 8 Jul 1189

9 **Matilda, Empress of Germany**

Born: 7 Feb 1102
-CONTINUED AS #1,ROYAL CHART 1502
Died: 10 Sep 1167

2 **John, King of Eng.**

Born: 24 Dec 1167

Married:

Died: 19 Oct 1216

10 **Guillaume X, Duke Aquitaine**

Born: 1099
-CONTINUED AS #1,ROYAL CHART 1503
Married: 1121

Died: 9 Apr 1137

5 **Eleanor, Queen of Eng.**

Born: Abt 1122

Died: 31 Mar 1204

11 **Eleanor, Duchess of Aquitaine**

Born: Abt 1103
-CONTINUED AS #1,ROYAL CHART 1504
Died: Aft Mar 1130

1 **Joan PLANTAGENET**

Born: Abt 1188
-SAME AS #15,ROYAL CHART 73
Married: Bef 23 Mar 1204/1205

Died: 2 Feb 1237

12

Born:

Married:

Died:

Llewelyn Ap IORWERTH

Spouse

6

Born:

Married:

Died:

13

Born:

Died:

3 **Clemence DAUNTSEY**

Born: Abt 1170

Died:

14

Born:

Married:

Died:

7

Born:

Died:

15

Born:

Died:

Sources include: *Royal Ancestors* (1989), chart 11347; *Ancestral Roots* 236, 27; Roberts *500*, p. 305 (#3 Clemence). Note: #1 Joan was illegitimate by #3 Clemence, possibly Clemence Dauntsey, wife of Nicholas De Verdun (see chart 1655).

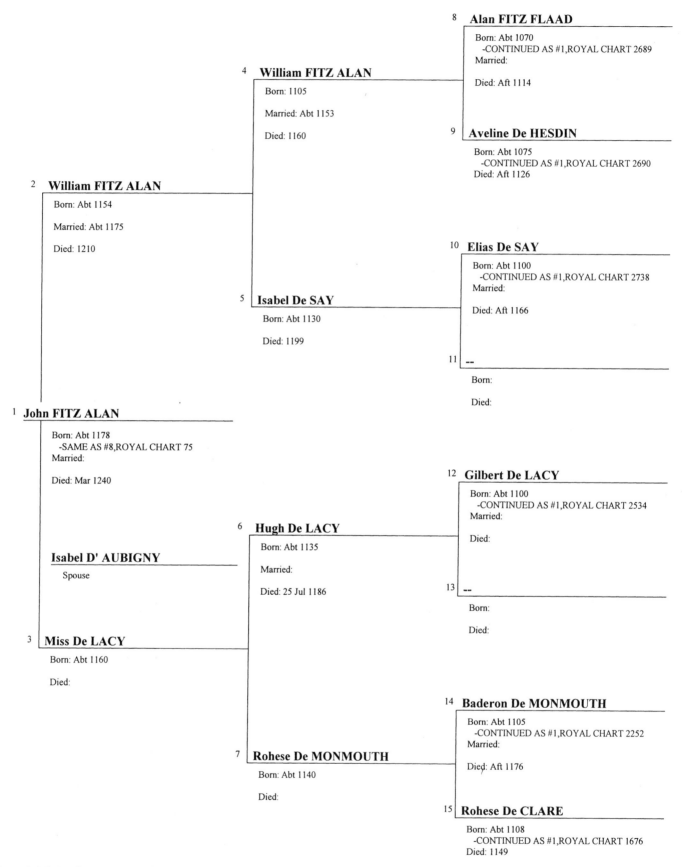

8 Alan FITZ FLAAD

Born: Abt 1070
-CONTINUED AS #1,ROYAL CHART 2689
Married:

Died: Aft 1114

4 William FITZ ALAN

Born: 1105

Married: Abt 1153

Died: 1160

9 Aveline De HESDIN

Born: Abt 1075
-CONTINUED AS #1,ROYAL CHART 2690
Died: Aft 1126

2 William FITZ ALAN

Born: Abt 1154

Married: Abt 1175

Died: 1210

10 Elias De SAY

Born: Abt 1100
-CONTINUED AS #1,ROYAL CHART 2738
Married:

Died: Aft 1166

5 Isabel De SAY

Born: Abt 1130

Died: 1199

11 --

Born:

Died:

1 John FITZ ALAN

Born: Abt 1178
-SAME AS #8,ROYAL CHART 75
Married:

Died: Mar 1240

12 Gilbert De LACY

Born: Abt 1100
-CONTINUED AS #1,ROYAL CHART 2534
Married:

Died:

6 Hugh De LACY

Born: Abt 1135

Married:

Died: 25 Jul 1186

13 --

Born:

Died:

Isabel D' AUBIGNY

Spouse

3 Miss De LACY

Born: Abt 1160

Died:

14 Baderon De MONMOUTH

Born: Abt 1105
-CONTINUED AS #1,ROYAL CHART 2252
Married:

Died: Aft 1176

7 Rohese De MONMOUTH

Born: Abt 1140

Died:

15 Rohese De CLARE

Born: Abt 1108
-CONTINUED AS #1,ROYAL CHART 1676
Died: 1149

Sources include: *Royal Ancestors* (1989), charts 11348, 11470-72; Faris preliminary baronial manuscript (1998), pp. 600-601 (Fitz Alan), 929-930 (Lacy); *Ancestral Roots* 149-27.

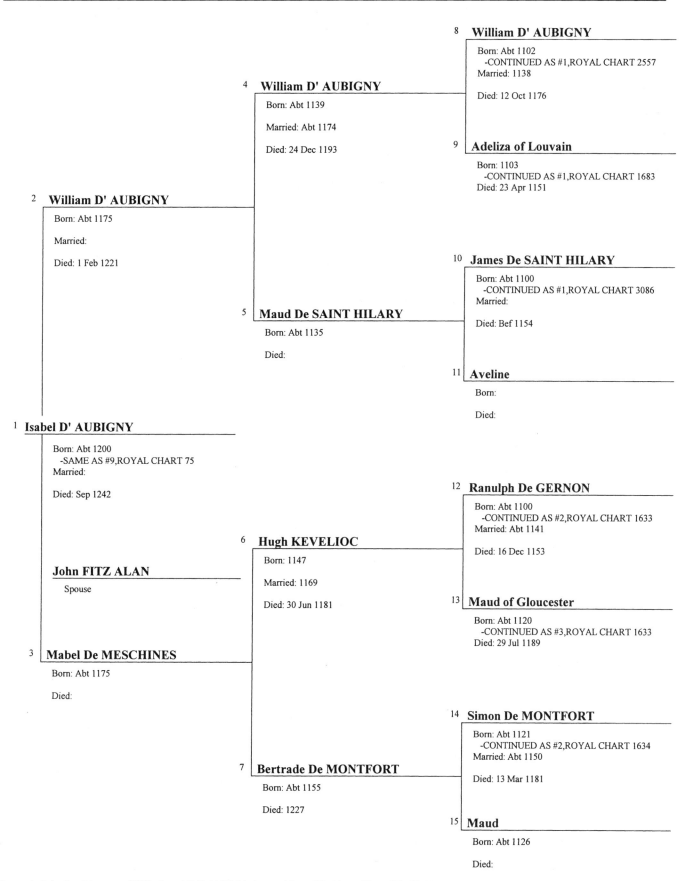

8 William D' AUBIGNY

Born: Abt 1102
-CONTINUED AS #1,ROYAL CHART 2557
Married: 1138

Died: 12 Oct 1176

4 William D' AUBIGNY

Born: Abt 1139

Married: Abt 1174

Died: 24 Dec 1193

9 Adeliza of Louvain

Born: 1103
-CONTINUED AS #1,ROYAL CHART 1683
Died: 23 Apr 1151

2 William D' AUBIGNY

Born: Abt 1175

Married:

Died: 1 Feb 1221

10 James De SAINT HILARY

Born: Abt 1100
-CONTINUED AS #1,ROYAL CHART 3086
Married:

Died: Bef 1154

5 Maud De SAINT HILARY

Born: Abt 1135

Died:

11 Aveline

Born:

Died:

1 Isabel D' AUBIGNY

Born: Abt 1200
-SAME AS #9,ROYAL CHART 75
Married:

Died: Sep 1242

12 Ranulph De GERNON

Born: Abt 1100
-CONTINUED AS #2,ROYAL CHART 1633
Married: Abt 1141

Died: 16 Dec 1153

6 Hugh KEVELIOC

Born: 1147

Married: 1169

Died: 30 Jun 1181

13 Maud of Gloucester

Born: Abt 1120
-CONTINUED AS #3,ROYAL CHART 1633
Died: 29 Jul 1189

John FITZ ALAN

Spouse

3 Mabel De MESCHINES

Born: Abt 1175

Died:

14 Simon De MONTFORT

Born: Abt 1121
-CONTINUED AS #2,ROYAL CHART 1634
Married: Abt 1150

Died: 13 Mar 1181

7 Bertrade De MONTFORT

Born: Abt 1155

Died: 1227

15 Maud

Born: Abt 1126

Died:

Sources include: *Royal Ancestors* (1989), charts 11348, 11473-74; *Ancestral Roots* 149; *Magna Charta* 134, 129; Turton 107; *TAG* 73:308 (#6 & 7 ancestry).

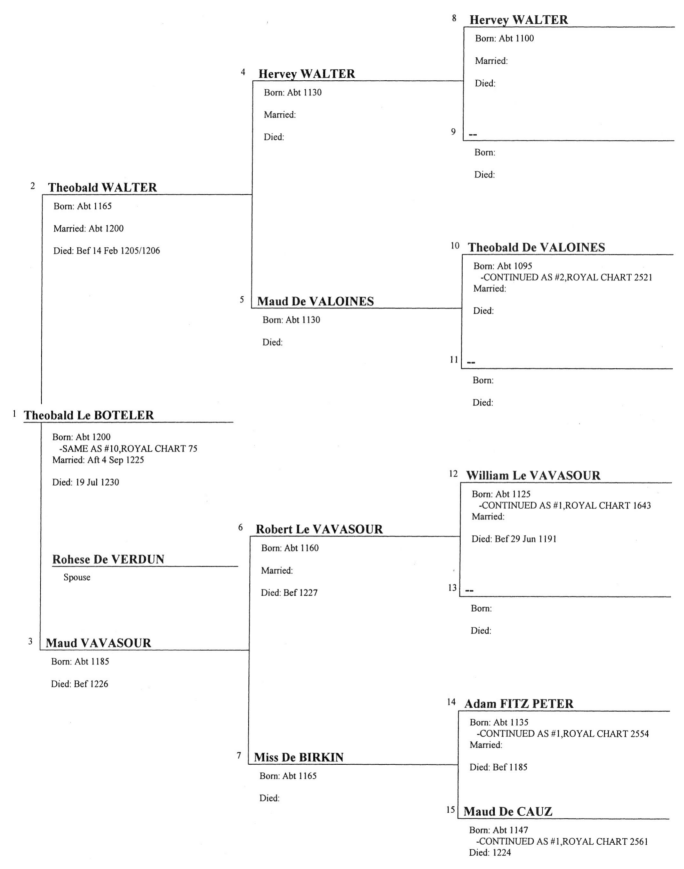

8 Hervey WALTER
Born: Abt 1100
Married:
Died:

4 Hervey WALTER
Born: Abt 1130
Married:
Died:

9 --
Born:
Died:

2 Theobald WALTER
Born: Abt 1165
Married: Abt 1200
Died: Bef 14 Feb 1205/1206

10 Theobald De VALOINES
Born: Abt 1095
  -CONTINUED AS #2,ROYAL CHART 2521
Married:
Died:

5 Maud De VALOINES
Born: Abt 1130
Died:

11 --
Born:
Died:

1 Theobald Le BOTELER
Born: Abt 1200
  -SAME AS #10,ROYAL CHART 75
Married: Aft 4 Sep 1225
Died: 19 Jul 1230

Rohese De VERDUN
Spouse

12 William Le VAVASOUR
Born: Abt 1125
  -CONTINUED AS #1,ROYAL CHART 1643
Married:
Died: Bef 29 Jun 1191

6 Robert Le VAVASOUR
Born: Abt 1160
Married:
Died: Bef 1227

13 --
Born:
Died:

3 Maud VAVASOUR
Born: Abt 1185
Died: Bef 1226

14 Adam FITZ PETER
Born: Abt 1135
  -CONTINUED AS #1,ROYAL CHART 2554
Married:
Died: Bef 1185

7 Miss De BIRKIN
Born: Abt 1165
Died:

15 Maud De CAUZ
Born: Abt 1147
  -CONTINUED AS #1,ROYAL CHART 2561
Died: 1224

Sources include: *Royal Ancestors* (1989), charts 11348, 11337; Faris preliminary baronial manuscript (1998), pp. 274-275 (Butler), 1578-79 (Vavasour), 127-128 (Birkin); *Ancestral Roots* 149-28. Notes: The identity shown for #7 (a 1st wife) is not certain. #8 Hervey was probably son of Walter (man of Robert Malet in 1086, held Stradbrook, Suffolk).

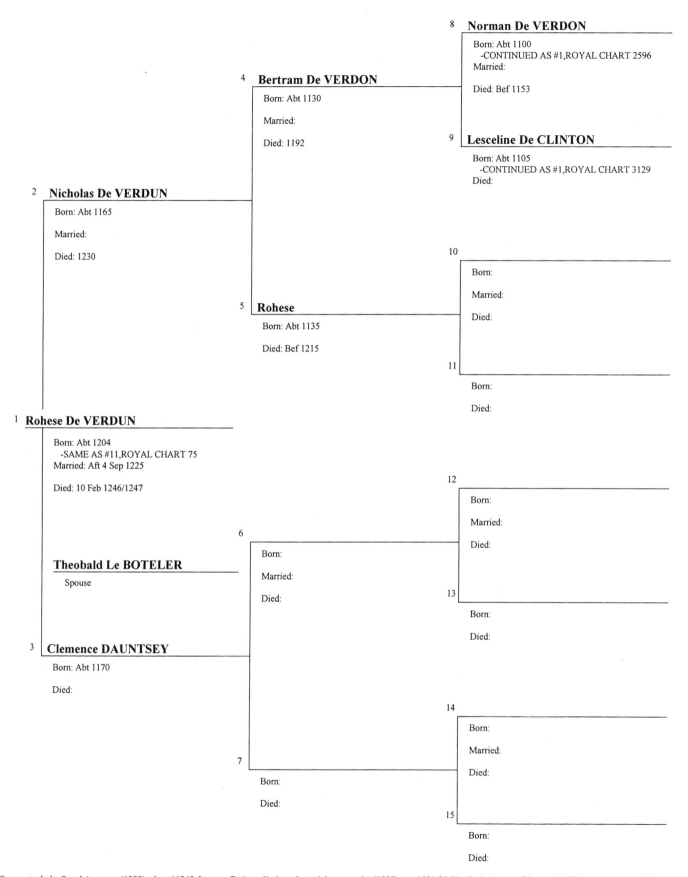

8 **Norman De VERDON**

Born: Abt 1100
   -CONTINUED AS #1,ROYAL CHART 2596
Married:

Died: Bef 1153

4 **Bertram De VERDON**

Born: Abt 1130

Married:

Died: 1192

9 **Lesceline De CLINTON**

Born: Abt 1105
   -CONTINUED AS #1,ROYAL CHART 3129
Died:

2 **Nicholas De VERDUN**

Born: Abt 1165

Married:

Died: 1230

10

Born:

Married:

Died:

5 **Rohese**

Born: Abt 1135

Died: Bef 1215

11

Born:

Died:

1 **Rohese De VERDUN**

Born: Abt 1204
   -SAME AS #11,ROYAL CHART 75
Married: Aft 4 Sep 1225

Died: 10 Feb 1246/1247

12

Born:

Married:

Died:

6

Born:

Married:

Died:

13

Born:

Died:

Theobald Le BOTELER

Spouse

3 **Clemence DAUNTSEY**

Born: Abt 1170

Died:

14

Born:

Married:

Died:

7

Born:

Died:

15

Born:

Died:

Sources include: *Royal Ancestors* (1989), chart 11348 & notes; Faris preliminary baronial manuscript (1998), pp. 1584-85 (Verdun); *Ancestral Roots* 149-28; See note chart 1651 regarding #3 Clemence.

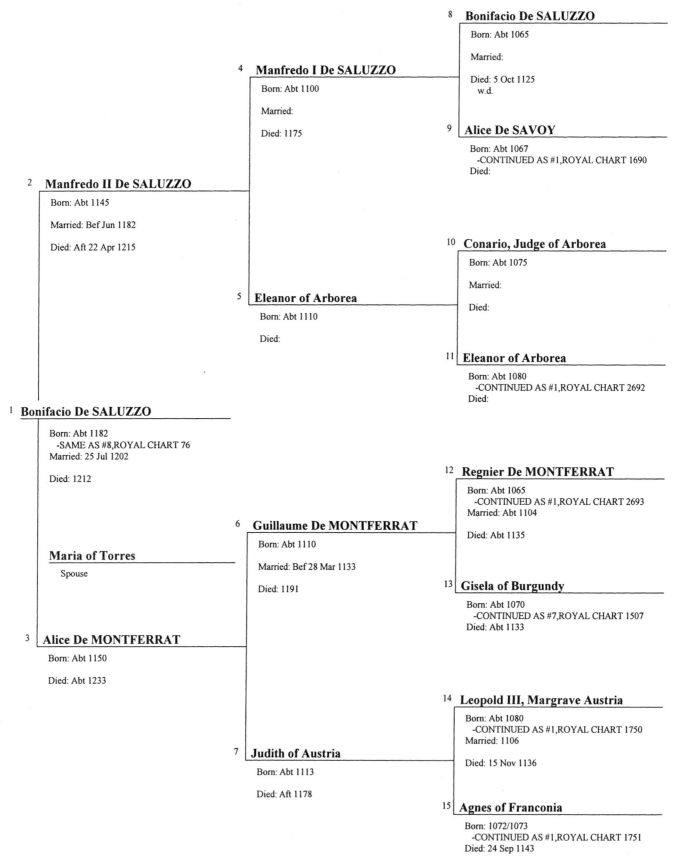

8 **Bonifacio De SALUZZO**

Born: Abt 1065

Married:

Died: 5 Oct 1125
w.d.

4 **Manfredo I De SALUZZO**

Born: Abt 1100

Married:

Died: 1175

9 **Alice De SAVOY**

Born: Abt 1067
  -CONTINUED AS #1,ROYAL CHART 1690
Died:

2 **Manfredo II De SALUZZO**

Born: Abt 1145

Married: Bef Jun 1182

Died: Aft 22 Apr 1215

10 **Conario, Judge of Arborea**

Born: Abt 1075

Married:

Died:

5 **Eleanor of Arborea**

Born: Abt 1110

Died:

11 **Eleanor of Arborea**

Born: Abt 1080
  -CONTINUED AS #1,ROYAL CHART 2692
Died:

1 **Bonifacio De SALUZZO**

Born: Abt 1182
  -SAME AS #8,ROYAL CHART 76
Married: 25 Jul 1202

Died: 1212

12 **Regnier De MONTFERRAT**

Born: Abt 1065
  -CONTINUED AS #1,ROYAL CHART 2693
Married: Abt 1104

Died: Abt 1135

6 **Guillaume De MONTFERRAT**

Born: Abt 1110

Married: Bef 28 Mar 1133

Died: 1191

13 **Gisela of Burgundy**

Born: Abt 1070
  -CONTINUED AS #7,ROYAL CHART 1507
Died: Abt 1133

Maria of Torres

Spouse

3 **Alice De MONTFERRAT**

Born: Abt 1150

Died: Abt 1233

14 **Leopold III, Margrave Austria**

Born: Abt 1080
  -CONTINUED AS #1,ROYAL CHART 1750
Married: 1106

Died: 15 Nov 1136

7 **Judith of Austria**

Born: Abt 1113

Died: Aft 1178

15 **Agnes of Franconia**

Born: 1072/1073
  -CONTINUED AS #1,ROYAL CHART 1751
Died: 24 Sep 1143

Sources include: *Royal Ancestors* (1989), charts 11388, 11829-31; Faris preliminary Charlemagne manuscript (June 1995), pp. 186-187; Schwennicke 2:199-200 (#3 ancestry); Turton 109-110; Kraentzler 1127. Note: The ancestry Turton gives for #8 Bonifacio contradicts other sources and appears to be incorrect.

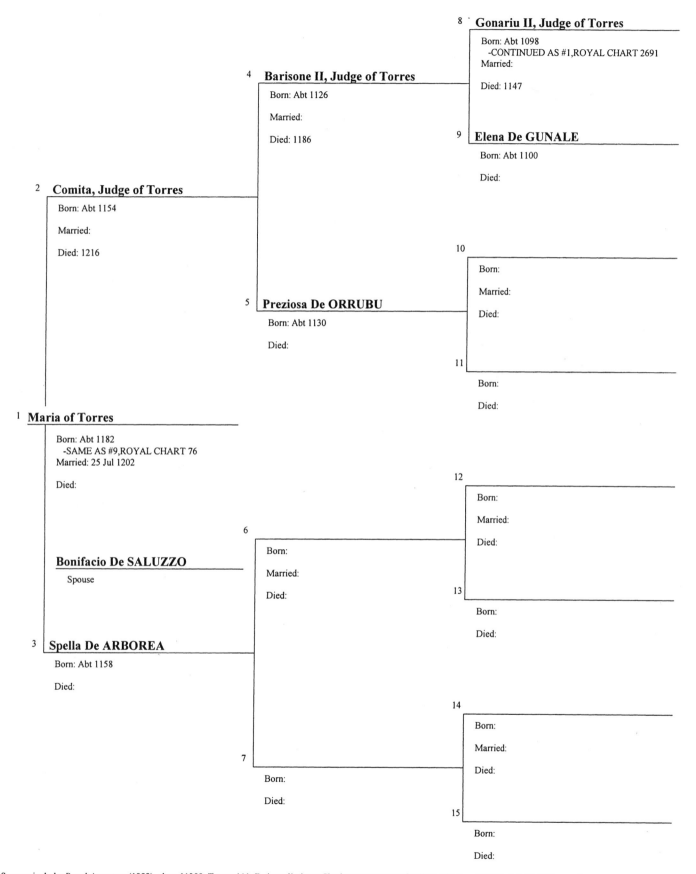

8 Gonariu II, Judge of Torres

Born: Abt 1098
　-CONTINUED AS #1,ROYAL CHART 2691
Married:

Died: 1147

4 Barisone II, Judge of Torres

Born: Abt 1126

Married:

Died: 1186

9 Elena De GUNALE

Born: Abt 1100

Died:

2 Comita, Judge of Torres

Born: Abt 1154

Married:

Died: 1216

10

Born:

Married:

Died:

5 Preziosa De ORRUBU

Born: Abt 1130

Died:

11

Born:

Died:

1 Maria of Torres

Born: Abt 1182
　-SAME AS #9,ROYAL CHART 76
Married: 25 Jul 1202

Died:

12

Born:

Married:

Died:

6

Born:

Married:

Died:

13

Born:

Died:

Bonifacio De SALUZZO

Spouse

3 Spella De ARBOREA

Born: Abt 1158

Died:

14

Born:

Married:

Died:

7

Born:

Died:

15

Born:

Died:

Sources include: *Royal Ancestors* (1989), chart 11388; Turton 111; Faris preliminary Charlemagne manuscript (June 1995), p. 187 (#1, 2 & 3); LDS records.

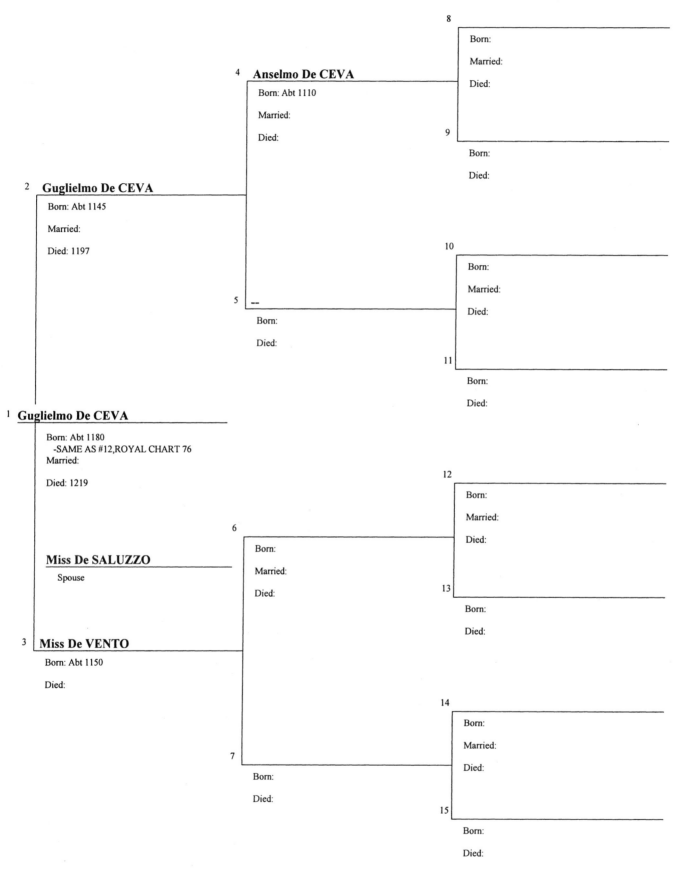

8

Born:

Married:

Died:

4 **Anselmo De CEVA**

Born: Abt 1110

Married:

Died:

9

Born:

Died:

2 **Guglielmo De CEVA**

Born: Abt 1145

Married:

Died: 1197

10

Born:

Married:

Died:

5 --

Born:

Died:

11

Born:

Died:

1 **Guglielmo De CEVA**

Born: Abt 1180
    -SAME AS #12,ROYAL CHART 76
Married:

Died: 1219

12

Born:

Married:

Died:

6

Born:

Married:

Died:

13

Born:

Died:

Miss De SALUZZO

Spouse

3 **Miss De VENTO**

Born: Abt 1150

Died:

14

Born:

Married:

Died:

7

Born:

Died:

15

Born:

Died:

Sources include: *Royal Ancestors* (1989), charts 11365, 11997; Turton 99; LDS records (#1, 2 & 3). Note: #4 Anselmo is uncertain. The parentage and ancestry Turton claims for him contradicts other reliable work and appears to be incorrect.

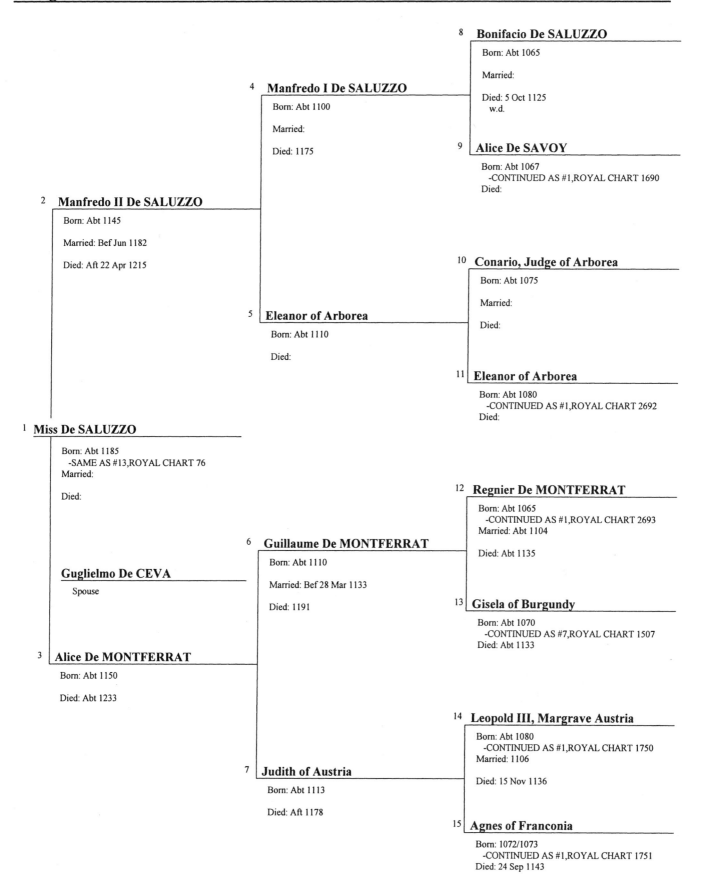

8 **Bonifacio De SALUZZO**

Born: Abt 1065

Married:

Died: 5 Oct 1125
w.d.

4 **Manfredo I De SALUZZO**

Born: Abt 1100

Married:

Died: 1175

9 **Alice De SAVOY**

Born: Abt 1067
-CONTINUED AS #1,ROYAL CHART 1690
Died:

2 **Manfredo II De SALUZZO**

Born: Abt 1145

Married: Bef Jun 1182

Died: Aft 22 Apr 1215

10 **Conario, Judge of Arborea**

Born: Abt 1075

Married:

Died:

5 **Eleanor of Arborea**

Born: Abt 1110

Died:

11 **Eleanor of Arborea**

Born: Abt 1080
-CONTINUED AS #1,ROYAL CHART 2692
Died:

1 **Miss De SALUZZO**

Born: Abt 1185
-SAME AS #13,ROYAL CHART 76
Married:

Died:

12 **Regnier De MONTFERRAT**

Born: Abt 1065
-CONTINUED AS #1,ROYAL CHART 2693
Married: Abt 1104

Died: Abt 1135

6 **Guillaume De MONTFERRAT**

Born: Abt 1110

Married: Bef 28 Mar 1133

Died: 1191

13 **Gisela of Burgundy**

Born: Abt 1070
-CONTINUED AS #7,ROYAL CHART 1507
Died: Abt 1133

Guglielmo De CEVA

Spouse

3 **Alice De MONTFERRAT**

Born: Abt 1150

Died: Abt 1233

14 **Leopold III, Margrave Austria**

Born: Abt 1080
-CONTINUED AS #1,ROYAL CHART 1750
Married: 1106

Died: 15 Nov 1136

7 **Judith of Austria**

Born: Abt 1113

Died: Aft 1178

15 **Agnes of Franconia**

Born: 1072/1073
-CONTINUED AS #1,ROYAL CHART 1751
Died: 24 Sep 1143

Sources include: *Royal Ancestors* (1989), chart 11365; Turton 99, 109-110; Chart 1656 & sources. Note: The ancestry Turton gives for #8 Bonifacio contradicts other sources and appears to be incorrect.

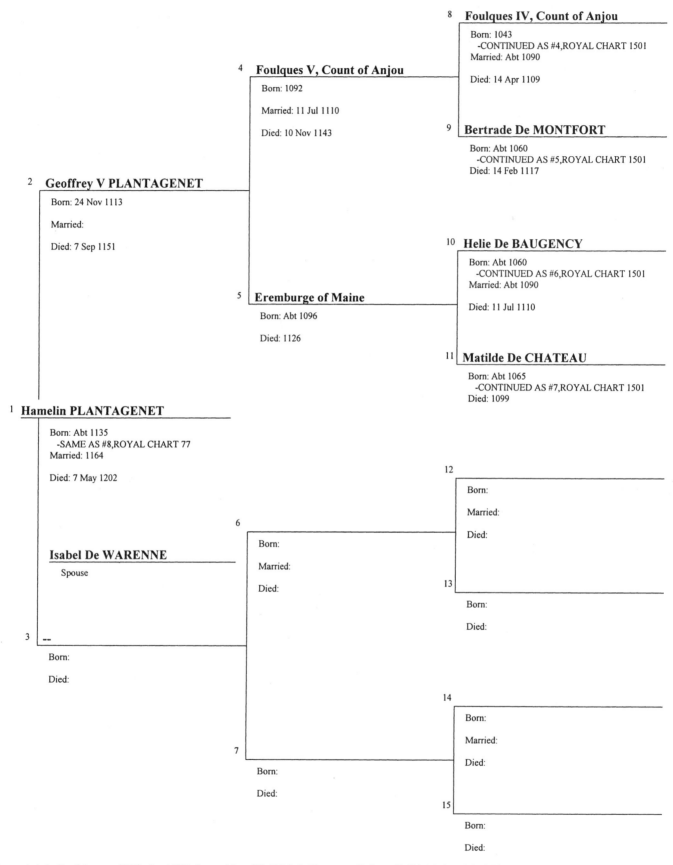

8 Foulques IV, Count of Anjou

Born: 1043
-CONTINUED AS #4,ROYAL CHART 1501
Married: Abt 1090

Died: 14 Apr 1109

4 Foulques V, Count of Anjou

Born: 1092

Married: 11 Jul 1110

Died: 10 Nov 1143

9 Bertrade De MONTFORT

Born: Abt 1060
-CONTINUED AS #5,ROYAL CHART 1501
Died: 14 Feb 1117

2 Geoffrey V PLANTAGENET

Born: 24 Nov 1113

Married:

Died: 7 Sep 1151

10 Helie De BAUGENCY

Born: Abt 1060
-CONTINUED AS #6,ROYAL CHART 1501
Married: Abt 1090

Died: 11 Jul 1110

5 Eremburge of Maine

Born: Abt 1096

Died: 1126

11 Matilde De CHATEAU

Born: Abt 1065
-CONTINUED AS #7,ROYAL CHART 1501
Died: 1099

1 Hamelin PLANTAGENET

Born: Abt 1135
-SAME AS #8,ROYAL CHART 77
Married: 1164

Died: 7 May 1202

12

Born:

Married:

Died:

6

Born:

Married:

Died:

13

Born:

Died:

Isabel De WARENNE

Spouse

3 --

Born:

Died:

14

Born:

Married:

Died:

7

Born:

Died:

15

Born:

Died:

Sources include: *Royal Ancestors* (1989), chart 11355; *Ancestral Roots* 123, 118; Faris--Plantagenet 18; Stuart 53, 313; Moriarty 1-4, 10-12. Note: #1 Hamelin was son of Geoffrey by an unknown mistress.

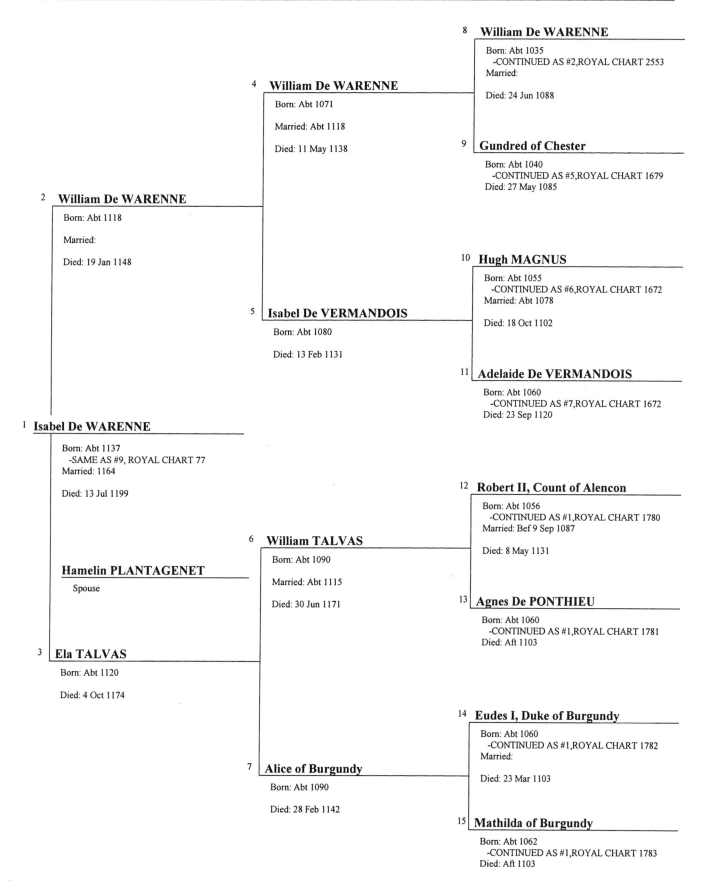

8   **William De WARENNE**

Born: Abt 1035
  -CONTINUED AS #2,ROYAL CHART 2553
Married:

Died: 24 Jun 1088

4   **William De WARENNE**

Born: Abt 1071

Married: Abt 1118

Died: 11 May 1138

9   **Gundred of Chester**

Born: Abt 1040
  -CONTINUED AS #5,ROYAL CHART 1679
Died: 27 May 1085

2   **William De WARENNE**

Born: Abt 1118

Married:

Died: 19 Jan 1148

10   **Hugh MAGNUS**

Born: Abt 1055
  -CONTINUED AS #6,ROYAL CHART 1672
Married: Abt 1078

Died: 18 Oct 1102

5   **Isabel De VERMANDOIS**

Born: Abt 1080

Died: 13 Feb 1131

11   **Adelaide De VERMANDOIS**

Born: Abt 1060
  -CONTINUED AS #7,ROYAL CHART 1672
Died: 23 Sep 1120

1   **Isabel De WARENNE**

Born: Abt 1137
  -SAME AS #9, ROYAL CHART 77
Married: 1164

Died: 13 Jul 1199

Hamelin PLANTAGENET

Spouse

12   **Robert II, Count of Alencon**

Born: Abt 1056
  -CONTINUED AS #1,ROYAL CHART 1780
Married: Bef 9 Sep 1087

Died: 8 May 1131

6   **William TALVAS**

Born: Abt 1090

Married: Abt 1115

Died: 30 Jun 1171

13   **Agnes De PONTHIEU**

Born: Abt 1060
  -CONTINUED AS #1,ROYAL CHART 1781
Died: Aft 1103

3   **Ela TALVAS**

Born: Abt 1120

Died: 4 Oct 1174

14   **Eudes I, Duke of Burgundy**

Born: Abt 1060
  -CONTINUED AS #1,ROYAL CHART 1782
Married:

Died: 23 Mar 1103

7   **Alice of Burgundy**

Born: Abt 1090

Died: 28 Feb 1142

15   **Mathilda of Burgundy**

Born: Abt 1062
  -CONTINUED AS #1,ROYAL CHART 1783
Died: Aft 1103

Sources include: *Royal Ancestors* 11355; *Ancestral Roots* 83, 108; Chart 1525 and sources.

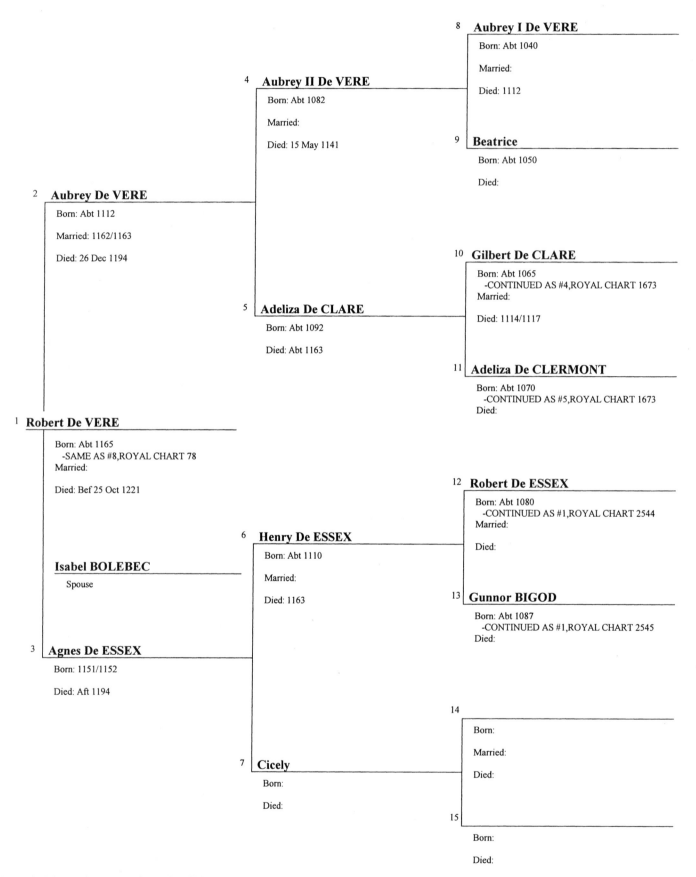

8 | **Aubrey I De VERE**
Born: Abt 1040
Married:
Died: 1112

4 | **Aubrey II De VERE**
Born: Abt 1082
Married:
Died: 15 May 1141

9 | **Beatrice**
Born: Abt 1050
Died:

2 | **Aubrey De VERE**
Born: Abt 1112
Married: 1162/1163
Died: 26 Dec 1194

10 | **Gilbert De CLARE**
Born: Abt 1065
-CONTINUED AS #4,ROYAL CHART 1673
Married:
Died: 1114/1117

5 | **Adeliza De CLARE**
Born: Abt 1092
Died: Abt 1163

11 | **Adeliza De CLERMONT**
Born: Abt 1070
-CONTINUED AS #5,ROYAL CHART 1673
Died:

1 | **Robert De VERE**
Born: Abt 1165
-SAME AS #8,ROYAL CHART 78
Married:
Died: Bef 25 Oct 1221

Isabel BOLEBEC
Spouse

12 | **Robert De ESSEX**
Born: Abt 1080
-CONTINUED AS #1,ROYAL CHART 2544
Married:
Died:

6 | **Henry De ESSEX**
Born: Abt 1110
Married:
Died: 1163

13 | **Gunnor BIGOD**
Born: Abt 1087
-CONTINUED AS #1,ROYAL CHART 2545
Died:

3 | **Agnes De ESSEX**
Born: 1151/1152
Died: Aft 1194

14
Born:
Married:
Died:

7 | **Cicely**
Born:
Died:

15
Born:
Died:

Sources include: *Royal Ancestors* 11350; Faris preliminary baronial manuscript (1998), pp. 1588-92 (Vere); *Complete Peerage* 10:193-207; *Ancestral Roots* 246.

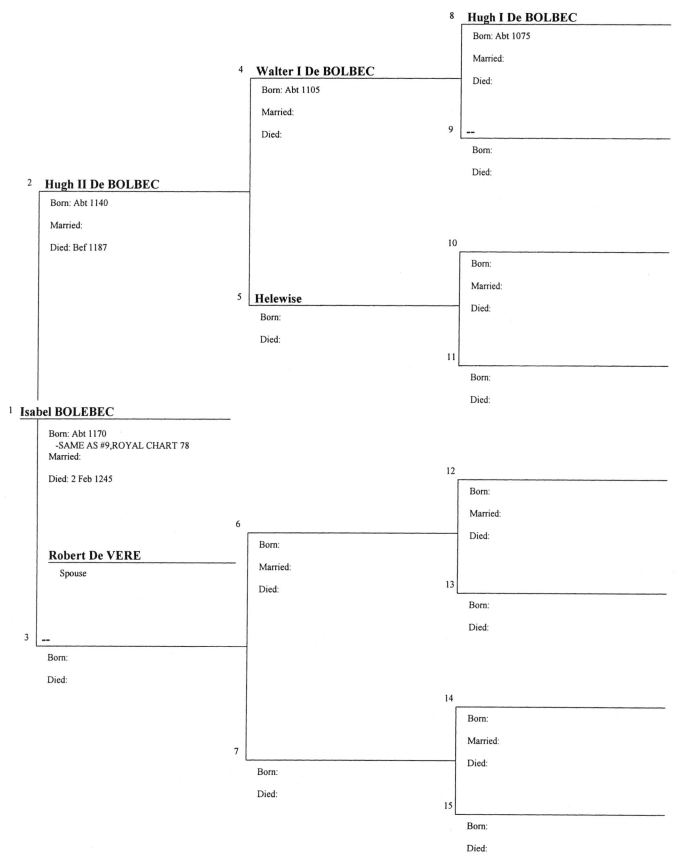

8 Hugh I De BOLBEC
Born: Abt 1075
Married:
Died:

4 Walter I De BOLBEC
Born: Abt 1105
Married:
Died:

9 --
Born:
Died:

2 Hugh II De BOLBEC
Born: Abt 1140
Married:
Died: Bef 1187

10
Born:
Married:
Died:

5 Helewise
Born:
Died:

11
Born:
Died:

1 Isabel BOLEBEC
Born: Abt 1170
-SAME AS #9,ROYAL CHART 78
Married:
Died: 2 Feb 1245

12
Born:
Married:
Died:

6
Born:
Married:
Died:

13
Born:
Died:

Robert De VERE
Spouse

3 --
Born:
Died:

14
Born:
Married:
Died:

7
Born:
Died:

15
Born:
Died:

Sources include: *Royal Ancestors* (1989), chart 11350; *Ancestral Roots* 246-27; Turton 113.

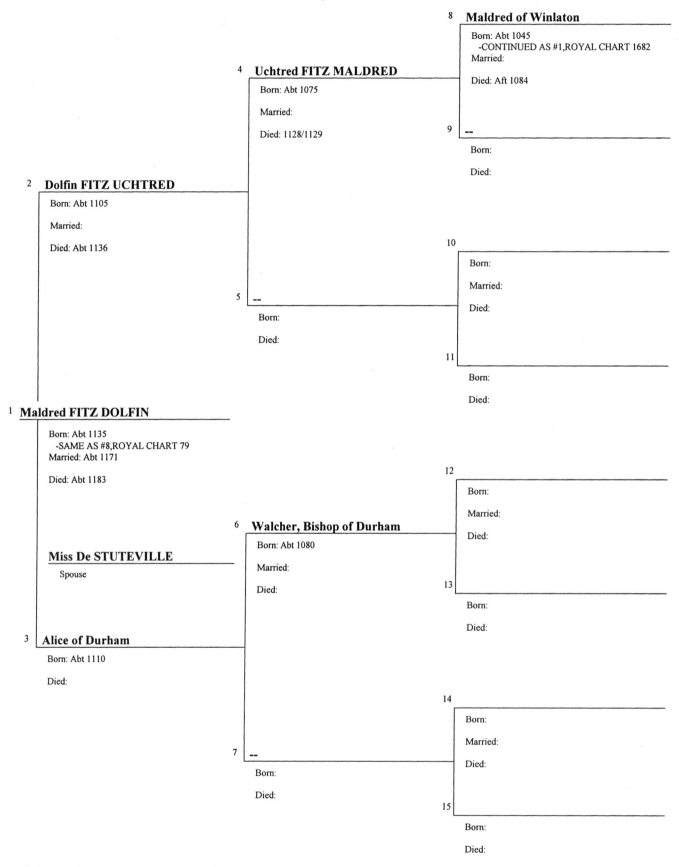

8 Maldred of Winlaton

Born: Abt 1045
  -CONTINUED AS #1,ROYAL CHART 1682
Married:

Died: Aft 1084

4 Uchtred FITZ MALDRED

Born: Abt 1075

Married:

Died: 1128/1129

9 --

Born:

Died:

2 Dolfin FITZ UCHTRED

Born: Abt 1105

Married:

Died: Abt 1136

10

Born:

Married:

Died:

5 --

Born:

Died:

11

Born:

Died:

1 Maldred FITZ DOLFIN

Born: Abt 1135
  -SAME AS #8,ROYAL CHART 79
Married: Abt 1171

Died: Abt 1183

12

Born:

Married:

Died:

6 Walcher, Bishop of Durham

Born: Abt 1080

Married:

Died:

13

Born:

Died:

Miss De STUTEVILLE

Spouse

3 Alice of Durham

Born: Abt 1110

Died:

14

Born:

Married:

Died:

7 --

Born:

Died:

15

Born:

Died:

Sources include: *Royal Ancestors* 11352, 11487; *Ancestral Roots* 247.

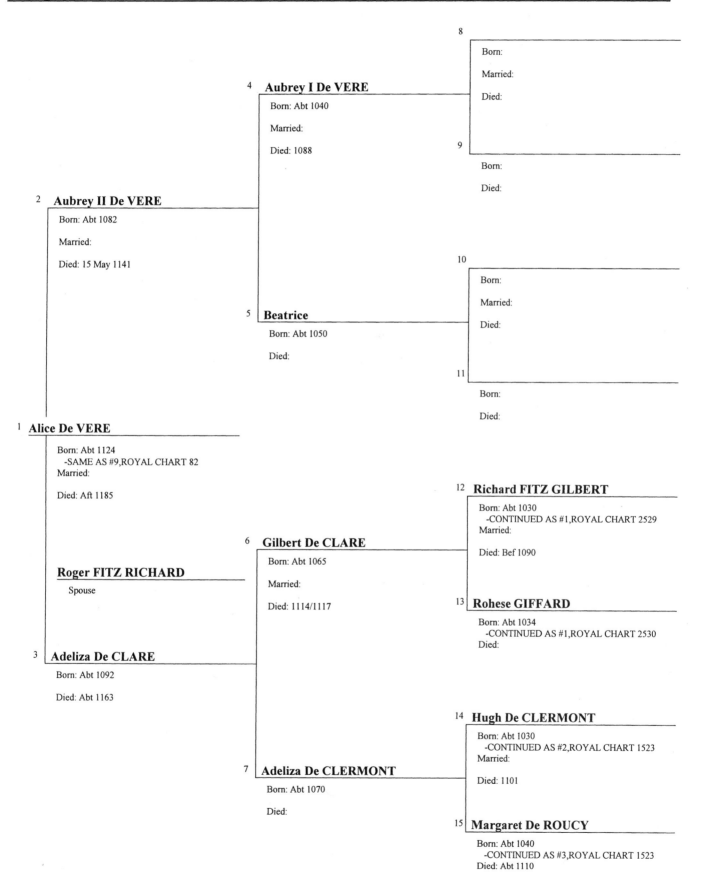

8

4 **Aubrey I De VERE**

Born: Abt 1040

Married:

Died: 1088

Born:

Married:

Died:

9

Born:

Died:

2 **Aubrey II De VERE**

Born: Abt 1082

Married:

Died: 15 May 1141

10

Born:

Married:

Died:

5 **Beatrice**

Born: Abt 1050

Died:

11

Born:

Died:

1 **Alice De VERE**

Born: Abt 1124
    -SAME AS #9,ROYAL CHART 82
Married:

Died: Aft 1185

12 **Richard FITZ GILBERT**

Born: Abt 1030
    -CONTINUED AS #1,ROYAL CHART 2529
Married:

Died: Bef 1090

6 **Gilbert De CLARE**

Born: Abt 1065

Married:

Died: 1114/1117

13 **Rohese GIFFARD**

Born: Abt 1034
    -CONTINUED AS #1,ROYAL CHART 2530
Died:

Roger FITZ RICHARD

Spouse

3 **Adeliza De CLARE**

Born: Abt 1092

Died: Abt 1163

14 **Hugh De CLERMONT**

Born: Abt 1030
    -CONTINUED AS #2,ROYAL CHART 1523
Married:

Died: 1101

7 **Adeliza De CLERMONT**

Born: Abt 1070

Died:

15 **Margaret De ROUCY**

Born: Abt 1040
    -CONTINUED AS #3,ROYAL CHART 1523
Died: Abt 1110

Sources include: *Royal Ancestors* 11391, 11457; Faris preliminary baronial manuscript (1998), pp. 1588-90 (Vere); *Complete Peerage* 10:193-199; *Ancestral Roots* 246D; *Magna Charta* 156, 154.

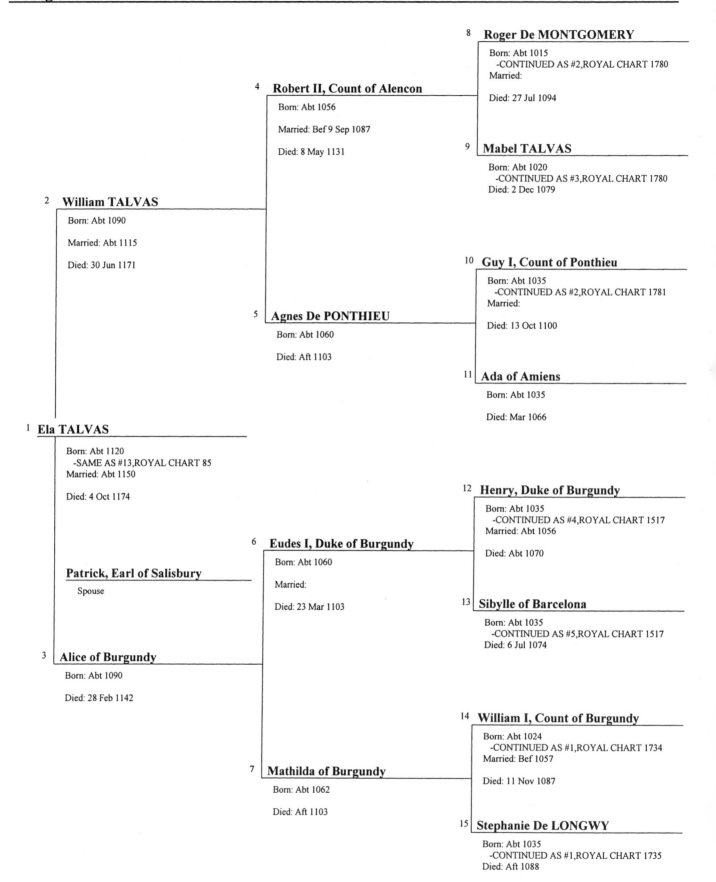

2 William TALVAS

Born: Abt 1090

Married: Abt 1115

Died: 30 Jun 1171

4 Robert II, Count of Alencon

Born: Abt 1056

Married: Bef 9 Sep 1087

Died: 8 May 1131

8 Roger De MONTGOMERY

Born: Abt 1015
  -CONTINUED AS #2,ROYAL CHART 1780
Married:

Died: 27 Jul 1094

9 Mabel TALVAS

Born: Abt 1020
  -CONTINUED AS #3,ROYAL CHART 1780
Died: 2 Dec 1079

5 Agnes De PONTHIEU

Born: Abt 1060

Died: Aft 1103

10 Guy I, Count of Ponthieu

Born: Abt 1035
  -CONTINUED AS #2,ROYAL CHART 1781
Married:

Died: 13 Oct 1100

11 Ada of Amiens

Born: Abt 1035

Died: Mar 1066

1 Ela TALVAS

Born: Abt 1120
  -SAME AS #13,ROYAL CHART 85
Married: Abt 1150

Died: 4 Oct 1174

Patrick, Earl of Salisbury

Spouse

3 Alice of Burgundy

Born: Abt 1090

Died: 28 Feb 1142

6 Eudes I, Duke of Burgundy

Born: Abt 1060

Married:

Died: 23 Mar 1103

12 Henry, Duke of Burgundy

Born: Abt 1035
  -CONTINUED AS #4,ROYAL CHART 1517
Married: Abt 1056

Died: Abt 1070

13 Sibylle of Barcelona

Born: Abt 1035
  -CONTINUED AS #5,ROYAL CHART 1517
Died: 6 Jul 1074

7 Mathilda of Burgundy

Born: Abt 1062

Died: Aft 1103

14 William I, Count of Burgundy

Born: Abt 1024
  -CONTINUED AS #1,ROYAL CHART 1734
Married: Bef 1057

Died: 11 Nov 1087

15 Stephanie De LONGWY

Born: Abt 1035
  -CONTINUED AS #1,ROYAL CHART 1735
Died: Aft 1088

Sources include: *Royal Ancestors* (1989), chart 11466; *Ancestral Roots* 108; Stuart 148; Moriarty 112-114.

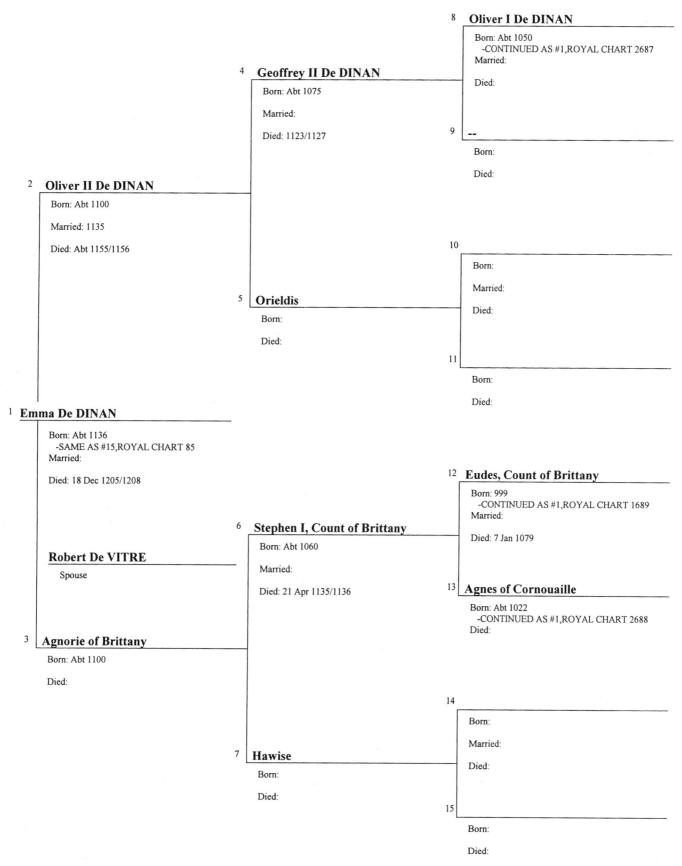

8 Oliver I De DINAN

Born: Abt 1050
  -CONTINUED AS #1,ROYAL CHART 2687
Married:

Died:

4 Geoffrey II De DINAN

Born: Abt 1075

Married:

Died: 1123/1127

9 --

Born:

Died:

2 Oliver II De DINAN

Born: Abt 1100

Married: 1135

Died: Abt 1155/1156

10

Born:

Married:

Died:

5 Orieldis

Born:

Died:

11

Born:

Died:

1 Emma De DINAN

Born: Abt 1136
  -SAME AS #15,ROYAL CHART 85
Married:

Died: 18 Dec 1205/1208

12 Eudes, Count of Brittany

Born: 999
  -CONTINUED AS #1,ROYAL CHART 1689
Married:

Died: 7 Jan 1079

6 Stephen I, Count of Brittany

Born: Abt 1060

Married:

Died: 21 Apr 1135/1136

13 Agnes of Cornouaille

Born: Abt 1022
  -CONTINUED AS #1,ROYAL CHART 2688
Died:

Robert De VITRE

Spouse

3 Agnorie of Brittany

Born: Abt 1100

Died:

14

Born:

Married:

Died:

7 Hawise

Born:

Died:

15

Born:

Died:

Sources include: *Royal Ancestors* (1989), chart 11488; Faris preliminary Charlemagne manuscript (June 1995), pp. 122, 76-77; *Ancestral Roots* 8 (2004), Lines 108-27, 214; *Ancestral Roots* 108-27, 214; Turton 126. Note: The ancestry of #1 Emma is not clear. #2 is also claimed as Alan, a brother of Oliver II. #13 is also called Orguen. Faris accepts the line through #3, 6 & 12 as shown.

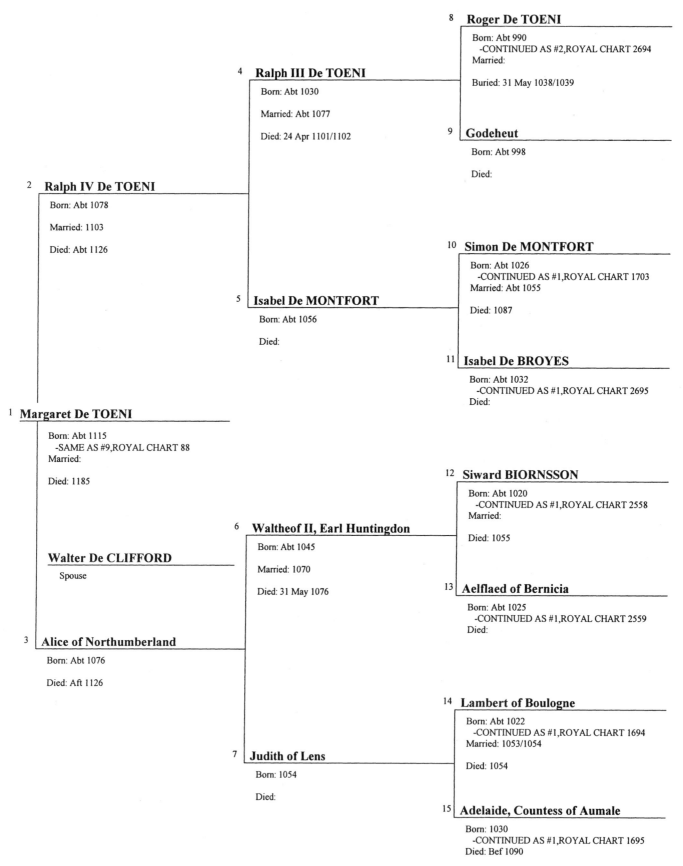

8 Roger De TOENI
Born: Abt 990
  -CONTINUED AS #2,ROYAL CHART 2694
Married:

Buried: 31 May 1038/1039

4 Ralph III De TOENI
Born: Abt 1030

Married: Abt 1077

Died: 24 Apr 1101/1102

9 Godeheut
Born: Abt 998

Died:

2 Ralph IV De TOENI
Born: Abt 1078

Married: 1103

Died: Abt 1126

10 Simon De MONTFORT
Born: Abt 1026
  -CONTINUED AS #1,ROYAL CHART 1703
Married: Abt 1055

Died: 1087

5 Isabel De MONTFORT
Born: Abt 1056

Died:

11 Isabel De BROYES
Born: Abt 1032
  -CONTINUED AS #1,ROYAL CHART 2695
Died:

1 Margaret De TOENI
Born: Abt 1115
  -SAME AS #9,ROYAL CHART 88
Married:

Died: 1185

12 Siward BIORNSSON
Born: Abt 1020
  -CONTINUED AS #1,ROYAL CHART 2558
Married:

Died: 1055

6 Waltheof II, Earl Huntingdon
Born: Abt 1045

Married: 1070

Died: 31 May 1076

13 Aelflaed of Bernicia
Born: Abt 1025
  -CONTINUED AS #1,ROYAL CHART 2559
Died:

Walter De CLIFFORD
Spouse

3 Alice of Northumberland
Born: Abt 1076

Died: Aft 1126

14 Lambert of Boulogne
Born: Abt 1022
  -CONTINUED AS #1,ROYAL CHART 1694
Married: 1053/1054

Died: 1054

7 Judith of Lens
Born: 1054

Died:

15 Adelaide, Countess of Aumale
Born: 1030
  -CONTINUED AS #1,ROYAL CHART 1695
Died: Bef 1090

Sources include: *Royal Ancestors* (1989), chart 11357; Collett family group sheets (Toeni, Montfort); Turton 141; *Ancestral Roots* 98A (#2 & 3 ancestry).

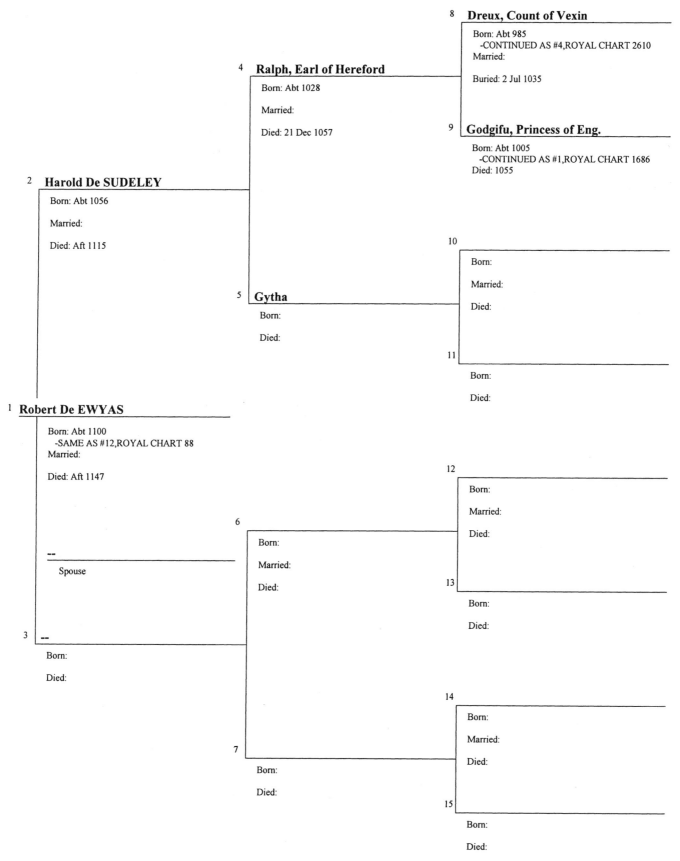

2 **Harold De SUDELEY**

Born: Abt 1056

Married:

Died: Aft 1115

4 **Ralph, Earl of Hereford**

Born: Abt 1028

Married:

Died: 21 Dec 1057

8 **Dreux, Count of Vexin**

Born: Abt 985
 -CONTINUED AS #4,ROYAL CHART 2610
Married:

Buried: 2 Jul 1035

9 **Godgifu, Princess of Eng.**

Born: Abt 1005
 -CONTINUED AS #1,ROYAL CHART 1686
Died: 1055

5 **Gytha**

Born:

Died:

10

Born:

Married:

Died:

11

Born:

Died:

1 **Robert De EWYAS**

Born: Abt 1100
 -SAME AS #12,ROYAL CHART 88
Married:

Died: Aft 1147

--

Spouse

3 --

Born:

Died:

6

Born:

Married:

Died:

12

Born:

Married:

Died:

13

Born:

Died:

7

Born:

Died:

14

Born:

Married:

Died:

15

Born:

Died:

Sources include: *Royal Ancestors* 11448; *Ancestral Roots* 255, 235, 250; Turton 141; Moriarty 135 (#8 ancestry).

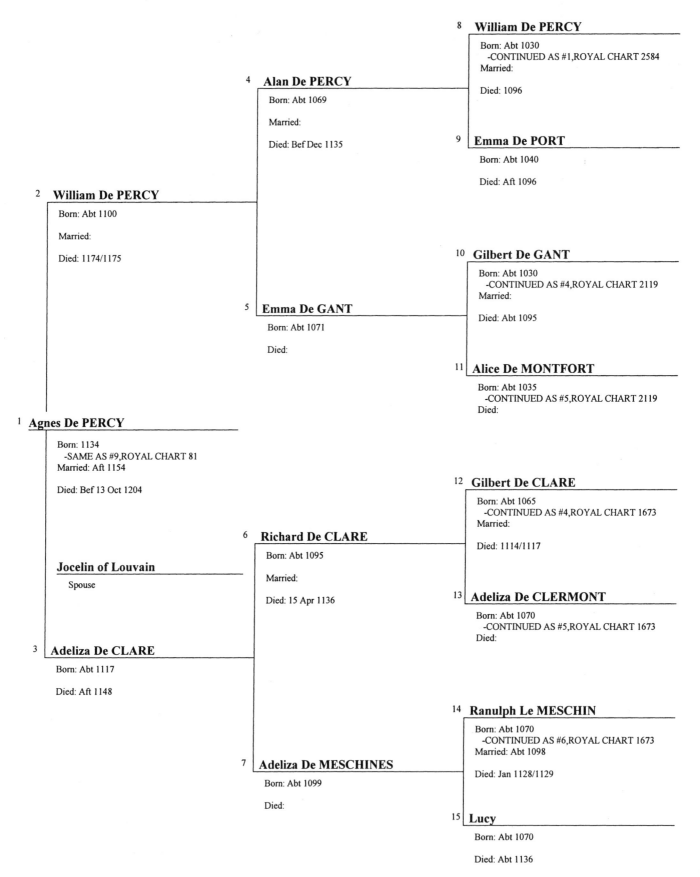

8 William De PERCY

Born: Abt 1030
-CONTINUED AS #1,ROYAL CHART 2584
Married:

Died: 1096

4 Alan De PERCY

Born: Abt 1069

Married:

Died: Bef Dec 1135

9 Emma De PORT

Born: Abt 1040

Died: Aft 1096

2 William De PERCY

Born: Abt 1100

Married:

Died: 1174/1175

10 Gilbert De GANT

Born: Abt 1030
-CONTINUED AS #4,ROYAL CHART 2119
Married:

Died: Abt 1095

5 Emma De GANT

Born: Abt 1071

Died:

11 Alice De MONTFORT

Born: Abt 1035
-CONTINUED AS #5,ROYAL CHART 2119
Died:

1 Agnes De PERCY

Born: 1134
-SAME AS #9,ROYAL CHART 81
Married: Aft 1154

Died: Bef 13 Oct 1204

12 Gilbert De CLARE

Born: Abt 1065
-CONTINUED AS #4,ROYAL CHART 1673
Married:

Died: 1114/1117

6 Richard De CLARE

Born: Abt 1095

Married:

Died: 15 Apr 1136

Jocelin of Louvain

Spouse

13 Adeliza De CLERMONT

Born: Abt 1070
-CONTINUED AS #5,ROYAL CHART 1673
Died:

3 Adeliza De CLARE

Born: Abt 1117

Died: Aft 1148

14 Ranulph Le MESCHIN

Born: Abt 1070
-CONTINUED AS #6,ROYAL CHART 1673
Married: Abt 1098

Died: Jan 1128/1129

7 Adeliza De MESCHINES

Born: Abt 1099

Died:

15 Lucy

Born: Abt 1070

Died: Abt 1136

Sources include: *Royal Ancestors* (1989), chart 11353; *Ancestral Roots* 161-24, 246B; Kraentzler 1137; LDS records; Turton 140 (wrongly inserts an extra generation between #2 William and #4 Alan). Note:The parentage of #9 Emma is disputed.

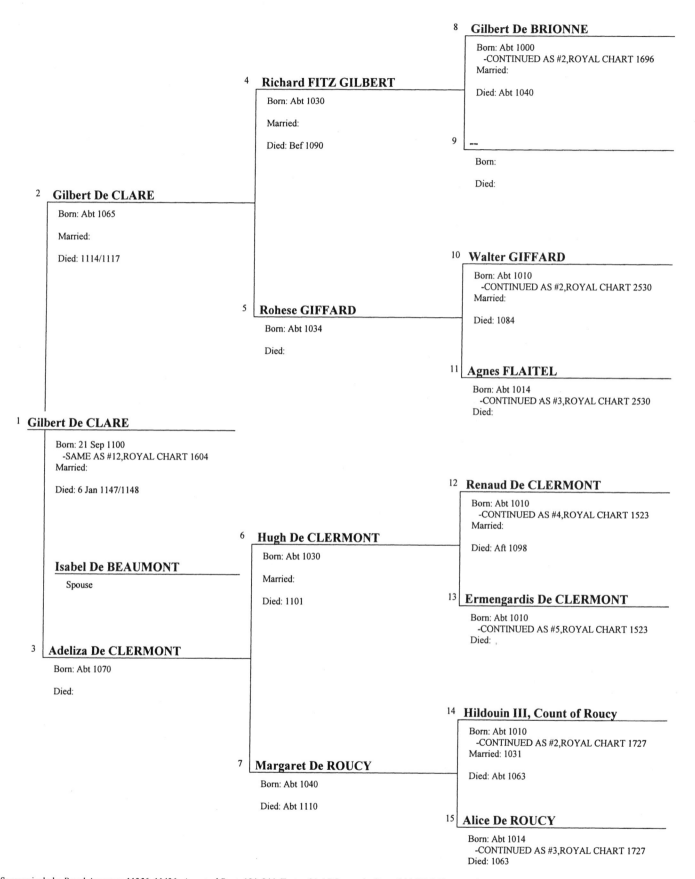

8 Gilbert De BRIONNE

Born: Abt 1000
-CONTINUED AS #2,ROYAL CHART 1696
Married:

Died: Abt 1040

4 Richard FITZ GILBERT

Born: Abt 1030

Married:

Died: Bef 1090

9 --

Born:

Died:

2 Gilbert De CLARE

Born: Abt 1065

Married:

Died: 1114/1117

10 Walter GIFFARD

Born: Abt 1010
-CONTINUED AS #2,ROYAL CHART 2530
Married:

Died: 1084

5 Rohese GIFFARD

Born: Abt 1034

Died:

11 Agnes FLAITEL

Born: Abt 1014
-CONTINUED AS #3,ROYAL CHART 2530
Died:

1 Gilbert De CLARE

Born: 21 Sep 1100
-SAME AS #12,ROYAL CHART 1604
Married:

Died: 6 Jan 1147/1148

12 Renaud De CLERMONT

Born: Abt 1010
-CONTINUED AS #4,ROYAL CHART 1523
Married:

Died: Aft 1098

6 Hugh De CLERMONT

Born: Abt 1030

Married:

Died: 1101

Isabel De BEAUMONT

Spouse

13 Ermengardis De CLERMONT

Born: Abt 1010
-CONTINUED AS #5,ROYAL CHART 1523
Died: ,

3 Adeliza De CLERMONT

Born: Abt 1070

Died:

14 Hildouin III, Count of Roucy

Born: Abt 1010
-CONTINUED AS #2,ROYAL CHART 1727
Married: 1031

Died: Abt 1063

7 Margaret De ROUCY

Born: Abt 1040

Died: Abt 1110

15 Alice De ROUCY

Born: Abt 1014
-CONTINUED AS #3,ROYAL CHART 1727
Died: 1063

Sources include: *Royal Ancestors* 11356, 11436; *Ancestral Roots* 184, 246; Turton 94; LDS records; Stuart 344 (#6 & 7 ancestry).

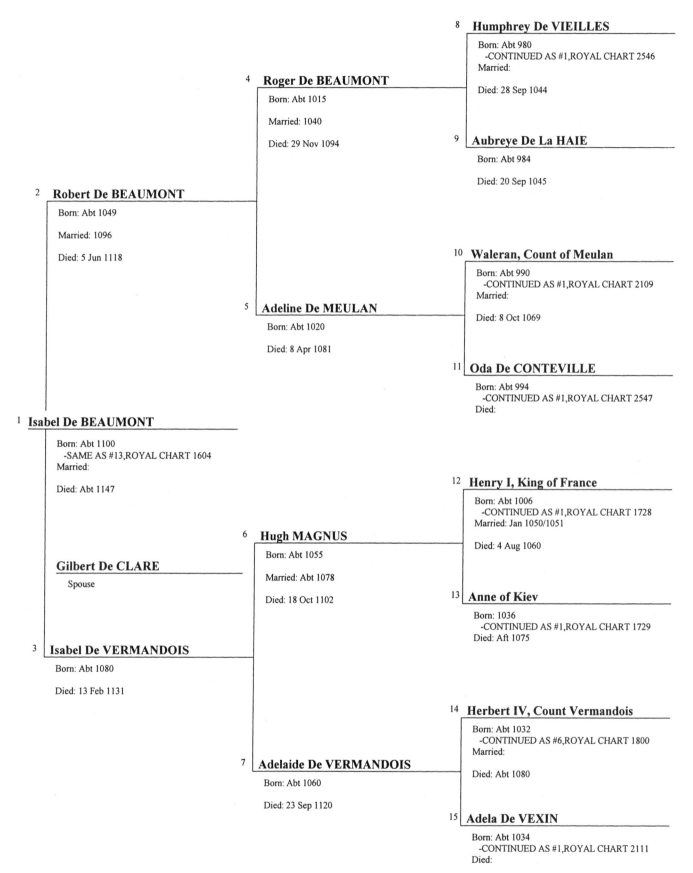

2 Robert De BEAUMONT

Born: Abt 1049

Married: 1096

Died: 5 Jun 1118

4 Roger De BEAUMONT

Born: Abt 1015

Married: 1040

Died: 29 Nov 1094

8 Humphrey De VIEILLES

Born: Abt 980
 -CONTINUED AS #1,ROYAL CHART 2546
Married:

Died: 28 Sep 1044

9 Aubreye De La HAIE

Born: Abt 984

Died: 20 Sep 1045

5 Adeline De MEULAN

Born: Abt 1020

Died: 8 Apr 1081

10 Waleran, Count of Meulan

Born: Abt 990
 -CONTINUED AS #1,ROYAL CHART 2109
Married:

Died: 8 Oct 1069

11 Oda De CONTEVILLE

Born: Abt 994
 -CONTINUED AS #1,ROYAL CHART 2547
Died:

1 Isabel De BEAUMONT

Born: Abt 1100
 -SAME AS #13,ROYAL CHART 1604
Married:

Died: Abt 1147

Gilbert De CLARE

Spouse

3 Isabel De VERMANDOIS

Born: Abt 1080

Died: 13 Feb 1131

6 Hugh MAGNUS

Born: Abt 1055

Married: Abt 1078

Died: 18 Oct 1102

12 Henry I, King of France

Born: Abt 1006
 -CONTINUED AS #1,ROYAL CHART 1728
Married: Jan 1050/1051

Died: 4 Aug 1060

13 Anne of Kiev

Born: 1036
 -CONTINUED AS #1,ROYAL CHART 1729
Died: Aft 1075

7 Adelaide De VERMANDOIS

Born: Abt 1060

Died: 23 Sep 1120

14 Herbert IV, Count Vermandois

Born: Abt 1032
 -CONTINUED AS #6,ROYAL CHART 1800
Married:

Died: Abt 1080

15 Adela De VEXIN

Born: Abt 1034
 -CONTINUED AS #1,ROYAL CHART 2111
Died:

Sources include: *Royal Ancestors* 11356, 11443, 11425, 11544-45; *Ancestral Roots* 66, 50; Schwennicke 3:700; Faris preliminary Charlemagne manuscript (June 1995), pp. 183-184, 273-274 (#2 & 3 ancestry); Turton 114, 100.

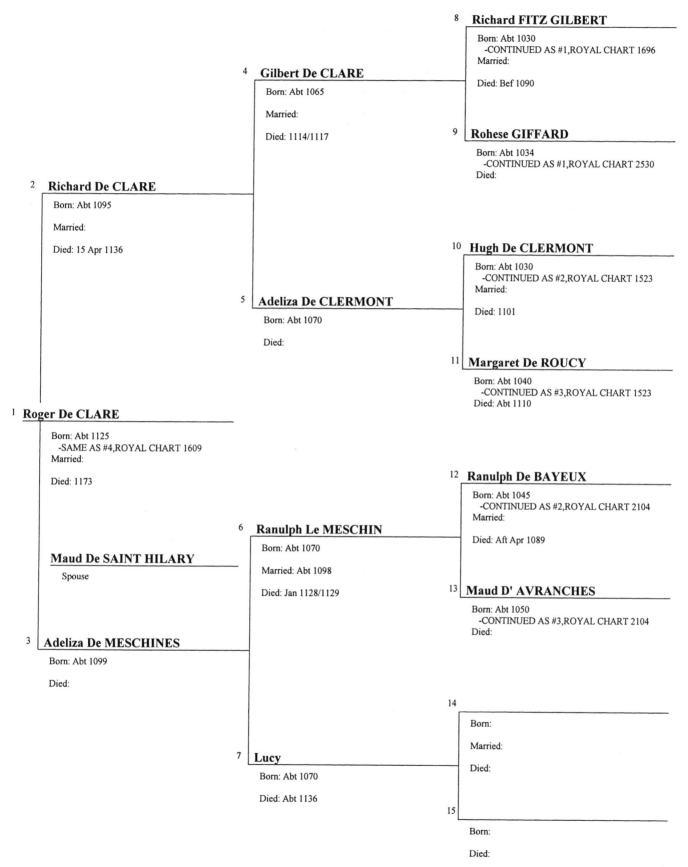

8 Richard FITZ GILBERT
Born: Abt 1030
-CONTINUED AS #1,ROYAL CHART 1696
Married:

Died: Bef 1090

4 Gilbert De CLARE
Born: Abt 1065

Married:

Died: 1114/1117

9 Rohese GIFFARD
Born: Abt 1034
-CONTINUED AS #1,ROYAL CHART 2530
Died:

2 Richard De CLARE
Born: Abt 1095

Married:

Died: 15 Apr 1136

10 Hugh De CLERMONT
Born: Abt 1030
-CONTINUED AS #2,ROYAL CHART 1523
Married:

Died: 1101

5 Adeliza De CLERMONT
Born: Abt 1070

Died:

11 Margaret De ROUCY
Born: Abt 1040
-CONTINUED AS #3,ROYAL CHART 1523
Died: Abt 1110

1 Roger De CLARE
Born: Abt 1125
-SAME AS #4,ROYAL CHART 1609
Married:

Died: 1173

12 Ranulph De BAYEUX
Born: Abt 1045
-CONTINUED AS #2,ROYAL CHART 2104
Married:

Died: Aft Apr 1089

6 Ranulph Le MESCHIN
Born: Abt 1070

Married: Abt 1098

Died: Jan 1128/1129

Maud De SAINT HILARY
Spouse

13 Maud D' AVRANCHES
Born: Abt 1050
-CONTINUED AS #3,ROYAL CHART 2104
Died:

3 Adeliza De MESCHINES
Born: Abt 1099

Died:

14
Born:

Married:

Died:

7 Lucy
Born: Abt 1070

Died: Abt 1136

15
Born:

Died:

Sources include: *Royal Ancestors* 11438; *Ancestral Roots* 246B, 132A.

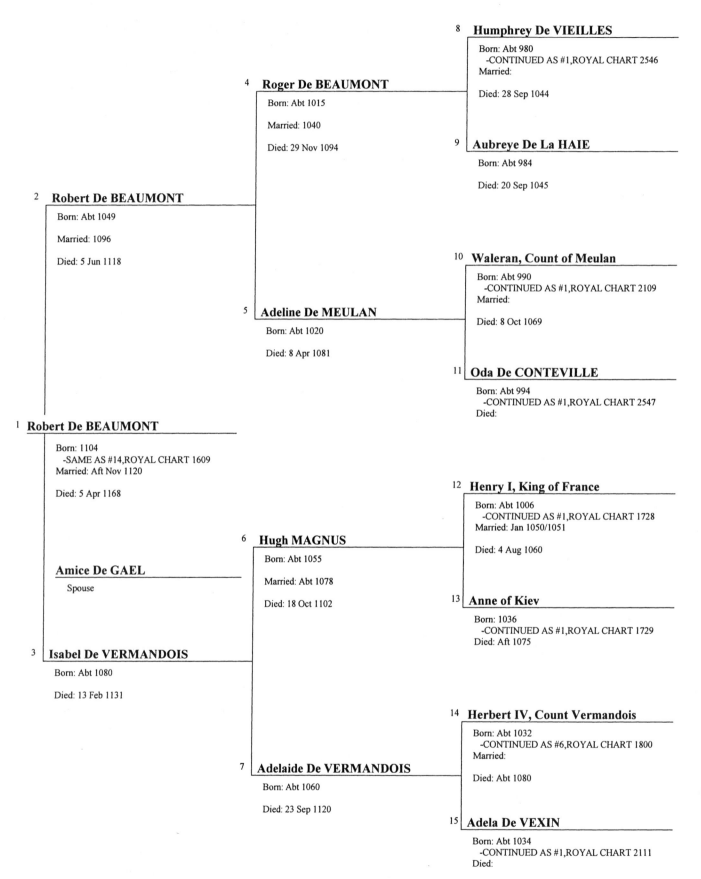

8 Humphrey De VIEILLES
Born: Abt 980
-CONTINUED AS #1,ROYAL CHART 2546
Married:

Died: 28 Sep 1044

4 Roger De BEAUMONT
Born: Abt 1015
Married: 1040
Died: 29 Nov 1094

9 Aubreye De La HAIE
Born: Abt 984

Died: 20 Sep 1045

2 Robert De BEAUMONT
Born: Abt 1049
Married: 1096
Died: 5 Jun 1118

10 Waleran, Count of Meulan
Born: Abt 990
-CONTINUED AS #1,ROYAL CHART 2109
Married:

Died: 8 Oct 1069

5 Adeline De MEULAN
Born: Abt 1020
Died: 8 Apr 1081

11 Oda De CONTEVILLE
Born: Abt 994
-CONTINUED AS #1,ROYAL CHART 2547
Died:

1 Robert De BEAUMONT
Born: 1104
-SAME AS #14,ROYAL CHART 1609
Married: Aft Nov 1120

Died: 5 Apr 1168

12 Henry I, King of France
Born: Abt 1006
-CONTINUED AS #1,ROYAL CHART 1728
Married: Jan 1050/1051

Died: 4 Aug 1060

6 Hugh MAGNUS
Born: Abt 1055
Married: Abt 1078
Died: 18 Oct 1102

13 Anne of Kiev
Born: 1036
-CONTINUED AS #1,ROYAL CHART 1729
Died: Aft 1075

Amice De GAEL
Spouse

3 Isabel De VERMANDOIS
Born: Abt 1080
Died: 13 Feb 1131

14 Herbert IV, Count Vermandois
Born: Abt 1032
-CONTINUED AS #6,ROYAL CHART 1800
Married:

Died: Abt 1080

7 Adelaide De VERMANDOIS
Born: Abt 1060
Died: 23 Sep 1120

15 Adela De VEXIN
Born: Abt 1034
-CONTINUED AS #1,ROYAL CHART 2111
Died:

Sources include: *Royal Ancestors* 11439; *Ancestral Roots* 53; Schwennicke 3:700; Faris preliminary Charlemagne manuscript (June 1995), pp. 183-184, 273-274 (#2 & 3 ancestry).

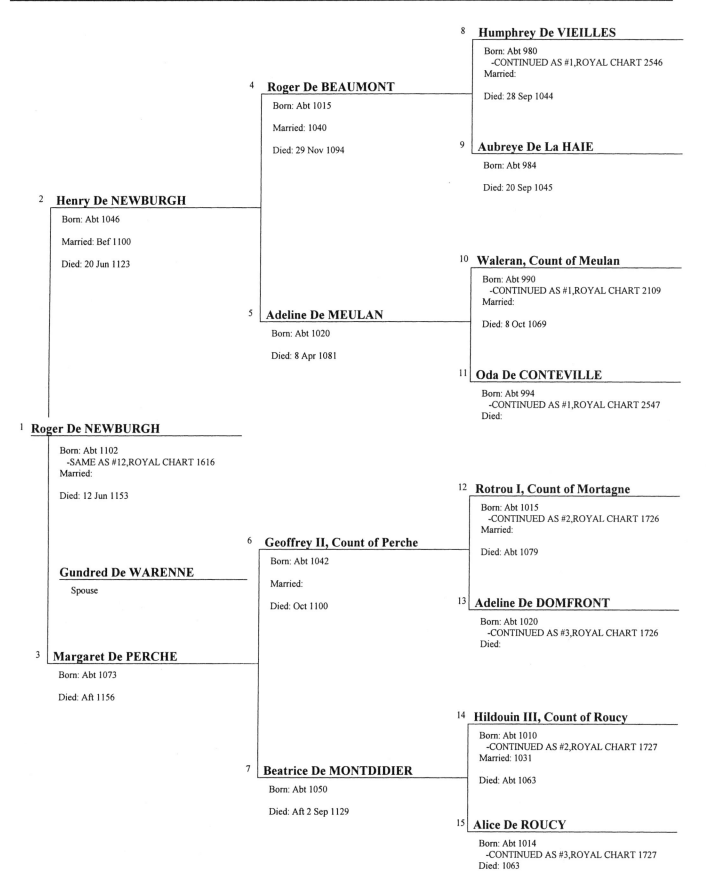

8 Humphrey De VIEILLES
Born: Abt 980
  -CONTINUED AS #1,ROYAL CHART 2546
Married:

Died: 28 Sep 1044

4 Roger De BEAUMONT
Born: Abt 1015

Married: 1040

Died: 29 Nov 1094

9 Aubreye De La HAIE
Born: Abt 984

Died: 20 Sep 1045

2 Henry De NEWBURGH
Born: Abt 1046

Married: Bef 1100

Died: 20 Jun 1123

10 Waleran, Count of Meulan
Born: Abt 990
  -CONTINUED AS #1,ROYAL CHART 2109
Married:

Died: 8 Oct 1069

5 Adeline De MEULAN
Born: Abt 1020

Died: 8 Apr 1081

11 Oda De CONTEVILLE
Born: Abt 994
  -CONTINUED AS #1,ROYAL CHART 2547
Died:

1 Roger De NEWBURGH
Born: Abt 1102
  -SAME AS #12,ROYAL CHART 1616
Married:

Died: 12 Jun 1153

12 Rotrou I, Count of Mortagne
Born: Abt 1015
  -CONTINUED AS #2,ROYAL CHART 1726
Married:

Died: Abt 1079

6 Geoffrey II, Count of Perche
Born: Abt 1042

Married:

Died: Oct 1100

Gundred De WARENNE
Spouse

13 Adeline De DOMFRONT
Born: Abt 1020
  -CONTINUED AS #3,ROYAL CHART 1726
Died:

3 Margaret De PERCHE
Born: Abt 1073

Died: Aft 1156

14 Hildouin III, Count of Roucy
Born: Abt 1010
  -CONTINUED AS #2,ROYAL CHART 1727
Married: 1031

Died: Abt 1063

7 Beatrice De MONTDIDIER
Born: Abt 1050

Died: Aft 2 Sep 1129

15 Alice De ROUCY
Born: Abt 1014
  -CONTINUED AS #3,ROYAL CHART 1727
Died: 1063

Sources include: *Royal Ancestors* 11455; *Ancestral Roots* 151; Stuart 249 (#6 & 7 ancestry); Moriarty 49 (#6 & 7 ancestry).

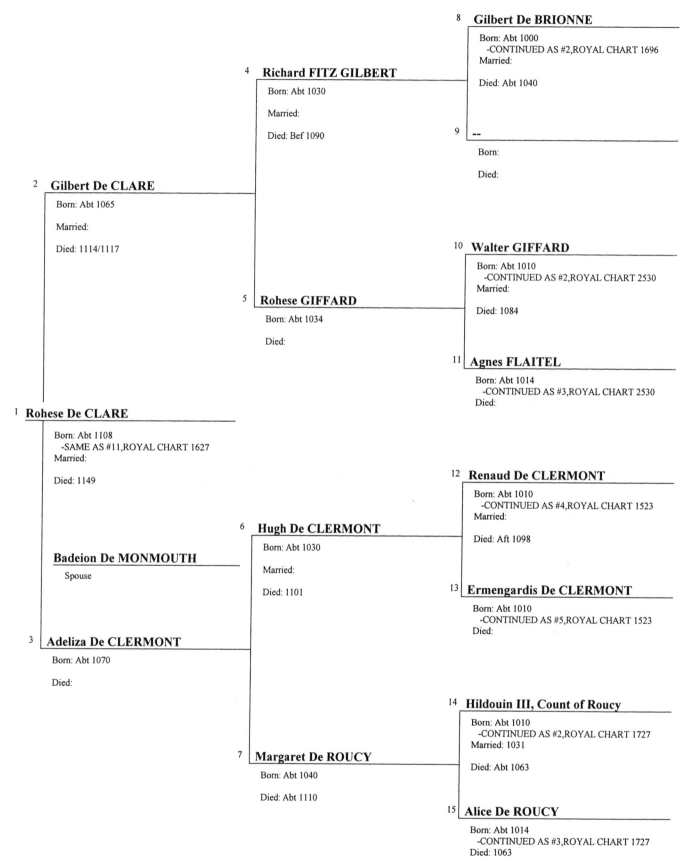

8 Gilbert De BRIONNE
Born: Abt 1000
 -CONTINUED AS #2,ROYAL CHART 1696
Married:

Died: Abt 1040

4 Richard FITZ GILBERT
Born: Abt 1030

Married:

Died: Bef 1090

9 --
Born:

Died:

2 Gilbert De CLARE
Born: Abt 1065

Married:

Died: 1114/1117

10 Walter GIFFARD
Born: Abt 1010
 -CONTINUED AS #2,ROYAL CHART 2530
Married:

Died: 1084

5 Rohese GIFFARD
Born: Abt 1034

Died:

11 Agnes FLAITEL
Born: Abt 1014
 -CONTINUED AS #3,ROYAL CHART 2530
Died:

1 Rohese De CLARE
Born: Abt 1108
 -SAME AS #11,ROYAL CHART 1627
Married:

Died: 1149

12 Renaud De CLERMONT
Born: Abt 1010
 -CONTINUED AS #4,ROYAL CHART 1523
Married:

Died: Aft 1098

6 Hugh De CLERMONT
Born: Abt 1030

Married:

Died: 1101

13 Ermengardis De CLERMONT
Born: Abt 1010
 -CONTINUED AS #5,ROYAL CHART 1523
Died:

Badeion De MONMOUTH
Spouse

3 Adeliza De CLERMONT
Born: Abt 1070

Died:

14 Hildouin III, Count of Roucy
Born: Abt 1010
 -CONTINUED AS #2,ROYAL CHART 1727
Married: 1031

Died: Abt 1063

7 Margaret De ROUCY
Born: Abt 1040

Died: Abt 1110

15 Alice De ROUCY
Born: Abt 1014
 -CONTINUED AS #3,ROYAL CHART 1727
Died: 1063

Sources include: *Ancestral Roots* 177A-7; *Royal Ancestors* 11436. See chart 1671 for additional sources.

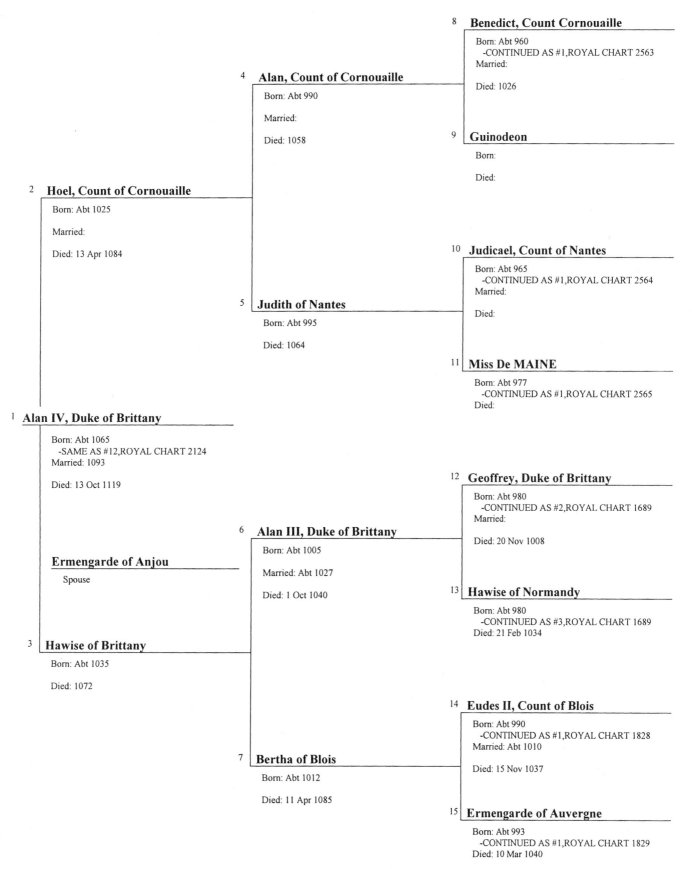

8 **Benedict, Count Cornouaille**

Born: Abt 960
-CONTINUED AS #1,ROYAL CHART 2563
Married:

Died: 1026

4 **Alan, Count of Cornouaille**

Born: Abt 990

Married:

Died: 1058

9 **Guinodeon**

Born:

Died:

2 **Hoel, Count of Cornouaille**

Born: Abt 1025

Married:

Died: 13 Apr 1084

10 **Judicael, Count of Nantes**

Born: Abt 965
-CONTINUED AS #1,ROYAL CHART 2564
Married:

Died:

5 **Judith of Nantes**

Born: Abt 995

Died: 1064

11 **Miss De MAINE**

Born: Abt 977
-CONTINUED AS #1,ROYAL CHART 2565
Died:

1 **Alan IV, Duke of Brittany**

Born: Abt 1065
-SAME AS #12,ROYAL CHART 2124
Married: 1093

Died: 13 Oct 1119

12 **Geoffrey, Duke of Brittany**

Born: Abt 980
-CONTINUED AS #2,ROYAL CHART 1689
Married:

Died: 20 Nov 1008

6 **Alan III, Duke of Brittany**

Born: Abt 1005

Married: Abt 1027

Died: 1 Oct 1040

13 **Hawise of Normandy**

Born: Abt 980
-CONTINUED AS #3,ROYAL CHART 1689
Died: 21 Feb 1034

Ermengarde of Anjou

Spouse

3 **Hawise of Brittany**

Born: Abt 1035

Died: 1072

14 **Eudes II, Count of Blois**

Born: Abt 990
-CONTINUED AS #1,ROYAL CHART 1828
Married: Abt 1010

Died: 15 Nov 1037

7 **Bertha of Blois**

Born: Abt 1012

Died: 11 Apr 1085

15 **Ermengarde of Auvergne**

Born: Abt 993
-CONTINUED AS #1,ROYAL CHART 1829
Died: 10 Mar 1040

Sources include: *Royal Ancestors* (1989), chart 11459; *Ancestral Roots* 39, 136; *Complete Peerage* 3:427, 10:780, 786 (#2 ancestry); Turton 188.

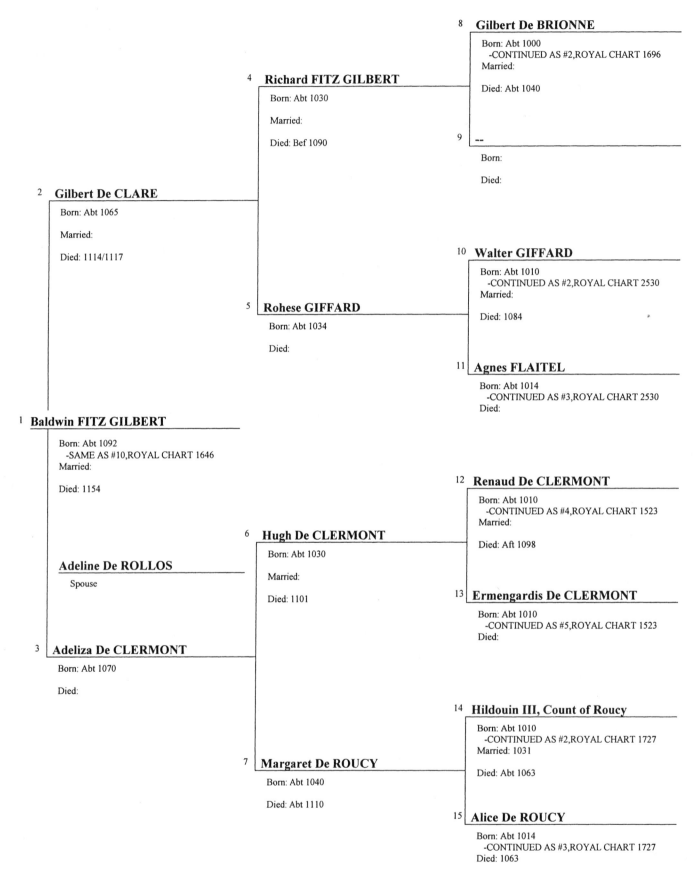

8 | Gilbert De BRIONNE

Born: Abt 1000
  -CONTINUED AS #2,ROYAL CHART 1696
Married:

Died: Abt 1040

4 | Richard FITZ GILBERT

Born: Abt 1030

Married:

Died: Bef 1090

9 | --

Born:

Died:

2 | Gilbert De CLARE

Born: Abt 1065

Married:

Died: 1114/1117

10 | Walter GIFFARD

Born: Abt 1010
  -CONTINUED AS #2,ROYAL CHART 2530
Married:

Died: 1084

5 | Rohese GIFFARD

Born: Abt 1034

Died:

11 | Agnes FLAITEL

Born: Abt 1014
  -CONTINUED AS #3,ROYAL CHART 2530
Died:

1 | Baldwin FITZ GILBERT

Born: Abt 1092
  -SAME AS #10,ROYAL CHART 1646
Married:

Died: 1154

12 | Renaud De CLERMONT

Born: Abt 1010
  -CONTINUED AS #4,ROYAL CHART 1523
Married:

Died: Aft 1098

6 | Hugh De CLERMONT

Born: Abt 1030

Married:

Died: 1101

13 | Ermengardis De CLERMONT

Born: Abt 1010
  -CONTINUED AS #5,ROYAL CHART 1523
Died:

Adeline De ROLLOS

Spouse

3 | Adeliza De CLERMONT

Born: Abt 1070

Died:

14 | Hildouin III, Count of Roucy

Born: Abt 1010
  -CONTINUED AS #2,ROYAL CHART 1727
Married: 1031

Died: Abt 1063

7 | Margaret De ROUCY

Born: Abt 1040

Died: Abt 1110

15 | Alice De ROUCY

Born: Abt 1014
  -CONTINUED AS #3,ROYAL CHART 1727
Died: 1063

Sources include: *Royal Ancestors* (1989), chart 11469; *Ancestral Roots* 184A; See chart 1671 for additional sources.

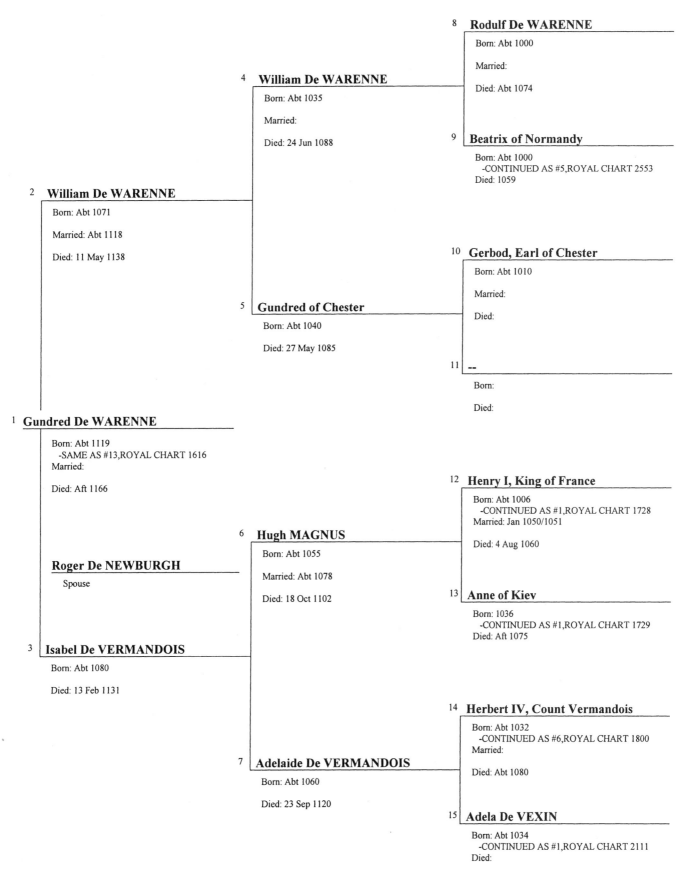

8 Rodulf De WARENNE
Born: Abt 1000
Married:
Died: Abt 1074

4 William De WARENNE
Born: Abt 1035
Married:
Died: 24 Jun 1088

9 Beatrix of Normandy
Born: Abt 1000
  -CONTINUED AS #5,ROYAL CHART 2553
Died: 1059

2 William De WARENNE
Born: Abt 1071
Married: Abt 1118
Died: 11 May 1138

10 Gerbod, Earl of Chester
Born: Abt 1010
Married:
Died:

5 Gundred of Chester
Born: Abt 1040
Died: 27 May 1085

11 --
Born:
Died:

1 Gundred De WARENNE
Born: Abt 1119
  -SAME AS #13,ROYAL CHART 1616
Married:
Died: Aft 1166

12 Henry I, King of France
Born: Abt 1006
  -CONTINUED AS #1,ROYAL CHART 1728
Married: Jan 1050/1051
Died: 4 Aug 1060

6 Hugh MAGNUS
Born: Abt 1055
Married: Abt 1078
Died: 18 Oct 1102

13 Anne of Kiev
Born: 1036
  -CONTINUED AS #1,ROYAL CHART 1729
Died: Aft 1075

Roger De NEWBURGH
Spouse

3 Isabel De VERMANDOIS
Born: Abt 1080
Died: 13 Feb 1131

14 Herbert IV, Count Vermandois
Born: Abt 1032
  -CONTINUED AS #6,ROYAL CHART 1800
Married:
Died: Abt 1080

7 Adelaide De VERMANDOIS
Born: Abt 1060
Died: 23 Sep 1120

15 Adela De VEXIN
Born: Abt 1034
  -CONTINUED AS #1,ROYAL CHART 2111
Died:

Sources include: *Royal Ancestors* (1989), charts 11455, 11424 and notes; *Ancestral Roots* 84, 50; Moriarty 184; Stuart 135; Sir Anthony Wagner, *Pedigree and Progress*, p. 205, pedigree 46. Note: The parentage of #5 Gundred is disputed. She was <u>not</u> daughter of William I the Conqueror (see *NGSQ* 59:317). #10 Gerbod was hereditary Advocate of St. Bertin at St. Omer, Earl of Chester, and <u>possible</u> father (according to Moriarty) of Gerbod the Fleming, Earl of Chester, and of #5 Gundred.

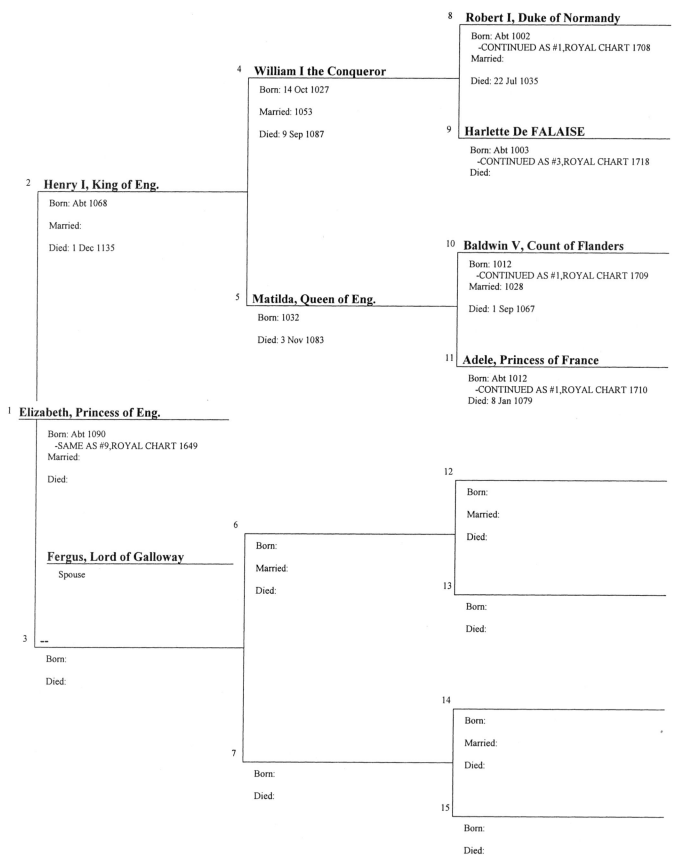

8 **Robert I, Duke of Normandy**

Born: Abt 1002
-CONTINUED AS #1,ROYAL CHART 1708
Married:

Died: 22 Jul 1035

4 **William I the Conqueror**

Born: 14 Oct 1027

Married: 1053

Died: 9 Sep 1087

9 **Harlette De FALAISE**

Born: Abt 1003
-CONTINUED AS #3,ROYAL CHART 1718
Died:

2 **Henry I, King of Eng.**

Born: Abt 1068

Married:

Died: 1 Dec 1135

10 **Baldwin V, Count of Flanders**

Born: 1012
-CONTINUED AS #1,ROYAL CHART 1709
Married: 1028

Died: 1 Sep 1067

5 **Matilda, Queen of Eng.**

Born: 1032

Died: 3 Nov 1083

11 **Adele, Princess of France**

Born: Abt 1012
-CONTINUED AS #1,ROYAL CHART 1710
Died: 8 Jan 1079

1 **Elizabeth, Princess of Eng.**

Born: Abt 1090
-SAME AS #9,ROYAL CHART 1649
Married:

Died:

12

Born:

Married:

Died:

6

Born:

Married:

Died:

13

Born:

Died:

Fergus, Lord of Galloway

Spouse

3 --

Born:

Died:

14

Born:

Married:

Died:

7

Born:

Died:

15

Born:

Died:

Sources include: *Royal Ancestors* (1989), chart 11462; *Ancestral Roots* 38-24, 121-25, 121B; See chart 1502 for additional sources. Note: #1 Elizabeth was illegitimate by an unknown mistress of Henry I, according to *Ancestral Roots*. However, Douglas Richardson doubts that Elizabeth was a daughter of Henry.

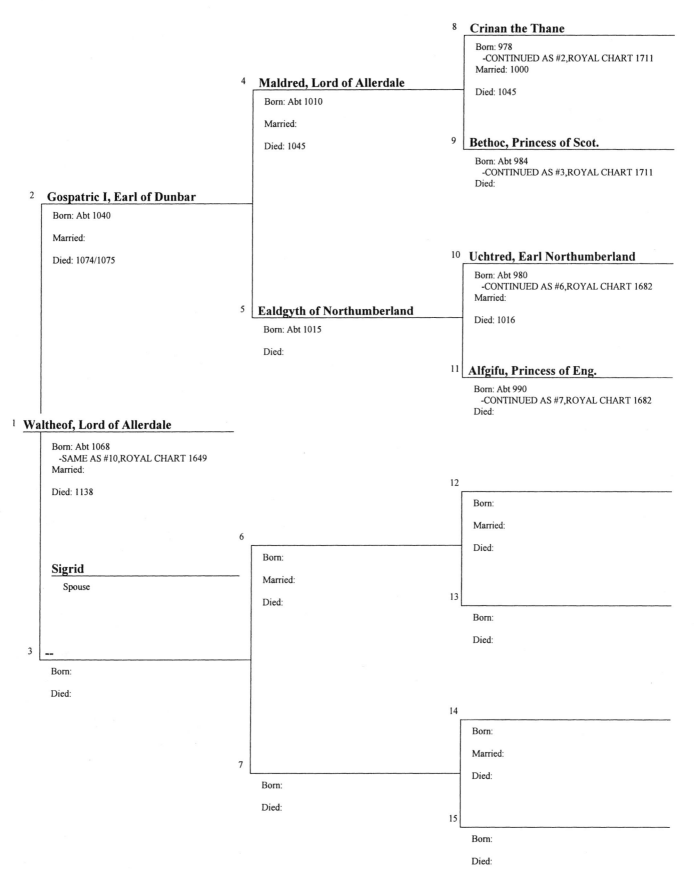

8 **Crinan the Thane**
Born: 978
-CONTINUED AS #2,ROYAL CHART 1711
Married: 1000

Died: 1045

4 **Maldred, Lord of Allerdale**
Born: Abt 1010

Married:

Died: 1045

9 **Bethoc, Princess of Scot.**
Born: Abt 984
-CONTINUED AS #3,ROYAL CHART 1711
Died:

2 **Gospatric I, Earl of Dunbar**
Born: Abt 1040

Married:

Died: 1074/1075

10 **Uchtred, Earl Northumberland**
Born: Abt 980
-CONTINUED AS #6,ROYAL CHART 1682
Married:

Died: 1016

5 **Ealdgyth of Northumberland**
Born: Abt 1015

Died:

11 **Alfgifu, Princess of Eng.**
Born: Abt 990
-CONTINUED AS #7,ROYAL CHART 1682
Died:

1 **Waltheof, Lord of Allerdale**
Born: Abt 1068
-SAME AS #10,ROYAL CHART 1649
Married:

Died: 1138

12
Born:

Married:

Died:

6
Born:

Married:

Died:

13
Born:

Died:

Sigrid
Spouse

3 **--**
Born:

Died:

14
Born:

Married:

Died:

7
Born:

Died:

15
Born:

Died:

Sources include: *Royal Ancestors* 11462, 11562-63; *Ancestral Roots* 38, 34, 247-20. Note: #3 was "a sister of Edmund". This could not be King Edmund.

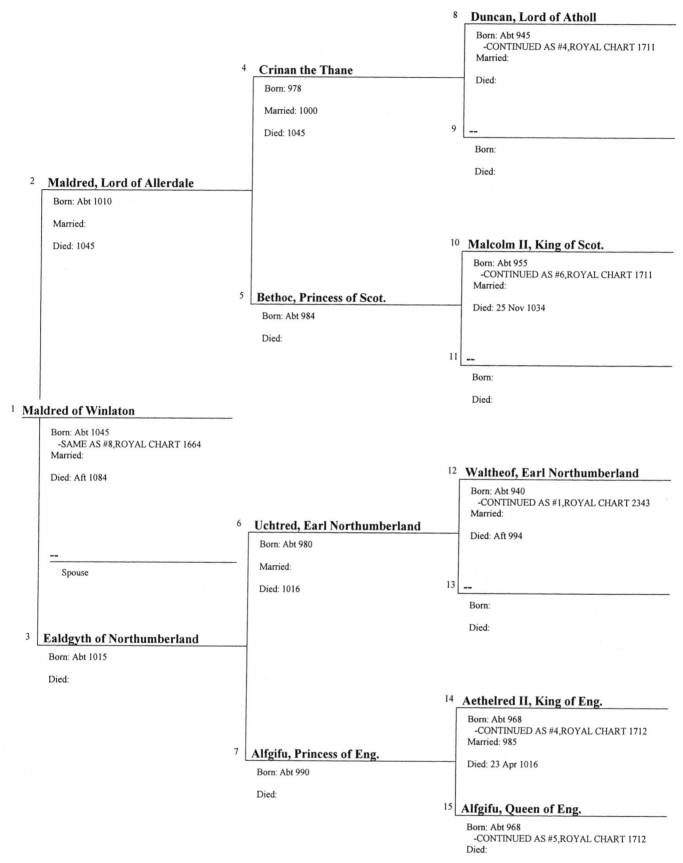

8 Duncan, Lord of Atholl
Born: Abt 945
-CONTINUED AS #4,ROYAL CHART 1711
Married:

Died:

4 Crinan the Thane
Born: 978

Married: 1000

Died: 1045

9 --
Born:

Died:

2 Maldred, Lord of Allerdale
Born: Abt 1010

Married:

Died: 1045

10 Malcolm II, King of Scot.
Born: Abt 955
-CONTINUED AS #6,ROYAL CHART 1711
Married:

Died: 25 Nov 1034

5 Bethoc, Princess of Scot.
Born: Abt 984

Died:

11 --
Born:

Died:

1 Maldred of Winlaton
Born: Abt 1045
-SAME AS #8,ROYAL CHART 1664
Married:

Died: Aft 1084

12 Waltheof, Earl Northumberland
Born: Abt 940
-CONTINUED AS #1,ROYAL CHART 2343
Married:

Died: Aft 994

6 Uchtred, Earl Northumberland
Born: Abt 980

Married:

Died: 1016

13 --
Born:

Died:

**-- **
Spouse

3 Ealdgyth of Northumberland
Born: Abt 1015

Died:

14 Aethelred II, King of Eng.
Born: Abt 968
-CONTINUED AS #4,ROYAL CHART 1712
Married: 985

Died: 23 Apr 1016

7 Alfgifu, Princess of Eng.
Born: Abt 990

Died:

15 Alfgifu, Queen of Eng.
Born: Abt 968
-CONTINUED AS #5,ROYAL CHART 1712
Died:

Sources include: *Royal Ancestors* (1989), chart 11487; *Ancestral Roots* 247.

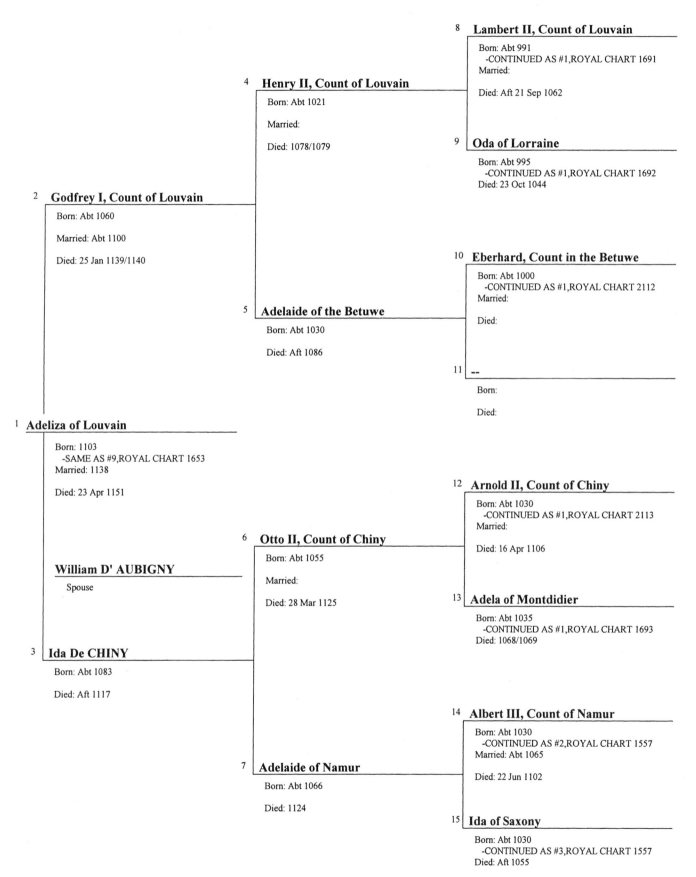

8 Lambert II, Count of Louvain

Born: Abt 991
-CONTINUED AS #1,ROYAL CHART 1691
Married:

Died: Aft 21 Sep 1062

4 Henry II, Count of Louvain

Born: Abt 1021

Married:

Died: 1078/1079

9 Oda of Lorraine

Born: Abt 995
-CONTINUED AS #1,ROYAL CHART 1692
Died: 23 Oct 1044

2 Godfrey I, Count of Louvain

Born: Abt 1060

Married: Abt 1100

Died: 25 Jan 1139/1140

10 Eberhard, Count in the Betuwe

Born: Abt 1000
-CONTINUED AS #1,ROYAL CHART 2112
Married:

Died:

5 Adelaide of the Betuwe

Born: Abt 1030

Died: Aft 1086

11 --

Born:

Died:

1 Adeliza of Louvain

Born: 1103
-SAME AS #9,ROYAL CHART 1653
Married: 1138

Died: 23 Apr 1151

12 Arnold II, Count of Chiny

Born: Abt 1030
-CONTINUED AS #1,ROYAL CHART 2113
Married:

Died: 16 Apr 1106

6 Otto II, Count of Chiny

Born: Abt 1055

Married:

Died: 28 Mar 1125

13 Adela of Montdidier

Born: Abt 1035
-CONTINUED AS #1,ROYAL CHART 1693
Died: 1068/1069

William D' AUBIGNY

Spouse

14 Albert III, Count of Namur

Born: Abt 1030
-CONTINUED AS #2,ROYAL CHART 1557
Married: Abt 1065

Died: 22 Jun 1102

3 Ida De CHINY

Born: Abt 1083

Died: Aft 1117

7 Adelaide of Namur

Born: Abt 1066

Died: 1124

15 Ida of Saxony

Born: Abt 1030
-CONTINUED AS #3,ROYAL CHART 1557
Died: Aft 1055

Sources include: *Royal Ancestors* (1989), chart 11473; *Ancestral Roots* 149, 155; Stuart 68, 120 (#2 & 3 ancestry), 389 (#5 ancestry); Moriarty 154-156, 125-126. Note: The ancestry shown for #5 Adelaide (or Adele) is not certain.

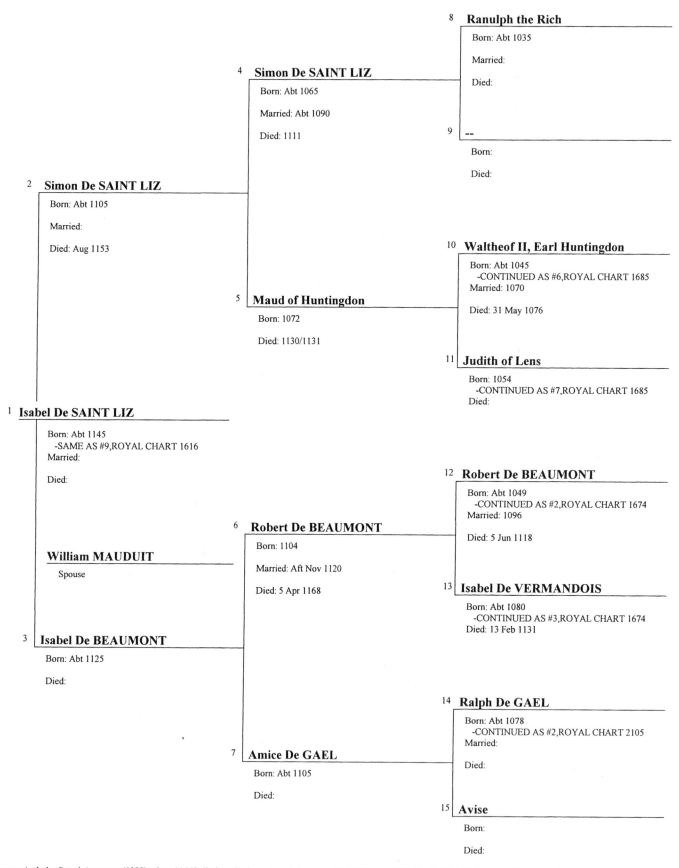

8 Ranulph the Rich
Born: Abt 1035
Married:
Died:

4 Simon De SAINT LIZ
Born: Abt 1065
Married: Abt 1090
Died: 1111

9 --
Born:
Died:

2 Simon De SAINT LIZ
Born: Abt 1105
Married:
Died: Aug 1153

10 Waltheof II, Earl Huntingdon
Born: Abt 1045
  -CONTINUED AS #6,ROYAL CHART 1685
Married: 1070
Died: 31 May 1076

5 Maud of Huntingdon
Born: 1072
Died: 1130/1131

11 Judith of Lens
Born: 1054
  -CONTINUED AS #7,ROYAL CHART 1685
Died:

1 Isabel De SAINT LIZ
Born: Abt 1145
  -SAME AS #9,ROYAL CHART 1616
Married:
Died:

William MAUDUIT
Spouse

12 Robert De BEAUMONT
Born: Abt 1049
  -CONTINUED AS #2,ROYAL CHART 1674
Married: 1096
Died: 5 Jun 1118

6 Robert De BEAUMONT
Born: 1104
Married: Aft Nov 1120
Died: 5 Apr 1168

13 Isabel De VERMANDOIS
Born: Abt 1080
  -CONTINUED AS #3,ROYAL CHART 1674
Died: 13 Feb 1131

3 Isabel De BEAUMONT
Born: Abt 1125
Died:

14 Ralph De GAEL
Born: Abt 1078
  -CONTINUED AS #2,ROYAL CHART 2105
Married:
Died:

7 Amice De GAEL
Born: Abt 1105
Died:

15 Avise
Born:
Died:

Sources include: *Royal Ancestors* (1989), chart 11453; Faris preliminary baronial manuscript (1998), pp. 1360 (St. Liz), 84-86 (Beaumont); *Ancestral Roots* 84-27 (#2 Simon grandfather of Robert Mauduit, died 1222); Turton 117.

Pedigree Chart

Chart 1685

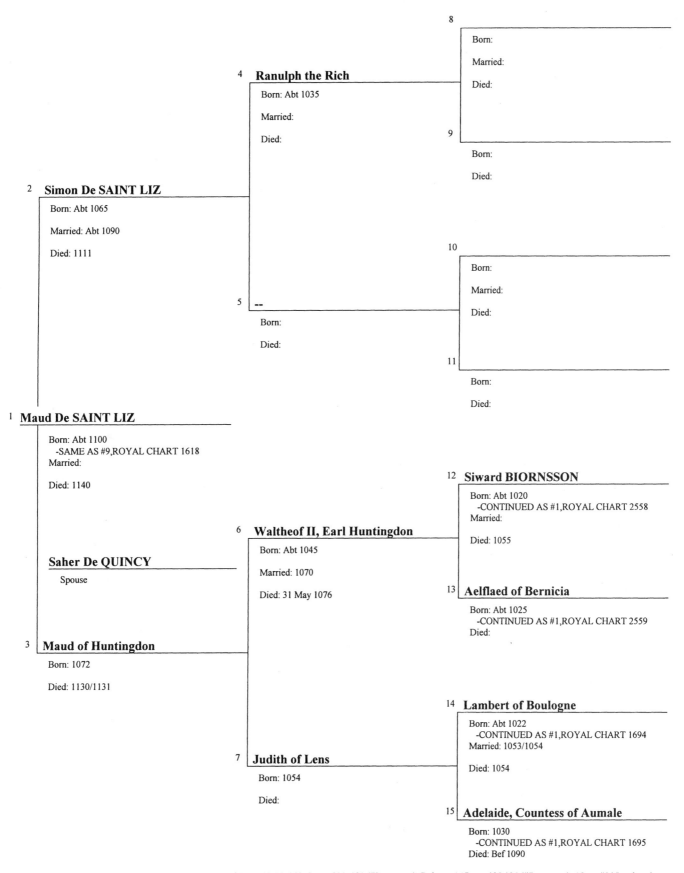

8

Born:

Married:

Died:

4   **Ranulph the Rich**

Born: Abt 1035

Married:

Died:

9

Born:

Died:

2   **Simon De SAINT LIZ**

Born: Abt 1065

Married: Abt 1090

Died: 1111

10

Born:

Married:

Died:

5   **--**

Born:

Died:

11

Born:

Died:

1   **Maud De SAINT LIZ**

Born: Abt 1100
   -SAME AS #9,ROYAL CHART 1618
Married:

Died: 1140

12   **Siward BIORNSSON**

Born: Abt 1020
   -CONTINUED AS #1,ROYAL CHART 2558
Married:

Died: 1055

6   **Waltheof II, Earl Huntingdon**

Born: Abt 1045

Married: 1070

Died: 31 May 1076

13   **Aelflaed of Bernicia**

Born: Abt 1025
   -CONTINUED AS #1,ROYAL CHART 2559
Died:

Saher De QUINCY

Spouse

3   **Maud of Huntingdon**

Born: 1072

Died: 1130/1131

14   **Lambert of Boulogne**

Born: Abt 1022
   -CONTINUED AS #1,ROYAL CHART 1694
Married: 1053/1054

Died: 1054

7   **Judith of Lens**

Born: 1054

Died:

15   **Adelaide, Countess of Aumale**

Born: 1030
   -CONTINUED AS #1,ROYAL CHART 1695
Died: Bef 1090

Sources include: *Royal Ancestors* (1989), chart 11442; *Ancestral Roots* 53-27, 148; Stuart 221, 131 (#3 ancestry); Roberts *AAP*, pp. 195-196 (#7 ancestry). Note: #14 Lambert is not certain. #7 might be daughter of Enguerrand II, Count of Ponthieu, 1st husband of #15 Adelaide. Lambert was the 2nd husband. Enguerrand II was son of Hugh II & Bertha (continued chart 1781, #4 & 5).

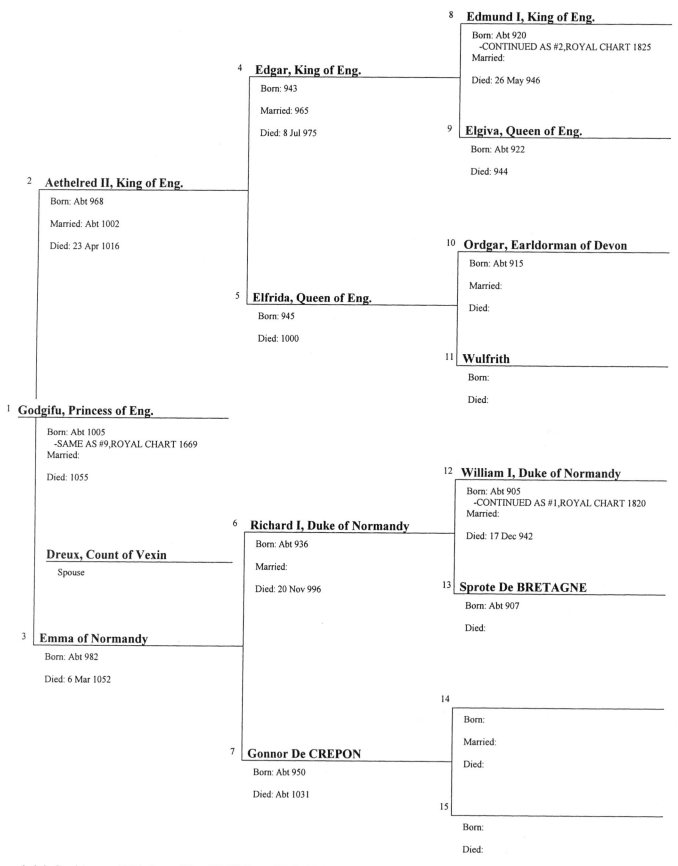

8 **Edmund I, King of Eng.**

Born: Abt 920
-CONTINUED AS #2,ROYAL CHART 1825
Married:

Died: 26 May 946

4 **Edgar, King of Eng.**

Born: 943

Married: 965

Died: 8 Jul 975

9 **Elgiva, Queen of Eng.**

Born: Abt 922

Died: 944

2 **Aethelred II, King of Eng.**

Born: Abt 968

Married: Abt 1002

Died: 23 Apr 1016

10 **Ordgar, Earldorman of Devon**

Born: Abt 915

Married:

Died:

5 **Elfrida, Queen of Eng.**

Born: 945

Died: 1000

11 **Wulfrith**

Born:

Died:

1 **Godgifu, Princess of Eng.**

Born: Abt 1005
-SAME AS #9,ROYAL CHART 1669
Married:

Died: 1055

12 **William I, Duke of Normandy**

Born: Abt 905
-CONTINUED AS #1,ROYAL CHART 1820
Married:

Died: 17 Dec 942

6 **Richard I, Duke of Normandy**

Born: Abt 936

Married:

Died: 20 Nov 996

13 **Sprote De BRETAGNE**

Born: Abt 907

Died:

Dreux, Count of Vexin

Spouse

3 **Emma of Normandy**

Born: Abt 982

Died: 6 Mar 1052

14

Born:

Married:

Died:

7 **Gonnor De CREPON**

Born: Abt 950

Died: Abt 1031

15

Born:

Died:

Sources include: *Royal Ancestors* 11546; *Ancestral Roots* 250, 235; Turton 175; *TAG* 72:187-204 (#6 ancestry).

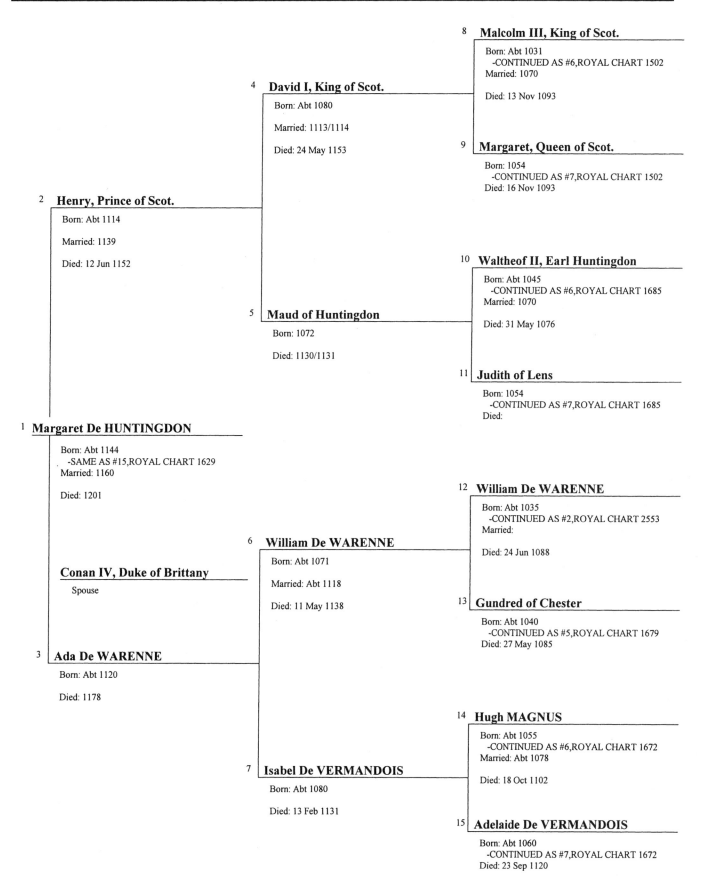

8 **Malcolm III, King of Scot.**

Born: Abt 1031
  -CONTINUED AS #6,ROYAL CHART 1502
Married: 1070

Died: 13 Nov 1093

4 **David I, King of Scot.**

Born: Abt 1080

Married: 1113/1114

Died: 24 May 1153

9 **Margaret, Queen of Scot.**

Born: 1054
  -CONTINUED AS #7,ROYAL CHART 1502
Died: 16 Nov 1093

2 **Henry, Prince of Scot.**

Born: Abt 1114

Married: 1139

Died: 12 Jun 1152

10 **Waltheof II, Earl Huntingdon**

Born: Abt 1045
  -CONTINUED AS #6,ROYAL CHART 1685
Married: 1070

Died: 31 May 1076

5 **Maud of Huntingdon**

Born: 1072

Died: 1130/1131

11 **Judith of Lens**

Born: 1054
  -CONTINUED AS #7,ROYAL CHART 1685
Died:

1 **Margaret De HUNTINGDON**

Born: Abt 1144
  -SAME AS #15,ROYAL CHART 1629
Married: 1160

Died: 1201

12 **William De WARENNE**

Born: Abt 1035
  -CONTINUED AS #2,ROYAL CHART 2553
Married:

Died: 24 Jun 1088

6 **William De WARENNE**

Born: Abt 1071

Married: Abt 1118

Died: 11 May 1138

13 **Gundred of Chester**

Born: Abt 1040
  -CONTINUED AS #5,ROYAL CHART 1679
Died: 27 May 1085

Conan IV, Duke of Brittany

Spouse

3 **Ada De WARENNE**

Born: Abt 1120

Died: 1178

14 **Hugh MAGNUS**

Born: Abt 1055
  -CONTINUED AS #6,ROYAL CHART 1672
Married: Abt 1078

Died: 18 Oct 1102

7 **Isabel De VERMANDOIS**

Born: Abt 1080

Died: 13 Feb 1131

15 **Adelaide De VERMANDOIS**

Born: Abt 1060
  -CONTINUED AS #7,ROYAL CHART 1672
Died: 23 Sep 1120

Sources include: *Royal Ancestors* (1989), chart 11490; *Ancestral Roots* 96; Chart 1550 and sources.

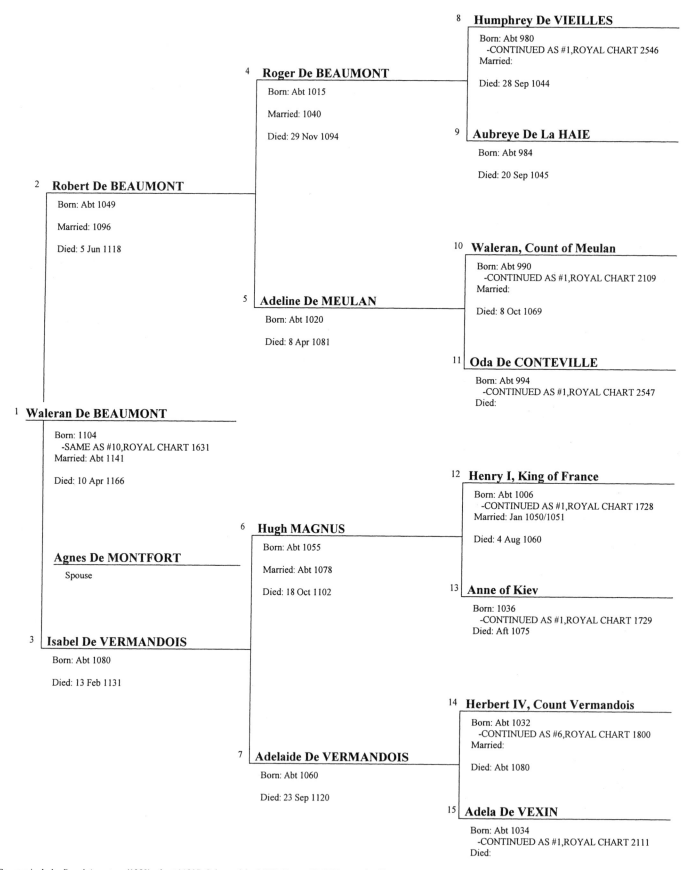

8 Humphrey De VIEILLES

Born: Abt 980
 -CONTINUED AS #1,ROYAL CHART 2546
Married:

Died: 28 Sep 1044

4 Roger De BEAUMONT

Born: Abt 1015

Married: 1040

Died: 29 Nov 1094

9 Aubreye De La HAIE

Born: Abt 984

Died: 20 Sep 1045

2 Robert De BEAUMONT

Born: Abt 1049

Married: 1096

Died: 5 Jun 1118

10 Waleran, Count of Meulan

Born: Abt 990
 -CONTINUED AS #1,ROYAL CHART 2109
Married:

Died: 8 Oct 1069

5 Adeline De MEULAN

Born: Abt 1020

Died: 8 Apr 1081

11 Oda De CONTEVILLE

Born: Abt 994
 -CONTINUED AS #1,ROYAL CHART 2547
Died:

1 Waleran De BEAUMONT

Born: 1104
 -SAME AS #10,ROYAL CHART 1631
Married: Abt 1141

Died: 10 Apr 1166

12 Henry I, King of France

Born: Abt 1006
 -CONTINUED AS #1,ROYAL CHART 1728
Married: Jan 1050/1051

Died: 4 Aug 1060

6 Hugh MAGNUS

Born: Abt 1055

Married: Abt 1078

Died: 18 Oct 1102

Agnes De MONTFORT

Spouse

13 Anne of Kiev

Born: 1036
 -CONTINUED AS #1,ROYAL CHART 1729
Died: Aft 1075

3 Isabel De VERMANDOIS

Born: Abt 1080

Died: 13 Feb 1131

14 Herbert IV, Count Vermandois

Born: Abt 1032
 -CONTINUED AS #6,ROYAL CHART 1800
Married:

Died: Abt 1080

7 Adelaide De VERMANDOIS

Born: Abt 1060

Died: 23 Sep 1120

15 Adela De VEXIN

Born: Abt 1034
 -CONTINUED AS #1,ROYAL CHART 2111
Died:

Sources include: *Royal Ancestors* (1989), chart 11907; Schwennicke 3:700; Turton 83; LDS records; Chart 1672 and sources.

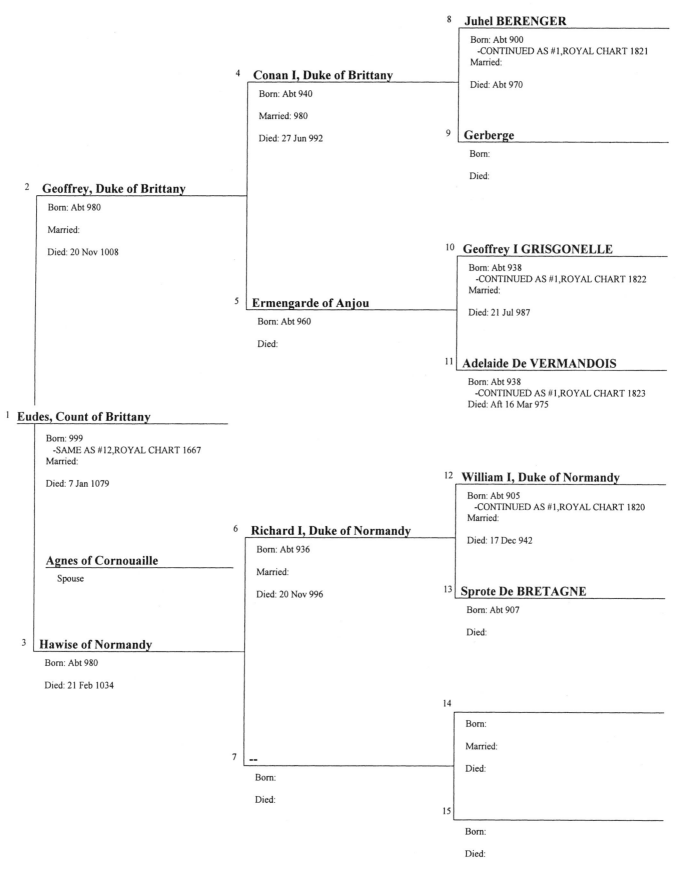

8   **Juhel BERENGER**

Born: Abt 900
   -CONTINUED AS #1,ROYAL CHART 1821
Married:

Died: Abt 970

4   **Conan I, Duke of Brittany**

Born: Abt 940

Married: 980

Died: 27 Jun 992

9   **Gerberge**

Born:

Died:

2   **Geoffrey, Duke of Brittany**

Born: Abt 980

Married:

Died: 20 Nov 1008

10   **Geoffrey I GRISGONELLE**

Born: Abt 938
   -CONTINUED AS #1,ROYAL CHART 1822
Married:

Died: 21 Jul 987

5   **Ermengarde of Anjou**

Born: Abt 960

Died:

11   **Adelaide De VERMANDOIS**

Born: Abt 938
   -CONTINUED AS #1,ROYAL CHART 1823
Died: Aft 16 Mar 975

1   **Eudes, Count of Brittany**

Born: 999
   -SAME AS #12,ROYAL CHART 1667
Married:

Died: 7 Jan 1079

12   **William I, Duke of Normandy**

Born: Abt 905
   -CONTINUED AS #1,ROYAL CHART 1820
Married:

Died: 17 Dec 942

6   **Richard I, Duke of Normandy**

Born: Abt 936

Married:

Died: 20 Nov 996

13   **Sprote De BRETAGNE**

Born: Abt 907

Died:

Agnes of Cornouaille

Spouse

3   **Hawise of Normandy**

Born: Abt 980

Died: 21 Feb 1034

14

Born:

Married:

Died:

7   **--**

Born:

Died:

15

Born:

Died:

Sources include: *Royal Ancestors* (1989), charts 11488, 11560-61; *Ancestral Roots* 214; *TAG* 72:187-204 (#6 ancestry).

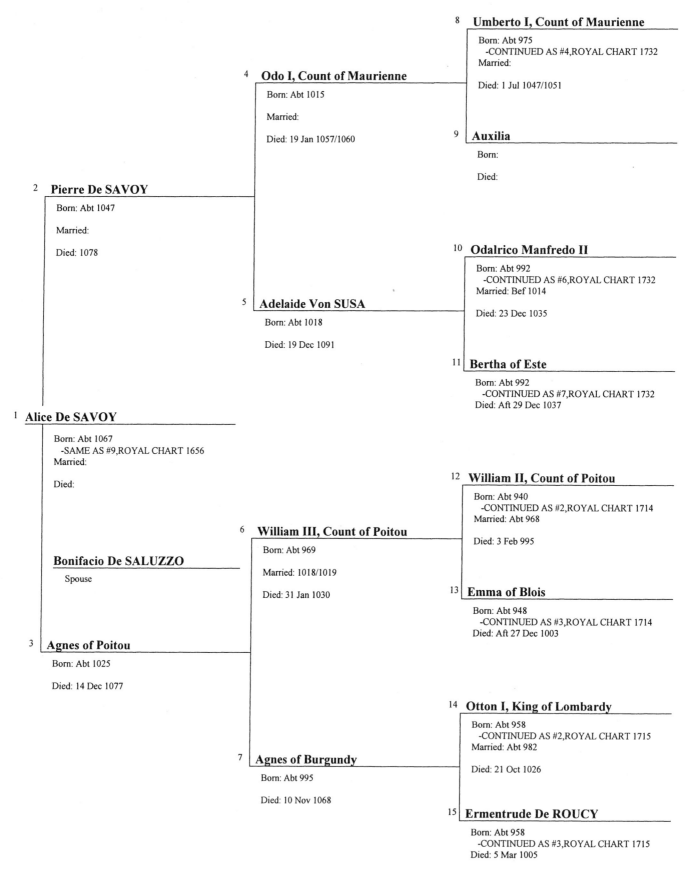

8 Umberto I, Count of Maurienne

Born: Abt 975
-CONTINUED AS #4,ROYAL CHART 1732
Married:

Died: 1 Jul 1047/1051

4 Odo I, Count of Maurienne

Born: Abt 1015

Married:

Died: 19 Jan 1057/1060

9 Auxilia

Born:

Died:

2 Pierre De SAVOY

Born: Abt 1047

Married:

Died: 1078

10 Odalrico Manfredo II

Born: Abt 992
-CONTINUED AS #6,ROYAL CHART 1732
Married: Bef 1014

Died: 23 Dec 1035

5 Adelaide Von SUSA

Born: Abt 1018

Died: 19 Dec 1091

11 Bertha of Este

Born: Abt 992
-CONTINUED AS #7,ROYAL CHART 1732
Died: Aft 29 Dec 1037

1 Alice De SAVOY

Born: Abt 1067
-SAME AS #9,ROYAL CHART 1656
Married:

Died:

12 William II, Count of Poitou

Born: Abt 940
-CONTINUED AS #2,ROYAL CHART 1714
Married: Abt 968

Died: 3 Feb 995

6 William III, Count of Poitou

Born: Abt 969

Married: 1018/1019

Died: 31 Jan 1030

Bonifacio De SALUZZO

Spouse

13 Emma of Blois

Born: Abt 948
-CONTINUED AS #3,ROYAL CHART 1714
Died: Aft 27 Dec 1003

3 Agnes of Poitou

Born: Abt 1025

Died: 14 Dec 1077

14 Otton I, King of Lombardy

Born: Abt 958
-CONTINUED AS #2,ROYAL CHART 1715
Married: Abt 982

Died: 21 Oct 1026

7 Agnes of Burgundy

Born: Abt 995

Died: 10 Nov 1068

15 Ermentrude De ROUCY

Born: Abt 958
-CONTINUED AS #3,ROYAL CHART 1715
Died: 5 Mar 1005

Sources include: *Royal Ancestors* (1989), chart 11831, family group sheets for #4 Odo (Eudes) and #6 William III (Guillaume V of Aquitaine); Turton 109. Notes: If #2 Pierre (Pietro) is correctly identified (chronology would appear to make this uncertain), he would have to be about 20 years younger than his wife Agnes. Turton gives #3 as the same Agnes who earlier married Emperor Henry III (see chart 1751, #4 & 5). *Tableaux Genealogiques des Souverans de la France* 2:39 gives #3 as a sister of that Agnes, also named Agnes.

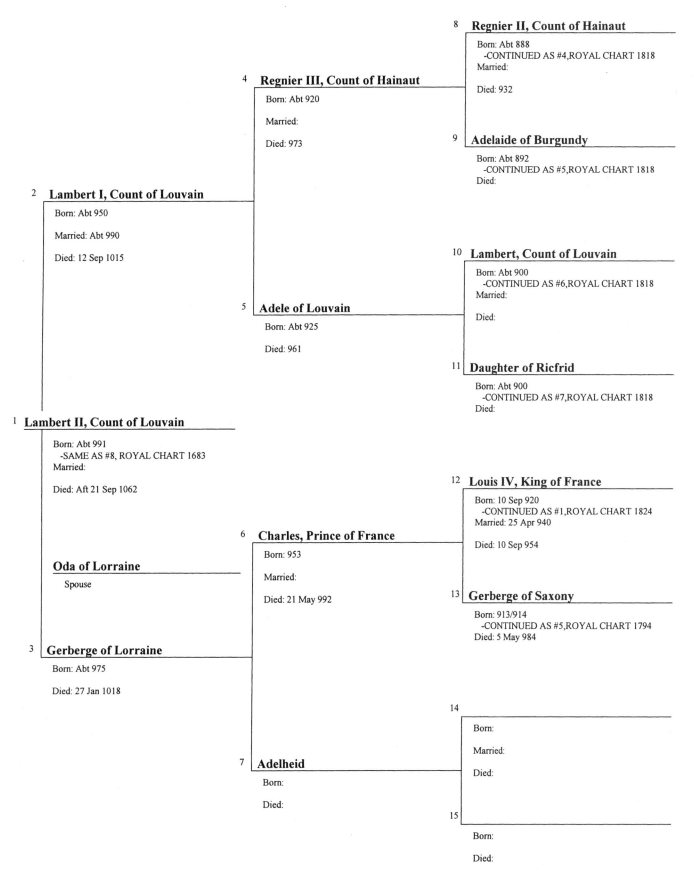

8 Regnier II, Count of Hainaut

Born: Abt 888
-CONTINUED AS #4,ROYAL CHART 1818
Married:

Died: 932

4 Regnier III, Count of Hainaut

Born: Abt 920

Married:

Died: 973

9 Adelaide of Burgundy

Born: Abt 892
-CONTINUED AS #5,ROYAL CHART 1818
Died:

2 Lambert I, Count of Louvain

Born: Abt 950

Married: Abt 990

Died: 12 Sep 1015

10 Lambert, Count of Louvain

Born: Abt 900
-CONTINUED AS #6,ROYAL CHART 1818
Married:

Died:

5 Adele of Louvain

Born: Abt 925

Died: 961

11 Daughter of Ricfrid

Born: Abt 900
-CONTINUED AS #7,ROYAL CHART 1818
Died:

1 Lambert II, Count of Louvain

Born: Abt 991
-SAME AS #8, ROYAL CHART 1683
Married:

Died: Aft 21 Sep 1062

12 Louis IV, King of France

Born: 10 Sep 920
-CONTINUED AS #1,ROYAL CHART 1824
Married: 25 Apr 940

Died: 10 Sep 954

6 Charles, Prince of France

Born: 953

Married:

Died: 21 May 992

Oda of Lorraine

Spouse

13 Gerberge of Saxony

Born: 913/914
-CONTINUED AS #5,ROYAL CHART 1794
Died: 5 May 984

3 Gerberge of Lorraine

Born: Abt 975

Died: 27 Jan 1018

14

Born:

Married:

Died:

7 Adelheid

Born:

Died:

15

Born:

Died:

Sources include: *Royal Ancestors* 11760, 11519-20; *Ancestral Roots* 155, 148, 240; Stuart 68, 135, 310; Moriarty 125, 50, 26. Notes: #10 is not certain. #5 is also claimed as Adele of Dagsbourg, daughter of Hugh II.

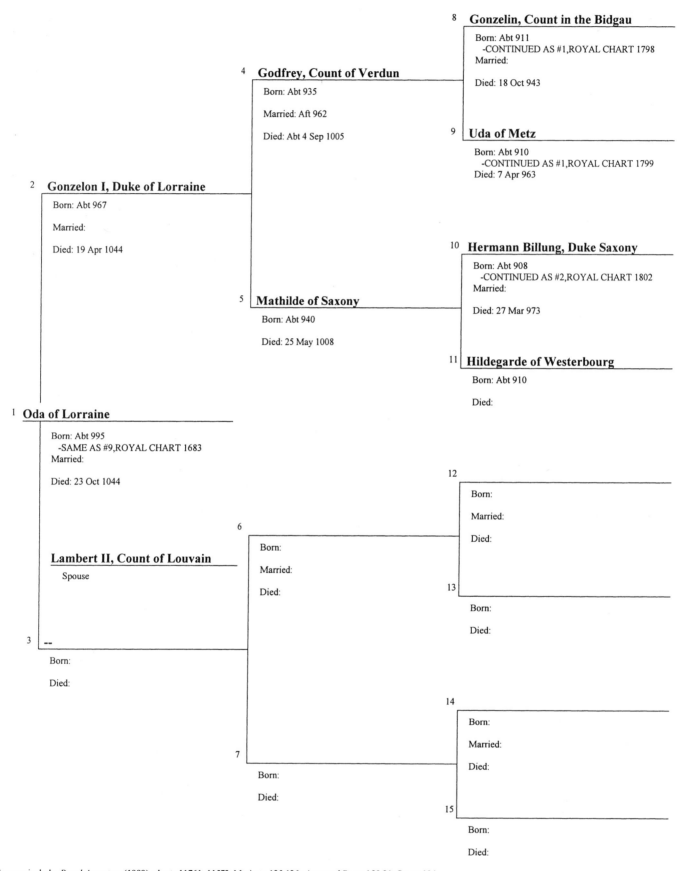

8 Gonzelin, Count in the Bidgau

Born: Abt 911
-CONTINUED AS #1, ROYAL CHART 1798
Married:

Died: 18 Oct 943

4 Godfrey, Count of Verdun

Born: Abt 935

Married: Aft 962

Died: Abt 4 Sep 1005

9 Uda of Metz

Born: Abt 910
-CONTINUED AS #1, ROYAL CHART 1799
Died: 7 Apr 963

2 Gonzelon I, Duke of Lorraine

Born: Abt 967

Married:

Died: 19 Apr 1044

10 Hermann Billung, Duke Saxony

Born: Abt 908
-CONTINUED AS #2, ROYAL CHART 1802
Married:

Died: 27 Mar 973

5 Mathilde of Saxony

Born: Abt 940

Died: 25 May 1008

11 Hildegarde of Westerbourg

Born: Abt 910

Died:

1 Oda of Lorraine

Born: Abt 995
-SAME AS #9, ROYAL CHART 1683
Married:

Died: 23 Oct 1044

Lambert II, Count of Louvain

Spouse

3 --

Born:

Died:

6

Born:

Married:

Died:

12

Born:

Married:

Died:

13

Born:

Died:

7

Born:

Died:

14

Born:

Married:

Died:

15

Born:

Died:

Sources include: *Royal Ancestors* (1989), charts 11761, 11572; Moriarty 125-126; *Ancestral Roots* 155-21; Stuart 104.

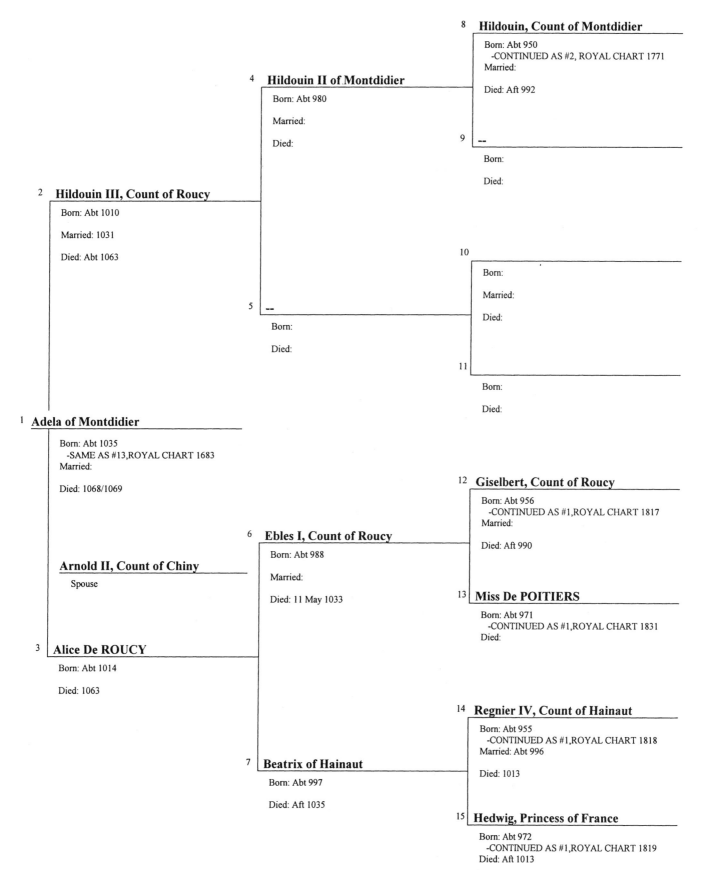

8 **Hildouin, Count of Montdidier**
Born: Abt 950
-CONTINUED AS #2, ROYAL CHART 1771
Married:

Died: Aft 992

4 **Hildouin II of Montdidier**
Born: Abt 980

Married:

Died:

9 --
Born:

Died:

2 **Hildouin III, Count of Roucy**
Born: Abt 1010

Married: 1031

Died: Abt 1063

10
Born:

Married:

Died:

5 --
Born:

Died:

11
Born:

Died:

1 **Adela of Montdidier**
Born: Abt 1035
-SAME AS #13, ROYAL CHART 1683
Married:

Died: 1068/1069

12 **Giselbert, Count of Roucy**
Born: Abt 956
-CONTINUED AS #1, ROYAL CHART 1817
Married:

Died: Aft 990

6 **Ebles I, Count of Roucy**
Born: Abt 988

Married:

Died: 11 May 1033

13 **Miss De POITIERS**
Born: Abt 971
-CONTINUED AS #1, ROYAL CHART 1831
Died:

Arnold II, Count of Chiny
Spouse

3 **Alice De ROUCY**
Born: Abt 1014

Died: 1063

14 **Regnier IV, Count of Hainaut**
Born: Abt 955
-CONTINUED AS #1, ROYAL CHART 1818
Married: Abt 996

Died: 1013

7 **Beatrix of Hainaut**
Born: Abt 997

Died: Aft 1035

15 **Hedwig, Princess of France**
Born: Abt 972
-CONTINUED AS #1, ROYAL CHART 1819
Died: Aft 1013

Sources include: Stuart 66, 266, 170; *Ancestral Roots* 149-22A, 151, 106; Moriarty 155, 49-50; *Royal Ancestors* 11473, 11685, 11538. Note: #1 Adela should not be confused with a claimed sister Adele (Ada) De Roucy who is claimed to have married 1st Godfrey De Guise and 2nd Walter De Ath (see charts 1548 & 2116).

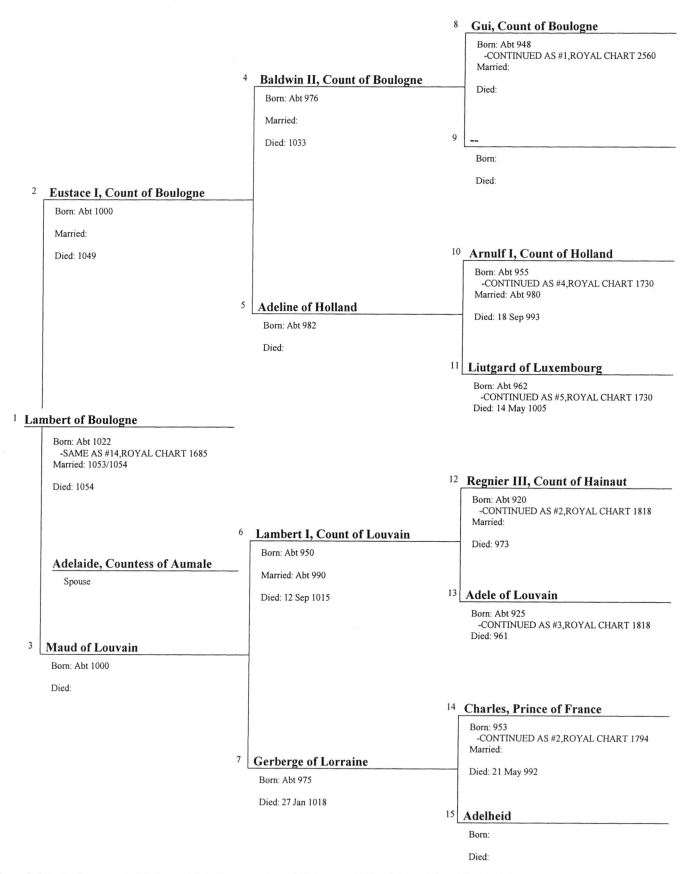

8 **Gui, Count of Boulogne**

Born: Abt 948
-CONTINUED AS #1,ROYAL CHART 2560
Married:

Died:

4 **Baldwin II, Count of Boulogne**

Born: Abt 976

Married:

Died: 1033

9 **--**

Born:

Died:

2 **Eustace I, Count of Boulogne**

Born: Abt 1000

Married:

Died: 1049

10 **Arnulf I, Count of Holland**

Born: Abt 955
-CONTINUED AS #4,ROYAL CHART 1730
Married: Abt 980

Died: 18 Sep 993

5 **Adeline of Holland**

Born: Abt 982

Died:

11 **Liutgard of Luxembourg**

Born: Abt 962
-CONTINUED AS #5,ROYAL CHART 1730
Died: 14 May 1005

1 **Lambert of Boulogne**

Born: Abt 1022
-SAME AS #14,ROYAL CHART 1685
Married: 1053/1054

Died: 1054

12 **Regnier III, Count of Hainaut**

Born: Abt 920
-CONTINUED AS #2,ROYAL CHART 1818
Married:

Died: 973

6 **Lambert I, Count of Louvain**

Born: Abt 950

Married: Abt 990

Died: 12 Sep 1015

13 **Adele of Louvain**

Born: Abt 925
-CONTINUED AS #3,ROYAL CHART 1818
Died: 961

Adelaide, Countess of Aumale

Spouse

3 **Maud of Louvain**

Born: Abt 1000

Died:

14 **Charles, Prince of France**

Born: 953
-CONTINUED AS #2,ROYAL CHART 1794
Married:

Died: 21 May 992

7 **Gerberge of Lorraine**

Born: Abt 975

Died: 27 Jan 1018

15 **Adelheid**

Born:

Died:

Sources include: *Royal Ancestors* (1989), charts 11423, 11574; *Ancestral Roots* 148; Stuart 131, 77, 242, 312-35; Moriarty 165, 113, 55; Paget 7 (#2 ancestry); Roberts *AAP*, pp. 195-196. Note: The ancestry shown for #2 Eustace is not proven. See Moriarty 165 note. In a preliminary Charlemagne manuscript (June 1995), p. 58, Faris gives #2 Eustace as perhaps the son of Arnulf, grandson of Adalolf De Boulogne (d. 13 Nov 933), and great grandson of Baldwin II & Alfthryth (see chart 1801, #4 & 5), but that claim is chronologically difficult.

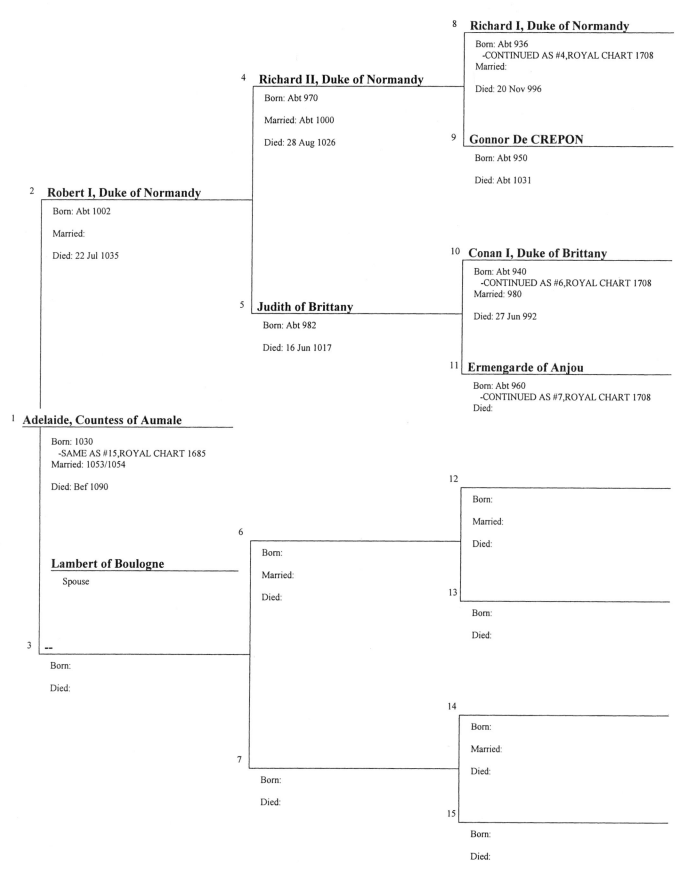

8 Richard I, Duke of Normandy

Born: Abt 936
-CONTINUED AS #4,ROYAL CHART 1708
Married:

Died: 20 Nov 996

4 Richard II, Duke of Normandy

Born: Abt 970

Married: Abt 1000

Died: 28 Aug 1026

9 Gonnor De CREPON

Born: Abt 950

Died: Abt 1031

2 Robert I, Duke of Normandy

Born: Abt 1002

Married:

Died: 22 Jul 1035

10 Conan I, Duke of Brittany

Born: Abt 940
-CONTINUED AS #6,ROYAL CHART 1708
Married: 980

Died: 27 Jun 992

5 Judith of Brittany

Born: Abt 982

Died: 16 Jun 1017

11 Ermengarde of Anjou

Born: Abt 960
-CONTINUED AS #7,ROYAL CHART 1708
Died:

1 Adelaide, Countess of Aumale

Born: 1030
-SAME AS #15,ROYAL CHART 1685
Married: 1053/1054

Died: Bef 1090

12

Born:

Married:

Died:

Lambert of Boulogne

Spouse

6

Born:

Married:

Died:

13

Born:

Died:

3 --

Born:

Died:

14

Born:

Married:

Died:

7

Born:

Died:

15

Born:

Died:

Sources include: *Royal Ancestors* (1989), chart 11423; Stuart 131; Faris preliminary Charlemagne manuscript (June 1995), pp. 26-27; *Ancestral Roots* 148; Roberts *AAP*, pp. 195-196; *TAG* 72:187-204 (#8 ancestry). Note: Faris states that #3 (mother of Adelaide) probably was <u>not</u> Harlette (Herleve) De Falais (mother of William I the Conqueror). See chart 1502.

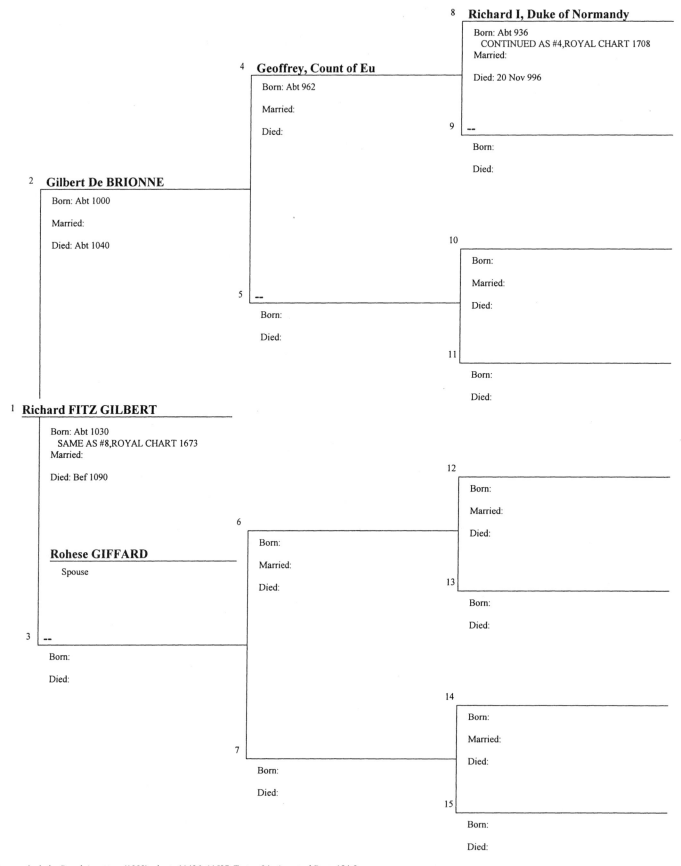

8 Richard I, Duke of Normandy
Born: Abt 936
CONTINUED AS #4, ROYAL CHART 1708
Married:

Died: 20 Nov 996

4 Geoffrey, Count of Eu
Born: Abt 962

Married:

Died:

9 --
Born:

Died:

2 Gilbert De BRIONNE
Born: Abt 1000

Married:

Died: Abt 1040

10
Born:

Married:

Died:

5 --
Born:

Died:

11
Born:

Died:

1 Richard FITZ GILBERT
Born: Abt 1030
SAME AS #8, ROYAL CHART 1673
Married:

Died: Bef 1090

12
Born:

Married:

Died:

6
Born:

Married:

Died:

13
Born:

Died:

Rohese GIFFARD
Spouse

3 --
Born:

Died:

14
Born:

Married:

Died:

7
Born:

Died:

15
Born:

Died:

Sources include: *Royal Ancestors* (1989), charts 11436, 11537; Turton 94; *Ancestral Roots* 184-2.

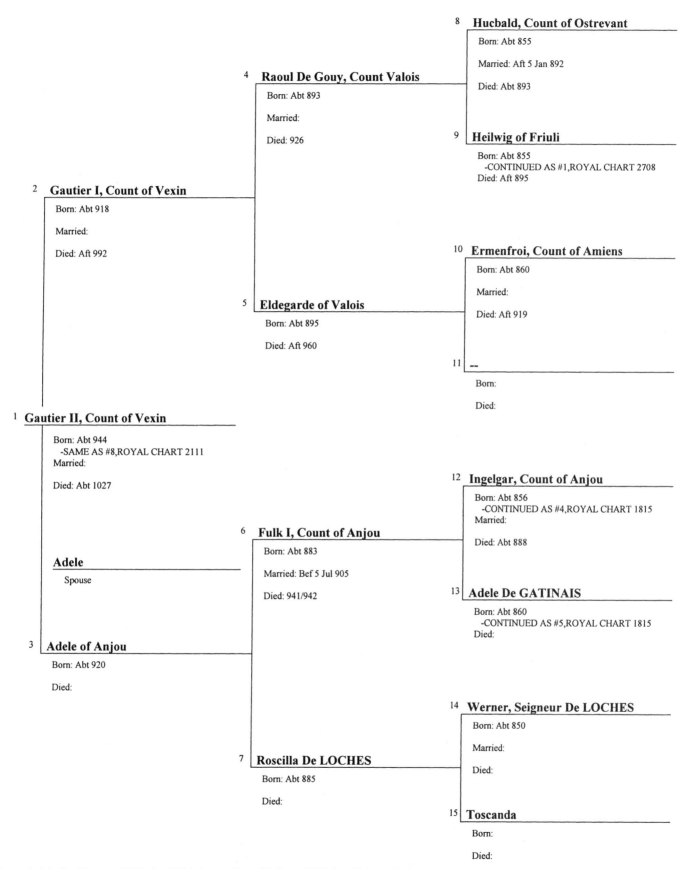

8 Hucbald, Count of Ostrevant

Born: Abt 855

Married: Aft 5 Jan 892

Died: Abt 893

4 Raoul De Gouy, Count Valois

Born: Abt 893

Married:

Died: 926

9 Heilwig of Friuli

Born: Abt 855
-CONTINUED AS #1,ROYAL CHART 2708
Died: Aft 895

2 Gautier I, Count of Vexin

Born: Abt 918

Married:

Died: Aft 992

10 Ermenfroi, Count of Amiens

Born: Abt 860

Married:

Died: Aft 919

5 Eldegarde of Valois

Born: Abt 895

Died: Aft 960

11 --

Born:

Died:

1 Gautier II, Count of Vexin

Born: Abt 944
-SAME AS #8,ROYAL CHART 2111
Married:

Died: Abt 1027

12 Ingelgar, Count of Anjou

Born: Abt 856
-CONTINUED AS #4,ROYAL CHART 1815
Married:

Died: Abt 888

6 Fulk I, Count of Anjou

Born: Abt 883

Married: Bef 5 Jul 905

Died: 941/942

13 Adele De GATINAIS

Born: Abt 860
-CONTINUED AS #5,ROYAL CHART 1815
Died:

Adele

Spouse

3 Adele of Anjou

Born: Abt 920

Died:

14 Werner, Seigneur De LOCHES

Born: Abt 850

Married:

Died:

7 Roscilla De LOCHES

Born: Abt 885

Died:

15 Toscanda

Born:

Died:

Sources include: *Royal Ancestors* (1989), chart 11524; *Ancestral Roots* 250; Stuart 185; Faris preliminary Charlemagne manuscript (June 1995), pp. 274-276; Schwennicke 3:657; Moriarty 135. Notes: The ancestry of both #3 Adele and #4 Raoul is disputed and uncertain. Stuart, citing Schwennicke, inserts an additional Raoul (md Liegard) between #4 and Hucbold & Heiliwich, but this claim is unacceptable chronologically. David H. Kelly thinks it more likely that Raoul was son of Theuderic the Nibelung (Count of Valois & Vexin), who was of the male line of Childebrand I (see chart 2019, #4). #5 Eldegarde may have been a niece or sister of Ermenfroi (Ermenfrid) instead of a daughter. Chronology suggest she was more likely a daughter.

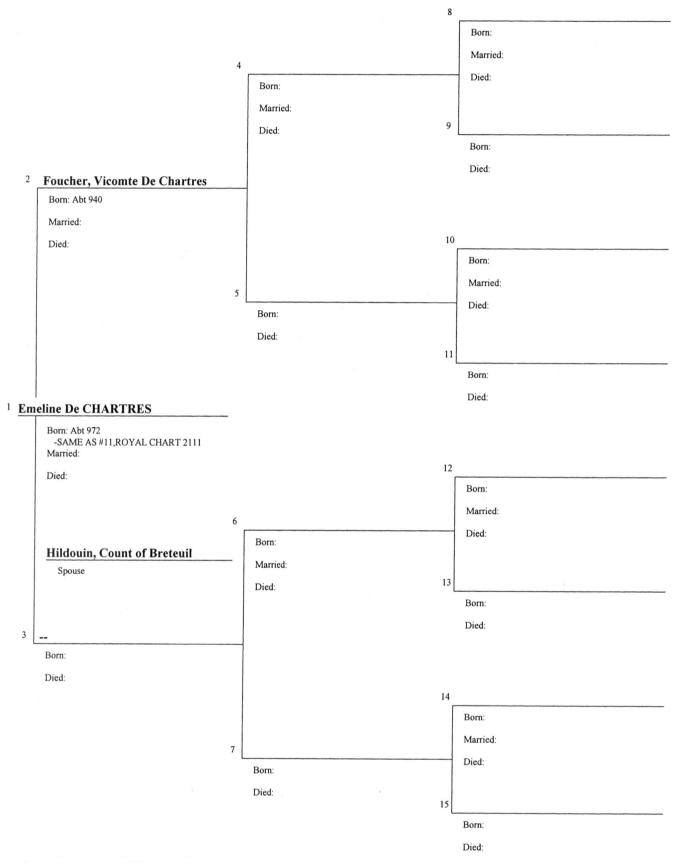

8

Born:

Married:

Died:

4

Born:

Married:

Died:

9

Born:

Died:

2 Foucher, Vicomte De Chartres

Born: Abt 940

Married:

Died:

10

Born:

Married:

Died:

5

Born:

Died:

11

Born:

Died:

1 Emeline De CHARTRES

Born: Abt 972
  -SAME AS #11,ROYAL CHART 2111
Married:

Died:

12

Born:

Married:

Died:

6

Born:

Married:

Died:

13

Born:

Died:

Hildouin, Count of Breteuil

Spouse

3 --

Born:

Died:

14

Born:

Married:

Died:

7

Born:

Died:

15

Born:

Died:

Sources include: *Royal Ancestors* (1989), chart 11525; Stuart 168-34; Moriarty 136.

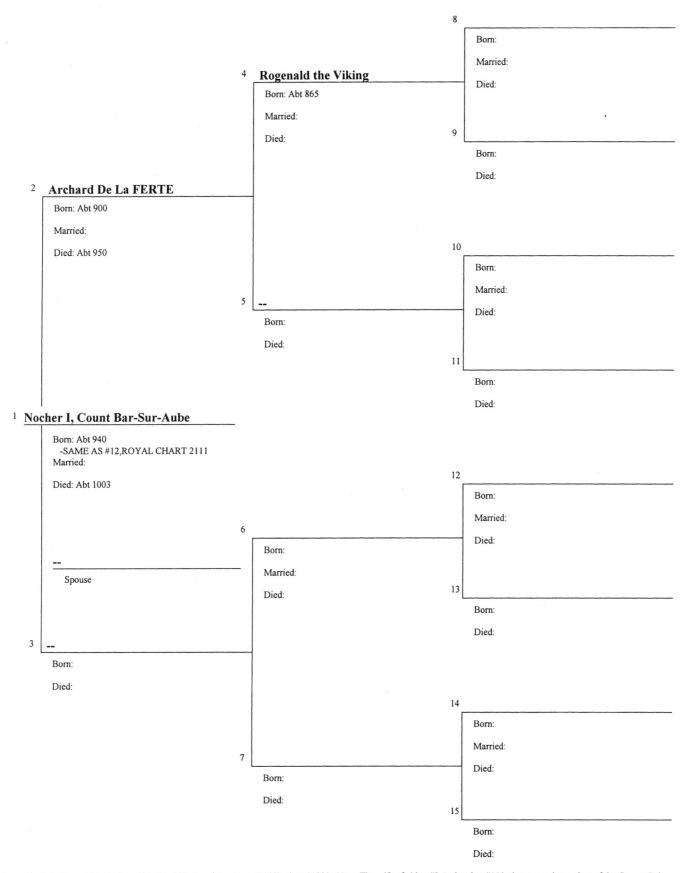

8

Born:

Married:

Died:

4   **Rogenald the Viking**

Born: Abt 865

Married:

Died:

9

Born:

Died:

2   **Archard De La FERTE**

Born: Abt 900

Married:

Died: Abt 950

10

Born:

Married:

Died:

5   **--**

Born:

Died:

11

Born:

Died:

1   **Nocher I, Count Bar-Sur-Aube**

Born: Abt 940
  -SAME AS #12,ROYAL CHART 2111
Married:

Died: Abt 1003

--

    Spouse

3   **--**

Born:

Died:

6

Born:

Married:

Died:

12

Born:

Married:

Died:

13

Born:

Died:

7

Born:

Died:

14

Born:

Married:

Died:

15

Born:

Died:

Sources include: Stuart 108; Moriarty 136-137, 267; *Royal Ancestors* (1989), chart 11939. Note: The wife of either #2 Archaud or #1 Nocher was a descendant of the Counts Gui and Fulk of Bar-Sur-Aube at the end of the 9th century.

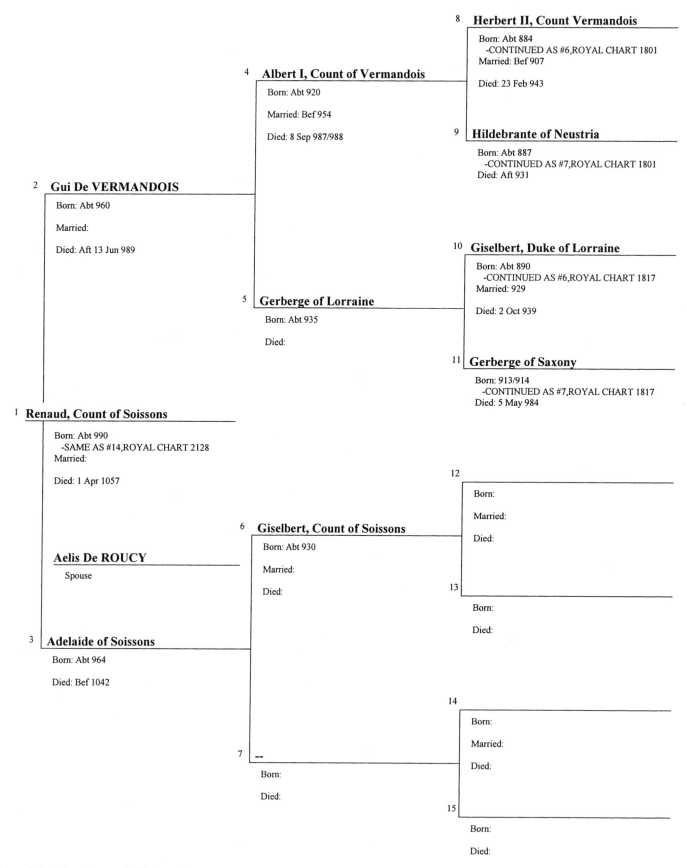

8 Herbert II, Count Vermandois
Born: Abt 884
-CONTINUED AS #6,ROYAL CHART 1801
Married: Bef 907

Died: 23 Feb 943

4 Albert I, Count of Vermandois
Born: Abt 920

Married: Bef 954

Died: 8 Sep 987/988

9 Hildebrante of Neustria
Born: Abt 887
-CONTINUED AS #7,ROYAL CHART 1801
Died: Aft 931

2 Gui De VERMANDOIS
Born: Abt 960

Married:

Died: Aft 13 Jun 989

10 Giselbert, Duke of Lorraine
Born: Abt 890
-CONTINUED AS #6,ROYAL CHART 1817
Married: 929

Died: 2 Oct 939

5 Gerberge of Lorraine
Born: Abt 935

Died:

11 Gerberge of Saxony
Born: 913/914
-CONTINUED AS #7,ROYAL CHART 1817
Died: 5 May 984

1 Renaud, Count of Soissons
Born: Abt 990
-SAME AS #14,ROYAL CHART 2128
Married:

Died: 1 Apr 1057

12
Born:

Married:

Died:

6 Giselbert, Count of Soissons
Born: Abt 930

Married:

Died:

Aelis De ROUCY
Spouse

13
Born:

Died:

3 Adelaide of Soissons
Born: Abt 964

Died: Bef 1042

14
Born:

Married:

Died:

7 --
Born:

Died:

15
Born:

Died:

Sources include: *Royal Ancestors* (1989), chart 12114; Stuart 188; Moriarty 267-268. Note: An alternate claim that #1 Renaud was son of Nocher II & Aelis of Soissons (see chart 2111) is difficult chronologically. This Aelis was daughter of #2 & 3 Gui & Adelaide above. Brandenburg makes Renaud the son of Gui & Adelaide (see Moriarty 268).

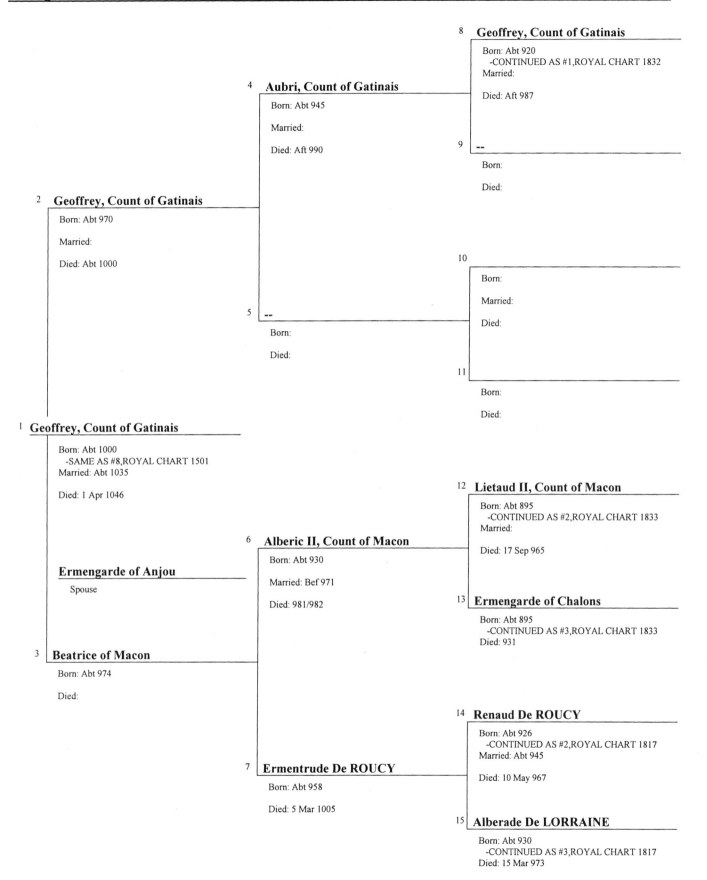

8 Geoffrey, Count of Gatinais

Born: Abt 920
-CONTINUED AS #1,ROYAL CHART 1832
Married:

Died: Aft 987

4 Aubri, Count of Gatinais

Born: Abt 945

Married:

Died: Aft 990

9 --

Born:

Died:

2 Geoffrey, Count of Gatinais

Born: Abt 970

Married:

Died: Abt 1000

10

Born:

Married:

Died:

5 --

Born:

Died:

11

Born:

Died:

1 Geoffrey, Count of Gatinais

Born: Abt 1000
-SAME AS #8,ROYAL CHART 1501
Married: Abt 1035

Died: 1 Apr 1046

12 Lietaud II, Count of Macon

Born: Abt 895
-CONTINUED AS #2,ROYAL CHART 1833
Married:

Died: 17 Sep 965

6 Alberic II, Count of Macon

Born: Abt 930

Married: Bef 971

Died: 981/982

13 Ermengarde of Chalons

Born: Abt 895
-CONTINUED AS #3,ROYAL CHART 1833
Died: 931

Ermengarde of Anjou

Spouse

3 Beatrice of Macon

Born: Abt 974

Died:

14 Renaud De ROUCY

Born: Abt 926
-CONTINUED AS #2,ROYAL CHART 1817
Married: Abt 945

Died: 10 May 967

7 Ermentrude De ROUCY

Born: Abt 958

Died: 5 Mar 1005

15 Alberade De LORRAINE

Born: Abt 930
-CONTINUED AS #3,ROYAL CHART 1817
Died: 15 Mar 973

Sources include: *Royal Ancestors* (1989), chart 11401; *Ancestral Roots* 118-22; Stuart 53, 92, 101; Moriarty 1-2. Note: #13 Ermengarde (1st wife of Lietaud) may not be the mother of #6 Alberic (Aubri). The mother might be Berta (2nd wife) or Richilde (3rd wife). Moriarty accepts Ermengarde.

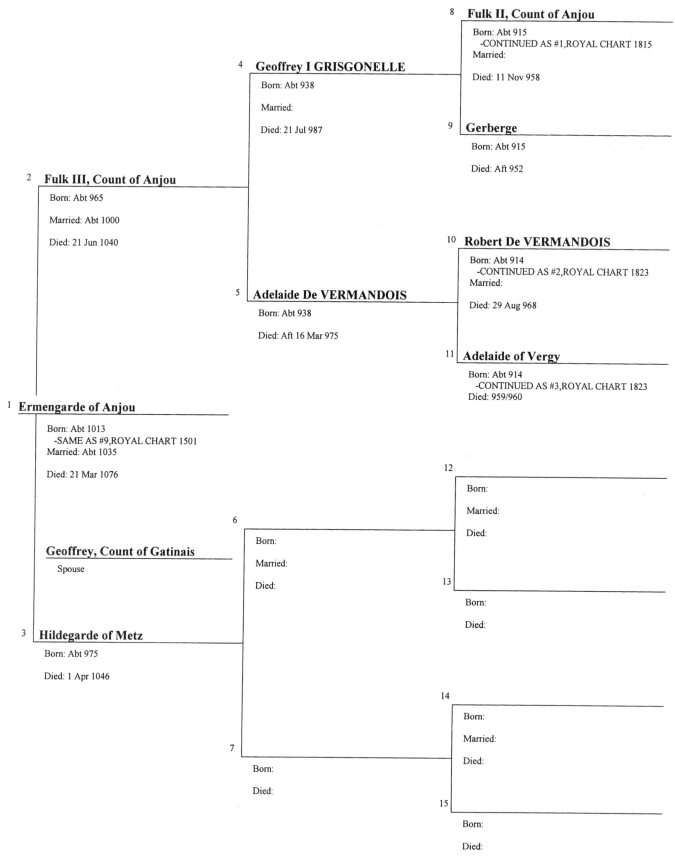

8 Fulk II, Count of Anjou

Born: Abt 915
-CONTINUED AS #1,ROYAL CHART 1815
Married:

Died: 11 Nov 958

9 Gerberge

Born: Abt 915

Died: Aft 952

4 Geoffrey I GRISGONELLE

Born: Abt 938

Married:

Died: 21 Jul 987

10 Robert De VERMANDOIS

Born: Abt 914
-CONTINUED AS #2,ROYAL CHART 1823
Married:

Died: 29 Aug 968

11 Adelaide of Vergy

Born: Abt 914
-CONTINUED AS #3,ROYAL CHART 1823
Died: 959/960

5 Adelaide De VERMANDOIS

Born: Abt 938

Died: Aft 16 Mar 975

2 Fulk III, Count of Anjou

Born: Abt 965

Married: Abt 1000

Died: 21 Jun 1040

1 Ermengarde of Anjou

Born: Abt 1013
-SAME AS #9,ROYAL CHART 1501
Married: Abt 1035

Died: 21 Mar 1076

Geoffrey, Count of Gatinais

Spouse

3 Hildegarde of Metz

Born: Abt 975

Died: 1 Apr 1046

12

Born:

Married:

Died:

13

Born:

Died:

6

Born:

Married:

Died:

14

Born:

Married:

Died:

15

Born:

Died:

7

Born:

Died:

Sources include: *Royal Ancestors* (1989), chart 11401; *Ancestral Roots* 118; Stuart 91; Moriarty 4.

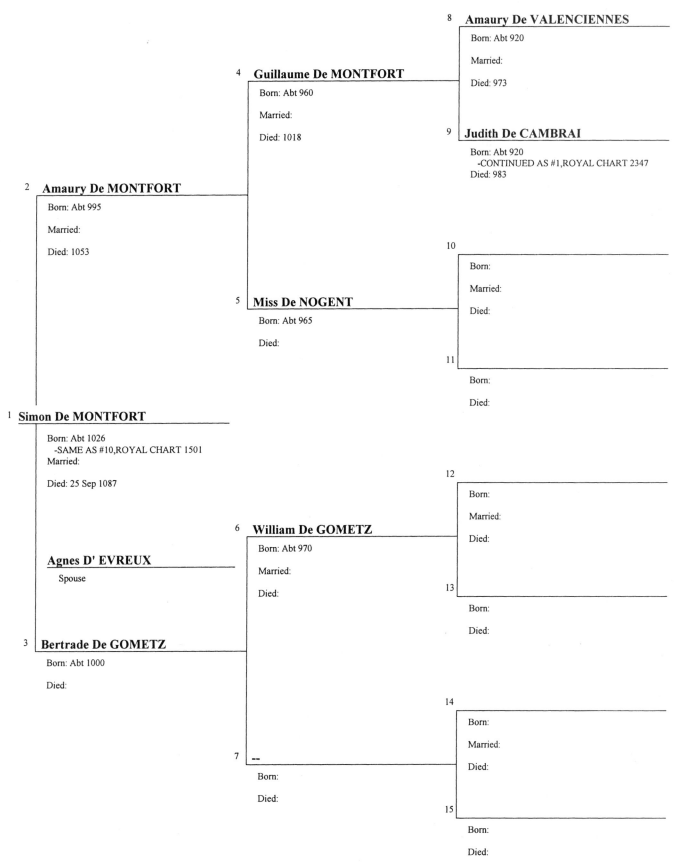

8 **Amaury De VALENCIENNES**

Born: Abt 920

Married:

Died: 973

4 **Guillaume De MONTFORT**

Born: Abt 960

Married:

Died: 1018

9 **Judith De CAMBRAI**

Born: Abt 920
 -CONTINUED AS #1,ROYAL CHART 2347
Died: 983

2 **Amaury De MONTFORT**

Born: Abt 995

Married:

Died: 1053

10

Born:

Married:

Died:

5 **Miss De NOGENT**

Born: Abt 965

Died:

11

Born:

Died:

1 **Simon De MONTFORT**

Born: Abt 1026
 -SAME AS #10,ROYAL CHART 1501
Married:

Died: 25 Sep 1087

12

Born:

Married:

Died:

6 **William De GOMETZ**

Born: Abt 970

Married:

Died:

13

Born:

Died:

Agnes D' EVREUX

Spouse

3 **Bertrade De GOMETZ**

Born: Abt 1000

Died:

14

Born:

Married:

Died:

7 **--**

Born:

Died:

15

Born:

Died:

Sources include: *Royal Ancestors* (1989), chart 11402; Faris preliminary Charlemagne manuscript (June 1995), p. 188; Stuart 90; Moriarty 10; Turton 230; Collett (family group sheet for #2 Amauri).

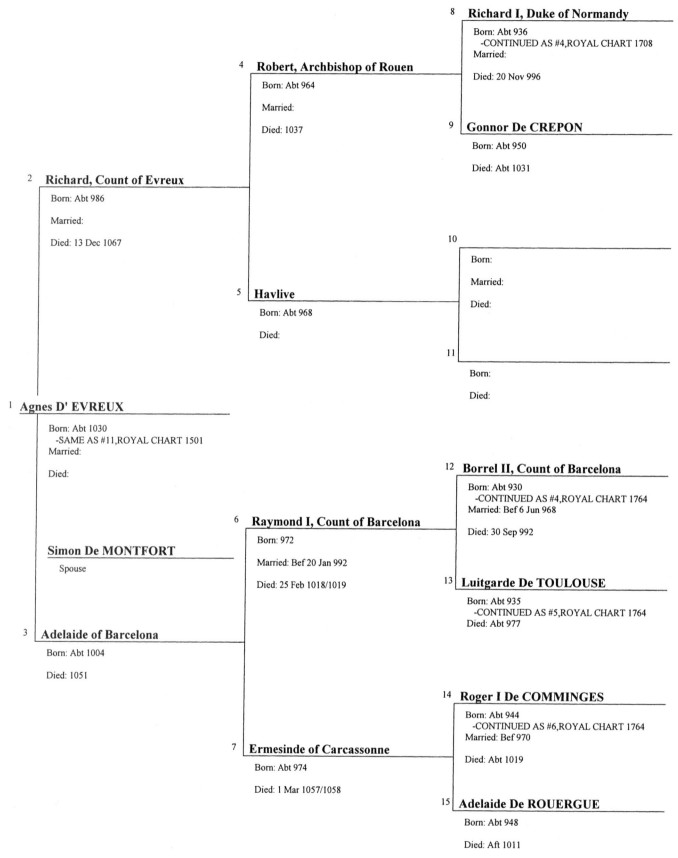

8 Richard I, Duke of Normandy

Born: Abt 936
-CONTINUED AS #4,ROYAL CHART 1708
Married:

Died: 20 Nov 996

4 Robert, Archbishop of Rouen

Born: Abt 964

Married:

Died: 1037

9 Gonnor De CREPON

Born: Abt 950

Died: Abt 1031

2 Richard, Count of Evreux

Born: Abt 986

Married:

Died: 13 Dec 1067

10

Born:

Married:

Died:

5 Havlive

Born: Abt 968

Died:

11

Born:

Died:

1 Agnes D' EVREUX

Born: Abt 1030
-SAME AS #11,ROYAL CHART 1501
Married:

Died:

12 Borrel II, Count of Barcelona

Born: Abt 930
-CONTINUED AS #4,ROYAL CHART 1764
Married: Bef 6 Jun 968

Died: 30 Sep 992

6 Raymond I, Count of Barcelona

Born: 972

Married: Bef 20 Jan 992

Died: 25 Feb 1018/1019

13 Luitgarde De TOULOUSE

Born: Abt 935
-CONTINUED AS #5,ROYAL CHART 1764
Died: Abt 977

Simon De MONTFORT

Spouse

3 Adelaide of Barcelona

Born: Abt 1004

Died: 1051

14 Roger I De COMMINGES

Born: Abt 944
-CONTINUED AS #6,ROYAL CHART 1764
Married: Bef 970

Died: Abt 1019

7 Ermesinde of Carcassonne

Born: Abt 974

Died: 1 Mar 1057/1058

15 Adelaide De ROUERGUE

Born: Abt 948

Died: Aft 1011

Sources include: *Royal Ancestors* (1989), chart 11402; *Ancestral Roots* 118-23; Stuart 168; Moriarty 10-11; *TAG* 72:187-204 (#8 ancestry).

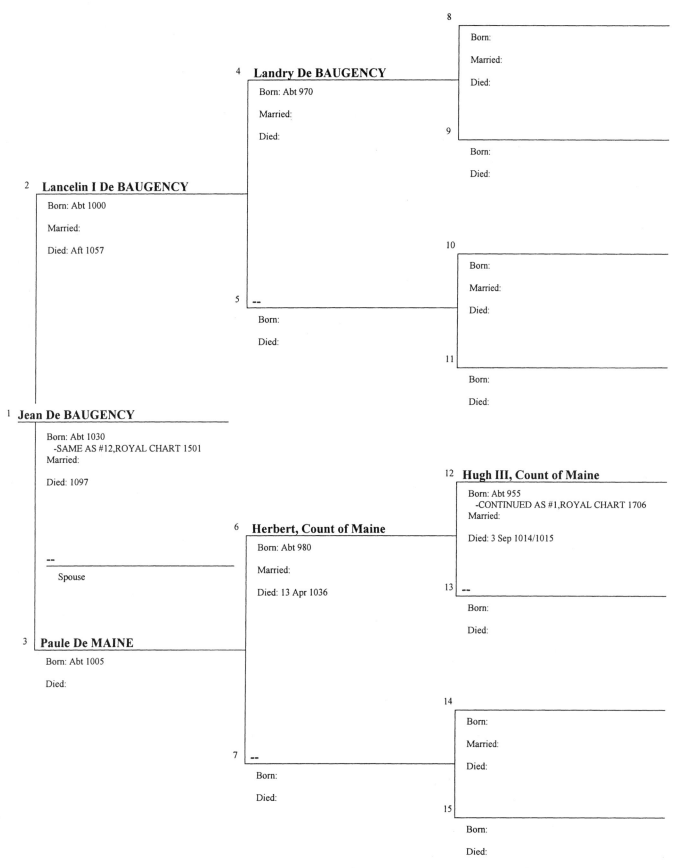

8

Born:

Married:

Died:

4 **Landry De BAUGENCY**

Born: Abt 970

Married:

Died:

9

Born:

Died:

2 **Lancelin I De BAUGENCY**

Born: Abt 1000

Married:

Died: Aft 1057

10

Born:

Married:

Died:

5 --

Born:

Died:

11

Born:

Died:

1 **Jean De BAUGENCY**

Born: Abt 1030
 -SAME AS #12,ROYAL CHART 1501
Married:

Died: 1097

12 **Hugh III, Count of Maine**

Born: Abt 955
 -CONTINUED AS #1,ROYAL CHART 1706
Married:

Died: 3 Sep 1014/1015

6 **Herbert, Count of Maine**

Born: Abt 980

Married:

Died: 13 Apr 1036

13 --

Born:

Died:

--

Spouse

3 **Paule De MAINE**

Born: Abt 1005

Died:

14

Born:

Married:

Died:

7 --

Born:

Died:

15

Born:

Died:

Sources include: *Royal Ancestors* (1989), chart 11692; Faris preliminary Charlemagne manuscript (June 1995), pp. 180-181. Stuart 313, 4; Moriarty 11; Turton 175. Note: Faris corrects other sources that claim #3 Paule (Paula) as the wife of #1 Jean.

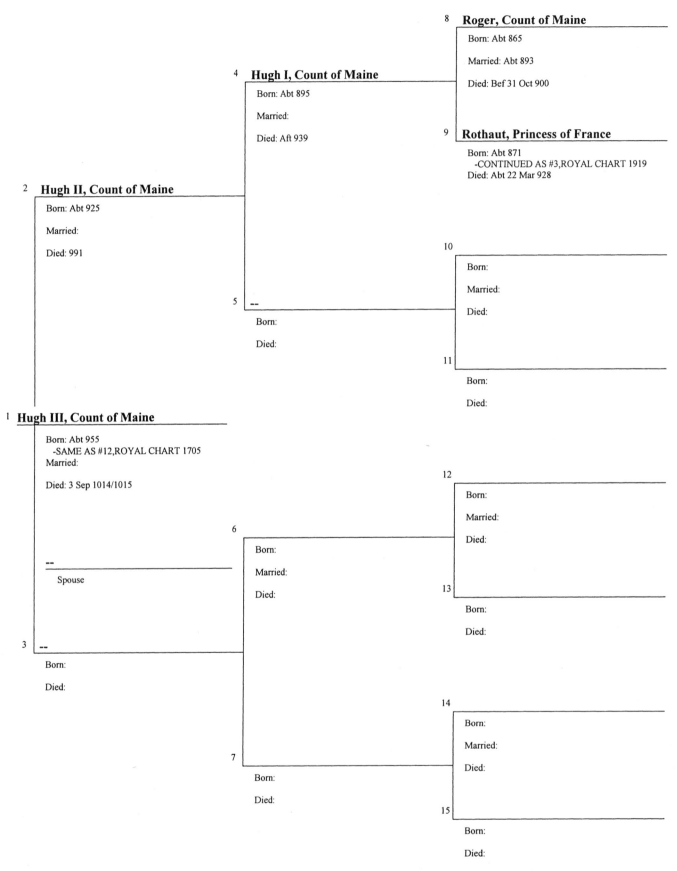

8 Roger, Count of Maine
Born: Abt 865
Married: Abt 893
Died: Bef 31 Oct 900

4 Hugh I, Count of Maine
Born: Abt 895
Married:
Died: Aft 939

9 Rothaut, Princess of France
Born: Abt 871
  -CONTINUED AS #3,ROYAL CHART 1919
Died: Abt 22 Mar 928

2 Hugh II, Count of Maine
Born: Abt 925
Married:
Died: 991

10
Born:
Married:
Died:

5 --
Born:
Died:

11
Born:
Died:

1 Hugh III, Count of Maine
Born: Abt 955
  -SAME AS #12,ROYAL CHART 1705
Married:
Died: 3 Sep 1014/1015

12
Born:
Married:
Died:

6
Born:
Married:
Died:

13
Born:
Died:

**-- **
Spouse

3 --
Born:
Died:

14
Born:
Married:
Died:

7
Born:
Died:

15
Born:
Died:

Sources include: *Royal Ancestors* (1989), charts 11692, 11937; Faris preliminary Charlemagne manuscript (June 1995), p. 180; Stuart 357; Moriarty 11, 37.

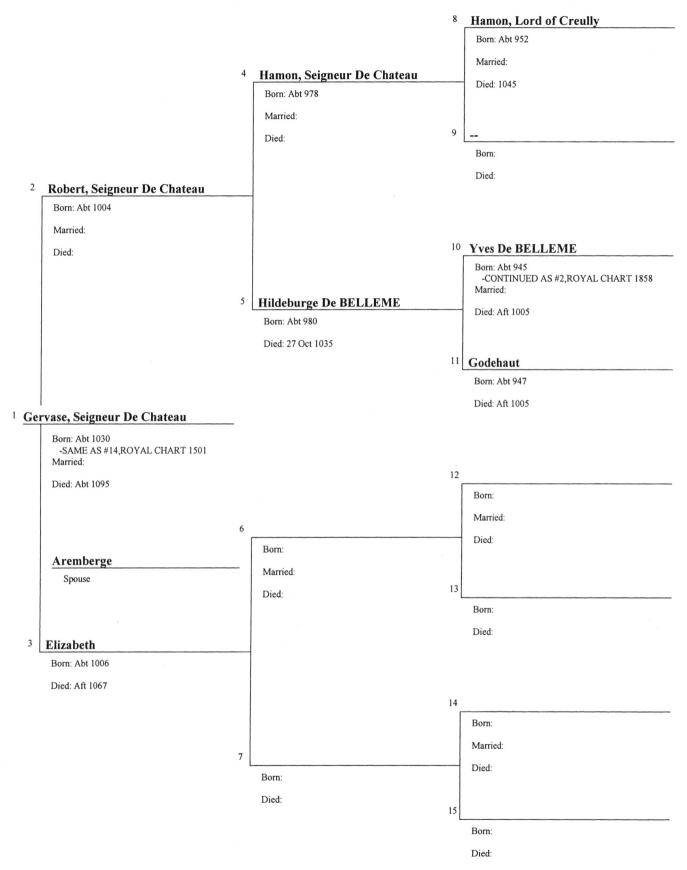

8 **Hamon, Lord of Creully**

Born: Abt 952

Married:

Died: 1045

4 **Hamon, Seigneur De Chateau**

Born: Abt 978

Married:

Died:

9 **--**

Born:

Died:

2 **Robert, Seigneur De Chateau**

Born: Abt 1004

Married:

Died:

10 **Yves De BELLEME**

Born: Abt 945
-CONTINUED AS #2,ROYAL CHART 1858
Married:

Died: Aft 1005

5 **Hildeburge De BELLEME**

Born: Abt 980

Died: 27 Oct 1035

11 **Godehaut**

Born: Abt 947

Died: Aft 1005

1 **Gervase, Seigneur De Chateau**

Born: Abt 1030
-SAME AS #14,ROYAL CHART 1501
Married:

Died: Abt 1095

12

Born:

Married:

Died:

6

Born:

Married:

Died:

13

Born:

Died:

Aremberge

Spouse

3 **Elizabeth**

Born: Abt 1006

Died: Aft 1067

14

Born:

Married:

Died:

7

Born:

Died:

15

Born:

Died:

Sources include: *Royal Ancestors* (1989), chart 11693; Stuart 354; Moriarty 12. Note: #5 is called either Hildeburge or Godehaut.

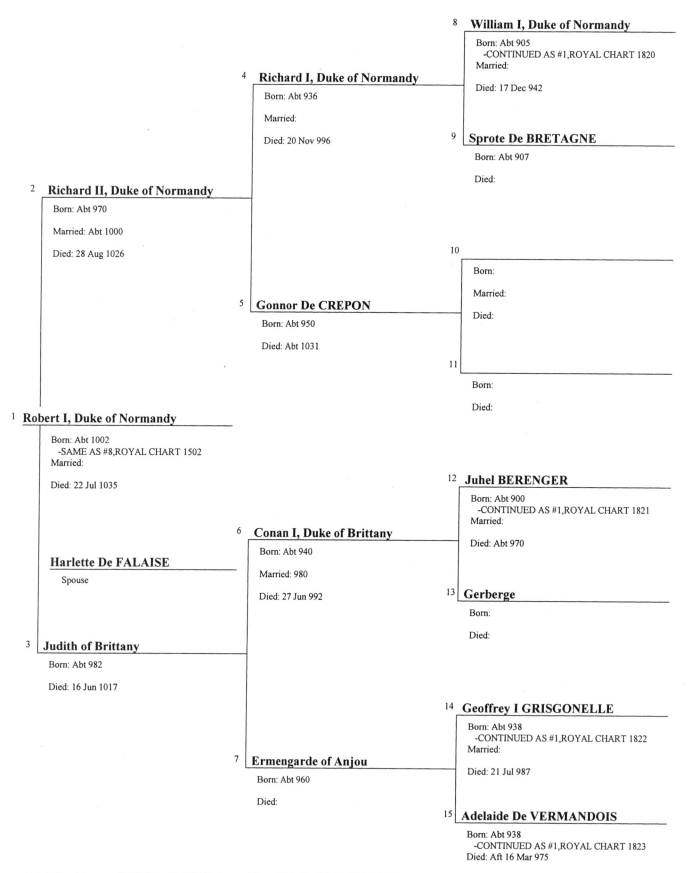

8 William I, Duke of Normandy
Born: Abt 905
-CONTINUED AS #1,ROYAL CHART 1820
Married:

Died: 17 Dec 942

4 Richard I, Duke of Normandy
Born: Abt 936

Married:

Died: 20 Nov 996

9 Sprote De BRETAGNE
Born: Abt 907

Died:

2 Richard II, Duke of Normandy
Born: Abt 970

Married: Abt 1000

Died: 28 Aug 1026

10
Born:

Married:

Died:

5 Gonnor De CREPON
Born: Abt 950

Died: Abt 1031

11
Born:

Died:

1 Robert I, Duke of Normandy
Born: Abt 1002
-SAME AS #8,ROYAL CHART 1502
Married:

Died: 22 Jul 1035

12 Juhel BERENGER
Born: Abt 900
-CONTINUED AS #1,ROYAL CHART 1821
Married:

Died: Abt 970

6 Conan I, Duke of Brittany
Born: Abt 940

Married: 980

Died: 27 Jun 992

13 Gerberge
Born:

Died:

Harlette De FALAISE
Spouse

3 Judith of Brittany
Born: Abt 982

Died: 16 Jun 1017

14 Geoffrey I GRISGONELLE
Born: Abt 938
-CONTINUED AS #1,ROYAL CHART 1822
Married:

Died: 21 Jul 987

7 Ermengarde of Anjou
Born: Abt 960

Died:

15 Adelaide De VERMANDOIS
Born: Abt 938
-CONTINUED AS #1,ROYAL CHART 1823
Died: Aft 16 Mar 975

Sources include: *Royal Ancestors* 11403; Stuart 89, 166-167; *Ancestral Roots* 121E, 121; *TAG* 72:187-204 (#4 ancestry); Moriarty 11, 13-14, 4; LDS records. Note: The chronology is very tight for the ancestry shown for #7 Ermengarde, although all sources seem to agree on the ancestry as given.

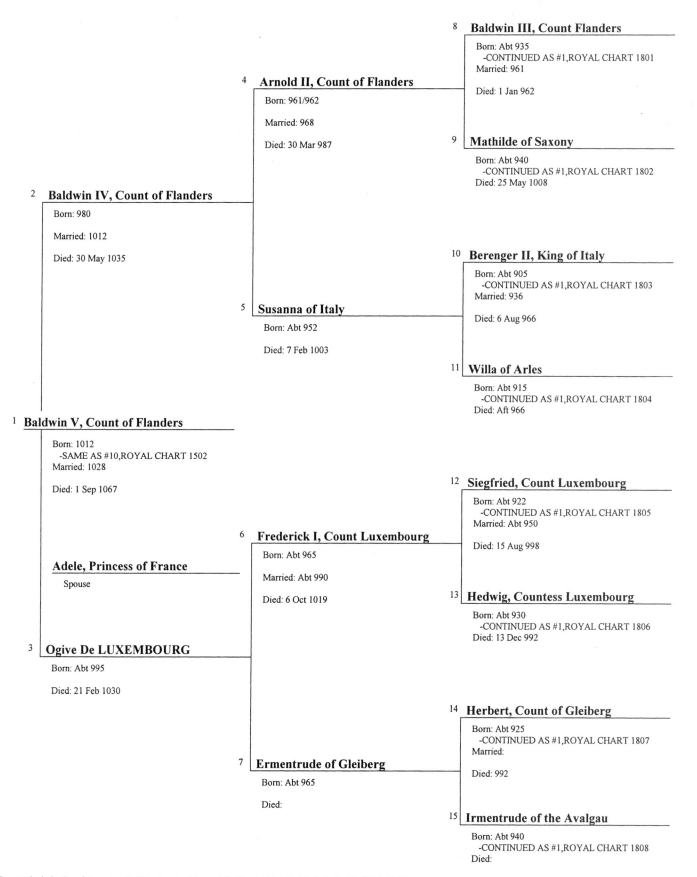

8 **Baldwin III, Count Flanders**

Born: Abt 935
  -CONTINUED AS #1,ROYAL CHART 1801
Married: 961

Died: 1 Jan 962

4 **Arnold II, Count of Flanders**

Born: 961/962

Married: 968

Died: 30 Mar 987

9 **Mathilde of Saxony**

Born: Abt 940
  -CONTINUED AS #1,ROYAL CHART 1802
Died: 25 May 1008

2 **Baldwin IV, Count of Flanders**

Born: 980

Married: 1012

Died: 30 May 1035

10 **Berenger II, King of Italy**

Born: Abt 905
  -CONTINUED AS #1,ROYAL CHART 1803
Married: 936

Died: 6 Aug 966

5 **Susanna of Italy**

Born: Abt 952

Died: 7 Feb 1003

11 **Willa of Arles**

Born: Abt 915
  -CONTINUED AS #1,ROYAL CHART 1804
Died: Aft 966

1 **Baldwin V, Count of Flanders**

Born: 1012
  -SAME AS #10,ROYAL CHART 1502
Married: 1028

Died: 1 Sep 1067

12 **Siegfried, Count Luxembourg**

Born: Abt 922
  -CONTINUED AS #1,ROYAL CHART 1805
Married: Abt 950

Died: 15 Aug 998

6 **Frederick I, Count Luxembourg**

Born: Abt 965

Married: Abt 990

Died: 6 Oct 1019

Adele, Princess of France

Spouse

13 **Hedwig, Countess Luxembourg**

Born: Abt 930
  -CONTINUED AS #1,ROYAL CHART 1806
Died: 13 Dec 992

3 **Ogive De LUXEMBOURG**

Born: Abt 995

Died: 21 Feb 1030

14 **Herbert, Count of Gleiberg**

Born: Abt 925
  -CONTINUED AS #1,ROYAL CHART 1807
Married:

Died: 992

7 **Ermentrude of Gleiberg**

Born: Abt 965

Died:

15 **Irmentrude of the Avalgau**

Born: Abt 940
  -CONTINUED AS #1,ROYAL CHART 1808
Died:

Sources include: *Royal Ancestors* 11404; *Ancestral Roots* 162; Stuart 141, 353; Moriarty 14-15, 17-18, 21-24.

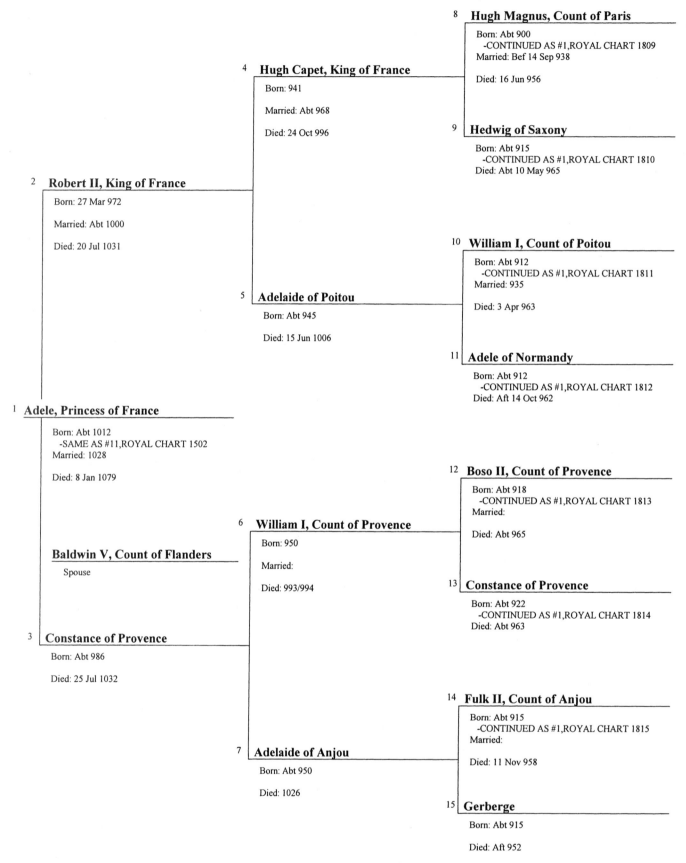

8   **Hugh Magnus, Count of Paris**

Born: Abt 900
  -CONTINUED AS #1,ROYAL CHART 1809
Married: Bef 14 Sep 938

Died: 16 Jun 956

4   **Hugh Capet, King of France**

Born: 941

Married: Abt 968

Died: 24 Oct 996

9   **Hedwig of Saxony**

Born: Abt 915
  -CONTINUED AS #1,ROYAL CHART 1810
Died: Abt 10 May 965

2   **Robert II, King of France**

Born: 27 Mar 972

Married: Abt 1000

Died: 20 Jul 1031

10   **William I, Count of Poitou**

Born: Abt 912
  -CONTINUED AS #1,ROYAL CHART 1811
Married: 935

Died: 3 Apr 963

5   **Adelaide of Poitou**

Born: Abt 945

Died: 15 Jun 1006

11   **Adele of Normandy**

Born: Abt 912
  -CONTINUED AS #1,ROYAL CHART 1812
Died: Aft 14 Oct 962

1   **Adele, Princess of France**

Born: Abt 1012
  -SAME AS #11,ROYAL CHART 1502
Married: 1028

Died: 8 Jan 1079

12   **Boso II, Count of Provence**

Born: Abt 918
  -CONTINUED AS #1,ROYAL CHART 1813
Married:

Died: Abt 965

6   **William I, Count of Provence**

Born: 950

Married:

Died: 993/994

Baldwin V, Count of Flanders

Spouse

13   **Constance of Provence**

Born: Abt 922
  -CONTINUED AS #1,ROYAL CHART 1814
Died: Abt 963

3   **Constance of Provence**

Born: Abt 986

Died: 25 Jul 1032

14   **Fulk II, Count of Anjou**

Born: Abt 915
  -CONTINUED AS #1,ROYAL CHART 1815
Married:

Died: 11 Nov 958

7   **Adelaide of Anjou**

Born: Abt 950

Died: 1026

15   **Gerberge**

Born: Abt 915

Died: Aft 952

Sources include: *Royal Ancestors* 11404; *Ancestral Roots* 128, 141A; Stuart 140; Moriarty 24, 27-28; Faris preliminary Charlemagne manuscript (June 1995), pp. 88-89.

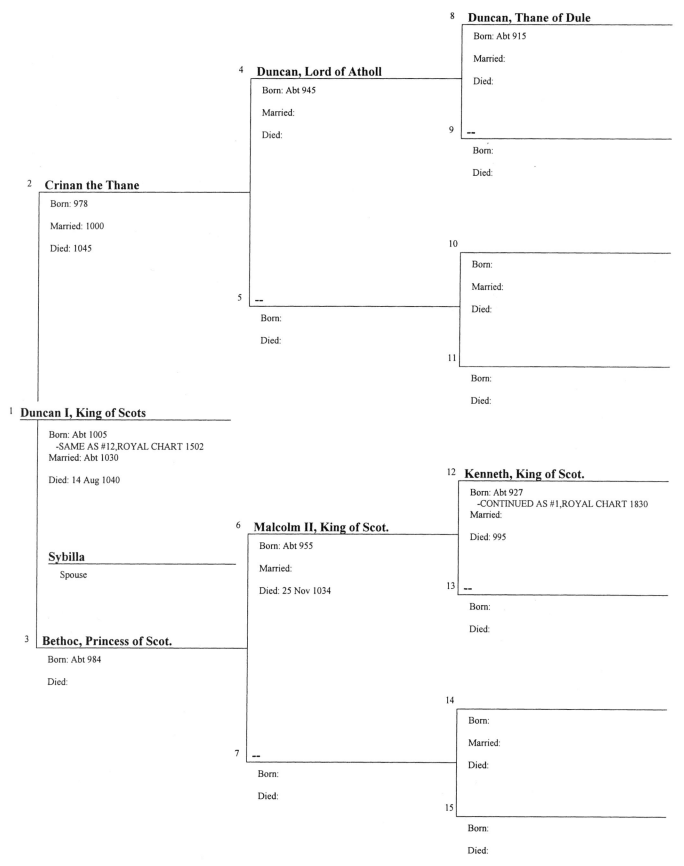

8 Duncan, Thane of Dule
Born: Abt 915
Married:
Died:

4 Duncan, Lord of Atholl
Born: Abt 945
Married:
Died:

9 --
Born:
Died:

2 Crinan the Thane
Born: 978
Married: 1000
Died: 1045

10
Born:
Married:
Died:

5 --
Born:
Died:

11
Born:
Died:

1 Duncan I, King of Scots
Born: Abt 1005
  -SAME AS #12,ROYAL CHART 1502
Married: Abt 1030
Died: 14 Aug 1040

12 Kenneth, King of Scot.
Born: Abt 927
  -CONTINUED AS #1,ROYAL CHART 1830
Married:
Died: 995

6 Malcolm II, King of Scot.
Born: Abt 955
Married:
Died: 25 Nov 1034

13 --
Born:
Died:

Sybilla
Spouse

14
Born:
Married:
Died:

3 Bethoc, Princess of Scot.
Born: Abt 984
Died:

7 --
Born:
Died:

15
Born:
Died:

Sources include: *Royal Ancestors* (1989), chart 11405; *Ancestral Roots* 170; Stuart 165, 252.

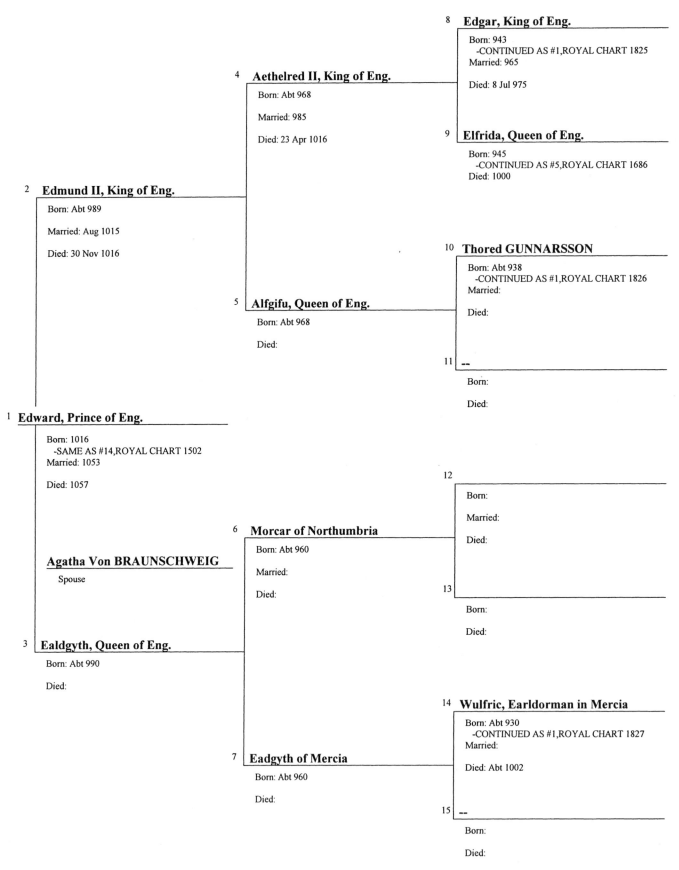

8   **Edgar, King of Eng.**

Born: 943
  -CONTINUED AS #1,ROYAL CHART 1825
Married: 965

Died: 8 Jul 975

4   **Aethelred II, King of Eng.**

Born: Abt 968

Married: 985

Died: 23 Apr 1016

9   **Elfrida, Queen of Eng.**

Born: 945
  -CONTINUED AS #5,ROYAL CHART 1686
Died: 1000

2   **Edmund II, King of Eng.**

Born: Abt 989

Married: Aug 1015

Died: 30 Nov 1016

10   **Thored GUNNARSSON**

Born: Abt 938
  -CONTINUED AS #1,ROYAL CHART 1826
Married:

Died:

5   **Alfgifu, Queen of Eng.**

Born: Abt 968

Died:

11   **--**

Born:

Died:

1   **Edward, Prince of Eng.**

Born: 1016
  -SAME AS #14,ROYAL CHART 1502
Married: 1053

Died: 1057

12

Born:

Married:

Died:

6   **Morcar of Northumbria**

Born: Abt 960

Married:

Died:

13

Born:

Died:

Agatha Von BRAUNSCHWEIG

Spouse

3   **Ealdgyth, Queen of Eng.**

Born: Abt 990

Died:

14   **Wulfric, Earldorman in Mercia**

Born: Abt 930
  -CONTINUED AS #1,ROYAL CHART 1827
Married:

Died: Abt 1002

7   **Eadgyth of Mercia**

Born: Abt 960

Died:

15   **--**

Born:

Died:

Sources include: *Royal Ancestors* 11406; *Ancestral Roots* 1; Stuart 233, 22; Moriarty 31, 249.

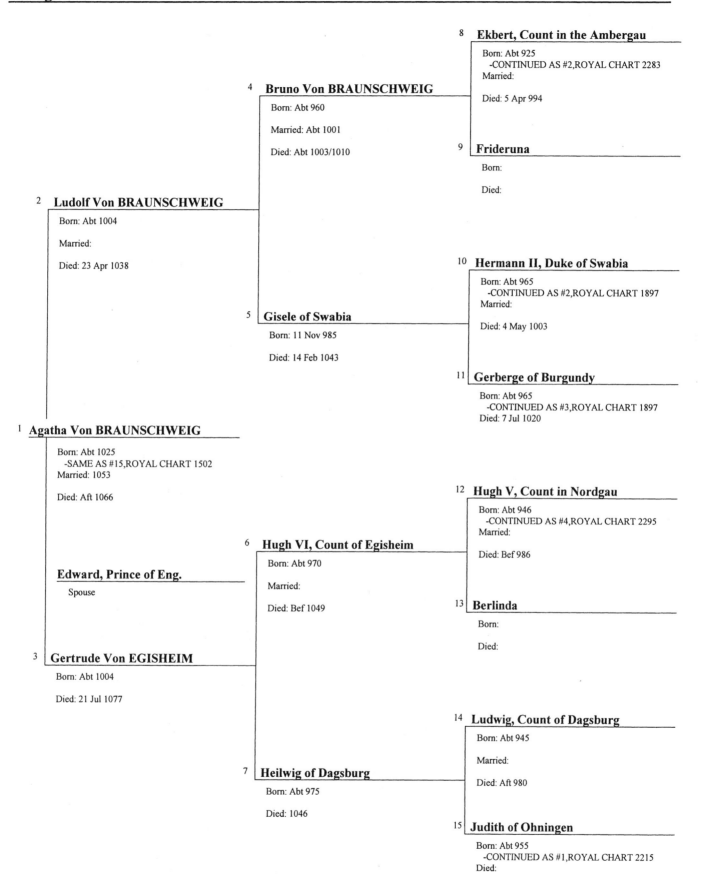

8 Ekbert, Count in the Ambergau

Born: Abt 925
  -CONTINUED AS #2,ROYAL CHART 2283
Married:

Died: 5 Apr 994

4 Bruno Von BRAUNSCHWEIG

Born: Abt 960

Married: Abt 1001

Died: Abt 1003/1010

9 Frideruna

Born:

Died:

2 Ludolf Von BRAUNSCHWEIG

Born: Abt 1004

Married:

Died: 23 Apr 1038

10 Hermann II, Duke of Swabia

Born: Abt 965
  -CONTINUED AS #2,ROYAL CHART 1897
Married:

Died: 4 May 1003

5 Gisele of Swabia

Born: 11 Nov 985

Died: 14 Feb 1043

11 Gerberge of Burgundy

Born: Abt 965
  -CONTINUED AS #3,ROYAL CHART 1897
Died: 7 Jul 1020

1 Agatha Von BRAUNSCHWEIG

Born: Abt 1025
  -SAME AS #15,ROYAL CHART 1502
Married: 1053

Died: Aft 1066

12 Hugh V, Count in Nordgau

Born: Abt 946
  -CONTINUED AS #4,ROYAL CHART 2295
Married:

Died: Bef 986

6 Hugh VI, Count of Egisheim

Born: Abt 970

Married:

Died: Bef 1049

13 Berlinda

Born:

Died:

Edward, Prince of Eng.

Spouse

3 Gertrude Von EGISHEIM

Born: Abt 1004

Died: 21 Jul 1077

14 Ludwig, Count of Dagsburg

Born: Abt 945

Married:

Died: Aft 980

7 Heilwig of Dagsburg

Born: Abt 975

Died: 1046

15 Judith of Ohningen

Born: Abt 955
  -CONTINUED AS #1,ROYAL CHART 2215
Died:

Sources include: *Royal Ancestors* (1989), chart 11406; Faris preliminary Charlemagne manuscript (June 1995), pp. 16, 283-284, 125-126; *NEHGR* 152:215-235, 150:417-432; Stuart 318; Moriarty 31. Note: The identification and parentage of #1 Agatha is uncertain and heavily disputed. The version argued in *NEHGR* 152 and accepted by Faris and Richardson is accepted here.

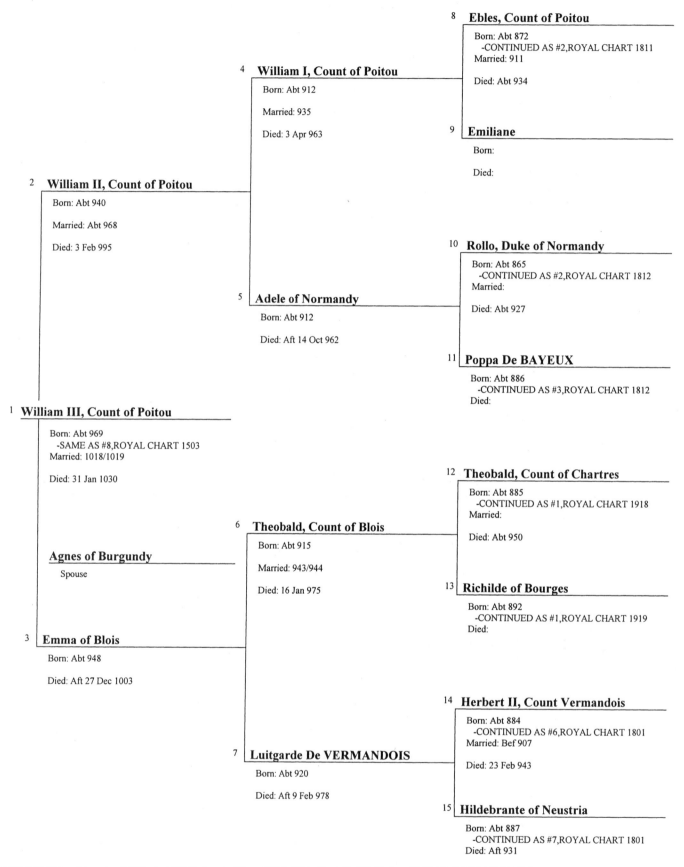

8 **Ebles, Count of Poitou**

Born: Abt 872
-CONTINUED AS #2,ROYAL CHART 1811
Married: 911

Died: Abt 934

4 **William I, Count of Poitou**

Born: Abt 912

Married: 935

Died: 3 Apr 963

9 **Emiliane**

Born:

Died:

2 **William II, Count of Poitou**

Born: Abt 940

Married: Abt 968

Died: 3 Feb 995

10 **Rollo, Duke of Normandy**

Born: Abt 865
-CONTINUED AS #2,ROYAL CHART 1812
Married:

Died: Abt 927

5 **Adele of Normandy**

Born: Abt 912

Died: Aft 14 Oct 962

11 **Poppa De BAYEUX**

Born: Abt 886
-CONTINUED AS #3,ROYAL CHART 1812
Died:

1 **William III, Count of Poitou**

Born: Abt 969
-SAME AS #8,ROYAL CHART 1503
Married: 1018/1019

Died: 31 Jan 1030

12 **Theobald, Count of Chartres**

Born: Abt 885
-CONTINUED AS #1,ROYAL CHART 1918
Married:

Died: Abt 950

6 **Theobald, Count of Blois**

Born: Abt 915

Married: 943/944

Died: 16 Jan 975

13 **Richilde of Bourges**

Born: Abt 892
-CONTINUED AS #1,ROYAL CHART 1919
Died:

Agnes of Burgundy

Spouse

3 **Emma of Blois**

Born: Abt 948

Died: Aft 27 Dec 1003

14 **Herbert II, Count Vermandois**

Born: Abt 884
-CONTINUED AS #6,ROYAL CHART 1801
Married: Bef 907

Died: 23 Feb 943

7 **Luitgarde De VERMANDOIS**

Born: Abt 920

Died: Aft 9 Feb 978

15 **Hildebrante of Neustria**

Born: Abt 887
-CONTINUED AS #7,ROYAL CHART 1801
Died: Aft 931

Sources include: *Royal Ancestors* (1989), chart 11407; *Ancestral Roots* 110-23, 144A; Stuart 88, 340; Moriarty 35-36, 27; *TAG* 72:187-204 (#11 ancestry).

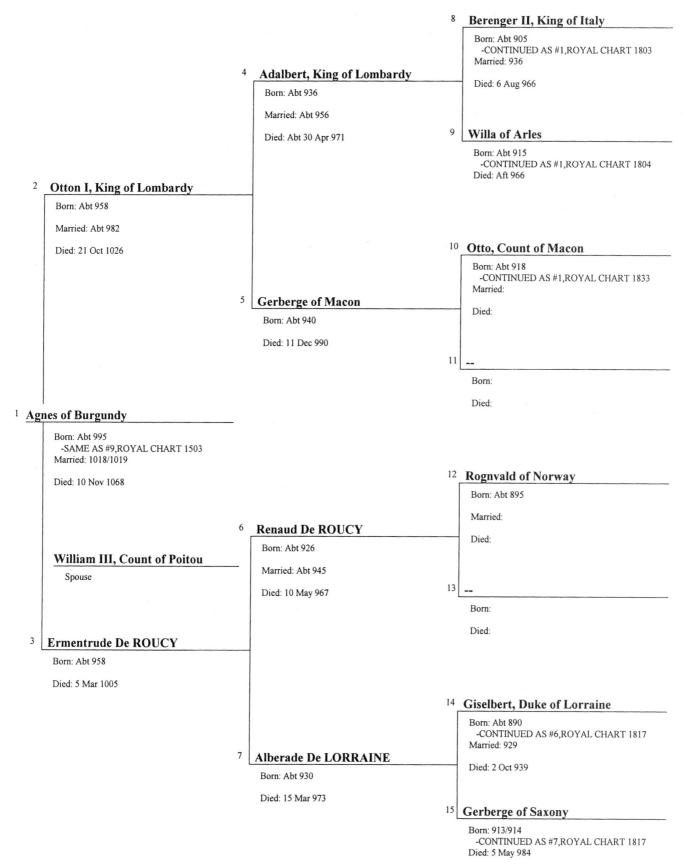

8 Berenger II, King of Italy

Born: Abt 905
  -CONTINUED AS #1,ROYAL CHART 1803
Married: 936

Died: 6 Aug 966

4 Adalbert, King of Lombardy

Born: Abt 936

Married: Abt 956

Died: Abt 30 Apr 971

9 Willa of Arles

Born: Abt 915
  -CONTINUED AS #1,ROYAL CHART 1804
Died: Aft 966

2 Otton I, King of Lombardy

Born: Abt 958

Married: Abt 982

Died: 21 Oct 1026

10 Otto, Count of Macon

Born: Abt 918
  -CONTINUED AS #1,ROYAL CHART 1833
Married:

Died:

5 Gerberge of Macon

Born: Abt 940

Died: 11 Dec 990

11 --

Born:

Died:

1 Agnes of Burgundy

Born: Abt 995
  -SAME AS #9,ROYAL CHART 1503
Married: 1018/1019

Died: 10 Nov 1068

12 Rognvald of Norway

Born: Abt 895

Married:

Died:

6 Renaud De ROUCY

Born: Abt 926

Married: Abt 945

Died: 10 May 967

13 --

Born:

Died:

William III, Count of Poitou

Spouse

3 Ermentrude De ROUCY

Born: Abt 958

Died: 5 Mar 1005

14 Giselbert, Duke of Lorraine

Born: Abt 890
  -CONTINUED AS #6,ROYAL CHART 1817
Married: 929

Died: 2 Oct 939

7 Alberade De LORRAINE

Born: Abt 930

Died: 15 Mar 973

15 Gerberge of Saxony

Born: 913/914
  -CONTINUED AS #7,ROYAL CHART 1817
Died: 5 May 984

Sources include: *Royal Ancestors* (1989), chart 11407; Stuart 161, 94, 170; Moriarty 37-39; Charles Evans in *TAG* 52:25 (corrects Moriarty on parentage of #5 Gerberge, adding one generation -- Otto). Note: #12 Rognvald is not certain.

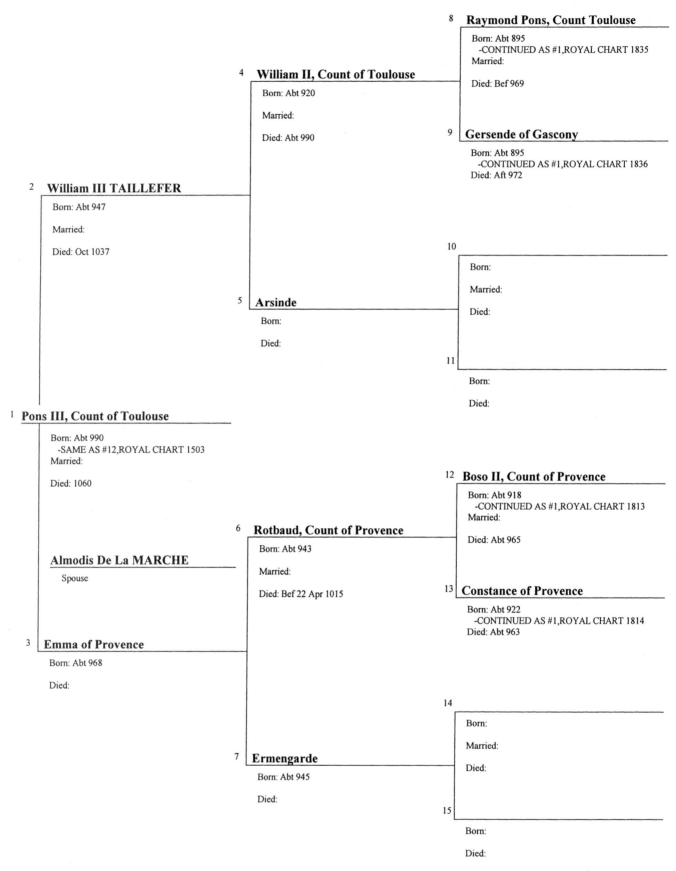

8 **Raymond Pons, Count Toulouse**

Born: Abt 895
-CONTINUED AS #1,ROYAL CHART 1835
Married:

Died: Bef 969

4 **William II, Count of Toulouse**

Born: Abt 920

Married:

Died: Abt 990

9 **Gersende of Gascony**

Born: Abt 895
-CONTINUED AS #1,ROYAL CHART 1836
Died: Aft 972

2 **William III TAILLEFER**

Born: Abt 947

Married:

Died: Oct 1037

10

Born:

Married:

Died:

5 **Arsinde**

Born:

Died:

11

Born:

Died:

1 **Pons III, Count of Toulouse**

Born: Abt 990
-SAME AS #12,ROYAL CHART 1503
Married:

Died: 1060

12 **Boso II, Count of Provence**

Born: Abt 918
-CONTINUED AS #1,ROYAL CHART 1813
Married:

Died: Abt 965

6 **Rotbaud, Count of Provence**

Born: Abt 943

Married:

Died: Bef 22 Apr 1015

13 **Constance of Provence**

Born: Abt 922
-CONTINUED AS #1,ROYAL CHART 1814
Died: Abt 963

Almodis De La MARCHE

Spouse

3 **Emma of Provence**

Born: Abt 968

Died:

14

Born:

Married:

Died:

7 **Ermengarde**

Born: Abt 945

Died:

15

Born:

Died:

Sources include: *Royal Ancestors* (1989), charts 11409, 11747; Moriarty 41-42, 27-28; Faris preliminary Charlemagne manuscript (June 1995), pp. 262-263; Stuart 374-375, 326 (information missing or in error). Notes: Many sources give #2 William III as son of #8 Raymond Pons (Raymond III). Moriarty inserts an additional generation (William II), as shown above. Faris inserts an additional generation (another Rotbaud or Rotbald who married Eimildis De Gevaudan) between #6 & 12. This makes the chronology too tight to be acceptable. It appears more likely that #6 Rotbaud married 1st Ermengarde and 2nd Eimilde De Gevaudun. Compare chart 2208, #6 & 7.

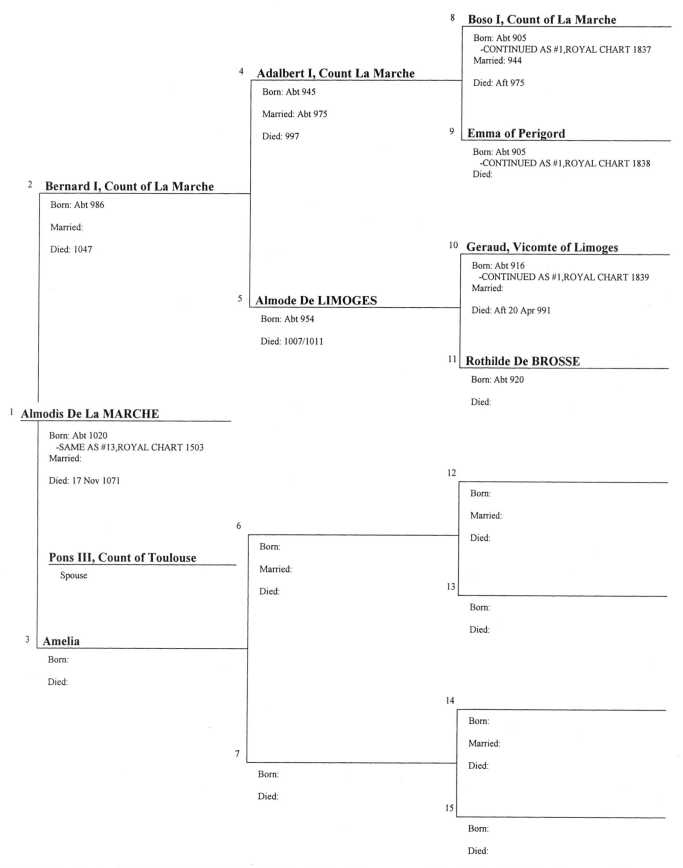

8   **Boso I, Count of La Marche**

Born: Abt 905
   -CONTINUED AS #1,ROYAL CHART 1837
Married: 944

Died: Aft 975

4   **Adalbert I, Count La Marche**

Born: Abt 945

Married: Abt 975

Died: 997

9   **Emma of Perigord**

Born: Abt 905
   -CONTINUED AS #1,ROYAL CHART 1838
Died:

2   **Bernard I, Count of La Marche**

Born: Abt 986

Married:

Died: 1047

10   **Geraud, Vicomte of Limoges**

Born: Abt 916
   -CONTINUED AS #1,ROYAL CHART 1839
Married:

Died: Aft 20 Apr 991

5   **Almode De LIMOGES**

Born: Abt 954

Died: 1007/1011

11   **Rothilde De BROSSE**

Born: Abt 920

Died:

1   **Almodis De La MARCHE**

Born: Abt 1020
   -SAME AS #13,ROYAL CHART 1503
Married:

Died: 17 Nov 1071

12

Born:

Married:

Died:

6

Born:

Married:

Died:

13

Born:

Died:

Pons III, Count of Toulouse

Spouse

3   **Amelia**

Born:

Died:

14

Born:

Married:

Died:

7

Born:

Died:

15

Born:

Died:

Sources include: *Royal Ancestors* (1989), chart 11409; Stuart 327; Moriarty 42; Faris preliminary Charlemagne manuscript (June 1995), pp. 165-166. Note: The parentage of #3 Amelia and of #11 Rothilde is disputed.

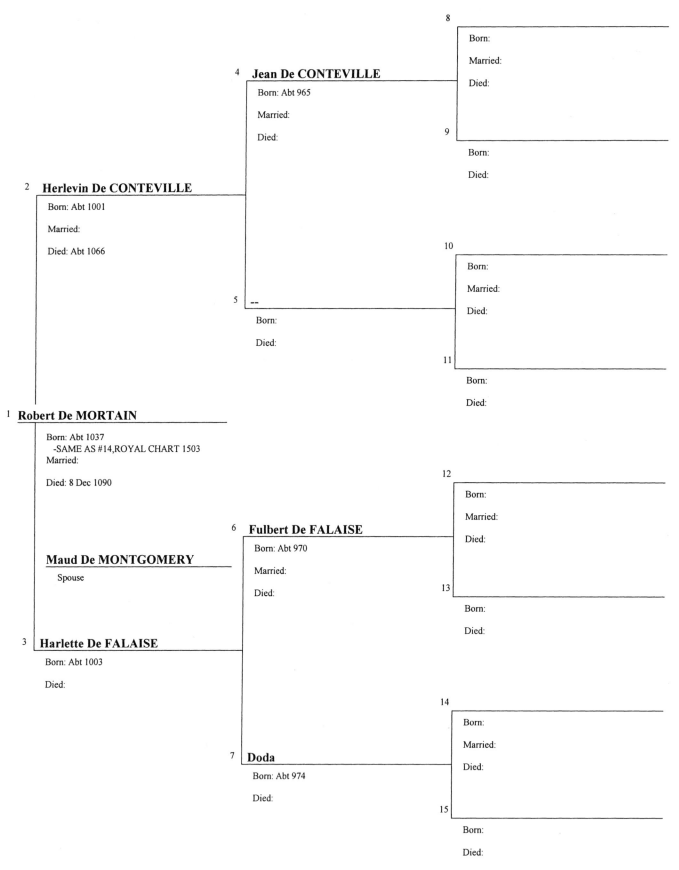

8
Born:
Married:
Died:

4 Jean De CONTEVILLE
Born: Abt 965
Married:
Died:

9
Born:
Died:

2 Herlevin De CONTEVILLE
Born: Abt 1001
Married:
Died: Abt 1066

10
Born:
Married:
Died:

5 --
Born:
Died:

11
Born:
Died:

1 Robert De MORTAIN
Born: Abt 1037
  -SAME AS #14,ROYAL CHART 1503
Married:
Died: 8 Dec 1090

12
Born:
Married:
Died:

6 Fulbert De FALAISE
Born: Abt 970
Married:
Died:

13
Born:
Died:

Maud De MONTGOMERY
Spouse

3 Harlette De FALAISE
Born: Abt 1003
Died:

14
Born:
Married:
Died:

7 Doda
Born: Abt 974
Died:

15
Born:
Died:

Sources include: *Royal Ancestors* (1989), chart 11409; Stuart 160; *Ancestral Roots* 185-1.

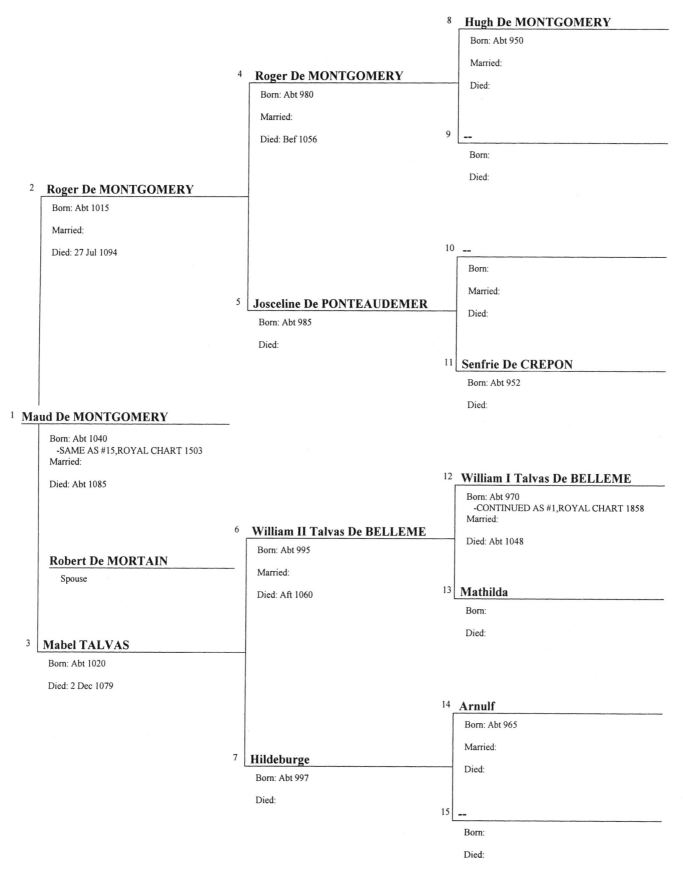

8 **Hugh De MONTGOMERY**

Born: Abt 950

Married:

Died:

4 **Roger De MONTGOMERY**

Born: Abt 980

Married:

Died: Bef 1056

9 **--**

Born:

Died:

2 **Roger De MONTGOMERY**

Born: Abt 1015

Married:

Died: 27 Jul 1094

10 **--**

Born:

Married:

Died:

5 **Josceline De PONTEAUDEMER**

Born: Abt 985

Died:

11 **Senfrie De CREPON**

Born: Abt 952

Died:

1 **Maud De MONTGOMERY**

Born: Abt 1040
-SAME AS #15,ROYAL CHART 1503
Married:

Died: Abt 1085

12 **William I Talvas De BELLEME**

Born: Abt 970
-CONTINUED AS #1,ROYAL CHART 1858
Married:

Died: Abt 1048

6 **William II Talvas De BELLEME**

Born: Abt 995

Married:

Died: Aft 1060

13 **Mathilda**

Born:

Died:

Robert De MORTAIN

Spouse

3 **Mabel TALVAS**

Born: Abt 1020

Died: 2 Dec 1079

14 **Arnulf**

Born: Abt 965

Married:

Died:

7 **Hildeburge**

Born: Abt 997

Died:

15 **--**

Born:

Died:

Sources include: *Royal Ancestors* (1989), charts 11409, 11662, 11527 & 11403 notes; *Ancestral Roots* 185-1; Stuart 335 (contains numerous errors); Moriarty 44-45, 12; Sir Anthony Wagner, *Pedigree and Progress*, p. 205, pedigree 46; Turton 13. Notes: There are several areas of disagreement on the above lines. Moriarty appears to remain the most reliable guide and has been followed where there are disputes. Moriarty and Wagner agree on #5 Josceline and #11 Senfrie as shown. #8 Hugh is not certain. Additional ancestry claimed for him by Stuart and Turton appears to be unreliable.

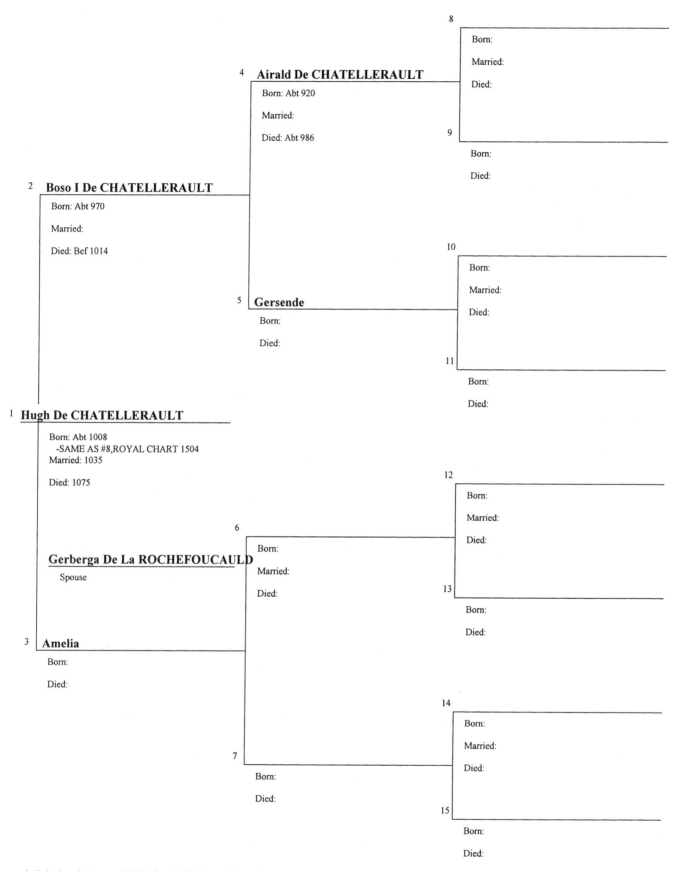

8

Born:

Married:

Died:

4   **Airald De CHATELLERAULT**

Born: Abt 920

Married:

Died: Abt 986

9

Born:

Died:

2   **Boso I De CHATELLERAULT**

Born: Abt 970

Married:

Died: Bef 1014

10

Born:

Married:

Died:

5   **Gersende**

Born:

Died:

11

Born:

Died:

1   **Hugh De CHATELLERAULT**

Born: Abt 1008
  -SAME AS #8,ROYAL CHART 1504
Married: 1035

Died: 1075

12

Born:

Married:

Died:

6

Born:

Married:

Died:

13

Born:

Died:

Gerberga De La ROCHEFOUCAULD

Spouse

3   **Amelia**

Born:

Died:

14

Born:

Married:

Died:

7

Born:

Died:

15

Born:

Died:

Sources include: *Royal Ancestors* (1989), chart 11498; Stuart 305; Moriarty 45, 243-244; Turton 9; *Ancestral Roots* 183-2.

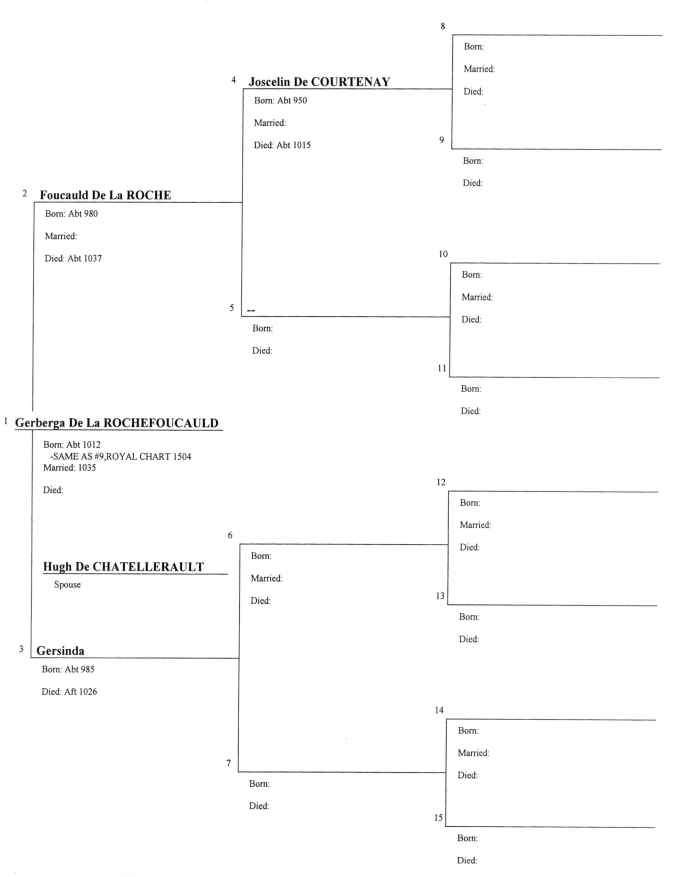

4 Joscelin De **COURTENAY**

Born: Abt 950

Married:

Died: Abt 1015

2 Foucauld De La **ROCHE**

Born: Abt 980

Married:

Died: Abt 1037

5 --

Born:

Died:

1 Gerberga De La **ROCHEFOUCAULD**

Born: Abt 1012
-SAME AS #9,ROYAL CHART 1504
Married: 1035

Died:

Hugh De **CHATELLERAULT**

Spouse

3 **Gersinda**

Born: Abt 985

Died: Aft 1026

6

Born:

Married:

Died:

7

Born:

Died:

8

Born:

Married:

Died:

9

Born:

Died:

10

Born:

Married:

Died:

11

Born:

Died:

12

Born:

Married:

Died:

13

Born:

Died:

14

Born:

Married:

Died:

15

Born:

Died:

Sources include: *Royal Ancestors* (1989), chart 11498; Stuart 306; Moriarty 45; Turton 9; *Ancestral Roots* 183-2.

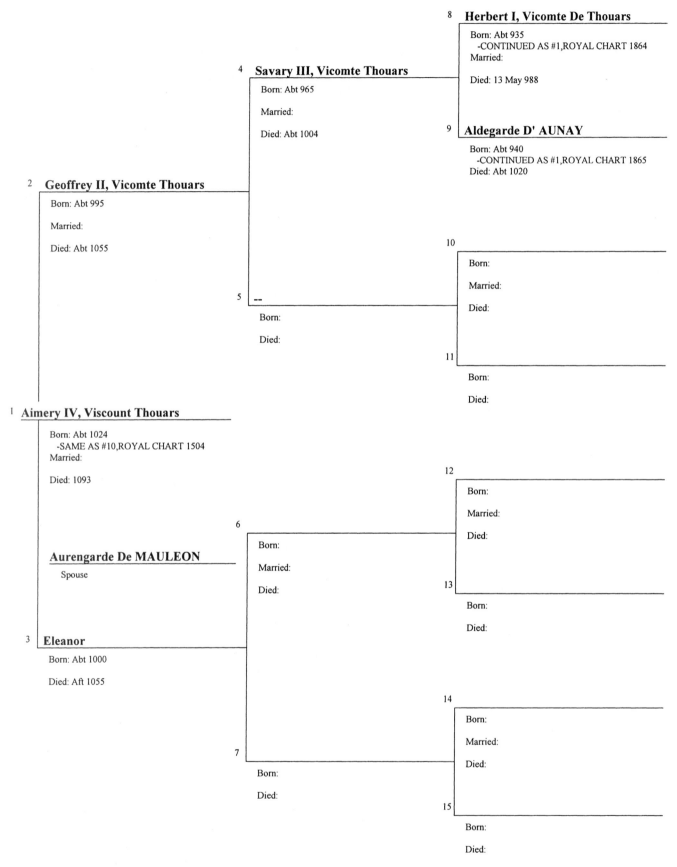

8 Herbert I, Vicomte De Thouars

Born: Abt 935
-CONTINUED AS #1,ROYAL CHART 1864
Married:

Died: 13 May 988

4 Savary III, Vicomte Thouars

Born: Abt 965

Married:

Died: Abt 1004

9 Aldegarde D' AUNAY

Born: Abt 940
-CONTINUED AS #1,ROYAL CHART 1865
Died: Abt 1020

2 Geoffrey II, Vicomte Thouars

Born: Abt 995

Married:

Died: Abt 1055

10

Born:

Married:

Died:

5 --

Born:

Died:

11

Born:

Died:

1 Aimery IV, Viscount Thouars

Born: Abt 1024
-SAME AS #10,ROYAL CHART 1504
Married:

Died: 1093

12

Born:

Married:

Died:

6

Born:

Married:

Died:

13

Born:

Died:

Aurengarde De MAULEON

Spouse

3 Eleanor

Born: Abt 1000

Died: Aft 1055

14

Born:

Married:

Died:

7

Born:

Died:

15

Born:

Died:

Sources include: *Royal Ancestors* (1989), chart 11498; Stuart 159; Moriarty 46; *Ancestral Roots* 183.

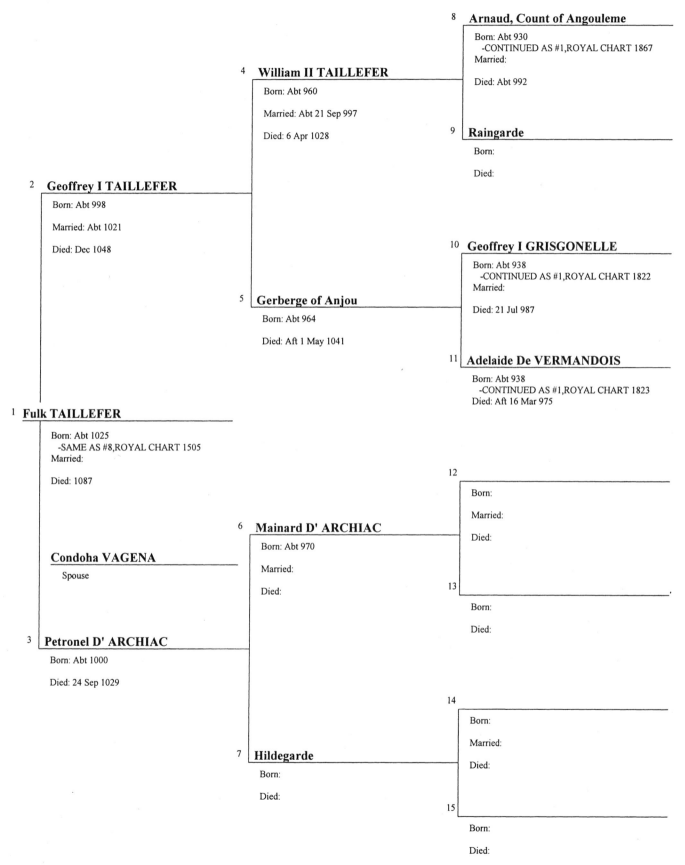

8 Arnaud, Count of Angouleme
Born: Abt 930
-CONTINUED AS #1,ROYAL CHART 1867
Married:

Died: Abt 992

4 William II TAILLEFER
Born: Abt 960

Married: Abt 21 Sep 997

Died: 6 Apr 1028

9 Raingarde
Born:

Died:

2 Geoffrey I TAILLEFER
Born: Abt 998

Married: Abt 1021

Died: Dec 1048

10 Geoffrey I GRISGONELLE
Born: Abt 938
-CONTINUED AS #1,ROYAL CHART 1822
Married:

Died: 21 Jul 987

5 Gerberge of Anjou
Born: Abt 964

Died: Aft 1 May 1041

11 Adelaide De VERMANDOIS
Born: Abt 938
-CONTINUED AS #1,ROYAL CHART 1823
Died: Aft 16 Mar 975

1 Fulk TAILLEFER
Born: Abt 1025
-SAME AS #8,ROYAL CHART 1505
Married:

Died: 1087

Condoha VAGENA
Spouse

12
Born:

Married:

Died:

6 Mainard D' ARCHIAC
Born: Abt 970

Married:

Died:

13
Born:

Died:

3 Petronel D' ARCHIAC
Born: Abt 1000

Died: 24 Sep 1029

14
Born:

Married:

Died:

7 Hildegarde
Born:

Died:

15
Born:

Died:

Sources include: *Royal Ancestors* (1989), chart 11410; Stuart 87; Moriarty 46-47, 4; Faris preliminary Charlemagne manuscript (June 1995), p. 18.

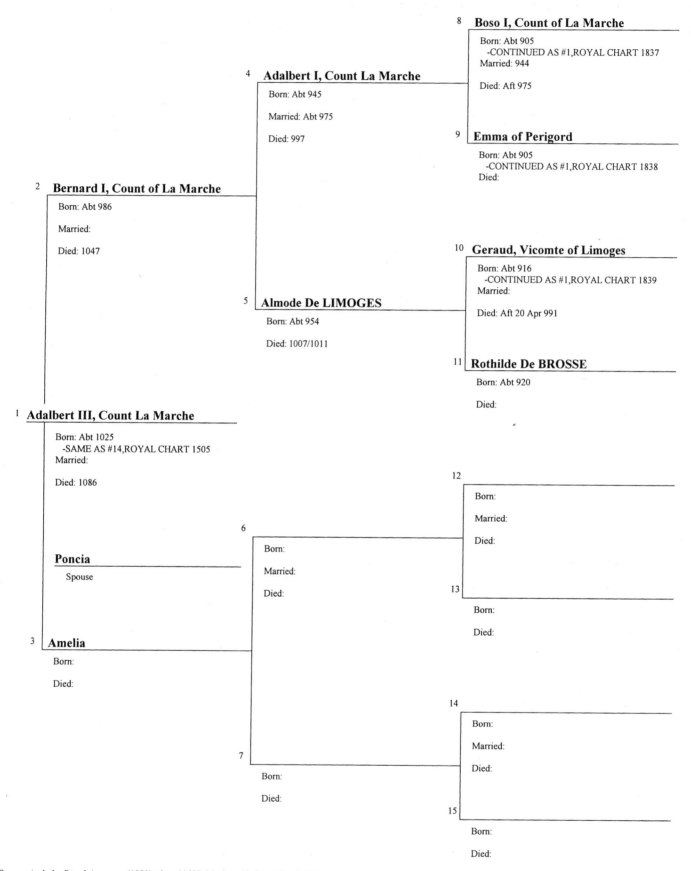

8 **Boso I, Count of La Marche**

Born: Abt 905
 -CONTINUED AS #1,ROYAL CHART 1837
Married: 944

Died: Aft 975

4 **Adalbert I, Count La Marche**

Born: Abt 945

Married: Abt 975

Died: 997

9 **Emma of Perigord**

Born: Abt 905
 -CONTINUED AS #1,ROYAL CHART 1838
Died:

2 **Bernard I, Count of La Marche**

Born: Abt 986

Married:

Died: 1047

10 **Geraud, Vicomte of Limoges**

Born: Abt 916
 -CONTINUED AS #1,ROYAL CHART 1839
Married:

Died: Aft 20 Apr 991

5 **Almode De LIMOGES**

Born: Abt 954

Died: 1007/1011

11 **Rothilde De BROSSE**

Born: Abt 920

Died:

1 **Adalbert III, Count La Marche**

Born: Abt 1025
 -SAME AS #14,ROYAL CHART 1505
Married:

Died: 1086

12

Born:

Married:

Died:

6

Born:

Married:

Died:

13

Born:

Died:

Poncia

Spouse

3 **Amelia**

Born:

Died:

14

Born:

Married:

Died:

7

Born:

Died:

15

Born:

Died:

Sources include: *Royal Ancestors* (1989), chart 11687; Moriarty 42; Stuart 87-29 (#1); 327 (#2 & 3 ancestry). Note: The parentage of #3 Amelia is disputed.

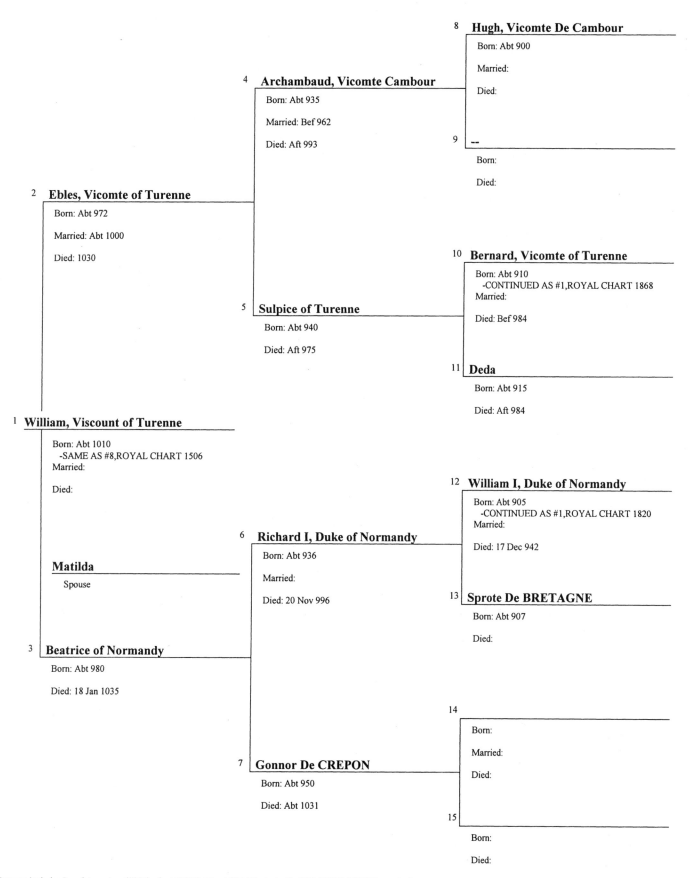

8 **Hugh, Vicomte De Cambour**
Born: Abt 900
Married:
Died:

4 **Archambaud, Vicomte Cambour**
Born: Abt 935
Married: Bef 962
Died: Aft 993

9 **--**
Born:
Died:

2 **Ebles, Vicomte of Turenne**
Born: Abt 972
Married: Abt 1000
Died: 1030

10 **Bernard, Vicomte of Turenne**
Born: Abt 910
-CONTINUED AS #1,ROYAL CHART 1868
Married:
Died: Bef 984

5 **Sulpice of Turenne**
Born: Abt 940
Died: Aft 975

11 **Deda**
Born: Abt 915
Died: Aft 984

1 **William, Viscount of Turenne**
Born: Abt 1010
-SAME AS #8,ROYAL CHART 1506
Married:
Died:

Matilda
Spouse

12 **William I, Duke of Normandy**
Born: Abt 905
-CONTINUED AS #1,ROYAL CHART 1820
Married:
Died: 17 Dec 942

6 **Richard I, Duke of Normandy**
Born: Abt 936
Married:
Died: 20 Nov 996

13 **Sprote De BRETAGNE**
Born: Abt 907
Died:

3 **Beatrice of Normandy**
Born: Abt 980
Died: 18 Jan 1035

14
Born:
Married:
Died:

7 **Gonnor De CREPON**
Born: Abt 950
Died: Abt 1031

15
Born:
Died:

Sources include: *Royal Ancestors* (1989), chart 11745; Stuart 156; Moriarty 48; *TAG* 72:187-204 (#6 ancestry).

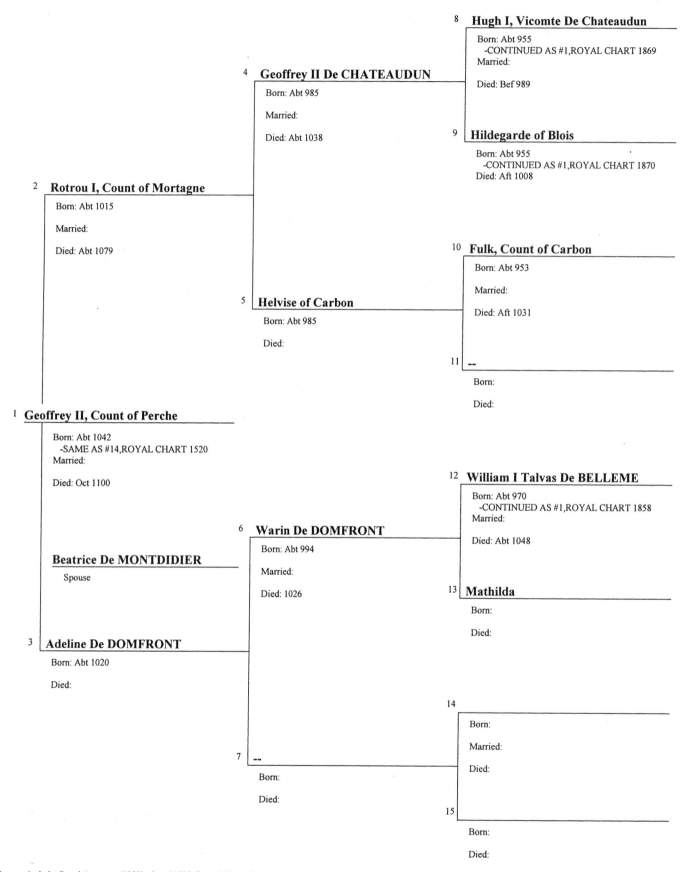

8 Hugh I, Vicomte De Chateaudun

Born: Abt 955
-CONTINUED AS #1, ROYAL CHART 1869
Married:

Died: Bef 989

4 Geoffrey II De CHATEAUDUN

Born: Abt 985

Married:

Died: Abt 1038

9 Hildegarde of Blois

Born: Abt 955
-CONTINUED AS #1, ROYAL CHART 1870
Died: Aft 1008

2 Rotrou I, Count of Mortagne

Born: Abt 1015

Married:

Died: Abt 1079

10 Fulk, Count of Carbon

Born: Abt 953

Married:

Died: Aft 1031

5 Helvise of Carbon

Born: Abt 985

Died:

11 --

Born:

Died:

1 Geoffrey II, Count of Perche

Born: Abt 1042
-SAME AS #14, ROYAL CHART 1520
Married:

Died: Oct 1100

12 William I Talvas De BELLEME

Born: Abt 970
-CONTINUED AS #1, ROYAL CHART 1858
Married:

Died: Abt 1048

6 Warin De DOMFRONT

Born: Abt 994

Married:

Died: 1026

13 Mathilda

Born:

Died:

Beatrice De MONTDIDIER

Spouse

3 Adeline De DOMFRONT

Born: Abt 1020

Died:

14

Born:

Married:

Died:

7 --

Born:

Died:

15

Born:

Died:

Sources include: *Royal Ancestors* (1989), chart 11685; Stuart 249; Moriarty 48-49, 12; Schwennicke 3:689; *Ancestral Roots* 151-24. Notes: Moriarty inserts an additional Geoffrey between #2 Rotrou and #8 Hugh. The Stuart version shown above seems more acceptable chronologically. Schwennicke gives #4 Geoffrey II as a nephew of #8 Hugh I. Moriarty shows #10 Fulk as possibly son of Herve (died 954).

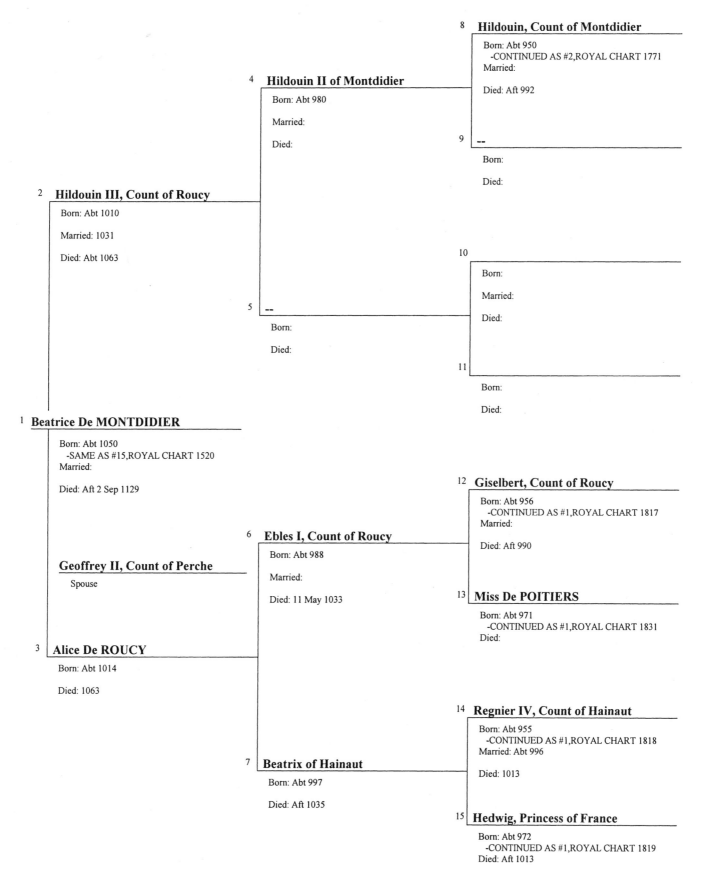

8 **Hildouin, Count of Montdidier**
Born: Abt 950
-CONTINUED AS #2,ROYAL CHART 1771
Married:

Died: Aft 992

4 **Hildouin II of Montdidier**
Born: Abt 980

Married:

Died:

9 --
Born:

Died:

2 **Hildouin III, Count of Roucy**
Born: Abt 1010

Married: 1031

Died: Abt 1063

10
Born:

Married:

Died:

5 --
Born:

Died:

11
Born:

Died:

1 **Beatrice De MONTDIDIER**
Born: Abt 1050
-SAME AS #15,ROYAL CHART 1520
Married:

Died: Aft 2 Sep 1129

12 **Giselbert, Count of Roucy**
Born: Abt 956
-CONTINUED AS #1,ROYAL CHART 1817
Married:

Died: Aft 990

6 **Ebles I, Count of Roucy**
Born: Abt 988

Married:

Died: 11 May 1033

13 **Miss De POITIERS**
Born: Abt 971
-CONTINUED AS #1,ROYAL CHART 1831
Died:

Geoffrey II, Count of Perche
Spouse

3 **Alice De ROUCY**
Born: Abt 1014

Died: 1063

14 **Regnier IV, Count of Hainaut**
Born: Abt 955
-CONTINUED AS #1,ROYAL CHART 1818
Married: Abt 996

Died: 1013

7 **Beatrix of Hainaut**
Born: Abt 997

Died: Aft 1035

15 **Hedwig, Princess of France**
Born: Abt 972
-CONTINUED AS #1,ROYAL CHART 1819
Died: Aft 1013

Sources include: *Royal Ancestors* 11685, 11538; Stuart 266, 170; *Ancestral Roots* 151, 106; Moriarty 49-50.

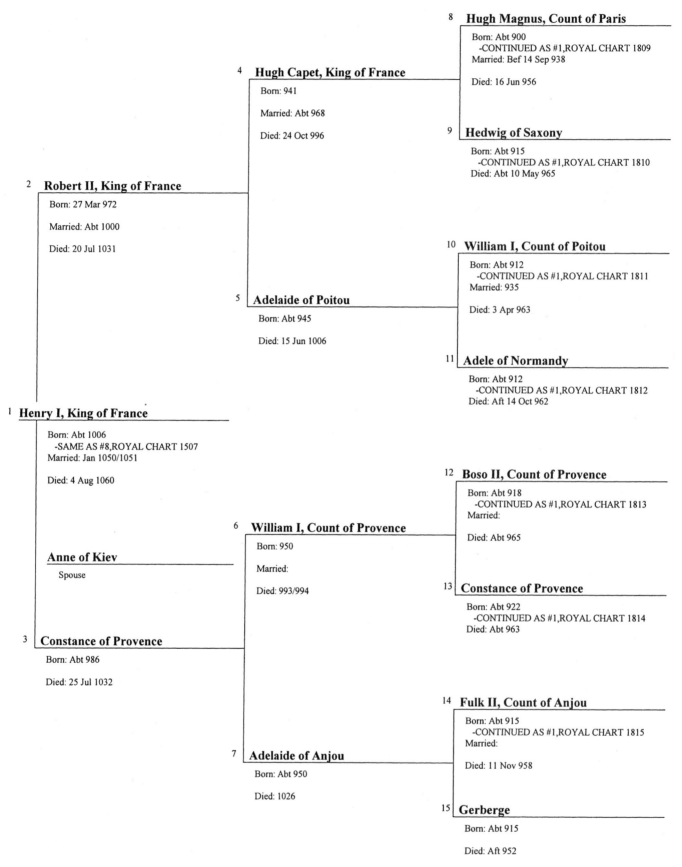

8 Hugh Magnus, Count of Paris

Born: Abt 900
-CONTINUED AS #1,ROYAL CHART 1809
Married: Bef 14 Sep 938

Died: 16 Jun 956

4 Hugh Capet, King of France

Born: 941

Married: Abt 968

Died: 24 Oct 996

9 Hedwig of Saxony

Born: Abt 915
-CONTINUED AS #1,ROYAL CHART 1810
Died: Abt 10 May 965

2 Robert II, King of France

Born: 27 Mar 972

Married: Abt 1000

Died: 20 Jul 1031

10 William I, Count of Poitou

Born: Abt 912
-CONTINUED AS #1,ROYAL CHART 1811
Married: 935

Died: 3 Apr 963

5 Adelaide of Poitou

Born: Abt 945

Died: 15 Jun 1006

11 Adele of Normandy

Born: Abt 912
-CONTINUED AS #1,ROYAL CHART 1812
Died: Aft 14 Oct 962

1 Henry I, King of France

Born: Abt 1006
-SAME AS #8,ROYAL CHART 1507
Married: Jan 1050/1051

Died: 4 Aug 1060

12 Boso II, Count of Provence

Born: Abt 918
-CONTINUED AS #1,ROYAL CHART 1813
Married:

Died: Abt 965

6 William I, Count of Provence

Born: 950

Married:

Died: 993/994

13 Constance of Provence

Born: Abt 922
-CONTINUED AS #1,ROYAL CHART 1814
Died: Abt 963

Anne of Kiev

Spouse

3 Constance of Provence

Born: Abt 986

Died: 25 Jul 1032

14 Fulk II, Count of Anjou

Born: Abt 915
-CONTINUED AS #1,ROYAL CHART 1815
Married:

Died: 11 Nov 958

7 Adelaide of Anjou

Born: Abt 950

Died: 1026

15 Gerberge

Born: Abt 915

Died: Aft 952

Sources include: *Royal Ancestors* 11412; *Ancestral Roots* 101, 141A; Stuart 134; Moriarty 51, 24.

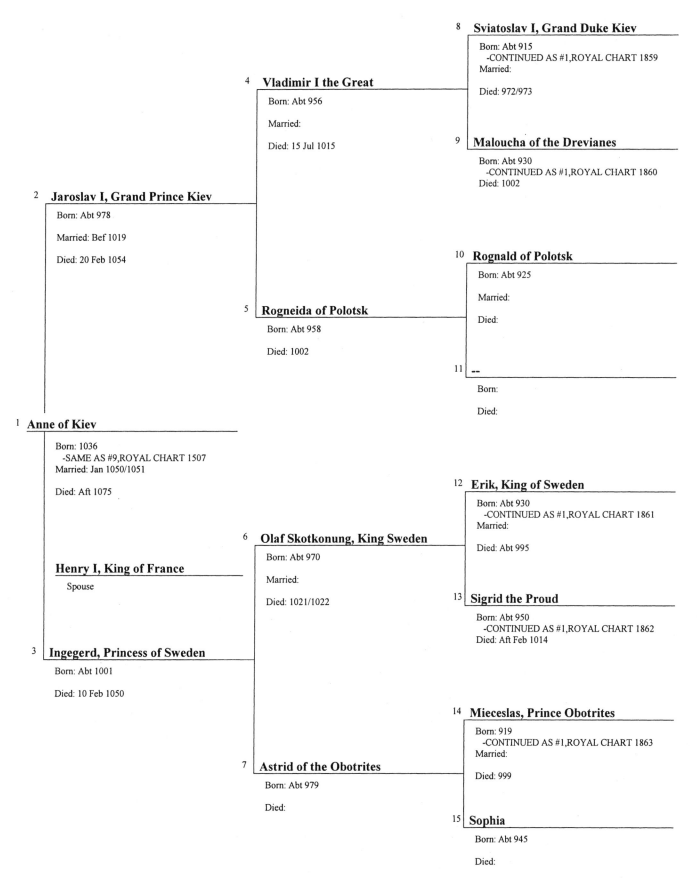

8 **Sviatoslav I, Grand Duke Kiev**

Born: Abt 915
    -CONTINUED AS #1,ROYAL CHART 1859
Married:

Died: 972/973

4 **Vladimir I the Great**

Born: Abt 956

Married:

Died: 15 Jul 1015

9 **Maloucha of the Drevianes**

Born: Abt 930
    -CONTINUED AS #1,ROYAL CHART 1860
Died: 1002

2 **Jaroslav I, Grand Prince Kiev**

Born: Abt 978

Married: Bef 1019

Died: 20 Feb 1054

10 **Rognald of Polotsk**

Born: Abt 925

Married:

Died:

5 **Rogneida of Polotsk**

Born: Abt 958

Died: 1002

11 **--**

Born:

Died:

1 **Anne of Kiev**

Born: 1036
    -SAME AS #9,ROYAL CHART 1507
Married: Jan 1050/1051

Died: Aft 1075

12 **Erik, King of Sweden**

Born: Abt 930
    -CONTINUED AS #1,ROYAL CHART 1861
Married:

Died: Abt 995

6 **Olaf Skotkonung, King Sweden**

Born: Abt 970

Married:

Died: 1021/1022

Henry I, King of France

Spouse

13 **Sigrid the Proud**

Born: Abt 950
    -CONTINUED AS #1,ROYAL CHART 1862
Died: Aft Feb 1014

3 **Ingegerd, Princess of Sweden**

Born: Abt 1001

Died: 10 Feb 1050

14 **Mieceslas, Prince Obotrites**

Born: 919
    -CONTINUED AS #1,ROYAL CHART 1863
Married:

Died: 999

7 **Astrid of the Obotrites**

Born: Abt 979

Died:

15 **Sophia**

Born: Abt 945

Died:

Sources include: *Royal Ancestors* (1989), charts 11425, 11412; *Ancestral Roots* 241; Stuart 143, 240; Moriarty 52-54, 221; LDS records.

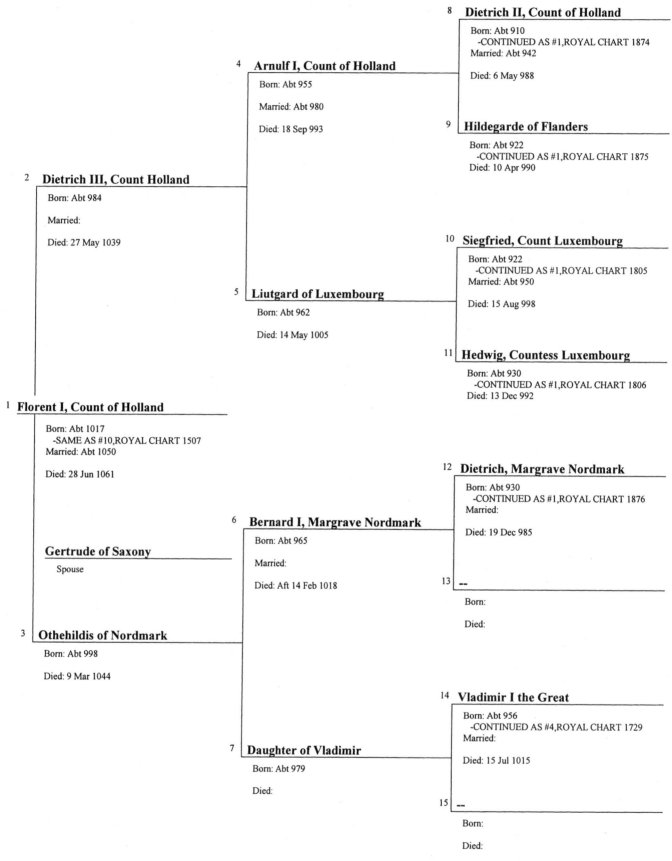

8 Dietrich II, Count of Holland

Born: Abt 910
-CONTINUED AS #1,ROYAL CHART 1874
Married: Abt 942

Died: 6 May 988

4 Arnulf I, Count of Holland

Born: Abt 955

Married: Abt 980

Died: 18 Sep 993

9 Hildegarde of Flanders

Born: Abt 922
-CONTINUED AS #1,ROYAL CHART 1875
Died: 10 Apr 990

2 Dietrich III, Count Holland

Born: Abt 984

Married:

Died: 27 May 1039

10 Siegfried, Count Luxembourg

Born: Abt 922
-CONTINUED AS #1,ROYAL CHART 1805
Married: Abt 950

Died: 15 Aug 998

5 Liutgard of Luxembourg

Born: Abt 962

Died: 14 May 1005

11 Hedwig, Countess Luxembourg

Born: Abt 930
-CONTINUED AS #1,ROYAL CHART 1806
Died: 13 Dec 992

1 Florent I, Count of Holland

Born: Abt 1017
-SAME AS #10,ROYAL CHART 1507
Married: Abt 1050

Died: 28 Jun 1061

12 Dietrich, Margrave Nordmark

Born: Abt 930
-CONTINUED AS #1,ROYAL CHART 1876
Married:

Died: 19 Dec 985

6 Bernard I, Margrave Nordmark

Born: Abt 965

Married:

Died: Aft 14 Feb 1018

13 --

Born:

Died:

Gertrude of Saxony

Spouse

3 Othehildis of Nordmark

Born: Abt 998

Died: 9 Mar 1044

14 Vladimir I the Great

Born: Abt 956
-CONTINUED AS #4,ROYAL CHART 1729
Married:

Died: 15 Jul 1015

7 Daughter of Vladimir

Born: Abt 979

Died:

15 --

Born:

Died:

Sources include: *Royal Ancestors* (1989), chart 11491; Stuart 311, 27; Faris preliminary Charlemagne manuscript (June 1995), pp. 157-158; Moriarty 55, 97-98. Note: #15 was Vladimir's 6th wife, a Bulgarian, name unknown.

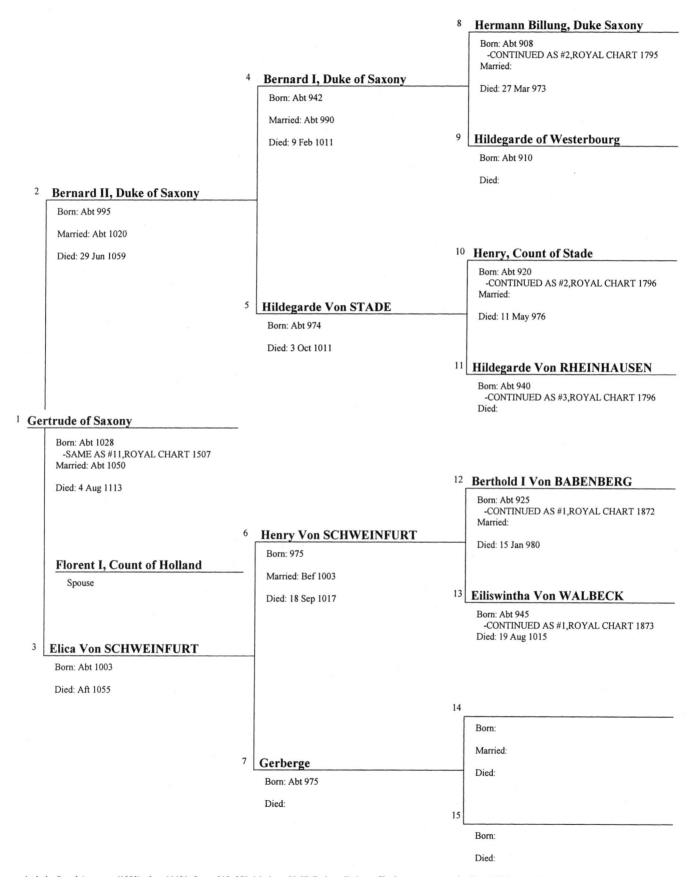

8 Hermann Billung, Duke Saxony

Born: Abt 908
-CONTINUED AS #2,ROYAL CHART 1795
Married:

Died: 27 Mar 973

4 Bernard I, Duke of Saxony

Born: Abt 942

Married: Abt 990

Died: 9 Feb 1011

9 Hildegarde of Westerbourg

Born: Abt 910

Died:

2 Bernard II, Duke of Saxony

Born: Abt 995

Married: Abt 1020

Died: 29 Jun 1059

10 Henry, Count of Stade

Born: Abt 920
-CONTINUED AS #2,ROYAL CHART 1796
Married:

Died: 11 May 976

5 Hildegarde Von STADE

Born: Abt 974

Died: 3 Oct 1011

11 Hildegarde Von RHEINHAUSEN

Born: Abt 940
-CONTINUED AS #3,ROYAL CHART 1796
Died:

1 Gertrude of Saxony

Born: Abt 1028
-SAME AS #11,ROYAL CHART 1507
Married: Abt 1050

Died: 4 Aug 1113

12 Berthold I Von BABENBERG

Born: Abt 925
-CONTINUED AS #1,ROYAL CHART 1872
Married:

Died: 15 Jan 980

6 Henry Von SCHWEINFURT

Born: 975

Married: Bef 1003

Died: 18 Sep 1017

13 Eiliswintha Von WALBECK

Born: Abt 945
-CONTINUED AS #1,ROYAL CHART 1873
Died: 19 Aug 1015

Florent I, Count of Holland

Spouse

3 Elica Von SCHWEINFURT

Born: Abt 1003

Died: Aft 1055

14

Born:

Married:

Died:

7 Gerberge

Born: Abt 975

Died:

15

Born:

Died:

Sources include: *Royal Ancestors* (1989), chart 11491; Stuart 312, 270; Moriarty 56-57; Faris preliminary Charlemagne manuscript (June 1995), pp. 158, 144-145, 285; *Ancestral Roots* 101-23. Note: Stuart and Moriarty disagree on the ancestry of #7 Gerberge. Faris presents both claims.

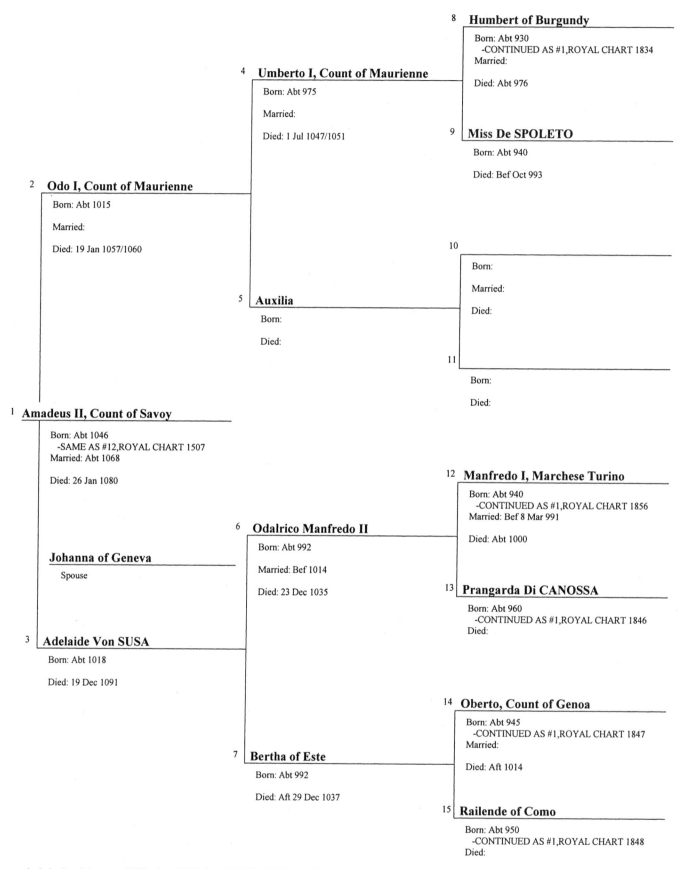

8 Humbert of Burgundy
Born: Abt 930
-CONTINUED AS #1,ROYAL CHART 1834
Married:
Died: Abt 976

4 Umberto I, Count of Maurienne
Born: Abt 975
Married:
Died: 1 Jul 1047/1051

9 Miss De SPOLETO
Born: Abt 940
Died: Bef Oct 993

2 Odo I, Count of Maurienne
Born: Abt 1015
Married:
Died: 19 Jan 1057/1060

10
Born:
Married:
Died:

5 Auxilia
Born:
Died:

11
Born:
Died:

1 Amadeus II, Count of Savoy
Born: Abt 1046
-SAME AS #12,ROYAL CHART 1507
Married: Abt 1068
Died: 26 Jan 1080

12 Manfredo I, Marchese Turino
Born: Abt 940
-CONTINUED AS #1,ROYAL CHART 1856
Married: Bef 8 Mar 991
Died: Abt 1000

6 Odalrico Manfredo II
Born: Abt 992
Married: Bef 1014
Died: 23 Dec 1035

Johanna of Geneva
Spouse

13 Prangarda Di CANOSSA
Born: Abt 960
-CONTINUED AS #1,ROYAL CHART 1846
Died:

3 Adelaide Von SUSA
Born: Abt 1018
Died: 19 Dec 1091

14 Oberto, Count of Genoa
Born: Abt 945
-CONTINUED AS #1,ROYAL CHART 1847
Married:
Died: Aft 1014

7 Bertha of Este
Born: Abt 992
Died: Aft 29 Dec 1037

15 Railende of Como
Born: Abt 950
-CONTINUED AS #1,ROYAL CHART 1848
Died:

Sources include: *Royal Ancestors* (1989), chart 11663; Stuart 93, 173, 315; Moriarty 59-62, 58 (discussion of #4 ancestry). Notes: The parentage of #5 Auxilia is disputed and uncertain. #9 is uncertain but may have been a daughter of Amadeo of Spoleto.

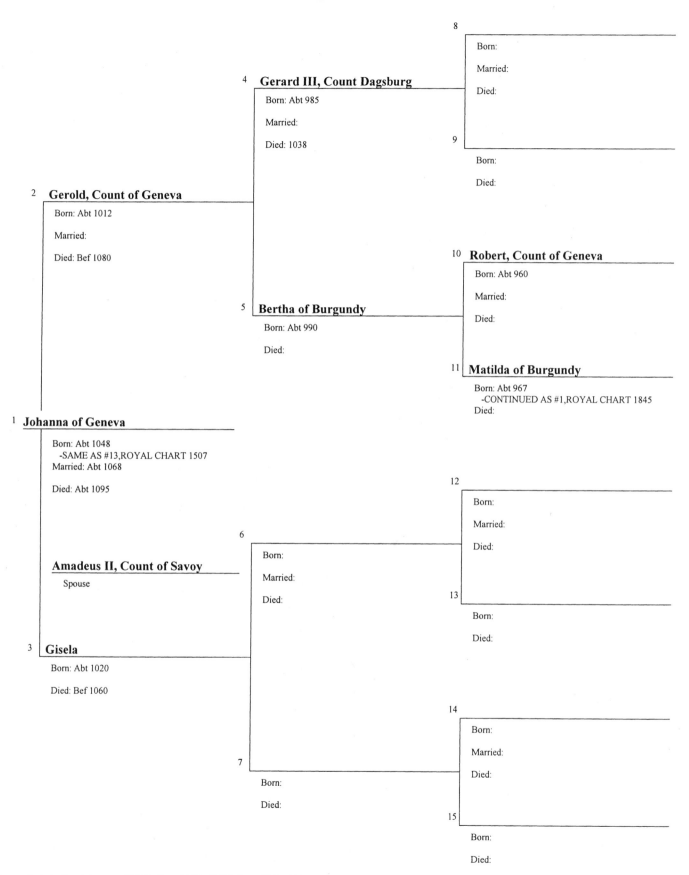

8

Born:

Married:

Died:

4 Gerard III, Count Dagsburg

Born: Abt 985

Married:

Died: 1038

9

Born:

Died:

2 Gerold, Count of Geneva

Born: Abt 1012

Married:

Died: Bef 1080

10 Robert, Count of Geneva

Born: Abt 960

Married:

Died:

5 Bertha of Burgundy

Born: Abt 990

Died:

11 Matilda of Burgundy

Born: Abt 967
   -CONTINUED AS #1, ROYAL CHART 1845
Died:

1 Johanna of Geneva

Born: Abt 1048
   -SAME AS #13, ROYAL CHART 1507
Married: Abt 1068

Died: Abt 1095

12

Born:

Married:

Died:

6

Born:

Married:

Died:

13

Born:

Died:

Amadeus II, Count of Savoy

Spouse

3 Gisela

Born: Abt 1020

Died: Bef 1060

14

Born:

Married:

Died:

7

Born:

Died:

15

Born:

Died:

Sources include: *Royal Ancestors* (1989), charts 11663, 11447; Stuart 93-31, 175; *Ancestral Roots* 8 (2004), Line 133 (#2 ancestry); *Ancestral Roots* 133 (#2 ancestry).

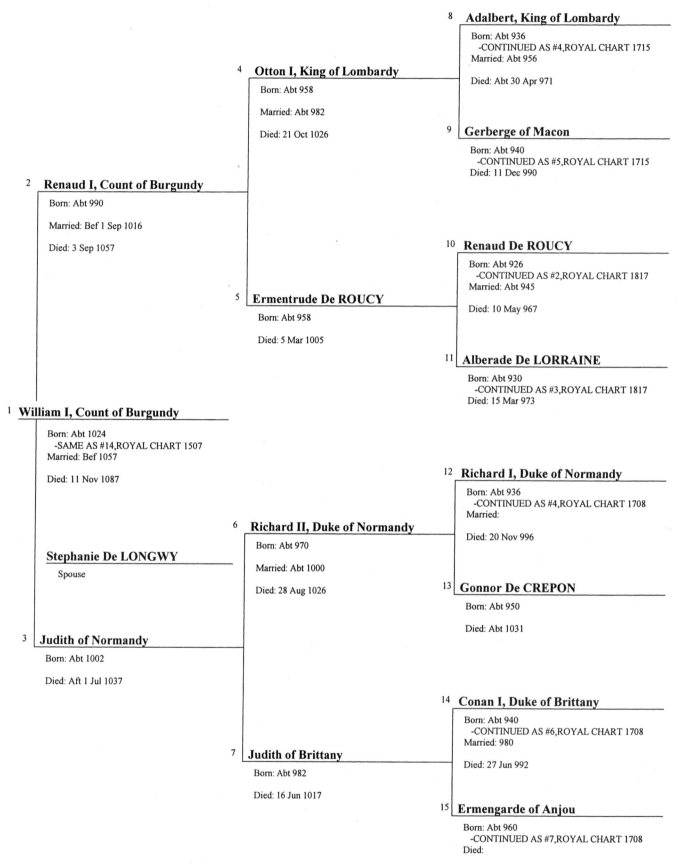

8 Adalbert, King of Lombardy

Born: Abt 936
  -CONTINUED AS #4,ROYAL CHART 1715
Married: Abt 956

Died: Abt 30 Apr 971

4 Otton I, King of Lombardy

Born: Abt 958

Married: Abt 982

Died: 21 Oct 1026

9 Gerberge of Macon

Born: Abt 940
  -CONTINUED AS #5,ROYAL CHART 1715
Died: 11 Dec 990

2 Renaud I, Count of Burgundy

Born: Abt 990

Married: Bef 1 Sep 1016

Died: 3 Sep 1057

10 Renaud De ROUCY

Born: Abt 926
  -CONTINUED AS #2,ROYAL CHART 1817
Married: Abt 945

Died: 10 May 967

5 Ermentrude De ROUCY

Born: Abt 958

Died: 5 Mar 1005

11 Alberade De LORRAINE

Born: Abt 930
  -CONTINUED AS #3,ROYAL CHART 1817
Died: 15 Mar 973

1 William I, Count of Burgundy

Born: Abt 1024
  -SAME AS #14,ROYAL CHART 1507
Married: Bef 1057

Died: 11 Nov 1087

12 Richard I, Duke of Normandy

Born: Abt 936
  -CONTINUED AS #4,ROYAL CHART 1708
Married:

Died: 20 Nov 996

6 Richard II, Duke of Normandy

Born: Abt 970

Married: Abt 1000

Died: 28 Aug 1026

13 Gonnor De CREPON

Born: Abt 950

Died: Abt 1031

Stephanie De LONGWY

Spouse

3 Judith of Normandy

Born: Abt 1002

Died: Aft 1 Jul 1037

14 Conan I, Duke of Brittany

Born: Abt 940
  -CONTINUED AS #6,ROYAL CHART 1708
Married: 980

Died: 27 Jun 992

7 Judith of Brittany

Born: Abt 982

Died: 16 Jun 1017

15 Ermengarde of Anjou

Born: Abt 960
  -CONTINUED AS #7,ROYAL CHART 1708
Died:

Sources include: *Royal Ancestors* (1989), chart 11418; Stuart 94; *Ancestral Roots* 144-22, 132; Moriarty 62, 37; Faris preliminary Charlemagne manuscript (June 1995), pp. 63-64, 208; *TAG* 72:187-204 (#12 ancestry). Note: #3 is also given as Aelis, Adalaide, or Alice (same parentage).

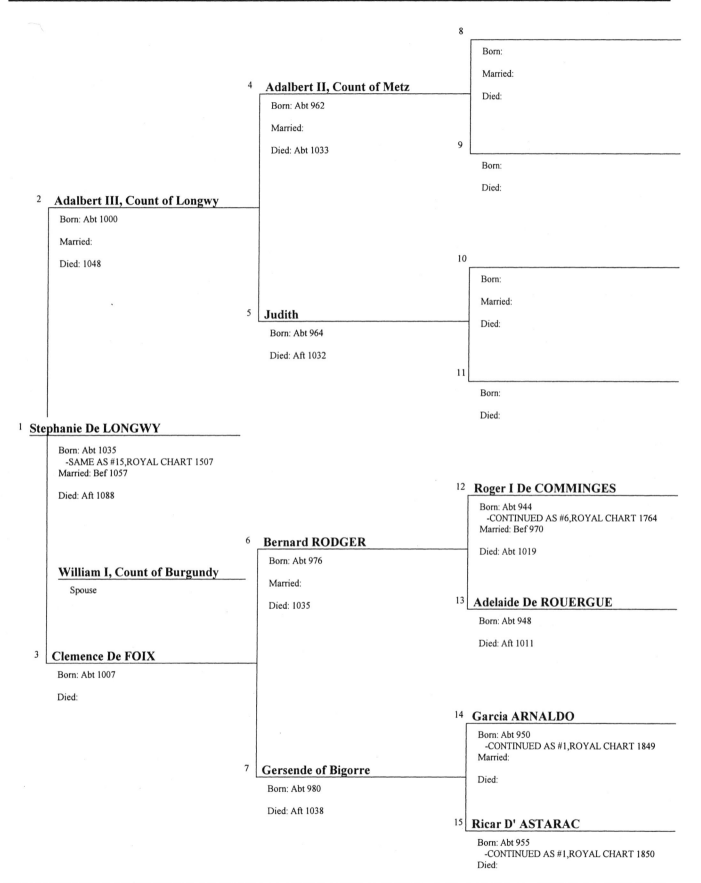

8

Born:

Married:

Died:

4 Adalbert II, Count of Metz

Born: Abt 962

Married:

Died: Abt 1033

9

Born:

Died:

2 Adalbert III, Count of Longwy

Born: Abt 1000

Married:

Died: 1048

10

Born:

Married:

Died:

5 Judith

Born: Abt 964

Died: Aft 1032

11

Born:

Died:

1 Stephanie De LONGWY

Born: Abt 1035
  -SAME AS #15,ROYAL CHART 1507
Married: Bef 1057

Died: Aft 1088

12 Roger I De COMMINGES

Born: Abt 944
  -CONTINUED AS #6,ROYAL CHART 1764
Married: Bef 970

Died: Abt 1019

6 Bernard RODGER

Born: Abt 976

Married:

Died: 1035

13 Adelaide De ROUERGUE

Born: Abt 948

Died: Aft 1011

William I, Count of Burgundy

Spouse

3 Clemence De FOIX

Born: Abt 1007

Died:

14 Garcia ARNALDO

Born: Abt 950
  -CONTINUED AS #1,ROYAL CHART 1849
Married:

Died:

7 Gersende of Bigorre

Born: Abt 980

Died: Aft 1038

15 Ricar D' ASTARAC

Born: Abt 955
  -CONTINUED AS #1,ROYAL CHART 1850
Died:

Sources include: Stuart 94-31, 105, 227; Faris preliminary Charlemagne manuscript (June 1995), pp. 64, 168; *Ancestral Roots* 144-22 & notes, 132-24; Moriarty 62 (#1), 129 (#2 ancestry), 69 (#6 ancestry), 80 (#7 ancestry); *Royal Ancestors* (1989), charts 11418 & notes, 11650 (#4 & 5); Turton 200 (#4 & 5 ancestry). Note: The parentage of #1 Stephanie has long been disputed and is not certain. The version shown above, argued by De Vajay, is accepted by Stuart and Faris. The parentage and ancestry of #4 & 5 Adalbert II & Judith is also disputed. Three different versions are given by Stuart, Moriarty and Turton, and a fourth version is suggested by Faris (p. 168 list).

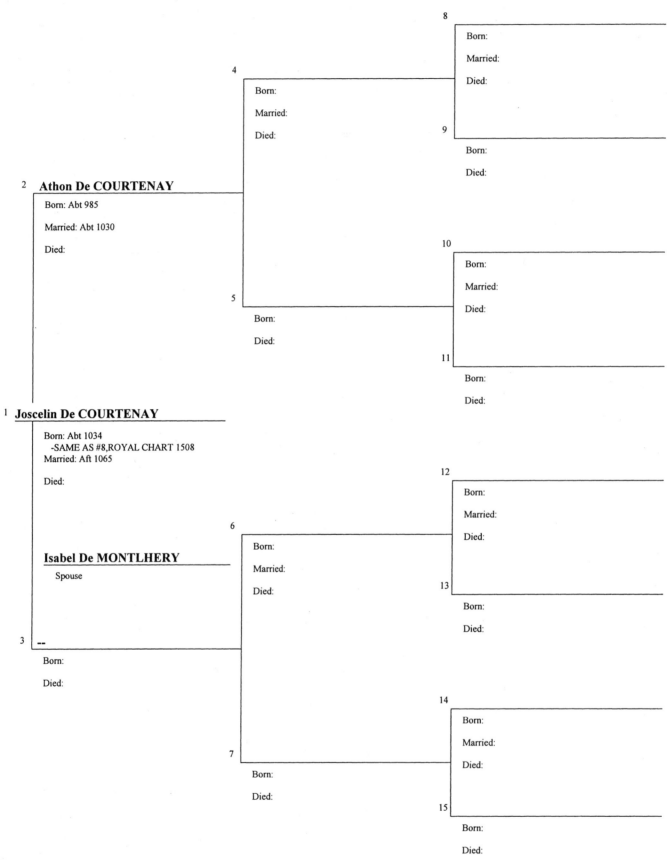

8

Born:

Married:

Died:

4

Born:

Married:

Died:

9

Born:

Died:

2 Athon De COURTENAY

Born: Abt 985

Married: Abt 1030

Died:

10

Born:

Married:

Died:

5

Born:

Died:

11

Born:

Died:

1 Joscelin De COURTENAY

Born: Abt 1034
  -SAME AS #8,ROYAL CHART 1508
Married: Aft 1065

Died:

12

Born:

Married:

Died:

6

Born:

Married:

Died:

13

Born:

Died:

Isabel De MONTLHERY

Spouse

3 --

Born:

Died:

14

Born:

Married:

Died:

7

Born:

Died:

15

Born:

Died:

Sources include: *Royal Ancestors* (1989), chart 11414; Stuart 241, 144; Moriarty 63; *Ancestral Roots* 107-23.

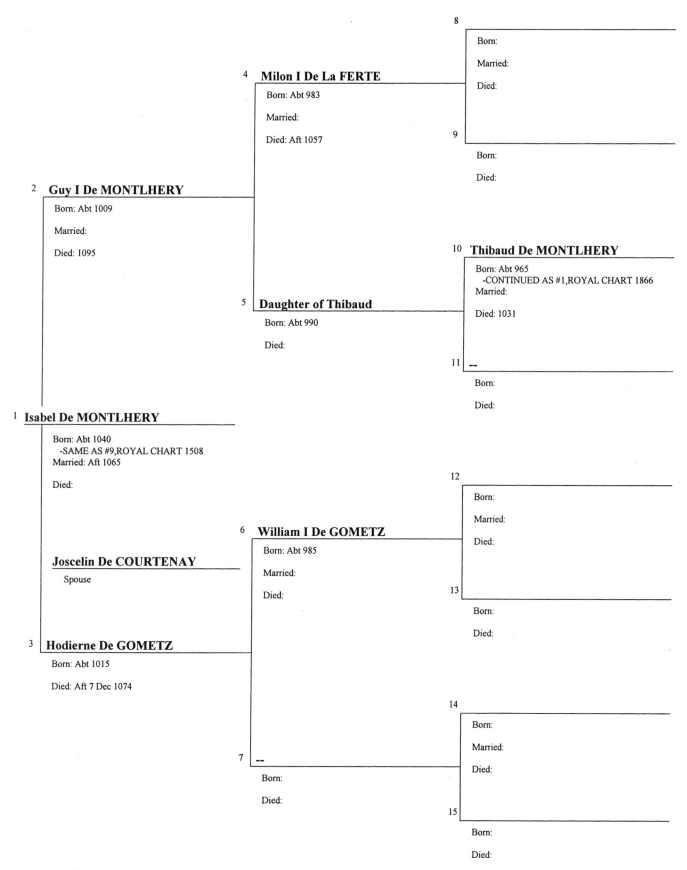

8

Born:

Married:

Died:

4 **Milon I De La FERTE**

Born: Abt 983

Married:

Died: Aft 1057

9

Born:

Died:

2 **Guy I De MONTLHERY**

Born: Abt 1009

Married:

Died: 1095

10 **Thibaud De MONTLHERY**

Born: Abt 965
  -CONTINUED AS #1,ROYAL CHART 1866
Married:

Died: 1031

5 **Daughter of Thibaud**

Born: Abt 990

Died:

11 --

Born:

Died:

1 **Isabel De MONTLHERY**

Born: Abt 1040
  -SAME AS #9,ROYAL CHART 1508
Married: Aft 1065

Died:

12

Born:

Married:

Died:

6 **William I De GOMETZ**

Born: Abt 985

Married:

Died:

13

Born:

Died:

Joscelin De COURTENAY

Spouse

3 **Hodierne De GOMETZ**

Born: Abt 1015

Died: Aft 7 Dec 1074

14

Born:

Married:

Died:

7 --

Born:

Died:

15

Born:

Died:

Sources include: *Royal Ancestors* (1989), chart 11414; Stuart 241; Moriarty 63, 265-266; *Ancestral Roots* 107-23.

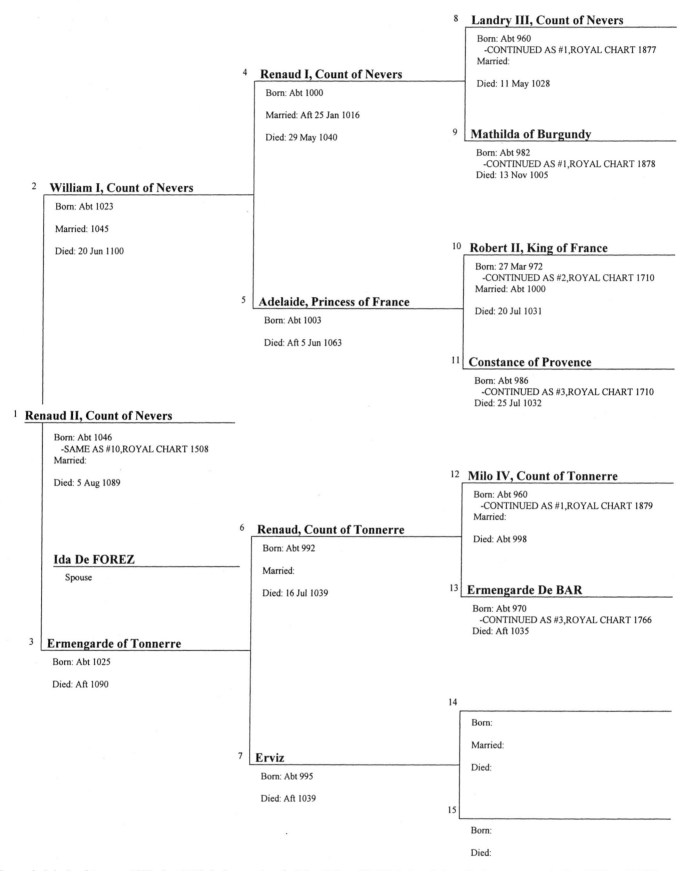

8 **Landry III, Count of Nevers**

Born: Abt 960
-CONTINUED AS #1,ROYAL CHART 1877
Married:

Died: 11 May 1028

4 **Renaud I, Count of Nevers**

Born: Abt 1000

Married: Aft 25 Jan 1016

Died: 29 May 1040

9 **Mathilda of Burgundy**

Born: Abt 982
-CONTINUED AS #1,ROYAL CHART 1878
Died: 13 Nov 1005

2 **William I, Count of Nevers**

Born: Abt 1023

Married: 1045

Died: 20 Jun 1100

10 **Robert II, King of France**

Born: 27 Mar 972
-CONTINUED AS #2,ROYAL CHART 1710
Married: Abt 1000

Died: 20 Jul 1031

5 **Adelaide, Princess of France**

Born: Abt 1003

Died: Aft 5 Jun 1063

11 **Constance of Provence**

Born: Abt 986
-CONTINUED AS #3,ROYAL CHART 1710
Died: 25 Jul 1032

1 **Renaud II, Count of Nevers**

Born: Abt 1046
-SAME AS #10,ROYAL CHART 1508
Married:

Died: 5 Aug 1089

12 **Milo IV, Count of Tonnerre**

Born: Abt 960
-CONTINUED AS #1,ROYAL CHART 1879
Married:

Died: Abt 998

6 **Renaud, Count of Tonnerre**

Born: Abt 992

Married:

Died: 16 Jul 1039

Ida De FOREZ

Spouse

13 **Ermengarde De BAR**

Born: Abt 970
-CONTINUED AS #3,ROYAL CHART 1766
Died: Aft 1035

3 **Ermengarde of Tonnerre**

Born: Abt 1025

Died: Aft 1090

14

Born:

Married:

Died:

7 **Erviz**

Born: Abt 995

Died: Aft 1039

15

Born:

Died:

Sources include: *Royal Ancestors* (1989), chart 11415, family group sheet for Robert II; Stuart 232, 254; Faris preliminary Charlemagne manuscript (June 1995), pp. 204-205; Schwennicke 3:716; *Ancestral Roots* 107; Moriarty 64. Notes: Moriarty gives #5 Adelaide as daughter of Hugh Capet. She is now accepted as daughter of Robert II and granddaughter of Hugh Capet. She should not be confused with a sister Adele who married Baldwin V (see chart 1710, #1).

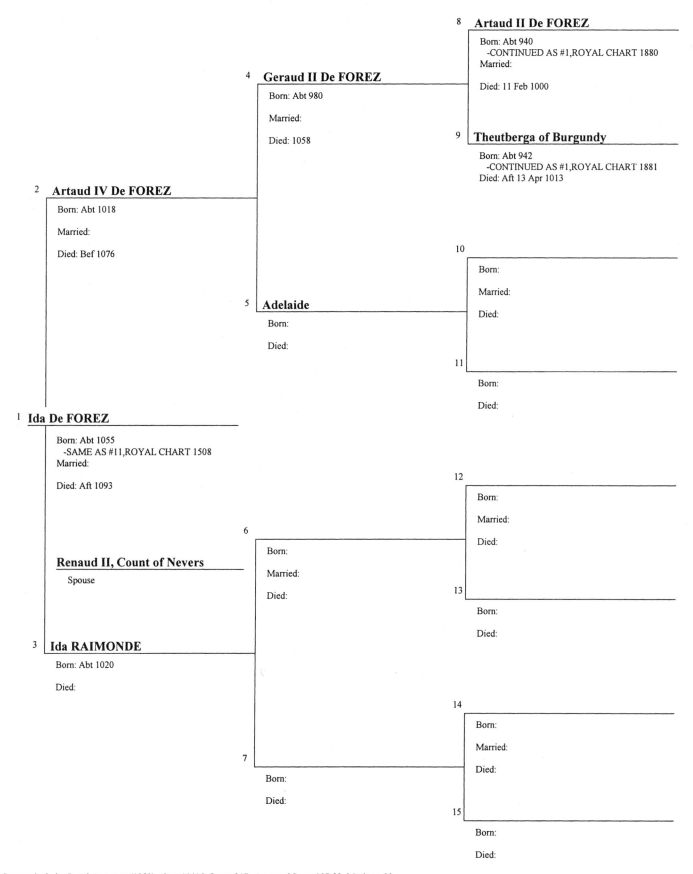

8 **Artaud II De FOREZ**

Born: Abt 940
 -CONTINUED AS #1,ROYAL CHART 1880
Married:

Died: 11 Feb 1000

4 **Geraud II De FOREZ**

Born: Abt 980

Married:

Died: 1058

9 **Theutberga of Burgundy**

Born: Abt 942
 -CONTINUED AS #1,ROYAL CHART 1881
Died: Aft 13 Apr 1013

2 **Artaud IV De FOREZ**

Born: Abt 1018

Married:

Died: Bef 1076

10

Born:

Married:

Died:

5 **Adelaide**

Born:

Died:

11

Born:

Died:

1 **Ida De FOREZ**

Born: Abt 1055
 -SAME AS #11,ROYAL CHART 1508
Married:

Died: Aft 1093

12

Born:

Married:

Died:

6

Born:

Married:

Died:

13

Born:

Died:

Renaud II, Count of Nevers

Spouse

3 **Ida RAIMONDE**

Born: Abt 1020

Died:

14

Born:

Married:

Died:

7

Born:

Died:

15

Born:

Died:

Sources include: *Royal Ancestors* (1989), chart 11415; Stuart 317; *Ancestral Roots* 107-22; Moriarty 66.

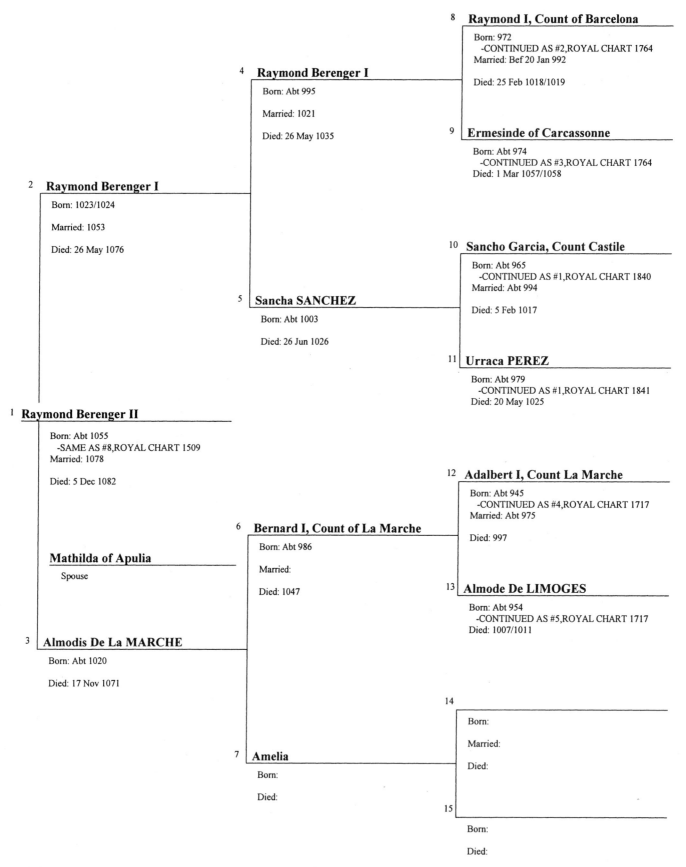

8 Raymond I, Count of Barcelona

Born: 972
 -CONTINUED AS #2,ROYAL CHART 1764
Married: Bef 20 Jan 992

Died: 25 Feb 1018/1019

4 Raymond Berenger I

Born: Abt 995

Married: 1021

Died: 26 May 1035

9 Ermesinde of Carcassonne

Born: Abt 974
 -CONTINUED AS #3,ROYAL CHART 1764
Died: 1 Mar 1057/1058

2 Raymond Berenger I

Born: 1023/1024

Married: 1053

Died: 26 May 1076

10 Sancho Garcia, Count Castile

Born: Abt 965
 -CONTINUED AS #1,ROYAL CHART 1840
Married: Abt 994

Died: 5 Feb 1017

5 Sancha SANCHEZ

Born: Abt 1003

Died: 26 Jun 1026

11 Urraca PEREZ

Born: Abt 979
 -CONTINUED AS #1,ROYAL CHART 1841
Died: 20 May 1025

1 Raymond Berenger II

Born: Abt 1055
 -SAME AS #8,ROYAL CHART 1509
Married: 1078

Died: 5 Dec 1082

12 Adalbert I, Count La Marche

Born: Abt 945
 -CONTINUED AS #4,ROYAL CHART 1717
Married: Abt 975

Died: 997

6 Bernard I, Count of La Marche

Born: Abt 986

Married:

Died: 1047

Mathilda of Apulia

Spouse

13 Almode De LIMOGES

Born: Abt 954
 -CONTINUED AS #5,ROYAL CHART 1717
Died: 1007/1011

3 Almodis De La MARCHE

Born: Abt 1020

Died: 17 Nov 1071

14

Born:

Married:

Died:

7 Amelia

Born:

Died:

15

Born:

Died:

Sources include: *Royal Ancestors* (1989), chart 11680; Stuart 54, 327; Moriarty 67, 42, 241, 245, 79. Note: The parentage of #7 Amelia is disputed.

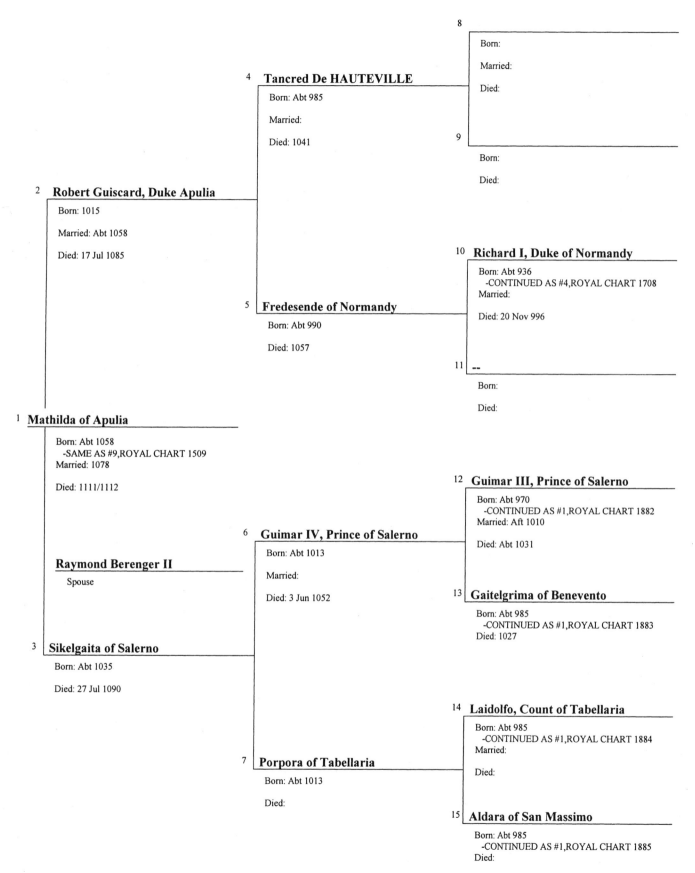

8

Born:

Married:

Died:

4 Tancred De HAUTEVILLE

Born: Abt 985

Married:

Died: 1041

9

Born:

Died:

2 Robert Guiscard, Duke Apulia

Born: 1015

Married: Abt 1058

Died: 17 Jul 1085

10 Richard I, Duke of Normandy

Born: Abt 936
-CONTINUED AS #4,ROYAL CHART 1708
Married:

Died: 20 Nov 996

5 Fredesende of Normandy

Born: Abt 990

Died: 1057

11 --

Born:

Died:

1 Mathilda of Apulia

Born: Abt 1058
-SAME AS #9,ROYAL CHART 1509
Married: 1078

Died: 1111/1112

12 Guimar III, Prince of Salerno

Born: Abt 970
-CONTINUED AS #1,ROYAL CHART 1882
Married: Aft 1010

Died: Abt 1031

6 Guimar IV, Prince of Salerno

Born: Abt 1013

Married:

Died: 3 Jun 1052

13 Gaitelgrima of Benevento

Born: Abt 985
-CONTINUED AS #1,ROYAL CHART 1883
Died: 1027

Raymond Berenger II

Spouse

3 Sikelgaita of Salerno

Born: Abt 1035

Died: 27 Jul 1090

14 Laidolfo, Count of Tabellaria

Born: Abt 985
-CONTINUED AS #1,ROYAL CHART 1884
Married:

Died:

7 Porpora of Tabellaria

Born: Abt 1013

Died:

15 Aldara of San Massimo

Born: Abt 985
-CONTINUED AS #1,ROYAL CHART 1885
Died:

Sources include: *Royal Ancestors* (1989), chart 11680; Stuart 296-297; *TAG* 52:23-26; 72:187-204 (#10 ancestry); Moriarty 67, 71-72. Note: #5 (2nd wife of Tancred) is not certain and may instead be Muriella (1st wife). #5 is also claimed as an illegitimate daughter of Richard II (chart 1708, #2). The Stuart version is followed above.

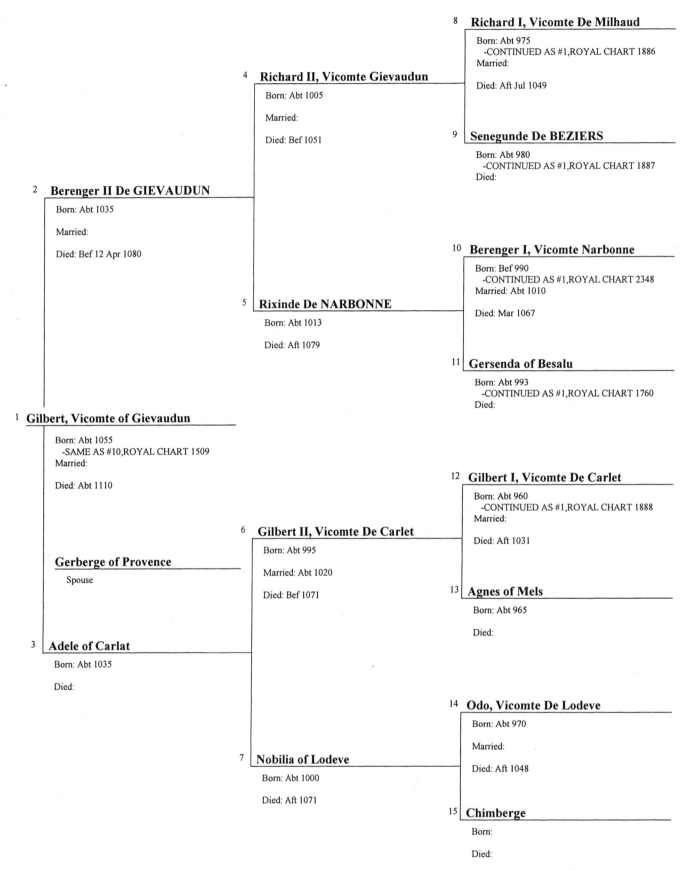

8 Richard I, Vicomte De Milhaud
Born: Abt 975
-CONTINUED AS #1,ROYAL CHART 1886
Married:

Died: Aft Jul 1049

4 Richard II, Vicomte Gievaudun
Born: Abt 1005

Married:

Died: Bef 1051

9 Senegunde De BEZIERS
Born: Abt 980
-CONTINUED AS #1,ROYAL CHART 1887
Died:

2 Berenger II De GIEVAUDUN
Born: Abt 1035

Married:

Died: Bef 12 Apr 1080

10 Berenger I, Vicomte Narbonne
Born: Bef 990
-CONTINUED AS #1,ROYAL CHART 2348
Married: Abt 1010

Died: Mar 1067

5 Rixinde De NARBONNE
Born: Abt 1013

Died: Aft 1079

11 Gersenda of Besalu
Born: Abt 993
-CONTINUED AS #1,ROYAL CHART 1760
Died:

1 Gilbert, Vicomte of Gievaudun
Born: Abt 1055
-SAME AS #10,ROYAL CHART 1509
Married:

Died: Abt 1110

12 Gilbert I, Vicomte De Carlet
Born: Abt 960
-CONTINUED AS #1,ROYAL CHART 1888
Married:

Died: Aft 1031

6 Gilbert II, Vicomte De Carlet
Born: Abt 995

Married: Abt 1020

Died: Bef 1071

13 Agnes of Mels
Born: Abt 965

Died:

Gerberge of Provence
Spouse

3 Adele of Carlat
Born: Abt 1035

Died:

14 Odo, Vicomte De Lodeve
Born: Abt 970

Married:

Died: Aft 1048

7 Nobilia of Lodeve
Born: Abt 1000

Died: Aft 1071

15 Chimberge
Born:

Died:

Sources include: *Royal Ancestors* (1989), chart 11666; Stuart 257, 226; Faris preliminary Charlemagne manuscript (June 1995), p. 46; Moriarty 75-76; Turton 218. Note: The parentage of #14 Odo (Odon) is uncertain. Moriarty gives Odo as <u>perhaps</u> son of Antgarius (Vicomte De Lodeve) & Gariberge. Turton gives Odo as son of Hildin and grandson of Antgarius & Gariberge, both of whose ancestry is unknown.

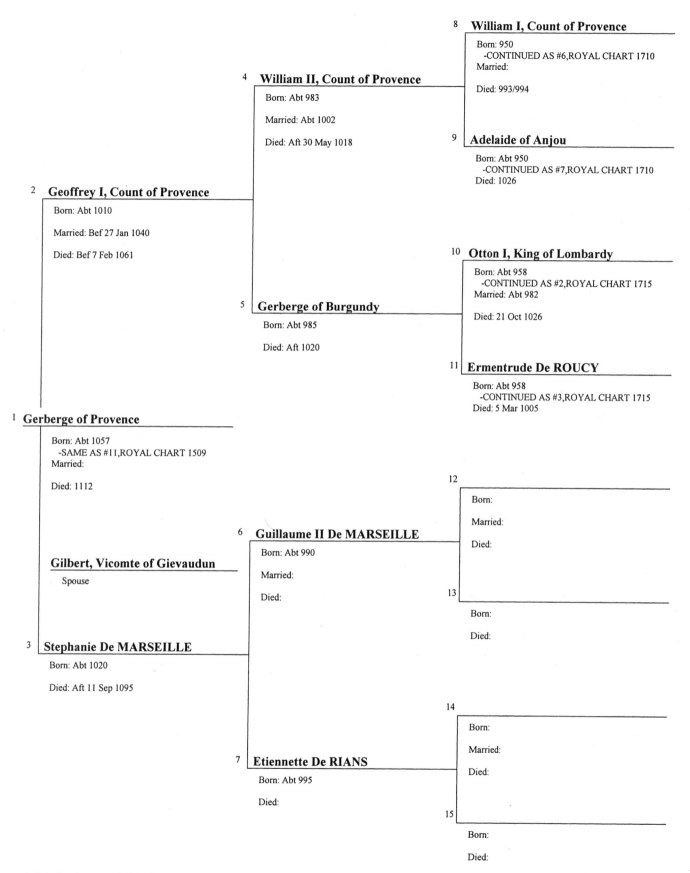

8 **William I, Count of Provence**

Born: 950
  -CONTINUED AS #6,ROYAL CHART 1710
Married:

Died: 993/994

4 **William II, Count of Provence**

Born: Abt 983

Married: Abt 1002

Died: Aft 30 May 1018

9 **Adelaide of Anjou**

Born: Abt 950
  -CONTINUED AS #7,ROYAL CHART 1710
Died: 1026

2 **Geoffrey I, Count of Provence**

Born: Abt 1010

Married: Bef 27 Jan 1040

Died: Bef 7 Feb 1061

10 **Otton I, King of Lombardy**

Born: Abt 958
  -CONTINUED AS #2,ROYAL CHART 1715
Married: Abt 982

Died: 21 Oct 1026

5 **Gerberge of Burgundy**

Born: Abt 985

Died: Aft 1020

11 **Ermentrude De ROUCY**

Born: Abt 958
  -CONTINUED AS #3,ROYAL CHART 1715
Died: 5 Mar 1005

1 **Gerberge of Provence**

Born: Abt 1057
  -SAME AS #11,ROYAL CHART 1509
Married:

Died: 1112

12

Born:

Married:

Died:

6 **Guillaume II De MARSEILLE**

Born: Abt 990

Married:

Died:

13

Born:

Died:

Gilbert, Vicomte of Gievaudun

Spouse

3 **Stephanie De MARSEILLE**

Born: Abt 1020

Died: Aft 11 Sep 1095

14

Born:

Married:

Died:

7 **Etiennette De RIANS**

Born: Abt 995

Died:

15

Born:

Died:

Sources include: *Royal Ancestors* (1989), chart 11666; Moriarty 77; Stuart 298; Faris preliminary Charlemagne manuscript (June 1995), pp. 46, 255-226; Turton 218. Note: Stuart claims #1 Gerberge as daughter of Fulk Bertrand (died about 27 Apr 1051), a brother of #2 Geoffrey. See chart 1755, #12 & 13.

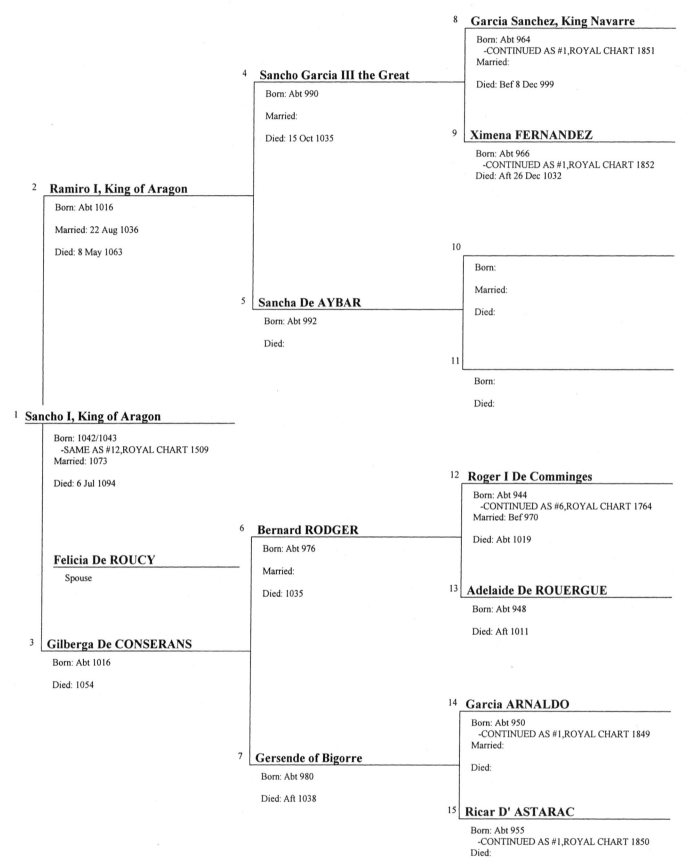

8 **Garcia Sanchez, King Navarre**

Born: Abt 964
-CONTINUED AS #1,ROYAL CHART 1851
Married:

Died: Bef 8 Dec 999

4 **Sancho Garcia III the Great**

Born: Abt 990

Married:

Died: 15 Oct 1035

9 **Ximena FERNANDEZ**

Born: Abt 966
-CONTINUED AS #1,ROYAL CHART 1852
Died: Aft 26 Dec 1032

2 **Ramiro I, King of Aragon**

Born: Abt 1016

Married: 22 Aug 1036

Died: 8 May 1063

10

Born:

Married:

Died:

5 **Sancha De AYBAR**

Born: Abt 992

Died:

11

Born:

Died:

1 **Sancho I, King of Aragon**

Born: 1042/1043
-SAME AS #12,ROYAL CHART 1509
Married: 1073

Died: 6 Jul 1094

12 **Roger I De Comminges**

Born: Abt 944
-CONTINUED AS #6,ROYAL CHART 1764
Married: Bef 970

Died: Abt 1019

6 **Bernard RODGER**

Born: Abt 976

Married:

Died: 1035

Felicia De ROUCY

Spouse

13 **Adelaide De ROUERGUE**

Born: Abt 948

Died: Aft 1011

3 **Gilberga De CONSERANS**

Born: Abt 1016

Died: 1054

14 **Garcia ARNALDO**

Born: Abt 950
-CONTINUED AS #1,ROYAL CHART 1849
Married:

Died:

7 **Gersende of Bigorre**

Born: Abt 980

Died: Aft 1038

15 **Ricar D' ASTARAC**

Born: Abt 955
-CONTINUED AS #1,ROYAL CHART 1850
Died:

Sources include: *Royal Ancestors* (1989), chart 11679; Stuart 95; Moriarty 78; *Ancestral Roots* 111-25 (#1 Sancho).

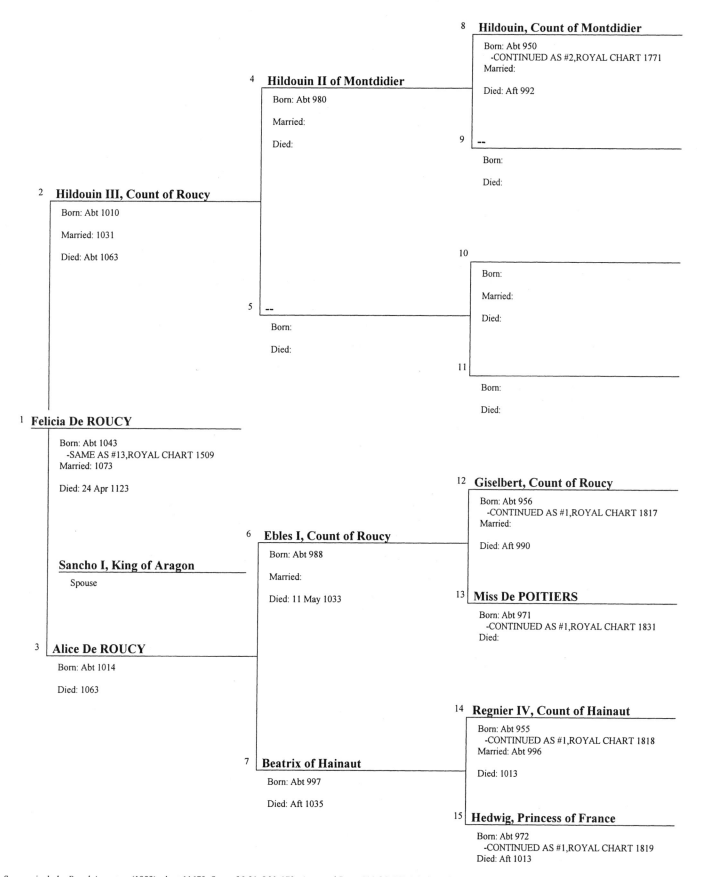

8 **Hildouin, Count of Montdidier**

Born: Abt 950
-CONTINUED AS #2,ROYAL CHART 1771
Married:

Died: Aft 992

4 **Hildouin II of Montdidier**

Born: Abt 980

Married:

Died:

9 **--**

Born:

Died:

2 **Hildouin III, Count of Roucy**

Born: Abt 1010

Married: 1031

Died: Abt 1063

10

Born:

Married:

Died:

5 **--**

Born:

Died:

11

Born:

Died:

1 **Felicia De ROUCY**

Born: Abt 1043
-SAME AS #13,ROYAL CHART 1509
Married: 1073

Died: 24 Apr 1123

12 **Giselbert, Count of Roucy**

Born: Abt 956
-CONTINUED AS #1,ROYAL CHART 1817
Married:

Died: Aft 990

6 **Ebles I, Count of Roucy**

Born: Abt 988

Married:

Died: 11 May 1033

13 **Miss De POITIERS**

Born: Abt 971
-CONTINUED AS #1,ROYAL CHART 1831
Died:

Sancho I, King of Aragon

Spouse

3 **Alice De ROUCY**

Born: Abt 1014

Died: 1063

14 **Regnier IV, Count of Hainaut**

Born: Abt 955
-CONTINUED AS #1,ROYAL CHART 1818
Married: Abt 996

Died: 1013

7 **Beatrix of Hainaut**

Born: Abt 997

Died: Aft 1035

15 **Hedwig, Princess of France**

Born: Abt 972
-CONTINUED AS #1,ROYAL CHART 1819
Died: Aft 1013

Sources include: *Royal Ancestors* (1989), chart 11679; Stuart 95-31, 266, 170; *Ancestral Roots* 111-25, 151; Moriarty 49.

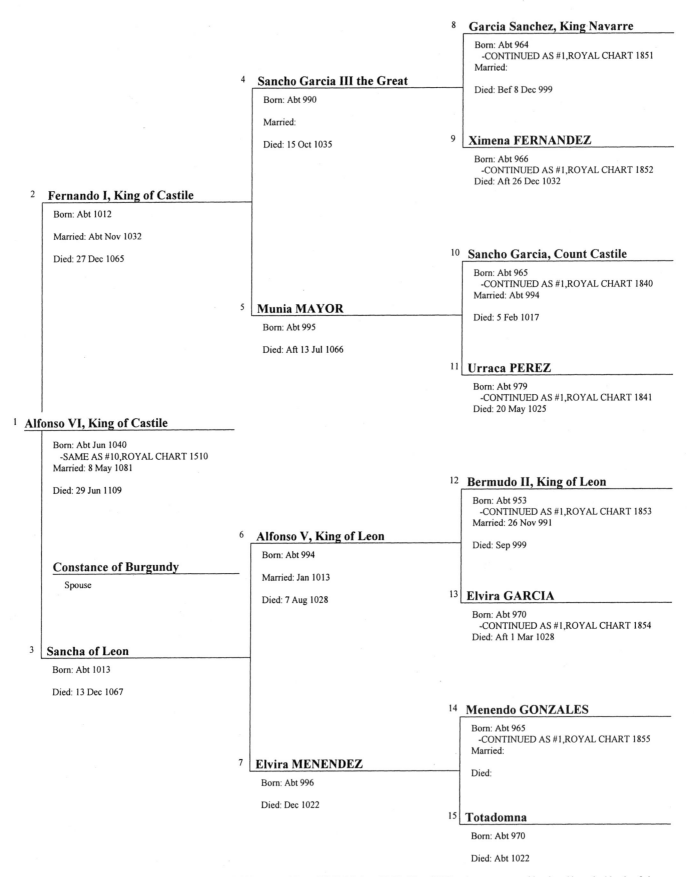

8 Garcia Sanchez, King Navarre
Born: Abt 964
  -CONTINUED AS #1,ROYAL CHART 1851
Married:

Died: Bef 8 Dec 999

4 Sancho Garcia III the Great
Born: Abt 990

Married:

Died: 15 Oct 1035

9 Ximena FERNANDEZ
Born: Abt 966
  -CONTINUED AS #1,ROYAL CHART 1852
Died: Aft 26 Dec 1032

2 Fernando I, King of Castile
Born: Abt 1012

Married: Abt Nov 1032

Died: 27 Dec 1065

10 Sancho Garcia, Count Castile
Born: Abt 965
  -CONTINUED AS #1,ROYAL CHART 1840
Married: Abt 994

Died: 5 Feb 1017

5 Munia MAYOR
Born: Abt 995

Died: Aft 13 Jul 1066

11 Urraca PEREZ
Born: Abt 979
  -CONTINUED AS #1,ROYAL CHART 1841
Died: 20 May 1025

1 Alfonso VI, King of Castile
Born: Abt Jun 1040
  -SAME AS #10,ROYAL CHART 1510
Married: 8 May 1081

Died: 29 Jun 1109

12 Bermudo II, King of Leon
Born: Abt 953
  -CONTINUED AS #1,ROYAL CHART 1853
Married: 26 Nov 991

Died: Sep 999

6 Alfonso V, King of Leon
Born: Abt 994

Married: Jan 1013

Died: 7 Aug 1028

Constance of Burgundy
Spouse

13 Elvira GARCIA
Born: Abt 970
  -CONTINUED AS #1,ROYAL CHART 1854
Died: Aft 1 Mar 1028

3 Sancha of Leon
Born: Abt 1013

Died: 13 Dec 1067

14 Menendo GONZALES
Born: Abt 965
  -CONTINUED AS #1,ROYAL CHART 1855
Married:

Died:

7 Elvira MENENDEZ
Born: Abt 996

Died: Dec 1022

15 Totadomna
Born: Abt 970

Died: Abt 1022

Sources include: *Royal Ancestors* (1989), chart 11419; Stuart 248, 276; *Ancestral Roots* 113-23; Moriarty 82, 78. Note: #15 Totadomna was granddaughter (through either her father or mother, names unknown) of Froila Gutierrez, son of Gutierre Menendez & Ilduara Eriz (see chart 1855, #14 & 15).

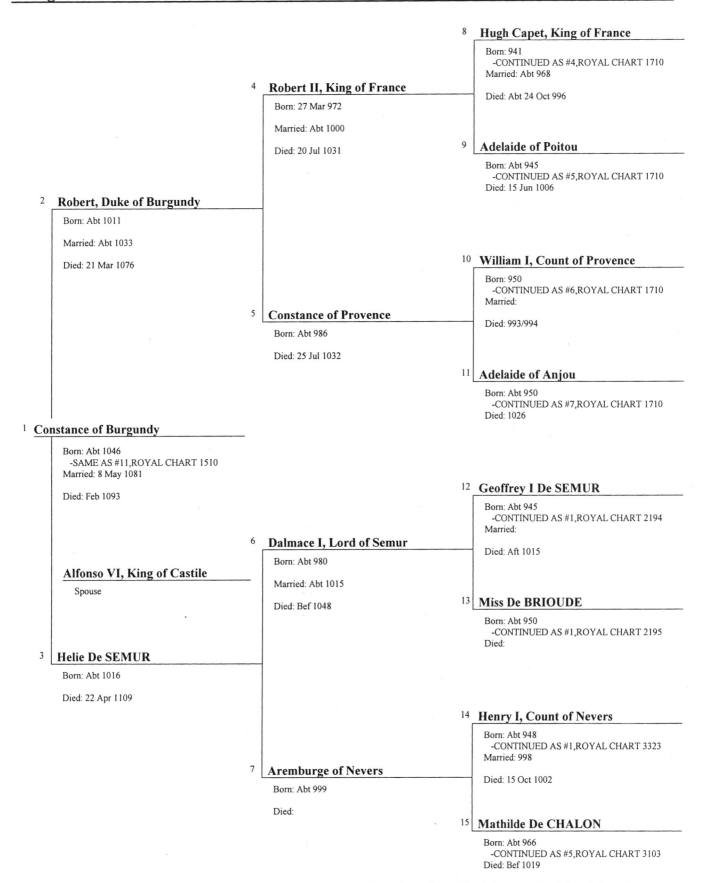

8 **Hugh Capet, King of France**
Born: 941
  -CONTINUED AS #4,ROYAL CHART 1710
Married: Abt 968

Died: Abt 24 Oct 996

4 **Robert II, King of France**
Born: 27 Mar 972

Married: Abt 1000

Died: 20 Jul 1031

9 **Adelaide of Poitou**
Born: Abt 945
  -CONTINUED AS #5,ROYAL CHART 1710
Died: 15 Jun 1006

2 **Robert, Duke of Burgundy**
Born: Abt 1011

Married: Abt 1033

Died: 21 Mar 1076

10 **William I, Count of Provence**
Born: 950
  -CONTINUED AS #6,ROYAL CHART 1710
Married:

Died: 993/994

5 **Constance of Provence**
Born: Abt 986

Died: 25 Jul 1032

11 **Adelaide of Anjou**
Born: Abt 950
  -CONTINUED AS #7,ROYAL CHART 1710
Died: 1026

1 **Constance of Burgundy**
Born: Abt 1046
  -SAME AS #11,ROYAL CHART 1510
Married: 8 May 1081

Died: Feb 1093

12 **Geoffrey I De SEMUR**
Born: Abt 945
  -CONTINUED AS #1,ROYAL CHART 2194
Married:

Died: Aft 1015

6 **Dalmace I, Lord of Semur**
Born: Abt 980

Married: Abt 1015

Died: Bef 1048

13 **Miss De BRIOUDE**
Born: Abt 950
  -CONTINUED AS #1,ROYAL CHART 2195
Died:

Alfonso VI, King of Castile
Spouse

3 **Helie De SEMUR**
Born: Abt 1016

Died: 22 Apr 1109

14 **Henry I, Count of Nevers**
Born: Abt 948
  -CONTINUED AS #1,ROYAL CHART 3323
Married: 998

Died: 15 Oct 1002

7 **Aremburge of Nevers**
Born: Abt 999

Died:

15 **Mathilde De CHALON**
Born: Abt 966
  -CONTINUED AS #5,ROYAL CHART 3103
Died: Bef 1019

Sources include: *Royal Ancestors* (1989), charts 11419, 11408; Stuart 155, 154, 134, 333, 85, 348-36 (contradicts 85-33); Moriarty 40-41, 24; Faris preliminary Charlemagne manuscript (June 1995), pp. 99, 80, 249-250; *Ancestral Roots* 8 (2004), Lines 113, 108; Schwennicke 3:433-434, 2:11 (#3 ancestry). Notes: The parentage of both #6 & 7 is disputed. #6 Dalmace is also claimed as the son of Geoffrey II & Mathilde (see cht. 3103, #4 & 5) and grandson of #12 & 13 above. Stuart 85-32 cites the 1987 work of Constance B. Bouchard (Sword, Miter and Cloister pp. 356-361), saying that the ancestry of #7 Aremburge is unknown.

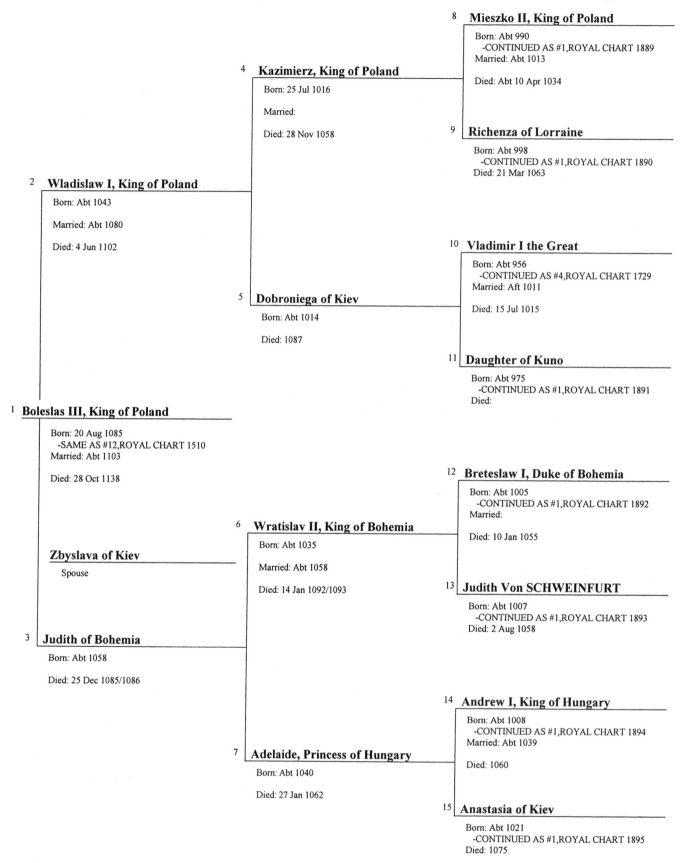

8 Mieszko II, King of Poland
Born: Abt 990
-CONTINUED AS #1,ROYAL CHART 1889
Married: Abt 1013

Died: Abt 10 Apr 1034

4 Kazimierz, King of Poland
Born: 25 Jul 1016

Married:

Died: 28 Nov 1058

9 Richenza of Lorraine
Born: Abt 998
-CONTINUED AS #1,ROYAL CHART 1890
Died: 21 Mar 1063

2 Wladislaw I, King of Poland
Born: Abt 1043

Married: Abt 1080

Died: 4 Jun 1102

10 Vladimir I the Great
Born: Abt 956
-CONTINUED AS #4,ROYAL CHART 1729
Married: Aft 1011

Died: 15 Jul 1015

5 Dobroniega of Kiev
Born: Abt 1014

Died: 1087

11 Daughter of Kuno
Born: Abt 975
-CONTINUED AS #1,ROYAL CHART 1891
Died:

1 Boleslas III, King of Poland
Born: 20 Aug 1085
-SAME AS #12,ROYAL CHART 1510
Married: Abt 1103

Died: 28 Oct 1138

12 Breteslaw I, Duke of Bohemia
Born: Abt 1005
-CONTINUED AS #1,ROYAL CHART 1892
Married:

Died: 10 Jan 1055

6 Wratislav II, King of Bohemia
Born: Abt 1035

Married: Abt 1058

Died: 14 Jan 1092/1093

13 Judith Von SCHWEINFURT
Born: Abt 1007
-CONTINUED AS #1,ROYAL CHART 1893
Died: 2 Aug 1058

Zbyslava of Kiev
Spouse

3 Judith of Bohemia
Born: Abt 1058

Died: 25 Dec 1085/1086

14 Andrew I, King of Hungary
Born: Abt 1008
-CONTINUED AS #1,ROYAL CHART 1894
Married: Abt 1039

Died: 1060

7 Adelaide, Princess of Hungary
Born: Abt 1040

Died: 27 Jan 1062

15 Anastasia of Kiev
Born: Abt 1021
-CONTINUED AS #1,ROYAL CHART 1895
Died: 1075

Sources include: *Royal Ancestors* (1989), chart 11499; *Ancestral Roots* 147, 244; Stuart 378, 362; Moriarty 84-85.

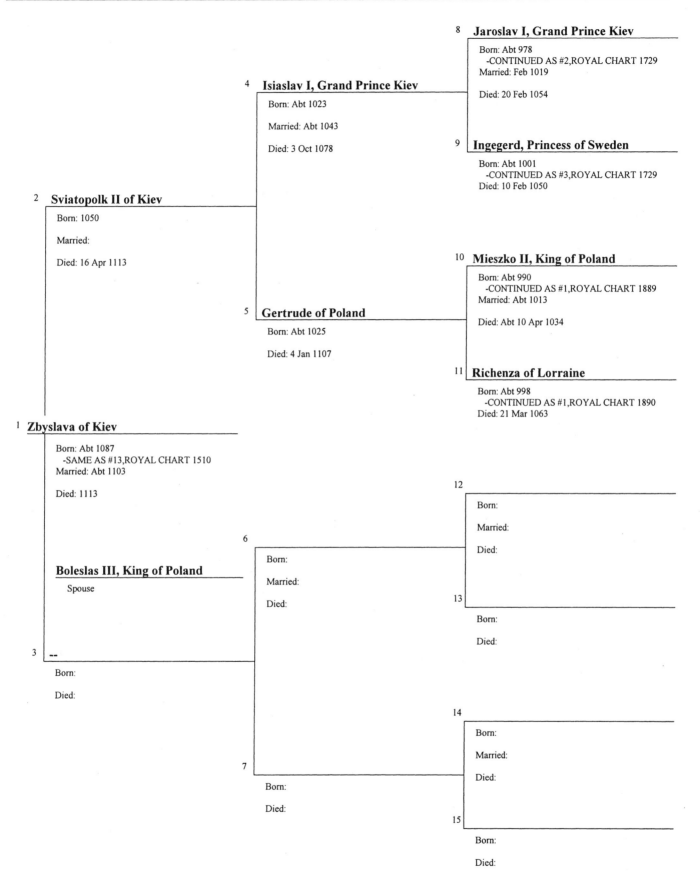

8 Jaroslav I, Grand Prince Kiev

Born: Abt 978
-CONTINUED AS #2,ROYAL CHART 1729
Married: Feb 1019

Died: 20 Feb 1054

4 Isiaslav I, Grand Prince Kiev

Born: Abt 1023

Married: Abt 1043

Died: 3 Oct 1078

9 Ingegerd, Princess of Sweden

Born: Abt 1001
-CONTINUED AS #3,ROYAL CHART 1729
Died: 10 Feb 1050

2 Sviatopolk II of Kiev

Born: 1050

Married:

Died: 16 Apr 1113

10 Mieszko II, King of Poland

Born: Abt 990
-CONTINUED AS #1,ROYAL CHART 1889
Married: Abt 1013

Died: Abt 10 Apr 1034

5 Gertrude of Poland

Born: Abt 1025

Died: 4 Jan 1107

11 Richenza of Lorraine

Born: Abt 998
-CONTINUED AS #1,ROYAL CHART 1890
Died: 21 Mar 1063

1 Zbyslava of Kiev

Born: Abt 1087
-SAME AS #13,ROYAL CHART 1510
Married: Abt 1103

Died: 1113

12

Born:

Married:

Died:

6

Born:

Married:

Died:

13

Born:

Died:

Boleslas III, King of Poland

Spouse

3 --

Born:

Died:

14

Born:

Married:

Died:

7

Born:

Died:

15

Born:

Died:

Sources include: *Royal Ancestors* (1989), chart 11499; *Ancestral Roots* 241; Stuart 363; Moriarty 87.

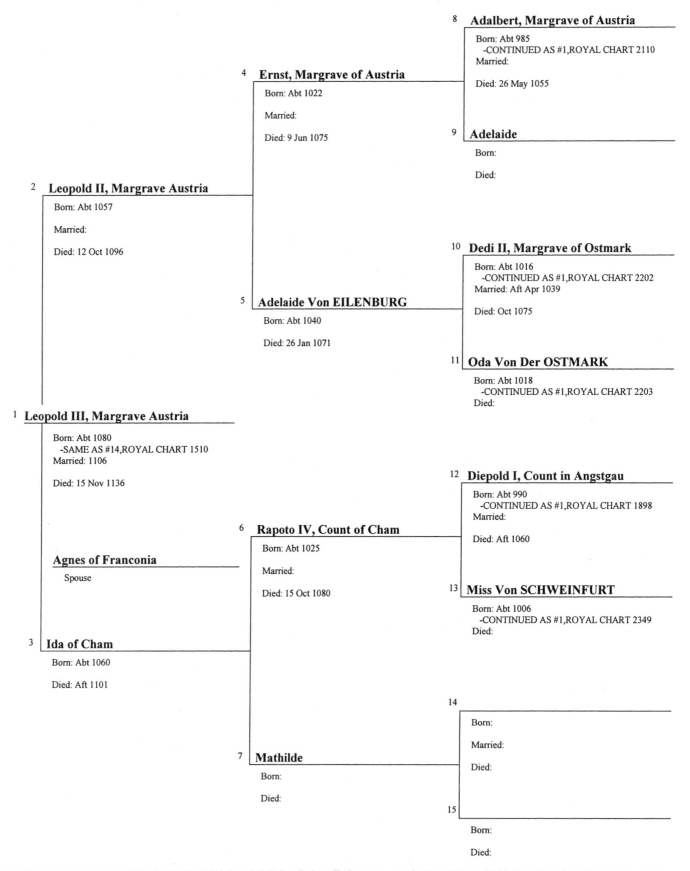

8 Adalbert, Margrave of Austria

Born: Abt 985
   -CONTINUED AS #1,ROYAL CHART 2110
Married:

Died: 26 May 1055

4 Ernst, Margrave of Austria

Born: Abt 1022

Married:

Died: 9 Jun 1075

9 Adelaide

Born:

Died:

2 Leopold II, Margrave Austria

Born: Abt 1057

Married:

Died: 12 Oct 1096

10 Dedi II, Margrave of Ostmark

Born: Abt 1016
   -CONTINUED AS #1,ROYAL CHART 2202
Married: Aft Apr 1039

Died: Oct 1075

5 Adelaide Von EILENBURG

Born: Abt 1040

Died: 26 Jan 1071

11 Oda Von Der OSTMARK

Born: Abt 1018
   -CONTINUED AS #1,ROYAL CHART 2203
Died:

1 Leopold III, Margrave Austria

Born: Abt 1080
   -SAME AS #14,ROYAL CHART 1510
Married: 1106

Died: 15 Nov 1136

12 Diepold I, Count in Angstgau

Born: Abt 990
   -CONTINUED AS #1,ROYAL CHART 1898
Married:

Died: Aft 1060

6 Rapoto IV, Count of Cham

Born: Abt 1025

Married:

Died: 15 Oct 1080

Agnes of Franconia

Spouse

13 Miss Von SCHWEINFURT

Born: Abt 1006
   -CONTINUED AS #1,ROYAL CHART 2349
Died:

3 Ida of Cham

Born: Abt 1060

Died: Aft 1101

14

Born:

Married:

Died:

7 Mathilde

Born:

Died:

15

Born:

Died:

Sources include: *Royal Ancestors* (1989), charts 11499, 11830; Stuart 279; Faris preliminary Charlemagne manuscript (June 1995), pp. 27-28, 101-102; Moriarty 90, 95-96; *Ancestral Roots* 147-26. Notes: #5 Adelaide might be the sister instead of the daughter of #10 Dedi. Moriarty considered this alternate claim and opted for the version charted above, but it is very tight chronologically. The claim by Stuart that #7 (wife of Rapoto) was a daughter of Hermann I, Count of Castile, is unacceptable chronologically. He was born about 1036-38. Faris gives #7 as Mathilde (perhaps Von Wels-Lambach).

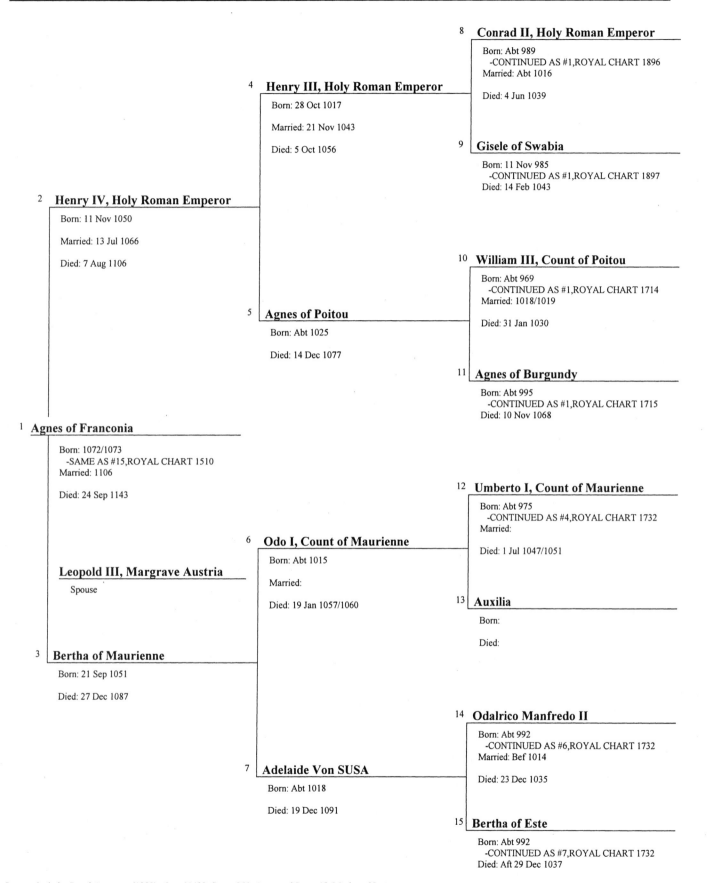

8 **Conrad II, Holy Roman Emperor**

Born: Abt 989
-CONTINUED AS #1,ROYAL CHART 1896
Married: Abt 1016

Died: 4 Jun 1039

4 **Henry III, Holy Roman Emperor**

Born: 28 Oct 1017

Married: 21 Nov 1043

Died: 5 Oct 1056

9 **Gisele of Swabia**

Born: 11 Nov 985
-CONTINUED AS #1,ROYAL CHART 1897
Died: 14 Feb 1043

2 **Henry IV, Holy Roman Emperor**

Born: 11 Nov 1050

Married: 13 Jul 1066

Died: 7 Aug 1106

10 **William III, Count of Poitou**

Born: Abt 969
-CONTINUED AS #1,ROYAL CHART 1714
Married: 1018/1019

Died: 31 Jan 1030

5 **Agnes of Poitou**

Born: Abt 1025

Died: 14 Dec 1077

11 **Agnes of Burgundy**

Born: Abt 995
-CONTINUED AS #1,ROYAL CHART 1715
Died: 10 Nov 1068

1 **Agnes of Franconia**

Born: 1072/1073
-SAME AS #15,ROYAL CHART 1510
Married: 1106

Died: 24 Sep 1143

12 **Umberto I, Count of Maurienne**

Born: Abt 975
-CONTINUED AS #4,ROYAL CHART 1732
Married:

Died: 1 Jul 1047/1051

6 **Odo I, Count of Maurienne**

Born: Abt 1015

Married:

Died: 19 Jan 1057/1060

Leopold III, Margrave Austria

Spouse

13 **Auxilia**

Born:

Died:

3 **Bertha of Maurienne**

Born: 21 Sep 1051

Died: 27 Dec 1087

14 **Odalrico Manfredo II**

Born: Abt 992
-CONTINUED AS #6,ROYAL CHART 1732
Married: Bef 1014

Died: 23 Dec 1035

7 **Adelaide Von SUSA**

Born: Abt 1018

Died: 19 Dec 1091

15 **Bertha of Este**

Born: Abt 992
-CONTINUED AS #7,ROYAL CHART 1732
Died: Aft 29 Dec 1037

Sources include: *Royal Ancestors* (1989), chart 11499; Stuart 359; *Ancestral Roots* 45; Moriarty 92.

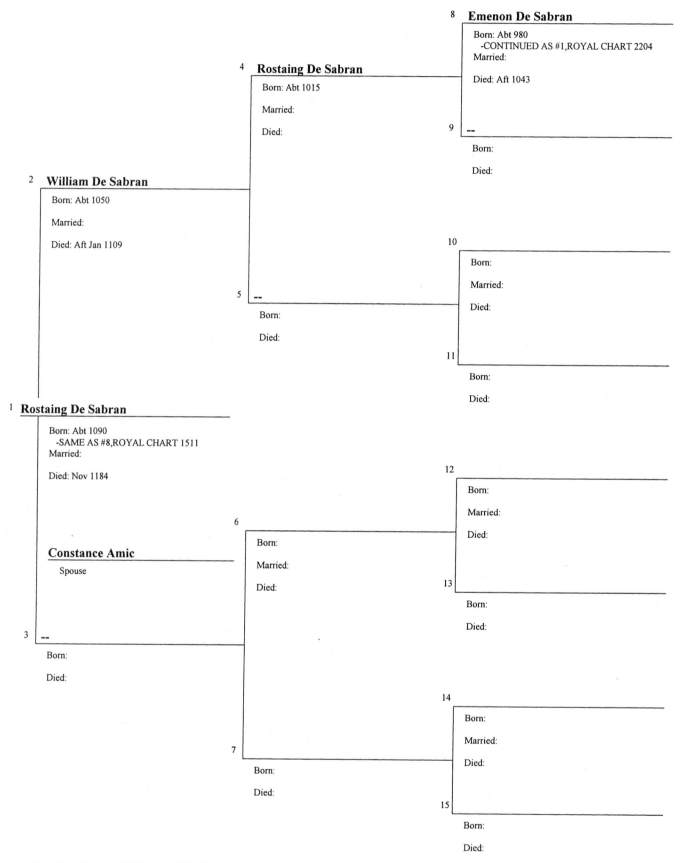

8

Emenon De Sabran

Born: Abt 980
-CONTINUED AS #1, ROYAL CHART 2204
Married:

Died: Aft 1043

4

Rostaing De Sabran

Born: Abt 1015

Married:

Died:

9

--

Born:

Died:

2

William De Sabran

Born: Abt 1050

Married:

Died: Aft Jan 1109

10

Born:

Married:

Died:

5

--

Born:

Died:

11

Born:

Died:

1

Rostaing De Sabran

Born: Abt 1090
-SAME AS #8, ROYAL CHART 1511
Married:

Died: Nov 1184

12

Born:

Married:

Died:

6

Born:

Married:

Died:

Constance Amic

Spouse

13

Born:

Died:

3

--

Born:

Died:

14

Born:

Married:

Died:

7

Born:

Died:

15

Born:

Died:

Sources include: *Royal Ancestors* (1989), chart 11841; Moriarty 98; Stuart 116.

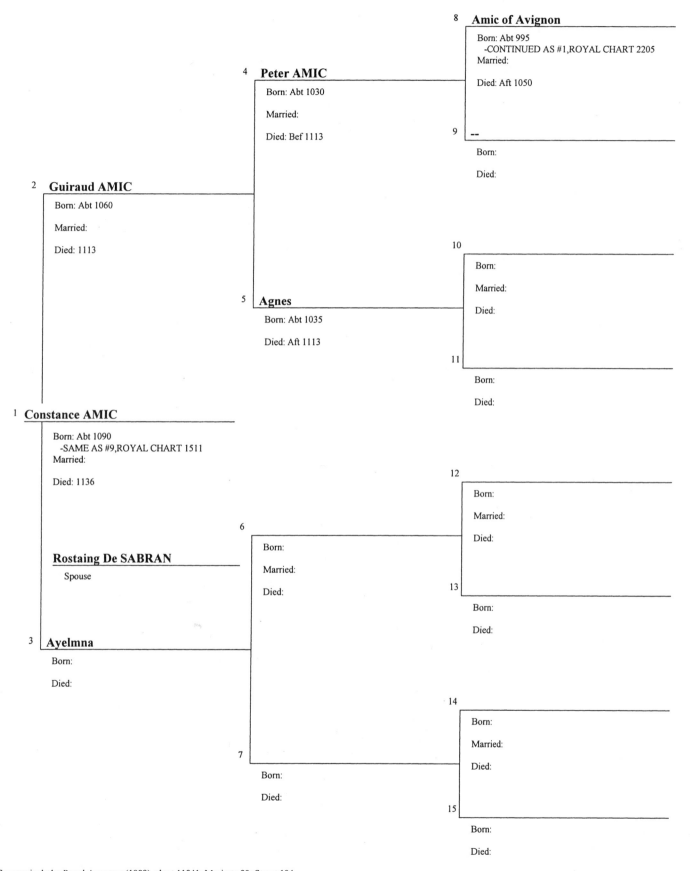

8 **Amic of Avignon**
Born: Abt 995
  -CONTINUED AS #1, ROYAL CHART 2205
Married:

Died: Aft 1050

4 **Peter AMIC**
Born: Abt 1030

Married:

Died: Bef 1113

9 **--**
Born:

Died:

2 **Guiraud AMIC**
Born: Abt 1060

Married:

Died: 1113

10
Born:

Married:

Died:

5 **Agnes**
Born: Abt 1035

Died: Aft 1113

11
Born:

Died:

1 **Constance AMIC**
Born: Abt 1090
  -SAME AS #9, ROYAL CHART 1511
Married:

Died: 1136

12
Born:

Married:

Died:

6
Born:

Married:

Died:

13
Born:

Died:

Rostaing De SABRAN
Spouse

3 **Ayelmna**
Born:

Died:

14
Born:

Married:

Died:

7
Born:

Died:

15
Born:

Died:

Sources include: *Royal Ancestors* (1989), chart 11841; Moriarty 99; Stuart 194.

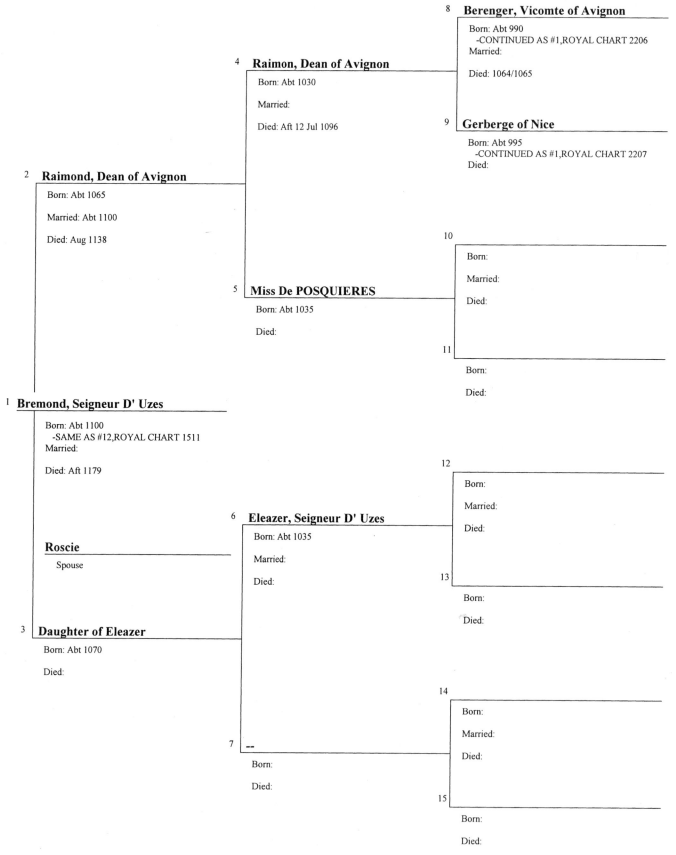

4 **Raimon, Dean of Avignon**

Born: Abt 1030

Married:

Died: Aft 12 Jul 1096

9 **Gerberge of Nice**

Born: Abt 995
  -CONTINUED AS #1,ROYAL CHART 2207
Died:

2 **Raimond, Dean of Avignon**

Born: Abt 1065

Married: Abt 1100

Died: Aug 1138

10

Born:

Married:

Died:

5 **Miss De POSQUIERES**

Born: Abt 1035

Died:

11

Born:

Died:

1 **Bremond, Seigneur D' Uzes**

Born: Abt 1100
  -SAME AS #12,ROYAL CHART 1511
Married:

Died: Aft 1179

12

Born:

Married:

Died:

6 **Eleazer, Seigneur D' Uzes**

Born: Abt 1035

Married:

Died:

13

Born:

Died:

Roscie

Spouse

3 **Daughter of Eleazer**

Born: Abt 1070

Died:

14

Born:

Married:

Died:

7 **--**

Born:

Died:

15

Born:

Died:

Sources include: *Royal Ancestors* (1989), chart 11843; Stuart 193; Moriarty 100.

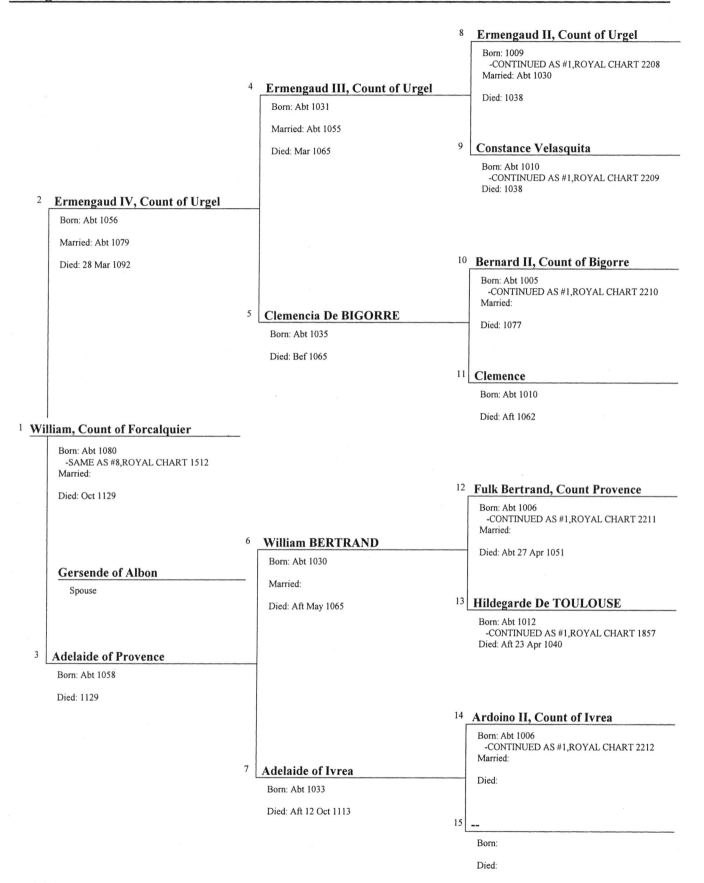

1 William, Count of Forcalquier

Born: Abt 1080
-SAME AS #8,ROYAL CHART 1512
Married:

Died: Oct 1129

2 Ermengaud IV, Count of Urgel

Born: Abt 1056

Married: Abt 1079

Died: 28 Mar 1092

4 Ermengaud III, Count of Urgel

Born: Abt 1031

Married: Abt 1055

Died: Mar 1065

8 Ermengaud II, Count of Urgel

Born: 1009
-CONTINUED AS #1,ROYAL CHART 2208
Married: Abt 1030

Died: 1038

9 Constance Velasquita

Born: Abt 1010
-CONTINUED AS #1,ROYAL CHART 2209
Died: 1038

5 Clemencia De BIGORRE

Born: Abt 1035

Died: Bef 1065

10 Bernard II, Count of Bigorre

Born: Abt 1005
-CONTINUED AS #1,ROYAL CHART 2210
Married:

Died: 1077

11 Clemence

Born: Abt 1010

Died: Aft 1062

Gersende of Albon

Spouse

3 Adelaide of Provence

Born: Abt 1058

Died: 1129

6 William BERTRAND

Born: Abt 1030

Married:

Died: Aft May 1065

12 Fulk Bertrand, Count Provence

Born: Abt 1006
-CONTINUED AS #1,ROYAL CHART 2211
Married:

Died: Abt 27 Apr 1051

13 Hildegarde De TOULOUSE

Born: Abt 1012
-CONTINUED AS #1,ROYAL CHART 1857
Died: Aft 23 Apr 1040

7 Adelaide of Ivrea

Born: Abt 1033

Died: Aft 12 Oct 1113

14 Ardoino II, Count of Ivrea

Born: Abt 1006
-CONTINUED AS #1,ROYAL CHART 2212
Married:

Died:

15 --

Born:

Died:

Sources include: *Royal Ancestors* (1989), chart 11838; Stuart 195, 197; Faris preliminary Charlemagne manuscript (June 1995), pp. 267, 226; Moriarty 100-101, 103. Notes: Moriarty gives #5 as Adoleta, ancestry unknown. The Stuart and Faris version (Clemencia De Bigorre) is followed above. #11 is also given as Estefania. Faris gives #7 as Adelaide De Righino, daughter of Guy De Righino & Gerberge De Saluces. The Moriarty and Stuart version (Ivrea) is followed above.

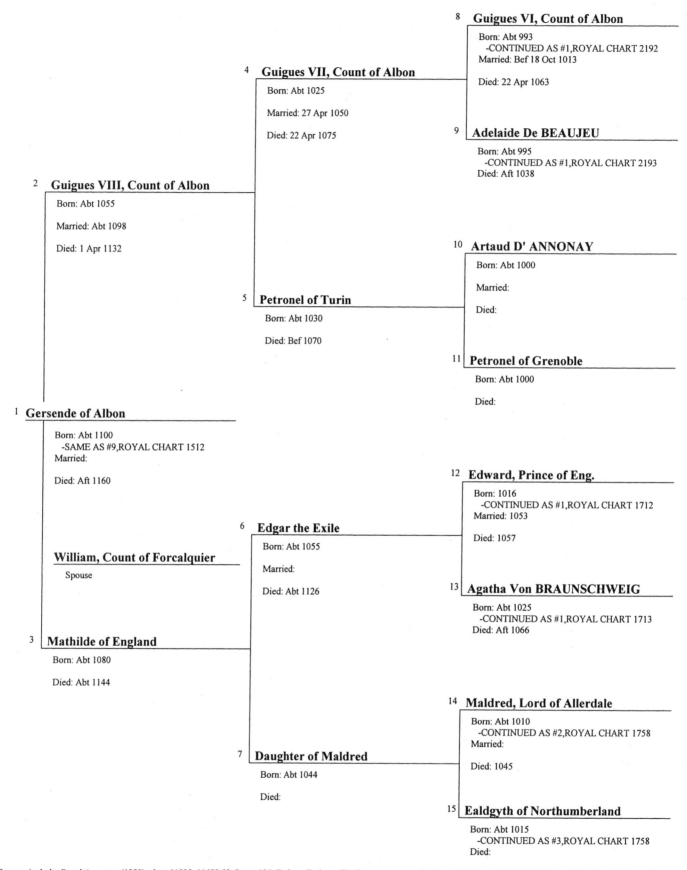

8 Guigues VI, Count of Albon

Born: Abt 993
 -CONTINUED AS #1,ROYAL CHART 2192
Married: Bef 18 Oct 1013

Died: 22 Apr 1063

4 Guigues VII, Count of Albon

Born: Abt 1025

Married: 27 Apr 1050

Died: 22 Apr 1075

9 Adelaide De BEAUJEU

Born: Abt 995
 -CONTINUED AS #1,ROYAL CHART 2193
Died: Aft 1038

2 Guigues VIII, Count of Albon

Born: Abt 1055

Married: Abt 1098

Died: 1 Apr 1132

10 Artaud D' ANNONAY

Born: Abt 1000

Married:

Died:

5 Petronel of Turin

Born: Abt 1030

Died: Bef 1070

11 Petronel of Grenoble

Born: Abt 1000

Died:

1 Gersende of Albon

Born: Abt 1100
 -SAME AS #9,ROYAL CHART 1512
Married:

Died: Aft 1160

12 Edward, Prince of Eng.

Born: 1016
 -CONTINUED AS #1,ROYAL CHART 1712
Married: 1053

Died: 1057

6 Edgar the Exile

Born: Abt 1055

Married:

Died: Abt 1126

13 Agatha Von BRAUNSCHWEIG

Born: Abt 1025
 -CONTINUED AS #1,ROYAL CHART 1713
Died: Aft 1066

William, Count of Forcalquier

Spouse

3 Mathilde of England

Born: Abt 1080

Died: Abt 1144

14 Maldred, Lord of Allerdale

Born: Abt 1010
 -CONTINUED AS #2,ROYAL CHART 1758
Married:

Died: 1045

7 Daughter of Maldred

Born: Abt 1044

Died:

15 Ealdgyth of Northumberland

Born: Abt 1015
 -CONTINUED AS #3,ROYAL CHART 1758
Died:

Sources include: *Royal Ancestors* (1989), chart 11838, 11682-83; Stuart 196; Faris preliminary Charlemagne manuscript (June 1995), pp. 278-279; Moriarty 102. Note: #1 Gersende may have been the daughter of Guigues VIII and an unknown 1st wife. Very tight chronology is required to make Gersende the daughter of Mathilde, as shown above and as given in all of the cited sources. The identification and ancestry of Mathilde is disputed. See Stuart 196, Faris 279, and Moriarty 102 & 259 notes. Moriarty concluded that Mathilde was probably the daughter of Edgar the Exile.

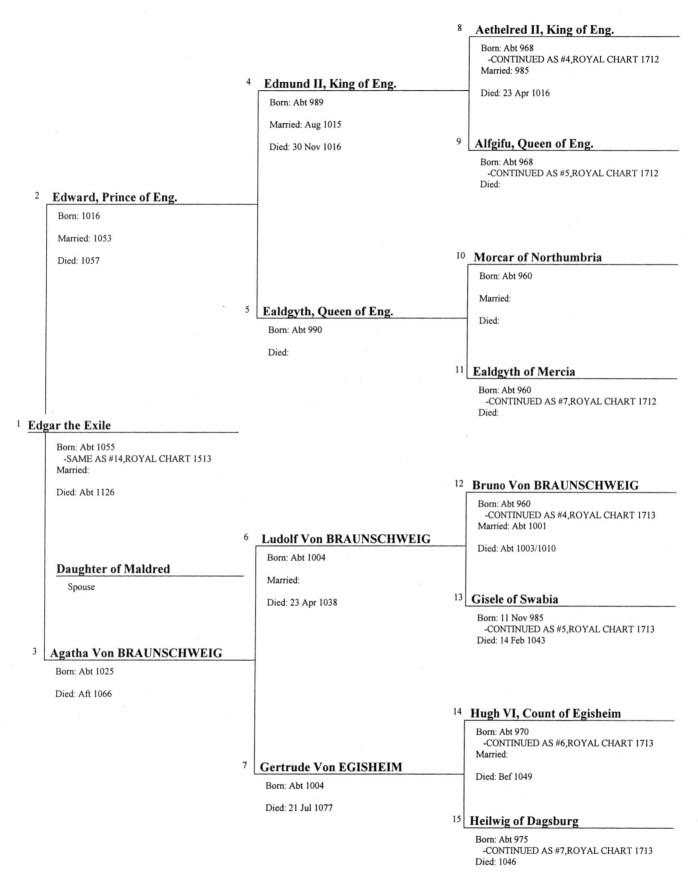

8 **Aethelred II, King of Eng.**

Born: Abt 968
  -CONTINUED AS #4,ROYAL CHART 1712
Married: 985

Died: 23 Apr 1016

4 **Edmund II, King of Eng.**

Born: Abt 989

Married: Aug 1015

Died: 30 Nov 1016

9 **Alfgifu, Queen of Eng.**

Born: Abt 968
  -CONTINUED AS #5,ROYAL CHART 1712
Died:

2 **Edward, Prince of Eng.**

Born: 1016

Married: 1053

Died: 1057

10 **Morcar of Northumbria**

Born: Abt 960

Married:

Died:

5 **Ealdgyth, Queen of Eng.**

Born: Abt 990

Died:

11 **Ealdgyth of Mercia**

Born: Abt 960
  -CONTINUED AS #7,ROYAL CHART 1712
Died:

1 **Edgar the Exile**

Born: Abt 1055
  -SAME AS #14,ROYAL CHART 1513
Married:

Died: Abt 1126

12 **Bruno Von BRAUNSCHWEIG**

Born: Abt 960
  -CONTINUED AS #4,ROYAL CHART 1713
Married: Abt 1001

Died: Abt 1003/1010

6 **Ludolf Von BRAUNSCHWEIG**

Born: Abt 1004

Married:

Died: 23 Apr 1038

13 **Gisele of Swabia**

Born: 11 Nov 985
  -CONTINUED AS #5,ROYAL CHART 1713
Died: 14 Feb 1043

Daughter of Maldred

Spouse

3 **Agatha Von BRAUNSCHWEIG**

Born: Abt 1025

Died: Aft 1066

14 **Hugh VI, Count of Egisheim**

Born: Abt 970
  -CONTINUED AS #6,ROYAL CHART 1713
Married:

Died: Bef 1049

7 **Gertrude Von EGISHEIM**

Born: Abt 1004

Died: 21 Jul 1077

15 **Heilwig of Dagsburg**

Born: Abt 975
  -CONTINUED AS #7,ROYAL CHART 1713
Died: 1046

Sources include: *Royal Ancestors* (1989), charts 11683, 11406; Stuart 196-32; Faris preliminary Charlemagne manuscript (1995), pp. 16, 284; *NEHGR* 150:417-432, 152:215-235 (#3 identification and ancestry). Note: The parentage of #3 Agatha is heavily disputed. The version argued in *NEHGR* 152 and accepted by Faris and Richardson is accepted here.

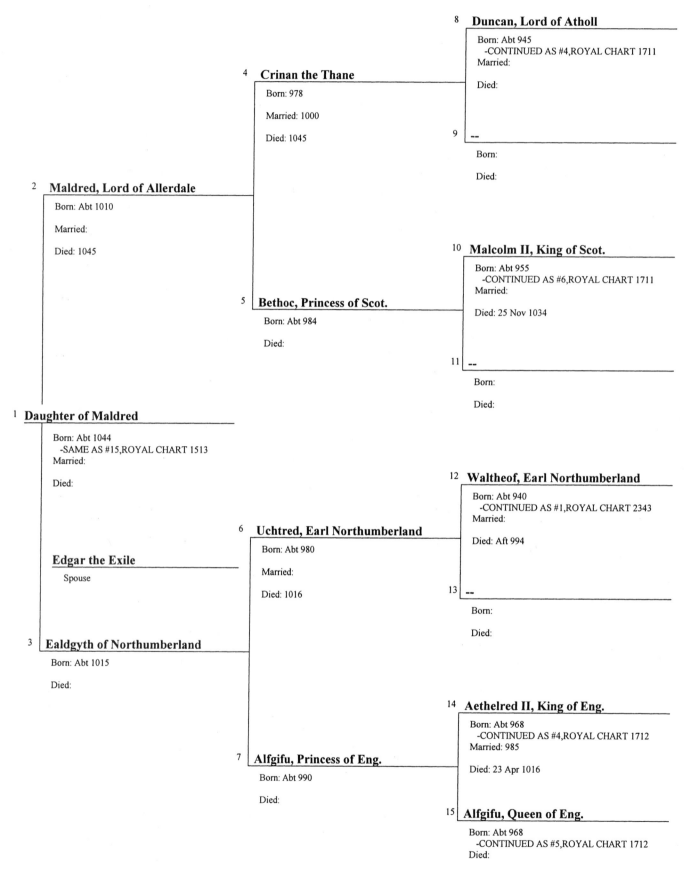

8 Duncan, Lord of Atholl

Born: Abt 945
-CONTINUED AS #4,ROYAL CHART 1711
Married:

Died:

4 Crinan the Thane

Born: 978

Married: 1000

Died: 1045

9 --

Born:

Died:

2 Maldred, Lord of Allerdale

Born: Abt 1010

Married:

Died: 1045

10 Malcolm II, King of Scot.

Born: Abt 955
-CONTINUED AS #6,ROYAL CHART 1711
Married:

Died: 25 Nov 1034

5 Bethoc, Princess of Scot.

Born: Abt 984

Died:

11 --

Born:

Died:

1 Daughter of Maldred

Born: Abt 1044
-SAME AS #15,ROYAL CHART 1513
Married:

Died:

12 Waltheof, Earl Northumberland

Born: Abt 940
-CONTINUED AS #1,ROYAL CHART 2343
Married:

Died: Aft 994

6 Uchtred, Earl Northumberland

Born: Abt 980

Married:

Died: 1016

13 --

Born:

Died:

Edgar the Exile

Spouse

3 Ealdgyth of Northumberland

Born: Abt 1015

Died:

14 Aethelred II, King of Eng.

Born: Abt 968
-CONTINUED AS #4,ROYAL CHART 1712
Married: 985

Died: 23 Apr 1016

7 Alfgifu, Princess of Eng.

Born: Abt 990

Died:

15 Alfgifu, Queen of Eng.

Born: Abt 968
-CONTINUED AS #5,ROYAL CHART 1712
Died:

Sources include: *Royal Ancestors* (1989), chart 11487; Stuart 196-32; *Ancestral Roots* 172-20, 247-20 (#2 & 3 ancestry).

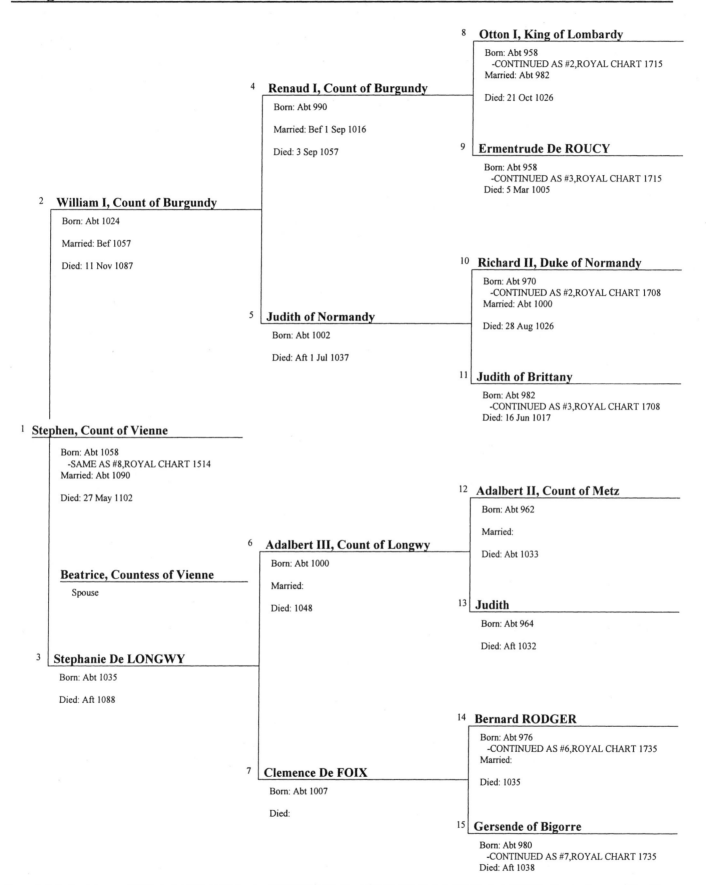

2   **William I, Count of Burgundy**

Born: Abt 1024

Married: Bef 1057

Died: 11 Nov 1087

4   **Renaud I, Count of Burgundy**

Born: Abt 990

Married: Bef 1 Sep 1016

Died: 3 Sep 1057

8   **Otton I, King of Lombardy**

Born: Abt 958
-CONTINUED AS #2,ROYAL CHART 1715
Married: Abt 982

Died: 21 Oct 1026

9   **Ermentrude De ROUCY**

Born: Abt 958
-CONTINUED AS #3,ROYAL CHART 1715
Died: 5 Mar 1005

5   **Judith of Normandy**

Born: Abt 1002

Died: Aft 1 Jul 1037

10   **Richard II, Duke of Normandy**

Born: Abt 970
-CONTINUED AS #2,ROYAL CHART 1708
Married: Abt 1000

Died: 28 Aug 1026

11   **Judith of Brittany**

Born: Abt 982
-CONTINUED AS #3,ROYAL CHART 1708
Died: 16 Jun 1017

1   **Stephen, Count of Vienne**

Born: Abt 1058
-SAME AS #8,ROYAL CHART 1514
Married: Abt 1090

Died: 27 May 1102

Beatrice, Countess of Vienne

Spouse

3   **Stephanie De LONGWY**

Born: Abt 1035

Died: Aft 1088

6   **Adalbert III, Count of Longwy**

Born: Abt 1000

Married:

Died: 1048

12   **Adalbert II, Count of Metz**

Born: Abt 962

Married:

Died: Abt 1033

13   **Judith**

Born: Abt 964

Died: Aft 1032

7   **Clemence De FOIX**

Born: Abt 1007

Died:

14   **Bernard RODGER**

Born: Abt 976
-CONTINUED AS #6,ROYAL CHART 1735
Married:

Died: 1035

15   **Gersende of Bigorre**

Born: Abt 980
-CONTINUED AS #7,ROYAL CHART 1735
Died: Aft 1038

Sources include: *Royal Ancestors* (1989), charts 11694, 11418 & notes, 11650 (#12 & 13); Stuart 187, 94, 105; Moriarty 105, 62; charts 1734-35 with notes & sources. Note: The parentage and ancestry of #12 & 13 Adalbert II & Judith is disputed. Three different versions are given by Stuart, Moriarty, and Turton.

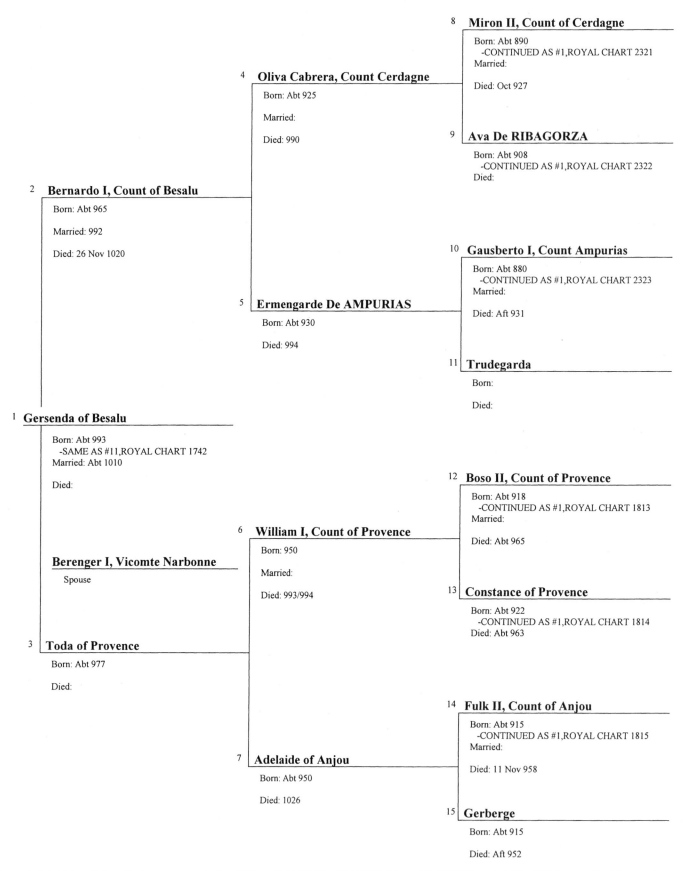

8 **Miron II, Count of Cerdagne**

Born: Abt 890
-CONTINUED AS #1,ROYAL CHART 2321
Married:

Died: Oct 927

4 **Oliva Cabrera, Count Cerdagne**

Born: Abt 925

Married:

Died: 990

9 **Ava De RIBAGORZA**

Born: Abt 908
-CONTINUED AS #1,ROYAL CHART 2322
Died:

2 **Bernardo I, Count of Besalu**

Born: Abt 965

Married: 992

Died: 26 Nov 1020

10 **Gausberto I, Count Ampurias**

Born: Abt 880
-CONTINUED AS #1,ROYAL CHART 2323
Married:

Died: Aft 931

5 **Ermengarde De AMPURIAS**

Born: Abt 930

Died: 994

11 **Trudegarda**

Born:

Died:

1 **Gersenda of Besalu**

Born: Abt 993
-SAME AS #11,ROYAL CHART 1742
Married: Abt 1010

Died:

12 **Boso II, Count of Provence**

Born: Abt 918
-CONTINUED AS #1,ROYAL CHART 1813
Married:

Died: Abt 965

6 **William I, Count of Provence**

Born: 950

Married:

Died: 993/994

13 **Constance of Provence**

Born: Abt 922
-CONTINUED AS #1,ROYAL CHART 1814
Died: Abt 963

Berenger I, Vicomte Narbonne

Spouse

3 **Toda of Provence**

Born: Abt 977

Died:

14 **Fulk II, Count of Anjou**

Born: Abt 915
-CONTINUED AS #1,ROYAL CHART 1815
Married:

Died: 11 Nov 958

7 **Adelaide of Anjou**

Born: Abt 950

Died: 1026

15 **Gerberge**

Born: Abt 915

Died: Aft 952

Sources include: Faris preliminary Charlemagne manuscript (June 1995), pp. 45-46, 225; Stuart 226-33 (#1); Schwennicke 3:137 (#2 ancestry); Chart 2209 & sources (#2 & 3 ancestry).

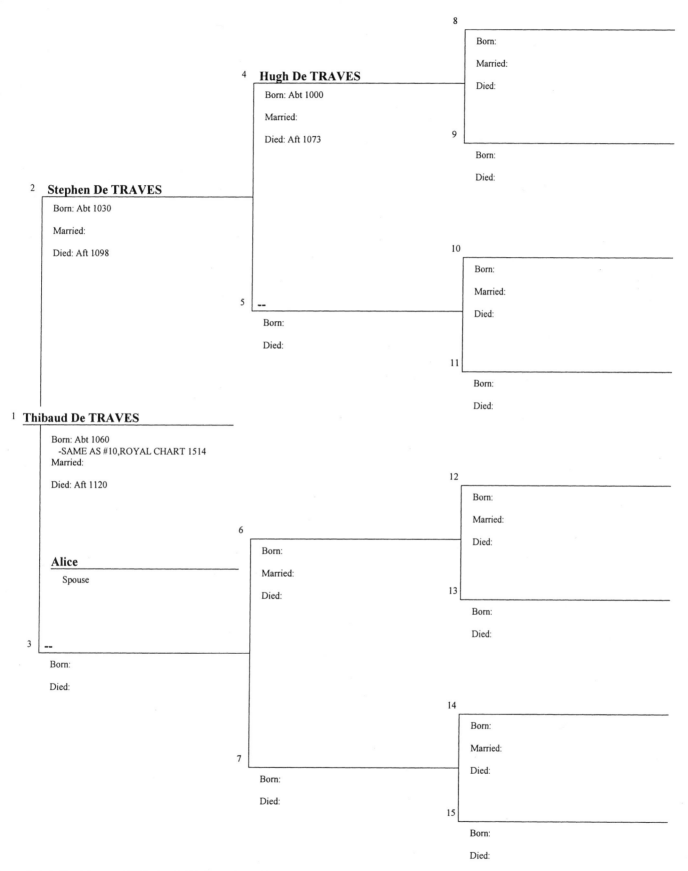

8

Born:

Married:

Died:

4 **Hugh De TRAVES**

Born: Abt 1000

Married:

Died: Aft 1073

9

Born:

Died:

2 **Stephen De TRAVES**

Born: Abt 1030

Married:

Died: Aft 1098

10

Born:

Married:

Died:

5 --

Born:

Died:

11

Born:

Died:

1 **Thibaud De TRAVES**

Born: Abt 1060
  -SAME AS #10,ROYAL CHART 1514
Married:

Died: Aft 1120

12

Born:

Married:

Died:

6

Born:

Married:

Died:

13

Born:

Died:

Alice

Spouse

3 --

Born:

Died:

14

Born:

Married:

Died:

7

Born:

Died:

15

Born:

Died:

Sources include: *Royal Ancestors* (1989), chart 11695; Stuart 190; Moriarty 105.

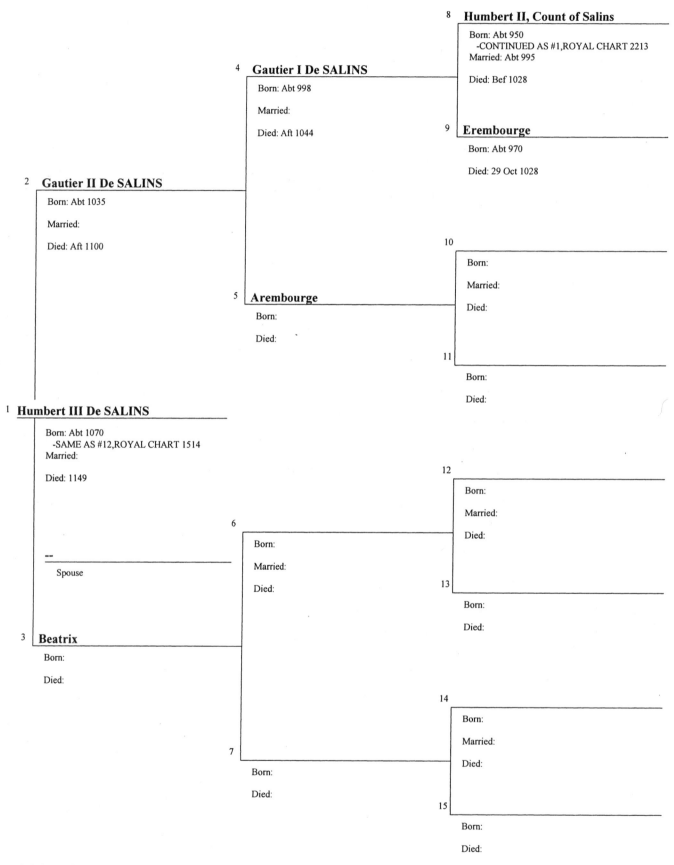

8 Humbert II, Count of Salins
Born: Abt 950
 -CONTINUED AS #1,ROYAL CHART 2213
Married: Abt 995

Died: Bef 1028

4 Gautier I De SALINS
Born: Abt 998

Married:

Died: Aft 1044

9 Erembourge
Born: Abt 970

Died: 29 Oct 1028

2 Gautier II De SALINS
Born: Abt 1035

Married:

Died: Aft 1100

5 Arembourge
Born:

Died:

10
Born:

Married:

Died:

11
Born:

Died:

1 Humbert III De SALINS
Born: Abt 1070
 -SAME AS #12,ROYAL CHART 1514
Married:

Died: 1149

--
Spouse

3 Beatrix
Born:

Died:

6
Born:

Married:

Died:

12
Born:

Married:

Died:

13
Born:

Died:

7
Born:

Died:

14
Born:

Married:

Died:

15
Born:

Died:

Sources include: *Royal Ancestors* (1989), charts 11828, 11845; Stuart 189, 191, 348; Moriarty 106, 40-41; *TAG* 74:152; Turton 61. Note: The tentative ancestry given by Moriarty and Stuart for #9 Erembourge is chronologically unacceptable. Also, Stuart 85-33 contradicts Stuart 348-36 on the claimed line.

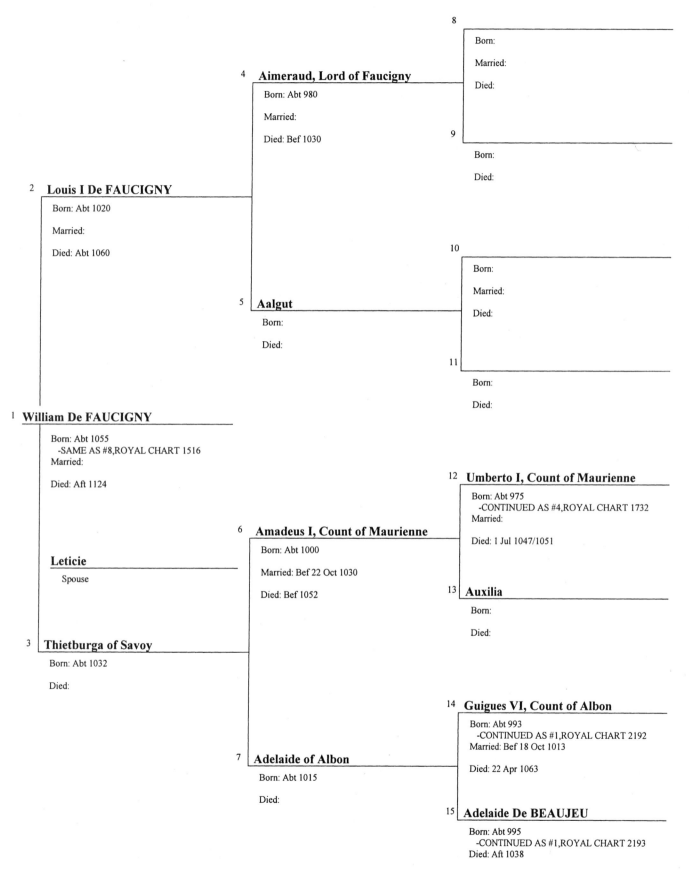

8

Born:

Married:

Died:

4   Aimeraud, Lord of Faucigny

Born: Abt 980

Married:

Died: Bef 1030

9

Born:

Died:

2   Louis I De FAUCIGNY

Born: Abt 1020

Married:

Died: Abt 1060

10

Born:

Married:

Died:

5   Aalgut

Born:

Died:

11

Born:

Died:

1   William De FAUCIGNY

Born: Abt 1055
  -SAME AS #8,ROYAL CHART 1516
Married:

Died: Aft 1124

12   Umberto I, Count of Maurienne

Born: Abt 975
  -CONTINUED AS #4,ROYAL CHART 1732
Married:

Died: 1 Jul 1047/1051

6   Amadeus I, Count of Maurienne

Born: Abt 1000

Married: Bef 22 Oct 1030

Died: Bef 1052

13   Auxilia

Born:

Died:

Leticie

Spouse

3   Thietburga of Savoy

Born: Abt 1032

Died:

14   Guigues VI, Count of Albon

Born: Abt 993
  -CONTINUED AS #1,ROYAL CHART 2192
Married: Bef 18 Oct 1013

Died: 22 Apr 1063

7   Adelaide of Albon

Born: Abt 1015

Died:

15   Adelaide De BEAUJEU

Born: Abt 995
  -CONTINUED AS #1,ROYAL CHART 2193
Died: Aft 1038

Sources include: Stuart 288, 175-31; Moriarty 107, 59; Faris preliminary Charlemagne manuscript (June 1995), pp. 130, 278-279.

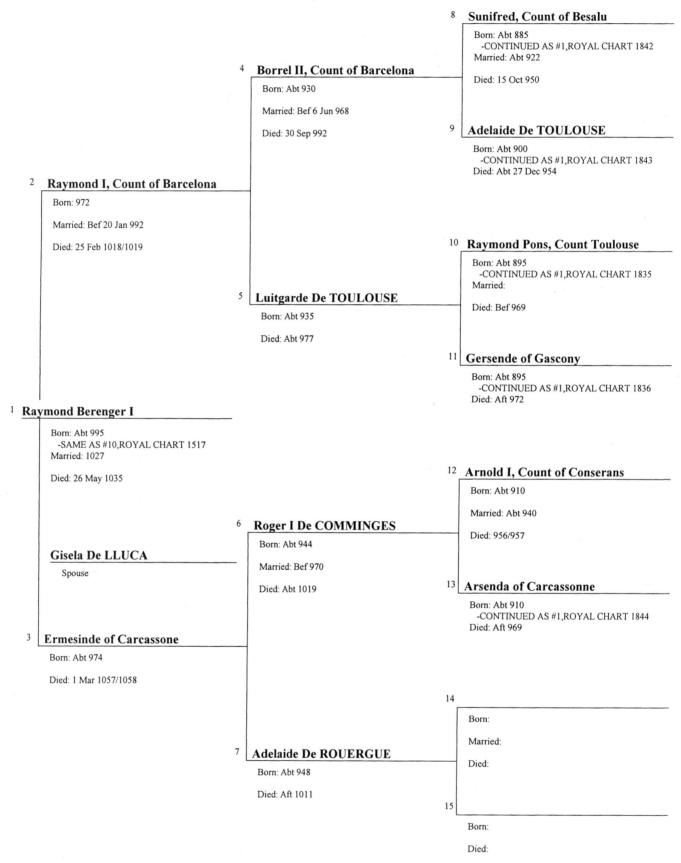

8 **Sunifred, Count of Besalu**

Born: Abt 885
-CONTINUED AS #1,ROYAL CHART 1842
Married: Abt 922

Died: 15 Oct 950

4 **Borrel II, Count of Barcelona**

Born: Abt 930

Married: Bef 6 Jun 968

Died: 30 Sep 992

9 **Adelaide De TOULOUSE**

Born: Abt 900
-CONTINUED AS #1,ROYAL CHART 1843
Died: Abt 27 Dec 954

2 **Raymond I, Count of Barcelona**

Born: 972

Married: Bef 20 Jan 992

Died: 25 Feb 1018/1019

10 **Raymond Pons, Count Toulouse**

Born: Abt 895
-CONTINUED AS #1,ROYAL CHART 1835
Married:

Died: Bef 969

5 **Luitgarde De TOULOUSE**

Born: Abt 935

Died: Abt 977

11 **Gersende of Gascony**

Born: Abt 895
-CONTINUED AS #1,ROYAL CHART 1836
Died: Aft 972

1 **Raymond Berenger I**

Born: Abt 995
-SAME AS #10,ROYAL CHART 1517
Married: 1027

Died: 26 May 1035

12 **Arnold I, Count of Conserans**

Born: Abt 910

Married: Abt 940

Died: 956/957

6 **Roger I De COMMINGES**

Born: Abt 944

Married: Bef 970

Died: Abt 1019

Gisela De LLUCA

Spouse

13 **Arsenda of Carcassonne**

Born: Abt 910
-CONTINUED AS #1,ROYAL CHART 1844
Died: Aft 969

3 **Ermesinde of Carcassone**

Born: Abt 974

Died: 1 Mar 1057/1058

14

Born:

Married:

Died:

7 **Adelaide De ROUERGUE**

Born: Abt 948

Died: Aft 1011

15

Born:

Died:

Sources include: *Royal Ancestors* (1989), chart 11680; Stuart 54, 291; Moriarty 67; *Ancestral Roots* 108-23; Turton 55. Note: Stuart states #12 Arnold is probably son of Aznar.

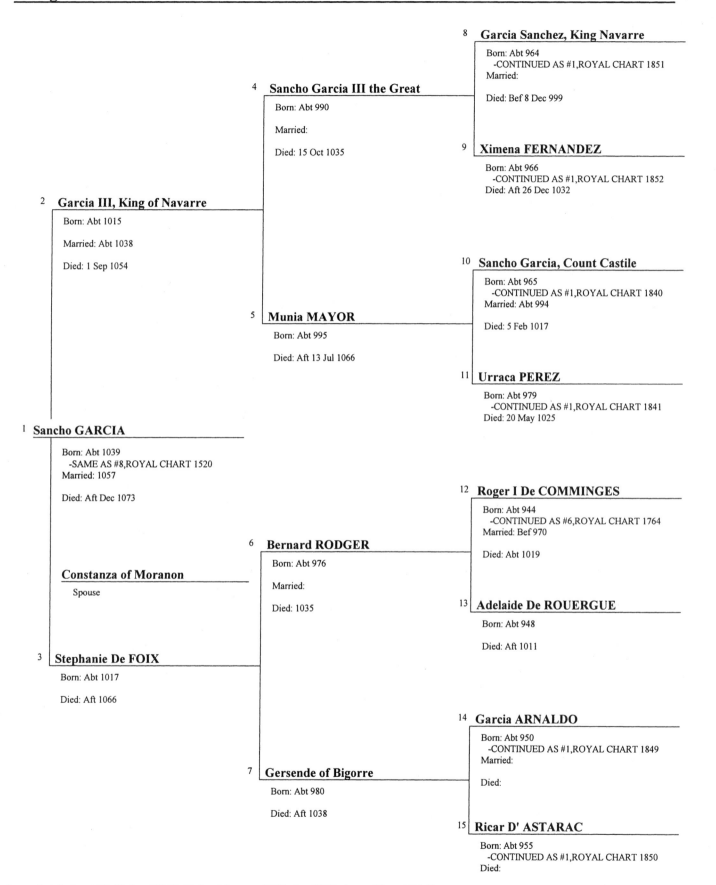

Pedigree Chart   Chart 1765

8 **Garcia Sanchez, King Navarre**

Born: Abt 964
-CONTINUED AS #1,ROYAL CHART 1851
Married:

Died: Bef 8 Dec 999

4 **Sancho Garcia III the Great**

Born: Abt 990

Married:

Died: 15 Oct 1035

9 **Ximena FERNANDEZ**

Born: Abt 966
-CONTINUED AS #1,ROYAL CHART 1852
Died: Aft 26 Dec 1032

2 **Garcia III, King of Navarre**

Born: Abt 1015

Married: Abt 1038

Died: 1 Sep 1054

10 **Sancho Garcia, Count Castile**

Born: Abt 965
-CONTINUED AS #1,ROYAL CHART 1840
Married: Abt 994

Died: 5 Feb 1017

5 **Munia MAYOR**

Born: Abt 995

Died: Aft 13 Jul 1066

11 **Urraca PEREZ**

Born: Abt 979
-CONTINUED AS #1,ROYAL CHART 1841
Died: 20 May 1025

1 **Sancho GARCIA**

Born: Abt 1039
-SAME AS #8,ROYAL CHART 1520
Married: 1057

Died: Aft Dec 1073

12 **Roger I De COMMINGES**

Born: Abt 944
-CONTINUED AS #6,ROYAL CHART 1764
Married: Bef 970

Died: Abt 1019

6 **Bernard RODGER**

Born: Abt 976

Married:

Died: 1035

13 **Adelaide De ROUERGUE**

Born: Abt 948

Died: Aft 1011

Constanza of Moranon

Spouse

3 **Stephanie De FOIX**

Born: Abt 1017

Died: Aft 1066

14 **Garcia ARNALDO**

Born: Abt 950
-CONTINUED AS #1,ROYAL CHART 1849
Married:

Died:

7 **Gersende of Bigorre**

Born: Abt 980

Died: Aft 1038

15 **Ricar D' ASTARAC**

Born: Abt 955
-CONTINUED AS #1,ROYAL CHART 1850
Died:

Sources include: Stuart 151; Moriarty 109, 78, 80; *Royal Ancestors* (1989), chart 11667; *Ancestral Roots* 113A-24.

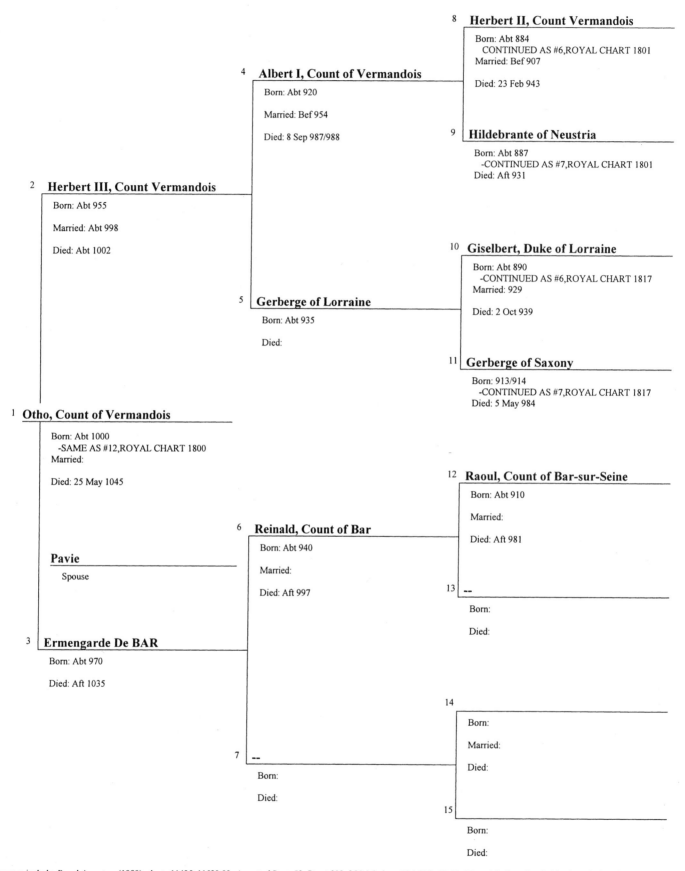

8 **Herbert II, Count Vermandois**

Born: Abt 884
  CONTINUED AS #6,ROYAL CHART 1801
Married: Bef 907

Died: 23 Feb 943

4 **Albert I, Count of Vermandois**

Born: Abt 920

Married: Bef 954

Died: 8 Sep 987/988

9 **Hildebrante of Neustria**

Born: Abt 887
  -CONTINUED AS #7,ROYAL CHART 1801
Died: Aft 931

2 **Herbert III, Count Vermandois**

Born: Abt 955

Married: Abt 998

Died: Abt 1002

10 **Giselbert, Duke of Lorraine**

Born: Abt 890
  -CONTINUED AS #6,ROYAL CHART 1817
Married: 929

Died: 2 Oct 939

5 **Gerberge of Lorraine**

Born: Abt 935

Died:

11 **Gerberge of Saxony**

Born: 913/914
  -CONTINUED AS #7,ROYAL CHART 1817
Died: 5 May 984

1 **Otho, Count of Vermandois**

Born: Abt 1000
  -SAME AS #12,ROYAL CHART 1800
Married:

Died: 25 May 1045

12 **Raoul, Count of Bar-sur-Seine**

Born: Abt 910

Married:

Died: Aft 981

6 **Reinald, Count of Bar**

Born: Abt 940

Married:

Died: Aft 997

13 **--**

Born:

Died:

Pavie

Spouse

3 **Ermengarde De BAR**

Born: Abt 970

Died: Aft 1035

14

Born:

Married:

Died:

7 **--**

Born:

Died:

15

Born:

Died:

Sources include: *Royal Ancestors* (1989), charts 11425, 11522-23; *Ancestral Roots* 50; Stuart 239, 256; Moriarty 134-135, 65-66. Note: Moriarty (copied by Stuart) gives #12 Raoul as a great-grandson of Renaud, Vicomte of Auxerre and Count of Bar-sur-Seine (died after 924), whose wife (name unknown) may have been a daughter of Raoul of Laesoie, son of Raoul, Count of Ponthieu (died 866). The father and grandfather of #12 Raoul are unknown.

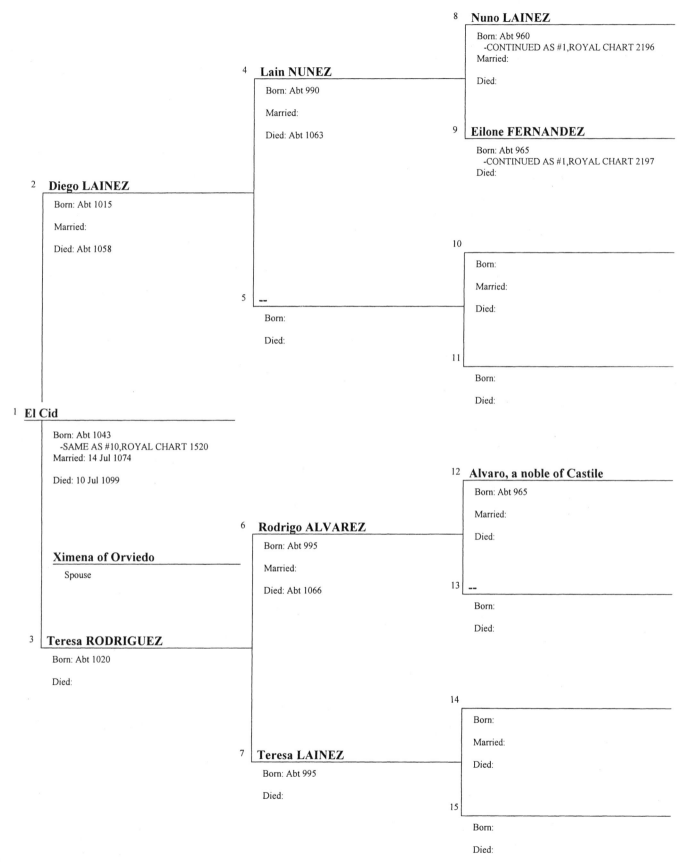

8 Nuno LAINEZ
Born: Abt 960
-CONTINUED AS #1,ROYAL CHART 2196
Married:

Died:

4 Lain NUNEZ
Born: Abt 990

Married:

Died: Abt 1063

9 Eilone FERNANDEZ
Born: Abt 965
-CONTINUED AS #1,ROYAL CHART 2197
Died:

2 Diego LAINEZ
Born: Abt 1015

Married:

Died: Abt 1058

10
Born:

Married:

Died:

5 --
Born:

Died:

11
Born:

Died:

1 El Cid
Born: Abt 1043
-SAME AS #10,ROYAL CHART 1520
Married: 14 Jul 1074

Died: 10 Jul 1099

12 Alvaro, a noble of Castile
Born: Abt 965

Married:

Died:

6 Rodrigo ALVAREZ
Born: Abt 995

Married:

Died: Abt 1066

13 --
Born:

Died:

Ximena of Orviedo
Spouse

3 Teresa RODRIGUEZ
Born: Abt 1020

Died:

14
Born:

Married:

Died:

7 Teresa LAINEZ
Born: Abt 995

Died:

15
Born:

Died:

Sources include: *Royal Ancestors* (1989), chart 11668; *Ancestral Roots* 8 (2004), Line 113A; *Ancestral Roots* 113A-23; Stuart 179-180; Moriarty 110; *NEHGR* 117:94-96. Note: #1 "El Cid" is Rodrigo Diaz De Vivar (Bivar) or De Castro.

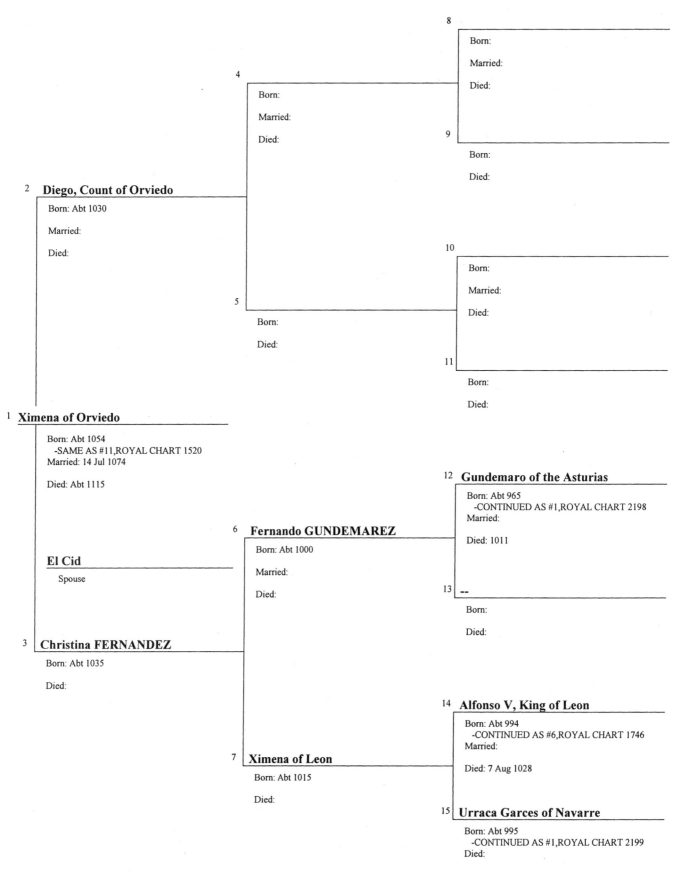

8

Born:

Married:

Died:

4

Born:

Married:

Died:

9

Born:

Died:

2 **Diego, Count of Orviedo**

Born: Abt 1030

Married:

Died:

10

Born:

Married:

Died:

5

Born:

Died:

11

Born:

Died:

1 **Ximena of Orviedo**

Born: Abt 1054
-SAME AS #11,ROYAL CHART 1520
Married: 14 Jul 1074

Died: Abt 1115

12 **Gundemaro of the Asturias**

Born: Abt 965
-CONTINUED AS #1,ROYAL CHART 2198
Married:

Died: 1011

6 **Fernando GUNDEMAREZ**

Born: Abt 1000

Married:

Died:

13 **--**

Born:

Died:

El Cid

Spouse

3 **Christina FERNANDEZ**

Born: Abt 1035

Died:

14 **Alfonso V, King of Leon**

Born: Abt 994
-CONTINUED AS #6,ROYAL CHART 1746
Married:

Died: 7 Aug 1028

7 **Ximena of Leon**

Born: Abt 1015

Died:

15 **Urraca Garces of Navarre**

Born: Abt 995
-CONTINUED AS #1,ROYAL CHART 2199
Died:

Sources include: *Royal Ancestors* (1989), chart 11668; Stuart 180; Moriarty 110, 82; *NEHGR* 117:94-96; *Ancestral Roots* 113A-23.

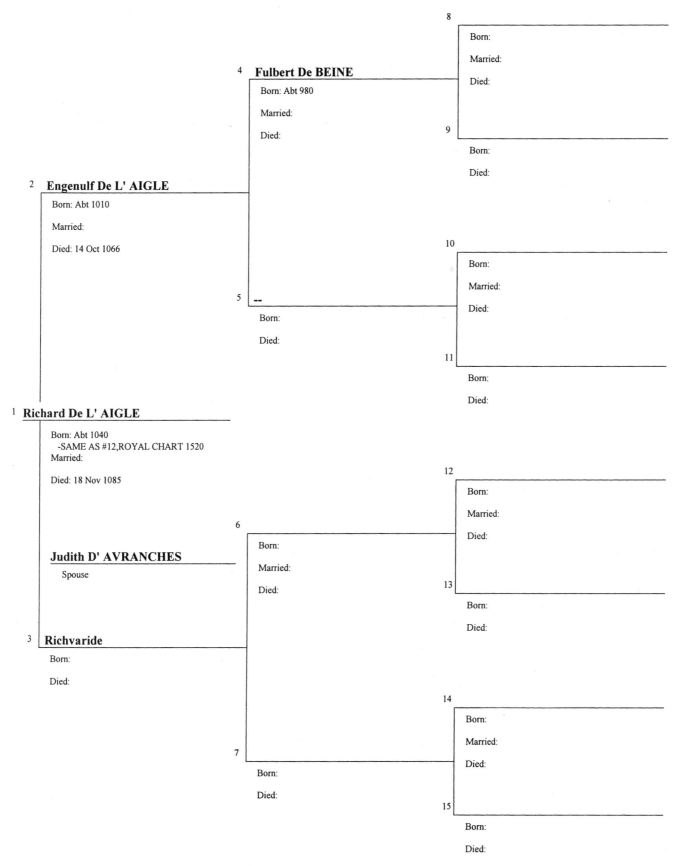

8

Born:

Married:

Died:

4   **Fulbert De BEINE**

Born: Abt 980

Married:

Died:

9

Born:

Died:

2   **Engenulf De L' AIGLE**

Born: Abt 1010

Married:

Died: 14 Oct 1066

10

Born:

Married:

Died:

5   --

Born:

Died:

11

Born:

Died:

1   **Richard De L' AIGLE**

Born: Abt 1040
   -SAME AS #12,ROYAL CHART 1520
Married:

Died: 18 Nov 1085

12

Born:

Married:

Died:

6

Born:

Married:

Died:

13

Born:

Died:

Judith D' AVRANCHES

Spouse

3   **Richvaride**

Born:

Died:

14

Born:

Married:

Died:

7

Born:

Died:

15

Born:

Died:

Sources include: *Royal Ancestors* (1989), chart 11684; Stuart 178; Moriarty 110-111.

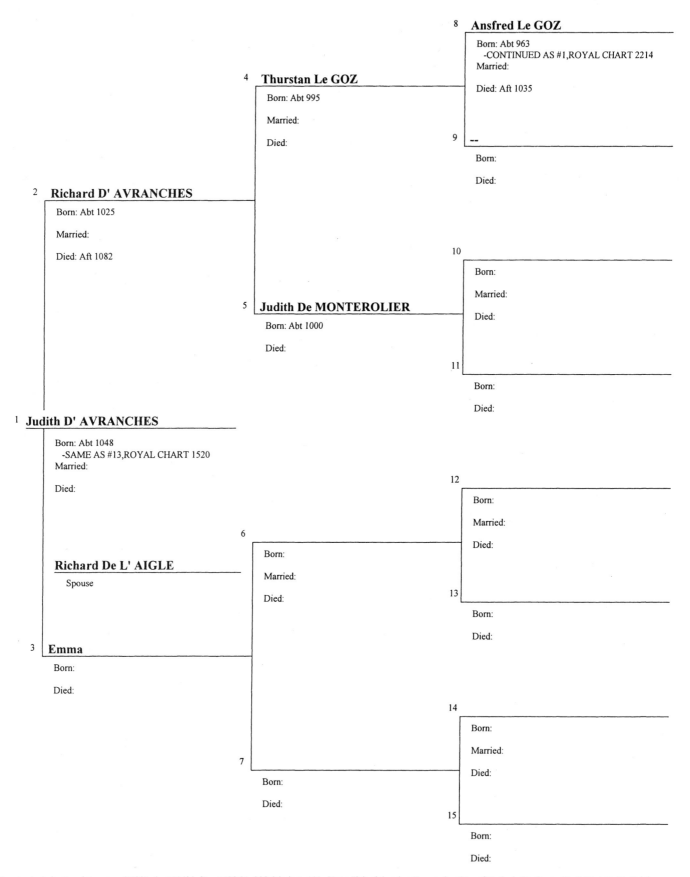

8 Ansfred Le GOZ

Born: Abt 963
  -CONTINUED AS #1,ROYAL CHART 2214
Married:

Died: Aft 1035

4 Thurstan Le GOZ

Born: Abt 995

Married:

Died:

9 --

Born:

Died:

2 Richard D' AVRANCHES

Born: Abt 1025

Married:

Died: Aft 1082

10

Born:

Married:

Died:

5 Judith De MONTEROLIER

Born: Abt 1000

Died:

11

Born:

Died:

1 Judith D' AVRANCHES

Born: Abt 1048
  -SAME AS #13,ROYAL CHART 1520
Married:

Died:

12

Born:

Married:

Died:

6

Born:

Married:

Died:

13

Born:

Died:

Richard De L' AIGLE

Spouse

3 Emma

Born:

Died:

14

Born:

Married:

Died:

7

Born:

Died:

15

Born:

Died:

Sources include: *Royal Ancestors* (1989), chart 11684; Stuart 178-31, 295; Moriarty 111. Note: #3 is claimed as Emma, daughter of Herlevin De Conteville & Harlette De Falaise (see chart 1718, #2 & 3). Moriarty states that this claim is probably unfounded.

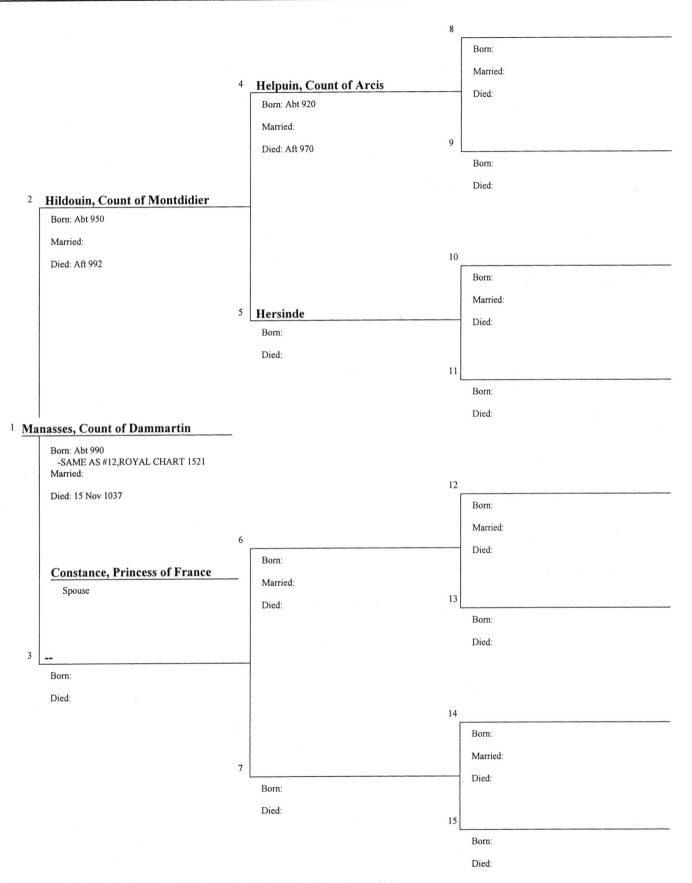

4 | **Helpuin, Count of Arcis**
Born: Abt 920
Married:
Died: Aft 970

8
Born:
Married:
Died:

9
Born:
Died:

2 | **Hildouin, Count of Montdidier**
Born: Abt 950
Married:
Died: Aft 992

5 | **Hersinde**
Born:
Died:

10
Born:
Married:
Died:

11
Born:
Died:

1 | **Manasses, Count of Dammartin**
Born: Abt 990
  -SAME AS #12,ROYAL CHART 1521
Married:
Died: 15 Nov 1037

Constance, Princess of France
  Spouse

3 | --
Born:
Died:

6
Born:
Married:
Died:

7
Born:
Died:

12
Born:
Married:
Died:

13
Born:
Died:

14
Born:
Married:
Died:

15
Born:
Died:

Sources include: *Royal Ancestors* (1989), chart 12121; Stuart 397, 266; *The Genealogists' Magazine* 21:94.

Pedigree Chart

Chart 1772

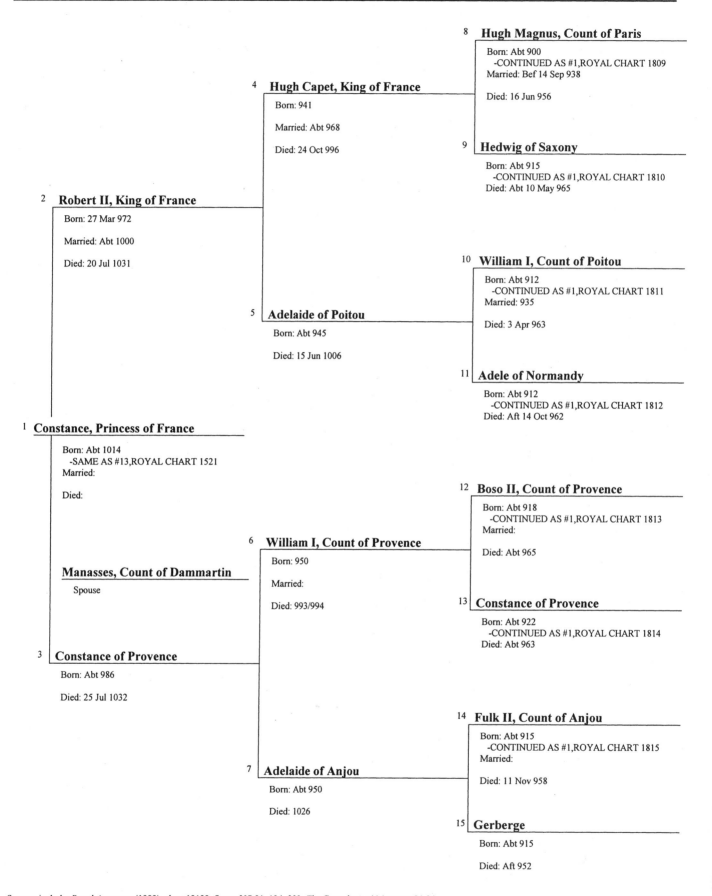

8 **Hugh Magnus, Count of Paris**

Born: Abt 900
-CONTINUED AS #1,ROYAL CHART 1809
Married: Bef 14 Sep 938

Died: 16 Jun 956

4 **Hugh Capet, King of France**

Born: 941

Married: Abt 968

Died: 24 Oct 996

9 **Hedwig of Saxony**

Born: Abt 915
-CONTINUED AS #1,ROYAL CHART 1810
Died: Abt 10 May 965

2 **Robert II, King of France**

Born: 27 Mar 972

Married: Abt 1000

Died: 20 Jul 1031

10 **William I, Count of Poitou**

Born: Abt 912
-CONTINUED AS #1,ROYAL CHART 1811
Married: 935

Died: 3 Apr 963

5 **Adelaide of Poitou**

Born: Abt 945

Died: 15 Jun 1006

11 **Adele of Normandy**

Born: Abt 912
-CONTINUED AS #1,ROYAL CHART 1812
Died: Aft 14 Oct 962

1 **Constance, Princess of France**

Born: Abt 1014
-SAME AS #13,ROYAL CHART 1521
Married:

Died:

12 **Boso II, Count of Provence**

Born: Abt 918
-CONTINUED AS #1,ROYAL CHART 1813
Married:

Died: Abt 965

6 **William I, Count of Provence**

Born: 950

Married:

Died: 993/994

Manasses, Count of Dammartin

Spouse

13 **Constance of Provence**

Born: Abt 922
-CONTINUED AS #1,ROYAL CHART 1814
Died: Abt 963

3 **Constance of Provence**

Born: Abt 986

Died: 25 Jul 1032

14 **Fulk II, Count of Anjou**

Born: Abt 915
-CONTINUED AS #1,ROYAL CHART 1815
Married:

Died: 11 Nov 958

7 **Adelaide of Anjou**

Born: Abt 950

Died: 1026

15 **Gerberge**

Born: Abt 915

Died: Aft 952

Sources include: *Royal Ancestors* (1989), chart 12122; Stuart 397-31, 134, 333; *The Genealogists' Magazine* 21:94.

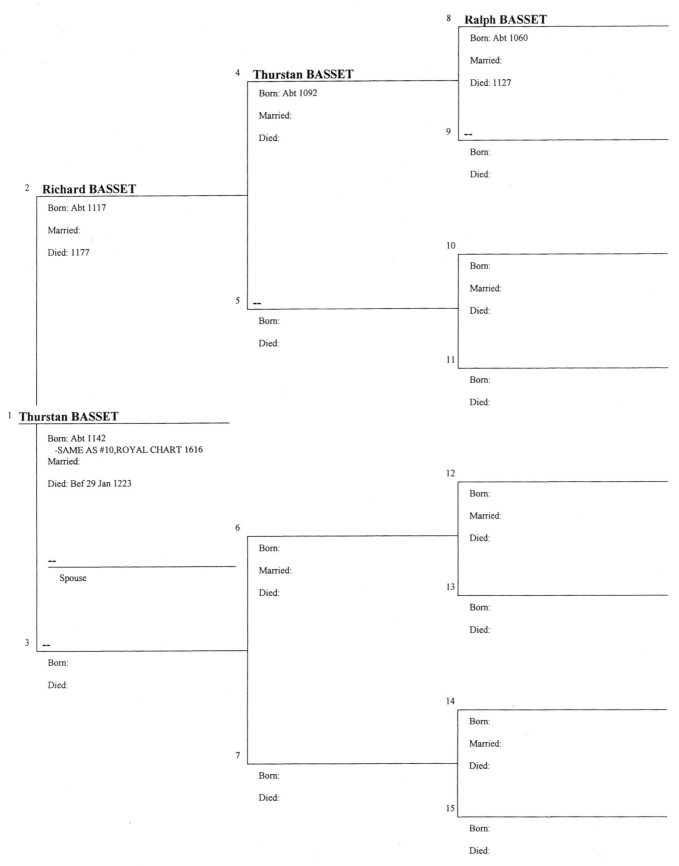

8 Ralph BASSET

Born: Abt 1060

Married:

Died: 1127

4 Thurstan BASSET

Born: Abt 1092

Married:

Died:

9 --

Born:

Died:

2 Richard BASSET

Born: Abt 1117

Married:

Died: 1177

10

Born:

Married:

Died:

5 --

Born:

Died:

11

Born:

Died:

1 Thurstan BASSET

Born: Abt 1142
  -SAME AS #10,ROYAL CHART 1616
Married:

Died: Bef 29 Jan 1223

12

Born:

Married:

Died:

6

Born:

Married:

Died:

13

Born:

Died:

--

Spouse

3 --

Born:

Died:

14

Born:

Married:

Died:

7

Born:

Died:

15

Born:

Died:

Sources include: Paget (1957) 26:1-2; *Royal Ancestors* (1989), chart 11454. Note: #8 Ralph is claimed as son of Thurstan (living 1080) and might be grandson of Osmund Basset (living 1050).

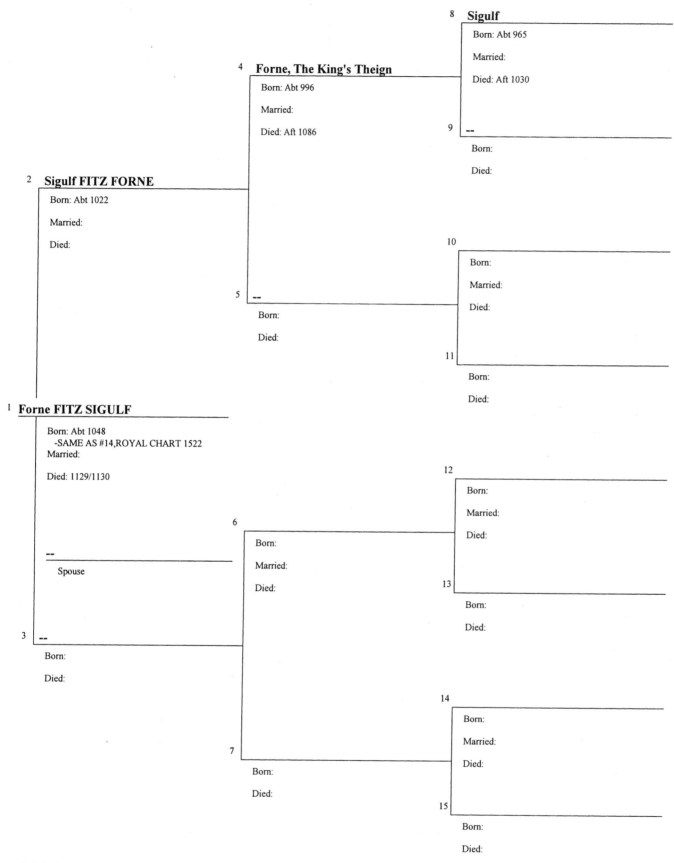

8 **Sigulf**
Born: Abt 965
Married:
Died: Aft 1030

4 **Forne, The King's Theign**
Born: Abt 996
Married:
Died: Aft 1086

9 --
Born:
Died:

2 **Sigulf FITZ FORNE**
Born: Abt 1022
Married:
Died:

10
Born:
Married:
Died:

5 --
Born:
Died:

11
Born:
Died:

1 **Forne FITZ SIGULF**
Born: Abt 1048
    -SAME AS #14, ROYAL CHART 1522
Married:
Died: 1129/1130

12
Born:
Married:
Died:

6
Born:
Married:
Died:

13
Born:
Died:

--
Spouse

3 --
Born:
Died:

14
Born:
Married:
Died:

7
Born:
Died:

15
Born:
Died:

Sources include: Stuart 396; LDS records.

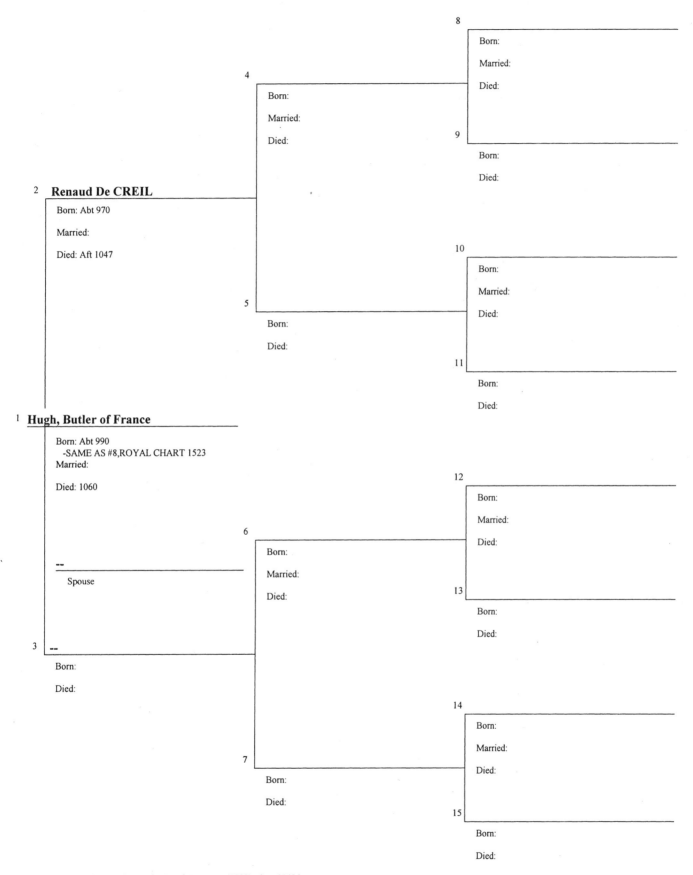

2 Renaud De CREIL
Born: Abt 970
Married:
Died: Aft 1047

4
Born:
Married:
Died:

8
Born:
Married:
Died:

9
Born:
Died:

5
Born:
Died:

10
Born:
Married:
Died:

11
Born:
Died:

1 Hugh, Butler of France
Born: Abt 990
  -SAME AS #8, ROYAL CHART 1523
Married:
Died: 1060

--
Spouse

3 --
Born:
Died:

6
Born:
Married:
Died:

12
Born:
Married:
Died:

13
Born:
Died:

7
Born:
Died:

14
Born:
Married:
Died:

15
Born:
Died:

Sources include: Stuart 344; LDS records; *Royal Ancestors* (1989), chart 11436.

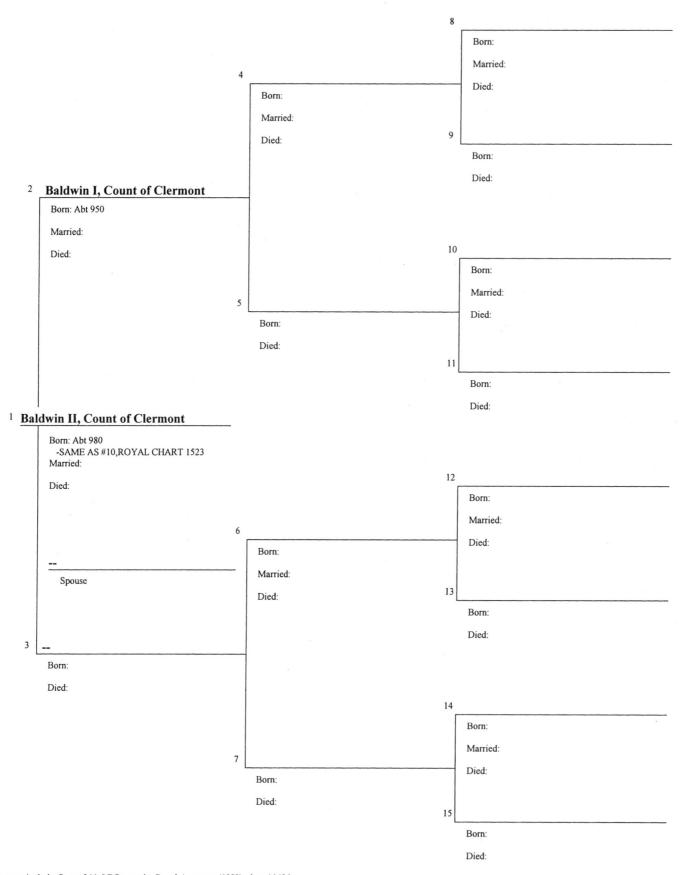

8

Born:

Married:

Died:

4

Born:

Married:

Died:

9

Born:

Died:

2   **Baldwin I, Count of Clermont**

Born: Abt 950

Married:

Died:

10

Born:

Married:

Died:

5

Born:

Died:

11

Born:

Died:

1   **Baldwin II, Count of Clermont**

Born: Abt 980
-SAME AS #10,ROYAL CHART 1523
Married:

Died:

12

Born:

Married:

Died:

6

Born:

Married:

Died:

13

Born:

Died:

--

Spouse

3   --

Born:

Died:

14

Born:

Married:

Died:

7

Born:

Married:

Died:

15

Born:

Died:

Sources include: Stuart 344; LDS records; *Royal Ancestors* (1989), chart 11436.

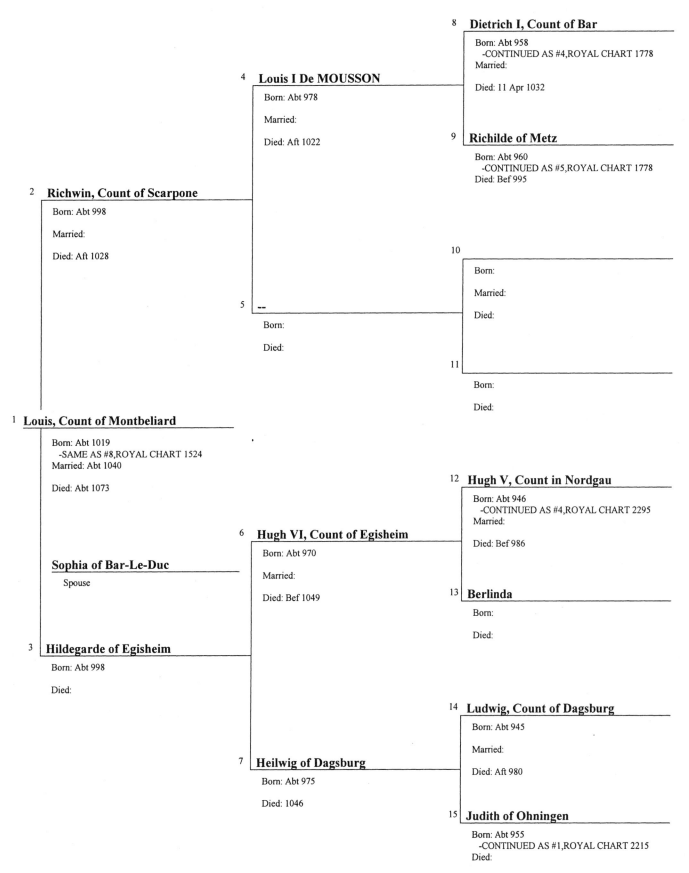

8 **Dietrich I, Count of Bar**

Born: Abt 958
-CONTINUED AS #4,ROYAL CHART 1778
Married:

Died: 11 Apr 1032

4 **Louis I De MOUSSON**

Born: Abt 978

Married:

Died: Aft 1022

9 **Richilde of Metz**

Born: Abt 960
-CONTINUED AS #5,ROYAL CHART 1778
Died: Bef 995

2 **Richwin, Count of Scarpone**

Born: Abt 998

Married:

Died: Aft 1028

10

Born:

Married:

Died:

5 **--**

Born:

Died:

11

Born:

Died:

1 **Louis, Count of Montbeliard**

Born: Abt 1019
-SAME AS #8,ROYAL CHART 1524
Married: Abt 1040

Died: Abt 1073

12 **Hugh V, Count in Nordgau**

Born: Abt 946
-CONTINUED AS #4,ROYAL CHART 2295
Married:

Died: Bef 986

6 **Hugh VI, Count of Egisheim**

Born: Abt 970

Married:

Died: Bef 1049

13 **Berlinda**

Born:

Died:

Sophia of Bar-Le-Duc

Spouse

3 **Hildegarde of Egisheim**

Born: Abt 998

Died:

14 **Ludwig, Count of Dagsburg**

Born: Abt 945

Married:

Died: Aft 980

7 **Heilwig of Dagsburg**

Born: Abt 975

Died: 1046

15 **Judith of Ohningen**

Born: Abt 955
-CONTINUED AS #1,ROYAL CHART 2215
Died:

Sources include: *Royal Ancestors* (1989), chart 11655; Stuart 149, 33; *Ancestral Roots* 167-22; Moriarty 193, 182. Note: Stuart's apparent identification of the parentage of #4 Louis as shown above is chronologically difficult and appears uncertain. See also *TAG* 74:148.

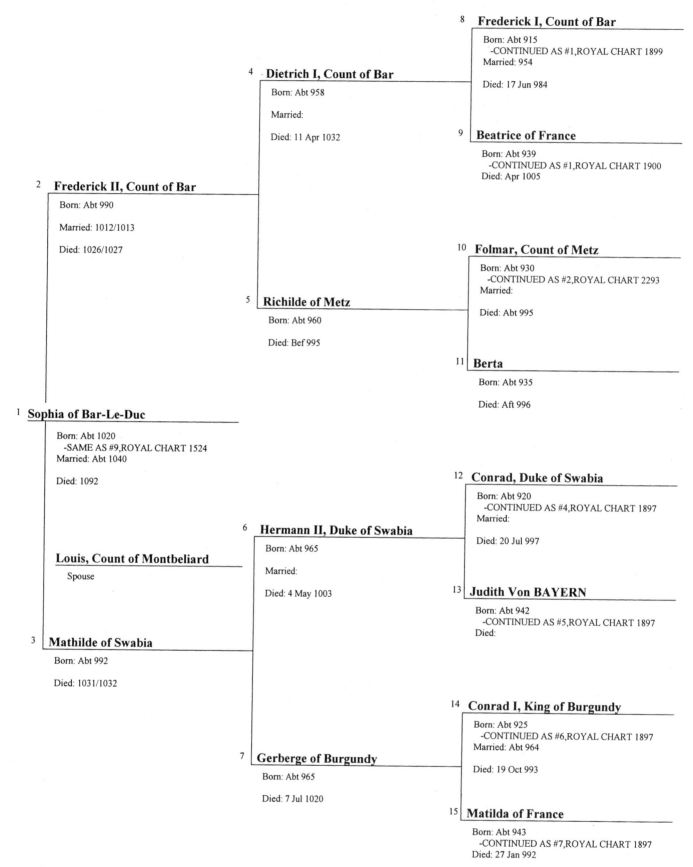

2 Frederick II, Count of Bar

Born: Abt 990

Married: 1012/1013

Died: 1026/1027

4 Dietrich I, Count of Bar

Born: Abt 958

Married:

Died: 11 Apr 1032

8 Frederick I, Count of Bar

Born: Abt 915
   -CONTINUED AS #1,ROYAL CHART 1899
Married: 954

Died: 17 Jun 984

9 Beatrice of France

Born: Abt 939
   -CONTINUED AS #1,ROYAL CHART 1900
Died: Apr 1005

5 Richilde of Metz

Born: Abt 960

Died: Bef 995

10 Folmar, Count of Metz

Born: Abt 930
   -CONTINUED AS #2,ROYAL CHART 2293
Married:

Died: Abt 995

11 Berta

Born: Abt 935

Died: Aft 996

1 Sophia of Bar-Le-Duc

Born: Abt 1020
   -SAME AS #9,ROYAL CHART 1524
Married: Abt 1040

Died: 1092

Louis, Count of Montbeliard

Spouse

3 Mathilde of Swabia

Born: Abt 992

Died: 1031/1032

6 Hermann II, Duke of Swabia

Born: Abt 965

Married:

Died: 4 May 1003

12 Conrad, Duke of Swabia

Born: Abt 920
   -CONTINUED AS #4,ROYAL CHART 1897
Married:

Died: 20 Jul 997

13 Judith Von BAYERN

Born: Abt 942
   -CONTINUED AS #5,ROYAL CHART 1897
Died:

7 Gerberge of Burgundy

Born: Abt 965

Died: 7 Jul 1020

14 Conrad I, King of Burgundy

Born: Abt 925
   -CONTINUED AS #6,ROYAL CHART 1897
Married: Abt 964

Died: 19 Oct 993

15 Matilda of France

Born: Abt 943
   -CONTINUED AS #7,ROYAL CHART 1897
Died: 27 Jan 992

Sources include: *Royal Ancestors* (1989), chart 11655; *Stuart* 247; *Ancestral Roots* 167; Moriarty 160, 94.

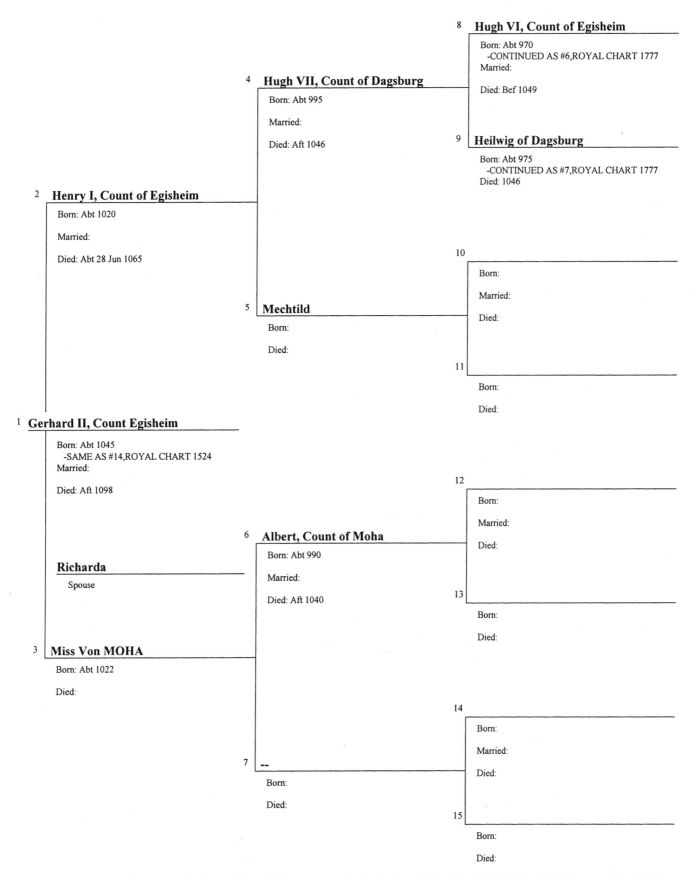

8   **Hugh VI, Count of Egisheim**

Born: Abt 970
   -CONTINUED AS #6, ROYAL CHART 1777
Married:

Died: Bef 1049

4   **Hugh VII, Count of Dagsburg**

Born: Abt 995

Married:

Died: Aft 1046

9   **Heilwig of Dagsburg**

Born: Abt 975
   -CONTINUED AS #7, ROYAL CHART 1777
Died: 1046

2   **Henry I, Count of Egisheim**

Born: Abt 1020

Married:

Died: Abt 28 Jun 1065

10

Born:

Married:

Died:

5   **Mechtild**

Born:

Died:

11

Born:

Died:

1   **Gerhard II, Count Egisheim**

Born: Abt 1045
   -SAME AS #14, ROYAL CHART 1524
Married:

Died: Aft 1098

12

Born:

Married:

Died:

6   **Albert, Count of Moha**

Born: Abt 990

Married:

Died: Aft 1040

13

Born:

Died:

Richarda

Spouse

3   **Miss Von MOHA**

Born: Abt 1022

Died:

14

Born:

Married:

Died:

7   **--**

Born:

Died:

15

Born:

Died:

Sources include: *Royal Ancestors* (1989), chart 11657; Faris preliminary Charlemagne manuscript (June 1995), pp. 125-126; Stuart 246, 33; Moriarty 195, 182; *Ancestral Roots* 144-24.
Note: The parentage and ancestry of #1 Gerhard is disputed. The Faris version is followed above.

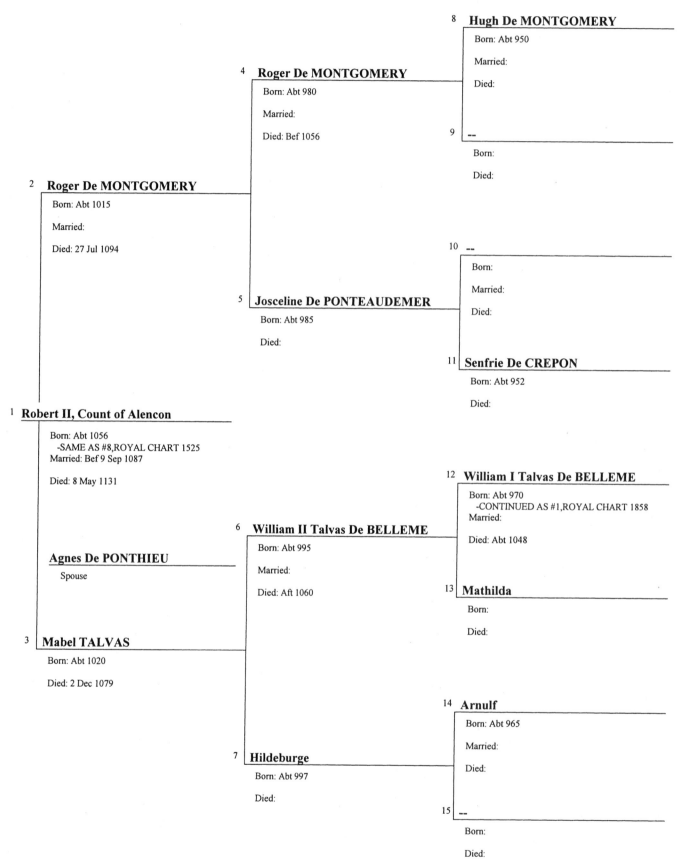

8 | **Hugh De MONTGOMERY**
Born: Abt 950
Married:
Died:

4 | **Roger De MONTGOMERY**
Born: Abt 980
Married:
Died: Bef 1056

9 | **--**
Born:
Died:

2 | **Roger De MONTGOMERY**
Born: Abt 1015
Married:
Died: 27 Jul 1094

10 | **--**
Born:
Married:
Died:

5 | **Josceline De PONTEAUDEMER**
Born: Abt 985
Died:

11 | **Senfrie De CREPON**
Born: Abt 952
Died:

1 | **Robert II, Count of Alencon**
Born: Abt 1056
    -SAME AS #8,ROYAL CHART 1525
Married: Bef 9 Sep 1087
Died: 8 May 1131

12 | **William I Talvas De BELLEME**
Born: Abt 970
    -CONTINUED AS #1,ROYAL CHART 1858
Married:
Died: Abt 1048

6 | **William II Talvas De BELLEME**
Born: Abt 995
Married:
Died: Aft 1060

13 | **Mathilda**
Born:
Died:

Agnes De PONTHIEU
Spouse

3 | **Mabel TALVAS**
Born: Abt 1020
Died: 2 Dec 1079

14 | **Arnulf**
Born: Abt 965
Married:
Died:

7 | **Hildeburge**
Born: Abt 997
Died:

15 | **--**
Born:
Died:

Sources include: *Royal Ancestors* (1989), chart 11527; Moriarty 112, 44-45, 12; Stuart 183, 335, 360; Chart 1719 with notes and sources.

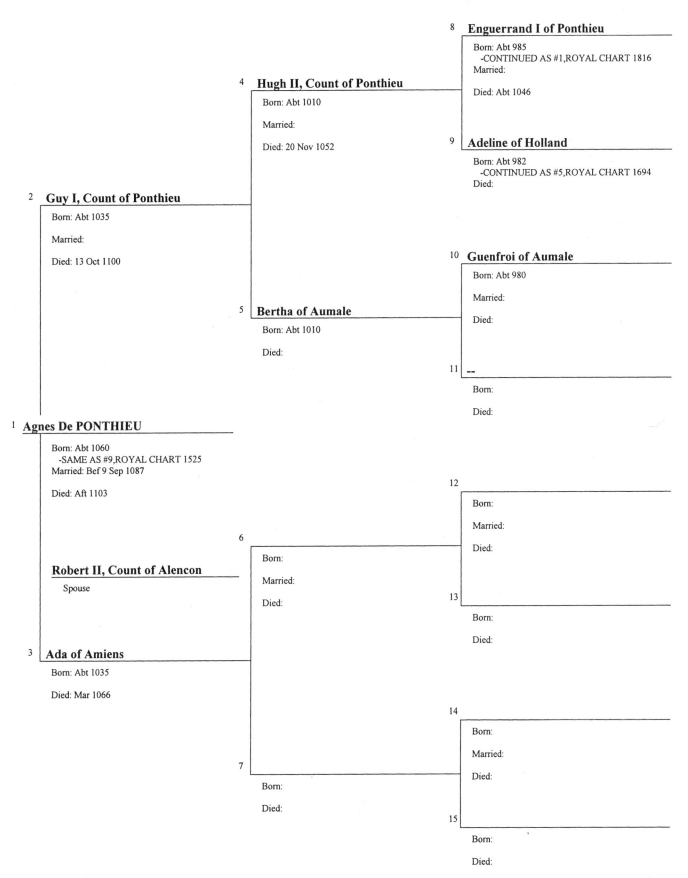

8 **Enguerrand I of Ponthieu**

Born: Abt 985
-CONTINUED AS #1,ROYAL CHART 1816
Married:

Died: Abt 1046

4 **Hugh II, Count of Ponthieu**

Born: Abt 1010

Married:

Died: 20 Nov 1052

9 **Adeline of Holland**

Born: Abt 982
-CONTINUED AS #5,ROYAL CHART 1694
Died:

2 **Guy I, Count of Ponthieu**

Born: Abt 1035

Married:

Died: 13 Oct 1100

10 **Guenfroi of Aumale**

Born: Abt 980

Married:

Died:

5 **Bertha of Aumale**

Born: Abt 1010

Died:

11 **__**

Born:

Died:

1 **Agnes De PONTHIEU**

Born: Abt 1060
-SAME AS #9,ROYAL CHART 1525
Married: Bef 9 Sep 1087

Died: Aft 1103

12

Born:

Married:

Died:

6

Born:

Married:

Died:

13

Born:

Died:

Robert II, Count of Alencon

Spouse

3 **Ada of Amiens**

Born: Abt 1035

Died: Mar 1066

14

Born:

Married:

Died:

7

Born:

Died:

15

Born:

Died:

Sources include: *Royal Ancestors* (1989), charts 11466, 11778-79; Stuart 244; Moriarty 113-114; *Ancestral Roots* 108-25; Roberts *AAP*, p.195 (#4 ancestry).

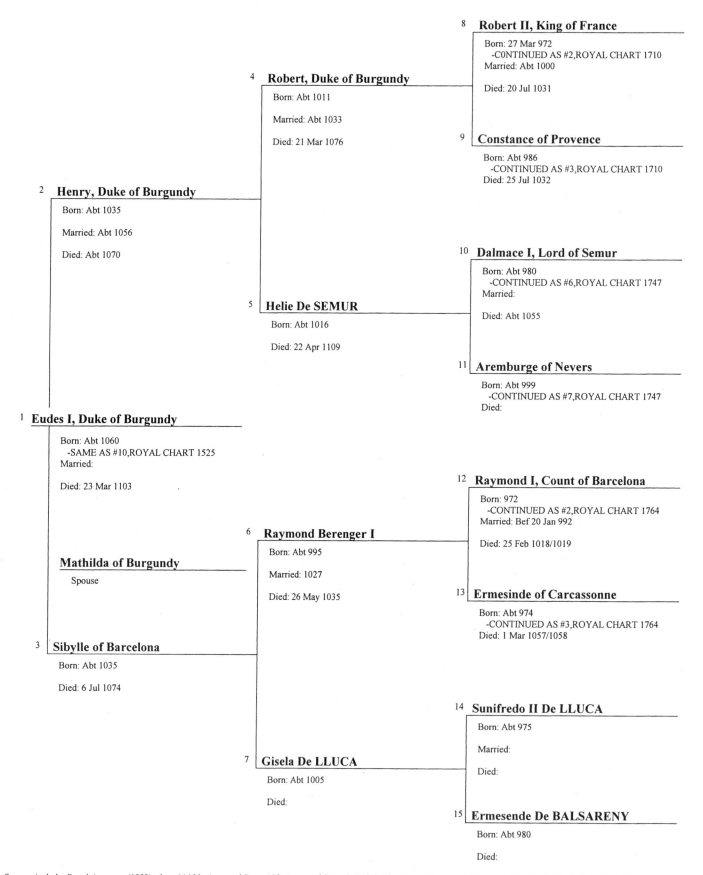

8 **Robert II, King of France**

Born: 27 Mar 972
-CONTINUED AS #2,ROYAL CHART 1710
Married: Abt 1000

Died: 20 Jul 1031

4 **Robert, Duke of Burgundy**

Born: Abt 1011

Married: Abt 1033

Died: 21 Mar 1076

9 **Constance of Provence**

Born: Abt 986
-CONTINUED AS #3,ROYAL CHART 1710
Died: 25 Jul 1032

2 **Henry, Duke of Burgundy**

Born: Abt 1035

Married: Abt 1056

Died: Abt 1070

10 **Dalmace I, Lord of Semur**

Born: Abt 980
-CONTINUED AS #6,ROYAL CHART 1747
Married:

Died: Abt 1055

5 **Helie De SEMUR**

Born: Abt 1016

Died: 22 Apr 1109

11 **Aremburge of Nevers**

Born: Abt 999
-CONTINUED AS #7,ROYAL CHART 1747
Died:

1 **Eudes I, Duke of Burgundy**

Born: Abt 1060
-SAME AS #10,ROYAL CHART 1525
Married:

Died: 23 Mar 1103

12 **Raymond I, Count of Barcelona**

Born: 972
-CONTINUED AS #2,ROYAL CHART 1764
Married: Bef 20 Jan 992

Died: 25 Feb 1018/1019

6 **Raymond Berenger I**

Born: Abt 995

Married: 1027

Died: 26 May 1035

13 **Ermesinde of Carcassonne**

Born: Abt 974
-CONTINUED AS #3,ROYAL CHART 1764
Died: 1 Mar 1057/1058

Mathilda of Burgundy

Spouse

3 **Sibylle of Barcelona**

Born: Abt 1035

Died: 6 Jul 1074

14 **Sunifredo II De LLUCA**

Born: Abt 975

Married:

Died:

7 **Gisela De LLUCA**

Born: Abt 1005

Died:

15 **Ermesende De BALSARENY**

Born: Abt 980

Died:

Sources include: *Royal Ancestors* (1989), chart 11466; *Ancestral Roots* 108; *Ancestral Roots* 8 (2004), Line 108; Schwennicke 2:20, 69; Stuart 245; Moriarty 114, 83. Note: #6 is also given as Berenger Ramon I.

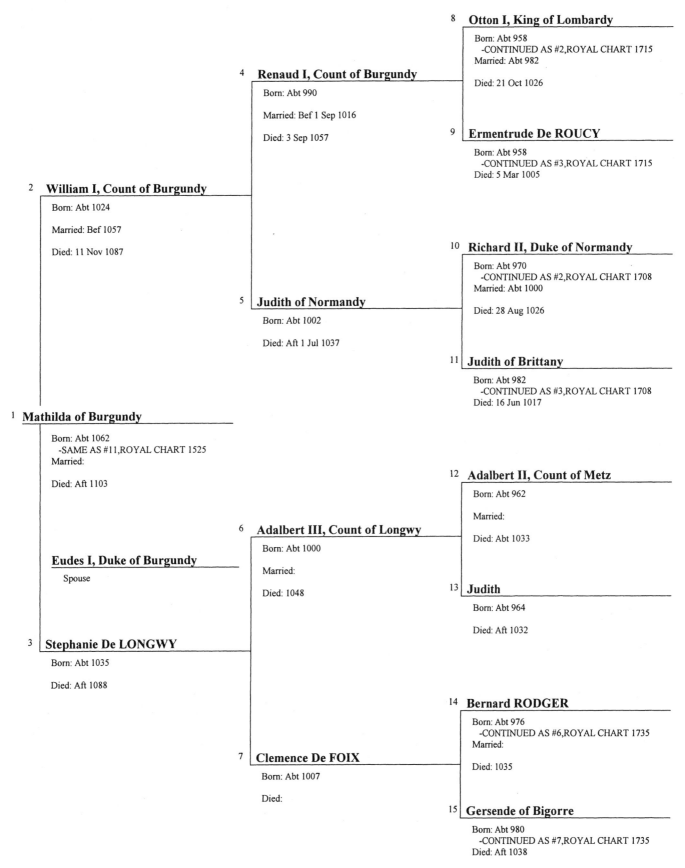

8 Otton I, King of Lombardy

Born: Abt 958
-CONTINUED AS #2,ROYAL CHART 1715
Married: Abt 982

Died: 21 Oct 1026

4 Renaud I, Count of Burgundy

Born: Abt 990

Married: Bef 1 Sep 1016

Died: 3 Sep 1057

9 Ermentrude De ROUCY

Born: Abt 958
-CONTINUED AS #3,ROYAL CHART 1715
Died: 5 Mar 1005

2 William I, Count of Burgundy

Born: Abt 1024

Married: Bef 1057

Died: 11 Nov 1087

10 Richard II, Duke of Normandy

Born: Abt 970
-CONTINUED AS #2,ROYAL CHART 1708
Married: Abt 1000

Died: 28 Aug 1026

5 Judith of Normandy

Born: Abt 1002

Died: Aft 1 Jul 1037

11 Judith of Brittany

Born: Abt 982
-CONTINUED AS #3,ROYAL CHART 1708
Died: 16 Jun 1017

1 Mathilda of Burgundy

Born: Abt 1062
-SAME AS #11,ROYAL CHART 1525
Married:

Died: Aft 1103

12 Adalbert II, Count of Metz

Born: Abt 962

Married:

Died: Abt 1033

6 Adalbert III, Count of Longwy

Born: Abt 1000

Married:

Died: 1048

13 Judith

Born: Abt 964

Died: Aft 1032

Eudes I, Duke of Burgundy

Spouse

3 Stephanie De LONGWY

Born: Abt 1035

Died: Aft 1088

14 Bernard RODGER

Born: Abt 976
-CONTINUED AS #6,ROYAL CHART 1735
Married:

Died: 1035

7 Clemence De FOIX

Born: Abt 1007

Died:

15 Gersende of Bigorre

Born: Abt 980
-CONTINUED AS #7,ROYAL CHART 1735
Died: Aft 1038

Sources include: *Royal Ancestors* (1989), chart 11466; Stuart 245-31, 94, 105; Moriarty 114, 62; *Ancestral Roots* 108-24, 132; Charts 1734-35 with notes & sources. Note: The parentage and ancestry of #12 &13 Adalbert & Judith is disputed. Three different versions are given by Stuart, Moriarty, and Turton.

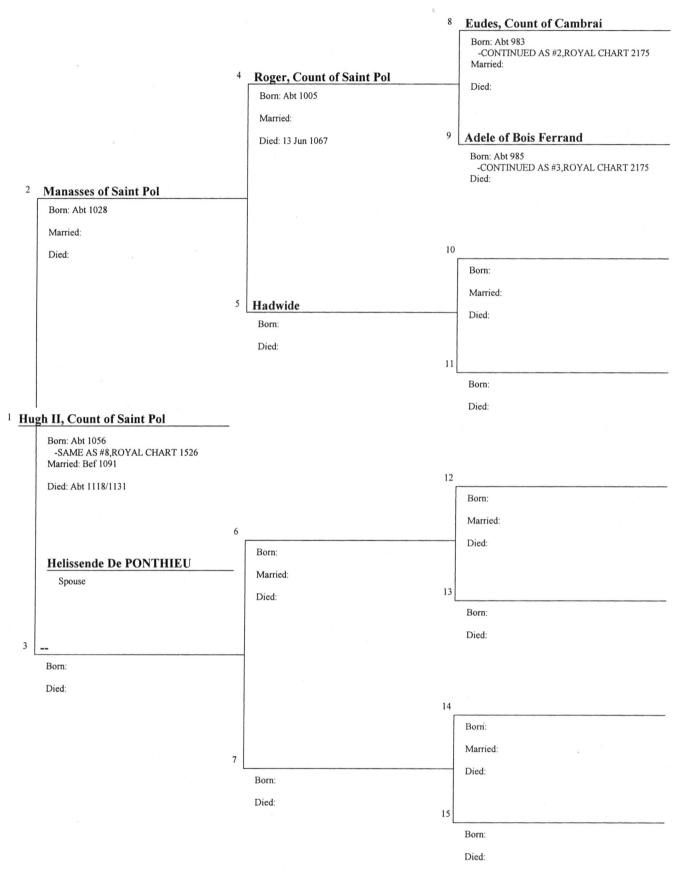

8 Eudes, Count of Cambrai

Born: Abt 983
  -CONTINUED AS #2,ROYAL CHART 2175
Married:

Died:

4 Roger, Count of Saint Pol

Born: Abt 1005

Married:

Died: 13 Jun 1067

9 Adele of Bois Ferrand

Born: Abt 985
  -CONTINUED AS #3,ROYAL CHART 2175
Died:

2 Manasses of Saint Pol

Born: Abt 1028

Married:

Died:

10

Born:

Married:

Died:

5 Hadwide

Born:

Died:

11

Born:

Died:

1 Hugh II, Count of Saint Pol

Born: Abt 1056
  -SAME AS #8,ROYAL CHART 1526
Married: Bef 1091

Died: Abt 1118/1131

12

Born:

Married:

Died:

6

Born:

Married:

Died:

13

Born:

Died:

Helissende De PONTHIEU

Spouse

3 --

Born:

Died:

14

Born:

Married:

Died:

7

Born:

Died:

15

Born:

Died:

Sources include: *Royal Ancestors* 11686; Stuart 184; Faris preliminary Charlemagne manuscript (June 1995), pp. 242-243, 72; Moriarty 115. Note: Sources agree that #1 Hugh was the grandson of #4 Roger, but #2 is uncertain. #2 was formerly claimed as Hugh I but is now believed to be either Manasses or a brother Robert.

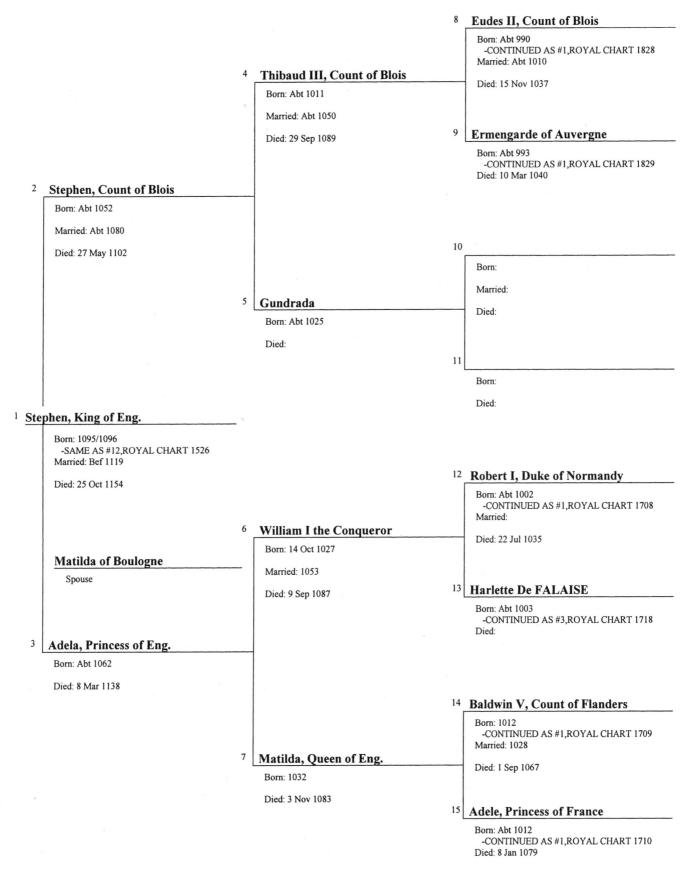

8 Eudes II, Count of Blois

Born: Abt 990
-CONTINUED AS #1,ROYAL CHART 1828
Married: Abt 1010

Died: 15 Nov 1037

4 **Thibaud III, Count of Blois**

Born: Abt 1011

Married: Abt 1050

Died: 29 Sep 1089

9 Ermengarde of Auvergne

Born: Abt 993
-CONTINUED AS #1,ROYAL CHART 1829
Died: 10 Mar 1040

2 **Stephen, Count of Blois**

Born: Abt 1052

Married: Abt 1080

Died: 27 May 1102

10

Born:

Married:

Died:

5 **Gundrada**

Born: Abt 1025

Died:

11

Born:

Died:

1 **Stephen, King of Eng.**

Born: 1095/1096
-SAME AS #12,ROYAL CHART 1526
Married: Bef 1119

Died: 25 Oct 1154

12 **Robert I, Duke of Normandy**

Born: Abt 1002
-CONTINUED AS #1,ROYAL CHART 1708
Married:

Died: 22 Jul 1035

6 **William I the Conqueror**

Born: 14 Oct 1027

Married: 1053

Died: 9 Sep 1087

13 Harlette De FALAISE

Born: Abt 1003
-CONTINUED AS #3,ROYAL CHART 1718
Died:

Matilda of Boulogne

Spouse

3 **Adela, Princess of Eng.**

Born: Abt 1062

Died: 8 Mar 1138

14 **Baldwin V, Count of Flanders**

Born: 1012
-CONTINUED AS #1,ROYAL CHART 1709
Married: 1028

Died: 1 Sep 1067

7 **Matilda, Queen of Eng.**

Born: 1032

Died: 3 Nov 1083

15 **Adele, Princess of France**

Born: Abt 1012
-CONTINUED AS #1,ROYAL CHART 1710
Died: 8 Jan 1079

Sources include: *Royal Ancestors* (1989), chart 11420; Stuart 133; Faris preliminary Charlemagne manuscript (June 1995), pp. 50-51; *Ancestral Roots* 137; Moriarty 117. Note: #5 Gundrada (Gondree, Gunnor) is disputed. #4 Thibaud is believed to have had three wives. #5 has also been claimed as Gersende or Gersinda of Maine (1st wife) and as Alix De Crepi (3rd wife).

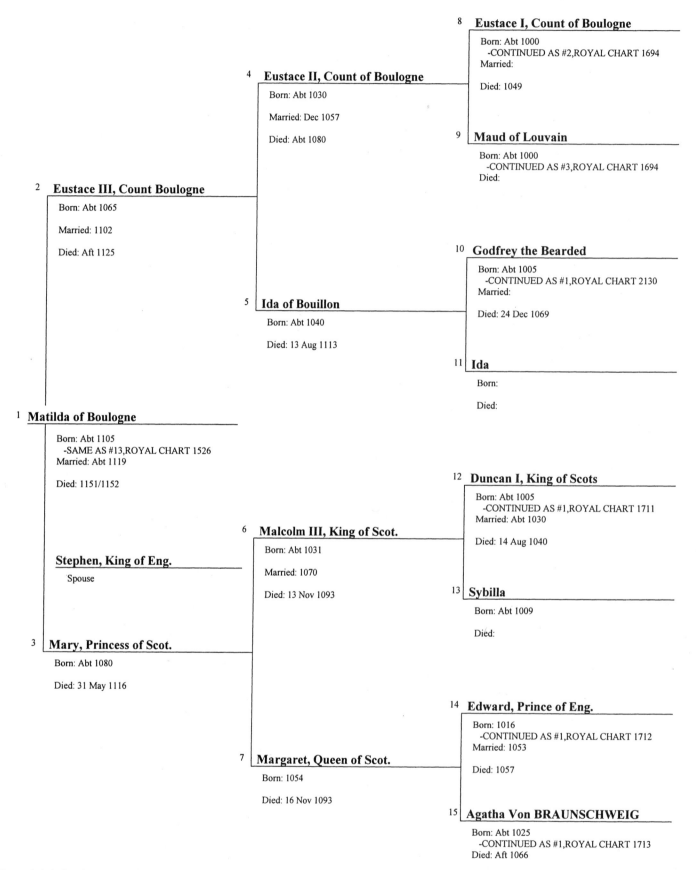

8 Eustace I, Count of Boulogne

Born: Abt 1000
-CONTINUED AS #2,ROYAL CHART 1694
Married:

Died: 1049

4 Eustace II, Count of Boulogne

Born: Abt 1030

Married: Dec 1057

Died: Abt 1080

9 Maud of Louvain

Born: Abt 1000
-CONTINUED AS #3,ROYAL CHART 1694
Died:

2 Eustace III, Count Boulogne

Born: Abt 1065

Married: 1102

Died: Aft 1125

10 Godfrey the Bearded

Born: Abt 1005
-CONTINUED AS #1,ROYAL CHART 2130
Married:

Died: 24 Dec 1069

5 Ida of Bouillon

Born: Abt 1040

Died: 13 Aug 1113

11 Ida

Born:

Died:

1 Matilda of Boulogne

Born: Abt 1105
-SAME AS #13,ROYAL CHART 1526
Married: Abt 1119

Died: 1151/1152

12 Duncan I, King of Scots

Born: Abt 1005
-CONTINUED AS #1,ROYAL CHART 1711
Married: Abt 1030

Died: 14 Aug 1040

6 Malcolm III, King of Scot.

Born: Abt 1031

Married: 1070

Died: 13 Nov 1093

Stephen, King of Eng.

Spouse

13 Sybilla

Born: Abt 1009

Died:

3 Mary, Princess of Scot.

Born: Abt 1080

Died: 31 May 1116

14 Edward, Prince of Eng.

Born: 1016
-CONTINUED AS #1,ROYAL CHART 1712
Married: 1053

Died: 1057

7 Margaret, Queen of Scot.

Born: 1054

Died: 16 Nov 1093

15 Agatha Von BRAUNSCHWEIG

Born: Abt 1025
-CONTINUED AS #1,ROYAL CHART 1713
Died: Aft 1066

Sources include: *Royal Ancestors* (1989), chart 11421; Faris preliminary Charlemagne manuscript (June 1995), pp. 58-59, 16-17; *Ancestral Roots* 158; Stuart 242; Moriarty 165-166, 126 (#10 ancestry).

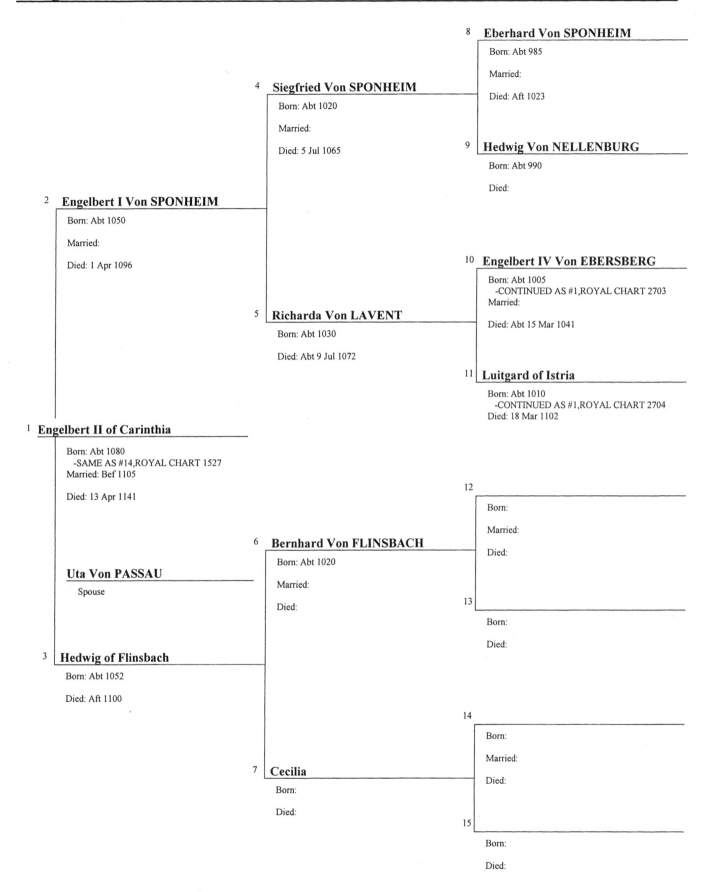

8 Eberhard Von SPONHEIM
Born: Abt 985
Married:
Died: Aft 1023

4 Siegfried Von SPONHEIM
Born: Abt 1020
Married:
Died: 5 Jul 1065

9 Hedwig Von NELLENBURG
Born: Abt 990
Died:

2 Engelbert I Von SPONHEIM
Born: Abt 1050
Married:
Died: 1 Apr 1096

10 Engelbert IV Von EBERSBERG
Born: Abt 1005
  -CONTINUED AS #1,ROYAL CHART 2703
Married:
Died: Abt 15 Mar 1041

5 Richarda Von LAVENT
Born: Abt 1030
Died: Abt 9 Jul 1072

11 Luitgard of Istria
Born: Abt 1010
  -CONTINUED AS #1,ROYAL CHART 2704
Died: 18 Mar 1102

1 Engelbert II of Carinthia
Born: Abt 1080
  -SAME AS #14,ROYAL CHART 1527
Married: Bef 1105
Died: 13 Apr 1141

12
Born:
Married:
Died:

6 Bernhard Von FLINSBACH
Born: Abt 1020
Married:
Died:

13
Born:
Died:

Uta Von PASSAU
Spouse

3 Hedwig of Flinsbach
Born: Abt 1052
Died: Aft 1100

14
Born:
Married:
Died:

7 Cecilia
Born:
Died:

15
Born:
Died:

Sources include: *Royal Ancestors* (1989), chart 11400; Faris preliminary Charlemagne manuscript (June 1995), p. 42; Stuart 228, 129; Moriarty 119-120; Turton 205; *Ancestral Roots* 137-24 (#1 Engelbert). Notes: There is much uncertainty on the above lines. The parentage of #3 Hedwig and of #4 Siegfried is uncertain. Turton makes #8 Eberhard the son of Aribo IV and continues the line. The identity of #11 Luitgard is uncertain.

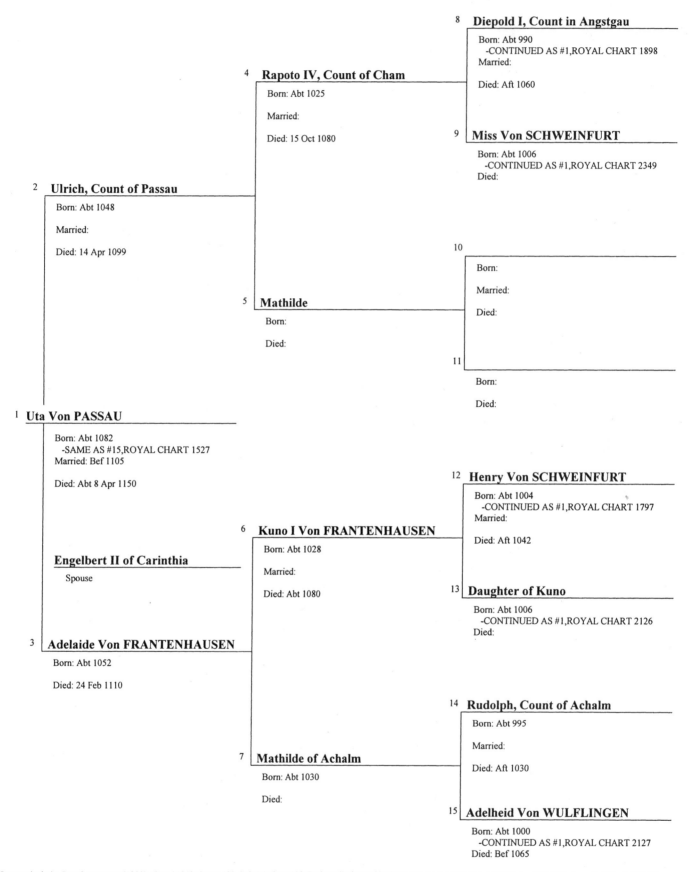

8 Diepold I, Count in Angstgau

Born: Abt 990
  -CONTINUED AS #1,ROYAL CHART 1898
Married:

Died: Aft 1060

4 Rapoto IV, Count of Cham

Born: Abt 1025

Married:

Died: 15 Oct 1080

9 Miss Von SCHWEINFURT

Born: Abt 1006
  -CONTINUED AS #1,ROYAL CHART 2349
Died:

2 Ulrich, Count of Passau

Born: Abt 1048

Married:

Died: 14 Apr 1099

10

Born:

Married:

Died:

5 Mathilde

Born:

Died:

11

Born:

Died:

1 Uta Von PASSAU

Born: Abt 1082
  -SAME AS #15,ROYAL CHART 1527
Married: Bef 1105

Died: Abt 8 Apr 1150

12 Henry Von SCHWEINFURT

Born: Abt 1004
  -CONTINUED AS #1,ROYAL CHART 1797
Married:

Died: Aft 1042

6 Kuno I Von FRANTENHAUSEN

Born: Abt 1028

Married:

Died: Abt 1080

13 Daughter of Kuno

Born: Abt 1006
  -CONTINUED AS #1,ROYAL CHART 2126
Died:

Engelbert II of Carinthia

Spouse

3 Adelaide Von FRANTENHAUSEN

Born: Abt 1052

Died: 24 Feb 1110

14 Rudolph, Count of Achalm

Born: Abt 995

Married:

Died: Aft 1030

7 Mathilde of Achalm

Born: Abt 1030

Died:

15 Adelheid Von WULFLINGEN

Born: Abt 1000
  -CONTINUED AS #1,ROYAL CHART 2127
Died: Bef 1065

Sources include: *Royal Ancestors* (1989), chart 11840; Stuart 128, 213; Moriarty 123; Faris preliminary Charlemagne manuscript (June 1995), pp. 101-102; *Ancestral Roots* 137-24.
Note: The parentage of #2 Ulrich is not certain. Faris (citing West Winter, in whose work he has expressed low confidence) gives Rapoto and Mathilde, as shown. Moriarty and Stuart give #4 as an unknown brother of this Rapoto.

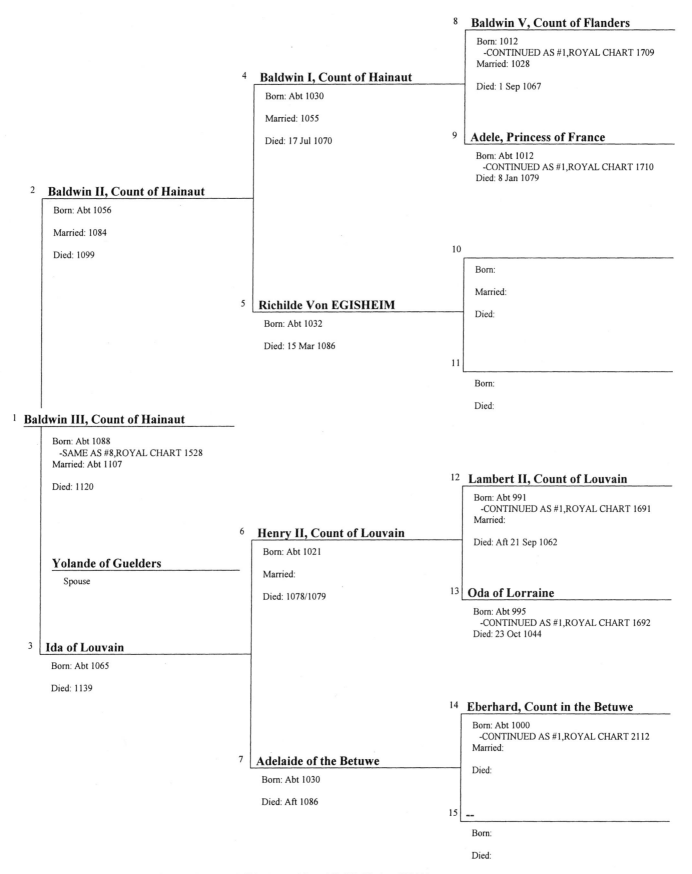

Pedigree Chart

8 **Baldwin V, Count of Flanders**
- Born: 1012
  - -CONTINUED AS #1,ROYAL CHART 1709
- Married: 1028
- Died: 1 Sep 1067

4 **Baldwin I, Count of Hainaut**
- Born: Abt 1030
- Married: 1055
- Died: 17 Jul 1070

9 **Adele, Princess of France**
- Born: Abt 1012
  - -CONTINUED AS #1,ROYAL CHART 1710
- Died: 8 Jan 1079

2 **Baldwin II, Count of Hainaut**
- Born: Abt 1056
- Married: 1084
- Died: 1099

10
- Born:
- Married:
- Died:

5 **Richilde Von EGISHEIM**
- Born: Abt 1032
- Died: 15 Mar 1086

11
- Born:
- Died:

1 **Baldwin III, Count of Hainaut**
- Born: Abt 1088
  - -SAME AS #8,ROYAL CHART 1528
- Married: Abt 1107
- Died: 1120

12 **Lambert II, Count of Louvain**
- Born: Abt 991
  - -CONTINUED AS #1,ROYAL CHART 1691
- Married:
- Died: Aft 21 Sep 1062

6 **Henry II, Count of Louvain**
- Born: Abt 1021
- Married:
- Died: 1078/1079

Yolande of Guelders
- Spouse

13 **Oda of Lorraine**
- Born: Abt 995
  - -CONTINUED AS #1,ROYAL CHART 1692
- Died: 23 Oct 1044

3 **Ida of Louvain**
- Born: Abt 1065
- Died: 1139

14 **Eberhard, Count in the Betuwe**
- Born: Abt 1000
  - -CONTINUED AS #1,ROYAL CHART 2112
- Married:
- Died:

7 **Adelaide of the Betuwe**
- Born: Abt 1030
- Died: Aft 1086

15 **--**
- Born:
- Died:

Sources include: *Royal Ancestors* (1989), chart 11658; Stuart 73, 138; *Ancestral Roots* 163, 160; Moriarty 124-125.

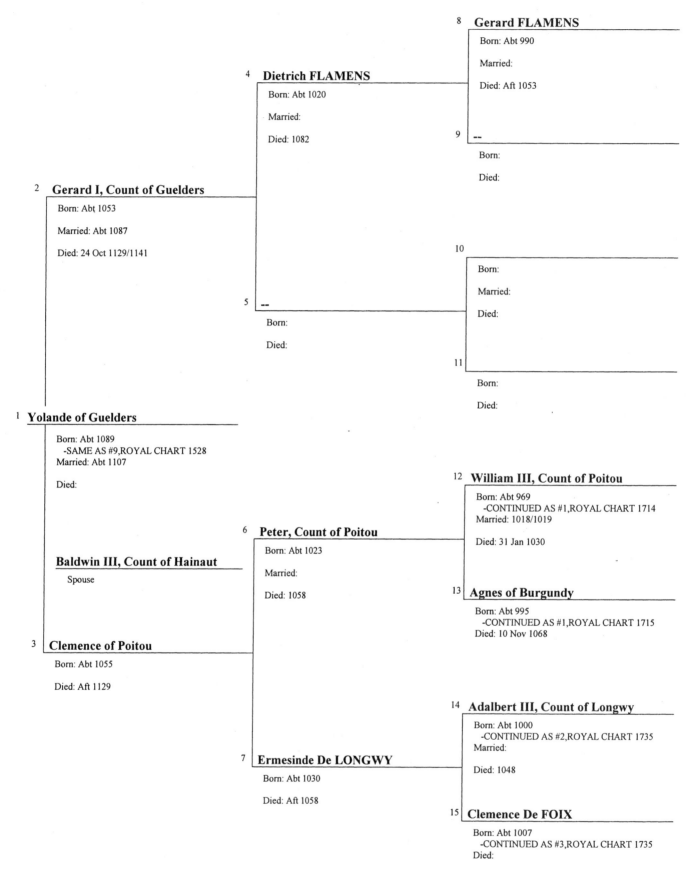

8 **Gerard FLAMENS**

Born: Abt 990

Married:

Died: Aft 1053

4 **Dietrich FLAMENS**

Born: Abt 1020

Married:

Died: 1082

9 --

Born:

Died:

2 **Gerard I, Count of Guelders**

Born: Abt 1053

Married: Abt 1087

Died: 24 Oct 1129/1141

10

Born:

Married:

Died:

5 --

Born:

Died:

11

Born:

Died:

1 **Yolande of Guelders**

Born: Abt 1089
　-SAME AS #9,ROYAL CHART 1528
Married: Abt 1107

Died:

12 **William III, Count of Poitou**

Born: Abt 969
　-CONTINUED AS #1,ROYAL CHART 1714
Married: 1018/1019

Died: 31 Jan 1030

6 **Peter, Count of Poitou**

Born: Abt 1023

Married:

Died: 1058

13 **Agnes of Burgundy**

Born: Abt 995
　-CONTINUED AS #1,ROYAL CHART 1715
Died: 10 Nov 1068

Baldwin III, Count of Hainaut

Spouse

3 **Clemence of Poitou**

Born: Abt 1055

Died: Aft 1129

14 **Adalbert III, Count of Longwy**

Born: Abt 1000
　-CONTINUED AS #2,ROYAL CHART 1735
Married:

Died: 1048

7 **Ermesinde De LONGWY**

Born: Abt 1030

Died: Aft 1058

15 **Clemence De FOIX**

Born: Abt 1007
　-CONTINUED AS #3,ROYAL CHART 1735
Died:

Sources include: *Royal Ancestors* (1989), chart 11658; Stuart 119; *Ancestral Roots* 163-25 (#1 & 2); Moriarty 127, 36; Faris preliminary Charlemagne manuscript (June 1995), p. 217 (#3 ancestry). Notes: #6 Peter is also called William. Stuart and Faris agree with the parentage shown for #7 Ermesinde. Moriarty (36, 246) states that the parentage of Ermesinde is unknown. Faris (pp. 217, 245) gives #3 (wife of #2 Gerard) as unknown, rejecting the claim of Clemence of Poitou. Moriarty (note pp. 127-128) accepts #3 as Clemence (md 1st Conrad I--see chart 1558--and 2nd Gerard). The Moriarty conclusion is being accepted here.

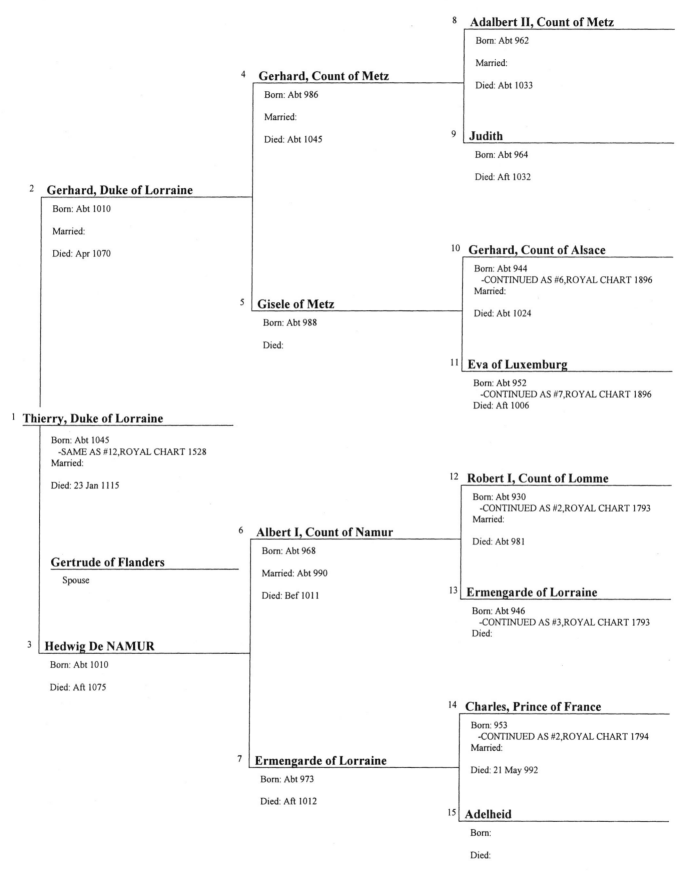

8 **Adalbert II, Count of Metz**

Born: Abt 962

Married:

Died: Abt 1033

4 **Gerhard, Count of Metz**

Born: Abt 986

Married:

Died: Abt 1045

9 **Judith**

Born: Abt 964

Died: Aft 1032

2 **Gerhard, Duke of Lorraine**

Born: Abt 1010

Married:

Died: Apr 1070

10 **Gerhard, Count of Alsace**

Born: Abt 944
-CONTINUED AS #6,ROYAL CHART 1896
Married:

Died: Abt 1024

5 **Gisele of Metz**

Born: Abt 988

Died:

11 **Eva of Luxemburg**

Born: Abt 952
-CONTINUED AS #7,ROYAL CHART 1896
Died: Aft 1006

1 **Thierry, Duke of Lorraine**

Born: Abt 1045
-SAME AS #12,ROYAL CHART 1528
Married:

Died: 23 Jan 1115

12 **Robert I, Count of Lomme**

Born: Abt 930
-CONTINUED AS #2,ROYAL CHART 1793
Married:

Died: Abt 981

6 **Albert I, Count of Namur**

Born: Abt 968

Married: Abt 990

Died: Bef 1011

Gertrude of Flanders

Spouse

13 **Ermengarde of Lorraine**

Born: Abt 946
-CONTINUED AS #3,ROYAL CHART 1793
Died:

3 **Hedwig De NAMUR**

Born: Abt 1010

Died: Aft 1075

14 **Charles, Prince of France**

Born: 953
-CONTINUED AS #2,ROYAL CHART 1794
Married:

Died: 21 May 992

7 **Ermengarde of Lorraine**

Born: Abt 973

Died: Aft 1012

15 **Adelheid**

Born:

Died:

Sources include: *Royal Ancestors* (1989), chart 11664; Stuart 158; *Ancestral Roots* 164-24; Moriarty 128-130; Turton 200. Notes: #1 is also called Dietrich. The parentage and ancestry of #8 & 9 Adalbert II & Judith is disputed. Three different versions are given by Stuart, Moriarty, and Turton. The parentage of #5 Gisele is also disputed. The Stuart version is shown above.

8 **Baldwin IV, Count of Flanders**

Born: 980
-CONTINUED AS #2,ROYAL CHART 1709
Married: 1012

Died: 30 May 1035

4 **Baldwin V, Count of Flanders**

Born: 1012

Married: 1028

Died: 1 Sep 1067

9 **Ogive De LUXEMBOURG**

Born: Abt 995
-CONTINUED AS #3,ROYAL CHART 1709
Died: 21 Feb 1030

2 **Robert Le FRISON**

Born: Abt 1035

Married: 1063

Died: 3 Oct 1093

10 **Robert II, King of France**

Born: 27 Mar 972
-CONTINUED AS #2,ROYAL CHART 1710
Married: Abt 1000

Died: 20 Jul 1031

5 **Adele, Princess of France**

Born: Abt 1012

Died: 8 Jan 1079

11 **Constance of Provence**

Born: Abt 986
-CONTINUED AS #3,ROYAL CHART 1710
Died: 25 Jul 1032

1 **Gertrude of Flanders**

Born: Abt 1070
-SAME AS #13,ROYAL CHART 1528
Married:

Died: 1117

12 **Bernard I, Duke of Saxony**

Born: Abt 942
-CONTINUED AS #1,ROYAL CHART 1795
Married: Abt 990

Died: 9 Feb 1011

6 **Bernard II, Duke of Saxony**

Born: Abt 995

Married: Abt 1020

Died: 29 Jun 1059

Thierry, Duke of Lorraine

Spouse

13 **Hildegarde Von STADE**

Born: Abt 974
-CONTINUED AS #1,ROYAL CHART 1796
Died: 3 Oct 1011

3 **Gertrude of Saxony**

Born: Abt 1028

Died: 4 Aug 1113

14 **Henry Von SCHWEINFURT**

Born: 975
-CONTINUED AS #2,ROYAL CHART 1797
Married: Bef 1003

Died: 18 Sep 1017

7 **Elica Von SCHWEINFURT**

Born: Abt 1003

Died: Aft 1055

15 **Gerberge**

Born: Abt 975

Died:

Sources include: *Royal Ancestors* (1989), chart 11653; Stuart 205, 312; *Ancestral Roots* 164; Moriarty 130, 15, 56.

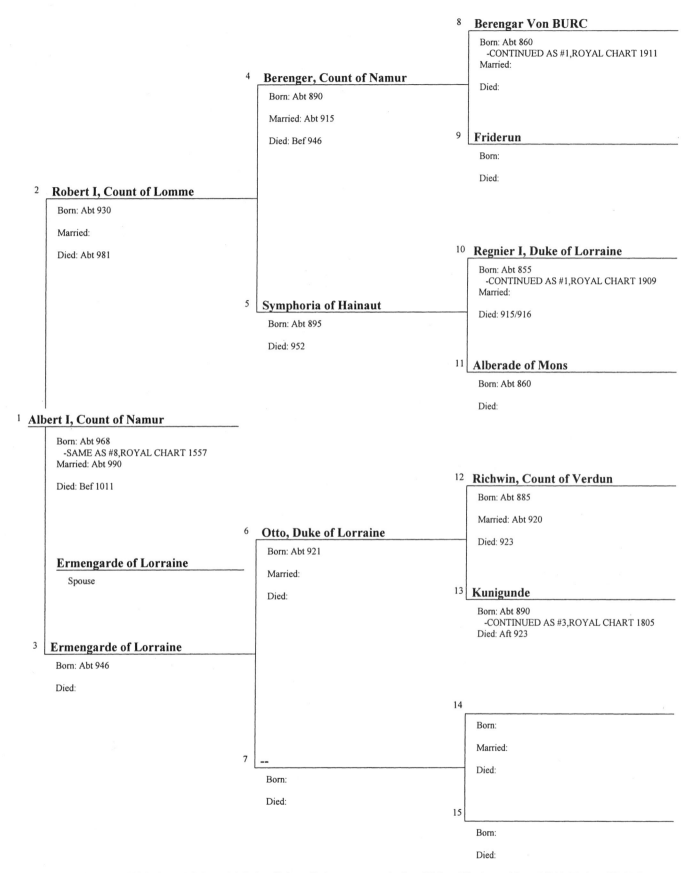

8 Berengar Von BURC

Born: Abt 860
    -CONTINUED AS #1,ROYAL CHART 1911
Married:

Died:

4 Berenger, Count of Namur

Born: Abt 890

Married: Abt 915

Died: Bef 946

9 Friderun

Born:

Died:

2 Robert I, Count of Lomme

Born: Abt 930

Married:

Died: Abt 981

10 Regnier I, Duke of Lorraine

Born: Abt 855
    -CONTINUED AS #1,ROYAL CHART 1909
Married:

Died: 915/916

5 Symphoria of Hainaut

Born: Abt 895

Died: 952

11 Alberade of Mons

Born: Abt 860

Died:

1 Albert I, Count of Namur

Born: Abt 968
    -SAME AS #8,ROYAL CHART 1557
Married: Abt 990

Died: Bef 1011

12 Richwin, Count of Verdun

Born: Abt 885

Married: Abt 920

Died: 923

6 Otto, Duke of Lorraine

Born: Abt 921

Married:

Died:

13 Kunigunde

Born: Abt 890
    -CONTINUED AS #3,ROYAL CHART 1805
Died: Aft 923

Ermengarde of Lorraine

Spouse

3 Ermengarde of Lorraine

Born: Abt 946

Died:

14

Born:

Married:

Died:

7 --

Born:

Died:

15

Born:

Died:

Sources include: *Royal Ancestors* (1989), chart 11572; Stuart 403; Faris preliminary Charlemagne manuscript (June 1995), p. 200; *Ancestral Roots* 149-20; Moriarty 128, 21; Turton 171. Notes: The ancestry shown for #2 Robert is not certain, and the identity and ancestry of #3 is not certain. Faris gives #3 as unknown. The parentage of #4 Berenger is not certain.

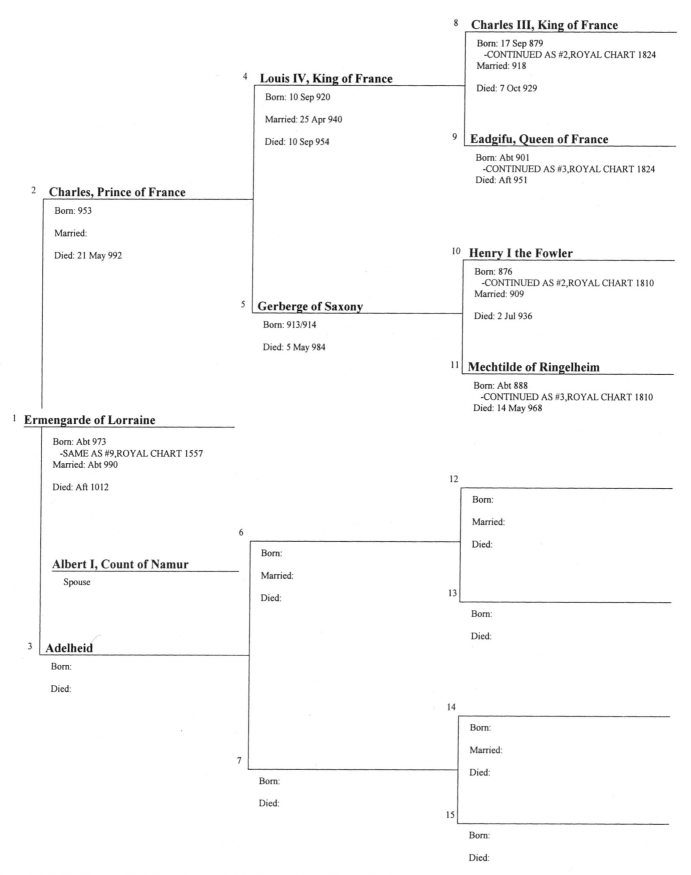

8 **Charles III, King of France**

Born: 17 Sep 879
  -CONTINUED AS #2,ROYAL CHART 1824
Married: 918

Died: 7 Oct 929

4 **Louis IV, King of France**

Born: 10 Sep 920

Married: 25 Apr 940

Died: 10 Sep 954

9 **Eadgifu, Queen of France**

Born: Abt 901
  -CONTINUED AS #3,ROYAL CHART 1824
Died: Aft 951

2 **Charles, Prince of France**

Born: 953

Married:

Died: 21 May 992

10 **Henry I the Fowler**

Born: 876
  -CONTINUED AS #2,ROYAL CHART 1810
Married: 909

Died: 2 Jul 936

5 **Gerberge of Saxony**

Born: 913/914

Died: 5 May 984

11 **Mechtilde of Ringelheim**

Born: Abt 888
  -CONTINUED AS #3,ROYAL CHART 1810
Died: 14 May 968

1 **Ermengarde of Lorraine**

Born: Abt 973
  -SAME AS #9,ROYAL CHART 1557
Married: Abt 990

Died: Aft 1012

12

Born:

Married:

Died:

6

Born:

Married:

Died:

13

Born:

Died:

Albert I, Count of Namur

Spouse

3 **Adelheid**

Born:

Died:

14

Born:

Married:

Died:

7

Born:

Died:

15

Born:

Died:

Sources include: *Royal Ancestors* 11572, 11520; *Ancestral Roots* 148-149; Moriarty 125, 35; Stuart 120, 171.

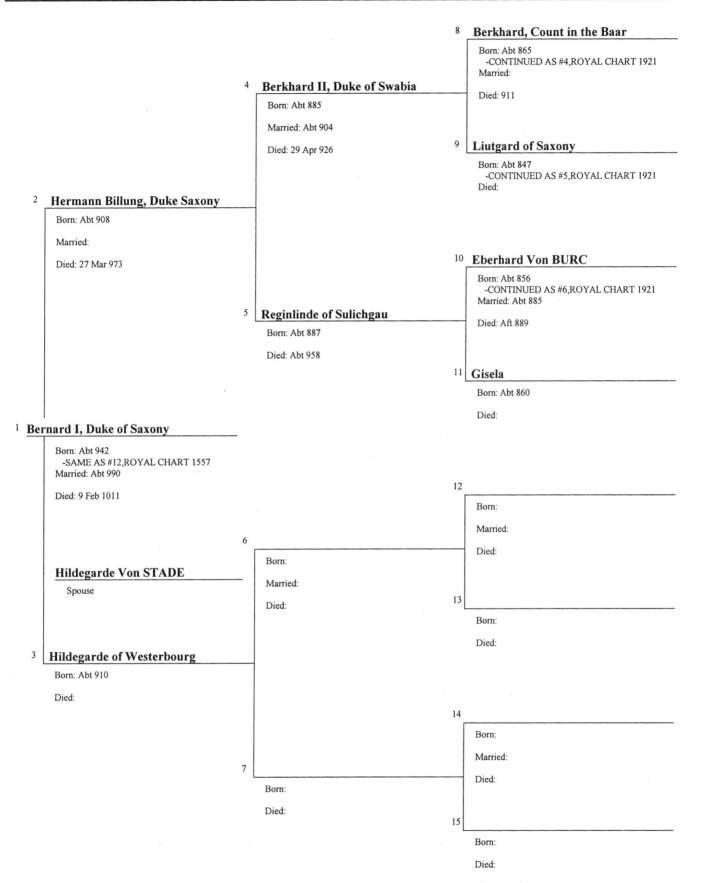

8 Berkhard, Count in the Baar

Born: Abt 865
-CONTINUED AS #4, ROYAL CHART 1921
Married:

Died: 911

4 Berkhard II, Duke of Swabia

Born: Abt 885

Married: Abt 904

Died: 29 Apr 926

9 Liutgard of Saxony

Born: Abt 847
-CONTINUED AS #5, ROYAL CHART 1921
Died:

2 Hermann Billung, Duke Saxony

Born: Abt 908

Married:

Died: 27 Mar 973

10 Eberhard Von BURC

Born: Abt 856
-CONTINUED AS #6, ROYAL CHART 1921
Married: Abt 885

Died: Aft 889

5 Reginlinde of Sulichgau

Born: Abt 887

Died: Abt 958

11 Gisela

Born: Abt 860

Died:

1 Bernard I, Duke of Saxony

Born: Abt 942
-SAME AS #12, ROYAL CHART 1557
Married: Abt 990

Died: 9 Feb 1011

12

Born:

Married:

Died:

6

Born:

Married:

Died:

13

Born:

Died:

Hildegarde Von STADE

Spouse

3 Hildegarde of Westerbourg

Born: Abt 910

Died:

14

Born:

Married:

Died:

7

Born:

Died:

15

Born:

Died:

Sources include: *Royal Ancestors* (1989), chart 11573; Stuart 312; Moriarty 56, 17; Faris preliminary Charlemagne manuscript (June 1995), pp. 143-145.

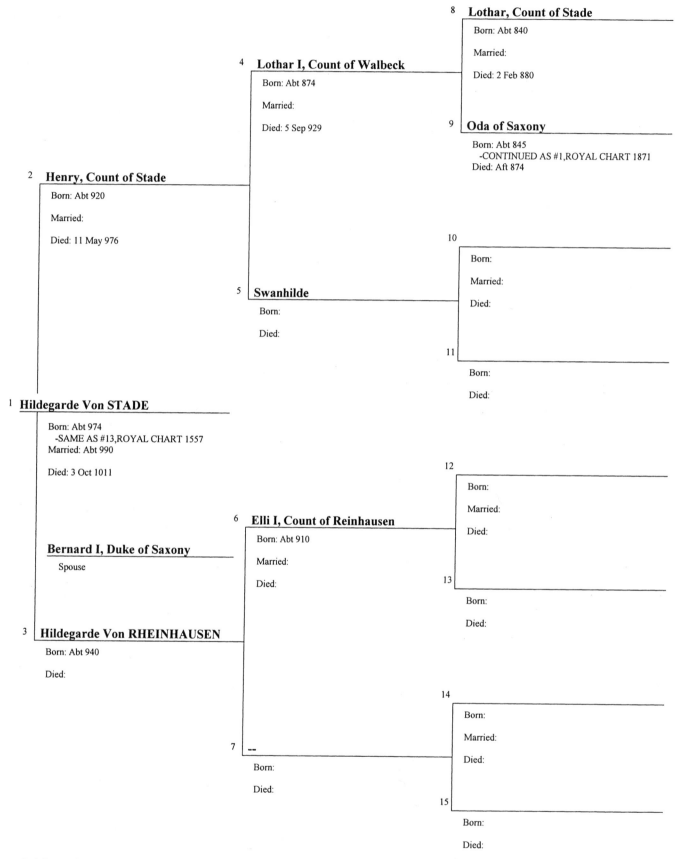

8 Lothar, Count of Stade
Born: Abt 840
Married:
Died: 2 Feb 880

4 Lothar I, Count of Walbeck
Born: Abt 874
Married:
Died: 5 Sep 929

9 Oda of Saxony
Born: Abt 845
-CONTINUED AS #1,ROYAL CHART 1871
Died: Aft 874

2 Henry, Count of Stade
Born: Abt 920
Married:
Died: 11 May 976

10
Born:
Married:
Died:

5 Swanhilde
Born:
Died:

11
Born:
Died:

1 Hildegarde Von STADE
Born: Abt 974
-SAME AS #13,ROYAL CHART 1557
Married: Abt 990
Died: 3 Oct 1011

Bernard I, Duke of Saxony
Spouse

12
Born:
Married:
Died:

6 Elli I, Count of Reinhausen
Born: Abt 910
Married:
Died:

13
Born:
Died:

3 Hildegarde Von RHEINHAUSEN
Born: Abt 940
Died:

14
Born:
Married:
Died:

7 --
Born:
Died:

15
Born:
Died:

Sources include: *Royal Ancestors* (1989), chart 11573; Stuart 301; Moriarty 56.

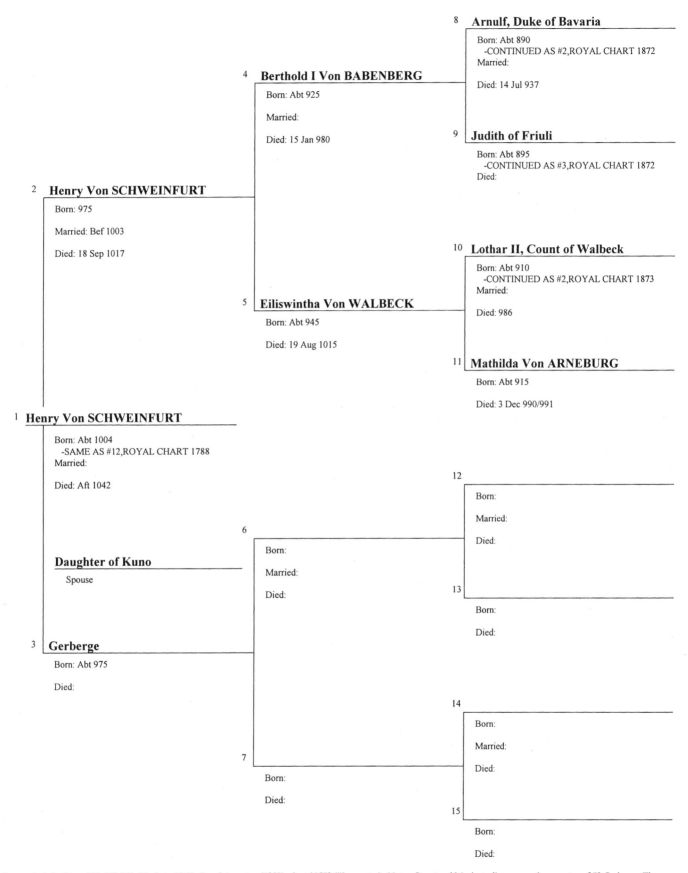

8 Arnulf, Duke of Bavaria

Born: Abt 890
-CONTINUED AS #2,ROYAL CHART 1872
Married:

Died: 14 Jul 937

4 Berthold I Von BABENBERG

Born: Abt 925

Married:

Died: 15 Jan 980

9 Judith of Friuli

Born: Abt 895
-CONTINUED AS #3,ROYAL CHART 1872
Died:

2 Henry Von SCHWEINFURT

Born: 975

Married: Bef 1003

Died: 18 Sep 1017

10 Lothar II, Count of Walbeck

Born: Abt 910
-CONTINUED AS #2,ROYAL CHART 1873
Married:

Died: 986

5 Eiliswintha Von WALBECK

Born: Abt 945

Died: 19 Aug 1015

11 Mathilda Von ARNEBURG

Born: Abt 915

Died: 3 Dec 990/991

1 Henry Von SCHWEINFURT

Born: Abt 1004
-SAME AS #12,ROYAL CHART 1788
Married:

Died: Aft 1042

12

Born:

Married:

Died:

6

Born:

Married:

Died:

Daughter of Kuno

Spouse

13

Born:

Died:

3 Gerberge

Born: Abt 975

Died:

14

Born:

Married:

Died:

7

Born:

Died:

15

Born:

Died:

Sources include: Stuart 213, 270-271; Moriarty 56-57; *Royal Ancestors* (1989), chart 11573 (#2 ancestry). Notes: Stuart and Moriarty disagree on the ancestry of #3 Gerberge. They show #11 Mathilda as daughter of Bruno, Count of Arneburg (died 19 Oct 1009-17), which is difficult chronologically.

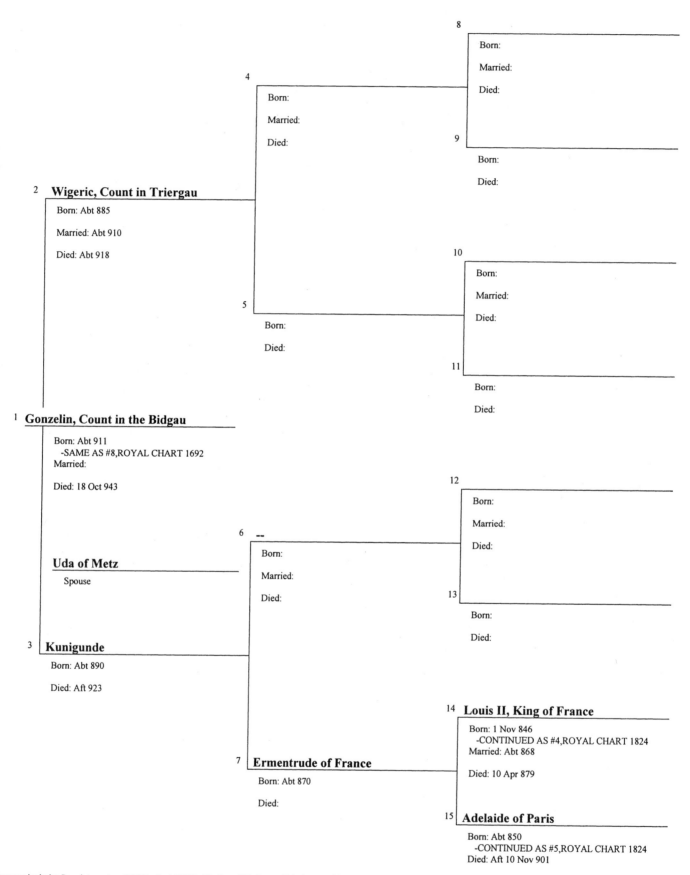

8

Born:

Married:

Died:

4

Born:

Married:

Died:

9

Born:

Died:

2 Wigeric, Count in Triergau

Born: Abt 885

Married: Abt 910

Died: Abt 918

10

Born:

Married:

Died:

5

Born:

Died:

11

Born:

Died:

1 Gonzelin, Count in the Bidgau

Born: Abt 911
    -SAME AS #8,ROYAL CHART 1692
Married:

Died: 18 Oct 943

12

Born:

Married:

Died:

6 --

Born:

Married:

Died:

13

Born:

Died:

Uda of Metz

Spouse

3 Kunigunde

Born: Abt 890

Died: Aft 923

14 Louis II, King of France

Born: 1 Nov 846
    -CONTINUED AS #4,ROYAL CHART 1824
Married: Abt 868

Died: 10 Apr 879

7 Ermentrude of France

Born: Abt 870

Died:

15 Adelaide of Paris

Born: Abt 850
    -CONTINUED AS #5,ROYAL CHART 1824
Died: Aft 10 Nov 901

Sources include: *Royal Ancestors* (1989), chart 11761; Moriarty 126; Stuart 104; *Ancestral Roots* 155-21, 143.

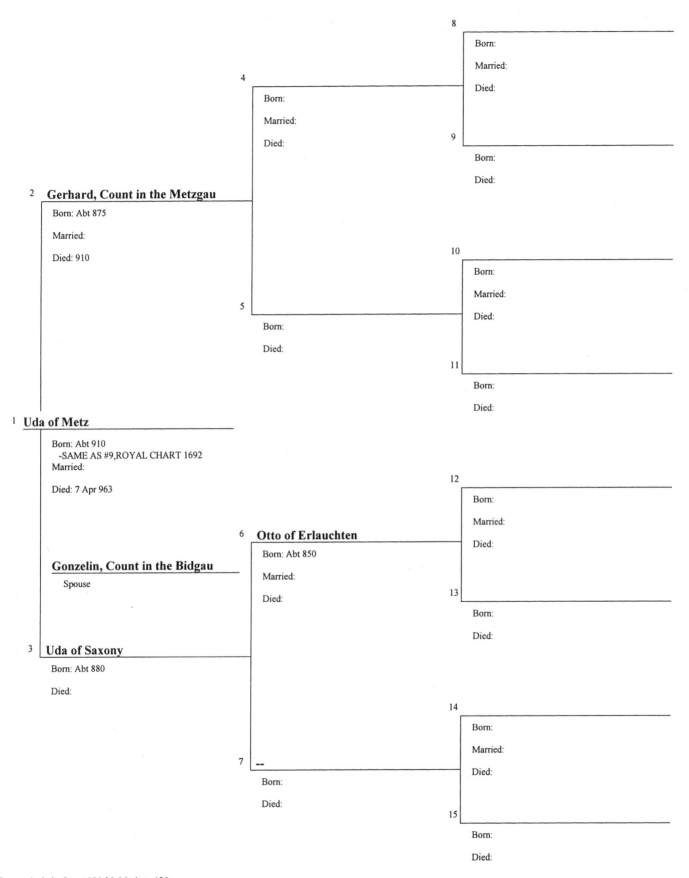

8

Born:

Married:

Died:

4

Born:

Married:

Died:

9

Born:

Died:

2 **Gerhard, Count in the Metzgau**

Born: Abt 875

Married:

Died: 910

10

Born:

Married:

Died:

5

Born:

Died:

11

Born:

Died:

1 **Uda of Metz**

Born: Abt 910
-SAME AS #9,ROYAL CHART 1692
Married:

Died: 7 Apr 963

12

Born:

Married:

Died:

6 **Otto of Erlauchten**

Born: Abt 850

Married:

Died:

13

Born:

Died:

Gonzelin, Count in the Bidgau

Spouse

3 **Uda of Saxony**

Born: Abt 880

Died:

14

Born:

Married:

Died:

7 --

Born:

Died:

15

Born:

Died:

Sources include: Stuart 104-36; Moriarty 126.

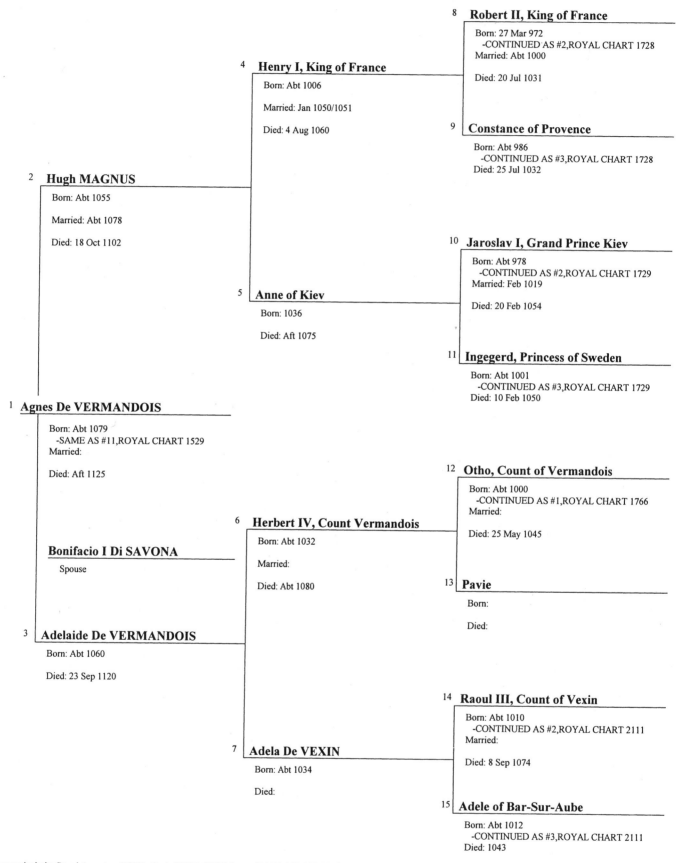

8 **Robert II, King of France**

Born: 27 Mar 972
  -CONTINUED AS #2,ROYAL CHART 1728
Married: Abt 1000

Died: 20 Jul 1031

4 **Henry I, King of France**

Born: Abt 1006

Married: Jan 1050/1051

Died: 4 Aug 1060

9 **Constance of Provence**

Born: Abt 986
  -CONTINUED AS #3,ROYAL CHART 1728
Died: 25 Jul 1032

2 **Hugh MAGNUS**

Born: Abt 1055

Married: Abt 1078

Died: 18 Oct 1102

10 **Jaroslav I, Grand Prince Kiev**

Born: Abt 978
  -CONTINUED AS #2,ROYAL CHART 1729
Married: Feb 1019

Died: 20 Feb 1054

5 **Anne of Kiev**

Born: 1036

Died: Aft 1075

11 **Ingegerd, Princess of Sweden**

Born: Abt 1001
  -CONTINUED AS #3,ROYAL CHART 1729
Died: 10 Feb 1050

1 **Agnes De VERMANDOIS**

Born: Abt 1079
  -SAME AS #11,ROYAL CHART 1529
Married:

Died: Aft 1125

12 **Otho, Count of Vermandois**

Born: Abt 1000
  -CONTINUED AS #1,ROYAL CHART 1766
Married:

Died: 25 May 1045

6 **Herbert IV, Count Vermandois**

Born: Abt 1032

Married:

Died: Abt 1080

Bonifacio I Di SAVONA

Spouse

13 **Pavie**

Born:

Died:

3 **Adelaide De VERMANDOIS**

Born: Abt 1060

Died: 23 Sep 1120

14 **Raoul III, Count of Vexin**

Born: Abt 1010
  -CONTINUED AS #2,ROYAL CHART 2111
Married:

Died: 8 Sep 1074

7 **Adela De VEXIN**

Born: Abt 1034

Died:

15 **Adele of Bar-Sur-Aube**

Born: Abt 1012
  -CONTINUED AS #3,ROYAL CHART 2111
Died: 1043

Sources include: *Royal Ancestors* (1989), charts 11846, 11425; Stuart 106-31, 143, 239; Moriarty 133; *Ancestral Roots* 50, 53 (#2 & 3 ancestry).

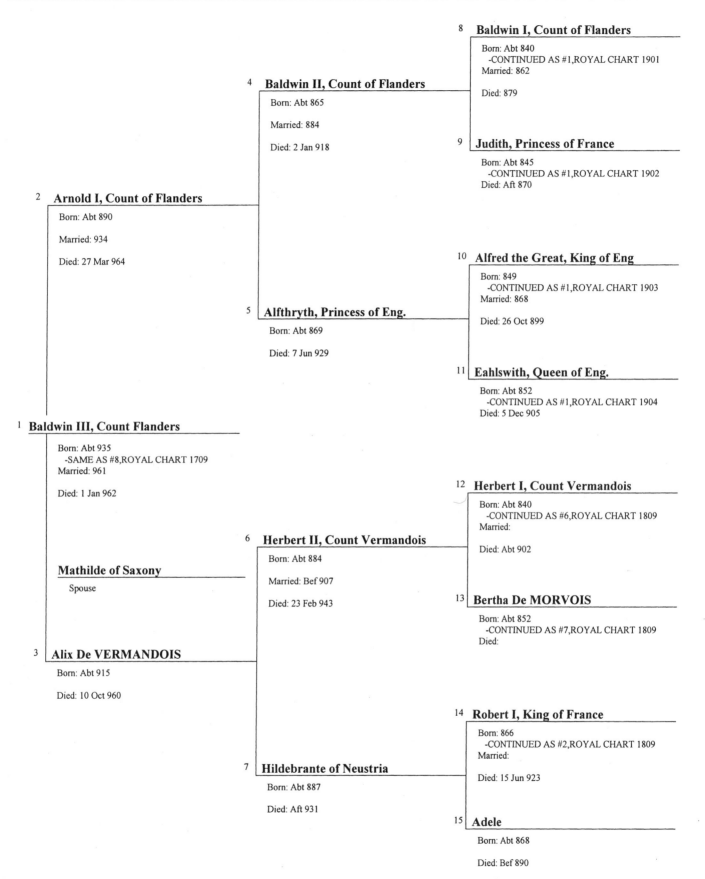

8   **Baldwin I, Count of Flanders**

Born: Abt 840
  -CONTINUED AS #1,ROYAL CHART 1901
Married: 862

Died: 879

4   **Baldwin II, Count of Flanders**

Born: Abt 865

Married: 884

Died: 2 Jan 918

9   **Judith, Princess of France**

Born: Abt 845
  -CONTINUED AS #1,ROYAL CHART 1902
Died: Aft 870

2   **Arnold I, Count of Flanders**

Born: Abt 890

Married: 934

Died: 27 Mar 964

10   **Alfred the Great, King of Eng**

Born: 849
  -CONTINUED AS #1,ROYAL CHART 1903
Married: 868

Died: 26 Oct 899

5   **Alfthryth, Princess of Eng.**

Born: Abt 869

Died: 7 Jun 929

11   **Eahlswith, Queen of Eng.**

Born: Abt 852
  -CONTINUED AS #1,ROYAL CHART 1904
Died: 5 Dec 905

1   **Baldwin III, Count Flanders**

Born: Abt 935
  -SAME AS #8,ROYAL CHART 1709
Married: 961

Died: 1 Jan 962

12   **Herbert I, Count Vermandois**

Born: Abt 840
  -CONTINUED AS #6,ROYAL CHART 1809
Married:

Died: Abt 902

6   **Herbert II, Count Vermandois**

Born: Abt 884

Married: Bef 907

Died: 23 Feb 943

13   **Bertha De MORVOIS**

Born: Abt 852
  -CONTINUED AS #7,ROYAL CHART 1809
Died:

Mathilde of Saxony

Spouse

3   **Alix De VERMANDOIS**

Born: Abt 915

Died: 10 Oct 960

14   **Robert I, King of France**

Born: 866
  -CONTINUED AS #2,ROYAL CHART 1809
Married:

Died: 15 Jun 923

7   **Hildebrante of Neustria**

Born: Abt 887

Died: Aft 931

15   **Adele**

Born: Abt 868

Died: Bef 890

Sources include: *Royal Ancestors* 11505; *Ancestral Roots* 162; Stuart 141; Moriarty 14.

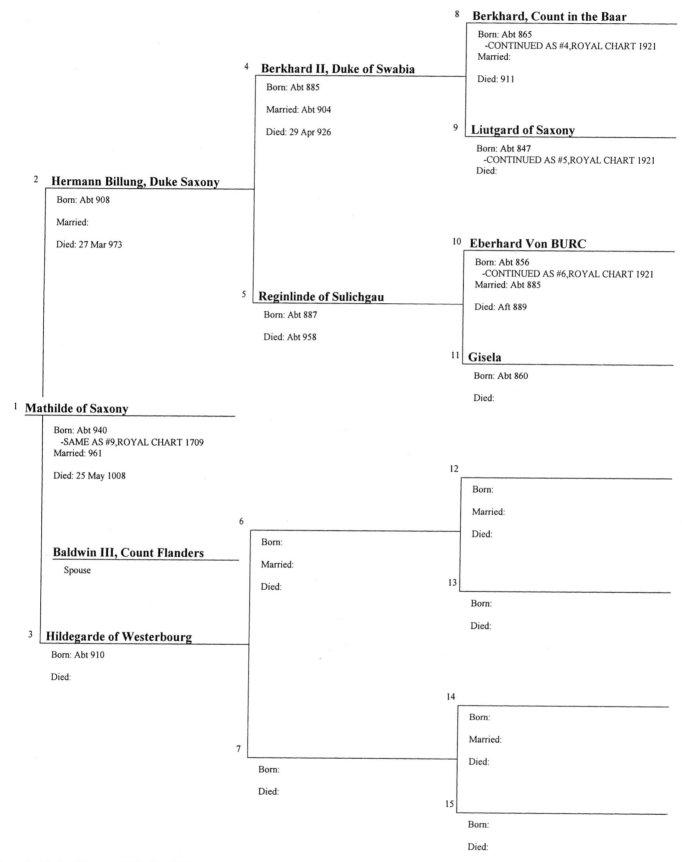

8 **Berkhard, Count in the Baar**

Born: Abt 865
 -CONTINUED AS #4,ROYAL CHART 1921
Married:

Died: 911

4 **Berkhard II, Duke of Swabia**

Born: Abt 885

Married: Abt 904

Died: 29 Apr 926

9 **Liutgard of Saxony**

Born: Abt 847
 -CONTINUED AS #5,ROYAL CHART 1921
Died:

2 **Hermann Billung, Duke Saxony**

Born: Abt 908

Married:

Died: 27 Mar 973

10 **Eberhard Von BURC**

Born: Abt 856
 -CONTINUED AS #6,ROYAL CHART 1921
Married: Abt 885

Died: Aft 889

5 **Reginlinde of Sulichgau**

Born: Abt 887

Died: Abt 958

11 **Gisela**

Born: Abt 860

Died:

1 **Mathilde of Saxony**

Born: Abt 940
 -SAME AS #9,ROYAL CHART 1709
Married: 961

Died: 25 May 1008

12

Born:

Married:

Died:

6

Born:

Married:

Died:

13

Born:

Died:

Baldwin III, Count Flanders

Spouse

3 **Hildegarde of Westerbourg**

Born: Abt 910

Died:

14

Born:

Married:

Died:

7

Born:

Died:

15

Born:

Died:

Sources include: *Royal Ancestors* (1989), chart 11761; *Ancestral Roots* 162-19; Moriarty 126, 17; Stuart 104-35, 312; Faris preliminary Charlemagne manuscript (June 1995), pp. 143-145.

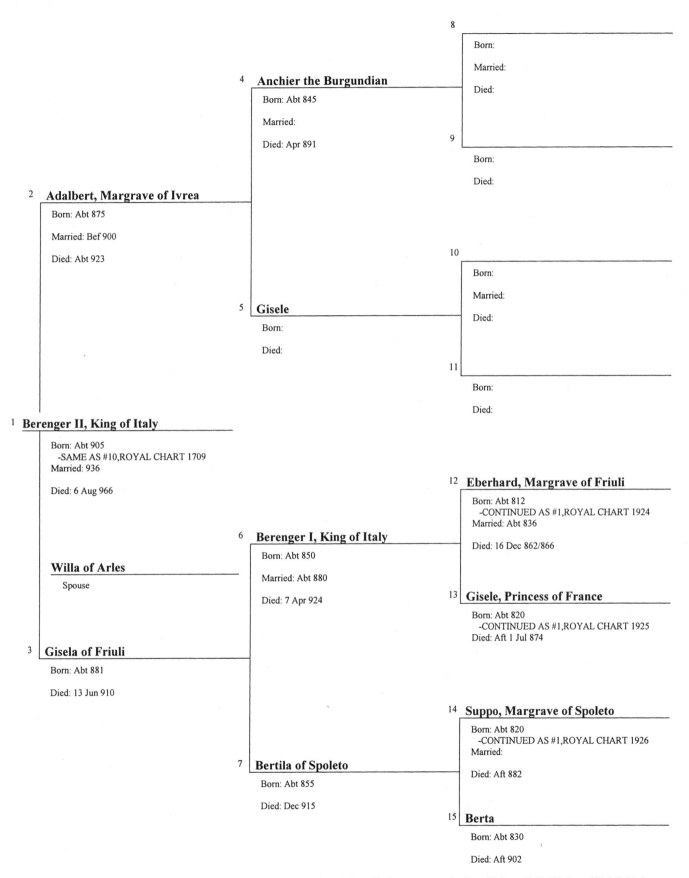

8

Born:

Married:

Died:

4 Anchier the Burgundian

Born: Abt 845

Married:

Died: Apr 891

9

Born:

Died:

2 Adalbert, Margrave of Ivrea

Born: Abt 875

Married: Bef 900

Died: Abt 923

10

Born:

Married:

Died:

5 Gisele

Born:

Died:

11

Born:

Died:

1 Berenger II, King of Italy

Born: Abt 905
-SAME AS #10,ROYAL CHART 1709
Married: 936

Died: 6 Aug 966

12 Eberhard, Margrave of Friuli

Born: Abt 812
-CONTINUED AS #1,ROYAL CHART 1924
Married: Abt 836

Died: 16 Dec 862/866

6 Berenger I, King of Italy

Born: Abt 850

Married: Abt 880

Died: 7 Apr 924

13 Gisele, Princess of France

Born: Abt 820
-CONTINUED AS #1,ROYAL CHART 1925
Died: Aft 1 Jul 874

Willa of Arles

Spouse

3 Gisela of Friuli

Born: Abt 881

Died: 13 Jun 910

14 Suppo, Margrave of Spoleto

Born: Abt 820
-CONTINUED AS #1,ROYAL CHART 1926
Married:

Died: Aft 882

7 Bertila of Spoleto

Born: Abt 855

Died: Dec 915

15 Berta

Born: Abt 830

Died: Aft 902

Sources include: *Royal Ancestors* (1989), charts 11569-70; *Ancestral Roots* 146, 145; Faris preliminary Charlemagne manuscript (June 1995), pp. 62-63, 143; Stuart 332, 269; Moriarty 18. Notes: The parentage and ancestry of #4 Anchier is disputed and uncertain. #15 Berta was daughter of a Count Wilfred.

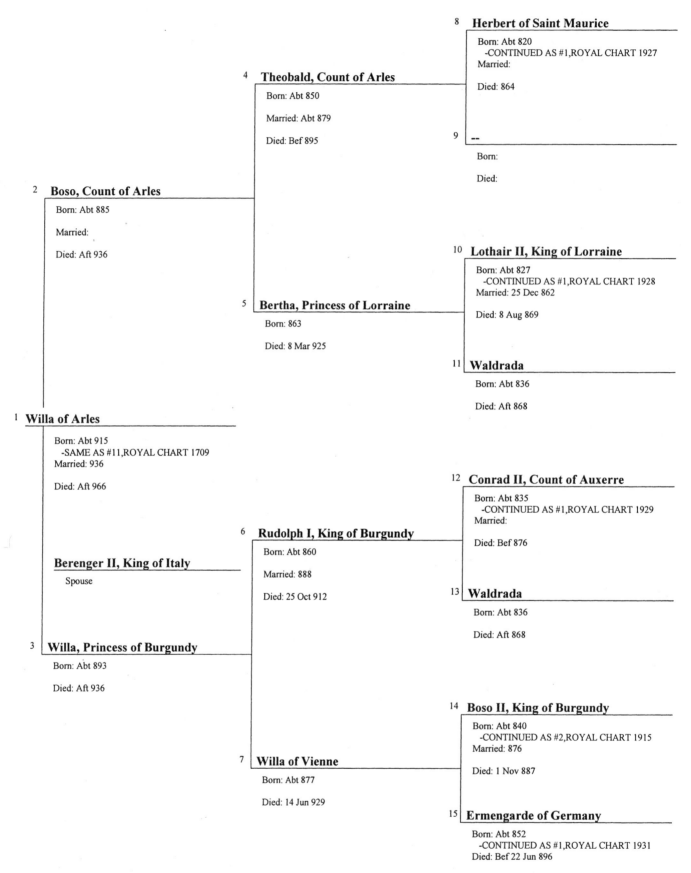

8 Herbert of Saint Maurice
Born: Abt 820
-CONTINUED AS #1,ROYAL CHART 1927
Married:
Died: 864

4 Theobald, Count of Arles
Born: Abt 850
Married: Abt 879
Died: Bef 895

9 --
Born:
Died:

2 Boso, Count of Arles
Born: Abt 885
Married:
Died: Aft 936

10 Lothair II, King of Lorraine
Born: Abt 827
-CONTINUED AS #1,ROYAL CHART 1928
Married: 25 Dec 862
Died: 8 Aug 869

5 Bertha, Princess of Lorraine
Born: 863
Died: 8 Mar 925

11 Waldrada
Born: Abt 836
Died: Aft 868

1 Willa of Arles
Born: Abt 915
-SAME AS #11,ROYAL CHART 1709
Married: 936
Died: Aft 966

12 Conrad II, Count of Auxerre
Born: Abt 835
-CONTINUED AS #1,ROYAL CHART 1929
Married:
Died: Bef 876

6 Rudolph I, King of Burgundy
Born: Abt 860
Married: 888
Died: 25 Oct 912

Berenger II, King of Italy
Spouse

13 Waldrada
Born: Abt 836
Died: Aft 868

3 Willa, Princess of Burgundy
Born: Abt 893
Died: Aft 936

14 Boso II, King of Burgundy
Born: Abt 840
-CONTINUED AS #2,ROYAL CHART 1915
Married: 876
Died: 1 Nov 887

7 Willa of Vienne
Born: Abt 877
Died: 14 Jun 929

15 Ermengarde of Germany
Born: Abt 852
-CONTINUED AS #1,ROYAL CHART 1931
Died: Bef 22 Jun 896

Sources include: *Royal Ancestors* (1989), charts 11569-70; *Ancestral Roots* 145; Stuart 263, 175; Moriarty 18-20, 33. Note: The parentage shown for #3 Willa is not certain. Moriarty gives it as probable.

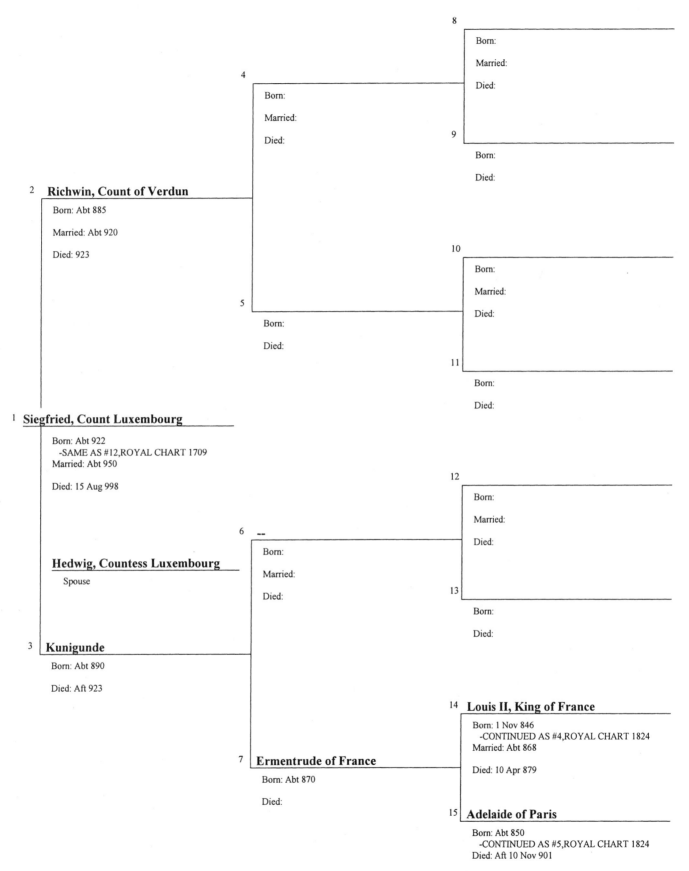

8

Born:

Married:

Died:

4

Born:

Married:

Died:

9

Born:

Died:

2 Richwin, Count of Verdun

Born: Abt 885

Married: Abt 920

Died: 923

10

Born:

Married:

Died:

5

Born:

Died:

11

Born:

Died:

1 Siegfried, Count Luxembourg

Born: Abt 922
   -SAME AS #12,ROYAL CHART 1709
Married: Abt 950

Died: 15 Aug 998

12

Born:

Married:

Died:

6 --

Born:

Married:

Died:

13

Born:

Died:

Hedwig, Countess Luxembourg

Spouse

3 Kunigunde

Born: Abt 890

Died: Aft 923

14 Louis II, King of France

Born: 1 Nov 846
   -CONTINUED AS #4,ROYAL CHART 1824
Married: Abt 868

Died: 10 Apr 879

7 Ermentrude of France

Born: Abt 870

Died:

15 Adelaide of Paris

Born: Abt 850
   -CONTINUED AS #5,ROYAL CHART 1824
Died: Aft 10 Nov 901

Sources include: *Royal Ancestors* (1989), chart 11583; *Ancestral Roots* 143; Stuart 353; Moriarty 21-22; Faris preliminary Charlemagne manuscript (June 1995), pp. 244, 167. Note: #2 (the father of Siegfried) is disputed. The version shown above (Richwin, 2nd husband of Kunigunde) was accepted by Brandenburg and Moriarty. Many later scholars give Siegfried as the son of Wigeric (Wigerich), 1st husband. See chart 1798.

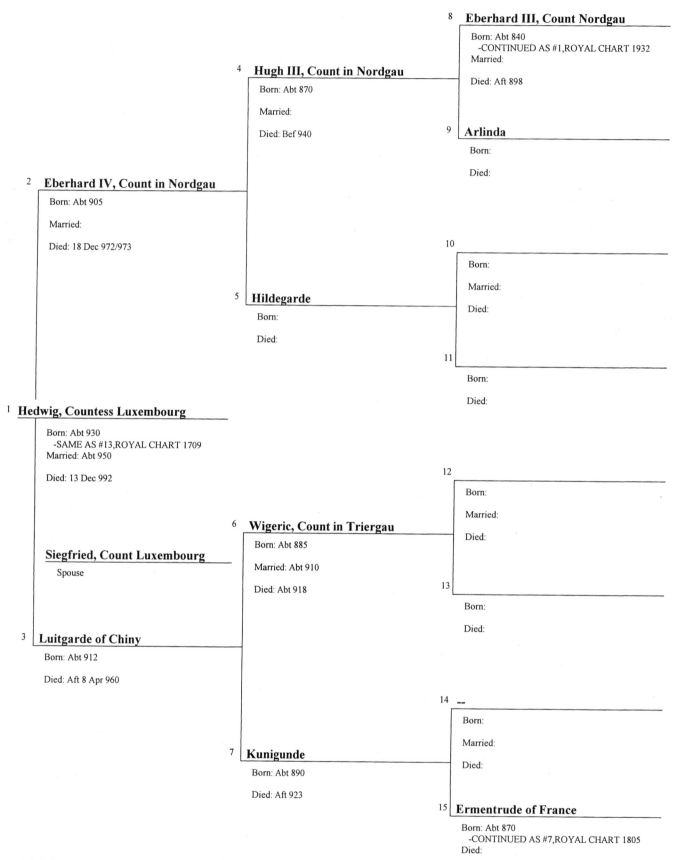

8 **Eberhard III, Count Nordgau**

Born: Abt 840
  -CONTINUED AS #1,ROYAL CHART 1932
Married:

Died: Aft 898

4 **Hugh III, Count in Nordgau**

Born: Abt 870

Married:

Died: Bef 940

9 **Arlinda**

Born:

Died:

2 **Eberhard IV, Count in Nordgau**

Born: Abt 905

Married:

Died: 18 Dec 972/973

10

Born:

Married:

Died:

5 **Hildegarde**

Born:

Died:

11

Born:

Died:

1 **Hedwig, Countess Luxembourg**

Born: Abt 930
  -SAME AS #13,ROYAL CHART 1709
Married: Abt 950

Died: 13 Dec 992

12

Born:

Married:

Died:

6 **Wigeric, Count in Triergau**

Born: Abt 885

Married: Abt 910

Died: Abt 918

13

Born:

Died:

Siegfried, Count Luxembourg

Spouse

3 **Luitgarde of Chiny**

Born: Abt 912

Died: Aft 8 Apr 960

14 **--**

Born:

Married:

Died:

7 **Kunigunde**

Born: Abt 890

Died: Aft 923

15 **Ermentrude of France**

Born: Abt 870
  -CONTINUED AS #7,ROYAL CHART 1805
Died:

Sources include: *Royal Ancestors* (1989), chart 11583; *Ancestral Roots* 143-19; Stuart 353-36, 202; Moriarty 22, 126, 93-94, 181-182; Faris preliminary Charlemagne manuscript (June 1995), pp. 244, 167. Note: #2 & 3 Eberhard & Luitgarde had only one certain child, Hugh V (see charts 1777, 2295). They may also have been parents of Gerhard (see chart 1896) and of Hedwig (#1 above, wife of Siegfried). Faris states that #2 Eberhard was a 2nd husband of Luitgarde and that her 1st husband (Adalbert) was slain in 944. If this date is correct, then the claimed daughter Hedwig would likely be born about 945 or later, and the descent shown for her on chart 1896 would be chronologically untenable. See chart 2241 and note for another claimed marriage of #3 Luitgarde.

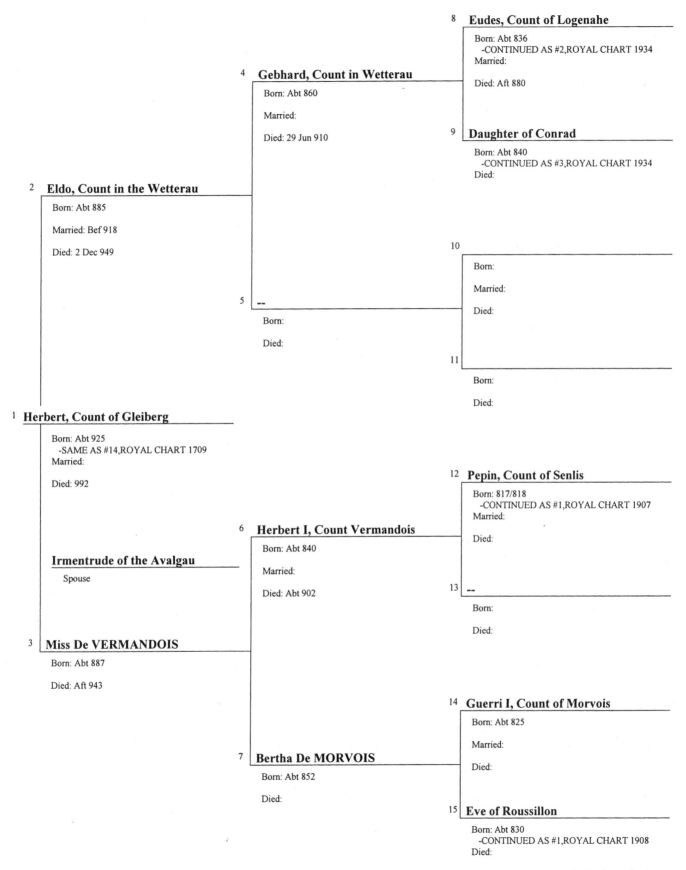

8 Eudes, Count of Logenahe

Born: Abt 836
  -CONTINUED AS #2,ROYAL CHART 1934
Married:

Died: Aft 880

4 Gebhard, Count in Wetterau

Born: Abt 860

Married:

Died: 29 Jun 910

9 Daughter of Conrad

Born: Abt 840
  -CONTINUED AS #3,ROYAL CHART 1934
Died:

2 Eldo, Count in the Wetterau

Born: Abt 885

Married: Bef 918

Died: 2 Dec 949

10

Born:

Married:

Died:

5 --

Born:

Died:

11

Born:

Died:

1 Herbert, Count of Gleiberg

Born: Abt 925
  -SAME AS #14,ROYAL CHART 1709
Married:

Died: 992

12 Pepin, Count of Senlis

Born: 817/818
  -CONTINUED AS #1,ROYAL CHART 1907
Married:

Died:

6 Herbert I, Count Vermandois

Born: Abt 840

Married:

Died: Abt 902

13 --

Born:

Died:

Irmentrude of the Avalgau

Spouse

3 Miss De VERMANDOIS

Born: Abt 887

Died: Aft 943

14 Guerri I, Count of Morvois

Born: Abt 825

Married:

Died:

7 Bertha De MORVOIS

Born: Abt 852

Died:

15 Eve of Roussillon

Born: Abt 830
  -CONTINUED AS #1,ROYAL CHART 1908
Died:

Sources include: *Royal Ancestors* (1989), chart 11584; *Ancestral Roots* 143-20, 50, 192; Stuart 353, 351; Moriarty 23. Note: Stuart eliminates one generation (Eudes) and makes #4 Gebhard the son of Gebhard (#2, chart 1933). Moriarty gives the line as shown above.

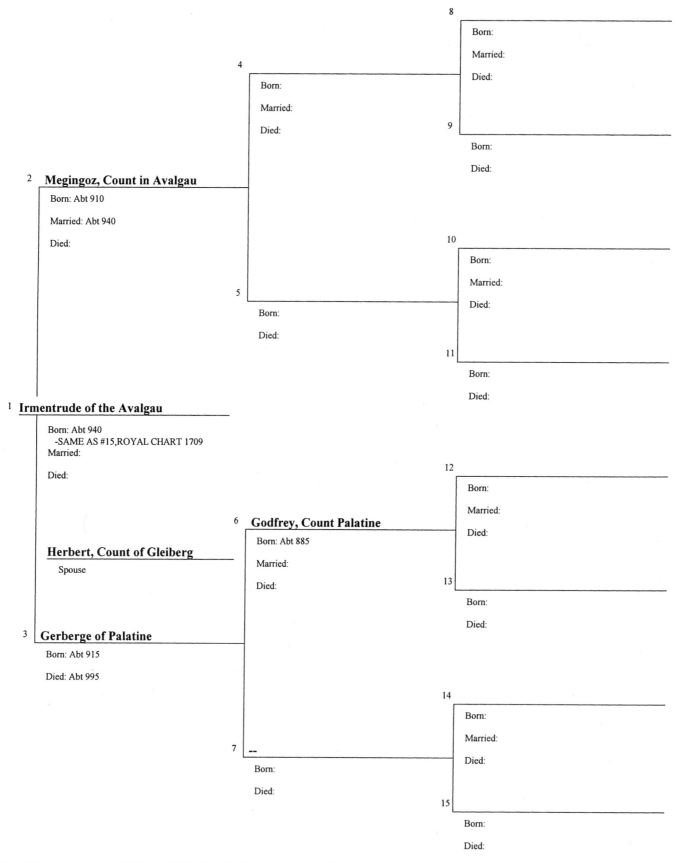

8
Born:
Married:
Died:

4
Born:
Married:
Died:

9
Born:
Died:

2 Megingoz, Count in Avalgau
Born: Abt 910
Married: Abt 940
Died:

10
Born:
Married:
Died:

5
Born:
Died:

11
Born:
Died:

1 Irmentrude of the Avalgau
Born: Abt 940
  -SAME AS #15,ROYAL CHART 1709
Married:
Died:

12
Born:
Married:
Died:

6 Godfrey, Count Palatine
Born: Abt 885
Married:
Died:

13
Born:
Died:

Herbert, Count of Gleiberg
Spouse

3 Gerberge of Palatine
Born: Abt 915
Died: Abt 995

14
Born:
Married:
Died:

7 --
Born:
Died:

15
Born:
Died:

Sources include: *Royal Ancestors* (1989), chart 11584; Stuart 351-36; Moriarty 206; Paget 2.

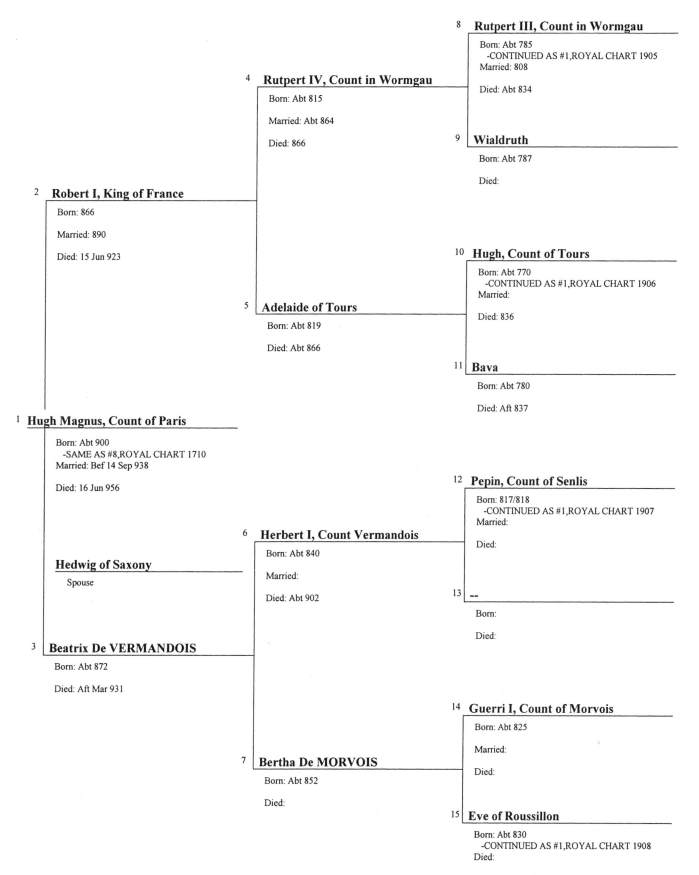

8 Rutpert III, Count in Wormgau

Born: Abt 785
-CONTINUED AS #1,ROYAL CHART 1905
Married: 808

Died: Abt 834

4 Rutpert IV, Count in Wormgau

Born: Abt 815

Married: Abt 864

Died: 866

9 Wialdruth

Born: Abt 787

Died:

2 Robert I, King of France

Born: 866

Married: 890

Died: 15 Jun 923

10 Hugh, Count of Tours

Born: Abt 770
-CONTINUED AS #1,ROYAL CHART 1906
Married:

Died: 836

5 Adelaide of Tours

Born: Abt 819

Died: Abt 866

11 Bava

Born: Abt 780

Died: Aft 837

1 Hugh Magnus, Count of Paris

Born: Abt 900
-SAME AS #8,ROYAL CHART 1710
Married: Bef 14 Sep 938

Died: 16 Jun 956

12 Pepin, Count of Senlis

Born: 817/818
-CONTINUED AS #1,ROYAL CHART 1907
Married:

Died:

6 Herbert I, Count Vermandois

Born: Abt 840

Married:

Died: Abt 902

13 --

Born:

Died:

Hedwig of Saxony

Spouse

3 Beatrix De VERMANDOIS

Born: Abt 872

Died: Aft Mar 931

14 Guerri I, Count of Morvois

Born: Abt 825

Married:

Died:

7 Bertha De MORVOIS

Born: Abt 852

Died:

15 Eve of Roussillon

Born: Abt 830
-CONTINUED AS #1,ROYAL CHART 1908
Died:

Sources include: *Royal Ancestors* 11506; *Ancestral Roots* 48, 50; Stuart 134, 169; Faris preliminary Charlemagne manuscript (June 1995), pp. 88, 272; Moriarty 9, 211, 215-216, 226-227, 281-282; *NEHGR* 117:268-271; *TAG* 49:85-88, 58:164-165. Notes: The parentage of #4 Rutpert IV (Robert the Stong) has been disputed and is discussed at length by Moriarty, who concludes that the controversy is now settled, with the ancestry as continued above. The parentage of #9 Wialdruth (Waldrada) is disputed (see *Ancestral Roots* 48-16; Moriarty 281; Stuart 169-39). The identification and parentage of #5 (a 2nd wife) is not certain.

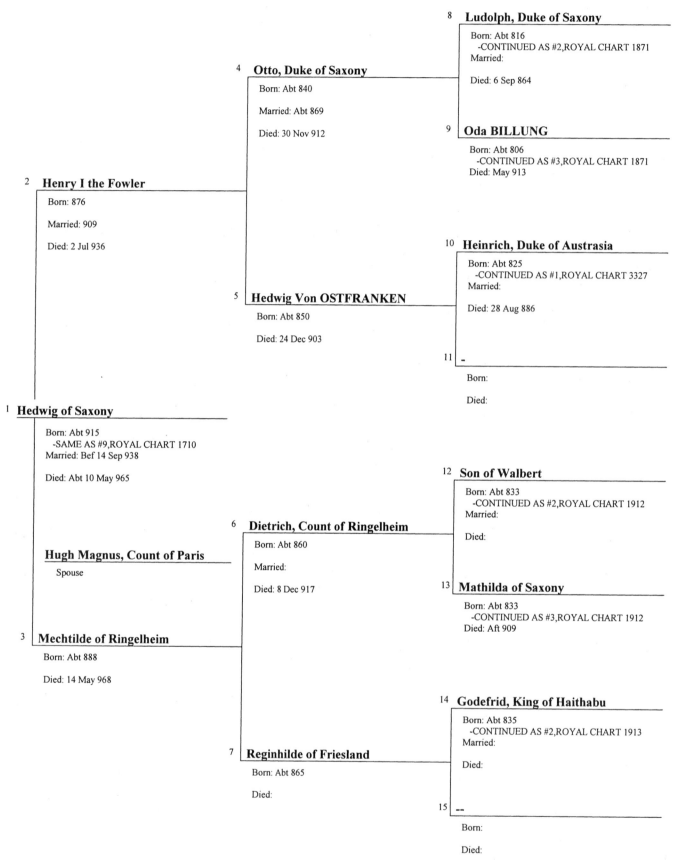

8 Ludolph, Duke of Saxony

Born: Abt 816
 -CONTINUED AS #2, ROYAL CHART 1871
Married:

Died: 6 Sep 864

4 Otto, Duke of Saxony

Born: Abt 840

Married: Abt 869

Died: 30 Nov 912

9 Oda BILLUNG

Born: Abt 806
 -CONTINUED AS #3, ROYAL CHART 1871
Died: May 913

2 Henry I the Fowler

Born: 876

Married: 909

Died: 2 Jul 936

10 Heinrich, Duke of Austrasia

Born: Abt 825
 -CONTINUED AS #1, ROYAL CHART 3327
Married:

Died: 28 Aug 886

5 Hedwig Von OSTFRANKEN

Born: Abt 850

Died: 24 Dec 903

11 _

Born:

Died:

1 Hedwig of Saxony

Born: Abt 915
 -SAME AS #9, ROYAL CHART 1710
Married: Bef 14 Sep 938

Died: Abt 10 May 965

12 Son of Walbert

Born: Abt 833
 -CONTINUED AS #2, ROYAL CHART 1912
Married:

Died:

6 Dietrich, Count of Ringelheim

Born: Abt 860

Married:

Died: 8 Dec 917

13 Mathilda of Saxony

Born: Abt 833
 -CONTINUED AS #3, ROYAL CHART 1912
Died: Aft 909

Hugh Magnus, Count of Paris

Spouse

3 Mechtilde of Ringelheim

Born: Abt 888

Died: 14 May 968

14 Godefrid, King of Haithabu

Born: Abt 835
 -CONTINUED AS #2, ROYAL CHART 1913
Married:

Died:

7 Reginhilde of Friesland

Born: Abt 865

Died:

15 --

Born:

Died:

Sources include: *Royal Ancestors* (1989), chart 11507; *Ancestral Roots* 8 (2004), Line 141; *Ancestral Roots* 141; Faris preliminary Charlemagne manuscript (June 1995), pp. 88, 248-249; Stuart 134, 92, 338; Moriarty 24-26; Schwennicke 3:54 (#4, 5 & 10); Turton 23; LDS records. Note: The parentage of #5 Hedwig is heavily disputed. The claim that she was daughter of Arnulf (King of Germany) & Oda of Bavaria is unacceptable chronologically. A claim by Faris (citing Decker-Hauff) that #11 was Judith of Friuli (see chart 2022, #1) also appears questionable. Faris, Schwennicke, and *Ancestral Roots* 8 all accept #10 Heinrich.

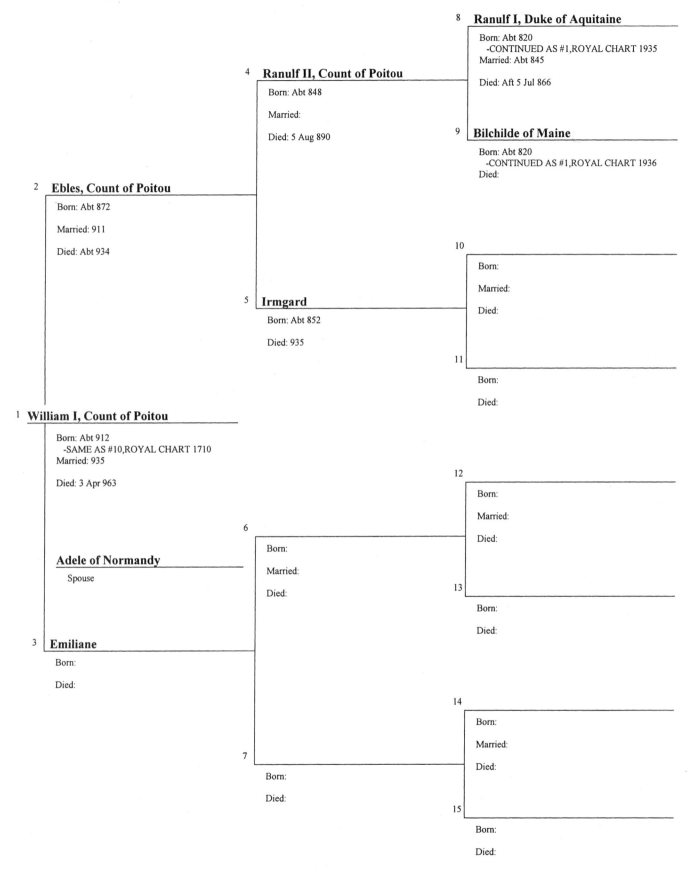

8 Ranulf I, Duke of Aquitaine

Born: Abt 820
-CONTINUED AS #1,ROYAL CHART 1935
Married: Abt 845

Died: Aft 5 Jul 866

4 Ranulf II, Count of Poitou

Born: Abt 848

Married:

Died: 5 Aug 890

9 Bilchilde of Maine

Born: Abt 820
-CONTINUED AS #1,ROYAL CHART 1936
Died:

2 Ebles, Count of Poitou

Born: Abt 872

Married: 911

Died: Abt 934

10

Born:

Married:

Died:

5 Irmgard

Born: Abt 852

Died: 935

11

Born:

Died:

1 William I, Count of Poitou

Born: Abt 912
-SAME AS #10,ROYAL CHART 1710
Married: 935

Died: 3 Apr 963

12

Born:

Married:

Died:

6

Born:

Married:

Died:

13

Born:

Died:

Adele of Normandy

Spouse

3 Emiliane

Born:

Died:

14

Born:

Married:

Died:

7

Born:

Died:

15

Born:

Died:

Sources include: *Royal Ancestors* (1989), chart 11512; *Ancestral Roots* 144A; Stuart 163; Moriarty 26-27; Faris preliminary Charlemagne manuscript (June 1995), pp. 216-217. Note: #3 (a 2nd wife) is disputed. Faris gives #3 as a 1st wife Aremburge (md. abt. 892), with their son William (#1) born about 900. #5 Irmgard (Ermengarde) was probably a concubine.

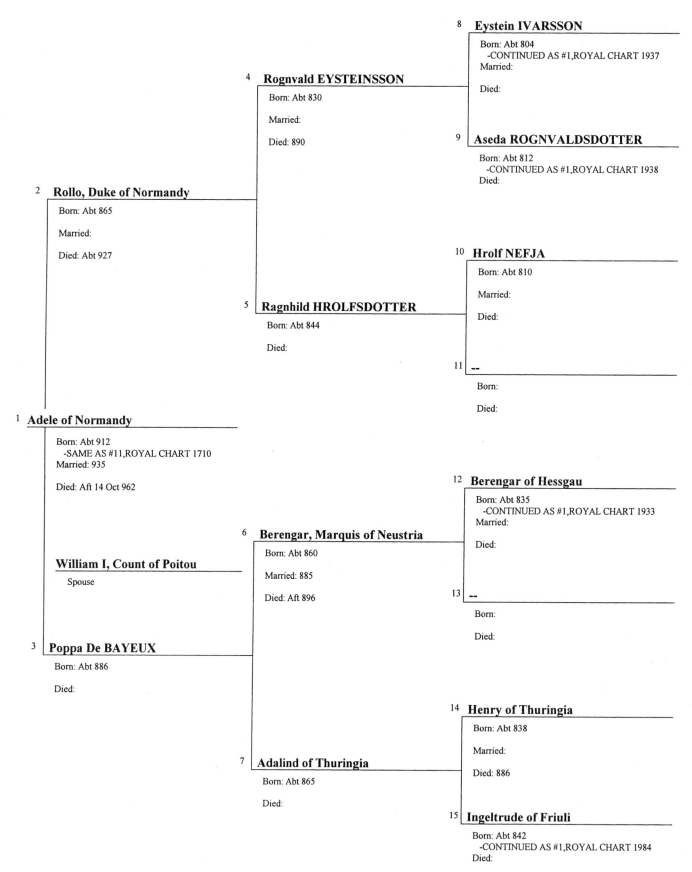

8 **Eystein IVARSSON**

Born: Abt 804
-CONTINUED AS #1,ROYAL CHART 1937
Married:

Died:

4 **Rognvald EYSTEINSSON**

Born: Abt 830

Married:

Died: 890

9 **Aseda ROGNVALDSDOTTER**

Born: Abt 812
-CONTINUED AS #1,ROYAL CHART 1938
Died:

2 **Rollo, Duke of Normandy**

Born: Abt 865

Married:

Died: Abt 927

10 **Hrolf NEFJA**

Born: Abt 810

Married:

Died:

5 **Ragnhild HROLFSDOTTER**

Born: Abt 844

Died:

11 **--**

Born:

Died:

1 **Adele of Normandy**

Born: Abt 912
-SAME AS #11,ROYAL CHART 1710
Married: 935

Died: Aft 14 Oct 962

12 **Berengar of Hessgau**

Born: Abt 835
-CONTINUED AS #1,ROYAL CHART 1933
Married:

Died:

6 **Berengar, Marquis of Neustria**

Born: Abt 860

Married: 885

Died: Aft 896

13 **--**

Born:

Died:

William I, Count of Poitou

Spouse

3 **Poppa De BAYEUX**

Born: Abt 886

Died:

14 **Henry of Thuringia**

Born: Abt 838

Married:

Died: 886

7 **Adalind of Thuringia**

Born: Abt 865

Died:

15 **Ingeltrude of Friuli**

Born: Abt 842
-CONTINUED AS #1,ROYAL CHART 1984
Died:

Sources include: *Royal Ancestors* (1989), chart 11512; *Ancestral Roots* 121E-18; Stuart 162, 166; Moriarty 11, 226; *TAG* 52:25; 72:187-204. Notes: The parentage and ancestry of #3 Poppa is disputed. Moriarty 226 and Evans (*TAG* 52) favored the claim that #3 Poppa was daughter of Gui, Count of Senlis, by an unknown daughter of Pepin, Count of Senlis (see chart 1907). However, the current consensus is that Poppa was daughter of Berengar. A recently-proposed ancestry for Poppa (see *TAG* 72) is shown above. #14 Henry is suggested to be the son of an Adalbert.

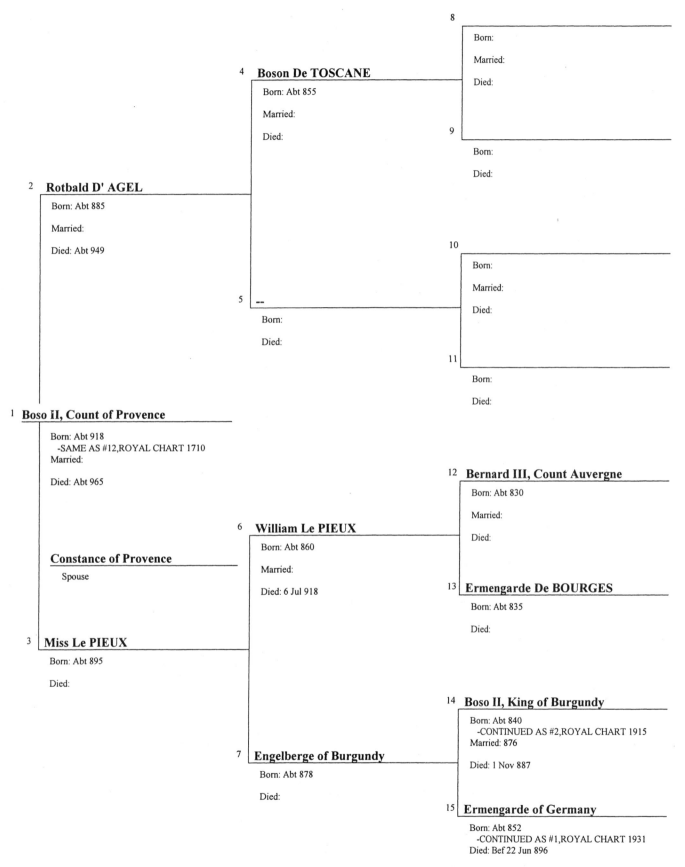

8

Born:

Married:

Died:

4 Boson De TOSCANE

Born: Abt 855

Married:

Died:

9

Born:

Died:

2 Rotbald D' AGEL

Born: Abt 885

Married:

Died: Abt 949

10

Born:

Married:

Died:

5 --

Born:

Died:

11

Born:

Died:

1 Boso II, Count of Provence

Born: Abt 918
  -SAME AS #12,ROYAL CHART 1710
Married:

Died: Abt 965

12 Bernard III, Count Auvergne

Born: Abt 830

Married:

Died:

6 William Le PIEUX

Born: Abt 860

Married:

Died: 6 Jul 918

13 Ermengarde De BOURGES

Born: Abt 835

Died:

Constance of Provence

Spouse

3 Miss Le PIEUX

Born: Abt 895

Died:

14 Boso II, King of Burgundy

Born: Abt 840
  -CONTINUED AS #2,ROYAL CHART 1915
Married: 876

Died: 1 Nov 887

7 Engelberge of Burgundy

Born: Abt 878

Died:

15 Ermengarde of Germany

Born: Abt 852
  -CONTINUED AS #1,ROYAL CHART 1931
Died: Bef 22 Jun 896

Sources include: *Royal Ancestors* (1989), chart 11785; Faris preliminary Charlemagne manuscript (June 1995), pp. 224-225; *Ancestral Roots* 141A-19; Stuart 333; Moriarty 27.

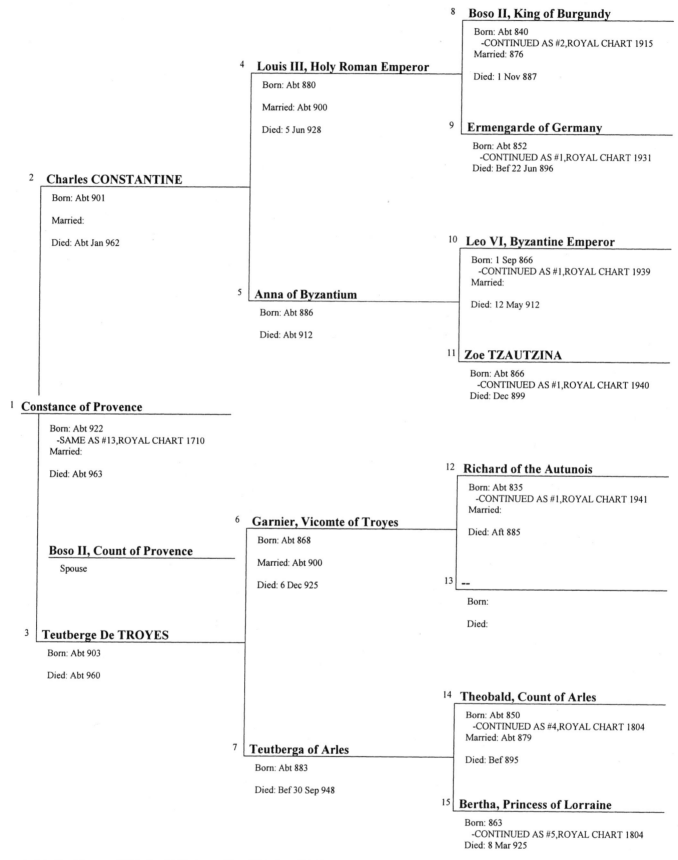

2 Charles CONSTANTINE
Born: Abt 901
Married:
Died: Abt Jan 962

4 Louis III, Holy Roman Emperor
Born: Abt 880
Married: Abt 900
Died: 5 Jun 928

8 Boso II, King of Burgundy
Born: Abt 840
-CONTINUED AS #2,ROYAL CHART 1915
Married: 876
Died: 1 Nov 887

9 Ermengarde of Germany
Born: Abt 852
-CONTINUED AS #1,ROYAL CHART 1931
Died: Bef 22 Jun 896

5 Anna of Byzantium
Born: Abt 886
Died: Abt 912

10 Leo VI, Byzantine Emperor
Born: 1 Sep 866
-CONTINUED AS #1,ROYAL CHART 1939
Married:
Died: 12 May 912

11 Zoe TZAUTZINA
Born: Abt 866
-CONTINUED AS #1,ROYAL CHART 1940
Died: Dec 899

1 Constance of Provence
Born: Abt 922
-SAME AS #13,ROYAL CHART 1710
Married:
Died: Abt 963

Boso II, Count of Provence
Spouse

3 Teutberge De TROYES
Born: Abt 903
Died: Abt 960

6 Garnier, Vicomte of Troyes
Born: Abt 868
Married: Abt 900
Died: 6 Dec 925

12 Richard of the Autunois
Born: Abt 835
-CONTINUED AS #1,ROYAL CHART 1941
Married:
Died: Aft 885

13 --
Born:
Died:

7 Teutberga of Arles
Born: Abt 883
Died: Bef 30 Sep 948

14 Theobald, Count of Arles
Born: Abt 850
-CONTINUED AS #4,ROYAL CHART 1804
Married: Abt 879
Died: Bef 895

15 Bertha, Princess of Lorraine
Born: 863
-CONTINUED AS #5,ROYAL CHART 1804
Died: 8 Mar 925

Sources include: *Royal Ancestors* (1989), chart 11785; *Ancestral Roots* 141A; Stuart 333-36, 25; Faris preliminary Charlemagne manuscript (June 1995), pp. 277-278; Moriarty 27, 19, 59, 257 (#3 ancestry), 259-260 (#2 ancestry); *The Genealogist* 2:5-7, 27-28.

Pedigree Chart

Chart 1815

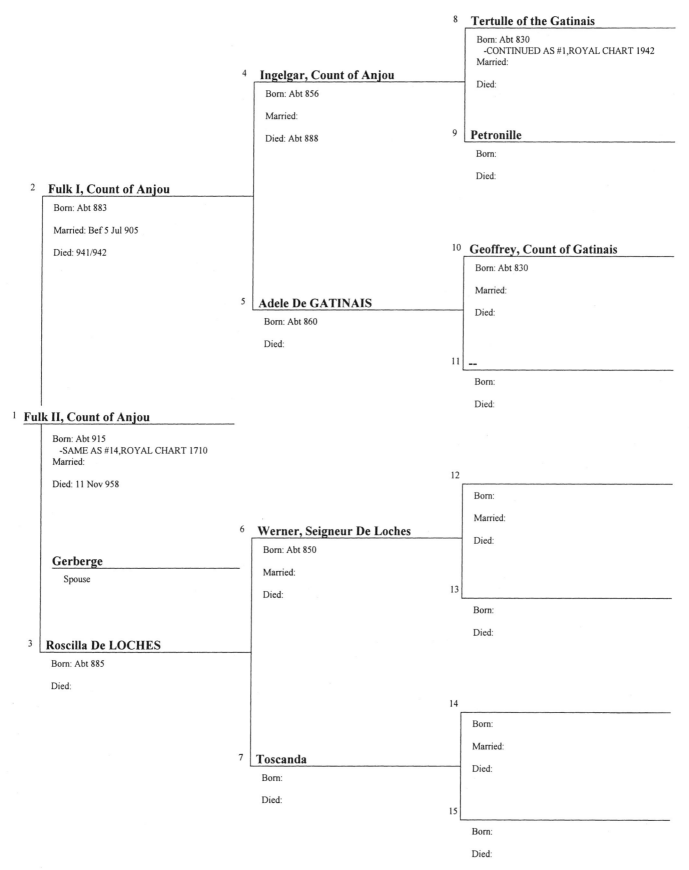

8 **Tertulle of the Gatinais**

Born: Abt 830
  -CONTINUED AS #1,ROYAL CHART 1942
Married:

Died:

4 **Ingelgar, Count of Anjou**

Born: Abt 856

Married:

Died: Abt 888

9 **Petronille**

Born:

Died:

2 **Fulk I, Count of Anjou**

Born: Abt 883

Married: Bef 5 Jul 905

Died: 941/942

10 **Geoffrey, Count of Gatinais**

Born: Abt 830

Married:

Died:

5 **Adele De GATINAIS**

Born: Abt 860

Died:

11 **--**

Born:

Died:

1 **Fulk II, Count of Anjou**

Born: Abt 915
  -SAME AS #14,ROYAL CHART 1710
Married:

Died: 11 Nov 958

Gerberge

Spouse

12

Born:

Married:

Died:

6 **Werner, Seigneur De Loches**

Born: Abt 850

Married:

Died:

13

Born:

Died:

3 **Roscilla De LOCHES**

Born: Abt 885

Died:

14

Born:

Married:

Died:

7 **Toscanda**

Born:

Died:

15

Born:

Died:

Sources include: *Royal Ancestors* (1989), chart 11502; Stuart 167; Moriarty 4, 37; LDS records.

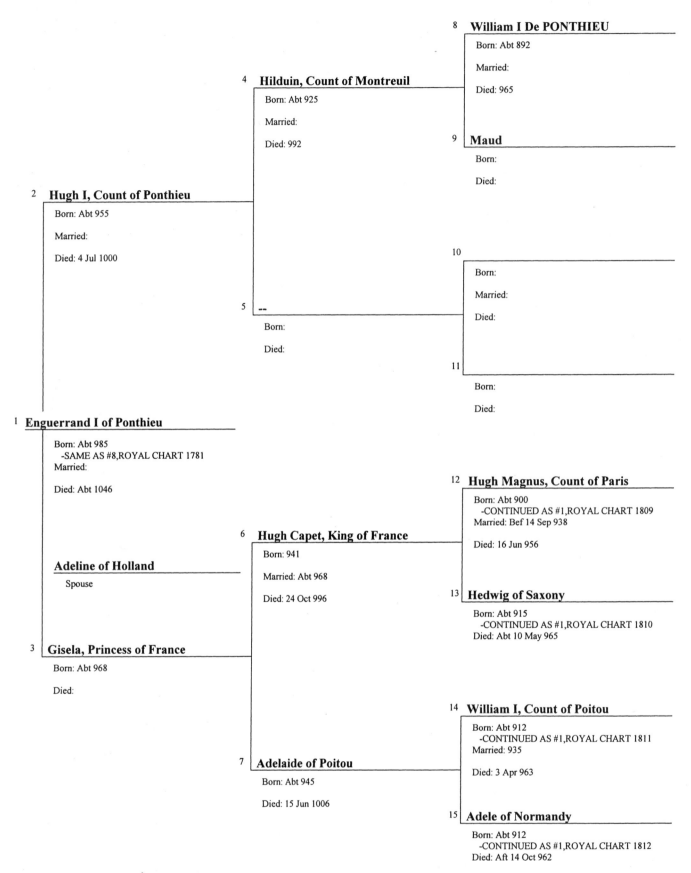

8 **William I De PONTHIEU**
Born: Abt 892
Married:
Died: 965

4 **Hilduin, Count of Montreuil**
Born: Abt 925
Married:
Died: 992

9 **Maud**
Born:
Died:

2 **Hugh I, Count of Ponthieu**
Born: Abt 955
Married:
Died: 4 Jul 1000

10
Born:
Married:
Died:

5 **--**
Born:
Died:

11
Born:
Died:

1 **Enguerrand I of Ponthieu**
Born: Abt 985
  -SAME AS #8,ROYAL CHART 1781
Married:
Died: Abt 1046

12 **Hugh Magnus, Count of Paris**
Born: Abt 900
  -CONTINUED AS #1,ROYAL CHART 1809
Married: Bef 14 Sep 938
Died: 16 Jun 956

6 **Hugh Capet, King of France**
Born: 941
Married: Abt 968
Died: 24 Oct 996

13 **Hedwig of Saxony**
Born: Abt 915
  -CONTINUED AS #1,ROYAL CHART 1810
Died: Abt 10 May 965

Adeline of Holland
Spouse

3 **Gisela, Princess of France**
Born: Abt 968
Died:

14 **William I, Count of Poitou**
Born: Abt 912
  -CONTINUED AS #1,ROYAL CHART 1811
Married: 935
Died: 3 Apr 963

7 **Adelaide of Poitou**
Born: Abt 945
Died: 15 Jun 1006

15 **Adele of Normandy**
Born: Abt 912
  -CONTINUED AS #1,ROYAL CHART 1812
Died: Aft 14 Oct 962

Sources include: *Royal Ancestors* (1989), chart 11778; Stuart 244; Moriarty 113, 24, 227; Roberts *AAP*, p.195; Turton 13. Note: The specific ancestry of #2 Hugh is disputed. Moriarty 227 agrees with Turton in giving #4 as Hilduin. Stuart gives #4 as Hugh (died 961), son of Roger, son of Herlouin (died 13 Aug 945). Turton gives #8 William (Guillaume) as son of Roger, son of Herlouin (died 945), which seems unacceptable chronologically. Moriarty agrees there is descent from an earlier Heligaud and son Herlouin, but the exact descent is not clear.

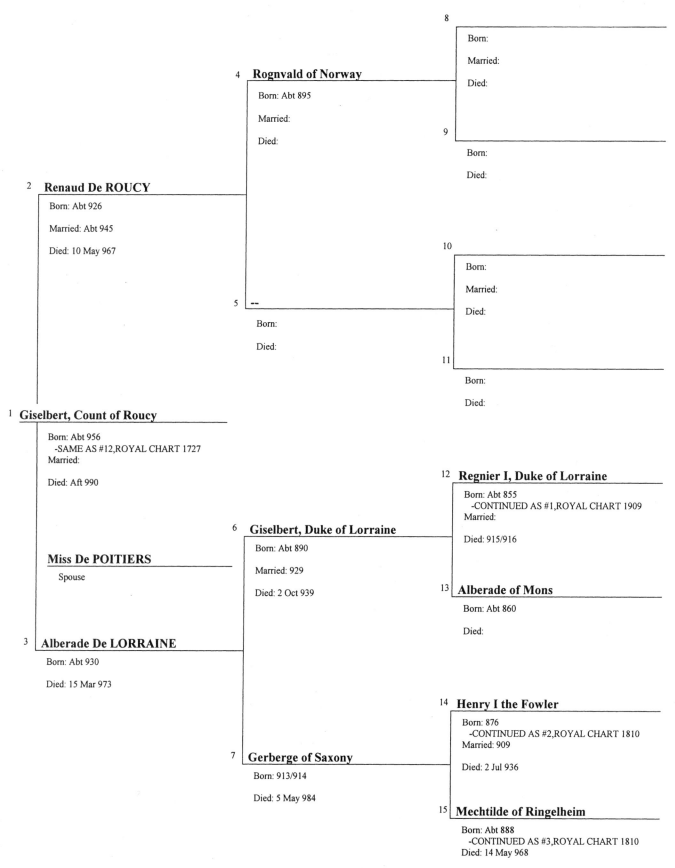

8

Born:

Married:

Died:

4 **Rognvald of Norway**

Born: Abt 895

Married:

Died:

9

Born:

Died:

2 **Renaud De ROUCY**

Born: Abt 926

Married: Abt 945

Died: 10 May 967

10

Born:

Married:

Died:

5 **--**

Born:

Died:

11

Born:

Died:

1 **Giselbert, Count of Roucy**

Born: Abt 956
-SAME AS #12,ROYAL CHART 1727
Married:

Died: Aft 990

12 **Regnier I, Duke of Lorraine**

Born: Abt 855
-CONTINUED AS #1,ROYAL CHART 1909
Married:

Died: 915/916

6 **Giselbert, Duke of Lorraine**

Born: Abt 890

Married: 929

Died: 2 Oct 939

13 **Alberade of Mons**

Born: Abt 860

Died:

Miss De POITIERS

Spouse

3 **Alberade De LORRAINE**

Born: Abt 930

Died: 15 Mar 973

14 **Henry I the Fowler**

Born: 876
-CONTINUED AS #2,ROYAL CHART 1810
Married: 909

Died: 2 Jul 936

7 **Gerberge of Saxony**

Born: 913/914

Died: 5 May 984

15 **Mechtilde of Ringelheim**

Born: Abt 888
-CONTINUED AS #3,ROYAL CHART 1810
Died: 14 May 968

Sources include: *Royal Ancestors* (1989), chart 11538; *Ancestral Roots* 151, 140, 240; Stuart 170, 92; Moriarty 39. Notes: The parentage shown for #2 Renaud is not certain. #13 Alberade (2nd wife) is uncertain. #13 might be Hersent (1st wife), daughter of Charles II (see chart 1902, #2).

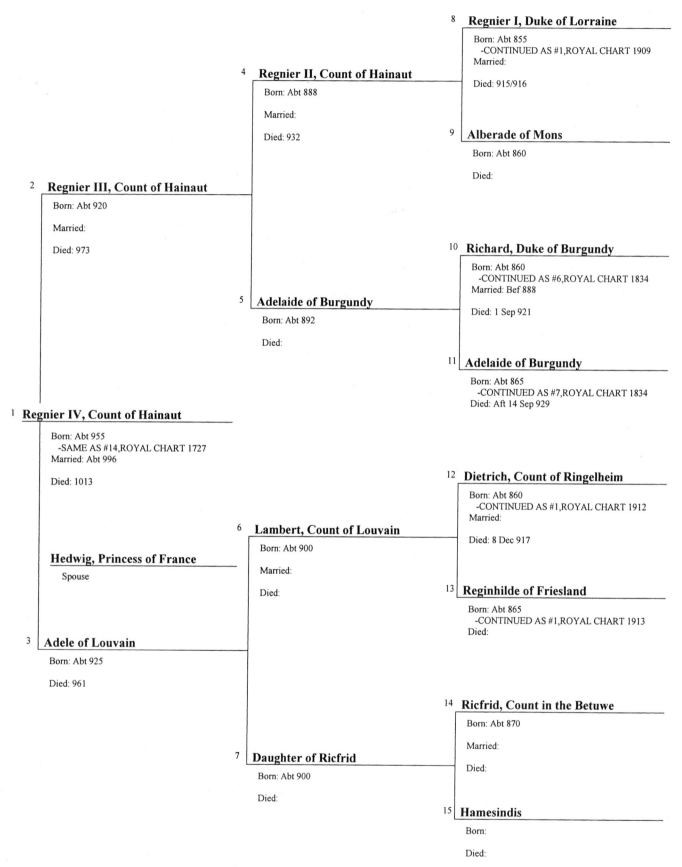

8 **Regnier I, Duke of Lorraine**

Born: Abt 855
-CONTINUED AS #1,ROYAL CHART 1909
Married:

Died: 915/916

4 **Regnier II, Count of Hainaut**

Born: Abt 888

Married:

Died: 932

9 **Alberade of Mons**

Born: Abt 860

Died:

2 **Regnier III, Count of Hainaut**

Born: Abt 920

Married:

Died: 973

10 **Richard, Duke of Burgundy**

Born: Abt 860
-CONTINUED AS #6,ROYAL CHART 1834
Married: Bef 888

Died: 1 Sep 921

5 **Adelaide of Burgundy**

Born: Abt 892

Died:

11 **Adelaide of Burgundy**

Born: Abt 865
-CONTINUED AS #7,ROYAL CHART 1834
Died: Aft 14 Sep 929

1 **Regnier IV, Count of Hainaut**

Born: Abt 955
-SAME AS #14,ROYAL CHART 1727
Married: Abt 996

Died: 1013

12 **Dietrich, Count of Ringelheim**

Born: Abt 860
-CONTINUED AS #1,ROYAL CHART 1912
Married:

Died: 8 Dec 917

6 **Lambert, Count of Louvain**

Born: Abt 900

Married:

Died:

Hedwig, Princess of France

Spouse

13 **Reginhilde of Friesland**

Born: Abt 865
-CONTINUED AS #1,ROYAL CHART 1913
Died:

3 **Adele of Louvain**

Born: Abt 925

Died: 961

14 **Ricfrid, Count in the Betuwe**

Born: Abt 870

Married:

Died:

7 **Daughter of Ricfrid**

Born: Abt 900

Died:

15 **Hamesindis**

Born:

Died:

Sources include: *Royal Ancestors* (1989), charts 11538, 11519; Moriarty 50, 39; Stuart 139, 68; Faris preliminary Charlemagne manuscript (June 1995), p. 67; *Ancestral Roots* 106, 155, 140, 240. Notes: #9 Alberade (2nd wife) is uncertain. #9 might be Hersent (1st wife), daughter of King Charles II (see chart 1902, #2). Moriarty gives Alberade. The identification and parentage shown for #5 is not certain. *Ancestral Roots* 8 (2004), Line 155 gives #5 as unknown, possibly daughter of a Count Boso. #3 is disputed. Faris gives #3 as Alix or Adela, daughter of Hugues III, Count of Dabo and Egisheim.

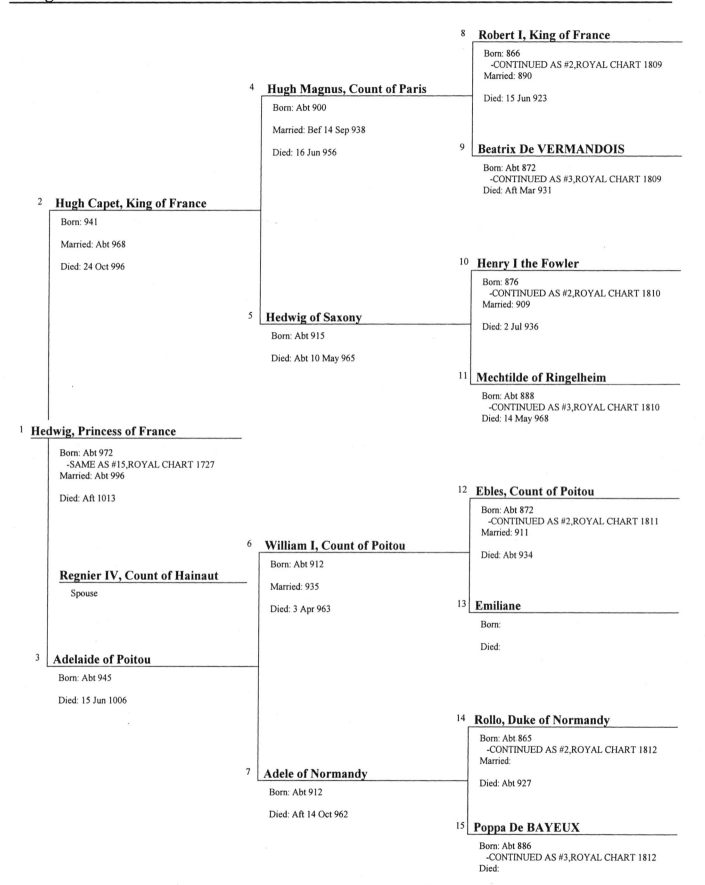

8 Robert I, King of France
Born: 866
 -CONTINUED AS #2,ROYAL CHART 1809
Married: 890

Died: 15 Jun 923

4 Hugh Magnus, Count of Paris
Born: Abt 900

Married: Bef 14 Sep 938

Died: 16 Jun 956

9 Beatrix De VERMANDOIS
Born: Abt 872
 -CONTINUED AS #3,ROYAL CHART 1809
Died: Aft Mar 931

2 Hugh Capet, King of France
Born: 941

Married: Abt 968

Died: 24 Oct 996

10 Henry I the Fowler
Born: 876
 -CONTINUED AS #2,ROYAL CHART 1810
Married: 909

Died: 2 Jul 936

5 Hedwig of Saxony
Born: Abt 915

Died: Abt 10 May 965

11 Mechtilde of Ringelheim
Born: Abt 888
 -CONTINUED AS #3,ROYAL CHART 1810
Died: 14 May 968

1 Hedwig, Princess of France
Born: Abt 972
 -SAME AS #15,ROYAL CHART 1727
Married: Abt 996

Died: Aft 1013

12 Ebles, Count of Poitou
Born: Abt 872
 -CONTINUED AS #2,ROYAL CHART 1811
Married: 911

Died: Abt 934

6 William I, Count of Poitou
Born: Abt 912

Married: 935

Died: 3 Apr 963

13 Emiliane
Born:

Died:

Regnier IV, Count of Hainaut
Spouse

3 Adelaide of Poitou
Born: Abt 945

Died: 15 Jun 1006

14 Rollo, Duke of Normandy
Born: Abt 865
 -CONTINUED AS #2,ROYAL CHART 1812
Married:

Died: Abt 927

7 Adele of Normandy
Born: Abt 912

Died: Aft 14 Oct 962

15 Poppa De BAYEUX
Born: Abt 886
 -CONTINUED AS #3,ROYAL CHART 1812
Died:

Sources include: *Royal Ancestors* 11538, 11504 and notes (#14 & 15); Stuart 163; *Ancestral Roots* 106, 144A, 121E-18; Moriarty 50, 24; *TAG* 72:187-204 (#15 ancestry).

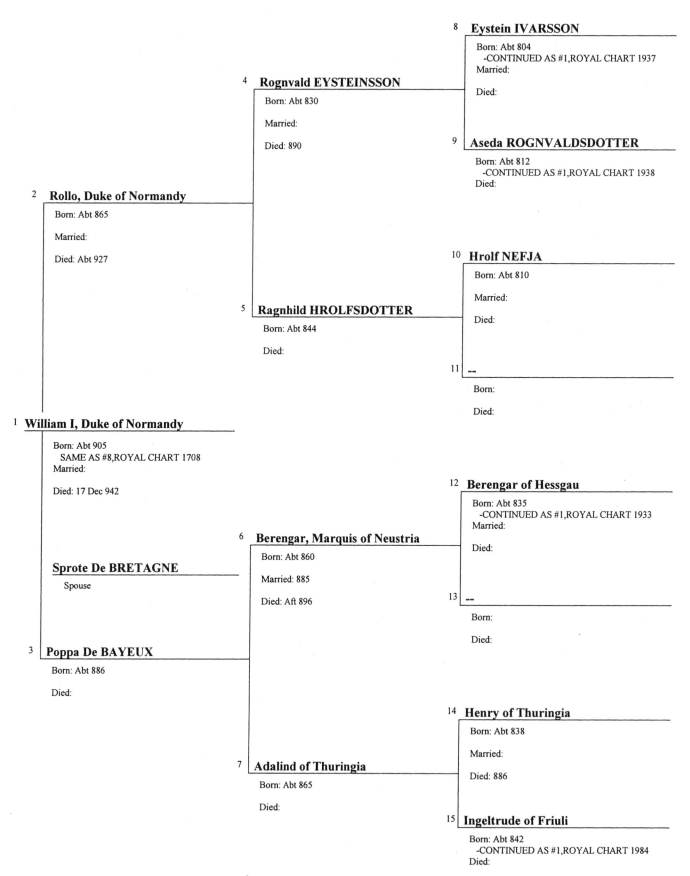

8 Eystein IVARSSON

Born: Abt 804
  -CONTINUED AS #1,ROYAL CHART 1937
Married:

Died:

4 Rognvald EYSTEINSSON

Born: Abt 830

Married:

Died: 890

9 Aseda ROGNVALDSDOTTER

Born: Abt 812
  -CONTINUED AS #1,ROYAL CHART 1938
Died:

2 Rollo, Duke of Normandy

Born: Abt 865

Married:

Died: Abt 927

10 Hrolf NEFJA

Born: Abt 810

Married:

Died:

5 Ragnhild HROLFSDOTTER

Born: Abt 844

Died:

11 --

Born:

Died:

1 William I, Duke of Normandy

Born: Abt 905
  SAME AS #8,ROYAL CHART 1708
Married:

Died: 17 Dec 942

12 Berengar of Hessgau

Born: Abt 835
  -CONTINUED AS #1,ROYAL CHART 1933
Married:

Died:

6 Berengar, Marquis of Neustria

Born: Abt 860

Married: 885

Died: Aft 896

13 --

Born:

Died:

Sprote De BRETAGNE

Spouse

3 Poppa De BAYEUX

Born: Abt 886

Died:

14 Henry of Thuringia

Born: Abt 838

Married:

Died: 886

7 Adalind of Thuringia

Born: Abt 865

Died:

15 Ingeltrude of Friuli

Born: Abt 842
  -CONTINUED AS #1,ROYAL CHART 1984
Died:

Sources include: *Royal Ancestors* (1989), chart 11504; *TAG* 72:187-204; 52:25; *Ancestral Roots* 121E; Stuart 166; Moriarty 11, 226. Notes: The parentage and ancestry of #3 Poppa is disputed. Moriarty 226 and Evans (*TAG* 52) favored the claim that #3 Poppa was daughter of Gui, Count of Senlis, by an unknown daughter of Pepin, Count of Senlis (see chart 1907). However, the current consensus is that Poppa was daughter of Berengar. A recently-proposed ancestry for Poppa (see *TAG* 72) is shown above. #14 Henry is suggested to be the son of an Adalbert.

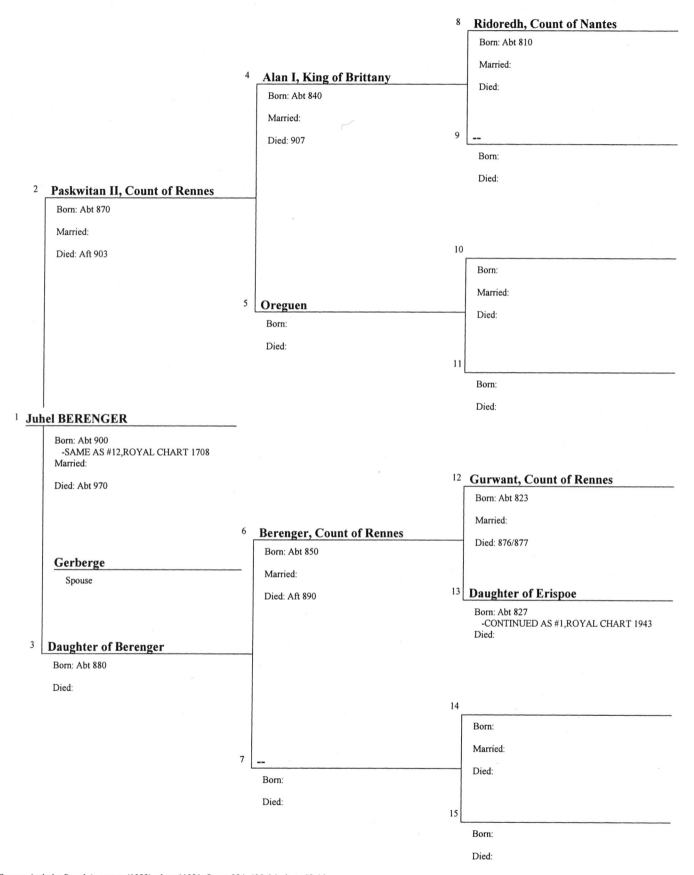

8 **Ridoredh, Count of Nantes**

Born: Abt 810

Married:

Died:

4 **Alan I, King of Brittany**

Born: Abt 840

Married:

Died: 907

9 **--**

Born:

Died:

2 **Paskwitan II, Count of Rennes**

Born: Abt 870

Married:

Died: Aft 903

10

Born:

Married:

Died:

5 **Oreguen**

Born:

Died:

11

Born:

Died:

1 **Juhel BERENGER**

Born: Abt 900
-SAME AS #12,ROYAL CHART 1708
Married:

Died: Abt 970

Gerberge

Spouse

12 **Gurwant, Count of Rennes**

Born: Abt 823

Married:

Died: 876/877

6 **Berenger, Count of Rennes**

Born: Abt 850

Married:

Died: Aft 890

13 **Daughter of Erispoe**

Born: Abt 827
-CONTINUED AS #1,ROYAL CHART 1943
Died:

3 **Daughter of Berenger**

Born: Abt 880

Died:

14

Born:

Married:

Died:

7 **--**

Born:

Died:

15

Born:

Died:

Sources include: *Royal Ancestors* (1989), chart 11931; Stuart 334, 405; Moriarty 13-14.

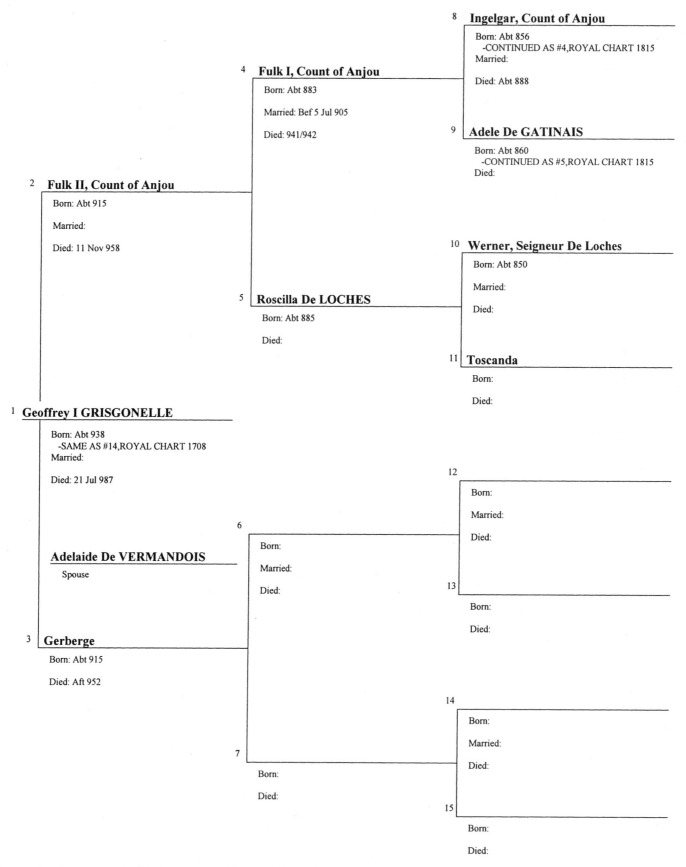

8 Ingelgar, Count of Anjou

Born: Abt 856
 -CONTINUED AS #4,ROYAL CHART 1815
Married:

Died: Abt 888

4 Fulk I, Count of Anjou

Born: Abt 883

Married: Bef 5 Jul 905

Died: 941/942

9 Adele De GATINAIS

Born: Abt 860
 -CONTINUED AS #5,ROYAL CHART 1815
Died:

2 Fulk II, Count of Anjou

Born: Abt 915

Married:

Died: 11 Nov 958

10 Werner, Seigneur De Loches

Born: Abt 850

Married:

Died:

5 Roscilla De LOCHES

Born: Abt 885

Died:

11 Toscanda

Born:

Died:

1 Geoffrey I GRISGONELLE

Born: Abt 938
 -SAME AS #14,ROYAL CHART 1708
Married:

Died: 21 Jul 987

12

Born:

Married:

Died:

6

Born:

Married:

Died:

13

Born:

Died:

Adelaide De VERMANDOIS

Spouse

3 Gerberge

Born: Abt 915

Died: Aft 952

14

Born:

Married:

Died:

7

Born:

Died:

15

Born:

Died:

Sources include: *Royal Ancestors* (1989), charts 11401, 11502; Stuart 167; Moriarty 4.

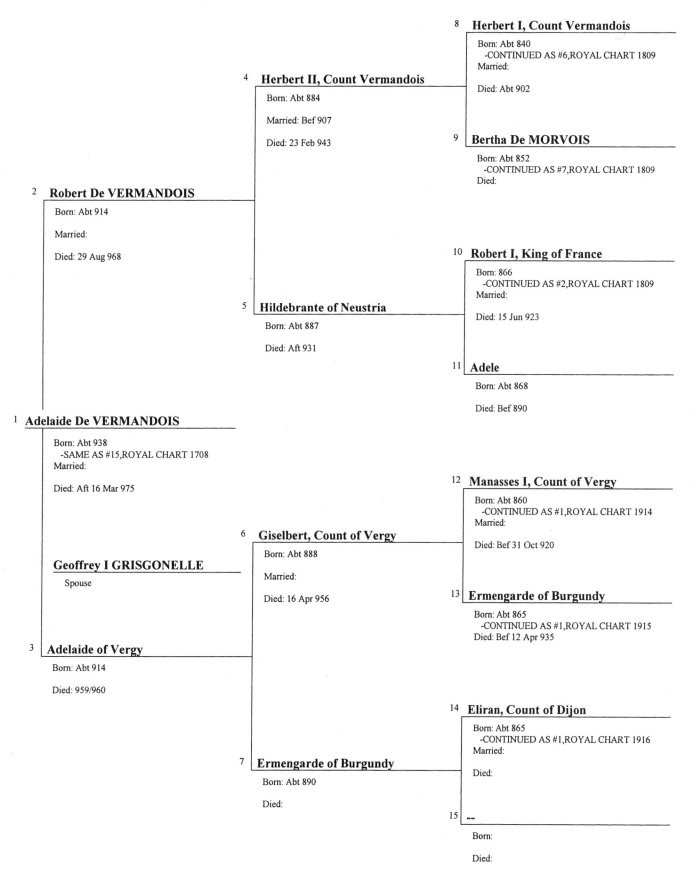

8 **Herbert I, Count Vermandois**

Born: Abt 840
-CONTINUED AS #6,ROYAL CHART 1809
Married:

Died: Abt 902

4 **Herbert II, Count Vermandois**

Born: Abt 884

Married: Bef 907

Died: 23 Feb 943

9 **Bertha De MORVOIS**

Born: Abt 852
-CONTINUED AS #7,ROYAL CHART 1809
Died:

2 **Robert De VERMANDOIS**

Born: Abt 914

Married:

Died: 29 Aug 968

10 **Robert I, King of France**

Born: 866
-CONTINUED AS #2,ROYAL CHART 1809
Married:

Died: 15 Jun 923

5 **Hildebrante of Neustria**

Born: Abt 887

Died: Aft 931

11 **Adele**

Born: Abt 868

Died: Bef 890

1 **Adelaide De VERMANDOIS**

Born: Abt 938
-SAME AS #15,ROYAL CHART 1708
Married:

Died: Aft 16 Mar 975

12 **Manasses I, Count of Vergy**

Born: Abt 860
-CONTINUED AS #1,ROYAL CHART 1914
Married:

Died: Bef 31 Oct 920

6 **Giselbert, Count of Vergy**

Born: Abt 888

Married:

Died: 16 Apr 956

13 **Ermengarde of Burgundy**

Born: Abt 865
-CONTINUED AS #1,ROYAL CHART 1915
Died: Bef 12 Apr 935

Geoffrey I GRISGONELLE

Spouse

3 **Adelaide of Vergy**

Born: Abt 914

Died: 959/960

14 **Eliran, Count of Dijon**

Born: Abt 865
-CONTINUED AS #1,ROYAL CHART 1916
Married:

Died:

7 **Ermengarde of Burgundy**

Born: Abt 890

Died:

15 **--**

Born:

Died:

Sources include: *Royal Ancestors* 11401, 11503, 11758; Stuart 258; *Ancestral Roots* 118; Moriarty 4, 6, 10, 38; LDS records.

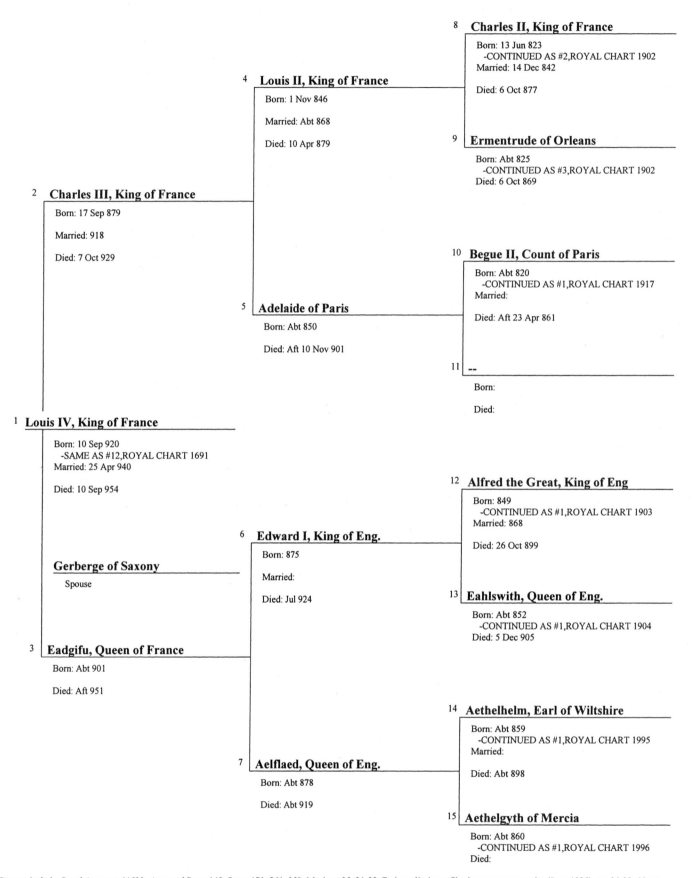

8 **Charles II, King of France**

Born: 13 Jun 823
  -CONTINUED AS #2,ROYAL CHART 1902
Married: 14 Dec 842

Died: 6 Oct 877

4 **Louis II, King of France**

Born: 1 Nov 846

Married: Abt 868

Died: 10 Apr 879

9 **Ermentrude of Orleans**

Born: Abt 825
  -CONTINUED AS #3,ROYAL CHART 1902
Died: 6 Oct 869

2 **Charles III, King of France**

Born: 17 Sep 879

Married: 918

Died: 7 Oct 929

10 **Begue II, Count of Paris**

Born: Abt 820
  -CONTINUED AS #1,ROYAL CHART 1917
Married:

Died: Aft 23 Apr 861

5 **Adelaide of Paris**

Born: Abt 850

Died: Aft 10 Nov 901

11 **--**

Born:

Died:

1 **Louis IV, King of France**

Born: 10 Sep 920
  -SAME AS #12,ROYAL CHART 1691
Married: 25 Apr 940

Died: 10 Sep 954

12 **Alfred the Great, King of Eng**

Born: 849
  -CONTINUED AS #1,ROYAL CHART 1903
Married: 868

Died: 26 Oct 899

6 **Edward I, King of Eng.**

Born: 875

Married:

Died: Jul 924

Gerberge of Saxony

Spouse

13 **Eahlswith, Queen of Eng.**

Born: Abt 852
  -CONTINUED AS #1,ROYAL CHART 1904
Died: 5 Dec 905

3 **Eadgifu, Queen of France**

Born: Abt 901

Died: Aft 951

14 **Aethelhelm, Earl of Wiltshire**

Born: Abt 859
  -CONTINUED AS #1,ROYAL CHART 1995
Married:

Died: Abt 898

7 **Aelflaed, Queen of Eng.**

Born: Abt 878

Died: Abt 919

15 **Aethelgyth of Mercia**

Born: Abt 860
  -CONTINUED AS #1,ROYAL CHART 1996
Died:

Sources include: *Royal Ancestors* 11520; *Ancestral Roots* 148; Stuart 171, 261, 350; Moriarty 35, 21-23; Faris preliminary Charlemagne manuscript (June 1995), pp. 96-98. Note: The parentage of #5 Adelaide is disputed, with at least four different versions claimed. The above version is one of two alternate versions suggested by Moriarty that both descend from Begue and Aupals, daughter of Charlemagne (see chart 1917). Faris gives #5 as daughter of Adalhard de Paris, Seigneur de Sennecey.

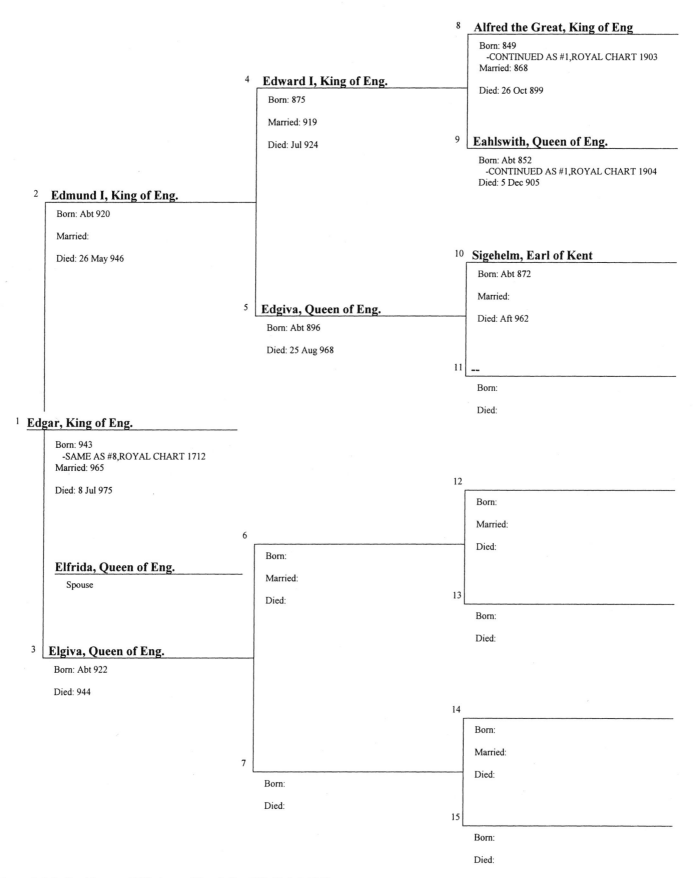

8 **Alfred the Great, King of Eng**

Born: 849
-CONTINUED AS #1,ROYAL CHART 1903
Married: 868

Died: 26 Oct 899

4 **Edward I, King of Eng.**

Born: 875

Married: 919

Died: Jul 924

9 **Eahlswith, Queen of Eng.**

Born: Abt 852
-CONTINUED AS #1,ROYAL CHART 1904
Died: 5 Dec 905

2 **Edmund I, King of Eng.**

Born: Abt 920

Married:

Died: 26 May 946

10 **Sigehelm, Earl of Kent**

Born: Abt 872

Married:

Died: Aft 962

5 **Edgiva, Queen of Eng.**

Born: Abt 896

Died: 25 Aug 968

11 **--**

Born:

Died:

1 **Edgar, King of Eng.**

Born: 943
-SAME AS #8,ROYAL CHART 1712
Married: 965

Died: 8 Jul 975

12

Born:

Married:

Died:

6

Born:

Married:

Died:

13

Born:

Died:

Elfrida, Queen of Eng.

Spouse

3 **Elgiva, Queen of Eng.**

Born: Abt 922

Died: 944

14

Born:

Married:

Died:

7

Born:

Died:

15

Born:

Died:

Sources include: *Royal Ancestors* 11511; *Ancestral Roots* 1; Stuart 233; Moriarty 30-31.

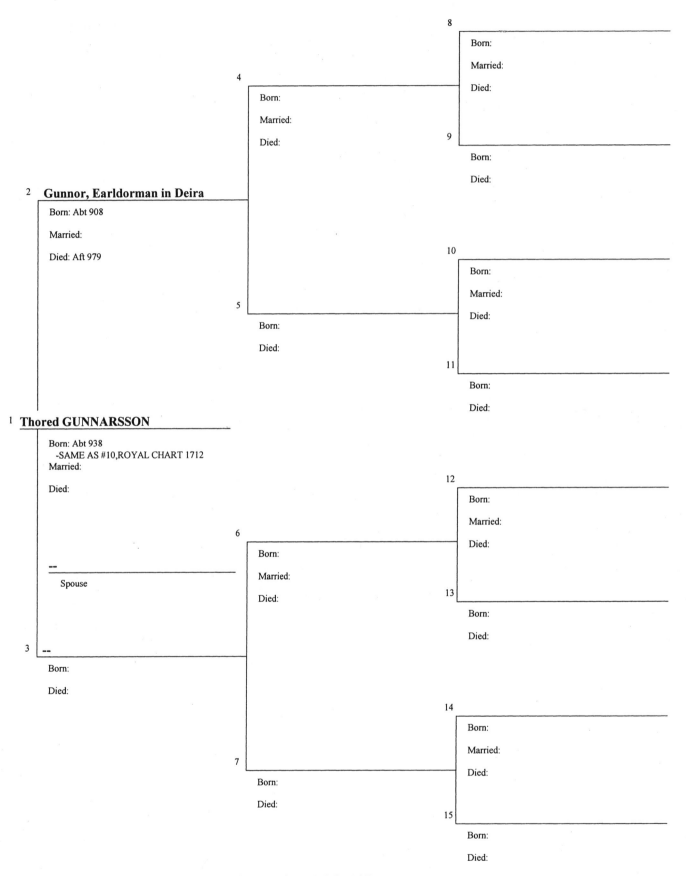

8

Born:

Married:

Died:

4

Born:

Married:

Died:

9

Born:

Died:

2 Gunnor, Earldorman in Deira

Born: Abt 908

Married:

Died: Aft 979

10

Born:

Married:

Died:

5

Born:

Died:

11

Born:

Died:

1 Thored GUNNARSSON

Born: Abt 938
  -SAME AS #10,ROYAL CHART 1712
Married:

Died:

12

Born:

Married:

Died:

6

Born:

Married:

Died:

13

Born:

Died:

--
   Spouse

3 --

Born:

Died:

14

Born:

Married:

Died:

7

Born:

Died:

15

Born:

Died:

Sources include: *Royal Ancestors* (1989), chart 11511; Moriarty 31; *Ancestral Roots* 1-19; Stuart 342.

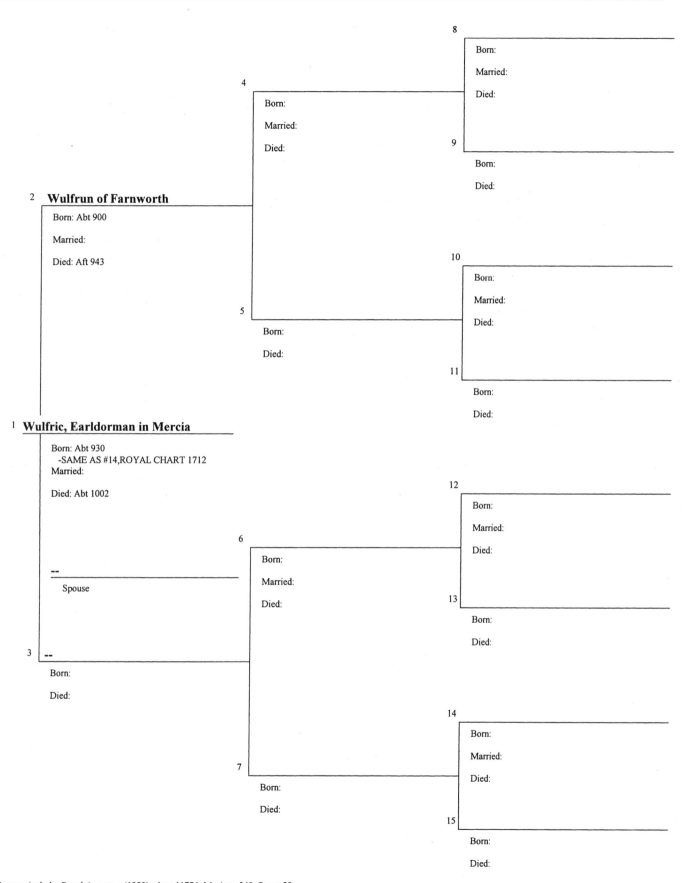

8

Born:

Married:

Died:

4

Born:

Married:

Died:

9

Born:

Died:

2 Wulfrun of Farnworth

Born: Abt 900

Married:

Died: Aft 943

10

Born:

Married:

Died:

5

Born:

Died:

11

Born:

Died:

1 Wulfric, Earldorman in Mercia

Born: Abt 930
  -SAME AS #14, ROYAL CHART 1712
Married:

Died: Abt 1002

12

Born:

Married:

Died:

6

Born:

Married:

Died:

13

Born:

Died:

--

Spouse

3 --

Born:

Died:

14

Born:

Married:

Died:

7

Born:

Died:

15

Born:

Died:

Sources include: *Royal Ancestors* (1989), chart 11774; Moriarty 249; Stuart 22.

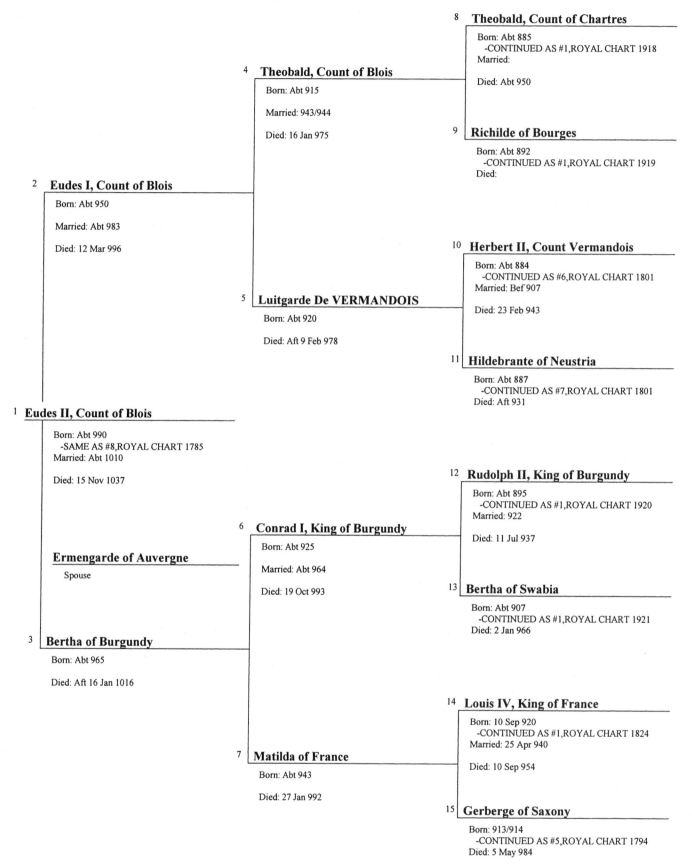

Pedigree Chart   Chart 1828

8 **Theobald, Count of Chartres**
Born: Abt 885
-CONTINUED AS #1,ROYAL CHART 1918
Married:

Died: Abt 950

4 **Theobald, Count of Blois**
Born: Abt 915

Married: 943/944

Died: 16 Jan 975

9 **Richilde of Bourges**
Born: Abt 892
-CONTINUED AS #1,ROYAL CHART 1919
Died:

2 **Eudes I, Count of Blois**
Born: Abt 950

Married: Abt 983

Died: 12 Mar 996

10 **Herbert II, Count Vermandois**
Born: Abt 884
-CONTINUED AS #6,ROYAL CHART 1801
Married: Bef 907

Died: 23 Feb 943

5 **Luitgarde De VERMANDOIS**
Born: Abt 920

Died: Aft 9 Feb 978

11 **Hildebrante of Neustria**
Born: Abt 887
-CONTINUED AS #7,ROYAL CHART 1801
Died: Aft 931

1 **Eudes II, Count of Blois**
Born: Abt 990
-SAME AS #8,ROYAL CHART 1785
Married: Abt 1010

Died: 15 Nov 1037

12 **Rudolph II, King of Burgundy**
Born: Abt 895
-CONTINUED AS #1,ROYAL CHART 1920
Married: 922

Died: 11 Jul 937

6 **Conrad I, King of Burgundy**
Born: Abt 925

Married: Abt 964

Died: 19 Oct 993

13 **Bertha of Swabia**
Born: Abt 907
-CONTINUED AS #1,ROYAL CHART 1921
Died: 2 Jan 966

Ermengarde of Auvergne
Spouse

3 **Bertha of Burgundy**
Born: Abt 965

Died: Aft 16 Jan 1016

14 **Louis IV, King of France**
Born: 10 Sep 920
-CONTINUED AS #1,ROYAL CHART 1824
Married: 25 Apr 940

Died: 10 Sep 954

7 **Matilda of France**
Born: Abt 943

Died: 27 Jan 992

15 **Gerberge of Saxony**
Born: 913/914
-CONTINUED AS #5,ROYAL CHART 1794
Died: 5 May 984

Sources include: *Royal Ancestors* 11420, 11580-81; Moriarty 117, 36, 33-34; *Ancestral Roots* 136, 159; Stuart 133, 230; LDS records.

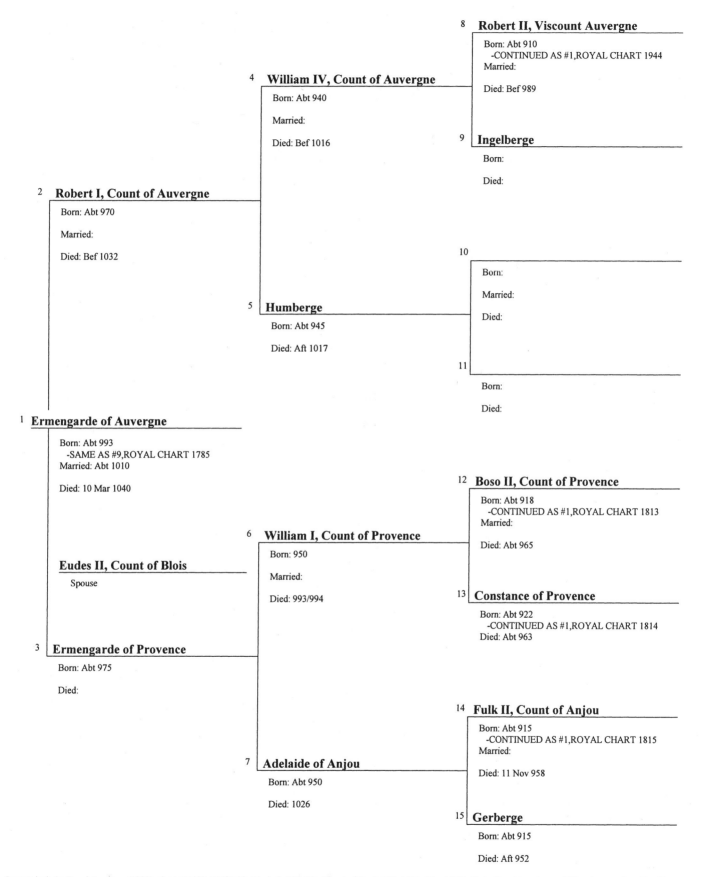

8 **Robert II, Viscount Auvergne**

Born: Abt 910
-CONTINUED AS #1,ROYAL CHART 1944
Married:

Died: Bef 989

4 **William IV, Count of Auvergne**

Born: Abt 940

Married:

Died: Bef 1016

9 **Ingelberge**

Born:

Died:

2 **Robert I, Count of Auvergne**

Born: Abt 970

Married:

Died: Bef 1032

10

Born:

Married:

Died:

5 **Humberge**

Born: Abt 945

Died: Aft 1017

11

Born:

Died:

1 **Ermengarde of Auvergne**

Born: Abt 993
-SAME AS #9,ROYAL CHART 1785
Married: Abt 1010

Died: 10 Mar 1040

Eudes II, Count of Blois

Spouse

12 **Boso II, Count of Provence**

Born: Abt 918
-CONTINUED AS #1,ROYAL CHART 1813
Married:

Died: Abt 965

6 **William I, Count of Provence**

Born: 950

Married:

Died: 993/994

13 **Constance of Provence**

Born: Abt 922
-CONTINUED AS #1,ROYAL CHART 1814
Died: Abt 963

3 **Ermengarde of Provence**

Born: Abt 975

Died:

14 **Fulk II, Count of Anjou**

Born: Abt 915
-CONTINUED AS #1,ROYAL CHART 1815
Married:

Died: 11 Nov 958

7 **Adelaide of Anjou**

Born: Abt 950

Died: 1026

15 **Gerberge**

Born: Abt 915

Died: Aft 952

Sources include: *Royal Ancestors* (1989), charts 11420, 11591-92; Moriarty 118, 28; *Ancestral Roots* 137, 141A; Stuart 127. Note: Stuart inserts an additional generation (Guy I) between #4 William and #8 Robert. The Moriarty version fits better chronologically and has been followed above.

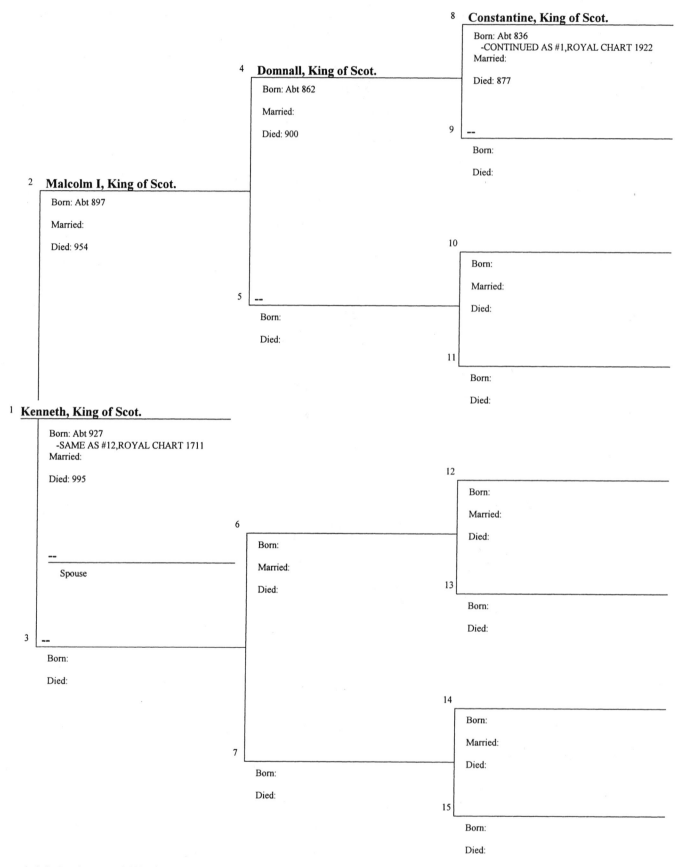

8 Constantine, King of Scot.
Born: Abt 836
    -CONTINUED AS #1,ROYAL CHART 1922
Married:

Died: 877

4 Domnall, King of Scot.
Born: Abt 862

Married:

Died: 900

9 --
Born:

Died:

2 Malcolm I, King of Scot.
Born: Abt 897

Married:

Died: 954

5 --
Born:

Died:

10
Born:

Married:

Died:

11
Born:

Died:

1 Kenneth, King of Scot.
Born: Abt 927
    -SAME AS #12,ROYAL CHART 1711
Married:

Died: 995

--
Spouse

3 --
Born:

Died:

6
Born:

Married:

Died:

12
Born:

Married:

Died:

13
Born:

Died:

7
Born:

Died:

14
Born:

Married:

Died:

15
Born:

Died:

Sources include: *Royal Ancestors* (1989), chart 11510; *Ancestral Roots* 170; Stuart 165.

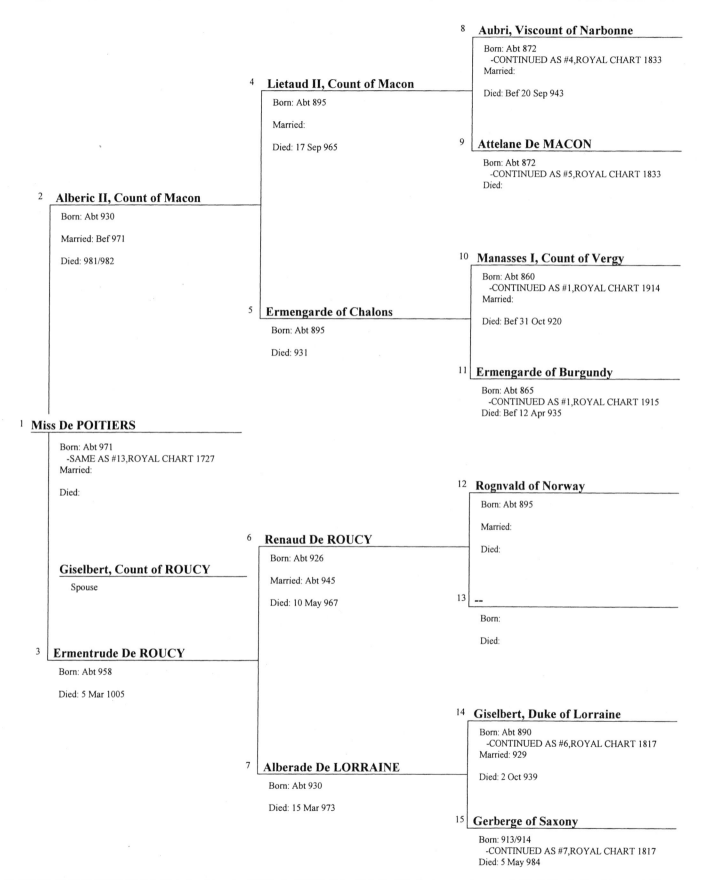

8 Aubri, Viscount of Narbonne

Born: Abt 872
  -CONTINUED AS #4,ROYAL CHART 1833
Married:

Died: Bef 20 Sep 943

4 Lietaud II, Count of Macon

Born: Abt 895

Married:

Died: 17 Sep 965

9 Attelane De MACON

Born: Abt 872
  -CONTINUED AS #5,ROYAL CHART 1833
Died:

2 Alberic II, Count of Macon

Born: Abt 930

Married: Bef 971

Died: 981/982

10 Manasses I, Count of Vergy

Born: Abt 860
  -CONTINUED AS #1,ROYAL CHART 1914
Married:

Died: Bef 31 Oct 920

5 Ermengarde of Chalons

Born: Abt 895

Died: 931

11 Ermengarde of Burgundy

Born: Abt 865
  -CONTINUED AS #1,ROYAL CHART 1915
Died: Bef 12 Apr 935

1 Miss De POITIERS

Born: Abt 971
  -SAME AS #13,ROYAL CHART 1727
Married:

Died:

12 Rognvald of Norway

Born: Abt 895

Married:

Died:

6 Renaud De ROUCY

Born: Abt 926

Married: Abt 945

Died: 10 May 967

13 --

Born:

Died:

Giselbert, Count of ROUCY

Spouse

3 Ermentrude De ROUCY

Born: Abt 958

Died: 5 Mar 1005

14 Giselbert, Duke of Lorraine

Born: Abt 890
  -CONTINUED AS #6,ROYAL CHART 1817
Married: 929

Died: 2 Oct 939

7 Alberade De LORRAINE

Born: Abt 930

Died: 15 Mar 973

15 Gerberge of Saxony

Born: 913/914
  -CONTINUED AS #7,ROYAL CHART 1817
Died: 5 May 984

Sources include: Stuart 170-33; Moriarty 50, 1; *Royal Ancestors* (1989), chart 11538. Notes: #1 (wife of Giselbert, name unknown, called <u>De Poitiers</u> by Stuart) is suggested by Moriarty to <u>possibly</u> be the daughter of Alberic (Aubri), Count of Macon, as tentatively accepted above. #5 Ermengarde (1st wife) is not certain. #2 Alberic may have been son of Berta (2nd wife) or Richilde (3rd wife). Moriarty accepts Ermengarde. See also chart 1701.

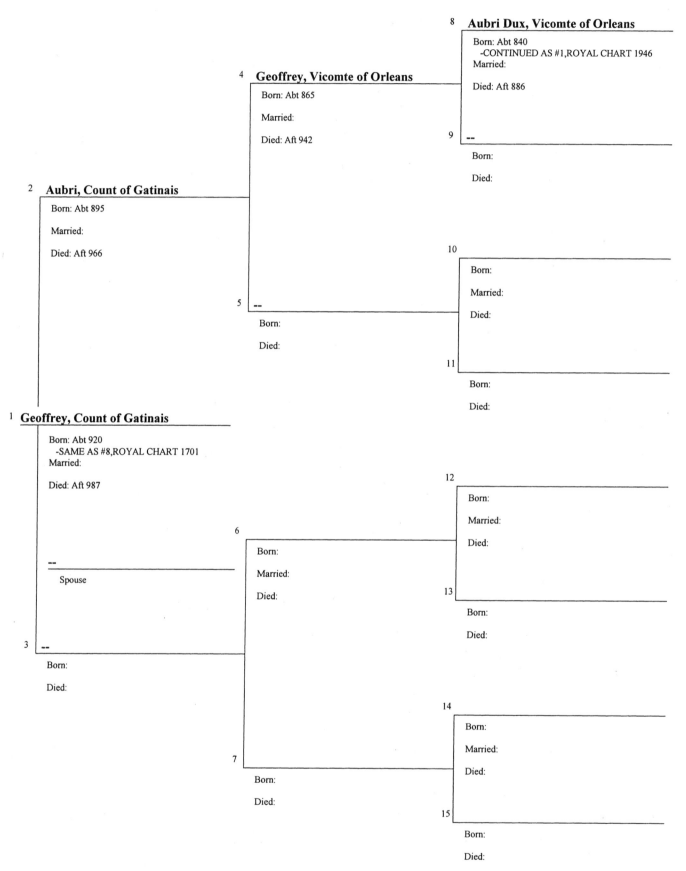

8   **Aubri Dux, Vicomte of Orleans**

Born: Abt 840
  -CONTINUED AS #1,ROYAL CHART 1946
Married:

Died: Aft 886

4   **Geoffrey, Vicomte of Orleans**

Born: Abt 865

Married:

Died: Aft 942

9   --

Born:

Died:

2   **Aubri, Count of Gatinais**

Born: Abt 895

Married:

Died: Aft 966

10

Born:

Married:

Died:

5   --

Born:

Died:

11

Born:

Died:

1   **Geoffrey, Count of Gatinais**

Born: Abt 920
  -SAME AS #8,ROYAL CHART 1701
Married:

Died: Aft 987

--

Spouse

12

Born:

Married:

Died:

6

Born:

Married:

Died:

13

Born:

Died:

3   --

Born:

Died:

14

Born:

Married:

Died:

7

Born:

Died:

15

Born:

Died:

Sources include: *Royal Ancestors* (1989), chart 11965; Moriarty 1; Stuart 53.

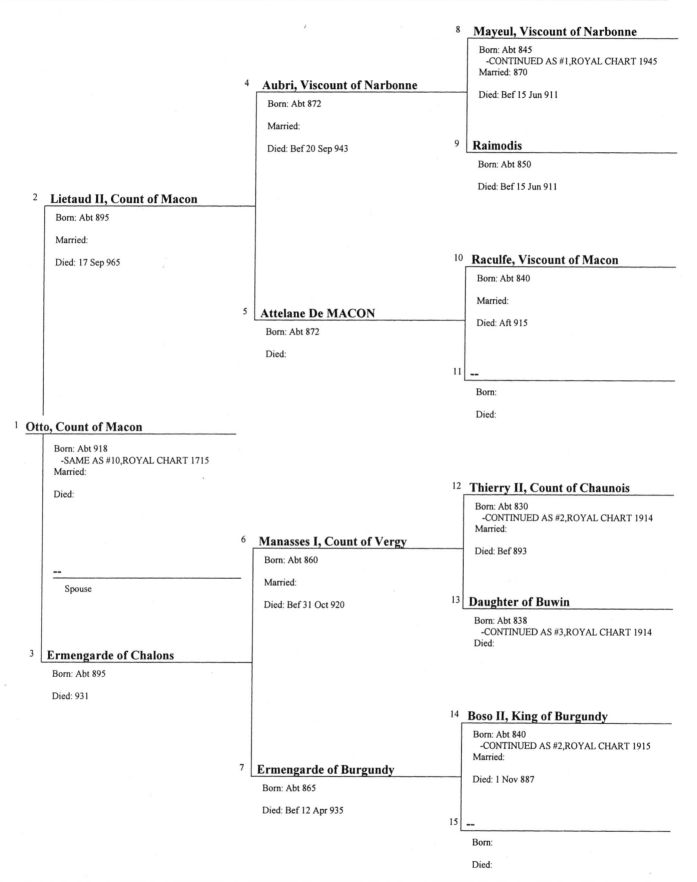

8 Mayeul, Viscount of Narbonne

Born: Abt 845
-CONTINUED AS #1,ROYAL CHART 1945
Married: 870

Died: Bef 15 Jun 911

4 Aubri, Viscount of Narbonne

Born: Abt 872

Married:

Died: Bef 20 Sep 943

9 Raimodis

Born: Abt 850

Died: Bef 15 Jun 911

2 Lietaud II, Count of Macon

Born: Abt 895

Married:

Died: 17 Sep 965

10 Raculfe, Viscount of Macon

Born: Abt 840

Married:

Died: Aft 915

5 Attelane De MACON

Born: Abt 872

Died:

11 --

Born:

Died:

1 Otto, Count of Macon

Born: Abt 918
-SAME AS #10,ROYAL CHART 1715
Married:

Died:

12 Thierry II, Count of Chaunois

Born: Abt 830
-CONTINUED AS #2,ROYAL CHART 1914
Married:

Died: Bef 893

6 Manasses I, Count of Vergy

Born: Abt 860

Married:

Died: Bef 31 Oct 920

13 Daughter of Buwin

Born: Abt 838
-CONTINUED AS #3,ROYAL CHART 1914
Died:

--

Spouse

3 Ermengarde of Chalons

Born: Abt 895

Died: 931

14 Boso II, King of Burgundy

Born: Abt 840
-CONTINUED AS #2,ROYAL CHART 1915
Married:

Died: 1 Nov 887

7 Ermengarde of Burgundy

Born: Abt 865

Died: Bef 12 Apr 935

15 --

Born:

Died:

Sources include: *Royal Ancestors* (1989), charts 11858, 11407 notes, 11757, 11964; Stuart 94-34, 101; Charles Evans in *TAG* 52:25 (identification of #1 Otto, adding that generation to Moriarty version); Moriarty 37, 1, 10; Turton 6.

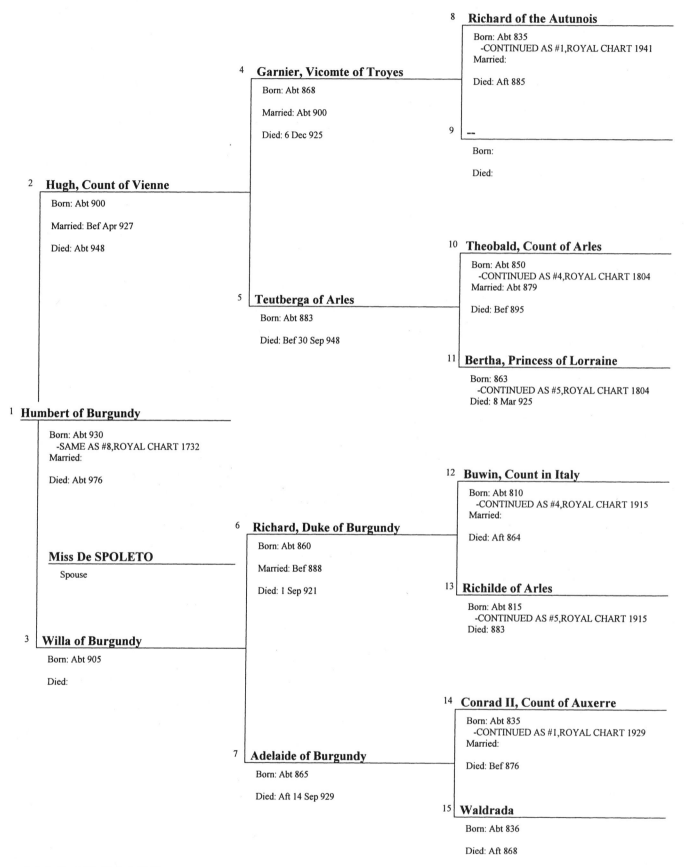

8 | **Richard of the Autunois**

Born: Abt 835
  -CONTINUED AS #1,ROYAL CHART 1941
Married:

Died: Aft 885

4 | **Garnier, Vicomte of Troyes**

Born: Abt 868

Married: Abt 900

Died: 6 Dec 925

9 | **--**

Born:

Died:

2 | **Hugh, Count of Vienne**

Born: Abt 900

Married: Bef Apr 927

Died: Abt 948

10 | **Theobald, Count of Arles**

Born: Abt 850
  -CONTINUED AS #4,ROYAL CHART 1804
Married: Abt 879

Died: Bef 895

5 | **Teutberga of Arles**

Born: Abt 883

Died: Bef 30 Sep 948

11 | **Bertha, Princess of Lorraine**

Born: 863
  -CONTINUED AS #5,ROYAL CHART 1804
Died: 8 Mar 925

1 | **Humbert of Burgundy**

Born: Abt 930
  -SAME AS #8,ROYAL CHART 1732
Married:

Died: Abt 976

12 | **Buwin, Count in Italy**

Born: Abt 810
  -CONTINUED AS #4,ROYAL CHART 1915
Married:

Died: Aft 864

6 | **Richard, Duke of Burgundy**

Born: Abt 860

Married: Bef 888

Died: 1 Sep 921

Miss De SPOLETO

Spouse

13 | **Richilde of Arles**

Born: Abt 815
  -CONTINUED AS #5,ROYAL CHART 1915
Died: 883

3 | **Willa of Burgundy**

Born: Abt 905

Died:

14 | **Conrad II, Count of Auxerre**

Born: Abt 835
  -CONTINUED AS #1,ROYAL CHART 1929
Married:

Died: Bef 876

7 | **Adelaide of Burgundy**

Born: Abt 865

Died: Aft 14 Sep 929

15 | **Waldrada**

Born: Abt 836

Died: Aft 868

Sources include: Stuart 173; Moriarty 59, 51.

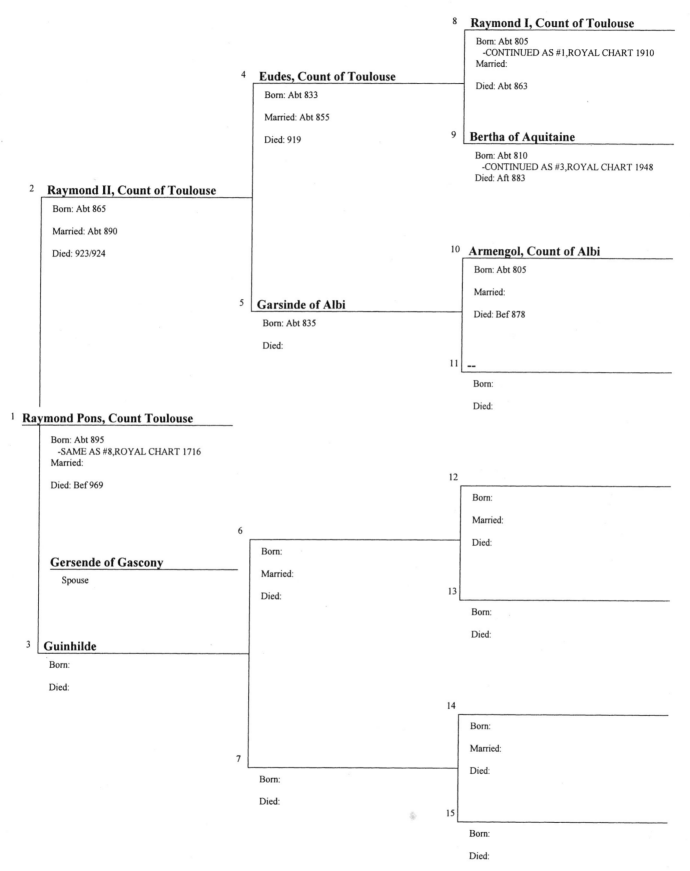

8 Raymond I, Count of Toulouse

Born: Abt 805
    -CONTINUED AS #1,ROYAL CHART 1910
Married:

Died: Abt 863

4 Eudes, Count of Toulouse

Born: Abt 833

Married: Abt 855

Died: 919

9 Bertha of Aquitaine

Born: Abt 810
    -CONTINUED AS #3,ROYAL CHART 1948
Died: Aft 883

2 Raymond II, Count of Toulouse

Born: Abt 865

Married: Abt 890

Died: 923/924

10 Armengol, Count of Albi

Born: Abt 805

Married:

Died: Bef 878

5 Garsinde of Albi

Born: Abt 835

Died:

11 --

Born:

Died:

1 Raymond Pons, Count Toulouse

Born: Abt 895
    -SAME AS #8,ROYAL CHART 1716
Married:

Died: Bef 969

12

Born:

Married:

Died:

6

Born:

Married:

Died:

13

Born:

Died:

Gersende of Gascony

Spouse

3 Guinhilde

Born:

Died:

14

Born:

Married:

Died:

7

Born:

Died:

15

Born:

Died:

Sources include: *Royal Ancestors* (1989), chart 11593; Moriarty 41; Stuart 329. Note: The parentage of #3 Guinhilde is disputed.

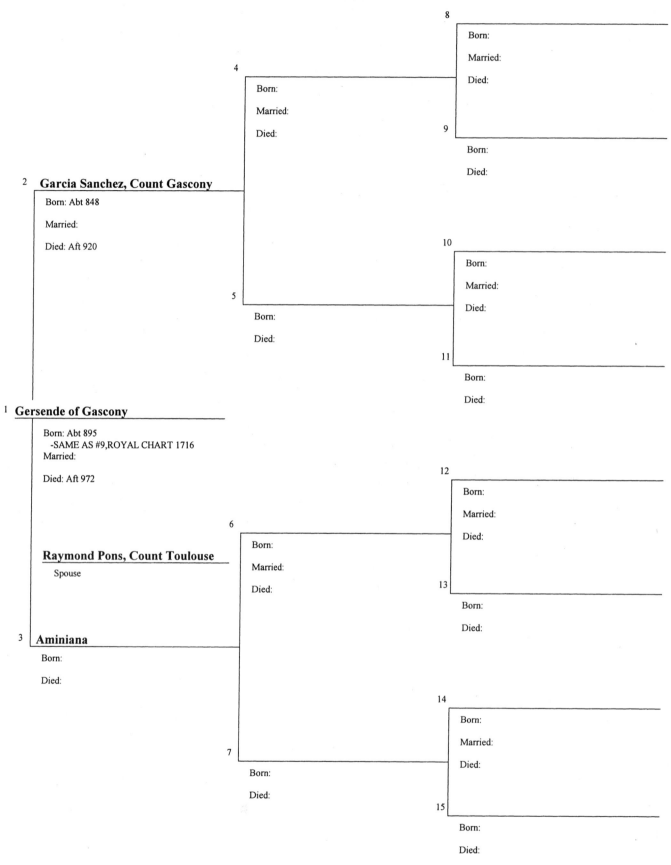

8

Born:

Married:

Died:

4

Born:

Married:

Died:

9

Born:

Died:

2 **Garcia Sanchez, Count Gascony**

Born: Abt 848

Married:

Died: Aft 920

10

Born:

Married:

Died:

5

Born:

Died:

11

Born:

Died:

1 **Gersende of Gascony**

Born: Abt 895
  -SAME AS #9,ROYAL CHART 1716
Married:

Died: Aft 972

12

Born:

Married:

Died:

6

Born:

Married:

Died:

13

Born:

Died:

Raymond Pons, Count Toulouse

Spouse

3 **Aminiana**

Born:

Died:

14

Born:

Married:

Died:

7

Born:

Died:

15

Born:

Died:

Sources include: *Royal Ancestors* (1989), chart 11593; Moriarty 41, 79, 255; Stuart 329-35. Note: The parentage of #1 Gersende is disputed, but Moriarty concludes that the version shown above is most probable.

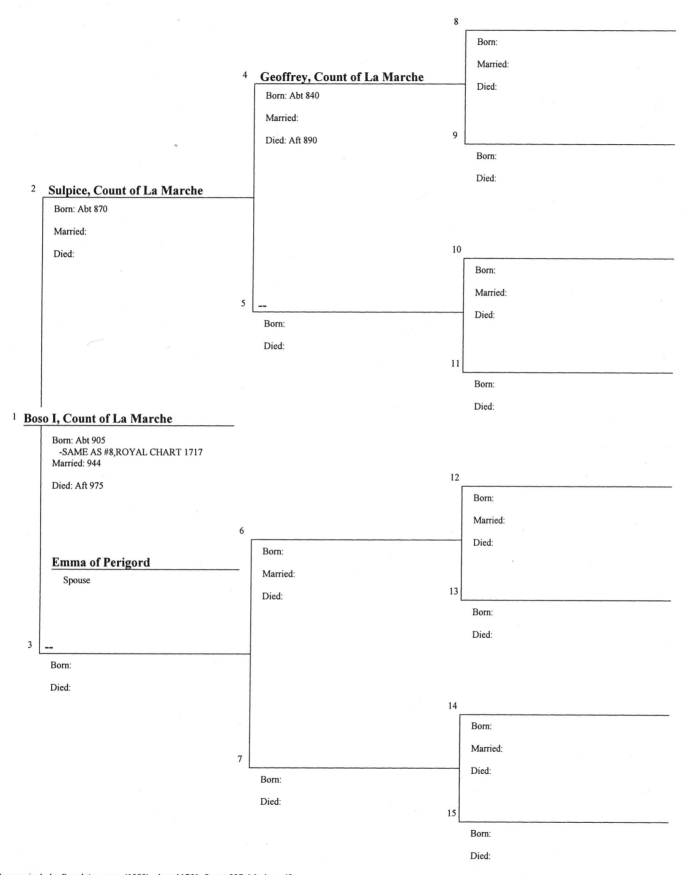

8
Born:
Married:
Died:

4 Geoffrey, Count of La Marche
Born: Abt 840
Married:
Died: Aft 890

9
Born:
Died:

2 Sulpice, Count of La Marche
Born: Abt 870
Married:
Died:

5 --
Born:
Died:

10
Born:
Married:
Died:

11
Born:
Died:

1 Boso I, Count of La Marche
Born: Abt 905
-SAME AS #8,ROYAL CHART 1717
Married: 944
Died: Aft 975

12
Born:
Married:
Died:

6
Born:
Married:
Died:

13
Born:
Died:

Emma of Perigord
Spouse

3 --
Born:
Died:

14
Born:
Married:
Died:

7
Born:
Died:

15
Born:
Died:

Sources include: *Royal Ancestors* (1989), chart 11751; Stuart 327; Moriarty 42.

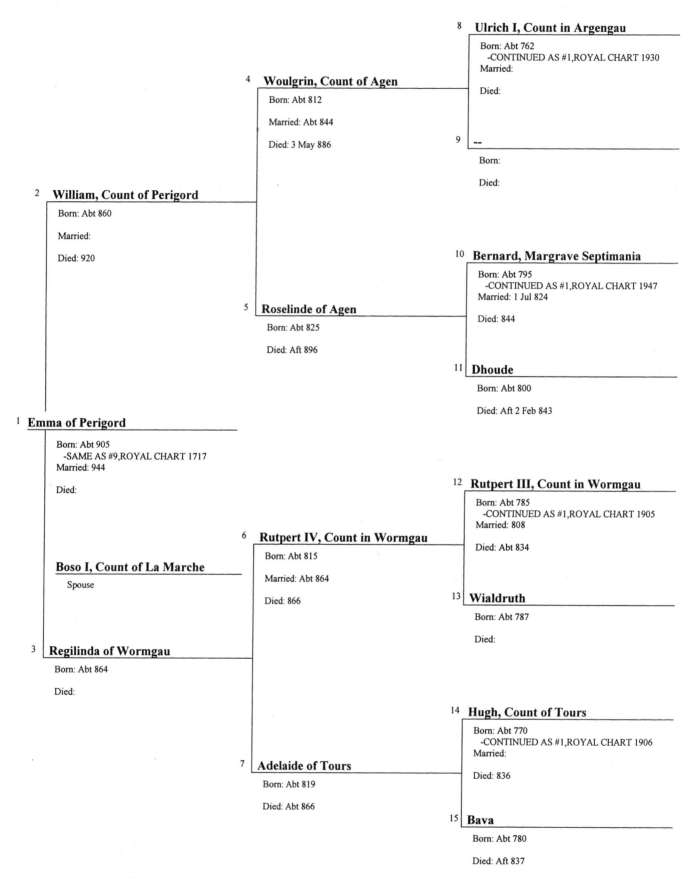

8 Ulrich I, Count in Argengau

Born: Abt 762
  -CONTINUED AS #1,ROYAL CHART 1930
Married:

Died:

4 Woulgrin, Count of Agen

Born: Abt 812

Married: Abt 844

Died: 3 May 886

9 --

Born:

Died:

2 William, Count of Perigord

Born: Abt 860

Married:

Died: 920

10 Bernard, Margrave Septimania

Born: Abt 795
  -CONTINUED AS #1,ROYAL CHART 1947
Married: 1 Jul 824

Died: 844

5 Roselinde of Agen

Born: Abt 825

Died: Aft 896

11 Dhoude

Born: Abt 800

Died: Aft 2 Feb 843

1 Emma of Perigord

Born: Abt 905
  -SAME AS #9,ROYAL CHART 1717
Married: 944

Died:

12 Rutpert III, Count in Wormgau

Born: Abt 785
  -CONTINUED AS #1,ROYAL CHART 1905
Married: 808

Died: Abt 834

6 Rutpert IV, Count in Wormgau

Born: Abt 815

Married: Abt 864

Died: 866

Boso I, Count of La Marche

Spouse

13 Wialdruth

Born: Abt 787

Died:

3 Regilinda of Wormgau

Born: Abt 864

Died:

14 Hugh, Count of Tours

Born: Abt 770
  -CONTINUED AS #1,ROYAL CHART 1906
Married:

Died: 836

7 Adelaide of Tours

Born: Abt 819

Died: Abt 866

15 Bava

Born: Abt 780

Died: Aft 837

Sources include: *Royal Ancestors* (1989), chart 11751; Moriarty 42-43; Stuart 326. Note: The parentage of #1 Emma and the chronology on this line is disputed and uncertain. In a preliminary Charlemagne manuscript (June 1995), p. 165 Faris states that #1 Emma was daughter of Bernard II, Count of Perigord. This Bernard II appears to be the son of Bernard I (md. Garsinde) and the <u>grandson</u> of #2 & 3 William & Regilinda above.

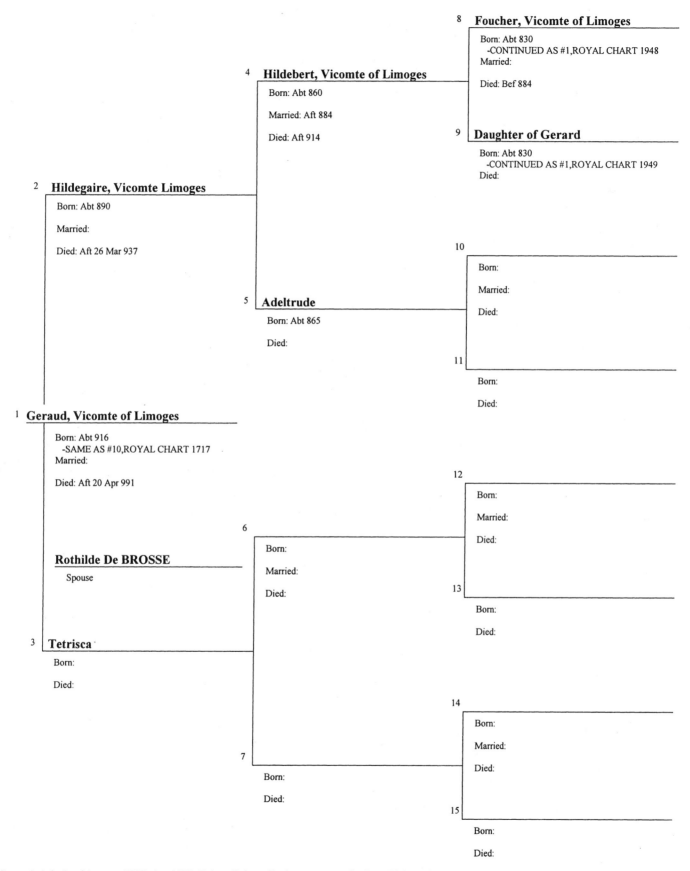

8 Foucher, Vicomte of Limoges

Born: Abt 830
-CONTINUED AS #1,ROYAL CHART 1948
Married:

Died: Bef 884

4 Hildebert, Vicomte of Limoges

Born: Abt 860

Married: Aft 884

Died: Aft 914

9 Daughter of Gerard

Born: Abt 830
-CONTINUED AS #1,ROYAL CHART 1949
Died:

2 Hildegaire, Vicomte Limoges

Born: Abt 890

Married:

Died: Aft 26 Mar 937

10

Born:

Married:

Died:

5 Adeltrude

Born: Abt 865

Died:

11

Born:

Died:

1 Geraud, Vicomte of Limoges

Born: Abt 916
-SAME AS #10,ROYAL CHART 1717
Married:

Died: Aft 20 Apr 991

12

Born:

Married:

Died:

6

Born:

Married:

Died:

13

Born:

Died:

Rothilde De BROSSE

Spouse

3 Tetrisca

Born:

Died:

14

Born:

Married:

Died:

7

Born:

Died:

15

Born:

Died:

Sources include: *Royal Ancestors* (1989), chart 11752; Faris preliminary Charlemagne manuscript (June 1995), p. 165; Stuart 328; Moriarty 43, 234-235. Note: #3 is also claimed as Tetberga (Tietberga, Teutberge), daughter of Geraud, Count of Bourges, son of Boso of Parthois. Faris (the version followed above) makes this Tetberga a 1st wife of #4 Hildebert, with #5 Adeltrude being a 2nd wife.

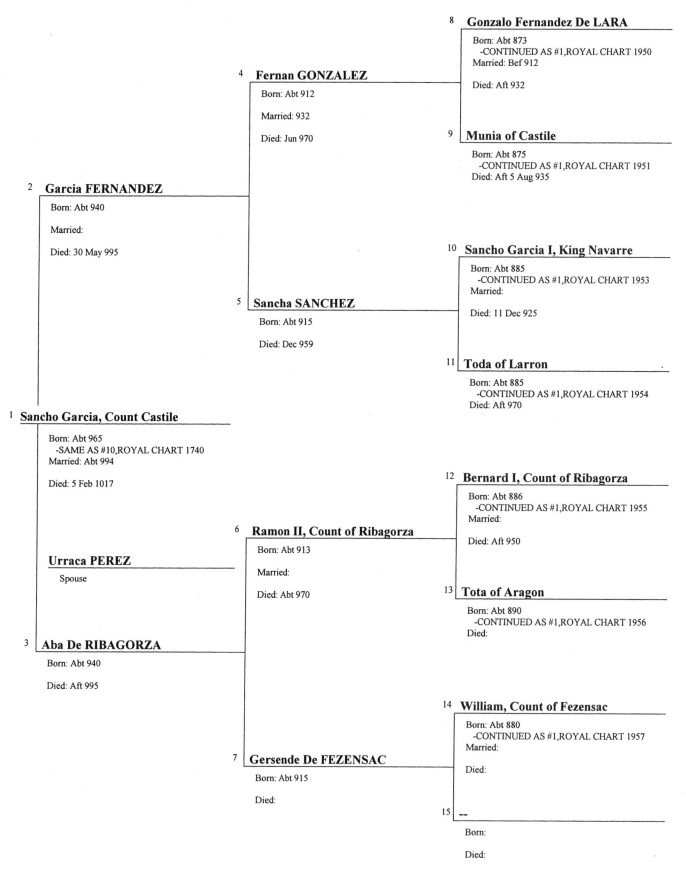

8 Gonzalo Fernandez De LARA

Born: Abt 873
 -CONTINUED AS #1,ROYAL CHART 1950
Married: Bef 912

Died: Aft 932

4 Fernan GONZALEZ

Born: Abt 912

Married: 932

Died: Jun 970

9 Munia of Castile

Born: Abt 875
 -CONTINUED AS #1,ROYAL CHART 1951
Died: Aft 5 Aug 935

2 Garcia FERNANDEZ

Born: Abt 940

Married:

Died: 30 May 995

10 Sancho Garcia I, King Navarre

Born: Abt 885
 -CONTINUED AS #1,ROYAL CHART 1953
Married:

Died: 11 Dec 925

5 Sancha SANCHEZ

Born: Abt 915

Died: Dec 959

11 Toda of Larron

Born: Abt 885
 -CONTINUED AS #1,ROYAL CHART 1954
Died: Aft 970

1 Sancho Garcia, Count Castile

Born: Abt 965
 -SAME AS #10,ROYAL CHART 1740
Married: Abt 994

Died: 5 Feb 1017

12 Bernard I, Count of Ribagorza

Born: Abt 886
 -CONTINUED AS #1,ROYAL CHART 1955
Married:

Died: Aft 950

6 Ramon II, Count of Ribagorza

Born: Abt 913

Married:

Died: Abt 970

13 Tota of Aragon

Born: Abt 890
 -CONTINUED AS #1,ROYAL CHART 1956
Died:

Urraca PEREZ

Spouse

3 Aba De RIBAGORZA

Born: Abt 940

Died: Aft 995

14 William, Count of Fezensac

Born: Abt 880
 -CONTINUED AS #1,ROYAL CHART 1957
Married:

Died:

7 Gersende De FEZENSAC

Born: Abt 915

Died:

15 --

Born:

Died:

Sources include: *Royal Ancestors* (1989), chart 11762; Stuart 285-286; Moriarty 79.

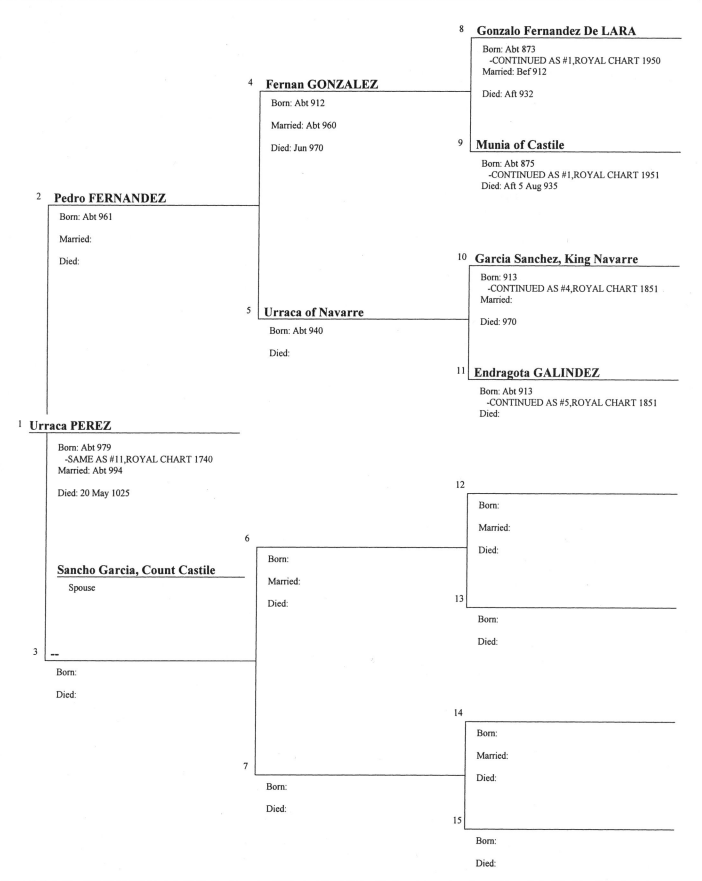

8 Gonzalo Fernandez De LARA

Born: Abt 873
  -CONTINUED AS #1,ROYAL CHART 1950
Married: Bef 912

Died: Aft 932

4 Fernan GONZALEZ

Born: Abt 912

Married: Abt 960

Died: Jun 970

9 Munia of Castile

Born: Abt 875
  -CONTINUED AS #1,ROYAL CHART 1951
Died: Aft 5 Aug 935

2 Pedro FERNANDEZ

Born: Abt 961

Married:

Died:

10 Garcia Sanchez, King Navarre

Born: 913
  -CONTINUED AS #4,ROYAL CHART 1851
Married:

Died: 970

5 Urraca of Navarre

Born: Abt 940

Died:

11 Endragota GALINDEZ

Born: Abt 913
  -CONTINUED AS #5,ROYAL CHART 1851
Died:

1 Urraca PEREZ

Born: Abt 979
  -SAME AS #11,ROYAL CHART 1740
Married: Abt 994

Died: 20 May 1025

12

Born:

Married:

Died:

6

Born:

Married:

Died:

Sancho Garcia, Count Castile

Spouse

13

Born:

Died:

3 --

Born:

Died:

14

Born:

Married:

Died:

7

Born:

Died:

15

Born:

Died:

Sources include: Stuart 285-34, 55, 292; Moriarty 79, 70; *Royal Ancestors* (1989), chart 11419. Notes: The descent shown above from #5 Urraca (2nd wife), claimed by both Moriarty and Stuart, is very tight chronologically. Perhaps #5 should be Sancha, 1st wife (see chart 1840). Stuart erroneously inserts an extra generation between #1 Urraca and #2 Pedro. #11 is disputed. Moriarty gives #11 as Teresa, 2nd wife of #10 Garcia. Endragota was a 1st wife.

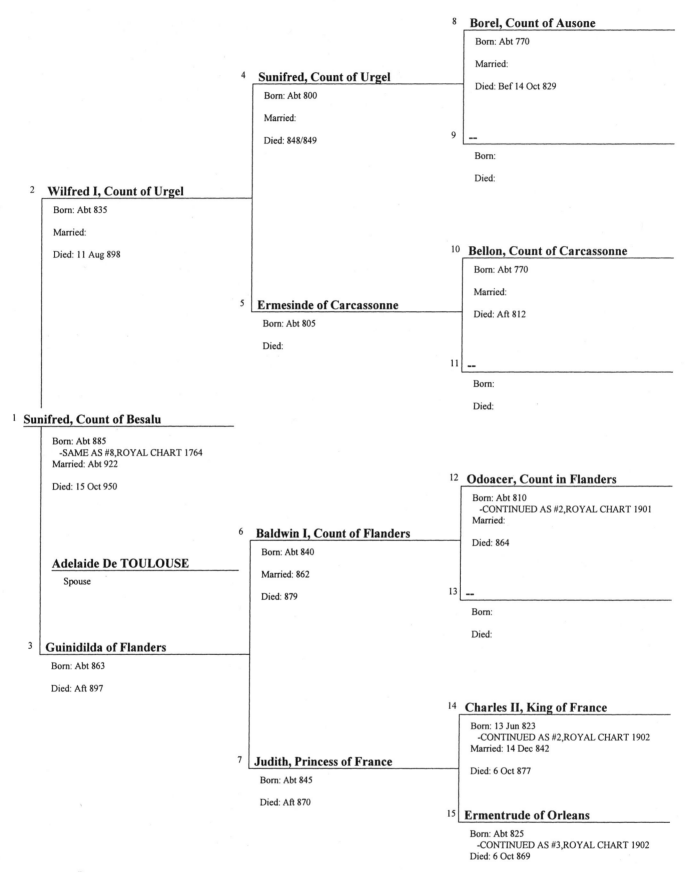

8 Borel, Count of Ausone
Born: Abt 770
Married:
Died: Bef 14 Oct 829

4 Sunifred, Count of Urgel
Born: Abt 800
Married:
Died: 848/849

9 --
Born:
Died:

2 Wilfred I, Count of Urgel
Born: Abt 835
Married:
Died: 11 Aug 898

10 Bellon, Count of Carcassonne
Born: Abt 770
Married:
Died: Aft 812

5 Ermesinde of Carcassonne
Born: Abt 805
Died:

11 --
Born:
Died:

1 Sunifred, Count of Besalu
Born: Abt 885
  -SAME AS #8,ROYAL CHART 1764
Married: Abt 922
Died: 15 Oct 950

12 Odoacer, Count in Flanders
Born: Abt 810
  -CONTINUED AS #2,ROYAL CHART 1901
Married:
Died: 864

6 Baldwin I, Count of Flanders
Born: Abt 840
Married: 862
Died: 879

13 --
Born:
Died:

Adelaide De TOULOUSE
Spouse

3 Guinidilda of Flanders
Born: Abt 863
Died: Aft 897

14 Charles II, King of France
Born: 13 Jun 823
  -CONTINUED AS #2,ROYAL CHART 1902
Married: 14 Dec 842
Died: 6 Oct 877

7 Judith, Princess of France
Born: Abt 845
Died: Aft 870

15 Ermentrude of Orleans
Born: Abt 825
  -CONTINUED AS #3,ROYAL CHART 1902
Died: 6 Oct 869

Sources include: *Royal Ancestors* (1989), charts 11765, 12075; Moriarty 67, 216-218; Stuart 54. Note: Stuart confuses the parentage of #'s 4 & 5 Sunifred & Ermesinde. The Moriarty version is well-studied and is accepted above.

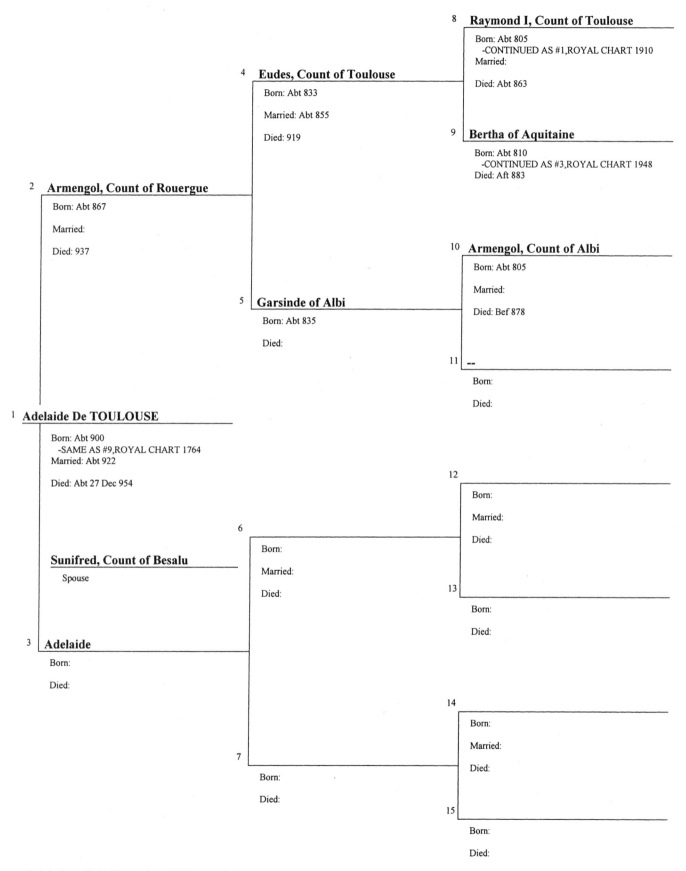

8 Raymond I, Count of Toulouse

Born: Abt 805
-CONTINUED AS #1,ROYAL CHART 1910
Married:

Died: Abt 863

4 Eudes, Count of Toulouse

Born: Abt 833

Married: Abt 855

Died: 919

9 Bertha of Aquitaine

Born: Abt 810
-CONTINUED AS #3,ROYAL CHART 1948
Died: Aft 883

2 Armengol, Count of Rouergue

Born: Abt 867

Married:

Died: 937

10 Armengol, Count of Albi

Born: Abt 805

Married:

Died: Bef 878

5 Garsinde of Albi

Born: Abt 835

Died:

11 --

Born:

Died:

1 Adelaide De TOULOUSE

Born: Abt 900
-SAME AS #9,ROYAL CHART 1764
Married: Abt 922

Died: Abt 27 Dec 954

12

Born:

Married:

Died:

Sunifred, Count of Besalu

Spouse

6

Born:

Married:

Died:

13

Born:

Died:

3 Adelaide

Born:

Died:

14

Born:

Married:

Died:

7

Born:

Died:

15

Born:

Died:

Sources include: Stuart 54-36, 329; Moriarty 41 (#2 ancestry).

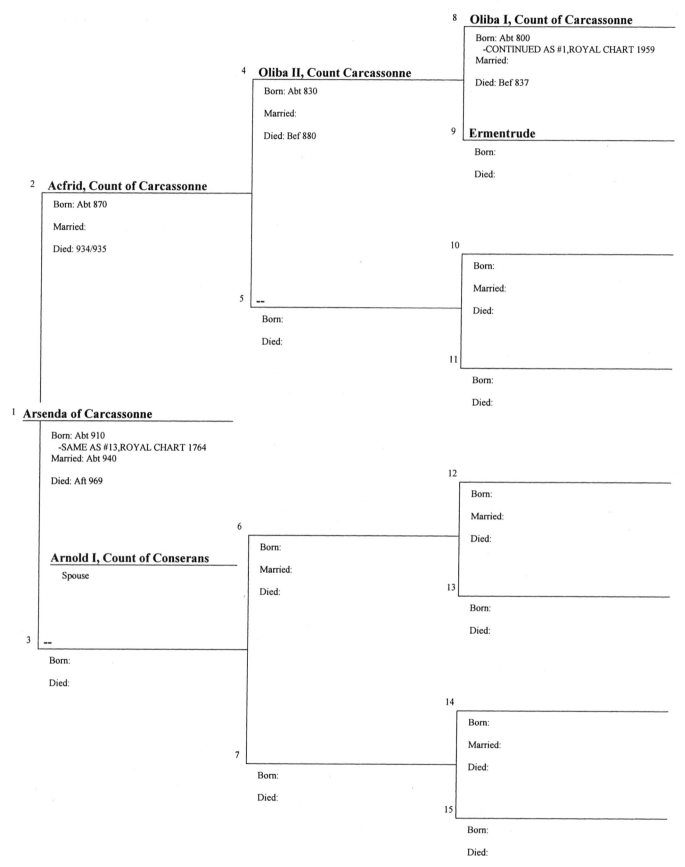

8   **Oliba I, Count of Carcassonne**

Born: Abt 800
    -CONTINUED AS #1, ROYAL CHART 1959
Married:

Died: Bef 837

4   **Oliba II, Count Carcassonne**

Born: Abt 830

Married:

Died: Bef 880

9   **Ermentrude**

Born:

Died:

2   **Acfrid, Count of Carcassonne**

Born: Abt 870

Married:

Died: 934/935

10

Born:

Married:

Died:

5   --

Born:

Died:

11

Born:

Died:

1   **Arsenda of Carcassonne**

Born: Abt 910
    -SAME AS #13, ROYAL CHART 1764
Married: Abt 940

Died: Aft 969

12

Born:

Married:

Died:

6

Born:

Married:

Died:

13

Born:

Died:

Arnold I, Count of Conserans

Spouse

3   --

Born:

Died:

14

Born:

Married:

Died:

7

Born:

Died:

15

Born:

Died:

Sources include: Stuart 291; Moriarty 68-69; *Royal Ancestors* (1989), chart 11688. Note: #9 is disputed. Moriarty gives #9 as Richilde, 2nd wife. Ermentrude was a 1st wife.

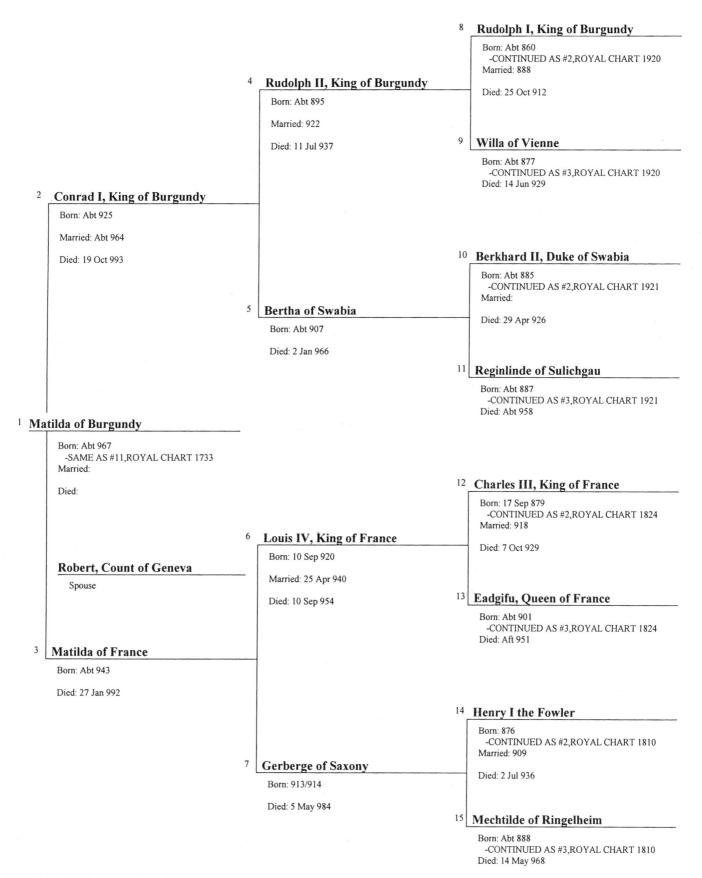

8 Rudolph I, King of Burgundy

Born: Abt 860
-CONTINUED AS #2,ROYAL CHART 1920
Married: 888

Died: 25 Oct 912

4 Rudolph II, King of Burgundy

Born: Abt 895

Married: 922

Died: 11 Jul 937

9 Willa of Vienne

Born: Abt 877
-CONTINUED AS #3,ROYAL CHART 1920
Died: 14 Jun 929

2 Conrad I, King of Burgundy

Born: Abt 925

Married: Abt 964

Died: 19 Oct 993

10 Berkhard II, Duke of Swabia

Born: Abt 885
-CONTINUED AS #2,ROYAL CHART 1921
Married:

Died: 29 Apr 926

5 Bertha of Swabia

Born: Abt 907

Died: 2 Jan 966

11 Reginlinde of Sulichgau

Born: Abt 887
-CONTINUED AS #3,ROYAL CHART 1921
Died: Abt 958

1 Matilda of Burgundy

Born: Abt 967
-SAME AS #11,ROYAL CHART 1733
Married:

Died:

12 Charles III, King of France

Born: 17 Sep 879
-CONTINUED AS #2,ROYAL CHART 1824
Married: 918

Died: 7 Oct 929

6 Louis IV, King of France

Born: 10 Sep 920

Married: 25 Apr 940

Died: 10 Sep 954

13 Eadgifu, Queen of France

Born: Abt 901
-CONTINUED AS #3,ROYAL CHART 1824
Died: Aft 951

Robert, Count of Geneva

Spouse

3 Matilda of France

Born: Abt 943

Died: 27 Jan 992

14 Henry I the Fowler

Born: 876
-CONTINUED AS #2,ROYAL CHART 1810
Married: 909

Died: 2 Jul 936

7 Gerberge of Saxony

Born: 913/914

Died: 5 May 984

15 Mechtilde of Ringelheim

Born: Abt 888
-CONTINUED AS #3,ROYAL CHART 1810
Died: 14 May 968

Sources include: *Royal Ancestors* (1989), charts 11447, 11566; *Ancestral Roots* 133; Moriarty 107, 34; Stuart 175.

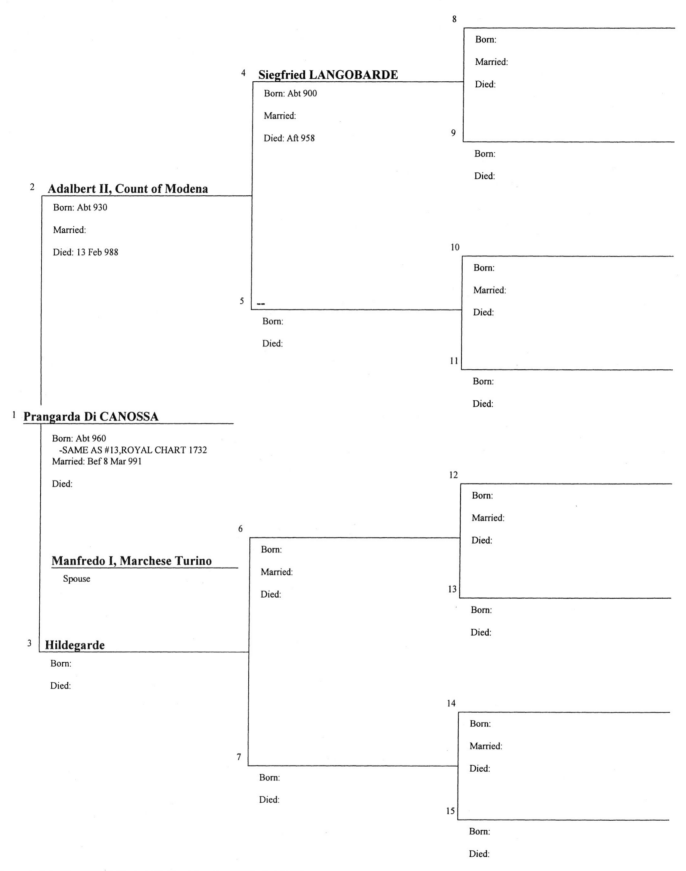

8

Born:

Married:

Died:

4 Siegfried LANGOBARDE

Born: Abt 900

Married:

Died: Aft 958

9

Born:

Died:

2 Adalbert II, Count of Modena

Born: Abt 930

Married:

Died: 13 Feb 988

10

Born:

Married:

Died:

5 --

Born:

Died:

11

Born:

Died:

1 Prangarda Di CANOSSA

Born: Abt 960
  -SAME AS #13,ROYAL CHART 1732
Married: Bef 8 Mar 991

Died:

12

Born:

Married:

Died:

6

Born:

Married:

Died:

13

Born:

Died:

Manfredo I, Marchese Turino

Spouse

3 Hildegarde

Born:

Died:

14

Born:

Married:

Died:

7

Born:

Died:

15

Born:

Died:

Sources include: Stuart 315-35; Moriarty 61; *Royal Ancestors* (1989), chart 11663.

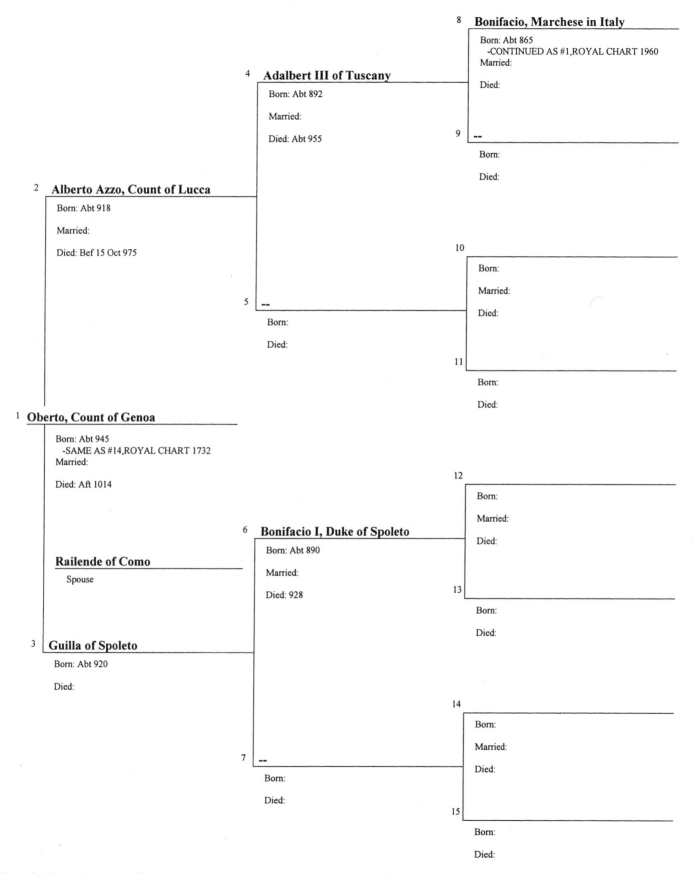

8 Bonifacio, Marchese in Italy

Born: Abt 865
  -CONTINUED AS #1,ROYAL CHART 1960
Married:

Died:

4 Adalbert III of Tuscany

Born: Abt 892

Married:

Died: Abt 955

9 --

Born:

Died:

2 Alberto Azzo, Count of Lucca

Born: Abt 918

Married:

Died: Bef 15 Oct 975

10

Born:

Married:

Died:

5 --

Born:

Died:

11

Born:

Died:

1 Oberto, Count of Genoa

Born: Abt 945
  -SAME AS #14,ROYAL CHART 1732
Married:

Died: Aft 1014

12

Born:

Married:

Died:

Railende of Como

Spouse

6 Bonifacio I, Duke of Spoleto

Born: Abt 890

Married:

Died: 928

13

Born:

Died:

3 Guilla of Spoleto

Born: Abt 920

Died:

14

Born:

Married:

Died:

7 --

Born:

Died:

15

Born:

Died:

Sources include: *Royal Ancestors* (1989), chart 11851; Stuart 93; Moriarty 61-62. Note: The parentage of #4 Adalbert is uncertain and disputed. Stuart makes #4 Adalbert a son of Gui and grandson of Adalbert II (who was a brother of #8 Bonifacio). The tentative Moriarty version shown above is more acceptable chronologically.

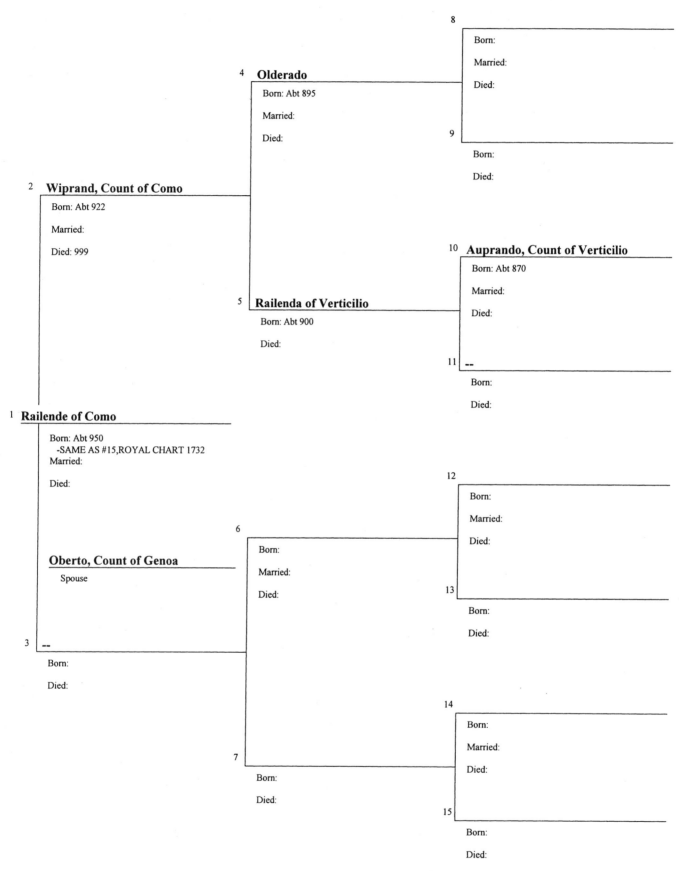

8

Born:

Married:

Died:

4 Olderado

Born: Abt 895

Married:

Died:

9

Born:

Died:

2 Wiprand, Count of Como

Born: Abt 922

Married:

Died: 999

10 Auprando, Count of Verticilio

Born: Abt 870

Married:

Died:

5 Railenda of Verticilio

Born: Abt 900

Died:

11 --

Born:

Died:

1 Railende of Como

Born: Abt 950
  -SAME AS #15,ROYAL CHART 1732
Married:

Died:

12

Born:

Married:

Died:

6

Born:

Married:

Died:

13

Born:

Died:

Oberto, Count of Genoa

Spouse

3 --

Born:

Died:

14

Born:

Married:

Died:

7

Born:

Died:

15

Born:

Died:

Sources include: *Royal Ancestors* (1989), chart 11851; Stuart 93-34; Moriarty 62. Note: The ancestry shown for #2 Wiprand is not certain.

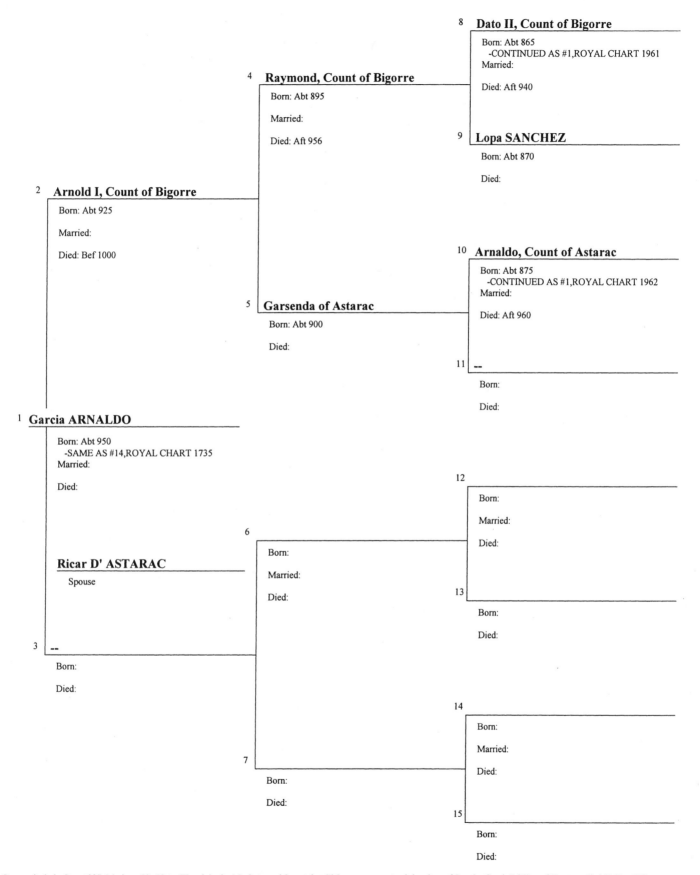

8 Dato II, Count of Bigorre

Born: Abt 865
-CONTINUED AS #1,ROYAL CHART 1961
Married:

Died: Aft 940

4 Raymond, Count of Bigorre

Born: Abt 895

Married:

Died: Aft 956

9 Lopa SANCHEZ

Born: Abt 870

Died:

2 Arnold I, Count of Bigorre

Born: Abt 925

Married:

Died: Bef 1000

10 Arnaldo, Count of Astarac

Born: Abt 875
-CONTINUED AS #1,ROYAL CHART 1962
Married:

Died: Aft 960

5 Garsenda of Astarac

Born: Abt 900

Died:

11 --

Born:

Died:

1 Garcia ARNALDO

Born: Abt 950
-SAME AS #14,ROYAL CHART 1735
Married:

Died:

12

Born:

Married:

Died:

6

Born:

Married:

Died:

Ricar D' ASTARAC

Spouse

13

Born:

Died:

3 --

Born:

Died:

14

Born:

Married:

Died:

7

Born:

Died:

15

Born:

Died:

Sources include: Stuart 227; Moriarty 80. Note: The claim by Moriarty and Stuart that #9 Lopa was a natural daughter of Sancho Garcia I (King of Navarre, died 11 Dec 925, see chart 1953, #1) cannot be reconciled chronologically with the maternal ancestry claimed for him on chart 1953. Stuart claims that #8 Dato was a brother of #9 Lopa's claimed grandmother Dadildi, which appears to be incorrect.

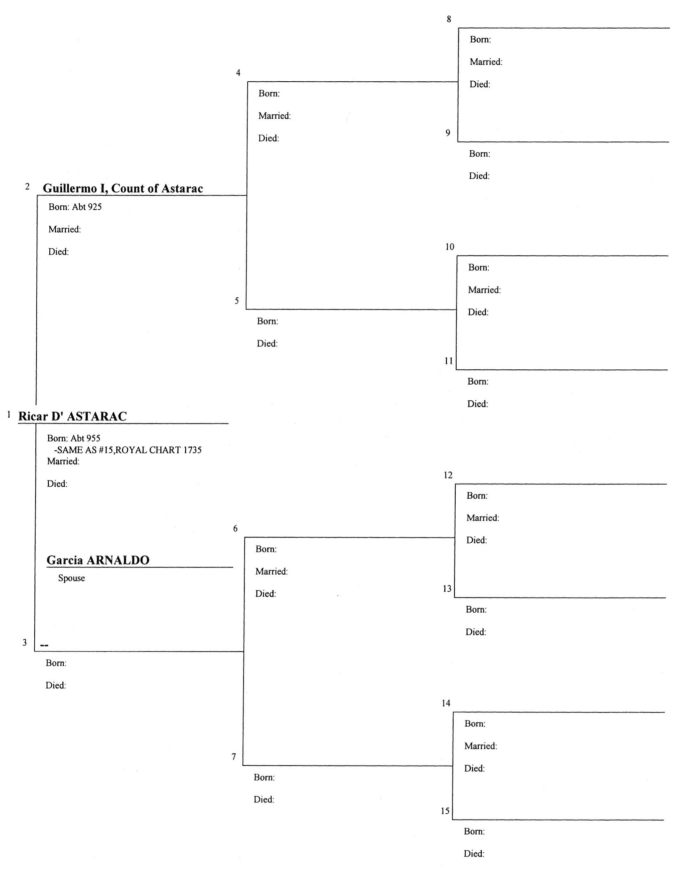

8

Born:

Married:

Died:

4

Born:

Married:

Died:

9

Born:

Died:

2   **Guillermo I, Count of Astarac**

Born: Abt 925

Married:

Died:

10

Born:

Married:

Died:

5

Born:

Died:

11

Born:

Died:

1   **Ricar D' ASTARAC**

Born: Abt 955
   -SAME AS #15,ROYAL CHART 1735
Married:

Died:

12

Born:

Married:

Died:

6

Born:

Married:

Died:

13

Born:

Died:

Garcia ARNALDO

Spouse

3   **--**

Born:

Died:

14

Born:

Married:

Died:

7

Born:

Died:

15

Born:

Died:

Sources include: Stuart 227-34.

Pedigree Chart

Chart 1851

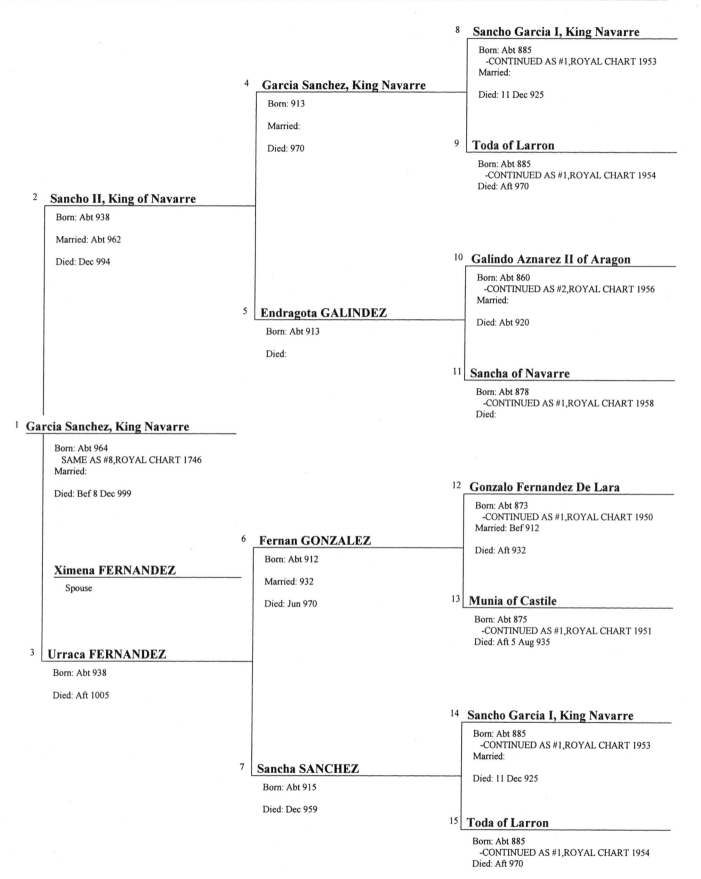

8 Sancho Garcia I, King Navarre

Born: Abt 885
 -CONTINUED AS #1,ROYAL CHART 1953
Married:

Died: 11 Dec 925

4 Garcia Sanchez, King Navarre

Born: 913

Married:

Died: 970

9 Toda of Larron

Born: Abt 885
 -CONTINUED AS #1,ROYAL CHART 1954
Died: Aft 970

2 Sancho II, King of Navarre

Born: Abt 938

Married: Abt 962

Died: Dec 994

10 Galindo Aznarez II of Aragon

Born: Abt 860
 -CONTINUED AS #2,ROYAL CHART 1956
Married:

Died: Abt 920

5 Endragota GALINDEZ

Born: Abt 913

Died:

11 Sancha of Navarre

Born: Abt 878
 -CONTINUED AS #1,ROYAL CHART 1958
Died:

1 Garcia Sanchez, King Navarre

Born: Abt 964
 SAME AS #8,ROYAL CHART 1746
Married:

Died: Bef 8 Dec 999

12 Gonzalo Fernandez De Lara

Born: Abt 873
 -CONTINUED AS #1,ROYAL CHART 1950
Married: Bef 912

Died: Aft 932

6 Fernan GONZALEZ

Born: Abt 912

Married: 932

Died: Jun 970

13 Munia of Castile

Born: Abt 875
 -CONTINUED AS #1,ROYAL CHART 1951
Died: Aft 5 Aug 935

Ximena FERNANDEZ

Spouse

3 Urraca FERNANDEZ

Born: Abt 938

Died: Aft 1005

14 Sancho Garcia I, King Navarre

Born: Abt 885
 -CONTINUED AS #1,ROYAL CHART 1953
Married:

Died: 11 Dec 925

7 Sancha SANCHEZ

Born: Abt 915

Died: Dec 959

15 Toda of Larron

Born: Abt 885
 -CONTINUED AS #1,ROYAL CHART 1954
Died: Aft 970

Sources include: *Royal Ancestors* (1989), chart 11589; Moriarty 78, 70, 79; Stuart 223. Note: Stuart erroneously gives #7 as Urraca, 2nd wife of Fernan. (See also chart 1841 & note).

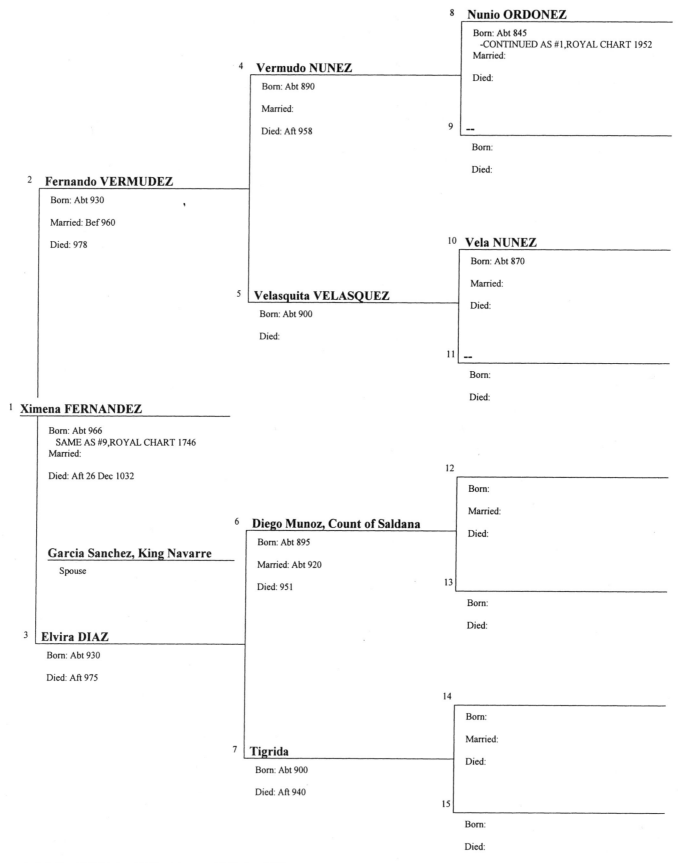

8 Nunio ORDONEZ

Born: Abt 845
    -CONTINUED AS #1, ROYAL CHART 1952
Married:

Died:

4 Vermudo NUNEZ

Born: Abt 890

Married:

Died: Aft 958

9 --

Born:

Died:

2 Fernando VERMUDEZ

Born: Abt 930

Married: Bef 960

Died: 978

10 Vela NUNEZ

Born: Abt 870

Married:

Died:

5 Velasquita VELASQUEZ

Born: Abt 900

Died:

11 --

Born:

Died:

1 Ximena FERNANDEZ

Born: Abt 966
    SAME AS #9, ROYAL CHART 1746
Married:

Died: Aft 26 Dec 1032

Garcia Sanchez, King Navarre

Spouse

12

Born:

Married:

Died:

6 Diego Munoz, Count of Saldana

Born: Abt 895

Married: Abt 920

Died: 951

13

Born:

Died:

3 Elvira DIAZ

Born: Abt 930

Died: Aft 975

14

Born:

Married:

Died:

7 Tigrida

Born: Abt 900

Died: Aft 940

15

Born:

Died:

Sources include: Stuart 267; Moriarty 78; *Royal Ancestors* (1989), chart 11768.

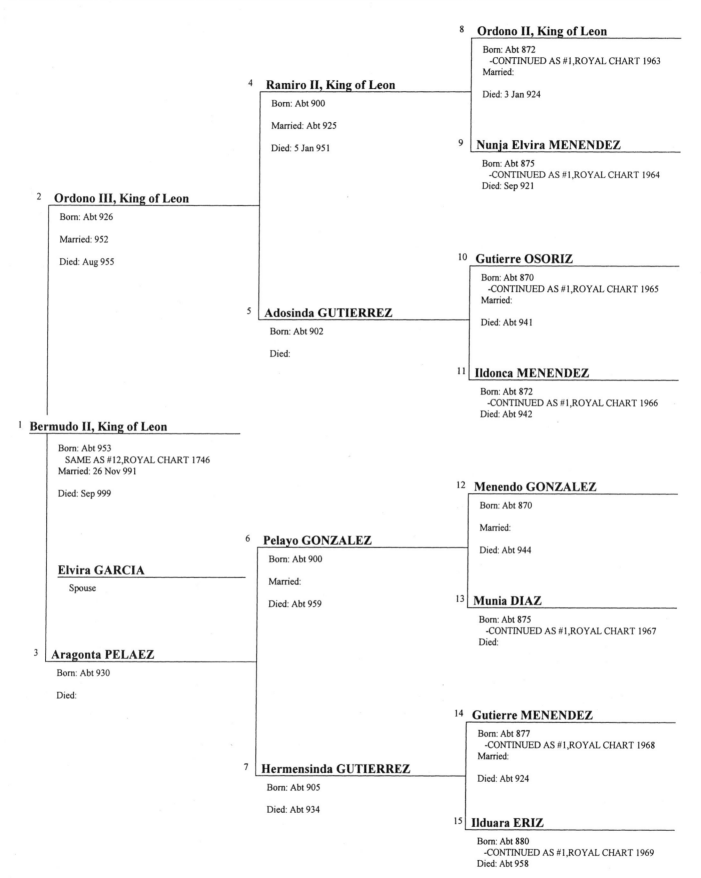

2 Ordono III, King of Leon
Born: Abt 926
Married: 952
Died: Aug 955

4 Ramiro II, King of Leon
Born: Abt 900
Married: Abt 925
Died: 5 Jan 951

8 Ordono II, King of Leon
Born: Abt 872
-CONTINUED AS #1,ROYAL CHART 1963
Married:
Died: 3 Jan 924

9 Nunja Elvira MENENDEZ
Born: Abt 875
-CONTINUED AS #1,ROYAL CHART 1964
Died: Sep 921

5 Adosinda GUTIERREZ
Born: Abt 902
Died:

10 Gutierre OSORIZ
Born: Abt 870
-CONTINUED AS #1,ROYAL CHART 1965
Married:
Died: Abt 941

11 Ildonca MENENDEZ
Born: Abt 872
-CONTINUED AS #1,ROYAL CHART 1966
Died: Abt 942

1 Bermudo II, King of Leon
Born: Abt 953
SAME AS #12,ROYAL CHART 1746
Married: 26 Nov 991
Died: Sep 999

Elvira GARCIA
Spouse

3 Aragonta PELAEZ
Born: Abt 930
Died:

6 Pelayo GONZALEZ
Born: Abt 900
Married:
Died: Abt 959

12 Menendo GONZALEZ
Born: Abt 870
Married:
Died: Abt 944

13 Munia DIAZ
Born: Abt 875
-CONTINUED AS #1,ROYAL CHART 1967
Died:

7 Hermensinda GUTIERREZ
Born: Abt 905
Died: Abt 934

14 Gutierre MENENDEZ
Born: Abt 877
-CONTINUED AS #1,ROYAL CHART 1968
Married:
Died: Abt 924

15 Ilduara ERIZ
Born: Abt 880
-CONTINUED AS #1,ROYAL CHART 1969
Died: Abt 958

Sources include: *Royal Ancestors* (1989), chart 11763; Stuart 276-277; Moriarty 82, 223; Von Isenburg 2:46; Charts prepared for Moriarty by Charles Evans. Note: The ancestry of #6 Pelayo is disputed. The Stuart version is tentatively accepted above.

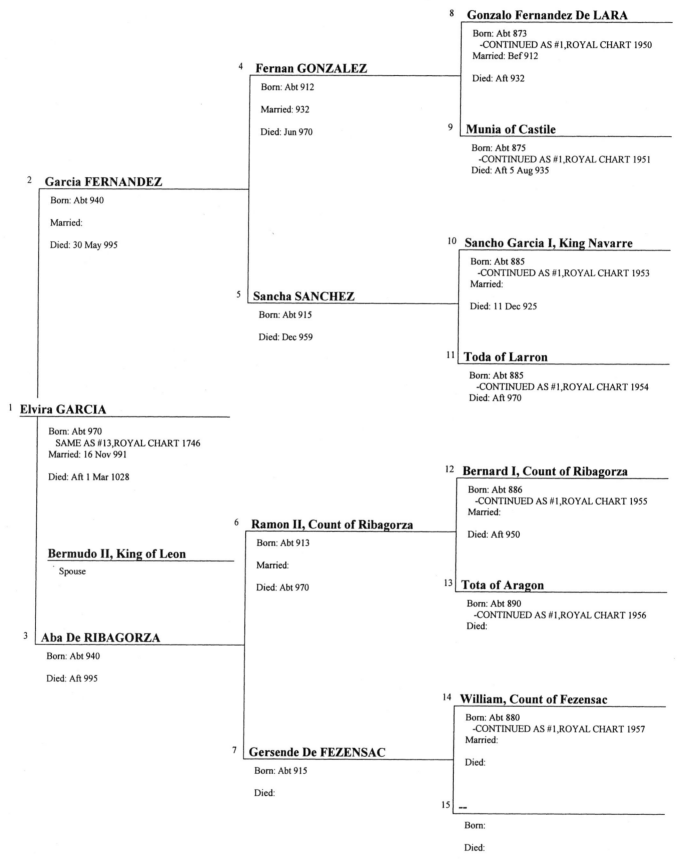

8 **Gonzalo Fernandez De LARA**

Born: Abt 873
   -CONTINUED AS #1,ROYAL CHART 1950
Married: Bef 912

Died: Aft 932

4 **Fernan GONZALEZ**

Born: Abt 912

Married: 932

Died: Jun 970

9 **Munia of Castile**

Born: Abt 875
   -CONTINUED AS #1,ROYAL CHART 1951
Died: Aft 5 Aug 935

2 **Garcia FERNANDEZ**

Born: Abt 940

Married:

Died: 30 May 995

10 **Sancho Garcia I, King Navarre**

Born: Abt 885
   -CONTINUED AS #1,ROYAL CHART 1953
Married:

Died: 11 Dec 925

5 **Sancha SANCHEZ**

Born: Abt 915

Died: Dec 959

11 **Toda of Larron**

Born: Abt 885
   -CONTINUED AS #1,ROYAL CHART 1954
Died: Aft 970

1 **Elvira GARCIA**

Born: Abt 970
   SAME AS #13,ROYAL CHART 1746
Married: 16 Nov 991

Died: Aft 1 Mar 1028

12 **Bernard I, Count of Ribagorza**

Born: Abt 886
   -CONTINUED AS #1,ROYAL CHART 1955
Married:

Died: Aft 950

6 **Ramon II, Count of Ribagorza**

Born: Abt 913

Married:

Died: Abt 970

Bermudo II, King of Leon

   Spouse

13 **Tota of Aragon**

Born: Abt 890
   -CONTINUED AS #1,ROYAL CHART 1956
Died:

3 **Aba De RIBAGORZA**

Born: Abt 940

Died: Aft 995

14 **William, Count of Fezensac**

Born: Abt 880
   -CONTINUED AS #1,ROYAL CHART 1957
Married:

Died:

7 **Gersende De FEZENSAC**

Born: Abt 915

Died:

15 **--**

Born:

Died:

Sources include: *Royal Ancestors* (1989), charts 11764, 11762; Stuart 276-34, 285-286; Moriarty 82, 79.

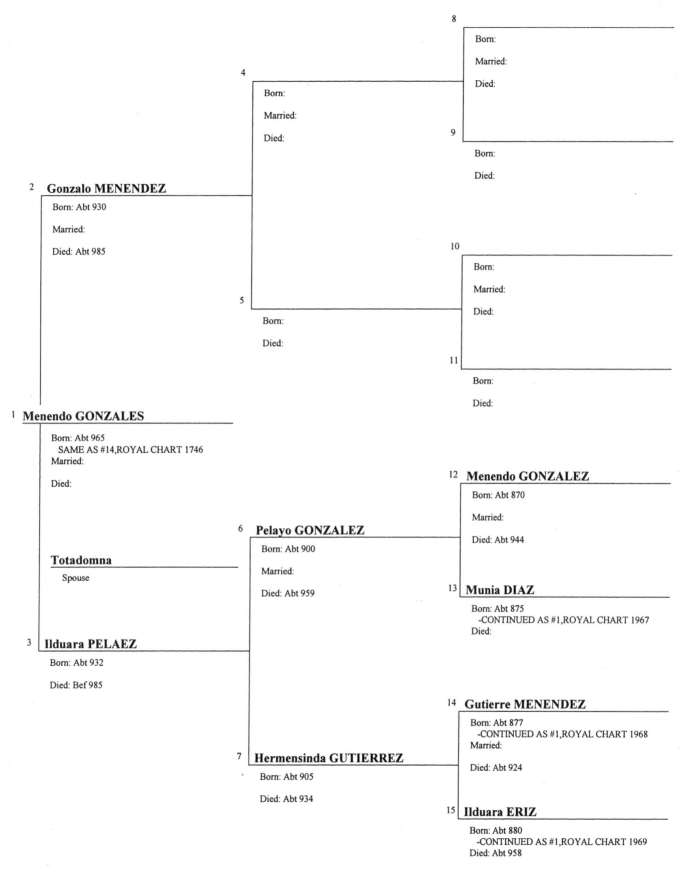

8

Born:

Married:

Died:

4

Born:

Married:

Died:

9

Born:

Died:

2 Gonzalo MENENDEZ

Born: Abt 930

Married:

Died: Abt 985

10

Born:

Married:

Died:

5

Born:

Died:

11

Born:

Died:

1 Menendo GONZALES

Born: Abt 965
    SAME AS #14,ROYAL CHART 1746
Married:

Died:

12 Menendo GONZALEZ

Born: Abt 870

Married:

Died: Abt 944

6 Pelayo GONZALEZ

Born: Abt 900

Married:

Died: Abt 959

13 Munia DIAZ

Born: Abt 875
    -CONTINUED AS #1,ROYAL CHART 1967
Died:

Totadomna

    Spouse

3 Ilduara PELAEZ

Born: Abt 932

Died: Bef 985

14 Gutierre MENENDEZ

Born: Abt 877
    -CONTINUED AS #1,ROYAL CHART 1968
Married:

Died: Abt 924

7 Hermensinda GUTIERREZ

Born: Abt 905

Died: Abt 934

15 Ilduara ERIZ

Born: Abt 880
    -CONTINUED AS #1,ROYAL CHART 1969
Died: Abt 958

Sources include: *Royal Ancestors* (1989), chart 11767; Stuart 277; Moriarty 223. Note: The ancestry of #6 Pelayo is disputed. The Stuart version is tentatively accepted above.

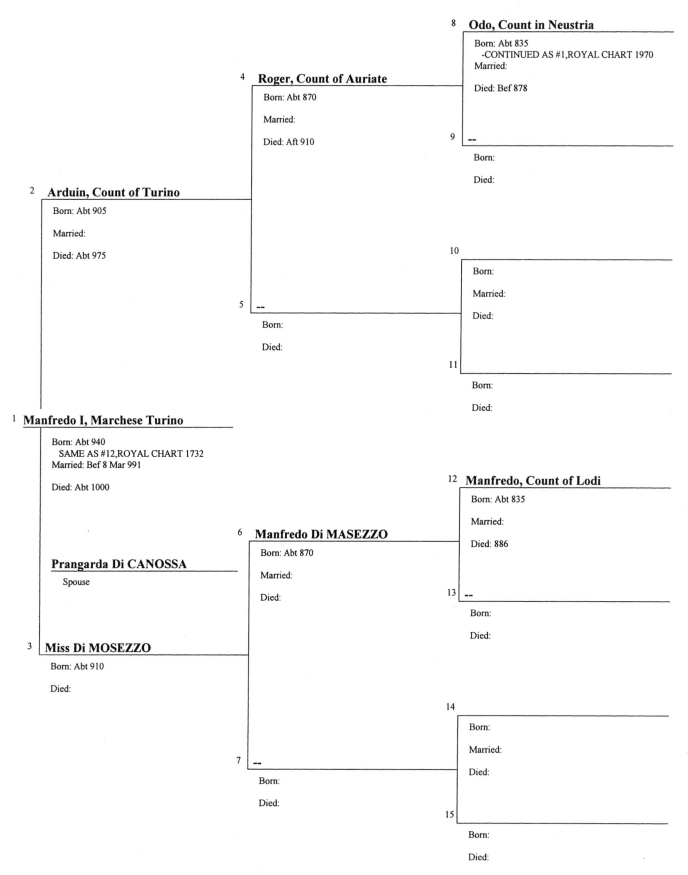

8 Odo, Count in Neustria

Born: Abt 835
-CONTINUED AS #1,ROYAL CHART 1970
Married:

Died: Bef 878

9 --

Born:

Died:

4 Roger, Count of Auriate

Born: Abt 870

Married:

Died: Aft 910

10

Born:

Married:

Died:

11

Born:

Died:

2 Arduin, Count of Turino

Born: Abt 905

Married:

Died: Abt 975

5 --

Born:

Died:

1 Manfredo I, Marchese Turino

Born: Abt 940
    SAME AS #12,ROYAL CHART 1732
Married: Bef 8 Mar 991

Died: Abt 1000

12 Manfredo, Count of Lodi

Born: Abt 835

Married:

Died: 886

13 --

Born:

Died:

6 Manfredo Di MASEZZO

Born: Abt 870

Married:

Died:

14

Born:

Married:

Died:

15

Born:

Died:

Prangarda Di CANOSSA

Spouse

3 Miss Di MOSEZZO

Born: Abt 910

Died:

7 --

Born:

Died:

Sources include: *Royal Ancestors* (1989), chart 11850; Stuart 315; Moriarty 60.

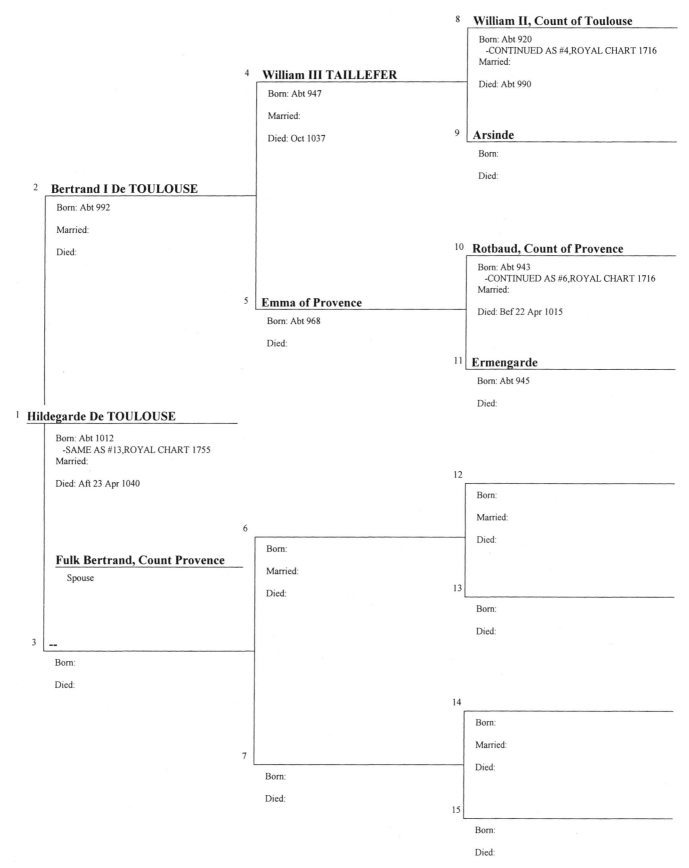

8 William II, Count of Toulouse

Born: Abt 920
    -CONTINUED AS #4, ROYAL CHART 1716
Married:

Died: Abt 990

4 William III TAILLEFER

Born: Abt 947

Married:

Died: Oct 1037

9 Arsinde

Born:

Died:

2 Bertrand I De TOULOUSE

Born: Abt 992

Married:

Died:

10 Rotbaud, Count of Provence

Born: Abt 943
    -CONTINUED AS #6, ROYAL CHART 1716
Married:

Died: Bef 22 Apr 1015

5 Emma of Provence

Born: Abt 968

Died:

11 Ermengarde

Born: Abt 945

Died:

1 Hildegarde De TOULOUSE

Born: Abt 1012
    -SAME AS #13, ROYAL CHART 1755
Married:

Died: Aft 23 Apr 1040

12

Born:

Married:

Died:

6

Born:

Married:

Died:

Fulk Bertrand, Count Provence

Spouse

13

Born:

Died:

3 --

Born:

Died:

14

Born:

Married:

Died:

7

Born:

Died:

15

Born:

Died:

Sources include: Faris preliminary Charlemagne manuscript (June 1995), pp. 226, 262-263; Stuart 197-34 (#1 & 2); Moriarty 101 (#1). Note: #1 is also called Eveza De Toulouse, same parentage.

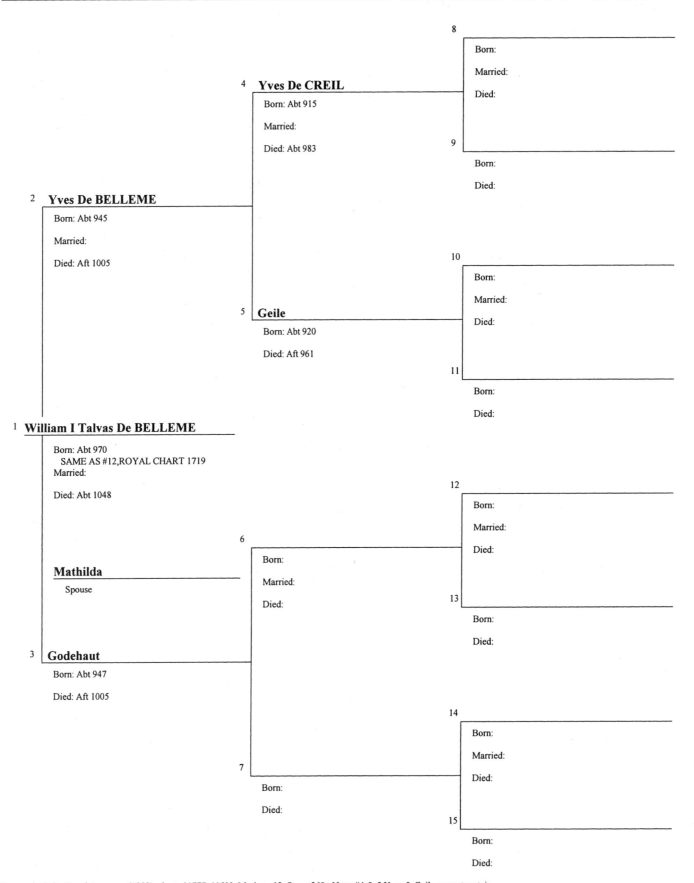

8

4 Yves De CREIL
Born: Abt 915
Married:
Died: Abt 983

9

Born:
Married:
Died:

Born:
Died:

2 Yves De BELLEME
Born: Abt 945
Married:
Died: Aft 1005

10

Born:
Married:
Died:

5 Geile
Born: Abt 920
Died: Aft 961

11

Born:
Died:

1 William I Talvas De BELLEME
Born: Abt 970
    SAME AS #12,ROYAL CHART 1719
Married:
Died: Abt 1048

Mathilda
    Spouse

12

Born:
Married:
Died:

6
Born:
Married:
Died:

13

Born:
Died:

3 Godehaut
Born: Abt 947
Died: Aft 1005

14

Born:
Married:
Died:

7
Born:
Died:

15

Born:
Died:

Sources include: *Royal Ancestors* (1989), charts 11777, 11500; Moriarty 12; Stuart 360. Note: #4 & 5 Yves & Geile are not certain.

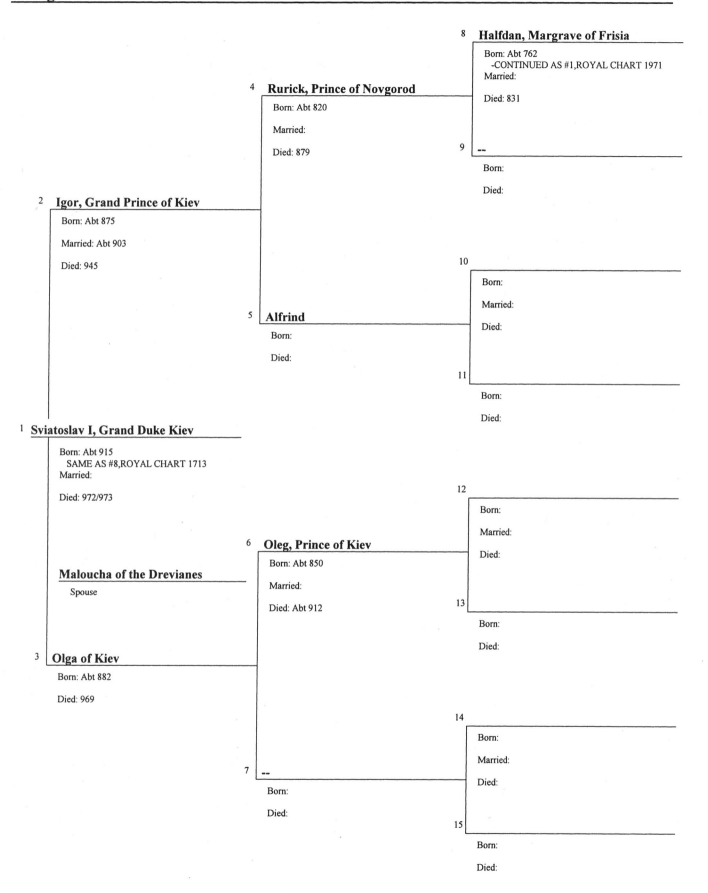

8 Halfdan, Margrave of Frisia

Born: Abt 762
-CONTINUED AS #1,ROYAL CHART 1971
Married:

Died: 831

9 --

Born:

Died:

4 Rurick, Prince of Novgorod

Born: Abt 820

Married:

Died: 879

10

Born:

Married:

Died:

5 Alfrind

Born:

Died:

11

Born:

Died:

2 Igor, Grand Prince of Kiev

Born: Abt 875

Married: Abt 903

Died: 945

1 Sviatoslav I, Grand Duke Kiev

Born: Abt 915
    SAME AS #8,ROYAL CHART 1713
Married:

Died: 972/973

Maloucha of the Drevianes

Spouse

12

Born:

Married:

Died:

6 Oleg, Prince of Kiev

Born: Abt 850

Married:

Died: Abt 912

13

Born:

Died:

3 Olga of Kiev

Born: Abt 882

Died: 969

14

Born:

Married:

Died:

7 --

Born:

Died:

15

Born:

Died:

Sources include: *Royal Ancestors* (1989), chart 11514; Stuart 143; Moriarty 52, 221; *Ancestral Roots* 241. Note: The ancestry shown for #2 & 3 Igor & Olga is not certain. It requires a long chronological stretch. Moriarty discusses three different claims for the parentage and ancestry of #2. The version shown above is the one followed by Stuart.

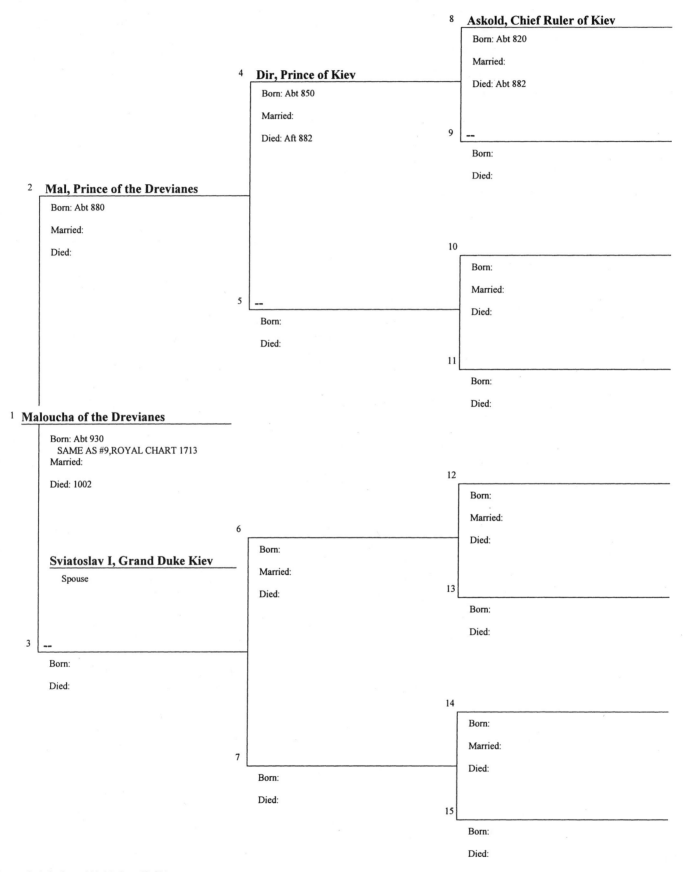

8 Askold, Chief Ruler of Kiev
Born: Abt 820
Married:
Died: Abt 882

4 Dir, Prince of Kiev
Born: Abt 850
Married:
Died: Aft 882

9 --
Born:
Died:

2 Mal, Prince of the Drevianes
Born: Abt 880
Married:
Died:

10
Born:
Married:
Died:

5 --
Born:
Died:

11
Born:
Died:

1 Maloucha of the Drevianes
Born: Abt 930
   SAME AS #9,ROYAL CHART 1713
Married:
Died: 1002

12
Born:
Married:
Died:

6
Born:
Married:
Died:

13
Born:
Died:

Sviatoslav I, Grand Duke Kiev
   Spouse

3 --
Born:
Died:

14
Born:
Married:
Died:

7
Born:
Died:

15
Born:
Died:

Sources include: Stuart 209; Moriarty 52, 221.

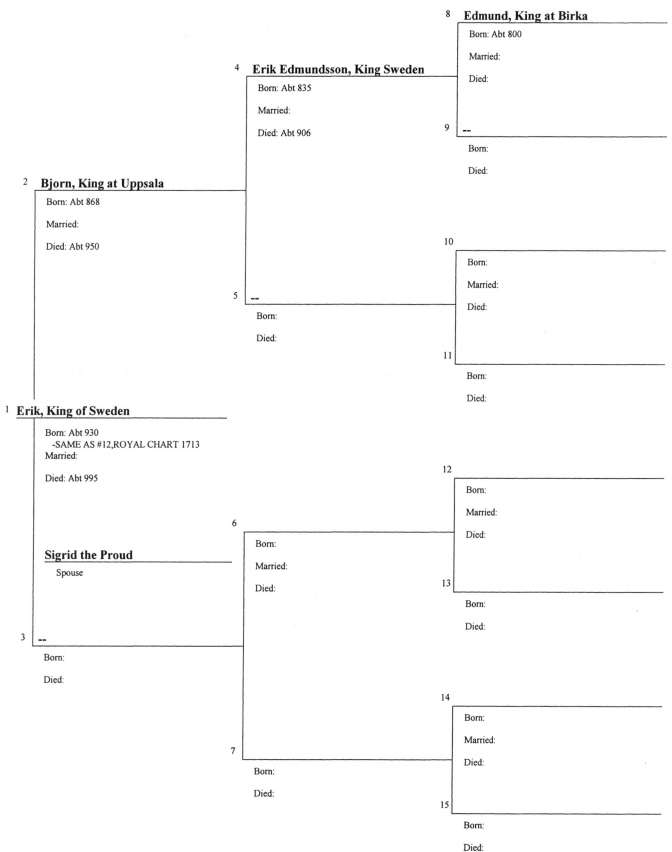

8 Edmund, King at Birka

Born: Abt 800

Married:

Died:

4 Erik Edmundsson, King Sweden

Born: Abt 835

Married:

Died: Abt 906

9 --

Born:

Died:

2 Bjorn, King at Uppsala

Born: Abt 868

Married:

Died: Abt 950

10

Born:

Married:

Died:

5 --

Born:

Died:

11

Born:

Died:

1 Erik, King of Sweden

Born: Abt 930
  -SAME AS #12,ROYAL CHART 1713
Married:

Died: Abt 995

Sigrid the Proud

Spouse

12

Born:

Married:

Died:

6

Born:

Married:

Died:

13

Born:

Died:

3 --

Born:

Died:

14

Born:

Married:

Died:

7

Born:

Died:

15

Born:

Died:

Sources include: *Royal Ancestors* (1989), chart 11515; Stuart 240; Moriarty 54. Note: Moriarty ends the above line with #8 Edmund, whom he states was king in 829. Stuart extends the line 24 more generations in Sweden and Denmark to Odin of Asgard in Asia (born about 215 A.D.--see chart 2098). Names and dates for these 24 generations are virtually identical to LDS Archive records created about half a century ago, except that those records insert two additional generations. Chronological considerations make it doubtful that the immediate ancestry claimed for #8 Edmund above is correct. He must have been born long before 832, the approximate birth date assigned to him, if he was king in 829, and it is unlikely therefore that his grandfather was leading a Viking expedition in 859 or his great-grandfather was alive until 845, as claimed.

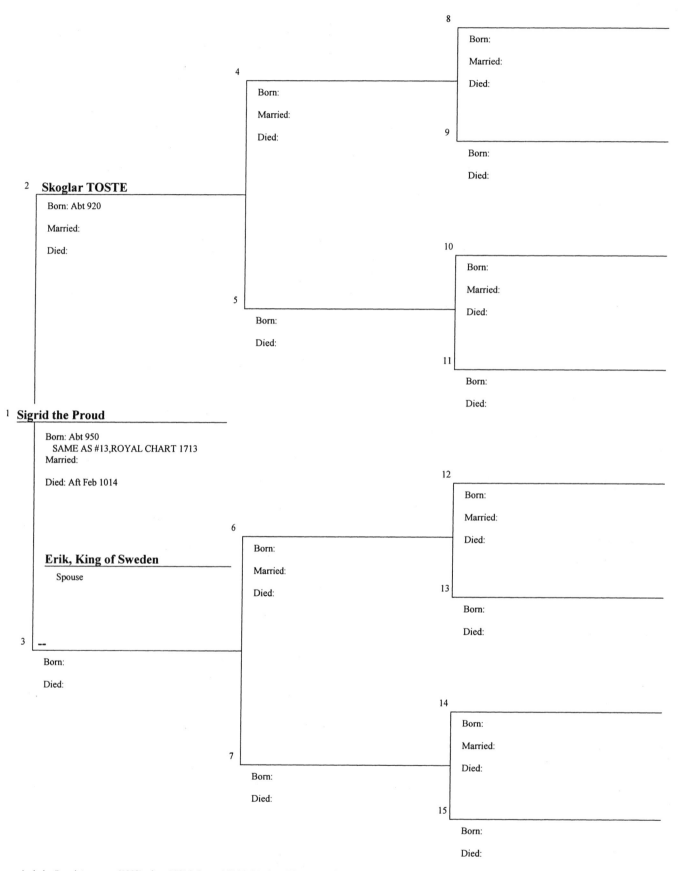

8

Born:

Married:

Died:

4

Born:

Married:

Died:

9

Born:

Died:

2 Skoglar TOSTE

Born: Abt 920

Married:

Died:

10

Born:

Married:

Died:

5

Born:

Died:

11

Born:

Died:

1 Sigrid the Proud

Born: Abt 950
    SAME AS #13,ROYAL CHART 1713
Married:

Died: Aft Feb 1014

12

Born:

Married:

Died:

6

Born:

Married:

Died:

13

Born:

Died:

Erik, King of Sweden

Spouse

3 --

Born:

Died:

14

Born:

Married:

Died:

7

Born:

Died:

15

Born:

Died:

Sources include: *Royal Ancestors* (1989), chart 11516; Stuart 240-34; Moriarty 54; *Ancestral Roots* 241-5.

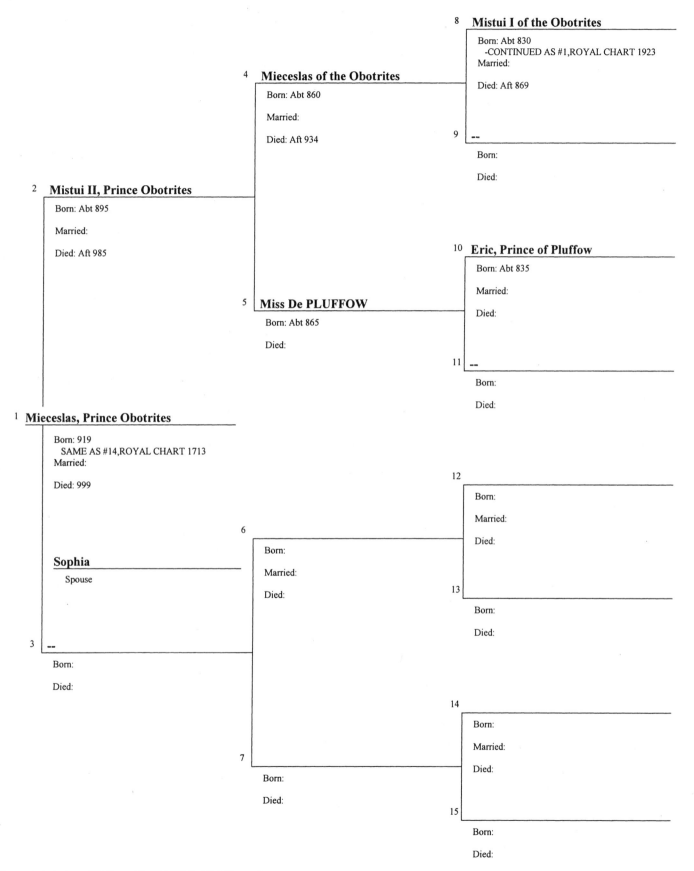

8 **Mistui I of the Obotrites**

Born: Abt 830
   -CONTINUED AS #1,ROYAL CHART 1923
Married:

Died: Aft 869

9 --

Born:

Died:

4 **Mieceslas of the Obotrites**

Born: Abt 860

Married:

Died: Aft 934

2 **Mistui II, Prince Obotrites**

Born: Abt 895

Married:

Died: Aft 985

10 **Eric, Prince of Pluffow**

Born: Abt 835

Married:

Died:

11 --

Born:

Died:

5 **Miss De PLUFFOW**

Born: Abt 865

Died:

1 **Mieceslas, Prince Obotrites**

Born: 919
   SAME AS #14,ROYAL CHART 1713
Married:

Died: 999

Sophia
   Spouse

3 --

Born:

Died:

12

Born:

Married:

Died:

13

Born:

Died:

6

Born:

Married:

Died:

14

Born:

Married:

Died:

15

Born:

Died:

7

Born:

Died:

Sources include: Stuart 380; Turton 27; *TAG* 74:148-149; LDS records.

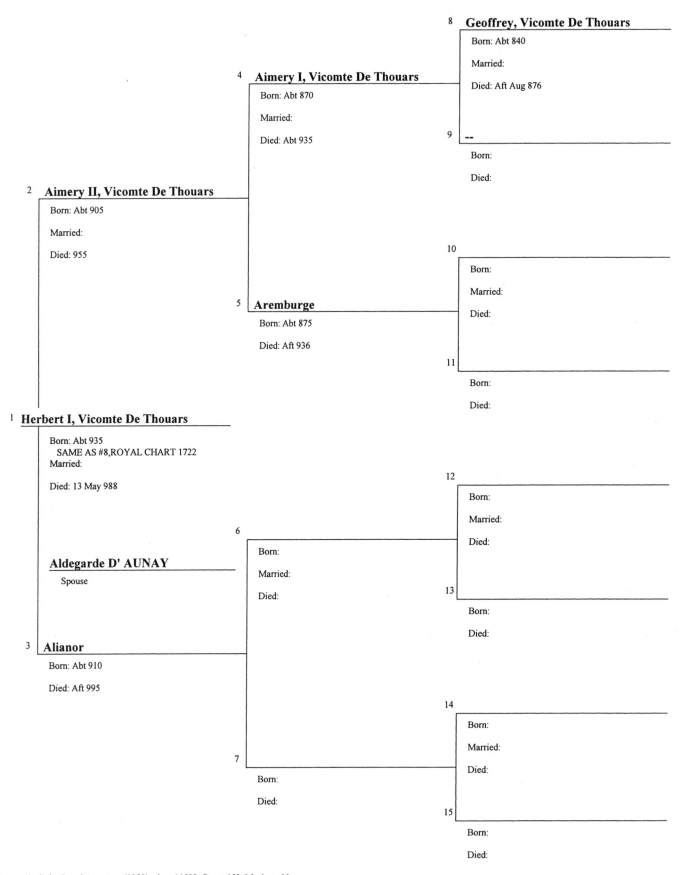

8 Geoffrey, Vicomte De Thouars

Born: Abt 840

Married:

Died: Aft Aug 876

9 --

Born:

Died:

4 Aimery I, Vicomte De Thouars

Born: Abt 870

Married:

Died: Abt 935

10

Born:

Married:

Died:

11

Born:

Died:

2 Aimery II, Vicomte De Thouars

Born: Abt 905

Married:

Died: 955

5 Aremburge

Born: Abt 875

Died: Aft 936

1 Herbert I, Vicomte De Thouars

Born: Abt 935
   SAME AS #8, ROYAL CHART 1722
Married:

Died: 13 May 988

Aldegarde D' AUNAY
   Spouse

6

Born:

Married:

Died:

12

Born:

Married:

Died:

13

Born:

Died:

3 Alianor

Born: Abt 910

Died: Aft 995

7

Born:

Died:

14

Born:

Married:

Died:

15

Born:

Died:

Sources include: *Royal Ancestors* (1989), chart 11599; Stuart 159; Moriarty 46.

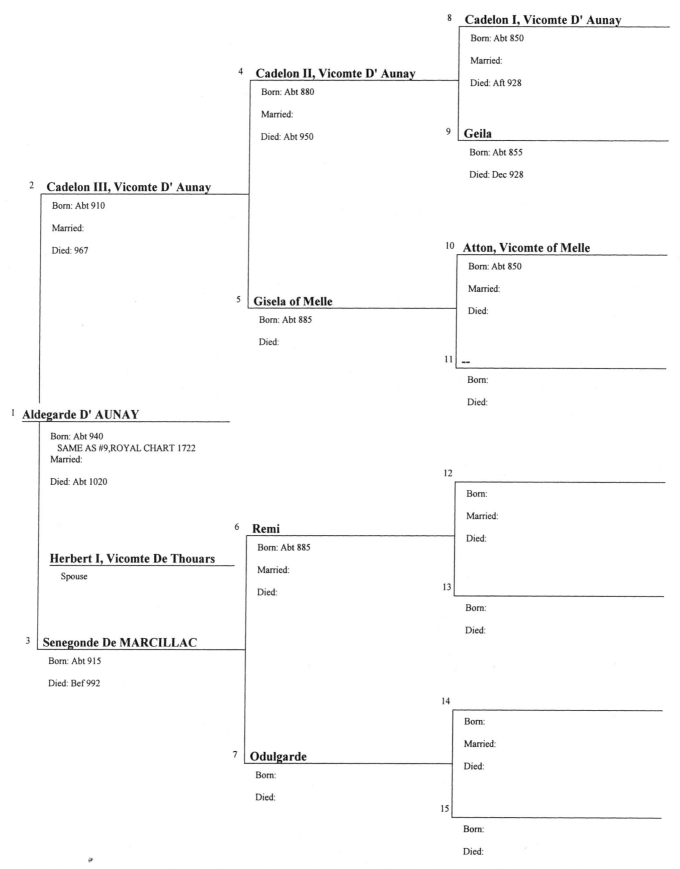

8 **Cadelon I, Vicomte D' Aunay**

Born: Abt 850

Married:

Died: Aft 928

4 **Cadelon II, Vicomte D' Aunay**

Born: Abt 880

Married:

Died: Abt 950

9 **Geila**

Born: Abt 855

Died: Dec 928

2 **Cadelon III, Vicomte D' Aunay**

Born: Abt 910

Married:

Died: 967

10 **Atton, Vicomte of Melle**

Born: Abt 850

Married:

Died:

5 **Gisela of Melle**

Born: Abt 885

Died:

11 **--**

Born:

Died:

1 **Aldegarde D' AUNAY**

Born: Abt 940
    SAME AS #9,ROYAL CHART 1722
Married:

Died: Abt 1020

12

Born:

Married:

Died:

6 **Remi**

Born: Abt 885

Married:

Died:

13

Born:

Died:

Herbert I, Vicomte De Thouars

Spouse

3 **Senegonde De MARCILLAC**

Born: Abt 915

Died: Bef 992

14

Born:

Married:

Died:

7 **Odulgarde**

Born:

Died:

15

Born:

Died:

Sources include : *Royal Ancestors* (1989), chart 11599; Stuart 331; Moriarty 46, 271. Note: The parentage of #4 is disputed. Moriarty gives #8 as Maingau, wife unknown. The Stuart version is tentatively accepted above.

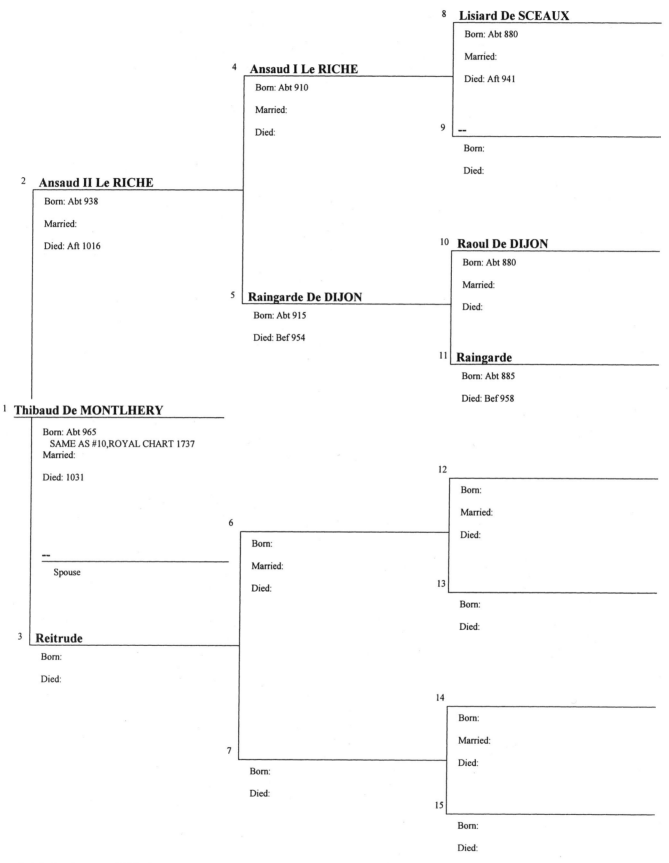

8 Lisiard De SCEAUX
Born: Abt 880
Married:
Died: Aft 941

4 Ansaud I Le RICHE
Born: Abt 910
Married:
Died:

9 --
Born:
Died:

2 Ansaud II Le RICHE
Born: Abt 938
Married:
Died: Aft 1016

10 Raoul De DIJON
Born: Abt 880
Married:
Died:

5 Raingarde De DIJON
Born: Abt 915
Died: Bef 954

11 Raingarde
Born: Abt 885
Died: Bef 958

1 Thibaud De MONTLHERY
Born: Abt 965
    SAME AS #10,ROYAL CHART 1737
Married:
Died: 1031

--
Spouse

12
Born:
Married:
Died:

6
Born:
Married:
Died:

13
Born:
Died:

3 Reitrude
Born:
Died:

14
Born:
Married:
Died:

7
Born:
Died:

15
Born:
Died:

Sources include: *Royal Ancestors* (1989), chart 11748; Stuart 241; Moriarty 63, 256-266.

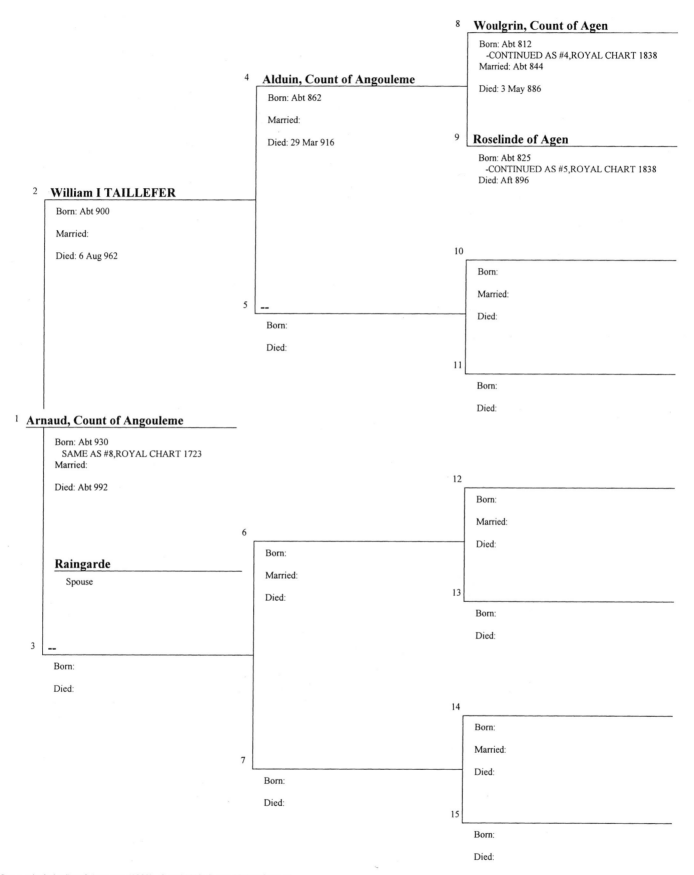

8 Woulgrin, Count of Agen

Born: Abt 812
    -CONTINUED AS #4,ROYAL CHART 1838
Married: Abt 844

Died: 3 May 886

4 Alduin, Count of Angouleme

Born: Abt 862

Married:

Died: 29 Mar 916

9 Roselinde of Agen

Born: Abt 825
    -CONTINUED AS #5,ROYAL CHART 1838
Died: Aft 896

2 William I TAILLEFER

Born: Abt 900

Married:

Died: 6 Aug 962

5 --

Born:

Died:

10

Born:

Married:

Died:

11

Born:

Died:

1 Arnaud, Count of Angouleme

Born: Abt 930
    SAME AS #8,ROYAL CHART 1723
Married:

Died: Abt 992

Raingarde

Spouse

3 --

Born:

Died:

6

Born:

Married:

Died:

12

Born:

Married:

Died:

13

Born:

Died:

7

Born:

Died:

14

Born:

Married:

Died:

15

Born:

Died:

Sources include: *Royal Ancestors* (1989), chart 11513; Stuart 87; Moriarty 46.

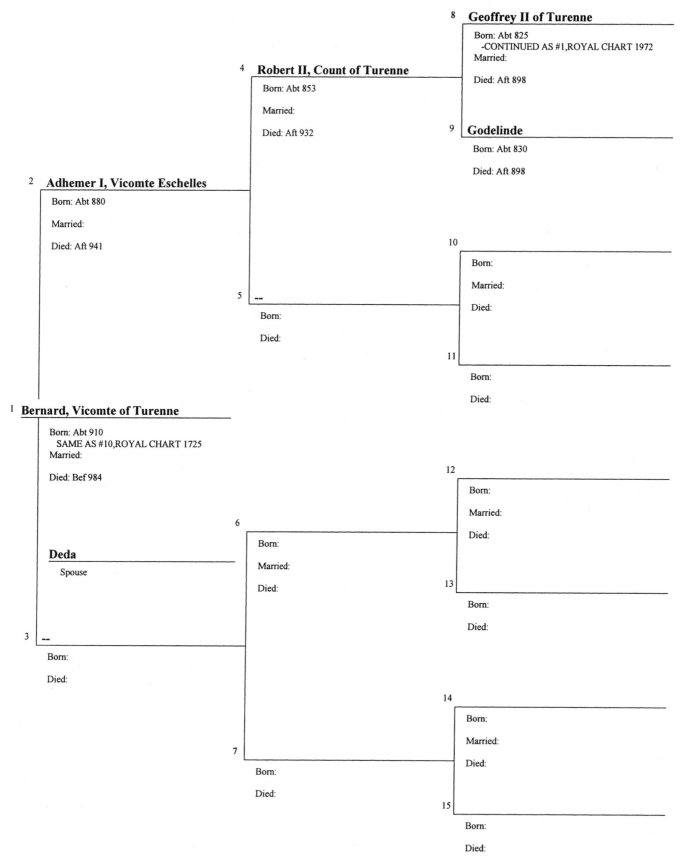

8 Geoffrey II of Turenne

Born: Abt 825
-CONTINUED AS #1,ROYAL CHART 1972
Married:

Died: Aft 898

4 Robert II, Count of Turenne

Born: Abt 853

Married:

Died: Aft 932

9 Godelinde

Born: Abt 830

Died: Aft 898

2 Adhemer I, Vicomte Eschelles

Born: Abt 880

Married:

Died: Aft 941

10

Born:

Married:

Died:

5 --

Born:

Died:

11

Born:

Died:

1 Bernard, Vicomte of Turenne

Born: Abt 910
    SAME AS #10,ROYAL CHART 1725
Married:

Died: Bef 984

12

Born:

Married:

Died:

6

Born:

Married:

Died:

13

Born:

Died:

Deda

Spouse

3 --

Born:

Died:

14

Born:

Married:

Died:

7

Born:

Died:

15

Born:

Died:

Sources include: Stuart 308; Moriarty 47-48.

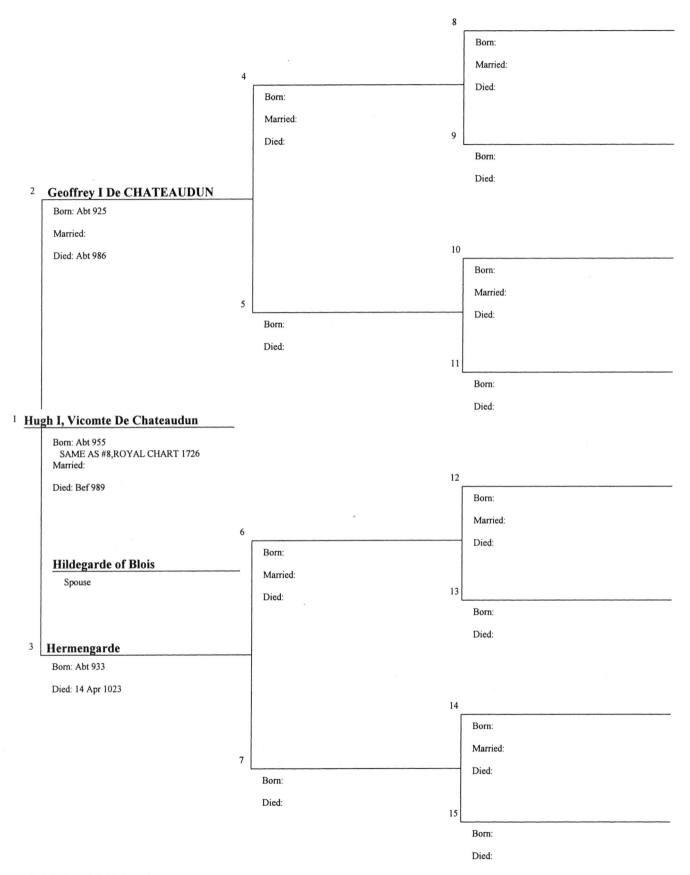

8
Born:
Married:
Died:

4
Born:
Married:
Died:

9
Born:
Died:

2 **Geoffrey I De CHATEAUDUN**
Born: Abt 925
Married:
Died: Abt 986

10
Born:
Married:
Died:

5
Born:
Died:

11
Born:
Died:

1 **Hugh I, Vicomte De Chateaudun**
Born: Abt 955
  SAME AS #8,ROYAL CHART 1726
Married:
Died: Bef 989

12
Born:
Married:
Died:

6
Born:
Married:
Died:

13
Born:
Died:

Hildegarde of Blois
  Spouse

3 **Hermengarde**
Born: Abt 933
Died: 14 Apr 1023

14
Born:
Married:
Died:

7
Born:
Died:

15
Born:
Died:

Sources include: Stuart 249; Moriarty 48.

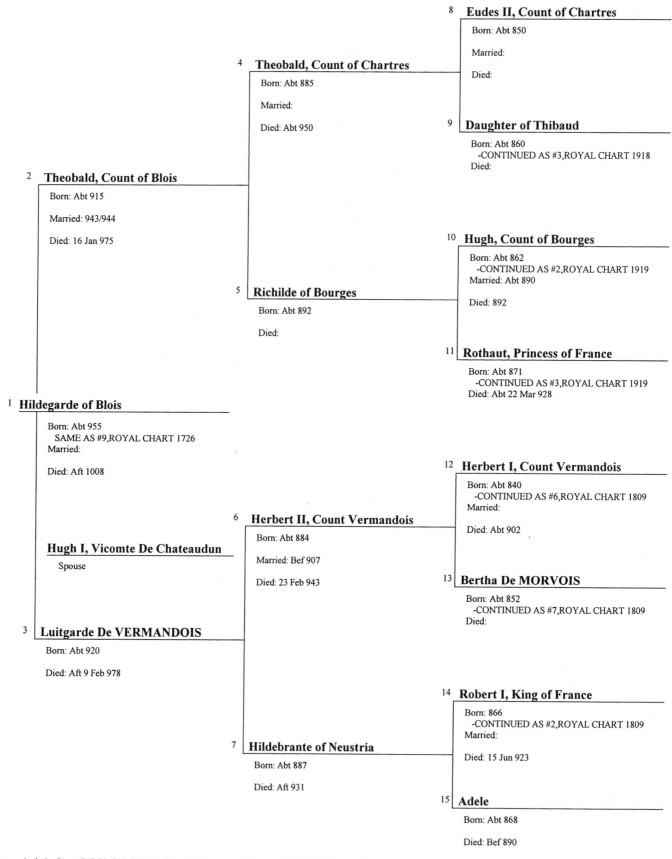

1 Hildegarde of Blois

Born: Abt 955
    SAME AS #9,ROYAL CHART 1726
Married:

Died: Aft 1008

Hugh I, Vicomte De Chateaudun

Spouse

2 Theobald, Count of Blois

Born: Abt 915

Married: 943/944

Died: 16 Jan 975

3 Luitgarde De VERMANDOIS

Born: Abt 920

Died: Aft 9 Feb 978

4 Theobald, Count of Chartres

Born: Abt 885

Married:

Died: Abt 950

5 Richilde of Bourges

Born: Abt 892

Died:

6 Herbert II, Count Vermandois

Born: Abt 884

Married: Bef 907

Died: 23 Feb 943

7 Hildebrante of Neustria

Born: Abt 887

Died: Aft 931

8 Eudes II, Count of Chartres

Born: Abt 850

Married:

Died:

9 Daughter of Thibaud

Born: Abt 860
    -CONTINUED AS #3,ROYAL CHART 1918
Died:

10 Hugh, Count of Bourges

Born: Abt 862
    -CONTINUED AS #2,ROYAL CHART 1919
Married: Abt 890

Died: 892

11 Rothaut, Princess of France

Born: Abt 871
    -CONTINUED AS #3,ROYAL CHART 1919
Died: Abt 22 Mar 928

12 Herbert I, Count Vermandois

Born: Abt 840
    -CONTINUED AS #6,ROYAL CHART 1809
Married:

Died: Abt 902

13 Bertha De MORVOIS

Born: Abt 852
    -CONTINUED AS #7,ROYAL CHART 1809
Died:

14 Robert I, King of France

Born: 866
    -CONTINUED AS #2,ROYAL CHART 1809
Married:

Died: 15 Jun 923

15 Adele

Born: Abt 868

Died: Bef 890

Sources include: Stuart 249-33, 340, 231; Moriarty 48, 36; *Ancestral Roots* 49, 136 (#2 & 3 ancestry).

Pedigree Chart

Chart 1871

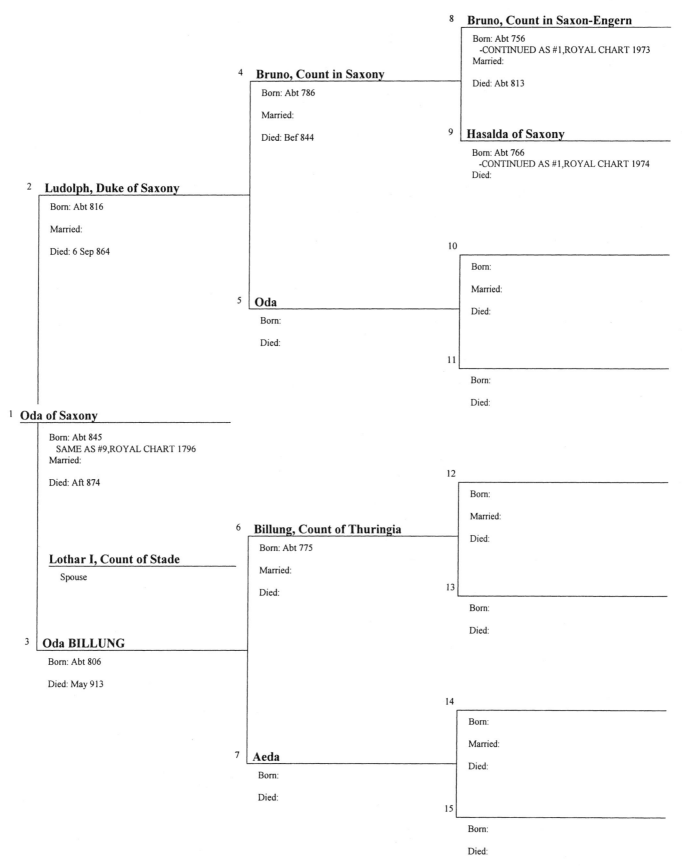

8   **Bruno, Count in Saxon-Engern**

Born: Abt 756
   -CONTINUED AS #1,ROYAL CHART 1973
Married:

Died: Abt 813

4   **Bruno, Count in Saxony**

Born: Abt 786

Married:

Died: Bef 844

9   **Hasalda of Saxony**

Born: Abt 766
   -CONTINUED AS #1,ROYAL CHART 1974
Died:

2   **Ludolph, Duke of Saxony**

Born: Abt 816

Married:

Died: 6 Sep 864

10

Born:

Married:

Died:

5   **Oda**

Born:

Died:

11

Born:

Died:

1   **Oda of Saxony**

Born: Abt 845
   SAME AS #9,ROYAL CHART 1796
Married:

Died: Aft 874

12

Born:

Married:

Died:

6   **Billung, Count of Thuringia**

Born: Abt 775

Married:

Died:

Lothar I, Count of Stade

   Spouse

13

Born:

Died:

3   **Oda BILLUNG**

Born: Abt 806

Died: May 913

14

Born:

Married:

Died:

7   **Aeda**

Born:

Died:

15

Born:

Died:

Sources include: Stuart 301, 92; *Royal Ancestors* (1989), chart 11507 (#2 & 3 ancestry); Moriarty 25 (#2 & 3 ancestry). Note: Moriarty states that #3 Oda died at age 107.

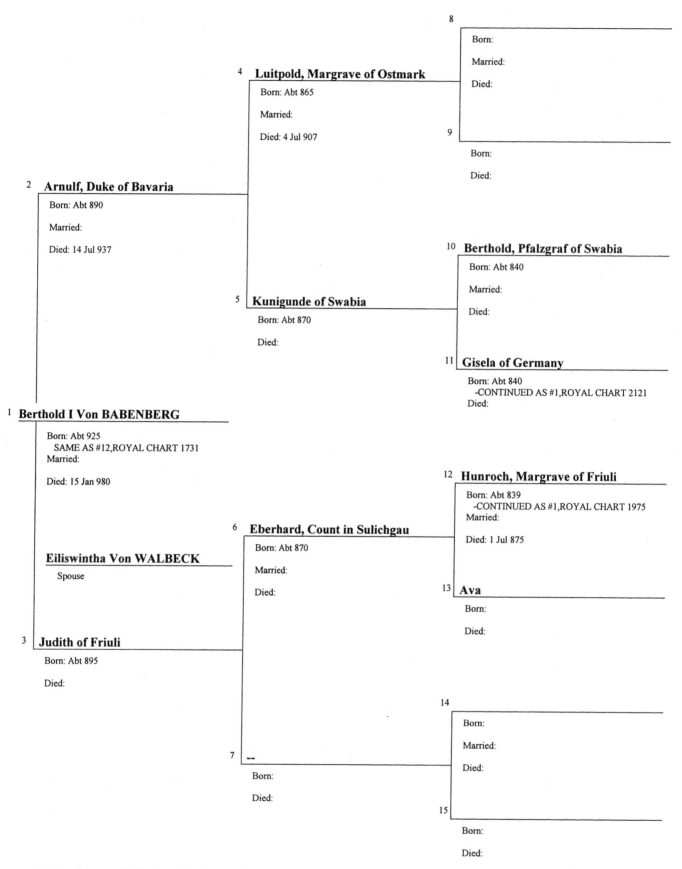

8

Born:

Married:

Died:

4 Luitpold, Margrave of Ostmark

Born: Abt 865

Married:

Died: 4 Jul 907

9

Born:

Died:

2 Arnulf, Duke of Bavaria

Born: Abt 890

Married:

Died: 14 Jul 937

10 Berthold, Pfalzgraf of Swabia

Born: Abt 840

Married:

Died:

5 Kunigunde of Swabia

Born: Abt 870

Died:

11 Gisela of Germany

Born: Abt 840
   -CONTINUED AS #1,ROYAL CHART 2121
Died:

1 Berthold I Von BABENBERG

Born: Abt 925
   SAME AS #12,ROYAL CHART 1731
Married:

Died: 15 Jan 980

12 Hunroch, Margrave of Friuli

Born: Abt 839
   -CONTINUED AS #1,ROYAL CHART 1975
Married:

Died: 1 Jul 875

6 Eberhard, Count in Sulichgau

Born: Abt 870

Married:

Died:

Eiliswintha Von WALBECK

Spouse

13 Ava

Born:

Died:

3 Judith of Friuli

Born: Abt 895

Died:

14

Born:

Married:

Died:

7 --

Born:

Died:

15

Born:

Died:

Sources include: *Royal Ancestors* (1989), chart 11874; Stuart 270, 272; Moriarty 57, 33, 18; Faris preliminary Charlemagne manuscript (June 1995), p. 41. Notes: #3 Judith is uncertain. Faris gives #3 as unknown, while proposing two other possibilities. #11 is uncertain. #13 Ava was daughter of a Duke Liutfried.

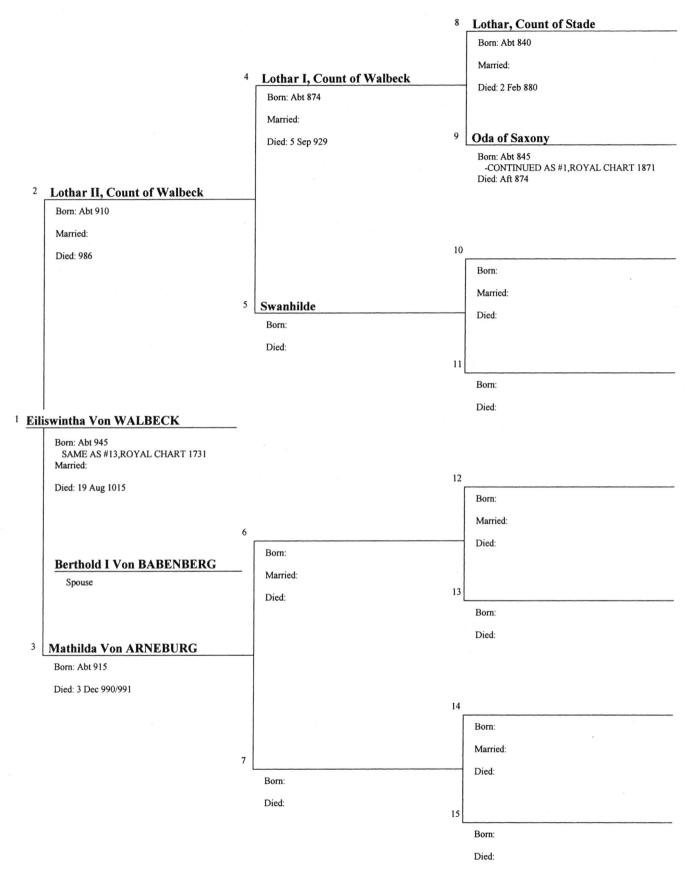

8 **Lothar, Count of Stade**

Born: Abt 840

Married:

Died: 2 Feb 880

4 **Lothar I, Count of Walbeck**

Born: Abt 874

Married:

Died: 5 Sep 929

9 **Oda of Saxony**

Born: Abt 845
 -CONTINUED AS #1,ROYAL CHART 1871
Died: Aft 874

2 **Lothar II, Count of Walbeck**

Born: Abt 910

Married:

Died: 986

10

Born:

Married:

Died:

5 **Swanhilde**

Born:

Died:

11

Born:

Died:

1 **Eiliswintha Von WALBECK**

Born: Abt 945
 SAME AS #13,ROYAL CHART 1731
Married:

Died: 19 Aug 1015

12

Born:

Married:

Died:

6

Born:

Married:

Died:

Berthold I Von BABENBERG

Spouse

13

Born:

Died:

3 **Mathilda Von ARNEBURG**

Born: Abt 915

Died: 3 Dec 990/991

14

Born:

Married:

Died:

7

Born:

Died:

15

Born:

Died:

Sources include: *Royal Ancestors* (1989), chart 11875; Stuart 271, 15; Moriarty 57. Note: Stuart and Moriarty show #3 Mathilda as a daughter of Bruno, Count of Arneburg (died 19 Oct 1009-17), which is difficult chronologically.

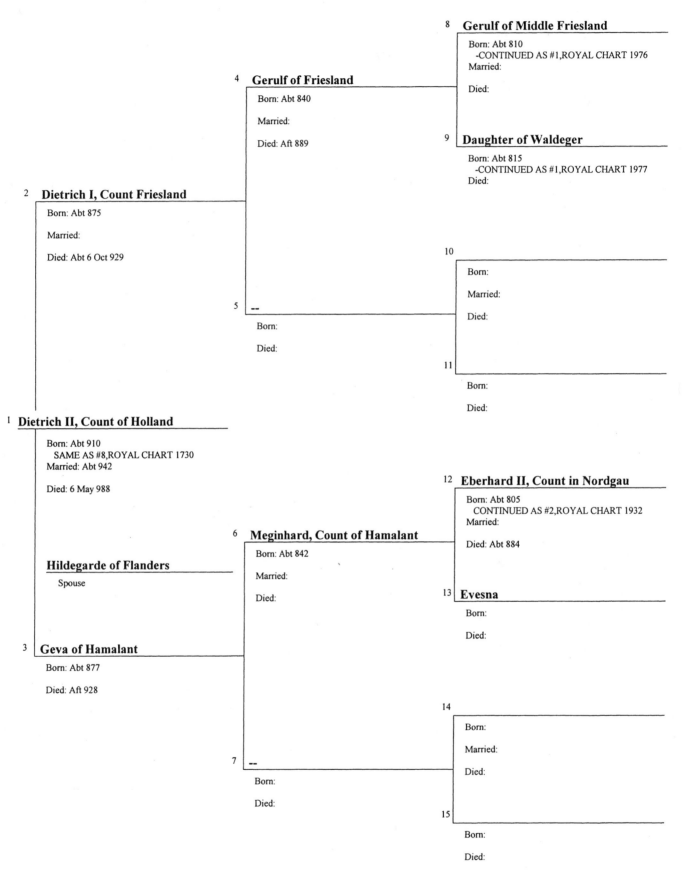

8 Gerulf of Middle Friesland

Born: Abt 810
-CONTINUED AS #1,ROYAL CHART 1976
Married:

Died:

4 Gerulf of Friesland

Born: Abt 840

Married:

Died: Aft 889

9 Daughter of Waldeger

Born: Abt 815
-CONTINUED AS #1,ROYAL CHART 1977
Died:

2 Dietrich I, Count Friesland

Born: Abt 875

Married:

Died: Abt 6 Oct 929

10

Born:

Married:

Died:

5 --

Born:

Died:

11

Born:

Died:

1 Dietrich II, Count of Holland

Born: Abt 910
   SAME AS #8,ROYAL CHART 1730
Married: Abt 942

Died: 6 May 988

12 Eberhard II, Count in Nordgau

Born: Abt 805
   CONTINUED AS #2,ROYAL CHART 1932
Married:

Died: Abt 884

6 Meginhard, Count of Hamalant

Born: Abt 842

Married:

Died:

Hildegarde of Flanders

Spouse

13 Evesna

Born:

Died:

3 Geva of Hamalant

Born: Abt 877

Died: Aft 928

14

Born:

Married:

Died:

7 --

Born:

Died:

15

Born:

Died:

Sources include: *Royal Ancestors* (1989), chart 11643; Stuart 311; Moriarty 55. Note: The tentative ancestry shown for #4 Gerulf is not certain, but Moriarty accepts it as quite probable.

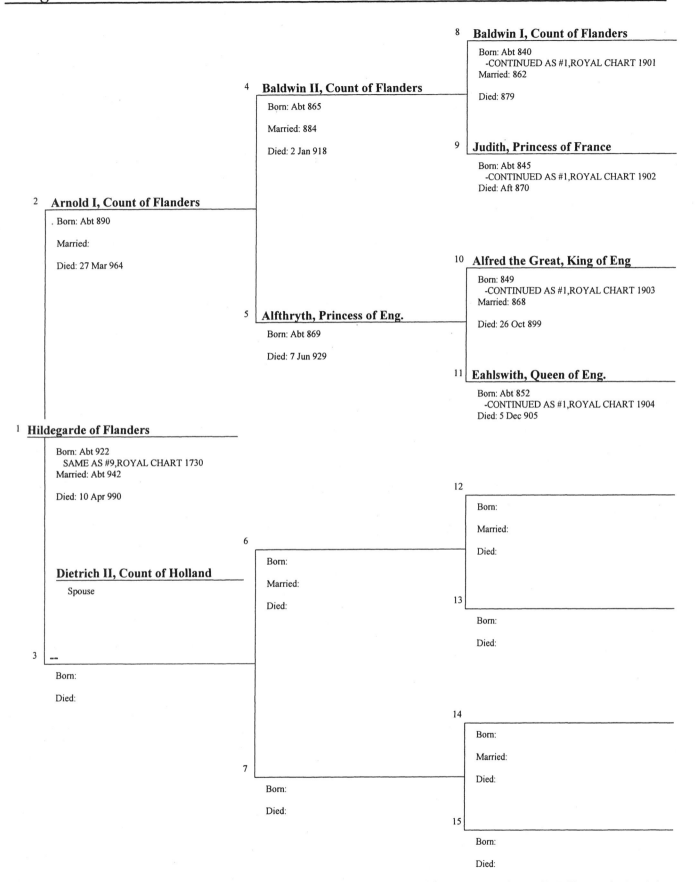

8 Baldwin I, Count of Flanders

Born: Abt 840
 -CONTINUED AS #1,ROYAL CHART 1901
Married: 862

Died: 879

4 Baldwin II, Count of Flanders

Born: Abt 865

Married: 884

Died: 2 Jan 918

9 Judith, Princess of France

Born: Abt 845
 -CONTINUED AS #1,ROYAL CHART 1902
Died: Aft 870

2 Arnold I, Count of Flanders

. Born: Abt 890

Married:

Died: 27 Mar 964

10 Alfred the Great, King of Eng

Born: 849
 -CONTINUED AS #1,ROYAL CHART 1903
Married: 868

Died: 26 Oct 899

5 Alfthryth, Princess of Eng.

Born: Abt 869

Died: 7 Jun 929

11 Eahlswith, Queen of Eng.

Born: Abt 852
 -CONTINUED AS #1,ROYAL CHART 1904
Died: 5 Dec 905

1 Hildegarde of Flanders

Born: Abt 922
 SAME AS #9,ROYAL CHART 1730
Married: Abt 942

Died: 10 Apr 990

12

Born:

Married:

Died:

6

Born:

Married:

Died:

Dietrich II, Count of Holland

Spouse

13

Born:

Died:

3 --

Born:

Died:

14

Born:

Married:

Died:

7

Born:

Died:

15

Born:

Died:

Sources include: Faris preliminary Charlemagne manuscript (June 1995), pp. 131, 157; Stuart 311-36, 141, 169; Moriarty 55, 14; *Ancestral Roots* 162, 48 (#2 ancestry). Note: Faris gives the mother of #1 Hildegarde as an unknown 1st wife of #2 Arnold (Arnulphe, Arnoul). Stuart gives #3 as Aliz (Adele, Adelaide) De Vermandois, a 2nd wife (see chart 1801).

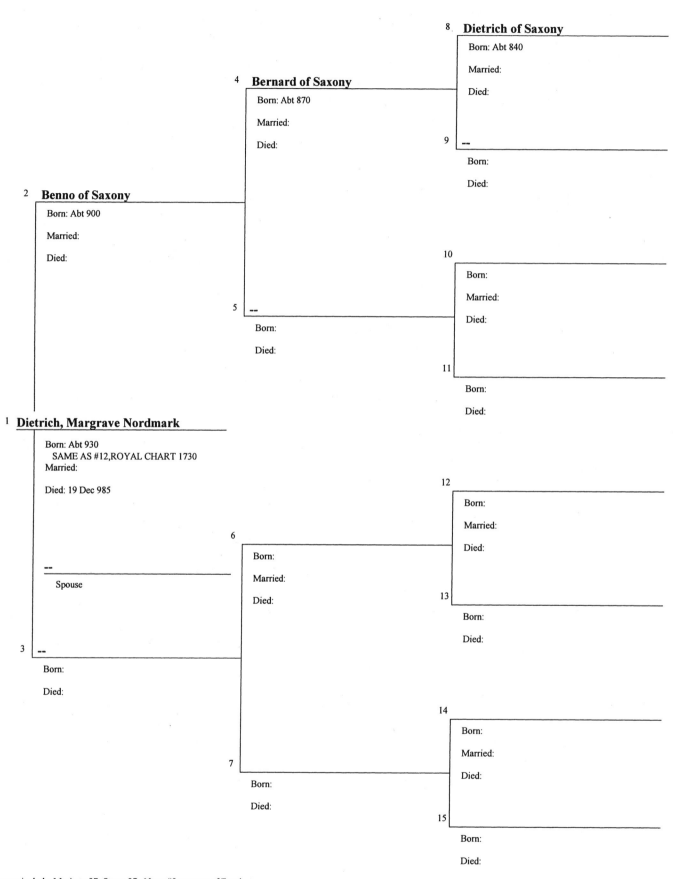

8 **Dietrich of Saxony**
Born: Abt 840
Married:
Died:

4 **Bernard of Saxony**
Born: Abt 870
Married:
Died:

9 --
Born:
Died:

2 **Benno of Saxony**
Born: Abt 900
Married:
Died:

5 --
Born:
Died:

10
Born:
Married:
Died:

11
Born:
Died:

1 **Dietrich, Margrave Nordmark**
Born: Abt 930
   SAME AS #12,ROYAL CHART 1730
Married:

Died: 19 Dec 985

--
Spouse

3 --
Born:
Died:

6
Born:
Married:
Died:

12
Born:
Married:
Died:

13
Born:
Died:

7
Born:
Died:

14
Born:
Married:
Died:

15
Born:
Died:

Sources include: Moriarty 97; Stuart 27. Note: #8 was son of Ezard.

Pedigree Chart

Chart 1877

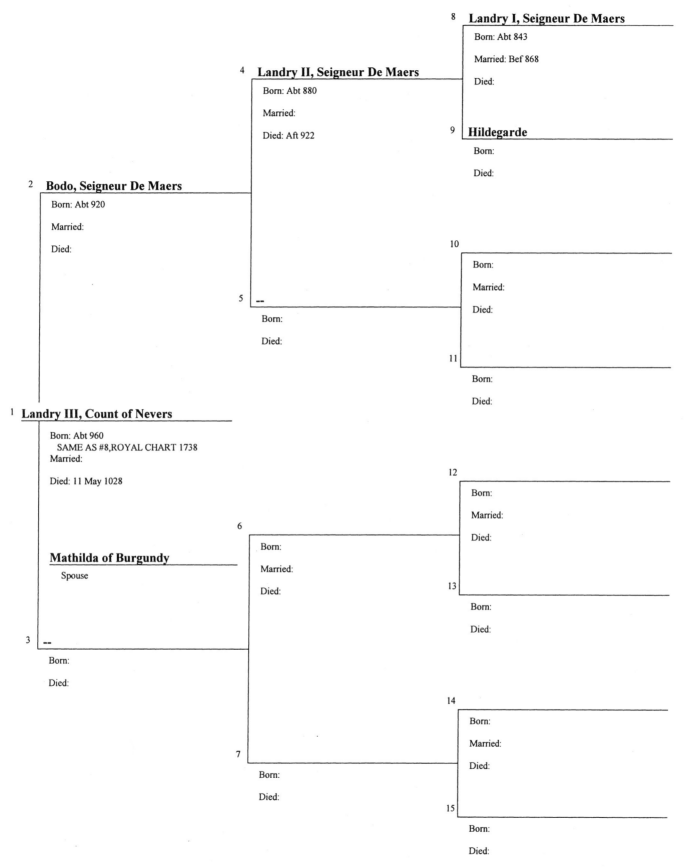

8 **Landry I, Seigneur De Maers**

Born: Abt 843

Married: Bef 868

Died:

4 **Landry II, Seigneur De Maers**

Born: Abt 880

Married:

Died: Aft 922

9 **Hildegarde**

Born:

Died:

2 **Bodo, Seigneur De Maers**

Born: Abt 920

Married:

Died:

5 **--**

Born:

Died:

10

Born:

Married:

Died:

11

Born:

Died:

1 **Landry III, Count of Nevers**

Born: Abt 960
     SAME AS #8,ROYAL CHART 1738
Married:

Died: 11 May 1028

6

Born:

Married:

Died:

12

Born:

Married:

Died:

13

Born:

Died:

Mathilda of Burgundy

     Spouse

3 **--**

Born:

Died:

7

Born:

Died:

14

Born:

Married:

Died:

15

Born:

Died:

Sources include: *Royal Ancestors* (1989), chart 11782; Stuart 255; Moriarty 64.

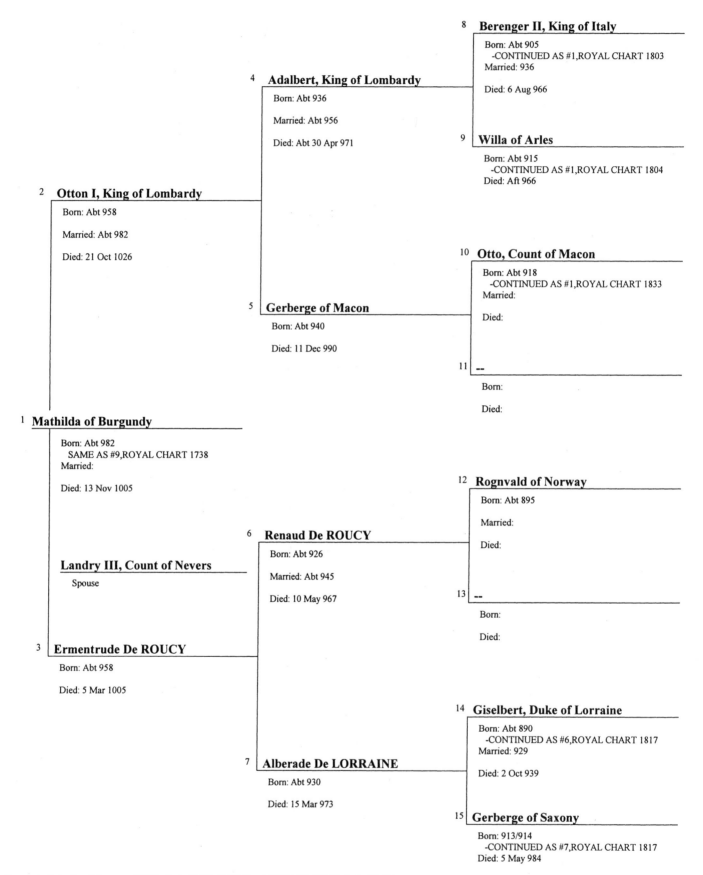

2 Otton I, King of Lombardy

Born: Abt 958

Married: Abt 982

Died: 21 Oct 1026

4 Adalbert, King of Lombardy

Born: Abt 936

Married: Abt 956

Died: Abt 30 Apr 971

8 Berenger II, King of Italy

Born: Abt 905
   -CONTINUED AS #1,ROYAL CHART 1803
Married: 936

Died: 6 Aug 966

9 Willa of Arles

Born: Abt 915
   -CONTINUED AS #1,ROYAL CHART 1804
Died: Aft 966

5 Gerberge of Macon

Born: Abt 940

Died: 11 Dec 990

10 Otto, Count of Macon

Born: Abt 918
   -CONTINUED AS #1,ROYAL CHART 1833
Married:

Died:

11 --

Born:

Died:

1 Mathilda of Burgundy

Born: Abt 982
   SAME AS #9,ROYAL CHART 1738
Married:

Died: 13 Nov 1005

Landry III, Count of Nevers

Spouse

3 Ermentrude De ROUCY

Born: Abt 958

Died: 5 Mar 1005

6 Renaud De ROUCY

Born: Abt 926

Married: Abt 945

Died: 10 May 967

12 Rognvald of Norway

Born: Abt 895

Married:

Died:

13 --

Born:

Died:

7 Alberade De LORRAINE

Born: Abt 930

Died: 15 Mar 973

14 Giselbert, Duke of Lorraine

Born: Abt 890
   -CONTINUED AS #6,ROYAL CHART 1817
Married: 929

Died: 2 Oct 939

15 Gerberge of Saxony

Born: 913/914
   -CONTINUED AS #7,ROYAL CHART 1817
Died: 5 May 984

Sources include: *Royal Ancestors* (1989), charts 11783, 11407; Stuart 255-34, 94, 161; Moriarty 64, 37.

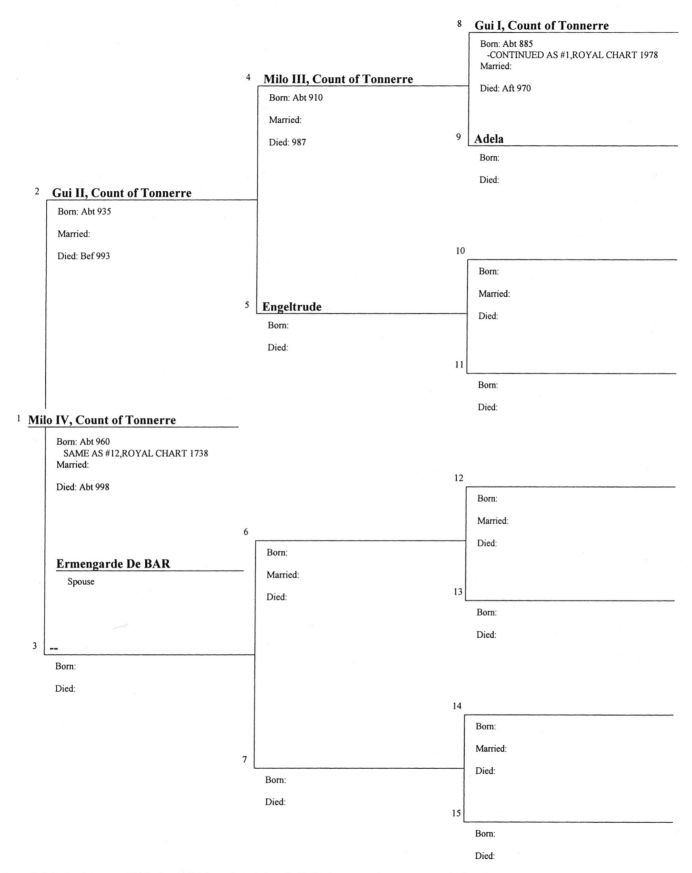

8 **Gui I, Count of Tonnerre**

Born: Abt 885
  -CONTINUED AS #1,ROYAL CHART 1978
Married:

Died: Aft 970

4 **Milo III, Count of Tonnerre**

Born: Abt 910

Married:

Died: 987

9 **Adela**

Born:

Died:

2 **Gui II, Count of Tonnerre**

Born: Abt 935

Married:

Died: Bef 993

10

Born:

Married:

Died:

5 **Engeltrude**

Born:

Died:

11

Born:

Died:

1 **Milo IV, Count of Tonnerre**

Born: Abt 960
  SAME AS #12,ROYAL CHART 1738
Married:

Died: Abt 998

12

Born:

Married:

Died:

6

Born:

Married:

Died:

13

Born:

Died:

Ermengarde De BAR

Spouse

3 **--**

Born:

Died:

14

Born:

Married:

Died:

7

Born:

Died:

15

Born:

Died:

Sources include: *Royal Ancestors* (1989), chart 11784; Stuart 254; Moriarty 64-65, 239-240. Note: The ancestry shown for #1 Milo is not certain. Moriarty outlines both this and an alternate version. Stuart gives incorrect ancestry for #5 Engeltrude and #9 Adela. Moriarty gives #9 Adela as daughter of Aubri.

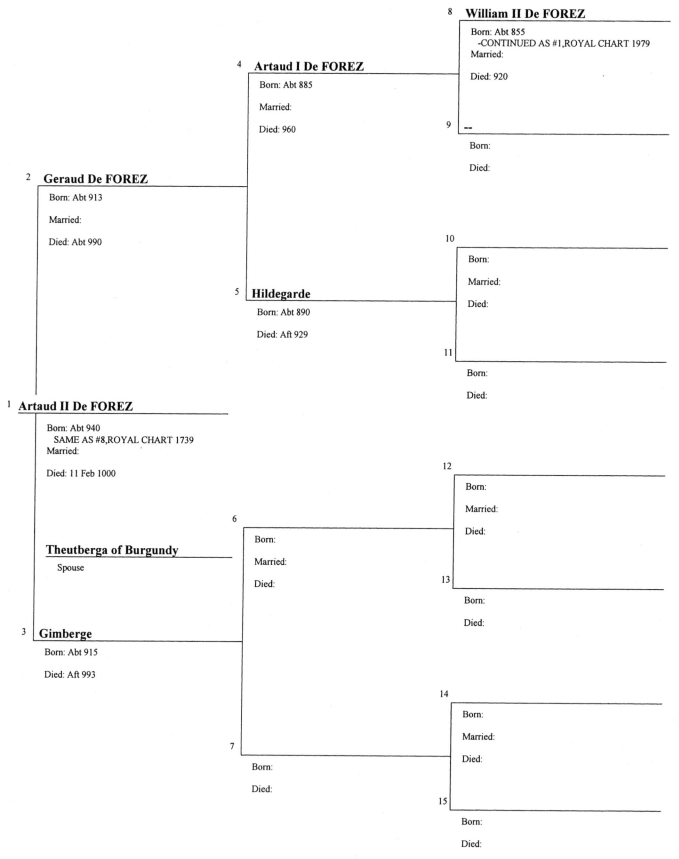

8 William II De FOREZ
Born: Abt 855
-CONTINUED AS #1,ROYAL CHART 1979
Married:

Died: 920

4 Artaud I De FOREZ
Born: Abt 885

Married:

Died: 960

9 --
Born:

Died:

2 Geraud De FOREZ
Born: Abt 913

Married:

Died: Abt 990

10
Born:

Married:

Died:

5 Hildegarde
Born: Abt 890

Died: Aft 929

11
Born:

Died:

1 Artaud II De FOREZ
Born: Abt 940
    SAME AS #8,ROYAL CHART 1739
Married:

Died: 11 Feb 1000

12
Born:

Married:

Died:

6
Born:

Married:

Died:

13
Born:

Died:

Theutberga of Burgundy
    Spouse

3 Gimberge
Born: Abt 915

Died: Aft 993

14
Born:

Married:

Died:

7
Born:

Died:

15
Born:

Died:

Sources include: *Royal Ancestors* 11517; Stuart 317; Moriarty 66.

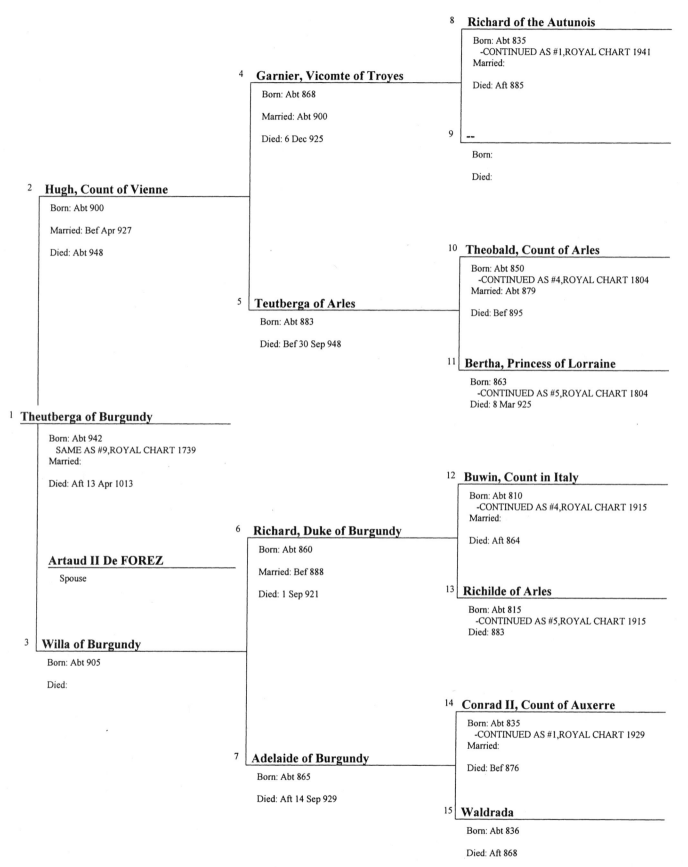

8 **Richard of the Autunois**

Born: Abt 835
-CONTINUED AS #1,ROYAL CHART 1941
Married:

Died: Aft 885

4 **Garnier, Vicomte of Troyes**

Born: Abt 868

Married: Abt 900

Died: 6 Dec 925

9 **--**

Born:

Died:

2 **Hugh, Count of Vienne**

Born: Abt 900

Married: Bef Apr 927

Died: Abt 948

10 **Theobald, Count of Arles**

Born: Abt 850
-CONTINUED AS #4,ROYAL CHART 1804
Married: Abt 879

Died: Bef 895

5 **Teutberga of Arles**

Born: Abt 883

Died: Bef 30 Sep 948

11 **Bertha, Princess of Lorraine**

Born: 863
-CONTINUED AS #5,ROYAL CHART 1804
Died: 8 Mar 925

1 **Theutberga of Burgundy**

Born: Abt 942
SAME AS #9,ROYAL CHART 1739
Married:

Died: Aft 13 Apr 1013

12 **Buwin, Count in Italy**

Born: Abt 810
-CONTINUED AS #4,ROYAL CHART 1915
Married:

Died: Aft 864

6 **Richard, Duke of Burgundy**

Born: Abt 860

Married: Bef 888

Died: 1 Sep 921

Artaud II De FOREZ

Spouse

13 **Richilde of Arles**

Born: Abt 815
-CONTINUED AS #5,ROYAL CHART 1915
Died: 883

3 **Willa of Burgundy**

Born: Abt 905

Died:

14 **Conrad II, Count of Auxerre**

Born: Abt 835
-CONTINUED AS #1,ROYAL CHART 1929
Married:

Died: Bef 876

7 **Adelaide of Burgundy**

Born: Abt 865

Died: Aft 14 Sep 929

15 **Waldrada**

Born: Abt 836

Died: Aft 868

Sources include: Stuart 317-34, 173; Moriarty 66, 59.

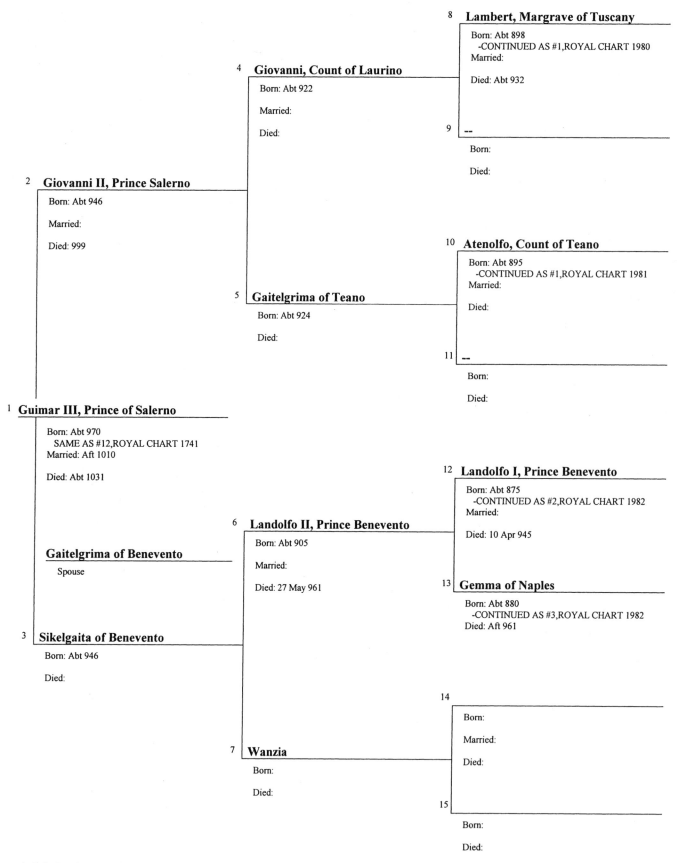

8 Lambert, Margrave of Tuscany

Born: Abt 898
-CONTINUED AS #1, ROYAL CHART 1980
Married:

Died: Abt 932

9 --

Born:

Died:

4 Giovanni, Count of Laurino

Born: Abt 922

Married:

Died:

2 Giovanni II, Prince Salerno

Born: Abt 946

Married:

Died: 999

10 Atenolfo, Count of Teano

Born: Abt 895
-CONTINUED AS #1, ROYAL CHART 1981
Married:

Died:

11 --

Born:

Died:

5 Gaitelgrima of Teano

Born: Abt 924

Died:

1 Guimar III, Prince of Salerno

Born: Abt 970
SAME AS #12, ROYAL CHART 1741
Married: Aft 1010

Died: Abt 1031

Gaitelgrima of Benevento

Spouse

12 Landolfo I, Prince Benevento

Born: Abt 875
-CONTINUED AS #2, ROYAL CHART 1982
Married:

Died: 10 Apr 945

6 Landolfo II, Prince Benevento

Born: Abt 905

Married:

Died: 27 May 961

13 Gemma of Naples

Born: Abt 880
-CONTINUED AS #3, ROYAL CHART 1982
Died: Aft 961

3 Sikelgaita of Benevento

Born: Abt 946

Died:

14

Born:

Married:

Died:

7 Wanzia

Born:

Died:

15

Born:

Died:

Sources include: *Royal Ancestors* (1989), chart 12093; Stuart 297; *TAG* 52:23-26; Moriarty 71.

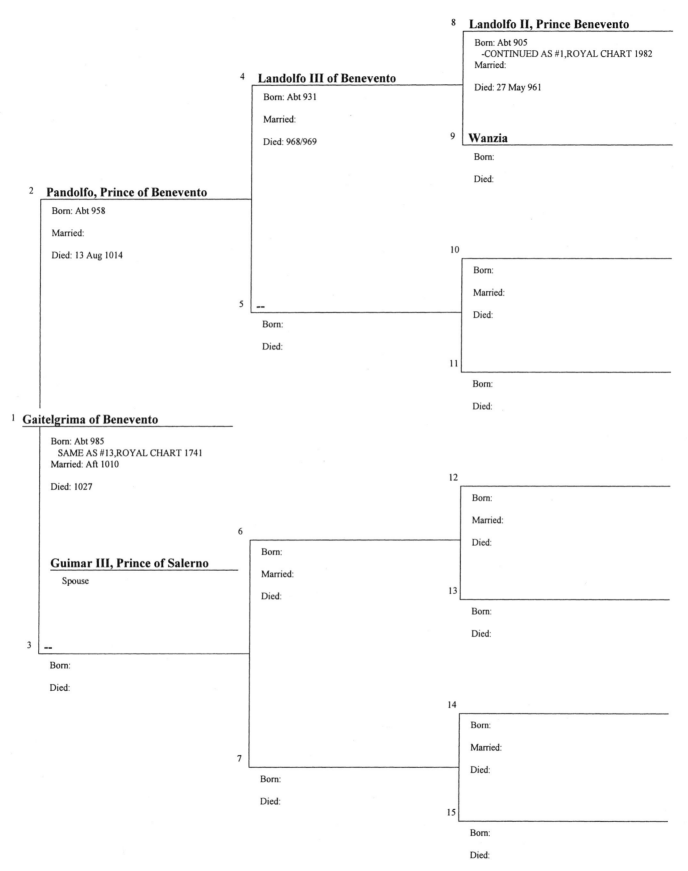

8 Landolfo II, Prince Benevento

Born: Abt 905
  -CONTINUED AS #1,ROYAL CHART 1982
Married:

Died: 27 May 961

4 Landolfo III of Benevento

Born: Abt 931

Married:

Died: 968/969

9 Wanzia

Born:

Died:

2 Pandolfo, Prince of Benevento

Born: Abt 958

Married:

Died: 13 Aug 1014

10

Born:

Married:

Died:

5 --

Born:

Died:

11

Born:

Died:

1 Gaitelgrima of Benevento

Born: Abt 985
  SAME AS #13,ROYAL CHART 1741
Married: Aft 1010

Died: 1027

12

Born:

Married:

Died:

6

Born:

Married:

Died:

13

Born:

Died:

Guimar III, Prince of Salerno

Spouse

3 --

Born:

Died:

14

Born:

Married:

Died:

7

Born:

Died:

15

Born:

Died:

Sources include: *Royal Ancestors* (1989), chart 12094; Stuart 283; *TAG* 52:23-26; Moriarty 72.

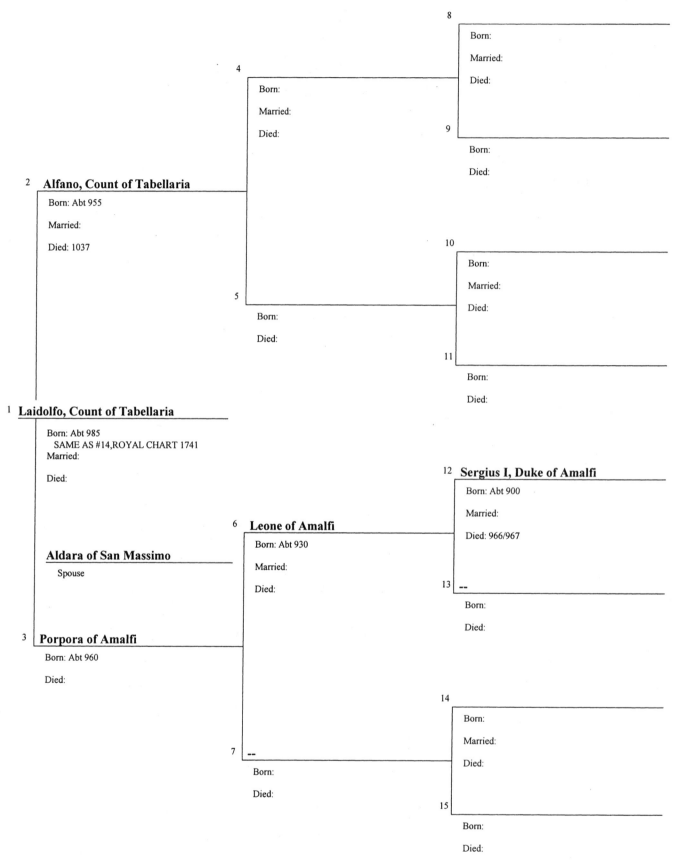

8

Born:

Married:

Died:

4

Born:

Married:

Died:

9

Born:

Died:

2 Alfano, Count of Tabellaria

Born: Abt 955

Married:

Died: 1037

10

Born:

Married:

Died:

5

Born:

Died:

11

Born:

Died:

1 Laidolfo, Count of Tabellaria

Born: Abt 985
    SAME AS #14,ROYAL CHART 1741
Married:

Died:

12 Sergius I, Duke of Amalfi

Born: Abt 900

Married:

Died: 966/967

6 Leone of Amalfi

Born: Abt 930

Married:

Died:

13 --

Born:

Died:

Aldara of San Massimo

Spouse

3 Porpora of Amalfi

Born: Abt 960

Died:

14

Born:

Married:

Died:

7 --

Born:

Died:

15

Born:

Died:

Sources include: *Royal Ancestors* (1989), chart 12091; Stuart 325; *TAG* 52:23-26.

Pedigree Chart

Chart 1885

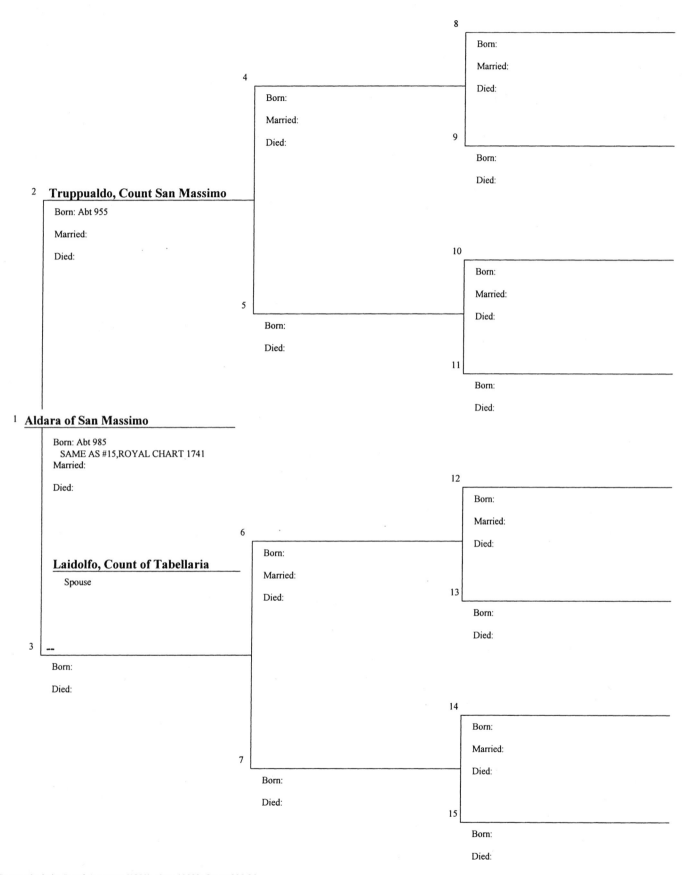

8
Born:
Married:
Died:

4
Born:
Married:
Died:

9
Born:
Died:

2 **Truppualdo, Count San Massimo**
Born: Abt 955
Married:
Died:

10
Born:
Married:
Died:

5
Born:
Died:

11
Born:
Died:

1 **Aldara of San Massimo**
Born: Abt 985
  SAME AS #15, ROYAL CHART 1741
Married:
Died:

12
Born:
Married:
Died:

6
Born:
Married:
Died:

13
Born:
Died:

Laidolfo, Count of Tabellaria
Spouse

3 --
Born:
Died:

14
Born:
Married:
Died:

7
Born:
Died:

15
Born:
Died:

Sources include: *Royal Ancestors* (1989), chart 12092; Stuart 325-34.

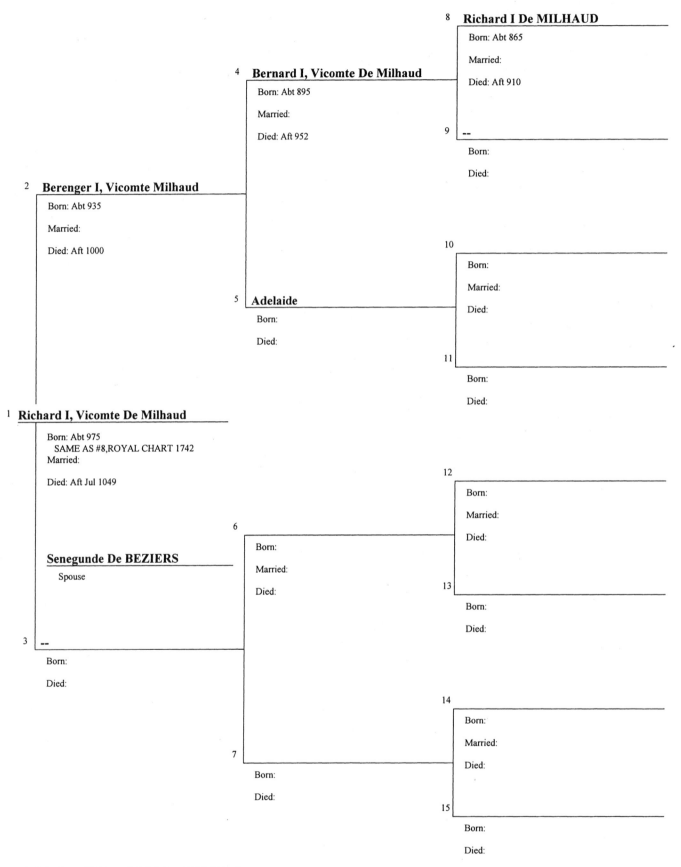

8 Richard I De MILHAUD

Born: Abt 865

Married:

Died: Aft 910

4 Bernard I, Vicomte De Milhaud

Born: Abt 895

Married:

Died: Aft 952

9 --

Born:

Died:

2 Berenger I, Vicomte Milhaud

Born: Abt 935

Married:

Died: Aft 1000

10

Born:

Married:

Died:

5 Adelaide

Born:

Died:

11

Born:

Died:

1 Richard I, Vicomte De Milhaud

Born: Abt 975
  SAME AS #8, ROYAL CHART 1742
Married:

Died: Aft Jul 1049

12

Born:

Married:

Died:

6

Born:

Married:

Died:

13

Born:

Died:

Senegunde De BEZIERS
  Spouse

3 --

Born:

Died:

14

Born:

Married:

Died:

7

Born:

Died:

15

Born:

Died:

Sources include: Stuart 402; Turton 218; Moriarty 76 (#1 Richard).

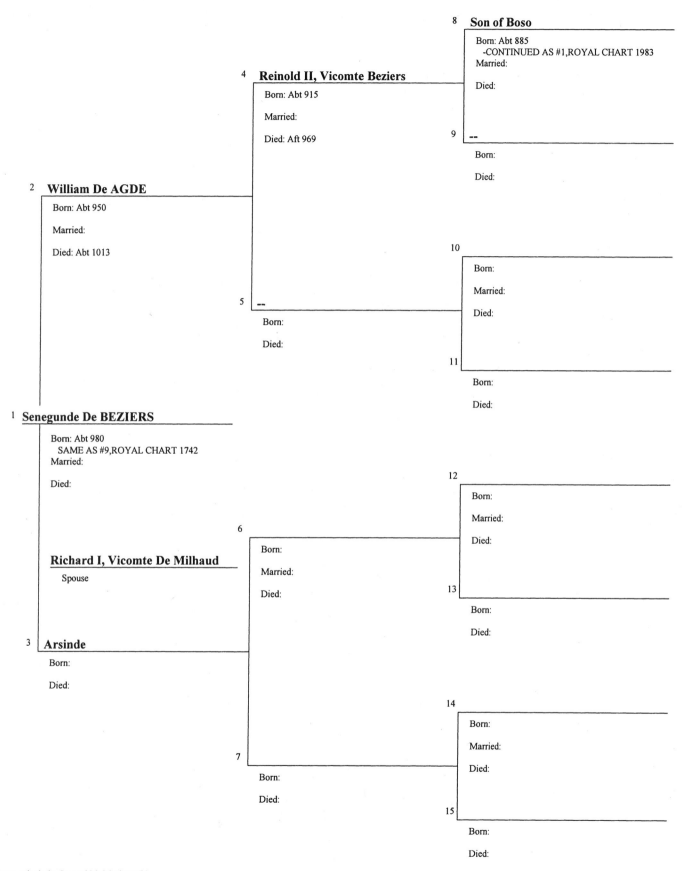

8   **Son of Boso**

Born: Abt 885
  -CONTINUED AS #1,ROYAL CHART 1983
Married:

Died:

4   **Reinold II, Vicomte Beziers**

Born: Abt 915

Married:

Died: Aft 969

9   **--**

Born:

Died:

2   **William De AGDE**

Born: Abt 950

Married:

Died: Abt 1013

10

Born:

Married:

Died:

5   **--**

Born:

Died:

11

Born:

Died:

1   **Senegunde De BEZIERS**

Born: Abt 980
  SAME AS #9,ROYAL CHART 1742
Married:

Died:

12

Born:

Married:

Died:

Richard I, Vicomte De Milhaud

Spouse

6

Born:

Married:

Died:

13

Born:

Died:

3   **Arsinde**

Born:

Died:

14

Born:

Married:

Died:

7

Born:

Died:

15

Born:

Died:

Sources include: Stuart 226; Moriarty 76.

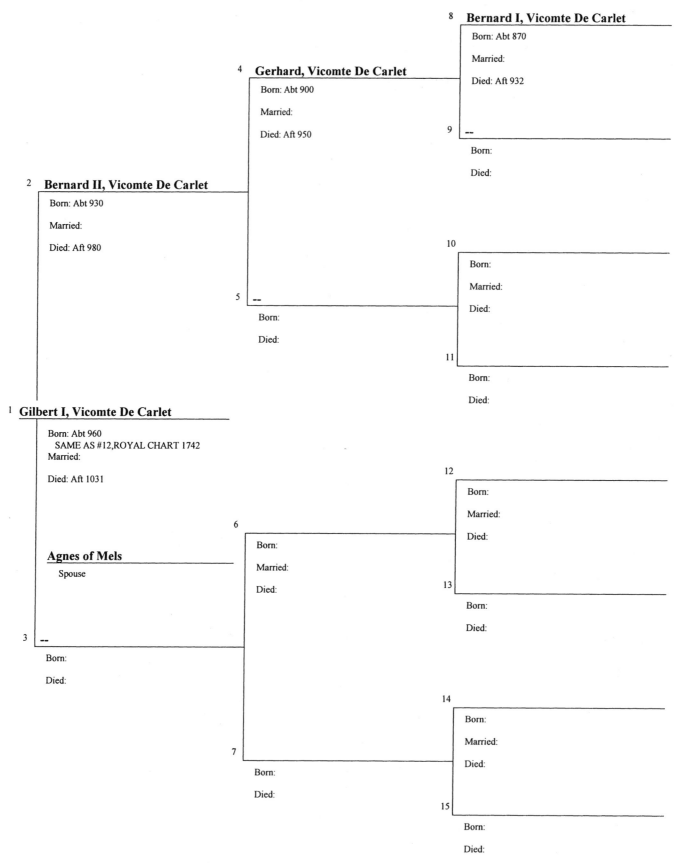

8 **Bernard I, Vicomte De Carlet**
Born: Abt 870
Married:
Died: Aft 932

4 **Gerhard, Vicomte De Carlet**
Born: Abt 900
Married:
Died: Aft 950

9 --
Born:
Died:

2 **Bernard II, Vicomte De Carlet**
Born: Abt 930
Married:
Died: Aft 980

10
Born:
Married:
Died:

5 --
Born:
Died:

11
Born:
Died:

1 **Gilbert I, Vicomte De Carlet**
Born: Abt 960
   SAME AS #12,ROYAL CHART 1742
Married:
Died: Aft 1031

12
Born:
Married:
Died:

6
Born:
Married:
Died:

13
Born:
Died:

Agnes of Mels
   Spouse

3 --
Born:
Died:

14
Born:
Married:
Died:

7
Born:
Died:

15
Born:
Died:

Sources include: Moriarty 75; Stuart 257.

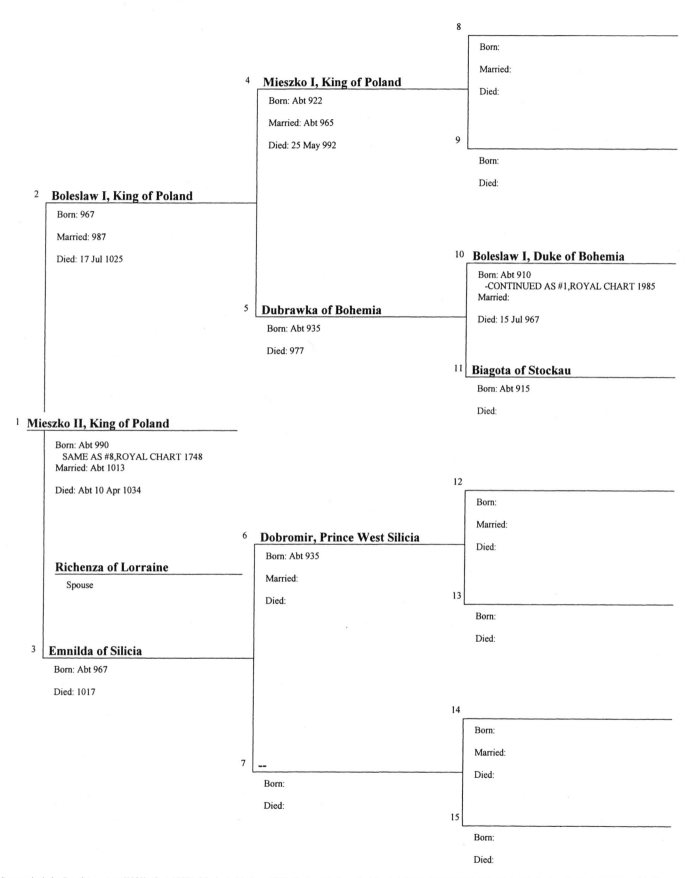

8

Born:

Married:

Died:

4 **Mieszko I, King of Poland**

Born: Abt 922

Married: Abt 965

Died: 25 May 992

9

Born:

Died:

2 **Boleslaw I, King of Poland**

Born: 967

Married: 987

Died: 17 Jul 1025

10 **Boleslaw I, Duke of Bohemia**

Born: Abt 910
  -CONTINUED AS #1,ROYAL CHART 1985
Married:

Died: 15 Jul 967

5 **Dubrawka of Bohemia**

Born: Abt 935

Died: 977

11 **Biagota of Stockau**

Born: Abt 915

Died:

1 **Mieszko II, King of Poland**

Born: Abt 990
  SAME AS #8,ROYAL CHART 1748
Married: Abt 1013

Died: Abt 10 Apr 1034

12

Born:

Married:

Died:

6 **Dobromir, Prince West Silicia**

Born: Abt 935

Married:

Died:

13

Born:

Died:

Richenza of Lorraine

Spouse

3 **Emnilda of Silicia**

Born: Abt 967

Died: 1017

14

Born:

Married:

Died:

7 **--**

Born:

Died:

15

Born:

Died:

Sources include: *Royal Ancestors* (1989), chart 11575; Moriarty 84; Stuart 378; Turton 57; *Ancestral Roots* 147-22; *TAG* 74:148, 151. Note: Moriarty ends the Polish line with #4 Mieszko (Miescyslaw), a Danish viking originally named Dag, who founded the Polish state about 960. Stuart and Turton make #4 the son of Ziemomysl (Ziemosmyl), and Stuart adds 3 additional generations to Piast, but Moriarty states that the traditional descent from Piast (a peasant) is false.

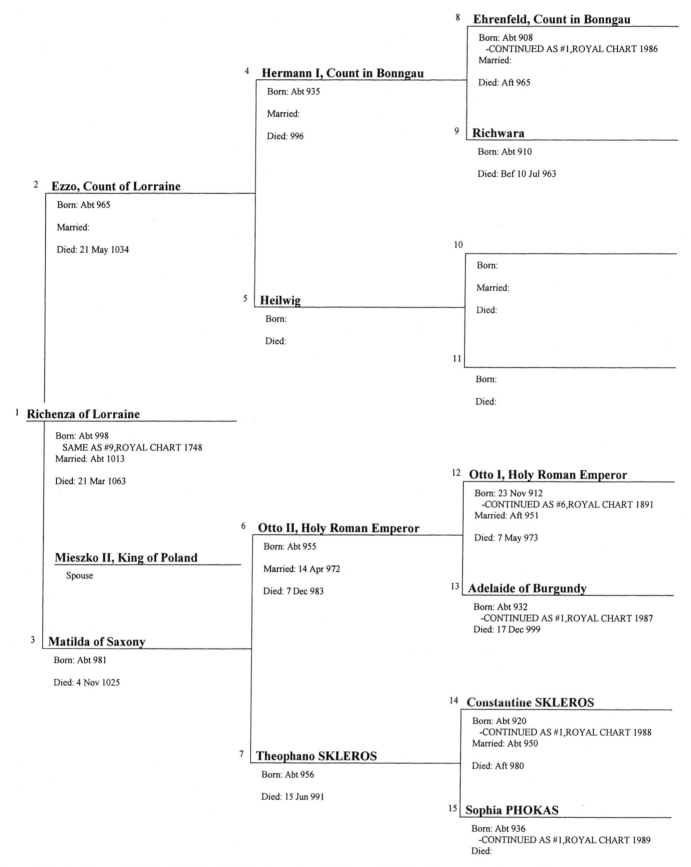

8 Ehrenfeld, Count in Bonngau

Born: Abt 908
  -CONTINUED AS #1, ROYAL CHART 1986
Married:

Died: Aft 965

4 Hermann I, Count in Bonngau

Born: Abt 935

Married:

Died: 996

9 Richwara

Born: Abt 910

Died: Bef 10 Jul 963

2 Ezzo, Count of Lorraine

Born: Abt 965

Married:

Died: 21 May 1034

10

Born:

Married:

Died:

5 Heilwig

Born:

Died:

11

Born:

Died:

1 Richenza of Lorraine

Born: Abt 998
  SAME AS #9, ROYAL CHART 1748
Married: Abt 1013

Died: 21 Mar 1063

12 Otto I, Holy Roman Emperor

Born: 23 Nov 912
  -CONTINUED AS #6, ROYAL CHART 1891
Married: Aft 951

Died: 7 May 973

6 Otto II, Holy Roman Emperor

Born: Abt 955

Married: 14 Apr 972

Died: 7 Dec 983

13 Adelaide of Burgundy

Born: Abt 932
  -CONTINUED AS #1, ROYAL CHART 1987
Died: 17 Dec 999

Mieszko II, King of Poland

Spouse

3 Matilda of Saxony

Born: Abt 981

Died: 4 Nov 1025

14 Constantine SKLEROS

Born: Abt 920
  -CONTINUED AS #1, ROYAL CHART 1988
Married: Abt 950

Died: Aft 980

7 Theophano SKLEROS

Born: Abt 956

Died: 15 Jun 991

15 Sophia PHOKAS

Born: Abt 936
  -CONTINUED AS #1, ROYAL CHART 1989
Died:

Sources include: *Royal Ancestors* (1989), chart 11575; Stuart 237, 208; *Ancestral Roots* 147; Moriarty 86-89. Note: The parentage and ancestry of #7 Theophano is disputed (see *The Genealogist* 2:6-7; Wagner, *Pedigree and Progress*, pedigree 43, p 202). However, Moriarty (88-89) discusses the problem and the evidence at length, and his conclusion is accepted as shown above.

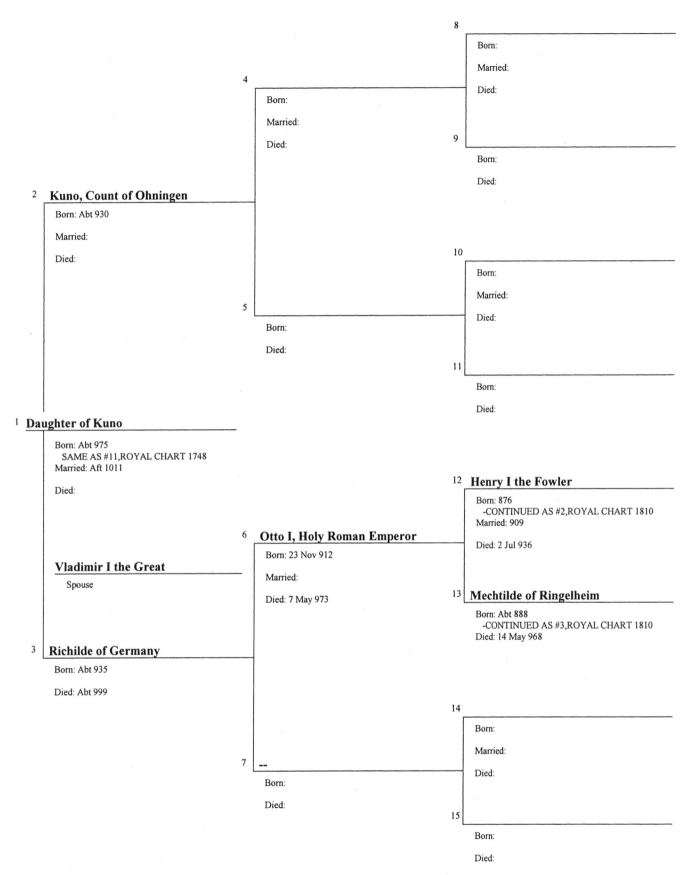

8

Born:

Married:

Died:

4

Born:

Married:

Died:

9

Born:

Died:

2 Kuno, Count of Ohningen

Born: Abt 930

Married:

Died:

10

Born:

Married:

Died:

5

Born:

Died:

11

Born:

Died:

1 Daughter of Kuno

Born: Abt 975
    SAME AS #11, ROYAL CHART 1748
Married: Aft 1011

Died:

12 Henry I the Fowler

Born: 876
    -CONTINUED AS #2, ROYAL CHART 1810
Married: 909

Died: 2 Jul 936

6 Otto I, Holy Roman Emperor

Born: 23 Nov 912

Married:

Died: 7 May 973

13 Mechtilde of Ringelheim

Born: Abt 888
    -CONTINUED AS #3, ROYAL CHART 1810
Died: 14 May 968

Vladimir I the Great

Spouse

3 Richilde of Germany

Born: Abt 935

Died: Abt 999

14

Born:

Married:

Died:

7 --

Born:

Died:

15

Born:

Died:

Sources include: *Royal Ancestors* (1989), chart 11576; Stuart 361-33, 321; Moriarty 53; *Ancestral Roots* 241-4; *TAG* 28:91-95.

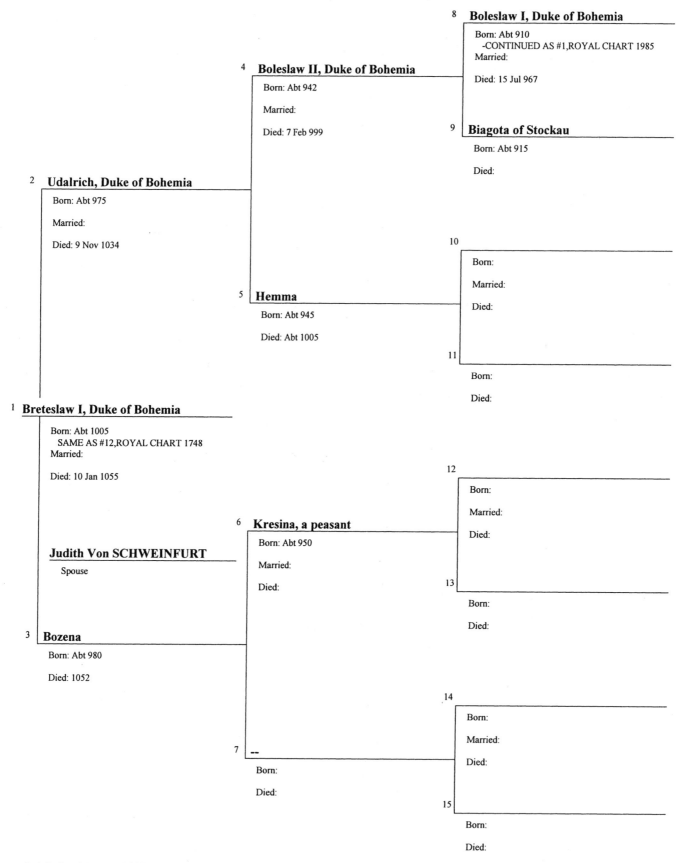

8 Boleslaw I, Duke of Bohemia

Born: Abt 910
   -CONTINUED AS #1,ROYAL CHART 1985
Married:

Died: 15 Jul 967

4 Boleslaw II, Duke of Bohemia

Born: Abt 942

Married:

Died: 7 Feb 999

9 Biagota of Stockau

Born: Abt 915

Died:

2 Udalrich, Duke of Bohemia

Born: Abt 975

Married:

Died: 9 Nov 1034

10

Born:

Married:

Died:

5 Hemma

Born: Abt 945

Died: Abt 1005

11

Born:

Died:

1 Breteslaw I, Duke of Bohemia

Born: Abt 1005
   SAME AS #12,ROYAL CHART 1748
Married:

Died: 10 Jan 1055

Judith Von SCHWEINFURT

Spouse

12

Born:

Married:

Died:

6 Kresina, a peasant

Born: Abt 950

Married:

Died:

13

Born:

Died:

3 Bozena

Born: Abt 980

Died: 1052

14

Born:

Married:

Died:

7 --

Born:

Died:

15

Born:

Died:

Sources include: *Royal Ancestors* (1989), chart 11915; Stuart 362; Moriarty 85.

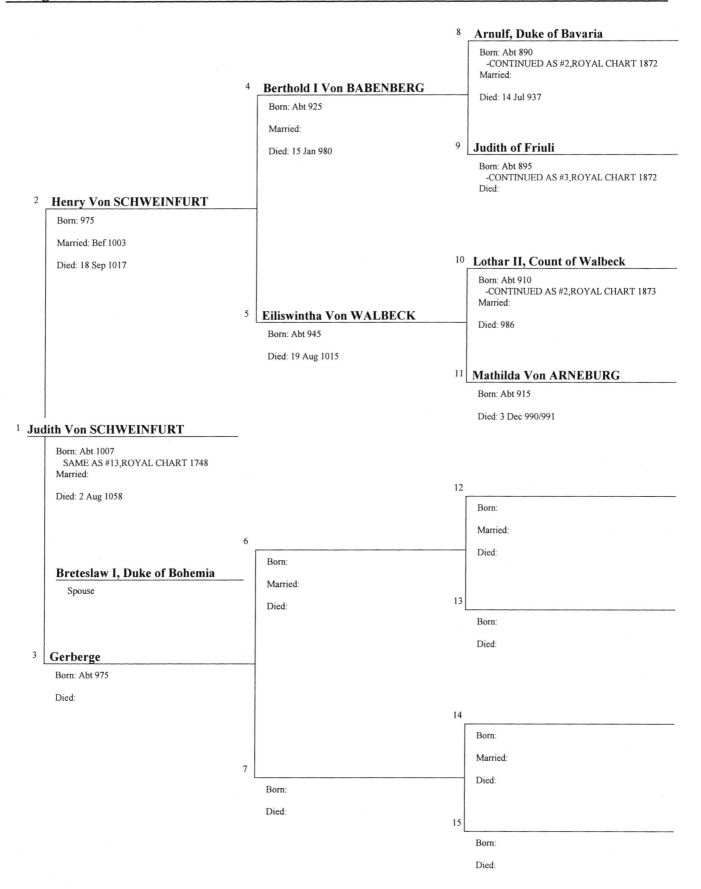

8 **Arnulf, Duke of Bavaria**

Born: Abt 890
-CONTINUED AS #2,ROYAL CHART 1872
Married:

Died: 14 Jul 937

4 **Berthold I Von BABENBERG**

Born: Abt 925

Married:

Died: 15 Jan 980

9 **Judith of Friuli**

Born: Abt 895
-CONTINUED AS #3,ROYAL CHART 1872
Died:

2 **Henry Von SCHWEINFURT**

Born: 975

Married: Bef 1003

Died: 18 Sep 1017

10 **Lothar II, Count of Walbeck**

Born: Abt 910
-CONTINUED AS #2,ROYAL CHART 1873
Married:

Died: 986

5 **Eiliswintha Von WALBECK**

Born: Abt 945

Died: 19 Aug 1015

11 **Mathilda Von ARNEBURG**

Born: Abt 915

Died: 3 Dec 990/991

1 **Judith Von SCHWEINFURT**

Born: Abt 1007
SAME AS #13,ROYAL CHART 1748
Married:

Died: 2 Aug 1058

12

Born:

Married:

Died:

Breteslaw I, Duke of Bohemia

Spouse

6

Born:

Married:

Died:

13

Born:

Died:

3 **Gerberge**

Born: Abt 975

Died:

14

Born:

Married:

Died:

7

Born:

Died:

15

Born:

Died:

Sources include: *Royal Ancestors* (1989), chart 11915; Stuart 362-34, 270; Moriarty 85, 57.

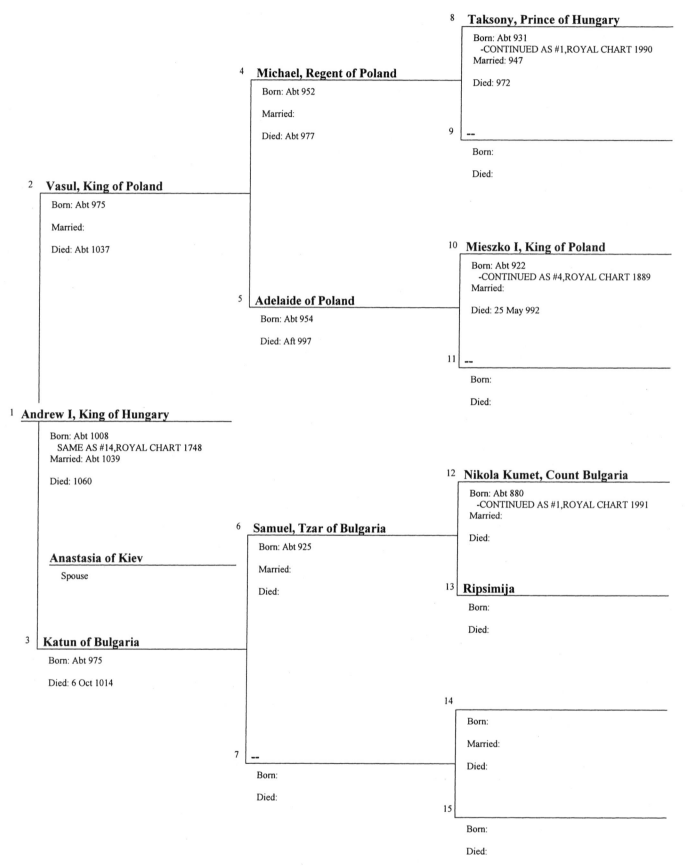

8 Taksony, Prince of Hungary

Born: Abt 931
-CONTINUED AS #1,ROYAL CHART 1990
Married: 947

Died: 972

4 Michael, Regent of Poland

Born: Abt 952

Married:

Died: Abt 977

9 --

Born:

Died:

2 Vasul, King of Poland

Born: Abt 975

Married:

Died: Abt 1037

10 Mieszko I, King of Poland

Born: Abt 922
-CONTINUED AS #4,ROYAL CHART 1889
Married:

Died: 25 May 992

5 Adelaide of Poland

Born: Abt 954

Died: Aft 997

11 --

Born:

Died:

1 Andrew I, King of Hungary

Born: Abt 1008
SAME AS #14,ROYAL CHART 1748
Married: Abt 1039

Died: 1060

Anastasia of Kiev

Spouse

12 Nikola Kumet, Count Bulgaria

Born: Abt 880
-CONTINUED AS #1,ROYAL CHART 1991
Married:

Died:

6 Samuel, Tzar of Bulgaria

Born: Abt 925

Married:

Died:

13 Ripsimija

Born:

Died:

3 Katun of Bulgaria

Born: Abt 975

Died: 6 Oct 1014

14

Born:

Married:

Died:

7 --

Born:

Died:

15

Born:

Died:

Sources include: *Royal Ancestors* (1989), chart 11577; Stuart 225, 51, 378, 309; Moriarty 86, 32; *Ancestral Roots* 243-244. Note: The identification and ancestry of #3 Katun is a tentative one.

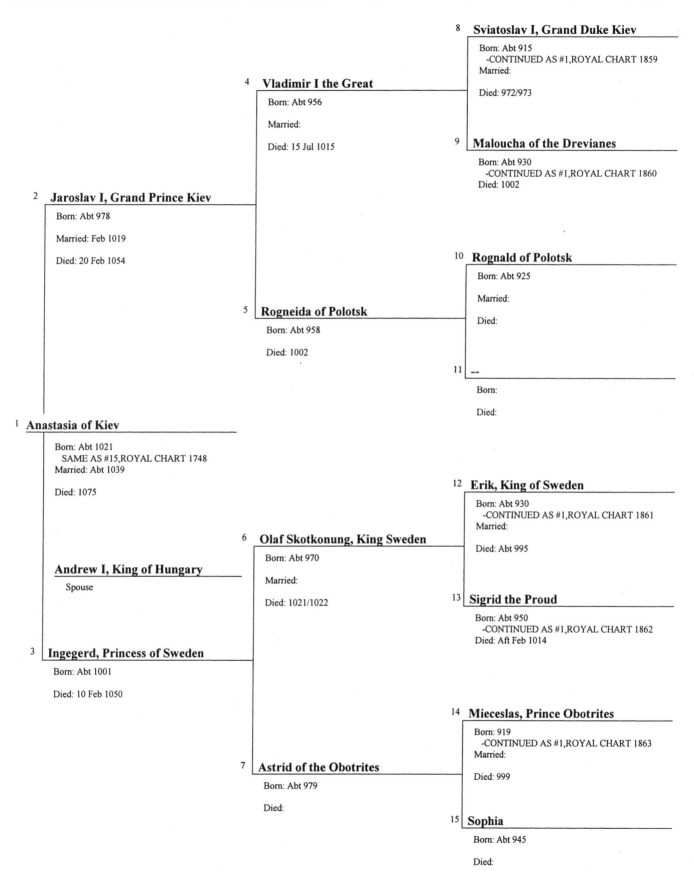

8 Sviatoslav I, Grand Duke Kiev

Born: Abt 915
-CONTINUED AS #1,ROYAL CHART 1859
Married:

Died: 972/973

4 Vladimir I the Great

Born: Abt 956

Married:

Died: 15 Jul 1015

9 Maloucha of the Drevianes

Born: Abt 930
-CONTINUED AS #1,ROYAL CHART 1860
Died: 1002

2 Jaroslav I, Grand Prince Kiev

Born: Abt 978

Married: Feb 1019

Died: 20 Feb 1054

10 Rognald of Polotsk

Born: Abt 925

Married:

Died:

5 Rogneida of Polotsk

Born: Abt 958

Died: 1002

11 __

Born:

Died:

1 Anastasia of Kiev

Born: Abt 1021
SAME AS #15,ROYAL CHART 1748
Married: Abt 1039

Died: 1075

Andrew I, King of Hungary

Spouse

12 Erik, King of Sweden

Born: Abt 930
-CONTINUED AS #1,ROYAL CHART 1861
Married:

Died: Abt 995

6 Olaf Skotkonung, King Sweden

Born: Abt 970

Married:

Died: 1021/1022

13 Sigrid the Proud

Born: Abt 950
-CONTINUED AS #1,ROYAL CHART 1862
Died: Aft Feb 1014

3 Ingegerd, Princess of Sweden

Born: Abt 1001

Died: 10 Feb 1050

14 Mieceslas, Prince Obotrites

Born: 919
-CONTINUED AS #1,ROYAL CHART 1863
Married:

Died: 999

7 Astrid of the Obotrites

Born: Abt 979

Died:

15 Sophia

Born: Abt 945

Died:

Sources include: *Royal Ancestors* (1989), chart 11577; Stuart 225-34, 134, 240; Moriarty 53; *Ancestral Roots* 244-6, 241.

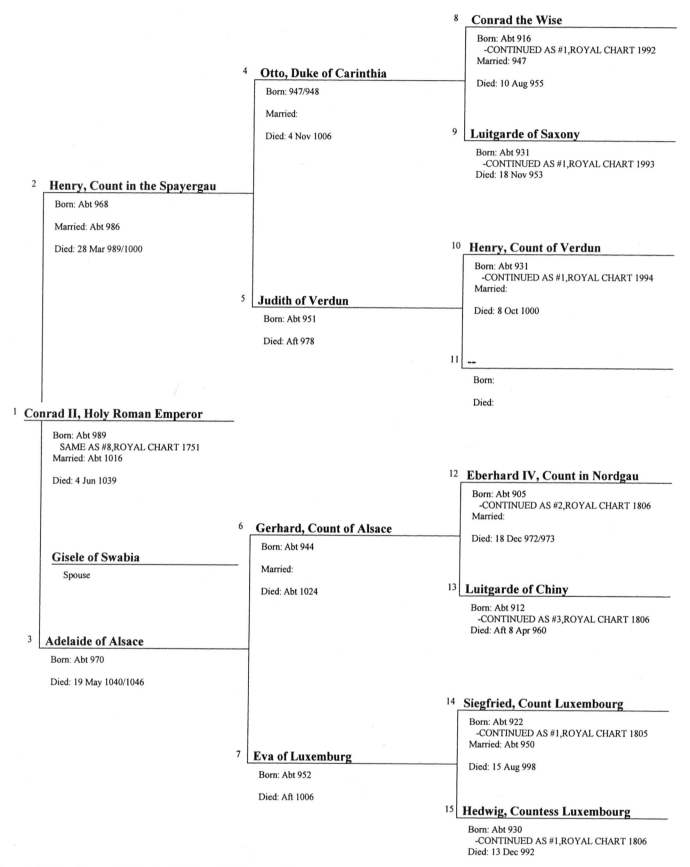

8 Conrad the Wise
Born: Abt 916
  -CONTINUED AS #1,ROYAL CHART 1992
Married: 947

Died: 10 Aug 955

4 Otto, Duke of Carinthia
Born: 947/948

Married:

Died: 4 Nov 1006

9 Luitgarde of Saxony
Born: Abt 931
  -CONTINUED AS #1,ROYAL CHART 1993
Died: 18 Nov 953

2 Henry, Count in the Spayergau
Born: Abt 968

Married: Abt 986

Died: 28 Mar 989/1000

10 Henry, Count of Verdun
Born: Abt 931
  -CONTINUED AS #1,ROYAL CHART 1994
Married:

Died: 8 Oct 1000

5 Judith of Verdun
Born: Abt 951

Died: Aft 978

11 --
Born:

Died:

1 Conrad II, Holy Roman Emperor
Born: Abt 989
  SAME AS #8,ROYAL CHART 1751
Married: Abt 1016

Died: 4 Jun 1039

12 Eberhard IV, Count in Nordgau
Born: Abt 905
  -CONTINUED AS #2,ROYAL CHART 1806
Married:

Died: 18 Dec 972/973

6 Gerhard, Count of Alsace
Born: Abt 944

Married:

Died: Abt 1024

13 Luitgarde of Chiny
Born: Abt 912
  -CONTINUED AS #3,ROYAL CHART 1806
Died: Aft 8 Apr 960

Gisele of Swabia
Spouse

3 Adelaide of Alsace
Born: Abt 970

Died: 19 May 1040/1046

14 Siegfried, Count Luxembourg
Born: Abt 922
  -CONTINUED AS #1,ROYAL CHART 1805
Married: Abt 950

Died: 15 Aug 998

7 Eva of Luxemburg
Born: Abt 952

Died: Aft 1006

15 Hedwig, Countess Luxembourg
Born: Abt 930
  -CONTINUED AS #1,ROYAL CHART 1806
Died: 13 Dec 992

Sources include: *Royal Ancestors* (1989), chart 11565; Stuart 359, 202; *Ancestral Roots* 45; Moriarty 92; Faris preliminary Charlemagne manuscript (June 1995), pp. 140-141. Notes: The ancestry of #5 Judith is disputed. Faris shows her as daughter of Henry of Bavaria (Heinrich Von Bayern), son of Arnulf, Duke of Bavaria (see chart 1872, #2). The parentage shown for #3 Adelaide and for #6 Gerhard is not certain. The maternal ancestry shown for #3 through Eva and Hedwig may be chronologically untenable. See note chart 1806.

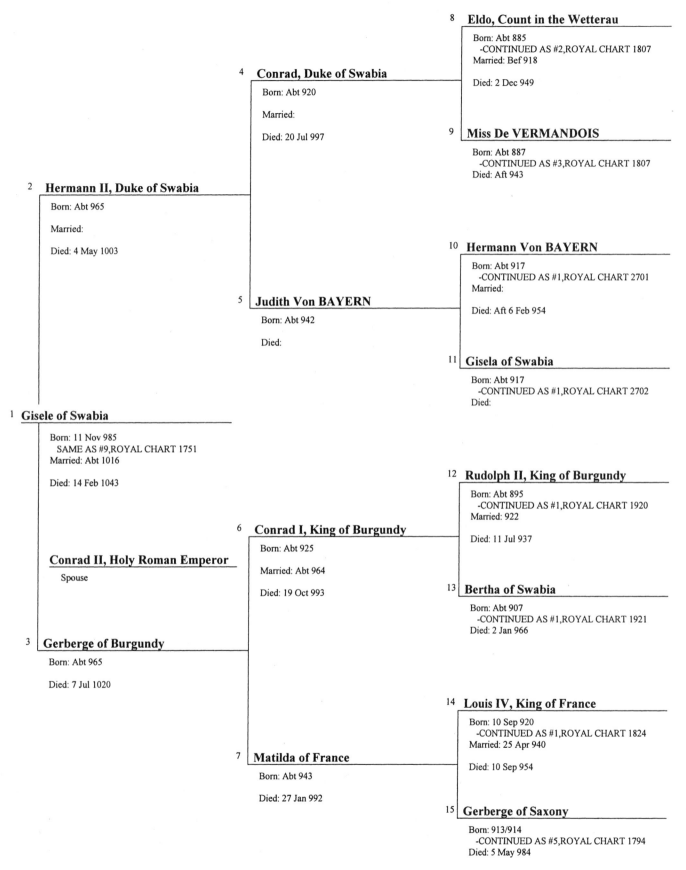

2 Hermann II, Duke of Swabia
Born: Abt 965
Married:
Died: 4 May 1003

4 Conrad, Duke of Swabia
Born: Abt 920
Married:
Died: 20 Jul 997

8 Eldo, Count in the Wetterau
Born: Abt 885
-CONTINUED AS #2,ROYAL CHART 1807
Married: Bef 918
Died: 2 Dec 949

9 Miss De VERMANDOIS
Born: Abt 887
-CONTINUED AS #3,ROYAL CHART 1807
Died: Aft 943

5 Judith Von BAYERN
Born: Abt 942
Died:

10 Hermann Von BAYERN
Born: Abt 917
-CONTINUED AS #1,ROYAL CHART 2701
Married:
Died: Aft 6 Feb 954

11 Gisela of Swabia
Born: Abt 917
-CONTINUED AS #1,ROYAL CHART 2702
Died:

1 Gisele of Swabia
Born: 11 Nov 985
SAME AS #9,ROYAL CHART 1751
Married: Abt 1016
Died: 14 Feb 1043

Conrad II, Holy Roman Emperor
Spouse

3 Gerberge of Burgundy
Born: Abt 965
Died: 7 Jul 1020

6 Conrad I, King of Burgundy
Born: Abt 925
Married: Abt 964
Died: 19 Oct 993

12 Rudolph II, King of Burgundy
Born: Abt 895
-CONTINUED AS #1,ROYAL CHART 1920
Married: 922
Died: 11 Jul 937

13 Bertha of Swabia
Born: Abt 907
-CONTINUED AS #1,ROYAL CHART 1921
Died: 2 Jan 966

7 Matilda of France
Born: Abt 943
Died: 27 Jan 992

14 Louis IV, King of France
Born: 10 Sep 920
-CONTINUED AS #1,ROYAL CHART 1824
Married: 25 Apr 940
Died: 10 Sep 954

15 Gerberge of Saxony
Born: 913/914
-CONTINUED AS #5,ROYAL CHART 1794
Died: 5 May 984

Sources include: *Royal Ancestors* (1989), chart 11566; Stuart 199; *Ancestral Roots* 157; Moriarty 94; Faris preliminary Charlemagne manuscript (June 1995), pp. 283-284. Note: #1 Gisele was born 11-13 Nov about 985-990.

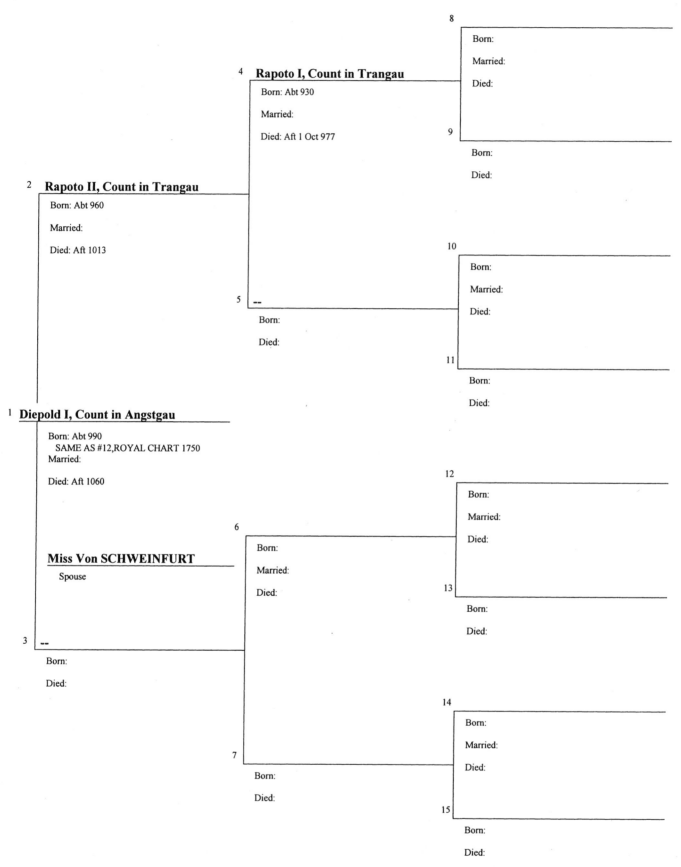

8

Born:

Married:

Died:

4 **Rapoto I, Count in Trangau**

Born: Abt 930

Married:

Died: Aft 1 Oct 977

9

Born:

Died:

2 **Rapoto II, Count in Trangau**

Born: Abt 960

Married:

Died: Aft 1013

10

Born:

Married:

Died:

5 --

Born:

Died:

11

Born:

Died:

1 **Diepold I, Count in Angstgau**

Born: Abt 990
SAME AS #12,ROYAL CHART 1750
Married:

Died: Aft 1060

12

Born:

Married:

Died:

6

Born:

Married:

Died:

13

Born:

Died:

Miss Von SCHWEINFURT

Spouse

3 --

Born:

Died:

14

Born:

Married:

Died:

7

Born:

Died:

15

Born:

Died:

Sources include: *Royal Ancestors* (1989), charts 11840, 11798; Moriarty 123; Stuart 128.

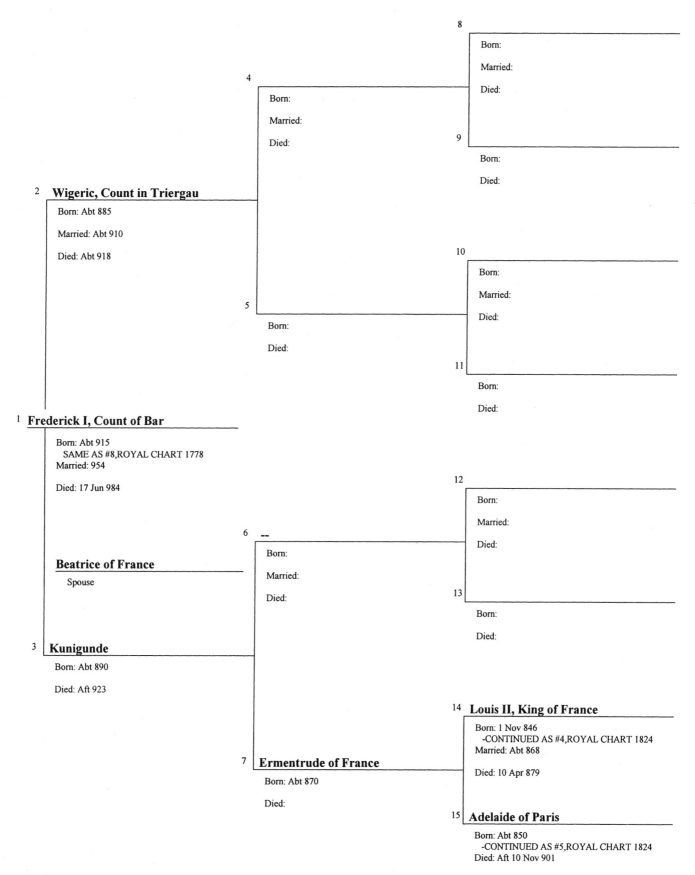

8
Born:
Married:
Died:

4
Born:
Married:
Died:

9
Born:
Died:

2 Wigeric, Count in Triergau
Born: Abt 885
Married: Abt 910
Died: Abt 918

10
Born:
Married:
Died:

5
Born:
Died:

11
Born:
Died:

1 Frederick I, Count of Bar
Born: Abt 915
  SAME AS #8,ROYAL CHART 1778
Married: 954
Died: 17 Jun 984

12
Born:
Married:
Died:

6 --
Born:
Married:
Died:

13
Born:
Died:

Beatrice of France
  Spouse

3 Kunigunde
Born: Abt 890
Died: Aft 923

14 Louis II, King of France
Born: 1 Nov 846
  -CONTINUED AS #4,ROYAL CHART 1824
Married: Abt 868
Died: 10 Apr 879

7 Ermentrude of France
Born: Abt 870
Died:

15 Adelaide of Paris
Born: Abt 850
  -CONTINUED AS #5,ROYAL CHART 1824
Died: Aft 10 Nov 901

Sources include: *Royal Ancestors* (1989), chart 11775; Stuart 319; Moriarty 160, 126. Note: #1 Frederick died 18 May 978 or 17 Jun 984.

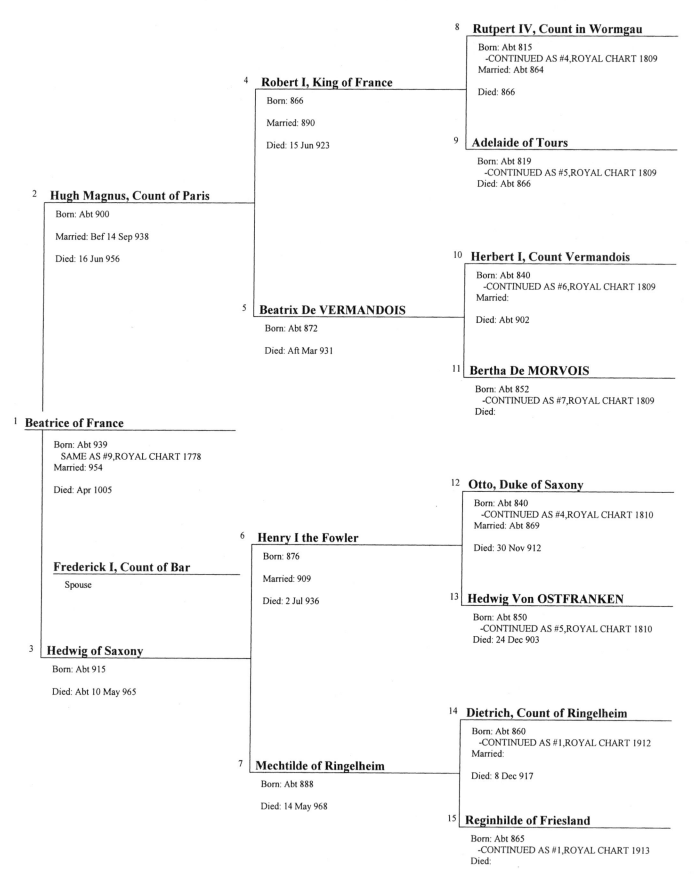

8   **Rutpert IV, Count in Wormgau**

Born: Abt 815
  -CONTINUED AS #4,ROYAL CHART 1809
Married: Abt 864

Died: 866

4   **Robert I, King of France**

Born: 866

Married: 890

Died: 15 Jun 923

9   **Adelaide of Tours**

Born: Abt 819
  -CONTINUED AS #5,ROYAL CHART 1809
Died: Abt 866

2   **Hugh Magnus, Count of Paris**

Born: Abt 900

Married: Bef 14 Sep 938

Died: 16 Jun 956

10   **Herbert I, Count Vermandois**

Born: Abt 840
  -CONTINUED AS #6,ROYAL CHART 1809
Married:

Died: Abt 902

5   **Beatrix De VERMANDOIS**

Born: Abt 872

Died: Aft Mar 931

11   **Bertha De MORVOIS**

Born: Abt 852
  -CONTINUED AS #7,ROYAL CHART 1809
Died:

1   **Beatrice of France**

Born: Abt 939
  SAME AS #9,ROYAL CHART 1778
Married: 954

Died: Apr 1005

12   **Otto, Duke of Saxony**

Born: Abt 840
  -CONTINUED AS #4,ROYAL CHART 1810
Married: Abt 869

Died: 30 Nov 912

6   **Henry I the Fowler**

Born: 876

Married: 909

Died: 2 Jul 936

Frederick I, Count of Bar

  Spouse

13   **Hedwig Von OSTFRANKEN**

Born: Abt 850
  -CONTINUED AS #5,ROYAL CHART 1810
Died: 24 Dec 903

3   **Hedwig of Saxony**

Born: Abt 915

Died: Abt 10 May 965

14   **Dietrich, Count of Ringelheim**

Born: Abt 860
  -CONTINUED AS #1,ROYAL CHART 1912
Married:

Died: 8 Dec 917

7   **Mechtilde of Ringelheim**

Born: Abt 888

Died: 14 May 968

15   **Reginhilde of Friesland**

Born: Abt 865
  -CONTINUED AS #1,ROYAL CHART 1913
Died:

Sources include: *Royal Ancestors* (1989), chart 11776; Stuart 319-36, 134; Moriarty 160, 24.

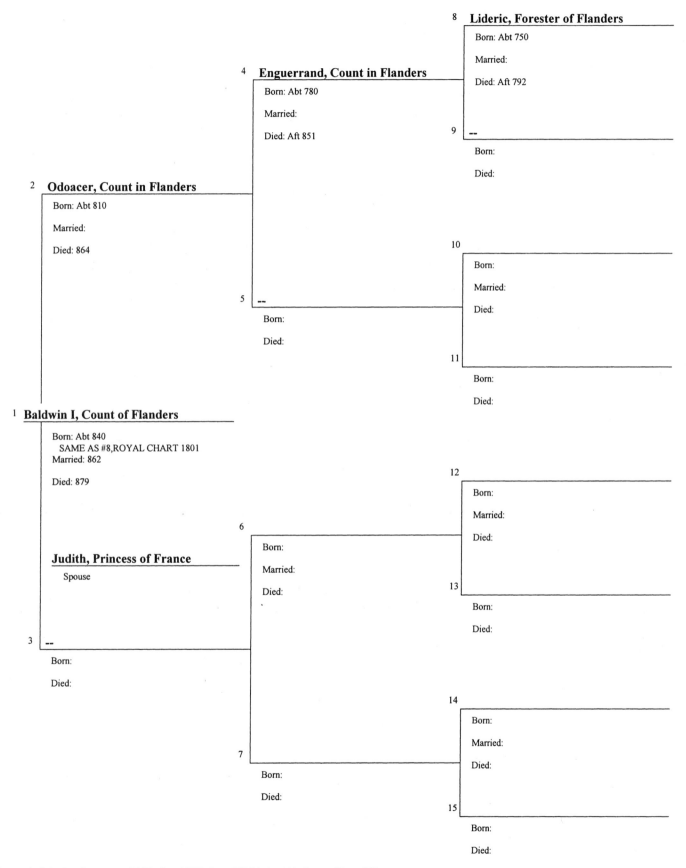

8 Lideric, Forester of Flanders

Born: Abt 750

Married:

Died: Aft 792

4 Enguerrand, Count in Flanders

Born: Abt 780

Married:

Died: Aft 851

9 --

Born:

Died:

2 Odoacer, Count in Flanders

Born: Abt 810

Married:

Died: 864

10

Born:

Married:

Died:

5 --

Born:

Died:

11

Born:

Died:

1 Baldwin I, Count of Flanders

Born: Abt 840
  SAME AS #8,ROYAL CHART 1801
Married: 862

Died: 879

12

Born:

Married:

Died:

6

Born:

Married:

Died:

13

Born:

Died:

Judith, Princess of France

Spouse

3 --

Born:

Died:

14

Born:

Married:

Died:

7

Born:

Died:

15

Born:

Died:

Sources include: *Royal Ancestors* (1989), chart 11505; Stuart 235; Moriarty 14; *Ancestral Roots* 162.

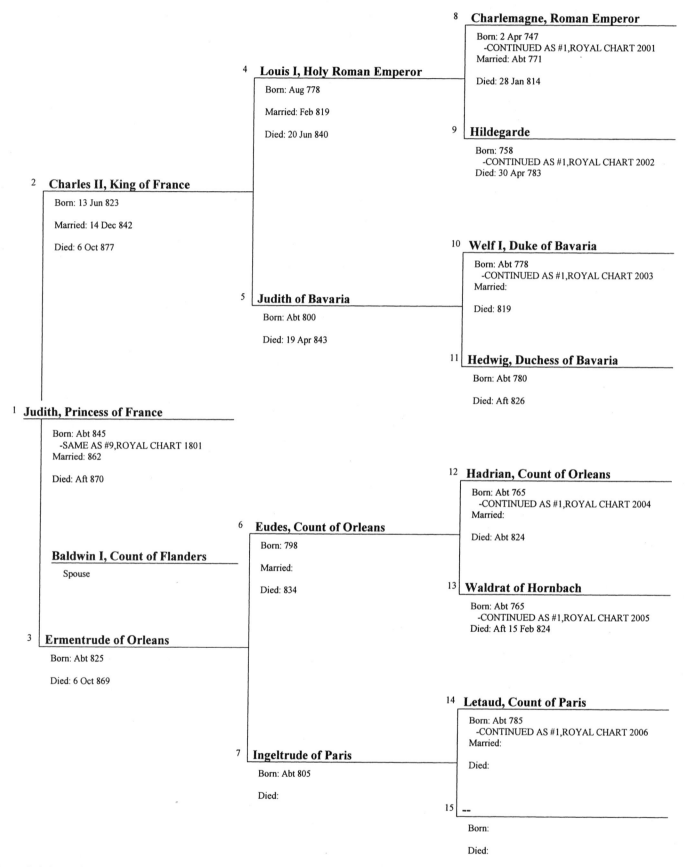

8 Charlemagne, Roman Emperor

Born: 2 Apr 747
-CONTINUED AS #1,ROYAL CHART 2001
Married: Abt 771

Died: 28 Jan 814

4 Louis I, Holy Roman Emperor

Born: Aug 778

Married: Feb 819

Died: 20 Jun 840

9 Hildegarde

Born: 758
-CONTINUED AS #1,ROYAL CHART 2002
Died: 30 Apr 783

2 Charles II, King of France

Born: 13 Jun 823

Married: 14 Dec 842

Died: 6 Oct 877

10 Welf I, Duke of Bavaria

Born: Abt 778
-CONTINUED AS #1,ROYAL CHART 2003
Married:

Died: 819

5 Judith of Bavaria

Born: Abt 800

Died: 19 Apr 843

11 Hedwig, Duchess of Bavaria

Born: Abt 780

Died: Aft 826

1 Judith, Princess of France

Born: Abt 845
-SAME AS #9,ROYAL CHART 1801
Married: 862

Died: Aft 870

12 Hadrian, Count of Orleans

Born: Abt 765
-CONTINUED AS #1,ROYAL CHART 2004
Married:

Died: Abt 824

6 Eudes, Count of Orleans

Born: 798

Married:

Died: 834

Baldwin I, Count of Flanders

Spouse

13 Waldrat of Hornbach

Born: Abt 765
-CONTINUED AS #1,ROYAL CHART 2005
Died: Aft 15 Feb 824

3 Ermentrude of Orleans

Born: Abt 825

Died: 6 Oct 869

14 Letaud, Count of Paris

Born: Abt 785
-CONTINUED AS #1,ROYAL CHART 2006
Married:

Died:

7 Ingeltrude of Paris

Born: Abt 805

Died:

15 --

Born:

Died:

Sources include: *Royal Ancestors* 11505, 11604; *Ancestral Roots* 162, 148, 140; Stuart 250, 171, 336; Moriarty 14, 16-17, 9, 23, 233.

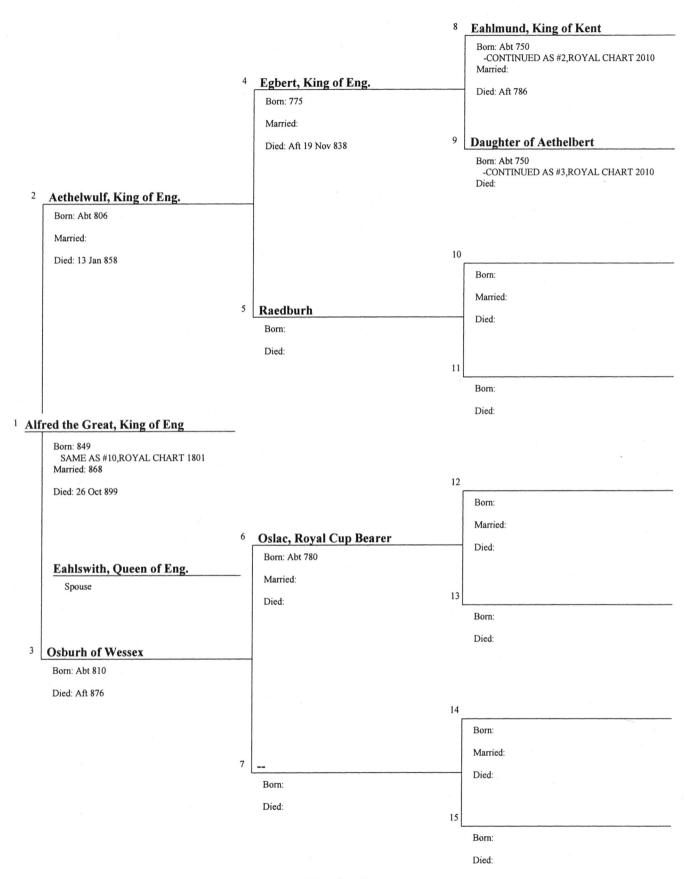

8 Eahlmund, King of Kent

Born: Abt 750
  -CONTINUED AS #2,ROYAL CHART 2010
Married:

Died: Aft 786

4 Egbert, King of Eng.

Born: 775

Married:

Died: Aft 19 Nov 838

9 Daughter of Aethelbert

Born: Abt 750
  -CONTINUED AS #3,ROYAL CHART 2010
Died:

2 Aethelwulf, King of Eng.

Born: Abt 806

Married:

Died: 13 Jan 858

10

Born:

Married:

Died:

5 Raedburh

Born:

Died:

11

Born:

Died:

1 Alfred the Great, King of Eng

Born: 849
  SAME AS #10,ROYAL CHART 1801
Married: 868

Died: 26 Oct 899

12

Born:

Married:

Died:

6 Oslac, Royal Cup Bearer

Born: Abt 780

Married:

Died:

13

Born:

Died:

Eahlswith, Queen of Eng.

Spouse

3 Osburh of Wessex

Born: Abt 810

Died: Aft 876

14

Born:

Married:

Died:

7 --

Born:

Died:

15

Born:

Died:

Sources include: *Royal Ancestors* (1989), chart 11605; *Ancestral Roots* 1; Stuart 233; Moriarty 16.

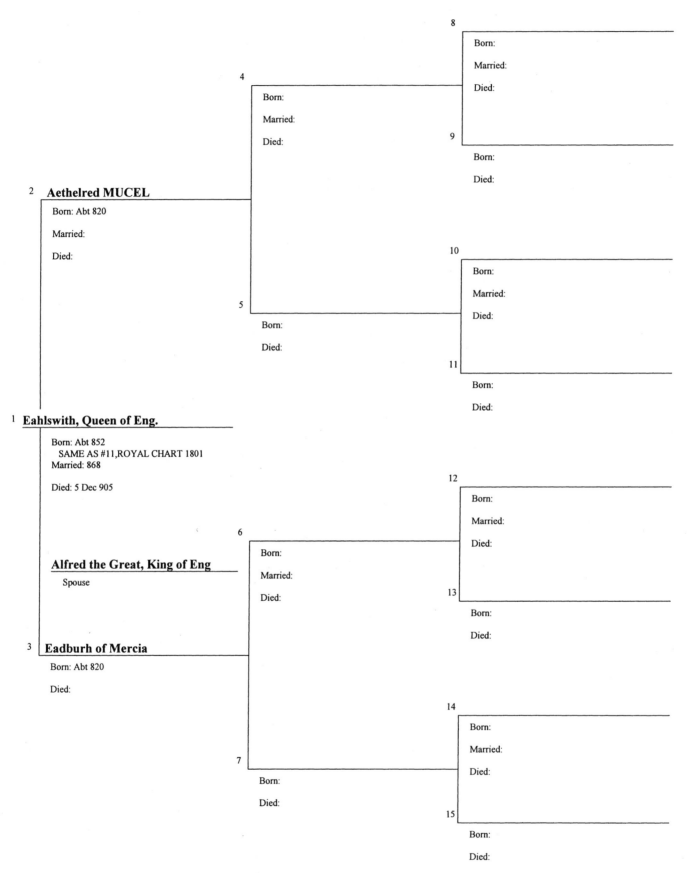

8

Born:

Married:

Died:

4

Born:

Married:

Died:

9

Born:

Died:

2   **Aethelred MUCEL**

Born: Abt 820

Married:

Died:

10

Born:

Married:

Died:

5

Born:

Died:

11

Born:

Died:

1   **Eahlswith, Queen of Eng.**

Born: Abt 852
   SAME AS #11,ROYAL CHART 1801
Married: 868

Died: 5 Dec 905

12

Born:

Married:

Died:

6

Born:

Married:

Died:

13

Born:

Died:

Alfred the Great, King of Eng

Spouse

3   **Eadburh of Mercia**

Born: Abt 820

Died:

14

Born:

Married:

Died:

7

Born:

Died:

15

Born:

Died:

Sources include: *Royal Ancestors* (1989), chart 11505; *Ancestral Roots* 1; Stuart 233-39, 238, 367-41; Moriarty 16, 254. Note: Moriarty states that #3 Eadburh was of the royal Mercian line. Stuart states that she descends from Wigmund, son of Witgraff, King of Mercia.

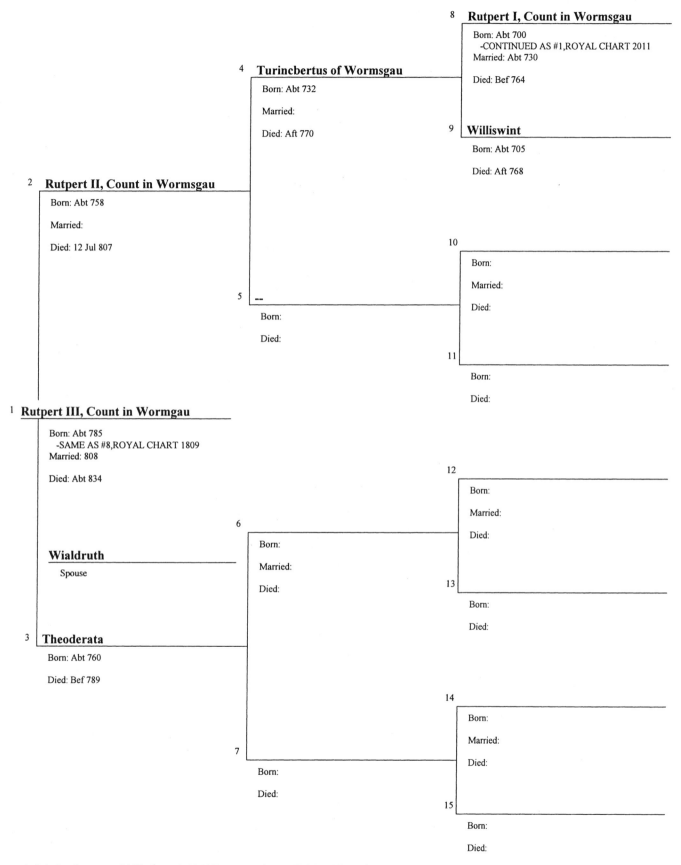

8 **Rutpert I, Count in Wormsgau**

Born: Abt 700
  -CONTINUED AS #1,ROYAL CHART 2011
Married: Abt 730

Died: Bef 764

4 **Turincbertus of Wormsgau**

Born: Abt 732

Married:

Died: Aft 770

9 **Williswint**

Born: Abt 705

Died: Aft 768

2 **Rutpert II, Count in Wormsgau**

Born: Abt 758

Married:

Died: 12 Jul 807

10

Born:

Married:

Died:

5 --

Born:

Died:

11

Born:

Died:

1 **Rutpert III, Count in Wormgau**

Born: Abt 785
  -SAME AS #8,ROYAL CHART 1809
Married: 808

Died: Abt 834

12

Born:

Married:

Died:

6

Born:

Married:

Died:

13

Born:

Died:

Wialdruth

Spouse

3 **Theoderata**

Born: Abt 760

Died: Bef 789

14

Born:

Married:

Died:

7

Born:

Died:

15

Born:

Died:

Sources include: *Royal Ancestors* (1989), charts 11506, 11615; *Ancestral Roots* 48; Stuart 169; Moriarty 211, 215-216, 226-227, 281-282. Note: #9 Williswint was daughter of a Count Adelhelm.

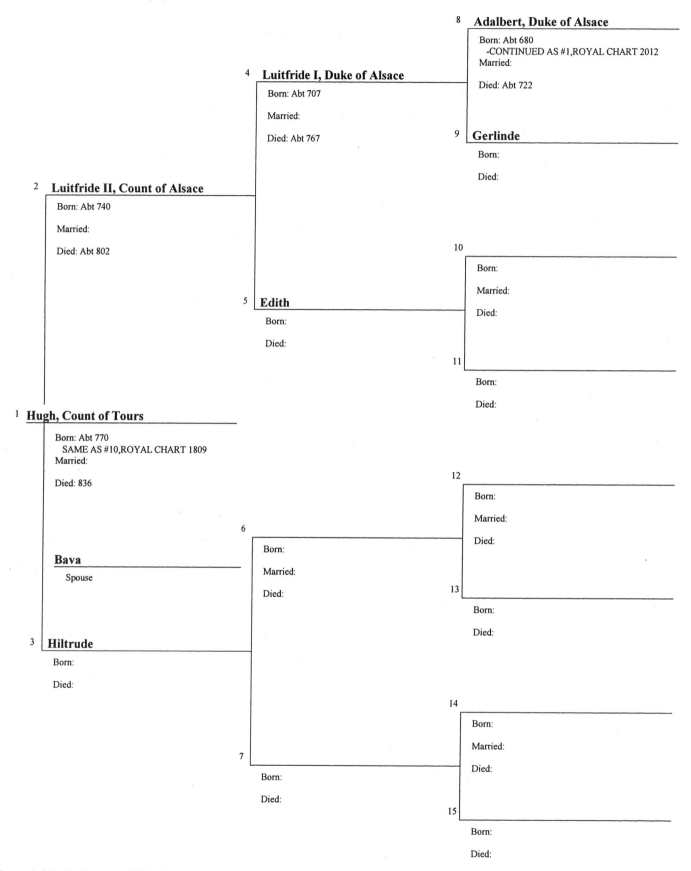

8 Adalbert, Duke of Alsace

Born: Abt 680
  -CONTINUED AS #1,ROYAL CHART 2012
Married:

Died: Abt 722

4 Luitfride I, Duke of Alsace

Born: Abt 707

Married:

Died: Abt 767

9 Gerlinde

Born:

Died:

2 Luitfride II, Count of Alsace

Born: Abt 740

Married:

Died: Abt 802

10

Born:

Married:

Died:

5 Edith

Born:

Died:

11

Born:

Died:

1 Hugh, Count of Tours

Born: Abt 770
  SAME AS #10,ROYAL CHART 1809
Married:

Died: 836

12

Born:

Married:

Died:

6

Born:

Married:

Died:

13

Born:

Died:

Bava

Spouse

3 Hiltrude

Born:

Died:

14

Born:

Married:

Died:

7

Born:

Died:

15

Born:

Died:

Sources include: *Royal Ancestors* (1989), chart 11621; *Ancestral Roots* 181; Stuart 224; Moriarty 21 note (discussion of #1 ancestry).

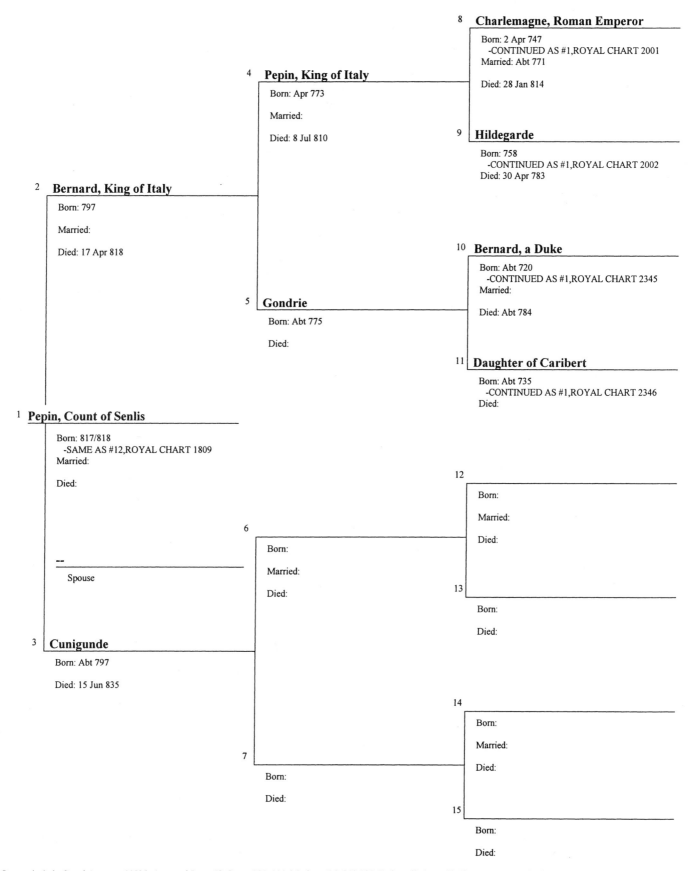

8 **Charlemagne, Roman Emperor**

Born: 2 Apr 747
-CONTINUED AS #1,ROYAL CHART 2001
Married: Abt 771

Died: 28 Jan 814

4 **Pepin, King of Italy**

Born: Apr 773

Married:

Died: 8 Jul 810

9 **Hildegarde**

Born: 758
-CONTINUED AS #1,ROYAL CHART 2002
Died: 30 Apr 783

2 **Bernard, King of Italy**

Born: 797

Married:

Died: 17 Apr 818

10 **Bernard, a Duke**

Born: Abt 720
-CONTINUED AS #1,ROYAL CHART 2345
Married:

Died: Abt 784

5 **Gondrie**

Born: Abt 775

Died:

11 **Daughter of Caribert**

Born: Abt 735
-CONTINUED AS #1,ROYAL CHART 2346
Died:

1 **Pepin, Count of Senlis**

Born: 817/818
-SAME AS #12,ROYAL CHART 1809
Married:

Died:

12

Born:

Married:

Died:

6

Born:

Married:

Died:

13

Born:

Died:

--

Spouse

3 **Cunigunde**

Born: Abt 797

Died: 15 Jun 835

14

Born:

Married:

Died:

7

Born:

Died:

15

Born:

Died:

Sources include: *Royal Ancestors* 11506; *Ancestral Roots* 50; Stuart 231, 114; Moriarty 5-8, 219-220; Faris preliminary Charlemagne manuscript (June 1995), pp. 271-272. Note: #5 is uncertain and disputed. Moriarty concluded that #5 was most likely a daughter of Duke Bernard--either Gondrie (Gondres, Gondree) or her sister Thierrie (Therese, Thierree)--as tentatively followed above.

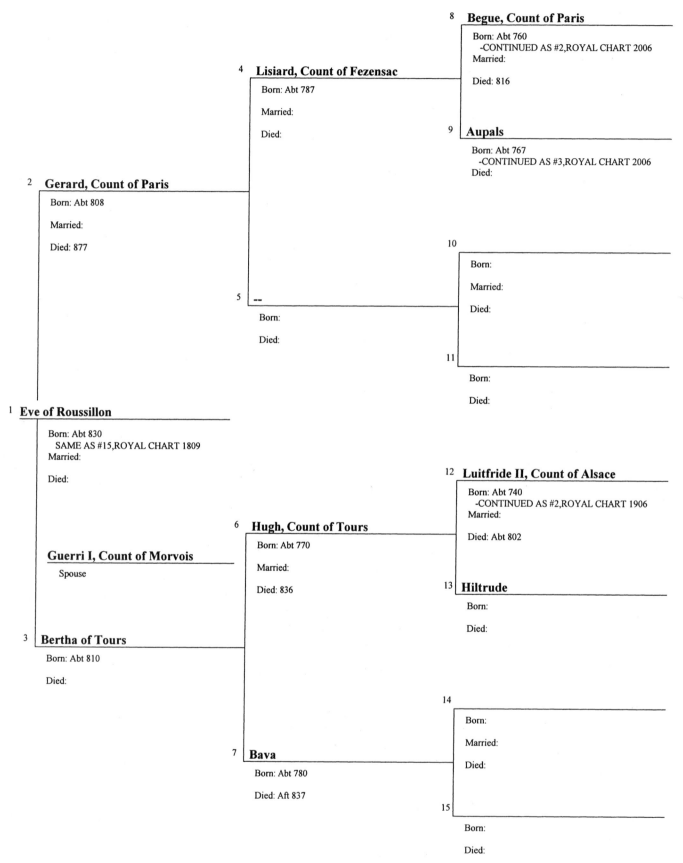

8 **Begue, Count of Paris**

Born: Abt 760
  -CONTINUED AS #2,ROYAL CHART 2006
Married:

Died: 816

4 **Lisiard, Count of Fezensac**

Born: Abt 787

Married:

Died:

9 **Aupals**

Born: Abt 767
  -CONTINUED AS #3,ROYAL CHART 2006
Died:

2 **Gerard, Count of Paris**

Born: Abt 808

Married:

Died: 877

10

Born:

Married:

Died:

5 **--**

Born:

Died:

11

Born:

Died:

1 **Eve of Roussillon**

Born: Abt 830
  SAME AS #15,ROYAL CHART 1809
Married:

Died:

12 **Luitfride II, Count of Alsace**

Born: Abt 740
  -CONTINUED AS #2,ROYAL CHART 1906
Married:

Died: Abt 802

6 **Hugh, Count of Tours**

Born: Abt 770

Married:

Died: 836

13 **Hiltrude**

Born:

Died:

Guerri I, Count of Morvois

Spouse

3 **Bertha of Tours**

Born: Abt 810

Died:

14

Born:

Married:

Died:

7 **Bava**

Born: Abt 780

Died: Aft 837

15

Born:

Died:

Sources include: Stuart 264; *Royal Ancestors* (1989), chart 11506.

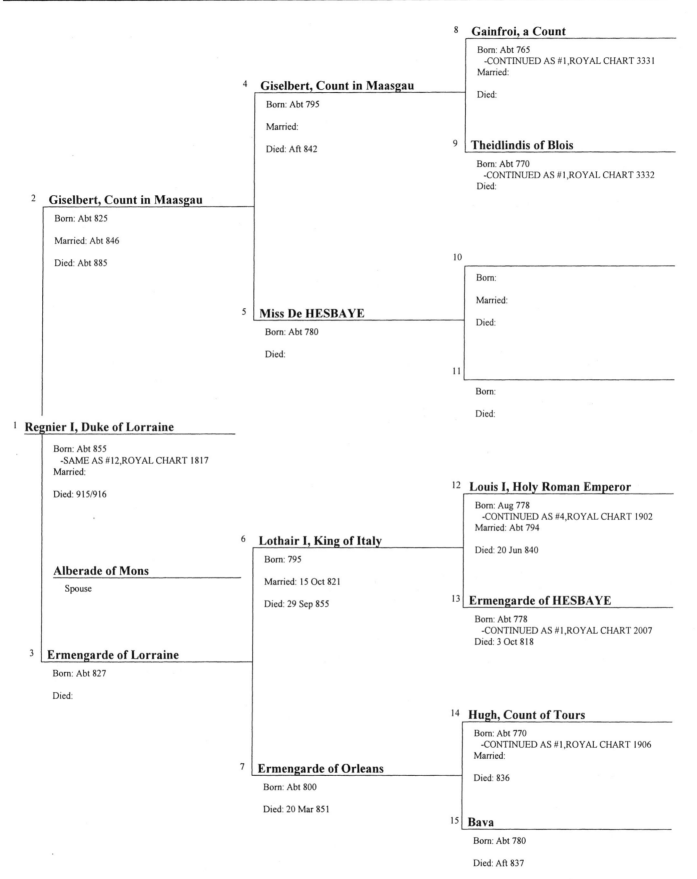

8 Gainfroi, a Count

Born: Abt 765
   -CONTINUED AS #1,ROYAL CHART 3331
Married:

Died:

4 Giselbert, Count in Maasgau

Born: Abt 795

Married:

Died: Aft 842

9 Theidlindis of Blois

Born: Abt 770
   -CONTINUED AS #1,ROYAL CHART 3332
Died:

2 Giselbert, Count in Maasgau

Born: Abt 825

Married: Abt 846

Died: Abt 885

10

Born:

Married:

Died:

5 Miss De HESBAYE

Born: Abt 780

Died:

11

Born:

Died:

1 Regnier I, Duke of Lorraine

Born: Abt 855
   -SAME AS #12,ROYAL CHART 1817
Married:

Died: 915/916

12 Louis I, Holy Roman Emperor

Born: Aug 778
   -CONTINUED AS #4,ROYAL CHART 1902
Married: Abt 794

Died: 20 Jun 840

6 Lothair I, King of Italy

Born: 795

Married: 15 Oct 821

Died: 29 Sep 855

13 Ermengarde of HESBAYE

Born: Abt 778
   -CONTINUED AS #1,ROYAL CHART 2007
Died: 3 Oct 818

Alberade of Mons

Spouse

3 Ermengarde of Lorraine

Born: Abt 827

Died:

14 Hugh, Count of Tours

Born: Abt 770
   -CONTINUED AS #1,ROYAL CHART 1906
Married:

Died: 836

7 Ermengarde of Orleans

Born: Abt 800

Died: 20 Mar 851

15 Bava

Born: Abt 780

Died: Aft 837

Sources include: *Royal Ancestors* 11501, 11601, 11621; *Ancestral Roots* 8 (2004), Lines 240, 140; *Ancestral Roots* 240, 140; Stuart 207; Faris preliminary Charlemagne manuscript (June 1995), pp. 66-67, 94-95; Moriarty 39. Notes: The ancestry of #2 Giselbert is uncertain. The tentative Moriarty version shows #2 Giselbert as son of Regnier of Echternach, son of Giselbert of the Bidgau. The *Ancestral Roots* version (also accepted by Faris) is charted above.

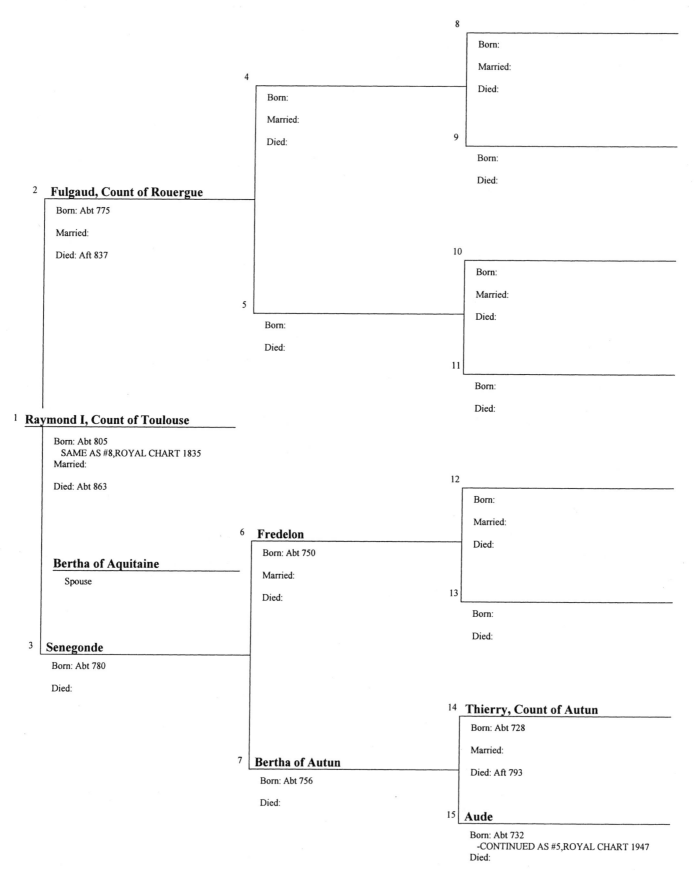

8

Born:

Married:

Died:

4

Born:

Married:

Died:

9

Born:

Died:

2   Fulgaud, Count of Rouergue

Born: Abt 775

Married:

Died: Aft 837

10

Born:

Married:

Died:

5

Born:

Died:

11

Born:

Died:

1   Raymond I, Count of Toulouse

Born: Abt 805
  SAME AS #8,ROYAL CHART 1835
Married:

Died: Abt 863

12

Born:

Married:

Died:

6   Fredelon

Born: Abt 750

Married:

Died:

13

Born:

Died:

Bertha of Aquitaine

Spouse

3   Senegonde

Born: Abt 780

Died:

14   Thierry, Count of Autun

Born: Abt 728

Married:

Died: Aft 793

7   Bertha of Autun

Born: Abt 756

Died:

15   Aude

Born: Abt 732
  -CONTINUED AS #5,ROYAL CHART 1947
Died:

Sources include: *Royal Ancestors* (1989), chart 11627; Stuart 329; Moriarty 41, 232. Note: The theory that #14 Thierry was identical with Makhir (who descends from a long ling of Jewish exilarchs at Babylon with biblical descent) has recently been disproved in a Nathaniel L. Taylor article (see *TAG* 72:205-223, 74:148, 150). Moriarty shows #14 Thierry as a possible son of Rolande (married Bernier) and grandson of Bertha (a Merovingian princess). Bertha was perhaps the daughter of Thierry III, King of Austrasia (see chart 2057).

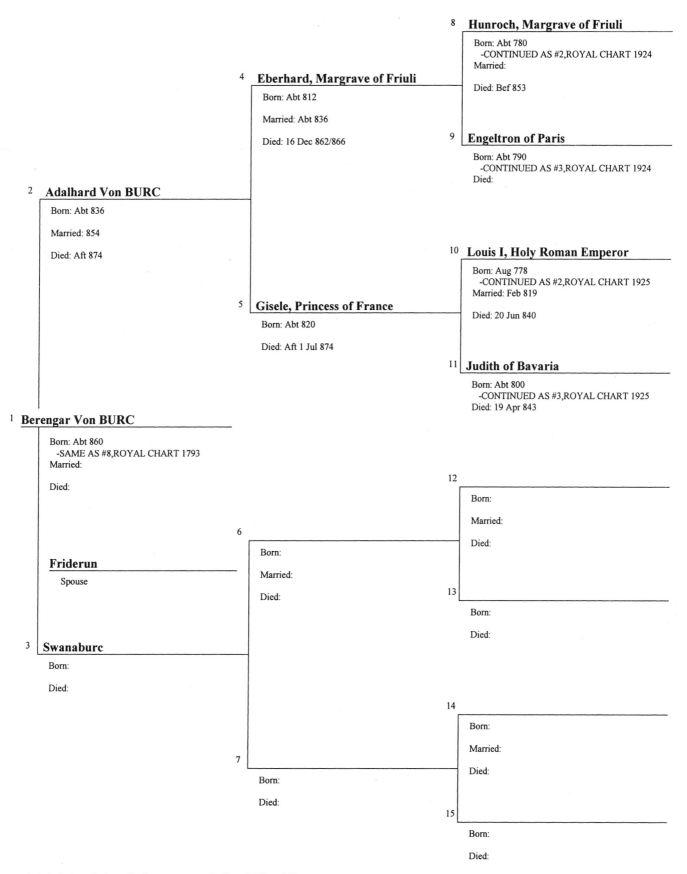

8 **Hunroch, Margrave of Friuli**

Born: Abt 780
-CONTINUED AS #2,ROYAL CHART 1924
Married:

Died: Bef 853

4 **Eberhard, Margrave of Friuli**

Born: Abt 812

Married: Abt 836

Died: 16 Dec 862/866

9 **Engeltron of Paris**

Born: Abt 790
-CONTINUED AS #3,ROYAL CHART 1924
Died:

2 **Adalhard Von BURC**

Born: Abt 836

Married: 854

Died: Aft 874

10 **Louis I, Holy Roman Emperor**

Born: Aug 778
-CONTINUED AS #2,ROYAL CHART 1925
Married: Feb 819

Died: 20 Jun 840

5 **Gisele, Princess of France**

Born: Abt 820

Died: Aft 1 Jul 874

11 **Judith of Bavaria**

Born: Abt 800
-CONTINUED AS #3,ROYAL CHART 1925
Died: 19 Apr 843

1 **Berengar Von BURC**

Born: Abt 860
-SAME AS #8,ROYAL CHART 1793
Married:

Died:

Friderun

Spouse

12

Born:

Married:

Died:

6

Born:

Married:

Died:

13

Born:

Died:

3 **Swanaburc**

Born:

Died:

14

Born:

Married:

Died:

7

Born:

Died:

15

Born:

Died:

Sources include: Faris preliminary Charlemagne manuscript (June 1995), p. 143.

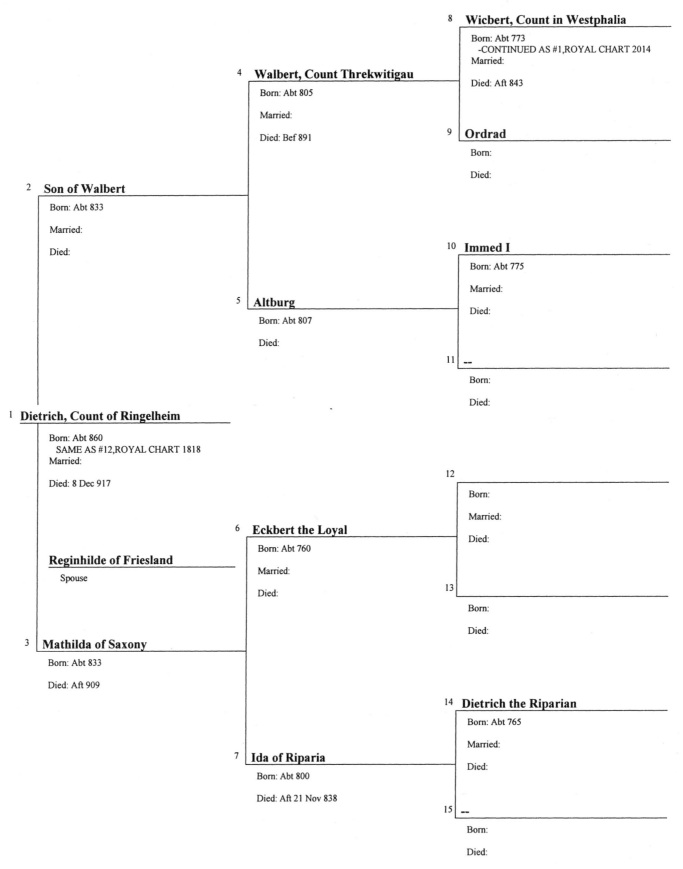

8 **Wicbert, Count in Westphalia**

Born: Abt 773
  -CONTINUED AS #1,ROYAL CHART 2014
Married:

Died: Aft 843

4 **Walbert, Count Threkwitigau**

Born: Abt 805

Married:

Died: Bef 891

9 **Ordrad**

Born:

Died:

2 **Son of Walbert**

Born: Abt 833

Married:

Died:

10 **Immed I**

Born: Abt 775

Married:

Died:

5 **Altburg**

Born: Abt 807

Died:

11 **--**

Born:

Died:

1 **Dietrich, Count of Ringelheim**

Born: Abt 860
  SAME AS #12,ROYAL CHART 1818
Married:

Died: 8 Dec 917

12

Born:

Married:

Died:

6 **Eckbert the Loyal**

Born: Abt 760

Married:

Died:

Reginhilde of Friesland

Spouse

13

Born:

Died:

3 **Mathilda of Saxony**

Born: Abt 833

Died: Aft 909

14 **Dietrich the Riparian**

Born: Abt 765

Married:

Died:

7 **Ida of Riparia**

Born: Abt 800

Died: Aft 21 Nov 838

15 **--**

Born:

Died:

Sources include: *Royal Ancestors* (1989), charts 11507, 11636; Stuart 338-339; Moriarty 26; Turton 23; LDS records. Note: Turton gives #2 as Reginhart (son of Walbert & Altburg).

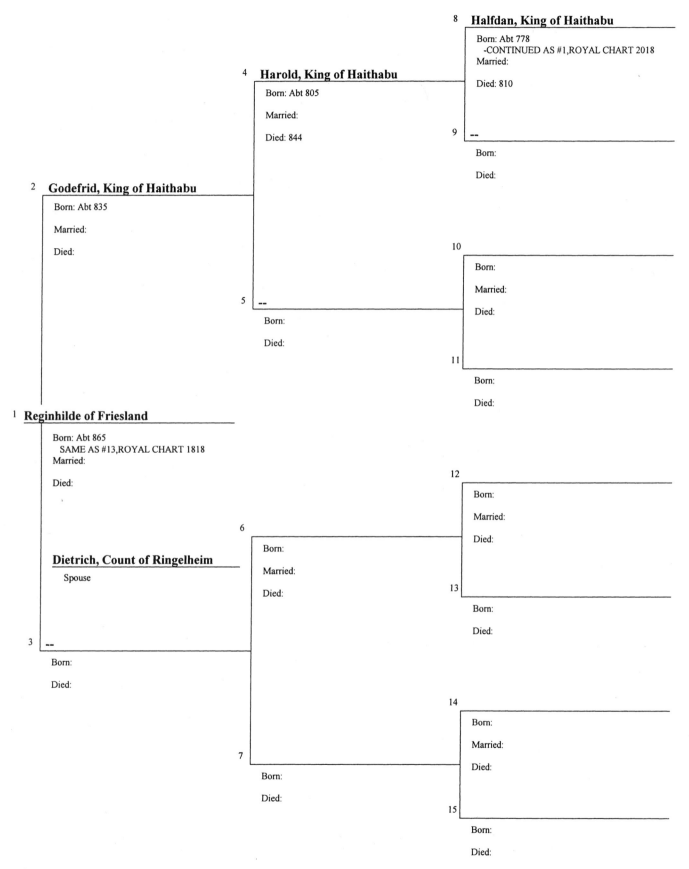

8 Halfdan, King of Haithabu

Born: Abt 778
-CONTINUED AS #1,ROYAL CHART 2018
Married:

Died: 810

4 Harold, King of Haithabu

Born: Abt 805

Married:

Died: 844

9 --

Born:

Died:

2 Godefrid, King of Haithabu

Born: Abt 835

Married:

Died:

10

Born:

Married:

Died:

5 --

Born:

Died:

11

Born:

Died:

1 Reginhilde of Friesland

Born: Abt 865
SAME AS #13,ROYAL CHART 1818
Married:

Died:

12

Born:

Married:

Died:

6

Born:

Married:

Died:

13

Born:

Died:

Dietrich, Count of Ringelheim

Spouse

3 --

Born:

Died:

14

Born:

Married:

Died:

7

Born:

Died:

15

Born:

Died:

Sources include: Stuart 310, 217; Moriarty 26; *Royal Ancestors* (1989), chart 11507. Note: Stuart gives #3 as Gisela, daughter of Lothair II & Waldrada (see chart 1804, #10 & 11). This is difficult chronologically. Perhaps #2 Godefrid had an earlier unknown wife who was mother of Reginhilde.

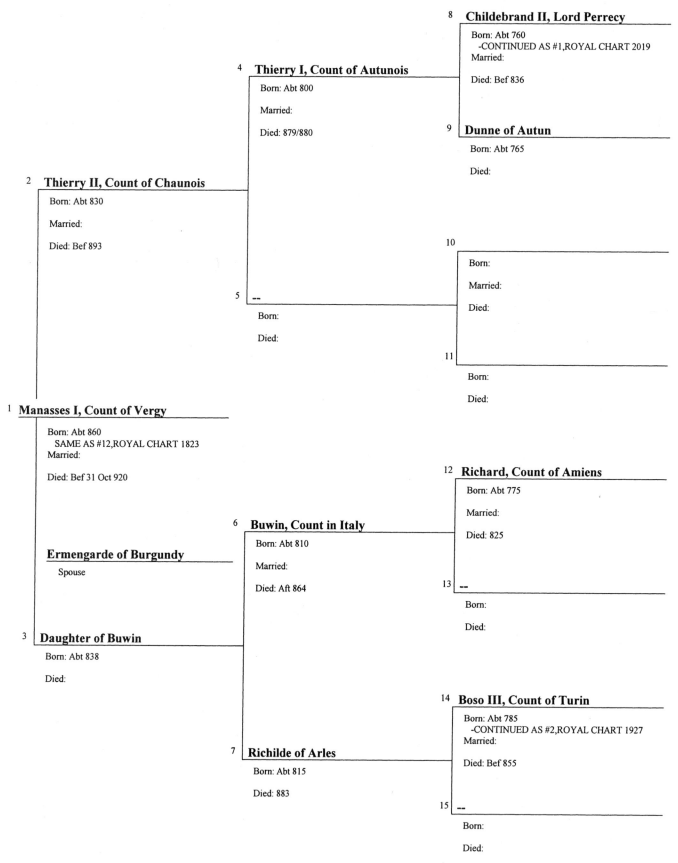

8 **Childebrand II, Lord Perrecy**

Born: Abt 760
-CONTINUED AS #1,ROYAL CHART 2019
Married:

Died: Bef 836

4 **Thierry I, Count of Autunois**

Born: Abt 800

Married:

Died: 879/880

9 **Dunne of Autun**

Born: Abt 765

Died:

2 **Thierry II, Count of Chaunois**

Born: Abt 830

Married:

Died: Bef 893

10

Born:

Married:

Died:

5 --

Born:

Died:

11

Born:

Died:

1 **Manasses I, Count of Vergy**

Born: Abt 860
    SAME AS #12,ROYAL CHART 1823
Married:

Died: Bef 31 Oct 920

12 **Richard, Count of Amiens**

Born: Abt 775

Married:

Died: 825

6 **Buwin, Count in Italy**

Born: Abt 810

Married:

Died: Aft 864

13 --

Born:

Died:

Ermengarde of Burgundy

Spouse

3 **Daughter of Buwin**

Born: Abt 838

Died:

14 **Boso III, Count of Turin**

Born: Abt 785
-CONTINUED AS #2,ROYAL CHART 1927
Married:

Died: Bef 855

7 **Richilde of Arles**

Born: Abt 815

Died: 883

15 --

Born:

Died:

Sources include: *Royal Ancestors* (1989), chart 11758 & notes; Stuart 258, 173; Moriarty 10, 255.

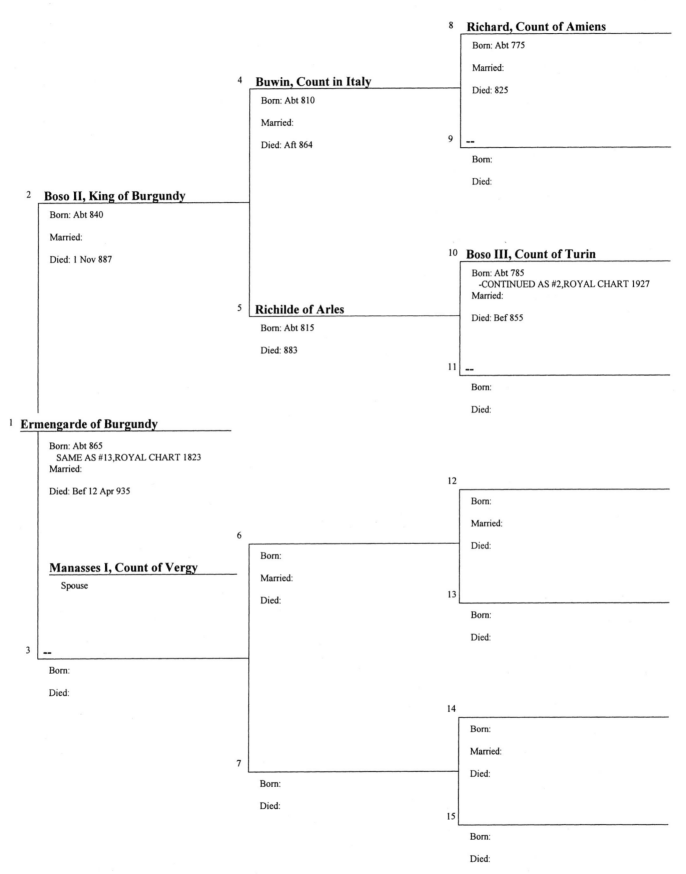

8 **Richard, Count of Amiens**

Born: Abt 775

Married:

Died: 825

4 **Buwin, Count in Italy**

Born: Abt 810

Married:

Died: Aft 864

9 --

Born:

Died:

2 **Boso II, King of Burgundy**

Born: Abt 840

Married:

Died: 1 Nov 887

10 **Boso III, Count of Turin**

Born: Abt 785
    -CONTINUED AS #2,ROYAL CHART 1927
Married:

Died: Bef 855

5 **Richilde of Arles**

Born: Abt 815

Died: 883

11 --

Born:

Died:

1 **Ermengarde of Burgundy**

Born: Abt 865
    SAME AS #13,ROYAL CHART 1823
Married:

Died: Bef 12 Apr 935

12

Born:

Married:

Died:

6

Born:

Married:

Died:

13

Born:

Died:

Manasses I, Count of Vergy

    Spouse

3 --

Born:

Died:

14

Born:

Married:

Died:

7

Born:

Died:

15

Born:

Died:

Sources include: *Royal Ancestors* (1989), chart 11758 & notes, 11570, 11964, 11992, family group sheet for #4 Buwin; Stuart 258, 343; Moriarty 10, 51; Von Isenburg 2:23 (#1 ancestry). Note: The parentage of #1 Ermengarde is uncertain. The cited sources give her as a likely daughter of Boso II as shown by an unknown 1st wife, but Faris in a preliminary Charlemagne manuscript (June 1995), p. 277 states that the 1st wife died childless. See chart 1814 for Boso II and his 2nd wife Ermengarde.

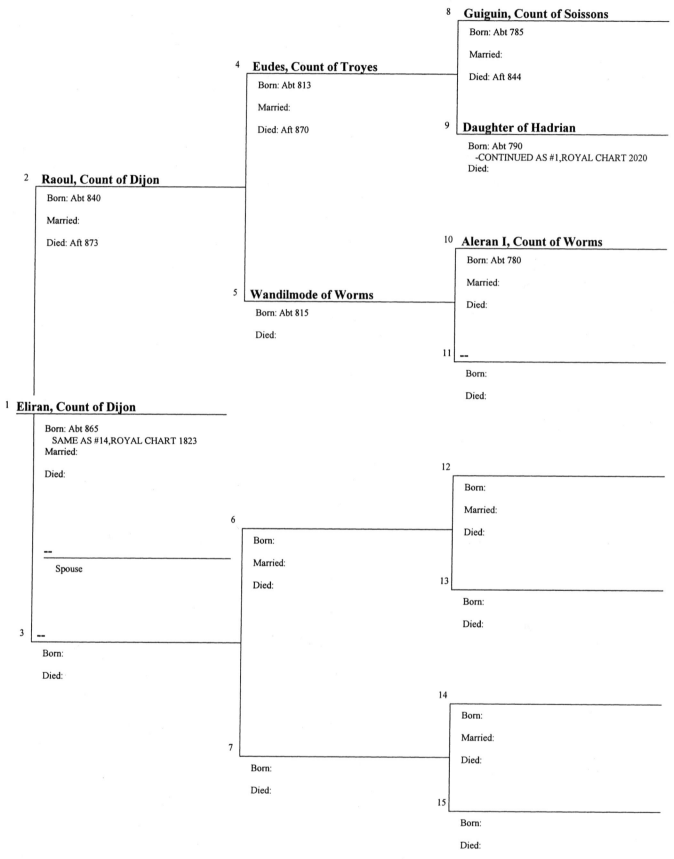

2 Raoul, Count of Dijon
Born: Abt 840
Married:
Died: Aft 873

4 Eudes, Count of Troyes
Born: Abt 813
Married:
Died: Aft 870

8 Guiguin, Count of Soissons
Born: Abt 785
Married:
Died: Aft 844

9 Daughter of Hadrian
Born: Abt 790
-CONTINUED AS #1,ROYAL CHART 2020
Died:

5 Wandilmode of Worms
Born: Abt 815
Died:

10 Aleran I, Count of Worms
Born: Abt 780
Married:
Died:

11 --
Born:
Died:

1 Eliran, Count of Dijon
Born: Abt 865
SAME AS #14,ROYAL CHART 1823
Married:
Died:

--
Spouse

3 --
Born:
Died:

6
Born:
Married:
Died:

12
Born:
Married:
Died:

13
Born:
Died:

7
Born:
Died:

14
Born:
Married:
Died:

15
Born:
Died:

Sources include: *Royal Ancestors* (1989), chart 11758; Moriarty 38; Stuart 258-37 (#1), 348 (#2 ancestry).

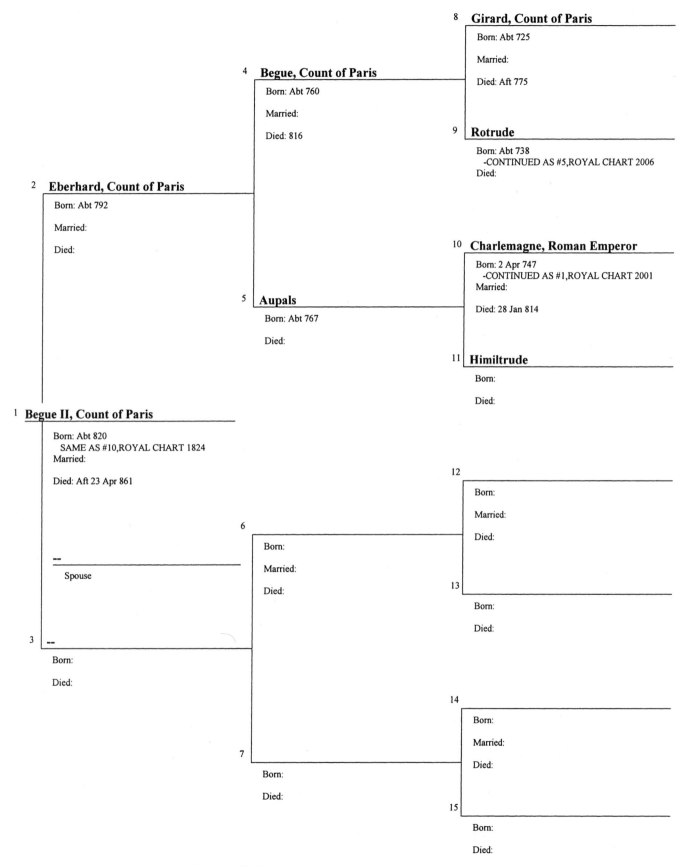

8 **Girard, Count of Paris**

Born: Abt 725

Married:

Died: Aft 775

4 **Begue, Count of Paris**

Born: Abt 760

Married:

Died: 816

9 **Rotrude**

Born: Abt 738
  -CONTINUED AS #5,ROYAL CHART 2006
Died:

2 **Eberhard, Count of Paris**

Born: Abt 792

Married:

Died:

10 **Charlemagne, Roman Emperor**

Born: 2 Apr 747
  -CONTINUED AS #1,ROYAL CHART 2001
Married:

Died: 28 Jan 814

5 **Aupals**

Born: Abt 767

Died:

11 **Himiltrude**

Born:

Died:

1 **Begue II, Count of Paris**

Born: Abt 820
  SAME AS #10,ROYAL CHART 1824
Married:

Died: Aft 23 Apr 861

12

Born:

Married:

Died:

6

Born:

Married:

Died:

13

Born:

Died:

--

Spouse

3 **--**

Born:

Died:

14

Born:

Married:

Died:

7

Born:

Died:

15

Born:

Died:

Sources include: *Royal Ancestors* (1989), chart 11609; Moriarty 22-23; Stuart 350.

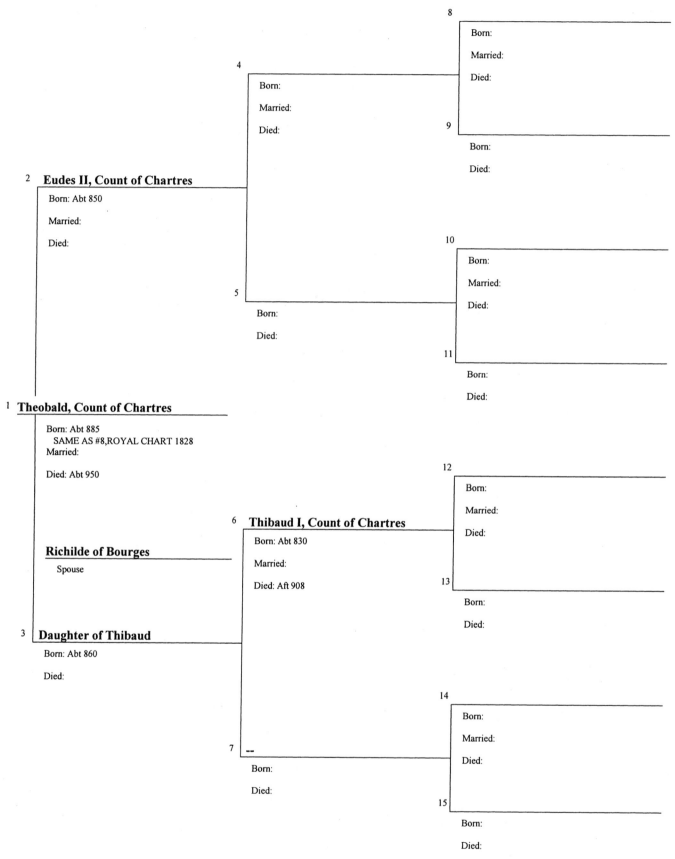

8
Born:
Married:
Died:

4
Born:
Married:
Died:

9
Born:
Died:

2 Eudes II, Count of Chartres
Born: Abt 850
Married:
Died:

10
Born:
Married:
Died:

5
Born:
Died:

11
Born:
Died:

1 Theobald, Count of Chartres
Born: Abt 885
    SAME AS #8,ROYAL CHART 1828
Married:
Died: Abt 950

12
Born:
Married:
Died:

6 Thibaud I, Count of Chartres
Born: Abt 830
Married:
Died: Aft 908

13
Born:
Died:

Richilde of Bourges
Spouse

3 Daughter of Thibaud
Born: Abt 860
Died:

14
Born:
Married:
Died:

7 --
Born:
Died:

15
Born:
Died:

Sources include: *Royal Ancestors* (1989), chart 11580; Moriarty 36; Stuart 340; *Ancestral Roots* 49.

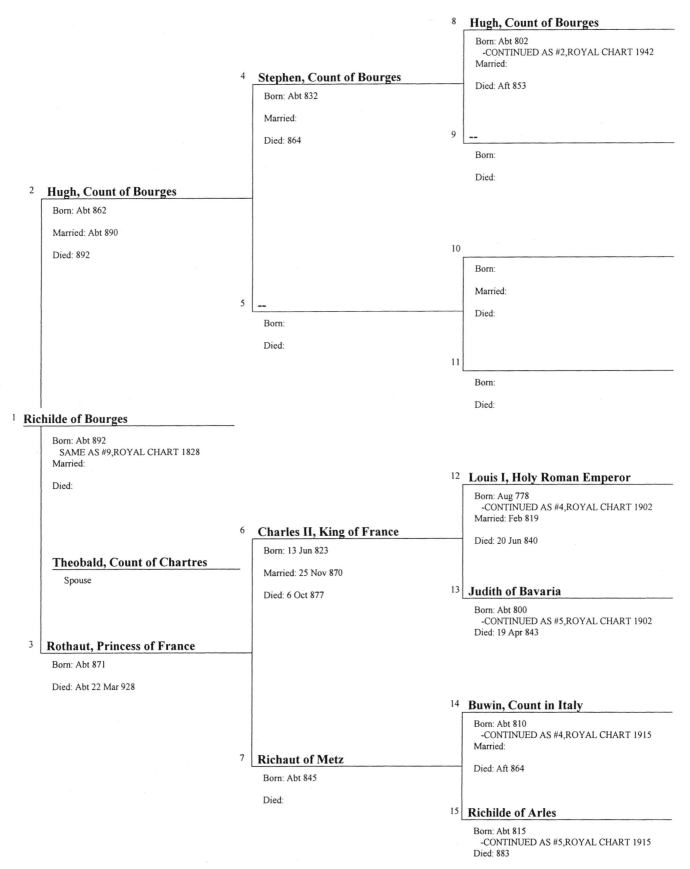

8 **Hugh, Count of Bourges**

Born: Abt 802
-CONTINUED AS #2,ROYAL CHART 1942
Married:

Died: Aft 853

4 **Stephen, Count of Bourges**

Born: Abt 832

Married:

Died: 864

9 **--**

Born:

Died:

2 **Hugh, Count of Bourges**

Born: Abt 862

Married: Abt 890

Died: 892

10

Born:

Married:

Died:

5 **--**

Born:

Died:

11

Born:

Died:

1 **Richilde of Bourges**

Born: Abt 892
SAME AS #9,ROYAL CHART 1828
Married:

Died:

12 **Louis I, Holy Roman Emperor**

Born: Aug 778
-CONTINUED AS #4,ROYAL CHART 1902
Married: Feb 819

Died: 20 Jun 840

6 **Charles II, King of France**

Born: 13 Jun 823

Married: 25 Nov 870

Died: 6 Oct 877

13 **Judith of Bavaria**

Born: Abt 800
-CONTINUED AS #5,ROYAL CHART 1902
Died: 19 Apr 843

Theobald, Count of Chartres

Spouse

3 **Rothaut, Princess of France**

Born: Abt 871

Died: Abt 22 Mar 928

14 **Buwin, Count in Italy**

Born: Abt 810
-CONTINUED AS #4,ROYAL CHART 1915
Married:

Died: Aft 864

7 **Richaut of Metz**

Born: Abt 845

Died:

15 **Richilde of Arles**

Born: Abt 815
-CONTINUED AS #5,ROYAL CHART 1915
Died: 883

Sources include: *Royal Ancestors* (1989), chart 11582; Stuart 346; Moriarty 37; *Ancestral Roots* 49. Note: *Ancestral Roots* 8 (2004), Line 49 changes #2 to Roger, Count of Maine (see chart 1706, # 8). The Moriarty version is retained above, tentatively assigning both husbands to #3 Rothaut.

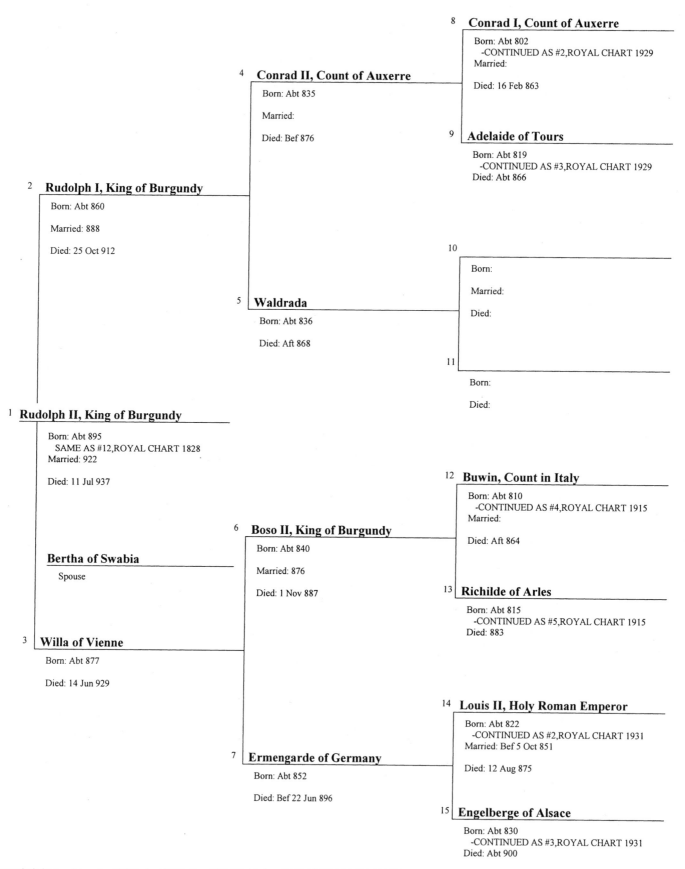

8 **Conrad I, Count of Auxerre**

Born: Abt 802
-CONTINUED AS #2,ROYAL CHART 1929
Married:

Died: 16 Feb 863

4 **Conrad II, Count of Auxerre**

Born: Abt 835

Married:

Died: Bef 876

9 **Adelaide of Tours**

Born: Abt 819
-CONTINUED AS #3,ROYAL CHART 1929
Died: Abt 866

2 **Rudolph I, King of Burgundy**

Born: Abt 860

Married: 888

Died: 25 Oct 912

10

Born:

Married:

Died:

5 **Waldrada**

Born: Abt 836

Died: Aft 868

11

Born:

Died:

1 **Rudolph II, King of Burgundy**

Born: Abt 895
SAME AS #12,ROYAL CHART 1828
Married: 922

Died: 11 Jul 937

12 **Buwin, Count in Italy**

Born: Abt 810
-CONTINUED AS #4,ROYAL CHART 1915
Married:

Died: Aft 864

6 **Boso II, King of Burgundy**

Born: Abt 840

Married: 876

Died: 1 Nov 887

13 **Richilde of Arles**

Born: Abt 815
-CONTINUED AS #5,ROYAL CHART 1915
Died: 883

Bertha of Swabia

Spouse

3 **Willa of Vienne**

Born: Abt 877

Died: 14 Jun 929

14 **Louis II, Holy Roman Emperor**

Born: Abt 822
-CONTINUED AS #2,ROYAL CHART 1931
Married: Bef 5 Oct 851

Died: 12 Aug 875

7 **Ermengarde of Germany**

Born: Abt 852

Died: Bef 22 Jun 896

15 **Engelberge of Alsace**

Born: Abt 830
-CONTINUED AS #3,ROYAL CHART 1931
Died: Abt 900

Sources include: *Royal Ancestors* (1989), chart 11581; Stuart 175, 343; Moriarty 33, 51, 21 (#9 Adelaide), 259 (#7 ancestry); Von Isenburg 2:23; *Ancestral Roots* 141B (#7 ancestry).

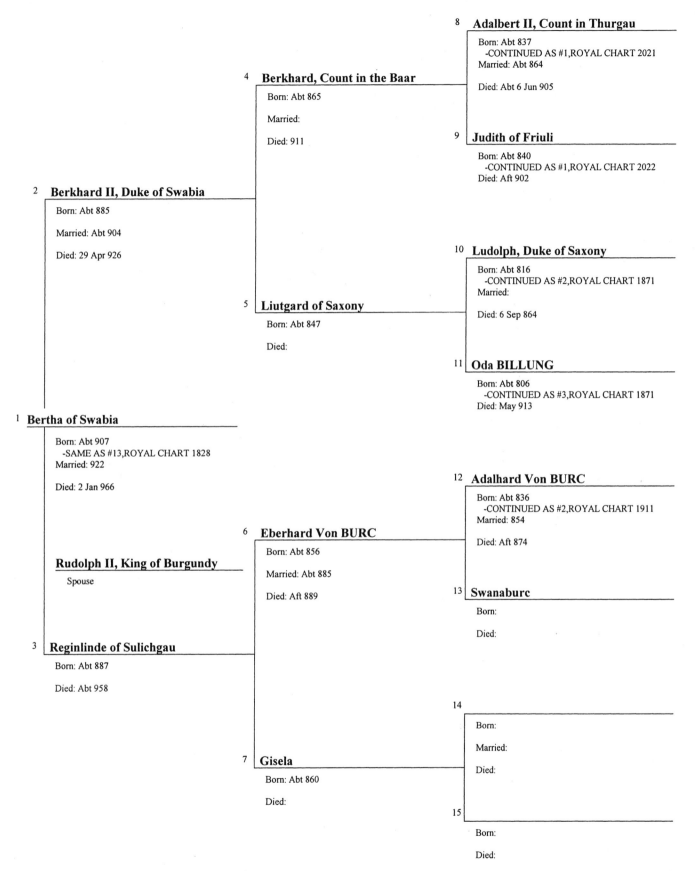

8 Adalbert II, Count in Thurgau

Born: Abt 837
-CONTINUED AS #1,ROYAL CHART 2021
Married: Abt 864

Died: Abt 6 Jun 905

4 Berkhard, Count in the Baar

Born: Abt 865

Married:

Died: 911

9 Judith of Friuli

Born: Abt 840
-CONTINUED AS #1,ROYAL CHART 2022
Died: Aft 902

2 Berkhard II, Duke of Swabia

Born: Abt 885

Married: Abt 904

Died: 29 Apr 926

10 Ludolph, Duke of Saxony

Born: Abt 816
-CONTINUED AS #2,ROYAL CHART 1871
Married:

Died: 6 Sep 864

5 Liutgard of Saxony

Born: Abt 847

Died:

11 Oda BILLUNG

Born: Abt 806
-CONTINUED AS #3,ROYAL CHART 1871
Died: May 913

1 Bertha of Swabia

Born: Abt 907
-SAME AS #13,ROYAL CHART 1828
Married: 922

Died: 2 Jan 966

12 Adalhard Von BURC

Born: Abt 836
-CONTINUED AS #2,ROYAL CHART 1911
Married: 854

Died: Aft 874

6 Eberhard Von BURC

Born: Abt 856

Married: Abt 885

Died: Aft 889

Rudolph II, King of Burgundy

Spouse

13 Swanaburc

Born:

Died:

3 Reginlinde of Sulichgau

Born: Abt 887

Died: Abt 958

14

Born:

Married:

Died:

7 Gisela

Born: Abt 860

Died:

15

Born:

Died:

Sources include: *Royal Ancestors* (1989), chart 11581; Stuart 345; Moriarty 33-35, 206; Turton 181; Faris preliminary Charlemagne manuscript (June 1995), pp. 84, 143-144. Note: The ancestry shown for #4, 5, & 6 is all uncertain. Faris vacillates on the identification of #9 Judith (compare pp. 84, 248), which requires #4 Berkhard to be much younger than the wife (#5 Liutgard) Faris claims for him. The ancestry given by Faris for #6 Eberhard, as shown above, requires very tight chronology.

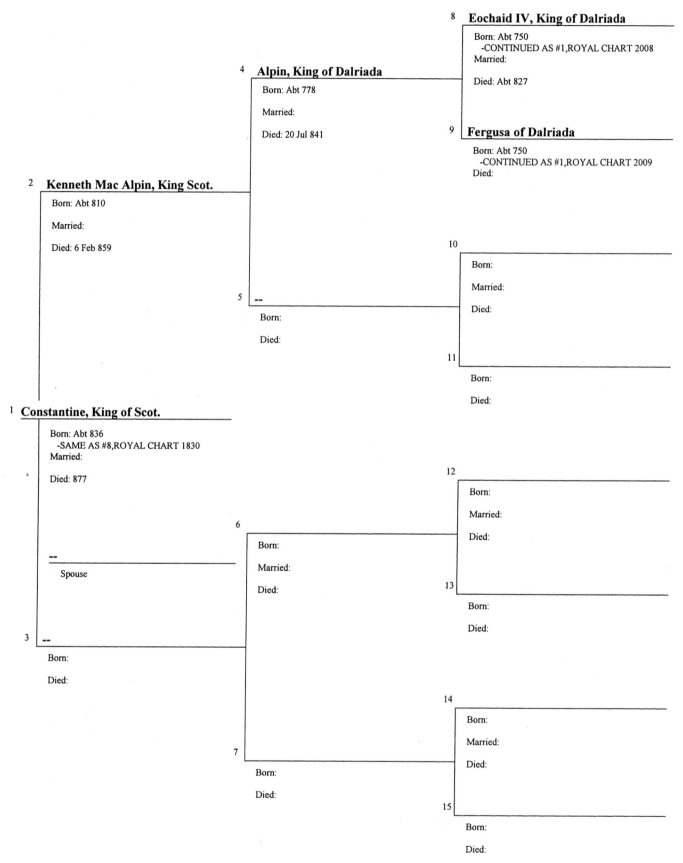

8 **Eochaid IV, King of Dalriada**

Born: Abt 750
-CONTINUED AS #1,ROYAL CHART 2008
Married:

Died: Abt 827

4 **Alpin, King of Dalriada**

Born: Abt 778

Married:

Died: 20 Jul 841

9 **Fergusa of Dalriada**

Born: Abt 750
-CONTINUED AS #1,ROYAL CHART 2009
Died:

2 **Kenneth Mac Alpin, King Scot.**

Born: Abt 810

Married:

Died: 6 Feb 859

10

Born:

Married:

Died:

5 **--**

Born:

Died:

11

Born:

Died:

1 **Constantine, King of Scot.**

Born: Abt 836
-SAME AS #8,ROYAL CHART 1830
Married:

Died: 877

12

Born:

Married:

Died:

6

Born:

Married:

Died:

13

Born:

Died:

--

Spouse

3 **--**

Born:

Died:

14

Born:

Married:

Died:

7

Born:

Died:

15

Born:

Died:

Sources include: *Royal Ancestors* (1989), charts 11510, 11606; *Ancestral Roots* 170; Stuart 165; Moriarty 29, 278.

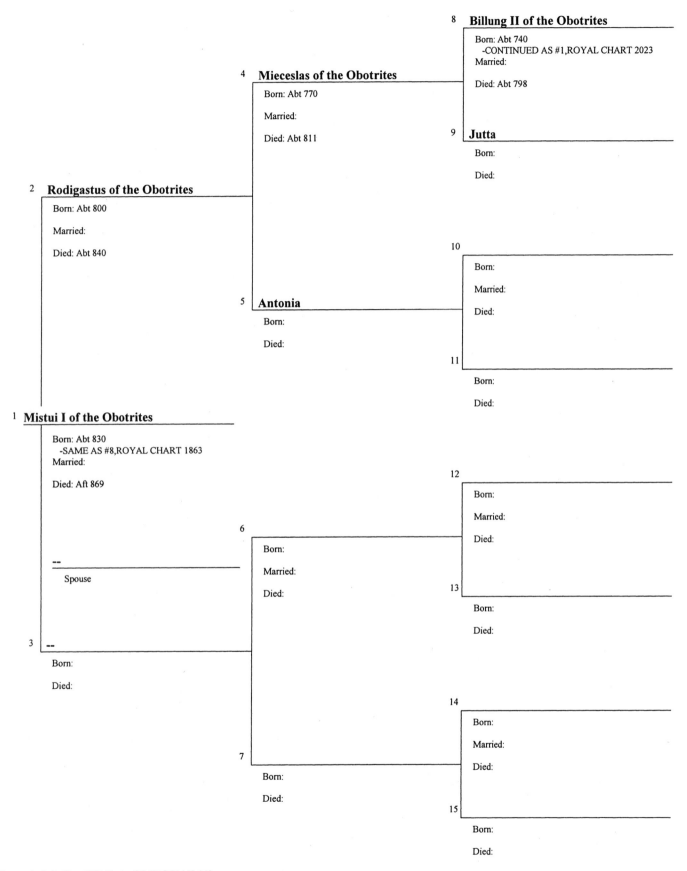

8 Billung II of the Obotrites

Born: Abt 740
  -CONTINUED AS #1,ROYAL CHART 2023
Married:

Died: Abt 798

4 Mieceslas of the Obotrites

Born: Abt 770

Married:

Died: Abt 811

9 Jutta

Born:

Died:

2 Rodigastus of the Obotrites

Born: Abt 800

Married:

Died: Abt 840

10

Born:

Married:

Died:

5 Antonia

Born:

Died:

11

Born:

Died:

1 Mistui I of the Obotrites

Born: Abt 830
  -SAME AS #8,ROYAL CHART 1863
Married:

Died: Aft 869

--
  Spouse

12

Born:

Married:

Died:

6

Born:

Married:

Died:

13

Born:

Died:

3 --

Born:

Died:

14

Born:

Married:

Died:

7

Born:

Died:

15

Born:

Died:

Sources include: Stuart 380; Turton 27; *TAG* 74:148-149.

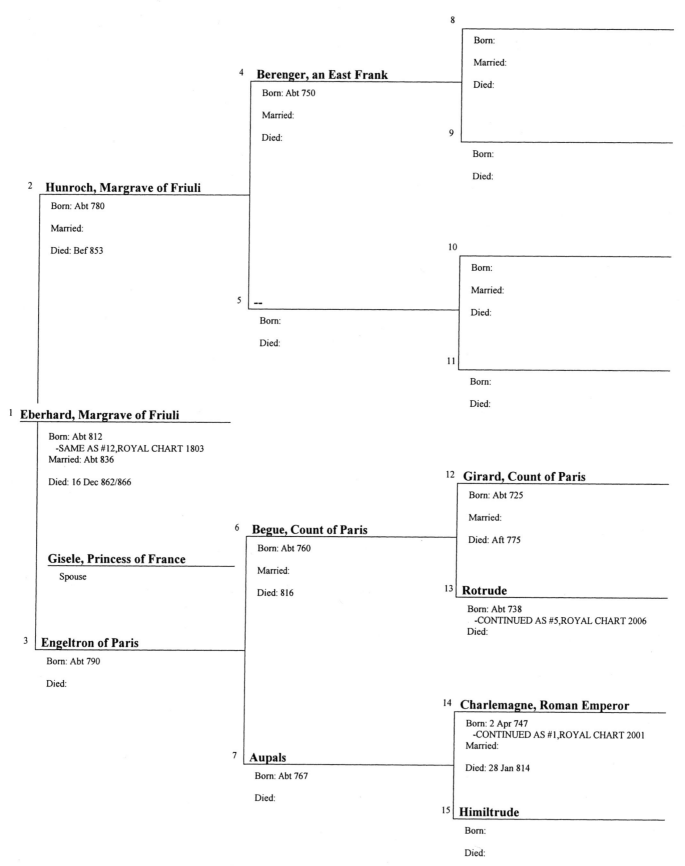

8

Born:

Married:

Died:

4 **Berenger, an East Frank**

Born: Abt 750

Married:

Died:

9

Born:

Died:

2 **Hunroch, Margrave of Friuli**

Born: Abt 780

Married:

Died: Bef 853

10

Born:

Married:

Died:

5 **--**

Born:

Died:

11

Born:

Died:

1 **Eberhard, Margrave of Friuli**

Born: Abt 812
  -SAME AS #12,ROYAL CHART 1803
Married: Abt 836

Died: 16 Dec 862/866

12 **Girard, Count of Paris**

Born: Abt 725

Married:

Died: Aft 775

6 **Begue, Count of Paris**

Born: Abt 760

Married:

Died: 816

13 **Rotrude**

Born: Abt 738
  -CONTINUED AS #5,ROYAL CHART 2006
Died:

Gisele, Princess of France

Spouse

3 **Engeltron of Paris**

Born: Abt 790

Died:

14 **Charlemagne, Roman Emperor**

Born: 2 Apr 747
  -CONTINUED AS #1,ROYAL CHART 2001
Married:

Died: 28 Jan 814

7 **Aupals**

Born: Abt 767

Died:

15 **Himiltrude**

Born:

Died:

Sources include: *Royal Ancestors* (1989), chart 11634; Stuart 269; *Ancestral Roots* 191; Moriarty 18, 229, 22-23.

Pedigree Chart

Chart 1925

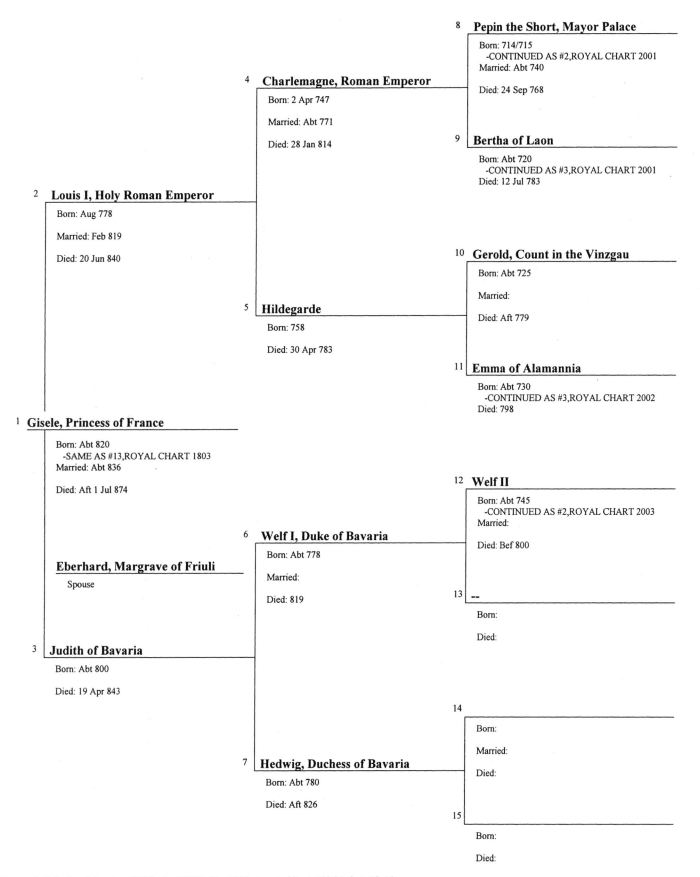

8 Pepin the Short, Mayor Palace
Born: 714/715
-CONTINUED AS #2,ROYAL CHART 2001
Married: Abt 740

Died: 24 Sep 768

4 Charlemagne, Roman Emperor
Born: 2 Apr 747

Married: Abt 771

Died: 28 Jan 814

9 Bertha of Laon
Born: Abt 720
-CONTINUED AS #3,ROYAL CHART 2001
Died: 12 Jul 783

2 Louis I, Holy Roman Emperor
Born: Aug 778

Married: Feb 819

Died: 20 Jun 840

10 Gerold, Count in the Vinzgau
Born: Abt 725

Married:

Died: Aft 779

5 Hildegarde
Born: 758

Died: 30 Apr 783

11 Emma of Alamannia
Born: Abt 730
-CONTINUED AS #3,ROYAL CHART 2002
Died: 798

1 Gisele, Princess of France
Born: Abt 820
-SAME AS #13,ROYAL CHART 1803
Married: Abt 836

Died: Aft 1 Jul 874

12 Welf II
Born: Abt 745
-CONTINUED AS #2,ROYAL CHART 2003
Married:

Died: Bef 800

6 Welf I, Duke of Bavaria
Born: Abt 778

Married:

Died: 819

Eberhard, Margrave of Friuli
Spouse

13 --
Born:

Died:

3 Judith of Bavaria
Born: Abt 800

Died: 19 Apr 843

14
Born:

Married:

Died:

7 Hedwig, Duchess of Bavaria
Born: Abt 780

Died: Aft 826

15
Born:

Died:

Sources include: *Royal Ancestors* (1989), chart 11634; Stuart 185; *Ancestral Roots* 146; Moriarty 18, 16.

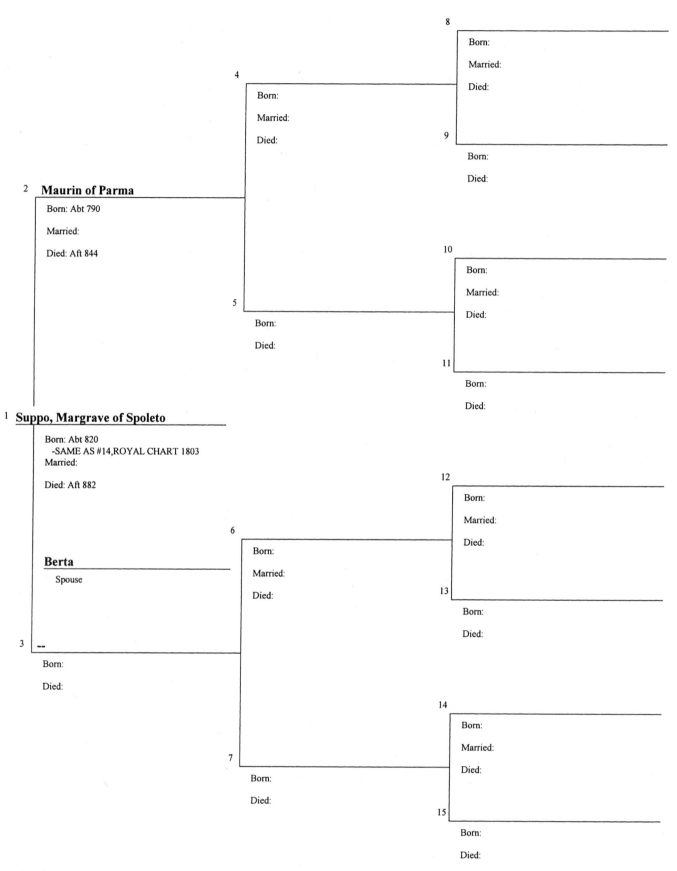

8
Born:
Married:
Died:

4
Born:
Married:
Died:

9
Born:
Died:

2 Maurin of Parma
Born: Abt 790
Married:
Died: Aft 844

10
Born:
Married:
Died:

5
Born:
Died:

11
Born:
Died:

1 Suppo, Margrave of Spoleto
Born: Abt 820
  -SAME AS #14,ROYAL CHART 1803
Married:
Died: Aft 882

12
Born:
Married:
Died:

6
Born:
Married:
Died:

13
Born:
Died:

Berta
Spouse

3 --
Born:
Died:

14
Born:
Married:
Died:

7
Born:
Died:

15
Born:
Died:

Sources include: *Royal Ancestors* (1989), chart 11569; Moriarty 18-19; Stuart 269-38.

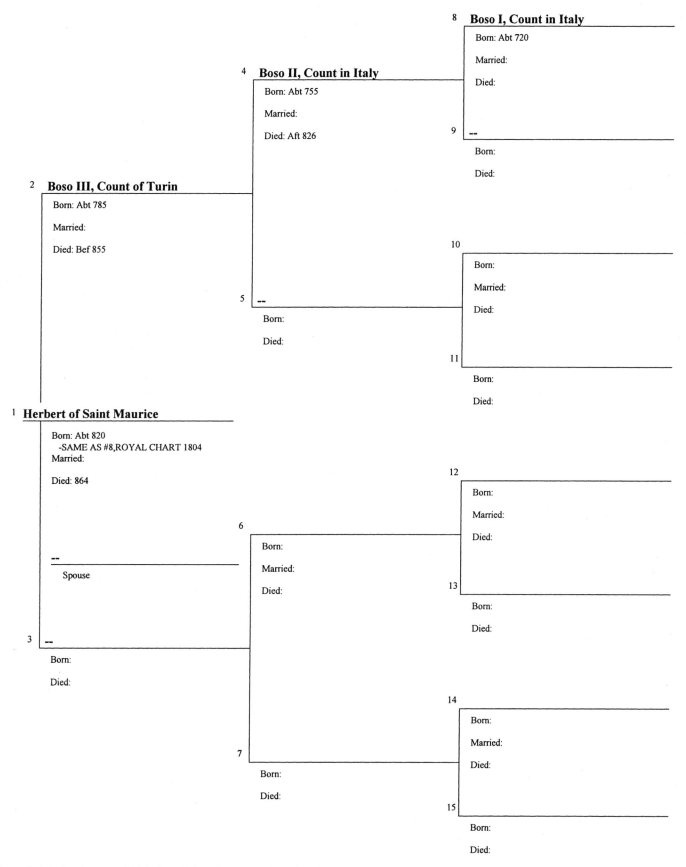

8 Boso I, Count in Italy
Born: Abt 720
Married:
Died:

4 Boso II, Count in Italy
Born: Abt 755
Married:
Died: Aft 826

9 --
Born:
Died:

2 Boso III, Count of Turin
Born: Abt 785
Married:
Died: Bef 855

5 --
Born:
Died:

10
Born:
Married:
Died:

11
Born:
Died:

1 Herbert of Saint Maurice
Born: Abt 820
 -SAME AS #8,ROYAL CHART 1804
Married:
Died: 864

**-- **
Spouse

3 --
Born:
Died:

6
Born:
Married:
Died:

12
Born:
Married:
Died:

13
Born:
Died:

7
Born:
Died:

14
Born:
Married:
Died:

15
Born:
Died:

Sources include: *Royal Ancestors* (1989), charts 11570, 11992; Stuart 174; Moriarty 19.

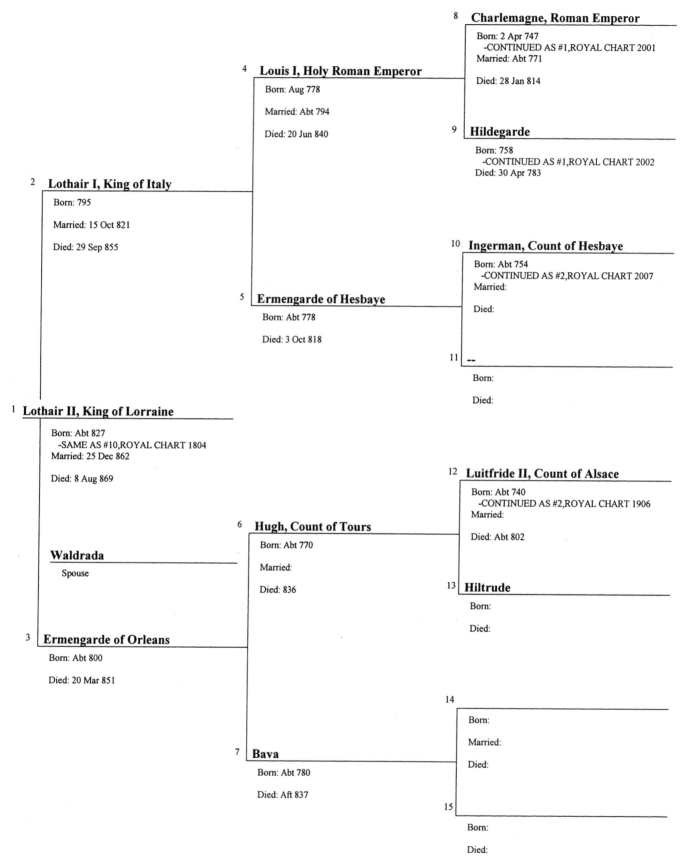

8 Charlemagne, Roman Emperor
Born: 2 Apr 747
-CONTINUED AS #1,ROYAL CHART 2001
Married: Abt 771

Died: 28 Jan 814

4 Louis I, Holy Roman Emperor
Born: Aug 778

Married: Abt 794

Died: 20 Jun 840

9 Hildegarde
Born: 758
-CONTINUED AS #1,ROYAL CHART 2002
Died: 30 Apr 783

2 Lothair I, King of Italy
Born: 795

Married: 15 Oct 821

Died: 29 Sep 855

10 Ingerman, Count of Hesbaye
Born: Abt 754
-CONTINUED AS #2,ROYAL CHART 2007
Married:

Died:

5 Ermengarde of Hesbaye
Born: Abt 778

Died: 3 Oct 818

11 --
Born:

Died:

1 Lothair II, King of Lorraine
Born: Abt 827
-SAME AS #10,ROYAL CHART 1804
Married: 25 Dec 862

Died: 8 Aug 869

12 Luitfride II, Count of Alsace
Born: Abt 740
-CONTINUED AS #2,ROYAL CHART 1906
Married:

Died: Abt 802

6 Hugh, Count of Tours
Born: Abt 770

Married:

Died: 836

13 Hiltrude
Born:

Died:

Waldrada
Spouse

3 Ermengarde of Orleans
Born: Abt 800

Died: 20 Mar 851

14
Born:

Married:

Died:

7 Bava
Born: Abt 780

Died: Aft 837

15
Born:

Died:

Sources include: *Royal Ancestors* (1989), charts 11570, 11601-02; *Ancestral Roots* 145, 140; Stuart 263; Moriarty 20.

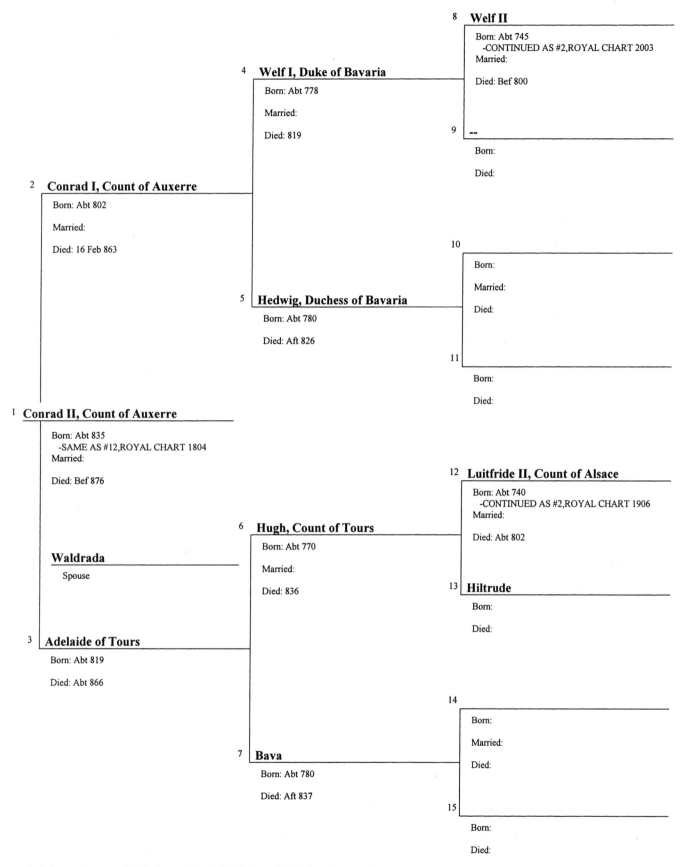

8 Welf II

Born: Abt 745
-CONTINUED AS #2,ROYAL CHART 2003
Married:

Died: Bef 800

4 Welf I, Duke of Bavaria

Born: Abt 778

Married:

Died: 819

9 --

Born:

Died:

2 Conrad I, Count of Auxerre

Born: Abt 802

Married:

Died: 16 Feb 863

10

Born:

Married:

Died:

5 Hedwig, Duchess of Bavaria

Born: Abt 780

Died: Aft 826

11

Born:

Died:

1 Conrad II, Count of Auxerre

Born: Abt 835
-SAME AS #12,ROYAL CHART 1804
Married:

Died: Bef 876

12 Luitfride II, Count of Alsace

Born: Abt 740
-CONTINUED AS #2,ROYAL CHART 1906
Married:

Died: Abt 802

6 Hugh, Count of Tours

Born: Abt 770

Married:

Died: 836

13 Hiltrude

Born:

Died:

Waldrada

Spouse

3 Adelaide of Tours

Born: Abt 819

Died: Abt 866

14

Born:

Married:

Died:

7 Bava

Born: Abt 780

Died: Aft 837

15

Born:

Died:

Sources include: *Royal Ancestors* (1989), charts 11570, 11630-31; Stuart 300; Moriarty 33.

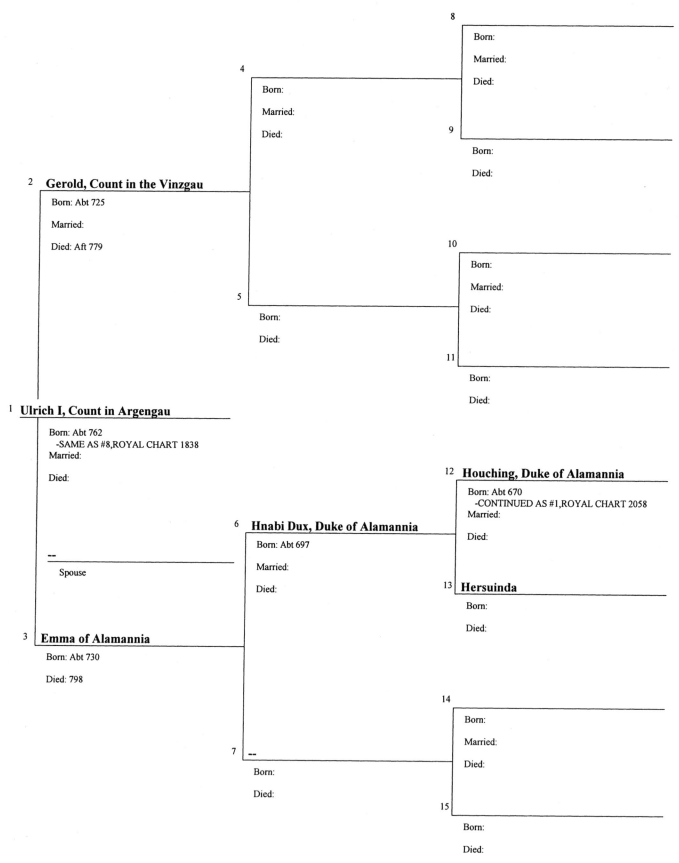

8
Born:
Married:
Died:

4
Born:
Married:
Died:

9
Born:
Died:

2 Gerold, Count in the Vinzgau
Born: Abt 725
Married:
Died: Aft 779

10
Born:
Married:
Died:

5
Born:
Died:

11
Born:
Died:

1 Ulrich I, Count in Argengau
Born: Abt 762
-SAME AS #8,ROYAL CHART 1838
Married:
Died:

12 Houching, Duke of Alamannia
Born: Abt 670
-CONTINUED AS #1,ROYAL CHART 2058
Married:
Died:

6 Hnabi Dux, Duke of Alamannia
Born: Abt 697
Married:
Died:

13 Hersuinda
Born:
Died:

--
Spouse

3 Emma of Alamannia
Born: Abt 730
Died: 798

14
Born:
Married:
Died:

7 --
Born:
Died:

15
Born:
Died:

Sources include: *Royal Ancestors* (1989), chart 11944; Stuart 364; Moriarty 212; *Ancestral Roots* 182 (#2 &3 ancestry).

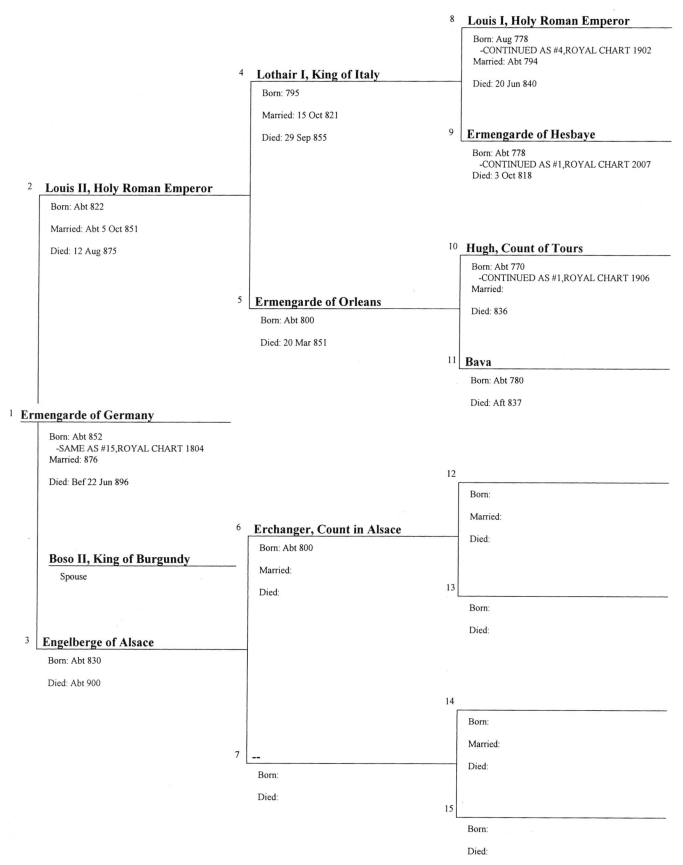

8 Louis I, Holy Roman Emperor

Born: Aug 778
-CONTINUED AS #4,ROYAL CHART 1902
Married: Abt 794

Died: 20 Jun 840

4 Lothair I, King of Italy

Born: 795

Married: 15 Oct 821

Died: 29 Sep 855

9 Ermengarde of Hesbaye

Born: Abt 778
-CONTINUED AS #1,ROYAL CHART 2007
Died: 3 Oct 818

2 Louis II, Holy Roman Emperor

Born: Abt 822

Married: Abt 5 Oct 851

Died: 12 Aug 875

10 Hugh, Count of Tours

Born: Abt 770
-CONTINUED AS #1,ROYAL CHART 1906
Married:

Died: 836

5 Ermengarde of Orleans

Born: Abt 800

Died: 20 Mar 851

11 Bava

Born: Abt 780

Died: Aft 837

1 Ermengarde of Germany

Born: Abt 852
-SAME AS #15,ROYAL CHART 1804
Married: 876

Died: Bef 22 Jun 896

12

Born:

Married:

Died:

6 Erchanger, Count in Alsace

Born: Abt 800

Married:

Died:

13

Born:

Died:

Boso II, King of Burgundy

Spouse

3 Engelberge of Alsace

Born: Abt 830

Died: Abt 900

14

Born:

Married:

Died:

7 --

Born:

Died:

15

Born:

Died:

Sources include: *Royal Ancestors* (1989), chart 12073; Stuart 25; *Ancestral Roots* 141B; Moriarty 51, 259. Note: The ancestry of #3 Engelburge is disputed. In a preliminary Charlemagne manuscript (June 1995), Faris gives #3 as daughter of Gui I De Spolete (Spoleto) & Itana De Benavent, with Gui I given as a grandson of Pepin, King of Italy (see chart 1907, #4). This requires very tight chronology and appears questionable.

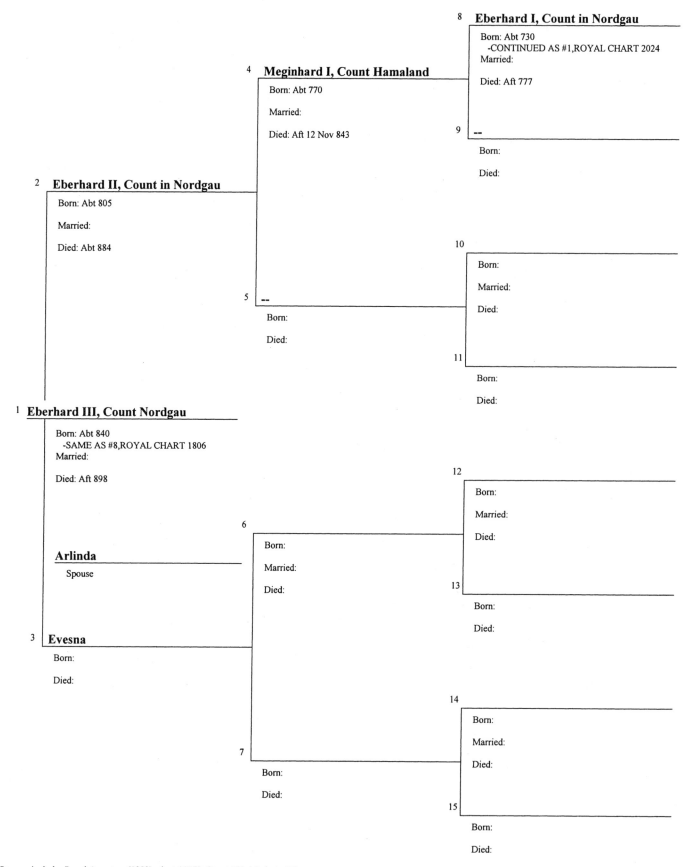

8 Eberhard I, Count in Nordgau
Born: Abt 730
   -CONTINUED AS #1,ROYAL CHART 2024
Married:

Died: Aft 777

4 Meginhard I, Count Hamaland
Born: Abt 770

Married:

Died: Aft 12 Nov 843

9 --
Born:

Died:

2 Eberhard II, Count in Nordgau
Born: Abt 805

Married:

Died: Abt 884

10
Born:

Married:

Died:

5 --
Born:

Died:

11
Born:

Died:

1 Eberhard III, Count Nordgau
Born: Abt 840
   -SAME AS #8,ROYAL CHART 1806
Married:

Died: Aft 898

Arlinda
Spouse

12
Born:

Married:

Died:

6
Born:

Married:

Died:

13
Born:

Died:

3 Evesna
Born:

Died:

14
Born:

Married:

Died:

7
Born:

Died:

15
Born:

Died:

Sources include: *Royal Ancestors* (1989), chart 11773; Stuart 202; Moriarty 181.

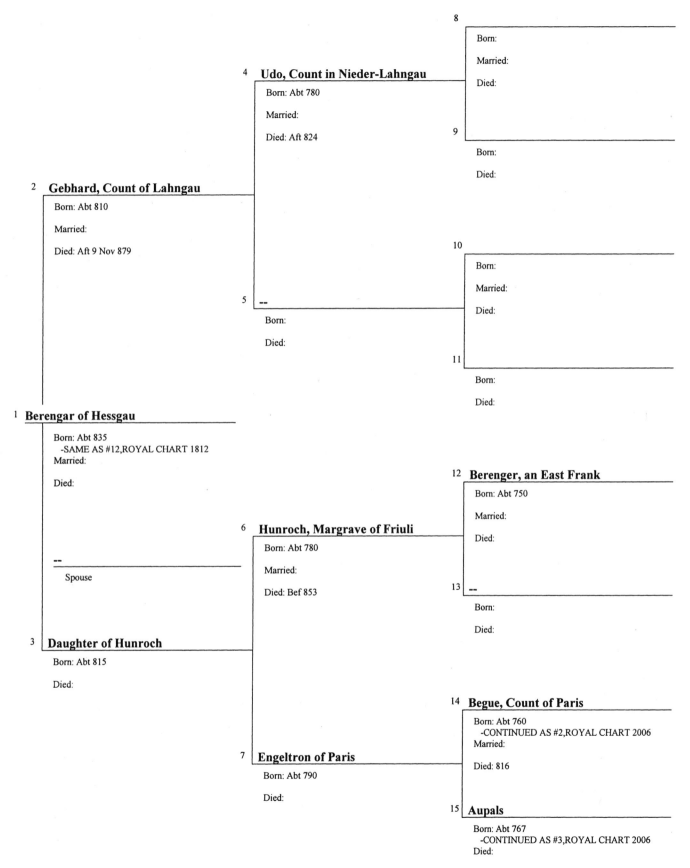

8

Born:

Married:

Died:

4 Udo, Count in Nieder-Lahngau

Born: Abt 780

Married:

Died: Aft 824

9

Born:

Died:

2 Gebhard, Count of Lahngau

Born: Abt 810

Married:

Died: Aft 9 Nov 879

10

Born:

Married:

Died:

5 --

Born:

Died:

11

Born:

Died:

1 Berengar of Hessgau

Born: Abt 835
-SAME AS #12,ROYAL CHART 1812
Married:

Died:

12 Berenger, an East Frank

Born: Abt 750

Married:

Died:

6 Hunroch, Margrave of Friuli

Born: Abt 780

Married:

Died: Bef 853

13 --

Born:

Died:

**-- **

Spouse

3 Daughter of Hunroch

Born: Abt 815

Died:

14 Begue, Count of Paris

Born: Abt 760
-CONTINUED AS #2,ROYAL CHART 2006
Married:

Died: 816

7 Engeltron of Paris

Born: Abt 790

Died:

15 Aupals

Born: Abt 767
-CONTINUED AS #3,ROYAL CHART 2006
Died:

Sources include: *Royal Ancestors* (1989), chart 11617; *Ancestral Roots* 192; Moriarty 23; Stuart 351; *TAG* 72:187-204. Note: The parentage of #2 Gebhard is disputed. Moriarty and Stuart give #4 Udo as shown. #4 is also suggested *(TAG* 72:202*)* to be Eudes (Odo), Count of Orleans (continued chart 1902, #6).

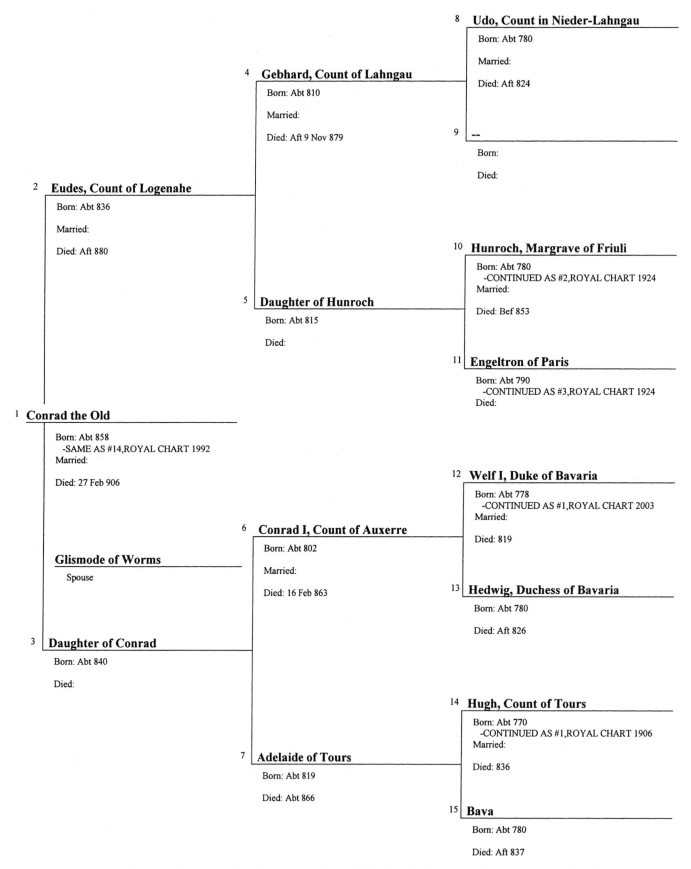

8 | **Udo, Count in Nieder-Lahngau**
Born: Abt 780
Married:
Died: Aft 824

4 | **Gebhard, Count of Lahngau**
Born: Abt 810
Married:
Died: Aft 9 Nov 879

9 | **--**
Born:
Died:

2 | **Eudes, Count of Logenahe**
Born: Abt 836
Married:
Died: Aft 880

10 | **Hunroch, Margrave of Friuli**
Born: Abt 780
-CONTINUED AS #2, ROYAL CHART 1924
Married:
Died: Bef 853

5 | **Daughter of Hunroch**
Born: Abt 815
Died:

11 | **Engeltron of Paris**
Born: Abt 790
-CONTINUED AS #3, ROYAL CHART 1924
Died:

1 | **Conrad the Old**
Born: Abt 858
-SAME AS #14, ROYAL CHART 1992
Married:
Died: 27 Feb 906

Glismode of Worms
Spouse

12 | **Welf I, Duke of Bavaria**
Born: Abt 778
-CONTINUED AS #1, ROYAL CHART 2003
Married:
Died: 819

6 | **Conrad I, Count of Auxerre**
Born: Abt 802
Married:
Died: 16 Feb 863

13 | **Hedwig, Duchess of Bavaria**
Born: Abt 780
Died: Aft 826

3 | **Daughter of Conrad**
Born: Abt 840
Died:

14 | **Hugh, Count of Tours**
Born: Abt 770
-CONTINUED AS #1, ROYAL CHART 1906
Married:
Died: 836

7 | **Adelaide of Tours**
Born: Abt 819
Died: Abt 866

15 | **Bava**
Born: Abt 780
Died: Aft 837

Sources include: *Royal Ancestors* (1989), chart 11617; *Ancestral Roots* 192; Moriarty 23; *TAG* 72:187-204 (#4 Gebhard); Stuart 351 (#4 ancestry), 300, 224 (#6 & 7 ancestry). Note: The parentage of #4 Gebhard is disputed. Moriarty and Stuart give #8 Udo as shown. #8 is also suggested (*TAG* 72:202) to be Eudes (Odo), Count of Orleans (see chart 1902, #6).

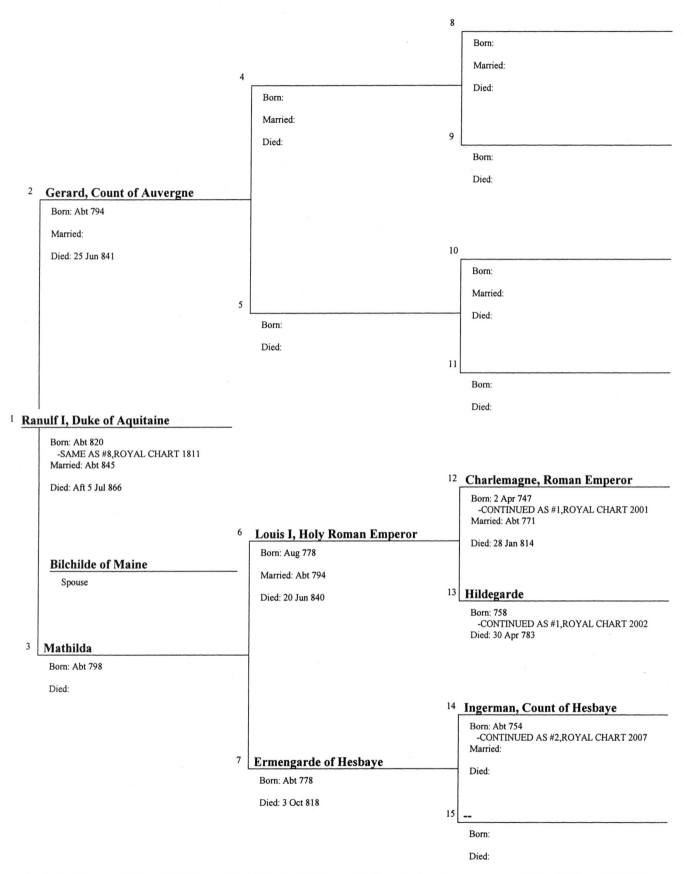

8

Born:

Married:

Died:

4

Born:

Married:

Died:

9

Born:

Died:

2 Gerard, Count of Auvergne

Born: Abt 794

Married:

Died: 25 Jun 841

10

Born:

Married:

Died:

5

Born:

Died:

11

Born:

Died:

1 Ranulf I, Duke of Aquitaine

Born: Abt 820
  -SAME AS #8,ROYAL CHART 1811
Married: Abt 845

Died: Aft 5 Jul 866

12 Charlemagne, Roman Emperor

Born: 2 Apr 747
  -CONTINUED AS #1,ROYAL CHART 2001
Married: Abt 771

Died: 28 Jan 814

6 Louis I, Holy Roman Emperor

Born: Aug 778

Married: Abt 794

Died: 20 Jun 840

13 Hildegarde

Born: 758
  -CONTINUED AS #1,ROYAL CHART 2002
Died: 30 Apr 783

Bilchilde of Maine

Spouse

3 Mathilda

Born: Abt 798

Died:

14 Ingerman, Count of Hesbaye

Born: Abt 754
  -CONTINUED AS #2,ROYAL CHART 2007
Married:

Died:

7 Ermengarde of Hesbaye

Born: Abt 778

Died: 3 Oct 818

15 --

Born:

Died:

Sources include: *Royal Ancestors* (1989), chart 11619; *Ancestral Roots* 144A; Stuart 163; Moriarty 26; Faris preliminary Charlemagne manuscript (June 1995), pp. 215-216. Note: #3 was an unknown daughter (<u>perhaps</u> Mathilda or Rotrude) of Louis I and Ermengarde.

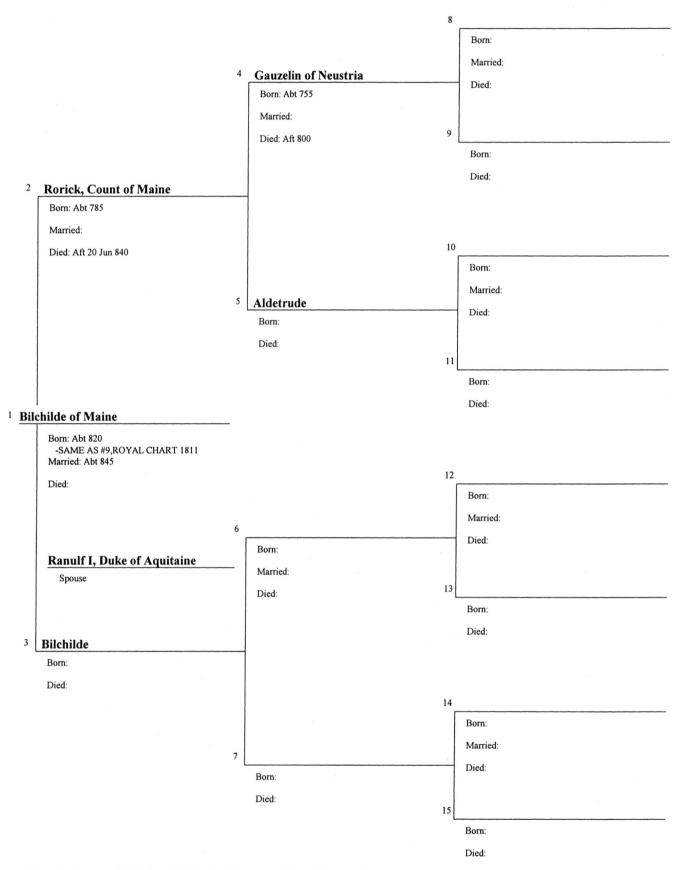

8

Born:

Married:

Died:

4 Gauzelin of Neustria

Born: Abt 755

Married:

Died: Aft 800

9

Born:

Died:

2 Rorick, Count of Maine

Born: Abt 785

Married:

Died: Aft 20 Jun 840

10

Born:

Married:

Died:

5 Aldetrude

Born:

Died:

11

Born:

Died:

1 Bilchilde of Maine

Born: Abt 820
-SAME AS #9,ROYAL CHART 1811
Married: Abt 845

Died:

12

Born:

Married:

Died:

6

Born:

Married:

Died:

Ranulf I, Duke of Aquitaine

Spouse

13

Born:

Died:

3 Bilchilde

Born:

Died:

14

Born:

Married:

Died:

7

Born:

Died:

15

Born:

Died:

Sources include: *Royal Ancestors* (1989), chart 11620; Moriarty 26-27; *Ancestral Roots* 144A; Stuart 163-38. Note: #1 was a daughter of Rorick, <u>probably</u> Bilchilde, who had married first Bernard, Count of Poitou.

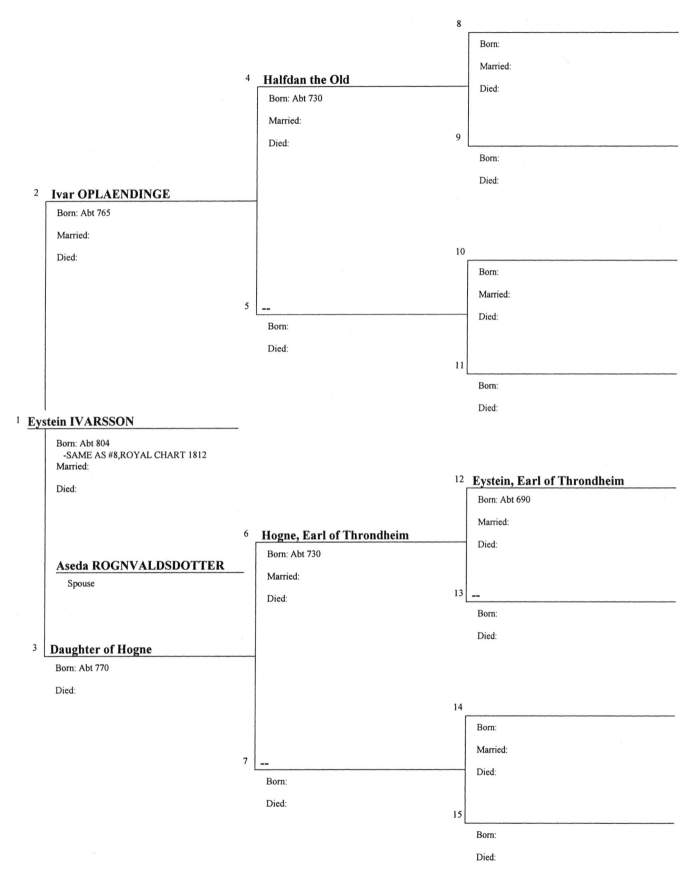

8

Born:

Married:

Died:

4 **Halfdan the Old**

Born: Abt 730

Married:

Died:

9

Born:

Died:

2 **Ivar OPLAENDINGE**

Born: Abt 765

Married:

Died:

10

Born:

Married:

Died:

5 --

Born:

Died:

11

Born:

Died:

1 **Eystein IVARSSON**

Born: Abt 804
-SAME AS #8,ROYAL CHART 1812
Married:

Died:

12 **Eystein, Earl of Throndheim**

Born: Abt 690

Married:

Died:

6 **Hogne, Earl of Throndheim**

Born: Abt 730

Married:

Died:

Aseda ROGNVALDSDOTTER

Spouse

13 --

Born:

Died:

3 **Daughter of Hogne**

Born: Abt 770

Died:

14

Born:

Married:

Died:

7 --

Born:

Died:

15

Born:

Died:

Sources include: *Royal Ancestors* (1989), chart 11623; Stuart 44, 386; Moriarty 10; *Ancestral Roots* 121E. Note: #12 Eystein was son of Thrond.

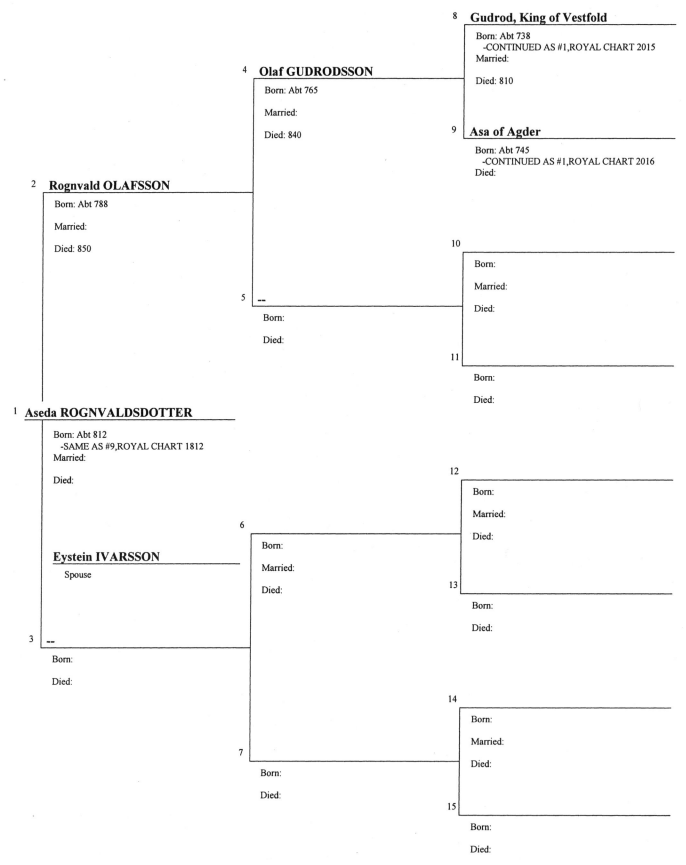

8 **Gudrod, King of Vestfold**

Born: Abt 738
-CONTINUED AS #1,ROYAL CHART 2015
Married:

Died: 810

4 **Olaf GUDRODSSON**

Born: Abt 765

Married:

Died: 840

9 **Asa of Agder**

Born: Abt 745
-CONTINUED AS #1,ROYAL CHART 2016
Died:

2 **Rognvald OLAFSSON**

Born: Abt 788

Married:

Died: 850

10

Born:

Married:

Died:

5 --

Born:

Died:

11

Born:

Died:

1 **Aseda ROGNVALDSDOTTER**

Born: Abt 812
-SAME AS #9,ROYAL CHART 1812
Married:

Died:

12

Born:

Married:

Died:

6

Born:

Married:

Died:

13

Born:

Died:

Eystein IVARSSON

Spouse

3 --

Born:

Died:

14

Born:

Married:

Died:

7

Born:

Died:

15

Born:

Died:

Sources include: *Royal Ancestors* (1989), chart 11603; Stuart 166. Note: Chronological considerations suggest that the descent claimed above from #8 Gudrod is very uncertain. Gudrod may have been born much later than the date assigned above. Compare chart 2269.

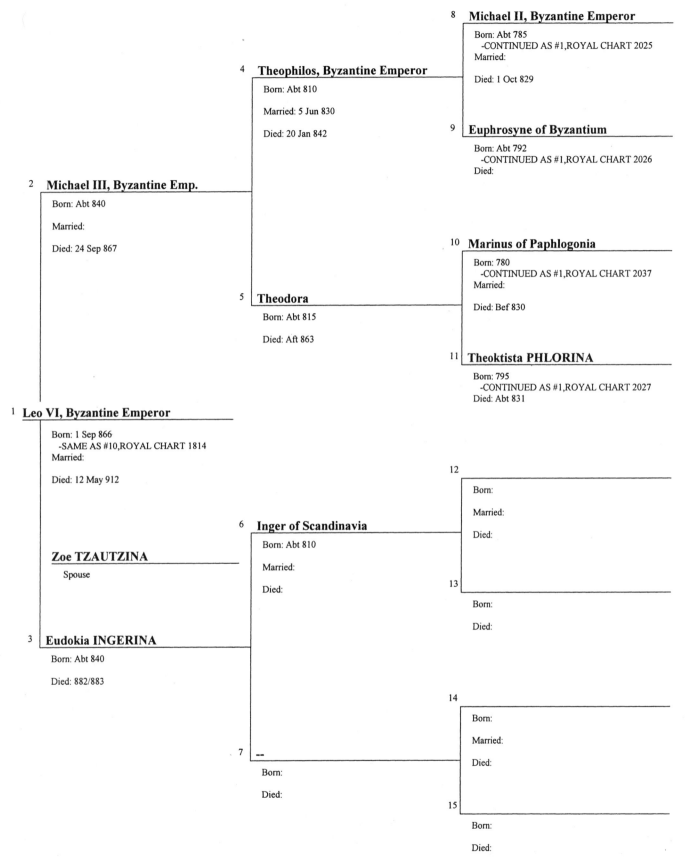

8 Michael II, Byzantine Emperor

Born: Abt 785
  -CONTINUED AS #1,ROYAL CHART 2025
Married:

Died: 1 Oct 829

4 Theophilos, Byzantine Emperor

Born: Abt 810

Married: 5 Jun 830

Died: 20 Jan 842

9 Euphrosyne of Byzantium

Born: Abt 792
  -CONTINUED AS #1,ROYAL CHART 2026
Died:

2 Michael III, Byzantine Emp.

Born: Abt 840

Married:

Died: 24 Sep 867

10 Marinus of Paphlogonia

Born: 780
  -CONTINUED AS #1,ROYAL CHART 2037
Married:

Died: Bef 830

5 Theodora

Born: Abt 815

Died: Aft 863

11 Theoktista PHLORINA

Born: 795
  -CONTINUED AS #1,ROYAL CHART 2027
Died: Abt 831

1 Leo VI, Byzantine Emperor

Born: 1 Sep 866
  -SAME AS #10,ROYAL CHART 1814
Married:

Died: 12 May 912

Zoe TZAUTZINA

Spouse

12

Born:

Married:

Died:

6 Inger of Scandinavia

Born: Abt 810

Married:

Died:

13

Born:

Died:

3 Eudokia INGERINA

Born: Abt 840

Died: 882/883

14

Born:

Married:

Died:

7 --

Born:

Died:

15

Born:

Died:

Sources include: *Royal Ancestors* (1989), chart 12058; *The Genealogist* 2:5-7, 21; Stuart 253, 322A; *Ancestral Roots* 141A. Notes: #3 Eudokia was a mistress of #2 Michael. She married Basil I. It is uncertain which was the father of #1 Leo. Anthony R. Wagner (*Pedigree and Progress*, pedigree 43, p. 202) follows the Basil I line. Stuart, citing Brook (*The Genealogist*) and Settipani, concludes that the weight of evidence leans toward Michael, as followed above. Basil I was son of Konstantinos and Pancalo (see chart 2038). #9 is also claimed to be Thekla, 1st wife. Euphrosyne was a 2nd wife.

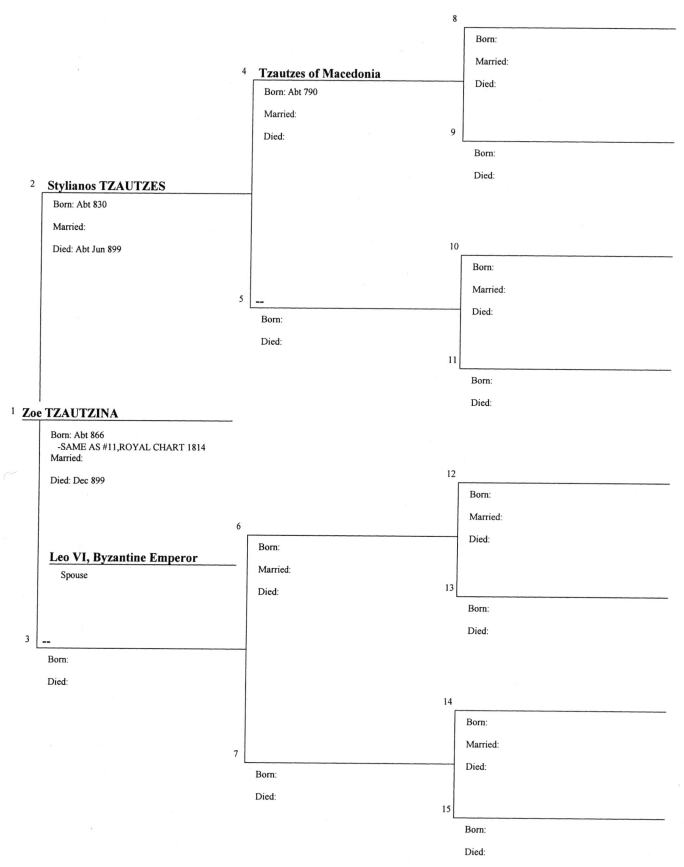

8

Born:

Married:

Died:

4 Tzautzes of Macedonia

Born: Abt 790

Married:

Died:

9

Born:

Died:

2 Stylianos TZAUTZES

Born: Abt 830

Married:

Died: Abt Jun 899

10

Born:

Married:

Died:

5 --

Born:

Died:

11

Born:

Died:

1 Zoe TZAUTZINA

Born: Abt 866
  -SAME AS #11,ROYAL CHART 1814
Married:

Died: Dec 899

12

Born:

Married:

Died:

6

Born:

Married:

Died:

13

Born:

Died:

Leo VI, Byzantine Emperor

Spouse

3 --

Born:

Died:

14

Born:

Married:

Died:

7

Born:

Died:

15

Born:

Died:

Sources include: *Royal Ancestors* (1989), chart 12070; *The Genealogist* 2:27; Stuart 253-39.

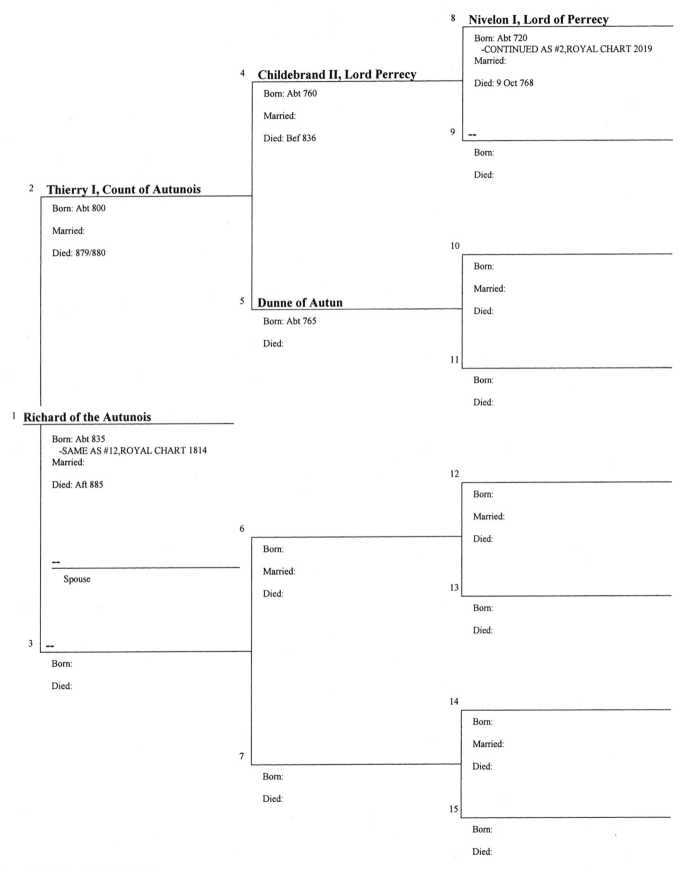

8   **Nivelon I, Lord of Perrecy**

Born: Abt 720
  -CONTINUED AS #2,ROYAL CHART 2019
Married:

Died: 9 Oct 768

9   --

Born:

Died:

4   **Childebrand II, Lord Perrecy**

Born: Abt 760

Married:

Died: Bef 836

2   **Thierry I, Count of Autunois**

Born: Abt 800

Married:

Died: 879/880

10

Born:

Married:

Died:

5   **Dunne of Autun**

Born: Abt 765

Died:

11

Born:

Died:

1   **Richard of the Autunois**

Born: Abt 835
  -SAME AS #12,ROYAL CHART 1814
Married:

Died: Aft 885

12

Born:

Married:

Died:

6

Born:

Married:

Died:

13

Born:

Died:

3   --

Born:

Died:

--   Spouse

14

Born:

Married:

Died:

7

Born:

Died:

15

Born:

Died:

Sources include: Stuart 173; Moriarty 257.

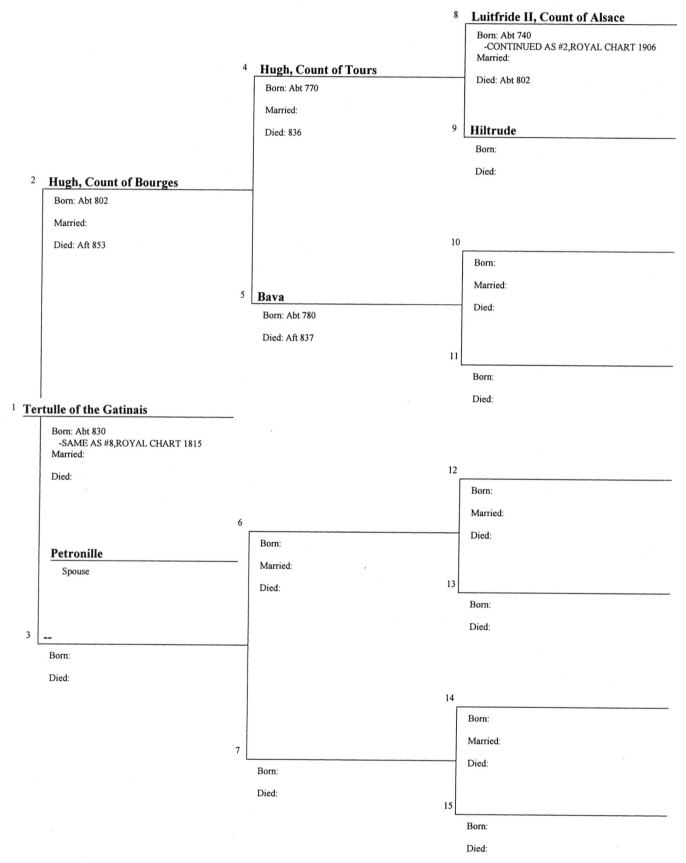

8 Luitfride II, Count of Alsace
Born: Abt 740
    -CONTINUED AS #2, ROYAL CHART 1906
Married:

Died: Abt 802

4 Hugh, Count of Tours
Born: Abt 770

Married:

Died: 836

9 Hiltrude
Born:

Died:

2 Hugh, Count of Bourges
Born: Abt 802

Married:

Died: Aft 853

10
Born:

Married:

Died:

5 Bava
Born: Abt 780

Died: Aft 837

11
Born:

Died:

1 Tertulle of the Gatinais
Born: Abt 830
    -SAME AS #8, ROYAL CHART 1815
Married:

Died:

12
Born:

Married:

Died:

6
Born:

Married:

Died:

13
Born:

Died:

Petronille
Spouse

3 --
Born:

Died:

14
Born:

Married:

Died:

7
Born:

Died:

15
Born:

Died:

Sources include: Stuart 167; Moriarty 37; *Royal Ancestors* (1989), chart 11502.

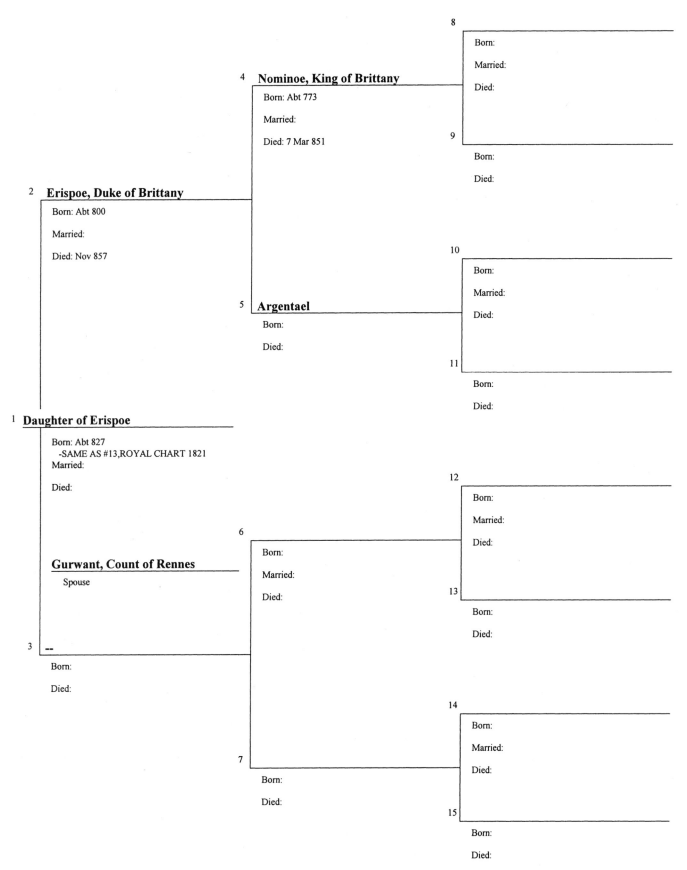

8

Born:

Married:

Died:

4 **Nominoe, King of Brittany**

Born: Abt 773

Married:

Died: 7 Mar 851

9

Born:

Died:

2 **Erispoe, Duke of Brittany**

Born: Abt 800

Married:

Died: Nov 857

10

Born:

Married:

Died:

5 **Argentael**

Born:

Died:

11

Born:

Died:

1 **Daughter of Erispoe**

Born: Abt 827
  -SAME AS #13,ROYAL CHART 1821
Married:

Died:

12

Born:

Married:

Died:

Gurwant, Count of Rennes

Spouse

6

Born:

Married:

Died:

13

Born:

Died:

3 **--**

Born:

Died:

14

Born:

Married:

Died:

7

Born:

Died:

15

Born:

Died:

Sources include: *Royal Ancestors* (1989), charts 11931-32; Moriarty 13; Stuart 405; *TAG* 74:149 (parentage and ancestry of #4 Nominoe unknown).

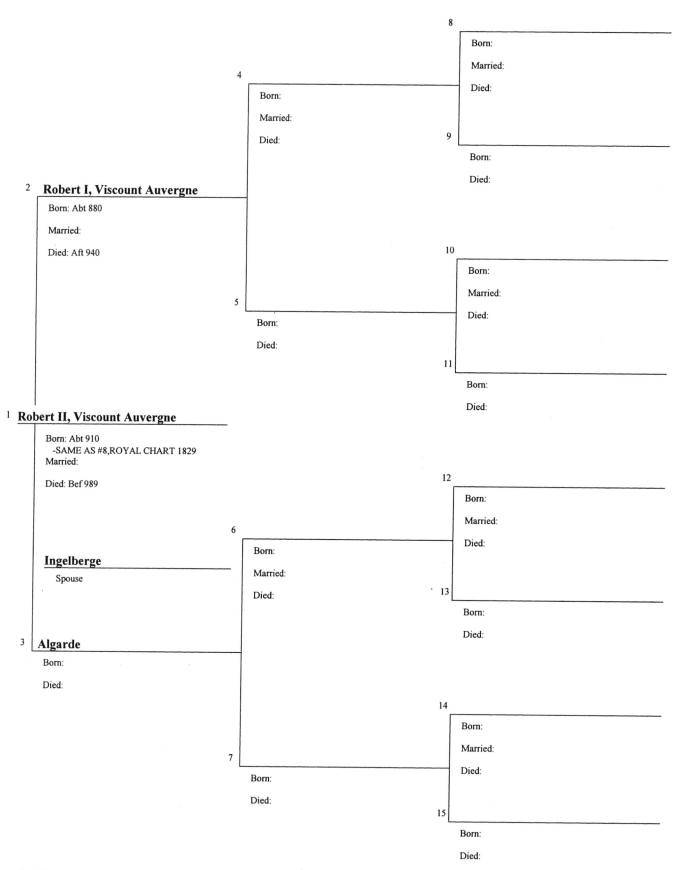

8

Born:

Married:

Died:

4

Born:

Married:

Died:

9

Born:

Died:

2 Robert I, Viscount Auvergne

Born: Abt 880

Married:

Died: Aft 940

10

Born:

Married:

Died:

5

Born:

Died:

11

Born:

Died:

1 Robert II, Viscount Auvergne

Born: Abt 910
  -SAME AS #8,ROYAL CHART 1829
Married:

Died: Bef 989

12

Born:

Married:

Died:

6

Born:

Married:

Died:

13

Born:

Died:

Ingelberge

Spouse

3 Algarde

Born:

Died:

14

Born:

Married:

Died:

7

Born:

Died:

15

Born:

Died:

Sources include: *Royal Ancestors* (1989), chart 11591; Moriarty 118; Stuart 127. Note: The parentage of #2 & 3 are both disputed.

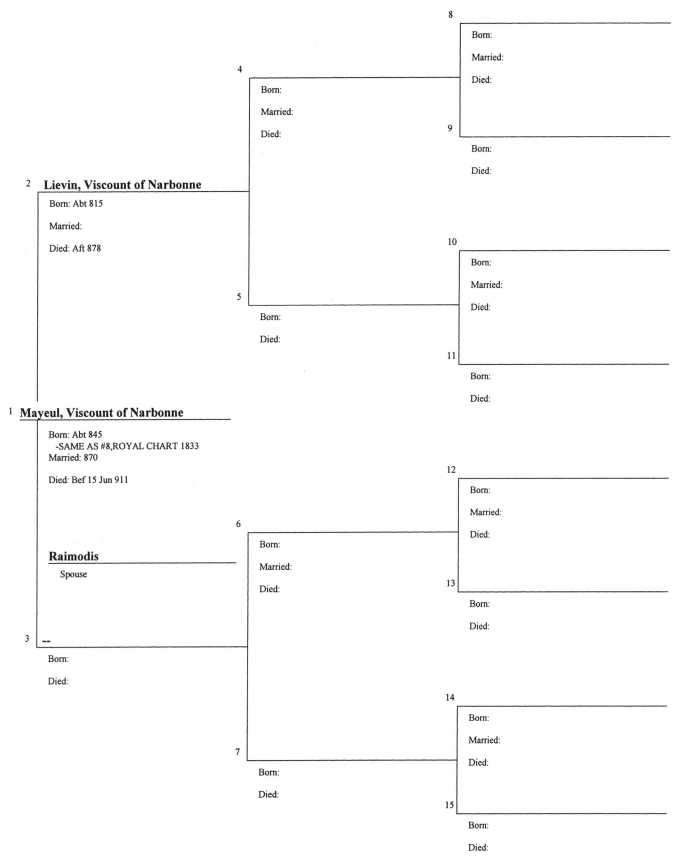

8

Born:

Married:

Died:

4

Born:

Married:

Died:

9

Born:

Died:

2 Lievin, Viscount of Narbonne

Born: Abt 815

Married:

Died: Aft 878

10

Born:

Married:

Died:

5

Born:

Died:

11

Born:

Died:

1 Mayeul, Viscount of Narbonne

Born: Abt 845
  -SAME AS #8,ROYAL CHART 1833
Married: 870

Died: Bef 15 Jun 911

12

Born:

Married:

Died:

6

Born:

Married:

Died:

13

Born:

Died:

Raimodis

Spouse

3 --

Born:

Died:

14

Born:

Married:

Died:

7

Born:

Died:

15

Born:

Died:

Sources include: *Royal Ancestors* (1989), chart 11757; Stuart 101, 53; Moriarty 1. Note: #2 Lievin is not certain. His parentage and grandparentage is unknown. Moriarty (copied by Stuart) gives him as a possible great-grandson of Milo (Count of Narbonne, died after 782), who was son of Guerin and Adelindis (continued chart 2065).

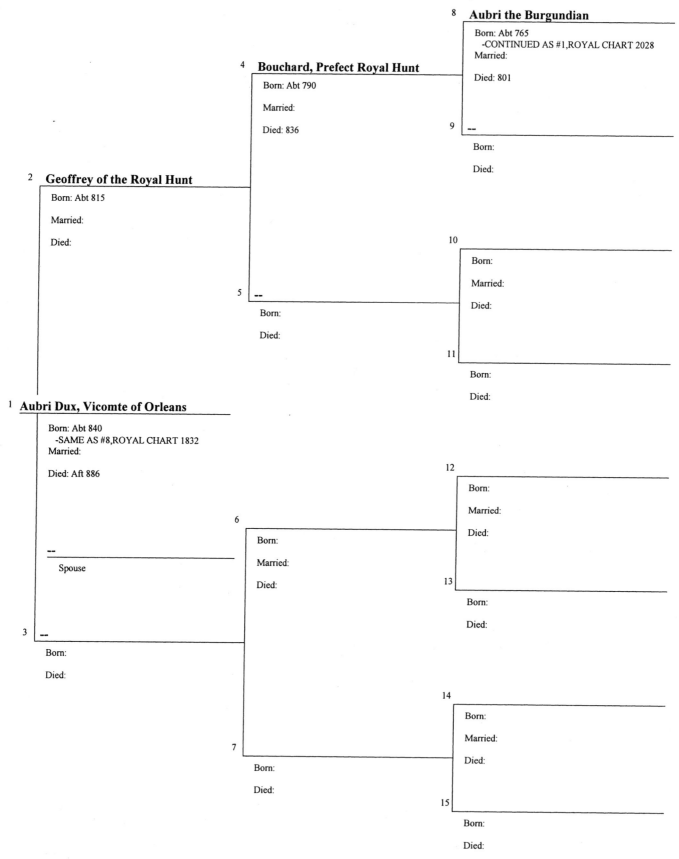

8 Aubri the Burgundian

Born: Abt 765
  -CONTINUED AS #1,ROYAL CHART 2028
Married:

Died: 801

4 Bouchard, Prefect Royal Hunt

Born: Abt 790

Married:

Died: 836

9 --

Born:

Died:

2 Geoffrey of the Royal Hunt

Born: Abt 815

Married:

Died:

10

Born:

Married:

Died:

5 --

Born:

Died:

11

Born:

Died:

1 Aubri Dux, Vicomte of Orleans

Born: Abt 840
  -SAME AS #8,ROYAL CHART 1832
Married:

Died: Aft 886

12

Born:

Married:

Died:

6

Born:

Married:

Died:

13

Born:

Died:

--

Spouse

3 --

Born:

Died:

14

Born:

Married:

Died:

7

Born:

Died:

15

Born:

Died:

Sources include: *Royal Ancestors* (1989), charts 11965-66; Stuart 53; Moriarty 1. Note: #2 is uncertain, perhaps Geoffrey, perhaps son of Bouchard.

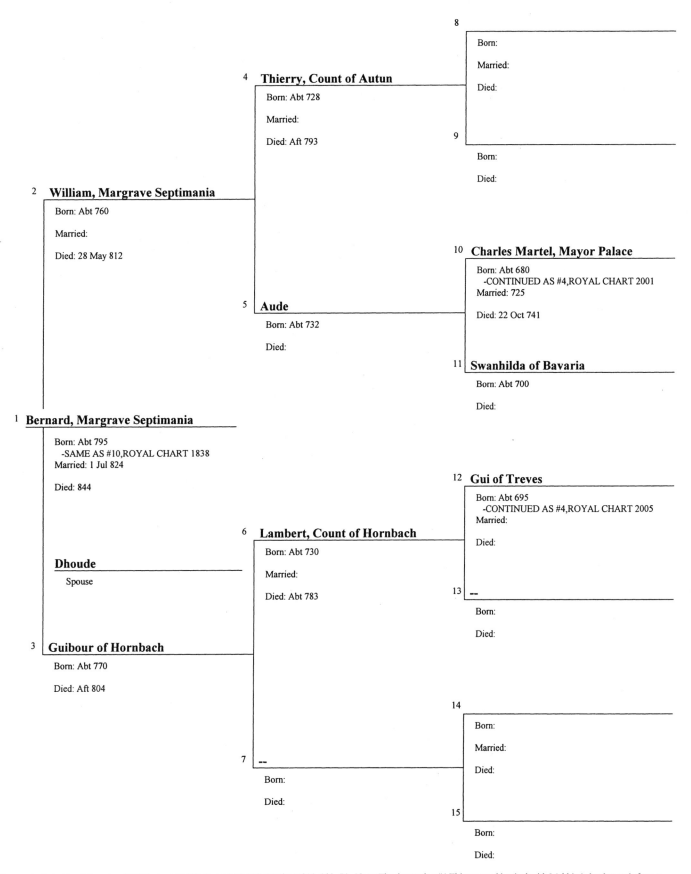

8

Born:

Married:

Died:

4 Thierry, Count of Autun

Born: Abt 728

Married:

Died: Aft 793

9

Born:

Died:

2 William, Margrave Septimania

Born: Abt 760

Married:

Died: 28 May 812

10 Charles Martel, Mayor Palace

Born: Abt 680
  -CONTINUED AS #4,ROYAL CHART 2001
Married: 725

Died: 22 Oct 741

5 Aude

Born: Abt 732

Died:

11 Swanhilda of Bavaria

Born: Abt 700

Died:

1 Bernard, Margrave Septimania

Born: Abt 795
  -SAME AS #10,ROYAL CHART 1838
Married: 1 Jul 824

Died: 844

12 Gui of Treves

Born: Abt 695
  -CONTINUED AS #4,ROYAL CHART 2005
Married:

Died:

6 Lambert, Count of Hornbach

Born: Abt 730

Married:

Died: Abt 783

13 --

Born:

Died:

Dhoude

Spouse

3 Guibour of Hornbach

Born: Abt 770

Died: Aft 804

14

Born:

Married:

Died:

7 --

Born:

Died:

15

Born:

Died:

Sources include: *Royal Ancestors* (1989), chart 11624; Stuart 326, 330; Moriarty 215, 232, 74. Note: The theory that #4 Thierry was identical with Makhir (who descends from a long line of Jewish exilarchs at Babylon with biblical descent) has recently been disproved in a Nathaniel L. Taylor article (see *TAG* 72:205-223; 74:148, 150). Moriarty suggests that #4 Thierry may be a son of Rolande (married Bernier) and grandson of Bertha (a Merovingian princess). Bertha was perhaps the daughter of Thierry III, King of Austrasia (see chart 2057).

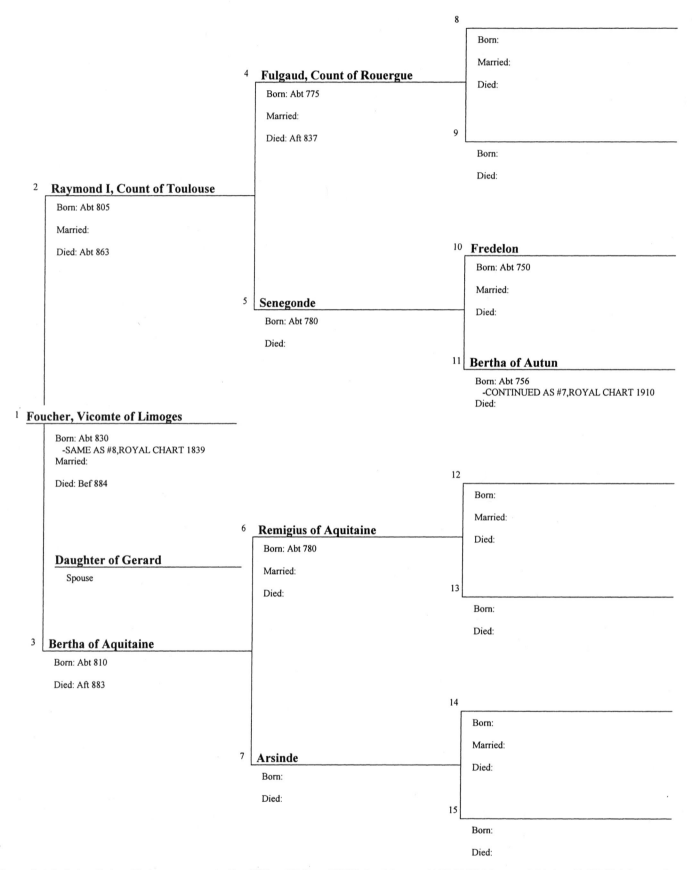

4 Fulgaud, Count of Rouergue
Born: Abt 775
Married:
Died: Aft 837

8
Born:
Married:
Died:

9
Born:
Died:

2 Raymond I, Count of Toulouse
Born: Abt 805
Married:
Died: Abt 863

10 Fredelon
Born: Abt 750
Married:
Died:

5 Senegonde
Born: Abt 780
Died:

11 Bertha of Autun
Born: Abt 756
    -CONTINUED AS #7,ROYAL CHART 1910
Died:

1 Foucher, Vicomte of Limoges
Born: Abt 830
    -SAME AS #8,ROYAL CHART 1839
Married:
Died: Bef 884

Daughter of Gerard
Spouse

6 Remigius of Aquitaine
Born: Abt 780
Married:
Died:

12
Born:
Married:
Died:

13
Born:
Died:

3 Bertha of Aquitaine
Born: Abt 810
Died: Aft 883

7 Arsinde
Born:
Died:

14
Born:
Married:
Died:

15
Born:
Died:

Sources include: Faris preliminary Charlemagne manuscript (June 1995), p. 165; Stuart 328-329; *Royal Ancestors* 11627-28 (#2 & 3 ancestry); Moriarty 41, 232 (#2 & 3 ancestry).

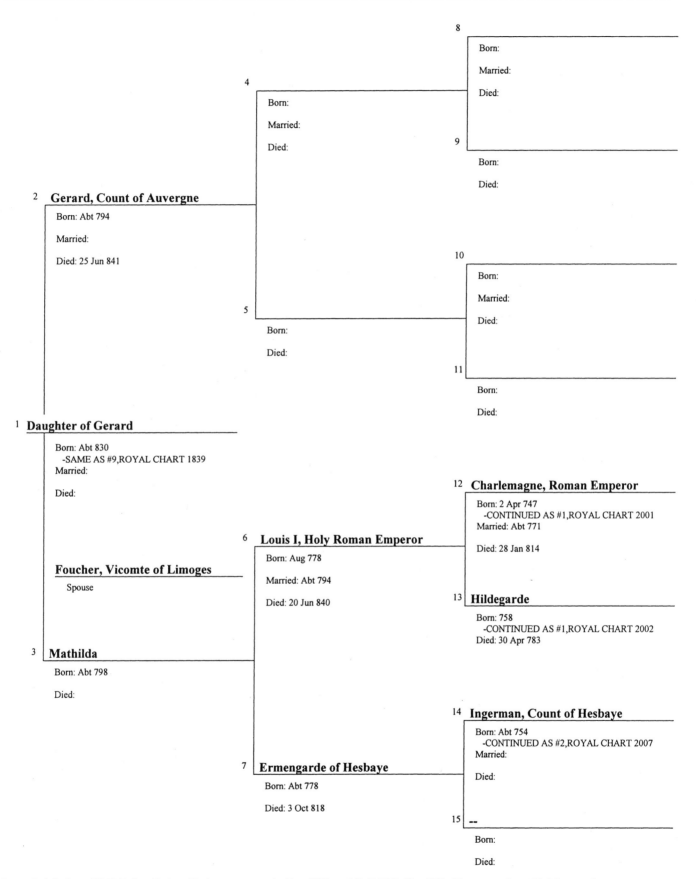

8

Born:

Married:

Died:

4

Born:

Married:

Died:

9

Born:

Died:

2 Gerard, Count of Auvergne

Born: Abt 794

Married:

Died: 25 Jun 841

10

Born:

Married:

Died:

5

Born:

Died:

11

Born:

Died:

1 Daughter of Gerard

Born: Abt 830
-SAME AS #9,ROYAL CHART 1839
Married:

Died:

12 Charlemagne, Roman Emperor

Born: 2 Apr 747
-CONTINUED AS #1,ROYAL CHART 2001
Married: Abt 771

Died: 28 Jan 814

6 Louis I, Holy Roman Emperor

Born: Aug 778

Married: Abt 794

Died: 20 Jun 840

Foucher, Vicomte of Limoges

Spouse

13 Hildegarde

Born: 758
-CONTINUED AS #1,ROYAL CHART 2002
Died: 30 Apr 783

3 Mathilda

Born: Abt 798

Died:

14 Ingerman, Count of Hesbaye

Born: Abt 754
-CONTINUED AS #2,ROYAL CHART 2007
Married:

Died:

7 Ermengarde of Hesbaye

Born: Abt 778

Died: 3 Oct 818

15 --

Born:

Died:

Sources include: Stuart 328-39; Faris preliminary Charlemagne manuscript (June 1995), pp. 165, 215-216; Chart 1935 with sources and note (#2 & 3 ancestry).

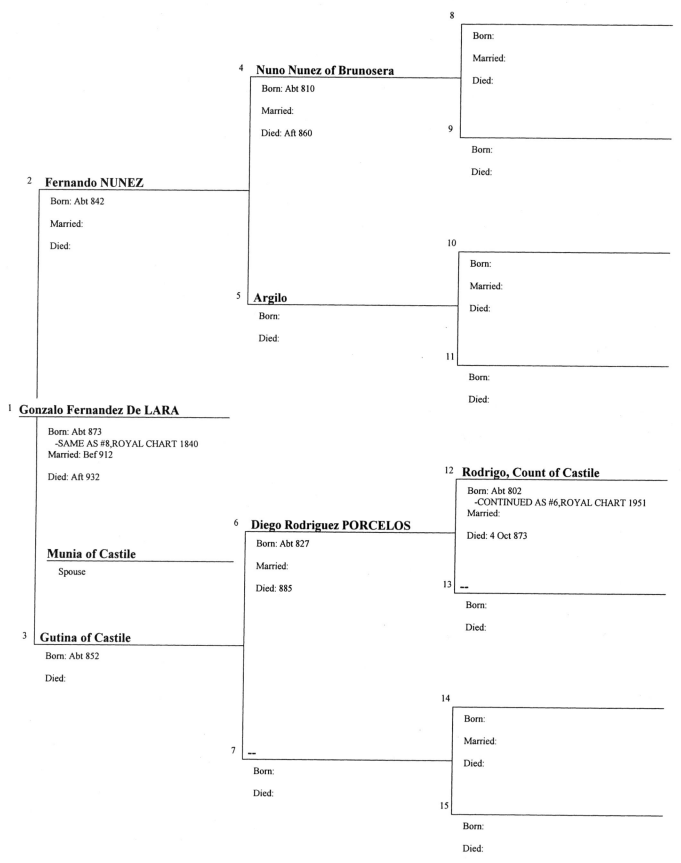

8

Born:

Married:

Died:

4 | **Nuno Nunez of Brunosera**

Born: Abt 810

Married:

Died: Aft 860

9

Born:

Died:

2 | **Fernando NUNEZ**

Born: Abt 842

Married:

Died:

10

Born:

Married:

Died:

5 | **Argilo**

Born:

Died:

11

Born:

Died:

1 | **Gonzalo Fernandez De LARA**

Born: Abt 873
  -SAME AS #8,ROYAL CHART 1840
Married: Bef 912

Died: Aft 932

12 | **Rodrigo, Count of Castile**

Born: Abt 802
  -CONTINUED AS #6,ROYAL CHART 1951
Married:

Died: 4 Oct 873

6 | **Diego Rodriguez PORCELOS**

Born: Abt 827

Married:

Died: 885

13 | --

Born:

Died:

Munia of Castile

Spouse

3 | **Gutina of Castile**

Born: Abt 852

Died:

14

Born:

Married:

Died:

7 | --

Born:

Died:

15

Born:

Died:

Sources include: *Royal Ancestors* (1989), charts 11762, 11933; Stuart 285; Moriarty 79, 225.

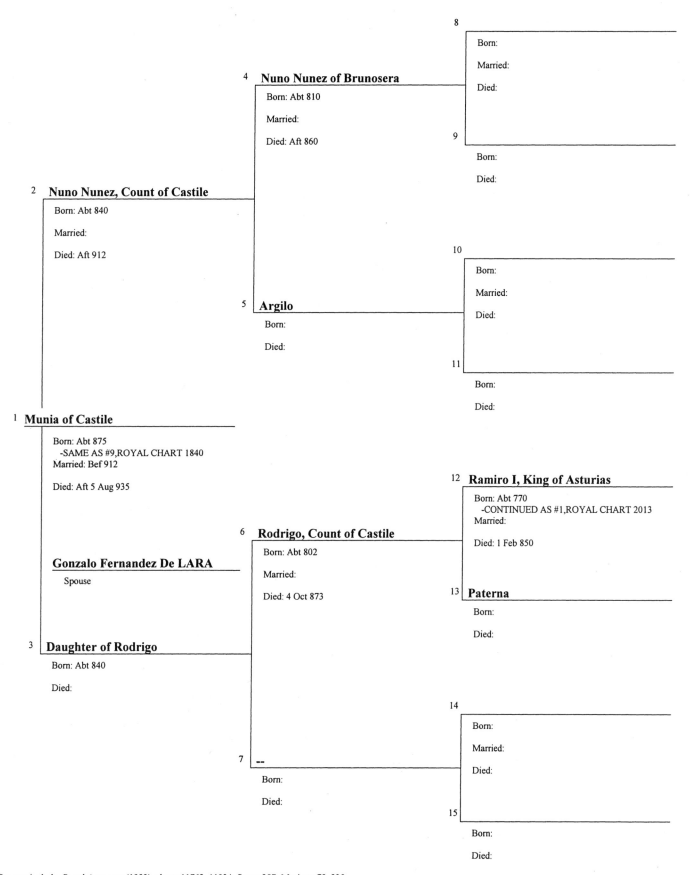

8

Born:

Married:

Died:

4 Nuno Nunez of Brunosera

Born: Abt 810

Married:

Died: Aft 860

9

Born:

Died:

2 Nuno Nunez, Count of Castile

Born: Abt 840

Married:

Died: Aft 912

10

Born:

Married:

Died:

5 Argilo

Born:

Died:

11

Born:

Died:

1 Munia of Castile

Born: Abt 875
-SAME AS #9,ROYAL CHART 1840
Married: Bef 912

Died: Aft 5 Aug 935

Gonzalo Fernandez De LARA

Spouse

12 Ramiro I, King of Asturias

Born: Abt 770
-CONTINUED AS #1,ROYAL CHART 2013
Married:

Died: 1 Feb 850

6 Rodrigo, Count of Castile

Born: Abt 802

Married:

Died: 4 Oct 873

13 Paterna

Born:

Died:

3 Daughter of Rodrigo

Born: Abt 840

Died:

14

Born:

Married:

Died:

7 --

Born:

Died:

15

Born:

Died:

Sources include: *Royal Ancestors* (1989), charts 11762, 11934; Stuart 287; Moriarty 79, 225.

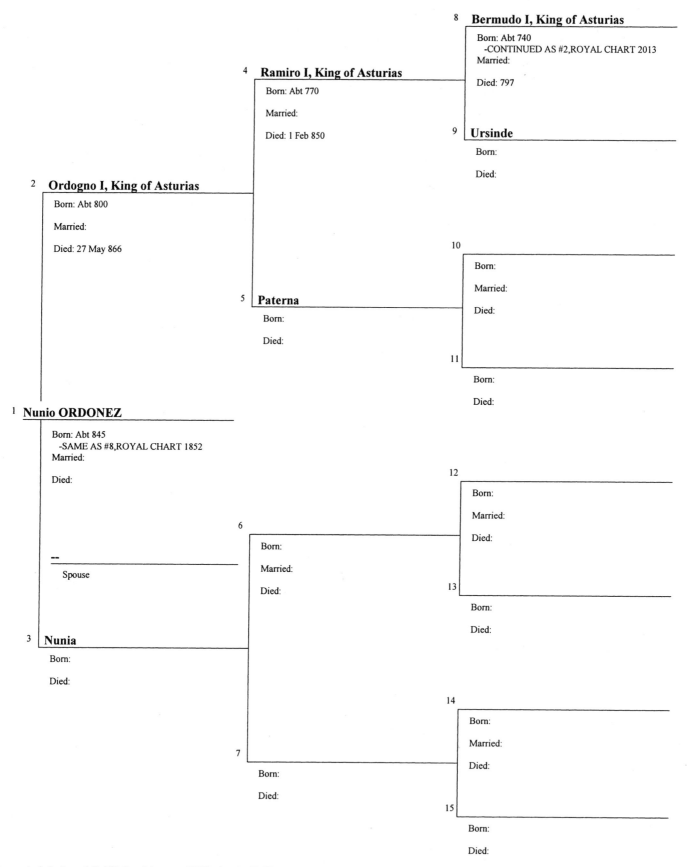

8 Bermudo I, King of Asturias
Born: Abt 740
  -CONTINUED AS #2,ROYAL CHART 2013
Married:

Died: 797

4 Ramiro I, King of Asturias
Born: Abt 770

Married:

Died: 1 Feb 850

9 Ursinde
Born:

Died:

2 Ordogno I, King of Asturias
Born: Abt 800

Married:

Died: 27 May 866

10
Born:

Married:

Died:

5 Paterna
Born:

Died:

11
Born:

Died:

1 Nunio ORDONEZ
Born: Abt 845
  -SAME AS #8,ROYAL CHART 1852
Married:

Died:

12
Born:

Married:

Died:

6
Born:

Married:

Died:

13
Born:

Died:

--
  Spouse

3 Nunia
Born:

Died:

14
Born:

Married:

Died:

7
Born:

Died:

15
Born:

Died:

Sources include: Stuart 267, 276; *Royal Ancestors* (1989), chart 11590 (#2 ancestry); Moriarty 82 (#2 ancestry).

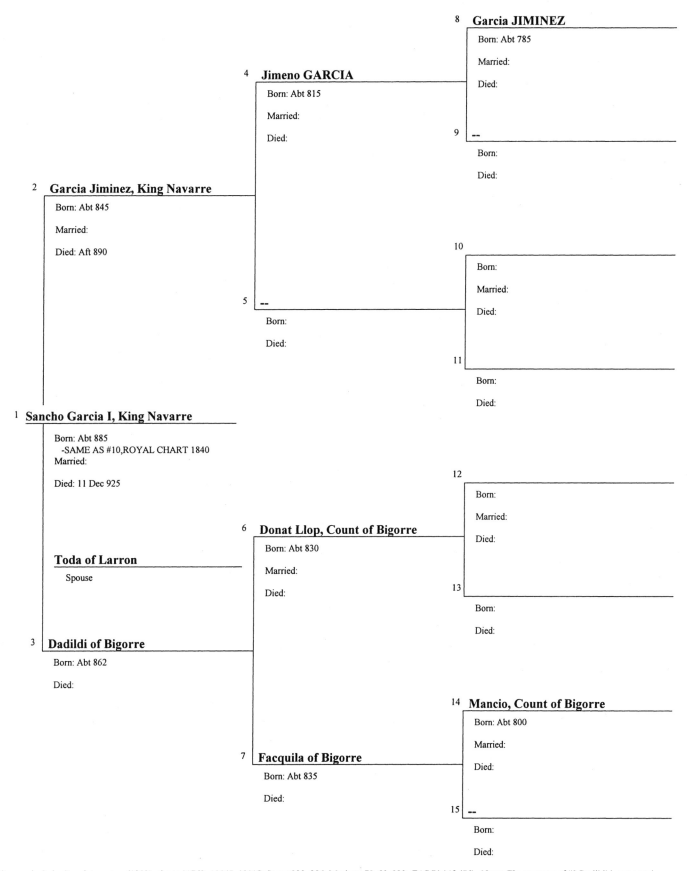

8 Garcia JIMINEZ

Born: Abt 785

Married:

Died:

4 Jimeno GARCIA

Born: Abt 815

Married:

Died:

9 --

Born:

Died:

2 Garcia Jiminez, King Navarre

Born: Abt 845

Married:

Died: Aft 890

10

Born:

Married:

Died:

5 --

Born:

Died:

11

Born:

Died:

1 Sancho Garcia I, King Navarre

Born: Abt 885
    -SAME AS #10,ROYAL CHART 1840
Married:

Died: 11 Dec 925

12

Born:

Married:

Died:

6 Donat Llop, Count of Bigorre

Born: Abt 830

Married:

Died:

13

Born:

Died:

Toda of Larron

Spouse

3 Dadildi of Bigorre

Born: Abt 862

Died:

14 Mancio, Count of Bigorre

Born: Abt 800

Married:

Died:

7 Facquila of Bigorre

Born: Abt 835

Died:

15 --

Born:

Died:

Sources include: *Royal Ancestors* (1989), charts 11762, 11567, 12117; Stuart 223, 286; Moriarty 70, 80, 222; *TAG* 74:148 (#6). Notes: The ancestry of #3 Dadildi is not certain. Moriarty and Stuart claim additional ancestry for #6 Donat, and they insert an additional Llop between #3 & 6, which has been omitted here to place #6 Donat nearer the end of the 9th century. His parentage is unknown. See *TAG* 74:148.

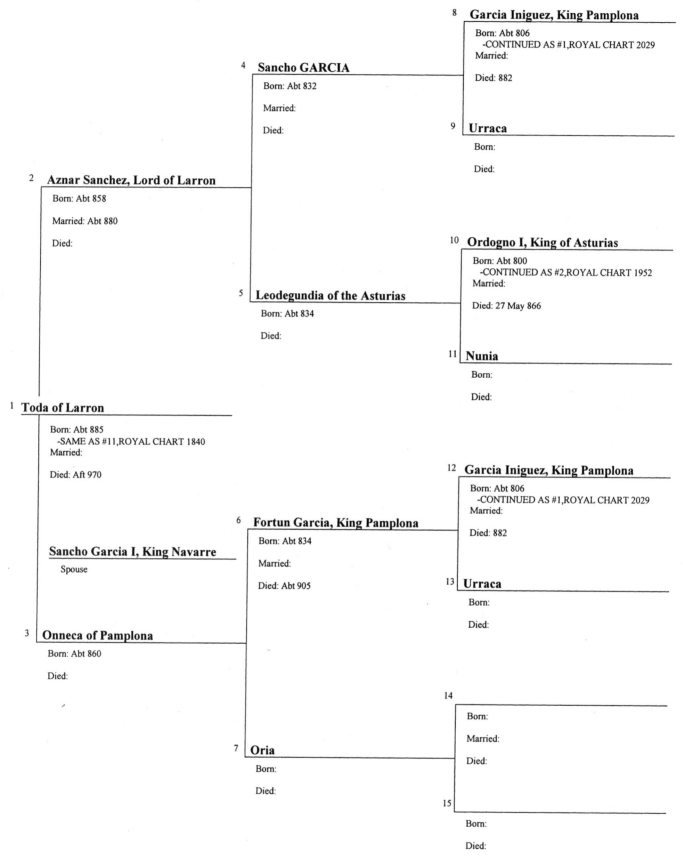

8 **Garcia Iniguez, King Pamplona**

Born: Abt 806
-CONTINUED AS #1,ROYAL CHART 2029
Married:

Died: 882

4 **Sancho GARCIA**

Born: Abt 832

Married:

Died:

9 **Urraca**

Born:

Died:

2 **Aznar Sanchez, Lord of Larron**

Born: Abt 858

Married: Abt 880

Died:

10 **Ordogno I, King of Asturias**

Born: Abt 800
-CONTINUED AS #2,ROYAL CHART 1952
Married:

Died: 27 May 866

5 **Leodegundia of the Asturias**

Born: Abt 834

Died:

11 **Nunia**

Born:

Died:

1 **Toda of Larron**

Born: Abt 885
-SAME AS #11,ROYAL CHART 1840
Married:

Died: Aft 970

Sancho Garcia I, King Navarre

Spouse

3 **Onneca of Pamplona**

Born: Abt 860

Died:

12 **Garcia Iniguez, King Pamplona**

Born: Abt 806
-CONTINUED AS #1,ROYAL CHART 2029
Married:

Died: 882

6 **Fortun Garcia, King Pamplona**

Born: Abt 834

Married:

Died: Abt 905

13 **Urraca**

Born:

Died:

14

Born:

Married:

Died:

7 **Oria**

Born:

Died:

15

Born:

Died:

Sources include: *Royal Ancestors* (1989), charts 11762, 11590, 11596; Stuart 293-294; Moriarty 70.

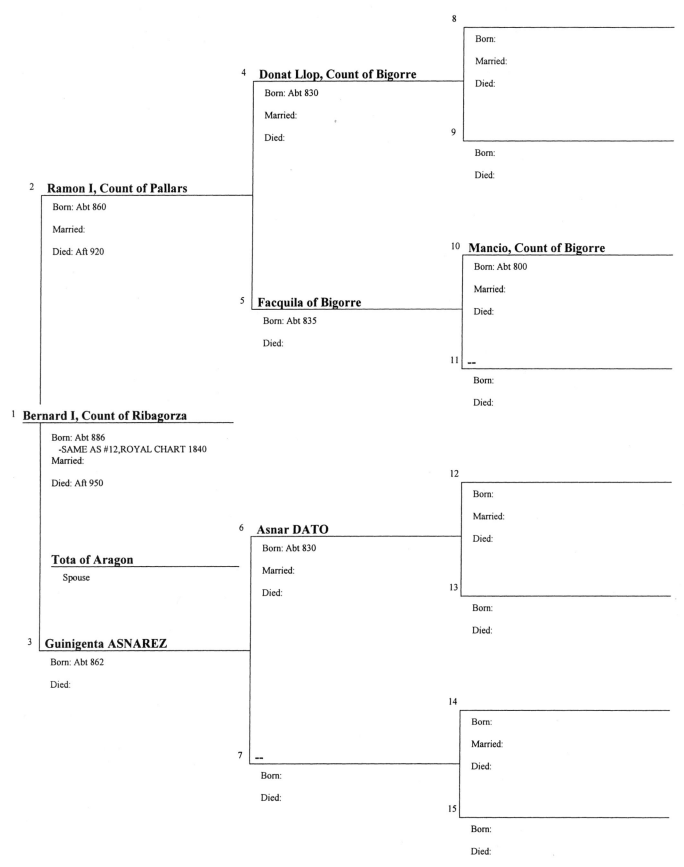

8 _____

Born:

Married:

Died:

4 Donat Llop, Count of Bigorre

Born: Abt 830

Married:

Died:

9 _____

Born:

Died:

2 Ramon I, Count of Pallars

Born: Abt 860

Married:

Died: Aft 920

10 Mancio, Count of Bigorre

Born: Abt 800

Married:

Died:

5 Facquila of Bigorre

Born: Abt 835

Died:

11 -- _____

Born:

Died:

1 Bernard I, Count of Ribagorza

Born: Abt 886
    -SAME AS #12,ROYAL CHART 1840
Married:

Died: Aft 950

12 _____

Born:

Married:

Died:

6 Asnar DATO

Born: Abt 830

Married:

Died:

13 _____

Born:

Died:

Tota of Aragon

    Spouse

3 Guinigenta ASNAREZ

Born: Abt 862

Died:

14 _____

Born:

Married:

Died:

7 -- _____

Born:

Died:

15 _____

Born:

Died:

Sources include: _Royal Ancestors_ (1989), chart 11762; Stuart 286; Moriarty 80; _TAG_ 74:148 (#4). Note: Moriarty and Stuart claim additional ancestry for #4 Donat, and they insert an additional Llop between #2 & 4, which has been omitted here to place #4 Donat nearer the end of the 9th century. His parentage is unknown. See _TAG_ 74:148.

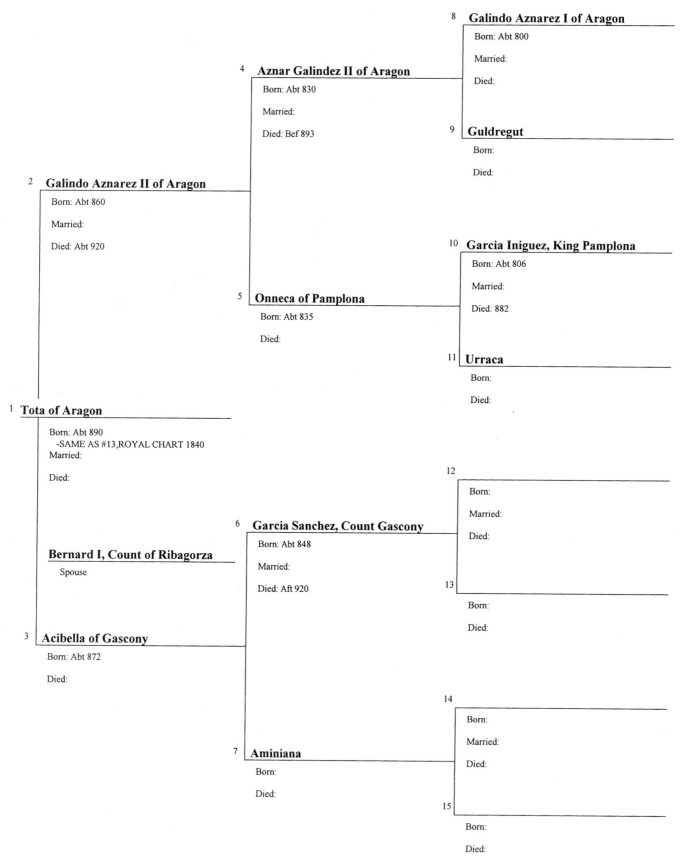

8 Galindo Aznarez I of Aragon
Born: Abt 800
Married:
Died:

4 Aznar Galindez II of Aragon
Born: Abt 830
Married:
Died: Bef 893

9 Guldregut
Born:
Died:

2 Galindo Aznarez II of Aragon
Born: Abt 860
Married:
Died: Abt 920

10 Garcia Iniguez, King Pamplona
Born: Abt 806
Married:
Died: 882

5 Onneca of Pamplona
Born: Abt 835
Died:

11 Urraca
Born:
Died:

1 Tota of Aragon
Born: Abt 890
-SAME AS #13,ROYAL CHART 1840
Married:
Died:

12
Born:
Married:
Died:

6 Garcia Sanchez, Count Gascony
Born: Abt 848
Married:
Died: Aft 920

13
Born:
Died:

Bernard I, Count of Ribagorza
Spouse

3 Acibella of Gascony
Born: Abt 872
Died:

14
Born:
Married:
Died:

7 Aminiana
Born:
Died:

15
Born:
Died:

Sources include: *Royal Ancestors* (1989), chart 11762; Stuart 290; Moriarty 79.

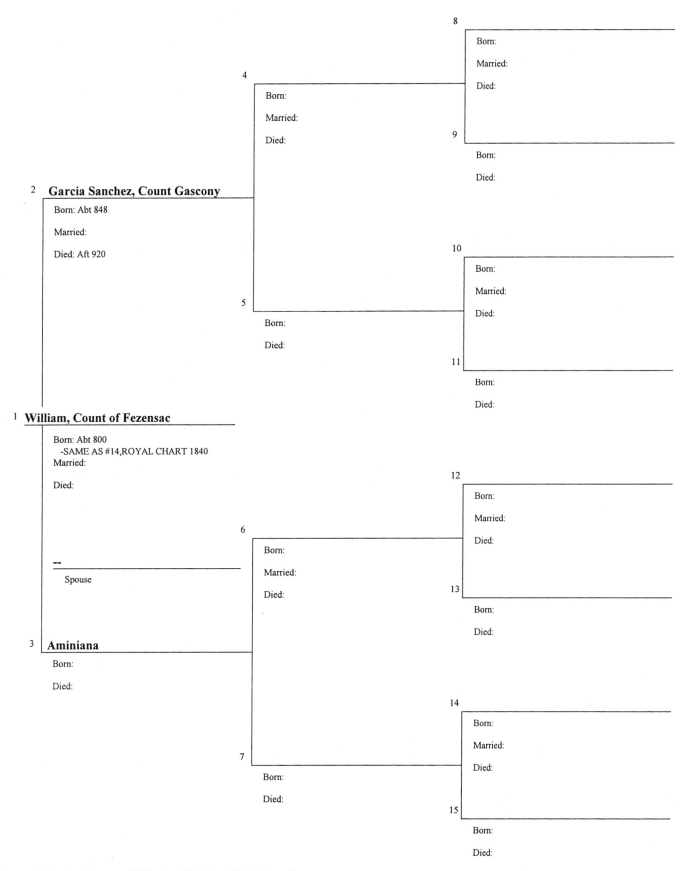

8

Born:

Married:

Died:

4

Born:

Married:

Died:

9

Born:

Died:

2 Garcia Sanchez, Count Gascony

Born: Abt 848

Married:

Died: Aft 920

10

Born:

Married:

Died:

5

Born:

Died:

11

Born:

Died:

1 William, Count of Fezensac

Born: Abt 800
-SAME AS #14,ROYAL CHART 1840
Married:

Died:

12

Born:

Married:

Died:

6

Born:

Married:

Died:

13

Born:

Died:

--

Spouse

3 Aminiana

Born:

Died:

14

Born:

Married:

Died:

7

Born:

Died:

15

Born:

Died:

Sources include: *Royal Ancestors* (1989), chart 11762; Stuart 289; Moriarty 79.

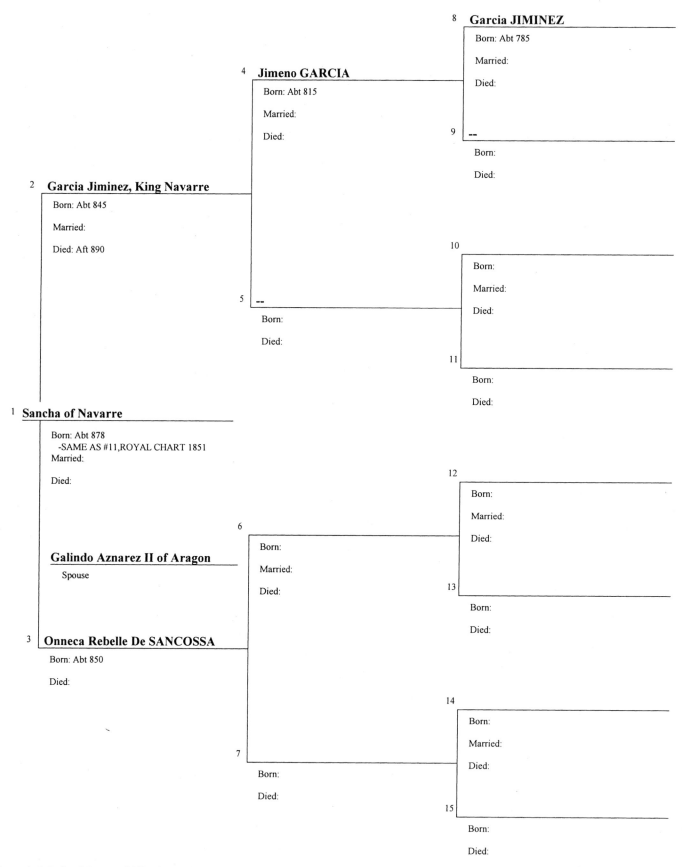

8 **Garcia JIMINEZ**

Born: Abt 785

Married:

Died:

4 **Jimeno GARCIA**

Born: Abt 815

Married:

Died:

9 --

Born:

Died:

2 **Garcia Jiminez, King Navarre**

Born: Abt 845

Married:

Died: Aft 890

10

Born:

Married:

Died:

5 --

Born:

Died:

11

Born:

Died:

1 **Sancha of Navarre**

Born: Abt 878
-SAME AS #11, ROYAL CHART 1851
Married:

Died:

12

Born:

Married:

Died:

6

Born:

Married:

Died:

13

Born:

Died:

Galindo Aznarez II of Aragon

Spouse

3 **Onneca Rebelle De SANCOSSA**

Born: Abt 850

Died:

14

Born:

Married:

Died:

7

Born:

Died:

15

Born:

Died:

Sources include: *Royal Ancestors* (1989), chart 11589; Stuart 292-40, 223; Moriarty 77, 70.

Pedigree Chart

Chart 1959

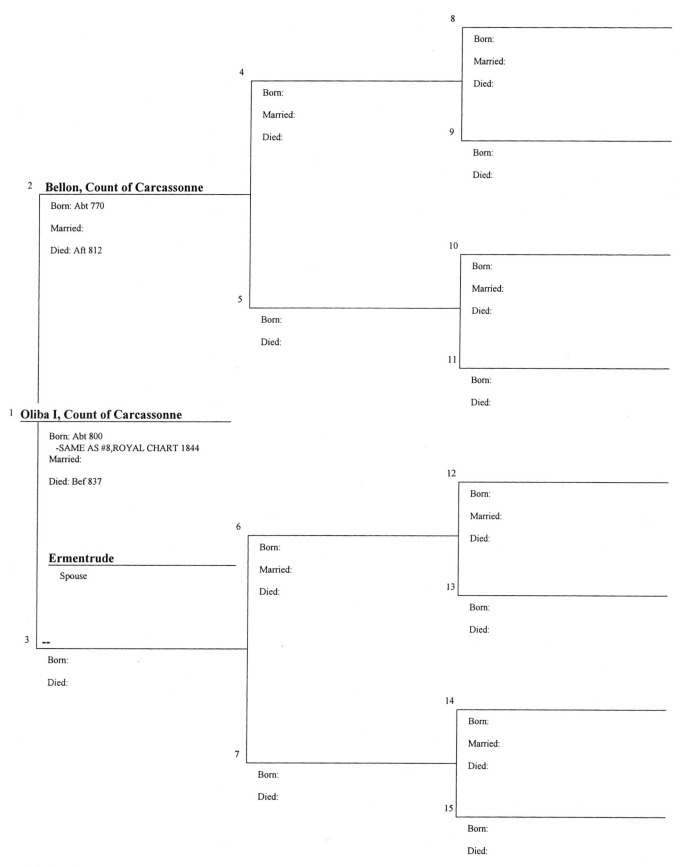

8

Born:

Married:

Died:

4

Born:

Married:

Died:

9

Born:

Died:

2   **Bellon, Count of Carcassonne**

Born: Abt 770

Married:

Died: Aft 812

10

Born:

Married:

Died:

5

Born:

Died:

11

Born:

Died:

1   **Oliba I, Count of Carcassonne**

Born: Abt 800
   -SAME AS #8,ROYAL CHART 1844
Married:

Died: Bef 837

12

Born:

Married:

Died:

6

Born:

Married:

Died:

13

Born:

Died:

Ermentrude

Spouse

3   **--**

Born:

Died:

14

Born:

Married:

Died:

7

Born:

Died:

15

Born:

Died:

Sources include: Moriarty 68; Stuart 291.

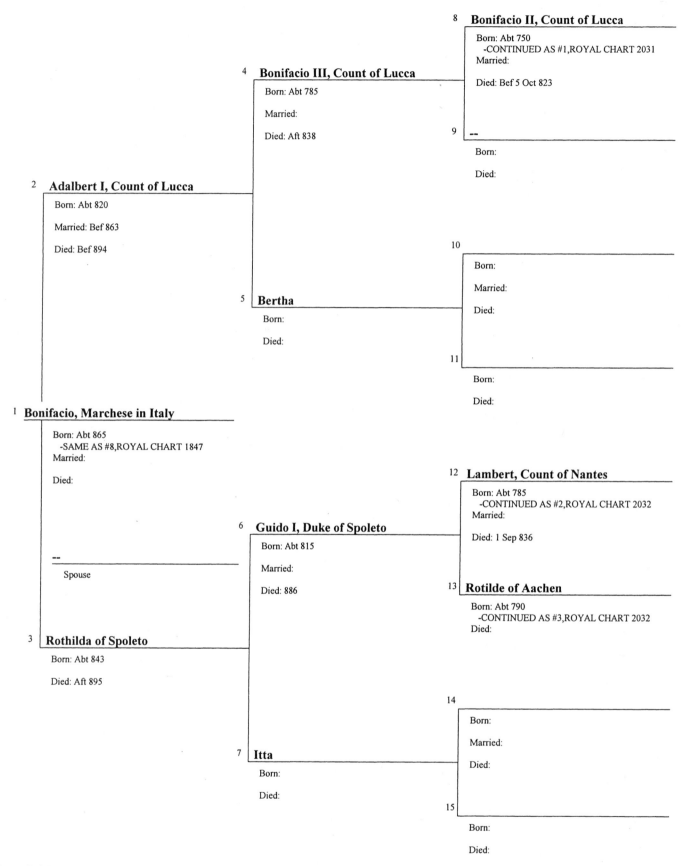

8 Bonifacio II, Count of Lucca
Born: Abt 750
-CONTINUED AS #1,ROYAL CHART 2031
Married:

Died: Bef 5 Oct 823

4 Bonifacio III, Count of Lucca
Born: Abt 785

Married:

Died: Aft 838

9 --
Born:

Died:

2 Adalbert I, Count of Lucca
Born: Abt 820

Married: Bef 863

Died: Bef 894

10
Born:

Married:

Died:

5 Bertha
Born:

Died:

11
Born:

Died:

1 Bonifacio, Marchese in Italy
Born: Abt 865
-SAME AS #8,ROYAL CHART 1847
Married:

Died:

12 Lambert, Count of Nantes
Born: Abt 785
-CONTINUED AS #2,ROYAL CHART 2032
Married:

Died: 1 Sep 836

6 Guido I, Duke of Spoleto
Born: Abt 815

Married:

Died: 886

13 Rotilde of Aachen
Born: Abt 790
-CONTINUED AS #3,ROYAL CHART 2032
Died:

--
Spouse

3 Rothilda of Spoleto
Born: Abt 843

Died: Aft 895

14
Born:

Married:

Died:

7 Itta
Born:

Died:

15
Born:

Died:

Sources include: *Royal Ancestors* (1989), chart 11994; Moriarty 61, 74; Stuart 93, 265 (#2 & 3 ancestry); *TAG* 52:26 (#3 ancestry). Notes: It is uncertain whether there were one or two generations named Guido (Gui) between #3 Rothilda and #12 Lambert. #13 is also claimed as an unknown daughter of Pepin (King of Italy), making her a granddaughter (instead of a daughter) of Charlemagne. The Charles Evans version (*TAG* 52:26) works best chronologically and is followed above on the ancestry of #3.

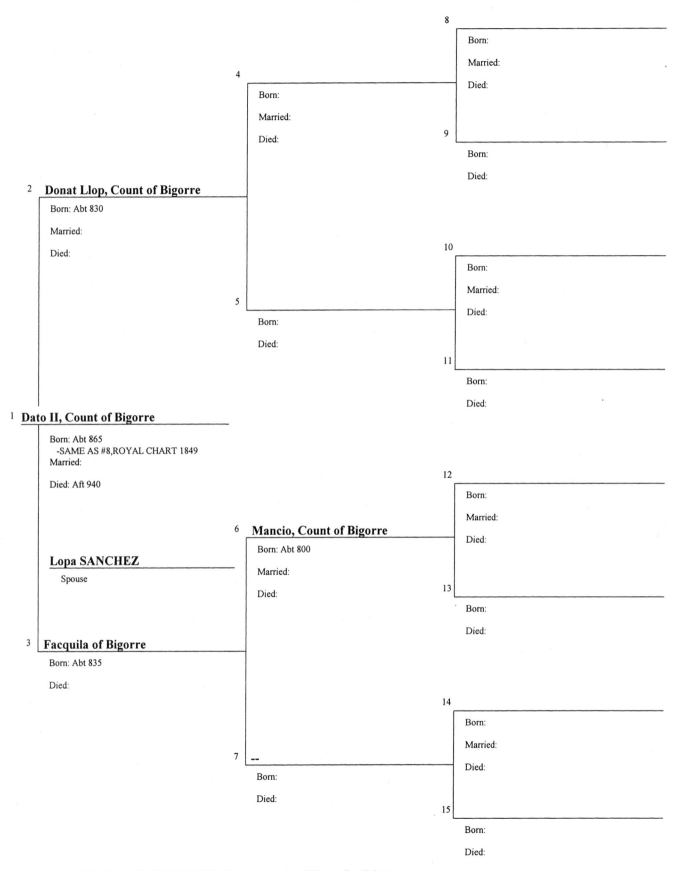

2 Donat Llop, Count of Bigorre
Born: Abt 830
Married:
Died:

1 Dato II, Count of Bigorre
Born: Abt 865
 -SAME AS #8,ROYAL CHART 1849
Married:
Died: Aft 940

Lopa SANCHEZ
Spouse

3 Facquila of Bigorre
Born: Abt 835
Died:

4
Born:
Married:
Died:

5
Born:
Died:

6 Mancio, Count of Bigorre
Born: Abt 800
Married:
Died:

7 --
Born:
Died:

8
Born:
Married:
Died:

9
Born:
Died:

10
Born:
Married:
Died:

11
Born:
Died:

12
Born:
Married:
Died:

13
Born:
Died:

14
Born:
Married:
Died:

15
Born:
Died:

Sources include: Stuart 227; Moriarty 80; *TAG* 74:148 (#2).   Note: See note chart 1955 regarding #2 Donat.

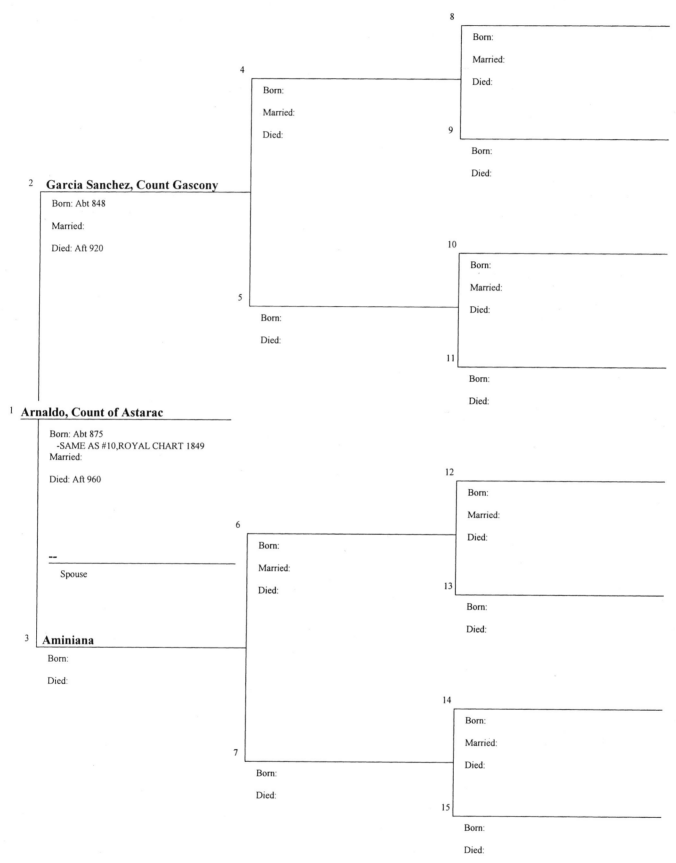

8

Born:

Married:

Died:

4

Born:

Married:

Died:

9

Born:

Died:

2 Garcia Sanchez, Count Gascony

Born: Abt 848

Married:

Died: Aft 920

10

Born:

Married:

Died:

5

Born:

Died:

11

Born:

Died:

1 Arnaldo, Count of Astarac

Born: Abt 875
   -SAME AS #10,ROYAL CHART 1849
Married:

Died: Aft 960

12

Born:

Married:

Died:

6

Born:

Married:

Died:

13

Born:

Died:

--
   Spouse

3 Aminiana

Born:

Died:

14

Born:

Married:

Died:

7

Born:

Died:

15

Born:

Died:

Sources include: Stuart 216; Moriarty 80.

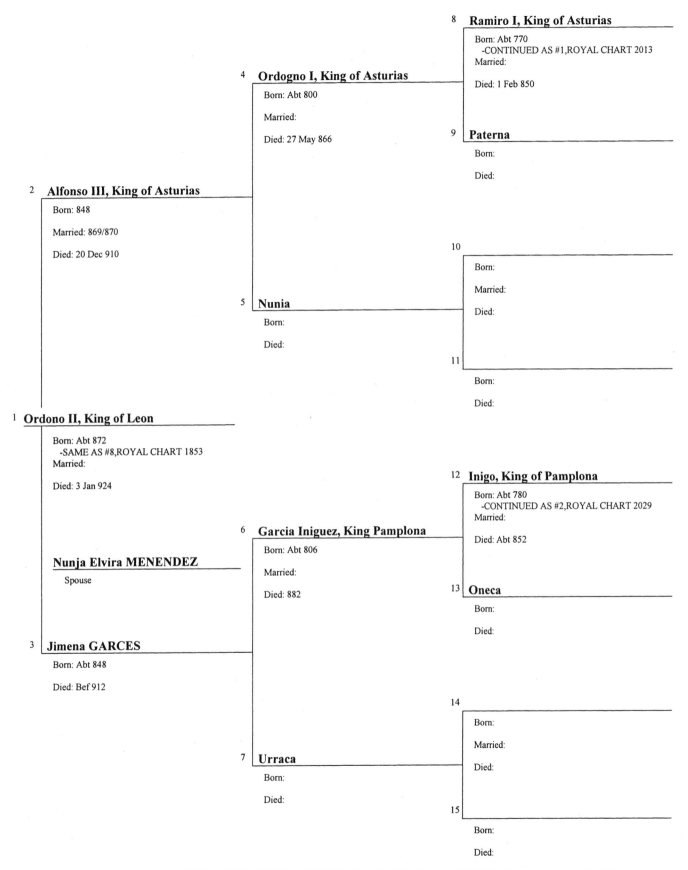

8 Ramiro I, King of Asturias

Born: Abt 770
  -CONTINUED AS #1,ROYAL CHART 2013
Married:

Died: 1 Feb 850

4 Ordogno I, King of Asturias

Born: Abt 800

Married:

Died: 27 May 866

9 Paterna

Born:

Died:

2 Alfonso III, King of Asturias

Born: 848

Married: 869/870

Died: 20 Dec 910

10

Born:

Married:

Died:

5 Nunia

Born:

Died:

11

Born:

Died:

1 Ordono II, King of Leon

Born: Abt 872
  -SAME AS #8,ROYAL CHART 1853
Married:

Died: 3 Jan 924

12 Inigo, King of Pamplona

Born: Abt 780
  -CONTINUED AS #2,ROYAL CHART 2029
Married:

Died: Abt 852

6 Garcia Iniguez, King Pamplona

Born: Abt 806

Married:

Died: 882

13 Oneca

Born:

Died:

Nunja Elvira MENENDEZ

Spouse

3 Jimena GARCES

Born: Abt 848

Died: Bef 912

14

Born:

Married:

Died:

7 Urraca

Born:

Died:

15

Born:

Died:

Sources include: *Royal Ancestors* (1989), charts 11763, 12102-03, 11590; Stuart 276, 76; Moriarty 82, 70; Von Isenburg 2:46; Charles Evans charts prepared in 1955.

Pedigree Chart

Chart 1964

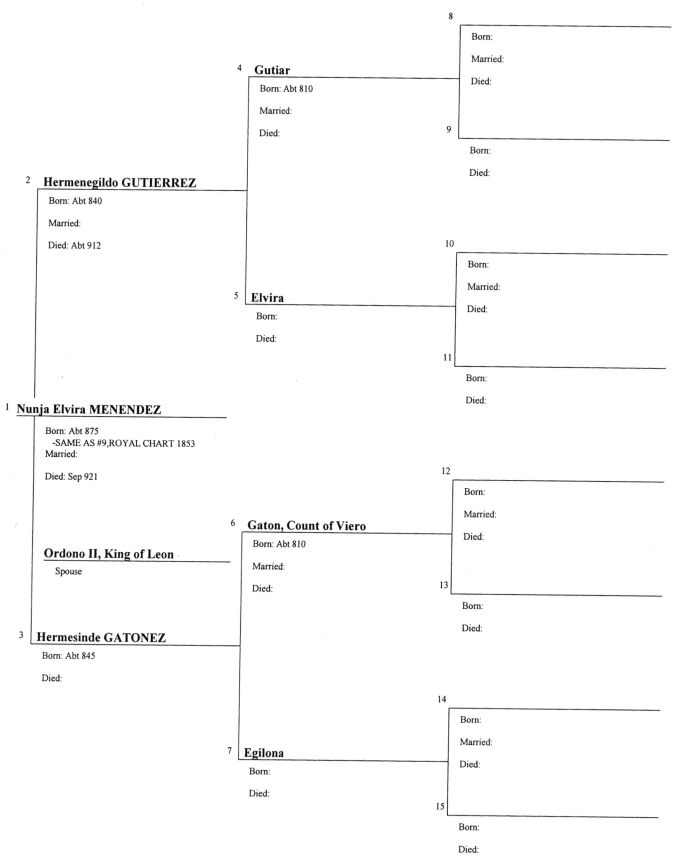

4 Gutiar
Born: Abt 810
Married:
Died:

8
Born:
Married:
Died:

9
Born:
Died:

2 Hermenegildo GUTIERREZ
Born: Abt 840
Married:
Died: Abt 912

5 Elvira
Born:
Died:

10
Born:
Married:
Died:

11
Born:
Died:

1 Nunja Elvira MENENDEZ
Born: Abt 875
-SAME AS #9,ROYAL CHART 1853
Married:
Died: Sep 921

Ordono II, King of Leon
Spouse

6 Gaton, Count of Viero
Born: Abt 810
Married:
Died:

12
Born:
Married:
Died:

13
Born:
Died:

3 Hermesinde GATONEZ
Born: Abt 845
Died:

7 Egilona
Born:
Died:

14
Born:
Married:
Died:

15
Born:
Died:

Sources include: Stuart 276-37, 21; Moriarty 82, 223; *Royal Ancestors* (1989), chart 12102.

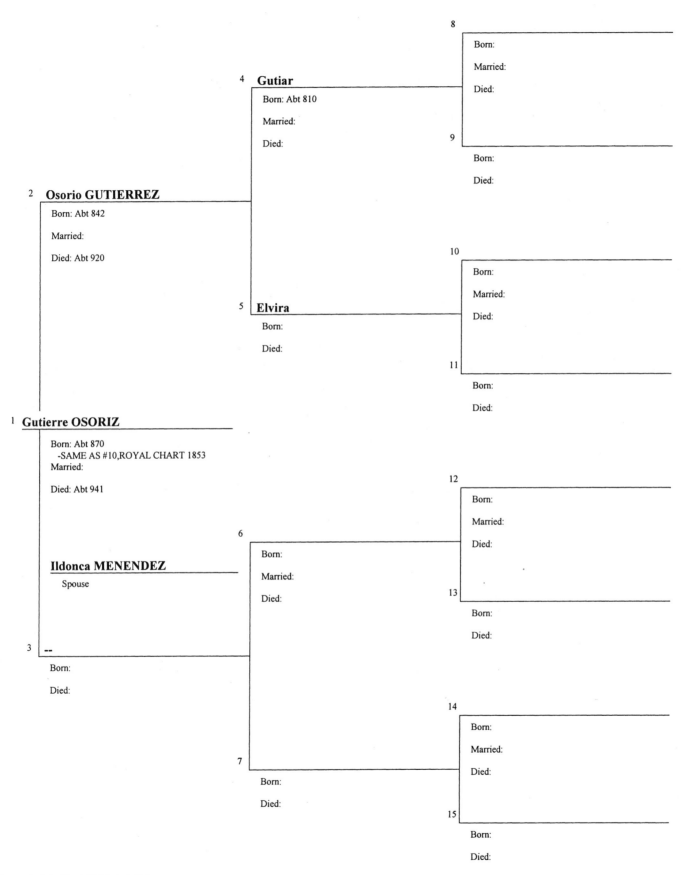

4 Gutiar
Born: Abt 810
Married:
Died:

8
Born:
Married:
Died:

9
Born:
Died:

2 Osorio GUTIERREZ
Born: Abt 842
Married:
Died: Abt 920

5 Elvira
Born:
Died:

10
Born:
Married:
Died:

11
Born:
Died:

1 Gutierre OSORIZ
Born: Abt 870
-SAME AS #10,ROYAL CHART 1853
Married:
Died: Abt 941

Ildonca MENENDEZ
Spouse

3 --
Born:
Died:

6
Born:
Married:
Died:

12
Born:
Married:
Died:

13
Born:
Died:

7
Born:
Died:

14
Born:
Married:
Died:

15
Born:
Died:

Sources include: Stuart 20; Moriarty 223.

Pedigree Chart

Chart 1966

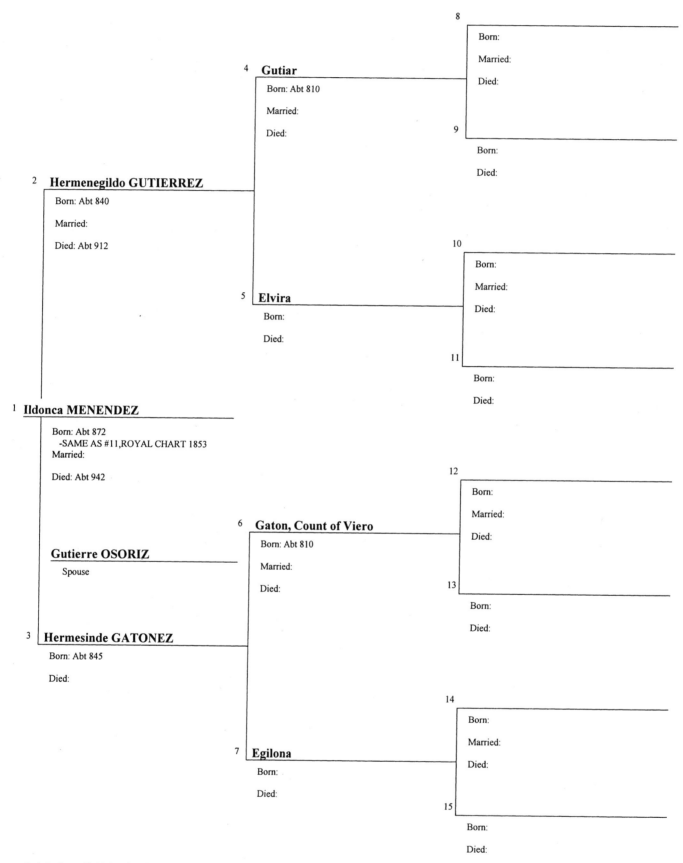

8

Born:

Married:

Died:

4 Gutiar

Born: Abt 810

Married:

Died:

9

Born:

Died:

2 Hermenegildo GUTIERREZ

Born: Abt 840

Married:

Died: Abt 912

10

Born:

Married:

Died:

5 Elvira

Born:

Died:

11

Born:

Died:

1 Ildonca MENENDEZ

Born: Abt 872
 -SAME AS #11,ROYAL CHART 1853
Married:

Died: Abt 942

12

Born:

Married:

Died:

6 Gaton, Count of Viero

Born: Abt 810

Married:

Died:

13

Born:

Died:

Gutierre OSORIZ

Spouse

3 Hermesinde GATONEZ

Born: Abt 845

Died:

14

Born:

Married:

Died:

7 Egilona

Born:

Died:

15

Born:

Died:

Sources include: Stuart 20-21; Moriarty 223.

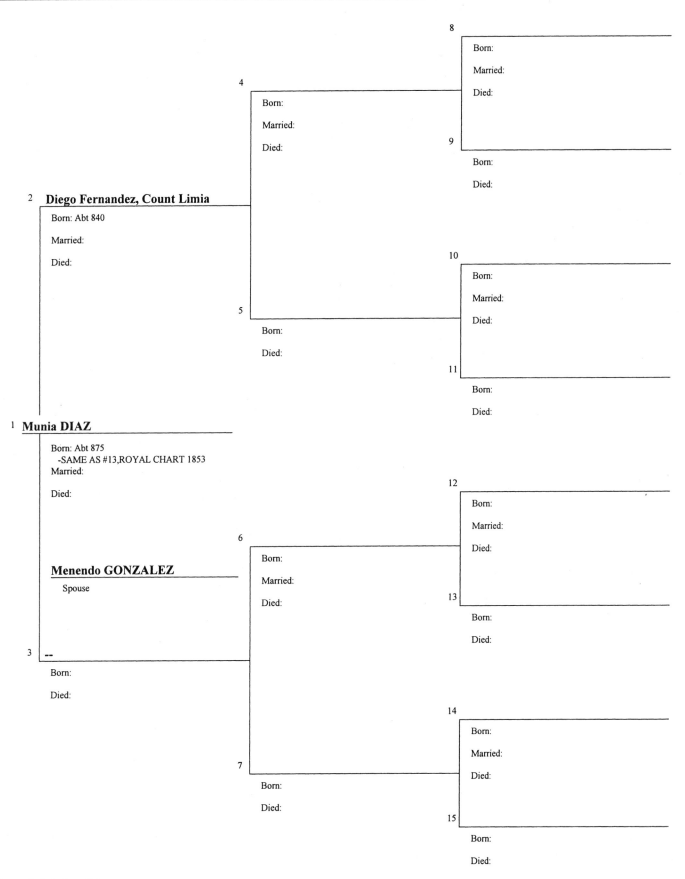

2   **Diego Fernandez, Count Limia**

Born: Abt 840

Married:

Died:

1   **Munia DIAZ**

Born: Abt 875
   -SAME AS #13,ROYAL CHART 1853
Married:

Died:

Menendo GONZALEZ

Spouse

3   **--**

Born:

Died:

4

Born:

Married:

Died:

5

Born:

Died:

6

Born:

Married:

Died:

7

Born:

Died:

8

Born:

Married:

Died:

9

Born:

Died:

10

Born:

Married:

Died:

11

Born:

Died:

12

Born:

Married:

Died:

13

Born:

Died:

14

Born:

Married:

Died:

15

Born:

Died:

Sources include: Stuart 277.

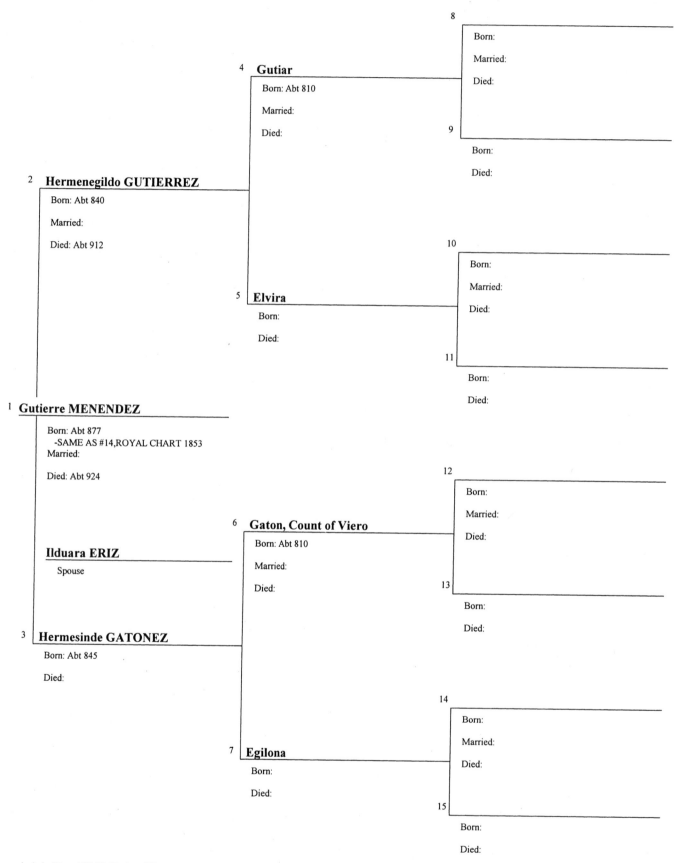

8

Born:

Married:

Died:

4 Gutiar

Born: Abt 810

Married:

Died:

9

Born:

Died:

2 Hermenegildo GUTIERREZ

Born: Abt 840

Married:

Died: Abt 912

10

Born:

Married:

Died:

5 Elvira

Born:

Died:

11

Born:

Died:

1 Gutierre MENENDEZ

Born: Abt 877
    -SAME AS #14,ROYAL CHART 1853
Married:

Died: Abt 924

12

Born:

Married:

Died:

6 Gaton, Count of Viero

Born: Abt 810

Married:

Died:

13

Born:

Died:

Ilduara ERIZ

Spouse

3 Hermesinde GATONEZ

Born: Abt 845

Died:

14

Born:

Married:

Died:

7 Egilona

Born:

Died:

15

Born:

Died:

Sources include: Stuart 277-36; Moriarty 223.

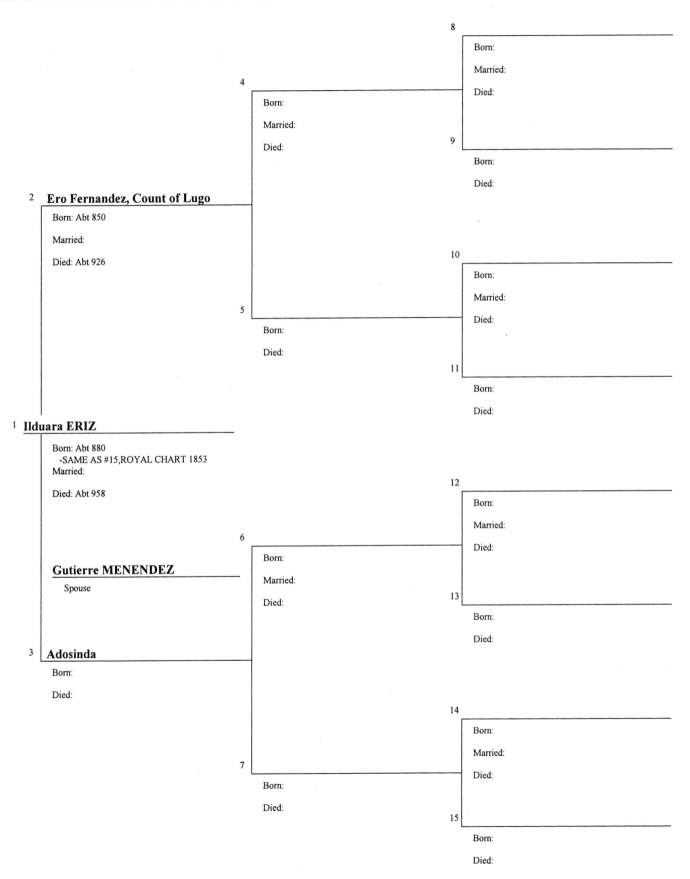

8

Born:

Married:

Died:

4

Born:

Married:

Died:

9

Born:

Died:

2 Ero Fernandez, Count of Lugo

Born: Abt 850

Married:

Died: Abt 926

10

Born:

Married:

Died:

5

Born:

Died:

11

Born:

Died:

1 Ilduara ERIZ

Born: Abt 880
  -SAME AS #15,ROYAL CHART 1853
Married:

Died: Abt 958

12

Born:

Married:

Died:

6

Born:

Married:

Died:

Gutierre MENENDEZ

Spouse

13

Born:

Died:

3 Adosinda

Born:

Died:

14

Born:

Married:

Died:

7

Born:

Died:

15

Born:

Died:

Sources include: Moriarty 223; Stuart 277-36.

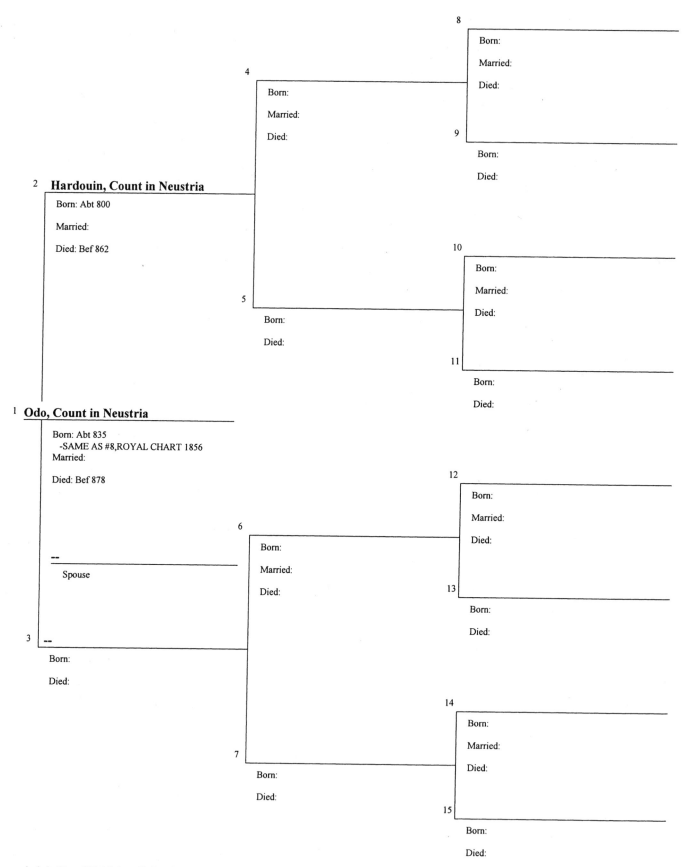

8

Born:

Married:

Died:

4

Born:

Married:

Died:

9

Born:

Died:

2 **Hardouin, Count in Neustria**

Born: Abt 800

Married:

Died: Bef 862

10

Born:

Married:

Died:

5

Born:

Died:

11

Born:

Died:

1 **Odo, Count in Neustria**

Born: Abt 835
    -SAME AS #8,ROYAL CHART 1856
Married:

Died: Bef 878

12

Born:

Married:

Died:

6

Born:

Married:

Died:

13

Born:

Died:

--
      Spouse

3 --

Born:

Died:

14

Born:

Married:

Died:

7

Born:

Died:

15

Born:

Died:

Sources include: Stuart 315; Moriarty 60; *Royal Ancestors* (1989), chart 11850.

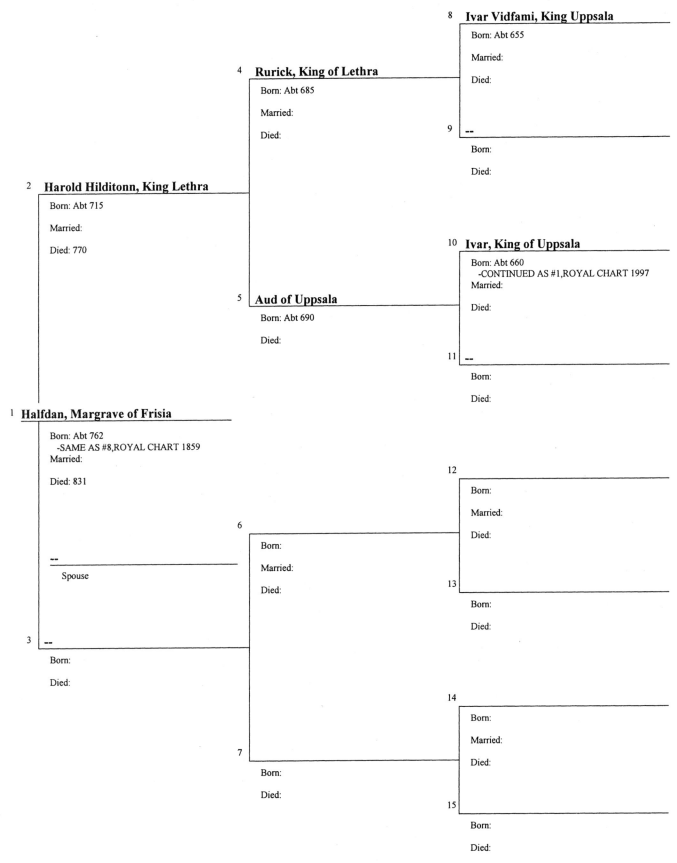

8   **Ivar Vidfami, King Uppsala**

Born: Abt 655

Married:

Died:

4   **Rurick, King of Lethra**

Born: Abt 685

Married:

Died:

9   --

Born:

Died:

2   **Harold Hilditonn, King Lethra**

Born: Abt 715

Married:

Died: 770

10   **Ivar, King of Uppsala**

Born: Abt 660
   -CONTINUED AS #1,ROYAL CHART 1997
Married:

Died:

5   **Aud of Uppsala**

Born: Abt 690

Died:

11   --

Born:

Died:

1   **Halfdan, Margrave of Frisia**

Born: Abt 762
   -SAME AS #8,ROYAL CHART 1859
Married:

Died: 831

--

Spouse

3   --

Born:

Died:

6

Born:

Married:

Died:

12

Born:

Married:

Died:

13

Born:

Died:

7

Born:

Died:

14

Born:

Married:

Died:

15

Born:

Died:

Sources include: Stuart 143, 240; Moriarty 52; *Royal Ancestors* (1989), chart 11719. Note: #8 Ivar, whose parentage is unknown, is claimed as a grandson of Rurick, Skioldung Prince of Lethra.

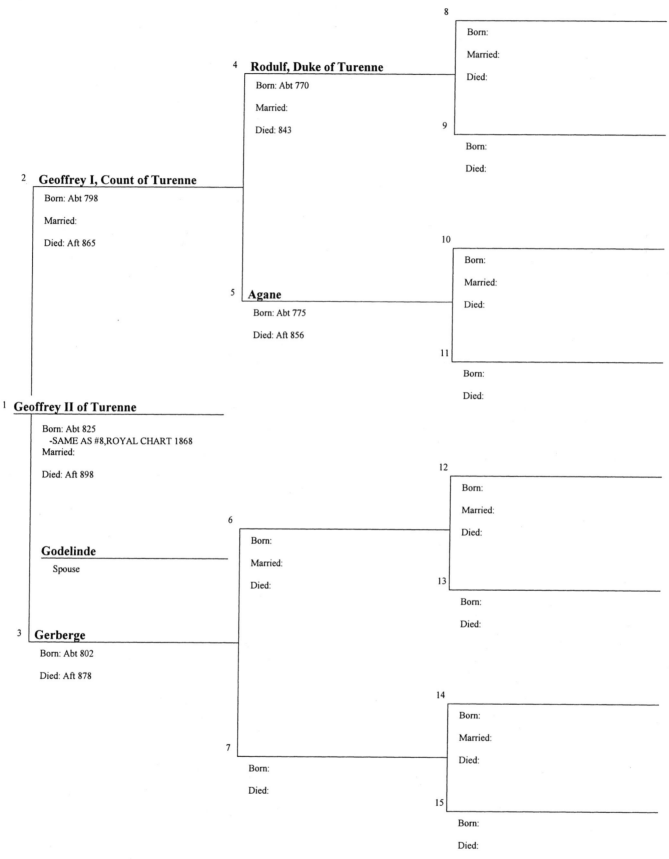

8

Born:

Married:

Died:

4 Rodulf, Duke of Turenne

Born: Abt 770

Married:

Died: 843

9

Born:

Died:

2 Geoffrey I, Count of Turenne

Born: Abt 798

Married:

Died: Aft 865

10

Born:

Married:

Died:

5 Agane

Born: Abt 775

Died: Aft 856

11

Born:

Died:

1 Geoffrey II of Turenne

Born: Abt 825
 -SAME AS #8,ROYAL CHART 1868
Married:

Died: Aft 898

12

Born:

Married:

Died:

6

Born:

Married:

Died:

13

Born:

Died:

Godelinde

Spouse

3 Gerberge

Born: Abt 802

Died: Aft 878

14

Born:

Married:

Died:

7

Born:

Died:

15

Born:

Died:

Sources include: Stuart 308; Moriarty 47.

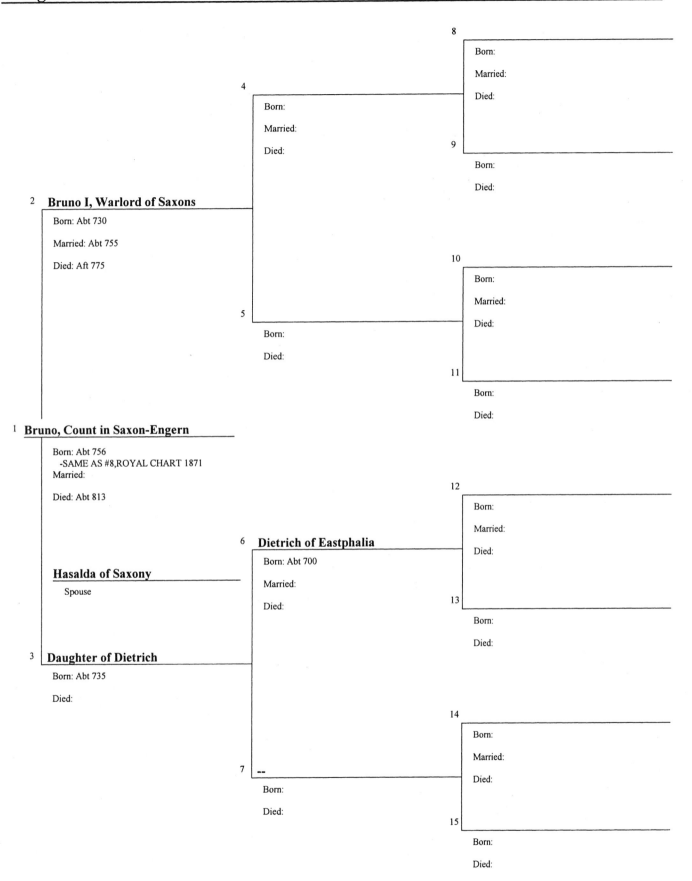

2 Bruno I, Warlord of Saxons

Born: Abt 730

Married: Abt 755

Died: Aft 775

4

Born:

Married:

Died:

8

Born:

Married:

Died:

9

Born:

Died:

5

Born:

Died:

10

Born:

Married:

Died:

11

Born:

Died:

1 Bruno, Count in Saxon-Engern

Born: Abt 756
-SAME AS #8, ROYAL CHART 1871
Married:

Died: Abt 813

Hasalda of Saxony

Spouse

3 Daughter of Dietrich

Born: Abt 735

Died:

6 Dietrich of Eastphalia

Born: Abt 700

Married:

Died:

12

Born:

Married:

Died:

13

Born:

Died:

7 --

Born:

Died:

14

Born:

Married:

Died:

15

Born:

Died:

Sources include: Stuart 92; Moriarty 25; *Royal Ancestors* (1989), chart 11635.

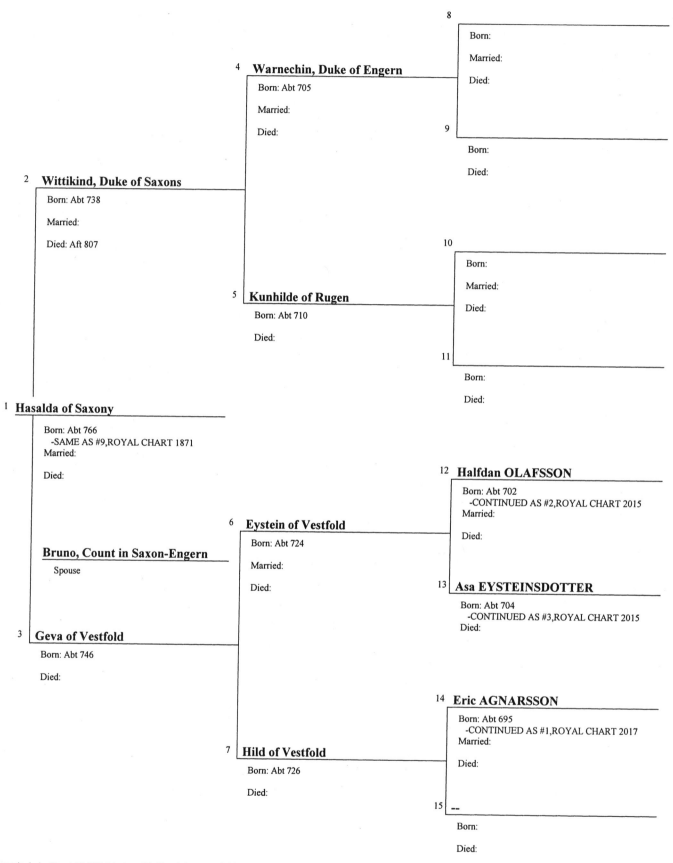

8

Born:

Married:

Died:

4 Warnechin, Duke of Engern

Born: Abt 705

Married:

Died:

9

Born:

Died:

2 Wittikind, Duke of Saxons

Born: Abt 738

Married:

Died: Aft 807

10

Born:

Married:

Died:

5 Kunhilde of Rugen

Born: Abt 710

Died:

11

Born:

Died:

1 Hasalda of Saxony

Born: Abt 766
  -SAME AS #9,ROYAL CHART 1871
Married:

Died:

12 Halfdan OLAFSSON

Born: Abt 702
  -CONTINUED AS #2,ROYAL CHART 2015
Married:

Died:

6 Eystein of Vestfold

Born: Abt 724

Married:

Died:

13 Asa EYSTEINSDOTTER

Born: Abt 704
  -CONTINUED AS #3,ROYAL CHART 2015
Died:

Bruno, Count in Saxon-Engern

Spouse

3 Geva of Vestfold

Born: Abt 746

Died:

14 Eric AGNARSSON

Born: Abt 695
  -CONTINUED AS #1,ROYAL CHART 2017
Married:

Died:

7 Hild of Vestfold

Born: Abt 726

Died:

15 --

Born:

Died:

Sources include: Stuart 92, 339; Moriarty 25; *Royal Ancestors* (1989), chart 11635.

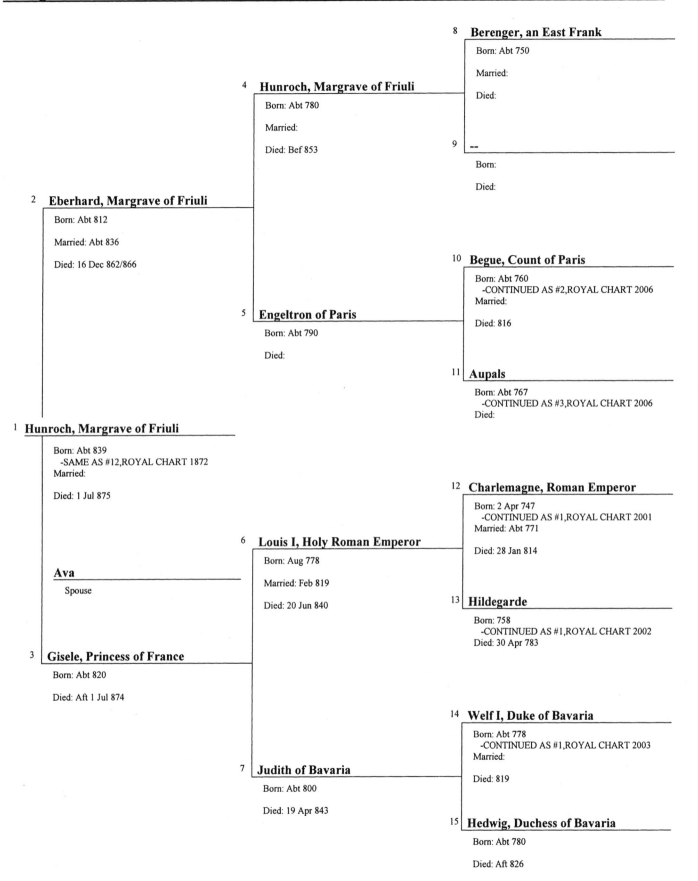

8 Berenger, an East Frank

Born: Abt 750

Married:

Died:

4 Hunroch, Margrave of Friuli

Born: Abt 780

Married:

Died: Bef 853

9 --

Born:

Died:

2 Eberhard, Margrave of Friuli

Born: Abt 812

Married: Abt 836

Died: 16 Dec 862/866

10 Begue, Count of Paris

Born: Abt 760
 -CONTINUED AS #2,ROYAL CHART 2006
Married:

Died: 816

5 Engeltron of Paris

Born: Abt 790

Died:

11 Aupals

Born: Abt 767
 -CONTINUED AS #3,ROYAL CHART 2006
Died:

1 Hunroch, Margrave of Friuli

Born: Abt 839
 -SAME AS #12,ROYAL CHART 1872
Married:

Died: 1 Jul 875

12 Charlemagne, Roman Emperor

Born: 2 Apr 747
 -CONTINUED AS #1,ROYAL CHART 2001
Married: Abt 771

Died: 28 Jan 814

6 Louis I, Holy Roman Emperor

Born: Aug 778

Married: Feb 819

Died: 20 Jun 840

13 Hildegarde

Born: 758
 -CONTINUED AS #1,ROYAL CHART 2002
Died: 30 Apr 783

Ava

Spouse

3 Gisele, Princess of France

Born: Abt 820

Died: Aft 1 Jul 874

14 Welf I, Duke of Bavaria

Born: Abt 778
 -CONTINUED AS #1,ROYAL CHART 2003
Married:

Died: 819

7 Judith of Bavaria

Born: Abt 800

Died: 19 Apr 843

15 Hedwig, Duchess of Bavaria

Born: Abt 780

Died: Aft 826

Sources include: *Royal Ancestors* (1989), chart 11874; Stuart 272; Moriarty 18.

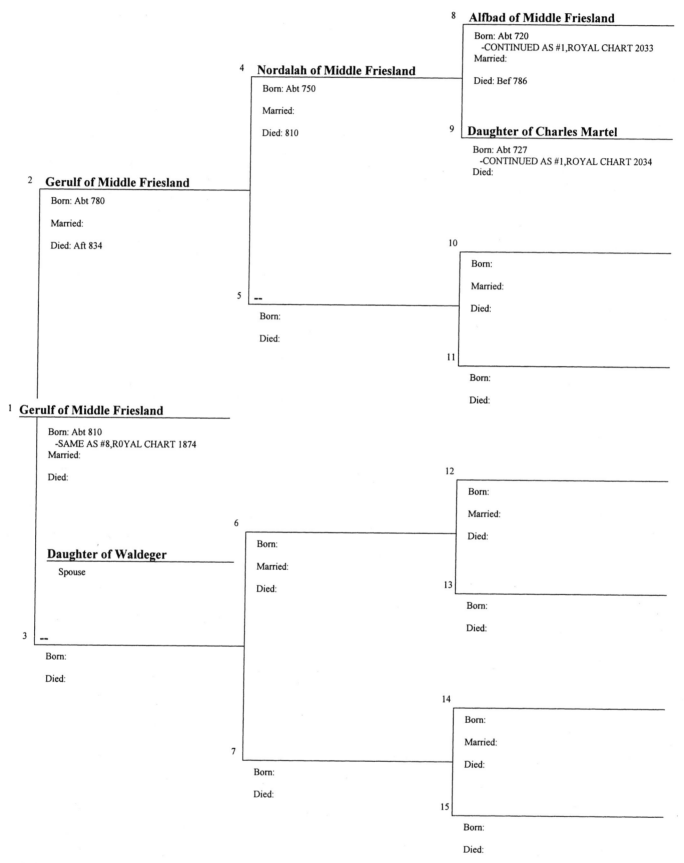

Pedigree Chart

Chart 1976

8 **Alfbad of Middle Friesland**

Born: Abt 720
-CONTINUED AS #1,ROYAL CHART 2033
Married:

Died: Bef 786

4 **Nordalah of Middle Friesland**

Born: Abt 750

Married:

Died: 810

9 **Daughter of Charles Martel**

Born: Abt 727
-CONTINUED AS #1,ROYAL CHART 2034
Died:

2 **Gerulf of Middle Friesland**

Born: Abt 780

Married:

Died: Aft 834

10

Born:

Married:

Died:

5 --

Born:

Died:

11

Born:

Died:

1 **Gerulf of Middle Friesland**

Born: Abt 810
-SAME AS #8,R0YAL CHART 1874
Married:

Died:

12

Born:

Married:

Died:

6

Born:

Married:

Died:

13

Born:

Died:

Daughter of Waldeger

Spouse

3 --

Born:

Died:

14

Born:

Married:

Died:

7

Born:

Died:

15

Born:

Died:

Sources include: Moriatry 54-55; *Royal Ancestors* (1989), chart 11643.

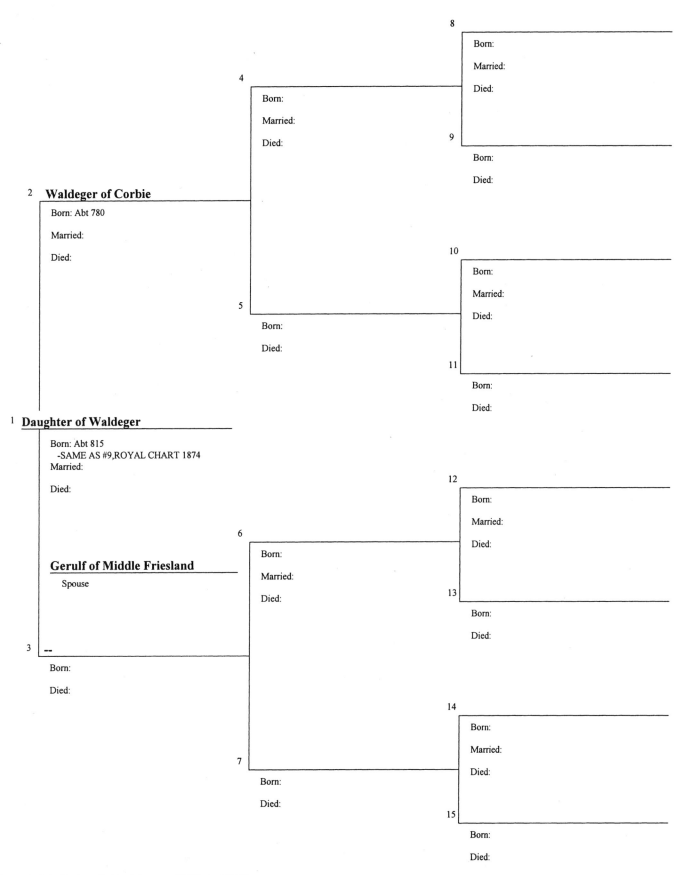

8
Born:
Married:
Died:

4
Born:
Married:
Died:

9
Born:
Died:

2 Waldeger of Corbie
Born: Abt 780
Married:
Died:

10
Born:
Married:
Died:

5
Born:
Died:

11
Born:
Died:

1 Daughter of Waldeger
Born: Abt 815
 -SAME AS #9,ROYAL CHART 1874
Married:
Died:

12
Born:
Married:
Died:

6
Born:
Married:
Died:

13
Born:
Died:

Gerulf of Middle Friesland
Spouse

3 --
Born:
Died:

14
Born:
Married:
Died:

7
Born:
Died:

15
Born:
Died:

Sources include: Moriarty 55; *Royal Ancestors* (1989), chart 11643.

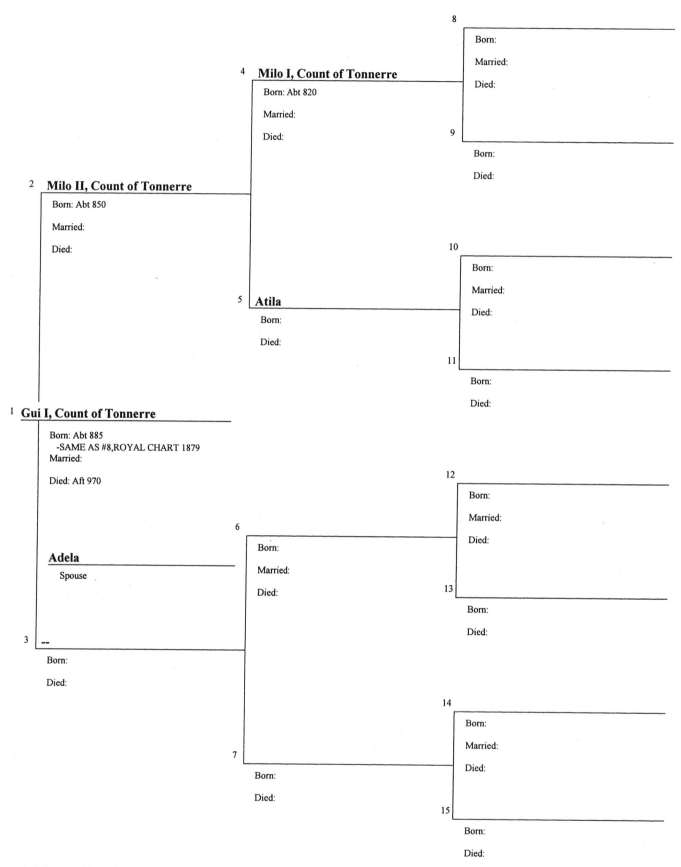

4 Milo I, Count of Tonnerre
Born: Abt 820
Married:
Died:

8
Born:
Married:
Died:

9
Born:
Died:

2 Milo II, Count of Tonnerre
Born: Abt 850
Married:
Died:

5 Atila
Born:
Died:

10
Born:
Married:
Died:

11
Born:
Died:

1 Gui I, Count of Tonnerre
Born: Abt 885
  -SAME AS #8,ROYAL CHART 1879
Married:
Died: Aft 970

Adela
  Spouse

3 --
Born:
Died:

6
Born:
Married:
Died:

12
Born:
Married:
Died:

13
Born:
Died:

7
Born:
Died:

14
Born:
Married:
Died:

15
Born:
Died:

Sources include: Stuart 254; Moriarty 239-240, 64-65.

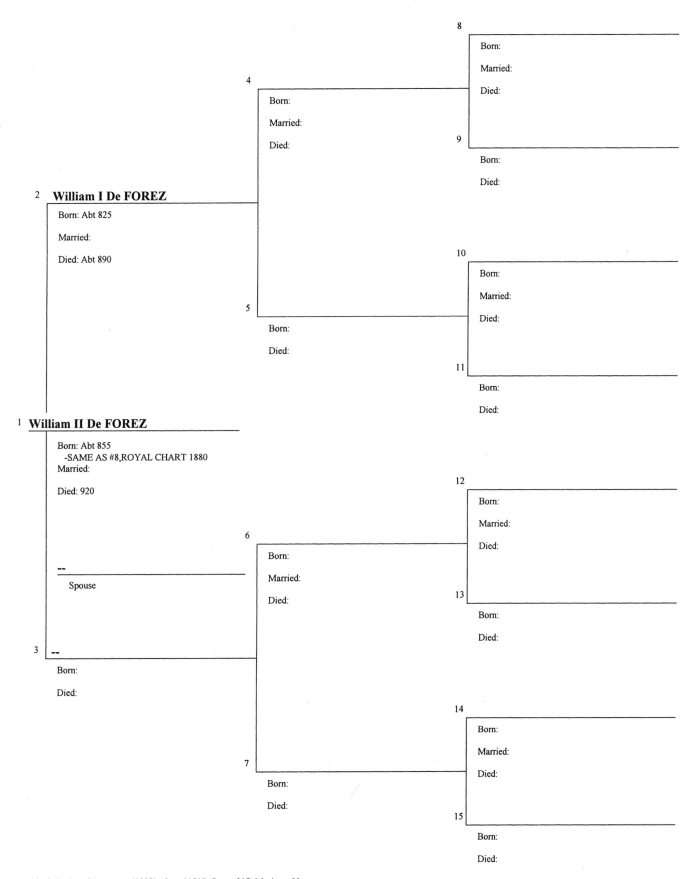

8

Born:

Married:

Died:

4

Born:

Married:

Died:

9

Born:

Died:

2 William I De FOREZ

Born: Abt 825

Married:

Died: Abt 890

10

Born:

Married:

Died:

5

Born:

Died:

11

Born:

Died:

1 William II De FOREZ

Born: Abt 855
  -SAME AS #8,ROYAL CHART 1880
Married:

Died: 920

12

Born:

Married:

Died:

6

Born:

Married:

Died:

13

Born:

Died:

--

Spouse

3 --

Born:

Died:

14

Born:

Married:

Died:

7

Born:

Died:

15

Born:

Died:

Sources include: *Royal Ancestors* (1989), chart 11517; Stuart 317; Moriarty 66.

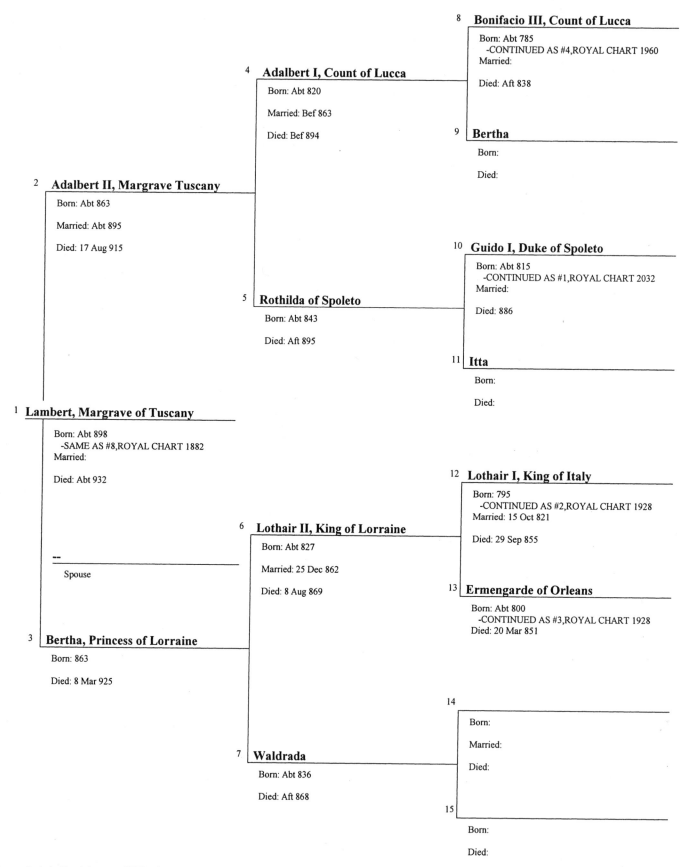

8 Bonifacio III, Count of Lucca
Born: Abt 785
  -CONTINUED AS #4,ROYAL CHART 1960
Married:
Died: Aft 838

4 Adalbert I, Count of Lucca
Born: Abt 820
Married: Bef 863
Died: Bef 894

9 Bertha
Born:
Died:

2 Adalbert II, Margrave Tuscany
Born: Abt 863
Married: Abt 895
Died: 17 Aug 915

10 Guido I, Duke of Spoleto
Born: Abt 815
  -CONTINUED AS #1,ROYAL CHART 2032
Married:
Died: 886

5 Rothilda of Spoleto
Born: Abt 843
Died: Aft 895

11 Itta
Born:
Died:

1 Lambert, Margrave of Tuscany
Born: Abt 898
  -SAME AS #8,ROYAL CHART 1882
Married:
Died: Abt 932

-- Spouse

12 Lothair I, King of Italy
Born: 795
  -CONTINUED AS #2,ROYAL CHART 1928
Married: 15 Oct 821
Died: 29 Sep 855

6 Lothair II, King of Lorraine
Born: Abt 827
Married: 25 Dec 862
Died: 8 Aug 869

13 Ermengarde of Orleans
Born: Abt 800
  -CONTINUED AS #3,ROYAL CHART 1928
Died: 20 Mar 851

3 Bertha, Princess of Lorraine
Born: 863
Died: 8 Mar 925

14
Born:
Married:
Died:

7 Waldrada
Born: Abt 836
Died: Aft 868

15
Born:
Died:

Sources include: *Royal Ancestors* (1989), chart 12093; Stuart 31; *TAG* 52:23-26. Note: See notes chart 1960 concerning the ancestry of #5 Rothilda.

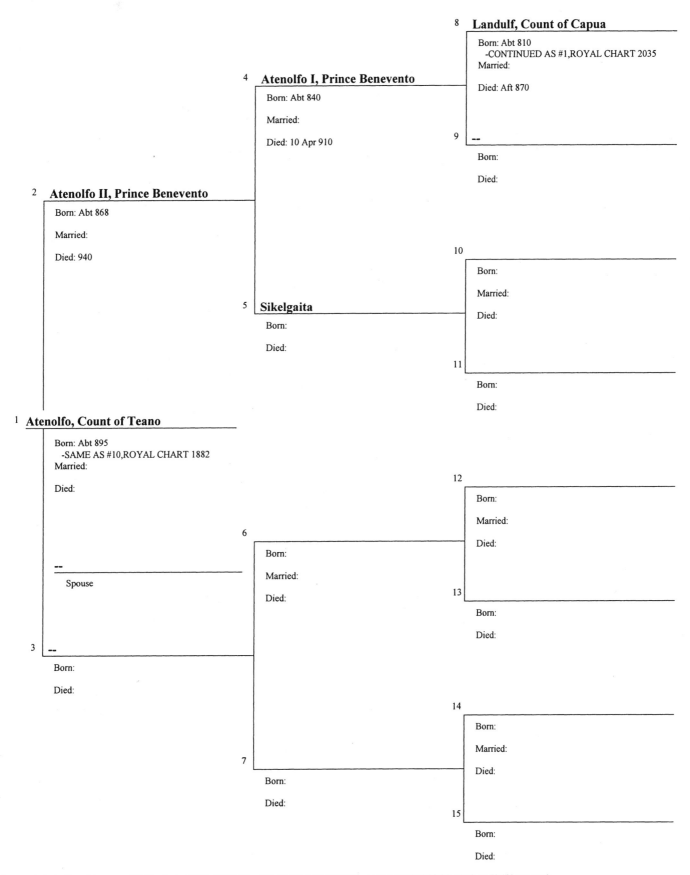

8 Landulf, Count of Capua

Born: Abt 810
-CONTINUED AS #1,ROYAL CHART 2035
Married:

Died: Aft 870

4 Atenolfo I, Prince Benevento

Born: Abt 840

Married:

Died: 10 Apr 910

9 --

Born:

Died:

2 Atenolfo II, Prince Benevento

Born: Abt 868

Married:

Died: 940

10

Born:

Married:

Died:

5 Sikelgaita

Born:

Died:

11

Born:

Died:

1 Atenolfo, Count of Teano

Born: Abt 895
-SAME AS #10,ROYAL CHART 1882
Married:

Died:

12

Born:

Married:

Died:

6

Born:

Married:

Died:

13

Born:

Died:

--
Spouse

3 --

Born:

Died:

14

Born:

Married:

Died:

7

Born:

Died:

15

Born:

Died:

Sources include: *Royal Ancestors* (1989), charts 12093, 12096; Stuart 31-36 (#1 & 2), 283 (#4 ancestry); *TAG* 52:23-26; Moriarty 72 (#4 ancestry).

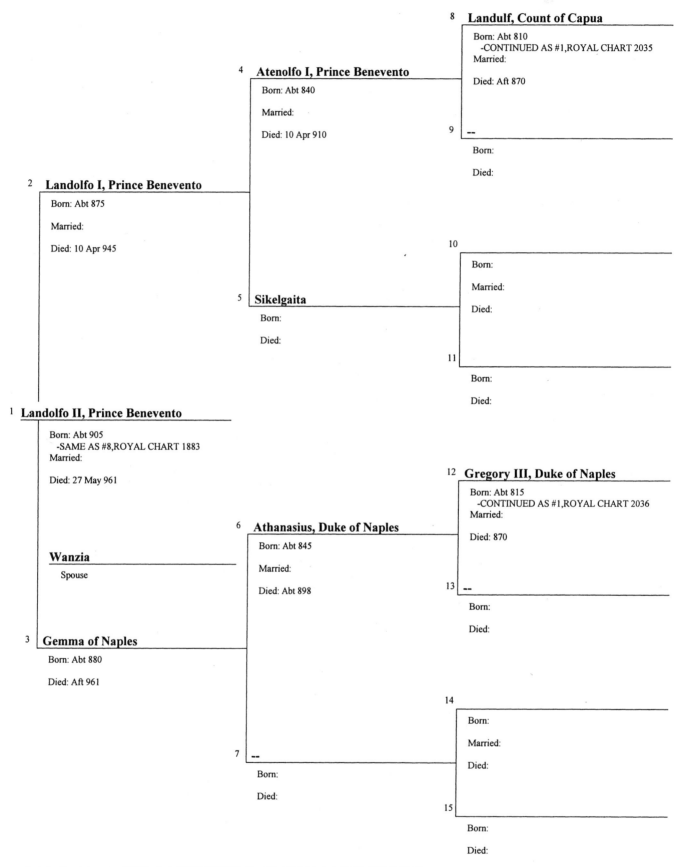

8 **Landulf, Count of Capua**

Born: Abt 810
-CONTINUED AS #1,ROYAL CHART 2035
Married:

Died: Aft 870

4 **Atenolfo I, Prince Benevento**

Born: Abt 840

Married:

Died: 10 Apr 910

9 --

Born:

Died:

2 **Landolfo I, Prince Benevento**

Born: Abt 875

Married:

Died: 10 Apr 945

10

Born:

Married:

Died:

5 **Sikelgaita**

Born:

Died:

11

Born:

Died:

1 **Landolfo II, Prince Benevento**

Born: Abt 905
-SAME AS #8,ROYAL CHART 1883
Married:

Died: 27 May 961

12 **Gregory III, Duke of Naples**

Born: Abt 815
-CONTINUED AS #1,ROYAL CHART 2036
Married:

Died: 870

6 **Athanasius, Duke of Naples**

Born: Abt 845

Married:

Died: Abt 898

13 --

Born:

Died:

Wanzia

Spouse

3 **Gemma of Naples**

Born: Abt 880

Died: Aft 961

14

Born:

Married:

Died:

7 --

Born:

Died:

15

Born:

Died:

Sources include: *Royal Ancestors* (1989), charts 12093, 12096-97; Stuart 283, 280; Moriarty 72-73; *TAG* 52:23-26.

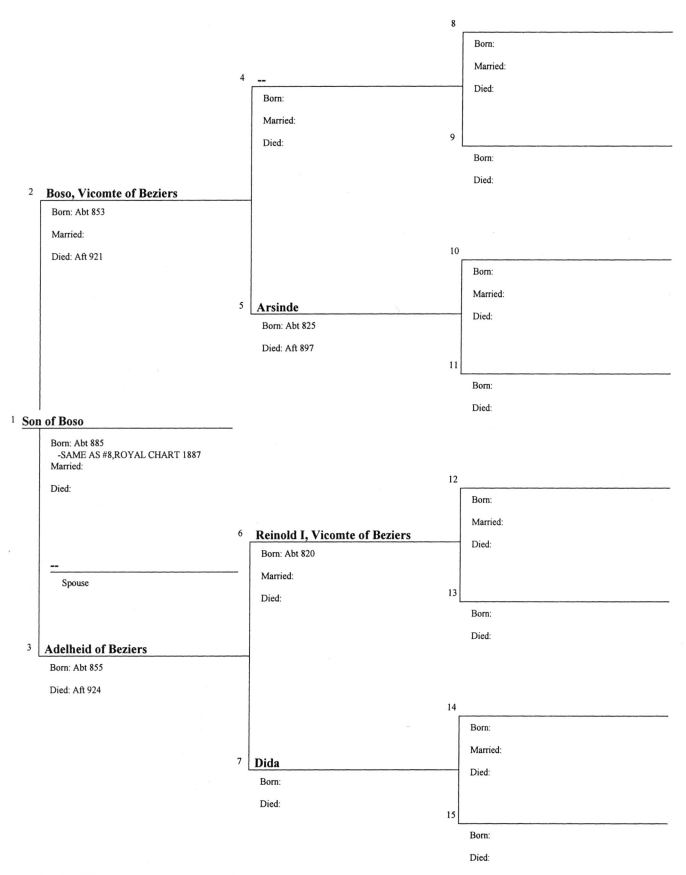

8

Born:

Married:

Died:

4 --

Born:

Married:

Died:

9

Born:

Died:

2 **Boso, Vicomte of Beziers**

Born: Abt 853

Married:

Died: Aft 921

10

Born:

Married:

Died:

5 **Arsinde**

Born: Abt 825

Died: Aft 897

11

Born:

Died:

1 **Son of Boso**

Born: Abt 885
  -SAME AS #8,ROYAL CHART 1887
Married:

Died:

12

Born:

Married:

Died:

6 **Reinold I, Vicomte of Beziers**

Born: Abt 820

Married:

Died:

13

Born:

Died:

--

Spouse

3 **Adelheid of Beziers**

Born: Abt 855

Died: Aft 924

14

Born:

Married:

Died:

7 **Dida**

Born:

Died:

15

Born:

Died:

Sources include: Stuart 226.

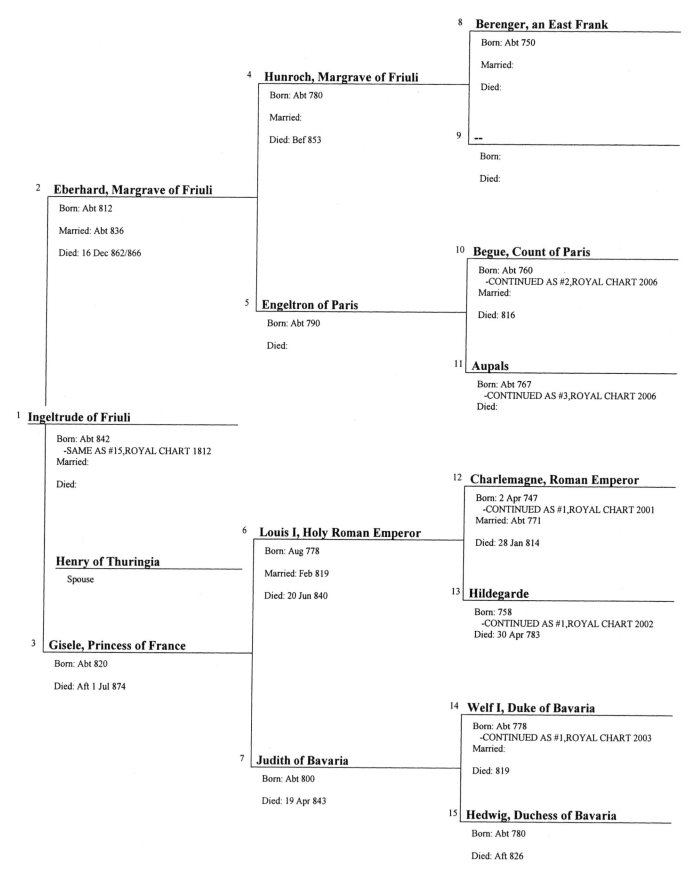

8 Berenger, an East Frank
Born: Abt 750
Married:
Died:

4 Hunroch, Margrave of Friuli
Born: Abt 780
Married:
Died: Bef 853

9 --
Born:
Died:

2 Eberhard, Margrave of Friuli
Born: Abt 812
Married: Abt 836
Died: 16 Dec 862/866

10 Begue, Count of Paris
Born: Abt 760
-CONTINUED AS #2,ROYAL CHART 2006
Married:
Died: 816

5 Engeltron of Paris
Born: Abt 790
Died:

11 Aupals
Born: Abt 767
-CONTINUED AS #3,ROYAL CHART 2006
Died:

1 Ingeltrude of Friuli
Born: Abt 842
-SAME AS #15,ROYAL CHART 1812
Married:
Died:

12 Charlemagne, Roman Emperor
Born: 2 Apr 747
-CONTINUED AS #1,ROYAL CHART 2001
Married: Abt 771
Died: 28 Jan 814

6 Louis I, Holy Roman Emperor
Born: Aug 778
Married: Feb 819
Died: 20 Jun 840

13 Hildegarde
Born: 758
-CONTINUED AS #1,ROYAL CHART 2002
Died: 30 Apr 783

Henry of Thuringia
Spouse

3 Gisele, Princess of France
Born: Abt 820
Died: Aft 1 Jul 874

14 Welf I, Duke of Bavaria
Born: Abt 778
-CONTINUED AS #1,ROYAL CHART 2003
Married:
Died: 819

7 Judith of Bavaria
Born: Abt 800
Died: 19 Apr 843

15 Hedwig, Duchess of Bavaria
Born: Abt 780
Died: Aft 826

Sources include: *TAG* 72:187-204; *Royal Ancestors* (1989), chart 11634 (#2 & 3 ancestry); Stuart 269, 185 (#2 & 3 ancestry); *Ancestral Roots* 191, 146 (#2 & 3 ancestry); Moriarty 16, 18, 22-23, 229 (#2 & 3 ancestry).

Pedigree Chart

Chart 1985

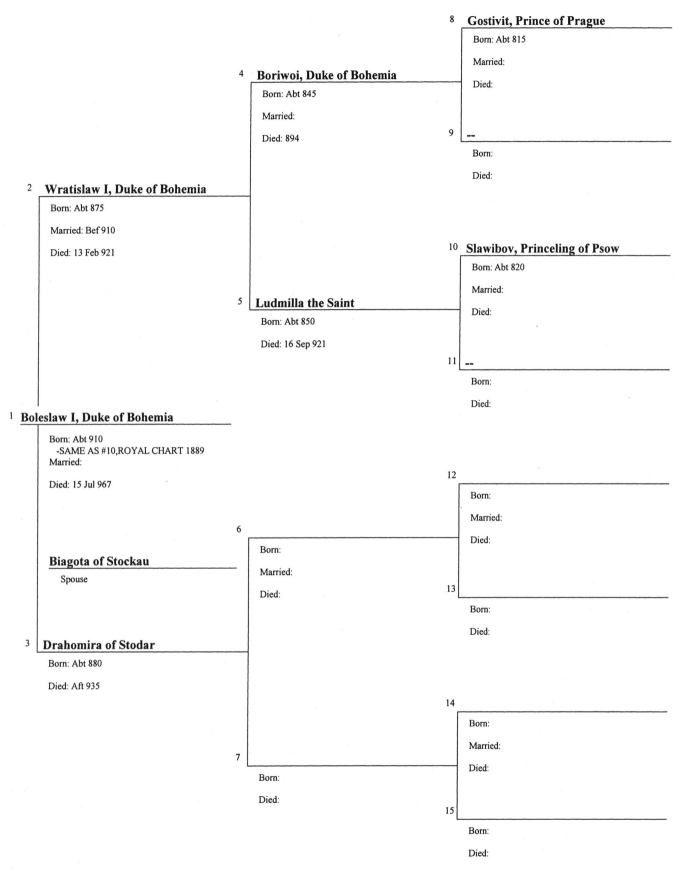

8 Gostivit, Prince of Prague

Born: Abt 815

Married:

Died:

4 Boriwoi, Duke of Bohemia

Born: Abt 845

Married:

Died: 894

9 --

Born:

Died:

2 Wratislaw I, Duke of Bohemia

Born: Abt 875

Married: Bef 910

Died: 13 Feb 921

10 Slawibov, Princeling of Psow

Born: Abt 820

Married:

Died:

5 Ludmilla the Saint

Born: Abt 850

Died: 16 Sep 921

11 --

Born:

Died:

1 Boleslaw I, Duke of Bohemia

Born: Abt 910
-SAME AS #10,ROYAL CHART 1889
Married:

Died: 15 Jul 967

12

Born:

Married:

Died:

6

Born:

Married:

Died:

13

Born:

Died:

Biagota of Stockau

Spouse

3 Drahomira of Stodar

Born: Abt 880

Died: Aft 935

14

Born:

Married:

Died:

7

Born:

Died:

15

Born:

Died:

Sources include: *Royal Ancestors* (1989), chart 11852; Stuart 362; Moriarty 85.

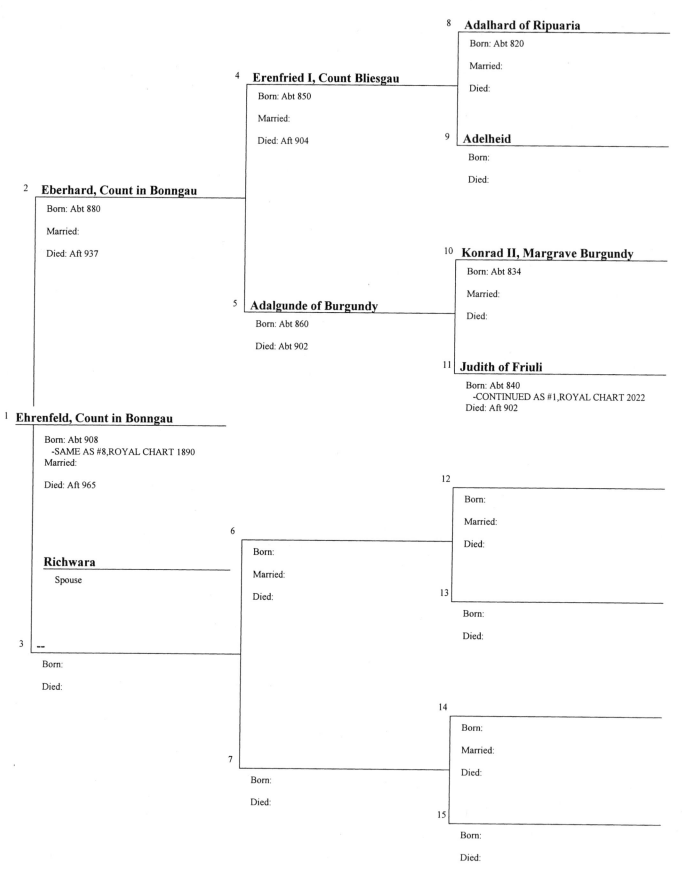

8 Adalhard of Ripuaria

Born: Abt 820

Married:

Died:

4 Erenfried I, Count Bliesgau

Born: Abt 850

Married:

Died: Aft 904

9 Adelheid

Born:

Died:

2 Eberhard, Count in Bonngau

Born: Abt 880

Married:

Died: Aft 937

10 Konrad II, Margrave Burgundy

Born: Abt 834

Married:

Died:

5 Adalgunde of Burgundy

Born: Abt 860

Died: Abt 902

11 Judith of Friuli

Born: Abt 840
-CONTINUED AS #1,ROYAL CHART 2022
Died: Aft 902

1 Ehrenfeld, Count in Bonngau

Born: Abt 908
-SAME AS #8,ROYAL CHART 1890
Married:

Died: Aft 965

12

Born:

Married:

Died:

6

Born:

Married:

Died:

13

Born:

Died:

Richwara

Spouse

3 --

Born:

Died:

14

Born:

Married:

Died:

7

Born:

Died:

15

Born:

Died:

Sources include: *Ancestral Roots* 8 (2004), line 147A; Stuart 208, 389; Moriarty 86. Notes: The parentage of #1 Ehrenfeld is not certain. The Stuart and *Ancestral Roots* version is shown above. Moriarty shows #1 as possibly the son of Hermann, Count in the Avalgau. #8 Adalhard appears questionable if he was living in the 920s, as claimed in *Ancestral Roots*.

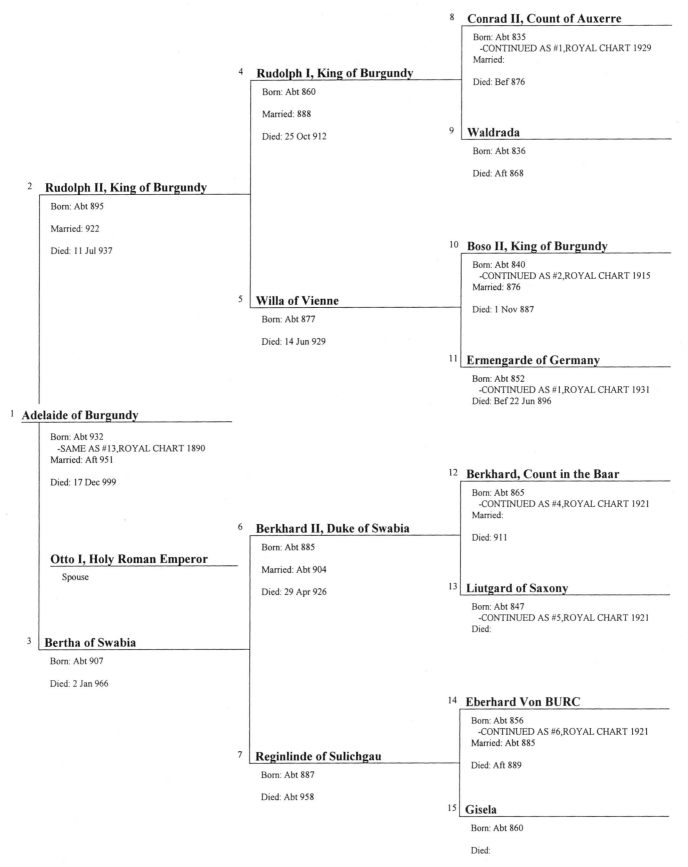

8 Conrad II, Count of Auxerre

Born: Abt 835
-CONTINUED AS #1, ROYAL CHART 1929
Married:

Died: Bef 876

4 Rudolph I, King of Burgundy

Born: Abt 860

Married: 888

Died: 25 Oct 912

9 Waldrada

Born: Abt 836

Died: Aft 868

2 Rudolph II, King of Burgundy

Born: Abt 895

Married: 922

Died: 11 Jul 937

10 Boso II, King of Burgundy

Born: Abt 840
-CONTINUED AS #2, ROYAL CHART 1915
Married: 876

Died: 1 Nov 887

5 Willa of Vienne

Born: Abt 877

Died: 14 Jun 929

11 Ermengarde of Germany

Born: Abt 852
-CONTINUED AS #1, ROYAL CHART 1931
Died: Bef 22 Jun 896

1 Adelaide of Burgundy

Born: Abt 932
-SAME AS #13, ROYAL CHART 1890
Married: Aft 951

Died: 17 Dec 999

12 Berkhard, Count in the Baar

Born: Abt 865
-CONTINUED AS #4, ROYAL CHART 1921
Married:

Died: 911

6 Berkhard II, Duke of Swabia

Born: Abt 885

Married: Abt 904

Died: 29 Apr 926

Otto I, Holy Roman Emperor

Spouse

13 Liutgard of Saxony

Born: Abt 847
-CONTINUED AS #5, ROYAL CHART 1921
Died:

3 Bertha of Swabia

Born: Abt 907

Died: 2 Jan 966

14 Eberhard Von BURC

Born: Abt 856
-CONTINUED AS #6, ROYAL CHART 1921
Married: Abt 885

Died: Aft 889

7 Reginlinde of Sulichgau

Born: Abt 887

Died: Abt 958

15 Gisela

Born: Abt 860

Died:

Sources include: *Royal Ancestors* (1989), chart 11509; Stuart 323; Moriarty 33-34; *Ancestral Roots* 147-19.

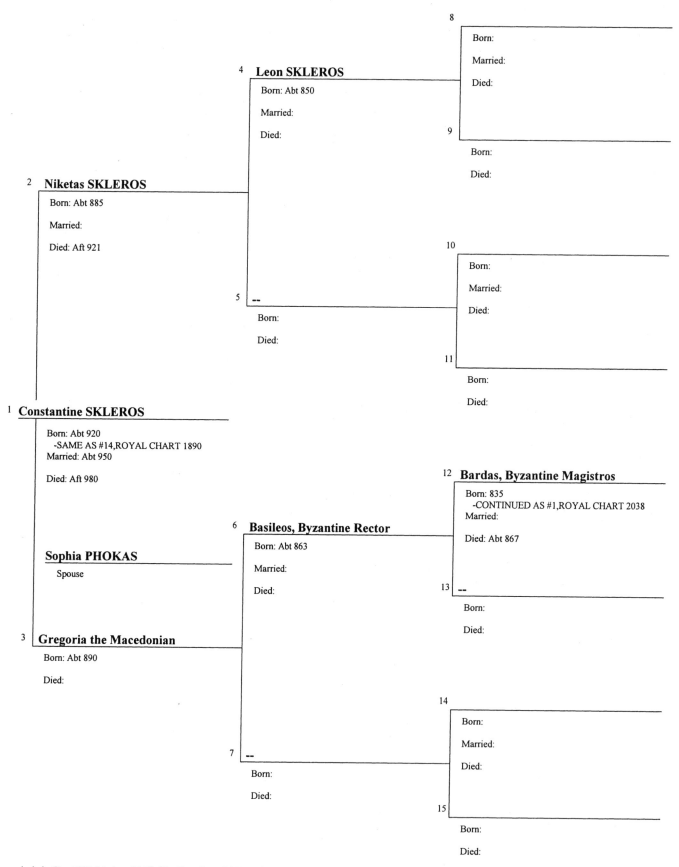

8

Born:

Married:

Died:

4 Leon SKLEROS

Born: Abt 850

Married:

Died:

9

Born:

Died:

2 Niketas SKLEROS

Born: Abt 885

Married:

Died: Aft 921

10

Born:

Married:

Died:

5 --

Born:

Died:

11

Born:

Died:

1 Constantine SKLEROS

Born: Abt 920
-SAME AS #14,ROYAL CHART 1890
Married: Abt 950

Died: Aft 980

12 Bardas, Byzantine Magistros

Born: 835
-CONTINUED AS #1,ROYAL CHART 2038
Married:

Died: Abt 867

6 Basileos, Byzantine Rector

Born: Abt 863

Married:

Died:

13 --

Born:

Died:

Sophia PHOKAS

Spouse

3 Gregoria the Macedonian

Born: Abt 890

Died:

14

Born:

Married:

Died:

7 --

Born:

Died:

15

Born:

Died:

Sources include: Stuart 322; Moriarty 88-89; *The Genealogist* 2:19-20 (#3 ancestry); *Royal Ancestors* (1989), charts 11575, 12065 (#3 ancestry).

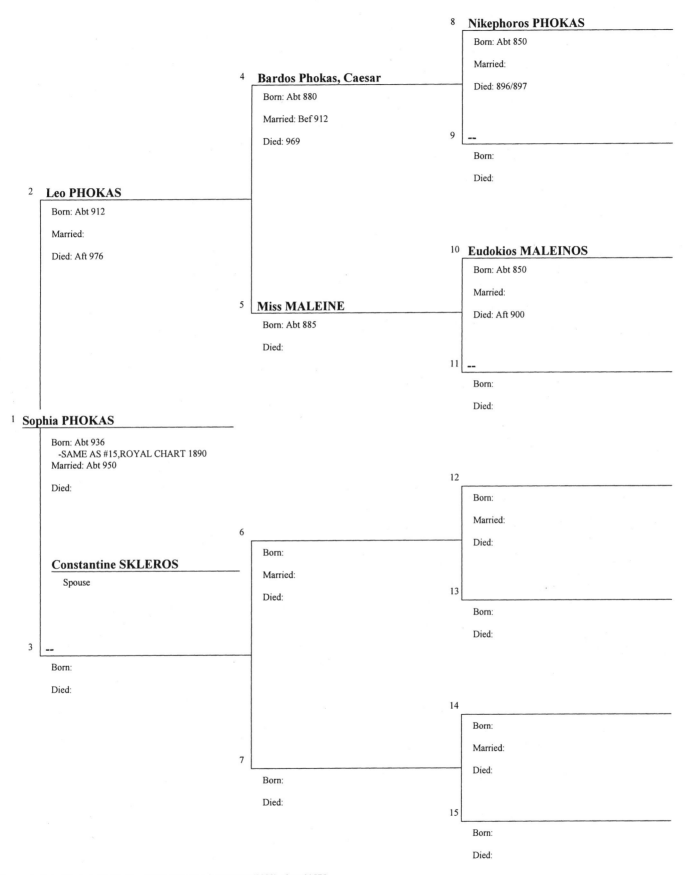

8 Nikephoros PHOKAS
Born: Abt 850
Married:
Died: 896/897

9 --
Born:
Died:

4 Bardos Phokas, Caesar
Born: Abt 880
Married: Bef 912
Died: 969

10 Eudokios MALEINOS
Born: Abt 850
Married:
Died: Aft 900

11 --
Born:
Died:

2 Leo PHOKAS
Born: Abt 912
Married:
Died: Aft 976

5 Miss MALEINE
Born: Abt 885
Died:

1 Sophia PHOKAS
Born: Abt 936
  -SAME AS #15,ROYAL CHART 1890
Married: Abt 950
Died:

Constantine SKLEROS
Spouse

3 --
Born:
Died:

6
Born:
Married:
Died:

12
Born:
Married:
Died:

13
Born:
Died:

7
Born:
Died:

14
Born:
Married:
Died:

15
Born:
Died:

Sources include: Moriarty 88-89; Stuart 219, 275; *Royal Ancestors* (1989), chart 11575.

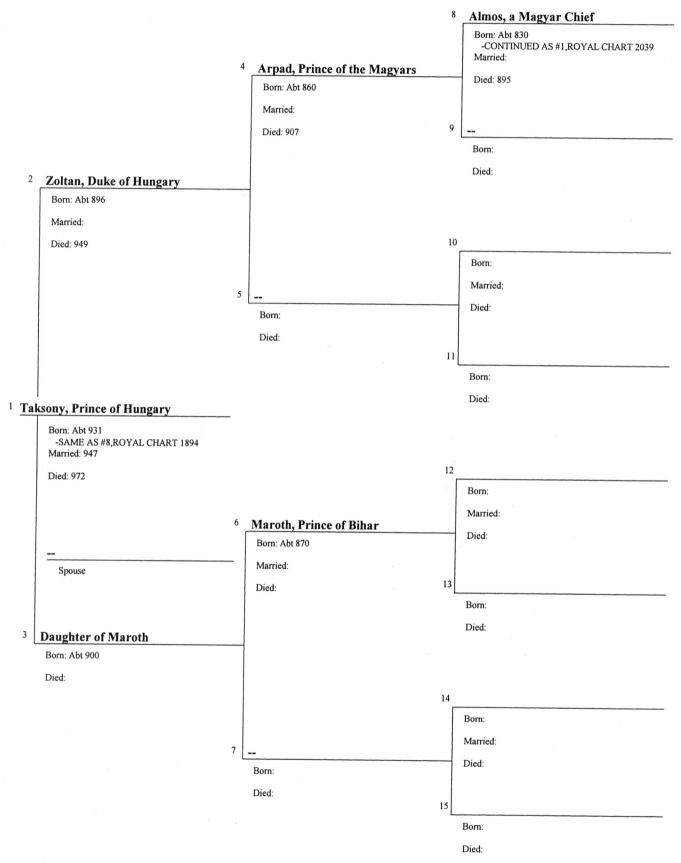

8 Almos, a Magyar Chief
Born: Abt 830
 -CONTINUED AS #1,ROYAL CHART 2039
Married:

Died: 895

4 Arpad, Prince of the Magyars
Born: Abt 860

Married:

Died: 907

9 --
Born:

Died:

2 Zoltan, Duke of Hungary
Born: Abt 896

Married:

Died: 949

10
Born:

Married:

Died:

5 --
Born:

Died:

11
Born:

Died:

1 Taksony, Prince of Hungary
Born: Abt 931
 -SAME AS #8,ROYAL CHART 1894
Married: 947

Died: 972

12
Born:

Married:

Died:

6 Maroth, Prince of Bihar
Born: Abt 870

Married:

Died:

13
Born:

Died:

--
Spouse

3 Daughter of Maroth
Born: Abt 900

Died:

14
Born:

Married:

Died:

7 --
Born:

Died:

15
Born:

Died:

Sources include: *Royal Ancestors* (1989), chart 11947; Stuart 51; Moriarty 31-32; Von Isenburg 2:103.

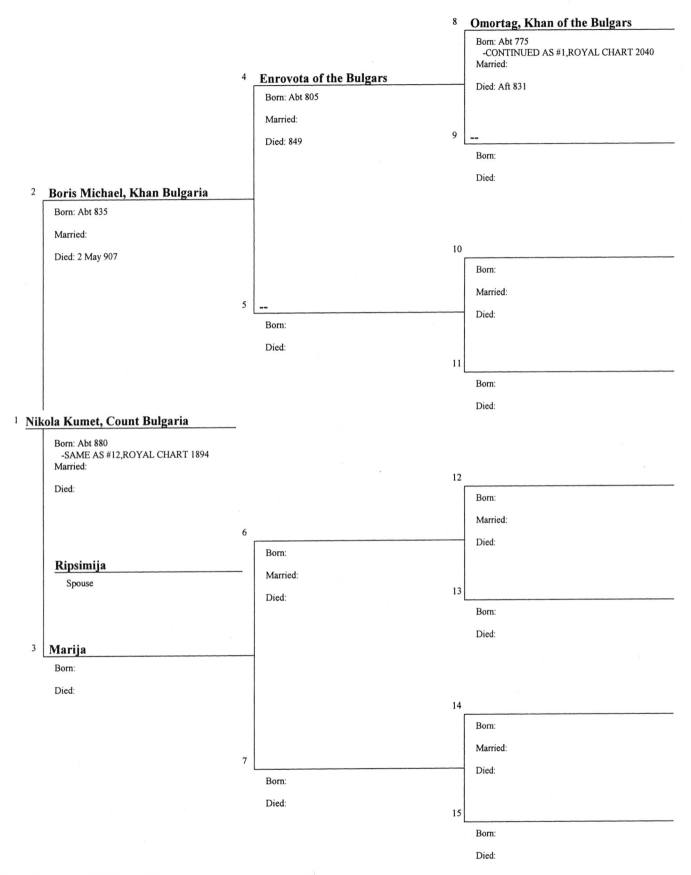

8 Omortag, Khan of the Bulgars
Born: Abt 775
-CONTINUED AS #1,ROYAL CHART 2040
Married:
Died: Aft 831

4 Enrovota of the Bulgars
Born: Abt 805
Married:
Died: 849

9 --
Born:
Died:

2 Boris Michael, Khan Bulgaria
Born: Abt 835
Married:
Died: 2 May 907

10
Born:
Married:
Died:

5 --
Born:
Died:

11
Born:
Died:

1 Nikola Kumet, Count Bulgaria
Born: Abt 880
-SAME AS #12,ROYAL CHART 1894
Married:
Died:

12
Born:
Married:
Died:

6
Born:
Married:
Died:

Ripsimija
Spouse

13
Born:
Died:

3 Marija
Born:
Died:

14
Born:
Married:
Died:

7
Born:
Died:

15
Born:
Died:

Sources include: Stuart 309; Moriarty 139.

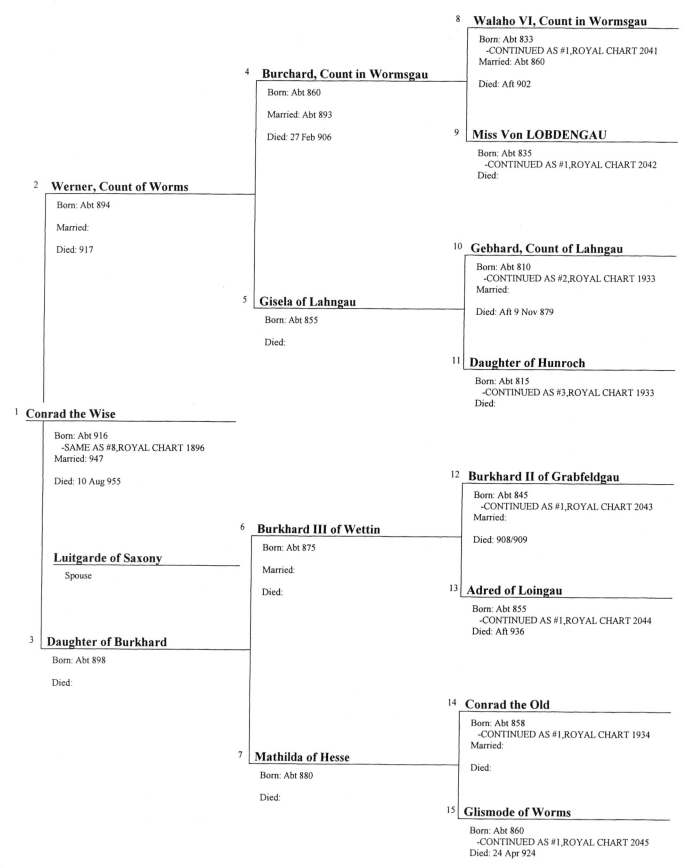

Pedigree Chart structure:

8 Walaho VI, Count in Wormsgau
Born: Abt 833
-CONTINUED AS #1,ROYAL CHART 2041
Married: Abt 860
Died: Aft 902

4 Burchard, Count in Wormsgau
Born: Abt 860
Married: Abt 893
Died: 27 Feb 906

9 Miss Von LOBDENGAU
Born: Abt 835
-CONTINUED AS #1,ROYAL CHART 2042
Died:

2 Werner, Count of Worms
Born: Abt 894
Married:
Died: 917

10 Gebhard, Count of Lahngau
Born: Abt 810
-CONTINUED AS #2,ROYAL CHART 1933
Married:
Died: Aft 9 Nov 879

5 Gisela of Lahngau
Born: Abt 855
Died:

11 Daughter of Hunroch
Born: Abt 815
-CONTINUED AS #3,ROYAL CHART 1933
Died:

1 Conrad the Wise
Born: Abt 916
-SAME AS #8,ROYAL CHART 1896
Married: 947
Died: 10 Aug 955

12 Burkhard II of Grabfeldgau
Born: Abt 845
-CONTINUED AS #1,ROYAL CHART 2043
Married:
Died: 908/909

6 Burkhard III of Wettin
Born: Abt 875
Married:
Died:

13 Adred of Loingau
Born: Abt 855
-CONTINUED AS #1,ROYAL CHART 2044
Died: Aft 936

Luitgarde of Saxony
Spouse

3 Daughter of Burkhard
Born: Abt 898
Died:

14 Conrad the Old
Born: Abt 858
-CONTINUED AS #1,ROYAL CHART 1934
Married:
Died:

7 Mathilda of Hesse
Born: Abt 880
Died:

15 Glismode of Worms
Born: Abt 860
-CONTINUED AS #1,ROYAL CHART 2045
Died: 24 Apr 924

Sources include: *Royal Ancestors* (1989), charts 11565, 11617; Stuart 359; Moriarty 91, 23; *Ancestral Roots* 192. Note: The parentage and ancestry of #2 & 3 Werner and his unknown wife is disputed. The Moriarty version is given above. The *Ancestral Roots* version makes #2 Werner the son of Conrad the Old & Glismode (see #14 & 15 above). In a preliminary Charlemagne manuscript (June 1995), p. 140, Faris makes #2 the son of another Werner and gives #3 as Hicha Von Schwaben, daughter of Berkhard & Reginlinde (see chart 1921, #2 & 3). Schwennicke 1:4 terminates the line with #2 Werner & #3 unknown.

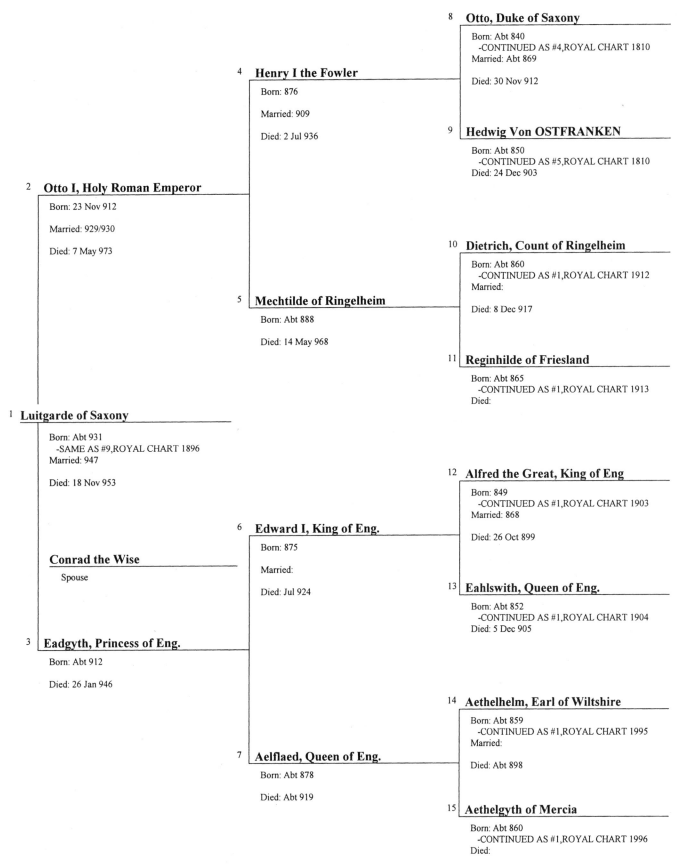

8 Otto, Duke of Saxony
Born: Abt 840
-CONTINUED AS #4,ROYAL CHART 1810
Married: Abt 869

Died: 30 Nov 912

4 Henry I the Fowler
Born: 876
Married: 909
Died: 2 Jul 936

9 Hedwig Von OSTFRANKEN
Born: Abt 850
-CONTINUED AS #5,ROYAL CHART 1810
Died: 24 Dec 903

2 Otto I, Holy Roman Emperor
Born: 23 Nov 912
Married: 929/930
Died: 7 May 973

10 Dietrich, Count of Ringelheim
Born: Abt 860
-CONTINUED AS #1,ROYAL CHART 1912
Married:

Died: 8 Dec 917

5 Mechtilde of Ringelheim
Born: Abt 888
Died: 14 May 968

11 Reginhilde of Friesland
Born: Abt 865
-CONTINUED AS #1,ROYAL CHART 1913
Died:

1 Luitgarde of Saxony
Born: Abt 931
-SAME AS #9,ROYAL CHART 1896
Married: 947
Died: 18 Nov 953

12 Alfred the Great, King of Eng
Born: 849
-CONTINUED AS #1,ROYAL CHART 1903
Married: 868

Died: 26 Oct 899

6 Edward I, King of Eng.
Born: 875
Married:
Died: Jul 924

Conrad the Wise
Spouse

13 Eahlswith, Queen of Eng.
Born: Abt 852
-CONTINUED AS #1,ROYAL CHART 1904
Died: 5 Dec 905

3 Eadgyth, Princess of Eng.
Born: Abt 912
Died: 26 Jan 946

14 Aethelhelm, Earl of Wiltshire
Born: Abt 859
-CONTINUED AS #1,ROYAL CHART 1995
Married:

Died: Abt 898

7 Aelflaed, Queen of Eng.
Born: Abt 878
Died: Abt 919

15 Aethelgyth of Mercia
Born: Abt 860
-CONTINUED AS #1,ROYAL CHART 1996
Died:

Sources include: *Royal Ancestors* (1989), chart 11565; *Ancestral Roots* 45; Stuart 359-37, 321, 376; Moriarty 87, 30-31, 254.

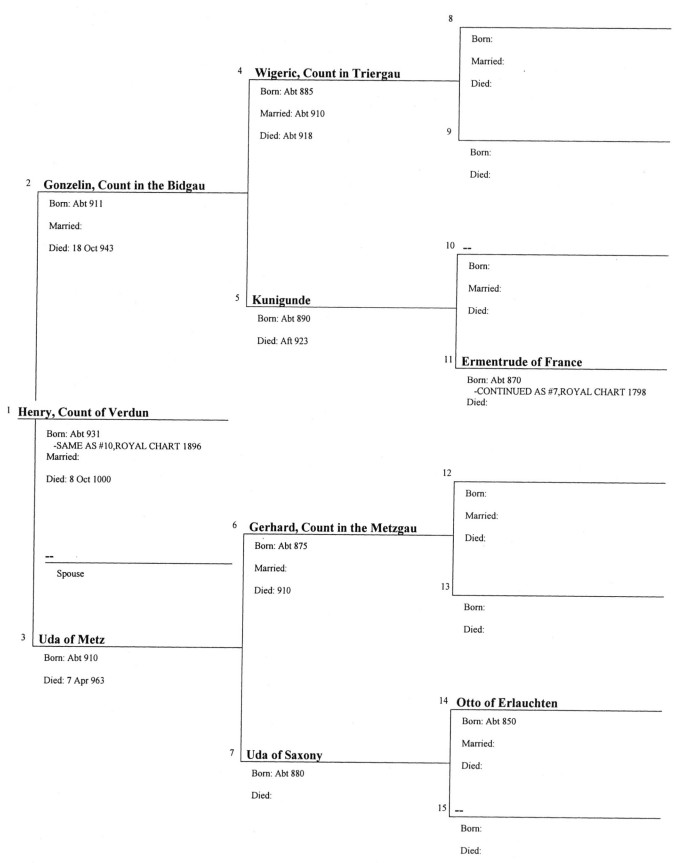

8

Born:

Married:

Died:

4 | **Wigeric, Count in Triergau**

Born: Abt 885

Married: Abt 910

Died: Abt 918

9

Born:

Died:

2 | **Gonzelin, Count in the Bidgau**

Born: Abt 911

Married:

Died: 18 Oct 943

10 | --

Born:

Married:

Died:

5 | **Kunigunde**

Born: Abt 890

Died: Aft 923

11 | **Ermentrude of France**

Born: Abt 870
  -CONTINUED AS #7,ROYAL CHART 1798
Died:

1 | **Henry, Count of Verdun**

Born: Abt 931
  -SAME AS #10,ROYAL CHART 1896
Married:

Died: 8 Oct 1000

12

Born:

Married:

Died:

6 | **Gerhard, Count in the Metzgau**

Born: Abt 875

Married:

Died: 910

13

Born:

Died:

--

Spouse

3 | **Uda of Metz**

Born: Abt 910

Died: 7 Apr 963

14 | **Otto of Erlauchten**

Born: Abt 850

Married:

Died:

7 | **Uda of Saxony**

Born: Abt 880

Died:

15 | --

Born:

Died:

Sources include: Stuart 359-36, 104; Moriarty 92, 126; *Royal Ancestors* (1989), chart 11565; *Ancestral Roots* 45-19.

Pedigree Chart

Chart 1995

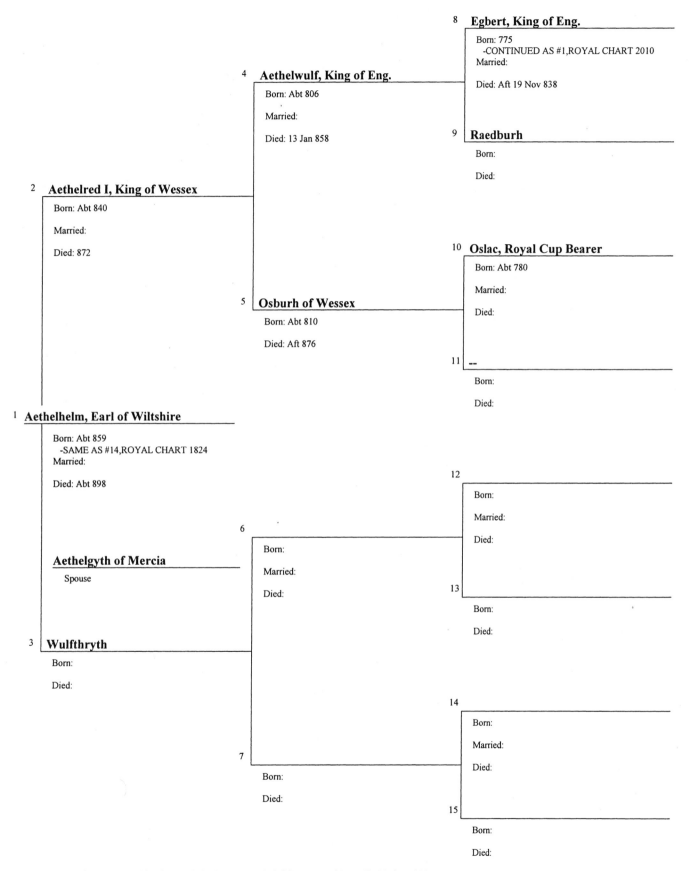

8 Egbert, King of Eng.

Born: 775
   -CONTINUED AS #1,ROYAL CHART 2010
Married:

Died: Aft 19 Nov 838

4 Aethelwulf, King of Eng.

Born: Abt 806

Married:

Died: 13 Jan 858

9 Raedburh

Born:

Died:

2 Aethelred I, King of Wessex

Born: Abt 840

Married:

Died: 872

10 Oslac, Royal Cup Bearer

Born: Abt 780

Married:

Died:

5 Osburh of Wessex

Born: Abt 810

Died: Aft 876

11 --

Born:

Died:

1 Aethelhelm, Earl of Wiltshire

Born: Abt 859
   -SAME AS #14,ROYAL CHART 1824
Married:

Died: Abt 898

12

Born:

Married:

Died:

6

Born:

Married:

Died:

13

Born:

Died:

Aethelgyth of Mercia

Spouse

3 Wulfthryth

Born:

Died:

14

Born:

Married:

Died:

7

Born:

Died:

15

Born:

Died:

Sources include: *Royal Ancestors* (1989), charts 11616, 12082; Stuart 376, 367; *Ancestral Roots* 1B; Moriarty 254.

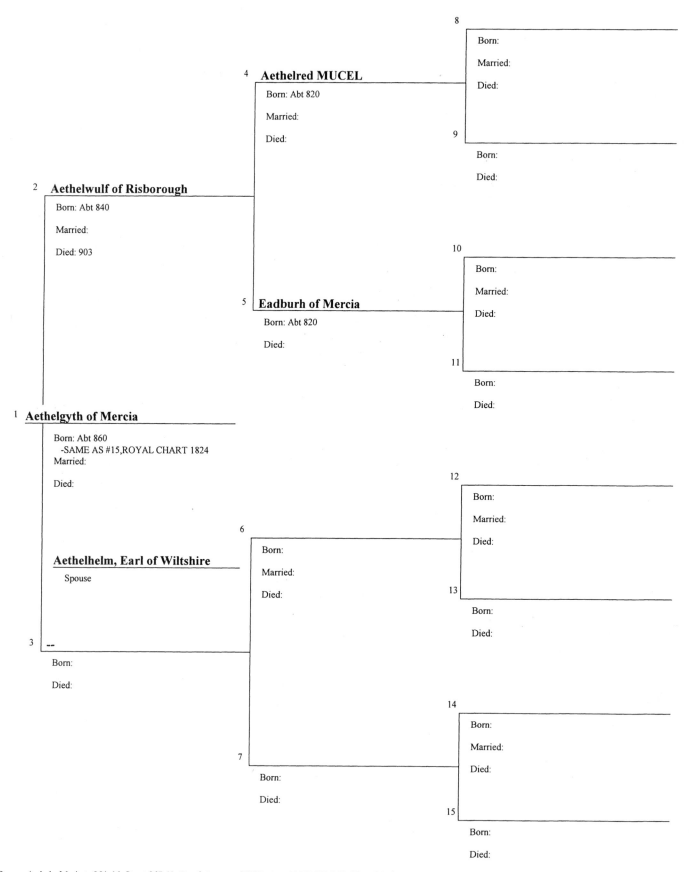

8
Born:
Married:
Died:

4 Aethelred MUCEL
Born: Abt 820
Married:
Died:

9
Born:
Died:

2 Aethelwulf of Risborough
Born: Abt 840
Married:
Died: 903

10
Born:
Married:
Died:

5 Eadburh of Mercia
Born: Abt 820
Died:

11
Born:
Died:

1 Aethelgyth of Mercia
Born: Abt 860
-SAME AS #15,ROYAL CHART 1824
Married:
Died:

Aethelhelm, Earl of Wiltshire
Spouse

12
Born:
Married:
Died:

6
Born:
Married:
Died:

13
Born:
Died:

3 --
Born:
Died:

14
Born:
Married:
Died:

7
Born:
Died:

15
Born:
Died:

Sources include: Moriarty 254, 16; Stuart 367-41; *Royal Ancestors* (1989), chart 11605 (#4 & 5). Note: Moriarty states that #5 Eadburh was of the royal Mercian line. Stuart states that she descends from Wigmund, son of Witgraff, King of Mercia.

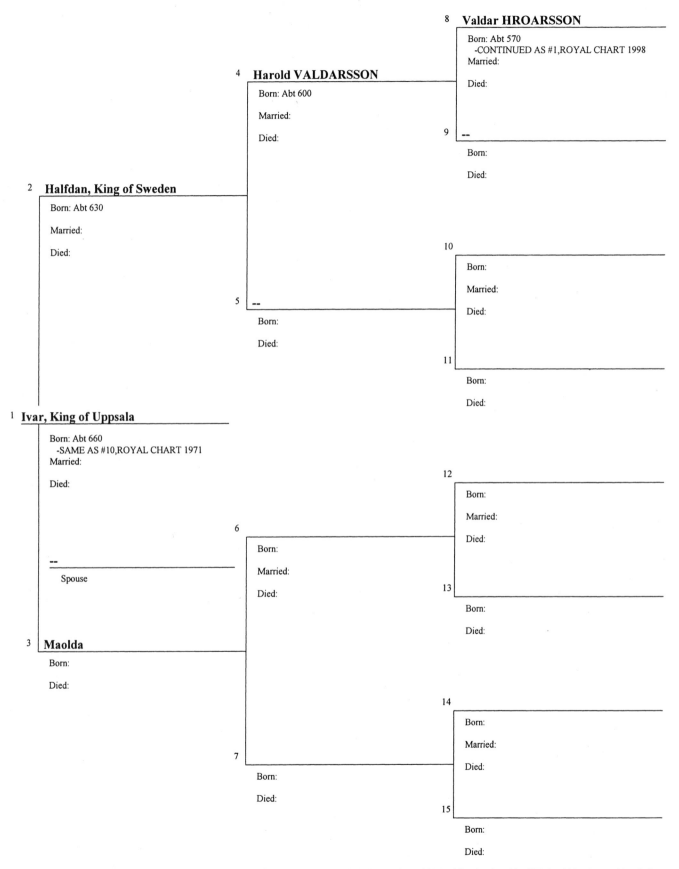

8 **Valdar HROARSSON**

Born: Abt 570
-CONTINUED AS #1,ROYAL CHART 1998
Married:

Died:

4 **Harold VALDARSSON**

Born: Abt 600

Married:

Died:

9 --

Born:

Died:

2 **Halfdan, King of Sweden**

Born: Abt 630

Married:

Died:

10

Born:

Married:

Died:

5 --

Born:

Died:

11

Born:

Died:

1 **Ivar, King of Uppsala**

Born: Abt 660
-SAME AS #10,ROYAL CHART 1971
Married:

Died:

12

Born:

Married:

Died:

6

Born:

Married:

Died:

13

Born:

Died:

--

Spouse

3 **Maolda**

Born:

Died:

14

Born:

Married:

Died:

7

Born:

Died:

15

Born:

Died:

Sources include: *Royal Ancestors* (1989), charts 11719-20; Stuart 240; LDS records. Note: Hildis (Princess of Vandals) is claimed as the wife of #4 Harold (LDS records) and of #8 Valdar (Stuart version). She may have been the daughter of Hilderic, King of Vandals, a descendant of Genseric, a Vandal who conquered much of Africa about 425-455 AD.

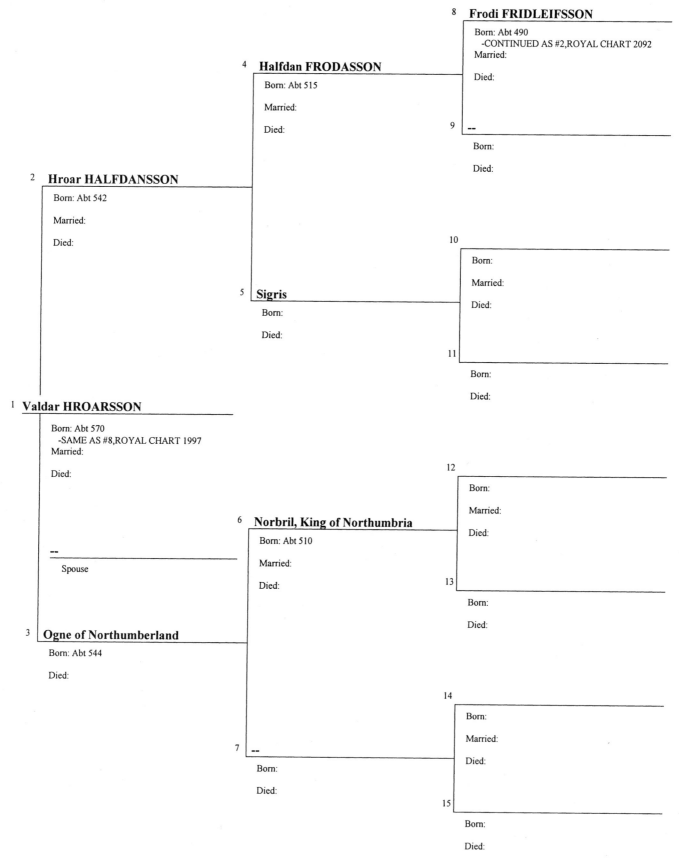

8 Frodi FRIDLEIFSSON

Born: Abt 490
  -CONTINUED AS #2,ROYAL CHART 2092
Married:

Died:

4 Halfdan FRODASSON

Born: Abt 515

Married:

Died:

9 --

Born:

Died:

2 Hroar HALFDANSSON

Born: Abt 542

Married:

Died:

10

Born:

Married:

Died:

5 Sigris

Born:

Died:

11

Born:

Died:

1 Valdar HROARSSON

Born: Abt 570
  -SAME AS #8,ROYAL CHART 1997
Married:

Died:

--

Spouse

12

Born:

Married:

Died:

6 Norbril, King of Northumbria

Born: Abt 510

Married:

Died:

13

Born:

Died:

3 Ogne of Northumberland

Born: Abt 544

Died:

14

Born:

Married:

Died:

7 --

Born:

Died:

15

Born:

Died:

Sources include: *Royal Ancestors* (1989), chart 11720; Stuart 240.

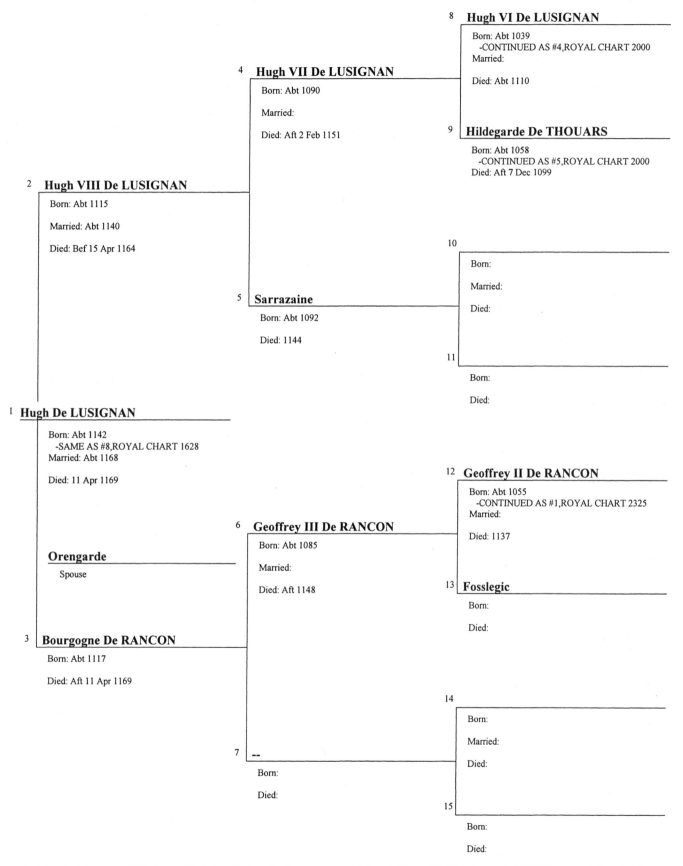

8 Hugh VI De LUSIGNAN
Born: Abt 1039
-CONTINUED AS #4,ROYAL CHART 2000
Married:

Died: Abt 1110

4 Hugh VII De LUSIGNAN
Born: Abt 1090

Married:

Died: Aft 2 Feb 1151

9 Hildegarde De THOUARS
Born: Abt 1058
-CONTINUED AS #5,ROYAL CHART 2000
Died: Aft 7 Dec 1099

2 Hugh VIII De LUSIGNAN
Born: Abt 1115

Married: Abt 1140

Died: Bef 15 Apr 1164

10
Born:

Married:

Died:

5 Sarrazaine
Born: Abt 1092

Died: 1144

11
Born:

Died:

1 Hugh De LUSIGNAN
Born: Abt 1142
-SAME AS #8,ROYAL CHART 1628
Married: Abt 1168

Died: 11 Apr 1169

12 Geoffrey II De RANCON
Born: Abt 1055
-CONTINUED AS #1,ROYAL CHART 2325
Married:

Died: 1137

6 Geoffrey III De RANCON
Born: Abt 1085

Married:

Died: Aft 1148

13 Fosslegic
Born:

Died:

Orengarde
Spouse

3 Bourgogne De RANCON
Born: Abt 1117

Died: Aft 11 Apr 1169

14
Born:

Married:

Died:

7 --
Born:

Died:

15
Born:

Died:

Sources include: *Royal Ancestors* (1989), chart 11674; Faris preliminary Charlemagne manuscript (June 1995), pp. 169-171; Schwennicke 3:815-816; *Ancestral Roots* 123-28; Turton 81.

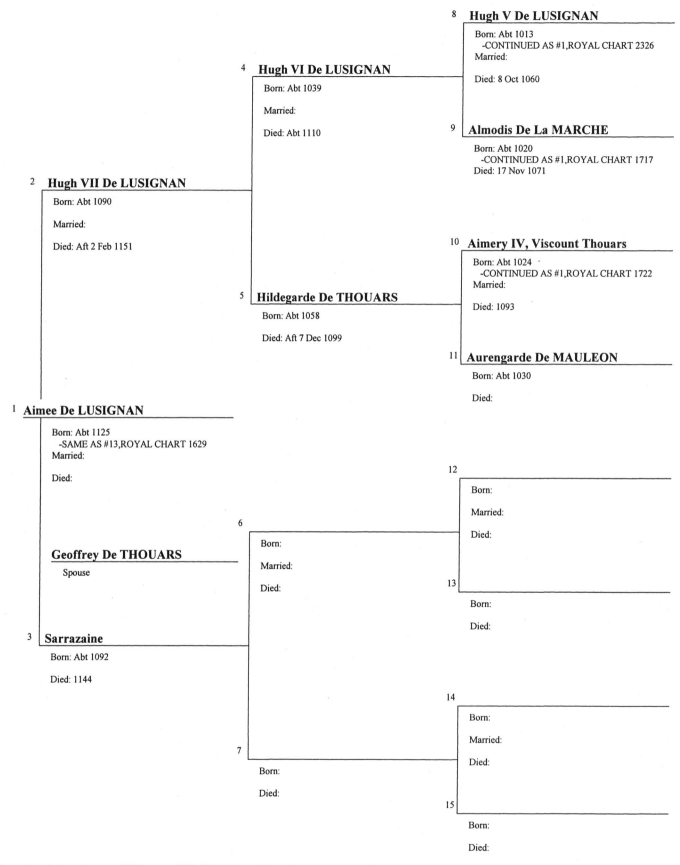

Pedigree Chart

Chart 2000

8 **Hugh V De LUSIGNAN**

Born: Abt 1013
-CONTINUED AS #1,ROYAL CHART 2326
Married:

Died: 8 Oct 1060

4 **Hugh VI De LUSIGNAN**

Born: Abt 1039

Married:

Died: Abt 1110

9 **Almodis De La MARCHE**

Born: Abt 1020
-CONTINUED AS #1,ROYAL CHART 1717
Died: 17 Nov 1071

2 **Hugh VII De LUSIGNAN**

Born: Abt 1090

Married:

Died: Aft 2 Feb 1151

10 **Aimery IV, Viscount Thouars**

Born: Abt 1024
-CONTINUED AS #1,ROYAL CHART 1722
Married:

Died: 1093

5 **Hildegarde De THOUARS**

Born: Abt 1058

Died: Aft 7 Dec 1099

11 **Aurengarde De MAULEON**

Born: Abt 1030

Died:

1 **Aimee De LUSIGNAN**

Born: Abt 1125
-SAME AS #13,ROYAL CHART 1629
Married:

Died:

12

Born:

Married:

Died:

6

Born:

Married:

Died:

13

Born:

Died:

Geoffrey De THOUARS

Spouse

3 **Sarrazaine**

Born: Abt 1092

Died: 1144

14

Born:

Married:

Died:

7

Born:

Died:

15

Born:

Died:

Sources include: *Royal Ancestors* (1989), charts 11906, 11674; Faris preliminary Charlemagne manuscript (June 1995), pp. 260, 169-170; Schwennicke 3:815 (#2 ancestry); Turton 187, 81; *Ancestral Roots* 96-27 (#1 Aenor).

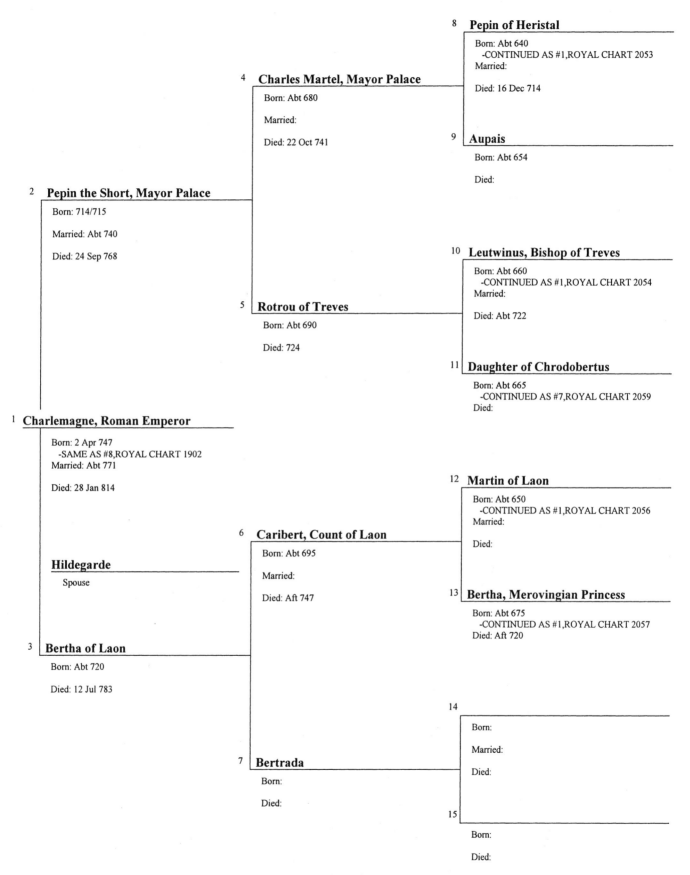

8 Pepin of Heristal

Born: Abt 640
-CONTINUED AS #1,ROYAL CHART 2053
Married:

Died: 16 Dec 714

4 Charles Martel, Mayor Palace

Born: Abt 680

Married:

Died: 22 Oct 741

9 Aupais

Born: Abt 654

Died:

2 Pepin the Short, Mayor Palace

Born: 714/715

Married: Abt 740

Died: 24 Sep 768

10 Leutwinus, Bishop of Treves

Born: Abt 660
-CONTINUED AS #1,ROYAL CHART 2054
Married:

Died: Abt 722

5 Rotrou of Treves

Born: Abt 690

Died: 724

11 Daughter of Chrodobertus

Born: Abt 665
-CONTINUED AS #7,ROYAL CHART 2059
Died:

1 Charlemagne, Roman Emperor

Born: 2 Apr 747
-SAME AS #8,ROYAL CHART 1902
Married: Abt 771

Died: 28 Jan 814

12 Martin of Laon

Born: Abt 650
-CONTINUED AS #1,ROYAL CHART 2056
Married:

Died:

6 Caribert, Count of Laon

Born: Abt 695

Married:

Died: Aft 747

Hildegarde

Spouse

13 Bertha, Merovingian Princess

Born: Abt 675
-CONTINUED AS #1,ROYAL CHART 2057
Died: Aft 720

3 Bertha of Laon

Born: Abt 720

Died: 12 Jul 783

14

Born:

Married:

Died:

7 Bertrada

Born:

Died:

15

Born:

Died:

Sources include: *Royal Ancestors* (1989), chart 11601; *Ancestral Roots* 50; Stuart 171, 214; Moriarty 5, 8, 232.

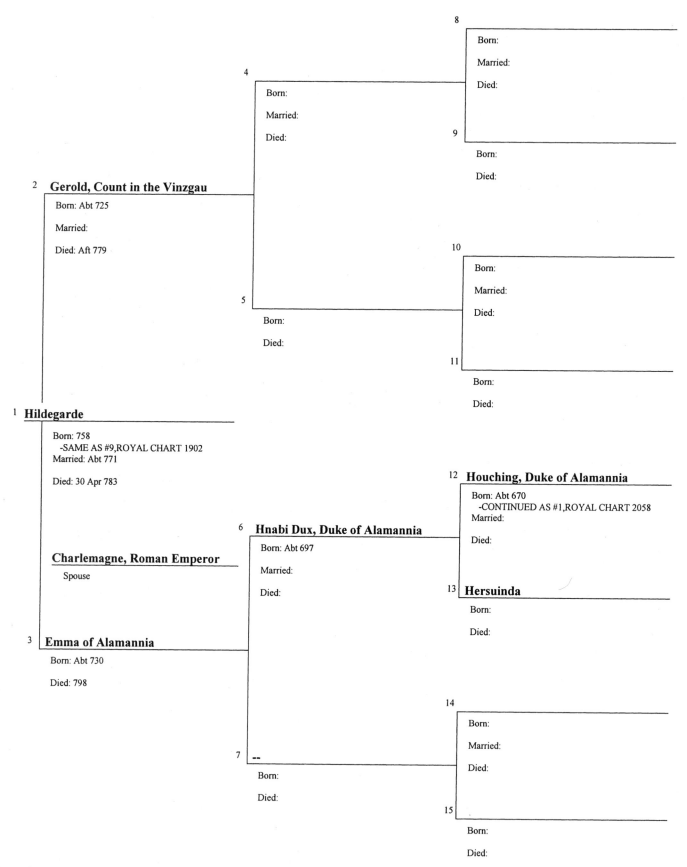

8

Born:

Married:

Died:

4

Born:

Married:

Died:

9

Born:

Died:

2 Gerold, Count in the Vinzgau

Born: Abt 725

Married:

Died: Aft 779

10

Born:

Married:

Died:

5

Born:

Died:

11

Born:

Died:

1 Hildegarde

Born: 758
    -SAME AS #9,ROYAL CHART 1902
Married: Abt 771

Died: 30 Apr 783

12 Houching, Duke of Alamannia

Born: Abt 670
    -CONTINUED AS #1,ROYAL CHART 2058
Married:

Died:

6 Hnabi Dux, Duke of Alamannia

Born: Abt 697

Married:

Died:

13 Hersuinda

Born:

Died:

Charlemagne, Roman Emperor

Spouse

3 Emma of Alamannia

Born: Abt 730

Died: 798

14

Born:

Married:

Died:

7 --

Born:

Died:

15

Born:

Died:

Sources include: *Royal Ancestors* (1989), chart 11601; *Ancestral Roots* 182; Stuart 262; Moriarty 8-9.

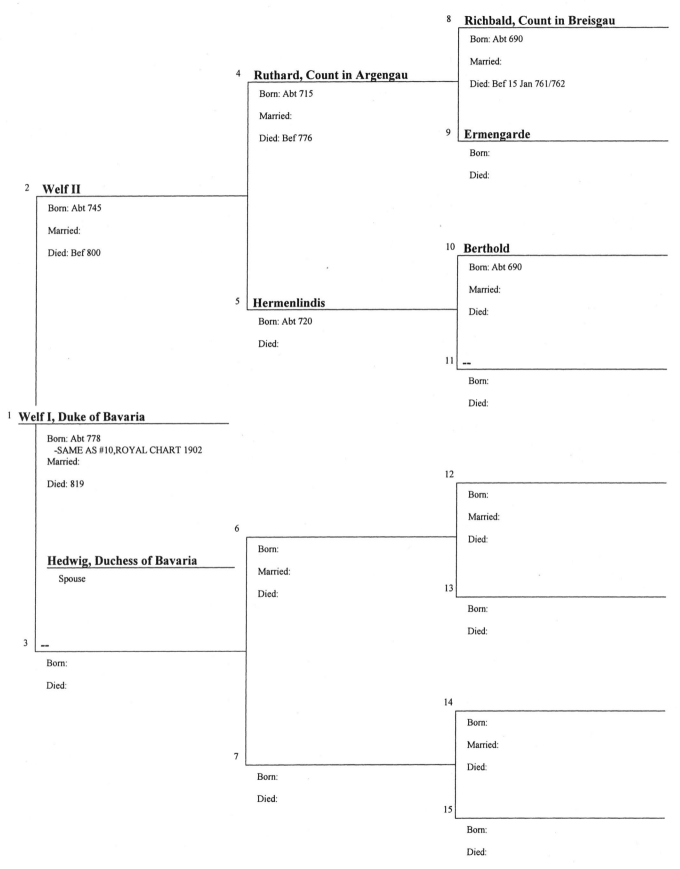

8 **Richbald, Count in Breisgau**

Born: Abt 690

Married:

Died: Bef 15 Jan 761/762

4 **Ruthard, Count in Argengau**

Born: Abt 715

Married:

Died: Bef 776

9 **Ermengarde**

Born:

Died:

2 **Welf II**

Born: Abt 745

Married:

Died: Bef 800

10 **Berthold**

Born: Abt 690

Married:

Died:

5 **Hermenlindis**

Born: Abt 720

Died:

11 **--**

Born:

Died:

1 **Welf I, Duke of Bavaria**

Born: Abt 778
  -SAME AS #10, ROYAL CHART 1902
Married:

Died: 819

12

Born:

Married:

Died:

6

Born:

Married:

Died:

13

Born:

Died:

Hedwig, Duchess of Bavaria

Spouse

3 **--**

Born:

Died:

14

Born:

Married:

Died:

7

Born:

Died:

15

Born:

Died:

Sources include: *Royal Ancestors* (1989), chart 11630; Stuart 300; Moriarty 17. Note: The parentage and ancestry of #1 Welf is disputed and uncertain. The tentative Moriarty version is given above.

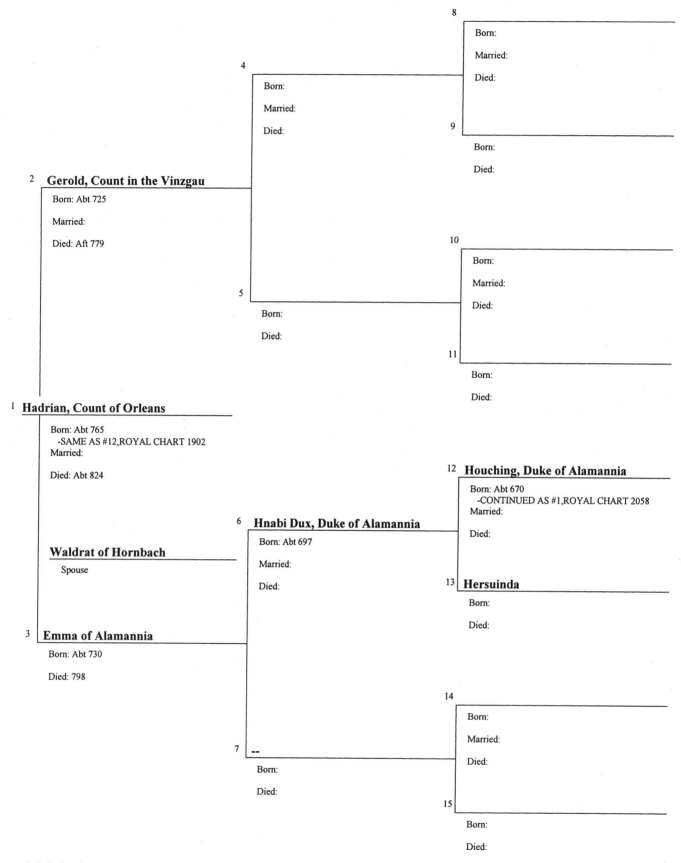

8

Born:

Married:

Died:

4

Born:

Married:

Died:

9

Born:

Died:

2 **Gerold, Count in the Vinzgau**

Born: Abt 725

Married:

Died: Aft 779

10

Born:

Married:

Died:

5

Born:

Died:

11

Born:

Died:

1 **Hadrian, Count of Orleans**

Born: Abt 765
 -SAME AS #12,ROYAL CHART 1902
Married:

Died: Abt 824

12 **Houching, Duke of Alamannia**

Born: Abt 670
 -CONTINUED AS #1,ROYAL CHART 2058
Married:

Died:

6 **Hnabi Dux, Duke of Alamannia**

Born: Abt 697

Married:

Died:

13 **Hersuinda**

Born:

Died:

Waldrat of Hornbach

Spouse

3 **Emma of Alamannia**

Born: Abt 730

Died: 798

14

Born:

Married:

Died:

7 **--**

Born:

Died:

15

Born:

Died:

Sources include: *Royal Ancestors* (1989), chart 11604; Stuart 336; Moriarty 233.

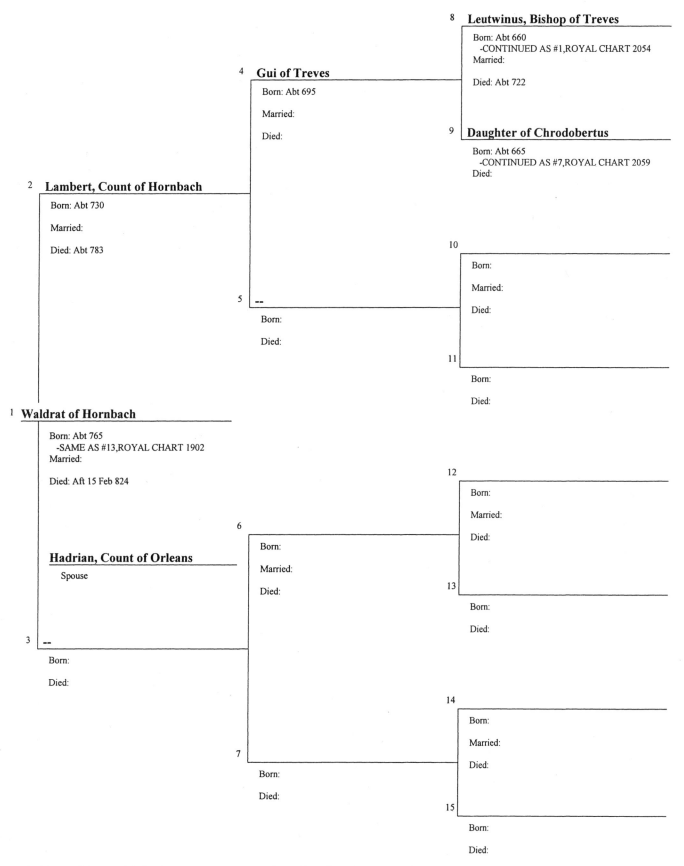

8 Leutwinus, Bishop of Treves

Born: Abt 660
  -CONTINUED AS #1,ROYAL CHART 2054
Married:

Died: Abt 722

4 Gui of Treves

Born: Abt 695

Married:

Died:

9 Daughter of Chrodobertus

Born: Abt 665
  -CONTINUED AS #7,ROYAL CHART 2059
Died:

2 Lambert, Count of Hornbach

Born: Abt 730

Married:

Died: Abt 783

10

Born:

Married:

Died:

5 --

Born:

Died:

11

Born:

Died:

1 Waldrat of Hornbach

Born: Abt 765
  -SAME AS #13,ROYAL CHART 1902
Married:

Died: Aft 15 Feb 824

12

Born:

Married:

Died:

6

Born:

Married:

Died:

13

Born:

Died:

Hadrian, Count of Orleans

Spouse

3 --

Born:

Died:

14

Born:

Married:

Died:

7

Born:

Died:

15

Born:

Died:

Sources include: *Royal Ancestors* (1989) , charts 11604, 11995; Stuart 336-42, 330; Moriarty 233, 74. Note: The parentage and ancestry shown for #1 Waldrat is not certain.

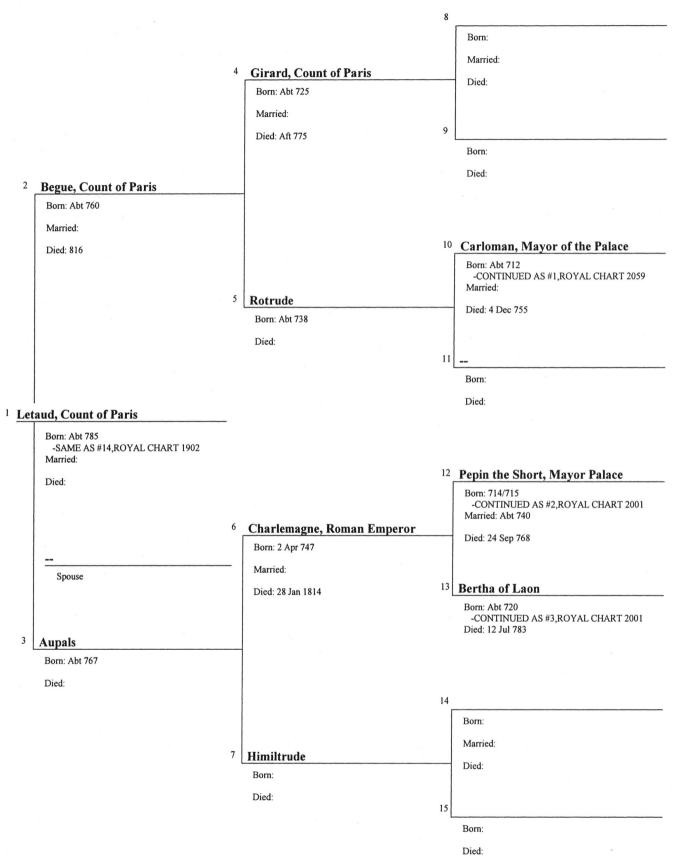

8

Born:

Married:

Died:

4 Girard, Count of Paris

Born: Abt 725

Married:

Died: Aft 775

9

Born:

Died:

2 Begue, Count of Paris

Born: Abt 760

Married:

Died: 816

10 Carloman, Mayor of the Palace

Born: Abt 712
  -CONTINUED AS #1,ROYAL CHART 2059
Married:

Died: 4 Dec 755

5 Rotrude

Born: Abt 738

Died:

11 --

Born:

Died:

1 Letaud, Count of Paris

Born: Abt 785
  -SAME AS #14,ROYAL CHART 1902
Married:

Died:

12 Pepin the Short, Mayor Palace

Born: 714/715
  -CONTINUED AS #2,ROYAL CHART 2001
Married: Abt 740

Died: 24 Sep 768

6 Charlemagne, Roman Emperor

Born: 2 Apr 747

Married:

Died: 28 Jan 1814

13 Bertha of Laon

Born: Abt 720
  -CONTINUED AS #3,ROYAL CHART 2001
Died: 12 Jul 783

--

Spouse

3 Aupals

Born: Abt 767

Died:

14

Born:

Married:

Died:

7 Himiltrude

Born:

Died:

15

Born:

Died:

Sources include: *Royal Ancestors* (1989), charts 11604, 11725; Stuart 250-39, 269, 171; Moriarty 22-23; *Ancestral Roots* 191 (#2 & 3 ancestry). Note: #11 (wife of Carloman) is disputed.

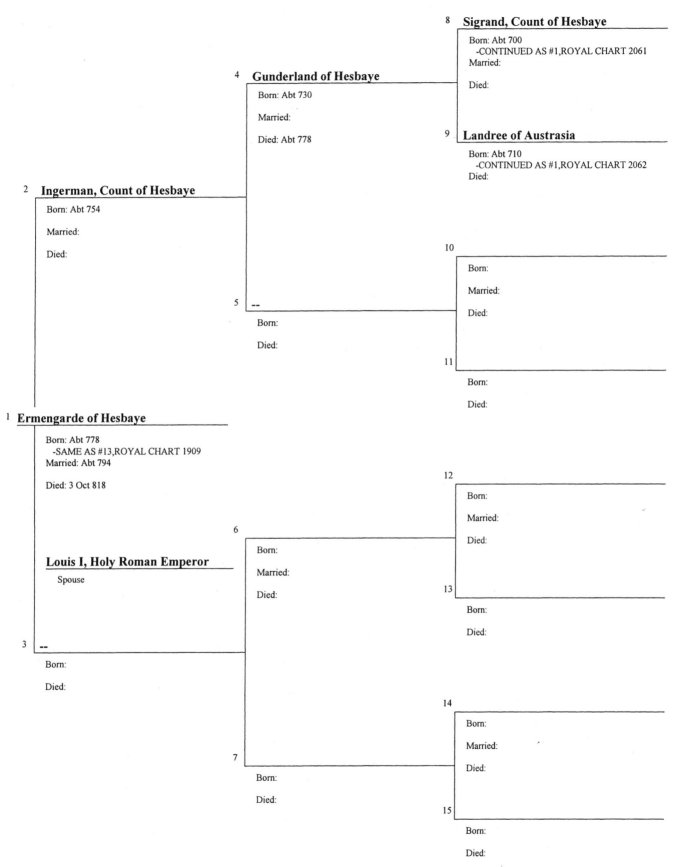

8 Sigrand, Count of Hesbaye

Born: Abt 700
  -CONTINUED AS #1,ROYAL CHART 2061
Married:

Died:

9 Landree of Austrasia

Born: Abt 710
  -CONTINUED AS #1,ROYAL CHART 2062
Died:

4 Gunderland of Hesbaye

Born: Abt 730

Married:

Died: Abt 778

10

Born:

Married:

Died:

11

Born:

Died:

2 Ingerman, Count of Hesbaye

Born: Abt 754

Married:

Died:

5 --

Born:

Died:

1 Ermengarde of Hesbaye

Born: Abt 778
  -SAME AS #13,ROYAL CHART 1909
Married: Abt 794

Died: 3 Oct 818

12

Born:

Married:

Died:

6

Born:

Married:

Died:

13

Born:

Died:

Louis I, Holy Roman Emperor

Spouse

3 --

Born:

Died:

14

Born:

Married:

Died:

7

Born:

Died:

15

Born:

Died:

Sources include: *Royal Ancestors* (1989), chart 11601; Moriarty 20-21, 1, 5; Stuart 352; *Ancestral Roots* 140-14. Note: #4 was an unknown son of Sigrand, perhaps Gunderland.

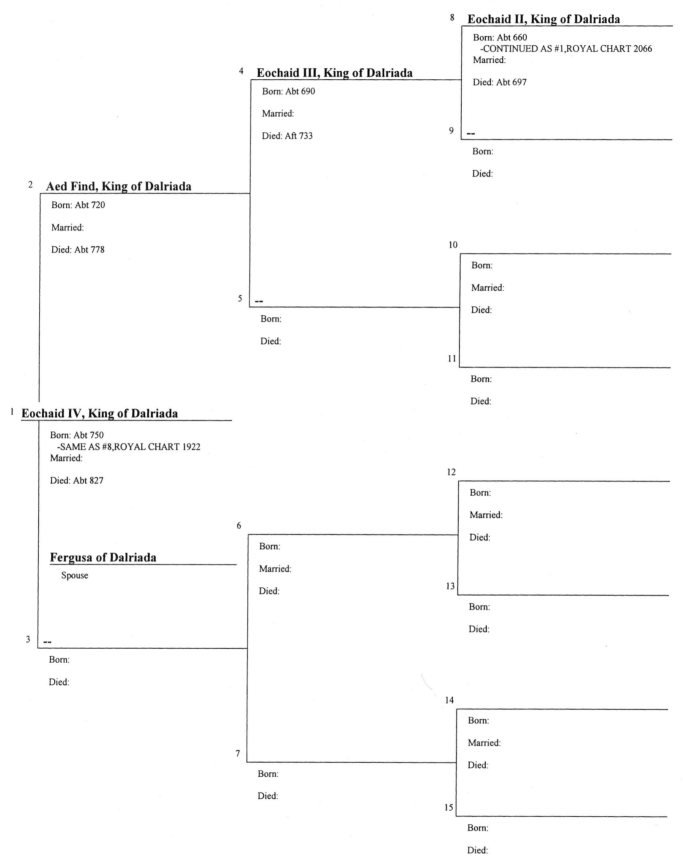

8 Eochaid II, King of Dalriada

Born: Abt 660
 -CONTINUED AS #1,ROYAL CHART 2066
Married:

Died: Abt 697

4 Eochaid III, King of Dalriada

Born: Abt 690

Married:

Died: Aft 733

9 --

Born:

Died:

2 Aed Find, King of Dalriada

Born: Abt 720

Married:

Died: Abt 778

10

Born:

Married:

Died:

5 --

Born:

Died:

11

Born:

Died:

1 Eochaid IV, King of Dalriada

Born: Abt 750
 -SAME AS #8,ROYAL CHART 1922
Married:

Died: Abt 827

12

Born:

Married:

Died:

6

Born:

Married:

Died:

13

Born:

Died:

Fergusa of Dalriada

Spouse

3 --

Born:

Died:

14

Born:

Married:

Died:

7

Born:

Died:

15

Born:

Died:

Sources include: *Royal Ancestors* (1989), chart 11606; *Ancestral Roots* 170; Stuart 165; Moriarty 29.

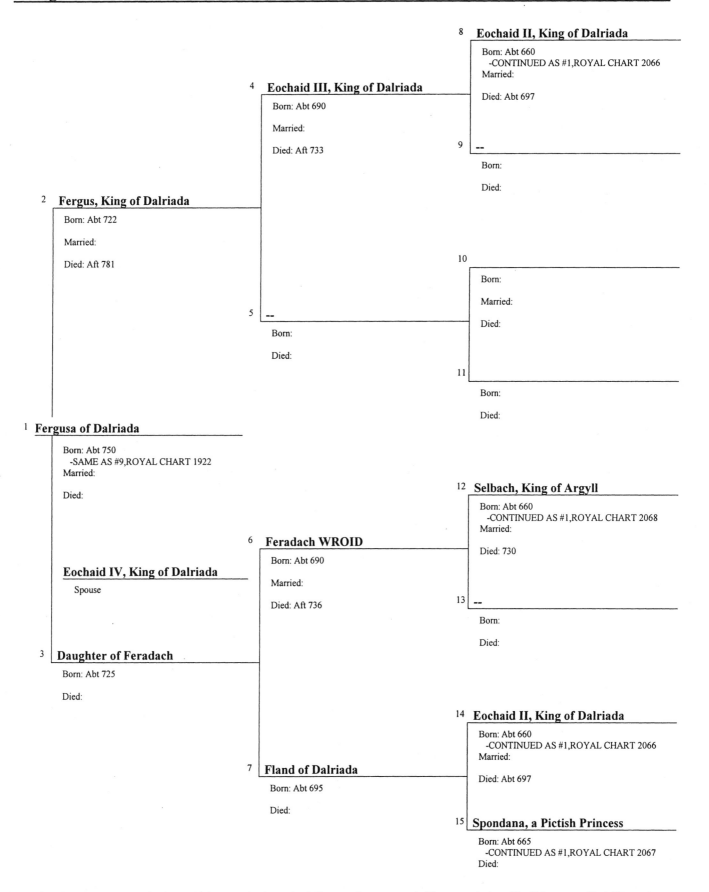

8 Eochaid II, King of Dalriada

Born: Abt 660
-CONTINUED AS #1,ROYAL CHART 2066
Married:

Died: Abt 697

4 Eochaid III, King of Dalriada

Born: Abt 690

Married:

Died: Aft 733

9 --

Born:

Died:

2 Fergus, King of Dalriada

Born: Abt 722

Married:

Died: Aft 781

10

Born:

Married:

Died:

5 --

Born:

Died:

11

Born:

Died:

1 Fergusa of Dalriada

Born: Abt 750
-SAME AS #9,ROYAL CHART 1922
Married:

Died:

12 Selbach, King of Argyll

Born: Abt 660
-CONTINUED AS #1,ROYAL CHART 2068
Married:

Died: 730

6 Feradach WROID

Born: Abt 690

Married:

Died: Aft 736

13 --

Born:

Died:

Eochaid IV, King of Dalriada

Spouse

3 Daughter of Feradach

Born: Abt 725

Died:

14 Eochaid II, King of Dalriada

Born: Abt 660
-CONTINUED AS #1,ROYAL CHART 2066
Married:

Died: Abt 697

7 Fland of Dalriada

Born: Abt 695

Died:

15 Spondana, a Pictish Princess

Born: Abt 665
-CONTINUED AS #1,ROYAL CHART 2067
Died:

Sources include: *Royal Ancestors* (1989), chart 11606; Stuart 355; Moriarty 278-279, 29. Notes: Stuart erroneously skips a generation by making #2 Fergus son of Eochaid II. Moriarty states that #7 Fland was a half-sister of #4 Eochaid III.

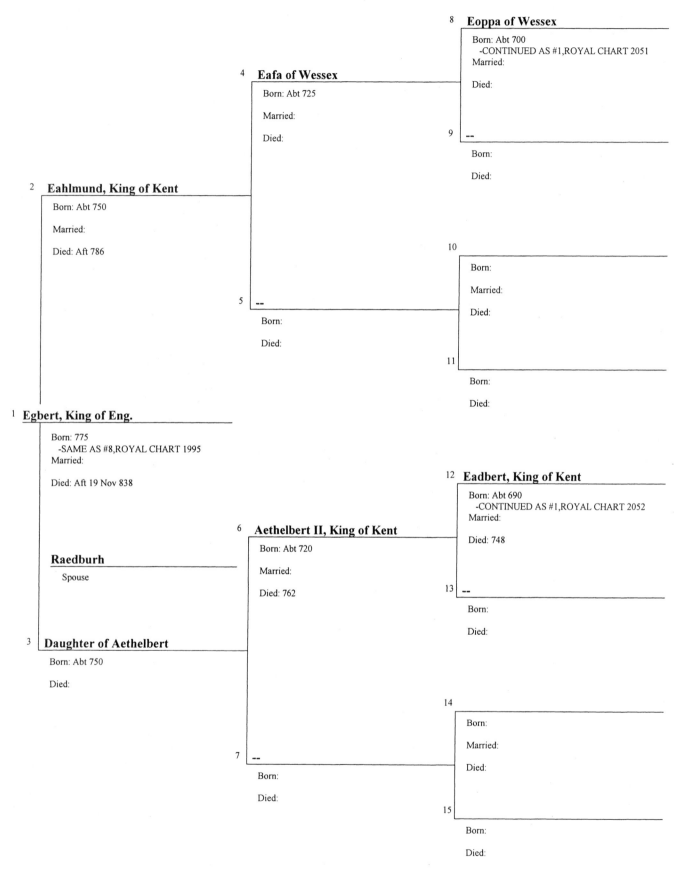

8 **Eoppa of Wessex**

Born: Abt 700
  -CONTINUED AS #1,ROYAL CHART 2051
Married:

Died:

4 **Eafa of Wessex**

Born: Abt 725

Married:

Died:

9 --

Born:

Died:

2 **Eahlmund, King of Kent**

Born: Abt 750

Married:

Died: Aft 786

5 --

Born:

Died:

10

Born:

Married:

Died:

11

Born:

Died:

1 **Egbert, King of Eng.**

Born: 775
  -SAME AS #8,ROYAL CHART 1995
Married:

Died: Aft 19 Nov 838

Raedburh

Spouse

12 **Eadbert, King of Kent**

Born: Abt 690
  -CONTINUED AS #1,ROYAL CHART 2052
Married:

Died: 748

6 **Aethelbert II, King of Kent**

Born: Abt 720

Married:

Died: 762

13 --

Born:

Died:

3 **Daughter of Aethelbert**

Born: Abt 750

Died:

7 --

Born:

Died:

14

Born:

Married:

Died:

15

Born:

Died:

Sources include: *Royal Ancestors* (1989), charts 11605, 11714; Stuart 233, 233A; *Ancestral Roots* 1; Moriarty 15-16; Wagner, *Pedigree and Progress*, p.53 (Kelley proposal for #3 ancestry); *TAG* 78:130-137 (Apr 2003)--discussion of alternative descents of #1 Egbert from the kings of Kent.

Pedigree Chart

Chart 2011

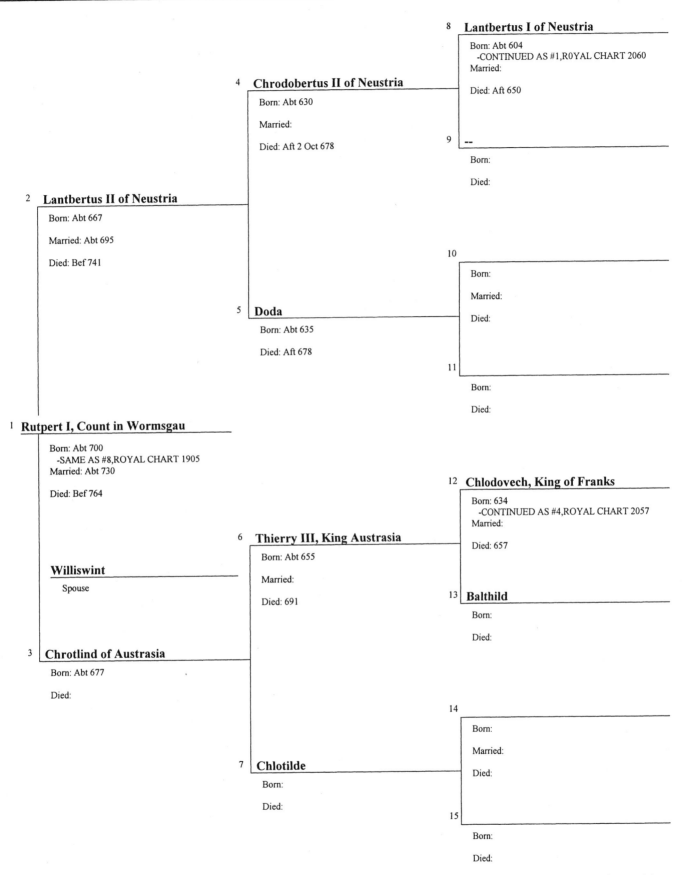

8   **Lantbertus I of Neustria**

Born: Abt 604
  -CONTINUED AS #1,R0YAL CHART 2060
Married:

Died: Aft 650

4   **Chrodobertus II of Neustria**

Born: Abt 630

Married:

Died: Aft 2 Oct 678

9   **--**

Born:

Died:

2   **Lantbertus II of Neustria**

Born: Abt 667

Married: Abt 695

Died: Bef 741

10

Born:

Married:

Died:

5   **Doda**

Born: Abt 635

Died: Aft 678

11

Born:

Died:

1   **Rutpert I, Count in Wormsgau**

Born: Abt 700
  -SAME AS #8,ROYAL CHART 1905
Married: Abt 730

Died: Bef 764

12   **Chlodovech, King of Franks**

Born: 634
  -CONTINUED AS #4,ROYAL CHART 2057
Married:

Died: 657

6   **Thierry III, King Austrasia**

Born: Abt 655

Married:

Died: 691

13   **Balthild**

Born:

Died:

Williswint

Spouse

3   **Chrotlind of Austrasia**

Born: Abt 677

Died:

14

Born:

Married:

Died:

7   **Chlotilde**

Born:

Died:

15

Born:

Died:

Sources include: *Royal Ancestors* (1989), chart 11615; Stuart 169, 123; Moriarty 281, 8 (#6 Thierry); *Ancestral Roots* 48. Note: The ancestry shown for #2 Lantbertus and the identification and ancestry of #3 Chrotlind is not certain.

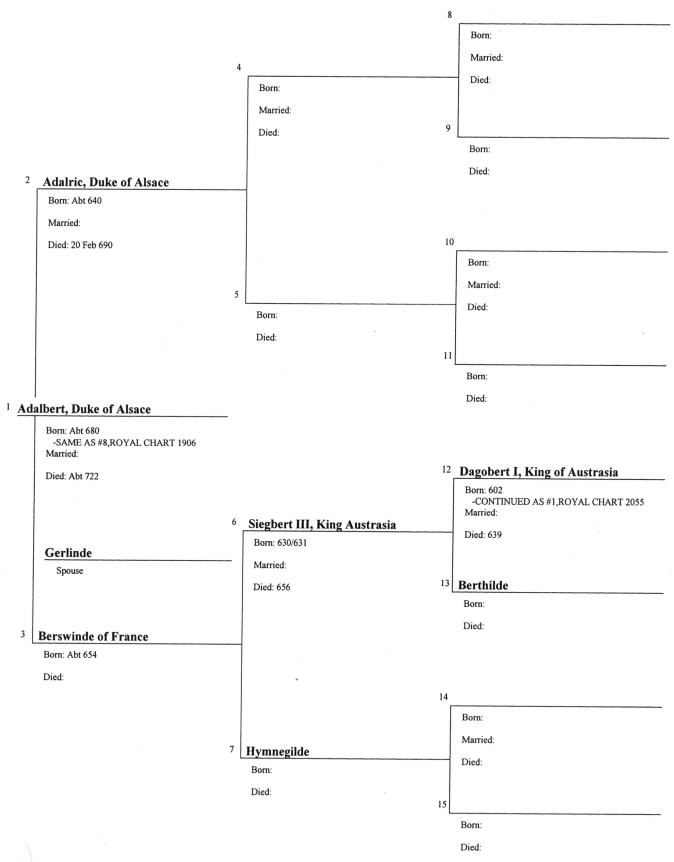

8

Born:

Married:

Died:

4

Born:

Married:

Died:

9

Born:

Died:

2 **Adalric, Duke of Alsace**

Born: Abt 640

Married:

Died: 20 Feb 690

10

Born:

Married:

Died:

5

Born:

Died:

11

Born:

Died:

1 **Adalbert, Duke of Alsace**

Born: Abt 680
  -SAME AS #8,ROYAL CHART 1906
Married:

Died: Abt 722

12 **Dagobert I, King of Austrasia**

Born: 602
  -CONTINUED AS #1,ROYAL CHART 2055
Married:

Died: 639

6 **Siegbert III, King Austrasia**

Born: 630/631

Married:

Died: 656

13 **Berthilde**

Born:

Died:

Gerlinde

Spouse

3 **Berswinde of France**

Born: Abt 654

Died:

14

Born:

Married:

Died:

7 **Hymnegilde**

Born:

Died:

15

Born:

Died:

Sources include: *Royal Ancestors* (1989), chart 11736; Stuart 224, 303; *Ancestral Roots* 181; Moriarty 21 note (#3 ancestry).

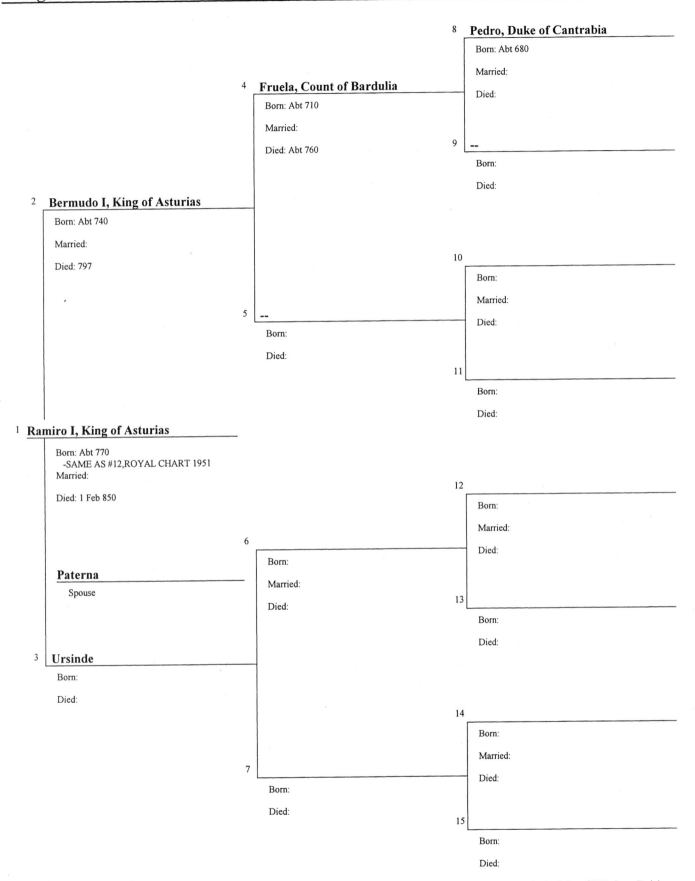

8 Pedro, Duke of Cantrabia

Born: Abt 680

Married:

Died:

4 Fruela, Count of Bardulia

Born: Abt 710

Married:

Died: Abt 760

9 --

Born:

Died:

2 Bermudo I, King of Asturias

Born: Abt 740

Married:

Died: 797

10

Born:

Married:

Died:

5 --

Born:

Died:

11

Born:

Died:

1 Ramiro I, King of Asturias

Born: Abt 770
   -SAME AS #12, ROYAL CHART 1951
Married:

Died: 1 Feb 850

12

Born:

Married:

Died:

6

Born:

Married:

Died:

13

Born:

Died:

Paterna

Spouse

3 Ursinde

Born:

Died:

14

Born:

Married:

Died:

7

Born:

Died:

15

Born:

Died:

Sources include: *Royal Ancestors* (1989), charts 11590, 11600; Stuart 276; Moriarty 82; Turton 38. Note: Stuart and Turton erroneously claim the father of #8 Pedro as Ervigio (d. 687) & Liubigotona. Moriarty (citing correspondence from Charles Evans) gives #8 Pedro as perhaps son of Diego (md. Gulvira), son of Divigra (md. Aguilo), dau. of Benedicto & Ellesinda. Gulvira was dau. of Osilia, dau. of Benedicto & Ellesinda.

Pedigree Chart

Chart 2014

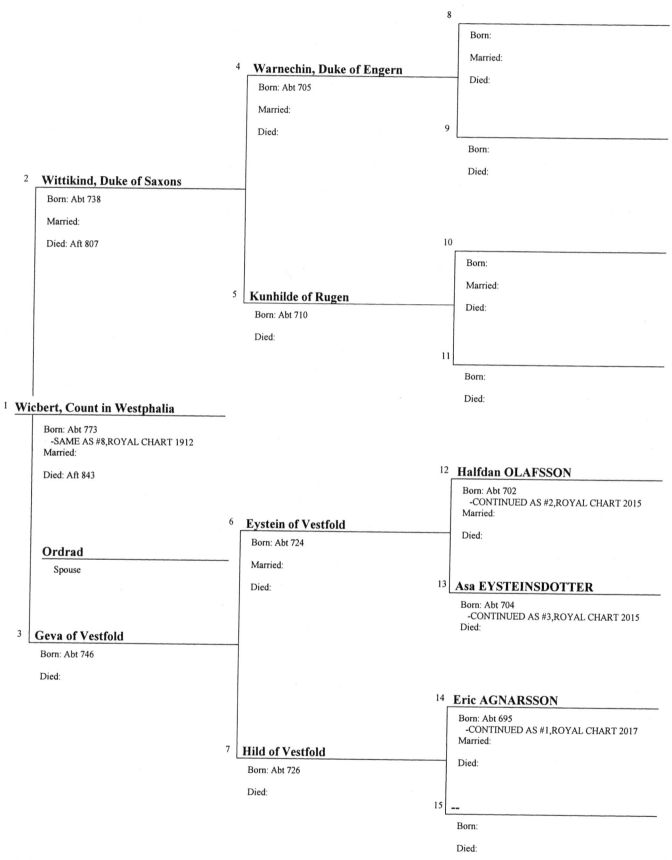

8

Born:

Married:

Died:

4 **Warnechin, Duke of Engern**

Born: Abt 705

Married:

Died:

9

Born:

Died:

2 **Wittikind, Duke of Saxons**

Born: Abt 738

Married:

Died: Aft 807

10

Born:

Married:

Died:

5 **Kunhilde of Rugen**

Born: Abt 710

Died:

11

Born:

Died:

1 **Wicbert, Count in Westphalia**

Born: Abt 773
-SAME AS #8,ROYAL CHART 1912
Married:

Died: Aft 843

12 **Halfdan OLAFSSON**

Born: Abt 702
-CONTINUED AS #2,ROYAL CHART 2015
Married:

Died:

6 **Eystein of Vestfold**

Born: Abt 724

Married:

Died:

13 **Asa EYSTEINSDOTTER**

Born: Abt 704
-CONTINUED AS #3,ROYAL CHART 2015
Died:

Ordrad

Spouse

3 **Geva of Vestfold**

Born: Abt 746

Died:

14 **Eric AGNARSSON**

Born: Abt 695
-CONTINUED AS #1,ROYAL CHART 2017
Married:

Died:

7 **Hild of Vestfold**

Born: Abt 726

Died:

15 **--**

Born:

Died:

Sources include: *Royal Ancestors* (1989), chart 11636; Stuart 339; Moriarty 25-26.

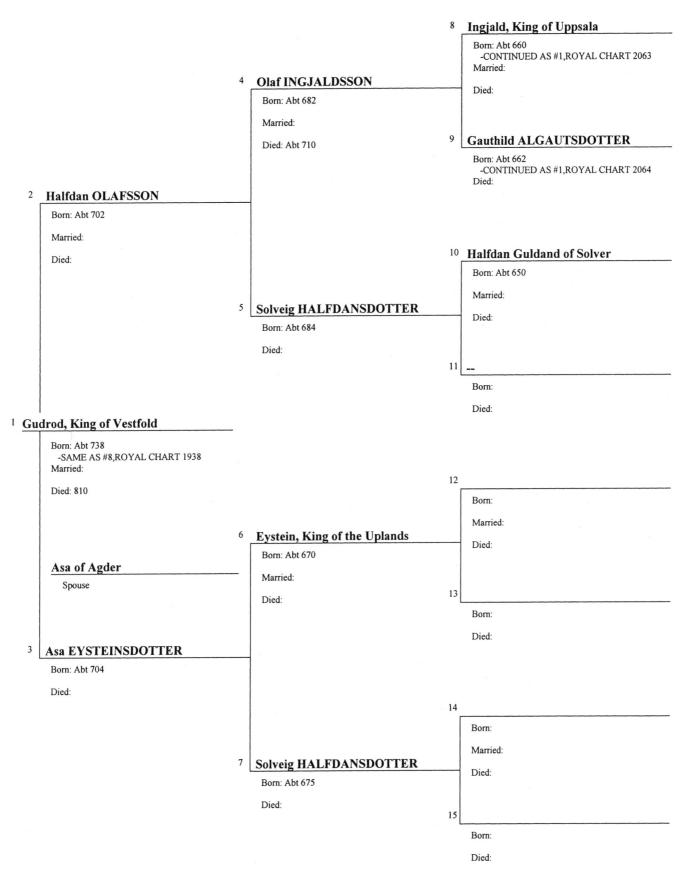

8 Ingjald, King of Uppsala

Born: Abt 660
  -CONTINUED AS #1,ROYAL CHART 2063
Married:

Died:

4 Olaf INGJALDSSON

Born: Abt 682

Married:

Died: Abt 710

9 Gauthild ALGAUTSDOTTER

Born: Abt 662
  -CONTINUED AS #1,ROYAL CHART 2064
Died:

2 Halfdan OLAFSSON

Born: Abt 702

Married:

Died:

10 Halfdan Guldand of Solver

Born: Abt 650

Married:

Died:

5 Solveig HALFDANSDOTTER

Born: Abt 684

Died:

11 __

Born:

Died:

1 Gudrod, King of Vestfold

Born: Abt 738
  -SAME AS #8,ROYAL CHART 1938
Married:

Died: 810

12

Born:

Married:

Died:

6 Eystein, King of the Uplands

Born: Abt 670

Married:

Died:

13

Born:

Died:

Asa of Agder

Spouse

3 Asa EYSTEINSDOTTER

Born: Abt 704

Died:

14

Born:

Married:

Died:

7 Solveig HALFDANSDOTTER

Born: Abt 675

Died:

15

Born:

Died:

Sources include: *Royal Ancestors* (1989), charts 11603, 11703-04; Stuart 166, Moriarty 170.

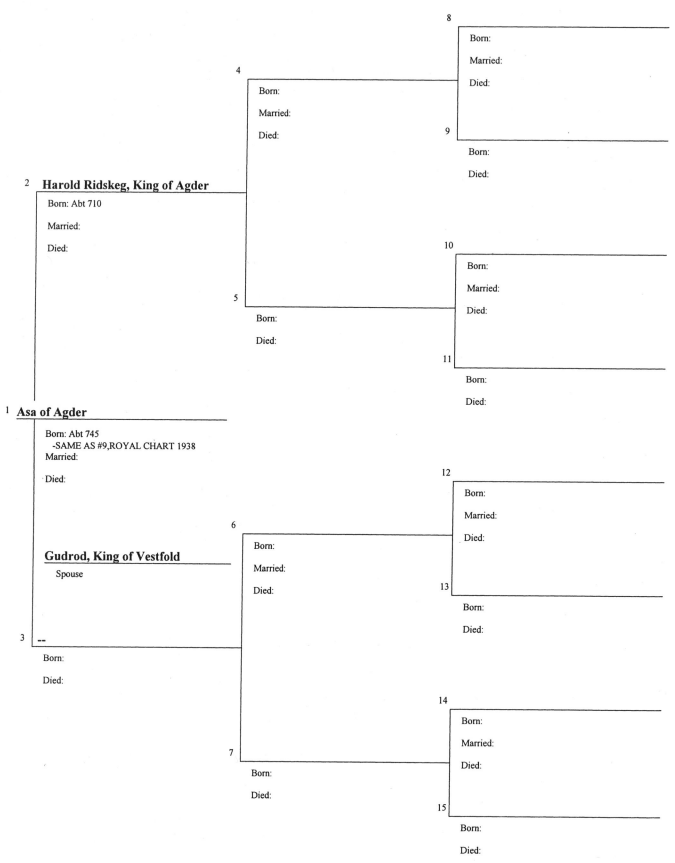

2 Harold Ridskeg, King of Agder

Born: Abt 710

Married:

Died:

1 Asa of Agder

Born: Abt 745
-SAME AS #9,ROYAL CHART 1938

Married:

Died:

Gudrod, King of Vestfold

Spouse

3 --

Born:

Died:

4

Born:

Married:

Died:

5

Born:

Died:

6

Born:

Married:

Died:

7

Born:

Died:

8

Born:

Married:

Died:

9

Born:

Died:

10

Born:

Married:

Died:

11

Born:

Died:

12

Born:

Married:

Died:

13

Born:

Died:

14

Born:

Married:

Died:

15

Born:

Died:

Sources include: Stuart 166-40; Moriarty 170.

Pedigree Chart

Chart 2017

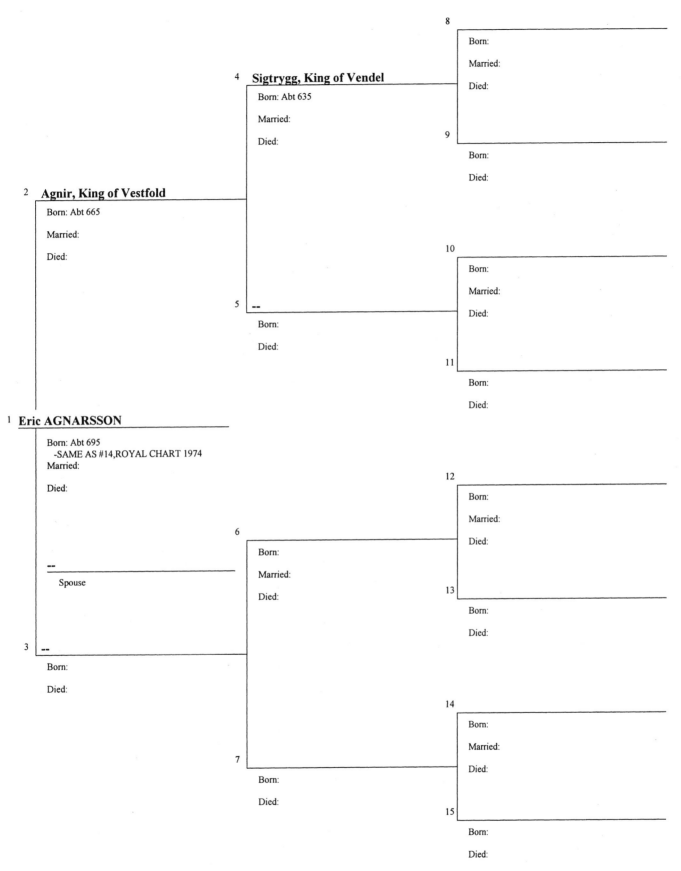

8

Born:

Married:

Died:

4 Sigtrygg, King of Vendel

Born: Abt 635

Married:

Died:

9

Born:

Died:

2 Agnir, King of Vestfold

Born: Abt 665

Married:

Died:

10

Born:

Married:

Died:

5 --

Born:

Died:

11

Born:

Died:

1 Eric AGNARSSON

Born: Abt 695
   -SAME AS #14, ROYAL CHART 1974
Married:

Died:

12

Born:

Married:

Died:

6

Born:

Married:

Died:

13

Born:

Died:

--

Spouse

3 --

Born:

Died:

14

Born:

Married:

Died:

7

Born:

Died:

15

Born:

Died:

Sources include: Stuart 339-42; Moriarty 170.

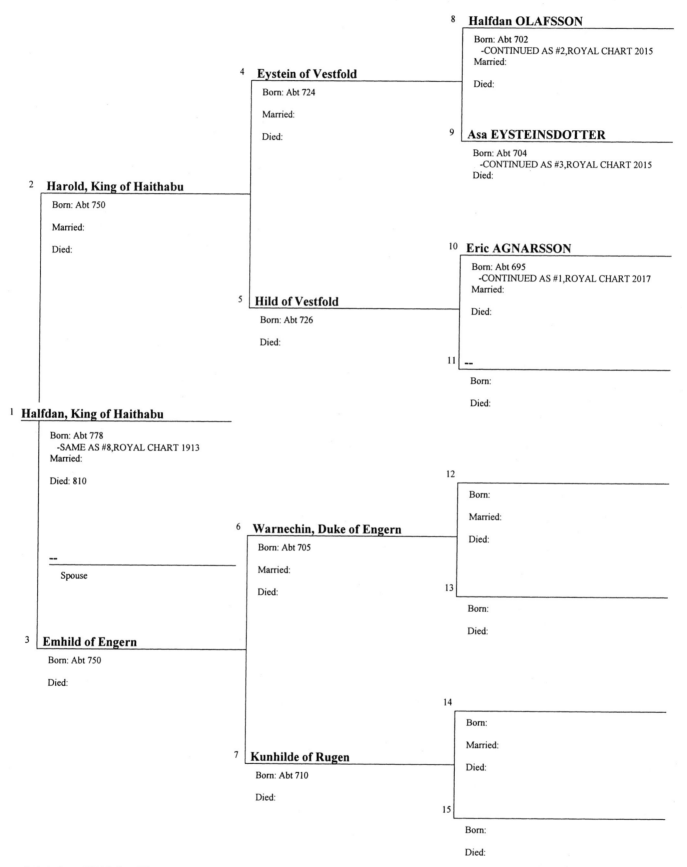

2   **Harold, King of Haithabu**

Born: Abt 750

Married:

Died:

4   **Eystein of Vestfold**

Born: Abt 724

Married:

Died:

8   **Halfdan OLAFSSON**

Born: Abt 702
   -CONTINUED AS #2,ROYAL CHART 2015
Married:

Died:

9   **Asa EYSTEINSDOTTER**

Born: Abt 704
   -CONTINUED AS #3,ROYAL CHART 2015
Died:

5   **Hild of Vestfold**

Born: Abt 726

Died:

10   **Eric AGNARSSON**

Born: Abt 695
   -CONTINUED AS #1,ROYAL CHART 2017
Married:

Died:

11   **--**

Born:

Died:

1   **Halfdan, King of Haithabu**

Born: Abt 778
   -SAME AS #8,ROYAL CHART 1913
Married:

Died: 810

--
    Spouse

3   **Emhild of Engern**

Born: Abt 750

Died:

6   **Warnechin, Duke of Engern**

Born: Abt 705

Married:

Died:

12

Born:

Married:

Died:

13

Born:

Died:

7   **Kunhilde of Rugen**

Born: Abt 710

Died:

14

Born:

Married:

Died:

15

Born:

Died:

Sources include: Stuart 217; Moriarty 170.

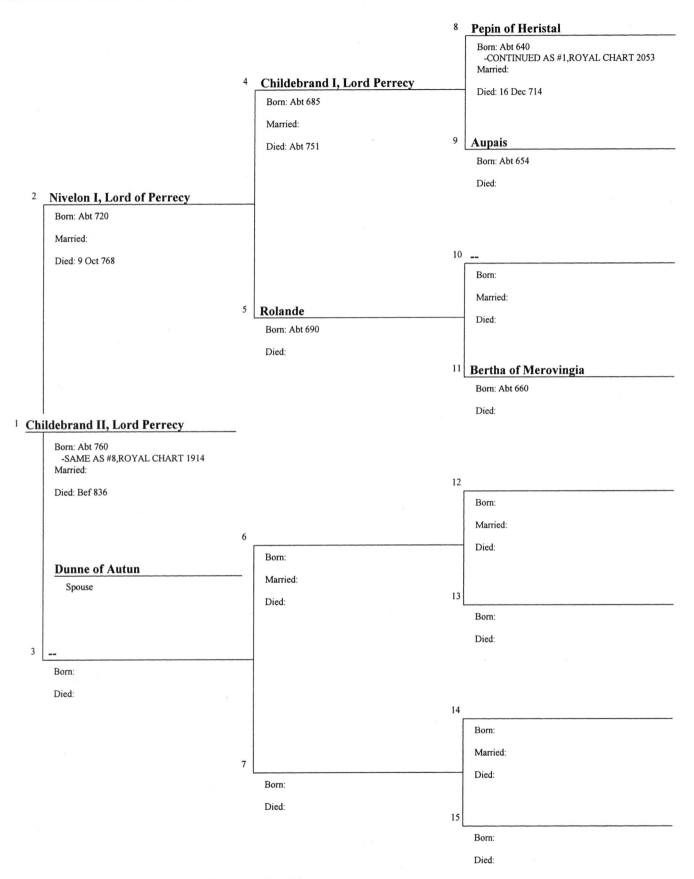

8 Pepin of Heristal

Born: Abt 640
   -CONTINUED AS #1,ROYAL CHART 2053
Married:

Died: 16 Dec 714

4 Childebrand I, Lord Perrecy

Born: Abt 685

Married:

Died: Abt 751

9 Aupais

Born: Abt 654

Died:

2 Nivelon I, Lord of Perrecy

Born: Abt 720

Married:

Died: 9 Oct 768

10 --

Born:

Married:

Died:

5 Rolande

Born: Abt 690

Died:

11 Bertha of Merovingia

Born: Abt 660

Died:

1 Childebrand II, Lord Perrecy

Born: Abt 760
   -SAME AS #8,ROYAL CHART 1914
Married:

Died: Bef 836

12

Born:

Married:

Died:

6

Born:

Married:

Died:

13

Born:

Died:

Dunne of Autun

Spouse

3 --

Born:

Died:

14

Born:

Married:

Died:

7

Born:

Died:

15

Born:

Died:

Sources include: *Royal Ancestors* (1989), chart 11998; Stuart 173; Moriarty 255.

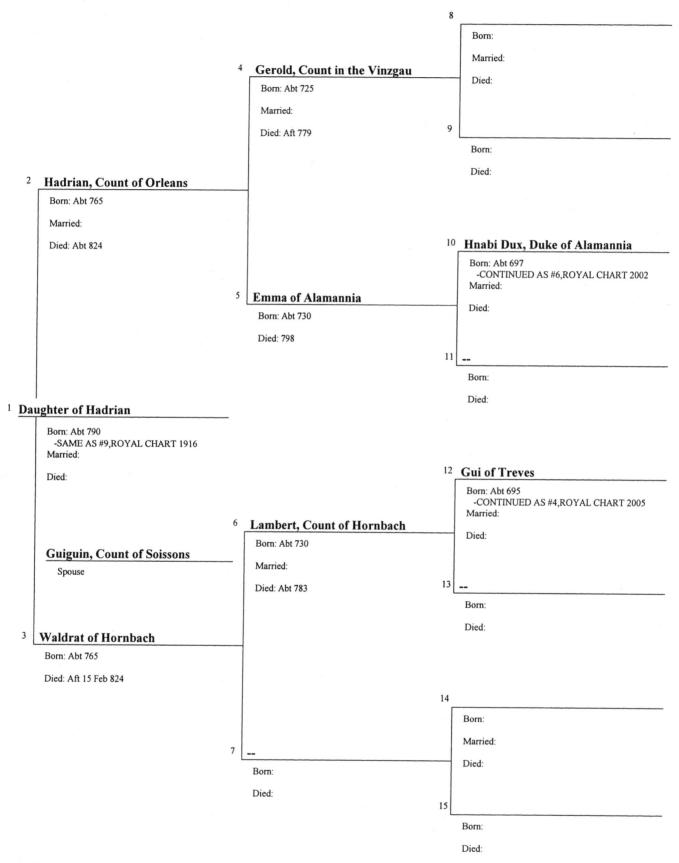

8

Born:

Married:

Died:

4   Gerold, Count in the Vinzgau

Born: Abt 725

Married:

Died: Aft 779

9

Born:

Died:

2   Hadrian, Count of Orleans

Born: Abt 765

Married:

Died: Abt 824

10   Hnabi Dux, Duke of Alamannia

Born: Abt 697
   -CONTINUED AS #6,ROYAL CHART 2002
Married:

Died:

5   Emma of Alamannia

Born: Abt 730

Died: 798

11   --

Born:

Died:

1   Daughter of Hadrian

Born: Abt 790
   -SAME AS #9,ROYAL CHART 1916
Married:

Died:

12   Gui of Treves

Born: Abt 695
   -CONTINUED AS #4,ROYAL CHART 2005
Married:

Died:

6   Lambert, Count of Hornbach

Born: Abt 730

Married:

Died: Abt 783

13   --

Born:

Died:

Guiguin, Count of Soissons

Spouse

3   Waldrat of Hornbach

Born: Abt 765

Died: Aft 15 Feb 824

14

Born:

Married:

Died:

7   --

Born:

Died:

15

Born:

Died:

Sources include: Moriarty 38, 9; Stuart 336 (#2 & 3 ancestry); *Royal Ancestors* (1989), chart 11604 (#2 & 3 ancestry).

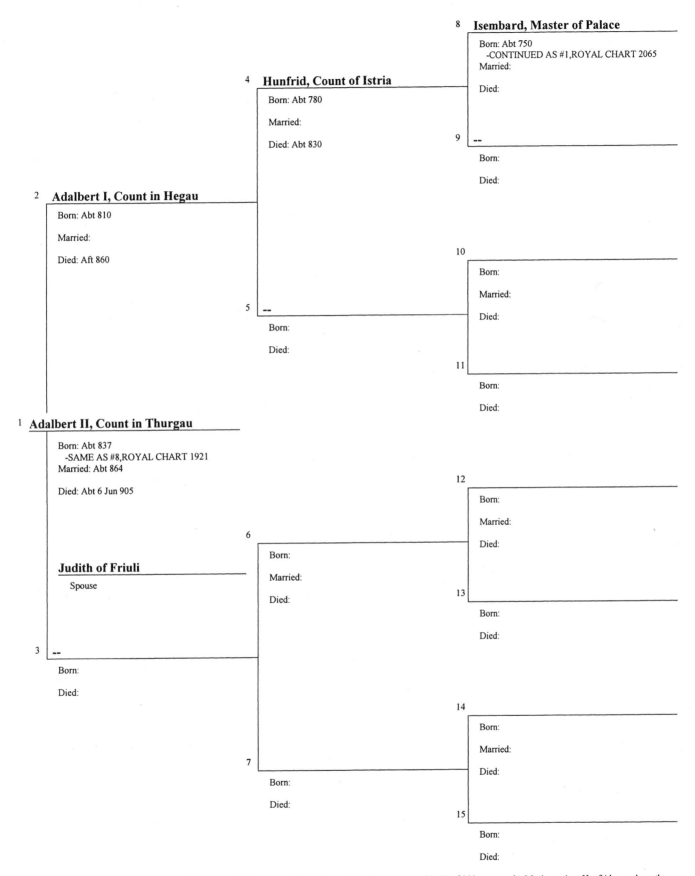

8 **Isembard, Master of Palace**

Born: Abt 750
  -CONTINUED AS #1,ROYAL CHART 2065
Married:

Died:

4 **Hunfrid, Count of Istria**

Born: Abt 780

Married:

Died: Abt 830

9 --

Born:

Died:

2 **Adalbert I, Count in Hegau**

Born: Abt 810

Married:

Died: Aft 860

10

Born:

Married:

Died:

5 --

Born:

Died:

11

Born:

Died:

1 **Adalbert II, Count in Thurgau**

Born: Abt 837
  -SAME AS #8,ROYAL CHART 1921
Married: Abt 864

Died: Abt 6 Jun 905

12

Born:

Married:

Died:

6

Born:

Married:

Died:

13

Born:

Died:

Judith of Friuli

Spouse

3 --

Born:

Died:

14

Born:

Married:

Died:

7

Born:

Died:

15

Born:

Died:

Sources include: *Royal Ancestors* (1989), chart 11633; Stuart 345; Moriarty 34, 205-206, 1. Note: The ancestry of #4 Hunfrid is not certain. Moriarty gives Hunfrid as perhaps the son of either Isembard or an unknown brother.

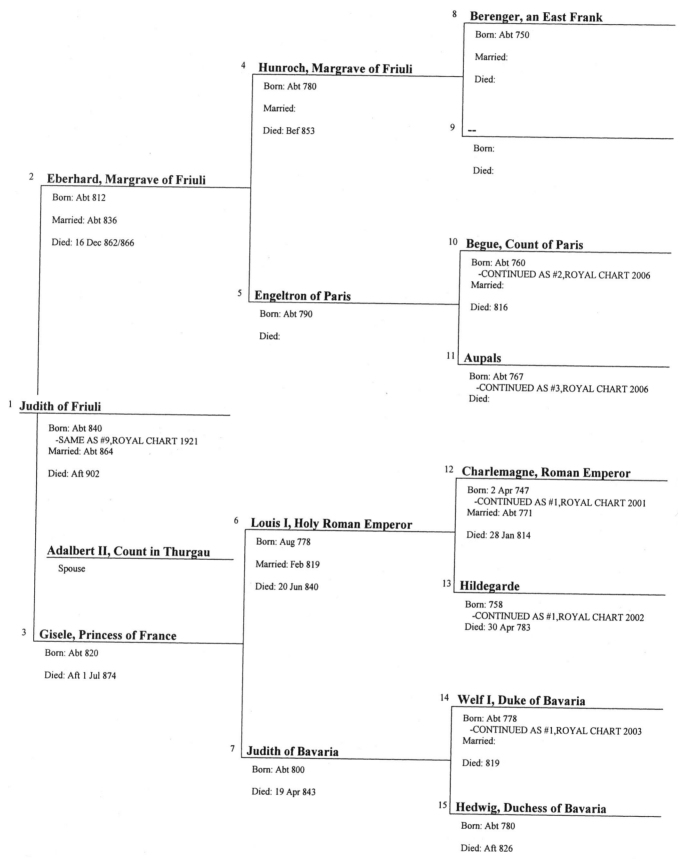

8 Berenger, an East Frank
Born: Abt 750
Married:
Died:

4 Hunroch, Margrave of Friuli
Born: Abt 780
Married:
Died: Bef 853

9 --
Born:
Died:

2 Eberhard, Margrave of Friuli
Born: Abt 812
Married: Abt 836
Died: 16 Dec 862/866

10 Begue, Count of Paris
Born: Abt 760
-CONTINUED AS #2,ROYAL CHART 2006
Married:
Died: 816

5 Engeltron of Paris
Born: Abt 790
Died:

11 Aupals
Born: Abt 767
-CONTINUED AS #3,ROYAL CHART 2006
Died:

1 Judith of Friuli
Born: Abt 840
-SAME AS #9,ROYAL CHART 1921
Married: Abt 864
Died: Aft 902

12 Charlemagne, Roman Emperor
Born: 2 Apr 747
-CONTINUED AS #1,ROYAL CHART 2001
Married: Abt 771
Died: 28 Jan 814

6 Louis I, Holy Roman Emperor
Born: Aug 778
Married: Feb 819
Died: 20 Jun 840

13 Hildegarde
Born: 758
-CONTINUED AS #1,ROYAL CHART 2002
Died: 30 Apr 783

Adalbert II, Count in Thurgau
Spouse

3 Gisele, Princess of France
Born: Abt 820
Died: Aft 1 Jul 874

14 Welf I, Duke of Bavaria
Born: Abt 778
-CONTINUED AS #1,ROYAL CHART 2003
Married:
Died: 819

7 Judith of Bavaria
Born: Abt 800
Died: 19 Apr 843

15 Hedwig, Duchess of Bavaria
Born: Abt 780
Died: Aft 826

Sources include: *Royal Ancestors* (1989), chart 11634; Stuart 345-40, 269, 389-39; Moriarty 18.

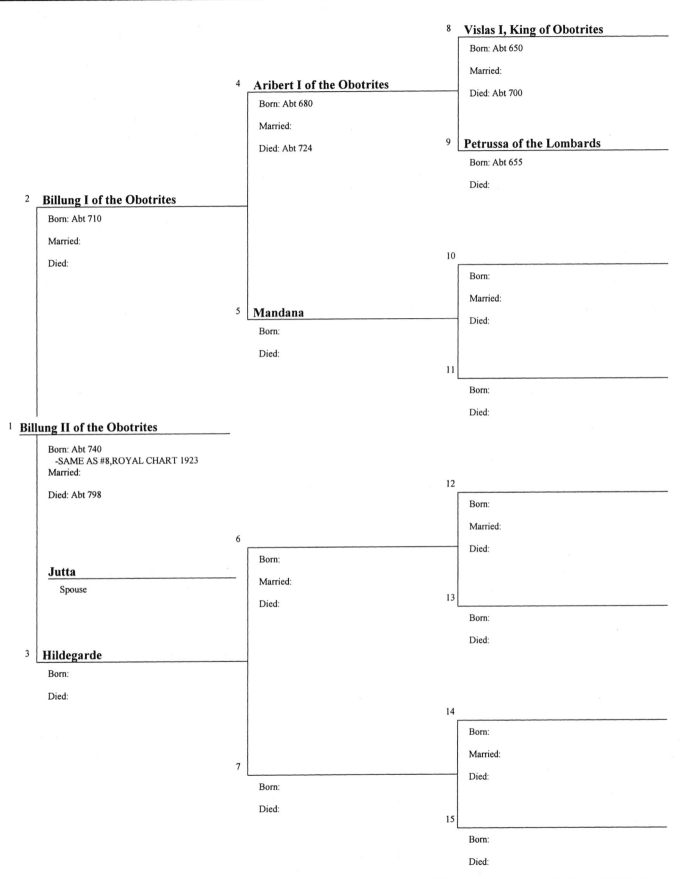

8 Vislas I, King of Obotrites
Born: Abt 650
Married:
Died: Abt 700

4 Aribert I of the Obotrites
Born: Abt 680
Married:
Died: Abt 724

9 Petrussa of the Lombards
Born: Abt 655
Died:

2 Billung I of the Obotrites
Born: Abt 710
Married:
Died:

10
Born:
Married:
Died:

5 Mandana
Born:
Died:

11
Born:
Died:

1 Billung II of the Obotrites
Born: Abt 740
  -SAME AS #8,ROYAL CHART 1923
Married:
Died: Abt 798

12
Born:
Married:
Died:

Jutta
Spouse

6
Born:
Married:
Died:

13
Born:
Died:

3 Hildegarde
Born:
Died:

14
Born:
Married:
Died:

7
Born:
Died:

15
Born:
Died:

Sources include: Stuart 380; Turton 27; *TAG* 74:148-149. Note: Stuart and Turton continue #9 Petrussa for ten or more additional generations. However, Paul C. Reed (*TAG* 74:148-149) states that the connection to the Lombards from the rulers of the Obotrites is problematic, and he suggests there are reasons that Schwennicke and Wagner do not include the connection.

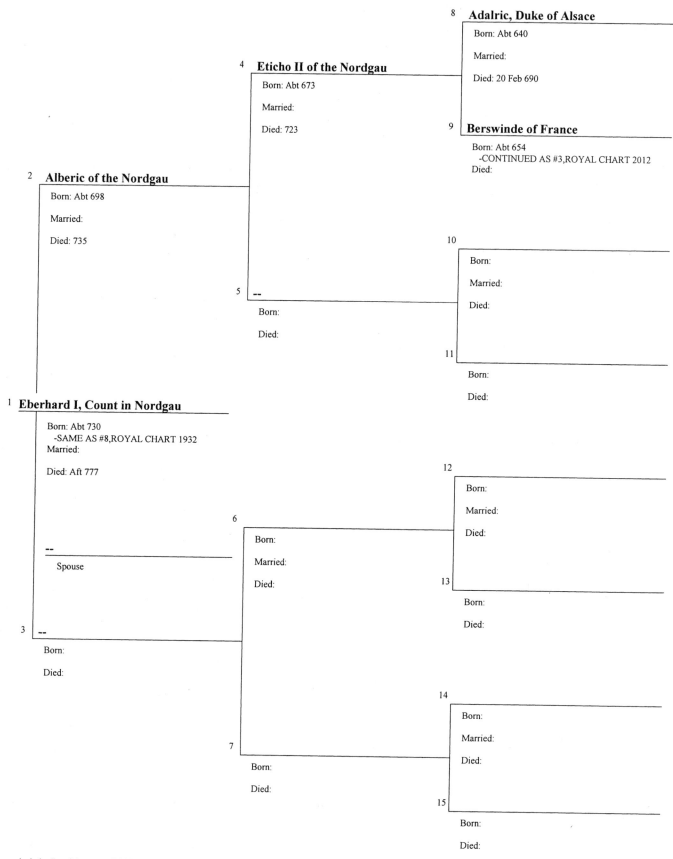

8 **Adalric, Duke of Alsace**
Born: Abt 640
Married:
Died: 20 Feb 690

4 **Eticho II of the Nordgau**
Born: Abt 673
Married:
Died: 723

9 **Berswinde of France**
Born: Abt 654
-CONTINUED AS #3,ROYAL CHART 2012
Died:

2 **Alberic of the Nordgau**
Born: Abt 698
Married:
Died: 735

10
Born:
Married:
Died:

5 --
Born:
Died:

11
Born:
Died:

1 **Eberhard I, Count in Nordgau**
Born: Abt 730
-SAME AS #8,ROYAL CHART 1932
Married:
Died: Aft 777

12
Born:
Married:
Died:

6
Born:
Married:
Died:

13
Born:
Died:

--
Spouse

3 --
Born:
Died:

14
Born:
Married:
Died:

7
Born:
Died:

15
Born:
Died:

Sources include: *Royal Ancestors* (1989), chart 11945; Stuart 202, 224-42; Moriarty 181, 93 note (states that the claimed descent of #1 Eberhard from #8 & 9 Adalric (Eticho I) & Berswinde, as shown above, is quite uncertain); Turton 182.

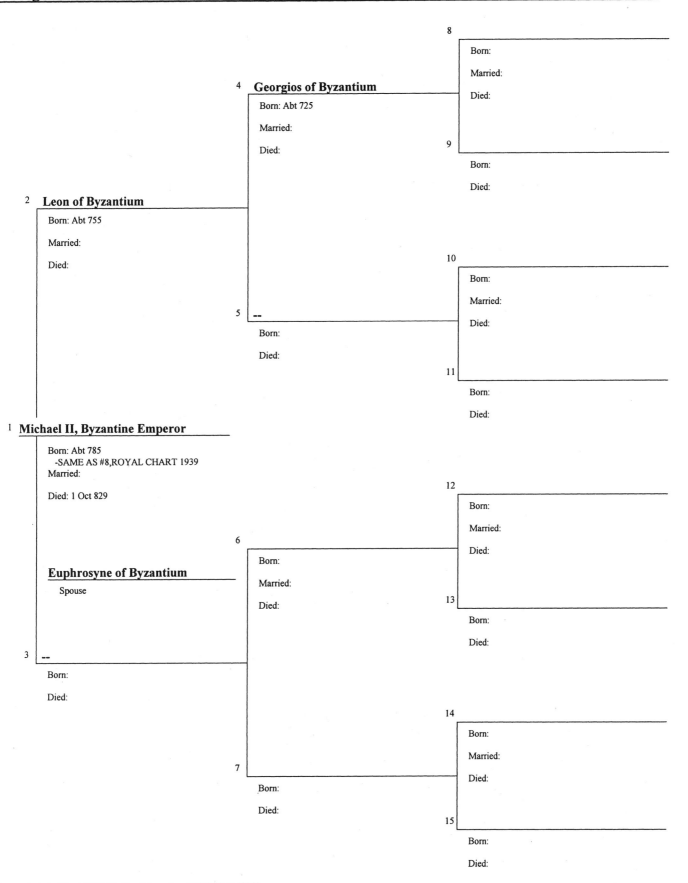

4 Georgios of Byzantium
Born: Abt 725
Married:
Died:

2 Leon of Byzantium
Born: Abt 755
Married:
Died:

5 --
Born:
Died:

8
Born:
Married:
Died:

9
Born:
Died:

10
Born:
Married:
Died:

11
Born:
Died:

1 Michael II, Byzantine Emperor
Born: Abt 785
-SAME AS #8,ROYAL CHART 1939
Married:
Died: 1 Oct 829

Euphrosyne of Byzantium
Spouse

3 --
Born:
Died:

6
Born:
Married:
Died:

7
Born:
Died:

12
Born:
Married:
Died:

13
Born:
Died:

14
Born:
Married:
Died:

15
Born:
Died:

Sources include: Stuart 322A-41; *Royal Ancestors* (1989), chart 12058.

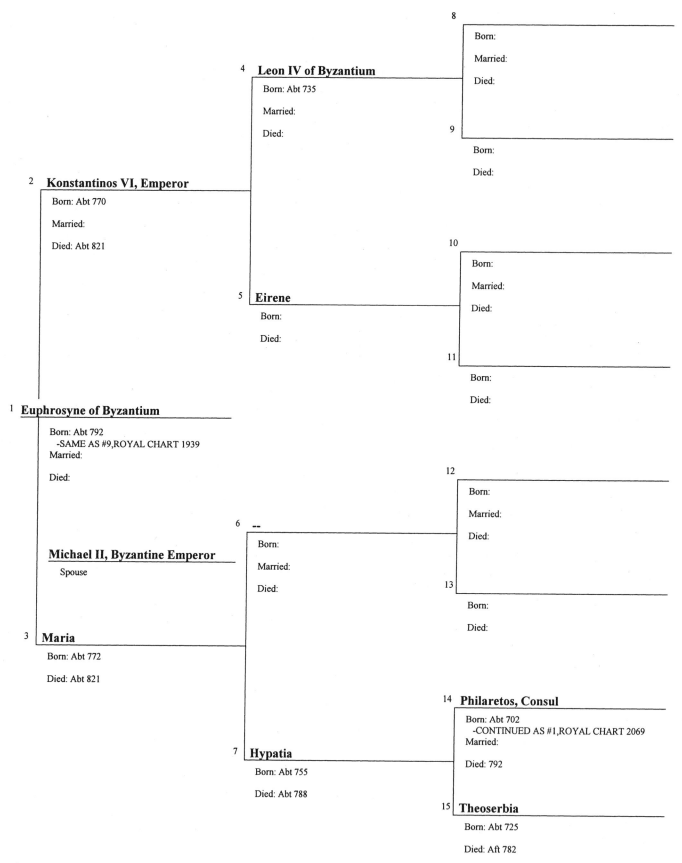

8

Born:

Married:

Died:

4 **Leon IV of Byzantium**

Born: Abt 735

Married:

Died:

9

Born:

Died:

2 **Konstantinos VI, Emperor**

Born: Abt 770

Married:

Died: Abt 821

10

Born:

Married:

Died:

5 **Eirene**

Born:

Died:

11

Born:

Died:

1 **Euphrosyne of Byzantium**

Born: Abt 792
-SAME AS #9,ROYAL CHART 1939
Married:

Died:

12

Born:

Married:

Died:

Michael II, Byzantine Emperor

Spouse

6 **--**

Born:

Married:

Died:

13

Born:

Died:

3 **Maria**

Born: Abt 772

Died: Abt 821

14 **Philaretos, Consul**

Born: Abt 702
-CONTINUED AS #1,ROYAL CHART 2069
Married:

Died: 792

7 **Hypatia**

Born: Abt 755

Died: Abt 788

15 **Theoserbia**

Born: Abt 725

Died: Aft 782

Sources include: Stuart 322B.

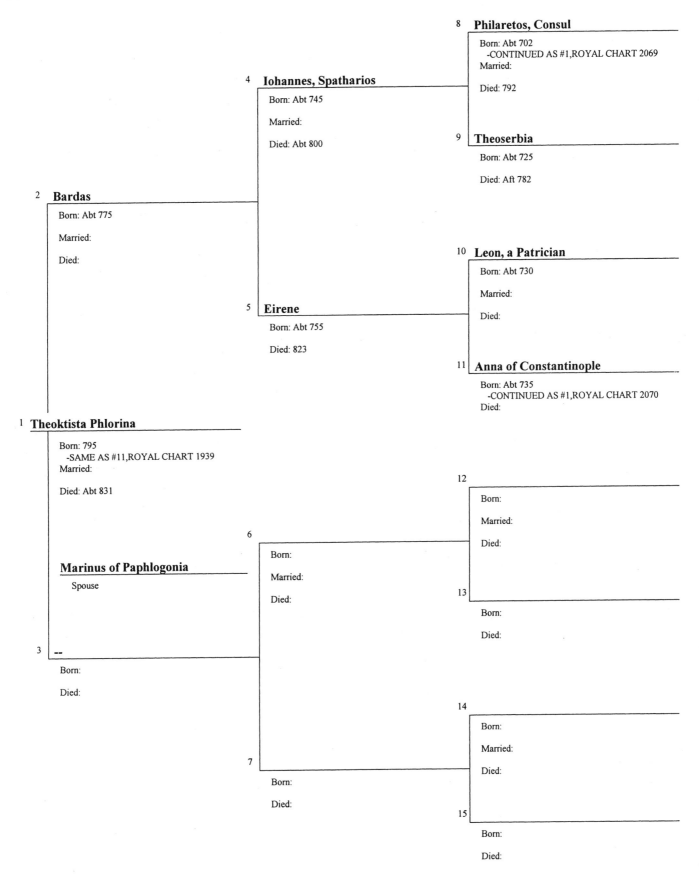

8 Philaretos, Consul
Born: Abt 702
-CONTINUED AS #1,ROYAL CHART 2069
Married:

Died: 792

9 Theoserbia
Born: Abt 725

Died: Aft 782

4 Iohannes, Spatharios
Born: Abt 745

Married:

Died: Abt 800

10 Leon, a Patrician
Born: Abt 730

Married:

Died:

5 Eirene
Born: Abt 755

Died: 823

11 Anna of Constantinople
Born: Abt 735
-CONTINUED AS #1,ROYAL CHART 2070
Died:

2 Bardas
Born: Abt 775

Married:

Died:

1 Theoktista Phlorina
Born: 795
-SAME AS #11,ROYAL CHART 1939
Married:

Died: Abt 831

Marinus of Paphlogonia
Spouse

3 --
Born:

Died:

6
Born:

Married:

Died:

12
Born:

Married:

Died:

13
Born:

Died:

7
Born:

Died:

14
Born:

Married:

Died:

15
Born:

Died:

Sources include: Stuart 322A; *Royal Ancestors* (1989), chart 12058.

Pedigree Chart

Chart 2028

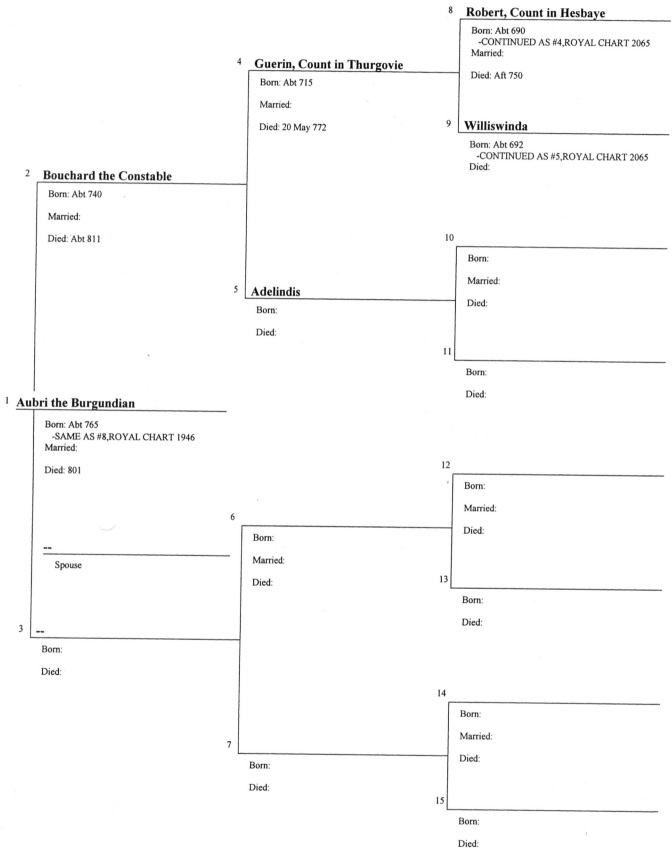

8 **Robert, Count in Hesbaye**

Born: Abt 690
-CONTINUED AS #4, ROYAL CHART 2065
Married:

Died: Aft 750

4 **Guerin, Count in Thurgovie**

Born: Abt 715

Married:

Died: 20 May 772

9 **Williswinda**

Born: Abt 692
-CONTINUED AS #5, ROYAL CHART 2065
Died:

2 **Bouchard the Constable**

Born: Abt 740

Married:

Died: Abt 811

10

Born:

Married:

Died:

5 **Adelindis**

Born:

Died:

11

Born:

Died:

1 **Aubri the Burgundian**

Born: Abt 765
-SAME AS #8, ROYAL CHART 1946
Married:

Died: 801

12

Born:

Married:

Died:

6

Born:

Married:

Died:

13

Born:

Died:

--

Spouse

3 **--**

Born:

Died:

14

Born:

Married:

Died:

7

Born:

Died:

15

Born:

Died:

Sources include: *Royal Ancestors* (1989), charts 11966-67; Stuart 53; Moriarty 1.

Pedigree Chart

Chart 2029

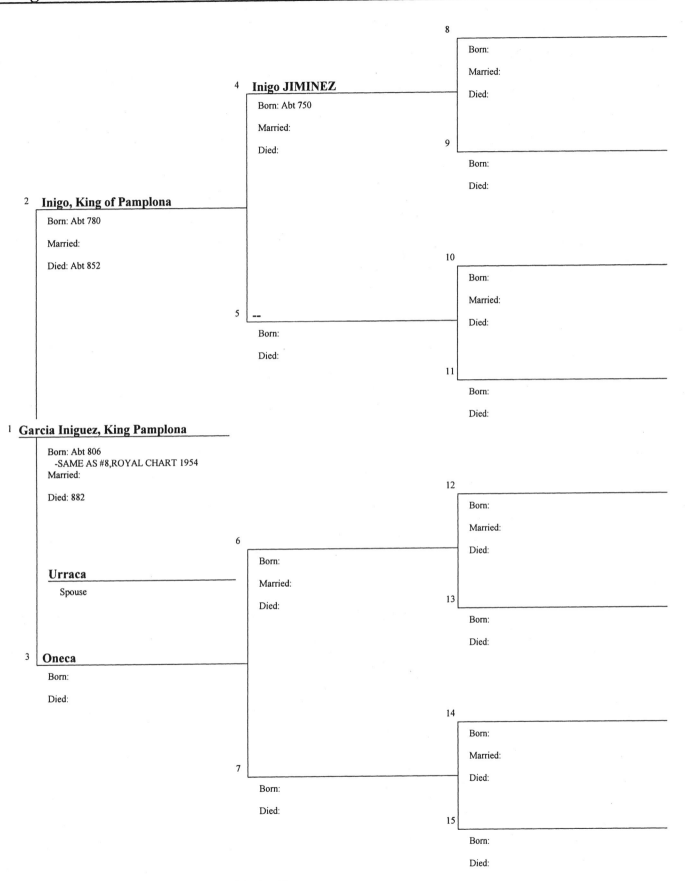

8

Born:

Married:

Died:

4 Inigo JIMINEZ

Born: Abt 750

Married:

Died:

9

Born:

Died:

2 Inigo, King of Pamplona

Born: Abt 780

Married:

Died: Abt 852

10

Born:

Married:

Died:

5 --

Born:

Died:

11

Born:

Died:

1 Garcia Iniguez, King Pamplona

Born: Abt 806
  -SAME AS #8,ROYAL CHART 1954
Married:

Died: 882

12

Born:

Married:

Died:

6

Born:

Married:

Died:

13

Born:

Died:

Urraca
  Spouse

3 Oneca

Born:

Died:

14

Born:

Married:

Died:

7

Born:

Died:

15

Born:

Died:

Sources include: *Royal Ancestors* (1989), chart 11590; Stuart 76; Moriarty 70.

Pedigree Chart

Chart 2030

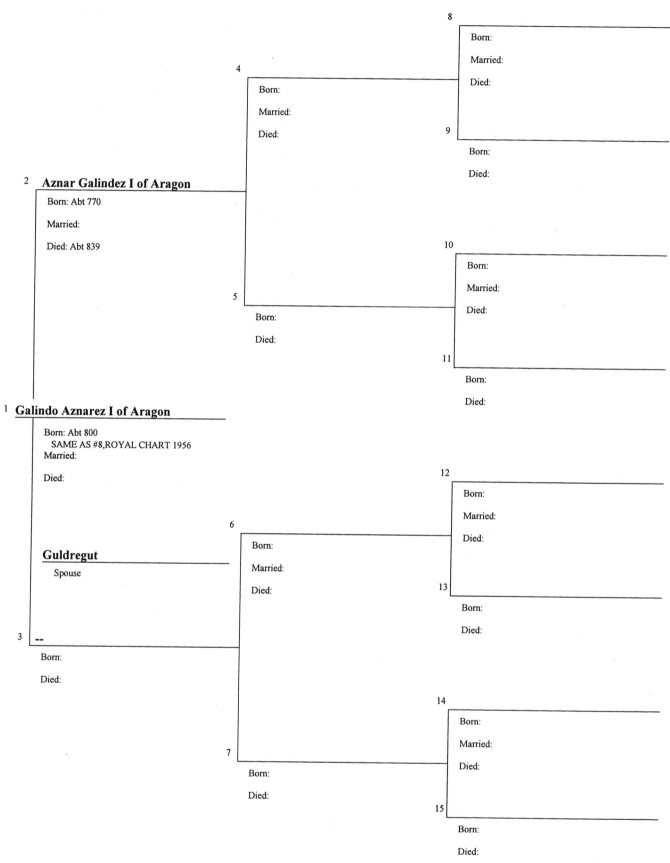

8

Born:

Married:

Died:

4

Born:

Married:

Died:

9

Born:

Died:

2 Aznar Galindez I of Aragon

Born: Abt 770

Married:

Died: Abt 839

10

Born:

Married:

Died:

5

Born:

Died:

11

Born:

Died:

1 Galindo Aznarez I of Aragon

Born: Abt 800
    SAME AS #8,ROYAL CHART 1956
Married:

Died:

12

Born:

Married:

Died:

6

Born:

Married:

Died:

13

Born:

Died:

Guldregut

Spouse

3 --

Born:

Died:

14

Born:

Married:

Died:

7

Born:

Died:

15

Born:

Died:

Sources include: *Royal Ancestors* (1989), chart 11597; Stuart 292; Moriarty 77.

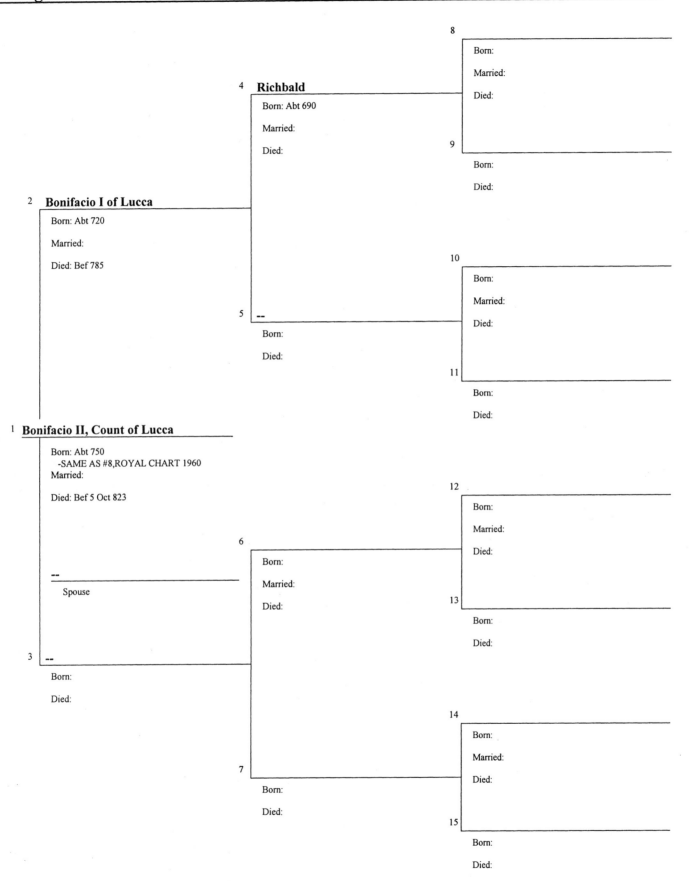

8

Born:

Married:

Died:

4 Richbald

Born: Abt 690

Married:

Died:

9

Born:

Died:

2 Bonifacio I of Lucca

Born: Abt 720

Married:

Died: Bef 785

10

Born:

Married:

Died:

5 --

Born:

Died:

11

Born:

Died:

1 Bonifacio II, Count of Lucca

Born: Abt 750

  -SAME AS #8,ROYAL CHART 1960

Married:

Died: Bef 5 Oct 823

12

Born:

Married:

Died:

6

Born:

Married:

Died:

13

Born:

Died:

**-- **

Spouse

3 --

Born:

Died:

14

Born:

Married:

Died:

7

Born:

Died:

15

Born:

Died:

Sources include: *Royal Ancestors* (1989), chart 11994; Stuart 93; Moriarty 61.

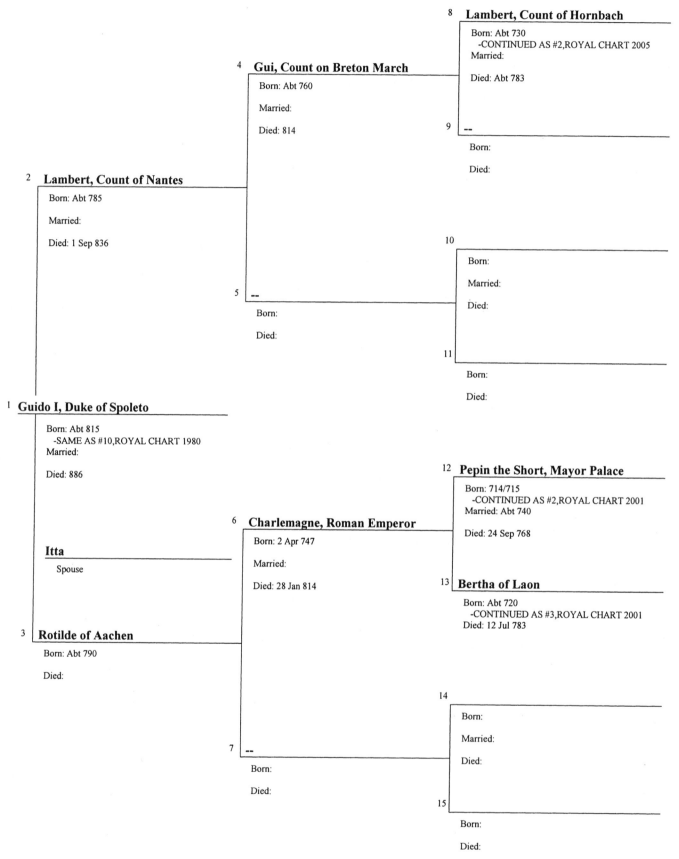

Pedigree Chart

8 **Lambert, Count of Hornbach**
Born: Abt 730
-CONTINUED AS #2,ROYAL CHART 2005
Married:
Died: Abt 783

4 **Gui, Count on Breton March**
Born: Abt 760
Married:
Died: 814

9 --
Born:
Died:

2 **Lambert, Count of Nantes**
Born: Abt 785
Married:
Died: 1 Sep 836

10
Born:
Married:
Died:

5 --
Born:
Died:

11
Born:
Died:

1 **Guido I, Duke of Spoleto**
Born: Abt 815
-SAME AS #10,ROYAL CHART 1980
Married:
Died: 886

12 **Pepin the Short, Mayor Palace**
Born: 714/715
-CONTINUED AS #2,ROYAL CHART 2001
Married: Abt 740
Died: 24 Sep 768

6 **Charlemagne, Roman Emperor**
Born: 2 Apr 747
Married:
Died: 28 Jan 814

13 **Bertha of Laon**
Born: Abt 720
-CONTINUED AS #3,ROYAL CHART 2001
Died: 12 Jul 783

Itta
Spouse

14
Born:
Married:
Died:

3 **Rotilde of Aachen**
Born: Abt 790
Died:

7 --
Born:
Died:

15
Born:
Died:

Sources include: *Royal Ancestors* (1989), charts 11994-95; *TAG* 52:26; Stuart 265; Moriarty 74.

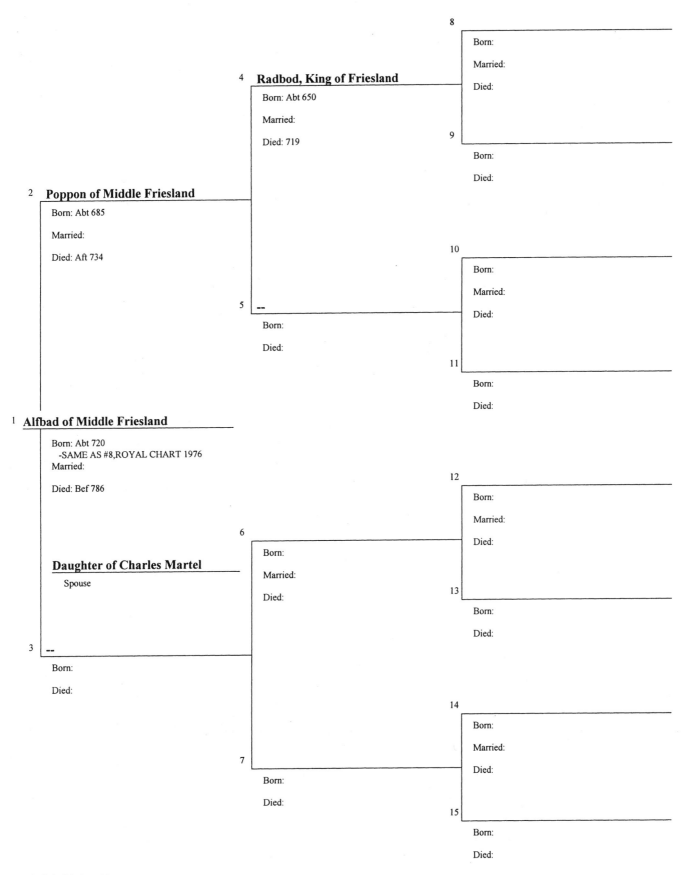

4   **Radbod, King of Friesland**

Born: Abt 650

Married:

Died: 719

8

Born:

Married:

Died:

9

Born:

Died:

2   **Poppon of Middle Friesland**

Born: Abt 685

Married:

Died: Aft 734

5   --

Born:

Died:

10

Born:

Married:

Died:

11

Born:

Died:

1   **Alfbad of Middle Friesland**

Born: Abt 720
  -SAME AS #8,ROYAL CHART 1976
Married:

Died: Bef 786

Daughter of Charles Martel
  Spouse

3   --

Born:

Died:

6

Born:

Married:

Died:

12

Born:

Married:

Died:

13

Born:

Died:

7

Born:

Died:

14

Born:

Married:

Died:

15

Born:

Died:

Sources include: Moriarty 54.

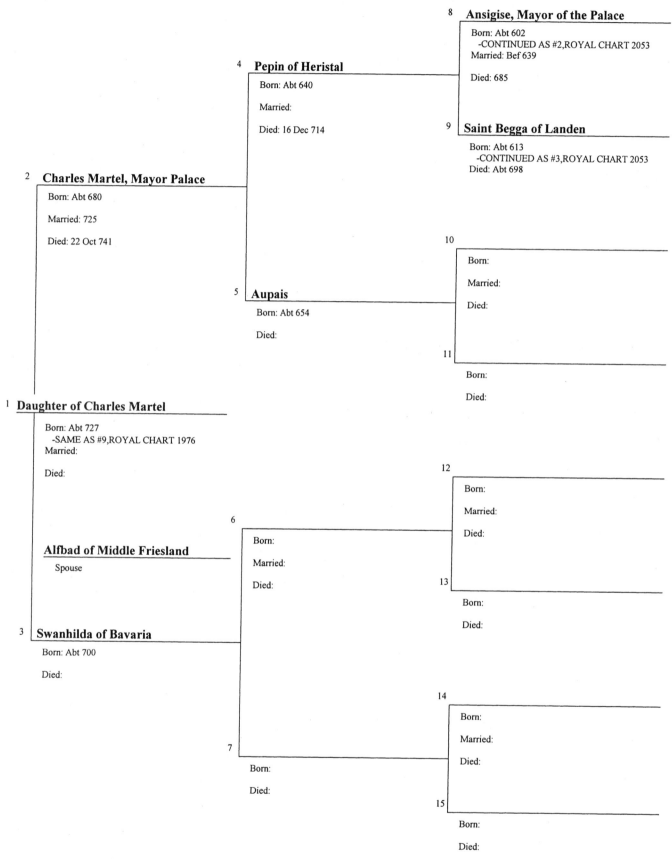

8   **Ansigise, Mayor of the Palace**

Born: Abt 602
-CONTINUED AS #2,ROYAL CHART 2053
Married: Bef 639

Died: 685

4   **Pepin of Heristal**

Born: Abt 640

Married:

Died: 16 Dec 714

9   **Saint Begga of Landen**

Born: Abt 613
-CONTINUED AS #3,ROYAL CHART 2053
Died: Abt 698

2   **Charles Martel, Mayor Palace**

Born: Abt 680

Married: 725

Died: 22 Oct 741

10

Born:

Married:

Died:

5   **Aupais**

Born: Abt 654

Died:

11

Born:

Died:

1   **Daughter of Charles Martel**

Born: Abt 727
-SAME AS #9,ROYAL CHART 1976
Married:

Died:

12

Born:

Married:

Died:

6

Born:

Married:

Died:

13

Born:

Died:

Alfbad of Middle Friesland

Spouse

3   **Swanhilda of Bavaria**

Born: Abt 700

Died:

14

Born:

Married:

Died:

7

Born:

Died:

15

Born:

Died:

Sources include: Moriarty 54; Stuart 171 (#2 ancestry); *Royal Ancestors* (1989), charts 11624, 11701 (#2 ancestry).

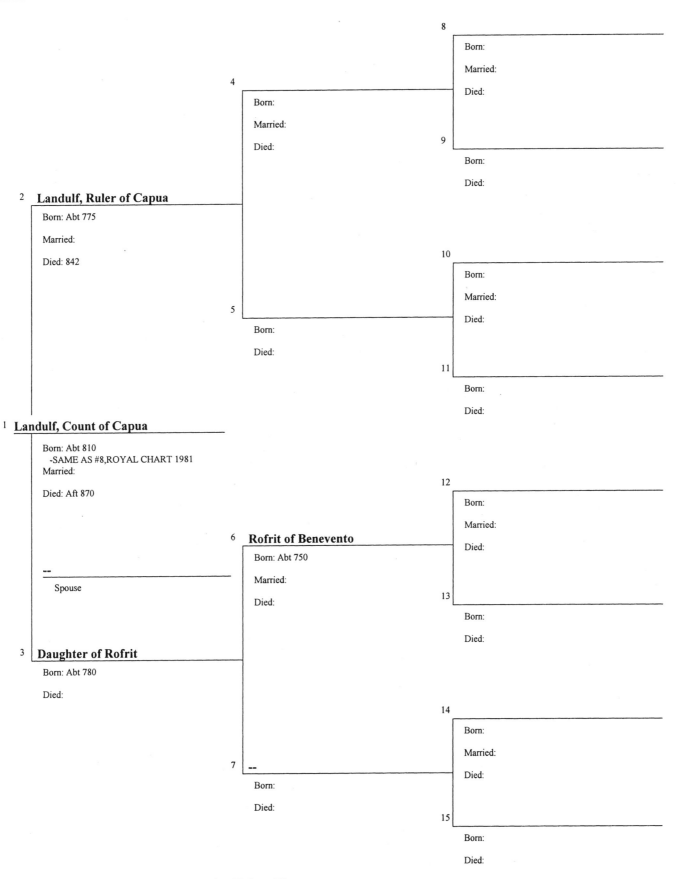

8

Born:

Married:

Died:

4

Born:

Married:

Died:

9

Born:

Died:

2 | **Landulf, Ruler of Capua**

Born: Abt 775

Married:

Died: 842

10

Born:

Married:

Died:

5

Born:

Died:

11

Born:

Died:

1 | **Landulf, Count of Capua**

Born: Abt 810
  -SAME AS #8,ROYAL CHART 1981
Married:

Died: Aft 870

12

Born:

Married:

Died:

6 | **Rofrit of Benevento**

Born: Abt 750

Married:

Died:

13

Born:

Died:

--

Spouse

14

Born:

Married:

Died:

3 | **Daughter of Rofrit**

Born: Abt 780

Died:

7 | **--**

Born:

Died:

15

Born:

Died:

Sources include: *Royal Ancestors* (1989), chart 12096; Moriarty 72; Stuart 283.

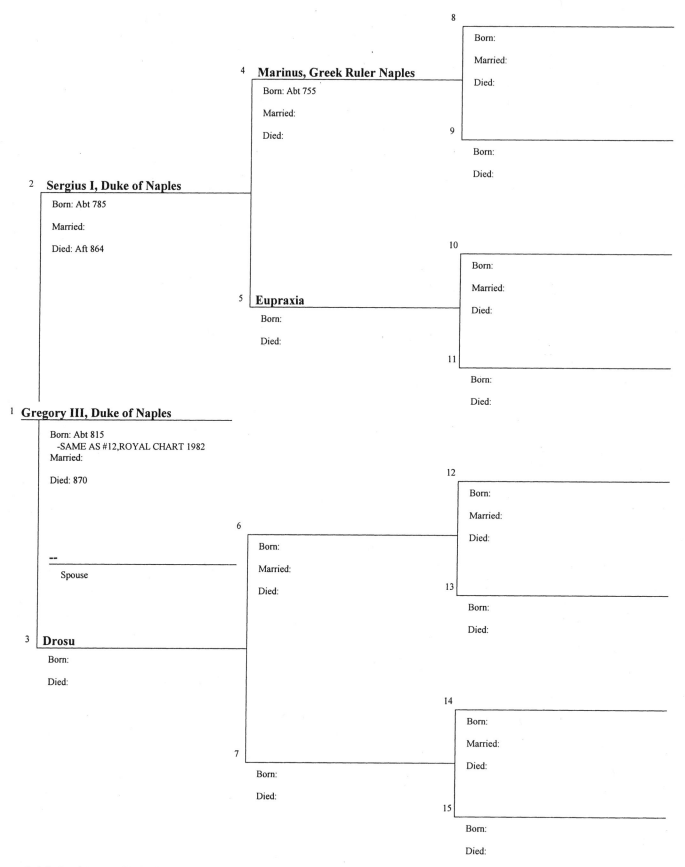

8
Born:
Married:
Died:

4 **Marinus, Greek Ruler Naples**
Born: Abt 755
Married:
Died:

9
Born:
Died:

2 **Sergius I, Duke of Naples**
Born: Abt 785
Married:
Died: Aft 864

10
Born:
Married:
Died:

5 **Eupraxia**
Born:
Died:

11
Born:
Died:

1 **Gregory III, Duke of Naples**
Born: Abt 815
  -SAME AS #12,ROYAL CHART 1982
Married:
Died: 870

12
Born:
Married:
Died:

6
Born:
Married:
Died:

13
Born:
Died:

--
Spouse

3 **Drosu**
Born:
Died:

14
Born:
Married:
Died:

7
Born:
Died:

15
Born:
Died:

Sources include: *Royal Ancestors* (1989), chart 12097; Stuart 280; Moriarty 73; *TAG* 52:23-26.

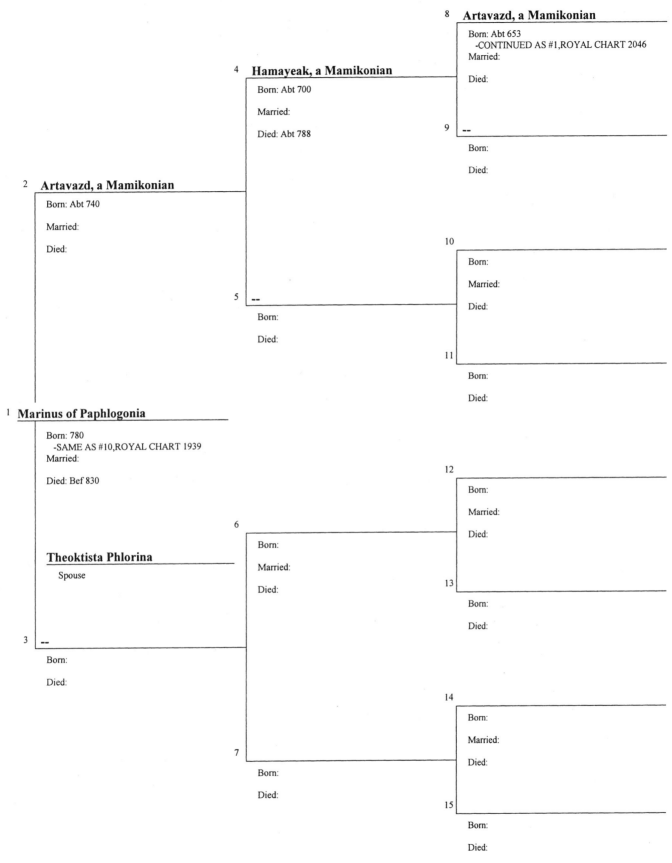

8 Artavazd, a Mamikonian

Born: Abt 653
  -CONTINUED AS #1,ROYAL CHART 2046
Married:

Died:

4 Hamayeak, a Mamikonian

Born: Abt 700

Married:

Died: Abt 788

9 --

Born:

Died:

2 Artavazd, a Mamikonian

Born: Abt 740

Married:

Died:

10

Born:

Married:

Died:

5 --

Born:

Died:

11

Born:

Died:

1 Marinus of Paphlogonia

Born: 780
  -SAME AS #10,ROYAL CHART 1939
Married:

Died: Bef 830

12

Born:

Married:

Died:

6

Born:

Married:

Died:

Theoktista Phlorina

Spouse

13

Born:

Died:

3 --

Born:

Died:

14

Born:

Married:

Died:

7

Born:

Died:

15

Born:

Died:

Sources include: *Royal Ancestors* (1989), chart 12060; Stuart 322A-42, 322; *The Genealogist* 2:21. Note: The parentage and ancestry of #2 Artavazd is uncertain. The Stuart version is followed above.

Pedigree Chart

Chart 2038

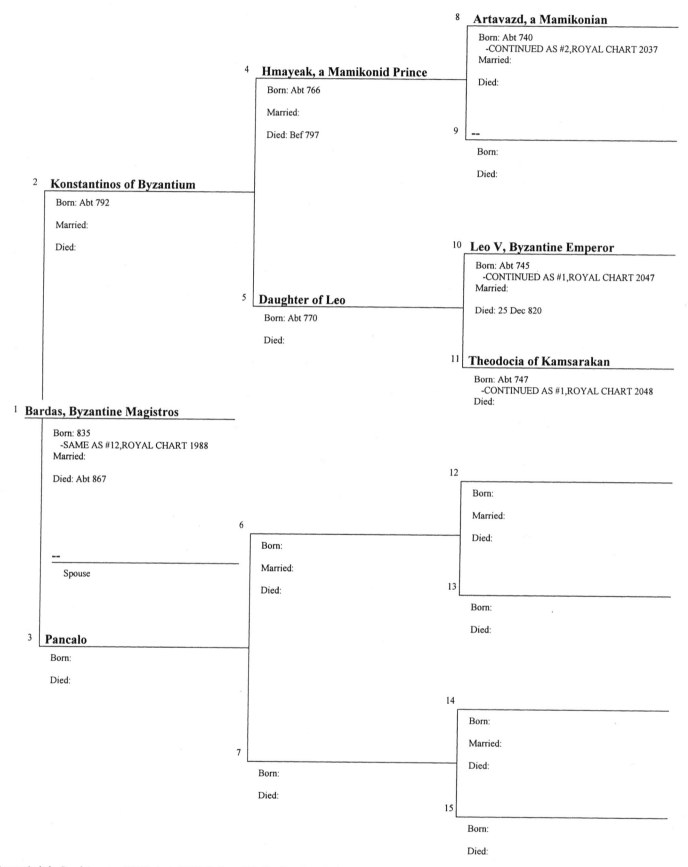

8 Artavazd, a Mamikonian

Born: Abt 740
-CONTINUED AS #2,ROYAL CHART 2037
Married:

Died:

4 Hmayeak, a Mamikonid Prince

Born: Abt 766

Married:

Died: Bef 797

9 --

Born:

Died:

2 Konstantinos of Byzantium

Born: Abt 792

Married:

Died:

10 Leo V, Byzantine Emperor

Born: Abt 745
-CONTINUED AS #1,ROYAL CHART 2047
Married:

Died: 25 Dec 820

5 Daughter of Leo

Born: Abt 770

Died:

11 Theodocia of Kamsarakan

Born: Abt 747
-CONTINUED AS #1,ROYAL CHART 2048
Died:

1 Bardas, Byzantine Magistros

Born: 835
-SAME AS #12,ROYAL CHART 1988
Married:

Died: Abt 867

--

Spouse

12

Born:

Married:

Died:

6

Born:

Married:

Died:

13

Born:

Died:

3 Pancalo

Born:

Died:

14

Born:

Married:

Died:

7

Born:

Died:

15

Born:

Died:

Sources include: *Royal Ancestors* (1989), charts 12065-66; Stuart 322; *The Genealogist* 2:19-20.

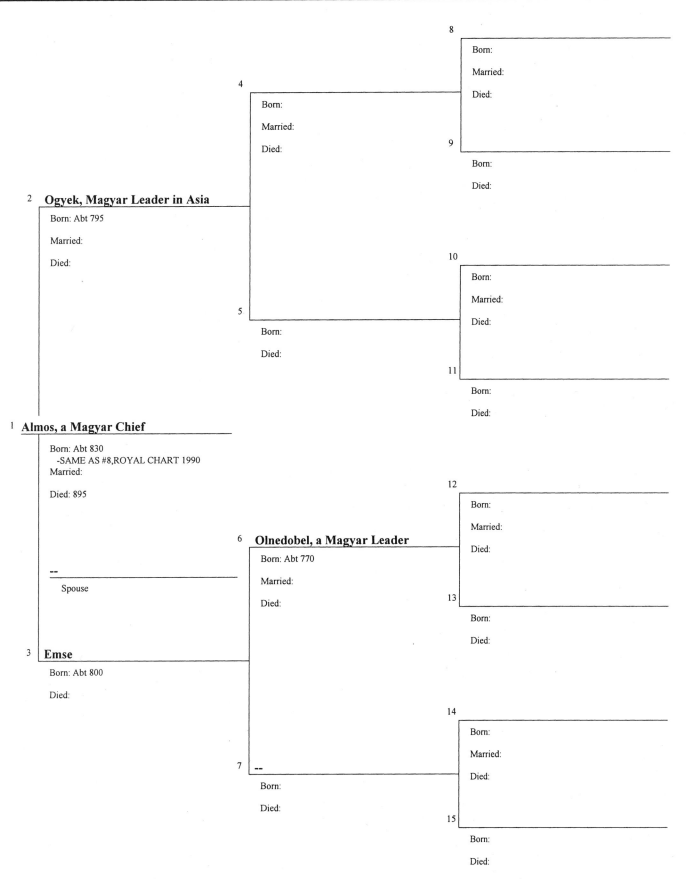

8

Born:

Married:

Died:

4

Born:

Married:

Died:

9

Born:

Died:

2 Ogyek, Magyar Leader in Asia

Born: Abt 795

Married:

Died:

10

Born:

Married:

Died:

5

Born:

Died:

11

Born:

Died:

1 Almos, a Magyar Chief

Born: Abt 830
  -SAME AS #8,ROYAL CHART 1990
Married:

Died: 895

12

Born:

Married:

Died:

6 Olnedobel, a Magyar Leader

Born: Abt 770

Married:

Died:

13

Born:

Died:

--

Spouse

3 Emse

Born: Abt 800

Died:

7 --

Born:

Died:

14

Born:

Married:

Died:

15

Born:

Died:

Sources include: *Royal Ancestors* (1989), charts 11947, 11996; Stuart 51; Moriarty 31.

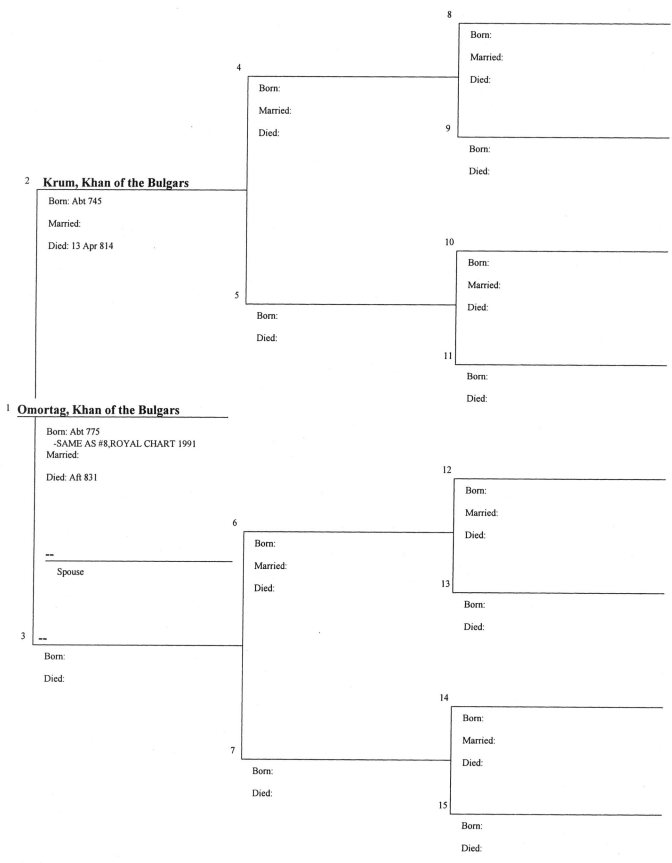

8

Born:

Married:

Died:

4

Born:

Married:

Died:

9

Born:

Died:

2 Krum, Khan of the Bulgars

Born: Abt 745

Married:

Died: 13 Apr 814

10

Born:

Married:

Died:

5

Born:

Died:

11

Born:

Died:

1 Omortag, Khan of the Bulgars

Born: Abt 775
  -SAME AS #8,ROYAL CHART 1991
Married:

Died: Aft 831

12

Born:

Married:

Died:

6

Born:

Married:

Died:

13

Born:

Died:

--

Spouse

3 --

Born:

Died:

14

Born:

Married:

Died:

7

Born:

Died:

15

Born:

Died:

Sources include: Stuart 309; Moriarty 139.

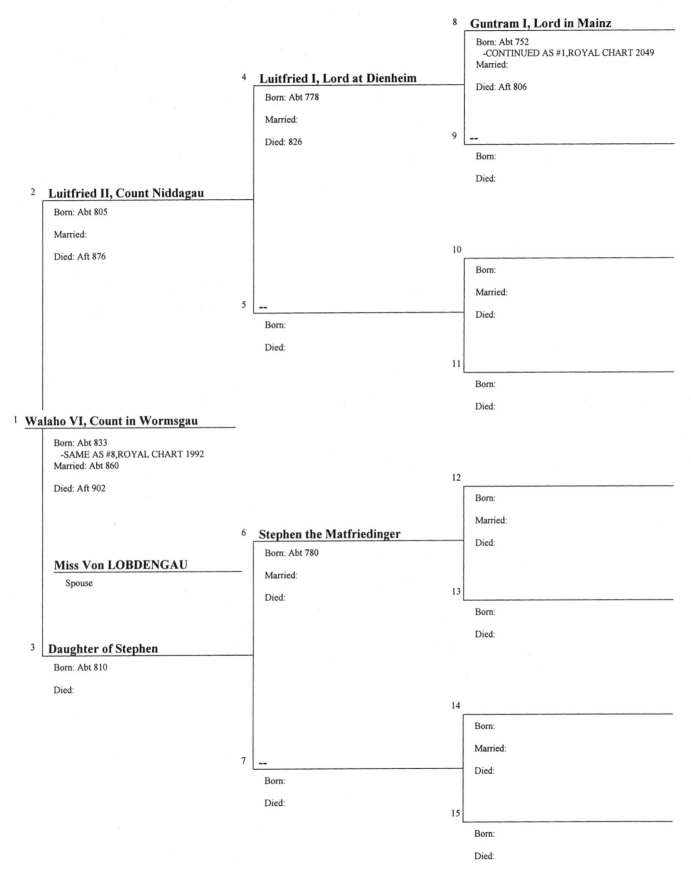

8 **Guntram I, Lord in Mainz**

Born: Abt 752
-CONTINUED AS #1, ROYAL CHART 2049
Married:

Died: Aft 806

4 **Luitfried I, Lord at Dienheim**

Born: Abt 778

Married:

Died: 826

9 --

Born:

Died:

2 **Luitfried II, Count Niddagau**

Born: Abt 805

Married:

Died: Aft 876

10

Born:

Married:

Died:

5 --

Born:

Died:

11

Born:

Died:

1 **Walaho VI, Count in Wormsgau**

Born: Abt 833
-SAME AS #8, ROYAL CHART 1992
Married: Abt 860

Died: Aft 902

12

Born:

Married:

Died:

6 **Stephen the Matfriedinger**

Born: Abt 780

Married:

Died:

13

Born:

Died:

Miss Von LOBDENGAU

Spouse

14

Born:

Married:

Died:

3 **Daughter of Stephen**

Born: Abt 810

Died:

7 --

Born:

Died:

15

Born:

Died:

Sources include: Stuart 359; Moriarty 91.

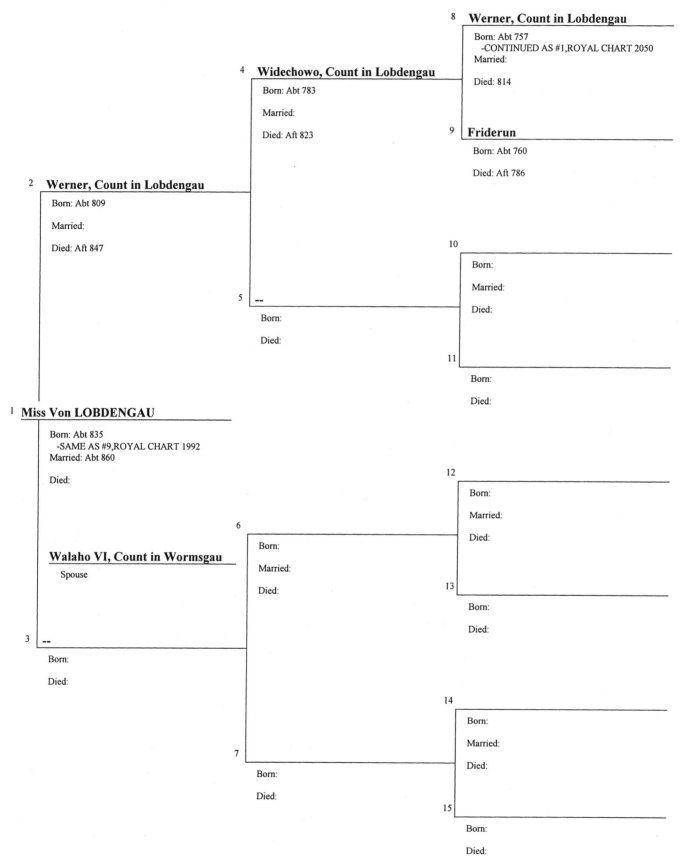

8 Werner, Count in Lobdengau

Born: Abt 757
   -CONTINUED AS #1,ROYAL CHART 2050
Married:

Died: 814

4 Widechowo, Count in Lobdengau

Born: Abt 783

Married:

Died: Aft 823

9 Friderun

Born: Abt 760

Died: Aft 786

2 Werner, Count in Lobdengau

Born: Abt 809

Married:

Died: Aft 847

5 --

Born:

Died:

10

Born:

Married:

Died:

11

Born:

Died:

1 Miss Von LOBDENGAU

Born: Abt 835
   -SAME AS #9,ROYAL CHART 1992
Married: Abt 860

Died:

Walaho VI, Count in Wormsgau

Spouse

12

Born:

Married:

Died:

6

Born:

Married:

Died:

13

Born:

Died:

3 --

Born:

Died:

14

Born:

Married:

Died:

7

Born:

Died:

15

Born:

Died:

Sources include: Stuart 200; Moriarty 93.

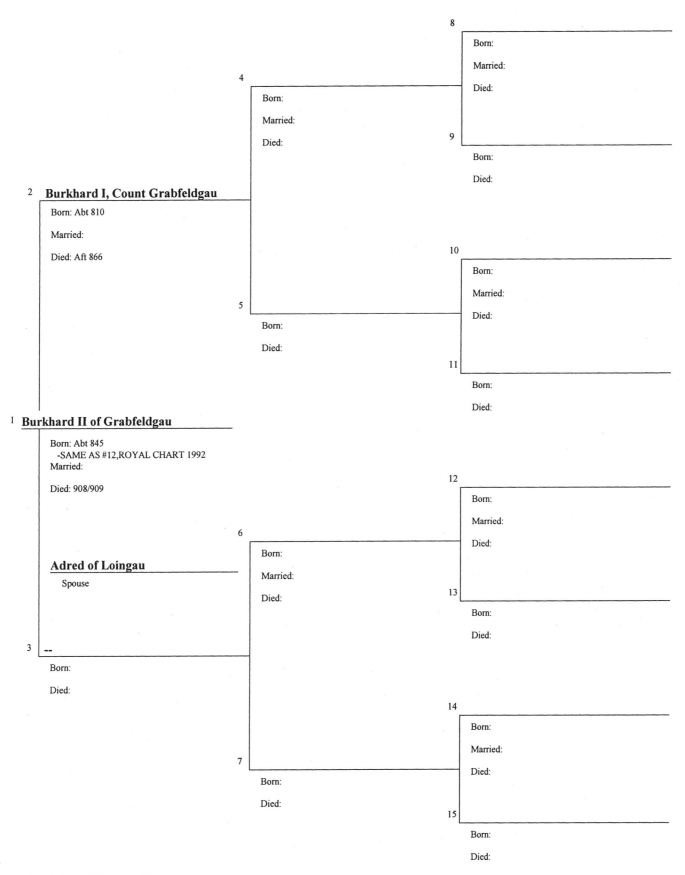

8

Born:

Married:

Died:

4

Born:

Married:

Died:

9

Born:

Died:

2 Burkhard I, Count Grabfeldgau

Born: Abt 810

Married:

Died: Aft 866

10

Born:

Married:

Died:

5

Born:

Died:

11

Born:

Died:

1 Burkhard II of Grabfeldgau

Born: Abt 845
   -SAME AS #12,ROYAL CHART 1992
Married:

Died: 908/909

12

Born:

Married:

Died:

6

Born:

Married:

Died:

13

Born:

Died:

Adred of Loingau

Spouse

3 --

Born:

Died:

14

Born:

Married:

Died:

7

Born:

Died:

15

Born:

Died:

Sources include: Stuart 210; Moriarty 95.

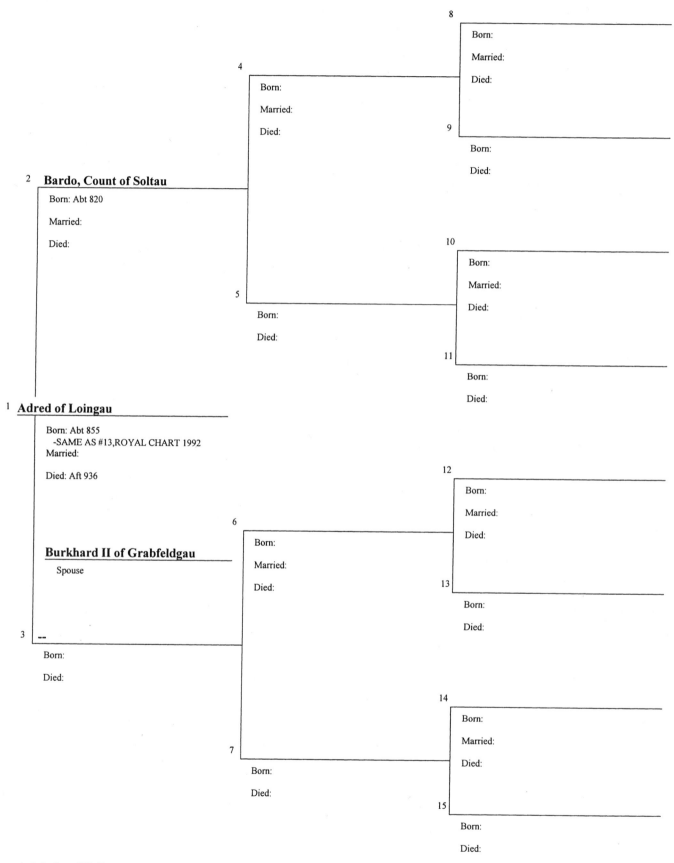

8

Born:

Married:

Died:

4

Born:

Married:

Died:

9

Born:

Died:

2 **Bardo, Count of Soltau**

Born: Abt 820

Married:

Died:

10

Born:

Married:

Died:

5

Born:

Died:

11

Born:

Died:

1 **Adred of Loingau**

Born: Abt 855
-SAME AS #13,ROYAL CHART 1992
Married:

Died: Aft 936

12

Born:

Married:

Died:

6

Born:

Married:

Died:

13

Born:

Died:

Burkhard II of Grabfeldgau

Spouse

3 --

Born:

Died:

14

Born:

Married:

Died:

7

Born:

Died:

15

Born:

Died:

Sources include: Stuart 210-40.

Pedigree Chart

Chart 2045

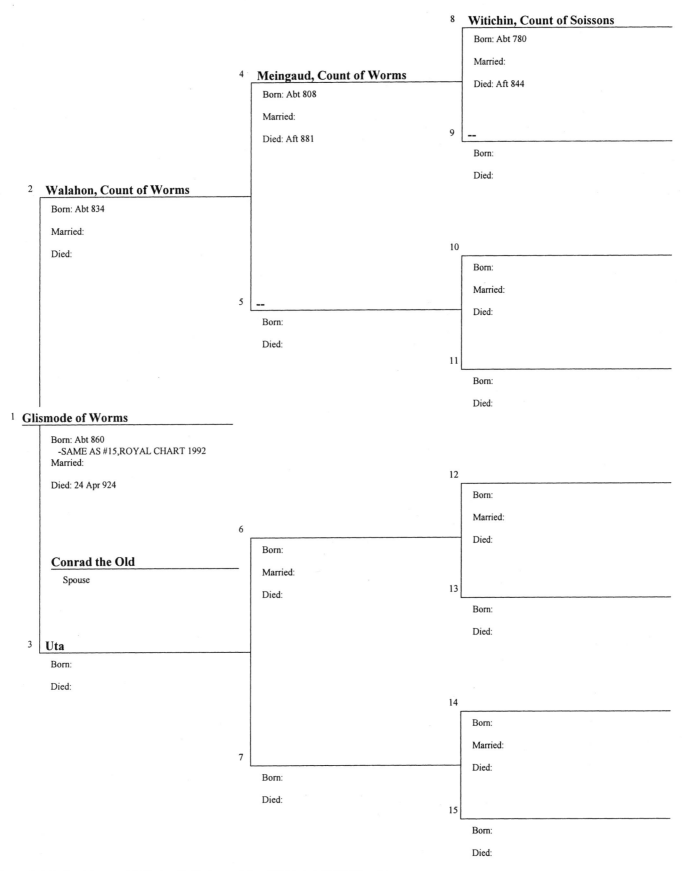

8 Witichin, Count of Soissons

Born: Abt 780

Married:

Died: Aft 844

4 Meingaud, Count of Worms

Born: Abt 808

Married:

Died: Aft 881

9 --

Born:

Died:

2 Walahon, Count of Worms

Born: Abt 834

Married:

Died:

10

Born:

Married:

Died:

5 --

Born:

Died:

11

Born:

Died:

1 Glismode of Worms

Born: Abt 860
-SAME AS #15,ROYAL CHART 1992
Married:

Died: 24 Apr 924

12

Born:

Married:

Died:

6

Born:

Married:

Died:

13

Born:

Died:

Conrad the Old

Spouse

3 Uta

Born:

Died:

14

Born:

Married:

Died:

7

Born:

Died:

15

Born:

Died:

Sources include: *Royal Ancestors* (1989), chart 11617; *Ancestral Roots* 192; Moriarty 23 (#1 Glismode).

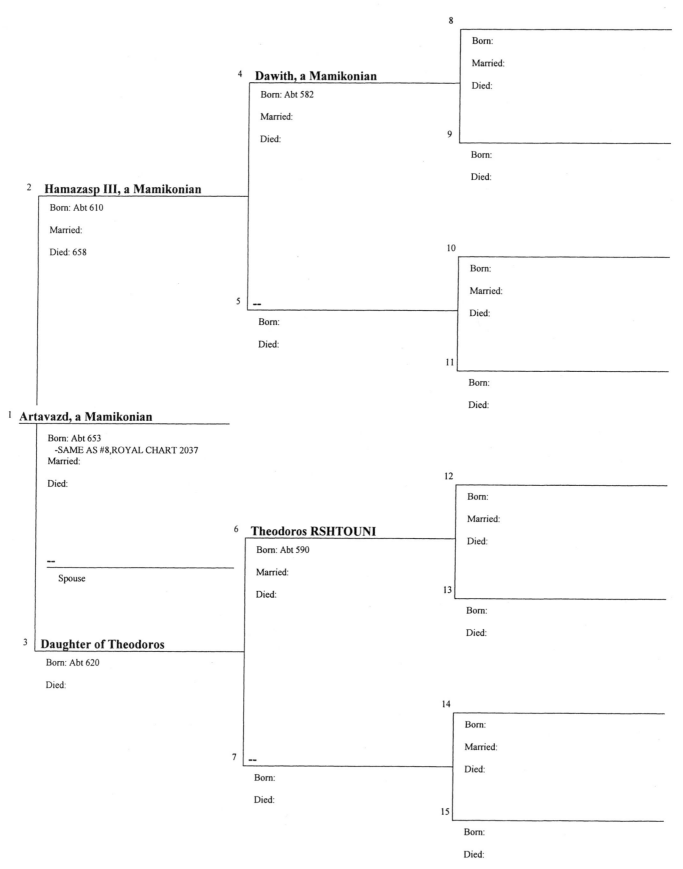

8

4 Dawith, a Mamikonian

Born:

Married:

Died:

Born: Abt 582

Married:

Died:

9

Born:

Died:

2 Hamazasp III, a Mamikonian

Born: Abt 610

Married:

Died: 658

10

Born:

Married:

Died:

5 --

Born:

Died:

11

Born:

Died:

1 Artavazd, a Mamikonian

Born: Abt 653
  -SAME AS #8,ROYAL CHART 2037
Married:

Died:

12

Born:

Married:

Died:

6 Theodoros RSHTOUNI

Born: Abt 590

Married:

Died:

13

Born:

Died:

--
  Spouse

3 Daughter of Theodoros

Born: Abt 620

Died:

14

Born:

Married:

Died:

7 --

Born:

Died:

15

Born:

Died:

Sources include: Stuart 322. Note: The parentage of #4 Dawith is disputed. Stuart gives #8 as Vahan and continues that line to the 7th century B.C. and beyond on some branches, including ties to Syrian and Persian kings and Egyptian pharaohs. The claimed line through the Mamikonians is problematic at many points, with some connections being assumed (see *TAG* 74:148, 150). The line is therefore not being included here.

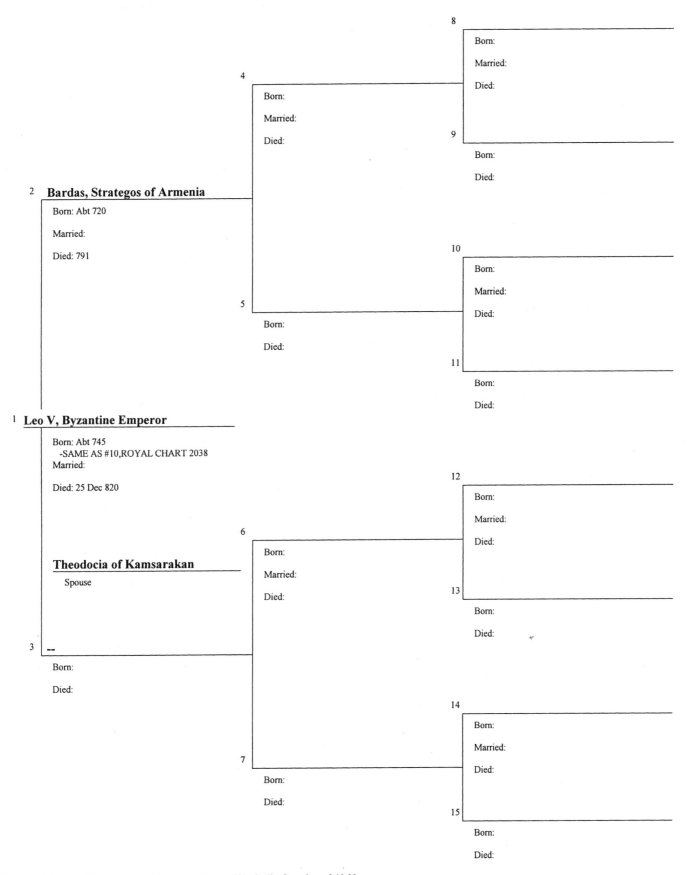

8

Born:

Married:

Died:

4

Born:

Married:

Died:

9

Born:

Died:

2   **Bardas, Strategos of Armenia**

Born: Abt 720

Married:

Died: 791

10

Born:

Married:

Died:

5

Born:

Died:

11

Born:

Died:

1 **Leo V, Byzantine Emperor**

Born: Abt 745
  -SAME AS #10,ROYAL CHART 2038
Married:

Died: 25 Dec 820

12

Born:

Married:

Died:

6

Born:

Married:

Died:

13

Born:

Died:

Theodocia of Kamsarakan

Spouse

3 --

Born:

Died:

14

Born:

Married:

Died:

7

Born:

Died:

15

Born:

Died:

Sources include: *Royal Ancestors* (1989), chart 12066; Stuart 322-42; *The Genealogist* 2:19-20.

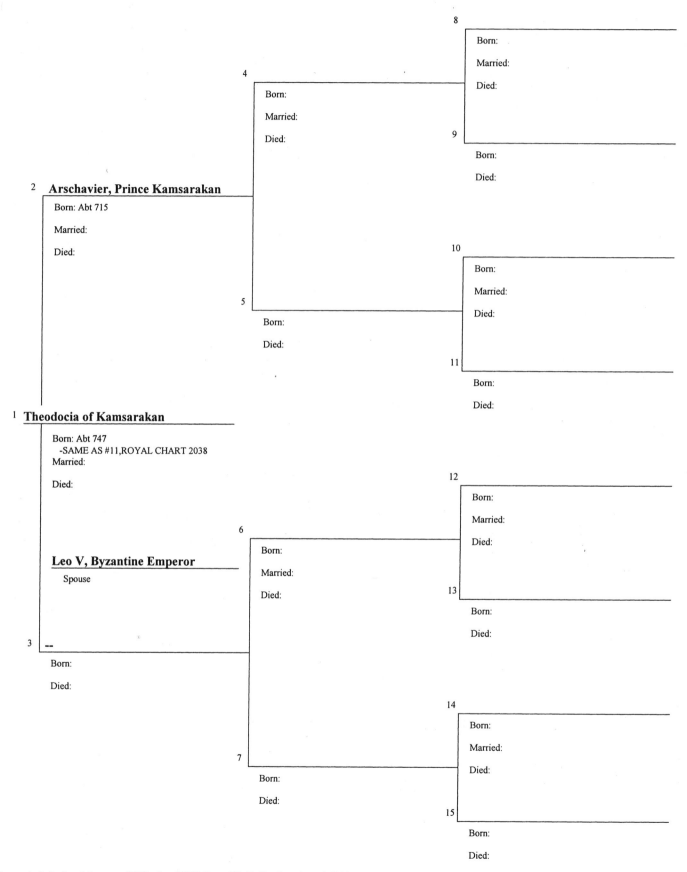

8

Born:

Married:

Died:

4

Born:

Married:

Died:

9

Born:

Died:

2   Arschavier, Prince Kamsarakan

Born: Abt 715

Married:

Died:

10

Born:

Married:

Died:

5

Born:

Died:

11

Born:

Died:

1   Theodocia of Kamsarakan

Born: Abt 747

   -SAME AS #11,ROYAL CHART 2038

Married:

Died:

12

Born:

Married:

Died:

6

Born:

Married:

Died:

13

Born:

Died:

Leo V, Byzantine Emperor

   Spouse

3   --

Born:

Died:

14

Born:

Married:

Died:

7

Born:

Died:

15

Born:

Died:

Sources include: *Royal Ancestors* (1989), chart 12066; Stuart 322-42; *The Genealogist* 2:19-20.

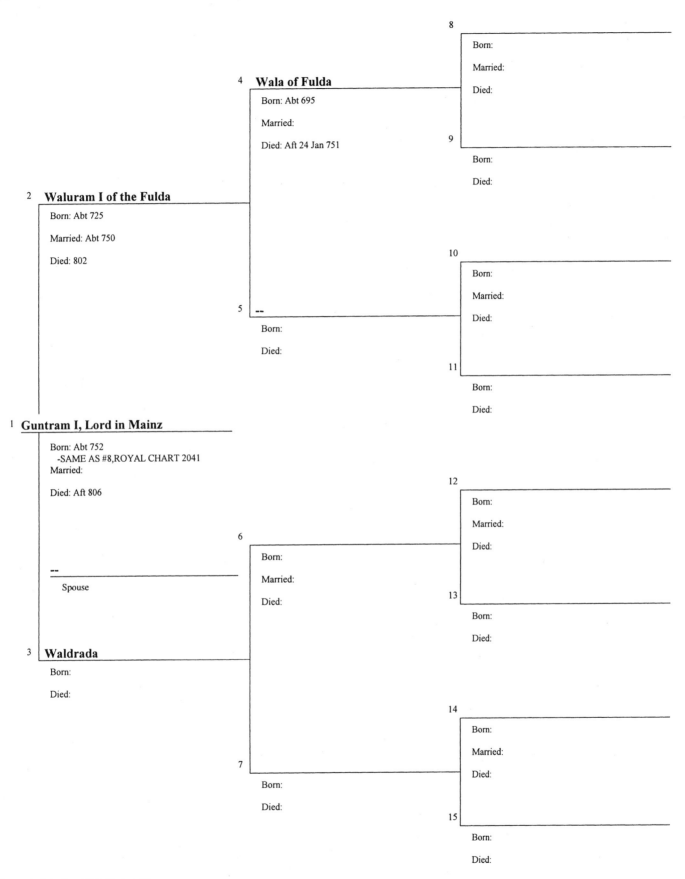

8

Born:

Married:

Died:

4 Wala of Fulda

Born: Abt 695

Married:

Died: Aft 24 Jan 751

9

Born:

Died:

2 Waluram I of the Fulda

Born: Abt 725

Married: Abt 750

Died: 802

10

Born:

Married:

Died:

5 --

Born:

Died:

11

Born:

Died:

1 Guntram I, Lord in Mainz

Born: Abt 752
  -SAME AS #8,ROYAL CHART 2041
Married:

Died: Aft 806

12

Born:

Married:

Died:

6

Born:

Married:

Died:

13

Born:

Died:

--

Spouse

3 Waldrada

Born:

Died:

14

Born:

Married:

Died:

7

Born:

Died:

15

Born:

Died:

Sources include: Stuart 359; Moriarty 91.

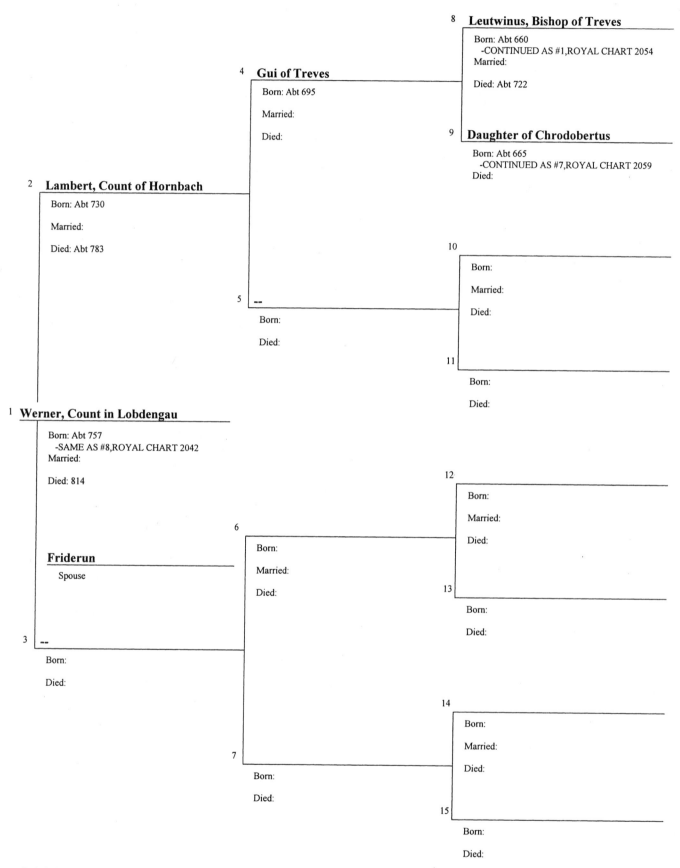

8 **Leutwinus, Bishop of Treves**

Born: Abt 660
-CONTINUED AS #1,ROYAL CHART 2054
Married:

Died: Abt 722

4 **Gui of Treves**

Born: Abt 695

Married:

Died:

9 **Daughter of Chrodobertus**

Born: Abt 665
-CONTINUED AS #7,ROYAL CHART 2059
Died:

2 **Lambert, Count of Hornbach**

Born: Abt 730

Married:

Died: Abt 783

10

Born:

Married:

Died:

5 --

Born:

Died:

11

Born:

Died:

1 **Werner, Count in Lobdengau**

Born: Abt 757
-SAME AS #8,ROYAL CHART 2042
Married:

Died: 814

12

Born:

Married:

Died:

6

Born:

Married:

Died:

13

Born:

Died:

Friderun

Spouse

3 --

Born:

Died:

14

Born:

Married:

Died:

7

Born:

Died:

15

Born:

Died:

Sources include: Stuart 200; Moriarty 93, 74.

Pedigree Chart

Chart 2051

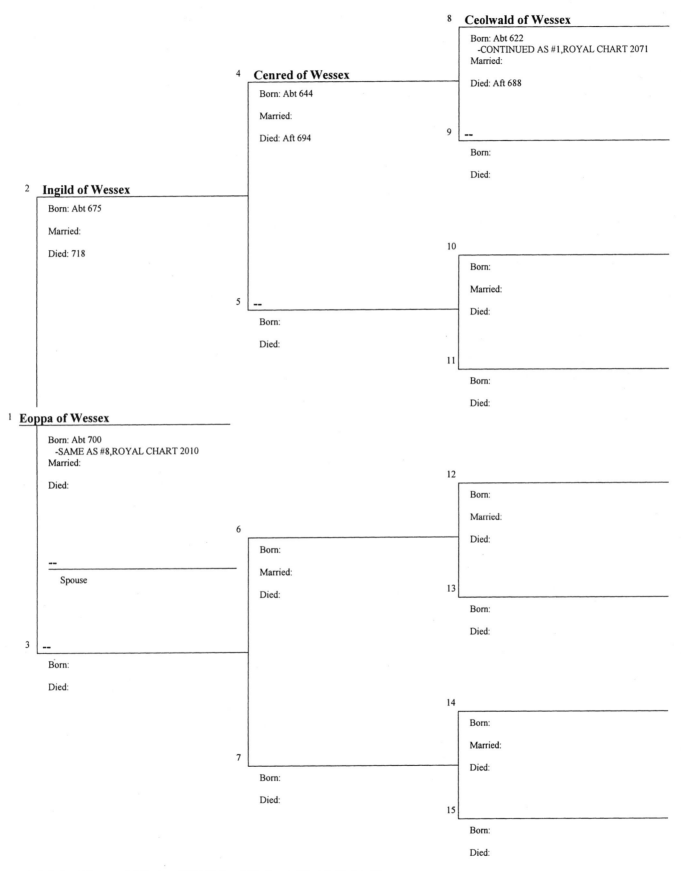

8 Ceolwald of Wessex

Born: Abt 622
 -CONTINUED AS #1,ROYAL CHART 2071
Married:

Died: Aft 688

4 Cenred of Wessex

Born: Abt 644

Married:

Died: Aft 694

9 --

Born:

Died:

2 Ingild of Wessex

Born: Abt 675

Married:

Died: 718

5 --

Born:

Died:

10

Born:

Married:

Died:

11

Born:

Died:

1 Eoppa of Wessex

Born: Abt 700
 -SAME AS #8,ROYAL CHART 2010
Married:

Died:

**-- **
Spouse

12

Born:

Married:

Died:

6

Born:

Married:

Died:

13

Born:

Died:

3 --

Born:

Died:

14

Born:

Married:

Died:

7

Born:

Died:

15

Born:

Died:

Sources include: *Royal Ancestors* (1989), charts 11714-15; Stuart 233; *Ancestral Roots* 1; Moriarty 15.

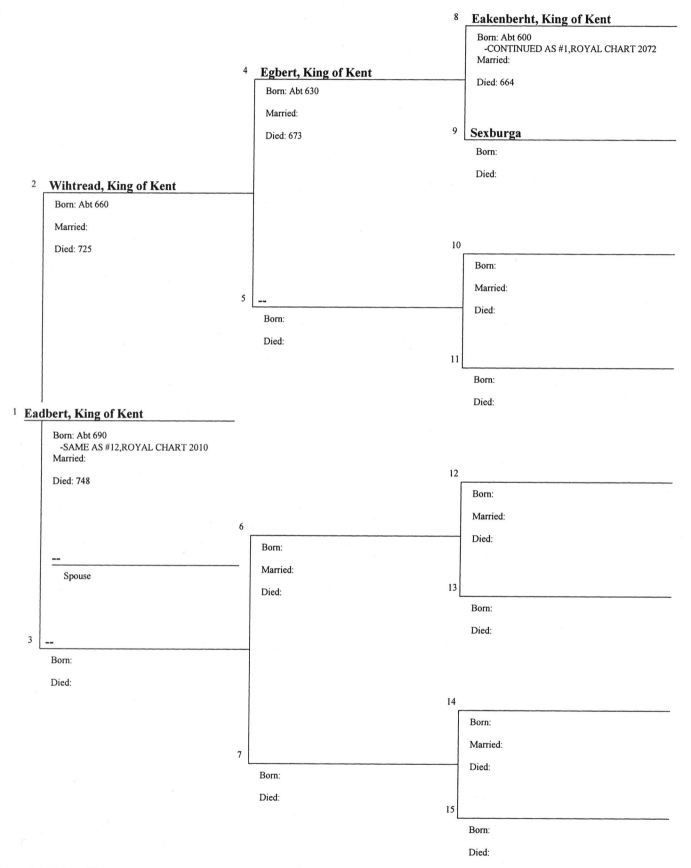

8 Eakenberht, King of Kent
Born: Abt 600
-CONTINUED AS #1,ROYAL CHART 2072
Married:

Died: 664

4 Egbert, King of Kent
Born: Abt 630

Married:

Died: 673

9 Sexburga
Born:

Died:

2 Wihtread, King of Kent
Born: Abt 660

Married:

Died: 725

5 --
Born:

Died:

10
Born:

Married:

Died:

11
Born:

Died:

1 Eadbert, King of Kent
Born: Abt 690
-SAME AS #12,ROYAL CHART 2010
Married:

Died: 748

--
Spouse

3 --
Born:

Died:

6
Born:

Married:

Died:

12
Born:

Married:

Died:

13
Born:

Died:

7
Born:

Died:

14
Born:

Married:

Died:

15
Born:

Died:

Sources include: Stuart 233A.

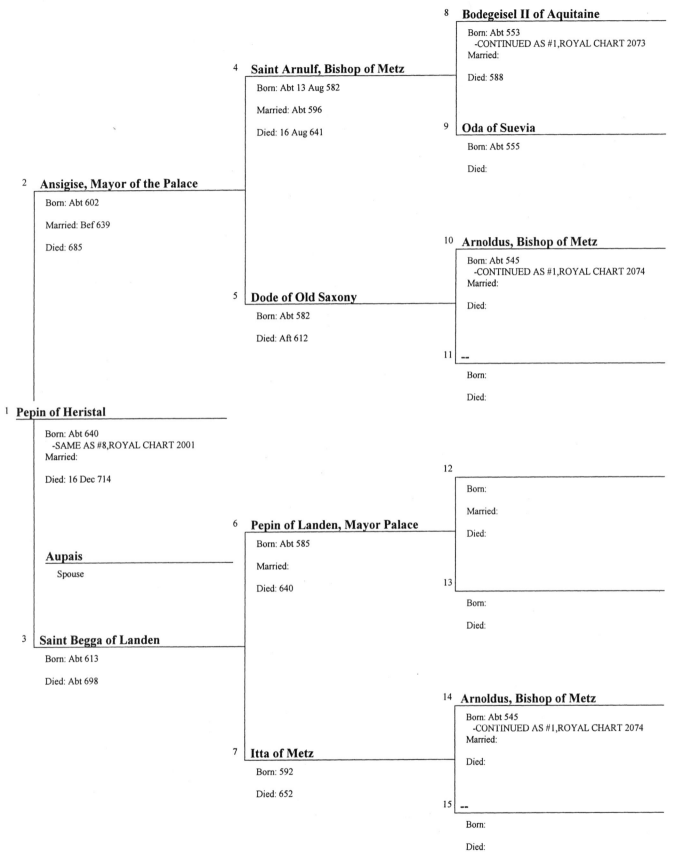

8 Bodegeisel II of Aquitaine

Born: Abt 553
 -CONTINUED AS #1,ROYAL CHART 2073
Married:

Died: 588

4 Saint Arnulf, Bishop of Metz

Born: Abt 13 Aug 582

Married: Abt 596

Died: 16 Aug 641

9 Oda of Suevia

Born: Abt 555

Died:

2 Ansigise, Mayor of the Palace

Born: Abt 602

Married: Bef 639

Died: 685

10 Arnoldus, Bishop of Metz

Born: Abt 545
 -CONTINUED AS #1,ROYAL CHART 2074
Married:

Died:

5 Dode of Old Saxony

Born: Abt 582

Died: Aft 612

11 --

Born:

Died:

1 Pepin of Heristal

Born: Abt 640
 -SAME AS #8,ROYAL CHART 2001
Married:

Died: 16 Dec 714

12

Born:

Married:

Died:

6 Pepin of Landen, Mayor Palace

Born: Abt 585

Married:

Died: 640

Aupais

Spouse

13

Born:

Died:

3 Saint Begga of Landen

Born: Abt 613

Died: Abt 698

14 Arnoldus, Bishop of Metz

Born: Abt 545
 -CONTINUED AS #1,ROYAL CHART 2074
Married:

Died:

7 Itta of Metz

Born: 592

Died: 652

15 --

Born:

Died:

Sources include: *Royal Ancestors* (1989), chart 11701; *Ancestral Roots* 190; Stuart 171; Moriarty 5, 8, 224.

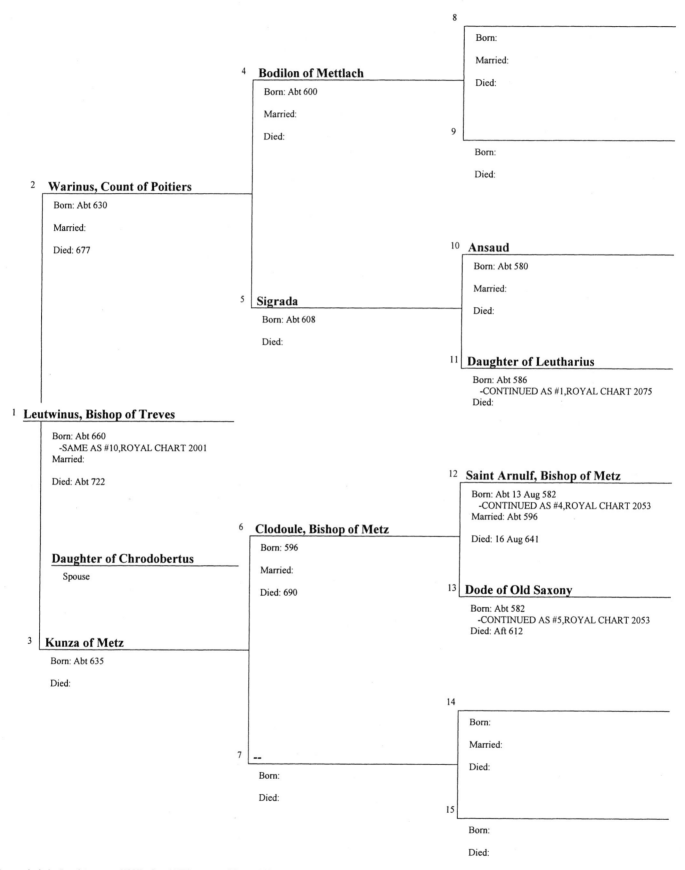

8

Born:

Married:

Died:

4 Bodilon of Mettlach

Born: Abt 600

Married:

Died:

9

Born:

Died:

2 Warinus, Count of Poitiers

Born: Abt 630

Married:

Died: 677

10 Ansaud

Born: Abt 580

Married:

Died:

5 Sigrada

Born: Abt 608

Died:

11 Daughter of Leutharius

Born: Abt 586
   -CONTINUED AS #1,ROYAL CHART 2075
Died:

1 Leutwinus, Bishop of Treves

Born: Abt 660
   -SAME AS #10,ROYAL CHART 2001
Married:

Died: Abt 722

12 Saint Arnulf, Bishop of Metz

Born: Abt 13 Aug 582
   -CONTINUED AS #4,ROYAL CHART 2053
Married: Abt 596

Died: 16 Aug 641

6 Clodoule, Bishop of Metz

Born: 596

Married:

Died: 690

13 Dode of Old Saxony

Born: Abt 582
   -CONTINUED AS #5,ROYAL CHART 2053
Died: Aft 612

Daughter of Chrodobertus

Spouse

3 Kunza of Metz

Born: Abt 635

Died:

14

Born:

Married:

Died:

7 --

Born:

Died:

15

Born:

Died:

Sources include: *Royal Ancestors* (1989), chart 11702; *Ancestral Roots* 50; Stuart 171-43, 330, 53 (same as 2); Moriarty 1, 5, 8, 74. Note: The ancestry shown for #2 Warinus (Warin) is not certain.

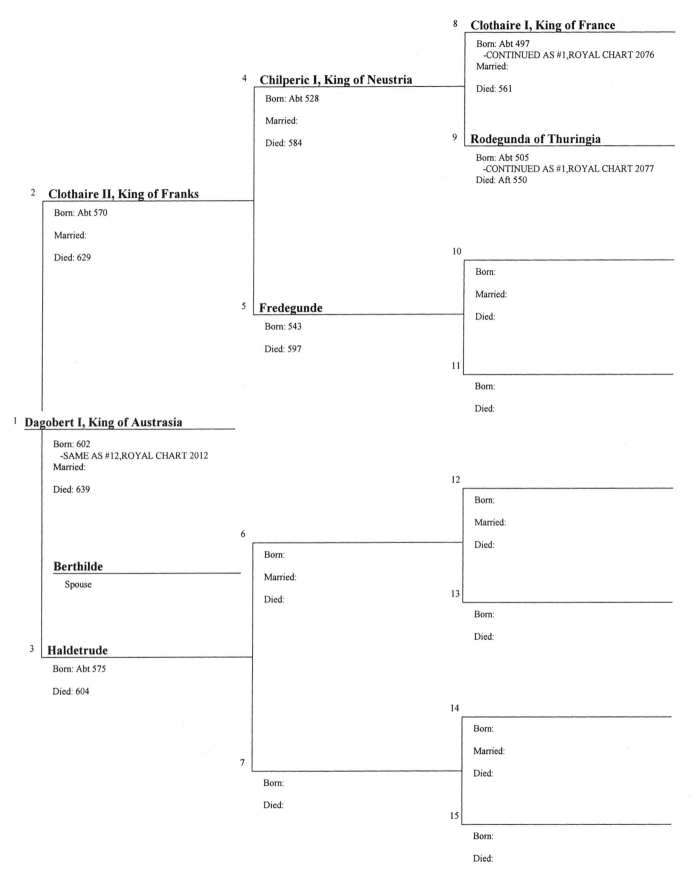

8 Clothaire I, King of France

Born: Abt 497
  -CONTINUED AS #1,ROYAL CHART 2076
Married:

Died: 561

4 Chilperic I, King of Neustria

Born: Abt 528

Married:

Died: 584

9 Rodegunda of Thuringia

Born: Abt 505
  -CONTINUED AS #1,ROYAL CHART 2077
Died: Aft 550

2 Clothaire II, King of Franks

Born: Abt 570

Married:

Died: 629

10

Born:

Married:

Died:

5 Fredegunde

Born: 543

Died: 597

11

Born:

Died:

1 Dagobert I, King of Austrasia

Born: 602
  -SAME AS #12,ROYAL CHART 2012
Married:

Died: 639

12

Born:

Married:

Died:

6

Born:

Married:

Died:

13

Born:

Died:

Berthilde

Spouse

3 Haldetrude

Born: Abt 575

Died: 604

14

Born:

Married:

Died:

7

Born:

Died:

15

Born:

Died:

Sources include: Stuart 303; Turton 54-55; Moriarty 21 note (#1); *Royal Ancestors* (1989), chart 11736 (#1).

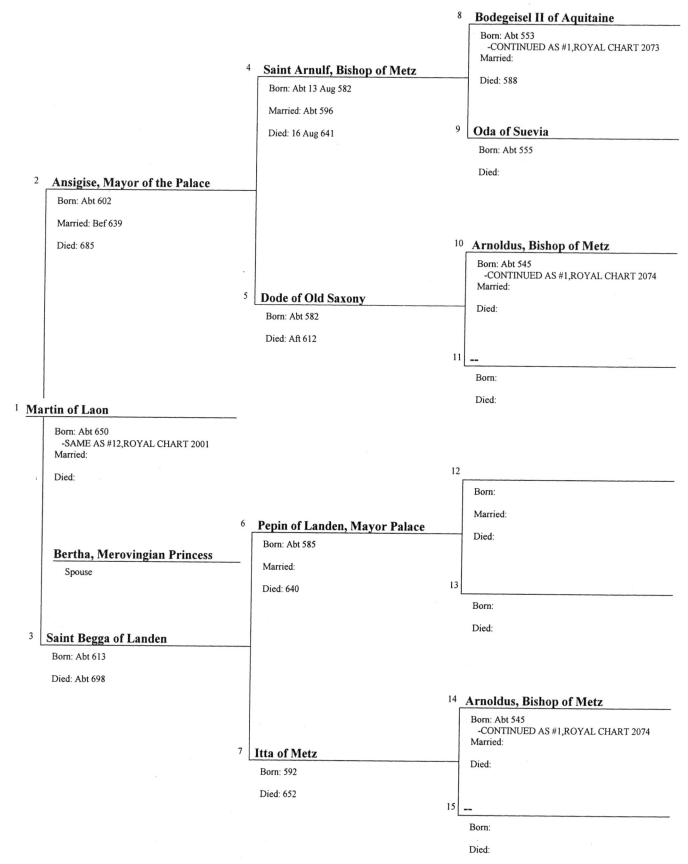

8 Bodegeisel II of Aquitaine

Born: Abt 553
-CONTINUED AS #1,ROYAL CHART 2073
Married:

Died: 588

4 Saint Arnulf, Bishop of Metz

Born: Abt 13 Aug 582

Married: Abt 596

Died: 16 Aug 641

9 Oda of Suevia

Born: Abt 555

Died:

2 Ansigise, Mayor of the Palace

Born: Abt 602

Married: Bef 639

Died: 685

10 Arnoldus, Bishop of Metz

Born: Abt 545
-CONTINUED AS #1,ROYAL CHART 2074
Married:

Died:

5 Dode of Old Saxony

Born: Abt 582

Died: Aft 612

11 --

Born:

Died:

1 Martin of Laon

Born: Abt 650
-SAME AS #12,ROYAL CHART 2001
Married:

Died:

12

Born:

Married:

Died:

Bertha, Merovingian Princess

Spouse

6 Pepin of Landen, Mayor Palace

Born: Abt 585

Married:

Died: 640

13

Born:

Died:

3 Saint Begga of Landen

Born: Abt 613

Died: Abt 698

14 Arnoldus, Bishop of Metz

Born: Abt 545
-CONTINUED AS #1,ROYAL CHART 2074
Married:

Died:

7 Itta of Metz

Born: 592

Died: 652

15 --

Born:

Died:

Sources include: Stuart 214-44, 171, 260; *Royal Ancestors* (1989), chart 11993.

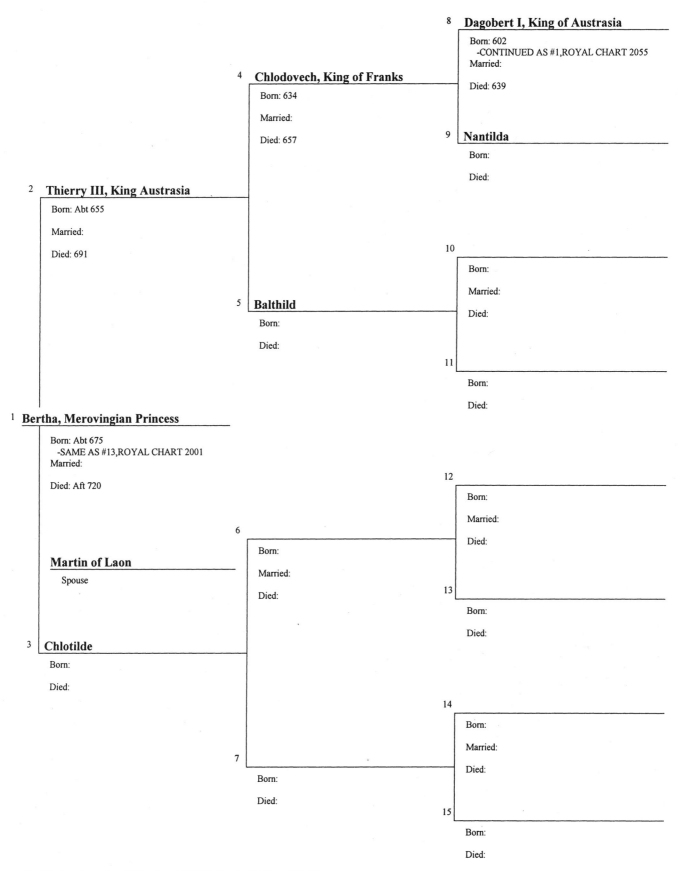

8 Dagobert I, King of Austrasia

Born: 602
  -CONTINUED AS #1, ROYAL CHART 2055
Married:

Died: 639

4 Chlodovech, King of Franks

Born: 634

Married:

Died: 657

9 Nantilda

Born:

Died:

2 Thierry III, King Austrasia

Born: Abt 655

Married:

Died: 691

10

Born:

Married:

Died:

5 Balthild

Born:

Died:

11

Born:

Died:

1 Bertha, Merovingian Princess

Born: Abt 675
  -SAME AS #13, ROYAL CHART 2001
Married:

Died: Aft 720

12

Born:

Married:

Died:

6

Born:

Married:

Died:

Martin of Laon

Spouse

13

Born:

Died:

3 Chlotilde

Born:

Died:

14

Born:

Married:

Died:

7

Born:

Died:

15

Born:

Died:

Sources include: *Royal Ancestors* (1989), chart 11993; Moriarty 8, 232; Stuart 214, 123.

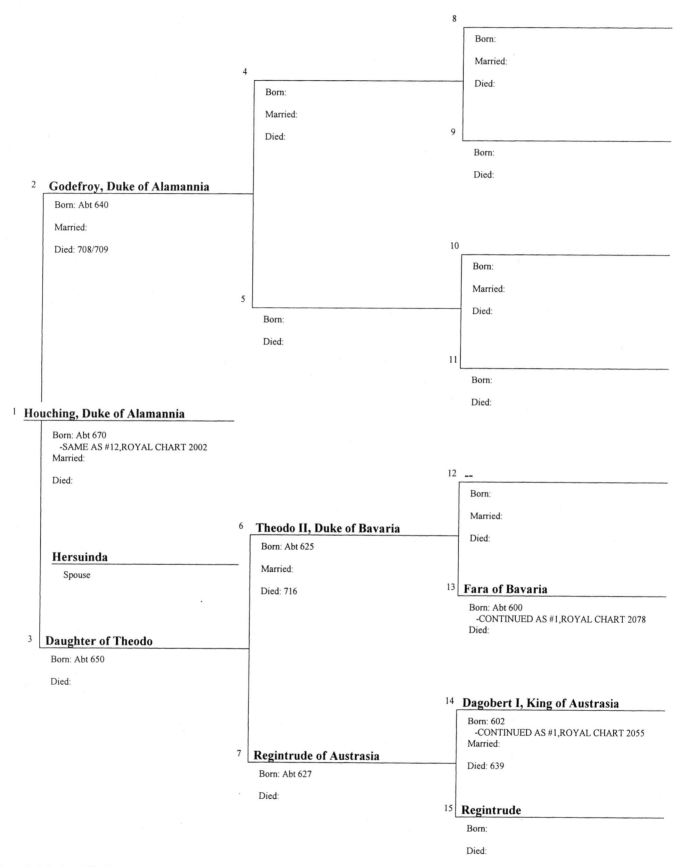

8
Born:
Married:
Died:

4
Born:
Married:
Died:

9
Born:
Died:

2 Godefroy, Duke of Alamannia
Born: Abt 640
Married:
Died: 708/709

10
Born:
Married:
Died:

5
Born:
Died:

11
Born:
Died:

1 Houching, Duke of Alamannia
Born: Abt 670
-SAME AS #12, ROYAL CHART 2002
Married:
Died:

12 --
Born:
Married:
Died:

6 Theodo II, Duke of Bavaria
Born: Abt 625
Married:
Died: 716

13 Fara of Bavaria
Born: Abt 600
-CONTINUED AS #1, ROYAL CHART 2078
Died:

Hersuinda
Spouse

3 Daughter of Theodo
Born: Abt 650
Died:

14 Dagobert I, King of Austrasia
Born: 602
-CONTINUED AS #1, ROYAL CHART 2055
Married:
Died: 639

7 Regintrude of Austrasia
Born: Abt 627
Died:

15 Regintrude
Born:
Died:

Sources include: Stuart 262, 303; *Royal Ancestors* (1989), chart 11728; *Ancestral Roots* 182; Moriarty 8. Note: Stuart shows #6 Theodo died 716 and # 13 Fara died 611. The two dates cannot be reconciled.

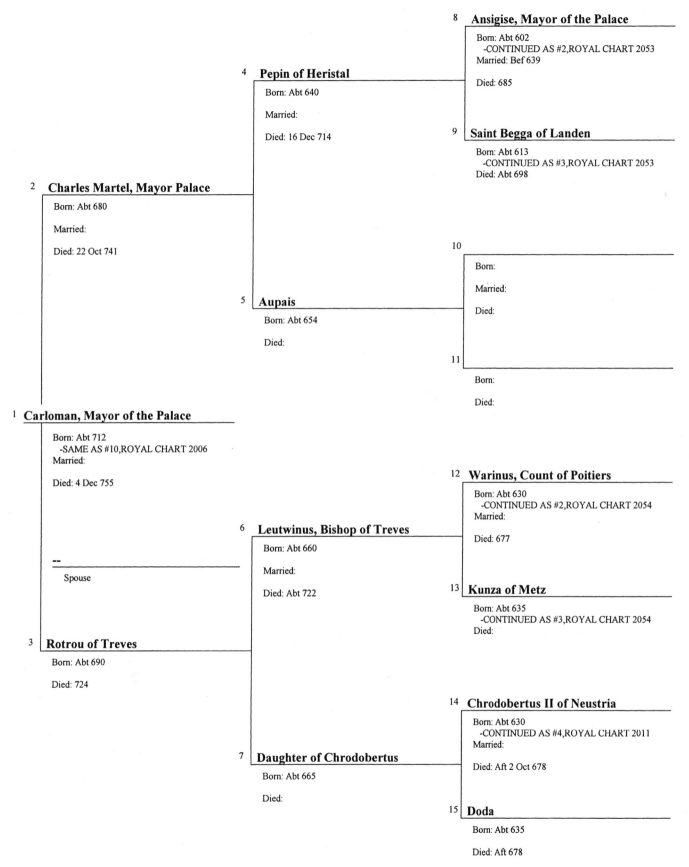

8 **Ansigise, Mayor of the Palace**

Born: Abt 602
-CONTINUED AS #2,ROYAL CHART 2053
Married: Bef 639

Died: 685

4 **Pepin of Heristal**

Born: Abt 640

Married:

Died: 16 Dec 714

9 **Saint Begga of Landen**

Born: Abt 613
-CONTINUED AS #3,ROYAL CHART 2053
Died: Abt 698

2 **Charles Martel, Mayor Palace**

Born: Abt 680

Married:

Died: 22 Oct 741

10

Born:

Married:

Died:

5 **Aupais**

Born: Abt 654

Died:

11

Born:

Died:

1 **Carloman, Mayor of the Palace**

Born: Abt 712
-SAME AS #10,ROYAL CHART 2006
Married:

Died: 4 Dec 755

12 **Warinus, Count of Poitiers**

Born: Abt 630
-CONTINUED AS #2,ROYAL CHART 2054
Married:

Died: 677

6 **Leutwinus, Bishop of Treves**

Born: Abt 660

Married:

Died: Abt 722

13 **Kunza of Metz**

Born: Abt 635
-CONTINUED AS #3,ROYAL CHART 2054
Died:

--

Spouse

3 **Rotrou of Treves**

Born: Abt 690

Died: 724

14 **Chrodobertus II of Neustria**

Born: Abt 630
-CONTINUED AS #4,ROYAL CHART 2011
Married:

Died: Aft 2 Oct 678

7 **Daughter of Chrodobertus**

Born: Abt 665

Died:

15 **Doda**

Born: Abt 635

Died: Aft 678

Sources include: *Royal Ancestors* (1989), charts 11725, 11701-02; *Ancestral Roots* 191; Stuart 269; Moriarty 5 (#2 & 3 ancestry).

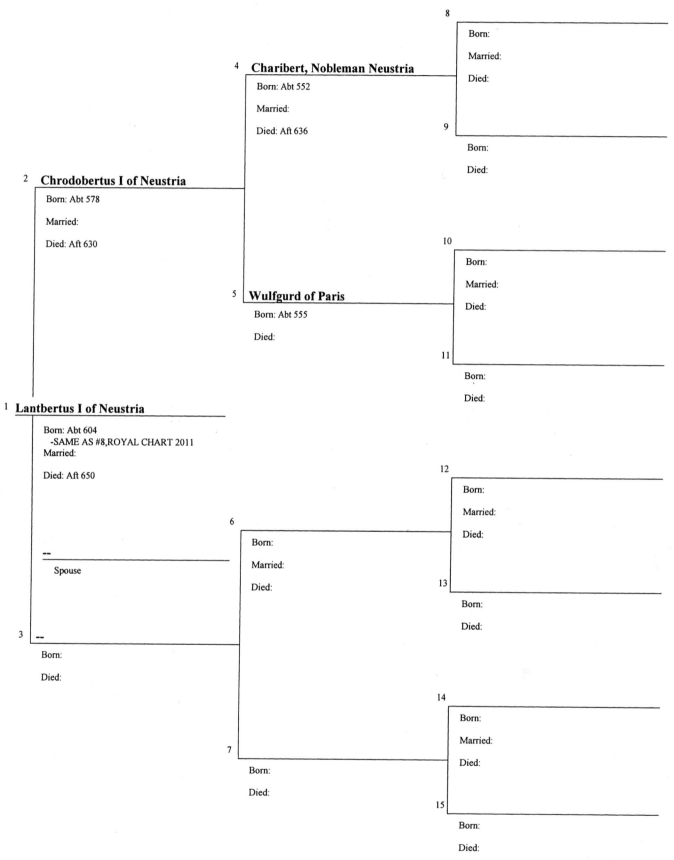

4 Charibert, Nobleman Neustria

Born: Abt 552

Married:

Died: Aft 636

8

Born:

Married:

Died:

9

Born:

Died:

2 Chrodobertus I of Neustria

Born: Abt 578

Married:

Died: Aft 630

5 Wulfgurd of Paris

Born: Abt 555

Died:

10

Born:

Married:

Died:

11

Born:

Died:

1 Lantbertus I of Neustria

Born: Abt 604
    -SAME AS #8,ROYAL CHART 2011
Married:

Died: Aft 650

--
    Spouse

3 --

Born:

Died:

6

Born:

Married:

Died:

12

Born:

Married:

Died:

13

Born:

Died:

7

Born:

Died:

14

Born:

Married:

Died:

15

Born:

Died:

Sources include: Stuart 169; *Royal Ancestors* (1989), chart 11724; Moriarty 281.

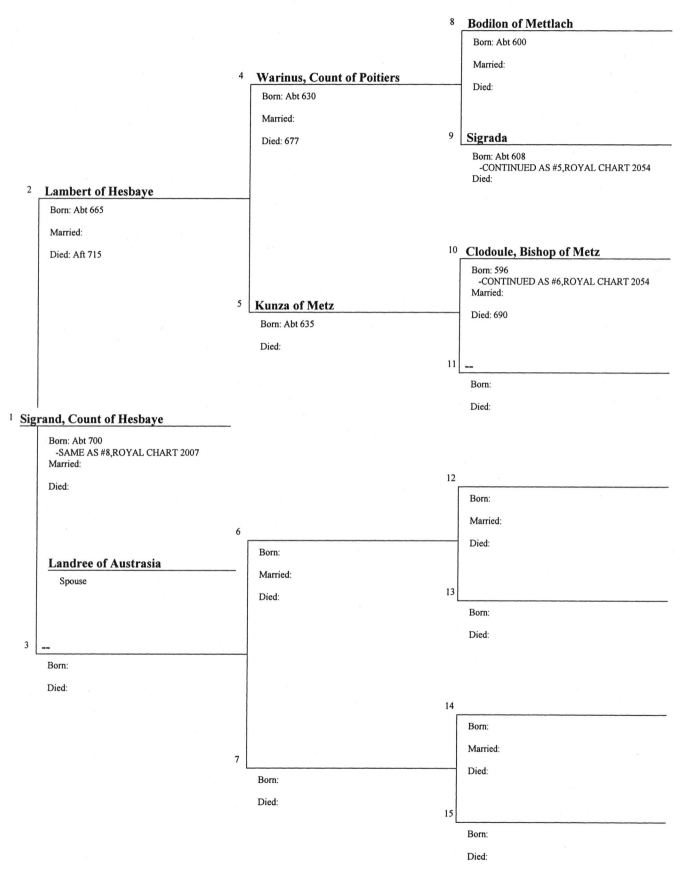

8 **Bodilon of Mettlach**

Born: Abt 600

Married:

Died:

4 **Warinus, Count of Poitiers**

Born: Abt 630

Married:

Died: 677

9 **Sigrada**

Born: Abt 608
   -CONTINUED AS #5,ROYAL CHART 2054
Died:

2 **Lambert of Hesbaye**

Born: Abt 665

Married:

Died: Aft 715

10 **Clodoule, Bishop of Metz**

Born: 596
   -CONTINUED AS #6,ROYAL CHART 2054
Married:

Died: 690

5 **Kunza of Metz**

Born: Abt 635

Died:

11 **--**

Born:

Died:

1 **Sigrand, Count of Hesbaye**

Born: Abt 700
   -SAME AS #8,ROYAL CHART 2007
Married:

Died:

12

Born:

Married:

Died:

6

Born:

Married:

Died:

13

Born:

Died:

Landree of Austrasia

Spouse

3 **--**

Born:

Died:

14

Born:

Married:

Died:

7

Born:

Died:

15

Born:

Died:

Sources include: Moriarty 20, 1; Stuart 352-24, 53.

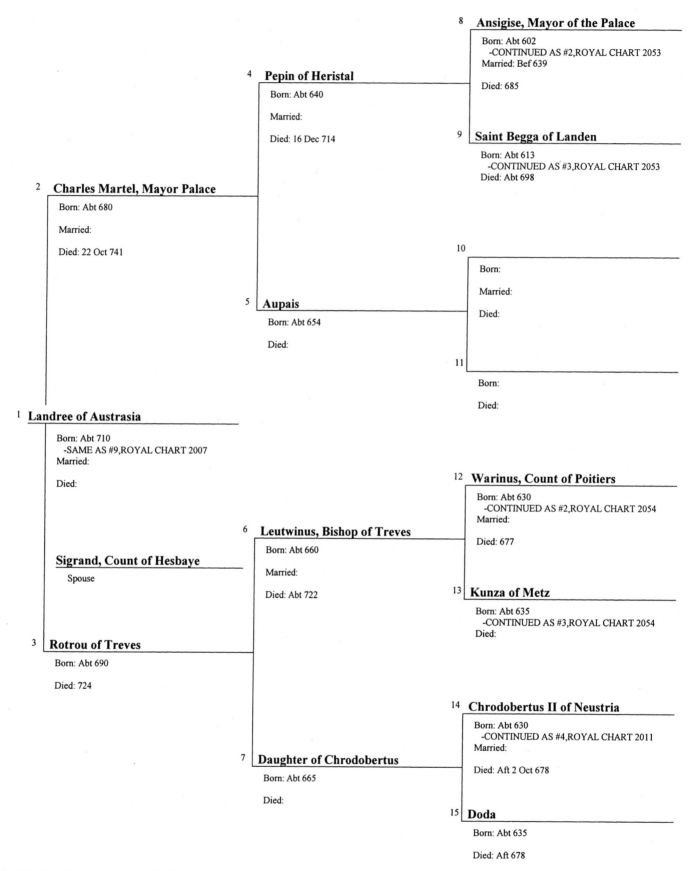

8 Ansigise, Mayor of the Palace

Born: Abt 602
-CONTINUED AS #2,ROYAL CHART 2053
Married: Bef 639

Died: 685

4 Pepin of Heristal

Born: Abt 640

Married:

Died: 16 Dec 714

9 Saint Begga of Landen

Born: Abt 613
-CONTINUED AS #3,ROYAL CHART 2053
Died: Abt 698

2 Charles Martel, Mayor Palace

Born: Abt 680

Married:

Died: 22 Oct 741

10

Born:

Married:

Died:

5 Aupais

Born: Abt 654

Died:

11

Born:

Died:

1 Landree of Austrasia

Born: Abt 710
-SAME AS #9,ROYAL CHART 2007
Married:

Died:

12 Warinus, Count of Poitiers

Born: Abt 630
-CONTINUED AS #2,ROYAL CHART 2054
Married:

Died: 677

6 Leutwinus, Bishop of Treves

Born: Abt 660

Married:

Died: Abt 722

13 Kunza of Metz

Born: Abt 635
-CONTINUED AS #3,ROYAL CHART 2054
Died:

Sigrand, Count of Hesbaye

Spouse

3 Rotrou of Treves

Born: Abt 690

Died: 724

14 Chrodobertus II of Neustria

Born: Abt 630
-CONTINUED AS #4,ROYAL CHART 2011
Married:

Died: Aft 2 Oct 678

7 Daughter of Chrodobertus

Born: Abt 665

Died:

15 Doda

Born: Abt 635

Died: Aft 678

Sources include: Moriarty 20, 5; Stuart 352, 171.

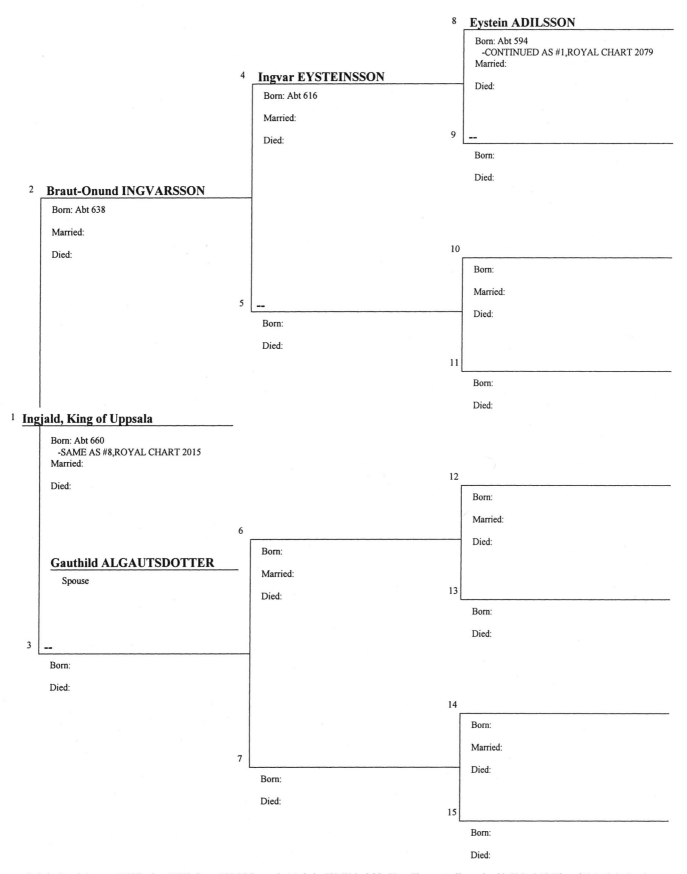

8 Eystein ADILSSON

Born: Abt 594
-CONTINUED AS #1, ROYAL CHART 2079
Married:

Died:

4 Ingvar EYSTEINSSON

Born: Abt 616

Married:

Died:

9 --

Born:

Died:

2 Braut-Onund INGVARSSON

Born: Abt 638

Married:

Died:

10

Born:

Married:

Died:

5 --

Born:

Died:

11

Born:

Died:

1 Ingjald, King of Uppsala

Born: Abt 660
-SAME AS #8, ROYAL CHART 2015
Married:

Died:

12

Born:

Married:

Died:

6

Born:

Married:

Died:

13

Born:

Died:

Gauthild ALGAUTSDOTTER

Spouse

3 --

Born:

Died:

14

Born:

Married:

Died:

7

Born:

Died:

15

Born:

Died:

Sources include: *Royal Ancestors* (1989), chart 11703; Stuart 166; LDS records; Moriarity 170 (#1 Ingjald). Note: The proven line ends with #1 Ingjald, King of Uppsala in Sweden, whose descendants ruled in Norway. Moriarty ends the line with #1. The line beyond that point is given as commonly accepted, but it relies heavily on tradition, is undocumentable, and is probably not entirely correct. The tight chronology required is not credible.

Pedigree Chart

Chart 2064

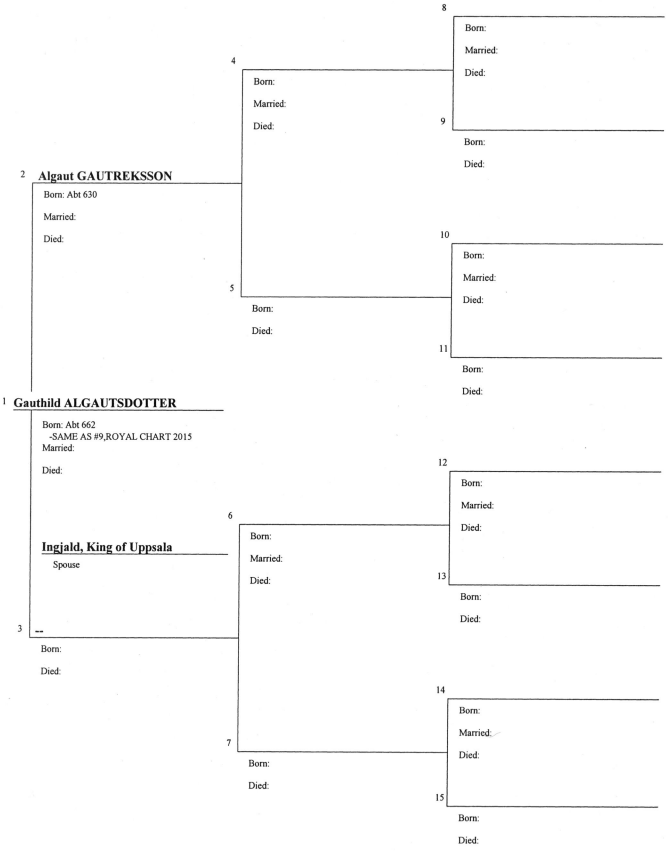

8

Born:

Married:

Died:

4

Born:

Married:

Died:

9

Born:

Died:

2 Algaut GAUTREKSSON

Born: Abt 630

Married:

Died:

10

Born:

Married:

Died:

5

Born:

Died:

11

Born:

Died:

1 Gauthild ALGAUTSDOTTER

Born: Abt 662
  -SAME AS #9,ROYAL CHART 2015
Married:

Died:

12

Born:

Married:

Died:

Ingjald, King of Uppsala

Spouse

6

Born:

Married:

Died:

13

Born:

Died:

3 --

Born:

Died:

14

Born:

Married:

Died:

7

Born:

Died:

15

Born:

Died:

Sources include: *Royal Ancestors* (1989), chart 11703; Stuart 166-43; Moriarty 170.

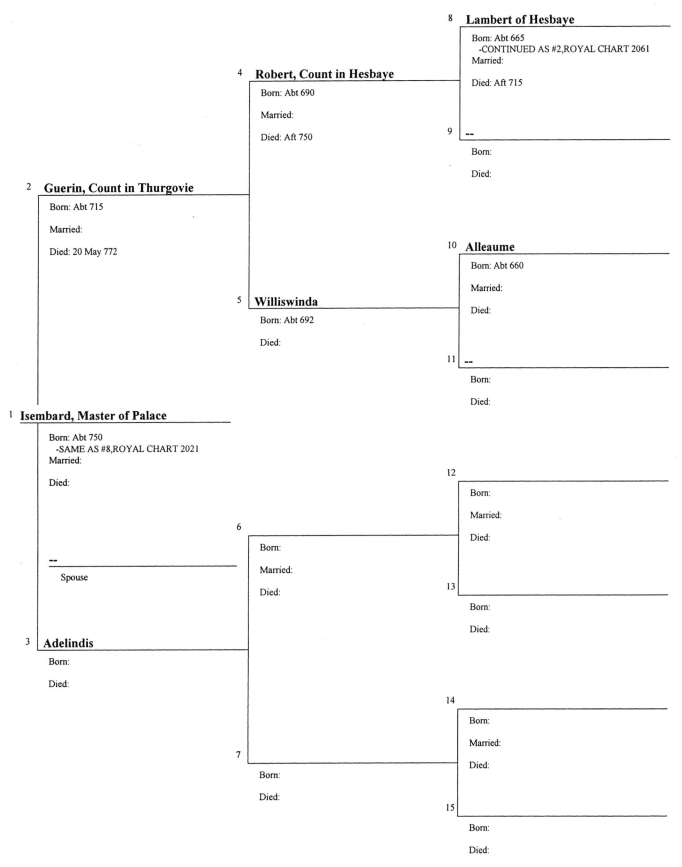

8 Lambert of Hesbaye

Born: Abt 665
  -CONTINUED AS #2,ROYAL CHART 2061
Married:

Died: Aft 715

9 --

Born:

Died:

4 Robert, Count in Hesbaye

Born: Abt 690

Married:

Died: Aft 750

2 Guerin, Count in Thurgovie

Born: Abt 715

Married:

Died: 20 May 772

10 Alleaume

Born: Abt 660

Married:

Died:

11 --

Born:

Died:

5 Williswinda

Born: Abt 692

Died:

1 Isembard, Master of Palace

Born: Abt 750
  -SAME AS #8,ROYAL CHART 2021
Married:

Died:

--

Spouse

12

Born:

Married:

Died:

6

Born:

Married:

Died:

13

Born:

Died:

3 Adelindis

Born:

Died:

14

Born:

Married:

Died:

7

Born:

Died:

15

Born:

Died:

Sources include: Stuart 345, 53; Moriarty 1.

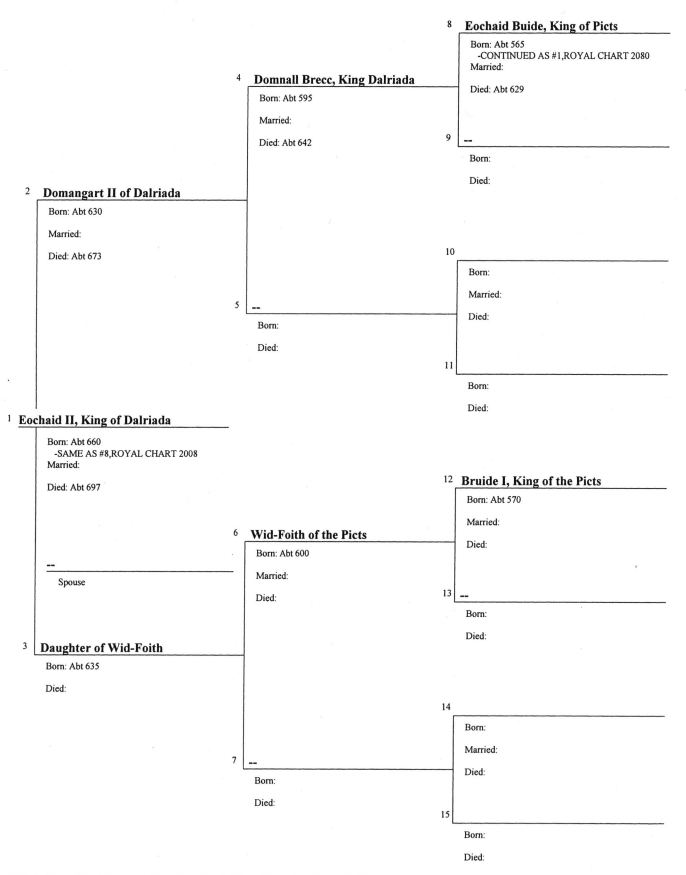

8 Eochaid Buide, King of Picts

Born: Abt 565
-CONTINUED AS #1,ROYAL CHART 2080
Married:

Died: Abt 629

4 Domnall Brecc, King Dalriada

Born: Abt 595

Married:

Died: Abt 642

9 --

Born:

Died:

2 Domangart II of Dalriada

Born: Abt 630

Married:

Died: Abt 673

10

Born:

Married:

Died:

5 --

Born:

Died:

11

Born:

Died:

1 Eochaid II, King of Dalriada

Born: Abt 660
-SAME AS #8,ROYAL CHART 2008
Married:

Died: Abt 697

12 Bruide I, King of the Picts

Born: Abt 570

Married:

Died:

6 Wid-Foith of the Picts

Born: Abt 600

Married:

Died:

13 --

Born:

Died:

--

Spouse

14

Born:

Married:

Died:

3 Daughter of Wid-Foith

Born: Abt 635

Died:

7 --

Born:

Died:

15

Born:

Died:

Sources include: *Royal Ancestors* (1989), chart 11729; *Ancestral Roots* 170; Stuart 165; Moriarty 29.

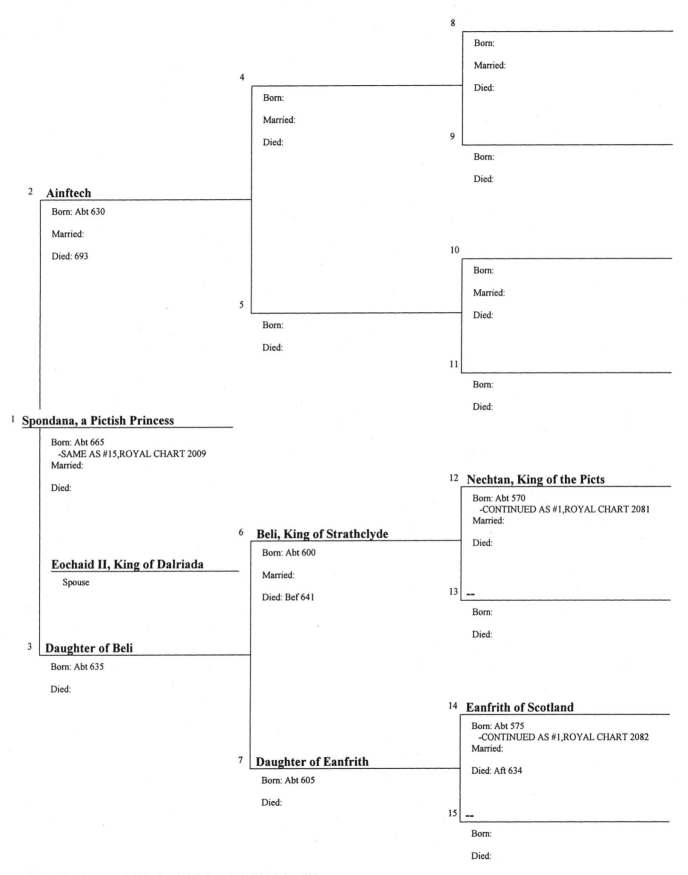

8
Born:
Married:
Died:

9
Born:
Died:

4
Born:
Married:
Died:

2 Ainftech
Born: Abt 630
Married:
Died: 693

10
Born:
Married:
Died:

11
Born:
Died:

5
Born:
Died:

1 Spondana, a Pictish Princess
Born: Abt 665
    -SAME AS #15,ROYAL CHART 2009
Married:
Died:

12 Nechtan, King of the Picts
Born: Abt 570
    -CONTINUED AS #1,ROYAL CHART 2081
Married:
Died:

13 --
Born:
Died:

6 Beli, King of Strathclyde
Born: Abt 600
Married:
Died: Bef 641

Eochaid II, King of Dalriada
    Spouse

3 Daughter of Beli
Born: Abt 635
Died:

14 Eanfrith of Scotland
Born: Abt 575
    -CONTINUED AS #1,ROYAL CHART 2082
Married:
Died: Aft 634

15 --
Born:
Died:

7 Daughter of Eanfrith
Born: Abt 605
Died:

Sources include: *Royal Ancestors* (1989), chart 11859; Stuart 341, 406; Moriarty 279.

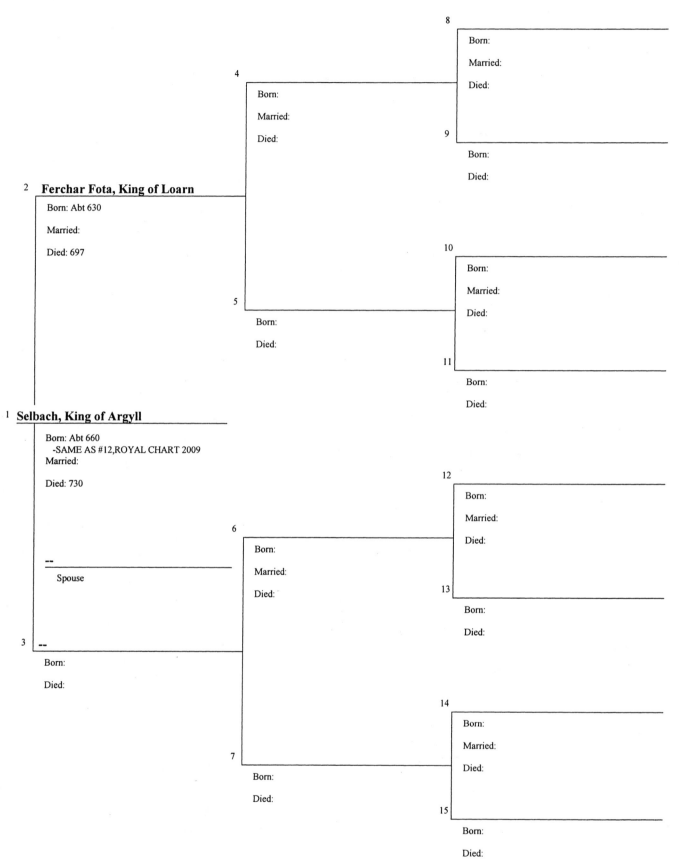

8

Born:

Married:

Died:

4

Born:

Married:

Died:

9

Born:

Died:

2 **Ferchar Fota, King of Loarn**

Born: Abt 630

Married:

Died: 697

10

Born:

Married:

Died:

5

Born:

Died:

11

Born:

Died:

1 **Selbach, King of Argyll**

Born: Abt 660
-SAME AS #12,ROYAL CHART 2009
Married:

Died: 730

12

Born:

Married:

Died:

6

Born:

Married:

Died:

13

Born:

Died:

--
Spouse

3 --

Born:

Died:

14

Born:

Married:

Died:

7

Born:

Died:

15

Born:

Died:

Sources include: *Royal Ancestors* (1989), chart 11800; Stuart 355; Moriarty 278.

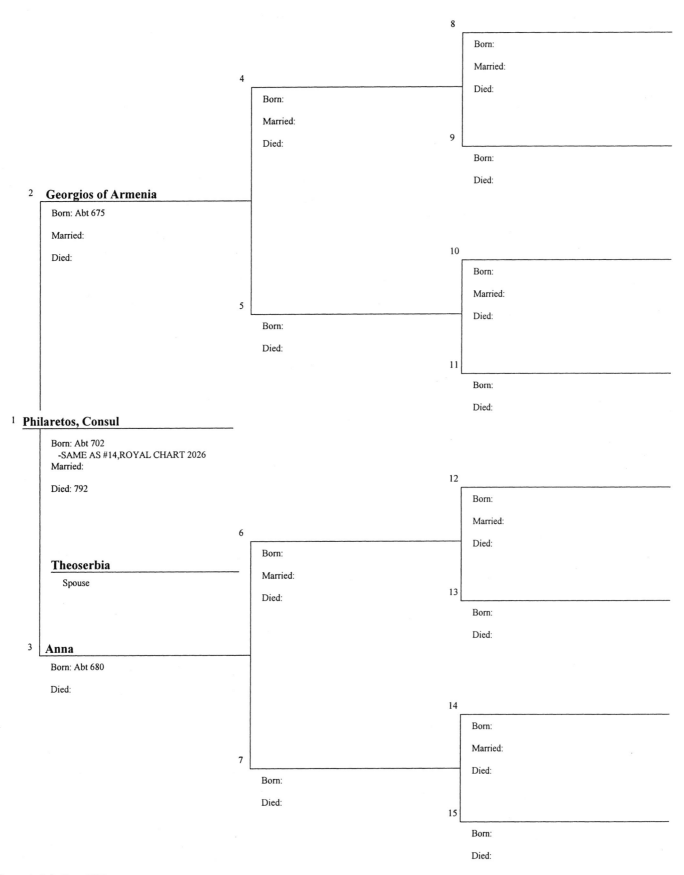

8

Born:

Married:

Died:

4

Born:

Married:

Died:

9

Born:

Died:

2 **Georgios of Armenia**

Born: Abt 675

Married:

Died:

10

Born:

Married:

Died:

5

Born:

Died:

11

Born:

Died:

1 **Philaretos, Consul**

Born: Abt 702
   -SAME AS #14,ROYAL CHART 2026
Married:

Died: 792

12

Born:

Married:

Died:

6

Born:

Married:

Died:

13

Born:

Died:

Theoserbia

Spouse

3 **Anna**

Born: Abt 680

Died:

14

Born:

Married:

Died:

7

Born:

Died:

15

Born:

Died:

Sources include: Stuart 322A.

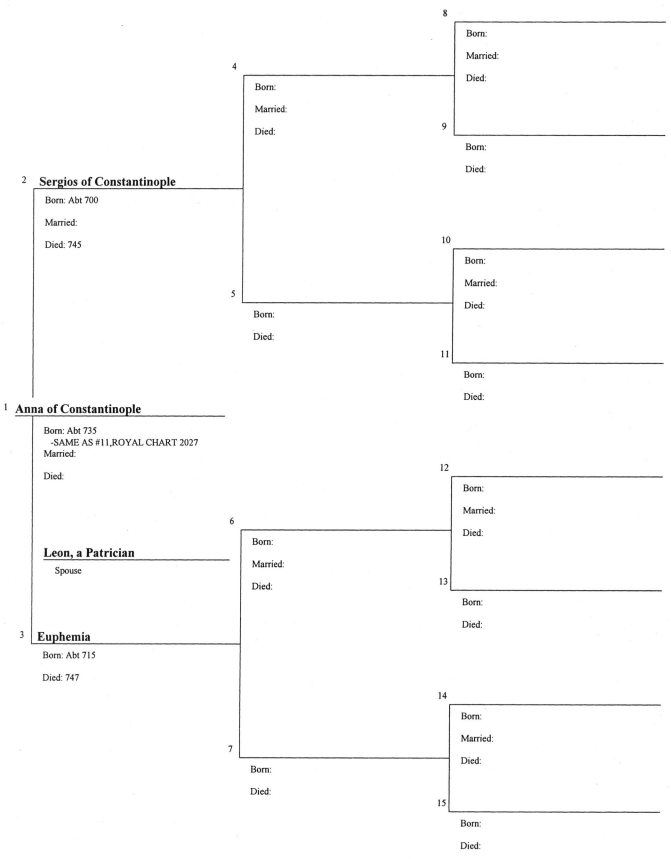

8

Born:

Married:

Died:

4

Born:

Married:

Died:

9

Born:

Died:

2 Sergios of Constantinople

Born: Abt 700

Married:

Died: 745

10

Born:

Married:

Died:

5

Born:

Died:

11

Born:

Died:

1 Anna of Constantinople

Born: Abt 735
  -SAME AS #11,ROYAL CHART 2027
Married:

Died:

12

Born:

Married:

Died:

6

Born:

Married:

Died:

13

Born:

Died:

Leon, a Patrician

Spouse

3 Euphemia

Born: Abt 715

Died: 747

14

Born:

Married:

Died:

7

Born:

Died:

15

Born:

Died:

Sources include: Stuart 322A-44.

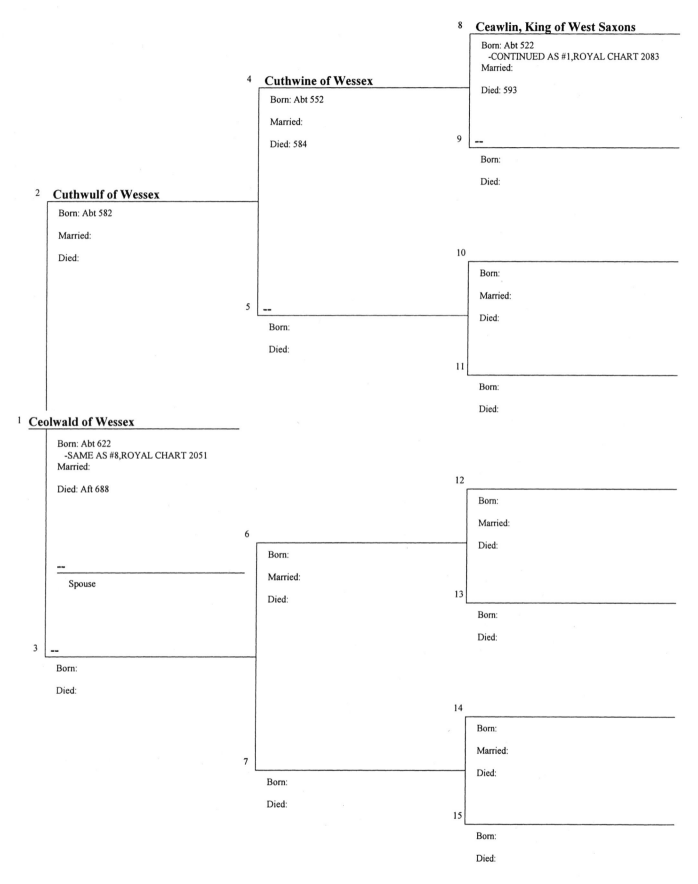

8 **Ceawlin, King of West Saxons**

Born: Abt 522
   -CONTINUED AS #1,ROYAL CHART 2083
Married:

Died: 593

4 **Cuthwine of Wessex**

Born: Abt 552

Married:

Died: 584

9 --

Born:

Died:

2 **Cuthwulf of Wessex**

Born: Abt 582

Married:

Died:

10

Born:

Married:

Died:

5 --

Born:

Died:

11

Born:

Died:

1 **Ceolwald of Wessex**

Born: Abt 622
   -SAME AS #8,ROYAL CHART 2051
Married:

Died: Aft 688

12

Born:

Married:

Died:

6

Born:

Married:

Died:

13

Born:

Died:

--

Spouse

3 --

Born:

Died:

14

Born:

Married:

Died:

7

Born:

Died:

15

Born:

Died:

Sources include: *Royal Ancestors* (1989), chart 11715; Stuart 233; *Ancestral Roots* 1; Moriarty 15.

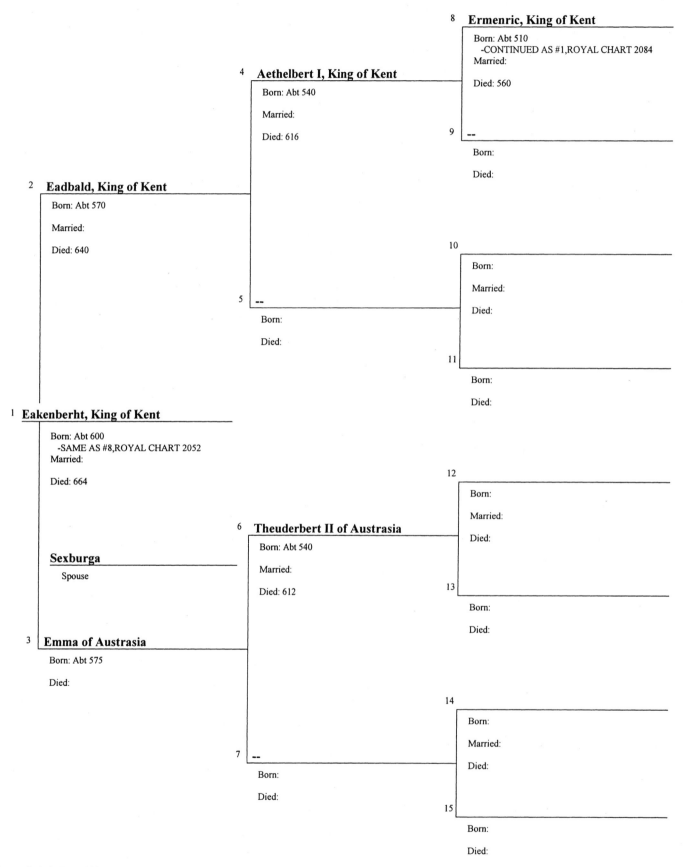

8   Ermenric, King of Kent

Born: Abt 510
-CONTINUED AS #1,ROYAL CHART 2084
Married:

Died: 560

4   Aethelbert I, King of Kent

Born: Abt 540

Married:

Died: 616

9 --

Born:

Died:

2   Eadbald, King of Kent

Born: Abt 570

Married:

Died: 640

10

Born:

Married:

Died:

5 --

Born:

Died:

11

Born:

Died:

1   Eakenberht, King of Kent

Born: Abt 600
-SAME AS #8,ROYAL CHART 2052
Married:

Died: 664

Sexburga

Spouse

12

Born:

Married:

Died:

6   Theuderbert II of Austrasia

Born: Abt 540

Married:

Died: 612

13

Born:

Died:

3   Emma of Austrasia

Born: Abt 575

Died:

14

Born:

Married:

Died:

7 --

Born:

Died:

15

Born:

Died:

Sources include: Stuart 233A.

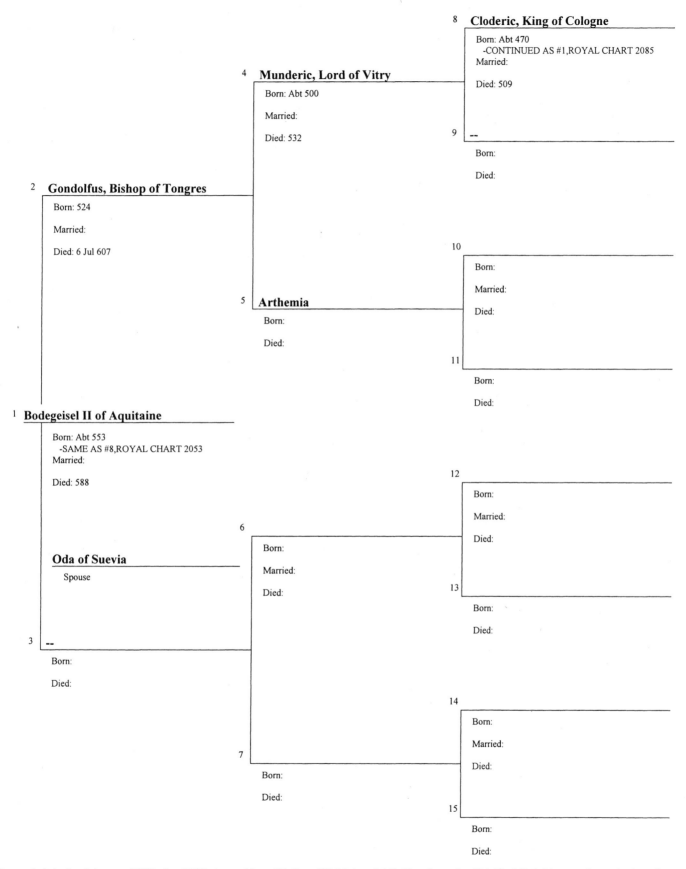

8 Cloderic, King of Cologne

Born: Abt 470
-CONTINUED AS #1,ROYAL CHART 2085
Married:

Died: 509

4 Munderic, Lord of Vitry

Born: Abt 500

Married:

Died: 532

9 --

Born:

Died:

2 Gondolfus, Bishop of Tongres

Born: 524

Married:

Died: 6 Jul 607

10

Born:

Married:

Died:

5 Arthemia

Born:

Died:

11

Born:

Died:

1 Bodegeisel II of Aquitaine

Born: Abt 553
-SAME AS #8,ROYAL CHART 2053
Married:

Died: 588

12

Born:

Married:

Died:

6

Born:

Married:

Died:

13

Born:

Died:

Oda of Suevia

Spouse

3 --

Born:

Died:

14

Born:

Married:

Died:

7

Born:

Died:

15

Born:

Died:

Sources include: *Royal Ancestors* (1989), chart 11968; *Ancestral Roots* 190; Stuart 171; Moriarty 5, 241. Note: Stuart gives #9 (wife of Cloderic) as an unknown daughter of Agilolfinges. *Ancestral Roots* states that the identity of #9 is unknown.

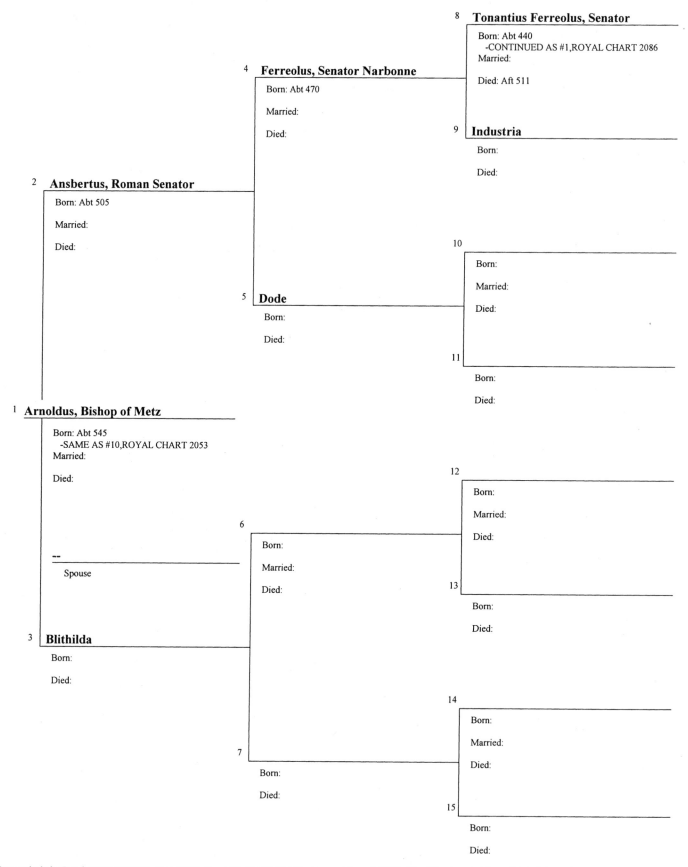

8 **Tonantius Ferreolus, Senator**

Born: Abt 440
-CONTINUED AS #1,ROYAL CHART 2086
Married:

Died: Aft 511

4 **Ferreolus, Senator Narbonne**

Born: Abt 470

Married:

Died:

9 **Industria**

Born:

Died:

2 **Ansbertus, Roman Senator**

Born: Abt 505

Married:

Died:

10

Born:

Married:

Died:

5 **Dode**

Born:

Died:

11

Born:

Died:

1 **Arnoldus, Bishop of Metz**

Born: Abt 545
-SAME AS #10,ROYAL CHART 2053
Married:

Died:

12

Born:

Married:

Died:

6

Born:

Married:

Died:

13

Born:

Died:

--

Spouse

3 **Blithilda**

Born:

Died:

14

Born:

Married:

Died:

7

Born:

Died:

15

Born:

Died:

Sources include: *Royal Ancestors* (1989), chart 11726; Stuart 171-46, 260-46, 236; *Ancestral Roots* 8 (2004), Line 180; *Ancestral Roots* 190-9, 180; Moriarty 7-8.

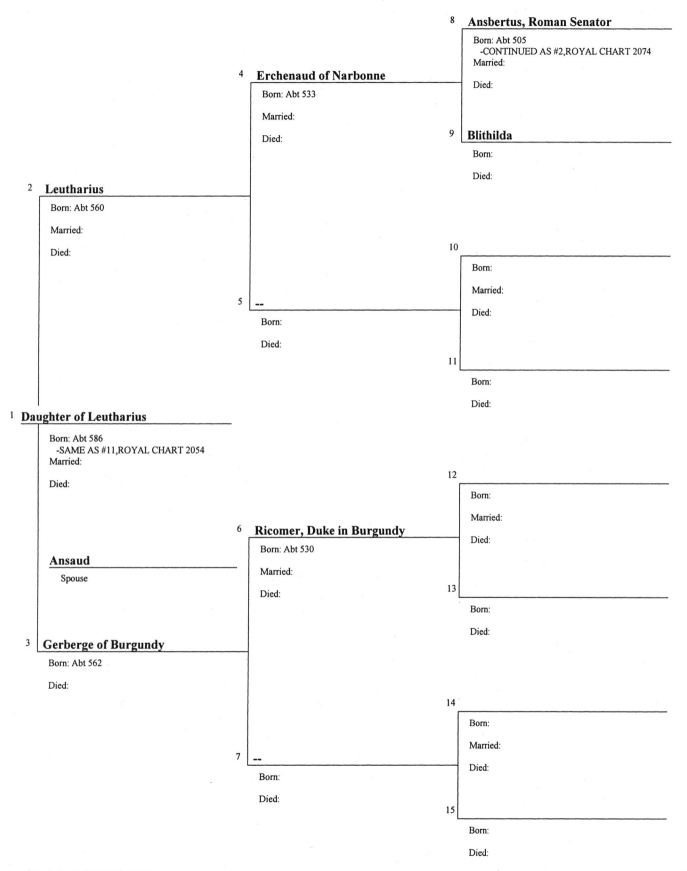

8 Ansbertus, Roman Senator

Born: Abt 505
   -CONTINUED AS #2,ROYAL CHART 2074
Married:

Died:

9 Blithilda

Born:

Died:

4 Erchenaud of Narbonne

Born: Abt 533

Married:

Died:

10

Born:

Married:

Died:

11

Born:

Died:

2 Leutharius

Born: Abt 560

Married:

Died:

5 --

Born:

Died:

1 Daughter of Leutharius

Born: Abt 586
   -SAME AS #11,ROYAL CHART 2054
Married:

Died:

Ansaud

Spouse

12

Born:

Married:

Died:

13

Born:

Died:

6 Ricomer, Duke in Burgundy

Born: Abt 530

Married:

Died:

3 Gerberge of Burgundy

Born: Abt 562

Died:

14

Born:

Married:

Died:

15

Born:

Died:

7 --

Born:

Died:

Sources include: Stuart 236; Moriarty 7-8.

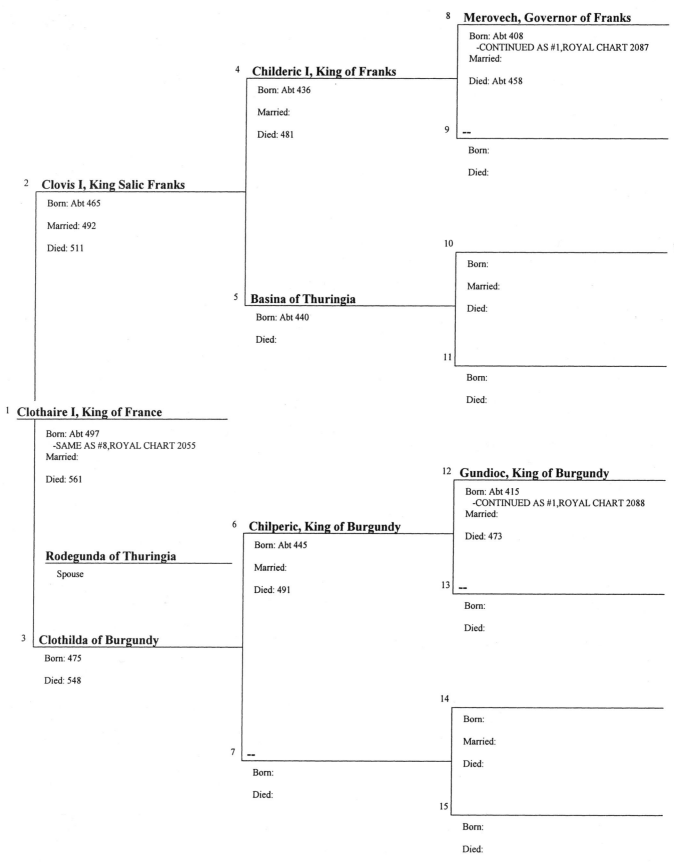

8 Merovech, Governor of Franks

Born: Abt 408
-CONTINUED AS #1,ROYAL CHART 2087
Married:

Died: Abt 458

4 Childeric I, King of Franks

Born: Abt 436

Married:

Died: 481

9 --

Born:

Died:

2 Clovis I, King Salic Franks

Born: Abt 465

Married: 492

Died: 511

10

Born:

Married:

Died:

5 Basina of Thuringia

Born: Abt 440

Died:

11

Born:

Died:

1 Clothaire I, King of France

Born: Abt 497
-SAME AS #8,ROYAL CHART 2055
Married:

Died: 561

Rodegunda of Thuringia

Spouse

12 Gundioc, King of Burgundy

Born: Abt 415
-CONTINUED AS #1,ROYAL CHART 2088
Married:

Died: 473

6 Chilperic, King of Burgundy

Born: Abt 445

Married:

Died: 491

13 --

Born:

Died:

3 Clothilda of Burgundy

Born: 475

Died: 548

14

Born:

Married:

Died:

7 --

Born:

Died:

15

Born:

Died:

Sources include: Stuart 303, 349; Turton 54. Note: The ancestry shown for #6 Chilperic is tentative.

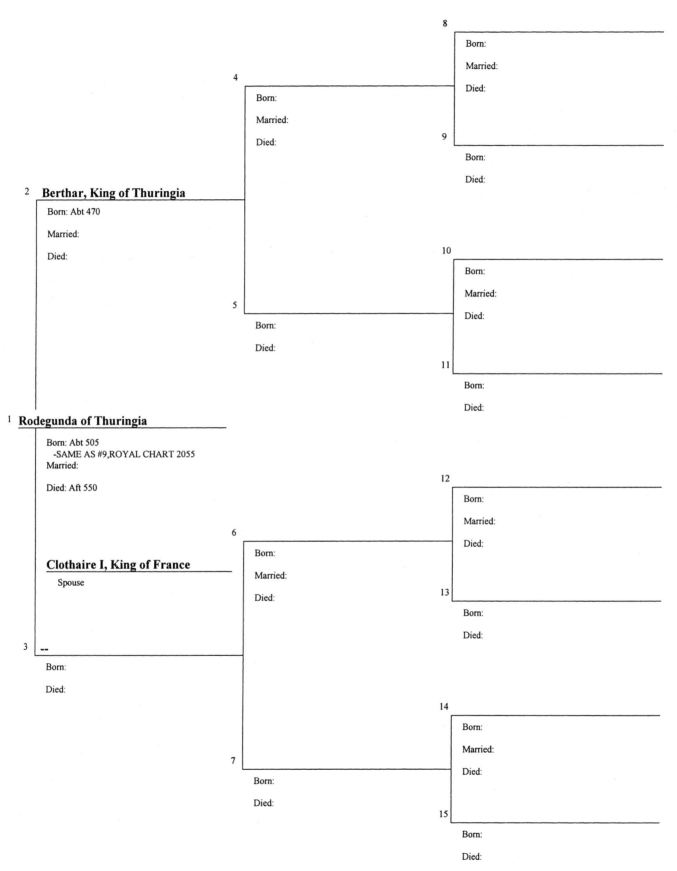

2 Berthar, King of Thuringia
Born: Abt 470
Married:
Died:

4
Born:
Married:
Died:

8
Born:
Married:
Died:

9
Born:
Died:

5
Born:
Died:

10
Born:
Married:
Died:

11
Born:
Died:

1 Rodegunda of Thuringia
Born: Abt 505
  -SAME AS #9,ROYAL CHART 2055
Married:

Died: Aft 550

Clothaire I, King of France
Spouse

3 --
Born:
Died:

6
Born:
Married:
Died:

12
Born:
Married:
Died:

13
Born:
Died:

7
Born:
Died:

14
Born:
Married:
Died:

15
Born:
Died:

Sources include: Stuart 303-50.

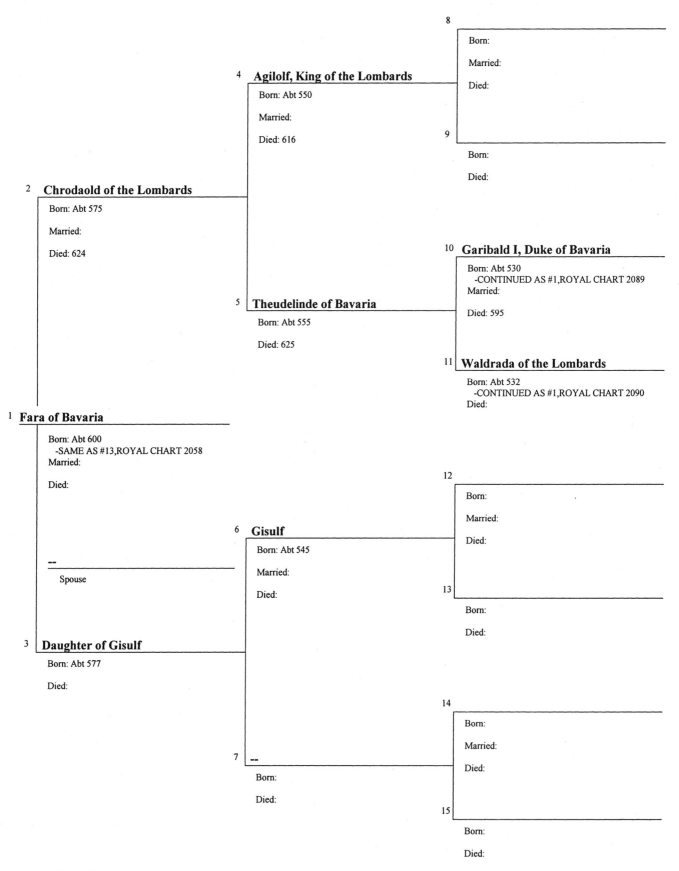

8

Born:

Married:

Died:

---

4 Agilolf, King of the Lombards

Born: Abt 550

Married:

Died: 616

9

Born:

Died:

---

2 Chrodaold of the Lombards

Born: Abt 575

Married:

Died: 624

---

10 Garibald I, Duke of Bavaria

Born: Abt 530
    -CONTINUED AS #1,ROYAL CHART 2089
Married:

Died: 595

---

5 Theudelinde of Bavaria

Born: Abt 555

Died: 625

11 Waldrada of the Lombards

Born: Abt 532
    -CONTINUED AS #1,ROYAL CHART 2090
Died:

---

1 Fara of Bavaria

Born: Abt 600
    -SAME AS #13,ROYAL CHART 2058
Married:

Died:

--
Spouse

12

Born:

Married:

Died:

---

6 Gisulf

Born: Abt 545

Married:

Died:

13

Born:

Died:

---

3 Daughter of Gisulf

Born: Abt 577

Died:

14

Born:

Married:

Died:

---

7 --

Born:

Died:

15

Born:

Died:

Sources include: Stuart 262.

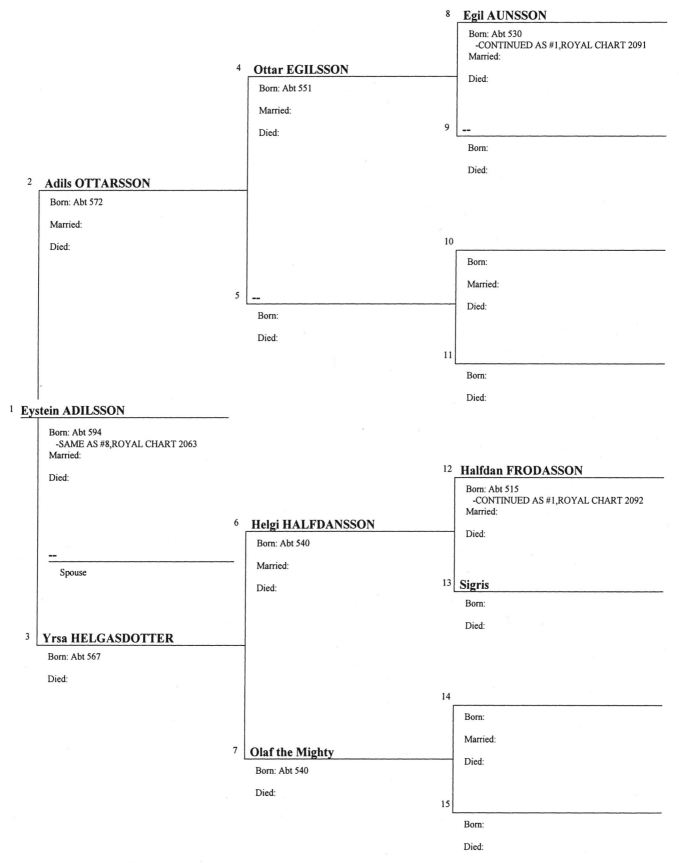

8 Egil AUNSSON

Born: Abt 530
   -CONTINUED AS #1,ROYAL CHART 2091
Married:

Died:

4 Ottar EGILSSON

Born: Abt 551

Married:

Died:

9 --

Born:

Died:

2 Adils OTTARSSON

Born: Abt 572

Married:

Died:

10

Born:

Married:

Died:

5 --

Born:

Died:

11

Born:

Died:

1 Eystein ADILSSON

Born: Abt 594
   -SAME AS #8,ROYAL CHART 2063
Married:

Died:

--

Spouse

12 Halfdan FRODASSON

Born: Abt 515
   -CONTINUED AS #1,ROYAL CHART 2092
Married:

Died:

6 Helgi HALFDANSSON

Born: Abt 540

Married:

Died:

13 Sigris

Born:

Died:

3 Yrsa HELGASDOTTER

Born: Abt 567

Died:

14

Born:

Married:

Died:

7 Olaf the Mighty

Born: Abt 540

Died:

15

Born:

Died:

Sources include: *Royal Ancestors* (1989), chart 11705; Stuart 166, 324; LDS records.

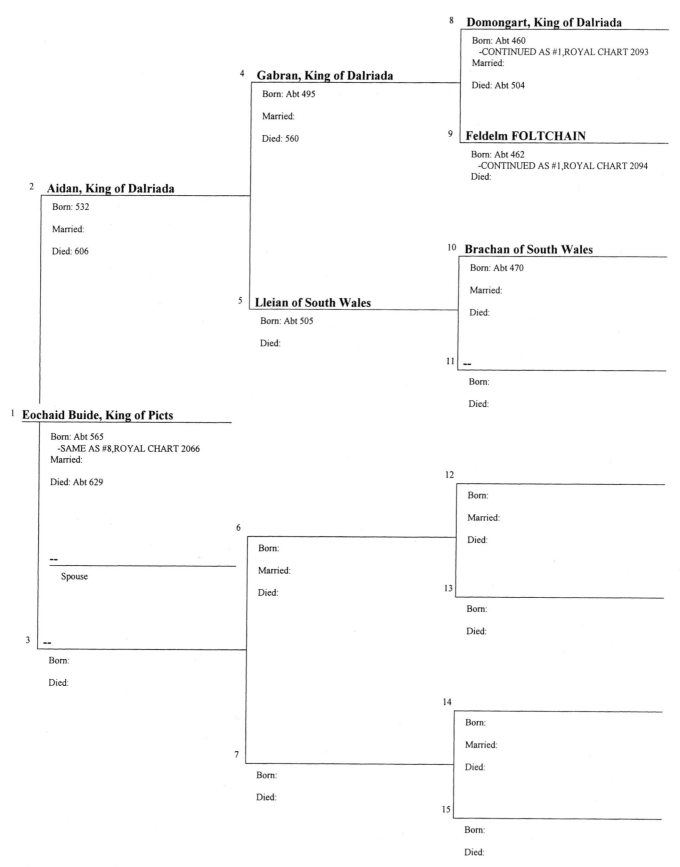

8 Domongart, King of Dalriada

Born: Abt 460
-CONTINUED AS #1,ROYAL CHART 2093
Married:

Died: Abt 504

4 Gabran, King of Dalriada

Born: Abt 495

Married:

Died: 560

9 Feldelm FOLTCHAIN

Born: Abt 462
-CONTINUED AS #1,ROYAL CHART 2094
Died:

2 Aidan, King of Dalriada

Born: 532

Married:

Died: 606

10 Brachan of South Wales

Born: Abt 470

Married:

Died:

5 Lleian of South Wales

Born: Abt 505

Died:

11 --

Born:

Died:

1 Eochaid Buide, King of Picts

Born: Abt 565
-SAME AS #8,ROYAL CHART 2066
Married:

Died: Abt 629

12

Born:

Married:

Died:

6

Born:

Married:

Died:

13

Born:

Died:

--

Spouse

3 --

Born:

Died:

14

Born:

Married:

Died:

7

Born:

Died:

15

Born:

Died:

Sources include: *Royal Ancestors* (1989), chart 11730; *Ancestral Roots* 170; Stuart 165; Moriarty 28-29.

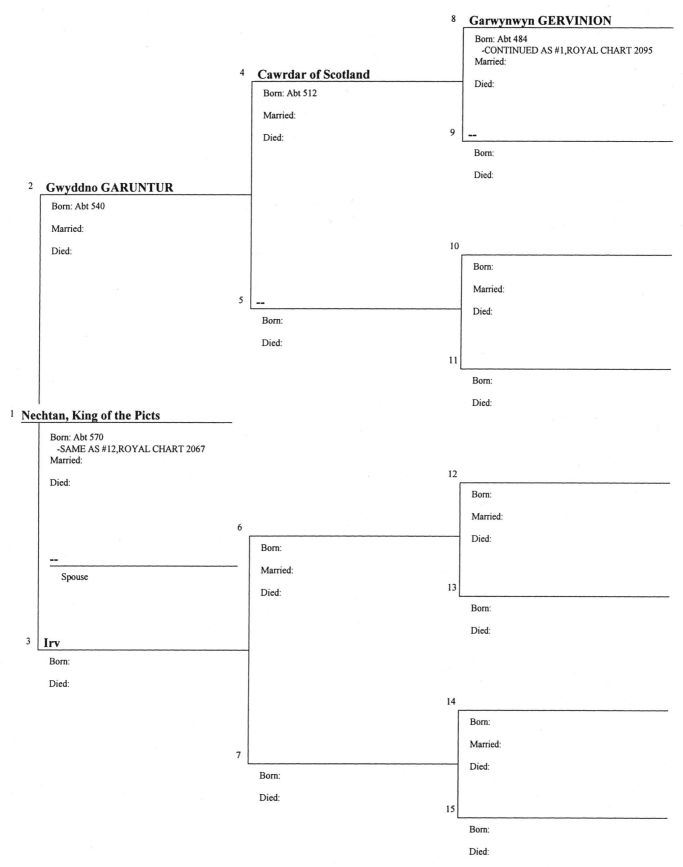

8 Garwynwyn GERVINION

Born: Abt 484
 -CONTINUED AS #1,ROYAL CHART 2095
Married:

Died:

4 Cawrdar of Scotland

Born: Abt 512

Married:

Died:

9 --

Born:

Died:

2 Gwyddno GARUNTUR

Born: Abt 540

Married:

Died:

10

Born:

Married:

Died:

5 --

Born:

Died:

11

Born:

Died:

1 Nechtan, King of the Picts

Born: Abt 570
 -SAME AS #12,ROYAL CHART 2067
Married:

Died:

12

Born:

Married:

Died:

6

Born:

Married:

Died:

13

Born:

Died:

--
    Spouse

3 Irv

Born:

Died:

14

Born:

Married:

Died:

7

Born:

Died:

15

Born:

Died:

Sources include: *Royal Ancestors* (1989), chart 11925; Stuart 341; Moriarty 279.

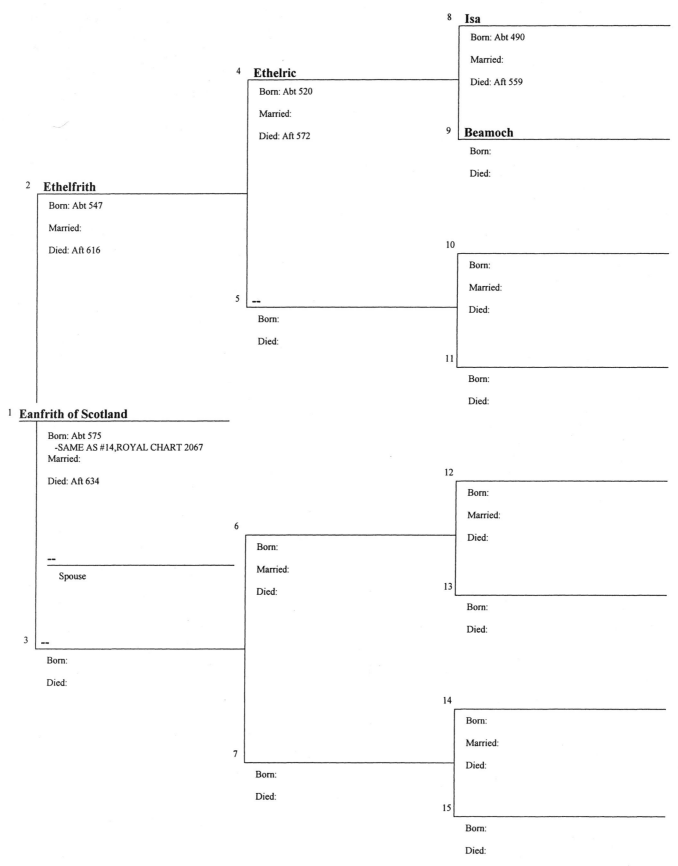

8 **Isa**
Born: Abt 490
Married:
Died: Aft 559

4 **Ethelric**
Born: Abt 520
Married:
Died: Aft 572

9 **Beamoch**
Born:
Died:

2 **Ethelfrith**
Born: Abt 547
Married:
Died: Aft 616

5 **--**
Born:
Died:

10
Born:
Married:
Died:

11
Born:
Died:

1 **Eanfrith of Scotland**
Born: Abt 575
  -SAME AS #14,ROYAL CHART 2067
Married:
Died: Aft 634

--
Spouse

6
Born:
Married:
Died:

12
Born:
Married:
Died:

13
Born:
Died:

3 **--**
Born:
Died:

7
Born:
Died:

14
Born:
Married:
Died:

15
Born:
Died:

Sources include: Stuart 406. Note: Stuart gives #8 Isa as son of Eoppa, son of Esa, son of Ingui, son of Augewit, son of Aloc, son of Benoc, son of Brand of Scandinavia (born about 271, continued chart 2098, #1). The claim fits well chronologically but cannot be proven or disproven. See note chart 2098.

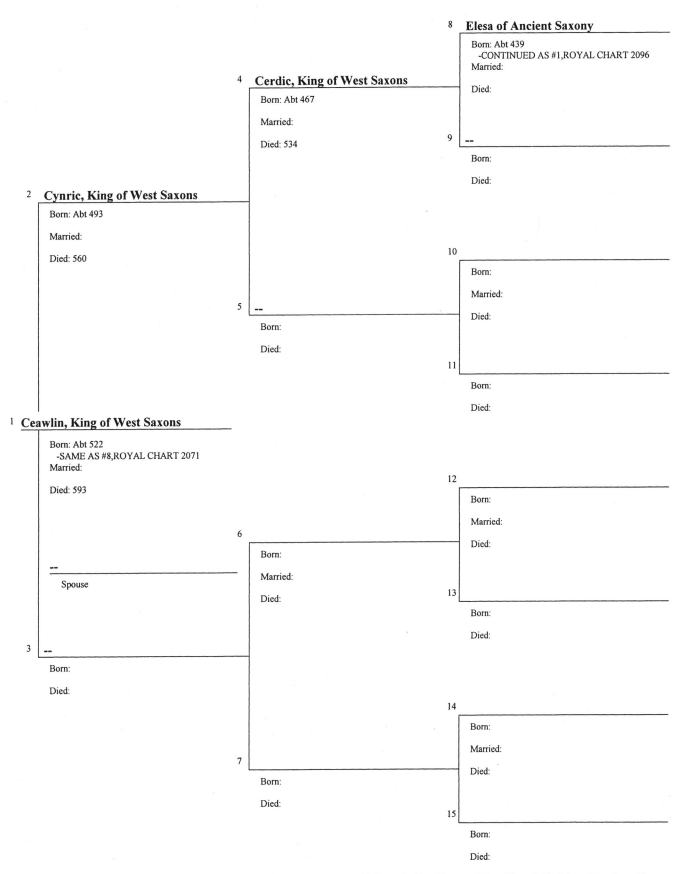

8 **Elesa of Ancient Saxony**

Born: Abt 439
  -CONTINUED AS #1,ROYAL CHART 2096
Married:

Died:

4 **Cerdic, King of West Saxons**

Born: Abt 467

Married:

Died: 534

9 --

Born:

Died:

2 **Cynric, King of West Saxons**

Born: Abt 493

Married:

Died: 560

10

Born:

Married:

Died:

5 --

Born:

Died:

11

Born:

Died:

1 **Ceawlin, King of West Saxons**

Born: Abt 522
  -SAME AS #8,ROYAL CHART 2071
Married:

Died: 593

12

Born:

Married:

Died:

6

Born:

Married:

Died:

13

Born:

Died:

--

Spouse

3 --

Born:

Died:

14

Born:

Married:

Died:

7

Born:

Died:

15

Born:

Died:

Sources include: *Royal Ancestors* (1989), chart 11716; *Ancestral Roots* 1; Stuart 233; Moriarty 15; LDS records. Note: The proved line of the early English and West Saxon kings ends with #4 Cerdic above. Moriarty ends with #8 Elesa. The line beyond that point to Odin (see chart 2098) is shown here as commonly accepted. It may be correct but cannot be proven or disproven. See additional note chart 2098.

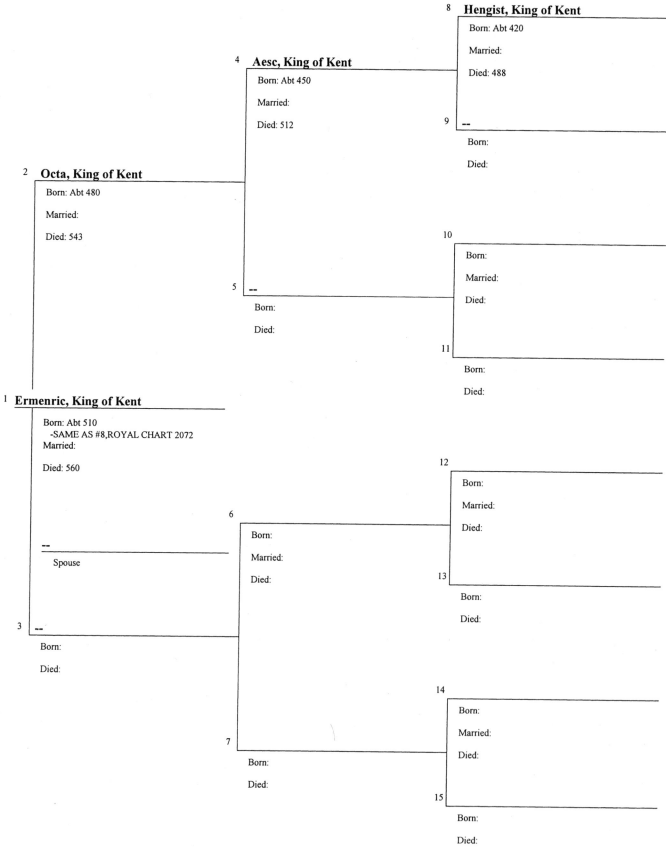

4 **Aesc, King of Kent**
Born: Abt 450
Married:
Died: 512

9 --
Born:
Died:

2 **Octa, King of Kent**
Born: Abt 480
Married:
Died: 543

10
Born:
Married:
Died:

5 --
Born:
Died:

11
Born:
Died:

1 **Ermenric, King of Kent**
Born: Abt 510
  -SAME AS #8,ROYAL CHART 2072
Married:
Died: 560

12
Born:
Married:
Died:

6
Born:
Married:
Died:

13
Born:
Died:

--
Spouse

3 --
Born:
Died:

14
Born:
Married:
Died:

7
Born:
Died:

15
Born:
Died:

Sources include: Stuart 233A.

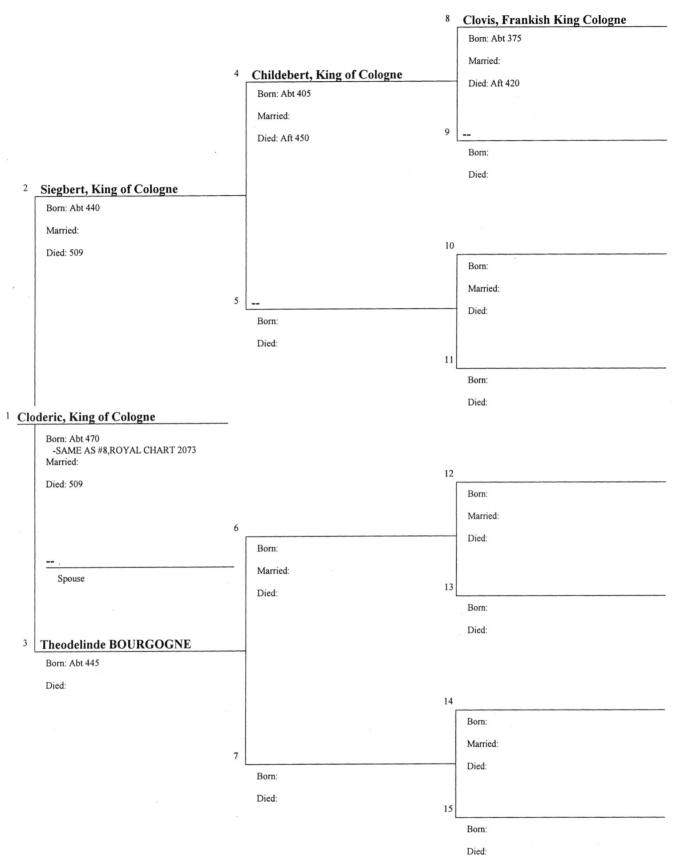

8 Clovis, Frankish King Cologne

Born: Abt 375

Married:

Died: Aft 420

4 Childebert, King of Cologne

Born: Abt 405

Married:

Died: Aft 450

9 --

Born:

Died:

2 Siegbert, King of Cologne

Born: Abt 440

Married:

Died: 509

10

Born:

Married:

Died:

5 --

Born:

Died:

11

Born:

Died:

1 Cloderic, King of Cologne

Born: Abt 470
-SAME AS #8,ROYAL CHART 2073
Married:

Died: 509

12

Born:

Married:

Died:

6

Born:

Married:

Died:

13

Born:

Died:

--

Spouse

3 Theodelinde BOURGOGNE

Born: Abt 445

Died:

14

Born:

Married:

Died:

7

Born:

Died:

15

Born:

Died:

Sources include: *Royal Ancestors* (1989), charts 11968-69; *Ancestral Roots* 190; Stuart 171; Moriarty 5.

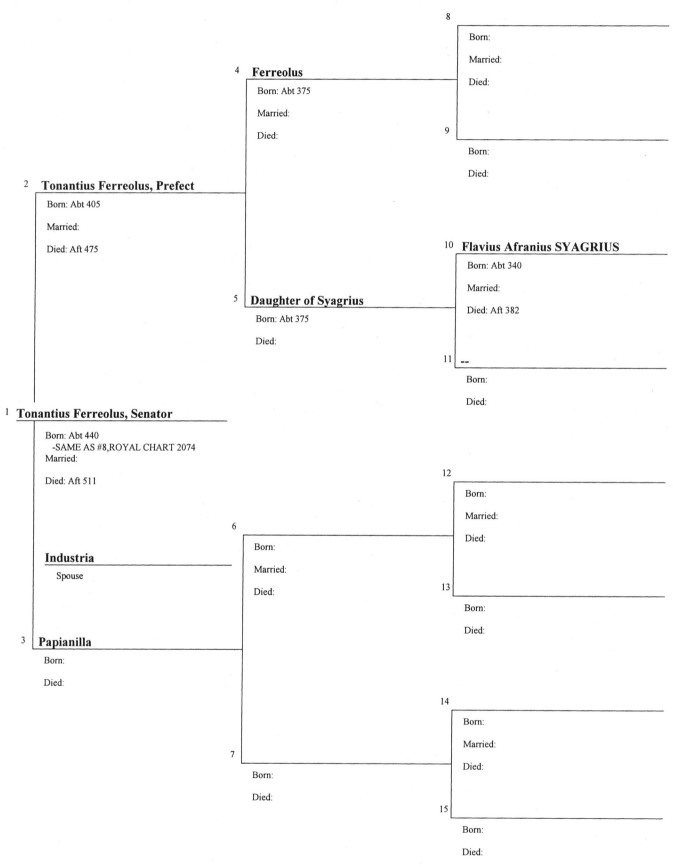

8

Born:

Married:

Died:

4 **Ferreolus**

Born: Abt 375

Married:

Died:

9

Born:

Died:

2 **Tonantius Ferreolus, Prefect**

Born: Abt 405

Married:

Died: Aft 475

10 **Flavius Afranius SYAGRIUS**

Born: Abt 340

Married:

Died: Aft 382

5 **Daughter of Syagrius**

Born: Abt 375

Died:

11 --

Born:

Died:

1 **Tonantius Ferreolus, Senator**

Born: Abt 440

  -SAME AS #8,ROYAL CHART 2074

Married:

Died: Aft 511

12

Born:

Married:

Died:

6

Born:

Married:

Died:

13

Born:

Died:

Industria

Spouse

3 **Papianilla**

Born:

Died:

14

Born:

Married:

Died:

7

Born:

Died:

15

Born:

Died:

Sources include: *Royal Ancestors* (1989), charts 11726-27; *Ancestral Roots* 8 (2004), Line 180; *Ancestral Roots* 180; Moriarty 7.

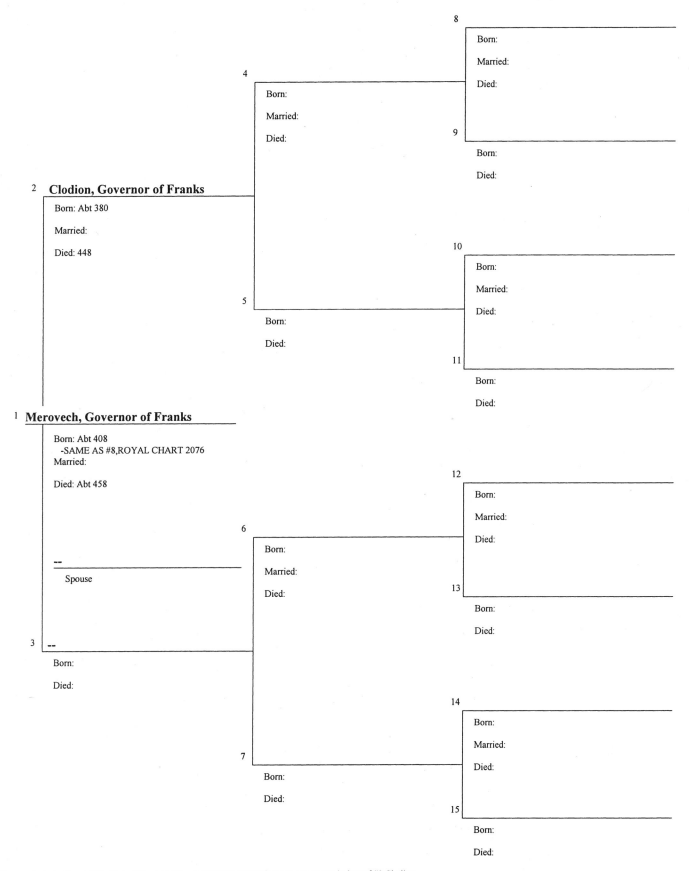

8

Born:

Married:

Died:

4

Born:

Married:

Died:

9

Born:

Died:

2 Clodion, Governor of Franks

Born: Abt 380

Married:

Died: 448

10

Born:

Married:

Died:

5

Born:

Died:

11

Born:

Died:

1 Merovech, Governor of Franks

Born: Abt 408
 -SAME AS #8,ROYAL CHART 2076
Married:

Died: Abt 458

12

Born:

Married:

Died:

6

Born:

Married:

Died:

13

Born:

Died:

--
  Spouse

3 --

Born:

Died:

14

Born:

Married:

Died:

7

Born:

Died:

15

Born:

Died:

Sources include: Stuart 303. Note: It is uncertain whether #1 Merovech was a son or son-in-law of #2 Clodion.

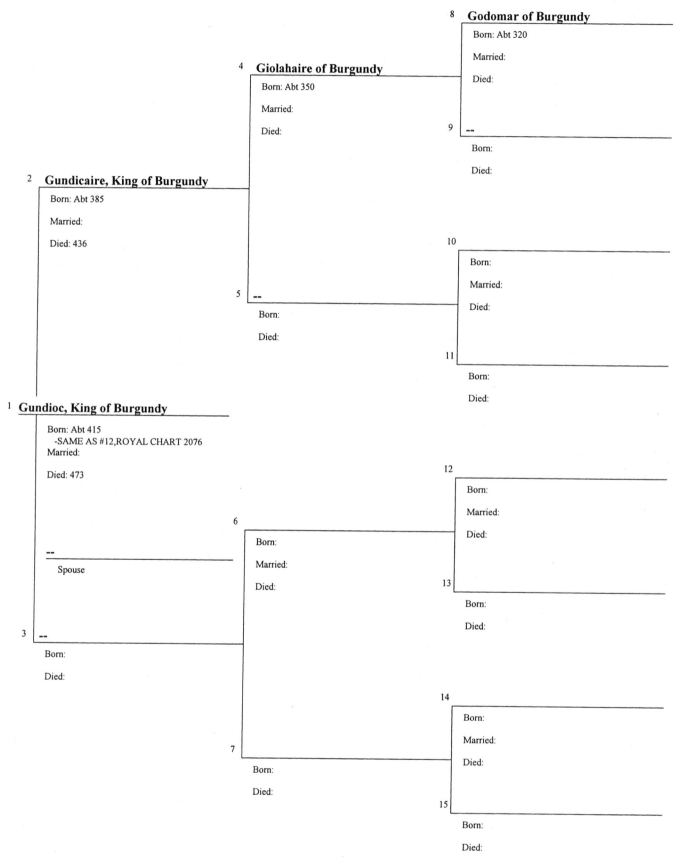

8 Godomar of Burgundy
Born: Abt 320
Married:
Died:

4 Giolahaire of Burgundy
Born: Abt 350
Married:
Died:

9 --
Born:
Died:

2 Gundicaire, King of Burgundy
Born: Abt 385
Married:
Died: 436

10
Born:
Married:
Died:

5 --
Born:
Died:

11
Born:
Died:

1 Gundioc, King of Burgundy
Born: Abt 415
 -SAME AS #12, ROYAL CHART 2076
Married:
Died: 473

12
Born:
Married:
Died:

6
Born:
Married:
Died:

13
Born:
Died:

--
Spouse

3 --
Born:
Died:

14
Born:
Married:
Died:

7
Born:
Died:

15
Born:
Died:

Sources include: Stuart 349; Turton 54. Note: Turton (copied by Stuart) gives #8 Godomar as son of Gibica. The above line is all tentative.

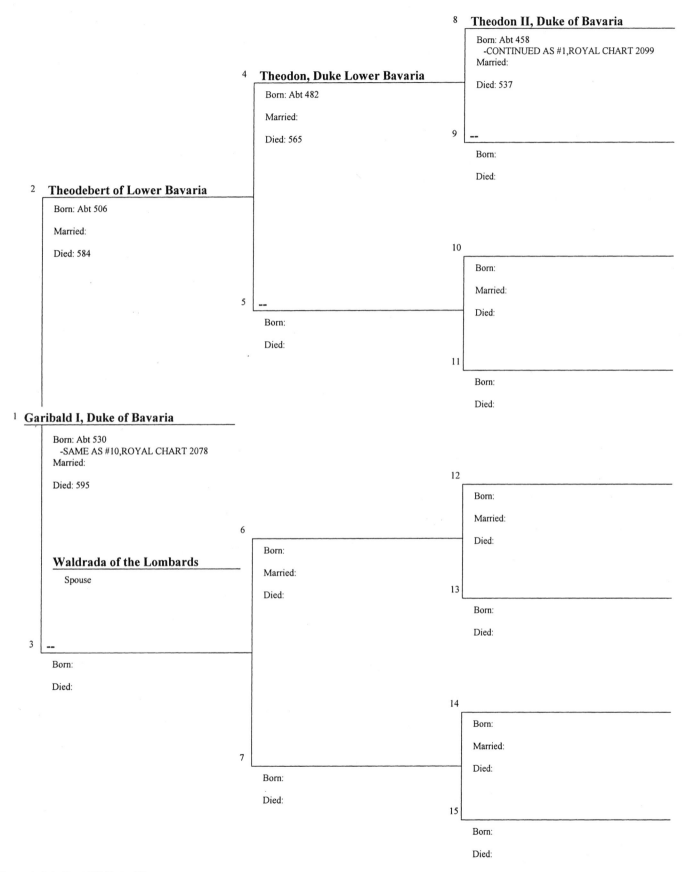

8 Theodon II, Duke of Bavaria

Born: Abt 458
-CONTINUED AS #1,ROYAL CHART 2099
Married:

Died: 537

4 Theodon, Duke Lower Bavaria

Born: Abt 482

Married:

Died: 565

9 --

Born:

Died:

2 Theodebert of Lower Bavaria

Born: Abt 506

Married:

Died: 584

10

Born:

Married:

Died:

5 --

Born:

Died:

11

Born:

Died:

1 Garibald I, Duke of Bavaria

Born: Abt 530
-SAME AS #10,ROYAL CHART 2078
Married:

Died: 595

12

Born:

Married:

Died:

6

Born:

Married:

Died:

13

Born:

Died:

Waldrada of the Lombards

Spouse

3 --

Born:

Died:

14

Born:

Married:

Died:

7

Born:

Died:

15

Born:

Died:

Sources include: Stuart 262; Turton 27.

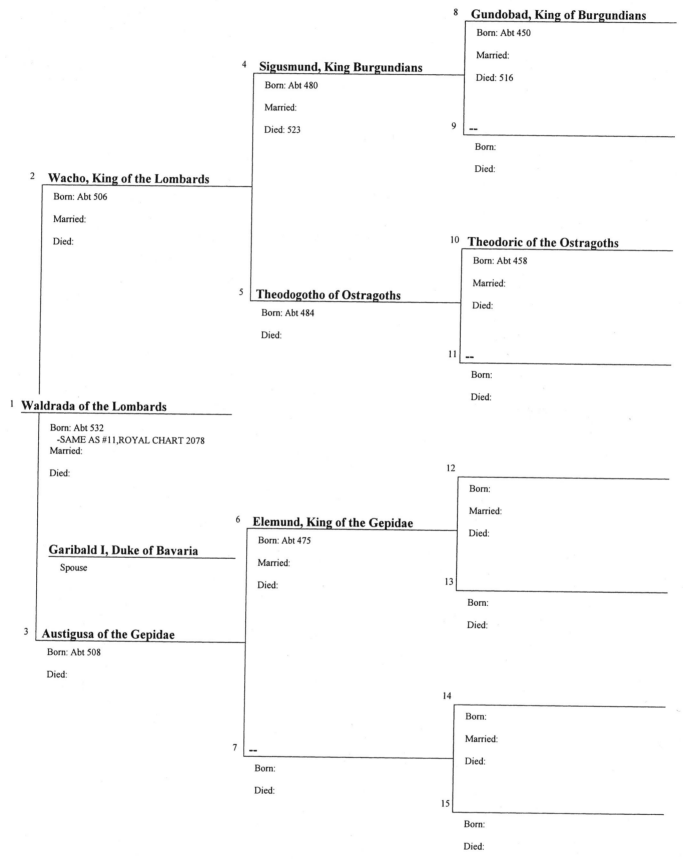

8 **Gundobad, King of Burgundians**
Born: Abt 450
Married:
Died: 516

4 **Sigusmund, King Burgundians**
Born: Abt 480
Married:
Died: 523

9 --
Born:
Died:

2 **Wacho, King of the Lombards**
Born: Abt 506
Married:
Died:

10 **Theodoric of the Ostragoths**
Born: Abt 458
Married:
Died:

5 **Theodogotho of Ostragoths**
Born: Abt 484
Died:

11 --
Born:
Died:

1 **Waldrada of the Lombards**
Born: Abt 532
      -SAME AS #11,ROYAL CHART 2078
Married:
Died:

12
Born:
Married:
Died:

6 **Elemund, King of the Gepidae**
Born: Abt 475
Married:
Died:

13
Born:
Died:

Garibald I, Duke of Bavaria
Spouse

3 **Austigusa of the Gepidae**
Born: Abt 508
Died:

14
Born:
Married:
Died:

7 --
Born:
Died:

15
Born:
Died:

Sources include: Stuart 380; Turton 27. Note: Stuart and Turton disagree on the parentage of #2. The Stuart version is tentatively followed above. The whole line is problematic (see *TAG* 74:148-149) so is not being charted further. Stuart gives the father of #8 as Gundick, King of the Burgundians (died 473), whose wife's maternal grandfather was Walia, King of the Visagoths (died 419). He gives #10 as son of another Theodoric (died 526) and grandson of Theudimir (died 474) and Erelicia.

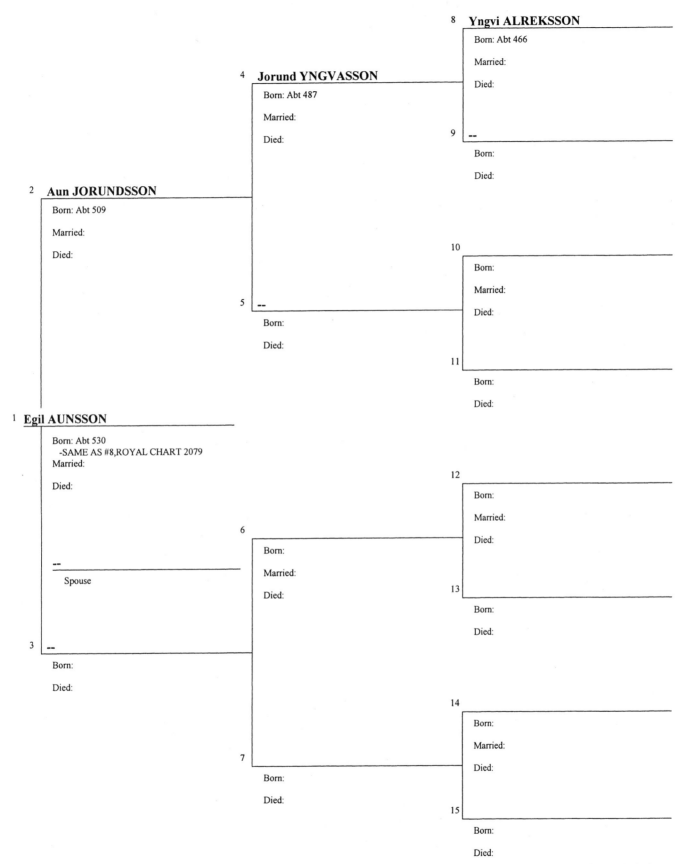

8 Yngvi ALREKSSON

Born: Abt 466

Married:

Died:

4 Jorund YNGVASSON

Born: Abt 487

Married:

Died:

9 --

Born:

Died:

2 Aun JORUNDSSON

Born: Abt 509

Married:

Died:

10

Born:

Married:

Died:

5 --

Born:

Died:

11

Born:

Died:

1 Egil AUNSSON

Born: Abt 530
    -SAME AS #8,ROYAL CHART 2079
Married:

Died:

12

Born:

Married:

Died:

6

Born:

Married:

Died:

13

Born:

Died:

--

Spouse

3 --

Born:

Died:

14

Born:

Married:

Died:

7

Born:

Died:

15

Born:

Died:

Sources include: *Royal Ancestors* (1989), charts 11706-09; Stuart 166; LDS records. Note: Stuart and LDS records both show a 13-generation descent for #8 Yngvi from Njord, King of the Swedes, as follows: 1. Yngvi (#8 above); 2. Alrek (md Dagreid Dagsdotter); 3. Agni (md Skjalf Frostasdotter); 4. Dag (b. abt 403); 5. Dyggvi; 6. Domar (md Drott); 7. Domaldi (b. abt 340); 8. Visbur; 9. Vanlandi (md Driva, dau of Snaer, King of Finland); 10. Svegdi (b. abt 277; md Vana); 11. Fjolnar; 12. Yngvi-Frey, King of Sweden (md Gerd Gymersdotter); 13. Njord, King of the Swedes (b. abt 214). There is no way to either prove or disprove this line. However, since only 21 years per generation is allowed, the line is probably not entirely correct.

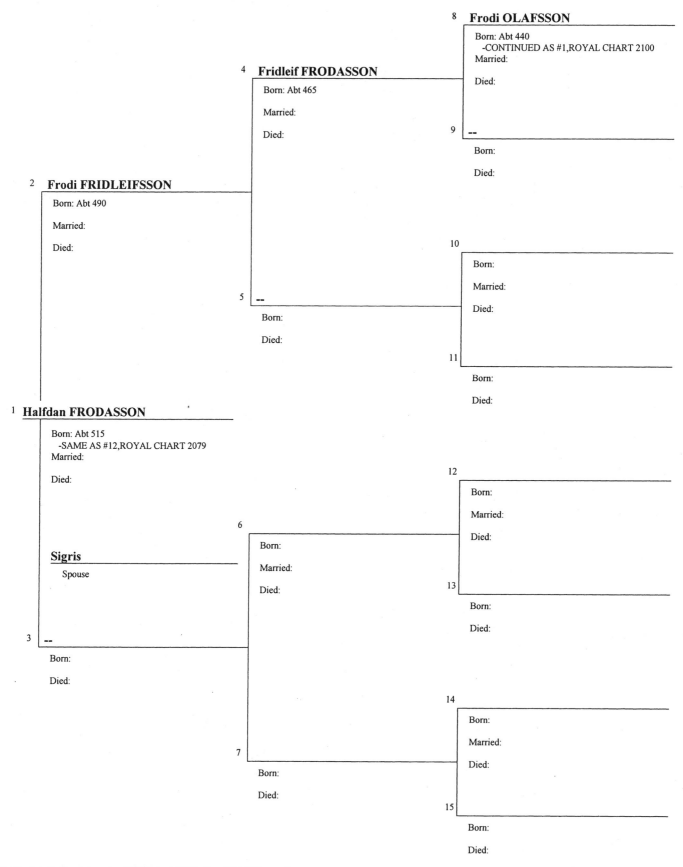

8 Frodi OLAFSSON

Born: Abt 440
  -CONTINUED AS #1,ROYAL CHART 2100
Married:

Died:

4 Fridleif FRODASSON

Born: Abt 465

Married:

Died:

9 --

Born:

Died:

2 Frodi FRIDLEIFSSON

Born: Abt 490

Married:

Died:

10

Born:

Married:

Died:

5 --

Born:

Died:

11

Born:

Died:

1 Halfdan FRODASSON

Born: Abt 515
  -SAME AS #12,ROYAL CHART 2079
Married:

Died:

Sigris

Spouse

12

Born:

Married:

Died:

6

Born:

Married:

Died:

13

Born:

Died:

3 --

Born:

Died:

14

Born:

Married:

Died:

7

Born:

Died:

15

Born:

Died:

Sources include: *Royal Ancestors* (1989), chart 11710; Stuart 324; LDS records.

Chart 2093

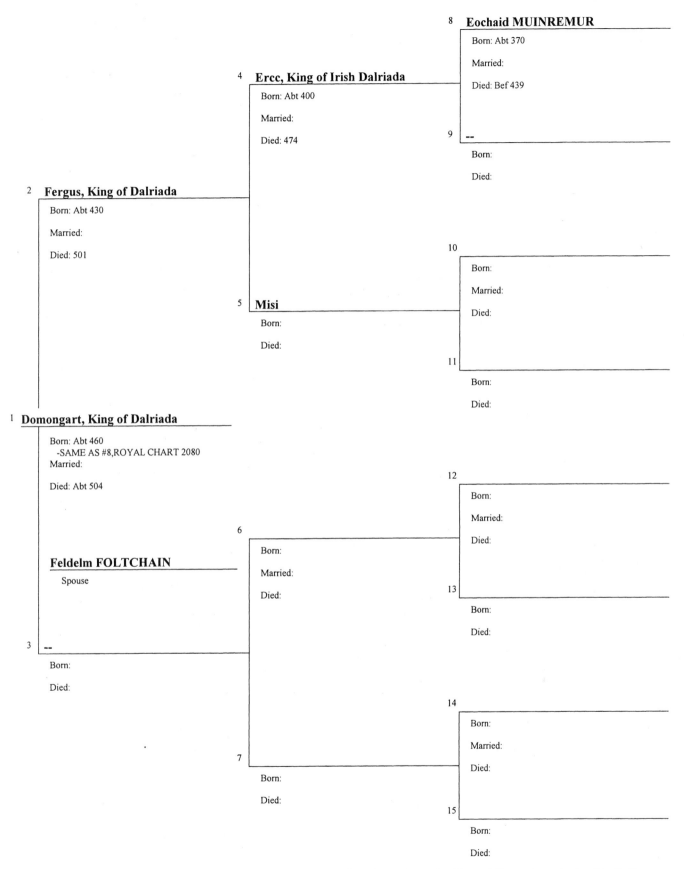

8 Eochaid MUINREMUR
- Born: Abt 370
- Married:
- Died: Bef 439

9 --
- Born:
- Died:

4 Ercc, King of Irish Dalriada
- Born: Abt 400
- Married:
- Died: 474

10
- Born:
- Married:
- Died:

11
- Born:
- Died:

2 Fergus, King of Dalriada
- Born: Abt 430
- Married:
- Died: 501

5 Misi
- Born:
- Died:

12
- Born:
- Married:
- Died:

13
- Born:
- Died:

1 Domongart, King of Dalriada
- Born: Abt 460
  - -SAME AS #8,ROYAL CHART 2080
- Married:
- Died: Abt 504

Feldelm FOLTCHAIN
- Spouse

3 --
- Born:
- Died:

6
- Born:
- Married:
- Died:

7
- Born:
- Died:

14
- Born:
- Married:
- Died:

15
- Born:
- Died:

Sources include: *Royal Ancestors* (1989), charts 11730-31; *Ancestral Roots* 170; Stuart 165; Moriarty 28. Note: Stuart gives #9 as probably an unknown daughter (Erca?) of Laorn, son of Eru.

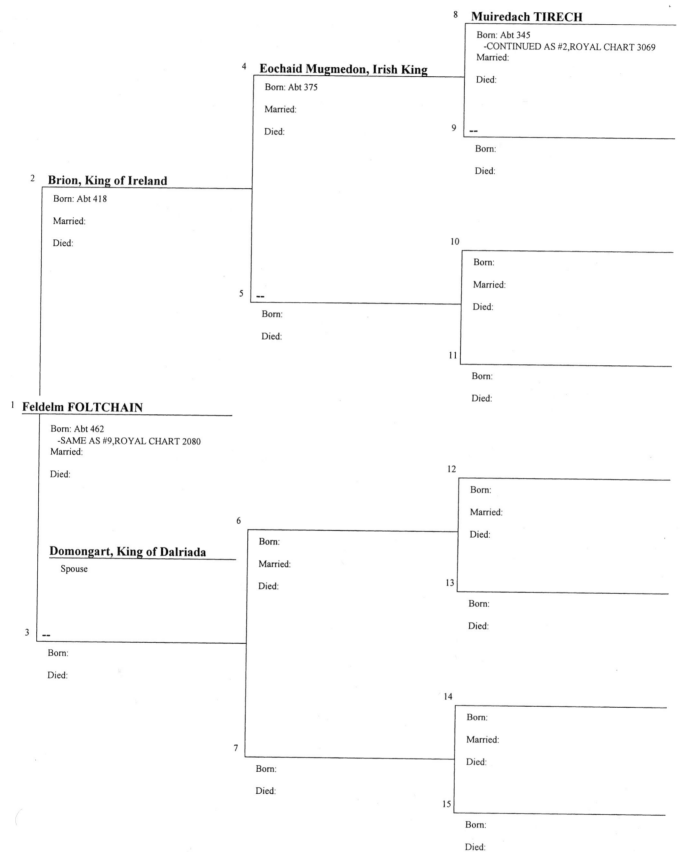

8 **Muiredach TIRECH**

Born: Abt 345
 -CONTINUED AS #2,ROYAL CHART 3069
Married:

Died:

4 **Eochaid Mugmedon, Irish King**

Born: Abt 375

Married:

Died:

9 --

Born:

Died:

2 **Brion, King of Ireland**

Born: Abt 418

Married:

Died:

10

Born:

Married:

Died:

5 --

Born:

Died:

11

Born:

Died:

1 **Feldelm FOLTCHAIN**

Born: Abt 462
 -SAME AS #9,ROYAL CHART 2080
Married:

Died:

12

Born:

Married:

Died:

Domongart, King of Dalriada

Spouse

6

Born:

Married:

Died:

13

Born:

Died:

3 --

Born:

Died:

14

Born:

Married:

Died:

7

Born:

Died:

15

Born:

Died:

Sources include: *Royal Ancestors* (1989), charts 11730, 11732; *Ancestral Roots* 170-3; Stuart 251; Moriarty 28.

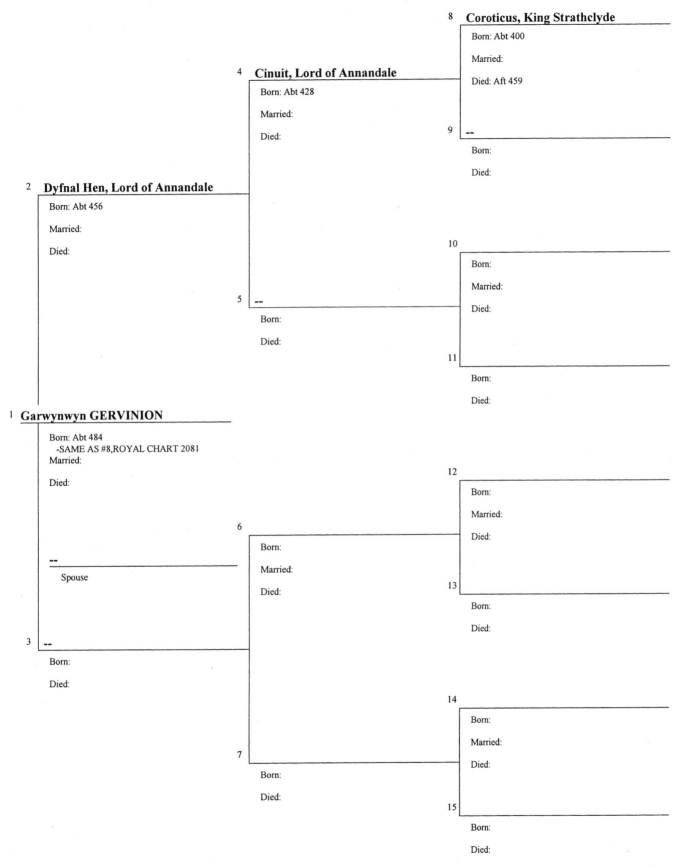

8 Coroticus, King Strathclyde
Born: Abt 400
Married:
Died: Aft 459

4 Cinuit, Lord of Annandale
Born: Abt 428
Married:
Died:

9 --
Born:
Died:

2 Dyfnal Hen, Lord of Annandale
Born: Abt 456
Married:
Died:

10
Born:
Married:
Died:

5 --
Born:
Died:

11
Born:
Died:

1 Garwynwyn GERVINION
Born: Abt 484
    -SAME AS #8, ROYAL CHART 2081
Married:
Died:

12
Born:
Married:
Died:

6
Born:
Married:
Died:

13
Born:
Died:

**-- **
Spouse

3 --
Born:
Died:

14
Born:
Married:
Died:

7
Born:
Died:

15
Born:
Died:

Sources include: *Royal Ancestors* (1989), charts 11925, 11956; Stuart 341; Moriarty 279. Note: Stuart gives #8 Croticus as son of Cynloup, son of Cinhil. Moriarty ends with #8.

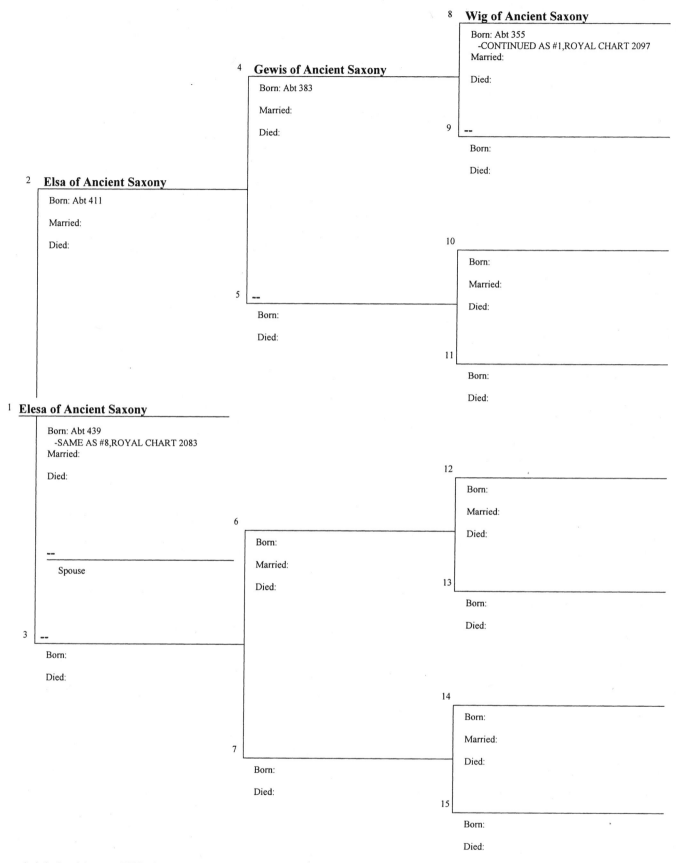

8 **Wig of Ancient Saxony**

Born: Abt 355
   -CONTINUED AS #1,ROYAL CHART 2097
Married:

Died:

4 **Gewis of Ancient Saxony**

Born: Abt 383

Married:

Died:

9 --

Born:

Died:

2 **Elsa of Ancient Saxony**

Born: Abt 411

Married:

Died:

10

Born:

Married:

Died:

5 --

Born:

Died:

11

Born:

Died:

1 **Elesa of Ancient Saxony**

Born: Abt 439
   -SAME AS #8,ROYAL CHART 2083
Married:

Died:

12

Born:

Married:

Died:

--

Spouse

6

Born:

Married:

Died:

13

Born:

Died:

3 --

Born:

Died:

14

Born:

Married:

Died:

7

Born:

Died:

15

Born:

Died:

Sources include: *Royal Ancestors* (1989), charts 11716-17; Stuart 233; LDS records; Moriarty 15 (ends with #1 Elesa).

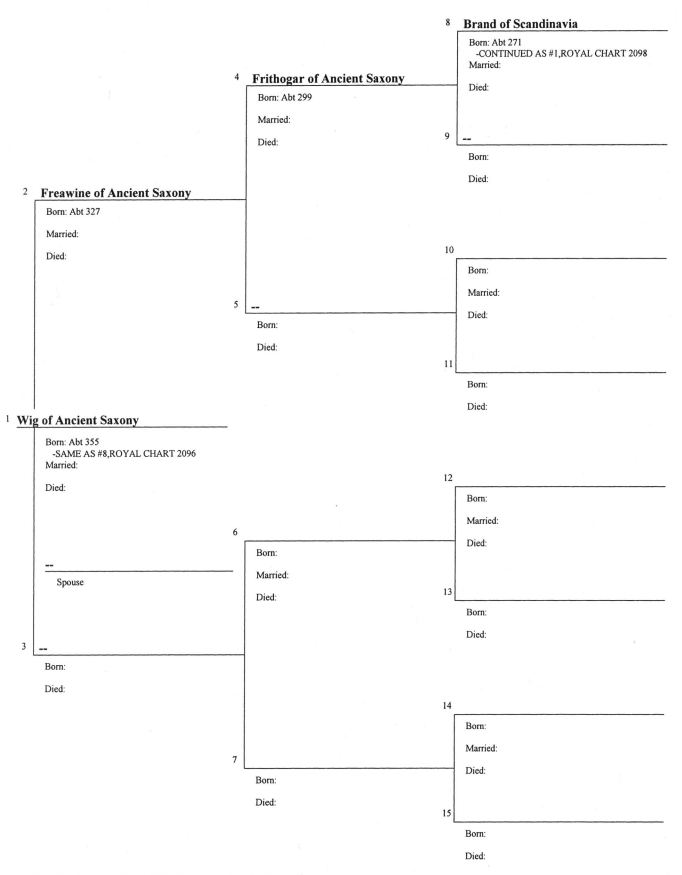

8 Brand of Scandinavia

Born: Abt 271
  -CONTINUED AS #1,ROYAL CHART 2098
Married:

Died:

4 Frithogar of Ancient Saxony

Born: Abt 299

Married:

Died:

9 --

Born:

Died:

2 Freawine of Ancient Saxony

Born: Abt 327

Married:

Died:

10

Born:

Married:

Died:

5 --

Born:

Died:

11

Born:

Died:

1 Wig of Ancient Saxony

Born: Abt 355
  -SAME AS #8,ROYAL CHART 2096
Married:

Died:

12

Born:

Married:

Died:

6

Born:

Married:

Died:

13

Born:

Died:

--

Spouse

14

Born:

Married:

Died:

3 --

Born:

Died:

7

Born:

Died:

15

Born:

Died:

Sources include: *Royal Ancestors* (1989), charts 11717-18; Stuart 233; LDS records.

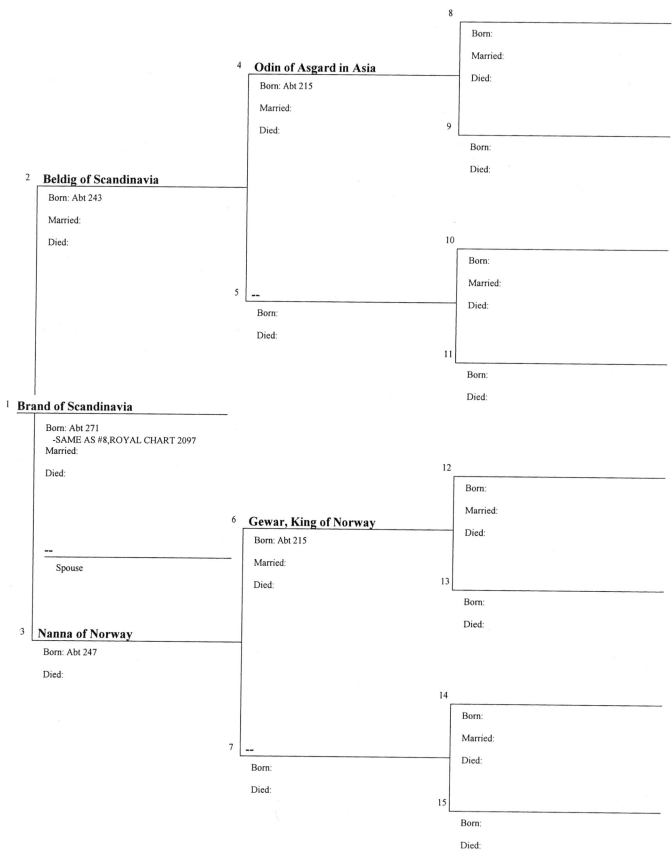

8

Born:

Married:

Died:

4 Odin of Asgard in Asia

Born: Abt 215

Married:

Died:

9

Born:

Died:

2 Beldig of Scandinavia

Born: Abt 243

Married:

Died:

10

Born:

Married:

Died:

5 --

Born:

Died:

11

Born:

Died:

1 Brand of Scandinavia

Born: Abt 271
  -SAME AS #8,ROYAL CHART 2097
Married:

Died:

12

Born:

Married:

Died:

6 Gewar, King of Norway

Born: Abt 215

Married:

Died:

13

Born:

Died:

--

Spouse

14

Born:

Married:

Died:

3 Nanna of Norway

Born: Abt 247

Died:

7 --

Born:

Died:

15

Born:

Died:

Sources include: *Royal Ancestors* (1989), charts 11718, 11713; Stuart 233; LDS records. Notes: Various claimed descents from #4 Odin may be correct but cannot be proven. An argument for the claims, as stated on an LDS Archive family group sheet for Odin prepared in about 1953--nearly half a century ago--is that "ancient chronologers independent of each other and without contact or knowledge of each other have claimed and recorded lineal descent for their rulers from Odin." A common claim for Odin's ancestry (Odin son of Frithuwald, son of Freothelaf, son of Finn, etc.) is believed to be fictitious (see *TAG* 74:148).

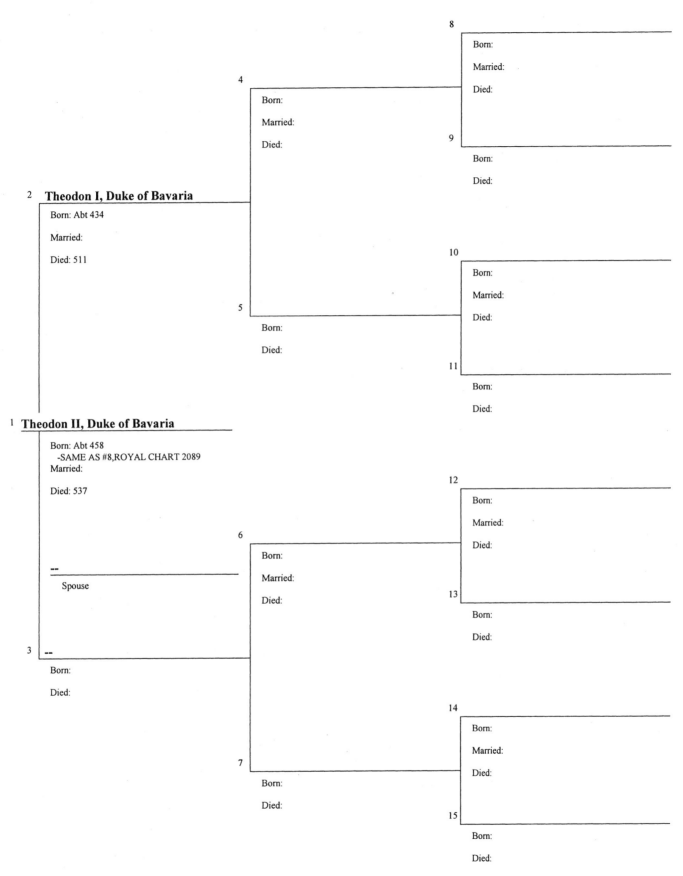

8

Born:

Married:

Died:

4

Born:

Married:

Died:

9

Born:

Died:

2 Theodon I, Duke of Bavaria

Born: Abt 434

Married:

Died: 511

10

Born:

Married:

Died:

5

Born:

Died:

11

Born:

Died:

1 Theodon II, Duke of Bavaria

Born: Abt 458
  -SAME AS #8,ROYAL CHART 2089
Married:

Died: 537

12

Born:

Married:

Died:

6

Born:

Married:

Died:

13

Born:

Died:

--
  Spouse

3 --

Born:

Died:

14

Born:

Married:

Died:

7

Born:

Died:

15

Born:

Died:

Sources include: Stuart 262; Turton 8.

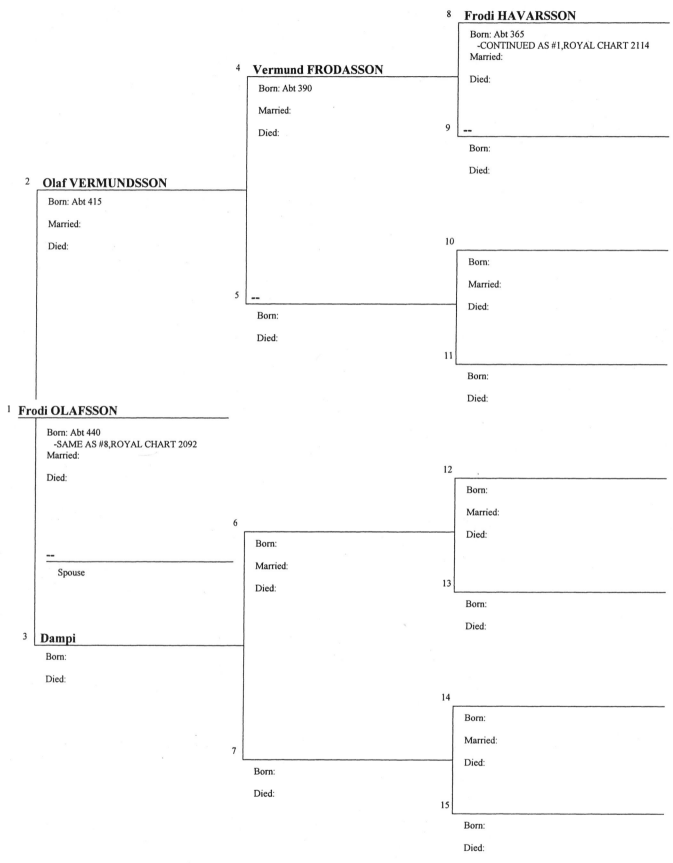

8 **Frodi HAVARSSON**

Born: Abt 365
  -CONTINUED AS #1,ROYAL CHART 2114
Married:

Died:

4 **Vermund FRODASSON**

Born: Abt 390

Married:

Died:

9 --

Born:

Died:

2 **Olaf VERMUNDSSON**

Born: Abt 415

Married:

Died:

10

Born:

Married:

Died:

5 --

Born:

Died:

11

Born:

Died:

1 **Frodi OLAFSSON**

Born: Abt 440
  -SAME AS #8,ROYAL CHART 2092
Married:

Died:

12

Born:

Married:

Died:

6

Born:

Married:

Died:

13

Born:

Died:

--

Spouse

3 **Dampi**

Born:

Died:

14

Born:

Married:

Died:

7

Born:

Died:

15

Born:

Died:

Sources include: *Royal Ancestors* (1989), charts 11710-11; Stuart 324; LDS records. Note: LDS records show #1 Frodi as son of Dan and grandson of Olaf. Stuart skips Dan, as followed above.

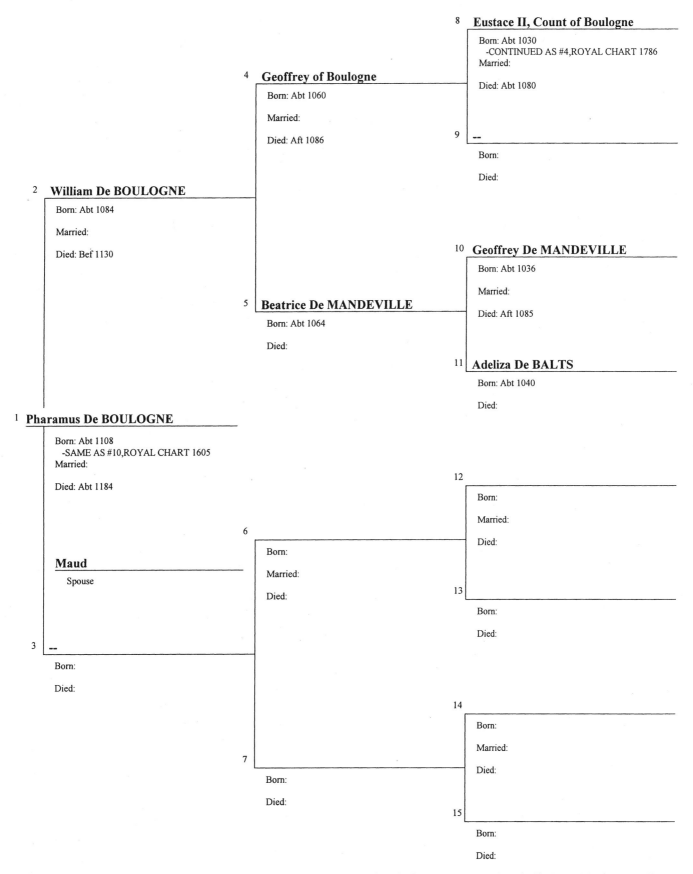

8 **Eustace II, Count of Boulogne**

Born: Abt 1030
   -CONTINUED AS #4,ROYAL CHART 1786
Married:

Died: Abt 1080

4 **Geoffrey of Boulogne**

Born: Abt 1060

Married:

Died: Aft 1086

9 --

Born:

Died:

2 **William De BOULOGNE**

Born: Abt 1084

Married:

Died: Bef 1130

10 **Geoffrey De MANDEVILLE**

Born: Abt 1036

Married:

Died: Aft 1085

5 **Beatrice De MANDEVILLE**

Born: Abt 1064

Died:

11 **Adeliza De BALTS**

Born: Abt 1040

Died:

1 **Pharamus De BOULOGNE**

Born: Abt 1108
   -SAME AS #10,ROYAL CHART 1605
Married:

Died: Abt 1184

12

Born:

Married:

Died:

6

Born:

Married:

Died:

13

Born:

Died:

Maud

Spouse

3 --

Born:

Died:

14

Born:

Married:

Died:

7

Born:

Died:

15

Born:

Died:

Sources include: *Royal Ancestors* (1989), chart 11433; *Ancestral Roots* 158A; Research report by Douglas Richardson on the Lucy & Boulogne families (July 2004). Note: #4 Geoffrey was an illegitimate son of #8 Eustace. #4 has previously been claimed as Godfrey, a legitimate son of Eustace and Ida (see chart 1786, #4 & 5). Richardson states that Geoffrey (illegitimate) is definitely correct (August 2004).

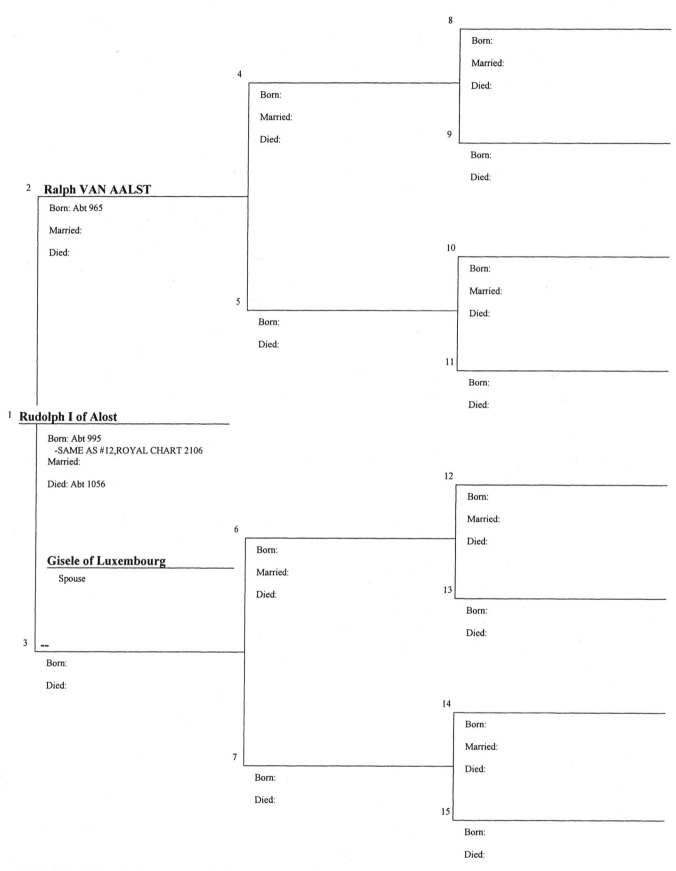

8

Born:

Married:

Died:

4

Born:

Married:

Died:

9

Born:

Died:

2 **Ralph VAN AALST**

Born: Abt 965

Married:

Died:

10

Born:

Married:

Died:

5

Born:

Died:

11

Born:

Died:

1 **Rudolph I of Alost**

Born: Abt 995
-SAME AS #12,ROYAL CHART 2106
Married:

Died: Abt 1056

12

Born:

Married:

Died:

6

Born:

Married:

Died:

13

Born:

Died:

Gisele of Luxembourg

Spouse

3 --

Born:

Died:

14

Born:

Married:

Died:

7

Born:

Died:

15

Born:

Died:

Sources include: Faris preliminary Charlemagne manuscript (June 1995), p. 1; Faris preliminary baronial manuscript (1998), p. 688 (Gant); Schwennicke 7:22a (#1 Rudolph); *Ancestral Roots* 143-21 (#1 Rudolph). Notes: #1 Rudolph is also called Ralph De Gand. #2 is also claimed (Faris baronial, citing *Carleton*) as Adalbert De Alost, son of Arnulf & Liutgard (continued chart 1730, #4 & 5).

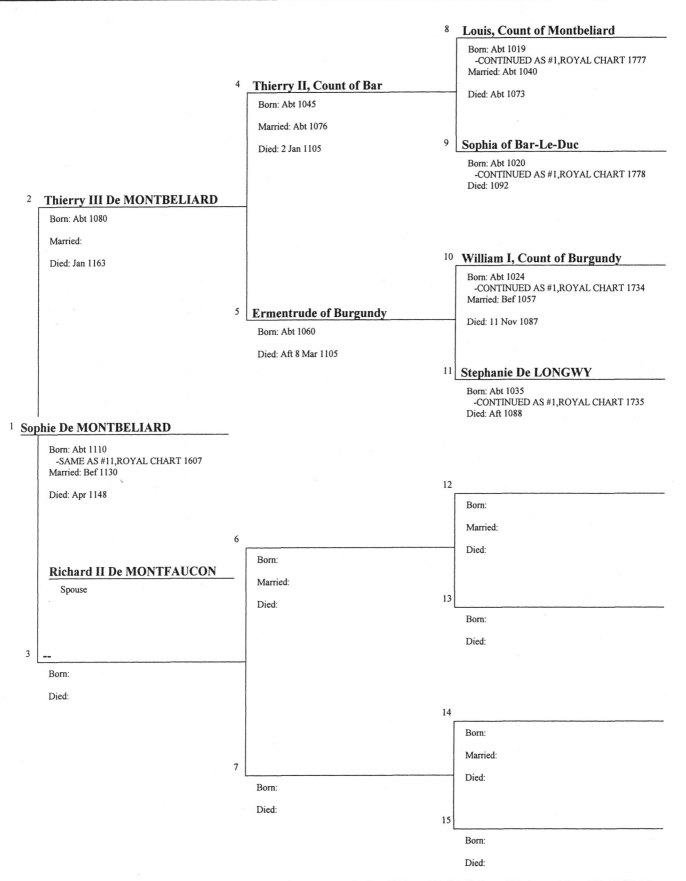

8 **Louis, Count of Montbeliard**

Born: Abt 1019
-CONTINUED AS #1,ROYAL CHART 1777
Married: Abt 1040

Died: Abt 1073

4 **Thierry II, Count of Bar**

Born: Abt 1045

Married: Abt 1076

Died: 2 Jan 1105

9 **Sophia of Bar-Le-Duc**

Born: Abt 1020
-CONTINUED AS #1,ROYAL CHART 1778
Died: 1092

2 **Thierry III De MONTBELIARD**

Born: Abt 1080

Married:

Died: Jan 1163

10 **William I, Count of Burgundy**

Born: Abt 1024
-CONTINUED AS #1,ROYAL CHART 1734
Married: Bef 1057

Died: 11 Nov 1087

5 **Ermentrude of Burgundy**

Born: Abt 1060

Died: Aft 8 Mar 1105

11 **Stephanie De LONGWY**

Born: Abt 1035
-CONTINUED AS #1,ROYAL CHART 1735
Died: Aft 1088

1 **Sophie De MONTBELIARD**

Born: Abt 1110
-SAME AS #11,ROYAL CHART 1607
Married: Bef 1130

Died: Apr 1148

12

Born:

Married:

Died:

6

Born:

Married:

Died:

13

Born:

Died:

Richard II De MONTFAUCON

Spouse

3 **--**

Born:

Died:

14

Born:

Married:

Died:

7

Born:

Died:

15

Born:

Died:

Sources include: *Royal Ancestors* (1989), chart 11652; Faris preliminary Charlemagne manuscript (June 1995), pp. 185-186, 34; Turton 206; *Ancestral Roots* 167, 144 (#4 & 5 ancestry); Stuart 149 (#4 & 5 ancestry).

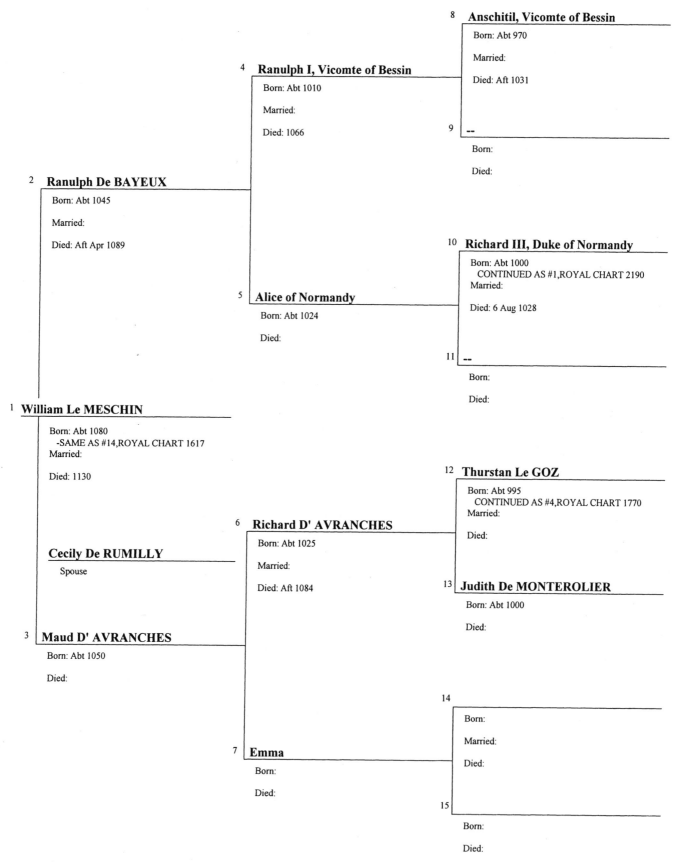

8 **Anschitil, Vicomte of Bessin**

Born: Abt 970

Married:

Died: Aft 1031

4 **Ranulph I, Vicomte of Bessin**

Born: Abt 1010

Married:

Died: 1066

9 --

Born:

Died:

2 **Ranulph De BAYEUX**

Born: Abt 1045

Married:

Died: Aft Apr 1089

10 **Richard III, Duke of Normandy**

Born: Abt 1000
    CONTINUED AS #1,ROYAL CHART 2190
Married:

Died: 6 Aug 1028

5 **Alice of Normandy**

Born: Abt 1024

Died:

11 --

Born:

Died:

1 **William Le MESCHIN**

Born: Abt 1080
    -SAME AS #14,ROYAL CHART 1617
Married:

Died: 1130

12 **Thurstan Le GOZ**

Born: Abt 995
    CONTINUED AS #4,ROYAL CHART 1770
Married:

Died:

6 **Richard D' AVRANCHES**

Born: Abt 1025

Married:

Died: Aft 1084

Cecily De RUMILLY

Spouse

13 **Judith De MONTEROLIER**

Born: Abt 1000

Died:

3 **Maud D' AVRANCHES**

Born: Abt 1050

Died:

14

Born:

Married:

Died:

7 **Emma**

Born:

Died:

15

Born:

Died:

Sources include: *Royal Ancestors* (1989), charts 11461, 11541-42; Faris preliminary baronial manuscript (1998), p. 336 (Chester); *Ancestral Roots* 132B, 132A, 40-24; Kraentzler 1309; Stuart 295 (#6 ancestry). Note: #7 is claimed as Emma, daughter of Herlevin De Conteville & Harlette De Falaise (see chart 1718, #2 & 3). Moriarty states that this claim is probably unfounded.

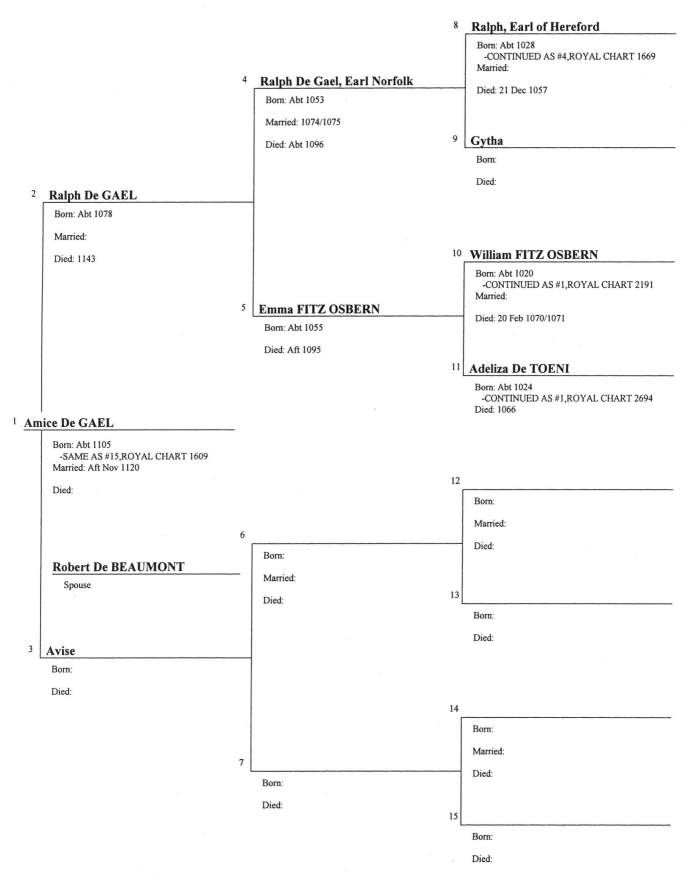

8 Ralph, Earl of Hereford
Born: Abt 1028
  -CONTINUED AS #4,ROYAL CHART 1669
Married:

Died: 21 Dec 1057

4 Ralph De Gael, Earl Norfolk
Born: Abt 1053

Married: 1074/1075

Died: Abt 1096

9 Gytha
Born:

Died:

2 Ralph De GAEL
Born: Abt 1078

Married:

Died: 1143

10 William FITZ OSBERN
Born: Abt 1020
  -CONTINUED AS #1,ROYAL CHART 2191
Married:

Died: 20 Feb 1070/1071

5 Emma FITZ OSBERN
Born: Abt 1055

Died: Aft 1095

11 Adeliza De TOENI
Born: Abt 1024
  -CONTINUED AS #1,ROYAL CHART 2694
Died: 1066

1 Amice De GAEL
Born: Abt 1105
  -SAME AS #15,ROYAL CHART 1609
Married: Aft Nov 1120

Died:

Robert De BEAUMONT
Spouse

3 Avise
Born:

Died:

6
Born:

Married:

Died:

12
Born:

Married:

Died:

13
Born:

Died:

7
Born:

Died:

14
Born:

Married:

Died:

15
Born:

Died:

Sources include: *Royal Ancestors* (1989), chart 11439; *Ancestral Roots* 53-25; Turton 100.

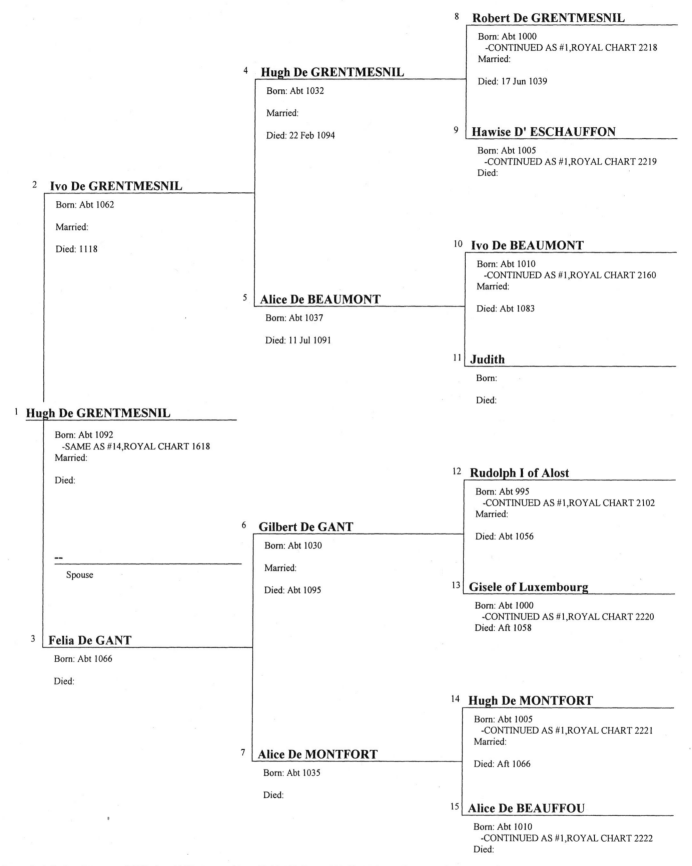

2 Ivo De GRENTMESNIL

Born: Abt 1062

Married:

Died: 1118

---

1 Hugh De GRENTMESNIL

Born: Abt 1092
-SAME AS #14,ROYAL CHART 1618
Married:

Died:

--

Spouse

---

3 Felia De GANT

Born: Abt 1066

Died:

---

4 Hugh De GRENTMESNIL

Born: Abt 1032

Married:

Died: 22 Feb 1094

---

5 Alice De BEAUMONT

Born: Abt 1037

Died: 11 Jul 1091

---

6 Gilbert De GANT

Born: Abt 1030

Married:

Died: Abt 1095

---

7 Alice De MONTFORT

Born: Abt 1035

Died:

---

8 Robert De GRENTMESNIL

Born: Abt 1000
-CONTINUED AS #1,ROYAL CHART 2218
Married:

Died: 17 Jun 1039

---

9 Hawise D' ESCHAUFFON

Born: Abt 1005
-CONTINUED AS #1,ROYAL CHART 2219
Died:

---

10 Ivo De BEAUMONT

Born: Abt 1010
-CONTINUED AS #1,ROYAL CHART 2160
Married:

Died: Abt 1083

---

11 Judith

Born:

Died:

---

12 Rudolph I of Alost

Born: Abt 995
-CONTINUED AS #1,ROYAL CHART 2102
Married:

Died: Abt 1056

---

13 Gisele of Luxembourg

Born: Abt 1000
-CONTINUED AS #1,ROYAL CHART 2220
Died: Aft 1058

---

14 Hugh De MONTFORT

Born: Abt 1005
-CONTINUED AS #1,ROYAL CHART 2221
Married:

Died: Aft 1066

---

15 Alice De BEAUFFOU

Born: Abt 1010
-CONTINUED AS #1,ROYAL CHART 2222
Died:

Sources include: *Royal Ancestors* (1989), chart 11443; *Ancestral Roots* 53-26, 143; Turton 100, 88; LDS records. Note: The ancestry given for #12 Rudolph (Ralph) by Turton and LDS records is chronologically unacceptable.

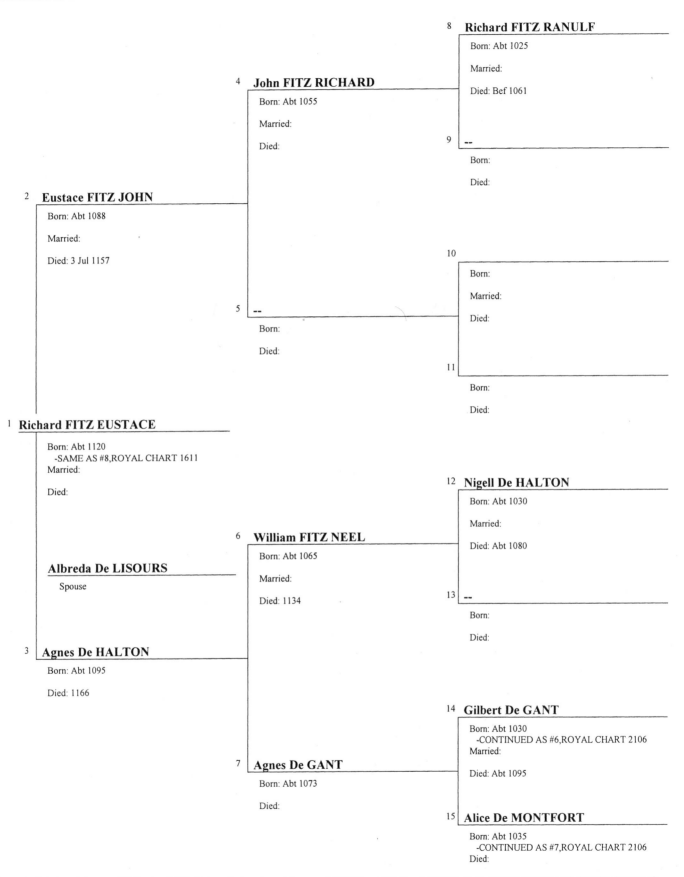

8 **Richard FITZ RANULF**

Born: Abt 1025

Married:

Died: Bef 1061

4 **John FITZ RICHARD**

Born: Abt 1055

Married:

Died:

9 --

Born:

Died:

2 **Eustace FITZ JOHN**

Born: Abt 1088

Married:

Died: 3 Jul 1157

10

Born:

Married:

Died:

5 --

Born:

Died:

11

Born:

Died:

1 **Richard FITZ EUSTACE**

Born: Abt 1120
-SAME AS #8,ROYAL CHART 1611
Married:

Died:

12 **Nigell De HALTON**

Born: Abt 1030

Married:

Died: Abt 1080

6 **William FITZ NEEL**

Born: Abt 1065

Married:

Died: 1134

Albreda De LISOURS

Spouse

13 --

Born:

Died:

3 **Agnes De HALTON**

Born: Abt 1095

Died: 1166

14 **Gilbert De GANT**

Born: Abt 1030
-CONTINUED AS #6,ROYAL CHART 2106
Married:

Died: Abt 1095

7 **Agnes De GANT**

Born: Abt 1073

Died:

15 **Alice De MONTFORT**

Born: Abt 1035
-CONTINUED AS #7,ROYAL CHART 2106
Died:

Sources include: *Royal Ancestors* (1989), chart 11440; Faris preliminary baronial manuscript (1998), pp. 926 (Lacy), 627 (Fitz Neel), 689 (Gant); Turton 95; Complete Peerage 12 (part 2):7-11 (ancestry of #2 Eustace). Note: The father of #8, Ranulf or Ralph the Moneyer, lived in Normandy in 1035 and died by 1061.

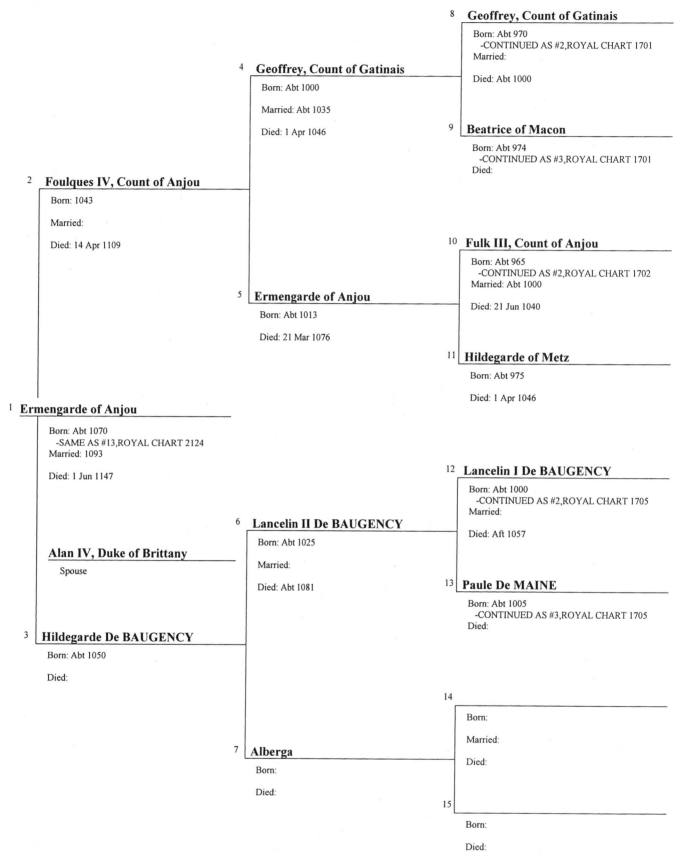

8 **Geoffrey, Count of Gatinais**

Born: Abt 970
-CONTINUED AS #2,ROYAL CHART 1701
Married:

Died: Abt 1000

4 **Geoffrey, Count of Gatinais**

Born: Abt 1000

Married: Abt 1035

Died: 1 Apr 1046

9 **Beatrice of Macon**

Born: Abt 974
-CONTINUED AS #3,ROYAL CHART 1701
Died:

2 **Foulques IV, Count of Anjou**

Born: 1043

Married:

Died: 14 Apr 1109

10 **Fulk III, Count of Anjou**

Born: Abt 965
-CONTINUED AS #2,ROYAL CHART 1702
Married: Abt 1000

Died: 21 Jun 1040

5 **Ermengarde of Anjou**

Born: Abt 1013

Died: 21 Mar 1076

11 **Hildegarde of Metz**

Born: Abt 975

Died: 1 Apr 1046

1 **Ermengarde of Anjou**

Born: Abt 1070
-SAME AS #13,ROYAL CHART 2124
Married: 1093

Died: 1 Jun 1147

Alan IV, Duke of Brittany

Spouse

12 **Lancelin I De BAUGENCY**

Born: Abt 1000
-CONTINUED AS #2,ROYAL CHART 1705
Married:

Died: Aft 1057

6 **Lancelin II De BAUGENCY**

Born: Abt 1025

Married:

Died: Abt 1081

13 **Paule De MAINE**

Born: Abt 1005
-CONTINUED AS #3,ROYAL CHART 1705
Died:

3 **Hildegarde De BAUGENCY**

Born: Abt 1050

Died:

14

Born:

Married:

Died:

7 **Alberga**

Born:

Died:

15

Born:

Died:

Sources include: *Royal Ancestors* (1989), chart 11459; *Ancestral Roots* 119; Moriarty 197, 11 (#6 ancestry); Stuart 4 (#6 ancestry).

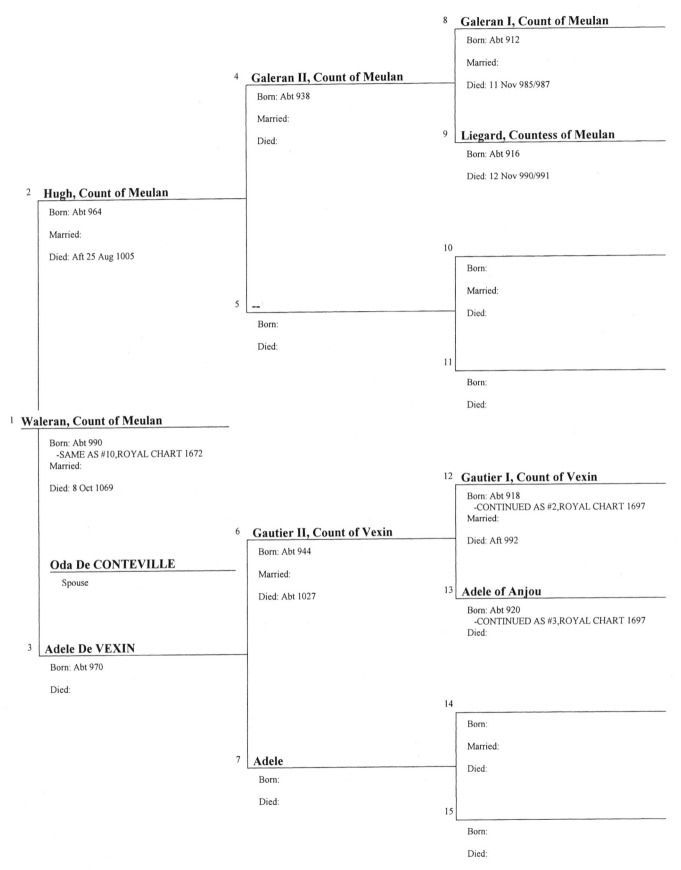

8 Galeran I, Count of Meulan
Born: Abt 912
Married:
Died: 11 Nov 985/987

4 Galeran II, Count of Meulan
Born: Abt 938
Married:
Died:

9 Liegard, Countess of Meulan
Born: Abt 916
Died: 12 Nov 990/991

2 Hugh, Count of Meulan
Born: Abt 964
Married:
Died: Aft 25 Aug 1005

10
Born:
Married:
Died:

5 --
Born:
Died:

11
Born:
Died:

1 Waleran, Count of Meulan
Born: Abt 990
 -SAME AS #10,ROYAL CHART 1672
Married:
Died: 8 Oct 1069

12 Gautier I, Count of Vexin
Born: Abt 918
 -CONTINUED AS #2,ROYAL CHART 1697
Married:
Died: Aft 992

6 Gautier II, Count of Vexin
Born: Abt 944
Married:
Died: Abt 1027

13 Adele of Anjou
Born: Abt 920
 -CONTINUED AS #3,ROYAL CHART 1697
Died:

Oda De CONTEVILLE
Spouse

3 Adele De VEXIN
Born: Abt 970
Died:

14
Born:
Married:
Died:

7 Adele
Born:
Died:

15
Born:
Died:

Sources include: *Royal Ancestors* (1989), chart 11545; Stuart 185, 234; Moriarty 135 (#6 ancestry); *Ancestral Roots* 50-24 (#1), 250 (#6 ancestry); Turton 100; Collett family group sheets; LDS records. Notes: #2 & 4 are disputed by Turton. The Stuart version is accepted above. The ancestry shown for #13 Adele is probable but not certain. Turton gives #7 as Adele De Senlis, daughter of Bernard (Bormard) and descendant of Pepin, Count of Senlis (see chart 1907). Moriarty, Stuart, and *Ancestral Roots* all end with #7 Adele.

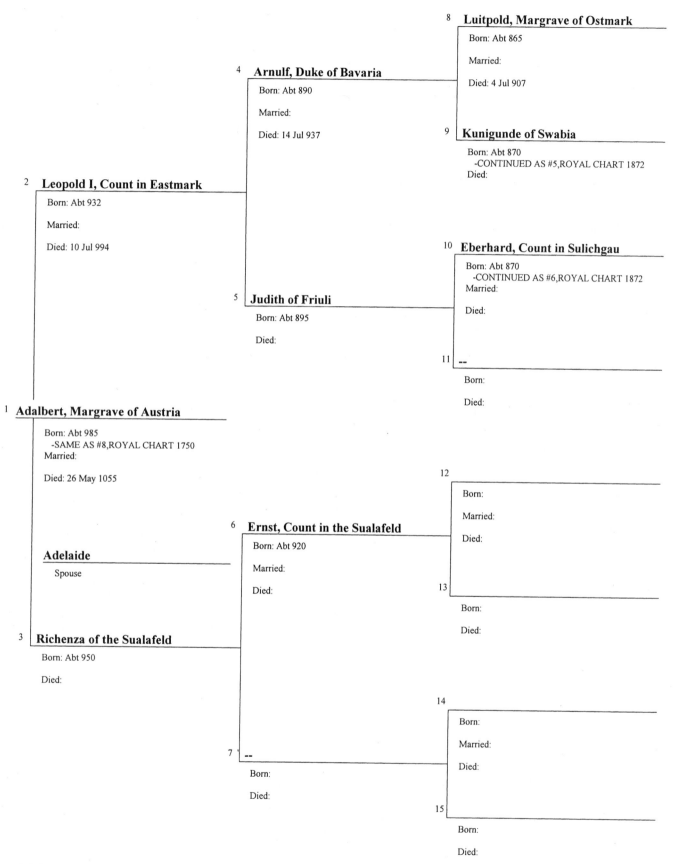

8 Luitpold, Margrave of Ostmark

Born: Abt 865

Married:

Died: 4 Jul 907

4 Arnulf, Duke of Bavaria

Born: Abt 890

Married:

Died: 14 Jul 937

9 Kunigunde of Swabia

Born: Abt 870
   -CONTINUED AS #5,ROYAL CHART 1872
Died:

2 Leopold I, Count in Eastmark

Born: Abt 932

Married:

Died: 10 Jul 994

10 Eberhard, Count in Sulichgau

Born: Abt 870
   -CONTINUED AS #6,ROYAL CHART 1872
Married:

Died:

5 Judith of Friuli

Born: Abt 895

Died:

11 --

Born:

Died:

1 Adalbert, Margrave of Austria

Born: Abt 985
   -SAME AS #8,ROYAL CHART 1750
Married:

Died: 26 May 1055

12

Born:

Married:

Died:

6 Ernst, Count in the Sualafeld

Born: Abt 920

Married:

Died:

13

Born:

Died:

Adelaide

Spouse

3 Richenza of the Sualafeld

Born: Abt 950

Died:

14

Born:

Married:

Died:

7 --

Born:

Died:

15

Born:

Died:

Sources include: *Royal Ancestors* (1989), chart 12118; Stuart 279; Moriarty 90.

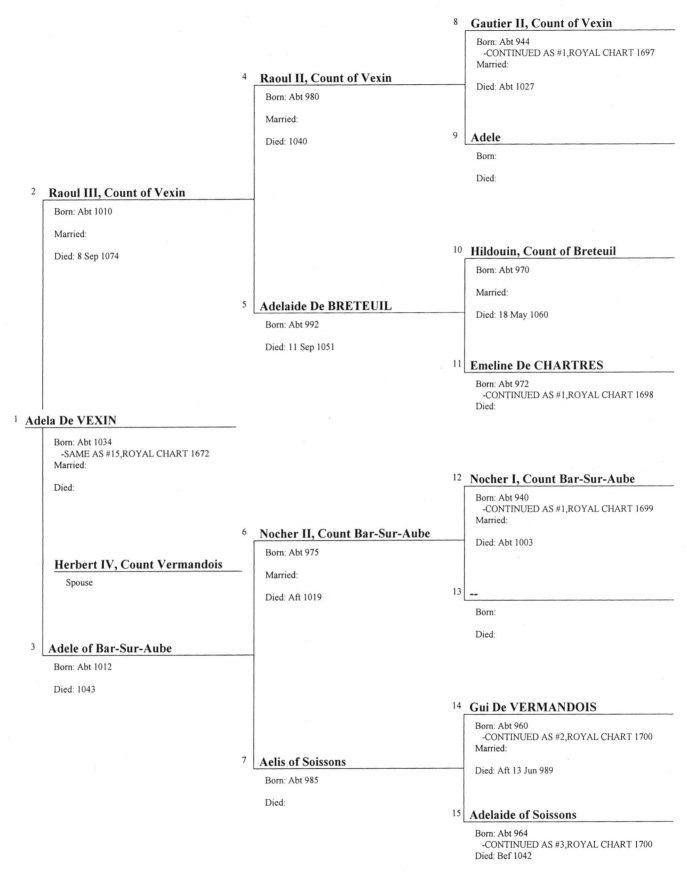

8 **Gautier II, Count of Vexin**

Born: Abt 944
-CONTINUED AS #1,ROYAL CHART 1697
Married:

Died: Abt 1027

4 **Raoul II, Count of Vexin**

Born: Abt 980

Married:

Died: 1040

9 **Adele**

Born:

Died:

2 **Raoul III, Count of Vexin**

Born: Abt 1010

Married:

Died: 8 Sep 1074

10 **Hildouin, Count of Breteuil**

Born: Abt 970

Married:

Died: 18 May 1060

5 **Adelaide De BRETEUIL**

Born: Abt 992

Died: 11 Sep 1051

11 **Emeline De CHARTRES**

Born: Abt 972
-CONTINUED AS #1,ROYAL CHART 1698
Died:

1 **Adela De VEXIN**

Born: Abt 1034
-SAME AS #15,ROYAL CHART 1672
Married:

Died:

12 **Nocher I, Count Bar-Sur-Aube**

Born: Abt 940
-CONTINUED AS #1,ROYAL CHART 1699
Married:

Died: Abt 1003

6 **Nocher II, Count Bar-Sur-Aube**

Born: Abt 975

Married:

Died: Aft 1019

13 **--**

Born:

Died:

Herbert IV, Count Vermandois

Spouse

3 **Adele of Bar-Sur-Aube**

Born: Abt 1012

Died: 1043

14 **Gui De VERMANDOIS**

Born: Abt 960
-CONTINUED AS #2,ROYAL CHART 1700
Married:

Died: Aft 13 Jun 989

7 **Aelis of Soissons**

Born: Abt 985

Died:

15 **Adelaide of Soissons**

Born: Abt 964
-CONTINUED AS #3,ROYAL CHART 1700
Died: Bef 1042

Sources include: *Royal Ancestors* (1989), chart 11425; *Ancestral Roots* 50-22; Stuart 268; Moriarty 134-137, 267; Turton 112; Collett 21-5A. Notes: The parentage of #3 Adele is uncertain. Moriarty (followed by Stuart) gives her as <u>perhaps</u> the daughter of Nocher III, son of Nocher II and Aelis. Collett gives her as daughter of Nocher I. Both claims present chronological problems. She is being tentatively assigned here as daughter of Nocher II and Aelis, which fits well chronologically. See note chart 2109 regarding #9 Adele. #10 Hildouin is claimed as son of Hildouin, Count of Ponthieu (died 981), and Turton 13 extends that line to Charlemagne, but both the claim and the extension appear to be unreliable.

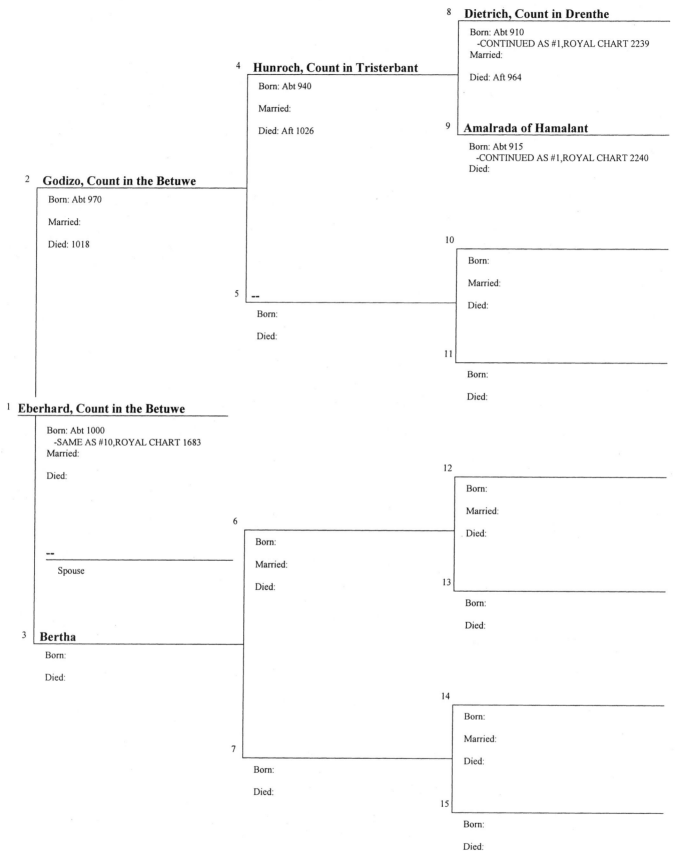

8 **Dietrich, Count in Drenthe**

Born: Abt 910
-CONTINUED AS #1,ROYAL CHART 2239
Married:

Died: Aft 964

4 **Hunroch, Count in Tristerbant**

Born: Abt 940

Married:

Died: Aft 1026

9 **Amalrada of Hamalant**

Born: Abt 915
-CONTINUED AS #1,ROYAL CHART 2240
Died:

2 **Godizo, Count in the Betuwe**

Born: Abt 970

Married:

Died: 1018

10

Born:

Married:

Died:

5 --

Born:

Died:

11

Born:

Died:

1 **Eberhard, Count in the Betuwe**

Born: Abt 1000
-SAME AS #10,ROYAL CHART 1683
Married:

Died:

12

Born:

Married:

Died:

6

Born:

Married:

Died:

13

Born:

Died:

--

Spouse

3 **Bertha**

Born:

Died:

14

Born:

Married:

Died:

7

Born:

Died:

15

Born:

Died:

Sources include: Stuart 389; Moriarty 125 (#1); *Ancestral Roots* 155-22 (#1); *Royal Ancestors* (1989), chart 11473.

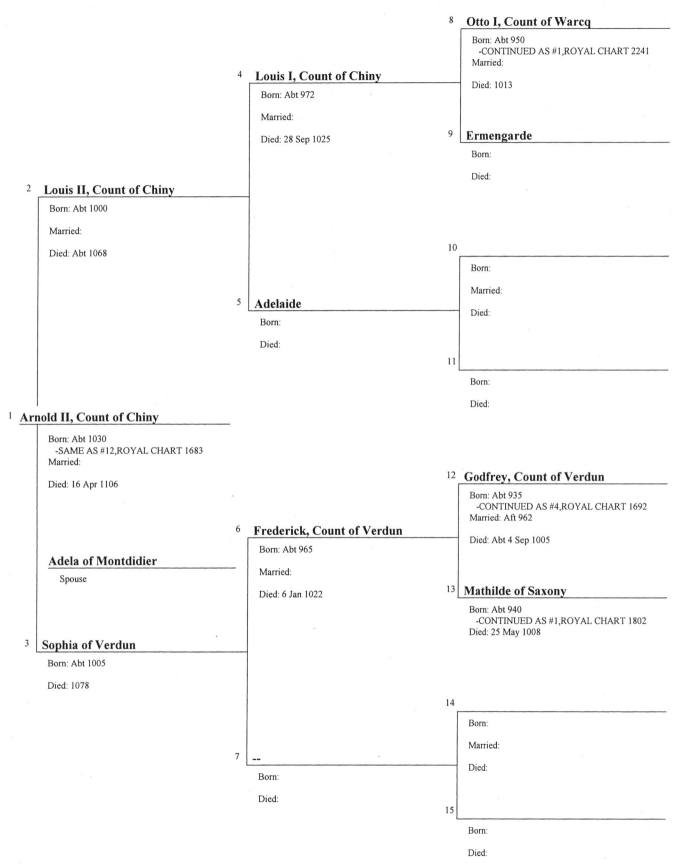

8 Otto I, Count of Warcq

Born: Abt 950
-CONTINUED AS #1, ROYAL CHART 2241
Married:

Died: 1013

4 Louis I, Count of Chiny

Born: Abt 972

Married:

Died: 28 Sep 1025

9 Ermengarde

Born:

Died:

2 Louis II, Count of Chiny

Born: Abt 1000

Married:

Died: Abt 1068

10

Born:

Married:

Died:

5 Adelaide

Born:

Died:

11

Born:

Died:

1 Arnold II, Count of Chiny

Born: Abt 1030
-SAME AS #12, ROYAL CHART 1683
Married:

Died: 16 Apr 1106

12 Godfrey, Count of Verdun

Born: Abt 935
-CONTINUED AS #4, ROYAL CHART 1692
Married: Aft 962

Died: Abt 4 Sep 1005

6 Frederick, Count of Verdun

Born: Abt 965

Married:

Died: 6 Jan 1022

Adela of Montdidier

Spouse

13 Mathilde of Saxony

Born: Abt 940
-CONTINUED AS #1, ROYAL CHART 1802
Died: 25 May 1008

3 Sophia of Verdun

Born: Abt 1005

Died: 1078

14

Born:

Married:

Died:

7 --

Born:

Died:

15

Born:

Died:

Sources include: Moriarty 155, 126; Stuart 65; *Royal Ancestors* (1989), chart 11473. Notes: The ancestry shown for #3 Sophia is not certain. #9 (wife of Otto I) was not the daughter of Albert I (Count of Namur, born about 968) and Ermengarde of Lorraine (see charts 1793-94), as claimed by Stuart and as shown (but questioned) by Moriarty. This is not possible chronologically.

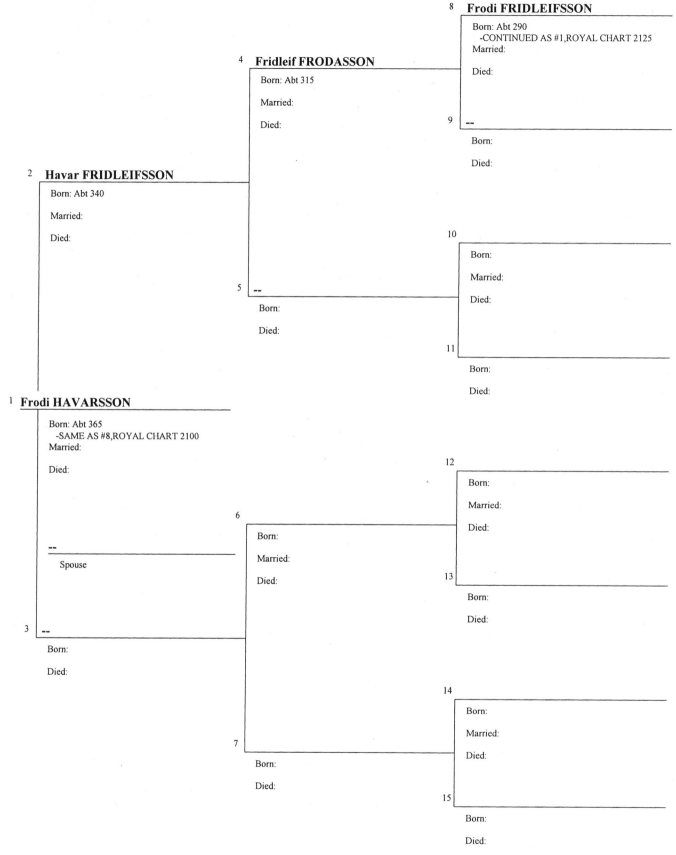

8 Frodi FRIDLEIFSSON

Born: Abt 290
   -CONTINUED AS #1,ROYAL CHART 2125
Married:

Died:

4 Fridleif FRODASSON

Born: Abt 315

Married:

Died:

9 --

Born:

Died:

2 Havar FRIDLEIFSSON

Born: Abt 340

Married:

Died:

10

Born:

Married:

Died:

5 --

Born:

Died:

11

Born:

Died:

1 Frodi HAVARSSON

Born: Abt 365
   -SAME AS #8,ROYAL CHART 2100
Married:

Died:

12

Born:

Married:

Died:

--

Spouse

6

Born:

Married:

Died:

13

Born:

Died:

3 --

Born:

Died:

14

Born:

Married:

Died:

7

Born:

Died:

15

Born:

Died:

Sources include: *Royal Ancestors* (1989), charts 11711-12; Stuart 324; LDS records.

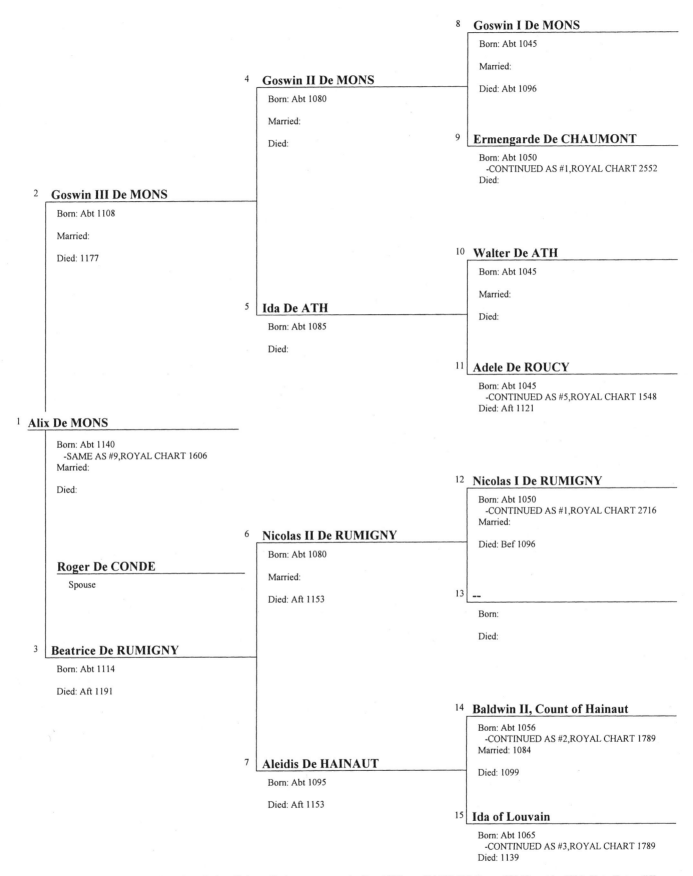

8 Goswin I De MONS
Born: Abt 1045
Married:
Died: Abt 1096

4 Goswin II De MONS
Born: Abt 1080
Married:
Died:

9 Ermengarde De CHAUMONT
Born: Abt 1050
-CONTINUED AS #1,ROYAL CHART 2552
Died:

2 Goswin III De MONS
Born: Abt 1108
Married:
Died: 1177

10 Walter De ATH
Born: Abt 1045
Married:
Died:

5 Ida De ATH
Born: Abt 1085
Died:

11 Adele De ROUCY
Born: Abt 1045
-CONTINUED AS #5,ROYAL CHART 1548
Died: Aft 1121

1 Alix De MONS
Born: Abt 1140
-SAME AS #9,ROYAL CHART 1606
Married:
Died:

12 Nicolas I De RUMIGNY
Born: Abt 1050
-CONTINUED AS #1,ROYAL CHART 2716
Married:
Died: Bef 1096

6 Nicolas II De RUMIGNY
Born: Abt 1080
Married:
Died: Aft 1153

13 --
Born:
Died:

Roger De CONDE
Spouse

3 Beatrice De RUMIGNY
Born: Abt 1114
Died: Aft 1191

14 Baldwin II, Count of Hainaut
Born: Abt 1056
-CONTINUED AS #2,ROYAL CHART 1789
Married: 1084
Died: 1099

7 Aleidis De HAINAUT
Born: Abt 1095
Died: Aft 1153

15 Ida of Louvain
Born: Abt 1065
-CONTINUED AS #3,ROYAL CHART 1789
Died: 1139

Sources include: *Royal Ancestors* (1989), chart 11957; Faris preliminary Charlemagne manuscript (June 1995), pp. 184-185, 239; Turton 191; Kraentzler 1316. Note: Turton differs somewhat on the Mons (#4) and Rumigny (#6) ancestry. He gives extensive ancestry for #8 Goswin that appears to be unreliable.

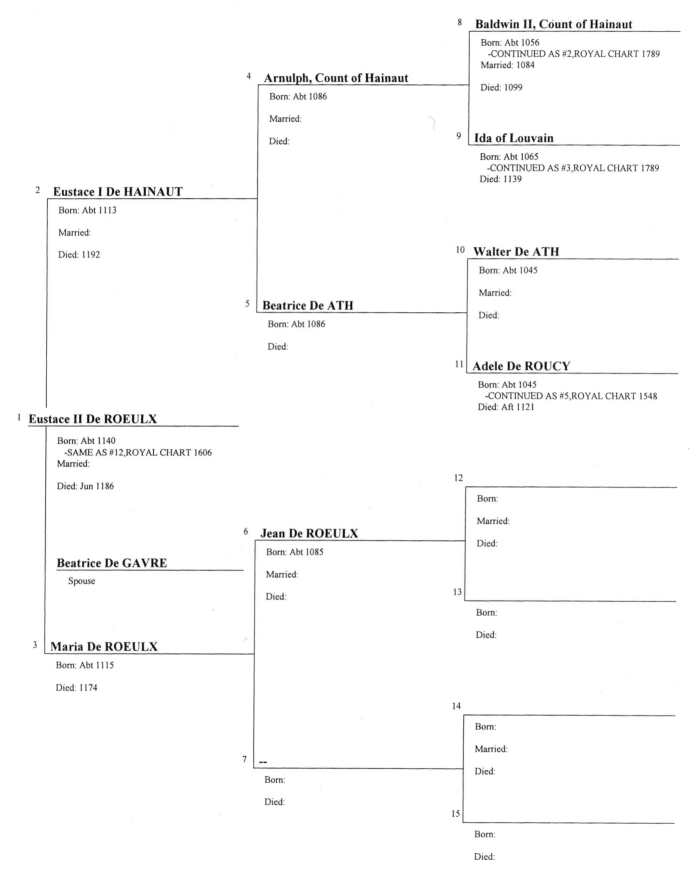

8 Baldwin II, Count of Hainaut

Born: Abt 1056
-CONTINUED AS #2,ROYAL CHART 1789
Married: 1084

Died: 1099

4 Arnulph, Count of Hainaut

Born: Abt 1086

Married:

Died:

9 Ida of Louvain

Born: Abt 1065
-CONTINUED AS #3,ROYAL CHART 1789
Died: 1139

2 Eustace I De HAINAUT

Born: Abt 1113

Married:

Died: 1192

10 Walter De ATH

Born: Abt 1045

Married:

Died:

5 Beatrice De ATH

Born: Abt 1086

Died:

11 Adele De ROUCY

Born: Abt 1045
-CONTINUED AS #5,ROYAL CHART 1548
Died: Aft 1121

1 Eustace II De ROEULX

Born: Abt 1140
-SAME AS #12,ROYAL CHART 1606
Married:

Died: Jun 1186

12

Born:

Married:

Died:

6 Jean De ROEULX

Born: Abt 1085

Married:

Died:

13

Born:

Died:

Beatrice De GAVRE

Spouse

3 Maria De ROEULX

Born: Abt 1115

Died: 1174

14

Born:

Married:

Died:

7 --

Born:

Died:

15

Born:

Died:

Sources include: *Royal Ancestors* (1989), chart 11959; Faris preliminary Charlemagne manuscript (June 1995), p. 232; Kraentzler 1318; Turton 191.

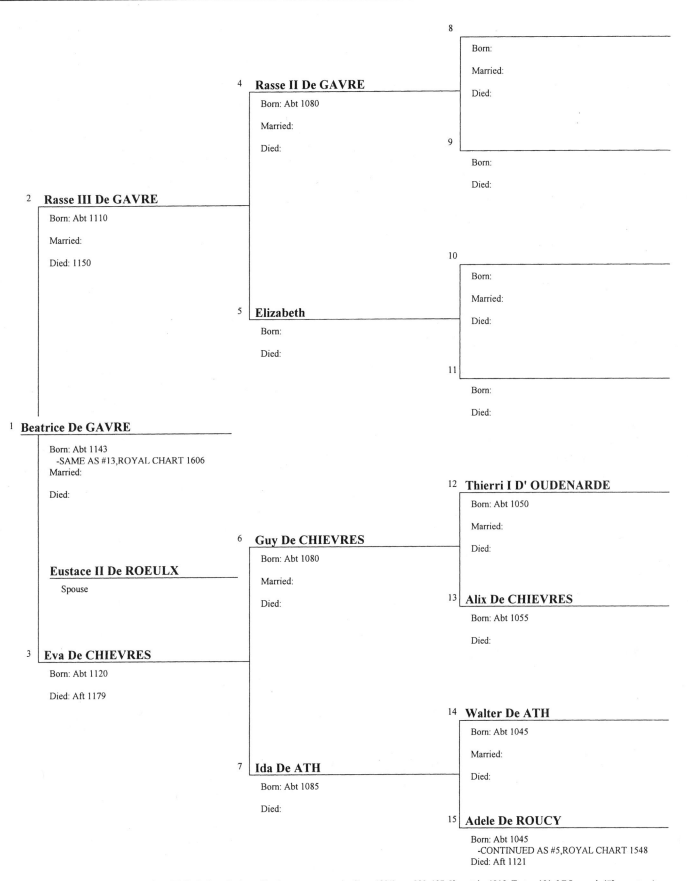

8

Born:

Married:

Died:

4 Rasse II De GAVRE

Born: Abt 1080

Married:

Died:

9

Born:

Died:

2 Rasse III De GAVRE

Born: Abt 1110

Married:

Died: 1150

10

Born:

Married:

Died:

5 Elizabeth

Born:

Died:

11

Born:

Died:

1 Beatrice De GAVRE

Born: Abt 1143
  -SAME AS #13,ROYAL CHART 1606
Married:

Died:

12 Thierri I D' OUDENARDE

Born: Abt 1050

Married:

Died:

6 Guy De CHIEVRES

Born: Abt 1080

Married:

Died:

13 Alix De CHIEVRES

Born: Abt 1055

Died:

Eustace II De ROEULX

Spouse

3 Eva De CHIEVRES

Born: Abt 1120

Died: Aft 1179

14 Walter De ATH

Born: Abt 1045

Married:

Died:

7 Ida De ATH

Born: Abt 1085

Died:

15 Adele De ROUCY

Born: Abt 1045
  -CONTINUED AS #5,ROYAL CHART 1548
Died: Aft 1121

Sources include: *Royal Ancestors* (1989), chart 11959; Faris preliminary Charlemagne manuscript (June 1995), pp. 232, 107; Kraentzler 1318; Turton 191; LDS records (#3 parentage).
Note: Turton gives ancestry for #4 that appears to be unreliable.

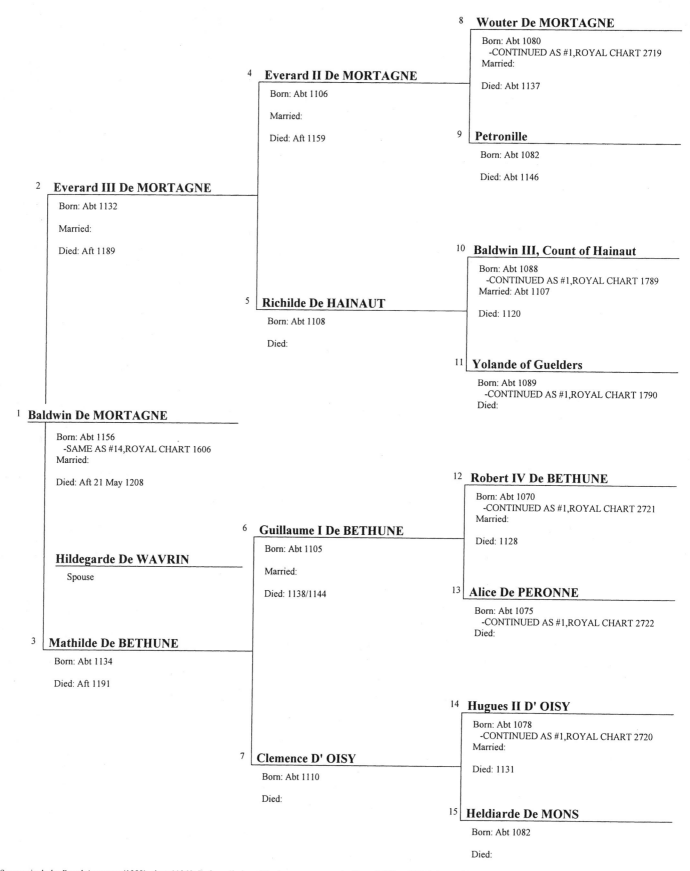

8 **Wouter De MORTAGNE**
Born: Abt 1080
 -CONTINUED AS #1,ROYAL CHART 2719
Married:

Died: Abt 1137

4 **Everard II De MORTAGNE**
Born: Abt 1106

Married:

Died: Aft 1159

9 **Petronille**
Born: Abt 1082

Died: Abt 1146

2 **Everard III De MORTAGNE**
Born: Abt 1132

Married:

Died: Aft 1189

10 **Baldwin III, Count of Hainaut**
Born: Abt 1088
 -CONTINUED AS #1,ROYAL CHART 1789
Married: Abt 1107

Died: 1120

5 **Richilde De HAINAUT**
Born: Abt 1108

Died:

11 **Yolande of Guelders**
Born: Abt 1089
 -CONTINUED AS #1,ROYAL CHART 1790
Died:

1 **Baldwin De MORTAGNE**
Born: Abt 1156
 -SAME AS #14,ROYAL CHART 1606
Married:

Died: Aft 21 May 1208

12 **Robert IV De BETHUNE**
Born: Abt 1070
 -CONTINUED AS #1,ROYAL CHART 2721
Married:

Died: 1128

6 **Guillaume I De BETHUNE**
Born: Abt 1105

Married:

Died: 1138/1144

Hildegarde De WAVRIN
Spouse

13 **Alice De PERONNE**
Born: Abt 1075
 -CONTINUED AS #1,ROYAL CHART 2722
Died:

3 **Mathilde De BETHUNE**
Born: Abt 1134

Died: Aft 1191

14 **Hugues II D' OISY**
Born: Abt 1078
 -CONTINUED AS #1,ROYAL CHART 2720
Married:

Died: 1131

7 **Clemence D' OISY**
Born: Abt 1110

Died:

15 **Heldiarde De MONS**
Born: Abt 1082

Died:

Sources include: *Royal Ancestors* (1989), chart 11960; Faris preliminary Charlemagne manuscript (June 1995), p. 264; Schwennicke 7:88 (#2 ancestry), 7:57 (#3 ancestry); Kraentzler 1319; Turton 191, 174, 198. Notes: The parentage of #4 Eberhard is disputed. #3 is also claimed as a 2nd wife Gertrude, who is claimed as daughter of Lambert De Montagu, but that parentage is disputed. The Faris version is followed above.

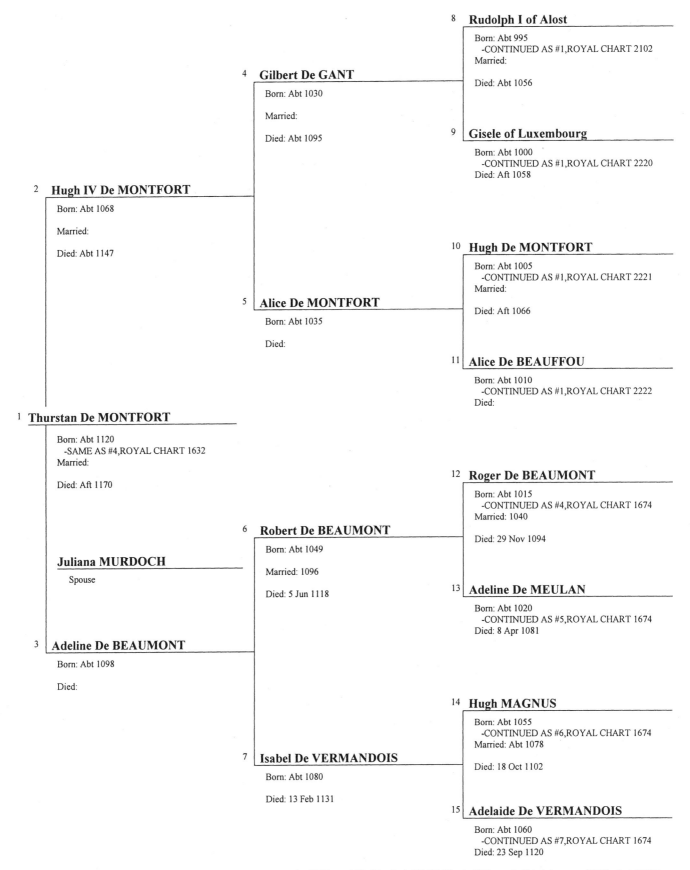

8 Rudolph I of Alost

Born: Abt 995
  -CONTINUED AS #1,ROYAL CHART 2102
Married:

Died: Abt 1056

4 Gilbert De GANT

Born: Abt 1030

Married:

Died: Abt 1095

9 Gisele of Luxembourg

Born: Abt 1000
  -CONTINUED AS #1,ROYAL CHART 2220
Died: Aft 1058

2 Hugh IV De MONTFORT

Born: Abt 1068

Married:

Died: Abt 1147

10 Hugh De MONTFORT

Born: Abt 1005
  -CONTINUED AS #1,ROYAL CHART 2221
Married:

Died: Aft 1066

5 Alice De MONTFORT

Born: Abt 1035

Died:

11 Alice De BEAUFFOU

Born: Abt 1010
  -CONTINUED AS #1,ROYAL CHART 2222
Died:

1 Thurstan De MONTFORT

Born: Abt 1120
  -SAME AS #4,ROYAL CHART 1632
Married:

Died: Aft 1170

12 Roger De BEAUMONT

Born: Abt 1015
  -CONTINUED AS #4,ROYAL CHART 1674
Married: 1040

Died: 29 Nov 1094

6 Robert De BEAUMONT

Born: Abt 1049

Married: 1096

Died: 5 Jun 1118

13 Adeline De MEULAN

Born: Abt 1020
  -CONTINUED AS #5,ROYAL CHART 1674
Died: 8 Apr 1081

Juliana MURDOCH

Spouse

3 Adeline De BEAUMONT

Born: Abt 1098

Died:

14 Hugh MAGNUS

Born: Abt 1055
  -CONTINUED AS #6,ROYAL CHART 1674
Married: Abt 1078

Died: 18 Oct 1102

7 Isabel De VERMANDOIS

Born: Abt 1080

Died: 13 Feb 1131

15 Adelaide De VERMANDOIS

Born: Abt 1060
  -CONTINUED AS #7,ROYAL CHART 1674
Died: 23 Sep 1120

Sources include: Paget (1957) 377:1-2, 378:1; Faris preliminary baronial manuscript (1998), pp. 1113 (Montfort), 688-689 (Gant); LDS records; *Royal Ancestors* (1989), chart 11908; Turton 88; *Ancestral Roots* 143 (#4 & 5 ancestry). Note: The parentage of #1 Thurstan is not certain. Paget gives #1 as possibly son of Hugh IV, as shown above. Faris gives #1 as perhaps son of a Thurstan who died in 1097. Both versions are problematic.

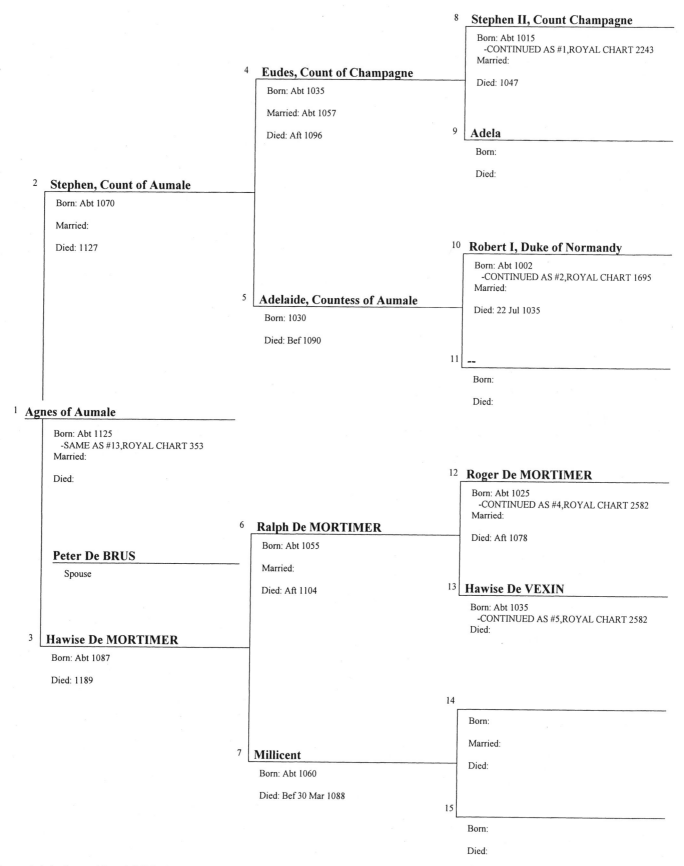

8 **Stephen II, Count Champagne**

Born: Abt 1015
   -CONTINUED AS #1,ROYAL CHART 2243
Married:

Died: 1047

4 **Eudes, Count of Champagne**

Born: Abt 1035

Married: Abt 1057

Died: Aft 1096

9 **Adela**

Born:

Died:

2 **Stephen, Count of Aumale**

Born: Abt 1070

Married:

Died: 1127

10 **Robert I, Duke of Normandy**

Born: Abt 1002
   -CONTINUED AS #2,ROYAL CHART 1695
Married:

Died: 22 Jul 1035

5 **Adelaide, Countess of Aumale**

Born: 1030

Died: Bef 1090

11 **--**

Born:

Died:

1 **Agnes of Aumale**

Born: Abt 1125
   -SAME AS #13,ROYAL CHART 353
Married:

Died:

12 **Roger De MORTIMER**

Born: Abt 1025
   -CONTINUED AS #4,ROYAL CHART 2582
Married:

Died: Aft 1078

6 **Ralph De MORTIMER**

Born: Abt 1055

Married:

Died: Aft 1104

Peter De BRUS

Spouse

13 **Hawise De VEXIN**

Born: Abt 1035
   -CONTINUED AS #5,ROYAL CHART 2582
Died:

3 **Hawise De MORTIMER**

Born: Abt 1087

Died: 1189

14

Born:

Married:

Died:

7 **Millicent**

Born: Abt 1060

Died: Bef 30 Mar 1088

15

Born:

Died:

Sources include: *Ancestral Roots* 8 (2004), Line 136; *Ancestral Roots* 136; Schwennicke 2:46; *Royal Ancestors* (1989), charts 11353, 12085-86; Faris preliminary Charlemagne manuscript (June 1995), pp. 26-27 (#2 ancestry); Consultation with Douglas Richardson. Notes: Richardson (July 2000) rejects the claim that #1 Agnes was the wife of Adam II De Brus (see charts 81, 2583). The correction adopted in *Ancestral Roots* 8 (#1 Agnes md. Peter De Brus, son of Adam De Brus & Joan Le Grammaire) is accepted here. Schwennicke shows Agnes md. Peter. Faris states that #11 (mother of Adelaide) was probably not Harlette (Herleve) De Falaise (mother of William I the Conqueror). See chart 1502.

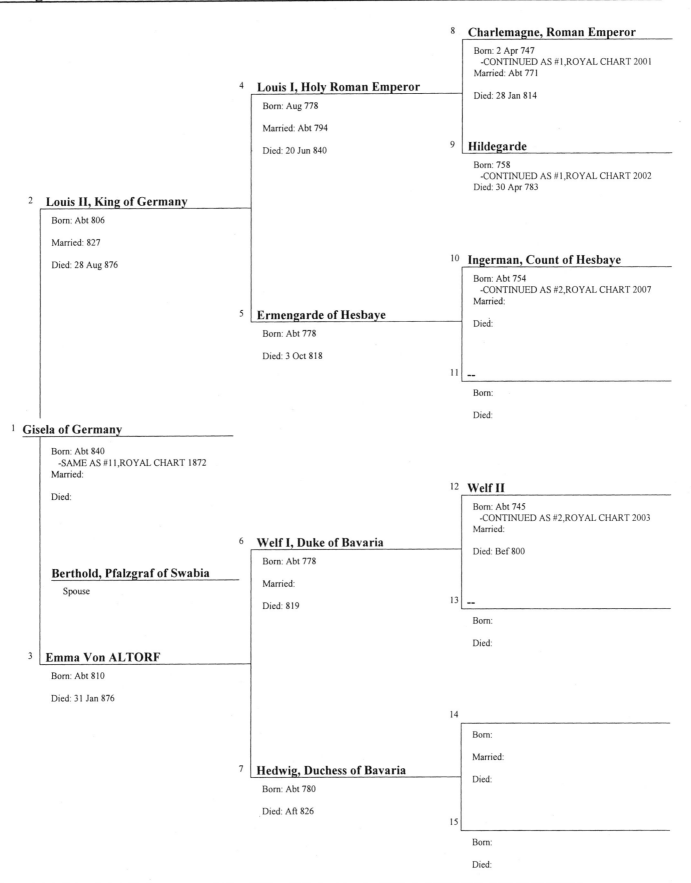

8 Charlemagne, Roman Emperor
Born: 2 Apr 747
  -CONTINUED AS #1,ROYAL CHART 2001
Married: Abt 771

Died: 28 Jan 814

4 Louis I, Holy Roman Emperor
Born: Aug 778

Married: Abt 794

Died: 20 Jun 840

9 Hildegarde
Born: 758
  -CONTINUED AS #1,ROYAL CHART 2002
Died: 30 Apr 783

2 Louis II, King of Germany
Born: Abt 806

Married: 827

Died: 28 Aug 876

10 Ingerman, Count of Hesbaye
Born: Abt 754
  -CONTINUED AS #2,ROYAL CHART 2007
Married:

Died:

5 Ermengarde of Hesbaye
Born: Abt 778

Died: 3 Oct 818

11 --
Born:

Died:

1 Gisela of Germany
Born: Abt 840
  -SAME AS #11,ROYAL CHART 1872
Married:

Died:

12 Welf II
Born: Abt 745
  -CONTINUED AS #2,ROYAL CHART 2003
Married:

Died: Bef 800

6 Welf I, Duke of Bavaria
Born: Abt 778

Married:

Died: 819

Berthold, Pfalzgraf of Swabia
Spouse

13 --
Born:

Died:

3 Emma Von ALTORF
Born: Abt 810

Died: 31 Jan 876

14
Born:

Married:

Died:

7 Hedwig, Duchess of Bavaria
Born: Abt 780

Died: Aft 826

15
Born:

Died:

Sources include: Faris preliminary Charlemagne manuscript (June 1995), pp. 40-41; *Royal Ancestors* (1989), charts 11508, 11601, 11630 (#2 & 3 ancestry).

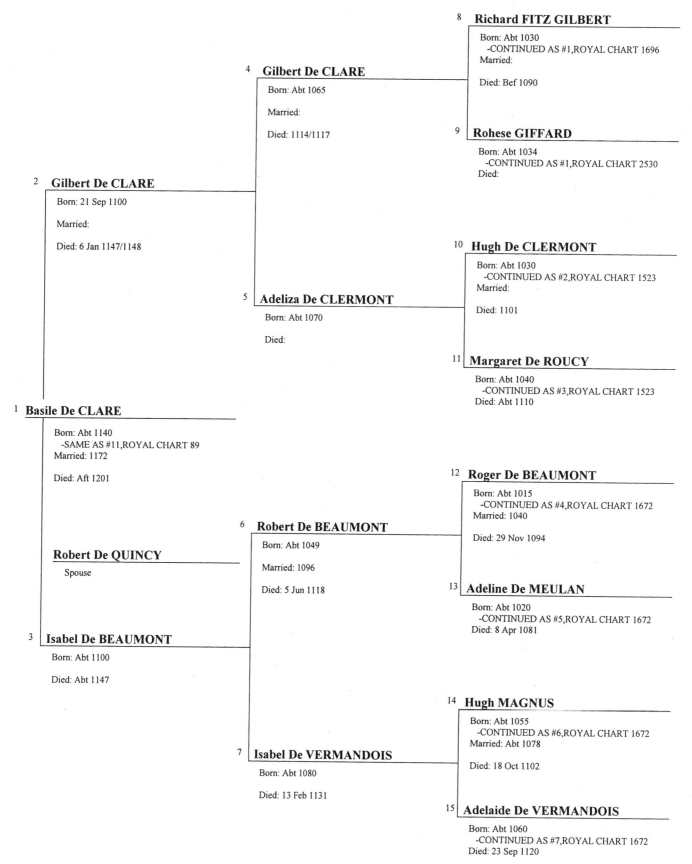

8 **Richard FITZ GILBERT**

Born: Abt 1030
  -CONTINUED AS #1,ROYAL CHART 1696
Married:

Died: Bef 1090

---

4 **Gilbert De CLARE**

Born: Abt 1065

Married:

Died: 1114/1117

---

9 **Rohese GIFFARD**

Born: Abt 1034
  -CONTINUED AS #1,ROYAL CHART 2530
Died:

---

2 **Gilbert De CLARE**

Born: 21 Sep 1100

Married:

Died: 6 Jan 1147/1148

---

10 **Hugh De CLERMONT**

Born: Abt 1030
  -CONTINUED AS #2,ROYAL CHART 1523
Married:

Died: 1101

---

5 **Adeliza De CLERMONT**

Born: Abt 1070

Died:

---

11 **Margaret De ROUCY**

Born: Abt 1040
  -CONTINUED AS #3,ROYAL CHART 1523
Died: Abt 1110

---

1 **Basile De CLARE**

Born: Abt 1140
  -SAME AS #11,ROYAL CHART 89
Married: 1172

Died: Aft 1201

Robert De QUINCY

Spouse

---

12 **Roger De BEAUMONT**

Born: Abt 1015
  -CONTINUED AS #4,ROYAL CHART 1672
Married: 1040

Died: 29 Nov 1094

---

6 **Robert De BEAUMONT**

Born: Abt 1049

Married: 1096

Died: 5 Jun 1118

---

13 **Adeline De MEULAN**

Born: Abt 1020
  -CONTINUED AS #5,ROYAL CHART 1672
Died: 8 Apr 1081

---

3 **Isabel De BEAUMONT**

Born: Abt 1100

Died: Abt 1147

---

14 **Hugh MAGNUS**

Born: Abt 1055
  -CONTINUED AS #6,ROYAL CHART 1672
Married: Abt 1078

Died: 18 Oct 1102

---

7 **Isabel De VERMANDOIS**

Born: Abt 1080

Died: 13 Feb 1131

---

15 **Adelaide De VERMANDOIS**

Born: Abt 1060
  -CONTINUED AS #7,ROYAL CHART 1672
Died: 23 Sep 1120

Sources include: Research report on Ancestry of Maud De Prendergast by Douglas Richardson, dated 16 July 2000; Turton 143. Note: #1 Basile might be daughter of Richard De Clare by an unknown lst wife (not by Eve of Leinster--see chart 1604) and granddaughter of # 2 & 3 Gilbert & Isabel above.

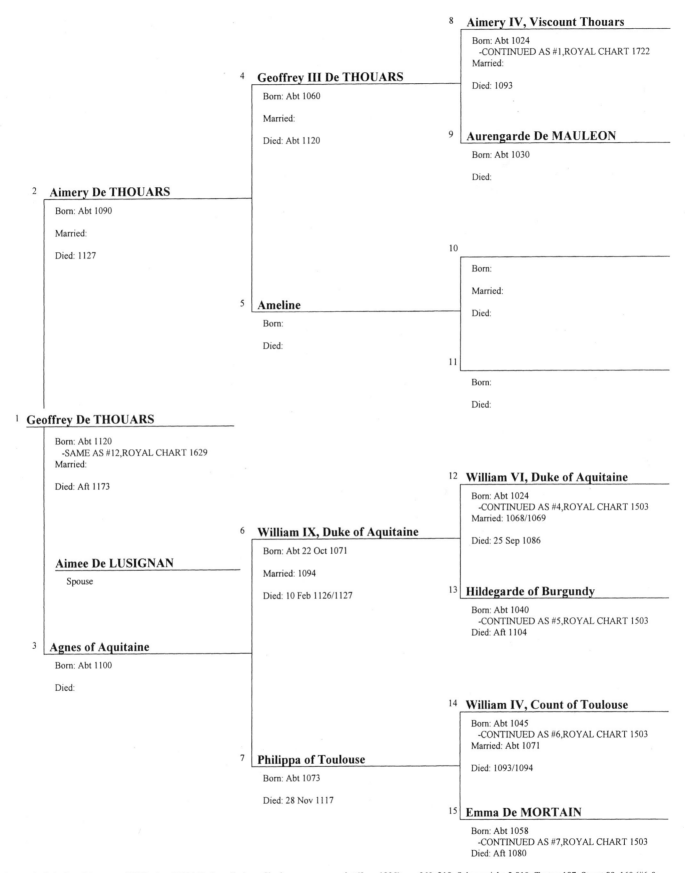

Pedigree Chart

8 **Aimery IV, Viscount Thouars**

Born: Abt 1024
-CONTINUED AS #1,ROYAL CHART 1722
Married:

Died: 1093

4 **Geoffrey III De THOUARS**

Born: Abt 1060

Married:

Died: Abt 1120

9 **Aurengarde De MAULEON**

Born: Abt 1030

Died:

2 **Aimery De THOUARS**

Born: Abt 1090

Married:

Died: 1127

10

Born:

Married:

Died:

5 **Ameline**

Born:

Died:

11

Born:

Died:

1 **Geoffrey De THOUARS**

Born: Abt 1120
-SAME AS #12,ROYAL CHART 1629
Married:

Died: Aft 1173

12 **William VI, Duke of Aquitaine**

Born: Abt 1024
-CONTINUED AS #4,ROYAL CHART 1503
Married: 1068/1069

Died: 25 Sep 1086

6 **William IX, Duke of Aquitaine**

Born: Abt 22 Oct 1071

Married: 1094

Died: 10 Feb 1126/1127

13 **Hildegarde of Burgundy**

Born: Abt 1040
-CONTINUED AS #5,ROYAL CHART 1503
Died: Aft 1104

Aimee De LUSIGNAN

Spouse

3 **Agnes of Aquitaine**

Born: Abt 1100

Died:

14 **William IV, Count of Toulouse**

Born: Abt 1045
-CONTINUED AS #6,ROYAL CHART 1503
Married: Abt 1071

Died: 1093/1094

7 **Philippa of Toulouse**

Born: Abt 1073

Died: 28 Nov 1117

15 **Emma De MORTAIN**

Born: Abt 1058
-CONTINUED AS #7,ROYAL CHART 1503
Died: Aft 1080

Sources include: *Royal Ancestors* (1989), chart 11906; Faris preliminary Charlemagne manuscript (June 1995), pp. 260, 218; Schwennicke 3:810; Turton 187; Stuart 88, 160 (#6 & 7 ancestry); *Ancestral Roots* 96-27 (#1 William), 111 (ancestry of #3 Agnes).

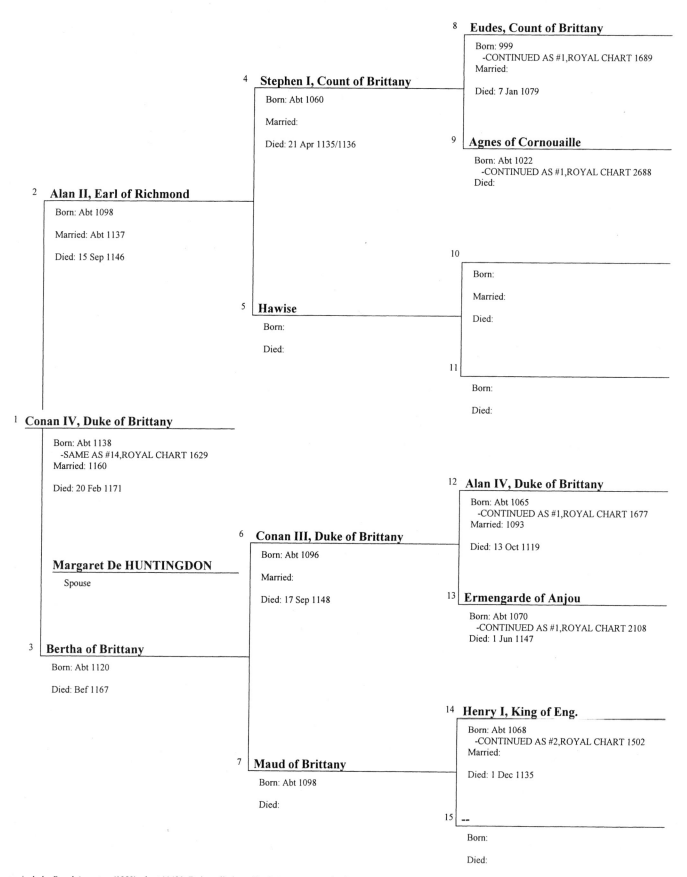

8 **Eudes, Count of Brittany**

Born: 999
  -CONTINUED AS #1,ROYAL CHART 1689
Married:

Died: 7 Jan 1079

4 **Stephen I, Count of Brittany**

Born: Abt 1060

Married:

Died: 21 Apr 1135/1136

9 **Agnes of Cornouaille**

Born: Abt 1022
  -CONTINUED AS #1,ROYAL CHART 2688
Died:

2 **Alan II, Earl of Richmond**

Born: Abt 1098

Married: Abt 1137

Died: 15 Sep 1146

10

Born:

Married:

Died:

5 **Hawise**

Born:

Died:

11

Born:

Died:

1 **Conan IV, Duke of Brittany**

Born: Abt 1138
  -SAME AS #14,ROYAL CHART 1629
Married: 1160

Died: 20 Feb 1171

12 **Alan IV, Duke of Brittany**

Born: Abt 1065
  -CONTINUED AS #1,ROYAL CHART 1677
Married: 1093

Died: 13 Oct 1119

6 **Conan III, Duke of Brittany**

Born: Abt 1096

Married:

Died: 17 Sep 1148

13 **Ermengarde of Anjou**

Born: Abt 1070
  -CONTINUED AS #1,ROYAL CHART 2108
Died: 1 Jun 1147

Margaret De HUNTINGDON

Spouse

3 **Bertha of Brittany**

Born: Abt 1120

Died: Bef 1167

14 **Henry I, King of Eng.**

Born: Abt 1068
  -CONTINUED AS #2,ROYAL CHART 1502
Married:

Died: 1 Dec 1135

7 **Maud of Brittany**

Born: Abt 1098

Died:

15 --

Born:

Died:

Sources include: *Royal Ancestors* (1989), chart 11490; Faris preliminary Charlemagne manuscript (June 1995), pp. 76-79; Schwennicke 2:75; *Ancestral Roots* 119, 227. Note: #9 Agnes is not certain. The mother of #4 Stephen is also given as Orguen--, who may have been a 1st wife of #8 Eudes, with Agnes being a 2nd wife.

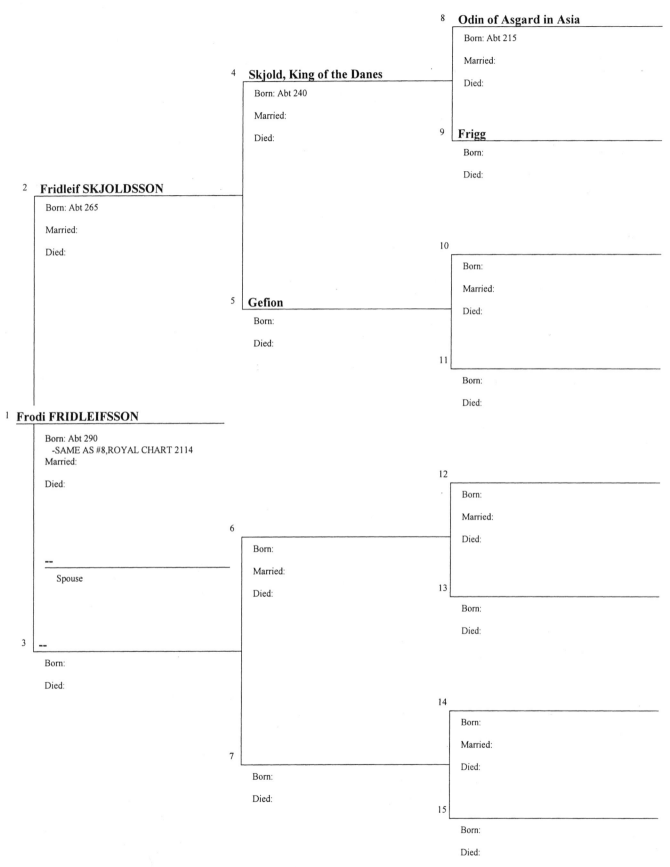

8 Odin of Asgard in Asia
Born: Abt 215
Married:
Died:

4 Skjold, King of the Danes
Born: Abt 240
Married:
Died:

9 Frigg
Born:
Died:

2 Fridleif SKJOLDSSON
Born: Abt 265
Married:
Died:

10
Born:
Married:
Died:

5 Gefion
Born:
Died:

11
Born:
Died:

1 Frodi FRIDLEIFSSON
Born: Abt 290
  -SAME AS #8,ROYAL CHART 2114
Married:
Died:

--
Spouse

12
Born:
Married:
Died:

6
Born:
Married:
Died:

13
Born:
Died:

3 --
Born:
Died:

14
Born:
Married:
Died:

7
Born:
Died:

15
Born:
Died:

Sources include: *Royal Ancestors* (1989), charts 11712-13; Stuart 324; LDS records. Note: See notes chart 2098 regarding claimed descents and claimed ancestry for #8 Odin.

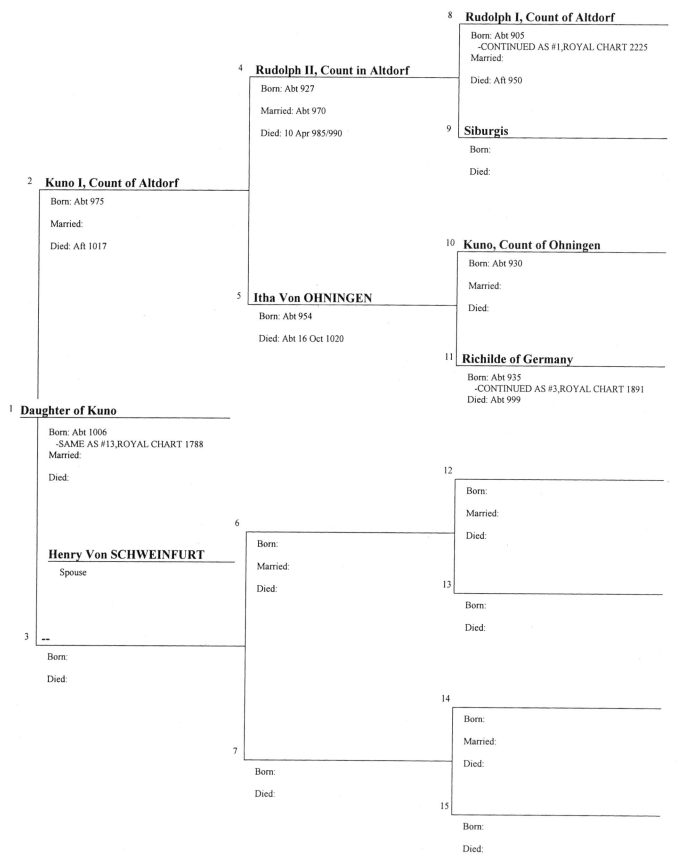

8 Rudolph I, Count of Altdorf

Born: Abt 905
-CONTINUED AS #1,ROYAL CHART 2225
Married:

Died: Aft 950

4 Rudolph II, Count in Altdorf

Born: Abt 927

Married: Abt 970

Died: 10 Apr 985/990

9 Siburgis

Born:

Died:

2 Kuno I, Count of Altdorf

Born: Abt 975

Married:

Died: Aft 1017

10 Kuno, Count of Ohningen

Born: Abt 930

Married:

Died:

5 Itha Von OHNINGEN

Born: Abt 954

Died: Abt 16 Oct 1020

11 Richilde of Germany

Born: Abt 935
-CONTINUED AS #3,ROYAL CHART 1891
Died: Abt 999

1 Daughter of Kuno

Born: Abt 1006
-SAME AS #13,ROYAL CHART 1788
Married:

Died:

12

Born:

Married:

Died:

6

Born:

Married:

Died:

13

Born:

Died:

Henry Von SCHWEINFURT

Spouse

3 --

Born:

Died:

14

Born:

Married:

Died:

7

Born:

Died:

15

Born:

Died:

Sources include: Stuart 213; Moriarty 168; *Royal Ancestors* (1989), chart 11788 (#4 & 5 ancestry).

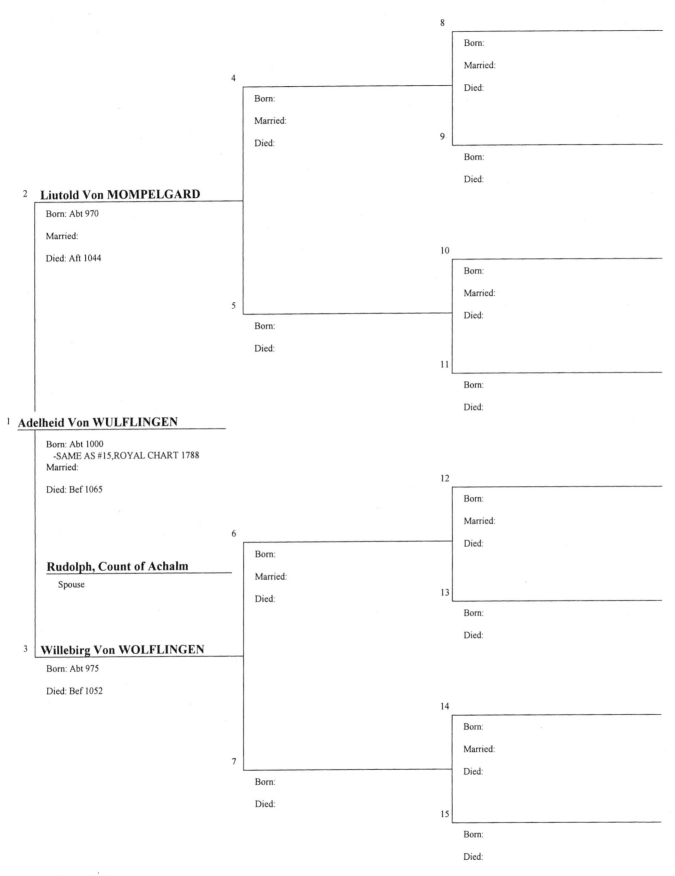

8

Born:

Married:

Died:

4

Born:

Married:

Died:

9

Born:

Died:

2 **Liutold Von MOMPELGARD**

Born: Abt 970

Married:

Died: Aft 1044

10

Born:

Married:

Died:

5

Born:

Died:

11

Born:

Died:

1 **Adelheid Von WULFLINGEN**

Born: Abt 1000
-SAME AS #15,ROYAL CHART 1788
Married:

Died: Bef 1065

12

Born:

Married:

Died:

6

Born:

Married:

Died:

13

Born:

Died:

Rudolph, Count of Achalm

Spouse

3 **Willebirg Von WOLFLINGEN**

Born: Abt 975

Died: Bef 1052

14

Born:

Married:

Died:

7

Born:

Died:

15

Born:

Died:

Sources include: Stuart 213-33.

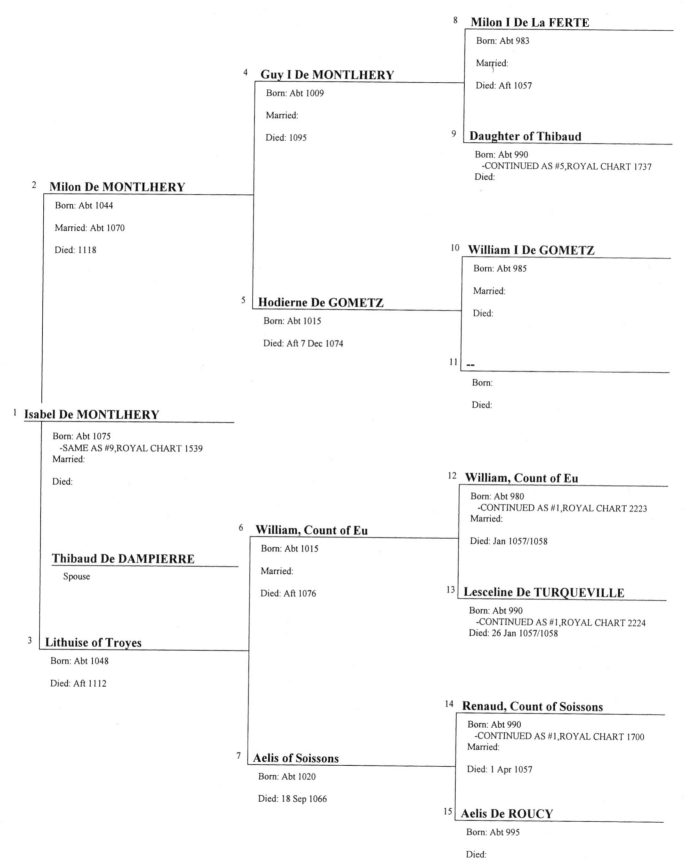

8 Milon I De La FERTE

Born: Abt 983

Married:

Died: Aft 1057

4 Guy I De MONTLHERY

Born: Abt 1009

Married:

Died: 1095

9 Daughter of Thibaud

Born: Abt 990
  -CONTINUED AS #5,ROYAL CHART 1737
Died:

2 Milon De MONTLHERY

Born: Abt 1044

Married: Abt 1070

Died: 1118

10 William I De GOMETZ

Born: Abt 985

Married:

Died:

5 Hodierne De GOMETZ

Born: Abt 1015

Died: Aft 7 Dec 1074

11 --

Born:

Died:

1 Isabel De MONTLHERY

Born: Abt 1075
  -SAME AS #9,ROYAL CHART 1539
Married:

Died:

12 William, Count of Eu

Born: Abt 980
  -CONTINUED AS #1,ROYAL CHART 2223
Married:

Died: Jan 1057/1058

6 William, Count of Eu

Born: Abt 1015

Married:

Died: Aft 1076

13 Lesceline De TURQUEVILLE

Born: Abt 990
  -CONTINUED AS #1,ROYAL CHART 2224
Died: 26 Jan 1057/1058

Thibaud De DAMPIERRE

Spouse

14 Renaud, Count of Soissons

Born: Abt 990
  -CONTINUED AS #1,ROYAL CHART 1700
Married:

Died: 1 Apr 1057

3 Lithuise of Troyes

Born: Abt 1048

Died: Aft 1112

7 Aelis of Soissons

Born: Abt 1020

Died: 18 Sep 1066

15 Aelis De ROUCY

Born: Abt 995

Died:

Sources include: *Royal Ancestors* (1989), chart 11823; Stuart 57; Moriarty 150, 63, 265, 267.

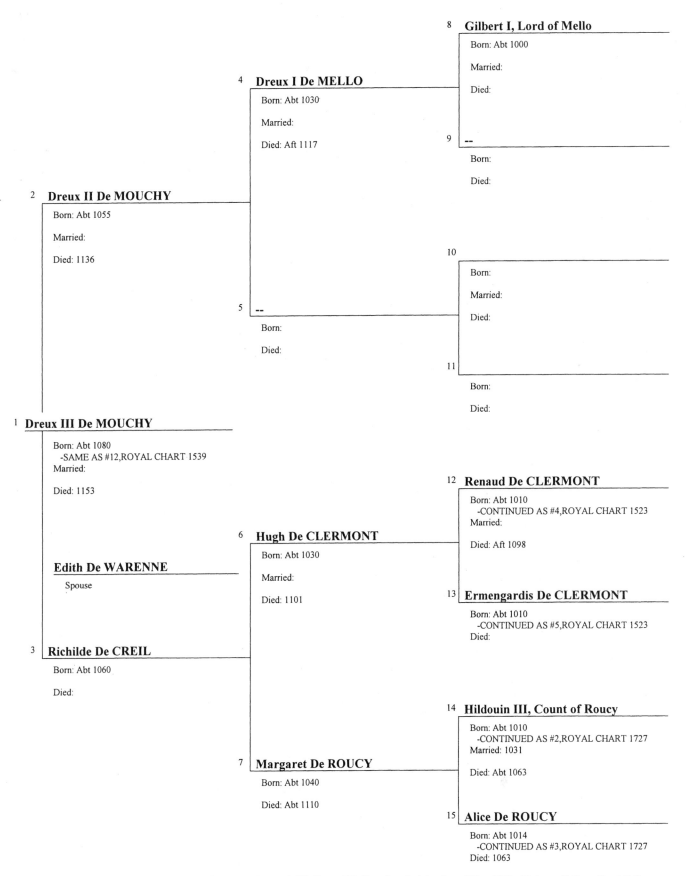

8 **Gilbert I, Lord of Mello**

Born: Abt 1000

Married:

Died:

4 **Dreux I De MELLO**

Born: Abt 1030

Married:

Died: Aft 1117

9 **--**

Born:

Died:

2 **Dreux II De MOUCHY**

Born: Abt 1055

Married:

Died: 1136

10

Born:

Married:

Died:

5 **--**

Born:

Died:

11

Born:

Died:

1 **Dreux III De MOUCHY**

Born: Abt 1080
    -SAME AS #12,ROYAL CHART 1539
Married:

Died: 1153

12 **Renaud De CLERMONT**

Born: Abt 1010
    -CONTINUED AS #4,ROYAL CHART 1523
Married:

Died: Aft 1098

6 **Hugh De CLERMONT**

Born: Abt 1030

Married:

Died: 1101

13 **Ermengardis De CLERMONT**

Born: Abt 1010
    -CONTINUED AS #5,ROYAL CHART 1523
Died:

Edith De WARENNE

    Spouse

3 **Richilde De CREIL**

Born: Abt 1060

Died:

14 **Hildouin III, Count of Roucy**

Born: Abt 1010
    -CONTINUED AS #2,ROYAL CHART 1727
Married: 1031

Died: Abt 1063

7 **Margaret De ROUCY**

Born: Abt 1040

Died: Abt 1110

15 **Alice De ROUCY**

Born: Abt 1014
    -CONTINUED AS #3,ROYAL CHART 1727
Died: 1063

Sources include: *Royal Ancestors* (1989), chart 11946; Stuart 56; Moriarty 151, 269; Turton 210. Note: Stuart's claim of an additional Gilbert between #2 Dreux II and #4 Dreux I is chronologically untenable.

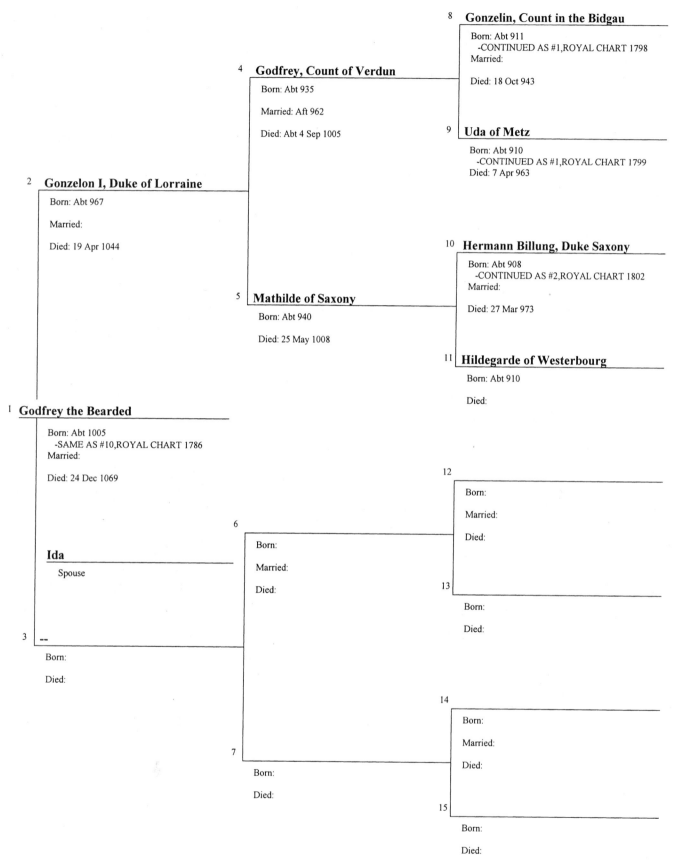

8 Gonzelin, Count in the Bidgau

Born: Abt 911
  -CONTINUED AS #1,ROYAL CHART 1798
Married:

Died: 18 Oct 943

4 Godfrey, Count of Verdun

Born: Abt 935

Married: Aft 962

Died: Abt 4 Sep 1005

9 Uda of Metz

Born: Abt 910
  -CONTINUED AS #1,ROYAL CHART 1799
Died: 7 Apr 963

2 Gonzelon I, Duke of Lorraine

Born: Abt 967

Married:

Died: 19 Apr 1044

10 Hermann Billung, Duke Saxony

Born: Abt 908
  -CONTINUED AS #2,ROYAL CHART 1802
Married:

Died: 27 Mar 973

5 Mathilde of Saxony

Born: Abt 940

Died: 25 May 1008

11 Hildegarde of Westerbourg

Born: Abt 910

Died:

1 Godfrey the Bearded

Born: Abt 1005
  -SAME AS #10,ROYAL CHART 1786
Married:

Died: 24 Dec 1069

12

Born:

Married:

Died:

6

Born:

Married:

Died:

13

Born:

Died:

Ida

Spouse

3 --

Born:

Died:

14

Born:

Married:

Died:

7

Born:

Died:

15

Born:

Died:

Sources include: *Royal Ancestors* (1989), charts 11421, 11761; Moriarty 126; Stuart 104 (#2 ancestry); Collett (family group sheet for #2 Gonzelon).

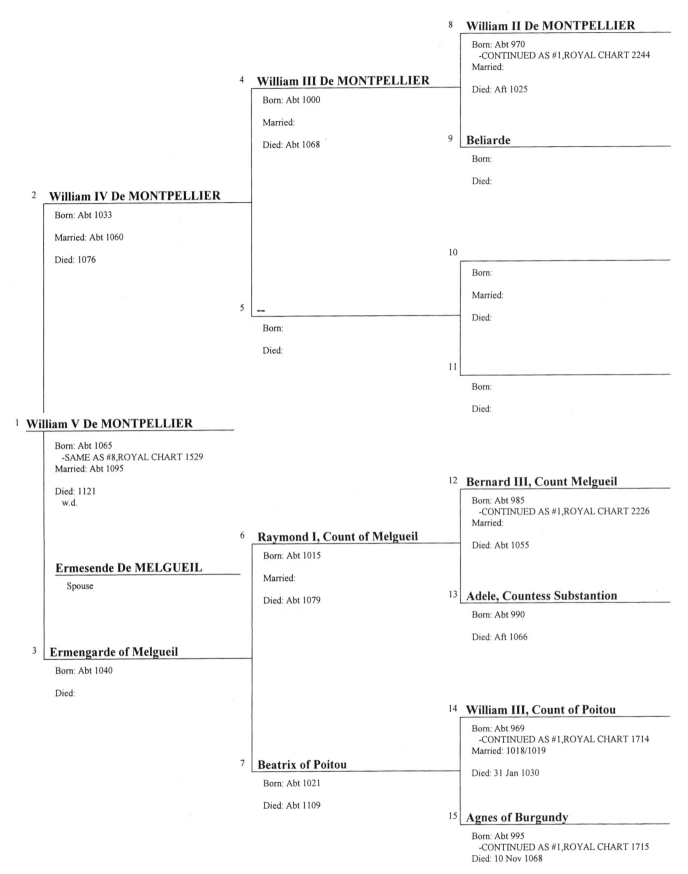

8   **William II De MONTPELLIER**

Born: Abt 970
-CONTINUED AS #1,ROYAL CHART 2244
Married:

Died: Aft 1025

4   **William III De MONTPELLIER**

Born: Abt 1000

Married:

Died: Abt 1068

9   **Beliarde**

Born:

Died:

2   **William IV De MONTPELLIER**

Born: Abt 1033

Married: Abt 1060

Died: 1076

10

Born:

Married:

Died:

5   **--**

Born:

Died:

11

Born:

Died:

1   **William V De MONTPELLIER**

Born: Abt 1065
-SAME AS #8,ROYAL CHART 1529
Married: Abt 1095

Died: 1121
w.d.

12   **Bernard III, Count Melgueil**

Born: Abt 985
-CONTINUED AS #1,ROYAL CHART 2226
Married:

Died: Abt 1055

6   **Raymond I, Count of Melgueil**

Born: Abt 1015

Married:

Died: Abt 1079

13   **Adele, Countess Substantion**

Born: Abt 990

Died: Aft 1066

Ermesende De MELGUEIL

Spouse

3   **Ermengarde of Melgueil**

Born: Abt 1040

Died:

14   **William III, Count of Poitou**

Born: Abt 969
-CONTINUED AS #1,ROYAL CHART 1714
Married: 1018/1019

Died: 31 Jan 1030

7   **Beatrix of Poitou**

Born: Abt 1021

Died: Abt 1109

15   **Agnes of Burgundy**

Born: Abt 995
-CONTINUED AS #1,ROYAL CHART 1715
Died: 10 Nov 1068

Sources include: *Royal Ancestors* (1989), charts 11846, 11853; Stuart 150; Moriarty 131; Faris preliminary Charlemagne manuscript (June 1995), p. 192; Turton 58. Note: There is disagreement on #2. Faris, citing West Winter, omits William IV and makes #2 William III (Guillaume III Guilhem De Montpellier) the husband of Ermengarde of Melgueil.

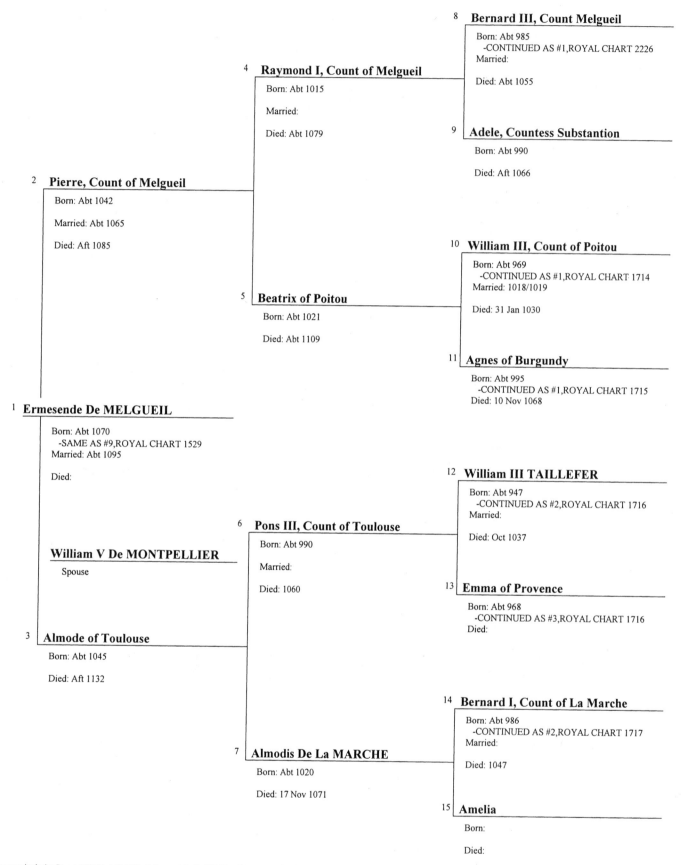

8 Bernard III, Count Melgueil
Born: Abt 985
-CONTINUED AS #1,ROYAL CHART 2226
Married:

Died: Abt 1055

4 Raymond I, Count of Melgueil
Born: Abt 1015

Married:

Died: Abt 1079

9 Adele, Countess Substantion
Born: Abt 990

Died: Aft 1066

2 Pierre, Count of Melgueil
Born: Abt 1042

Married: Abt 1065

Died: Aft 1085

10 William III, Count of Poitou
Born: Abt 969
-CONTINUED AS #1,ROYAL CHART 1714
Married: 1018/1019

Died: 31 Jan 1030

5 Beatrix of Poitou
Born: Abt 1021

Died: Abt 1109

11 Agnes of Burgundy
Born: Abt 995
-CONTINUED AS #1,ROYAL CHART 1715
Died: 10 Nov 1068

1 Ermesende De MELGUEIL
Born: Abt 1070
-SAME AS #9,ROYAL CHART 1529
Married: Abt 1095

Died:

12 William III TAILLEFER
Born: Abt 947
-CONTINUED AS #2,ROYAL CHART 1716
Married:

Died: Oct 1037

6 Pons III, Count of Toulouse
Born: Abt 990

Married:

Died: 1060

13 Emma of Provence
Born: Abt 968
-CONTINUED AS #3,ROYAL CHART 1716
Died:

William V De MONTPELLIER
Spouse

3 Almode of Toulouse
Born: Abt 1045

Died: Aft 1132

14 Bernard I, Count of La Marche
Born: Abt 986
-CONTINUED AS #2,ROYAL CHART 1717
Married:

Died: 1047

7 Almodis De La MARCHE
Born: Abt 1020

Died: 17 Nov 1071

15 Amelia
Born:

Died:

Sources include: Stuart 150-31, 142, 203; Schwennicke 3:444; *Royal Ancestors* (1989), charts 11846 (#1), 11409 (#6 & 7 ancestry); Moriarty 131 (#1), 42 (#3 ancestry). Note: The identification and parentage shown for #1 Ermesende is disputed and uncertain. In a preliminary Charlemagne manuscript (June 1995, p. 192), Faris gives her parentage as unknown and cites West Winter's statement that she was not of Melgueil. Schwennicke accepts Melgueil, with ancestry as shown.

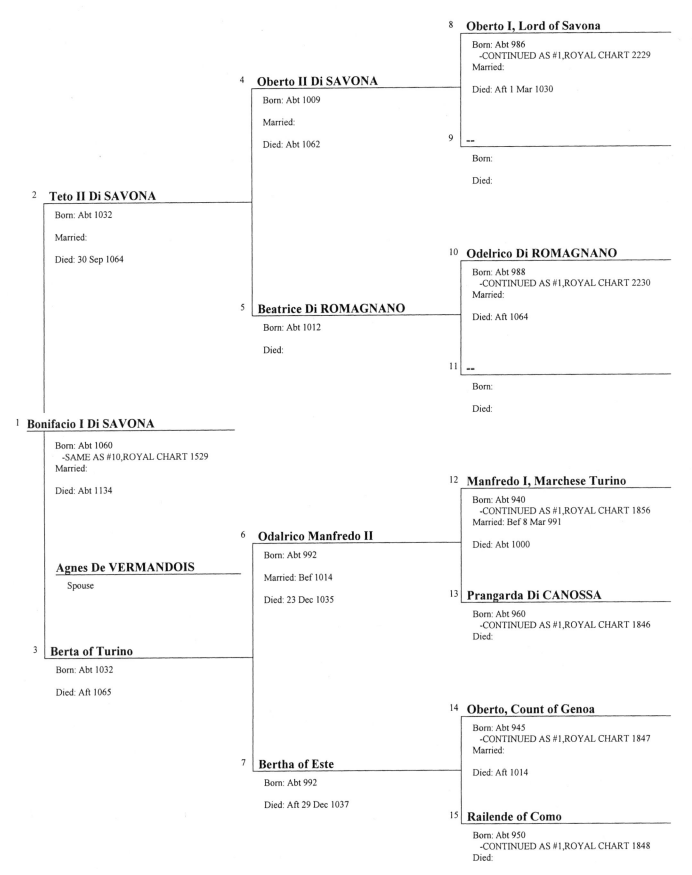

8 Oberto I, Lord of Savona

Born: Abt 986
-CONTINUED AS #1,ROYAL CHART 2229
Married:

Died: Aft 1 Mar 1030

4 Oberto II Di SAVONA

Born: Abt 1009

Married:

Died: Abt 1062

9 --

Born:

Died:

2 Teto II Di SAVONA

Born: Abt 1032

Married:

Died: 30 Sep 1064

10 Odelrico Di ROMAGNANO

Born: Abt 988
-CONTINUED AS #1,ROYAL CHART 2230
Married:

Died: Aft 1064

5 Beatrice Di ROMAGNANO

Born: Abt 1012

Died:

11 --

Born:

Died:

1 Bonifacio I Di SAVONA

Born: Abt 1060
-SAME AS #10,ROYAL CHART 1529
Married:

Died: Abt 1134

12 Manfredo I, Marchese Turino

Born: Abt 940
-CONTINUED AS #1,ROYAL CHART 1856
Married: Bef 8 Mar 991

Died: Abt 1000

6 Odalrico Manfredo II

Born: Abt 992

Married: Bef 1014

Died: 23 Dec 1035

13 Prangarda Di CANOSSA

Born: Abt 960
-CONTINUED AS #1,ROYAL CHART 1846
Died:

Agnes De VERMANDOIS

Spouse

3 Berta of Turino

Born: Abt 1032

Died: Aft 1065

14 Oberto, Count of Genoa

Born: Abt 945
-CONTINUED AS #1,ROYAL CHART 1847
Married:

Died: Aft 1014

7 Bertha of Este

Born: Abt 992

Died: Aft 29 Dec 1037

15 Railende of Como

Born: Abt 950
-CONTINUED AS #1,ROYAL CHART 1848
Died:

Sources include: *Royal Ancestors* (1989), chart 11846; Stuart 106; Moriarty 133.

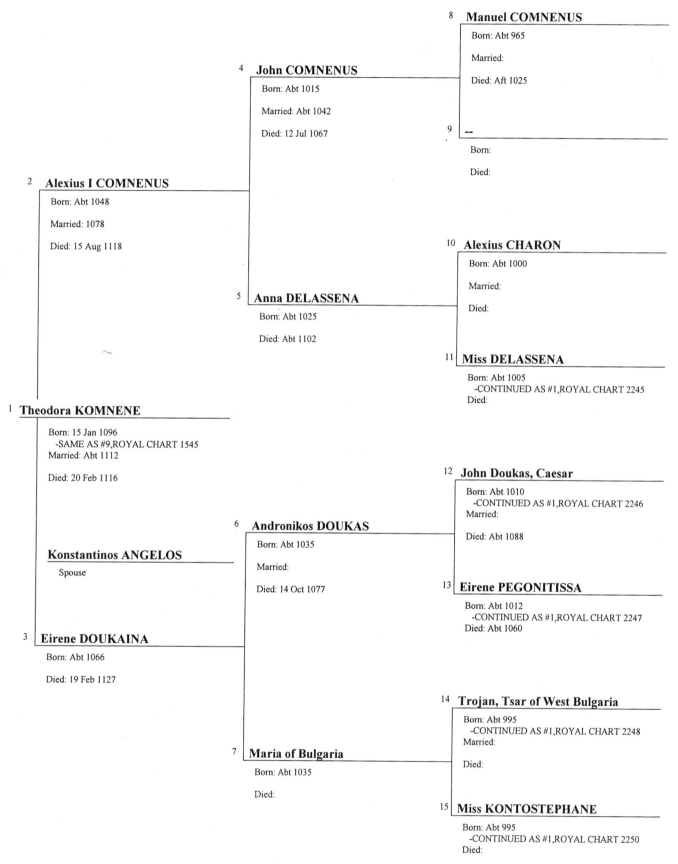

8 **Manuel COMNENUS**

Born: Abt 965

Married:

Died: Aft 1025

4 **John COMNENUS**

Born: Abt 1015

Married: Abt 1042

Died: 12 Jul 1067

9 **--**

Born:

Died:

2 **Alexius I COMNENUS**

Born: Abt 1048

Married: 1078

Died: 15 Aug 1118

10 **Alexius CHARON**

Born: Abt 1000

Married:

Died:

5 **Anna DELASSENA**

Born: Abt 1025

Died: Abt 1102

11 **Miss DELASSENA**

Born: Abt 1005
-CONTINUED AS #1,ROYAL CHART 2245
Died:

1 **Theodora KOMNENE**

Born: 15 Jan 1096
-SAME AS #9,ROYAL CHART 1545
Married: Abt 1112

Died: 20 Feb 1116

12 **John Doukas, Caesar**

Born: Abt 1010
-CONTINUED AS #1,ROYAL CHART 2246
Married:

Died: Abt 1088

6 **Andronikos DOUKAS**

Born: Abt 1035

Married:

Died: 14 Oct 1077

Konstantinos ANGELOS

Spouse

13 **Eirene PEGONITISSA**

Born: Abt 1012
-CONTINUED AS #1,ROYAL CHART 2247
Died: Abt 1060

3 **Eirene DOUKAINA**

Born: Abt 1066

Died: 19 Feb 1127

14 **Trojan, Tsar of West Bulgaria**

Born: Abt 995
-CONTINUED AS #1,ROYAL CHART 2248
Married:

Died:

7 **Maria of Bulgaria**

Born: Abt 1035

Died:

15 **Miss KONTOSTEPHANE**

Born: Abt 995
-CONTINUED AS #1,ROYAL CHART 2250
Died:

Sources include: *Royal Ancestors* (1989), charts 11486, 11848, 11861; Stuart 111, 215, 42; *Ancestral Roots* 45-27, 105A-24; Moriarty 137-138, 174; *The Genealogist* 2:3-33.

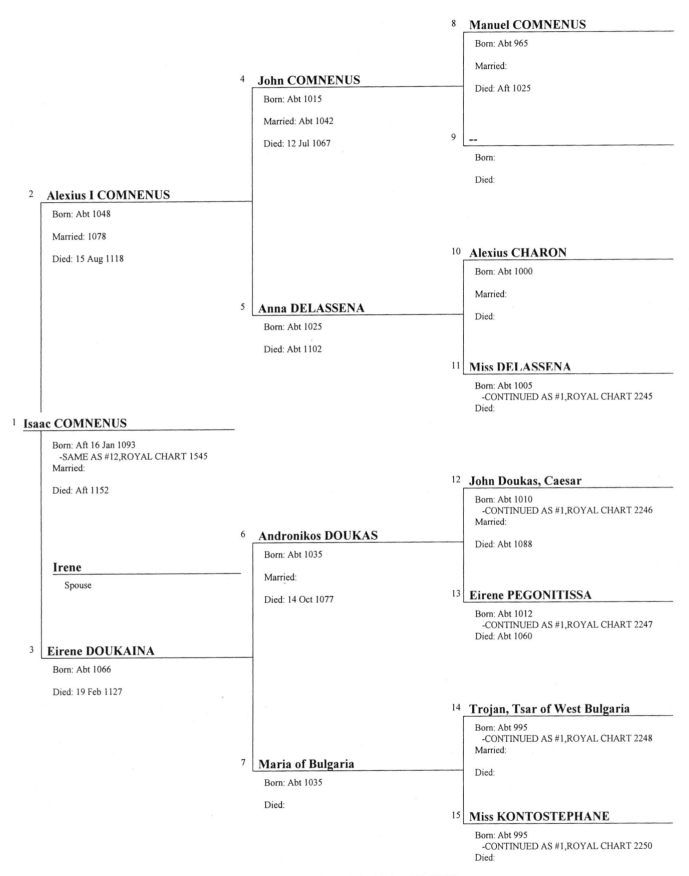

8 Manuel COMNENUS
Born: Abt 965
Married:
Died: Aft 1025

4 John COMNENUS
Born: Abt 1015
Married: Abt 1042
Died: 12 Jul 1067

9 --
Born:
Died:

2 Alexius I COMNENUS
Born: Abt 1048
Married: 1078
Died: 15 Aug 1118

10 Alexius CHARON
Born: Abt 1000
Married:
Died:

5 Anna DELASSENA
Born: Abt 1025
Died: Abt 1102

11 Miss DELASSENA
Born: Abt 1005
-CONTINUED AS #1,ROYAL CHART 2245
Died:

1 Isaac COMNENUS
Born: Aft 16 Jan 1093
-SAME AS #12,ROYAL CHART 1545
Married:
Died: Aft 1152

Irene
Spouse

12 John Doukas, Caesar
Born: Abt 1010
-CONTINUED AS #1,ROYAL CHART 2246
Married:
Died: Abt 1088

6 Andronikos DOUKAS
Born: Abt 1035
Married:
Died: 14 Oct 1077

13 Eirene PEGONITISSA
Born: Abt 1012
-CONTINUED AS #1,ROYAL CHART 2247
Died: Abt 1060

3 Eirene DOUKAINA
Born: Abt 1066
Died: 19 Feb 1127

14 Trojan, Tsar of West Bulgaria
Born: Abt 995
-CONTINUED AS #1,ROYAL CHART 2248
Married:
Died:

7 Maria of Bulgaria
Born: Abt 1035
Died:

15 Miss KONTOSTEPHANE
Born: Abt 995
-CONTINUED AS #1,ROYAL CHART 2250
Died:

Sources include: *Royal Ancestors* (1989), chart 11861; Stuart 42, 111, 215; *Ancestral Roots* 45-27; Moriarty 174, 137-138.

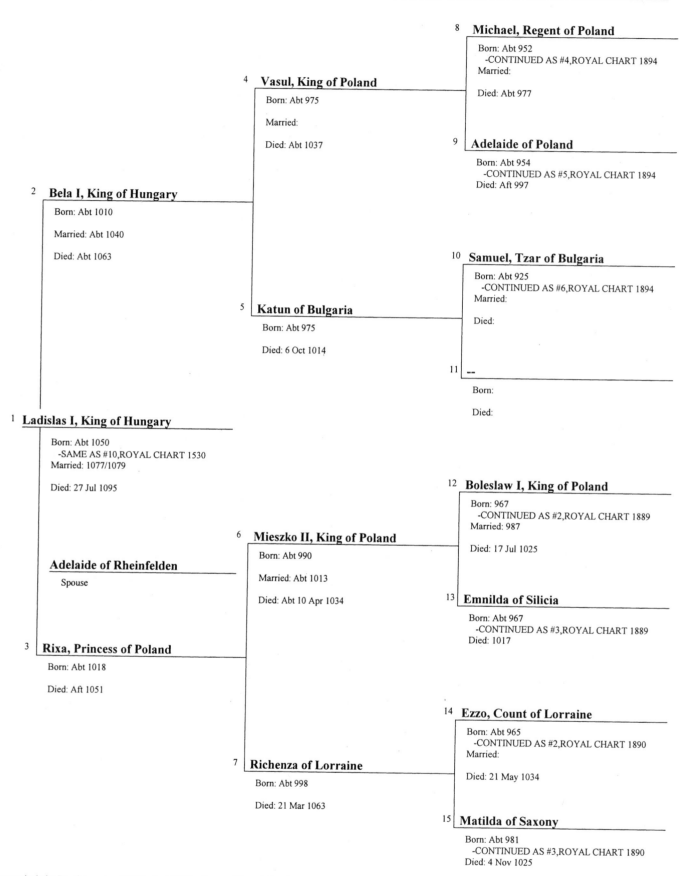

8 Michael, Regent of Poland
Born: Abt 952
-CONTINUED AS #4,ROYAL CHART 1894
Married:

Died: Abt 977

4 Vasul, King of Poland
Born: Abt 975

Married:

Died: Abt 1037

9 Adelaide of Poland
Born: Abt 954
-CONTINUED AS #5,ROYAL CHART 1894
Died: Aft 997

2 Bela I, King of Hungary
Born: Abt 1010

Married: Abt 1040

Died: Abt 1063

10 Samuel, Tzar of Bulgaria
Born: Abt 925
-CONTINUED AS #6,ROYAL CHART 1894
Married:

Died:

5 Katun of Bulgaria
Born: Abt 975

Died: 6 Oct 1014

11 --
Born:

Died:

1 Ladislas I, King of Hungary
Born: Abt 1050
-SAME AS #10,ROYAL CHART 1530
Married: 1077/1079

Died: 27 Jul 1095

12 Boleslaw I, King of Poland
Born: 967
-CONTINUED AS #2,ROYAL CHART 1889
Married: 987

Died: 17 Jul 1025

6 Mieszko II, King of Poland
Born: Abt 990

Married: Abt 1013

Died: Abt 10 Apr 1034

13 Emnilda of Silicia
Born: Abt 967
-CONTINUED AS #3,ROYAL CHART 1889
Died: 1017

Adelaide of Rheinfelden
Spouse

3 Rixa, Princess of Poland
Born: Abt 1018

Died: Aft 1051

14 Ezzo, Count of Lorraine
Born: Abt 965
-CONTINUED AS #2,ROYAL CHART 1890
Married:

Died: 21 May 1034

7 Richenza of Lorraine
Born: Abt 998

Died: 21 Mar 1063

15 Matilda of Saxony
Born: Abt 981
-CONTINUED AS #3,ROYAL CHART 1890
Died: 4 Nov 1025

Sources include: *Royal Ancestors* (1989), chart 11848; *Ancestral Roots* 244A, 243, 147; Stuart 75, 51; Moriarty 140.

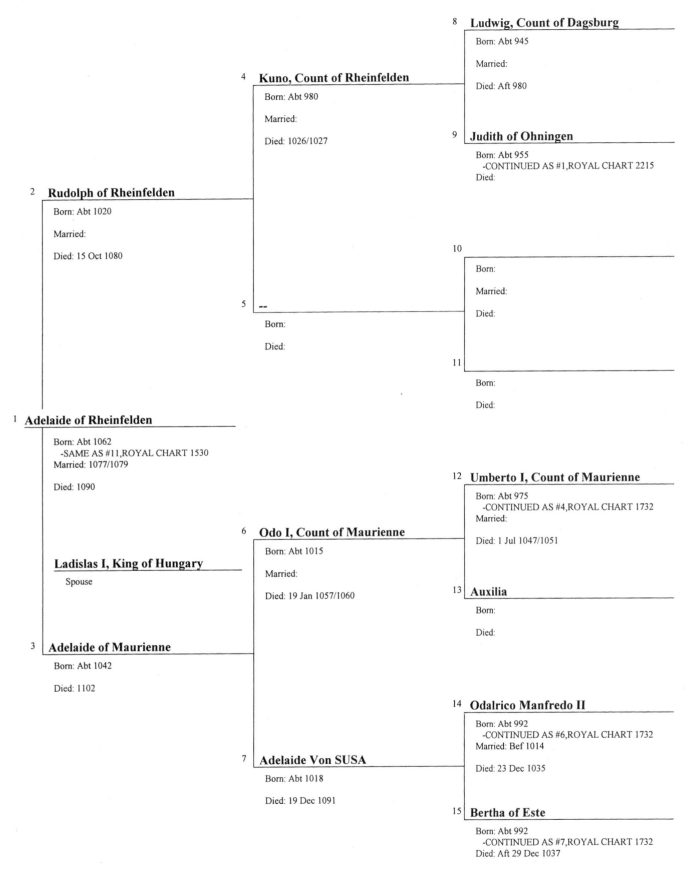

8 Ludwig, Count of Dagsburg

Born: Abt 945

Married:

Died: Aft 980

4 Kuno, Count of Rheinfelden

Born: Abt 980

Married:

Died: 1026/1027

9 Judith of Ohningen

Born: Abt 955
-CONTINUED AS #1,ROYAL CHART 2215
Died:

2 Rudolph of Rheinfelden

Born: Abt 1020

Married:

Died: 15 Oct 1080

10

Born:

Married:

Died:

5 --

Born:

Died:

11

Born:

Died:

1 Adelaide of Rheinfelden

Born: Abt 1062
-SAME AS #11,ROYAL CHART 1530
Married: 1077/1079

Died: 1090

12 Umberto I, Count of Maurienne

Born: Abt 975
-CONTINUED AS #4,ROYAL CHART 1732
Married:

Died: 1 Jul 1047/1051

6 Odo I, Count of Maurienne

Born: Abt 1015

Married:

Died: 19 Jan 1057/1060

13 Auxilia

Born:

Died:

Ladislas I, King of Hungary

Spouse

3 Adelaide of Maurienne

Born: Abt 1042

Died: 1102

14 Odalrico Manfredo II

Born: Abt 992
-CONTINUED AS #6,ROYAL CHART 1732
Married: Bef 1014

Died: 23 Dec 1035

7 Adelaide Von SUSA

Born: Abt 1018

Died: 19 Dec 1091

15 Bertha of Este

Born: Abt 992
-CONTINUED AS #7,ROYAL CHART 1732
Died: Aft 29 Dec 1037

Sources include: *Royal Ancestors* (1989), chart 11848; Stuart 381; *The Genealogist* 1:131; *Ancestral Roots* 244A-7; Moriarty 140; Turton 12. Notes: The parentage of #1 Adelaide is disputed. The version shown here agrees with Charles Evans (*The Genealogist* 1:131), who corrects the Moriarty and *Ancestral Roots* version. Turton claims #5 as Richilde of Ohningen, daughter of Kuno and Richilde (see chart 2215, #2 & 3). The Stuart version, followed here, gives them instead as the parents of #9 Judith.

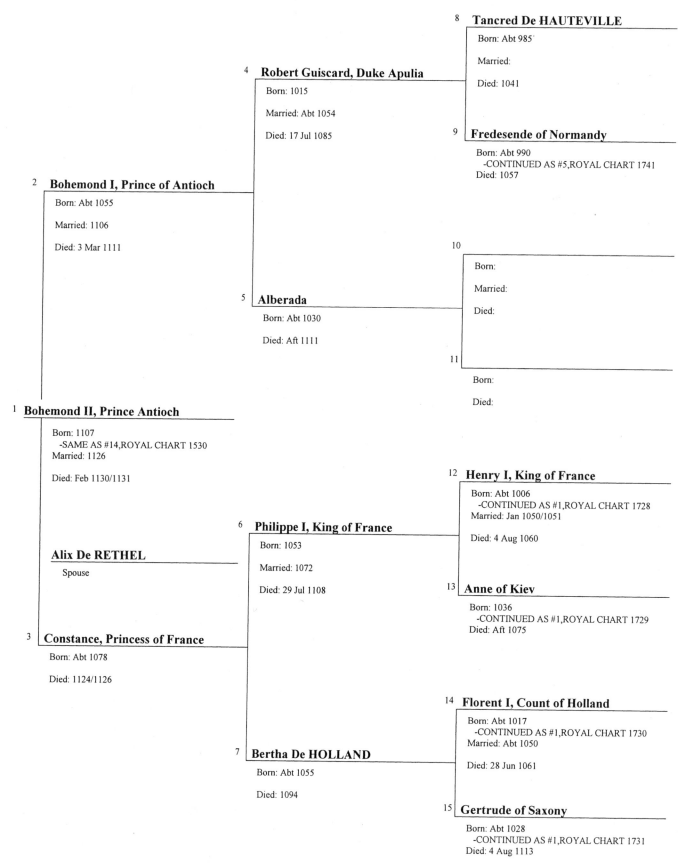

8 Tancred De HAUTEVILLE

Born: Abt 985'

Married:

Died: 1041

4 Robert Guiscard, Duke Apulia

Born: 1015

Married: Abt 1054

Died: 17 Jul 1085

9 Fredesende of Normandy

Born: Abt 990
-CONTINUED AS #5,ROYAL CHART 1741
Died: 1057

2 Bohemond I, Prince of Antioch

Born: Abt 1055

Married: 1106

Died: 3 Mar 1111

10

Born:

Married:

Died:

5 Alberada

Born: Abt 1030

Died: Aft 1111

11

Born:

Died:

1 Bohemond II, Prince Antioch

Born: 1107
-SAME AS #14,ROYAL CHART 1530
Married: 1126

Died: Feb 1130/1131

12 Henry I, King of France

Born: Abt 1006
-CONTINUED AS #1,ROYAL CHART 1728
Married: Jan 1050/1051

Died: 4 Aug 1060

6 Philippe I, King of France

Born: 1053

Married: 1072

Died: 29 Jul 1108

13 Anne of Kiev

Born: 1036
-CONTINUED AS #1,ROYAL CHART 1729
Died: Aft 1075

Alix De RETHEL

Spouse

3 Constance, Princess of France

Born: Abt 1078

Died: 1124/1126

14 Florent I, Count of Holland

Born: Abt 1017
-CONTINUED AS #1,ROYAL CHART 1730
Married: Abt 1050

Died: 28 Jun 1061

7 Bertha De HOLLAND

Born: Abt 1055

Died: 1094

15 Gertrude of Saxony

Born: Abt 1028
-CONTINUED AS #1,ROYAL CHART 1731
Died: 4 Aug 1113

Sources include: *Royal Ancestors* (1989), chart 11495; *Ancestral Roots* 103; Stuart 80; Moriarty 142.

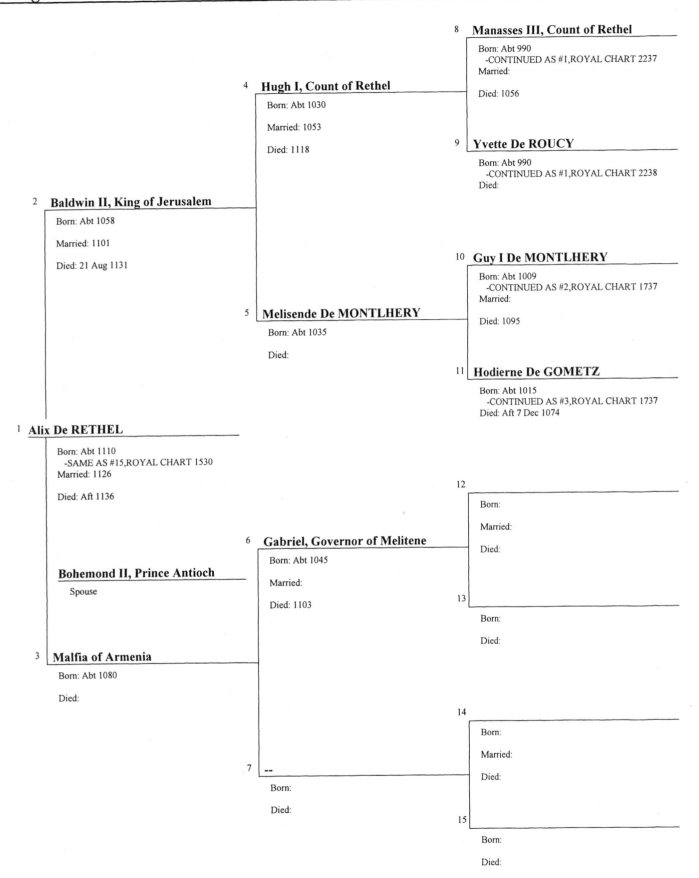

8 Manasses III, Count of Rethel
Born: Abt 990
-CONTINUED AS #1,ROYAL CHART 2237
Married:

Died: 1056

4 Hugh I, Count of Rethel
Born: Abt 1030

Married: 1053

Died: 1118

9 Yvette De ROUCY
Born: Abt 990
-CONTINUED AS #1,ROYAL CHART 2238
Died:

2 Baldwin II, King of Jerusalem
Born: Abt 1058

Married: 1101

Died: 21 Aug 1131

10 Guy I De MONTLHERY
Born: Abt 1009
-CONTINUED AS #2,ROYAL CHART 1737
Married:

Died: 1095

5 Melisende De MONTLHERY
Born: Abt 1035

Died:

11 Hodierne De GOMETZ
Born: Abt 1015
-CONTINUED AS #3,ROYAL CHART 1737
Died: Aft 7 Dec 1074

1 Alix De RETHEL
Born: Abt 1110
-SAME AS #15,ROYAL CHART 1530
Married: 1126

Died: Aft 1136

12
Born:

Married:

Died:

6 Gabriel, Governor of Melitene
Born: Abt 1045

Married:

Died: 1103

13
Born:

Died:

Bohemond II, Prince Antioch
Spouse

3 Malfia of Armenia
Born: Abt 1080

Died:

14
Born:

Married:

Died:

7 --
Born:

Died:

15
Born:

Died:

Sources include: *Royal Ancestors* (1989), chart 11495; *Ancestral Roots* 103-25, 103A; Stuart 145; Faris preliminary Charlemagne manuscript (June 1995), pp. 230-231; Moriarty 142-143. Note: Moriarty agrees with the ancestry of #4 Hugh as shown above. Stuart and Faris add an additional Manasses between #4 & 8 above.

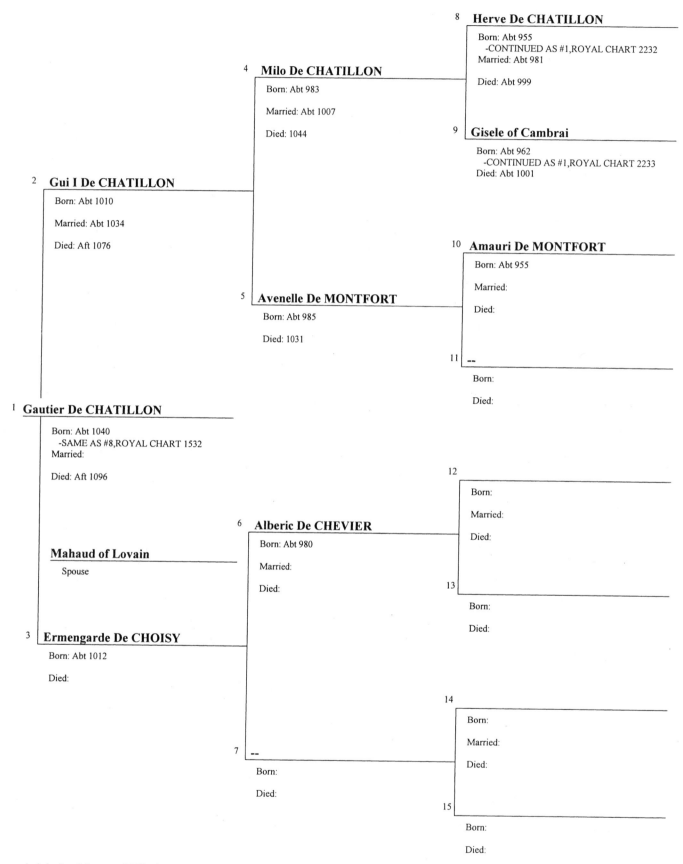

8 **Herve De CHATILLON**

Born: Abt 955
-CONTINUED AS #1,ROYAL CHART 2232
Married: Abt 981

Died: Abt 999

4 **Milo De CHATILLON**

Born: Abt 983

Married: Abt 1007

Died: 1044

9 **Gisele of Cambrai**

Born: Abt 962
-CONTINUED AS #1,ROYAL CHART 2233
Died: Abt 1001

2 **Gui I De CHATILLON**

Born: Abt 1010

Married: Abt 1034

Died: Aft 1076

10 **Amauri De MONTFORT**

Born: Abt 955

Married:

Died:

5 **Avenelle De MONTFORT**

Born: Abt 985

Died: 1031

11 **--**

Born:

Died:

1 **Gautier De CHATILLON**

Born: Abt 1040
-SAME AS #8,ROYAL CHART 1532
Married:

Died: Aft 1096

12

Born:

Married:

Died:

6 **Alberic De CHEVIER**

Born: Abt 980

Married:

Died:

Mahaud of Lovain

Spouse

13

Born:

Died:

3 **Ermengarde De CHOISY**

Born: Abt 1012

Died:

14

Born:

Married:

Died:

7 **--**

Born:

Died:

15

Born:

Died:

Sources include: *Royal Ancestors* (1989), chart 11494; Stuart 99; Moriarty 147, 262, 272-273; Turton 184. Note: The parentage and ancestry shown for #4 Milo is not certain.

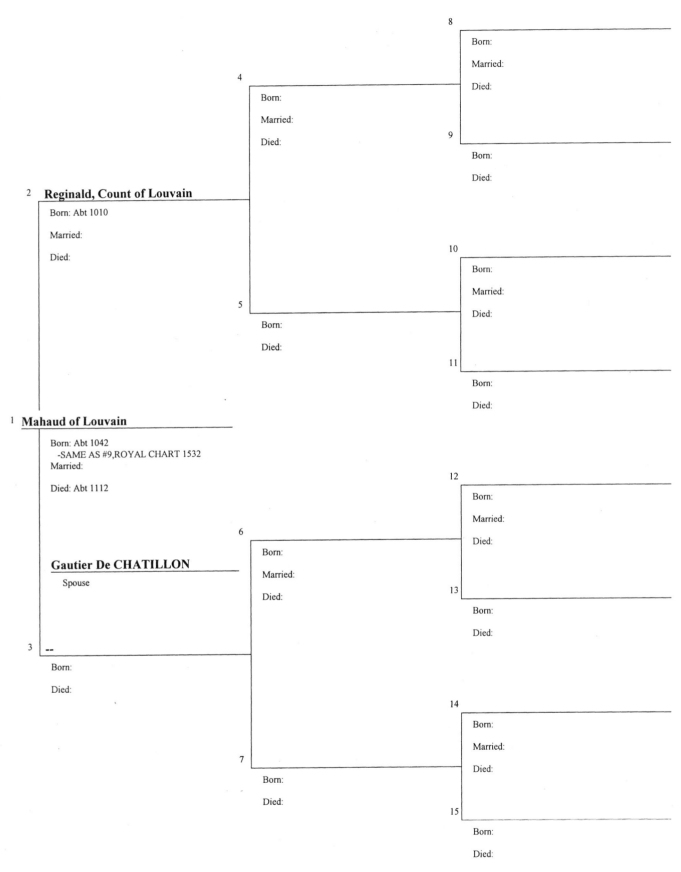

8

Born:

Married:

Died:

4

Born:

Married:

Died:

9

Born:

Died:

2 **Reginald, Count of Louvain**

Born: Abt 1010

Married:

Died:

10

Born:

Married:

Died:

5

Born:

Died:

11

Born:

Died:

1 **Mahaud of Louvain**

Born: Abt 1042
-SAME AS #9,ROYAL CHART 1532
Married:

Died: Abt 1112

12

Born:

Married:

Died:

6

Born:

Married:

Died:

13

Born:

Died:

Gautier De CHATILLON

Spouse

3 **--**

Born:

Died:

14

Born:

Married:

Died:

7

Born:

Died:

15

Born:

Died:

Sources include: Stuart 99-31.

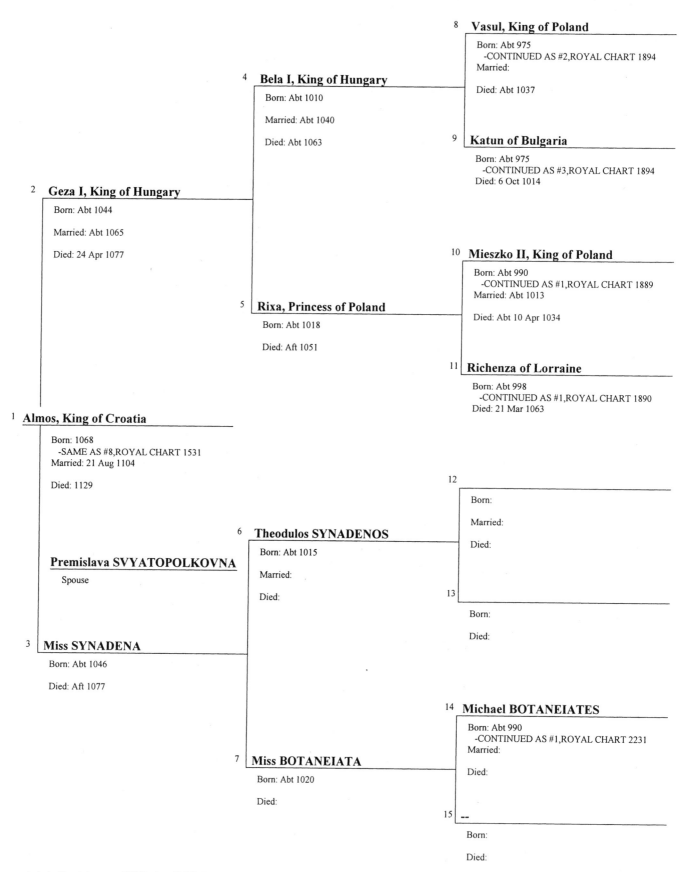

8   **Vasul, King of Poland**

Born: Abt 975
-CONTINUED AS #2,ROYAL CHART 1894
Married:

Died: Abt 1037

4   **Bela I, King of Hungary**

Born: Abt 1010

Married: Abt 1040

Died: Abt 1063

9   **Katun of Bulgaria**

Born: Abt 975
-CONTINUED AS #3,ROYAL CHART 1894
Died: 6 Oct 1014

2   **Geza I, King of Hungary**

Born: Abt 1044

Married: Abt 1065

Died: 24 Apr 1077

10   **Mieszko II, King of Poland**

Born: Abt 990
-CONTINUED AS #1,ROYAL CHART 1889
Married: Abt 1013

Died: Abt 10 Apr 1034

5   **Rixa, Princess of Poland**

Born: Abt 1018

Died: Aft 1051

11   **Richenza of Lorraine**

Born: Abt 998
-CONTINUED AS #1,ROYAL CHART 1890
Died: 21 Mar 1063

1   **Almos, King of Croatia**

Born: 1068
-SAME AS #8,ROYAL CHART 1531
Married: 21 Aug 1104

Died: 1129

12

Born:

Married:

Died:

6   **Theodulos SYNADENOS**

Born: Abt 1015

Married:

Died:

13

Born:

Died:

Premislava SVYATOPOLKOVNA

Spouse

3   **Miss SYNADENA**

Born: Abt 1046

Died: Aft 1077

14   **Michael BOTANEIATES**

Born: Abt 990
-CONTINUED AS #1,ROYAL CHART 2231
Married:

Died:

7   **Miss BOTANEIATA**

Born: Abt 1020

Died:

15   --

Born:

Died:

Sources include: *Royal Ancestors* (1989), chart 11492; Stuart 51; *Ancestral Roots* 242-9, 243; Moriarty 143; *The Genealogist* 2:11, 22, 26.

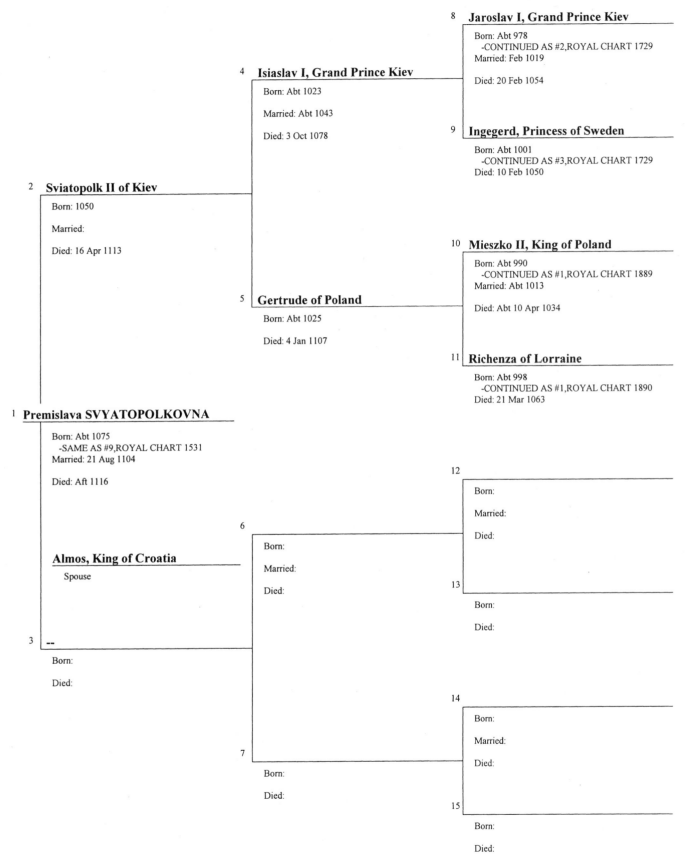

8 **Jaroslav I, Grand Prince Kiev**

Born: Abt 978
-CONTINUED AS #2, ROYAL CHART 1729
Married: Feb 1019

Died: 20 Feb 1054

4 **Isiaslav I, Grand Prince Kiev**

Born: Abt 1023

Married: Abt 1043

Died: 3 Oct 1078

9 **Ingegerd, Princess of Sweden**

Born: Abt 1001
-CONTINUED AS #3, ROYAL CHART 1729
Died: 10 Feb 1050

2 **Sviatopolk II of Kiev**

Born: 1050

Married:

Died: 16 Apr 1113

10 **Mieszko II, King of Poland**

Born: Abt 990
-CONTINUED AS #1, ROYAL CHART 1889
Married: Abt 1013

Died: Abt 10 Apr 1034

5 **Gertrude of Poland**

Born: Abt 1025

Died: 4 Jan 1107

11 **Richenza of Lorraine**

Born: Abt 998
-CONTINUED AS #1, ROYAL CHART 1890
Died: 21 Mar 1063

1 **Premislava SVYATOPOLKOVNA**

Born: Abt 1075
-SAME AS #9, ROYAL CHART 1531
Married: 21 Aug 1104

Died: Aft 1116

12

Born:

Married:

Died:

6

Born:

Married:

Died:

13

Born:

Died:

Almos, King of Croatia

Spouse

3 **--**

Born:

Died:

14

Born:

Married:

Died:

7

Born:

Died:

15

Born:

Died:

Sources include: Stuart 51; Von Isenburg 2:104; LDS records; *Royal Ancestors* (1989), chart 11492; Moriarty 143 (disputes #1).

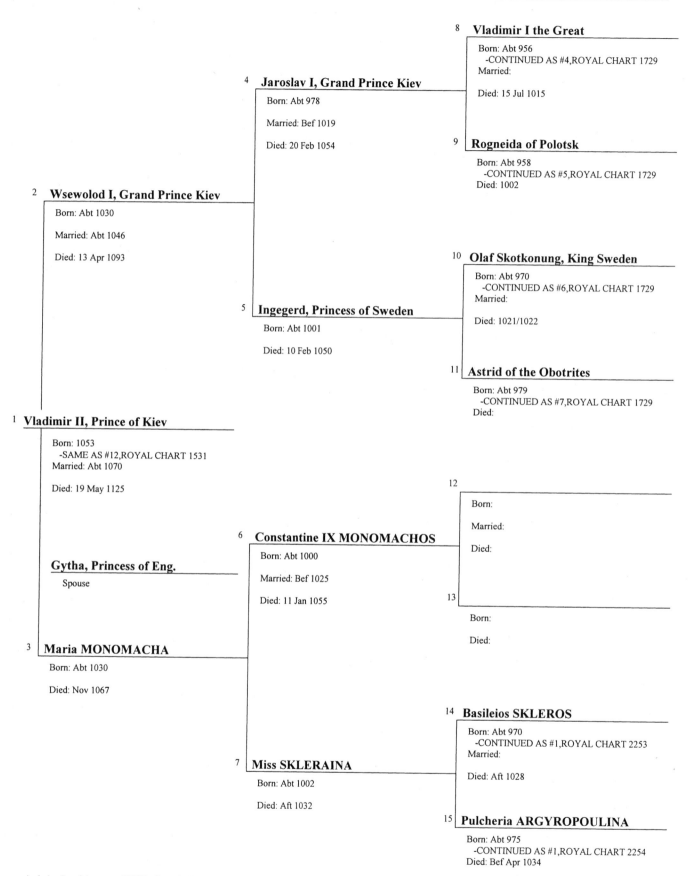

8 Vladimir I the Great
Born: Abt 956
-CONTINUED AS #4,ROYAL CHART 1729
Married:
Died: 15 Jul 1015

4 Jaroslav I, Grand Prince Kiev
Born: Abt 978
Married: Bef 1019
Died: 20 Feb 1054

9 Rogneida of Polotsk
Born: Abt 958
-CONTINUED AS #5,ROYAL CHART 1729
Died: 1002

2 Wsewolod I, Grand Prince Kiev
Born: Abt 1030
Married: Abt 1046
Died: 13 Apr 1093

10 Olaf Skotkonung, King Sweden
Born: Abt 970
-CONTINUED AS #6,ROYAL CHART 1729
Married:
Died: 1021/1022

5 Ingegerd, Princess of Sweden
Born: Abt 1001
Died: 10 Feb 1050

11 Astrid of the Obotrites
Born: Abt 979
-CONTINUED AS #7,ROYAL CHART 1729
Died:

1 Vladimir II, Prince of Kiev
Born: 1053
-SAME AS #12,ROYAL CHART 1531
Married: Abt 1070
Died: 19 May 1125

12
Born:
Married:
Died:

6 Constantine IX MONOMACHOS
Born: Abt 1000
Married: Bef 1025
Died: 11 Jan 1055

13
Born:
Died:

Gytha, Princess of Eng.
Spouse

3 Maria MONOMACHA
Born: Abt 1030
Died: Nov 1067

14 Basileios SKLEROS
Born: Abt 970
-CONTINUED AS #1,ROYAL CHART 2253
Married:
Died: Aft 1028

7 Miss SKLERAINA
Born: Abt 1002
Died: Aft 1032

15 Pulcheria ARGYROPOULINA
Born: Abt 975
-CONTINUED AS #1,ROYAL CHART 2254
Died: Bef Apr 1034

Sources include: *Royal Ancestors* (1989), charts 11493, 11412, 12064; Stuart 240, 115; Moriarty 144; *Ancestral Roots* 242; *The Genealogist* 2:21, 26, 32.

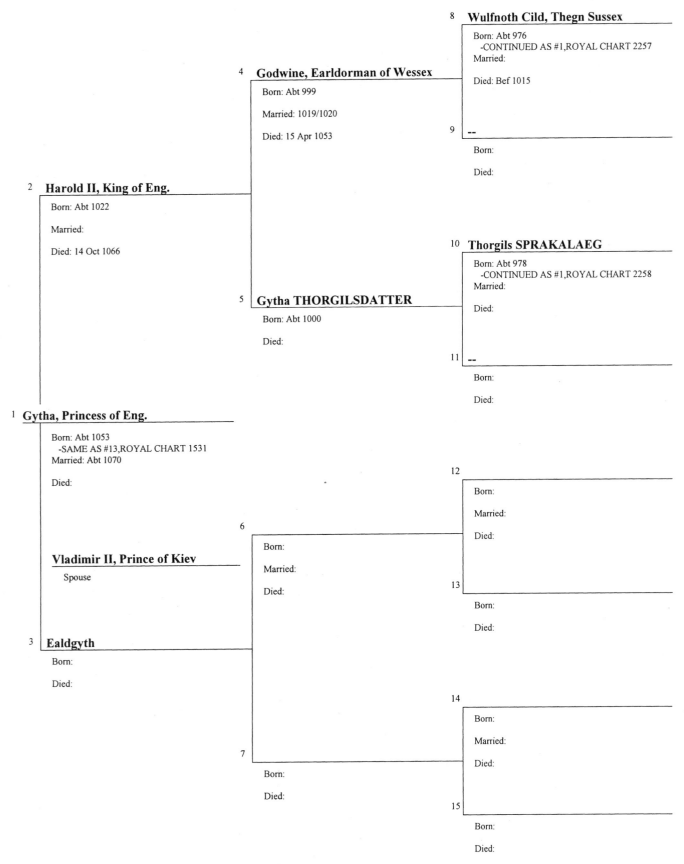

8 Wulfnoth Cild, Thegn Sussex

Born: Abt 976
 -CONTINUED AS #1,ROYAL CHART 2257
Married:

Died: Bef 1015

4 Godwine, Earldorman of Wessex

Born: Abt 999

Married: 1019/1020

Died: 15 Apr 1053

9 --

Born:

Died:

2 Harold II, King of Eng.

Born: Abt 1022

Married:

Died: 14 Oct 1066

10 Thorgils SPRAKALAEG

Born: Abt 978
 -CONTINUED AS #1,ROYAL CHART 2258
Married:

Died:

5 Gytha THORGILSDATTER

Born: Abt 1000

Died:

11 --

Born:

Died:

1 Gytha, Princess of Eng.

Born: Abt 1053
 -SAME AS #13,ROYAL CHART 1531
Married: Abt 1070

Died:

12

Born:

Married:

Died:

6

Born:

Married:

Died:

Vladimir II, Prince of Kiev

Spouse

13

Born:

Died:

3 Ealdgyth

Born:

Died:

14

Born:

Married:

Died:

7

Born:

Died:

15

Born:

Died:

Sources include: *Royal Ancestors* (1989), charts 11493, 11594-95; Stuart 368; *Ancestral Roots* 1B; Moriarty 145-146, 150-152.

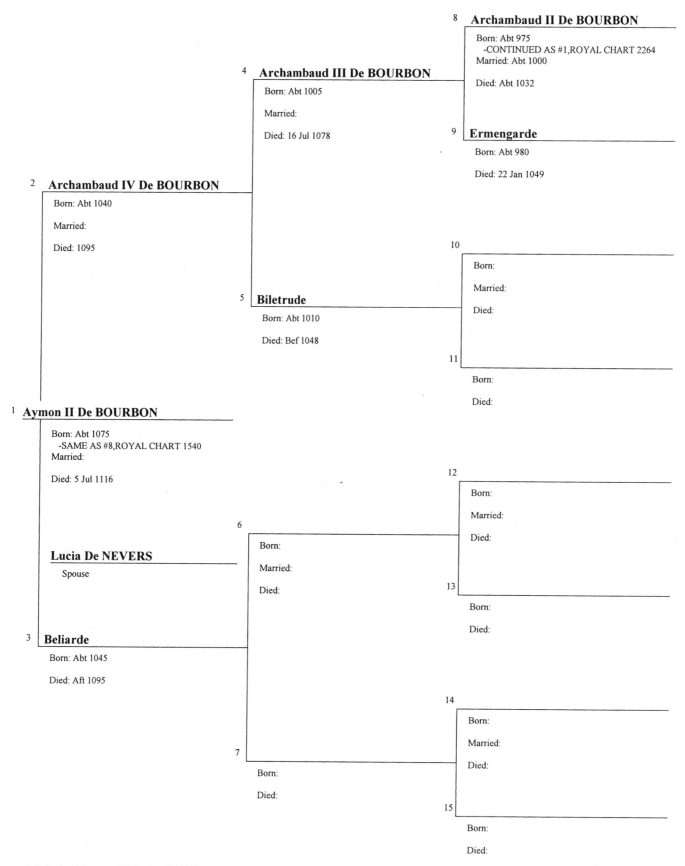

8 **Archambaud II De BOURBON**

Born: Abt 975
  -CONTINUED AS #1, ROYAL CHART 2264
Married: Abt 1000

Died: Abt 1032

4 **Archambaud III De BOURBON**

Born: Abt 1005

Married:

Died: 16 Jul 1078

9 **Ermengarde**

Born: Abt 980

Died: 22 Jan 1049

2 **Archambaud IV De BOURBON**

Born: Abt 1040

Married:

Died: 1095

10

Born:

Married:

Died:

5 **Biletrude**

Born: Abt 1010

Died: Bef 1048

11

Born:

Died:

1 **Aymon II De BOURBON**

Born: Abt 1075
  -SAME AS #8, ROYAL CHART 1540
Married:

Died: 5 Jul 1116

12

Born:

Married:

Died:

Lucia De NEVERS

Spouse

6

Born:

Married:

Died:

13

Born:

Died:

3 **Beliarde**

Born: Abt 1045

Died: Aft 1095

14

Born:

Married:

Died:

7

Born:

Died:

15

Born:

Died:

Sources include: *Royal Ancestors* (1989), chart 11824; Stuart 59; Moriarty 152-153. Note: #9 Ermengarde might be the daughter of Herbert or Hubert De Sully, but Moriarty states this is quite uncertain.

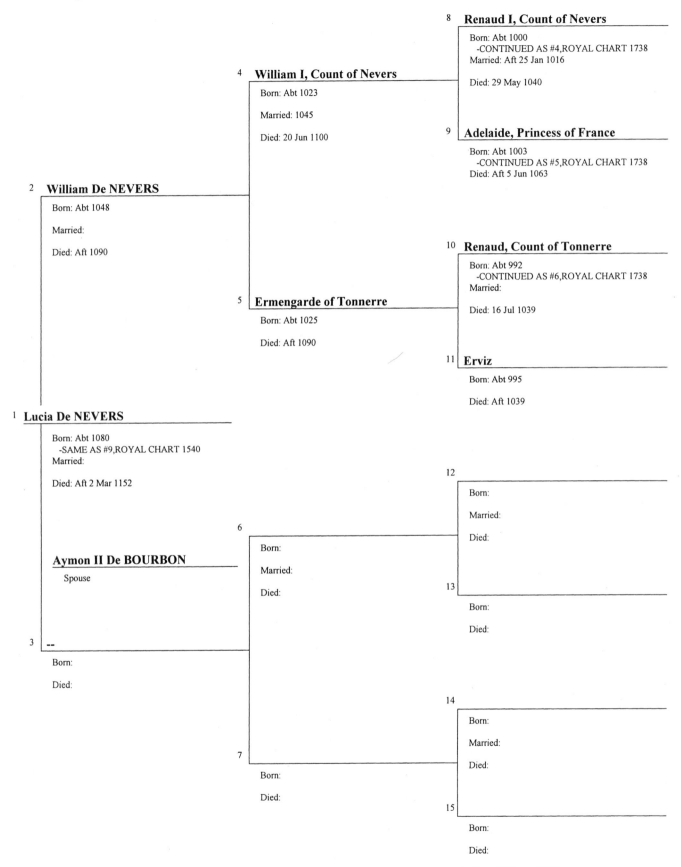

8 Renaud I, Count of Nevers

Born: Abt 1000
  -CONTINUED AS #4,ROYAL CHART 1738
Married: Aft 25 Jan 1016

Died: 29 May 1040

4 William I, Count of Nevers

Born: Abt 1023

Married: 1045

Died: 20 Jun 1100

9 Adelaide, Princess of France

Born: Abt 1003
  -CONTINUED AS #5,ROYAL CHART 1738
Died: Aft 5 Jun 1063

2 William De NEVERS

Born: Abt 1048

Married:

Died: Aft 1090

10 Renaud, Count of Tonnerre

Born: Abt 992
  -CONTINUED AS #6,ROYAL CHART 1738
Married:

Died: 16 Jul 1039

5 Ermengarde of Tonnerre

Born: Abt 1025

Died: Aft 1090

11 Erviz

Born: Abt 995

Died: Aft 1039

1 Lucia De NEVERS

Born: Abt 1080
  -SAME AS #9,ROYAL CHART 1540
Married:

Died: Aft 2 Mar 1152

12

Born:

Married:

Died:

6

Born:

Married:

Died:

13

Born:

Died:

Aymon II De BOURBON

Spouse

3 --

Born:

Died:

14

Born:

Married:

Died:

7

Born:

Died:

15

Born:

Died:

Sources include: *Royal Ancestors* (1989), chart 11824; Stuart 61; Moriarty 153, 64; Faris preliminary Charlemagne manuscript (June 1995), pp. 60, 204.

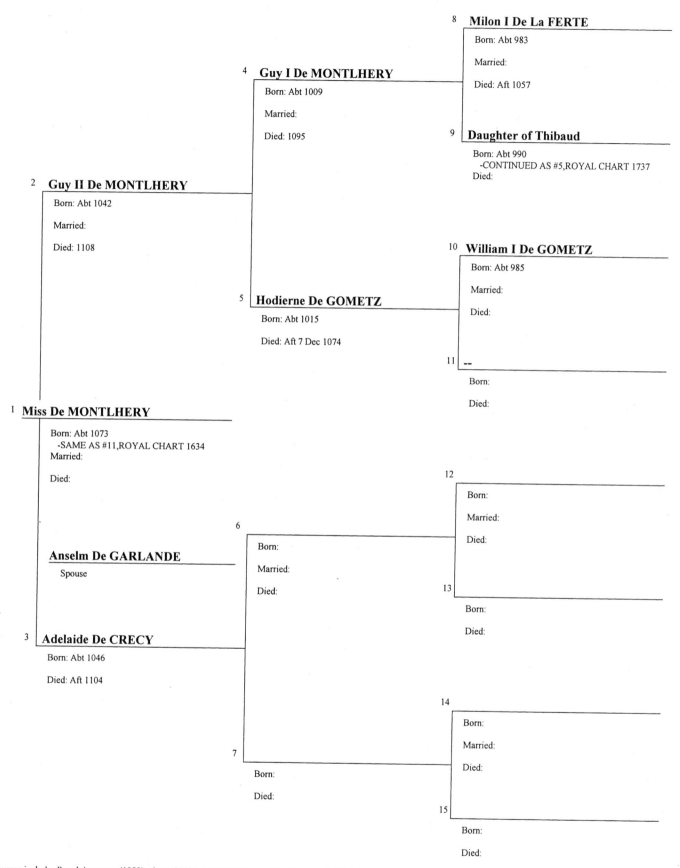

8 **Milon I De La FERTE**
Born: Abt 983
Married:
Died: Aft 1057

4 **Guy I De MONTLHERY**
Born: Abt 1009
Married:
Died: 1095

9 **Daughter of Thibaud**
Born: Abt 990
    -CONTINUED AS #5, ROYAL CHART 1737
Died:

2 **Guy II De MONTLHERY**
Born: Abt 1042
Married:
Died: 1108

10 **William I De GOMETZ**
Born: Abt 985
Married:
Died:

5 **Hodierne De GOMETZ**
Born: Abt 1015
Died: Aft 7 Dec 1074

11 **--**
Born:
Died:

1 **Miss De MONTLHERY**
Born: Abt 1073
    -SAME AS #11, ROYAL CHART 1634
Married:
Died:

12
Born:
Married:
Died:

6
Born:
Married:
Died:

13
Born:
Died:

Anselm De GARLANDE
    Spouse

3 **Adelaide De CRECY**
Born: Abt 1046
Died: Aft 1104

14
Born:
Married:
Died:

7
Born:
Died:

15
Born:
Died:

Sources include: *Royal Ancestors* (1989), charts 11445, 11550-51; Turton 230; Moriarty 63 (#2 & 3 ancestry); Stuart 5 (#2 & 3 ancestry).

8 Frederick, Lord of Buren

Born: Abt 1020
  -CONTINUED AS #2,ROYAL CHART 2152
Married: Abt 1042

Died: Bef 1094

4 Frederick I, Duke of Swabia

Born: Abt 1050

Married: 1089

Died: 20 Jan 1105

9 Hildegarde of Swabia

Born: Abt 1022
  -CONTINUED AS #3,ROYAL CHART 2152
Died: Bef 4 Feb 1095

2 Frederick II, Duke of Swabia

Born: 1090

Married: 1121

Died: 6 Apr 1147

10 Henry IV, Holy Roman Emperor

Born: 11 Nov 1050
  -CONTINUED AS #2,ROYAL CHART 1751
Married: 13 Jul 1066

Died: 7 Aug 1106

5 Agnes of Franconia

Born: 1072/1073

Died: 24 Sep 1143

11 Bertha of Maurienne

Born: 21 Sep 1051
  -CONTINUED AS #3,ROYAL CHART 1751
Died: 27 Dec 1087

1 Bertha of Swabia

Born: Abt 1123
  -SAME AS #11,ROYAL CHART 1621
Married:

Died: Abt 25 Mar 1195

Mathieu I, Duke of Lorraine

Spouse

12 Welf IV, Duke of Bavaria

Born: 1037
  -CONTINUED AS #2,ROYAL CHART 2153
Married: Abt 1071

Died: 9 Nov 1101

6 Henry I, Duke of Bavaria

Born: 1074

Married: Abt 1100

Died: 13 Dec 1126

13 Judith of Flanders

Born: Abt 1033
  -CONTINUED AS #3,ROYAL CHART 2153
Died: 5 Mar 1094

3 Judith of Bavaria

Born: Abt 1100

Died: 22 Feb 1130

14 Magnus, Duke of Saxony

Born: Abt 1045
  -CONTINUED AS #2,ROYAL CHART 2154
Married: Abt 1071

Died: 23 Aug 1106

7 Wulfhilda of Saxony

Born: Abt 1075

Died: 29 Dec 1126

15 Sophia, Princess of Hungary

Born: Abt 1043
  -CONTINUED AS #3,ROYAL CHART 2154
Died: 18 Jun 1095

Sources include: *Royal Ancestors* (1989), chart 11697; Turton 200, 39; LDS records; Stuart 40, 43 (#2 & 3 ancestry).

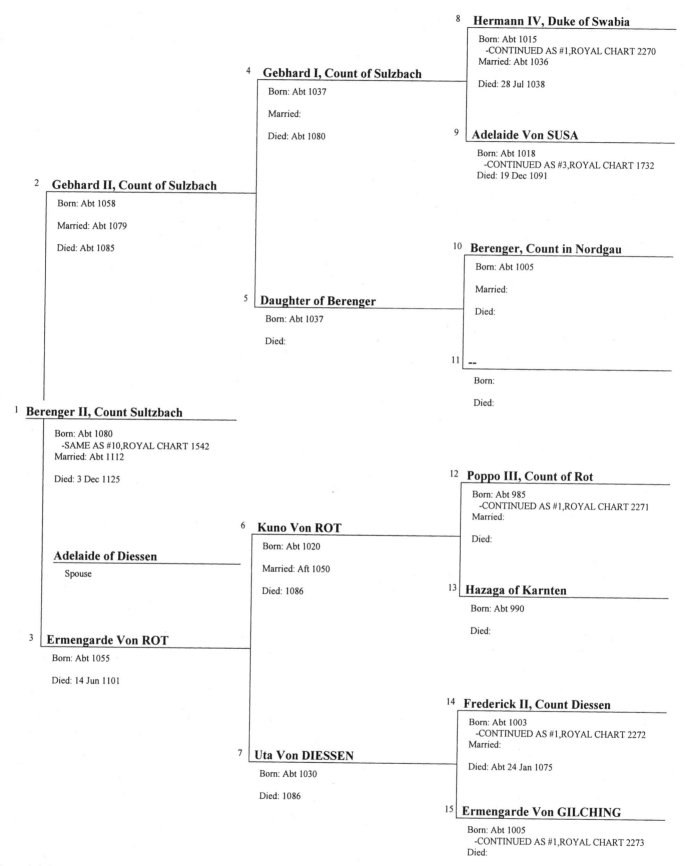

8 Hermann IV, Duke of Swabia
Born: Abt 1015
-CONTINUED AS #1,ROYAL CHART 2270
Married: Abt 1036

Died: 28 Jul 1038

4 Gebhard I, Count of Sulzbach
Born: Abt 1037

Married:

Died: Abt 1080

9 Adelaide Von SUSA
Born: Abt 1018
-CONTINUED AS #3,ROYAL CHART 1732
Died: 19 Dec 1091

2 Gebhard II, Count of Sulzbach
Born: Abt 1058

Married: Abt 1079

Died: Abt 1085

10 Berenger, Count in Nordgau
Born: Abt 1005

Married:

Died:

5 Daughter of Berenger
Born: Abt 1037

Died:

11 --
Born:

Died:

1 Berenger II, Count Sultzbach
Born: Abt 1080
-SAME AS #10,ROYAL CHART 1542
Married: Abt 1112

Died: 3 Dec 1125

12 Poppo III, Count of Rot
Born: Abt 985
-CONTINUED AS #1,ROYAL CHART 2271
Married:

Died:

6 Kuno Von ROT
Born: Abt 1020

Married: Aft 1050

Died: 1086

Adelaide of Diessen
Spouse

13 Hazaga of Karnten
Born: Abt 990

Died:

3 Ermengarde Von ROT
Born: Abt 1055

Died: 14 Jun 1101

14 Frederick II, Count Diessen
Born: Abt 1003
-CONTINUED AS #1,ROYAL CHART 2272
Married:

Died: Abt 24 Jan 1075

7 Uta Von DIESSEN
Born: Abt 1030

Died: 1086

15 Ermengarde Von GILCHING
Born: Abt 1005
-CONTINUED AS #1,ROYAL CHART 2273
Died:

Sources include: *Royal Ancestors* (1989), chart 11892; Stuart 63, 49; Moriarty 156-157; Faris preliminary Charlemagne manuscript (June 1995), pp. 251-252, 121. Note: Faris gives #6 Kuno as the son (instead of the grandson) of Poppo II Von Rot.

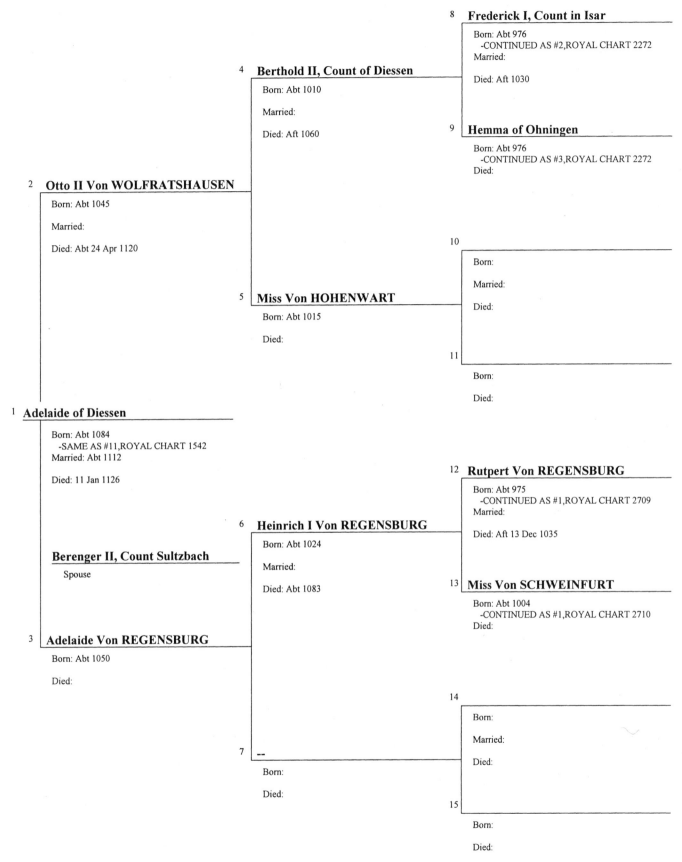

8   **Frederick I, Count in Isar**

Born: Abt 976
    -CONTINUED AS #2, ROYAL CHART 2272
Married:

Died: Aft 1030

4   **Berthold II, Count of Diessen**

Born: Abt 1010

Married:

Died: Aft 1060

9   **Hemma of Ohningen**

Born: Abt 976
    -CONTINUED AS #3, ROYAL CHART 2272
Died:

2   **Otto II Von WOLFRATSHAUSEN**

Born: Abt 1045

Married:

Died: Abt 24 Apr 1120

10

Born:

Married:

Died:

5   **Miss Von HOHENWART**

Born: Abt 1015

Died:

11

Born:

Died:

1   **Adelaide of Diessen**

Born: Abt 1084
    -SAME AS #11, ROYAL CHART 1542
Married: Abt 1112

Died: 11 Jan 1126

Berenger II, Count Sultzbach

Spouse

12   **Rutpert Von REGENSBURG**

Born: Abt 975
    -CONTINUED AS #1, ROYAL CHART 2709
Married:

Died: Aft 13 Dec 1035

6   **Heinrich I Von REGENSBURG**

Born: Abt 1024

Married:

Died: Abt 1083

13   **Miss Von SCHWEINFURT**

Born: Abt 1004
    -CONTINUED AS #1, ROYAL CHART 2710
Died:

3   **Adelaide Von REGENSBURG**

Born: Abt 1050

Died:

14

Born:

Married:

Died:

7   **--**

Born:

Died:

15

Born:

Died:

Sources include: *Royal Ancestors* (1989), chart 11893; Stuart 64; Moriarty 156, 158; Faris preliminary Charlemagne manuscript (June 1995), pp. 252, 287, 230.

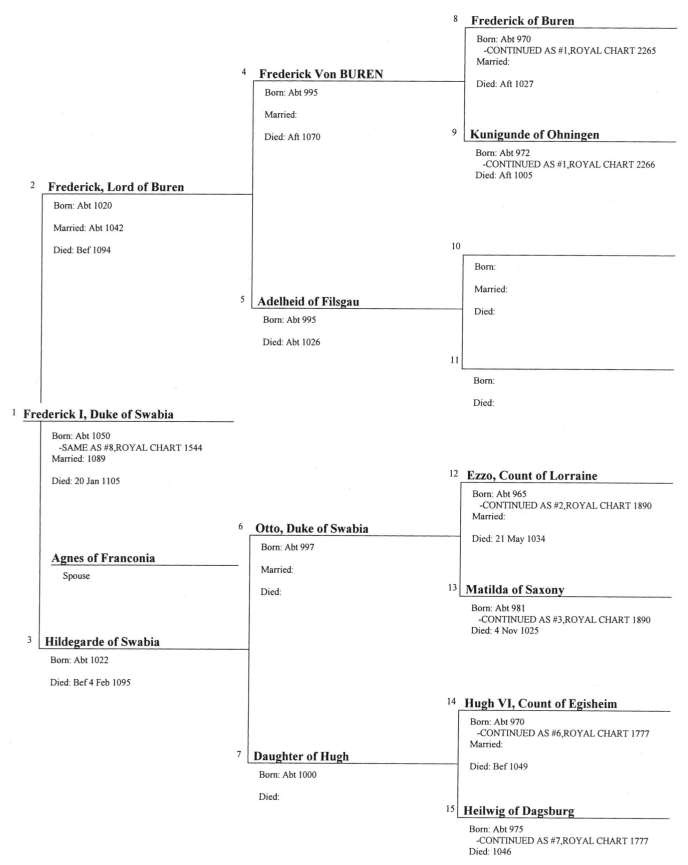

8 Frederick of Buren
Born: Abt 970
-CONTINUED AS #1,ROYAL CHART 2265
Married:

Died: Aft 1027

4 Frederick Von BUREN
Born: Abt 995

Married:

Died: Aft 1070

9 Kunigunde of Ohningen
Born: Abt 972
-CONTINUED AS #1,ROYAL CHART 2266
Died: Aft 1005

2 Frederick, Lord of Buren
Born: Abt 1020

Married: Abt 1042

Died: Bef 1094

10
Born:

Married:

Died:

5 Adelheid of Filsgau
Born: Abt 995

Died: Abt 1026

11
Born:

Died:

1 Frederick I, Duke of Swabia
Born: Abt 1050
-SAME AS #8,ROYAL CHART 1544
Married: 1089

Died: 20 Jan 1105

12 Ezzo, Count of Lorraine
Born: Abt 965
-CONTINUED AS #2,ROYAL CHART 1890
Married:

Died: 21 May 1034

6 Otto, Duke of Swabia
Born: Abt 997

Married:

Died:

13 Matilda of Saxony
Born: Abt 981
-CONTINUED AS #3,ROYAL CHART 1890
Died: 4 Nov 1025

Agnes of Franconia
Spouse

3 Hildegarde of Swabia
Born: Abt 1022

Died: Bef 4 Feb 1095

14 Hugh VI, Count of Egisheim
Born: Abt 970
-CONTINUED AS #6,ROYAL CHART 1777
Married:

Died: Bef 1049

7 Daughter of Hugh
Born: Abt 1000

Died:

15 Heilwig of Dagsburg
Born: Abt 975
-CONTINUED AS #7,ROYAL CHART 1777
Died: 1046

Sources include: *Royal Ancestors* (1989), chart 11484; Stuart 40; Moriarty 166; *Ancestral Roots* 45-24. Note: The given names of #5 (Adelheid) and #9 (Kunigunde) are not certain.

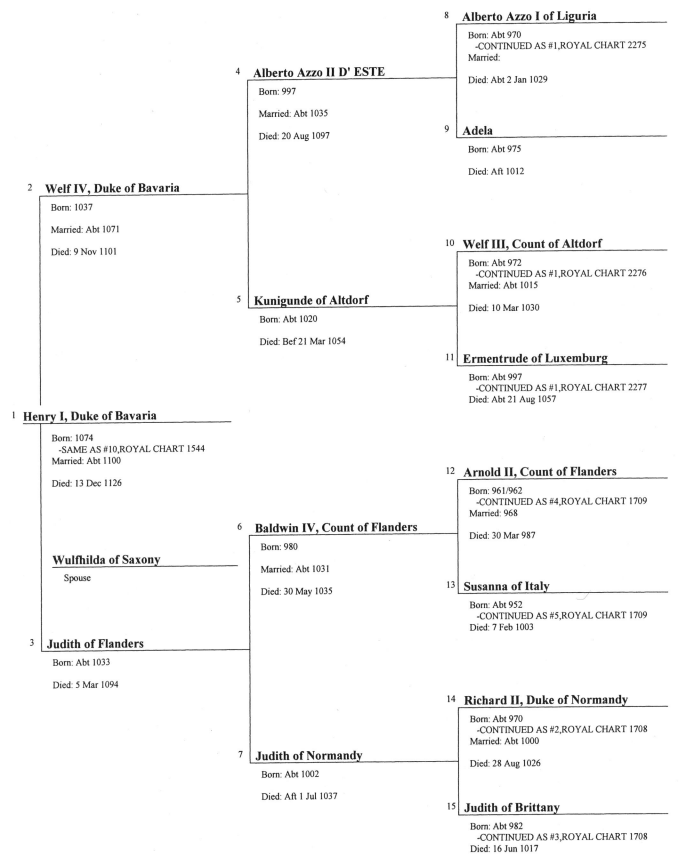

8 Alberto Azzo I of Liguria

Born: Abt 970
-CONTINUED AS #1,ROYAL CHART 2275
Married:

Died: Abt 2 Jan 1029

4 Alberto Azzo II D' ESTE

Born: 997

Married: Abt 1035

Died: 20 Aug 1097

9 Adela

Born: Abt 975

Died: Aft 1012

2 Welf IV, Duke of Bavaria

Born: 1037

Married: Abt 1071

Died: 9 Nov 1101

10 Welf III, Count of Altdorf

Born: Abt 972
-CONTINUED AS #1,ROYAL CHART 2276
Married: Abt 1015

Died: 10 Mar 1030

5 Kunigunde of Altdorf

Born: Abt 1020

Died: Bef 21 Mar 1054

11 Ermentrude of Luxemburg

Born: Abt 997
-CONTINUED AS #1,ROYAL CHART 2277
Died: Abt 21 Aug 1057

1 Henry I, Duke of Bavaria

Born: 1074
-SAME AS #10,ROYAL CHART 1544
Married: Abt 1100

Died: 13 Dec 1126

Wulfhilda of Saxony

Spouse

12 Arnold II, Count of Flanders

Born: 961/962
-CONTINUED AS #4,ROYAL CHART 1709
Married: 968

Died: 30 Mar 987

6 Baldwin IV, Count of Flanders

Born: 980

Married: Abt 1031

Died: 30 May 1035

13 Susanna of Italy

Born: Abt 952
-CONTINUED AS #5,ROYAL CHART 1709
Died: 7 Feb 1003

3 Judith of Flanders

Born: Abt 1033

Died: 5 Mar 1094

14 Richard II, Duke of Normandy

Born: Abt 970
-CONTINUED AS #2,ROYAL CHART 1708
Married: Abt 1000

Died: 28 Aug 1026

7 Judith of Normandy

Born: Abt 1002

Died: Aft 1 Jul 1037

15 Judith of Brittany

Born: Abt 982
-CONTINUED AS #3,ROYAL CHART 1708
Died: 16 Jun 1017

Sources include: *Royal Ancestors* (1989), chart 11485; *Ancestral Roots* 166; Stuart 43; Moriarty 167. Note: The origin and parentage of #3 Judith (of Flanders?) is disputed. The sources cited all give #3 as Judith of Flanders, with parentage as shown. However, Faris disputes this claim and gives #3 as Judith of Normandy (born 1028), daughter of Richard III, Duke of Normandy (see chart 2190, #1) & Adele, Princess of France (see chart 1710, #1). Faris also states that #6 Baldwin IV did not have a 2nd wife Judith. The Faris version requires #3 Judith to be 9 years older than her husband Welf and 46 years older than their son Henry, which is unusual and somewhat difficult. See Faris preliminary Charlemagne manuscript (June 1995), pp.4, 132, 208. *Ancestral Roots* 8 (2004), Line 166 now agrees with Faris. Moriarty gives #7 as Baldwin's 2nd wife Judith or Eleanor of Normandy.

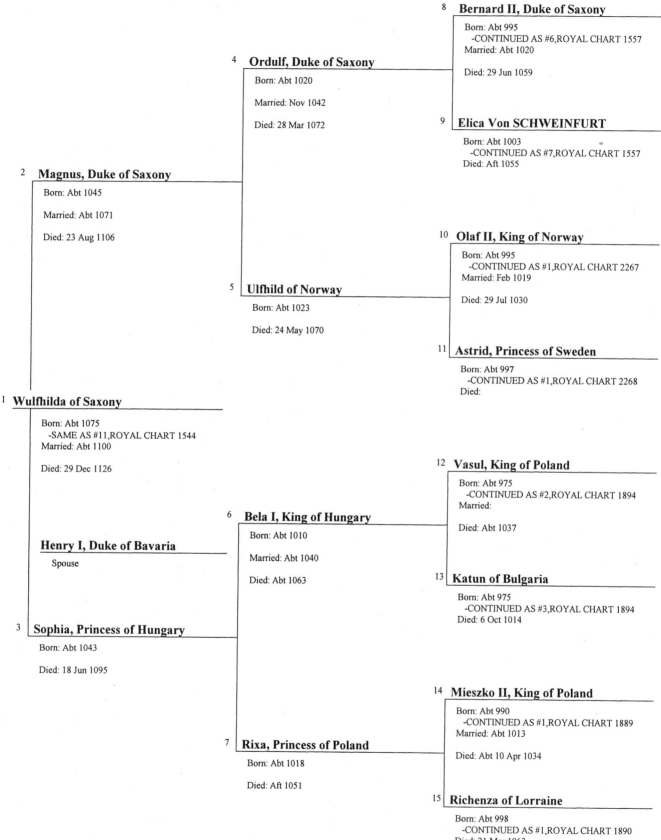

8 **Bernard II, Duke of Saxony**
Born: Abt 995
-CONTINUED AS #6,ROYAL CHART 1557
Married: Abt 1020

Died: 29 Jun 1059

4 **Ordulf, Duke of Saxony**
Born: Abt 1020

Married: Nov 1042

Died: 28 Mar 1072

9 **Elica Von SCHWEINFURT**
Born: Abt 1003
-CONTINUED AS #7,ROYAL CHART 1557
Died: Aft 1055

2 **Magnus, Duke of Saxony**
Born: Abt 1045

Married: Abt 1071

Died: 23 Aug 1106

10 **Olaf II, King of Norway**
Born: Abt 995
-CONTINUED AS #1,ROYAL CHART 2267
Married: Feb 1019

Died: 29 Jul 1030

5 **Ulfhild of Norway**
Born: Abt 1023

Died: 24 May 1070

11 **Astrid, Princess of Sweden**
Born: Abt 997
-CONTINUED AS #1,ROYAL CHART 2268
Died:

1 **Wulfhilda of Saxony**
Born: Abt 1075
-SAME AS #11,ROYAL CHART 1544
Married: Abt 1100

Died: 29 Dec 1126

12 **Vasul, King of Poland**
Born: Abt 975
-CONTINUED AS #2,ROYAL CHART 1894
Married:

Died: Abt 1037

6 **Bela I, King of Hungary**
Born: Abt 1010

Married: Abt 1040

Died: Abt 1063

Henry I, Duke of Bavaria
Spouse

13 **Katun of Bulgaria**
Born: Abt 975
-CONTINUED AS #3,ROYAL CHART 1894
Died: 6 Oct 1014

3 **Sophia, Princess of Hungary**
Born: Abt 1043

Died: 18 Jun 1095

14 **Mieszko II, King of Poland**
Born: Abt 990
-CONTINUED AS #1,ROYAL CHART 1889
Married: Abt 1013

Died: Abt 10 Apr 1034

7 **Rixa, Princess of Poland**
Born: Abt 1018

Died: Aft 1051

15 **Richenza of Lorraine**
Born: Abt 998
-CONTINUED AS #1,ROYAL CHART 1890
Died: 21 Mar 1063

Sources include: *Royal Ancestors* (1989), chart 11485; *Ancestral Roots* 243, 243A; Stuart 28; Moriarty 169; Faris preliminary Charlemagne manuscript (June 1995), pp. 145-146, 138. Note: The mother of #3 Sophia is disputed. Faris, citing Wegener, gives #7 as Tuta Von Formbach. All other sources give Rixa, as shown.

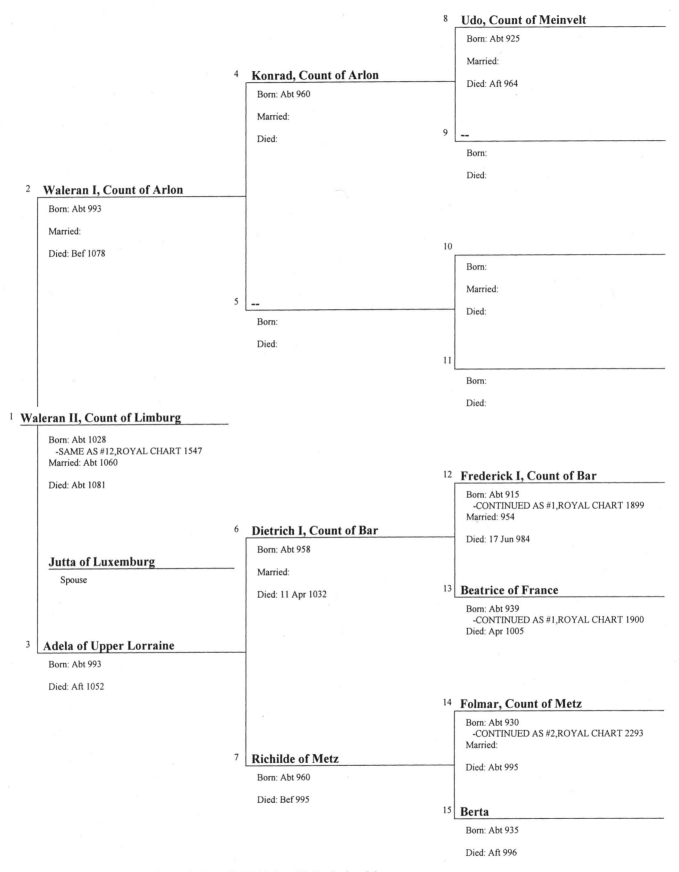

8 Udo, Count of Meinvelt
Born: Abt 925
Married:
Died: Aft 964

4 Konrad, Count of Arlon
Born: Abt 960
Married:
Died:

9 --
Born:
Died:

2 Waleran I, Count of Arlon
Born: Abt 993
Married:
Died: Bef 1078

10
Born:
Married:
Died:

5 --
Born:
Died:

11
Born:
Died:

1 Waleran II, Count of Limburg
Born: Abt 1028
 -SAME AS #12,ROYAL CHART 1547
Married: Abt 1060

Died: Abt 1081

12 Frederick I, Count of Bar
Born: Abt 915
 -CONTINUED AS #1,ROYAL CHART 1899
Married: 954

Died: 17 Jun 984

6 Dietrich I, Count of Bar
Born: Abt 958
Married:
Died: 11 Apr 1032

Jutta of Luxemburg
Spouse

13 Beatrice of France
Born: Abt 939
 -CONTINUED AS #1,ROYAL CHART 1900
Died: Apr 1005

3 Adela of Upper Lorraine
Born: Abt 993
Died: Aft 1052

14 Folmar, Count of Metz
Born: Abt 930
 -CONTINUED AS #2,ROYAL CHART 2293
Married:

Died: Abt 995

7 Richilde of Metz
Born: Abt 960
Died: Bef 995

15 Berta
Born: Abt 935
Died: Aft 996

Sources include: *Royal Ancestors* (1989), chart 11698; Stuart 62, 319; Moriarty 159; Von Isenburg 2:6.

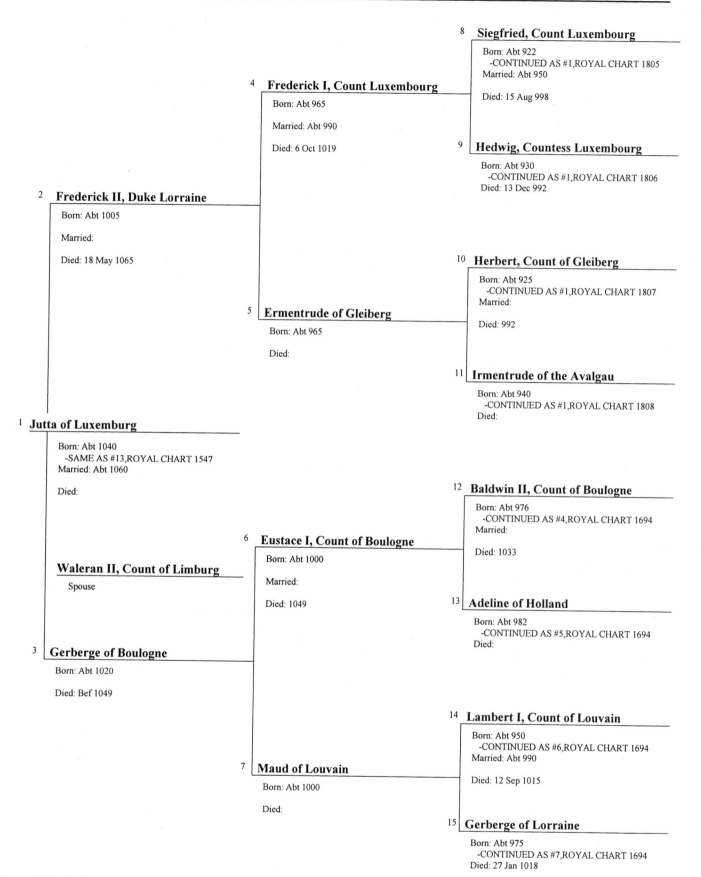

8 Siegfried, Count Luxembourg

Born: Abt 922
-CONTINUED AS #1,ROYAL CHART 1805
Married: Abt 950

Died: 15 Aug 998

4 Frederick I, Count Luxembourg

Born: Abt 965

Married: Abt 990

Died: 6 Oct 1019

9 Hedwig, Countess Luxembourg

Born: Abt 930
-CONTINUED AS #1,ROYAL CHART 1806
Died: 13 Dec 992

2 Frederick II, Duke Lorraine

Born: Abt 1005

Married:

Died: 18 May 1065

10 Herbert, Count of Gleiberg

Born: Abt 925
-CONTINUED AS #1,ROYAL CHART 1807
Married:

Died: 992

5 Ermentrude of Gleiberg

Born: Abt 965

Died:

11 Irmentrude of the Avalgau

Born: Abt 940
-CONTINUED AS #1,ROYAL CHART 1808
Died:

1 Jutta of Luxemburg

Born: Abt 1040
-SAME AS #13,ROYAL CHART 1547
Married: Abt 1060

Died:

Waleran II, Count of Limburg

Spouse

12 Baldwin II, Count of Boulogne

Born: Abt 976
-CONTINUED AS #4,ROYAL CHART 1694
Married:

Died: 1033

6 Eustace I, Count of Boulogne

Born: Abt 1000

Married:

Died: 1049

13 Adeline of Holland

Born: Abt 982
-CONTINUED AS #5,ROYAL CHART 1694
Died:

3 Gerberge of Boulogne

Born: Abt 1020

Died: Bef 1049

14 Lambert I, Count of Louvain

Born: Abt 950
-CONTINUED AS #6,ROYAL CHART 1694
Married: Abt 990

Died: 12 Sep 1015

7 Maud of Louvain

Born: Abt 1000

Died:

15 Gerberge of Lorraine

Born: Abt 975
-CONTINUED AS #7,ROYAL CHART 1694
Died: 27 Jan 1018

Sources include: *Royal Ancestors* (1989), chart 11698; Stuart 58, 242; Moriarty 161.

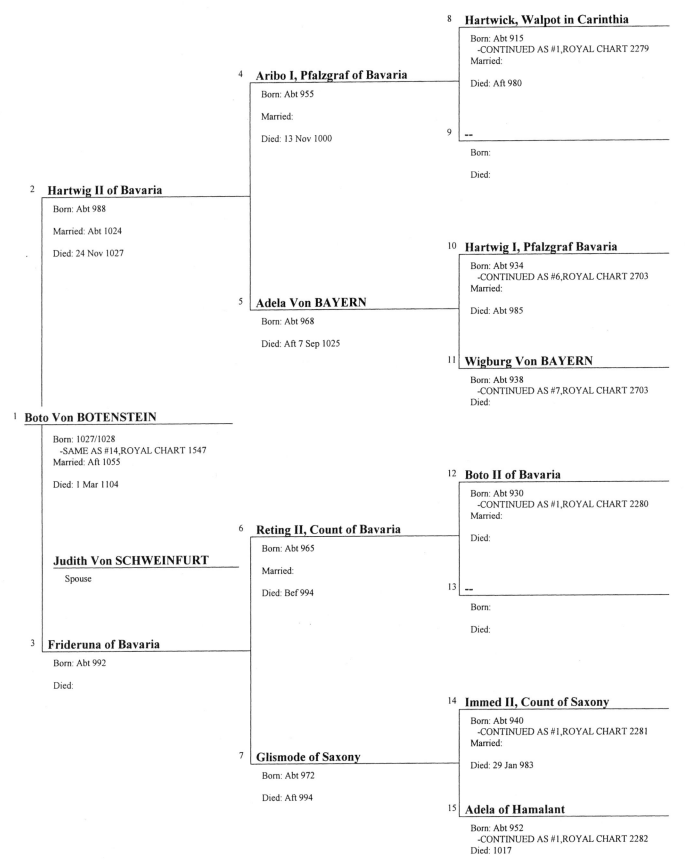

2 Hartwig II of Bavaria

Born: Abt 988

Married: Abt 1024

Died: 24 Nov 1027

4 Aribo I, Pfalzgraf of Bavaria

Born: Abt 955

Married:

Died: 13 Nov 1000

8 Hartwick, Walpot in Carinthia

Born: Abt 915
-CONTINUED AS #1,ROYAL CHART 2279
Married:

Died: Aft 980

9 --

Born:

Died:

5 Adela Von BAYERN

Born: Abt 968

Died: Aft 7 Sep 1025

10 Hartwig I, Pfalzgraf Bavaria

Born: Abt 934
-CONTINUED AS #6,ROYAL CHART 2703
Married:

Died: Abt 985

11 Wigburg Von BAYERN

Born: Abt 938
-CONTINUED AS #7,ROYAL CHART 2703
Died:

1 Boto Von BOTENSTEIN

Born: 1027/1028
-SAME AS #14,ROYAL CHART 1547
Married: Aft 1055

Died: 1 Mar 1104

Judith Von SCHWEINFURT

Spouse

3 Frideruna of Bavaria

Born: Abt 992

Died:

6 Reting II, Count of Bavaria

Born: Abt 965

Married:

Died: Bef 994

12 Boto II of Bavaria

Born: Abt 930
-CONTINUED AS #1,ROYAL CHART 2280
Married:

Died:

13 --

Born:

Died:

7 Glismode of Saxony

Born: Abt 972

Died: Aft 994

14 Immed II, Count of Saxony

Born: Abt 940
-CONTINUED AS #1,ROYAL CHART 2281
Married:

Died: 29 Jan 983

15 Adela of Hamalant

Born: Abt 952
-CONTINUED AS #1,ROYAL CHART 2282
Died: 1017

Sources include: *Royal Ancestors* (1989), chart 11864; Stuart 48, 136; Moriarty 162.

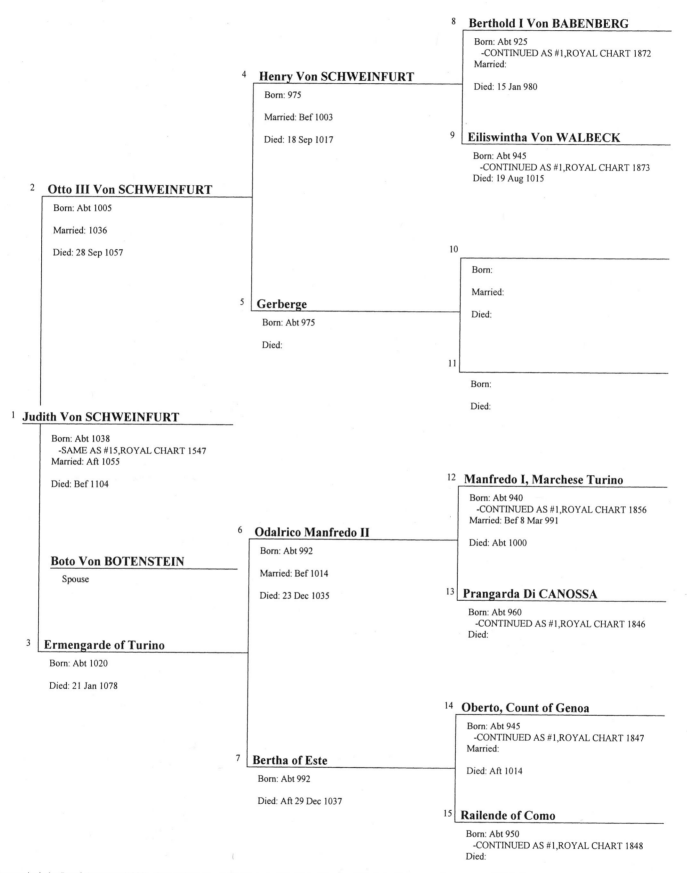

8   **Berthold I Von BABENBERG**

Born: Abt 925
    -CONTINUED AS #1,ROYAL CHART 1872
Married:

Died: 15 Jan 980

4   **Henry Von SCHWEINFURT**

Born: 975

Married: Bef 1003

Died: 18 Sep 1017

9   **Eiliswintha Von WALBECK**

Born: Abt 945
    -CONTINUED AS #1,ROYAL CHART 1873
Died: 19 Aug 1015

2   **Otto III Von SCHWEINFURT**

Born: Abt 1005

Married: 1036

Died: 28 Sep 1057

10

Born:

Married:

Died:

5   **Gerberge**

Born: Abt 975

Died:

11

Born:

Died:

1   **Judith Von SCHWEINFURT**

Born: Abt 1038
    -SAME AS #15,ROYAL CHART 1547
Married: Aft 1055

Died: Bef 1104

12   **Manfredo I, Marchese Turino**

Born: Abt 940
    -CONTINUED AS #1,ROYAL CHART 1856
Married: Bef 8 Mar 991

Died: Abt 1000

6   **Odalrico Manfredo II**

Born: Abt 992

Married: Bef 1014

Died: 23 Dec 1035

Boto Von BOTENSTEIN

    Spouse

13   **Prangarda Di CANOSSA**

Born: Abt 960
    -CONTINUED AS #1,ROYAL CHART 1846
Died:

3   **Ermengarde of Turino**

Born: Abt 1020

Died: 21 Jan 1078

14   **Oberto, Count of Genoa**

Born: Abt 945
    -CONTINUED AS #1,ROYAL CHART 1847
Married:

Died: Aft 1014

7   **Bertha of Este**

Born: Abt 992

Died: Aft 29 Dec 1037

15   **Railende of Como**

Born: Abt 950
    -CONTINUED AS #1,ROYAL CHART 1848
Died:

Sources include: *Royal Ancestors* (1989), chart 11864; Stuart 47; Moriarty 163. Note: Stuart and Moriarty disagree on the ancestry of #5 Gerberge.

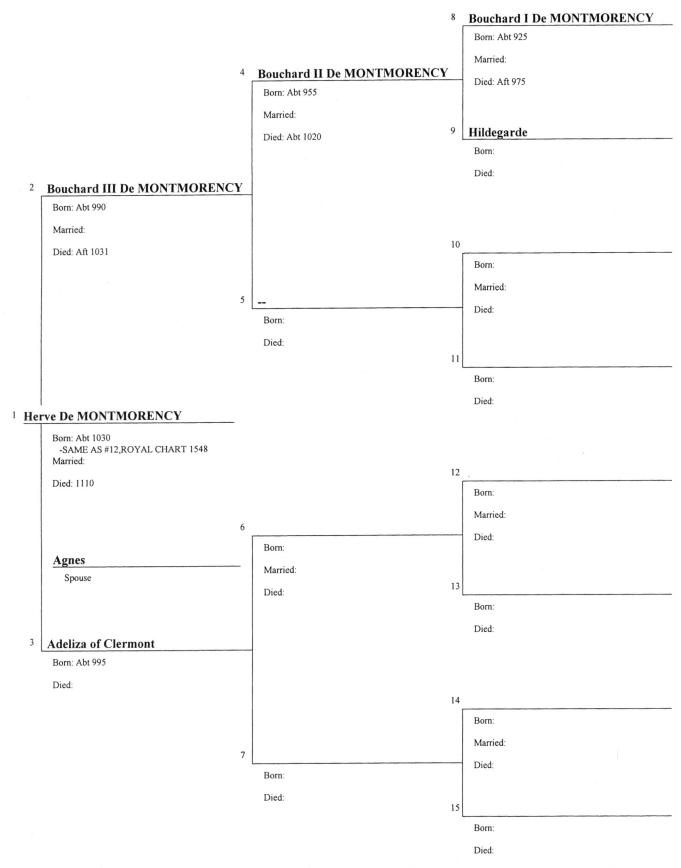

8 Bouchard I De MONTMORENCY
Born: Abt 925
Married:
Died: Aft 975

4 Bouchard II De MONTMORENCY
Born: Abt 955
Married:
Died: Abt 1020

9 Hildegarde
Born:
Died:

2 Bouchard III De MONTMORENCY
Born: Abt 990
Married:
Died: Aft 1031

10
Born:
Married:
Died:

5 --
Born:
Died:

11
Born:
Died:

1 Herve De MONTMORENCY
Born: Abt 1030
 -SAME AS #12,ROYAL CHART 1548
Married:
Died: 1110

12
Born:
Married:
Died:

6
Born:
Married:
Died:

Agnes
Spouse

13
Born:
Died:

3 Adeliza of Clermont
Born: Abt 995
Died:

14
Born:
Married:
Died:

7
Born:
Died:

15
Born:
Died:

Sources include: *Royal Ancestors* (1989), chart 11867; Moriarty 177; Stuart 34; *TAG* 74:148; Turton 231. Note: There is some confusion and uncertainty on the above Montmorency line. Claims are made for additional ancestry, but Moriarty ends the line with #8 & 9 Bouchard I & Hildegarde.

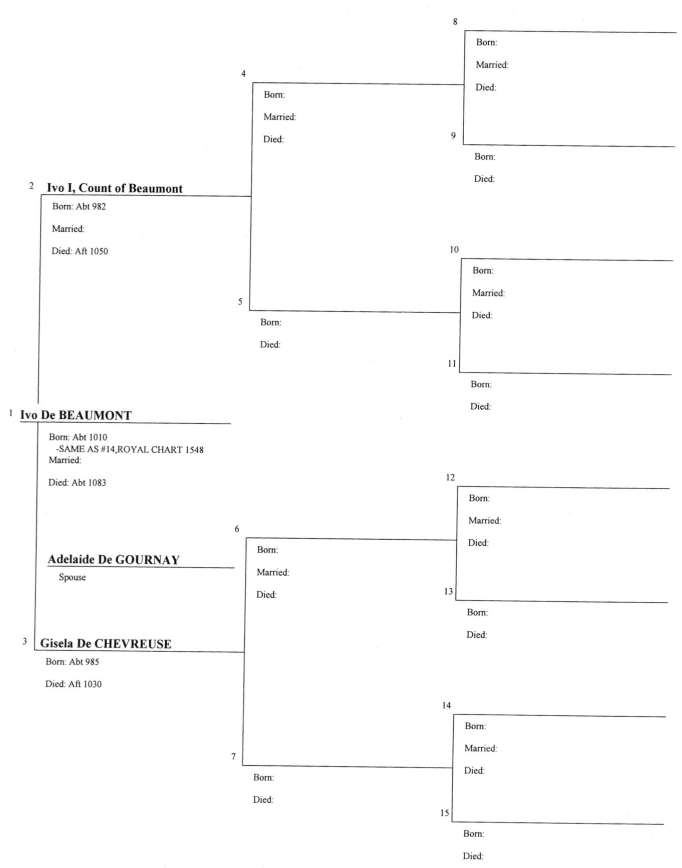

8
Born:
Married:
Died:

4
Born:
Married:
Died:

9
Born:
Died:

2   **Ivo I, Count of Beaumont**
Born: Abt 982
Married:
Died: Aft 1050

10
Born:
Married:
Died:

5
Born:
Died:

11
Born:
Died:

1   **Ivo De BEAUMONT**
Born: Abt 1010
  -SAME AS #14,ROYAL CHART 1548
Married:
Died: Abt 1083

12
Born:
Married:
Died:

6
Born:
Married:
Died:

13
Born:
Died:

Adelaide De GOURNAY
Spouse

3   **Gisela De CHEVREUSE**
Born: Abt 985
Died: Aft 1030

14
Born:
Married:
Died:

7
Born:
Died:

15
Born:
Died:

Sources include: *Royal Ancestors* (1989), charts 11868, 11549; Stuart 274; Moriarty 177; LDS records; Turton 100, 231. Note: Stuart inserts two additional generations (both named Ivo) between #1 & 2, and he adds parentage for #2. The added information contains conflicting dates and poses chronological problems. The Moriarty version is accepted and shown above.

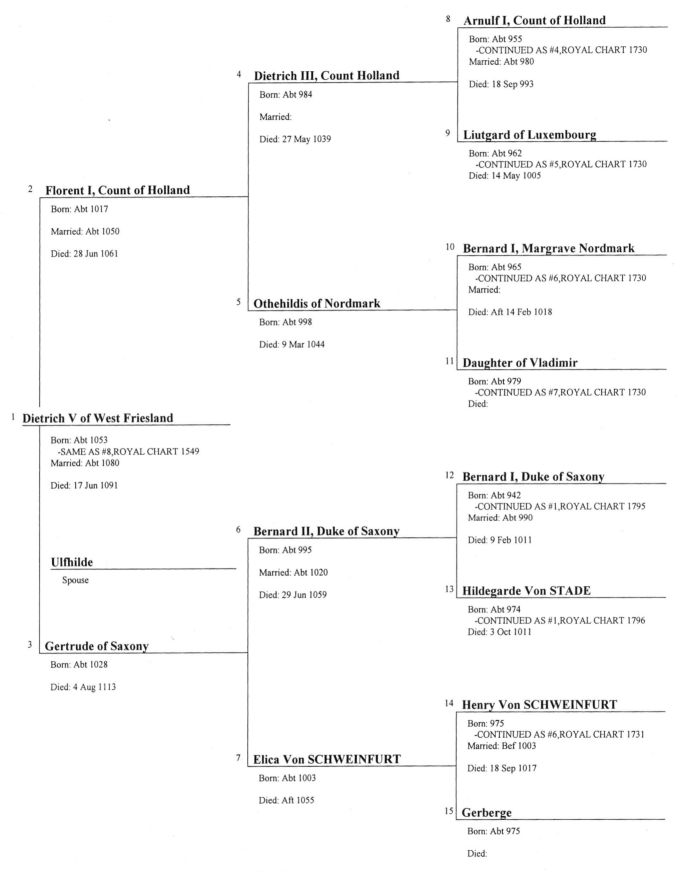

8 Arnulf I, Count of Holland

Born: Abt 955
 -CONTINUED AS #4,ROYAL CHART 1730
Married: Abt 980

Died: 18 Sep 993

4 Dietrich III, Count Holland

Born: Abt 984

Married:

Died: 27 May 1039

9 Liutgard of Luxembourg

Born: Abt 962
 -CONTINUED AS #5,ROYAL CHART 1730
Died: 14 May 1005

2 Florent I, Count of Holland

Born: Abt 1017

Married: Abt 1050

Died: 28 Jun 1061

10 Bernard I, Margrave Nordmark

Born: Abt 965
 -CONTINUED AS #6,ROYAL CHART 1730
Married:

Died: Aft 14 Feb 1018

5 Othehildis of Nordmark

Born: Abt 998

Died: 9 Mar 1044

11 Daughter of Vladimir

Born: Abt 979
 -CONTINUED AS #7,ROYAL CHART 1730
Died:

1 Dietrich V of West Friesland

Born: Abt 1053
 -SAME AS #8,ROYAL CHART 1549
Married: Abt 1080

Died: 17 Jun 1091

12 Bernard I, Duke of Saxony

Born: Abt 942
 -CONTINUED AS #1,ROYAL CHART 1795
Married: Abt 990

Died: 9 Feb 1011

6 Bernard II, Duke of Saxony

Born: Abt 995

Married: Abt 1020

Died: 29 Jun 1059

13 Hildegarde Von STADE

Born: Abt 974
 -CONTINUED AS #1,ROYAL CHART 1796
Died: 3 Oct 1011

Ulfhilde

Spouse

3 Gertrude of Saxony

Born: Abt 1028

Died: 4 Aug 1113

14 Henry Von SCHWEINFURT

Born: 975
 -CONTINUED AS #6,ROYAL CHART 1731
Married: Bef 1003

Died: 18 Sep 1017

7 Elica Von SCHWEINFURT

Born: Abt 1003

Died: Aft 1055

15 Gerberge

Born: Abt 975

Died:

Sources include: *Royal Ancestors* (1989), chart 11869; Stuart 38; Moriarty 55.

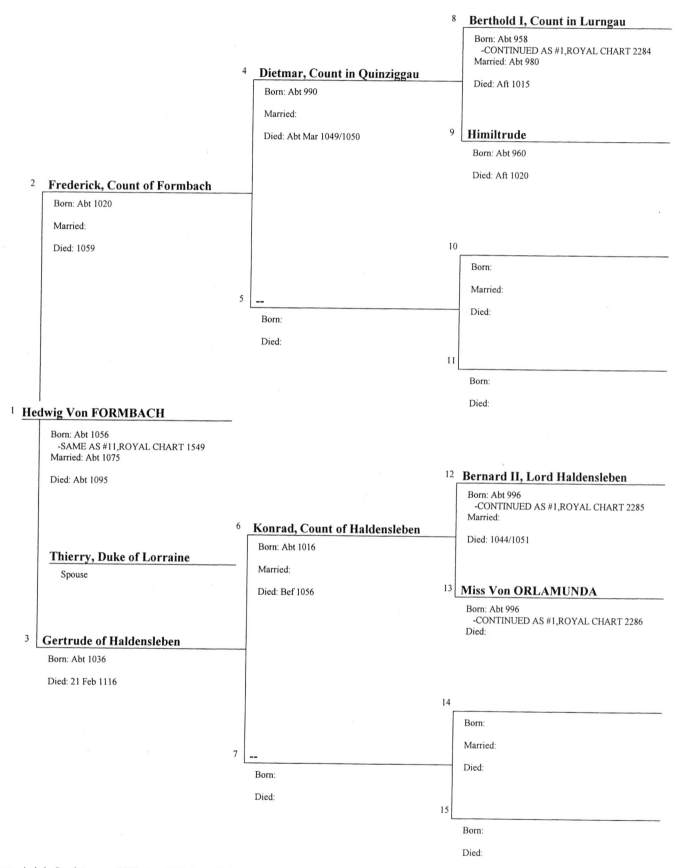

8 Berthold I, Count in Lurngau
Born: Abt 958
-CONTINUED AS #1,ROYAL CHART 2284
Married: Abt 980

Died: Aft 1015

4 Dietmar, Count in Quinziggau
Born: Abt 990

Married:

Died: Abt Mar 1049/1050

9 Himiltrude
Born: Abt 960

Died: Aft 1020

2 Frederick, Count of Formbach
Born: Abt 1020

Married:

Died: 1059

10
Born:

Married:

Died:

5 --
Born:

Died:

11
Born:

Died:

1 Hedwig Von FORMBACH
Born: Abt 1056
-SAME AS #11,ROYAL CHART 1549
Married: Abt 1075

Died: Abt 1095

12 Bernard II, Lord Haldensleben
Born: Abt 996
-CONTINUED AS #1,ROYAL CHART 2285
Married:

Died: 1044/1051

6 Konrad, Count of Haldensleben
Born: Abt 1016

Married:

Died: Bef 1056

13 Miss Von ORLAMUNDA
Born: Abt 996
-CONTINUED AS #1,ROYAL CHART 2286
Died:

Thierry, Duke of Lorraine
Spouse

3 Gertrude of Haldensleben
Born: Abt 1036

Died: 21 Feb 1116

14
Born:

Married:

Died:

7 --
Born:

Died:

15
Born:

Died:

Sources include: *Royal Ancestors* (1989), chart 11870; Stuart 41, 27; Moriarty 172; Faris preliminary Charlemagne manuscript (June 1995), pp. 2, 138. Note: #4 is also called Thiemo.

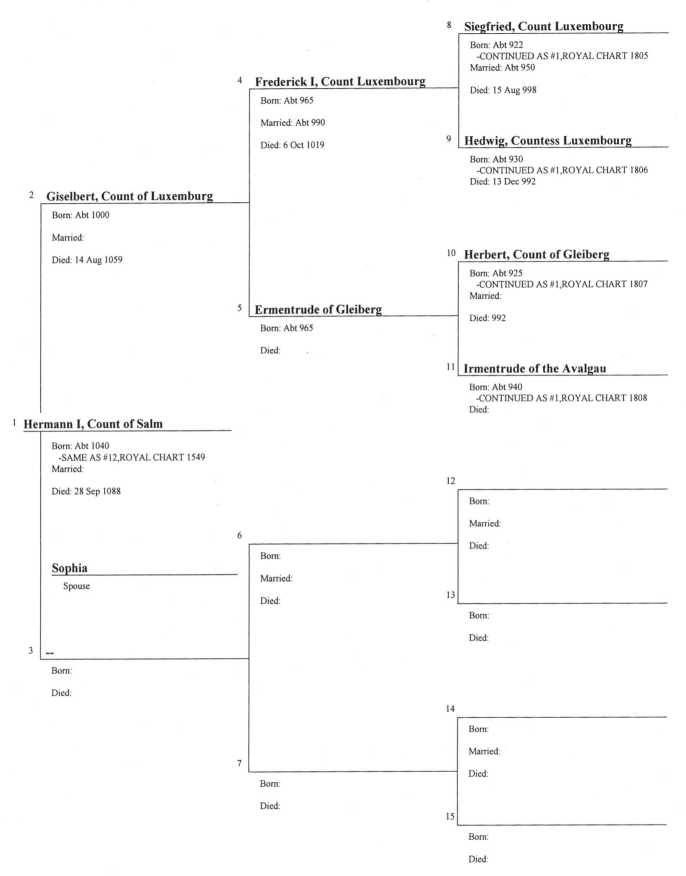

8 **Siegfried, Count Luxembourg**

Born: Abt 922
    -CONTINUED AS #1,ROYAL CHART 1805
Married: Abt 950

Died: 15 Aug 998

4 **Frederick I, Count Luxembourg**

Born: Abt 965

Married: Abt 990

Died: 6 Oct 1019

9 **Hedwig, Countess Luxembourg**

Born: Abt 930
    -CONTINUED AS #1,ROYAL CHART 1806
Died: 13 Dec 992

2 **Giselbert, Count of Luxemburg**

Born: Abt 1000

Married:

Died: 14 Aug 1059

10 **Herbert, Count of Gleiberg**

Born: Abt 925
    -CONTINUED AS #1,ROYAL CHART 1807
Married:

Died: 992

5 **Ermentrude of Gleiberg**

Born: Abt 965

Died:

11 **Irmentrude of the Avalgau**

Born: Abt 940
    -CONTINUED AS #1,ROYAL CHART 1808
Died:

1 **Hermann I, Count of Salm**

Born: Abt 1040
    -SAME AS #12,ROYAL CHART 1549
Married:

Died: 28 Sep 1088

12

Born:

Married:

Died:

6

Born:

Married:

Died:

Sophia
    Spouse

13

Born:

Died:

3 **--**

Born:

Died:

14

Born:

Married:

Died:

7

Born:

Died:

15

Born:

Died:

Sources include: *Royal Ancestors* (1989), chart 11876; Stuart 391; Moriarty 179, 129.

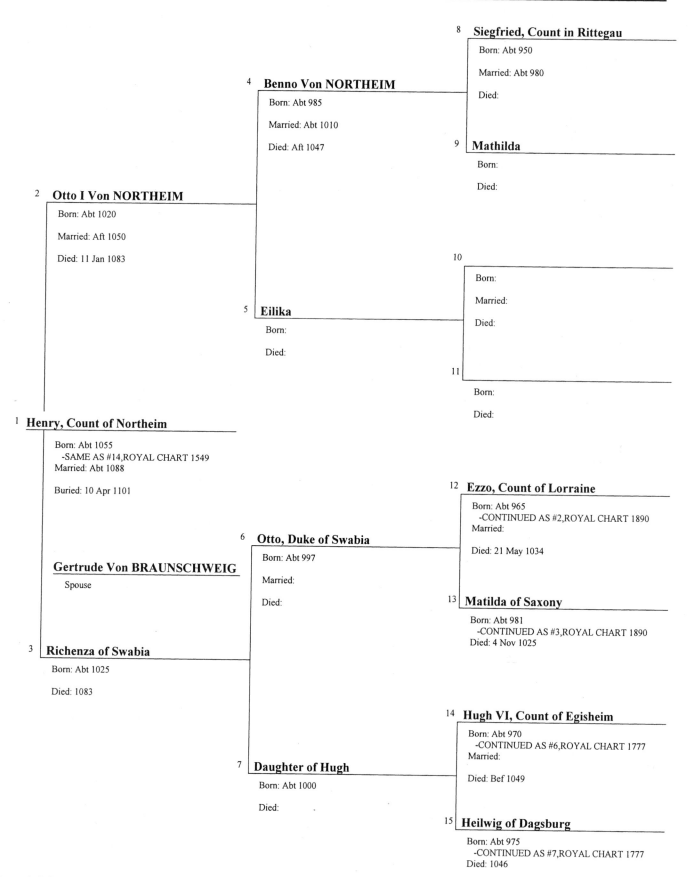

8 Siegfried, Count in Rittegau

Born: Abt 950

Married: Abt 980

Died:

4 Benno Von NORTHEIM

Born: Abt 985

Married: Abt 1010

Died: Aft 1047

9 Mathilda

Born:

Died:

2 Otto I Von NORTHEIM

Born: Abt 1020

Married: Aft 1050

Died: 11 Jan 1083

10

Born:

Married:

Died:

5 Eilika

Born:

Died:

11

Born:

Died:

1 Henry, Count of Northeim

Born: Abt 1055
-SAME AS #14,ROYAL CHART 1549
Married: Abt 1088

Buried: 10 Apr 1101

12 Ezzo, Count of Lorraine

Born: Abt 965
-CONTINUED AS #2,ROYAL CHART 1890
Married:

Died: 21 May 1034

6 Otto, Duke of Swabia

Born: Abt 997

Married:

Died:

13 Matilda of Saxony

Born: Abt 981
-CONTINUED AS #3,ROYAL CHART 1890
Died: 4 Nov 1025

Gertrude Von BRAUNSCHWEIG

Spouse

3 Richenza of Swabia

Born: Abt 1025

Died: 1083

14 Hugh VI, Count of Egisheim

Born: Abt 970
-CONTINUED AS #6,ROYAL CHART 1777
Married:

Died: Bef 1049

7 Daughter of Hugh

Born: Abt 1000

Died:

15 Heilwig of Dagsburg

Born: Abt 975
-CONTINUED AS #7,ROYAL CHART 1777
Died: 1046

Sources include: *Royal Ancestors* (1989), chart 11877; Moriarty 179, 166; Stuart 392 (ends with #1), 26 (#2 & 3 ancestry).

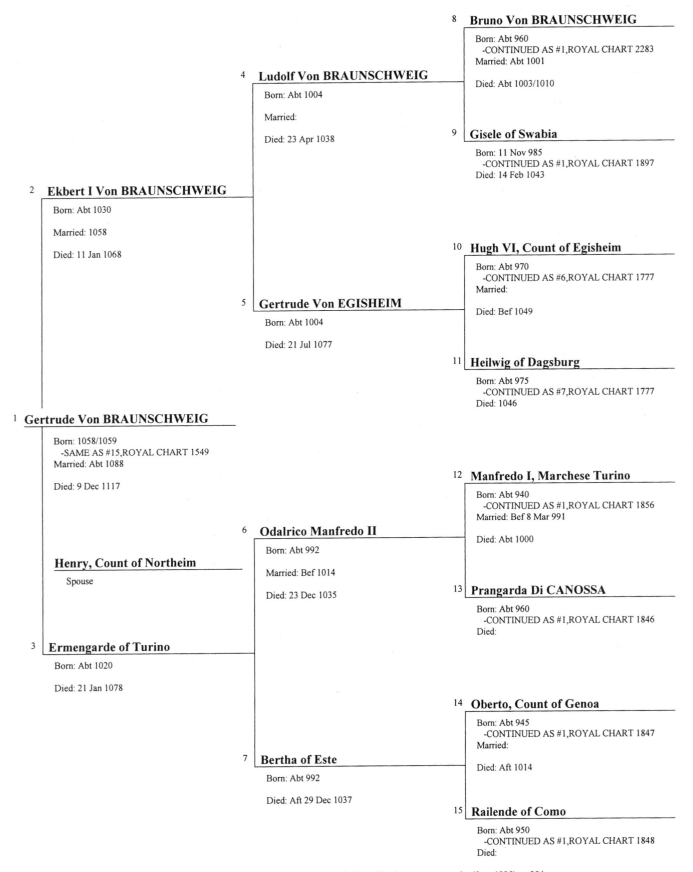

8 **Bruno Von BRAUNSCHWEIG**

Born: Abt 960
-CONTINUED AS #1,ROYAL CHART 2283
Married: Abt 1001

Died: Abt 1003/1010

4 **Ludolf Von BRAUNSCHWEIG**

Born: Abt 1004

Married:

Died: 23 Apr 1038

9 **Gisele of Swabia**

Born: 11 Nov 985
-CONTINUED AS #1,ROYAL CHART 1897
Died: 14 Feb 1043

2 **Ekbert I Von BRAUNSCHWEIG**

Born: Abt 1030

Married: 1058

Died: 11 Jan 1068

10 **Hugh VI, Count of Egisheim**

Born: Abt 970
-CONTINUED AS #6,ROYAL CHART 1777
Married:

Died: Bef 1049

5 **Gertrude Von EGISHEIM**

Born: Abt 1004

Died: 21 Jul 1077

11 **Heilwig of Dagsburg**

Born: Abt 975
-CONTINUED AS #7,ROYAL CHART 1777
Died: 1046

1 **Gertrude Von BRAUNSCHWEIG**

Born: 1058/1059
-SAME AS #15,ROYAL CHART 1549
Married: Abt 1088

Died: 9 Dec 1117

12 **Manfredo I, Marchese Turino**

Born: Abt 940
-CONTINUED AS #1,ROYAL CHART 1856
Married: Bef 8 Mar 991

Died: Abt 1000

6 **Odalrico Manfredo II**

Born: Abt 992

Married: Bef 1014

Died: 23 Dec 1035

13 **Prangarda Di CANOSSA**

Born: Abt 960
-CONTINUED AS #1,ROYAL CHART 1846
Died:

Henry, Count of Northeim

Spouse

3 **Ermengarde of Turino**

Born: Abt 1020

Died: 21 Jan 1078

14 **Oberto, Count of Genoa**

Born: Abt 945
-CONTINUED AS #1,ROYAL CHART 1847
Married:

Died: Aft 1014

7 **Bertha of Este**

Born: Abt 992

Died: Aft 29 Dec 1037

15 **Railende of Como**

Born: Abt 950
-CONTINUED AS #1,ROYAL CHART 1848
Died:

Sources include: *Royal Ancestors* (1989), chart 11877; Stuart 393; Moriarty 180; Faris preliminary Charlemagne manuscript (June 1995), p. 284.

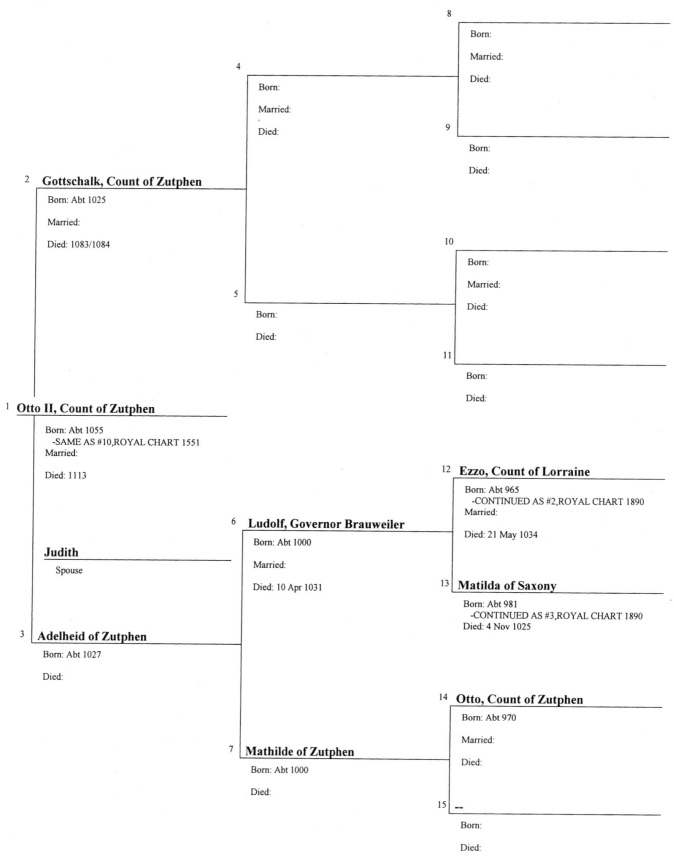

8

Born:

Married:

Died:

4

Born:

Married:

Died:

9

Born:

Died:

2 **Gottschalk, Count of Zutphen**

Born: Abt 1025

Married:

Died: 1083/1084

10

Born:

Married:

Died:

5

Born:

Died:

11

Born:

Died:

1 **Otto II, Count of Zutphen**

Born: Abt 1055
-SAME AS #10,ROYAL CHART 1551
Married:

Died: 1113

12 **Ezzo, Count of Lorraine**

Born: Abt 965
-CONTINUED AS #2,ROYAL CHART 1890
Married:

Died: 21 May 1034

6 **Ludolf, Governor Brauweiler**

Born: Abt 1000

Married:

Died: 10 Apr 1031

13 **Matilda of Saxony**

Born: Abt 981
-CONTINUED AS #3,ROYAL CHART 1890
Died: 4 Nov 1025

Judith

Spouse

3 **Adelheid of Zutphen**

Born: Abt 1027

Died:

14 **Otto, Count of Zutphen**

Born: Abt 970

Married:

Died:

7 **Mathilde of Zutphen**

Born: Abt 1000

Died:

15 **--**

Born:

Died:

Sources include: Stuart 379.

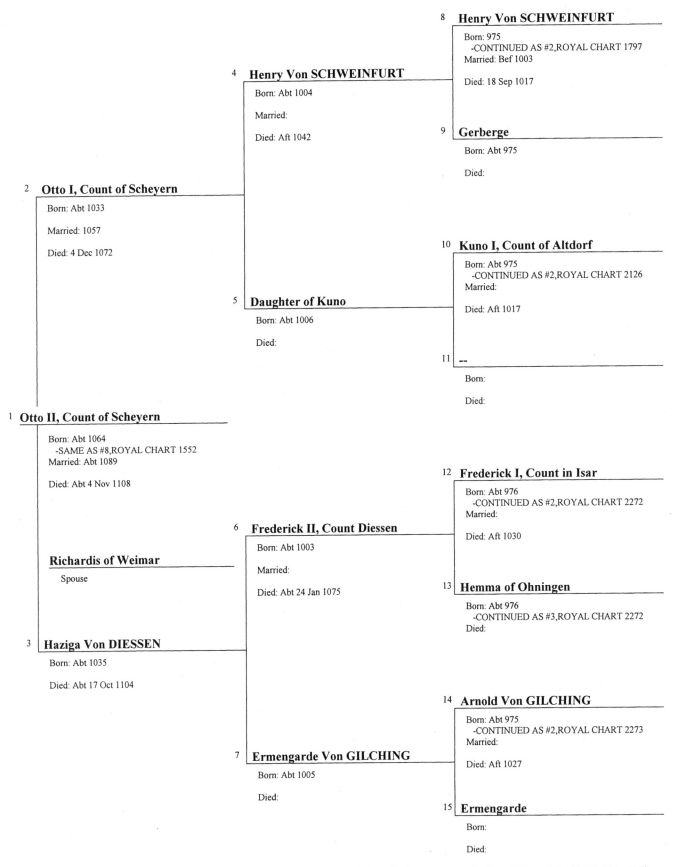

2 **Otto I, Count of Scheyern**
Born: Abt 1033
Married: 1057
Died: 4 Dec 1072

4 **Henry Von SCHWEINFURT**
Born: Abt 1004
Married:
Died: Aft 1042

8 **Henry Von SCHWEINFURT**
Born: 975
-CONTINUED AS #2,ROYAL CHART 1797
Married: Bef 1003
Died: 18 Sep 1017

9 **Gerberge**
Born: Abt 975
Died:

5 **Daughter of Kuno**
Born: Abt 1006
Died:

10 **Kuno I, Count of Altdorf**
Born: Abt 975
-CONTINUED AS #2,ROYAL CHART 2126
Married:
Died: Aft 1017

11 **--**
Born:
Died:

1 **Otto II, Count of Scheyern**
Born: Abt 1064
-SAME AS #8,ROYAL CHART 1552
Married: Abt 1089
Died: Abt 4 Nov 1108

Richardis of Weimar
Spouse

3 **Haziga Von DIESSEN**
Born: Abt 1035
Died: Abt 17 Oct 1104

6 **Frederick II, Count Diessen**
Born: Abt 1003
Married:
Died: Abt 24 Jan 1075

12 **Frederick I, Count in Isar**
Born: Abt 976
-CONTINUED AS #2,ROYAL CHART 2272
Married:
Died: Aft 1030

13 **Hemma of Ohningen**
Born: Abt 976
-CONTINUED AS #3,ROYAL CHART 2272
Died:

7 **Ermengarde Von GILCHING**
Born: Abt 1005
Died:

14 **Arnold Von GILCHING**
Born: Abt 975
-CONTINUED AS #2,ROYAL CHART 2273
Married:
Died: Aft 1027

15 **Ermengarde**
Born:
Died:

Sources include: *Royal Ancestors* (1989), chart 11880; Stuart 307, 46; Moriarty 186-187; Faris preliminary Charlemagne manuscript (June 1995), pp. 285-286, 121. Note: #7 (the mother of Haziga) is disputed and uncertain. Faris gives #7 as a 1st wife Hadamut Von Eppenstein, daughter of Ezzo (Count in the Isar) & Richgardis Sieghardingerin. Stuart and Moriarty give #7 as Ermengarde Von Gilching, as shown, although Moriarty acknowledges the Eppenstein claim. It is agreed that #7 Ermengarde was the mother of a daughter Uta (see chart 2150, #7).

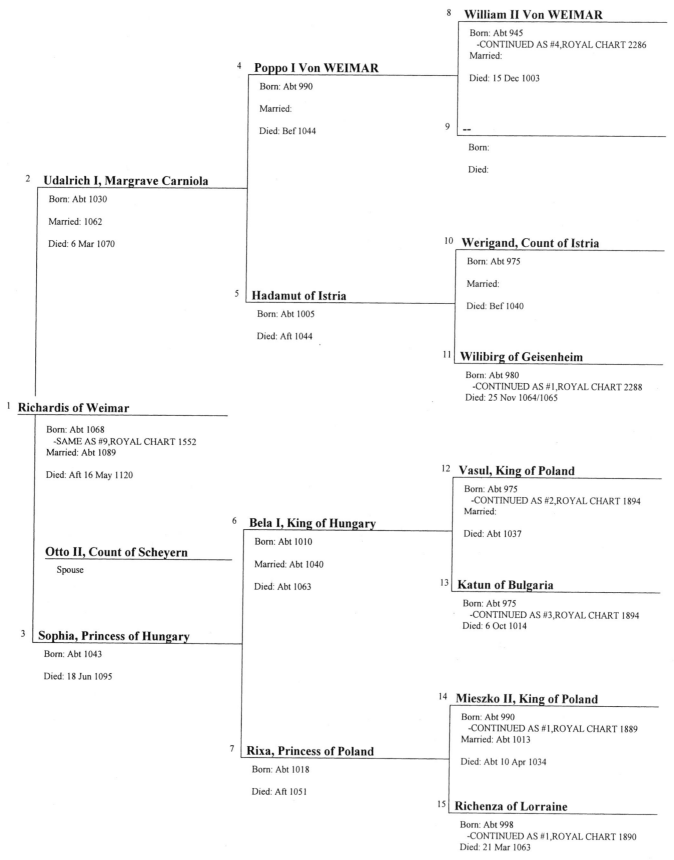

8 William II Von WEIMAR

Born: Abt 945
-CONTINUED AS #4,ROYAL CHART 2286
Married:

Died: 15 Dec 1003

4 Poppo I Von WEIMAR

Born: Abt 990

Married:

Died: Bef 1044

9 --

Born:

Died:

2 Udalrich I, Margrave Carniola

Born: Abt 1030

Married: 1062

Died: 6 Mar 1070

10 Werigand, Count of Istria

Born: Abt 975

Married:

Died: Bef 1040

5 Hadamut of Istria

Born: Abt 1005

Died: Aft 1044

11 Wilibirg of Geisenheim

Born: Abt 980
-CONTINUED AS #1,ROYAL CHART 2288
Died: 25 Nov 1064/1065

1 Richardis of Weimar

Born: Abt 1068
-SAME AS #9,ROYAL CHART 1552
Married: Abt 1089

Died: Aft 16 May 1120

12 Vasul, King of Poland

Born: Abt 975
-CONTINUED AS #2,ROYAL CHART 1894
Married:

Died: Abt 1037

6 Bela I, King of Hungary

Born: Abt 1010

Married: Abt 1040

Died: Abt 1063

Otto II, Count of Scheyern

Spouse

13 Katun of Bulgaria

Born: Abt 975
-CONTINUED AS #3,ROYAL CHART 1894
Died: 6 Oct 1014

3 Sophia, Princess of Hungary

Born: Abt 1043

Died: 18 Jun 1095

14 Mieszko II, King of Poland

Born: Abt 990
-CONTINUED AS #1,ROYAL CHART 1889
Married: Abt 1013

Died: Abt 10 Apr 1034

7 Rixa, Princess of Poland

Born: Abt 1018

Died: Aft 1051

15 Richenza of Lorraine

Born: Abt 998
-CONTINUED AS #1,ROYAL CHART 1890
Died: 21 Mar 1063

Sources include: *Royal Ancestors* (1989), chart 11880; Stuart 281; Moriarty 188.

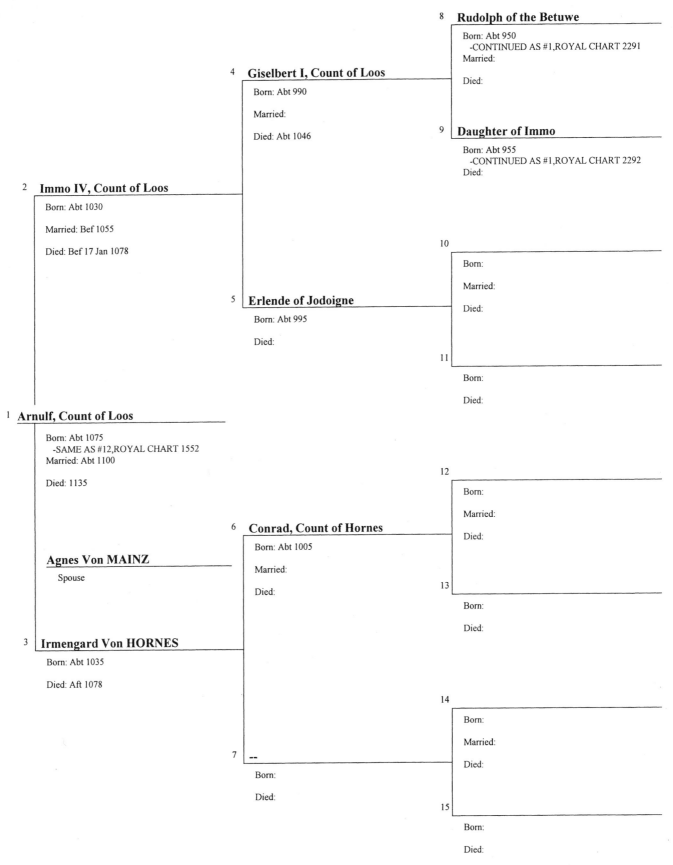

8 | **Rudolph of the Betuwe**
Born: Abt 950
 -CONTINUED AS #1, ROYAL CHART 2291
Married:

Died:

4 | **Giselbert I, Count of Loos**
Born: Abt 990

Married:

Died: Abt 1046

9 | **Daughter of Immo**
Born: Abt 955
 -CONTINUED AS #1, ROYAL CHART 2292
Died:

2 | **Immo IV, Count of Loos**
Born: Abt 1030

Married: Bef 1055

Died: Bef 17 Jan 1078

10
Born:

Married:

Died:

5 | **Erlende of Jodoigne**
Born: Abt 995

Died:

11
Born:

Died:

1 | **Arnulf, Count of Loos**
Born: Abt 1075
 -SAME AS #12, ROYAL CHART 1552
Married: Abt 1100

Died: 1135

12
Born:

Married:

Died:

6 | **Conrad, Count of Hornes**
Born: Abt 1005

Married:

Died:

13
Born:

Died:

Agnes Von MAINZ
Spouse

3 | **Irmengard Von HORNES**
Born: Abt 1035

Died: Aft 1078

14
Born:

Married:

Died:

7 | **--**
Born:

Died:

15
Born:

Died:

Sources include: *Royal Ancestors* (1989), chart 11882; Stuart 100; Moriarty 189. Note: Moriarty differs in several respects with the above pedigree. He adds an additional generation (another Arnulf who married Alheidis of Holland) between #1 & #2 above. He gives #5 as Luitgarde of Namur, and he gives a different tentative ancestry for #4 Giselbert. The Stuart version (following Schwennicke) is tentatively followed above.

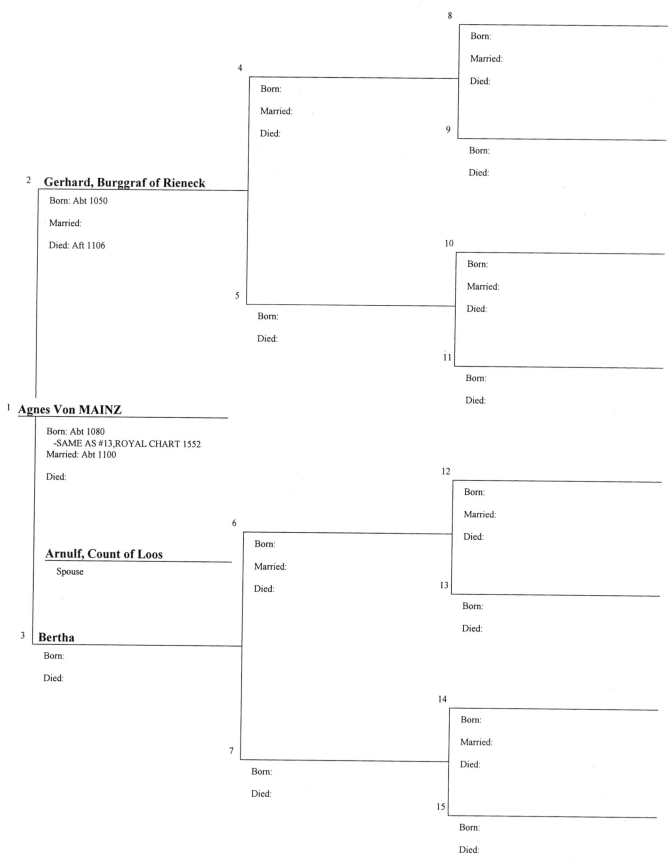

8
Born:
Married:
Died:

4
Born:
Married:
Died:

9
Born:
Died:

2 Gerhard, Burggraf of Rieneck
Born: Abt 1050
Married:
Died: Aft 1106

10
Born:
Married:
Died:

5
Born:
Died:

11
Born:
Died:

1 Agnes Von MAINZ
Born: Abt 1080
  -SAME AS #13,ROYAL CHART 1552
Married: Abt 1100
Died:

12
Born:
Married:
Died:

6
Born:
Married:
Died:

13
Born:
Died:

Arnulf, Count of Loos
Spouse

3 Bertha
Born:
Died:

14
Born:
Married:
Died:

7
Born:
Died:

15
Born:
Died:

Sources include: *Royal Ancestors* (1989), chart 11882; Moriarty 189; Stuart 320-29, 278. Note: Stuart gives #3 as Hedwig of Blieskastel and claims extensive ancestry that is clearly incorrect.

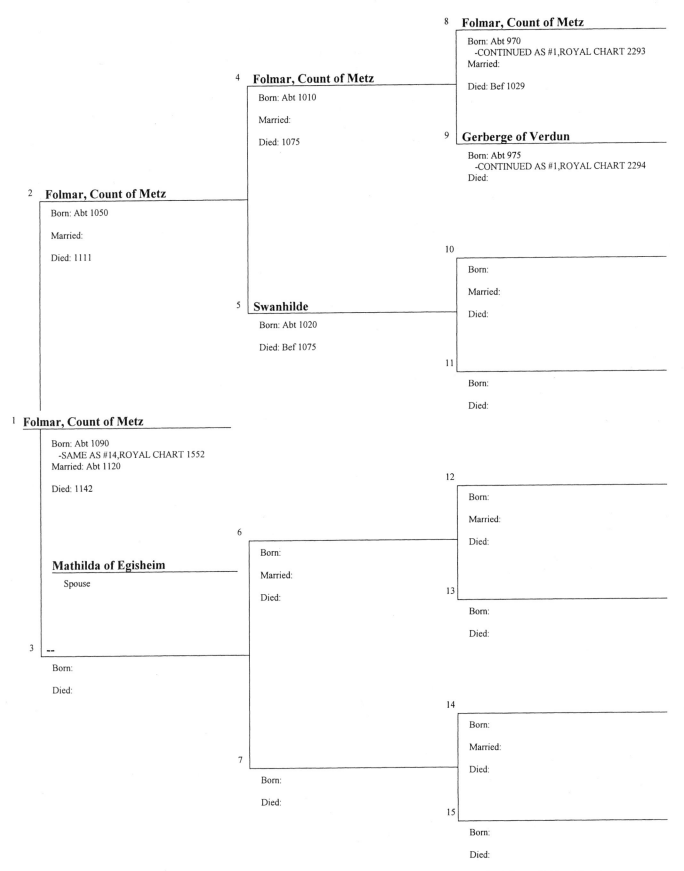

8 **Folmar, Count of Metz**

Born: Abt 970
-CONTINUED AS #1,ROYAL CHART 2293
Married:

Died: Bef 1029

4 **Folmar, Count of Metz**

Born: Abt 1010

Married:

Died: 1075

9 **Gerberge of Verdun**

Born: Abt 975
-CONTINUED AS #1,ROYAL CHART 2294
Died:

2 **Folmar, Count of Metz**

Born: Abt 1050

Married:

Died: 1111

10

Born:

Married:

Died:

5 **Swanhilde**

Born: Abt 1020

Died: Bef 1075

11

Born:

Died:

1 **Folmar, Count of Metz**

Born: Abt 1090
-SAME AS #14,ROYAL CHART 1552
Married: Abt 1120

Died: 1142

12

Born:

Married:

Died:

6

Born:

Married:

Died:

13

Born:

Died:

Mathilda of Egisheim

Spouse

3 --

Born:

Died:

14

Born:

Married:

Died:

7

Born:

Died:

15

Born:

Died:

Sources include: *Royal Ancestors* (1989), chart 11883; Moriarty 190-191; Faris preliminary Charlemagne manuscript (June 1995), pp. 48-49; Stuart 45. Note: There is disagreement on the precise descent of #1 Folmar from the Folmar who married Gerberge and who died before 1029 (see #8 & 9 above). The Moriarty version is tentatively retained above. Faris and Stuart follow Schwennicke 6:156, giving #1 Folmar as son of Folmar (md. Swanehilde), son of Folmar (md. Judith), son of Gottfried, son of #8 & 9 Folmar & Gerberge.

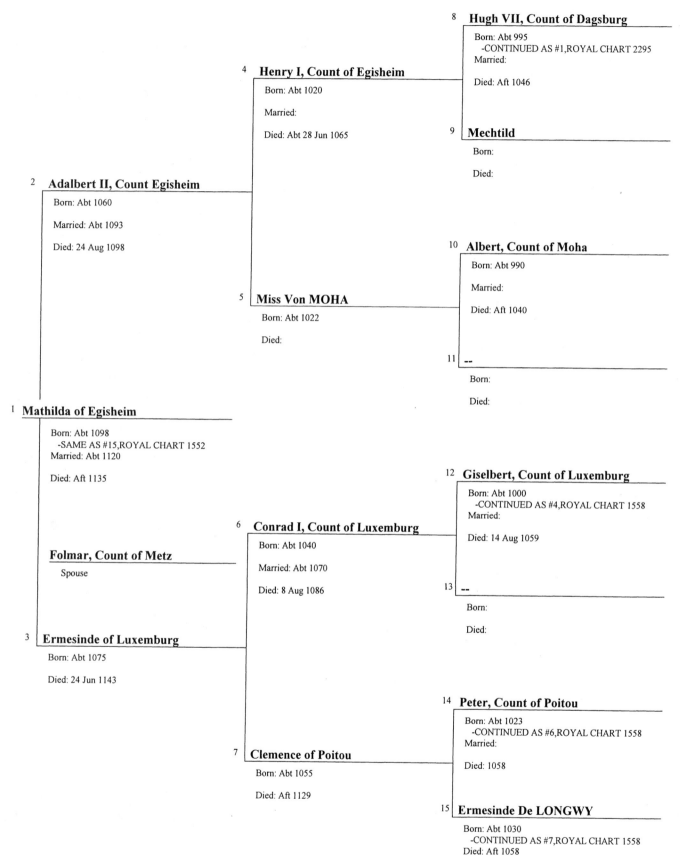

8 Hugh VII, Count of Dagsburg

Born: Abt 995
  -CONTINUED AS #1,ROYAL CHART 2295
Married:

Died: Aft 1046

4 Henry I, Count of Egisheim

Born: Abt 1020

Married:

Died: Abt 28 Jun 1065

9 Mechtild

Born:

Died:

2 Adalbert II, Count Egisheim

Born: Abt 1060

Married: Abt 1093

Died: 24 Aug 1098

10 Albert, Count of Moha

Born: Abt 990

Married:

Died: Aft 1040

5 Miss Von MOHA

Born: Abt 1022

Died:

11 --

Born:

Died:

1 Mathilda of Egisheim

Born: Abt 1098
  -SAME AS #15,ROYAL CHART 1552
Married: Abt 1120

Died: Aft 1135

12 Giselbert, Count of Luxemburg

Born: Abt 1000
  -CONTINUED AS #4,ROYAL CHART 1558
Married:

Died: 14 Aug 1059

6 Conrad I, Count of Luxemburg

Born: Abt 1040

Married: Abt 1070

Died: 8 Aug 1086

Folmar, Count of Metz

Spouse

13 --

Born:

Died:

3 Ermesinde of Luxemburg

Born: Abt 1075

Died: 24 Jun 1143

14 Peter, Count of Poitou

Born: Abt 1023
  -CONTINUED AS #6,ROYAL CHART 1558
Married:

Died: 1058

7 Clemence of Poitou

Born: Abt 1055

Died: Aft 1129

15 Ermesinde De LONGWY

Born: Abt 1030
  -CONTINUED AS #7,ROYAL CHART 1558
Died: Aft 1058

Sources include: *Royal Ancestors* (1989), chart 11883; Stuart 30; Faris preliminary Charlemagne manuscript (June 1995), pp. 48-49, 126, 245; Moriarty 191. Note: Moriarty omits one generation (#4 Henry) from the above line.

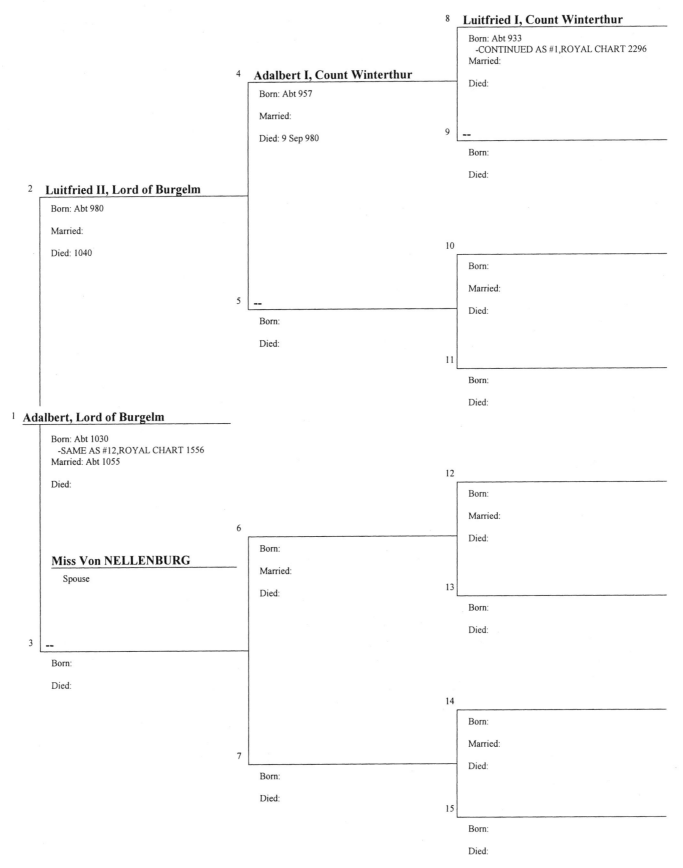

8 **Luitfried I, Count Winterthur**

Born: Abt 933
-CONTINUED AS #1,ROYAL CHART 2296
Married:

Died:

4 **Adalbert I, Count Winterthur**

Born: Abt 957

Married:

Died: 9 Sep 980

9 --

Born:

Died:

2 **Luitfried II, Lord of Burgelm**

Born: Abt 980

Married:

Died: 1040

10

Born:

Married:

Died:

5 --

Born:

Died:

11

Born:

Died:

1 **Adalbert, Lord of Burgelm**

Born: Abt 1030
-SAME AS #12,ROYAL CHART 1556
Married: Abt 1055

Died:

12

Born:

Married:

Died:

6

Born:

Married:

Died:

13

Born:

Died:

Miss Von NELLENBURG

Spouse

3 --

Born:

Died:

14

Born:

Married:

Died:

7

Born:

Married:

Died:

15

Born:

Died:

Sources include: *Royal Ancestors* (1989), chart 11941; Stuart 364; Moriarty 213.

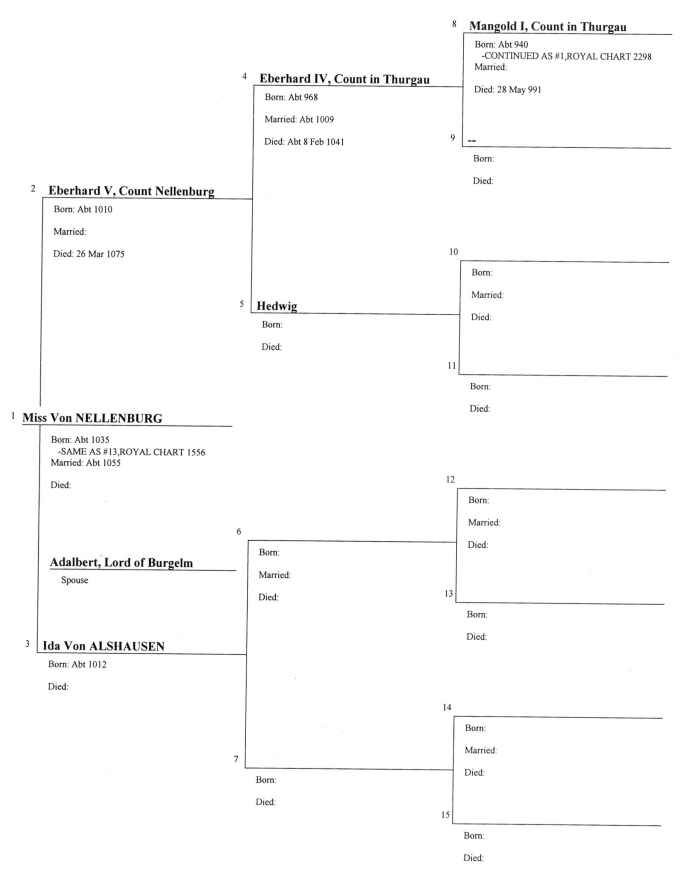

8 **Mangold I, Count in Thurgau**

Born: Abt 940
   -CONTINUED AS #1,ROYAL CHART 2298
Married:

Died: 28 May 991

4 **Eberhard IV, Count in Thurgau**

Born: Abt 968

Married: Abt 1009

Died: Abt 8 Feb 1041

9 --

Born:

Died:

2 **Eberhard V, Count Nellenburg**

Born: Abt 1010

Married:

Died: 26 Mar 1075

10

Born:

Married:

Died:

5 **Hedwig**

Born:

Died:

11

Born:

Died:

1 **Miss Von NELLENBURG**

Born: Abt 1035
   -SAME AS #13,ROYAL CHART 1556
Married: Abt 1055

Died:

12

Born:

Married:

Died:

6

Born:

Married:

Died:

13

Born:

Died:

Adalbert, Lord of Burgelm

Spouse

3 **Ida Von ALSHAUSEN**

Born: Abt 1012

Died:

14

Born:

Married:

Died:

7

Born:

Died:

15

Born:

Died:

Sources include: *Royal Ancestors* (1989), chart 11941; Stuart 18; Moriarty 206.

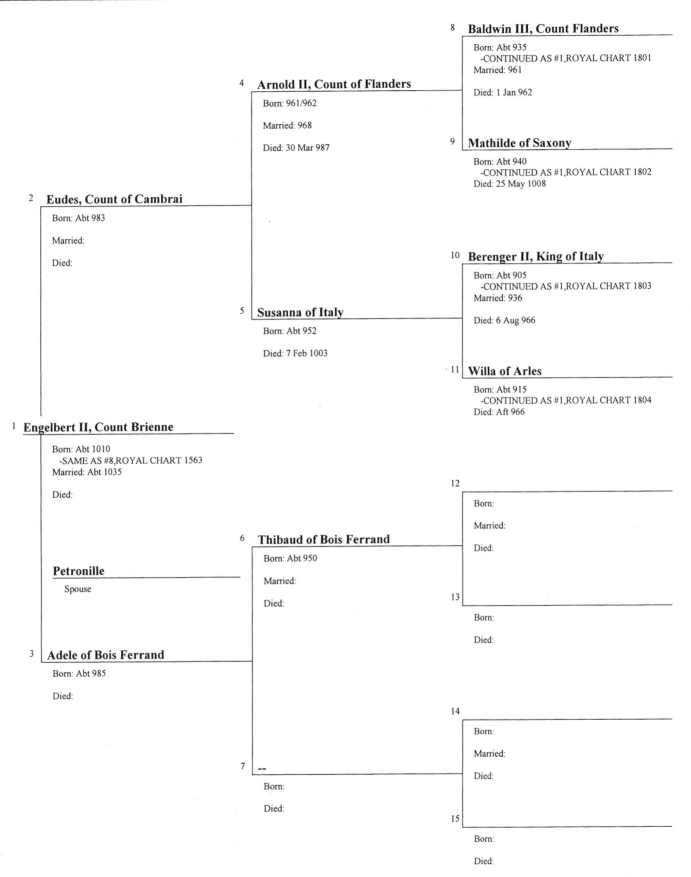

8 Baldwin III, Count Flanders

Born: Abt 935
 -CONTINUED AS #1,ROYAL CHART 1801
Married: 961

Died: 1 Jan 962

4 Arnold II, Count of Flanders

Born: 961/962

Married: 968

Died: 30 Mar 987

9 Mathilde of Saxony

Born: Abt 940
 -CONTINUED AS #1,ROYAL CHART 1802
Died: 25 May 1008

2 Eudes, Count of Cambrai

Born: Abt 983

Married:

Died:

10 Berenger II, King of Italy

Born: Abt 905
 -CONTINUED AS #1,ROYAL CHART 1803
Married: 936

Died: 6 Aug 966

5 Susanna of Italy

Born: Abt 952

Died: 7 Feb 1003

11 Willa of Arles

Born: Abt 915
 -CONTINUED AS #1,ROYAL CHART 1804
Died: Aft 966

1 Engelbert II, Count Brienne

Born: Abt 1010
 -SAME AS #8,ROYAL CHART 1563
Married: Abt 1035

Died:

12

Born:

Married:

Died:

6 Thibaud of Bois Ferrand

Born: Abt 950

Married:

Died:

Petronille

Spouse

13

Born:

Died:

3 Adele of Bois Ferrand

Born: Abt 985

Died:

14

Born:

Married:

Died:

7 --

Born:

Died:

15

Born:

Died:

Sources include: Faris preliminary Charlemagne manuscript (June 1995), pp. 72, 132; Moriarty 277; Stuart 383. Note: Stuart gives #1 as Engelbert IV, son of Engelbert III & Windesmode of Salins (following Schwennicke 3:681), but this is believed to be in error.

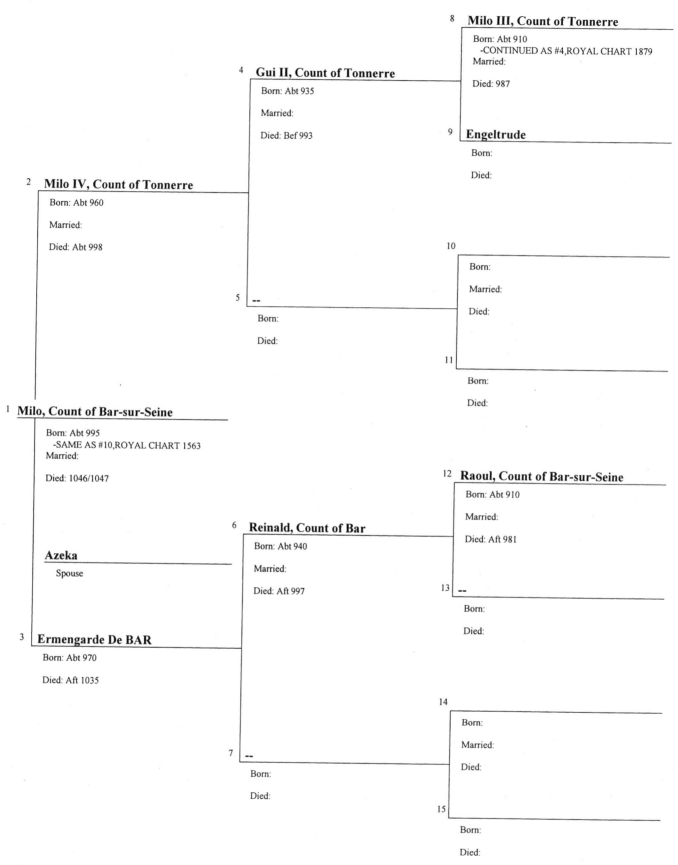

8 Milo III, Count of Tonnerre

Born: Abt 910
  -CONTINUED AS #4,ROYAL CHART 1879
Married:

Died: 987

4 Gui II, Count of Tonnerre

Born: Abt 935

Married:

Died: Bef 993

9 Engeltrude

Born:

Died:

2 Milo IV, Count of Tonnerre

Born: Abt 960

Married:

Died: Abt 998

10

Born:

Married:

Died:

5 --

Born:

Died:

11

Born:

Died:

1 Milo, Count of Bar-sur-Seine

Born: Abt 995
  -SAME AS #10,ROYAL CHART 1563
Married:

Died: 1046/1047

12 Raoul, Count of Bar-sur-Seine

Born: Abt 910

Married:

Died: Aft 981

6 Reinald, Count of Bar

Born: Abt 940

Married:

Died: Aft 997

13 --

Born:

Died:

Azeka

Spouse

3 Ermengarde De BAR

Born: Abt 970

Died: Aft 1035

14

Born:

Married:

Died:

7 --

Born:

Died:

15

Born:

Died:

Sources include: *Royal Ancestors* (1989), chart 11784; Stuart 383-30, 254; Turton 204, 206. Note: See note chart 1766 regarding the ancestry of #12 Raoul.

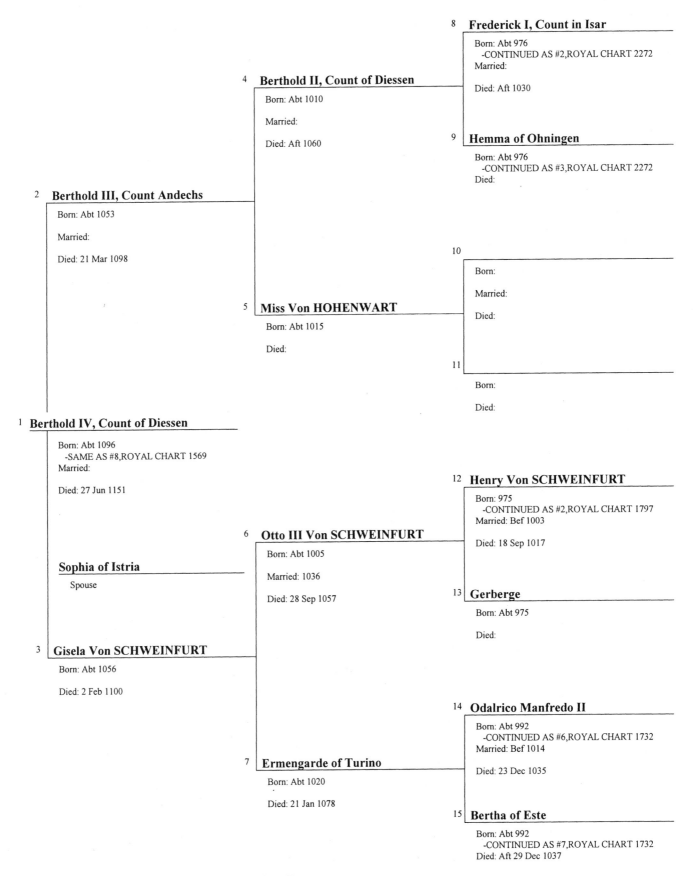

8 Frederick I, Count in Isar

Born: Abt 976
  -CONTINUED AS #2,ROYAL CHART 2272
Married:

Died: Aft 1030

4 Berthold II, Count of Diessen

Born: Abt 1010

Married:

Died: Aft 1060

9 Hemma of Ohningen

Born: Abt 976
  -CONTINUED AS #3,ROYAL CHART 2272
Died:

2 Berthold III, Count Andechs

Born: Abt 1053

Married:

Died: 21 Mar 1098

10

Born:

Married:

Died:

5 Miss Von HOHENWART

Born: Abt 1015

Died:

11

Born:

Died:

1 Berthold IV, Count of Diessen

Born: Abt 1096
  -SAME AS #8,ROYAL CHART 1569
Married:

Died: 27 Jun 1151

12 Henry Von SCHWEINFURT

Born: 975
  -CONTINUED AS #2,ROYAL CHART 1797
Married: Bef 1003

Died: 18 Sep 1017

6 Otto III Von SCHWEINFURT

Born: Abt 1005

Married: 1036

Died: 28 Sep 1057

13 Gerberge

Born: Abt 975

Died:

Sophia of Istria

Spouse

3 Gisela Von SCHWEINFURT

Born: Abt 1056

Died: 2 Feb 1100

14 Odalrico Manfredo II

Born: Abt 992
  -CONTINUED AS #6,ROYAL CHART 1732
Married: Bef 1014

Died: 23 Dec 1035

7 Ermengarde of Turino

Born: Abt 1020

Died: 21 Jan 1078

15 Bertha of Este

Born: Abt 992
  -CONTINUED AS #7,ROYAL CHART 1732
Died: Aft 29 Dec 1037

Sources include: *Royal Ancestors* (1989), chart 11890; Stuart 7; Moriarty 198.

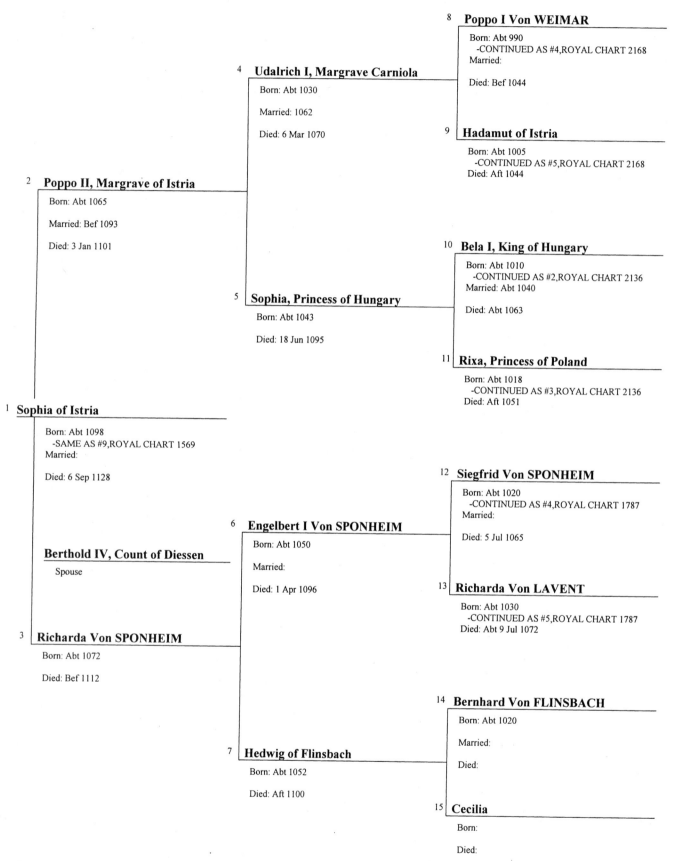

8 Poppo I Von WEIMAR

Born: Abt 990
-CONTINUED AS #4,ROYAL CHART 2168
Married:

Died: Bef 1044

4 Udalrich I, Margrave Carniola

Born: Abt 1030

Married: 1062

Died: 6 Mar 1070

9 Hadamut of Istria

Born: Abt 1005
-CONTINUED AS #5,ROYAL CHART 2168
Died: Aft 1044

2 Poppo II, Margrave of Istria

Born: Abt 1065

Married: Bef 1093

Died: 3 Jan 1101

10 Bela I, King of Hungary

Born: Abt 1010
-CONTINUED AS #2,ROYAL CHART 2136
Married: Abt 1040

Died: Abt 1063

5 Sophia, Princess of Hungary

Born: Abt 1043

Died: 18 Jun 1095

11 Rixa, Princess of Poland

Born: Abt 1018
-CONTINUED AS #3,ROYAL CHART 2136
Died: Aft 1051

1 Sophia of Istria

Born: Abt 1098
-SAME AS #9,ROYAL CHART 1569
Married:

Died: 6 Sep 1128

12 Siegfrid Von SPONHEIM

Born: Abt 1020
-CONTINUED AS #4,ROYAL CHART 1787
Married:

Died: 5 Jul 1065

6 Engelbert I Von SPONHEIM

Born: Abt 1050

Married:

Died: 1 Apr 1096

Berthold IV, Count of Diessen

Spouse

13 Richarda Von LAVENT

Born: Abt 1030
-CONTINUED AS #5,ROYAL CHART 1787
Died: Abt 9 Jul 1072

3 Richarda Von SPONHEIM

Born: Abt 1072

Died: Bef 1112

14 Bernhard Von FLINSBACH

Born: Abt 1020

Married:

Died:

7 Hedwig of Flinsbach

Born: Abt 1052

Died: Aft 1100

15 Cecilia

Born:

Died:

Sources include: *Royal Ancestors* (1989), chart 11890; Stuart 10; Moriarty 188.